This Bible belongs to

____

PRESENTED BY

____

____

DATE

____

My Church Record

BAPTISM, FIRST COMMUNION, CONFIRMATION,
AND OTHER MEMORABLE EVENTS

EVENT ____

____________________________________ DATE ____________

EVENT ____

____________________________________ DATE ____________

EVENT ____

____________________________________ DATE ____________

EVENT ____

____________________________________ DATE ____________

EVENT ____

____________________________________ DATE ____________

My Family History

MY NAME ______________________________

WHEN I WAS BORN ______________________________

MY FATHER ______________________________

MY FATHER'S PARENTS ______________________________

MY MOTHER ______________________________

MY MOTHER'S PARENTS ______________________________

MY BROTHERS AND SISTERS

NAME ______________________________

NAME ______________________________

NAME ______________________________

NAME ______________________________

NAME ______________________________

**Your word is a lamp to my feet
and a light to my path.**

PSALM 119:105

Precious Moments Holy Bible

NRSV

Precious Moments Holy Bible

NRSV

New Revised Standard Version
Catholic Edition, Anglicized Text

Catholic Bible Press

An imprint of HarperCollins Christian Publishers

Catholic Bible Press is an imprint of HarperCollins Christian Publishing, Inc.
Published in Nashville, Tennessee, by Catholic Bible Press

Library of Congress Control Number: 2020940713

Imprimatur
Most Rev. Daniel E. Pilarczyk, President, National Conference of Catholic Bishops
Washington, DC, September 12, 1991

Imprimatur
Canadian Conference of Catholic Bishops Ottawa, October 15, 1991

This Bible was set in the NRSV Typeface, created exclusively for HarperCollins Christian Publishing at the 2K/DENMARK type foundry.

Printed in India

25 26 27 28 29 30 31 /BPI/ 15 14 13 12 11 10 9 8 7 6 5

TABLE OF CONTENTS

MORE HELP

ABBREVIATIONS

The following abbreviations are used for the books of the Bible:

OT = Old Testament
NT = New Testament

Abbr.	Book	Testament
1 Chr.	1 Chronicles	OT
1 Cor.	1 Corinthians	NT
1 Jn.	1 John	NT
1 Kings	1 Kings	OT
1 Macc	1 Maccabees	OT
1 Pet	1 Peter	NT
1 Sam.	1 Samuel	OT
1 Thess	1 Thessalonians	NT
1 Tim	1 Timothy	NT
2 Chr	2 Chronicles	OT
2 Cor.	2 Corinthians	NT
2 Jn.	2 John	NT
2 Kings	2 Kings	OT
2 Macc	2 Maccabees	OT
2 Pet.	2 Peter	NT
2 Sam.	2 Samuel	OT
2 Thess	2 Thessalonians	NT
2 Tim	2 Timothy	NT
3 Jn.	3 John	NT
Acts	Acts of the Apostles	NT
Am.	Amos	OT
Bar	Baruch	OT
Col	Colossians	NT
Dan	Daniel	OT
Deut.	Deuteronomy	OT
Eccl	Ecclesiastes	OT
Eph	Ephesians	NT
Esth	Esther	OT
Ex.	Exodus	OT
Ezek	Ezekiel	OT
Ezra	Ezra	OT
Gal	Galatians	NT
Gen.	Genesis	OT
Hab	Habakkuk	OT
Hag	Haggai	OT
Heb	Hebrews	NT
Hos.	Hosea	OT
Isa	Isaiah	OT
Jas	James	NT
Jdt	Judith	OT
Jer.	Jeremiah	OT
Jn	John	NT
Job	Job	OT
Joel	Joel	OT
Jon	Jonah	OT
Josh	Joshua	OT
Jude	Jude	NT
Judg	Judges	OT
Lam	Lamentations	OT
Lev	Leviticus	OT
Lk.	Luke	NT
Mal.	Malachi	OT
Mic.	Micah	OT
Mk	Mark	NT
Mt	Matthew	NT
Nah	Nahum	OT
Neh	Nehemiah	OT
Num	Numbers	OT
Ob	Obadiah	OT
Phil	Philippians	NT
Philem.	Philemon	NT
Prov	Proverbs	OT
Ps(s)	Psalms	OT
Rev.	Revelation	NT
Rom.	Romans	NT
Ruth	Ruth	OT
Sir	Sirach (Ecclesiasticus)	OT
Song	Song of Solomon	OT
Titus	Titus	NT
Tob.	Tobit	OT
Wis.	Wisdom of Solomon	OT
Zech	Zechariah	OT
Zeph.	Zephaniah	OT

In the notes to the books of the Old Testament the following abbreviations are used:

- *Ant.* . . . . . . Josephus, *Antiquities of the Jews*
- Aram . . . . Aramaic
- Ch(s). . . . . Chapter(s)
- Cn. . . . . Correction; made where the text has suffered in transmission and the versions provide no satisfactory restoration, but where the Standard Bible Committee agrees with the judgment of competent scholars as to the most probable reconstruction of the original text.
- Gk. . . . . Septuagint, Greek version of the OT
- Heb . . . . Hebrew of the consonantal Masoretic Text of the OT
- Josephus . . . . Flavius Josephus (Jewish historian, ca. 37–95 CE)
- Macc. . . . . The book(s) of the Maccabees
- Ms(s) . . . . Manuscript(s)
- MT . . . . The Hebrew of the pointed Masoretic Text of the OT
- OL . . . . Old Latin
- Q Ms(s) . . . . Manuscript(s) found at Qumran by the Dead Sea
- Sam . . . . Samaritan Hebrew text of the OT
- Syr . . . . Syriac Version of the OT
- Syr H . . . . Syriac Version of Origen's Hexapla
- Tg. . . . . Targum
- Vg. . . . Vulgate, Latin Version of the OT

Preface to the

NEW REVISED STANDARD VERSION

Catholic Edition

This Catholic edition of the New Revised Standard Version of the Bible has been authorized by the National Conference of Catholic Bishops in the U.S.A. and by the National Council of the Churches of Christ in the U.S.A. It has received the ecclesiastical approval of the Catholic Bishops of both the United States and Canada. The undersigned, who prepared this edition, is a member of the Revised Standard Version Bible Translation Committee as well as an active member and past president of the Catholic Biblical Association of America.

Roman Catholics are already familiar with the accuracy and elegance of the New Revised Standard Version, first published in 1990. It has previously appeared in two major types of edition: an edition of the Old and New Testaments alone, the Bible of most Protestants; and an edition of the Old and New Testaments with the Apocryphal/Deuterocanonical Books placed between the two Testaments. The text of the latter edition received the Imprimatur (official approbation) of the United States and Canadian Catholic Bishops. The New Revised Standard Version is truly an ecumenical translation, for it was produced by Roman Catholic, Eastern Orthodox, Protestant, and Jewish scholars. Because of this Catholic presence no change in the translation was requested for this edition. The only exceptions are the Book of Esther, which exists in two different forms that are explained below, and the Book of Daniel, which includes the deuterocanonical portions that are listed below.

Regarding the number of the books of the Old Testament canon and their arrangement, however, Protestants and Jews on the one hand, and Roman Catholics and Orthodox Christians on the other, hold different beliefs. From the time of the Reformation in the sixteenth century, Protestants have adopted the Jewish canon of the Old Testament, which was established by the rabbis at the end of the first century of the Common Era. This canon includes only those books that were written in Hebrew and Aramaic. In addition to these books, however, Roman Catholics, following the ancient tradition of the Christian church, also hold the Deuterocanonical Books of the Old Testament to be sacred and inspired, and therefore canonical. Protestants and Jews call these books Apocrypha, a word that means "hidden or concealed," an inappropriate title for works that were part of the Greek Old Testament (the Septuagint) from pre-Christian times. The Roman Catholic canon, which was fixed by the time of the Council of Hippo in 393 and reaffirmed by the two Councils of Carthage in 397 and 419, was formally defined by the Council of Trent in 1546. This canon contains seven Deuterocanonical Books: Tobit, Judith, the Wisdom of Solomon, Sirach (the Wisdom of Ben Sira, also known as Ecclesiasticus), Baruch including the Letter of Jeremiah as chapter 6, and 1 and 2 Maccabees; and extra portions of two other books: the Additions to Esther; and the Prayer of Azariah and the Song of the Three Jews inserted between verses 23 and 24 of Daniel 3, Susanna as Daniel 13, and Bel and the Dragon as Daniel 14. Over and above these books and extra portions, the Bible of Greek and Slavonic Orthodox Christians includes 1 Esdras, the Prayer of Manasseh, Psalm 151, and 3 Maccabees. The Slavonic Bible also contains 2 Esdras, and an appendix to the Greek Bible includes 4 Maccabees.

Several of the Deuterocanonical Books were written originally in Hebrew or Aramaic, the rest in Greek. More than two-thirds of the Book of

Sirach is now extant in Hebrew, and four fragments of the Book of Tobit in Hebrew and Aramaic were recovered from Qumran Cave IV. It seems certain that Judith and the additions to Daniel were also written originally in Hebrew. Hebrew is the original language of the prose parts of Baruch; the poetic parts were composed in Greek. The Wisdom of Solomon was written completely in Greek. The original language of 1 Maccabees was Hebrew while 2 Maccabees was composed in Greek.

The Book of Esther has two different forms: the short Hebrew original; and the longer Greek version that contains one hundred and seven additional verses comprising six distinct portions, A through F. It is the translation of the entire Greek version that appears in the Deuterocanonical section of the New Revised Standard Version. In this Catholic edition, however, the translation of the Greek portions has been inserted at the appropriate places of the translation of the Hebrew form of the book. Some of the Greek portions apparently had a Hebrew origin; the others were written in Greek.

What is distinctive about this Catholic edition—as well as every other edition published by Roman Catholics—is that the Deuterocanonical Books and portions are placed in their proper order among the other books of the Old Testament. Thus, Tobit, Judith, the long form of Esther, and 1 and 2 Maccabees are found among the so-called historical books directly after Nehemiah. The Wisdom of Solomon and the Book of Sirach follow after the Song of Solomon among the wisdom books. Because Baruch, the well-known secretary of Jeremiah, is said to be the author of the work that bears his name, the book is placed after Jeremiah and Lamentations. This order of books comes from the Latin Vulgate translated by St. Jerome in the late fourth and early fifth centuries. It is essentially the same order as that found in the fourth-century Codex Vaticanus, one of the oldest extant manuscripts of the Septuagint.

Roman Catholics will welcome this edition of the New Revised Standard Version of the Bible for personal reading and study as well as liturgical usage. Based on the latest manuscript discoveries and critical editions, it offers the fruits of the best biblical scholarship in the idiom of today while being sensitive to the contemporary concern for inclusive language when referring to human beings.

ALEXANDER A. DI LELLA, O.F.M.
Andrews-Kelly-Ryan Distinguished
Professor of Biblical Studies
The Catholic University of America

September 30, 1992
Feast of St. Jerome

Preface to the

NEW REVISED STANDARD VERSION

Anglicized Edition

The publication of the New Revised Standard Version of the Bible in 1990 marked the latest stage in the development of an authoritative English language text, a process that started in England with the translation commonly known as the Authorized or King James Version of 1611. The ongoing task of translation had already resulted in the Revised Standard Version of 1952, and a fuller account of this developmental process can be found in the preface To the Reader.

The RSV rapidly found favour throughout the English-speaking world, and in the United Kingdom the translation was quickly adopted by churches, theological colleges, and university faculties as their standard version. In all these places, the RSV was recognized as being authoritative and accurate, impartial in its scholarship, and well-suited to the needs of the Christian community of that period.

The continuance of the Translation Committee's work after the RSV first appeared is a testimony to the fluid nature of the labour with which it is concerned. Bible translators must try to reflect the language of the people for whom they are writing, and the NRSV, recognizing that the English language was evolving rapidly, adopted terms that are familiar to contemporary readers. Yet the English language has developed in different ways in separate countries, and there has been an ongoing divergence between the language as it is used in the United States of America, and the form most commonly used in the British Isles and other countries where British usage is preferred. Therefore, whilst the appearance of the NRSV was warmly welcomed, it soon became apparent that there was a sufficient number of variances between American and British usage to suggest that an edition embodying British usage would be appreciated. The task of producing a text that would meet this need was therefore undertaken, with the convenient (if not strictly accurate) description of an Anglicized Edition.

All those participating in the process of 'anglicization' accepted that no attempt could be made to alter the basic translation in any way; their responsibility was simply to render words that might otherwise be uncertain or awkward into the best generally acceptable equivalent in British usage, whilst at the same time adjusting appropriate points of spelling, grammar, and punctuation.

It is the spelling of various words that will for many present the most obvious examples of change. (Readers may care to note that the verb ending *-ize*, in Britain sometimes regarded as American usage, has been retained where this is etymologically permissible). Other common changes include: the insertion of 'and' into numbers higher than one hundred; the replacement of obsolete (in British usage) past participles such as 'gotten'; the avoidance of subjunctive verbs, still familiar in American but much rarer in British usage; the reinstatement of prepositions such as 'to' and 'for' often elided in US idiom.

The Anglicized Edition's editors also found that words in common use could sometimes have different meanings in various English-speaking cultures, which must affect understanding and interpretation of the text. Thus, references to the (freshwater) Sea of Galilee retain this form, but where the proper name is not given in full, 'sea' is replaced by 'lake', a more unmistakable description for readers to whom sea implies salt water, corresponding to the American 'ocean'. The 'tone' of a particular word may also vary between countries;

what is an acceptable 'informal' use in the USA may sometimes be seen as a vulgarism in Britain and other places.

Many smaller alterations have been made, apparently insignificant in themselves, yet which contribute to the overall rendition of the biblical narrative in what may be termed British style.

The intention that lies behind the publication of the New Revised Standard Version Anglicized Edition has been to present an already excellent version of the Scriptures in the form most accessible to its intended readers, so reinforcing their understanding. The editorial work was carried out in Great Britain, but the active support and encouragement of members of the original Translation Committee has ensured that the foundational scholarship which undergirds the NRSV has been retained and enhanced for those who prefer British usage. It is the earnest hope of all involved in the task that their efforts will enable still more readers to gain fresh insights into the written Word of God.

Oxford
October 1995

WHY READ THE BIBLE?

Imagine having a best friend who never listened to what you had to say. You had great and exciting things to share, but she didn't pay any attention to you. How well would she actually know you? How strong do you think your friendship would be?

God is the best friend we could ever wish for. To help our friendship with him grow, we need to know what he has to say to us. He has written things that matter to him in the pages of the Bible. When we take time to read it, we are not just reading a bunch of stories. We are hearing God's heart and growing closer to the One who loves us! As we learn what is important to God, we begin to value those things too. We learn to live our lives by his directions and not our own thinking. God uses his Word to teach us, renew our minds, and help us become more like Jesus.

> All scripture is inspired by God and is useful for teaching, for reproof, for correction, and for training in righteousness.
>
> 2 Timothy 3.16

If you want to read through sections of the Bible, use one of the reading plans found in the back of this Bible.

THE OLD TESTAMENT

GENESIS

The first book of the Bible is not a scientific narrative about the origin of the universe. Rather, it is the story of the beginning of humanity's relationship with God. The literary context of the book is the origin of everything, of the world, of humanity, of the people of God. The narrative is an accumulation of oral traditions told from generation to generation over the centuries about the dependence of all things on God and about humanity's purpose and destiny as creatures made in the image and likeness of God.

Genesis contains four major divisions: the creation narratives (ch. 1.1—11.32); the stories of Abraham (12.1—25.18); the stories of Jacob (25.19—36.43); and the stories of Joseph (37.1—50.26). The first creation story is read every year in the liturgy at the Easter Vigil. Also, each year on the Vigil of Pentecost, the story of the Tower of Babel is read. Other parts of Genesis are read during the liturgy in Year I of the weekday liturgical calendar starting on Monday of the Fifth Week of the Year through Saturday of the Fourteenth Week.

SIX DAYS OF CREATION AND THE SABBATH

1 In the beginning when God created[a] the heavens and the earth,
2the earth was a formless void and darkness covered the face of the deep, while
a wind from God[b] swept over the face of
the waters. 3Then God said, 'Let there
be light'; and there was light. 4And God
saw that the light was good; and God
separated the light from the darkness.
5God called the light Day, and the darkness he called Night. And there was evening and there was morning, the first
day.
6 And God said, 'Let there be a dome
in the midst of the waters, and let it separate the waters from the waters.' 7So
God made the dome and separated the
waters that were under the dome from
the waters that were above the dome.
And it was so. 8God called the dome
Sky. And there was evening and there
was morning, the second day.
9 And God said, 'Let the waters under the sky be gathered together into
one place, and let the dry land appear.'
And it was so. 10God called the dry land
Earth, and the waters that were gathered together he called Seas. And God
saw that it was good. 11Then God said,
'Let the earth put forth vegetation:
plants yielding seed, and fruit trees of
every kind on earth that bear fruit with
the seed in it.' And it was so. 12The earth
brought forth vegetation: plants yielding seed of every kind, and trees of every kind bearing fruit with the seed in
it. And God saw that it was good. 13And
there was evening and there was morning, the third day.
14 And God said, 'Let there be lights
in the dome of the sky to separate the
day from the night; and let them be
for signs and for seasons and for days
and years, 15and let them be lights in
the dome of the sky to give light upon
the earth.' And it was so. 16God made
the two great lights—the greater light
to rule the day and the lesser light to
rule the night—and the stars. 17God
set them in the dome of the sky to give
light upon the earth, 18to rule over the
day and over the night, and to separate
the light from the darkness. And God

[a] **1.1** *Or when God began to create or In the beginning God created* [b] **1.2** *Or while the spirit of God or while a mighty wind*

saw that it was good. 19And there was
evening and there was morning, the
fourth day.

20 And God said, 'Let the waters
bring forth swarms of living creatures,
and let birds fly above the earth across
the dome of the sky.' 21So God created
the great sea monsters and every living
creature that moves, of every kind, with
which the waters swarm, and every
winged bird of every kind. And God saw
that it was good. 22God blessed them,
saying, 'Be fruitful and multiply and
fill the waters in the seas, and let birds
multiply on the earth.' 23And there was
evening and there was morning, the
fifth day.

24 And God said, 'Let the earth bring
forth living creatures of every kind: cattle and creeping things and wild animals of the earth of every kind.' And it
was so. 25God made the wild animals of
the earth of every kind, and the cattle of
every kind, and everything that creeps
upon the ground of every kind. And God
saw that it was good.

26 Then God said, 'Let us make humankind[c] in our image, according to
our likeness; and let them have dominion over the fish of the sea, and over the
birds of the air, and over the cattle, and
over all the wild animals of the earth,[d]
and over every creeping thing that
creeps upon the earth.'

27 So God created humankind[e]
in his image,
in the image of God he
created them;[f]
male and female he created them.

28God blessed them, and God said to
them, 'Be fruitful and multiply, and fill
the earth and subdue it; and have dominion over the fish of the sea and over
the birds of the air and over every living
thing that moves upon the earth.' 29God
said, 'See, I have given you every plant
yielding seed that is upon the face of all
the earth, and every tree with seed in
its fruit; you shall have them for food.
30And to every beast of the earth, and
to every bird of the air, and to everything that creeps on the earth, everything that has the breath of life, I have
given every green plant for food.' And
it was so. 31God saw everything that he
had made, and indeed, it was very good.
And there was evening and there was
morning, the sixth day.

2 Thus the heavens and the earth
were finished, and all their multitude. 2And on the seventh day God finished the work that he had done, and he
rested on the seventh day from all the
work that he had done. 3So God blessed
the seventh day and hallowed it, because on it God rested from all the work
that he had done in creation.

4 These are the generations of the
heavens and the earth when they were
created.

ANOTHER ACCOUNT OF THE CREATION

In the day that the LORD[g] God made
the earth and the heavens, 5when no
plant of the field was yet in the earth
and no herb of the field had yet sprung
up—for the LORD God had not caused
it to rain upon the earth, and there
was no one to till the ground; 6but a
stream would rise from the earth, and
water the whole face of the ground—
7then the LORD God formed man from
the dust of the ground,[h] and breathed
into his nostrils the breath of life; and
the man became a living being. 8And
the LORD God planted a garden in
Eden, in the east; and there he put the
man whom he had formed. 9Out of the
ground the LORD God made to grow every tree that is pleasant to the sight and
good for food, the tree of life also in the
midst of the garden, and the tree of the
knowledge of good and evil.

10 A river flows out of Eden to water
the garden, and from there it divides
and becomes four branches. 11The name
of the first is Pishon; it is the one that
flows around the whole land of Havilah, where there is gold; 12and the gold
of that land is good; bdellium and onyx
stone are there. 13The name of the second river is Gihon; it is the one that
flows around the whole land of Cush.
14The name of the third river is Tigris,
which flows east of Assyria. And the
fourth river is the Euphrates.

15 The LORD God took the man and
put him in the garden of Eden to till it
and keep it. 16And the LORD God commanded the man, 'You may freely eat of
every tree of the garden; 17but of the tree
of the knowledge of good and evil you
shall not eat, for in the day that you eat
of it you shall die.'

[c] 1.26 Heb *adam* [d] 1.26 Syr: Heb *and over all the earth* [e] 1.27 Heb *adam* [f] 1.27 Heb *him*
[g] 2.4 Heb *YHWH*, as in other places where 'LORD' is spelled with capital letters (see also Ex 3.14–15 with notes). [h] 2.7 Or *formed a man* (Heb *adam*) *of dust from the ground* (Heb *adamah*)

18 Then the LORD God said, 'It is not
good that the man should be alone;
I will make him a helper as his partner.' 19 So out of the ground the LORD
God formed every animal of the field
and every bird of the air, and brought
them to the man to see what he would
call them; and whatever the man called
each living creature, that was its name.
20 The man gave names to all cattle, and
to the birds of the air, and to every animal of the field; but for the man[i] there
was not found a helper as his partner.
21 So the LORD God caused a deep sleep
to fall upon the man, and he slept; then
he took one of his ribs and closed up its
place with flesh. 22 And the rib that the
LORD God had taken from the man he
made into a woman and brought her to
the man. 23 Then the man said,

'This at last is bone of my bones
  and flesh of my flesh;
this one shall be called Woman,[j]
  for out of Man[k] this one
    was taken.'

24 Therefore a man leaves his father and
his mother and clings to his wife, and
they become one flesh. 25 And the man
and his wife were both naked, and were
not ashamed.

THE FIRST SIN AND ITS PUNISHMENT

3 Now the serpent was more crafty
than any other wild animal that
the LORD God had made. He said to the
woman, 'Did God say, "You shall not
eat from any tree in the garden"?' 2 The
woman said to the serpent, 'We may
eat of the fruit of the trees in the garden; 3 but God said, "You shall not eat of
the fruit of the tree that is in the middle of the garden, nor shall you touch
it, or you shall die." ' 4 But the serpent
said to the woman, 'You will not die;
5 for God knows that when you eat of it
your eyes will be opened, and you will
be like God,[l] knowing good and evil.' 6 So
when the woman saw that the tree was
good for food, and that it was a delight
to the eyes, and that the tree was to be
desired to make one wise, she took of its
fruit and ate; and she also gave some to
her husband, who was with her, and he
ate. 7 Then the eyes of both were opened,
and they knew that they were naked;
and they sewed fig leaves together and
made loincloths for themselves.

8 They heard the sound of the LORD
God walking in the garden at the time
of the evening breeze, and the man and
his wife hid themselves from the presence of the LORD God among the trees
of the garden. 9 But the LORD God called
to the man, and said to him, 'Where
are you?' 10 He said, 'I heard the sound
of you in the garden, and I was afraid,
because I was naked; and I hid myself.'
11 He said, 'Who told you that you were
naked? Have you eaten from the tree
of which I commanded you not to eat?'
12 The man said, 'The woman whom you
gave to be with me, she gave me fruit
from the tree, and I ate.' 13 Then the
LORD God said to the woman, 'What is
this that you have done?' The woman
said, 'The serpent tricked me, and I ate.'
14 The LORD God said to the serpent,

'Because you have done this,
  cursed are you among all animals
  and among all wild creatures;
upon your belly you shall go,
  and dust you shall eat
  all the days of your life.
15 I will put enmity between you
    and the woman,
  and between your offspring
    and hers;
he will strike your head,
  and you will strike his heel.'

16 To the woman he said,

'I will greatly increase your
    pangs in childbearing;
  in pain you shall bring
    forth children,
yet your desire shall be for
    your husband,
  and he shall rule over you.'

17 And to the man[m] he said,

'Because you have listened to
    the voice of your wife,
  and have eaten of the tree
about which I commanded you,
  "You shall not eat of it",
cursed is the ground because of you;
  in toil you shall eat of it all
    the days of your life;
18 thorns and thistles it shall
    bring forth for you;
  and you shall eat the
    plants of the field.
19 By the sweat of your face
  you shall eat bread
until you return to the ground,
  for out of it you were taken;
you are dust,
  and to dust you shall return.'

i 2.20 Or *for Adam* j 2.23 Heb *ishshah*
k 2.23 Heb *ish* l 3.5 Or *gods* m 3.17 Or *to Adam*

20 The man named his wife Eve,[n] because she was the mother of all who live.
21And the LORD God made garments of
skins for the man[o] and for his wife, and
clothed them.
22 Then the LORD God said, 'See, the
man has become like one of us, knowing good and evil; and now, he might
reach out his hand and take also from
the tree of life, and eat, and live for ever'— 23therefore the LORD God sent him
forth from the garden of Eden, to till the
ground from which he was taken. 24He
drove out the man; and at the east of the
garden of Eden he placed the cherubim,
and a sword flaming and turning to
guard the way to the tree of life.

CAIN MURDERS ABEL

4 Now the man knew his wife Eve,
and she conceived and bore Cain,
saying, 'I have produced[p] a man with
the help of the LORD.' 2Next she bore his
brother Abel. Now Abel was a keeper of
sheep, and Cain a tiller of the ground.
3In the course of time Cain brought to
the LORD an offering of the fruit of the
ground, 4and Abel for his part brought
of the firstlings of his flock, their fat
portions. And the LORD had regard for
Abel and his offering, 5but for Cain and
his offering he had no regard. So Cain
was very angry, and his countenance
fell. 6The LORD said to Cain, 'Why are
you angry, and why has your countenance fallen? 7If you do well, will you
not be accepted? And if you do not do
well, sin is lurking at the door; its desire
is for you, but you must master it.'
8 Cain said to his brother Abel, 'Let
us go out to the field.'[q] And when they
were in the field, Cain rose up against
his brother Abel and killed him. 9Then
the LORD said to Cain, 'Where is your
brother Abel?' He said, 'I do not know;
am I my brother's keeper?' 10And the
LORD said, 'What have you done? Listen; your brother's blood is crying out
to me from the ground! 11And now you
are cursed from the ground, which has
opened its mouth to receive your brother's blood from your hand. 12When you
till the ground, it will no longer yield
to you its strength; you will be a fugitive and a wanderer on the earth.' 13Cain
said to the LORD, 'My punishment is
greater than I can bear! 14Today you
have driven me away from the soil, and
I shall be hidden from your face; I shall
be a fugitive and a wanderer on the
earth, and anyone who meets me may
kill me.' 15Then the LORD said to him,
'Not so![r] Whoever kills Cain will suffer
a sevenfold vengeance.' And the LORD
put a mark on Cain, so that no one who
came upon him would kill him. 16Then
Cain went away from the presence of
the LORD, and settled in the land of
Nod,[s] east of Eden.

BEGINNINGS OF CIVILIZATION

17 Cain knew his wife, and she conceived and bore Enoch; and he built a
city, and named it Enoch after his son
Enoch. 18To Enoch was born Irad; and
Irad was the father of Mehujael, and
Mehujael the father of Methushael, and
Methushael the father of Lamech. 19La-
mech took two wives; the name of one
was Adah, and the name of the other
Zillah. 20Adah bore Jabal; he was the
ancestor of those who live in tents and
have livestock. 21His brother's name
was Jubal; he was the ancestor of all
those who play the lyre and pipe. 22Zil-
lah bore Tubal-cain, who made all kinds
of bronze and iron tools. The sister of
Tubal-cain was Naamah.
23 Lamech said to his wives:
'Adah and Zillah, hear my voice;
you wives of Lamech, listen
to what I say:
I have killed a man for
wounding me,
a young man for striking me.
24 If Cain is avenged sevenfold,
truly Lamech seventy-sevenfold.'
25 Adam knew his wife again, and
she bore a son and named him Seth, for
she said, 'God has appointed[t] for me another child instead of Abel, because Cain
killed him.' 26To Seth also a son was
born, and he named him Enosh. At that
time people began to invoke the name
of the LORD.

ADAM'S DESCENDANTS TO NOAH AND HIS SONS

5 This is the list of the descendants of
Adam. When God created human-
kind,[u] he made them[v] in the likeness of
God. 2Male and female he created them,
and he blessed them and named them
'Humankind'[w] when they were created.

[n] **3.20** In Heb *Eve* resembles the word for *living* [o] **3.21** Or *for Adam* [p] **4.1** The verb in Heb resembles the word for *Cain* [q] **4.8** Sam Gk Syr Compare Vg: MT lacks *Let us go out to the field* [r] **4.15** Gk Syr Vg: Heb *Therefore* [s] **4.16** That is *Wandering* [t] **4.25** The verb in Heb resembles the word for *Seth* [u] **5.1** Heb *adam* [v] **5.1** Heb *him* [w] **5.2** Heb *adam*

3 When Adam had lived for one hundred and thirty years, he became the father of a son in his likeness, according
to his image, and named him Seth. 4The
days of Adam after he became the father
of Seth were eight hundred years; and
he had other sons and daughters. 5Thus
all the days that Adam lived were nine
hundred and thirty years; and he died.
6 When Seth had lived for one hundred and five years, he became the father of Enosh. 7Seth lived after the birth
of Enosh for eight hundred and seven
years, and had other sons and daughters. 8Thus all the days of Seth were nine
hundred and twelve years; and he died.
9 When Enosh had lived for ninety
years, he became the father of Kenan.
10Enosh lived after the birth of Kenan
for eight hundred and fifteen years, and
had other sons and daughters. 11Thus all
the days of Enosh were nine hundred
and five years; and he died.
12 When Kenan had lived for seventy years, he became the father of Mahalalel. 13Kenan lived after the birth of
Mahalalel for eight hundred and forty
years, and had other sons and daughters. 14Thus all the days of Kenan were
nine hundred and ten years; and he
died.
15 When Mahalalel had lived for
sixty-five years, he became the father of
Jared. 16Mahalalel lived after the birth
of Jared for eight hundred and thirty
years, and had other sons and daughters. 17Thus all the days of Mahalalel
were eight hundred and ninety-five
years; and he died.
18 When Jared had lived for one hundred and sixty-two years he became
the father of Enoch. 19Jared lived after
the birth of Enoch for eight hundred
years, and had other sons and daughters. 20Thus all the days of Jared were
nine hundred and sixty-two years; and
he died.
21 When Enoch had lived for sixty-
five years, he became the father of Methuselah. 22Enoch walked with God
after the birth of Methuselah for three
hundred years, and had other sons and
daughters. 23Thus all the days of Enoch
were three hundred and sixty-five
years. 24Enoch walked with God; then
he was no more, because God took him.
25 When Methuselah had lived for
one hundred and eighty-seven years, he
became the father of Lamech. 26Methu-
selah lived after the birth of Lamech for
seven hundred and eighty-two years,
and had other sons and daughters.
27Thus all the days of Methuselah were
nine hundred and sixty-nine years; and
he died.
28 When Lamech had lived for one
hundred and eighty-two years, he became the father of a son; 29he named
him Noah, saying, 'Out of the ground
that the LORD has cursed this one shall
bring us relief from our work and from
the toil of our hands.' 30Lamech lived after the birth of Noah for five hundred
and ninety-five years, and had other
sons and daughters. 31Thus all the days
of Lamech were seven hundred and
seventy-seven years; and he died.
32 After Noah was five hundred
years old, Noah became the father of
Shem, Ham, and Japheth.

THE WICKEDNESS OF HUMANKIND

6 When people began to multiply on
the face of the ground, and daughters were born to them, 2the sons of God
saw that they were fair; and they took
wives for themselves of all that they
chose. 3Then the LORD said, 'My spirit
shall not abide[x] in mortals for ever, for
they are flesh; their days shall be one
hundred and twenty years.' 4The Nephilim were on the earth in those days—
and also afterwards—when the sons
of God went in to the daughters of humans, who bore children to them. These
were the heroes that were of old, warriors of renown.
5 The LORD saw that the wickedness of humankind was great in the
earth, and that every inclination of the
thoughts of their hearts was only evil
continually. 6And the LORD was sorry
that he had made humankind on the
earth, and it grieved him to his heart.
7So the LORD said, 'I will blot out from
the earth the human beings I have
created—people together with animals
and creeping things and birds of the air,
for I am sorry that I have made them.'
8But Noah found favour in the sight of
the LORD.

NOAH PLEASES GOD

9 These are the descendants of Noah.
Noah was a righteous man, blameless
in his generation; Noah walked with
God. 10And Noah had three sons, Shem,
Ham, and Japheth.
11 Now the earth was corrupt in
God's sight, and the earth was filled

[x] 6.3 Meaning of Heb uncertain

with violence. 12 And God saw that the earth was corrupt; for all flesh had corrupted its ways upon the earth. 13 And God said to Noah, 'I have determined to make an end of all flesh, for the earth is filled with violence because of them; now I am going to destroy them along with the earth. 14 Make yourself an ark of cypress[y] wood; make rooms in the ark, and cover it inside and out with pitch. 15 This is how you are to make it: the length of the ark three hundred cubits, its width fifty cubits, and its height thirty cubits. 16 Make a roof[z] for the ark, and finish it to a cubit above; and put the door of the ark in its side; make it with lower, second, and third decks. 17 For my part, I am going to bring a flood of waters on the earth, to destroy from under heaven all flesh in which is the breath of life; everything that is on the earth shall die. 18 But I will establish my covenant with you; and you shall come into the ark, you, your sons, your wife, and your sons' wives with you. 19 And of every living thing, of all flesh, you shall bring two of every kind into the ark, to keep them alive with you; they shall be male and female. 20 Of the birds according to their kinds, and of the animals according to their kinds, of every creeping thing of the ground according to its kind, two of every kind shall come in to you, to keep them alive. 21 Also take with you every kind of food that is eaten, and store it up; and it shall serve as food for you and for them.' 22 Noah did this; he did all that God commanded him.

THE GREAT FLOOD

7 Then the LORD said to Noah, 'Go into the ark, you and all your household, for I have seen that you alone are righteous before me in this generation. 2 Take with you seven pairs of all clean animals, the male and its mate; and a pair of the animals that are not clean, the male and its mate; 3 and seven pairs of the birds of the air also, male and female, to keep their kind alive on the face of all the earth. 4 For in seven days I will send rain on the earth for forty days and forty nights; and every living thing that I have made I will blot out from the face of the ground.' 5 And Noah did all that the LORD had commanded him.

6 Noah was six hundred years old when the flood of waters came on the earth. 7 And Noah with his sons and his wife and his sons' wives went into the ark to escape the waters of the flood. 8 Of clean animals, and of animals that are not clean, and of birds, and of everything that creeps on the ground, 9 two and two, male and female, went into the ark with Noah, as God had commanded Noah. 10 And after seven days the waters of the flood came on the earth.

11 In the six-hundredth year of Noah's life, in the second month, on the seventeenth day of the month, on that day all the fountains of the great deep burst forth, and the windows of the heavens were opened. 12 The rain fell on the earth for forty days and forty nights. 13 On the very same day Noah with his sons, Shem and Ham and Japheth, and Noah's wife and the three wives of his sons, entered the ark, 14 they and every wild animal of every kind, and all domestic animals of every kind, and every creeping thing that creeps on the earth, and every bird of every kind—every bird, every winged creature. 15 They went into the ark with Noah, two and two of all flesh in which there was the breath of life. 16 And those that entered, male and female of all flesh, went in as God had commanded him; and the LORD shut him in.

17 The flood continued for forty days on the earth; and the waters increased, and bore up the ark, and it rose high above the earth. 18 The waters swelled and increased greatly on the earth; and the ark floated on the face of the waters. 19 The waters swelled so mightily on the earth that all the high mountains under the whole heaven were covered; 20 the waters swelled above the mountains, covering them fifteen cubits deep. 21 And all flesh died that moved on the earth, birds, domestic animals, wild animals, all swarming creatures that swarm on the earth, and all human beings; 22 everything on dry land in whose nostrils was the breath of life died. 23 He blotted out every living thing that was on the face of the ground, human beings and animals and creeping things and birds of the air; they were blotted out from the earth. Only Noah was left, and those that were with him in the ark. 24 And the waters swelled on the earth for one hundred and fifty days.

THE FLOOD SUBSIDES

8 But God remembered Noah and all the wild animals and all the do-

[y] 6.14 Meaning of Heb uncertain [z] 6.16 Or *window*

mestic animals that were with him in
the ark. And God made a wind blow over
the earth, and the waters subsided; 2the
fountains of the deep and the windows
of the heavens were closed, the rain from
the heavens was restrained, 3and the waters gradually receded from the earth. At
the end of one hundred and fifty days the
waters had abated; 4and in the seventh
month, on the seventeenth day of the
month, the ark came to rest on the mountains of Ararat. 5The waters continued to
abate until the tenth month; in the tenth
month, on the first day of the month, the
tops of the mountains appeared.

6 At the end of forty days Noah opened
the window of the ark that he had made
7and sent out the raven; and it went to
and fro until the waters were dried up
from the earth. 8Then he sent out the
dove from him, to see if the waters had
subsided from the face of the ground;
9but the dove found no place to set its
foot, and it returned to him to the ark,
for the waters were still on the face of the
whole earth. So he put out his hand and
took it and brought it into the ark with
him. 10He waited another seven days,
and again he sent out the dove from the
ark; 11and the dove came back to him in
the evening, and there in its beak was a
freshly plucked olive leaf; so Noah knew
that the waters had subsided from the
earth. 12Then he waited another seven
days, and sent out the dove; and it did not
return to him any more.

13 In the six hundred and first year,
in the first month, on the first day of the
month, the waters were dried up from the
earth; and Noah removed the covering of
the ark, and looked, and saw that the face
of the ground was drying. 14In the second month, on the twenty-seventh day
of the month, the earth was dry. 15Then
God said to Noah, 16'Go out of the ark, you
and your wife, and your sons and your
sons' wives with you. 17Bring out with
you every living thing that is with you
of all flesh—birds and animals and every
creeping thing that creeps on the earth—
so that they may abound on the earth,
and be fruitful and multiply on the earth.'
18So Noah went out with his sons and
his wife and his sons' wives. 19And every
animal, every creeping thing, and every
bird, everything that moves on the earth,
went out of the ark by families.

GOD'S PROMISE TO NOAH

20 Then Noah built an altar to the
LORD, and took of every clean animal
and of every clean bird, and offered
burnt-offerings on the altar. 21And
when the LORD smelt the pleasing
odour, the LORD said in his heart, 'I will
never again curse the ground because of
humankind, for the inclination of the
human heart is evil from youth; nor will
I ever again destroy every living creature as I have done.
22 As long as the earth endures,
seedtime and harvest,
cold and heat,
summer and winter, day and night,
shall not cease.'

THE COVENANT WITH NOAH

9 God blessed Noah and his sons, and
said to them, 'Be fruitful and multiply, and fill the earth. 2The fear and
dread of you shall rest on every animal
of the earth, and on every bird of the
air, on everything that creeps on the
ground, and on all the fish of the sea;
into your hand they are delivered. 3Ev-
ery moving thing that lives shall be food
for you; and just as I gave you the green
plants, I give you everything. 4Only,
you shall not eat flesh with its life, that
is, its blood. 5For your own lifeblood I
will surely require a reckoning: from
every animal I will require it and from
human beings, each one for the blood of
another, I will require a reckoning for
human life.
6 Whoever sheds the blood
of a human,
by a human shall that person's
blood be shed;
for in his own image
God made humankind.
7And you, be fruitful and multiply,
abound on the earth and multiply in it.'

8 Then God said to Noah and to his
sons with him, 9'As for me, I am establishing my covenant with you and your
descendants after you, 10and with every living creature that is with you, the
birds, the domestic animals, and every
animal of the earth with you, as many
as came out of the ark.[a] 11I establish my
covenant with you, that never again
shall all flesh be cut off by the waters of
a flood, and never again shall there be
a flood to destroy the earth.' 12God said,
'This is the sign of the covenant that I
make between me and you and every
living creature that is with you, for
all future generations: 13I have set my
bow in the clouds, and it shall be a sign

[a] 9.10 Gk: Heb adds *every animal of the earth*

of the covenant between me and the earth. 14 When I bring clouds over the earth and the bow is seen in the clouds, 15 I will remember my covenant that is between me and you and every living creature of all flesh; and the waters shall never again become a flood to destroy all flesh. 16 When the bow is in the clouds, I will see it and remember the everlasting covenant between God and every living creature of all flesh that is on the earth.' 17 God said to Noah, 'This is the sign of the covenant that I have established between me and all flesh that is on the earth.'

NOAH AND HIS SONS

18 The sons of Noah who went out of the ark were Shem, Ham, and Japheth. Ham was the father of Canaan. 19 These three were the sons of Noah; and from these the whole earth was peopled.

20 Noah, a man of the soil, was the first to plant a vineyard. 21 He drank some of the wine and became drunk, and he lay uncovered in his tent. 22 And Ham, the father of Canaan, saw the nakedness of his father, and told his two brothers outside. 23 Then Shem and Japheth took a garment, laid it on both their shoulders, and walked backwards and covered the nakedness of their father; their faces were turned away, and they did not see their father's nakedness. 24 When Noah awoke from his wine and knew what his youngest son had done to him, 25 he said,

'Cursed be Canaan;
lowest of slaves shall he be
to his brothers.'

26 He also said,

'Blessed by the LORD my
God be Shem;
and let Canaan be his slave.
27 May God make space for[b] Japheth,
and let him live in the
tents of Shem;
and let Canaan be his slave.'

28 After the flood Noah lived for three hundred and fifty years. 29 All the days of Noah were nine hundred and fifty years; and he died.

NATIONS DESCENDED FROM NOAH

10 These are the descendants of Noah's sons, Shem, Ham, and Japheth; children were born to them after the flood.

2 The descendants of Japheth: Gomer, Magog, Madai, Javan, Tubal, Meshech, and Tiras. 3 The descendants of Gomer: Ashkenaz, Riphath, and Togarmah. 4 The descendants of Javan: Elishah, Tarshish, Kittim, and Rodanim.[c] 5 From these the coastland peoples spread. These are the descendants of Japheth[d] in their lands, with their own language, by their families, in their nations.

6 The descendants of Ham: Cush, Egypt, Put, and Canaan. 7 The descendants of Cush: Seba, Havilah, Sabtah, Raamah, and Sabteca. The descendants of Raamah: Sheba and Dedan. 8 Cush became the father of Nimrod; he was the first on earth to become a mighty warrior. 9 He was a mighty hunter before the LORD; therefore it is said, 'Like Nimrod a mighty hunter before the LORD.' 10 The beginning of his kingdom was Babel, Erech, and Accad, all of them in the land of Shinar. 11 From that land he went into Assyria, and built Nineveh, Rehoboth-ir, Calah, and 12 Resen between Nineveh and Calah; that is the great city. 13 Egypt became the father of Ludim, Anamim, Lehabim, Naphtuhim, 14 Pathrusim, Casluhim, and Caphtorim, from which the Philistines come.[e]

15 Canaan became the father of Sidon his firstborn, and Heth, 16 and the Jebusites, the Amorites, the Girgashites, 17 the Hivites, the Arkites, the Sinites, 18 the Arvadites, the Zemarites, and the Hamathites. Afterwards the families of the Canaanites spread abroad. 19 And the territory of the Canaanites extended from Sidon, in the direction of Gerar, as far as Gaza, and in the direction of Sodom, Gomorrah, Admah, and Zeboiim, as far as Lasha. 20 These are the descendants of Ham, by their families, their languages, their lands, and their nations.

21 To Shem also, the father of all the children of Eber, the elder brother of Japheth, children were born. 22 The descendants of Shem: Elam, Asshur, Arpachshad, Lud, and Aram. 23 The descendants of Aram: Uz, Hul, Gether, and Mash. 24 Arpachshad became the father of Shelah; and Shelah became the father of Eber. 25 To Eber were born two sons: the name of one was Peleg,[f] for in his days the earth was divided, and his brother's name was Joktan. 26 Joktan became the father of Almodad, Sheleph, Hazarmaveth, Jerah, 27 Hadoram, Uzal, Diklah,

[b] **9.27** Heb *yapht*, a play on *Japheth* [c] **10.4** Heb Mss Sam Gk See 1 Chr 1.7: MT *Dodanim*
[d] **10.5** Compare verses 20, 31. Heb lacks *These are the descendants of Japheth* [e] **10.14** Cn: Heb *Casluhim, from which the Philistines come, and Caphtorim* [f] **10.25** That is *Division*

28 Obal, Abimael, Sheba, 29 Ophir, Havilah, and Jobab; all these were the descendants of Joktan. 30 The territory in which they lived extended from Mesha in the direction of Sephar, the hill country of the east. 31 These are the descendants of Shem, by their families, their languages, their lands, and their nations.

32 These are the families of Noah's sons, according to their genealogies, in their nations; and from these the nations spread abroad on the earth after the flood.

THE TOWER OF BABEL

11 Now the whole earth had one language and the same words. 2 And as they migrated from the east,[g] they came upon a plain in the land of Shinar and settled there. 3 And they said to one another, 'Come, let us make bricks, and burn them thoroughly.' And they had brick for stone, and bitumen for mortar. 4 Then they said, 'Come, let us build ourselves a city, and a tower with its top in the heavens, and let us make a name for ourselves; otherwise we shall be scattered abroad upon the face of the whole earth.' 5 The LORD came down to see the city and the tower, which mortals had built. 6 And the LORD said, 'Look, they are one people, and they have all one language; and this is only the beginning of what they will do; nothing that they propose to do will now be impossible for them. 7 Come, let us go down, and confuse their language there, so that they will not understand one another's speech.' 8 So the LORD scattered them abroad from there over the face of all the earth, and they left off building the city. 9 Therefore it was called Babel, because there the LORD confused[h] the language of all the earth; and from there the LORD scattered them abroad over the face of all the earth.

DESCENDANTS OF SHEM

10 These are the descendants of Shem. When Shem was one hundred years old, he became the father of Arpachshad two years after the flood; 11 and Shem lived after the birth of Arpachshad for five hundred years, and had other sons and daughters.

12 When Arpachshad had lived for thirty-five years, he became the father of Shelah; 13 and Arpachshad lived after the birth of Shelah for four hundred and three years, and had other sons and daughters.

14 When Shelah had lived for thirty years, he became the father of Eber; 15 and Shelah lived after the birth of Eber for four hundred and three years, and had other sons and daughters.

16 When Eber had lived for thirty-four years, he became the father of Peleg; 17 and Eber lived after the birth of Peleg for four hundred and thirty years, and had other sons and daughters.

18 When Peleg had lived for thirty years, he became the father of Reu; 19 and Peleg lived after the birth of Reu for two hundred and nine years, and had other sons and daughters.

20 When Reu had lived for thirty-two years, he became the father of Serug; 21 and Reu lived after the birth of Serug for two hundred and seven years, and had other sons and daughters.

22 When Serug had lived for thirty years, he became the father of Nahor; 23 and Serug lived after the birth of Nahor for two hundred years, and had other sons and daughters.

24 When Nahor had lived for twenty-nine years, he became the father of Terah; 25 and Nahor lived after the birth of Terah for one hundred and nineteen years, and had other sons and daughters.

26 When Terah had lived for seventy years, he became the father of Abram, Nahor, and Haran.

DESCENDANTS OF TERAH

27 Now these are the descendants of Terah. Terah was the father of Abram, Nahor, and Haran; and Haran was the father of Lot. 28 Haran died before his father Terah in the land of his birth, in Ur of the Chaldeans. 29 Abram and Nahor took wives; the name of Abram's wife was Sarai, and the name of Nahor's wife was Milcah. She was the daughter of Haran the father of Milcah and Iscah. 30 Now Sarai was barren; she had no child.

31 Terah took his son Abram and his grandson Lot son of Haran, and his daughter-in-law Sarai, his son Abram's wife, and they went out together from Ur of the Chaldeans to go into the land of Canaan; but when they came to Haran, they settled there. 32 The days of Terah were two hundred and five years; and Terah died in Haran.

[g] **11.2** Or *migrated eastward* [h] **11.9** Heb *balal*, meaning *to confuse*

THE CALL OF ABRAM

12 Now the LORD said to Abram,
'Go from your country and your
kindred and your father's house to the
land that I will show you. 2 I will make of
you a great nation, and I will bless you,
and make your name great, so that you
will be a blessing. 3 I will bless those who
bless you, and the one who curses you I
will curse; and in you all the families of
the earth shall be blessed.'[i]

4 So Abram went, as the LORD
had told him; and Lot went with him.
Abram was seventy-five years old when
he departed from Haran. 5 Abram took
his wife Sarai and his brother's son Lot,
and all the possessions that they had
gathered, and the persons whom they
had acquired in Haran; and they set
forth to go to the land of Canaan. When
they had come to the land of Canaan,
6 Abram passed through the land to the
place at Shechem, to the oak[j] of Moreh.
At that time the Canaanites were in
the land. 7 Then the LORD appeared to
Abram, and said, 'To your offspring[k] I
will give this land.' So he built there an
altar to the LORD, who had appeared to
him. 8 From there he moved on to the
hill country on the east of Bethel, and
pitched his tent, with Bethel on the west
and Ai on the east; and there he built an
altar to the LORD and invoked the name
of the LORD. 9 And Abram journeyed on
by stages towards the Negeb.

ABRAM AND SARAI IN EGYPT

10 Now there was a famine in the
land. So Abram went down to Egypt to
reside there as an alien, for the famine
was severe in the land. 11 When he was
about to enter Egypt, he said to his wife
Sarai, 'I know well that you are a woman
beautiful in appearance; 12 and when the
Egyptians see you, they will say, "This
is his wife"; then they will kill me, but
they will let you live. 13 Say you are my
sister, so that it may go well with me
because of you, and that my life may be
spared on your account.' 14 When Abram
entered Egypt the Egyptians saw that
the woman was very beautiful. 15 When
the officials of Pharaoh saw her, they
praised her to Pharaoh. And the woman
was taken into Pharaoh's house. 16 And
for her sake he dealt well with Abram;
and he had sheep, oxen, male donkeys,
male and female slaves, female donkeys,
and camels.

17 But the LORD afflicted Pharaoh
and his house with great plagues because of Sarai, Abram's wife. 18 So Pharaoh called Abram, and said, 'What is this
you have done to me? Why did you not
tell me that she was your wife? 19 Why
did you say, "She is my sister", so that I
took her for my wife? Now then, here is
your wife; take her, and be gone.' 20 And
Pharaoh gave his men orders concerning him; and they set him on the way,
with his wife and all that he had.

ABRAM AND LOT SEPARATE

13 So Abram went up from Egypt,
he and his wife and all that he
had, and Lot with him, into the Negeb.

2 Now Abram was very rich in livestock, in silver, and in gold. 3 He journeyed on by stages from the Negeb as
far as Bethel, to the place where his tent
had been at the beginning, between
Bethel and Ai, 4 to the place where he
had made an altar at the first; and there
Abram called on the name of the LORD.
5 Now Lot, who went with Abram, also
had flocks and herds and tents, 6 so that
the land could not support both of them
living together; for their possessions
were so great that they could not live
together, 7 and there was strife between
the herders of Abram's livestock and the
herders of Lot's livestock. At that time
the Canaanites and the Perizzites lived
in the land.

8 Then Abram said to Lot, 'Let there
be no strife between you and me, and between your herders and my herders; for
we are kindred. 9 Is not the whole land
before you? Separate yourself from me.
If you take the left hand, then I will go to
the right; or if you take the right hand,
then I will go to the left.' 10 Lot looked
about him, and saw that the plain of the
Jordan was well watered everywhere
like the garden of the LORD, like the
land of Egypt, in the direction of Zoar;
this was before the LORD had destroyed
Sodom and Gomorrah. 11 So Lot chose
for himself all the plain of the Jordan,
and Lot journeyed eastwards; thus they
separated from each other. 12 Abram settled in the land of Canaan, while Lot
settled among the cities of the Plain and
moved his tent as far as Sodom. 13 Now
the people of Sodom were wicked, great
sinners against the LORD.

14 The LORD said to Abram, after Lot
had separated from him, 'Raise your
eyes now, and look from the place where

[i] **12.3** *Or by you all the families of the earth shall bless themselves* [j] **12.6** *Or terebinth*
[k] **12.7** Heb *seed*

you are, northwards and southwards
and eastwards and westwards; 15for all
the land that you see I will give to you
and to your offspring[l] for ever. 16I will
make your offspring like the dust of the
earth; so that if one can count the dust
of the earth, your offspring also can be
counted. 17Rise up, walk through the
length and the breadth of the land, for
I will give it to you.' 18So Abram moved
his tent, and came and settled by the
oaks[m] of Mamre, which are at Hebron;
and there he built an altar to the LORD.

LOT'S CAPTIVITY AND RESCUE

14 In the days of King Amraphel of
Shinar, King Arioch of Ellasar,
King Chedorlaomer of Elam, and King
Tidal of Goiim, 2these kings made war
with King Bera of Sodom, King Birsha
of Gomorrah, King Shinab of Admah,
King Shemeber of Zeboiim, and the
king of Bela (that is, Zoar). 3All these
joined forces in the Valley of Siddim
(that is, the Dead Sea).[n] 4For twelve
years they had served Chedorlaomer,
but in the thirteenth year they rebelled. 5In the fourteenth year Chedorlaomer and the kings who were with
him came and subdued the Rephaim
in Ashteroth-karnaim, the Zuzim in
Ham, the Emim in Shaveh-kiriathaim,
6and the Horites in the hill country of
Seir as far as El-paran on the edge of the
wilderness; 7then they turned back and
came to En-mishpat (that is, Kadesh),
and subdued all the country of the Amalekites, and also the Amorites who lived
in Hazazon-tamar. 8Then the king of
Sodom, the king of Gomorrah, the king
of Admah, the king of Zeboiim, and the
king of Bela (that is, Zoar) went out, and
they joined battle in the Valley of Siddim 9with King Chedorlaomer of Elam,
King Tidal of Goiim, King Amraphel of
Shinar, and King Arioch of Ellasar, four
kings against five. 10Now the Valley of
Siddim was full of bitumen pits; and as
the kings of Sodom and Gomorrah fled,
some fell into them, and the rest fled to
the hill country. 11So the enemy took all
the goods of Sodom and Gomorrah, and
all their provisions, and went their way;
12they also took Lot, the son of Abram's
brother, who lived in Sodom, and his
goods, and departed.

13 Then one who had escaped came
and told Abram the Hebrew, who was
living by the oaks[o] of Mamre the Amorite, brother of Eshcol and of Aner;
these were allies of Abram. 14When
Abram heard that his nephew had been
taken captive, he led forth his trained
men, born in his house, three hundred
and eighteen of them, and went in pursuit as far as Dan. 15He divided his forces
against them by night, he and his servants, and routed them and pursued
them to Hobah, north of Damascus.
16Then he brought back all the goods,
and also brought back his nephew Lot
with his goods, and the women and the
people.

ABRAM BLESSED BY MELCHIZEDEK

17 After his return from the defeat of
Chedorlaomer and the kings who were
with him, the king of Sodom went out
to meet him at the Valley of Shaveh
(that is, the King's Valley). 18And King
Melchizedek of Salem brought out bread
and wine; he was priest of God Most
High.[p] 19He blessed him and said,

'Blessed be Abram by God
Most High,[q]
maker of heaven and earth;
20 and blessed be God Most High,[r]
who has delivered your enemies
into your hand!'

And Abram gave him one-tenth of everything. 21Then the king of Sodom said
to Abram, 'Give me the people, but take
the goods for yourself.' 22But Abram
said to the king of Sodom, 'I have sworn
to the LORD, God Most High,[s] maker of
heaven and earth, 23that I would not
take a thread or a sandal-thong or anything that is yours, so that you might
not say, "I have made Abram rich." 24I
will take nothing but what the young
men have eaten, and the share of the
men who went with me—Aner, Eshcol,
and Mamre. Let them take their share.'

GOD'S COVENANT WITH ABRAM

15 After these things the word of
the LORD came to Abram in a
vision, 'Do not be afraid, Abram, I am
your shield; your reward shall be very
great.' 2But Abram said, 'O Lord GOD,
what will you give me, for I continue
childless, and the heir of my house is Eliezer of Damascus?'[t] 3And Abram said,
'You have given me no offspring, and
so a slave born in my house is to be my
heir.' 4But the word of the LORD came
to him, 'This man shall not be your heir;

[l] 13.15 Heb *seed* [m] 13.18 Or *terebinths*
[n] 14.3 Heb *Salt Sea* [o] 14.13 Or *terebinths*
[p] 14.18 Heb *El Elyon* [q] 14.19 Heb *El Elyon*
[r] 14.20 Heb *El Elyon* [s] 14.22 Heb *El Elyon*
[t] 15.2 Meaning of Heb uncertain

no one but your very own issue shall be
your heir.' 5He brought him outside and
said, 'Look towards heaven and count
the stars, if you are able to count them.'
Then he said to him, 'So shall your descendants be.' 6And he believed the
LORD; and the LORD[u] reckoned it to him
as righteousness.

7 Then he said to him, 'I am the LORD
who brought you from Ur of the Chaldeans, to give you this land to possess.'
8But he said, 'O Lord GOD, how am I to
know that I shall possess it?' 9He said to
him, 'Bring me a heifer three years old, a
female goat three years old, a ram three
years old, a turtle-dove, and a young pigeon.' 10He brought him all these and
cut them in two, laying each half over
against the other; but he did not cut the
birds in two. 11And when birds of prey
came down on the carcasses, Abram
drove them away.

12 As the sun was going down, a
deep sleep fell upon Abram, and a deep
and terrifying darkness descended upon
him. 13Then the LORD[v] said to Abram,
'Know this for certain, that your offspring shall be aliens in a land that is
not theirs, and shall be slaves there, and
they shall be oppressed for four hundred
years; 14but I will bring judgement on
the nation that they serve, and afterwards they shall come out with great
possessions. 15As for yourself, you shall
go to your ancestors in peace; you shall
be buried in a good old age. 16And they
shall come back here in the fourth generation; for the iniquity of the Amorites
is not yet complete.'

17 When the sun had gone down
and it was dark, a smoking fire-pot and
a flaming torch passed between these
pieces. 18On that day the LORD made a
covenant with Abram, saying, 'To your
descendants I give this land, from the
river of Egypt to the great river, the
river Euphrates, 19the land of the Kenites, the Kenizzites, the Kadmonites,
20the Hittites, the Perizzites, the Rephaim, 21the Amorites, the Canaanites,
the Girgashites, and the Jebusites.'

THE BIRTH OF ISHMAEL

16 Now Sarai, Abram's wife, bore
him no children. She had an
Egyptian slave-girl whose name was
Hagar, 2and Sarai said to Abram, 'You
see that the LORD has prevented me
from bearing children; go in to my
slave-girl; it may be that I shall obtain
children by her.' And Abram listened
to the voice of Sarai. 3So, after Abram
had lived for ten years in the land of Canaan, Sarai, Abram's wife, took Hagar
the Egyptian, her slave-girl, and gave
her to her husband Abram as a wife.
4He went in to Hagar, and she conceived; and when she saw that she had
conceived, she looked with contempt on
her mistress. 5Then Sarai said to Abram,
'May the wrong done to me be on you! I
gave my slave-girl to your embrace, and
when she saw that she had conceived,
she looked on me with contempt. May
the LORD judge between you and me!'
6But Abram said to Sarai, 'Your slave-
girl is in your power; do to her as you
please.' Then Sarai dealt harshly with
her, and she ran away from her.

7 The angel of the LORD found her
by a spring of water in the wilderness,
the spring on the way to Shur. 8And he
said, 'Hagar, slave-girl of Sarai, where
have you come from and where are you
going?' She said, 'I am running away
from my mistress Sarai.' 9The angel of
the LORD said to her, 'Return to your
mistress, and submit to her.' 10The angel of the LORD also said to her, 'I will
so greatly multiply your offspring that
they cannot be counted for multitude.'
11And the angel of the LORD said to her,

'Now you have conceived and
shall bear a son;
you shall call him Ishmael,[w]
for the LORD has given heed
to your affliction.
12 He shall be a wild ass of a man,
with his hand against everyone,
and everyone's hand against him;
and he shall live at odds
with all his kin.'

13So she named the LORD who spoke to
her, 'You are El-roi';[x] for she said, 'Have I
really seen God and remained alive after
seeing him?'[y] 14Therefore the well was
called Beer-lahai-roi;[z] it lies between
Kadesh and Bered.

15 Hagar bore Abram a son; and
Abram named his son, whom Hagar
bore, Ishmael. 16Abram was eighty-six
years old when Hagar bore him[a] Ishmael.

THE SIGN OF THE COVENANT

17 When Abram was ninety-nine
years old, the LORD appeared to
Abram, and said to him, 'I am God Al-

[u] 15.6 Heb *he* [v] 15.13 Heb *he* [w] 16.11 That is *God hears* [x] 16.13 Perhaps *God of seeing* or *God who sees* [y] 16.13 Meaning of Heb uncertain [z] 16.14 That is *the Well of the Living One who sees me* [a] 16.16 Heb *Abram*

mighty;[b] walk before me, and be blameless. 2And I will make my covenant between me and you, and will make you
exceedingly numerous.' 3Then Abram
fell on his face; and God said to him,
4'As for me, this is my covenant with
you: You shall be the ancestor of a multitude of nations. 5No longer shall your
name be Abram,[c] but your name shall
be Abraham;[d] for I have made you the
ancestor of a multitude of nations. 6I
will make you exceedingly fruitful; and
I will make nations of you, and kings
shall come from you. 7I will establish
my covenant between me and you, and
your offspring after you throughout
their generations, for an everlasting
covenant, to be God to you and to your
offspring[e] after you. 8And I will give to
you, and to your offspring after you, the
land where you are now an alien, all the
land of Canaan, for a perpetual holding;
and I will be their God.'

9 God said to Abraham, 'As for you,
you shall keep my covenant, you and
your offspring after you throughout
their generations. 10This is my covenant, which you shall keep, between
me and you and your offspring after
you: Every male among you shall be
circumcised. 11You shall circumcise the
flesh of your foreskins, and it shall be a
sign of the covenant between me and
you. 12Throughout your generations
every male among you shall be circumcised when he is eight days old, including the slave born in your house and the
one bought with your money from any
foreigner who is not of your offspring.
13Both the slave born in your house and
the one bought with your money must
be circumcised. So shall my covenant be
in your flesh an everlasting covenant.
14Any uncircumcised male who is not
circumcised in the flesh of his foreskin
shall be cut off from his people; he has
broken my covenant.'

15 God said to Abraham, 'As for Sarai your wife, you shall not call her Sarai, but Sarah shall be her name. 16I will
bless her, and moreover I will give you a
son by her. I will bless her, and she shall
give rise to nations; kings of peoples
shall come from her.' 17Then Abraham
fell on his face and laughed, and said to
himself, 'Can a child be born to a man
who is a hundred years old? Can Sarah,
who is ninety years old, bear a child?'
18And Abraham said to God, 'O that
Ishmael might live in your sight!' 19God
said, 'No, but your wife Sarah shall bear
you a son, and you shall name him
Isaac.[f] I will establish my covenant with
him as an everlasting covenant for his
offspring after him. 20As for Ishmael,
I have heard you; I will bless him and
make him fruitful and exceedingly numerous; he shall be the father of twelve
princes, and I will make him a great
nation. 21But my covenant I will establish with Isaac, whom Sarah shall bear
to you at this season next year.' 22And
when he had finished talking with him,
God went up from Abraham.

23 Then Abraham took his son Ishmael and all the slaves born in his house
or bought with his money, every male
among the men of Abraham's house,
and he circumcised the flesh of their
foreskins that very day, as God had said
to him. 24Abraham was ninety-nine
years old when he was circumcised in
the flesh of his foreskin. 25And his son
Ishmael was thirteen years old when he
was circumcised in the flesh of his foreskin. 26That very day Abraham and his
son Ishmael were circumcised; 27and all
the men of his house, slaves born in the
house and those bought with money
from a foreigner, were circumcised with
him.

A SON PROMISED TO ABRAHAM AND SARAH

18 The LORD appeared to Abraham[g] by the oaks[h] of Mamre, as
he sat at the entrance of his tent in the
heat of the day. 2He looked up and saw
three men standing near him. When he
saw them, he ran from the tent entrance
to meet them, and bowed down to the
ground. 3He said, 'My lord, if I find favour with you, do not pass by your
servant. 4Let a little water be brought,
and wash your feet, and rest yourselves
under the tree. 5Let me bring a little
bread, that you may refresh yourselves,
and after that you may pass on—since
you have come to your servant.' So they
said, 'Do as you have said.' 6And Abraham hastened into the tent to Sarah,
and said, 'Make ready quickly three
measures[i] of choice flour, knead it, and
make cakes.' 7Abraham ran to the herd,
and took a calf, tender and good, and
gave it to the servant, who hastened to

[b] 17.1 Traditional rendering of Heb *El Shaddai*
[c] 17.5 That is *exalted ancestor* [d] 17.5 Here taken to mean *ancestor of a multitude*
[e] 17.7 Heb *seed* [f] 17.19 That is *he laughs*
[g] 18.1 Heb *him* [h] 18.1 Or *terebinths*
[i] 18.6 Heb *seahs*

prepare it. 8 Then he took curds and milk
and the calf that he had prepared, and
set it before them; and he stood by them
under the tree while they ate.

9 They said to him, 'Where is your
wife Sarah?' And he said, 'There, in the
tent.' 10 Then one said, 'I will surely return to you in due season, and your wife
Sarah shall have a son.' And Sarah was
listening at the tent entrance behind
him. 11 Now Abraham and Sarah were
old, advanced in age; it had ceased to be
with Sarah after the manner of women.
12 So Sarah laughed to herself, saying,
'After I have grown old, and my husband is old, shall I have pleasure?' 13 The
LORD said to Abraham, 'Why did Sarah
laugh, and say, "Shall I indeed bear a
child, now that I am old?" 14 Is anything
too wonderful for the LORD? At the set
time I will return to you, in due season, and Sarah shall have a son.' 15 But
Sarah denied, saying, 'I did not laugh';
for she was afraid. He said, 'Oh yes, you
did laugh.'

JUDGEMENT PRONOUNCED ON SODOM

16 Then the men set out from there,
and they looked towards Sodom; and
Abraham went with them to set them
on their way. 17 The LORD said, 'Shall I
hide from Abraham what I am about
to do, 18 seeing that Abraham shall become a great and mighty nation, and all
the nations of the earth shall be blessed
in him?[j] 19 No, for I have chosen[k] him,
that he may charge his children and his
household after him to keep the way of
the LORD by doing righteousness and
justice; so that the LORD may bring about
for Abraham what he has promised him.'
20 Then the LORD said, 'How great is the
outcry against Sodom and Gomorrah
and how very grave their sin! 21 I must go
down and see whether they have done altogether according to the outcry that has
come to me; and if not, I will know.'

22 So the men turned from there, and
went towards Sodom, while Abraham
remained standing before the LORD.[l]
23 Then Abraham came near and said,
'Will you indeed sweep away the righteous with the wicked? 24 Suppose there
are fifty righteous within the city; will
you then sweep away the place and not
forgive it for the fifty righteous who are
in it? 25 Far be it from you to do such a
thing, to slay the righteous with the
wicked, so that the righteous fare as the
wicked! Far be that from you! Shall not
the Judge of all the earth do what is just?'
26 And the LORD said, 'If I find at Sodom
fifty righteous in the city, I will forgive
the whole place for their sake.' 27 Abraham answered, 'Let me take it upon myself to speak to the Lord, I who am but
dust and ashes. 28 Suppose five of the fifty
righteous are lacking? Will you destroy
the whole city for lack of five?' And he
said, 'I will not destroy it if I find forty-
five there.' 29 Again he spoke to him,
'Suppose forty are found there.' He answered, 'For the sake of forty I will not do
it.' 30 Then he said, 'Oh do not let the Lord
be angry if I speak. Suppose thirty are
found there.' He answered, 'I will not do
it, if I find thirty there.' 31 He said, 'Let me
take it upon myself to speak to the Lord.
Suppose twenty are found there.' He answered, 'For the sake of twenty I will not
destroy it.' 32 Then he said, 'Oh do not let
the Lord be angry if I speak just once
more. Suppose ten are found there.' He
answered, 'For the sake of ten I will not
destroy it.' 33 And the LORD went his way,
when he had finished speaking to Abraham; and Abraham returned to his place.

THE DEPRAVITY OF SODOM

19 The two angels came to Sodom
in the evening, and Lot was sitting in the gateway of Sodom. When
Lot saw them, he rose to meet them,
and bowed down with his face to the
ground. 2 He said, 'Please, my lords, turn
aside to your servant's house and spend
the night, and wash your feet; then you
can rise early and go on your way.' They
said, 'No; we will spend the night in the
square.' 3 But he urged them strongly; so
they turned aside to him and entered
his house; and he made them a feast,
and baked unleavened bread, and they
ate. 4 But before they lay down, the men
of the city, the men of Sodom, both
young and old, all the people to the last
man, surrounded the house; 5 and they
called to Lot, 'Where are the men who
came to you tonight? Bring them out
to us, so that we may know them.' 6 Lot
went out of the door to the men, shut
the door after him, 7 and said, 'I beg you,
my brothers, do not act so wickedly.
8 Look, I have two daughters who have
not known a man; let me bring them
out to you, and do to them as you please;
only do nothing to these men, for they

[j] **18.18** Or *and all the nations of the earth shall bless themselves by him* [k] **18.19** Heb *known*
[l] **18.22** Another ancient tradition reads *while the LORD remained standing before Abraham*

have come under the shelter of my roof.'
9But they replied, 'Stand back!' And
they said, 'This fellow came here as an
alien, and he would play the judge! Now
we will deal worse with you than with
them.' Then they pressed hard against
the man Lot, and came near the door
to break it down. 10But the men inside
reached out their hands and brought
Lot into the house with them, and shut
the door. 11And they struck with blindness the men who were at the door of
the house, both small and great, so that
they were unable to find the door.

SODOM AND GOMORRAH DESTROYED

12 Then the men said to Lot, 'Have
you anyone else here? Sons-in-law,
sons, daughters, or anyone you have in
the city—bring them out of the place.
13For we are about to destroy this place,
because the outcry against its people
has become great before the LORD, and
the LORD has sent us to destroy it.' 14So
Lot went out and said to his sons-in-
law, who were to marry his daughters,
'Up, get out of this place; for the LORD is
about to destroy the city.' But he seemed
to his sons-in-law to be jesting.

15 When morning dawned, the angels urged Lot, saying, 'Get up, take
your wife and your two daughters who
are here, or else you will be consumed
in the punishment of the city.' 16But he
lingered; so the men seized him and his
wife and his two daughters by the hand,
the LORD being merciful to him, and
they brought him out and left him outside the city. 17When they had brought
them outside, they[m] said, 'Flee for your
life; do not look back or stop anywhere
in the Plain; flee to the hills, or else
you will be consumed.' 18And Lot said
to them, 'Oh, no, my lords; 19your servant has found favour with you, and
you have shown me great kindness in
saving my life; but I cannot flee to the
hills, for fear the disaster will overtake
me and I die. 20Look, that city is near
enough to flee to, and it is a little one.
Let me escape there—is it not a little
one?—and my life will be saved!' 21He
said to him, 'Very well, I grant you this
favour too, and will not overthrow the
city of which you have spoken. 22Hurry,
escape there, for I can do nothing until
you arrive there.' Therefore the city was
called Zoar.[n] 23The sun had risen on the
earth when Lot came to Zoar.

24 Then the LORD rained on Sodom
and Gomorrah sulphur and fire from
the LORD out of heaven; 25and he overthrew those cities, and all the Plain,
and all the inhabitants of the cities, and
what grew on the ground. 26But Lot's
wife, behind him, looked back, and she
became a pillar of salt.

27 Abraham went early in the morning to the place where he had stood before the LORD; 28and he looked down
towards Sodom and Gomorrah and towards all the land of the Plain, and saw
the smoke of the land going up like the
smoke of a furnace.

29 So it was that, when God destroyed the cities of the Plain, God remembered Abraham, and sent Lot out
of the midst of the overthrow, when he
overthrew the cities in which Lot had
settled.

THE SHAMEFUL ORIGIN OF MOAB AND AMMON

30 Now Lot went up out of Zoar and
settled in the hills with his two daughters, for he was afraid to stay in Zoar; so
he lived in a cave with his two daughters. 31And the firstborn said to the
younger, 'Our father is old, and there is
not a man on earth to come in to us after the manner of all the world. 32Come,
let us make our father drink wine, and
we will lie with him, so that we may
preserve offspring through our father.'
33So they made their father drink wine
that night; and the firstborn went in,
and lay with her father; he did not know
when she lay down or when she rose.
34On the next day, the firstborn said
to the younger, 'Look, I lay last night
with my father; let us make him drink
wine tonight also; then you go in and
lie with him, so that we may preserve
offspring through our father.' 35So they
made their father drink wine that night
also; and the younger rose, and lay with
him; and he did not know when she lay
down or when she rose. 36Thus both the
daughters of Lot became pregnant by
their father. 37The firstborn bore a son,
and named him Moab; he is the ancestor of the Moabites to this day. 38The
younger also bore a son and named him
Ben-ammi; he is the ancestor of the
Ammonites to this day.

ABRAHAM AND SARAH AT GERAR

20 From there Abraham journeyed towards the region of
the Negeb, and settled between Kadesh

[m] 19.17 Gk Syr Vg: Heb *he*   [n] 19.22 That is *Little*

and Shur. While residing in Gerar as an alien, 2Abraham said of his wife Sarah, 'She is my sister.' And King Abimelech of Gerar sent and took Sarah. 3But God came to Abimelech in a dream by night, and said to him, 'You are about to die because of the woman whom you have taken; for she is a married woman.' 4Now Abimelech had not approached her; so he said, 'Lord, will you destroy an innocent people? 5Did he not himself say to me, "She is my sister"? And she herself said, "He is my brother." I did this in the integrity of my heart and the innocence of my hands.' 6Then God said to him in the dream, 'Yes, I know that you did this in the integrity of your heart; furthermore it was I who kept you from sinning against me. Therefore I did not let you touch her. 7Now then, return the man's wife; for he is a prophet, and he will pray for you and you shall live. But if you do not restore her, know that you shall surely die, you and all that are yours.'

8 So Abimelech rose early in the morning, and called all his servants and told them all these things; and the men were very much afraid. 9Then Abimelech called Abraham, and said to him, 'What have you done to us? How have I sinned against you, that you have brought such great guilt on me and my kingdom? You have done things to me that ought not to be done.' 10And Abimelech said to Abraham, 'What were you thinking of, that you did this thing?' 11Abraham said, 'I did it because I thought, There is no fear of God at all in this place, and they will kill me because of my wife. 12Besides, she is indeed my sister, the daughter of my father but not the daughter of my mother; and she became my wife. 13And when God caused me to wander from my father's house, I said to her, "This is the kindness you must do me: at every place to which we come, say of me, He is my brother." ' 14Then Abimelech took sheep and oxen, and male and female slaves, and gave them to Abraham, and restored his wife Sarah to him. 15Abimelech said, 'My land is before you; settle where it pleases you.' 16To Sarah he said, 'Look, I have given your brother a thousand pieces of silver; it is your exoneration before all who are with you; you are completely vindicated.' 17Then Abraham prayed to God; and God healed Abimelech, and also healed his wife and female slaves so that they bore children. 18For the LORD had closed fast all the wombs of the house of Abimelech because of Sarah, Abraham's wife.

THE BIRTH OF ISAAC

21 The LORD dealt with Sarah as he had said, and the LORD did for Sarah as he had promised. 2Sarah conceived and bore Abraham a son in his old age, at the time of which God had spoken to him. 3Abraham gave the name Isaac to his son whom Sarah bore him. 4And Abraham circumcised his son Isaac when he was eight days old, as God had commanded him. 5Abraham was a hundred years old when his son Isaac was born to him. 6Now Sarah said, 'God has brought laughter for me; everyone who hears will laugh with me.' 7And she said, 'Who would ever have said to Abraham that Sarah would nurse children? Yet I have borne him a son in his old age.'

HAGAR AND ISHMAEL SENT AWAY

8 The child grew, and was weaned; and Abraham made a great feast on the day that Isaac was weaned. 9But Sarah saw the son of Hagar the Egyptian, whom she had borne to Abraham, playing with her son Isaac.[o] 10So she said to Abraham, 'Cast out this slave woman with her son; for the son of this slave woman shall not inherit along with my son Isaac.' 11The matter was very distressing to Abraham on account of his son. 12But God said to Abraham, 'Do not be distressed because of the boy and because of your slave woman; whatever Sarah says to you, do as she tells you, for it is through Isaac that offspring shall be named after you. 13As for the son of the slave woman, I will make a nation of him also, because he is your offspring.' 14So Abraham rose early in the morning, and took bread and a skin of water, and gave it to Hagar, putting it on her shoulder, along with the child, and sent her away. And she departed, and wandered about in the wilderness of Beer-sheba.

15 When the water in the skin was gone, she cast the child under one of the bushes. 16Then she went and sat down opposite him a good way off, about the distance of a bowshot; for she said, 'Do not let me look on the death of the child.' And as she sat opposite him, she lifted up her voice and wept. 17And God heard the voice of the boy; and the angel

[o] 21.9 Gk Vg: Heb lacks *with her son Isaac*

of God called to Hagar from heaven, and
said to her, 'What troubles you, Hagar?
Do not be afraid; for God has heard the
voice of the boy where he is. 18Come, lift
up the boy and hold him fast with your
hand, for I will make a great nation of
him.' 19Then God opened her eyes, and
she saw a well of water. She went, and
filled the skin with water, and gave the
boy a drink.

20 God was with the boy, and he
grew up; he lived in the wilderness, and
became an expert with the bow. 21He
lived in the wilderness of Paran; and his
mother got a wife for him from the land
of Egypt.

ABRAHAM AND ABIMELECH MAKE A COVENANT

22 At that time Abimelech, with Phicol the commander of his army, said to
Abraham, 'God is with you in all that you
do; 23now therefore swear to me here by
God that you will not deal falsely with
me or with my offspring or with my
posterity, but as I have dealt loyally with
you, you will deal with me and with the
land where you have resided as an alien.'
24And Abraham said, 'I swear it.'

25 When Abraham complained to
Abimelech about a well of water that
Abimelech's servants had seized,
26Abimelech said, 'I do not know who
has done this; you did not tell me, and
I have not heard of it until today.' 27So
Abraham took sheep and oxen and gave
them to Abimelech, and the two men
made a covenant. 28Abraham set apart
seven ewe lambs of the flock. 29And
Abimelech said to Abraham, 'What is
the meaning of these seven ewe lambs
that you have set apart?' 30He said,
'These seven ewe lambs you shall accept from my hand, in order that you
may be a witness for me that I dug this
well.' 31Therefore that place was called
Beer-sheba;[p] because there both of them
swore an oath. 32When they had made
a covenant at Beer-sheba, Abimelech,
with Phicol the commander of his army,
left and returned to the land of the Philistines. 33Abraham[q] planted a tamarisk
tree in Beer-sheba, and called there on
the name of the LORD, the Everlasting
God.[r] 34And Abraham resided as an
alien for many days in the land of the
Philistines.

THE COMMAND TO SACRIFICE ISAAC

22 After these things God tested
Abraham. He said to him, 'Abraham!' And he said, 'Here I am.' 2He said,
'Take your son, your only son Isaac,
whom you love, and go to the land of
Moriah, and offer him there as a burnt-
offering on one of the mountains that I
shall show you.' 3So Abraham rose early
in the morning, saddled his donkey,
and took two of his young men with
him, and his son Isaac; he cut the wood
for the burnt-offering, and set out and
went to the place in the distance that
God had shown him. 4On the third day
Abraham looked up and saw the place
far away. 5Then Abraham said to his
young men, 'Stay here with the donkey; the boy and I will go over there;
we will worship, and then we will come
back to you.' 6Abraham took the wood
of the burnt-offering and laid it on his
son Isaac, and he himself carried the
fire and the knife. So the two of them
walked on together. 7Isaac said to his
father Abraham, 'Father!' And he said,
'Here I am, my son.' He said, 'The fire
and the wood are here, but where is the
lamb for a burnt-offering?' 8Abraham
said, 'God himself will provide the lamb
for a burnt-offering, my son.' So the two
of them walked on together.

9 When they came to the place that
God had shown him, Abraham built an
altar there and laid the wood in order.
He bound his son Isaac, and laid him
on the altar, on top of the wood. 10Then
Abraham reached out his hand and took
the knife to kill[s] his son. 11But the angel
of the LORD called to him from heaven,
and said, 'Abraham, Abraham!' And he
said, 'Here I am.' 12He said, 'Do not lay
your hand on the boy or do anything to
him; for now I know that you fear God,
since you have not withheld your son,
your only son, from me.' 13And Abraham looked up and saw a ram, caught
in a thicket by its horns. Abraham went
and took the ram and offered it up as a
burnt-offering instead of his son. 14So
Abraham called that place 'The LORD
will provide';[t] as it is said to this day,
'On the mount of the LORD it shall be
provided.'[u]

15 The angel of the LORD called to
Abraham a second time from heaven,
16and said, 'By myself I have sworn, says
the LORD: Because you have done this,
and have not withheld your son, your

p 21.31 That is *Well of seven* or *Well of the oath*
q 21.33 Heb *He* r 21.33 Or *the LORD, El Olam*
s 22.10 Or *to slaughter* t 22.14 Or *will see*; Heb traditionally transliterated *Jehovah Jireh*
u 22.14 Or *he shall be seen*

only son, [17]I will indeed bless you, and
I will make your offspring as numerous
as the stars of heaven and as the sand
that is on the seashore. And your offspring shall possess the gate of their enemies, [18]and by your offspring shall all
the nations of the earth gain blessing
for themselves, because you have obeyed
my voice.' [19]So Abraham returned to his
young men, and they arose and went
together to Beer-sheba; and Abraham
lived at Beer-sheba.

THE CHILDREN OF NAHOR

20 Now after these things it was told
Abraham, 'Milcah also has borne children, to your brother Nahor: [21]Uz the
firstborn, Buz his brother, Kemuel the
father of Aram, [22]Chesed, Hazo, Pildash,
Jidlaph, and Bethuel.' [23]Bethuel became
the father of Rebekah. These eight Milcah bore to Nahor, Abraham's brother.
[24]Moreover, his concubine, whose name
was Reumah, bore Tebah, Gaham, Ta-
hash, and Maacah.

SARAH'S DEATH AND BURIAL

23 Sarah lived for one hundred and
twenty-seven years; this was
the length of Sarah's life. [2]And Sarah
died at Kiriath-arba (that is, Hebron) in
the land of Canaan; and Abraham went
in to mourn for Sarah and to weep for
her. [3]Abraham rose up from beside his
dead, and said to the Hittites, [4]'I am a
stranger and an alien residing among
you; give me property among you for a
burying-place, so that I may bury my
dead out of my sight.' [5]The Hittites answered Abraham, [6]'Hear us, my lord;
you are a mighty prince among us.
Bury your dead in the choicest of our
burial places; none of us will withhold
from you any burial ground for burying
your dead.' [7]Abraham rose and bowed
to the Hittites, the people of the land.
[8]He said to them, 'If you are willing that
I should bury my dead out of my sight,
hear me, and entreat for me Ephron son
of Zohar, [9]so that he may give me the
cave of Machpelah, which he owns; it is
at the end of his field. For the full price
let him give it to me in your presence as
a possession for a burying-place.' [10]Now
Ephron was sitting among the Hittites;
and Ephron the Hittite answered Abraham in the hearing of the Hittites, of
all who went in at the gate of his city,
[11]'No, my lord, hear me; I give you the
field, and I give you the cave that is in it;
in the presence of my people I give it to
you; bury your dead.' [12]Then Abraham
bowed down before the people of the
land. [13]He said to Ephron in the hearing of the people of the land, 'If you only
will listen to me! I will give the price
of the field; accept it from me, so that I
may bury my dead there.' [14]Ephron answered Abraham, [15]'My lord, listen to
me; a piece of land worth four hundred
shekels of silver—what is that between
you and me? Bury your dead.' [16]Abra-
ham agreed with Ephron; and Abraham
weighed out for Ephron the silver that
he had named in the hearing of the Hittites, four hundred shekels of silver, according to the weights current among
the merchants.

17 So the field of Ephron in Machpelah, which was to the east of Mamre, the
field with the cave that was in it and all
the trees that were in the field, throughout its whole area, passed [18]to Abraham
as a possession in the presence of the
Hittites, in the presence of all who went
in at the gate of his city. [19]After this,
Abraham buried Sarah his wife in the
cave of the field of Machpelah facing
Mamre (that is, Hebron) in the land of
Canaan. [20]The field and the cave that is
in it passed from the Hittites into Abraham's possession as a burying-place.

THE MARRIAGE OF ISAAC AND REBEKAH

24 Now Abraham was old, well advanced in years; and the LORD
had blessed Abraham in all things.
[2]Abraham said to his servant, the oldest of his house, who had charge of all
that he had, 'Put your hand under my
thigh [3]and I will make you swear by the
LORD, the God of heaven and earth, that
you will not get a wife for my son from
the daughters of the Canaanites, among
whom I live, [4]but will go to my country and to my kindred and get a wife
for my son Isaac.' [5]The servant said to
him, 'Perhaps the woman may not be
willing to follow me to this land; must
I then take your son back to the land
from which you came?' [6]Abraham said
to him, 'See to it that you do not take my
son back there. [7]The LORD, the God of
heaven, who took me from my father's
house and from the land of my birth,
and who spoke to me and swore to me,
"To your offspring I will give this land",
he will send his angel before you; you
shall take a wife for my son from there.
[8]But if the woman is not willing to follow you, then you will be free from this

oath of mine; only you must not take my son back there.' 9 So the servant put his hand under the thigh of Abraham his master and swore to him concerning this matter.

10 Then the servant took ten of his master's camels and departed, taking all kinds of choice gifts from his master; and he set out and went to Aram-naharaim, to the city of Nahor. 11 He made the camels kneel down outside the city by the well of water; it was towards evening, the time when women go out to draw water. 12 And he said, 'O LORD, God of my master Abraham, please grant me success today and show steadfast love to my master Abraham. 13 I am standing here by the spring of water, and the daughters of the townspeople are coming out to draw water. 14 Let the girl to whom I shall say, "Please offer your jar that I may drink", and who shall say, "Drink, and I will water your camels"—let her be the one whom you have appointed for your servant Isaac. By this I shall know that you have shown steadfast love to my master.'

15 Before he had finished speaking, there was Rebekah, who was born to Bethuel son of Milcah, the wife of Nahor, Abraham's brother, coming out with her water-jar on her shoulder. 16 The girl was very fair to look upon, a virgin whom no man had known. She went down to the spring, filled her jar, and came up. 17 Then the servant ran to meet her and said, 'Please let me sip a little water from your jar.' 18 'Drink, my lord,' she said, and quickly lowered her jar upon her hand and gave him a drink. 19 When she had finished giving him a drink, she said, 'I will draw for your camels also, until they have finished drinking.' 20 So she quickly emptied her jar into the trough and ran again to the well to draw, and she drew for all his camels. 21 The man gazed at her in silence to learn whether or not the LORD had made his journey successful.

22 When the camels had finished drinking, the man took a gold nose-ring weighing a half-shekel, and two bracelets for her arms weighing ten gold shekels, 23 and said, 'Tell me whose daughter you are. Is there room in your father's house for us to spend the night?' 24 She said to him, 'I am the daughter of Bethuel son of Milcah, whom she bore to Nahor.' 25 She added, 'We have plenty of straw and fodder and a place to spend the night.' 26 The man bowed his head and worshipped the LORD 27 and said, 'Blessed be the LORD, the God of my master Abraham, who has not forsaken his steadfast love and his faithfulness towards my master. As for me, the LORD has led me on the way to the house of my master's kin.'

28 Then the girl ran and told her mother's household about these things. 29 Rebekah had a brother whose name was Laban; and Laban ran out to the man, to the spring. 30 As soon as he had seen the nose-ring, and the bracelets on his sister's arms, and when he heard the words of his sister Rebekah, 'Thus the man spoke to me', he went to the man; and there he was, standing by the camels at the spring. 31 He said, 'Come in, O blessed of the LORD. Why do you stand outside when I have prepared the house and a place for the camels?' 32 So the man came into the house; and Laban unloaded the camels, and gave him straw and fodder for the camels, and water to wash his feet and the feet of the men who were with him. 33 Then food was set before him to eat; but he said, 'I will not eat until I have told my errand.' He said, 'Speak on.'

34 So he said, 'I am Abraham's servant. 35 The LORD has greatly blessed my master, and he has become wealthy; he has given him flocks and herds, silver and gold, male and female slaves, camels and donkeys. 36 And Sarah my master's wife bore a son to my master when she was old; and he has given him all that he has. 37 My master made me swear, saying, "You shall not take a wife for my son from the daughters of the Canaanites, in whose land I live; 38 but you shall go to my father's house, to my kindred, and get a wife for my son." 39 I said to my master, "Perhaps the woman will not follow me." 40 But he said to me, "The LORD, before whom I walk, will send his angel with you and make your way successful. You shall get a wife for my son from my kindred, from my father's house. 41 Then you will be free from my oath, when you come to my kindred; even if they will not give her to you, you will be free from my oath."

42 'I came today to the spring, and said, "O LORD, the God of my master Abraham, if now you will only make successful the way I am going! 43 I am standing here by the spring of water; let the young woman who comes out to draw, to whom I shall say, 'Please give me a little water from your jar to drink,'

44 and who will say to me, 'Drink, and I
will draw for your camels also'—let her
be the woman whom the LORD has appointed for my master's son."
45 'Before I had finished speaking in
my heart, there was Rebekah coming
out with her water-jar on her shoulder;
and she went down to the spring, and
drew. I said to her, "Please let me drink."
46 She quickly let down her jar from her
shoulder, and said, "Drink, and I will
also water your camels." So I drank, and
she also watered the camels. 47 Then I
asked her, "Whose daughter are you?"
She said, "The daughter of Bethuel, Nahor's son, whom Milcah bore to him."
So I put the ring on her nose, and the
bracelets on her arms. 48 Then I bowed
my head and worshipped the LORD, and
blessed the LORD, the God of my master
Abraham, who had led me by the right
way to obtain the daughter of my master's kinsman for his son. 49 Now then, if
you will deal loyally and truly with my
master, tell me; and if not, tell me, so
that I may turn either to the right hand
or to the left.'
50 Then Laban and Bethuel answered, 'The thing comes from the
LORD; we cannot speak to you anything
bad or good. 51 Look, Rebekah is before
you; take her and go, and let her be the
wife of your master's son, as the LORD
has spoken.'
52 When Abraham's servant heard
their words, he bowed himself to the
ground before the LORD. 53 And the servant brought out jewellery of silver and
of gold, and garments, and gave them to
Rebekah; he also gave to her brother and
to her mother costly ornaments. 54 Then
he and the men who were with him ate
and drank, and they spent the night
there. When they rose in the morning,
he said, 'Send me back to my master.'
55 Her brother and her mother said, 'Let
the girl remain with us a while, at least
ten days; after that she may go.' 56 But he
said to them, 'Do not delay me, since the
LORD has made my journey successful;
let me go, that I may go to my master.'
57 They said, 'We will call the girl, and
ask her.' 58 And they called Rebekah,
and said to her, 'Will you go with this
man?' She said, 'I will.' 59 So they sent
away their sister Rebekah and her nurse
along with Abraham's servant and his
men. 60 And they blessed Rebekah and
said to her,

'May you, our sister, become
thousands of myriads;
may your offspring gain possession
of the gates of their foes.'

61 Then Rebekah and her maids rose up,
mounted the camels, and followed the
man; thus the servant took Rebekah,
and went his way.
62 Now Isaac had come from[v] Beer-
lahai-roi, and was settled in the Negeb.
63 Isaac went out in the evening to walk[w]
in the field; and looking up, he saw camels
coming. 64 And Rebekah looked up, and
when she saw Isaac, she slipped quickly
from the camel, 65 and said to the servant,
'Who is the man over there, walking in
the field to meet us?' The servant said, 'It
is my master.' So she took her veil and covered herself. 66 And the servant told Isaac
all the things that he had done. 67 Then
Isaac brought her into his mother Sarah's
tent. He took Rebekah, and she became
his wife; and he loved her. So Isaac was
comforted after his mother's death.

ABRAHAM MARRIES KETURAH

25 Abraham took another wife,
whose name was Keturah. 2 She
bore him Zimran, Jokshan, Medan,
Midian, Ishbak, and Shuah. 3 Jokshan
was the father of Sheba and Dedan.
The sons of Dedan were Asshurim, Le-
tushim, and Leummim. 4 The sons of
Midian were Ephah, Epher, Hanoch,
Abida, and Eldaah. All these were the
children of Keturah. 5 Abraham gave all
he had to Isaac. 6 But to the sons of his
concubines Abraham gave gifts, while
he was still living, and he sent them
away from his son Isaac, eastwards to
the east country.

THE DEATH OF ABRAHAM

7 This is the length of Abraham's life,
one hundred and seventy-five years.
8 Abraham breathed his last and died in a
good old age, an old man and full of years,
and was gathered to his people. 9 His sons
Isaac and Ishmael buried him in the cave
of Machpelah, in the field of Ephron son
of Zohar the Hittite, east of Mamre, 10 the
field that Abraham purchased from the
Hittites. There Abraham was buried,
with his wife Sarah. 11 After the death of
Abraham God blessed his son Isaac. And
Isaac settled at Beer-lahai-roi.

ISHMAEL'S DESCENDANTS

12 These are the descendants of Ishmael, Abraham's son, whom Hagar the

[v] 24.62 Syr Tg: Heb *from coming to*
[w] 24.63 Meaning of Heb word is uncertain

Egyptian, Sarah's slave-girl, bore to
Abraham. 13 These are the names of the
sons of Ishmael, named in the order of
their birth: Nebaioth, the firstborn of
Ishmael; and Kedar, Adbeel, Mibsam,
14 Mishma, Dumah, Massa, 15 Hadad,
Tema, Jetur, Naphish, and Kedemah.
16 These are the sons of Ishmael and
these are their names, by their villages
and by their encampments, twelve
princes according to their tribes. 17 (This
is the length of the life of Ishmael,
one hundred and thirty-seven years;
he breathed his last and died, and was
gathered to his people.) 18 They settled
from Havilah to Shur, which is opposite
Egypt in the direction of Assyria; he settled down[x] alongside[y] all his people.

THE BIRTH AND YOUTH OF ESAU AND JACOB

19 These are the descendants of Isaac,
Abraham's son: Abraham was the father of Isaac, 20 and Isaac was forty years
old when he married Rebekah, daughter of Bethuel the Aramean of Paddan-
aram, sister of Laban the Aramean.
21 Isaac prayed to the LORD for his wife,
because she was barren; and the LORD
granted his prayer, and his wife Rebekah conceived. 22 The children struggled together within her; and she said,
'If it is to be this way, why do I live?'[z] So
she went to inquire of the LORD. 23 And
the LORD said to her,

'Two nations are in your womb,
and two peoples born of you
shall be divided;
one shall be stronger than the other,
the elder shall serve the younger.'

24 When her time to give birth was at
hand, there were twins in her womb.
25 The first came out red, all his body
like a hairy mantle; so they named him
Esau. 26 Afterwards his brother came
out, with his hand gripping Esau's heel;
so he was named Jacob.[a] Isaac was sixty
years old when she bore them.

27 When the boys grew up, Esau was
a skilful hunter, a man of the field, while
Jacob was a quiet man, living in tents.
28 Isaac loved Esau, because he was fond
of game; but Rebekah loved Jacob.

ESAU SELLS HIS BIRTHRIGHT

29 Once when Jacob was cooking a
stew, Esau came in from the field, and
he was famished. 30 Esau said to Jacob,
'Let me eat some of that red stuff, for I
am famished!' (Therefore he was called
Edom.[b]) 31 Jacob said, 'First sell me your
birthright.' 32 Esau said, 'I am about to
die; of what use is a birthright to me?'
33 Jacob said, 'Swear to me first.'[c] So he
swore to him, and sold his birthright to
Jacob. 34 Then Jacob gave Esau bread and
lentil stew, and he ate and drank, and
rose and went his way. Thus Esau despised his birthright.

ISAAC AND ABIMELECH

26 Now there was a famine in the
land, besides the former famine
that had occurred in the days of Abraham. And Isaac went to Gerar, to King
Abimelech of the Philistines. 2 The LORD
appeared to Isaac[d] and said, 'Do not go
down to Egypt; settle in the land that
I shall show you. 3 Reside in this land
as an alien, and I will be with you, and
will bless you; for to you and to your
descendants I will give all these lands,
and I will fulfil the oath that I swore to
your father Abraham. 4 I will make your
offspring as numerous as the stars of
heaven, and will give to your offspring
all these lands; and all the nations of
the earth shall gain blessing for themselves through your offspring, 5 because
Abraham obeyed my voice and kept my
charge, my commandments, my statutes, and my laws.'

6 So Isaac settled in Gerar. 7 When
the men of the place asked him about
his wife, he said, 'She is my sister'; for
he was afraid to say, 'My wife,' thinking, 'or else the men of the place might
kill me for the sake of Rebekah, because
she is attractive in appearance.' 8 When
Isaac had been there a long time, King
Abimelech of the Philistines looked out
of a window and saw him fondling his
wife Rebekah. 9 So Abimelech called for
Isaac, and said, 'So she is your wife! Why
then did you say, "She is my sister"?'
Isaac said to him, 'Because I thought I
might die because of her.' 10 Abimelech
said, 'What is this you have done to us?
One of the people might easily have lain
with your wife, and you would have
brought guilt upon us.' 11 So Abimelech
warned all the people, saying, 'Whoever
touches this man or his wife shall be put
to death.'

12 Isaac sowed seed in that land, and
in the same year reaped a hundredfold.
The LORD blessed him, 13 and the man

[x] **25.18** Heb *he fell* [y] **25.18** Or *down in opposition to* [z] **25.22** Syr: Meaning of Heb uncertain [a] **25.26** That is *He takes by the heel* or *He supplants* [b] **25.30** That is *Red* [c] **25.33** Heb *today* [d] **26.2** Heb *him*

became rich; he prospered more and more until he became very wealthy. 14He had possessions of flocks and herds, and a great household, so that the Philistines envied him. 15(Now the Philistines had stopped up and filled with earth all the wells that his father's servants had dug in the days of his father Abraham.) 16And Abimelech said to Isaac, 'Go away from us; you have become too powerful for us.'

17 So Isaac departed from there and camped in the valley of Gerar and settled there. 18Isaac dug again the wells of water that had been dug in the days of his father Abraham; for the Philistines had stopped them up after the death of Abraham; and he gave them the names that his father had given them. 19But when Isaac's servants dug in the valley and found there a well of spring water, 20the herders of Gerar quarrelled with Isaac's herders, saying, 'The water is ours.' So he called the well Esek,[e] because they contended with him. 21Then they dug another well, and they quarrelled over that one also; so he called it Sitnah.[f] 22He moved from there and dug another well, and they did not quarrel over it; so he called it Rehoboth,[g] saying, 'Now the LORD has made room for us, and we shall be fruitful in the land.'

23 From there he went up to Beersheba. 24And that very night the LORD appeared to him and said, 'I am the God of your father Abraham; do not be afraid, for I am with you and will bless you and make your offspring numerous for my servant Abraham's sake.' 25So he built an altar there, called on the name of the LORD, and pitched his tent there. And there Isaac's servants dug a well.

26 Then Abimelech went to him from Gerar, with Ahuzzath his adviser and Phicol the commander of his army. 27Isaac said to them, 'Why have you come to me, seeing that you hate me and have sent me away from you?' 28They said, 'We see plainly that the LORD has been with you; so we say, let there be an oath between you and us, and let us make a covenant with you 29so that you will do us no harm, just as we have not touched you and have done to you nothing but good and have sent you away in peace. You are now the blessed of the LORD.' 30So he made them a feast, and they ate and drank. 31In the morning they rose early and exchanged oaths; and Isaac set them on their way, and they departed from him in peace. 32That same day Isaac's servants came and told him about the well that they had dug, and said to him, 'We have found water!' 33He called it Shibah;[h] therefore the name of the city is Beersheba[i] to this day.

ESAU'S HITTITE WIVES

34 When Esau was forty years old, he married Judith daughter of Beeri the Hittite, and Basemath daughter of Elon the Hittite; 35and they made life bitter for Isaac and Rebekah.

ISAAC BLESSES JACOB

27 When Isaac was old and his eyes were dim so that he could not see, he called his elder son Esau and said to him, 'My son'; and he answered, 'Here I am.' 2He said, 'See, I am old; I do not know the day of my death. 3Now then, take your weapons, your quiver and your bow, and go out to the field, and hunt game for me. 4Then prepare for me savoury food, such as I like, and bring it to me to eat, so that I may bless you before I die.'

5 Now Rebekah was listening when Isaac spoke to his son Esau. So when Esau went to the field to hunt for game and bring it, 6Rebekah said to her son Jacob, 'I heard your father say to your brother Esau, 7"Bring me game, and prepare for me savoury food to eat, that I may bless you before the LORD before I die." 8Now therefore, my son, obey my word as I command you. 9Go to the flock, and get me two choice kids, so that I may prepare from them savoury food for your father, such as he likes; 10and you shall take it to your father to eat, so that he may bless you before he dies.' 11But Jacob said to his mother Rebekah, 'Look, my brother Esau is a hairy man, and I am a man of smooth skin. 12Perhaps my father will feel me, and I shall seem to be mocking him, and bring a curse on myself and not a blessing.' 13His mother said to him, 'Let your curse be on me, my son; only obey my word, and go, get them for me.' 14So he went and got them and brought them to his mother; and his mother prepared savoury food, such as his father loved. 15Then Rebekah took the best garments of her elder son Esau, which were with her in the house, and put them on her

[e] **26.20** That is *Contention* [f] **26.21** That is *Enmity* [g] **26.22** That is *Broad places* or *Room*
[h] **26.33** A word resembling the word for *oath*
[i] **26.33** That is *Well of the oath* or *Well of seven*

younger son Jacob; 16and she put the
skins of the kids on his hands and on
the smooth part of his neck. 17Then she
handed the savoury food, and the bread
that she had prepared, to her son Jacob.

18 So he went in to his father, and
said, 'My father'; and he said, 'Here I am;
who are you, my son?' 19Jacob said to his
father, 'I am Esau your firstborn. I have
done as you told me; now sit up and eat
of my game, so that you may bless me.'
20But Isaac said to his son, 'How is it that
you have found it so quickly, my son?'
He answered, 'Because the LORD your
God granted me success.' 21Then Isaac
said to Jacob, 'Come near, that I may
feel you, my son, to know whether you
are really my son Esau or not.' 22So Jacob went up to his father Isaac, who felt
him and said, 'The voice is Jacob's voice,
but the hands are the hands of Esau.'
23He did not recognize him, because his
hands were hairy like his brother Esau's
hands; so he blessed him. 24He said, 'Are
you really my son Esau?' He answered,
'I am.' 25Then he said, 'Bring it to me,
that I may eat of my son's game and
bless you.' So he brought it to him, and
he ate; and he brought him wine, and
he drank. 26Then his father Isaac said to
him, 'Come near and kiss me, my son.'
27So he came near and kissed him; and
he smelled the smell of his garments,
and blessed him, and said,

'Ah, the smell of my son
  is like the smell of a field that
    the LORD has blessed.
28 May God give you of the
    dew of heaven,
  and of the fatness of the earth,
  and plenty of grain and wine.
29 Let peoples serve you,
  and nations bow down to you.
Be lord over your brothers,
  and may your mother's sons
    bow down to you.
Cursed be everyone who curses you,
  and blessed be everyone
    who blesses you!'

ESAU'S LOST BLESSING

30 As soon as Isaac had finished
blessing Jacob, when Jacob had scarcely
gone out from the presence of his father
Isaac, his brother Esau came in from
his hunting. 31He also prepared savoury
food, and brought it to his father. And
he said to his father, 'Let my father sit
up and eat of his son's game, so that you
may bless me.' 32His father Isaac said to
him, 'Who are you?' He answered, 'I am
your firstborn son, Esau.' 33Then Isaac
trembled violently, and said, 'Who was
it then that hunted game and brought it
to me, and I ate it all[j] before you came,
and I have blessed him?—yes, and
blessed he shall be!' 34When Esau heard
his father's words, he cried out with an
exceedingly great and bitter cry, and
said to his father, 'Bless me, me also, father!' 35But he said, 'Your brother came
deceitfully, and he has taken away your
blessing.' 36Esau said, 'Is he not rightly
named Jacob?[k] For he has supplanted
me these two times. He took away my
birthright; and look, now he has taken
away my blessing.' Then he said, 'Have
you not reserved a blessing for me?'
37Isaac answered Esau, 'I have already
made him your lord, and I have given
him all his brothers as servants, and
with grain and wine I have sustained
him. What then can I do for you, my
son?' 38Esau said to his father, 'Have
you only one blessing, father? Bless me,
me also, father!' And Esau lifted up his
voice and wept.

39 Then his father Isaac answered
him:

'See, away from[l] the fatness of the
    earth shall your home be,
  and away from[m] the dew
    of heaven on high.
40 By your sword you shall live,
  and you shall serve your brother;
but when you break loose,[n]
  you shall break his yoke
    from your neck.'

JACOB ESCAPES ESAU'S FURY

41 Now Esau hated Jacob because of
the blessing with which his father had
blessed him, and Esau said to himself,
'The days of mourning for my father are
approaching; then I will kill my brother
Jacob.' 42But the words of her elder son
Esau were told to Rebekah; so she sent
and called her younger son Jacob and
said to him, 'Your brother Esau is consoling himself by planning to kill you.
43Now therefore, my son, obey my voice;
flee at once to my brother Laban in Haran, 44and stay with him for a while,
until your brother's fury turns away—
45until your brother's anger against you
turns away, and he forgets what you
have done to him; then I will send, and

[j] 27.33 Cn: Heb *of all* [k] 27.36 That is *He supplants* or *He takes by the heel* [l] 27.39 Or *See, of* [m] 27.39 Or *and of* [n] 27.40 Meaning of Heb uncertain

bring you back from there. Why should
I lose both of you in one day?'
46 Then Rebekah said to Isaac, 'I am
weary of my life because of the Hittite
women. If Jacob marries one of the Hittite women such as these, one of the
women of the land, what good will my
life be to me?'

28 Then Isaac called Jacob and
blessed him, and charged him,
'You shall not marry one of the Canaanite women. 2 Go at once to Paddan-aram
to the house of Bethuel, your mother's
father; and take as wife from there one
of the daughters of Laban, your mother's brother. 3 May God Almighty[o] bless
you and make you fruitful and numerous, that you may become a company of
peoples. 4 May he give to you the blessing of Abraham, to you and to your offspring with you, so that you may take
possession of the land where you now
live as an alien—land that God gave to
Abraham.' 5 Thus Isaac sent Jacob away;
and he went to Paddan-aram, to Laban son of Bethuel the Aramean, the
brother of Rebekah, Jacob's and Esau's
mother.

ESAU MARRIES ISHMAEL'S DAUGHTER

6 Now Esau saw that Isaac had
blessed Jacob and sent him away to
Paddan-aram to take a wife from there,
and that as he blessed him he charged
him, 'You shall not marry one of the
Canaanite women', 7 and that Jacob had
obeyed his father and his mother and
gone to Paddan-aram. 8 So when Esau
saw that the Canaanite women did not
please his father Isaac, 9 Esau went to
Ishmael and took Mahalath daughter
of Abraham's son Ishmael, and sister of
Nebaioth, to be his wife in addition to
the wives he had.

JACOB'S DREAM AT BETHEL

10 Jacob left Beer-sheba and went
towards Haran. 11 He came to a certain
place and stayed there for the night, because the sun had set. Taking one of the
stones of the place, he put it under his
head and lay down in that place. 12 And
he dreamed that there was a ladder[p] set
up on the earth, the top of it reaching
to heaven; and the angels of God were
ascending and descending on it. 13 And
the LORD stood beside him[q] and said, 'I
am the LORD, the God of Abraham your
father and the God of Isaac; the land
on which you lie I will give to you and
to your offspring; 14 and your offspring
shall be like the dust of the earth, and
you shall spread abroad to the west and
to the east and to the north and to the
south; and all the families of the earth
shall be blessed[r] in you and in your offspring. 15 Know that I am with you and
will keep you wherever you go, and will
bring you back to this land; for I will not
leave you until I have done what I have
promised you.' 16 Then Jacob woke from
his sleep and said, 'Surely the LORD is
in this place—and I did not know it!'
17 And he was afraid, and said, 'How
awesome is this place! This is none other
than the house of God, and this is the
gate of heaven.'
18 So Jacob rose early in the morning, and he took the stone that he had
put under his head and set it up for a pillar and poured oil on the top of it. 19 He
called that place Bethel;[s] but the name
of the city was Luz at the first. 20 Then
Jacob made a vow, saying, 'If God will be
with me, and will keep me in this way
that I go, and will give me bread to eat
and clothing to wear, 21 so that I come
again to my father's house in peace,
then the LORD shall be my God, 22 and
this stone, which I have set up for a pillar, shall be God's house; and of all that
you give me I will surely give one-tenth
to you.'

JACOB MEETS RACHEL

29 Then Jacob went on his journey,
and came to the land of the people of the east. 2 As he looked, he saw a
well in the field and three flocks of sheep
lying there beside it; for out of that well
the flocks were watered. The stone on
the well's mouth was large, 3 and when
all the flocks were gathered there, the
shepherds would roll the stone from the
mouth of the well, and water the sheep,
and put the stone back in its place on
the mouth of the well.
4 Jacob said to them, 'My brothers,
where do you come from?' They said,
'We are from Haran.' 5 He said to them,
'Do you know Laban son of Nahor?'
They said, 'We do.' 6 He said to them,
'Is it well with him?' 'Yes,' they replied,
'and here is his daughter Rachel, coming with the sheep.' 7 He said, 'Look, it is
still broad daylight; it is not time for the
animals to be gathered together. Water

[o] **28.3** Traditional rendering of Heb *El Shaddai*
[p] **28.12** Or *stairway* or *ramp* [q] **28.13** Or *stood above it* [r] **28.14** Or *shall bless themselves*
[s] **28.19** That is *House of God*

the sheep, and go, pasture them.' 8But
they said, 'We cannot until all the flocks
are gathered together, and the stone is
rolled from the mouth of the well; then
we water the sheep.'

9 While he was still speaking with
them, Rachel came with her father's
sheep; for she kept them. 10Now when
Jacob saw Rachel, the daughter of his
mother's brother Laban, and the sheep
of his mother's brother Laban, Jacob
went up and rolled the stone from the
well's mouth, and watered the flock of
his mother's brother Laban. 11Then Jacob kissed Rachel, and wept aloud.
12And Jacob told Rachel that he was her
father's kinsman, and that he was Rebekah's son; and she ran and told her
father.

13 When Laban heard the news
about his sister's son Jacob, he ran to
meet him; he embraced him and kissed
him, and brought him to his house. Jacob[t] told Laban all these things, 14and
Laban said to him, 'Surely you are my
bone and my flesh!' And he stayed with
him for a month.

JACOB MARRIES LABAN'S DAUGHTERS

15 Then Laban said to Jacob, 'Because
you are my kinsman, should you therefore serve me for nothing? Tell me, what
shall your wages be?' 16Now Laban had
two daughters; the name of the elder
was Leah, and the name of the younger
was Rachel. 17Leah's eyes were lovely,[u]
and Rachel was graceful and beautiful.
18Jacob loved Rachel; so he said, 'I will
serve you seven years for your younger
daughter Rachel.' 19Laban said, 'It is
better that I give her to you than that
I should give her to any other man; stay
with me.' 20So Jacob served seven years
for Rachel, and they seemed to him but
a few days because of the love he had for
her.

21 Then Jacob said to Laban, 'Give me
my wife that I may go in to her, for my
time is completed.' 22So Laban gathered
together all the people of the place, and
made a feast. 23But in the evening he
took his daughter Leah and brought her
to Jacob; and he went in to her. 24(Laban gave his maid Zilpah to his daughter Leah to be her maid.) 25When morning came, it was Leah! And Jacob said
to Laban, 'What is this you have done
to me? Did I not serve with you for Rachel? Why then have you deceived me?'
26Laban said, 'This is not done in our
country—giving the younger before the
firstborn. 27Complete the week of this
one, and we will give you the other also
in return for serving me for another
seven years.' 28Jacob did so, and completed her week; then Laban gave him
his daughter Rachel as a wife. 29(Laban
gave his maid Bilhah to his daughter
Rachel to be her maid.) 30So Jacob went
in to Rachel also, and he loved Rachel
more than Leah. He served Laban[v] for
another seven years.

31 When the LORD saw that Leah
was unloved, he opened her womb;
but Rachel was barren. 32Leah conceived and bore a son, and she named
him Reuben;[w] for she said, 'Because
the LORD has looked on my affliction;
surely now my husband will love me.'
33She conceived again and bore a son,
and said, 'Because the LORD has heard[x]
that I am hated, he has given me this
son also'; and she named him Simeon.
34Again she conceived and bore a son,
and said, 'Now this time my husband
will be joined[y] to me, because I have
borne him three sons'; therefore he was
named Levi. 35She conceived again and
bore a son, and said, 'This time I will
praise[z] the LORD'; therefore she named
him Judah; then she ceased bearing.

30 When Rachel saw that she bore
Jacob no children, she envied
her sister; and she said to Jacob, 'Give
me children, or I shall die!' 2Jacob became very angry with Rachel and said,
'Am I in the place of God, who has withheld from you the fruit of the womb?'
3Then she said, 'Here is my maid Bilhah;
go in to her, that she may bear upon my
knees and that I too may have children
through her.' 4So she gave him her maid
Bilhah as a wife; and Jacob went in to
her. 5And Bilhah conceived and bore
Jacob a son. 6Then Rachel said, 'God
has judged me, and has also heard my
voice and given me a son'; therefore she
named him Dan.[a] 7Rachel's maid Bilhah
conceived again and bore Jacob a second
son. 8Then Rachel said, 'With mighty
wrestlings I have wrestled[b] with my sister, and have prevailed'; so she named
him Naphtali.

9 When Leah saw that she had ceased
bearing children, she took her maid
Zilpah and gave her to Jacob as a wife.

[t] 29.13 Heb *He* [u] 29.17 Meaning of Heb uncertain [v] 29.30 Heb *him* [w] 29.32 That is *See, a son* [x] 29.33 Heb *shama* [y] 29.34 Heb *lawah* [z] 29.35 Heb *hodah* [a] 30.6 That is *He judged* [b] 30.8 Heb *niphtal*

10Then Leah's maid Zilpah bore Jacob
a son. 11And Leah said, 'Good fortune!'
so she named him Gad.[c] 12Leah's maid
Zilpah bore Jacob a second son. 13And
Leah said, 'Happy am I! For the women
will call me happy'; so she named him
Asher.[d]

14 In the days of wheat harvest Reuben went and found mandrakes in the
field, and brought them to his mother
Leah. Then Rachel said to Leah, 'Please
give me some of your son's mandrakes.'
15But she said to her, 'Is it a small matter that you have taken away my husband? Would you take away my son's
mandrakes also?' Rachel said, 'Then he
may lie with you tonight for your son's
mandrakes.' 16When Jacob came from
the field in the evening, Leah went out
to meet him, and said, 'You must come
in to me; for I have hired you with my
son's mandrakes.' So he lay with her
that night. 17And God heeded Leah, and
she conceived and bore Jacob a fifth son.
18Leah said, 'God has given me my hire[e]
because I gave my maid to my husband';
so she named him Issachar. 19And Leah
conceived again, and she bore Jacob a
sixth son. 20Then Leah said, 'God has
endowed me with a good dowry; now
my husband will honour[f] me, because I
have borne him six sons'; so she named
him Zebulun. 21Afterwards she bore a
daughter, and named her Dinah.

22 Then God remembered Rachel,
and God heeded her and opened her
womb. 23She conceived and bore a son,
and said, 'God has taken away my reproach'; 24and she named him Joseph,[g]
saying, 'May the LORD add to me another son!'

JACOB PROSPERS AT LABAN'S EXPENSE

25 When Rachel had borne Joseph,
Jacob said to Laban, 'Send me away,
that I may go to my own home and
country. 26Give me my wives and my
children for whom I have served you,
and let me go; for you know very well
the service I have given you.' 27But Laban said to him, 'If you will allow me
to say so, I have learned by divination
that the LORD has blessed me because of
you; 28name your wages, and I will give
them.' 29Jacob said to him, 'You yourself
know how I have served you, and how
your cattle have fared with me. 30For
you had little before I came, and it has
increased abundantly; and the LORD
has blessed you wherever I turned. But
now when shall I provide for my own
household also?' 31He said, 'What shall I
give you?' Jacob said, 'You shall not give
me anything; if you will do this for me,
I will again feed your flock and keep it:
32let me pass through all your flock today, removing from it every speckled
and spotted sheep and every black lamb,
and the spotted and speckled among the
goats; and such shall be my wages. 33So
my honesty will answer for me later,
when you come to look into my wages
with you. Every one that is not speckled
and spotted among the goats and black
among the lambs, if found with me,
shall be counted stolen.' 34Laban said,
'Good! Let it be as you have said.' 35But
that day Laban removed the male goats
that were striped and spotted, and all
the female goats that were speckled and
spotted, every one that had white on
it, and every lamb that was black, and
put them in charge of his sons; 36and
he set a distance of three days' journey
between himself and Jacob, while Jacob
was pasturing the rest of Laban's flock.

37 Then Jacob took fresh rods of poplar and almond and plane, and peeled
white streaks in them, exposing the
white of the rods. 38He set the rods
that he had peeled in front of the flocks
in the troughs, that is, the watering-
places, where the flocks came to drink.
And since they bred when they came to
drink, 39the flocks bred in front of the
rods, and so the flocks produced young
that were striped, speckled, and spotted.
40Jacob separated the lambs, and set the
faces of the flocks toward the striped
and the completely black animals in
the flock of Laban; and he put his own
droves apart, and did not put them with
Laban's flock. 41Whenever the stronger
of the flock were breeding, Jacob laid the
rods in the troughs before the eyes of
the flock, that they might breed among
the rods, 42but for the feebler of the flock
he did not lay them there; so the feebler
were Laban's, and the stronger Jacob's.
43Thus the man grew exceedingly rich,
and had large flocks, and male and female slaves, and camels and donkeys.

JACOB FLEES WITH FAMILY AND FLOCKS

31 Now Jacob heard that the sons
of Laban were saying, 'Jacob
has taken all that was our father's; he

[c] 30.11 That is *Fortune* [d] 30.13 That is *Happy*
[e] 30.18 Heb *sakar* [f] 30.20 Heb *zabal*
[g] 30.24 That is *He adds*

has gained all this wealth from what
belonged to our father.' 2And Jacob
saw that Laban did not regard him as
favourably as he did before. 3Then the
LORD said to Jacob, 'Return to the land
of your ancestors and to your kindred,
and I will be with you.' 4So Jacob sent
and called Rachel and Leah into the
field where his flock was, 5and said to
them, 'I see that your father does not regard me as favourably as he did before.
But the God of my father has been with
me. 6You know that I have served your
father with all my strength; 7yet your
father has cheated me and changed my
wages ten times, but God did not permit him to harm me. 8If he said, "The
speckled shall be your wages", then all
the flock bore speckled; and if he said,
"The striped shall be your wages", then
all the flock bore striped. 9Thus God has
taken away the livestock of your father,
and given them to me.

10 'During the mating of the flock I
once had a dream in which I looked up
and saw that the male goats that leaped
upon the flock were striped, speckled,
and mottled. 11Then the angel of God
said to me in the dream, "Jacob," and I
said, "Here I am!" 12And he said, "Look
up and see that all the goats that leap
on the flock are striped, speckled, and
mottled; for I have seen all that Laban is
doing to you. 13I am the God of Bethel,[h]
where you anointed a pillar and made a
vow to me. Now leave this land at once
and return to the land of your birth." '
14Then Rachel and Leah answered him,
'Is there any portion or inheritance left
to us in our father's house? 15Are we not
regarded by him as foreigners? For he
has sold us, and he has been using up the
money given for us. 16All the property
that God has taken away from our father
belongs to us and to our children; now
then, do whatever God has said to you.'

17 So Jacob arose, and set his children and his wives on camels; 18and he
drove away all his livestock, all the property that he had gained, the livestock in
his possession that he had acquired in
Paddan-aram, to go to his father Isaac
in the land of Canaan.

19 Now Laban had gone to shear
his sheep, and Rachel stole her father's
household gods. 20And Jacob deceived
Laban the Aramean, in that he did not
tell him that he intended to flee. 21So he
fled with all that he had; starting out he
crossed the Euphrates,[i] and set his face
towards the hill country of Gilead.

LABAN OVERTAKES JACOB

22 On the third day Laban was told
that Jacob had fled. 23So he took his
kinsfolk with him and pursued him for
seven days until he caught up with him
in the hill country of Gilead. 24But God
came to Laban the Aramean in a dream
by night, and said to him, 'Take heed
that you say not a word to Jacob, either
good or bad.'

25 Laban overtook Jacob. Now Jacob
had pitched his tent in the hill country,
and Laban with his kinsfolk camped in
the hill country of Gilead. 26Laban said
to Jacob, 'What have you done? You
have deceived me, and carried away my
daughters like captives of the sword.
27Why did you flee secretly and deceive
me and not tell me? I would have sent
you away with mirth and songs, with
tambourine and lyre. 28And why did
you not permit me to kiss my sons and
my daughters farewell? What you have
done is foolish. 29It is in my power to
do you harm; but the God of your father
spoke to me last night, saying, "Take
heed that you speak to Jacob neither
good nor bad." 30Even though you had
to go because you longed greatly for
your father's house, why did you steal
my gods?' 31Jacob answered Laban, 'Because I was afraid, for I thought that
you would take your daughters from
me by force. 32But anyone with whom
you find your gods shall not live. In the
presence of our kinsfolk, point out what
I have that is yours, and take it.' Now Jacob did not know that Rachel had stolen
the gods.[j]

33 So Laban went into Jacob's tent,
and into Leah's tent, and into the tent
of the two maids, but he did not find
them. And he went out of Leah's tent,
and entered Rachel's. 34Now Rachel had
taken the household gods and put them
in the camel's saddle, and sat on them.
Laban felt all about in the tent, but did
not find them. 35And she said to her
father, 'Let not my lord be angry that
I cannot rise before you, for the way of
women is upon me.' So he searched, but
did not find the household gods.

36 Then Jacob became angry, and
upbraided Laban. Jacob said to Laban,
'What is my offence? What is my sin,
that you have hotly pursued me? 37Al-
though you have felt about through all
my goods, what have you found of all

[h] **31.13** Cn: Meaning of Heb uncertain
[i] **31.21** Heb *the river* [j] **31.32** Heb *them*

your household goods? Set it here before my kinsfolk and your kinsfolk, so
that they may decide between us two.
38 These twenty years I have been with
you; your ewes and your female goats
have not miscarried, and I have not
eaten the rams of your flocks. 39 That
which was torn by wild beasts I did not
bring to you; I bore the loss of it myself;
of my hand you required it, whether
stolen by day or stolen by night. 40 It
was like this with me: by day the heat
consumed me, and the cold by night,
and my sleep fled from my eyes. 41 These
twenty years I have been in your house;
I served you for fourteen years for your
two daughters, and six years for your
flock, and you have changed my wages
ten times. 42 If the God of my father, the
God of Abraham and the Fear[k] of Isaac,
had not been on my side, surely now
you would have sent me away empty-
handed. God saw my affliction and the
labour of my hands, and rebuked you
last night.'

LABAN AND JACOB MAKE A COVENANT

43 Then Laban answered and said
to Jacob, 'The daughters are my daughters, the children are my children, the
flocks are my flocks, and all that you
see is mine. But what can I do today
about these daughters of mine, or about
their children whom they have borne?
44 Come now, let us make a covenant,
you and I; and let it be a witness between you and me.' 45 So Jacob took a
stone, and set it up as a pillar. 46 And Jacob said to his kinsfolk, 'Gather stones,'
and they took stones, and made a heap;
and they ate there by the heap. 47 Laban called it Jegar-sahadutha:[l] but Jacob called it Galeed.[m] 48 Laban said, 'This
heap is a witness between you and me
today.' Therefore he called it Galeed,
49 and the pillar[n] Mizpah,[o] for he said,
'The LORD watch between you and me,
when we are absent one from the other.
50 If you ill-treat my daughters, or if you
take wives in addition to my daughters,
though no one else is with us, remember that God is witness between you and
me.'

51 Then Laban said to Jacob, 'See this
heap and see the pillar, which I have set
between you and me. 52 This heap is a
witness, and the pillar is a witness, that
I will not pass beyond this heap to you,
and you will not pass beyond this heap
and this pillar to me, for harm. 53 May
the God of Abraham and the God of
Nahor'—the God of their father—'judge
between us.' So Jacob swore by the Fear[p]
of his father Isaac, 54 and Jacob offered
a sacrifice on the height and called his
kinsfolk to eat bread; and they ate bread
and tarried all night in the hill country.

55 [q]Early in the morning Laban rose
up, and kissed his grandchildren and
his daughters and blessed them; then
he departed and returned home.

32 Jacob went on his way and the
angels of God met him; 2 and
when Jacob saw them he said, 'This is
God's camp!' So he called that place Mahanaim.[r]

JACOB SENDS PRESENTS TO APPEASE ESAU

3 Jacob sent messengers before him
to his brother Esau in the land of Seir,
the country of Edom, 4 instructing
them, 'Thus you shall say to my lord
Esau: Thus says your servant Jacob, "I
have lived with Laban as an alien, and
stayed until now; 5 and I have oxen, donkeys, flocks, male and female slaves; and
I have sent to tell my lord, in order that
I may find favour in your sight."'

6 The messengers returned to Jacob,
saying, 'We came to your brother Esau,
and he is coming to meet you, and four
hundred men are with him.' 7 Then Jacob was greatly afraid and distressed;
and he divided the people that were
with him, and the flocks and herds and
camels, into two companies, 8 thinking,
'If Esau comes to one company and destroys it, then the company that is left
will escape.'

9 And Jacob said, 'O God of my father
Abraham and God of my father Isaac,
O LORD who said to me, "Return to
your country and to your kindred, and
I will do you good", 10 I am not worthy
of the least of all the steadfast love and
all the faithfulness that you have shown
to your servant, for with only my staff
I crossed this Jordan; and now I have
become two companies. 11 Deliver me,
please, from the hand of my brother,
from the hand of Esau, for I am afraid
of him; he may come and kill us all, the
mothers with the children. 12 Yet you

[k] 31.42 Meaning of Heb uncertain [l] 31.47 In Aramaic *The heap of witness* [m] 31.47 In Hebrew *The heap of witness* [n] 31.49 Compare Sam: MT lacks *the pillar* [o] 31.49 That is *Watchpost* [p] 31.53 Meaning of Heb uncertain [q] 31.55 Ch 32.1 in Heb [r] 32.2 Here taken to mean *Two camps*

have said, "I will surely do you good,
and make your offspring as the sand of
the sea, which cannot be counted because of their number." '
13 So he spent that night there, and
from what he had with him he took a
present for his brother Esau, 14two hundred female goats and twenty male
goats, two hundred ewes and twenty
rams, 15thirty milch camels and their
colts, forty cows and ten bulls, twenty
female donkeys and ten male donkeys.
16These he delivered into the hand of
his servants, each drove by itself, and
said to his servants, 'Pass on ahead of
me, and put a space between drove and
drove.' 17He instructed the foremost,
'When Esau my brother meets you, and
asks you, "To whom do you belong?
Where are you going? And whose are
these ahead of you?" 18then you shall
say, "They belong to your servant Jacob;
they are a present sent to my lord Esau;
and moreover he is behind us." ' 19He
likewise instructed the second and the
third and all who followed the droves,
'You shall say the same thing to Esau
when you meet him, 20and you shall
say, "Moreover your servant Jacob is
behind us." ' For he thought, 'I may appease him with the present that goes
ahead of me, and afterwards I shall see
his face; perhaps he will accept me.' 21So
the present passed on ahead of him; and
he himself spent that night in the camp.

JACOB WRESTLES AT PENIEL

22 The same night he got up and took
his two wives, his two maids, and his
eleven children, and crossed the ford
of the Jabbok. 23He took them and sent
them across the stream, and likewise
everything that he had. 24Jacob was left
alone; and a man wrestled with him
until daybreak. 25When the man saw
that he did not prevail against Jacob, he
struck him on the hip socket; and Jacob's
hip was put out of joint as he wrestled
with him. 26Then he said, 'Let me go,
for the day is breaking.' But Jacob said,
'I will not let you go, unless you bless
me.' 27So he said to him, 'What is your
name?' And he said, 'Jacob.' 28Then the
man[s] said, 'You shall no longer be called
Jacob, but Israel,[t] for you have striven
with God and with humans,[u] and have
prevailed.' 29Then Jacob asked him,
'Please tell me your name.' But he said,
'Why is it that you ask my name?' And
there he blessed him. 30So Jacob called
the place Peniel,[v] saying, 'For I have
seen God face to face, and yet my life is
preserved.' 31The sun rose upon him as
he passed Penuel, limping because of his
hip. 32Therefore to this day the Israelites
do not eat the thigh muscle that is on
the hip socket, because he struck Jacob
on the hip socket at the thigh muscle.

JACOB AND ESAU MEET

33 Now Jacob looked up and saw
Esau coming, and four hundred
men with him. So he divided the children among Leah and Rachel and the
two maids. 2He put the maids with
their children in front, then Leah with
her children, and Rachel and Joseph
last of all. 3He himself went on ahead
of them, bowing himself to the ground
seven times, until he came near his
brother.
4 But Esau ran to meet him, and
embraced him, and fell on his neck
and kissed him, and they wept. 5When
Esau looked up and saw the women and
children, he said, 'Who are these with
you?' Jacob said, 'The children whom
God has graciously given your servant.' 6Then the maids drew near, they
and their children, and bowed down;
7Leah likewise and her children drew
near and bowed down; and finally Joseph and Rachel drew near, and they
bowed down. 8Esau said, 'What do you
mean by all this company that I met?'
Jacob answered, 'To find favour with my
lord.' 9But Esau said, 'I have enough, my
brother; keep what you have for yourself.' 10Jacob said, 'No, please; if I find
favour with you, then accept my present from my hand; for truly to see your
face is like seeing the face of God—since
you have received me with such favour.
11Please accept my gift that is brought
to you, because God has dealt graciously
with me, and because I have everything
I want.' So he urged him, and he took it.
12 Then Esau said, 'Let us journey on
our way, and I will go alongside you.'
13But Jacob said to him, 'My lord knows
that the children are frail and that the
flocks and herds, which are nursing, are
a care to me; and if they are overdriven
for one day, all the flocks will die. 14Let
my lord pass on ahead of his servant,
and I will lead on slowly, according to
the pace of the cattle that are before me

[s] **32.28** Heb *he* [t] **32.28** That is *The one who strives with God* or *God strives* [u] **32.28** Or *with divine and human beings* [v] **32.30** That is *The face of God*

and according to the pace of the children, until I come to my lord in Seir.'
15 So Esau said, 'Let me leave with
you some of the people who are with
me.' But he said, 'Why should my lord be
so kind to me?' 16So Esau returned that
day on his way to Seir. 17But Jacob journeyed to Succoth,[w] and built himself a
house, and made booths for his cattle;
therefore the place is called Succoth.

JACOB REACHES SHECHEM

18 Jacob came safely to the city of
Shechem, which is in the land of Canaan, on his way from Paddan-aram;
and he camped before the city. 19And
from the sons of Hamor, Shechem's father, he bought for one hundred pieces
of money[x] the plot of land on which he
had pitched his tent. 20There he erected
an altar and called it El-Elohe-Israel.[y]

THE RAPE OF DINAH

34 Now Dinah the daughter of
Leah, whom she had borne to
Jacob, went out to visit the women of
the region. 2When Shechem son of Hamor the Hivite, prince of the region,
saw her, he seized her and lay with her
by force. 3And his soul was drawn to Dinah daughter of Jacob; he loved the girl,
and spoke tenderly to her. 4So Shechem
spoke to his father Hamor, saying, 'Get
me this girl to be my wife.'
5 Now Jacob heard that Shechem[z]
had defiled his daughter Dinah; but his
sons were with his cattle in the field, so
Jacob held his peace until they came.
6And Hamor the father of Shechem
went out to Jacob to speak with him,
7just as the sons of Jacob came in from
the field. When they heard of it, the men
were indignant and very angry, because
he had committed an outrage in Israel
by lying with Jacob's daughter, for such
a thing ought not to be done.
8 But Hamor spoke with them, saying, 'The heart of my son Shechem longs
for your daughter; please give her to him
in marriage. 9Make marriages with us;
give your daughters to us, and take our
daughters for yourselves. 10You shall
live with us; and the land shall be open
to you; live and trade in it, and get property in it.' 11Shechem also said to her father and to her brothers, 'Let me find favour with you, and whatever you say to
me I will give. 12Put the marriage present and gift as high as you like, and I
will give whatever you ask me; only give
me the girl to be my wife.'
13 The sons of Jacob answered Shechem and his father Hamor deceitfully,
because he had defiled their sister Dinah. 14They said to them, 'We cannot
do this thing, to give our sister to one
who is uncircumcised, for that would
be a disgrace to us. 15Only on this condition will we consent to you: that you
will become as we are and every male
among you be circumcised. 16Then we
will give our daughters to you, and we
will take your daughters for ourselves,
and we will live among you and become
one people. 17But if you will not listen to
us and be circumcised, then we will take
our daughter and be gone.'
18 Their words pleased Hamor and
Hamor's son Shechem. 19And the young
man did not delay to do the thing, because he was delighted with Jacob's
daughter. Now he was the most honoured of all his family. 20So Hamor and
his son Shechem came to the gate of
their city and spoke to the men of their
city, saying, 21'These people are friendly
with us; let them live in the land and
trade in it, for the land is large enough
for them; let us take their daughters
in marriage, and let us give them our
daughters. 22Only on this condition will
they agree to live among us, to become
one people: that every male among us
be circumcised as they are circumcised.
23Will not their livestock, their property, and all their animals be ours? Only
let us agree with them, and they will
live among us.' 24And all who went out
of the city gate heeded Hamor and his
son Shechem; and every male was circumcised, all who went out of the gate
of his city.

DINAH'S BROTHERS AVENGE THEIR SISTER

25 On the third day, when they were
still in pain, two of the sons of Jacob,
Simeon and Levi, Dinah's brothers,
took their swords and came against the
city unawares, and killed all the males.
26They killed Hamor and his son Shechem with the sword, and took Dinah
out of Shechem's house, and went away.
27And the other sons of Jacob came
upon the slain, and plundered the city,
because their sister had been defiled.
28They took their flocks and their herds,
their donkeys, and whatever was in the
city and in the field. 29All their wealth,

[w] **33.17** That is *Booths* [x] **33.19** Heb *one hundred qesitah* [y] **33.20** That is *God, the God of Israel* [z] **34.5** Heb *he*

all their little ones and their wives, all that was in the houses, they captured and made their prey. 30 Then Jacob said to Simeon and Levi, 'You have brought trouble on me by making me odious to the inhabitants of the land, the Canaanites and the Perizzites; my numbers are few, and if they gather themselves against me and attack me, I shall be destroyed, both I and my household.' 31 But they said, 'Should our sister be treated like a whore?'

JACOB RETURNS TO BETHEL

35 God said to Jacob, 'Arise, go up to Bethel, and settle there. Make an altar there to the God who appeared to you when you fled from your brother Esau.' 2 So Jacob said to his household and to all who were with him, 'Put away the foreign gods that are among you, and purify yourselves, and change your clothes; 3 then come, let us go up to Bethel, that I may make an altar there to the God who answered me in the day of my distress and has been with me wherever I have gone.' 4 So they gave to Jacob all the foreign gods that they had, and the rings that were in their ears; and Jacob hid them under the oak that was near Shechem.

5 As they journeyed, a terror from God fell upon the cities all around them, so that no one pursued them. 6 Jacob came to Luz (that is, Bethel), which is in the land of Canaan, he and all the people who were with him, 7 and there he built an altar and called the place El-bethel,[a] because it was there that God had revealed himself to him when he fled from his brother. 8 And Deborah, Rebekah's nurse, died, and she was buried under an oak below Bethel. So it was called Allon-bacuth.[b]

9 God appeared to Jacob again when he came from Paddan-aram, and he blessed him. 10 God said to him, 'Your name is Jacob; no longer shall you be called Jacob, but Israel shall be your name.' So he was called Israel. 11 God said to him, 'I am God Almighty:[c] be fruitful and multiply; a nation and a company of nations shall come from you, and kings shall spring from you. 12 The land that I gave to Abraham and Isaac I will give to you, and I will give the land to your offspring after you.' 13 Then God went up from him at the place where he had spoken with him. 14 Jacob set up a pillar in the place where he had spoken with him, a pillar of stone; and he poured out a drink-offering on it, and poured oil on it. 15 So Jacob called the place where God had spoken with him Bethel.

THE BIRTH OF BENJAMIN AND THE DEATH OF RACHEL

16 Then they journeyed from Bethel; and when they were still some distance from Ephrath, Rachel was in childbirth, and she had a difficult labour. 17 When she was in her difficult labour, the midwife said to her, 'Do not be afraid; for now you will have another son.' 18 As her soul was departing (for she died), she named him Ben-oni;[d] but his father called him Benjamin.[e] 19 So Rachel died, and she was buried on the way to Ephrath (that is, Bethlehem), 20 and Jacob set up a pillar at her grave; it is the pillar of Rachel's tomb, which is there to this day. 21 Israel journeyed on, and pitched his tent beyond the tower of Eder.

22 While Israel lived in that land, Reuben went and lay with Bilhah his father's concubine; and Israel heard of it.

Now the sons of Jacob were twelve. 23 The sons of Leah: Reuben (Jacob's firstborn), Simeon, Levi, Judah, Issachar, and Zebulun. 24 The sons of Rachel: Joseph and Benjamin. 25 The sons of Bilhah, Rachel's maid: Dan and Naphtali. 26 The sons of Zilpah, Leah's maid: Gad and Asher. These were the sons of Jacob who were born to him in Paddan-aram.

THE DEATH OF ISAAC

27 Jacob came to his father Isaac at Mamre, or Kiriath-arba (that is, Hebron), where Abraham and Isaac had resided as aliens. 28 Now the days of Isaac were one hundred and eighty years. 29 And Isaac breathed his last; he died and was gathered to his people, old and full of days; and his sons Esau and Jacob buried him.

ESAU'S DESCENDANTS

36 These are the descendants of Esau (that is, Edom). 2 Esau took his wives from the Canaanites: Adah daughter of Elon the Hittite, Oholibamah daughter of Anah son[f] of Zibeon the Hivite, 3 and Basemath, Ishmael's daughter, sister of Nebaioth. 4 Adah bore Eliphaz to Esau; Basemath bore Reuel; 5 and Oholibamah bore Jeush, Jalam,

[a] 35.7 That is *God of Bethel* [b] 35.8 That is *Oak of weeping* [c] 35.11 Traditional rendering of Heb *El Shaddai* [d] 35.18 That is *Son of my sorrow* [e] 35.18 That is *Son of the right hand* or *Son of the South* [f] 36.2 Sam Gk Syr: Heb *daughter*

and Korah. These are the sons of Esau
who were born to him in the land of Canaan.
6 Then Esau took his wives, his sons,
his daughters, and all the members of
his household, his cattle, all his livestock, and all the property he had acquired in the land of Canaan; and he
moved to a land some distance from his
brother Jacob. 7For their possessions
were too great for them to live together;
the land where they were living could
not support them because of their livestock. 8So Esau settled in the hill country of Seir; Esau is Edom.
9 These are the descendants of Esau,
ancestor of the Edomites, in the hill
country of Seir. 10These are the names
of Esau's sons: Eliphaz, son of Adah the
wife of Esau; Reuel, the son of Esau's
wife Basemath. 11The sons of Eliphaz
were Teman, Omar, Zepho, Gatam, and
Kenaz. 12(Timna was a concubine of Eliphaz, Esau's son; she bore Amalek to
Eliphaz.) These were the sons of Adah,
Esau's wife. 13These were the sons of
Reuel: Nahath, Zerah, Shammah, and
Mizzah. These were the sons of Esau's
wife Basemath. 14These were the sons
of Esau's wife Oholibamah, daughter of
Anah son[g] of Zibeon: she bore to Esau
Jeush, Jalam, and Korah.

CLANS AND KINGS OF EDOM

15 These are the clans[h] of the sons of
Esau. The sons of Eliphaz the firstborn
of Esau: the clans[i] Teman, Omar, Zepho, Kenaz, 16Korah, Gatam, and Amalek; these are the clans[j] of Eliphaz in the
land of Edom; they are the sons of Adah.
17These are the sons of Esau's son Reuel:
the clans[k] Nahath, Zerah, Shammah,
and Mizzah; these are the clans[l] of Reuel
in the land of Edom; they are the sons
of Esau's wife Basemath. 18These are
the sons of Esau's wife Oholibamah: the
clans[m] Jeush, Jalam, and Korah; these
are the clans[n] born of Esau's wife Oholibamah, the daughter of Anah. 19These
are the sons of Esau (that is, Edom), and
these are their clans.[o]
20 These are the sons of Seir the Ho-
rite, the inhabitants of the land: Lotan,
Shobal, Zibeon, Anah, 21Dishon, Ezer,
and Dishan; these are the clans[p] of the
Horites, the sons of Seir in the land of
Edom. 22The sons of Lotan were Hori
and Heman; and Lotan's sister was
Timna. 23These are the sons of Shobal:
Alvan, Manahath, Ebal, Shepho, and
Onam. 24These are the sons of Zibeon:
Aiah and Anah; he is the Anah who
found the springs[q] in the wilderness,
as he pastured the donkeys of his father Zibeon. 25These are the children of
Anah: Dishon and Oholibamah daughter of Anah. 26These are the sons of Dishon: Hemdan, Eshban, Ithran, and
Cheran. 27These are the sons of Ezer: Bilhan, Zaavan, and Akan. 28These are the
sons of Dishan: Uz and Aran. 29These
are the clans[r] of the Horites: the clans[s]
Lotan, Shobal, Zibeon, Anah, 30Dishon,
Ezer, and Dishan; these are the clans[t] of
the Horites, clan by clan[u] in the land of
Seir.
31 These are the kings who reigned
in the land of Edom, before any king
reigned over the Israelites. 32Bela son of
Beor reigned in Edom, the name of his
city being Dinhabah. 33Bela died, and
Jobab son of Zerah of Bozrah succeeded
him as king. 34Jobab died, and Husham
of the land of the Temanites succeeded
him as king. 35Husham died, and Hadad
son of Bedad, who defeated Midian in
the country of Moab, succeeded him as
king, the name of his city being Avith.
36Hadad died, and Samlah of Masrekah succeeded him as king. 37Samlah
died, and Shaul of Rehoboth on the Euphrates succeeded him as king. 38Shaul
died, and Baal-hanan son of Achbor succeeded him as king. 39Baal-hanan son
of Achbor died, and Hadar succeeded
him as king, the name of his city being
Pau; his wife's name was Mehetabel, the
daughter of Matred, daughter of Me-
zahab.
40 These are the names of the clans[v]
of Esau, according to their families
and their localities by their names: the
clans[w] Timna, Alvah, Jetheth, 41Oholi-
bamah, Elah, Pinon, 42Kenaz, Teman,
Mibzar, 43Magdiel, and Iram; these are
the clans[x] of Edom (that is, Esau, the father of Edom), according to their settlements in the land that they held.

JOSEPH DREAMS OF GREATNESS

37 Jacob settled in the land where
his father had lived as an alien,
the land of Canaan. 2This is the story of
the family of Jacob.

[g] 36.14 Gk Syr: Heb *daughter* [h] 36.15 Or *chiefs*
[i] 36.15 Or *chiefs* [j] 36.16 Or *chiefs* [k] 36.17 Or
chiefs [l] 36.17 Or *chiefs* [m] 36.18 Or *chiefs*
[n] 36.18 Or *chiefs* [o] 36.19 Or *chiefs*
[p] 36.21 Or *chiefs* [q] 36.24 Meaning of Heb
uncertain [r] 36.29 Or *chiefs* [s] 36.29 Or *chiefs*
[t] 36.30 Or *chiefs* [u] 36.30 Or *chief by chief*
[v] 36.40 Or *chiefs* [w] 36.40 Or *chiefs*
[x] 36.43 Or *chiefs*

Joseph, being seventeen years old,
was shepherding the flock with his
brothers; he was a helper to the sons of
Bilhah and Zilpah, his father's wives;
and Joseph brought a bad report of
them to their father. 3Now Israel loved
Joseph more than any other of his children, because he was the son of his old
age; and he had made him a long robe
with sleeves.[y] 4But when his brothers
saw that their father loved him more
than all his brothers, they hated him,
and could not speak peaceably to him.

5 Once Joseph had a dream, and
when he told it to his brothers, they
hated him even more. 6He said to them,
'Listen to this dream that I dreamed.
7There we were, binding sheaves in the
field. Suddenly my sheaf rose and stood
upright; then your sheaves gathered
around it, and bowed down to my sheaf.'
8His brothers said to him, 'Are you indeed to reign over us? Are you indeed to
have dominion over us?' So they hated
him even more because of his dreams
and his words.

9 He had another dream, and told it
to his brothers, saying, 'Look, I have had
another dream: the sun, the moon, and
eleven stars were bowing down to me.'
10But when he told it to his father and
to his brothers, his father rebuked him,
and said to him, 'What kind of dream
is this that you have had? Shall we indeed come, I and your mother and your
brothers, and bow to the ground before
you?' 11So his brothers were jealous of
him, but his father kept the matter in
mind.

JOSEPH IS SOLD BY HIS BROTHERS

12 Now his brothers went to pasture
their father's flock near Shechem. 13And
Israel said to Joseph, 'Are not your
brothers pasturing the flock at Shechem? Come, I will send you to them.'
He answered, 'Here I am.' 14So he said to
him, 'Go now, see if it is well with your
brothers and with the flock; and bring
word back to me.' So he sent him from
the valley of Hebron.

He came to Shechem, 15and a man
found him wandering in the fields; the
man asked him, 'What are you seeking?'
16'I am seeking my brothers,' he said;
'tell me, please, where they are pasturing the flock.' 17The man said, 'They have
gone away, for I heard them say, "Let
us go to Dothan."' So Joseph went after his brothers, and found them at Dothan. 18They saw him from a distance,
and before he came near to them, they
conspired to kill him. 19They said to
one another, 'Here comes this dreamer.
20Come now, let us kill him and throw
him into one of the pits; then we shall
say that a wild animal has devoured
him, and we shall see what will become
of his dreams.' 21But when Reuben
heard it, he delivered him out of their
hands, saying, 'Let us not take his life.'
22Reuben said to them, 'Shed no blood;
throw him into this pit here in the wilderness, but lay no hand on him'—that
he might rescue him out of their hand
and restore him to his father. 23So
when Joseph came to his brothers, they
stripped him of his robe, the long robe
with sleeves[z] that he wore; 24and they
took him and threw him into a pit. The
pit was empty; there was no water in it.

25 Then they sat down to eat; and
looking up they saw a caravan of Ishmaelites coming from Gilead, with their
camels carrying gum, balm, and resin,
on their way to carry it down to Egypt.
26Then Judah said to his brothers, 'What
profit is there if we kill our brother and
conceal his blood? 27Come, let us sell
him to the Ishmaelites, and not lay our
hands on him, for he is our brother, our
own flesh.' And his brothers agreed.
28When some Midianite traders passed
by, they drew Joseph up, lifting him out
of the pit, and sold him to the Ishmaelites for twenty pieces of silver. And they
took Joseph to Egypt.

29 When Reuben returned to the pit
and saw that Joseph was not in the pit,
he tore his clothes. 30He returned to his
brothers, and said, 'The boy is gone; and
I, where can I turn?' 31Then they took
Joseph's robe, slaughtered a goat, and
dipped the robe in the blood. 32They
had the long robe with sleeves[a] taken to
their father, and they said, 'This we have
found; see now whether it is your son's
robe or not.' 33He recognized it, and
said, 'It is my son's robe! A wild animal
has devoured him; Joseph is without
doubt torn to pieces.' 34Then Jacob tore
his garments, and put sackcloth on his
loins, and mourned for his son for many
days. 35All his sons and all his daughters
sought to comfort him; but he refused
to be comforted, and said, 'No, I shall
go down to Sheol to my son, mourning.' Thus his father bewailed him.

[y] **37.3** Traditional rendering (compare Gk): *a coat of many colours*; meaning of Heb uncertain
[z] **37.23** See note on 37.3 [a] **37.32** See note on 37.3

36 Meanwhile the Midianites had sold him in Egypt to Potiphar, one of Pharaoh's officials, the captain of the guard.

JUDAH AND TAMAR

38 It happened at that time that Judah went down from his brothers and settled near a certain Adullamite whose name was Hirah. 2 There Judah saw the daughter of a certain Canaanite whose name was Shua; he married her and went in to her. 3 She conceived and bore a son; and he named him Er. 4 Again she conceived and bore a son whom she named Onan. 5 Yet again she bore a son, and she named him Shelah. She[b] was in Chezib when she bore him. 6 Judah took a wife for Er his firstborn; her name was Tamar. 7 But Er, Judah's firstborn, was wicked in the sight of the LORD, and the LORD put him to death. 8 Then Judah said to Onan, 'Go in to your brother's wife and perform the duty of a brother-in-law to her; raise up offspring for your brother.' 9 But since Onan knew that the offspring would not be his, he spilled his semen on the ground whenever he went in to his brother's wife, so that he would not give offspring to his brother. 10 What he did was displeasing in the sight of the LORD, and he put him to death also. 11 Then Judah said to his daughter-in-law Tamar, 'Remain a widow in your father's house until my son Shelah grows up'—for he feared that he too would die, like his brothers. So Tamar went to live in her father's house.

12 In course of time the wife of Judah, Shua's daughter, died; when Judah's time of mourning was over,[c] he went up to Timnah to his sheep-shearers, he and his friend Hirah the Adullamite. 13 When Tamar was told, 'Your father-in-law is going up to Timnah to shear his sheep', 14 she put off her widow's garments, put on a veil, wrapped herself up, and sat down at the entrance to Enaim, which is on the road to Timnah. She saw that Shelah was grown up, yet she had not been given to him in marriage. 15 When Judah saw her, he thought her to be a prostitute, for she had covered her face. 16 He went over to her at the roadside, and said, 'Come, let me come in to you', for he did not know that she was his daughter-in-law. She said, 'What will you give me, that you may come in to me?' 17 He answered, 'I will send you a kid from the flock.' And she said, 'Only if you give me a pledge, until you send it.' 18 He said, 'What pledge shall I give you?' She replied, 'Your signet and your cord, and the staff that is in your hand.' So he gave them to her, and went in to her, and she conceived by him. 19 Then she got up and went away, and taking off her veil she put on the garments of her widowhood.

20 When Judah sent the kid by his friend the Adullamite, to recover the pledge from the woman, he could not find her. 21 He asked the townspeople, 'Where is the temple prostitute who was at Enaim by the wayside?' But they said, 'No prostitute has been here.' 22 So he returned to Judah, and said, 'I have not found her; moreover, the townspeople said, "No prostitute has been here."' 23 Judah replied, 'Let her keep the things as her own, otherwise we will be laughed at; you see, I sent this kid, and you could not find her.'

24 About three months later Judah was told, 'Your daughter-in-law Tamar has played the whore; moreover she is pregnant as a result of whoredom.' And Judah said, 'Bring her out, and let her be burned.' 25 As she was being brought out, she sent word to her father-in-law, 'It was the owner of these who made me pregnant.' And she said, 'Take note, please, whose these are, the signet and the cord and the staff.' 26 Then Judah acknowledged them and said, 'She is more in the right than I, since I did not give her to my son Shelah.' And he did not lie with her again.

27 When the time of her delivery came, there were twins in her womb. 28 While she was in labour, one put out a hand; and the midwife took and bound on his hand a crimson thread, saying, 'This one came out first.' 29 But just then he drew back his hand, and out came his brother; and she said, 'What a breach you have made for yourself!' Therefore he was named Perez.[d] 30 Afterwards his brother came out with the crimson thread on his hand; and he was named Zerah.[e]

JOSEPH AND POTIPHAR'S WIFE

39 Now Joseph was taken down to Egypt, and Potiphar, an officer of Pharaoh, the captain of the guard, an Egyptian, bought him from the Ishmaelites who had brought him down there.

[b] **38.5** Gk: Heb *He* [c] **38.12** Heb *when Judah was comforted* [d] **38.29** That is *A breach*
[e] **38.30** That is *Brightness*; perhaps alluding to the crimson thread

2The LORD was with Joseph, and he became a successful man; he was in the house of his Egyptian master. 3His master saw that the LORD was with him, and that the LORD caused all that he did to prosper in his hands. 4So Joseph found favour in his sight and attended him; he made him overseer of his house and put him in charge of all that he had. 5From the time that he made him overseer in his house and over all that he had, the LORD blessed the Egyptian's house for Joseph's sake; the blessing of the LORD was on all that he had, in house and field. 6So he left all that he had in Joseph's charge; and, with him there, he had no concern for anything but the food that he ate.

Now Joseph was handsome and good-looking. 7And after a time his master's wife cast her eyes on Joseph and said, 'Lie with me.' 8But he refused and said to his master's wife, 'Look, with me here, my master has no concern about anything in the house, and he has put everything that he has in my hand. 9He is not greater in this house than I am, nor has he kept back anything from me except yourself, because you are his wife. How then could I do this great wickedness, and sin against God?' 10And although she spoke to Joseph day after day, he would not consent to lie beside her or to be with her. 11One day, however, when he went into the house to do his work, and while no one else was in the house, 12she caught hold of his garment, saying, 'Lie with me!' But he left his garment in her hand, and fled and ran outside. 13When she saw that he had left his garment in her hand and had fled outside, 14she called out to the members of her household and said to them, 'See, my husband[f] has brought among us a Hebrew to insult us! He came in to me to lie with me, and I cried out with a loud voice; 15and when he heard me raise my voice and cry out, he left his garment beside me, and fled outside.' 16Then she kept his garment by her until his master came home, 17and she told him the same story, saying, 'The Hebrew servant, whom you have brought among us, came in to me to insult me; 18but as soon as I raised my voice and cried out, he left his garment beside me, and fled outside.'

19 When his master heard the words that his wife spoke to him, saying, 'This is the way your servant treated me', he became enraged. 20And Joseph's master took him and put him into the prison, the place where the king's prisoners were confined; he remained there in prison. 21But the LORD was with Joseph and showed him steadfast love; he gave him favour in the sight of the chief jailer. 22The chief jailer committed to Joseph's care all the prisoners who were in the prison, and whatever was done there, he was the one who did it. 23The chief jailer paid no heed to anything that was in Joseph's care, because the LORD was with him; and whatever he did, the LORD made it prosper.

THE DREAMS OF TWO PRISONERS

40 Some time after this, the cupbearer of the king of Egypt and his baker offended their lord the king of Egypt. 2Pharaoh was angry with his two officers, the chief cupbearer and the chief baker, 3and he put them in custody in the house of the captain of the guard, in the prison where Joseph was confined. 4The captain of the guard charged Joseph with them, and he waited on them; and they continued for some time in custody. 5One night they both dreamed—the cupbearer and the baker of the king of Egypt, who were confined in the prison—each his own dream, and each dream with its own meaning. 6When Joseph came to them in the morning, he saw that they were troubled. 7So he asked Pharaoh's officers, who were with him in custody in his master's house, 'Why are your faces downcast today?' 8They said to him, 'We have had dreams, and there is no one to interpret them.' And Joseph said to them, 'Do not interpretations belong to God? Please tell them to me.'

9 So the chief cupbearer told his dream to Joseph, and said to him, 'In my dream there was a vine before me, 10and on the vine there were three branches. As soon as it budded, its blossoms came out and the clusters ripened into grapes. 11Pharaoh's cup was in my hand; and I took the grapes and pressed them into Pharaoh's cup, and placed the cup in Pharaoh's hand.' 12Then Joseph said to him, 'This is its interpretation: the three branches are three days; 13within three days Pharaoh will lift up your head and restore you to your office; and you shall place Pharaoh's cup in his hand, just as you used to do when you were his cupbearer. 14But remember me when it is

f 39.14 Heb *he*

well with you; please do me the kindness to make mention of me to Pharaoh,
and so get me out of this place. 15For in
fact I was stolen out of the land of the
Hebrews; and here also I have done
nothing that they should have put me
into the dungeon.'

16 When the chief baker saw that the
interpretation was favourable, he said to
Joseph, 'I also had a dream: there were
three cake baskets on my head, 17and
in the uppermost basket there were all
sorts of baked food for Pharaoh, but the
birds were eating it out of the basket
on my head.' 18And Joseph answered,
'This is its interpretation: the three baskets are three days; 19within three days
Pharaoh will lift up your head—from
you!—and hang you on a pole; and the
birds will eat the flesh from you.'

20 On the third day, which was Pharaoh's birthday, he made a feast for all
his servants, and lifted up the head of
the chief cupbearer and the head of the
chief baker among his servants. 21He
restored the chief cupbearer to his cup-
bearing, and he placed the cup in Pharaoh's hand; 22but the chief baker he
hanged, just as Joseph had interpreted
to them. 23Yet the chief cupbearer did
not remember Joseph, but forgot him.

JOSEPH INTERPRETS PHARAOH'S DREAM

41 After two whole years, Pharaoh
dreamed that he was standing
by the Nile, 2and there came up out of
the Nile seven sleek and fat cows, and
they grazed in the reed grass. 3Then
seven other cows, ugly and thin, came
up out of the Nile after them, and stood
by the other cows on the bank of the
Nile. 4The ugly and thin cows ate up
the seven sleek and fat cows. And Pharaoh awoke. 5Then he fell asleep and
dreamed a second time; seven ears of
grain, plump and good, were growing
on one stalk. 6Then seven ears, thin and
blighted by the east wind, sprouted after them. 7The thin ears swallowed up
the seven plump and full ears. Pharaoh awoke, and it was a dream. 8In the
morning his spirit was troubled; so he
sent and called for all the magicians of
Egypt and all its wise men. Pharaoh
told them his dreams, but there was no
one who could interpret them to Pharaoh.

9 Then the chief cupbearer said to
Pharaoh, 'I remember my faults today.
10Once Pharaoh was angry with his servants, and put me and the chief baker in
custody in the house of the captain of
the guard. 11We dreamed on the same
night, he and I, each having a dream
with its own meaning. 12A young Hebrew was there with us, a servant of the
captain of the guard. When we told him,
he interpreted our dreams to us, giving
an interpretation to each according to
his dream. 13As he interpreted to us, so
it turned out; I was restored to my office, and the baker was hanged.'

14 Then Pharaoh sent for Joseph,
and he was hurriedly brought out of
the dungeon. When he had shaved
himself and changed his clothes, he
came in before Pharaoh. 15And Pharaoh said to Joseph, 'I have had a dream,
and there is no one who can interpret
it. I have heard it said of you that when
you hear a dream you can interpret it.'
16Joseph answered Pharaoh, 'It is not I;
God will give Pharaoh a favourable answer.' 17Then Pharaoh said to Joseph, 'In
my dream I was standing on the banks
of the Nile; 18and seven cows, fat and
sleek, came up out of the Nile and fed in
the reed grass. 19Then seven other cows
came up after them, poor, very ugly, and
thin. Never had I seen such ugly ones
in all the land of Egypt. 20The thin and
ugly cows ate up the first seven fat cows,
21but when they had eaten them no one
would have known that they had done
so, for they were still as ugly as before.
Then I awoke. 22I fell asleep a second
time[9] and I saw in my dream seven ears
of grain, full and good, growing on one
stalk, 23and seven ears, withered, thin,
and blighted by the east wind, sprouting after them; 24and the thin ears swallowed up the seven good ears. But when
I told it to the magicians, there was no
one who could explain it to me.'

25 Then Joseph said to Pharaoh, 'Pharaoh's dreams are one and the same; God
has revealed to Pharaoh what he is
about to do. 26The seven good cows are
seven years, and the seven good ears are
seven years; the dreams are one. 27The
seven lean and ugly cows that came up
after them are seven years, as are the
seven empty ears blighted by the east
wind. They are seven years of famine.
28It is as I told Pharaoh; God has shown
to Pharaoh what he is about to do.
29There will come seven years of great
plenty throughout all the land of Egypt.

9 41.22 Gk Syr Vg: Heb lacks *I fell asleep a second time*

30 After them there will arise seven years of famine, and all the plenty will be forgotten in the land of Egypt; the famine will consume the land. 31 The plenty will no longer be known in the land because of the famine that will follow, for it will be very grievous. 32 And the doubling of Pharaoh's dream means that the thing is fixed by God, and God will shortly bring it about. 33 Now therefore let Pharaoh select a man who is discerning and wise, and set him over the land of Egypt. 34 Let Pharaoh proceed to appoint overseers over the land, and take one-fifth of the produce of the land of Egypt during the seven plenteous years. 35 Let them gather all the food of these good years that are coming, and lay up grain under the authority of Pharaoh for food in the cities, and let them keep it. 36 That food shall be a reserve for the land against the seven years of famine that are to befall the land of Egypt, so that the land may not perish through the famine.'

JOSEPH'S RISE TO POWER

37 The proposal pleased Pharaoh and all his servants. 38 Pharaoh said to his servants, 'Can we find anyone else like this—one in whom is the spirit of God?' 39 So Pharaoh said to Joseph, 'Since God has shown you all this, there is no one so discerning and wise as you. 40 You shall be over my house, and all my people shall order themselves as you command; only with regard to the throne will I be greater than you.' 41 And Pharaoh said to Joseph, 'See, I have set you over all the land of Egypt.' 42 Removing his signet ring from his hand, Pharaoh put it on Joseph's hand; he arrayed him in garments of fine linen, and put a gold chain around his neck. 43 He had him ride in the chariot of his second-in-command; and they cried out in front of him, 'Bow the knee!'[h] Thus he set him over all the land of Egypt. 44 Moreover, Pharaoh said to Joseph, 'I am Pharaoh, and without your consent no one shall lift up hand or foot in all the land of Egypt.' 45 Pharaoh gave Joseph the name Zaphenath-paneah; and he gave him Asenath daughter of Potiphera, priest of On, as his wife. Thus Joseph gained authority over the land of Egypt.

46 Joseph was thirty years old when he entered the service of Pharaoh king of Egypt. And Joseph went out from the presence of Pharaoh, and went through all the land of Egypt. 47 During the seven plenteous years the earth produced abundantly. 48 He gathered up all the food of the seven years when there was plenty[i] in the land of Egypt, and stored up food in the cities; he stored up in every city the food from the fields around it. 49 So Joseph stored up grain in such abundance—like the sand of the sea—that he stopped measuring it; it was beyond measure.

50 Before the years of famine came, Joseph had two sons, whom Asenath daughter of Potiphera, priest of On, bore to him. 51 Joseph named the firstborn Manasseh,[j] 'For', he said, 'God has made me forget all my hardship and all my father's house.' 52 The second he named Ephraim,[k] 'For God has made me fruitful in the land of my misfortunes.'

53 The seven years of plenty that prevailed in the land of Egypt came to an end; 54 and the seven years of famine began to come, just as Joseph had said. There was famine in every country, but throughout the land of Egypt there was bread. 55 When all the land of Egypt was famished, the people cried to Pharaoh for bread. Pharaoh said to all the Egyptians, 'Go to Joseph; what he says to you, do.' 56 And since the famine had spread over all the land, Joseph opened all the storehouses,[l] and sold to the Egyptians, for the famine was severe in the land of Egypt. 57 Moreover, all the world came to Joseph in Egypt to buy grain, because the famine became severe throughout the world.

JOSEPH'S BROTHERS GO TO EGYPT

42 When Jacob learned that there was grain in Egypt, he said to his sons, 'Why do you keep looking at one another? 2 I have heard', he said, 'that there is grain in Egypt; go down and buy grain for us there, that we may live and not die.' 3 So ten of Joseph's brothers went down to buy grain in Egypt. 4 But Jacob did not send Joseph's brother Benjamin with his brothers, for he feared that harm might come to him. 5 Thus the sons of Israel were among the other people who came to buy grain, for the famine had reached the land of Canaan.

[h] 41.43 *Abrek*, apparently an Egyptian word similar in sound to the Hebrew word meaning *to kneel* [i] 41.48 Sam Gk: MT *the seven years that were* [j] 41.51 That is *Making to forget* [k] 41.52 From a Hebrew word meaning *to be fruitful* [l] 41.56 Gk Vg Compare Syr: Heb *opened all that was in* (or, *among*) *them*

6 Now Joseph was governor over the
land; it was he who sold to all the people of the land. And Joseph's brothers
came and bowed themselves before him
with their faces to the ground. 7When
Joseph saw his brothers, he recognized
them, but he treated them like strangers and spoke harshly to them. 'Where
do you come from?' he said. They said,
'From the land of Canaan, to buy food.'
8Although Joseph had recognized his
brothers, they did not recognize him.
9Joseph also remembered the dreams
that he had dreamed about them. He
said to them, 'You are spies; you have
come to see the nakedness of the land!'
10They said to him, 'No, my lord; your
servants have come to buy food. 11We
are all sons of one man; we are honest
men; your servants have never been
spies.' 12But he said to them, 'No, you
have come to see the nakedness of the
land!' 13They said, 'We, your servants,
are twelve brothers, the sons of a certain man in the land of Canaan; the
youngest, however, is now with our father, and one is no more.' 14But Joseph
said to them, 'It is just as I have said to
you; you are spies! 15Here is how you
shall be tested: as Pharaoh lives, you
shall not leave this place unless your
youngest brother comes here! 16Let
one of you go and bring your brother,
while the rest of you remain in prison,
in order that your words may be tested,
whether there is truth in you; or else,
as Pharaoh lives, surely you are spies.'
17And he put them all together in
prison for three days.

18 On the third day Joseph said to
them, 'Do this and you will live, for I
fear God: 19if you are honest men, let one
of your brothers stay here where you
are imprisoned. The rest of you shall go
and carry grain for the famine of your
households, 20and bring your youngest
brother to me. Thus your words will be
verified, and you shall not die.' And they
agreed to do so. 21They said to one another, 'Alas, we are paying the penalty
for what we did to our brother; we saw
his anguish when he pleaded with us,
but we would not listen. That is why
this anguish has come upon us.' 22Then
Reuben answered them, 'Did I not tell
you not to wrong the boy? But you
would not listen. So now there comes a
reckoning for his blood.' 23They did not
know that Joseph understood them,
since he spoke with them through an
interpreter. 24He turned away from
them and wept; then he returned and
spoke to them. And he picked out Simeon and had him bound before their
eyes. 25Joseph then gave orders to fill
their bags with grain, to return every
man's money to his sack, and to give
them provisions for their journey. This
was done for them.

JOSEPH'S BROTHERS RETURN TO CANAAN

26 They loaded their donkeys with
their grain, and departed. 27When one
of them opened his sack to give his donkey fodder at the lodging-place, he saw
his money at the top of the sack. 28He
said to his brothers, 'My money has
been put back; here it is in my sack!' At
this they lost heart and turned trembling to one another, saying, 'What is
this that God has done to us?'

29 When they came to their father
Jacob in the land of Canaan, they told
him all that had happened to them,
saying, 30'The man, the lord of the
land, spoke harshly to us, and charged
us with spying on the land. 31But we
said to him, "We are honest men, we
are not spies. 32We are twelve brothers,
sons of our father; one is no more, and
the youngest is now with our father in
the land of Canaan." 33Then the man,
the lord of the land, said to us, "By
this I shall know that you are honest
men: leave one of your brothers with
me, take grain for the famine of your
households, and go your way. 34Bring
your youngest brother to me, and I
shall know that you are not spies but
honest men. Then I will release your
brother to you, and you may trade in
the land." '

35 As they were emptying their
sacks, there in each one's sack was his
bag of money. When they and their father saw their bundles of money, they
were dismayed. 36And their father
Jacob said to them, 'I am the one you
have bereaved of children: Joseph is no
more, and Simeon is no more, and now
you would take Benjamin. All this has
happened to me!' 37Then Reuben said
to his father, 'You may kill my two sons
if I do not bring him back to you. Put
him in my hands, and I will bring him
back to you.' 38But he said, 'My son shall
not go down with you, for his brother
is dead, and he alone is left. If harm
should come to him on the journey that
you are to make, you would bring down
my grey hairs with sorrow to Sheol.'

THE BROTHERS COME AGAIN, BRINGING BENJAMIN

43 Now the famine was severe in the land. 2 And when they had eaten up the grain that they had brought from Egypt, their father said to them, 'Go again, buy us a little more food.' 3 But Judah said to him, 'The man solemnly warned us, saying, "You shall not see my face unless your brother is with you." 4 If you will send our brother with us, we will go down and buy you food; 5 but if you will not send him, we will not go down, for the man said to us, "You shall not see my face, unless your brother is with you."' 6 Israel said, 'Why did you treat me so badly as to tell the man that you had another brother?' 7 They replied, 'The man questioned us carefully about ourselves and our kindred, saying, "Is your father still alive? Have you another brother?" What we told him was in answer to these questions. Could we in any way know that he would say, "Bring your brother down"?' 8 Then Judah said to his father Israel, 'Send the boy with me, and let us be on our way, so that we may live and not die—you and we and also our little ones. 9 I myself will be surety for him; you can hold me accountable for him. If I do not bring him back to you and set him before you, then let me bear the blame for ever. 10 If we had not delayed, we would now have returned twice.'

11 Then their father Israel said to them, 'If it must be so, then do this: take some of the choice fruits of the land in your bags, and carry them down as a present to the man—a little balm and a little honey, gum, resin, pistachio nuts, and almonds. 12 Take double the money with you. Carry back with you the money that was returned in the top of your sacks; perhaps it was an oversight. 13 Take your brother also, and be on your way again to the man; 14 may God Almighty[m] grant you mercy before the man, so that he may send back your other brother and Benjamin. As for me, if I am bereaved of my children, I am bereaved.' 15 So the men took the present, and they took double the money with them, as well as Benjamin. Then they went on their way down to Egypt, and stood before Joseph.

16 When Joseph saw Benjamin with them, he said to the steward of his house, 'Bring the men into the house, and slaughter an animal and make ready, for the men are to dine with me at noon.' 17 The man did as Joseph said, and brought the men to Joseph's house. 18 Now the men were afraid because they were brought to Joseph's house, and they said, 'It is because of the money, replaced in our sacks the first time, that we have been brought in, so that he may have an opportunity to fall upon us, to make slaves of us and take our donkeys.' 19 So they went up to the steward of Joseph's house and spoke with him at the entrance to the house. 20 They said, 'Oh, my lord, we came down the first time to buy food; 21 and when we came to the lodging-place we opened our sacks, and there was each one's money in the top of his sack, our money in full weight. So we have brought it back with us. 22 Moreover, we have brought down with us additional money to buy food. We do not know who put our money in our sacks.' 23 He replied, 'Rest assured, do not be afraid; your God and the God of your father must have put treasure in your sacks for you; I received your money.' Then he brought Simeon out to them. 24 When the steward[n] had brought the men into Joseph's house, and given them water, and they had washed their feet, and when he had given their donkeys fodder, 25 they made the present ready for Joseph's coming at noon, for they had heard that they would dine there.

26 When Joseph came home, they brought him the present that they had carried into the house, and bowed to the ground before him. 27 He inquired about their welfare, and said, 'Is your father well, the old man of whom you spoke? Is he still alive?' 28 They said, 'Your servant our father is well; he is still alive.' And they bowed their heads and did obeisance. 29 Then he looked up and saw his brother Benjamin, his mother's son, and said, 'Is this your youngest brother, of whom you spoke to me? God be gracious to you, my son!' 30 With that, Joseph hurried out, because he was overcome with affection for his brother, and he was about to weep. So he went into a private room and wept there. 31 Then he washed his face and came out; and controlling himself he said, 'Serve the meal.' 32 They served him by himself, and them by themselves, and the Egyptians who ate with him by themselves, because the Egyptians could not eat with the

[m] 43.14 Traditional rendering of Heb *El Shaddai*
[n] 43.24 Heb *the man*

Hebrews, for that is an abomination to
the Egyptians. 33When they were seated
before him, the firstborn according to
his birthright and the youngest according to his youth, the men looked at one
another in amazement. 34Portions were
taken to them from Joseph's table, but
Benjamin's portion was five times as
much as any of theirs. So they drank
and were merry with him.

JOSEPH DETAINS BENJAMIN

44 Then he commanded the steward of his house, 'Fill the men's
sacks with food, as much as they can
carry, and put each man's money in the
top of his sack. 2Put my cup, the silver
cup, in the top of the sack of the youngest, with his money for the grain.' And
he did as Joseph told him. 3As soon as
the morning was light, the men were
sent away with their donkeys. 4When
they had gone only a short distance
from the city, Joseph said to his steward, 'Go, follow after the men; and when
you overtake them, say to them, "Why
have you returned evil for good? Why
have you stolen my silver cup?[o] 5Is it
not from this that my lord drinks? Does
he not indeed use it for divination? You
have done wrong in doing this." '

6 When he overtook them, he repeated these words to them. 7They said
to him, 'Why does my lord speak such
words as these? Far be it from your servants that they should do such a thing!
8Look, the money that we found at the
top of our sacks, we brought back to
you from the land of Canaan; why then
would we steal silver or gold from your
lord's house? 9Should it be found with
any one of your servants, let him die;
moreover, the rest of us will become my
lord's slaves.' 10He said, 'Even so; in accordance with your words, let it be: he
with whom it is found shall become my
slave, but the rest of you shall go free.'
11Then each one quickly lowered his sack
to the ground, and each opened his sack.
12He searched, beginning with the eldest and ending with the youngest; and
the cup was found in Benjamin's sack.
13At this they tore their clothes. Then
each one loaded his donkey, and they
returned to the city.

14 Judah and his brothers came to
Joseph's house while he was still there;
and they fell to the ground before him.
15Joseph said to them, 'What deed is this
that you have done? Do you not know
that one such as I can practise divination?' 16And Judah said, 'What can we
say to my lord? What can we speak?
How can we clear ourselves? God has
found out the guilt of your servants;
here we are then, my lord's slaves, both
we and also the one in whose possession
the cup has been found.' 17But he said,
'Far be it from me that I should do so!
Only the one in whose possession the
cup was found shall be my slave; but as
for you, go up in peace to your father.'

JUDAH PLEADS FOR BENJAMIN'S RELEASE

18 Then Judah stepped up to him and
said, 'O my lord, let your servant please
speak a word in my lord's ears, and do
not be angry with your servant; for
you are like Pharaoh himself. 19My lord
asked his servants, saying, "Have you a
father or a brother?" 20And we said to
my lord, "We have a father, an old man,
and a young brother, the child of his old
age. His brother is dead; he alone is left
of his mother's children, and his father
loves him." 21Then you said to your servants, "Bring him down to me, so that I
may set my eyes on him." 22We said to
my lord, "The boy cannot leave his father, for if he should leave his father,
his father would die." 23Then you said
to your servants, "Unless your youngest brother comes down with you, you
shall see my face no more." 24When we
went back to your servant my father we
told him the words of my lord. 25And
when our father said, "Go again, buy us
a little food", 26we said, "We cannot go
down. Only if our youngest brother goes
with us, will we go down; for we cannot
see the man's face unless our youngest
brother is with us." 27Then your servant
my father said to us, "You know that
my wife bore me two sons; 28one left
me, and I said, Surely he has been torn
to pieces; and I have never seen him
since. 29If you take this one also from
me, and harm comes to him, you will
bring down my grey hairs in sorrow to
Sheol." 30Now therefore, when I come to
your servant my father and the boy is
not with us, then, as his life is bound up
in the boy's life, 31when he sees that the
boy is not with us, he will die; and your
servants will bring down the grey hairs
of your servant our father with sorrow
to Sheol. 32For your servant became
surety for the boy to my father, saying,

[o] 44.4 Gk Compare Vg: Heb lacks *Why have you stolen my silver cup?*

"If I do not bring him back to you, then I
will bear the blame in the sight of my father all my life." 33 Now therefore, please
let your servant remain as a slave to my
lord in place of the boy; and let the boy
go back with his brothers. 34 For how
can I go back to my father if the boy is
not with me? I fear to see the suffering
that would come upon my father.'

JOSEPH REVEALS HIMSELF TO HIS BROTHERS

45 Then Joseph could no longer
control himself before all those
who stood by him, and he cried out,
'Send everyone away from me.' So no
one stayed with him when Joseph made
himself known to his brothers. 2 And he
wept so loudly that the Egyptians heard
it, and the household of Pharaoh heard
it. 3 Joseph said to his brothers, 'I am Joseph. Is my father still alive?' But his
brothers could not answer him, so dismayed were they at his presence.

4 Then Joseph said to his brothers,
'Come closer to me.' And they came
closer. He said, 'I am your brother Joseph, whom you sold into Egypt. 5 And
now do not be distressed, or angry
with yourselves, because you sold me
here; for God sent me before you to preserve life. 6 For the famine has been in
the land these two years; and there are
five more years in which there will be
neither ploughing nor harvest. 7 God
sent me before you to preserve for you
a remnant on earth, and to keep alive
for you many survivors. 8 So it was not
you who sent me here, but God; he has
made me a father to Pharaoh, and lord
of all his house and ruler over all the
land of Egypt. 9 Hurry and go up to my
father and say to him, "Thus says your
son Joseph, God has made me lord of all
Egypt; come down to me, do not delay.
10 You shall settle in the land of Goshen,
and you shall be near me, you and your
children and your children's children, as
well as your flocks, your herds, and all
that you have. 11 I will provide for you
there—since there are five more years
of famine to come—so that you and
your household, and all that you have,
will not come to poverty." 12 And now
your eyes and the eyes of my brother
Benjamin see that it is my own mouth
that speaks to you. 13 You must tell my
father how greatly I am honoured in
Egypt, and all that you have seen. Hurry
and bring my father down here.' 14 Then
he fell upon his brother Benjamin's
neck and wept, while Benjamin wept
upon his neck. 15 And he kissed all his
brothers and wept upon them; and after
that his brothers talked with him.

16 When the report was heard in
Pharaoh's house, 'Joseph's brothers have
come', Pharaoh and his servants were
pleased. 17 Pharaoh said to Joseph, 'Say
to your brothers, "Do this: load your animals and go back to the land of Canaan.
18 Take your father and your households
and come to me, so that I may give you
the best of the land of Egypt, and you
may enjoy the fat of the land." 19 You
are further charged to say, "Do this:
take wagons from the land of Egypt for
your little ones and for your wives, and
bring your father, and come. 20 Give no
thought to your possessions, for the best
of all the land of Egypt is yours." '

21 The sons of Israel did so. Joseph
gave them wagons according to the instruction of Pharaoh, and he gave them
provisions for the journey. 22 To each
one of them he gave a set of garments;
but to Benjamin he gave three hundred
pieces of silver and five sets of garments.
23 To his father he sent the following: ten
donkeys loaded with the good things of
Egypt, and ten female donkeys loaded
with grain, bread, and provision for his
father on the journey. 24 Then he sent his
brothers on their way, and as they were
leaving he said to them, 'Do not quarrel[p] along the way.'

25 So they went up out of Egypt and
came to their father Jacob in the land of
Canaan. 26 And they told him, 'Joseph is
still alive! He is even ruler over all the
land of Egypt.' He was stunned; he could
not believe them. 27 But when they told
him all the words of Joseph that he had
said to them, and when he saw the wagons that Joseph had sent to carry him,
the spirit of their father Jacob revived.
28 Israel said, 'Enough! My son Joseph is
still alive. I must go and see him before
I die.'

JACOB BRINGS HIS WHOLE FAMILY TO EGYPT

46 When Israel set out on his journey with all that he had and
came to Beer-sheba, he offered sacrifices to the God of his father Isaac. 2 God
spoke to Israel in visions of the night,
and said, 'Jacob, Jacob.' And he said,
'Here I am.' 3 Then he said, 'I am God,[q]
the God of your father; do not be afraid

[p] 45.24 Or *be agitated* [q] 46.3 Heb *the God*

to go down to Egypt, for I will make of you a great nation there. 4I myself will go down with you to Egypt, and I will also bring you up again; and Joseph's own hand shall close your eyes.'

5 Then Jacob set out from Beer-sheba; and the sons of Israel carried their father Jacob, their little ones, and their wives, in the wagons that Pharaoh had sent to carry him. 6They also took their livestock and the goods that they had acquired in the land of Canaan, and they came into Egypt, Jacob and all his offspring with him, 7his sons, and his sons' sons with him, his daughters, and his sons' daughters; all his offspring he brought with him into Egypt.

8 Now these are the names of the Israelites, Jacob and his offspring, who came to Egypt. Reuben, Jacob's firstborn, 9and the children of Reuben: Hanoch, Pallu, Hezron, and Carmi. 10The children of Simeon: Jemuel, Jamin, Ohad, Jachin, Zohar, and Shaul,[r] the son of a Canaanite woman. 11The children of Levi: Gershon, Kohath, and Merari. 12The children of Judah: Er, Onan, Shelah, Perez, and Zerah (but Er and Onan died in the land of Canaan); and the children of Perez were Hezron and Hamul. 13The children of Issachar: Tola, Puvah, Jashub,[s] and Shimron. 14The children of Zebulun: Sered, Elon, and Jahleel 15(these are the sons of Leah, whom she bore to Jacob in Paddan-aram, together with his daughter Dinah; in all his sons and his daughters numbered thirty-three). 16The children of Gad: Ziphion, Haggi, Shuni, Ezbon, Eri, Arodi, and Areli. 17The children of Asher: Imnah, Ishvah, Ishvi, Beriah, and their sister Serah. The children of Beriah: Heber and Malchiel 18(these are the children of Zilpah, whom Laban gave to his daughter Leah; and these she bore to Jacob—sixteen persons). 19The children of Jacob's wife Rachel: Joseph and Benjamin. 20To Joseph in the land of Egypt were born Manasseh and Ephraim, whom Asenath daughter of Potiphera, priest of On, bore to him. 21The children of Benjamin: Bela, Becher, Ashbel, Gera, Naaman, Ehi, Rosh, Muppim, Huppim, and Ard 22(these are the children of Rachel, who were born to Jacob—fourteen persons in all). 23The children of Dan: Hashum.[t] 24The children of Naphtali: Jahzeel, Guni, Jezer, and Shillem 25(these are the children of Bilhah, whom Laban gave to his daughter Rachel, and these she bore to Jacob—seven persons in all). 26All the persons belonging to Jacob who came into Egypt, who were his own offspring, not including the wives of his sons, were sixty-six persons in all. 27The children of Joseph, who were born to him in Egypt, were two; all the persons of the house of Jacob who came into Egypt were seventy.

JACOB SETTLES IN GOSHEN

28 Israel[u] sent Judah ahead to Joseph to lead the way before him into Goshen. When they came to the land of Goshen, 29Joseph made ready his chariot and went up to meet his father Israel in Goshen. He presented himself to him, fell on his neck, and wept on his neck a good while. 30Israel said to Joseph, 'I can die now, having seen for myself that you are still alive.' 31Joseph said to his brothers and to his father's household, 'I will go up and tell Pharaoh, and will say to him, "My brothers and my father's household, who were in the land of Canaan, have come to me. 32The men are shepherds, for they have been keepers of livestock; and they have brought their flocks, and their herds, and all that they have." 33When Pharaoh calls you, and says, "What is your occupation?" 34you shall say, "Your servants have been keepers of livestock from our youth even until now, both we and our ancestors"—in order that you may settle in the land of Goshen, because all shepherds are abhorrent to the Egyptians.'

47 So Joseph went and told Pharaoh, 'My father and my brothers, with their flocks and herds and all that they possess, have come from the land of Canaan; they are now in the land of Goshen.' 2From among his brothers he took five men and presented them to Pharaoh. 3Pharaoh said to his brothers, 'What is your occupation?' And they said to Pharaoh, 'Your servants are shepherds, as our ancestors were.' 4They said to Pharaoh, 'We have come to reside as aliens in the land; for there is no pasture for your servants' flocks because the famine is severe in the land of Canaan. Now, we ask you, let your servants settle in the land of Goshen.' 5Then Pharaoh said to Joseph, 'Your father and your brothers have come to you. 6The land of Egypt is before you; settle your father and your brothers in the best part of the land; let them live in the land of

[r] **46.10** Or *Saul* [s] **46.13** Compare Sam Gk Num 26.24; 1 Chr 7.1: MT *Iob* [t] **46.23** Gk: Heb *Hushim* [u] **46.28** Heb *He*

Goshen; and if you know that there are capable men among them, put them in charge of my livestock.'

7 Then Joseph brought in his father Jacob, and presented him before Pharaoh, and Jacob blessed Pharaoh. 8 Pharaoh said to Jacob, 'How many are the years of your life?' 9 Jacob said to Pharaoh, 'The years of my earthly sojourn are one hundred and thirty; few and hard have been the years of my life. They do not compare with the years of the life of my ancestors during their long sojourn.' 10 Then Jacob blessed Pharaoh, and went out from the presence of Pharaoh. 11 Joseph settled his father and his brothers, and granted them a holding in the land of Egypt, in the best part of the land, in the land of Rameses, as Pharaoh had instructed. 12 And Joseph provided his father, his brothers, and all his father's household with food, according to the number of their dependants.

THE FAMINE IN EGYPT

13 Now there was no food in all the land, for the famine was very severe. The land of Egypt and the land of Canaan languished because of the famine. 14 Joseph collected all the money to be found in the land of Egypt and in the land of Canaan, in exchange for the grain that they bought; and Joseph brought the money into Pharaoh's house. 15 When the money from the land of Egypt and from the land of Canaan was spent, all the Egyptians came to Joseph, and said, 'Give us food! Why should we die before your eyes? For our money is gone.' 16 And Joseph answered, 'Give me your livestock, and I will give you food in exchange for your livestock, if your money is gone.' 17 So they brought their livestock to Joseph; and Joseph gave them food in exchange for the horses, the flocks, the herds, and the donkeys. That year he supplied them with food in exchange for all their livestock. 18 When that year was ended, they came to him the following year, and said to him, 'We cannot hide from my lord that our money is all spent; and the herds of cattle are my lord's. There is nothing left in the sight of my lord but our bodies and our lands. 19 Shall we die before your eyes, both we and our land? Buy us and our land in exchange for food. We with our land will become slaves to Pharaoh; just give us seed, so that we may live and not die, and that the land may not become desolate.'

20 So Joseph bought all the land of Egypt for Pharaoh. All the Egyptians sold their fields, because the famine was severe upon them; and the land became Pharaoh's. 21 As for the people, he made slaves of them[v] from one end of Egypt to the other. 22 Only the land of the priests he did not buy; for the priests had a fixed allowance from Pharaoh, and lived on the allowance that Pharaoh gave them; therefore they did not sell their land. 23 Then Joseph said to the people, 'Now that I have this day bought you and your land for Pharaoh, here is seed for you; sow the land. 24 And at the harvests you shall give one-fifth to Pharaoh, and four-fifths shall be your own, as seed for the field and as food for yourselves and your households, and as food for your little ones.' 25 They said, 'You have saved our lives; may it please my lord, we will be slaves to Pharaoh.' 26 So Joseph made it a statute concerning the land of Egypt, and it stands to this day, that Pharaoh should have the fifth. The land of the priests alone did not become Pharaoh's.

THE LAST DAYS OF JACOB

27 Thus Israel settled in the land of Egypt, in the region of Goshen; and they gained possessions in it, and were fruitful and multiplied exceedingly. 28 Jacob lived in the land of Egypt for seventeen years; so the days of Jacob, the years of his life, were one hundred and forty-seven years.

29 When the time of Israel's death drew near, he called his son Joseph and said to him, 'If I have found favour with you, put your hand under my thigh and promise to deal loyally and truly with me. Do not bury me in Egypt. 30 When I lie down with my ancestors, carry me out of Egypt and bury me in their burial place.' He answered, 'I will do as you have said.' 31 And he said, 'Swear to me'; and he swore to him. Then Israel bowed himself on the head of his bed.

JACOB BLESSES JOSEPH'S SONS

48 After this Joseph was told, 'Your father is ill.' So he took with him his two sons Manasseh and Ephraim. 2 When Jacob was told, 'Your son Joseph has come to you', he[w] summoned his strength and sat up in bed. 3 And Jacob said to Joseph, 'God Almighty[x] appeared

[v] **47.21** Sam Gk Compare Vg: MT *He removed them to the cities* [w] **48.2** Heb *Israel*
[x] **48.3** Traditional rendering of Heb *El Shaddai*

to me at Luz in the land of Canaan, and
he blessed me, 4and said to me, "I am
going to make you fruitful and increase
your numbers; I will make of you a company of peoples, and will give this land
to your offspring after you for a perpetual holding." 5Therefore your two sons,
who were born to you in the land of
Egypt before I came to you in Egypt, are
now mine; Ephraim and Manasseh shall
be mine, just as Reuben and Simeon
are. 6As for the offspring born to you after them, they shall be yours. They shall
be recorded under the names of their
brothers with regard to their inheritance. 7For when I came from Paddan,
Rachel, alas, died in the land of Canaan
on the way, while there was still some
distance to go to Ephrath; and I buried
her there on the way to Ephrath' (that
is, Bethlehem).

8 When Israel saw Joseph's sons, he
said, 'Who are these?' 9Joseph said to
his father, 'They are my sons, whom God
has given me here.' And he said, 'Bring
them to me, please, that I may bless
them.' 10Now the eyes of Israel were dim
with age, and he could not see well. So
Joseph brought them near him; and he
kissed them and embraced them. 11Is-
rael said to Joseph, 'I did not expect to
see your face; and here God has let me
see your children also.' 12Then Joseph removed them from his father's knees,[y]
and he bowed himself with his face to
the earth. 13Joseph took them both,
Ephraim in his right hand towards Israel's left, and Manasseh in his left hand
towards Israel's right, and brought
them near him. 14But Israel stretched
out his right hand and laid it on the
head of Ephraim, who was the younger,
and his left hand on the head of Manasseh, crossing his hands, for Manasseh
was the firstborn. 15He blessed Joseph,
and said,

'The God before whom my ancestors
Abraham and Isaac walked,
the God who has been my shepherd
all my life to this day,
16 the angel who has redeemed me
from all harm, bless the boys;
and in them let my name be
perpetuated, and the
name of my ancestors
Abraham and Isaac;
and let them grow into a
multitude on the earth.'

17 When Joseph saw that his father laid his right hand on the head of
Ephraim, it displeased him; so he took
his father's hand, to remove it from
Ephraim's head to Manasseh's head.
18Joseph said to his father, 'Not so, my
father! Since this one is the firstborn,
put your right hand on his head.' 19But
his father refused, and said, 'I know, my
son, I know; he also shall become a people, and he also shall be great. Nevertheless, his younger brother shall be greater
than he, and his offspring shall become
a multitude of nations.' 20So he blessed
them that day, saying,

'By you[z] Israel will invoke
blessings, saying,
"God make you[a] like Ephraim
and like Manasseh." '

So he put Ephraim ahead of Manasseh.
21Then Israel said to Joseph, 'I am about
to die, but God will be with you and will
bring you again to the land of your ancestors. 22I now give to you one portion[b]
more than to your brothers, the portion[c]
that I took from the hand of the Amorites with my sword and with my bow.'

JACOB'S LAST WORDS TO HIS SONS

49 Then Jacob called his sons, and
said: 'Gather around, that I may
tell you what will happen to you in days
to come.

2 Assemble and hear, O sons of Jacob;
listen to Israel your father.

3 'Reuben, you are my firstborn,
my might and the first
fruits of my vigour,
excelling in rank and
excelling in power.
4 Unstable as water, you shall
no longer excel
because you went up on to
your father's bed;
then you defiled it—you[d] went
up on to my couch!

5 'Simeon and Levi are brothers;
weapons of violence are
their swords.
6 May I never come into their council;
may I not be joined to
their company—
for in their anger they killed men,
and at their whim they
hamstrung oxen.

[y] 48.12 Heb *from his knees* [z] 48.20 *you* here is singular in Heb [a] 48.20 *you* here is singular in Heb [b] 48.22 Or *mountain-slope* (Heb *shekem*, a play on the name of the town and district of Shechem) [c] 48.22 Or *mountain-slope* (Heb *shekem*, a play on the name of the town and district of Shechem) [d] 49.4 Gk Syr Tg: Heb *he*

7 Cursed be their anger, for it is fierce,
and their wrath, for it is cruel!
I will divide them in Jacob,
and scatter them in Israel.

8 'Judah, your brothers shall
praise you;
your hand shall be on the
neck of your enemies;
your father's sons shall bow
down before you.
9 Judah is a lion's whelp;
from the prey, my son,
you have gone up.
He crouches down, he stretches
out like a lion,
like a lioness—who dares
rouse him up?
10 The sceptre shall not depart
from Judah,
nor the ruler's staff from
between his feet,
until tribute comes to him;[e]
and the obedience of the
peoples is his.
11 Binding his foal to the vine
and his donkey's colt to
the choice vine,
he washes his garments in wine
and his robe in the blood
of grapes;
12 his eyes are darker than wine,
and his teeth whiter than milk.

13 'Zebulun shall settle at the
shore of the sea;
he shall be a haven for ships,
and his border shall be at Sidon.

14 'Issachar is a strong donkey,
lying down between the
sheepfolds;
15 he saw that a resting-place was good,
and that the land was pleasant;
so he bowed his shoulder
to the burden,
and became a slave at
forced labour.

16 'Dan shall judge his people
as one of the tribes of Israel.
17 Dan shall be a snake
by the roadside,
a viper along the path,
that bites the horse's heels
so that its rider falls backwards.

18 'I wait for your salvation, O LORD.

19 'Gad shall be raided by raiders,
but he shall raid at their heels.

20 'Asher's[f] food shall be rich,
and he shall provide
royal delicacies.

21 'Naphtali is a doe let loose
that bears lovely fawns.[g]

22 'Joseph is a fruitful bough,
a fruitful bough by a spring;
his branches run over the wall.[h]
23 The archers fiercely attacked him;
they shot at him and
pressed him hard.
24 Yet his bow remained taut,
and his arms[i] were made agile
by the hands of the Mighty
One of Jacob,
by the name of the Shepherd,
the Rock of Israel,
25 by the God of your father,
who will help you,
by the Almighty[j] who
will bless you
with blessings of heaven above,
blessings of the deep that
lies beneath,
blessings of the breasts
and of the womb.
26 The blessings of your father
are stronger than the blessings
of the eternal mountains,
the bounties[k] of the
everlasting hills;
may they be on the head of Joseph,
on the brow of him who was set
apart from his brothers.

27 'Benjamin is a ravenous wolf,
in the morning devouring
the prey,
and at evening dividing the spoil.'

28 All these are the twelve tribes of Israel, and this is what their father said to them when he blessed them, blessing each one of them with a suitable blessing.

JACOB'S DEATH AND BURIAL

29 Then he charged them, saying to
them, 'I am about to be gathered to my
people. Bury me with my ancestors—in
the cave in the field of Ephron the Hittite,
30 in the cave in the field at Machpelah,

[e] **49.10** Or *until Shiloh comes* or *until he comes to Shiloh* or (with Syr) *until he comes to whom it belongs* [f] **49.20** Gk Vg Syr: Heb *From Asher*
[g] **49.21** Or *that gives beautiful words*
[h] **49.22** Meaning of Heb uncertain [i] **49.24** Heb *the arms of his hands* [j] **49.25** Traditional rendering of Heb *Shaddai* [k] **49.26** Cn Compare Gk: Heb *of my progenitors to the boundaries*

near Mamre, in the land of Canaan, in
the field that Abraham bought from
Ephron the Hittite as a burial site.
31 There Abraham and his wife Sarah
were buried; there Isaac and his wife
Rebekah were buried; and there I buried Leah— 32 the field and the cave that
is in it were purchased from the Hittites.' 33 When Jacob ended his charge
to his sons, he drew up his feet into the
bed, breathed his last, and was gathered
to his people.

50 Then Joseph threw himself on
his father's face and wept over
him and kissed him. 2 Joseph commanded the physicians in his service
to embalm his father. So the physicians
embalmed Israel; 3 they spent forty days
in doing this, for that is the time required for embalming. And the Egyptians wept for him for seventy days.

4 When the days of weeping for him
were past, Joseph addressed the household of Pharaoh, 'If now I have found favour with you, please speak to Pharaoh
as follows: 5 My father made me swear
an oath; he said, "I am about to die. In
the tomb that I hewed out for myself
in the land of Canaan, there you shall
bury me." Now therefore let me go up,
so that I may bury my father; then I will
return.' 6 Pharaoh answered, 'Go up, and
bury your father, as he made you swear
to do.'

7 So Joseph went up to bury his father. With him went up all the servants
of Pharaoh, the elders of his household,
and all the elders of the land of Egypt,
8 as well as all the household of Joseph,
his brothers, and his father's household. Only their children, their flocks,
and their herds were left in the land
of Goshen. 9 Both chariots and charioteers went up with him. It was a very
great company. 10 When they came to
the threshing-floor of Atad, which is
beyond the Jordan, they held there a
very great and sorrowful lamentation;
and he observed a time of mourning
for his father for seven days. 11 When
the Canaanite inhabitants of the land
saw the mourning on the threshing-
floor of Atad, they said, 'This is a grievous mourning on the part of the Egyptians.' Therefore the place was named
Abel-mizraim;[l] it is beyond the Jordan.
12 Thus his sons did for him as he had instructed them. 13 They carried him to the
land of Canaan and buried him in the
cave of the field at Machpelah, the field
near Mamre, which Abraham bought
as a burial site from Ephron the Hittite.
14 After he had buried his father, Joseph
returned to Egypt with his brothers and
all who had gone up with him to bury
his father.

JOSEPH FORGIVES HIS BROTHERS

15 Realizing that their father was
dead, Joseph's brothers said, 'What if Joseph still bears a grudge against us and
pays us back in full for all the wrong that
we did to him?' 16 So they approached[m]
Joseph, saying, 'Your father gave this
instruction before he died, 17 "Say to
Joseph: I beg you, forgive the crime of
your brothers and the wrong they did in
harming you." Now therefore please forgive the crime of the servants of the God
of your father.' Joseph wept when they
spoke to him. 18 Then his brothers also
wept,[n] fell down before him, and said,
'We are here as your slaves.' 19 But Joseph
said to them, 'Do not be afraid! Am I in
the place of God? 20 Even though you intended to do harm to me, God intended
it for good, in order to preserve a numerous people, as he is doing today.
21 So have no fear; I myself will provide
for you and your little ones.' In this way
he reassured them, speaking kindly to
them.

JOSEPH'S LAST DAYS AND DEATH

22 So Joseph remained in Egypt, he
and his father's household; and Joseph
lived for one hundred and ten years.
23 Joseph saw Ephraim's children of the
third generation; the children of Machir
son of Manasseh were also born on Joseph's knees.

24 Then Joseph said to his brothers,
'I am about to die; but God will surely
come to you, and bring you up out of
this land to the land that he swore to
Abraham, to Isaac, and to Jacob.' 25 So
Joseph made the Israelites swear, saying, 'When God comes to you, you shall
carry up my bones from here.' 26 And Joseph died, being one hundred and ten
years old; he was embalmed and placed
in a coffin in Egypt.

[l] **50.11** That is *mourning* (or *meadow*) *of Egypt*
[m] **50.16** Gk Syr: Heb *they commanded*
[n] **50.18** Cn: Heb *also came*

EXODUS

The book of Exodus tells the central story of the Old Testament. It narrates how God freed the Israelites from oppression in Egypt and led them miraculously across the Red Sea into the desert to form them into an independent people. Moses is the main character in this story and is the one through whom God leads the people out of Egypt to Mt. Sinai, where God gives the Ten Commandments (ch. 20) and establishes the covenant relationship with the Israelites.

Exodus has four main sections: the enslavement of the Israelites in Egypt (1.1–13.22); the exodus from Egypt and the journey to Sinai (14.1–18.27); the covenant at Mt. Sinai and the Ten Commandments (19.1–24.18); the tabernacle and the golden calf (25.1–40.38). The story from Exodus about the Passover meal (12.1–8, 11–14) is read every year at Mass on Holy Thursday. Also, the story about the crossing of the Red Sea is read at the Easter Vigil (14.15–15.1). The theophany of God at Mt. Sinai is offered as an optional reading every year at the Vigil of Pentecost (19.3–8, 16–20). Exodus is also read as the First Reading at Mass during Year I of the weekday calendar from Monday of the Fifteenth Week through Thursday of the Seventeenth Week.

1 These are the names of the sons of
Israel who came to Egypt with Jacob, each with his household: 2Reuben,
Simeon, Levi, and Judah, 3Issachar, Zebulun, and Benjamin, 4Dan and Naphtali, Gad and Asher. 5The total number
of people born to Jacob was seventy.
Joseph was already in Egypt. 6Then Joseph died, and all his brothers, and that
whole generation. 7But the Israelites
were fruitful and prolific; they multiplied and grew exceedingly strong, so
that the land was filled with them.

THE ISRAELITES ARE OPPRESSED

8 Now a new king arose over Egypt,
who did not know Joseph. 9He said to
his people, 'Look, the Israelite people
are more numerous and more powerful
than we. 10Come, let us deal shrewdly
with them, or they will increase and, in
the event of war, join our enemies and
fight against us and escape from the
land.' 11Therefore they set taskmasters
over them to oppress them with forced
labour. They built supply cities, Pithom
and Rameses, for Pharaoh. 12But the
more they were oppressed, the more
they multiplied and spread, so that the
Egyptians came to dread the Israelites.
13The Egyptians became ruthless in
imposing tasks on the Israelites, 14and
made their lives bitter with hard service
in mortar and brick and in every kind
of field labour. They were ruthless in all
the tasks that they imposed on them.

15 The king of Egypt said to the Hebrew midwives, one of whom was
named Shiphrah and the other Puah,
16'When you act as midwives to the
Hebrew women, and see them on the
birthstool, if it is a boy, kill him; but if
it is a girl, she shall live.' 17But the midwives feared God; they did not do as the
king of Egypt commanded them, but
they let the boys live. 18So the king of
Egypt summoned the midwives and
said to them, 'Why have you done this,
and allowed the boys to live?' 19The midwives said to Pharaoh, 'Because the
Hebrew women are not like the Egyptian women; for they are vigorous and
give birth before the midwife comes
to them.' 20So God dealt well with the
midwives; and the people multiplied
and became very strong. 21And because

the midwives feared God, he gave them
families. 22 Then Pharaoh commanded
all his people, 'Every boy that is born to
the Hebrews[a] you shall throw into the
Nile, but you shall let every girl live.'

BIRTH AND YOUTH OF MOSES

2 Now a man from the house of Levi
went and married a Levite woman.
2 The woman conceived and bore a son;
and when she saw that he was a fine
baby, she hid him for three months.
3 When she could hide him no longer
she got a papyrus basket for him, and
plastered it with bitumen and pitch; she
put the child in it and placed it among
the reeds on the bank of the river. 4 His
sister stood at a distance, to see what
would happen to him.

5 The daughter of Pharaoh came
down to bathe at the river, while her
attendants walked beside the river. She
saw the basket among the reeds and
sent her maid to bring it. 6 When she
opened it, she saw the child. He was
crying, and she took pity on him. 'This
must be one of the Hebrews' children,'
she said. 7 Then his sister said to Pharaoh's daughter, 'Shall I go and get you a
nurse from the Hebrew women to nurse
the child for you?' 8 Pharaoh's daughter
said to her, 'Yes.' So the girl went and
called the child's mother. 9 Pharaoh's
daughter said to her, 'Take this child
and nurse it for me, and I will give you
your wages.' So the woman took the
child and nursed it. 10 When the child
grew up, she brought him to Pharaoh's
daughter, and she took him as her son.
She named him Moses,[b] 'because', she
said, 'I drew him out[c] of the water.'

MOSES FLEES TO MIDIAN

11 One day, after Moses had grown up,
he went out to his people and saw their
forced labour. He saw an Egyptian beating a Hebrew, one of his kinsfolk. 12 He
looked this way and that, and seeing no
one he killed the Egyptian and hid him
in the sand. 13 When he went out the next
day, he saw two Hebrews fighting; and
he said to the one who was in the wrong,
'Why do you strike your fellow Hebrew?'
14 He answered, 'Who made you a ruler
and judge over us? Do you mean to kill
me as you killed the Egyptian?' Then Moses was afraid and thought, 'Surely the
thing is known.' 15 When Pharaoh heard
of it, he sought to kill Moses.

But Moses fled from Pharaoh. He settled in the land of Midian, and sat down
by a well. 16 The priest of Midian had
seven daughters. They came to draw water, and filled the troughs to water their
father's flock. 17 But some shepherds
came and drove them away. Moses got
up and came to their defence and watered their flock. 18 When they returned
to their father Reuel, he said, 'How is
it that you have come back so soon today?' 19 They said, 'An Egyptian helped
us against the shepherds; he even drew
water for us and watered the flock.' 20 He
said to his daughters, 'Where is he?
Why did you leave the man? Invite him
to break bread.' 21 Moses agreed to stay
with the man, and he gave Moses his
daughter Zipporah in marriage. 22 She
bore a son, and he named him Gershom;
for he said, 'I have been an alien[d] residing in a foreign land.'

23 After a long time the king of Egypt
died. The Israelites groaned under their
slavery, and cried out. Out of the slavery their cry for help rose up to God.
24 God heard their groaning, and God remembered his covenant with Abraham,
Isaac, and Jacob. 25 God looked upon the
Israelites, and God took notice of them.

MOSES AT THE BURNING BUSH

3 Moses was keeping the flock of his
father-in-law Jethro, the priest of
Midian; he led his flock beyond the wilderness, and came to Horeb, the mountain of God. 2 There the angel of the
LORD appeared to him in a flame of fire
out of a bush; he looked, and the bush
was blazing, yet it was not consumed.
3 Then Moses said, 'I must turn aside and
look at this great sight, and see why the
bush is not burned up.' 4 When the LORD
saw that he had turned aside to see, God
called to him out of the bush, 'Moses,
Moses!' And he said, 'Here I am.' 5 Then
he said, 'Come no closer! Remove the
sandals from your feet, for the place on
which you are standing is holy ground.'
6 He said further, 'I am the God of your
father, the God of Abraham, the God of
Isaac, and the God of Jacob.' And Moses
hid his face, for he was afraid to look at
God.

7 Then the LORD said, 'I have observed the misery of my people who
are in Egypt; I have heard their cry on
account of their taskmasters. Indeed,
I know their sufferings, 8 and I have
come down to deliver them from the

[a] 1.22 Sam Gk Tg: Heb lacks *to the Hebrews*
[b] 2.10 Heb *Mosheh* [c] 2.10 Heb *mashah*
[d] 2.22 Heb *ger*

Egyptians, and to bring them up out
of that land to a good and broad land,
a land flowing with milk and honey,
to the country of the Canaanites, the
Hittites, the Amorites, the Perizzites,
the Hivites, and the Jebusites. 9The cry
of the Israelites has now come to me; I
have also seen how the Egyptians oppress them. 10So come, I will send you
to Pharaoh to bring my people, the Israelites, out of Egypt.' 11But Moses said
to God, 'Who am I that I should go to
Pharaoh, and bring the Israelites out
of Egypt?' 12He said, 'I will be with you;
and this shall be the sign for you that
it is I who sent you: when you have
brought the people out of Egypt, you
shall worship God on this mountain.'

THE DIVINE NAME REVEALED

13 But Moses said to God, 'If I come
to the Israelites and say to them, "The
God of your ancestors has sent me to
you", and they ask me, "What is his
name?" what shall I say to them?' 14God
said to Moses, 'I AM WHO I AM.'[e] He said
further, 'Thus you shall say to the Israelites, "I AM has sent me to you."' 15God
also said to Moses, 'Thus you shall say
to the Israelites, "The LORD,[f] the God
of your ancestors, the God of Abraham,
the God of Isaac, and the God of Jacob,
has sent me to you":

This is my name for ever,
and this my title for all generations.

16Go and assemble the elders of Israel,
and say to them, "The LORD, the God of
your ancestors, the God of Abraham, of
Isaac, and of Jacob, has appeared to me,
saying: I have given heed to you and to
what has been done to you in Egypt. 17I
declare that I will bring you up out of
the misery of Egypt, to the land of the
Canaanites, the Hittites, the Amorites,
the Perizzites, the Hivites, and the Jebusites, a land flowing with milk and
honey." 18They will listen to your voice;
and you and the elders of Israel shall
go to the king of Egypt and say to him,
"The LORD, the God of the Hebrews, has
met with us; let us now go a three days'
journey into the wilderness, so that we
may sacrifice to the LORD our God." 19I
know, however, that the king of Egypt
will not let you go unless compelled by
a mighty hand.[g] 20So I will stretch out
my hand and strike Egypt with all my
wonders that I will perform in it; after
that he will let you go. 21I will bring this
people into such favour with the Egyptians that, when you go, you will not go
empty-handed; 22each woman shall ask
her neighbour and any woman living in
the neighbour's house for jewellery of
silver and of gold, and clothing, and you
shall put them on your sons and on your
daughters; and so you shall plunder the
Egyptians.'

MOSES' MIRACULOUS POWER

4 Then Moses answered, 'But suppose
they do not believe me or listen to
me, but say, "The LORD did not appear
to you."' 2The LORD said to him, 'What
is that in your hand?' He said, 'A staff.'
3And he said, 'Throw it on the ground.'
So he threw the staff on the ground, and
it became a snake; and Moses drew back
from it. 4Then the LORD said to Moses,
'Reach out your hand, and seize it by the
tail'—so he reached out his hand and
grasped it, and it became a staff in his
hand— 5'so that they may believe that
the LORD, the God of their ancestors,
the God of Abraham, the God of Isaac,
and the God of Jacob, has appeared to
you.'

6 Again, the LORD said to him, 'Put
your hand inside your cloak.' He put his
hand into his cloak; and when he took
it out, his hand was leprous,[h] as white
as snow. 7Then God said, 'Put your hand
back into your cloak'—so he put his
hand back into his cloak, and when he
took it out, it was restored like the rest of
his body— 8'If they will not believe you
or heed the first sign, they may believe
the second sign. 9If they will not believe
even these two signs or heed you, you
shall take some water from the Nile and
pour it on the dry ground; and the water
that you shall take from the Nile will become blood on the dry ground.'

10 But Moses said to the LORD, 'O my
Lord, I have never been eloquent, neither in the past nor even now that you
have spoken to your servant; but I am
slow of speech and slow of tongue.'
11Then the LORD said to him, 'Who gives
speech to mortals? Who makes them
mute or deaf, seeing or blind? Is it not I,
the LORD? 12Now go, and I will be with
your mouth and teach you what you
are to speak.' 13But he said, 'O my Lord,
please send someone else.' 14Then the

[e] **3.14** Or *I AM WHAT I AM* or *I WILL BE WHAT I WILL BE* [f] **3.15** The word 'LORD' when spelled with capital letters stands for the divine name, *YHWH*, which is here connected with the verb *hayah*, 'to be' [g] **3.19** Gk Vg: Heb *no, not by a mighty hand* [h] **4.6** A term for several skin diseases; precise meaning uncertain

anger of the LORD was kindled against
Moses and he said, 'What of your brother
Aaron the Levite? I know that he can
speak fluently; even now he is coming
out to meet you, and when he sees you
his heart will be glad. 15You shall speak
to him and put the words in his mouth;
and I will be with your mouth and with
his mouth, and will teach you what you
shall do. 16He indeed shall speak for you
to the people; he shall serve as a mouth
for you, and you shall serve as God for
him. 17Take in your hand this staff, with
which you shall perform the signs.'

MOSES RETURNS TO EGYPT

18 Moses went back to his father-in-
law Jethro and said to him, 'Please let
me go back to my kindred in Egypt and
see whether they are still living.' And
Jethro said to Moses, 'Go in peace.' 19The
LORD said to Moses in Midian, 'Go back
to Egypt; for all those who were seeking
your life are dead.' 20So Moses took his
wife and his sons, put them on a donkey, and went back to the land of Egypt;
and Moses carried the staff of God in his
hand.

21 And the LORD said to Moses,
'When you go back to Egypt, see that you
perform before Pharaoh all the wonders
that I have put in your power; but I will
harden his heart, so that he will not let
the people go. 22Then you shall say to
Pharaoh, "Thus says the LORD: Israel
is my firstborn son. 23I said to you, 'Let
my son go that he may worship me.' But
you refused to let him go; now I will kill
your firstborn son." '

24 On the way, at a place where they
spent the night, the LORD met him and
tried to kill him. 25But Zipporah took a
flint and cut off her son's foreskin, and
touched Moses'[i] feet with it, and said,
'Truly you are a bridegroom of blood to
me!' 26So he let him alone. It was then
she said, 'A bridegroom of blood by circumcision.'

27 The LORD said to Aaron, 'Go into
the wilderness to meet Moses.' So he
went; and he met him at the mountain
of God and kissed him. 28Moses told
Aaron all the words of the LORD with
which he had sent him, and all the signs
with which he had charged him. 29Then
Moses and Aaron went and assembled
all the elders of the Israelites. 30Aaron
spoke all the words that the LORD had
spoken to Moses, and performed the
signs in the sight of the people. 31The
people believed; and when they heard
that the LORD had given heed to the Israelites and that he had seen their misery, they bowed down and worshipped.

BRICKS WITHOUT STRAW

5 Afterwards Moses and Aaron went
to Pharaoh and said, 'Thus says the
LORD, the God of Israel, "Let my people go, so that they may celebrate a
festival to me in the wilderness." ' 2But
Pharaoh said, 'Who is the LORD, that I
should heed him and let Israel go? I do
not know the LORD, and I will not let
Israel go.' 3Then they said, 'The God of
the Hebrews has revealed himself to us;
let us go a three days' journey into the
wilderness to sacrifice to the LORD our
God, or he will fall upon us with pestilence or sword.' 4But the king of Egypt
said to them, 'Moses and Aaron, why
are you taking the people away from
their work? Get to your labours!' 5Phar-
aoh continued, 'Now they are more numerous than the people of the land[j] and
yet you want them to stop working!'
6That same day Pharaoh commanded
the taskmasters of the people, as well as
their supervisors, 7'You shall no longer
give the people straw to make bricks,
as before; let them go and gather straw
for themselves. 8But you shall require
of them the same quantity of bricks as
they have made previously; do not diminish it, for they are lazy; that is why
they cry, "Let us go and offer sacrifice to
our God." 9Let heavier work be laid on
them; then they will labour at it and pay
no attention to deceptive words.'

10 So the taskmasters and the supervisors of the people went out and
said to the people, 'Thus says Pharaoh,
"I will not give you straw. 11Go and get
straw yourselves, wherever you can find
it; but your work will not be lessened
in the least." ' 12So the people scattered
throughout the land of Egypt, to gather
stubble for straw. 13The taskmasters
were urgent, saying, 'Complete your
work, the same daily assignment as
when you were given straw.' 14And the
supervisors of the Israelites, whom Pharaoh's taskmasters had set over them,
were beaten, and were asked, 'Why did
you not finish the required quantity of
bricks yesterday and today, as you did
before?'

15 Then the Israelite supervisors
came to Pharaoh and cried, 'Why do

[i] **4.25** Heb *his* [j] **5.5** Sam: Heb *The people of the land are now many*

you treat your servants like this? 16 No straw is given to your servants, yet they say to us, "Make bricks!" Look how your servants are beaten! You are unjust to your own people.'[k] 17 He said, 'You are lazy, lazy; that is why you say, "Let us go and sacrifice to the LORD." 18 Go now, and work; for no straw shall be given you, but you shall still deliver the same number of bricks.' 19 The Israelite supervisors saw that they were in trouble when they were told, 'You shall not lessen your daily number of bricks.' 20 As they left Pharaoh, they came upon Moses and Aaron who were waiting to meet them. 21 They said to them, 'The LORD look upon you and judge! You have brought us into bad odour with Pharaoh and his officials, and have put a sword in their hand to kill us.'

22 Then Moses turned again to the LORD and said, 'O LORD, why have you mistreated this people? Why did you ever send me? 23 Since I first came to Pharaoh to speak in your name, he has mistreated this people, and you have done nothing at all to deliver your people.'

ISRAEL'S DELIVERANCE ASSURED

6 Then the LORD said to Moses, 'Now you shall see what I will do to Pharaoh: Indeed, by a mighty hand he will let them go; by a mighty hand he will drive them out of his land.'

2 God also spoke to Moses and said to him: 'I am the LORD. 3 I appeared to Abraham, Isaac, and Jacob as God Almighty,[l] but by my name "The LORD"[m] I did not make myself known to them. 4 I also established my covenant with them, to give them the land of Canaan, the land in which they resided as aliens. 5 I have also heard the groaning of the Israelites, whom the Egyptians are holding as slaves, and I have remembered my covenant. 6 Say therefore to the Israelites, "I am the LORD, and I will free you from the burdens of the Egyptians and deliver you from slavery to them. I will redeem you with an outstretched arm and with mighty acts of judgement. 7 I will take you as my people, and I will be your God. You shall know that I am the LORD your God, who has freed you from the burdens of the Egyptians. 8 I will bring you into the land that I swore to give to Abraham, Isaac, and Jacob; I will give it to you for a possession. I am the LORD."' 9 Moses told this to the Israelites; but they would not listen to Moses, because of their broken spirit and their cruel slavery.

10 Then the LORD spoke to Moses, 11 'Go and tell Pharaoh king of Egypt to let the Israelites go out of his land.' 12 But Moses spoke to the LORD, 'The Israelites have not listened to me; how then shall Pharaoh listen to me, poor speaker that I am?'[n] 13 Thus the LORD spoke to Moses and Aaron, and gave them orders regarding the Israelites and Pharaoh king of Egypt, charging them to free the Israelites from the land of Egypt.

THE GENEALOGY OF MOSES AND AARON

14 The following are the heads of their ancestral houses: the sons of Reuben, the firstborn of Israel: Hanoch, Pallu, Hezron, and Carmi; these are the families of Reuben. 15 The sons of Simeon: Jemuel, Jamin, Ohad, Jachin, Zohar, and Shaul,[o] the son of a Canaanite woman; these are the families of Simeon. 16 The following are the names of the sons of Levi according to their genealogies: Gershon,[p] Kohath, and Merari, and the length of Levi's life was one hundred and thirty-seven years. 17 The sons of Gershon:[q] Libni and Shimei, by their families. 18 The sons of Kohath: Amram, Izhar, Hebron, and Uzziel, and the length of Kohath's life was one hundred and thirty-three years. 19 The sons of Merari: Mahli and Mushi. These are the families of the Levites according to their genealogies. 20 Amram married Jochebed his father's sister and she bore him Aaron and Moses, and the length of Amram's life was one hundred and thirty-seven years. 21 The sons of Izhar: Korah, Nepheg, and Zichri. 22 The sons of Uzziel: Mishael, Elzaphan, and Sithri. 23 Aaron married Elisheba, daughter of Amminadab and sister of Nahshon, and she bore him Nadab, Abihu, Eleazar, and Ithamar. 24 The sons of Korah: Assir, Elkanah, and Abiasaph; these are the families of the Korahites. 25 Aaron's son Eleazar married one of the daughters of Putiel, and she bore him Phinehas. These are the heads of the ancestral houses of the Levites by their families.

26 It was this same Aaron and Moses to whom the LORD said, 'Bring the

[k] **5.16** Gk Compare Syr Vg: Heb *beaten, and the sin of your people* [l] **6.3** Traditional rendering of Heb *El Shaddai* [m] **6.3** Heb *YHWH*; see note at 3.15 [n] **6.12** Heb *me? I am uncircumcised of lips* [o] **6.15** Or *Saul* [p] **6.16** Also spelled *Gershom*; see 2.22 [q] **6.17** Also spelled *Gershom*; see 2.22

Israelites out of the land of Egypt, company by company.' 27It was they who spoke to Pharaoh king of Egypt to bring the Israelites out of Egypt, the same Moses and Aaron.

MOSES AND AARON OBEY GOD'S COMMANDS

28 On the day when the LORD spoke to Moses in the land of Egypt, 29he said to him, 'I am the LORD; tell Pharaoh king of Egypt all that I am speaking to you.' 30But Moses said in the LORD's presence, 'Since I am a poor speaker,[r] why would Pharaoh listen to me?'

7 The LORD said to Moses, 'See, I have made you like God to Pharaoh, and your brother Aaron shall be your prophet. 2You shall speak all that I command you, and your brother Aaron shall tell Pharaoh to let the Israelites go out of his land. 3But I will harden Pharaoh's heart, and I will multiply my signs and wonders in the land of Egypt. 4When Pharaoh does not listen to you, I will lay my hand upon Egypt and bring my people the Israelites, company by company, out of the land of Egypt by great acts of judgement. 5The Egyptians shall know that I am the LORD, when I stretch out my hand against Egypt and bring the Israelites out from among them.' 6Moses and Aaron did so; they did just as the LORD commanded them. 7Moses was eighty years old and Aaron eighty-three when they spoke to Pharaoh.

AARON'S MIRACULOUS ROD

8 The LORD said to Moses and Aaron, 9'When Pharaoh says to you, "Perform a wonder", then you shall say to Aaron, "Take your staff and throw it down before Pharaoh, and it will become a snake."' 10So Moses and Aaron went to Pharaoh and did as the LORD had commanded; Aaron threw down his staff before Pharaoh and his officials, and it became a snake. 11Then Pharaoh summoned the wise men and the sorcerers; and they also, the magicians of Egypt, did the same by their secret arts. 12Each one threw down his staff, and they became snakes; but Aaron's staff swallowed up theirs. 13Still Pharaoh's heart was hardened, and he would not listen to them, as the LORD had said.

THE FIRST PLAGUE: WATER TURNED TO BLOOD

14 Then the LORD said to Moses, 'Pharaoh's heart is hardened; he refuses to let the people go. 15Go to Pharaoh in the morning, as he is going out to the water; stand by at the river bank to meet him, and take in your hand the staff that was turned into a snake. 16Say to him, "The LORD, the God of the Hebrews, sent me to you to say, 'Let my people go, so that they may worship me in the wilderness.' But until now you have not listened. 17Thus says the LORD, 'By this you shall know that I am the LORD.' See, with the staff that is in my hand I will strike the water that is in the Nile, and it shall be turned to blood. 18The fish in the river shall die, the river itself shall stink, and the Egyptians shall be unable to drink water from the Nile."' 19The LORD said to Moses, 'Say to Aaron, "Take your staff and stretch out your hand over the waters of Egypt—over its rivers, its canals, and its ponds, and all its pools of water—so that they may become blood; and there shall be blood throughout the whole land of Egypt, even in vessels of wood and in vessels of stone."'

20 Moses and Aaron did just as the LORD commanded. In the sight of Pharaoh and of his officials he lifted up the staff and struck the water in the river, and all the water in the river was turned into blood, 21and the fish in the river died. The river stank so that the Egyptians could not drink its water, and there was blood throughout the whole land of Egypt. 22But the magicians of Egypt did the same by their secret arts; so Pharaoh's heart remained hardened, and he would not listen to them, as the LORD had said. 23Pharaoh turned and went into his house, and he did not take even this to heart. 24And all the Egyptians had to dig along the Nile for water to drink, for they could not drink the water of the river.

25 Seven days passed after the LORD had struck the Nile.

THE SECOND PLAGUE: FROGS

8[s] Then the LORD said to Moses, 'Go to Pharaoh and say to him, "Thus says the LORD: Let my people go, so that they may worship me. 2If you refuse to let them go, I will plague your whole country with frogs. 3The river shall swarm with frogs; they shall come up into your palace, into your bedchamber and your bed, and into the houses of your officials and of your people,[t] and into your

[r] 6.30 Heb *am uncircumcised of lips*; see 6.12
[s] 8.1 Ch 7.26 in Heb [t] 8.3 Gk: Heb *upon your people*

ovens and your kneading bowls. 4The
frogs shall come up on you and on your
people and on all your officials." ' 5[u]And
the LORD said to Moses, 'Say to Aaron,
"Stretch out your hand with your staff
over the rivers, the canals, and the
pools, and make frogs come up on the
land of Egypt." ' 6So Aaron stretched out
his hand over the waters of Egypt; and
the frogs came up and covered the land
of Egypt. 7But the magicians did the
same by their secret arts, and brought
frogs up on the land of Egypt.

8 Then Pharaoh called Moses and
Aaron, and said, 'Pray to the LORD to
take away the frogs from me and my
people, and I will let the people go to
sacrifice to the LORD.' 9Moses said to
Pharaoh, 'Kindly tell me when I am to
pray for you and for your officials and
for your people, that the frogs may be
removed from you and your houses
and be left only in the Nile.' 10And he
said, 'Tomorrow.' Moses said, 'As you
say! So that you may know that there
is no one like the LORD our God, 11the
frogs shall leave you and your houses
and your officials and your people; they
shall be left only in the Nile.' 12Then Moses and Aaron went out from Pharaoh;
and Moses cried out to the LORD concerning the frogs that he had brought
upon Pharaoh.[v] 13And the LORD did as
Moses requested: the frogs died in the
houses, the courtyards, and the fields.
14And they gathered them together in
heaps, and the land stank. 15But when
Pharaoh saw that there was a respite,
he hardened his heart, and would not
listen to them, just as the LORD had
said.

THE THIRD PLAGUE: GNATS

16 Then the LORD said to Moses,
'Say to Aaron, "Stretch out your staff
and strike the dust of the earth, so that
it may become gnats throughout the
whole land of Egypt." ' 17And they did
so; Aaron stretched out his hand with
his staff and struck the dust of the earth,
and gnats came on humans and animals
alike; all the dust of the earth turned
into gnats throughout the whole land of
Egypt. 18The magicians tried to produce
gnats by their secret arts, but they could
not. There were gnats on both humans
and animals. 19And the magicians said
to Pharaoh, 'This is the finger of God!'
But Pharaoh's heart was hardened, and
he would not listen to them, just as the
LORD had said.

THE FOURTH PLAGUE: FLIES

20 Then the LORD said to Moses,
'Rise early in the morning and present
yourself before Pharaoh, as he goes
out to the water, and say to him, "Thus
says the LORD: Let my people go, so
that they may worship me. 21For if you
will not let my people go, I will send
swarms of flies on you, your officials,
and your people, and into your houses;
and the houses of the Egyptians shall
be filled with swarms of flies; so also
the land where they live. 22But on
that day I will set apart the land of Goshen, where my people live, so that no
swarms of flies shall be there, that you
may know that I the LORD am in this
land. 23Thus I will make a distinction[w]
between my people and your people.
This sign shall appear tomorrow." '
24The LORD did so, and great swarms
of flies came into the house of Pharaoh
and into his officials' houses; in all of
Egypt the land was ruined because of
the flies.

25 Then Pharaoh summoned Moses
and Aaron, and said, 'Go, sacrifice to
your God within the land.' 26But Moses
said, 'It would not be right to do so; for
the sacrifices that we offer to the LORD
our God are offensive to the Egyptians.
If we offer in the sight of the Egyptians
sacrifices that are offensive to them,
will they not stone us? 27We must go a
three days' journey into the wilderness
and sacrifice to the LORD our God as
he commands us.' 28So Pharaoh said, 'I
will let you go to sacrifice to the LORD
your God in the wilderness, provided
you do not go very far away. Pray for
me.' 29Then Moses said, 'As soon as I
leave you, I will pray to the LORD that
the swarms of flies may depart tomorrow from Pharaoh, from his officials,
and from his people; only do not let
Pharaoh again deal falsely by not letting the people go to sacrifice to the
LORD.'

30 So Moses went out from Pharaoh and prayed to the LORD. 31And the
LORD did as Moses asked: he removed
the swarms of flies from Pharaoh, from
his officials, and from his people; not
one remained. 32But Pharaoh hardened
his heart this time also, and would not
let the people go.

[u] **8.5** Ch 8.1 in Heb [v] **8.12** Or *frogs, as he had agreed with Pharaoh* [w] **8.23** Gk Vg: Heb *will set redemption*

THE FIFTH PLAGUE: LIVESTOCK DISEASED

9 Then the LORD said to Moses, 'Go to Pharaoh, and say to him, "Thus says the LORD, the God of the Hebrews: Let my people go, so that they may worship me. 2For if you refuse to let them go and still hold them, 3the hand of the LORD will strike with a deadly pestilence your livestock in the field: the horses, the donkeys, the camels, the herds, and the flocks. 4But the LORD will make a distinction between the livestock of Israel and the livestock of Egypt, so that nothing shall die of all that belongs to the Israelites." ' 5The LORD set a time, saying, 'Tomorrow the LORD will do this thing in the land.' 6And on the next day the LORD did so; all the livestock of the Egyptians died, but of the livestock of the Israelites not one died. 7Pharaoh inquired and found that not one of the livestock of the Israelites was dead. But the heart of Pharaoh was hardened, and he would not let the people go.

THE SIXTH PLAGUE: BOILS

8 Then the LORD said to Moses and Aaron, 'Take handfuls of soot from the kiln, and let Moses throw it in the air in the sight of Pharaoh. 9It shall become fine dust all over the land of Egypt, and shall cause festering boils on humans and animals throughout the whole land of Egypt.' 10So they took soot from the kiln, and stood before Pharaoh, and Moses threw it in the air, and it caused festering boils on humans and animals. 11The magicians could not stand before Moses because of the boils, for the boils afflicted the magicians as well as all the Egyptians. 12But the LORD hardened the heart of Pharaoh, and he would not listen to them, just as the LORD had spoken to Moses.

THE SEVENTH PLAGUE: THUNDER AND HAIL

13 Then the LORD said to Moses, 'Rise up early in the morning and present yourself before Pharaoh, and say to him, "Thus says the LORD, the God of the Hebrews: Let my people go, so that they may worship me. 14For this time I will send all my plagues upon you yourself, and upon your officials, and upon your people, so that you may know that there is no one like me in all the earth. 15For by now I could have stretched out my hand and struck you and your people with pestilence, and you would have been cut off from the earth. 16But this is why I have let you live: to show you my power, and to make my name resound through all the earth. 17You are still exalting yourself against my people, and will not let them go. 18Tomorrow at this time I will cause the heaviest hail to fall that has ever fallen in Egypt from the day it was founded until now. 19Send, therefore, and have your livestock and everything that you have in the open field brought to a secure place; every human or animal that is in the open field and is not brought under shelter will die when the hail comes down upon them." ' 20Those officials of Pharaoh who feared the word of the LORD hurried their slaves and livestock off to a secure place. 21Those who did not regard the word of the LORD left their slaves and livestock in the open field.

22 The LORD said to Moses, 'Stretch out your hand towards heaven so that hail may fall on the whole land of Egypt, on humans and animals and all the plants of the field in the land of Egypt.' 23Then Moses stretched out his staff towards heaven, and the LORD sent thunder and hail, and fire came down on the earth. And the LORD rained hail on the land of Egypt; 24there was hail with fire flashing continually in the midst of it, such heavy hail as had never fallen in all the land of Egypt since it became a nation. 25The hail struck down everything that was in the open field throughout all the land of Egypt, both human and animal; the hail also struck down all the plants of the field, and shattered every tree in the field. 26Only in the land of Goshen, where the Israelites were, there was no hail.

27 Then Pharaoh summoned Moses and Aaron, and said to them, 'This time I have sinned; the LORD is in the right, and I and my people are in the wrong. 28Pray to the LORD! Enough of God's thunder and hail! I will let you go; you need stay no longer.' 29Moses said to him, 'As soon as I have gone out of the city, I will stretch out my hands to the LORD; the thunder will cease, and there will be no more hail, so that you may know that the earth is the LORD's. 30But as for you and your officials, I know that you do not yet fear the LORD God.' 31(Now the flax and the barley were ruined, for the barley was in the ear and the flax was in bud. 32But the wheat and the spelt were not ruined, for they are late in coming up.) 33So Moses left Pharaoh,

went out of the city, and stretched out
his hands to the LORD; then the thunder and the hail ceased, and the rain
no longer poured down on the earth.
34But when Pharaoh saw that the
rain and the hail and the thunder had
ceased, he sinned once more and hardened his heart, he and his officials. 35So
the heart of Pharaoh was hardened, and
he would not let the Israelites go, just as
the LORD had spoken through Moses.

THE EIGHTH PLAGUE: LOCUSTS

10 Then the LORD said to Moses,
'Go to Pharaoh; for I have hardened his heart and the heart of his officials, in order that I may show these
signs of mine among them, 2and that
you may tell your children and grandchildren how I have made fools of the
Egyptians and what signs I have done
among them—so that you may know
that I am the LORD.'

3 So Moses and Aaron went to Pharaoh, and said to him, 'Thus says the
LORD, the God of the Hebrews, "How
long will you refuse to humble yourself
before me? Let my people go, so that
they may worship me. 4For if you refuse
to let my people go, tomorrow I will
bring locusts into your country. 5They
shall cover the surface of the land, so
that no one will be able to see the land.
They shall devour the last remnant left
you after the hail, and they shall devour
every tree of yours that grows in the
field. 6They shall fill your houses, and
the houses of all your officials and of all
the Egyptians—something that neither
your parents nor your grandparents
have seen, from the day they came on
earth to this day." ' Then he turned and
went out from Pharaoh.

7 Pharaoh's officials said to him,
'How long shall this fellow be a snare to
us? Let the people go, so that they may
worship the LORD their God; do you not
yet understand that Egypt is ruined?'
8So Moses and Aaron were brought
back to Pharaoh, and he said to them,
'Go, worship the LORD your God! But
which ones are to go?' 9Moses said, 'We
will go with our young and our old; we
will go with our sons and daughters and
with our flocks and herds, because we
have the LORD's festival to celebrate.'
10He said to them, 'The LORD indeed will
be with you, if ever I let your little ones
go with you! Plainly you have some evil
purpose in mind. 11No, never! Your men
may go and worship the LORD, for that
is what you are asking.' And they were
driven out from Pharaoh's presence.

12 Then the LORD said to Moses,
'Stretch out your hand over the land
of Egypt, so that the locusts may come
upon it and eat every plant in the land,
all that the hail has left.' 13So Moses
stretched out his staff over the land of
Egypt, and the LORD brought an east
wind upon the land all that day and
all that night; when morning came,
the east wind had brought the locusts.
14The locusts came upon all the land of
Egypt and settled on the whole country
of Egypt, such a dense swarm of locusts
as had never been before, nor ever shall
be again. 15They covered the surface of
the whole land, so that the land was
black; and they ate all the plants in the
land and all the fruit of the trees that
the hail had left; nothing green was
left, no tree, no plant in the field, in all
the land of Egypt. 16Pharaoh hurriedly
summoned Moses and Aaron and said,
'I have sinned against the LORD your
God, and against you. 17Do forgive my
sin just this once, and pray to the LORD
your God that at the least he remove
this deadly thing from me.' 18So he went
out from Pharaoh and prayed to the
LORD. 19The LORD changed the wind
into a very strong west wind, which
lifted the locusts and drove them into
the Red Sea;[x] not a single locust was left
in all the country of Egypt. 20But the
LORD hardened Pharaoh's heart, and he
would not let the Israelites go.

THE NINTH PLAGUE: DARKNESS

21 Then the LORD said to Moses,
'Stretch out your hand towards heaven
so that there may be darkness over the
land of Egypt, a darkness that can be
felt.' 22So Moses stretched out his hand
towards heaven, and there was dense
darkness in all the land of Egypt for
three days. 23People could not see one
another, and for three days they could
not move from where they were; but all
the Israelites had light where they lived.
24Then Pharaoh summoned Moses, and
said, 'Go, worship the LORD. Only your
flocks and your herds shall remain behind. Even your children may go with
you.' 25But Moses said, 'You must also let
us have sacrifices and burnt-offerings
to sacrifice to the LORD our God. 26Our
livestock also must go with us; not a
hoof shall be left behind, for we must

[x] **10.19** Or *Sea of Reeds*

choose some of them for the worship of the LORD our God, and we will not know what to use to worship the LORD until we arrive there.' 27But the LORD hardened Pharaoh's heart, and he was unwilling to let them go. 28Then Pharaoh said to him, 'Get away from me! Take care that you do not see my face again, for on the day you see my face you shall die.' 29Moses said, 'Just as you say! I will never see your face again.'

WARNING OF THE FINAL PLAGUE

11 The LORD said to Moses, 'I will bring one more plague upon Pharaoh and upon Egypt; afterwards he will let you go from here; indeed, when he lets you go, he will drive you away. 2Tell the people that every man is to ask his neighbour and every woman is to ask her neighbour for objects of silver and gold.' 3The LORD gave the people favour in the sight of the Egyptians. Moreover, Moses himself was a man of great importance in the land of Egypt, in the sight of Pharaoh's officials, and in the sight of the people.

4 Moses said, 'Thus says the LORD: About midnight I will go out through Egypt. 5Every firstborn in the land of Egypt shall die, from the firstborn of Pharaoh who sits on his throne to the firstborn of the female slave who is behind the handmill, and all the firstborn of the livestock. 6Then there will be a loud cry throughout the whole land of Egypt, such as has never been nor will ever be again. 7But not a dog shall growl at any of the Israelites—not at people, not at animals—so that you may know that the LORD makes a distinction between Egypt and Israel. 8Then all these officials of yours shall come down to me, and bow low to me, saying, "Leave us, you and all the people who follow you." After that I will leave.' And in hot anger he left Pharaoh.

9 The LORD said to Moses, 'Pharaoh will not listen to you, in order that my wonders may be multiplied in the land of Egypt.' 10Moses and Aaron performed all these wonders before Pharaoh; but the LORD hardened Pharaoh's heart, and he did not let the people of Israel go out of his land.

THE FIRST PASSOVER INSTITUTED

12 The LORD said to Moses and Aaron in the land of Egypt: 2This month shall mark for you the beginning of months; it shall be the first month of the year for you. 3Tell the whole congregation of Israel that on the tenth of this month they are to take a lamb for each family, a lamb for each household. 4If a household is too small for a whole lamb, it shall join its closest neighbour in obtaining one; the lamb shall be divided in proportion to the number of people who eat of it. 5Your lamb shall be without blemish, a year-old male; you may take it from the sheep or from the goats. 6You shall keep it until the fourteenth day of this month; then the whole assembled congregation of Israel shall slaughter it at twilight. 7They shall take some of the blood and put it on the two doorposts and the lintel of the houses in which they eat it. 8They shall eat the lamb that same night; they shall eat it roasted over the fire with unleavened bread and bitter herbs. 9Do not eat any of it raw or boiled in water, but roasted over the fire, with its head, legs, and inner organs. 10You shall let none of it remain until the morning; anything that remains until the morning you shall burn. 11This is how you shall eat it: your loins girded, your sandals on your feet, and your staff in your hand; and you shall eat it hurriedly. It is the passover of the LORD. 12For I will pass through the land of Egypt that night, and I will strike down every firstborn in the land of Egypt, both human beings and animals; on all the gods of Egypt I will execute judgements: I am the LORD. 13The blood shall be a sign for you on the houses where you live: when I see the blood, I will pass over you, and no plague shall destroy you when I strike the land of Egypt.

14 This day shall be a day of remembrance for you. You shall celebrate it as a festival to the LORD; throughout your generations you shall observe it as a perpetual ordinance. 15Seven days you shall eat unleavened bread; on the first day you shall remove leaven from your houses, for whoever eats leavened bread from the first day until the seventh day shall be cut off from Israel. 16On the first day you shall hold a solemn assembly, and on the seventh day a solemn assembly; no work shall be done on those days; only what everyone must eat, that alone may be prepared by you. 17You shall observe the festival of unleavened bread, for on this very day I brought your companies out of the land of Egypt: you shall observe this day throughout your generations as a perpetual ordinance. 18In

the first month, from the evening of the
fourteenth day until the evening of the
twenty-first day, you shall eat unleavened bread. 19 For seven days no leaven
shall be found in your houses; for whoever eats what is leavened shall be cut off
from the congregation of Israel, whether
an alien or a native of the land. 20 You
shall eat nothing leavened; in all your settlements you shall eat unleavened bread.

21 Then Moses called all the elders of
Israel and said to them, 'Go, select lambs
for your families, and slaughter the passover lamb. 22 Take a bunch of hyssop, dip
it in the blood that is in the basin, and
touch the lintel and the two doorposts
with the blood in the basin. None of you
shall go outside the door of your house
until morning. 23 For the LORD will pass
through to strike down the Egyptians;
when he sees the blood on the lintel
and on the two doorposts, the LORD
will pass over that door and will not allow the destroyer to enter your houses
to strike you down. 24 You shall observe
this rite as a perpetual ordinance for you
and your children. 25 When you come to
the land that the LORD will give you, as
he has promised, you shall keep this observance. 26 And when your children ask
you, "What do you mean by this observance?" 27 you shall say, "It is the passover sacrifice to the LORD, for he passed
over the houses of the Israelites in
Egypt, when he struck down the Egyptians but spared our houses." ' And the
people bowed down and worshipped.

28 The Israelites went and did just as
the LORD had commanded Moses and
Aaron.

THE TENTH PLAGUE: DEATH OF THE FIRSTBORN

29 At midnight the LORD struck
down all the firstborn in the land of
Egypt, from the firstborn of Pharaoh
who sat on his throne to the firstborn of
the prisoner who was in the dungeon,
and all the firstborn of the livestock.
30 Pharaoh arose in the night, he and all
his officials and all the Egyptians; and
there was a loud cry in Egypt, for there
was not a house without someone dead.
31 Then he summoned Moses and Aaron
in the night, and said, 'Rise up, go away
from my people, both you and the Israelites! Go, worship the LORD, as you
said. 32 Take your flocks and your herds,
as you said, and be gone. And bring a
blessing on me too!'

THE EXODUS: FROM RAMESES TO SUCCOTH

33 The Egyptians urged the people to hasten their departure from the
land, for they said, 'We shall all be dead.'
34 So the people took their dough before
it was leavened, with their kneading-
bowls wrapped up in their cloaks on
their shoulders. 35 The Israelites had
done as Moses told them; they had
asked the Egyptians for jewellery of silver and gold, and for clothing, 36 and the
LORD had given the people favour in
the sight of the Egyptians, so that they
let them have what they asked. And so
they plundered the Egyptians.

37 The Israelites journeyed from
Rameses to Succoth, about six hundred
thousand men on foot, besides children.
38 A mixed crowd also went up with
them, and livestock in great numbers,
both flocks and herds. 39 They baked unleavened cakes of the dough that they
had brought out of Egypt; it was not
leavened, because they were driven out
of Egypt and could not wait, nor had
they prepared any provisions for themselves.

40 The time that the Israelites had
lived in Egypt was four hundred and
thirty years. 41 At the end of four hundred and thirty years, on that very day,
all the companies of the LORD went out
from the land of Egypt. 42 That was for
the LORD a night of vigil, to bring them
out of the land of Egypt. That same
night is a vigil to be kept for the LORD
by all the Israelites throughout their
generations.

DIRECTIONS FOR THE PASSOVER

43 The LORD said to Moses and
Aaron: This is the ordinance for the
passover: no foreigner shall eat of it,
44 but any slave who has been purchased
may eat of it after he has been circumcised; 45 no bound or hired servant may
eat of it. 46 It shall be eaten in one house;
you shall not take any of the animal outside the house, and you shall not break
any of its bones. 47 The whole congregation of Israel shall celebrate it. 48 If an
alien who resides with you wants to
celebrate the passover to the LORD, all
his males shall be circumcised; then he
may draw near to celebrate it; he shall
be regarded as a native of the land. But
no uncircumcised person shall eat of it;
49 there shall be one law for the native
and for the alien who resides among
you.

50 All the Israelites did just as the
LORD had commanded Moses and
Aaron. 51That very day the LORD
brought the Israelites out of the land of
Egypt, company by company.

13 The LORD said to Moses: 2Con-
secrate to me all the firstborn;
whatever is the first to open the womb
among the Israelites, of human beings
and animals, is mine.

THE FESTIVAL OF UNLEAVENED BREAD

3 Moses said to the people, 'Remember this day on which you came out of
Egypt, out of the house of slavery, because the LORD brought you out from
there by strength of hand; no leavened bread shall be eaten. 4Today, in
the month of Abib, you are going out.
5When the LORD brings you into the
land of the Canaanites, the Hittites, the
Amorites, the Hivites, and the Jebusites, which he swore to your ancestors
to give you, a land flowing with milk
and honey, you shall keep this observance in this month. 6For seven days you
shall eat unleavened bread, and on the
seventh day there shall be a festival to
the LORD. 7Unleavened bread shall be
eaten for seven days; no leavened bread
shall be seen in your possession, and
no leaven shall be seen among you in
all your territory. 8You shall tell your
child on that day, "It is because of what
the LORD did for me when I came out
of Egypt." 9It shall serve for you as a
sign on your hand and as a reminder
on your forehead, so that the teaching
of the LORD may be on your lips; for
with a strong hand the LORD brought
you out of Egypt. 10You shall keep this
ordinance at its proper time from year
to year.

THE CONSECRATION OF THE FIRSTBORN

11 'When the LORD has brought
you into the land of the Canaanites,
as he swore to you and your ancestors,
and has given it to you, 12you shall set
apart to the LORD all that first opens
the womb. All the firstborn of your livestock that are males shall be the LORD's.
13But every firstborn donkey you shall
redeem with a sheep; if you do not redeem it, you must break its neck. Every
firstborn male among your children you
shall redeem. 14When in the future your
child asks you, "What does this mean?"
you shall answer, "By strength of hand
the LORD brought us out of Egypt, from
the house of slavery. 15When Pharaoh
stubbornly refused to let us go, the
LORD killed all the firstborn in the land
of Egypt, from human firstborn to the
firstborn of animals. Therefore I sacrifice to the LORD every male that first
opens the womb, but every firstborn of
my sons I redeem." 16It shall serve as a
sign on your hand and as an emblem[y]
on your forehead that by strength of
hand the LORD brought us out of Egypt.'

THE PILLARS OF CLOUD AND FIRE

17 When Pharaoh let the people go,
God did not lead them by way of the
land of the Philistines, although that
was nearer; for God thought, 'If the
people face war, they may change their
minds and return to Egypt.' 18So God led
the people by the roundabout way of the
wilderness towards the Red Sea.[z] The Israelites went up out of the land of Egypt
prepared for battle. 19And Moses took
with him the bones of Joseph, who had
required a solemn oath of the Israelites,
saying, 'God will surely take notice of
you, and then you must carry my bones
with you from here.' 20They set out from
Succoth, and camped at Etham, on the
edge of the wilderness. 21The LORD went
in front of them in a pillar of cloud by
day, to lead them along the way, and in a
pillar of fire by night, to give them light,
so that they might travel by day and by
night. 22Neither the pillar of cloud by
day nor the pillar of fire by night left its
place in front of the people.

CROSSING THE RED SEA

14 Then the LORD said to Moses:
2'Tell the Israelites to turn back
and camp in front of Pi-hahiroth, between Migdol and the sea, in front of
Baal-zephon; you shall camp opposite it,
by the sea. 3Pharaoh will say of the Israelites, 'They are wandering aimlessly in
the land; the wilderness has closed in on
them.' 4I will harden Pharaoh's heart,
and he will pursue them, so that I will
gain glory for myself over Pharaoh and
all his army; and the Egyptians shall
know that I am the LORD. And they
did so.'

5 When the king of Egypt was told
that the people had fled, the minds of
Pharaoh and his officials were changed
towards the people, and they said, 'What
have we done, letting Israel leave our

[y] 13.16 Or *as a frontlet*; meaning of Heb uncertain
[z] 13.18 Or *Sea of Reeds*

service?' 6So he had his chariot made
ready, and took his army with him; 7he
took six hundred picked chariots and all
the other chariots of Egypt with officers
over all of them. 8The LORD hardened
the heart of Pharaoh king of Egypt and
he pursued the Israelites, who were going out boldly. 9The Egyptians pursued
them, all Pharaoh's horses and chariots,
his chariot drivers and his army; they
overtook them camped by the sea, by
Pi-hahiroth, in front of Baal-zephon.

10 As Pharaoh drew near, the Israelites looked back, and there were the
Egyptians advancing on them. In great
fear the Israelites cried out to the LORD.
11They said to Moses, 'Was it because
there were no graves in Egypt that you
have taken us away to die in the wilderness? What have you done to us, bringing us out of Egypt? 12Is this not the
very thing we told you in Egypt, "Let us
alone and let us serve the Egyptians"?
For it would have been better for us to
serve the Egyptians than to die in the
wilderness.' 13But Moses said to the people, 'Do not be afraid, stand firm, and
see the deliverance that the LORD will
accomplish for you today; for the Egyptians whom you see today you shall
never see again. 14The LORD will fight
for you, and you have only to keep still.'

15 Then the LORD said to Moses, 'Why
do you cry out to me? Tell the Israelites
to go forward. 16But you lift up your
staff, and stretch out your hand over the
sea and divide it, that the Israelites may
go into the sea on dry ground. 17Then I
will harden the hearts of the Egyptians
so that they will go in after them; and
so I will gain glory for myself over Pharaoh and all his army, his chariots, and
his chariot drivers. 18And the Egyptians
shall know that I am the LORD, when I
have gained glory for myself over Pharaoh, his chariots, and his chariot drivers.'

19 The angel of God who was going
before the Israelite army moved and
went behind them; and the pillar of
cloud moved from in front of them and
took its place behind them. 20It came
between the army of Egypt and the
army of Israel. And so the cloud was
there with the darkness, and it lit up the
night; one did not come near the other
all night.

21 Then Moses stretched out his
hand over the sea. The LORD drove the
sea back by a strong east wind all night,
and turned the sea into dry land; and
the waters were divided. 22The Israelites went into the sea on dry ground,
the waters forming a wall for them
on their right and on their left. 23The
Egyptians pursued, and went into the
sea after them, all of Pharaoh's horses,
chariots, and chariot drivers. 24At the
morning watch the LORD in the pillar
of fire and cloud looked down upon the
Egyptian army, and threw the Egyptian
army into panic. 25He clogged[a] their
chariot wheels so that they turned with
difficulty. The Egyptians said, 'Let us
flee from the Israelites, for the LORD is
fighting for them against Egypt.'

THE PURSUERS DROWNED

26 Then the LORD said to Moses,
'Stretch out your hand over the sea, so
that the water may come back upon
the Egyptians, upon their chariots and
chariot drivers.' 27So Moses stretched
out his hand over the sea, and at dawn
the sea returned to its normal depth. As
the Egyptians fled before it, the LORD
tossed the Egyptians into the sea. 28The
waters returned and covered the chariots and the chariot drivers, the entire
army of Pharaoh that had followed
them into the sea; not one of them remained. 29But the Israelites walked on
dry ground through the sea, the waters
forming a wall for them on their right
and on their left.

30 Thus the LORD saved Israel that
day from the Egyptians; and Israel saw
the Egyptians dead on the seashore.
31Israel saw the great work that the
LORD did against the Egyptians. So the
people feared the LORD and believed in
the LORD and in his servant Moses.

THE SONG OF MOSES

15 Then Moses and the Israelites
sang this song to the LORD:

'I will sing to the LORD, for he has
triumphed gloriously;
horse and rider he has
thrown into the sea.

2 The LORD is my strength
and my might,[b]
and he has become my salvation;
this is my God, and I will praise him,
my father's God, and I
will exalt him.

3 The LORD is a warrior;
the LORD is his name.

[a] **14.25** Sam Gk Syr: MT *removed*
[b] **15.2** Or *song*

4 ‘Pharaoh’s chariots and his army
he cast into the sea;
his picked officers were sunk
in the Red Sea.[c]
5 The floods covered them;
they went down into the
depths like a stone.
6 Your right hand, O LORD,
glorious in power—
your right hand, O LORD,
shattered the enemy.
7 In the greatness of your majesty you
overthrew your adversaries;
you sent out your fury, it
consumed them like stubble.
8 At the blast of your nostrils
the waters piled up,
the floods stood up in a heap;
the deeps congealed in the
heart of the sea.
9 The enemy said, “I will pursue,
I will overtake,
I will divide the spoil, my desire
shall have its fill of them.
I will draw my sword, my hand
shall destroy them.”
10 You blew with your wind, the
sea covered them;
they sank like lead in the
mighty waters.

11 ‘Who is like you, O LORD,
among the gods?
Who is like you, majestic
in holiness,
awesome in splendour,
doing wonders?
12 You stretched out your
right hand,
the earth swallowed them.

13 ‘In your steadfast love you led the
people whom you redeemed;
you guided them by your strength
to your holy abode.
14 The peoples heard, they trembled;
pangs seized the inhabitants
of Philistia.
15 Then the chiefs of Edom
were dismayed;
trembling seized the
leaders of Moab;
all the inhabitants of Canaan
melted away.
16 Terror and dread fell upon them;
by the might of your arm, they
became still as a stone
until your people, O LORD,
passed by,
until the people whom you
acquired passed by.
17 You brought them in and planted
them on the mountain of
your own possession,
the place, O LORD, that you
made your abode,
the sanctuary, O LORD, that your
hands have established.
18 The LORD will reign for ever and ever.’

19 When the horses of Pharaoh with
his chariots and his chariot drivers went
into the sea, the LORD brought back the
waters of the sea upon them; but the Israelites walked through the sea on dry
ground.

THE SONG OF MIRIAM

20 Then the prophet Miriam, Aaron’s
sister, took a tambourine in her hand;
and all the women went out after her
with tambourines and with dancing.
21 And Miriam sang to them:

‘Sing to the LORD, for he has
triumphed gloriously;
horse and rider he has thrown
into the sea.’

BITTER WATER MADE SWEET

22 Then Moses ordered Israel to set
out from the Red Sea,[d] and they went
into the wilderness of Shur. They went
for three days in the wilderness and
found no water. 23 When they came to
Marah, they could not drink the water
of Marah because it was bitter. That is
why it was called Marah.[e] 24 And the
people complained against Moses, saying, ‘What shall we drink?’ 25 He cried
out to the LORD; and the LORD showed
him a piece of wood;[f] he threw it into
the water, and the water became sweet.

There the LORD[g] made for them a
statute and an ordinance and there he
put them to the test. 26 He said, ‘If you
will listen carefully to the voice of the
LORD your God, and do what is right
in his sight, and give heed to his commandments and keep all his statutes,
I will not bring upon you any of the
diseases that I brought upon the Egyptians; for I am the LORD who heals you.’

27 Then they came to Elim, where
there were twelve springs of water and
seventy palm trees; and they camped
there by the water.

BREAD FROM HEAVEN

16 The whole congregation of the Israelites set out from Elim; and

[c] 15.4 Or *Sea of Reeds* [d] 15.22 Or *Sea of Reeds*
[e] 15.23 That is *Bitterness* [f] 15.25 Or *a tree*
[g] 15.25 Heb *he*

Israel came to the wilderness of Sin,
which is between Elim and Sinai, on
the fifteenth day of the second month
after they had departed from the land
of Egypt. 2The whole congregation of
the Israelites complained against Moses and Aaron in the wilderness. 3The
Israelites said to them, 'If only we had
died by the hand of the LORD in the land
of Egypt, when we sat by the fleshpots
and ate our fill of bread; for you have
brought us out into this wilderness to
kill this whole assembly with hunger.'

4 Then the LORD said to Moses, 'I
am going to rain bread from heaven for
you, and each day the people shall go
out and gather enough for that day. In
that way I will test them, whether they
will follow my instruction or not. 5On
the sixth day, when they prepare what
they bring in, it will be twice as much
as they gather on other days.' 6So Moses and Aaron said to all the Israelites,
'In the evening you shall know that it
was the LORD who brought you out of
the land of Egypt, 7and in the morning
you shall see the glory of the LORD, because he has heard your complaining
against the LORD. For what are we, that
you complain against us?' 8And Moses
said, 'When the LORD gives you meat to
eat in the evening and your fill of bread
in the morning, because the LORD has
heard the complaining that you utter
against him—what are we? Your complaining is not against us but against
the LORD.'

9 Then Moses said to Aaron, 'Say to
the whole congregation of the Israelites, "Draw near to the LORD, for he
has heard your complaining." ' 10And as
Aaron spoke to the whole congregation
of the Israelites, they looked towards
the wilderness, and the glory of the
LORD appeared in the cloud. 11The LORD
spoke to Moses and said, 12'I have heard
the complaining of the Israelites; say to
them, "At twilight you shall eat meat,
and in the morning you shall have your
fill of bread; then you shall know that I
am the LORD your God." '

13 In the evening quails came up and
covered the camp; and in the morning
there was a layer of dew around the
camp. 14When the layer of dew lifted,
there on the surface of the wilderness
was a fine flaky substance, as fine as
frost on the ground. 15When the Israelites saw it, they said to one another,
'What is it?'[h] For they did not know
what it was. Moses said to them, 'It is
the bread that the LORD has given you
to eat. 16This is what the LORD has commanded: "Gather as much of it as each
of you needs, an omer to a person according to the number of persons, all
providing for those in their own tents." '
17The Israelites did so, some gathering
more, some less. 18But when they measured it with an omer, those who gathered much had nothing over, and those
who gathered little had no shortage;
they gathered as much as each of them
needed. 19And Moses said to them, 'Let
no one leave any of it over until morning.' 20But they did not listen to Moses;
some left part of it until morning, and it
bred worms and became foul. And Moses was angry with them. 21Morning
by morning they gathered it, as much
as each needed; but when the sun grew
hot, it melted.

22 On the sixth day they gathered
twice as much food, two omers apiece.
When all the leaders of the congregation came and told Moses, 23he said to
them, 'This is what the LORD has commanded: "Tomorrow is a day of solemn
rest, a holy sabbath to the LORD; bake
what you want to bake and boil what
you want to boil, and all that is left over
put aside to be kept until morning." '
24So they put it aside until morning, as
Moses commanded them; and it did not
become foul, and there were no worms
in it. 25Moses said, 'Eat it today, for today is a sabbath to the LORD; today you
will not find it in the field. 26For six
days you shall gather it; but on the seventh day, which is a sabbath, there will
be none.'

27 On the seventh day some of the
people went out to gather, and they
found none. 28The LORD said to Moses, 'How long will you refuse to keep
my commandments and instructions?
29See! The LORD has given you the sabbath, therefore on the sixth day he gives
you food for two days; each of you stay
where you are; do not leave your place
on the seventh day.' 30So the people
rested on the seventh day.

31 The house of Israel called it manna;
it was like coriander seed, white, and
the taste of it was like wafers made with
honey. 32Moses said, 'This is what the
LORD has commanded: "Let an omer of
it be kept throughout your generations,
in order that they may see the food
with which I fed you in the wilderness,

[h] **16.15** Or *'It is manna'* (Heb *man hu*, see verse 31)

when I brought you out of the land of
Egypt." ' 33 And Moses said to Aaron,
'Take a jar, and put an omer of manna
in it, and place it before the LORD, to be
kept throughout your generations.' 34 As
the LORD commanded Moses, so Aaron
placed it before the covenant,[i] for safekeeping. 35 The Israelites ate manna for
forty years, until they came to a habitable land; they ate manna, until they
came to the border of the land of Canaan. 36 An omer is a tenth of an ephah.

WATER FROM THE ROCK

17 From the wilderness of Sin the
whole congregation of the Israelites journeyed by stages, as the LORD
commanded. They camped at Rephidim, but there was no water for the people to drink. 2 The people quarrelled with
Moses, and said, 'Give us water to drink.'
Moses said to them, 'Why do you quarrel with me? Why do you test the LORD?'
3 But the people thirsted there for water;
and the people complained against Moses and said, 'Why did you bring us out
of Egypt, to kill us and our children and
livestock with thirst?' 4 So Moses cried
out to the LORD, 'What shall I do with
this people? They are almost ready to
stone me.' 5 The LORD said to Moses, 'Go
on ahead of the people, and take some
of the elders of Israel with you; take
in your hand the staff with which you
struck the Nile, and go. 6 I will be standing there in front of you on the rock at
Horeb. Strike the rock, and water will
come out of it, so that the people may
drink.' Moses did so, in the sight of the
elders of Israel. 7 He called the place
Massah[j] and Meribah,[k] because the Israelites quarrelled and tested the LORD,
saying, 'Is the LORD among us or not?'

AMALEK ATTACKS ISRAEL AND IS DEFEATED

8 Then Amalek came and fought
with Israel at Rephidim. 9 Moses said
to Joshua, 'Choose some men for us and
go out; fight with Amalek. Tomorrow
I will stand on the top of the hill with
the staff of God in my hand.' 10 So Joshua
did as Moses told him, and fought with
Amalek, while Moses, Aaron, and Hur
went up to the top of the hill. 11 Whenever Moses held up his hand, Israel prevailed; and whenever he lowered his
hand, Amalek prevailed. 12 But Moses'
hands grew weary; so they took a stone
and put it under him, and he sat on it.
Aaron and Hur held up his hands, one
on one side, and the other on the other
side; so his hands were steady until the
sun set. 13 And Joshua defeated Amalek
and his people with the sword.

14 Then the LORD said to Moses,
'Write this as a reminder in a book and
recite it in the hearing of Joshua: I will
utterly blot out the remembrance of
Amalek from under heaven.' 15 And Moses built an altar and called it, The LORD
is my banner. 16 He said, 'A hand upon
the banner of the LORD![l] The LORD will
have war with Amalek from generation
to generation.'

JETHRO'S ADVICE

18 Jethro, the priest of Midian, Moses' father-in-law, heard of all
that God had done for Moses and for
his people Israel, how the LORD had
brought Israel out of Egypt. 2 After Moses had sent away his wife Zipporah,
his father-in-law Jethro took her back,
3 along with her two sons. The name of
one was Gershom (for he said, 'I have
been an alien[m] in a foreign land'), 4 and
the name of the other, Eliezer[n] (for
he said, 'The God of my father was my
help, and delivered me from the sword
of Pharaoh'). 5 Jethro, Moses' father-in-
law, came into the wilderness where
Moses was encamped at the mountain
of God, bringing Moses' sons and wife
to him. 6 He sent word to Moses, 'I, your
father-in-law Jethro, am coming to you,
with your wife and her two sons.' 7 Moses went out to meet his father-in-law;
he bowed down and kissed him; each
asked after the other's welfare, and they
went into the tent. 8 Then Moses told
his father-in-law all that the LORD had
done to Pharaoh and to the Egyptians
for Israel's sake, all the hardship that
had beset them on the way, and how
the LORD had delivered them. 9 Jethro
rejoiced for all the good that the LORD
had done to Israel, in delivering them
from the Egyptians.

10 Jethro said, 'Blessed be the LORD,
who has delivered you from the Egyptians and from Pharaoh. 11 Now I know
that the LORD is greater than all gods,
because he delivered the people from
the Egyptians,[o] when they dealt arrogantly with them.' 12 And Jethro, Moses'

[i] 16.34 Or *treaty* or *testimony*; Heb *eduth*
[j] 17.7 That is *Test* [k] 17.7 That is *Quarrel*
[l] 17.16 Cn: Meaning of Heb uncertain
[m] 18.3 Heb *ger* [n] 18.4 Heb *Eli*, my God; *ezer*, help [o] 18.11 The clause *because . . . Egyptians* has been transposed from verse 10

father-in-law, brought a burnt-offering
and sacrifices to God; and Aaron came
with all the elders of Israel to eat bread
with Moses' father-in-law in the presence of God.

13 The next day Moses sat as judge
for the people, while the people stood
around him from morning until evening.
14 When Moses' father-in-law saw all that
he was doing for the people, he said,
'What is this that you are doing for the
people? Why do you sit alone, while all
the people stand around you from morning until evening?' 15 Moses said to his
father-in-law, 'Because the people come
to me to inquire of God. 16 When they
have a dispute, they come to me and I
decide between one person and another,
and I make known to them the statutes
and instructions of God.' 17 Moses' father-
in-law said to him, 'What you are doing is
not good. 18 You will surely wear yourself
out, both you and these people with you.
For the task is too heavy for you; you cannot do it alone. 19 Now listen to me. I will
give you counsel, and God be with you!
You should represent the people before
God, and you should bring their cases before God; 20 teach them the statutes and
instructions and make known to them
the way they are to go and the things
they are to do. 21 You should also look for
able men among all the people, men who
fear God, are trustworthy, and hate dishonest gain; set such men over them as
officers over thousands, hundreds, fifties, and tens. 22 Let them sit as judges
for the people at all times; let them bring
every important case to you, but decide
every minor case themselves. So it will
be easier for you, and they will bear the
burden with you. 23 If you do this, and
God so commands you, then you will be
able to endure, and all these people will
go to their home in peace.'

24 So Moses listened to his father-in-
law and did all that he had said. 25 Moses
chose able men from all Israel and appointed them as heads over the people,
as officers over thousands, hundreds,
fifties, and tens. 26 And they judged
the people at all times; hard cases they
brought to Moses, but any minor case
they decided themselves. 27 Then Moses
let his father-in-law depart, and he went
off to his own country.

THE ISRAELITES REACH MOUNT SINAI

19 At the third new moon after the
Israelites had gone out of the
land of Egypt, on that very day, they
came into the wilderness of Sinai. 2 They
had journeyed from Rephidim, entered
the wilderness of Sinai, and camped
in the wilderness; Israel camped there
in front of the mountain. 3 Then Moses went up to God; the LORD called to
him from the mountain, saying, 'Thus
you shall say to the house of Jacob, and
tell the Israelites: 4 You have seen what
I did to the Egyptians, and how I bore
you on eagles' wings and brought you to
myself. 5 Now therefore, if you obey my
voice and keep my covenant, you shall
be my treasured possession out of all
the peoples. Indeed, the whole earth is
mine, 6 but you shall be for me a priestly
kingdom and a holy nation. These are
the words that you shall speak to the Israelites.'

7 So Moses came, summoned the elders of the people, and set before them
all these words that the LORD had commanded him. 8 The people all answered
as one: 'Everything that the LORD has
spoken we will do.' Moses reported the
words of the people to the LORD. 9 Then
the LORD said to Moses, 'I am going to
come to you in a dense cloud, in order
that the people may hear when I speak
with you and so trust you ever after.'

THE PEOPLE CONSECRATED

When Moses had told the words of
the people to the LORD, 10 the LORD said
to Moses: 'Go to the people and consecrate them today and tomorrow. Have
them wash their clothes 11 and prepare
for the third day, because on the third
day the LORD will come down upon
Mount Sinai in the sight of all the people. 12 You shall set limits for the people
all around, saying, "Be careful not to go
up the mountain or to touch the edge of
it. Any who touch the mountain shall
be put to death. 13 No hand shall touch
them, but they shall be stoned or shot
with arrows;[p] whether animal or human being, they shall not live." When
the trumpet sounds a long blast, they
may go up on the mountain.' 14 So Moses
went down from the mountain to the
people. He consecrated the people, and
they washed their clothes. 15 And he said
to the people, 'Prepare for the third day;
do not go near a woman.'

16 On the morning of the third day
there was thunder and lightning, as
well as a thick cloud on the mountain,

[p] 19.13 Heb lacks *with arrows*

and a blast of a trumpet so loud that all
the people who were in the camp trembled. 17Moses brought the people out of
the camp to meet God. They took their
stand at the foot of the mountain. 18Now
Mount Sinai was wrapped in smoke,
because the LORD had descended upon
it in fire; the smoke went up like the
smoke of a kiln, while the whole mountain shook violently. 19As the blast of
the trumpet grew louder and louder,
Moses would speak and God would answer him in thunder. 20When the LORD
descended upon Mount Sinai, to the top
of the mountain, the LORD summoned
Moses to the top of the mountain, and
Moses went up. 21Then the LORD said
to Moses, 'Go down and warn the people not to break through to the LORD to
look; otherwise many of them will perish. 22Even the priests who approach the
LORD must consecrate themselves or
the LORD will break out against them.'
23Moses said to the LORD, 'The people
are not permitted to come up to Mount
Sinai; for you yourself warned us, saying, "Set limits around the mountain
and keep it holy." ' 24The LORD said to
him, 'Go down, and come up bringing
Aaron with you; but do not let either
the priests or the people break through
to come up to the LORD; otherwise he
will break out against them.' 25So Moses
went down to the people and told them.

THE TEN COMMANDMENTS

20 Then God spoke all these words:
2 I am the LORD your God, who
brought you out of the land of Egypt,
out of the house of slavery; 3you shall
have no other gods before[q] me.

4 You shall not make for yourself an
idol, whether in the form of anything
that is in heaven above, or that is on the
earth beneath, or that is in the water under the earth. 5You shall not bow down
to them or worship them; for I the LORD
your God am a jealous God, punishing
children for the iniquity of parents, to
the third and the fourth generation
of those who reject me, 6but showing
steadfast love to the thousandth generation[r] of those who love me and keep my
commandments.

7 You shall not make wrongful use of
the name of the LORD your God, for the
LORD will not acquit anyone who misuses his name.

8 Remember the sabbath day, and
keep it holy. 9For six days you shall labour and do all your work. 10But the
seventh day is a sabbath to the LORD
your God; you shall not do any work—
you, your son or your daughter, your
male or female slave, your livestock, or
the alien resident in your towns. 11For
in six days the LORD made heaven and
earth, the sea, and all that is in them,
but rested the seventh day; therefore
the LORD blessed the sabbath day and
consecrated it.

12 Honour your father and your
mother, so that your days may be long
in the land that the LORD your God is
giving you.

13 You shall not murder.[s]

14 You shall not commit adultery.

15 You shall not steal.

16 You shall not bear false witness
against your neighbour.

17 You shall not covet your neighbour's house; you shall not covet your
neighbour's wife, or male or female
slave, or ox, or donkey, or anything that
belongs to your neighbour.

18 When all the people witnessed the
thunder and lightning, the sound of
the trumpet, and the mountain smoking, they were afraid[t] and trembled and
stood at a distance, 19and said to Moses,
'You speak to us, and we will listen; but
do not let God speak to us, or we will
die.' 20Moses said to the people, 'Do not
be afraid; for God has come only to test
you and to put the fear of him upon
you so that you do not sin.' 21Then the
people stood at a distance, while Moses
drew near to the thick darkness where
God was.

THE LAW CONCERNING THE ALTAR

22 The LORD said to Moses: Thus you
shall say to the Israelites: 'You have seen
for yourselves that I spoke with you
from heaven. 23You shall not make gods
of silver alongside me, nor shall you
make for yourselves gods of gold. 24You
need make for me only an altar of earth
and sacrifice on it your burnt-offerings
and your offerings of well-being, your
sheep and your oxen; in every place
where I cause my name to be remembered I will come to you and bless you.
25But if you make for me an altar of
stone, do not build it of hewn stones; for
if you use a chisel upon it you profane
it. 26You shall not go up by steps to my
altar, so that your nakedness may not be
exposed on it.'

[q] 20.3 Or *besides* [r] 20.6 Or *to thousands*
[s] 20.13 Or *kill* [t] 20.18 Sam Gk Syr Vg: MT
they saw

THE LAW CONCERNING SLAVES

21 These are the ordinances that you shall set before them:

2 When you buy a male Hebrew slave, he shall serve for six years, but in the seventh he shall go out a free person, without debt. [3]If he comes in single, he shall go out single; if he comes in married, then his wife shall go out with him. [4]If his master gives him a wife and she bears him sons or daughters, the wife and her children shall be her master's and he shall go out alone. [5]But if the slave declares, 'I love my master, my wife, and my children; I will not go out a free person', [6]then his master shall bring him before God.[u] He shall be brought to the door or the doorpost; and his master shall pierce his ear with an awl; and he shall serve him for life.

7 When a man sells his daughter as a slave, she shall not go out as the male slaves do. [8]If she does not please her master, who designated her for himself, then he shall let her be redeemed; he shall have no right to sell her to a foreign people, since he has dealt unfairly with her. [9]If he designates her for his son, he shall deal with her as with a daughter. [10]If he takes another wife to himself, he shall not diminish the food, clothing, or marital rights of the first wife.[v] [11]And if he does not do these three things for her, she shall go out without debt, without payment of money.

THE LAW CONCERNING VIOLENCE

12 Whoever strikes a person mortally shall be put to death. [13]If it was not premeditated, but came about by an act of God, then I will appoint for you a place to which the killer may flee. [14]But if someone wilfully attacks and kills another by treachery, you shall take the killer from my altar for execution.

15 Whoever strikes father or mother shall be put to death.

16 Whoever kidnaps a person, whether that person has been sold or is still held in possession, shall be put to death.

17 Whoever curses father or mother shall be put to death.

18 When individuals quarrel and one strikes the other with a stone or fist so that the injured party, though not dead, is confined to bed, [19]but recovers and walks around outside with the help of a staff, then the assailant shall be free of liability, except to pay for the loss of time, and to arrange for full recovery.

20 When a slave-owner strikes a male or female slave with a rod and the slave dies immediately, the owner shall be punished. [21]But if the slave survives for a day or two, there is no punishment; for the slave is the owner's property.

22 When people who are fighting injure a pregnant woman so that there is a miscarriage, and yet no further harm follows, the one responsible shall be fined what the woman's husband demands, paying as much as the judges determine. [23]If any harm follows, then you shall give life for life, [24]eye for eye, tooth for tooth, hand for hand, foot for foot, [25]burn for burn, wound for wound, stripe for stripe.

26 When a slave-owner strikes the eye of a male or female slave, destroying it, the owner shall let the slave go, a free person, to compensate for the eye. [27]If the owner knocks out a tooth of a male or female slave, the slave shall be let go, a free person, to compensate for the tooth.

LAWS CONCERNING PROPERTY

28 When an ox gores a man or a woman to death, the ox shall be stoned, and its flesh shall not be eaten; but the owner of the ox shall not be liable. [29]If the ox has been accustomed to gore in the past, and its owner has been warned but has not restrained it, and it kills a man or a woman, the ox shall be stoned, and its owner also shall be put to death. [30]If a ransom is imposed on the owner, then the owner shall pay whatever is imposed for the redemption of the victim's life. [31]If it gores a boy or a girl, the owner shall be dealt with according to this same rule. [32]If the ox gores a male or female slave, the owner shall pay to the slave-owner thirty shekels of silver, and the ox shall be stoned.

33 If someone leaves a pit open, or digs a pit and does not cover it, and an ox or a donkey falls into it, [34]the owner of the pit shall make restitution, giving money to its owner, but keeping the dead animal.

35 If someone's ox hurts the ox of another, so that it dies, then they shall sell the live ox and divide the price of it; and the dead animal they shall also divide. [36]But if it was known that the ox was accustomed to gore in the past, and its owner has not restrained it, the owner shall restore ox for ox, but keep the dead animal.

[u] **21.6** *Or to the judges* [v] **21.10** Heb *of her*

LAWS OF RESTITUTION

22 [w]When someone steals an ox or a sheep, and slaughters it or sells it, the thief shall pay five oxen for an ox, and four sheep for a sheep.[x] The thief shall make restitution, but if unable to do so, shall be sold for the theft. 4When the animal, whether ox or donkey or sheep, is found alive in the thief's possession, the thief shall pay double.

2[y] If a thief is found breaking in, and is beaten to death, no blood-guilt is incurred; 3but if it happens after sunrise, blood-guilt is incurred.

5 When someone causes a field or vineyard to be grazed over, or lets livestock loose to graze in someone else's field, restitution shall be made from the best in the owner's field or vineyard.

6 When fire breaks out and catches in thorns so that the stacked grain or the standing grain or the field is consumed, the one who started the fire shall make full restitution.

7 When someone delivers to a neighbour money or goods for safe keeping, and they are stolen from the neighbour's house, then the thief, if caught, shall pay double. 8If the thief is not caught, the owner of the house shall be brought before God,[z] to determine whether or not the owner had laid hands on the neighbour's goods.

9 In any case of disputed ownership involving ox, donkey, sheep, clothing, or any other loss, of which one party says, 'This is mine', the case of both parties shall come before God;[a] the one whom God condemns[b] shall pay double to the other.

10 When someone delivers to another a donkey, ox, sheep, or any other animal for safekeeping, and it dies or is injured or is carried off, without anyone seeing it, 11an oath before the LORD shall decide between the two of them that the one has not laid hands on the property of the other; the owner shall accept the oath, and no restitution shall be made. 12But if it was stolen, restitution shall be made to its owner. 13If it was mangled by beasts, let it be brought as evidence; restitution shall not be made for the mangled remains.

14 When someone borrows an animal from another and it is injured or dies, the owner not being present, full restitution shall be made. 15If the owner was present, there shall be no restitution; if it was hired, only the hiring fee is due.

SOCIAL AND RELIGIOUS LAWS

16 When a man seduces a virgin who is not engaged to be married, and lies with her, he shall give the bride-price for her and make her his wife. 17But if her father refuses to give her to him, he shall pay an amount equal to the bride-price for virgins.

18 You shall not permit a female sorcerer to live.

19 Whoever lies with an animal shall be put to death.

20 Whoever sacrifices to any god, other than the LORD alone, shall be devoted to destruction.

21 You shall not wrong or oppress a resident alien, for you were aliens in the land of Egypt. 22You shall not abuse any widow or orphan. 23If you do abuse them, when they cry out to me, I will surely heed their cry; 24my wrath will burn, and I will kill you with the sword, and your wives shall become widows and your children orphans.

25 If you lend money to my people, to the poor among you, you shall not deal with them as a creditor; you shall not exact interest from them. 26If you take your neighbour's cloak in pawn, you shall restore it before the sun goes down; 27for it may be your neighbour's only clothing to use as cover; in what else shall that person sleep? And if your neighbour cries out to me, I will listen, for I am compassionate.

28 You shall not revile God, or curse a leader of your people.

29 You shall not delay to make offerings from the fullness of your harvest and from the outflow of your presses.[c]

The firstborn of your sons you shall give to me. 30You shall do the same with your oxen and with your sheep: for seven days it shall remain with its mother; on the eighth day you shall give it to me.

31 You shall be people consecrated to me; therefore you shall not eat any meat that is mangled by beasts in the field; you shall throw it to the dogs.

JUSTICE FOR ALL

23 You shall not spread a false report. You shall not join hands with the wicked to act as a malicious witness. 2You shall not follow a majority

[w] **22.1** Ch 21.37 in Heb [x] **22.1** Verses 2, 3, and 4 rearranged thus: 3b, 4, 2, 3a [y] **22.2** Ch 22.1 in Heb [z] **22.8** Or *before the judges* [a] **22.9** Or *before the judges* [b] **22.9** Or *the judges condemn* [c] **22.29** Meaning of Heb uncertain

in wrongdoing; when you bear witness
in a lawsuit, you shall not side with the
majority so as to pervert justice; 3nor
shall you be partial to the poor in a lawsuit.
4 When you come upon your enemy's
ox or donkey going astray, you shall
bring it back.
5 When you see the donkey of one
who hates you lying under its burden
and you would hold back from setting it
free, you must help to set it free.[d]
6 You shall not pervert the justice
due to your poor in their lawsuits. 7Keep
far from a false charge, and do not kill
the innocent or those in the right, for
I will not acquit the guilty. 8You shall
take no bribe, for a bribe blinds the officials, and subverts the cause of those
who are in the right.
9 You shall not oppress a resident
alien; you know the heart of an alien,
for you were aliens in the land of Egypt.

SABBATICAL YEAR AND SABBATH

10 For six years you shall sow your
land and gather in its yield; 11but the
seventh year you shall let it rest and lie
fallow, so that the poor of your people
may eat; and what they leave the wild
animals may eat. You shall do the same
with your vineyard, and with your olive
orchard.
12 For six days you shall do your
work, but on the seventh day you shall
rest, so that your ox and your donkey
may have relief, and your home-born
slave and the resident alien may be refreshed. 13Be attentive to all that I have
said to you. Do not invoke the names of
other gods; do not let them be heard on
your lips.

THE ANNUAL FESTIVALS

14 Three times in the year you shall
hold a festival for me. 15You shall observe the festival of unleavened bread;
as I commanded you, you shall eat unleavened bread for seven days at the appointed time in the month of Abib, for
in it you came out of Egypt.
No one shall appear before me empty-
handed.
16 You shall observe the festival of
harvest, of the first fruits of your labour,
of what you sow in the field. You shall
observe the festival of ingathering at
the end of the year, when you gather in
from the field the fruit of your labour.
17Three times in the year all your males
shall appear before the Lord GOD.
18 You shall not offer the blood of my
sacrifice with anything leavened, or let
the fat of my festival remain until the
morning.
19 The choicest of the first fruits of
your ground you shall bring into the
house of the LORD your God.
You shall not boil a kid in its mother's
milk.

THE CONQUEST OF CANAAN PROMISED

20 I am going to send an angel in
front of you, to guard you on the way
and to bring you to the place that I have
prepared. 21Be attentive to him and listen to his voice; do not rebel against
him, for he will not pardon your transgression; for my name is in him.
22 But if you listen attentively to his
voice and do all that I say, then I will be
an enemy to your enemies and a foe to
your foes.
23 When my angel goes in front of
you, and brings you to the Amorites,
the Hittites, the Perizzites, the Canaanites, the Hivites, and the Jebusites, and I
blot them out, 24you shall not bow down
to their gods, or worship them, or follow
their practices, but you shall utterly demolish them and break their pillars in
pieces. 25You shall worship the LORD
your God, and I[e] will bless your bread
and your water; and I will take sickness
away from among you. 26No one shall
miscarry or be barren in your land; I
will fulfil the number of your days. 27I
will send my terror in front of you, and
will throw into confusion all the people
against whom you shall come, and I will
make all your enemies turn their backs
to you. 28And I will send the pestilence[f]
in front of you, which shall drive out the
Hivites, the Canaanites, and the Hittites from before you. 29I will not drive
them out from before you in one year, or
the land would become desolate and the
wild animals would multiply against
you. 30Little by little I will drive them
out from before you, until you have increased and possess the land. 31I will set
your borders from the Red Sea[g] to the
sea of the Philistines, and from the wilderness to the Euphrates; for I will hand
over to you the inhabitants of the land,
and you shall drive them out before
you. 32You shall make no covenant with
them and their gods. 33They shall not

[d] **23.5** Meaning of Heb uncertain [e] **23.25** Gk Vg: Heb *he* [f] **23.28** Or *hornets*: Meaning of Heb uncertain [g] **23.31** Or *Sea of Reeds*

live in your land, or they will make you
sin against me; for if you worship their
gods, it will surely be a snare to you.

THE BLOOD OF THE COVENANT

24 Then he said to Moses, 'Come up
to the LORD, you and Aaron, Nadab, and Abihu, and seventy of the elders of Israel, and worship at a distance.
2 Moses alone shall come near the LORD;
but the others shall not come near, and
the people shall not come up with him.'
3 Moses came and told the people all
the words of the LORD and all the ordinances; and all the people answered
with one voice, and said, 'All the words
that the LORD has spoken we will do.'
4 And Moses wrote down all the words
of the LORD. He rose early in the morning, and built an altar at the foot of the
mountain, and set up twelve pillars,
corresponding to the twelve tribes of Israel. 5 He sent young men of the people
of Israel, who offered burnt-offerings
and sacrificed oxen as offerings of well-
being to the LORD. 6 Moses took half of
the blood and put it in basins, and half
of the blood he dashed against the altar.
7 Then he took the book of the covenant,
and read it in the hearing of the people;
and they said, 'All that the LORD has spoken we will do, and we will be obedient.'
8 Moses took the blood and dashed it on
the people, and said, 'See the blood of the
covenant that the LORD has made with
you in accordance with all these words.'

ON THE MOUNTAIN WITH GOD

9 Then Moses and Aaron, Nadab,
and Abihu, and seventy of the elders
of Israel went up, 10 and they saw the
God of Israel. Under his feet there was
something like a pavement of sapphire
stone, like the very heaven for clearness.
11 God[h] did not lay his hand on the chief
men of the people of Israel; also they beheld God, and they ate and drank.
12 The LORD said to Moses, 'Come up
to me on the mountain, and wait there;
and I will give you the tablets of stone,
with the law and the commandment,
which I have written for their instruction.' 13 So Moses set out with his assistant Joshua, and Moses went up into the
mountain of God. 14 To the elders he had
said, 'Wait here for us, until we come to
you again; for Aaron and Hur are with
you; whoever has a dispute may go to
them.'
15 Then Moses went up on the mountain, and the cloud covered the mountain. 16 The glory of the LORD settled
on Mount Sinai, and the cloud covered
it for six days; on the seventh day he
called to Moses out of the cloud. 17 Now
the appearance of the glory of the LORD
was like a devouring fire on the top of
the mountain in the sight of the people
of Israel. 18 Moses entered the cloud, and
went up on the mountain. Moses was
on the mountain for forty days and forty
nights.

OFFERINGS FOR THE TABERNACLE

25 The LORD said to Moses: 2 Tell
the Israelites to take for me an
offering; from all whose hearts prompt
them to give you shall receive the offering for me. 3 This is the offering that
you shall receive from them: gold, silver,
and bronze, 4 blue, purple, and crimson yarns and fine linen, goats' hair,
5 tanned rams' skins, fine leather,[i] acacia wood, 6 oil for the lamps, spices for
the anointing-oil and for the fragrant
incense, 7 onyx stones and gems to be
set in the ephod and for the breastpiece.
8 And have them make me a sanctuary,
so that I may dwell among them. 9 In accordance with all that I show you concerning the pattern of the tabernacle
and of all its furniture, so you shall
make it.

THE ARK OF THE COVENANT

10 They shall make an ark of acacia
wood; it shall be two and a half cubits
long, a cubit and a half wide, and a cubit and a half high. 11 You shall overlay
it with pure gold, inside and outside
you shall overlay it, and you shall make
a moulding of gold upon it all round.
12 You shall cast four rings of gold for it
and put them on its four feet, two rings
on one side of it, and two rings on the
other side. 13 You shall make poles of acacia wood, and overlay them with gold.
14 And you shall put the poles into the
rings on the sides of the ark, by which
to carry the ark. 15 The poles shall remain
in the rings of the ark; they shall not be
taken from it. 16 You shall put into the
ark the covenant[j] that I shall give you.
17 Then you shall make a mercy-
seat[k] of pure gold; two cubits and a
half shall be its length, and a cubit and
a half its width. 18 You shall make two
cherubim of gold; you shall make them
of hammered work, at the two ends of

[h] **24.11** Heb *He* [i] **25.5** Meaning of Heb uncertain [j] **25.16** Or *treaty, or testimony*; Heb *eduth* [k] **25.17** Or *a cover*

the mercy-seat.[l] 19 Make one cherub at
one end, and one cherub at the other;
of one piece with the mercy-seat[m] you
shall make the cherubim at its two
ends. 20 The cherubim shall spread out
their wings above, overshadowing the
mercy-seat[n] with their wings. They
shall face each other; the faces of the
cherubim shall be turned towards the
mercy-seat.[o] 21 You shall put the mercy-
seat[p] on the top of the ark; and in the
ark you shall put the covenant[q] that I
shall give you. 22 There I will meet you,
and from above the mercy-seat,[r] from
between the two cherubim that are on
the ark of the covenant,[s] I will deliver to
you all my commands for the Israelites.

THE TABLE FOR THE BREAD OF THE PRESENCE

23 You shall make a table of acacia
wood, two cubits long, one cubit wide,
and a cubit and a half high. 24 You shall
overlay it with pure gold, and make a
moulding of gold round it. 25 You shall
make round it a rim a handbreadth
wide, and a moulding of gold round the
rim. 26 You shall make for it four rings
of gold, and fasten the rings to the four
corners at its four legs. 27 The rings that
hold the poles used for carrying the table shall be close to the rim. 28 You shall
make the poles of acacia wood, and
overlay them with gold, and the table
shall be carried with these. 29 You shall
make its plates and dishes for incense,
and its flagons and bowls with which
to pour drink-offerings; you shall make
them of pure gold. 30 And you shall set
the bread of the Presence on the table
before me always.

THE LAMPSTAND

31 You shall make a lampstand of
pure gold. The base and the shaft of the
lampstand shall be made of hammered
work; its cups, its calyxes, and its petals
shall be of one piece with it; 32 and there
shall be six branches going out of its
sides, three branches of the lampstand
out of one side of it and three branches
of the lampstand out of the other side
of it; 33 three cups shaped like almond
blossoms, each with calyx and petals,
on one branch, and three cups shaped
like almond blossoms, each with calyx
and petals, on the other branch—so for
the six branches going out of the lampstand. 34 On the lampstand itself there
shall be four cups shaped like almond
blossoms, each with its calyxes and petals. 35 There shall be a calyx of one piece
with it under the first pair of branches,
a calyx of one piece with it under the
next pair of branches, and a calyx of
one piece with it under the last pair of
branches—so for the six branches that
go out of the lampstand. 36 Their calyxes
and their branches shall be of one piece
with it, the whole of it one hammered
piece of pure gold. 37 You shall make the
seven lamps for it; and the lamps shall
be set up so as to give light on the space
in front of it. 38 Its snuffers and trays
shall be of pure gold. 39 It, and all these
utensils, shall be made from a talent
of pure gold. 40 And see that you make
them according to the pattern for them,
which is being shown you on the mountain.

THE TABERNACLE

26 Moreover, you shall make the
tabernacle with ten curtains of
fine twisted linen, and blue, purple, and
crimson yarns; you shall make them
with cherubim skilfully worked into
them. 2 The length of each curtain shall
be twenty-eight cubits, and the width of
each curtain four cubits; all the curtains
shall be of the same size. 3 Five curtains
shall be joined to one another; and the
other five curtains shall be joined to one
another. 4 You shall make loops of blue
on the edge of the outermost curtain in
the first set; and likewise you shall make
loops on the edge of the outermost curtain in the second set. 5 You shall make
fifty loops on the one curtain, and you
shall make fifty loops on the edge of
the curtain that is in the second set;
the loops shall be opposite one another.
6 You shall make fifty clasps of gold, and
join the curtains to one another with
the clasps, so that the tabernacle may
be one whole.

7 You shall also make curtains of
goats' hair for a tent over the tabernacle;
you shall make eleven curtains. 8 The
length of each curtain shall be thirty cubits, and the width of each curtain four
cubits; the eleven curtains shall be of
the same size. 9 You shall join five curtains by themselves, and six curtains
by themselves, and the sixth curtain
you shall double over at the front of the
tent. 10 You shall make fifty loops on the

[l] 25.18 Or *the cover* [m] 25.19 Or *the cover* [n] 25.20 Or *the cover* [o] 25.20 Or *the cover* [p] 25.21 Or *the cover* [q] 25.21 Or *treaty*, or *testimony*; Heb *eduth* [r] 25.22 Or *the cover* [s] 25.22 Or *treaty, or testimony*; Heb *eduth*

edge of the curtain that is outermost in one set, and fifty loops on the edge of the curtain that is outermost in the second set.

11 You shall make fifty clasps of bronze, and put the clasps into the loops, and join the tent together, so that it may be one whole. 12 The part that remains of the curtains of the tent, the half-curtain that remains, shall hang over the back of the tabernacle. 13 The cubit on one side, and the cubit on the other side, of what remains in the length of the curtains of the tent, shall hang over the sides of the tabernacle, on this side and that side, to cover it. 14 You shall make for the tent a covering of tanned rams' skins and an outer covering of fine leather.[t]

THE FRAMEWORK

15 You shall make upright frames of acacia wood for the tabernacle. 16 Ten cubits shall be the length of a frame, and a cubit and a half the width of each frame. 17 There shall be two pegs in each frame to fit the frames together; you shall make these for all the frames of the tabernacle. 18 You shall make the frames for the tabernacle: twenty frames for the south side; 19 and you shall make forty bases of silver under the twenty frames, two bases under the first frame for its two pegs, and two bases under the next frame for its two pegs; 20 and for the second side of the tabernacle, on the north side twenty frames, 21 and their forty bases of silver, two bases under the first frame, and two bases under the next frame; 22 and for the rear of the tabernacle westward you shall make six frames. 23 You shall make two frames for corners of the tabernacle in the rear; 24 they shall be separate beneath, but joined at the top, at the first ring; it shall be the same with both of them; they shall form the two corners. 25 And so there shall be eight frames, with their bases of silver, sixteen bases; two bases under the first frame, and two bases under the next frame.

26 You shall make bars of acacia wood, five for the frames of one side of the tabernacle, 27 and five bars for the frames of the other side of the tabernacle, and five bars for the frames of the side of the tabernacle at the rear to the west. 28 The middle bar, halfway up the frames, shall pass through from end to end. 29 You shall overlay the frames with gold, and shall make their rings of gold to hold the bars; and you shall overlay the bars with gold. 30 Then you shall erect the tabernacle according to the plan for it that you were shown on the mountain.

THE CURTAIN

31 You shall make a curtain of blue, purple, and crimson yarns, and of fine twisted linen; it shall be made with cherubim skilfully worked into it. 32 You shall hang it on four pillars of acacia overlaid with gold, which have hooks of gold and rest on four bases of silver. 33 You shall hang the curtain under the clasps, and bring the ark of the covenant[u] inside, within the curtain; and the curtain shall separate for you the holy place from the most holy. 34 You shall put the mercy-seat[v] on the ark of the covenant[w] in the most holy place. 35 You shall set the table outside the curtain, and the lampstand on the south side of the tabernacle opposite the table; and you shall put the table on the north side.

36 You shall make a screen for the entrance of the tent, of blue, purple, and crimson yarns, and of fine twisted linen, embroidered with needlework. 37 You shall make for the screen five pillars of acacia, and overlay them with gold; their hooks shall be of gold, and you shall cast five bases of bronze for them.

THE ALTAR OF BURNT-OFFERING

27 You shall make the altar of acacia wood, five cubits long and five cubits wide; the altar shall be square, and it shall be three cubits high. 2 You shall make horns for it on its four corners; its horns shall be of one piece with it, and you shall overlay it with bronze. 3 You shall make pots for it to receive its ashes, and shovels and basins and forks and firepans; you shall make all its utensils of bronze. 4 You shall also make for it a grating, a network of bronze; and on the net you shall make four bronze rings at its four corners. 5 You shall set it under the ledge of the altar so that the net shall extend half-way down the altar. 6 You shall make poles for the altar, poles of acacia wood, and overlay them with bronze; 7 the poles shall be put through the rings, so that the poles shall be on

[t] **26.14** Meaning of Heb uncertain [u] **26.33** Or *treaty*, or *testimony*; Heb *eduth* [v] **26.34** Or *the cover* [w] **26.34** Or *treaty*, or *testimony*; Heb *eduth*

the two sides of the altar when it is carried. 8 You shall make it hollow, with
boards. They shall be made just as you
were shown on the mountain.

THE COURT AND ITS HANGINGS

9 You shall make the court of the tabernacle. On the south side the court shall
have hangings of fine twisted linen one
hundred cubits long for that side; 10 its
twenty pillars and their twenty bases
shall be of bronze, but the hooks of the
pillars and their bands shall be of silver.
11 Likewise, for its length on the north
side there shall be hangings one hundred cubits long, their pillars twenty
and their bases twenty, of bronze, but
the hooks of the pillars and their bands
shall be of silver. 12 For the width of the
court on the west side there shall be fifty
cubits of hangings, with ten pillars and
ten bases. 13 The width of the court on
the front to the east shall be fifty cubits.
14 There shall be fifteen cubits of hangings on one side, with three pillars and
three bases. 15 There shall be fifteen cubits of hangings on the other side, with
three pillars and three bases. 16 For the
gate of the court there shall be a screen
twenty cubits long, of blue, purple,
and crimson yarns, and of fine twisted
linen, embroidered with needlework;
it shall have four pillars and with them
four bases. 17 All the pillars around the
court shall be banded with silver; their
hooks shall be of silver, and their bases of
bronze. 18 The length of the court shall be
one hundred cubits, the width fifty, and
the height five cubits, with hangings of
fine twisted linen and bases of bronze.
19 All the utensils of the tabernacle for
every use, and all its pegs and all the
pegs of the court, shall be of bronze.

THE OIL FOR THE LAMP

20 You shall further command the
Israelites to bring you pure oil of beaten
olives for the light, so that a lamp may
be set up to burn regularly. 21 In the tent
of meeting, outside the curtain that is
before the covenant,[x] Aaron and his
sons shall tend it from evening to morning before the LORD. It shall be a perpetual ordinance to be observed throughout their generations by the Israelites.

VESTMENTS FOR THE PRIESTHOOD

28 Then bring near to you your
brother Aaron, and his sons
with him, from among the Israelites, to
serve me as priests—Aaron and Aaron's
sons, Nadab and Abihu, Eleazar and Ithamar. 2 You shall make sacred vestments
for the glorious adornment of your
brother Aaron. 3 And you shall speak to
all who have ability, whom I have endowed with skill, that they make Aaron's vestments to consecrate him for my
priesthood. 4 These are the vestments
that they shall make: a breastpiece,
an ephod, a robe, a chequered tunic, a
turban, and a sash. When they make
these sacred vestments for your brother
Aaron and his sons to serve me as
priests, 5 they shall use gold, blue, purple, and crimson yarns, and fine linen.

THE EPHOD

6 They shall make the ephod of gold,
of blue, purple, and crimson yarns, and
of fine twisted linen, skilfully worked.
7 It shall have two shoulder-pieces attached to its two edges, so that it may
be joined together. 8 The decorated band
on it shall be of the same workmanship
and materials, of gold, of blue, purple,
and crimson yarns, and of fine twisted
linen. 9 You shall take two onyx stones,
and engrave on them the names of
the sons of Israel, 10 six of their names
on one stone, and the names of the remaining six on the other stone, in the
order of their birth. 11 As a gem-cutter
engraves signets, so you shall engrave
the two stones with the names of the
sons of Israel; you shall mount them in
settings of gold filigree. 12 You shall set
the two stones on the shoulder-pieces of
the ephod, as stones of remembrance for
the sons of Israel; and Aaron shall bear
their names before the LORD on his two
shoulders for remembrance. 13 You shall
make settings of gold filigree, 14 and two
chains of pure gold, twisted like cords;
and you shall attach the corded chains
to the settings.

THE BREASTPLATE

15 You shall make a breastpiece of
judgement, in skilled work; you shall
make it in the style of the ephod; of
gold, of blue and purple and crimson
yarns, and of fine twisted linen you
shall make it. 16 It shall be square and
doubled, a span in length and a span in
width. 17 You shall set in it four rows of
stones. A row of carnelian,[y] chrysolite,
and emerald shall be the first row; 18 and
the second row a turquoise, a sapphire,[z]

[x] **27.21** Or *treaty*, or *testimony*; Heb *eduth*
[y] **28.17** The identity of several of these stones is uncertain
[z] **28.18** Or *lapis lazuli*

and a moonstone; 19 and the third row
a jacinth, an agate, and an amethyst;
20 and the fourth row a beryl, an onyx,
and a jasper; they shall be set in gold
filigree. 21 There shall be twelve stones
with names corresponding to the names
of the sons of Israel; they shall be like
signets, each engraved with its name,
for the twelve tribes. 22 You shall make
for the breastpiece chains of pure gold,
twisted like cords; 23 and you shall make
for the breastpiece two rings of gold, and
put the two rings on the two edges of
the breastpiece. 24 You shall put the two
cords of gold in the two rings at the edges
of the breastpiece; 25 the two ends of the
two cords you shall attach to the two
settings, and so attach it in front to the
shoulder-pieces of the ephod. 26 You shall
make two rings of gold, and put them
at the two ends of the breastpiece, on
its inside edge next to the ephod. 27 You
shall make two rings of gold, and attach
them in front to the lower part of the
two shoulder-pieces of the ephod, at its
joining above the decorated band of the
ephod. 28 The breastpiece shall be bound
by its rings to the rings of the ephod with
a blue cord, so that it may lie on the decorated band of the ephod, and so that the
breastpiece shall not come loose from the
ephod. 29 So Aaron shall bear the names
of the sons of Israel in the breastpiece of
judgement on his heart when he goes
into the holy place, for a continual remembrance before the LORD. 30 In the
breastpiece of judgement you shall put
the Urim and the Thummim, and they
shall be on Aaron's heart when he goes
in before the LORD; thus Aaron shall bear
the judgement of the Israelites on his
heart before the LORD continually.

OTHER PRIESTLY VESTMENTS

31 You shall make the robe of the
ephod all of blue. 32 It shall have an
opening for the head in the middle of it,
with a woven binding round the opening, like the opening in a coat of mail,[a]
so that it may not be torn. 33 On its
lower hem you shall make pomegranates of blue, purple, and crimson yarns,
all round the lower hem, with bells
of gold between them all round— 34 a
golden bell and a pomegranate alternat-
ing all round the lower hem of the robe.
35 Aaron shall wear it when he ministers, and its sound shall be heard when
he goes into the holy place before the
LORD, and when he comes out, so that
he may not die.

36 You shall make a rosette of pure
gold, and engrave on it, like the engraving of a signet, 'Holy to the LORD.' 37 You
shall fasten it on the turban with a blue
cord; it shall be on the front of the turban. 38 It shall be on Aaron's forehead,
and Aaron shall take on himself any
guilt incurred in the holy offering that
the Israelites consecrate as their sacred
donations; it shall always be on his forehead, in order that they may find favour
before the LORD.

39 You shall make the chequered tunic of fine linen, and you shall make a
turban of fine linen, and you shall make
a sash embroidered with needlework.

40 For Aaron's sons you shall make
tunics and sashes and head-dresses;
you shall make them for their glorious
adornment. 41 You shall put them on
your brother Aaron, and on his sons
with him, and shall anoint them and
ordain them and consecrate them, so
that they may serve me as priests. 42 You
shall make for them linen undergarments to cover their naked flesh; they
shall reach from the hips to the thighs;
43 Aaron and his sons shall wear them
when they go into the tent of meeting,
or when they come near the altar to
minister in the holy place; or they will
bring guilt on themselves and die. This
shall be a perpetual ordinance for him
and for his descendants after him.

THE ORDINATION OF THE PRIESTS

29 Now this is what you shall do to
them to consecrate them, so that
they may serve me as priests. Take one
young bull and two rams without blemish, 2 and unleavened bread, unleavened
cakes mixed with oil, and unleavened
wafers spread with oil. You shall make
them of choice wheat flour. 3 You shall
put them in one basket and bring them
in the basket, and bring the bull and
the two rams. 4 You shall bring Aaron
and his sons to the entrance of the tent
of meeting, and wash them with water. 5 Then you shall take the vestments,
and put on Aaron the tunic and the
robe of the ephod, and the ephod, and
the breastpiece, and gird him with the
decorated band of the ephod; 6 and you
shall set the turban on his head, and put
the holy diadem on the turban. 7 You
shall take the anointing-oil, and pour it
on his head and anoint him. 8 Then you
shall bring his sons, and put tunics on

[a] 28.32 Meaning of Heb uncertain

them, [9]and you shall gird them with sashes[b] and tie head-dresses on them; and the priesthood shall be theirs by a perpetual ordinance. You shall then ordain Aaron and his sons.

10 You shall bring the bull in front of the tent of meeting. Aaron and his sons shall lay their hands on the head of the bull, [11]and you shall slaughter the bull before the LORD, at the entrance of the tent of meeting, [12]and shall take some of the blood of the bull and put it on the horns of the altar with your finger, and all the rest of the blood you shall pour out at the base of the altar. [13]You shall take all the fat that covers the entrails, and the appendage of the liver, and the two kidneys with the fat that is on them, and turn them into smoke on the altar. [14]But the flesh of the bull, and its skin, and its dung, you shall burn with fire outside the camp; it is a sin-offering.

15 Then you shall take one of the rams, and Aaron and his sons shall lay their hands on the head of the ram, [16]and you shall slaughter the ram, and shall take its blood and dash it against all sides of the altar. [17]Then you shall cut the ram into its parts, and wash its entrails and its legs, and put them with its parts and its head, [18]and turn the whole ram into smoke on the altar; it is a burnt-offering to the LORD; it is a pleasing odour, an offering by fire to the LORD.

19 You shall take the other ram; and Aaron and his sons shall lay their hands on the head of the ram, [20]and you shall slaughter the ram, and take some of its blood and put it on the lobe of Aaron's right ear and on the lobes of the right ears of his sons, and on the thumbs of their right hands, and on the big toes of their right feet, and dash the rest of the blood against all sides of the altar. [21]Then you shall take some of the blood that is on the altar, and some of the anointing-oil, and sprinkle it on Aaron and his vestments and on his sons and his sons' vestments with him; then he and his vestments shall be holy, as well as his sons and his sons' vestments.

22 You shall also take the fat of the ram, the fat-tail, the fat that covers the entrails, the appendage of the liver, the two kidneys with the fat that is on them, and the right thigh (for it is a ram of ordination), [23]and one loaf of bread, one cake of bread made with oil, and one wafer, out of the basket of unleavened bread that is before the LORD; [24]and you shall place all these on the palms of Aaron and on the palms of his sons, and raise them as an elevation-offering before the LORD. [25]Then you shall take them from their hands, and turn them into smoke on the altar on top of the burnt-offering of pleasing odour before the LORD; it is an offering by fire to the LORD.

26 You shall take the breast of the ram of Aaron's ordination and raise it as an elevation-offering before the LORD; and it shall be your portion. [27]You shall consecrate the breast that was raised as an elevation-offering and the thigh that was raised as an elevation-offering from the ram of ordination, from that which belonged to Aaron and his sons. [28]These things shall be a perpetual ordinance for Aaron and his sons from the Israelites, for this is an offering; and it shall be an offering by the Israelites from their sacrifice of offerings of well-being, their offering to the LORD.

29 The sacred vestments of Aaron shall be passed on to his sons after him; they shall be anointed in them and ordained in them. [30]The son who is priest in his place shall wear them for seven days, when he comes into the tent of meeting to minister in the holy place.

31 You shall take the ram of ordination, and boil its flesh in a holy place; [32]and Aaron and his sons shall eat the flesh of the ram and the bread that is in the basket, at the entrance of the tent of meeting. [33]They themselves shall eat the food by which atonement is made, to ordain and consecrate them, but no one else shall eat of them, because they are holy. [34]If any of the flesh for the ordination, or of the bread, remains until the morning, then you shall burn the remainder with fire; it shall not be eaten, because it is holy.

35 Thus you shall do to Aaron and to his sons, just as I have commanded you; over seven days you shall ordain them. [36]Also every day you shall offer a bull as a sin-offering for atonement. Also you shall offer a sin-offering for the altar, when you make atonement for it, and shall anoint it, to consecrate it. [37]For seven days you shall make atonement for the altar, and consecrate it, and the altar shall be most holy; whatever touches the altar shall become holy.

THE DAILY OFFERINGS

38 Now this is what you shall offer on the altar: two lambs a year old regularly

[b] **29.9** Gk: Heb *sashes, Aaron and his sons*

each day. 39 One lamb you shall offer in
the morning, and the other lamb you
shall offer in the evening; 40 and with
the first lamb one-tenth of a measure
of choice flour mixed with one-fourth
of a hin of beaten oil, and one-fourth
of a hin of wine for a drink-offering.
41 And the other lamb you shall offer
in the evening, and shall offer with it a
grain-offering and its drink-offering, as
in the morning, for a pleasing odour, an
offering by fire to the LORD. 42 It shall
be a regular burnt-offering throughout
your generations at the entrance of the
tent of meeting before the LORD, where
I will meet you, to speak to you there.
43 I will meet the Israelites there, and it
shall be sanctified by my glory; 44 I will
consecrate the tent of meeting and the
altar; Aaron also and his sons I will consecrate, to serve me as priests. 45 I will
dwell among the Israelites, and I will be
their God. 46 And they shall know that
I am the LORD their God, who brought
them out of the land of Egypt that I
might dwell among them; I am the
LORD their God.

THE ALTAR OF INCENSE

30 You shall make an altar on
which to offer incense; you
shall make it of acacia wood. 2 It shall
be one cubit long, and one cubit wide;
it shall be square, and shall be two cubits high; its horns shall be of one piece
with it. 3 You shall overlay it with pure
gold, its top, and its sides all round and
its horns; and you shall make for it a
moulding of gold all round. 4 And you
shall make two golden rings for it; under its moulding on two opposite sides
of it you shall make them, and they
shall hold the poles with which to carry
it. 5 You shall make the poles of acacia wood, and overlay them with gold.
6 You shall place it in front of the curtain
that is above the ark of the covenant,[c]
in front of the mercy-seat[d] that is over
the covenant,[e] where I will meet you.
7 Aaron shall offer fragrant incense on
it; every morning when he dresses the
lamps he shall offer it, 8 and when Aaron
sets up the lamps in the evening he shall
offer it, a regular incense-offering before
the LORD throughout your generations.
9 You shall not offer unholy incense
on it, or a burnt-offering, or a grain-
offering; and you shall not pour a drink-
offering on it. 10 Once a year Aaron shall
perform the rite of atonement on its
horns. Throughout your generations he
shall perform the atonement for it once
a year with the blood of the atoning sin-
offering. It is most holy to the LORD.

THE HALF-SHEKEL FOR THE SANCTUARY

11 The LORD spoke to Moses: 12 When
you take a census of the Israelites to register them, at registration all of them
shall give a ransom for their lives to the
LORD, so that no plague may come upon
them for being registered. 13 This is what
each one who is registered shall give:
half a shekel according to the shekel of
the sanctuary (the shekel is twenty gerahs), half a shekel as an offering to the
LORD. 14 Each one who is registered,
from twenty years old and upwards,
shall give the LORD's offering. 15 The rich
shall not give more, and the poor shall
not give less, than the half-shekel, when
you bring this offering to the LORD to
make atonement for your lives. 16 You
shall take the atonement money from
the Israelites and shall designate it for
the service of the tent of meeting; before the LORD it will be a reminder to
the Israelites of the ransom given for
your lives.

THE BRONZE BASIN

17 The LORD spoke to Moses: 18 You
shall make a bronze basin with a bronze
stand for washing. You shall put it between the tent of meeting and the altar,
and you shall put water in it; 19 with the
water[f] Aaron and his sons shall wash
their hands and their feet. 20 When they
go into the tent of meeting, or when
they come near the altar to minister, to
make an offering by fire to the LORD,
they shall wash with water, so that they
may not die. 21 They shall wash their
hands and their feet, so that they may
not die: it shall be a perpetual ordinance
for them, for him and for his descendants throughout their generations.

THE ANOINTING-OIL AND INCENSE

22 The LORD spoke to Moses: 23 Take
the finest spices: of liquid myrrh five
hundred shekels, and of sweet-smelling
cinnamon half as much, that is, two
hundred and fifty, and two hundred
and fifty of aromatic cane, 24 and five
hundred of cassia—measured by the
sanctuary shekel—and a hin of olive oil;
25 and you shall make of these a sacred

[c] **30.6** Or *treaty, or testimony*; Heb *eduth*
[d] **30.6** Or *the cover* [e] **30.6** Or *treaty, or testimony*; Heb *eduth* [f] **30.19** Heb *it*

anointing-oil blended as by the perfumer; it shall be a holy anointing-oil.
26With it you shall anoint the tent of
meeting and the ark of the covenant,[g]
27and the table and all its utensils, and
the lampstand and its utensils, and
the altar of incense, 28and the altar of
burnt-offering with all its utensils, and
the basin with its stand; 29you shall
consecrate them, so that they may be
most holy; whatever touches them will
become holy. 30You shall anoint Aaron
and his sons, and consecrate them, in
order that they may serve me as priests.
31You shall say to the Israelites, 'This
shall be my holy anointing-oil throughout your generations. 32It shall not be
used in any ordinary anointing of the
body, and you shall make no other like it
in composition; it is holy, and it shall be
holy to you. 33Whoever compounds any
like it or whoever puts any of it on an
unqualified person shall be cut off from
the people.'

34 The LORD said to Moses: Take
sweet spices, stacte, and onycha, and
galbanum, sweet spices with pure
frankincense (an equal part of each),
35and make an incense blended as by
the perfumer, seasoned with salt, pure
and holy; 36and you shall beat some of
it into powder, and put part of it before the covenant[h] in the tent of meeting where I shall meet you; it shall be
for you most holy. 37When you make
incense according to this composition,
you shall not make it for yourselves; it
shall be regarded by you as holy to the
LORD. 38Whoever makes any like it to
use as perfume shall be cut off from the
people.

BEZALEL AND OHOLIAB

31 The LORD spoke to Moses: 2See, I
have called by name Bezalel son
of Uri son of Hur, of the tribe of Judah:
3and I have filled him with divine spirit,[i] with ability, intelligence, and knowledge in every kind of craft, 4to devise
artistic designs, to work in gold, silver,
and bronze, 5in cutting stones for setting, and in carving wood, in every kind
of craft. 6Moreover, I have appointed
with him Oholiab son of Ahisamach, of
the tribe of Dan; and I have given skill to
all the skilful, so that they may make all
that I have commanded you: 7the tent of
meeting, and the ark of the covenant,[j]
and the mercy-seat[k] that is on it, and all
the furnishings of the tent, 8the table
and its utensils, and the pure lampstand
with all its utensils, and the altar of incense, 9and the altar of burnt-offering
with all its utensils, and the basin with
its stand, 10and the finely worked vestments, the holy vestments for the priest
Aaron and the vestments of his sons,
for their service as priests, 11and the
anointing-oil and the fragrant incense
for the holy place. They shall do just as I
have commanded you.

THE SABBATH LAW

12 The LORD said to Moses: 13You
yourself are to speak to the Israelites:
'You shall keep my sabbaths, for this is
a sign between me and you throughout
your generations, given in order that
you may know that I, the LORD, sanctify you. 14You shall keep the sabbath,
because it is holy for you; everyone who
profanes it shall be put to death; whoever does any work on it shall be cut
off from among the people. 15For six
days shall work be done, but the seventh day is a sabbath of solemn rest,
holy to the LORD; whoever does any
work on the sabbath day shall be put
to death. 16Therefore the Israelites shall
keep the sabbath, observing the sabbath throughout their generations, as a
perpetual covenant. 17It is a sign for ever
between me and the people of Israel
that in six days the LORD made heaven
and earth, and on the seventh day he
rested, and was refreshed.'

THE TWO TABLETS OF THE COVENANT

18 When God[l] finished speaking with
Moses on Mount Sinai, he gave him the
two tablets of the covenant,[m] tablets of
stone, written with the finger of God.

THE GOLDEN CALF

32 When the people saw that Moses
delayed to come down from the
mountain, the people gathered around
Aaron and said to him, 'Come, make
gods for us, who shall go before us; as for
this Moses, the man who brought us up
out of the land of Egypt, we do not know
what has become of him.' 2Aaron said to
them, 'Take off the gold rings that are
on the ears of your wives, your sons,
and your daughters, and bring them to

[g] 30.26 Or *treaty, or testimony*; Heb *eduth*
[h] 30.36 Or *treaty, or testimony*; Heb *eduth*
[i] 31.3 Or *with the spirit of God* [j] 31.7 Or *treaty, or testimony*; Heb *eduth* [k] 31.7 Or *the cover*
[l] 31.18 Heb *he* [m] 31.18 Or *treaty, or testimony*; Heb *eduth*

me.' 3So all the people took off the gold
rings from their ears, and brought them
to Aaron. 4He took the gold from them,
formed it in a mould,[n] and cast an image of a calf; and they said, 'These are
your gods, O Israel, who brought you up
out of the land of Egypt!' 5When Aaron
saw this, he built an altar before it; and
Aaron made proclamation and said, 'Tomorrow shall be a festival to the LORD.'
6They rose early the next day, and offered burnt-offerings and brought sacrifices of well-being; and the people sat
down to eat and drink, and rose up to
revel.

7 The LORD said to Moses, 'Go
down at once! Your people, whom you
brought up out of the land of Egypt,
have acted perversely; 8they have been
quick to turn aside from the way that
I commanded them; they have cast for
themselves an image of a calf, and have
worshipped it and sacrificed to it, and
said, "These are your gods, O Israel,
who brought you up out of the land of
Egypt!" ' 9The LORD said to Moses, 'I
have seen this people, how stiff-necked
they are. 10Now let me alone, so that my
wrath may burn hot against them and
I may consume them; and of you I will
make a great nation.'

11 But Moses implored the LORD
his God, and said, 'O LORD, why does
your wrath burn hot against your people, whom you brought out of the land
of Egypt with great power and with a
mighty hand? 12Why should the Egyptians say, "It was with evil intent that
he brought them out to kill them in
the mountains, and to consume them
from the face of the earth"? Turn from
your fierce wrath; change your mind
and do not bring disaster on your people. 13Remember Abraham, Isaac, and
Israel, your servants, how you swore to
them by your own self, saying to them,
"I will multiply your descendants like
the stars of heaven, and all this land
that I have promised I will give to your
descendants, and they shall inherit it
for ever." ' 14And the LORD changed his
mind about the disaster that he planned
to bring on his people.

15 Then Moses turned and went
down from the mountain, carrying
the two tablets of the covenant[o] in his
hands, tablets that were written on
both sides, written on the front and on
the back. 16The tablets were the work of
God, and the writing was the writing of
God, engraved upon the tablets. 17When
Joshua heard the noise of the people as
they shouted, he said to Moses, 'There
is a noise of war in the camp.' 18But he
said,

'It is not the sound made by victors,
or the sound made by losers;
it is the sound of revellers
that I hear.'

19As soon as he came near the camp and
saw the calf and the dancing, Moses' anger burned hot, and he threw the tablets
from his hands and broke them at the
foot of the mountain. 20He took the calf
that they had made, burned it with fire,
ground it to powder, scattered it on the
water, and made the Israelites drink it.

21 Moses said to Aaron, 'What did
this people do to you that you have
brought so great a sin upon them?'
22And Aaron said, 'Do not let the anger
of my lord burn hot; you know the people, that they are bent on evil. 23They
said to me, "Make us gods, who shall
go before us; as for this Moses, the man
who brought us up out of the land of
Egypt, we do not know what has become of him." 24So I said to them, "Whoever has gold, take it off"; so they gave it
to me, and I threw it into the fire, and
out came this calf!'

25 When Moses saw that the people
were running wild (for Aaron had let
them run wild, to the derision of their
enemies), 26then Moses stood in the
gate of the camp, and said, 'Who is on
the LORD's side? Come to me!' And all
the sons of Levi gathered around him.
27He said to them, 'Thus says the LORD,
the God of Israel, "Put your sword on
your side, each of you! Go back and forth
from gate to gate throughout the camp,
and each of you kill your brother, your
friend, and your neighbour." ' 28The sons
of Levi did as Moses commanded, and
about three thousand of the people fell
on that day. 29Moses said, 'Today you
have ordained yourselves[p] for the service of the LORD, each one at the cost of a
son or a brother, and so have brought a
blessing on yourselves this day.'

30 On the next day Moses said to the
people, 'You have sinned a great sin. But
now I will go up to the LORD; perhaps I
can make atonement for your sin.' 31So
Moses returned to the LORD and said,
'Alas, this people has sinned a great sin;
they have made for themselves gods

[n] **32.4** Or *fashioned it with a graving-tool*; Meaning of Heb uncertain [o] **32.15** Or *treaty*, or *testimony*; Heb *eduth* [p] **32.29** Gk Vg Compare Tg: Heb *Today ordain yourselves*

of gold. 32 But now, if you will only forgive their sin—but if not, blot me out of the book that you have written.' 33 But the LORD said to Moses, 'Whoever has sinned against me I will blot out of my book. 34 But now go, lead the people to the place about which I have spoken to you; see, my angel shall go in front of you. Nevertheless, when the day comes for punishment, I will punish them for their sin.'

35 Then the LORD sent a plague on the people, because they made the calf—the one that Aaron made.

THE COMMAND TO LEAVE SINAI

33 The LORD said to Moses, 'Go, leave this place, you and the people whom you have brought up out of the land of Egypt, and go to the land of which I swore to Abraham, Isaac, and Jacob, saying, "To your descendants I will give it." 2 I will send an angel before you, and I will drive out the Canaanites, the Amorites, the Hittites, the Perizzites, the Hivites, and the Jebusites. 3 Go up to a land flowing with milk and honey; but I will not go up among you, or I would consume you on the way, for you are a stiff-necked people.'

4 When the people heard these harsh words, they mourned, and no one put on ornaments. 5 For the LORD had said to Moses, 'Say to the Israelites, "You are a stiff-necked people; if for a single moment I should go up among you, I would consume you. So now take off your ornaments, and I will decide what to do to you." ' 6 Therefore the Israelites stripped themselves of their ornaments, from Mount Horeb onwards.

THE TENT OUTSIDE THE CAMP

7 Now Moses used to take the tent and pitch it outside the camp, far off from the camp; he called it the tent of meeting. And everyone who sought the LORD would go out to the tent of meeting, which was outside the camp. 8 Whenever Moses went out to the tent, all the people would rise and stand, each of them, at the entrance of their tents and watch Moses until he had gone into the tent. 9 When Moses entered the tent, the pillar of cloud would descend and stand at the entrance of the tent, and the LORD would speak with Moses. 10 When all the people saw the pillar of cloud standing at the entrance of the tent, all the people would rise and bow down, all of them, at the entrance of their tents. 11 Thus the LORD used to speak to Moses face to face, as one speaks to a friend. Then he would return to the camp; but his young assistant, Joshua son of Nun, would not leave the tent.

MOSES' INTERCESSION

12 Moses said to the LORD, 'See, you have said to me, "Bring up this people"; but you have not let me know whom you will send with me. Yet you have said, "I know you by name, and you have also found favour in my sight." 13 Now if I have found favour in your sight, show me your ways, so that I may know you and find favour in your sight. Consider too that this nation is your people.' 14 He said, 'My presence will go with you, and I will give you rest.' 15 And he said to him, 'If your presence will not go, do not carry us up from here. 16 For how shall it be known that I have found favour in your sight, I and your people, unless you go with us? In this way, we shall be distinct, I and your people, from every people on the face of the earth.'

17 The LORD said to Moses, 'I will do the very thing that you have asked; for you have found favour in my sight, and I know you by name.' 18 Moses said, 'Show me your glory, I pray.' 19 And he said, 'I will make all my goodness pass before you, and will proclaim before you the name, "The LORD";[q] and I will be gracious to whom I will be gracious, and will show mercy on whom I will show mercy. 20 But', he said, 'you cannot see my face; for no one shall see me and live.' 21 And the LORD continued, 'See, there is a place by me where you shall stand on the rock; 22 and while my glory passes by I will put you in a cleft of the rock, and I will cover you with my hand until I have passed by; 23 then I will take away my hand, and you shall see my back; but my face shall not be seen.'

MOSES MAKES NEW TABLETS

34 The LORD said to Moses, 'Cut two tablets of stone like the former ones, and I will write on the tablets the words that were on the former tablets, which you broke. 2 Be ready in the morning, and come up in the morning to Mount Sinai and present yourself there to me, on the top of the mountain. 3 No one shall come up with you, and do not let anyone be seen throughout all the mountain; and do not let flocks or

q 33.19 Heb *YHWH*; see note at 3.15

herds graze in front of that mountain.'
4So Moses cut two tablets of stone like
the former ones; and he rose early in
the morning and went up on Mount
Sinai, as the LORD had commanded
him, and took in his hand the two tablets of stone. 5The LORD descended in
the cloud and stood with him there,
and proclaimed the name, 'The LORD.'[r]
6The LORD passed before him, and proclaimed,

'The LORD, the LORD,
a God merciful and gracious,
slow to anger,
and abounding in steadfast love
and faithfulness,
7 keeping steadfast love for the
thousandth generation,[s]
forgiving iniquity and
transgression and sin,
yet by no means clearing the guilty,
but visiting the iniquity
of the parents
upon the children
and the children's children,
to the third and the fourth
generation.'

8And Moses quickly bowed his head towards the earth, and worshipped. 9He
said, 'If now I have found favour in your
sight, O Lord, I pray, let the Lord go
with us. Although this is a stiff-necked
people, pardon our iniquity and our sin,
and take us for your inheritance.'

THE COVENANT RENEWED

10 He said: I hereby make a covenant. Before all your people I will perform marvels, such as have not been
performed in all the earth or in any nation; and all the people among whom
you live shall see the work of the LORD;
for it is an awesome thing that I will do
with you.

11 Observe what I command you today. See, I will drive out before you the
Amorites, the Canaanites, the Hittites,
the Perizzites, the Hivites, and the Jebusites. 12Take care not to make a covenant with the inhabitants of the land
to which you are going, or it will become
a snare among you. 13You shall tear
down their altars, break their pillars,
and cut down their sacred poles[t] 14(for
you shall worship no other god, because the LORD, whose name is Jealous,
is a jealous God). 15You shall not make
a covenant with the inhabitants of the
land, for when they prostitute themselves to their gods and sacrifice to their
gods, someone among them will invite
you, and you will eat of the sacrifice.
16And you will take wives from among
their daughters for your sons, and their
daughters who prostitute themselves
to their gods will make your sons also
prostitute themselves to their gods.

17 You shall not make cast idols.

18 You shall keep the festival of unleavened bread. For seven days you shall
eat unleavened bread, as I commanded
you, at the time appointed in the month
of Abib; for in the month of Abib you
came out from Egypt.

19 All that first opens the womb is
mine, all your male[u] livestock, the firstborn of cow and sheep. 20The firstborn
of a donkey you shall redeem with a
lamb, or if you will not redeem it you
shall break its neck. All the firstborn of
your sons you shall redeem.

No one shall appear before me empty-
handed.

21 For six days you shall work, but on
the seventh day you shall rest; even in
ploughing time and in harvest time you
shall rest. 22You shall observe the festival of weeks, the first fruits of wheat
harvest, and the festival of ingathering
at the turn of the year. 23Three times
in the year all your males shall appear
before the LORD God, the God of Israel.
24For I will cast out nations before you,
and enlarge your borders; no one shall
covet your land when you go up to appear before the LORD your God three
times in the year.

25 You shall not offer the blood of my
sacrifice with leaven, and the sacrifice
of the festival of the passover shall not
be left until the morning.

26 The best of the first fruits of your
ground you shall bring to the house of
the LORD your God.

You shall not boil a kid in its mother's
milk.

27 The LORD said to Moses: Write
these words; in accordance with these
words I have made a covenant with you
and with Israel. 28He was there with the
LORD for forty days and forty nights; he
neither ate bread nor drank water. And
he wrote on the tablets the words of the
covenant, the ten commandments.[v]

THE SHINING FACE OF MOSES

29 Moses came down from Mount Sinai. As he came down from the moun-

[r] **34.5** Heb *YHWH*; see note at 3.15 [s] **34.7** Or *for thousands* [t] **34.13** Heb *Asherim* [u] **34.19** Gk Theodotion Vg Tg: Meaning of Heb uncertain
[v] **34.28** Heb *words*

tain with the two tablets of the covenant[w] in his hand, Moses did not know
that the skin of his face shone because
he had been talking with God. 30When
Aaron and all the Israelites saw Moses,
the skin of his face was shining, and they
were afraid to come near him. 31But Moses called to them; and Aaron and all the
leaders of the congregation returned to
him, and Moses spoke with them. 32Af-
terwards all the Israelites came near,
and he gave them in commandment
all that the LORD had spoken with him
on Mount Sinai. 33When Moses had finished speaking with them, he put a veil
on his face; 34but whenever Moses went
in before the LORD to speak with him,
he would take the veil off, until he came
out; and when he came out, and told
the Israelites what he had been commanded, 35the Israelites would see the
face of Moses, that the skin of his face
was shining; and Moses would put the
veil on his face again, until he went in
to speak with him.

SABBATH REGULATIONS

35 Moses assembled all the congregation of the Israelites and said
to them: These are the things that the
LORD has commanded you to do:

2 For six days shall work be done,
but on the seventh day you shall have a
holy sabbath of solemn rest to the LORD;
whoever does any work on it shall be
put to death. 3You shall kindle no fire
in all your dwellings on the sabbath day.

PREPARATIONS FOR MAKING THE TABERNACLE

4 Moses said to all the congregation
of the Israelites: This is the thing that
the LORD has commanded: 5Take from
among you an offering to the LORD;
let whoever is of a generous heart
bring the LORD's offering: gold, silver,
and bronze; 6blue, purple, and crimson yarns, and fine linen; goats' hair,
7tanned rams' skins, and fine leather;[x]
acacia wood, 8oil for the light, spices for
the anointing-oil and for the fragrant
incense, 9and onyx stones and gems to
be set in the ephod and the breastpiece.

10 All who are skilful among you
shall come and make all that the LORD
has commanded: the tabernacle, 11its
tent and its covering, its clasps and its
frames, its bars, its pillars, and its bases;
12the ark with its poles, the mercy-seat,[y]
and the curtain for the screen; 13the table with its poles and all its utensils, and
the bread of the Presence; 14the lampstand also for the light, with its utensils
and its lamps, and the oil for the light;
15and the altar of incense, with its poles,
and the anointing-oil and the fragrant
incense, and the screen for the entrance,
the entrance of the tabernacle; 16the altar of burnt-offering, with its grating of
bronze, its poles, and all its utensils, the
basin with its stand; 17the hangings of
the court, its pillars and its bases, and
the screen for the gate of the court; 18the
pegs of the tabernacle and the pegs of
the court, and their cords; 19the finely
worked vestments for ministering in
the holy place, the holy vestments for
the priest Aaron, and the vestments of
his sons, for their service as priests.

OFFERINGS FOR THE TABERNACLE

20 Then all the congregation of the
Israelites withdrew from the presence
of Moses. 21And they came, everyone
whose heart was stirred, and everyone
whose spirit was willing, and brought
the LORD's offering to be used for the
tent of meeting, and for all its service,
and for the sacred vestments. 22So they
came, both men and women; all who
were of a willing heart brought brooches
and earings and signet rings and pendants, all sorts of gold objects, everyone
bringing an offering of gold to the LORD.
23And everyone who possessed blue or
purple or crimson yarn or fine linen
or goats' hair or tanned rams' skins or
fine leather,[z] brought them. 24Everyone
who could make an offering of silver or
bronze brought it as the LORD's offering; and everyone who possessed acacia
wood of any use in the work, brought it.
25All the skilful women spun with their
hands, and brought what they had spun
in blue and purple and crimson yarns
and fine linen; 26all the women whose
hearts moved them to use their skill
spun the goats' hair. 27And the leaders
brought onyx stones and gems to be
set in the ephod and the breastpiece,
28and spices and oil for the light, and for
the anointing-oil, and for the fragrant
incense. 29All the Israelite men and
women whose hearts made them willing to bring anything for the work that
the LORD had commanded by Moses to
be done, brought it as a freewill-offering
to the LORD.

[w] 34.29 Or *treaty*, or *testimony*; Heb *eduth*
[x] 35.7 Meaning of Heb uncertain [y] 35.12 Or *the cover* [z] 35.23 Meaning of Heb uncertain

BEZALEL AND OHOLIAB

30 Then Moses said to the Israelites:
See, the LORD has called by name Bezalel son of Uri son of Hur, of the tribe
of Judah; 31he has filled him with divine spirit,[a] with skill, intelligence, and
knowledge in every kind of craft, 32to
devise artistic designs, to work in gold,
silver, and bronze, 33in cutting stones
for setting, and in carving wood, in every kind of craft. 34And he has inspired
him to teach, both him and Oholiab son
of Ahisamach, of the tribe of Dan. 35He
has filled them with skill to do every
kind of work done by an artisan or by a
designer or by an embroiderer in blue,
purple, and crimson yarns, and in fine
linen, or by a weaver—by any sort of artisan or skilled designer.

36 Bezalel and Oholiab and everyone skilful to whom the LORD
has given skill and understanding to
know how to do any work in the construction of the sanctuary shall work in
accordance with all that the LORD has
commanded.

2 Moses then called Bezalel and
Oholiab and everyone skilful to whom
the LORD had given skill, everyone
whose heart was stirred to come to do
the work; 3and they received from Moses all the freewill-offerings that the
Israelites had brought for doing the
work on the sanctuary. They still kept
bringing him freewill-offerings every
morning, 4so that all the artisans who
were doing every sort of task on the
sanctuary came, each from the task being performed, 5and said to Moses, 'The
people are bringing much more than
enough for doing the work that the
LORD has commanded us to do.' 6So
Moses gave command, and word was
proclaimed throughout the camp: 'No
man or woman is to make anything
else as an offering for the sanctuary.'
So the people were restrained from
bringing; 7for what they had already
brought was more than enough to do
all the work.

CONSTRUCTION OF THE TABERNACLE

8 All those with skill among the
workers made the tabernacle with ten
curtains; they were made of fine twisted
linen, and blue, purple, and crimson
yarns, with cherubim skilfully worked
into them. 9The length of each curtain
was twenty-eight cubits, and the width
of each curtain four cubits; all the curtains were of the same size.

10 He joined five curtains to one another, and the other five curtains he
joined to one another. 11He made loops
of blue on the edge of the outermost
curtain of the first set; likewise he made
them on the edge of the outermost curtain of the second set; 12he made fifty
loops on the one curtain, and he made
fifty loops on the edge of the curtain
that was in the second set; the loops
were opposite one another. 13And he
made fifty clasps of gold, and joined the
curtains one to the other with clasps; so
the tabernacle was one whole.

14 He also made curtains of goats'
hair for a tent over the tabernacle; he
made eleven curtains. 15The length of
each curtain was thirty cubits, and
the width of each curtain four cubits;
the eleven curtains were of the same
size. 16He joined five curtains by themselves, and six curtains by themselves.
17He made fifty loops on the edge of the
outermost curtain of one set, and fifty
loops on the edge of the other connect-
ing curtain. 18He made fifty clasps of
bronze to join the tent together so that it
might be one whole. 19And he made for
the tent a covering of tanned rams' skins
and an outer covering of fine leather.[b]

20 Then he made the upright frames
for the tabernacle of acacia wood. 21Ten
cubits was the length of a frame, and
a cubit and a half the width of each
frame. 22Each frame had two pegs for
fitting together; he did this for all the
frames of the tabernacle. 23The frames
for the tabernacle he made in this way:
twenty frames for the south side; 24and
he made forty bases of silver under the
twenty frames, two bases under the
first frame for its two pegs, and two
bases under the next frame for its two
pegs. 25For the second side of the tabernacle, on the north side, he made
twenty frames 26and their forty bases of
silver, two bases under the first frame
and two bases under the next frame.
27For the rear of the tabernacle westward he made six frames. 28He made
two frames for corners of the tabernacle in the rear. 29They were separate
beneath, but joined at the top, at the
first ring; he made two of them in this
way, for the two corners. 30There were
eight frames with their bases of silver:
sixteen bases, under every frame two
bases.

[a] **35.31** Or *the spirit of God* [b] **36.19** Meaning of Heb uncertain

31 He made bars of acacia wood, five for the frames of one side of the tabernacle, 32and five bars for the frames of the other side of the tabernacle, and five bars for the frames of the tabernacle at the rear westward. 33He made the middle bar to pass through from end to end half-way up the frames. 34And he overlaid the frames with gold, and made rings of gold for them to hold the bars, and overlaid the bars with gold.

35 He made the curtain of blue, purple, and crimson yarns, and fine twisted linen, with cherubim skilfully worked into it. 36For it he made four pillars of acacia, and overlaid them with gold; their hooks were of gold, and he cast for them four bases of silver. 37He also made a screen for the entrance to the tent, of blue, purple, and crimson yarns, and fine twisted linen, embroidered with needlework; 38and its five pillars with their hooks. He overlaid their capitals and their bases with gold, but their five bases were of bronze.

MAKING THE ARK OF THE COVENANT

37 Bezalel made the ark of acacia wood; it was two and a half cubits long, a cubit and a half wide, and a cubit and a half high. 2He overlaid it with pure gold inside and outside, and made a moulding of gold round it. 3He cast for it four rings of gold for its four feet, two rings on one side of it and two rings on its other side. 4He made poles of acacia wood, and overlaid them with gold, 5and put the poles into the rings on the sides of the ark, to carry the ark. 6He made a mercy-seat[c] of pure gold; two cubits and a half was its length, and a cubit and a half its width. 7He made two cherubim of hammered gold; at the two ends of the mercy-seat[d] he made them, 8one cherub at one end, and one cherub at the other end; of one piece with the mercy-seat[e] he made the cherubim at its two ends. 9The cherubim spread out their wings above, overshadowing the mercy-seat[f] with their wings. They faced one another; the faces of the cherubim were turned towards the mercy-seat.[g]

MAKING THE TABLE FOR THE BREAD OF THE PRESENCE

10 He also made the table of acacia wood, two cubits long, one cubit wide, and a cubit and a half high. 11He overlaid it with pure gold, and made a moulding of gold round it. 12He made around it a rim a handbreadth wide, and made a moulding of gold round the rim. 13He cast for it four rings of gold, and fastened the rings to the four corners at its four legs. 14The rings that held the poles used for carrying the table were close to the rim. 15He made the poles of acacia wood to carry the table, and overlaid them with gold. 16And he made the vessels of pure gold that were to be on the table, its plates and dishes for incense, and its bowls and flagons with which to pour drink-offerings.

MAKING THE LAMPSTAND

17 He also made the lampstand of pure gold. The base and the shaft of the lampstand were made of hammered work; its cups, its calyxes, and its petals were of one piece with it. 18There were six branches going out of its sides, three branches of the lampstand out of one side of it and three branches of the lampstand out of the other side of it; 19three cups shaped like almond blossoms, each with calyx and petals, on one branch, and three cups shaped like almond blossoms, each with calyx and petals, on the other branch—so for the six branches going out of the lampstand. 20On the lampstand itself there were four cups shaped like almond blossoms, each with its calyxes and petals. 21There was a calyx of one piece with it under the first pair of branches, a calyx of one piece with it under the next pair of branches, and a calyx of one piece with it under the last pair of branches. 22Their calyxes and their branches were of one piece with it, the whole of it one hammered piece of pure gold. 23He made its seven lamps and its snuffers and its trays of pure gold. 24He made it and all its utensils of a talent of pure gold.

MAKING THE ALTAR OF INCENSE

25 He made the altar of incense of acacia wood, one cubit long, and one cubit wide; it was square, and was two cubits high; its horns were of one piece with it. 26He overlaid it with pure gold, its top, and its sides all round, and its horns; and he made for it a moulding of gold all round, 27and made two golden rings for it under its moulding, on two opposite sides of it, to hold the poles with which to carry it. 28And he made

[c] **37.6** Or *a cover* [d] **37.7** Or *the cover*
[e] **37.8** Or *the cover* [f] **37.9** Or *the cover*
[g] **37.9** Or *the cover*

the poles of acacia wood, and overlaid them with gold.

MAKING THE ANOINTING-OIL AND THE INCENSE

29 He made the holy anointing-oil also, and the pure fragrant incense, blended as by the perfumer.

MAKING THE ALTAR OF BURNT-OFFERING

38 He made the altar of burnt-offering also of acacia wood; it was five cubits long, and five cubits wide; it was square, and three cubits high. 2 He made horns for it on its four corners; its horns were of one piece with it, and he overlaid it with bronze. 3 He made all the utensils of the altar, the pots, the shovels, the basins, the forks, and the firepans: all its utensils he made of bronze. 4 He made for the altar a grating, a network of bronze, under its ledge, extending half-way down. 5 He cast four rings on the four corners of the bronze grating to hold the poles; 6 he made the poles of acacia wood, and overlaid them with bronze. 7 And he put the poles through the rings on the sides of the altar, to carry it with them; he made it hollow, with boards.

8 He made the basin of bronze, with its stand of bronze, from the mirrors of the women who served at the entrance to the tent of meeting.

MAKING THE COURT OF THE TABERNACLE

9 He made the court; for the south side the hangings of the court were of fine twisted linen, one hundred cubits long; 10 its twenty pillars and their twenty bases were of bronze, but the hooks of the pillars and their bands were of silver. 11 For the north side there were hangings one hundred cubits long; its twenty pillars and their twenty bases were of bronze, but the hooks of the pillars and their bands were of silver. 12 For the west side there were hangings fifty cubits long, with ten pillars and ten bases; the hooks of the pillars and their bands were of silver. 13 And for the front to the east, fifty cubits. 14 The hangings for one side of the gate were fifteen cubits, with three pillars and three bases. 15 And so for the other side; on each side of the gate of the court were hangings of fifteen cubits, with three pillars and three bases. 16 All the hangings around the court were of fine twisted linen. 17 The bases for the pillars were of bronze, but the hooks of the pillars and their bands were of silver; the overlaying of their capitals was also of silver, and all the pillars of the court were banded with silver. 18 The screen for the entrance to the court was embroidered with needlework in blue, purple, and crimson yarns and fine twisted linen. It was twenty cubits long and, along the width of it, five cubits high, corresponding to the hangings of the court. 19 There were four pillars; their four bases were of bronze, their hooks of silver, and the overlaying of their capitals and their bands of silver. 20 All the pegs for the tabernacle and for the court all around were of bronze.

MATERIALS OF THE TABERNACLE

21 These are the records of the tabernacle, the tabernacle of the covenant,[h] which were drawn up at the commandment of Moses, the work of the Levites being under the direction of Ithamar son of the priest Aaron. 22 Bezalel son of Uri son of Hur, of the tribe of Judah, made all that the LORD commanded Moses; 23 and with him was Oholiab son of Ahisamach, of the tribe of Dan, engraver, designer, and embroiderer in blue, purple, and crimson yarns, and in fine linen.

24 All the gold that was used for the work, in all the construction of the sanctuary, the gold from the offering, was twenty-nine talents and seven hundred and thirty shekels, measured by the sanctuary shekel. 25 The silver from those of the congregation who were counted was one hundred talents and one thousand seven hundred and seventy-five shekels, measured by the sanctuary shekel; 26 a beka a head (that is, half a shekel, measured by the sanctuary shekel), for everyone who was counted in the census, from twenty years old and upwards, for six hundred and three thousand, five hundred and fifty men. 27 The hundred talents of silver were for casting the bases of the sanctuary and the bases of the curtain: one hundred bases for the hundred talents, a talent for a base. 28 Of the one thousand seven hundred and seventy-five shekels he made hooks for the pillars, and overlaid their capitals and made bands for them. 29 The bronze that was contributed was seventy talents and two thou-

[h] **38.21** Or *treaty*, or *testimony*; Heb *eduth*

sand four hundred shekels; 30 with it he
made the bases for the entrance of the
tent of meeting, the bronze altar and the
bronze grating for it and all the utensils
of the altar, 31 the bases all around the
court, and the bases of the gate of the
court, all the pegs of the tabernacle, and
all the pegs around the court.

MAKING THE VESTMENTS FOR THE PRIESTHOOD

39 Of the blue, purple, and crimson
yarns they made finely worked
vestments, for ministering in the holy
place; they made the sacred vestments
for Aaron; as the LORD had commanded
Moses.

2 He made the ephod of gold, of
blue, purple, and crimson yarns, and
of fine twisted linen. 3 Gold leaf was
hammered out and cut into threads to
work into the blue, purple, and crimson
yarns and into the fine twisted linen, in
skilled design. 4 They made for the ephod
shoulder-pieces, joined to it at its two
edges. 5 The decorated band on it was of
the same materials and workmanship,
of gold, of blue, purple, and crimson
yarns, and of fine twisted linen; as the
LORD had commanded Moses.

6 The onyx stones were prepared, enclosed in settings of gold filigree and engraved like the engravings of a signet,
according to the names of the sons of
Israel. 7 He set them on the shoulder-
pieces of the ephod, to be stones of remembrance for the sons of Israel; as the
LORD had commanded Moses.

8 He made the breastpiece, in skilled
work, like the work of the ephod, of
gold, of blue, purple, and crimson
yarns, and of fine twisted linen. 9 It was
square; the breastpiece was made double, a span in length and a span in width
when doubled. 10 They set in it four rows
of stones. A row of carnelian,[i] chrysolite, and emerald was the first row;
11 and the second row, a turquoise, a sapphire,[j] and a moonstone; 12 and the third
row, a jacinth, an agate, and an amethyst; 13 and the fourth row, a beryl, an
onyx, and a jasper; they were enclosed
in settings of gold filigree. 14 There were
twelve stones with names corresponding to the names of the sons of Israel;
they were like signets, each engraved
with its name, for the twelve tribes.
15 They made on the breastpiece chains
of pure gold, twisted like cords; 16 and
they made two settings of gold filigree
and two gold rings, and put the two
rings on the two edges of the breastpiece; 17 and they put the two cords of
gold in the two rings at the edges of the
breastpiece. 18 Two ends of the two cords
they had attached to the two settings
of filigree; in this way they attached it
in front to the shoulder-pieces of the
ephod. 19 Then they made two rings of
gold, and put them at the two ends of
the breastpiece, on its inside edge next
to the ephod. 20 They made two rings of
gold, and attached them in front to the
lower part of the two shoulder-pieces of
the ephod, at its joining above the decorated band of the ephod. 21 They bound
the breastpiece by its rings to the rings
of the ephod with a blue cord, so that it
should lie on the decorated band of the
ephod, and that the breastpiece should
not come loose from the ephod; as the
LORD had commanded Moses.

22 He also made the robe of the
ephod woven all of blue yarn; 23 and the
opening of the robe in the middle of it
was like the opening in a coat of mail,[k]
with a binding round the opening,
so that it might not be torn. 24 On the
lower hem of the robe they made pomegranates of blue, purple, and crimson
yarns, and of fine twisted linen. 25 They
also made bells of pure gold, and put
the bells between the pomegranates on
the lower hem of the robe all round, between the pomegranates; 26 a bell and a
pomegranate, a bell and a pomegranate
all round on the lower hem of the robe
for ministering; as the LORD had commanded Moses.

27 They also made the tunics, woven
of fine linen, for Aaron and his sons,
28 and the turban of fine linen, and the
head-dresses of fine linen, and the linen
undergarments of fine twisted linen,
29 and the sash of fine twisted linen,
and of blue, purple, and crimson yarns,
embroidered with needlework; as the
LORD had commanded Moses.

30 They made the rosette of the holy
diadem of pure gold, and wrote on it an
inscription, like the engraving of a signet, 'Holy to the LORD.' 31 They tied to it
a blue cord, to fasten it on the turban
above; as the LORD had commanded
Moses.

THE WORK COMPLETED

32 In this way all the work of the
tabernacle of the tent of meeting was

[i] **39.10** The identification of several of these stones is uncertain [j] **39.11** Or *lapis lazuli*
[k] **39.23** Meaning of Heb uncertain

finished; the Israelites had done everything just as the LORD had commanded
Moses. 33 Then they brought the tabernacle to Moses, the tent and all its
utensils, its hooks, its frames, its bars,
its pillars, and its bases; 34 the covering
of tanned rams' skins and the covering
of fine leather,[l] and the curtain for the
screen; 35 the ark of the covenant[m] with
its poles and the mercy-seat;[n] 36 the table
with all its utensils, and the bread of the
Presence; 37 the pure lampstand with its
lamps set on it and all its utensils, and
the oil for the light; 38 the golden altar,
the anointing-oil and the fragrant incense, and the screen for the entrance
of the tent; 39 the bronze altar, and its
grating of bronze, its poles, and all its
utensils; the basin with its stand; 40 the
hangings of the court, its pillars, and its
bases, and the screen for the gate of the
court, its cords, and its pegs; and all the
utensils for the service of the tabernacle, for the tent of meeting; 41 the finely
worked vestments for ministering in
the holy place, the sacred vestments for
the priest Aaron, and the vestments of
his sons to serve as priests. 42 The Israelites had done all of the work just as the
LORD had commanded Moses. 43 When
Moses saw that they had done all the
work just as the LORD had commanded,
he blessed them.

THE TABERNACLE ERECTED AND ITS EQUIPMENT INSTALLED

40 The LORD spoke to Moses: 2 On
the first day of the first month
you shall set up the tabernacle of the
tent of meeting. 3 You shall put in it
the ark of the covenant,[o] and you shall
screen the ark with the curtain. 4 You
shall bring in the table, and arrange its
setting; and you shall bring in the lampstand, and set up its lamps. 5 You shall
put the golden altar for incense before
the ark of the covenant,[p] and set up the
screen for the entrance of the tabernacle.
6 You shall set the altar of burnt-offering
before the entrance of the tabernacle of
the tent of meeting, 7 and place the basin between the tent of meeting and the
altar, and put water in it. 8 You shall set
up the court all around, and hang up the
screen for the gate of the court. 9 Then
you shall take the anointing-oil, and
anoint the tabernacle and all that is in
it, and consecrate it and all its furniture,
so that it shall become holy. 10 You shall
also anoint the altar of burnt-offering
and all its utensils, and consecrate the
altar, so that the altar shall be most holy.
11 You shall also anoint the basin with its
stand, and consecrate it. 12 Then you shall
bring Aaron and his sons to the entrance
of the tent of meeting, and shall wash
them with water, 13 and put on Aaron the
sacred vestments, and you shall anoint
him and consecrate him, so that he may
serve me as priest. 14 You shall bring his
sons also and put tunics on them, 15 and
anoint them, as you anointed their father, that they may serve me as priests:
and their anointing shall admit them to
a perpetual priesthood throughout all
generations to come.

16 Moses did everything just as the
LORD had commanded him. 17 In the
first month in the second year, on the
first day of the month, the tabernacle
was set up. 18 Moses set up the tabernacle; he laid its bases, and set up its
frames, and put in its poles, and raised
up its pillars; 19 and he spread the tent
over the tabernacle, and put the covering of the tent over it; as the LORD had
commanded Moses. 20 He took the covenant[q] and put it into the ark, and put
the poles on the ark, and set the mercy-
seat[r] above the ark; 21 and he brought the
ark into the tabernacle, and set up the
curtain for screening, and screened the
ark of the covenant;[s] as the LORD had
commanded Moses. 22 He put the table
in the tent of meeting, on the north side
of the tabernacle, outside the curtain,
23 and set the bread in order on it before
the LORD; as the LORD had commanded
Moses. 24 He put the lampstand in the
tent of meeting, opposite the table on
the south side of the tabernacle, 25 and
set up the lamps before the LORD; as the
LORD had commanded Moses. 26 He put
the golden altar in the tent of meeting
before the curtain, 27 and offered fragrant incense on it; as the LORD had
commanded Moses. 28 He also put in
place the screen for the entrance of the
tabernacle. 29 He set the altar of burnt-
offering at the entrance of the tabernacle of the tent of meeting, and offered
on it the burnt-offering and the grain-
offering as the LORD had commanded
Moses. 30 He set the basin between the
tent of meeting and the altar, and put

[l] **39.34** Meaning of Heb uncertain [m] **39.35** Or *treaty, or testimony*; Heb *eduth* [n] **39.35** Or *the cover* [o] **40.3** Or *treaty, or testimony*; Heb *eduth* [p] **40.5** Or *treaty, or testimony*; Heb *eduth* [q] **40.20** Or *treaty, or testimony*; Heb *eduth* [r] **40.20** Or *the cover* [s] **40.21** Or *treaty, or testimony*; Heb *eduth*

water in it for washing, [31]with which
Moses and Aaron and his sons washed
their hands and their feet. [32]When they
went into the tent of meeting, and
when they approached the altar, they
washed; as the LORD had commanded
Moses. [33]He set up the court around the
tabernacle and the altar, and put up the
screen at the gate of the court. So Moses
finished the work.

THE CLOUD AND THE GLORY

34 Then the cloud covered the tent
of meeting, and the glory of the LORD
filled the tabernacle. [35]Moses was not
able to enter the tent of meeting because the cloud settled upon it, and
the glory of the LORD filled the tabernacle. [36]Whenever the cloud was taken
up from the tabernacle, the Israelites
would set out on each stage of their
journey; [37]but if the cloud was not taken
up, then they did not set out until the
day that it was taken up. [38]For the cloud
of the LORD was on the tabernacle by
day, and fire was in the cloud[t] by night,
before the eyes of all the house of Israel
at each stage of their journey.

[t] **40.38** Heb *it*

LEVITICUS

Sacrificial and ritual laws attributed to the tribe of Levi descending from the high priest, Aaron, are contained in the book of Leviticus. Leviticus is made up of legislation that teaches the Israelites how to maintain purity and sanctity appropriate for the people of God. The key theme of Leviticus is expressed by the repeated admonition: "You shall be holy, for I am holy" (see 11.44–45; 19.2; 20.26).

Leviticus is difficult for many readers because of the lack of narrative and many unfamiliar laws and rituals. However, chapter 19 deals with issues of holiness, including the famous injunction: "You shall love your neighbour as yourself" (19.18). Also in Leviticus are laws about the use of land, treatment of the poor, and periodic cancellation of debt, which have provoked ideas for environmental and economic policies in contemporary times.

Selected passages are read from the book of Leviticus at the Sunday liturgy in Year B of the Sixth Sunday of Ordinary Time (13.1–2, 44–46) and in Year A of the Seventh Sunday of Ordinary Time (19.1–2, 17–18). The famous passage from Leviticus 19 is also read on the Monday of the First Week of Lent in both Year I and II of the liturgical calendar.

THE BURNT-OFFERING

1 The LORD summoned Moses and
spoke to him from the tent of meeting, saying: 2Speak to the people of Israel and say to them: When any of you
bring an offering of livestock to the
LORD, you shall bring your offering
from the herd or from the flock.

3 If the offering is a burnt-offering
from the herd, you shall offer a male
without blemish; you shall bring it to
the entrance of the tent of meeting, for
acceptance in your behalf before the
LORD. 4You shall lay your hand on the
head of the burnt-offering, and it shall
be acceptable in your behalf as atonement for you. 5The bull shall be slaughtered before the LORD; and Aaron's sons
the priests shall offer the blood, dashing the blood against all sides of the
altar that is at the entrance of the tent
of meeting. 6The burnt-offering shall
be flayed and cut up into its parts. 7The
sons of the priest Aaron shall put fire on
the altar and arrange wood on the fire.
8Aaron's sons the priests shall arrange
the parts, with the head and the suet,
on the wood that is on the fire on the
altar; 9but its entrails and its legs shall
be washed with water. Then the priest
shall turn the whole into smoke on the
altar as a burnt-offering, an offering by
fire of pleasing odour to the LORD.

10 If your gift for a burnt-offering is
from the flock, from the sheep or goats,
your offering shall be a male without
blemish. 11It shall be slaughtered on the
north side of the altar before the LORD,
and Aaron's sons the priests shall dash
its blood against all sides of the altar.
12It shall be cut up into its parts, with
its head and its suet, and the priest shall
arrange them on the wood that is on
the fire on the altar; 13but the entrails
and the legs shall be washed with water. Then the priest shall offer the whole
and turn it into smoke on the altar; it
is a burnt-offering, an offering by fire of
pleasing odour to the LORD.

14 If your offering to the LORD is
a burnt-offering of birds, you shall
choose your offering from turtle-doves

or pigeons. 15The priest shall bring it to the altar and wring off its head, and turn it into smoke on the altar; and its blood shall be drained out against the side of the altar. 16He shall remove its crop with its contents[a] and throw it at the east side of the altar, in the place for ashes. 17He shall tear it open by its wings without severing it. Then the priest shall turn it into smoke on the altar, on the wood that is on the fire; it is a burnt-offering, an offering by fire of pleasing odour to the LORD.

GRAIN-OFFERINGS

2 When anyone presents a grain-offering to the LORD, the offering shall be of choice flour; the worshipper shall pour oil on it, and put frankincense on it, 2and bring it to Aaron's sons the priests. After taking from it a handful of the choice flour and oil, with all its frankincense, the priest shall turn this token portion into smoke on the altar, an offering by fire of pleasing odour to the LORD. 3And what is left of the grain-offering shall be for Aaron and his sons, a most holy part of the offerings by fire to the LORD.

4 When you present a grain-offering baked in the oven, it shall be of choice flour: unleavened cakes mixed with oil, or unleavened wafers spread with oil. 5If your offering is grain prepared on a griddle, it shall be of choice flour mixed with oil, unleavened; 6break it in pieces, and pour oil on it; it is a grain-offering. 7If your offering is grain prepared in a pan, it shall be made of choice flour in oil. 8You shall bring to the LORD the grain-offering that is prepared in any of these ways; and when it is presented to the priest, he shall take it to the altar. 9The priest shall remove from the grain-offering its token portion and turn this into smoke on the altar, an offering by fire of pleasing odour to the LORD. 10And what is left of the grain-offering shall be for Aaron and his sons; it is a most holy part of the offerings by fire to the LORD.

11 No grain-offering that you bring to the LORD shall be made with leaven, for you must not turn any leaven or honey into smoke as an offering by fire to the LORD. 12You may bring them to the LORD as an offering of choice products, but they shall not be offered on the altar for a pleasing odour. 13You shall not omit from your grain-offerings the salt of the covenant with your God; with all your offerings you shall offer salt.

14 If you bring a grain-offering of first fruits to the LORD, you shall bring as the grain-offering of your first fruits coarse new grain from fresh ears, parched with fire. 15You shall add oil to it and lay frankincense on it; it is a grain-offering. 16And the priest shall turn a token portion of it into smoke—some of the coarse grain and oil with all its frankincense; it is an offering by fire to the LORD.

OFFERINGS OF WELL-BEING

3 If the offering is a sacrifice of well-being, if you offer an animal of the herd, whether male or female, you shall offer one without blemish before the LORD. 2You shall lay your hand on the head of the offering and slaughter it at the entrance of the tent of meeting; and Aaron's sons the priests shall dash the blood against all sides of the altar. 3You shall offer from the sacrifice of well-being, as an offering by fire to the LORD, the fat that covers the entrails and all the fat that is around the entrails; 4the two kidneys with the fat that is on them at the loins, and the appendage of the liver, which he shall remove with the kidneys. 5Then Aaron's sons shall turn these into smoke on the altar, with the burnt-offering that is on the wood on the fire, as an offering by fire of pleasing odour to the LORD.

6 If your offering for a sacrifice of well-being to the LORD is from the flock, male or female, you shall offer one without blemish. 7If you present a sheep as your offering, you shall bring it before the LORD 8and lay your hand on the head of the offering. It shall be slaughtered before the tent of meeting, and Aaron's sons shall dash its blood against all sides of the altar. 9You shall present its fat from the sacrifice of well-being, as an offering by fire to the LORD: the whole broad tail, which shall be removed close to the backbone, the fat that covers the entrails, and all the fat that is around the entrails; 10the two kidneys with the fat that is on them at the loins, and the appendage of the liver, which you shall remove with the kidneys. 11Then the priest shall turn these into smoke on the altar as a food-offering by fire to the LORD.

12 If your offering is a goat, you shall bring it before the LORD 13and lay your hand on its head; it shall be slaughtered

[a] 1.16 Meaning of Heb uncertain

before the tent of meeting; and the sons
of Aaron shall dash its blood against all
sides of the altar. 14You shall present as
your offering from it, as an offering by
fire to the LORD, the fat that covers the
entrails, and all the fat that is around
the entrails; 15the two kidneys with the
fat that is on them at the loins, and the
appendage of the liver, which you shall
remove with the kidneys. 16Then the
priest shall turn these into smoke on
the altar as a food-offering by fire for a
pleasing odour.
All fat is the LORD's. 17It shall be a
perpetual statute throughout your generations, in all your settlements: you
must not eat any fat or any blood.

SIN-OFFERINGS

4 The LORD spoke to Moses, saying,
2Speak to the people of Israel, saying: When anyone sins unintentionally
in any of the LORD's commandments
about things not to be done, and does
any one of them:
3 If it is the anointed priest who sins,
thus bringing guilt on the people, he
shall offer for the sin that he has committed a bull of the herd without blemish as a sin-offering to the LORD. 4He
shall bring the bull to the entrance of
the tent of meeting before the LORD
and lay his hand on the head of the bull;
the bull shall be slaughtered before the
LORD. 5The anointed priest shall take
some of the blood of the bull and bring
it into the tent of meeting. 6The priest
shall dip his finger in the blood and
sprinkle some of the blood seven times
before the LORD in front of the curtain
of the sanctuary. 7The priest shall put
some of the blood on the horns of the altar of fragrant incense that is in the tent
of meeting before the LORD; and the rest
of the blood of the bull he shall pour out
at the base of the altar of burnt-offering,
which is at the entrance of the tent of
meeting. 8He shall remove all the fat
from the bull of sin-offering: the fat that
covers the entrails and all the fat that is
around the entrails; 9the two kidneys
with the fat that is on them at the loins;
and the appendage of the liver, which
he shall remove with the kidneys, 10just
as these are removed from the ox of the
sacrifice of well-being. The priest shall
turn them into smoke upon the altar of
burnt-offering. 11But the skin of the bull
and all its flesh, as well as its head, its
legs, its entrails, and its dung— 12all the
rest of the bull—he shall carry out to a
clean place outside the camp, to the ash
heap, and shall burn it on a wood fire; at
the ash heap it shall be burned.
13 If the whole congregation of Israel errs unintentionally and the matter
escapes the notice of the assembly, and
they do any one of the things that by
the LORD's commandments ought not
to be done, and incur guilt; 14when the
sin that they have committed becomes
known, the assembly shall offer a bull of
the herd for a sin-offering and bring it
before the tent of meeting. 15The elders
of the congregation shall lay their hands
on the head of the bull before the LORD,
and the bull shall be slaughtered before
the LORD. 16The anointed priest shall
bring some of the blood of the bull into
the tent of meeting, 17and the priest
shall dip his finger in the blood and
sprinkle it seven times before the LORD,
in front of the curtain. 18He shall put
some of the blood on the horns of the
altar that is before the LORD in the tent
of meeting; and the rest of the blood he
shall pour out at the base of the altar of
burnt-offering that is at the entrance of
the tent of meeting. 19He shall remove
all its fat and turn it into smoke on the
altar. 20He shall do with the bull just as
is done with the bull of sin-offering; he
shall do the same with this. The priest
shall make atonement for them, and
they shall be forgiven. 21He shall carry
the bull outside the camp, and burn it
as he burned the first bull; it is the sin-
offering for the assembly.
22 When a ruler sins, doing unintentionally any one of all the things that by
commandments of the LORD his God
ought not to be done, and incurs guilt,
23once the sin that he has committed is
made known to him, he shall bring as
his offering a male goat without blemish. 24He shall lay his hand on the head
of the goat; it shall be slaughtered at
the spot where the burnt-offering is
slaughtered before the LORD; it is a sin-
offering. 25The priest shall take some of
the blood of the sin-offering with his
finger and put it on the horns of the altar of burnt-offering, and pour out the
rest of its blood at the base of the altar
of burnt-offering. 26All its fat he shall
turn into smoke on the altar, like the fat
of the sacrifice of well-being. Thus the
priest shall make atonement on his behalf for his sin, and he shall be forgiven.
27 If anyone of the ordinary people
among you sins unintentionally in doing any one of the things that by the

LORD's commandments ought not to be done, and incurs guilt, 28 when the sin that you have committed is made known to you, you shall bring a female goat without blemish as your offering, for the sin that you have committed. 29 You shall lay your hand on the head of the sin-offering; and the sin-offering shall be slaughtered at the place of the burnt-offering. 30 The priest shall take some of its blood with his finger and put it on the horns of the altar of burnt-offering, and he shall pour out the rest of its blood at the base of the altar. 31 He shall remove all its fat, as the fat is removed from the offering of well-being, and the priest shall turn it into smoke on the altar for a pleasing odour to the LORD. Thus the priest shall make atonement on your behalf, and you shall be forgiven.

32 If the offering you bring as a sin-offering is a sheep, you shall bring a female without blemish. 33 You shall lay your hand on the head of the sin-offering; and it shall be slaughtered as a sin-offering at the spot where the burnt-offering is slaughtered. 34 The priest shall take some of the blood of the sin-offering with his finger and put it on the horns of the altar of burnt-offering, and pour out the rest of its blood at the base of the altar. 35 You shall remove all its fat, as the fat of the sheep is removed from the sacrifice of well-being, and the priest shall turn it into smoke on the altar, with the offerings by fire to the LORD. Thus the priest shall make atonement on your behalf for the sin that you have committed, and you shall be forgiven.

5 When any of you sin in that you have heard a public adjuration to testify and—though able to testify as one who has seen or learned of the matter—do not speak up, you are subject to punishment. 2 Or when any of you touch any unclean thing—whether the carcass of an unclean beast or the carcass of unclean livestock or the carcass of an unclean swarming thing—and are unaware of it, you have become unclean, and are guilty. 3 Or when you touch human uncleanness—any uncleanness by which one can become unclean—and are unaware of it, when you come to know it, you shall be guilty. 4 Or when any of you utter aloud a rash oath for a bad or a good purpose, whatever people utter in an oath, and are unaware of it, when you come to know it, you shall in any of these be guilty. 5 When you realize your guilt in any of these, you shall confess the sin that you have committed. 6 And you shall bring to the LORD, as your penalty for the sin that you have committed, a female from the flock, a sheep or a goat, as a sin-offering; and the priest shall make atonement on your behalf for your sin.

7 But if you cannot afford a sheep, you shall bring to the LORD, as your penalty for the sin that you have committed, two turtle-doves or two pigeons, one for a sin-offering and the other for a burnt-offering. 8 You shall bring them to the priest, who shall offer first the one for the sin-offering, wringing its head at the nape without severing it. 9 He shall sprinkle some of the blood of the sin-offering on the side of the altar, while the rest of the blood shall be drained out at the base of the altar; it is a sin-offering. 10 And the second he shall offer for a burnt-offering according to the regulation. Thus the priest shall make atonement on your behalf for the sin that you have committed, and you shall be forgiven.

11 But if you cannot afford two turtle-doves or two pigeons, you shall bring as your offering for the sin that you have committed one-tenth of an ephah of choice flour for a sin-offering; you shall not put oil on it or lay frankincense on it, for it is a sin-offering. 12 You shall bring it to the priest, and the priest shall scoop up a handful of it as its memorial portion, and turn this into smoke on the altar, with the offerings by fire to the LORD; it is a sin-offering. 13 Thus the priest shall make atonement on your behalf for whichever of these sins you have committed, and you shall be forgiven. Like the grain-offering, the rest shall be for the priest.

OFFERINGS WITH RESTITUTION

14 The LORD spoke to Moses, saying: 15 When any of you commit a trespass and sin unintentionally in any of the holy things of the LORD, you shall bring, as your guilt-offering to the LORD, a ram without blemish from the flock, convertible into silver by the sanctuary shekel; it is a guilt-offering. 16 And you shall make restitution for the holy thing in which you were remiss, and shall add one-fifth to it and give it to the priest. The priest shall make atonement on your behalf with the ram of the guilt-offering, and you shall be forgiven.

17 If any of you sin without knowing it, doing any of the things that by the LORD's commandments ought not to be done, you have incurred guilt, and are subject to punishment. 18 You shall bring to the priest a ram without blemish from the flock, or the equivalent, as a guilt-offering; and the priest shall make atonement on your behalf for the error that you committed unintentionally, and you shall be forgiven. 19 It is a guilt-offering; you have incurred guilt before the LORD.

6[b] The LORD spoke to Moses, saying: 2 When any of you sin and commit a trespass against the LORD by deceiving a neighbour in a matter of a deposit or a pledge, or by robbery, or if you have defrauded a neighbour, 3 or have found something lost and lied about it—if you swear falsely regarding any of the various things that one may do and sin thereby— 4 when you have sinned and realize your guilt, and would restore what you took by robbery or by fraud or the deposit that was committed to you, or the lost thing that you found, 5 or anything else about which you have sworn falsely, you shall repay the principal amount and shall add one-fifth to it. You shall pay it to its owner when you realize your guilt. 6 And you shall bring to the priest, as your guilt-offering to the LORD, a ram without blemish from the flock, or its equivalent, for a guilt-offering. 7 The priest shall make atonement on your behalf before the LORD, and you shall be forgiven for any of the things that one may do and incur guilt thereby.

INSTRUCTIONS CONCERNING SACRIFICES

8 [c]The LORD spoke to Moses, saying: 9 Command Aaron and his sons, saying: This is the ritual of the burnt-offering. The burnt-offering itself shall remain on the hearth upon the altar all night until the morning, while the fire on the altar shall be kept burning. 10 The priest shall put on his linen vestments after putting on his linen undergarments next to his body; and he shall take up the ashes to which the fire has reduced the burnt-offering on the altar, and place them beside the altar. 11 Then he shall take off his vestments and put on other garments, and carry the ashes out to a clean place outside the camp. 12 The fire on the altar shall be kept burning; it shall not go out. Every morning the priest shall add wood to it, lay out the burnt-offering on it, and turn into smoke the fat pieces of the offerings of well-being. 13 A perpetual fire shall be kept burning on the altar; it shall not go out.

14 This is the ritual of the grain-offering: The sons of Aaron shall offer it before the LORD, in front of the altar. 15 They shall take from it a handful of the choice flour and oil of the grain-offering, with all the frankincense that is on the offering, and they shall turn its memorial portion into smoke on the altar as a pleasing odour to the LORD. 16 Aaron and his sons shall eat what is left of it; it shall be eaten as unleavened cakes in a holy place; in the court of the tent of meeting they shall eat it. 17 It shall not be baked with leaven. I have given it as their portion of my offerings by fire; it is most holy, like the sin-offering and the guilt-offering. 18 Every male among the descendants of Aaron shall eat of it, as their perpetual due throughout your generations, from the LORD's offerings by fire; anything that touches them shall become holy.

19 The LORD spoke to Moses, saying: 20 This is the offering that Aaron and his sons shall offer to the LORD on the day when he is anointed: one-tenth of an ephah of choice flour as a regular offering, half of it in the morning and half in the evening. 21 It shall be made with oil on a griddle; you shall bring it well soaked, as a grain-offering of baked[d] pieces, and you shall present it as a pleasing odour to the LORD. 22 And so the priest, anointed from among Aaron's descendants as a successor, shall prepare it; it is the LORD's—a perpetual due—to be turned entirely into smoke. 23 Every grain-offering of a priest shall be wholly burned; it shall not be eaten.

24 The LORD spoke to Moses, saying: 25 Speak to Aaron and his sons, saying: This is the ritual of the sin-offering. The sin-offering shall be slaughtered before the LORD at the spot where the burnt-offering is slaughtered; it is most holy. 26 The priest who offers it as a sin-offering shall eat of it; it shall be eaten in a holy place, in the court of the tent of meeting. 27 Whatever touches its flesh shall become holy; and when any of its blood is spattered on a garment, you shall wash the bespattered part in a holy place. 28 An earthen vessel in which

[b] **6.1** Ch 5.20 in Heb [c] **6.8** Ch 6.1 in Heb
[d] **6.21** Meaning of Heb uncertain

it was boiled shall be broken; but if it is
boiled in a bronze vessel, that shall be
scoured and rinsed in water. 29 Every
male among the priests shall eat of it;
it is most holy. 30 But no sin-offering
shall be eaten from which any blood
is brought into the tent of meeting for
atonement in the holy place; it shall be
burned with fire.

7 This is the ritual of the guilt-
offering. It is most holy; 2 at the spot
where the burnt-offering is slaughtered,
they shall slaughter the guilt-offering,
and its blood shall be dashed against all
sides of the altar. 3 All its fat shall be offered: the broad tail, the fat that covers
the entrails, 4 the two kidneys with the
fat that is on them at the loins, and the
appendage of the liver, which shall be
removed with the kidneys. 5 The priest
shall turn them into smoke on the altar
as an offering by fire to the LORD; it is
a guilt-offering. 6 Every male among the
priests shall eat of it; it shall be eaten in
a holy place; it is most holy.

7 The guilt-offering is like the sin-
offering, there is the same ritual for
them; the priest who makes atonement
with it shall have it. 8 So, too, the priest
who offers anyone's burnt-offering
shall keep the skin of the burnt-offering
that he has offered. 9 And every grain-
offering baked in the oven, and all that
is prepared in a pan or on a griddle, shall
belong to the priest who offers it. 10 But
every other grain-offering, mixed with
oil or dry, shall belong to all the sons of
Aaron equally.

FURTHER INSTRUCTIONS

11 This is the ritual of the sacrifice of
the offering of well-being that one may
offer to the LORD. 12 If you offer it for
thanksgiving, you shall offer with the
thank-offering unleavened cakes mixed
with oil, unleavened wafers spread with
oil, and cakes of choice flour well soaked
in oil. 13 With your thanksgiving sacrifice of well-being you shall bring your
offering with cakes of leavened bread.
14 From this you shall offer one cake
from each offering, as a gift to the LORD;
it shall belong to the priest who dashes
the blood of the offering of well-being.
15 And the flesh of your thanksgiving
sacrifice of well-being shall be eaten on
the day it is offered; you shall not leave
any of it until morning. 16 But if the sacrifice you offer is a votive offering or a
freewill-offering, it shall be eaten on the
day that you offer your sacrifice, and
what is left of it shall be eaten the next
day; 17 but what is left of the flesh of the
sacrifice shall be burned on the third
day. 18 If any of the flesh of your sacrifice
of well-being is eaten on the third day,
it shall not be acceptable, nor shall it be
credited to the one who offers it; it shall
be an abomination, and the one who
eats of it shall incur guilt.

19 Flesh that touches any unclean
thing shall not be eaten; it shall be
burned. As for other flesh, all who are
clean may eat such flesh. 20 But those
who eat flesh from the LORD's sacrifice of well-being while in a state of
uncleanness shall be cut off from their
kin. 21 When any one of you touches any
unclean thing—human uncleanness
or an unclean animal or any unclean
creature—and then eats flesh from the
LORD's sacrifice of well-being, you shall
be cut off from your kin.

22 The LORD spoke to Moses, saying:
23 Speak to the people of Israel, saying:
You shall eat no fat of ox or sheep or
goat. 24 The fat of an animal that died or
was torn by wild animals may be put to
any use, except that you must not eat
it. 25 If any one of you eats the fat from
an animal of which an offering by fire
may be made to the LORD, you who eat
it shall be cut off from your kin. 26 You
must not eat any blood whatever, either
of bird or of animal, in any of your settlements. 27 Any one of you who eats any
blood shall be cut off from your kin.

28 The LORD spoke to Moses, saying:
29 Speak to the people of Israel, saying:
Any one of you who would offer to the
LORD your sacrifice of well-being must
yourself bring to the LORD your offering
from your sacrifice of well-being. 30 Your
own hands shall bring the LORD's offering by fire; you shall bring the fat with
the breast, so that the breast may be
raised as an elevation-offering before
the LORD. 31 The priest shall turn the fat
into smoke on the altar, but the breast
shall belong to Aaron and his sons.
32 And the right thigh from your sacrifices of well-being you shall give to the
priest as an offering; 33 the one among
the sons of Aaron who offers the blood
and fat of the offering of well-being
shall have the right thigh for a portion. 34 For I have taken the breast of the
elevation-offering, and the thigh that is
offered, from the people of Israel, from
their sacrifices of well-being, and have
given them to Aaron the priest and to
his sons, as a perpetual due from the

people of Israel. 35 This is the portion allotted to Aaron and to his sons from the offerings made by fire to the LORD, once they have been brought forward to serve the LORD as priests; 36 these the LORD commanded to be given them, when he anointed them, as a perpetual due from the people of Israel throughout their generations.

37 This is the ritual of the burnt-offering, the grain-offering, the sin-offering, the guilt-offering, the offering of ordination, and the sacrifice of well-being, 38 which the LORD commanded Moses on Mount Sinai, when he commanded the people of Israel to bring their offerings to the LORD, in the wilderness of Sinai.

THE RITES OF ORDINATION

8 The LORD spoke to Moses, saying: 2 Take Aaron and his sons with him, the vestments, the anointing-oil, the bull of sin-offering, the two rams, and the basket of unleavened bread; 3 and assemble the whole congregation at the entrance of the tent of meeting. 4 And Moses did as the LORD commanded him. When the congregation was assembled at the entrance of the tent of meeting, 5 Moses said to the congregation, 'This is what the LORD has commanded to be done.'

6 Then Moses brought Aaron and his sons forward, and washed them with water. 7 He put the tunic on him, fastened the sash around him, clothed him with the robe, and put the ephod on him. He then put the decorated band of the ephod around him, tying the ephod to him with it. 8 He placed the breast-piece on him, and in the breastpiece he put the Urim and the Thummim. 9 And he set the turban on his head, and on the turban, in front, he set the golden ornament, the holy crown, as the LORD commanded Moses.

10 Then Moses took the anointing-oil and anointed the tabernacle and all that was in it, and consecrated them. 11 He sprinkled some of it on the altar seven times, and anointed the altar and all its utensils, and the basin and its base, to consecrate them. 12 He poured some of the anointing-oil on Aaron's head and anointed him, to consecrate him. 13 And Moses brought forward Aaron's sons, and clothed them with tunics, and fastened sashes around them, and tied head-dresses on them, as the LORD commanded Moses.

14 He led forward the bull of sin-offering; and Aaron and his sons laid their hands upon the head of the bull of sin-offering, 15 and it was slaughtered. Moses took the blood and with his finger put some on each of the horns of the altar, purifying the altar; then he poured out the blood at the base of the altar. Thus he consecrated it, to make atonement for it. 16 Moses took all the fat that was around the entrails, and the appendage of the liver, and the two kidneys with their fat, and turned them into smoke on the altar. 17 But the bull itself, its skin and flesh and its dung, he burned with fire outside the camp, as the LORD commanded Moses.

18 Then he brought forward the ram of burnt-offering. Aaron and his sons laid their hands on the head of the ram, 19 and it was slaughtered. Moses dashed the blood against all sides of the altar. 20 The ram was cut into its parts, and Moses turned into smoke the head and the parts and the suet. 21 And after the entrails and the legs were washed with water, Moses turned into smoke the whole ram on the altar; it was a burnt-offering for a pleasing odour, an offering by fire to the LORD, as the LORD commanded Moses.

22 Then he brought forward the second ram, the ram of ordination. Aaron and his sons laid their hands on the head of the ram, 23 and it was slaughtered. Moses took some of its blood and put it on the lobe of Aaron's right ear and on the thumb of his right hand and on the big toe of his right foot. 24 After Aaron's sons were brought forward, Moses put some of the blood on the lobes of their right ears and on the thumbs of their right hands and on the big toes of their right feet; and Moses dashed the rest of the blood against all sides of the altar. 25 He took the fat—the broad tail, all the fat that was around the entrails, the appendage of the liver, and the two kidneys with their fat—and the right thigh. 26 From the basket of unleavened bread that was before the LORD, he took one cake of unleavened bread, one cake of bread with oil, and one wafer, and placed them on the fat and on the right thigh. 27 He placed all these on the palms of Aaron and on the palms of his sons, and raised them as an elevation-offering before the LORD. 28 Then Moses took them from their hands and turned them into smoke on the altar with the burnt-offering. This was an ordination-offering for a pleasing odour, an offering by fire to the LORD. [29]Moses took the breast and raised it as an elevation-offering before the LORD; it was Moses' portion of the ram of ordination, as the LORD commanded Moses.

30 Then Moses took some of the anointing-oil and some of the blood that was on the altar and sprinkled them on Aaron and his vestments, and also on his sons and their vestments. Thus he consecrated Aaron and his vestments, and also his sons and their vestments.

31 And Moses said to Aaron and his sons, 'Boil the flesh at the entrance of the tent of meeting, and eat it there with the bread that is in the basket of ordination-offerings, as I was commanded, "Aaron and his sons shall eat it"; [32]and what remains of the flesh and the bread you shall burn with fire. [33]You shall not go outside the entrance of the tent of meeting for seven days, until the day when your period of ordination is completed. For it will take seven days to ordain you; [34]as has been done today, the LORD has commanded to be done to make atonement for you. [35]You shall remain at the entrance of the tent of meeting day and night for seven days, keeping the LORD's charge so that you do not die; for so I am commanded.' [36]Aaron and his sons did all the things that the LORD commanded through Moses.

AARON'S PRIESTHOOD INAUGURATED

9 On the eighth day Moses summoned Aaron and his sons and the elders of Israel. [2]He said to Aaron, 'Take a bull calf for a sin-offering and a ram for a burnt-offering, without blemish, and offer them before the LORD. [3]And say to the people of Israel, "Take a male goat for a sin-offering; a calf and a lamb, yearlings without blemish, for a burnt-offering; [4]and an ox and a ram for an offering of well-being to sacrifice before the LORD; and a grain-offering mixed with oil. For today the LORD will appear to you." ' [5]They brought what Moses commanded to the front of the tent of meeting; and the whole congregation drew near and stood before the LORD. [6]And Moses said, 'This is the thing that the LORD commanded you to do, so that the glory of the LORD may appear to you.' [7]Then Moses said to Aaron, 'Draw near to the altar and sacrifice your sin-offering and your burnt-offering, and make atonement for yourself and for the people; and sacrifice the offering of the people, and make atonement for them; as the LORD has commanded.'

8 Aaron drew near to the altar, and slaughtered the calf of the sin-offering, which was for himself. [9]The sons of Aaron presented the blood to him, and he dipped his finger in the blood and put it on the horns of the altar; and the rest of the blood he poured out at the base of the altar. [10]But the fat, the kidneys, and the appendage of the liver from the sin-offering he turned into smoke on the altar, as the LORD commanded Moses; [11]and the flesh and the skin he burned with fire outside the camp.

12 Then he slaughtered the burnt-offering. Aaron's sons brought him the blood, and he dashed it against all sides of the altar. [13]And they brought him the burnt-offering piece by piece, and the head, which he turned into smoke on the altar. [14]He washed the entrails and the legs and, with the burnt-offering, turned them into smoke on the altar.

15 Next he presented the people's offering. He took the goat of the sin-offering that was for the people, and slaughtered it, and presented it as a sin-offering like the first one. [16]He presented the burnt-offering, and sacrificed it according to regulation. [17]He presented the grain-offering, and, taking a handful of it, he turned it into smoke on the altar, in addition to the burnt-offering of the morning.

18 He slaughtered the ox and the ram as a sacrifice of well-being for the people. Aaron's sons brought him the blood, which he dashed against all sides of the altar, [19]and the fat of the ox and of the ram—the broad tail, the fat that covers the entrails, the two kidneys and the fat on them,[e] and the appendage of the liver. [20]They first laid the fat on the breasts, and the fat was turned into smoke on the altar; [21]and the breasts and the right thigh Aaron raised as an elevation-offering before the LORD, as Moses had commanded.

22 Aaron lifted his hands towards the people and blessed them; and he came down after sacrificing the sin-offering, the burnt-offering, and the offering of well-being. [23]Moses and Aaron entered the tent of meeting, and then came out and blessed the people; and the glory

[e] 9.19 Gk: Heb *the broad tail, and that which covers, and the kidneys*

of the LORD appeared to all the people. 24 Fire came out from the LORD and consumed the burnt-offering and the fat on the altar; and when all the people saw it, they shouted and fell on their faces.

NADAB AND ABIHU

10 Now Aaron's sons, Nadab and Abihu, each took his censer, put fire in it, and laid incense on it; and they offered unholy fire before the LORD, such as he had not commanded them. 2 And fire came out from the presence of the LORD and consumed them, and they died before the LORD. 3 Then Moses said to Aaron, 'This is what the LORD meant when he said,

"Through those who are near me
  I will show myself holy,
and before all the people
  I will be glorified." '

And Aaron was silent.

4 Moses summoned Mishael and Elzaphan, sons of Uzziel the uncle of Aaron, and said to them, 'Come forward, and carry your kinsmen away from the front of the sanctuary to a place outside the camp.' 5 They came forward and carried them by their tunics out of the camp, as Moses had ordered. 6 And Moses said to Aaron and to his sons Eleazar and Ithamar, 'Do not dishevel your hair, and do not tear your vestments, or you will die and wrath will strike all the congregation; but your kindred, the whole house of Israel, may mourn the burning that the LORD has sent. 7 You shall not go outside the entrance of the tent of meeting, or you will die; for the anointing-oil of the LORD is on you.' And they did as Moses had ordered.

8 And the LORD spoke to Aaron: 9 Drink no wine or strong drink, neither you nor your sons, when you enter the tent of meeting, that you may not die; it is a statute for ever throughout your generations. 10 You are to distinguish between the holy and the common, and between the unclean and the clean; 11 and you are to teach the people of Israel all the statutes that the LORD has spoken to them through Moses.

12 Moses spoke to Aaron and to his remaining sons, Eleazar and Ithamar: Take the grain-offering that is left from the LORD's offerings by fire, and eat it unleavened beside the altar, for it is most holy; 13 you shall eat it in a holy place, because it is your due and your sons' due, from the offerings by fire to the LORD; for so I am commanded. 14 But the breast that is elevated and the thigh that is raised, you and your sons and daughters as well may eat in any clean place; for they have been assigned to you and your children from the sacrifices of the offerings of well-being of the people of Israel. 15 The thigh that is raised and the breast that is elevated they shall bring, together with the offerings by fire of the fat, to raise for an elevation-offering before the LORD; they are to be your due and that of your children for ever, as the LORD has commanded.

16 Then Moses made inquiry about the goat of the sin-offering, and—it had already been burned! He was angry with Eleazar and Ithamar, Aaron's remaining sons, and said, 17 'Why did you not eat the sin-offering in the sacred area? For it is most holy, and God[f] has given it to you that you may remove the guilt of the congregation, to make atonement on their behalf before the LORD. 18 Its blood was not brought into the inner part of the sanctuary. You should certainly have eaten it in the sanctuary, as I commanded.' 19 And Aaron spoke to Moses, 'See, today they offered their sin-offering and their burnt-offering before the LORD; and yet such things as these have befallen me! If I had eaten the sin-offering today, would it have been agreeable to the LORD?' 20 And when Moses heard that, he agreed.

CLEAN AND UNCLEAN FOODS

11 The LORD spoke to Moses and Aaron, saying to them: 2 Speak to the people of Israel, saying:

From among all the land animals, these are the creatures that you may eat. 3 Any animal that has divided hoofs and is cloven-footed and chews the cud—such you may eat. 4 But among those that chew the cud or have divided hoofs, you shall not eat the following: the camel, for even though it chews the cud, it does not have divided hoofs; it is unclean for you. 5 The rock-badger, for even though it chews the cud, it does not have divided hoofs; it is unclean for you. 6 The hare, for even though it chews the cud, it does not have divided hoofs; it is unclean for you. 7 The pig, for even though it has divided hoofs and is cloven-footed, it does not chew the cud; it is unclean for you. 8 Of their flesh you shall not eat, and their carcasses you shall not touch; they are unclean for you.

[f] 10.17 Heb *he*

9 These you may eat, of all that are
in the waters. Everything in the waters that has fins and scales, whether
in the seas or in the streams—such you
may eat. 10But anything in the seas or
the streams that does not have fins and
scales, of the swarming creatures in the
waters and among all the other living
creatures that are in the waters—they
are detestable to you 11and detestable
they shall remain. Of their flesh you
shall not eat, and their carcasses you
shall regard as detestable. 12Everything
in the waters that does not have fins
and scales is detestable to you.

13 These you shall regard as detestable among the birds. They shall not
be eaten; they are an abomination: the
eagle, the vulture, the osprey, 14the buzzard, the kite of any kind; 15every raven
of any kind; 16the ostrich, the nighthawk, the seagull, the hawk of any kind;
17the little owl, the cormorant, the great
owl, 18the water-hen, the desert-owl,[g]
the carrion vulture, 19the stork, the
heron of any kind, the hoopoe, and the
bat.[h]

20 All winged insects that walk upon
all fours are detestable to you. 21But
among the winged insects that walk on
all fours you may eat those that have
jointed legs above their feet, with which
to leap on the ground. 22Of them you
may eat: the locust according to its kind,
the bald locust according to its kind, the
cricket according to its kind, and the
grasshopper according to its kind. 23But
all other winged insects that have four
feet are detestable to you.

UNCLEAN ANIMALS

24 By these you shall become unclean; whoever touches the carcass of
any of them shall be unclean until the
evening, 25and whoever carries any part
of the carcass of any of them shall wash
his clothes and be unclean until the evening. 26Every animal that has divided
hoofs but is not cloven-footed or does
not chew the cud is unclean for you; everyone who touches one of them shall
be unclean. 27All that walk on their
paws, among the animals that walk on
all fours, are unclean for you; whoever
touches the carcass of any of them shall
be unclean until the evening, 28and the
one who carries the carcass shall wash
his clothes and be unclean until the evening; they are unclean for you.

29 These are unclean for you among
the creatures that swarm upon the
earth: the weasel, the mouse, the great
lizard according to its kind, 30the gecko,
the land-crocodile, the lizard, the sand-
lizard, and the chameleon. 31These are
unclean for you among all that swarm;
whoever touches one of them when
they are dead shall be unclean until the
evening. 32And anything upon which
any of them falls when they are dead
shall be unclean, whether an article of
wood or cloth or skin or sacking, any article that is used for any purpose; it shall
be dipped into water, and it shall be unclean until the evening, and then it shall
be clean. 33And if any of them falls into
any earthen vessel, all that is in it shall
be unclean, and you shall break the vessel. 34Any food that could be eaten shall
be unclean if water from any such vessel
comes upon it; and any liquid that could
be drunk shall be unclean if it was in
any such vessel. 35Everything on which
any part of the carcass falls shall be unclean; whether an oven or stove, it shall
be broken in pieces; they are unclean,
and shall remain unclean for you. 36But
a spring or a cistern holding water shall
be clean, while whatever touches the
carcass in it shall be unclean. 37If any
part of their carcass falls upon any seed
set aside for sowing, it is clean; 38but if
water is put on the seed and any part of
their carcass falls on it, it is unclean for
you.

39 If an animal of which you may
eat dies, anyone who touches its carcass shall be unclean until the evening.
40Those who eat of its carcass shall wash
their clothes and be unclean until the
evening; and those who carry the carcass shall wash their clothes and be unclean until the evening.

41 All creatures that swarm upon
the earth are detestable; they shall not
be eaten. 42Whatever moves on its belly,
and whatever moves on all fours, or
whatever has many feet, all the creatures that swarm upon the earth, you
shall not eat; for they are detestable.
43You shall not make yourselves detestable with any creature that swarms;
you shall not defile yourselves with
them, and so become unclean. 44For I
am the LORD your God; sanctify yourselves therefore, and be holy, for I am
holy. You shall not defile yourselves
with any swarming creature that moves
on the earth. 45For I am the LORD who

g **11.18** Or *pelican* h **11.19** Identification of several of the birds in verses 13–19 is uncertain

brought you up from the land of Egypt, to be your God; you shall be holy, for I am holy.

46 This is the law pertaining to land animal and bird and every living creature that moves through the waters and every creature that swarms upon the earth, 47to make a distinction between the unclean and the clean, and between the living creature that may be eaten and the living creature that may not be eaten.

PURIFICATION OF WOMEN AFTER CHILDBIRTH

12 The LORD spoke to Moses, saying: 2Speak to the people of Israel, saying:

If a woman conceives and bears a male child, she shall be ceremonially unclean for seven days; as at the time of her menstruation, she shall be unclean. 3On the eighth day the flesh of his foreskin shall be circumcised. 4Her time of blood purification shall be thirty-three days; she shall not touch any holy thing, or come into the sanctuary, until the days of her purification are completed. 5If she bears a female child, she shall be unclean for two weeks, as in her menstruation; her time of blood purification shall be sixty-six days.

6 When the days of her purification are completed, whether for a son or for a daughter, she shall bring to the priest at the entrance of the tent of meeting a lamb in its first year for a burnt-offering, and a pigeon or a turtle-dove for a sin-offering. 7He shall offer it before the LORD, and make atonement on her behalf; then she shall be clean from her flow of blood. This is the law for her who bears a child, male or female. 8If she cannot afford a sheep, she shall take two turtle-doves or two pigeons, one for a burnt-offering and the other for a sin-offering; and the priest shall make atonement on her behalf, and she shall be clean.

LEPROSY: VARIETIES AND SYMPTOMS

13 The LORD spoke to Moses and Aaron, saying:

2 When a person has on the skin of his body a swelling or an eruption or a spot, and it turns into a leprous[i] disease on the skin of his body, he shall be brought to Aaron the priest or to one of his sons the priests. 3The priest shall examine the disease on the skin of his body, and if the hair in the diseased area has turned white and the disease appears to be deeper than the skin of his body, it is a leprous[j] disease; after the priest has examined him he shall pronounce him ceremonially unclean. 4But if the spot is white in the skin of his body, and appears no deeper than the skin, and the hair in it has not turned white, the priest shall confine the diseased person for seven days. 5The priest shall examine him on the seventh day, and if he sees that the disease is checked and the disease has not spread in the skin, then the priest shall confine him for seven days more. 6The priest shall examine him again on the seventh day, and if the disease has abated and the disease has not spread in the skin, the priest shall pronounce him clean; it is only an eruption; and he shall wash his clothes, and be clean. 7But if the eruption spreads in the skin after he has shown himself to the priest for his cleansing, he shall appear again before the priest. 8The priest shall make an examination, and if the eruption has spread in the skin, the priest shall pronounce him unclean; it is a leprous[k] disease.

9 When a person contracts a leprous[l] disease, he shall be brought to the priest. 10The priest shall make an examination, and if there is a white swelling in the skin that has turned the hair white, and there is quick raw flesh in the swelling, 11it is a chronic leprous[m] disease in the skin of his body. The priest shall pronounce him unclean; he shall not confine him, for he is unclean. 12But if the disease breaks out in the skin, so that it covers all the skin of the diseased person from head to foot, so far as the priest can see, 13then the priest shall make an examination, and if the disease has covered all his body, he shall pronounce him clean of the disease; since it has all turned white, he is clean. 14But if raw flesh ever appears on him, he shall be unclean; 15the priest shall examine the raw flesh and pronounce him unclean. Raw flesh is unclean, for it is a leprous[n] disease. 16But if the raw flesh again turns white, he shall come to the

[i] 13.2 A term for several skin diseases; precise meaning uncertain [j] 13.3 A term for several skin diseases; precise meaning uncertain [k] 13.8 A term for several skin diseases; precise meaning uncertain [l] 13.9 A term for several skin diseases; precise meaning uncertain [m] 13.11 A term for several skin diseases; precise meaning uncertain [n] 13.15 A term for several skin diseases; precise meaning uncertain

priest; 17 the priest shall examine him,
and if the disease has turned white, the
priest shall pronounce the diseased person clean. He is clean.

18 When there is on the skin of one's
body a boil that has healed, 19 and in the
place of the boil there appears a white
swelling or a reddish-white spot, it shall
be shown to the priest. 20 The priest
shall make an examination, and if it appears deeper than the skin and its hair
has turned white, the priest shall pronounce him unclean; this is a leprous[o]
disease, broken out in the boil. 21 But if
the priest examines it and the hair on
it is not white, nor is it deeper than the
skin but has abated, the priest shall confine him for seven days. 22 If it spreads
in the skin, the priest shall pronounce
him unclean; it is diseased. 23 But if the
spot remains in one place and does not
spread, it is the scar of the boil; the
priest shall pronounce him clean.

24 Or, when the body has a burn on
the skin and the raw flesh of the burn
becomes a spot, reddish-white or white,
25 the priest shall examine it. If the hair
in the spot has turned white and it appears deeper than the skin, it is a leprous[p] disease; it has broken out in the
burn, and the priest shall pronounce
him unclean. This is a leprous[q] disease.
26 But if the priest examines it and the
hair in the spot is not white, and it is
no deeper than the skin but has abated,
the priest shall confine him for seven
days. 27 The priest shall examine him on
the seventh day; if it is spreading in the
skin, the priest shall pronounce him unclean. This is a leprous[r] disease. 28 But if
the spot remains in one place and does
not spread in the skin but has abated,
it is a swelling from the burn, and the
priest shall pronounce him clean; for it
is the scar of the burn.

29 When a man or woman has a disease on the head or in the beard, 30 the
priest shall examine the disease. If it appears deeper than the skin and the hair
in it is yellow and thin, the priest shall
pronounce him unclean; it is an itch,
a leprous[s] disease of the head or the
beard. 31 If the priest examines the itching disease, and it appears no deeper
than the skin and there is no black hair
in it, the priest shall confine the person
with the itching disease for seven days.
32 On the seventh day the priest shall
examine the itch; if the itch has not
spread, and there is no yellow hair in
it, and the itch appears to be no deeper
than the skin, 33 he shall shave, but the
itch he shall not shave. The priest shall
confine the person with the itch for
seven days more. 34 On the seventh day
the priest shall examine the itch; if the
itch has not spread in the skin and it
appears to be no deeper than the skin,
the priest shall pronounce him clean.
He shall wash his clothes and be clean.
35 But if the itch spreads in the skin after he was pronounced clean, 36 the
priest shall examine him. If the itch has
spread in the skin, the priest need not
seek for the yellow hair; he is unclean.
37 But if in his eyes the itch is checked,
and black hair has grown in it, the itch
is healed, he is clean; and the priest shall
pronounce him clean.

38 When a man or a woman has spots
on the skin of the body, white spots,
39 the priest shall make an examination,
and if the spots on the skin of the body
are of a dull white, it is a rash that has
broken out on the skin; he is clean.

40 If anyone loses the hair from his
head, he is bald but he is clean. 41 If he
loses the hair from his forehead and
temples, he has baldness of the forehead but he is clean. 42 But if there is
on the bald head or the bald forehead a
reddish-white diseased spot, it is a leprous[t] disease breaking out on his bald
head or his bald forehead. 43 The priest
shall examine him; if the diseased swelling is reddish-white on his bald head or
on his bald forehead, which resembles a
leprous[u] disease in the skin of the body,
44 he is leprous,[v] he is unclean. The priest
shall pronounce him unclean; the disease is on his head.

45 The person who has the leprous[w]
disease shall wear torn clothes and let
the hair of his head be dishevelled; and
he shall cover his upper lip and cry out,
'Unclean, unclean.' 46 He shall remain
unclean as long as he has the disease; he
is unclean. He shall live alone; his dwelling shall be outside the camp.

[o] **13.20** A term for several skin diseases; precise meaning uncertain [p] **13.25** A term for several skin diseases; precise meaning uncertain
[q] **13.25** A term for several skin diseases; precise meaning uncertain [r] **13.27** A term for several skin diseases; precise meaning uncertain
[s] **13.30** A term for several skin diseases; precise meaning uncertain [t] **13.42** A term for several skin diseases; precise meaning uncertain
[u] **13.43** A term for several skin diseases; precise meaning uncertain [v] **13.44** A term for several skin diseases; precise meaning uncertain
[w] **13.45** A term for several skin diseases; precise meaning uncertain

47 Concerning clothing: when a leprous[x] disease appears in it, in woollen or linen cloth, 48 in warp or woof of linen or wool, or in a skin or in anything made of skin, 49 if the disease shows greenish or reddish in the garment, whether in warp or woof or in skin or in anything made of skin, it is a leprous[y] disease and shall be shown to the priest. 50 The priest shall examine the disease, and put the diseased article aside for seven days. 51 He shall examine the disease on the seventh day. If the disease has spread in the cloth, in warp or woof, or in the skin, whatever be the use of the skin, this is a spreading leprous[z] disease; it is unclean. 52 He shall burn the clothing, whether diseased in warp or woof, woollen or linen, or anything of skin, for it is a spreading leprous[a] disease; it shall be burned in fire.

53 If the priest makes an examination, and the disease has not spread in the clothing, in warp or woof or in anything of skin, 54 the priest shall command them to wash the article in which the disease appears, and he shall put it aside for seven days more. 55 The priest shall examine the diseased article after it has been washed. If the diseased spot has not changed colour, though the disease has not spread, it is unclean; you shall burn it in fire, whether the leprous[b] spot is on the inside or on the outside.

56 If the priest makes an examination, and the disease has abated after it is washed, he shall tear the spot out of the cloth, in warp or woof, or out of skin. 57 If it appears again in the garment, in warp or woof, or in anything of skin, it is spreading; you shall burn with fire that in which the disease appears. 58 But the cloth, warp or woof, or anything of skin from which the disease disappears when you have washed it, shall then be washed a second time, and it shall be clean.

59 This is the ritual for a leprous[c] disease in a cloth of wool or linen, either in warp or woof, or in anything of skin, to decide whether it is clean or unclean.

PURIFICATION OF LEPERS AND LEPROUS HOUSES

14 The LORD spoke to Moses, saying: 2 This shall be the ritual for the leprous[d] person at the time of his cleansing:

He shall be brought to the priest; 3 the priest shall go out of the camp, and the priest shall make an examination. If the disease is healed in the leprous[e] person, 4 the priest shall command that two living clean birds and cedar wood and crimson yarn and hyssop be brought for the one who is to be cleansed. 5 The priest shall command that one of the birds be slaughtered over fresh water in an earthen vessel. 6 He shall take the living bird with the cedar wood and the crimson yarn and the hyssop, and dip them and the living bird in the blood of the bird that was slaughtered over the fresh water. 7 He shall sprinkle it seven times upon the one who is to be cleansed of the leprous[f] disease; then he shall pronounce him clean, and he shall let the living bird go into the open field. 8 The one who is to be cleansed shall wash his clothes, and shave off all his hair, and bathe himself in water, and he shall be clean. After that he shall come into the camp, but shall live outside his tent for seven days. 9 On the seventh day he shall shave all his hair: of head, beard, eyebrows; he shall shave all his hair. Then he shall wash his clothes, and bathe his body in water, and he shall be clean.

10 On the eighth day he shall take two male lambs without blemish, and one ewe lamb in its first year without blemish, and a grain-offering of three-tenths of an ephah of choice flour mixed with oil, and one log[g] of oil. 11 The priest who cleanses shall set the person to be cleansed, along with these things, before the LORD, at the entrance of the tent of meeting. 12 The priest shall take one of the lambs, and offer it as a guilt-offering, along with the log[h] of oil, and raise them as an elevation-offering before the LORD. 13 He shall slaughter the lamb in the place where the sin-offering and the burnt-offering are slaughtered in the holy place; for the guilt-offering, like the sin-offering, belongs to the priest: it is most holy. 14 The priest shall take some of the blood of the guilt-

[x] **13.47** A term for several skin diseases; precise meaning uncertain [y] **13.49** A term for several skin diseases; precise meaning uncertain
[z] **13.51** A term for several skin diseases; precise meaning uncertain [a] **13.52** A term for several skin diseases; precise meaning uncertain
[b] **13.55** A term for several skin diseases; precise meaning uncertain [c] **13.59** A term for several skin diseases; precise meaning uncertain
[d] **14.2** A term for several skin diseases; precise meaning uncertain [e] **14.3** A term for several skin diseases; precise meaning uncertain
[f] **14.7** A term for several skin diseases; precise meaning uncertain [g] **14.10** A liquid measure
[h] **14.12** A liquid measure

offering and put it on the lobe of the
right ear of the one to be cleansed, and
on the thumb of the right hand, and
on the big toe of the right foot. 15The
priest shall take some of the log[i] of oil
and pour it into the palm of his own left
hand, 16and dip his right finger in the
oil that is in his left hand and sprinkle
some oil with his finger seven times
before the LORD. 17Some of the oil that
remains in his hand the priest shall
put on the lobe of the right ear of the
one to be cleansed, and on the thumb
of the right hand, and on the big toe of
the right foot, on top of the blood of the
guilt-offering. 18The rest of the oil that is
in the priest's hand he shall put on the
head of the one to be cleansed. Then the
priest shall make atonement on his behalf before the LORD: 19the priest shall
offer the sin-offering, to make atonement for the one to be cleansed from
his uncleanness. Afterwards he shall
slaughter the burnt-offering; 20and the
priest shall offer the burnt-offering and
the grain-offering on the altar. Thus the
priest shall make atonement on his behalf and he shall be clean.

21 But if he is poor and cannot afford
so much, he shall take one male lamb
for a guilt-offering to be elevated, to
make atonement on his behalf, and one-
tenth of an ephah of choice flour mixed
with oil for a grain-offering, and a log[j]
of oil; 22also two turtle-doves or two pigeons, such as he can afford, one for a
sin-offering and the other for a burnt-
offering. 23On the eighth day he shall
bring them for his cleansing to the priest,
to the entrance of the tent of meeting, before the LORD; 24and the priest shall take
the lamb of the guilt-offering and the
log[k] of oil, and the priest shall raise them
as an elevation-offering before the LORD.
25The priest shall slaughter the lamb of
the guilt-offering and shall take some
of the blood of the guilt-offering, and
put it on the lobe of the right ear of the
one to be cleansed, and on the thumb of
the right hand, and on the big toe of the
right foot. 26The priest shall pour some
of the oil into the palm of his own left
hand, 27and shall sprinkle with his right
finger some of the oil that is in his left
hand seven times before the LORD. 28The
priest shall put some of the oil that is in
his hand on the lobe of the right ear of
the one to be cleansed, and on the thumb
of the right hand, and the big toe of the
right foot, where the blood of the guilt-
offering was placed. 29The rest of the oil
that is in the priest's hand he shall put
on the head of the one to be cleansed, to
make atonement on his behalf before the
LORD. 30And he shall offer, of the turtle-
doves or pigeons such as he can afford,
31one[l] for a sin-offering and the other
for a burnt-offering, along with a grain-
offering; and the priest shall make atonement before the LORD on behalf of the
one being cleansed. 32This is the ritual for
one who has a leprous[m] disease, who cannot afford the offerings for his cleansing.

33 The LORD spoke to Moses and
Aaron, saying:

34 When you come into the land of
Canaan, which I give you for a possession, and I put a leprous[n] disease in a
house in the land of your possession,
35the owner of the house shall come and
tell the priest, saying, 'There seems to me
to be some sort of disease in my house.'
36The priest shall command that they
empty the house before the priest goes
to examine the disease, or all that is in
the house will become unclean; and afterwards the priest shall go in to inspect
the house. 37He shall examine the disease; if the disease is in the walls of the
house with greenish or reddish spots,
and if it appears to be deeper than the
surface, 38the priest shall go outside to
the door of the house and shut up the
house for seven days. 39The priest shall
come again on the seventh day and make
an inspection; if the disease has spread
in the walls of the house, 40the priest
shall command that the stones in which
the disease appears be taken out and
thrown into an unclean place outside
the city. 41He shall have the inside of the
house scraped thoroughly, and the plaster that is scraped off shall be dumped in
an unclean place outside the city. 42They
shall take other stones and put them in
the place of those stones, and take other
plaster and plaster the house.

43 If the disease breaks out again in
the house, after he has taken out the
stones and scraped the house and plastered it, 44the priest shall go and make
inspection; if the disease has spread in
the house, it is a spreading leprous[o]
disease in the house; it is unclean.
45He shall have the house torn down,

[i] **14.15** A liquid measure [j] **14.21** A liquid measure [k] **14.24** A liquid measure [l] **14.31** Gk Syr: Heb *afford, 31such as he can afford, one*
[m] **14.32** A term for several skin diseases; precise meaning uncertain [n] **14.34** A term for several skin diseases; precise meaning uncertain
[o] **14.44** A term for several skin diseases; precise meaning uncertain

its stones and timber and all the plaster of the house, and taken outside the city to an unclean place. 46All who enter the house while it is shut up shall be unclean until the evening; 47and all who sleep in the house shall wash their clothes; and all who eat in the house shall wash their clothes.

48 If the priest comes and makes an inspection, and the disease has not spread in the house after the house was plastered, the priest shall pronounce the house clean; the disease is healed. 49For the cleansing of the house he shall take two birds, with cedar wood and crimson yarn and hyssop, 50and shall slaughter one of the birds over fresh water in an earthen vessel, 51and shall take the cedar wood and the hyssop and the crimson yarn, along with the living bird, and dip them in the blood of the slaughtered bird and the fresh water, and sprinkle the house seven times. 52Thus he shall cleanse the house with the blood of the bird, and with the fresh water, and with the living bird, and with the cedar wood and hyssop and crimson yarn; 53and he shall let the living bird go out of the city into the open field; so he shall make atonement for the house, and it shall be clean.

54 This is the ritual for any leprous[p] disease: for an itch, 55for leprous[q] diseases in clothing and houses, 56and for a swelling or an eruption or a spot, 57to determine when it is unclean and when it is clean. This is the ritual for leprous[r] diseases.

CONCERNING BODILY DISCHARGES

15 The LORD spoke to Moses and Aaron, saying: 2Speak to the people of Israel and say to them:

When any man has a discharge from his member,[s] his discharge makes him ceremonially unclean. 3The uncleanness of his discharge is this: whether his member[t] flows with his discharge, or his member[u] is stopped from discharging, it is uncleanness for him. 4Every bed on which the one with the discharge lies shall be unclean; and everything on which he sits shall be unclean. 5Anyone who touches his bed shall wash his clothes, and bathe in water, and be unclean until the evening. 6All who sit on anything on which the one with the discharge has sat shall wash their clothes, and bathe in water, and be unclean until the evening. 7All who touch the body of the one with the discharge shall wash their clothes, and bathe in water, and be unclean until the evening. 8If the one with the discharge spits on persons who are clean, then they shall wash their clothes, and bathe in water, and be unclean until the evening. 9Any saddle on which the one with the discharge rides shall be unclean. 10All who touch anything that was under him shall be unclean until the evening, and all who carry such a thing shall wash their clothes, and bathe in water, and be unclean until the evening. 11All those whom the one with the discharge touches without his having rinsed his hands in water shall wash their clothes, and bathe in water, and be unclean until the evening. 12Any earthen vessel that the one with the discharge touches shall be broken; and every vessel of wood shall be rinsed in water.

13 When the one with a discharge is cleansed of his discharge, he shall count seven days for his cleansing; he shall wash his clothes and bathe his body in fresh water, and he shall be clean. 14On the eighth day he shall take two turtledoves or two pigeons and come before the LORD to the entrance of the tent of meeting and give them to the priest. 15The priest shall offer them, one for a sin-offering and the other for a burnt-offering; and the priest shall make atonement on his behalf before the LORD for his discharge.

16 If a man has an emission of semen, he shall bathe his whole body in water, and be unclean until the evening. 17Everything made of cloth or of skin on which the semen falls shall be washed with water, and be unclean until the evening. 18If a man lies with a woman and has an emission of semen, both of them shall bathe in water, and be unclean until the evening.

19 When a woman has a discharge of blood that is her regular discharge from her body, she shall be in her impurity for seven days, and whoever touches her shall be unclean until the evening. 20Everything upon which she lies during her impurity shall be unclean; everything also upon which she sits shall be unclean. 21Whoever touches her bed

[p] 14.54 A term for several skin diseases; precise meaning uncertain [q] 14.55 A term for several skin diseases; precise meaning uncertain [r] 14.57 A term for several skin diseases; precise meaning uncertain [s] 15.2 Heb *flesh* [t] 15.3 Heb *flesh* [u] 15.3 Heb *flesh*

shall wash his clothes, and bathe in water, and be unclean until the evening. 22 Whoever touches anything upon which she sits shall wash his clothes, and bathe in water, and be unclean until the evening; 23 whether it is the bed or anything upon which she sits, when he touches it he shall be unclean until the evening. 24 If any man lies with her, and her impurity falls on him, he shall be unclean for seven days; and every bed on which he lies shall be unclean.

25 If a woman has a discharge of blood for many days, not at the time of her impurity, or if she has a discharge beyond the time of her impurity, for all the days of the discharge she shall continue in uncleanness; as in the days of her impurity, she shall be unclean. 26 Every bed on which she lies during all the days of her discharge shall be treated as the bed of her impurity; and everything on which she sits shall be unclean, as in the uncleanness of her impurity. 27 Whoever touches these things shall be unclean, and shall wash his clothes, and bathe in water, and be unclean until the evening. 28 If she is cleansed of her discharge, she shall count seven days, and after that she shall be clean. 29 On the eighth day she shall take two turtle-doves or two pigeons and bring them to the priest at the entrance of the tent of meeting. 30 The priest shall offer one for a sin-offering and the other for a burnt-offering; and the priest shall make atonement on her behalf before the LORD for her unclean discharge.

31 Thus you shall keep the people of Israel separate from their uncleanness, so that they do not die in their uncleanness by defiling my tabernacle that is in their midst.

32 This is the ritual for those who have a discharge: for him who has an emission of semen, becoming unclean thereby, 33 for her who is in the infirmity of her period, for anyone, male or female, who has a discharge, and for the man who lies with a woman who is unclean.

THE DAY OF ATONEMENT

16 The LORD spoke to Moses after the death of the two sons of Aaron, when they drew near before the LORD and died. 2 The LORD said to Moses:

Tell your brother Aaron not to come just at any time into the sanctuary inside the curtain before the mercy-seat[v] that is upon the ark, or he will die; for I appear in the cloud upon the mercy-seat.[w] 3 Thus shall Aaron come into the holy place: with a young bull for a sin-offering and a ram for a burnt-offering. 4 He shall put on the holy linen tunic, and shall have the linen undergarments next to his body, fasten the linen sash, and wear the linen turban; these are the holy vestments. He shall bathe his body in water, and then put them on. 5 He shall take from the congregation of the people of Israel two male goats for a sin-offering, and one ram for a burnt-offering.

6 Aaron shall offer the bull as a sin-offering for himself, and shall make atonement for himself and for his house. 7 He shall take the two goats and set them before the LORD at the entrance of the tent of meeting; 8 and Aaron shall cast lots on the two goats, one lot for the LORD and the other lot for Azazel.[x] 9 Aaron shall present the goat on which the lot fell for the LORD, and offer it as a sin-offering; 10 but the goat on which the lot fell for Azazel[y] shall be presented alive before the LORD to make atonement over it, so that it may be sent away into the wilderness to Azazel.[z]

11 Aaron shall present the bull as a sin-offering for himself, and shall make atonement for himself and for his house; he shall slaughter the bull as a sin-offering for himself. 12 He shall take a censer full of coals of fire from the altar before the LORD, and two handfuls of crushed sweet incense, and he shall bring it inside the curtain 13 and put the incense on the fire before the LORD, so that the cloud of the incense may cover the mercy-seat[a] that is upon the covenant,[b] or he will die. 14 He shall take some of the blood of the bull, and sprinkle it with his finger on the front of the mercy-seat,[c] and before the mercy-seat[d] he shall sprinkle the blood with his finger seven times.

15 He shall slaughter the goat of the sin-offering that is for the people and bring its blood inside the curtain, and do with its blood as he did with the blood of the bull, sprinkling it upon the mercy-seat[e] and before the mercy-seat.[f]

[v] 16.2 Or *the cover* [w] 16.2 Or *the cover*
[x] 16.8 Traditionally rendered *a scapegoat*
[y] 16.10 Traditionally rendered *a scapegoat*
[z] 16.10 Traditionally rendered *a scapegoat*
[a] 16.13 Or *the cover* [b] 16.13 Or *treaty*, or *testament*; Heb *eduth* [c] 16.14 Or *the cover*
[d] 16.14 Or *the cover* [e] 16.15 Or *the cover*
[f] 16.15 Or *the cover*

16 Thus he shall make atonement for the
sanctuary, because of the uncleannesses of the people of Israel, and because of
their transgressions, all their sins; and
so he shall do for the tent of meeting,
which remains with them in the midst
of their uncleannesses. 17 No one shall be
in the tent of meeting from the time he
enters to make atonement in the sanctuary until he comes out and has made
atonement for himself and for his house
and for all the assembly of Israel. 18 Then
he shall go out to the altar that is before
the LORD and make atonement on its
behalf, and shall take some of the blood
of the bull and of the blood of the goat,
and put it on each of the horns of the
altar. 19 He shall sprinkle some of the
blood on it with his finger seven times,
and cleanse it and hallow it from the uncleannesses of the people of Israel.

20 When he has finished atoning for
the holy place and the tent of meeting
and the altar, he shall present the live
goat. 21 Then Aaron shall lay both his
hands on the head of the live goat, and
confess over it all the iniquities of the
people of Israel, and all their transgressions, all their sins, putting them on the
head of the goat, and sending it away
into the wilderness by means of someone designated for the task.[g] 22 The goat
shall bear on itself all their iniquities to
a barren region; and the goat shall be set
free in the wilderness.

23 Then Aaron shall enter the tent
of meeting, and shall take off the linen
vestments that he put on when he went
into the holy place, and shall leave them
there. 24 He shall bathe his body in water
in a holy place, and put on his vestments;
then he shall come out and offer his
burnt-offering and the burnt-offering of
the people, making atonement for himself and for the people. 25 The fat of the
sin-offering he shall turn into smoke on
the altar. 26 The one who sets the goat free
for Azazel[h] shall wash his clothes and
bathe his body in water, and afterwards
may come into the camp. 27 The bull of
the sin-offering and the goat of the sin-
offering, whose blood was brought in to
make atonement in the holy place, shall
be taken outside the camp; their skin
and their flesh and their dung shall be
consumed in fire. 28 The one who burns
them shall wash his clothes and bathe
his body in water, and afterwards may
come into the camp.

29 This shall be a statute to you for
ever: In the seventh month, on the tenth
day of the month, you shall deny yourselves,[i] and shall do no work, neither the
citizen nor the alien who resides among
you. 30 For on this day atonement shall
be made for you, to cleanse you; from all
your sins you shall be clean before the
LORD. 31 It is a sabbath of complete rest
to you, and you shall deny yourselves;[j]
it is a statute for ever. 32 The priest who
is anointed and consecrated as priest in
his father's place shall make atonement,
wearing the linen vestments, the holy
vestments. 33 He shall make atonement
for the sanctuary, and he shall make
atonement for the tent of meeting and
for the altar, and he shall make atonement for the priests and for all the people of the assembly. 34 This shall be an
everlasting statute for you, to make
atonement for the people of Israel once
in the year for all their sins. And Moses
did as the LORD had commanded him.

THE SLAUGHTERING OF ANIMALS

17 The LORD spoke to Moses:
2 Speak to Aaron and his sons
and to all the people of Israel and say to
them: This is what the LORD has commanded. 3 If anyone of the house of Israel slaughters an ox or a lamb or a goat
in the camp, or slaughters it outside the
camp, 4 and does not bring it to the entrance of the tent of meeting, to present
it as an offering to the LORD before the
tabernacle of the LORD, he shall be held
guilty of bloodshed; he has shed blood,
and he shall be cut off from the people.
5 This is in order that the people of Israel may bring their sacrifices that they
offer in the open field, that they may
bring them to the LORD, to the priest at
the entrance of the tent of meeting, and
offer them as sacrifices of well-being
to the LORD. 6 The priest shall dash the
blood against the altar of the LORD at
the entrance of the tent of meeting, and
turn the fat into smoke as a pleasing
odour to the LORD, 7 so that they may
no longer offer their sacrifices for goat-
demons, to whom they prostitute themselves. This shall be a statute for ever to
them throughout their generations.

8 And say to them further: Anyone of
the house of Israel or of the aliens who
reside among them who offers a burnt-
offering or sacrifice, 9 and does not bring
it to the entrance of the tent of meeting,

[g] **16.21** Meaning of Heb uncertain
[h] **16.26** Traditionally rendered *a scapegoat*
[i] **16.29** Or *shall fast* [j] **16.31** Or *shall fast*

to sacrifice it to the LORD, shall be cut
off from the people.

EATING BLOOD PROHIBITED

10 If anyone of the house of Israel or
of the aliens who reside among them
eats any blood, I will set my face against
that person who eats blood, and will cut
that person off from the people. 11 For
the life of the flesh is in the blood; and
I have given it to you for making atonement for your lives on the altar; for, as
life, it is the blood that makes atonement. 12 Therefore I have said to the
people of Israel: No person among you
shall eat blood, nor shall any alien who
resides among you eat blood. 13 And
anyone of the people of Israel, or of the
aliens who reside among them, who
hunts down an animal or bird that may
be eaten shall pour out its blood and
cover it with earth.

14 For the life of every creature—its
blood is its life; therefore I have said to
the people of Israel: You shall not eat
the blood of any creature, for the life of
every creature is its blood; whoever eats
it shall be cut off. 15 All persons, citizens
or aliens, who eat what dies of itself or
what has been torn by wild animals,
shall wash their clothes, and bathe
themselves in water, and be unclean until the evening; then they shall be clean.
16 But if they do not wash themselves or
bathe their body, they shall bear their
guilt.

SEXUAL RELATIONS

18 The LORD spoke to Moses, saying:

2 Speak to the people of Israel and
say to them: I am the LORD your God.
3 You shall not do as they do in the land
of Egypt, where you lived, and you shall
not do as they do in the land of Canaan,
to which I am bringing you. You shall
not follow their statutes. 4 My ordinances you shall observe and my statutes you shall keep, following them: I
am the LORD your God. 5 You shall keep
my statutes and my ordinances; by doing so one shall live: I am the LORD.

6 None of you shall approach anyone near of kin to uncover nakedness:
I am the LORD. 7 You shall not uncover
the nakedness of your father, which is
the nakedness of your mother; she is
your mother, you shall not uncover her
nakedness. 8 You shall not uncover the
nakedness of your father's wife; it is the
nakedness of your father. 9 You shall not
uncover the nakedness of your sister,
your father's daughter or your mother's daughter, whether born at home
or born abroad. 10 You shall not uncover
the nakedness of your son's daughter or
of your daughter's daughter, for their
nakedness is your own nakedness. 11 You
shall not uncover the nakedness of your
father's wife's daughter, begotten by
your father, since she is your sister.
12 You shall not uncover the nakedness
of your father's sister; she is your father's flesh. 13 You shall not uncover the
nakedness of your mother's sister, for
she is your mother's flesh. 14 You shall
not uncover the nakedness of your father's brother, that is, you shall not approach his wife; she is your aunt. 15 You
shall not uncover the nakedness of your
daughter-in-law: she is your son's wife;
you shall not uncover her nakedness.
16 You shall not uncover the nakedness
of your brother's wife; it is your brother's nakedness. 17 You shall not uncover
the nakedness of a woman and her
daughter, and you shall not take[k] her
son's daughter or her daughter's daughter to uncover her nakedness; they are
your[l] flesh; it is depravity. 18 And you
shall not take[m] a woman as a rival to her
sister, uncovering her nakedness while
her sister is still alive.

19 You shall not approach a woman
to uncover her nakedness while she is
in her menstrual uncleanness. 20 You
shall not have sexual relations with
your kinsman's wife, and defile yourself with her. 21 You shall not give any of
your offspring to sacrifice them[n] to Molech, and so profane the name of your
God: I am the LORD. 22 You shall not lie
with a male as with a woman; it is an
abomination. 23 You shall not have sexual relations with any animal and defile
yourself with it, nor shall any woman
give herself to an animal to have sexual
relations with it: it is perversion.

24 Do not defile yourselves in any
of these ways, for by all these practices
the nations I am casting out before you
have defiled themselves. 25 Thus the land
became defiled; and I punished it for its
iniquity, and the land vomited out its
inhabitants. 26 But you shall keep my
statutes and my ordinances and commit
none of these abominations, either the
citizen or the alien who resides among
you 27 (for the inhabitants of the land,

[k] 18.17 Or *marry* [l] 18.17 Gk: Heb lacks *your*
[m] 18.18 Or *marry* [n] 18.21 Heb *to pass them over*

who were before you, committed all of
these abominations, and the land became defiled); 28 otherwise the land
will vomit you out for defiling it, as it
vomited out the nation that was before you. 29 For whoever commits any of
these abominations shall be cut off from
their people. 30 So keep my charge not to
commit any of these abominations that
were done before you, and not to defile
yourselves by them: I am the LORD your
God.

RITUAL AND MORAL HOLINESS

19 The LORD spoke to Moses, saying:
2 Speak to all the congregation of the
people of Israel and say to them: You
shall be holy, for I the LORD your God
am holy. 3 You shall each revere your
mother and father, and you shall keep
my sabbaths: I am the LORD your God.
4 Do not turn to idols or make cast images for yourselves: I am the LORD your
God.
5 When you offer a sacrifice of well-
being to the LORD, offer it in such a
way that it is acceptable in your behalf.
6 It shall be eaten on the same day you
offer it, or on the next day; and anything left over until the third day shall
be consumed in fire. 7 If it is eaten at all
on the third day, it is an abomination;
it will not be acceptable. 8 All who eat it
shall be subject to punishment, because
they have profaned what is holy to the
LORD; and any such person shall be cut
off from the people.
9 When you reap the harvest of your
land, you shall not reap to the very
edges of your field, or gather the gleanings of your harvest. 10 You shall not
strip your vineyard bare, or gather the
fallen grapes of your vineyard; you shall
leave them for the poor and the alien: I
am the LORD your God.
11 You shall not steal; you shall not
deal falsely; and you shall not lie to one
another. 12 And you shall not swear
falsely by my name, profaning the name
of your God: I am the LORD.
13 You shall not defraud your neighbour; you shall not steal; and you shall
not keep for yourself the wages of a labourer until morning. 14 You shall not
revile the deaf or put a stumbling-block
before the blind; you shall fear your God:
I am the LORD.
15 You shall not render an unjust
judgement; you shall not be partial to
the poor or defer to the great: with justice you shall judge your neighbour.
16 You shall not go around as a slanderer[o] among your people, and you shall
not profit by the blood[p] of your neighbour: I am the LORD.
17 You shall not hate in your heart
anyone of your kin; you shall reprove
your neighbour, or you will incur guilt
yourself. 18 You shall not take vengeance
or bear a grudge against any of your
people, but you shall love your neighbour as yourself: I am the LORD.
19 You shall keep my statutes. You
shall not let your animals breed with a
different kind; you shall not sow your
field with two kinds of seed; nor shall
you put on a garment made of two different materials.
20 If a man has sexual relations with
a woman who is a slave, designated for
another man but not ransomed or given
her freedom, an inquiry shall be held.
They shall not be put to death, since she
has not been freed; 21 but he shall bring
a guilt-offering for himself to the LORD,
at the entrance of the tent of meeting, a
ram as guilt-offering. 22 And the priest
shall make atonement for him with the
ram of guilt-offering before the LORD
for his sin that he committed; and the
sin he committed shall be forgiven him.
23 When you come into the land and
plant all kinds of trees for food, then you
shall regard their fruit as forbidden;[q] for
three years it shall be forbidden[r] to you;
it must not be eaten. 24 In the fourth
year all their fruit shall be set apart for
rejoicing in the LORD. 25 But in the fifth
year you may eat of their fruit, that
their yield may be increased for you: I
am the LORD your God.
26 You shall not eat anything with
its blood. You shall not practise augury or witchcraft. 27 You shall not round
off the hair on your temples or mar the
edges of your beard. 28 You shall not
make any gashes in your flesh for the
dead or tattoo any marks upon you: I
am the LORD.
29 Do not profane your daughter by
making her a prostitute, so that the
land may not become prostituted and
full of depravity. 30 You shall keep my
sabbaths and reverence my sanctuary: I
am the LORD.
31 Do not turn to mediums or wizards; do not seek them out, to be defiled
by them: I am the LORD your God.

[o] **19.16** Meaning of Heb uncertain [p] **19.16** Heb *stand against the blood* [q] **19.23** Heb *as their uncircumcision* [r] **19.23** Heb *uncircumcision*

32 You shall rise before the aged, and
defer to the old; and you shall fear your
God: I am the LORD.
33 When an alien resides with you
in your land, you shall not oppress the
alien. 34The alien who resides with you
shall be to you as the citizen among you;
you shall love the alien as yourself, for
you were aliens in the land of Egypt: I
am the LORD your God.
35 You shall not cheat in measuring
length, weight, or quantity. 36You shall
have honest balances, honest weights,
an honest ephah, and an honest hin: I
am the LORD your God, who brought
you out of the land of Egypt. 37You
shall keep all my statutes and all my ordinances, and observe them: I am the
LORD.

PENALTIES FOR VIOLATIONS OF HOLINESS

20 The LORD spoke to Moses, saying: 2Say further to the people
of Israel:
Any of the people of Israel, or of the
aliens who reside in Israel, who give
any of their offspring to Molech shall
be put to death; the people of the land
shall stone them to death. 3I myself will
set my face against them, and will cut
them off from the people, because they
have given of their offspring to Molech,
defiling my sanctuary and profaning
my holy name. 4And if the people of
the land should ever close their eyes to
them, when they give of their offspring
to Molech, and do not put them to
death, 5I myself will set my face against
them and against their family, and will
cut them off from among their people,
them and all who follow them in prostituting themselves to Molech.
6 If any turn to mediums and wizards, prostituting themselves to them, I
will set my face against them, and will
cut them off from the people. 7Conse-
crate yourselves therefore, and be holy;
for I am the LORD your God. 8Keep my
statutes, and observe them; I am the
LORD; I sanctify you. 9All who curse
father or mother shall be put to death;
having cursed father or mother, their
blood is upon them.
10 If a man commits adultery with
the wife of[s] his neighbour, both the
adulterer and the adulteress shall be
put to death. 11The man who lies with
his father's wife has uncovered his father's nakedness; both of them shall be
put to death; their blood is upon them.
12If a man lies with his daughter-in-
law, both of them shall be put to death;
they have committed perversion; their
blood is upon them. 13If a man lies with
a male as with a woman, both of them
have committed an abomination; they
shall be put to death; their blood is upon
them. 14If a man takes a wife and her
mother also, it is depravity; they shall
be burned to death, both he and they,
that there may be no depravity among
you. 15If a man has sexual relations with
an animal, he shall be put to death; and
you shall kill the animal. 16If a woman
approaches any animal and has sexual relations with it, you shall kill the
woman and the animal; they shall be
put to death, their blood is upon them.
17 If a man takes his sister, a daughter of his father or a daughter of his
mother, and sees her nakedness, and
she sees his nakedness, it is a disgrace,
and they shall be cut off in the sight
of their people; he has uncovered his
sister's nakedness, he shall be subject
to punishment. 18If a man lies with a
woman having her sickness and uncovers her nakedness, he has laid bare her
flow and she has laid bare her flow of
blood; both of them shall be cut off from
their people. 19You shall not uncover the
nakedness of your mother's sister or of
your father's sister, for that is to lay bare
one's own flesh; they shall be subject to
punishment. 20If a man lies with his
uncle's wife, he has uncovered his uncle's nakedness; they shall be subject to
punishment; they shall die childless. 21If
a man takes his brother's wife, it is impurity; he has uncovered his brother's
nakedness; they shall be childless.
22 You shall keep all my statutes and
all my ordinances, and observe them,
so that the land to which I bring you to
settle in may not vomit you out. 23You
shall not follow the practices of the nation that I am driving out before you.
Because they did all these things, I abhorred them. 24But I have said to you:
You shall inherit their land, and I will
give it to you to possess, a land flowing
with milk and honey. I am the LORD
your God; I have separated you from
the peoples. 25You shall therefore make
a distinction between the clean animal
and the unclean, and between the unclean bird and the clean; you shall not
bring abomination on yourselves by

[s] **20.10** Heb repeats *if a man commits adultery with the wife of*

animal or by bird or by anything with which the ground teems, which I have set apart for you to hold unclean. 26You shall be holy to me; for I the LORD am holy, and I have separated you from the other peoples to be mine.

27 A man or a woman who is a medium or a wizard shall be put to death; they shall be stoned to death, their blood is upon them.

THE HOLINESS OF PRIESTS

21 The LORD said to Moses: Speak to the priests, the sons of Aaron, and say to them:

No one shall defile himself for a dead person among his relatives, 2except for his nearest kin: his mother, his father, his son, his daughter, his brother; 3likewise, for a virgin sister, close to him because she has had no husband, he may defile himself for her. 4But he shall not defile himself as a husband among his people and so profane himself. 5They shall not make bald spots upon their heads, or shave off the edges of their beards, or make any gashes in their flesh. 6They shall be holy to their God, and not profane the name of their God; for they offer the LORD's offerings by fire, the food of their God; therefore they shall be holy. 7They shall not marry a prostitute or a woman who has been defiled; neither shall they marry a woman divorced from her husband. For they are holy to their God, 8and you shall treat them as holy, since they offer the food of your God; they shall be holy to you, for I the LORD, I who sanctify you, am holy. 9When the daughter of a priest profanes herself through prostitution, she profanes her father; she shall be burned to death.

10 The priest who is exalted above his fellows, on whose head the anointing-oil has been poured and who has been consecrated to wear the vestments, shall not dishevel his hair, nor tear his vestments. 11He shall not go where there is a dead body; he shall not defile himself even for his father or mother. 12He shall not go outside the sanctuary and thus profane the sanctuary of his God; for the consecration of the anointing-oil of his God is upon him: I am the LORD. 13He shall marry only a woman who is a virgin. 14A widow, or a divorced woman, or a woman who has been defiled, a prostitute, these he shall not marry. He shall marry a virgin of his own kin, 15that he may not profane his offspring among his kin; for I am the LORD; I sanctify him.

16 The LORD spoke to Moses, saying: 17Speak to Aaron and say: No one of your offspring throughout their generations who has a blemish may approach to offer the food of his God. 18For no one who has a blemish shall draw near, one who is blind or lame, or one who has a mutilated face or a limb too long, 19or one who has a broken foot or a broken hand, 20or a hunchback, or a dwarf, or a man with a blemish in his eyes or an itching disease or scabs or crushed testicles. 21No descendant of Aaron the priest who has a blemish shall come near to offer the LORD's offerings by fire; since he has a blemish, he shall not come near to offer the food of his God. 22He may eat the food of his God, of the most holy as well as of the holy. 23But he shall not come near the curtain or approach the altar, because he has a blemish, that he may not profane my sanctuaries; for I am the LORD; I sanctify them. 24Thus Moses spoke to Aaron and to his sons and to all the people of Israel.

THE USE OF HOLY OFFERINGS

22 The LORD spoke to Moses, saying: 2Direct Aaron and his sons to deal carefully with the sacred donations of the people of Israel, which they dedicate to me, so that they may not profane my holy name; I am the LORD. 3Say to them: If anyone among all your offspring throughout your generations comes near the sacred donations, which the people of Israel dedicate to the LORD, while he is in a state of uncleanness, that person shall be cut off from my presence: I am the LORD. 4No one of Aaron's offspring who has a leprous[t] disease or suffers a discharge may eat of the sacred donations until he is clean. Whoever touches anything made unclean by a corpse or a man who has had an emission of semen, 5and whoever touches any swarming thing by which he may be made unclean or any human being by whom he may be made unclean—whatever his uncleanness may be— 6the person who touches any such shall be unclean until evening and shall not eat of the sacred donations unless he has washed his body in water. 7When the sun sets he shall be clean; and afterwards he may eat of the sacred donations, for they are his food. 8That

[t] 22.4 A term for several skin diseases; precise meaning uncertain

which died or was torn by wild animals
he shall not eat, becoming unclean by
it: I am the LORD. 9They shall keep my
charge, so that they may not incur guilt
and die in the sanctuary[u] for having
profaned it: I am the LORD; I sanctify
them.

10 No lay person shall eat of the sacred donations. No bound or hired
servant of the priest shall eat of the
sacred donations; 11but if a priest acquires anyone by purchase, the person
may eat of them; and those that are
born in his house may eat of his food.
12If a priest's daughter marries a layman, she shall not eat of the offering of
the sacred donations; 13but if a priest's
daughter is widowed or divorced, without offspring, and returns to her father's house, as in her youth, she may
eat of her father's food. No lay person
shall eat of it. 14If a man eats of the sacred donation unintentionally, he shall
add one-fifth of its value to it, and give
the sacred donation to the priest. 15No
one shall profane the sacred donations
of the people of Israel, which they offer to the LORD, 16causing them to bear
guilt requiring a guilt-offering, by eating their sacred donations: for I am the
LORD; I sanctify them.

ACCEPTABLE OFFERINGS

17 The LORD spoke to Moses, saying: 18Speak to Aaron and his sons and
all the people of Israel and say to them:
When anyone of the house of Israel or of
the aliens residing in Israel presents an
offering, whether in payment of a vow
or as a freewill-offering that is offered to
the LORD as a burnt-offering, 19to be acceptable in your behalf it shall be a male
without blemish, of the cattle or the
sheep or the goats. 20You shall not offer
anything that has a blemish, for it will
not be acceptable in your behalf.

21 When anyone offers a sacrifice of
well-being to the LORD, in fulfilment
of a vow or as a freewill-offering, from
the herd or from the flock, to be acceptable it must be perfect; there shall be no
blemish in it. 22Anything blind, or injured, or maimed, or having a discharge
or an itch or scabs—these you shall not
offer to the LORD or put any of them on
the altar as offerings by fire to the LORD.
23An ox or a lamb that has a limb too
long or too short you may present for a
freewill-offering; but it will not be accepted for a vow. 24Any animal that has
its testicles bruised or crushed or torn or
cut, you shall not offer to the LORD; such
you shall not do within your land, 25nor
shall you accept any such animals from
a foreigner to offer as food to your God;
since they are mutilated, with a blemish in them, they shall not be accepted
in your behalf.

26 The LORD spoke to Moses, saying: 27When an ox or a sheep or a goat
is born, it shall remain for seven days
with its mother, and from the eighth
day onwards it shall be acceptable as
the LORD's offering by fire. 28But you
shall not slaughter, from the herd or
the flock, an animal with its young on
the same day. 29When you sacrifice a
thanksgiving-offering to the LORD, you
shall sacrifice it so that it may be acceptable in your behalf. 30It shall be eaten on
the same day; you shall not leave any of
it until morning: I am the LORD.

31 Thus you shall keep my commandments and observe them: I am the
LORD. 32You shall not profane my holy
name, that I may be sanctified among
the people of Israel: I am the LORD; I
sanctify you, 33I who brought you out of
the land of Egypt to be your God: I am
the LORD.

APPOINTED FESTIVALS

23 The LORD spoke to Moses, saying: 2Speak to the people of Israel and say to them: These are the appointed festivals of the LORD that you
shall proclaim as holy convocations, my
appointed festivals.

THE SABBATH, PASSOVER, AND UNLEAVENED BREAD

3 For six days shall work be done; but
the seventh day is a sabbath of complete rest, a holy convocation; you shall
do no work: it is a sabbath to the LORD
throughout your settlements.

4 These are the appointed festivals
of the LORD, the holy convocations,
which you shall celebrate at the time appointed for them. 5In the first month,
on the fourteenth day of the month,
at twilight,[v] there shall be a passover-
offering to the LORD, 6and on the fifteenth day of the same month is the festival of unleavened bread to the LORD;
for seven days you shall eat unleavened
bread. 7On the first day you shall have a
holy convocation; you shall not work at
your occupations. 8For seven days you

[u] 22.9 Vg: Heb *incur guilt for it and die in it*
[v] 23.5 Heb *between the two evenings*

shall present the LORD's offerings by
fire; on the seventh day there shall be a
holy convocation: you shall not work at
your occupations.

THE OFFERING OF FIRST FRUITS

9 The LORD spoke to Moses: 10 Speak
to the people of Israel and say to them:
When you enter the land that I am giving you and you reap its harvest, you
shall bring the sheaf of the first fruits
of your harvest to the priest. 11 He shall
raise the sheaf before the LORD, so that
you may find acceptance; on the day after the sabbath the priest shall raise it.
12 On the day when you raise the sheaf,
you shall offer a lamb a year old, without blemish, as a burnt-offering to the
LORD. 13 And the grain-offering with
it shall be two-tenths of an ephah of
choice flour mixed with oil, an offering
by fire of pleasing odour to the LORD;
and the drink-offering with it shall be
of wine, one-fourth of a hin. 14 You shall
eat no bread or parched grain or fresh
ears until that very day, until you have
brought the offering of your God: it is a
statute for ever throughout your generations in all your settlements.

THE FESTIVAL OF WEEKS

15 And from the day after the sabbath, from the day on which you bring
the sheaf of the elevation-offering, you
shall count off seven weeks; they shall
be complete. 16 You shall count until
the day after the seventh sabbath, fifty
days; then you shall present an offering of new grain to the LORD. 17 You
shall bring from your settlements two
loaves of bread as an elevation-offering,
each made of two-tenths of an ephah;
they shall be of choice flour, baked with
leaven, as first fruits to the LORD. 18 You
shall present with the bread seven
lambs a year old without blemish, one
young bull, and two rams; they shall be
a burnt-offering to the LORD, along with
their grain-offering and their drink-
offerings, an offering by fire of pleasing
odour to the LORD. 19 You shall also offer one male goat for a sin-offering, and
two male lambs a year old as a sacrifice
of well-being. 20 The priest shall raise
them with the bread of the first fruits as
an elevation-offering before the LORD,
together with the two lambs; they shall
be holy to the LORD for the priest. 21 On
that same day you shall make proclamation; you shall hold a holy convocation;
you shall not work at your occupations.
This is a statute for ever in all your settlements throughout your generations.
22 When you reap the harvest of
your land, you shall not reap to the very
edges of your field, or gather the gleanings of your harvest; you shall leave
them for the poor and for the alien: I am
the LORD your God.

THE FESTIVAL OF TRUMPETS

23 The LORD spoke to Moses, saying:
24 Speak to the people of Israel, saying:
In the seventh month, on the first day
of the month, you shall observe a day of
complete rest, a holy convocation com-
memorated with trumpet blasts. 25 You
shall not work at your occupations; and
you shall present the LORD's offering by
fire.

THE DAY OF ATONEMENT

26 The LORD spoke to Moses, saying: 27 Now, the tenth day of this seventh month is the day of atonement; it
shall be a holy convocation for you: you
shall deny yourselves[w] and present the
LORD's offering by fire; 28 and you shall
do no work during that entire day; for
it is a day of atonement, to make atonement on your behalf before the LORD
your God. 29 For anyone who does not
practise self-denial[x] during that entire day shall be cut off from the people. 30 And anyone who does any work
during that entire day, such a one I will
destroy from the midst of the people.
31 You shall do no work: it is a statute for
ever throughout your generations in all
your settlements. 32 It shall be to you a
sabbath of complete rest, and you shall
deny yourselves;[y] on the ninth day of
the month at evening, from evening to
evening you shall keep your sabbath.

THE FESTIVAL OF BOOTHS

33 The LORD spoke to Moses, saying:
34 Speak to the people of Israel, saying:
On the fifteenth day of this seventh
month, and lasting seven days, there
shall be the festival of booths[z] to the
LORD. 35 The first day shall be a holy
convocation; you shall not work at your
occupations. 36 For seven days you shall
present the LORD's offerings by fire; on
the eighth day you shall observe a holy
convocation and present the LORD's offerings by fire; it is a solemn assembly;
you shall not work at your occupations.

[w] **23.27** Or *shall fast* [x] **23.29** Or *does not fast*
[y] **23.32** Or *shall fast* [z] **23.34** Or *tabernacles*:
Heb *succoth*

37 These are the appointed festivals
of the LORD, which you shall celebrate
as times of holy convocation, for presenting to the LORD offerings by fire—
burnt-offerings and grain-offerings,
sacrifices and drink-offerings, each on
its proper day— 38 apart from the sabbaths of the LORD, and apart from your
gifts, and apart from all your votive offerings, and apart from all your freewill-
offerings, which you give to the LORD.
39 Now, the fifteenth day of the seventh month, when you have gathered
in the produce of the land, you shall
keep the festival of the LORD, lasting
seven days; a complete rest on the first
day, and a complete rest on the eighth
day. 40 On the first day you shall take
the fruit of majestic[a] trees, branches of
palm trees, boughs of leafy trees, and
willows of the brook; and you shall rejoice before the LORD your God for seven
days. 41 You shall keep it as a festival to
the LORD seven days in the year; you
shall keep it in the seventh month as a
statute for ever throughout your generations. 42 You shall live in booths for
seven days; all that are citizens in Israel shall live in booths, 43 so that your
generations may know that I made the
people of Israel live in booths when I
brought them out of the land of Egypt: I
am the LORD your God.
44 Thus Moses declared to the people
of Israel the appointed festivals of the
LORD.

THE LAMP

24 The LORD spoke to Moses, saying: 2 Command the people of
Israel to bring you pure oil of beaten
olives for the lamp, that a light may be
kept burning regularly. 3 Aaron shall set
it up in the tent of meeting, outside the
curtain of the covenant,[b] to burn from
evening to morning before the LORD
regularly; it shall be a statute for ever
throughout your generations. 4 He shall
set up the lamps on the lampstand of
pure gold[c] before the LORD regularly.

THE BREAD FOR THE TABERNACLE

5 You shall take choice flour, and
bake twelve loaves of it; two-tenths of
an ephah shall be in each loaf. 6 You shall
place them in two rows, six in a row, on
the table of pure gold.[d] 7 You shall put
pure frankincense with each row, to be a
token offering for the bread, as an offering by fire to the LORD. 8 Every sabbath
day Aaron shall set them in order before
the LORD regularly as a commitment of
the people of Israel, as a covenant for
ever. 9 They shall be for Aaron and his
descendants, who shall eat them in a
holy place, for they are most holy portions for him from the offerings by fire
to the LORD, a perpetual due.

BLASPHEMY AND ITS PUNISHMENT

10 A man whose mother was an Israelite and whose father was an Egyptian came out among the people of Israel; and the Israelite woman's son and
a certain Israelite began fighting in the
camp. 11 The Israelite woman's son blasphemed the Name in a curse. And they
brought him to Moses—now his mother's name was Shelomith, daughter of
Dibri, of the tribe of Dan— 12 and they
put him in custody, until the decision of
the LORD should be made clear to them.
13 The LORD said to Moses, saying: 14 Take the blasphemer outside the
camp; and let all who were within hearing lay their hands on his head, and
let the whole congregation stone him.
15 And speak to the people of Israel, saying: Anyone who curses God shall bear
the sin. 16 One who blasphemes the
name of the LORD shall be put to death;
the whole congregation shall stone the
blasphemer. Aliens as well as citizens,
when they blaspheme the Name, shall
be put to death. 17 Anyone who kills a human being shall be put to death. 18 Anyone who kills an animal shall make restitution for it, life for life. 19 Anyone who
maims another shall suffer the same
injury in return: 20 fracture for fracture,
eye for eye, tooth for tooth; the injury
inflicted is the injury to be suffered.
21 One who kills an animal shall make
restitution for it; but one who kills a human being shall be put to death. 22 You
shall have one law for the alien and for
the citizen: for I am the LORD your God.
23 Moses spoke thus to the people of Israel; and they took the blasphemer outside the camp, and stoned him to death.
The people of Israel did as the LORD had
commanded Moses.

THE SABBATICAL YEAR

25 The LORD spoke to Moses on
Mount Sinai, saying: 2 Speak to
the people of Israel and say to them:
When you enter the land that I am giving you, the land shall observe a sabbath

[a] 23.40 Meaning of Heb uncertain [b] 24.3 Or *treaty, or testament*; Heb *eduth* [c] 24.4 Heb *pure lampstand* [d] 24.6 Heb *pure table*

for the LORD. 3For six years you shall sow your field, and for six years you shall prune your vineyard, and gather in their yield; 4but in the seventh year there shall be a sabbath of complete rest for the land, a sabbath for the LORD: you shall not sow your field or prune your vineyard. 5You shall not reap the aftergrowth of your harvest or gather the grapes of your unpruned vine: it shall be a year of complete rest for the land. 6You may eat what the land yields during its sabbath—you, your male and female slaves, your hired and your bound labourers who live with you; 7for your livestock also, and for the wild animals in your land all its yield shall be for food.

THE YEAR OF JUBILEE

8 You shall count off seven weeks[e] of years, seven times seven years, so that the period of seven weeks of years gives forty-nine years. 9Then you shall have the trumpet sounded loud; on the tenth day of the seventh month—on the day of atonement—you shall have the trumpet sounded throughout all your land. 10And you shall hallow the fiftieth year and you shall proclaim liberty throughout the land to all its inhabitants. It shall be a jubilee for you: you shall return, every one of you, to your property and every one of you to your family. 11That fiftieth year shall be a jubilee for you: you shall not sow, or reap the aftergrowth, or harvest the unpruned vines. 12For it is a jubilee; it shall be holy to you: you shall eat only what the field itself produces.

13 In this year of jubilee you shall return, every one of you, to your property. 14When you make a sale to your neighbour or buy from your neighbour, you shall not cheat one another. 15When you buy from your neighbour, you shall pay only for the number of years since the jubilee; the seller shall charge you only for the remaining crop-years. 16If the years are more, you shall increase the price, and if the years are fewer, you shall diminish the price; for it is a certain number of harvests that are being sold to you. 17You shall not cheat one another, but you shall fear your God; for I am the LORD your God.

18 You shall observe my statutes and faithfully keep my ordinances, so that you may live on the land securely. 19The land will yield its fruit, and you will eat your fill and live on it securely. 20Should you ask, 'What shall we eat in the seventh year, if we may not sow or gather in our crop?' 21I will order my blessing for you in the sixth year, so that it will yield a crop for three years. 22When you sow in the eighth year, you will be eating from the old crop; until the ninth year, when its produce comes in, you shall eat the old. 23The land shall not be sold in perpetuity, for the land is mine; with me you are but aliens and tenants. 24Throughout the land that you hold, you shall provide for the redemption of the land.

25 If anyone of your kin falls into difficulty and sells a piece of property, then the next-of-kin shall come and redeem what the relative has sold. 26If the person has no one to redeem it, but then prospers and finds sufficient means to do so, 27the years since its sale shall be computed and the difference shall be refunded to the person to whom it was sold, and the property shall be returned. 28But if there are not sufficient means to recover it, what was sold shall remain with the purchaser until the year of jubilee; in the jubilee it shall be released, and the property shall be returned.

29 If anyone sells a dwelling-house in a walled city, it may be redeemed until a year has elapsed since its sale; the right of redemption shall be for one year. 30If it is not redeemed before a full year has elapsed, a house that is in a walled city shall pass in perpetuity to the purchaser, throughout the generations; it shall not be released in the jubilee. 31But houses in villages that have no walls around them shall be classed as open country; they may be redeemed, and they shall be released in the jubilee. 32As for the cities of the Levites, the Levites shall for ever have the right of redemption of the houses in the cities belonging to them. 33Such property as may be redeemed from the Levites—houses sold in a city belonging to them—shall be released in the jubilee; because the houses in the cities of the Levites are their possession among the people of Israel. 34But the open land around their cities may not be sold; for that is their possession for all time.

35 If any of your kin fall into difficulty and become dependent on you,[f] you shall support them; they shall live with you as though resident aliens. 36Do not take interest in advance or otherwise make a profit from them, but

[e] 25.8 Or *sabbaths* [f] 25.35 Meaning of Heb uncertain

fear your God; let them live with you.
37You shall not lend them your money
at interest taken in advance, or provide
them food at a profit. 38I am the LORD
your God, who brought you out of the
land of Egypt, to give you the land of Canaan, to be your God.

39 If any who are dependent on you
become so impoverished that they sell
themselves to you, you shall not make
them serve as slaves. 40They shall remain with you as hired or bound labourers. They shall serve with you until the year of the jubilee. 41Then they
and their children with them shall be
free from your authority; they shall go
back to their own family and return to
their ancestral property. 42For they are
my servants, whom I brought out of the
land of Egypt; they shall not be sold as
slaves are sold. 43You shall not rule over
them with harshness, but shall fear
your God. 44As for the male and female
slaves whom you may have, it is from
the nations around you that you may
acquire male and female slaves. 45You
may also acquire them from among the
aliens residing with you, and from their
families that are with you, who have
been born in your land; and they may be
your property. 46You may keep them as
a possession for your children after you,
for them to inherit as property. These
you may treat as slaves, but as for your
fellow Israelites, no one shall rule over
the other with harshness.

47 If resident aliens among you prosper, and if any of your kin fall into difficulty with one of them and sell themselves to an alien, or to a branch of the
alien's family, 48after they have sold
themselves they shall have the right
of redemption; one of their brothers
may redeem them, 49or their uncle or
their uncle's son may redeem them, or
anyone of their family who is of their
own flesh may redeem them; or if they
prosper they may redeem themselves.
50They shall compute with the purchaser the total from the year when they
sold themselves to the alien until the jubilee year; the price of the sale shall be
applied to the number of years: the time
they were with the owner shall be rated
as the time of a hired labourer. 51If many
years remain, they shall pay for their redemption in proportion to the purchase
price; 52and if few years remain until the jubilee year, they shall compute
thus: according to the years involved
they shall make payment for their redemption. 53As a labourer hired by the
year they shall be under the alien's authority, who shall not, however, rule
with harshness over them in your sight.
54And if they have not been redeemed
in any of these ways, they and their
children with them shall go free in the
jubilee year. 55For to me the people of Israel are servants; they are my servants
whom I brought out from the land of
Egypt: I am the LORD your God.

REWARDS FOR OBEDIENCE

26 You shall make for yourselves no
idols and erect no carved images
or pillars, and you shall not place figured stones in your land, to worship at
them; for I am the LORD your God. 2You
shall keep my sabbaths and reverence
my sanctuary: I am the LORD.

3 If you follow my statutes and keep
my commandments and observe them
faithfully, 4I will give you your rains in
their season, and the land shall yield its
produce, and the trees of the field shall
yield their fruit. 5Your threshing shall
overtake the vintage, and the vintage
shall overtake the sowing; you shall eat
your bread to the full, and live securely
in your land. 6And I will grant peace in
the land, and you shall lie down, and no
one shall make you afraid; I will remove
dangerous animals from the land, and
no sword shall go through your land.
7You shall give chase to your enemies,
and they shall fall before you by the
sword. 8Five of you shall give chase to
a hundred, and a hundred of you shall
give chase to ten thousand; your enemies shall fall before you by the sword.
9I will look with favour upon you and
make you fruitful and multiply you; and
I will maintain my covenant with you.
10You shall eat old grain long stored,
and you shall have to clear out the old
to make way for the new. 11I will place
my dwelling in your midst, and I shall
not abhor you. 12And I will walk among
you, and will be your God, and you shall
be my people. 13I am the LORD your
God who brought you out of the land of
Egypt, to be their slaves no more; I have
broken the bars of your yoke and made
you walk erect.

PENALTIES FOR DISOBEDIENCE

14 But if you will not obey me, and
do not observe all these commandments, 15if you spurn my statutes, and
abhor my ordinances, so that you will
not observe all my commandments,

and you break my covenant, 16 I in turn
will do this to you: I will bring terror on
you; consumption and fever that waste
the eyes and cause life to pine away.
You shall sow your seed in vain, for your
enemies shall eat it. 17 I will set my face
against you, and you shall be struck
down by your enemies; your foes shall
rule over you, and you shall flee though
no one pursues you. 18 And if in spite of
this you will not obey me, I will continue to punish you sevenfold for your
sins. 19 I will break your proud glory, and
I will make your sky like iron and your
earth like copper. 20 Your strength shall
be spent to no purpose: your land shall
not yield its produce, and the trees of
the land shall not yield their fruit.

21 If you continue hostile to me,
and will not obey me, I will continue to
plague you sevenfold for your sins. 22 I
will let loose wild animals against you,
and they shall bereave you of your children and destroy your livestock; they
shall make you few in number, and your
roads shall be deserted.

23 If in spite of these punishments
you have not turned back to me, but
continue hostile to me, 24 then I too
will continue hostile to you: I myself
will strike you sevenfold for your sins.
25 I will bring the sword against you,
executing vengeance for the covenant;
and if you withdraw within your cities, I will send pestilence among you,
and you shall be delivered into enemy hands. 26 When I break your staff
of bread, ten women shall bake your
bread in a single oven, and they shall
dole out your bread by weight; and
though you eat, you shall not be satisfied.

27 But if, despite this, you disobey
me, and continue hostile to me, 28 I will
continue hostile to you in fury; I in turn
will punish you myself sevenfold for
your sins. 29 You shall eat the flesh of
your sons, and you shall eat the flesh
of your daughters. 30 I will destroy your
high places and cut down your incense-
altars; I will heap your carcasses on the
carcasses of your idols. I will abhor you.
31 I will lay your cities waste, will make
your sanctuaries desolate, and I will not
smell your pleasing odours. 32 I will dev-
astate the land, so that your enemies
who come to settle in it shall be appalled
at it. 33 And you I will scatter among the
nations, and I will unsheathe the sword
against you; your land shall be a desolation, and your cities a waste.

34 Then the land shall enjoy[g] its sabbath years as long as it lies desolate,
while you are in the land of your enemies; then the land shall rest, and enjoy[h] its sabbath years. 35 As long as it lies
desolate, it shall have the rest it did not
have on your sabbaths when you were
living on it. 36 And as for those of you
who survive, I will send faintness into
their hearts in the lands of their enemies; the sound of a driven leaf shall
put them to flight, and they shall flee
as one flees from the sword, and they
shall fall though no one pursues. 37 They
shall stumble over one another, as if to
escape a sword, though no one pursues;
and you shall have no power to stand
against your enemies. 38 You shall perish among the nations, and the land of
your enemies shall devour you. 39 And
those of you who survive shall languish
in the land of your enemies because of
their iniquities; also they shall languish
because of the iniquities of their ancestors.

40 But if they confess their iniquity
and the iniquity of their ancestors, in
that they committed treachery against
me and, moreover, that they continued hostile to me— 41 so that I, in turn,
continued hostile to them and brought
them into the land of their enemies; if
then their uncircumcised heart is humbled and they make amends for their iniquity, 42 then will I remember my covenant with Jacob; I will remember also
my covenant with Isaac and also my
covenant with Abraham, and I will remember the land. 43 For the land shall be
deserted by them, and enjoy[i] its sabbath
years by lying desolate without them,
while they shall make amends for their
iniquity, because they dared to spurn
my ordinances, and they abhorred my
statutes. 44 Yet for all that, when they
are in the land of their enemies, I will
not spurn them, or abhor them so as
to destroy them utterly and break my
covenant with them; for I am the LORD
their God; 45 but I will remember in their
favour the covenant with their ancestors whom I brought out of the land of
Egypt in the sight of the nations, to be
their God: I am the LORD.

46 These are the statutes and ordinances and laws that the LORD established between himself and the people
of Israel on Mount Sinai through Moses.

[g] **26.34** Or *make up for* [h] **26.34** Or *make up for*
[i] **26.43** Or *make up for*

VOTIVE OFFERINGS

27 The LORD spoke to Moses, saying: 2Speak to the people of Israel
and say to them: When a person makes
an explicit vow to the LORD concerning the equivalent for a human being,
3the equivalent for a male shall be: from
twenty to sixty years of age the equivalent shall be fifty shekels of silver by
the sanctuary shekel. 4If the person is a
female, the equivalent is thirty shekels.
5If the age is from five to twenty years of
age, the equivalent is twenty shekels for
a male and ten shekels for a female. 6If
the age is from one month to five years,
the equivalent for a male is five shekels
of silver, and for a female the equivalent
is three shekels of silver. 7And if the person is sixty years old or over, then the
equivalent for a male is fifteen shekels,
and for a female ten shekels. 8If any cannot afford the equivalent, they shall be
brought before the priest and the priest
shall assess them; the priest shall assess
them according to what each one making a vow can afford.

9 If it concerns an animal that may
be brought as an offering to the LORD,
any such that may be given to the LORD
shall be holy. 10Another shall not be
exchanged or substituted for it, either
good for bad or bad for good; and if one
animal is substituted for another, both
that one and its substitute shall be holy.
11If it concerns any unclean animal that
may not be brought as an offering to the
LORD, the animal shall be presented before the priest. 12The priest shall assess
it: whether good or bad, according to
the assessment of the priest, so it shall
be. 13But if it is to be redeemed, one-
fifth must be added to the assessment.

14 If a person consecrates a house
to the LORD, the priest shall assess it:
whether good or bad, as the priest as-
sesses it, so it shall stand. 15And if the
one who consecrates the house wishes
to redeem it, one-fifth shall be added to
its assessed value, and it shall revert to
the original owner.

16 If a person consecrates to the
LORD any inherited land-holding, its assessment shall be in accordance with its
seed requirements: fifty shekels of silver
to a homer of barley seed. 17If the person
consecrates the field as of the year of jubilee, that assessment shall stand; 18but
if the field is consecrated after the jubilee, the priest shall compute the price
for it according to the years that remain
until the year of jubilee, and the assessment shall be reduced. 19And if the one
who consecrates the field wishes to redeem it, then one-fifth shall be added
to its assessed value, and it shall revert
to the original owner; 20but if the field
is not redeemed, or if it has been sold
to someone else, it shall no longer be
redeemable. 21But when the field is released in the jubilee, it shall be holy to
the LORD as a devoted field; it becomes
the priest's holding. 22If someone consecrates to the LORD a field that has
been purchased, which is not a part of
the inherited land-holding, 23the priest
shall compute for it the proportionate
assessment up to the year of jubilee, and
the assessment shall be paid as of that
day, a sacred donation to the LORD. 24In
the year of jubilee the field shall return
to the one from whom it was bought,
whose holding the land is. 25All assess-
ments shall be by the sanctuary shekel:
twenty gerahs shall make a shekel.

26 A firstling of animals, however,
which as a firstling belongs to the
LORD, cannot be consecrated by anyone;
whether ox or sheep, it is the LORD's.
27If it is an unclean animal, it shall be
ransomed at its assessment, with one-
fifth added; if it is not redeemed, it shall
be sold at its assessment.

28 Nothing that a person owns that
has been devoted to destruction for the
LORD, be it human or animal, or inherited land-holding, may be sold or
redeemed; every devoted thing is most
holy to the LORD. 29No human beings
who have been devoted to destruction
can be ransomed; they shall be put to
death.

30 All tithes from the land, whether
the seed from the ground or the fruit
from the tree, are the LORD's; they are
holy to the LORD. 31If persons wish to
redeem any of their tithes, they must
add one-fifth to them. 32All tithes of
herd and flock, every tenth one that
passes under the shepherd's staff, shall
be holy to the LORD. 33Let no one inquire whether it is good or bad, or make
substitution for it; if one makes substitution for it, then both it and the substitute shall be holy and cannot be redeemed.

34 These are the commandments
that the LORD gave to Moses for the
people of Israel on Mount Sinai.

NUMBERS

The book of Numbers continues the story of the people of Israel as they journey in the wilderness between Mt. Sinai and the promised land of Canaan. Numbers provides a census of the twelve tribes of Israel as they depart for their journey in the wilderness (ch. 1) and at the end of their journey as they anticipate their entry into the promised land (ch. 26). The underlying theme of the narrative is renewed hope in a new generation that is preparing to enter the land of Canaan.

The famous priestly blessing from the book of Numbers is read every year during the Feast of the Octave of Christmas, the Solemnity of Mary, Mother of God: "The LORD bless you and keep you; the LORD make his face to shine upon you, and be gracious to you; the LORD lift up his countenance upon you, and give you peace" (6.24–26).

THE FIRST CENSUS OF ISRAEL

1 The LORD spoke to Moses in the
wilderness of Sinai, in the tent of
meeting, on the first day of the second
month, in the second year after they
had come out of the land of Egypt, saying: 2Take a census of the whole congregation of Israelites, in their clans, by
ancestral houses, according to the number of names, every male individually;
3from twenty years old and upwards,
everyone in Israel able to go to war. You
and Aaron shall enrol them, company
by company. 4A man from each tribe
shall be with you, each man the head
of his ancestral house. 5These are the
names of the men who shall assist you:

From Reuben, Elizur son of Shedeur.
6 From Simeon, Shelumiel son of Zurishaddai.
7 From Judah, Nahshon son of Amminadab.
8 From Issachar, Nethanel son of Zuar.
9 From Zebulun, Eliab son of Helon.
10 From the sons of Joseph:
from Ephraim, Elishama son of Ammihud;
from Manasseh, Gamaliel son of Pedahzur.
11 From Benjamin, Abidan son of Gideoni.
12 From Dan, Ahiezer son of Ammishaddai.
13 From Asher, Pagiel son of Ochran.
14 From Gad, Eliasaph son of Deuel.
15 From Naphtali, Ahira son of Enan.

16These were the ones chosen from the
congregation, the leaders of their ancestral tribes, the heads of the divisions of
Israel.

17 Moses and Aaron took these men
who had been designated by name,
18and on the first day of the second
month they assembled the whole congregation together. They registered
themselves in their clans, by their ancestral houses, according to the number
of names from twenty years old and upwards, individually, 19as the LORD commanded Moses. So he enrolled them in
the wilderness of Sinai.

20 The descendants of Reuben, Israel's firstborn, their lineage, in their
clans, by their ancestral houses, according to the number of names, individually, every male from twenty years old
and upwards, everyone able to go to
war: 21those enrolled of the tribe of Reuben were forty-six thousand five hundred.

22 The descendants of Simeon, their
lineage, in their clans, by their ancestral houses, those of them that were
numbered, according to the number of
names, individually, every male from
twenty years old and upwards, every-

one able to go to war: 23 those enrolled
of the tribe of Simeon were fifty-nine
thousand three hundred.
24 The descendants of Gad, their
lineage, in their clans, by their ancestral houses, according to the number of
the names, from twenty years old and
upwards, everyone able to go to war:
25 those enrolled of the tribe of Gad were
forty-five thousand six hundred and
fifty.
26 The descendants of Judah, their
lineage, in their clans, by their ancestral houses, according to the number
of names, from twenty years old and
upwards, everyone able to go to war:
27 those enrolled of the tribe of Judah
were seventy-four thousand six hundred.
28 The descendants of Issachar, their
lineage, in their clans, by their ancestral houses, according to the number
of names, from twenty years old and
upwards, everyone able to go to war:
29 those enrolled of the tribe of Issachar
were fifty-four thousand four hundred.
30 The descendants of Zebulun, their
lineage, in their clans, by their ancestral houses, according to the number
of names, from twenty years old and
upwards, everyone able to go to war:
31 those enrolled of the tribe of Zebulun
were fifty-seven thousand four hundred.
32 The descendants of Joseph, namely,
the descendants of Ephraim, their
lineage, in their clans, by their ancestral houses, according to the number
of names, from twenty years old and
upwards, everyone able to go to war:
33 those enrolled of the tribe of Ephraim
were forty thousand five hundred.
34 The descendants of Manasseh,
their lineage, in their clans, by their ancestral houses, according to the number
of names, from twenty years old and
upwards, everyone able to go to war:
35 those enrolled of the tribe of Manasseh were thirty-two thousand two hundred.
36 The descendants of Benjamin,
their lineage, in their clans, by their ancestral houses, according to the number
of names, from twenty years old and
upwards, everyone able to go to war:
37 those enrolled of the tribe of Benjamin
were thirty-five thousand four hundred.
38 The descendants of Dan, their
lineage, in their clans, by their ancestral houses, according to the number
of names, from twenty years old and
upwards, everyone able to go to war:
39 those enrolled of the tribe of Dan were
sixty-two thousand seven hundred.
40 The descendants of Asher, their
lineage, in their clans, by their ancestral houses, according to the number
of names, from twenty years old and
upwards, everyone able to go to war:
41 those enrolled of the tribe of Asher
were forty-one thousand five hundred.
42 The descendants of Naphtali, their
lineage, in their clans, by their ancestral houses, according to the number
of names, from twenty years old and
upwards, everyone able to go to war:
43 those enrolled of the tribe of Naphtali were fifty-three thousand four hundred.
44 These are those who were enrolled, whom Moses and Aaron enrolled
with the help of the leaders of Israel,
twelve men, each representing his ancestral house. 45 So the whole number of
the Israelites, by their ancestral houses,
from twenty years old and upwards,
everyone able to go to war in Israel—
46 their whole number was six hundred
and three thousand five hundred and
fifty. 47 The Levites, however, were not
numbered by their ancestral tribe along
with them.
48 The LORD had said to Moses:
49 Only the tribe of Levi you shall not
enrol, and you shall not take a census of them with the other Israelites.
50 Rather you shall appoint the Levites
over the tabernacle of the covenant,[a]
and over all its equipment, and over
all that belongs to it; they are to carry
the tabernacle and all its equipment,
and they shall tend it, and shall camp
around the tabernacle. 51 When the tabernacle is to set out, the Levites shall
take it down; and when the tabernacle
is to be pitched, the Levites shall set it
up. And any outsider who comes near
shall be put to death. 52 The other Israelites shall camp in their respective
regimental camps, by companies; 53 but
the Levites shall camp around the tabernacle of the covenant,[b] so that there
may be no wrath on the congregation
of the Israelites; and the Levites shall
perform the guard duty of the tabernacle of the covenant.[c] 54 The Israelites
did so; they did just as the LORD commanded Moses.

[a] **1.50** Or *treaty*, or *testimony*; Heb *eduth* [b] **1.53** Or *treaty*, or *testimony*; Heb *eduth* [c] **1.53** Or *treaty*, or *testimony*; Heb *eduth*

THE ORDER OF ENCAMPMENT AND MARCHING

2 The LORD spoke to Moses and
Aaron, saying: 2The Israelites shall
camp each in their respective regiments, under ensigns by their ancestral houses; they shall camp facing the
tent of meeting on every side. 3Those to
camp on the east side towards the sunrise shall be of the regimental encampment of Judah by companies. The leader
of the people of Judah shall be Nahshon
son of Amminadab, 4with a company
as enrolled of seventy-four thousand six
hundred. 5Those to camp next to him
shall be the tribe of Issachar. The leader
of the Issacharites shall be Nethanel son
of Zuar, 6with a company as enrolled of
fifty-four thousand four hundred. 7Then
the tribe of Zebulun: The leader of the
Zebulunites shall be Eliab son of Helon,
8with a company as enrolled of fifty-
seven thousand four hundred. 9The total enrolment of the camp of Judah, by
companies, is one hundred and eighty-
six thousand four hundred. They shall
set out first on the march.

10 On the south side shall be the regimental encampment of Reuben by companies. The leader of the Reubenites shall
be Elizur son of Shedeur, 11with a company as enrolled of forty-six thousand five
hundred. 12And those to camp next to him
shall be the tribe of Simeon. The leader of
the Simeonites shall be Shelumiel son
of Zurishaddai, 13with a company as enrolled of fifty-nine thousand three hundred. 14Then the tribe of Gad: The leader of
the Gadites shall be Eliasaph son of Reuel,
15with a company as enrolled of forty-five
thousand six hundred and fifty. 16The total enrolment of the camp of Reuben, by
companies, is one hundred and fifty-one
thousand four hundred and fifty. They
shall set out second.

17 The tent of meeting, with the
camp of the Levites, shall set out in the
centre of the camps; they shall set out
just as they camp, each in position, by
their regiments.

18 On the west side shall be the regimental encampment of Ephraim by
companies. The leader of the people of
Ephraim shall be Elishama son of Ammihud, 19with a company as enrolled of forty
thousand five hundred. 20Next to him
shall be the tribe of Manasseh. The leader
of the people of Manasseh shall be Gamaliel son of Pedahzur, 21with a company as
enrolled of thirty-two thousand two hundred. 22Then the tribe of Benjamin: The
leader of the Benjaminites shall be Abidan son of Gideoni, 23with a company as
enrolled of thirty-five thousand four hundred. 24The total enrolment of the camp of
Ephraim, by companies, is one hundred
and eight thousand one hundred. They
shall set out third on the march.

25 On the north side shall be the regimental encampment of Dan by companies. The leader of the Danites shall be
Ahiezer son of Ammishaddai, 26with a
company as enrolled of sixty-two thousand seven hundred. 27Those to camp
next to him shall be the tribe of Asher.
The leader of the Asherites shall be Pagiel son of Ochran, 28with a company
as enrolled of forty-one thousand five
hundred. 29Then the tribe of Naphtali:
The leader of the Naphtalites shall be
Ahira son of Enan, 30with a company
as enrolled of fifty-three thousand four
hundred. 31The total enrolment of the
camp of Dan is one hundred and fifty-
seven thousand six hundred. They shall
set out last, by companies.[d]

32 This was the enrolment of the Israelites by their ancestral houses; the
total enrolment in the camps by their
companies was six hundred and three
thousand five hundred and fifty. 33Just
as the LORD had commanded Moses,
the Levites were not enrolled among
the other Israelites.

34 The Israelites did just as the LORD
had commanded Moses: They camped
by regiments, and they set out the same
way, everyone by clans, according to ancestral houses.

THE SONS OF AARON

3 This is the lineage of Aaron and Moses at the time when the LORD spoke
with Moses on Mount Sinai. 2These are
the names of the sons of Aaron: Nadab
the firstborn, and Abihu, Eleazar, and
Ithamar; 3these are the names of the
sons of Aaron, the anointed priests,
whom he ordained to minister as
priests. 4Nadab and Abihu died before
the LORD when they offered unholy
fire before the LORD in the wilderness
of Sinai, and they had no children. Eleazar and Ithamar served as priests in the
lifetime of their father Aaron.

THE DUTIES OF THE LEVITES

5 Then the LORD spoke to Moses, saying: 6Bring the tribe of Levi near, and

[d] **2.31** Compare verses 9, 16, 24: Heb *by their regiments*

set them before Aaron the priest, so that they may assist him. 7They shall perform duties for him and for the whole congregation in front of the tent of meeting, doing service at the tabernacle; 8they shall be in charge of all the furnishings of the tent of meeting, and attend to the duties for the Israelites as they do service at the tabernacle. 9You shall give the Levites to Aaron and his descendants; they are unreservedly given to him from among the Israelites. 10But you shall make a register of Aaron and his descendants; it is they who shall attend to the priesthood, and any outsider who comes near shall be put to death.

11 Then the LORD spoke to Moses, saying: 12I hereby accept the Levites from among the Israelites as substitutes for all the firstborn that open the womb among the Israelites. The Levites shall be mine, 13for all the firstborn are mine; when I killed all the firstborn in the land of Egypt, I consecrated for my own all the firstborn in Israel, both human and animal; they shall be mine. I am the LORD.

A CENSUS OF THE LEVITES

14 Then the LORD spoke to Moses in the wilderness of Sinai, saying: 15Enrol the Levites by ancestral houses and by clans. You shall enrol every male from a month old and upwards. 16So Moses enrolled them according to the word of the LORD, as he was commanded. 17The following were the sons of Levi, by their names: Gershon, Kohath, and Merari. 18These are the names of the sons of Gershon by their clans: Libni and Shimei. 19The sons of Kohath by their clans: Amram, Izhar, Hebron, and Uzziel. 20The sons of Merari by their clans: Mahli and Mushi. These are the clans of the Levites, by their ancestral houses.

21 To Gershon belonged the clan of the Libnites and the clan of the Shimeites; these were the clans of the Gershonites. 22Their enrolment, counting all the males from a month old and upwards, was seven thousand five hundred. 23The clans of the Gershonites were to camp behind the tabernacle on the west, 24with Eliasaph son of Lael as head of the ancestral house of the Gershonites. 25The responsibility of the sons of Gershon in the tent of meeting was to be the tabernacle, the tent with its covering, the screen for the entrance of the tent of meeting, 26the hangings of the court, the screen for the entrance of the court that is around the tabernacle and the altar, and its cords—all the service pertaining to these.

27 To Kohath belonged the clan of the Amramites, the clan of the Izharites, the clan of the Hebronites, and the clan of the Uzzielites; these are the clans of the Kohathites. 28Counting all the males, from a month old and upwards, there were eight thousand six hundred, attending to the duties of the sanctuary. 29The clans of the Kohathites were to camp on the south side of the tabernacle, 30with Elizaphan son of Uzziel as head of the ancestral house of the clans of the Kohathites. 31Their responsibility was to be the ark, the table, the lampstand, the altars, the vessels of the sanctuary with which the priests minister, and the screen—all the service pertaining to these. 32Eleazar son of Aaron the priest was to be chief over the leaders of the Levites, and to have oversight of those who had charge of the sanctuary.

33 To Merari belonged the clan of the Mahlites and the clan of the Mushites: these are the clans of Merari. 34Their enrolment, counting all the males from a month old and upwards, was six thousand two hundred. 35The head of the ancestral house of the clans of Merari was Zuriel son of Abihail; they were to camp on the north side of the tabernacle. 36The responsibility assigned to the sons of Merari was to be the frames of the tabernacle, the bars, the pillars, the bases, and all their accessories—all the service pertaining to these; 37also the pillars of the court all around, with their bases and pegs and cords.

38 Those who were to camp in front of the tabernacle on the east—in front of the tent of meeting towards the east—were Moses and Aaron and Aaron's sons, having charge of the rites within the sanctuary, whatever had to be done for the Israelites; and any outsider who came near was to be put to death. 39The total enrolment of the Levites whom Moses and Aaron enrolled at the commandment of the LORD, by their clans, all the males from a month old and upwards, was twenty-two thousand.

THE REDEMPTION OF THE FIRSTBORN

40 Then the LORD said to Moses: Enrol all the firstborn males of the Israelites, from a month old and upwards, and count their names. 41But you shall

accept the Levites for me—I am the
LORD—as substitutes for all the firstborn among the Israelites, and the livestock of the Levites as substitutes for
all the firstborn among the livestock of
the Israelites. 42So Moses enrolled all
the firstborn among the Israelites, as
the LORD commanded him. 43The total
enrolment, all the firstborn males from
a month old and upwards, counting
the number of names, was twenty-two
thousand two hundred and seventy-
three.

44 Then the LORD spoke to Moses,
saying: 45Accept the Levites as substitutes for all the firstborn among the Israelites, and the livestock of the Levites
as substitutes for their livestock; and the
Levites shall be mine. I am the LORD.
46As the price of redemption of the two
hundred and seventy-three of the firstborn of the Israelites, over and above
the number of the Levites, 47you shall
accept five shekels apiece, reckoning
by the shekel of the sanctuary, a shekel
of twenty gerahs. 48Give to Aaron and
his sons the money by which the excess
number of them is redeemed. 49So Moses took the redemption money from
those who were over and above those
redeemed by the Levites; 50from the
firstborn of the Israelites he took the
money, one thousand three hundred
and sixty-five shekels, reckoned by the
shekel of the sanctuary; 51and Moses
gave the redemption money to Aaron
and his sons, according to the word of
the LORD, as the LORD had commanded
Moses.

THE KOHATHITES

4 The LORD spoke to Moses and
Aaron, saying: 2Take a census of
the Kohathites separate from the other
Levites, by their clans and their ancestral houses, 3from thirty years old up
to fifty years old, all who qualify to do
work relating to the tent of meeting.
4The service of the Kohathites relating to the tent of meeting concerns the
most holy things.

5 When the camp is to set out, Aaron
and his sons shall go in and take down
the screening curtain, and cover the
ark of the covenant[e] with it; 6then they
shall put on it a covering of fine leather,[f]
and spread over that a cloth all of blue,
and shall put its poles in place. 7Over
the table of the bread of the Presence
they shall spread a blue cloth, and put
on it the plates, the dishes for incense,
the bowls, and the flagons for the drink-
offering; the regular bread also shall be
on it; 8then they shall spread over them
a crimson cloth, and cover it with a covering of fine leather,[g] and shall put its
poles in place. 9They shall take a blue
cloth, and cover the lampstand for the
light, with its lamps, its snuffers, its
trays, and all the vessels for oil with
which it is supplied; 10and they shall put
it with all its utensils in a covering of
fine leather,[h] and put it on the carrying-
frame. 11Over the golden altar they shall
spread a blue cloth, and cover it with a
covering of fine leather,[i] and shall put
its poles in place; 12and they shall take
all the utensils of the service that are
used in the sanctuary, and put them
in a blue cloth, and cover them with a
covering of fine leather,[j] and put them
on the carrying-frame. 13They shall
take away the ashes from the altar, and
spread a purple cloth over it; 14and they
shall put on it all the utensils of the altar, which are used for the service there,
the firepans, the forks, the shovels, and
the basins, all the utensils of the altar;
and they shall spread on it a covering of
fine leather,[k] and shall put its poles in
place. 15When Aaron and his sons have
finished covering the sanctuary and all
the furnishings of the sanctuary, as the
camp sets out, after that the Kohathites shall come to carry these, but they
must not touch the holy things, or they
will die. These are the things of the tent
of meeting that the Kohathites are to
carry.

16 Eleazar son of Aaron the priest
shall have charge of the oil for the light,
the fragrant incense, the regular grain-
offering, and the anointing-oil, the
oversight of all the tabernacle and all
that is in it, in the sanctuary and in its
utensils.

17 Then the LORD spoke to Moses
and Aaron, saying: 18You must not let
the tribe of the clans of the Kohathites
be destroyed from among the Levites.
19This is how you must deal with them
in order that they may live and not die
when they come near to the most holy
things: Aaron and his sons shall go in
and assign each to a particular task or
burden. 20But the Kohathites[l] must not

[e] 4.5 Or *treaty*, or *testimony*; Heb *eduth*
[f] 4.6 Meaning of Heb uncertain [g] 4.8 Meaning of Heb uncertain [h] 4.10 Meaning of Heb uncertain [i] 4.11 Meaning of Heb uncertain [j] 4.12 Meaning of Heb uncertain [k] 4.14 Meaning of Heb uncertain [l] 4.20 Heb *they*

go in to look on the holy things even for
a moment; otherwise they will die.

THE GERSHONITES AND MERARITES

21 The then the LORD spoke to Moses,
saying: 22 Take a census of the Gershonites also, by their ancestral houses and
by their clans; 23 from thirty years old up
to fifty years old you shall enrol them,
all who qualify to do work in the tent
of meeting. 24 This is the service of the
clans of the Gershonites, in serving and
bearing burdens: 25 They shall carry the
curtains of the tabernacle, and the tent
of meeting with its covering, and the
outer covering of fine leather[m] that is on
top of it, and the screen for the entrance
of the tent of meeting, 26 and the hangings of the court, and the screen for the
entrance of the gate of the court that is
around the tabernacle and the altar, and
their cords, and all the equipment for
their service; and they shall do all that
needs to be done with regard to them.
27 All the service of the Gershonites shall
be at the command of Aaron and his
sons, in all that they are to carry, and
in all that they have to do; and you shall
assign to their charge all that they are
to carry. 28 This is the service of the clans
of the Gershonites relating to the tent of
meeting, and their responsibilities are
to be under the oversight of Ithamar
son of Aaron the priest.

29 As for the Merarites, you shall enrol them by their clans and their ancestral houses; 30 from thirty years old up
to fifty years old you shall enrol them,
everyone who qualifies to do the work
of the tent of meeting. 31 This is what
they are charged to carry, as the whole
of their service in the tent of meeting:
the frames of the tabernacle, with its
bars, pillars, and bases, 32 and the pillars
of the court all around with their bases,
pegs, and cords, with all their equipment and all their related service; and
you shall assign by name the objects
that they are required to carry. 33 This is
the service of the clans of the Merarites,
the whole of their service relating to the
tent of meeting, under the hand of Ithamar son of Aaron the priest.

CENSUS OF THE LEVITES

34 So Moses and Aaron and the leaders of the congregation enrolled the Kohathites, by their clans and their ancestral houses, 35 from thirty years old up to
fifty years old, everyone who qualified
for work relating to the tent of meeting; 36 and their enrolment by clans was
two thousand seven hundred and fifty.
37 This was the enrolment of the clans
of the Kohathites, all who served at
the tent of meeting, whom Moses and
Aaron enrolled according to the commandment of the LORD by Moses.

38 The enrolment of the Gershonites, by their clans and their ancestral
houses, 39 from thirty years old up to
fifty years old, everyone who qualified
for work relating to the tent of meeting— 40 their enrolment by their clans
and their ancestral houses was two
thousand six hundred and thirty. 41 This
was the enrolment of the clans of the
Gershonites, all who served at the tent
of meeting, whom Moses and Aaron enrolled according to the commandment
of the LORD.

42 The enrolment of the clans of the
Merarites, by their clans and their ancestral houses, 43 from thirty years old
up to fifty years old, everyone who qualified for work relating to the tent of
meeting— 44 their enrolment by their
clans was three thousand two hundred.
45 This is the enrolment of the clans of
the Merarites, whom Moses and Aaron
enrolled according to the commandment of the LORD by Moses.

46 All those who were enrolled of the
Levites, whom Moses and Aaron and
the leaders of Israel enrolled, by their
clans and their ancestral houses, 47 from
thirty years old up to fifty years old, everyone who qualified to do the work of
service and the work of bearing burdens
relating to the tent of meeting, 48 their
enrolment was eight thousand five
hundred and eighty. 49 According to the
commandment of the LORD through
Moses they were appointed to their several tasks of serving or carrying; thus
they were enrolled by him, as the LORD
commanded Moses.

UNCLEAN PERSONS

5 The LORD spoke to Moses, saying:
2 Command the Israelites to put out
of the camp everyone who is leprous,[n]
or has a discharge, and everyone who is
unclean through contact with a corpse;
3 you shall put out both male and female, putting them outside the camp;
they must not defile their camp, where
I dwell among them. 4 The Israelites did
so, putting them outside the camp; as

[m] **4.25** Meaning of Heb uncertain [n] **5.2** A term for several skin diseases; precise meaning uncertain

the LORD had spoken to Moses, so the
Israelites did.

CONFESSION AND RESTITUTION

5 The LORD spoke to Moses, saying:
6Speak to the Israelites: When a man
or a woman wrongs another, breaking
faith with the LORD, that person incurs
guilt 7and shall confess the sin that has
been committed. The person shall make
full restitution for the wrong, adding
one-fifth to it, and giving it to the one
who was wronged. 8If the injured party
has no next-of-kin to whom restitution
may be made for the wrong, the restitution for wrong shall go to the LORD
for the priest, in addition to the ram of
atonement with which atonement is
made for the guilty party. 9Among all
the sacred donations of the Israelites,
every gift that they bring to the priest
shall be his. 10The sacred donations of all
are their own; whatever anyone gives to
the priest shall be his.

CONCERNING AN UNFAITHFUL WIFE

11 The LORD spoke to Moses, saying: 12Speak to the Israelites and say to
them: If any man's wife goes astray and
is unfaithful to him, 13if a man has had
intercourse with her but it is hidden
from her husband, so that she is unde-
tected though she has defiled herself,
and there is no witness against her since
she was not caught in the act; 14if a spirit
of jealousy comes on him, and he is jealous of his wife who has defiled herself;
or if a spirit of jealousy comes on him,
and he is jealous of his wife, though she
has not defiled herself; 15then the man
shall bring his wife to the priest. And
he shall bring the offering required for
her, one-tenth of an ephah of barley
flour. He shall pour no oil on it and put
no frankincense on it, for it is a grain-
offering of jealousy, a grain-offering of
remembrance, bringing iniquity to remembrance.

16 Then the priest shall bring her
near, and set her before the LORD;
17the priest shall take holy water in an
earthen vessel, and take some of the
dust that is on the floor of the tabernacle and put it into the water. 18The
priest shall set the woman before the
LORD, dishevel the woman's hair, and
place in her hands the grain-offering
of remembrance, which is the grain-
offering of jealousy. In his own hand the
priest shall have the water of bitterness
that brings the curse. 19Then the priest
shall make her take an oath, saying, 'If
no man has lain with you, if you have
not turned aside to uncleanness while
under your husband's authority, be immune to this water of bitterness that
brings the curse. 20But if you have gone
astray while under your husband's authority, if you have defiled yourself and
some man other than your husband has
had intercourse with you'— 21let the
priest make the woman take the oath
of the curse and say to the woman—
'the LORD make you an execration and
an oath among your people, when the
LORD makes your uterus drop, your
womb discharge; 22now may this water
that brings the curse enter your bowels
and make your womb discharge, your
uterus drop!' And the woman shall say,
'Amen. Amen.'

23 Then the priest shall put these
curses in writing, and wash them off
into the water of bitterness. 24He shall
make the woman drink the water of
bitterness that brings the curse, and
the water that brings the curse shall
enter her and cause bitter pain. 25The
priest shall take the grain-offering of
jealousy out of the woman's hand, and
shall elevate the grain-offering before the LORD and bring it to the altar;
26and the priest shall take a handful of
the grain-offering, as its memorial portion, and turn it into smoke on the altar,
and afterwards shall make the woman
drink the water. 27When he has made
her drink the water, then, if she has defiled herself and has been unfaithful to
her husband, the water that brings the
curse shall enter into her and cause bitter pain, and her womb shall discharge,
her uterus drop, and the woman shall
become an execration among her people. 28But if the woman has not defiled
herself and is clean, then she shall be
immune and be able to conceive children.

29 This is the law in cases of jealousy,
when a wife, while under her husband's
authority, goes astray and defiles herself, 30or when a spirit of jealousy comes
on a man and he is jealous of his wife;
then he shall set the woman before the
LORD, and the priest shall apply this entire law to her. 31The man shall be free
from iniquity, but the woman shall bear
her iniquity.

THE NAZIRITES

6 The LORD spoke to Moses, saying:
2Speak to the Israelites and say

to them: When either men or women
make a special vow, the vow of a nazirite,[o] to separate themselves to the
LORD, 3 they shall separate themselves
from wine and strong drink; they shall
drink no wine vinegar or other vinegar,
and shall not drink any grape juice or
eat grapes, fresh or dried. 4 All their days
as nazirites[p] they shall eat nothing that
is produced by the grape-vine, not even
the seeds or the skins.

5 All the days of their nazirite vow
no razor shall come upon the head; until the time is completed for which they
separate themselves to the LORD, they
shall be holy; they shall let the locks of
the head grow long.

6 All the days that they separate
themselves to the LORD they shall not
go near a corpse. 7 Even if their father
or mother, brother or sister, should die,
they may not defile themselves; because
their consecration to God is upon the
head. 8 All their days as nazirites[q] they
are holy to the LORD.

9 If someone dies very suddenly
nearby, defiling the consecrated head,
then they shall shave the head on the
day of their cleansing; on the seventh
day they shall shave it. 10 On the eighth
day they shall bring two turtle-doves or
two young pigeons to the priest at the
entrance of the tent of meeting, 11 and
the priest shall offer one as a sin-offering
and the other as a burnt-offering, and
make atonement for them, because they
incurred guilt by reason of the corpse.
They shall sanctify the head that same
day, 12 and separate themselves to the
LORD for their days as nazirites,[r] and
bring a male lamb a year old as a guilt-
offering. The former time shall be void,
because the consecrated head was defiled.

13 This is the law for the nazirites[s]
when the time of their consecration has
been completed: they shall be brought
to the entrance of the tent of meeting,
14 and they shall offer their gift to the
LORD, one male lamb a year old without blemish as a burnt-offering, one
ewe lamb a year old without blemish as
a sin-offering, one ram without blemish
as an offering of well-being, 15 and a basket of unleavened bread, cakes of choice
flour mixed with oil, and unleavened
wafers spread with oil, with their grain-
offering and their drink-offerings. 16 The
priest shall present them before the
LORD and offer their sin-offering and
burnt-offering, 17 and shall offer the ram
as a sacrifice of well-being to the LORD,
with the basket of unleavened bread;
the priest also shall make the accompa-
nying grain-offering and drink-offering.
18 Then the nazirites[t] shall shave the
consecrated head at the entrance of the
tent of meeting, and shall take the hair
from the consecrated head and put it on
the fire under the sacrifice of well-being.
19 The priest shall take the shoulder of
the ram, when it is boiled, and one unleavened cake out of the basket, and one
unleavened wafer, and shall put them
in the palms of the nazirites,[u] after
they have shaved the consecrated head.
20 Then the priest shall elevate them as
an elevation-offering before the LORD;
they are a holy portion for the priest, together with the breast that is elevated
and the thigh that is offered. After that
the nazirites[v] may drink wine.

21 This is the law for the nazirites[w]
who take a vow. Their offering to the
LORD must be in accordance with the
nazirite[x] vow, apart from what else they
can afford. In accordance with whatever
vow they take, so they shall do, following the law for their consecration.

THE PRIESTLY BENEDICTION

22 The LORD spoke to Moses, saying:
23 Speak to Aaron and his sons, saying,
Thus you shall bless the Israelites: You
shall say to them,

24 The LORD bless you and keep you;
25 the LORD make his face to
shine upon you, and
be gracious to you;
26 the LORD lift up his countenance
upon you, and give
you peace.

27 So they shall put my name on the
Israelites, and I will bless them.

OFFERINGS OF THE LEADERS

7 On the day when Moses had finished setting up the tabernacle, and
had anointed and consecrated it with
all its furnishings, and had anointed
and consecrated the altar with all its

[o] 6.2 That is *one separated* or *one consecrated* [p] 6.4 That is *those separated* or *those consecrated* [q] 6.8 That is *those separated* or *those consecrated* [r] 6.12 That is *those separated* or *those consecrated* [s] 6.13 That is *those separated* or *those consecrated* [t] 6.18 That is *those separated* or *those consecrated* [u] 6.19 That is *those separated* or *those consecrated* [v] 6.20 That is *those separated* or *those consecrated* [w] 6.21 That is *those separated* or *those consecrated* [x] 6.21 That is *one separated* or *one consecrated*

utensils, 2the leaders of Israel, heads of their ancestral houses, the leaders of the tribes, who were over those who were enrolled, made offerings. 3They brought their offerings before the LORD, six covered wagons and twelve oxen, a wagon for every two of the leaders, and for each one an ox; they presented them before the tabernacle. 4Then the LORD said to Moses: 5Accept these from them, that they may be used in performing the service of the tent of meeting, and give them to the Levites, to each according to his service. 6So Moses took the wagons and the oxen, and gave them to the Levites. 7Two wagons and four oxen he gave to the Gershonites, according to their service; 8and four wagons and eight oxen he gave to the Merarites, according to their service, under the direction of Ithamar son of Aaron the priest. 9But to the Kohathites he gave none, because they were charged with the care of the holy things that had to be carried on the shoulders.

10 The leaders also presented offerings for the dedication of the altar at the time when it was anointed; the leaders presented their offering before the altar. 11The LORD said to Moses: They shall present their offerings, one leader each day, for the dedication of the altar.

12 The one who presented his offering on the first day was Nahshon son of Amminadab, of the tribe of Judah; 13his offering was one silver plate weighing one hundred and thirty shekels, one silver basin weighing seventy shekels, according to the shekel of the sanctuary, both of them full of choice flour mixed with oil for a grain-offering; 14one golden dish weighing ten shekels, full of incense; 15one young bull, one ram, one male lamb a year old, for a burnt-offering; 16one male goat for a sin-offering; 17and for the sacrifice of well-being, two oxen, five rams, five male goats, and five male lambs a year old. This was the offering of Nahshon son of Amminadab.

18 On the second day Nethanel son of Zuar, the leader of Issachar, presented an offering; 19he presented for his offering one silver plate weighing one hundred and thirty shekels, one silver basin weighing seventy shekels, according to the shekel of the sanctuary, both of them full of choice flour mixed with oil for a grain-offering; 20one golden dish weighing ten shekels, full of incense; 21one young bull, one ram, one male lamb a year old, as a burnt-offering; 22one male goat as a sin-offering; 23and for the sacrifice of well-being, two oxen, five rams, five male goats, and five male lambs a year old. This was the offering of Nethanel son of Zuar.

24 On the third day Eliab son of Helon, the leader of the Zebulunites: 25his offering was one silver plate weighing one hundred and thirty shekels, one silver basin weighing seventy shekels, according to the shekel of the sanctuary, both of them full of choice flour mixed with oil for a grain-offering; 26one golden dish weighing ten shekels, full of incense; 27one young bull, one ram, one male lamb a year old, for a burnt-offering; 28one male goat for a sin-offering; 29and for the sacrifice of well-being, two oxen, five rams, five male goats, and five male lambs a year old. This was the offering of Eliab son of Helon.

30 On the fourth day Elizur son of Shedeur, the leader of the Reubenites: 31his offering was one silver plate weighing one hundred and thirty shekels, one silver basin weighing seventy shekels, according to the shekel of the sanctuary, both of them full of choice flour mixed with oil for a grain-offering; 32one golden dish weighing ten shekels, full of incense; 33one young bull, one ram, one male lamb a year old, for a burnt-offering; 34one male goat for a sin-offering; 35and for the sacrifice of well-being, two oxen, five rams, five male goats, and five male lambs a year old. This was the offering of Elizur son of Shedeur.

36 On the fifth day Shelumiel son of Zurishaddai, the leader of the Simeonites: 37his offering was one silver plate weighing one hundred and thirty shekels, one silver basin weighing seventy shekels, according to the shekel of the sanctuary, both of them full of choice flour mixed with oil for a grain-offering; 38one golden dish weighing ten shekels, full of incense; 39one young bull, one ram, one male lamb a year old, for a burnt-offering; 40one male goat for a sin-offering; 41and for the sacrifice of well-being, two oxen, five rams, five male goats, and five male lambs a year old. This was the offering of Shelumiel son of Zurishaddai.

42 On the sixth day Eliasaph son of Deuel, the leader of the Gadites: 43his offering was one silver plate weighing one hundred and thirty shekels, one

silver basin weighing seventy shekels,
according to the shekel of the sanctuary, both of them full of choice flour
mixed with oil for a grain-offering;
44one golden dish weighing ten shekels, full of incense; 45one young bull,
one ram, one male lamb a year old, for
a burnt-offering; 46one male goat for a
sin-offering; 47and for the sacrifice of
well-being, two oxen, five rams, five
male goats, and five male lambs a year
old. This was the offering of Eliasaph
son of Deuel.

48 On the seventh day Elishama son
of Ammihud, the leader of the Ephraimites: 49his offering was one silver
plate weighing one hundred and thirty
shekels, one silver basin weighing seventy shekels, according to the shekel
of the sanctuary, both of them full of
choice flour mixed with oil for a grain-
offering; 50one golden dish weighing
ten shekels, full of incense; 51one young
bull, one ram, one male lamb a year old,
for a burnt-offering; 52one male goat for
a sin-offering; 53and for the sacrifice of
well-being, two oxen, five rams, five
male goats, and five male lambs a year
old. This was the offering of Elishama
son of Ammihud.

54 On the eighth day Gamaliel son
of Pedahzur, the leader of the Manassites: 55his offering was one silver plate
weighing one hundred and thirty shekels, one silver basin weighing seventy
shekels, according to the shekel of the
sanctuary, both of them full of choice
flour mixed with oil for a grain-offering;
56one golden dish weighing ten shekels, full of incense; 57one young bull,
one ram, one male lamb a year old, for
a burnt-offering; 58one male goat for a
sin-offering; 59and for the sacrifice of
well-being, two oxen, five rams, five
male goats, and five male lambs a year
old. This was the offering of Gamaliel
son of Pedahzur.

60 On the ninth day Abidan son of
Gideoni, the leader of the Benjaminites: 61his offering was one silver plate
weighing one hundred and thirty shekels, one silver basin weighing seventy
shekels, according to the shekel of the
sanctuary, both of them full of choice
flour mixed with oil for a grain-offering;
62one golden dish weighing ten shekels, full of incense; 63one young bull,
one ram, one male lamb a year old, for
a burnt-offering; 64one male goat for a
sin-offering; 65and for the sacrifice of
well-being, two oxen, five rams, five
male goats, and five male lambs a year
old. This was the offering of Abidan son
of Gideoni.

66 On the tenth day Ahiezer son of
Ammishaddai, the leader of the Danites: 67his offering was one silver plate
weighing one hundred and thirty shekels, one silver basin weighing seventy
shekels, according to the shekel of the
sanctuary, both of them full of choice
flour mixed with oil for a grain-offering;
68one golden dish weighing ten shekels, full of incense; 69one young bull,
one ram, one male lamb a year old, for
a burnt-offering; 70one male goat for a
sin-offering; 71and for the sacrifice of
well-being, two oxen, five rams, five
male goats, and five male lambs a year
old. This was the offering of Ahiezer son
of Ammishaddai.

72 On the eleventh day Pagiel son
of Ochran, the leader of the Asherites: 73his offering was one silver plate
weighing one hundred and thirty shekels, one silver basin weighing seventy
shekels, according to the shekel of the
sanctuary, both of them full of choice
flour mixed with oil for a grain-offering;
74one golden dish weighing ten shekels, full of incense; 75one young bull,
one ram, one male lamb a year old, for
a burnt-offering; 76one male goat for a
sin-offering; 77and for the sacrifice of
well-being, two oxen, five rams, five
male goats, and five male lambs a year
old. This was the offering of Pagiel son
of Ochran.

78 On the twelfth day Ahira son
of Enan, the leader of the Naphtalites: 79his offering was one silver plate
weighing one hundred and thirty shekels, one silver basin weighing seventy
shekels, according to the shekel of the
sanctuary, both of them full of choice
flour mixed with oil for a grain-offering;
80one golden dish weighing ten shekels, full of incense; 81one young bull,
one ram, one male lamb a year old, for
a burnt-offering; 82one male goat for a
sin-offering; 83and for the sacrifice of
well-being, two oxen, five rams, five
male goats, and five male lambs a year
old. This was the offering of Ahira son
of Enan.

84 This was the dedication-offering
for the altar, at the time when it was
anointed, from the leaders of Israel:
twelve silver plates, twelve silver basins, twelve golden dishes, 85each silver
plate weighing one hundred and thirty
shekels and each basin seventy, all the

silver of the vessels two thousand four
hundred shekels according to the shekel
of the sanctuary, 86the twelve golden
dishes, full of incense, weighing ten
shekels apiece according to the shekel of
the sanctuary, all the gold of the dishes
being one hundred and twenty shekels;
87all the livestock for the burnt-offering
twelve bulls, twelve rams, twelve male
lambs a year old, with their grain-
offering; and twelve male goats for a
sin-offering; 88and all the livestock for
the sacrifice of well-being twenty-four
bulls, the rams sixty, the male goats
sixty, the male lambs a year old sixty.
This was the dedication-offering for the
altar, after it was anointed.

89 When Moses went into the tent
of meeting to speak with the LORD,[y] he
would hear the voice speaking to him
from above the mercy-seat[z] that was on
the ark of the covenant[a] from between
the two cherubim; thus it spoke to him.

THE SEVEN LAMPS

8 The LORD spoke to Moses, saying:
2Speak to Aaron and say to him:
When you set up the lamps, the seven
lamps shall give light in front of the
lampstand. 3Aaron did so; he set up its
lamps to give light in front of the lampstand, as the LORD had commanded
Moses. 4Now this was how the lampstand was made, out of hammered work
of gold. From its base to its flowers, it
was hammered work; according to the
pattern that the LORD had shown Moses, so he made the lampstand.

CONSECRATION AND SERVICE OF THE LEVITES

5 The LORD spoke to Moses, saying:
6Take the Levites from among the Israelites and cleanse them. 7Thus you
shall do to them, to cleanse them: sprinkle the water of purification on them,
have them shave their whole body with
a razor and wash their clothes, and so
cleanse themselves. 8Then let them
take a young bull and its grain-offering
of choice flour mixed with oil, and you
shall take another young bull for a sin-
offering. 9You shall bring the Levites
before the tent of meeting, and assemble the whole congregation of the Israelites. 10When you bring the Levites
before the LORD, the Israelites shall lay
their hands on the Levites, 11and Aaron
shall present the Levites before the
LORD as an elevation-offering from the
Israelites, that they may perform the
service of the LORD. 12The Levites shall
lay their hands on the heads of the bulls,
and he shall offer one for a sin-offering
and the other for a burnt-offering to the
LORD, to make atonement for the Levites. 13Then you shall have the Levites
stand before Aaron and his sons, and
you shall present them as an elevation-
offering to the LORD.

14 Thus you shall separate the Levites from among the other Israelites,
and the Levites shall be mine. 15There-
after the Levites may go in to perform
service at the tent of meeting, once you
have cleansed them and presented them
as an elevation-offering. 16For they are
unreservedly given to me from among
the Israelites; I have taken them for myself, in place of all that open the womb,
the firstborn of all the Israelites. 17For
all the firstborn among the Israelites are
mine, both human and animal. On the
day that I struck down all the firstborn
in the land of Egypt I consecrated them
for myself, 18but I have taken the Levites in place of all the firstborn among
the Israelites. 19Moreover, I have given
the Levites as a gift to Aaron and his
sons from among the Israelites, to do
the service for the Israelites at the tent
of meeting, and to make atonement for
the Israelites, in order that there may be
no plague among the Israelites for coming too close to the sanctuary.

20 Moses and Aaron and the whole
congregation of the Israelites did with
the Levites accordingly; the Israelites
did with the Levites just as the LORD
had commanded Moses concerning
them. 21The Levites purified themselves
from sin and washed their clothes; then
Aaron presented them as an elevation-
offering before the LORD, and Aaron
made atonement for them to cleanse
them. 22Thereafter the Levites went in
to perform their service in the tent of
meeting in attendance on Aaron and
his sons. As the LORD had commanded
Moses concerning the Levites, so they
dealt with them.

23 The LORD spoke to Moses, saying: 24This applies to the Levites: from
twenty-five years old and upwards they
shall begin to do duty in the service of
the tent of meeting; 25and from the age
of fifty years they shall retire from the
duty of the service and serve no more.
26They may assist their brothers in the
tent of meeting in carrying out their du-

[y] 7.89 Heb *him* [z] 7.89 Or *the cover* [a] 7.89 Or *treaty*, or *testimony*; Heb *eduth*

ties, but they shall perform no service.
Thus you shall deal with the Levites in
assigning their duties.

THE PASSOVER AT SINAI

9 The LORD spoke to Moses in the wilderness of Sinai, in the first month
of the second year after they had come
out of the land of Egypt, saying: 2Let
the Israelites keep the passover at its appointed time. 3On the fourteenth day of
this month, at twilight,[b] you shall keep it
at its appointed time; according to all its
statutes and all its regulations you shall
keep it. 4So Moses told the Israelites that
they should keep the passover. 5They
kept the passover in the first month, on
the fourteenth day of the month, at twilight,[c] in the wilderness of Sinai. Just as
the LORD had commanded Moses, so the
Israelites did. 6Now there were certain
people who were unclean through touching a corpse, so that they could not keep
the passover on that day. They came before Moses and Aaron on that day, 7and
said to him, 'Although we are unclean
through touching a corpse, why must
we be kept from presenting the LORD's
offering at its appointed time among the
Israelites?' 8Moses spoke to them, 'Wait,
so that I may hear what the LORD will
command concerning you.'

9 The LORD spoke to Moses, saying:
10Speak to the Israelites, saying: Anyone of you or your descendants who is
unclean through touching a corpse, or
is away on a journey, shall still keep the
passover to the LORD. 11In the second
month on the fourteenth day, at twilight,[d] they shall keep it; they shall eat it
with unleavened bread and bitter herbs.
12They shall leave none of it until morning, nor break a bone of it; according to
all the statute for the passover they shall
keep it. 13But anyone who is clean and is
not on a journey, and yet refrains from
keeping the passover, shall be cut off
from the people for not presenting the
LORD's offering at its appointed time;
such a one shall bear the consequences
for the sin. 14Any alien residing among
you who wishes to keep the passover to
the LORD shall do so according to the
statute of the passover and according to
its regulation; you shall have one statute for both the resident alien and the
native.

THE CLOUD AND THE FIRE

15 On the day the tabernacle was set
up, the cloud covered the tabernacle,
the tent of the covenant;[e] and from evening until morning it was over the tabernacle, having the appearance of fire.
16It was always so: the cloud covered it
by day[f] and the appearance of fire by
night. 17Whenever the cloud lifted from
over the tent, then the Israelites would
set out; and in the place where the cloud
settled down, there the Israelites would
camp. 18At the command of the LORD
the Israelites would set out, and at
the command of the LORD they would
camp. As long as the cloud rested over
the tabernacle, they would remain in
camp. 19Even when the cloud continued
over the tabernacle for many days, the
Israelites would keep the charge of the
LORD, and would not set out. 20Some-
times the cloud would remain for a few
days over the tabernacle, and according
to the command of the LORD they would
remain in camp; then according to the
command of the LORD they would set
out. 21Sometimes the cloud would remain from evening until morning; and
when the cloud lifted in the morning,
they would set out, or if it continued for
a day and a night, when the cloud lifted
they would set out. 22Whether it was
two days, or a month, or a longer time,
that the cloud continued over the tabernacle, resting upon it, the Israelites
would remain in camp and would not
set out; but when it lifted they would
set out. 23At the command of the LORD
they would camp, and at the command
of the LORD they would set out. They
kept the charge of the LORD, at the command of the LORD by Moses.

THE SILVER TRUMPETS

10 The LORD spoke to Moses, saying: 2Make two silver trumpets;
you shall make them of hammered
work; and you shall use them for summoning the congregation, and for
breaking camp. 3When both are blown,
the whole congregation shall assemble
before you at the entrance of the tent
of meeting. 4But if only one is blown,
then the leaders, the heads of the tribes
of Israel, shall assemble before you.
5When you blow an alarm, the camps
on the east side shall set out; 6when you
blow a second alarm, the camps on the
south side shall set out. An alarm is to
be blown whenever they are to set out.

[b] 9.3 Heb *between the two evenings* [c] 9.5 Heb *between the two evenings* [d] 9.11 Heb *between the two evenings* [e] 9.15 Or *treaty*, or *testimony*; Heb *eduth* [f] 9.16 Gk Syr Vg: Heb lacks *by day*

7 But when the assembly is to be gathered, you shall blow, but you shall not
sound an alarm. 8 The sons of Aaron, the
priests, shall blow the trumpets; this
shall be a perpetual institution for you
throughout your generations. 9 When
you go to war in your land against the
adversary who oppresses you, you shall
sound an alarm with the trumpets, so
that you may be remembered before
the LORD your God and be saved from
your enemies. 10 Also on your days of
rejoicing, at your appointed festivals,
and at the beginnings of your months,
you shall blow the trumpets over your
burnt-offerings and over your sacrifices
of well-being; they shall serve as a reminder on your behalf before the LORD
your God: I am the LORD your God.

DEPARTURE FROM SINAI

11 In the second year, in the second month, on the twentieth day of
the month, the cloud lifted from over
the tabernacle of the covenant.[g] 12 Then
the Israelites set out by stages from the
wilderness of Sinai, and the cloud settled down in the wilderness of Paran.
13 They set out for the first time at the
command of the LORD by Moses. 14 The
standard of the camp of Judah set out
first, company by company, and over
the whole company was Nahshon son
of Amminadab. 15 Over the company of
the tribe of Issachar was Nethanel son
of Zuar; 16 and over the company of the
tribe of Zebulun was Eliab son of Helon.

17 Then the tabernacle was taken
down, and the Gershonites and the Merarites, who carried the tabernacle, set
out. 18 Next the standard of the camp of
Reuben set out, company by company;
and over the whole company was Elizur
son of Shedeur. 19 Over the company of
the tribe of Simeon was Shelumiel son
of Zurishaddai, 20 and over the company
of the tribe of Gad was Eliasaph son of
Deuel.

21 Then the Kohathites, who carried
the holy things, set out; and the tabernacle was set up before their arrival.
22 Next the standard of the Ephraimite
camp set out, company by company,
and over the whole company was Elishama son of Ammihud. 23 Over the company of the tribe of Manasseh was Gamaliel son of Pedahzur, 24 and over the
company of the tribe of Benjamin was
Abidan son of Gideoni.

25 Then the standard of the camp of
Dan, acting as the rearguard of all the
camps, set out, company by company,
and over the whole company was Ahiezer son of Ammishaddai. 26 Over the
company of the tribe of Asher was Pagiel son of Ochran, 27 and over the company of the tribe of Naphtali was Ahira
son of Enan. 28 This was the order of
march of the Israelites, company by
company, when they set out.

29 Moses said to Hobab son of Reuel
the Midianite, Moses' father-in-law, 'We
are setting out for the place of which the
LORD said, "I will give it to you"; come
with us, and we will treat you well; for
the LORD has promised good to Israel.'
30 But he said to him, 'I will not go, but I
will go back to my own land and to my
kindred.' 31 He said, 'Do not leave us, for
you know where we should camp in the
wilderness, and you will serve as eyes
for us. 32 Moreover, if you go with us,
whatever good the LORD does for us, the
same we will do for you.'

33 So they set out from the mount of
the LORD on three days' journey with
the ark of the covenant of the LORD going before them for three days' journey,
to seek out a resting-place for them,
34 the cloud of the LORD being over them
by day when they set out from the camp.

35 Whenever the ark set out, Moses
would say,

'Arise, O LORD, let your enemies
be scattered,
and your foes flee before you.'

36 And whenever it came to rest, he
would say,

'Return, O LORD of the ten thousand
thousands of Israel.'[h]

COMPLAINING IN THE DESERT

11 Now when the people complained in the hearing of the
LORD about their misfortunes, the
LORD heard it and his anger was kindled. Then the fire of the LORD burned
against them, and consumed some out-
lying parts of the camp. 2 But the people
cried out to Moses; and Moses prayed to
the LORD, and the fire abated. 3 So that
place was called Taberah,[i] because the
fire of the LORD burned against them.

4 The rabble among them had a
strong craving; and the Israelites also
wept again, and said, 'If only we had
meat to eat! 5 We remember the fish we
used to eat in Egypt for nothing, the
cucumbers, the melons, the leeks, the

[g] **10.11** Or *treaty*, or *testimony*; Heb *eduth*
[h] **10.36** Meaning of Heb uncertain [i] **11.3** That is *Burning*

onions, and the garlic; 6 but now our strength is dried up, and there is nothing at all but this manna to look at.'

7 Now the manna was like coriander seed, and its colour was like the colour of gum resin. 8 The people went around and gathered it, ground it in mills or beat it in mortars, then boiled it in pots and made cakes of it; and the taste of it was like the taste of cakes baked with oil. 9 When the dew fell on the camp in the night, the manna would fall with it.

10 Moses heard the people weeping throughout their families, all at the entrances of their tents. Then the LORD became very angry, and Moses was displeased. 11 So Moses said to the LORD, 'Why have you treated your servant so badly? Why have I not found favour in your sight, that you lay the burden of all this people on me? 12 Did I conceive all this people? Did I give birth to them, that you should say to me, "Carry them in your bosom, as a nurse carries a sucking child, to the land that you promised on oath to their ancestors"? 13 Where am I to get meat to give to all this people? For they come weeping to me and say, "Give us meat to eat!" 14 I am not able to carry all this people alone, for they are too heavy for me. 15 If this is the way you are going to treat me, put me to death at once—if I have found favour in your sight—and do not let me see my misery.'

THE SEVENTY ELDERS

16 So the LORD said to Moses, 'Gather for me seventy of the elders of Israel, whom you know to be the elders of the people and officers over them; bring them to the tent of meeting, and have them take their place there with you. 17 I will come down and talk with you there; and I will take some of the spirit that is on you and put it on them; and they shall bear the burden of the people along with you so that you will not bear it all by yourself. 18 And say to the people: Consecrate yourselves for tomorrow, and you shall eat meat; for you have wailed in the hearing of the LORD, saying, "If only we had meat to eat! Surely it was better for us in Egypt." Therefore the LORD will give you meat, and you shall eat. 19 You shall eat not only one day, or two days, or five days, or ten days, or twenty days, 20 but for a whole month—until it comes out of your nostrils and becomes loathsome to you—because you have rejected the LORD who is among you, and have wailed before him, saying, "Why did we ever leave Egypt?" ' 21 But Moses said, 'The people I am with number six hundred thousand on foot; and you say, "I will give them meat, that they may eat for a whole month"! 22 Are there enough flocks and herds to slaughter for them? Are there enough fish in the sea to catch for them?' 23 The LORD said to Moses, 'Is the LORD's power limited?[j] Now you shall see whether my word will come true for you or not.'

24 So Moses went out and told the people the words of the LORD; and he gathered seventy elders of the people, and placed them all around the tent. 25 Then the LORD came down in the cloud and spoke to him, and took some of the spirit that was on him and put it on the seventy elders; and when the spirit rested upon them, they prophesied. But they did not do so again.

26 Two men remained in the camp, one named Eldad, and the other named Medad, and the spirit rested on them; they were among those registered, but they had not gone out to the tent, and so they prophesied in the camp. 27 And a young man ran and told Moses, 'Eldad and Medad are prophesying in the camp.' 28 And Joshua son of Nun, the assistant of Moses, one of his chosen men,[k] said, 'My lord Moses, stop them!' 29 But Moses said to him, 'Are you jealous for my sake? Would that all the LORD's people were prophets, and that the LORD would put his spirit on them!' 30 And Moses and the elders of Israel returned to the camp.

THE QUAILS

31 Then a wind went out from the LORD, and it brought quails from the sea and let them fall beside the camp, about a day's journey on this side and a day's journey on the other side, all around the camp, about two cubits deep on the ground. 32 So the people worked all that day and night and all the next day, gathering the quails; the least anyone gathered was ten homers; and they spread them out for themselves all around the camp. 33 But while the meat was still between their teeth, before it was consumed, the anger of the LORD was kindled against the people, and the LORD struck the people with a very great plague. 34 So that place was called Kibroth-hattaavah,[l] because there they

[j] **11.23** Heb *LORD's hand too short?* [k] **11.28** Or *of Moses from his youth* [l] **11.34** That is *Graves of craving*

buried the people who had the craving. 35 From Kibroth-hattaavah the people journeyed to Hazeroth.

AARON AND MIRIAM JEALOUS OF MOSES

12 While they were at Hazeroth, Miriam and Aaron spoke against Moses because of the Cushite woman whom he had married (for he had indeed married a Cushite woman); 2 and they said, 'Has the LORD spoken only through Moses? Has he not spoken through us also?' And the LORD heard it. 3 Now the man Moses was very humble,[m] more so than anyone else on the face of the earth. 4 Suddenly the LORD said to Moses, Aaron, and Miriam, 'Come out, you three, to the tent of meeting.' So the three of them came out. 5 Then the LORD came down in a pillar of cloud, and stood at the entrance of the tent, and called Aaron and Miriam; and they both came forward. 6 And he said, 'Hear my words:

When there are prophets among you,
  I the LORD make myself known
    to them in visions;
  I speak to them in dreams.
7 Not so with my servant Moses;
  he is entrusted with all my house.
8 With him I speak face to face—
    clearly, not in riddles;
  and he beholds the form
    of the LORD.

Why then were you not afraid to speak against my servant Moses?' 9 And the anger of the LORD was kindled against them, and he departed.

10 When the cloud went away from over the tent, Miriam had become leprous,[n] as white as snow. And Aaron turned towards Miriam and saw that she was leprous. 11 Then Aaron said to Moses, 'Oh, my lord, do not punish us[o] for a sin that we have so foolishly committed. 12 Do not let her be like one stillborn, whose flesh is half consumed when it comes out of its mother's womb.' 13 And Moses cried to the LORD, 'O God, please heal her.' 14 But the LORD said to Moses, 'If her father had but spat in her face, would she not bear her shame for seven days? Let her be shut out of the camp for seven days, and after that she may be brought in again.' 15 So Miriam was shut out of the camp for seven days; and the people did not set out on the march until Miriam had been brought in again. 16 After that the people set out from Hazeroth, and camped in the wilderness of Paran.

SPIES SENT INTO CANAAN

13 The LORD said to Moses, 2 'Send men to spy out the land of Canaan, which I am giving to the Israelites; from each of their ancestral tribes you shall send a man, every one a leader among them.' 3 So Moses sent them from the wilderness of Paran, according to the command of the LORD, all of them leading men among the Israelites. 4 These were their names: From the tribe of Reuben, Shammua son of Zaccur; 5 from the tribe of Simeon, Shaphat son of Hori; 6 from the tribe of Judah, Caleb son of Jephunneh; 7 from the tribe of Issachar, Igal son of Joseph; 8 from the tribe of Ephraim, Hoshea son of Nun; 9 from the tribe of Benjamin, Palti son of Raphu; 10 from the tribe of Zebulun, Gaddiel son of Sodi; 11 from the tribe of Joseph (that is, from the tribe of Manasseh), Gaddi son of Susi; 12 from the tribe of Dan, Ammiel son of Gemalli; 13 from the tribe of Asher, Sethur son of Michael; 14 from the tribe of Naphtali, Nahbi son of Vophsi; 15 from the tribe of Gad, Geuel son of Machi. 16 These were the names of the men whom Moses sent to spy out the land. And Moses changed the name of Hoshea son of Nun to Joshua.

17 Moses sent them to spy out the land of Canaan, and said to them, 'Go up there into the Negeb, and go up into the hill country, 18 and see what the land is like, and whether the people who live in it are strong or weak, whether they are few or many, 19 and whether the land they live in is good or bad, and whether the towns that they live in are unwalled or fortified, 20 and whether the land is rich or poor, and whether there are trees in it or not. Be bold, and bring some of the fruit of the land.' Now it was the season of the first ripe grapes.

21 So they went up and spied out the land from the wilderness of Zin to Rehob, near Lebo-hamath. 22 They went up into the Negeb, and came to Hebron; and Ahiman, Sheshai, and Talmai, the Anakites, were there. (Hebron was built seven years before Zoan in Egypt.) 23 And they came to the Wadi Eshcol, and cut down from there a branch with a single cluster of grapes, and they carried it on a pole between two of them. They also brought some pomegranates and figs. 24 That place was called the

[m] 12.3 Or *devout* [n] 12.10 A term for several skin diseases; precise meaning uncertain
[o] 12.11 Heb *do not lay sin upon us*

Wadi Eshcol,[p] because of the cluster that
the Israelites cut down from there.

THE REPORT OF THE SPIES

25 At the end of forty days they returned from spying out the land. 26 And
they came to Moses and Aaron and to
all the congregation of the Israelites in
the wilderness of Paran, at Kadesh; they
brought back word to them and to all
the congregation, and showed them the
fruit of the land. 27 And they told him,
'We came to the land to which you sent
us; it flows with milk and honey, and
this is its fruit. 28 Yet the people who live
in the land are strong, and the towns
are fortified and very large; and besides,
we saw the descendants of Anak there.
29 The Amalekites live in the land of the
Negeb; the Hittites, the Jebusites, and
the Amorites live in the hill country;
and the Canaanites live by the sea, and
along the Jordan.'

30 But Caleb quieted the people before Moses, and said, 'Let us go up at
once and occupy it, for we are well able
to overcome it.' 31 Then the men who had
gone up with him said, 'We are not able
to go up against this people, for they are
stronger than we are.' 32 So they brought
to the Israelites an unfavourable report of the land that they had spied
out, saying, 'The land that we have gone
through as spies is a land that devours
its inhabitants; and all the people that
we saw in it are of great size. 33 There we
saw the Nephilim (the Anakites come
from the Nephilim); and to ourselves
we seemed like grasshoppers, and so we
seemed to them.'

THE PEOPLE REBEL

14 Then all the congregation raised
a loud cry, and the people wept
that night. 2 And all the Israelites complained against Moses and Aaron;
the whole congregation said to them,
'Would that we had died in the land
of Egypt! Or would that we had died
in this wilderness! 3 Why is the LORD
bringing us into this land to fall by the
sword? Our wives and our little ones
will become booty; would it not be better for us to go back to Egypt?' 4 So they
said to one another, 'Let us choose a captain, and go back to Egypt.'

5 Then Moses and Aaron fell on their
faces before all the assembly of the congregation of the Israelites. 6 And Joshua
son of Nun and Caleb son of Jephunneh,
who were among those who had spied
out the land, tore their clothes 7 and said
to all the congregation of the Israelites, 'The land that we went through as
spies is an exceedingly good land. 8 If the
LORD is pleased with us, he will bring
us into this land and give it to us, a land
that flows with milk and honey. 9 Only,
do not rebel against the LORD; and do
not fear the people of the land, for they
are no more than bread for us; their protection is removed from them, and the
LORD is with us; do not fear them.' 10 But
the whole congregation threatened to
stone them.

Then the glory of the LORD appeared
at the tent of meeting to all the Israelites. 11 And the LORD said to Moses,
'How long will this people despise me?
And how long will they refuse to believe
in me, in spite of all the signs that I have
done among them? 12 I will strike them
with pestilence and disinherit them,
and I will make of you a nation greater
and mightier than they.'

MOSES INTERCEDES FOR THE PEOPLE

13 But Moses said to the LORD, 'Then
the Egyptians will hear of it, for in
your might you brought up this people
from among them, 14 and they will tell
the inhabitants of this land. They have
heard that you, O LORD, are in the midst
of this people; for you, O LORD, are seen
face to face, and your cloud stands over
them and you go in front of them, in a
pillar of cloud by day and in a pillar of
fire by night. 15 Now if you kill this people all at one time, then the nations who
have heard about you will say, 16 "It is
because the LORD was not able to bring
this people into the land he swore to
give them that he has slaughtered them
in the wilderness." 17 And now, therefore, let the power of the LORD be great
in the way that you promised when you
spoke, saying,

18 "The LORD is slow to anger,
and abounding in steadfast love,
forgiving iniquity and transgression,
but by no means clearing the guilty,
visiting the iniquity of the parents
upon the children
to the third and the fourth
generation."

19 Forgive the iniquity of this people according to the greatness of your steadfast love, just as you have pardoned this
people, from Egypt even until now.'

[p] 13.24 That is *Cluster*

20 Then the LORD said, 'I do forgive,
just as you have asked; 21 nevertheless—
as I live, and as all the earth shall be filled
with the glory of the LORD— 22 none of
the people who have seen my glory and
the signs that I did in Egypt and in the
wilderness, and yet have tested me these
ten times and have not obeyed my voice,
23 shall see the land that I swore to give
to their ancestors; none of those who despised me shall see it. 24 But my servant
Caleb, because he has a different spirit
and has followed me wholeheartedly, I
will bring into the land into which he
went, and his descendants shall possess
it. 25 Now, since the Amalekites and the
Canaanites live in the valleys, turn tomorrow and set out for the wilderness
by the way to the Red Sea.'[q]

AN ATTEMPTED INVASION IS REPULSED

26 And the LORD spoke to Moses and
to Aaron, saying: 27 How long shall this
wicked congregation complain against
me? I have heard the complaints of the
Israelites, which they complain against
me. 28 Say to them, 'As I live', says the
LORD, 'I will do to you the very things I
heard you say: 29 your dead bodies shall
fall in this very wilderness; and of all
your number, included in the census,
from twenty years old and upwards,
who have complained against me, 30 not
one of you shall come into the land in
which I swore to settle you, except Caleb son of Jephunneh and Joshua son
of Nun. 31 But your little ones, who you
said would become booty, I will bring
in, and they shall know the land that
you have despised. 32 But as for you, your
dead bodies shall fall in this wilderness.
33 And your children shall be shepherds
in the wilderness for forty years, and
shall suffer for your faithlessness, until
the last of your dead bodies lies in the
wilderness. 34 According to the number
of the days in which you spied out the
land, forty days, for every day a year, you
shall bear your iniquity, forty years, and
you shall know my displeasure.' 35 I the
LORD have spoken; surely I will do thus
to all this wicked congregation gathered
together against me: in this wilderness
they shall come to a full end, and there
they shall die.

36 And the men whom Moses sent
to spy out the land, who returned and
made all the congregation complain
against him by bringing a bad report about the land— 37 the men who
brought an unfavourable report about
the land died by a plague before the
LORD. 38 But Joshua son of Nun and Caleb son of Jephunneh alone remained
alive, of those men who went to spy out
the land.

39 When Moses told these words to
all the Israelites, the people mourned
greatly. 40 They rose early in the morning and went up to the heights of the
hill country, saying, 'Here we are. We
will go up to the place that the LORD
has promised, for we have sinned.' 41 But
Moses said, 'Why do you continue to
transgress the command of the LORD?
That will not succeed. 42 Do not go up,
for the LORD is not with you; do not let
yourselves be struck down before your
enemies. 43 For the Amalekites and the
Canaanites will confront you there, and
you shall fall by the sword; because you
have turned back from following the
LORD, the LORD will not be with you.'
44 But they presumed to go up to the
heights of the hill country, even though
the ark of the covenant of the LORD, and
Moses, had not left the camp. 45 Then
the Amalekites and the Canaanites who
lived in that hill country came down
and defeated them, pursuing them as
far as Hormah.

VARIOUS OFFERINGS

15 The LORD spoke to Moses, saying: 2 Speak to the Israelites and
say to them: When you come into the
land you are to inhabit, which I am giving you, 3 and you make an offering by
fire to the LORD from the herd or from
the flock—whether a burnt-offering or
a sacrifice, to fulfil a vow or as a freewill-
offering or at your appointed festivals—
to make a pleasing odour for the LORD,
4 then whoever presents such an offering to the LORD shall present also a
grain-offering, one-tenth of an ephah
of choice flour, mixed with one-fourth
of a hin of oil. 5 Moreover, you shall offer
one-fourth of a hin of wine as a drink-
offering with the burnt-offering or the
sacrifice, for each lamb. 6 For a ram,
you shall offer a grain-offering, two-
tenths of an ephah of choice flour mixed
with one-third of a hin of oil; 7 and as a
drink-offering you shall offer one-third
of a hin of wine, a pleasing odour to
the LORD. 8 When you offer a bull as a
burnt-offering or a sacrifice, to fulfil a
vow or as an offering of well-being to

[q] **14.25** Or *Sea of Reeds*

the LORD, 9 then you shall present with the bull a grain-offering, three-tenths of an ephah of choice flour, mixed with half a hin of oil, 10 and you shall present as a drink-offering half a hin of wine, as an offering by fire, a pleasing odour to the LORD.

11 Thus it shall be done for each ox or ram, or for each of the male lambs or the kids. 12 According to the number that you offer, so you shall do with each and every one. 13 Every native Israelite shall do these things in this way, in presenting an offering by fire, a pleasing odour to the LORD. 14 An alien who lives with you, or who takes up permanent residence among you, and wishes to offer an offering by fire, a pleasing odour to the LORD, shall do as you do. 15 As for the assembly, there shall be for both you and the resident alien a single statute, a perpetual statute throughout your generations; you and the alien shall be alike before the LORD. 16 You and the alien who resides with you shall have the same law and the same ordinance.

17 The LORD spoke to Moses, saying: 18 Speak to the Israelites and say to them: After you come into the land to which I am bringing you, 19 whenever you eat of the bread of the land, you shall present a donation to the LORD. 20 From your first batch of dough you shall present a loaf as a donation; you shall present it just as you present a donation from the threshing-floor. 21 Throughout your generations you shall give to the LORD a donation from the first of your batch of dough.

22 But if you unintentionally fail to observe all these commandments that the LORD has spoken to Moses— 23 everything that the LORD has commanded you by Moses, from the day the LORD gave commandment and thereafter, throughout your generations— 24 then if it was done unintentionally without the knowledge of the congregation, the whole congregation shall offer one young bull for a burnt-offering, a pleasing odour to the LORD, together with its grain-offering and its drink-offering, according to the ordinance, and one male goat for a sin-offering. 25 The priest shall make atonement for all the congregation of the Israelites, and they shall be forgiven; it was unintentional, and they have brought their offering, an offering by fire to the LORD, and their sin-offering before the LORD, for their error. 26 All the congregation of the Israelites shall be forgiven, as well as the aliens residing among them, because the whole people was involved in the error.

27 An individual who sins unintentionally shall present a female goat a year old for a sin-offering. 28 And the priest shall make atonement before the LORD for the one who commits an error, when it is unintentional, to make atonement for the person, who then shall be forgiven. 29 For both the native among the Israelites and the alien residing among them—you shall have the same law for anyone who acts in error. 30 But whoever acts high-handedly, whether a native or an alien, affronts the LORD, and shall be cut off from among the people. 31 Because of having despised the word of the LORD and broken his commandment, such a person shall be utterly cut off and bear the guilt.

PENALTY FOR VIOLATING THE SABBATH

32 When the Israelites were in the wilderness, they found a man gathering sticks on the sabbath day. 33 Those who found him gathering sticks brought him to Moses, Aaron, and to the whole congregation. 34 They put him in custody, because it was not clear what should be done to him. 35 Then the LORD said to Moses, 'The man shall be put to death; all the congregation shall stone him outside the camp.' 36 The whole congregation brought him outside the camp and stoned him to death, just as the LORD had commanded Moses.

FRINGES ON GARMENTS

37 The LORD said to Moses: 38 Speak to the Israelites, and tell them to make fringes on the corners of their garments throughout their generations and to put a blue cord on the fringe at each corner. 39 You have the fringe so that, when you see it, you will remember all the commandments of the LORD and do them, and not follow the lust of your own heart and your own eyes. 40 So you shall remember and do all my commandments, and you shall be holy to your God. 41 I am the LORD your God, who brought you out of the land of Egypt, to be your God: I am the LORD your God.

REVOLT OF KORAH, DATHAN, AND ABIRAM

16 Now Korah son of Izhar son of Kohath son of Levi, along

with Dathan and Abiram sons of Eliab,
and On son of Peleth—descendants of
Reuben—took 2two hundred and fifty
Israelite men, leaders of the congregation, chosen from the assembly, well-
known men,[r] and they confronted Moses. 3They assembled against Moses and
against Aaron, and said to them, 'You
have gone too far! All the congregation
are holy, every one of them, and the
LORD is among them. So why then do
you exalt yourselves above the assembly
of the LORD?' 4When Moses heard it, he
fell on his face. 5Then he said to Korah
and all his company, 'In the morning
the LORD will make known who is his,
and who is holy, and who will be allowed to approach him; the one whom
he will choose he will allow to approach
him. 6Do this: take censers, Korah and
all your[s] company, 7and tomorrow put
fire in them, and lay incense on them
before the LORD; and the man whom
the LORD chooses shall be the holy one.
You Levites have gone too far!' 8Then
Moses said to Korah, 'Hear now, you
Levites! 9Is it too little for you that the
God of Israel has separated you from the
congregation of Israel, to allow you to
approach him in order to perform the
duties of the LORD's tabernacle, and to
stand before the congregation and serve
them? 10He has allowed you to approach
him, and all your brother Levites with
you; yet you seek the priesthood as
well! 11Therefore you and all your company have gathered together against
the LORD. What is Aaron that you rail
against him?'

12 Moses sent for Dathan and Abiram sons of Eliab; but they said, 'We will
not come! 13Is it too little that you have
brought us up out of a land flowing with
milk and honey to kill us in the wilderness, that you must also lord it over us?
14It is clear you have not brought us into
a land flowing with milk and honey, or
given us an inheritance of fields and
vineyards. Would you put out the eyes
of these men? We will not come!'

15 Moses was very angry and said
to the LORD, 'Pay no attention to their
offering. I have not taken one donkey
from them, and I have not harmed any
one of them.' 16And Moses said to Korah, 'As for you and all your company,
be present tomorrow before the LORD,
you and they and Aaron; 17and let each
one of you take his censer, and put incense on it, and each one of you present
his censer before the LORD, two hundred and fifty censers; you also, and
Aaron, each his censer.' 18So each man
took his censer, and they put fire in the
censers and laid incense on them, and
they stood at the entrance of the tent of
meeting with Moses and Aaron. 19Then
Korah assembled the whole congregation against them at the entrance of the
tent of meeting. And the glory of the
LORD appeared to the whole congregation.

20 Then the LORD spoke to Moses and
to Aaron, saying: 21Separate yourselves
from this congregation, so that I may
consume them in a moment. 22They fell
on their faces, and said, 'O God, the God
of the spirits of all flesh, shall one person sin and you become angry with the
whole congregation?'

23 And the LORD spoke to Moses,
saying: 24Say to the congregation: Get
away from the dwellings of Korah, Dathan, and Abiram. 25So Moses got up
and went to Dathan and Abiram; the
elders of Israel followed him. 26He said
to the congregation, 'Turn away from
the tents of these wicked men, and
touch nothing of theirs, or you will be
swept away for all their sins.' 27So they
got away from the dwellings of Korah,
Dathan, and Abiram; and Dathan and
Abiram came out and stood at the entrance of their tents, together with their
wives, their children, and their little
ones. 28And Moses said, 'This is how you
shall know that the LORD has sent me to
do all these works; it has not been of my
own accord: 29If these people die a natural death, or if a natural fate comes on
them, then the LORD has not sent me.
30But if the LORD creates something
new, and the ground opens its mouth
and swallows them up, with all that belongs to them, and they go down alive
into Sheol, then you shall know that
these men have despised the LORD.'

31 As soon as he finished speaking
all these words, the ground under them
was split apart. 32The earth opened its
mouth and swallowed them up, along
with their households—everyone who
belonged to Korah and all their goods.
33So they with all that belonged to them
went down alive into Sheol; the earth
closed over them, and they perished
from the midst of the assembly. 34All
Israel around them fled at their outcry,
for they said, 'The earth will swallow us

[r] 16.2 Cn: Heb *and they confronted Moses, and two hundred and fifty men . . . well-known men*
[s] 16.6 Heb *his*

too!' 35And fire came out from the LORD
and consumed the two hundred and
fifty men offering the incense.
36[t] Then the LORD spoke to Moses,
saying: 37Tell Eleazar son of Aaron the
priest to take the censers out of the
blaze; then scatter the fire far and wide.
38For the censers of these sinners have
become holy at the cost of their lives.
Make them into hammered plates as
a covering for the altar, for they presented them before the LORD and they
became holy. Thus they shall be a sign
to the Israelites. 39So Eleazar the priest
took the bronze censers that had been
presented by those who were burned;
and they were hammered out as a covering for the altar— 40a reminder to the
Israelites that no outsider, who is not
of the descendants of Aaron, shall approach to offer incense before the LORD,
so as not to become like Korah and his
company—just as the LORD had said to
him through Moses.
41 On the next day, however, the
whole congregation of the Israelites
rebelled against Moses and against
Aaron, saying, 'You have killed the people of the LORD.' 42And when the congregation had assembled against them,
Moses and Aaron turned towards the
tent of meeting; the cloud had covered
it and the glory of the LORD appeared.
43Then Moses and Aaron came to the
front of the tent of meeting, 44and the
LORD spoke to Moses, saying, 45'Get
away from this congregation, so that I
may consume them in a moment.' And
they fell on their faces. 46Moses said to
Aaron, 'Take your censer, put fire on it
from the altar and lay incense on it, and
carry it quickly to the congregation and
make atonement for them. For wrath
has gone out from the LORD; the plague
has begun.' 47So Aaron took it as Moses
had ordered, and ran into the middle of
the assembly, where the plague had already begun among the people. He put
on the incense, and made atonement
for the people. 48He stood between the
dead and the living; and the plague was
stopped. 49Those who died by the plague
were fourteen thousand seven hundred,
besides those who died in the affair of
Korah. 50When the plague was stopped,
Aaron returned to Moses at the entrance of the tent of meeting.

THE BUDDING OF AARON'S ROD

17[u] The LORD spoke to Moses, saying: 2Speak to the Israelites,
and get twelve staffs from them, one
for each ancestral house, from all the
leaders of their ancestral houses. Write
each man's name on his staff, 3and write
Aaron's name on the staff of Levi. For
there shall be one staff for the head of
each ancestral house. 4Place them in the
tent of meeting before the covenant,[v]
where I meet with you. 5And the staff
of the man whom I choose shall sprout;
thus I will put a stop to the complaints
of the Israelites that they continually
make against you. 6Moses spoke to the
Israelites; and all their leaders gave him
staffs, one for each leader, according to
their ancestral houses, twelve staffs; and
the staff of Aaron was among theirs. 7So
Moses placed the staffs before the LORD
in the tent of the covenant.[w]
8 When Moses went into the tent
of the covenant[x] on the next day, the
staff of Aaron for the house of Levi had
sprouted. It put forth buds, produced
blossoms, and bore ripe almonds. 9Then
Moses brought out all the staffs from
before the LORD to all the Israelites;
and they looked, and each man took
his staff. 10And the LORD said to Moses, 'Put back the staff of Aaron before
the covenant,[y] to be kept as a warning
to rebels, so that you may make an end
of their complaints against me, or else
they will die.' 11Moses did so; just as the
LORD commanded him, so he did.
12 The Israelites said to Moses, 'We
are perishing; we are lost, all of us are
lost! 13Everyone who approaches the
tabernacle of the LORD will die. Are we
all to perish?'

RESPONSIBILITY OF PRIESTS AND LEVITES

18 The LORD said to Aaron: You
and your sons and your ancestral house with you shall bear responsibility for offences connected with the
sanctuary, while you and your sons
alone shall bear responsibility for offences connected with the priesthood.
2So bring with you also your brothers
of the tribe of Levi, your ancestral tribe,
in order that they may be joined to you,
and serve you while you and your sons
with you are in front of the tent of the
covenant.[z] 3They shall perform duties

[t] 16.36 Ch 17.1 in Heb [u] 17.1 Ch 17.16 in Heb
[v] 17.4 Or *treaty, or testimony*; Heb *eduth*
[w] 17.7 Or *treaty, or testimony*; Heb *eduth*
[x] 17.8 Or *treaty, or testimony*; Heb *eduth*
[y] 17.10 Or *treaty, or testimony*; Heb *eduth*
[z] 18.2 Or *treaty, or testimony*; Heb *eduth*

for you and for the whole tent. But they must not approach either the utensils of the sanctuary or the altar, otherwise both they and you will die. 4 They are attached to you in order to perform the duties of the tent of meeting, for all the service of the tent; no outsider shall approach you. 5 You yourselves shall perform the duties of the sanctuary and the duties of the altar, so that wrath may never again come upon the Israelites. 6 It is I who now take your brother Levites from among the Israelites; they are now yours as a gift, dedicated to the LORD, to perform the service of the tent of meeting. 7 But you and your sons with you shall diligently perform your priestly duties in all that concerns the altar and the area behind the curtain. I give your priesthood as a gift;[a] any outsider who approaches shall be put to death.

THE PRIESTS' PORTION

8 The LORD spoke to Aaron: I have given you charge of the offerings made to me, all the holy gifts of the Israelites; I have given them to you and your sons as a priestly portion due to you in perpetuity. 9 This shall be yours from the most holy things, reserved from the fire: every offering of theirs that they render to me as a most holy thing, whether grain-offering, sin-offering, or guilt-offering, shall belong to you and your sons. 10 As a most holy thing you shall eat it; every male may eat it; it shall be holy to you. 11 This also is yours: I have given to you, together with your sons and daughters, as a perpetual due, whatever is set aside from the gifts of all the elevation-offerings of the Israelites; everyone who is clean in your house may eat them. 12 All the best of the oil and all the best of the wine and of the grain, the choice produce that they give to the LORD, I have given to you. 13 The first fruits of all that is in their land, which they bring to the LORD, shall be yours; everyone who is clean in your house may eat of it. 14 Every devoted thing in Israel shall be yours. 15 The first issue of the womb of all creatures, human and animal, which is offered to the LORD, shall be yours; but the firstborn of human beings you shall redeem, and the firstborn of unclean animals you shall redeem. 16 Their redemption price, reckoned from one month of age, you shall fix at five shekels of silver, according to the shekel of the sanctuary (that is, twenty gerahs). 17 But the firstborn of a cow, or the firstborn of a sheep, or the firstborn of a goat, you shall not redeem; they are holy. You shall dash their blood on the altar, and shall turn their fat into smoke as an offering by fire for a pleasing odour to the LORD; 18 but their flesh shall be yours, just as the breast that is elevated and as the right thigh are yours. 19 All the holy offerings that the Israelites present to the LORD I have given to you, together with your sons and daughters, as a perpetual due; it is a covenant of salt for ever before the LORD for you and your descendants as well. 20 Then the LORD said to Aaron: You shall have no allotment in their land, nor shall you have any share among them; I am your share and your possession among the Israelites.

21 To the Levites I have given every tithe in Israel for a possession in return for the service that they perform, the service in the tent of meeting. 22 From now on the Israelites shall no longer approach the tent of meeting, or else they will incur guilt and die. 23 But the Levites shall perform the service of the tent of meeting, and they shall bear responsibility for their own offences; it shall be a perpetual statute throughout your generations. But among the Israelites they shall have no allotment, 24 because I have given to the Levites as their portion the tithe of the Israelites, which they set apart as an offering to the LORD. Therefore I have said of them that they shall have no allotment among the Israelites.

25 Then the LORD spoke to Moses, saying: 26 You shall speak to the Levites, saying: When you receive from the Israelites the tithe that I have given you from them for your portion, you shall set apart an offering from it to the LORD, a tithe of the tithe. 27 It shall be reckoned to you as your gift, the same as the grain of the threshing-floor and the fullness of the wine press. 28 Thus you also shall set apart an offering to the LORD from all the tithes that you receive from the Israelites; and from them you shall give the LORD's offering to the priest Aaron. 29 Out of all the gifts to you, you shall set apart every offering due to the LORD; the best of all of them is the part to be consecrated. 30 Say also to them: When you have set apart the best of it, then the rest shall be reckoned to the Levites as produce of the threshing-floor, and

[a] **18.7** Heb *as a service of gift*

as produce of the wine press. 31 You may
eat it in any place, you and your households; for it is your payment for your
service in the tent of meeting. 32 You
shall incur no guilt by reason of it, when
you have offered the best of it. But you
shall not profane the holy gifts of the Israelites, on pain of death.

CEREMONY OF THE RED HEIFER

19 The LORD spoke to Moses and
Aaron, saying: 2 This is a statute of the law that the LORD has commanded: Tell the Israelites to bring you
a red heifer without defect, in which
there is no blemish and on which no
yoke has been laid. 3 You shall give it to
the priest Eleazar, and it shall be taken
outside the camp and slaughtered in his
presence. 4 The priest Eleazar shall take
some of its blood with his finger and
sprinkle it seven times towards the front
of the tent of meeting. 5 Then the heifer
shall be burned in his sight; its skin, its
flesh, and its blood, with its dung, shall
be burned. 6 The priest shall take cedar
wood, hyssop, and crimson material,
and throw them into the fire in which
the heifer is burning. 7 Then the priest
shall wash his clothes and bathe his
body in water, and afterwards he may
come into the camp; but the priest shall
remain unclean until evening. 8 The one
who burns the heifer[b] shall wash his
clothes in water and bathe his body in
water; he shall remain unclean until
evening. 9 Then someone who is clean
shall gather up the ashes of the heifer,
and deposit them outside the camp in
a clean place; and they shall be kept for
the congregation of the Israelites for the
water for cleansing. It is a purification-
offering. 10 The one who gathers the
ashes of the heifer shall wash his clothes
and be unclean until evening.

This shall be a perpetual statute for
the Israelites and for the alien residing
among them. 11 Those who touch the
dead body of any human being shall be
unclean for seven days. 12 They shall purify themselves with the water on the
third day and on the seventh day, and
so be clean; but if they do not purify
themselves on the third day and on the
seventh day, they will not become clean.
13 All who touch a corpse, the body of a
human being who has died, and do not
purify themselves, defile the tabernacle
of the LORD; such persons shall be cut
off from Israel. Since water for cleansing
was not dashed on them, they remain
unclean; their uncleanness is still on
them.

14 This is the law when someone dies
in a tent: everyone who comes into the
tent, and everyone who is in the tent,
shall be unclean for seven days. 15 And
every open vessel with no cover fastened
on it is unclean. 16 Whoever in the open
field touches one who has been killed by
a sword, or who has died naturally,[c] or
a human bone, or a grave, shall be unclean for seven days. 17 For the unclean
they shall take some ashes of the burnt
purification-offering, and running water shall be added in a vessel; 18 then a
clean person shall take hyssop, dip it in
the water, and sprinkle it on the tent, on
all the furnishings, on the persons who
were there, and on whoever touched the
bone, the slain, the corpse, or the grave.
19 The clean person shall sprinkle the unclean ones on the third day and on the
seventh day, thus purifying them on
the seventh day. Then they shall wash
their clothes and bathe themselves
in water, and at evening they shall be
clean. 20 Any who are unclean but do not
purify themselves, those persons shall
be cut off from the assembly, for they
have defiled the sanctuary of the LORD.
Since the water for cleansing has not
been dashed on them, they are unclean.

21 It shall be a perpetual statute for
them. The one who sprinkles the water
for cleansing shall wash his clothes, and
whoever touches the water for cleansing
shall be unclean until evening. 22 Whatever the unclean person touches shall
be unclean, and anyone who touches it
shall be unclean until evening.

THE WATERS OF MERIBAH

20 The Israelites, the whole congregation, came into the wilderness of Zin in the first month, and the
people stayed in Kadesh. Miriam died
there, and was buried there.

2 Now there was no water for the
congregation; so they gathered together
against Moses and against Aaron. 3 The
people quarrelled with Moses and said,
'Would that we had died when our kindred died before the LORD! 4 Why have
you brought the assembly of the LORD
into this wilderness for us and our
livestock to die here? 5 Why have you
brought us up out of Egypt, to bring us
to this wretched place? It is no place for
grain, or figs, or vines, or pomegranates;

[b] 19.8 Heb *it* [c] 19.16 Heb lacks *naturally*

and there is no water to drink.' 6Then
Moses and Aaron went away from the
assembly to the entrance of the tent of
meeting; they fell on their faces, and the
glory of the LORD appeared to them.
7The LORD spoke to Moses, saying:
8Take the staff, and assemble the congregation, you and your brother Aaron,
and command the rock before their eyes
to yield its water. Thus you shall bring
water out of the rock for them; thus you
shall provide drink for the congregation
and their livestock.

9 So Moses took the staff from before the LORD, as he had commanded
him. 10Moses and Aaron gathered the
assembly together before the rock,
and he said to them, 'Listen, you rebels, shall we bring water for you out of
this rock?' 11Then Moses lifted up his
hand and struck the rock twice with his
staff; water came out abundantly, and
the congregation and their livestock
drank. 12But the LORD said to Moses
and Aaron, 'Because you did not trust in
me, to show my holiness before the eyes
of the Israelites, therefore you shall not
bring this assembly into the land that I
have given them.' 13These are the waters
of Meribah,[d] where the people of Israel
quarrelled with the LORD, and by which
he showed his holiness.

PASSAGE THROUGH EDOM REFUSED

14 Moses sent messengers from Kadesh to the king of Edom, 'Thus says
your brother Israel: You know all the
adversity that has befallen us: 15how
our ancestors went down to Egypt,
and we lived in Egypt for a long time;
and the Egyptians oppressed us and
our ancestors; 16and when we cried to
the LORD, he heard our voice, and sent
an angel and brought us out of Egypt;
and here we are in Kadesh, a town on
the edge of your territory. 17Now let
us pass through your land. We will not
pass through field or vineyard, or drink
water from any well; we will go along
the King's Highway, not turning aside
to the right hand or to the left until we
have passed through your territory.'

18 But Edom said to him, 'You shall
not pass through, or we will come out
with the sword against you.' 19The Israelites said to him, 'We will stay on the
highway; and if we drink of your water,
we and our livestock, then we will pay
for it. It is only a small matter; just let
us pass through on foot.' 20But he said,
'You shall not pass through.' And Edom
came out against them with a large
force, heavily armed. 21Thus Edom refused to give Israel passage through
their territory; so Israel turned away
from them.

THE DEATH OF AARON

22 They set out from Kadesh, and
the Israelites, the whole congregation,
came to Mount Hor. 23Then the LORD
said to Moses and Aaron at Mount Hor,
on the border of the land of Edom, 24'Let
Aaron be gathered to his people. For
he shall not enter the land that I have
given to the Israelites, because you rebelled against my command at the waters of Meribah. 25Take Aaron and his
son Eleazar, and bring them up Mount
Hor; 26strip Aaron of his vestments, and
put them on his son Eleazar. But Aaron
shall be gathered to his people,[e] and
shall die there.' 27Moses did as the LORD
had commanded; they went up Mount
Hor in the sight of the whole congregation. 28Moses stripped Aaron of his
vestments, and put them on his son Eleazar; and Aaron died there on the top of
the mountain. Moses and Eleazar came
down from the mountain. 29When all
the congregation saw that Aaron had
died, all the house of Israel mourned for
Aaron for thirty days.

THE BRONZE SERPENT

21 When the Canaanite, the king
of Arad, who lived in the Negeb,
heard that Israel was coming by the way
of Atharim, he fought against Israel and
took some of them captive. 2Then Israel
made a vow to the LORD and said, 'If
you will indeed give this people into our
hands, then we will utterly destroy their
towns.' 3The LORD listened to the voice
of Israel, and handed over the Canaanites; and they utterly destroyed them
and their towns; so the place was called
Hormah.[f]

4 From Mount Hor they set out by
the way to the Red Sea,[g] to go around
the land of Edom; but the people became
impatient on the way. 5The people spoke
against God and against Moses, 'Why
have you brought us up out of Egypt to
die in the wilderness? For there is no
food and no water, and we detest this
miserable food.' 6Then the LORD sent poisonous[h] serpents among the people, and
they bit the people, so that many Israel-

[d] **20.13** That is *Quarrel* [e] **20.26** Heb lacks *to his people* [f] **21.3** Heb *Destruction* [g] **21.4** Or *Sea of Reeds* [h] **21.6** Or *fiery*; Heb *seraphim*

ites died. 7The people came to Moses and
said, 'We have sinned by speaking against
the LORD and against you; pray to the
LORD to take away the serpents from us.'
So Moses prayed for the people. 8And the
LORD said to Moses, 'Make a poisonous[i]
serpent, and set it on a pole; and everyone who is bitten shall look at it and live.'
9So Moses made a serpent of bronze, and
put it upon a pole; and whenever a serpent bit someone, that person would
look at the serpent of bronze and live.

THE JOURNEY TO MOAB

10 The Israelites set out, and camped
in Oboth. 11They set out from Oboth,
and camped at Iye-abarim, in the wilderness bordering Moab towards the
sunrise. 12From there they set out, and
camped in the Wadi Zered. 13From there
they set out, and camped on the other
side of the Arnon, in[j] the wilderness
that extends from the boundary of the
Amorites; for the Arnon is the boundary of Moab, between Moab and the
Amorites. 14Wherefore it is said in the
Book of the Wars of the LORD,

'Waheb in Suphah and the wadis.
The Arnon 15and the slopes
of the wadis
that extend to the seat of Ar,
and lie along the border of Moab.'[k]

16 From there they continued to
Beer;[l] that is the well of which the
LORD said to Moses, 'Gather the people
together, and I will give them water.'
17Then Israel sang this song:

'Spring up, O well!—Sing to it!—
18 the well that the leaders sank,
that the nobles of the people dug,
with the sceptre, with the staff.'

From the wilderness to Mattanah,
19from Mattanah to Nahaliel, from Nahaliel to Bamoth, 20and from Bamoth
to the valley lying in the region of Moab
by the top of Pisgah that overlooks the
waste-land.[m]

KING SIHON DEFEATED

21 Then Israel sent messengers to
King Sihon of the Amorites, saying,
22'Let me pass through your land; we
will not turn aside into field or vineyard;
we will not drink the water of any well;
we will go by the King's Highway until
we have passed through your territory.'
23But Sihon would not allow Israel to
pass through his territory. Sihon gathered all his people together, and went
out against Israel to the wilderness; he
came to Jahaz, and fought against Israel.
24Israel put him to the sword, and took
possession of his land from the Arnon to
the Jabbok, as far as to the Ammonites;
for the boundary of the Ammonites was
strong. 25Israel took all these towns, and
Israel settled in all the towns of the Amorites, in Heshbon, and in all its villages.
26For Heshbon was the city of King Sihon of the Amorites, who had fought
against the former king of Moab and
captured all his land as far as the Arnon.
27Therefore the ballad-singers say,

'Come to Heshbon, let it be built;
let the city of Sihon be established.
28 For fire came out from Heshbon,
flame from the city of Sihon.
It devoured Ar of Moab,
and swallowed up[n] the
heights of the Arnon.
29 Woe to you, O Moab!
You are undone, O people
of Chemosh!
He has made his sons fugitives,
and his daughters captives,
to an Amorite king, Sihon.
30 So their posterity perished
from Heshbon[o] to Dibon,
and we laid waste until fire
spread to Medeba.'[p]

31 Thus Israel settled in the land of
the Amorites. 32Moses sent to spy out
Jazer; and they captured its villages, and
dispossessed the Amorites who were
there.

KING OG DEFEATED

33 Then they turned and went up
the road to Bashan; and King Og of Bashan came out against them, he and all
his people, to battle at Edrei. 34But the
LORD said to Moses, 'Do not be afraid
of him; for I have given him into your
hand, with all his people, and all his
land. You shall do to him as you did to
King Sihon of the Amorites, who ruled
in Heshbon.' 35So they killed him, his
sons, and all his people, until there was
no survivor left; and they took possession of his land.

BALAK SUMMONS BALAAM TO CURSE ISRAEL

22 The Israelites set out, and
camped in the plains of Moab

[i] 21.8 Or *fiery*; Heb *seraph* [j] 21.13 Gk: Heb *which is in* [k] 21.15 Meaning of Heb uncertain [l] 21.16 That is *Well* [m] 21.20 Or *Jeshimon* [n] 21.28 Gk: Heb *and the lords of* [o] 21.30 Gk: Heb *we have shot at them; Heshbon has perished* [p] 21.30 Compare Sam Gk: Meaning of MT uncertain

across the Jordan from Jericho. 2Now
Balak son of Zippor saw all that Israel
had done to the Amorites. 3Moab was in
great dread of the people, because they
were so numerous; Moab was overcome
with fear of the people of Israel. 4And
Moab said to the elders of Midian, 'This
horde will now lick up all that is around
us, as an ox licks up the grass of the
field.' Now Balak son of Zippor was king
of Moab at that time. 5He sent messengers to Balaam son of Beor at Pethor,
which is on the Euphrates, in the land
of Amaw,[q] to summon him, saying, 'A
people has come out of Egypt; they have
spread over the face of the earth, and
they have settled next to me. 6Come
now, curse this people for me, since
they are stronger than I; perhaps I shall
be able to defeat them and drive them
from the land; for I know that whomsoever you bless is blessed, and whomsoever you curse is cursed.'

7 So the elders of Moab and the elders
of Midian departed with the fees for divination in their hand; and they came to
Balaam, and gave him Balak's message.
8He said to them, 'Stay here tonight, and
I will bring back word to you, just as the
LORD speaks to me'; so the officials of
Moab stayed with Balaam. 9God came
to Balaam and said, 'Who are these men
with you?' 10Balaam said to God, 'King
Balak son of Zippor of Moab has sent me
this message: 11"A people has come out of
Egypt and has spread over the face of the
earth; now come, curse them for me; perhaps I shall be able to fight against them
and drive them out." ' 12God said to Balaam, 'You shall not go with them; you
shall not curse the people, for they are
blessed.' 13So Balaam rose in the morning, and said to the officials of Balak, 'Go
to your own land, for the LORD has refused to let me go with you.' 14So the officials of Moab rose and went to Balak, and
said, 'Balaam refuses to come with us.'

15 Once again Balak sent officials,
more numerous and more distinguished
than these. 16They came to Balaam and
said to him, 'Thus says Balak son of Zippor: "Do not let anything hinder you
from coming to me; 17for I will surely
do you great honour, and whatever you
say to me I will do; come, curse this people for me." ' 18But Balaam replied to the
servants of Balak, 'Although Balak were
to give me his house full of silver and
gold, I could not go beyond the command of the LORD my God, to do less or
more. 19You remain here, as the others
did, so that I may learn what more the
LORD may say to me.' 20That night God
came to Balaam and said to him, 'If the
men have come to summon you, get up
and go with them; but do only what I
tell you to do.' 21So Balaam got up in the
morning, saddled his donkey, and went
with the officials of Moab.

BALAAM, THE DONKEY, AND THE ANGEL

22 God's anger was kindled because
he was going, and the angel of the LORD
took his stand in the road as his adversary. Now he was riding on the donkey, and his two servants were with
him. 23The donkey saw the angel of the
LORD standing in the road, with a drawn
sword in his hand; so the donkey turned
off the road, and went into the field; and
Balaam struck the donkey, to turn it back
on to the road. 24Then the angel of the
LORD stood in a narrow path between
the vineyards, with a wall on either side.
25When the donkey saw the angel of the
LORD, it scraped against the wall, and
scraped Balaam's foot against the wall;
so he struck it again. 26Then the angel
of the LORD went ahead, and stood in a
narrow place, where there was no way
to turn either to the right or to the left.
27When the donkey saw the angel of the
LORD, it lay down under Balaam; and Balaam's anger was kindled, and he struck
the donkey with his staff. 28Then the
LORD opened the mouth of the donkey,
and it said to Balaam, 'What have I done
to you, that you have struck me these
three times?' 29Balaam said to the donkey, 'Because you have made a fool of me!
I wish I had a sword in my hand! I would
kill you right now!' 30But the donkey said
to Balaam, 'Am I not your donkey, which
you have ridden all your life to this day?
Have I been in the habit of treating you
in this way?' And he said, 'No.'

31 Then the LORD opened the eyes
of Balaam, and he saw the angel of the
LORD standing in the road, with his
drawn sword in his hand; and he bowed
down, falling on his face. 32The angel of
the LORD said to him, 'Why have you
struck your donkey these three times?
I have come out as an adversary, because your way is perverse[r] before me.
33The donkey saw me, and turned away
from me these three times. If it had not
turned away from me, surely I would
by now have killed you and let it live.'

[q] 22.5 Or *land of his kinsfolk* [r] 22.32 Meaning of Heb uncertain

34Then Balaam said to the angel of the
LORD, 'I have sinned, for I did not know
that you were standing in the road to
oppose me. Now therefore, if it is displeasing to you, I will return home.'
35The angel of the LORD said to Balaam,
'Go with the men; but speak only what
I tell you to speak.' So Balaam went on
with the officials of Balak.

36 When Balak heard that Balaam
had come, he went out to meet him at
Ir-moab, on the boundary formed by
the Arnon, at the farthest point of the
boundary. 37Balak said to Balaam, 'Did I
not send to summon you? Why did you
not come to me? Am I not able to honour you?' 38Balaam said to Balak, 'I have
come to you now, but do I have power
to say just anything? The word God puts
in my mouth, that is what I must say.'
39Then Balaam went with Balak, and
they came to Kiriath-huzoth. 40Ba-
lak sacrificed oxen and sheep, and sent
them to Balaam and to the officials who
were with him.

BALAAM'S FIRST ORACLE

41 On the next day Balak took Balaam and brought him up to Bamoth-
baal; and from there he could see part of
23 the people of Israel.[s] 1Then Balaam said to Balak, 'Build me
seven altars here, and prepare seven
bulls and seven rams for me.' 2Balak did
as Balaam had said; and Balak and Balaam offered a bull and a ram on each
altar. 3Then Balaam said to Balak, 'Stay
here beside your burnt-offerings while I
go aside. Perhaps the LORD will come to
meet me. Whatever he shows me I will
tell you.' And he went to a bare height.

4 Then God met Balaam; and Balaam
said to him, 'I have arranged the seven
altars, and have offered a bull and a ram
on each altar.' 5The LORD put a word in
Balaam's mouth, and said, 'Return to
Balak, and this is what you must say.'
6So he returned to Balak,[t] who was
standing beside his burnt-offerings
with all the officials of Moab. 7Then Balaam[u] uttered his oracle, saying:

'Balak has brought me from Aram,
the king of Moab from the
eastern mountains:
"Come, curse Jacob for me;
Come, denounce Israel!"
8 How can I curse whom God
has not cursed?
How can I denounce those
whom the LORD has
not denounced?
9 For from the top of the
crags I see him,
from the hills I behold him.
Here is a people living alone,
and not reckoning itself
among the nations!
10 Who can count the dust of Jacob,
or number the dust-cloud[v]
of Israel?
Let me die the death of the upright,
and let my end be like his!'

11 Then Balak said to Balaam, 'What
have you done to me? I brought you to
curse my enemies, but now you have
done nothing but bless them.' 12He answered, 'Must I not take care to say what
the LORD puts into my mouth?'

BALAAM'S SECOND ORACLE

13 So Balak said to him, 'Come with
me to another place from which you
may see them; you shall see only part of
them, and shall not see them all; then
curse them for me from there.' 14So he
took him to the field of Zophim, to the
top of Pisgah. He built seven altars, and
offered a bull and a ram on each altar.
15Balaam said to Balak, 'Stand here beside your burnt-offerings, while I meet
the LORD over there.' 16The LORD met
Balaam, put a word into his mouth, and
said, 'Return to Balak, and this is what
you shall say.' 17When he came to him, he
was standing beside his burnt-offerings
with the officials of Moab. Balak said to
him, 'What has the LORD said?' 18Then
Balaam uttered his oracle, saying:

'Rise, Balak, and hear;
listen to me, O son of Zippor:
19 God is not a human being,
that he should lie,
or a mortal, that he should
change his mind.
Has he promised, and will
he not do it?
Has he spoken, and will
he not fulfil it?
20 See, I received a command to bless;
he has blessed, and I
cannot revoke it.
21 He has not beheld misfortune
in Jacob;
nor has he seen trouble in Israel.
The LORD their God is with them,
acclaimed as a king among them.
22 God, who brings them out of Egypt,
is like the horns of a wild
ox for them.

[s] 22.41 Heb lacks *of Israel* [t] 23.6 Heb *him*
[u] 23.7 Heb *he* [v] 23.10 Or *fourth part*

23 Surely there is no enchantment
against Jacob,
no divination against Israel;
now it shall be said of Jacob
and Israel,
"See what God has done!"
24 Look, a people rising up
like a lioness,
and rousing itself like a lion!
It does not lie down until it
has eaten the prey
and drunk the blood of the slain.'

25 Then Balak said to Balaam, 'Do
not curse them at all, and do not bless
them at all.' 26But Balaam answered Balak, 'Did I not tell you, "Whatever the
LORD says, that is what I must do"?'
27 So Balak said to Balaam, 'Come
now, I will take you to another place;
perhaps it will please God that you may
curse them for me from there.' 28So
Balak took Balaam to the top of Peor,
which overlooks the waste-land.[w] 29Ba-
laam said to Balak, 'Build me seven altars here, and prepare seven bulls and
seven rams for me.' 30So Balak did as
Balaam had said, and offered a bull and
a ram on each altar.

BALAAM'S THIRD ORACLE

24 Now Balaam saw that it pleased
the LORD to bless Israel, so he
did not go, as at other times, to look
for omens, but set his face towards the
wilderness. 2Balaam looked up and saw
Israel camping tribe by tribe. Then the
spirit of God came upon him, 3and he
uttered his oracle, saying:

'The oracle of Balaam son of Beor,
the oracle of the man whose
eye is clear,[x]
4 the oracle of one who hears
the words of God,
who sees the vision of
the Almighty,[y]
who falls down, but with
eyes uncovered:
5 how fair are your tents, O Jacob,
your encampments, O Israel!
6 Like palm groves that stretch far away,
like gardens beside a river,
like aloes that the LORD has planted,
like cedar trees beside the waters.
7 Water shall flow from his buckets,
and his seed shall have
abundant water,
his king shall be higher than Agag,
and his kingdom shall be exalted.
8 God, who brings him out of Egypt,
is like the horns of a wild
ox for him;
he shall devour the nations
that are his foes
and break their bones.
He shall strike with his arrows.[z]
9 He crouched, he lay down like a lion,
and like a lioness; who will
rouse him up?
Blessed is everyone who blesses you,
and cursed is everyone
who curses you.'

10 Then Balak's anger was kindled
against Balaam, and he struck his hands
together. Balak said to Balaam, 'I summoned you to curse my enemies, but instead you have blessed them these three
times. 11Now be off with you! Go home!
I said, "I will reward you richly", but the
LORD has denied you any reward.' 12And
Balaam said to Balak, 'Did I not tell your
messengers whom you sent to me, 13"If
Balak should give me his house full of
silver and gold, I would not be able to
go beyond the word of the LORD, to do
either good or bad of my own will; what
the LORD says, that is what I will say"?
14So now, I am going to my people; let
me advise you what this people will do
to your people in days to come.'

BALAAM'S FOURTH ORACLE

15 So he uttered his oracle, saying:
'The oracle of Balaam son of Beor,
the oracle of the man
whose eye is clear,[a]
16 the oracle of one who hears
the words of God,
and knows the knowledge
of the Most High,[b]
who sees the vision of the Almighty,[c]
who falls down, but with
his eyes uncovered:
17 I see him, but not now;
I behold him, but not near—
a star shall come out of Jacob,
and a sceptre shall rise
out of Israel;
it shall crush the borderlands[d]
of Moab,
and the territory[e] of all
the Shethites.
18 Edom will become a possession,
Seir a possession of its enemies,[f]
while Israel does valiantly.

[w] 23.28 Or *overlooks Jeshimon* [x] 24.3 Or *closed or open* [y] 24.4 Traditional rendering of Heb *Shaddai* [z] 24.8 Meaning of Heb uncertain
[a] 24.15 Or *closed or open* [b] 24.16 Or *of Elyon*
[c] 24.16 Traditional rendering of Heb *Shaddai*
[d] 24.17 Or *forehead* [e] 24.17 Some Mss read *skull* [f] 24.18 Heb *Seir, its enemies, a possession*

19 One out of Jacob shall rule,
and destroy the survivors of Ir.'
20 Then he looked on Amalek, and
uttered his oracle, saying:
'First among the nations
was Amalek,
but its end is to perish for ever.'
21 Then he looked on the Kenite, and
uttered his oracle, saying:
'Enduring is your dwelling-place,
and your nest is set in the rock;
22 yet Kain is destined for burning.
How long shall Asshur take
you away captive?'
23 Again he uttered his oracle, saying:
'Alas, who shall live when
God does this?
24 But ships shall come from Kittim
and shall afflict Asshur and Eber;
and he also shall perish for ever.'
25 Then Balaam got up and went
back to his place, and Balak also went
his way.

WORSHIP OF BAAL OF PEOR

25 While Israel was staying at
Shittim, the people began to
have sexual relations with the women
of Moab. 2These invited the people to
the sacrifices of their gods, and the people ate and bowed down to their gods.
3Thus Israel yoked itself to the Baal of
Peor, and the LORD's anger was kindled
against Israel. 4The LORD said to Moses, 'Take all the chiefs of the people,
and impale them in the sun before the
LORD, in order that the fierce anger of
the LORD may turn away from Israel.'
5And Moses said to the judges of Israel,
'Each of you shall kill any of your people
who have yoked themselves to the Baal
of Peor.'
6 Just then one of the Israelites came
and brought a Midianite woman into
his family, in the sight of Moses and in
the sight of the whole congregation of
the Israelites, while they were weeping
at the entrance of the tent of meeting.
7When Phinehas son of Eleazar, son of
Aaron the priest, saw it, he got up and
left the congregation. Taking a spear in
his hand, 8he went after the Israelite
man into the tent, and pierced the two
of them, the Israelite and the woman,
through the belly. So the plague was
stopped among the people of Israel.
9Nevertheless, those that died by the
plague were twenty-four thousand.
10 The LORD spoke to Moses, saying:
11'Phinehas son of Eleazar, son of Aaron
the priest, has turned back my wrath
from the Israelites by manifesting such
zeal among them on my behalf that in
my jealousy I did not consume the Israelites. 12Therefore say, "I hereby grant
him my covenant of peace. 13It shall be
for him and for his descendants after
him a covenant of perpetual priesthood,
because he was zealous for his God, and
made atonement for the Israelites."'
14 The name of the slain Israelite
man, who was killed with the Midianite woman, was Zimri son of Salu, head
of an ancestral house belonging to the
Simeonites. 15The name of the Midianite woman who was killed was Cozbi
daughter of Zur, who was the head of a
clan, an ancestral house in Midian.
16 The LORD said to Moses, 17'Harass
the Midianites, and defeat them; 18for
they have harassed you by the trickery
with which they deceived you in the affair of Peor, and in the affair of Cozbi,
the daughter of a leader of Midian, their
sister; she was killed on the day of the
plague that resulted from Peor.'

A CENSUS OF THE NEW GENERATION

26 After the plague the LORD said
to Moses and to Eleazar son of
Aaron the priest, 2'Take a census of the
whole congregation of the Israelites,
from twenty years old and upwards, by
their ancestral houses, everyone in Israel able to go to war.' 3Moses and Eleazar the priest spoke with them in the
plains of Moab by the Jordan opposite
Jericho, saying, 4'Take a census of the
people,[9] from twenty years old and upwards', as the LORD commanded Moses.
The Israelites, who came out of the
land of Egypt, were:
5 Reuben, the firstborn of Israel. The
descendants of Reuben: of Hanoch, the
clan of the Hanochites; of Pallu, the clan
of the Palluites; 6of Hezron, the clan of
the Hezronites; of Carmi, the clan of the
Carmites. 7These are the clans of the
Reubenites; the number of those enrolled was forty-three thousand seven
hundred and thirty. 8And the descendants of Pallu: Eliab. 9The descendants
of Eliab: Nemuel, Dathan, and Abiram.
These are the same Dathan and Abiram, chosen from the congregation,
who rebelled against Moses and Aaron
in the company of Korah, when they
rebelled against the LORD, 10and the

[9] 26.4 Heb lacks *take a census of the people*: Compare verse 2

earth opened its mouth and swallowed
them up along with Korah, when that
company died, when the fire devoured
two hundred and fifty men; and they
became a warning. 11 Notwithstanding,
the sons of Korah did not die.

12 The descendants of Simeon by
their clans: of Nemuel, the clan of
the Nemuelites; of Jamin, the clan
of the Jaminites; of Jachin, the clan of
the Jachinites; 13 of Zerah, the clan of
the Zerahites; of Shaul, the clan of the
Shaulites.[h] 14 These are the clans of the
Simeonites, twenty-two thousand two
hundred.

15 The children of Gad by their clans:
of Zephon, the clan of the Zephonites;
of Haggi, the clan of the Haggites; of
Shuni, the clan of the Shunites; 16 of
Ozni, the clan of the Oznites; of Eri, the
clan of the Erites; 17 of Arod, the clan of
the Arodites; of Areli, the clan of the
Arelites. 18 These are the clans of the
Gadites: the number of those enrolled
was forty thousand five hundred.

19 The sons of Judah: Er and Onan;
Er and Onan died in the land of Canaan. 20 The descendants of Judah by
their clans were: of Shelah, the clan of
the Shelanites; of Perez, the clan of the
Perezites; of Zerah, the clan of the Zerahites. 21 The descendants of Perez were:
of Hezron, the clan of the Hezronites;
of Hamul, the clan of the Hamulites.
22 These are the clans of Judah: the number of those enrolled was seventy-six
thousand five hundred.

23 The descendants of Issachar by
their clans: of Tola, the clan of the To-
laites; of Puvah, the clan of the Punites;
24 of Jashub, the clan of the Jashubites;
of Shimron, the clan of the Shimronites.
25 These are the clans of Issachar: sixty-
four thousand three hundred enrolled.

26 The descendants of Zebulun by
their clans: of Sered, the clan of the Se-
redites; of Elon, the clan of the Elonites;
of Jahleel, the clan of the Jahleelites.
27 These are the clans of the Zebulunites;
the number of those enrolled was sixty
thousand five hundred.

28 The sons of Joseph by their clans:
Manasseh and Ephraim. 29 The descendants of Manasseh: of Machir, the clan
of the Machirites; and Machir was the
father of Gilead; of Gilead, the clan of
the Gileadites. 30 These are the descendants of Gilead: of Iezer, the clan of the
Iezerites; of Helek, the clan of the Helek-
ites; 31 and of Asriel, the clan of the
Asrielites; and of Shechem, the clan of
the Shechemites; 32 and of Shemida, the
clan of the Shemidaites; and of Hepher,
the clan of the Hepherites. 33 Now Zelophehad son of Hepher had no sons, but
daughters: and the names of the daughters of Zelophehad were Mahlah, Noah,
Hoglah, Milcah, and Tirzah. 34 These are
the clans of Manasseh; the number of
those enrolled was fifty-two thousand
seven hundred.

35 These are the descendants of
Ephraim according to their clans: of
Shuthelah, the clan of the Shuthela-
hites; of Becher, the clan of the Becher-
ites; of Tahan, the clan of the Tahanites.
36 And these are the descendants of Shuthelah: of Eran, the clan of the Eranites.
37 These are the clans of the Ephraimites: the number of those enrolled was
thirty-two thousand five hundred.
These are the descendants of Joseph by
their clans.

38 The descendants of Benjamin by
their clans: of Bela, the clan of the Be-
laites; of Ashbel, the clan of the Ash-
belites; of Ahiram, the clan of the Ahi-
ramites; 39 of Shephupham, the clan of
the Shuphamites; of Hupham, the clan
of the Huphamites. 40 And the sons of
Bela were Ard and Naaman: of Ard, the
clan of the Ardites; of Naaman, the clan
of the Naamites. 41 These are the descendants of Benjamin by their clans; the
number of those enrolled was forty-five
thousand six hundred.

42 These are the descendants of Dan
by their clans: of Shuham, the clan of
the Shuhamites. These are the clans of
Dan by their clans. 43 All the clans of the
Shuhamites: sixty-four thousand four
hundred enrolled.

44 The descendants of Asher by their
families: of Imnah, the clan of the Im-
nites; of Ishvi, the clan of the Ishvites;
of Beriah, the clan of the Beriites. 45 Of
the descendants of Beriah: of Heber,
the clan of the Heberites; of Malchiel,
the clan of the Malchielites. 46 And the
name of the daughter of Asher was Serah. 47 These are the clans of the Asherites: the number of those enrolled was
fifty-three thousand four hundred.

48 The descendants of Naphtali by
their clans: of Jahzeel, the clan of the
Jahzeelites; of Guni, the clan of the
Gunites; 49 of Jezer, the clan of the Jez-
erites; of Shillem, the clan of the Shil-
lemites. 50 These are the Naphtalites[i] by

[h] **26.13** Or *Saul . . . Saulites* [i] **26.50** Heb *clans of Naphtali*

their clans: the number of those enrolled
was forty-five thousand four hundred.
51 This was the number of the Israelites enrolled: six hundred and one thousand seven hundred and thirty.
52 The LORD spoke to Moses, saying:
53To these the land shall be apportioned
for inheritance according to the number of names. 54To a large tribe you shall
give a large inheritance, and to a small
tribe you shall give a small inheritance;
every tribe shall be given its inheritance according to its enrolment. 55But
the land shall be apportioned by lot; according to the names of their ancestral
tribes they shall inherit. 56Their inheritance shall be apportioned according to
lot between the larger and the smaller.
57 This is the enrolment of the Levites by their clans: of Gershon, the clan
of the Gershonites; of Kohath, the clan
of the Kohathites; of Merari, the clan of
the Merarites. 58These are the clans of
Levi: the clan of the Libnites, the clan of
the Hebronites, the clan of the Mahlites,
the clan of the Mushites, the clan of the
Korahites. Now Kohath was the father
of Amram. 59The name of Amram's wife
was Jochebed daughter of Levi, who was
born to Levi in Egypt; and she bore to
Amram: Aaron, Moses, and their sister
Miriam. 60To Aaron were born Nadab,
Abihu, Eleazar, and Ithamar. 61But Nadab and Abihu died when they offered
unholy fire before the LORD. 62The number of those enrolled was twenty-three
thousand, every male one month old
and upwards; for they were not enrolled
among the Israelites because there was
no allotment given to them among the
Israelites.
63 These were those enrolled by Moses and Eleazar the priest, who enrolled
the Israelites in the plains of Moab by
the Jordan opposite Jericho. 64Among
these there was not one of those enrolled by Moses and Aaron the priest,
who had enrolled the Israelites in the
wilderness of Sinai. 65For the LORD had
said of them, 'They shall die in the wilderness.' Not one of them was left, except Caleb son of Jephunneh and Joshua
son of Nun.

THE DAUGHTERS OF ZELOPHEHAD

27 Then the daughters of Zelophehad came forward. Zelophehad
was son of Hepher son of Gilead son of
Machir son of Manasseh son of Joseph,
a member of the Manassite clans. The
names of his daughters were: Mahlah, Noah, Hoglah, Milcah, and Tirzah.
2They stood before Moses, Eleazar the
priest, the leaders, and all the congregation, at the entrance of the tent of meeting, and they said, 3'Our father died in
the wilderness; he was not among the
company of those who gathered themselves together against the LORD in the
company of Korah, but died for his own
sin; and he had no sons. 4Why should
the name of our father be taken away
from his clan because he had no son?
Give to us a possession among our father's brothers.'
5 Moses brought their case before the
LORD. 6And the LORD spoke to Moses,
saying: 7The daughters of Zelophehad
are right in what they are saying; you
shall indeed let them possess an inheritance among their father's brothers and
pass the inheritance of their father on
to them. 8You shall also say to the Israelites, 'If a man dies, and has no son,
then you shall pass his inheritance on
to his daughter. 9If he has no daughter, then you shall give his inheritance
to his brothers. 10If he has no brothers,
then you shall give his inheritance to
his father's brothers. 11And if his father
has no brothers, then you shall give his
inheritance to the nearest kinsman of
his clan, and he shall possess it. It shall
be for the Israelites a statute and ordinance, as the LORD commanded Moses.'

JOSHUA APPOINTED MOSES' SUCCESSOR

12 The LORD said to Moses, 'Go up
this mountain of the Abarim range,
and see the land that I have given to the
Israelites. 13When you have seen it, you
also shall be gathered to your people, as
your brother Aaron was, 14because you
rebelled against my word in the wilderness of Zin when the congregation
quarrelled with me.[j] You did not show
my holiness before their eyes at the waters.' (These are the waters of Meribath-
kadesh in the wilderness of Zin.) 15Mo-
ses spoke to the LORD, saying, 16'Let the
LORD, the God of the spirits of all flesh,
appoint someone over the congregation 17who shall go out before them and
come in before them, who shall lead
them out and bring them in, so that the
congregation of the LORD may not be
like sheep without a shepherd.' 18So the
LORD said to Moses, 'Take Joshua son
of Nun, a man in whom is the spirit,

j 27.14 Heb lacks *with me*

and lay your hand upon him; 19 have him stand before Eleazar the priest and all the congregation, and commission him in their sight. 20 You shall give him some of your authority, so that all the congregation of the Israelites may obey. 21 But he shall stand before Eleazar the priest, who shall inquire for him by the decision of the Urim before the LORD; at his word they shall go out, and at his word they shall come in, both he and all the Israelites with him, the whole congregation.' 22 So Moses did as the LORD commanded him. He took Joshua and had him stand before Eleazar the priest and the whole congregation; 23 he laid his hands on him and commissioned him—as the LORD had directed through Moses.

DAILY OFFERINGS

28 The LORD spoke to Moses, saying: 2 Command the Israelites, and say to them: My offering, the food for my offerings by fire, my pleasing odour, you shall take care to offer to me at its appointed time. 3 And you shall say to them, This is the offering by fire that you shall offer to the LORD: two male lambs a year old without blemish, daily, as a regular offering. 4 One lamb you shall offer in the morning, and the other lamb you shall offer at twilight;[k] 5 also one-tenth of an ephah of choice flour for a grain-offering, mixed with one-fourth of a hin of beaten oil. 6 It is a regular burnt-offering, ordained at Mount Sinai for a pleasing odour, an offering by fire to the LORD. 7 Its drink-offering shall be one-fourth of a hin for each lamb; in the sanctuary you shall pour out a drink-offering of strong drink to the LORD. 8 The other lamb you shall offer at twilight[l] with a grain-offering and a drink-offering like the one in the morning; you shall offer it as an offering by fire, a pleasing odour to the LORD.

SABBATH OFFERINGS

9 On the sabbath day: two male lambs a year old without blemish, and two-tenths of an ephah of choice flour for a grain-offering, mixed with oil, and its drink-offering— 10 this is the burnt-offering for every sabbath, in addition to the regular burnt-offering and its drink-offering.

MONTHLY OFFERINGS

11 At the beginnings of your months you shall offer a burnt-offering to the LORD: two young bulls, one ram, seven male lambs a year old without blemish; 12 also three-tenths of an ephah of choice flour for a grain-offering, mixed with oil, for each bull; and two-tenths of choice flour for a grain-offering, mixed with oil, for the one ram; 13 and one-tenth of choice flour mixed with oil as a grain-offering for every lamb—a burnt-offering of pleasing odour, an offering by fire to the LORD. 14 Their drink-offerings shall be half a hin of wine for a bull, one-third of a hin for a ram, and one-fourth of a hin for a lamb. This is the burnt-offering of every month throughout the months of the year. 15 And there shall be one male goat for a sin-offering to the LORD; it shall be offered in addition to the regular burnt-offering and its drink-offering.

OFFERINGS AT PASSOVER

16 On the fourteenth day of the first month there shall be a passover-offering to the LORD. 17 And on the fifteenth day of this month is a festival; for seven days shall unleavened bread be eaten. 18 On the first day there shall be a holy convocation. You shall not work at your occupations. 19 You shall offer an offering by fire, a burnt-offering to the LORD: two young bulls, one ram, and seven male lambs a year old; see that they are without blemish. 20 Their grain-offering shall be of choice flour mixed with oil: three-tenths of an ephah shall you offer for a bull, and two-tenths for a ram; 21 one-tenth shall you offer for each of the seven lambs; 22 also one male goat for a sin-offering, to make atonement for you. 23 You shall offer these in addition to the burnt-offering of the morning, which belongs to the regular burnt-offering. 24 In the same way you shall offer daily, for seven days, the food of an offering by fire, a pleasing odour to the LORD; it shall be offered in addition to the regular burnt-offering and its drink-offering. 25 And on the seventh day you shall have a holy convocation; you shall not work at your occupations.

OFFERINGS AT THE FESTIVAL OF WEEKS

26 On the day of the first fruits, when you offer a grain-offering of new grain to the LORD at your festival of weeks, you shall have a holy convocation; you shall

[k] 28.4 Heb *between the two evenings*
[l] 28.8 Heb *between the two evenings*

not work at your occupations. [27]You shall offer a burnt-offering, a pleasing odour to the LORD: two young bulls, one ram, seven male lambs a year old. [28]Their grain-offering shall be of choice flour mixed with oil, three-tenths of an ephah for each bull, two-tenths for one ram, [29]one-tenth for each of the seven lambs; [30]with one male goat, to make atonement for you. [31]In addition to the regular burnt-offering with its grain-offering, you shall offer them and their drink-offering. They shall be without blemish.

OFFERINGS AT THE FESTIVAL OF TRUMPETS

29 On the first day of the seventh month you shall have a holy convocation; you shall not work at your occupations. It is a day for you to blow the trumpets, [2]and you shall offer a burnt-offering, a pleasing odour to the LORD: one young bull, one ram, seven male lambs a year old without blemish. [3]Their grain-offering shall be of choice flour mixed with oil, three-tenths of one ephah for the bull, two-tenths for the ram, [4]and one-tenth for each of the seven lambs; [5]with one male goat for a sin-offering, to make atonement for you. [6]These are in addition to the burnt-offering of the new moon and its grain-offering, and the regular burnt-offering and its grain-offering, and their drink-offerings, according to the ordinance for them, a pleasing odour, an offering by fire to the LORD.

OFFERINGS ON THE DAY OF ATONEMENT

7 On the tenth day of this seventh month you shall have a holy convocation, and deny yourselves;[m] you shall do no work. [8]You shall offer a burnt-offering to the LORD, a pleasing odour: one young bull, one ram, seven male lambs a year old. They shall be without blemish. [9]Their grain-offering shall be of choice flour mixed with oil, three-tenths of an ephah for the bull, two-tenths for the one ram, [10]one-tenth for each of the seven lambs; [11]with one male goat for a sin-offering, in addition to the sin-offering of atonement, and the regular burnt-offering and its grain-offering, and their drink-offerings.

OFFERINGS AT THE FESTIVAL OF BOOTHS

12 On the fifteenth day of the seventh month you shall have a holy convocation; you shall not work at your occupations. You shall celebrate a festival to the LORD for seven days. [13]You shall offer a burnt-offering, an offering by fire, a pleasing odour to the LORD: thirteen young bulls, two rams, fourteen male lambs a year old. They shall be without blemish. [14]Their grain-offering shall be of choice flour mixed with oil, three-tenths of an ephah for each of the thirteen bulls, two-tenths for each of the two rams, [15]and one-tenth for each of the fourteen lambs; [16]also one male goat for a sin-offering, in addition to the regular burnt-offering, its grain-offering and its drink-offering.

17 On the second day: twelve young bulls, two rams, fourteen male lambs a year old without blemish, [18]with the grain-offering and the drink-offerings for the bulls, for the rams, and for the lambs, as prescribed in accordance with their number; [19]also one male goat for a sin-offering, in addition to the regular burnt-offering and its grain-offering, and their drink-offerings.

20 On the third day: eleven bulls, two rams, fourteen male lambs a year old without blemish, [21]with the grain-offering and the drink-offerings for the bulls, for the rams, and for the lambs, as prescribed in accordance with their number; [22]also one male goat for a sin-offering, in addition to the regular burnt-offering and its grain-offering and its drink-offering.

23 On the fourth day: ten bulls, two rams, fourteen male lambs a year old without blemish, [24]with the grain-offering and the drink-offerings for the bulls, for the rams, and for the lambs, as prescribed in accordance with their number; [25]also one male goat for a sin-offering, in addition to the regular burnt-offering, its grain-offering and its drink-offering.

26 On the fifth day: nine bulls, two rams, fourteen male lambs a year old without blemish, [27]with the grain-offering and the drink-offerings for the bulls, for the rams, and for the lambs, as prescribed in accordance with their number; [28]also one male goat for a sin-offering, in addition to the regular burnt-offering and its grain-offering and its drink-offering.

29 On the sixth day: eight bulls, two rams, fourteen male lambs a year old without blemish, [30]with the grain-offering

[m] **29.7** Or *and fast*

and the drink-offerings for the bulls,
for the rams, and for the lambs, as
prescribed in accordance with their
number; 31 also one male goat for a
sin-offering, in addition to the regular
burnt-offering, its grain-offering, and
its drink-offerings.
32 On the seventh day: seven bulls,
two rams, fourteen male lambs a year
old without blemish, 33 with the grain-
offering and the drink-offerings for the
bulls, for the rams, and for the lambs,
as prescribed in accordance with their
number; 34 also one male goat for a
sin-offering, besides the regular burnt-
offering, its grain-offering, and its
drink-offering.
35 On the eighth day you shall have
a solemn assembly; you shall not work
at your occupations. 36 You shall offer
a burnt-offering, an offering by fire, a
pleasing odour to the LORD: one bull,
one ram, seven male lambs a year old
without blemish, 37 and the grain-
offering and the drink-offerings for the
bull, for the ram, and for the lambs, as
prescribed in accordance with their
number; 38 also one male goat for a
sin-offering, in addition to the regular
burnt-offering and its grain-offering
and its drink-offering.
39 These you shall offer to the LORD at
your appointed festivals, in addition to
your votive offerings and your freewill-
offerings, as your burnt-offerings, your
grain-offerings, your drink-offerings,
and your offerings of well-being.
40[n] So Moses told the Israelites everything just as the LORD had commanded Moses.

VOWS MADE BY WOMEN

30 Then Moses said to the heads
of the tribes of the Israelites:
This is what the LORD has commanded.
2 When a man makes a vow to the LORD,
or swears an oath to bind himself by a
pledge, he shall not break his word; he
shall do according to all that proceeds
out of his mouth.
3 When a woman makes a vow to
the LORD, or binds herself by a pledge,
while within her father's house, in her
youth, 4 and her father hears of her vow
or her pledge by which she has bound
herself, and says nothing to her; then all
her vows shall stand, and any pledge by
which she has bound herself shall stand.
5 But if her father expresses disapproval
to her at the time that he hears of it, no
vow of hers, and no pledge by which she
has bound herself, shall stand; and the
LORD will forgive her, because her father
had expressed to her his disapproval.
6 If she marries, while obligated by
her vows or any thoughtless utterance
of her lips by which she has bound herself, 7 and her husband hears of it and
says nothing to her at the time that he
hears, then her vows shall stand, and
her pledges by which she has bound herself shall stand. 8 But if, at the time that
her husband hears of it, he expresses
disapproval to her, then he shall nullify
the vow by which she was obligated, or
the thoughtless utterance of her lips,
by which she bound herself; and the
LORD will forgive her. 9 (But every vow
of a widow or of a divorced woman, by
which she has bound herself, shall be
binding upon her.) 10 And if she made a
vow in her husband's house, or bound
herself by a pledge with an oath, 11 and
her husband heard it and said nothing
to her, and did not express disapproval
to her, then all her vows shall stand, and
any pledge by which she bound herself
shall stand. 12 But if her husband nullifies them at the time that he hears
them, then whatever proceeds out of
her lips concerning her vows, or concerning her pledge of herself, shall not
stand. Her husband has nullified them,
and the LORD will forgive her. 13 Any
vow or any binding oath to deny herself,[o] her husband may allow to stand,
or her husband may nullify. 14 But if her
husband says nothing to her from day
to day,[p] then he validates all her vows,
or all her pledges, by which she is obligated; he has validated them, because
he said nothing to her at the time that
he heard of them. 15 But if he nullifies
them some time after he has heard of
them, then he shall bear her guilt.
16 These are the statutes that the
LORD commanded Moses concerning a
husband and his wife, and a father and
his daughter while she is still young and
in her father's house.

WAR AGAINST MIDIAN

31 The LORD spoke to Moses, saying, 2 'Avenge the Israelites on
the Midianites; afterwards you shall be
gathered to your people.' 3 So Moses said
to the people, 'Arm some of your number for the war, so that they may go
against Midian, to execute the LORD's

[n] **29.40** Ch 30.1 in Heb [o] **30.13** Or *to fast*
[p] **30.14** Or *from that day to the next*

vengeance on Midian. [4]You shall send a thousand from each of the tribes of Israel to the war.' [5]So out of the thousands of Israel, a thousand from each tribe were conscripted, twelve thousand armed for battle. [6]Moses sent them to the war, a thousand from each tribe, along with Phinehas son of Eleazar the priest,[q] with the vessels of the sanctuary and the trumpets for sounding the alarm in his hand. [7]They did battle against Midian, as the LORD had commanded Moses, and killed every male. [8]They killed the kings of Midian: Evi, Rekem, Zur, Hur, and Reba, the five kings of Midian, in addition to others who were slain by them; and they also killed Balaam son of Beor with the sword. [9]The Israelites took the women of Midian and their little ones captive; and they took all their cattle, their flocks, and all their goods as booty. [10]All their towns where they had settled, and all their encampments, they burned, [11]but they took all the spoil and all the booty, both people and animals. [12]Then they brought the captives and the booty and the spoil to Moses, to Eleazar the priest, and to the congregation of the Israelites, at the camp on the plains of Moab by the Jordan at Jericho.

RETURN FROM THE WAR

13 Moses, Eleazar the priest, and all the leaders of the congregation went to meet them outside the camp. [14]Moses became angry with the officers of the army, the commanders of thousands and the commanders of hundreds, who had come from service in the war. [15]Moses said to them, 'Have you allowed all the women to live? [16]These women here, on Balaam's advice, made the Israelites act treacherously against the LORD in the affair of Peor, so that the plague came among the congregation of the LORD. [17]Now therefore, kill every male among the little ones, and kill every woman who has known a man by sleeping with him. [18]But all the young girls who have not known a man by sleeping with him, keep alive for yourselves. [19]Camp outside the camp for seven days; whoever of you has killed any person or touched a corpse, purify yourselves and your captives on the third and on the seventh day. [20]You shall purify every garment, every article of skin, everything made of goats' hair, and every article of wood.'

21 Eleazar the priest said to the troops who had gone to battle: 'This is the statute of the law that the LORD has commanded Moses: [22]gold, silver, bronze, iron, tin, and lead— [23]everything that can withstand fire, shall be passed through fire, and it shall be clean. Nevertheless it shall also be purified with the water for purification; and whatever cannot withstand fire, shall be passed through the water. [24]You must wash your clothes on the seventh day, and you shall be clean; afterwards you may come into the camp.'

DISPOSITION OF CAPTIVES AND BOOTY

25 The LORD spoke to Moses, saying, [26]'You and Eleazar the priest and the heads of the ancestral houses of the congregation make an inventory of the booty captured, both human and animal. [27]Divide the booty into two parts, between the warriors who went out to battle and all the congregation. [28]From the share of the warriors who went out to battle, set aside as tribute for the LORD one item out of every five hundred, whether persons, oxen, donkeys, sheep, or goats. [29]Take it from their half and give it to Eleazar the priest as an offering to the LORD. [30]But from the Israelites' half you shall take one out of every fifty, whether persons, oxen, donkeys, sheep, or goats—all the animals—and give them to the Levites who have charge of the tabernacle of the LORD.'

31 Then Moses and Eleazar the priest did as the LORD had commanded Moses:

32 The booty remaining from the spoil that the troops had taken totalled six hundred and seventy-five thousand sheep, [33]seventy-two thousand oxen, [34]sixty-one thousand donkeys, [35]and thirty-two thousand persons in all, women who had not known a man by sleeping with him.

36 The half-share, the portion of those who had gone out to war, was in number three hundred and thirty-seven thousand five hundred sheep and goats, [37]and the LORD's tribute of sheep and goats was six hundred and seventy-five. [38]The oxen were thirty-six thousand, of which the LORD's tribute was seventy-two. [39]The donkeys were thirty thousand five hundred, of which the LORD's tribute was sixty-one. [40]The persons were sixteen thousand, of which the LORD's tribute was thirty-two persons. [41]Moses gave the tribute, the offering

[q] 31.6 Gk: Heb adds *to the war*

for the LORD, to Eleazar the priest, as
the LORD had commanded Moses.
42 As for the Israelites' half, which
Moses separated from that of the troops,
43the congregation's half was three hundred and thirty-seven thousand five
hundred sheep and goats, 44thirty-six
thousand oxen, 45thirty thousand five
hundred donkeys, 46and sixteen thousand persons. 47From the Israelites' half
Moses took one of every fifty, both of
persons and of animals, and gave them
to the Levites who had charge of the
tabernacle of the LORD; as the LORD had
commanded Moses.
48 Then the officers who were over
the thousands of the army, the commanders of thousands and the commanders of hundreds, approached Moses, 49and said to Moses, 'Your servants
have counted the warriors who are under our command, and not one of us is
missing. 50And we have brought the
LORD's offering, what each of us found,
articles of gold, armlets and bracelets,
signet rings, ear-rings, and pendants,
to make atonement for ourselves before the LORD.' 51Moses and Eleazar the
priest received the gold from them, all
in the form of crafted articles. 52And all
the gold of the offering that they offered
to the LORD, from the commanders of
thousands and the commanders of hundreds, was sixteen thousand seven hundred and fifty shekels. 53(The troops had
all taken plunder for themselves.) 54So
Moses and Eleazar the priest received
the gold from the commanders of thousands and of hundreds, and brought it
into the tent of meeting as a memorial
for the Israelites before the LORD.

CONQUEST AND DIVISION OF TRANSJORDAN

32 Now the Reubenites and the
Gadites owned a very great
number of cattle. When they saw that
the land of Jazer and the land of Gilead
was a good place for cattle, 2the Gadites
and the Reubenites came and spoke to
Moses, to Eleazar the priest, and to the
leaders of the congregation, saying,
3'Ataroth, Dibon, Jazer, Nimrah, Heshbon, Elealeh, Sebam, Nebo, and Beon—
4the land that the LORD subdued before
the congregation of Israel—is a land for
cattle; and your servants have cattle.'
5They continued, 'If we have found favour in your sight, let this land be given
to your servants for a possession; do not
make us cross the Jordan.'
6 But Moses said to the Gadites and
to the Reubenites, 'Shall your brothers
go to war while you sit here? 7Why will
you discourage the hearts of the Israelites from going over into the land that
the LORD has given them? 8Your fathers did this, when I sent them from
Kadesh-barnea to see the land. 9When
they went up to the Wadi Eshcol and
saw the land, they discouraged the
hearts of the Israelites from going into
the land that the LORD had given them.
10The LORD's anger was kindled on that
day and he swore, saying, 11"Surely
none of the people who came up out of
Egypt, from twenty years old and upwards, shall see the land that I swore
to give to Abraham, to Isaac, and to Jacob, because they have not unreservedly
followed me— 12none except Caleb son
of Jephunneh the Kenizzite and Joshua
son of Nun, for they have unreservedly
followed the LORD." 13And the LORD's
anger was kindled against Israel, and he
made them wander in the wilderness
for forty years, until all the generation
that had done evil in the sight of the
LORD had disappeared. 14And now you,
a brood of sinners, have risen in place
of your fathers, to increase the LORD's
fierce anger against Israel! 15If you turn
away from following him, he will again
abandon them in the wilderness; and
you will destroy all this people.'
16 Then they came up to him and
said, 'We will build sheepfolds here for
our flocks, and towns for our little ones,
17but we will take up arms as a vanguard[r] before the Israelites, until we
have brought them to their place. Meanwhile our little ones will stay in the fortified towns because of the inhabitants
of the land. 18We will not return to our
homes until all the Israelites have obtained their inheritance. 19We will not
inherit with them on the other side of
the Jordan and beyond, because our inheritance has come to us on this side of
the Jordan to the east.'
20 So Moses said to them, 'If you do
this—if you take up arms to go before
the LORD for the war, 21and all those of
you who bear arms cross the Jordan before the LORD, until he has driven out
his enemies from before him 22and the
land is subdued before the LORD—then
after that you may return and be free
of obligation to the LORD and to Israel,
and this land shall be your possession

[r] **32.17** Cn: Heb *hurrying*

before the LORD. 23But if you do not do this, you have sinned against the LORD; and be sure your sin will find you out. 24Build towns for your little ones, and folds for your flocks; but do what you have promised.'

25 Then the Gadites and the Reubenites said to Moses, 'Your servants will do as my lord commands. 26Our little ones, our wives, our flocks, and all our livestock shall remain there in the towns of Gilead; 27but your servants will cross over, everyone armed for war, to do battle for the LORD, just as my lord orders.'

28 So Moses gave command concerning them to Eleazar the priest, to Joshua son of Nun, and to the heads of the ancestral houses of the Israelite tribes. 29And Moses said to them, 'If the Gadites and the Reubenites, everyone armed for battle before the LORD, will cross over the Jordan with you and the land shall be subdued before you, then you shall give them the land of Gilead for a possession; 30but if they will not cross over with you armed, they shall have possessions among you in the land of Canaan.' 31The Gadites and the Reubenites answered, 'As the LORD has spoken to your servants, so we will do. 32We will cross over armed before the LORD into the land of Canaan, but the possession of our inheritance shall remain with us on this side of[s] the Jordan.'

33 Moses gave to them—to the Gadites and to the Reubenites and to the half-tribe of Manasseh son of Joseph—the kingdom of King Sihon of the Amorites and the kingdom of King Og of Bashan, the land and its towns, with the territories of the surrounding towns. 34And the Gadites rebuilt Dibon, Ataroth, Aroer, 35Atroth-shophan, Jazer, Jogbehah, 36Beth-nimrah, and Beth-haran, fortified cities, and folds for sheep. 37And the Reubenites rebuilt Heshbon, Elealeh, Kiriathaim, 38Nebo, and Baal-meon (some names being changed), and Sibmah; and they gave names to the towns that they rebuilt. 39The descendants of Machir son of Manasseh went to Gilead, captured it, and dispossessed the Amorites who were there; 40so Moses gave Gilead to Machir son of Manasseh, and he settled there. 41Jair son of Manasseh went and captured their villages, and renamed them Havvoth-jair.[t] 42And Nobah went and captured Kenath and its villages, and renamed it Nobah after himself.

THE STAGES OF ISRAEL'S JOURNEY FROM EGYPT

33 These are the stages by which the Israelites went out of the land of Egypt in military formation under the leadership of Moses and Aaron. 2Moses wrote down their starting points, stage by stage, by command of the LORD; and these are their stages according to their starting places. 3They set out from Rameses in the first month, on the fifteenth day of the first month; on the day after the passover the Israelites went out boldly in the sight of all the Egyptians, 4while the Egyptians were burying all their firstborn, whom the LORD had struck down among them. The LORD executed judgements even against their gods.

5 So the Israelites set out from Rameses, and camped at Succoth. 6They set out from Succoth, and camped at Etham, which is on the edge of the wilderness. 7They set out from Etham, and turned back to Pi-hahiroth, which faces Baal-zephon; and they camped before Migdol. 8They set out from Pi-hahiroth, passed through the sea into the wilderness, went a three days' journey in the wilderness of Etham, and camped at Marah. 9They set out from Marah and came to Elim; at Elim there were twelve springs of water and seventy palm trees, and they camped there. 10They set out from Elim and camped by the Red Sea.[u] 11They set out from the Red Sea[v] and camped in the wilderness of Sin. 12They set out from the wilderness of Sin and camped at Dophkah. 13They set out from Dophkah and camped at Alush. 14They set out from Alush and camped at Rephidim, where there was no water for the people to drink. 15They set out from Rephidim and camped in the wilderness of Sinai. 16They set out from the wilderness of Sinai and camped at Kibroth-hattaavah. 17They set out from Kibroth-hattaavah and camped at Hazeroth. 18They set out from Hazeroth and camped at Rithmah. 19They set out from Rithmah and camped at Rimmon-perez. 20They set out from Rimmon-perez and camped at Libnah. 21They set out from Libnah and camped at Rissah. 22They set out from Rissah and camped at Kehelathah. 23They set out from Kehelathah and camped at Mount Shepher. 24They set out from Mount Shepher and camped

[s] **32.32** Heb *beyond* [t] **32.41** That is *the villages of Jair* [u] **33.10** Or *Sea of Reeds* [v] **33.11** Or *Sea of Reeds*

at Haradah. 25They set out from Haradah and camped at Makheloth. 26They
set out from Makheloth and camped at
Tahath. 27They set out from Tahath and
camped at Terah. 28They set out from Terah and camped at Mithkah. 29They set
out from Mithkah and camped at Hashmonah. 30They set out from Hashmonah
and camped at Moseroth. 31They set out
from Moseroth and camped at Bene-
jaakan. 32They set out from Bene-jaakan
and camped at Hor-haggidgad. 33They
set out from Hor-haggidgad and camped
at Jotbathah. 34They set out from Jotbathah and camped at Abronah. 35They set
out from Abronah and camped at Ezion-
geber. 36They set out from Ezion-geber
and camped in the wilderness of Zin
(that is, Kadesh). 37They set out from Kadesh and camped at Mount Hor, on the
edge of the land of Edom.

38 Aaron the priest went up Mount
Hor at the command of the LORD and
died there in the fortieth year after
the Israelites had come out of the land
of Egypt, on the first day of the fifth
month. 39Aaron was one hundred and
twenty-three years old when he died on
Mount Hor.

40 The Canaanite, the king of Arad,
who lived in the Negeb in the land of
Canaan, heard of the coming of the Israelites.

41 They set out from Mount Hor and
camped at Zalmonah. 42They set out
from Zalmonah and camped at Punon.
43They set out from Punon and camped
at Oboth. 44They set out from Oboth and
camped at Iye-abarim, in the territory
of Moab. 45They set out from Iyim and
camped at Dibon-gad. 46They set out
from Dibon-gad and camped at Almon-
diblathaim. 47They set out from Almon-
diblathaim and camped in the mountains of Abarim, before Nebo. 48They
set out from the mountains of Abarim
and camped in the plains of Moab by the
Jordan at Jericho; 49they camped by the
Jordan from Beth-jeshimoth as far as
Abel-shittim in the plains of Moab.

DIRECTIONS FOR THE CONQUEST OF CANAAN

50 In the plains of Moab by the Jordan at Jericho, the LORD spoke to Moses, saying: 51Speak to the Israelites, and
say to them: When you cross over the
Jordan into the land of Canaan, 52you
shall drive out all the inhabitants of the
land from before you, destroy all their
figured stones, destroy all their cast images, and demolish all their high places.
53You shall take possession of the land
and settle in it, for I have given you the
land to possess. 54You shall apportion
the land by lot according to your clans;
to a large one you shall give a large inheritance, and to a small one you shall
give a small inheritance; the inheritance shall belong to the person on
whom the lot falls; according to your
ancestral tribes you shall inherit. 55But
if you do not drive out the inhabitants
of the land from before you, then those
whom you let remain shall be as barbs
in your eyes and thorns in your sides;
they shall trouble you in the land where
you are settling. 56And I will do to you
as I thought to do to them.

THE BOUNDARIES OF THE LAND

34 The LORD spoke to Moses, saying: 2Command the Israelites,
and say to them: When you enter the
land of Canaan (this is the land that
shall fall to you for an inheritance, the
land of Canaan, defined by its boundaries), 3your south sector shall extend
from the wilderness of Zin along the
side of Edom. Your southern boundary
shall begin from the end of the Dead
Sea[w] on the east; 4your boundary shall
turn south of the ascent of Akrabbim,
and cross to Zin, and its outer limit shall
be south of Kadesh-barnea; then it shall
go on to Hazar-addar, and cross to Az-
mon; 5the boundary shall turn from Az-
mon to the Wadi of Egypt, and its termi-
nation shall be at the Sea.

6 For the western boundary, you
shall have the Great Sea and its[x] coast;
this shall be your western boundary.

7 This shall be your northern boundary: from the Great Sea you shall mark
out your line to Mount Hor; 8from
Mount Hor you shall mark it out to
Lebo-hamath, and the outer limit of the
boundary shall be at Zedad; 9then the
boundary shall extend to Ziphron, and
its end shall be at Hazar-enan; this shall
be your northern boundary.

10 You shall mark out your eastern
boundary from Hazar-enan to Shepham; 11and the boundary shall continue down from Shepham to Riblah on
the east side of Ain; and the boundary
shall go down, and reach the eastern
slope of the sea of Chinnereth; 12and the
boundary shall go down to the Jordan,
and its end shall be at the Dead Sea.[y]

[w] **34.3** Heb *Salt Sea* [x] **34.6** Syr: Heb lacks *its*
[y] **34.12** Heb *Salt Sea*

This shall be your land with its boundaries all round.
13 Moses commanded the Israelites,
saying: This is the land that you shall inherit by lot, which the LORD has commanded to give to the nine tribes and
to the half-tribe; 14for the tribe of the
Reubenites by their ancestral houses
and the tribe of the Gadites by their ancestral houses have taken their inheritance, and also the half-tribe of Manasseh; 15the two tribes and the half-tribe
have taken their inheritance beyond the
Jordan at Jericho eastwards, towards
the sunrise.

TRIBAL LEADERS

16 The LORD spoke to Moses, saying:
17These are the names of the men who
shall apportion the land to you for inheritance: the priest Eleazar and Joshua
son of Nun. 18You shall take one leader
of every tribe to apportion the land for
inheritance. 19These are the names of
the men: Of the tribe of Judah, Caleb
son of Jephunneh. 20Of the tribe of the
Simeonites, Shemuel son of Ammihud.
21Of the tribe of Benjamin, Elidad son of
Chislon. 22Of the tribe of the Danites a
leader, Bukki son of Jogli. 23Of the Josephites: of the tribe of the Manassites a
leader, Hanniel son of Ephod, 24and of
the tribe of the Ephraimites a leader,
Kemuel son of Shiphtan. 25Of the tribe
of the Zebulunites a leader, Eli-zaphan
son of Parnach. 26Of the tribe of the
Issacharites a leader, Paltiel son of Az-
zan. 27And of the tribe of the Asherites a
leader, Ahihud son of Shelomi. 28Of the
tribe of the Naphtalites a leader, Peda-
hel son of Ammihud. 29These were the
ones whom the LORD commanded to
apportion the inheritance for the Israelites in the land of Canaan.

CITIES FOR THE LEVITES

35 In the plains of Moab by the Jordan at Jericho, the LORD spoke
to Moses, saying: 2Command the Israelites to give, from the inheritance
that they possess, towns for the Levites
to live in; you shall also give to the Levites pasture lands surrounding the
towns. 3The towns shall be theirs to live
in, and their pasture lands shall be for
their cattle, for their livestock, and for
all their animals. 4The pasture lands of
the towns, which you shall give to the
Levites, shall reach from the wall of the
town outwards a thousand cubits all
around. 5You shall measure, outside the
town, for the east side two thousand
cubits, for the south side two thousand
cubits, for the west side two thousand
cubits, and for the north side two thousand cubits, with the town in the middle; this shall belong to them as pasture
land for their towns.
6 The towns that you give to the Levites shall include the six cities of refuge, where you shall permit a slayer to
flee, and in addition to them you shall
give forty-two towns. 7The towns that
you give to the Levites shall total forty-
eight, with their pasture lands. 8And as
for the towns that you shall give from
the possession of the Israelites, from
the larger tribes you shall take many,
and from the smaller tribes you shall
take few; each, in proportion to the inheritance that it obtains, shall give of its
towns to the Levites.

CITIES OF REFUGE

9 The LORD spoke to Moses, saying:
10Speak to the Israelites, and say to
them: When you cross the Jordan into
the land of Canaan, 11then you shall select cities to be cities of refuge for you, so
that a slayer who kills a person without
intent may flee there. 12The cities shall
be for you a refuge from the avenger, so
that the slayer may not die until there is
a trial before the congregation.
13 The cities that you designate shall
be six cities of refuge for you: 14you shall
designate three cities beyond the Jordan, and three cities in the land of Canaan, to be cities of refuge. 15These six
cities shall serve as refuge for the Israelites, for the resident or transient alien
among them, so that anyone who kills
a person without intent may flee there.

CONCERNING MURDER AND BLOOD-REVENGE

16 But anyone who strikes another
with an iron object, and death ensues,
is a murderer; the murderer shall be put
to death. 17Or anyone who strikes another with a stone in hand that could
cause death, and death ensues, is a murderer; the murderer shall be put to death.
18Or anyone who strikes another with a
weapon of wood in hand that could cause
death, and death ensues, is a murderer;
the murderer shall be put to death. 19The
avenger of blood is the one who shall put
the murderer to death; when they meet,
the avenger of blood shall execute the
sentence. 20Likewise, if someone pushes
another from hatred, or hurls something

at another, lying in wait, and death ensues, 21 or in enmity strikes another with
the hand, and death ensues, then the
one who struck the blow shall be put
to death; that person is a murderer; the
avenger of blood shall put the murderer
to death when they meet.

22 But if someone pushes another suddenly without enmity, or hurls any object
without lying in wait, 23 or, while handling any stone that could cause death,
unintentionally[z] drops it on another and
death ensues, though they were not enemies, and no harm was intended, 24 then
the congregation shall judge between the
slayer and the avenger of blood, in accordance with these ordinances; 25 and the
congregation shall rescue the slayer from
the avenger of blood. Then the congregation shall send the slayer back to the original city of refuge. The slayer shall live in
it until the death of the high priest who
was anointed with the holy oil. 26 But if
the slayer shall at any time go outside the
bounds of the original city of refuge, 27 and
is found by the avenger of blood outside
the bounds of the city of refuge, and is
killed by the avenger, no blood-guilt shall
be incurred. 28 For the slayer must remain
in the city of refuge until the death of the
high priest; but after the death of the high
priest the slayer may return home.

29 These things shall be a statute and
ordinance for you throughout your generations wherever you live.

30 If anyone kills another, the murderer shall be put to death on the evidence of witnesses; but no one shall be
put to death on the testimony of a single
witness. 31 Moreover, you shall accept no
ransom for the life of a murderer who
is subject to the death penalty; a murderer must be put to death. 32 Nor shall
you accept ransom for one who has fled
to a city of refuge, enabling the fugitive to return to live in the land before
the death of the high priest. 33 You shall
not pollute the land in which you live;
for blood pollutes the land, and no expiation can be made for the land, for the
blood that is shed in it, except by the
blood of the one who shed it. 34 You shall
not defile the land in which you live, in
which I also dwell; for I the LORD dwell
among the Israelites.

MARRIAGE OF FEMALE HEIRS

36 The heads of the ancestral houses
of the clans of the descendants of
Gilead son of Machir son of Manasseh,
of the Josephite clans, came forward
and spoke in the presence of Moses and
the leaders, the heads of the ancestral
houses of the Israelites; 2 they said, 'The
LORD commanded my lord to give the
land for inheritance by lot to the Israelites; and my lord was commanded by
the LORD to give the inheritance of our
brother Zelophehad to his daughters.
3 But if they are married into another Israelite tribe, then their inheritance will
be taken from the inheritance of our
ancestors and added to the inheritance
of the tribe into which they marry; so
it will be taken away from the allotted
portion of our inheritance. 4 And when
the jubilee of the Israelites comes, then
their inheritance will be added to the
inheritance of the tribe into which they
have married; and their inheritance will
be taken from the inheritance of our ancestral tribe.'

5 Then Moses commanded the Israelites according to the word of the
LORD, saying, 'The descendants of the
tribe of Joseph are right in what they
are saying. 6 This is what the LORD commands concerning the daughters of
Zelophehad, "Let them marry whom
they think best; only it must be into a
clan of their father's tribe that they are
married, 7 so that no inheritance of the
Israelites shall be transferred from one
tribe to another; for all Israelites shall
retain the inheritance of their ancestral
tribes. 8 Every daughter who possesses
an inheritance in any tribe of the Israelites shall marry one from the clan of
her father's tribe, so that all Israelites
may continue to possess their ancestral
inheritance. 9 No inheritance shall be
transferred from one tribe to another;
for each of the tribes of the Israelites
shall retain its own inheritance."'

10 The daughters of Zelophehad did
as the LORD had commanded Moses.
11 Mahlah, Tirzah, Hoglah, Milcah, and
Noah, the daughters of Zelophehad,
married sons of their father's brothers.
12 They were married into the clans of
the descendants of Manasseh son of Joseph, and their inheritance remained in
the tribe of their father's clan.

13 These are the commandments
and the ordinances that the LORD commanded through Moses to the Israelites
in the plains of Moab by the Jordan at
Jericho.

[z] **35.23** Heb *without seeing*

DEUTERONOMY

The book of Deuteronomy is an extended testimony or address of Moses to the people of Israel just prior to their entry into the promised land. Moses recounts the law (the Torah) by which the people must live in order to remain faithful to God. The law challenges the people to reform, to centralize their worship, and to become a humane and just people by caring for the poor and disadvantaged. The special style, themes, and language of Deuteronomy greatly influenced the biblical works of Joshua, Judges, 1 and 2 Samuel, and 1 and 2 Kings.

Deuteronomy is divided into three discourses of Moses followed by an appendix that recounts the death of Moses. Passages from Deuteronomy are read at various Sundays during the liturgical year. An important passage that is a central theme of the story line echoed in the biblical books from Joshua to Kings is the text read every year on the Thursday after Ash Wednesday. In this passage the Israelites are told: "If you obey the commandments of the LORD your God . . . then you shall live and become numerous . . . But if your heart turns away . . . you shall perish" (30.16–18). The Israelites would prosper only if they remained faithful to God.

EVENTS AT HOREB RECALLED

1 These are the words that Moses spoke to all Israel beyond the
Jordan—in the wilderness, on the plain
opposite Suph, between Paran and To-
phel, Laban, Hazeroth, and Di-zahab.
2(By the way of Mount Seir it takes
eleven days to reach Kadesh-barnea
from Horeb.) 3In the fortieth year, on
the first day of the eleventh month,
Moses spoke to the Israelites just as the
LORD had commanded him to speak
to them. 4This was after he had defeated King Sihon of the Amorites, who
reigned in Heshbon, and King Og of Bashan, who reigned in Ashtaroth and[a] in
Edrei. 5Beyond the Jordan in the land of
Moab, Moses undertook to expound this
law as follows:
6 The LORD our God spoke to us at
Horeb, saying, 'You have stayed long
enough at this mountain. 7Resume
your journey, and go into the hill country of the Amorites as well as into the
neighbouring regions—the Arabah, the
hill country, the Shephelah, the Negeb,
and the sea coast—the land of the Canaanites and the Lebanon, as far as the
great river, the river Euphrates. 8See, I
have set the land before you; go in and
take possession of the land that I[b] swore
to your ancestors, to Abraham, to Isaac,
and to Jacob, to give to them and to
their descendants after them.'

APPOINTMENT OF TRIBAL LEADERS

9 At that time I said to you, 'I am unable by myself to bear you. 10The LORD
your God has multiplied you, so that
today you are as numerous as the stars
of heaven. 11May the LORD, the God of
your ancestors, increase you a thousand times more and bless you, as he
has promised you! 12But how can I bear
the heavy burden of your disputes all by
myself? 13Choose for each of your tribes
individuals who are wise, discerning,
and reputable to be your leaders.' 14You
answered me, 'The plan you have proposed is a good one.' 15So I took the leaders of your tribes, wise and reputable

[a] 1.4 Gk Syr Vg Compare Josh 12.4: Heb lacks *and*
[b] 1.8 Sam Gk: MT *the LORD*

individuals, and installed them as leaders over you, commanders of thousands, commanders of hundreds, commanders of fifties, commanders of tens, and officials, throughout your tribes. 16 I charged your judges at that time: 'Give the members of your community a fair hearing, and judge rightly between one person and another, whether citizen or resident alien. 17 You must not be partial in judging: hear out the small and the great alike; you shall not be intimidated by anyone, for the judgement is God's. Any case that is too hard for you, bring to me, and I will hear it.' 18 So I charged you at that time with all the things that you should do.

ISRAEL'S REFUSAL TO ENTER THE LAND

19 Then, just as the LORD our God had ordered us, we set out from Horeb and went through all that great and terrible wilderness that you saw, on the way to the hill country of the Amorites, until we reached Kadesh-barnea. 20 I said to you, 'You have reached the hill country of the Amorites, which the LORD our God is giving us. 21 See, the LORD your God has given the land to you; go up, take possession, as the LORD, the God of your ancestors, has promised you; do not fear or be dismayed.'

22 All of you came to me and said, 'Let us send men ahead of us to explore the land for us and bring back a report to us regarding the route by which we should go up and the cities we will come to.' 23 The plan seemed good to me, and I selected twelve of you, one from each tribe. 24 They set out and went up into the hill country, and when they reached the Valley of Eshcol they spied it out 25 and gathered some of the land's produce, which they brought down to us. They brought back a report to us, and said, 'It is a good land that the LORD our God is giving us.'

26 But you were unwilling to go up. You rebelled against the command of the LORD your God; 27 you grumbled in your tents and said, 'It is because the LORD hates us that he has brought us out of the land of Egypt, to hand us over to the Amorites to destroy us. 28 Where are we heading? Our kindred have made our hearts fail by reporting, "The people are stronger and taller than we are; the cities are large and fortified up to heaven! We actually saw there the offspring of the Anakim!"' 29 I said to you, 'Have no dread or fear of them. 30 The LORD your God, who goes before you, is the one who will fight for you, just as he did for you in Egypt before your very eyes, 31 and in the wilderness, where you saw how the LORD your God carried you, just as one carries a child, all the way that you travelled until you reached this place. 32 But in spite of this, you have no trust in the LORD your God, 33 who goes before you on the way to seek out a place for you to camp, in fire by night, and in the cloud by day, to show you the route you should take.'

THE PENALTY FOR ISRAEL'S REBELLION

34 When the LORD heard your words, he was wrathful and swore: 35 'Not one of these—not one of this evil generation—shall see the good land that I swore to give to your ancestors, 36 except Caleb son of Jephunneh. He shall see it, and to him and to his descendants I will give the land on which he set foot, because of his complete fidelity to the LORD.' 37 Even with me the LORD was angry on your account, saying, 'You also shall not enter there. 38 Joshua son of Nun, your assistant, shall enter there; encourage him, for he is the one who will secure Israel's possession of it. 39 And as for your little ones, who you thought would become booty, your children, who today do not yet know right from wrong, they shall enter there; to them I will give it, and they shall take possession of it. 40 But as for you, journey back into the wilderness, in the direction of the Red Sea.'[c]

41 You answered me, 'We have sinned against the LORD! We are ready to go up and fight, just as the LORD our God commanded us.' So all of you strapped on your battle gear, and thought it easy to go up into the hill country. 42 The LORD said to me, 'Say to them, "Do not go up and do not fight, for I am not in the midst of you; otherwise you will be defeated by your enemies."' 43 Although I told you, you would not listen. You rebelled against the command of the LORD and presumptuously went up into the hill country. 44 The Amorites who lived in that hill country then came out against you and chased you as bees do. They beat you down in Seir as far as Hormah. 45 When you returned and wept before the LORD, the LORD would neither heed your voice nor pay you any attention.

[c] 1.40 Or *Sea of Reeds*

THE DESERT YEARS

46 After you had stayed at Kadesh as many days as you did,

2 1we journeyed back into the wilderness, in the direction of the Red Sea,[d] as the LORD had told me, and skirted Mount Seir for many days. 2Then the LORD said to me: 3'You have been skirting this hill country long enough. Head north, 4and charge the people as follows: You are about to pass through the territory of your kindred, the descendants of Esau, who live in Seir. They will be afraid of you, so be very careful 5not to engage in battle with them, for I will not give you even so much as a foot's length of their land, since I have given Mount Seir to Esau as a possession. 6You shall purchase food from them for money, so that you may eat; and you shall also buy water from them for money, so that you may drink. 7Surely the LORD your God has blessed you in all your undertakings; he knows your going through this great wilderness. These forty years the LORD your God has been with you; you have lacked nothing.' 8So we passed by our kin, the descendants of Esau who live in Seir, leaving behind the route of the Arabah, and leaving behind Elath and Ezion-geber.

When we had headed out along the route of the wilderness of Moab, 9the LORD said to me: 'Do not harass Moab or engage them in battle, for I will not give you any of its land as a possession, since I have given Ar as a possession to the descendants of Lot.' 10(The Emim—a large and numerous people, as tall as the Anakim—had formerly inhabited it. 11Like the Anakim, they are usually reckoned as Rephaim, though the Moabites call them Emim. 12Moreover, the Horim had formerly inhabited Seir, but the descendants of Esau dispossessed them, destroying them and settling in their place, as Israel has done in the land that the LORD gave them as a possession.) 13'Now then, proceed to cross over the Wadi Zered.'

So we crossed over the Wadi Zered. 14And the length of time we had travelled from Kadesh-barnea until we crossed the Wadi Zered was thirty-eight years, until the entire generation of warriors had perished from the camp, as the LORD had sworn concerning them. 15Indeed, the LORD's own hand was against them, to root them out from the camp, until all had perished.

16 Just as soon as all the warriors had died from among the people, 17the LORD spoke to me, saying, 18'Today you are going to cross the boundary of Moab at Ar. 19When you approach the frontier of the Ammonites, do not harass them or engage them in battle, for I will not give the land of the Ammonites to you as a possession, because I have given it to the descendants of Lot.' 20(It also is usually reckoned as a land of Rephaim. Rephaim formerly inhabited it, though the Ammonites call them Zamzummim, 21a strong and numerous people, as tall as the Anakim. But the LORD destroyed them from before the Ammonites so that they could dispossess them and settle in their place. 22He did the same for the descendants of Esau, who live in Seir, by destroying the Horim before them so that they could dispossess them and settle in their place even to this day. 23As for the Avvim, who had lived in settlements in the vicinity of Gaza, the Caphtorim, who came from Caphtor, destroyed them and settled in their place.) 24'Proceed on your journey and cross the Wadi Arnon. See, I have handed over to you King Sihon the Amorite of Heshbon, and his land. Begin to take possession by engaging him in battle. 25This day I will begin to put the dread and fear of you upon the peoples everywhere under heaven; when they hear report of you, they will tremble and be in anguish because of you.'

DEFEAT OF KING SIHON

26 So I sent messengers from the wilderness of Kedemoth to King Sihon of Heshbon with the following terms of peace: 27'If you let me pass through your land, I will travel only along the road; I will turn aside neither to the right nor to the left. 28You shall sell me food for money, so that I may eat, and supply me water for money, so that I may drink. Only allow me to pass through on foot—29just as the descendants of Esau who live in Seir have done for me and likewise the Moabites who live in Ar—until I cross the Jordan into the land that the LORD our God is giving us.' 30But King Sihon of Heshbon was not willing to let us pass through, for the LORD your God had hardened his spirit and made his heart defiant in order to hand him over to you, as he has now done.

31 The LORD said to me, 'See, I have begun to give Sihon and his land over to you. Begin now to take possession of his

d 2.1 Or *Sea of Reeds*

land.’ 32So when Sihon came out against
us, he and all his people for battle at
Jahaz, 33the LORD our God gave him
over to us; and we struck him down,
along with his offspring and all his people. 34At that time we captured all his
towns, and in each town we utterly destroyed men, women, and children. We
left not a single survivor. 35Only the
livestock we kept as spoil for ourselves,
as well as the plunder of the towns that
we had captured. 36From Aroer on the
edge of the Wadi Arnon (including the
town that is in the wadi itself) as far as
Gilead, there was no citadel too high for
us. The LORD our God gave everything
to us. 37You did not encroach, however,
on the land of the Ammonites, avoid-
ing the whole upper region of the Wadi
Jabbok as well as the towns of the hill
country, just as[e] the LORD our God had
charged.

DEFEAT OF KING OG

3 When we headed up the road to Bashan, King Og of Bashan came out
against us, he and all his people, for battle at Edrei. 2The LORD said to me, ‘Do
not fear him, for I have handed him
over to you, along with his people and
his land. Do to him as you did to King
Sihon of the Amorites, who reigned in
Heshbon.’ 3So the LORD our God also
handed over to us King Og of Bashan
and all his people. We struck him down
until not a single survivor was left. 4At
that time we captured all his towns;
there was no citadel that we did not take
from them—sixty towns, the whole region of Argob, the kingdom of Og in
Bashan. 5All these were fortress towns
with high walls, double gates, and bars,
besides a great many villages. 6And we
utterly destroyed them, as we had done
to King Sihon of Heshbon, in each city
utterly destroying men, women, and
children. 7But all the livestock and the
plunder of the towns we kept as spoil for
ourselves.

8 So at that time we took from the
two kings of the Amorites the land beyond the Jordan, from the Wadi Arnon
to Mount Hermon 9(the Sidonians call
Hermon Sirion, while the Amorites call
it Senir), 10all the towns of the tableland, the whole of Gilead, and all of Bashan, as far as Salecah and Edrei, towns
of Og’s kingdom in Bashan. 11(Now only
King Og of Bashan was left of the remnant of the Rephaim. In fact his bed, an
iron bed, can still be seen in Rabbah of
the Ammonites. By the common cubit it
is nine cubits long and four cubits wide.)
12As for the land that we took possession of at that time, I gave to the Reubenites and Gadites the territory north
of Aroer[f] that is on the edge of the Wadi
Arnon, as well as half the hill country
of Gilead with its towns, 13and I gave to
the half-tribe of Manasseh the rest of
Gilead and all of Bashan, Og’s kingdom.
(The whole region of Argob: all that portion of Bashan used to be called a land of
Rephaim; 14Jair the Manassite acquired
the whole region of Argob as far as the
border of the Geshurites and the Maacathites, and he named them—that is,
Bashan—after himself, Havvoth-jair,[g]
as it is to this day.) 15To Machir I gave
Gilead. 16And to the Reubenites and the
Gadites I gave the territory from Gilead as far as the Wadi Arnon, with the
middle of the wadi as a boundary, and
up to the Jabbok, the wadi being the
boundary of the Ammonites; 17the Arabah also, with the Jordan and its banks,
from Chinnereth down to the sea of the
Arabah, the Dead Sea,[h] with the lower
slopes of Pisgah on the east.

18 At that time, I charged you as follows: ‘Although the LORD your God has
given you this land to occupy, all your
troops shall cross over armed as the
vanguard of your Israelite kin. 19Only
your wives, your children, and your
livestock—I know that you have much
livestock—shall stay behind in the
towns that I have given to you. 20When
the LORD gives rest to your kindred, as
to you, and they too have occupied the
land that the LORD your God is giving
them beyond the Jordan, then each of
you may return to the property that
I have given to you.’ 21And I charged
Joshua as well at that time, saying:
‘Your own eyes have seen everything
that the LORD your God has done to
these two kings; so the LORD will do
to all the kingdoms into which you are
about to cross. 22Do not fear them, for
it is the LORD your God who fights for
you.’

MOSES VIEWS CANAAN FROM PISGAH

23 At that time, too, I entreated the
LORD, saying: 24‘O Lord GOD, you have
only begun to show your servant your
greatness and your might; what god in

[e] 2.37 Gk Tg: Heb *and all* [f] 3.12 Heb *territory from Aroer* [g] 3.14 That is *Settlement of Jair* [h] 3.17 Heb *Salt Sea*

heaven or on earth can perform deeds
and mighty acts like yours! 25Let me
cross over to see the good land beyond
the Jordan, that good hill country and
the Lebanon.' 26But the LORD was angry
with me on your account and would not
heed me. The LORD said to me, 'Enough
from you! Never speak to me of this
matter again! 27Go up to the top of Pisgah and look around you to the west, to
the north, to the south, and to the east.
Look well, for you shall not cross over
this Jordan. 28But charge Joshua, and
encourage and strengthen him, because
it is he who shall cross over at the head
of this people and who shall secure their
possession of the land that you will see.'
29So we remained in the valley opposite
Beth-peor.

MOSES COMMANDS OBEDIENCE

4 So now, Israel, give heed to the
statutes and ordinances that I am
teaching you to observe, so that you
may live to enter and occupy the land
that the LORD, the God of your ancestors, is giving you. 2You must neither
add anything to what I command you
nor take away anything from it, but
keep the commandments of the LORD
your God with which I am charging
you. 3You have seen for yourselves what
the LORD did with regard to the Baal
of Peor—how the LORD your God destroyed from among you everyone who
followed the Baal of Peor, 4while those
of you who held fast to the LORD your
God are all alive today.

5 See, just as the LORD my God has
charged me, I now teach you statutes
and ordinances for you to observe in
the land that you are about to enter and
occupy. 6You must observe them diligently, for this will show your wisdom
and discernment to the peoples, who,
when they hear all these statutes, will
say, 'Surely this great nation is a wise
and discerning people!' 7For what other
great nation has a god so near to it as
the LORD our God is whenever we call
to him? 8And what other great nation
has statutes and ordinances as just as
this entire law that I am setting before
you today?

9 But take care and watch yourselves
closely, so as neither to forget the things
that your eyes have seen nor to let them
slip from your mind all the days of your
life; make them known to your children
and your children's children— 10how
you once stood before the LORD your
God at Horeb, when the LORD said to
me, 'Assemble the people for me, and
I will let them hear my words, so that
they may learn to fear me as long as they
live on the earth, and may teach their
children to do so'; 11you approached
and stood at the foot of the mountain
while the mountain was blazing up
to the very heavens, shrouded in dark
clouds. 12Then the LORD spoke to you
out of the fire. You heard the sound of
words but saw no form; there was only
a voice. 13He declared to you his covenant, which he charged you to observe,
that is, the ten commandments;[i] and he
wrote them on two stone tablets. 14And
the LORD charged me at that time to
teach you statutes and ordinances for
you to observe in the land that you are
about to cross into and occupy.

15 Since you saw no form when the
LORD spoke to you at Horeb out of the
fire, take care and watch yourselves
closely, 16so that you do not act corruptly by making an idol for yourselves,
in the form of any figure—the likeness
of male or female, 17the likeness of any
animal that is on the earth, the likeness
of any winged bird that flies in the air,
18the likeness of anything that creeps on
the ground, the likeness of any fish that
is in the water under the earth. 19And
when you look up to the heavens and
see the sun, the moon, and the stars, all
the host of heaven, do not be led astray
and bow down to them and serve them,
things that the LORD your God has allotted to all the peoples everywhere under
heaven. 20But the LORD has taken you
and brought you out of the iron-smelter,
out of Egypt, to become a people of his
very own possession, as you are now.

21 The LORD was angry with me
because of you, and he vowed that I
should not cross the Jordan and that I
should not enter the good land that the
LORD your God is giving for your possession. 22For I am going to die in this
land without crossing over the Jordan,
but you are going to cross over to take
possession of that good land. 23So be
careful not to forget the covenant that
the LORD your God made with you, and
not to make for yourselves an idol in the
form of anything that the LORD your
God has forbidden you. 24For the LORD
your God is a devouring fire, a jealous
God.

[i] 4.13 Heb *the ten words*

25 When you have had children and
children's children, and become complacent in the land, if you act corruptly by
making an idol in the form of anything,
thus doing what is evil in the sight of
the LORD your God, and provoking him
to anger, 26 I call heaven and earth to
witness against you today that you will
soon utterly perish from the land that
you are crossing the Jordan to occupy;
you will not live long on it, but will be
utterly destroyed. 27 The LORD will scatter you among the peoples; only a few
of you will be left among the nations
where the LORD will lead you. 28 There
you will serve other gods made by human hands, objects of wood and stone
that neither see, nor hear, nor eat, nor
smell. 29 From there you will seek the
LORD your God, and you will find him
if you search after him with all your
heart and soul. 30 In your distress, when
all these things have happened to you
in time to come, you will return to the
LORD your God and heed him. 31 Because the LORD your God is a merciful
God, he will neither abandon you nor
destroy you; he will not forget the covenant with your ancestors that he swore
to them.

32 For ask now about former ages,
long before your own, ever since the day
that God created human beings on the
earth; ask from one end of heaven to
the other: has anything so great as this
ever happened or has its like ever been
heard of? 33 Has any people ever heard
the voice of a god speaking out of a fire,
as you have heard, and lived? 34 Or has
any god ever attempted to go and take
a nation for himself from the midst of
another nation, by trials, by signs and
wonders, by war, by a mighty hand
and an outstretched arm, and by terrifying displays of power, as the LORD
your God did for you in Egypt before
your very eyes? 35 To you it was shown
so that you would acknowledge that the
LORD is God; there is no other besides
him. 36 From heaven he made you hear
his voice to discipline you. On earth he
showed you his great fire, while you
heard his words coming out of the fire.
37 And because he loved your ancestors,
he chose their descendants after them.
He brought you out of Egypt with
his own presence, by his great power,
38 driving out before you nations greater
and mightier than yourselves, to bring
you in, giving you their land for a possession, as it is still today. 39 So acknowledge today and take to heart that the
LORD is God in heaven above and on the
earth beneath; there is no other. 40 Keep
his statutes and his commandments,
which I am commanding you today for
your own well-being and that of your
descendants after you, so that you may
long remain in the land that the LORD
your God is giving you for all time.

CITIES OF REFUGE EAST OF THE JORDAN

41 Then Moses set apart on the east
side of the Jordan three cities 42 to which
a homicide could flee, someone who unintentionally kills another person, the
two not having been at enmity before;
the homicide could flee to one of these
cities and live: 43 Bezer in the wilderness
on the tableland belonging to the Reubenites, Ramoth in Gilead belonging to
the Gadites, and Golan in Bashan belonging to the Manassites.

TRANSITION TO THE SECOND ADDRESS

44 This is the law that Moses set before the Israelites. 45 These are the decrees and the statutes and ordinances
that Moses spoke to the Israelites when
they had come out of Egypt, 46 beyond
the Jordan in the valley opposite Beth-
peor, in the land of King Sihon of the
Amorites, who reigned at Heshbon,
whom Moses and the Israelites defeated
when they came out of Egypt. 47 They
occupied his land and the land of King
Og of Bashan, the two kings of the Amorites on the eastern side of the Jordan:
48 from Aroer, which is on the edge of
the Wadi Arnon, as far as Mount Sirion[j]
(that is, Hermon), 49 together with all
the Arabah on the east side of the Jordan as far as the Sea of the Arabah, under the slopes of Pisgah.

THE TEN COMMANDMENTS

5 Moses convened all Israel, and said
to them:

Hear, O Israel, the statutes and ordinances that I am addressing to you today; you shall learn them and observe
them diligently. 2 The LORD our God
made a covenant with us at Horeb. 3 Not
with our ancestors did the LORD make
this covenant, but with us, who are all
of us here alive today. 4 The LORD spoke
with you face to face at the mountain,
out of the fire. 5 (At that time I was

j 4.48 Syr: Heb *Sion*

standing between the LORD and you to
declare to you the words[k] of the LORD;
for you were afraid because of the fire
and did not go up the mountain.) And
he said:

6 I am the LORD your God, who
brought you out of the land of Egypt,
out of the house of slavery; 7you shall
have no other gods before[l] me.

8 You shall not make for yourself an
idol, whether in the form of anything
that is in heaven above, or that is on
the earth beneath, or that is in the water under the earth. 9You shall not bow
down to them or worship them; for I the
LORD your God am a jealous God, punishing children for the iniquity of parents, to the third and fourth generation
of those who reject me, 10but showing
steadfast love to the thousandth generation[m] of those who love me and keep my
commandments.

11 You shall not make wrongful use
of the name of the LORD your God, for
the LORD will not acquit anyone who
misuses his name.

12 Observe the sabbath day and
keep it holy, as the LORD your God commanded you. 13For six days you shall labour and do all your work. 14But the seventh day is a sabbath to the LORD your
God; you shall not do any work—you, or
your son or your daughter, or your male
or female slave, or your ox or your donkey, or any of your livestock, or the resident alien in your towns, so that your
male and female slave may rest as well
as you. 15Remember that you were a
slave in the land of Egypt, and the LORD
your God brought you out from there
with a mighty hand and an outstretched
arm; therefore the LORD your God commanded you to keep the sabbath day.

16 Honour your father and your
mother, as the LORD your God commanded you, so that your days may be
long and that it may go well with you
in the land that the LORD your God is
giving you.

17 You shall not murder.[n]

18 Neither shall you commit adultery.

19 Neither shall you steal.

20 Neither shall you bear false witness against your neighbour.

21 Neither shall you covet your
neighbour's wife.

Neither shall you desire your neighbour's house, or field, or male or female
slave, or ox, or donkey, or anything that
belongs to your neighbour.

MOSES THE MEDIATOR OF GOD'S WILL

22 These words the LORD spoke with
a loud voice to your whole assembly at
the mountain, out of the fire, the cloud,
and the thick darkness, and he added
no more. He wrote them on two stone
tablets, and gave them to me. 23When
you heard the voice out of the darkness,
while the mountain was burning with
fire, you approached me, all the heads
of your tribes and your elders; 24and
you said, 'Look, the LORD our God has
shown us his glory and greatness, and
we have heard his voice out of the fire.
Today we have seen that God may speak
to someone and the person may still
live. 25So now why should we die? For
this great fire will consume us; if we
hear the voice of the LORD our God any
longer, we shall die. 26For who is there
of all flesh that has heard the voice of
the living God speaking out of fire, as
we have, and remained alive? 27Go near,
you yourself, and hear all that the LORD
our God will say. Then tell us everything
that the LORD our God tells you, and we
will listen and do it.'

28 The LORD heard your words when
you spoke to me, and the LORD said to
me: 'I have heard the words of this people, which they have spoken to you; they
are right in all that they have spoken.
29If only they had such a mind as this,
to fear me and to keep all my commandments always, so that it might go well
with them and with their children for
ever! 30Go, say to them, "Return to your
tents." 31But you, stand here by me, and
I will tell you all the commandments,
the statutes and the ordinances, that
you shall teach them, so that they may
do them in the land that I am giving
them to possess.' 32You must therefore
be careful to do as the LORD your God
has commanded you; you shall not turn
to the right or to the left. 33You must
follow exactly the path that the LORD
your God has commanded you, so that
you may live, and that it may go well
with you, and that you may live long in
the land that you are to possess.

THE GREAT COMMANDMENT

6 Now this is the commandment—
the statutes and the ordinances—
that the LORD your God charged me to
teach you to observe in the land that
you are about to cross into and occupy,

k 5.5 Q Mss Sam Gk Syr Vg Tg: MT *word* l 5.7 Or *besides* m 5.10 Or *to thousands* n 5.17 Or *kill*

2so that you and your children and your
children's children may fear the LORD
your God all the days of your life, and
keep all his decrees and his commandments that I am commanding you, so
that your days may be long. 3Hear therefore, O Israel, and observe them diligently, so that it may go well with you,
and so that you may multiply greatly in
a land flowing with milk and honey, as
the LORD, the God of your ancestors, has
promised you.

4 Hear, O Israel: The LORD is our
God, the LORD alone.[o] 5You shall love
the LORD your God with all your heart,
and with all your soul, and with all your
might. 6Keep these words that I am
commanding you today in your heart.
7Recite them to your children and talk
about them when you are at home and
when you are away, when you lie down
and when you rise. 8Bind them as a sign
on your hand, fix them as an emblem[p]
on your forehead, 9and write them on
the doorposts of your house and on your
gates.

CAUTION AGAINST DISOBEDIENCE

10 When the LORD your God has
brought you into the land that he swore
to your ancestors, to Abraham, to Isaac,
and to Jacob, to give you—a land with
fine, large cities that you did not build,
11houses filled with all sorts of goods that
you did not fill, hewn cisterns that you
did not hew, vineyards and olive groves
that you did not plant—and when you
have eaten your fill, 12take care that you
do not forget the LORD, who brought
you out of the land of Egypt, out of the
house of slavery. 13The LORD your God
you shall fear; him you shall serve, and
by his name alone you shall swear. 14Do
not follow other gods, any of the gods
of the peoples who are all around you,
15because the LORD your God, who is
present with you, is a jealous God. The
anger of the LORD your God would be
kindled against you and he would destroy you from the face of the earth.

16 Do not put the LORD your God to
the test, as you tested him at Massah.
17You must diligently keep the commandments of the LORD your God, and
his decrees, and his statutes that he has
commanded you. 18Do what is right and
good in the sight of the LORD, so that it
may go well with you, and so that you
may go in and occupy the good land
that the LORD swore to your ancestors
to give you, 19thrusting out all your enemies from before you, as the LORD has
promised.

20 When your children ask you in
time to come, 'What is the meaning of
the decrees and the statutes and the
ordinances that the LORD our God has
commanded you?' 21then you shall say
to your children, 'We were Pharaoh's
slaves in Egypt, but the LORD brought
us out of Egypt with a mighty hand.
22The LORD displayed before our eyes
great and awesome signs and wonders
against Egypt, against Pharaoh and
all his household. 23He brought us out
from there in order to bring us in, to
give us the land that he promised on
oath to our ancestors. 24Then the LORD
commanded us to observe all these statutes, to fear the LORD our God, for our
lasting good, so as to keep us alive, as is
now the case. 25If we diligently observe
this entire commandment before the
LORD our God, as he has commanded
us, we will be in the right.'

A CHOSEN PEOPLE

7 When the LORD your God brings
you into the land that you are about
to enter and occupy, and he clears away
many nations before you—the Hittites,
the Girgashites, the Amorites, the Canaanites, the Perizzites, the Hivites, and
the Jebusites, seven nations mightier
and more numerous than you— 2and
when the LORD your God gives them
over to you and you defeat them, then
you must utterly destroy them. Make no
covenant with them and show them no
mercy. 3Do not intermarry with them,
giving your daughters to their sons or
taking their daughters for your sons,
4for that would turn away your children
from following me, to serve other gods.
Then the anger of the LORD would be
kindled against you, and he would destroy you quickly. 5But this is how you
must deal with them: break down their
altars, smash their pillars, hew down
their sacred poles,[q] and burn their idols
with fire. 6For you are a people holy to
the LORD your God; the LORD your God
has chosen you out of all the peoples on
earth to be his people, his treasured possession.

7 It was not because you were more
numerous than any other people that
the LORD set his heart on you and chose

[o] 6.4 Or *The LORD our God is one LORD*, or *The LORD our God, the LORD is one*, or *The LORD is our God, the LORD is one* [p] 6.8 Or *as a frontlet*
[q] 7.5 Heb *Asherim*

you—for you were the fewest of all peoples. 8It was because the LORD loved you
and kept the oath that he swore to your
ancestors, that the LORD has brought
you out with a mighty hand, and redeemed you from the house of slavery,
from the hand of Pharaoh king of Egypt.
9Know therefore that the LORD your
God is God, the faithful God who maintains covenant loyalty with those who
love him and keep his commandments,
to a thousand generations, 10and who
repays in their own person those who
reject him. He does not delay but repays
in their own person those who reject
him. 11Therefore, observe diligently the
commandment—the statutes and the
ordinances—that I am commanding
you today.

BLESSINGS FOR OBEDIENCE

12 If you heed these ordinances, by
diligently observing them, the LORD
your God will maintain with you the
covenant loyalty that he swore to your
ancestors; 13he will love you, bless you,
and multiply you; he will bless the fruit
of your womb and the fruit of your
ground, your grain and your wine and
your oil, the increase of your cattle and
the issue of your flock, in the land that
he swore to your ancestors to give you.
14You shall be the most blessed of peoples, with neither sterility nor barrenness among you or your livestock. 15The
LORD will turn away from you every
illness; all the dread diseases of Egypt
that you experienced, he will not inflict
on you, but he will lay them on all who
hate you. 16You shall devour all the peoples that the LORD your God is giving
over to you, showing them no pity; you
shall not serve their gods, for that would
be a snare to you.

17 If you say to yourself, 'These nations are more numerous than I; how
can I dispossess them?' 18do not be
afraid of them. Just remember what the
LORD your God did to Pharaoh and to all
Egypt, 19the great trials that your eyes
saw, the signs and wonders, the mighty
hand and the outstretched arm by which
the LORD your God brought you out. The
LORD your God will do the same to all
the peoples of whom you are afraid.
20Moreover, the LORD your God will
send the pestilence[r] against them, until
even the survivors and the fugitives are
destroyed. 21Have no dread of them, for
the LORD your God, who is present with
you, is a great and awesome God. 22The
LORD your God will clear away these nations before you little by little; you will
not be able to make a quick end of them,
otherwise the wild animals would become too numerous for you. 23But the
LORD your God will give them over to
you, and throw them into great panic,
until they are destroyed. 24He will hand
their kings over to you and you shall
blot out their name from under heaven;
no one will be able to stand against you,
until you have destroyed them. 25The
images of their gods you shall burn with
fire. Do not covet the silver or the gold
that is on them and take it for yourself,
because you could be ensnared by it; for
it is abhorrent to the LORD your God.
26Do not bring an abhorrent thing into
your house, or you will be set apart for
destruction like it. You must utterly detest and abhor it, for it is set apart for
destruction.

A WARNING NOT TO FORGET GOD IN PROSPERITY

8 This entire commandment that I
command you today you must diligently observe, so that you may live
and increase, and go in and occupy the
land that the LORD promised on oath
to your ancestors. 2Remember the long
way that the LORD your God has led
you these forty years in the wilderness,
in order to humble you, testing you to
know what was in your heart, whether
or not you would keep his commandments. 3He humbled you by letting
you hunger, then by feeding you with
manna, with which neither you nor
your ancestors were acquainted, in order to make you understand that one
does not live by bread alone, but by every word that comes from the mouth of
the LORD.[s] 4The clothes on your back did
not wear out and your feet did not swell
these forty years. 5Know then in your
heart that as a parent disciplines a child
so the LORD your God disciplines you.
6Therefore keep the commandments
of the LORD your God, by walking in
his ways and by fearing him. 7For the
LORD your God is bringing you into a
good land, a land with flowing streams,
with springs and underground waters
welling up in valleys and hills, 8a land
of wheat and barley, of vines and fig
trees and pomegranates, a land of olive
trees and honey, 9a land where you may

[r] **7.20** Or *hornets*: Meaning of Heb uncertain
[s] **8.3** Or *by anything that the LORD decrees*

eat bread without scarcity, where you will lack nothing, a land whose stones are iron and from whose hills you may mine copper. 10 You shall eat your fill and bless the LORD your God for the good land that he has given you.

11 Take care that you do not forget the LORD your God, by failing to keep his commandments, his ordinances, and his statutes, which I am commanding you today. 12 When you have eaten your fill and have built fine houses and live in them, 13 and when your herds and flocks have multiplied, and your silver and gold is multiplied, and all that you have is multiplied, 14 then do not exalt yourself, forgetting the LORD your God, who brought you out of the land of Egypt, out of the house of slavery, 15 who led you through the great and terrible wilderness, an arid waste-land with poisonous[t] snakes and scorpions. He made water flow for you from flint rock, 16 and fed you in the wilderness with manna that your ancestors did not know, to humble you and to test you, and in the end to do you good. 17 Do not say to yourself, 'My power and the might of my own hand have gained me this wealth.' 18 But remember the LORD your God, for it is he who gives you power to get wealth, so that he may confirm his covenant that he swore to your ancestors, as he is doing today. 19 If you do forget the LORD your God and follow other gods to serve and worship them, I solemnly warn you today that you shall surely perish. 20 Like the nations that the LORD is destroying before you, so shall you perish, because you would not obey the voice of the LORD your God.

THE CONSEQUENCES OF REBELLING AGAINST GOD

9 Hear, O Israel! You are about to cross the Jordan today, to go in and dispossess nations larger and mightier than you, great cities, fortified to the heavens, 2 a strong and tall people, the offspring of the Anakim, whom you know. You have heard it said of them, 'Who can stand up to the Anakim?' 3 Know then today that the LORD your God is the one who crosses over before you as a devouring fire; he will defeat them and subdue them before you, so that you may dispossess and destroy them quickly, as the LORD has promised you.

4 When the LORD your God thrusts them out before you, do not say to yourself, 'It is because of my righteousness that the LORD has brought me in to occupy this land'; it is rather because of the wickedness of these nations that the LORD is dispossessing them before you. 5 It is not because of your righteousness or the uprightness of your heart that you are going in to occupy their land; but because of the wickedness of those nations that the LORD your God is dispossessing them before you, in order to fulfil the promise that the LORD made on oath to your ancestors, to Abraham, to Isaac, and to Jacob.

6 Know, then, that the LORD your God is not giving you this good land to occupy because of your righteousness; for you are a stubborn people. 7 Remember and do not forget how you provoked the LORD your God to wrath in the wilderness; you have been rebellious against the LORD from the day you came out of the land of Egypt until you came to this place.

8 Even at Horeb you provoked the LORD to wrath, and the LORD was so angry with you that he was ready to destroy you. 9 When I went up the mountain to receive the stone tablets, the tablets of the covenant that the LORD made with you, I remained on the mountain for forty days and forty nights; I neither ate bread nor drank water. 10 And the LORD gave me the two stone tablets written with the finger of God; on them were all the words that the LORD had spoken to you at the mountain out of the fire on the day of the assembly. 11 At the end of forty days and forty nights the LORD gave me the two stone tablets, the tablets of the covenant. 12 Then the LORD said to me, 'Get up, go down quickly from here, for your people whom you have brought from Egypt have acted corruptly. They have been quick to turn from the way that I commanded them; they have cast an image for themselves.' 13 Furthermore, the LORD said to me, 'I have seen that this people is indeed a stubborn people. 14 Let me alone that I may destroy them and blot out their name from under heaven; and I will make of you a nation mightier and more numerous than they.'

15 So I turned and went down from the mountain, while the mountain was ablaze; the two tablets of the covenant were in my two hands. 16 Then I saw that you had indeed sinned against

[t] **8.15** Or *fiery*; Heb *seraph*

the LORD your God, by casting for yourselves an image of a calf; you had been
quick to turn from the way that the
LORD had commanded you. 17So I took
hold of the two tablets and flung them
from my two hands, smashing them
before your eyes. 18Then I lay prostrate
before the LORD as before, for forty days
and forty nights; I neither ate bread nor
drank water, because of all the sin you
had committed, provoking the LORD by
doing what was evil in his sight. 19For I
was afraid that the anger that the LORD
bore against you was so fierce that he
would destroy you. But the LORD listened to me that time also. 20The LORD
was so angry with Aaron that he was
ready to destroy him, but I interceded
also on behalf of Aaron at that same
time. 21Then I took the sinful thing you
had made, the calf, and burned it with
fire and crushed it, grinding it thoroughly, until it was reduced to dust; and
I threw the dust of it into the stream
that runs down the mountain.

22 At Taberah also, and at Massah,
and at Kibroth-hattaavah, you provoked the LORD to wrath. 23And when
the LORD sent you from Kadesh-barnea,
saying, 'Go up and occupy the land that
I have given you', you rebelled against
the command of the LORD your God,
neither trusting him nor obeying him.
24You have been rebellious against the
LORD as long as he has[u] known you.

25 Throughout the forty days and
forty nights that I lay prostrate before
the LORD when the LORD intended to
destroy you, 26I prayed to the LORD and
said, 'Lord GOD, do not destroy the people who are your very own possession,
whom you redeemed in your greatness,
whom you brought out of Egypt with a
mighty hand. 27Remember your servants, Abraham, Isaac, and Jacob; pay
no attention to the stubbornness of this
people, their wickedness and their sin,
28otherwise the land from which you
have brought us might say, "Because
the LORD was not able to bring them
into the land that he promised them,
and because he hated them, he has
brought them out to let them die in the
wilderness." 29For they are the people of
your very own possession, whom you
brought out by your great power and by
your outstretched arm.'

THE SECOND PAIR OF TABLETS

10 At that time the LORD said to
me, 'Carve out two tablets of
stone like the former ones, and come up
to me on the mountain, and make an
ark of wood. 2I will write on the tablets
the words that were on the former tablets, which you smashed, and you shall
put them in the ark.' 3So I made an ark
of acacia wood, cut two tablets of stone
like the former ones, and went up the
mountain with the two tablets in my
hand. 4Then he wrote on the tablets
the same words as before, the ten commandments[v] that the LORD had spoken to you on the mountain out of the
fire on the day of the assembly; and the
LORD gave them to me. 5So I turned and
came down from the mountain, and put
the tablets in the ark that I had made;
and there they are, as the LORD commanded me.

6 (The Israelites journeyed from Beeroth-
bene-jaakan[w] to Moserah. There Aaron
died, and there he was buried; his son
Eleazar succeeded him as priest. 7From
there they journeyed to Gudgodah, and
from Gudgodah to Jotbathah, a land
with flowing streams. 8At that time the
LORD set apart the tribe of Levi to carry
the ark of the covenant of the LORD, to
stand before the LORD to minister to
him, and to bless in his name, to this
day. 9Therefore Levi has no allotment or
inheritance with his kindred; the LORD
is his inheritance, as the LORD your God
promised him.)

10 I stayed on the mountain for forty
days and forty nights, as I had done the
first time. And once again the LORD listened to me. The LORD was unwilling to
destroy you. 11The LORD said to me, 'Get
up, go on your journey at the head of the
people, that they may go in and occupy
the land that I swore to their ancestors
to give them.'

THE ESSENCE OF THE LAW

12 So now, O Israel, what does the
LORD your God require of you? Only to
fear the LORD your God, to walk in all
his ways, to love him, to serve the LORD
your God with all your heart and with all
your soul, 13and to keep the commandments of the LORD your God[x] and his decrees that I am commanding you today,
for your own well-being. 14Although
heaven and the heaven of heavens belong to the LORD your God, the earth
with all that is in it, 15yet the LORD set
his heart in love on your ancestors alone

[u] 9.24 Sam Gk: MT *I have* [v] 10.4 Heb *the ten words* [w] 10.6 Or *the wells of the Bene-jaakan*
[x] 10.13 Q Ms Gk Syr: MT lacks *your God*

and chose you, their descendants after them, out of all the peoples, as it is today. 16 Circumcise, then, the foreskin of your heart, and do not be stubborn any longer. 17 For the LORD your God is God of gods and Lord of lords, the great God, mighty and awesome, who is not partial and takes no bribe, 18 who executes justice for the orphan and the widow, and who loves the strangers, providing them with food and clothing. 19 You shall also love the stranger, for you were strangers in the land of Egypt. 20 You shall fear the LORD your God; him alone you shall worship; to him you shall hold fast, and by his name you shall swear. 21 He is your praise; he is your God, who has done for you these great and awesome things that your own eyes have seen. 22 Your ancestors went down to Egypt seventy persons; and now the LORD your God has made you as numerous as the stars in heaven.

REWARDS FOR OBEDIENCE

11 You shall love the LORD your God, therefore, and keep his charge, his decrees, his ordinances, and his commandments always. 2 Remember today that it was not your children (who have not known or seen the discipline of the LORD your God), but it is you who must acknowledge his greatness, his mighty hand and his outstretched arm, 3 his signs and his deeds that he did in Egypt to Pharaoh, the king of Egypt, and to all his land; 4 what he did to the Egyptian army, to their horses and chariots, how he made the water of the Red Sea[y] flow over them as they pursued you, so that the LORD has destroyed them to this day; 5 what he did to you in the wilderness, until you came to this place; 6 and what he did to Dathan and Abiram, sons of Eliab son of Reuben, how in the midst of all Israel the earth opened its mouth and swallowed them up, along with their households, their tents, and every living being in their company; 7 for it is your own eyes that have seen every great deed that the LORD did.

8 Keep, then, this entire commandment that I am commanding you today, so that you may have strength to go in and occupy the land that you are crossing over to occupy, 9 and so that you may live long in the land that the LORD swore to your ancestors to give to them and their descendants, a land flowing with milk and honey. 10 For the land that you are about to enter to occupy is not like the land of Egypt, from which you have come, where you sow your seed and irrigate by foot like a vegetable garden. 11 But the land that you are crossing over to occupy is a land of hills and valleys, watered by rain from the sky, 12 a land that the LORD your God looks after. The eyes of the LORD your God are always on it, from the beginning of the year to the end of the year.

13 If you will only heed his every commandment[z] that I am commanding you today—loving the LORD your God, and serving him with all your heart and with all your soul— 14 then he[a] will give the rain for your land in its season, the early rain and the later rain, and you will gather in your grain, your wine, and your oil; 15 and he[b] will give grass in your fields for your livestock, and you will eat your fill. 16 Take care, or you will be seduced into turning away, serving other gods and worshipping them, 17 for then the anger of the LORD will be kindled against you and he will shut up the heavens, so that there will be no rain and the land will yield no fruit; then you will perish quickly from the good land that the LORD is giving you.

18 You shall put these words of mine in your heart and soul, and you shall bind them as a sign on your hand, and fix them as an emblem[c] on your forehead. 19 Teach them to your children, talking about them when you are at home and when you are away, when you lie down and when you rise. 20 Write them on the doorposts of your house and on your gates, 21 so that your days and the days of your children may be multiplied in the land that the LORD swore to your ancestors to give them, as long as the heavens are above the earth.

22 If you will diligently observe this entire commandment that I am commanding you, loving the LORD your God, walking in all his ways, and holding fast to him, 23 then the LORD will drive out all these nations before you, and you will dispossess nations larger and mightier than yourselves. 24 Every place on which you set foot shall be yours; your territory shall extend from the wilderness to the Lebanon and from the River, the river Euphrates, to the Western Sea. 25 No one will be able to stand against you;

[y] **11.4** Or *Sea of Reeds* [z] **11.13** Compare Gk: Heb *my commandments* [a] **11.14** Sam Gk Vg: MT *I* [b] **11.15** Sam Gk Vg: MT *I* [c] **11.18** Or *as a frontlet*

the LORD your God will put the fear and
dread of you on all the land on which you
set foot, as he promised you.

26 See, I am setting before you today
a blessing and a curse: 27the blessing,
if you obey the commandments of the
LORD your God that I am commanding
you today; 28and the curse, if you do not
obey the commandments of the LORD
your God, but turn from the way that
I am commanding you today, to follow
other gods that you have not known.

29 When the LORD your God has
brought you into the land that you are
entering to occupy, you shall set the
blessing on Mount Gerizim and the
curse on Mount Ebal. 30As you know,
they are beyond the Jordan, some distance to the west, in the land of the Canaanites who live in the Arabah, opposite Gilgal, beside the oak[d] of Moreh.

31 When you cross the Jordan to go in
to occupy the land that the LORD your
God is giving you, and when you occupy
it and live in it, 32you must diligently
observe all the statutes and ordinances
that I am setting before you today.

PAGAN SHRINES TO BE DESTROYED

12 These are the statutes and ordinances that you must diligently
observe in the land that the LORD, the
God of your ancestors, has given you to
occupy all the days that you live on the
earth.

2 You must demolish completely all
the places where the nations whom
you are about to dispossess served their
gods, on the mountain heights, on the
hills, and under every leafy tree. 3Break
down their altars, smash their pillars,
burn their sacred poles[e] with fire, and
hew down the idols of their gods, and
thus blot out their name from their
places. 4You shall not worship the LORD
your God in such ways. 5But you shall
seek the place that the LORD your God
will choose out of all your tribes as his
habitation to put his name there. You
shall go there, 6bringing there your
burnt-offerings and your sacrifices,
your tithes and your donations, your
votive gifts, your freewill-offerings, and
the firstlings of your herds and flocks.
7And you shall eat there in the presence
of the LORD your God, you and your
households together, rejoicing in all the
undertakings in which the LORD your
God has blessed you.

8 You shall not act as we are acting
here today, all of us according to our
own desires, 9for you have not yet come
into the rest and the possession that the
LORD your God is giving you. 10When
you cross over the Jordan and live in the
land that the LORD your God is allotting
to you, and when he gives you rest from
your enemies all around so that you live
in safety, 11then you shall bring everything that I command you to the place
that the LORD your God will choose as
a dwelling for his name: your burnt-
offerings and your sacrifices, your tithes
and your donations, and all your choice
votive gifts that you vow to the LORD.
12And you shall rejoice before the LORD
your God, you together with your sons
and your daughters, your male and female slaves, and the Levites who reside
in your towns (since they have no allotment or inheritance with you).

A PRESCRIBED PLACE OF WORSHIP

13 Take care that you do not offer
your burnt-offerings at any place you
happen to see. 14But only at the place
that the LORD will choose in one of your
tribes—there you shall offer your burnt-
offerings and there you shall do everything I command you.

15 Yet whenever you desire you may
slaughter and eat meat within any of
your towns, according to the blessing
that the LORD your God has given you;
the unclean and the clean may eat of it,
as they would of gazelle or deer. 16The
blood, however, you must not eat; you
shall pour it out on the ground like
water. 17Nor may you eat within your
towns the tithe of your grain, your wine,
or your oil, the firstlings of your herds
or your flocks, any of your votive gifts
that you vow, your freewill-offerings,
or your donations; 18these you shall eat
in the presence of the LORD your God at
the place that the LORD your God will
choose, you together with your son and
your daughter, your male and female
slaves, and the Levites resident in your
towns, rejoicing in the presence of the
LORD your God in all your undertakings.
19Take care that you do not neglect the
Levite as long as you live in your land.

20 When the LORD your God enlarges
your territory, as he has promised you,
and you say, 'I am going to eat some
meat', because you wish to eat meat,
you may eat meat whenever you have
the desire. 21If the place where the LORD

[d] 11.30 Gk Syr: Compare Gen 12.6; Heb *oaks* or *terebinths* [e] 12.3 Heb *Asherim*

your God will choose to put his name is
too far from you, and you slaughter as I
have commanded you any of your herd
or flock that the LORD has given you,
then you may eat within your towns
whenever you desire. 22 Indeed, just as
gazelle or deer is eaten, so you may eat
it; the unclean and the clean alike may
eat it. 23 Only be sure that you do not eat
the blood; for the blood is the life, and
you shall not eat the life with the meat.
24 Do not eat it; you shall pour it out on
the ground like water. 25 Do not eat it, so
that all may go well with you and your
children after you, because you do what
is right in the sight of the LORD. 26 But
the sacred donations that are due from
you, and your votive gifts, you shall
bring to the place that the LORD will
choose. 27 You shall present your burnt-
offerings, both the meat and the blood,
on the altar of the LORD your God; the
blood of your other sacrifices shall be
poured out beside[f] the altar of the LORD
your God, but the meat you may eat.

28 Be careful to obey all these words
that I command you today,[g] so that it
may go well with you and with your
children after you for ever, because you
will be doing what is good and right in
the sight of the LORD your God.

WARNING AGAINST IDOLATRY

29 When the LORD your God has cut
off before you the nations whom you are
about to enter to dispossess them, when
you have dispossessed them and live in
their land, 30 take care that you are not
ensnared into imitating them, after
they have been destroyed before you:
do not inquire concerning their gods,
saying, 'How did these nations worship their gods? I also want to do the
same.' 31 You must not do the same for
the LORD your God, because every abhorrent thing that the LORD hates they
have done for their gods. They would
even burn their sons and their daughters in the fire to their gods. 32 [h]You
must diligently observe everything that
I command you; do not add to it or take
anything from it.

13 [i]If prophets or those who divine by dreams appear among
you and promise you omens or portents, 2 and the omens or the portents
declared by them take place, and they
say, 'Let us follow other gods' (whom
you have not known) 'and let us serve
them', 3 you must not heed the words
of those prophets or those who divine
by dreams; for the LORD your God is
testing you, to know whether you indeed love the LORD your God with all
your heart and soul. 4 The LORD your
God you shall follow, him alone you
shall fear, his commandments you shall
keep, his voice you shall obey, him you
shall serve, and to him you shall hold
fast. 5 But those prophets or those who
divine by dreams shall be put to death
for having spoken treason against the
LORD your God—who brought you out
of the land of Egypt and redeemed you
from the house of slavery—to turn you
from the way in which the LORD your
God commanded you to walk. So you
shall purge the evil from your midst.

6 If anyone secretly entices you—
even if it is your brother, your father's
son or[j] your mother's son, or your own
son or daughter, or the wife you embrace, or your most intimate friend—
saying, 'Let us go and worship other
gods', whom neither you nor your ancestors have known, 7 any of the gods of the
peoples that are around you, whether
near you or far away from you, from
one end of the earth to the other, 8 you
must not yield to or heed any such persons. Show them no pity or compassion
and do not shield them. 9 But you shall
surely kill them; your own hand shall be
first against them to execute them, and
afterwards the hand of all the people.
10 Stone them to death for trying to turn
you away from the LORD your God, who
brought you out of the land of Egypt,
out of the house of slavery. 11 Then all Israel shall hear and be afraid, and never
again do any such wickedness.

12 If you hear it said about one of
the towns that the LORD your God is
giving you to live in, 13 that scoundrels
from among you have gone out and led
the inhabitants of the town astray, saying, 'Let us go and worship other gods',
whom you have not known, 14 then you
shall inquire and make a thorough investigation. If the charge is established
that such an abhorrent thing has been
done among you, 15 you shall put the
inhabitants of that town to the sword,
utterly destroying it and everything
in it—even putting its livestock to the
sword. 16 All of its spoil you shall gather
into its public square; then burn the
town and all its spoil with fire, as a

[f] **12.27** Or *on* [g] **12.28** Gk Sam Syr: MT lacks *today* [h] **12.32** Ch 13.1 in Heb [i] **13.1** Ch 13.2 in Heb [j] **13.6** Sam Gk Compare Tg: MT lacks *your father's son or*

whole burnt-offering to the LORD your God. It shall remain a perpetual ruin, never to be rebuilt. 17 Do not let anything devoted to destruction stick to your hand, so that the LORD may turn from his fierce anger and show you compassion, and in his compassion multiply you, as he swore to your ancestors, 18 if you obey the voice of the LORD your God by keeping all his commandments that I am commanding you today, doing what is right in the sight of the LORD your God.

PAGAN PRACTICES FORBIDDEN

14 You are children of the LORD your God. You must not lacerate yourselves or shave your forelocks for the dead. 2 For you are a people holy to the LORD your God; it is you the LORD has chosen out of all the peoples on earth to be his people, his treasured possession.

CLEAN AND UNCLEAN FOODS

3 You shall not eat any abhorrent thing. 4 These are the animals you may eat: the ox, the sheep, the goat, 5 the deer, the gazelle, the roebuck, the wild goat, the ibex, the antelope, and the mountain-sheep. 6 Any animal that divides the hoof and has the hoof cloven in two, and chews the cud, among the animals, you may eat. 7 Yet of those that chew the cud or have the hoof cloven you shall not eat these: the camel, the hare, and the rock-badger, because they chew the cud but do not divide the hoof; they are unclean for you. 8 And the pig, because it divides the hoof but does not chew the cud, is unclean for you. You shall not eat their meat, and you shall not touch their carcasses.

9 Of all that live in water you may eat these: whatever has fins and scales you may eat. 10 And whatever does not have fins and scales you shall not eat; it is unclean for you.

11 You may eat any clean birds. 12 But these are the ones that you shall not eat: the eagle, the vulture, the osprey, 13 the buzzard, the kite of any kind; 14 every raven of any kind; 15 the ostrich, the nighthawk, the seagull, the hawk of any kind; 16 the little owl and the great owl, the water-hen 17 and the desert-owl,[k] the carrion vulture and the cormorant, 18 the stork, the heron of any kind; the hoopoe and the bat.[l] 19 And all winged insects are unclean for you; they shall not be eaten. 20 You may eat any clean winged creature.

21 You shall not eat anything that dies of itself; you may give it to aliens residing in your towns for them to eat, or you may sell it to a foreigner. For you are a people holy to the LORD your God.

You shall not boil a kid in its mother's milk.

REGULATIONS CONCERNING TITHES

22 Set apart a tithe of all the yield of your seed that is brought in yearly from the field. 23 In the presence of the LORD your God, in the place that he will choose as a dwelling for his name, you shall eat the tithe of your grain, your wine, and your oil, as well as the firstlings of your herd and flock, so that you may learn to fear the LORD your God always. 24 But if, when the LORD your God has blessed you, the distance is so great that you are unable to transport it, because the place where the LORD your God will choose to set his name is too far away from you, 25 then you may turn it into money. With the money secure in hand, go to the place that the LORD your God will choose; 26 spend the money for whatever you wish—oxen, sheep, wine, strong drink, or whatever you desire. And you shall eat there in the presence of the LORD your God, you and your household rejoicing together. 27 As for the Levites resident in your towns, do not neglect them, because they have no allotment or inheritance with you.

28 Every third year you shall bring out the full tithe of your produce for that year, and store it within your towns; 29 the Levites, because they have no allotment or inheritance with you, as well as the resident aliens, the orphans, and the widows in your towns, may come and eat their fill so that the LORD your God may bless you in all the work that you undertake.

LAWS CONCERNING THE SABBATICAL YEAR

15 Every seventh year you shall grant a remission of debts. 2 And this is the manner of the remission: every creditor shall remit the claim that is held against a neighbour, not exacting it from a neighbour who is a member of the community, because the LORD's remission has been proclaimed. 3 From a foreigner you may exact it, but you must remit your claim on whatever any member of your community owes you.

[k] **14.17** Or *pelican* [l] **14.18** Identification of several of the birds in verses 12–18 is uncertain

4 There will, however, be no one in need
among you, because the LORD is sure
to bless you in the land that the LORD
your God is giving you as a possession to
occupy, 5 if only you will obey the LORD
your God by diligently observing this
entire commandment that I command
you today. 6 When the LORD your God
has blessed you, as he promised you,
you will lend to many nations, but you
will not borrow; you will rule over many
nations, but they will not rule over you.

7 If there is among you anyone in
need, a member of your community in
any of your towns within the land that
the LORD your God is giving you, do not
be hard-hearted or tight-fisted towards
your needy neighbour. 8 You should
rather open your hand, willingly lending enough to meet the need, whatever
it may be. 9 Be careful that you do not
entertain a mean thought, thinking,
'The seventh year, the year of remission,
is near', and therefore view your needy
neighbour with hostility and give nothing; your neighbour might cry to the
LORD against you, and you would incur
guilt. 10 Give liberally and be ungrudg-
ing when you do so, for on this account
the LORD your God will bless you in all
your work and in all that you undertake.
11 Since there will never cease to be some
in need on the earth, I therefore command you, 'Open your hand to the poor
and needy neighbour in your land.'

12 If a member of your community,
whether a Hebrew man or a Hebrew
woman, is sold[m] to you and works for
you for six years, in the seventh year
you shall set that person free. 13 And
when you send a male slave[n] out from
you a free person, you shall not send
him out empty-handed. 14 Provide liberally out of your flock, your threshing-
floor, and your wine press, thus giving
to him some of the bounty with which
the LORD your God has blessed you.
15 Remember that you were a slave in
the land of Egypt, and the LORD your
God redeemed you; for this reason I lay
this command upon you today. 16 But if
he says to you, 'I will not go out from
you', because he loves you and your
household, since he is well off with you,
17 then you shall take an awl and thrust
it through his earlobe into the door, and
he shall be your slave[o] for ever.

You shall do the same with regard to
your female slave.[p]

18 Do not consider it a hardship
when you send them out from you free
persons, because for six years they have
given you services worth the wages of
hired labourers; and the LORD your God
will bless you in all that you do.

THE FIRSTBORN OF LIVESTOCK

19 Every firstling male born of your
herd and flock you shall consecrate to
the LORD your God; you shall not do
work with your firstling ox nor shear
the firstling of your flock. 20 You shall eat
it, you together with your household,
in the presence of the LORD your God
year by year at the place that the LORD
will choose. 21 But if it has any defect—
any serious defect, such as lameness
or blindness—you shall not sacrifice it
to the LORD your God; 22 within your
towns you may eat it, the unclean and
the clean alike, as you would a gazelle or
deer. 23 Its blood, however, you must not
eat; you shall pour it out on the ground
like water.

THE PASSOVER REVIEWED

16 Observe the month[q] of Abib
by keeping the passover to the
LORD your God, for in the month of Abib
the LORD your God brought you out
of Egypt by night. 2 You shall offer the
passover sacrifice to the LORD your God,
from the flock and the herd, at the place
that the LORD will choose as a dwelling
for his name. 3 You must not eat with it
anything leavened. For seven days you
shall eat unleavened bread with it—the
bread of affliction—because you came
out of the land of Egypt in great haste,
so that all the days of your life you may
remember the day of your departure
from the land of Egypt. 4 No leaven shall
be seen with you in all your territory for
seven days; and none of the meat of what
you slaughter on the evening of the first
day shall remain until morning. 5 You
are not permitted to offer the passover
sacrifice within any of your towns that
the LORD your God is giving you. 6 But
at the place that the LORD your God will
choose as a dwelling for his name, only
there shall you offer the passover sacrifice, in the evening at sunset, the time
of day when you departed from Egypt.
7 You shall cook it and eat it at the place
that the LORD your God will choose; the
next morning you may go back to your
tents. 8 For six days you shall continue
to eat unleavened bread, and on the sev-

[m] 15.12 Or *sells himself or herself* [n] 15.13 Heb *him* [o] 15.17 Or *bondman* [p] 15.17 Or *bondwoman* [q] 16.1 Or *new moon*

enth day there shall be a solemn assembly for the LORD your God, when you shall do no work.

THE FESTIVAL OF WEEKS REVIEWED

9 You shall count seven weeks; begin to count the seven weeks from the time the sickle is first put to the standing grain. 10 Then you shall keep the festival of weeks to the LORD your God, contributing a freewill-offering in proportion to the blessing that you have received from the LORD your God. 11 Rejoice before the LORD your God—you and your sons and your daughters, your male and female slaves, the Levites resident in your towns, as well as the strangers, the orphans, and the widows who are among you—at the place that the LORD your God will choose as a dwelling for his name. 12 Remember that you were a slave in Egypt, and diligently observe these statutes.

THE FESTIVAL OF BOOTHS REVIEWED

13 You shall keep the festival of booths[r] for seven days, when you have gathered in the produce from your threshing-floor and your wine press. 14 Rejoice during your festival, you and your sons and your daughters, your male and female slaves, as well as the Levites, the strangers, the orphans, and the widows resident in your towns. 15 For seven days you shall keep the festival to the LORD your God at the place that the LORD will choose; for the LORD your God will bless you in all your produce and in all your undertakings, and you shall surely celebrate.

16 Three times a year all your males shall appear before the LORD your God at the place that he will choose: at the festival of unleavened bread, at the festival of weeks, and at the festival of booths.[s] They shall not appear before the LORD empty-handed; 17 all shall give as they are able, according to the blessing of the LORD your God that he has given you.

MUNICIPAL JUDGES AND OFFICERS

18 You shall appoint judges and officials throughout your tribes, in all your towns that the LORD your God is giving you, and they shall render just decisions for the people. 19 You must not distort justice; you must not show partiality; and you must not accept bribes, for a bribe blinds the eyes of the wise and subverts the cause of those who are in the right. 20 Justice, and only justice, you shall pursue, so that you may live and occupy the land that the LORD your God is giving you.

FORBIDDEN FORMS OF WORSHIP

21 You shall not plant any tree as a sacred pole[t] beside the altar that you make for the LORD your God; 22 nor shall you set up a stone pillar—things that the LORD your God hates.

17 You must not sacrifice to the LORD your God an ox or a sheep that has a defect, anything seriously wrong; for that is abhorrent to the LORD your God.

2 If there is found among you, in one of your towns that the LORD your God is giving you, a man or woman who does what is evil in the sight of the LORD your God, and transgresses his covenant 3 by going to serve other gods and worshipping them—whether the sun or the moon or any of the host of heaven, which I have forbidden— 4 and if it is reported to you or you hear of it, and you make a thorough inquiry, and the charge is proved true that such an abhorrent thing has occurred in Israel, 5 then you shall bring out to your gates that man or that woman who has committed this crime and you shall stone the man or woman to death. 6 On the evidence of two or three witnesses the death sentence shall be executed; a person must not be put to death on the evidence of only one witness. 7 The hands of the witnesses shall be the first raised against the person to execute the death penalty, and afterwards the hands of all the people. So you shall purge the evil from your midst.

LEGAL DECISIONS BY PRIESTS AND JUDGES

8 If a judicial decision is too difficult for you to make between one kind of bloodshed and another, one kind of legal right and another, or one kind of assault and another—any such matters of dispute in your towns—then you shall immediately go up to the place that the LORD your God will choose, 9 where you shall consult with the levitical priests and the judge who is in office in those days; they shall announce to you the decision in the case. 10 Carry out exactly the decision that they announce to

[r] 16.13 Or *tabernacles*; Heb *succoth* [s] 16.16 Or *tabernacles*; Heb *succoth* [t] 16.21 Heb *Asherah*

you from the place that the LORD will choose, diligently observing everything they instruct you. 11 You must carry out fully the law that they interpret for you or the ruling that they announce to you; do not turn aside from the decision that they announce to you, either to the right or to the left. 12 As for anyone who presumes to disobey the priest appointed to minister there to the LORD your God, or the judge, that person shall die. So you shall purge the evil from Israel. 13 All the people will hear and be afraid, and will not act presumptuously again.

LIMITATIONS OF ROYAL AUTHORITY

14 When you have come into the land that the LORD your God is giving you, and have taken possession of it and settled in it, and you say, 'I will set a king over me, like all the nations that are around me', 15 you may indeed set over you a king whom the LORD your God will choose. One of your own community you may set as king over you; you are not permitted to put a foreigner over you, who is not of your own community. 16 Even so, he must not acquire many horses for himself, or return the people to Egypt in order to acquire more horses, since the LORD has said to you, 'You must never return that way again.' 17 And he must not acquire many wives for himself, or else his heart will turn away; also silver and gold he must not acquire in great quantity for himself. 18 When he has taken the throne of his kingdom, he shall have a copy of this law written for him in the presence of the levitical priests. 19 It shall remain with him and he shall read in it all the days of his life, so that he may learn to fear the LORD his God, diligently observing all the words of this law and these statutes, 20 neither exalting himself above other members of the community nor turning aside from the commandment, either to the right or to the left, so that he and his descendants may reign long over his kingdom in Israel.

PRIVILEGES OF PRIESTS AND LEVITES

18 The levitical priests, the whole tribe of Levi, shall have no allotment or inheritance within Israel. They may eat the sacrifices that are the LORD's portion[u] 2 but they shall have no inheritance among the other members of the community; the LORD is their inheritance, as he promised them.

3 This shall be the priests' due from the people, from those offering a sacrifice, whether an ox or a sheep: they shall give to the priest the shoulder, the two jowls, and the stomach. 4 The first fruits of your grain, your wine, and your oil, as well as the first of the fleece of your sheep, you shall give him. 5 For the LORD your God has chosen Levi[v] out of all your tribes, to stand and minister in the name of the LORD, him and his sons for all time.

6 If a Levite leaves any of your towns, from wherever he has been residing in Israel, and comes to the place that the LORD will choose (and he may come whenever he wishes), 7 then he may minister in the name of the LORD his God, like all his fellow-Levites who stand to minister there before the LORD. 8 They shall have equal portions to eat, even though they have income from the sale of family possessions.[w]

CHILD-SACRIFICE, DIVINATION, AND MAGIC PROHIBITED

9 When you come into the land that the LORD your God is giving you, you must not learn to imitate the abhorrent practices of those nations. 10 No one shall be found among you who makes a son or daughter pass through fire, or who practises divination, or is a soothsayer, or an augur, or a sorcerer, 11 or one who casts spells, or who consults ghosts or spirits, or who seeks oracles from the dead. 12 For whoever does these things is abhorrent to the LORD; it is because of such abhorrent practices that the LORD your God is driving them out before you. 13 You must remain completely loyal to the LORD your God. 14 Although these nations that you are about to dispossess do give heed to soothsayers and diviners, as for you, the LORD your God does not permit you to do so.

A NEW PROPHET LIKE MOSES

15 The LORD your God will raise up for you a prophet[x] like me from among your own people; you shall heed such a prophet.[y] 16 This is what you requested of the LORD your God at Horeb on the day of the assembly when you said: 'If I hear the voice of the LORD my God any more, or ever again see this great fire, I will die.' 17 Then the LORD replied to me: 'They are right in what they have said.

[u] **18.1** Meaning of Heb uncertain [v] **18.5** Heb *him* [w] **18.8** Meaning of Heb uncertain
[x] **18.15** Or *prophets* [y] **18.15** Or *such prophets*

18 I will raise up for them a prophet[z]
like you from among their own people;
I will put my words in the mouth of
the prophet,[a] who shall speak to them
everything that I command. 19 Anyone who does not heed the words that
the prophet[b] shall speak in my name,
I myself will hold accountable. 20 But
any prophet who speaks in the name of
other gods, or who presumes to speak
in my name a word that I have not
commanded the prophet to speak—
that prophet shall die.' 21 You may say
to yourself, 'How can we recognize a
word that the LORD has not spoken?'
22 If a prophet speaks in the name of the
LORD but the thing does not take place
or prove true, it is a word that the LORD
has not spoken. The prophet has spoken
it presumptuously; do not be frightened
by it.

LAWS CONCERNING THE CITIES OF REFUGE

19 When the LORD your God has
cut off the nations whose land
the LORD your God is giving you, and
you have dispossessed them and settled in their towns and in their houses,
2 you shall set apart three cities in the
land that the LORD your God is giving
you to possess. 3 You shall calculate the
distances[c] and divide into three regions
the land that the LORD your God gives
you as a possession, so that any homicide can flee to one of them.

4 Now this is the case of a homicide
who might flee there and live, that is,
someone who has killed another person
unintentionally when the two had not
been at enmity before: 5 Suppose someone goes into the forest with another to
cut wood, and when one of them swings
the axe to cut down a tree, the head slips
from the handle and strikes the other
person who then dies; the killer may
flee to one of these cities and live. 6 But
if the distance is too great, the avenger
of blood in hot anger might pursue and
overtake and put the killer to death,
although a death sentence was not deserved, since the two had not been at
enmity before. 7 Therefore I command
you: You shall set apart three cities.

8 If the LORD your God enlarges
your territory, as he swore to your
ancestors—and he will give you all the
land that he promised your ancestors to
give you, 9 provided you diligently observe this entire commandment that
I command you today, by loving the
LORD your God and walking always
in his ways—then you shall add three
more cities to these three, 10 so that the
blood of an innocent person may not be
shed in the land that the LORD your God
is giving you as an inheritance, thereby
bringing blood-guilt upon you.

11 But if someone at enmity with another lies in wait and attacks and takes
the life of that person, and flees into one
of these cities, 12 then the elders of the
killer's city shall send to have the culprit
taken from there and handed over to
the avenger of blood to be put to death.
13 Show no pity; you shall purge the guilt
of innocent blood from Israel, so that it
may go well with you.

PROPERTY BOUNDARIES

14 You must not move your neighbour's boundary marker, set up by former generations, on the property that
will be allotted to you in the land that
the LORD your God is giving you to possess.

LAW CONCERNING WITNESSES

15 A single witness shall not suffice to convict a person of any crime or
wrongdoing in connection with any offence that may be committed. Only on
the evidence of two or three witnesses
shall a charge be sustained. 16 If a malicious witness comes forward to accuse
someone of wrongdoing, 17 then both
parties to the dispute shall appear before the LORD, before the priests and the
judges who are in office in those days,
18 and the judges shall make a thorough
inquiry. If the witness is a false witness,
having testified falsely against another,
19 then you shall do to the false witness
just as the false witness had meant to do
to the other. So you shall purge the evil
from your midst. 20 The rest shall hear
and be afraid, and a crime such as this
shall never again be committed among
you. 21 Show no pity: life for life, eye for
eye, tooth for tooth, hand for hand, foot
for foot.

RULES OF WARFARE

20 When you go out to war against
your enemies, and see horses
and chariots, an army larger than your
own, you shall not be afraid of them;
for the LORD your God is with you,
who brought you up from the land of

[z] 18.18 Or *prophets* [a] 18.18 Or *mouths of the prophets* [b] 18.19 Heb *he* [c] 19.3 Or *prepare roads to them*

Egypt. [2]Before you engage in battle, the priest shall come forward and speak to the troops, [3]and shall say to them: 'Hear, O Israel! Today you are drawing near to do battle against your enemies. Do not lose heart, or be afraid, or panic, or be in dread of them; [4]for it is the LORD your God who goes with you, to fight for you against your enemies, to give you victory.' [5]Then the officials shall address the troops, saying, 'Has anyone built a new house but not dedicated it? He should go back to his house, or he might die in the battle and another dedicate it. [6]Has anyone planted a vineyard but not yet enjoyed its fruit? He should go back to his house, or he might die in the battle and another be first to enjoy its fruit. [7]Has anyone become engaged to a woman but not yet married her? He should go back to his house, or he might die in the battle and another marry her.' [8]The officials shall continue to address the troops, saying, 'Is anyone afraid or disheartened? He should go back to his house, or he might cause the heart of his comrades to fail like his own.' [9]When the officials have finished addressing the troops, then the commanders shall take charge of them.

10 When you draw near to a town to fight against it, offer it terms of peace. [11]If it accepts your terms of peace and surrenders to you, then all the people in it shall serve you in forced labour. [12]If it does not submit to you peacefully, but makes war against you, then you shall besiege it; [13]and when the LORD your God gives it into your hand, you shall put all its males to the sword. [14]You may, however, take as your booty the women, the children, livestock, and everything else in the town, all its spoil. You may enjoy the spoil of your enemies, which the LORD your God has given you. [15]Thus you shall treat all the towns that are very far from you, which are not towns of the nations here. [16]But as for the towns of these peoples that the LORD your God is giving you as an inheritance, you must not let anything that breathes remain alive. [17]You shall annihilate them—the Hittites and the Amorites, the Canaanites and the Perizzites, the Hivites and the Jebusites—just as the LORD your God has commanded, [18]so that they may not teach you to do all the abhorrent things that they do for their gods, and you thus sin against the LORD your God.

19 If you besiege a town for a long time, making war against it in order to take it, you must not destroy its trees by wielding an axe against them. Although you may take food from them, you must not cut them down. Are trees in the field human beings that they should come under siege from you? [20]You may destroy only the trees that you know do not produce food; you may cut them down for use in building siegeworks against the town that makes war with you, until it falls.

LAW CONCERNING MURDER BY PERSONS UNKNOWN

21 If, in the land that the LORD your God is giving you to possess, a body is found lying in open country, and it is not known who struck the person down, [2]then your elders and your judges shall come out to measure the distances to the towns that are near the body. [3]The elders of the town nearest the body shall take a heifer that has never been worked, one that has not pulled in the yoke; [4]the elders of that town shall bring the heifer down to a wadi with running water, which is neither ploughed nor sown, and shall break the heifer's neck there in the wadi. [5]Then the priests, the sons of Levi, shall come forward, for the LORD your God has chosen them to minister to him and to pronounce blessings in the name of the LORD, and by their decision all cases of dispute and assault shall be settled. [6]All the elders of that town nearest the body shall wash their hands over the heifer whose neck was broken in the wadi, [7]and they shall declare: 'Our hands did not shed this blood, nor were we witnesses to it. [8]Absolve, O LORD, your people Israel, whom you redeemed; do not let the guilt of innocent blood remain in the midst of your people Israel.' Then they will be absolved of blood-guilt. [9]So you shall purge the guilt of innocent blood from your midst, because you must do what is right in the sight of the LORD.

FEMALE CAPTIVES

10 When you go out to war against your enemies, and the LORD your God hands them over to you and you take them captive, [11]suppose you see among the captives a beautiful woman whom you desire and want to marry, [12]and so you bring her home to your house: she shall shave her head, pare her nails, [13]discard her captive's garb, and shall remain in your house for a full month,

mourning for her father and mother;
after that you may go in to her and be
her husband, and she shall be your wife.
14But if you are not satisfied with her,
you shall let her go free and not sell her
for money. You must not treat her as a
slave, since you have dishonoured her.

THE RIGHT OF THE FIRSTBORN

15 If a man has two wives, one of
them loved and the other disliked, and
if both the loved and the disliked have
borne him sons, the firstborn being the
son of the one who is disliked, 16then on
the day when he wills his possessions to
his sons, he is not permitted to treat the
son of the loved as the firstborn in pref-
erence to the son of the disliked, who is
the firstborn. 17He must acknowledge as
firstborn the son of the one who is disliked, giving him a double portion[d] of all
that he has; since he is the first issue of
his virility, the right of the firstborn is
his.

REBELLIOUS CHILDREN

18 If someone has a stubborn and rebellious son who will not obey his father
and mother, who does not heed them
when they discipline him, 19then his
father and his mother shall take hold of
him and bring him out to the elders of
his town at the gate of that place. 20They
shall say to the elders of his town, 'This
son of ours is stubborn and rebellious.
He will not obey us. He is a glutton and
a drunkard.' 21Then all the men of the
town shall stone him to death. So you
shall purge the evil from your midst;
and all Israel will hear, and be afraid.

MISCELLANEOUS LAWS

22 When someone is convicted of a
crime punishable by death and is executed, and you hang him on a tree, 23his
corpse must not remain all night upon
the tree; you shall bury him that same
day, for anyone hung on a tree is under God's curse. You must not defile the
land that the LORD your God is giving
you for possession.

22 You shall not watch your neighbour's ox or sheep straying away
and ignore them; you shall take them
back to their owner. 2If the owner does
not reside near you or you do not know
who the owner is, you shall bring it to
your own house, and it shall remain
with you until the owner claims it; then
you shall return it. 3You shall do the
same with a neighbour's donkey; you
shall do the same with a neighbour's
garment; and you shall do the same
with anything else that your neighbour
loses and you find. You may not withhold your help.

4 You shall not see your neighbour's
donkey or ox fallen on the road and ignore it; you shall help to lift it up.

5 A woman shall not wear a man's apparel, nor shall a man put on a woman's
garment; for whoever does such things
is abhorrent to the LORD your God.

6 If you come on a bird's nest, in any
tree or on the ground, with fledglings
or eggs, with the mother sitting on the
fledglings or on the eggs, you shall not
take the mother with the young. 7Let
the mother go, taking only the young
for yourself, in order that it may go well
with you and you may live long.

8 When you build a new house, you
shall make a parapet for your roof; otherwise you might have blood-guilt on
your house, if anyone should fall from it.

9 You shall not sow your vineyard
with a second kind of seed, or the whole
yield will have to be forfeited, both the
crop that you have sown and the yield
of the vineyard itself.

10 You shall not plough with an ox
and a donkey yoked together.

11 You shall not wear clothes made
of wool and linen woven together.

12 You shall make tassels on the four
corners of the cloak with which you
cover yourself.

LAWS CONCERNING SEXUAL RELATIONS

13 Suppose a man marries a woman,
but after going in to her, he dislikes her
14and makes up charges against her,
slandering her by saying, 'I married this
woman; but when I lay with her, I did
not find evidence of her virginity.' 15The
father of the young woman and her
mother shall then submit the evidence
of the young woman's virginity to the
elders of the city at the gate. 16The father of the young woman shall say to the
elders: 'I gave my daughter in marriage
to this man but he dislikes her; 17now
he has made up charges against her,
saying, "I did not find evidence of your
daughter's virginity." But here is the evidence of my daughter's virginity.' Then
they shall spread out the cloth before the
elders of the town. 18The elders of that
town shall take the man and punish

[d] 21.17 Heb *two-thirds*

him; [19]they shall fine him one hundred
shekels of silver (which they shall give to
the young woman's father) because he
has slandered a virgin of Israel. She shall
remain his wife; he shall not be permitted to divorce her as long as he lives.

20 If, however, this charge is true,
that evidence of the young woman's virginity was not found, [21]then they shall
bring the young woman out to the entrance of her father's house and the men
of her town shall stone her to death, because she committed a disgraceful act in
Israel by prostituting herself in her father's house. So you shall purge the evil
from your midst.

22 If a man is caught lying with the
wife of another man, both of them shall
die, the man who lay with the woman
as well as the woman. So you shall
purge the evil from Israel.

23 If there is a young woman, a virgin already engaged to be married, and
a man meets her in the town and lies
with her, [24]you shall bring both of them
to the gate of that town and stone them
to death, the young woman because
she did not cry for help in the town and
the man because he violated his neighbour's wife. So you shall purge the evil
from your midst.

25 But if the man meets the engaged woman in the open country, and
the man seizes her and lies with her,
then only the man who lay with her
shall die. [26]You shall do nothing to the
young woman; the young woman has
not committed an offence punishable
by death, because this case is like that
of someone who attacks and murders a
neighbour. [27]Since he found her in the
open country, the engaged woman may
have cried for help, but there was no one
to rescue her.

28 If a man meets a virgin who is not
engaged, and seizes her and lies with
her, and they are caught in the act, [29]the
man who lay with her shall give fifty
shekels of silver to the young woman's
father, and she shall become his wife.
Because he violated her he shall not be
permitted to divorce her as long as he
lives.

30[e] A man shall not marry his father's wife, thereby violating his father's rights.[f]

THOSE EXCLUDED FROM THE ASSEMBLY

23 No one whose testicles are
crushed or whose penis is cut off
shall be admitted to the assembly of the
LORD.

2 Those born of an illicit union shall
not be admitted to the assembly of the
LORD. Even to the tenth generation,
none of their descendants shall be admitted to the assembly of the LORD.

3 No Ammonite or Moabite shall be
admitted to the assembly of the LORD.
Even to the tenth generation, none of
their descendants shall be admitted
to the assembly of the LORD, [4]because
they did not meet you with food and
water on your journey out of Egypt, and
because they hired against you Balaam
son of Beor, from Pethor of Mesopotamia, to curse you. [5](Yet the LORD your
God refused to heed Balaam; the LORD
your God turned the curse into a blessing for you, because the LORD your God
loved you.) [6]You shall never promote
their welfare or their prosperity as long
as you live.

7 You shall not abhor any of the
Edomites, for they are your kin. You
shall not abhor any of the Egyptians, because you were an alien residing in their
land. [8]The children of the third generation that are born to them may be admitted to the assembly of the LORD.

SANITARY, RITUAL, AND HUMANITARIAN PRECEPTS

9 When you are encamped against
your enemies you shall guard against
any impropriety.

10 If one of you becomes unclean because of a nocturnal emission, then he
shall go outside the camp; he must not
come within the camp. [11]When evening
comes, he shall wash himself with water, and when the sun has set, he may
come back into the camp.

12 You shall have a designated area
outside the camp to which you shall
go. [13]With your utensils you shall have
a trowel; when you relieve yourself outside, you shall dig a hole with it and
then cover up your excrement. [14]Be-
cause the LORD your God travels along
with your camp, to save you and to
hand over your enemies to you, therefore your camp must be holy, so that he
may not see anything indecent among
you and turn away from you.

15 Slaves who have escaped to you
from their owners shall not be given
back to them. [16]They shall reside with
you, in your midst, in any place they

[e] **22.30** Ch 23.1 in Heb [f] **22.30** Heb *uncovering his father's skirt*

choose in any one of your towns, wherever they please; you shall not oppress
them.
17 None of the daughters of Israel
shall be a temple prostitute; none of the
sons of Israel shall be a temple prostitute. 18 You shall not bring the fee of a
prostitute or the wages of a male prostitute[g] into the house of the LORD your
God in payment for any vow, for both of
these are abhorrent to the LORD your
God.
19 You shall not charge interest on
loans to another Israelite, interest on
money, interest on provisions, interest on anything that is lent. 20 On loans
to a foreigner you may charge interest,
but on loans to another Israelite you
may not charge interest, so that the
LORD your God may bless you in all your
undertakings in the land that you are
about to enter and possess.
21 If you make a vow to the LORD
your God, do not postpone fulfilling it;
for the LORD your God will surely require it of you, and you would incur
guilt. 22 But if you refrain from vow-
ing, you will not incur guilt. 23 Whatever your lips utter you must diligently
perform, just as you have freely vowed
to the LORD your God with your own
mouth.
24 If you go into your neighbour's
vineyard, you may eat your fill of grapes,
as many as you wish, but you shall not
put any in a container.
25 If you go into your neighbour's
standing grain, you may pluck the ears
with your hand, but you shall not put
a sickle to your neighbour's standing
grain.

LAWS CONCERNING MARRIAGE AND DIVORCE

24 Suppose a man enters into marriage with a woman, but she
does not please him because he finds
something objectionable about her, and
so he writes her a certificate of divorce,
puts it in her hand, and sends her out
of his house; she then leaves his house
2 and goes off to become another man's
wife. 3 Then suppose the second man
dislikes her, writes her a bill of divorce,
puts it in her hand, and sends her out
of his house (or the second man who
married her dies); 4 her first husband,
who sent her away, is not permitted to
take her again to be his wife after she
has been defiled; for that would be abhorrent to the LORD, and you shall not
bring guilt on the land that the LORD
your God is giving you as a possession.

MISCELLANEOUS LAWS

5 When a man is newly married, he
shall not go out with the army or be
charged with any related duty. He shall
be free at home for one year, to be happy
with the wife whom he has married.
6 No one shall take a mill or an upper
millstone in pledge, for that would be
taking a life in pledge.
7 If someone is caught kidnapping
another Israelite, enslaving or selling
the Israelite, then that kidnapper shall
die. So you shall purge the evil from
your midst.
8 Guard against an outbreak of a leprous[h] skin disease by being very careful;
you shall carefully observe whatever the
levitical priests instruct you, just as I
have commanded them. 9 Remember
what the LORD your God did to Miriam
on your journey out of Egypt.
10 When you make your neighbour a
loan of any kind, you shall not go into
the house to take the pledge. 11 You
shall wait outside, while the person to
whom you are making the loan brings
the pledge out to you. 12 If the person is
poor, you shall not sleep in the garment
given you as[i] the pledge. 13 You shall give
the pledge back by sunset, so that your
neighbour may sleep in the cloak and
bless you; and it will be to your credit
before the LORD your God.
14 You shall not withhold the wages
of poor and needy labourers, whether
other Israelites or aliens who reside in
your land in one of your towns. 15 You
shall pay them their wages daily before
sunset, because they are poor and their
livelihood depends on them; otherwise
they might cry to the LORD against you,
and you would incur guilt.
16 Parents shall not be put to death
for their children, nor shall children be
put to death for their parents; only for
their own crimes may persons be put to
death.
17 You shall not deprive a resident
alien or an orphan of justice; you shall
not take a widow's garment in pledge.
18 Remember that you were a slave in
Egypt and the LORD your God redeemed
you from there; therefore I command
you to do this.

g 23.18 Heb *a dog* h 24.8 A term for several skin diseases; precise meaning uncertain
i 24.12 Heb lacks *the garment given you as*

19 When you reap your harvest in
your field and forget a sheaf in the field,
you shall not go back to get it; it shall
be left for the alien, the orphan, and
the widow, so that the LORD your God
may bless you in all your undertakings.
20 When you beat your olive trees, do not
strip what is left; it shall be for the alien,
the orphan, and the widow.

21 When you gather the grapes of
your vineyard, do not glean what is left;
it shall be for the alien, the orphan, and
the widow. 22 Remember that you were
a slave in the land of Egypt; therefore I
am commanding you to do this.

25 Suppose two persons have a dispute and enter into litigation,
and the judges decide between them,
declaring one to be in the right and the
other to be in the wrong. 2 If the one in
the wrong deserves to be flogged, the
judge shall make that person lie down
and be beaten in his presence with the
number of lashes proportionate to the
offence. 3 Forty lashes may be given but
not more; if more lashes than these are
given, your neighbour will be degraded
in your sight.

4 You shall not muzzle an ox while it
is treading out the grain.

LEVIRATE MARRIAGE

5 When brothers reside together, and
one of them dies and has no son, the
wife of the deceased shall not be married outside the family to a stranger.
Her husband's brother shall go in to her,
taking her in marriage, and performing
the duty of a husband's brother to her,
6 and the firstborn whom she bears shall
succeed to the name of the deceased
brother, so that his name may not be
blotted out of Israel. 7 But if the man has
no desire to marry his brother's widow,
then his brother's widow shall go up to
the elders at the gate and say, 'My husband's brother refuses to perpetuate his
brother's name in Israel; he will not
perform the duty of a husband's brother
to me.' 8 Then the elders of his town
shall summon him and speak to him.
If he persists, saying, 'I have no desire
to marry her', 9 then his brother's wife
shall go up to him in the presence of the
elders, pull his sandal off his foot, spit
in his face, and declare, 'This is what is
done to the man who does not build up
his brother's house.' 10 Throughout Israel his family shall be known as 'the
house of him whose sandal was pulled
off.'

VARIOUS COMMANDS

11 If men get into a fight with one
another, and the wife of one intervenes
to rescue her husband from the grip of
his opponent by reaching out and seizing his genitals, 12 you shall cut off her
hand; show no pity.

13 You shall not have in your bag two
kinds of weights, large and small. 14 You
shall not have in your house two kinds
of measures, large and small. 15 You shall
have only a full and honest weight; you
shall have only a full and honest measure, so that your days may be long in the
land that the LORD your God is giving
you. 16 For all who do such things, all
who act dishonestly, are abhorrent to
the LORD your God.

17 Remember what Amalek did to
you on your journey out of Egypt, 18 how
he attacked you on the way, when you
were faint and weary, and struck down
all who lagged behind you; he did not
fear God. 19 Therefore when the LORD
your God has given you rest from all
your enemies on every hand, in the land
that the LORD your God is giving you as
an inheritance to possess, you shall blot
out the remembrance of Amalek from
under heaven; do not forget.

FIRST FRUITS AND TITHES

26 When you have come into the
land that the LORD your God
is giving you as an inheritance to possess, and you possess it, and settle in
it, 2 you shall take some of the first of
all the fruit of the ground, which you
harvest from the land that the LORD
your God is giving you, and you shall
put it in a basket and go to the place
that the LORD your God will choose
as a dwelling for his name. 3 You shall
go to the priest who is in office at that
time, and say to him, 'Today I declare
to the LORD your God that I have come
into the land that the LORD swore to
our ancestors to give us.' 4 When the
priest takes the basket from your hand
and sets it down before the altar of the
LORD your God, 5 you shall make this
response before the LORD your God:
'A wandering Aramean was my ancestor; he went down into Egypt and lived
there as an alien, few in number, and
there he became a great nation, mighty
and populous. 6 When the Egyptians
treated us harshly and afflicted us,
by imposing hard labour on us, 7 we
cried to the LORD, the God of our ancestors; the LORD heard our voice and

Names of God

No *one* name can describe all God is and all that he does. So he shows us who he is through his different names. Here are some of his names that you will find in the Bible:

1. God Most High .... *Genesis 14:19*
2. I Am Who I Am .... *Exodus 3:14*
3. Wonderful Counsellor .... *Isaiah 9:6*
4. Prince of Peace .... *Isaiah 9:6*
5. God Is with Us .... *Matthew 1:23*
6. Saviour .... *Luke 2:11*
7. The Word .... *John 1:1*
8. The Light of the World .... *John 8:12*
9. The Way, and the Truth, and the Life .... *John 14:6*
10. The Author of Life .... *Acts 3:15*
11. Abba; Father .... *Romans 8:15*
12. Great Shepherd of the Sheep .... *Hebrews 13:20*
13. Love .... *1 John 4:8*
14. King of Kings and Lord of Lords .... *1 Timothy 6:15*
15. The Beginning and the End .... *Revelation 22:13*

Days of Creation

In the beginning . . . God created the heavens and the earth.

Genesis 1:1

DAY 1 • Day and Night *Genesis 1:3–5*
God said, "Let there be light"; and there was light . . . God called the light Day, and the darkness he called Night.

DAY 2 • Sky *Genesis 1:6–8*
God said, "Let there be a dome in the midst of the waters, and let it separate the waters from the waters" . . . God called the dome Sky.

DAY 3 • Land, Sea, and Plants *Genesis 1:9–13*
God said, "Let the waters under the sky be gathered together into one place, and let the dry land appear" . . . Then God said, "Let the earth put forth vegetation: plants yielding seed, and fruit trees of every kind."

DAY 4 • Stars, Moon, and Sun *Genesis 1:14–19*
God said, "Let there be lights in the dome of the sky to separate the day from the night" . . . God made the two great lights . . . and the stars.

DAY 5 • Sea Animals and Birds *Genesis 1:20–23*

God said, "Let the waters bring forth swarms of living creatures, and let birds fly above the earth across the dome of the sky" . . . God blessed them, saying, "Be fruitful and multiply."

DAY 6 • Land Animals and Humans

Genesis 1:24–31

God said, "Let the earth bring forth living creatures of every kind" . . . Then God said, "Let us make humankind in our image, according to our likeness" . . . So God created humankind in his image . . . male and female he created them.

DAY 7 • Rest *Genesis 2:1–3*

God finished the work that he had done, and he rested on the seventh day.

It is the LORD your God who goes with you; he will not fail you or forsake you.

DEUTERONOMY 31:6

saw our affliction, our toil, and our oppression. 8 The LORD brought us out of
Egypt with a mighty hand and an outstretched arm, with a terrifying display
of power, and with signs and wonders;
9 and he brought us into this place and
gave us this land, a land flowing with
milk and honey. 10 So now I bring the
first of the fruit of the ground that you,
O LORD, have given me.' You shall set
it down before the LORD your God and
bow down before the LORD your God.
11 Then you, together with the Levites
and the aliens who reside among you,
shall celebrate with all the bounty that
the LORD your God has given to you
and to your house.

12 When you have finished paying
all the tithe of your produce in the third
year (which is the year of the tithe),
giving it to the Levites, the aliens, the
orphans, and the widows, so that they
may eat their fill within your towns,
13 then you shall say before the LORD
your God: 'I have removed the sacred
portion from the house, and I have given
it to the Levites, the resident aliens, the
orphans, and the widows, in accordance
with your entire commandment that
you commanded me; I have neither
transgressed nor forgotten any of your
commandments: 14 I have not eaten of it
while in mourning; I have not removed
any of it while I was unclean; and I have
not offered any of it to the dead. I have
obeyed the LORD my God, doing just as
you commanded me. 15 Look down from
your holy habitation, from heaven, and
bless your people Israel and the ground
that you have given us, as you swore
to our ancestors—a land flowing with
milk and honey.'

CONCLUDING EXHORTATION

16 This very day the LORD your God is
commanding you to observe these statutes and ordinances; so observe them
diligently with all your heart and with
all your soul. 17 Today you have obtained
the LORD's agreement: to be your God;
and for you to walk in his ways, to keep
his statutes, his commandments, and
his ordinances, and to obey him. 18 Today the LORD has obtained your agreement: to be his treasured people, as he
promised you, and to keep his commandments; 19 for him to set you high
above all nations that he has made, in
praise and in fame and in honour; and
for you to be a people holy to the LORD
your God, as he promised.

THE INSCRIBED STONES AND ALTAR ON MOUNT EBAL

27 Then Moses and the elders of
Israel charged all the people as
follows: Keep the entire commandment
that I am commanding you today. 2 On
the day that you cross over the Jordan
into the land that the LORD your God is
giving you, you shall set up large stones
and cover them with plaster. 3 You shall
write on them all the words of this law
when you have crossed over, to enter
the land that the LORD your God is giving you, a land flowing with milk and
honey, as the LORD, the God of your
ancestors, promised you. 4 So when
you have crossed over the Jordan, you
shall set up these stones, about which I
am commanding you today, on Mount
Ebal, and you shall cover them with
plaster. 5 And you shall build an altar
there to the LORD your God, an altar of
stones on which you have not used an
iron tool. 6 You must build the altar of
the LORD your God of unhewn[j] stones.
Then offer up burnt-offerings on it to
the LORD your God, 7 make sacrifices of
well-being, and eat them there, rejoicing before the LORD your God. 8 You
shall write on the stones all the words of
this law very clearly.

9 Then Moses and the levitical priests
spoke to all Israel, saying: Keep silence
and hear, O Israel! This very day you
have become the people of the LORD
your God. 10 Therefore obey the LORD
your God, observing his commandments and his statutes that I am commanding you today.

TWELVE CURSES

11 The same day Moses charged the
people as follows: 12 When you have
crossed over the Jordan, these shall
stand on Mount Gerizim for the blessing
of the people: Simeon, Levi, Judah, Issachar, Joseph, and Benjamin. 13 And these
shall stand on Mount Ebal for the curse:
Reuben, Gad, Asher, Zebulun, Dan, and
Naphtali. 14 Then the Levites shall declare in a loud voice to all the Israelites:

15 'Cursed be anyone who makes an
idol or casts an image, anything abhorrent to the LORD, the work of an artisan,
and sets it up in secret.' All the people
shall respond, saying, 'Amen!'

16 'Cursed be anyone who dishonours father or mother.' All the people
shall say, 'Amen!'

[j] 27.6 Heb *whole*

17 'Cursed be anyone who moves a
neighbour's boundary marker.' All the
people shall say, 'Amen!'
18 'Cursed be anyone who misleads a
blind person on the road.' All the people
shall say, 'Amen!'
19 'Cursed be anyone who deprives
the alien, the orphan, and the widow of
justice.' All the people shall say, 'Amen!'
20 'Cursed be anyone who lies with
his father's wife, because he has violated
his father's rights.'[k] All the people shall
say, 'Amen!'
21 'Cursed be anyone who lies with
any animal.' All the people shall say,
'Amen!'
22 'Cursed be anyone who lies with
his sister, whether the daughter of his
father or the daughter of his mother.' All
the people shall say, 'Amen!'
23 'Cursed be anyone who lies with
his mother-in-law.' All the people shall
say, 'Amen!'
24 'Cursed be anyone who strikes
down a neighbour in secret.' All the people shall say, 'Amen!'
25 'Cursed be anyone who takes a
bribe to shed innocent blood.' All the
people shall say, 'Amen!'
26 'Cursed be anyone who does not
uphold the words of this law by observing them.' All the people shall say,
'Amen!'

BLESSINGS FOR OBEDIENCE

28 If you will only obey the LORD
your God, by diligently observing all his commandments that I am
commanding you today, the LORD your
God will set you high above all the nations of the earth; 2all these blessings
shall come upon you and overtake you,
if you obey the LORD your God:
3 Blessed shall you be in the city, and
blessed shall you be in the field.
4 Blessed shall be the fruit of your
womb, the fruit of your ground, and the
fruit of your livestock, both the increase
of your cattle and the issue of your flock.
5 Blessed shall be your basket and
your kneading-bowl.
6 Blessed shall you be when you come
in, and blessed shall you be when you go
out.
7 The LORD will cause your enemies
who rise against you to be defeated before you; they shall come out against
you one way, and flee before you seven
ways. 8The LORD will command the
blessing upon you in your barns, and
in all that you undertake; he will bless
you in the land that the LORD your God
is giving you. 9The LORD will establish
you as his holy people, as he has sworn
to you, if you keep the commandments
of the LORD your God and walk in his
ways. 10All the peoples of the earth shall
see that you are called by the name of
the LORD, and they shall be afraid of
you. 11The LORD will make you abound
in prosperity, in the fruit of your womb,
in the fruit of your livestock, and in the
fruit of your ground in the land that the
LORD swore to your ancestors to give
you. 12The LORD will open for you his
rich storehouse, the heavens, to give
the rain of your land in its season and
to bless all your undertakings. You will
lend to many nations, but you will not
borrow. 13The LORD will make you the
head, and not the tail; you shall be only
at the top, and not at the bottom—if you
obey the commandments of the LORD
your God, which I am commanding you
today, by diligently observing them,
14and if you do not turn aside from any
of the words that I am commanding you
today, either to the right or to the left,
following other gods to serve them.

WARNINGS AGAINST DISOBEDIENCE

15 But if you will not obey the LORD
your God by diligently observing all his
commandments and decrees, which I
am commanding you today, then all
these curses shall come upon you and
overtake you:
16 Cursed shall you be in the city,
and cursed shall you be in the field.
17 Cursed shall be your basket and
your kneading-bowl.
18 Cursed shall be the fruit of your
womb, the fruit of your ground, the
increase of your cattle, and the issue of
your flock.
19 Cursed shall you be when you
come in, and cursed shall you be when
you go out.
20 The LORD will send upon you disaster, panic, and frustration in everything you attempt to do, until you are
destroyed and perish quickly, on account of the evil of your deeds, because
you have forsaken me. 21The LORD will
make the pestilence cling to you until
it has consumed you from the land that
you are entering to possess. 22The LORD
will afflict you with consumption, fever, inflammation, with fiery heat and
drought, and with blight and mildew;

[k] 27.20 Heb *uncovered his father's skirt*

they shall pursue you until you perish. 23 The sky over your head shall be
bronze, and the earth under you iron.
24 The LORD will change the rain of your
land into powder, and only dust shall
come down upon you from the sky until
you are destroyed.
25 The LORD will cause you to be defeated before your enemies; you shall go
out against them one way and flee before them seven ways. You shall become
an object of horror to all the kingdoms
of the earth. 26 Your corpses shall be food
for every bird of the air and animal of
the earth, and there shall be no one to
frighten them away. 27 The LORD will
afflict you with the boils of Egypt, with
ulcers, scurvy, and itch, of which you
cannot be healed. 28 The LORD will afflict you with madness, blindness, and
confusion of mind; 29 you shall grope
about at noon as blind people grope in
darkness, but you shall be unable to find
your way; and you shall be continually
abused and robbed, without anyone to
help. 30 You shall become engaged to a
woman, but another man shall lie with
her. You shall build a house, but not live
in it. You shall plant a vineyard, but not
enjoy its fruit. 31 Your ox shall be butchered before your eyes, but you shall not
eat of it. Your donkey shall be stolen in
front of you, and shall not be restored
to you. Your sheep shall be given to
your enemies, without anyone to help
you. 32 Your sons and daughters shall
be given to another people, while you
look on; you will strain your eyes looking for them all day but be powerless to
do anything. 33 A people whom you do
not know shall eat up the fruit of your
ground and of all your labours; you shall
be continually abused and crushed,
34 and driven mad by the sight that your
eyes shall see. 35 The LORD will strike you
on the knees and on the legs with grievous boils of which you cannot be healed,
from the sole of your foot to the crown
of your head. 36 The LORD will bring you,
and the king whom you set over you, to
a nation that neither you nor your ancestors have known, where you shall
serve other gods, of wood and stone.
37 You shall become an object of horror,
a proverb, and a byword among all the
peoples where the LORD will lead you.
38 You shall carry much seed into the
field but shall gather little in, for the locust shall consume it. 39 You shall plant
vineyards and dress them, but you shall
neither drink the wine nor gather the
grapes, for the worm shall eat them.
40 You shall have olive trees throughout all your territory, but you shall not
anoint yourself with the oil, for your
olives shall drop off. 41 You shall have
sons and daughters, but they shall not
remain yours, for they shall go into captivity. 42 All your trees and the fruit of
your ground the cicada shall take over.
43 Aliens residing among you shall ascend above you higher and higher,
while you shall descend lower and
lower. 44 They shall lend to you but you
shall not lend to them; they shall be the
head and you shall be the tail.
45 All these curses shall come upon
you, pursuing and overtaking you until
you are destroyed, because you did not
obey the LORD your God, by observing
the commandments and the decrees
that he commanded you. 46 They shall
be among you and your descendants as
a sign and a portent for ever.
47 Because you did not serve the
LORD your God joyfully and with gladness of heart for the abundance of everything, 48 therefore you shall serve
your enemies whom the LORD will send
against you, in hunger and thirst, in
nakedness and lack of everything. He
will put an iron yoke on your neck until
he has destroyed you. 49 The LORD will
bring a nation from far away, from the
end of the earth, to swoop down on you
like an eagle, a nation whose language
you do not understand, 50 a grim-faced
nation showing no respect to the old or
favour to the young. 51 It shall consume
the fruit of your livestock and the fruit
of your ground until you are destroyed,
leaving you neither grain, wine, and
oil, nor the increase of your cattle and
the issue of your flock, until it has made
you perish. 52 It shall besiege you in all
your towns until your high and fortified walls, in which you trusted, come
down throughout your land; it shall
besiege you in all your towns throughout the land that the LORD your God
has given you. 53 In the desperate straits
to which the enemy siege reduces you,
you will eat the fruit of your womb, the
flesh of your own sons and daughters
whom the LORD your God has given
you. 54 Even the most refined and gentle
of men among you will begrudge food to
his own brother, to the wife whom he
embraces, and to the last of his remaining children, 55 giving to none of them
any of the flesh of his children whom he
is eating, because nothing else remains

to him, in the desperate straits to which the enemy siege will reduce you in all your towns. 56 She who is the most refined and gentle among you, so gentle and refined that she does not venture to set the sole of her foot on the ground, will begrudge food to the husband whom she embraces, to her own son, and to her own daughter, 57 begrudging even the afterbirth that comes out from between her thighs, and the children that she bears, because she is eating them in secret for lack of anything else, in the desperate straits to which the enemy siege will reduce you in your towns.

58 If you do not diligently observe all the words of this law that are written in this book, fearing this glorious and awesome name, the LORD your God, 59 then the LORD will overwhelm both you and your offspring with severe and lasting afflictions and grievous and lasting maladies. 60 He will bring back upon you all the diseases of Egypt, of which you were in dread, and they shall cling to you. 61 Every other malady and affliction, even though not recorded in the book of this law, the LORD will inflict on you until you are destroyed. 62 Although once you were as numerous as the stars in heaven, you shall be left few in number, because you did not obey the LORD your God. 63 And just as the LORD took delight in making you prosperous and numerous, so the LORD will take delight in bringing you to ruin and destruction; you shall be plucked off the land that you are entering to possess. 64 The LORD will scatter you among all peoples, from one end of the earth to the other; and there you shall serve other gods, of wood and stone, which neither you nor your ancestors have known. 65 Among those nations you shall find no ease, no resting-place for the sole of your foot. There the LORD will give you a trembling heart, failing eyes, and a languishing spirit. 66 Your life shall hang in doubt before you; night and day you shall be in dread, with no assurance of your life. 67 In the morning you shall say, 'If only it were evening!' and at evening you shall say, 'If only it were morning!'—because of the dread that your heart shall feel and the sights that your eyes shall see. 68 The LORD will bring you back in ships to Egypt, by a route that I promised you would never see again; and there you shall offer yourselves for sale to your enemies as male and female slaves, but there will be no buyer.

29 [l]These are the words of the covenant that the LORD commanded Moses to make with the Israelites in the land of Moab, in addition to the covenant that he had made with them at Horeb.

THE COVENANT RENEWED IN MOAB

2[m] Moses summoned all Israel and said to them: You have seen all that the LORD did before your eyes in the land of Egypt, to Pharaoh and to all his servants and to all his land, 3 the great trials that your eyes saw, the signs, and those great wonders. 4 But to this day the LORD has not given you a mind to understand, or eyes to see, or ears to hear. 5 I have led you for forty years in the wilderness. The clothes on your back have not worn out, and the sandals on your feet have not worn out; 6 you have not eaten bread, and you have not drunk wine or strong drink—so that you may know that I am the LORD your God. 7 When you came to this place, King Sihon of Heshbon and King Og of Bashan came out against us for battle, but we defeated them. 8 We took their land and gave it as an inheritance to the Reubenites, the Gadites, and the half-tribe of Manasseh. 9 Therefore diligently observe the words of this covenant, in order that you may succeed[n] in everything that you do.

10 You stand assembled today, all of you, before the LORD your God—the leaders of your tribes,[o] your elders, and your officials, all the men of Israel, 11 your children, your women, and the aliens who are in your camp, both those who cut your wood and those who draw your water— 12 to enter into the covenant of the LORD your God, sworn by an oath, which the LORD your God is making with you today; 13 in order that he may establish you today as his people, and that he may be your God, as he promised you and as he swore to your ancestors, to Abraham, to Isaac, and to Jacob. 14 I am making this covenant, sworn by an oath, not only with you who stand here with us today before the LORD our God, 15 but also with those who are not here with us today. 16 You know how we lived in the land of Egypt, and how we came through the midst of the nations through which you passed. 17 You have seen their detestable things, the filthy idols of wood and stone, of sil-

[l] **29.1** Ch 28.69 in Heb [m] **29.2** Ch 29.1 in Heb
[n] **29.9** Or *deal wisely* [o] **29.10** Gk Syr: Heb *your leaders, your tribes*

ver and gold, that were among them.
18It may be that there is among you a
man or woman, or a family or tribe,
whose heart is already turning away
from the LORD our God to serve the gods
of those nations. It may be that there
is among you a root sprouting poisonous and bitter growth. 19All who hear
the words of this oath and bless themselves, thinking in their hearts, 'We are
safe even though we go our own stubborn ways' (thus bringing disaster on
moist and dry alike)[p]— 20the LORD will
be unwilling to pardon them, for the
LORD's anger and passion will smoke
against them. All the curses written in
this book will descend on them, and the
LORD will blot out their names from under heaven. 21The LORD will single them
out from all the tribes of Israel for calamity, in accordance with all the curses
of the covenant written in this book of
the law. 22The next generation, your
children who rise up after you, as well
as the foreigner who comes from a distant country, will see the devastation of
that land and the afflictions with which
the LORD has afflicted it— 23all its soil
burned out by sulphur and salt, nothing planted, nothing sprouting, unable
to support any vegetation, like the destruction of Sodom and Gomorrah, Admah and Zeboiim, which the LORD destroyed in his fierce anger— 24they and
indeed all the nations will wonder, 'Why
has the LORD done thus to this land?
What caused this great display of anger?' 25They will conclude, 'It is because
they abandoned the covenant of the
LORD, the God of their ancestors, which
he made with them when he brought
them out of the land of Egypt. 26They
turned and served other gods, worshipping them, gods whom they had not
known and whom he had not allotted
to them; 27so the anger of the LORD was
kindled against that land, bringing on it
every curse written in this book. 28The
LORD uprooted them from their land in
anger, fury, and great wrath, and cast
them into another land, as is now the
case.' 29The secret things belong to the
LORD our God, but the revealed things
belong to us and to our children for ever,
to observe all the words of this law.

GOD'S FIDELITY ASSURED

30 When all these things have happened to you, the blessings and
the curses that I have set before you, if
you call them to mind among all the
nations where the LORD your God has
driven you, 2and return to the LORD
your God, and you and your children
obey him with all your heart and with
all your soul, just as I am commanding
you today, 3then the LORD your God will
restore your fortunes and have compassion on you, gathering you again from
all the peoples among whom the LORD
your God has scattered you. 4Even if you
are exiled to the ends of the world,[q] from
there the LORD your God will gather
you, and from there he will bring you
back. 5The LORD your God will bring
you into the land that your ancestors
possessed, and you will possess it; he
will make you more prosperous and numerous than your ancestors.

6 Moreover, the LORD your God will
circumcise your heart and the heart of
your descendants, so that you will love
the LORD your God with all your heart
and with all your soul, in order that you
may live. 7The LORD your God will put
all these curses on your enemies and
on the adversaries who took advantage
of you. 8Then you shall again obey the
LORD, observing all his commandments
that I am commanding you today, 9and
the LORD your God will make you abundantly prosperous in all your undertakings, in the fruit of your body, in the
fruit of your livestock, and in the fruit of
your soil. For the LORD will again take
delight in prospering you, just as he delighted in prospering your ancestors,
10when you obey the LORD your God
by observing his commandments and
decrees that are written in this book of
the law, because you turn to the LORD
your God with all your heart and with
all your soul.

EXHORTATION TO CHOOSE LIFE

11 Surely, this commandment that
I am commanding you today is not too
hard for you, nor is it too far away. 12It is
not in heaven, that you should say, 'Who
will go up to heaven for us, and get it for
us so that we may hear it and observe
it?' 13Neither is it beyond the sea, that
you should say, 'Who will cross to the
other side of the sea for us, and get it for
us so that we may hear it and observe
it?' 14No, the word is very near to you;
it is in your mouth and in your heart for
you to observe.

[p] 29.19 Meaning of Heb uncertain [q] 30.4 Heb *of heaven*

15 See, I have set before you today
life and prosperity, death and adversity.
16 If you obey the commandments of the
LORD your God[r] that I am commanding you today, by loving the LORD your
God, walking in his ways, and observing
his commandments, decrees, and ordinances, then you shall live and become
numerous, and the LORD your God will
bless you in the land that you are entering to possess. 17 But if your heart turns
away and you do not hear, but are led
astray to bow down to other gods and
serve them, 18 I declare to you today that
you shall perish; you shall not live long
in the land that you are crossing the Jordan to enter and possess. 19 I call heaven
and earth to witness against you today
that I have set before you life and death,
blessings and curses. Choose life so that
you and your descendants may live,
20 loving the LORD your God, obeying
him, and holding fast to him; for that
means life to you and length of days, so
that you may live in the land that the
LORD swore to give to your ancestors, to
Abraham, to Isaac, and to Jacob.

JOSHUA BECOMES MOSES' SUCCESSOR

31 When Moses had finished speaking all[s] these words to all Israel,
2 he said to them: 'I am now a hundred
and twenty years old. I am no longer
able to get about, and the LORD has told
me, "You shall not cross over this Jordan." 3 The LORD your God himself will
cross over before you. He will destroy
these nations before you, and you shall
dispossess them. Joshua also will cross
over before you, as the LORD promised.
4 The LORD will do to them as he did
to Sihon and Og, the kings of the Amorites, and to their land, when he destroyed them. 5 The LORD will give them
over to you and you shall deal with them
in full accord with the command that I
have given to you. 6 Be strong and bold;
have no fear or dread of them, because
it is the LORD your God who goes with
you; he will not fail you or forsake you.'

7 Then Moses summoned Joshua and
said to him in the sight of all Israel: 'Be
strong and bold, for you are the one who
will go with this people into the land
that the LORD has sworn to their ancestors to give them; and you will put them
in possession of it. 8 It is the LORD who
goes before you. He will be with you; he
will not fail you or forsake you. Do not
fear or be dismayed.'

THE LAW TO BE READ EVERY SEVENTH YEAR

9 Then Moses wrote down this law,
and gave it to the priests, the sons of
Levi, who carried the ark of the covenant of the LORD, and to all the elders
of Israel. 10 Moses commanded them:
'Every seventh year, in the scheduled
year of remission, during the festival of booths,[t] 11 when all Israel comes
to appear before the LORD your God
at the place that he will choose, you
shall read this law before all Israel in
their hearing. 12 Assemble the people—
men, women, and children, as well as
the aliens residing in your towns—so
that they may hear and learn to fear
the LORD your God and to observe diligently all the words of this law, 13 and
so that their children, who have not
known it, may hear and learn to fear the
LORD your God, as long as you live in
the land that you are crossing over the
Jordan to possess.'

MOSES AND JOSHUA RECEIVE GOD'S CHARGE

14 The LORD said to Moses, 'Your
time to die is near; call Joshua and present yourselves in the tent of meeting,
so that I may commission him.' So
Moses and Joshua went and presented
themselves in the tent of meeting, 15 and
the LORD appeared at the tent in a pillar
of cloud; the pillar of cloud stood at the
entrance to the tent.

16 The LORD said to Moses, 'Soon
you will lie down with your ancestors.
Then this people will begin to prostitute
themselves to the foreign gods in their
midst, the gods of the land into which
they are going; they will forsake me,
breaking my covenant that I have made
with them. 17 My anger will be kindled
against them on that day. I will forsake
them and hide my face from them; they
will become easy prey, and many terrible troubles will come upon them. On
that day they will say, "Have not these
troubles come upon us because our God
is not in our midst?" 18 On that day I will
surely hide my face on account of all the
evil they have done by turning to other
gods. 19 Now therefore write this song,
and teach it to the Israelites; put it in
their mouths, in order that this song
may be a witness for me against the

[r] **30.16** Gk: Heb lacks *If you obey the commandments of the LORD your God* [s] **31.1** Q Ms Gk: MT *Moses went and spoke* [t] **31.10** Or *tabernacles*; Heb *succoth*

Israelites. 20For when I have brought
them into the land flowing with milk
and honey, which I promised on oath
to their ancestors, and they have eaten
their fill and grown fat, they will turn
to other gods and serve them, despising
me and breaking my covenant. 21And
when many terrible troubles come upon
them, this song will confront them as a
witness, because it will not be lost from
the mouths of their descendants. For I
know what they are inclined to do even
now, before I have brought them into
the land that I promised them on oath.'
22That very day Moses wrote this song
and taught it to the Israelites.

23 Then the LORD commissioned
Joshua son of Nun and said, 'Be strong
and bold, for you shall bring the Israelites into the land that I promised them;
I will be with you.'

24 When Moses had finished writing
down in a book the words of this law to
the very end, 25Moses commanded the
Levites who carried the ark of the covenant of the LORD, saying, 26'Take this
book of the law and put it beside the ark
of the covenant of the LORD your God; let
it remain there as a witness against you.
27For I know well how rebellious and
stubborn you are. If you already have
been so rebellious towards the LORD
while I am still alive among you, how
much more after my death! 28Assem-
ble to me all the elders of your tribes and
your officials, so that I may recite these
words in their hearing and call heaven
and earth to witness against them.
29For I know that after my death you
will surely act corruptly, turning aside
from the way that I have commanded
you. In time to come trouble will befall
you, because you will do what is evil in
the sight of the LORD, provoking him to
anger through the work of your hands.'

THE SONG OF MOSES

30 Then Moses recited the words of
this song, to the very end, in the hearing of the whole assembly of Israel:

32 Give ear, O heavens,
and I will speak;
let the earth hear the words
of my mouth.
2 May my teaching drop like the rain,
my speech condense like the dew;
like gentle rain on grass,
like showers on new growth.
3 For I will proclaim the name
of the LORD;
ascribe greatness to our God!
4 The Rock, his work is perfect,
and all his ways are just.
A faithful God, without deceit,
just and upright is he;
5 yet his degenerate children have
dealt falsely with him,[u]
a perverse and crooked
generation.
6 Do you thus repay the LORD,
O foolish and senseless people?
Is not he your father, who
created you,
who made you and
established you?
7 Remember the days of old,
consider the years long past;
ask your father, and he will
inform you;
your elders, and they
will tell you.
8 When the Most High[v] apportioned
the nations,
when he divided humankind,
he fixed the boundaries of
the peoples
according to the number
of the gods;[w]
9 the LORD's own portion
was his people,
Jacob his allotted share.

10 He sustained[x] him in a
desert land,
in a howling wilderness waste;
he shielded him, cared for him,
guarded him as the apple
of his eye.
11 As an eagle stirs up its nest,
and hovers over its young;
as it spreads its wings,
takes them up,
and bears them aloft on
its pinions,
12 the LORD alone guided him;
no foreign god was with him.
13 He set him upon the heights
of the land,
and fed him with[y] produce
of the field;
he nursed him with honey
from the crags,
with oil from flinty rock;
14 curds from the herd, and milk
from the flock,
with fat of lambs and rams;

[u] 32.5 Meaning of Heb uncertain
[v] 32.8 Traditional rendering of Heb *Elyon*
[w] 32.8 Q Ms Compare Gk Tg: MT *the Israelites*
[x] 32.10 Sam Gk Compare Tg: MT *found*
[y] 32.13 Sam Gk Syr Tg: MT *he ate*

Bashan bulls and goats,
together with the choicest wheat—
you drank fine wine from
the blood of grapes.
15 Jacob ate his fill;[z]
Jeshurun grew fat, and kicked.
You grew fat, bloated, and gorged!
He abandoned God who made him,
and scoffed at the Rock
of his salvation.
16 They made him jealous with
strange gods,
with abhorrent things they
provoked him.
17 They sacrificed to demons, not God,
to deities they had never known,
to new ones recently arrived,
whom your ancestors
had not feared.
18 You were unmindful of the
Rock that bore you;[a]
you forgot the God who
gave you birth.

19 The LORD saw it, and was jealous;[b]
he spurned[c] his sons and
daughters.
20 He said: I will hide my face
from them,
I will see what their end will be;
for they are a perverse generation,
children in whom there is
no faithfulness.
21 They made me jealous with
what is no god,
provoked me with their idols.
So I will make them jealous with
what is no people,
provoke them with a
foolish nation.
22 For a fire is kindled by my anger,
and burns to the depths of Sheol;
it devours the earth and its increase,
and sets on fire the foundations
of the mountains.
23 I will heap disasters upon them,
spend my arrows against them:
24 wasting hunger,
burning consumption,
bitter pestilence.
The teeth of beasts I will send
against them,
with venom of things
crawling in the dust.
25 In the street the sword shall bereave,
and in the chambers terror,
for young man and woman alike,
nursing child and old grey head.
26 I thought to scatter them[d]
and blot out the memory of
them from humankind;
27 but I feared provocation
by the enemy,
for their adversaries might
misunderstand
and say, 'Our hand is triumphant;
it was not the LORD who
did all this.'
28 They are a nation void of sense;
there is no understanding
in them.
29 If they were wise, they would
understand this;
they would discern what
the end would be.
30 How could one have routed
a thousand,
and two put a myriad to flight,
unless their Rock had sold them,
the LORD had given them up?
31 Indeed their rock is not
like our Rock;
our enemies are fools.[e]
32 Their vine comes from the vine-stock
of Sodom,
from the vineyards of Gomorrah;
their grapes are grapes of poison,
their clusters are bitter;
33 their wine is the poison of serpents,
the cruel venom of asps.

34 Is not this laid up in store with me,
sealed up in my treasuries?
35 Vengeance is mine, and recompense,
for the time when their
foot shall slip;
because the day of their
calamity is at hand,
their doom comes swiftly.

36 Indeed the LORD will vindicate
his people,
have compassion on his servants,
when he sees that their
power is gone,
neither bond nor free remaining.
37 Then he will say: Where
are their gods,
the rock in which they
took refuge,
38 who ate the fat of their sacrifices,
and drank the wine of
their libations?
Let them rise up and help you,
let them be your protection!

[z] 32.15 Q Mss Sam Gk: MT lacks *Jacob ate his fill* [a] 32.18 Or *that begot you* [b] 32.19 Q Mss Gk: MT lacks *was jealous* [c] 32.19 Cn: Heb *he spurned because of provocation* [d] 32.26 Gk: Meaning of Heb uncertain [e] 32.31 Gk: Meaning of Heb uncertain

39 See now that I, even I, am he;
there is no god besides me.
I kill and I make alive;
I wound and I heal;
and no one can deliver
from my hand.
40 For I lift up my hand to heaven,
and swear: As I live for ever,
41 when I whet my flashing sword,
and my hand takes hold
on judgement;
I will take vengeance on my
adversaries,
and will repay those who hate me.
42 I will make my arrows drunk
with blood,
and my sword shall devour flesh—
with the blood of the slain
and the captives,
from the long-haired enemy.

43 Praise, O heavens,[f] his people,
worship him, all you gods![g]
For he will avenge the blood
of his children,[h]
and take vengeance on
his adversaries;
he will repay those who hate him,[i]
and cleanse the land for
his people.[j]

44 Moses came and recited all the
words of this song in the hearing of
the people, he and Joshua[k] son of Nun.
45 When Moses had finished reciting all
these words to all Israel, 46 he said to
them: 'Take to heart all the words that
I am giving in witness against you today; give them as a command to your
children, so that they may diligently
observe all the words of this law. 47 This
is no trifling matter for you, but rather
your very life; through it you may live
long in the land that you are crossing
over the Jordan to possess.'

MOSES' DEATH FORETOLD

48 On that very day the LORD addressed Moses as follows: 49 'Ascend
this mountain of the Abarim, Mount
Nebo, which is in the land of Moab,
across from Jericho, and view the land
of Canaan, which I am giving to the Israelites for a possession; 50 you shall die
there on the mountain that you ascend
and shall be gathered to your kin, as
your brother Aaron died on Mount Hor
and was gathered to his kin; 51 because
both of you broke faith with me among
the Israelites at the waters of Meribath-
kadesh in the wilderness of Zin, by failing to maintain my holiness among the
Israelites. 52 Although you may view the
land from a distance, you shall not enter it—the land that I am giving to the
Israelites.'

MOSES' FINAL BLESSING ON ISRAEL

33 This is the blessing with which
Moses, the man of God, blessed
the Israelites before his death. 2 He said:
The LORD came from Sinai,
and dawned from Seir upon us;[l]
he shone forth from Mount Paran.
With him were myriads of
holy ones;[m]
at his right, a host of his own.[n]
3 Indeed, O favourite among[o] peoples,
all his holy ones were in
your charge;
they marched at your heels,
accepted direction from you.
4 Moses charged us with the law,
as a possession for the
assembly of Jacob.
5 There arose a king in Jeshurun,
when the leaders of the
people assembled—
the united tribes of Israel.

6 May Reuben live, and not die out,
even though his numbers are few.

7 And this he said of Judah:
O LORD, give heed to Judah,
and bring him to his people;
strengthen his hands for him,[p]
and be a help against his
adversaries.

8 And of Levi he said:
Give to Levi[q] your Thummim,
and your Urim to your loyal one,
whom you tested at Massah,
with whom you contended at
the waters of Meribah;
9 who said of his father and mother,
'I regard them not';
he ignored his kin,
and did not acknowledge
his children.
For they observed your word,
and kept your covenant.

[f] **32.43** Q Ms Gk: MT *nations* [g] **32.43** Q Ms Gk: MT lacks this line [h] **32.43** Q Ms Gk: MT *his servants* [i] **32.43** Q Ms Gk: MT lacks this line [j] **32.43** Q Ms Sam Gk Vg: MT *his land his people* [k] **32.44** Sam Gk Syr Vg: MT *Hoshea* [l] **33.2** Gk Syr Vg Compare Tg: Heb *upon them* [m] **33.2** Cn Compare Gk Sam Syr Vg: MT *He came from Ribeboth-kodesh,* [n] **33.2** Cn Compare Gk: Meaning of Heb uncertain [o] **33.3** Or *O lover of the* [p] **33.7** Cn: Heb *with his hands he contended* [q] **33.8** Q Ms Gk: MT lacks *Give to Levi*

10 They teach Jacob your ordinances,
and Israel your law;
they place incense before you,
and whole burnt-offerings
on your altar.
11 Bless, O LORD, his substance,
and accept the work of his hands;
crush the loins of his adversaries,
of those that hate him, so that
they do not rise again.

12 Of Benjamin he said:
The beloved of the LORD
rests in safety—
the High God[r] surrounds him
all day long—
the beloved[s] rests between
his shoulders.

13 And of Joseph he said:
Blessed by the LORD be his land,
with the choice gifts of
heaven above,
and of the deep that lies beneath;
14 with the choice fruits of the sun,
and the rich yield of the months;
15 with the finest produce of the
ancient mountains,
and the abundance of the
everlasting hills;
16 with the choice gifts of the
earth and its fullness,
and the favour of the one
who dwells on Sinai.[t]
Let these come on the head
of Joseph,
on the brow of the prince
among his brothers.
17 A firstborn[u] bull—majesty is his!
His horns are the horns
of a wild ox;
with them he gores the peoples,
driving them to[v] the ends
of the earth;
such are the myriads of Ephraim,
such the thousands of Manasseh.

18 And of Zebulun he said:
Rejoice, Zebulun, in your going out;
and Issachar, in your tents.
19 They call peoples to the mountain;
there they offer the right
sacrifices;
for they suck the affluence of the seas
and the hidden treasures
of the sand.

20 And of Gad he said:
Blessed be the enlargement of Gad!
Gad lives like a lion;
he tears at arm and scalp.
21 He chose the best for himself,
for there a commander's
allotment was reserved;
he came at the head of the people,
he executed the justice
of the LORD,
and his ordinances for Israel.

22 And of Dan he said:
Dan is a lion's whelp
that leaps forth from Bashan.

23 And of Naphtali he said:
O Naphtali, sated with favour,
full of the blessing of the LORD,
possess the west and the south.

24 And of Asher he said:
Most blessed of sons be Asher;
may he be the favourite
of his brothers,
and may he dip his foot in oil.
25 Your bars are iron and bronze;
and as your days, so is
your strength.

26 There is none like God, O Jeshurun,
who rides through the
heavens to your help,
majestic through the skies.
27 He subdues the ancient gods,[w]
shatters[x] the forces of old;[y]
he drove out the enemy before you,
and said, 'Destroy!'
28 So Israel lives in safety,
untroubled is Jacob's abode[z]
in a land of grain and wine,
where the heavens drop
down dew.
29 Happy are you, O Israel!
Who is like you,
a people saved by the LORD,
the shield of your help,
and the sword of your triumph!
Your enemies shall come
fawning to you,
and you shall tread on their backs.

MOSES DIES AND IS BURIED IN THE LAND OF MOAB

34 Then Moses went up from the
plains of Moab to Mount Nebo,
to the top of Pisgah, which is opposite
Jericho, and the LORD showed him the

[r] 33.12 Heb *above him* [s] 33.12 Heb *he* [t] 33.16 Cn: Heb *in the bush* [u] 33.17 Q Ms Gk Syr Vg: MT *His firstborn* [v] 33.17 Cn: Heb *the peoples, together* [w] 33.27 Or *The eternal God is a dwelling-place* [x] 33.27 Cn: Heb *from underneath* [y] 33.27 Or *the everlasting arms* [z] 33.28 Or *fountain*

whole land: Gilead as far as Dan, [2]all
Naphtali, the land of Ephraim and Manasseh, all the land of Judah as far as
the Western Sea, [3]the Negeb, and the
Plain—that is, the valley of Jericho, the
city of palm trees—as far as Zoar. [4]The
LORD said to him, 'This is the land of
which I swore to Abraham, to Isaac, and
to Jacob, saying, "I will give it to your
descendants"; I have let you see it with
your eyes, but you shall not cross over
there.' [5]Then Moses, the servant of the
LORD, died there in the land of Moab, at
the LORD's command. [6]He was buried
in a valley in the land of Moab, opposite
Beth-peor, but no one knows his burial
place to this day. [7]Moses was one hundred and twenty years old when he died;
his sight was unimpaired and his vigour
had not abated. [8]The Israelites wept for
Moses in the plains of Moab for thirty
days; then the period of mourning for
Moses was ended.

9 Joshua son of Nun was full of the
spirit of wisdom, because Moses had
laid his hands on him; and the Israelites obeyed him, doing as the LORD had
commanded Moses.

10 Never since has there arisen a
prophet in Israel like Moses, whom the
LORD knew face to face. [11]He was un-
equalled for all the signs and wonders
that the LORD sent him to perform in
the land of Egypt, against Pharaoh and
all his servants and his entire land,
[12]and for all the mighty deeds and all the
terrifying displays of power that Moses
performed in the sight of all Israel.

JOSHUA

Whether one considers the book of Joshua as the sixth part of a Hexateuch (a collection of six books) that completes the story line of the patriarchal promises or sees it as the beginning of the story of the conquest of the promised land, it is the continuation of the history of God's people under the leadership of Joshua, the successor of Moses. The book shows God's fidelity in giving the Israelites the land promised in the book of Genesis (15.18ff.). To take possession of the land, the Israelites have to enter into a long period of invasion and conquest, but one that is destined to be successful to the extent that God's people remain faithful as enjoined by the perspective of Deuteronomy.

Passages from Joshua are read during the liturgy in Year I of the weekday calendar from Thursday through Saturday of the Nineteenth Week of the Year. In these passages the crossing of the Jordan into the promised land (3.7–17) and the renewal of the covenant at Shechem (24.1–29) are read.

GOD'S COMMISSION TO JOSHUA

1 After the death of Moses the servant of the LORD, the LORD spoke
to Joshua son of Nun, Moses' assistant,
saying, 2'My servant Moses is dead.
Now proceed to cross the Jordan, you
and all this people, into the land that
I am giving to them, to the Israelites.
3Every place that the sole of your foot
will tread upon I have given to you, as
I promised to Moses. 4From the wilderness and the Lebanon as far as the
great river, the river Euphrates, all the
land of the Hittites, to the Great Sea in
the west shall be your territory. 5No one
shall be able to stand against you all the
days of your life. As I was with Moses, so
I will be with you; I will not fail you or
forsake you. 6Be strong and courageous;
for you shall put this people in possession of the land that I swore to their
ancestors to give them. 7Only be strong
and very courageous, being careful to
act in accordance with all the law that
my servant Moses commanded you; do
not turn from it to the right hand or to
the left, so that you may be successful
wherever you go. 8This book of the law
shall not depart out of your mouth; you
shall meditate on it day and night, so
that you may be careful to act in accordance with all that is written in it. For
then you shall make your way prosperous, and then you shall be successful.
9I hereby command you: Be strong and
courageous; do not be frightened or dismayed, for the LORD your God is with
you wherever you go.'

PREPARATIONS FOR THE INVASION

10 Then Joshua commanded the officers of the people, 11'Pass through the
camp, and command the people: "Prepare your provisions; for in three days
you are to cross over the Jordan, to go
in to take possession of the land that the
LORD your God gives you to possess."'

12 To the Reubenites, the Gadites,
and the half-tribe of Manasseh Joshua
said, 13'Remember the word that Moses
the servant of the LORD commanded
you, saying, "The LORD your God is providing you a place of rest, and will give
you this land." 14Your wives, your little
ones, and your livestock shall remain in
the land that Moses gave you beyond
the Jordan. But all the warriors among
you shall cross over armed before your
kindred and shall help them, 15until the
LORD gives rest to your kindred as well
as to you, and they too take possession
of the land that the LORD your God is

giving them. Then you shall return to
your own land and take possession of it,
the land that Moses the servant of the
LORD gave you beyond the Jordan to the
east.'
16 They answered Joshua: 'All that
you have commanded us we will do, and
wherever you send us we will go. 17Just
as we obeyed Moses in all things, so we
will obey you. Only may the LORD your
God be with you, as he was with Moses!
18Whoever rebels against your orders
and disobeys your words, whatever you
command, shall be put to death. Only be
strong and courageous.'

SPIES SENT TO JERICHO

2 Then Joshua son of Nun sent two
men secretly from Shittim as spies,
saying, 'Go, view the land, especially
Jericho.' So they went, and entered the
house of a prostitute whose name was
Rahab, and spent the night there. 2The
king of Jericho was told, 'Some Israelites have come here tonight to search
out the land.' 3Then the king of Jericho
sent orders to Rahab, 'Bring out the
men who have come to you, who entered your house, for they have come
only to search out the whole land.' 4But
the woman took the two men and hid
them. Then she said, 'True, the men
came to me, but I did not know where
they came from. 5And when it was time
to close the gate at dark, the men went
out. Where the men went I do not know.
Pursue them quickly, for you can overtake them.' 6She had, however, brought
them up to the roof and hidden them
with the stalks of flax that she had laid
out on the roof. 7So the men pursued
them on the way to the Jordan as far as
the fords. As soon as the pursuers had
gone out, the gate was shut.
8 Before they went to sleep, she came
up to them on the roof 9and said to the
men: 'I know that the LORD has given
you the land, and that dread of you has
fallen on us, and that all the inhabitants
of the land melt in fear before you. 10For
we have heard how the LORD dried up
the water of the Red Sea[a] before you
when you came out of Egypt, and what
you did to the two kings of the Amorites
that were beyond the Jordan, to Sihon
and Og, whom you utterly destroyed.
11As soon as we heard it, our hearts
failed, and there was no courage left
in any of us because of you. The LORD
your God is indeed God in heaven above
and on earth below. 12Now then, since
I have dealt kindly with you, swear to
me by the LORD that you in turn will
deal kindly with my family. Give me a
sign of good faith 13that you will spare
my father and mother, my brothers and
sisters, and all who belong to them, and
deliver our lives from death.' 14The men
said to her, 'Our life for yours! If you do
not tell this business of ours, then we
will deal kindly and faithfully with you
when the LORD gives us the land.'
15 Then she let them down by a rope
through the window, for her house was
on the outer side of the city wall and she
resided within the wall itself. 16She said
to them, 'Go towards the hill country, so
that the pursuers may not come upon
you. Hide yourselves there for three
days, until the pursuers have returned;
then afterwards you may go on your
way.' 17The men said to her, 'We will be
released from this oath that you have
made us swear to you 18if we invade
the land and you do not tie this crimson cord in the window through which
you let us down, and you do not gather
into your house your father and mother,
your brothers, and all your family. 19If
any of you go out of the doors of your
house into the street, they shall be responsible for their own death, and we
shall be innocent; but if a hand is laid
upon any who are with you in the house,
we shall bear the responsibility for their
death. 20But if you tell this business of
ours, then we shall be released from this
oath that you made us swear to you.'
21She said, 'According to your words, so
be it.' She sent them away and they departed. Then she tied the crimson cord
in the window.
22 They departed and went into the
hill country and stayed there for three
days, until the pursuers returned. The
pursuers had searched all along the way
and found nothing. 23Then the two men
came down again from the hill country.
They crossed over, came to Joshua son
of Nun, and told him all that had happened to them. 24They said to Joshua,
'Truly the LORD has given all the land
into our hands; moreover, all the inhabitants of the land melt in fear before us.'

ISRAEL CROSSES THE JORDAN

3 Early in the morning Joshua rose
and set out from Shittim with all
the Israelites, and they came to the Jordan. They camped there before cross-

[a] 2.10 Or *Sea of Reeds*

ing over. 2At the end of three days the
officers went through the camp 3and
commanded the people, 'When you see
the ark of the covenant of the LORD
your God being carried by the levitical
priests, then you shall set out from your
place. Follow it, 4so that you may know
the way you should go, for you have not
passed this way before. Yet there shall
be a space between you and it, a distance of about two thousand cubits; do
not come any nearer to it.' 5Then Joshua
said to the people, 'Sanctify yourselves;
for tomorrow the LORD will do wonders
among you.' 6To the priests Joshua said,
'Take up the ark of the covenant, and
pass on in front of the people.' So they
took up the ark of the covenant and
went in front of the people.

7 The LORD said to Joshua, 'This day
I will begin to exalt you in the sight of
all Israel, so that they may know that
I will be with you as I was with Moses.
8You are the one who shall command
the priests who bear the ark of the covenant, "When you come to the edge of
the waters of the Jordan, you shall stand
still in the Jordan."' 9Joshua then said to
the Israelites, 'Draw near and hear the
words of the LORD your God.' 10Joshua
said, 'By this you shall know that among
you is the living God who without fail
will drive out from before you the Canaanites, Hittites, Hivites, Perizzites,
Girgashites, Amorites, and Jebusites:
11the ark of the covenant of the Lord of
all the earth is going to pass before you
into the Jordan. 12So now select twelve
men from the tribes of Israel, one from
each tribe. 13When the soles of the feet
of the priests who bear the ark of the
LORD, the Lord of all the earth, rest in
the waters of the Jordan, the waters of
the Jordan flowing from above shall be
cut off; they shall stand in a single heap.'

14 When the people set out from
their tents to cross over the Jordan, the
priests bearing the ark of the covenant
were in front of the people. 15Now the
Jordan overflows all its banks throughout the time of harvest. So when those
who bore the ark had come to the Jordan, and the feet of the priests bearing
the ark were dipped in the edge of the
water, 16the waters flowing from above
stood still, rising up in a single heap far
off at Adam, the city that is beside Zarethan, while those flowing towards the
sea of the Arabah, the Dead Sea,[b] were
wholly cut off. Then the people crossed
over opposite Jericho. 17While all Israel
were crossing over on dry ground, the
priests who bore the ark of the covenant
of the LORD stood on dry ground in the
middle of the Jordan, until the entire
nation finished crossing over the Jordan.

TWELVE STONES SET UP AT GILGAL

4 When the entire nation had finished
crossing over the Jordan, the LORD
said to Joshua: 2'Select twelve men from
the people, one from each tribe, 3and
command them, "Take twelve stones
from here out of the middle of the Jordan, from the place where the priests'
feet stood, carry them over with you,
and lay them down in the place where
you camp tonight."' 4Then Joshua summoned the twelve men from the Israelites, whom he had appointed, one from
each tribe. 5Joshua said to them, 'Pass
on before the ark of the LORD your God
into the middle of the Jordan, and each
of you take up a stone on his shoulder,
one for each of the tribes of the Israelites, 6so that this may be a sign among
you. When your children ask in time
to come, "What do those stones mean
to you?" 7then you shall tell them that
the waters of the Jordan were cut off in
front of the ark of the covenant of the
LORD. When it crossed over the Jordan,
the waters of the Jordan were cut off. So
these stones shall be to the Israelites a
memorial for ever.'

8 The Israelites did as Joshua commanded. They took up twelve stones out
of the middle of the Jordan, according
to the number of the tribes of the Israelites, as the LORD told Joshua, carried
them over with them to the place where
they camped, and laid them down
there. 9(Joshua set up twelve stones in
the middle of the Jordan, in the place
where the feet of the priests bearing the
ark of the covenant had stood; and they
are there to this day.)

10 The priests who bore the ark remained standing in the middle of the
Jordan, until everything was finished
that the LORD commanded Joshua to
tell the people, according to all that Moses had commanded Joshua. The people
crossed over in haste. 11As soon as all the
people had finished crossing over, the
ark of the LORD, and the priests, crossed
over in front of the people. 12The Reubenites, the Gadites, and the half-tribe
of Manasseh crossed over armed before

[b] **3.16** Heb *Salt Sea*

the Israelites, as Moses had ordered
them. 13About forty thousand armed for
war crossed over before the LORD to the
plains of Jericho for battle.
14 On that day the LORD exalted
Joshua in the sight of all Israel; and they
stood in awe of him, as they had stood
in awe of Moses, all the days of his life.
15 The LORD said to Joshua, 16'Command the priests who bear the ark of
the covenant[c] to come up out of the
Jordan.' 17Joshua therefore commanded
the priests, 'Come up out of the Jordan.'
18When the priests bearing the ark of
the covenant of the LORD came up from
the middle of the Jordan, and the soles
of the priests' feet touched dry ground,
the waters of the Jordan returned to
their place and overflowed all its banks,
as before.
19 The people came up out of the Jordan on the tenth day of the first month,
and they camped in Gilgal on the eastern border of Jericho. 20Those twelve
stones, which they had taken out of the
Jordan, Joshua set up in Gilgal, 21say-
ing to the Israelites, 'When your children ask their parents in time to come,
"What do these stones mean?" 22then
you shall let your children know, "Israel crossed over the Jordan here on dry
ground." 23For the LORD your God dried
up the waters of the Jordan for you until
you crossed over, as the LORD your God
did to the Red Sea,[d] which he dried up
for us until we crossed over, 24so that all
the peoples of the earth may know that
the hand of the LORD is mighty, and so
that you may fear the LORD your God for
ever.'

THE NEW GENERATION CIRCUMCISED

5 When all the kings of the Amorites
beyond the Jordan to the west, and
all the kings of the Canaanites by the
sea, heard that the LORD had dried up
the waters of the Jordan for the Israelites until they had crossed over, their
hearts failed, and there was no longer
any spirit in them, because of the Israelites.
2 At that time the LORD said to
Joshua, 'Make flint knives and circumcise the Israelites a second time.'
3So Joshua made flint knives, and circumcised the Israelites at Gibeath-
haaraloth.[e] 4This is the reason why
Joshua circumcised them: all the males
of the people who came out of Egypt, all
the warriors, had died during the journey through the wilderness after they
had come out of Egypt. 5Although all
the people who came out had been circumcised, yet all the people born on
the journey through the wilderness
after they had come out of Egypt had
not been circumcised. 6For the Israelites travelled for forty years in the wilderness, until all the nation, the warriors who came out of Egypt, perished,
not having listened to the voice of the
LORD. To them the LORD swore that he
would not let them see the land that he
had sworn to their ancestors to give us,
a land flowing with milk and honey. 7So
it was their children, whom he raised
up in their place, that Joshua circumcised; for they were uncircumcised, because they had not been circumcised on
the way.
8 When the circumcising of all the
nation was done, they remained in
their places in the camp until they were
healed. 9The LORD said to Joshua, 'Today I have rolled away from you the
disgrace of Egypt.' And so that place is
called Gilgal[f] to this day.

THE PASSOVER AT GILGAL

10 While the Israelites were encamped in Gilgal they kept the passover
in the evening on the fourteenth day of
the month in the plains of Jericho. 11On
the day after the passover, on that very
day, they ate the produce of the land,
unleavened cakes and parched grain.
12The manna ceased on the day they ate
the produce of the land, and the Israelites no longer had manna; they ate the
crops of the land of Canaan that year.

JOSHUA'S VISION

13 Once when Joshua was near Jericho, he looked up and saw a man standing before him with a drawn sword in
his hand. Joshua went to him and said
to him, 'Are you one of us, or one of our
adversaries?' 14He replied, 'Neither; but
as commander of the army of the LORD
I have now come.' And Joshua fell on his
face to the earth and worshipped, and
he said to him, 'What do you command
your servant, my lord?' 15The commander of the army of the LORD said to
Joshua, 'Remove the sandals from your
feet, for the place where you stand is
holy.' And Joshua did so.

[c] 4.16 Or *treaty*, or *testimony*; Heb *eduth*
[d] 4.23 Or *Sea of Reeds* [e] 5.3 That is *the Hill of the Foreskins* [f] 5.9 Related to Heb *galal* to roll

JERICHO TAKEN AND DESTROYED

6 Now Jericho was shut up inside and out because of the Israelites; no one came out and no one went in. 2 The LORD said to Joshua, 'See, I have handed Jericho over to you, along with its king and soldiers. 3 You shall march around the city, all the warriors circling the city once. Thus you shall do for six days, 4 with seven priests bearing seven trumpets of rams' horns before the ark. On the seventh day you shall march around the city seven times, the priests blowing the trumpets. 5 When they make a long blast with the ram's horn, as soon as you hear the sound of the trumpet, then all the people shall shout with a great shout; and the wall of the city will fall down flat, and all the people shall charge straight ahead.' 6 So Joshua son of Nun summoned the priests and said to them, 'Take up the ark of the covenant, and have seven priests carry seven trumpets of rams' horns in front of the ark of the LORD.' 7 To the people he said, 'Go forward and march around the city; have the armed men pass on before the ark of the LORD.'

8 As Joshua had commanded the people, the seven priests carrying the seven trumpets of rams' horns before the LORD went forward, blowing the trumpets, with the ark of the covenant of the LORD following them. 9 And the armed men went before the priests who blew the trumpets; the rearguard came after the ark, while the trumpets blew continually. 10 To the people Joshua gave this command: 'You shall not shout or let your voice be heard, nor shall you utter a word, until the day I tell you to shout. Then you shall shout.' 11 So the ark of the LORD went around the city, circling it once; and they came into the camp, and spent the night in the camp.

12 Then Joshua rose early in the morning, and the priests took up the ark of the LORD. 13 The seven priests carrying the seven trumpets of rams' horns before the ark of the LORD passed on, blowing the trumpets continually. The armed men went before them, and the rearguard came after the ark of the LORD, while the trumpets blew continually. 14 On the second day they marched around the city once and then returned to the camp. They did this for six days.

15 On the seventh day they rose early, at dawn, and marched around the city in the same manner seven times. It was only on that day that they marched around the city seven times. 16 And at the seventh time, when the priests had blown the trumpets, Joshua said to the people, 'Shout! For the LORD has given you the city. 17 The city and all that is in it shall be devoted to the LORD for destruction. Only Rahab the prostitute and all who are with her in her house shall live, because she hid the messengers we sent. 18 As for you, keep away from the things devoted to destruction, so as not to covet[g] and take any of the devoted things and make the camp of Israel an object for destruction, bringing trouble upon it. 19 But all silver and gold, and vessels of bronze and iron, are sacred to the LORD; they shall go into the treasury of the LORD.' 20 So the people shouted, and the trumpets were blown. As soon as the people heard the sound of the trumpets, they raised a great shout, and the wall fell down flat; so the people charged straight ahead into the city and captured it. 21 Then they devoted to destruction by the edge of the sword all in the city, both men and women, young and old, oxen, sheep, and donkeys.

22 Joshua said to the two men who had spied out the land, 'Go into the prostitute's house, and bring the woman out of it and all who belong to her, as you swore to her.' 23 So the young men who had been spies went in and brought Rahab out, along with her father, her mother, her brothers, and all who belonged to her—they brought all her kindred out—and set them outside the camp of Israel. 24 They burned down the city, and everything in it; only the silver and gold, and the vessels of bronze and iron, they put into the treasury of the house of the LORD. 25 But Rahab the prostitute, with her family and all who belonged to her, Joshua spared. Her family[h] has lived in Israel ever since. For she hid the messengers whom Joshua sent to spy out Jericho.

26 Joshua then pronounced this oath, saying,

'Cursed before the LORD be
    anyone who tries
  to build this city—this Jericho!
At the cost of his firstborn he
    shall lay its foundation,
  and at the cost of his youngest
    he shall set up its gates!'

27 So the LORD was with Joshua; and his fame was in all the land.

[g] 6.18 Gk: Heb *devote to destruction* Compare 7.21
[h] 6.25 Heb *She*

THE SIN OF ACHAN AND ITS PUNISHMENT

7 But the Israelites broke faith in regard to the devoted things: Achan
son of Carmi son of Zabdi son of Zerah,
of the tribe of Judah, took some of the
devoted things; and the anger of the
LORD burned against the Israelites.
2 Joshua sent men from Jericho to Ai,
which is near Beth-aven, east of Bethel,
and said to them, 'Go up and spy out the
land.' And the men went up and spied
out Ai. 3 Then they returned to Joshua
and said to him, 'Not all the people need
go up; about two or three thousand men
should go up and attack Ai. Since they
are so few, do not make the whole people toil up there.' 4 So about three thousand of the people went up there; and
they fled before the men of Ai. 5 The men
of Ai killed about thirty-six of them,
chasing them from outside the gate as
far as Shebarim and killing them on the
slope. The hearts of the people failed and
turned to water.
6 Then Joshua tore his clothes, and
fell to the ground on his face before the
ark of the LORD until the evening, he
and the elders of Israel; and they put
dust on their heads. 7 Joshua said, 'Ah,
Lord GOD! Why have you brought this
people across the Jordan at all, to hand
us over to the Amorites so as to destroy
us? Would that we had been content to
settle beyond the Jordan! 8 O Lord, what
can I say, now that Israel has turned
their backs to their enemies! 9 The Canaanites and all the inhabitants of the
land will hear of it, and surround us,
and cut off our name from the earth.
Then what will you do for your great
name?'
10 The LORD said to Joshua, 'Stand
up! Why have you fallen upon your face?
11 Israel has sinned; they have transgressed my covenant that I imposed
on them. They have taken some of the
devoted things; they have stolen, they
have acted deceitfully, and they have
put them among their own belongings.
12 Therefore the Israelites are unable to
stand before their enemies; they turn
their backs to their enemies, because
they have become a thing devoted for
destruction themselves. I will be with
you no more, unless you destroy the devoted things from among you. 13 Proceed
to sanctify the people, and say, "Sanctify
yourselves for tomorrow; for thus says
the LORD, the God of Israel, 'There are
devoted things among you, O Israel; you
will be unable to stand before your enemies until you take away the devoted
things from among you.' 14 In the morning therefore you shall come forward
tribe by tribe. The tribe that the LORD
takes shall come near by clans, the clan
that the LORD takes shall come near
by households, and the household that
the LORD takes shall come near one by
one. 15 And the one who is taken as having the devoted things shall be burned
with fire, together with all that he has,
for having transgressed the covenant of
the LORD, and for having done an outrageous thing in Israel." '
16 So Joshua rose early in the morning, and brought Israel near tribe by
tribe, and the tribe of Judah was taken.
17 He brought near the clans of Judah,
and the clan of the Zerahites was taken;
and he brought near the clan of the Zerahites, family by family,[i] and Zabdi
was taken. 18 And he brought near his
household one by one, and Achan son of
Carmi son of Zabdi son of Zerah, of the
tribe of Judah, was taken. 19 Then Joshua
said to Achan, 'My son, give glory to the
LORD God of Israel and make confession to him. Tell me now what you have
done; do not hide it from me.' 20 And
Achan answered Joshua, 'It is true; I am
the one who sinned against the LORD
God of Israel. This is what I did: 21 when
I saw among the spoil a beautiful mantle from Shinar, and two hundred shekels of silver, and a bar of gold weighing
fifty shekels, then I coveted them and
took them. They now lie hidden in the
ground inside my tent, with the silver
underneath.'
22 So Joshua sent messengers, and
they ran to the tent; and there it was,
hidden in his tent with the silver underneath. 23 They took them out of the tent
and brought them to Joshua and all the
Israelites; and they spread them out before the LORD. 24 Then Joshua and all Israel with him took Achan son of Zerah,
with the silver, the mantle, and the bar
of gold, with his sons and daughters,
with his oxen, donkeys, and sheep, and
his tent and all that he had; and they
brought them up to the Valley of Achor.
25 Joshua said, 'Why did you bring trouble on us? The LORD is bringing trouble
on you today.' And all Israel stoned him
to death; they burned them with fire,
cast stones on them, 26 and raised over
him a great heap of stones that remains

[i] 7.17 Mss Syr: MT *man by man*

to this day. Then the LORD turned from
his burning anger. Therefore that place
to this day is called the Valley of Achor.[j]

AI CAPTURED BY A STRATAGEM AND DESTROYED

8 Then the LORD said to Joshua, 'Do
not fear or be dismayed; take all the
fighting men with you, and go up now
to Ai. See, I have handed over to you the
king of Ai with his people, his city, and
his land. 2 You shall do to Ai and its king
as you did to Jericho and its king; only
its spoil and its livestock you may take
as booty for yourselves. Set an ambush
against the city, behind it.'

3 So Joshua and all the fighting men
set out to go up against Ai. Joshua chose
thirty thousand warriors and sent them
out by night 4 with the command, 'You
shall lie in ambush against the city, behind it; do not go very far from the city,
but all of you stay alert. 5 I and all the
people who are with me will approach
the city. When they come out against
us, as before, we shall flee from them.
6 They will come out after us until we
have drawn them away from the city;
for they will say, "They are fleeing from
us, as before." While we flee from them,
7 you shall rise up from the ambush and
seize the city; for the LORD your God
will give it into your hand. 8 And when
you have taken the city, you shall set the
city on fire, doing as the LORD has ordered; see, I have commanded you.' 9 So
Joshua sent them out; and they went to
the place of ambush, and lay between
Bethel and Ai, to the west of Ai; but
Joshua spent that night in the camp.[k]

10 In the morning Joshua rose early
and mustered the people, and went
up, with the elders of Israel, before the
people to Ai. 11 All the fighting men
who were with him went up, and drew
near before the city, and camped on the
north side of Ai, with a ravine between
them and Ai. 12 Taking about five thousand men, he set them in ambush between Bethel and Ai, to the west of the
city. 13 So they stationed the forces, the
main encampment that was north of
the city and its rearguard west of the
city. But Joshua spent that night in the
valley. 14 When the king of Ai saw this,
he and all his people, the inhabitants of
the city, hurried out early in the morning to the meeting-place facing the
Arabah to meet Israel in battle; but he
did not know that there was an ambush against him behind the city. 15 And
Joshua and all Israel made a pretence
of being beaten before them, and fled
in the direction of the wilderness. 16 So
all the people who were in the city were
called together to pursue them, and as
they pursued Joshua they were drawn
away from the city. 17 There was not a
man left in Ai or Bethel who did not go
out after Israel; they left the city open,
and pursued Israel.

18 Then the LORD said to Joshua,
'Stretch out the sword that is in your
hand towards Ai; for I will give it into
your hand.' And Joshua stretched out
the sword that was in his hand towards
the city. 19 As soon as he stretched out
his hand, the troops in ambush rose
quickly out of their place and rushed
forward. They entered the city, took it,
and at once set the city on fire. 20 So
when the men of Ai looked back, the
smoke of the city was rising to the sky.
They had no power to flee this way or
that, for the people who fled to the wilderness turned back against the pursuers. 21 When Joshua and all Israel saw
that the ambush had taken the city and
that the smoke of the city was rising,
then they turned back and struck down
the men of Ai. 22 And the others came
out from the city against them; so they
were surrounded by Israelites, some on
one side, and some on the other; and Israel struck them down until no one was
left who survived or escaped. 23 But the
king of Ai was taken alive and brought
to Joshua.

24 When Israel had finished slaughtering all the inhabitants of Ai in the
open wilderness where they pursued
them, and when all of them to the very
last had fallen by the edge of the sword,
all Israel returned to Ai, and attacked it
with the edge of the sword. 25 The total
of those who fell that day, both men and
women, was twelve thousand—all the
people of Ai. 26 For Joshua did not draw
back his hand, with which he stretched
out the sword, until he had utterly destroyed all the inhabitants of Ai. 27 Only
the livestock and the spoil of that city
Israel took as their booty, according to
the word of the LORD that he had issued
to Joshua. 28 So Joshua burned Ai, and
made it for ever a heap of ruins, as it is
to this day. 29 And he hanged the king of
Ai on a tree until evening; and at sunset
Joshua commanded, and they took his

[j] 7.26 That is *Trouble* [k] 8.9 Heb *among the people*

body down from the tree, threw it down
at the entrance of the gate of the city,
and raised over it a great heap of stones,
which stands there to this day.

JOSHUA RENEWS THE COVENANT

30 Then Joshua built on Mount Ebal
an altar to the LORD, the God of Israel,
31just as Moses the servant of the LORD
had commanded the Israelites, as it is
written in the book of the law of Moses,
'an altar of unhewn[l] stones, on which
no iron tool has been used'; and they offered on it burnt-offerings to the LORD,
and sacrificed offerings of well-being.
32And there, in the presence of the Israelites, Joshua[m] wrote on the stones
a copy of the law of Moses, which he
had written. 33All Israel, alien as well
as citizen, with their elders and officers and their judges, stood on opposite
sides of the ark in front of the levitical
priests who carried the ark of the covenant of the LORD, half of them in front
of Mount Gerizim and half of them in
front of Mount Ebal, as Moses the servant of the LORD had commanded at the
first, that they should bless the people of Israel. 34And afterwards he read
all the words of the law, blessings and
curses, according to all that is written in
the book of the law. 35There was not a
word of all that Moses commanded that
Joshua did not read before all the assembly of Israel, and the women, and the
little ones, and the aliens who resided
among them.

THE GIBEONITES SAVE THEMSELVES BY TRICKERY

9 Now when all the kings who were
beyond the Jordan in the hill country and in the lowland all along the coast
of the Great Sea towards Lebanon—the
Hittites, the Amorites, the Canaanites, the Perizzites, the Hivites, and the
Jebusites—heard of this, 2they gathered
together with one accord to fight Joshua
and Israel.

3 But when the inhabitants of Gibeon heard what Joshua had done to Jericho and to Ai, 4they on their part acted
with cunning: they went and prepared
provisions,[n] and took worn-out sacks
for their donkeys, and wineskins, worn-
out and torn and mended, 5with worn-
out, patched sandals on their feet, and
worn-out clothes; and all their provisions were dry and mouldy. 6They went
to Joshua in the camp at Gilgal, and said
to him and to the Israelites, 'We have
come from a far country; so now make
a treaty with us.' 7But the Israelites said
to the Hivites, 'Perhaps you live among
us; then how can we make a treaty with
you?' 8They said to Joshua, 'We are your
servants.' And Joshua said to them,
'Who are you? And where do you come
from?' 9They said to him, 'Your servants have come from a very far country, because of the name of the LORD
your God; for we have heard a report of
him, of all that he did in Egypt, 10and
of all that he did to the two kings of the
Amorites who were beyond the Jordan, King Sihon of Heshbon, and King
Og of Bashan who lived in Ashtaroth.
11So our elders and all the inhabitants
of our country said to us, "Take provisions in your hand for the journey; go
to meet them, and say to them, 'We are
your servants; come now, make a treaty
with us.'" 12Here is our bread; it was still
warm when we took it from our houses
as our food for the journey, on the day
we set out to come to you, but now, see,
it is dry and mouldy; 13these wineskins
were new when we filled them, and see,
they are burst; and these garments and
sandals of ours are worn out from the
very long journey.' 14So the leaders[o] par-
took of their provisions, and did not ask
direction from the LORD. 15And Joshua
made peace with them, guaranteeing
their lives by a treaty; and the leaders
of the congregation swore an oath to
them.

16 But when three days had passed
after they had made a treaty with them,
they heard that they were their neighbours and were living among them.
17So the Israelites set out and reached
their cities on the third day. Now their
cities were Gibeon, Chephirah, Beeroth,
and Kiriath-jearim. 18But the Israelites
did not attack them, because the leaders
of the congregation had sworn to them
by the LORD, the God of Israel. Then all
the congregation murmured against
the leaders. 19But all the leaders said to
all the congregation, 'We have sworn
to them by the LORD, the God of Israel, and now we must not touch them.
20This is what we will do to them: We
will let them live, so that wrath may not
come upon us, because of the oath that
we swore to them.' 21The leaders said to
them, 'Let them live.' So they became
hewers of wood and drawers of water for

[l] 8.31 Heb *whole* [m] 8.32 Heb *he* [n] 9.4 Cn: Meaning of Heb uncertain [o] 9.14 Gk: Heb *men*

all the congregation, as the leaders had
decided concerning them.
22 Joshua summoned them, and said
to them, 'Why did you deceive us, saying, "We are very far from you", while
in fact you are living among us? 23Now
therefore you are cursed, and some of
you shall always be slaves, hewers of
wood and drawers of water for the house
of my God.' 24They answered Joshua,
'Because it was told to your servants
for a certainty that the LORD your God
had commanded his servant Moses to
give you all the land, and to destroy all
the inhabitants of the land before you;
so we were in great fear for our lives because of you, and did this thing. 25And
now we are in your hand: do as it seems
good and right in your sight to do to us.'
26This is what he did for them: he saved
them from the Israelites; and they did
not kill them. 27But on that day Joshua
made them hewers of wood and drawers of water for the congregation and for
the altar of the LORD, to continue to this
day, in the place that he should choose.

THE SUN STANDS STILL

10 When King Adoni-zedek of Jerusalem heard how Joshua had
taken Ai, and had utterly destroyed it,
doing to Ai and its king as he had done
to Jericho and its king, and how the
inhabitants of Gibeon had made peace
with Israel and were among them, 2he[p]
became greatly frightened, because Gibeon was a large city, like one of the royal
cities, and was larger than Ai, and all
its men were warriors. 3So King Adoni-
zedek of Jerusalem sent a message to
King Hoham of Hebron, to King Piram
of Jarmuth, to King Japhia of Lachish,
and to King Debir of Eglon, saying,
4'Come up and help me, and let us attack Gibeon; for it has made peace with
Joshua and with the Israelites.' 5Then
the five kings of the Amorites—the
king of Jerusalem, the king of Hebron,
the king of Jarmuth, the king of Lachish, and the king of Eglon—gathered
their forces, and went up with all their
armies and encamped against Gibeon,
and made war against it.
6 And the Gibeonites sent to Joshua
at the camp in Gilgal, saying, 'Do not
abandon your servants; come up to us
quickly, and save us, and help us; for
all the kings of the Amorites who live
in the hill country are gathered against
us.' 7So Joshua went up from Gilgal, he
and all the fighting force with him, all
the mighty warriors. 8The LORD said
to Joshua, 'Do not fear them, for I have
handed them over to you; not one of
them shall stand before you.' 9So Joshua
came upon them suddenly, having
marched up all night from Gilgal. 10And
the LORD threw them into a panic before Israel, who inflicted a great slaughter on them at Gibeon, chased them by
the way of the ascent of Beth-horon, and
struck them down as far as Azekah and
Makkedah. 11As they fled before Israel,
while they were going down the slope of
Beth-horon, the LORD threw down huge
stones from heaven on them as far as
Azekah, and they died; there were more
who died because of the hailstones than
the Israelites killed with the sword.
12 On the day when the LORD gave
the Amorites over to the Israelites,
Joshua spoke to the LORD; and he said
in the sight of Israel,
'Sun, stand still at Gibeon,
and Moon, in the valley
of Aijalon.'
13 And the sun stood still, and
the moon stopped,
until the nation took vengeance
on their enemies.
Is this not written in the Book of Jashar?
The sun stopped in mid-heaven, and did
not hurry to set for about a whole day.
14There has been no day like it before or
since, when the LORD heeded a human
voice; for the LORD fought for Israel.
15 Then Joshua returned, and all Israel with him, to the camp at Gilgal.

FIVE KINGS DEFEATED

16 Meanwhile, these five kings fled
and hid themselves in the cave at Makkedah. 17And it was told Joshua, 'The five
kings have been found, hidden in the
cave at Makkedah.' 18Joshua said, 'Roll
large stones against the mouth of the
cave, and set men by it to guard them;
19but do not stay there yourselves; pursue your enemies, and attack them from
the rear. Do not let them enter their
towns, for the LORD your God has given
them into your hand.' 20When Joshua
and the Israelites had finished inflicting a very great slaughter on them, until they were wiped out, and when the
survivors had entered into the fortified
towns, 21all the people returned safe to
Joshua in the camp at Makkedah; no
one dared to speak[q] against any of the
Israelites.

[p] 10.2 Heb *they* [q] 10.21 Heb *moved his tongue*

22 Then Joshua said, 'Open the mouth
of the cave, and bring those five kings
out to me from the cave.' 23They did so,
and brought the five kings out to him
from the cave, the king of Jerusalem, the
king of Hebron, the king of Jarmuth, the
king of Lachish, and the king of Eglon.
24When they brought the kings out to
Joshua, Joshua summoned all the Israelites, and said to the chiefs of the warriors who had gone with him, 'Come
near, put your feet on the necks of these
kings.' Then they came near and put
their feet on their necks. 25And Joshua
said to them, 'Do not be afraid or dismayed; be strong and courageous; for
thus the LORD will do to all the enemies against whom you fight.' 26After-
wards Joshua struck them down and put
them to death, and he hung them on
five trees. And they hung on the trees
until evening. 27At sunset Joshua commanded, and they took them down from
the trees and threw them into the cave
where they had hidden themselves; they
set large stones against the mouth of the
cave, which remain to this very day.

28 Joshua took Makkedah on that
day, and struck it and its king with the
edge of the sword; he utterly destroyed
every person in it; he left no one remaining. And he did to the king of Makkedah
as he had done to the king of Jericho.

29 Then Joshua passed on from Makkedah, and all Israel with him, to Libnah, and fought against Libnah. 30The
LORD gave it also and its king into the
hand of Israel; and he struck it with the
edge of the sword, and every person in
it; he left no one remaining in it; and he
did to its king as he had done to the king
of Jericho.

31 Next Joshua passed on from Libnah, and all Israel with him, to Lachish,
and laid siege to it, and assaulted it.
32The LORD gave Lachish into the hand
of Israel, and he took it on the second
day, and struck it with the edge of the
sword, and every person in it, as he had
done to Libnah.

33 Then King Horam of Gezer came
up to help Lachish; and Joshua struck
him and his people, leaving him no survivors.

34 From Lachish Joshua passed on
with all Israel to Eglon; and they laid
siege to it, and assaulted it; 35and they
took it that day, and struck it with the
edge of the sword; and every person in it
he utterly destroyed that day, as he had
done to Lachish.

36 Then Joshua went up with all Israel from Eglon to Hebron; they assaulted it, 37and took it, and struck it with
the edge of the sword, and its king and
its towns, and every person in it; he left
no one remaining, just as he had done
to Eglon, and utterly destroyed it with
every person in it.

38 Then Joshua, with all Israel,
turned back to Debir and assaulted it,
39and he took it with its king and all its
towns; they struck them with the edge
of the sword, and utterly destroyed every person in it; he left no one remaining, just as he had done to Hebron, and,
as he had done to Libnah and its king,
so he did to Debir and its king.

40 So Joshua defeated the whole
land, the hill country and the Negeb
and the lowland and the slopes, and all
their kings; he left no one remaining,
but utterly destroyed all that breathed,
as the LORD God of Israel commanded.
41And Joshua defeated them from
Kadesh-barnea to Gaza, and all the
country of Goshen, as far as Gibeon.
42Joshua took all these kings and their
land at one time, because the LORD God
of Israel fought for Israel. 43Then Joshua
returned, and all Israel with him, to the
camp at Gilgal.

THE UNITED KINGS OF NORTHERN CANAAN DEFEATED

11 When King Jabin of Hazor heard
of this, he sent to King Jobab of
Madon, to the king of Shimron, to the
king of Achshaph, 2and to the kings
who were in the northern hill country,
and in the Arabah south of Chinneroth,
and in the lowland, and in Naphoth-dor
on the west, 3to the Canaanites in the
east and the west, the Amorites, the
Hittites, the Perizzites, and the Jebusites in the hill country, and the Hivites
under Hermon in the land of Mizpah.
4They came out, with all their troops,
a great army, in number like the sand
on the seashore, with very many horses
and chariots. 5All these kings joined
their forces, and came and camped together at the waters of Merom, to fight
with Israel.

6 And the LORD said to Joshua, 'Do
not be afraid of them, for tomorrow at
this time I will hand over all of them,
slain, to Israel; you shall hamstring
their horses, and burn their chariots
with fire.' 7So Joshua came suddenly
upon them with all his fighting force,
by the waters of Merom, and fell upon

them. 8And the LORD handed them
over to Israel, who attacked them and
chased them as far as Great Sidon and
Misrephoth-maim, and eastwards as
far as the valley of Mizpeh. They struck
them down, until they had left no one
remaining. 9And Joshua did to them
as the LORD commanded him; he hamstrung their horses, and burned their
chariots with fire.

10 Joshua turned back at that time,
and took Hazor, and struck its king
down with the sword. Before that time
Hazor was the head of all those kingdoms. 11And they put to the sword all
who were in it, utterly destroying them;
there was no one left who breathed, and
he burned Hazor with fire. 12And all
the towns of those kings, and all their
kings, Joshua took, and struck them
with the edge of the sword, utterly destroying them, as Moses the servant of
the LORD had commanded. 13But Israel
burned none of the towns that stood on
mounds except Hazor, which Joshua did
burn. 14All the spoil of these towns, and
the livestock, the Israelites took for their
booty; but all the people they struck
down with the edge of the sword, until
they had destroyed them, and they did
not leave any who breathed. 15As the
LORD had commanded his servant Moses, so Moses commanded Joshua, and
so Joshua did; he left nothing undone
of all that the LORD had commanded
Moses.

SUMMARY OF JOSHUA'S CONQUESTS

16 So Joshua took all that land: the
hill country and all the Negeb and all
the land of Goshen and the lowland and
the Arabah and the hill country of Israel and its lowland, 17from Mount Halak, which rises towards Seir, as far as
Baal-gad in the valley of Lebanon below
Mount Hermon. He took all their kings,
struck them down, and put them to
death. 18Joshua made war a long time
with all those kings. 19There was not a
town that made peace with the Israelites, except the Hivites, the inhabitants
of Gibeon; all were taken in battle. 20For
it was the LORD's doing to harden their
hearts so that they would come against
Israel in battle, in order that they might
be utterly destroyed, and might receive
no mercy, but be exterminated, just as
the LORD had commanded Moses.

21 At that time Joshua came and
wiped out the Anakim from the hill
country, from Hebron, from Debir,
from Anab, and from all the hill country of Judah, and from all the hill country of Israel; Joshua utterly destroyed
them with their towns. 22None of the
Anakim was left in the land of the Israelites; some remained only in Gaza, in
Gath, and in Ashdod. 23So Joshua took
the whole land, according to all that the
LORD had spoken to Moses; and Joshua
gave it for an inheritance to Israel according to their tribal allotments. And
the land had rest from war.

THE KINGS CONQUERED BY MOSES

12 Now these are the kings of the
land, whom the Israelites defeated, whose land they occupied beyond the Jordan towards the east, from
the Wadi Arnon to Mount Hermon,
with all the Arabah eastwards: 2King
Sihon of the Amorites who lived at
Heshbon, and ruled from Aroer, which
is on the edge of the Wadi Arnon, and
from the middle of the valley as far as
the river Jabbok, the boundary of the
Ammonites, that is, half of Gilead, 3and
the Arabah to the Sea of Chinneroth
eastwards, and in the direction of Beth-
jeshimoth, to the sea of the Arabah,
the Dead Sea,[r] southwards to the foot
of the slopes of Pisgah; 4and King Og[s]
of Bashan, one of the last of the Rephaim, who lived at Ashtaroth and at Edrei 5and ruled over Mount Hermon and
Salecah and all Bashan to the boundary
of the Geshurites and the Maacathites,
and over half of Gilead to the boundary
of King Sihon of Heshbon. 6Moses, the
servant of the LORD, and the Israelites
defeated them; and Moses the servant of
the LORD gave their land for a possession to the Reubenites and the Gadites
and the half-tribe of Manasseh.

THE KINGS CONQUERED BY JOSHUA

7 The following are the kings of the
land whom Joshua and the Israelites
defeated on the west side of the Jordan,
from Baal-gad in the valley of Lebanon
to Mount Halak, that rises towards Seir
(and Joshua gave their land to the tribes
of Israel as a possession according to
their allotments, 8in the hill country,
in the lowland, in the Arabah, in the
slopes, in the wilderness, and in the
Negeb, the land of the Hittites, Amorites, Canaanites, Perizzites, Hivites,
and Jebusites):

[r] 12.3 Heb *Salt Sea* [s] 12.4 Gk: Heb *the boundary of King Og*

9 the king of Jericho one
the king of Ai, which is next to Bethel one
10 the king of Jerusalem one
the king of Hebron one
11 the king of Jarmuth one
the king of Lachish one
12 the king of Eglon one
the king of Gezer one
13 the king of Debir one
the king of Geder one
14 the king of Hormah one
the king of Arad one
15 the king of Libnah one
the king of Adullam one
16 the king of Makkedah one
the king of Bethel one
17 the king of Tappuah one
the king of Hepher one
18 the king of Aphek one
the king of Lasharon one
19 the king of Madon one
the king of Hazor one
20 the king of Shimron-meron one
the king of Achshaph one
21 the king of Taanach one
the king of Megiddo one
22 the king of Kedesh one
the king of Jokneam in Carmel one
23 the king of Dor in Naphath-dor one
the king of Goiim in Galilee,[t] one
24 the king of Tirzah one
thirty-one kings in all.

THE PARTS OF CANAAN STILL UNCONQUERED

13 Now Joshua was old and advanced in years; and the LORD said to him, 'You are old and advanced in years, and very much of the land still remains to be possessed. 2This is the land that still remains: all the regions of the Philistines, and all those of the Geshurites 3(from the Shihor, which is east of Egypt, northwards to the boundary of Ekron, it is reckoned as Canaanite; there are five rulers of the Philistines, those of Gaza, Ashdod, Ashkelon, Gath, and Ekron), and those of the Avvim 4in the south; all the land of the Canaanites, and Mearah that belongs to the Sidonians, to Aphek, to the boundary of the Amorites, 5and the land of the Gebalites, and all Lebanon, towards the east, from Baal-gad below Mount Hermon to Lebo-hamath, 6all the inhabitants of the hill country from Lebanon to Misrephoth-maim, even all the Sidonians. I will myself drive them out from before the Israelites; only allot the land to Israel for an inheritance, as I have commanded you. 7Now therefore divide this land for an inheritance to the nine tribes and the half-tribe of Manasseh.'

THE TERRITORY EAST OF THE JORDAN

8 With the other half-tribe of Manasseh,[u] the Reubenites and the Gadites received their inheritance, which Moses gave them, beyond the Jordan eastwards, as Moses the servant of the LORD gave them: 9from Aroer, which is on the edge of the Wadi Arnon, and the town that is in the middle of the valley, and all the tableland from[v] Medeba as far as Dibon; 10and all the cities of King Sihon of the Amorites, who reigned in Heshbon, as far as the boundary of the Ammonites; 11and Gilead, and the region of the Geshurites and Maacathites, and all Mount Hermon, and all Bashan to Salecah; 12all the kingdom of Og in Bashan, who reigned in Ashtaroth and in Edrei (he alone was left of the survivors of the Rephaim); these Moses had defeated and driven out. 13Yet the Israelites did not drive out the Geshurites or the Maacathites; but Geshur and Maacath live within Israel to this day.

14 To the tribe of Levi alone Moses gave no inheritance; the offerings by fire to the LORD God of Israel are their inheritance, as he said to them.

THE TERRITORY OF REUBEN

15 Moses gave an inheritance to the tribe of the Reubenites according to their clans. 16Their territory was from Aroer, which is on the edge of the Wadi Arnon, and the town that is in the middle of the valley, and all the tableland by Medeba; 17with Heshbon, and all its towns that are in the tableland; Dibon, and Bamoth-baal, and Beth-baal-meon, 18and Jahaz, and Kedemoth, and Mephaath, 19and Kiriathaim, and Sibmah, and Zereth-shahar on the hill of the valley, 20and Beth-peor, and the slopes of Pisgah, and Beth-jeshimoth, 21that is, all the towns of the tableland, and all the kingdom of King Sihon of the Amorites, who reigned in Heshbon, whom Moses defeated with the leaders of Midian, Evi and Rekem and Zur and Hur and Reba, as princes of Sihon, who lived in the land. 22Along with the rest of those they put to death, the Israelites also put to the sword Balaam

[t] 12.23 Gk: Heb *Gilgal* [u] 13.8 Cn: Heb *With it*
[v] 13.9 Compare Gk: Heb lacks *from*

son of Beor, who practised divination.
23 And the border of the Reubenites was
the Jordan and its banks. This was the
inheritance of the Reubenites according
to their families, with their towns and
villages.

THE TERRITORY OF GAD

24 Moses gave an inheritance also
to the tribe of the Gadites, according
to their families. 25 Their territory was
Jazer, and all the towns of Gilead, and
half the land of the Ammonites, to
Aroer, which is east of Rabbah, 26 and
from Heshbon to Ramath-mizpeh and
Betonim, and from Mahanaim to the
territory of Debir,[w] 27 and in the valley
Beth-haram, Beth-nimrah, Succoth,
and Zaphon, the rest of the kingdom of
King Sihon of Heshbon, the Jordan and
its banks, as far as the lower end of the
Sea of Chinnereth, eastwards beyond
the Jordan. 28 This is the inheritance
of the Gadites according to their clans,
with their towns and villages.

THE TERRITORY OF THE HALF-TRIBE OF MANASSEH (EAST)

29 Moses gave an inheritance to the
half-tribe of Manasseh; it was allotted to
the half-tribe of the Manassites according to their families. 30 Their territory
extended from Mahanaim, through all
Bashan, the whole kingdom of King Og
of Bashan, and all the settlements of Jair,
which are in Bashan, sixty towns, 31 and
half of Gilead, and Ashtaroth, and Edrei,
the towns of the kingdom of Og in Bashan; these were allotted to the people
of Machir son of Manasseh according to
their clans—for half the Machirites.

32 These are the inheritances that
Moses distributed in the plains of Moab,
beyond the Jordan east of Jericho. 33 But
to the tribe of Levi Moses gave no inheritance; the LORD God of Israel is their
inheritance, as he said to them.

THE DISTRIBUTION OF TERRITORY WEST OF THE JORDAN

14 These are the inheritances that
the Israelites received in the
land of Canaan, which the priest Eleazar, and Joshua son of Nun, and the
heads of the families of the tribes of the
Israelites distributed to them. 2 Their inheritance was by lot, as the LORD had
commanded Moses for the nine and a
half tribes. 3 For Moses had given an inheritance to the two and a half tribes
beyond the Jordan; but to the Levites he
gave no inheritance among them. 4 For
the people of Joseph were two tribes,
Manasseh and Ephraim; and no portion
was given to the Levites in the land, but
only towns to live in, with their pasture
lands for their flocks and herds. 5 The
Israelites did as the LORD commanded
Moses; they allotted the land.

HEBRON ALLOTTED TO CALEB

6 Then the people of Judah came to
Joshua at Gilgal; and Caleb son of Jephunneh the Kenizzite said to him, 'You
know what the LORD said to Moses the
man of God in Kadesh-barnea concerning you and me. 7 I was forty years old
when Moses the servant of the LORD
sent me from Kadesh-barnea to spy out
the land; and I brought him an honest
report. 8 But my companions who went
up with me made the heart of the people fail; yet I wholeheartedly followed
the LORD my God. 9 And Moses swore
on that day, saying, "Surely the land on
which your foot has trodden shall be an
inheritance for you and your children for
ever, because you have wholeheartedly
followed the LORD my God." 10 And now,
as you see, the LORD has kept me alive,
as he said, these forty-five years since
the time that the LORD spoke this word
to Moses, while Israel was journeying
through the wilderness; and here I am
today, eighty-five years old. 11 I am still
as strong today as I was on the day that
Moses sent me; my strength now is as
my strength was then, for war, and for
going and coming. 12 So now give me
this hill country of which the LORD
spoke on that day; for you heard on that
day how the Anakim were there, with
great fortified cities; it may be that the
LORD will be with me, and I shall drive
them out, as the LORD said.'

13 Then Joshua blessed him, and gave
Hebron to Caleb son of Jephunneh for an
inheritance. 14 So Hebron became the inheritance of Caleb son of Jephunneh the
Kenizzite to this day, because he wholeheartedly followed the LORD, the God of
Israel. 15 Now the name of Hebron formerly was Kiriath-arba;[x] this Arba was[y]
the greatest man among the Anakim.
And the land had rest from war.

THE TERRITORY OF JUDAH

15 The lot for the tribe of the people
of Judah according to their fam-

[w] **13.26** Gk Syr Vg: Heb *Lidebir* [x] **14.15** That is *the city of Arba* [y] **14.15** Heb lacks *this Arba was*

ilies reached southwards to the boundary of Edom, to the wilderness of Zin at
the farthest south. 2And their southern
boundary ran from the end of the Dead
Sea,[z] from the bay that faces southwards; 3it goes out southwards of the
ascent of Akrabbim, passes along to Zin,
and goes up south of Kadesh-barnea,
along by Hezron, up to Addar, makes
a turn to Karka, 4passes along to Az-
mon, goes out by the Wadi of Egypt, and
comes to its end at the sea. This shall be
your southern boundary. 5And the eastern boundary is the Dead Sea,[a] to the
mouth of the Jordan. And the boundary
on the north side runs from the bay of
the sea at the mouth of the Jordan; 6and
the boundary goes up to Beth-hoglah,
and passes along north of Beth-arabah;
and the boundary goes up to the Stone
of Bohan, Reuben's son; 7and the boundary goes up to Debir from the Valley
of Achor, and so northwards, turning
towards Gilgal, which is opposite the
ascent of Adummim, which is on the
south side of the valley; and the boundary passes along to the waters of En-
shemesh, and ends at En-rogel; 8then
the boundary goes up by the valley of
the son of Hinnom at the southern slope
of the Jebusites (that is, Jerusalem); and
the boundary goes up to the top of the
mountain that lies over against the
valley of Hinnom, on the west, at the
northern end of the valley of Rephaim;
9then the boundary extends from the
top of the mountain to the spring of the
Waters of Nephtoah, and from there to
the towns of Mount Ephron; then the
boundary bends around to Baalah (that
is, Kiriath-jearim); 10and the boundary
circles west of Baalah to Mount Seir,
passes along to the northern slope of
Mount Jearim (that is, Chesalon), and
goes down to Beth-shemesh, and passes
along by Timnah; 11the boundary goes
out to the slope of the hill north of Ekron, then the boundary bends around to
Shikkeron, and passes along to Mount
Baalah, and goes out to Jabneel; then
the boundary comes to an end at the
sea. 12And the western boundary was
the Mediterranean with its coast. This is
the boundary surrounding the people of
Judah according to their families.

CALEB OCCUPIES HIS PORTION

13 According to the commandment
of the LORD to Joshua, he gave to Caleb
son of Jephunneh a portion among the
people of Judah, Kiriath-arba,[b] that is,
Hebron (Arba was the father of Anak).
14And Caleb drove out from there the
three sons of Anak: Sheshai, Ahiman,
and Talmai, the descendants of Anak.
15From there he went up against the
inhabitants of Debir; now the name
of Debir formerly was Kiriath-sepher.
16And Caleb said, 'Whoever attacks
Kiriath-sepher and takes it, to him I will
give my daughter Achsah as wife.' 17Oth-
niel son of Kenaz, the brother of Caleb,
took it; and he gave him his daughter
Achsah as wife. 18When she came to
him, she urged him to ask her father
for a field. As she dismounted from her
donkey, Caleb said to her, 'What do you
want?' 19She said to him, 'Give me a
present; since you have set me in the
land of the Negeb, give me springs of
water as well.' So Caleb gave her the upper springs and the lower springs.

THE TOWNS OF JUDAH

20 This is the inheritance of the tribe
of the people of Judah according to their
families. 21The towns belonging to the
tribe of the people of Judah in the extreme south, towards the boundary of
Edom, were Kabzeel, Eder, Jagur, 22Ki-
nah, Dimonah, Adadah, 23Kedesh, Hazor, Ithnan, 24Ziph, Telem, Bealoth,
25Hazor-hadattah, Kerioth-hezron (that
is, Hazor), 26Amam, Shema, Moladah,
27Hazar-gaddah, Heshmon, Beth-pelet,
28Hazar-shual, Beer-sheba, Biziothiah,
29Baalah, Iim, Ezem, 30Eltolad, Chesil,
Hormah, 31Ziklag, Madmannah, San-
sannah, 32Lebaoth, Shilhim, Ain, and
Rimmon: in all, twenty-nine towns,
with their villages.

33 And in the lowlands, Eshtaol, Zo-
rah, Ashnah, 34Zanoah, En-gannim,
Tappuah, Enam, 35Jarmuth, Adullam,
Socoh, Azekah, 36Shaaraim, Adithaim,
Gederah, Gederothaim: fourteen towns
with their villages.

37 Zenan, Hadashah, Migdal-gad,
38Dilan, Mizpeh, Jokthe-el, 39Lachish,
Bozkath, Eglon, 40Cabbon, Lahmam,
Chitlish, 41Gederoth, Beth-dagon, Naamah, and Makkedah: sixteen towns
with their villages.

42 Libnah, Ether, Ashan, 43Iphtah,
Ashnah, Nezib, 44Keilah, Achzib, and
Mareshah: nine towns with their vil-
lages.

45 Ekron, with its dependencies and
its villages; 46from Ekron to the sea, all

[z] 15.2 Heb *Salt Sea* [a] 15.5 Heb *Salt Sea*
[b] 15.13 That is *the city of Arba*

that were near Ashdod, with their villages.
47 Ashdod, its towns and its villages;
Gaza, its towns and its villages; to the
Wadi of Egypt, and the Great Sea with
its coast.
48 And in the hill country, Shamir, Jattir, Socoh, 49Dannah, Kiriath-
sannah (that is, Debir), 50Anab, Esh-
temoh, Anim, 51Goshen, Holon, and
Giloh: eleven towns with their villages.
52 Arab, Dumah, Eshan, 53Janim,
Beth-tappuah, Aphekah, 54Humtah,
Kiriath-arba (that is, Hebron), and Zior:
nine towns with their villages.
55 Maon, Carmel, Ziph, Juttah, 56Jez-
reel, Jokdeam, Zanoah, 57Kain, Gibeah,
and Timnah: ten towns with their villages.
58 Halhul, Beth-zur, Gedor, 59Ma-
arath, Beth-anoth, and Eltekon: six
towns with their villages.
60 Kiriath-baal (that is, Kiriath-
jearim) and Rabbah: two towns with
their villages.
61 In the wilderness, Beth-arabah,
Middin, Secacah, 62Nibshan, the City of
Salt, and En-gedi: six towns with their
villages.
63 But the people of Judah could not
drive out the Jebusites, the inhabitants
of Jerusalem; so the Jebusites live with
the people of Judah in Jerusalem to this
day.

THE TERRITORY OF EPHRAIM

16 The allotment of the Josephites
went from the Jordan by Jeri-
cho, east of the waters of Jericho, into
the wilderness, going up from Jericho
into the hill country to Bethel; 2then going from Bethel to Luz, it passes along
to Ataroth, the territory of the Archites;
3then it goes down westwards to the
territory of the Japhletites, as far as the
territory of Lower Beth-horon, then to
Gezer, and it ends at the sea.
4 The Josephites—Manasseh and
Ephraim—received their inheritance.
5 The territory of the Ephraimites by
their families was as follows: the boundary of their inheritance on the east was
Ataroth-addar as far as Upper Beth-
horon, 6and the boundary goes from
there to the sea; on the north is Michmethath; then on the east the boundary
makes a turn towards Taanath-shiloh,
and passes along beyond it on the east
to Janoah, 7then it goes down from Janoah to Ataroth and to Naarah, and
touches Jericho, ending at the Jordan.
8From Tappuah the boundary goes
westwards to the Wadi Kanah, and ends
at the sea. Such is the inheritance of the
tribe of the Ephraimites by their families, 9together with the towns that were
set apart for the Ephraimites within the
inheritance of the Manassites, all those
towns with their villages. 10They did
not, however, drive out the Canaanites
who lived in Gezer: so the Canaanites
have lived within Ephraim to this day
but have been made to do forced labour.

THE OTHER HALF-TRIBE OF MANASSEH (WEST)

17 Then allotment was made to the
tribe of Manasseh, for he was
the firstborn of Joseph. To Machir the
firstborn of Manasseh, the father of Gilead, were allotted Gilead and Bashan,
because he was a warrior. 2And allotments were made to the rest of the tribe
of Manasseh, by their families, Abiezer,
Helek, Asriel, Shechem, Hepher, and
Shemida; these were the male descendants of Manasseh son of Joseph, by their
families.
3 Now Zelophehad son of Hepher son
of Gilead son of Machir son of Manasseh
had no sons, but only daughters; and
these are the names of his daughters:
Mahlah, Noah, Hoglah, Milcah, and Tirzah. 4They came before the priest Eleazar and Joshua son of Nun and the leaders, and said, 'The LORD commanded
Moses to give us an inheritance along
with our male kin.' So according to the
commandment of the LORD he gave
them an inheritance among the kinsmen of their father. 5Thus there fell to
Manasseh ten portions, besides the land
of Gilead and Bashan, which is on the
other side of the Jordan, 6because the
daughters of Manasseh received an inheritance along with his sons. The land
of Gilead was allotted to the rest of the
Manassites.
7 The territory of Manasseh reached
from Asher to Michmethath, which is
east of Shechem; then the boundary
goes along southwards to the inhabitants of En-tappuah. 8The land of Tappuah belonged to Manasseh, but the
town of Tappuah on the boundary of
Manasseh belonged to the Ephraimites. 9Then the boundary went down to
the Wadi Kanah. The towns here, to the
south of the wadi, among the towns of
Manasseh, belong to Ephraim. Then the
boundary of Manasseh goes along the
north side of the wadi and ends at the

sea. 10The land to the south is Ephraim's
and that to the north is Manasseh's,
with the sea forming its boundary; on
the north Asher is reached, and on the
east Issachar. 11Within Issachar and
Asher, Manasseh had Beth-shean and
its villages, Ibleam and its villages, the
inhabitants of Dor and its villages, the
inhabitants of En-dor and its villages,
the inhabitants of Taanach and its villages, and the inhabitants of Megiddo
and its villages (the third is Naphath).[c]
12Yet the Manassites could not take possession of those towns; but the Canaanites continued to live in that land. 13But
when the Israelites grew strong, they
put the Canaanites to forced labour, but
did not utterly drive them out.

THE TRIBE OF JOSEPH PROTESTS

14 The tribe of Joseph spoke to
Joshua, saying, 'Why have you given me
but one lot and one portion as an inheritance, since we are a numerous people,
whom all along the LORD has blessed?'
15And Joshua said to them, 'If you are
a numerous people, go up to the forest,
and clear ground there for yourselves in
the land of the Perizzites and the Rephaim, since the hill country of Ephraim is
too narrow for you.' 16The tribe of Joseph
said, 'The hill country is not enough for
us; yet all the Canaanites who live in the
plain have chariots of iron, both those
in Beth-shean and its villages and those
in the Valley of Jezreel.' 17Then Joshua
said to the house of Joseph, to Ephraim
and Manasseh, 'You are indeed a numerous people, and have great power;
you shall not have one lot only, 18but the
hill country shall be yours, for though it
is a forest, you shall clear it and possess
it to its farthest borders; for you shall
drive out the Canaanites, though they
have chariots of iron, and though they
are strong.'

THE TERRITORIES OF THE REMAINING TRIBES

18 Then the whole congregation of
the Israelites assembled at Shiloh, and set up the tent of meeting there.
The land lay subdued before them.

2 There remained among the Israelites seven tribes whose inheritance had
not yet been apportioned. 3So Joshua
said to the Israelites, 'How long will you
be slack about going in and taking possession of the land that the LORD, the
God of your ancestors, has given you?
4Provide three men from each tribe,
and I will send them out that they may
begin to go throughout the land, writing a description of it with a view to
their inheritances. Then come back to
me. 5They shall divide it into seven portions, Judah continuing in its territory
on the south, and the house of Joseph in
their territory on the north. 6You shall
describe the land in seven divisions and
bring the description here to me; and
I will cast lots for you here before the
LORD our God. 7The Levites have no portion among you, for the priesthood of
the LORD is their heritage; and Gad and
Reuben and the half-tribe of Manasseh
have received their inheritance beyond
the Jordan eastwards, which Moses the
servant of the LORD gave them.'

8 So the men started on their way;
and Joshua charged those who went to
write the description of the land, saying, 'Go throughout the land and write
a description of it, and come back to me;
and I will cast lots for you here before
the LORD in Shiloh.' 9So the men went
and traversed the land and set down in
a book a description of it by towns in
seven divisions; then they came back
to Joshua in the camp at Shiloh, 10and
Joshua cast lots for them in Shiloh before the LORD; and there Joshua apportioned the land to the Israelites, to each
a portion.

THE TERRITORY OF BENJAMIN

11 The lot of the tribe of Benjamin according to its families came up, and the
territory allotted to it fell between the
tribe of Judah and the tribe of Joseph.
12On the north side their boundary began at the Jordan; then the boundary
goes up to the slope of Jericho on the
north, then up through the hill country westwards; and it ends at the wilderness of Beth-aven. 13From there
the boundary passes along southwards
in the direction of Luz, to the slope of
Luz (that is, Bethel), then the boundary goes down to Ataroth-addar, on the
mountain that lies south of Lower Beth-
horon. 14Then the boundary goes in another direction, turning on the western
side southwards from the mountain
that lies to the south, opposite Beth-
horon, and it ends at Kiriath-baal (that
is, Kiriath-jearim), a town belonging to
the tribe of Judah. This forms the western side. 15The southern side begins at
the outskirts of Kiriath-jearim; and the

[c] 17.11 Meaning of Heb uncertain

boundary goes from there to Ephron,[d]
to the spring of the Waters of Nephtoah;
16 then the boundary goes down to the
border of the mountain that overlooks
the valley of the son of Hinnom, which
is at the northern end of the valley of
Rephaim; and it then goes down the
valley of Hinnom, south of the slope of
the Jebusites, and downwards to En-
rogel; 17 then it bends in a northerly direction going on to En-shemesh, and
from there goes to Geliloth, which is opposite the ascent of Adummim; then it
goes down to the Stone of Bohan, Reuben's son; 18 and passing on to the north
of the slope of Beth-arabah[e] it goes
down to the Arabah; 19 then the boundary passes on to the north of the slope
of Beth-hoglah; and the boundary ends
at the northern bay of the Dead Sea,[f] at
the south end of the Jordan: this is the
southern border. 20 The Jordan forms its
boundary on the eastern side. This is the
inheritance of the tribe of Benjamin,
according to its families, boundary by
boundary all round.

21 Now the towns of the tribe of
Benjamin according to their families
were Jericho, Beth-hoglah, Emek-keziz,
22 Beth-arabah, Zemaraim, Bethel,
23 Avvim, Parah, Ophrah, 24 Chephar-
ammoni, Ophni, and Geba—twelve
towns with their villages: 25 Gibeon, Ramah, Beeroth, 26 Mizpeh, Chephirah,
Mozah, 27 Rekem, Irpeel, Taralah, 28 Zela,
Haeleph, Jebus[g] (that is, Jerusalem),
Gibeah,[h] and Kiriath-jearim[i]—fourteen
towns with their villages. This is the inheritance of the tribe of Benjamin according to its families.

THE TERRITORY OF SIMEON

19 The second lot came out for Simeon, for the tribe of Simeon, according to its families; its inheritance
lay within the inheritance of the tribe of
Judah. 2 It had for its inheritance Beer-
sheba, Sheba, Moladah, 3 Hazar-shual,
Balah, Ezem, 4 Eltolad, Bethul, Hormah, 5 Ziklag, Beth-marcaboth, Hazar-
susah, 6 Beth-lebaoth, and Sharuhen—
thirteen towns with their villages;
7 Ain, Rimmon, Ether, and Ashan—four
towns with their villages; 8 together
with all the villages all around these
towns as far as Baalath-beer, Ramah
of the Negeb. This was the inheritance
of the tribe of Simeon according to its
families. 9 The inheritance of the tribe of
Simeon formed part of the territory of
Judah; because the portion of the tribe
of Judah was too large for them, the
tribe of Simeon obtained an inheritance
within their inheritance.

THE TERRITORY OF ZEBULUN

10 The third lot came up for the tribe
of Zebulun, according to its families. The
boundary of its inheritance reached as
far as Sarid; 11 then its boundary goes
up westwards, and on to Maralah, and
touches Dabbesheth, then the wadi
that is east of Jokneam; 12 from Sarid it
goes in the other direction eastwards
towards the sunrise to the boundary
of Chisloth-tabor; from there it goes
to Daberath, then up to Japhia; 13 from
there it passes along on the east towards
the sunrise to Gath-hepher, to Eth-
kazin, and going on to Rimmon it bends
towards Neah; 14 then on the north the
boundary makes a turn to Hannathon,
and it ends at the valley of Iphtah-el;
15 and Kattath, Nahalal, Shimron, Id-
alah, and Bethlehem—twelve towns
with their villages. 16 This is the inheritance of the tribe of Zebulun, according
to its families—these towns with their
villages.

THE TERRITORY OF ISSACHAR

17 The fourth lot came out for Issachar, for the tribe of Issachar, according
to its families. 18 Its territory included
Jezreel, Chesulloth, Shunem, 19 Haph-
araim, Shion, Anaharath, 20 Rabbith,
Kishion, Ebez, 21 Remeth, En-gannim,
En-haddah, Beth-pazzez; 22 the boundary also touches Tabor, Shahazumah,
and Beth-shemesh, and its boundary
ends at the Jordan—sixteen towns with
their villages. 23 This is the inheritance
of the tribe of Issachar, according to its
families—the towns with their villages.

THE TERRITORY OF ASHER

24 The fifth lot came out for the tribe
of Asher according to its families. 25 Its
boundary included Helkath, Hali, Be-
ten, Achshaph, 26 Allammelech, Amad,
and Mishal; on the west it touches
Carmel and Shihor-libnath, 27 then it
turns eastwards, goes to Beth-dagon,
and touches Zebulun and the valley of
Iphtah-el northwards to Beth-emek and
Neiel; then it continues in the north to
Cabul, 28 Ebron, Rehob, Hammon, Ka-

[d] **18.15** Cn See 15.9. Heb *westwards* [e] **18.18** Gk: Heb *to the slope over against the Arabah*
[f] **18.19** Heb *Salt Sea* [g] **18.28** Gk Syr Vg: Heb *the Jebusite* [h] **18.28** Heb *Gibeath* [i] **18.28** Gk: Heb *Kiriath*

nah, as far as Great Sidon; 29then the
boundary turns to Ramah, reaching
to the fortified city of Tyre; then the
boundary turns to Hosah, and it ends
at the sea; Mahalab,[j] Achzib, 30Ummah,
Aphek, and Rehob—twenty-two towns
with their villages. 31This is the inheritance of the tribe of Asher according
to its families—these towns with their
villages.

THE TERRITORY OF NAPHTALI

32 The sixth lot came out for the tribe
of Naphtali, for the tribe of Naphtali, according to its families. 33And its boundary ran from Heleph, from the oak in
Zaanannim, and Adami-nekeb, and Jabneel, as far as Lakkum; and it ended at
the Jordan; 34then the boundary turns
westwards to Aznoth-tabor, and goes
from there to Hukkok, touching Zebulun at the south, and Asher on the
west, and Judah on the east at the Jordan. 35The fortified towns are Ziddim,
Zer, Hammath, Rakkath, Chinnereth,
36Adamah, Ramah, Hazor, 37Kedesh,
Edrei, En-hazor, 38Iron, Migdal-el, Ho-
rem, Beth-anath, and Beth-shemesh—
nineteen towns with their villages.
39This is the inheritance of the tribe of
Naphtali according to its families—the
towns with their villages.

THE TERRITORY OF DAN

40 The seventh lot came out for the
tribe of Dan, according to its families. 41The territory of its inheritance
included Zorah, Eshtaol, Ir-shemesh,
42Shaalabbin, Aijalon, Ithlah, 43Elon,
Timnah, Ekron, 44Eltekeh, Gibbethon,
Baalath, 45Jehud, Bene-berak, Gath-
rimmon, 46Me-jarkon, and Rakkon
at the border opposite Joppa. 47When
the territory of the Danites was lost to
them, the Danites went up and fought
against Leshem, and after capturing it
and putting it to the sword, they took
possession of it and settled in it, calling
Leshem, Dan, after their ancestor Dan.
48This is the inheritance of the tribe of
Dan, according to their families—these
towns with their villages.

JOSHUA'S INHERITANCE

49 When they had finished distribut-
ing the several territories of the land as
inheritances, the Israelites gave an inheritance among them to Joshua son of
Nun. 50By command of the LORD they
gave him the town that he asked for,
Timnath-serah in the hill country of
Ephraim; he rebuilt the town, and settled in it.

51 These are the inheritances that
the priest Eleazar and Joshua son of
Nun and the heads of the families of
the tribes of the Israelites distributed
by lot at Shiloh before the LORD, at the
entrance of the tent of meeting. So they
finished dividing the land.

THE CITIES OF REFUGE

20 Then the LORD spoke to Joshua,
saying, 2'Say to the Israelites,
"Appoint the cities of refuge, of which
I spoke to you through Moses, 3so that
anyone who kills a person without intent or by mistake may flee there;
they shall be for you a refuge from the
avenger of blood. 4The slayer shall flee to
one of these cities and shall stand at the
entrance of the gate of the city, and explain the case to the elders of that city;
then the fugitive shall be taken into the
city, and given a place, and shall remain
with them. 5And if the avenger of blood
is in pursuit, they shall not give up the
slayer, because the neighbour was killed
by mistake, there having been no enmity between them before. 6The slayer
shall remain in that city until there is a
trial before the congregation, until the
death of the one who is high priest at
the time: then the slayer may return
home, to the town in which the deed
was done."'

7 So they set apart Kedesh in Galilee
in the hill country of Naphtali, and Shechem in the hill country of Ephraim,
and Kiriath-arba (that is, Hebron) in
the hill country of Judah. 8And beyond
the Jordan east of Jericho, they appointed Bezer in the wilderness on the
tableland, from the tribe of Reuben, and
Ramoth in Gilead, from the tribe of Gad,
and Golan in Bashan, from the tribe of
Manasseh. 9These were the cities designated for all the Israelites, and for the
aliens residing among them, that anyone who killed a person without intent
could flee there, so as not to die by the
hand of the avenger of blood, until there
was a trial before the congregation.

CITIES ALLOTTED TO THE LEVITES

21 Then the heads of the families of
the Levites came to the priest Eleazar and to Joshua son of Nun and to the
heads of the families of the tribes of the
Israelites; 2they said to them at Shiloh

[j] 19.29 Cn Compare Gk: Heb *Mehebel*

in the land of Canaan, 'The LORD commanded through Moses that we be
given towns to live in, along with their
pasture lands for our livestock.' 3So by
command of the LORD the Israelites
gave to the Levites the following towns
and pasture lands out of their inheritance.

4 The lot came out for the families of
the Kohathites. So those Levites who
were descendants of Aaron the priest
received by lot thirteen towns from the
tribes of Judah, Simeon, and Benjamin.

5 The rest of the Kohathites received
by lot ten towns from the families of the
tribe of Ephraim, from the tribe of Dan,
and the half-tribe of Manasseh.

6 The Gershonites received by lot
thirteen towns from the families of the
tribe of Issachar, from the tribe of Asher,
from the tribe of Naphtali, and from the
half-tribe of Manasseh in Bashan.

7 The Merarites according to their
families received twelve towns from the
tribe of Reuben, the tribe of Gad, and
the tribe of Zebulun.

8 These towns and their pasture
lands the Israelites gave by lot to the
Levites, as the LORD had commanded
through Moses.

9 Out of the tribe of Judah and the
tribe of Simeon they gave the following towns mentioned by name, 10which
went to the descendants of Aaron, one
of the families of the Kohathites who
belonged to the Levites, since the lot fell
to them first. 11They gave them Kiriath-
arba (Arba being the father of Anak),
that is Hebron, in the hill country of
Judah, along with the pasture lands
around it. 12But the fields of the town
and its villages had been given to Caleb
son of Jephunneh as his holding.

13 To the descendants of Aaron the
priest they gave Hebron, the city of refuge for the slayer, with its pasture lands,
Libnah with its pasture lands, 14Jattir
with its pasture lands, Eshtemoa with
its pasture lands, 15Holon with its pasture lands, Debir with its pasture lands,
16Ain with its pasture lands, Juttah with
its pasture lands, and Beth-shemesh
with its pasture lands—nine towns
out of these two tribes. 17Out of the
tribe of Benjamin: Gibeon with its pasture lands, Geba with its pasture lands,
18Anathoth with its pasture lands, and
Almon with its pasture lands—four
towns. 19The towns of the descendants
of Aaron—the priests—were thirteen
in all, with their pasture lands.

20 As to the rest of the Kohathites belonging to the Kohathite families of the
Levites, the towns allotted to them were
out of the tribe of Ephraim. 21To them
were given Shechem, the city of refuge
for the slayer, with its pasture lands
in the hill country of Ephraim, Gezer
with its pasture lands, 22Kibzaim with
its pasture lands, and Beth-horon with
its pasture lands—four towns. 23Out of
the tribe of Dan: Elteke with its pasture
lands, Gibbethon with its pasture lands,
24Aijalon with its pasture lands, Gath-
rimmon with its pasture lands—four
towns. 25Out of the half-tribe of Manasseh: Taanach with its pasture lands, and
Gath-rimmon with its pasture lands—
two towns. 26The towns of the families
of the rest of the Kohathites were ten in
all, with their pasture lands.

27 To the Gershonites, one of the
families of the Levites, were given out
of the half-tribe of Manasseh, Golan in
Bashan with its pasture lands, the city
of refuge for the slayer, and Beeshte-
rah with its pasture lands—two towns.
28Out of the tribe of Issachar: Kishion
with its pasture lands, Daberath with its
pasture lands, 29Jarmuth with its pasture lands, En-gannim with its pasture
lands—four towns. 30Out of the tribe of
Asher: Mishal with its pasture lands,
Abdon with its pasture lands, 31Helkath
with its pasture lands, and Rehob with
its pasture lands—four towns. 32Out of
the tribe of Naphtali: Kedesh in Galilee
with its pasture lands, the city of refuge
for the slayer, Hammoth-dor with its
pasture lands, and Kartan with its pasture lands—three towns. 33The towns of
the several families of the Gershonites
were in all thirteen, with their pasture
lands.

34 To the rest of the Levites—the
Merarite families—were given out of
the tribe of Zebulun: Jokneam with its
pasture lands, Kartah with its pasture
lands, 35Dimnah with its pasture lands,
Nahalal with its pasture lands—four
towns. 36Out of the tribe of Reuben: Bezer with its pasture lands, Jahzah with
its pasture lands, 37Kedemoth with its
pasture lands, and Mephaath with its
pasture lands—four towns. 38Out of
the tribe of Gad: Ramoth in Gilead with
its pasture lands, the city of refuge for
the slayer, Mahanaim with its pasture
lands, 39Heshbon with its pasture lands,
Jazer with its pasture lands—four towns
in all. 40As for the towns of the several
Merarite families, that is, the remain-

der of the families of the Levites, those allotted to them were twelve in all.

41 The towns of the Levites within the holdings of the Israelites were in all forty-eight towns with their pasture lands. 42 Each of these towns had its pasture lands around it; so it was with all these towns.

43 Thus the LORD gave to Israel all the land that he swore to their ancestors that he would give them; and having taken possession of it, they settled there. 44 And the LORD gave them rest on every side just as he had sworn to their ancestors; not one of all their enemies had withstood them, for the LORD had given all their enemies into their hands. 45 Not one of all the good promises that the LORD had made to the house of Israel had failed; all came to pass.

THE EASTERN TRIBES RETURN TO THEIR TERRITORY

22 Then Joshua summoned the Reubenites, the Gadites, and the half-tribe of Manasseh, 2 and said to them, 'You have observed all that Moses the servant of the LORD commanded you, and have obeyed me in all that I have commanded you; 3 you have not forsaken your kindred these many days, down to this day, but have been careful to keep the charge of the LORD your God. 4 And now the LORD your God has given rest to your kindred, as he promised them; therefore turn and go to your tents in the land where your possession lies, which Moses the servant of the LORD gave you on the other side of the Jordan. 5 Take good care to observe the commandment and instruction that Moses the servant of the LORD commanded you, to love the LORD your God, to walk in all his ways, to keep his commandments, and to hold fast to him, and to serve him with all your heart and with all your soul.' 6 So Joshua blessed them and sent them away, and they went to their tents.

7 Now to one half of the tribe of Manasseh Moses had given a possession in Bashan; but to the other half Joshua had given a possession beside their fellow-Israelites in the land west of the Jordan. And when Joshua sent them away to their tents and blessed them, 8 he said to them, 'Go back to your tents with much wealth, and with very much livestock, with silver, gold, bronze, and iron, and with a great quantity of clothing; divide the spoil of your enemies with your kindred.' 9 So the Reubenites and the Gadites and the half-tribe of Manasseh returned home, parting from the Israelites at Shiloh, which is in the land of Canaan, to go to the land of Gilead, their own land of which they had taken possession by command of the LORD through Moses.

A MEMORIAL ALTAR EAST OF THE JORDAN

10 When they came to the region[k] near the Jordan that lies in the land of Canaan, the Reubenites and the Gadites and the half-tribe of Manasseh built there an altar by the Jordan, an altar of great size. 11 The Israelites heard that the Reubenites and the Gadites and the half-tribe of Manasseh had built an altar at the frontier of the land of Canaan, in the region[l] near the Jordan, on the side that belongs to the Israelites. 12 And when the people of Israel heard of it, the whole assembly of the Israelites gathered at Shiloh, to make war against them.

13 Then the Israelites sent the priest Phinehas son of Eleazar to the Reubenites and the Gadites and the half-tribe of Manasseh, in the land of Gilead, 14 and with him ten chiefs, one from each of the tribal families of Israel, every one of them the head of a family among the clans of Israel. 15 They came to the Reubenites, the Gadites, and the half-tribe of Manasseh in the land of Gilead, and they said to them, 16 'Thus says the whole congregation of the LORD, "What is this treachery that you have committed against the God of Israel in turning away today from following the LORD, by building yourselves an altar today in rebellion against the LORD? 17 Have we not had enough of the sin at Peor from which even yet we have not cleansed ourselves, and for which a plague came upon the congregation of the LORD, 18 that you must turn away today from following the LORD! If you rebel against the LORD today, he will be angry with the whole congregation of Israel tomorrow. 19 But now, if your land is unclean, cross over into the LORD's land where the LORD's tabernacle now stands, and take for yourselves a possession among us; only do not rebel against the LORD, or rebel against us[m] by building yourselves an altar other than the altar of

[k] 22.10 Or *to Geliloth* [l] 22.11 Or *at Geliloth*
[m] 22.19 Or *make rebels of us*

the LORD our God. 20 Did not Achan son
of Zerah break faith in the matter of the
devoted things, and wrath fell upon all
the congregation of Israel? And he did
not perish alone for his iniquity!"'

21 Then the Reubenites, the Gadites,
and the half-tribe of Manasseh said in
answer to the heads of the families of
Israel, 22 'The LORD, God of gods! The
LORD, God of gods! He knows; and let
Israel itself know! If it was in rebellion
or in breach of faith towards the LORD,
do not spare us today 23 for building an
altar to turn away from following the
LORD; or if we did so to offer burnt-
offerings or grain-offerings or offerings
of well-being on it, may the LORD himself take vengeance. 24 No! We did it from
fear that in time to come your children
might say to our children, "What have
you to do with the LORD, the God of Israel? 25 For the LORD has made the Jordan a boundary between us and you,
you Reubenites and Gadites; you have
no portion in the LORD." So your children might make our children cease
to worship the LORD. 26 Therefore we
said, "Let us now build an altar, not for
burnt-offering, nor for sacrifice, 27 but to
be a witness between us and you, and
between the generations after us, that
we do perform the service of the LORD
in his presence with our burnt-offerings
and sacrifices and offerings of well-
being; so that your children may never
say to our children in time to come, 'You
have no portion in the LORD.' " 28 And
we thought, If this should be said to us
or to our descendants in time to come,
we could say, "Look at this copy of the
altar of the LORD, which our ancestors
made, not for burnt-offerings, nor for
sacrifice, but to be a witness between
us and you." 29 Far be it from us that we
should rebel against the LORD, and turn
away this day from following the LORD
by building an altar for burnt-offering,
grain-offering, or sacrifice, other than
the altar of the LORD our God that
stands before his tabernacle!'

30 When the priest Phinehas and the
chiefs of the congregation, the heads
of the families of Israel who were with
him, heard the words that the Reubenites and the Gadites and the Manassites
spoke, they were satisfied. 31 The priest
Phinehas son of Eleazar said to the Reubenites and the Gadites and the Manassites, 'Today we know that the LORD is
among us, because you have not committed this treachery against the LORD;
now you have saved the Israelites from
the hand of the LORD.'

32 Then the priest Phinehas son of
Eleazar and the chiefs returned from
the Reubenites and the Gadites in the
land of Gilead to the land of Canaan, to
the Israelites, and brought back word to
them. 33 The report pleased the Israelites;
and the Israelites blessed God and spoke
no more of making war against them, to
destroy the land where the Reubenites
and the Gadites were settled. 34 The Reubenites and the Gadites called the altar
Witness;[n] 'For', said they, 'it is a witness
between us that the LORD is God.'

JOSHUA EXHORTS THE PEOPLE

23 A long time afterwards, when
the LORD had given rest to Israel from all their enemies all around,
and Joshua was old and well advanced
in years, 2 Joshua summoned all Israel,
their elders and heads, their judges and
officers, and said to them, 'I am now old
and well advanced in years; 3 and you
have seen all that the LORD your God
has done to all these nations for your
sake, for it is the LORD your God who
has fought for you. 4 I have allotted to
you as an inheritance for your tribes
those nations that remain, along with
all the nations that I have already cut
off, from the Jordan to the Great Sea in
the west. 5 The LORD your God will push
them back before you, and drive them
out of your sight; and you shall possess
their land, as the LORD your God promised you. 6 Therefore be very steadfast
to observe and do all that is written in
the book of the law of Moses, turning
aside from it neither to the right nor to
the left, 7 so that you may not be mixed
with these nations left here among you,
or make mention of the names of their
gods, or swear by them, or serve them,
or bow yourselves down to them, 8 but
hold fast to the LORD your God, as you
have done to this day. 9 For the LORD has
driven out before you great and strong
nations; and as for you, no one has been
able to withstand you to this day. 10 One
of you puts to flight a thousand, since it
is the LORD your God who fights for you,
as he promised you. 11 Be very careful,
therefore, to love the LORD your God.
12 For if you turn back, and join the survivors of these nations left here among
you, and intermarry with them, so that
you marry their women and they yours,

[n] **22.34** Cn Compare Syr: Heb lacks *Witness*

13 know assuredly that the LORD your God will not continue to drive out these nations before you; but they shall be a snare and a trap for you, a scourge on your sides, and thorns in your eyes, until you perish from this good land that the LORD your God has given you.

14 'And now I am about to go the way of all the earth, and you know in your hearts and souls, all of you, that not one thing has failed of all the good things that the LORD your God promised concerning you; all have come to pass for you, not one of them has failed. 15 But just as all the good things that the LORD your God promised concerning you have been fulfilled for you, so the LORD will bring upon you all the bad things, until he has destroyed you from this good land that the LORD your God has given you. 16 If you transgress the covenant of the LORD your God, which he enjoined on you, and go and serve other gods and bow down to them, then the anger of the LORD will be kindled against you, and you shall perish quickly from the good land that he has given to you.'

THE TRIBES RENEW THE COVENANT

24 Then Joshua gathered all the tribes of Israel to Shechem, and summoned the elders, the heads, the judges, and the officers of Israel; and they presented themselves before God. 2 And Joshua said to all the people, 'Thus says the LORD, the God of Israel: Long ago your ancestors—Terah and his sons Abraham and Nahor—lived beyond the Euphrates and served other gods. 3 Then I took your father Abraham from beyond the River and led him through all the land of Canaan and made his offspring many. I gave him Isaac; 4 and to Isaac I gave Jacob and Esau. I gave Esau the hill country of Seir to possess, but Jacob and his children went down to Egypt. 5 Then I sent Moses and Aaron, and I plagued Egypt with what I did in its midst; and afterwards I brought you out. 6 When I brought your ancestors out of Egypt, you came to the sea; and the Egyptians pursued your ancestors with chariots and horsemen to the Red Sea.[o] 7 When they cried out to the LORD, he put darkness between you and the Egyptians, and made the sea come upon them and cover them; and your eyes saw what I did to Egypt. Afterwards you lived in the wilderness for a long time. 8 Then I brought you to the land of the Amorites, who lived on the other side of the Jordan; they fought with you, and I handed them over to you, and you took possession of their land, and I destroyed them before you. 9 Then King Balak, son of Zippor of Moab, set out to fight against Israel. He sent and invited Balaam son of Beor to curse you, 10 but I would not listen to Balaam; therefore he blessed you; so I rescued you out of his hand. 11 When you went over the Jordan and came to Jericho, the citizens of Jericho fought against you, and also the Amorites, the Perizzites, the Canaanites, the Hittites, the Girgashites, the Hivites, and the Jebusites; and I handed them over to you. 12 I sent the hornet[p] ahead of you, which drove out before you the two kings of the Amorites; it was not by your sword or by your bow. 13 I gave you a land on which you had not laboured, and towns that you had not built, and you live in them; you eat the fruit of vineyards and olive groves that you did not plant.

14 'Now therefore revere the LORD, and serve him in sincerity and in faithfulness; put away the gods that your ancestors served beyond the River and in Egypt, and serve the LORD. 15 Now if you are unwilling to serve the LORD, choose this day whom you will serve, whether the gods your ancestors served in the region beyond the River or the gods of the Amorites in whose land you are living; but as for me and my household, we will serve the LORD.'

16 Then the people answered, 'Far be it from us that we should forsake the LORD to serve other gods; 17 for it is the LORD our God who brought us and our ancestors up from the land of Egypt, out of the house of slavery, and who did those great signs in our sight. He protected us along all the way that we went, and among all the peoples through whom we passed; 18 and the LORD drove out before us all the peoples, the Amorites who lived in the land. Therefore we also will serve the LORD, for he is our God.'

19 But Joshua said to the people, 'You cannot serve the LORD, for he is a holy God. He is a jealous God; he will not forgive your transgressions or your sins. 20 If you forsake the LORD and serve foreign gods, then he will turn and do you harm, and consume you, after having done you good.' 21 And the people said

[o] **24.6** Or *Sea of Reeds* [p] **24.12** Meaning of Heb uncertain

to Joshua, 'No, we will serve the LORD!'
22 Then Joshua said to the people, 'You
are witnesses against yourselves that
you have chosen the LORD, to serve
him.' And they said, 'We are witnesses.'
23 He said, 'Then put away the foreign
gods that are among you, and incline
your hearts to the LORD, the God of
Israel.' 24 The people said to Joshua,
'The LORD our God we will serve, and
him we will obey.' 25 So Joshua made
a covenant with the people that day,
and made statutes and ordinances for
them at Shechem. 26 Joshua wrote these
words in the book of the law of God;
and he took a large stone, and set it up
there under the oak in the sanctuary of
the LORD. 27 Joshua said to all the people, 'See, this stone shall be a witness
against us; for it has heard all the words
of the LORD that he spoke to us; therefore it shall be a witness against you,
if you deal falsely with your God.' 28 So
Joshua sent the people away to their inheritances.

DEATH OF JOSHUA AND ELEAZAR

29 After these things Joshua son of
Nun, the servant of the LORD, died, being
one hundred and ten years old. 30 They
buried him in his own inheritance at
Timnath-serah, which is in the hill country of Ephraim, north of Mount Gaash.
31 Israel served the LORD all the days
of Joshua, and all the days of the elders
who outlived Joshua and had known all
the work that the LORD did for Israel.
32 The bones of Joseph, which the
Israelites had brought up from Egypt,
were buried at Shechem, in the portion of ground that Jacob had bought
from the children of Hamor, the father
of Shechem, for one hundred pieces of
money;[q] it became an inheritance of the
descendants of Joseph.
33 Eleazar son of Aaron died; and
they buried him at Gibeah, the town of
his son Phinehas, which had been given
him in the hill country of Ephraim.

[q] 24.32 Heb *one hundred qesitah*

JUDGES

Judges derives its name from twelve warriors or judges who were leaders raised up by God to deliver the people from the threat of their enemies. The events of this narrative occurred from the time of the death of Joshua until just prior to the birth of Samuel. The series of various stories is set in the context of a recurring pattern of infidelity to God followed by oppression that, in turn, is reversed by repentance of the people and deliverance by the leadership of the warrior/judge. On the surface, the stories seem to portray the heroics of powerful regional leaders. On a deeper level, however, they highlight the prophetic role in which God raises up leaders to restore the people to obedience and fidelity to the covenant.

Passages from the book of Judges are read during Mass from Monday through Thursday of the Twentieth Week of Year I and during the Advent season anticipating Christmas, when the story of Samson's birth is recalled as a prefiguring or backdrop to the Gospel text from Luke depicting the birth of John the Baptist (13.2–7, 24–25).

ISRAEL'S FAILURE TO COMPLETE THE CONQUEST OF CANAAN

1 After the death of Joshua, the Israelites inquired of the LORD, 'Who
shall go up first for us against the Canaanites, to fight against them?' 2The
LORD said, 'Judah shall go up. I hereby
give the land into his hand.' 3Judah
said to his brother Simeon, 'Come up
with me into the territory allotted to
me, that we may fight against the Canaanites; then I too will go with you
into the territory allotted to you.' So
Simeon went with him. 4Then Judah
went up and the LORD gave the Canaanites and the Perizzites into their
hand; and they defeated ten thousand
of them at Bezek. 5They came upon
Adoni-bezek at Bezek, and fought
against him, and defeated the Canaanites and the Perizzites. 6Adoni-
bezek fled; but they pursued him, and
caught him, and cut off his thumbs
and big toes. 7Adoni-bezek said, 'Seventy kings with their thumbs and big
toes cut off used to pick up scraps under my table; as I have done, so God
has paid me back.' They brought him
to Jerusalem, and he died there.

8 Then the people of Judah fought
against Jerusalem and took it. They put
it to the sword and set the city on fire.
9Afterwards the people of Judah went
down to fight against the Canaanites
who lived in the hill country, in the
Negeb, and in the lowlands. 10Judah
went against the Canaanites who lived
in Hebron (the name of Hebron was formerly Kiriath-arba); and they defeated
Sheshai and Ahiman and Talmai.

11 From there they went against the
inhabitants of Debir (the name of Debir
was formerly Kiriath-sepher). 12Then Caleb said, 'Whoever attacks Kiriath-sepher
and takes it, I will give him my daughter
Achsah as wife.' 13And Othniel son of
Kenaz, Caleb's younger brother, took it;
and he gave him his daughter Achsah as
wife. 14When she came to him, she urged
him to ask her father for a field. As she
dismounted from her donkey, Caleb said
to her, 'What do you want?' 15She said to
him, 'Give me a present; since you have
set me in the land of the Negeb, give me
also Gulloth-mayim.'[a] So Caleb gave her
Upper Gulloth and Lower Gulloth.

[a] 1.15 That is *Basins of Water*

16 The descendants of Hobab[b] the Kenite, Moses' father-in-law, went up with the people of Judah from the city of palms into the wilderness of Judah, which lies in the Negeb near Arad. Then they went and settled with the Amalekites.[c] 17Judah went with his brother Simeon, and they defeated the Canaanites who inhabited Zephath, and devoted it to destruction. So the city was called Hormah. 18Judah took Gaza with its territory, Ashkelon with its territory, and Ekron with its territory. 19The LORD was with Judah, and he took possession of the hill country, but could not drive out the inhabitants of the plain, because they had chariots of iron. 20Hebron was given to Caleb, as Moses had said; and he drove out from it the three sons of Anak. 21But the Benjaminites did not drive out the Jebusites who lived in Jerusalem; so the Jebusites have lived in Jerusalem among the Benjaminites to this day.

22 The house of Joseph also went up against Bethel; and the LORD was with them. 23The house of Joseph sent out spies to Bethel (the name of the city was formerly Luz). 24When the spies saw a man coming out of the city, they said to him, 'Show us the way into the city, and we will deal kindly with you.' 25So he showed them the way into the city; and they put the city to the sword, but they let the man and all his family go. 26So the man went to the land of the Hittites and built a city, and named it Luz; that is its name to this day.

27 Manasseh did not drive out the inhabitants of Beth-shean and its villages, or Taanach and its villages, or the inhabitants of Dor and its villages, or the inhabitants of Ibleam and its villages, or the inhabitants of Megiddo and its villages; but the Canaanites continued to live in that land. 28When Israel grew strong, they put the Canaanites to forced labour, but did not in fact drive them out.

29 And Ephraim did not drive out the Canaanites who lived in Gezer; but the Canaanites lived among them in Gezer.

30 Zebulun did not drive out the inhabitants of Kitron, or the inhabitants of Nahalol; but the Canaanites lived among them, and became subject to forced labour.

31 Asher did not drive out the inhabitants of Acco, or the inhabitants of Sidon, or of Ahlab, or of Achzib, or of Helbah, or of Aphik, or of Rehob; 32but the Asherites lived among the Canaanites, the inhabitants of the land; for they did not drive them out.

33 Naphtali did not drive out the inhabitants of Beth-shemesh, or the inhabitants of Beth-anath, but lived among the Canaanites, the inhabitants of the land; nevertheless the inhabitants of Beth-shemesh and of Beth-anath became subject to forced labour for them.

34 The Amorites pressed the Danites back into the hill country; they did not allow them to come down to the plain. 35The Amorites continued to live in Harheres, in Aijalon, and in Shaalbim, but the hand of the house of Joseph rested heavily on them, and they became subject to forced labour. 36The border of the Amorites ran from the ascent of Akrabbim, from Sela and upwards.

ISRAEL'S DISOBEDIENCE

2 Now the angel of the LORD went up from Gilgal to Bochim, and said, 'I brought you up from Egypt, and brought you into the land that I had promised to your ancestors. I said, "I will never break my covenant with you. 2For your part, do not make a covenant with the inhabitants of this land; tear down their altars." But you have not obeyed my command. See what you have done! 3So now I say, I will not drive them out before you; but they shall become adversaries[d] to you, and their gods shall be a snare to you.' 4When the angel of the LORD spoke these words to all the Israelites, the people lifted up their voices and wept. 5So they named that place Bochim,[e] and there they sacrificed to the LORD.

DEATH OF JOSHUA

6 When Joshua dismissed the people, the Israelites all went to their own inheritances to take possession of the land. 7The people worshipped the LORD all the days of Joshua, and all the days of the elders who outlived Joshua, who had seen all the great work that the LORD had done for Israel. 8Joshua son of Nun, the servant of the LORD, died at the age of one hundred and ten years. 9So they buried him within the bounds of his inheritance in Timnath-heres, in the hill country of Ephraim, north of Mount Gaash. 10Moreover, that whole

[b] **1.16** Gk: Heb lacks *Hobab* [c] **1.16** See 1 Sam 15.6: Heb *people* [d] **2.3** OL Vg Compare Gk: Heb *sides* [e] **2.5** That is *Weepers*

generation was gathered to their ancestors, and another generation grew up
after them, who did not know the LORD
or the work that he had done for Israel.

ISRAEL'S UNFAITHFULNESS

11 Then the Israelites did what was
evil in the sight of the LORD and worshipped the Baals; 12and they abandoned the LORD, the God of their ancestors, who had brought them out of the
land of Egypt; they followed other gods,
from among the gods of the peoples
who were all around them, and bowed
down to them; and they provoked the
LORD to anger. 13They abandoned the
LORD, and worshipped Baal and the
Astartes. 14So the anger of the LORD
was kindled against Israel, and he gave
them over to plunderers who plundered
them, and he sold them into the power
of their enemies all around, so that they
could no longer withstand their enemies. 15Whenever they marched out,
the hand of the LORD was against them
to bring misfortune, as the LORD had
warned them and sworn to them; and
they were in great distress.

16 Then the LORD raised up judges,
who delivered them out of the power of
those who plundered them. 17Yet they
did not listen even to their judges; for
they lusted after other gods and bowed
down to them. They soon turned aside
from the way in which their ancestors
had walked, who had obeyed the commandments of the LORD; they did not
follow their example. 18Whenever the
LORD raised up judges for them, the
LORD was with the judge, and he delivered them from the hand of their enemies all the days of the judge; for the
LORD would be moved to pity by their
groaning because of those who persecuted and oppressed them. 19But whenever the judge died, they would relapse
and behave worse than their ancestors,
following other gods, worshipping
them and bowing down to them. They
would not drop any of their practices
or their stubborn ways. 20So the anger
of the LORD was kindled against Israel;
and he said, 'Because this people have
transgressed my covenant that I commanded their ancestors, and have not
obeyed my voice, 21I will no longer drive
out before them any of the nations that
Joshua left when he died.' 22In order to
test Israel, whether or not they would
take care to walk in the way of the LORD
as their ancestors did, 23the LORD had
left those nations, not driving them out
at once, and had not handed them over
to Joshua.

NATIONS REMAINING IN THE LAND

3 Now these are the nations that the
LORD left to test all those in Israel
who had no experience of any war in
Canaan 2(it was only that successive
generations of Israelites might know
war, to teach those who had no experience of it before): 3the five lords of the
Philistines, and all the Canaanites, and
the Sidonians, and the Hivites who
lived on Mount Lebanon, from Mount
Baal-hermon as far as Lebo-hamath.
4They were for the testing of Israel, to
know whether Israel would obey the
commandments of the LORD, which
he commanded their ancestors by Moses. 5So the Israelites lived among the
Canaanites, the Hittites, the Amorites,
the Perizzites, the Hivites, and the Jebusites; 6and they took their daughters
as wives for themselves, and their own
daughters they gave to their sons; and
they worshipped their gods.

OTHNIEL

7 The Israelites did what was evil in
the sight of the LORD, forgetting the
LORD their God, and worshipping the
Baals and the Asherahs. 8Therefore the
anger of the LORD was kindled against
Israel, and he sold them into the hand
of King Cushan-rishathaim of Aram-
naharaim; and the Israelites served
Cushan-rishathaim for eight years. 9But
when the Israelites cried out to the LORD,
the LORD raised up a deliverer for the Israelites, who delivered them, Othniel son
of Kenaz, Caleb's younger brother. 10The
spirit of the LORD came upon him, and
he judged Israel; he went out to war, and
the LORD gave King Cushan-rishathaim
of Aram into his hand; and his hand prevailed over Cushan-rishathaim. 11So the
land had rest for forty years. Then Othniel son of Kenaz died.

EHUD

12 The Israelites again did what was
evil in the sight of the LORD; and the
LORD strengthened King Eglon of Moab
against Israel, because they had done
what was evil in the sight of the LORD.
13In alliance with the Ammonites and
the Amalekites, he went and defeated
Israel; and they took possession of the
city of palms. 14So the Israelites served
King Eglon of Moab for eighteen years.

15 But when the Israelites cried out
to the LORD, the LORD raised up for
them a deliverer, Ehud son of Gera, the
Benjaminite, a left-handed man. The Israelites sent tribute by him to King Eglon of Moab. 16 Ehud made for himself a
sword with two edges, a cubit in length;
and he fastened it on his right thigh under his clothes. 17 Then he presented the
tribute to King Eglon of Moab. Now Eglon was a very fat man. 18 When Ehud
had finished presenting the tribute, he
sent the people who carried the tribute
on their way. 19 But he himself turned
back at the sculptured stones near Gilgal, and said, 'I have a secret message
for you, O king.' So the king said,[f] 'Silence!' and all his attendants went out
from his presence. 20 Ehud came to him,
while he was sitting alone in his cool
roof-chamber, and said, 'I have a message from God for you.' So he rose from
his seat. 21 Then Ehud reached with his
left hand, took the sword from his right
thigh, and thrust it into Eglon's[g] belly;
22 the hilt also went in after the blade,
and the fat closed over the blade, for he
did not draw the sword out of his belly;
and the dirt came out.[h] 23 Then Ehud
went out into the vestibule,[i] and closed
the doors of the roof-chamber on him,
and locked them.

24 After he had gone, the servants
came. When they saw that the doors
of the roof-chamber were locked, they
thought, 'He must be relieving himself[j]
in the cool chamber.' 25 So they waited
until they were embarrassed. When he
still did not open the doors of the roof-
chamber, they took the key and opened
them. There was their lord lying dead
on the floor.

26 Ehud escaped while they delayed, and passed beyond the sculptured
stones, and escaped to Seirah. 27 When
he arrived, he sounded the trumpet in
the hill country of Ephraim; and the Israelites went down with him from the
hill country, having him at their head.
28 He said to them, 'Follow after me; for
the LORD has given your enemies the
Moabites into your hand.' So they went
down after him, and seized the fords of
the Jordan against the Moabites, and
allowed no one to cross over. 29 At that
time they killed about ten thousand of
the Moabites, all strong, able-bodied
men; no one escaped. 30 So Moab was
subdued that day under the hand of Israel. And the land had rest for eighty
years.

SHAMGAR

31 After him came Shamgar son of
Anath, who killed six hundred of the
Philistines with an ox-goad. He too de-
livered Israel.

DEBORAH AND BARAK

4 The Israelites again did what was
evil in the sight of the LORD, after Ehud died. 2 So the LORD sold them
into the hand of King Jabin of Canaan,
who reigned in Hazor; the commander
of his army was Sisera, who lived in
Harosheth-ha-goiim. 3 Then the Israelites cried out to the LORD for help; for he
had nine hundred chariots of iron, and
had oppressed the Israelites cruelly for
twenty years.

4 At that time Deborah, a prophetess, wife of Lappidoth, was judging Israel. 5 She used to sit under the palm of
Deborah between Ramah and Bethel in
the hill country of Ephraim; and the Israelites came up to her for judgement.
6 She sent and summoned Barak son of
Abinoam from Kedesh in Naphtali, and
said to him, 'The LORD, the God of Israel, commands you, "Go, take position
at Mount Tabor, bringing ten thousand
from the tribe of Naphtali and the tribe
of Zebulun. 7 I will draw out Sisera, the
general of Jabin's army, to meet you by
the Wadi Kishon with his chariots and
his troops; and I will give him into your
hand." ' 8 Barak said to her, 'If you will go
with me, I will go; but if you will not go
with me, I will not go.' 9 And she said,
'I will surely go with you; nevertheless,
the road on which you are going will not
lead to your glory, for the LORD will sell
Sisera into the hand of a woman.' Then
Deborah got up and went with Barak
to Kedesh. 10 Barak summoned Zebulun
and Naphtali to Kedesh; and ten thousand warriors went up behind him; and
Deborah went up with him.

11 Now Heber the Kenite had separated from the other Kenites,[k] that is,
the descendants of Hobab the father-in-
law of Moses, and had encamped as far
away as Elon-bezaanannim, which is
near Kedesh.

12 When Sisera was told that Barak
son of Abinoam had gone up to Mount
Tabor, 13 Sisera called out all his chariots, nine hundred chariots of iron,
and all the troops who were with him,

[f] 3.19 Heb *he said* [g] 3.21 Heb *his* [h] 3.22 With Tg Vg: Meaning of Heb uncertain [i] 3.23 Meaning of Heb uncertain [j] 3.24 Heb *covering his feet*
[k] 4.11 Heb *from the Kain*

from Harosheth-ha-goiim to the Wadi
Kishon. 14Then Deborah said to Barak,
'Up! For this is the day on which the
LORD has given Sisera into your hand.
The LORD is indeed going out before
you.' So Barak went down from Mount
Tabor with ten thousand warriors following him. 15And the LORD threw Sisera and all his chariots and all his army
into a panic[l] before Barak; Sisera got
down from his chariot and fled away on
foot, 16while Barak pursued the chariots
and the army to Harosheth-ha-goiim.
All the army of Sisera fell by the sword;
no one was left.

17 Now Sisera had fled away on foot
to the tent of Jael wife of Heber the Kenite; for there was peace between King
Jabin of Hazor and the clan of Heber the
Kenite. 18Jael came out to meet Sisera,
and said to him, 'Turn aside, my lord,
turn aside to me; have no fear.' So he
turned aside to her into the tent, and she
covered him with a rug. 19Then he said
to her, 'Please give me a little water to
drink; for I am thirsty.' So she opened a
skin of milk and gave him a drink and
covered him. 20He said to her, 'Stand at
the entrance of the tent, and if anybody
comes and asks you, "Is anyone here?"
say, "No."' 21But Jael wife of Heber took
a tent-peg, and took a hammer in her
hand, and went softly to him and drove
the peg into his temple, until it went
down into the ground—he was lying
fast asleep from weariness—and he died.
22Then, as Barak came in pursuit of Sisera, Jael went out to meet him, and said
to him, 'Come, and I will show you the
man whom you are seeking.' So he went
into her tent; and there was Sisera lying
dead, with the tent-peg in his temple.

23 So on that day God subdued King
Jabin of Canaan before the Israelites.
24Then the hand of the Israelites bore
harder and harder on King Jabin of Canaan, until they destroyed King Jabin of
Canaan.

THE SONG OF DEBORAH

5 Then Deborah and Barak son of
Abinoam sang on that day, saying:
2 'When locks are long in Israel,
when the people offer
themselves willingly—
bless[m] the LORD!

3 'Hear, O kings; give ear, O princes;
to the LORD I will sing,
I will make melody to the
LORD, the God of Israel.

4 'LORD, when you went out from Seir,
when you marched from
the region of Edom,
the earth trembled,
and the heavens poured,
the clouds indeed poured water.
5 The mountains quaked before the
LORD, the One of Sinai,
before the LORD, the God of Israel.

6 'In the days of Shamgar son of Anath,
in the days of Jael, caravans ceased
and travellers kept to the byways.
7 The peasantry prospered in Israel,
they grew fat on plunder,
because you arose, Deborah,
arose as a mother in Israel.
8 When new gods were chosen,
then war was in the gates.
Was shield or spear to be seen
among forty thousand in Israel?
9 My heart goes out to the
commanders of Israel
who offered themselves willingly
among the people.
Bless the LORD.

10 'Tell of it, you who ride on
white donkeys,
you who sit on rich carpets,[n]
and you who walk by the way.
11 To the sound of musicians[o] at
the watering-places,
there they repeat the triumphs
of the LORD,
the triumphs of his
peasantry in Israel.

'Then down to the gates marched
the people of the LORD.

12 'Awake, awake, Deborah!
Awake, awake, utter a song!
Arise, Barak, lead away your captives,
O son of Abinoam.
13 Then down marched the
remnant of the noble;
the people of the LORD
marched down for him[p]
against the mighty.
14 From Ephraim they set out[q]
into the valley,[r]
following you, Benjamin,
with your kin;

[l] **4.15** Heb adds *to the sword*; compare verse 16
[m] **5.2** Or *You who offer yourselves willingly among the people, bless*
[n] **5.10** Meaning of Heb uncertain
[o] **5.11** Meaning of Heb uncertain
[p] **5.13** Gk: Heb *me*
[q] **5.14** Cn: Heb *From Ephraim their root*
[r] **5.14** Gk: Heb *in Amalek*

from Machir marched down
the commanders,
and from Zebulun those who
bear the marshal's staff;
15 the chiefs of Issachar came
with Deborah,
and Issachar faithful to Barak;
into the valley they rushed
out at his heels.
Among the clans of Reuben
there were great searchings
of heart.
16 Why did you tarry among
the sheepfolds,
to hear the piping for the flocks?
Among the clans of Reuben
there were great searchings
of heart.
17 Gilead stayed beyond the Jordan;
and Dan, why did he abide
with the ships?
Asher sat still at the coast of the sea,
settling down by his landings.
18 Zebulun is a people that
scorned death;
Naphtali too, on the heights
of the field.

19 'The kings came, they fought;
then fought the kings of Canaan,
at Taanach, by the waters
of Megiddo;
they got no spoils of silver.
20 The stars fought from heaven,
from their courses they
fought against Sisera.
21 The torrent Kishon swept them away,
the onrushing torrent, the
torrent Kishon.
March on, my soul, with might!

22 'Then loud beat the horses' hoofs
with the galloping, galloping
of his steeds.

23 'Curse Meroz, says the angel
of the LORD,
curse bitterly its inhabitants,
because they did not come to
the help of the LORD,
to the help of the LORD
against the mighty.

24 'Most blessed of women be Jael,
the wife of Heber the Kenite,
of tent-dwelling women
most blessed.
25 He asked water and she
gave him milk,
she brought him curds in
a lordly bowl.
26 She put her hand to the tent-peg
and her right hand to the
workmen's mallet;
she struck Sisera a blow,
she crushed his head,
she shattered and pierced
his temple.
27 He sank, he fell,
he lay still at her feet;
at her feet he sank, he fell;
where he sank, there he fell dead.

28 'Out of the window she peered,
the mother of Sisera gazed[s]
through the lattice:
"Why is his chariot so long
in coming?
Why tarry the hoofbeats
of his chariots?"
29 Her wisest ladies make answer,
indeed, she answers the
question herself:
30 "Are they not finding and
dividing the spoil?—
A girl or two for every man;
spoil of dyed stuffs for Sisera,
spoil of dyed stuffs embroidered,
two pieces of dyed work
embroidered for my
neck as spoil?"

31 'So perish all your enemies, O LORD!
But may your friends be like the
sun as it rises in its might.'

And the land had rest for forty years.

THE MIDIANITE OPPRESSION

6 The Israelites did what was evil in
the sight of the LORD, and the LORD
gave them into the hand of Midian for
seven years. 2 The hand of Midian prevailed over Israel; and because of Midian the Israelites provided for themselves hiding-places in the mountains,
caves and strongholds. 3 For whenever
the Israelites put in seed, the Midianites and the Amalekites and the people
of the east would come up against them.
4 They would encamp against them and
destroy the produce of the land, as far as
the neighbourhood of Gaza, and leave no
sustenance in Israel, and no sheep or ox
or donkey. 5 For they and their livestock
would come up, and they would even
bring their tents, as thick as locusts;
neither they nor their camels could be
counted; so they wasted the land as they
came in. 6 Thus Israel was greatly im-

[s] 5.28 Gk Compare Tg: Heb *exclaimed*

poverished because of Midian; and the
Israelites cried out to the LORD for help.
7 When the Israelites cried to the
LORD on account of the Midianites,
8the LORD sent a prophet to the Israelites; and he said to them, 'Thus says
the LORD, the God of Israel: I led you
up from Egypt, and brought you out of
the house of slavery; 9and I delivered
you from the hand of the Egyptians,
and from the hand of all who oppressed
you, and drove them out before you, and
gave you their land; 10and I said to you,
"I am the LORD your God; you shall not
pay reverence to the gods of the Amorites, in whose land you live." But you
have not given heed to my voice.'

THE CALLING OF GIDEON

11 Now the angel of the LORD came
and sat under the oak at Ophrah, which
belonged to Joash the Abiezrite, as his
son Gideon was beating out wheat
in the wine press, to hide it from the
Midianites. 12The angel of the LORD
appeared to him and said to him, 'The
LORD is with you, you mighty warrior.'
13Gideon answered him, 'But sir, if the
LORD is with us, why then has all this
happened to us? And where are all his
wonderful deeds that our ancestors
recounted to us, saying, "Did not the
LORD bring us up from Egypt?" But
now the LORD has cast us off, and given
us into the hand of Midian.' 14Then the
LORD turned to him and said, 'Go in this
might of yours and deliver Israel from
the hand of Midian; I hereby commission you.' 15He responded, 'But sir, how
can I deliver Israel? My clan is the weak-
est in Manasseh, and I am the least in
my family.' 16The LORD said to him,
'But I will be with you, and you shall
strike down the Midianites, every one
of them.' 17Then he said to him, 'If now I
have found favour with you, then show
me a sign that it is you who speak with
me. 18Do not depart from here until I
come to you, and bring out my present,
and set it before you.' And he said, 'I will
stay until you return.'
19 So Gideon went into his house
and prepared a kid, and unleavened
cakes from an ephah of flour; the meat
he put in a basket, and the broth he put
in a pot, and brought them to him under the oak and presented them. 20The
angel of God said to him, 'Take the meat
and the unleavened cakes, and put them
on this rock, and pour out the broth.'
And he did so. 21Then the angel of the
LORD reached out the tip of the staff
that was in his hand, and touched the
meat and the unleavened cakes; and fire
sprang up from the rock and consumed
the meat and the unleavened cakes; and
the angel of the LORD vanished from
his sight. 22Then Gideon perceived that
it was the angel of the LORD; and Gideon said, 'Help me, Lord GOD! For I have
seen the angel of the LORD face to face.'
23But the LORD said to him, 'Peace be
to you; do not fear, you shall not die.'
24Then Gideon built an altar there to the
LORD, and called it, The LORD is peace.
To this day it still stands at Ophrah,
which belongs to the Abiezrites.
25 That night the LORD said to him,
'Take your father's bull, the second bull
seven years old, and pull down the altar
of Baal that belongs to your father, and
cut down the sacred pole[t] that is beside
it; 26and build an altar to the LORD your
God on the top of the stronghold here, in
proper order; then take the second bull,
and offer it as a burnt-offering with the
wood of the sacred pole[u] that you shall
cut down.' 27So Gideon took ten of his
servants, and did as the LORD had told
him; but because he was too afraid of his
family and the townspeople to do it by
day, he did it by night.

GIDEON DESTROYS THE ALTAR OF BAAL

28 When the townspeople rose early
in the morning, the altar of Baal was
broken down, and the sacred pole[v] beside it was cut down, and the second bull
was offered on the altar that had been
built. 29So they said to one another,
'Who has done this?' After searching
and inquiring, they were told, 'Gideon
son of Joash did it.' 30Then the townspeople said to Joash, 'Bring out your
son, so that he may die, for he has pulled
down the altar of Baal and cut down the
sacred pole[w] beside it.' 31But Joash said
to all who were arrayed against him,
'Will you contend for Baal? Or will you
defend his cause? Whoever contends for
him shall be put to death by morning. If
he is a god, let him contend for himself,
because his altar has been pulled down.'
32Therefore on that day Gideon[x] was
called Jerubbaal, that is to say, 'Let Baal
contend against him', because he pulled
down his altar.

[t] **6.25** Heb *Asherah* [u] **6.26** Heb *Asherah*
[v] **6.28** Heb *Asherah* [w] **6.30** Heb *Asherah*
[x] **6.32** Heb *he*

33 Then all the Midianites and the
Amalekites and the people of the east
came together, and crossing the Jordan
they encamped in the Valley of Jezreel.
34 But the spirit of the LORD took possession of Gideon; and he sounded the
trumpet, and the Abiezrites were called
out to follow him. 35 He sent messengers
throughout all Manasseh, and they too
were called out to follow him. He also
sent messengers to Asher, Zebulun,
and Naphtali, and they went up to meet
them.

THE SIGN OF THE FLEECE

36 Then Gideon said to God, 'In order
to see whether you will deliver Israel by
my hand, as you have said, 37 I am going
to lay a fleece of wool on the threshing-
floor; if there is dew on the fleece alone,
and it is dry on all the ground, then I
shall know that you will deliver Israel
by my hand, as you have said.' 38 And it
was so. When he rose early next morning and squeezed the fleece, he wrung
enough dew from the fleece to fill a
bowl with water. 39 Then Gideon said to
God, 'Do not let your anger burn against
me, let me speak one more time; let
me, please, make trial with the fleece
just once more; let it be dry only on the
fleece, and on all the ground let there
be dew.' 40 And God did so that night. It
was dry on the fleece only, and on all the
ground there was dew.

GIDEON SURPRISES AND ROUTS THE MIDIANITES

7 Then Jerubbaal (that is, Gideon)
and all the troops that were with
him rose early and encamped beside the
spring of Harod; and the camp of Midian was north of them, below[y] the hill
of Moreh, in the valley.
2 The LORD said to Gideon, 'The
troops with you are too many for me
to give the Midianites into their hand.
Israel would only take the credit away
from me, saying, "My own hand has delivered me." 3 Now therefore proclaim
this in the hearing of the troops, "Whoever is fearful and trembling, let him
return home."' Thus Gideon sifted them
out;[z] twenty-two thousand returned,
and ten thousand remained.
4 Then the LORD said to Gideon, 'The
troops are still too many; take them
down to the water and I will sift them
out for you there. When I say, "This
one shall go with you", he shall go with
you; and when I say, "This one shall not
go with you", he shall not go.' 5 So he
brought the troops down to the water;
and the LORD said to Gideon, 'All those
who lap the water with their tongues,
as a dog laps, you shall put to one side;
all those who kneel down to drink, putting their hands to their mouths,[a] you
shall put to the other side.' 6 The number
of those that lapped was three hundred;
but all the rest of the troops knelt down
to drink water. 7 Then the LORD said to
Gideon, 'With the three hundred that
lapped I will deliver you, and give the
Midianites into your hand. Let all the
others go to their homes.' 8 So he took
the jars of the troops from their hands,[b]
and their trumpets; and he sent all the
rest of Israel back to their own tents, but
retained the three hundred. The camp of
Midian was below him in the valley.
9 That same night the LORD said to
him, 'Get up, attack the camp; for I have
given it into your hand. 10 But if you fear
to attack, go down to the camp with
your servant Purah; 11 and you shall hear
what they say, and afterwards your
hands shall be strengthened to attack
the camp.' Then he went down with
his servant Purah to the outposts of
the armed men that were in the camp.
12 The Midianites and the Amalekites
and all the people of the east lay along
the valley as thick as locusts; and their
camels were without number, countless as the sand on the seashore. 13 When
Gideon arrived, there was a man telling
a dream to his comrade; and he said, 'I
had a dream, and in it a cake of barley
bread tumbled into the camp of Midian,
and came to the tent, and struck it so
that it fell; it turned upside down, and
the tent collapsed.' 14 And his comrade
answered, 'This is no other than the
sword of Gideon son of Joash, a man of
Israel; into his hand God has given Midian and all the army.'
15 When Gideon heard the telling
of the dream and its interpretation,
he worshipped; and he returned to the
camp of Israel, and said, 'Get up; for the
LORD has given the army of Midian into
your hand.' 16 After he divided the three
hundred men into three companies,
and put trumpets into the hands of all
of them, and empty jars, with torches
inside the jars, 17 he said to them, 'Look

[y] **7.1** Heb *from* [z] **7.3** Cn: Heb *home, and depart from Mount Gilead"'* [a] **7.5** Heb places the words *putting their hands to their mouths* after the word *lapped* in verse 6 [b] **7.8** Cn: Heb *So the people took provisions in their hands*

at me, and do the same; when I come
to the outskirts of the camp, do as I do.
18When I blow the trumpet, I and all
who are with me, then you also blow
the trumpets around the whole camp,
and shout, "For the LORD and for Gideon!"'

19 So Gideon and the hundred who
were with him came to the outskirts
of the camp at the beginning of the
middle watch, when they had just set
the watch; and they blew the trumpets and smashed the jars that were in
their hands. 20So the three companies
blew the trumpets and broke the jars,
holding in their left hands the torches,
and in their right hands the trumpets to blow; and they cried, 'A sword
for the LORD and for Gideon!' 21Every
man stood in his place all around the
camp, and all the men in camp ran; they
cried out and fled. 22When they blew
the three hundred trumpets, the LORD
set every man's sword against his fellow and against all the army; and the
army fled as far as Beth-shittah towards
Zererah,[c] as far as the border of Abel-
meholah, by Tabbath. 23And the men of
Israel were called out from Naphtali and
from Asher and from all Manasseh, and
they pursued after the Midianites.

24 Then Gideon sent messengers
throughout all the hill country of
Ephraim, saying, 'Come down against
the Midianites and seize the waters
against them, as far as Beth-barah,
and also the Jordan.' So all the men
of Ephraim were called out, and they
seized the waters as far as Beth-barah,
and also the Jordan. 25They captured the
two captains of Midian, Oreb and Zeeb;
they killed Oreb at the rock of Oreb,
and Zeeb they killed at the wine press
of Zeeb, as they pursued the Midianites. They brought the heads of Oreb and
Zeeb to Gideon beyond the Jordan.

GIDEON'S TRIUMPH AND VENGEANCE

8 Then the Ephraimites said to him,
'What have you done to us, not to
call us when you went to fight against
the Midianites?' And they upbraided him violently. 2So he said to them,
'What have I done now in comparison
with you? Is not the gleaning of the
grapes of Ephraim better than the vintage of Abiezer? 3God has given into
your hands the captains of Midian, Oreb
and Zeeb; what have I been able to do
in comparison with you?' When he said
this, their anger against him subsided.

4 Then Gideon came to the Jordan
and crossed over, he and the three hundred who were with him, exhausted
and famished.[d] 5So he said to the people of Succoth, 'Please give some loaves
of bread to my followers, for they are
exhausted, and I am pursuing Zebah
and Zalmunna, the kings of Midian.'
6But the officials of Succoth said, 'Do
you already have in your possession the
hands of Zebah and Zalmunna, that we
should give bread to your army?' 7Gid-
eon replied, 'Well then, when the LORD
has given Zebah and Zalmunna into my
hand, I will trample your flesh on the
thorns of the wilderness and on briers.'
8From there he went up to Penuel, and
made the same request of them; and the
people of Penuel answered him as the
people of Succoth had answered. 9So
he said to the people of Penuel, 'When I
come back victorious, I will break down
this tower.'

10 Now Zebah and Zalmunna were
in Karkor with their army, about fifteen thousand men, all who were left
of all the army of the people of the east;
for one hundred and twenty thousand
men bearing arms had fallen. 11So Gideon went up by the caravan route east
of Nobah and Jogbehah, and attacked
the army; for the army was off its guard.
12Zebah and Zalmunna fled; and he
pursued them and took the two kings
of Midian, Zebah and Zalmunna, and
threw all the army into a panic.

13 When Gideon son of Joash returned from the battle by the ascent of
Heres, 14he caught a young man, one of
the people of Succoth, and questioned
him; and he listed for him the officials
and elders of Succoth, seventy-seven
people. 15Then he came to the people of
Succoth, and said, 'Here are Zebah and
Zalmunna, about whom you taunted
me, saying, "Do you already have in
your possession the hands of Zebah and
Zalmunna, that we should give bread
to your troops who are exhausted?"'
16So he took the elders of the city and
he took thorns of the wilderness and
briers and with them he trampled[e] the
people of Succoth. 17He also broke down
the tower of Penuel, and killed the men
of the city.

18 Then he said to Zebah and Zalmunna, 'What about the men whom
you killed at Tabor?' They answered,

[c] 7.22 Another reading is *Zeredah* [d] 8.4 Gk: Heb *pursuing* [e] 8.16 With verse 7, Compare Gk: Heb *he taught*

'As you are, so were they, every one
of them; they resembled the sons of a
king.' 19And he replied, 'They were my
brothers, the sons of my mother; as the
LORD lives, if you had saved them alive,
I would not kill you.' 20So he said to Jether his firstborn, 'Go, kill them!' But
the boy did not draw his sword, for he
was afraid, because he was still a boy.
21Then Zebah and Zalmunna said, 'You
come and kill us; for as the man is, so
is his strength.' So Gideon proceeded to
kill Zebah and Zalmunna; and he took
the crescents that were on the necks of
their camels.

GIDEON'S IDOLATRY

22 Then the Israelites said to Gideon,
'Rule over us, you and your son and your
grandson also; for you have delivered us
out of the hand of Midian.' 23Gideon
said to them, 'I will not rule over you,
and my son will not rule over you; the
LORD will rule over you.' 24Then Gideon
said to them, 'Let me make a request
of you; each of you give me an ear-ring
he has taken as booty.' (For the enemy[f]
had golden ear-rings, because they were
Ishmaelites.) 25'We will willingly give
them,' they answered. So they spread
a garment, and each threw into it an
ear-ring he had taken as booty. 26The
weight of the golden ear-rings that
he requested was one thousand seven
hundred shekels of gold (apart from
the crescents and the pendants and the
purple garments worn by the kings of
Midian, and the collars that were on the
necks of their camels). 27Gideon made
an ephod of it and put it in his town, in
Ophrah; and all Israel prostituted themselves to it there, and it became a snare
to Gideon and to his family. 28So Midian
was subdued before the Israelites, and
they lifted up their heads no more. So
the land had rest for forty years in the
days of Gideon.

DEATH OF GIDEON

29 Jerubbaal son of Joash went to live
in his own house. 30Now Gideon had
seventy sons, his own offspring, for he
had many wives. 31His concubine who
was in Shechem also bore him a son,
and he named him Abimelech. 32Then
Gideon son of Joash died at a good old
age, and was buried in the tomb of his
father Joash at Ophrah of the Abiezrites.

33 As soon as Gideon died, the Israelites relapsed and prostituted themselves
with the Baals, making Baal-berith
their god. 34The Israelites did not remember the LORD their God, who had
rescued them from the hand of all their
enemies on every side; 35and they did
not exhibit loyalty to the house of Jerubbaal (that is, Gideon) in return for all the
good that he had done to Israel.

ABIMELECH ATTEMPTS TO ESTABLISH A MONARCHY

9 Now Abimelech son of Jerubbaal
went to Shechem to his mother's
kinsfolk and said to them and to the
whole clan of his mother's family, 2'Say
in the hearing of all the lords of Shechem,
"Which is better for you, that all seventy
of the sons of Jerubbaal rule over you,
or that one rule over you?" Remember
also that I am your bone and your flesh.'
3So his mother's kinsfolk spoke all these
words on his behalf in the hearing of all
the lords of Shechem; and their hearts
inclined to follow Abimelech, for they
said, 'He is our brother.' 4They gave him
seventy pieces of silver out of the temple of Baal-berith with which Abimelech
hired worthless and reckless fellows, who
followed him. 5He went to his father's
house at Ophrah, and killed his brothers
the sons of Jerubbaal, seventy men, on
one stone; but Jotham, the youngest son
of Jerubbaal, survived, for he hid himself. 6Then all the lords of Shechem and
all Beth-millo came together, and they
went and made Abimelech king, by the
oak of the pillar[g] at Shechem.

THE PARABLE OF THE TREES

7 When it was told to Jotham, he
went and stood on the top of Mount Gerizim, and cried aloud and said to them,
'Listen to me, you lords of Shechem, so
that God may listen to you.

8 The trees once went out
    to anoint a king over themselves.
  So they said to the olive tree,
    "Reign over us."
9 The olive tree answered them,
    "Shall I stop producing my rich oil
      by which gods and mortals
        are honoured,
    and go to sway over the trees?"
10 Then the trees said to the fig tree,
    "You come and reign over us."
11 But the fig tree answered them,
    "Shall I stop producing
        my sweetness
      and my delicious fruit,
    and go to sway over the trees?"

[f] 8.24 Heb *they* [g] 9.6 Cn: Meaning of Heb uncertain

12 Then the trees said to the vine,
"You come and reign over us."
13 But the vine said to them,
"Shall I stop producing my wine
that cheers gods and mortals,
and go to sway over the trees?"
14 So all the trees said to the bramble,
"You come and reign over us."
15 And the bramble said to the trees,
"If in good faith you are anointing
me king over you,
then come and take
refuge in my shade;
but if not, let fire come out
of the bramble
and devour the cedars
of Lebanon."

16 'Now therefore, if you acted in
good faith and honour when you made
Abimelech king, and if you have dealt
well with Jerubbaal and his house,
and have done to him as his actions
deserved— 17 for my father fought for
you, and risked his life, and rescued
you from the hand of Midian; 18 but you
have risen up against my father's house
this day, and have killed his sons, seventy men on one stone, and have made
Abimelech, the son of his slave-woman,
king over the lords of Shechem, because
he is your kinsman— 19 if, I say, you
have acted in good faith and honour towards Jerubbaal and towards his house
this day, then rejoice in Abimelech, and
let him also rejoice in you; 20 but if not,
let fire come out from Abimelech, and
devour the lords of Shechem, and Beth-
millo; and let fire come out from the
lords of Shechem, and from Beth-millo,
and devour Abimelech.' 21 Then Jotham
ran away and fled, going to Beer, where
he remained for fear of his brother
Abimelech.

THE DOWNFALL OF ABIMELECH

22 Abimelech ruled over Israel for
three years. 23 But God sent an evil spirit
between Abimelech and the lords of
Shechem; and the lords of Shechem
dealt treacherously with Abimelech.
24 This happened so that the violence
done to the seventy sons of Jerubbaal
might be avenged[h] and their blood be
laid on their brother Abimelech, who
killed them, and on the lords of Shechem, who strengthened his hands to
kill his brothers. 25 So, out of hostility to
him, the lords of Shechem set ambushes
on the mountain tops. They robbed all
who passed by them along that way;
and it was reported to Abimelech.

26 When Gaal son of Ebed moved into
Shechem with his kinsfolk, the lords of
Shechem put confidence in him. 27 They
went out into the field and gathered the
grapes from their vineyards, trod them,
and celebrated. Then they went into the
temple of their god, ate and drank, and
ridiculed Abimelech. 28 Gaal son of Ebed
said, 'Who is Abimelech, and who are we
of Shechem, that we should serve him?
Did not the son of Jerubbaal and Zebul
his officer serve the men of Hamor father of Shechem? Why then should we
serve him? 29 If only this people were
under my command! Then I would remove Abimelech; I would say[i] to him,
"Increase your army, and come out."'

30 When Zebul the ruler of the city
heard the words of Gaal son of Ebed, his
anger was kindled. 31 He sent messengers to Abimelech at Arumah,[j] saying,
'Look, Gaal son of Ebed and his kinsfolk
have come to Shechem, and they are
stirring up[k] the city against you. 32 Now
therefore, go by night, you and the
troops that are with you, and lie in wait
in the fields. 33 Then early in the morning, as soon as the sun rises, get up
and rush on the city; and when he and
the troops that are with him come out
against you, you may deal with them as
best you can.'

34 So Abimelech and all the troops
with him got up by night and lay in
wait against Shechem in four companies. 35 When Gaal son of Ebed went out
and stood in the entrance of the gate
of the city, Abimelech and the troops
with him rose from the ambush. 36 And
when Gaal saw them, he said to Zebul,
'Look, people are coming down from
the mountain tops!' And Zebul said to
him, 'The shadows on the mountains
look like people to you.' 37 Gaal spoke
again and said, 'Look, people are coming down from Tabbur-erez, and one
company is coming from the direction
of Elon-meonenim.'[l] 38 Then Zebul said
to him, 'Where is your boast[m] now, you
who said, "Who is Abimelech, that we
should serve him?" Are not these the
troops you made light of? Go out now
and fight with them.' 39 So Gaal went
out at the head of the lords of Shechem,
and fought with Abimelech. 40 Abimelech chased him, and he fled before him.
Many fell wounded, up to the entrance

[h] **9.24** Heb *might come* [i] **9.29** Gk: Heb *and he said* [j] **9.31** Cn See 9.41. Heb *Tormah* [k] **9.31** Cn: Heb *are besieging* [l] **9.37** That is *Diviners' Oak* [m] **9.38** Heb *mouth*

of the gate. 41So Abimelech resided at Arumah; and Zebul drove out Gaal and his kinsfolk, so that they could not live on at Shechem.

42 On the following day the people went out into the fields. When Abimelech was told, 43he took his troops and divided them into three companies, and lay in wait in the fields. When he looked and saw the people coming out of the city, he rose against them and killed them. 44Abimelech and the company that was[n] with him rushed forward and stood at the entrance of the gate of the city, while the two companies rushed on all who were in the fields and killed them. 45Abimelech fought against the city all that day; he took the city, and killed the people that were in it; and he razed the city and sowed it with salt.

46 When all the lords of the Tower of Shechem heard of it, they entered the stronghold of the temple of El-berith. 47Abimelech was told that all the lords of the Tower of Shechem were gathered together. 48So Abimelech went up to Mount Zalmon, he and all the troops that were with him. Abimelech took an axe in his hand, cut down a bundle of brushwood, and took it up and laid it on his shoulder. Then he said to the troops with him, 'What you have seen me do, do quickly, as I have done.' 49So every one of the troops cut down a bundle and following Abimelech put it against the stronghold, and they set the stronghold on fire over them, so that all the people of the Tower of Shechem also died, about a thousand men and women.

50 Then Abimelech went to Thebez, and encamped against Thebez, and took it. 51But there was a strong tower within the city, and all the men and women and all the lords of the city fled to it and shut themselves in; and they went to the roof of the tower. 52Abimelech came to the tower, and fought against it, and came near to the entrance of the tower to burn it with fire. 53But a certain woman threw an upper millstone on Abimelech's head, and crushed his skull. 54Immediately he called to the young man who carried his armour and said to him, 'Draw your sword and kill me, so people will not say about me, "A woman killed him." ' So the young man thrust him through, and he died. 55When the Israelites saw that Abimelech was dead, they all went home. 56Thus God repaid Abimelech for the crime he committed against his father in killing his seventy brothers; 57and God also made all the wickedness of the people of Shechem fall back on their heads, and on them came the curse of Jotham son of Jerubbaal.

TOLA AND JAIR

10 After Abimelech, Tola son of Puah son of Dodo, a man of Issachar, who lived at Shamir in the hill country of Ephraim, rose to deliver Israel. 2He judged Israel for twenty-three years. Then he died, and was buried at Shamir.

3 After him came Jair the Gileadite, who judged Israel for twenty-two years. 4He had thirty sons who rode on thirty donkeys; and they had thirty towns, which are in the land of Gilead, and are called Havvoth-jair to this day. 5Jair died, and was buried in Kamon.

OPPRESSION BY THE AMMONITES

6 The Israelites again did what was evil in the sight of the LORD, worshipping the Baals and the Astartes, the gods of Aram, the gods of Sidon, the gods of Moab, the gods of the Ammonites, and the gods of the Philistines. Thus they abandoned the LORD, and did not worship him. 7So the anger of the LORD was kindled against Israel, and he sold them into the hand of the Philistines and into the hand of the Ammonites, 8and they crushed and oppressed the Israelites that year. For eighteen years they oppressed all the Israelites that were beyond the Jordan in the land of the Amorites, which is in Gilead. 9The Ammonites also crossed the Jordan to fight against Judah and against Benjamin and against the house of Ephraim; so that Israel was greatly distressed.

10 So the Israelites cried to the LORD, saying, 'We have sinned against you, because we have abandoned our God and have worshipped the Baals.' 11And the LORD said to the Israelites, 'Did I not deliver you[o] from the Egyptians and from the Amorites, from the Ammonites and from the Philistines? 12The Sidonians also, and the Amalekites, and the Maonites oppressed you; and you cried to me, and I delivered you out of their hand. 13Yet you have abandoned me and worshipped other gods; therefore I will deliver you no more. 14Go and cry to the gods whom you have chosen;

[n] **9.44** Vg and some Gk Mss: Heb *companies that were* [o] **10.11** Heb lacks *Did I not deliver you*

let them deliver you in the time of your distress.' 15 And the Israelites said to the LORD, 'We have sinned; do to us whatever seems good to you; but deliver us this day!' 16 So they put away the foreign gods from among them and worshipped the LORD; and he could no longer bear to see Israel suffer.

17 Then the Ammonites were called to arms, and they encamped in Gilead; and the Israelites came together, and they encamped at Mizpah. 18 The commanders of the people of Gilead said to one another, 'Who will begin the fight against the Ammonites? He shall be head over all the inhabitants of Gilead.'

JEPHTHAH

11 Now Jephthah the Gileadite, the son of a prostitute, was a mighty warrior. Gilead was the father of Jephthah. 2 Gilead's wife also bore him sons; and when his wife's sons grew up, they drove Jephthah away, saying to him, 'You shall not inherit anything in our father's house; for you are the son of another woman.' 3 Then Jephthah fled from his brothers and lived in the land of Tob. Outlaws collected around Jephthah and went raiding with him.

4 After a time the Ammonites made war against Israel. 5 And when the Ammonites made war against Israel, the elders of Gilead went to bring Jephthah from the land of Tob. 6 They said to Jephthah, 'Come and be our commander, so that we may fight with the Ammonites.' 7 But Jephthah said to the elders of Gilead, 'Are you not the very ones who rejected me and drove me out of my father's house? So why do you come to me now when you are in trouble?' 8 The elders of Gilead said to Jephthah, 'Nevertheless, we have now turned back to you, so that you may go with us and fight with the Ammonites, and become head over us, over all the inhabitants of Gilead.' 9 Jephthah said to the elders of Gilead, 'If you bring me home again to fight with the Ammonites, and the LORD gives them over to me, I will be your head.' 10 And the elders of Gilead said to Jephthah, 'The LORD will be witness between us; we will surely do as you say.' 11 So Jephthah went with the elders of Gilead, and the people made him head and commander over them; and Jephthah spoke all his words before the LORD at Mizpah.

12 Then Jephthah sent messengers to the king of the Ammonites and said, 'What is there between you and me, that you have come to me to fight against my land?' 13 The king of the Ammonites answered the messengers of Jephthah, 'Because Israel, on coming from Egypt, took away my land from the Arnon to the Jabbok and to the Jordan; now therefore restore it peaceably.' 14 Once again Jephthah sent messengers to the king of the Ammonites 15 and said to him: 'Thus says Jephthah: Israel did not take away the land of Moab or the land of the Ammonites, 16 but when they came up from Egypt, Israel went through the wilderness to the Red Sea[p] and came to Kadesh. 17 Israel then sent messengers to the king of Edom, saying, "Let us pass through your land"; but the king of Edom would not listen. They also sent to the king of Moab, but he would not consent. So Israel remained at Kadesh. 18 Then they journeyed through the wilderness, went around the land of Edom and the land of Moab, arrived on the eastern side of the land of Moab, and camped on the other side of the Arnon. They did not enter the territory of Moab, for the Arnon was the boundary of Moab. 19 Israel then sent messengers to King Sihon of the Amorites, king of Heshbon; and Israel said to him, "Let us pass through your land to our country." 20 But Sihon did not trust Israel to pass through his territory; so Sihon gathered all his people together, and encamped at Jahaz, and fought with Israel. 21 Then the LORD, the God of Israel, gave Sihon and all his people into the hand of Israel, and they defeated them; so Israel occupied all the land of the Amorites, who inhabited that country. 22 They occupied all the territory of the Amorites from the Arnon to the Jabbok and from the wilderness to the Jordan. 23 So now the LORD, the God of Israel, has conquered the Amorites for the benefit of his people Israel. Do you intend to take their place? 24 Should you not possess what your god Chemosh gives you to possess? And should we not be the ones to possess everything that the LORD our God has conquered for our benefit? 25 Now are you any better than King Balak son of Zippor of Moab? Did he ever enter into conflict with Israel, or did he ever go to war with them? 26 While Israel lived in Heshbon and its villages, and in Aroer and its villages, and in all the towns that are along the Arnon, for

[p] 11.16 Or *Sea of Reeds*

three hundred years, why did you not
recover them within that time? 27It is
not I who have sinned against you, but
you are the one who does me wrong by
making war on me. Let the LORD, who
is judge, decide today for the Israelites
or for the Ammonites.' 28But the king of
the Ammonites did not heed the message that Jephthah sent him.

JEPHTHAH'S VOW

29 Then the spirit of the LORD came
upon Jephthah, and he passed through
Gilead and Manasseh. He passed on
to Mizpah of Gilead, and from Mizpah
of Gilead he passed on to the Ammonites. 30And Jephthah made a vow to the
LORD, and said, 'If you will give the Ammonites into my hand, 31then whoever
comes out of the doors of my house to
meet me, when I return victorious from
the Ammonites, shall be the LORD's, to
be offered up by me as a burnt-offering.'
32So Jephthah crossed over to the Ammonites to fight against them; and the
LORD gave them into his hand. 33He inflicted a massive defeat on them from
Aroer to the neighbourhood of Minnith, twenty towns, and as far as Abel-
keramim. So the Ammonites were subdued before the people of Israel.

JEPHTHAH'S DAUGHTER

34 Then Jephthah came to his home
at Mizpah; and there was his daughter coming out to meet him with timbrels and with dancing. She was his
only child; he had no son or daughter
except her. 35When he saw her, he tore
his clothes, and said, 'Alas, my daughter! You have brought me very low; you
have become the cause of great trouble
to me. For I have opened my mouth to
the LORD, and I cannot take back my
vow.' 36She said to him, 'My father, if you
have opened your mouth to the LORD,
do to me according to what has gone out
of your mouth, now that the LORD has
given you vengeance against your enemies, the Ammonites.' 37And she said
to her father, 'Let this thing be done
for me: Grant me two months, so that I
may go and wander[q] on the mountains,
and bewail my virginity, my companions and I.' 38'Go,' he said and sent her
away for two months. So she departed,
she and her companions, and bewailed
her virginity on the mountains. 39At
the end of two months, she returned to
her father, who did with her according
to the vow he had made. She had never
slept with a man. So there arose an Israelite custom that 40for four days every
year the daughters of Israel would go
out to lament the daughter of Jephthah
the Gileadite.

INTERTRIBAL DISSENSION

12 The men of Ephraim were called
to arms, and they crossed to Zaphon and said to Jephthah, 'Why did
you cross over to fight against the Ammonites, and did not call us to go with
you? We will burn your house down
over you!' 2Jephthah said to them, 'My
people and I were engaged in conflict
with the Ammonites who oppressed us[r]
severely. But when I called you, you did
not deliver me from their hand. 3When
I saw that you would not deliver me, I
took my life in my hand, and crossed
over against the Ammonites, and the
LORD gave them into my hand. Why
then have you come up to me this day,
to fight against me?' 4Then Jephthah
gathered all the men of Gilead and
fought with Ephraim; and the men of
Gilead defeated Ephraim, because they
said, 'You are fugitives from Ephraim,
you Gileadites—in the heart of Ephraim
and Manasseh.'[s] 5Then the Gileadites
took the fords of the Jordan against the
Ephraimites. Whenever one of the fugitives of Ephraim said, 'Let me go over',
the men of Gilead would say to him,
'Are you an Ephraimite?' When he said,
'No', 6they said to him, 'Then say Shib-
boleth', and he said, 'Sibboleth', for he
could not pronounce it right. Then they
seized him and killed him at the fords of
the Jordan. Forty-two thousand of the
Ephraimites fell at that time.

7 Jephthah judged Israel for six years.
Then Jephthah the Gileadite died, and
was buried in his town in Gilead.[t]

IBZAN, ELON, AND ABDON

8 After him Ibzan of Bethlehem
judged Israel. 9He had thirty sons. He
gave his thirty daughters in marriage
outside his clan and brought in thirty
young women from outside for his sons.
He judged Israel for seven years. 10Then
Ibzan died, and was buried at Bethlehem.

11 After him Elon the Zebulunite
judged Israel; and he judged Israel for
ten years. 12Then Elon the Zebulunite

[q] 11.37 Cn: Heb *go down* [r] 12.2 Gk OL, Syr H: Heb lacks *who oppressed us* [s] 12.4 Meaning of Heb uncertain: Gk omits *because ... Manasseh* [t] 12.7 Gk: Heb *in the towns of Gilead*

died, and was buried at Aijalon in the
land of Zebulun.

13 After him Abdon son of Hillel the
Pirathonite judged Israel. 14He had forty
sons and thirty grandsons, who rode on
seventy donkeys; he judged Israel for
eight years. 15Then Abdon son of Hillel
the Pirathonite died, and was buried at
Pirathon in the land of Ephraim, in the
hill country of the Amalekites.

THE BIRTH OF SAMSON

13 The Israelites again did what
was evil in the sight of the LORD,
and the LORD gave them into the hand
of the Philistines for forty years.

2 There was a certain man of Zorah,
of the tribe of the Danites, whose name
was Manoah. His wife was barren, having borne no children. 3And the angel
of the LORD appeared to the woman
and said to her, 'Although you are barren, having borne no children, you shall
conceive and bear a son. 4Now be careful not to drink wine or strong drink, or
to eat anything unclean, 5for you shall
conceive and bear a son. No razor is to
come on his head, for the boy shall be
a nazirite[u] to God from birth. It is he
who shall begin to deliver Israel from
the hand of the Philistines.' 6Then the
woman came and told her husband, 'A
man of God came to me, and his appearance was like that of an angel[v] of God,
most awe-inspiring; I did not ask him
where he came from, and he did not tell
me his name; 7but he said to me, "You
shall conceive and bear a son. So then
drink no wine or strong drink, and eat
nothing unclean, for the boy shall be a
nazirite[w] to God from birth to the day
of his death." '

8 Then Manoah entreated the LORD,
and said, 'O LORD, I pray, let the man
of God whom you sent come to us again
and teach us what we are to do concerning the boy who will be born.' 9God listened to Manoah, and the angel of God
came again to the woman as she sat
in the field; but her husband Manoah
was not with her. 10So the woman ran
quickly and told her husband, 'The man
who came to me the other day has appeared to me.' 11Manoah got up and followed his wife, and came to the man
and said to him, 'Are you the man who
spoke to this woman?' And he said, 'I
am.' 12Then Manoah said, 'Now when
your words come true, what is to be the
boy's rule of life; what is he to do?' 13The
angel of the LORD said to Manoah, 'Let
the woman give heed to all that I said to
her. 14She may not eat of anything that
comes from the vine. She is not to drink
wine or strong drink, or eat any unclean
thing. She is to observe everything that
I commanded her.'

15 Manoah said to the angel of the
LORD, 'Allow us to detain you, and prepare a kid for you.' 16The angel of the
LORD said to Manoah, 'If you detain
me, I will not eat your food; but if you
want to prepare a burnt-offering, then
offer it to the LORD.' (For Manoah did
not know that he was the angel of the
LORD.) 17Then Manoah said to the angel
of the LORD, 'What is your name, so that
we may honour you when your words
come true?' 18But the angel of the LORD
said to him, 'Why do you ask my name?
It is too wonderful.'

19 So Manoah took the kid with the
grain-offering, and offered it on the rock
to the LORD, to him who works[x] wonders.[y] 20When the flame went up towards heaven from the altar, the angel
of the LORD ascended in the flame of the
altar while Manoah and his wife looked
on; and they fell on their faces to the
ground. 21The angel of the LORD did not
appear again to Manoah and his wife.
Then Manoah realized that it was the angel of the LORD. 22And Manoah said to
his wife, 'We shall surely die, for we have
seen God.' 23But his wife said to him, 'If
the LORD had meant to kill us, he would
not have accepted a burnt-offering and a
grain-offering at our hands, or shown us
all these things, or now announced to us
such things as these.'

24 The woman bore a son, and named
him Samson. The boy grew, and the
LORD blessed him. 25The spirit of the
LORD began to stir him in Mahaneh-
dan, between Zorah and Eshtaol.

SAMSON'S MARRIAGE

14 Once Samson went down to
Timnah, and at Timnah he saw
a Philistine woman. 2Then he came up,
and told his father and mother, 'I saw a
Philistine woman at Timnah; now get
her for me as my wife.' 3But his father
and mother said to him, 'Is there not a
woman among your kin, or among all
our[z] people, that you must go to take

[u] 13.5 That is *one separated* or *one consecrated*
[v] 13.6 Or *the angel* [w] 13.7 That is *one separated* or *one consecrated* [x] 13.19 Gk Vg: Heb *and working* [y] 13.19 Heb *wonders, while Manoah and his wife looked on* [z] 14.3 Cn: Heb *my*

a wife from the uncircumcised Philistines?' But Samson said to his father, 'Get her for me, because she pleases me.' 4 His father and mother did not know that this was from the LORD; for he was seeking a pretext to act against the Philistines. At that time the Philistines had dominion over Israel.

5 Then Samson went down with his father and mother to Timnah. When he came to the vineyards of Timnah, suddenly a young lion roared at him. 6 The spirit of the LORD rushed on him, and he tore the lion apart with his bare hands as one might tear apart a kid. But he did not tell his father or his mother what he had done. 7 Then he went down and talked with the woman, and she pleased Samson. 8 After a while he returned to marry her, and he turned aside to see the carcass of the lion, and there was a swarm of bees in the body of the lion, and honey. 9 He scraped it out into his hands, and went on, eating as he went. When he came to his father and mother, he gave some to them, and they ate it. But he did not tell them that he had taken the honey from the carcass of the lion.

10 His father went down to the woman, and Samson made a feast there as the young men were accustomed to do. 11 When the people saw him, they brought thirty companions to be with him. 12 Samson said to them, 'Let me now put a riddle to you. If you can explain it to me within the seven days of the feast, and find it out, then I will give you thirty linen garments and thirty festal garments. 13 But if you cannot explain it to me, then you shall give me thirty linen garments and thirty festal garments.' So they said to him, 'Ask your riddle; let us hear it.' 14 He said to them,

'Out of the eater came
something to eat.
Out of the strong came
something sweet.'

But for three days they could not explain the riddle.

15 On the fourth[a] day they said to Samson's wife, 'Coax your husband to explain the riddle to us, or we will burn you and your father's house with fire. Have you invited us here to impoverish us?' 16 So Samson's wife wept before him, saying, 'You hate me; you do not really love me. You have asked a riddle of my people, but you have not explained it to me.' He said to her, 'Look, I have not told my father or my mother. Why should I tell you?' 17 She wept before him for the seven days that their feast lasted; and because she nagged him, on the seventh day he told her. Then she explained the riddle to her people. 18 The men of the town said to him on the seventh day before the sun went down,

'What is sweeter than honey?
What is stronger than a lion?'

And he said to them,

'If you had not ploughed
with my heifer,
you would not have found
out my riddle.'

19 Then the spirit of the LORD rushed on him, and he went down to Ashkelon. He killed thirty men of the town, took their spoil, and gave the festal garments to those who had explained the riddle. In hot anger he went back to his father's house. 20 And Samson's wife was given to his companion, who had been his best man.

SAMSON DEFEATS THE PHILISTINES

15 After a while, at the time of the wheat harvest, Samson went to visit his wife, bringing along a kid. He said, 'I want to go into my wife's room.' But her father would not allow him to go in. 2 Her father said, 'I was sure that you had rejected her; so I gave her to your companion. Is not her younger sister prettier than she? Why not take her instead?' 3 Samson said to them, 'This time, when I do mischief to the Philistines, I will be without blame.' 4 So Samson went and caught three hundred foxes, and took some torches; and he turned the foxes[b] tail to tail, and put a torch between each pair of tails. 5 When he had set fire to the torches, he let the foxes go into the standing grain of the Philistines, and burned up the shocks and the standing grain, as well as the vineyards and[c] olive groves. 6 Then the Philistines asked, 'Who has done this?' And they said, 'Samson, the son-in-law of the Timnite, because he has taken Samson's wife and given her to his companion.' So the Philistines came up, and burned her and her father. 7 Samson said to them, 'If this is what you do, I swear I will not stop until I have taken revenge on you.' 8 He struck them down hip and thigh with great slaughter; and he went down and lived in the cleft of the rock of Etam.

[a] 14.15 Gk Syr: Heb *seventh* [b] 15.4 Heb *them*
[c] 15.5 Gk Tg Vg: Heb lacks *and*

9 Then the Philistines came up and
encamped in Judah, and made a raid
on Lehi. 10The men of Judah said, 'Why
have you come up against us?' They
said, 'We have come up to bind Samson,
to do to him as he did to us.' 11Then three
thousand men of Judah went down to
the cleft of the rock of Etam, and they
said to Samson, 'Do you not know that
the Philistines are rulers over us? What
then have you done to us?' He replied,
'As they did to me, so I have done to
them.' 12They said to him, 'We have come
down to bind you, so that we may give
you into the hands of the Philistines.'
Samson answered them, 'Swear to me
that you yourselves will not attack me.'
13They said to him, 'No, we will only
bind you and give you into their hands;
we will not kill you.' So they bound him
with two new ropes, and brought him
up from the rock.

14 When he came to Lehi, the Philistines came shouting to meet him; and
the spirit of the LORD rushed on him,
and the ropes that were on his arms became like flax that has caught fire, and
his bonds melted off his hands. 15Then
he found a fresh jawbone of a donkey,
reached down and took it, and with it
he killed a thousand men. 16And Samson said,

'With the jawbone of a donkey,
  heaps upon heaps,
with the jawbone of a donkey
  I have slain a thousand men.'

17When he had finished speaking, he
threw away the jawbone; and that place
was called Ramath-lehi.[d]

18 By then he was very thirsty, and
he called on the LORD, saying, 'You
have granted this great victory by the
hand of your servant. Am I now to die
of thirst, and fall into the hands of the
uncircumcised?' 19So God split open the
hollow place that is at Lehi, and water
came from it. When he drank, his spirit
returned, and he revived. Therefore it
was named En-hakkore,[e] which is at
Lehi to this day. 20And he judged Israel
in the days of the Philistines for twenty
years.

SAMSON AND DELILAH

16 Once Samson went to Gaza,
where he saw a prostitute and
went in to her. 2The Gazites were told,[f]
'Samson has come here.' So they encircled the place and lay in wait for him all
night at the city gate. They kept quiet
all night, thinking, 'Let us wait until
the light of the morning; then we will
kill him.' 3But Samson lay only until
midnight. Then at midnight he rose up,
took hold of the doors of the city gate
and the two posts, pulled them up, bar
and all, put them on his shoulders, and
carried them to the top of the hill that is
in front of Hebron.

4 After this he fell in love with a
woman in the valley of Sorek, whose
name was Delilah. 5The lords of the
Philistines came to her and said to her,
'Coax him, and find out what makes his
strength so great, and how we may over-
power him, so that we may bind him in
order to subdue him; and we will each
give you eleven hundred pieces of silver.'
6So Delilah said to Samson, 'Please tell
me what makes your strength so great,
and how you could be bound, so that
one could subdue you.' 7Samson said to
her, 'If they bind me with seven fresh
bowstrings that are not dried out, then
I shall become weak, and be like anyone
else.' 8Then the lords of the Philistines
brought her seven fresh bowstrings
that had not dried out, and she bound
him with them. 9While men were lying in wait in an inner chamber, she
said to him, 'The Philistines are upon
you, Samson!' But he snapped the bowstrings, as a strand of fibre snaps when
it touches the fire. So the secret of his
strength was not known.

10 Then Delilah said to Samson, 'You
have mocked me and told me lies; please
tell me how you could be bound.' 11He
said to her, 'If they bind me with new
ropes that have not been used, then I
shall become weak, and be like anyone
else.' 12So Delilah took new ropes and
bound him with them, and said to him,
'The Philistines are upon you, Samson!'
(The men lying in wait were in an inner
chamber.) But he snapped the ropes off
his arms like a thread.

13 Then Delilah said to Samson,
'Until now you have mocked me and
told me lies; tell me how you could be
bound.' He said to her, 'If you weave the
seven locks of my head with the web
and make it tight with the pin, then I
shall become weak, and be like anyone
else.' 14So while he slept, Delilah took
the seven locks of his head and wove
them into the web,[g] and made them

[d] **15.17** That is *The Hill of the Jawbone*
[e] **15.19** That is *The Spring of the One who Called*
[f] **16.2** Gk: Heb lacks *were told* [g] **16.14** Compare Gk: in verses 13–14, Heb lacks *and make it tight . . . into the web*

tight with the pin. Then she said to him,
'The Philistines are upon you, Samson!'
But he awoke from his sleep, and pulled
away the pin, the loom, and the web.
15 Then she said to him, 'How can
you say, "I love you", when your heart
is not with me? You have mocked me
three times now and have not told me
what makes your strength so great.'
16 Finally, after she had nagged him
with her words day after day, and pes-
tered him, he was tired to death. 17 So
he told her his whole secret, and said to
her, 'A razor has never come upon my
head; for I have been a nazirite[h] to God
from my mother's womb. If my head
were shaved, then my strength would
leave me; I would become weak, and be
like anyone else.'
18 When Delilah realized that he had
told her his whole secret, she sent and
called the lords of the Philistines, saying,
'This time come up, for he has told his
whole secret to me.' Then the lords of the
Philistines came up to her, and brought
the money in their hands. 19 She let him
fall asleep on her lap; and she called a
man, and had him shave off the seven
locks of his head. He began to weaken,[i]
and his strength left him. 20 Then she
said, 'The Philistines are upon you, Samson!' When he awoke from his sleep, he
thought, 'I will go out as at other times,
and shake myself free.' But he did not
know that the LORD had left him. 21 So
the Philistines seized him and gouged
out his eyes. They brought him down to
Gaza and bound him with bronze shackles; and he ground at the mill in the
prison. 22 But the hair of his head began
to grow again after it had been shaved.

SAMSON'S DEATH

23 Now the lords of the Philistines
gathered to offer a great sacrifice to
their god Dagon, and to rejoice; for they
said, 'Our god has given Samson our enemy into our hand.' 24 When the people
saw him, they praised their god; for they
said, 'Our god has given our enemy into
our hand, the ravager of our country,
who has killed many of us.' 25 And when
their hearts were merry, they said, 'Call
Samson, and let him entertain us.' So
they called Samson out of the prison,
and he performed for them. They made
him stand between the pillars; 26 and
Samson said to the attendant who held
him by the hand, 'Let me feel the pillars
on which the house rests, so that I may
lean against them.' 27 Now the house
was full of men and women; all the lords
of the Philistines were there, and on the
roof there were about three thousand
men and women, who looked on while
Samson performed.
28 Then Samson called to the LORD
and said, 'Lord GOD, remember me and
strengthen me only this once, O God,
so that with this one act of revenge I
may pay back the Philistines for my
two eyes.'[j] 29 And Samson grasped the
two middle pillars on which the house
rested, and he leaned his weight against
them, his right hand on the one and his
left hand on the other. 30 Then Samson
said, 'Let me die with the Philistines.'
He strained with all his might; and the
house fell on the lords and all the people who were in it. So those he killed at
his death were more than those he had
killed during his life. 31 Then his brothers
and all his family came down and took
him and brought him up and buried
him between Zorah and Eshtaol in the
tomb of his father Manoah. He had
judged Israel for twenty years.

MICAH AND THE LEVITE

17 There was a man in the hill country of Ephraim whose name was
Micah. 2 He said to his mother, 'The
eleven hundred pieces of silver that
were taken from you, about which you
uttered a curse, and even spoke it in my
hearing—that silver is in my possession; I took it; but now I will return it to
you.'[k] And his mother said, 'May my son
be blessed by the LORD!' 3 Then he returned the eleven hundred pieces of silver to his mother; and his mother said,
'I consecrate the silver to the LORD from
my hand for my son, to make an idol of
cast metal.' 4 So when he returned the
money to his mother, his mother took
two hundred pieces of silver, and gave
it to the silversmith, who made it into
an idol of cast metal; and it was in the
house of Micah. 5 This man Micah had a
shrine, and he made an ephod and teraphim, and installed one of his sons, who
became his priest. 6 In those days there
was no king in Israel; all the people did
what was right in their own eyes.
7 Now there was a young man of
Bethlehem in Judah, of the clan of Ju-

[h] **16.17** That is *one separated* or *one consecrated*
[i] **16.19** Gk: Heb *She began to torment him*
[j] **16.28** Or *so that I may be avenged upon the Philistines for one of my two eyes*
[k] **17.2** The words *but now I will return it to you* are transposed from the end of verse 3 in Heb

dah. He was a Levite residing there.
8This man left the town of Bethlehem
in Judah, to live wherever he could find
a place. He came to the house of Micah
in the hill country of Ephraim to carry
on his work.[l] 9Micah said to him, 'From
where do you come?' He replied, 'I am a
Levite of Bethlehem in Judah, and I am
going to live wherever I can find a place.'
10Then Micah said to him, 'Stay with me,
and be to me a father and a priest, and I
will give you ten pieces of silver a year,
a set of clothes, and your living.'[m] 11The
Levite agreed to stay with the man; and
the young man became to him like one
of his sons. 12So Micah installed the Levite, and the young man became his
priest, and was in the house of Micah.
13Then Micah said, 'Now I know that the
LORD will prosper me, because the Levite has become my priest.'

THE MIGRATION OF DAN

18 In those days there was no king
in Israel. And in those days the
tribe of the Danites was seeking for itself a territory to live in; for until then
no territory among the tribes of Israel had been allotted to them. 2So the
Danites sent five valiant men from the
whole number of their clan, from Zorah and from Eshtaol, to spy out the
land and to explore it; and they said to
them, 'Go, explore the land.' When they
came to the hill country of Ephraim, to
the house of Micah, they stayed there.
3While they were at Micah's house, they
recognized the voice of the young Levite; so they went over and asked him,
'Who brought you here? What are you
doing in this place? What is your business here?' 4He said to them, 'Micah
did such and such for me, and he hired
me, and I have become his priest.' 5Then
they said to him, 'Inquire of God that we
may know whether the mission we are
undertaking will succeed.' 6The priest
replied, 'Go in peace. The mission you
are on is under the eye of the LORD.'

7 The five men went on, and when
they came to Laish, they observed the
people who were there living securely,
after the manner of the Sidonians, quiet
and unsuspecting, lacking[n] nothing on
earth, and possessing wealth.[o] Furthermore, they were far from the Sidonians
and had no dealings with Aram.[p] 8When
they came to their kinsfolk at Zorah and
Eshtaol, they said to them, 'What do you
report?' 9They said, 'Come, let us go up
against them; for we have seen the land,
and it is very good. Will you do nothing? Do not be slow to go, but enter in
and possess the land. 10When you go,
you will come to an unsuspecting people. The land is broad—God has indeed
given it into your hands—a place where
there is no lack of anything on earth.'

11 Six hundred men of the Danite
clan, armed with weapons of war, set
out from Zorah and Eshtaol, 12and went
up and encamped at Kiriath-jearim
in Judah. On this account that place is
called Mahaneh-dan[q] to this day; it is
west of Kiriath-jearim. 13From there
they passed on to the hill country of
Ephraim, and came to the house of Micah.

14 Then the five men who had gone
to spy out the land (that is, Laish) said
to their comrades, 'Do you know that in
these buildings there are an ephod, teraphim, and an idol of cast metal? Now
therefore consider what you will do.'
15So they turned in that direction and
came to the house of the young Levite,
at the home of Micah, and greeted him.
16While the six hundred men of the
Danites, armed with their weapons of
war, stood by the entrance of the gate,
17the five men who had gone to spy out
the land proceeded to enter and take
the idol of cast metal, the ephod, and
the teraphim.[r] The priest was standing
by the entrance of the gate with the six
hundred men armed with weapons of
war. 18When the men went into Micah's
house and took the idol of cast metal,
the ephod, and the teraphim, the priest
said to them, 'What are you doing?'
19They said to him, 'Keep quiet! Put your
hand over your mouth, and come with
us, and be to us a father and a priest. Is
it better for you to be priest to the house
of one person, or to be priest to a tribe
and clan in Israel?' 20Then the priest accepted the offer. He took the ephod, the
teraphim, and the idol, and went along
with the people.

21 So they resumed their journey, putting the little ones, the livestock, and the goods in front of them.
22When they were some distance from
the home of Micah, the men who were
in the houses near Micah's house were

[l] **17.8** Or *Ephraim, continuing his journey*
[m] **17.10** Heb *living,' and the Levite went*
[n] **18.7** Cn Compare 18.10: Meaning of Heb uncertain
[o] **18.7** Meaning of Heb uncertain
[p] **18.7** Symmachus: Heb *with anyone*
[q] **18.12** That is *Camp of Dan*
[r] **18.17** Compare 17.4, 5; 18.14: Heb *teraphim and the cast metal*

called out, and they overtook the Danites. 23They shouted to the Danites, who
turned around and said to Micah, 'What
is the matter that you come with such
a company?' 24He replied, 'You take my
gods that I made, and the priest, and go
away, and what have I left? How then
can you ask me, "What is the matter?"'
25And the Danites said to him, 'You had
better not let your voice be heard among
us or else hot-tempered fellows will attack you, and you will lose your life and
the lives of your household.' 26Then the
Danites went on their way. When Micah
saw that they were too strong for him,
he turned and went back to his home.

THE DANITES SETTLE IN LAISH

27 The Danites, having taken what
Micah had made, and the priest who belonged to him, came to Laish, to a people quiet and unsuspecting, put them to
the sword, and burned down the city.
28There was no deliverer, because it was
far from Sidon and they had no dealings with Aram.[s] It was in the valley
that belongs to Beth-rehob. They rebuilt
the city, and lived in it. 29They named
the city Dan, after their ancestor Dan,
who was born to Israel; but the name
of the city was formerly Laish. 30Then
the Danites set up the idol for themselves. Jonathan son of Gershom, son
of Moses,[t] and his sons were priests to
the tribe of the Danites until the time
the land went into captivity. 31So they
maintained as their own Micah's idol
that he had made, as long as the house
of God was at Shiloh.

THE LEVITE'S CONCUBINE

19 In those days, when there was
no king in Israel, a certain Levite, residing in the remote parts of the
hill country of Ephraim, took to himself a concubine from Bethlehem in Judah. 2But his concubine became angry
with[u] him, and she went away from
him to her father's house at Bethlehem
in Judah, and was there for some four
months. 3Then her husband set out after her, to speak tenderly to her and
bring her back. He had with him his
servant and a couple of donkeys. When
he reached[v] her father's house, the girl's
father saw him and came with joy to
meet him. 4His father-in-law, the girl's
father, made him stay, and he remained
with him for three days; so they ate
and drank, and he[w] stayed there. 5On
the fourth day they got up early in the
morning, and he prepared to go; but
the girl's father said to his son-in-law,
'Fortify yourself with a bit of food, and
after that you may go.' 6So the two men
sat and ate and drank together; and the
girl's father said to the man, 'Why not
spend the night and enjoy yourself?'
7When the man got up to go, his father-
in-law kept urging him until he spent
the night there again. 8On the fifth
day he got up early in the morning to
leave; and the girl's father said, 'Fortify
yourself.' So they lingered[x] until the day
declined, and the two of them ate and
drank.[y] 9When the man with his concubine and his servant got up to leave, his
father-in-law, the girl's father, said to
him, 'Look, the day has worn on until it
is almost evening. Spend the night. See,
the day has drawn to a close. Spend the
night here and enjoy yourself. Tomorrow you can get up early in the morning
for your journey, and go home.'

10 But the man would not spend the
night; he got up and departed, and arrived opposite Jebus (that is, Jerusalem).
He had with him a couple of saddled
donkeys, and his concubine was with
him. 11When they were near Jebus, the
day was far spent, and the servant said
to his master, 'Come now, let us turn
aside to this city of the Jebusites, and
spend the night in it.' 12But his master
said to him, 'We will not turn aside into
a city of foreigners, who do not belong
to the people of Israel; but we will continue on to Gibeah.' 13Then he said to his
servant, 'Come, let us try to reach one
of these places, and spend the night at
Gibeah or at Ramah.' 14So they passed
by and went on their way; and the sun
went down on them near Gibeah, which
belongs to Benjamin. 15They turned
aside there, to go in and spend the night
at Gibeah. He went in and sat down in
the open square of the city, but no one
took them in to spend the night.

16 Then at evening there was an old
man coming from his work in the field.
The man was from the hill country of
Ephraim, and he was residing in Gibeah. (The people of the place were Benjaminites.) 17When the old man looked up
and saw the wayfarer in the open square

[s] **18.28** Cn Compare verse 7: Heb *with anyone*
[t] **18.30** Another reading is *son of Manasseh*
[u] **19.2** Gk OL: Heb *prostituted herself against*
[v] **19.3** Gk: Heb *she brought him to*
[w] **19.4** Compare verse 7 and Gk: Heb *they*
[x] **19.8** Cn: Heb *Linger* [y] **19.8** Gk: Heb lacks *and drank*

of the city, he said, 'Where are you going
and where do you come from?' 18He answered him, 'We are passing from Bethlehem in Judah to the remote parts of
the hill country of Ephraim, from which
I come. I went to Bethlehem in Judah;
and I am going to my home.[z] Nobody
has offered to take me in. 19We your servants have straw and fodder for our donkeys, with bread and wine for me and
the woman and the young man along
with us. We need nothing more.' 20The
old man said, 'Peace be to you. I will care
for all your wants; only do not spend the
night in the square.' 21So he brought him
into his house, and fed the donkeys; they
washed their feet, and ate and drank.

GIBEAH'S CRIME

22 While they were enjoying themselves, the men of the city, a depraved
lot, surrounded the house, and started
pounding on the door. They said to the
old man, the master of the house, 'Bring
out the man who came into your house,
so that we may have intercourse with
him.' 23And the man, the master of the
house, went out to them and said to
them, 'No, my brothers, do not act so
wickedly. Since this man is my guest,
do not do this vile thing. 24Here are my
virgin daughter and his concubine; let
me bring them out now. Ravish them
and do whatever you want to them; but
against this man do not do such a vile
thing.' 25But the men would not listen to him. So the man seized his concubine, and put her out to them. They
wantonly raped her, and abused her all
through the night until the morning.
And as the dawn began to break, they
let her go. 26As morning appeared, the
woman came and fell down at the door
of the man's house where her master
was, until it was light.

27 In the morning her master got
up, opened the doors of the house, and
when he went out to go on his way,
there was his concubine lying at the
door of the house, with her hands on
the threshold. 28'Get up,' he said to her,
'we are going.' But there was no answer.
Then he put her on the donkey; and the
man set out for his home. 29When he
had entered his house, he took a knife,
and grasping his concubine he cut her
into twelve pieces, limb by limb, and
sent her throughout all the territory
of Israel. 30Then he commanded the
men whom he sent, saying, 'Thus shall
you say to all the Israelites, "Has such a
thing ever happened[a] since the day that
the Israelites came up from the land of
Egypt until this day? Consider it, take
counsel, and speak out." '

THE OTHER TRIBES ATTACK BENJAMIN

20 Then all the Israelites came out,
from Dan to Beer-sheba, including the land of Gilead, and the congregation assembled in one body before the
LORD at Mizpah. 2The chiefs of all the
people, of all the tribes of Israel, presented themselves in the assembly of
the people of God, four hundred thousand foot-soldiers bearing arms. 3(Now
the Benjaminites heard that the people
of Israel had gone up to Mizpah.) And
the Israelites said, 'Tell us, how did this
criminal act come about?' 4The Levite,
the husband of the woman who was
murdered, answered, 'I came to Gibeah that belongs to Benjamin, I and
my concubine, to spend the night. 5The
lords of Gibeah rose up against me, and
surrounded the house at night. They intended to kill me, and they raped my
concubine until she died. 6Then I took
my concubine and cut her into pieces,
and sent her throughout the whole extent of Israel's territory; for they have
committed a vile outrage in Israel. 7So
now, you Israelites, all of you, give your
advice and counsel here and now.'

8 All the people got up as one, saying,
'We will not any of us go to our tents, nor
will any of us return to our houses. 9But
now this is what we will do to Gibeah:
we will go up[b] against it by lot. 10We will
take ten men of a hundred throughout
all the tribes of Israel, and a hundred of
a thousand, and a thousand of ten thousand, to bring provisions for the troops,
who are going to repay[c] Gibeah of Benjamin for all the disgrace that they have
done in Israel.' 11So all the men of Israel
gathered against the city, united as one.

12 The tribes of Israel sent men
through all the tribe of Benjamin, saying,
'What crime is this that has been committed among you? 13Now then, hand
over those scoundrels in Gibeah, so that
we may put them to death, and purge
the evil from Israel.' But the Benjaminites would not listen to their kinsfolk,
the Israelites. 14The Benjaminites came

[z] 19.18 Gk Compare 19.29. Heb *to the house of the* LORD [a] 19.30 Compare Gk: Heb [30]*And all who saw it said, 'Such a thing has not happened or been seen* [b] 20.9 Gk: Heb lacks *we will go up* [c] 20.10 Compare Gk: Meaning of Heb uncertain

together out of the towns to Gibeah, to
go out to battle against the Israelites.
15 On that day the Benjaminites mustered twenty-six thousand armed men
from their towns, besides the inhabitants of Gibeah. 16 Of all this force,
there were seven hundred picked men
who were left-handed; every one could
sling a stone at a hair, and not miss.
17 And the Israelites, apart from Benjamin, mustered four hundred thousand
armed men, all of them warriors.

18 The Israelites proceeded to go up
to Bethel, where they inquired of God,
'Which of us shall go up first to battle against the Benjaminites?' And the
LORD answered, 'Judah shall go up first.'

19 Then the Israelites got up in the
morning, and encamped against Gibeah. 20 The Israelites went out to battle
against Benjamin; and the Israelites
drew up the battle line against them at
Gibeah. 21 The Benjaminites came out
of Gibeah, and struck down on that day
twenty-two thousand of the Israelites.
23 [d] The Israelites went up and wept before the LORD until the evening; and they
inquired of the LORD, 'Shall we again
draw near to battle against our kinsfolk
the Benjaminites?' And the LORD said,
'Go up against them.' 22 The Israelites
took courage, and again formed the battle line in the same place where they had
formed it on the first day.

24 So the Israelites advanced against
the Benjaminites on the second day.
25 Benjamin moved out against them
from Gibeah the second day, and struck
down eighteen thousand of the Israelites, all of them armed men. 26 Then all
the Israelites, the whole army, went
back to Bethel and wept, sitting there
before the LORD; they fasted that day
until evening. Then they offered burnt-
offerings and sacrifices of well-being
before the LORD. 27 And the Israelites
inquired of the LORD (for the ark of
the covenant of God was there in those
days, 28 and Phinehas son of Eleazar, son
of Aaron, ministered before it in those
days), saying, 'Shall we go out once
more to battle against our kinsfolk the
Benjaminites, or shall we desist?' The
LORD answered, 'Go up, for tomorrow I
will give them into your hand.'

29 So Israel stationed men in ambush around Gibeah. 30 Then the Israelites went up against the Benjaminites
on the third day, and set themselves in
array against Gibeah, as before. 31 When
the Benjaminites went out against the
army, they were drawn away from the
city. As before they began to inflict casualties on the troops, along the main
roads, one of which goes up to Bethel
and the other to Gibeah, as well as in
the open country, killing about thirty
men of Israel. 32 The Benjaminites
thought, 'They are being routed before us, as previously.' But the Israelites said, 'Let us retreat and draw them
away from the city towards the roads.'
33 The main body of the Israelites drew
back its battle line to Baal-tamar, while
those Israelites who were in ambush
rushed out of their place west[e] of Geba.
34 There came against Gibeah ten thousand picked men out of all Israel, and
the battle was fierce. But the Benjaminites did not realize that disaster
was close upon them.

35 The LORD defeated Benjamin before Israel; and the Israelites destroyed
twenty-five thousand one hundred men
of Benjamin that day, all of them armed.

36 Then the Benjaminites saw that
they were defeated.[f]

The Israelites gave ground to Benjamin, because they trusted to the troops
in ambush that they had stationed
against Gibeah. 37 The troops in ambush
rushed quickly upon Gibeah. Then they
put the whole city to the sword. 38 Now
the agreement between the main body
of Israel and the men in ambush was
that when they sent up a cloud of smoke
out of the city 39 the main body of Israel
should turn in battle. But Benjamin had
begun to inflict casualties on the Israelites, killing about thirty of them; so they
thought, 'Surely they are defeated before
us, as in the first battle.' 40 But when the
cloud, a column of smoke, began to rise
out of the city, the Benjaminites looked
behind them—and there was the whole
city going up in smoke towards the sky!
41 Then the main body of Israel turned,
and the Benjaminites were dismayed,
for they saw that disaster was close upon
them. 42 Therefore they turned away
from the Israelites in the direction of the
wilderness; but the battle overtook them,
and those who came out of the city[g] were
slaughtering them in between.[h] 43 Cutting down[i] the Benjaminites, they pursued them from Nohah[j] and trod them

[d] **20.23** Verses 22 and 23 are transposed
[e] **20.33** Gk Vg: Heb *in the plain* [f] **20.36** This sentence is continued by verse 45.
[g] **20.42** Compare Vg and some Gk Mss: Heb *cities*
[h] **20.42** Compare Syr: Meaning of Heb uncertain
[i] **20.43** Gk: Heb *Surrounding* [j] **20.43** Gk: Heb *pursued them at their resting-place*

down as far as a place east of Gibeah.
44 Eighteen thousand Benjaminites fell,
all of them courageous fighters. 45 When
they turned and fled towards the wilderness to the rock of Rimmon, five thousand of them were cut down on the main
roads, and they were pursued as far as
Gidom, and two thousand of them were
slain. 46 So all who fell that day of Benjamin were twenty-five thousand arms-
bearing men, all of them courageous
fighters. 47 But six hundred turned and
fled towards the wilderness to the rock
of Rimmon, and remained at the rock
of Rimmon for four months. 48 Meanwhile, the Israelites turned back against
the Benjaminites, and put them to the
sword—the city, the people, the animals,
and all that remained. Also the remaining towns they set on fire.

THE BENJAMINITES SAVED FROM EXTINCTION

21 Now the Israelites had sworn
at Mizpah, 'No one of us shall
give his daughter in marriage to Benjamin.' 2 And the people came to Bethel,
and sat there until evening before God,
and they lifted up their voices and wept
bitterly. 3 They said, 'O LORD, the God of
Israel, why has it come to pass that today there should be one tribe lacking in
Israel?' 4 On the next day, the people got
up early, and built an altar there, and
offered burnt-offerings and sacrifices
of well-being. 5 Then the Israelites said,
'Which of all the tribes of Israel did not
come up in the assembly to the LORD?'
For a solemn oath had been taken concerning whoever did not come up to
the LORD to Mizpah, saying, 'That one
shall be put to death.' 6 But the Israelites
had compassion for Benjamin their kin,
and said, 'One tribe is cut off from Israel
this day. 7 What shall we do for wives for
those who are left, since we have sworn
by the LORD that we will not give them
any of our daughters as wives?'

8 Then they said, 'Is there anyone
from the tribes of Israel who did not
come up to the LORD to Mizpah?' It
turned out that no one from Jabesh-
gilead had come to the camp, to the assembly. 9 For when the roll was called
among the people, not one of the inhabitants of Jabesh-gilead was there. 10 So
the congregation sent twelve thousand
soldiers there and commanded them,
'Go, put the inhabitants of Jabesh-gilead
to the sword, including the women and
the little ones. 11 This is what you shall
do; every male and every woman that
has lain with a male you shall devote to
destruction.' 12 And they found among
the inhabitants of Jabesh-gilead four
hundred young virgins who had never
slept with a man and brought them to
the camp at Shiloh, which is in the land
of Canaan.

13 Then the whole congregation sent
word to the Benjaminites who were at
the rock of Rimmon, and proclaimed
peace to them. 14 Benjamin returned
at that time; and they gave them the
women whom they had saved alive of
the women of Jabesh-gilead; but they
did not suffice for them.

15 The people had compassion on
Benjamin because the LORD had made
a breach in the tribes of Israel. 16 So the
elders of the congregation said, 'What
shall we do for wives for those who are
left, since there are no women left in
Benjamin?' 17 And they said, 'There must
be heirs for the survivors of Benjamin,
in order that a tribe may not be blotted
out from Israel. 18 Yet we cannot give
any of our daughters to them as wives.'
For the Israelites had sworn, 'Cursed be
anyone who gives a wife to Benjamin.'
19 So they said, 'Look, the yearly festival
of the LORD is taking place at Shiloh,
which is north of Bethel, on the east of
the highway that goes up from Bethel to
Shechem, and south of Lebonah.' 20 And
they instructed the Benjaminites, saying, 'Go and lie in wait in the vineyards,
21 and watch; when the young women of
Shiloh come out to dance in the dances,
then come out of the vineyards and each
of you carry off a wife for himself from
the young women of Shiloh, and go to
the land of Benjamin. 22 Then if their fathers or their brothers come to complain
to us, we will say to them, "Be generous
and allow us to have them; because we
did not capture in battle a wife for each
man. But neither did you incur guilt by
giving your daughters to them." ' 23 The
Benjaminites did so; they took wives for
each of them from the dancers whom
they abducted. Then they went and returned to their territory, and rebuilt the
towns, and lived in them. 24 So the Israelites departed from there at that time
by tribes and families, and they went
out from there to their own territories.

25 In those days there was no king in
Israel; all the people did what was right
in their own eyes.

RUTH

A dramatic short story situated "in the days when the judges ruled" (1.1), the book of Ruth is about an Israelite woman, Naomi, and her Moabite daughter-in-law, Ruth, whose fortunes turn when Ruth becomes joined to the Israelite people through her marriage to Boaz. She bears a son, Obed, who becomes the father of Jesse, who in turn becomes the father of David. This story underscores the timeless values of loyalty, love of family, and openness to foreigners. It also marks an important step in the story of God's universal plan of salvation through the lineage of David.

Passages from Ruth are read during the liturgy on Friday and Saturday of the Twentieth Week of Year I.

ELIMELECH'S FAMILY GOES TO MOAB

1 In the days when the judges ruled,
there was a famine in the land, and
a certain man of Bethlehem in Judah
went to live in the country of Moab, he
and his wife and two sons. 2The name
of the man was Elimelech and the name
of his wife Naomi, and the names of
his two sons were Mahlon and Chilion;
they were Ephrathites from Bethlehem
in Judah. They went into the country of
Moab and remained there. 3But Elimelech, the husband of Naomi, died, and
she was left with her two sons. 4These
took Moabite wives; the name of one
was Orpah and the name of the other
Ruth. When they had lived there for
about ten years, 5both Mahlon and Chilion also died, so that the woman was left
without her two sons or her husband.

NAOMI AND HER MOABITE DAUGHTERS-IN-LAW

6 Then she started to return with
her daughters-in-law from the country of Moab, for she had heard in the
country of Moab that the LORD had
had consideration for his people and
given them food. 7So she set out from
the place where she had been living, she
and her two daughters-in-law, and they
went on their way to go back to the land
of Judah. 8But Naomi said to her two
daughters-in-law, 'Go back each of you
to your mother's house. May the LORD
deal kindly with you, as you have dealt
with the dead and with me. 9The LORD
grant that you may find security, each of
you in the house of your husband.' Then
she kissed them, and they wept aloud.
10They said to her, 'No, we will return
with you to your people.' 11But Naomi
said, 'Turn back, my daughters, why will
you go with me? Do I still have sons in
my womb that they may become your
husbands? 12Turn back, my daughters,
go your way, for I am too old to have a
husband. Even if I thought there was
hope for me, even if I should have a husband tonight and bear sons, 13would you
then wait until they were grown? Would
you then refrain from marrying? No,
my daughters, it has been far more bitter
for me than for you, because the hand of
the LORD has turned against me.' 14Then
they wept aloud again. Orpah kissed her
mother-in-law, but Ruth clung to her.

15 So she said, 'See, your sister-in-
law has gone back to her people and to
her gods; return after your sister-in-law.'
16But Ruth said,

'Do not press me to leave you
or to turn back from
following you!
Where you go, I will go;
where you lodge, I will lodge;
your people shall be my people,
and your God my God.
17 Where you die, I will die—
there will I be buried.

May the LORD do thus and so to me,
and more as well,
if even death parts me from you!'
18 When Naomi saw that she was determined to go with her, she said no more
to her.
19 So the two of them went on until they came to Bethlehem. When they
came to Bethlehem, the whole town
was stirred because of them; and the
women said, 'Is this Naomi?' 20 She said
to them,
'Call me no longer Naomi,[a]
call me Mara,[b]
for the Almighty[c] has dealt
bitterly with me.
21 I went away full,
but the LORD has brought
me back empty;
why call me Naomi
when the LORD has dealt
harshly with[d] me,
and the Almighty[e] has brought
calamity upon me?'
22 So Naomi returned together with
Ruth the Moabite, her daughter-in-law,
who came back with her from the country of Moab. They came to Bethlehem at
the beginning of the barley harvest.

RUTH MEETS BOAZ

2 Now Naomi had a kinsman on her
husband's side, a prominent rich
man, of the family of Elimelech, whose
name was Boaz. 2 And Ruth the Moabite said to Naomi, 'Let me go to the
field and glean among the ears of grain,
behind someone in whose sight I may
find favour.' She said to her, 'Go, my
daughter.' 3 So she went. She came and
gleaned in the field behind the reapers.
As it happened, she came to the part of
the field belonging to Boaz, who was
of the family of Elimelech. 4 Just then
Boaz came from Bethlehem. He said
to the reapers, 'The LORD be with you.'
They answered, 'The LORD bless you.'
5 Then Boaz said to his servant who was
in charge of the reapers, 'To whom does
this young woman belong?' 6 The servant who was in charge of the reapers
answered, 'She is the Moabite who came
back with Naomi from the country of
Moab. 7 She said, "Please let me glean
and gather among the sheaves behind
the reapers." So she came, and she has
been on her feet from early this morning until now, without resting even for
a moment.'[f]
8 Then Boaz said to Ruth, 'Now listen, my daughter, do not go to glean in
another field or leave this one, but keep
close to my young women. 9 Keep your
eyes on the field that is being reaped,
and follow behind them. I have ordered
the young men not to bother you. If you
get thirsty, go to the vessels and drink
from what the young men have drawn.'
10 Then she fell prostrate, with her face
to the ground, and said to him, 'Why
have I found favour in your sight, that
you should take notice of me, when I am
a foreigner?' 11 But Boaz answered her,
'All that you have done for your mother-
in-law since the death of your husband
has been fully told me, and how you left
your father and mother and your native
land and came to a people that you did
not know before. 12 May the LORD reward you for your deeds, and may you
have a full reward from the LORD, the
God of Israel, under whose wings you
have come for refuge!' 13 Then she said,
'May I continue to find favour in your
sight, my lord, for you have comforted
me and spoken kindly to your servant,
even though I am not one of your servants.'
14 At mealtime Boaz said to her,
'Come here, and eat some of this bread,
and dip your morsel in the sour wine.'
So she sat beside the reapers, and he
heaped up for her some parched grain.
She ate until she was satisfied, and she
had some left over. 15 When she got up to
glean, Boaz instructed his young men,
'Let her glean even among the standing
sheaves, and do not reproach her. 16 You
must also pull out some handfuls for her
from the bundles, and leave them for
her to glean, and do not rebuke her.'
17 So she gleaned in the field until
evening. Then she beat out what she had
gleaned, and it was about an ephah of
barley. 18 She picked it up and came into
the town, and her mother-in-law saw
how much she had gleaned. Then she
took out and gave her what was left over
after she herself had been satisfied. 19 Her
mother-in-law said to her, 'Where did
you glean today? And where have you
worked? Blessed be the man who took
notice of you.' So she told her mother-
in-law with whom she had worked, and
said, 'The name of the man with whom
I worked today is Boaz.' 20 Then Naomi
said to her daughter-in-law, 'Blessed be

[a] **1.20** That is *Pleasant* [b] **1.20** That is *Bitter*
[c] **1.20** Traditional rendering of Heb *Shaddai*
[d] **1.21** Or *has testified against* [e] **1.21** Traditional rendering of Heb *Shaddai* [f] **2.7** Compare Gk Vg: Meaning of Heb uncertain

he by the LORD, whose kindness has not
forsaken the living or the dead!' Naomi
also said to her, 'The man is a relative
of ours, one of our nearest kin.'[g] 21Then
Ruth the Moabite said, 'He even said
to me, "Stay close by my servants, until they have finished all my harvest." '
22Naomi said to Ruth, her daughter-in-
law, 'It is better, my daughter, that you
go out with his young women, otherwise you might be bothered in another
field.' 23So she stayed close to the young
women of Boaz, gleaning until the end
of the barley and wheat harvests; and
she lived with her mother-in-law.

RUTH AND BOAZ AT THE THRESHING-FLOOR

3 Naomi her mother-in-law said to
her, 'My daughter, I need to seek
some security for you, so that it may be
well with you. 2Now here is our kinsman Boaz, with whose young women
you have been working. See, he is win-
nowing barley tonight at the threshing-
floor. 3Now wash and anoint yourself,
and put on your best clothes and go
down to the threshing-floor; but do not
make yourself known to the man until
he has finished eating and drinking.
4When he lies down, observe the place
where he lies; then, go and uncover his
feet and lie down; and he will tell you
what to do.' 5She said to her, 'All that
you tell me I will do.'

6 So she went down to the threshing-
floor and did just as her mother-in-law
had instructed her. 7When Boaz had
eaten and drunk, and he was in a con-
tented mood, he went to lie down at the
end of the heap of grain. Then she came
quietly and uncovered his feet, and lay
down. 8At midnight the man was startled and turned over, and there, lying at
his feet, was a woman! 9He said, 'Who
are you?' And she answered, 'I am Ruth,
your servant; spread your cloak over
your servant, for you are next-of-kin.'[h]
10He said, 'May you be blessed by the
LORD, my daughter; this last instance of
your loyalty is better than the first; you
have not gone after young men, whether
poor or rich. 11And now, my daughter,
do not be afraid; I will do for you all that
you ask, for all the assembly of my people know that you are a worthy woman.
12But now, though it is true that I am
a near kinsman, there is another kinsman more closely related than I. 13Re-
main this night, and in the morning, if
he will act as next-of-kin[i] for you, good;
let him do so. If he is not willing to act as
next-of-kin[j] for you, then, as the LORD
lives, I will act as next-of-kin[k] for you.
Lie down until the morning.'

14 So she lay at his feet until morning, but got up before one person could
recognize another; for he said, 'It must
not be known that the woman came
to the threshing-floor.' 15Then he said,
'Bring the cloak you are wearing and
hold it out.' So she held it, and he measured out six measures of barley, and put
it on her back; then he went into the
city. 16She came to her mother-in-law,
who said, 'How did things go with you,[l]
my daughter?' Then she told her all that
the man had done for her, 17saying, 'He
gave me these six measures of barley, for
he said, "Do not go back to your mother-
in-law empty-handed." ' 18She replied,
'Wait, my daughter, until you learn how
the matter turns out, for the man will
not rest, but will settle the matter today.'

THE MARRIAGE OF BOAZ AND RUTH

4 No sooner had Boaz gone up to the
gate and sat down there than the
next-of-kin,[m] of whom Boaz had spoken,
came passing by. So Boaz said, 'Come
over, friend; sit down here.' And he went
over and sat down. 2Then Boaz took ten
men of the elders of the city, and said,
'Sit down here'; so they sat down. 3He
then said to the next-of-kin,[n] 'Naomi,
who has come back from the country of
Moab, is selling the parcel of land that
belonged to our kinsman Elimelech. 4So
I thought I would tell you of it, and say:
Buy it in the presence of those sitting
here, and in the presence of the elders of
my people. If you will redeem it, redeem
it; but if you will not, tell me, so that I
may know; for there is no one prior to
you to redeem it, and I come after you.'
So he said, 'I will redeem it.' 5Then Boaz
said, 'The day you acquire the field from
the hand of Naomi, you are also acquiring Ruth[o] the Moabite, the widow of the
dead man, to maintain the dead man's
name on his inheritance.' 6At this, the
next-of-kin[p] said, 'I cannot redeem it for
myself without damaging my own in-

[g] **2.20** *Or one with the right to redeem* [h] **3.9** *Or one with the right to redeem* [i] **3.13** *Or one with the right to redeem* [j] **3.13** *Or one with the right to redeem* [k] **3.13** *Or one with the right to redeem* [l] **3.16** *Or 'Who are you,* [m] **4.1** *Or one with the right to redeem* [n] **4.3** *Or one with the right to redeem* [o] **4.5** OL Vg: Heb *from the hand of Naomi and from Ruth* [p] **4.6** *Or one with the right to redeem*

heritance. Take my right of redemption
yourself, for I cannot redeem it.'
7 Now this was the custom in former
times in Israel concerning redeeming
and exchanging: to confirm a trans-
action, one party took off a sandal and
gave it to the other; this was the manner of attesting in Israel. 8 So when the
next-of-kin[q] said to Boaz, 'Acquire it for
yourself', he took off his sandal. 9 Then
Boaz said to the elders and all the people, 'Today you are witnesses that I
have acquired from the hand of Naomi
all that belonged to Elimelech and all
that belonged to Chilion and Mahlon.
10 I have also acquired Ruth the Moabite, the wife of Mahlon, to be my wife,
to maintain the dead man's name on
his inheritance, in order that the name
of the dead may not be cut off from his
kindred and from the gate of his native
place; today you are witnesses.' 11 Then
all the people who were at the gate,
along with the elders, said, 'We are witnesses. May the LORD make the woman
who is coming into your house like Rachel and Leah, who together built up
the house of Israel. May you produce
children in Ephrathah and bestow a
name in Bethlehem; 12 and, through the
children that the LORD will give you by
this young woman, may your house be
like the house of Perez, whom Tamar
bore to Judah.'

THE GENEALOGY OF DAVID

13 So Boaz took Ruth and she became
his wife. When they came together, the
LORD made her conceive, and she bore a
son. 14 Then the women said to Naomi,
'Blessed be the LORD, who has not left
you this day without next-of-kin;[r] and
may his name be renowned in Israel!
15 He shall be to you a restorer of life and
a nourisher of your old age; for your
daughter-in-law who loves you, who is
more to you than seven sons, has borne
him.' 16 Then Naomi took the child and
laid him in her bosom, and became his
nurse. 17 The women of the neighbourhood gave him a name, saying, 'A son
has been born to Naomi.' They named
him Obed; he became the father of Jesse,
the father of David.
18 Now these are the descendants of
Perez: Perez became the father of Hezron, 19 Hezron of Ram, Ram of Amminadab, 20 Amminadab of Nahshon, Nahshon of Salmon, 21 Salmon of Boaz, Boaz
of Obed, 22 Obed of Jesse, and Jesse of
David.

[q] 4.8 *Or one with the right to redeem* [r] 4.14 *Or one with the right to redeem*

1 SAMUEL

Samuel plays a prominent role in the first section of the story in 1 Samuel. Samuel was responsible for David being identified and eventually established as king. The book is the first part of a two-part narrative that carries the story of the Israelite history from the time of the judges to the beginnings of the monarchy in Israel under Saul and then under David. The Deuteronomistic perspective dominates the narrative as it stresses obedience to the covenant, Jerusalem as the central place of worship, and the kingship of David.

First Samuel is read consecutively during Year II of the weekday liturgical calendar from Monday of the First Week of the Year until Friday of the Second Week of the Year. In these passages, the birth of Samuel, his call to be prophet of Israel, his leadership over the people of Israel, the anointing of Saul as king, and the replacement of Saul with David as the anointed one are all remembered in the liturgical context.

SAMUEL'S BIRTH AND DEDICATION

1 There was a certain man of Ra-
mathaim, a Zuphite[a] from the hill
country of Ephraim, whose name was
Elkanah son of Jeroham son of Elihu
son of Tohu son of Zuph, an Ephraimite. 2He had two wives; the name of one
was Hannah, and the name of the other
Peninnah. Peninnah had children, but
Hannah had no children.

3 Now this man used to go up year
by year from his town to worship and to
sacrifice to the LORD of hosts at Shiloh,
where the two sons of Eli, Hophni and
Phinehas, were priests of the LORD. 4On
the day when Elkanah sacrificed, he
would give portions to his wife Peninnah and to all her sons and daughters;
5but to Hannah he gave a double portion,[b] because he loved her, though the
LORD had closed her womb. 6Her rival
used to provoke her severely, to irritate
her, because the LORD had closed her
womb. 7So it went on year after year;
as often as she went up to the house
of the LORD, she used to provoke her.
Therefore Hannah wept and would not
eat. 8Her husband Elkanah said to her,
'Hannah, why do you weep? Why do you
not eat? Why is your heart sad? Am I
not more to you than ten sons?'

9 After they had eaten and drunk at
Shiloh, Hannah rose and presented herself before the LORD.[c] Now Eli the priest
was sitting on the seat beside the doorpost of the temple of the LORD. 10She
was deeply distressed and prayed to the
LORD, and wept bitterly. 11She made
this vow: 'O LORD of hosts, if only you
will look on the misery of your servant,
and remember me, and not forget your
servant, but will give to your servant a
male child, then I will set him before
you as a nazirite[d] until the day of his
death. He shall drink neither wine nor
intoxicants,[e] and no razor shall touch
his head.'

12 As she continued praying before
the LORD, Eli observed her mouth.
13Hannah was praying silently; only her
lips moved, but her voice was not heard;
therefore Eli thought she was drunk.
14So Eli said to her, 'How long will you
make a drunken spectacle of yourself?
Put away your wine.' 15But Hannah an-

[a] 1.1 Compare Gk and 1 Chr 6.35–36: Heb *Ramathaim-zophim* [b] 1.5 Syr: Meaning of Heb uncertain [c] 1.9 Gk: Heb lacks *and presented herself before the LORD* [d] 1.11 That is one *separated* or *one consecrated* [e] 1.11 Cn Compare Gk Q Ms 1.22: MT *then I will give him to the LORD all the days of his life*

swered, 'No, my lord, I am a woman
deeply troubled; I have drunk neither
wine nor strong drink, but I have been
pouring out my soul before the LORD.
16Do not regard your servant as a worthless woman, for I have been speaking
out of my great anxiety and vexation all
this time.' 17Then Eli answered, 'Go in
peace; the God of Israel grant the petition you have made to him.' 18And she
said, 'Let your servant find favour in
your sight.' Then the woman went to
her quarters,[f] ate and drank with her
husband,[g] and her countenance was sad
no longer.[h]

19 They rose early in the morning
and worshipped before the LORD; then
they went back to their house at Ramah.
Elkanah knew his wife Hannah, and the
LORD remembered her. 20In due time
Hannah conceived and bore a son. She
named him Samuel, for she said, 'I have
asked him of the LORD.'

21 The man Elkanah and all his
household went up to offer to the LORD
the yearly sacrifice, and to pay his vow.
22But Hannah did not go up, for she said
to her husband, 'As soon as the child is
weaned, I will bring him, that he may
appear in the presence of the LORD, and
remain there for ever; I will offer him as
a nazirite[i] for all time.'[j] 23Her husband
Elkanah said to her, 'Do what seems
best to you, wait until you have weaned
him; only—may the LORD establish his
word.'[k] So the woman remained and
nursed her son, until she weaned him.
24When she had weaned him, she took
him up with her, along with a three-
year-old bull,[l] an ephah of flour, and a
skin of wine. She brought him to the
house of the LORD at Shiloh; and the
child was young. 25Then they slaughtered the bull, and they brought the
child to Eli. 26And she said, 'Oh, my lord!
As you live, my lord, I am the woman
who was standing here in your presence,
praying to the LORD. 27For this child I
prayed; and the LORD has granted me
the petition that I made to him. 28There-
fore I have lent him to the LORD; as long
as he lives, he is given to the LORD.'

She left him there for[m] the LORD.

HANNAH'S PRAYER

2 Hannah prayed and said,
'My heart exults in the LORD;
my strength is exalted in my God.[n]
My mouth derides my enemies,
because I rejoice in my[o] victory.

2 'There is no Holy One like the LORD,
no one besides you;
there is no Rock like our God.
3 Talk no more so very proudly,
let not arrogance come
from your mouth;
for the LORD is a God of knowledge,
and by him actions are weighed.
4 The bows of the mighty are broken,
but the feeble gird on strength.
5 Those who were full have hired
themselves out for bread,
but those who were hungry
are fat with spoil.
The barren has borne seven,
but she who has many
children is forlorn.
6 The LORD kills and brings to life;
he brings down to Sheol
and raises up.
7 The LORD makes poor and makes rich;
he brings low, he also exalts.
8 He raises up the poor from the dust;
he lifts the needy from
the ash heap,
to make them sit with princes
and inherit a seat of honour.[p]
For the pillars of the earth
are the LORD's,
and on them he has set the world.

9 'He will guard the feet of his
faithful ones,
but the wicked shall be cut
off in darkness;
for not by might does one prevail.
10 The LORD! His adversaries
shall be shattered;
the Most High[q] will thunder
in heaven.
The LORD will judge the ends
of the earth;
he will give strength to his king,
and exalt the power of
his anointed.'

ELI'S WICKED SONS

11 Then Elkanah went home to Ramah, while the boy remained to minister

[f] **1.18** Gk: Heb *went on her way* [g] **1.18** Gk: Heb lacks *and drank with her husband* [h] **1.18** Gk: Meaning of Heb uncertain [i] **1.22** That is *one separated* or *one consecrated* [j] **1.22** Cn Compare Q Ms: MT lacks *I will offer him as a nazirite for all time* [k] **1.23** MT: Q Ms Gk Compare Syr *that which goes out of your mouth* [l] **1.24** Q Ms Gk Syr: MT *three bulls* [m] **1.28** Gk (Compare Q Ms) and Gk at 2.11: MT *And he* (that is, Elkanah) *worshipped there before* [n] **2.1** Gk: Heb *the LORD* [o] **2.1** Q Ms: MT *your* [p] **2.8** Gk (Compare Q Ms) adds *He grants the vow of the one who vows, and blesses the years of the just* [q] **2.10** Cn Heb *against him he*

to the LORD, in the presence of the
priest Eli.
12 Now the sons of Eli were scoundrels; they had no regard for the LORD
13or for the duties of the priests to the
people. When anyone offered sacrifice, the priest's servant would come,
while the meat was boiling, with a
three-pronged fork in his hand, 14and
he would thrust it into the pan, or kettle, or cauldron, or pot; all that the fork
brought up the priest would take for
himself.[r] This is what they did at Shiloh to all the Israelites who came there.
15Moreover, before the fat was burned,
the priest's servant would come and say
to the one who was sacrificing, 'Give
meat for the priest to roast; for he will
not accept boiled meat from you, but
only raw.' 16And if the man said to him,
'Let them burn the fat first, and then
take whatever you wish', he would say,
'No, you must give it now; if not, I will
take it by force.' 17Thus the sin of the
young men was very great in the sight
of the LORD; for they treated the offerings of the LORD with contempt.

THE CHILD SAMUEL AT SHILOH

18 Samuel was ministering before
the LORD, a boy wearing a linen ephod.
19His mother used to make for him a
little robe and take it to him each year,
when she went up with her husband
to offer the yearly sacrifice. 20Then Eli
would bless Elkanah and his wife, and
say, 'May the LORD repay[s] you with
children by this woman for the gift that
she made to[t] the LORD'; and then they
would return to their home.
21 And[u] the LORD took note of Hannah; she conceived and bore three sons
and two daughters. And the boy Samuel
grew up in the presence of the LORD.

PROPHECY AGAINST ELI'S HOUSEHOLD

22 Now Eli was very old. He heard
all that his sons were doing to all Israel, and how they lay with the women
who served at the entrance to the tent
of meeting. 23He said to them, 'Why do
you do such things? For I hear of your
evil dealings from all these people. 24No,
my sons; it is not a good report that I
hear the people of the LORD spreading
abroad. 25If one person sins against another, someone can intercede for the
sinner with the LORD;[v] but if someone
sins against the LORD, who can make
intercession?' But they would not listen
to the voice of their father; for it was the
will of the LORD to kill them.
26 Now the boy Samuel continued to
grow both in stature and in favour with
the LORD and with the people.
27 A man of God came to Eli and said
to him, 'Thus the LORD has said, "I revealed[w] myself to the family of your ancestor in Egypt when they were slaves[x]
to the house of Pharaoh. 28I chose him
out of all the tribes of Israel to be my
priest, to go up to my altar, to offer incense, to wear an ephod before me; and
I gave to the family of your ancestor all
my offerings by fire from the people of
Israel. 29Why then look with greedy
eye[y] at my sacrifices and my offerings
that I commanded, and honour your
sons more than me by fattening yourselves on the choicest parts of every offering of my people Israel?" 30Therefore
the LORD the God of Israel declares: "I
promised that your family and the family of your ancestor should go in and out
before me for ever"; but now the LORD
declares: "Far be it from me; for those
who honour me I will honour, and
those who despise me shall be treated
with contempt. 31See, a time is coming
when I will cut off your strength and
the strength of your ancestor's family,
so that no one in your family will live to
old age. 32Then in distress you will look
with greedy eye[z] on all the prosperity
that shall be bestowed upon Israel; and
no one in your family shall ever live to
old age. 33The only one of you whom I
shall not cut off from my altar shall be
spared to weep out his[a] eyes and grieve
his[b] heart; all the members of your
household shall die by the sword.[c] 34The
fate of your two sons, Hophni and Phinehas, shall be the sign to you—both of
them shall die on the same day. 35I will
raise up for myself a faithful priest, who
shall do according to what is in my heart
and in my mind. I will build him a sure
house, and he shall go in and out before
my anointed one for ever. 36Everyone
who is left in your family shall come to
implore him for a piece of silver or a loaf
of bread, and shall say, Please put me in

[r] **2.14** Gk Syr Vg: Heb *with it* [s] **2.20** Q Ms Gk: MT *give* [t] **2.20** Q Ms Gk: MT *for the petition that she asked of* [u] **2.21** Q Ms Gk: MT *When* [v] **2.25** Gk Compare Q Ms: MT *another, God will mediate for him* [w] **2.27** Gk Tg Syr: Heb *Did I reveal* [x] **2.27** Q Ms Gk: MT lacks *slaves* [y] **2.29** Q Ms Gk: MT *then kick* [z] **2.32** Q Ms Gk: MT *will kick* [a] **2.33** Q Ms Gk: MT *your* [b] **2.33** Q Ms Gk: Heb *your* [c] **2.33** Q Ms See Gk: MT *die like mortals*

one of the priest's places, that I may eat
a morsel of bread." '

SAMUEL'S CALLING AND PROPHETIC ACTIVITY

3 Now the boy Samuel was ministering to the LORD under Eli. The word
of the LORD was rare in those days; visions were not widespread.
2 At that time Eli, whose eyesight
had begun to grow dim so that he could
not see, was lying down in his room;
3the lamp of God had not yet gone out,
and Samuel was lying down in the temple of the LORD, where the ark of God
was. 4Then the LORD called, 'Samuel!
Samuel!'[d] and he said, 'Here I am!' 5and
ran to Eli, and said, 'Here I am, for you
called me.' But he said, 'I did not call; lie
down again.' So he went and lay down.
6The LORD called again, 'Samuel!' Samuel got up and went to Eli, and said,
'Here I am, for you called me.' But he
said, 'I did not call, my son; lie down
again.' 7Now Samuel did not yet know
the LORD, and the word of the LORD
had not yet been revealed to him. 8The
LORD called Samuel again, a third time.
And he got up and went to Eli, and said,
'Here I am, for you called me.' Then Eli
perceived that the LORD was calling the
boy. 9Therefore Eli said to Samuel, 'Go,
lie down; and if he calls you, you shall
say, "Speak, LORD, for your servant is
listening." ' So Samuel went and lay
down in his place.
10 Now the LORD came and stood
there, calling as before, 'Samuel! Samuel!' And Samuel said, 'Speak, for your
servant is listening.' 11Then the LORD
said to Samuel, 'See, I am about to do
something in Israel that will make both
ears of anyone who hears of it tingle.
12On that day I will fulfil against Eli
all that I have spoken concerning his
house, from beginning to end. 13For I
have told him that I am about to punish
his house for ever, for the iniquity that
he knew, because his sons were blaspheming God,[e] and he did not restrain
them. 14Therefore I swear to the house
of Eli that the iniquity of Eli's house
shall not be expiated by sacrifice or offering for ever.'
15 Samuel lay there until morning;
then he opened the doors of the house
of the LORD. Samuel was afraid to tell
the vision to Eli. 16But Eli called Samuel and said, 'Samuel, my son.' He said,
'Here I am.' 17Eli said, 'What was it that
he told you? Do not hide it from me.
May God do so to you and more also, if
you hide anything from me of all that
he told you.' 18So Samuel told him everything and hid nothing from him.
Then he said, 'It is the LORD; let him do
what seems good to him.'
19 As Samuel grew up, the LORD was
with him and let none of his words fall
to the ground. 20And all Israel from Dan
to Beer-sheba knew that Samuel was a
trustworthy prophet of the LORD. 21The
LORD continued to appear at Shiloh, for
the LORD revealed himself to Samuel at
4 Shiloh by the word of the LORD.
1And the word of Samuel came to
all Israel.

THE ARK OF GOD CAPTURED

In those days the Philistines mustered for war against Israel,[f] and Israel
went out to battle against them;[g] they
encamped at Ebenezer, and the Philistines encamped at Aphek. 2The Philistines drew up in line against Israel, and
when the battle was joined,[h] Israel was
defeated by the Philistines, who killed
about four thousand men on the field
of battle. 3When the troops came to the
camp, the elders of Israel said, 'Why has
the LORD put us to rout today before the
Philistines? Let us bring the ark of the
covenant of the LORD here from Shiloh,
so that he may come among us and save
us from the power of our enemies.' 4So
the people sent to Shiloh, and brought
from there the ark of the covenant of
the LORD of hosts, who is enthroned
on the cherubim. The two sons of Eli,
Hophni and Phinehas, were there with
the ark of the covenant of God.
5 When the ark of the covenant of
the LORD came into the camp, all Israel
gave a mighty shout, so that the earth
resounded. 6When the Philistines heard
the noise of the shouting, they said,
'What does this great shouting in the
camp of the Hebrews mean?' When they
learned that the ark of the LORD had
come to the camp, 7the Philistines were
afraid; for they said, 'Gods have[i] come
into the camp.' They also said, 'Woe to us!
For nothing like this has happened before. 8Woe to us! Who can deliver us from
the power of these mighty gods? These
are the gods who struck the Egyptians

[d] **3.4** Q Ms Gk See 3.10: MT *the LORD called Samuel*
[e] **3.13** Another reading is *for themselves*
[f] **4.1** Gk: Heb lacks *In those days the Philistines mustered for war against Israel* [g] **4.1** Gk: Heb *against the Philistines* [h] **4.2** Meaning of Heb uncertain [i] **4.7** Or *A god has*

with every sort of plague in the wilderness. 9Take courage, and be men, O Philistines, in order not to become slaves to the Hebrews as they have been to you; be men and fight.'

10 So the Philistines fought; Israel was defeated, and they fled, everyone to his home. There was a very great slaughter, for there fell of Israel thirty thousand foot-soldiers. 11The ark of God was captured; and the two sons of Eli, Hophni and Phinehas, died.

DEATH OF ELI

12 A man of Benjamin ran from the battle line, and came to Shiloh the same day, with his clothes torn and with earth upon his head. 13When he arrived, Eli was sitting upon his seat by the road watching, for his heart trembled for the ark of God. When the man came into the city and told the news, all the city cried out. 14When Eli heard the sound of the outcry, he said, 'What is this uproar?' Then the man came quickly and told Eli. 15Now Eli was ninety-eight years old and his eyes were set, so that he could not see. 16The man said to Eli, 'I have just come from the battle; I fled from the battle today.' He said, 'How did it go, my son?' 17The messenger replied, 'Israel has fled before the Philistines, and there has also been a great slaughter among the troops; your two sons also, Hophni and Phinehas, are dead, and the ark of God has been captured.' 18When he mentioned the ark of God, Eli[j] fell over backwards from his seat by the side of the gate; and his neck was broken and he died, for he was an old man, and heavy. He had judged Israel for forty years.

19 Now his daughter-in-law, the wife of Phinehas, was pregnant, about to give birth. When she heard the news that the ark of God was captured, and that her father-in-law and her husband were dead, she bowed and gave birth; for her labour pains overwhelmed her. 20As she was about to die, the women attending her said to her, 'Do not be afraid, for you have borne a son.' But she did not answer or give heed. 21She named the child Ichabod, meaning, 'The glory has departed from Israel', because the ark of God had been captured and because of her father-in-law and her husband. 22She said, 'The glory has departed from Israel, for the ark of God has been captured.'

THE PHILISTINES AND THE ARK

5 When the Philistines captured the ark of God, they brought it from Ebenezer to Ashdod; 2then the Philistines took the ark of God and brought it into the house of Dagon and placed it beside Dagon. 3When the people of Ashdod rose early the next day, there was Dagon, fallen on his face to the ground before the ark of the LORD. So they took Dagon and put him back in his place. 4But when they rose early on the next morning, Dagon had fallen on his face to the ground before the ark of the LORD, and the head of Dagon and both his hands were lying cut off upon the threshold; only the trunk of[k] Dagon was left to him. 5This is why the priests of Dagon and all who enter the house of Dagon do not step on the threshold of Dagon in Ashdod to this day.

6 The hand of the LORD was heavy upon the people of Ashdod, and he terrified and struck them with tumours, both in Ashdod and in its territory. 7And when the inhabitants of Ashdod saw how things were, they said, 'The ark of the God of Israel must not remain with us; for his hand is heavy on us and on our god Dagon.' 8So they sent and gathered together all the lords of the Philistines, and said, 'What shall we do with the ark of the God of Israel?' The inhabitants of Gath replied, 'Let the ark of God be moved on to us.'[l] So they moved the ark of the God of Israel to Gath.[m] 9But after they had brought it to Gath,[n] the hand of the LORD was against the city, causing a very great panic; he struck the inhabitants of the city, both young and old, so that tumours broke out on them. 10So they sent the ark of the God of Israel[o] to Ekron. But when the ark of God came to Ekron, the people of Ekron cried out, 'Why[p] have they brought across to us[q] the ark of the God of Israel to kill us[r] and our[s] people?' 11They sent therefore and gathered together all the lords of the Philistines, and said, 'Send away the ark of the God of Israel, and let it return to its own place, that it may not kill us and our people.' For there was a deathly panic[t] throughout the whole city. The hand of God was very heavy

[j] 4.18 Heb *he* [k] 5.4 Heb lacks *the trunk of*
[l] 5.8 Gk Compare Q Ms: MT *They answered, 'Let the ark of the God of Israel be brought across to Gath.'* [m] 5.8 Gk: Heb lacks *to Gath* [n] 5.9 Q Ms: MT lacks *to Gath* [o] 5.10 Q Ms Gk: MT lacks *of Israel* [p] 5.10 Q Ms Gk: MT lacks *Why*
[q] 5.10 Heb *me* [r] 5.10 Heb *me* [s] 5.10 Heb *my*
[t] 5.11 Q Ms reads *a panic from the LORD*

there; 12 those who did not die were stricken with tumours, and the cry of the city went up to heaven.

THE ARK RETURNED TO ISRAEL

6 The ark of the LORD was in the country of the Philistines for seven months. 2 Then the Philistines called for the priests and the diviners and said, 'What shall we do with the ark of the LORD? Tell us what we should send with it to its place.' 3 They said, 'If you send away the ark of the God of Israel, do not send it empty, but by all means return him a guilt-offering. Then you will be healed and will be ransomed;[u] will not his hand then turn from you?' 4 And they said, 'What is the guilt-offering that we should return to him?' They answered, 'Five gold tumours and five gold mice, according to the number of the lords of the Philistines; for the same plague was upon all of you and upon your lords. 5 So you must make images of your tumours and images of your mice that ravage the land, and give glory to the God of Israel; perhaps he will lighten his hand on you and your gods and your land. 6 Why should you harden your hearts as the Egyptians and Pharaoh hardened their hearts? After he had made fools of them, did they not let the people go, and they departed? 7 Now then, get ready a new cart and two milch-cows that have never borne a yoke, and yoke the cows to the cart, but take their calves home, away from them. 8 Take the ark of the LORD and place it on the cart, and put in a box at its side the figures of gold, which you are returning to him as a guilt-offering. Then send it off, and let it go on its way. 9 And watch; if it goes up on the way to its own land, to Beth-shemesh, then it is he who has done us this great harm; but if not, then we shall know that it is not his hand that struck us; it happened to us by chance.'

10 The men did so; they took two milch-cows and yoked them to the cart, and shut up their calves at home. 11 They put the ark of the LORD on the cart, and the box with the gold mice and the images of their tumours. 12 The cows went straight in the direction of Beth-shemesh along one highway, lowing as they went; they turned neither to the right nor to the left, and the lords of the Philistines went after them as far as the border of Beth-shemesh.

13 Now the people of Beth-shemesh were reaping their wheat harvest in the valley. When they looked up and saw the ark, they went with rejoicing to meet it.[v] 14 The cart came into the field of Joshua of Beth-shemesh, and stopped there. A large stone was there; so they split up the wood of the cart and offered the cows as a burnt-offering to the LORD. 15 The Levites took down the ark of the LORD and the box that was beside it, in which were the gold objects, and set them upon the large stone. Then the people of Beth-shemesh offered burnt-offerings and presented sacrifices on that day to the LORD. 16 When the five lords of the Philistines saw it, they returned that day to Ekron.

17 These are the gold tumours, which the Philistines returned as a guilt-offering to the LORD: one for Ashdod, one for Gaza, one for Ashkelon, one for Gath, one for Ekron; 18 also the gold mice, according to the number of all the cities of the Philistines belonging to the five lords, both fortified cities and unwalled villages. The great stone, beside which they set down the ark of the LORD, is a witness to this day in the field of Joshua of Beth-shemesh.

THE ARK AT KIRIATH-JEARIM

19 The descendants of Jeconiah did not rejoice with the people of Beth-shemesh when they greeted[w] the ark of the LORD; and he killed seventy men of them.[x] The people mourned because the LORD had made a great slaughter among the people. 20 Then the people of Beth-shemesh said, 'Who is able to stand before the LORD, this holy God? To whom shall he go so that we may be rid of him?' 21 So they sent messengers to the inhabitants of Kiriath-jearim, saying, 'The Philistines have returned the ark of the LORD. Come down and

7 take it up to you.' 1 And the people of Kiriath-jearim came and took up the ark of the LORD, and brought it to the house of Abinadab on the hill. They consecrated his son, Eleazar, to have charge of the ark of the LORD.

2 From the day that the ark was lodged at Kiriath-jearim, a long time passed, some twenty years, and all the house of Israel lamented[y] after the LORD.

[u] **6.3** Q Ms Gk: MT *and it will be known to you*
[v] **6.13** Gk: Heb *rejoiced to see it*
[w] **6.19** Gk: Heb *And he killed some of the people of Beth-shemesh, because they looked into*
[x] **6.19** Heb *killed seventy men, fifty thousand men*
[y] **7.2** Meaning of Heb uncertain

SAMUEL AS JUDGE

3 Then Samuel said to all the house of
Israel, 'If you are returning to the LORD
with all your heart, then put away the
foreign gods and the Astartes from
among you. Direct your heart to the
LORD, and serve him only, and he will
deliver you out of the hand of the Philistines.' 4So Israel put away the Baals and
the Astartes, and they served the LORD
only.

5 Then Samuel said, 'Gather all Israel
at Mizpah, and I will pray to the LORD
for you.' 6So they gathered at Mizpah,
and drew water and poured it out before the LORD. They fasted that day, and
said, 'We have sinned against the LORD.'
And Samuel judged the people of Israel
at Mizpah.

7 When the Philistines heard that the
people of Israel had gathered at Mizpah, the lords of the Philistines went up
against Israel. And when the people of
Israel heard of it they were afraid of the
Philistines. 8The people of Israel said
to Samuel, 'Do not cease to cry out to
the LORD our God for us, and pray that
he may save us from the hand of the
Philistines.' 9So Samuel took a sucking
lamb and offered it as a whole burnt-
offering to the LORD; Samuel cried out
to the LORD for Israel, and the LORD answered him. 10As Samuel was offering
up the burnt-offering, the Philistines
drew near to attack Israel; but the LORD
thundered with a mighty voice that day
against the Philistines and threw them
into confusion; and they were routed
before Israel. 11And the men of Israel
went out of Mizpah and pursued the
Philistines, and struck them down as
far as beyond Beth-car.

12 Then Samuel took a stone and set
it up between Mizpah and Jeshanah,[z]
and named it Ebenezer;[a] for he said,
'Thus far the LORD has helped us.' 13So
the Philistines were subdued and did
not again enter the territory of Israel;
the hand of the LORD was against the
Philistines all the days of Samuel. 14The
towns that the Philistines had taken
from Israel were restored to Israel, from
Ekron to Gath; and Israel recovered
their territory from the hand of the
Philistines. There was peace also between Israel and the Amorites.

15 Samuel judged Israel all the days
of his life. 16He went on a circuit year
by year to Bethel, Gilgal, and Mizpah;
and he judged Israel in all these places.
17Then he would come back to Ramah,
for his home was there; he administered
justice there to Israel, and built there an
altar to the LORD.

ISRAEL DEMANDS A KING

8 When Samuel became old, he made
his sons judges over Israel. 2The
name of his firstborn son was Joel, and
the name of his second, Abijah; they
were judges in Beer-sheba. 3Yet his sons
did not follow in his ways, but turned
aside after gain; they took bribes and
perverted justice.

4 Then all the elders of Israel gathered together and came to Samuel at
Ramah, 5and said to him, 'You are old
and your sons do not follow in your
ways; appoint for us, then, a king to
govern us, like other nations.' 6But the
thing displeased Samuel when they
said, 'Give us a king to govern us.' Samuel prayed to the LORD, 7and the LORD
said to Samuel, 'Listen to the voice of
the people in all that they say to you;
for they have not rejected you, but they
have rejected me from being king over
them. 8Just as they have done to me,[b]
from the day I brought them up out
of Egypt to this day, forsaking me and
serving other gods, so also they are doing to you. 9Now then, listen to their
voice; only—you shall solemnly warn
them, and show them the ways of the
king who shall reign over them.'

10 So Samuel reported all the words
of the LORD to the people who were asking him for a king. 11He said, 'These will
be the ways of the king who will reign
over you: he will take your sons and appoint them to his chariots and to be his
horsemen, and to run before his chariots; 12and he will appoint for himself
commanders of thousands and commanders of fifties, and some to plough
his ground and to reap his harvest, and
to make his implements of war and the
equipment of his chariots. 13He will
take your daughters to be perfumers
and cooks and bakers. 14He will take the
best of your fields and vineyards and olive orchards and give them to his courtiers. 15He will take one-tenth of your
grain and of your vineyards and give
it to his officers and his courtiers. 16He
will take your male and female slaves,
and the best of your cattle[c] and donkeys,
and put them to his work. 17He will take
one-tenth of your flocks, and you shall

[z] 7.12 Gk Syr: Heb *Shen* [a] 7.12 That is *Stone of Help* [b] 8.8 Gk: Heb lacks *to me* [c] 8.16 Gk: Heb *young men*

be his slaves. 18And in that day you will
cry out because of your king, whom
you have chosen for yourselves; but the
LORD will not answer you in that day.'

ISRAEL'S REQUEST FOR A KING GRANTED

19 But the people refused to listen to
the voice of Samuel; they said, 'No! but
we are determined to have a king over
us, 20so that we also may be like other
nations, and that our king may govern us and go out before us and fight
our battles.' 21When Samuel had heard
all the words of the people, he repeated
them in the ears of the LORD. 22The
LORD said to Samuel, 'Listen to their
voice and set a king over them.' Samuel
then said to the people of Israel, 'Each of
you return home.'

SAUL CHOSEN TO BE KING

9 There was a man of Benjamin whose
name was Kish son of Abiel son of
Zeror son of Becorath son of Aphiah, a
Benjaminite, a man of wealth. 2He had
a son whose name was Saul, a handsome young man. There was not a man
among the people of Israel more handsome than he; he stood head and shoulders above everyone else.
3 Now the donkeys of Kish, Saul's father, had strayed. So Kish said to his son
Saul, 'Take one of the boys with you; go
and look for the donkeys.' 4He passed
through the hill country of Ephraim
and passed through the land of Shali-
shah, but they did not find them. And
they passed through the land of Shaa-
lim, but they were not there. Then he
passed through the land of Benjamin,
but they did not find them.
5 When they came to the land of
Zuph, Saul said to the boy who was with
him, 'Let us turn back, or my father will
stop worrying about the donkeys and
worry about us.' 6But he said to him,
'There is a man of God in this town; he is
a man held in honour. Whatever he says
always comes true. Let us go there now;
perhaps he will tell us about the journey
on which we have set out.' 7Then Saul replied to the boy, 'But if we go, what can
we bring the man? For the bread in our
sacks is gone, and there is no present to
bring to the man of God. What have we?'
8The boy answered Saul again, 'Here, I
have with me a quarter-shekel of silver;
I will give it to the man of God, to tell
us our way.' 9(Formerly in Israel, anyone who went to inquire of God would
say, 'Come, let us go to the seer'; for the
one who is now called a prophet was
formerly called a seer.) 10Saul said to the
boy, 'Good; come, let us go.' So they went
to the town where the man of God was.
11 As they went up the hill to the
town, they met some girls coming out
to draw water, and said to them, 'Is the
seer here?' 12They answered, 'Yes, there
he is just ahead of you. Hurry; he has
come just now to the town, because
the people have a sacrifice today at the
shrine. 13As soon as you enter the town,
you will find him, before he goes up to
the shrine to eat. For the people will
not eat until he comes, since he must
bless the sacrifice; afterwards those eat
who are invited. Now go up, for you will
meet him immediately.' 14So they went
up to the town. As they were entering
the town, they saw Samuel coming
out towards them on his way up to the
shrine.
15 Now the day before Saul came, the
LORD had revealed to Samuel: 16'Tomorrow about this time I will send to you
a man from the land of Benjamin, and
you shall anoint him to be ruler over my
people Israel. He shall save my people
from the hand of the Philistines; for I
have seen the suffering of[d] my people,
because their outcry has come to me.'
17When Samuel saw Saul, the LORD told
him, 'Here is the man of whom I spoke
to you. He it is who shall rule over my
people.' 18Then Saul approached Samuel inside the gate, and said, 'Tell me,
please, where is the house of the seer?'
19Samuel answered Saul, 'I am the seer;
go up before me to the shrine, for today
you shall eat with me, and in the morning I will let you go and will tell you all
that is on your mind. 20As for your donkeys that were lost three days ago, give
no further thought to them, for they
have been found. And on whom is all
Israel's desire fixed, if not on you and
on all your ancestral house?' 21Saul answered, 'I am only a Benjaminite, from
the least of the tribes of Israel, and my
family is the humblest of all the families
of the tribe of Benjamin. Why then have
you spoken to me in this way?'
22 Then Samuel took Saul and his
servant-boy and brought them into the
hall, and gave them a place at the head
of those who had been invited, of whom
there were about thirty. 23And Samuel said to the cook, 'Bring the portion

[d] 9.16 Gk: Heb lacks *the suffering of*

I gave you, the one I asked you to put
aside.' 24The cook took up the thigh and
what went with it[e] and set them before
Saul. Samuel said, 'See, what was kept
is set before you. Eat; for it is set[f] before
you at the appointed time, so that you
might eat with the guests.'[g]
So Saul ate with Samuel that day.
25When they came down from the
shrine into the town, a bed was spread
for Saul[h] on the roof, and he lay down
to sleep.[i] 26Then at the break of dawn[j]
Samuel called to Saul upon the roof, 'Get
up, so that I may send you on your way.'
Saul got up, and both he and Samuel
went out into the street.

SAMUEL ANOINTS SAUL

27 As they were going down to the
outskirts of the town, Samuel said to
Saul, 'Tell the boy to go on before us, and
when he has passed on, stop here yourself for a while, that I may make known
10 to you the word of God.' 1Sam-
uel took a phial of oil and poured
it on his head, and kissed him; he said,
'The LORD has anointed you ruler over
his people Israel. You shall reign over
the people of the LORD and you will
save them from the hand of their enemies all around. Now this shall be the
sign to you that the LORD has anointed
you ruler[k] over his heritage: 2When you
depart from me today you will meet two
men by Rachel's tomb in the territory of
Benjamin at Zelzah; they will say to you,
"The donkeys that you went to seek are
found, and now your father has stopped
worrying about them and is worrying about you, saying: What shall I do
about my son?" 3Then you shall go on
from there further and come to the oak
of Tabor; three men going up to God at
Bethel will meet you there, one carrying three kids, another carrying three
loaves of bread, and another carrying
a skin of wine. 4They will greet you and
give you two loaves of bread, which you
shall accept from them. 5After that you
shall come to Gibeath-elohim,[l] at the
place where the Philistine garrison is;
there, as you come to the town, you will
meet a band of prophets coming down
from the shrine with harp, tambourine, flute, and lyre playing in front of
them; they will be in a prophetic frenzy.
6Then the spirit of the LORD will possess you, and you will be in a prophetic
frenzy along with them and be turned
into a different person. 7Now when
these signs meet you, do whatever you
see fit to do, for God is with you. 8And
you shall go down to Gilgal ahead of me;
then I will come down to you to present burnt-offerings and offer sacrifices
of well-being. For seven days you shall
wait, until I come to you and show you
what you shall do.'

SAUL PROPHESIES

9 As he turned away to leave Samuel, God gave him another heart; and
all these signs were fulfilled that day.
10When they were going from there[m]
to Gibeah,[n] a band of prophets met
him; and the spirit of God possessed
him, and he fell into a prophetic frenzy
along with them. 11When all who knew
him before saw how he prophesied with
the prophets, the people said to one another, 'What has come over the son of
Kish? Is Saul also among the prophets?'
12A man of the place answered, 'And
who is their father?' Therefore it became a proverb, 'Is Saul also among the
prophets?' 13When his prophetic frenzy
had ended, he went home.[o]
14 Saul's uncle said to him and to the
boy, 'Where did you go?' And he replied,
'To seek the donkeys; and when we saw
they were not to be found, we went to
Samuel.' 15Saul's uncle said, 'Tell me
what Samuel said to you.' 16Saul said to
his uncle, 'He told us that the donkeys
had been found.' But about the matter of
the kingship, of which Samuel had spoken, he did not tell him anything.

SAUL PROCLAIMED KING

17 Samuel summoned the people
to the LORD at Mizpah 18and said to
them,[p] 'Thus says the LORD, the God of
Israel, "I brought up Israel out of Egypt,
and I rescued you from the hand of the
Egyptians and from the hand of all the
kingdoms that were oppressing you."
19But today you have rejected your God,
who saves you from all your calamities
and your distresses; and you have said,
"No! but set a king over us." Now therefore present yourselves before the LORD
by your tribes and by your clans.'

[e] **9.24** Meaning of Heb uncertain [f] **9.24** Q Ms Gk: MT *it was kept* [g] **9.24** Cn: Heb *it was kept for you, saying, I have invited the people* [h] **9.25** Gk: Heb *and he spoke with Saul* [i] **9.25** Gk: Heb lacks *and he lay down to sleep* [j] **9.26** Gk: Heb *and they arose early and at break of dawn* [k] **10.1** Gk: Heb lacks *over his people Israel. You shall . . . anointed you ruler* [l] **10.5** Or *the Hill of God* [m] **10.10** Gk: Heb *they came there* [n] **10.10** Or *the hill* [o] **10.13** Cn: Heb *he came to the shrine* [p] **10.18** Heb *to the people of Israel*

20 Then Samuel brought all the tribes
of Israel near, and the tribe of Benjamin
was taken by lot. 21He brought the tribe
of Benjamin near by its families, and
the family of the Matrites was taken by
lot. Finally he brought the family of the
Matrites near man by man,[q] and Saul
the son of Kish was taken by lot. But
when they sought him, he could not be
found. 22So they inquired again of the
LORD, 'Did the man come here?'[r] and
the LORD said, 'See, he has hidden himself among the baggage.' 23Then they
ran and brought him from there. When
he took his stand among the people, he
was head and shoulders taller than any
of them. 24Samuel said to all the people, 'Do you see the one whom the LORD
has chosen? There is no one like him
among all the people.' And all the people shouted, 'Long live the king!'

25 Samuel told the people the rights
and duties of the kingship; and he wrote
them in a book and laid it up before the
LORD. Then Samuel sent all the people
back to their homes. 26Saul also went to
his home at Gibeah, and with him went
warriors whose hearts God had touched.
27But some worthless fellows said, 'How
can this man save us?' They despised
him and brought him no present. But
he held his peace.

Now Nahash, king of the Ammonites, had been grievously oppressing the
Gadites and the Reubenites. He would
gouge out the right eye of each of them
and would not grant Israel a deliverer.
No one was left of the Israelites across
the Jordan whose right eye Nahash,
king of the Ammonites, had not gouged
out. But there were seven thousand
men who had escaped from the Ammonites and had entered Jabesh-gilead.[s]

SAUL DEFEATS THE AMMONITES

11 About a month later,[t] Nahash
the Ammonite went up and besieged Jabesh-gilead; and all the men of
Jabesh said to Nahash, 'Make a treaty
with us, and we will serve you.' 2But Nahash the Ammonite said to them, 'On
this condition I will make a treaty with
you, namely that I gouge out everyone's
right eye, and thus put disgrace upon
all Israel.' 3The elders of Jabesh said to
him, 'Give us seven days' respite that we
may send messengers through all the
territory of Israel. Then, if there is no
one to save us, we will give ourselves up
to you.' 4When the messengers came to
Gibeah of Saul, they reported the matter
in the hearing of the people; and all the
people wept aloud.

5 Now Saul was coming from the
field behind the oxen; and Saul said,
'What is the matter with the people,
that they are weeping?' So they told
him the message from the inhabitants
of Jabesh. 6And the spirit of God came
upon Saul in power when he heard
these words, and his anger was greatly
kindled. 7He took a yoke of oxen, and cut
them in pieces and sent them throughout all the territory of Israel by messengers, saying, 'Whoever does not come
out after Saul and Samuel, so shall it
be done to his oxen!' Then the dread of
the LORD fell upon the people, and they
came out as one. 8When he mustered
them at Bezek, those from Israel were
three hundred thousand, and those
from Judah seventy[u] thousand. 9They
said to the messengers who had come,
'Thus shall you say to the inhabitants
of Jabesh-gilead: "Tomorrow, by the
time the sun is hot, you shall have deliverance." ' When the messengers came
and told the inhabitants of Jabesh, they
rejoiced. 10So the inhabitants of Jabesh
said, 'Tomorrow we will give ourselves
up to you, and you may do to us whatever seems good to you.' 11The next day
Saul put the people in three companies.
At the morning watch they came into
the camp and cut down the Ammonites
until the heat of the day; and those who
survived were scattered, so that no two
of them were left together.

12 The people said to Samuel, 'Who is
it that said, "Shall Saul reign over us?"
Give them to us so that we may put them
to death.' 13But Saul said, 'No one shall be
put to death this day, for today the LORD
has brought deliverance to Israel.'

14 Samuel said to the people, 'Come,
let us go to Gilgal and there renew the
kingship.' 15So all the people went to
Gilgal, and there they made Saul king
before the LORD in Gilgal. There they
sacrificed offerings of well-being before
the LORD, and there Saul and all the Israelites rejoiced greatly.

SAMUEL'S FAREWELL ADDRESS

12 Samuel said to all Israel, 'I have
listened to you in all that you

[q] 10.21 Gk: Heb lacks *Finally . . . man by man*
[r] 10.22 Gk: Heb *Is there yet a man to come here?*
[s] 10.27 Q Ms Compare Josephus, *Antiquities* VI.v.1 (68–71): MT lacks *Now Nahash . . . entered Jabesh-gilead.*
[t] 11.1 Q Ms Gk: MT lacks *About a month later*
[u] 11.8 Q Ms Gk: MT *thirty*

have said to me, and have set a king over you. 2See, it is the king who leads you now; I am old and grey, but my sons are with you. I have led you from my youth until this day. 3Here I am; testify against me before the LORD and before his anointed. Whose ox have I taken? Or whose donkey have I taken? Or whom have I defrauded? Whom have I oppressed? Or from whose hand have I taken a bribe to blind my eyes with it? Testify against me[v] and I will restore it to you.' 4They said, 'You have not defrauded us or oppressed us or taken anything from the hand of anyone.' 5He said to them, 'The LORD is witness against you, and his anointed is witness this day, that you have not found anything in my hand.' And they said, 'He is witness.'

6 Samuel said to the people, 'The LORD is witness, who[w] appointed Moses and Aaron and brought your ancestors up out of the land of Egypt. 7Now therefore take your stand, so that I may enter into judgement with you before the LORD, and I will declare to you[x] all the saving deeds of the LORD that he performed for you and for your ancestors. 8When Jacob went into Egypt and the Egyptians oppressed them,[y] then your ancestors cried to the LORD and the LORD sent Moses and Aaron, who brought forth your ancestors out of Egypt, and settled them in this place. 9But they forgot the LORD their God; and he sold them into the hand of Sisera, commander of the army of King Jabin of[z] Hazor, and into the hand of the Philistines, and into the hand of the king of Moab; and they fought against them. 10Then they cried to the LORD, and said, "We have sinned, because we have forsaken the LORD, and have served the Baals and the Astartes; but now rescue us out of the hand of our enemies, and we will serve you." 11And the LORD sent Jerubbaal and Barak,[a] and Jephthah, and Samson,[b] and rescued you out of the hand of your enemies on every side; and you lived in safety. 12But when you saw that King Nahash of the Ammonites came against you, you said to me, "No, but a king shall reign over us", though the LORD your God was your king. 13See, here is the king whom you have chosen, for whom you have asked; see, the LORD has set a king over you. 14If you will fear the LORD and serve him and heed his voice and not rebel against the commandment of the LORD, and if both you and the king who reigns over you will follow the LORD your God, it will be well; 15but if you will not heed the voice of the LORD, but rebel against the commandment of the LORD, then the hand of the LORD will be against you and your king.[c] 16Now therefore take your stand and see this great thing that the LORD will do before your eyes. 17Is it not the wheat harvest today? I will call upon the LORD, that he may send thunder and rain; and you shall know and see that the wickedness that you have done in the sight of the LORD is great in demanding a king for yourselves.' 18So Samuel called upon the LORD, and the LORD sent thunder and rain that day; and all the people greatly feared the LORD and Samuel.

19 All the people said to Samuel, 'Pray to the LORD your God for your servants, so that we may not die; for we have added to all our sins the evil of demanding a king for ourselves.' 20And Samuel said to the people, 'Do not be afraid; you have done all this evil, yet do not turn aside from following the LORD, but serve the LORD with all your heart; 21and do not turn aside after useless things that cannot profit or save, for they are useless. 22For the LORD will not cast away his people, for his great name's sake, because it has pleased the LORD to make you a people for himself. 23Moreover as for me, far be it from me that I should sin against the LORD by ceasing to pray for you; and I will instruct you in the good and the right way. 24Only fear the LORD, and serve him faithfully with all your heart; for consider what great things he has done for you. 25But if you still do wickedly, you shall be swept away, both you and your king.'

SAUL'S UNLAWFUL SACRIFICE

13 Saul was . . .[d] years old when he began to reign; and he reigned for . . . and two[e] years over Israel.

2 Saul chose three thousand out of Israel; two thousand were with Saul in Michmash and the hill country of Bethel,

[v] 12.3 Gk: Heb lacks *Testify against me*
[w] 12.6 Gk: Heb lacks *is witness, who* [x] 12.7 Gk: Heb lacks *and I will declare to you* [y] 12.8 Gk: Heb lacks *and the Egyptians oppressed them*
[z] 12.9 Gk: Heb lacks *King Jabin of* [a] 12.11 Gk Syr: Heb *Bedan* [b] 12.11 Gk: Heb *Samuel*
[c] 12.15 Gk: Heb *and your ancestors* [d] 13.1 The number is lacking in the Heb text (the verse is lacking in the Septuagint). [e] 13.1 *Two* is not the entire number; something has dropped out.

and a thousand were with Jonathan in
Gibeah of Benjamin; the rest of the people he sent home to their tents. 3Jonathan
defeated the garrison of the Philistines
that was at Geba; and the Philistines
heard of it. And Saul blew the trumpet
throughout all the land, saying, 'Let the
Hebrews hear!' 4When all Israel heard
that Saul had defeated the garrison of the
Philistines, and also that Israel had become odious to the Philistines, the people
were called out to join Saul at Gilgal.

5 The Philistines mustered to fight
with Israel, thirty thousand chariots,
and six thousand horsemen, and troops
like the sand on the seashore in multitude; they came up and encamped at
Michmash, to the east of Beth-aven.
6When the Israelites saw that they were
in distress (for the troops were hard
pressed), the people hid themselves in
caves and in holes and in rocks and in
tombs and in cisterns. 7Some Hebrews
crossed the Jordan to the land of Gad
and Gilead. Saul was still at Gilgal, and
all the people followed him trembling.

8 He waited for seven days, the time
appointed by Samuel; but Samuel did
not come to Gilgal, and the people began
to slip away from Saul.[f] 9So Saul said,
'Bring the burnt-offering here to me,
and the offerings of well-being.' And he
offered the burnt-offering. 10As soon
as he had finished offering the burnt-
offering, Samuel arrived; and Saul went
out to meet him and salute him. 11Sam-
uel said, 'What have you done?' Saul replied, 'When I saw that the people were
slipping away from me, and that you did
not come within the days appointed,
and that the Philistines were mustering
at Michmash, 12I said, "Now the Philistines will come down upon me at Gilgal,
and I have not entreated the favour of
the LORD"; so I forced myself, and offered the burnt-offering.' 13Samuel said
to Saul, 'You have done foolishly; you
have not kept the commandment of the
LORD your God, which he commanded
you. The LORD would have established
your kingdom over Israel for ever, 14but
now your kingdom will not continue;
the LORD has sought out a man after his
own heart; and the LORD has appointed
him to be ruler over his people, because
you have not kept what the LORD commanded you.' 15And Samuel left and
went on his way from Gilgal.[g] The rest
of the people followed Saul to join the
army; they went up from Gilgal towards
Gibeah of Benjamin.[h]

PREPARATIONS FOR BATTLE

Saul counted the people who were
present with him, about six hundred
men. 16Saul, his son Jonathan, and the
people who were present with them
stayed in Geba of Benjamin; but the
Philistines encamped at Michmash.
17And raiders came out of the camp
of the Philistines in three companies;
one company turned towards Ophrah,
to the land of Shual, 18another company turned towards Beth-horon, and
another company turned towards the
mountain[i] that looks down upon the
valley of Zeboim towards the wilderness.

19 Now there was no blacksmith
to be found throughout all the land of
Israel; for the Philistines said, 'The Hebrews must not make swords or spears
for themselves'; 20so all the Israelites
went down to the Philistines to sharpen
their ploughshares, mattocks, axes, or
sickles;[j] 21The charge was two-thirds of a
shekel[k] for the ploughshares and for the
mattocks, and one-third of a shekel for
sharpening the axes and for setting the
goads.[l] 22So on the day of the battle neither sword nor spear was to be found in
the possession of any of the people with
Saul and Jonathan; but Saul and his son
Jonathan had them.

JONATHAN SURPRISES AND ROUTS THE PHILISTINES

23 Now a garrison of the Philistines
14 had gone out to the pass of
Michmash. 1One day Jonathan
son of Saul said to the young man who
carried his armour, 'Come, let us go over
to the Philistine garrison on the other
side.' But he did not tell his father. 2Saul
was staying in the outskirts of Gibeah
under the pomegranate tree that is at
Migron; the troops that were with him
were about six hundred men, 3along
with Ahijah son of Ahitub, Ichabod's
brother, son of Phinehas son of Eli, the
priest of the LORD in Shiloh, carrying
an ephod. Now the people did not know
that Jonathan had gone. 4In the pass,[m]
by which Jonathan tried to go over to
the Philistine garrison, there was a
rocky crag on one side and a rocky crag

[f] 13.8 Heb *him* [g] 13.15 Gk: Heb *went up from Gilgal to Gibeah of Benjamin* [h] 13.15 Gk: Heb lacks *The rest . . . of Benjamin* [i] 13.18 Cn Compare Gk: Heb *towards the border*
[j] 13.20 Gk: Heb *ploughshare* [k] 13.21 Heb *was a pim* [l] 13.21 Cn: Meaning of Heb uncertain
[m] 14.4 Heb *Between the passes*

on the other; the name of one was Bo-
zez, and the name of the other Seneh.
5One crag rose on the north in front of
Michmash, and the other on the south
in front of Geba.

6 Jonathan said to the young man
who carried his armour, 'Come, let us
go over to the garrison of these uncircumcised; it may be that the LORD will
act for us; for nothing can hinder the
LORD from saving by many or by few.'
7His armour-bearer said to him, 'Do all
that your mind inclines to.[n] I am with
you; as your mind is, so is mine.'[o] 8Then
Jonathan said, 'Now we will cross over
to those men and will show ourselves to
them. 9If they say to us, "Wait until we
come to you", then we will stand still in
our place, and we will not go up to them.
10But if they say, "Come up to us", then
we will go up; for the LORD has given
them into our hand. That will be the sign
for us.' 11So both of them showed themselves to the garrison of the Philistines;
and the Philistines said, 'Look, Hebrews
are coming out of the holes where they
have hidden themselves.' 12The men of
the garrison hailed Jonathan and his
armour-bearer, saying, 'Come up to us,
and we will show you something.' Jonathan said to his armour-bearer, 'Come
up after me; for the LORD has given
them into the hand of Israel.' 13Then
Jonathan climbed up on his hands and
feet, with his armour-bearer following
after him. The Philistines[p] fell before
Jonathan, and his armour-bearer, coming after him, killed them. 14In that first
slaughter Jonathan and his armour-
bearer killed about twenty men within
an area about half a furrow long in an
acre[q] of land. 15There was a panic in the
camp, in the field, and among all the
people; the garrison and even the raiders trembled; the earth quaked; and it
became a very great panic.

16 Saul's lookouts in Gibeah of Benjamin were watching as the multitude
was surging back and forth.[r] 17Then
Saul said to the troops that were with
him, 'Call the roll and see who has gone
from us.' When they had called the roll,
Jonathan and his armour-bearer were
not there. 18Saul said to Ahijah, 'Bring
the ark[s] of God here.' For at that time
the ark[t] of God went with the Israelites.
19While Saul was talking to the priest,
the tumult in the camp of the Philistines increased more and more; and
Saul said to the priest, 'Withdraw your
hand.' 20Then Saul and all the people
who were with him rallied and went
into the battle; and every sword was
against the other, so that there was very
great confusion. 21Now the Hebrews
who previously had been with the Philistines and had gone up with them into
the camp turned and joined the Israelites who were with Saul and Jonathan.
22Likewise, when all the Israelites who
had gone into hiding in the hill country
of Ephraim heard that the Philistines
were fleeing, they too followed closely
after them in the battle. 23So the LORD
gave Israel the victory that day.

The battle passed beyond Beth-aven,
and the troops with Saul numbered altogether about ten thousand men. The
battle spread out over the hill country of
Ephraim.

SAUL'S RASH OATH

24 Now Saul committed a very rash
act on that day.[u] He had laid an oath on
the troops, saying, 'Cursed be anyone
who eats food before it is evening and
I have been avenged on my enemies.'
So none of the troops tasted food. 25All
the troops[v] came upon a honeycomb;
and there was honey on the ground.
26When the troops came upon the
honeycomb, the honey was dripping
out; but they did not put their hands to
their mouths, for they feared the oath.
27But Jonathan had not heard his father
charge the troops with the oath; so he
extended the staff that was in his hand,
and dipped the tip of it in the honeycomb, and put his hand to his mouth;
and his eyes brightened. 28Then one of
the soldiers said, 'Your father strictly
charged the troops with an oath, saying, "Cursed be anyone who eats food
this day." And so the troops are faint.'
29Then Jonathan said, 'My father has
troubled the land; see how my eyes have
brightened because I tasted a little of
this honey. 30How much better if today
the troops had eaten freely of the spoil
taken from their enemies; for now the
slaughter among the Philistines has not
been great.'

31 After they had struck down the
Philistines that day from Michmash to
Aijalon, the troops were very faint; 32so

[n] 14.7 Gk: Heb *Do all that is in your mind. Turn*
[o] 14.7 Gk: Heb lacks *so is mine* [p] 14.13 Heb
They [q] 14.14 Heb *yoke* [r] 14.16 Gk: Heb *they
went and there* [s] 14.18 Gk *the ephod*
[t] 14.18 Gk *the ephod* [u] 14.24 Gk: Heb *The
Israelites were distressed that day*
[v] 14.25 Heb *land*

the troops flew upon the spoil, and took
sheep and oxen and calves, and slaughtered them on the ground; and the
troops ate them with the blood. 33 Then
it was reported to Saul, 'Look, the troops
are sinning against the LORD by eating
with the blood.' And he said, 'You have
dealt treacherously; roll a large stone
before me here.'[w] 34 Saul said, 'Disperse
yourselves among the troops, and say to
them, "Let all bring their oxen or their
sheep, and slaughter them here, and
eat; and do not sin against the LORD
by eating with the blood." ' So all of the
troops brought their oxen with them
that night, and slaughtered them there.
35 And Saul built an altar to the LORD;
it was the first altar that he built to the
LORD.

JONATHAN IN DANGER OF DEATH

36 Then Saul said, 'Let us go down after the Philistines by night and despoil
them until the morning light; let us not
leave one of them.' They said, 'Do whatever seems good to you.' But the priest
said, 'Let us draw near to God here.' 37 So
Saul inquired of God, 'Shall I go down
after the Philistines? Will you give them
into the hand of Israel?' But he did not
answer him that day. 38 Saul said, 'Come
here, all you leaders of the people; and
let us find out how this sin has arisen
today. 39 For as the LORD lives who saves
Israel, even if it is in my son Jonathan,
he shall surely die!' But there was no
one among all the people who answered
him. 40 He said to all Israel, 'You shall
be on one side, and I and my son Jonathan will be on the other side.' The people said to Saul, 'Do what seems good
to you.' 41 Then Saul said, 'O LORD God
of Israel, why have you not answered
your servant today? If this guilt is in
me or in my son Jonathan, O LORD God
of Israel, give Urim; but if this guilt is
in your people Israel,[x] give Thummim.'
And Jonathan and Saul were indicated
by the lot, but the people were cleared.
42 Then Saul said, 'Cast the lot between
me and my son Jonathan.' And Jonathan was taken.

43 Then Saul said to Jonathan, 'Tell
me what you have done.' Jonathan told
him, 'I tasted a little honey with the tip
of the staff that was in my hand; here
I am, I will die.' 44 Saul said, 'God do so
to me and more also; you shall surely
die, Jonathan!' 45 Then the people said
to Saul, 'Shall Jonathan die, who has accomplished this great victory in Israel?
Perish the thought! As the LORD lives,
not one hair of his head shall fall to the
ground; for he has worked with God today.' So the people ransomed Jonathan,
and he did not die. 46 Then Saul withdrew from pursuing the Philistines; and
the Philistines went to their own place.

SAUL'S CONTINUING WARS

47 When Saul had taken the kingship
over Israel, he fought against all his enemies on every side—against Moab,
against the Ammonites, against Edom,
against the kings of Zobah, and against
the Philistines; wherever he turned he
routed them. 48 He did valiantly, and
struck down the Amalekites, and rescued Israel out of the hands of those
who plundered them.

49 Now the sons of Saul were Jonathan, Ishvi, and Malchishua; and the
names of his two daughters were these:
the name of the firstborn was Merab,
and the name of the younger, Michal.
50 The name of Saul's wife was Ahinoam
daughter of Ahimaaz. And the name of
the commander of his army was Abner
son of Ner, Saul's uncle; 51 Kish was the
father of Saul, and Ner the father of Abner was the son of Abiel.

52 There was hard fighting against
the Philistines all the days of Saul; and
when Saul saw any strong or valiant
warrior, he took him into his service.

SAUL DEFEATS THE AMALEKITES BUT SPARES THEIR KING

15 Samuel said to Saul, 'The LORD
sent me to anoint you king over
his people Israel; now therefore listen to
the words of the LORD. 2 Thus says the
LORD of hosts, "I will punish the Amalekites for what they did in opposing
the Israelites when they came up out
of Egypt. 3 Now go and attack Amalek,
and utterly destroy all that they have; do
not spare them, but kill both man and
woman, child and infant, ox and sheep,
camel and donkey." '

4 So Saul summoned the people, and
numbered them in Telaim, two hundred thousand foot-soldiers, and ten
thousand soldiers of Judah. 5 Saul came
to the city of the Amalekites and lay in
wait in the valley. 6 Saul said to the Kenites, 'Go! Leave! Withdraw from among
the Amalekites, or I will destroy you
with them; for you showed kindness to

[w] 14.33 Gk: Heb *me this day* [x] 14.41 Vg Compare Gk: Heb *41Saul said to the LORD, the God of Israel*

all the people of Israel when they came
up out of Egypt.' So the Kenites withdrew from the Amalekites. 7 Saul defeated the Amalekites, from Havilah as
far as Shur, which is east of Egypt. 8 He
took King Agag of the Amalekites alive,
but utterly destroyed all the people with
the edge of the sword. 9 Saul and the
people spared Agag, and the best of the
sheep and of the cattle and of the fatlings, and the lambs, and all that was
valuable, and would not utterly destroy
them; all that was despised and worthless they utterly destroyed.

SAUL REJECTED AS KING

10 The word of the LORD came to
Samuel: 11 'I regret that I made Saul
king, for he has turned back from following me, and has not carried out my
commands.' Samuel was angry; and he
cried out to the LORD all night. 12 Samuel rose early in the morning to meet
Saul, and Samuel was told, 'Saul went
to Carmel, where he set up a monument
for himself, and on returning he passed
on down to Gilgal.' 13 When Samuel came
to Saul, Saul said to him, 'May you be
blessed by the LORD; I have carried out
the command of the LORD.' 14 But Samuel said, 'What then is this bleating of
sheep in my ears, and the lowing of cattle that I hear?' 15 Saul said, 'They have
brought them from the Amalekites; for
the people spared the best of the sheep
and the cattle, to sacrifice to the LORD
your God; but the rest we have utterly
destroyed.' 16 Then Samuel said to Saul,
'Stop! I will tell you what the LORD said
to me last night.' He replied, 'Speak.'

17 Samuel said, 'Though you are little in your own eyes, are you not the
head of the tribes of Israel? The LORD
anointed you king over Israel. 18 And
the LORD sent you on a mission, and
said, "Go, utterly destroy the sinners,
the Amalekites, and fight against them
until they are consumed." 19 Why then
did you not obey the voice of the LORD?
Why did you swoop down on the spoil,
and do what was evil in the sight of the
LORD?' 20 Saul said to Samuel, 'I have
obeyed the voice of the LORD, I have
gone on the mission on which the LORD
sent me, I have brought Agag the king
of Amalek, and I have utterly destroyed
the Amalekites. 21 But from the spoil the
people took sheep and cattle, the best
of the things devoted to destruction, to
sacrifice to the LORD your God in Gilgal.'
22 And Samuel said,

'Has the LORD as great delight
in burnt-offerings
and sacrifices,
as in obedience to the voice
of the LORD?
Surely, to obey is better
than sacrifice,
and to heed than the fat of rams.
23 For rebellion is no less a sin
than divination,
and stubbornness is like
iniquity and idolatry.
Because you have rejected the
word of the LORD,
he has also rejected you
from being king.'

24 Saul said to Samuel, 'I have
sinned; for I have transgressed the commandment of the LORD and your words,
because I feared the people and obeyed
their voice. 25 Now therefore, I pray,
pardon my sin, and return with me, so
that I may worship the LORD.' 26 Samuel said to Saul, 'I will not return with
you; for you have rejected the word of
the LORD, and the LORD has rejected
you from being king over Israel.' 27 As
Samuel turned to go away, Saul caught
hold of the hem of his robe, and it tore.
28 And Samuel said to him, 'The LORD
has torn the kingdom of Israel from
you this very day, and has given it to a
neighbour of yours, who is better than
you. 29 Moreover, the Glory of Israel will
not recant[y] or change his mind; for he is
not a mortal, that he should change his
mind.' 30 Then Saul[z] said, 'I have sinned;
yet honour me now before the elders
of my people and before Israel, and return with me, so that I may worship
the LORD your God.' 31 So Samuel turned
back after Saul; and Saul worshipped
the LORD.

32 Then Samuel said, 'Bring Agag
king of the Amalekites here to me.' And
Agag came to him haltingly.[a] Agag said,
'Surely this is the bitterness of death.'[b]
33 But Samuel said,

'As your sword has made
women childless,
so your mother shall be childless
among women.'

And Samuel hewed Agag in pieces before the LORD in Gilgal.

34 Then Samuel went to Ramah; and
Saul went up to his house in Gibeah of
Saul. 35 Samuel did not see Saul again

[y] 15.29 Q Ms Gk: MT *deceive* [z] 15.30 Heb *he*
[a] 15.32 Cn Compare Gk: Meaning of Heb uncertain
[b] 15.32 Q Ms Gk: MT *Surely the bitterness of death is past*

until the day of his death, but Samuel
grieved over Saul. And the LORD was
sorry that he had made Saul king over
Israel.

DAVID ANOINTED AS KING

16 The LORD said to Samuel, 'How
long will you grieve over Saul? I
have rejected him from being king over
Israel. Fill your horn with oil and set
out; I will send you to Jesse the Bethlehemite, for I have provided for myself
a king among his sons.' 2Samuel said,
'How can I go? If Saul hears of it, he
will kill me.' And the LORD said, 'Take
a heifer with you, and say, "I have come
to sacrifice to the LORD." 3Invite Jesse to
the sacrifice, and I will show you what
you shall do; and you shall anoint for me
the one whom I name to you.' 4Samuel
did what the LORD commanded, and
came to Bethlehem. The elders of the
city came to meet him trembling, and
said, 'Do you come peaceably?' 5He said,
'Peaceably; I have come to sacrifice to
the LORD; sanctify yourselves and come
with me to the sacrifice.' And he sanctified Jesse and his sons and invited them
to the sacrifice.

6 When they came, he looked on
Eliab and thought, 'Surely the LORD's
anointed is now before the LORD.'[c] 7But
the LORD said to Samuel, 'Do not look
on his appearance or on the height of
his stature, because I have rejected him;
for the LORD does not see as mortals see;
they look on the outward appearance,
but the LORD looks on the heart.' 8Then
Jesse called Abinadab, and made him
pass before Samuel. He said, 'Neither
has the LORD chosen this one.' 9Then
Jesse made Shammah pass by. And he
said, 'Neither has the LORD chosen this
one.' 10Jesse made seven of his sons pass
before Samuel, and Samuel said to Jesse,
'The LORD has not chosen any of these.'
11Samuel said to Jesse, 'Are all your sons
here?' And he said, 'There remains yet
the youngest, but he is keeping the
sheep.' And Samuel said to Jesse, 'Send
and bring him; for we will not sit down
until he comes here.' 12He sent and
brought him in. Now he was ruddy, and
had beautiful eyes, and was handsome.
The LORD said, 'Rise and anoint him;
for this is the one.' 13Then Samuel took
the horn of oil, and anointed him in the
presence of his brothers; and the spirit
of the LORD came mightily upon David
from that day forward. Samuel then set
out and went to Ramah.

DAVID PLAYS THE LYRE FOR SAUL

14 Now the spirit of the LORD departed from Saul, and an evil spirit
from the LORD tormented him. 15And
Saul's servants said to him, 'See now,
an evil spirit from God is tormenting
you. 16Let our lord now command the
servants who attend you to look for
someone who is skilful in playing the
lyre; and when the evil spirit from God
is upon you, he will play it, and you will
feel better.' 17So Saul said to his servants,
'Provide for me someone who can play
well, and bring him to me.' 18One of the
young men answered, 'I have seen a son
of Jesse the Bethlehemite who is skilful
in playing, a man of valour, a warrior,
prudent in speech, and a man of good
presence; and the LORD is with him.'
19So Saul sent messengers to Jesse, and
said, 'Send me your son David who is
with the sheep.' 20Jesse took a donkey
loaded with bread, a skin of wine, and
a kid, and sent them by his son David to
Saul. 21And David came to Saul, and entered his service. Saul loved him greatly,
and he became his armour-bearer.
22Saul sent to Jesse, saying, 'Let David
remain in my service, for he has found
favour in my sight.' 23And whenever the
evil spirit from God came upon Saul,
David took the lyre and played it with
his hand, and Saul would be relieved
and feel better, and the evil spirit would
depart from him.

DAVID AND GOLIATH

17 Now the Philistines gathered
their armies for battle; they were
gathered at Socoh, which belongs to Judah, and encamped between Socoh and
Azekah, in Ephes-dammim. 2Saul and
the Israelites gathered and encamped
in the valley of Elah, and formed ranks
against the Philistines. 3The Philistines
stood on the mountain on one side, and
Israel stood on the mountain on the
other side, with a valley between them.
4And there came out from the camp of
the Philistines a champion named Goliath, of Gath, whose height was six[d]
cubits and a span. 5He had a helmet
of bronze on his head, and he was ar-
moured with a coat of mail; the weight
of the coat was five thousand shekels of
bronze. 6He had greaves of bronze on
his legs and a javelin of bronze slung
between his shoulders. 7The shaft of his
spear was like a weaver's beam, and his

c 16.6 Heb *him* d 17.4 MT: Q Ms Gk *four*

spear's head weighed six hundred shekels of iron; and his shield-bearer went before him. 8He stood and shouted to the ranks of Israel, 'Why have you come out to draw up for battle? Am I not a Philistine, and are you not servants of Saul? Choose a man for yourselves, and let him come down to me. 9If he is able to fight with me and kill me, then we will be your servants; but if I prevail against him and kill him, then you shall be our servants and serve us.' 10And the Philistine said, 'Today I defy the ranks of Israel! Give me a man, that we may fight together.' 11When Saul and all Israel heard these words of the Philistine, they were dismayed and greatly afraid.

12 Now David was the son of an Ephrathite of Bethlehem in Judah, named Jesse, who had eight sons. In the days of Saul the man was already old and advanced in years.[e] 13The three eldest sons of Jesse had followed Saul to the battle; the names of his three sons who went to the battle were Eliab the firstborn, and next to him Abinadab, and the third Shammah. 14David was the youngest; the three eldest followed Saul, 15but David went back and forth from Saul to feed his father's sheep at Bethlehem. 16For forty days the Philistine came forward and took his stand, morning and evening.

17 Jesse said to his son David, 'Take for your brothers an ephah of this parched grain and these ten loaves, and carry them quickly to the camp to your brothers; 18also take these ten cheeses to the commander of their thousand. See how your brothers fare, and bring some token from them.'

19 Now Saul, and they, and all the men of Israel, were in the valley of Elah, fighting with the Philistines. 20David rose early in the morning, left someone in charge of the sheep, took the provisions, and went as Jesse had commanded him. He came to the encampment as the army was going forth to the battle line, shouting the war cry. 21Israel and the Philistines drew up for battle, army against army. 22David left the things in charge of the keeper of the baggage, ran to the ranks, and went and greeted his brothers. 23As he talked with them, the champion, the Philistine of Gath, Goliath by name, came up out of the ranks of the Philistines, and spoke the same words as before. And David heard him.

24 All the Israelites, when they saw the man, fled from him and were very much afraid. 25The Israelites said, 'Have you seen this man who has come up? Surely he has come up to defy Israel. The king will greatly enrich the man who kills him, and will give him his daughter and make his family free in Israel.' 26David said to the men who stood by him, 'What shall be done for the man who kills this Philistine, and takes away the reproach from Israel? For who is this uncircumcised Philistine that he should defy the armies of the living God?' 27The people answered him in the same way, 'So shall it be done for the man who kills him.'

28 His eldest brother Eliab heard him talking to the men; and Eliab's anger was kindled against David. He said, 'Why have you come down? With whom have you left those few sheep in the wilderness? I know your presumption and the evil of your heart; for you have come down just to see the battle.' 29David said, 'What have I done now? It was only a question.' 30He turned away from him towards another and spoke in the same way; and the people answered him again as before.

31 When the words that David spoke were heard, they repeated them before Saul; and he sent for him. 32David said to Saul, 'Let no one's heart fail because of him; your servant will go and fight with this Philistine.' 33Saul said to David, 'You are not able to go against this Philistine to fight with him; for you are just a boy, and he has been a warrior from his youth.' 34But David said to Saul, 'Your servant used to keep sheep for his father; and whenever a lion or a bear came, and took a lamb from the flock, 35I went after it and struck it down, rescuing the lamb from its mouth; and if it turned against me, I would catch it by the jaw, strike it down, and kill it. 36Your servant has killed both lions and bears; and this uncircumcised Philistine shall be like one of them, since he has defied the armies of the living God.' 37David said, 'The LORD, who saved me from the paw of the lion and from the paw of the bear, will save me from the hand of this Philistine.' So Saul said to David, 'Go, and may the LORD be with you!'

38 Saul clothed David with his armour; he put a bronze helmet on his head and clothed him with a coat of mail. 39David strapped Saul's sword

[e] **17.12** Gk Syr: Heb *among men*

over the armour, and he tried in vain to
walk, for he was not used to them. Then
David said to Saul, 'I cannot walk with
these; for I am not used to them.' So David removed them. 40Then he took his
staff in his hand, and chose five smooth
stones from the wadi, and put them in
his shepherd's bag, in the pouch; his
sling was in his hand, and he drew near
to the Philistine.

41 The Philistine came on and drew
near to David, with his shield-bearer
in front of him. 42When the Philistine
looked and saw David, he disdained
him, for he was only a youth, ruddy and
handsome in appearance. 43The Philistine said to David, 'Am I a dog, that you
come to me with sticks?' And the Philistine cursed David by his gods. 44The Philistine said to David, 'Come to me, and
I will give your flesh to the birds of the
air and to the wild animals of the field.'
45But David said to the Philistine, 'You
come to me with sword and spear and
javelin; but I come to you in the name of
the LORD of hosts, the God of the armies
of Israel, whom you have defied. 46This
very day the LORD will deliver you into
my hand, and I will strike you down and
cut off your head; and I will give the dead
bodies of the Philistine army this very
day to the birds of the air and to the wild
animals of the earth, so that all the earth
may know that there is a God in Israel,
47and that all this assembly may know
that the LORD does not save by sword
and spear; for the battle is the LORD's
and he will give you into our hand.'

48 When the Philistine drew nearer
to meet David, David ran quickly towards the battle line to meet the Philistine. 49David put his hand in his bag,
took out a stone, slung it, and struck
the Philistine on his forehead; the stone
sank into his forehead, and he fell face
down on the ground.

50 So David prevailed over the Philistine with a sling and a stone, striking
down the Philistine and killing him;
there was no sword in David's hand.
51Then David ran and stood over the
Philistine; he grasped his sword, drew it
out of its sheath, and killed him; then he
cut off his head with it.

When the Philistines saw that their
champion was dead, they fled. 52The
troops of Israel and Judah rose up with
a shout and pursued the Philistines as
far as Gath[f] and the gates of Ekron, so
that the wounded Philistines fell on the
way from Shaaraim as far as Gath and
Ekron. 53The Israelites came back from
chasing the Philistines, and they plundered their camp. 54David took the head
of the Philistine and brought it to Jerusalem; but he put his armour in his tent.

55 When Saul saw David go out
against the Philistine, he said to Abner,
the commander of the army, 'Abner,
whose son is this young man?' Abner
said, 'As your soul lives, O king, I do not
know.' 56The king said, 'Inquire whose
son the stripling is.' 57On David's return
from killing the Philistine, Abner took
him and brought him before Saul, with
the head of the Philistine in his hand.
58Saul said to him, 'Whose son are you,
young man?' And David answered, 'I
am the son of your servant Jesse the
Bethlehemite.'

JONATHAN'S COVENANT WITH DAVID

18 When David[g] had finished speaking to Saul, the soul of Jonathan
was bound to the soul of David, and Jonathan loved him as his own soul. 2Saul
took him that day and would not let
him return to his father's house. 3Then
Jonathan made a covenant with David,
because he loved him as his own soul.
4Jonathan stripped himself of the robe
that he was wearing, and gave it to David, and his armour, and even his sword
and his bow and his belt. 5David went
out and was successful wherever Saul
sent him; as a result, Saul set him over
the army. And all the people, even the
servants of Saul, approved.

6 As they were coming home, when
David returned from killing the Philistine, the women came out of all the
towns of Israel, singing and dancing,
to meet King Saul, with tambourines,
with songs of joy, and with musical instruments.[h] 7And the women sang to
one another as they made merry,

'Saul has killed his thousands,
and David his tens of thousands.'

8Saul was very angry, for this saying
displeased him. He said, 'They have ascribed to David tens of thousands, and to
me they have ascribed thousands; what
more can he have but the kingdom?' 9So
Saul eyed David from that day on.

SAUL TRIES TO KILL DAVID

10 The next day an evil spirit from
God rushed upon Saul, and he raved

[f] **17.52** Gk Syr: Heb *Gai* [g] **18.1** Heb *he*
[h] **18.6** Or *triangles*, or *three-stringed instruments*

within his house, while David was playing the lyre, as he did day by day. Saul
had his spear in his hand; 11and Saul
threw the spear, for he thought, 'I will
pin David to the wall.' But David eluded
him twice.
12 Saul was afraid of David, because
the LORD was with him but had departed
from Saul. 13So Saul removed him from
his presence, and made him a commander
of a thousand; and David marched out
and came in, leading the army. 14David
had success in all his undertakings; for
the LORD was with him. 15When Saul saw
that he had great success, he stood in awe
of him. 16But all Israel and Judah loved
David; for it was he who marched out and
came in leading them.

DAVID MARRIES MICHAL

17 Then Saul said to David, 'Here is
my elder daughter Merab; I will give her
to you as a wife; only be valiant for me
and fight the LORD's battles.' For Saul
thought, 'I will not raise a hand against
him; let the Philistines deal with him.'
18David said to Saul, 'Who am I and who
are my kinsfolk, my father's family in
Israel, that I should be son-in-law to
the king?' 19But at the time when Saul's
daughter Merab should have been given
to David, she was given to Adriel the
Meholathite as a wife.
20 Now Saul's daughter Michal
loved David. Saul was told, and the
thing pleased him. 21Saul thought, 'Let
me give her to him that she may be a
snare for him and that the hand of the
Philistines may be against him.' Therefore Saul said to David a second time,[i]
'You shall now be my son-in-law.' 22Saul
commanded his servants, 'Speak to David in private and say, "See, the king is
delighted with you, and all his servants
love you; now then, become the king's
son-in-law." ' 23So Saul's servants reported these words to David in private.
And David said, 'Does it seem to you a
little thing to become the king's son-in-
law, seeing that I am a poor man and of
no repute?' 24The servants of Saul told
him, 'This is what David said.' 25Then
Saul said, 'Thus shall you say to David,
"The king desires no marriage present
except a hundred foreskins of the Philistines, that he may be avenged on the
king's enemies." ' Now Saul planned to
make David fall by the hand of the Philistines. 26When his servants told David
these words, David was well pleased
to be the king's son-in-law. Before the
time had expired, 27David rose and
went, along with his men, and killed
one hundred[j] of the Philistines; and David brought their foreskins, which were
given in full number to the king, that
he might become the king's son-in-law.
Saul gave him his daughter Michal as a
wife. 28But when Saul realized that the
LORD was with David, and that Saul's
daughter Michal loved him, 29Saul was
still more afraid of David. So Saul was
David's enemy from that time forward.
30 Then the commanders of the Philistines came out to battle; and as often
as they came out, David had more success than all the servants of Saul, so that
his fame became very great.

JONATHAN INTERCEDES FOR DAVID

19 Saul spoke to his son Jonathan
and to all his servants about
killing David. But Saul's son Jonathan
took great delight in David. 2Jonathan
told David, 'My father Saul is trying to
kill you; therefore be on guard tomorrow morning; stay in a secret place and
hide yourself. 3I will go out and stand
beside my father in the field where you
are, and I will speak to my father about
you; if I learn anything I will tell you.'
4Jonathan spoke well of David to his
father Saul, saying to him, 'The king
should not sin against his servant David, because he has not sinned against
you, and because his deeds have been
of good service to you; 5for he took his
life in his hand when he attacked the
Philistine, and the LORD brought about
a great victory for all Israel. You saw
it, and rejoiced; why then will you sin
against an innocent person by killing
David without cause?' 6Saul heeded the
voice of Jonathan; Saul swore, 'As the
LORD lives, he shall not be put to death.'
7So Jonathan called David and related
all these things to him. Jonathan then
brought David to Saul, and he was in his
presence as before.

MICHAL HELPS DAVID ESCAPE FROM SAUL

8 Again there was war, and David
went out to fight the Philistines. He
launched a heavy attack on them, so
that they fled before him. 9Then an evil
spirit from the LORD came upon Saul, as
he sat in his house with his spear in his
hand, while David was playing music.

[i] **18.21** Heb *by two* [j] **18.27** Gk Compare 2 Sam 3.14: Heb *two hundred*

10Saul sought to pin David to the wall with the spear; but he eluded Saul, so that he struck the spear into the wall. David fled and escaped that night.

11 Saul sent messengers to David's house to keep watch over him, planning to kill him in the morning. David's wife Michal told him, 'If you do not save your life tonight, tomorrow you will be killed.' 12So Michal let David down through the window; he fled away and escaped. 13Michal took an idol[k] and laid it on the bed; she put a net[l] of goats' hair on its head, and covered it with the clothes. 14When Saul sent messengers to take David, she said, 'He is sick.' 15Then Saul sent the messengers to see David for themselves. He said, 'Bring him up to me in the bed, that I may kill him.' 16When the messengers came in, the idol[m] was in the bed, with the covering[n] of goats' hair on its head. 17Saul said to Michal, 'Why have you deceived me like this, and let my enemy go, so that he has escaped?' Michal answered Saul, 'He said to me, "Let me go; why should I kill you?"'

DAVID JOINS SAMUEL IN RAMAH

18 Now David fled and escaped; he came to Samuel at Ramah, and told him all that Saul had done to him. He and Samuel went and settled at Naioth. 19Saul was told, 'David is at Naioth in Ramah.' 20Then Saul sent messengers to take David. When they saw the company of the prophets in a frenzy, with Samuel standing in charge of[o] them, the spirit of God came upon the messengers of Saul, and they also fell into a prophetic frenzy. 21When Saul was told, he sent other messengers, and they also fell into a frenzy. Saul sent messengers again the third time, and they also fell into a frenzy. 22Then he himself went to Ramah. He came to the great well that is in Secu;[p] he asked, 'Where are Samuel and David?' And someone said, 'They are at Naioth in Ramah.' 23He went there, towards Naioth in Ramah; and the spirit of God came upon him. As he was going, he fell into a prophetic frenzy, until he came to Naioth in Ramah. 24He too stripped off his clothes, and he too fell into a frenzy before Samuel. He lay naked all that day and all that night. Therefore it is said, 'Is Saul also among the prophets?'

THE FRIENDSHIP OF DAVID AND JONATHAN

20 David fled from Naioth in Ramah. He came before Jonathan and said, 'What have I done? What is my guilt? And what is my sin against your father that he is trying to take my life?' 2He said to him, 'Perish the thought! You shall not die. My father does nothing either great or small without disclosing it to me; and why should my father hide this from me? Never!' 3But David also swore, 'Your father knows well that you like me; and he thinks, "Do not let Jonathan know this, or he will be grieved." But truly, as the LORD lives and as you yourself live, there is but a step between me and death.' 4Then Jonathan said to David, 'Whatever you say, I will do for you.' 5David said to Jonathan, 'Tomorrow is the new moon, and I should not fail to sit with the king at the meal; but let me go, so that I may hide in the field until the third evening. 6If your father misses me at all, then say, "David earnestly asked leave of me to run to Bethlehem his city; for there is a yearly sacrifice there for all the family." 7If he says, "Good!" it will be well with your servant; but if he is angry, then know that evil has been determined by him. 8Therefore deal kindly with your servant, for you have brought your servant into a sacred covenant[q] with you. But if there is guilt in me, kill me yourself; why should you bring me to your father?' 9Jonathan said, 'Far be it from you! If I knew that it was decided by my father that evil should come upon you, would I not tell you?' 10Then David said to Jonathan, 'Who will tell me if your father answers you harshly?' 11Jonathan replied to David, 'Come, let us go out into the field.' So they both went out into the field.

12 Jonathan said to David, 'By the LORD, the God of Israel! When I have sounded out my father, about this time tomorrow, or on the third day, if he is well disposed towards David, shall I not then send and disclose it to you? 13But if my father intends to do you harm, the LORD do so to Jonathan, and more also, if I do not disclose it to you, and send you away, so that you may go in safety. May the LORD be with you, as he has been with my father. 14If I am still alive, show me the faithful love of the LORD; but if I die,[r] 15never cut off your faithful

[k] 19.13 Heb *took the teraphim* [l] 19.13 Meaning of Heb uncertain [m] 19.16 Heb *the teraphim*
[n] 19.16 Meaning of Heb uncertain
[o] 19.20 Meaning of Heb uncertain [p] 19.22 Gk reads *to the well of the threshing-floor on the bare height* [q] 20.8 Heb *a covenant of the LORD*
[r] 20.14 Meaning of Heb uncertain

love from my house, even if the LORD
were to cut off every one of the enemies
of David from the face of the earth.'
16 Thus Jonathan made a covenant with
the house of David, saying, 'May the
LORD seek out the enemies of David.'
17 Jonathan made David swear again by
his love for him; for he loved him as he
loved his own life.

18 Jonathan said to him, 'Tomorrow
is the new moon; you will be missed,
because your place will be empty. 19 On
the day after tomorrow, you shall go a
long way down; go to the place where
you hid yourself earlier, and remain beside the stone there.[s] 20 I will shoot three
arrows to the side of it, as though I shot
at a mark. 21 Then I will send the boy,
saying, "Go, find the arrows." If I say to
the boy, "Look, the arrows are on this
side of you, collect them", then you are
to come, for, as the LORD lives, it is safe
for you and there is no danger. 22 But if I
say to the young man, "Look, the arrows
are beyond you", then go; for the LORD
has sent you away. 23 As for the matter
about which you and I have spoken, the
LORD is witness[t] between you and me
for ever.'

24 So David hid himself in the field.
When the new moon came, the king sat
at the feast to eat. 25 The king sat upon
his seat, as at other times, upon the seat
by the wall. Jonathan stood, while Abner sat by Saul's side; but David's place
was empty.

26 Saul did not say anything that
day; for he thought, 'Something has
befallen him; he is not clean, surely he
is not clean.' 27 But on the second day,
the day after the new moon, David's
place was empty. And Saul said to his
son Jonathan, 'Why has the son of Jesse
not come to the feast, either yesterday
or today?' 28 Jonathan answered Saul,
'David earnestly asked leave of me to go
to Bethlehem; 29 he said, "Let me go; for
our family is holding a sacrifice in the
city, and my brother has commanded
me to be there. So now, if I have found
favour in your sight, let me get away,
and see my brothers." For this reason he
has not come to the king's table.'

30 Then Saul's anger was kindled
against Jonathan. He said to him, 'You
son of a perverse, rebellious woman! Do
I not know that you have chosen the son
of Jesse to your own shame, and to the
shame of your mother's nakedness? 31 For
as long as the son of Jesse lives upon the
earth, neither you nor your kingdom
shall be established. Now send and bring
him to me, for he shall surely die.' 32 Then
Jonathan answered his father Saul, 'Why
should he be put to death? What has he
done?' 33 But Saul threw his spear at him
to strike him; so Jonathan knew that it
was the decision of his father to put David to death. 34 Jonathan rose from the
table in fierce anger and ate no food on
the second day of the month, for he was
grieved for David, and because his father
had disgraced him.

35 In the morning Jonathan went
out into the field to the appointment
with David, and with him was a little
boy. 36 He said to the boy, 'Run and find
the arrows that I shoot.' As the boy ran,
he shot an arrow beyond him. 37 When
the boy came to the place where Jonathan's arrow had fallen, Jonathan called
after the boy and said, 'Is the arrow not
beyond you?' 38 Jonathan called after the
boy, 'Hurry, be quick, do not linger.' So
Jonathan's boy gathered up the arrows
and came to his master. 39 But the boy
knew nothing; only Jonathan and David knew the arrangement. 40 Jonathan
gave his weapons to the boy and said
to him, 'Go and carry them to the city.'
41 As soon as the boy had gone, David
rose from beside the stone heap[u] and
prostrated himself with his face to the
ground. He bowed three times, and they
kissed each other, and wept with each
other; David wept the more.[v] 42 Then
Jonathan said to David, 'Go in peace,
since both of us have sworn in the name
of the LORD, saying, "The LORD shall be
between me and you, and between my
descendants and your descendants, for
ever." ' He got up and left; and Jonathan
went into the city.[w]

DAVID AND THE HOLY BREAD

21[x] David came to Nob to the priest
Ahimelech. Ahimelech came
trembling to meet David, and said to
him, 'Why are you alone, and no one
with you?' 2 David said to the priest
Ahimelech, 'The king has charged me
with a matter, and said to me, "No one
must know anything of the matter
about which I send you, and with which
I have charged you." I have made an
appointment[y] with the young men for

[s] 20.19 Meaning of Heb uncertain [t] 20.23 Gk: Heb lacks *witness* [u] 20.41 Gk: Heb *from beside the south* [v] 20.41 Vg: Meaning of Heb uncertain [w] 20.42 This sentence is 21.1 in Heb [x] 21.1 Ch 21.2 in Heb [y] 21.2 Q Ms Vg Compare Gk: Meaning of MT uncertain

such and such a place. 3Now then, what
have you at hand? Give me five loaves
of bread, or whatever is here.' 4The
priest answered David, 'I have no ordinary bread at hand, only holy bread—
provided that the young men have
kept themselves from women.' 5David
answered the priest, 'Indeed, women
have been kept from us as always when
I go on an expedition; the vessels of the
young men are holy even when it is a
common journey; how much more today will their vessels be holy?' 6So the
priest gave him the holy bread; for there
was no bread there except the bread of
the Presence, which is removed from
before the LORD to be replaced by hot
bread on the day it is taken away.

7 Now a certain man of the servants
of Saul was there that day, detained before the LORD; his name was Doeg the
Edomite, the chief of Saul's shepherds.

8 David said to Ahimelech, 'Is there
no spear or sword here with you? I did
not bring my sword or my weapons
with me, because the king's business
required haste.' 9The priest said, 'The
sword of Goliath the Philistine, whom
you killed in the valley of Elah, is here
wrapped in a cloth behind the ephod;
if you will take that, take it, for there is
none here except that one.' David said,
'There is none like it; give it to me.'

DAVID FLEES TO GATH

10 David rose and fled that day from
Saul; he went to King Achish of Gath.
11The servants of Achish said to him, 'Is
this not David the king of the land? Did
they not sing to one another of him in
dances,

"Saul has killed his thousands,
and David his tens of thousands"?'

12David took these words to heart and
was very much afraid of King Achish
of Gath. 13So he changed his behaviour
before them; he pretended to be mad
when in their presence.[z] He scratched
marks on the doors of the gate, and let
his spittle run down his beard. 14Achish
said to his servants, 'Look, you see the
man is mad; why then have you brought
him to me? 15Do I lack madmen, that
you have brought this fellow to play the
madman in my presence? Shall this fellow come into my house?'

DAVID AND HIS FOLLOWERS AT ADULLAM

22 David left there and escaped to
the cave of Adullam; when his
brothers and all his father's house heard
of it, they went down there to him. 2Ev-
eryone who was in distress, and everyone who was in debt, and everyone who
was discontented gathered to him; and
he became captain over them. Those
who were with him numbered about
four hundred.

3 David went from there to Mizpeh
of Moab. He said to the king of Moab,
'Please let my father and mother come[a]
to you, until I know what God will do
for me.' 4He left them with the king of
Moab, and they stayed with him all the
time that David was in the stronghold.
5Then the prophet Gad said to David,
'Do not remain in the stronghold; leave,
and go into the land of Judah.' So David
left, and went into the forest of Hereth.

SAUL SLAUGHTERS THE PRIESTS AT NOB

6 Saul heard that David and those
who were with him had been located.
Saul was sitting at Gibeah, under the
tamarisk tree on the height, with his
spear in his hand, and all his servants
were standing around him. 7Saul said
to his servants who stood around him,
'Hear now, you Benjaminites; will the
son of Jesse give every one of you fields
and vineyards, will he make you all
commanders of thousands and commanders of hundreds? 8Is that why all
of you have conspired against me? No
one discloses to me when my son makes
a league with the son of Jesse, none of
you is sorry for me or discloses to me
that my son has stirred up my servant
against me, to lie in wait, as he is doing
today.' 9Doeg the Edomite, who was in
charge of Saul's servants, answered, 'I
saw the son of Jesse coming to Nob, to
Ahimelech son of Ahitub; 10he inquired
of the LORD for him, gave him provisions, and gave him the sword of Goliath the Philistine.'

11 The king sent for the priest Ahimelech son of Ahitub and for all his father's house, the priests who were at
Nob; and all of them came to the king.
12Saul said, 'Listen now, son of Ahitub.' He answered, 'Here I am, my lord.'
13Saul said to him, 'Why have you conspired against me, you and the son of
Jesse, by giving him bread and a sword,
and by inquiring of God for him, so that
he has risen against me, to lie in wait, as
he is doing today?'

[z] **21.13** Heb *in their hands* [a] **22.3** Syr Vg: Heb *come out*

14 Then Ahimelech answered the
king, 'Who among all your servants is so
faithful as David? He is the king's son-
in-law, and is quick[b] to do your bidding,
and is honoured in your house. 15 Is today the first time that I have inquired
of God for him? By no means! Do not let
the king impute anything to his servant
or to any member of my father's house;
for your servant has known nothing of
all this, much or little.' 16 The king said,
'You shall surely die, Ahimelech, you
and all your father's house.' 17 The king
said to the guard who stood around
him, 'Turn and kill the priests of the
LORD, because their hand also is with
David; they knew that he fled, and did
not disclose it to me.' But the servants
of the king would not raise their hand
to attack the priests of the LORD. 18 Then
the king said to Doeg, 'You, Doeg, turn
and attack the priests.' Doeg the Edomite turned and attacked the priests; on
that day he killed eighty-five who wore
the linen ephod. 19 Nob, the city of the
priests, he put to the sword; men and
women, children and infants, oxen,
donkeys, and sheep, he put to the sword.

20 But one of the sons of Ahimelech
son of Ahitub, named Abiathar, escaped
and fled after David. 21 Abiathar told David that Saul had killed the priests of the
LORD. 22 David said to Abiathar, 'I knew
on that day, when Doeg the Edomite was there, that he would surely tell
Saul. I am responsible[c] for the lives of all
your father's house. 23 Stay with me, and
do not be afraid; for the one who seeks
my life seeks your life; you will be safe
with me.'

DAVID SAVES THE CITY OF KEILAH

23 Now they told David, 'The Philistines are fighting against
Keilah, and are robbing the threshing-
floors.' 2 David inquired of the LORD,
'Shall I go and attack these Philistines?'
The LORD said to David, 'Go and attack
the Philistines and save Keilah.' 3 But
David's men said to him, 'Look, we are
afraid here in Judah; how much more
then if we go to Keilah against the armies of the Philistines?' 4 Then David
inquired of the LORD again. The LORD
answered him, 'Yes, go down to Keilah;
for I will give the Philistines into your
hand.' 5 So David and his men went to
Keilah, fought with the Philistines,
brought away their livestock, and dealt
them a heavy defeat. Thus David rescued the inhabitants of Keilah.

6 When Abiathar son of Ahimelech
fled to David at Keilah, he came down
with an ephod in his hand. 7 Now it was
told Saul that David had come to Keilah.
And Saul said, 'God has given[d] him into
my hand; for he has shut himself in by
entering a town that has gates and bars.'
8 Saul summoned all the people to war,
to go down to Keilah, to besiege David
and his men. 9 When David learned that
Saul was plotting evil against him, he
said to the priest Abiathar, 'Bring the
ephod here.' 10 David said, 'O LORD, the
God of Israel, your servant has heard
that Saul seeks to come to Keilah, to
destroy the city on my account. 11 And
now, will[e] Saul come down as your servant has heard? O LORD, the God of Israel, I beseech you, tell your servant.'
The LORD said, 'He will come down.'
12 Then David said, 'Will the men of Keilah surrender me and my men into
the hand of Saul?' The LORD said, 'They
will surrender you.' 13 Then David and
his men, who were about six hundred,
set out and left Keilah; they wandered
wherever they could go. When Saul was
told that David had escaped from Keilah, he gave up the expedition. 14 David
remained in the strongholds in the wilderness, in the hill country of the Wilderness of Ziph. Saul sought him every
day, but the LORD[f] did not give him into
his hand.

DAVID ELUDES SAUL IN THE WILDERNESS

15 David was in the Wilderness of
Ziph at Horesh when he learned that[g]
Saul had come out to seek his life.
16 Saul's son Jonathan set out and came
to David at Horesh; there he strengthened his hand through the LORD.[h] 17 He
said to him, 'Do not be afraid; for the
hand of my father Saul shall not find
you; you shall be king over Israel, and
I shall be second to you; my father Saul
also knows that this is so.' 18 Then the
two of them made a covenant before the
LORD; David remained at Horesh, and
Jonathan went home.

19 Then some Ziphites went up to
Saul at Gibeah and said, 'David is hiding
among us in the strongholds of Horesh,

[b] **22.14** Heb *and turns aside* [c] **22.22** Gk Vg: Meaning of Heb uncertain [d] **23.7** Gk Tg: Heb *made a stranger of* [e] **23.11** Q Ms Compare Gk: MT *Will the men of Keilah surrender me into his hand? Will* [f] **23.14** Q Ms Gk: MT *God* [g] **23.15** Or *saw that* [h] **23.16** Compare Q Ms Gk: MT *God*

on the hill of Hachilah, which is south
of Jeshimon. 20Now, O king, whenever
you wish to come down, do so; and our
part will be to surrender him into the
king's hand.' 21Saul said, 'May you be
blessed by the LORD for showing me
compassion! 22Go and make sure once
more; find out exactly where he is, and
who has seen him there; for I am told
that he is very cunning. 23Look around
and learn all the hiding-places where he
lurks, and come back to me with sure
information. Then I will go with you;
and if he is in the land, I will search
him out among all the thousands of Judah.' 24So they set out and went to Ziph
ahead of Saul.

David and his men were in the wilderness of Maon, in the Arabah to the
south of Jeshimon. 25Saul and his men
went to search for him. When David
was told, he went down to the rock and
stayed in the wilderness of Maon. When
Saul heard that, he pursued David into
the wilderness of Maon. 26Saul went
on one side of the mountain, and David and his men on the other side of the
mountain. David was hurrying to get
away from Saul, while Saul and his men
were closing in on David and his men
to capture them. 27Then a messenger
came to Saul, saying, 'Hurry and come;
for the Philistines have made a raid on
the land.' 28So Saul stopped pursuing
David, and went against the Philistines;
therefore that place was called the Rock
of Escape.[i] 29[j]David then went up from
there, and lived in the strongholds of
En-gedi.

DAVID SPARES SAUL'S LIFE

24 When Saul returned from following the Philistines, he was
told, 'David is in the wilderness of En-
gedi.' 2Then Saul took three thousand
chosen men out of all Israel, and went to
look for David and his men in the direction of the Rocks of the Wild Goats. 3He
came to the sheepfolds beside the road,
where there was a cave; and Saul went
in to relieve himself.[k] Now David and
his men were sitting in the innermost
parts of the cave. 4The men of David said
to him, 'Here is the day of which the
LORD said to you, "I will give your enemy into your hand, and you shall do to
him as it seems good to you."' Then David went and stealthily cut off a corner
of Saul's cloak. 5Afterwards David was
stricken to the heart because he had cut
off a corner of Saul's cloak. 6He said to
his men, 'The LORD forbid that I should
do this thing to my lord, the LORD's
anointed, to raise my hand against him;
for he is the LORD's anointed.' 7So David scolded his men severely and did not
permit them to attack Saul. Then Saul
got up and left the cave, and went on his
way.

8 Afterwards David also rose up and
went out of the cave and called after Saul,
'My lord the king!' When Saul looked behind him, David bowed with his face to
the ground, and did obeisance. 9David
said to Saul, 'Why do you listen to the
words of those who say, "David seeks
to do you harm"? 10This very day your
eyes have seen how the LORD gave you
into my hand in the cave; and some
urged me to kill you, but I spared[l] you.
I said, "I will not raise my hand against
my lord; for he is the LORD's anointed."
11See, my father, see the corner of your
cloak in my hand; for by the fact that I
cut off the corner of your cloak, and did
not kill you, you may know for certain
that there is no wrong or treason in my
hands. I have not sinned against you,
though you are hunting me to take my
life. 12May the LORD judge between me
and you! May the LORD avenge me on
you; but my hand shall not be against
you. 13As the ancient proverb says, "Out
of the wicked comes forth wickedness";
but my hand shall not be against you.
14Against whom has the king of Israel
come out? Whom do you pursue? A
dead dog? A single flea? 15May the LORD
therefore be judge, and give sentence
between me and you. May he see to it,
and plead my cause, and vindicate me
against you.'

16 When David had finished speaking these words to Saul, Saul said, 'Is
that your voice, my son David?' Saul
lifted up his voice and wept. 17He said to
David, 'You are more righteous than I;
for you have repaid me good, whereas I
have repaid you evil. 18Today you have
explained how you have dealt well with
me, in that you did not kill me when the
LORD put me into your hands. 19For who
has ever found an enemy, and sent the
enemy safely away? So may the LORD
reward you with good for what you have
done to me this day. 20Now I know that
you shall surely be king, and that the
kingdom of Israel shall be established in

[i] **23.28** Or *Rock of Division*; meaning of Heb uncertain [j] **23.29** Ch 24.1 in Heb [k] **24.3** Heb *to cover his feet* [l] **24.10** Gk Syr Tg Vg: Heb *it* (my eye) *spared*

your hand. 21Swear to me therefore by
the LORD that you will not cut off my
descendants after me, and that you will
not wipe out my name from my father's
house.' 22So David swore this to Saul.
Then Saul went home; but David and
his men went up to the stronghold.

DEATH OF SAMUEL

25 Now Samuel died; and all Israel assembled and mourned for
him. They buried him at his home in
Ramah.

Then David got up and went down to
the wilderness of Paran.

DAVID AND THE WIFE OF NABAL

2 There was a man in Maon, whose
property was in Carmel. The man was very
rich; he had three thousand sheep and a
thousand goats. He was shearing his sheep
in Carmel. 3Now the name of the man was
Nabal, and the name of his wife Abigail.
The woman was clever and beautiful, but
the man was surly and mean; he was a Ca-
lebite. 4David heard in the wilderness that
Nabal was shearing his sheep. 5So David
sent ten young men; and David said to the
young men, 'Go up to Carmel, and go to
Nabal, and greet him in my name. 6Thus
you shall salute him: "Peace be to you, and
peace be to your house, and peace be to all
that you have. 7I hear that you have shearers; now your shepherds have been with
us, and we did them no harm, and they
missed nothing, all the time they were in
Carmel. 8Ask your young men, and they
will tell you. Therefore let my young men
find favour in your sight; for we have come
on a feast day. Please give whatever you
have at hand to your servants and to your
son David." '

9 When David's young men came,
they said all this to Nabal in the name
of David; and then they waited. 10But
Nabal answered David's servants, 'Who
is David? Who is the son of Jesse? There
are many servants today who are breaking away from their masters. 11Shall I
take my bread and my water and the
meat that I have butchered for my
shearers, and give it to men who come
from I do not know where?' 12So David's
young men turned away, and came back
and told him all this. 13David said to his
men, 'Every man strap on his sword!'
And every one of them strapped on
his sword; David also strapped on his
sword; and about four hundred men
went up after David, while two hundred
remained with the baggage.

14 But one of the young men told
Abigail, Nabal's wife, 'David sent messengers out of the wilderness to salute
our master; and he shouted insults at
them. 15Yet the men were very good to
us, and we suffered no harm, and we
never missed anything when we were
in the fields, as long as we were with
them; 16they were a wall to us both by
night and by day, all the while we were
with them keeping the sheep. 17Now
therefore know this and consider what
you should do; for evil has been decided
against our master and against all his
house; he is so ill-natured that no one
can speak to him.'

18 Then Abigail hurried and took
two hundred loaves, two skins of wine,
five sheep ready dressed, five measures
of parched grain, one hundred clusters
of raisins, and two hundred cakes of
figs. She loaded them on donkeys 19and
said to her young men, 'Go on ahead of
me; I am coming after you.' But she did
not tell her husband Nabal. 20As she
rode on the donkey and came down under cover of the mountain, David and
his men came down towards her; and
she met them. 21Now David had said,
'Surely it was in vain that I protected all
that this fellow has in the wilderness, so
that nothing was missed of all that belonged to him; but he has returned me
evil for good. 22God do so to David[m] and
more also, if by morning I leave as much
as one male of all who belong to him.'

23 When Abigail saw David, she
hurried and alighted from the donkey,
and fell before David on her face, bowing to the ground. 24She fell at his feet
and said, 'Upon me alone, my lord, be
the guilt; please let your servant speak
in your ears, and hear the words of your
servant. 25My lord, do not take seriously
this ill-natured fellow Nabal; for as his
name is, so is he; Nabal[n] is his name,
and folly is with him; but I, your servant, did not see the young men of my
lord, whom you sent.

26 'Now then, my lord, as the LORD
lives, and as you yourself live, since the
LORD has restrained you from blood-
guilt and from taking vengeance with
your own hand, now let your enemies
and those who seek to do evil to my lord
be like Nabal. 27And now let this present that your servant has brought to
my lord be given to the young men who

[m] **25.22** Gk Compare Syr: Heb *the enemies of David* [n] **25.25** That is *Fool*

follow my lord. 28 Please forgive the trespass of your servant; for the LORD will certainly make my lord a sure house, because my lord is fighting the battles of the LORD; and evil shall not be found in you as long as you live. 29 If anyone should rise up to pursue you and to seek your life, the life of my lord shall be bound in the bundle of the living under the care of the LORD your God; but the lives of your enemies he shall sling out as from the hollow of a sling. 30 When the LORD has done to my lord according to all the good that he has spoken concerning you, and has appointed you prince over Israel, 31 my lord shall have no cause of grief, or pangs of conscience, for having shed blood without cause or for having saved himself. And when the LORD has dealt well with my lord, then remember your servant.'

32 David said to Abigail, 'Blessed be the LORD, the God of Israel, who sent you to meet me today! 33 Blessed be your good sense, and blessed be you, who have kept me today from blood-guilt and from avenging myself by my own hand! 34 For as surely as the LORD the God of Israel lives, who has restrained me from hurting you, unless you had hurried and come to meet me, truly by morning there would not have been left to Nabal as much as one male.' 35 Then David received from her hand what she had brought him; he said to her, 'Go up to your house in peace; see, I have heeded your voice, and I have granted your petition.'

36 Abigail came to Nabal; he was holding a feast in his house, like the feast of a king. Nabal's heart was merry within him, for he was very drunk; so she told him nothing at all until the morning light. 37 In the morning, when the wine had gone out of Nabal, his wife told him these things, and his heart died within him; he became like a stone. 38 About ten days later the LORD struck Nabal, and he died.

39 When David heard that Nabal was dead, he said, 'Blessed be the LORD who has judged the case of Nabal's insult to me, and has kept back his servant from evil; the LORD has returned the evildoing of Nabal upon his own head.' Then David sent and wooed Abigail, to make her his wife. 40 When David's servants came to Abigail at Carmel, they said to her, 'David has sent us to you to take you to him as his wife.' 41 She rose and bowed down, with her face to the ground, and said, 'Your servant is a slave to wash the feet of the servants of my lord.' 42 Abigail got up hurriedly and rode away on a donkey; her five maids attended her. She went after the messengers of David and became his wife.

43 David also married Ahinoam of Jezreel; both of them became his wives. 44 Saul had given his daughter Michal, David's wife, to Palti son of Laish, who was from Gallim.

DAVID SPARES SAUL'S LIFE A SECOND TIME

26 Then the Ziphites came to Saul at Gibeah, saying, 'David is in hiding on the hill of Hachilah, which is opposite Jeshimon.'[o] 2 So Saul rose and went down to the Wilderness of Ziph, with three thousand chosen men of Israel, to seek David in the Wilderness of Ziph. 3 Saul encamped on the hill of Hachilah, which is opposite Jeshimon[p] beside the road. But David remained in the wilderness. When he learned that Saul had come after him into the wilderness, 4 David sent out spies, and learned that Saul had indeed arrived. 5 Then David set out and came to the place where Saul had encamped; and David saw the place where Saul lay, with Abner son of Ner, the commander of his army. Saul was lying within the encampment, while the army was encamped around him.

6 Then David said to Ahimelech the Hittite, and to Joab's brother Abishai son of Zeruiah, 'Who will go down with me into the camp to Saul?' Abishai said, 'I will go down with you.' 7 So David and Abishai went to the army by night; there Saul lay sleeping within the encampment, with his spear stuck in the ground at his head; and Abner and the army lay around him. 8 Abishai said to David, 'God has given your enemy into your hand today; now therefore let me pin him to the ground with one stroke of the spear; I will not strike him twice.' 9 But David said to Abishai, 'Do not destroy him; for who can raise his hand against the LORD's anointed, and be guiltless?' 10 David said, 'As the LORD lives, the LORD will strike him down; or his day will come to die; or he will go down into battle and perish. 11 The LORD forbid that I should raise my hand against the LORD's anointed; but

[o] **26.1** Or *opposite the waste-land* [p] **26.3** Or *opposite the waste-land*

now take the spear that is at his head,
and the water-jar, and let us go.' 12So
David took the spear that was at Saul's
head and the water-jar, and they went
away. No one saw it, or knew it, nor did
anyone awake; for they were all asleep,
because a deep sleep from the LORD had
fallen upon them.

13 Then David went over to the other
side, and stood on top of a hill far away,
with a great distance between them.
14David called to the army and to Abner son of Ner, saying, 'Abner! Will you
not answer?' Then Abner replied, 'Who
are you that calls to the king?' 15David
said to Abner, 'Are you not a man? Who
is like you in Israel? Why then have you
not kept watch over your lord the king?
For one of the people came in to destroy
your lord the king. 16This thing that
you have done is not good. As the LORD
lives, you deserve to die, because you
have not kept watch over your lord, the
LORD's anointed. See now, where is the
king's spear, or the water-jar that was at
his head?'

17 Saul recognized David's voice,
and said, 'Is that your voice, my son David?' David said, 'It is my voice, my lord,
O king.' 18And he added, 'Why does my
lord pursue his servant? For what have I
done? What guilt is on my hands? 19Now
therefore let my lord the king hear the
words of his servant. If it is the LORD
who has stirred you up against me, may
he accept an offering; but if it is mortals,
may they be cursed before the LORD,
for they have driven me out today from
my share in the heritage of the LORD,
saying, "Go, serve other gods." 20Now,
therefore, do not let my blood fall to the
ground, away from the presence of the
LORD; for the king of Israel has come
out to seek a single flea, like one who
hunts a partridge in the mountains.'

21 Then Saul said, 'I have done
wrong; come back, my son David, for
I will never harm you again, because
my life was precious in your sight today; I have been a fool, and have made a
great mistake.' 22David replied, 'Here is
the spear, O king! Let one of the young
men come over and get it. 23The LORD
rewards everyone for his righteousness
and his faithfulness; for the LORD gave
you into my hand today, but I would
not raise my hand against the LORD's
anointed. 24As your life was precious
today in my sight, so may my life be
precious in the sight of the LORD, and
may he rescue me from all tribulation.'
25Then Saul said to David, 'Blessed be
you, my son David! You will do many
things and will succeed in them.' So David went on his way, and Saul returned
to his place.

DAVID SERVES KING ACHISH OF GATH

27 David said in his heart, 'I shall
now perish one day by the hand
of Saul; there is nothing better for me
than to escape to the land of the Philistines; then Saul will despair of seeking me any longer within the borders
of Israel, and I shall escape out of his
hand.' 2So David set out and went over,
he and the six hundred men who were
with him, to King Achish son of Maoch
of Gath. 3David stayed with Achish at
Gath, he and his troops, every man with
his household, and David with his two
wives, Ahinoam of Jezreel, and Abigail
of Carmel, Nabal's widow. 4When Saul
was told that David had fled to Gath, he
no longer sought for him.

5 Then David said to Achish, 'If I have
found favour in your sight, let a place be
given me in one of the country towns,
so that I may live there; for why should
your servant live in the royal city with
you?' 6So that day Achish gave him Ziklag; therefore Ziklag has belonged to the
kings of Judah to this day. 7The length
of time that David lived in the country
of the Philistines was one year and four
months.

8 Now David and his men went up
and made raids on the Geshurites, the
Girzites, and the Amalekites; for these
were the landed settlements from Te-
lam[q] on the way to Shur and on to the
land of Egypt. 9David struck the land,
leaving neither man nor woman alive,
but took away the sheep, the oxen, the
donkeys, the camels, and the clothing, and came back to Achish. 10When
Achish asked, 'Against whom[r] have you
made a raid today?' David would say,
'Against the Negeb of Judah', or 'Against
the Negeb of the Jerahmeelites', or
'Against the Negeb of the Kenites.' 11Da-
vid left neither man nor woman alive to
be brought back to Gath, thinking, 'They
might tell about us, and say, "David has
done so and so."' Such was his practice
all the time he lived in the country of
the Philistines. 12Achish trusted David,
thinking, 'He has made himself utterly

[q] **27.8** Compare Gk 15.4: Heb *from of old*
[r] **27.10** Q Ms Gk Vg: MT lacks *whom*

abhorrent to his people Israel; therefore
he shall always be my servant.'

28 In those days the Philistines
gathered their forces for war, to
fight against Israel. Achish said to David, 'You know, of course, that you and
your men are to go out with me in the
army.' 2David said to Achish, 'Very well,
then you shall know what your servant
can do.' Achish said to David, 'Very well,
I will make you my bodyguard for life.'

SAUL CONSULTS A MEDIUM

3 Now Samuel had died, and all Israel
had mourned for him and buried him in
Ramah, his own city. Saul had expelled
the mediums and the wizards from the
land. 4The Philistines assembled, and
came and encamped at Shunem. Saul
gathered all Israel, and they encamped
at Gilboa. 5When Saul saw the army of
the Philistines, he was afraid, and his
heart trembled greatly. 6When Saul inquired of the LORD, the LORD did not answer him, not by dreams, nor by Urim,
nor by prophets. 7Then Saul said to his
servants, 'Seek out for me a woman who
is a medium, so that I may go to her and
inquire of her.' His servants said to him,
'There is a medium at Endor.'

8 So Saul disguised himself and put
on other clothes and went there, he and
two men with him. They came to the
woman by night. And he said, 'Consult
a spirit for me, and bring up for me the
one whom I name to you.' 9The woman
said to him, 'Surely you know what Saul
has done, how he has cut off the mediums and the wizards from the land.
Why then are you laying a snare for my
life to bring about my death?' 10But Saul
swore to her by the LORD, 'As the LORD
lives, no punishment shall come upon
you for this thing.' 11Then the woman
said, 'Whom shall I bring up for you?'
He answered, 'Bring up Samuel for
me.' 12When the woman saw Samuel,
she cried out with a loud voice; and the
woman said to Saul, 'Why have you deceived me? You are Saul!' 13The king said
to her, 'Have no fear; what do you see?'
The woman said to Saul, 'I see a divine
being[s] coming up out of the ground.'
14He said to her, 'What is his appearance?' She said, 'An old man is coming
up; he is wrapped in a robe.' So Saul
knew that it was Samuel, and he bowed
with his face to the ground, and did
obeisance.

15 Then Samuel said to Saul, 'Why
have you disturbed me by bringing me
up?' Saul answered, 'I am in great distress, for the Philistines are warring
against me, and God has turned away
from me and answers me no more, either by prophets or by dreams; so I have
summoned you to tell me what I should
do.' 16Samuel said, 'Why then do you ask
me, since the LORD has turned from you
and become your enemy? 17The LORD
has done to you just as he spoke by me;
for the LORD has torn the kingdom out
of your hand, and given it to your neighbour David. 18Because you did not obey
the voice of the LORD, and did not carry
out his fierce wrath against Amalek,
therefore the LORD has done this thing
to you today. 19Moreover, the LORD
will give Israel along with you into the
hands of the Philistines; and tomorrow
you and your sons shall be with me; the
LORD will also give the army of Israel
into the hands of the Philistines.'

20 Immediately Saul fell full length
on the ground, filled with fear because of
the words of Samuel; and there was no
strength in him, for he had eaten nothing all day and all night. 21The woman
came to Saul, and when she saw that
he was terrified, she said to him, 'Your
servant has listened to you; I have taken
my life in my hand, and have listened to
what you have said to me. 22Now therefore, you also listen to your servant; let
me set a morsel of bread before you.
Eat, that you may have strength when
you go on your way.' 23He refused, and
said, 'I will not eat.' But his servants,
together with the woman, urged him;
and he listened to their words. So he
got up from the ground and sat on the
bed. 24Now the woman had a fatted
calf in the house. She quickly slaughtered it, and she took flour, kneaded it,
and baked unleavened cakes. 25She put
them before Saul and his servants, and
they ate. Then they rose and went away
that night.

THE PHILISTINES REJECT DAVID

29 Now the Philistines gathered all
their forces at Aphek, while the
Israelites were encamped by the fountain that is in Jezreel. 2As the lords of
the Philistines were marching on by
hundreds and by thousands, and David and his men were marching in the
rear with Achish, 3the commanders of
the Philistines said, 'What are these Hebrews doing here?' Achish said to the

[s] 28.13 Or *a god*; or *gods*

commanders of the Philistines, 'Is this
not David, the servant of King Saul of
Israel, who has been with me now for
days and years? Since he deserted to me
I have found no fault in him to this day.'
4But the commanders of the Philistines
were angry with him; and the commanders of the Philistines said to him,
'Send the man back, so that he may return to the place that you have assigned
to him; he shall not go down with us to
battle, or else he may become an adversary to us in the battle. For how could
this fellow reconcile himself to his lord?
Would it not be with the heads of the
men here? 5Is this not David, of whom
they sing to one another in dances,

"Saul has killed his thousands,
and David his tens of thousands"?'

6 Then Achish called David and said
to him, 'As the LORD lives, you have
been honest, and to me it seems right
that you should march out and in with
me in the campaign; for I have found
nothing wrong in you from the day of
your coming to me until today. Nevertheless the lords do not approve of you.
7So go back now; and go peaceably; do
nothing to displease the lords of the
Philistines.' 8David said to Achish, 'But
what have I done? What have you found
in your servant from the day I entered
your service until now, that I should not
go and fight against the enemies of my
lord the king?' 9Achish replied to David, 'I know that you are as blameless in
my sight as an angel of God; nevertheless, the commanders of the Philistines
have said, "He shall not go up with us
to the battle." 10Now then rise early in
the morning, you and the servants of
your lord who came with you, and go to
the place that I appointed for you. As for
the evil report, do not take it to heart,
for you have done well before me.[t] Start
early in the morning, and leave as soon
as you have light.' 11So David set out
with his men early in the morning, to
return to the land of the Philistines. But
the Philistines went up to Jezreel.

DAVID AVENGES THE DESTRUCTION OF ZIKLAG

30 Now when David and his men
came to Ziklag on the third day,
the Amalekites had made a raid on the
Negeb and on Ziklag. They had attacked
Ziklag, burned it down, 2and taken
captive the women and all[u] who were
in it, both small and great; they killed
none of them, but carried them off, and
went on their way. 3When David and
his men came to the city, they found it
burnt down, and their wives and sons
and daughters taken captive. 4Then David and the people who were with him
raised their voices and wept, until they
had no more strength to weep. 5David's
two wives also had been taken captive,
Ahinoam of Jezreel, and Abigail the
widow of Nabal of Carmel. 6David was
in great danger; for the people spoke of
stoning him, because all the people were
bitter in spirit for their sons and daughters. But David strengthened himself in
the LORD his God.

7 David said to the priest Abiathar son of Ahimelech, 'Bring me the
ephod.' So Abiathar brought the ephod
to David. 8David inquired of the LORD,
'Shall I pursue this band? Shall I overtake them?' He answered him, 'Pursue; for you shall surely overtake and
shall surely rescue.' 9So David set out,
he and the six hundred men who were
with him. They came to the Wadi Besor, where those stayed who were left
behind. 10But David went on with the
pursuit, he and four hundred men; two
hundred stayed behind, too exhausted
to cross the Wadi Besor.

11 In the open country they found
an Egyptian, and brought him to David. They gave him bread and he ate;
they gave him water to drink; 12they
also gave him a piece of fig cake and two
clusters of raisins. When he had eaten,
his spirit revived; for he had not eaten
bread or drunk water for three days and
three nights. 13Then David said to him,
'To whom do you belong? Where are
you from?' He said, 'I am a young man
of Egypt, servant to an Amalekite. My
master left me behind because I fell sick
three days ago. 14We had made a raid
on the Negeb of the Cherethites and
on that which belongs to Judah and on
the Negeb of Caleb; and we burned Ziklag down.' 15David said to him, 'Will you
take me down to this raiding party?' He
said, 'Swear to me by God that you will
not kill me, or hand me over to my master, and I will take you down to them.'

16 When he had taken him down,
they were spread out all over the ground,
eating and drinking and dancing, because of the great amount of spoil they
had taken from the land of the Philistines and from the land of Judah. 17Da-

[t] **29.10** Gk: Heb lacks *and go to the place . . . done well before me* [u] **30.2** Gk: Heb lacks *and all*

vid attacked them from twilight until
the evening of the next day. Not one
of them escaped, except four hundred
young men, who mounted camels and
fled. 18David recovered all that the Amalekites had taken; and David rescued
his two wives. 19Nothing was missing,
whether small or great, sons or daughters, spoil or anything that had been
taken; David brought back everything.
20David also captured all the flocks and
herds, which were driven ahead of the
other cattle; people said, 'This is David's
spoil.'

21 Then David came to the two hundred men who had been too exhausted
to follow David, and who had been
left at the Wadi Besor. They went out
to meet David and to meet the people
who were with him. When David drew
near to the people he saluted them.
22Then all the corrupt and worthless
fellows among the men who had gone
with David said, 'Because they did not
go with us, we will not give them any
of the spoil that we have recovered, except that each man may take his wife
and children, and leave.' 23But David
said, 'You shall not do so, my brothers,
with what the LORD has given us; he
has preserved us and handed over to
us the raiding party that attacked us.
24Who would listen to you in this matter? For the share of the one who goes
down into the battle shall be the same
as the share of the one who stays by the
baggage; they shall share alike.' 25From
that day forward he made it a statute
and an ordinance for Israel; it continues
to the present day.

26 When David came to Ziklag, he
sent part of the spoil to his friends, the
elders of Judah, saying, 'Here is a present
for you from the spoil of the enemies of
the LORD'; 27it was for those in Bethel,
in Ramoth of the Negeb, in Jattir, 28in
Aroer, in Siphmoth, in Eshtemoa, 29in
Racal, in the towns of the Jerahmeelites, in the towns of the Kenites, 30in
Hormah, in Bor-ashan, in Athach, 31in
Hebron, all the places where David and
his men had roamed.

THE DEATH OF SAUL AND HIS SONS

31 Now the Philistines fought
against Israel; and the men of
Israel fled before the Philistines, and
many fell[v] on Mount Gilboa. 2The Philistines overtook Saul and his sons; and the
Philistines killed Jonathan and Abinadab and Malchishua, the sons of Saul.
3The battle pressed hard upon Saul; the
archers found him, and he was badly
wounded by them. 4Then Saul said to
his armour-bearer, 'Draw your sword
and thrust me through with it, so that
these uncircumcised may not come and
thrust me through, and make sport of
me.' But his armour-bearer was unwilling; for he was terrified. So Saul took his
own sword and fell upon it. 5When his
armour-bearer saw that Saul was dead,
he also fell upon his sword and died with
him. 6So Saul and his three sons and his
armour-bearer and all his men died together on the same day. 7When the men
of Israel who were on the other side of
the valley and those beyond the Jordan
saw that the men of Israel had fled and
that Saul and his sons were dead, they
forsook their towns and fled; and the
Philistines came and occupied them.

8 The next day, when the Philistines
came to strip the dead, they found Saul
and his three sons fallen on Mount Gilboa. 9They cut off his head, stripped
off his armour, and sent messengers
throughout the land of the Philistines
to carry the good news to the houses of
their idols and to the people. 10They put
his armour in the temple of Astarte;[w]
and they fastened his body to the wall of
Beth-shan. 11But when the inhabitants
of Jabesh-gilead heard what the Philistines had done to Saul, 12all the valiant
men set out, travelled all night long, and
took the body of Saul and the bodies of
his sons from the wall of Beth-shan.
They came to Jabesh and burned them
there. 13Then they took their bones and
buried them under the tamarisk tree in
Jabesh, and fasted for seven days.

[v] 31.1 Heb *and they fell slain* [w] 31.10 Heb
plural

2 SAMUEL

The second part of the book of Samuel (2 Samuel) does not speak of Samuel, but of David and the stories about his reign as king. This is not a systematic history of events leading up to the establishment of the monarchy, but a narration of stories surrounding the principal figure of the book, namely King David. First David becomes king of Judah (ch. 2), then king of Israel (ch. 5), and finally he establishes Jerusalem as the capital of a united kingdom (ch. 6). The Lord's promise of an eternal dynasty is a key passage in 2 Sam 7 and becomes the basis for the Jewish expectation of a messiah, a son of David.

Texts from 2 Samuel are read in the liturgy from Saturday of the Second Week of Year II until Wednesday of the Fourth Week of Year II. In these later texts the adultery with Bathsheba, the revolt and death of Absalom, and David's acknowledgment of his sin before the Lord are all told consecutively in the First Reading each day.

DAVID MOURNS FOR SAUL AND JONATHAN

1 After the death of Saul, when David had returned from defeating
the Amalekites, David remained two
days in Ziklag. 2On the third day, a man
came from Saul's camp, with his clothes
torn and dirt on his head. When he came
to David, he fell to the ground and did
obeisance. 3David said to him, 'Where
have you come from?' He said to him,
'I have escaped from the camp of Israel.'
4David said to him, 'How did things go?
Tell me!' He answered, 'The army fled
from the battle, but also many of the
army fell and died; and Saul and his son
Jonathan also died.' 5Then David asked
the young man who was reporting to
him, 'How do you know that Saul and
his son Jonathan died?' 6The young man
reporting to him said, 'I happened to be
on Mount Gilboa; and there was Saul
leaning on his spear, while the chariots
and the horsemen drew close to him.
7When he looked behind him, he saw
me, and called to me. I answered, "Here,
sir." 8And he said to me, "Who are you?"
I answered him, "I am an Amalekite."
9He said to me, "Come, stand over me
and kill me; for convulsions have seized
me, and yet my life still lingers." 10So
I stood over him, and killed him, for I
knew that he could not live after he had
fallen. I took the crown that was on his
head and the armlet that was on his
arm, and I have brought them here to
my lord.'

11 Then David took hold of his clothes
and tore them; and all the men who were
with him did the same. 12They mourned
and wept, and fasted until evening for
Saul and for his son Jonathan, and for
the army of the LORD and for the house
of Israel, because they had fallen by the
sword. 13David said to the young man
who had reported to him, 'Where do you
come from?' He answered, 'I am the son
of a resident alien, an Amalekite.' 14Da-
vid said to him, 'Were you not afraid
to lift your hand to destroy the LORD's
anointed?' 15Then David called one of
the young men and said, 'Come here and
strike him down.' So he struck him down
and he died. 16David said to him, 'Your
blood be on your head; for your own
mouth has testified against you, saying,
"I have killed the LORD's anointed."'

17 David intoned this lamentation
over Saul and his son Jonathan. 18(He
ordered that The Song of the Bow[a] be

[a] 1.18 Heb *that The Bow*

taught to the people of Judah; it is written in the Book of Jashar.) He said:

19 Your glory, O Israel, lies slain
upon your high places!
How the mighty have fallen!
20 Tell it not in Gath,
proclaim it not in the
streets of Ashkelon;
or the daughters of the
Philistines will rejoice,
the daughters of the
uncircumcised will exult.

21 You mountains of Gilboa,
let there be no dew or
rain upon you,
nor bounteous fields![b]
For there the shield of the
mighty was defiled,
the shield of Saul, anointed
with oil no more.

22 From the blood of the slain,
from the fat of the mighty,
the bow of Jonathan did
not turn back,
nor the sword of Saul
return empty.

23 Saul and Jonathan, beloved
and lovely!
In life and in death they
were not divided;
they were swifter than eagles,
they were stronger than lions.

24 O daughters of Israel, weep
over Saul,
who clothed you with
crimson, in luxury,
who put ornaments of gold
on your apparel.

25 How the mighty have fallen
in the midst of the battle!

Jonathan lies slain upon
your high places.
26 I am distressed for you, my
brother Jonathan;
greatly beloved were you to me;
your love to me was wonderful,
passing the love of women.

27 How the mighty have fallen,
and the weapons of war perished!

DAVID ANOINTED KING OF JUDAH

2 After this David inquired of the
LORD, 'Shall I go up into any of the
cities of Judah?' The LORD said to him, 'Go
up.' David said, 'To which shall I go up?'
He said, 'To Hebron.' 2So David went up
there, along with his two wives, Ahinoam of Jezreel, and Abigail the widow
of Nabal of Carmel. 3David brought up
the men who were with him, every one
with his household; and they settled in
the towns of Hebron. 4Then the people of
Judah came, and there they anointed David king over the house of Judah.

When they told David, 'It was the people of Jabesh-gilead who buried Saul',
5David sent messengers to the people
of Jabesh-gilead, and said to them, 'May
you be blessed by the LORD, because you
showed this loyalty to Saul your lord,
and buried him! 6Now may the LORD
show steadfast love and faithfulness to
you! And I too will reward you because
you have done this thing. 7Therefore let
your hands be strong, and be valiant; for
Saul your lord is dead, and the house of
Judah has anointed me king over them.'

ISHBAAL KING OF ISRAEL

8 But Abner son of Ner, commander
of Saul's army, had taken Ishbaal[c] son
of Saul, and brought him over to Mahanaim. 9He made him king over Gilead,
the Ashurites, Jezreel, Ephraim, Benjamin, and over all Israel. 10Ishbaal,[d] Saul's
son, was forty years old when he began
to reign over Israel, and he reigned for
two years. But the house of Judah followed David. 11The time that David was
king in Hebron over the house of Judah
was seven years and six months.

THE BATTLE OF GIBEON

12 Abner son of Ner, and the servants of Ishbaal[e] son of Saul, went out
from Mahanaim to Gibeon. 13Joab son
of Zeruiah, and the servants of David,
went out and met them at the pool of
Gibeon. One group sat on one side of the
pool, while the other sat on the other
side of the pool. 14Abner said to Joab,
'Let the young men come forward and
have a contest before us.' Joab said, 'Let
them come forward.' 15So they came forward and were counted as they passed
by, twelve for Benjamin and Ishbaal[f]
son of Saul, and twelve of the servants
of David. 16Each grasped his opponent

[b] 1.21 Meaning of Heb uncertain [c] 2.8 Gk Compare 1 Chr 8.33; 9.39: Heb *Ish-bosheth*, 'man of shame' [d] 2.10 Gk Compare 1 Chr 8.33; 9.39: Heb *Ish-bosheth*, 'man of shame' [e] 2.12 Gk Compare 1 Chr 8.33; 9.39: Heb *Ish-bosheth*, 'man of shame' [f] 2.15 Gk Compare 1 Chr 8.33; 9.39: Heb *Ish-bosheth*, 'man of shame'

by the head, and thrust his sword in his
opponent's side; so they fell down together. Therefore that place was called
Helkath-hazzurim,[g] which is at Gibeon.
17The battle was very fierce that day;
and Abner and the men of Israel were
beaten by the servants of David.

18 The three sons of Zeruiah were
there, Joab, Abishai, and Asahel. Now
Asahel was as swift of foot as a wild gazelle. 19Asahel pursued Abner, turning
neither to the right nor to the left as
he followed him. 20Then Abner looked
back and said, 'Is it you, Asahel?' He answered, 'Yes, it is.' 21Abner said to him,
'Turn to your right or to your left, and
seize one of the young men, and take his
spoil.' But Asahel would not turn away
from following him. 22Abner said again
to Asahel, 'Turn away from following me; why should I strike you to the
ground? How then could I show my face
to your brother Joab?' 23But he refused
to turn away. So Abner struck him in
the stomach with the butt of his spear,
so that the spear came out at his back.
He fell there, and died where he lay. And
all those who came to the place where
Asahel had fallen and died, stood still.

24 But Joab and Abishai pursued Abner. As the sun was going down they
came to the hill of Ammah, which lies
before Giah on the way to the wilderness of Gibeon. 25The Benjaminites rallied around Abner and formed a single
band; they took their stand on the top
of a hill. 26Then Abner called to Joab, 'Is
the sword to keep devouring for ever?
Do you not know that the end will be
bitter? How long will it be before you order your people to turn from the pursuit
of their kinsmen?' 27Joab said, 'As God
lives, if you had not spoken, the people
would have continued to pursue their
kinsmen, not stopping until morning.'
28Joab sounded the trumpet and all the
people stopped; they no longer pursued
Israel or engaged in battle any further.

29 Abner and his men travelled all
that night through the Arabah; they
crossed the Jordan, and, marching the
whole forenoon,[h] they came to Mahanaim. 30Joab returned from the pursuit
of Abner; and when he had gathered all
the people together, there were missing
of David's servants nineteen men besides Asahel. 31But the servants of David had killed of Benjamin three hundred and sixty of Abner's men. 32They
took up Asahel and buried him in the
tomb of his father, which was at Bethlehem. Joab and his men marched all
night, and the day broke upon them at
Hebron.

ABNER DEFECTS TO DAVID

3 There was a long war between the
house of Saul and the house of David; David grew stronger and stronger,
while the house of Saul became weaker
and weaker.

2 Sons were born to David at Hebron:
his firstborn was Amnon, of Ahinoam
of Jezreel; 3his second, Chileab, of Abigail the widow of Nabal of Carmel; the
third, Absalom son of Maacah, daughter of King Talmai of Geshur; 4the
fourth, Adonijah son of Haggith; the
fifth, Shephatiah son of Abital; 5and the
sixth, Ithream, of David's wife Eglah.
These were born to David in Hebron.

6 While there was war between the
house of Saul and the house of David,
Abner was making himself strong in
the house of Saul. 7Now Saul had a concubine whose name was Rizpah daughter of Aiah. And Ishbaal[i] said to Abner,
'Why have you gone in to my father's
concubine?' 8The words of Ishbaal[j]
made Abner very angry; he said, 'Am
I a dog's head for Judah? Today I keep
showing loyalty to the house of your
father Saul, to his brothers, and to his
friends, and have not given you into
the hand of David; and yet you charge
me now with a crime concerning this
woman. 9So may God do to Abner and
so may he add to it! For just what the
LORD has sworn to David, that will I accomplish for him, 10to transfer the kingdom from the house of Saul, and set up
the throne of David over Israel and over
Judah, from Dan to Beer-sheba.' 11And
Ishbaal[k] could not answer Abner another word, because he feared him.

12 Abner sent messengers to David
at Hebron,[l] saying, 'To whom does the
land belong? Make your covenant with
me, and I will give you my support to
bring all Israel over to you.' 13He said,
'Good; I will make a covenant with you.
But one thing I require of you: you shall
never appear in my presence unless
you bring Saul's daughter Michal when
you come to see me.' 14Then David sent
messengers to Saul's son Ishbaal,[m] say-

[g] **2.16** That is *Field of Sword-edges*
[h] **2.29** Meaning of Heb uncertain [i] **3.7** Heb *And he* [j] **3.8** Gk Compare 1 Chr 8.33; 9.39: Heb *Ish-bosheth*, 'man of shame' [k] **3.11** Heb *And he* [l] **3.12** Gk: Heb *where he was* [m] **3.14** Heb *Ish-bosheth*

ing, 'Give me my wife Michal, to whom
I became engaged at the price of one
hundred foreskins of the Philistines.'
15 Ishbaal[n] sent and took her from her
husband Paltiel the son of Laish. 16 But
her husband went with her, weeping as
he walked behind her all the way to Bahurim. Then Abner said to him, 'Go back
home!' So he went back.

17 Abner sent word to the elders of
Israel, saying, 'For some time past you
have been seeking David as king over
you. 18 Now then bring it about; for the
LORD has promised David: Through my
servant David I will save my people Israel from the hand of the Philistines,
and from all their enemies.' 19 Abner also
spoke directly to the Benjaminites; then
Abner went to tell David at Hebron all
that Israel and the whole house of Benjamin were ready to do.

20 When Abner came with twenty
men to David at Hebron, David made a
feast for Abner and the men who were
with him. 21 Abner said to David, 'Let
me go and rally all Israel to my lord the
king, in order that they may make a covenant with you, and that you may reign
over all that your heart desires.' So David dismissed Abner, and he went away
in peace.

ABNER IS KILLED BY JOAB

22 Just then the servants of David
arrived with Joab from a raid, bringing
much spoil with them. But Abner was
not with David at Hebron, for David[o]
had dismissed him, and he had gone
away in peace. 23 When Joab and all the
army that was with him came, it was
told Joab, 'Abner son of Ner came to the
king, and he has dismissed him, and he
has gone away in peace.' 24 Then Joab
went to the king and said, 'What have
you done? Abner came to you; why did
you dismiss him, so that he got away?
25 You know that Abner son of Ner came
to deceive you, and to learn your comings and goings and to learn all that you
are doing.'

26 When Joab came out from David's
presence, he sent messengers after Abner, and they brought him back from
the cistern of Sirah; but David did not
know about it. 27 When Abner returned
to Hebron, Joab took him aside in the
gateway to speak with him privately,
and there he stabbed him in the stomach. So he died for shedding[p] the blood
of Asahel, Joab's[q] brother. 28 Afterwards, when David heard of it, he said,
'I and my kingdom are for ever guiltless
before the LORD for the blood of Abner son of Ner. 29 May the guilt[r] fall on
the head of Joab, and on all his father's
house; and may the house of Joab never
be without one who has a discharge, or
who is leprous,[s] or who holds a spindle,
or who falls by the sword, or who lacks
food!' 30 So Joab and his brother Abishai
murdered Abner because he had killed
their brother Asahel in the battle at Gibeon.

31 Then David said to Joab and to all
the people who were with him, 'Tear
your clothes, and put on sackcloth, and
mourn over Abner.' And King David followed the bier. 32 They buried Abner at
Hebron. The king lifted up his voice and
wept at the grave of Abner, and all the
people wept. 33 The king lamented for
Abner, saying,

'Should Abner die as a fool dies?
34 Your hands were not bound,
your feet were not fettered;
as one falls before the wicked
you have fallen.'

And all the people wept over him again.
35 Then all the people came to persuade
David to eat something while it was still
day; but David swore, saying, 'So may
God do to me, and more, if I taste bread
or anything else before the sun goes
down!' 36 All the people took notice of it,
and it pleased them; just as everything
the king did pleased all the people. 37 So
all the people and all Israel understood
that day that the king had no part in the
killing of Abner son of Ner. 38 And the
king said to his servants, 'Do you not
know that a prince and a great man has
fallen this day in Israel? 39 Today I am
powerless, even though anointed king;
these men, the sons of Zeruiah, are too
violent for me. The LORD pay back the
one who does wickedly in accordance
with his wickedness!'

ISHBAAL ASSASSINATED

4 When Saul's son Ishbaal[t] heard that
Abner had died at Hebron, his courage failed, and all Israel was dismayed.
2 Saul's son had two captains of raiding
bands; the name of one was Baanah,
and the name of the other Rechab. They
were sons of Rimmon, a Benjaminite
from Beeroth—for Beeroth is considered

[n] 3.15 Heb *Ish-bosheth* [o] 3.22 Heb *he*
[p] 3.27 Heb lacks *shedding* [q] 3.27 Heb *his*
[r] 3.29 Heb *May it* [s] 3.29 A term for several skin diseases; precise meaning uncertain [t] 4.1 Heb lacks *Ishbaal*

to belong to Benjamin. 3(Now the people of Beeroth had fled to Gittaim and
are there as resident aliens to this day).
4 Saul's son Jonathan had a son who
was crippled in his feet. He was five
years old when the news about Saul
and Jonathan came from Jezreel. His
nurse picked him up and fled; and, in
her haste to flee, it happened that he fell
and became lame. His name was Mephibosheth.[u]
5 Now the sons of Rimmon the Beerothite, Rechab and Baanah, set out,
and about the heat of the day they came
to the house of Ishbaal,[v] while he was
taking his noonday rest. 6They came inside the house as though to take wheat,
and they struck him in the stomach;
then Rechab and his brother Baanah
escaped.[w] 7Now they had come into the
house while he was lying on his couch
in his bedchamber; they attacked him,
killed him, and beheaded him. Then
they took his head and travelled by
way of the Arabah all night long. 8They
brought the head of Ishbaal[x] to David
at Hebron and said to the king, 'Here
is the head of Ishbaal,[y] son of Saul your
enemy who sought your life; the LORD
has avenged my lord the king this day
on Saul and on his offspring.'
9 David answered Rechab and his
brother Baanah, the sons of Rimmon
the Beerothite, 'As the LORD lives, who
has redeemed my life out of every adversity, 10when the one who told me, "See,
Saul is dead", thought he was bringing
good news, I seized him and killed him
at Ziklag—this was the reward I gave
him for his news. 11How much more
then, when wicked men have killed a
righteous man on his bed in his own
house! And now shall I not require his
blood at your hand, and destroy you
from the earth?' 12So David commanded
the young men, and they killed them;
they cut off their hands and feet, and
hung their bodies beside the pool at Hebron. But the head of Ishbaal[z] they took
and buried in the tomb of Abner at Hebron.

DAVID ANOINTED KING OF ALL ISRAEL

5 Then all the tribes of Israel came to
David at Hebron, and said, 'Look,
we are your bone and flesh. 2For some
time, while Saul was king over us, it was
you who led out Israel and brought it in.
The LORD said to you: It is you who shall
be shepherd of my people Israel, you
who shall be ruler over Israel.' 3So all the
elders of Israel came to the king at Hebron; and King David made a covenant
with them at Hebron before the LORD,
and they anointed David king over Israel. 4David was thirty years old when
he began to reign, and he reigned for
forty years. 5At Hebron he reigned over
Judah for seven years and six months;
and at Jerusalem he reigned over all Israel and Judah for thirty-three years.

JERUSALEM MADE CAPITAL OF THE COMBINED KINGDOM

6 The king and his men marched to
Jerusalem against the Jebusites, the
inhabitants of the land, who said to David, 'You will not come in here, even
the blind and the lame will turn you
back'—thinking, 'David cannot come
in here.' 7Nevertheless, David took the
stronghold of Zion, which is now the
city of David. 8David had said on that
day, 'Whoever wishes to strike down the
Jebusites, let him get up the water shaft
to attack the lame and the blind, those
whom David hates.'[a] Therefore it is said,
'The blind and the lame shall not come
into the house.' 9David occupied the
stronghold, and named it the city of David. David built the city all around from
the Millo inwards. 10And David became
greater and greater, for the LORD, the
God of hosts, was with him.
11 King Hiram of Tyre sent messengers to David, along with cedar trees,
and carpenters and masons who built
David a house. 12David then perceived
that the LORD had established him king
over Israel, and that he had exalted his
kingdom for the sake of his people Israel.
13 In Jerusalem, after he came from
Hebron, David took more concubines
and wives; and more sons and daughters were born to David. 14These are the
names of those who were born to him in
Jerusalem: Shammua, Shobab, Nathan,
Solomon, 15Ibhar, Elishua, Nepheg, Japhia, 16Elishama, Eliada, and Eliphelet.

PHILISTINE ATTACK REPULSED

17 When the Philistines heard that
David had been anointed king over
Israel, all the Philistines went up in
search of David; but David heard about

[u] 4.4 In 1 Chr 8.34 and 9.40, *Merib-baal*
[v] 4.5 Heb *Ish-bosheth* [w] 4.6 Meaning of Heb of verse 6 uncertain [x] 4.8 Heb *Ish-bosheth*
[y] 4.8 Heb *Ish-bosheth* [z] 4.12 Heb *Ish-bosheth*
[a] 5.8 Another reading is *those who hate David*

it and went down to the stronghold. 18Now the Philistines had come and spread out in the valley of Rephaim. 19David inquired of the LORD, 'Shall I go up against the Philistines? Will you give them into my hand?' The LORD said to David, 'Go up; for I will certainly give the Philistines into your hand.' 20So David came to Baal-perazim, and David defeated them there. He said, 'The LORD has burst forth against[b] my enemies before me, like a bursting flood.' Therefore that place is called Baal-perazim.[c] 21The Philistines abandoned their idols there, and David and his men carried them away.

22 Once again the Philistines came up, and were spread out in the valley of Rephaim. 23When David inquired of the LORD, he said, 'You shall not go up; go round to their rear, and come upon them opposite the balsam trees. 24When you hear the sound of marching in the tops of the balsam trees, then be on the alert; for then the LORD has gone out before you to strike down the army of the Philistines.' 25David did just as the LORD had commanded him; and he struck down the Philistines from Geba all the way to Gezer.

DAVID BRINGS THE ARK TO JERUSALEM

6 David again gathered all the chosen men of Israel, thirty thousand. 2David and all the people with him set out and went from Baale-judah, to bring up from there the ark of God, which is called by the name of the LORD of hosts who is enthroned on the cherubim. 3They carried the ark of God on a new cart, and brought it out of the house of Abinadab, which was on the hill. Uzzah and Ahio,[d] the sons of Abinadab, were driving the new cart 4with the ark of God;[e] and Ahio[f] went in front of the ark. 5David and all the house of Israel were dancing before the LORD with all their might, with songs[g] and lyres and harps and tambourines and castanets and cymbals.

6 When they came to the threshing-floor of Nacon, Uzzah reached out his hand to the ark of God and took hold of it, for the oxen shook it. 7The anger of the LORD was kindled against Uzzah; and God struck him there because he reached out his hand to the ark;[h] and he died there beside the ark of God. 8David was angry because the LORD had burst forth with an outburst upon Uzzah; so that place is called Perez-uzzah[i] to this day. 9David was afraid of the LORD that day; he said, 'How can the ark of the LORD come into my care?' 10So David was unwilling to take the ark of the LORD into his care in the city of David; instead David took it to the house of Obed-edom the Gittite. 11The ark of the LORD remained in the house of Obed-edom the Gittite for three months; and the LORD blessed Obed-edom and all his household.

12 It was told King David, 'The LORD has blessed the household of Obed-edom and all that belongs to him, because of the ark of God.' So David went and brought up the ark of God from the house of Obed-edom to the city of David with rejoicing; 13and when those who bore the ark of the LORD had gone six paces, he sacrificed an ox and a fatling. 14David danced before the LORD with all his might; David was girded with a linen ephod. 15So David and all the house of Israel brought up the ark of the LORD with shouting, and with the sound of the trumpet.

16 As the ark of the LORD came into the city of David, Michal daughter of Saul looked out of the window, and saw King David leaping and dancing before the LORD; and she despised him in her heart.

17 They brought in the ark of the LORD, and set it in its place, inside the tent that David had pitched for it; and David offered burnt-offerings and offerings of well-being before the LORD. 18When David had finished offering the burnt-offerings and the offerings of well-being, he blessed the people in the name of the LORD of hosts, 19and distributed food among all the people, the whole multitude of Israel, both men and women, to each a cake of bread, a portion of meat,[j] and a cake of raisins. Then all the people went back to their homes.

20 David returned to bless his household. But Michal the daughter of Saul came out to meet David, and said, 'How the king of Israel honoured himself today, uncovering himself today before

[b] **5.20** Heb *paraz* [c] **5.20** That is *Lord of Bursting Forth* [d] **6.3** Or *and his brother* [e] **6.4** Compare Gk: Heb *and brought it out of the house of Abinadab, which was on the hill with the ark of God* [f] **6.4** Or *and his brother* [g] **6.5** Q Ms Gk 1 Chr 13.8: Heb *fir trees* [h] **6.7** 1 Chr 13.10 Compare Q Ms: Meaning of Heb uncertain [i] **6.8** That is *Bursting Out Against Uzzah* [j] **6.19** Vg: Meaning of Heb uncertain

the eyes of his servants' maids, as any vulgar fellow might shamelessly uncover himself!' 21 David said to Michal, 'It was before the LORD, who chose me in place of your father and all his household, to appoint me as prince over Israel, the people of the LORD, that I have danced before the LORD. 22 I will make myself yet more contemptible than this, and I will be abased in my own eyes; but by the maids of whom you have spoken, by them I shall be held in honour.' 23 And Michal the daughter of Saul had no child to the day of her death.

GOD'S COVENANT WITH DAVID

7 Now when the king was settled in his house, and the LORD had given him rest from all his enemies around him, 2 the king said to the prophet Nathan, 'See now, I am living in a house of cedar, but the ark of God stays in a tent.' 3 Nathan said to the king, 'Go, do all that you have in mind; for the LORD is with you.'

4 But that same night the word of the LORD came to Nathan: 5 Go and tell my servant David: Thus says the LORD: Are you the one to build me a house to live in? 6 I have not lived in a house since the day I brought up the people of Israel from Egypt to this day, but I have been moving about in a tent and a tabernacle. 7 Wherever I have moved about among all the people of Israel, did I ever speak a word with any of the tribal leaders[k] of Israel, whom I commanded to shepherd my people Israel, saying, 'Why have you not built me a house of cedar?' 8 Now therefore thus you shall say to my servant David: Thus says the LORD of hosts: I took you from the pasture, from following the sheep to be prince over my people Israel; 9 and I have been with you wherever you went, and have cut off all your enemies from before you; and I will make for you a great name, like the name of the great ones of the earth. 10 And I will appoint a place for my people Israel and will plant them, so that they may live in their own place, and be disturbed no more; and evildoers shall afflict them no more, as formerly, 11 from the time that I appointed judges over my people Israel; and I will give you rest from all your enemies. Moreover, the LORD declares to you that the LORD will make you a house. 12 When your days are fulfilled and you lie down with your ancestors, I will raise up your offspring after you, who shall come forth from your body, and I will establish his kingdom. 13 He shall build a house for my name, and I will establish the throne of his kingdom for ever. 14 I will be a father to him, and he shall be a son to me. When he commits iniquity, I will punish him with a rod such as mortals use, with blows inflicted by human beings. 15 But I will not take[l] my steadfast love from him, as I took it from Saul, whom I put away from before you. 16 Your house and your kingdom shall be made sure for ever before me;[m] your throne shall be established for ever. 17 In accordance with all these words and with all this vision, Nathan spoke to David.

DAVID'S PRAYER

18 Then King David went in and sat before the LORD, and said, 'Who am I, O Lord GOD, and what is my house, that you have brought me thus far? 19 And yet this was a small thing in your eyes, O Lord GOD; you have spoken also of your servant's house for a great while to come. May this be instruction for the people,[n] O Lord GOD! 20 And what more can David say to you? For you know your servant, O Lord GOD! 21 Because of your promise, and according to your own heart, you have wrought all this greatness, so that your servant may know it. 22 Therefore you are great, O LORD God; for there is no one like you, and there is no God besides you, according to all that we have heard with our ears. 23 Who is like your people, like Israel? Is there another[o] nation on earth whose God went to redeem it as a people, and to make a name for himself, doing great and awesome things for them,[p] by driving out[q] before his people nations and their gods?[r] 24 And you established your people Israel for yourself to be your people for ever; and you, O LORD, became their God. 25 And now, O LORD God, as for the word that you have spoken concerning your servant and concerning his house, confirm it for ever; do as you have promised. 26 Thus your name will be magnified for ever in the saying, "The LORD of hosts is God over Israel"; and the house of your servant David will be established before you. 27 For you, O LORD of

[k] 7.7 Or *any of the tribes* [l] 7.15 Gk Syr Vg 1 Chr 17.13: Heb *shall not depart* [m] 7.16 Gk Heb Mss: MT *before you*; Compare 2 Sam 7.26, 29 [n] 7.19 Meaning of Heb uncertain [o] 7.23 Gk: Heb *one* [p] 7.23 Heb *you* [q] 7.23 Gk 1 Chr 17.21: Heb *for your land* [r] 7.23 Cn: Heb *before your people, whom you redeemed for yourself from Egypt, nations and its gods*

hosts, the God of Israel, have made this
revelation to your servant, saying, "I
will build you a house"; therefore your
servant has found courage to pray this
prayer to you. 28And now, O Lord GOD,
you are God, and your words are true,
and you have promised this good thing
to your servant; 29now therefore may
it please you to bless the house of your
servant, so that it may continue for ever
before you; for you, O Lord GOD, have
spoken, and with your blessing shall
the house of your servant be blessed for
ever.'

DAVID'S WARS

8 Some time afterwards, David attacked the Philistines and subdued
them; David took Metheg-ammah out
of the hand of the Philistines.

2 He also defeated the Moabites and,
making them lie down on the ground,
measured them off with a cord; he measured two lengths of cord for those who
were to be put to death, and one length[s]
for those who were to be spared. And
the Moabites became servants to David
and brought tribute.

3 David also struck down King Hadadezer son of Rehob of Zobah, as he
went to restore his monument[t] at the
river Euphrates. 4David took from him
one thousand seven hundred horsemen,
and twenty thousand foot-soldiers. David hamstrung all the chariot horses,
but left enough for a hundred chariots. 5When the Arameans of Damascus
came to help King Hadadezer of Zobah,
David killed twenty-two thousand men
of the Arameans. 6Then David put garrisons among the Arameans of Damascus; and the Arameans became servants
to David and brought tribute. The LORD
gave victory to David wherever he went.
7David took the gold shields that were
carried by the servants of Hadadezer,
and brought them to Jerusalem. 8From
Betah and from Berothai, towns of Hadadezer, King David took a great amount
of bronze.

9 When King Toi of Hamath heard
that David had defeated the whole army
of Hadadezer, 10Toi sent his son Joram
to King David, to greet him and to congratulate him because he had fought
against Hadadezer and defeated him.
Now Hadadezer had often been at war
with Toi. Joram brought with him articles of silver, gold, and bronze; 11these
also King David dedicated to the LORD,
together with the silver and gold that
he dedicated from all the nations he
subdued, 12from Edom, Moab, the Ammonites, the Philistines, Amalek, and
from the spoil of King Hadadezer son of
Rehob of Zobah.

13 David won a name for himself.
When he returned, he killed eighteen thousand Edomites[u] in the Valley
of Salt. 14He put garrisons in Edom;
throughout all Edom he put garrisons,
and all the Edomites became David's
servants. And the LORD gave victory to
David wherever he went.

DAVID'S OFFICERS

15 So David reigned over all Israel;
and David administered justice and equity to all his people. 16Joab son of Zeruiah was over the army; Jehoshaphat son
of Ahilud was recorder; 17Zadok son of
Ahitub and Ahimelech son of Abiathar
were priests; Seraiah was secretary;
18Benaiah son of Jehoiada was over[v] the
Cherethites and the Pelethites; and David's sons were priests.

DAVID'S KINDNESS TO MEPHIBOSHETH

9 David asked, 'Is there still anyone
left of the house of Saul to whom
I may show kindness for Jonathan's
sake?' 2Now there was a servant of the
house of Saul whose name was Ziba,
and he was summoned to David. The
king said to him, 'Are you Ziba?' And he
said, 'At your service!' 3The king said, 'Is
there anyone remaining of the house of
Saul to whom I may show the kindness
of God?' Ziba said to the king, 'There
remains a son of Jonathan; he is crippled in his feet.' 4The king said to him,
'Where is he?' Ziba said to the king, 'He
is in the house of Machir son of Ammiel,
at Lo-debar.' 5Then King David sent and
brought him from the house of Machir
son of Ammiel, at Lo-debar. 6Mephibo-
sheth[w] son of Jonathan son of Saul came
to David, and fell on his face and did
obeisance. David said, 'Mephibosheth!'[x]
He answered, 'I am your servant.' 7David
said to him, 'Do not be afraid, for I will
show you kindness for the sake of your
father Jonathan; I will restore to you
all the land of your grandfather Saul,
and you yourself shall eat at my table

[s] **8.2** Heb *one full length* [t] **8.3** Compare 1 Sam 15.12 and 2 Sam 18.18 [u] **8.13** Gk: Heb *returned from striking down eighteen thousand Arameans* [v] **8.18** Syr Tg Vg 20.23; 1 Chr 18.17: Heb lacks *was over* [w] **9.6** Or *Merib-baal*: See 4.4 note [x] **9.6** Or *Merib-baal*: See 4.4 note

always.' 8He did obeisance and said,
'What is your servant, that you should
look upon a dead dog such as I am?'
9 Then the king summoned Saul's
servant Ziba, and said to him, 'All that
belonged to Saul and to all his house I
have given to your master's grandson.
10You and your sons and your servants
shall till the land for him, and shall
bring in the produce, so that your master's grandson may have food to eat; but
your master's grandson Mephibosheth[y]
shall always eat at my table.' Now Ziba
had fifteen sons and twenty servants.
11Then Ziba said to the king, 'According
to all that my lord the king commands
his servant, so your servant will do.' Mephibosheth[z] ate at David's[a] table, like
one of the king's sons. 12Mephibosheth[b]
had a young son whose name was Mica.
And all who lived in Ziba's house became Mephibosheth's[c] servants. 13Me-
phibosheth[d] lived in Jerusalem, for he
always ate at the king's table. Now he
was lame in both his feet.

THE AMMONITES AND ARAMEANS ARE DEFEATED

10 Some time afterwards the king
of the Ammonites died, and his
son Hanun succeeded him. 2David said,
'I will deal loyally with Hanun son of
Nahash, just as his father dealt loyally
with me.' So David sent envoys to console him concerning his father. When
David's envoys came into the land of the
Ammonites, 3the princes of the Ammonites said to their lord Hanun, 'Do
you really think that David is honouring your father just because he has sent
messengers with condolences to you?
Has not David sent his envoys to you to
search the city, to spy it out, and to overthrow it?' 4So Hanun seized David's envoys, shaved off half the beard of each,
cut off their garments in the middle at
their hips, and sent them away. 5When
David was told, he sent to meet them,
for the men were greatly ashamed. The
king said, 'Remain at Jericho until your
beards have grown, and then return.'
6 When the Ammonites saw that they
had become odious to David, the Ammonites sent and hired the Arameans of
Beth-rehob and the Arameans of Zobah,
twenty thousand foot-soldiers, as well as
the king of Maacah, one thousand men,
and the men of Tob, twelve thousand
men. 7When David heard of it, he sent
Joab and all the army with the warriors.
8The Ammonites came out and drew
up in battle array at the entrance of the
gate; but the Arameans of Zobah and of
Rehob, and the men of Tob and Maacah,
were by themselves in the open country.
9 When Joab saw that the battle was
set against him both in front and in the
rear, he chose some of the picked men
of Israel, and arrayed them against the
Arameans; 10the rest of his men he put
in charge of his brother Abishai, and he
arrayed them against the Ammonites.
11He said, 'If the Arameans are too strong
for me, then you shall help me; but if the
Ammonites are too strong for you, then
I will come and help you. 12Be strong,
and let us be courageous for the sake of
our people, and for the cities of our God;
and may the LORD do what seems good
to him.' 13So Joab and the people who
were with him moved forward into battle against the Arameans; and they fled
before him. 14When the Ammonites
saw that the Arameans fled, they likewise fled before Abishai, and entered the
city. Then Joab returned from fighting
against the Ammonites, and came to Jerusalem.
15 But when the Arameans saw that
they had been defeated by Israel, they
gathered themselves together. 16Had-
adezer sent and brought out the Arameans who were beyond the Euphrates;
and they came to Helam, with Shobach
the commander of the army of Hadadezer at their head. 17When it was told to
David, he gathered all Israel together,
and crossed the Jordan, and came to
Helam. The Arameans arrayed themselves against David and fought with
him. 18The Arameans fled before Israel;
and David killed of the Arameans seven
hundred chariot teams and forty thousand horsemen,[e] and wounded Shobach
the commander of their army, so that
he died there. 19When all the kings who
were servants of Hadadezer saw that
they had been defeated by Israel, they
made peace with Israel, and became
subject to them. So the Arameans were
afraid to help the Ammonites any more.

DAVID COMMITS ADULTERY WITH BATHSHEBA

11 In the spring of the year, the
time when kings go out to bat-

[y] 9.10 Or *Merib-baal*: See 4.4 note [z] 9.11 Or *Merib-baal*: See 4.4 note [a] 9.11 Gk: Heb *my* [b] 9.12 Or *Merib-baal*: See 4.4 note [c] 9.12 Or *Merib-baal's*: See 4.4 note [d] 9.13 Or *Merib-baal*: See 4.4 note [e] 10.18 1 Chr 19.18 and some Gk Mss read *foot-soldiers*

tle, David sent Joab with his officers and
all Israel with him; they ravaged the
Ammonites, and besieged Rabbah. But
David remained at Jerusalem.
2 It happened, late one afternoon,
when David rose from his couch and
was walking about on the roof of the
king's house, that he saw from the roof
a woman bathing; the woman was
very beautiful. 3 David sent someone
to inquire about the woman. It was reported, 'This is Bathsheba daughter of
Eliam, the wife of Uriah the Hittite.' 4 So
David sent messengers to fetch her, and
she came to him, and he lay with her.
(Now she was purifying herself after her
period.) Then she returned to her house.
5 The woman conceived; and she sent
and told David, 'I am pregnant.'
6 So David sent word to Joab, 'Send
me Uriah the Hittite.' And Joab sent
Uriah to David. 7 When Uriah came to
him, David asked how Joab and the people fared, and how the war was going.
8 Then David said to Uriah, 'Go down to
your house, and wash your feet.' Uriah
went out of the king's house, and there
followed him a present from the king.
9 But Uriah slept at the entrance of the
king's house with all the servants of his
lord, and did not go down to his house.
10 When they told David, 'Uriah did not
go down to his house', David said to
Uriah, 'You have just come from a journey. Why did you not go down to your
house?' 11 Uriah said to David, 'The ark
and Israel and Judah remain in booths;[f]
and my lord Joab and the servants of my
lord are camping in the open field; shall I
then go to my house, to eat and to drink,
and to lie with my wife? As you live, and
as your soul lives, I will not do such a
thing.' 12 Then David said to Uriah, 'Remain here today also, and tomorrow I
will send you back.' So Uriah remained
in Jerusalem that day. On the next day,
13 David invited him to eat and drink in
his presence and made him drunk; and
in the evening he went out to lie on his
couch with the servants of his lord, but
he did not go down to his house.

DAVID HAS URIAH KILLED

14 In the morning David wrote a
letter to Joab, and sent it by the hand
of Uriah. 15 In the letter he wrote, 'Set
Uriah in the forefront of the hardest
fighting, and then draw back from him,
so that he may be struck down and die.'
16 As Joab was besieging the city, he assigned Uriah to the place where he knew
there were valiant warriors. 17 The men
of the city came out and fought with
Joab; and some of the servants of David
among the people fell. Uriah the Hittite was killed as well. 18 Then Joab sent
and told David all the news about the
fighting; 19 and he instructed the messenger, 'When you have finished telling
the king all the news about the fighting,
20 then, if the king's anger rises, and if
he says to you, "Why did you go so near
the city to fight? Did you not know that
they would shoot from the wall? 21 Who
killed Abimelech son of Jerubbaal?[g] Did
not a woman throw an upper millstone
on him from the wall, so that he died
at Thebez? Why did you go so near the
wall?" then you shall say, "Your servant
Uriah the Hittite is dead too." '
22 So the messenger went, and came
and told David all that Joab had sent
him to tell. 23 The messenger said to David, 'The men gained an advantage over
us, and came out against us in the field;
but we drove them back to the entrance
of the gate. 24 Then the archers shot at
your servants from the wall; some of
the king's servants are dead; and your
servant Uriah the Hittite is dead also.'
25 David said to the messenger, 'Thus
you shall say to Joab, "Do not let this
matter trouble you, for the sword devours now one and now another; press
your attack on the city, and overthrow
it." And encourage him.'
26 When the wife of Uriah heard that
her husband was dead, she made lamentation for him. 27 When the mourning
was over, David sent and brought her to
his house, and she became his wife, and
bore him a son.

NATHAN CONDEMNS DAVID

But the thing that David had done
12 displeased the LORD, 1 and the
LORD sent Nathan to David. He
came to him, and said to him, 'There
were two men in a certain city, one rich
and the other poor. 2 The rich man had
very many flocks and herds; 3 but the
poor man had nothing but one little ewe
lamb, which he had bought. He brought
it up, and it grew up with him and with
his children; it used to eat of his meagre
fare, and drink from his cup, and lie in
his bosom, and it was like a daughter to
him. 4 Now there came a traveller to the
rich man, and he was loath to take one

[f] **11.11** Or *at Succoth* [g] **11.21** Gk Syr Judg 7.1: Heb *Jerubbesheth*

of his own flock or herd to prepare for
the wayfarer who had come to him, but
he took the poor man's lamb, and prepared that for the guest who had come
to him.' 5Then David's anger was greatly
kindled against the man. He said to Nathan, 'As the LORD lives, the man who
has done this deserves to die; 6he shall
restore the lamb fourfold, because he
did this thing, and because he had no
pity.'

7 Nathan said to David, 'You are the
man! Thus says the LORD, the God of
Israel: I anointed you king over Israel,
and I rescued you from the hand of Saul;
8I gave you your master's house, and
your master's wives into your bosom,
and gave you the house of Israel and of
Judah; and if that had been too little, I
would have added as much more. 9Why
have you despised the word of the LORD,
to do what is evil in his sight? You have
struck down Uriah the Hittite with the
sword, and have taken his wife to be
your wife, and have killed him with the
sword of the Ammonites. 10Now therefore the sword shall never depart from
your house, for you have despised me,
and have taken the wife of Uriah the
Hittite to be your wife. 11Thus says the
LORD: I will raise up trouble against you
from within your own house; and I will
take your wives before your eyes, and
give them to your neighbour, and he
shall lie with your wives in the sight of
this very sun. 12For you did it secretly;
but I will do this thing before all Israel,
and before the sun.' 13David said to Nathan, 'I have sinned against the LORD.'
Nathan said to David, 'Now the LORD
has put away your sin; you shall not die.
14Nevertheless, because by this deed
you have utterly scorned the LORD,[h]
the child that is born to you shall die.'
15Then Nathan went to his house.

BATHSHEBA'S CHILD DIES

The LORD struck the child that Uriah's wife bore to David, and it became
very ill. 16David therefore pleaded
with God for the child; David fasted,
and went in and lay all night on the
ground. 17The elders of his house stood
beside him, urging him to rise from the
ground; but he would not, nor did he eat
food with them. 18On the seventh day
the child died. And the servants of David were afraid to tell him that the child
was dead; for they said, 'While the child
was still alive, we spoke to him, and he
did not listen to us; how then can we tell
him the child is dead? He may do himself some harm.' 19But when David saw
that his servants were whispering together, he perceived that the child was
dead; and David said to his servants, 'Is
the child dead?' They said, 'He is dead.'

20 Then David rose from the ground,
washed, anointed himself, and changed
his clothes. He went into the house of
the LORD, and worshipped; he then
went to his own house; and when he
asked, they set food before him and he
ate. 21Then his servants said to him,
'What is this thing that you have done?
You fasted and wept for the child while
it was alive; but when the child died, you
rose and ate food.' 22He said, 'While the
child was still alive, I fasted and wept;
for I said, "Who knows? The LORD may
be gracious to me, and the child may
live." 23But now he is dead; why should I
fast? Can I bring him back again? I shall
go to him, but he will not return to me.'

SOLOMON IS BORN

24 Then David consoled his wife
Bathsheba, and went to her, and lay
with her; and she bore a son, and he
named him Solomon. The LORD loved
him, 25and sent a message by the
prophet Nathan; so he named him Jedi-
diah,[i] because of the LORD.

THE AMMONITES CRUSHED

26 Now Joab fought against Rabbah
of the Ammonites, and took the royal
city. 27Joab sent messengers to David,
and said, 'I have fought against Rabbah; moreover, I have taken the water
city. 28Now, then, gather the rest of the
people together, and encamp against
the city, and take it; or I myself will
take the city, and it will be called by my
name.' 29So David gathered all the people together and went to Rabbah, and
fought against it and took it. 30He took
the crown of Milcom[j] from his head; the
weight of it was a talent of gold, and
in it was a precious stone; and it was
placed on David's head. He also brought
forth the spoil of the city, a very great
amount. 31He brought out the people
who were in it, and set them to work
with saws and iron picks and iron axes,
or sent them to the brickworks. Thus he
did to all the cities of the Ammonites.

[h] **12.14** Ancient scribal tradition: Compare 1 Sam 25.22 note: Heb *scorned the enemies of the LORD*
[i] **12.25** That is *Beloved of the LORD* [j] **12.30** Gk See 1 Kings 11.5, 33: Heb *their kings*

Then David and all the people returned
to Jerusalem.

AMNON AND TAMAR

13 Some time passed. David's son
Absalom had a beautiful sister
whose name was Tamar; and David's
son Amnon fell in love with her. 2Am-
non was so tormented that he made
himself ill because of his sister Tamar,
for she was a virgin and it seemed impossible to Amnon to do anything to
her. 3But Amnon had a friend whose
name was Jonadab, the son of David's
brother Shimeah; and Jonadab was a
very crafty man. 4He said to him, 'O son
of the king, why are you so haggard
morning after morning? Will you not
tell me?' Amnon said to him, 'I love Tamar, my brother Absalom's sister.' 5Jon-
adab said to him, 'Lie down on your bed,
and pretend to be ill; and when your father comes to see you, say to him, "Let
my sister Tamar come and give me
something to eat, and prepare the food
in my sight, so that I may see it and
eat it from her hand." ' 6So Amnon lay
down, and pretended to be ill; and when
the king came to see him, Amnon said
to the king, 'Please let my sister Tamar
come and make a couple of cakes in my
sight, so that I may eat from her hand.'

7 Then David sent home to Tamar,
saying, 'Go to your brother Amnon's
house, and prepare food for him.' 8So
Tamar went to her brother Amnon's
house, where he was lying down. She
took dough, kneaded it, made cakes in
his sight, and baked the cakes. 9Then she
took the pan and set them[k] out before
him, but he refused to eat. Amnon said,
'Send out everyone from me.' So everyone went out from him. 10Then Amnon
said to Tamar, 'Bring the food into the
chamber, so that I may eat from your
hand.' So Tamar took the cakes she had
made, and brought them into the chamber to Amnon her brother. 11But when
she brought them near him to eat, he
took hold of her, and said to her, 'Come,
lie with me, my sister.' 12She answered
him, 'No, my brother, do not force me; for
such a thing is not done in Israel; do not
do anything so vile! 13As for me, where
could I carry my shame? And as for you,
you would be as one of the scoundrels in
Israel. Now therefore, I beg you, speak
to the king; for he will not withhold me
from you.' 14But he would not listen to
her; and being stronger than she was, he
forced her and lay with her.

15 Then Amnon was seized with a
very great loathing for her; indeed, his
loathing was even greater than the lust
he had felt for her. Amnon said to her,
'Get out!' 16But she said to him, 'No,
my brother;[l] for this wrong in sending
me away is greater than the other that
you did to me.' But he would not listen
to her. 17He called the young man who
served him and said, 'Put this woman
out of my presence, and bolt the door after her.' 18(Now she was wearing a long
robe with sleeves; for this is how the virgin daughters of the king were clothed
in earlier times.[m]) So his servant put
her out, and bolted the door after her.
19But Tamar put ashes on her head, and
tore the long robe that she was wearing;
she put her hand on her head, and went
away, crying aloud as she went.

20 Her brother Absalom said to her,
'Has Amnon your brother been with
you? Be quiet for now, my sister; he is
your brother; do not take this to heart.'
So Tamar remained, a desolate woman,
in her brother Absalom's house. 21When
King David heard of all these things,
he became very angry, but he would
not punish his son Amnon, because he
loved him, for he was his firstborn.[n]
22But Absalom spoke to Amnon neither good nor bad; for Absalom hated
Amnon, because he had raped his sister
Tamar.

ABSALOM AVENGES THE VIOLATION OF HIS SISTER

23 After two full years Absalom had
sheepshearers at Baal-hazor, which is
near Ephraim, and Absalom invited all
the king's sons. 24Absalom came to the
king, and said, 'Your servant has sheep-
shearers; will the king and his servants
please go with your servant?' 25But the
king said to Absalom, 'No, my son, let
us not all go, or else we will be burdensome to you.' He pressed him, but he
would not go but gave him his blessing. 26Then Absalom said, 'If not, please
let my brother Amnon go with us.' The
king said to him, 'Why should he go
with you?' 27But Absalom pressed him
until he let Amnon and all the king's
sons go with him. Absalom made a
feast like a king's feast.[o] 28Then Absalom

[k] 13.9 Heb *and poured* [l] 13.16 Cn Compare Gk Vg: Meaning of Heb uncertain [m] 13.18 Cn: Heb *were clothed in robes* [n] 13.21 Q Ms Gk: MT lacks *but he would not punish . . . firstborn* [o] 13.27 Gk Compare Q Ms: MT lacks *Absalom made a feast like a king's feast*

commanded his servants, 'Watch when
Amnon's heart is merry with wine, and
when I say to you, "Strike Amnon", then
kill him. Do not be afraid; have I not
myself commanded you? Be courageous
and valiant.' 29So the servants of Absalom did to Amnon as Absalom had commanded. Then all the king's sons rose,
and each mounted his mule and fled.

30 While they were on the way, the
report came to David that Absalom had
killed all the king's sons, and not one of
them was left. 31The king rose, tore his
garments, and lay on the ground; and
all his servants who were standing by
tore their garments. 32But Jonadab, the
son of David's brother Shimeah, said,
'Let not my lord suppose that they have
killed all the young men the king's sons;
Amnon alone is dead. This has been
determined by Absalom from the day
Amnon[p] raped his sister Tamar. 33Now
therefore, do not let my lord the king
take it to heart, as if all the king's sons
were dead; for Amnon alone is dead.'

34 But Absalom fled. When the
young man who kept watch looked
up, he saw many people coming from
the Horonaim road[q] by the side of the
mountain. 35Jonadab said to the king,
'See, the king's sons have come; as your
servant said, so it has come about.' 36As
soon as he had finished speaking, the
king's sons arrived, and raised their
voices and wept; and the king and all his
servants also wept very bitterly.

37 But Absalom fled, and went to
Talmai son of Ammihud, king of Geshur. David mourned for his son day
after day. 38Absalom, having fled to Geshur, stayed there for three years. 39And
the heart of[r] the king went out, yearning for Absalom; for he was now consoled over the death of Amnon.

ABSALOM RETURNS TO JERUSALEM

14 Now Joab son of Zeruiah perceived that the king's mind was
on Absalom. 2Joab sent to Tekoa and
brought from there a wise woman. He
said to her, 'Pretend to be in mourning; put on mourning garments, do
not anoint yourself with oil, but behave
like a woman who has been mourning
many days for the dead. 3Go to the king
and speak to him as follows.' And Joab
put the words into her mouth.

4 When the woman of Tekoa came
to the king, she fell on her face to the
ground and did obeisance, and said,
'Help, O king!' 5The king asked her,
'What is your trouble?' She answered,
'Alas, I am a widow; my husband is dead.
6Your servant had two sons, and they
fought with one another in the field;
there was no one to part them, and one
struck the other and killed him. 7Now
the whole family has risen against your
servant. They say, "Give up the man who
struck his brother, so that we may kill
him for the life of his brother whom he
murdered, even if we destroy the heir as
well." Thus they would quench my one
remaining ember, and leave to my husband neither name nor remnant on the
face of the earth.'

8 Then the king said to the woman,
'Go to your house, and I will give orders
concerning you.' 9The woman of Tekoa
said to the king, 'On me be the guilt, my
lord the king, and on my father's house;
let the king and his throne be guiltless.'
10The king said, 'If anyone says anything
to you, bring him to me, and he shall
never touch you again.' 11Then she said,
'Please, may the king keep the LORD
your God in mind, so that the avenger
of blood may kill no more, and my son
not be destroyed.' He said, 'As the LORD
lives, not one hair of your son shall fall
to the ground.'

12 Then the woman said, 'Please let
your servant speak a word to my lord
the king.' He said, 'Speak.' 13The woman
said, 'Why then have you planned such
a thing against the people of God? For
in giving this decision the king convicts
himself, inasmuch as the king does not
bring his banished one home again.
14We must all die; we are like water
spilled on the ground, which cannot be
gathered up. But God will not take away
a life; he will devise plans so as not to
keep an outcast banished for ever from
his presence.[s] 15Now I have come to say
this to my lord the king because the
people have made me afraid; your servant thought, "I will speak to the king; it
may be that the king will perform the
request of his servant. 16For the king
will hear, and deliver his servant from
the hand of the man who would cut
both me and my son off from the heritage of God." 17Your servant thought,
"The word of my lord the king will set
me at rest"; for my lord the king is like
the angel of God, discerning good and
evil. The LORD your God be with you!'

[p] **13.32** Heb *he* [q] **13.34** Cn Compare Gk: Heb *the road behind him* [r] **13.39** Q Ms Gk: MT *And David* [s] **14.14** Meaning of Heb uncertain

18 Then the king answered the woman, 'Do not withhold from me anything I ask you.' The woman said, 'Let my lord the king speak.' 19 The king said, 'Is the hand of Joab with you in all this?' The woman answered and said, 'As surely as you live, my lord the king, one cannot turn right or left from anything that my lord the king has said. For it was your servant Joab who commanded me; it was he who put all these words into the mouth of your servant. 20 In order to change the course of affairs your servant Joab did this. But my lord has wisdom like the wisdom of the angel of God to know all things that are on the earth.'

21 Then the king said to Joab, 'Very well, I grant this; go, bring back the young man Absalom.' 22 Joab prostrated himself with his face to the ground and did obeisance, and blessed the king; and Joab said, 'Today your servant knows that I have found favour in your sight, my lord the king, in that the king has granted the request of his servant.' 23 So Joab set off, went to Geshur, and brought Absalom to Jerusalem. 24 The king said, 'Let him go to his own house; he is not to come into my presence.' So Absalom went to his own house, and did not come into the king's presence.

DAVID FORGIVES ABSALOM

25 Now in all Israel there was no one to be praised so much for his beauty as Absalom; from the sole of his foot to the crown of his head there was no blemish in him. 26 When he cut the hair of his head (for at the end of every year he used to cut it; when it was heavy on him, he cut it), he weighed the hair of his head, two hundred shekels by the king's weight. 27 There were born to Absalom three sons, and one daughter whose name was Tamar; she was a beautiful woman.

28 So Absalom lived two full years in Jerusalem without coming into the king's presence. 29 Then Absalom sent for Joab to send him to the king; but Joab would not come to him. He sent a second time, but Joab would not come. 30 Then he said to his servants, 'Look, Joab's field is next to mine, and he has barley there; go and set it on fire.' So Absalom's servants set the field on fire. 31 Then Joab rose and went to Absalom at his house, and said to him, 'Why have your servants set my field on fire?' 32 Absalom answered Joab, 'Look, I sent word to you: Come here, that I may send you to the king with the question, "Why have I come from Geshur? It would be better for me to be there still." Now let me go into the king's presence; if there is guilt in me, let him kill me!' 33 Then Joab went to the king and told him; and he summoned Absalom. So he came to the king and prostrated himself with his face to the ground before the king; and the king kissed Absalom.

ABSALOM USURPS THE THRONE

15 After this Absalom got himself a chariot and horses, and fifty men to run ahead of him. 2 Absalom used to rise early and stand beside the road into the gate; and when anyone brought a suit before the king for judgement, Absalom would call out and say, 'From what city are you?' When the person said, 'Your servant is of such and such a tribe in Israel', 3 Absalom would say, 'See, your claims are good and right; but there is no one deputed by the king to hear you.' 4 Absalom said moreover, 'If only I were judge in the land! Then all who had a suit or cause might come to me, and I would give them justice.' 5 Whenever people came near to do obeisance to him, he would put out his hand and take hold of them, and kiss them. 6 Thus Absalom did to every Israelite who came to the king for judgement; so Absalom stole the hearts of the people of Israel.

7 At the end of four[t] years Absalom said to the king, 'Please let me go to Hebron and pay the vow that I have made to the LORD. 8 For your servant made a vow while I lived at Geshur in Aram: If the LORD will indeed bring me back to Jerusalem, then I will worship the LORD in Hebron.'[u] 9 The king said to him, 'Go in peace.' So he got up, and went to Hebron. 10 But Absalom sent secret messengers throughout all the tribes of Israel, saying, 'As soon as you hear the sound of the trumpet, then shout: Absalom has become king at Hebron!' 11 Two hundred men from Jerusalem went with Absalom; they were invited guests, and they went in their innocence, knowing nothing of the matter. 12 While Absalom was offering the sacrifices, he sent for[v] Ahithophel the Gilonite, David's counsellor, from his city Giloh. The conspiracy grew in strength, and the people with Absalom kept increasing.

[t] 15.7 Gk Syr: Heb *forty* [u] 15.8 Gk Mss: Heb lacks *in Hebron* [v] 15.12 Or *he sent*

DAVID FLEES FROM JERUSALEM

13 A messenger came to David, saying, 'The hearts of the Israelites have gone after Absalom.' 14Then David said to all his officials who were with him at Jerusalem, 'Get up! Let us flee, or there will be no escape for us from Absalom. Hurry, or he will soon overtake us, and bring disaster down upon us, and attack the city with the edge of the sword.' 15The king's officials said to the king, 'Your servants are ready to do whatever our lord the king decides.' 16So the king left, followed by all his household, except ten concubines whom he left behind to look after the house. 17The king left, followed by all the people; and they stopped at the last house. 18All his officials passed by him; and all the Cherethites, and all the Pelethites, and all the six hundred Gittites who had followed him from Gath, passed on before the king.

19 Then the king said to Ittai the Gittite, 'Why are you also coming with us? Go back, and stay with the king; for you are a foreigner, and also an exile from your home. 20You came only yesterday, and shall I today make you wander about with us, while I go wherever I can? Go back, and take your kinsfolk with you; and may the LORD show[w] steadfast love and faithfulness to you.' 21But Ittai answered the king, 'As the LORD lives, and as my lord the king lives, wherever my lord the king may be, whether for death or for life, there also your servant will be.' 22David said to Ittai, 'Go then, march on.' So Ittai the Gittite marched on, with all his men and all the little ones who were with him. 23The whole country wept aloud as all the people passed by; the king crossed the Wadi Kidron, and all the people moved on towards the wilderness.

24 Abiathar came up, and Zadok also, with all the Levites, carrying the ark of the covenant of God. They set down the ark of God, until the people had all passed out of the city. 25Then the king said to Zadok, 'Carry the ark of God back into the city. If I find favour in the eyes of the LORD, he will bring me back and let me see both it and the place where it remains. 26But if he says, "I take no pleasure in you", here I am, let him do to me what seems good to him.' 27The king also said to the priest Zadok, 'Look,[x] go back to the city in peace, you and Abiathar,[y] with your two sons, Ahimaaz your son, and Jonathan son of Abiathar. 28See, I will wait at the fords of the wilderness until word comes from you to inform me.' 29So Zadok and Abiathar carried the ark of God back to Jerusalem, and they remained there.

30 But David went up the ascent of the Mount of Olives, weeping as he went, with his head covered and walking barefoot; and all the people who were with him covered their heads and went up, weeping as they went. 31David was told that Ahithophel was among the conspirators with Absalom. And David said, 'O LORD, I pray you, turn the counsel of Ahithophel into foolishness.'

HUSHAI BECOMES DAVID'S SPY

32 When David came to the summit, where God was worshipped, Hushai the Archite came to meet him with his coat torn and earth on his head. 33David said to him, 'If you go on with me, you will be a burden to me. 34But if you return to the city and say to Absalom, "I will be your servant, O king; as I have been your father's servant in time past, so now I will be your servant", then you will defeat for me the counsel of Ahithophel. 35The priests Zadok and Abiathar will be with you there. So whatever you hear from the king's house, tell it to the priests Zadok and Abiathar. 36Their two sons are with them there, Zadok's son Ahimaaz and Abiathar's son Jonathan; and by them you shall report to me everything you hear.' 37So Hushai, David's friend, came into the city, just as Absalom was entering Jerusalem.

DAVID'S ADVERSARIES

16 When David had passed a little beyond the summit, Ziba the servant of Mephibosheth[z] met him, with a couple of donkeys saddled, carrying two hundred loaves of bread, one hundred bunches of raisins, one hundred of summer fruits, and one skin of wine. 2The king said to Ziba, 'Why have you brought these?' Ziba answered, 'The donkeys are for the king's household to ride, the bread and summer fruit for the young men to eat, and the wine is for those to drink who faint in the wilderness.' 3The king said, 'And where is your master's son?' Ziba said to the king, 'He remains in Jerusalem; for he said, "Today the house of Israel will give me back

[w] **15.20** Gk Compare 2.6: Heb lacks *may the LORD show* [x] **15.27** Gk: Heb *Are you a seer* or *Do you see?* [y] **15.27** Cn: Heb lacks *and Abiathar* [z] **16.1** Or *Merib-baal*: See 4.4 note

my grandfather's kingdom."' 4Then the
king said to Ziba, 'All that belonged to
Mephibosheth[a] is now yours.' Ziba said,
'I do obeisance; let me find favour in
your sight, my lord the king.'

SHIMEI CURSES DAVID

5 When King David came to Bahurim, a man of the family of the house of
Saul came out whose name was Shimei
son of Gera; he came out cursing. 6He
threw stones at David and at all the servants of King David; now all the people
and all the warriors were on his right
and on his left. 7Shimei shouted while
he cursed, 'Out! Out! Murderer! Scoundrel! 8The LORD has avenged on all of
you the blood of the house of Saul, in
whose place you have reigned; and the
LORD has given the kingdom into the
hand of your son Absalom. See, disaster
has overtaken you; for you are a man of
blood.'

9 Then Abishai son of Zeruiah said
to the king, 'Why should this dead dog
curse my lord the king? Let me go over
and take off his head.' 10But the king
said, 'What have I to do with you, you
sons of Zeruiah? If he is cursing because
the LORD has said to him, "Curse David", who then shall say, "Why have you
done so?"' 11David said to Abishai and
to all his servants, 'My own son seeks
my life; how much more now may this
Benjaminite! Let him alone, and let him
curse; for the LORD has bidden him.
12It may be that the LORD will look on
my distress,[b] and the LORD will repay
me with good for this cursing of me today.' 13So David and his men went on
the road, while Shimei went along on
the hillside opposite him and cursed as
he went, throwing stones and flinging
dust at him. 14The king and all the people who were with him arrived weary
at the Jordan;[c] and there he refreshed
himself.

THE COUNSEL OF AHITHOPHEL

15 Now Absalom and all the Israelites[d] came to Jerusalem; Ahithophel
was with him. 16When Hushai the Archite, David's friend, came to Absalom,
Hushai said to Absalom, 'Long live the
king! Long live the king!' 17Absalom
said to Hushai, 'Is this your loyalty to
your friend? Why did you not go with
your friend?' 18Hushai said to Absalom,
'No; but the one whom the LORD and
this people and all the Israelites have
chosen, his I will be, and with him I
will remain. 19Moreover, whom should
I serve? Should it not be his son? Just as
I have served your father, so I will serve
you.'

20 Then Absalom said to Ahithophel,
'Give us your counsel; what shall we
do?' 21Ahithophel said to Absalom, 'Go
in to your father's concubines, the ones
he has left to look after the house; and
all Israel will hear that you have made
yourself odious to your father, and the
hands of all who are with you will be
strengthened.' 22So they pitched a tent
for Absalom upon the roof; and Absalom went in to his father's concubines
in the sight of all Israel. 23Now in those
days the counsel that Ahithophel gave
was as if one consulted the oracle[e] of
God; so all the counsel of Ahithophel
was esteemed, both by David and by
Absalom.

17 Moreover, Ahithophel said to
Absalom, 'Let me choose twelve
thousand men, and I will set out and
pursue David tonight. 2I will come upon
him while he is weary and discouraged,
and throw him into a panic; and all
the people who are with him will flee.
I will strike down only the king, 3and I
will bring all the people back to you as
a bride comes home to her husband.
You seek the life of only one man,[f] and
all the people will be at peace.' 4The advice pleased Absalom and all the elders
of Israel.

THE COUNSEL OF HUSHAI

5 Then Absalom said, 'Call Hushai
the Archite also, and let us hear too
what he has to say.' 6When Hushai came
to Absalom, Absalom said to him, 'This
is what Ahithophel has said; shall we do
as he advises? If not, you tell us.' 7Then
Hushai said to Absalom, 'This time
the counsel that Ahithophel has given
is not good.' 8Hushai continued, 'You
know that your father and his men are
warriors, and that they are enraged, like
a bear robbed of her cubs in the field.
Besides, your father is expert in war;
he will not spend the night with the
troops. 9Even now he has hidden himself in one of the pits, or in some other
place. And when some of our troops[g] fall
at the first attack, whoever hears it will

[a] 16.4 Or *Merib-baal*: See 4.4 note [b] 16.12 Gk Vg: Heb *iniquity* [c] 16.14 Gk: Heb lacks *at the Jordan* [d] 16.15 Gk: Heb *all the people, the men of Israel* [e] 16.23 Heb *word* [f] 17.3 Gk: Heb *like the return of the whole (is) the man whom you seek* [g] 17.9 Gk Mss: Heb *some of them*

say, "There has been a slaughter among
the troops who follow Absalom." 10Then
even the valiant warrior, whose heart is
like the heart of a lion, will utterly melt
with fear; for all Israel knows that your
father is a warrior, and that those who
are with him are valiant warriors. 11But
my counsel is that all Israel be gathered
to you, from Dan to Beer-sheba, like
the sand by the sea for multitude, and
that you go to battle in person. 12So we
shall come upon him in whatever place
he may be found, and we shall light
on him as the dew falls on the ground;
and he will not survive, nor will any of
those with him. 13If he withdraws into
a city, then all Israel will bring ropes to
that city, and we shall drag it into the
valley, until not even a pebble is to be
found there.' 14Absalom and all the men
of Israel said, 'The counsel of Hushai the
Archite is better than the counsel of
Ahithophel.' For the LORD had ordained
to defeat the good counsel of Ahithophel, so that the LORD might bring ruin
on Absalom.

HUSHAI WARNS DAVID TO ESCAPE

15 Then Hushai said to the priests
Zadok and Abiathar, 'Thus and so did
Ahithophel counsel Absalom and the
elders of Israel; and thus and so I have
counselled. 16Therefore send quickly and
tell David, "Do not lodge tonight at the
fords of the wilderness, but by all means
cross over; otherwise the king and all
the people who are with him will be
swallowed up." ' 17Jonathan and Ahimaaz were waiting at En-rogel; a servant-
girl used to go and tell them, and they
would go and tell King David; for they
could not risk being seen entering the
city. 18But a boy saw them, and told
Absalom; so both of them went away
quickly, and came to the house of a man
at Bahurim, who had a well in his courtyard; and they went down into it. 19The
man's wife took a covering, stretched it
over the well's mouth, and spread out
grain on it; and nothing was known of
it. 20When Absalom's servants came
to the woman at the house, they said,
'Where are Ahimaaz and Jonathan?' The
woman said to them, 'They have crossed
over the brook[h] of water.' And when
they had searched and could not find
them, they returned to Jerusalem.

21 After they had gone, the men
came up out of the well, and went and
told King David. They said to David, 'Go
and cross the water quickly; for thus and
so has Ahithophel counselled against
you.' 22So David and all the people who
were with him set out and crossed the
Jordan; by daybreak not one was left
who had not crossed the Jordan.

23 When Ahithophel saw that his
counsel was not followed, he saddled
his donkey and went off home to his
own city. He set his house in order, and
hanged himself; he died and was buried
in the tomb of his father.

24 Then David came to Mahanaim,
while Absalom crossed the Jordan with
all the men of Israel. 25Now Absalom
had set Amasa over the army in the
place of Joab. Amasa was the son of a
man named Ithra the Ishmaelite,[i] who
had married Abigal daughter of Nahash, sister of Zeruiah, Joab's mother.
26The Israelites and Absalom encamped
in the land of Gilead.

27 When David came to Mahanaim,
Shobi son of Nahash from Rabbah of
the Ammonites, and Machir son of Ammiel from Lo-debar, and Barzillai the
Gileadite from Rogelim 28brought beds,
basins, and earthen vessels, wheat,
barley, meal, parched grain, beans and
lentils,[j] 29honey and curds, sheep, and
cheese from the herd, for David and the
people with him to eat; for they said,
'The troops are hungry and weary and
thirsty in the wilderness.'

THE DEFEAT AND DEATH OF ABSALOM

18 Then David mustered the men
who were with him, and set over
them commanders of thousands and
commanders of hundreds. 2And David
divided the army into three groups:[k]
one-third under the command of
Joab, one-third under the command of
Abishai son of Zeruiah, Joab's brother,
and one-third under the command of Ittai the Gittite. The king said to the men,
'I myself will also go out with you.' 3But
the men said, 'You shall not go out. For
if we flee, they will not care about us. If
half of us die, they will not care about
us. But you are worth ten thousand of
us;[l] therefore it is better that you send
us help from the city.' 4The king said to
them, 'Whatever seems best to you I will
do.' So the king stood at the side of the
gate, while all the army marched out by

[h] **17.20** Meaning of Heb uncertain [i] **17.25** 1 Chr 2.17: Heb *Israelite* [j] **17.28** Heb *and lentils and parched grain* [k] **18.2** Gk: Heb *sent forth the army* [l] **18.3** Gk Vg Symmachus: Heb *for now there are ten thousand such as we*

hundreds and by thousands. 5 The king gave orders to Joab and Abishai and Ittai, saying, 'Deal gently for my sake with the young man Absalom.' And all the people heard when the king gave orders to all the commanders concerning Absalom.

6 So the army went out into the field against Israel; and the battle was fought in the forest of Ephraim. 7 The men of Israel were defeated there by the servants of David, and the slaughter there was great on that day, twenty thousand men. 8 The battle spread over the face of all the country; and the forest claimed more victims that day than the sword.

9 Absalom happened to meet the servants of David. Absalom was riding on his mule, and the mule went under the thick branches of a great oak. His head caught fast in the oak, and he was left hanging[m] between heaven and earth, while the mule that was under him went on. 10 A man saw it, and told Joab, 'I saw Absalom hanging in an oak.' 11 Joab said to the man who told him, 'What, you saw him! Why then did you not strike him there to the ground? I would have been glad to give you ten pieces of silver and a belt.' 12 But the man said to Joab, 'Even if I felt in my hand the weight of a thousand pieces of silver, I would not raise my hand against the king's son; for in our hearing the king commanded you and Abishai and Ittai, saying: For my sake protect the young man Absalom! 13 On the other hand, if I had dealt treacherously against his life[n] (and there is nothing hidden from the king), then you yourself would have stood aloof.' 14 Joab said, 'I will not waste time like this with you.' He took three spears in his hand, and thrust them into the heart of Absalom, while he was still alive in the oak. 15 And ten young men, Joab's armour-bearers, surrounded Absalom and struck him, and killed him.

16 Then Joab sounded the trumpet, and the troops came back from pursuing Israel, for Joab restrained the troops. 17 They took Absalom, threw him into a great pit in the forest, and raised over him a very great heap of stones. Meanwhile all the Israelites fled to their homes. 18 Now Absalom in his lifetime had taken and set up for himself a pillar that is in the King's Valley, for he said, 'I have no son to keep my name in remembrance'; he called the pillar by his own name. It is called Absalom's Monument to this day.

DAVID HEARS OF ABSALOM'S DEATH

19 Then Ahimaaz son of Zadok said, 'Let me run, and carry tidings to the king that the LORD has delivered him from the power of his enemies.' 20 Joab said to him, 'You are not to carry tidings today; you may carry tidings another day, but today you shall not do so, because the king's son is dead.' 21 Then Joab said to a Cushite, 'Go, tell the king what you have seen.' The Cushite bowed before Joab, and ran. 22 Then Ahimaaz son of Zadok said again to Joab, 'Come what may, let me also run after the Cushite.' And Joab said, 'Why will you run, my son, seeing that you have no reward[o] for the tidings?' 23 'Come what may,' he said, 'I will run.' So he said to him, 'Run.' Then Ahimaaz ran by the way of the Plain, and outran the Cushite.

24 Now David was sitting between the two gates. The sentinel went up to the roof of the gate by the wall, and when he looked up, he saw a man running alone. 25 The sentinel shouted and told the king. The king said, 'If he is alone, there are tidings in his mouth.' He kept coming, and drew near. 26 Then the sentinel saw another man running; and the sentinel called to the gatekeeper and said, 'See, another man running alone!' The king said, 'He also is bringing tidings.' 27 The sentinel said, 'I think the running of the first one is like the running of Ahimaaz son of Zadok.' The king said, 'He is a good man, and comes with good tidings.'

28 Then Ahimaaz cried out to the king, 'All is well!' He prostrated himself before the king with his face to the ground, and said, 'Blessed be the LORD your God, who has delivered up the men who raised their hand against my lord the king.' 29 The king said, 'Is it well with the young man Absalom?' Ahimaaz answered, 'When Joab sent your servant,[p] I saw a great tumult, but I do not know what it was.' 30 The king said, 'Turn aside, and stand here.' So he turned aside, and stood still.

31 Then the Cushite came; and the Cushite said, 'Good tidings for my lord the king! For the LORD has vindicated you this day, delivering you from the power of all who rose up against you.' 32 The king said to the Cushite, 'Is it well with the young man Absalom?' The

[m] **18.9** Gk Syr Tg: Heb *was put* [n] **18.13** Another reading is *at the risk of my life* [o] **18.22** Meaning of Heb uncertain [p] **18.29** Heb *the king's servant, your servant*

Cushite answered, 'May the enemies of
my lord the king, and all who rise up to
do you harm, be like that young man.'

DAVID MOURNS FOR ABSALOM

33[q] The king was deeply moved, and
went up to the chamber over the gate,
and wept; and as he went, he said, 'O my
son Absalom, my son, my son Absalom!
Would that I had died instead of you,
O Absalom, my son, my son!'

19 It was told Joab, 'The king is
weeping and mourning for Absalom.' 2 So the victory that day was
turned into mourning for all the troops;
for the troops heard that day, 'The king
is grieving for his son.' 3 The troops stole
into the city that day as soldiers steal in
who are ashamed when they flee in battle. 4 The king covered his face, and the
king cried with a loud voice, 'O my son
Absalom, O Absalom, my son, my son!'
5 Then Joab came into the house to the
king, and said, 'Today you have covered
with shame the faces of all your officers
who have saved your life today, and the
lives of your sons and your daughters,
and the lives of your wives and your
concubines, 6 for love of those who hate
you and for hatred of those who love
you. You have made it clear today that
commanders and officers are nothing to
you; for I perceive that if Absalom were
alive and all of us were dead today, then
you would be pleased. 7 So go out at once
and speak kindly to your servants; for
I swear by the LORD, if you do not go,
not a man will stay with you this night;
and this will be worse for you than any
disaster that has come upon you from
your youth until now.' 8 Then the king
got up and took his seat in the gate. The
troops were all told, 'See, the king is sitting in the gate'; and all the troops came
before the king.

DAVID RECALLED TO JERUSALEM

Meanwhile, all the Israelites had fled
to their homes. 9 All the people were disputing throughout all the tribes of Israel, saying, 'The king delivered us from
the hand of our enemies, and saved us
from the hand of the Philistines; and
now he has fled out of the land because
of Absalom. 10 But Absalom, whom we
anointed over us, is dead in battle. Now
therefore why do you say nothing about
bringing the king back?'

11 King David sent this message to
the priests Zadok and Abiathar, 'Say to
the elders of Judah, "Why should you
be the last to bring the king back to his
house? The talk of all Israel has come
to the king.[r] 12 You are my kin, you are
my bone and my flesh; why then should
you be the last to bring back the king?"
13 And say to Amasa, "Are you not my
bone and my flesh? So may God do to
me, and more, if you are not the commander of my army from now on, in
place of Joab." ' 14 Amasa[s] swayed the
hearts of all the people of Judah as one,
and they sent word to the king, 'Return,
both you and all your servants.' 15 So the
king came back to the Jordan; and Judah
came to Gilgal to meet the king and to
bring him over the Jordan.

16 Shimei son of Gera, the Benjaminite, from Bahurim, hurried to come
down with the people of Judah to meet
King David; 17 with him were a thousand people from Benjamin. And Ziba,
the servant of the house of Saul, with
his fifteen sons and his twenty servants,
rushed down to the Jordan ahead of the
king, 18 while the crossing was taking
place,[t] to bring over the king's household, and to do his pleasure.

DAVID'S MERCY TO SHIMEI

Shimei son of Gera fell down before
the king, as he was about to cross the
Jordan, 19 and said to the king, 'May my
lord not hold me guilty or remember
how your servant did wrong on the day
my lord the king left Jerusalem; may
the king not bear it in mind. 20 For your
servant knows that I have sinned; therefore, see, I have come this day, the first
of all the house of Joseph to come down
to meet my lord the king.' 21 Abishai son
of Zeruiah answered, 'Shall not Shimei
be put to death for this, because he
cursed the LORD's anointed?' 22 But David said, 'What have I to do with you,
you sons of Zeruiah, that you should today become an adversary to me? Shall
anyone be put to death in Israel this
day? For do I not know that I am this
day king over Israel?' 23 The king said to
Shimei, 'You shall not die.' And the king
gave him his oath.

DAVID AND MEPHIBOSHETH MEET

24 Mephibosheth[u] grandson of Saul
came down to meet the king; he had not
taken care of his feet, or trimmed his
beard, or washed his clothes, from the

[q] **18.33** Ch 19.1 in Heb [r] **19.11** Gk: Heb *to the king, to his house* [s] **19.14** Heb *He* [t] **19.18** Cn: Heb *the ford crossed* [u] **19.24** Or *Merib-baal*: See 4.4 note

day the king left until the day he came
back in safety. 25When he came from Jerusalem to meet the king, the king said
to him, 'Why did you not go with me,
Mephibosheth?'[v] 26He answered, 'My
lord, O king, my servant deceived me;
for your servant said to him, "Saddle a
donkey for me,[w] so that I may ride on
it and go with the king." For your servant is lame. 27He has slandered your
servant to my lord the king. But my
lord the king is like the angel of God; do
therefore what seems good to you. 28For
all my father's house were doomed to
death before my lord the king; but you
set your servant among those who eat
at your table. What further right have
I, then, to appeal to the king?' 29The
king said to him, 'Why speak any more
of your affairs? I have decided: you and
Ziba shall divide the land.' 30Mephibo-
sheth[x] said to the king, 'Let him take it
all, since my lord the king has arrived
home safely.'

DAVID'S KINDNESS TO BARZILLAI

31 Now Barzillai the Gileadite had
come down from Rogelim; he went on
with the king to the Jordan, to escort
him over the Jordan. 32Barzillai was a
very aged man, eighty years old. He had
provided the king with food while he
stayed at Mahanaim, for he was a very
wealthy man. 33The king said to Barzillai, 'Come over with me, and I will provide for you in Jerusalem at my side.'
34But Barzillai said to the king, 'How
many years have I still to live, that I
should go up with the king to Jerusalem? 35Today I am eighty years old; can
I discern what is pleasant and what is
not? Can your servant taste what he
eats or what he drinks? Can I still listen
to the voice of singing men and singing
women? Why then should your servant
be an added burden to my lord the king?
36Your servant will go a little way over
the Jordan with the king. Why should
the king recompense me with such a reward? 37Please let your servant return,
so that I may die in my own town, near
the graves of my father and my mother.
But here is your servant Chimham; let
him go over with my lord the king; and
do for him whatever seems good to you.'
38The king answered, 'Chimham shall
go over with me, and I will do for him
whatever seems good to you; and all
that you desire of me I will do for you.'
39Then all the people crossed over the
Jordan, and the king crossed over; the
king kissed Barzillai and blessed him,
and he returned to his own home. 40The
king went on to Gilgal, and Chimham
went on with him; all the people of Judah, and also half the people of Israel,
brought the king on his way.

41 Then all the people of Israel came
to the king, and said to him, 'Why have
our kindred the people of Judah stolen you away, and brought the king
and his household over the Jordan,
and all David's men with him?' 42All
the people of Judah answered the people of Israel, 'Because the king is near
of kin to us. Why then are you angry
over this matter? Have we eaten at all
at the king's expense? Or has he given
us any gift?' 43But the people of Israel
answered the people of Judah, 'We have
ten shares in the king, and in David also
we have more than you. Why then did
you despise us? Were we not the first to
speak of bringing back our king?' But
the words of the people of Judah were
fiercer than the words of the people of
Israel.

THE REBELLION OF SHEBA

20 Now a scoundrel named Sheba
son of Bichri, a Benjaminite,
happened to be there. He sounded the
trumpet and cried out,

'We have no portion in David,
no share in the son of Jesse!
Everyone to your tents, O Israel!'

2So all the people of Israel withdrew
from David and followed Sheba son of
Bichri; but the people of Judah followed
their king steadfastly from the Jordan to
Jerusalem.

3 David came to his house at Jerusalem; and the king took the ten concubines whom he had left to look after the
house, and put them in a house under
guard, and provided for them, but did
not go in to them. So they were shut up
until the day of their death, living as if
in widowhood.

4 Then the king said to Amasa, 'Call
the men of Judah together to me within
three days, and be here yourself.' 5So
Amasa went to summon Judah; but he
delayed beyond the set time that had
been appointed him. 6David said to
Abishai, 'Now Sheba son of Bichri will
do us more harm than Absalom; take
your lord's servants and pursue him, or
he will find fortified cities for himself,

[v] **19.25** Or *Merib-baal*: See 4.4 note [w] **19.26** Gk Syr Vg: Heb *said, "I will saddle a donkey for myself*
[x] **19.30** Or *Merib-baal*: See 4.4 note

and escape from us.' 7Joab's men went out after him, along with the Cherethites, the Pelethites, and all the warriors; they went out from Jerusalem to pursue Sheba son of Bichri. 8When they were at the large stone that is in Gibeon, Amasa came to meet them. Now Joab was wearing a soldier's garment and over it was a belt with a sword in its sheath fastened at his waist; as he went forward it fell out. 9Joab said to Amasa, 'Is it well with you, my brother?' And Joab took Amasa by the beard with his right hand to kiss him. 10But Amasa did not notice the sword in Joab's hand; Joab struck him in the belly so that his entrails poured out on the ground, and he died. He did not strike a second blow.

Then Joab and his brother Abishai pursued Sheba son of Bichri. 11And one of Joab's men took his stand by Amasa, and said, 'Whoever favours Joab, and whoever is for David, let him follow Joab.' 12Amasa lay wallowing in his blood on the highway, and the man saw that all the people were stopping. Since he saw that all who came by him were stopping, he carried Amasa from the highway into a field, and threw a garment over him. 13Once he was removed from the highway, all the people went on after Joab to pursue Sheba son of Bichri.

14 Sheba[y] passed through all the tribes of Israel to Abel of Beth-maacah;[z] and all the Bichrites[a] assembled, and followed him inside. 15Joab's forces[b] came and besieged him in Abel of Beth-maacah; they threw up a siege-ramp against the city, and it stood against the rampart. Joab's forces were battering the wall to break it down. 16Then a wise woman called from the city, 'Listen! Listen! Tell Joab, "Come here, I want to speak to you." ' 17He came near her; and the woman said, 'Are you Joab?' He answered, 'I am.' Then she said to him, 'Listen to the words of your servant.' He answered, 'I am listening.' 18Then she said, 'They used to say in the old days, "Let them inquire at Abel"; and so they would settle a matter. 19I am one of those who are peaceable and faithful in Israel; you seek to destroy a city that is a mother in Israel; why will you swallow up the heritage of the LORD?' 20Joab answered, 'Far be it from me, far be it, that I should swallow up or destroy! 21That is not the case! But a man of the hill country of Ephraim, called Sheba son of Bichri, has lifted up his hand against King David; give him up alone, and I will withdraw from the city.' The woman said to Joab, 'His head shall be thrown over the wall to you.' 22Then the woman went to all the people with her wise plan. And they cut off the head of Sheba son of Bichri, and threw it out to Joab. So he blew the trumpet, and they dispersed from the city, and all went to their homes, while Joab returned to Jerusalem to the king.

23 Now Joab was in command of all the army of Israel;[c] Benaiah son of Jehoiada was in command of the Cherethites and the Pelethites; 24Adoram was in charge of the forced labour; Jehoshaphat son of Ahilud was the recorder; 25Sheva was secretary; Zadok and Abiathar were priests; 26and Ira the Jairite was also David's priest.

DAVID AVENGES THE GIBEONITES

21 Now there was a famine in the days of David for three years, year after year; and David inquired of the LORD. The LORD said, 'There is blood-guilt on Saul and on his house, because he put the Gibeonites to death.' 2So the king called the Gibeonites and spoke to them. (Now the Gibeonites were not of the people of Israel, but of the remnant of the Amorites; although the people of Israel had sworn to spare them, Saul had tried to wipe them out in his zeal for the people of Israel and Judah.) 3David said to the Gibeonites, 'What shall I do for you? How shall I make expiation, that you may bless the heritage of the LORD?' 4The Gibeonites said to him, 'It is not a matter of silver or gold between us and Saul or his house; neither is it for us to put anyone to death in Israel.' He said, 'What do you say that I should do for you?' 5They said to the king, 'The man who consumed us and planned to destroy us, so that we should have no place in all the territory of Israel— 6let seven of his sons be handed over to us, and we will impale them before the LORD at Gibeon on the mountain of the LORD.'[d] The king said, 'I will hand them over.'

7 But the king spared Mephibosheth,[e] the son of Saul's son Jonathan, because of the oath of the LORD that was be-

[y] **20.14** Heb *He* [z] **20.14** Compare 20.15: Heb *and Beth-maacah* [a] **20.14** Compare Gk Vg: Heb *Berites* [b] **20.15** Heb *They* [c] **20.23** Cn: Heb *Joab to all the army, Israel* [d] **21.6** Cn Compare Gk and 21.9: Heb *at Gibeah of Saul, the chosen of the LORD* [e] **21.7** Or *Merib-baal*: See 4.4 note

tween them, between David and Jonathan son of Saul. 8The king took the
two sons of Rizpah daughter of Aiah,
whom she bore to Saul, Armoni and
Mephibosheth;[f] and the five sons of Merab[g] daughter of Saul, whom she bore to
Adriel son of Barzillai the Meholathite;
9he gave them into the hands of the Gibeonites, and they impaled them on the
mountain before the LORD. The seven of
them perished together. They were put
to death in the first days of harvest, at
the beginning of the barley harvest.

10 Then Rizpah the daughter of Aiah
took sackcloth, and spread it on a rock
for herself, from the beginning of harvest until rain fell on them from the
heavens; she did not allow the birds of
the air to come on the bodies[h] by day,
or the wild animals by night. 11When
David was told what Rizpah daughter of Aiah, the concubine of Saul, had
done, 12David went and took the bones
of Saul and the bones of his son Jonathan from the people of Jabesh-gilead,
who had stolen them from the public
square of Beth-shan, where the Philistines had hung them up, on the day the
Philistines killed Saul on Gilboa. 13He
brought up from there the bones of Saul
and the bones of his son Jonathan; and
they gathered the bones of those who
had been impaled. 14They buried the
bones of Saul and of his son Jonathan
in the land of Benjamin in Zela, in the
tomb of his father Kish; they did all that
the king commanded. After that, God
heeded supplications for the land.

EXPLOITS OF DAVID'S MEN

15 The Philistines went to war again
with Israel, and David went down together with his servants. They fought
against the Philistines, and David grew
weary. 16Ishbi-benob, one of the descendants of the giants, whose spear
weighed three hundred shekels of
bronze, and who was fitted out with
new weapons,[i] said he would kill David. 17But Abishai son of Zeruiah came
to his aid, and attacked the Philistine
and killed him. Then David's men swore
to him, 'You shall not go out with us
to battle any longer, so that you do not
quench the lamp of Israel.'

18 After this a battle took place with
the Philistines, at Gob; then Sibbecai
the Hushathite killed Saph, who was
one of the descendants of the giants.
19Then there was another battle with
the Philistines at Gob; and Elhanan
son of Jaare-oregim, the Bethlehemite,
killed Goliath the Gittite, the shaft of
whose spear was like a weaver's beam.
20There was again war at Gath, where
there was a man of great size, who had
six fingers on each hand, and six toes
on each foot, twenty-four in number;
he too was descended from the giants.
21When he taunted Israel, Jonathan son
of David's brother Shimei, killed him.
22These four were descended from the
giants in Gath; they fell by the hands of
David and his servants.

DAVID'S SONG OF THANKSGIVING

22 David spoke to the LORD the
words of this song on the day
when the LORD delivered him from the
hand of all his enemies, and from the
hand of Saul. 2He said:

The LORD is my rock, my fortress,
and my deliverer,
3 my God, my rock, in whom
I take refuge,
my shield and the horn of
my salvation,
my stronghold and my refuge,
my saviour; you save me
from violence.
4 I call upon the LORD, who is
worthy to be praised,
and I am saved from my enemies.

5 For the waves of death
encompassed me,
the torrents of perdition
assailed me;
6 the cords of Sheol entangled me,
the snares of death
confronted me.

7 In my distress I called upon
the LORD;
to my God I called.
From his temple he heard my voice,
and my cry came to his ears.

8 Then the earth reeled and rocked;
the foundations of the
heavens trembled
and quaked, because he
was angry.
9 Smoke went up from his nostrils,
and devouring fire from
his mouth;
glowing coals flamed
forth from him.

[f] **21.8** Or *Merib-baal*: See 4.4 note [g] **21.8** Two Heb Mss Syr Compare Gk: MT *Michal*
[h] **21.10** Heb *them* [i] **21.16** Heb *was belted anew*

10 He bowed the heavens, and
came down;
thick darkness was under his feet.
11 He rode on a cherub, and flew;
he was seen upon the
wings of the wind.
12 He made darkness around
him a canopy,
thick clouds, a gathering of water.
13 Out of the brightness before him
coals of fire flamed forth.
14 The LORD thundered from heaven;
the Most High uttered his voice.
15 He sent out arrows, and
scattered them
—lightning, and routed them.
16 Then the channels of the
sea were seen,
the foundations of the world
were laid bare
at the rebuke of the LORD,
at the blast of the breath
of his nostrils.

17 He reached from on high, he took me,
he drew me out of mighty waters.
18 He delivered me from my
strong enemy,
from those who hated me;
for they were too mighty for me.
19 They came upon me in the day
of my calamity,
but the LORD was my stay.
20 He brought me out into a
broad place;
he delivered me, because he
delighted in me.

21 The LORD rewarded me according
to my righteousness;
according to the cleanness of my
hands he recompensed me.
22 For I have kept the ways of the LORD,
and have not wickedly
departed from my God.
23 For all his ordinances were
before me,
and from his statutes I did
not turn aside.
24 I was blameless before him,
and I kept myself from guilt.
25 Therefore the LORD has
recompensed me according
to my righteousness,
according to my cleanness
in his sight.

26 With the loyal you show
yourself loyal;
with the blameless you show
yourself blameless;
27 with the pure you show yourself
pure,
and with the crooked you
show yourself perverse.
28 You deliver a humble people,
but your eyes are upon
the haughty to bring
them down.
29 Indeed, you are my lamp, O LORD,
the LORD lightens my darkness.
30 By you I can crush a troop,
and by my God I can leap
over a wall.
31 This God—his way is perfect;
the promise of the LORD
proves true;
he is a shield for all who
take refuge in him.

32 For who is God, but the LORD?
And who is a rock, except
our God?
33 The God who has girded me
with strength[j]
has opened wide my path.[k]
34 He made my[l] feet like the
feet of deer,
and set me secure on the heights.
35 He trains my hands for war,
so that my arms can bend
a bow of bronze.
36 You have given me the shield
of your salvation,
and your help[m] has made
me great.
37 You have made me stride freely,
and my feet do not slip;
38 I pursued my enemies and
destroyed them,
and did not turn back until
they were consumed.
39 I consumed them; I struck
them down, so that
they did not rise;
they fell under my feet.
40 For you girded me with strength
for the battle;
you made my assailants
sink under me.
41 You made my enemies turn
their backs to me,
those who hated me, and
I destroyed them.
42 They looked, but there was no
one to save them;
they cried to the LORD, but he
did not answer them.

[j] 22.33 Q Ms Gk Syr Vg Compare Ps 18.32: MT *God is my strong refuge* [k] 22.33 Meaning of Heb uncertain [l] 22.34 Another reading is *his* [m] 22.36 Q Ms: MT *your answering*

43 I beat them fine like the dust
of the earth,
I crushed them and stamped
them down like the
mire of the streets.

44 You delivered me from strife
with the peoples;[n]
you kept me as the head
of the nations;
people whom I had not
known served me.
45 Foreigners came cringing to me;
as soon as they heard of me,
they obeyed me.
46 Foreigners lost heart,
and came trembling out of
their strongholds.

47 The LORD lives! Blessed
be my rock,
and exalted be my God, the
rock of my salvation,
48 the God who gave me vengeance
and brought down peoples
under me,
49 who brought me out from
my enemies;
you exalted me above
my adversaries,
you delivered me from
the violent.

50 For this I will extol you, O LORD,
among the nations,
and sing praises to your name.
51 He is a tower of salvation
for his king,
and shows steadfast love
to his anointed,
to David and his descendants
for ever.

THE LAST WORDS OF DAVID

23 Now these are the last words of
David:
The oracle of David, son of Jesse,
the oracle of the man whom
God exalted,[o]
the anointed of the God of Jacob,
the favourite of the Strong
One of Israel:

2 The spirit of the LORD speaks
through me,
his word is upon my tongue.
3 The God of Israel has spoken,
the Rock of Israel has
said to me:
One who rules over people justly,
ruling in the fear of God,
4 is like the light of morning,
like the sun rising on a
cloudless morning,
gleaming from the rain on
the grassy land.

5 Is not my house like this with God?
For he has made with me an
everlasting covenant,
ordered in all things and secure.
Will he not cause to prosper
all my help and my desire?
6 But the godless are[p] all like thorns
that are thrown away;
for they cannot be picked
up with the hand;
7 to touch them one uses an iron bar
or the shaft of a spear.
And they are entirely consumed
in fire on the spot.[q]

DAVID'S MIGHTY MEN

8 These are the names of the warriors
whom David had: Josheb-basshebeth
a Tahchemonite; he was chief of the
Three;[r] he wielded his spear[s] against
eight hundred whom he killed at one
time.
9 Next to him among the three warriors was Eleazar son of Dodo son of
Ahohi. He was with David when they
defied the Philistines who were gathered there for battle. The Israelites withdrew, 10 but he stood his ground. He
struck down the Philistines until his
arm grew weary, though his hand clung
to the sword. The LORD brought about
a great victory that day. Then the people came back to him—but only to strip
the dead.
11 Next to him was Shammah son
of Agee, the Hararite. The Philistines
gathered together at Lehi, where there
was a plot of ground full of lentils; and
the army fled from the Philistines. 12 But
he took his stand in the middle of the
plot, defended it, and killed the Philistines; and the LORD brought about a
great victory.
13 Towards the beginning of harvest
three of the thirty[t] chiefs went down to
join David at the cave of Adullam, while
a band of Philistines was encamped in
the valley of Rephaim. 14 David was then
in the stronghold; and the garrison of

[n] 22.44 Gk: Heb *from strife with my people*
[o] 23.1 Q Ms: MT *who was raised on high*
[p] 23.6 Heb *But worthlessness* [q] 23.7 Heb *in sitting* [r] 23.8 Gk Vg Compare 1 Chr 11.11: Meaning of Heb uncertain [s] 23.8 1 Chr 11.11: Meaning of Heb uncertain [t] 23.13 Heb adds *head*

the Philistines was then at Bethlehem.
15David said longingly, 'O that someone would give me water to drink from
the well of Bethlehem that is by the
gate!' 16Then the three warriors broke
through the camp of the Philistines,
drew water from the well of Bethlehem
that was by the gate, and brought it to
David. But he would not drink of it; he
poured it out to the LORD, 17for he said,
'The LORD forbid that I should do this.
Can I drink the blood of the men who
went at the risk of their lives?' Therefore
he would not drink it. The three warriors did these things.

18 Now Abishai son of Zeruiah, the
brother of Joab, was chief of the Thirty.[u]
With his spear he fought against three
hundred men and killed them, and won
a name beside the Three. 19He was the
most renowned of the Thirty,[v] and became their commander; but he did not
attain to the Three.

20 Benaiah son of Jehoiada was a valiant warrior[w] from Kabzeel, a doer of
great deeds; he struck down two sons of
Ariel[x] of Moab. He also went down and
killed a lion in a pit on a day when snow
had fallen. 21And he killed an Egyptian,
a handsome man. The Egyptian had
a spear in his hand; but Benaiah went
against him with a staff, snatched the
spear out of the Egyptian's hand, and
killed him with his own spear. 22Such
were the things Benaiah son of Jehoiada
did, and won a name beside the three
warriors. 23He was renowned among
the Thirty, but he did not attain to the
Three. And David put him in charge of
his bodyguard.

24 Among the Thirty were Asahel
brother of Joab; Elhanan son of Dodo of
Bethlehem; 25Shammah of Harod; Elika
of Harod; 26Helez the Paltite; Ira son of
Ikkesh of Tekoa; 27Abiezer of Anathoth;
Mebunnai the Hushathite; 28Zalmon
the Ahohite; Maharai of Netophah;
29Heleb son of Baanah of Netophah; Ittai son of Ribai of Gibeah of the Benjaminites; 30Benaiah of Pirathon; Hiddai
of the torrents of Gaash; 31Abi-albon the
Arbathite; Azmaveth of Bahurim; 32Eli-
ahba of Shaalbon; the sons of Jashen:
Jonathan 33son of[y] Shammah the Hararite; Ahiam son of Sharar the Hararite;
34Eliphelet son of Ahasbai of Maacah;
Eliam son of Ahithophel the Gilonite;
35Hezro[z] of Carmel; Paarai the Arbite;
36Igal son of Nathan of Zobah; Bani the
Gadite; 37Zelek the Ammonite; Naharai
of Beeroth, the armour-bearer of Joab
son of Zeruiah; 38Ira the Ithrite; Gareb
the Ithrite; 39Uriah the Hittite—thirty-
seven in all.

DAVID'S CENSUS OF ISRAEL AND JUDAH

24 Again the anger of the LORD
was kindled against Israel, and
he incited David against them, saying,
'Go, count the people of Israel and Judah.' 2So the king said to Joab and the
commanders of the army,[a] who were
with him, 'Go through all the tribes of
Israel, from Dan to Beer-sheba, and take
a census of the people, so that I may
know how many there are.' 3But Joab
said to the king, 'May the LORD your
God increase the number of the people
a hundredfold, while the eyes of my lord
the king can still see it! But why does my
lord the king want to do this?' 4But the
king's word prevailed against Joab and
the commanders of the army. So Joab
and the commanders of the army went
out from the presence of the king to take
a census of the people of Israel. 5They
crossed the Jordan, and began from[b]
Aroer and from the city that is in the
middle of the valley, towards Gad and
on to Jazer. 6Then they came to Gilead,
and to Kadesh in the land of the Hittites;[c] and they came to Dan, and from
Dan[d] they went round to Sidon, 7and
came to the fortress of Tyre and to all
the cities of the Hivites and Canaanites;
and they went out to the Negeb of Judah
at Beer-sheba. 8So when they had gone
through all the land, they came back to
Jerusalem at the end of nine months
and twenty days. 9Joab reported to the
king the number of those who had been
recorded: in Israel there were eight hundred thousand soldiers able to draw the
sword, and those of Judah were five
hundred thousand.

JUDGEMENT ON DAVID'S SIN

10 But afterwards, David was
stricken to the heart because he had
numbered the people. David said to the
LORD, 'I have sinned greatly in what

[u] **23.18** Two Heb Mss Syr: MT *Three* [v] **23.19** Syr Compare 1 Chr 11.25: Heb *Was he the most renowned of the Three?* [w] **23.20** Another reading is *the son of Ish-hai* [x] **23.20** Gk: Heb lacks *sons of* [y] **23.33** Gk: Heb lacks *son of* [z] **23.35** Another reading is *Hezrai* [a] **24.2** 1 Chr 21.2 Gk: Heb *to Joab the commander of the army* [b] **24.5** Gk Mss: Heb *encamped in Aroer south of* [c] **24.6** Gk: Heb *to the land of Tahtim-hodshi* [d] **24.6** Cn Compare Gk: Heb *they came to Dan-jaan and*

I have done. But now, O LORD, I pray
you, take away the guilt of your servant; for I have done very foolishly.'
11When David rose in the morning, the
word of the LORD came to the prophet
Gad, David's seer, saying, 12'Go and say
to David: Thus says the LORD: Three
things I offer[e] you; choose one of them,
and I will do it to you.' 13So Gad came
to David and told him; he asked him,
'Shall three[f] years of famine come to
you on your land? Or will you flee for
three months before your foes while
they pursue you? Or shall there be
three days' pestilence in your land?
Now consider, and decide what answer
I shall return to the one who sent me.'
14Then David said to Gad, 'I am in great
distress; let us fall into the hand of the
LORD, for his mercy is great; but let me
not fall into human hands.'

15 So the LORD sent a pestilence on
Israel from that morning until the appointed time; and seventy thousand
of the people died, from Dan to Beer-
sheba. 16But when the angel stretched
out his hand towards Jerusalem to destroy it, the LORD relented concerning
the evil, and said to the angel who was
bringing destruction among the people, 'It is enough; now stay your hand.'
The angel of the LORD was then by the
threshing-floor of Araunah the Jebusite. 17When David saw the angel who
was destroying the people, he said to
the LORD, 'I alone have sinned, and I
alone have done wickedly; but these
sheep, what have they done? Let your
hand, I pray, be against me and against
my father's house.'

DAVID'S ALTAR ON THE THRESHING-FLOOR

18 That day Gad came to David and
said to him, 'Go up and erect an altar
to the LORD on the threshing-floor of
Araunah the Jebusite.' 19Following Gad's
instructions, David went up, as the
LORD had commanded. 20When Araunah looked down, he saw the king and
his servants coming towards him; and
Araunah went out and prostrated himself before the king with his face to the
ground. 21Araunah said, 'Why has my
lord the king come to his servant?' David said, 'To buy the threshing-floor
from you in order to build an altar to the
LORD, so that the plague may be averted
from the people.' 22Then Araunah said
to David, 'Let my lord the king take and
offer up what seems good to him; here
are the oxen for the burnt-offering, and
the threshing-sledges and the yokes of
the oxen for the wood. 23All this, O king,
Araunah gives to the king.' And Araunah said to the king, 'May the LORD your
God respond favourably to you.'

24 But the king said to Araunah, 'No,
but I will buy them from you for a price;
I will not offer burnt-offerings to the
LORD my God that cost me nothing.' So
David bought the threshing-floor and
the oxen for fifty shekels of silver. 25Da-
vid built there an altar to the LORD, and
offered burnt-offerings and offerings
of well-being. So the LORD answered
his supplication for the land, and the
plague was averted from Israel.

[e] **24.12** Or *hold over* [f] **24.13** 1 Chr 21.12 Gk: Heb *seven*

1 KINGS

First and 2 Kings were originally one book in Hebrew, similar to 1 and 2 Samuel. First Kings continues the narrative by treating the events of the succession of Solomon to the throne of David. The subsequent building of the temple, stories about the reign of Solomon itself, and the subsequent division of the kingdom after Solomon's death are told with the characteristic Deuteronomistic point of view. The kingdom of Israel in the north and the kingdom of Judah in the south were governed by a series of successive kings. The Israelite kings are presented as wicked and eventually lead to the demise of the Northern Kingdom. The kings of Judah are not judged as harshly and continue a little longer the Davidic dynasty. The final chapters of 1 Kings treat the works of the prophets, particularly Elijah and his confrontation with Jezebel, the wife of King Ahab.

The narrative of 1 Kings is presented in the liturgy during Year II of the weekday liturgical calendar. The passages are read consecutively on Thursday of the Fourth Week of the Year through Tuesday of the Eleventh Week of the Year. Selected passages are also read on certain Sundays within the liturgical cycle.

THE STRUGGLE FOR THE SUCCESSION

1 King David was old and advanced
in years; and although they covered him with clothes, he could not get
warm. 2So his servants said to him, 'Let
a young virgin be sought for my lord
the king, and let her wait on the king,
and be his attendant; let her lie in your
bosom, so that my lord the king may be
warm.' 3So they searched for a beautiful girl throughout all the territory of
Israel, and found Abishag the Shunammite, and brought her to the king. 4The
girl was very beautiful. She became the
king's attendant and served him, but
the king did not know her sexually.

5 Now Adonijah son of Haggith exalted himself, saying, 'I will be king'; he
prepared for himself chariots and horsemen, and fifty men to run before him.
6His father had never at any time displeased him by asking, 'Why have you
done that?' He was also a very handsome man, and he was born next after
Absalom. 7He conferred with Joab son
of Zeruiah and with the priest Abiathar,
and they supported Adonijah. 8But the
priest Zadok, and Benaiah son of Jehoiada, and the prophet Nathan, and
Shimei, and Rei, and David's own warriors did not side with Adonijah.

9 Adonijah sacrificed sheep, oxen, and
fatted cattle by the stone Zoheleth, which
is beside En-rogel, and he invited all his
brothers, the king's sons, and all the
royal officials of Judah, 10but he did not
invite the prophet Nathan or Benaiah or
the warriors or his brother Solomon.

11 Then Nathan said to Bathsheba,
Solomon's mother, 'Have you not heard
that Adonijah son of Haggith has become king and our lord David does not
know it? 12Now therefore come, let me
give you advice, so that you may save
your own life and the life of your son
Solomon. 13Go in at once to King David,
and say to him, "Did you not, my lord
the king, swear to your servant, saying:
Your son Solomon shall succeed me as
king, and he shall sit on my throne?
Why then is Adonijah king?" 14Then
while you are still there speaking with
the king, I will come in after you and
confirm your words.'

15 So Bathsheba went to the king in
his room. The king was very old; Abishag the Shunammite was attending
the king. 16Bathsheba bowed and did
obeisance to the king, and the king said,
'What do you wish?' 17She said to him,
'My lord, you swore to your servant by
the LORD your God, saying: Your son
Solomon shall succeed me as king, and
he shall sit on my throne. 18But now
suddenly Adonijah has become king,
though you, my lord the king, do not
know it. 19He has sacrificed oxen, fatted cattle, and sheep in abundance, and
has invited all the children of the king,
the priest Abiathar, and Joab the commander of the army; but your servant
Solomon he has not invited. 20But you,
my lord the king—the eyes of all Israel
are on you to tell them who shall sit on
the throne of my lord the king after
him. 21Otherwise it will come to pass,
when my lord the king sleeps with his
ancestors, that my son Solomon and I
will be counted offenders.'

22 While she was still speaking with
the king, the prophet Nathan came in.
23The king was told, 'Here is the prophet
Nathan.' When he came in before the
king, he did obeisance to the king, with
his face to the ground. 24Nathan said,
'My lord the king, have you said, "Adonijah shall succeed me as king, and he
shall sit on my throne"? 25For today he
has gone down and has sacrificed oxen,
fatted cattle, and sheep in abundance,
and has invited all the king's children,
Joab the commander[a] of the army, and
the priest Abiathar, who are now eating
and drinking before him, and saying,
"Long live King Adonijah!" 26But he
did not invite me, your servant, and the
priest Zadok, and Benaiah son of Jehoiada, and your servant Solomon. 27Has
this thing been brought about by my
lord the king and you have not let your
servants know who should sit on the
throne of my lord the king after him?'

THE ACCESSION OF SOLOMON

28 King David answered, 'Summon
Bathsheba to me.' So she came into the
king's presence, and stood before the
king. 29The king swore, saying, 'As the
LORD lives, who has saved my life from
every adversity, 30as I swore to you by
the LORD, the God of Israel, "Your son
Solomon shall succeed me as king, and
he shall sit on my throne in my place",
so will I do this day.' 31Then Bathsheba
bowed with her face to the ground, and
did obeisance to the king, and said, 'May
my lord King David live for ever!'

32 King David said, 'Summon to me
the priest Zadok, the prophet Nathan,
and Benaiah son of Jehoiada.' When they
came before the king, 33the king said to
them, 'Take with you the servants of
your lord, and have my son Solomon
ride on my own mule, and bring him
down to Gihon. 34There let the priest
Zadok and the prophet Nathan anoint
him king over Israel; then blow the
trumpet, and say, "Long live King Solomon!" 35You shall go up following him.
Let him enter and sit on my throne; he
shall be king in my place; for I have appointed him to be ruler over Israel and
over Judah.' 36Benaiah son of Jehoiada
answered the king, 'Amen! May the
LORD, the God of my lord the king, so
ordain. 37As the LORD has been with
my lord the king, so may he be with
Solomon, and make his throne greater
than the throne of my lord King David.'

38 So the priest Zadok, the prophet
Nathan, and Benaiah son of Jehoiada,
and the Cherethites and the Pelethites,
went down and had Solomon ride on
King David's mule, and led him to Gihon. 39There the priest Zadok took the
horn of oil from the tent and anointed
Solomon. Then they blew the trumpet,
and all the people said, 'Long live King
Solomon!' 40And all the people went up
following him, playing on pipes and rejoicing with great joy, so that the earth
quaked at their noise.

41 Adonijah and all the guests who
were with him heard it as they finished
feasting. When Joab heard the sound of
the trumpet, he said, 'Why is the city in
an uproar?' 42While he was still speaking, Jonathan son of the priest Abiathar
arrived. Adonijah said, 'Come in, for
you are a worthy man and surely you
bring good news.' 43Jonathan answered
Adonijah, 'No, for our lord King David
has made Solomon king; 44the king has
sent with him the priest Zadok, the
prophet Nathan, and Benaiah son of
Jehoiada, and the Cherethites and the
Pelethites; and they had him ride on
the king's mule; 45the priest Zadok and
the prophet Nathan have anointed him
king at Gihon; and they have gone up
from there rejoicing, so that the city is
in an uproar. This is the noise that you
heard. 46Solomon now sits on the royal
throne. 47Moreover, the king's servants

[a] 1.25 Gk: Heb *the commanders*

came to congratulate our lord King David, saying, "May God make the name
of Solomon more famous than yours,
and make his throne greater than your
throne." The king bowed in worship on
the bed 48and went on to pray thus,
"Blessed be the LORD, the God of Israel,
who today has granted one of my offspring[b] to sit on my throne and permitted me to witness it." '

49 Then all the guests of Adonijah got
up trembling and went their own ways.
50Adonijah, fearing Solomon, got up
and went to grasp the horns of the altar.
51Solomon was informed, 'Adonijah is
afraid of King Solomon; see, he has laid
hold of the horns of the altar, saying,
"Let King Solomon swear to me first
that he will not kill his servant with the
sword." ' 52So Solomon responded, 'If he
proves to be a worthy man, not one of
his hairs shall fall to the ground; but if
wickedness is found in him, he shall die.'
53Then King Solomon sent to have him
brought down from the altar. He came
to do obeisance to King Solomon; and
Solomon said to him, 'Go home.'

DAVID'S INSTRUCTION TO SOLOMON

2 When David's time to die drew
near, he charged his son Solomon,
saying: 2'I am about to go the way of
all the earth. Be strong, be courageous,
3and keep the charge of the LORD your
God, walking in his ways and keeping
his statutes, his commandments, his
ordinances, and his testimonies, as it
is written in the law of Moses, so that
you may prosper in all that you do and
wherever you turn. 4Then the LORD will
establish his word that he spoke concerning me: "If your heirs take heed to
their way, to walk before me in faithfulness with all their heart and with all
their soul, there shall not fail you a successor on the throne of Israel."

5 'Moreover, you know also what Joab
son of Zeruiah did to me, how he dealt
with the two commanders of the armies
of Israel, Abner son of Ner, and Amasa
son of Jether, whom he murdered, retal-
iating in time of peace for blood that had
been shed in war, and putting the blood
of war on the belt around his waist, and
on the sandals on his feet. 6Act therefore according to your wisdom, but do
not let his grey head go down to Sheol in
peace. 7Deal loyally, however, with the
sons of Barzillai the Gileadite, and let
them be among those who eat at your
table; for with such loyalty they met
me when I fled from your brother Absalom. 8There is also with you Shimei
son of Gera, the Benjaminite from Bahurim, who cursed me with a terrible
curse on the day when I went to Mahanaim; but when he came down to meet
me at the Jordan, I swore to him by the
LORD, "I will not put you to death with
the sword." 9Therefore do not hold him
guiltless, for you are a wise man; you
will know what you ought to do to him,
and you must bring his grey head down
with blood to Sheol.'

DEATH OF DAVID

10 Then David slept with his ancestors, and was buried in the city of David. 11The time that David reigned over
Israel was forty years; he reigned for
seven years in Hebron, and thirty-three
years in Jerusalem. 12So Solomon sat on
the throne of his father David; and his
kingdom was firmly established.

SOLOMON CONSOLIDATES HIS REIGN

13 Then Adonijah son of Haggith
came to Bathsheba, Solomon's mother.
She asked, 'Do you come peaceably?' He
said, 'Peaceably.' 14Then he said, 'May I
have a word with you?' She said, 'Go on.'
15He said, 'You know that the kingdom
was mine, and that all Israel expected
me to reign; however, the kingdom has
turned about and become my brother's,
for it was his from the LORD. 16And now
I have one request to make of you; do not
refuse me.' She said to him, 'Go on.' 17He
said, 'Please ask King Solomon—he will
not refuse you—to give me Abishag the
Shunammite as my wife.' 18Bathsheba
said, 'Very well; I will speak to the king
on your behalf.'

19 So Bathsheba went to King Solomon, to speak to him on behalf of Adonijah. The king rose to meet her, and
bowed down to her; then he sat on his
throne, and had a throne brought for
the king's mother, and she sat on his
right. 20Then she said, 'I have one small
request to make of you; do not refuse
me.' And the king said to her, 'Make
your request, my mother; for I will not
refuse you.' 21She said, 'Let Abishag the
Shunammite be given to your brother
Adonijah as his wife.' 22King Solomon
answered his mother, 'And why do you
ask Abishag the Shunammite for Adonijah? Ask for him the kingdom as well!
For he is my elder brother; ask not only

[b] **1.48** Gk: Heb *one*

for him but also for the priest Abiathar
and for Joab son of Zeruiah!' 23 Then
King Solomon swore by the LORD, 'So
may God do to me, and more also, for
Adonijah has devised this scheme at the
risk of his life! 24 Now therefore as the
LORD lives, who has established me and
placed me on the throne of my father
David, and who has made me a house
as he promised, today Adonijah shall be
put to death.' 25 So King Solomon sent
Benaiah son of Jehoiada; he struck him
down, and he died.

26 The king said to the priest Abiathar, 'Go to Anathoth, to your estate; for
you deserve death. But I will not at this
time put you to death, because you carried the ark of the Lord GOD before my
father David, and because you shared
in all the hardships my father endured.'
27 So Solomon banished Abiathar from
being priest to the LORD, thus fulfilling the word of the LORD that he had
spoken concerning the house of Eli in
Shiloh.

28 When the news came to Joab—for
Joab had supported Adonijah though he
had not supported Absalom—Joab fled
to the tent of the LORD and grasped the
horns of the altar. 29 When it was told
King Solomon, 'Joab has fled to the tent
of the LORD and now is beside the altar', Solomon sent Benaiah son of Jehoiada, saying, 'Go, strike him down.' 30 So
Benaiah came to the tent of the LORD
and said to him, 'The king commands,
"Come out." ' But he said, 'No, I will die
here.' Then Benaiah brought the king
word again, saying, 'Thus said Joab, and
thus he answered me.' 31 The king replied
to him, 'Do as he has said, strike him
down and bury him; and thus take away
from me and from my father's house the
guilt for the blood that Joab shed without cause. 32 The LORD will bring back
his bloody deeds on his own head, because, without the knowledge of my father David, he attacked and killed with
the sword two men more righteous and
better than himself, Abner son of Ner,
commander of the army of Israel, and
Amasa son of Jether, commander of the
army of Judah. 33 So shall their blood
come back on the head of Joab and on
the head of his descendants for ever; but
to David, and to his descendants, and to
his house, and to his throne, there shall
be peace from the LORD for evermore.'
34 Then Benaiah son of Jehoiada went up
and struck him down and killed him;
and he was buried at his own house
near the wilderness. 35 The king put Benaiah son of Jehoiada over the army in
his place, and the king put the priest Zadok in the place of Abiathar.

36 Then the king sent and summoned Shimei, and said to him, 'Build
yourself a house in Jerusalem, and live
there, and do not go out from there to
any place whatever. 37 For on the day
you go out, and cross the Wadi Kidron,
know for certain that you shall die; your
blood shall be on your own head.' 38 And
Shimei said to the king, 'The sentence is
fair; as my lord the king has said, so will
your servant do.' So Shimei lived in Jerusalem for many days.

39 But it happened at the end of
three years that two of Shimei's slaves
ran away to King Achish son of Maacah
of Gath. When it was told Shimei, 'Your
slaves are in Gath', 40 Shimei arose and
saddled a donkey, and went to Achish
in Gath, to search for his slaves; Shimei
went and brought his slaves from Gath.
41 When Solomon was told that Shimei
had gone from Jerusalem to Gath and
returned, 42 the king sent and summoned Shimei, and said to him, 'Did I
not make you swear by the LORD, and
solemnly adjure you, saying, "Know
for certain that on the day you go out
and go to any place whatever, you shall
die"? And you said to me, "The sentence
is fair; I accept." 43 Why then have you
not kept your oath to the LORD and the
commandment with which I charged
you?' 44 The king also said to Shimei,
'You know in your own heart all the
evil that you did to my father David;
so the LORD will bring back your evil
on your own head. 45 But King Solomon shall be blessed, and the throne
of David shall be established before the
LORD for ever.' 46 Then the king commanded Benaiah son of Jehoiada; and
he went out and struck him down, and
he died.

So the kingdom was established in
the hand of Solomon.

SOLOMON'S PRAYER FOR WISDOM

3 Solomon made a marriage alliance
with Pharaoh king of Egypt; he
took Pharaoh's daughter and brought
her into the city of David, until he had
finished building his own house and the
house of the LORD and the wall around
Jerusalem. 2 The people were sacrificing
at the high places, however, because no
house had yet been built for the name of
the LORD.

3 Solomon loved the LORD, walking
in the statutes of his father David; only,
he sacrificed and offered incense at the
high places. 4The king went to Gibeon to
sacrifice there, for that was the principal high place; Solomon used to offer a
thousand burnt-offerings on that altar.
5At Gibeon the LORD appeared to Solomon in a dream by night; and God said,
'Ask what I should give you.' 6And Solomon said, 'You have shown great and
steadfast love to your servant my father
David, because he walked before you in
faithfulness, in righteousness, and in
uprightness of heart towards you; and
you have kept for him this great and
steadfast love, and have given him a son
to sit on his throne today. 7And now,
O LORD my God, you have made your
servant king in place of my father David, although I am only a little child; I
do not know how to go out or come in.
8And your servant is in the midst of the
people whom you have chosen, a great
people, so numerous they cannot be
numbered or counted. 9Give your servant therefore an understanding mind
to govern your people, able to discern
between good and evil; for who can govern this your great people?'

10 It pleased the Lord that Solomon
had asked this. 11God said to him, 'Because you have asked this, and have not
asked for yourself long life or riches, or
for the life of your enemies, but have
asked for yourself understanding to discern what is right, 12I now do according
to your word. Indeed I give you a wise
and discerning mind; no one like you
has been before you and no one like you
shall arise after you. 13I give you also
what you have not asked, both riches
and honour all your life; no other king
shall compare with you. 14If you will
walk in my ways, keeping my statutes
and my commandments, as your father
David walked, then I will lengthen your
life.'

15 Then Solomon awoke; it had been
a dream. He came to Jerusalem, where
he stood before the ark of the covenant
of the LORD. He offered up burnt-
offerings and offerings of well-being,
and provided a feast for all his servants.

SOLOMON'S WISDOM IN JUDGEMENT

16 Later, two women who were prostitutes came to the king and stood before him. 17One woman said, 'Please, my
lord, this woman and I live in the same
house; and I gave birth while she was in
the house. 18Then on the third day after I gave birth, this woman also gave
birth. We were together; there was no
one else with us in the house, only the
two of us were in the house. 19Then this
woman's son died in the night, because
she lay on him. 20She got up in the middle of the night and took my son from
beside me while your servant slept. She
laid him at her breast, and laid her dead
son at my breast. 21When I rose in the
morning to nurse my son, I saw that
he was dead; but when I looked at him
closely in the morning, clearly it was
not the son I had borne.' 22But the other
woman said, 'No, the living son is mine,
and the dead son is yours.' The first said,
'No, the dead son is yours, and the living son is mine.' So they argued before
the king.

23 Then the king said, 'One says,
"This is my son that is alive, and your
son is dead"; while the other says, "Not
so! Your son is dead, and my son is the
living one." ' 24So the king said, 'Bring
me a sword', and they brought a sword
before the king. 25The king said, 'Divide
the living boy in two; then give half to
one, and half to the other.' 26But the
woman whose son was alive said to the
king—because compassion for her son
burned within her—'Please, my lord,
give her the living boy; certainly do not
kill him!' The other said, 'It shall be neither mine nor yours; divide it.' 27Then
the king responded: 'Give the first
woman the living boy; do not kill him.
She is his mother.' 28All Israel heard of
the judgement that the king had rendered; and they stood in awe of the king,
because they perceived that the wisdom
of God was in him, to execute justice.

SOLOMON'S ADMINISTRATIVE OFFICERS

4 King Solomon was king over all
Israel, 2and these were his high
officials: Azariah son of Zadok was the
priest; 3Elihoreph and Ahijah sons of
Shisha were secretaries; Jehoshaphat
son of Ahilud was recorder; 4Benaiah
son of Jehoiada was in command of the
army; Zadok and Abiathar were priests;
5Azariah son of Nathan was over the
officials; Zabud son of Nathan was
priest and king's friend; 6Ahishar was
in charge of the palace; and Adoniram
son of Abda was in charge of the forced
labour.

7 Solomon had twelve officials over
all Israel, who provided food for the

king and his household; each one had to make provision for one month in the year. 8These were their names: Ben-hur, in the hill country of Ephraim; 9Ben-deker, in Makaz, Shaalbim, Beth-shemesh, and Elon-beth-hanan; 10Ben-hesed, in Arubboth (to him belonged Socoh and all the land of Hepher); 11Ben-abinadab, in all Naphath-dor (he had Taphath, Solomon's daughter, as his wife); 12Baana son of Ahilud, in Taanach, Megiddo, and all Beth-shean, which is beside Zarethan below Jezreel, and from Beth-shean to Abel-meholah, as far as the other side of Jokmeam; 13Ben-geber, in Ramoth-gilead (he had the villages of Jair son of Manasseh, which are in Gilead, and he had the region of Argob, which is in Bashan, sixty great cities with walls and bronze bars); 14Ahinadab son of Iddo, in Mahanaim; 15Ahimaaz, in Naphtali (he had taken Basemath, Solomon's daughter, as his wife); 16Baana son of Hushai, in Asher and Bealoth; 17Jehoshaphat son of Paruah, in Issachar; 18Shimei son of Ela, in Benjamin; 19Geber son of Uri, in the land of Gilead, the country of King Sihon of the Amorites and of King Og of Bashan. And there was one official in the land of Judah.

MAGNIFICENCE OF SOLOMON'S RULE

20 Judah and Israel were as numerous as the sand by the sea; they ate and drank and were happy. 21[c]Solomon was sovereign over all the kingdoms from the Euphrates to the land of the Philistines, even to the border of Egypt; they brought tribute and served Solomon all the days of his life.

22 Solomon's provision for one day was thirty cors of choice flour, and sixty cors of meal, 23ten fat oxen, and twenty pasture-fed cattle, one hundred sheep, besides deer, gazelles, roebucks, and fatted fowl. 24For he had dominion over all the region west of the Euphrates from Tiphsah to Gaza, over all the kings west of the Euphrates; and he had peace on all sides. 25During Solomon's lifetime Judah and Israel lived in safety, from Dan even to Beer-sheba, all of them under their vines and fig trees. 26Solomon also had forty thousand stalls of horses for his chariots, and twelve thousand horsemen. 27Those officials supplied provisions for King Solomon and for all who came to King Solomon's table, each one in his month; they let nothing be lacking. 28They also brought to the required place barley and straw for the horses and swift steeds, each according to his charge.

FAME OF SOLOMON'S WISDOM

29 God gave Solomon very great wisdom, discernment, and breadth of understanding as vast as the sand on the seashore, 30so that Solomon's wisdom surpassed the wisdom of all the people of the east, and all the wisdom of Egypt. 31He was wiser than anyone else, wiser than Ethan the Ezrahite, and Heman, Calcol, and Darda, children of Mahol; his fame spread throughout all the surrounding nations. 32He composed three thousand proverbs, and his songs numbered a thousand and five. 33He would speak of trees, from the cedar that is in the Lebanon to the hyssop that grows in the wall; he would speak of animals, and birds, and reptiles, and fish. 34People came from all the nations to hear the wisdom of Solomon; they came from all the kings of the earth who had heard of his wisdom.

PREPARATIONS AND MATERIALS FOR THE TEMPLE

5 [d]Now King Hiram of Tyre sent his servants to Solomon, when he heard that they had anointed him king in place of his father; for Hiram had always been a friend to David. 2Solomon sent word to Hiram, saying, 3'You know that my father David could not build a house for the name of the LORD his God because of the warfare with which his enemies surrounded him, until the LORD put them under the soles of his feet.[e] 4But now the LORD my God has given me rest on every side; there is neither adversary nor misfortune. 5So I intend to build a house for the name of the LORD my God, as the LORD said to my father David, "Your son, whom I will set on your throne in your place, shall build the house for my name." 6Therefore command that cedars from the Lebanon be cut for me. My servants will join your servants, and I will give you whatever wages you set for your servants; for you know that there is no one among us who knows how to cut timber like the Sidonians.'

7 When Hiram heard the words of Solomon, he rejoiced greatly, and said, 'Blessed be the LORD today, who has

[c] 4.21 Ch 5.1 in Heb [d] 5.1 Ch 5.15 in Heb
[e] 5.3 Gk Tg Vg: Heb *my feet* or *his feet*

given to David a wise son to be over this
great people.' 8Hiram sent word to Solomon, 'I have heard the message that
you have sent to me; I will fulfil all your
needs in the matter of cedar and cypress
timber. 9My servants shall bring it down
to the sea from the Lebanon; I will make
it into rafts to go by sea to the place you
indicate. I will have them broken up
there for you to take away. And you
shall meet my needs by providing food
for my household.' 10So Hiram supplied
Solomon's every need for timber of cedar and cypress. 11Solomon in turn gave
Hiram twenty thousand cors of wheat
as food for his household, and twenty
cors of fine oil. Solomon gave this to
Hiram year by year. 12So the LORD gave
Solomon wisdom, as he promised him.
There was peace between Hiram and
Solomon; and the two of them made a
treaty.

13 King Solomon conscripted forced
labour out of all Israel; the levy numbered thirty thousand men. 14He sent
them to the Lebanon, ten thousand a
month in shifts; they would be a month
in the Lebanon and two months at
home; Adoniram was in charge of the
forced labour. 15Solomon also had seventy thousand labourers and eighty
thousand stonecutters in the hill country, 16besides Solomon's three thousand three hundred supervisors who
were over the work, having charge of
the people who did the work. 17At the
king's command, they quarried out
great, costly stones in order to lay the
foundation of the house with dressed
stones. 18So Solomon's builders and Hiram's builders and the Gebalites did the
stonecutting and prepared the timber
and the stone to build the house.

SOLOMON BUILDS THE TEMPLE

6 In the four hundred and eighti-
eth year after the Israelites came
out of the land of Egypt, in the fourth
year of Solomon's reign over Israel, in
the month of Ziv, which is the second
month, he began to build the house of
the LORD. 2The house that King Solomon built for the LORD was sixty cubits long, twenty cubits wide, and thirty
cubits high. 3The vestibule in front of
the nave of the house was twenty cubits wide, across the width of the house.
Its depth was ten cubits in front of the
house. 4For the house he made windows
with recessed frames.[f] 5He also built a
structure against the wall of the house,
running around the walls of the house,
both the nave and the inner sanctuary;
and he made side chambers all round.
6The lowest story[g] was five cubits wide,
the middle one was six cubits wide, and
the third was seven cubits wide; for
round the outside of the house he made
offsets on the wall in order that the supporting beams should not be inserted
into the walls of the house.

7 The house was built with stone
finished at the quarry, so that neither
hammer nor axe nor any tool of iron
was heard in the temple while it was being built.

8 The entrance for the middle story
was on the south side of the house: one
went up by winding stairs to the middle story, and from the middle story to
the third. 9So he built the house, and
finished it; he roofed the house with
beams and planks of cedar. 10He built
the structure against the whole house,
each story[h] five cubits high, and it was
joined to the house with timbers of
cedar.

11 Now the word of the LORD came
to Solomon, 12'Concerning this house
that you are building, if you will walk in
my statutes, obey my ordinances, and
keep all my commandments by walking in them, then I will establish my
promise with you, which I made to your
father David. 13I will dwell among the
children of Israel, and will not forsake
my people Israel.'

14 So Solomon built the house, and
finished it. 15He lined the walls of the
house on the inside with boards of cedar; from the floor of the house to the
rafters of the ceiling, he covered them
on the inside with wood; and he covered the floor of the house with boards
of cypress. 16He built twenty cubits of
the rear of the house with boards of cedar from the floor to the rafters, and he
built this within as an inner sanctuary,
as the most holy place. 17The house, that
is, the nave in front of the inner sanctuary, was forty cubits long. 18The cedar within the house had carvings of
gourds and open flowers; all was cedar,
no stone was seen. 19The inner sanctuary he prepared in the innermost part of
the house, to set there the ark of the covenant of the LORD. 20The interior of the
inner sanctuary was twenty cubits long,
twenty cubits wide, and twenty cubits

[f] **6.4** Gk: Meaning of Heb uncertain [g] **6.6** Gk: Heb *structure* [h] **6.10** Heb lacks *each story*

high; he overlaid it with pure gold. He
also overlaid the altar with cedar.[i] 21Sol-
omon overlaid the inside of the house
with pure gold, then he drew chains of
gold across, in front of the inner sanctuary, and overlaid it with gold. 22Next
he overlaid the whole house with gold,
in order that the whole house might be
perfect; even the whole altar that belonged to the inner sanctuary he overlaid with gold.

THE FURNISHINGS OF THE TEMPLE

23 In the inner sanctuary he made
two cherubim of olive wood, each ten
cubits high. 24Five cubits was the length
of one wing of the cherub, and five cubits the length of the other wing of the
cherub; it was ten cubits from the tip of
one wing to the tip of the other. 25The
other cherub also measured ten cubits;
both cherubim had the same measure
and the same form. 26The height of one
cherub was ten cubits, and so was that
of the other cherub. 27He put the cherubim in the innermost part of the house;
the wings of the cherubim were spread
out so that a wing of one was touching
one wall, and a wing of the other cherub
was touching the other wall; their other
wings towards the centre of the house
were touching wing to wing. 28He also
overlaid the cherubim with gold.

29 He carved the walls of the house
all round about with carved engravings
of cherubim, palm trees, and open flowers, in the inner and outer rooms. 30The
floor of the house he overlaid with gold,
in the inner and outer rooms.

31 For the entrance to the inner
sanctuary he made doors of olive wood;
the lintel and the doorposts were five-
sided.[j] 32He covered the two doors of
olive wood with carvings of cherubim,
palm trees, and open flowers; he overlaid them with gold, and spread gold on
the cherubim and on the palm trees.

33 So also he made for the entrance
to the nave doorposts of olive wood,
each four-sided, 34and two doors of cypress wood; the two leaves of one door
were folding, and the two leaves of the
other door were folding. 35He carved
cherubim, palm trees, and open flowers, overlaying them with gold evenly
applied upon the carved work. 36He
built the inner court with three courses
of dressed stone to one course of cedar
beams.

37 In the fourth year the foundation
of the house of the LORD was laid, in the
month of Ziv. 38In the eleventh year, in
the month of Bul, which is the eighth
month, the house was finished in all its
parts, and according to all its specifica-
tions. He was seven years in building it.

SOLOMON'S PALACE AND OTHER BUILDINGS

7 Solomon was building his own
house for thirteen years, and he finished his entire house.

2 He built the House of the Forest of
the Lebanon one hundred cubits long,
fifty cubits wide, and thirty cubits
high, built on four rows of cedar pillars,
with cedar beams on the pillars. 3It was
roofed with cedar on the forty-five rafters, fifteen in each row, which were on
the pillars. 4There were window frames
in the three rows, facing each other in
the three rows. 5All the doorways and
doorposts had four-sided frames, opposite, facing each other in the three rows.

6 He made the Hall of Pillars fifty cubits long and thirty cubits wide. There
was a porch in front with pillars, and a
canopy in front of them.

7 He made the Hall of the Throne
where he was to pronounce judgement,
the Hall of Justice, covered with cedar
from floor to floor.

8 His own house where he would reside, in the other court behind the hall,
was of the same construction. Solomon
also made a house like this hall for Pharaoh's daughter, whom he had taken in
marriage.

9 All these were made of costly
stones, cut according to measure, sawed
with saws, back and front, from the
foundation to the coping, and from outside to the great court. 10The foundation
was of costly stones, huge stones, stones
of eight and ten cubits. 11There were
costly stones above, cut to measure, and
cedar wood. 12The great court had three
courses of dressed stone to one layer of
cedar beams all round; so had the inner
court of the house of the LORD, and the
vestibule of the house.

PRODUCTS OF HIRAM THE BRONZEWORKER

13 Now King Solomon invited and
received Hiram from Tyre. 14He was the
son of a widow of the tribe of Naphtali,
whose father, a man of Tyre, had been
an artisan in bronze; he was full of skill,

[i] 6.20 Meaning of Heb uncertain [j] 6.31 Meaning of Heb uncertain

intelligence, and knowledge in working bronze. He came to King Solomon, and did all his work.

15 He cast two pillars of bronze. Eighteen cubits was the height of one, and a cord of twelve cubits would encircle it; the second pillar was the same.[k] 16 He also made two capitals of cast bronze, to set on the tops of the pillars; the height of one capital was five cubits, and the height of the other capital was five cubits. 17 There were nets of chequer-work with wreaths of chain-work for the capitals on the tops of the pillars; seven[l] for one capital, and seven[m] for the other capital. 18 He made the columns with two rows round each lattice-work to cover the capitals that were above the pomegranates; he did the same with the other capital. 19 Now the capitals that were on the tops of the pillars in the vestibule were of lily-work, four cubits high. 20 The capitals were on the two pillars and also above the rounded projection that was beside the lattice-work; there were two hundred pomegranates in rows all round; and so with the other capital. 21 He set up the pillars at the vestibule of the temple; he set up the pillar on the south and called it Jachin; and he set up the pillar on the north and called it Boaz. 22 On the tops of the pillars was lily-work. Thus the work of the pillars was finished.

23 Then he made the cast sea; it was round, ten cubits from brim to brim, and five cubits high. A line of thirty cubits would encircle it completely. 24 Under its brim were panels all round it, each of ten cubits, surrounding the sea; there were two rows of panels, cast when it was cast. 25 It stood on twelve oxen, three facing north, three facing west, three facing south, and three facing east; the sea was set on them. The hindquarters of each were towards the inside. 26 Its thickness was a handbreadth; its brim was made like the brim of a cup, like the flower of a lily; it held two thousand baths.[n]

27 He also made the ten stands of bronze; each stand was four cubits long, four cubits wide, and three cubits high. 28 This was the construction of the stands: they had borders; the borders were within the frames; 29 on the borders that were set in the frames were lions, oxen, and cherubim. On the frames, both above and below the lions and oxen, there were wreaths of bevelled work. 30 Each stand had four bronze wheels and axles of bronze; at the four corners were supports for a basin. The supports were cast with wreaths at the side of each. 31 Its opening was within the crown whose height was one cubit; its opening was round, as a pedestal is made; it was a cubit and a half wide. At its opening there were carvings; its borders were four-sided, not round. 32 The four wheels were underneath the borders; the axles of the wheels were in the stands; and the height of a wheel was a cubit and a half. 33 The wheels were made like a chariot wheel; their axles, their rims, their spokes, and their hubs were all cast. 34 There were four supports at the four corners of each stand; the supports were of one piece with the stands. 35 On the top of the stand there was a round band half a cubit high; on the top of the stand, its stays and its borders were of one piece with it. 36 On the surfaces of its stays and on its borders he carved cherubim, lions, and palm trees, where each had space, with wreaths all round. 37 In this way he made the ten stands; all of them were cast alike, with the same size and the same form.

38 He made ten basins of bronze; each basin held forty baths,[o] each basin measured four cubits; there was a basin for each of the ten stands. 39 He set five of the stands on the south side of the house, and five on the north side of the house; he set the sea on the south-east corner of the house.

40 Hiram also made the pots, the shovels, and the basins. So Hiram finished all the work that he did for King Solomon on the house of the LORD: 41 the two pillars, the two bowls of the capitals that were on the tops of the pillars, the two lattice-works to cover the two bowls of the capitals that were on the tops of the pillars; 42 the four hundred pomegranates for the two lattice-works, two rows of pomegranates for each lattice-work, to cover the two bowls of the capitals that were on the pillars; 43 the ten stands, the ten basins on the stands; 44 the one sea, and the twelve oxen underneath the sea.

45 The pots, the shovels, and the basins, all these vessels that Hiram made for King Solomon for the house of the LORD were of burnished bronze. 46 In

[k] **7.15** Cn: Heb *and a cord of twelve cubits encircled the second pillar*; Compare Jer 52.21
[l] **7.17** Heb: Gk *a net* [m] **7.17** Heb: Gk *a net*
[n] **7.26** A Heb measure of volume [o] **7.38** A Heb measure of volume

the plain of the Jordan the king cast
them, in the clay ground between Succoth and Zarethan. 47 Solomon left all
the vessels unweighed, because there
were so many of them; the weight of the
bronze was not determined.
48 So Solomon made all the vessels
that were in the house of the LORD: the
golden altar, the golden table for the
bread of the Presence, 49 the lampstands
of pure gold, five on the south side and
five on the north, in front of the inner
sanctuary; the flowers, the lamps, and
the tongs, of gold; 50 the cups, snuffers,
basins, dishes for incense, and firepans,
of pure gold; the sockets for the doors
of the innermost part of the house, the
most holy place, and for the doors of the
nave of the temple, of gold.
51 Thus all the work that King Solomon did on the house of the LORD
was finished. Solomon brought in the
things that his father David had dedicated, the silver, the gold, and the vessels, and stored them in the treasuries
of the house of the LORD.

DEDICATION OF THE TEMPLE

8 Then Solomon assembled the elders of Israel and all the heads of
the tribes, the leaders of the ancestral
houses of the Israelites, before King
Solomon in Jerusalem, to bring up the
ark of the covenant of the LORD out of
the city of David, which is Zion. 2 All
the people of Israel assembled to King
Solomon at the festival in the month
Ethanim, which is the seventh month.
3 And all the elders of Israel came, and
the priests carried the ark. 4 So they
brought up the ark of the LORD, the tent
of meeting, and all the holy vessels that
were in the tent; the priests and the Levites brought them up. 5 King Solomon
and all the congregation of Israel, who
had assembled before him, were with
him before the ark, sacrificing so many
sheep and oxen that they could not be
counted or numbered. 6 Then the priests
brought the ark of the covenant of the
LORD to its place, in the inner sanctuary of the house, in the most holy place,
underneath the wings of the cherubim.
7 For the cherubim spread out their
wings over the place of the ark, so that
the cherubim made a covering above
the ark and its poles. 8 The poles were
so long that the ends of the poles were
seen from the holy place in front of the
inner sanctuary; but they could not be
seen from outside; they are there to this
day. 9 There was nothing in the ark except the two tablets of stone that Moses
had placed there at Horeb, where the
LORD made a covenant with the Israelites, when they came out of the land of
Egypt. 10 And when the priests came out
of the holy place, a cloud filled the house
of the LORD, 11 so that the priests could
not stand to minister because of the
cloud; for the glory of the LORD filled
the house of the LORD.
12 Then Solomon said,
'The LORD has said that he would
dwell in thick darkness.
13 I have built you an exalted house,
a place for you to dwell in for ever.'

SOLOMON'S SPEECH

14 Then the king turned round and
blessed all the assembly of Israel, while
all the assembly of Israel stood. 15 He
said, 'Blessed be the LORD, the God of
Israel, who with his hand has fulfilled
what he promised with his mouth to
my father David, saying, 16 "Since the
day that I brought my people Israel out
of Egypt, I have not chosen a city from
any of the tribes of Israel in which to
build a house, that my name might be
there; but I chose David to be over my
people Israel." 17 My father David had it
in mind to build a house for the name
of the LORD, the God of Israel. 18 But the
LORD said to my father David, "You did
well to consider building a house for
my name; 19 nevertheless, you shall not
build the house, but your son who shall
be born to you shall build the house for
my name." 20 Now the LORD has upheld
the promise that he made; for I have
risen in the place of my father David; I
sit on the throne of Israel, as the LORD
promised, and have built the house for
the name of the LORD, the God of Israel. 21 There I have provided a place for
the ark, in which is the covenant of the
LORD that he made with our ancestors
when he brought them out of the land
of Egypt.'

SOLOMON'S PRAYER OF DEDICATION

22 Then Solomon stood before the
altar of the LORD in the presence of all
the assembly of Israel, and spread out
his hands to heaven. 23 He said, 'O LORD,
God of Israel, there is no God like you
in heaven above or on earth beneath,
keeping covenant and steadfast love for
your servants who walk before you with
all their heart, 24 the covenant that you
kept for your servant my father David as

you declared to him; you promised with
your mouth and have this day fulfilled
with your hand. 25Therefore, O LORD,
God of Israel, keep for your servant my
father David that which you promised
him, saying, "There shall never fail you a
successor before me to sit on the throne
of Israel, if only your children look to
their way, to walk before me as you have
walked before me." 26Therefore, O God
of Israel, let your word be confirmed,
which you promised to your servant my
father David.

27 'But will God indeed dwell on the
earth? Even heaven and the highest
heaven cannot contain you, much less
this house that I have built! 28Have regard to your servant's prayer and his
plea, O LORD my God, heeding the cry
and the prayer that your servant prays
to you today; 29that your eyes may be
open night and day towards this house,
the place of which you said, "My name
shall be there", that you may heed the
prayer that your servant prays towards
this place. 30Hear the plea of your servant and of your people Israel when
they pray towards this place; O hear in
heaven your dwelling-place; heed and
forgive.

31 'If someone sins against a neighbour and is given an oath to swear, and
comes and swears before your altar in
this house, 32then hear in heaven, and
act, and judge your servants, condemning the guilty by bringing their conduct
on their own head, and vindicating the
righteous by rewarding them according
to their righteousness.

33 'When your people Israel, having
sinned against you, are defeated before
an enemy but turn again to you, confess
your name, pray, and plead with you in
this house, 34then hear in heaven, forgive the sin of your people Israel, and
bring them again to the land that you
gave to their ancestors.

35 'When heaven is shut up and there
is no rain because they have sinned
against you, and then they pray towards
this place, confess your name, and turn
from their sin, because you punish[p]
them, 36then hear in heaven, and forgive the sin of your servants, your people Israel, when you teach them the
good way in which they should walk;
and grant rain on your land, which you
have given to your people as an inheritance.

37 'If there is famine in the land, if
there is plague, blight, mildew, locust, or
caterpillar; if their enemy besieges them
in any[q] of their cities; whatever plague,
whatever sickness there is; 38whatever
prayer, whatever plea there is from any
individual or from all your people Israel, all knowing the afflictions of their
own hearts so that they stretch out their
hands towards this house; 39then hear
in heaven your dwelling-place, forgive,
act, and render to all whose hearts you
know—according to all their ways, for
only you know what is in every human
heart— 40so that they may fear you all
the days that they live in the land that
you gave to our ancestors.

41 'Likewise when a foreigner, who
is not of your people Israel, comes from
a distant land because of your name
42—for they shall hear of your great
name, your mighty hand, and your outstretched arm—when a foreigner comes
and prays towards this house, 43then
hear in heaven your dwelling-place, and
do according to all that the foreigner
calls to you, so that all the peoples of
the earth may know your name and fear
you, as do your people Israel, and so that
they may know that your name has been
invoked on this house that I have built.

44 'If your people go out to battle
against their enemy, by whatever way
you shall send them, and they pray to
the LORD towards the city that you have
chosen and the house that I have built
for your name, 45then hear in heaven
their prayer and their plea, and maintain their cause.

46 'If they sin against you—for there
is no one who does not sin—and you
are angry with them and give them to
an enemy, so that they are carried away
captive to the land of the enemy, far
off or near; 47and if they come to their
senses in the land to which they have
been taken captive, and repent, and
plead with you in the land of their captors, saying, "We have sinned, and have
done wrong; we have acted wickedly";
48if they repent with all their heart and
soul in the land of their enemies, who
took them captive, and pray to you towards their land, which you gave to
their ancestors, the city that you have
chosen, and the house that I have built
for your name; 49then hear in heaven
your dwelling-place their prayer and
their plea, maintain their cause, 50and
forgive your people who have sinned

[p] 8.35 *Or when you answer* [q] 8.37 Gk Syr: Heb *in the land*

against you, and all their transgressions that they have committed against
you; and grant them compassion in the
sight of their captors, so that they may
have compassion on them 51(for they
are your people and heritage, which you
brought out of Egypt, from the midst
of the iron-smelter). 52Let your eyes be
open to the plea of your servant, and to
the plea of your people Israel, listening
to them whenever they call to you. 53For
you have separated them from among
all the peoples of the earth, to be your
heritage, just as you promised through
Moses, your servant, when you brought
our ancestors out of Egypt, O Lord GOD.'

SOLOMON BLESSES THE ASSEMBLY

54 Now when Solomon finished offering all this prayer and this plea to
the LORD, he arose from facing the altar
of the LORD, where he had knelt with
hands outstretched towards heaven;
55he stood and blessed all the assembly
of Israel with a loud voice:

56 'Blessed be the LORD, who has
given rest to his people Israel according
to all that he promised; not one word
has failed of all his good promise, which
he spoke through his servant Moses.
57The LORD our God be with us, as he
was with our ancestors; may he not
leave us or abandon us, 58but incline our
hearts to him, to walk in all his ways,
and to keep his commandments, his
statutes, and his ordinances, which he
commanded our ancestors. 59Let these
words of mine, with which I pleaded before the LORD, be near to the LORD our
God day and night, and may he maintain the cause of his servant and the
cause of his people Israel, as each day
requires; 60so that all the peoples of the
earth may know that the LORD is God;
there is no other. 61Therefore devote
yourselves completely to the LORD our
God, walking in his statutes and keeping his commandments, as at this day.'

SOLOMON OFFERS SACRIFICES

62 Then the king, and all Israel with
him, offered sacrifice before the LORD.
63Solomon offered as sacrifices of well-
being to the LORD twenty-two thousand oxen and one hundred and twenty
thousand sheep. So the king and all the
people of Israel dedicated the house of
the LORD. 64The same day the king consecrated the middle of the court that
was in front of the house of the LORD;
for there he offered the burnt-offerings
and the grain-offerings and the fat
pieces of the sacrifices of well-being, because the bronze altar that was before
the LORD was too small to receive the
burnt-offerings and the grain-offerings
and the fat pieces of the sacrifices of
well-being.

65 So Solomon held the festival at
that time, and all Israel with him—a
great assembly, people from Lebo-
hamath to the Wadi of Egypt—before
the LORD our God, for seven days.[r] 66On
the eighth day he sent the people away;
and they blessed the king, and went to
their tents, joyful and in good spirits because of all the goodness that the LORD
had shown to his servant David and to
his people Israel.

GOD APPEARS AGAIN TO SOLOMON

9 When Solomon had finished building the house of the LORD and the
king's house and all that Solomon desired to build, 2the LORD appeared to
Solomon a second time, as he had appeared to him at Gibeon. 3The LORD
said to him, 'I have heard your prayer
and your plea, which you made before
me; I have consecrated this house that
you have built, and put my name there
for ever; my eyes and my heart will be
there for all time. 4As for you, if you will
walk before me, as David your father
walked, with integrity of heart and uprightness, doing according to all that I
have commanded you, and keeping my
statutes and my ordinances, 5then I will
establish your royal throne over Israel
for ever, as I promised your father David, saying, "There shall not fail you a
successor on the throne of Israel."

6 'If you turn aside from following
me, you or your children, and do not
keep my commandments and my statutes that I have set before you, but go
and serve other gods and worship them,
7then I will cut Israel off from the land
that I have given them; and the house
that I have consecrated for my name I
will cast out of my sight; and Israel will
become a proverb and a taunt among
all peoples. 8This house will become a
heap of ruins;[s] everyone passing by it
will be astonished, and will hiss; and
they will say, "Why has the LORD done
such a thing to this land and to this
house?" 9Then they will say, "Because
they have forsaken the LORD their God,

[r] **8.65** Compare Gk: Heb *seven days and seven days, fourteen days* [s] **9.8** Syr Old Latin: Heb *will become high*

who brought their ancestors out of the
land of Egypt, and embraced other gods,
worshipping them and serving them;
therefore the LORD has brought this disaster upon them." '
10 At the end of twenty years, in
which Solomon had built the two
houses, the house of the LORD and the
king's house, 11King Hiram of Tyre having supplied Solomon with cedar and
cypress timber and gold, as much as he
desired, King Solomon gave to Hiram
twenty cities in the land of Galilee. 12But
when Hiram came from Tyre to see the
cities that Solomon had given him, they
did not please him. 13Therefore he said,
'What kind of cities are these that you
have given me, my brother?' So they
are called the land of Cabul[t] to this day.
14But Hiram had sent to the king one
hundred and twenty talents of gold.

OTHER ACTS OF SOLOMON

15 This is the account of the forced
labour that King Solomon conscripted
to build the house of the LORD and his
own house, the Millo and the wall of Jerusalem, Hazor, Megiddo, Gezer 16(Pharaoh king of Egypt had gone up and captured Gezer and burned it down, had
killed the Canaanites who lived in the
city, and had given it as dowry to his
daughter, Solomon's wife; 17so Solomon
rebuilt Gezer), Lower Beth-horon, 18Ba-
alath, Tamar in the wilderness, within
the land, 19as well as all of Solomon's
storage cities, the cities for his chariots,
the cities for his cavalry, and whatever
Solomon desired to build, in Jerusalem,
in Lebanon, and in all the land of his dominion. 20All the people who were left
of the Amorites, the Hittites, the Perizzites, the Hivites, and the Jebusites, who
were not of the people of Israel— 21their
descendants who were still left in the
land, whom the Israelites were unable
to destroy completely—these Solomon
conscripted for slave labour, and so
they are to this day. 22But of the Israelites Solomon made no slaves; they were
the soldiers, they were his officials, his
commanders, his captains, and the commanders of his chariotry and cavalry.
23 These were the chief officers who
were over Solomon's work: five hundred
and fifty, who had charge of the people
who carried on the work.
24 But Pharaoh's daughter went up
from the city of David to her own house
that Solomon had built for her; then he
built the Millo.
25 Three times a year Solomon used
to offer up burnt-offerings and sacrifices
of well-being on the altar that he built
for the LORD, offering incense[u] before
the LORD. So he completed the house.

SOLOMON'S COMMERCIAL ACTIVITY

26 King Solomon built a fleet of ships
at Ezion-geber, which is near Eloth on
the shore of the Red Sea,[v] in the land of
Edom. 27Hiram sent his servants with
the fleet, sailors who were familiar with
the sea, together with the servants of
Solomon. 28They went to Ophir, and
imported from there four hundred and
twenty talents of gold, which they delivered to King Solomon.

VISIT OF THE QUEEN OF SHEBA

10 When the queen of Sheba heard
of the fame of Solomon, (fame
due to[w] the name of the LORD), she
came to test him with hard questions.
2She came to Jerusalem with a very
great retinue, with camels bearing
spices, and very much gold, and precious stones; and when she came to Solomon, she told him all that was on her
mind. 3Solomon answered all her questions; there was nothing hidden from
the king that he could not explain to
her. 4When the queen of Sheba had observed all the wisdom of Solomon, the
house that he had built, 5the food of his
table, the seating of his officials, and the
attendance of his servants, their clothing, his valets, and his burnt-offerings
that he offered at the house of the LORD,
there was no more spirit in her.
6 So she said to the king, 'The report
was true that I heard in my own land
of your accomplishments and of your
wisdom, 7but I did not believe the reports until I came and my own eyes had
seen it. Not even half had been told me;
your wisdom and prosperity far surpass
the report that I had heard. 8Happy
are your wives![x] Happy are these your
servants, who continually attend you
and hear your wisdom! 9Blessed be the
LORD your God, who has delighted in
you and set you on the throne of Israel!
Because the LORD loved Israel for ever,
he has made you king to execute justice
and righteousness.' 10Then she gave the
king one hundred and twenty talents
of gold, a great quantity of spices, and

[t] **9.13** Perhaps meaning *a land good for nothing*
[u] **9.25** Gk: Heb *offering incense with it that was*
[v] **9.26** Or *Sea of Reeds* [w] **10.1** Meaning of Heb uncertain [x] **10.8** Gk Syr: Heb *men*

precious stones; never again did spices
come in such quantity as that which the
queen of Sheba gave to King Solomon.
11 Moreover, the fleet of Hiram,
which carried gold from Ophir, brought
from Ophir a great quantity of almug
wood and precious stones. 12From the
almug wood the king made supports
for the house of the LORD, and for the
king's house, lyres also and harps for the
singers; no such almug wood has come
or been seen to this day.
13 Meanwhile, King Solomon gave
to the queen of Sheba every desire that
she expressed, as well as what he gave
her out of Solomon's royal bounty. Then
she returned to her own land, with her
servants.
14 The weight of gold that came to
Solomon in one year was six hundred
and sixty-six talents of gold, 15besides
that which came from the traders and
from the business of the merchants,
and from all the kings of Arabia and
the governors of the land. 16King Solomon made two hundred large shields
of beaten gold; six hundred shekels of
gold went into each large shield. 17He
made three hundred shields of beaten
gold; three minas of gold went into each
shield; and the king put them in the
House of the Forest of Lebanon. 18The
king also made a great ivory throne,
and overlaid it with the finest gold.
19The throne had six steps. The top of
the throne was rounded in the back,
and on each side of the seat were arm
rests and two lions standing beside the
arm rests, 20while twelve lions were
standing, one on each end of a step, on
the six steps. Nothing like it was ever
made in any kingdom. 21All King Solomon's drinking vessels were of gold, and
all the vessels of the House of the Forest of Lebanon were of pure gold; none
were of silver—it was not considered as
anything in the days of Solomon. 22For
the king had a fleet of ships of Tarshish
at sea with the fleet of Hiram. Once every three years the fleet of ships of Tarshish used to come bringing gold, silver,
ivory, apes, and peacocks.[y]
23 Thus King Solomon excelled all
the kings of the earth in riches and in
wisdom. 24The whole earth sought the
presence of Solomon to hear his wisdom, which God had put into his mind.
25Every one of them brought a present,
objects of silver and gold, garments,
weaponry, spices, horses, and mules, so
much year by year.
26 Solomon gathered together chariots and horses; he had fourteen hundred
chariots and twelve thousand horses,
which he stationed in the chariot cities and with the king in Jerusalem.
27The king made silver as common in
Jerusalem as stones, and he made cedars as numerous as the sycomores of
the Shephelah. 28Solomon's import of
horses was from Egypt and Kue, and the
king's traders received them from Kue
at a price. 29A chariot could be imported
from Egypt for six hundred shekels of
silver, and a horse for one hundred and
fifty; so through the king's traders they
were exported to all the kings of the
Hittites and the kings of Aram.

SOLOMON'S ERRORS

11 King Solomon loved many foreign women along with the
daughter of Pharaoh: Moabite, Ammonite, Edomite, Sidonian, and Hittite
women, 2from the nations concerning
which the LORD had said to the Israelites, 'You shall not enter into marriage
with them, neither shall they with you;
for they will surely incline your heart
to follow their gods;' Solomon clung to
these in love. 3Among his wives were
seven hundred princesses and three
hundred concubines; and his wives
turned away his heart. 4For when Solomon was old, his wives turned away
his heart after other gods; and his heart
was not true to the LORD his God, as
was the heart of his father David. 5For
Solomon followed Astarte the goddess of the Sidonians, and Milcom the
abomination of the Ammonites. 6So
Solomon did what was evil in the sight
of the LORD, and did not completely follow the LORD, as his father David had
done. 7Then Solomon built a high place
for Chemosh the abomination of Moab,
and for Molech the abomination of the
Ammonites, on the mountain east of
Jerusalem. 8He did the same for all his
foreign wives, who offered incense and
sacrificed to their gods.
9 Then the LORD was angry with
Solomon, because his heart had turned
away from the LORD, the God of Israel,
who had appeared to him twice, 10and
had commanded him concerning this
matter, that he should not follow other
gods; but he did not observe what the
LORD commanded. 11Therefore the
LORD said to Solomon, 'Since this has

y 10.22 Or *baboons*

been your mind and you have not kept
my covenant and my statutes that I
have commanded you, I will surely tear
the kingdom from you and give it to
your servant. 12Yet for the sake of your
father David I will not do it in your lifetime; I will tear it out of the hand of your
son. 13I will not, however, tear away the
entire kingdom; I will give one tribe to
your son, for the sake of my servant David and for the sake of Jerusalem, which
I have chosen.'

ADVERSARIES OF SOLOMON

14 Then the LORD raised up an adversary against Solomon, Hadad the
Edomite; he was of the royal house in
Edom. 15For when David was in Edom,
and Joab the commander of the army
went up to bury the dead, he killed every male in Edom 16(for Joab and all
Israel remained there for six months,
until he had eliminated every male in
Edom); 17but Hadad fled to Egypt with
some Edomites who were servants of
his father. He was a young boy at that
time. 18They set out from Midian and
came to Paran; they took people with
them from Paran and came to Egypt, to
Pharaoh king of Egypt, who gave him
a house, assigned him an allowance of
food, and gave him land. 19Hadad found
great favour in the sight of Pharaoh, so
that he gave him his sister-in-law for
a wife, the sister of Queen Tahpenes.
20The sister of Tahpenes gave birth by
him to his son Genubath, whom Tahpenes weaned in Pharaoh's house; Genubath was in Pharaoh's house among
the children of Pharaoh. 21When Hadad
heard in Egypt that David slept with
his ancestors and that Joab the commander of the army was dead, Hadad
said to Pharaoh, 'Let me depart, that I
may go to my own country.' 22But Pharaoh said to him, 'What do you lack with
me that you now seek to go to your
own country?' And he said, 'No, do let
me go.'

23 God raised up another adversary
against Solomon,[z] Rezon son of Eliada,
who had fled from his master, King
Hadadezer of Zobah. 24He gathered followers around him and became leader
of a marauding band, after the slaughter by David; they went to Damascus,
settled there, and made him king in Damascus. 25He was an adversary of Israel
all the days of Solomon, making trouble
as Hadad did; he despised Israel and
reigned over Aram.

JEROBOAM'S REBELLION

26 Jeroboam son of Nebat, an Ephraimite of Zeredah, a servant of Solomon,
whose mother's name was Zeruah, a
widow, rebelled against the king. 27The
following was the reason he rebelled
against the king. Solomon built the
Millo, and closed up the gap in the wall[a]
of the city of his father David. 28The
man Jeroboam was very able, and when
Solomon saw that the young man was
industrious he gave him charge over all
the forced labour of the house of Joseph.
29About that time, when Jeroboam was
leaving Jerusalem, the prophet Ahijah
the Shilonite found him on the road.
Ahijah had clothed himself with a new
garment. The two of them were alone
in the open country 30when Ahijah laid
hold of the new garment he was wearing and tore it into twelve pieces. 31He
then said to Jeroboam: Take for yourself
ten pieces; for thus says the LORD, the
God of Israel, 'See, I am about to tear the
kingdom from the hand of Solomon,
and will give you ten tribes. 32One tribe
will remain his, for the sake of my servant David and for the sake of Jerusalem,
the city that I have chosen out of all the
tribes of Israel. 33This is because he has[b]
forsaken me, worshipped Astarte the
goddess of the Sidonians, Chemosh the
god of Moab, and Milcom the god of the
Ammonites, and has[c] not walked in my
ways, doing what is right in my sight
and keeping my statutes and my ordinances, as his father David did. 34Nev-
ertheless, I will not take the whole kingdom away from him but will make him
ruler all the days of his life, for the sake
of my servant David whom I chose and
who did keep my commandments and
my statutes; 35but I will take the kingdom away from his son and give it to
you—that is, the ten tribes. 36Yet to
his son I will give one tribe, so that my
servant David may always have a lamp
before me in Jerusalem, the city where
I have chosen to put my name. 37I will
take you, and you shall reign over all
that your soul desires; you shall be king
over Israel. 38If you will listen to all that
I command you, walk in my ways, and
do what is right in my sight by keeping
my statutes and my commandments, as
David my servant did, I will be with you,
and will build you an enduring house,
as I built for David, and I will give Is-

[z] **11.23** Heb *him* [a] **11.27** Heb lacks *in the wall*
[b] **11.33** Gk Syr Vg: Heb *they have* [c] **11.33** Gk Syr Vg: Heb *they have*

rael to you. 39For this reason I will punish the descendants of David, but not for
ever.' 40Solomon sought therefore to kill
Jeroboam; but Jeroboam promptly fled
to Egypt, to King Shishak of Egypt, and
remained in Egypt until the death of
Solomon.

DEATH OF SOLOMON

41 Now the rest of the acts of Solomon, all that he did as well as his wisdom, are they not written in the Book
of the Acts of Solomon? 42The time that
Solomon reigned in Jerusalem over all
Israel was forty years. 43Solomon slept
with his ancestors and was buried in
the city of his father David; and his son
Rehoboam succeeded him.

THE NORTHERN TRIBES SECEDE

12 Rehoboam went to Shechem, for
all Israel had come to Shechem
to make him king. 2When Jeroboam son
of Nebat heard of it (for he was still in
Egypt, where he had fled from King Solomon), then Jeroboam returned from[d]
Egypt. 3And they sent and called him;
and Jeroboam and all the assembly of Israel came and said to Rehoboam, 4'Your
father made our yoke heavy. Now therefore lighten the hard service of your father and his heavy yoke that he placed
on us, and we will serve you.' 5He said
to them, 'Go away for three days, then
come again to me.' So the people went
away.

6 Then King Rehoboam took counsel
with the older men who had attended
his father Solomon while he was still
alive, saying, 'How do you advise me
to answer this people?' 7They answered
him, 'If you will be a servant to this people today and serve them, and speak
good words to them when you answer
them, then they will be your servants
for ever.' 8But he disregarded the advice
that the older men gave him, and consulted the young men who had grown
up with him and now attended him. 9He
said to them, 'What do you advise that
we answer this people who have said to
me, "Lighten the yoke that your father
put on us"?' 10The young men who had
grown up with him said to him, 'Thus
you should say to this people who spoke
to you, "Your father made our yoke
heavy, but you must lighten it for us";
thus you should say to them, "My little
finger is thicker than my father's loins.
11Now, whereas my father laid on you a
heavy yoke, I will add to your yoke. My
father disciplined you with whips, but I
will discipline you with scorpions."'

12 So Jeroboam and all the people
came to Rehoboam on the third day, as
the king had said, 'Come to me again on
the third day.' 13The king answered the
people harshly. He disregarded the advice that the older men had given him
14and spoke to them according to the advice of the young men, 'My father made
your yoke heavy, but I will add to your
yoke; my father disciplined you with
whips, but I will discipline you with
scorpions.' 15So the king did not listen to
the people, because it was a turn of affairs brought about by the LORD that he
might fulfil his word, which the LORD
had spoken by Ahijah the Shilonite to
Jeroboam son of Nebat.

16 When all Israel saw that the king
would not listen to them, the people answered the king,

'What share do we have in David?
  We have no inheritance in
    the son of Jesse.
To your tents, O Israel!
  Look now to your own
    house, O David.'

So Israel went away to their tents.
17But Rehoboam reigned over the Israelites who were living in the towns
of Judah. 18When King Rehoboam sent
Adoram, who was taskmaster over the
forced labour, all Israel stoned him to
death. King Rehoboam then hurriedly
mounted his chariot to flee to Jerusalem. 19So Israel has been in rebellion
against the house of David to this day.

FIRST DYNASTY: JEROBOAM REIGNS OVER ISRAEL

20 When all Israel heard that Jeroboam had returned, they sent and called
him to the assembly and made him king
over all Israel. There was no one who
followed the house of David, except the
tribe of Judah alone.

21 When Rehoboam came to Jerusalem, he assembled all the house of Judah
and the tribe of Benjamin, one hundred
and eighty thousand chosen troops to
fight against the house of Israel, to restore the kingdom to Rehoboam son of
Solomon. 22But the word of God came
to Shemaiah the man of God: 23Say to
King Rehoboam of Judah, son of Solomon, and to all the house of Judah and
Benjamin, and to the rest of the people, 24'Thus says the LORD, You shall

[d] **12.2** Gk Vg Compare 2 Chr 10.2: Heb *lived in*

not go up or fight against your kindred the people of Israel. Let everyone go home, for this thing is from me.' So they heeded the word of the LORD and went home again, according to the word of the LORD.

JEROBOAM'S GOLDEN CALVES

25 Then Jeroboam built Shechem in the hill country of Ephraim, and resided there; he went out from there and built Penuel. 26Then Jeroboam said to himself, 'Now the kingdom may well revert to the house of David. 27If this people continues to go up to offer sacrifices in the house of the LORD at Jerusalem, the heart of this people will turn again to their master, King Rehoboam of Judah; they will kill me and return to King Rehoboam of Judah.' 28So the king took counsel, and made two calves of gold. He said to the people,[e] 'You have gone up to Jerusalem long enough. Here are your gods, O Israel, who brought you up out of the land of Egypt.' 29He set one in Bethel, and the other he put in Dan. 30And this thing became a sin, for the people went to worship before the one at Bethel and before the other as far as Dan.[f] 31He also made houses[g] on high places, and appointed priests from among all the people, who were not Levites. 32Jeroboam appointed a festival on the fifteenth day of the eighth month like the festival that was in Judah, and he offered sacrifices on the altar; so he did in Bethel, sacrificing to the calves that he had made. And he placed in Bethel the priests of the high places that he had made. 33He went up to the altar that he had made in Bethel on the fifteenth day in the eighth month, in the month that he alone had prescribed; he appointed a festival for the people of Israel, and he went up to the altar to offer incense.

A MAN OF GOD FROM JUDAH

13 While Jeroboam was standing by the altar to offer incense, a man of God came out of Judah by the word of the LORD to Bethel 2and proclaimed against the altar by the word of the LORD, and said, 'O altar, altar, thus says the LORD: "A son shall be born to the house of David, Josiah by name; and he shall sacrifice on you the priests of the high places who offer incense on you, and human bones shall be burned on you."' 3He gave a sign the same day, saying, 'This is the sign that the LORD has spoken: "The altar shall be torn down, and the ashes that are on it shall be poured out."' 4When the king heard what the man of God cried out against the altar at Bethel, Jeroboam stretched out his hand from the altar, saying, 'Seize him!' But the hand that he stretched out against him withered so that he could not draw it back to himself. 5The altar also was torn down, and the ashes poured out from the altar, according to the sign that the man of God had given by the word of the LORD. 6The king said to the man of God, 'Entreat now the favour of the LORD your God, and pray for me, so that my hand may be restored to me.' So the man of God entreated the LORD; and the king's hand was restored to him, and became as it was before. 7Then the king said to the man of God, 'Come home with me and dine, and I will give you a gift.' 8But the man of God said to the king, 'If you give me half your kingdom, I will not go in with you; nor will I eat food or drink water in this place. 9For thus I was commanded by the word of the LORD: You shall not eat food, or drink water, or return by the way that you came.' 10So he went another way, and did not return by the way that he had come to Bethel.

11 Now there lived an old prophet in Bethel. One of his sons came and told him all that the man of God had done that day in Bethel; the words also that he had spoken to the king, they told to their father. 12Their father said to them, 'Which way did he go?' And his sons showed him the way that the man of God who came from Judah had gone. 13Then he said to his sons, 'Saddle a donkey for me.' So they saddled a donkey for him, and he mounted it. 14He went after the man of God, and found him sitting under an oak tree. He said to him, 'Are you the man of God who came from Judah?' He answered, 'I am.' 15Then he said to him, 'Come home with me and eat some food.' 16But he said, 'I cannot return with you, or go in with you; nor will I eat food or drink water with you in this place; 17for it was said to me by the word of the LORD: You shall not eat food or drink water there, or return by the way that you came.' 18Then the other[h] said to him, 'I also am a prophet as you are, and an angel spoke to me by the word of the LORD: Bring him back

[e] **12.28** Gk: Heb *to them* [f] **12.30** Compare Gk: Heb *went to the one as far as Dan* [g] **12.31** Gk Vg Compare 13.32: Heb *a house* [h] **13.18** Heb *he*

with you into your house so that he may
eat food and drink water.' But he was
deceiving him. 19 Then the man of God[i]
went back with him, and ate food and
drank water in his house.

20 As they were sitting at the table, the word of the LORD came to the
prophet who had brought him back;
21 and he proclaimed to the man of God
who came from Judah, 'Thus says the
LORD: Because you have disobeyed the
word of the LORD, and have not kept the
commandment that the LORD your God
commanded you, 22 but have come back
and have eaten food and drunk water in
the place of which he said to you, "Eat
no food, and drink no water", your body
shall not come to your ancestral tomb.'
23 After the man of God[j] had eaten food
and had drunk, they saddled for him a
donkey belonging to the prophet who
had brought him back. 24 Then as he
went away, a lion met him on the road
and killed him. His body was thrown in
the road, and the donkey stood beside
it; the lion also stood beside the body.
25 People passed by and saw the body
thrown in the road, with the lion standing by the body. And they came and told
it in the town where the old prophet
lived.

26 When the prophet who had
brought him back from the way heard
of it, he said, 'It is the man of God who
disobeyed the word of the LORD; therefore the LORD has given him to the lion,
which has torn him and killed him according to the word that the LORD
spoke to him.' 27 Then he said to his
sons, 'Saddle a donkey for me.' So they
saddled one, 28 and he went and found
the body thrown in the road, with the
donkey and the lion standing beside the
body. The lion had not eaten the body or
attacked the donkey. 29 The prophet took
up the body of the man of God, laid it on
the donkey, and brought it back to the
city,[k] to mourn and to bury him. 30 He
laid the body in his own grave; and they
mourned over him, saying, 'Alas, my
brother!' 31 After he had buried him, he
said to his sons, 'When I die, bury me
in the grave in which the man of God is
buried; lay my bones beside his bones.
32 For the saying that he proclaimed by
the word of the LORD against the altar
in Bethel, and against all the houses of
the high places that are in the cities of
Samaria, shall surely come to pass.'

33 Even after this event Jeroboam
did not turn from his evil way, but made
priests for the high places again from
among all the people; any who wanted
to be priests he consecrated for the high
places. 34 This matter became sin to the
house of Jeroboam, so as to cut it off and
to destroy it from the face of the earth.

JUDGEMENT ON THE HOUSE OF JEROBOAM

14 At that time Abijah son of Jeroboam fell sick. 2 Jeroboam said to
his wife, 'Go, disguise yourself, so that it
will not be known that you are the wife
of Jeroboam, and go to Shiloh; for the
prophet Ahijah is there, who said of me
that I should be king over this people.
3 Take with you ten loaves, some cakes,
and a jar of honey, and go to him; he will
tell you what shall happen to the child.'

4 Jeroboam's wife did so; she set out
and went to Shiloh, and came to the
house of Ahijah. Now Ahijah could not
see, for his eyes were dim because of his
age. 5 But the LORD said to Ahijah, 'The
wife of Jeroboam is coming to inquire
of you concerning her son; for he is sick.
Thus and thus you shall say to her.'

When she came, she pretended to
be another woman. 6 But when Ahijah
heard the sound of her feet, as she came
in at the door, he said, 'Come in, wife of
Jeroboam; why do you pretend to be another? For I am charged with heavy tidings for you. 7 Go, tell Jeroboam, "Thus
says the LORD, the God of Israel: Because
I exalted you from among the people,
made you leader over my people Israel,
8 and tore the kingdom away from the
house of David to give it to you; yet you
have not been like my servant David,
who kept my commandments and followed me with all his heart, doing only
that which was right in my sight, 9 but
you have done evil above all those who
were before you and have gone and made
for yourself other gods, and cast images,
provoking me to anger, and have thrust
me behind your back; 10 therefore, I will
bring evil upon the house of Jeroboam.
I will cut off from Jeroboam every male,
both bond and free, in Israel and will
consume the house of Jeroboam, just as
one burns up dung until it is all gone.
11 Anyone belonging to Jeroboam who
dies in the city, the dogs shall eat; and
anyone who dies in the open country,
the birds of the air shall eat; for the
LORD has spoken." 12 Therefore set out,

[i] 13.19 Heb *he* [j] 13.23 Heb *he* [k] 13.29 Gk: Heb *he came to the town of the old prophet*

go to your house. When your feet enter
the city, the child shall die. 13All Israel
shall mourn for him and bury him; for
he alone of Jeroboam's family shall come
to the grave, because in him there is
found something pleasing to the LORD,
the God of Israel, in the house of Jeroboam. 14Moreover, the LORD will raise
up for himself a king over Israel, who
shall cut off the house of Jeroboam today, even now![l]

15 'The LORD will strike Israel, as
a reed is shaken in the water; he will
root up Israel out of this good land that
he gave to their ancestors, and scatter
them beyond the Euphrates, because
they have made their sacred poles,[m]
provoking the LORD to anger. 16He will
give Israel up because of the sins of Jeroboam, which he sinned and which he
caused Israel to commit.'

17 Then Jeroboam's wife got up and
went away, and she came to Tirzah. As
she came to the threshold of the house,
the child died. 18All Israel buried him
and mourned for him, according to the
word of the LORD, which he spoke by his
servant the prophet Ahijah.

DEATH OF JEROBOAM

19 Now the rest of the acts of Jeroboam, how he warred and how he
reigned, are written in the Book of the
Annals of the Kings of Israel. 20The time
that Jeroboam reigned was twenty-two
years; then he slept with his ancestors,
and his son Nadab succeeded him.

REHOBOAM REIGNS OVER JUDAH

21 Now Rehoboam son of Solomon
reigned in Judah. Rehoboam was forty-
one years old when he began to reign,
and he reigned for seventeen years in
Jerusalem, the city that the LORD had
chosen out of all the tribes of Israel, to
put his name there. His mother's name
was Naamah the Ammonite. 22Judah
did what was evil in the sight of the
LORD; they provoked him to jealousy
with their sins that they committed,
more than all that their ancestors had
done. 23For they also built for themselves high places, pillars, and sacred
poles[n] on every high hill and under every green tree; 24there were also male
temple prostitutes in the land. They
committed all the abominations of the
nations that the LORD drove out before
the people of Israel.

25 In the fifth year of King Rehoboam, King Shishak of Egypt came up
against Jerusalem; 26he took away the
treasures of the house of the LORD and
the treasures of the king's house; he took
everything. He also took away all the
shields of gold that Solomon had made;
27so King Rehoboam made shields of
bronze instead, and committed them to
the hands of the officers of the guard,
who kept the door of the king's house.
28As often as the king went into the
house of the LORD, the guard carried
them and brought them back to the
guardroom.

29 Now the rest of the acts of Rehoboam, and all that he did, are they not
written in the Book of the Annals of the
Kings of Judah? 30There was war between Rehoboam and Jeroboam continually. 31Rehoboam slept with his ancestors and was buried with his ancestors
in the city of David. His mother's name
was Naamah the Ammonite. His son
Abijam succeeded him.

ABIJAM REIGNS OVER JUDAH: IDOLATRY AND WAR

15 Now in the eighteenth year of
King Jeroboam son of Nebat,
Abijam began to reign over Judah. 2He
reigned for three years in Jerusalem.
His mother's name was Maacah daughter of Abishalom. 3He committed all the
sins that his father did before him; his
heart was not true to the LORD his God,
like the heart of his father David. 4Nev-
ertheless, for David's sake the LORD his
God gave him a lamp in Jerusalem, setting up his son after him, and establishing Jerusalem; 5because David did what
was right in the sight of the LORD, and
did not turn aside from anything that
he commanded him all the days of his
life, except in the matter of Uriah the
Hittite. 6The war begun between Rehoboam and Jeroboam continued all the
days of his life. 7The rest of the acts of
Abijam, and all that he did, are they not
written in the Book of the Annals of the
Kings of Judah? There was war between
Abijam and Jeroboam. 8Abijam slept
with his ancestors, and they buried him
in the city of David. Then his son Asa
succeeded him.

ASA REIGNS OVER JUDAH

9 In the twentieth year of King Jeroboam of Israel, Asa began to reign over
Judah; 10he reigned for forty-one years

[l] 14.14 Meaning of Heb uncertain [m] 14.15 Heb *Asherim* [n] 14.23 Heb *Asherim*

in Jerusalem. His mother's name was
Maacah daughter of Abishalom. 11Asa
did what was right in the sight of the
LORD, as his father David had done.
12He put away the male temple prostitutes out of the land, and removed all
the idols that his ancestors had made.
13He also removed his mother Maacah
from being queen mother, because she
had made an abominable image for
Asherah; Asa cut down her image and
burned it at the Wadi Kidron. 14But the
high places were not taken away. Nevertheless, the heart of Asa was true to the
LORD all his days. 15He brought into the
house of the LORD the votive gifts of his
father and his own votive gifts—silver,
gold, and utensils.

ALLIANCE WITH ARAM AGAINST ISRAEL

16 There was war between Asa and
King Baasha of Israel all their days.
17King Baasha of Israel went up against
Judah, and built Ramah, to prevent anyone from going out or coming in to King
Asa of Judah. 18Then Asa took all the
silver and the gold that were left in the
treasures of the house of the LORD and
the treasures of the king's house, and
gave them into the hands of his servants. King Asa sent them to King Ben-
hadad son of Tabrimmon son of Hezion
of Aram, who resided in Damascus, saying, 19'Let there be an alliance between
me and you, like that between my father
and your father: I am sending you a
present of silver and gold; go, break your
alliance with King Baasha of Israel, so
that he may withdraw from me.' 20Ben-
hadad listened to King Asa, and sent the
commanders of his armies against the
cities of Israel. He conquered Ijon, Dan,
Abel-beth-maacah, and all Chinneroth,
with all the land of Naphtali. 21When
Baasha heard of it, he stopped building
Ramah and lived in Tirzah. 22Then King
Asa made a proclamation to all Judah;
none was exempt: they carried away the
stones of Ramah and its timber, with
which Baasha had been building; with
them King Asa built Geba of Benjamin
and Mizpah. 23Now the rest of all the
acts of Asa, all his power, all that he did,
and the cities that he built, are they not
written in the Book of the Annals of the
Kings of Judah? But in his old age he
was diseased in his feet. 24Then Asa slept
with his ancestors, and was buried with
his ancestors in the city of his father David; his son Jehoshaphat succeeded him.

NADAB REIGNS OVER ISRAEL

25 Nadab son of Jeroboam began to
reign over Israel in the second year of
King Asa of Judah; he reigned over Israel for two years. 26He did what was
evil in the sight of the LORD, walking
in the way of his ancestor and in the sin
that he caused Israel to commit.
27 Baasha son of Ahijah, of the house
of Issachar, conspired against him; and
Baasha struck him down at Gibbethon,
which belonged to the Philistines; for
Nadab and all Israel were laying siege
to Gibbethon. 28So Baasha killed Nadab[o] in the third year of King Asa of
Judah, and succeeded him. 29As soon
as he was king, he killed all the house
of Jeroboam; he left to the house of Jeroboam not one that breathed, until he
had destroyed it, according to the word
of the LORD that he spoke by his servant
Ahijah the Shilonite— 30because of the
sins of Jeroboam that he committed and
that he caused Israel to commit, and because of the anger to which he provoked
the LORD, the God of Israel.
31 Now the rest of the acts of Nadab,
and all that he did, are they not written
in the Book of the Annals of the Kings
of Israel? 32There was war between Asa
and King Baasha of Israel all their days.

SECOND DYNASTY: BAASHA REIGNS OVER ISRAEL

33 In the third year of King Asa of
Judah, Baasha son of Ahijah began
to reign over all Israel at Tirzah; he
reigned for twenty-four years. 34He did
what was evil in the sight of the LORD,
walking in the way of Jeroboam and in
the sin that he caused Israel to commit.
16 The word of the LORD came to
Jehu son of Hanani against Ba-
asha, saying, 2'Since I exalted you out of
the dust and made you leader over my
people Israel, and you have walked in
the way of Jeroboam, and have caused
my people Israel to sin, provoking me to
anger with their sins, 3therefore, I will
consume Baasha and his house, and I
will make your house like the house of
Jeroboam son of Nebat. 4Anyone belonging to Baasha who dies in the city
the dogs shall eat; and anyone of his
who dies in the field the birds of the air
shall eat.'
5 Now the rest of the acts of Baasha,
what he did, and his power, are they
not written in the Book of the Annals of

[o] 15.28 Heb *him*

the Kings of Israel? 6 Baasha slept with
his ancestors, and was buried at Tirzah;
and his son Elah succeeded him. 7 Moreover, the word of the LORD came by the
prophet Jehu son of Hanani against Baasha and his house, both because of all
the evil that he did in the sight of the
LORD, provoking him to anger with
the work of his hands, in being like the
house of Jeroboam, and also because he
destroyed it.

ELAH REIGNS OVER ISRAEL

8 In the twenty-sixth year of King
Asa of Judah, Elah son of Baasha began to reign over Israel in Tirzah; he
reigned for two years. 9 But his servant
Zimri, commander of half his chariots,
conspired against him. When he was at
Tirzah, drinking himself drunk in the
house of Arza, who was in charge of the
palace at Tirzah, 10 Zimri came in and
struck him down and killed him, in the
twenty-seventh year of King Asa of Judah, and succeeded him.

11 When he began to reign, as soon
as he had seated himself on his throne,
he killed all the house of Baasha; he did
not leave him a single male of his kindred or his friends. 12 Thus Zimri destroyed all the house of Baasha, according to the word of the LORD, which he
spoke against Baasha by the prophet Jehu— 13 because of all the sins of Baasha
and the sins of his son Elah that they
committed, and that they caused Israel
to commit, provoking the LORD God of
Israel to anger with their idols. 14 Now
the rest of the acts of Elah, and all that
he did, are they not written in the Book
of the Annals of the Kings of Israel?

THIRD DYNASTY: ZIMRI REIGNS OVER ISRAEL

15 In the twenty-seventh year of
King Asa of Judah, Zimri reigned for
seven days in Tirzah. Now the troops
were encamped against Gibbethon,
which belonged to the Philistines, 16 and
the troops who were encamped heard it
said, 'Zimri has conspired, and he has
killed the king'; therefore all Israel made
Omri, the commander of the army, king
over Israel that day in the camp. 17 So
Omri went up from Gibbethon, and all
Israel with him, and they besieged Tirzah. 18 When Zimri saw that the city was
taken, he went into the citadel of the
king's house; he burned down the king's
house over himself with fire, and died—
19 because of the sins that he committed, doing evil in the sight of the LORD,
walking in the way of Jeroboam, and for
the sin that he committed, causing Israel to sin. 20 Now the rest of the acts of
Zimri, and the conspiracy that he made,
are they not written in the Book of the
Annals of the Kings of Israel?

FOURTH DYNASTY: OMRI REIGNS OVER ISRAEL

21 Then the people of Israel were divided into two parts; half of the people
followed Tibni son of Ginath, to make
him king, and half followed Omri. 22 But
the people who followed Omri overcame
the people who followed Tibni son of Ginath; so Tibni died, and Omri became
king. 23 In the thirty-first year of King
Asa of Judah, Omri began to reign over
Israel; he reigned for twelve years, six of
them in Tirzah.

SAMARIA THE NEW CAPITAL

24 He bought the hill of Samaria
from Shemer for two talents of silver; he
fortified the hill, and called the city that
he built Samaria, after the name of Shemer, the owner of the hill.

25 Omri did what was evil in the
sight of the LORD; he did more evil
than all who were before him. 26 For he
walked in all the way of Jeroboam son
of Nebat, and in the sins that he caused
Israel to commit, provoking the LORD,
the God of Israel, to anger by their idols.
27 Now the rest of the acts of Omri that
he did, and the power that he showed,
are they not written in the Book of the
Annals of the Kings of Israel? 28 Omri
slept with his ancestors, and was buried in Samaria; his son Ahab succeeded
him.

AHAB REIGNS OVER ISRAEL

29 In the thirty-eighth year of King
Asa of Judah, Ahab son of Omri began to reign over Israel; Ahab son of
Omri reigned over Israel in Samaria for
twenty-two years. 30 Ahab son of Omri
did evil in the sight of the LORD more
than all who were before him.

AHAB MARRIES JEZEBEL AND WORSHIPS BAAL

31 And as if it had been a light thing
for him to walk in the sins of Jeroboam
son of Nebat, he took as his wife Jezebel
daughter of King Ethbaal of the Sidonians, and went and served Baal, and worshipped him. 32 He erected an altar for
Baal in the house of Baal, which he built

in Samaria. 33Ahab also made a sacred
pole.[p] Ahab did more to provoke the anger of the LORD, the God of Israel, than
had all the kings of Israel who were before him. 34In his days Hiel of Bethel
built Jericho; he laid its foundation at
the cost of Abiram his firstborn, and set
up its gates at the cost of his youngest
son Segub, according to the word of the
LORD, which he spoke by Joshua son of
Nun.

ELIJAH PREDICTS A DROUGHT

17 Now Elijah the Tishbite, of
Tishbe[q] in Gilead, said to Ahab,
'As the LORD the God of Israel lives, before whom I stand, there shall be neither dew nor rain these years, except
by my word.' 2The word of the LORD
came to him, saying, 3'Go from here
and turn eastwards, and hide yourself
by the Wadi Cherith, which is east of
the Jordan. 4You shall drink from the
wadi, and I have commanded the ravens to feed you there.' 5So he went and
did according to the word of the LORD;
he went and lived by the Wadi Cherith,
which is east of the Jordan. 6The ravens
brought him bread and meat in the
morning, and bread and meat in the
evening; and he drank from the wadi.
7But after a while the wadi dried up, because there was no rain in the land.

THE WIDOW OF ZAREPHATH

8 Then the word of the LORD came
to him, saying, 9'Go now to Zarephath,
which belongs to Sidon, and live there;
for I have commanded a widow there
to feed you.' 10So he set out and went to
Zarephath. When he came to the gate of
the town, a widow was there gathering
sticks; he called to her and said, 'Bring
me a little water in a vessel, so that I
may drink.' 11As she was going to bring
it, he called to her and said, 'Bring me
a morsel of bread in your hand.' 12But
she said, 'As the LORD your God lives, I
have nothing baked, only a handful of
meal in a jar, and a little oil in a jug; I
am now gathering a couple of sticks, so
that I may go home and prepare it for
myself and my son, that we may eat it,
and die.' 13Elijah said to her, 'Do not be
afraid; go and do as you have said; but
first make me a little cake of it and bring
it to me, and afterwards make something for yourself and your son. 14For
thus says the LORD the God of Israel:
The jar of meal will not be emptied and
the jug of oil will not fail until the day
that the LORD sends rain on the earth.'
15She went and did as Elijah said, so
that she as well as he and her household
ate for many days. 16The jar of meal was
not emptied, neither did the jug of oil
fail, according to the word of the LORD
that he spoke by Elijah.

ELIJAH REVIVES THE WIDOW'S SON

17 After this the son of the woman,
the mistress of the house, became ill;
his illness was so severe that there was
no breath left in him. 18She then said
to Elijah, 'What have you against me,
O man of God? You have come to me to
bring my sin to remembrance, and to
cause the death of my son!' 19But he said
to her, 'Give me your son.' He took him
from her bosom, carried him up into
the upper chamber where he was lodging, and laid him on his own bed. 20He
cried out to the LORD, 'O LORD my God,
have you brought calamity even upon
the widow with whom I am staying,
by killing her son?' 21Then he stretched
himself upon the child three times, and
cried out to the LORD, 'O LORD my God,
let this child's life come into him again.'
22The LORD listened to the voice of Elijah; the life of the child came into him
again, and he revived. 23Elijah took the
child, brought him down from the upper chamber into the house, and gave
him to his mother; then Elijah said,
'See, your son is alive.' 24So the woman
said to Elijah, 'Now I know that you are
a man of God, and that the word of the
LORD in your mouth is truth.'

ELIJAH'S MESSAGE TO AHAB

18 After many days the word of
the LORD came to Elijah, in the
third year of the drought,[r] saying, 'Go,
present yourself to Ahab; I will send
rain on the earth.' 2So Elijah went to
present himself to Ahab. The famine
was severe in Samaria. 3Ahab summoned Obadiah, who was in charge of
the palace. (Now Obadiah revered the
LORD greatly; 4when Jezebel was killing
off the prophets of the LORD, Obadiah
took a hundred prophets, hid them fifty
to a cave, and provided them with bread
and water.) 5Then Ahab said to Obadiah,
'Go through the land to all the springs
of water and to all the wadis; perhaps
we may find grass to keep the horses
and mules alive, and not lose some of

p **16.33** Heb *Asherah* q **17.1** Gk: Heb *of the settlers* r **18.1** Heb lacks *of the drought*

the animals.' 6So they divided the land
between them to pass through it; Ahab
went in one direction by himself, and
Obadiah went in another direction by
himself.
7 As Obadiah was on the way, Elijah met him; Obadiah recognized him,
fell on his face, and said, 'Is it you, my
lord Elijah?' 8He answered him, 'It is
I. Go, tell your lord that Elijah is here.'
9And he said, 'How have I sinned, that
you would hand your servant over to
Ahab, to kill me? 10As the LORD your
God lives, there is no nation or kingdom to which my lord has not sent to
seek you; and when they would say, "He
is not here", he would require an oath of
the kingdom or nation, that they had
not found you. 11But now you say, "Go,
tell your lord that Elijah is here." 12As
soon as I have gone from you, the spirit
of the LORD will carry you I know not
where; so, when I come and tell Ahab
and he cannot find you, he will kill me,
although I your servant have revered
the LORD from my youth. 13Has it not
been told my lord what I did when Jezebel killed the prophets of the LORD, how
I hid a hundred of the LORD's prophets
fifty to a cave, and provided them with
bread and water? 14Yet now you say,
"Go, tell your lord that Elijah is here";
he will surely kill me.' 15Elijah said, 'As
the LORD of hosts lives, before whom I
stand, I will surely show myself to him
today.' 16So Obadiah went to meet Ahab,
and told him; and Ahab went to meet
Elijah.
17 When Ahab saw Elijah, Ahab said
to him, 'Is it you, you troubler of Israel?'
18He answered, 'I have not troubled Israel; but you have, and your father's
house, because you have forsaken the
commandments of the LORD and followed the Baals. 19Now therefore have
all Israel assemble for me at Mount Carmel, with the four hundred and fifty
prophets of Baal and the four hundred
prophets of Asherah, who eat at Jezebel's table.'

ELIJAH'S TRIUMPH OVER THE PRIESTS OF BAAL

20 So Ahab sent to all the Israelites,
and assembled the prophets at Mount
Carmel. 21Elijah then came near to all
the people, and said, 'How long will you
go limping with two different opinions?
If the LORD is God, follow him; but if
Baal, then follow him.' The people did
not answer him a word. 22Then Elijah
said to the people, 'I, even I only, am left
a prophet of the LORD; but Baal's prophets number four hundred and fifty. 23Let
two bulls be given to us; let them choose
one bull for themselves, cut it in pieces,
and lay it on the wood, but put no fire
to it; I will prepare the other bull and
lay it on the wood, but put no fire to
it. 24Then you call on the name of your
god and I will call on the name of the
LORD; the god who answers by fire is
indeed God.' All the people answered,
'Well spoken!' 25Then Elijah said to the
prophets of Baal, 'Choose for yourselves
one bull and prepare it first, for you are
many; then call on the name of your
god, but put no fire to it.' 26So they took
the bull that was given them, prepared
it, and called on the name of Baal from
morning until noon, crying, 'O Baal,
answer us!' But there was no voice, and
no answer. They limped about the altar that they had made. 27At noon Elijah mocked them, saying, 'Cry aloud!
Surely he is a god; either he is meditating, or he has wandered away, or he is
on a journey, or perhaps he is asleep and
must be awakened.' 28Then they cried
aloud and, as was their custom, they cut
themselves with swords and lances until the blood gushed out over them. 29As
midday passed, they raved on until the
time of the offering of the oblation, but
there was no voice, no answer, and no
response.
30 Then Elijah said to all the people,
'Come closer to me'; and all the people
came closer to him. First he repaired the
altar of the LORD that had been thrown
down; 31Elijah took twelve stones, according to the number of the tribes of
the sons of Jacob, to whom the word of
the LORD came, saying, 'Israel shall be
your name'; 32with the stones he built
an altar in the name of the LORD. Then
he made a trench around the altar, large
enough to contain two measures of
seed. 33Next he put the wood in order,
cut the bull in pieces, and laid it on the
wood. He said, 'Fill four jars with water
and pour it on the burnt-offering and on
the wood.' 34Then he said, 'Do it a second time'; and they did it a second time.
Again he said, 'Do it a third time'; and
they did it a third time, 35so that the
water ran all round the altar, and filled
the trench also with water.
36 At the time of the offering of the
oblation, the prophet Elijah came near
and said, 'O LORD, God of Abraham,
Isaac, and Israel, let it be known this

day that you are God in Israel, that I am your servant, and that I have done all these things at your bidding. 37 Answer me, O LORD, answer me, so that this people may know that you, O LORD, are God, and that you have turned their hearts back.' 38 Then the fire of the LORD fell and consumed the burnt-offering, the wood, the stones, and the dust, and even licked up the water that was in the trench. 39 When all the people saw it, they fell on their faces and said, 'The LORD indeed is God; the LORD indeed is God.' 40 Elijah said to them, 'Seize the prophets of Baal; do not let one of them escape.' Then they seized them; and Elijah brought them down to the Wadi Kishon, and killed them there.

THE DROUGHT ENDS

41 Elijah said to Ahab, 'Go up, eat and drink; for there is a sound of rushing rain.' 42 So Ahab went up to eat and to drink. Elijah went up to the top of Carmel; there he bowed himself down upon the earth and put his face between his knees. 43 He said to his servant, 'Go up now, look towards the sea.' He went up and looked, and said, 'There is nothing.' Then he said, 'Go again seven times.' 44 At the seventh time he said, 'Look, a little cloud no bigger than a person's hand is rising out of the sea.' Then he said, 'Go and say to Ahab, "Harness your chariot and go down before the rain stops you."' 45 In a little while the heavens grew black with clouds and wind; there was heavy rain. Ahab rode off and went to Jezreel. 46 But the hand of the LORD was on Elijah; he girded up his loins and ran in front of Ahab to the entrance of Jezreel.

ELIJAH FLEES FROM JEZEBEL

19 Ahab told Jezebel all that Elijah had done, and how he had killed all the prophets with the sword. 2 Then Jezebel sent a messenger to Elijah, saying, 'So may the gods do to me, and more also, if I do not make your life like the life of one of them by this time tomorrow.' 3 Then he was afraid; he got up and fled for his life, and came to Beer-sheba, which belongs to Judah; he left his servant there.

4 But he himself went a day's journey into the wilderness, and came and sat down under a solitary broom tree. He asked that he might die: 'It is enough; now, O LORD, take away my life, for I am no better than my ancestors.' 5 Then he lay down under the broom tree and fell asleep. Suddenly an angel touched him and said to him, 'Get up and eat.' 6 He looked, and there at his head was a cake baked on hot stones, and a jar of water. He ate and drank, and lay down again. 7 The angel of the LORD came a second time, touched him, and said, 'Get up and eat, otherwise the journey will be too much for you.' 8 He got up, and ate and drank; then he went in the strength of that food for forty days and forty nights to Horeb the mount of God. 9 At that place he came to a cave, and spent the night there.

Then the word of the LORD came to him, saying, 'What are you doing here, Elijah?' 10 He answered, 'I have been very zealous for the LORD, the God of hosts; for the Israelites have forsaken your covenant, thrown down your altars, and killed your prophets with the sword. I alone am left, and they are seeking my life, to take it away.'

ELIJAH MEETS GOD AT HOREB

11 He said, 'Go out and stand on the mountain before the LORD, for the LORD is about to pass by.' Now there was a great wind, so strong that it was splitting mountains and breaking rocks in pieces before the LORD, but the LORD was not in the wind; and after the wind an earthquake, but the LORD was not in the earthquake; 12 and after the earthquake a fire, but the LORD was not in the fire; and after the fire a sound of sheer silence. 13 When Elijah heard it, he wrapped his face in his mantle and went out and stood at the entrance of the cave. Then there came a voice to him that said, 'What are you doing here, Elijah?' 14 He answered, 'I have been very zealous for the LORD, the God of hosts; for the Israelites have forsaken your covenant, thrown down your altars, and killed your prophets with the sword. I alone am left, and they are seeking my life, to take it away.' 15 Then the LORD said to him, 'Go, return on your way to the wilderness of Damascus; when you arrive, you shall anoint Hazael as king over Aram. 16 Also you shall anoint Jehu son of Nimshi as king over Israel; and you shall anoint Elisha son of Shaphat of Abel-meholah as prophet in your place. 17 Whoever escapes from the sword of Hazael, Jehu shall kill; and whoever escapes from the sword of Jehu, Elisha shall kill. 18 Yet I will leave seven thousand in Israel, all the knees

that have not bowed to Baal, and every
mouth that has not kissed him.'

ELISHA BECOMES ELIJAH'S DISCIPLE

19 So he set out from there, and
found Elisha son of Shaphat, who was
ploughing. There were twelve yoke of
oxen ahead of him, and he was with
the twelfth. Elijah passed by him and
threw his mantle over him. 20He left
the oxen, ran after Elijah, and said, 'Let
me kiss my father and my mother, and
then I will follow you.' Then Elijah[s] said
to him, 'Go back again; for what have I
done to you?' 21He returned from following him, took the yoke of oxen, and
slaughtered them; using the equipment
from the oxen, he boiled their flesh, and
gave it to the people, and they ate. Then
he set out and followed Elijah, and became his servant.

AHAB'S WARS WITH THE ARAMEANS

20 King Ben-hadad of Aram gathered all his army together;
thirty-two kings were with him, along
with horses and chariots. He marched
against Samaria, laid siege to it, and attacked it. 2Then he sent messengers into
the city to King Ahab of Israel, and said
to him: 'Thus says Ben-hadad: 3Your silver and gold are mine; your fairest wives
and children also are mine.' 4The king
of Israel answered, 'As you say, my lord,
O king, I am yours, and all that I have.'
5The messengers came again and said:
'Thus says Ben-hadad: I sent to you,
saying, "Deliver to me your silver and
gold, your wives and children"; 6never-
theless, I will send my servants to you
tomorrow about this time, and they
shall search your house and the houses
of your servants, and lay hands on whatever pleases them,[t] and take it away.'

7 Then the king of Israel called all the
elders of the land, and said, 'Look now!
See how this man is seeking trouble; for
he sent to me for my wives, my children,
my silver, and my gold; and I did not refuse him.' 8Then all the elders and all
the people said to him, 'Do not listen or
consent.' 9So he said to the messengers
of Ben-hadad, 'Tell my lord the king: All
that you first demanded of your servant
I will do; but this thing I cannot do.' The
messengers left and brought him word
again. 10Ben-hadad sent to him and said,
'The gods do so to me, and more also, if
the dust of Samaria will provide a handful for each of the people who follow me.'
11The king of Israel answered, 'Tell him:
One who puts on armour should not
brag like one who takes it off.' 12When
Ben-hadad heard this message—now
he had been drinking with the kings in
the booths—he said to his men, 'Take
your positions!' And they took their positions against the city.

PROPHETIC OPPOSITION TO AHAB

13 Then a certain prophet came up to
King Ahab of Israel and said, 'Thus says
the LORD, Have you seen all this great
multitude? Look, I will give it into your
hand today; and you shall know that I
am the LORD.' 14Ahab said, 'By whom?'
He said, 'Thus says the LORD, By the
young men who serve the district governors.' Then he said, 'Who shall begin
the battle?' He answered, 'You.' 15Then
he mustered the young men who served
the district governors, two hundred and
thirty-two; after them he mustered all
the people of Israel, seven thousand.

16 They went out at noon, while Ben-
hadad was drinking himself drunk in
the booths, he and the thirty-two kings
allied with him. 17The young men who
served the district governors went out
first. Ben-hadad had sent out scouts,[u]
and they reported to him, 'Men have
come out from Samaria.' 18He said, 'If
they have come out for peace, take them
alive; if they have come out for war, take
them alive.'

19 But these had already come out of
the city: the young men who served the
district governors, and the army that
followed them. 20Each killed his man;
the Arameans fled and Israel pursued
them, but King Ben-hadad of Aram escaped on a horse with the cavalry. 21The
king of Israel went out, attacked the
horses and chariots, and defeated the
Arameans with a great slaughter.

22 Then the prophet approached the
king of Israel and said to him, 'Come,
strengthen yourself, and consider well
what you have to do; for in the spring
the king of Aram will come up against
you.'

THE ARAMEANS ARE DEFEATED

23 The servants of the king of Aram
said to him, 'Their gods are gods of the
hills, and so they were stronger than
we; but let us fight against them in the
plain, and surely we shall be stronger than they. 24Also do this: remove

[s] 19.20 Heb *he* [t] 20.6 Gk Syr Vg: Heb *you*
[u] 20.17 Heb lacks *scouts*

the kings, each from his post, and put
commanders in place of them; 25 and
muster an army like the army that you
have lost, horse for horse, and chariot
for chariot; then we will fight against
them in the plain, and surely we shall
be stronger than they.' He heeded their
voice, and did so.

26 In the spring Ben-hadad mustered the Arameans and went up to
Aphek to fight against Israel. 27 After
the Israelites had been mustered and
provisioned, they went out to engage
them; the people of Israel encamped
opposite them like two little flocks of
goats, while the Arameans filled the
country. 28 A man of God approached
and said to the king of Israel, 'Thus says
the LORD: Because the Arameans have
said, "The LORD is a god of the hills but
he is not a god of the valleys", therefore
I will give all this great multitude into
your hand, and you shall know that I
am the LORD.' 29 They encamped opposite one another for seven days. Then on
the seventh day the battle began; the
Israelites killed one hundred thousand
Aramean foot-soldiers in one day. 30 The
rest fled into the city of Aphek; and the
wall fell on twenty-seven thousand men
that were left.

Ben-hadad also fled, and entered
the city to hide. 31 His servants said
to him, 'Look, we have heard that the
kings of the house of Israel are merciful kings; let us put sackcloth around
our waists and ropes on our heads, and
go out to the king of Israel; perhaps he
will spare your life.' 32 So they tied sackcloth around their waists, put ropes on
their heads, went to the king of Israel,
and said, 'Your servant Ben-hadad says,
"Please let me live."' And he said, 'Is he
still alive? He is my brother.' 33 Now the
men were watching for an omen; they
quickly took it up from him and said,
'Yes, Ben-hadad is your brother.' Then
he said, 'Go and bring him.' So Ben-
hadad came out to him; and he had him
come up into the chariot. 34 Ben-hadad[v]
said to him, 'I will restore the towns
that my father took from your father;
and you may establish bazaars for yourself in Damascus, as my father did in
Samaria.' The king of Israel responded,[w]
'I will let you go on those terms.' So he
made a treaty with him and let him go.

A PROPHET CONDEMNS AHAB

35 At the command of the LORD a
certain member of a company of prophets[x] said to another, 'Strike me!' But
the man refused to strike him. 36 Then
he said to him, 'Because you have not
obeyed the voice of the LORD, as soon
as you have left me, a lion will kill you.'
And when he had left him, a lion met
him and killed him. 37 Then he found another man and said, 'Strike me!' So the
man hit him, striking and wounding
him. 38 Then the prophet departed, and
waited for the king along the road, disguising himself with a bandage over his
eyes. 39 As the king passed by, he cried
to the king and said, 'Your servant went
out into the thick of the battle; then a
soldier turned and brought a man to me,
and said, "Guard this man; if he is missing, your life shall be given for his life,
or else you shall pay a talent of silver."
40 While your servant was busy here and
there, he was gone.' The king of Israel
said to him, 'So shall your judgement be;
you yourself have decided it.' 41 Then he
quickly took the bandage away from his
eyes. The king of Israel recognized him
as one of the prophets. 42 Then he said
to him, 'Thus says the LORD, "Because
you have let the man go whom I had devoted to destruction, therefore your life
shall be for his life, and your people for
his people."' 43 The king of Israel set out
towards home, resentful and sullen, and
came to Samaria.

NABOTH'S VINEYARD

21 Later the following events took
place: Naboth the Jezreelite had
a vineyard in Jezreel, beside the palace
of King Ahab of Samaria. 2 And Ahab
said to Naboth, 'Give me your vineyard,
so that I may have it for a vegetable garden, because it is near my house; I will
give you a better vineyard for it; or, if
it seems good to you, I will give you its
value in money.' 3 But Naboth said to
Ahab, 'The LORD forbid that I should
give you my ancestral inheritance.'
4 Ahab went home resentful and sullen
because of what Naboth the Jezreelite
had said to him; for he had said, 'I will
not give you my ancestral inheritance.'
He lay down on his bed, turned away his
face, and would not eat.

5 His wife Jezebel came to him and
said, 'Why are you so depressed that
you will not eat?' 6 He said to her, 'Because I spoke to Naboth the Jezreelite
and said to him, "Give me your vineyard

[v] **20.34** Heb *He* [w] **20.34** Heb lacks *The king of Israel responded* [x] **20.35** Heb *of the sons of the prophets*

for money; or else, if you prefer, I will
give you another vineyard for it"; but he
answered, "I will not give you my vineyard."' 7His wife Jezebel said to him, 'Do
you now govern Israel? Get up, eat some
food, and be cheerful; I will give you the
vineyard of Naboth the Jezreelite.'

8 So she wrote letters in Ahab's name
and sealed them with his seal; she sent
the letters to the elders and the nobles
who lived with Naboth in his city. 9She
wrote in the letters, 'Proclaim a fast, and
seat Naboth at the head of the assembly;
10seat two scoundrels opposite him, and
have them bring a charge against him,
saying, "You have cursed God and the
king." Then take him out, and stone him
to death.' 11The men of his city, the elders and the nobles who lived in his city,
did as Jezebel had sent word to them.
Just as it was written in the letters that
she had sent to them, 12they proclaimed
a fast and seated Naboth at the head
of the assembly. 13The two scoundrels
came in and sat opposite him; and the
scoundrels brought a charge against Naboth, in the presence of the people, saying, 'Naboth cursed God and the king.'
So they took him outside the city, and
stoned him to death. 14Then they sent
to Jezebel, saying, 'Naboth has been
stoned; he is dead.'

15 As soon as Jezebel heard that Naboth had been stoned and was dead, Jezebel said to Ahab, 'Go, take possession of
the vineyard of Naboth the Jezreelite,
which he refused to give you for money;
for Naboth is not alive, but dead.' 16As
soon as Ahab heard that Naboth was
dead, Ahab set out to go down to the
vineyard of Naboth the Jezreelite, to
take possession of it.

ELIJAH PRONOUNCES GOD'S SENTENCE

17 Then the word of the LORD came
to Elijah the Tishbite, saying: 18Go down
to meet King Ahab of Israel, who rules[y]
in Samaria; he is now in the vineyard
of Naboth, where he has gone to take
possession. 19You shall say to him, 'Thus
says the LORD: Have you killed, and also
taken possession?' You shall say to him,
'Thus says the LORD: In the place where
dogs licked up the blood of Naboth, dogs
will also lick up your blood.'

20 Ahab said to Elijah, 'Have you
found me, O my enemy?' He answered,
'I have found you. Because you have sold
yourself to do what is evil in the sight
of the LORD, 21I will bring disaster on
you; I will consume you, and will cut off
from Ahab every male, bond or free, in
Israel; 22and I will make your house like
the house of Jeroboam son of Nebat, and
like the house of Baasha son of Ahijah,
because you have provoked me to anger and have caused Israel to sin. 23Also
concerning Jezebel the LORD said, "The
dogs shall eat Jezebel within the bounds
of Jezreel." 24Anyone belonging to Ahab
who dies in the city the dogs shall eat;
and anyone of his who dies in the open
country the birds of the air shall eat.'

25 (Indeed, there was no one like
Ahab, who sold himself to do what was
evil in the sight of the LORD, urged on
by his wife Jezebel. 26He acted most
abominably in going after idols, as the
Amorites had done, whom the LORD
drove out before the Israelites.)

27 When Ahab heard those words, he
tore his clothes and put sackcloth over
his bare flesh; he fasted, lay in the sackcloth, and went about dejectedly. 28Then
the word of the LORD came to Elijah the
Tishbite: 29'Have you seen how Ahab
has humbled himself before me? Because he has humbled himself before
me, I will not bring the disaster in his
days; but in his son's days I will bring
the disaster on his house.'

JOINT CAMPAIGN WITH JUDAH AGAINST ARAM

22 For three years Aram and Israel
continued without war. 2But in
the third year King Jehoshaphat of Judah came down to the king of Israel.
3The king of Israel said to his servants,
'Do you know that Ramoth-gilead belongs to us, yet we are doing nothing
to take it out of the hand of the king of
Aram?' 4He said to Jehoshaphat, 'Will
you go with me to battle at Ramoth-
gilead?' Jehoshaphat replied to the king
of Israel, 'I am as you are; my people are
your people, my horses are your horses.'

5 But Jehoshaphat also said to the
king of Israel, 'Inquire first for the word
of the LORD.' 6Then the king of Israel
gathered the prophets together, about
four hundred of them, and said to them,
'Shall I go to battle against Ramoth-
gilead, or shall I refrain?' They said, 'Go
up; for the LORD will give it into the
hand of the king.' 7But Jehoshaphat
said, 'Is there no other prophet of the
LORD here of whom we may inquire?'
8The king of Israel said to Jehoshaphat,

[y] 21.18 Heb *who is*

'There is still one other by whom we
may inquire of the LORD, Micaiah son
of Imlah; but I hate him, for he never
prophesies anything favourable about
me, but only disaster.' Jehoshaphat said,
'Let the king not say such a thing.' 9Then
the king of Israel summoned an officer
and said, 'Bring quickly Micaiah son
of Imlah.' 10Now the king of Israel and
King Jehoshaphat of Judah were sitting
on their thrones, arrayed in their robes,
at the threshing-floor at the entrance of
the gate of Samaria; and all the prophets were prophesying before them.
11Zedekiah son of Chenaanah made for
himself horns of iron, and he said, 'Thus
says the LORD: With these you shall gore
the Arameans until they are destroyed.'
12All the prophets were prophesying
the same and saying, 'Go up to Ramoth-
gilead and triumph; the LORD will give
it into the hand of the king.'

MICAIAH PREDICTS FAILURE

13 The messenger who had gone to
summon Micaiah said to him, 'Look,
the words of the prophets with one accord are favourable to the king; let your
word be like the word of one of them,
and speak favourably.' 14But Micaiah
said, 'As the LORD lives, whatever the
LORD says to me, that I will speak.'

15 When he had come to the king,
the king said to him, 'Micaiah, shall we
go to Ramoth-gilead to battle, or shall
we refrain?' He answered him, 'Go up
and triumph; the LORD will give it into
the hand of the king.' 16But the king said
to him, 'How many times must I make
you swear to tell me nothing but the
truth in the name of the LORD?' 17Then
Micaiah[z] said, 'I saw all Israel scattered
on the mountains, like sheep that have
no shepherd; and the LORD said, "These
have no master; let each one go home in
peace." ' 18The king of Israel said to Jehoshaphat, 'Did I not tell you that he
would not prophesy anything favourable about me, but only disaster?'

19 Then Micaiah[a] said, 'Therefore
hear the word of the LORD: I saw the
LORD sitting on his throne, with all
the host of heaven standing beside
him to the right and to the left of him.
20And the LORD said, "Who will entice
Ahab, so that he may go up and fall at
Ramoth-gilead?" Then one said one
thing, and another said another, 21until
a spirit came forward and stood before
the LORD, saying, "I will entice him."
22"How?" the LORD asked him. He replied, "I will go out and be a lying spirit
in the mouth of all his prophets." Then
the LORD[b] said, "You are to entice him,
and you shall succeed; go out and do it."
23So you see, the LORD has put a lying
spirit in the mouth of all these your
prophets; the LORD has decreed disaster
for you.'

24 Then Zedekiah son of Chenaanah
came up to Micaiah, slapped him on
the cheek, and said, 'Which way did the
spirit of the LORD pass from me to speak
to you?' 25Micaiah replied, 'You will find
out on that day when you go in to hide
in an inner chamber.' 26The king of Israel then ordered, 'Take Micaiah, and
return him to Amon the governor of the
city and to Joash the king's son, 27and
say, "Thus says the king: Put this fellow
in prison, and feed him on reduced rations of bread and water until I come in
peace." ' 28Micaiah said, 'If you return in
peace, the LORD has not spoken by me.'
And he said, 'Hear, you peoples, all of
you!'

DEFEAT AND DEATH OF AHAB

29 So the king of Israel and King Jehoshaphat of Judah went up to Ramoth-
gilead. 30The king of Israel said to Jehoshaphat, 'I will disguise myself and
go into battle, but you wear your robes.'
So the king of Israel disguised himself
and went into battle. 31Now the king of
Aram had commanded the thirty-two
captains of his chariots, 'Fight with no
one small or great, but only with the
king of Israel.' 32When the captains of
the chariots saw Jehoshaphat, they said,
'It is surely the king of Israel.' So they
turned to fight against him; and Jehoshaphat cried out. 33When the captains of
the chariots saw that it was not the king
of Israel, they turned back from pursuing him. 34But a certain man drew his
bow and unknowingly struck the king
of Israel between the scale-armour and
the breastplate; so he said to the driver
of his chariot, 'Turn around, and carry
me out of the battle, for I am wounded.'
35The battle grew hot that day, and the
king was propped up in his chariot facing the Arameans, until at evening he
died; the blood from the wound had
flowed into the bottom of the chariot. 36Then about sunset a shout went
through the army, 'Every man to his
city, and every man to his country!'

[z] **22.17** Heb *he* [a] **22.19** Heb *he*
[b] **22.22** Heb *he*

37 So the king died, and was brought
to Samaria; they buried the king in Samaria. [38]They washed the chariot by
the pool of Samaria; the dogs licked up
his blood, and the prostitutes washed
themselves in it,[c] according to the word
of the LORD that he had spoken. [39]Now
the rest of the acts of Ahab, and all that
he did, and the ivory house that he built,
and all the cities that he built, are they
not written in the Book of the Annals
of the Kings of Israel? [40]So Ahab slept
with his ancestors; and his son Ahaziah
succeeded him.

JEHOSHAPHAT REIGNS OVER JUDAH

41 Jehoshaphat son of Asa began to
reign over Judah in the fourth year of
King Ahab of Israel. [42]Jehoshaphat was
thirty-five years old when he began to
reign, and he reigned for twenty-five
years in Jerusalem. His mother's name
was Azubah daughter of Shilhi. [43]He
walked in all the way of his father Asa;
he did not turn aside from it, doing
what was right in the sight of the LORD;
yet the high places were not taken away,
and the people still sacrificed and offered incense on the high places. [44]Je-
hoshaphat also made peace with the
king of Israel.

45 Now the rest of the acts of Jehoshaphat, and his power that he showed,
and how he waged war, are they not
written in the Book of the Annals of the
Kings of Judah? [46]The remnant of the
male temple prostitutes who were still
in the land from the days of his father
Asa, he exterminated.

47 There was no king in Edom; a
deputy was king. [48]Jehoshaphat made
ships of the Tarshish type to go to
Ophir for gold; but they did not go, for
the ships were wrecked at Ezion-geber.
[49]Then Ahaziah son of Ahab said to Jehoshaphat, 'Let my servants go with
your servants in the ships', but Jehoshaphat was not willing. [50]Jehoshaphat
slept with his ancestors and was buried
with his ancestors in the city of his father David; his son Jehoram succeeded
him.

AHAZIAH REIGNS OVER ISRAEL

51 Ahaziah son of Ahab began to
reign over Israel in Samaria in the seventeenth year of King Jehoshaphat of
Judah; he reigned for two years over Israel. [52]He did what was evil in the sight
of the LORD, and walked in the way of
his father and mother, and in the way
of Jeroboam son of Nebat, who caused
Israel to sin. [53]He served Baal and worshipped him; he provoked the LORD, the
God of Israel, to anger, just as his father
had done.

[c] **22.38** Heb lacks *in it*

2 KINGS

The second book of Kings is a continuation of 1 Kings and picks up on the narrative following King Ahab's death. The work and interventions of Elijah, Elisha, and Isaiah are interwoven into the story line. The eventual demise of the kings of Israel and Judah are narrated in this book. Despite the reform of King Josiah, the kingdom of Judah also succumbs eventually to the powerful King Nebuchadnezzar of Babylon. These events were interpreted in light of the Deuteronomistic history that said the people of Israel would flourish only if they and their leaders remained faithful to God.

Selected passages from 2 Kings are read in the liturgy from Wednesday of the Eleventh Week of Year II through Friday of the Twelfth Week. The story of the healing of the leprosy of Naaman the Syrian by Elisha and the raising of the son of the Shunammite woman by Elisha are read during the season of Lent each year.

ELIJAH DENOUNCES AHAZIAH

1 After the death of Ahab, Moab rebelled against Israel.
2 Ahaziah had fallen through the lattice in his upper chamber in Samaria,
and lay injured; so he sent messengers,
telling them, 'Go, inquire of Baal-zebub,
the god of Ekron, whether I shall recover
from this injury.' 3But the angel of the
LORD said to Elijah the Tishbite, 'Get up,
go to meet the messengers of the king of
Samaria, and say to them, "Is it because
there is no God in Israel that you are
going to inquire of Baal-zebub, the god
of Ekron?" 4Now therefore, thus says
the LORD, "You shall not leave the bed
to which you have gone, but you shall
surely die."' So Elijah went.
5 The messengers returned to the
king, who said to them, 'Why have you
returned?' 6They answered him, 'There
came a man to meet us, who said to us,
"Go back to the king who sent you, and
say to him: Thus says the LORD: Is it because there is no God in Israel that you
are sending to inquire of Baal-zebub,
the god of Ekron? Therefore you shall
not leave the bed to which you have
gone, but shall surely die."' 7He said to
them, 'What sort of man was he who
came to meet you and told you these
things?' 8They answered him, 'A hairy
man, with a leather belt around his
waist.' He said, 'It is Elijah the Tishbite.'
9 Then the king sent to him a captain
of fifty with his fifty men. He went up
to Elijah, who was sitting on the top of
a hill, and said to him, 'O man of God,
the king says, "Come down."' 10But Elijah answered the captain of fifty, 'If I am
a man of God, let fire come down from
heaven and consume you and your fifty.'
Then fire came down from heaven, and
consumed him and his fifty.
11 Again the king sent to him another captain of fifty with his fifty. He
went up[a] and said to him, 'O man of
God, this is the king's order: Come down
quickly!' 12But Elijah answered them, 'If
I am a man of God, let fire come down
from heaven and consume you and your
fifty.' Then the fire of God came down
from heaven and consumed him and his
fifty.
13 Again the king sent the captain
of a third fifty with his fifty. So the
third captain of fifty went up, and
came and fell on his knees before Elijah, and entreated him, 'O man of God,
please let my life, and the life of these

[a] 1.11 Gk Compare verses 9, 13: Heb *He answered*

fifty servants of yours, be precious in
your sight. 14Look, fire came down from
heaven and consumed the two former
captains of fifty men with their fifties;
but now let my life be precious in your
sight.' 15Then the angel of the LORD said
to Elijah, 'Go down with him; do not be
afraid of him.' So he set out and went
down with him to the king, 16and said
to him, 'Thus says the LORD: Because
you have sent messengers to inquire of
Baal-zebub, the god of Ekron,—is it because there is no God in Israel to inquire
of his word?—therefore you shall not
leave the bed to which you have gone,
but you shall surely die.'

DEATH OF AHAZIAH

17 So he died according to the word
of the LORD that Elijah had spoken.
His brother[b] Jehoram succeeded him as
king in the second year of King Jehoram
son of Jehoshaphat of Judah, because
Ahaziah had no son. 18Now the rest of
the acts of Ahaziah that he did, are they
not written in the Book of the Annals of
the Kings of Israel?

ELIJAH ASCENDS TO HEAVEN

2 Now when the LORD was about to
take Elijah up to heaven by a whirlwind, Elijah and Elisha were on their
way from Gilgal. 2Elijah said to Elisha,
'Stay here; for the LORD has sent me as
far as Bethel.' But Elisha said, 'As the
LORD lives, and as you yourself live, I
will not leave you.' So they went down
to Bethel. 3The company of prophets[c]
who were in Bethel came out to Elisha,
and said to him, 'Do you know that today the LORD will take your master
away from you?' And he said, 'Yes, I
know; keep silent.'

4 Elijah said to him, 'Elisha, stay
here; for the LORD has sent me to Jericho.' But he said, 'As the LORD lives,
and as you yourself live, I will not leave
you.' So they came to Jericho. 5The company of prophets[d] who were at Jericho
drew near to Elisha, and said to him, 'Do
you know that today the LORD will take
your master away from you?' And he
answered, 'Yes, I know; be silent.'

6 Then Elijah said to him, 'Stay here;
for the LORD has sent me to the Jordan.'
But he said, 'As the LORD lives, and as
you yourself live, I will not leave you.'
So the two of them went on. 7Fifty men
of the company of prophets[e] also went,
and stood at some distance from them,
as they both were standing by the Jordan. 8Then Elijah took his mantle and
rolled it up, and struck the water; the
water was parted to the one side and to
the other, until the two of them crossed
on dry ground.

9 When they had crossed, Elijah said
to Elisha, 'Tell me what I may do for you,
before I am taken from you.' Elisha said,
'Please let me inherit a double share of
your spirit.' 10He responded, 'You have
asked a hard thing; yet, if you see me
as I am being taken from you, it will be
granted you; if not, it will not.' 11As they
continued walking and talking, a chariot of fire and horses of fire separated
the two of them, and Elijah ascended in
a whirlwind into heaven. 12Elisha kept
watching and crying out, 'Father, father! The chariots of Israel and its horsemen!' But when he could no longer see
him, he grasped his own clothes and
tore them in two pieces.

ELISHA SUCCEEDS ELIJAH

13 He picked up the mantle of Elijah
that had fallen from him, and went back
and stood on the bank of the Jordan.
14He took the mantle of Elijah that had
fallen from him, and struck the water,
saying, 'Where is the LORD, the God of
Elijah?' When he had struck the water,
the water was parted to the one side and
to the other, and Elisha went over.

15 When the company of prophets[f]
who were at Jericho saw him at a distance, they declared, 'The spirit of Elijah
rests on Elisha.' They came to meet him
and bowed to the ground before him.
16They said to him, 'See now, we have
fifty strong men among your servants;
please let them go and seek your master;
it may be that the spirit of the LORD has
caught him up and thrown him down
on some mountain or into some valley.'
He responded, 'No, do not send them.'
17But when they urged him until he was
ashamed, he said, 'Send them.' So they
sent fifty men who searched for three
days but did not find him. 18When they
came back to him (he had remained at
Jericho), he said to them, 'Did I not say
to you, Do not go?'

ELISHA PERFORMS MIRACLES

19 Now the people of the city said to
Elisha, 'The location of this city is good,
as my lord sees; but the water is bad,

[b] **1.17** Gk Syr: Heb lacks *His brother* [c] **2.3** Heb *sons of the prophets* [d] **2.5** Heb *sons of the prophets* [e] **2.7** Heb *sons of the prophets* [f] **2.15** Heb *sons of the prophets*

and the land is unfruitful.' 20He said,
'Bring me a new bowl, and put salt in
it.' So they brought it to him. 21Then he
went to the spring of water and threw
the salt into it, and said, 'Thus says the
LORD, I have made this water wholesome; from now on neither death nor
miscarriage shall come from it.' 22So the
water has been wholesome to this day,
according to the word that Elisha spoke.
23 He went up from there to Bethel;
and while he was going up on the way,
some small boys came out of the city
and jeered at him, saying, 'Go away,
baldhead! Go away, baldhead!' 24When
he turned round and saw them, he
cursed them in the name of the LORD.
Then two she-bears came out of the
woods and mauled forty-two of the
boys. 25From there he went on to Mount
Carmel, and then returned to Samaria.

JEHORAM REIGNS OVER ISRAEL

3 In the eighteenth year of King Jehoshaphat of Judah, Jehoram son
of Ahab became king over Israel in Samaria; he reigned for twelve years. 2He
did what was evil in the sight of the
LORD, though not like his father and
mother, for he removed the pillar of
Baal that his father had made. 3Never-
theless he clung to the sin of Jeroboam
son of Nebat, which he caused Israel to
commit; he did not depart from it.

WAR WITH MOAB

4 Now King Mesha of Moab was a
sheep breeder, who used to deliver to
the king of Israel one hundred thousand lambs, and the wool of one hundred thousand rams. 5But when Ahab
died, the king of Moab rebelled against
the king of Israel. 6So King Jehoram
marched out of Samaria at that time
and mustered all Israel. 7As he went
he sent word to King Jehoshaphat of
Judah, 'The king of Moab has rebelled
against me; will you go with me to battle against Moab?' He answered, 'I will;
I am with you, my people are your people, my horses are your horses.' 8Then he
asked, 'By which way shall we march?'
Jehoram answered, 'By the way of the
wilderness of Edom.'
9 So the king of Israel, the king of
Judah, and the king of Edom set out;
and when they had made a roundabout
march of seven days, there was no water
for the army or for the animals that were
with them. 10Then the king of Israel
said, 'Alas! The LORD has summoned us,
three kings, only to be handed over to
Moab.' 11But Jehoshaphat said, 'Is there
no prophet of the LORD here, through
whom we may inquire of the LORD?'
Then one of the servants of the king of
Israel answered, 'Elisha son of Shaphat,
who used to pour water on the hands of
Elijah, is here.' 12Jehoshaphat said, 'The
word of the LORD is with him.' So the
king of Israel and Jehoshaphat and the
king of Edom went down to him.
13 Elisha said to the king of Israel,
'What have I to do with you? Go to your
father's prophets or to your mother's.'
But the king of Israel said to him, 'No;
it is the LORD who has summoned us,
three kings, only to be handed over to
Moab.' 14Elisha said, 'As the LORD of
hosts lives, whom I serve, were it not
that I have regard for King Jehoshaphat
of Judah, I would give you neither a look
nor a glance. 15But get me a musician.'
And then, while the musician was playing, the power of the LORD came on him.
16And he said, 'Thus says the LORD, "I
will make this wadi full of pools." 17For
thus says the LORD, "You shall see neither wind nor rain, but the wadi shall
be filled with water, so that you shall
drink, you, your cattle, and your animals." 18This is only a trifle in the sight
of the LORD, for he will also hand Moab
over to you. 19You shall conquer every
fortified city and every choice city; every good tree you shall fell, all springs of
water you shall stop up, and every good
piece of land you shall ruin with stones.'
20The next day, about the time of the
morning offering, suddenly water began to flow from the direction of Edom,
until the country was filled with water.
21 When all the Moabites heard that
the kings had come up to fight against
them, all who were able to put on armour, from the youngest to the oldest,
were called out and were drawn up at
the frontier. 22When they rose early in
the morning, and the sun shone upon
the water, the Moabites saw the water
opposite them as red as blood. 23They
said, 'This is blood; the kings must have
fought together, and killed one another.
Now then, Moab, to the spoil!' 24But
when they came to the camp of Israel,
the Israelites rose up and attacked the
Moabites, who fled before them; as they
entered Moab they continued the attack.[9] 25The cities they overturned, and
on every good piece of land everyone

[9] 3.24 Compare Gk Syr: Meaning of Heb uncertain

threw a stone, until it was covered; every spring of water they stopped up, and every good tree they felled. Only at Kir-hareseth did the stone walls remain, until the slingers surrounded and attacked it. [26]When the king of Moab saw that the battle was going against him, he took with him seven hundred swordsmen to break through, opposite the king of Edom; but they could not. [27]Then he took his firstborn son who was to succeed him, and offered him as a burnt-offering on the wall. And great wrath came upon Israel, so they withdrew from him and returned to their own land.

ELISHA AND THE WIDOW'S OIL

4 Now the wife of a member of the company of prophets[h] cried to Elisha, 'Your servant my husband is dead; and you know that your servant feared the LORD, but a creditor has come to take my two children as slaves.' [2]Elisha said to her, 'What shall I do for you? Tell me, what do you have in the house?' She answered, 'Your servant has nothing in the house, except a jar of oil.' [3]He said, 'Go outside, borrow vessels from all your neighbours, empty vessels and not just a few. [4]Then go in, and shut the door behind you and your children, and start pouring into all these vessels; when each is full, set it aside.' [5]So she left him and shut the door behind her and her children; they kept bringing vessels to her, and she kept pouring. [6]When the vessels were full, she said to her son, 'Bring me another vessel.' But he said to her, 'There are no more.' Then the oil stopped flowing. [7]She came and told the man of God, and he said, 'Go, sell the oil and pay your debts, and you and your children can live on the rest.'

ELISHA RAISES THE SHUNAMMITE'S SON

8 One day Elisha was passing through Shunem, where a wealthy woman lived, who urged him to have a meal. So whenever he passed that way, he would stop there for a meal. [9]She said to her husband, 'Look, I am sure that this man who regularly passes our way is a holy man of God. [10]Let us make a small roof chamber with walls, and put there for him a bed, a table, a chair, and a lamp, so that he can stay there whenever he comes to us.'

11 One day when he came there, he went up to the chamber and lay down there. [12]He said to his servant Gehazi, 'Call the Shunammite woman.' When he had called her, she stood before him. [13]He said to him, 'Say to her, Since you have taken all this trouble for us, what may be done for you? Would you have a word spoken on your behalf to the king or to the commander of the army?' She answered, 'I live among my own people.' [14]He said, 'What then may be done for her?' Gehazi answered, 'Well, she has no son, and her husband is old.' [15]He said, 'Call her.' When he had called her, she stood at the door. [16]He said, 'At this season, in due time, you shall embrace a son.' She replied, 'No, my lord, O man of God; do not deceive your servant.'

17 The woman conceived and bore a son at that season, in due time, as Elisha had declared to her.

18 When the child was older, he went out one day to his father among the reapers. [19]He complained to his father, 'Oh, my head, my head!' The father said to his servant, 'Carry him to his mother.' [20]He carried him and brought him to his mother; the child sat on her lap until noon, and he died. [21]She went up and laid him on the bed of the man of God, closed the door on him, and left. [22]Then she called to her husband, and said, 'Send me one of the servants and one of the donkeys, so that I may quickly go to the man of God and come back again.' [23]He said, 'Why go to him today? It is neither new moon nor sabbath.' She said, 'It will be all right.' [24]Then she saddled the donkey and said to her servant, 'Urge the animal on; do not hold back for me unless I tell you.' [25]So she set out, and came to the man of God at Mount Carmel.

When the man of God saw her coming, he said to Gehazi his servant, 'Look, there is the Shunammite woman; [26]run at once to meet her, and say to her, Are you all right? Is your husband all right? Is the child all right?' She answered, 'It is all right.' [27]When she came to the man of God at the mountain, she caught hold of his feet. Gehazi approached to push her away. But the man of God said, 'Let her alone, for she is in bitter distress; the LORD has hidden it from me and has not told me.' [28]Then she said, 'Did I ask my lord for a son? Did I not say, Do not mislead me?' [29]He said to Gehazi, 'Gird up your loins, and take my staff in your hand, and go. If you meet anyone, give

[h] 4.1 Heb *the sons of the prophets*

no greeting, and if anyone greets you,
do not answer; and lay my staff on the
face of the child.' 30Then the mother of
the child said, 'As the LORD lives, and as
you yourself live, I will not leave without you.' So he rose up and followed her.
31Gehazi went on ahead and laid the
staff on the face of the child, but there
was no sound or sign of life. He came
back to meet him and told him, 'The
child has not awakened.'

32 When Elisha came into the house,
he saw the child lying dead on his bed.
33So he went in and closed the door
on the two of them, and prayed to the
LORD. 34Then he got up on the bed[i]
and lay upon the child, putting his
mouth upon his mouth, his eyes upon
his eyes, and his hands upon his hands;
and while he lay bent over him, the
flesh of the child became warm. 35He
got down, walked once to and fro in
the room, then got up again and bent
over him; the child sneezed seven times,
and the child opened his eyes. 36Elisha[j]
summoned Gehazi and said, 'Call the
Shunammite woman.' So he called her.
When she came to him, he said, 'Take
your son.' 37She came and fell at his feet,
bowing to the ground; then she took her
son and left.

ELISHA PURIFIES THE POT OF STEW

38 When Elisha returned to Gilgal,
there was a famine in the land. As the
company of prophets was[k] sitting before him, he said to his servant, 'Put
the large pot on, and make some stew
for the company of prophets.'[l] 39One of
them went out into the field to gather
herbs; he found a wild vine and gathered from it a lapful of wild gourds,
and came and cut them up into the pot
of stew, not knowing what they were.
40They served some for the men to eat.
But while they were eating the stew,
they cried out, 'O man of God, there is
death in the pot!' They could not eat it.
41He said, 'Then bring some flour.' He
threw it into the pot, and said, 'Serve
the people and let them eat.' And there
was nothing harmful in the pot.

ELISHA FEEDS ONE HUNDRED MEN

42 A man came from Baal-shalishah,
bringing food from the first fruits to the
man of God: twenty loaves of barley and
fresh ears of grain in his sack. Elisha
said, 'Give it to the people and let them
eat.' 43But his servant said, 'How can I
set this before a hundred people?' So he
repeated, 'Give it to the people and let
them eat, for thus says the LORD, "They
shall eat and have some left." ' 44He set
it before them, they ate, and had some
left, according to the word of the LORD.

THE HEALING OF NAAMAN

5 Naaman, commander of the army
of the king of Aram, was a great
man and in high favour with his master, because by him the LORD had given
victory to Aram. The man, though a
mighty warrior, suffered from leprosy.[m] 2Now the Arameans on one of
their raids had taken a young girl captive from the land of Israel, and she
served Naaman's wife. 3She said to her
mistress, 'If only my lord were with the
prophet who is in Samaria! He would
cure him of his leprosy.'[n] 4So Naaman[o]
went in and told his lord just what the
girl from the land of Israel had said.
5And the king of Aram said, 'Go then,
and I will send along a letter to the king
of Israel.'

He went, taking with him ten talents
of silver, six thousand shekels of gold,
and ten sets of garments. 6He brought
the letter to the king of Israel, which
read, 'When this letter reaches you,
know that I have sent to you my servant
Naaman, that you may cure him of his
leprosy.'[p] 7When the king of Israel read
the letter, he tore his clothes and said,
'Am I God, to give death or life, that this
man sends word to me to cure a man of
his leprosy?[q] Just look and see how he is
trying to pick a quarrel with me.'

8 But when Elisha the man of God
heard that the king of Israel had torn his
clothes, he sent a message to the king,
'Why have you torn your clothes? Let
him come to me, that he may learn that
there is a prophet in Israel.' 9So Naaman
came with his horses and chariots, and
halted at the entrance of Elisha's house.
10Elisha sent a messenger to him, saying, 'Go, wash in the Jordan seven
times, and your flesh shall be restored
and you shall be clean.' 11But Naaman
became angry and went away, saying,
'I thought that for me he would surely
come out, and stand and call on the

[i] **4.34** Heb lacks *on the bed* [j] **4.36** Heb *he*
[k] **4.38** Heb *sons of the prophets were* [l] **4.38** Heb *sons of the prophets* [m] **5.1** A term for several skin diseases; precise meaning uncertain [n] **5.3** A term for several skin diseases; precise meaning uncertain [o] **5.4** Heb *he* [p] **5.6** A term for several skin diseases; precise meaning uncertain
[q] **5.7** A term for several skin diseases; precise meaning uncertain

name of the LORD his God, and would
wave his hand over the spot, and cure
the leprosy![r] 12Are not Abana[s] and Phar-
par, the rivers of Damascus, better than
all the waters of Israel? Could I not wash
in them, and be clean?' He turned and
went away in a rage. 13But his servants
approached and said to him, 'Father, if
the prophet had commanded you to do
something difficult, would you not have
done it? How much more, when all he
said to you was, "Wash, and be clean"?'
14So he went down and immersed himself seven times in the Jordan, according
to the word of the man of God; his flesh
was restored like the flesh of a young
boy, and he was clean.

15 Then he returned to the man of
God, he and all his company; he came
and stood before him and said, 'Now
I know that there is no God in all the
earth except in Israel; please accept a
present from your servant.' 16But he
said, 'As the LORD lives, whom I serve,
I will accept nothing!' He urged him to
accept, but he refused. 17Then Naaman
said, 'If not, please let two mule-loads
of earth be given to your servant; for
your servant will no longer offer burnt-
offering or sacrifice to any god except
the LORD. 18But may the LORD pardon
your servant on one count: when my
master goes into the house of Rimmon
to worship there, leaning on my arm,
and I bow down in the house of Rimmon, when I do bow down in the house
of Rimmon, may the LORD pardon your
servant on this one count.' 19He said to
him, 'Go in peace.'

GEHAZI'S GREED

But when Naaman had gone from
him a short distance, 20Gehazi, the servant of Elisha the man of God, thought,
'My master has let that Aramean Naaman off too lightly by not accepting
from him what he offered. As the LORD
lives, I will run after him and get something out of him.' 21So Gehazi went after
Naaman. When Naaman saw someone
running after him, he jumped down
from the chariot to meet him and said,
'Is everything all right?' 22He replied,
'Yes, but my master has sent me to say,
"Two members of a company of prophets[t] have just come to me from the hill
country of Ephraim; please give them a
talent of silver and two changes of clothing." ' 23Naaman said, 'Please accept two
talents.' He urged him, and tied up two
talents of silver in two bags, with two
changes of clothing, and gave them to
two of his servants, who carried them
in front of Gehazi.[u] 24When he came
to the citadel, he took the bags[v] from
them, and stored them inside; he dismissed the men, and they left.

25 He went in and stood before his
master; and Elisha said to him, 'Where
have you been, Gehazi?' He answered,
'Your servant has not gone anywhere
at all.' 26But he said to him, 'Did I not
go with you in spirit when someone left
his chariot to meet you? Is this a time
to accept money and to accept clothing, olive orchards and vineyards, sheep
and oxen, and male and female slaves?
27Therefore the leprosy[w] of Naaman
shall cling to you, and to your descendants for ever.' So he left his presence leprous,[x] as white as snow.

THE MIRACLE OF THE AXEHEAD

6 Now the company of prophets[y]
said to Elisha, 'As you see, the place
where we live under your charge is too
small for us. 2Let us go to the Jordan,
and let us collect logs there, one for each
of us, and build a place there for us to
live.' He answered, 'Do so.' 3Then one of
them said, 'Please come with your servants.' And he answered, 'I will.' 4So he
went with them. When they came to
the Jordan, they cut down trees. 5But
as one was felling a log, his axehead fell
into the water; he cried out, 'Alas, master! It was borrowed.' 6Then the man of
God said, 'Where did it fall?' When he
showed him the place, he cut off a stick,
and threw it in there, and made the iron
float. 7He said, 'Pick it up.' So he reached
out his hand and took it.

THE ARAMEAN ATTACK IS THWARTED

8 Once when the king of Aram was
at war with Israel, he took counsel with
his officers. He said, 'At such and such a
place shall be my camp.' 9But the man of
God sent word to the king of Israel, 'Take
care not to pass this place, because the
Arameans are going down there.' 10The
king of Israel sent word to the place of
which the man of God spoke. More than

[r] **5.11** A term for several skin diseases; precise meaning uncertain [s] **5.12** Another reading is *Amana* [t] **5.22** Heb *sons of the prophets*
[u] **5.23** Heb *him* [v] **5.24** Heb lacks *the bags*
[w] **5.27** A term for several skin diseases; precise meaning uncertain [x] **5.27** A term for several skin diseases; precise meaning uncertain
[y] **6.1** Heb *sons of the prophets*

once or twice he warned such a place[z] so
that it was on the alert.
11 The mind of the king of Aram
was greatly perturbed because of this;
he called his officers and said to them,
'Now tell me who among us sides with
the king of Israel?' 12 Then one of his officers said, 'No one, my lord king. It is Elisha, the prophet in Israel, who tells the
king of Israel the words that you speak
in your bedchamber.' 13 He said, 'Go and
find where he is; I will send and seize
him.' He was told, 'He is in Dothan.' 14 So
he sent horses and chariots there and
a great army; they came by night, and
surrounded the city.
15 When an attendant of the man
of God rose early in the morning and
went out, an army with horses and
chariots was all around the city. His
servant said, 'Alas, master! What shall
we do?' 16 He replied, 'Do not be afraid,
for there are more with us than there
are with them.' 17 Then Elisha prayed:
'O LORD, please open his eyes that he
may see.' So the LORD opened the eyes
of the servant, and he saw; the mountain was full of horses and chariots of
fire all around Elisha. 18 When the Arameans[a] came down against him, Elisha
prayed to the LORD, and said, 'Strike
this people, please, with blindness.' So
he struck them with blindness as Elisha
had asked. 19 Elisha said to them, 'This is
not the way, and this is not the city; follow me, and I will bring you to the man
whom you seek.' And he led them to Samaria.
20 As soon as they entered Samaria,
Elisha said, 'O LORD, open the eyes of
these men so that they may see.' The
LORD opened their eyes, and they saw
that they were inside Samaria. 21 When
the king of Israel saw them he said to
Elisha, 'Father, shall I kill them? Shall I
kill them?' 22 He answered, 'No! Did you
capture with your sword and your bow
those whom you want to kill? Set food
and water before them so that they may
eat and drink; and let them go to their
master.' 23 So he prepared for them a
great feast; after they ate and drank, he
sent them on their way, and they went
to their master. And the Arameans no
longer came raiding into the land of Israel.

BEN-HADAD'S SIEGE OF SAMARIA

24 Some time later King Ben-hadad
of Aram mustered his entire army; he
marched against Samaria and laid siege
to it. 25 As the siege continued, famine
in Samaria became so great that a donkey's head was sold for eighty shekels of
silver, and one-fourth of a kab of dove's
dung for five shekels of silver. 26 Now as
the king of Israel was walking on the
city wall, a woman cried out to him,
'Help, my lord king!' 27 He said, 'No! Let
the LORD help you. How can I help you?
From the threshing-floor or from the
wine press?' 28 But then the king asked
her, 'What is your complaint?' She answered, 'This woman said to me, "Give
up your son; we will eat him today, and
we will eat my son tomorrow." 29 So we
cooked my son and ate him. The next
day I said to her, "Give up your son and
we will eat him." But she has hidden her
son.' 30 When the king heard the words
of the woman he tore his clothes—now
since he was walking on the city wall,
the people could see that he had sackcloth on his body underneath— 31 and
he said, 'So may God do to me, and
more, if the head of Elisha son of Shaphat stays on his shoulders today.' 32 So
he dispatched a man from his presence.
Now Elisha was sitting in his house,
and the elders were sitting with him. Before the messenger arrived, Elisha said
to the elders, 'Are you aware that this
murderer has sent someone to take off
my head? When the messenger comes,
see that you shut the door and hold it
closed against him. Is not the sound of
his master's feet behind him?' 33 While
he was still speaking with them, the
king[b] came down to him and said, 'This
trouble is from the LORD! Why should I
7 hope in the LORD any longer?' 1 But
Elisha said, 'Hear the word of the
LORD: thus says the LORD, Tomorrow
about this time a measure of choice
meal shall be sold for a shekel, and two
measures of barley for a shekel, at the
gate of Samaria.' 2 Then the captain on
whose hand the king leaned said to the
man of God, 'Even if the LORD were to
make windows in the sky, could such a
thing happen?' But he said, 'You shall
see it with your own eyes, but you shall
not eat from it.'

THE ARAMEANS FLEE

3 Now there were four leprous[c] men
outside the city gate, who said to one
another, 'Why should we sit here until we die? 4 If we say, "Let us enter the

[z] 6.10 Heb *warned it* [a] 6.18 Heb *they*
[b] 6.33 See 7.2: Heb *messenger* [c] 7.3 A term for several skin diseases; precise meaning uncertain

city", the famine is in the city, and we
shall die there; but if we sit here, we
shall also die. Therefore, let us desert
to the Aramean camp; if they spare our
lives, we shall live; and if they kill us,
we shall but die.' 5So they arose at twilight to go to the Aramean camp; but
when they came to the edge of the Aramean camp, there was no one there at
all. 6For the Lord had caused the Aramean army to hear the sound of chariots and of horses, the sound of a great
army, so that they said to one another,
'The king of Israel has hired the kings of
the Hittites and the kings of Egypt to
fight against us.' 7So they fled away in
the twilight and abandoned their tents,
their horses, and their donkeys, leaving
the camp just as it was, and fled for their
lives. 8When these leprous[d] men had
come to the edge of the camp, they went
into a tent, ate and drank, carried off silver, gold, and clothing, and went and
hid them. Then they came back, entered
another tent, carried off things from it,
and went and hid them.

9 Then they said to one another,
'What we are doing is wrong. This is a
day of good news; if we are silent and
wait until the morning light, we will
be found guilty; therefore let us go and
tell the king's household.' 10So they
came and called to the gatekeepers of
the city, and told them, 'We went to the
Aramean camp, but there was no one
to be seen or heard there, nothing but
the horses tied, the donkeys tied, and
the tents as they were.' 11Then the gatekeepers called out and proclaimed it to
the king's household. 12The king got up
in the night, and said to his servants, 'I
will tell you what the Arameans have
prepared against us. They know that we
are starving; so they have left the camp
to hide themselves in the open country,
thinking, "When they come out of the
city, we shall take them alive and get
into the city."' 13One of his servants said,
'Let some men take five of the remaining horses, since those left here will suffer the fate of the whole multitude of Israel that have perished already;[e] let us
send and find out.' 14So they took two
mounted men, and the king sent them
after the Aramean army, saying, 'Go
and find out.' 15So they went after them
as far as the Jordan; the whole way was
littered with garments and equipment
that the Arameans had thrown away
in their haste. So the messengers returned, and told the king.

16 Then the people went out, and
plundered the camp of the Arameans.
So a measure of choice meal was sold
for a shekel, and two measures of barley for a shekel, according to the word
of the LORD. 17Now the king had appointed the captain on whose hand he
leaned to have charge of the gate; the
people trampled him to death in the
gate, just as the man of God had said
when the king came down to him.
18For when the man of God had said
to the king, 'Two measures of barley
shall be sold for a shekel, and a measure of choice meal for a shekel, about
this time tomorrow in the gate of Samaria', 19the captain had answered the
man of God, 'Even if the LORD were to
make windows in the sky, could such a
thing happen?' And he had answered,
'You shall see it with your own eyes,
but you shall not eat from it.' 20It did
indeed happen to him; the people trampled him to death in the gate.

THE SHUNAMMITE WOMAN'S LAND RESTORED

8 Now Elisha had said to the woman
whose son he had restored to life,
'Get up and go with your household,
and settle wherever you can; for the
LORD has called for a famine, and it will
come on the land for seven years.' 2So
the woman got up and did according to
the word of the man of God; she went
with her household and settled in the
land of the Philistines for seven years.
3At the end of the seven years, when
the woman returned from the land of
the Philistines, she set out to appeal
to the king for her house and her land.
4Now the king was talking with Gehazi
the servant of the man of God, saying,
'Tell me all the great things that Elisha
has done.' 5While he was telling the king
how Elisha had restored a dead person
to life, the woman whose son he had
restored to life appealed to the king for
her house and her land. Gehazi said, 'My
lord king, here is the woman, and here
is her son whom Elisha restored to life.'
6When the king questioned the woman,
she told him. So the king appointed an
official for her, saying, 'Restore all that
was hers, together with all the revenue
of the fields from the day that she left
the land until now.'

[d] 7.8 A term for several skin diseases; precise meaning uncertain [e] 7.13 Compare Gk Syr Vg: Meaning of Heb uncertain

DEATH OF BEN-HADAD

7 Elisha went to Damascus while
King Ben-hadad of Aram was ill. When
it was told him, 'The man of God has
come here', 8the king said to Hazael,
'Take a present with you and go to meet
the man of God. Inquire of the LORD
through him, whether I shall recover
from this illness.' 9So Hazael went to
meet him, taking a present with him,
all kinds of goods of Damascus, forty
camel loads. When he entered and stood
before him, he said, 'Your son King Ben-
hadad of Aram has sent me to you, saying, "Shall I recover from this illness?" '
10Elisha said to him, 'Go, say to him,
"You shall certainly recover"; but the
LORD has shown me that he shall certainly die.' 11He fixed his gaze and stared
at him, until he was ashamed. Then
the man of God wept. 12Hazael asked,
'Why does my lord weep?' He answered,
'Because I know the evil that you will
do to the people of Israel; you will set
their fortresses on fire, you will kill
their young men with the sword, dash
in pieces their little ones, and rip up
their pregnant women.' 13Hazael said,
'What is your servant, who is a mere
dog, that he should do this great thing?'
Elisha answered, 'The LORD has shown
me that you are to be king over Aram.'
14Then he left Elisha, and went to his
master Ben-hadad,[f] who said to him,
'What did Elisha say to you?' And he
answered, 'He told me that you would
certainly recover.' 15But the next day he
took the bed-cover and dipped it in water and spread it over the king's face, until he died. And Hazael succeeded him.

JEHORAM REIGNS OVER JUDAH

16 In the fifth year of King Joram son
of Ahab of Israel,[g] Jehoram son of King
Jehoshaphat of Judah began to reign.
17He was thirty-two years old when he
became king, and he reigned for eight
years in Jerusalem. 18He walked in the
way of the kings of Israel, as the house
of Ahab had done, for the daughter of
Ahab was his wife. He did what was evil
in the sight of the LORD. 19Yet the LORD
would not destroy Judah, for the sake of
his servant David, since he had promised to give a lamp to him and to his descendants for ever.

20 In his days Edom revolted against
the rule of Judah, and set up a king of
their own. 21Then Joram crossed over
to Zair with all his chariots. He set out
by night and attacked the Edomites and
their chariot commanders who had surrounded him;[h] but his army fled home.
22So Edom has been in revolt against
the rule of Judah to this day. Libnah also
revolted at the same time. 23Now the
rest of the acts of Joram, and all that he
did, are they not written in the Book of
the Annals of the Kings of Judah? 24So
Joram slept with his ancestors, and was
buried with them in the city of David;
his son Ahaziah succeeded him.

AHAZIAH REIGNS OVER JUDAH

25 In the twelfth year of King Joram
son of Ahab of Israel, Ahaziah son of
King Jehoram of Judah began to reign.
26Ahaziah was twenty-two years old
when he began to reign; he reigned for
one year in Jerusalem. His mother's
name was Athaliah, a granddaughter
of King Omri of Israel. 27He also walked
in the way of the house of Ahab, doing
what was evil in the sight of the LORD,
as the house of Ahab had done, for he
was son-in-law to the house of Ahab.

28 He went with Joram son of Ahab
to wage war against King Hazael of
Aram at Ramoth-gilead, where the
Arameans wounded Joram. 29King Joram returned to be healed in Jezreel
of the wounds that the Arameans had
inflicted on him at Ramah, when he
fought against King Hazael of Aram.
King Ahaziah son of Jehoram of Judah
went down to see Joram son of Ahab in
Jezreel, because he was wounded.

ANOINTING OF JEHU

9 Then the prophet Elisha called a
member of the company of proph-
ets[i] and said to him, 'Gird up your loins;
take this flask of oil in your hand, and
go to Ramoth-gilead. 2When you arrive,
look there for Jehu son of Jehoshaphat,
son of Nimshi; go in and get him to
leave his companions, and take him into
an inner chamber. 3Then take the flask
of oil, pour it on his head, and say, "Thus
says the LORD: I anoint you king over
Israel." Then open the door and flee; do
not linger.'

4 So the young man, the young
prophet, went to Ramoth-gilead. 5He arrived while the commanders of the army
were in council, and he announced, 'I
have a message for you, commander.'
'For which one of us?' asked Jehu. 'For

[f] **8.14** Heb lacks *Ben-hadad* [g] **8.16** Gk Syr: Heb adds *Jehoshaphat being king of Judah,*
[h] **8.21** Meaning of Heb uncertain [i] **9.1** Heb *sons of the prophets*

you, commander.' 6So Jehu[j] got up and
went inside; the young man poured the
oil on his head, saying to him, 'Thus
says the LORD the God of Israel: I anoint
you king over the people of the LORD,
over Israel. 7You shall strike down the
house of your master Ahab, so that I
may avenge on Jezebel the blood of my
servants the prophets, and the blood of
all the servants of the LORD. 8For the
whole house of Ahab shall perish; I will
cut off from Ahab every male, bond or
free, in Israel. 9I will make the house of
Ahab like the house of Jeroboam son of
Nebat, and like the house of Baasha son
of Ahijah. 10The dogs shall eat Jezebel in
the territory of Jezreel, and no one shall
bury her.' Then he opened the door and
fled.

11 When Jehu came back to his master's officers, they said to him, 'Is everything all right? Why did that madman
come to you?' He answered them, 'You
know the sort and how they babble.'
12They said, 'Liar! Come on, tell us!' So
he said, 'This is just what he said to me:
"Thus says the LORD, I anoint you king
over Israel."' 13Then hurriedly they all
took their cloaks and spread them for
him on the bare[k] steps; and they blew
the trumpet, and proclaimed, 'Jehu is
king.'

JORAM OF ISRAEL KILLED

14 Thus Jehu son of Jehoshaphat son
of Nimshi conspired against Joram. Joram with all Israel had been on guard
at Ramoth-gilead against King Hazael
of Aram; 15but King Joram had returned
to be healed in Jezreel of the wounds
that the Arameans had inflicted on
him, when he fought against King Hazael of Aram. So Jehu said, 'If this is your
wish, then let no one slip out of the city
to go and tell the news in Jezreel.' 16Then
Jehu mounted his chariot and went to
Jezreel, where Joram was lying ill. King
Ahaziah of Judah had come down to
visit Joram.

17 In Jezreel, the sentinel standing
on the tower spied the company of Jehu
arriving, and said, 'I see a company.' Joram said, 'Take a horseman; send him
to meet them, and let him say, "Is it
peace?"' 18So the horseman went to
meet him; he said, 'Thus says the king,
"Is it peace?"' Jehu responded, 'What
have you to do with peace? Fall in behind
me.' The sentinel reported, saying, 'The
messenger reached them, but he is not
coming back.' 19Then he sent out a second horseman, who came to them and
said, 'Thus says the king, "Is it peace?"'
Jehu answered, 'What have you to do
with peace? Fall in behind me.' 20Again
the sentinel reported, 'He reached them,
but he is not coming back. It looks like
the driving of Jehu son of Nimshi; for he
drives like a maniac.'

21 Joram said, 'Get ready.' And they
got his chariot ready. Then King Joram
of Israel and King Ahaziah of Judah set
out, each in his chariot, and went to
meet Jehu; they met him at the property
of Naboth the Jezreelite. 22When Joram
saw Jehu, he said, 'Is it peace, Jehu?' He
answered, 'What peace can there be,
so long as the many whoredoms and
sorceries of your mother Jezebel continue?' 23Then Joram reined about and
fled, saying to Ahaziah, 'Treason, Ahaziah!' 24Jehu drew his bow with all his
strength, and shot Joram between the
shoulders, so that the arrow pierced his
heart; and he sank in his chariot. 25Jehu
said to his aide Bidkar, 'Lift him out,
and throw him on the plot of ground
belonging to Naboth the Jezreelite; for
remember, when you and I rode side by
side behind his father Ahab, how the
LORD uttered this oracle against him:
26"For the blood of Naboth and for the
blood of his children that I saw yesterday, says the LORD, I swear I will repay
you on this very plot of ground." Now
therefore lift him out and throw him on
the plot of ground, in accordance with
the word of the LORD.'

AHAZIAH OF JUDAH KILLED

27 When King Ahaziah of Judah saw
this, he fled in the direction of Beth-haggan. Jehu pursued him, saying,
'Shoot him also!' And they shot him[l] in
the chariot at the ascent to Gur, which is
by Ibleam. Then he fled to Megiddo, and
died there. 28His officers carried him in
a chariot to Jerusalem, and buried him
in his tomb with his ancestors in the
city of David.

29 In the eleventh year of Joram son
of Ahab, Ahaziah began to reign over
Judah.

JEZEBEL'S VIOLENT DEATH

30 When Jehu came to Jezreel, Jezebel heard of it; she painted her eyes,
and adorned her head, and looked out of
the window. 31As Jehu entered the gate,

[j] 9.6 Heb *he* [k] 9.13 Meaning of Heb uncertain
[l] 9.27 Syr Vg Compare Gk: Heb lacks *and they shot him*

she said, 'Is it peace, Zimri, murderer
of your master?' 32He looked up to the
window and said, 'Who is on my side?
Who?' Two or three eunuchs looked out
at him. 33He said, 'Throw her down.'
So they threw her down; some of her
blood spattered on the wall and on the
horses, which trampled on her. 34Then
he went in and ate and drank; he said,
'See to that cursed woman and bury
her; for she is a king's daughter.' 35But
when they went to bury her, they found
no more of her than the skull and the
feet and the palms of her hands. 36When
they came back and told him, he said,
'This is the word of the LORD, which he
spoke by his servant Elijah the Tishbite,
"In the territory of Jezreel the dogs shall
eat the flesh of Jezebel; 37the corpse of
Jezebel shall be like dung on the field in
the territory of Jezreel, so that no one
can say, This is Jezebel."'

MASSACRE OF AHAB'S DESCENDANTS

10 Now Ahab had seventy sons in
Samaria. So Jehu wrote letters
and sent them to Samaria, to the rulers of Jezreel,[m] to the elders, and to the
guardians of the sons of[n] Ahab, saying,
2'Since your master's sons are with you
and you have at your disposal chariots
and horses, a fortified city, and weapons, 3select the son of your master who
is the best qualified, set him on his father's throne, and fight for your master's house.' 4But they were utterly terrified and said, 'Look, two kings could
not withstand him; how then can we
stand?' 5So the steward of the palace,
and the governor of the city, along with
the elders and the guardians, sent word
to Jehu: 'We are your servants; we will
do anything you say. We will not make
anyone king; do whatever you think
right.' 6Then he wrote them a second
letter, saying, 'If you are on my side,
and if you are ready to obey me, take the
heads of your master's sons and come
to me at Jezreel tomorrow at this time.'
Now the king's sons, seventy persons,
were with the leaders of the city, who
were charged with their upbringing.
7When the letter reached them, they
took the king's sons and killed them,
seventy persons; they put their heads
in baskets and sent them to him at Jezreel. 8When the messenger came and
told him, 'They have brought the heads
of the king's sons', he said, 'Lay them in
two heaps at the entrance of the gate
until the morning.' 9Then in the morning when he went out, he stood and said
to all the people, 'You are innocent. It
was I who conspired against my master
and killed him; but who struck down all
these? 10Know then that there shall fall
to the earth nothing of the word of the
LORD, which the LORD spoke concerning the house of Ahab; for the LORD has
done what he said through his servant
Elijah.' 11So Jehu killed all who were left
of the house of Ahab in Jezreel, all his
leaders, close friends, and priests, until
he left him no survivor.

12 Then he set out and went to Samaria. On the way, when he was at
Beth-eked of the Shepherds, 13Jehu met
relatives of King Ahaziah of Judah and
said, 'Who are you?' They answered, 'We
are kin of Ahaziah; we have come down
to visit the royal princes and the sons
of the queen mother.' 14He said, 'Take
them alive.' They took them alive, and
slaughtered them at the pit of Beth-
eked, forty-two in all; he spared none of
them.

15 When he left there, he met Jehonadab son of Rechab coming to meet
him; he greeted him, and said to him,
'Is your heart as true to mine as mine
is to yours?'[o] Jehonadab answered, 'It is.'
Jehu said,[p] 'If it is, give me your hand.'
So he gave him his hand. Jehu took him
up with him into the chariot. 16He said,
'Come with me, and see my zeal for the
LORD.' So he[q] had him ride in his chariot. 17When he came to Samaria, he
killed all who were left to Ahab in Samaria, until he had wiped them out, according to the word of the LORD that he
spoke to Elijah.

SLAUGHTER OF WORSHIPPERS OF BAAL

18 Then Jehu assembled all the people and said to them, 'Ahab offered Baal
small service; but Jehu will offer much
more. 19Now therefore summon to me
all the prophets of Baal, all his worshippers, and all his priests; let none be
missing, for I have a great sacrifice to offer to Baal; whoever is missing shall not
live.' But Jehu was acting with cunning
in order to destroy the worshippers of
Baal. 20Jehu decreed, 'Sanctify a solemn
assembly for Baal.' So they proclaimed
it. 21Jehu sent word throughout all

[m] 10.1 Or *of the city*; Vg Compare Gk [n] 10.1 Gk: Heb lacks *of the sons of* [o] 10.15 Gk: Heb *Is it right with your heart, as my heart is with your heart?* [p] 10.15 Gk: Heb lacks *Jehu said*
[q] 10.16 Gk Syr Tg: Heb *they*

Israel; all the worshippers of Baal came, so that there was no one left who did not come. They entered the temple of Baal, until the temple of Baal was filled from wall to wall. 22He said to the keeper of the wardrobe, 'Bring out the vestments for all the worshippers of Baal.' So he brought out the vestments for them. 23Then Jehu entered the temple of Baal with Jehonadab son of Rechab; he said to the worshippers of Baal, 'Search and see that there is no worshipper of the LORD here among you, but only worshippers of Baal.' 24Then they proceeded to offer sacrifices and burnt-offerings.

Now Jehu had stationed eighty men outside, saying, 'Whoever allows any of those to escape whom I deliver into your hands shall forfeit his life.' 25As soon as he had finished presenting the burnt-offering, Jehu said to the guards and to the officers, 'Come in and kill them; let no one escape.' So they put them to the sword. The guards and the officers threw them out, and then went into the citadel of the temple of Baal. 26They brought out the pillar[r] that was in the temple of Baal, and burned it. 27Then they demolished the pillar of Baal, and destroyed the temple of Baal, and made it a latrine to this day.

28 Thus Jehu wiped out Baal from Israel. 29But Jehu did not turn aside from the sins of Jeroboam son of Nebat, which he caused Israel to commit—the golden calves that were in Bethel and in Dan. 30The LORD said to Jehu, 'Because you have done well in carrying out what I consider right, and in accordance with all that was in my heart have dealt with the house of Ahab, your sons of the fourth generation shall sit on the throne of Israel.' 31But Jehu was not careful to follow the law of the LORD the God of Israel with all his heart; he did not turn from the sins of Jeroboam, which he caused Israel to commit.

DEATH OF JEHU

32 In those days the LORD began to trim off parts of Israel. Hazael defeated them throughout the territory of Israel: 33from the Jordan eastwards, all the land of Gilead, the Gadites, the Reubenites, and the Manassites, from Aroer, which is by the Wadi Arnon, that is, Gilead and Bashan. 34Now the rest of the acts of Jehu, all that he did, and all his power, are they not written in the Book of the Annals of the Kings of Israel? 35So Jehu slept with his ancestors, and they buried him in Samaria. His son Jehoahaz succeeded him. 36The time that Jehu reigned over Israel in Samaria was twenty-eight years.

ATHALIAH REIGNS OVER JUDAH

11 Now when Athaliah, Ahaziah's mother, saw that her son was dead, she set about to destroy all the royal family. 2But Jehosheba, King Joram's daughter, Ahaziah's sister, took Joash son of Ahaziah, and stole him away from among the king's children who were about to be killed; she put[s] him and his nurse in a bedroom. Thus she[t] hid him from Athaliah, so that he was not killed; 3he remained with her for six years, hidden in the house of the LORD, while Athaliah reigned over the land.

JEHOIADA ANOINTS THE CHILD JOASH

4 But in the seventh year Jehoiada summoned the captains of the Carites and of the guards and had them come to him in the house of the LORD. He made a covenant with them and put them under oath in the house of the LORD; then he showed them the king's son. 5He commanded them, 'This is what you are to do: one-third of you, those who go off duty on the sabbath and guard the king's house 6(another third being at the gate Sur and a third at the gate behind the guards), shall guard the palace; 7and your two divisions that come on duty in force on the sabbath and guard the house of the LORD[u] 8shall surround the king, each with weapons in hand; and whoever approaches the ranks is to be killed. Be with the king in his comings and goings.'

9 The captains did according to all that the priest Jehoiada commanded; each brought his men who were to go off duty on the sabbath, with those who were to come on duty on the sabbath, and came to the priest Jehoiada. 10The priest delivered to the captains the spears and shields that had been King David's, which were in the house of the LORD; 11the guards stood, every man with his weapons in his hand, from the south side of the house to the north side of the house, around the altar and the house, to guard the king on every side.

[r] **10.26** Gk Vg Syr Tg: Heb *pillars* [s] **11.2** With 2 Chr 22.11: Heb lacks *she put* [t] **11.2** Gk Syr Vg Compare 2 Chr 22.11: Heb *they* [u] **11.7** Heb *the LORD to the king*

12Then he brought out the king's son,
put the crown on him, and gave him the
covenant;[v] they proclaimed him king,
and anointed him; they clapped their
hands and shouted, 'Long live the king!'

DEATH OF ATHALIAH

13 When Athaliah heard the noise of
the guard and of the people, she went
into the house of the LORD to the people; 14when she looked, there was the
king standing by the pillar, according
to custom, with the captains and the
trumpeters beside the king, and all the
people of the land rejoicing and blowing trumpets. Athaliah tore her clothes
and cried, 'Treason! Treason!' 15Then the
priest Jehoiada commanded the captains who were set over the army, 'Bring
her out between the ranks, and kill with
the sword anyone who follows her.' For
the priest said, 'Let her not be killed in
the house of the LORD.' 16So they laid
hands on her; she went through the
horses' entrance to the king's house,
and there she was put to death.

17 Jehoiada made a covenant between the LORD and the king and people, that they should be the LORD's
people; also between the king and the
people. 18Then all the people of the land
went to the house of Baal, and tore it
down; his altars and his images they
broke in pieces, and they killed Mattan, the priest of Baal, before the altars.
The priest posted guards over the house
of the LORD. 19He took the captains,
the Carites, the guards, and all the
people of the land; then they brought
the king down from the house of the
LORD, marching through the gate of
the guards to the king's house. He took
his seat on the throne of the kings. 20So
all the people of the land rejoiced; and
the city was quiet after Athaliah had
been killed with the sword at the king's
house.

21 [w]Jehoash[x] was seven years old
when he began to reign.

THE TEMPLE REPAIRED

12 In the seventh year of Jehu, Jehoash began to reign; he reigned
for forty years in Jerusalem. His mother's name was Zibiah of Beer-sheba. 2Je-
hoash did what was right in the sight of
the LORD all his days, because the priest
Jehoiada instructed him. 3Nevertheless,
the high places were not taken away;
the people continued to sacrifice and
make offerings on the high places.

4 Jehoash said to the priests, 'All the
money offered as sacred donations that
is brought into the house of the LORD,
the money for which each person is
assessed—the money from the assessment of persons—and the money from
the voluntary offerings brought into
the house of the LORD, 5let the priests
receive from each of the donors; and let
them repair the house wherever any
need of repairs is discovered.' 6But by
the twenty-third year of King Jehoash
the priests had made no repairs to the
house. 7Therefore King Jehoash summoned the priest Jehoiada with the
other priests and said to them, 'Why
are you not repairing the house? Now
therefore do not accept any more money
from your donors but hand it over for
the repair of the house.' 8So the priests
agreed that they would neither accept
more money from the people nor repair
the house.

9 Then the priest Jehoiada took a
chest, made a hole in its lid, and set it
beside the altar on the right side as
one entered the house of the LORD; the
priests who guarded the threshold put
in it all the money that was brought
into the house of the LORD. 10Whenever
they saw that there was a great deal of
money in the chest, the king's secretary
and the high priest went up, counted
the money that was found in the house
of the LORD, and tied it up in bags.
11They would give the money that was
weighed out into the hands of the workers who had the oversight of the house
of the LORD; then they paid it out to the
carpenters and the builders who worked
on the house of the LORD, 12to the masons and the stonecutters, as well as to
buy timber and quarried stone for making repairs on the house of the LORD, as
well as for any outlay for repairs of the
house. 13But for the house of the LORD
no basins of silver, snuffers, bowls,
trumpets, or any vessels of gold, or of
silver, were made from the money that
was brought into the house of the LORD,
14for that was given to the workers who
were repairing the house of the LORD
with it. 15They did not ask for an account
from those into whose hand they delivered the money to pay out to the workers, for they dealt honestly. 16The money
from the guilt-offerings and the money
from the sin-offerings was not brought

[v] **11.12** Or *treaty or testimony*; Heb *eduth*
[w] **11.21** Ch 12.1 in Heb [x] **11.21** Another spelling is *Joash*; see verse 19

into the house of the LORD; it belonged
to the priests.

HAZAEL THREATENS JERUSALEM

17 At that time King Hazael of Aram
went up, fought against Gath, and took
it. But when Hazael set his face to go up
against Jerusalem, 18 King Jehoash of
Judah took all the votive gifts that Jehoshaphat, Jehoram, and Ahaziah, his
ancestors, the kings of Judah, had dedicated, as well as his own votive gifts,
all the gold that was found in the treasuries of the house of the LORD and of
the king's house, and sent these to King
Hazael of Aram. Then Hazael withdrew
from Jerusalem.

DEATH OF JOASH

19 Now the rest of the acts of Joash,
and all that he did, are they not written
in the Book of the Annals of the Kings
of Judah? 20 His servants arose, made a
conspiracy, and killed Joash in the house
of Millo, on the way that goes down to
Silla. 21 It was Jozacar son of Shimeath
and Jehozabad son of Shomer, his servants, who struck him down, so that he
died. He was buried with his ancestors
in the city of David; then his son Amaziah succeeded him.

JEHOAHAZ REIGNS OVER ISRAEL

13 In the twenty-third year of
King Joash son of Ahaziah of
Judah, Jehoahaz son of Jehu began to
reign over Israel in Samaria; he reigned
for seventeen years. 2 He did what was
evil in the sight of the LORD, and followed the sins of Jeroboam son of Nebat, which he caused Israel to sin; he
did not depart from them. 3 The anger
of the LORD was kindled against Israel,
so that he gave them repeatedly into
the hand of King Hazael of Aram, then
into the hand of Ben-hadad son of Hazael. 4 But Jehoahaz entreated the LORD,
and the LORD heeded him; for he saw
the oppression of Israel, how the king
of Aram oppressed them. 5 Therefore
the LORD gave Israel a saviour, so that
they escaped from the hand of the Arameans; and the people of Israel lived
in their homes as formerly. 6 Nevertheless, they did not depart from the sins of
the house of Jeroboam, which he caused
Israel to sin, but walked[y] in them; the
sacred pole[z] also remained in Samaria.
7 So Jehoahaz was left with an army of
not more than fifty horsemen, ten chariots and ten thousand foot-soldiers; for
the king of Aram had destroyed them
and made them like the dust at threshing. 8 Now the rest of the acts of Jehoahaz and all that he did, including his
might, are they not written in the Book
of the Annals of the Kings of Israel? 9 So
Jehoahaz slept with his ancestors, and
they buried him in Samaria; then his
son Joash succeeded him.

JEHOASH REIGNS OVER ISRAEL

10 In the thirty-seventh year of King
Joash of Judah, Jehoash son of Jehoahaz
began to reign over Israel in Samaria;
he reigned for sixteen years. 11 He also
did what was evil in the sight of the
LORD; he did not depart from all the
sins of Jeroboam son of Nebat, which
he caused Israel to sin, but he walked in
them. 12 Now the rest of the acts of Joash, and all that he did, as well as the
might with which he fought against
King Amaziah of Judah, are they not
written in the Book of the Annals of the
Kings of Israel? 13 So Joash slept with
his ancestors, and Jeroboam sat upon
his throne; Joash was buried in Samaria
with the kings of Israel.

DEATH OF ELISHA

14 Now when Elisha had fallen sick
with the illness of which he was to die,
King Joash of Israel went down to him,
and wept before him, crying, 'My father,
my father! The chariots of Israel and its
horsemen!' 15 Elisha said to him, 'Take a
bow and arrows'; so he took a bow and
arrows. 16 Then he said to the king of Israel, 'Draw the bow'; and he drew it. Elisha laid his hands on the king's hands.
17 Then he said, 'Open the window to
the east'; and he opened it. Elisha said,
'Shoot'; and he shot. Then he said, 'The
LORD's arrow of victory, the arrow of
victory over Aram! For you shall fight
the Arameans in Aphek until you have
made an end of them.' 18 He continued,
'Take the arrows'; and he took them.
He said to the king of Israel, 'Strike
the ground with them'; he struck three
times, and stopped. 19 Then the man of
God was angry with him, and said, 'You
should have struck five or six times; then
you would have struck down Aram until
you had made an end of it, but now you
will strike down Aram only three times.'

20 So Elisha died, and they buried
him. Now bands of Moabites used to in-

[y] **13.6** Gk Syr Tg Vg: Heb *he walked* [z] **13.6** Heb *Asherah*

vade the land in the spring of the year.
21 As a man was being buried, a marauding band was seen and the man was
thrown into the grave of Elisha; as soon
as the man touched the bones of Elisha,
he came to life and stood on his feet.

ISRAEL RECAPTURES CITIES FROM ARAM

22 Now King Hazael of Aram oppressed Israel all the days of Jehoahaz.
23 But the LORD was gracious to them
and had compassion on them; he turned
towards them, because of his covenant
with Abraham, Isaac, and Jacob, and
would not destroy them; nor has he banished them from his presence until now.
24 When King Hazael of Aram died,
his son Ben-hadad succeeded him.
25 Then Jehoash son of Jehoahaz took
again from Ben-hadad son of Hazael the
towns that he had taken from his father
Jehoahaz in war. Three times Joash defeated him and recovered the towns of
Israel.

AMAZIAH REIGNS OVER JUDAH

14 In the second year of King Joash son of Joahaz of Israel, King
Amaziah son of Joash of Judah, began
to reign. 2 He was twenty-five years old
when he began to reign, and he reigned
for twenty-nine years in Jerusalem. His
mother's name was Jehoaddin of Jerusalem. 3 He did what was right in the sight
of the LORD, yet not like his ancestor
David; in all things he did as his father
Joash had done. 4 But the high places
were not removed; the people still sacrificed and made offerings on the high
places. 5 As soon as the royal power was
firmly in his hand he killed his servants who had murdered his father the
king. 6 But he did not put to death the
children of the murderers; according to
what is written in the book of the law
of Moses, where the LORD commanded,
'The parents shall not be put to death
for the children, or the children be put
to death for the parents; but all shall be
put to death for their own sins.'
7 He killed ten thousand Edomites
in the Valley of Salt and took Sela by
storm; he called it Jokthe-el, which is its
name to this day.
8 Then Amaziah sent messengers to
King Jehoash son of Jehoahaz, son of
Jehu, of Israel, saying, 'Come, let us look
one another in the face.' 9 King Jehoash
of Israel sent word to King Amaziah of
Judah, 'A thornbush on Lebanon sent to
a cedar on Lebanon, saying, "Give your
daughter to my son for a wife"; but a
wild animal of Lebanon passed by and
trampled down the thornbush. 10 You
have indeed defeated Edom, and your
heart has lifted you up. Be content with
your glory, and stay at home; for why
should you provoke trouble so that you
fall, you and Judah with you?'
11 But Amaziah would not listen. So
King Jehoash of Israel went up; he and
King Amaziah of Judah faced one another in battle at Beth-shemesh, which
belongs to Judah. 12 Judah was defeated
by Israel; everyone fled home. 13 King Jehoash of Israel captured King Amaziah
of Judah son of Jehoash, son of Ahaziah,
at Beth-shemesh; he came to Jerusalem,
and broke down the wall of Jerusalem
from the Ephraim Gate to the Corner
Gate, a distance of four hundred cubits.
14 He seized all the gold and silver, and
all the vessels that were found in the
house of the LORD and in the treasuries
of the king's house, as well as hostages;
then he returned to Samaria.
15 Now the rest of the acts that Jehoash did, his might, and how he fought
with King Amaziah of Judah, are they
not written in the Book of the Annals
of the Kings of Israel? 16 Jehoash slept
with his ancestors, and was buried in
Samaria with the kings of Israel; then
his son Jeroboam succeeded him.
17 King Amaziah son of Joash of Judah lived for fifteen years after the death
of King Jehoash son of Jehoahaz of Israel. 18 Now the rest of the deeds of Amaziah, are they not written in the Book of
the Annals of the Kings of Judah? 19 They
made a conspiracy against him in Jerusalem, and he fled to Lachish. But they
sent after him to Lachish, and killed him
there. 20 They brought him on horses; he
was buried in Jerusalem with his ancestors in the city of David. 21 All the people
of Judah took Azariah, who was sixteen
years old, and made him king to succeed
his father Amaziah. 22 He rebuilt Elath
and restored it to Judah, after King Amaziah[a] slept with his ancestors.

JEROBOAM, SON OF JOASH, REIGNS OVER ISRAEL

23 In the fifteenth year of King
Amaziah son of Joash of Judah, King
Jeroboam son of Joash of Israel began to
reign in Samaria; he reigned for forty-
one years. 24 He did what was evil in

[a] 14.22 Heb *the king*

the sight of the LORD; he did not depart from all the sins of Jeroboam son of Nebat, which he caused Israel to sin. 25 He restored the border of Israel from Lebo-hamath as far as the Sea of the Arabah, according to the word of the LORD, the God of Israel, which he spoke by his servant Jonah son of Amittai, the prophet, who was from Gath-hepher. 26 For the LORD saw that the distress of Israel was very bitter; there was no one left, bond or free, and no one to help Israel. 27 But the LORD had not said that he would blot out the name of Israel from under heaven, so he saved them by the hand of Jeroboam son of Joash.

28 Now the rest of the acts of Jeroboam, and all that he did, and his might, how he fought, and how he recovered for Israel Damascus and Hamath, which had belonged to Judah, are they not written in the Book of the Annals of the Kings of Israel? 29 Jeroboam slept with his ancestors, the kings of Israel; his son Zechariah succeeded him.

AZARIAH REIGNS OVER JUDAH

15 In the twenty-seventh year of King Jeroboam of Israel King Azariah son of Amaziah of Judah began to reign. 2 He was sixteen years old when he began to reign, and he reigned for fifty-two years in Jerusalem. His mother's name was Jecoliah of Jerusalem. 3 He did what was right in the sight of the LORD, just as his father Amaziah had done. 4 Nevertheless, the high places were not taken away; the people still sacrificed and made offerings on the high places. 5 The LORD struck the king, so that he was leprous[b] to the day of his death, and lived in a separate house. Jotham the king's son was in charge of the palace, governing the people of the land. 6 Now the rest of the acts of Azariah, and all that he did, are they not written in the Book of the Annals of the Kings of Judah? 7 Azariah slept with his ancestors; they buried him with his ancestors in the city of David; his son Jotham succeeded him.

ZECHARIAH REIGNS OVER ISRAEL

8 In the thirty-eighth year of King Azariah of Judah, Zechariah son of Jeroboam reigned over Israel in Samaria for six months. 9 He did what was evil in the sight of the LORD, as his ancestors had done. He did not depart from the sins of Jeroboam son of Nebat, which he caused Israel to sin. 10 Shallum son of Jabesh conspired against him, and struck him down in public and killed him, and reigned in place of him. 11 Now the rest of the deeds of Zechariah are written in the Book of the Annals of the Kings of Israel. 12 This was the promise of the LORD that he gave to Jehu: 'Your sons shall sit on the throne of Israel to the fourth generation.' And so it happened.

SHALLUM REIGNS OVER ISRAEL

13 Shallum son of Jabesh began to reign in the thirty-ninth year of King Uzziah of Judah; he reigned for one month in Samaria. 14 Then Menahem son of Gadi came up from Tirzah and came to Samaria; he struck down Shallum son of Jabesh in Samaria and killed him; he reigned in place of him. 15 Now the rest of the deeds of Shallum, including the conspiracy that he made, are written in the Book of the Annals of the Kings of Israel. 16 At that time Menahem sacked Tiphsah, all who were in it and its territory from Tirzah on; because they did not open it to him, he sacked it. He ripped open all the pregnant women in it.

MENAHEM REIGNS OVER ISRAEL

17 In the thirty-ninth year of King Azariah of Judah, Menahem son of Gadi began to reign over Israel; he reigned for ten years in Samaria. 18 He did what was evil in the sight of the LORD; he did not depart all his days from any of the sins of Jeroboam son of Nebat, which he caused Israel to sin. 19 King Pul of Assyria came against the land; Menahem gave Pul a thousand talents of silver, so that he might help him confirm his hold on the royal power. 20 Menahem exacted the money from Israel, that is, from all the wealthy, fifty shekels of silver from each one, to give to the king of Assyria. So the king of Assyria turned back, and did not stay there in the land. 21 Now the rest of the deeds of Menahem, and all that he did, are they not written in the Book of the Annals of the Kings of Israel? 22 Menahem slept with his ancestors, and his son Pekahiah succeeded him.

PEKAHIAH REIGNS OVER ISRAEL

23 In the fiftieth year of King Azariah of Judah, Pekahiah son of Menahem began to reign over Israel in Samaria; he reigned for two years. 24 He did what

[b] 15.5 A term for several skin diseases; precise meaning uncertain

was evil in the sight of the LORD; he
did not turn away from the sins of Jeroboam son of Nebat, which he caused
Israel to sin. 25Pekah son of Remaliah,
his captain, conspired against him with
fifty of the Gileadites, and attacked him
in Samaria, in the citadel of the palace
along with Argob and Arieh; he killed
him, and reigned in place of him. 26Now
the rest of the deeds of Pekahiah, and all
that he did, are written in the Book of
the Annals of the Kings of Israel.

PEKAH REIGNS OVER ISRAEL

27 In the fifty-second year of King
Azariah of Judah, Pekah son of Remaliah began to reign over Israel in Samaria; he reigned for twenty years.
28He did what was evil in the sight of
the LORD; he did not depart from the
sins of Jeroboam son of Nebat, which he
caused Israel to sin.

29 In the days of King Pekah of Israel, King Tiglath-pileser of Assyria
came and captured Ijon, Abel-beth-
maacah, Janoah, Kedesh, Hazor, Gilead,
and Galilee, all the land of Naphtali; and
he carried the people captive to Assyria.
30Then Hoshea son of Elah made a conspiracy against Pekah son of Remaliah,
attacked him, and killed him; he reigned
in place of him, in the twentieth year of
Jotham son of Uzziah. 31Now the rest of
the acts of Pekah, and all that he did, are
written in the Book of the Annals of the
Kings of Israel.

JOTHAM REIGNS OVER JUDAH

32 In the second year of King Pekah
son of Remaliah of Israel, King Jotham
son of Uzziah of Judah began to reign.
33He was twenty-five years old when he
began to reign and he reigned for sixteen years in Jerusalem. His mother's
name was Jerusha daughter of Zadok.
34He did what was right in the sight of
the LORD, just as his father Uzziah had
done. 35Nevertheless, the high places
were not removed; the people still sacrificed and made offerings on the high
places. He built the upper gate of the
house of the LORD. 36Now the rest of
the acts of Jotham, and all that he did,
are they not written in the Book of the
Annals of the Kings of Judah? 37In those
days the LORD began to send King Rezin of Aram and Pekah son of Remaliah
against Judah. 38Jotham slept with his
ancestors, and was buried with his ancestors in the city of David, his ancestor;
his son Ahaz succeeded him.

AHAZ REIGNS OVER JUDAH

16 In the seventeenth year of Pekah son of Remaliah, King Ahaz
son of Jotham of Judah began to reign.
2Ahaz was twenty years old when he
began to reign; he reigned for sixteen
years in Jerusalem. He did not do what
was right in the sight of the LORD his
God, as his ancestor David had done,
3but he walked in the way of the kings
of Israel. He even made his son pass
through fire, according to the abominable practices of the nations whom the
LORD drove out before the people of Israel. 4He sacrificed and made offerings
on the high places, on the hills, and under every green tree.

5 Then King Rezin of Aram and King
Pekah son of Remaliah of Israel came up
to wage war on Jerusalem; they besieged
Ahaz but could not conquer him. 6At
that time the king of Edom[c] recovered
Elath for Edom,[d] and drove the Judeans
from Elath; and the Edomites came to
Elath, where they live to this day. 7Ahaz
sent messengers to King Tiglath-pileser
of Assyria, saying, 'I am your servant
and your son. Come up, and rescue me
from the hand of the king of Aram and
from the hand of the king of Israel, who
are attacking me.' 8Ahaz also took the
silver and gold found in the house of the
LORD and in the treasures of the king's
house, and sent a present to the king of
Assyria. 9The king of Assyria listened
to him; the king of Assyria marched up
against Damascus, and took it, carrying
its people captive to Kir; then he killed
Rezin.

10 When King Ahaz went to Damascus to meet King Tiglath-pileser
of Assyria, he saw the altar that was
at Damascus. King Ahaz sent to the
priest Uriah a model of the altar, and
its pattern, exact in all its details. 11The
priest Uriah built the altar; in accordance with all that King Ahaz had sent
from Damascus, just so did the priest
Uriah build it, before King Ahaz arrived
from Damascus. 12When the king came
from Damascus, the king viewed the
altar. Then the king drew near to the
altar, went up on it, 13and offered his
burnt-offering and his grain-offering,
poured his drink-offering, and dashed
the blood of his offerings of well-being
against the altar. 14The bronze altar that
was before the LORD he removed from

[c] **16.6** Cn: Heb *King Rezin of Aram* [d] **16.6** Cn: Heb *Aram*

the front of the house, from the place
between his altar and the house of the
LORD, and put it on the north side of
his altar. 15 King Ahaz commanded the
priest Uriah, saying, 'Upon the great
altar offer the morning burnt-offering,
and the evening grain-offering, and the
king's burnt-offering, and his grain-
offering, with the burnt-offering of
all the people of the land, their grain-
offering, and their drink-offering; then
dash against it all the blood of the
burnt-offering, and all the blood of the
sacrifice; but the bronze altar shall be
for me to inquire by.' 16 The priest Uriah
did everything that King Ahaz commanded.

17 Then King Ahaz cut off the frames
of the stands, and removed the laver
from them; he removed the sea from
the bronze oxen that were under it, and
put it on a pediment of stone. 18 The covered portal for use on the sabbath that
had been built inside the palace, and the
outer entrance for the king, he removed
from[e] the house of the LORD. He did this
because of the king of Assyria. 19 Now
the rest of the acts of Ahaz that he did,
are they not written in the Book of the
Annals of the Kings of Judah? 20 Ahaz
slept with his ancestors, and was buried
with his ancestors in the city of David;
his son Hezekiah succeeded him.

HOSHEA REIGNS OVER ISRAEL

17 In the twelfth year of King Ahaz
of Judah, Hoshea son of Elah began to reign in Samaria over Israel; he
reigned for nine years. 2 He did what was
evil in the sight of the LORD, yet not like
the kings of Israel who were before him.
3 King Shalmaneser of Assyria came up
against him; Hoshea became his vassal,
and paid him tribute. 4 But the king of
Assyria found treachery in Hoshea; for
he had sent messengers to King So of
Egypt, and offered no tribute to the king
of Assyria, as he had done year by year;
therefore the king of Assyria confined
him and imprisoned him.

ISRAEL CARRIED CAPTIVE TO ASSYRIA

5 Then the king of Assyria invaded all
the land and came to Samaria; for three
years he besieged it. 6 In the ninth year
of Hoshea, the king of Assyria captured
Samaria; he carried the Israelites away
to Assyria. He placed them in Halah, on
the Habor, the river of Gozan, and in the
cities of the Medes.

7 This occurred because the people
of Israel had sinned against the LORD
their God, who had brought them up
out of the land of Egypt from under the
hand of Pharaoh king of Egypt. They
had worshipped other gods 8 and walked
in the customs of the nations whom the
LORD drove out before the people of Israel, and in the customs that the kings
of Israel had introduced.[f] 9 The people of
Israel secretly did things that were not
right against the LORD their God. They
built for themselves high places at all
their towns, from watch-tower to fortified city; 10 they set up for themselves
pillars and sacred poles[g] on every high
hill and under every green tree; 11 there
they made offerings on all the high
places, as the nations did whom the
LORD carried away before them. They
did wicked things, provoking the LORD
to anger; 12 they served idols, of which
the LORD had said to them, 'You shall
not do this.' 13 Yet the LORD warned Israel and Judah by every prophet and
every seer, saying, 'Turn from your evil
ways and keep my commandments
and my statutes, in accordance with all
the law that I commanded your ancestors and that I sent to you by my servants the prophets.' 14 They would not
listen but were stubborn, as their ancestors had been, who did not believe
in the LORD their God. 15 They despised
his statutes, and his covenant that he
made with their ancestors, and the
warnings that he gave them. They went
after false idols and became false; they
followed the nations that were around
them, concerning whom the LORD had
commanded them that they should not
do as they did. 16 They rejected all the
commandments of the LORD their God
and made for themselves cast images
of two calves; they made a sacred pole,[h]
worshipped all the host of heaven, and
served Baal. 17 They made their sons and
their daughters pass through fire; they
used divination and augury; and they
sold themselves to do evil in the sight
of the LORD, provoking him to anger.
18 Therefore the LORD was very angry
with Israel and removed them out of
his sight; none was left but the tribe of
Judah alone.

19 Judah also did not keep the commandments of the LORD their God but
walked in the customs that Israel had

[e] 16.18 Cn: Heb lacks *from* [f] 17.8 Meaning of Heb uncertain [g] 17.10 Heb *Asherim*
[h] 17.16 Heb *Asherah*

introduced. 20 The LORD rejected all
the descendants of Israel; he punished
them and gave them into the hand of
plunderers, until he had banished them
from his presence.

21 When he had torn Israel from the
house of David, they made Jeroboam
son of Nebat king. Jeroboam drove Israel from following the LORD and made
them commit great sin. 22 The people of
Israel continued in all the sins that Jeroboam committed; they did not depart
from them 23 until the LORD removed
Israel out of his sight, as he had foretold
through all his servants the prophets.
So Israel was exiled from their own land
to Assyria until this day.

ASSYRIA RESETTLES SAMARIA

24 The king of Assyria brought people from Babylon, Cuthah, Avva, Hamath, and Sepharvaim, and placed
them in the cities of Samaria in place
of the people of Israel; they took possession of Samaria, and settled in its cities.
25 When they first settled there, they did
not worship the LORD; therefore the
LORD sent lions among them, which
killed some of them. 26 So the king of
Assyria was told, 'The nations that you
have carried away and placed in the
cities of Samaria do not know the law
of the god of the land; therefore he has
sent lions among them; they are killing
them, because they do not know the law
of the god of the land.' 27 Then the king
of Assyria commanded, 'Send there one
of the priests whom you carried away
from there; let him[i] go and live there,
and teach them the law of the god of the
land.' 28 So one of the priests whom they
had carried away from Samaria came
and lived in Bethel; he taught them how
they should worship the LORD.

29 But every nation still made gods
of its own and put them in the shrines
of the high places that the people of Samaria had made, every nation in the
cities in which they lived; 30 the people
of Babylon made Succoth-benoth, the
people of Cuth made Nergal, the people
of Hamath made Ashima; 31 the Avvites
made Nibhaz and Tartak; the Sephar-
vites burned their children in the fire
to Adrammelech and Anammelech, the
gods of Sepharvaim. 32 They also worshipped the LORD and appointed from
among themselves all sorts of people
as priests of the high places, who sacrificed for them in the shrines of the
high places. 33 So they worshipped the
LORD, but they also served their own
gods, after the manner of the nations
from among whom they had been carried away. 34 To this day they continue
to practise their former customs.

They do not worship the LORD and
they do not follow the statutes or the
ordinances or the law or the commandment that the LORD commanded the
children of Jacob, whom he named Israel. 35 The LORD had made a covenant
with them and commanded them, 'You
shall not worship other gods or bow
yourselves to them or serve them or
sacrifice to them, 36 but you shall worship the LORD, who brought you out of
the land of Egypt with great power and
with an outstretched arm; you shall bow
yourselves to him, and to him you shall
sacrifice. 37 The statutes and the ordinances and the law and the commandment that he wrote for you, you shall
always be careful to observe. You shall
not worship other gods; 38 you shall not
forget the covenant that I have made
with you. You shall not worship other
gods, 39 but you shall worship the LORD
your God; he will deliver you out of the
hand of all your enemies.' 40 They would
not listen, however, but they continued
to practise their former custom.

41 So these nations worshipped the
LORD, but also served their carved images; to this day their children and their
children's children continue to do as
their ancestors did.

HEZEKIAH'S REIGN OVER JUDAH

18 In the third year of King Hoshea son of Elah of Israel, Hezekiah son of King Ahaz of Judah began
to reign. 2 He was twenty-five years old
when he began to reign; he reigned for
twenty-nine years in Jerusalem. His
mother's name was Abi daughter of
Zechariah. 3 He did what was right in
the sight of the LORD just as his ancestor David had done. 4 He removed the
high places, broke down the pillars, and
cut down the sacred pole.[j] He broke in
pieces the bronze serpent that Moses
had made, for until those days the people of Israel had made offerings to it; it
was called Nehushtan. 5 He trusted in
the LORD the God of Israel; so that there
was no one like him among all the kings
of Judah after him, or among those who
were before him. 6 For he held fast to the
LORD; he did not depart from following

[i] 17.27 Syr Vg: Heb *them* [j] 18.4 Heb *Asherah*

him but kept the commandments that
the LORD commanded Moses. 7 The
LORD was with him; wherever he went,
he prospered. He rebelled against the
king of Assyria and would not serve
him. 8 He attacked the Philistines as far
as Gaza and its territory, from watch-
tower to fortified city.

9 In the fourth year of King Hezekiah, which was the seventh year of
King Hoshea son of Elah of Israel, King
Shalmaneser of Assyria came up against
Samaria, besieged it, 10 and at the end
of three years took it. In the sixth year
of Hezekiah, which was the ninth year
of King Hoshea of Israel, Samaria was
taken. 11 The king of Assyria carried the
Israelites away to Assyria, settled them
in Halah, on the Habor, the river of Gozan, and in the cities of the Medes, 12 because they did not obey the voice of the
LORD their God but transgressed his
covenant—all that Moses the servant of
the LORD had commanded; they neither
listened nor obeyed.

SENNACHERIB INVADES JUDAH

13 In the fourteenth year of King
Hezekiah, King Sennacherib of Assyria
came up against all the fortified cities of
Judah and captured them. 14 King Hezekiah of Judah sent to the king of Assyria
at Lachish, saying, 'I have done wrong;
withdraw from me; whatever you impose on me I will bear.' The king of Assyria demanded of King Hezekiah of Judah three hundred talents of silver and
thirty talents of gold. 15 Hezekiah gave
him all the silver that was found in the
house of the LORD and in the treasuries
of the king's house. 16 At that time Hezekiah stripped the gold from the doors
of the temple of the LORD, and from the
doorposts that King Hezekiah of Judah
had overlaid, and gave it to the king
of Assyria. 17 The king of Assyria sent
the Tartan, the Rabsaris, and the Rabshakeh with a great army from Lachish
to King Hezekiah at Jerusalem. They
went up and came to Jerusalem. When
they arrived, they came and stood by
the conduit of the upper pool, which
is on the highway to the Fuller's Field.
18 When they called for the king, there
came out to them Eliakim son of Hilkiah, who was in charge of the palace,
and Shebnah the secretary, and Joah
son of Asaph, the recorder.

19 The Rabshakeh said to them, 'Say
to Hezekiah: Thus says the great king,
the king of Assyria: On what do you
base this confidence of yours? 20 Do you
think that mere words are strategy and
power for war? On whom do you now
rely, that you have rebelled against me?
21 See, you are relying now on Egypt,
that broken reed of a staff, which will
pierce the hand of anyone who leans on
it. Such is Pharaoh king of Egypt to all
who rely on him. 22 But if you say to me,
"We rely on the LORD our God", is it not
he whose high places and altars Hezekiah has removed, saying to Judah and
to Jerusalem, "You shall worship before
this altar in Jerusalem"? 23 Come now,
make a wager with my master the king
of Assyria: I will give you two thousand
horses, if you are able on your part to set
riders on them. 24 How then can you repulse a single captain among the least
of my master's servants, when you rely
on Egypt for chariots and for horsemen?
25 Moreover, is it without the LORD that
I have come up against this place to destroy it? The LORD said to me, Go up
against this land, and destroy it.'

26 Then Eliakim son of Hilkiah, and
Shebnah, and Joah said to the Rabshakeh, 'Please speak to your servants
in the Aramaic language, for we understand it; do not speak to us in the language of Judah within the hearing of
the people who are on the wall.' 27 But
the Rabshakeh said to them, 'Has my
master sent me to speak these words
to your master and to you, and not to
the people sitting on the wall, who are
doomed with you to eat their own dung
and to drink their own urine?'

28 Then the Rabshakeh stood and
called out in a loud voice in the language
of Judah, 'Hear the word of the great
king, the king of Assyria! 29 Thus says
the king: "Do not let Hezekiah deceive
you, for he will not be able to deliver you
out of my hand. 30 Do not let Hezekiah
make you rely on the LORD by saying,
The LORD will surely deliver us, and this
city will not be given into the hand of
the king of Assyria." 31 Do not listen to
Hezekiah; for thus says the king of Assyria: "Make your peace with me and
come out to me; then every one of you
will eat from your own vine and your
own fig tree, and drink water from your
own cistern, 32 until I come and take you
away to a land like your own land, a land
of grain and wine, a land of bread and
vineyards, a land of olive oil and honey,
that you may live and not die. Do not
listen to Hezekiah when he misleads
you by saying, The LORD will deliver us.

33 Has any of the gods of the nations ever
delivered its land out of the hand of the
king of Assyria? 34 Where are the gods of
Hamath and Arpad? Where are the gods
of Sepharvaim, Hena, and Ivvah? Have
they delivered Samaria out of my hand?
35 Who among all the gods of the countries have delivered their countries out
of my hand, that the LORD should deliver Jerusalem out of my hand?" '

36 But the people were silent and answered him not a word, for the king's
command was, 'Do not answer him.'
37 Then Eliakim son of Hilkiah, who was
in charge of the palace, and Shebna the
secretary, and Joah son of Asaph, the
recorder, came to Hezekiah with their
clothes torn and told him the words of
the Rabshakeh.

HEZEKIAH CONSULTS ISAIAH

19 When King Hezekiah heard it, he
tore his clothes, covered himself
with sackcloth, and went into the house
of the LORD. 2 And he sent Eliakim, who
was in charge of the palace, and Shebna
the secretary, and the senior priests,
covered with sackcloth, to the prophet
Isaiah son of Amoz. 3 They said to him,
'Thus says Hezekiah, This day is a day
of distress, of rebuke, and of disgrace;
children have come to birth, and there
is no strength to bring them forth. 4 It
may be that the LORD your God heard
all the words of the Rabshakeh, whom
his master the king of Assyria has sent
to mock the living God, and will rebuke
the words that the LORD your God has
heard; therefore lift up your prayer for
the remnant that is left.' 5 When the
servants of King Hezekiah came to Isaiah, 6 Isaiah said to them, 'Say to your
master, "Thus says the LORD: Do not
be afraid because of the words that you
have heard, with which the servants of
the king of Assyria have reviled me. 7 I
myself will put a spirit in him, so that
he shall hear a rumour and return to his
own land; I will cause him to fall by the
sword in his own land." '

SENNACHERIB'S THREAT

8 The Rabshakeh returned, and found
the king of Assyria fighting against Libnah; for he had heard that the king had
left Lachish. 9 When the king[k] heard
concerning King Tirhakah of Ethiopia,[l]
'See, he has set out to fight against you',
he sent messengers again to Hezekiah,
saying, 10 'Thus shall you speak to King
Hezekiah of Judah: Do not let your God
on whom you rely deceive you by promising that Jerusalem will not be given
into the hand of the king of Assyria.
11 See, you have heard what the kings of
Assyria have done to all lands, destroying them utterly. Shall you be delivered?
12 Have the gods of the nations delivered
them, the nations that my predecessors
destroyed, Gozan, Haran, Rezeph, and
the people of Eden who were in Telassar? 13 Where is the king of Hamath,
the king of Arpad, the king of the city
of Sepharvaim, the king of Hena, or the
king of Ivvah?'

HEZEKIAH'S PRAYER

14 Hezekiah received the letter from
the hand of the messengers and read
it; then Hezekiah went up to the house
of the LORD and spread it before the
LORD. 15 And Hezekiah prayed before
the LORD, and said: 'O LORD the God
of Israel, who are enthroned above the
cherubim, you are God, you alone, of
all the kingdoms of the earth; you have
made heaven and earth. 16 Incline your
ear, O LORD, and hear; open your eyes,
O LORD, and see; hear the words of Sennacherib, which he has sent to mock the
living God. 17 Truly, O LORD, the kings
of Assyria have laid waste the nations
and their lands, 18 and have hurled their
gods into the fire, though they were no
gods but the work of human hands—
wood and stone—and so they were destroyed. 19 So now, O LORD our God, save
us, I pray you, from his hand, so that all
the kingdoms of the earth may know
that you, O LORD, are God alone.'

20 Then Isaiah son of Amoz sent to
Hezekiah, saying, 'Thus says the LORD,
the God of Israel: I have heard your
prayer to me about King Sennacherib
of Assyria. 21 This is the word that the
LORD has spoken concerning him:

She despises you, she scorns you—
  virgin daughter Zion;
she tosses her head—behind
    your back,
  daughter Jerusalem.

22 'Whom have you mocked
    and reviled?
  Against whom have you
    raised your voice
and haughtily lifted your eyes?
  Against the Holy One of Israel!

[k] 19.9 Heb *he* [l] 19.9 Or *Nubia*; Heb *Cush*

23 By your messengers you have
mocked the Lord,
and you have said, "With
my many chariots
I have gone up the heights of
the mountains,
to the far recesses of Lebanon;
I felled its tallest cedars,
its choicest cypresses;
I entered its farthest retreat,
its densest forest.
24 I dug wells
and drank foreign waters,
I dried up with the sole of my foot
all the streams of Egypt."

25 'Have you not heard
that I determined it long ago?
I planned from days of old
what now I bring to pass,
that you should make fortified cities
crash into heaps of ruins,
26 while their inhabitants,
shorn of strength,
are dismayed and confounded;
they have become like plants
of the field
and like tender grass,
like grass on the housetops,
blighted before it is grown.

27 'But I know your rising[m]
and your sitting,
your going out and coming in,
and your raging against me.
28 Because you have raged against me
and your arrogance has
come to my ears,
I will put my hook in your nose
and my bit in your mouth;
I will turn you back on the way
by which you came.

29 'And this shall be the sign for
you: This year you shall eat what grows
of itself, and in the second year what
springs from that; then in the third
year sow, reap, plant vineyards, and eat
their fruit. 30The surviving remnant of
the house of Judah shall again take root
downwards, and bear fruit upwards;
31for from Jerusalem a remnant shall
go out, and from Mount Zion a band of
survivors. The zeal of the LORD of hosts
will do this.

32 'Therefore thus says the LORD
concerning the king of Assyria: He shall
not come into this city, shoot an arrow
there, come before it with a shield, or
cast up a siege-ramp against it. 33By the
way that he came, by the same he shall
return; he shall not come into this city,
says the LORD. 34For I will defend this
city to save it, for my own sake and for
the sake of my servant David.'

SENNACHERIB'S DEFEAT AND DEATH

35 That very night the angel of the
LORD set out and struck down one hundred and eighty-five thousand in the
camp of the Assyrians; when morning dawned, they were all dead bodies.
36Then King Sennacherib of Assyria
left, went home, and lived at Nineveh.
37As he was worshipping in the house
of his god Nisroch, his sons Adrammelech and Sharezer killed him with the
sword, and they escaped into the land of
Ararat. His son Esar-haddon succeeded
him.

HEZEKIAH'S ILLNESS

20 In those days Hezekiah became
sick and was at the point of
death. The prophet Isaiah son of Amoz
came to him, and said to him, 'Thus
says the LORD: Set your house in order,
for you shall die; you shall not recover.'
2Then Hezekiah turned his face to the
wall and prayed to the LORD: 3'Remember now, O LORD, I implore you, how
I have walked before you in faithfulness with a whole heart, and have done
what is good in your sight.' Hezekiah
wept bitterly. 4Before Isaiah had gone
out of the middle court, the word of the
LORD came to him: 5'Turn back, and say
to Hezekiah prince of my people, Thus
says the LORD, the God of your ancestor
David: I have heard your prayer, I have
seen your tears; indeed, I will heal you;
on the third day you shall go up to the
house of the LORD. 6I will add fifteen
years to your life. I will deliver you and
this city out of the hand of the king of
Assyria; I will defend this city for my
own sake and for my servant David's
sake.' 7Then Isaiah said, 'Bring a lump of
figs. Let them take it and apply it to the
boil, so that he may recover.'

8 Hezekiah said to Isaiah, 'What shall
be the sign that the LORD will heal me,
and that I shall go up to the house of the
LORD on the third day?' 9Isaiah said,
'This is the sign to you from the LORD,
that the LORD will do the thing that he
has promised: the shadow has now advanced ten intervals; shall it retreat ten
intervals?' 10Hezekiah answered, 'It is

[m] 19.27 Gk Compare Isa 37.27 Q Ms: MT lacks *rising*

normal for the shadow to lengthen ten intervals; rather let the shadow retreat ten intervals.' 11The prophet Isaiah cried to the LORD; and he brought the shadow back the ten intervals, by which the sun[n] had declined on the dial of Ahaz.

ENVOYS FROM BABYLON

12 At that time King Merodach-baladan son of Baladan of Babylon sent envoys with letters and a present to Hezekiah, for he had heard that Hezekiah had been sick. 13Hezekiah welcomed them;[o] he showed them all his treasure house, the silver, the gold, the spices, the precious oil, his armoury, all that was found in his storehouses; there was nothing in his house or in all his realm that Hezekiah did not show them. 14Then the prophet Isaiah came to King Hezekiah, and said to him, 'What did these men say? From where did they come to you?' Hezekiah answered, 'They have come from a far country, from Babylon.' 15He said, 'What have they seen in your house?' Hezekiah answered, 'They have seen all that is in my house; there is nothing in my storehouses that I did not show them.'

16 Then Isaiah said to Hezekiah, 'Hear the word of the LORD: 17Days are coming when all that is in your house, and that which your ancestors have stored up until this day, shall be carried to Babylon; nothing shall be left, says the LORD. 18Some of your own sons who are born to you shall be taken away; they shall be eunuchs in the palace of the king of Babylon.' 19Then Hezekiah said to Isaiah, 'The word of the LORD that you have spoken is good.' For he thought, 'Why not, if there will be peace and security in my days?'

DEATH OF HEZEKIAH

20 The rest of the deeds of Hezekiah, all his power, how he made the pool and the conduit and brought water into the city, are they not written in the Book of the Annals of the Kings of Judah? 21Hezekiah slept with his ancestors; and his son Manasseh succeeded him.

MANASSEH REIGNS OVER JUDAH

21 Manasseh was twelve years old when he began to reign; he reigned for fifty-five years in Jerusalem. His mother's name was Hephzibah. 2He did what was evil in the sight of the LORD, following the abominable practices of the nations that the LORD drove out before the people of Israel. 3For he rebuilt the high places that his father Hezekiah had destroyed; he erected altars for Baal, made a sacred pole,[p] as King Ahab of Israel had done, worshipped all the host of heaven, and served them. 4He built altars in the house of the LORD, of which the LORD had said, 'In Jerusalem I will put my name.' 5He built altars for all the host of heaven in the two courts of the house of the LORD. 6He made his son pass through fire; he practised soothsaying and augury, and dealt with mediums and with wizards. He did much evil in the sight of the LORD, provoking him to anger. 7The carved image of Asherah that he had made he set in the house of which the LORD said to David and to his son Solomon, 'In this house, and in Jerusalem, which I have chosen out of all the tribes of Israel, I will put my name for ever; 8I will not cause the feet of Israel to wander any more out of the land that I gave to their ancestors, if only they will be careful to do according to all that I have commanded them, and according to all the law that my servant Moses commanded them.' 9But they did not listen; Manasseh misled them to do more evil than the nations had done that the LORD destroyed before the people of Israel.

10 The LORD said by his servants the prophets, 11'Because King Manasseh of Judah has committed these abominations, has done things more wicked than all that the Amorites did, who were before him, and has caused Judah also to sin with his idols; 12therefore thus says the LORD, the God of Israel, I am bringing upon Jerusalem and Judah such evil that the ears of everyone who hears of it will tingle. 13I will stretch over Jerusalem the measuring line for Samaria, and the plummet for the house of Ahab; I will wipe Jerusalem as one wipes a dish, wiping it and turning it upside down. 14I will cast off the remnant of my heritage, and give them into the hand of their enemies; they shall become a prey and a spoil to all their enemies, 15because they have done what is evil in my sight and have provoked me to anger, since the day their ancestors came out of Egypt, even to this day.'

16 Moreover, Manasseh shed very much innocent blood, until he had filled

[n] **20.11** Syr See Isa 38.8 and Tg: Heb *it*
[o] **20.13** Gk Vg Syr: Heb *When Hezekiah heard about them* [p] **21.3** Heb *Asherah*

Jerusalem from one end to another, besides the sin that he caused Judah to sin so that they did what was evil in the sight of the LORD.

17 Now the rest of the acts of Manasseh, all that he did, and the sin that he committed, are they not written in the Book of the Annals of the Kings of Judah? 18 Manasseh slept with his ancestors, and was buried in the garden of his house, in the garden of Uzza. His son Amon succeeded him.

AMON REIGNS OVER JUDAH

19 Amon was twenty-two years old when he began to reign; he reigned for two years in Jerusalem. His mother's name was Meshullemeth daughter of Haruz of Jotbah. 20 He did what was evil in the sight of the LORD, as his father Manasseh had done. 21 He walked in all the way in which his father walked, served the idols that his father served, and worshipped them; 22 he abandoned the LORD, the God of his ancestors, and did not walk in the way of the LORD. 23 The servants of Amon conspired against him, and killed the king in his house. 24 But the people of the land killed all those who had conspired against King Amon, and the people of the land made his son Josiah king in place of him. 25 Now the rest of the acts of Amon that he did, are they not written in the Book of the Annals of the Kings of Judah? 26 He was buried in his tomb in the garden of Uzza; then his son Josiah succeeded him.

JOSIAH REIGNS OVER JUDAH

22 Josiah was eight years old when he began to reign; he reigned for thirty-one years in Jerusalem. His mother's name was Jedidah daughter of Adaiah of Bozkath. 2 He did what was right in the sight of the LORD, and walked in all the way of his father David; he did not turn aside to the right or to the left.

HILKIAH FINDS THE BOOK OF THE LAW

3 In the eighteenth year of King Josiah, the king sent Shaphan son of Azaliah, son of Meshullam, the secretary, to the house of the LORD, saying, 4 'Go up to the high priest Hilkiah, and have him count the entire sum of the money that has been brought into the house of the LORD, which the keepers of the threshold have collected from the people; 5 let it be given into the hand of the workers who have the oversight of the house of the LORD; let them give it to the workers who are at the house of the LORD, repairing the house, 6 that is, to the carpenters, to the builders, to the masons; and let them use it to buy timber and quarried stone to repair the house. 7 But no account shall be asked from them for the money that is delivered into their hand, for they deal honestly.'

8 The high priest Hilkiah said to Shaphan the secretary, 'I have found the book of the law in the house of the LORD.' When Hilkiah gave the book to Shaphan, he read it. 9 Then Shaphan the secretary came to the king, and reported to the king, 'Your servants have emptied out the money that was found in the house, and have delivered it into the hand of the workers who have oversight of the house of the LORD.' 10 Shaphan the secretary informed the king, 'The priest Hilkiah has given me a book.' Shaphan then read it aloud to the king.

11 When the king heard the words of the book of the law, he tore his clothes. 12 Then the king commanded the priest Hilkiah, Ahikam son of Shaphan, Achbor son of Micaiah, Shaphan the secretary, and the king's servant Asaiah, saying, 13 'Go, inquire of the LORD for me, for the people, and for all Judah, concerning the words of this book that has been found; for great is the wrath of the LORD that is kindled against us, because our ancestors did not obey the words of this book, to do according to all that is written concerning us.'

14 So the priest Hilkiah, Ahikam, Achbor, Shaphan, and Asaiah went to the prophetess Huldah the wife of Shallum son of Tikvah, son of Harhas, keeper of the wardrobe; she resided in Jerusalem in the Second Quarter, where they consulted her. 15 She declared to them, 'Thus says the LORD, the God of Israel: Tell the man who sent you to me, 16 Thus says the LORD, I will indeed bring disaster on this place and on its inhabitants—all the words of the book that the king of Judah has read. 17 Because they have abandoned me and have made offerings to other gods, so that they have provoked me to anger with all the work of their hands, therefore my wrath will be kindled against this place, and it will not be quenched. 18 But as to the king of Judah, who sent you to inquire of the LORD, thus shall you say to him, Thus says the LORD, the

God of Israel: Regarding the words that you have heard, 19 because your heart was penitent, and you humbled yourself before the LORD, when you heard how I spoke against this place, and against its inhabitants, that they should become a desolation and a curse, and because you have torn your clothes and wept before me, I also have heard you, says the LORD. 20 Therefore, I will gather you to your ancestors, and you shall be gathered to your grave in peace; your eyes shall not see all the disaster that I will bring on this place.' They took the message back to the king.

JOSIAH'S REFORMATION

23 Then the king directed that all the elders of Judah and Jerusalem should be gathered to him. 2 The king went up to the house of the LORD, and with him went all the people of Judah, all the inhabitants of Jerusalem, the priests, the prophets, and all the people, both small and great; he read in their hearing all the words of the book of the covenant that had been found in the house of the LORD. 3 The king stood by the pillar and made a covenant before the LORD, to follow the LORD, keeping his commandments, his decrees, and his statutes, with all his heart and all his soul, to perform the words of this covenant that were written in this book. All the people joined in the covenant.

4 The king commanded the high priest Hilkiah, the priests of the second order, and the guardians of the threshold, to bring out of the temple of the LORD all the vessels made for Baal, for Asherah, and for all the host of heaven; he burned them outside Jerusalem in the fields of the Kidron, and carried their ashes to Bethel. 5 He deposed the idolatrous priests whom the kings of Judah had ordained to make offerings in the high places at the cities of Judah and around Jerusalem; those also who made offerings to Baal, to the sun, the moon, the constellations, and all the host of the heavens. 6 He brought out the image of[q] Asherah from the house of the LORD, outside Jerusalem, to the Wadi Kidron, burned it at the Wadi Kidron, beat it to dust and threw the dust of it upon the graves of the common people. 7 He broke down the houses of the male temple prostitutes that were in the house of the LORD, where the women did weaving for Asherah. 8 He brought all the priests out of the towns of Judah, and defiled the high places where the priests had made offerings, from Geba to Beer-sheba; he broke down the high places of the gates that were at the entrance of the gate of Joshua the governor of the city, which were on the left at the gate of the city. 9 The priests of the high places, however, did not come up to the altar of the LORD in Jerusalem, but ate unleavened bread among their kindred. 10 He defiled Topheth, which is in the valley of Ben-hinnom, so that no one would make a son or a daughter pass through fire as an offering to Molech. 11 He removed the horses that the kings of Judah had dedicated to the sun, at the entrance to the house of the LORD, by the chamber of the eunuch Nathan-melech, which was in the precincts;[r] then he burned the chariots of the sun with fire. 12 The altars on the roof of the upper chamber of Ahaz, which the kings of Judah had made, and the altars that Manasseh had made in the two courts of the house of the LORD, he pulled down from there and broke in pieces, and threw the rubble into the Wadi Kidron. 13 The king defiled the high places that were east of Jerusalem, to the south of the Mount of Destruction, which King Solomon of Israel had built for Astarte the abomination of the Sidonians, for Chemosh the abomination of Moab, and for Milcom the abomination of the Ammonites. 14 He broke the pillars in pieces, cut down the sacred poles,[s] and covered the sites with human bones.

15 Moreover, the altar at Bethel, the high place erected by Jeroboam son of Nebat, who caused Israel to sin—he pulled down that altar along with the high place. He burned the high place, crushing it to dust; he also burned the sacred pole.[t] 16 As Josiah turned, he saw the tombs there on the mount; and he sent and took the bones out of the tombs, and burned them on the altar, and defiled it, according to the word of the LORD that the man of God proclaimed,[u] when Jeroboam stood by the altar at the festival; he turned and looked up at the tomb of the man of God who had predicted these things. 17 Then he said, 'What is that monument that I see?' The people of the city told him, 'It is the tomb of the man of God who

[q] 23.6 Heb lacks *image of* [r] 23.11 Meaning of Heb uncertain [s] 23.14 Heb *Asherim*
[t] 23.15 Heb *Asherah* [u] 23.16 Gk: Heb *proclaimed, who had predicted these things*

came from Judah and predicted these
things that you have done against the
altar at Bethel.' 18He said, 'Let him rest;
let no one move his bones.' So they let
his bones alone, with the bones of the
prophet who came out of Samaria.
19Moreover, Josiah removed all the
shrines of the high places that were in
the towns of Samaria, which kings of
Israel had made, provoking the LORD
to anger; he did to them just as he had
done at Bethel. 20He slaughtered on the
altars all the priests of the high places
who were there, and burned human
bones on them. Then he returned to Jerusalem.

THE PASSOVER CELEBRATED

21 The king commanded all the people, 'Keep the passover to the LORD your
God as prescribed in this book of the
covenant.' 22No such passover had been
kept since the days of the judges who
judged Israel, even during all the days
of the kings of Israel and of the kings of
Judah; 23but in the eighteenth year of
King Josiah this passover was kept to
the LORD in Jerusalem.

24 Moreover, Josiah did away with
the mediums, wizards, teraphim,[v] idols,
and all the abominations that were seen
in the land of Judah and in Jerusalem, so
that he established the words of the law
that were written in the book that the
priest Hilkiah had found in the house
of the LORD. 25Before him there was no
king like him, who turned to the LORD
with all his heart, with all his soul, and
with all his might, according to all the
law of Moses; nor did any like him arise
after him.

26 Still the LORD did not turn from
the fierceness of his great wrath, by
which his anger was kindled against
Judah, because of all the provocations
with which Manasseh had provoked
him. 27The LORD said, 'I will remove Judah also out of my sight, as I have removed Israel; and I will reject this city
that I have chosen, Jerusalem, and the
house of which I said, My name shall be
there.'

JOSIAH DIES IN BATTLE

28 Now the rest of the acts of Josiah,
and all that he did, are they not written
in the Book of the Annals of the Kings
of Judah? 29In his days Pharaoh Neco
king of Egypt went up to the king of
Assyria to the river Euphrates. King Josiah went to meet him; but when Pharaoh Neco met him at Megiddo, he killed
him. 30His servants carried him dead in
a chariot from Megiddo, brought him to
Jerusalem, and buried him in his own
tomb. The people of the land took Jehoahaz son of Josiah, anointed him, and
made him king in place of his father.

REIGN AND CAPTIVITY OF JEHOAHAZ

31 Jehoahaz was twenty-three years
old when he began to reign; he reigned
for three months in Jerusalem. His mother's name was Hamutal daughter of Jeremiah of Libnah. 32He did what was evil
in the sight of the LORD, just as his ancestors had done. 33Pharaoh Neco confined
him at Riblah in the land of Hamath, so
that he might not reign in Jerusalem,
and imposed tribute on the land of one
hundred talents of silver and a talent of
gold. 34Pharaoh Neco made Eliakim son
of Josiah king in place of his father Josiah,
and changed his name to Jehoiakim.
But he took Jehoahaz away; he came to
Egypt, and died there. 35Jehoiakim gave
the silver and the gold to Pharaoh, but he
taxed the land in order to meet Pharaoh's
demand for money. He exacted the silver
and the gold from the people of the land,
from all according to their assessment, to
give it to Pharaoh Neco.

JEHOIAKIM REIGNS OVER JUDAH

36 Jehoiakim was twenty-five years
old when he began to reign; he reigned
for eleven years in Jerusalem. His mother's name was Zebidah daughter of Pedaiah of Rumah. 37He did what was evil
in the sight of the LORD, just as all his
ancestors had done.

JUDAH OVERRUN BY ENEMIES

24 In his days King Nebuchadnezzar of Babylon came up; Jehoiakim became his servant for three years;
then he turned and rebelled against
him. 2The LORD sent against him
bands of the Chaldeans, bands of the
Arameans, bands of the Moabites, and
bands of the Ammonites; he sent them
against Judah to destroy it, according to
the word of the LORD that he spoke by
his servants the prophets. 3Surely this
came upon Judah at the command of the
LORD, to remove them out of his sight,
for the sins of Manasseh, for all that he
had committed, 4and also for the innocent blood that he had shed; for he filled

v 23.24 *Or household gods*

Jerusalem with innocent blood, and the
LORD was not willing to pardon. 5 Now
the rest of the deeds of Jehoiakim, and
all that he did, are they not written in
the Book of the Annals of the Kings of
Judah? 6 So Jehoiakim slept with his
ancestors; then his son Jehoiachin succeeded him. 7 The king of Egypt did not
come again out of his land, for the king
of Babylon had taken over all that belonged to the king of Egypt from the
Wadi of Egypt to the River Euphrates.

REIGN AND CAPTIVITY OF JEHOIACHIN

8 Jehoiachin was eighteen years old
when he began to reign; he reigned for
three months in Jerusalem. His mother's name was Nehushta daughter of Elnathan of Jerusalem. 9 He did what was
evil in the sight of the LORD, just as his
father had done.

10 At that time the servants of King
Nebuchadnezzar of Babylon came up to
Jerusalem, and the city was besieged.
11 King Nebuchadnezzar of Babylon
came to the city, while his servants were
besieging it; 12 King Jehoiachin of Judah
gave himself up to the king of Babylon,
himself, his mother, his servants, his officers, and his palace officials. The king
of Babylon took him prisoner in the
eighth year of his reign.

CAPTURE OF JERUSALEM

13 He carried off all the treasures of
the house of the LORD, and the treasures
of the king's house; he cut in pieces all
the vessels of gold in the temple of the
LORD, which King Solomon of Israel had
made, all this as the LORD had foretold.
14 He carried away all Jerusalem, all the
officials, all the warriors, ten thousand
captives, all the artisans and the smiths;
no one remained, except the poorest
people of the land. 15 He carried away Jehoiachin to Babylon; the king's mother,
the king's wives, his officials, and the
elite of the land, he took into captivity
from Jerusalem to Babylon. 16 The king
of Babylon brought captive to Babylon
all the men of valour, seven thousand,
the artisans and the smiths, one thousand, all of them strong and fit for war.
17 The king of Babylon made Mattaniah,
Jehoiachin's uncle, king in his place, and
changed his name to Zedekiah.

ZEDEKIAH REIGNS OVER JUDAH

18 Zedekiah was twenty-one years
old when he began to reign; he reigned
for eleven years in Jerusalem. His mother's name was Hamutal daughter of Jeremiah of Libnah. 19 He did what was evil
in the sight of the LORD, just as Jehoiakim had done. 20 Indeed, Jerusalem and
Judah so angered the LORD that he expelled them from his presence.

THE FALL AND CAPTIVITY OF JUDAH

25 Zedekiah rebelled against the king of
Babylon. 1 And in the ninth year
of his reign, in the tenth month,
on the tenth day of the month, King
Nebuchadnezzar of Babylon came with
all his army against Jerusalem, and laid
siege to it; they built siege-works against
it all round. 2 So the city was besieged
until the eleventh year of King Zedekiah. 3 On the ninth day of the fourth
month the famine became so severe in
the city that there was no food for the
people of the land. 4 Then a breach was
made in the city wall;[w] the king with all
the soldiers fled[x] by night by the way of
the gate between the two walls, by the
king's garden, though the Chaldeans
were all round the city. They went in the
direction of the Arabah. 5 But the army
of the Chaldeans pursued the king, and
overtook him in the plains of Jericho;
all his army was scattered, deserting
him. 6 Then they captured the king and
brought him up to the king of Babylon
at Riblah, who passed sentence on him.
7 They slaughtered the sons of Zedekiah
before his eyes, then put out the eyes of
Zedekiah; they bound him in fetters and
took him to Babylon.

8 In the fifth month, on the seventh
day of the month—which was the nineteenth year of King Nebuchadnezzar,
king of Babylon—Nebuzaradan, the
captain of the bodyguard, a servant of
the king of Babylon, came to Jerusalem.
9 He burned the house of the LORD, the
king's house, and all the houses of Jerusalem; every great house he burned
down. 10 All the army of the Chaldeans
who were with the captain of the guard
broke down the walls around Jerusalem.
11 Nebuzaradan the captain of the guard
carried into exile the rest of the people
who were left in the city and the deserters who had defected to the king of
Babylon—all the rest of the population.
12 But the captain of the guard left some
of the poorest people of the land to be
vine-dressers and tillers of the soil.

[w] **25.4** Heb lacks *wall* [x] **25.4** Gk Compare Jer 39.4; 52.7: Heb lacks *the king* and lacks *fled*

13 The bronze pillars that were in
the house of the LORD, as well as the
stands and the bronze sea that were in
the house of the LORD, the Chaldeans
broke in pieces, and carried the bronze
to Babylon. 14 They took away the pots,
the shovels, the snuffers, the dishes
for incense, and all the bronze vessels
used in the temple service, 15 as well as
the firepans and the basins. What was
made of gold the captain of the guard
took away for the gold, and what was
made of silver, for the silver. 16 As for the
two pillars, the one sea, and the stands,
which Solomon had made for the house
of the LORD, the bronze of all these vessels was beyond weighing. 17 The height
of one pillar was eighteen cubits, and on
it was a bronze capital; the height of the
capital was three cubits; lattice-work
and pomegranates, all of bronze, were
on the capital all round. The second pillar had the same, with the lattice-work.

18 The captain of the guard took the
chief priest Seraiah, the second priest
Zephaniah, and the three guardians of
the threshold; 19 from the city he took an
officer who had been in command of the
soldiers, and five men of the king's council who were found in the city; the secretary who was the commander of the
army who mustered the people of the
land; and sixty men of the people of the
land who were found in the city. 20 Nebuzaradan the captain of the guard took
them, and brought them to the king of
Babylon at Riblah. 21 The king of Babylon struck them down and put them to
death at Riblah in the land of Hamath.
So Judah went into exile out of its land.

GEDALIAH MADE GOVERNOR OF JUDAH

22 He appointed Gedaliah son of
Ahikam son of Shaphan as governor
over the people who remained in the
land of Judah, whom King Nebuchadnezzar of Babylon had left. 23 Now
when all the captains of the forces and
their men heard that the king of Babylon had appointed Gedaliah as governor, they came with their men to
Gedaliah at Mizpah, namely, Ishmael
son of Nethaniah, Johanan son of Kareah, Seraiah son of Tanhumeth the
Netophathite, and Jaazaniah son of
the Maacathite. 24 Gedaliah swore to
them and their men, saying, 'Do not
be afraid because of the Chaldean officials; live in the land, serve the king of
Babylon, and it shall be well with you.'
25 But in the seventh month, Ishmael
son of Nethaniah son of Elishama, of
the royal family, came with ten men;
they struck down Gedaliah so that he
died, along with the Judeans and Chaldeans who were with him at Mizpah.
26 Then all the people, high and low,[y]
and the captains of the forces, set out
and went to Egypt; for they were afraid
of the Chaldeans.

JEHOIACHIN RELEASED FROM PRISON

27 In the thirty-seventh year of the
exile of King Jehoiachin of Judah, in
the twelfth month, on the twenty-
seventh day of the month, King Evil-
merodach of Babylon, in the year that
he began to reign, released King Jehoiachin of Judah from prison; 28 he spoke
kindly to him, and gave him a seat
above the other seats of the kings who
were with him in Babylon. 29 So Jehoiachin put aside his prison clothes.
Every day of his life he dined regularly
in the king's presence. 30 For his allowance, a regular allowance was given
him by the king, a portion every day,
as long as he lived.

[y] 25.26 Or *young and old*

1 CHRONICLES

First Chronicles is the first part of a more comprehensive work that originally included 2 Chronicles, Ezra, and Nehemiah. Compiled during the fifth century BCE, all four parts of the whole work are concerned with the arrangements of temple worship in Jerusalem. First Chronicles reviews historical events leading up to David and his subsequent preparation for the building of the temple in Jerusalem. David is the central figure of 1 Chronicles beginning with the genealogical history (chs. 1–9), his ascension to the throne of the monarchy (chs. 10–12), his placement of the ark in Jerusalem (chs. 13–16), his military conquests (chs. 17–20), and his preparation for the temple construction before his death (chs. 21–29). David is presented much more favorably in the history of the Chronicler than he is in the history of the Deuteronomist. The Chronicler's history, like that of the Deuteronomist, is an interpretation of events in light of God's action and providence.

There is only one passage from 1 Chronicles that is taken into the Roman Lectionary. It is a selection used as one of the choices for the First Reading in the Common of the Blessed Virgin Mary. The passage describes the Levites bringing the ark of the Lord to Jerusalem and placing it in the tent prepared for it, surrounded by music appropriate for a liturgical setting as authorized by David (15.3–4, 15–16; 16.1–2). This passage evokes a striking image in the context of the Christian liturgy, which interprets it as a prefiguring of the presence of the Word of God to his people through the motherhood of the Blessed Virgin Mary.

FROM ADAM TO ABRAHAM

1 Adam, Seth, Enosh; 2Kenan, Mahalalel, Jared; 3Enoch, Methuselah,
Lamech; 4Noah, Shem, Ham, and Japheth.
5 The descendants of Japheth: Gomer,
Magog, Madai, Javan, Tubal, Meshech,
and Tiras. 6The descendants of Gomer:
Ashkenaz, Diphath,[a] and Togarmah.
7The descendants of Javan: Elishah, Tarshish, Kittim, and Rodanim.[b]
8 The descendants of Ham: Cush,
Egypt, Put, and Canaan. 9The descendants of Cush: Seba, Havilah, Sabta,
Raama, and Sabteca. The descendants of
Raamah: Sheba and Dedan. 10Cush became the father of Nimrod; he was the
first to be a mighty one on the earth.
11 Egypt became the father of Ludim, Anamim, Lehabim, Naphtuhim,
12Pathrusim, Casluhim, and Caphtorim,
from whom the Philistines come.[c]
13 Canaan became the father of Sidon his firstborn, and Heth, 14and the
Jebusites, the Amorites, the Girgashites, 15the Hivites, the Arkites, the
Sinites, 16the Arvadites, the Zemarites,
and the Hamathites.
17 The descendants of Shem: Elam,
Asshur, Arpachshad, Lud, Aram, Uz,
Hul, Gether, and Meshech.[d] 18Arpach-
shad became the father of Shelah; and
Shelah became the father of Eber. 19To
Eber were born two sons: the name of
one was Peleg (for in his days the earth
was divided), and the name of his brother
Joktan. 20Joktan became the father of
Almodad, Sheleph, Hazarmaveth, Je-
rah, 21Hadoram, Uzal, Diklah, 22Ebal,
Abimael, Sheba, 23Ophir, Havilah,

[a] 1.6 Gen 10.3 *Ripath*; See Gk Vg [b] 1.7 Gen 10.4 *Dodanim*; See Syr Vg [c] 1.12 Heb *Casluhim, from which the Philistines come, Caphtorim*; See Am 9.7, Jer 47.4 [d] 1.17 *Mash* in Gen 10.23

and Jobab; all these were the descendants of Joktan.
24 Shem, Arpachshad, Shelah; 25 Eber,
Peleg, Reu; 26 Serug, Nahor, Terah;
27 Abram, that is, Abraham.

FROM ABRAHAM TO JACOB

28 The sons of Abraham: Isaac and
Ishmael. 29 These are their genealogies:
the firstborn of Ishmael, Nebaioth; and
Kedar, Adbeel, Mibsam, 30 Mishma,
Dumah, Massa, Hadad, Tema, 31 Jetur,
Naphish, and Kedemah. These are the
sons of Ishmael. 32 The sons of Keturah,
Abraham's concubine: she bore Zimran,
Jokshan, Medan, Midian, Ishbak, and
Shuah. The sons of Jokshan: Sheba and
Dedan. 33 The sons of Midian: Ephah,
Epher, Hanoch, Abida, and Eldaah. All
these were the descendants of Keturah.
34 Abraham became the father of
Isaac. The sons of Isaac: Esau and Is-
rael. 35 The sons of Esau: Eliphaz, Reuel,
Jeush, Jalam, and Korah. 36 The sons of
Eliphaz: Teman, Omar, Zephi, Gatam,
Kenaz, Timna, and Amalek. 37 The sons
of Reuel: Nahath, Zerah, Shammah,
and Mizzah.
38 The sons of Seir: Lotan, Shobal,
Zibeon, Anah, Dishon, Ezer, and Di-
shan. 39 The sons of Lotan: Hori and
Homam; and Lotan's sister was Timna.
40 The sons of Shobal: Alian, Manahath,
Ebal, Shephi, and Onam. The sons of
Zibeon: Aiah and Anah. 41 The sons
of Anah: Dishon. The sons of Dishon:
Hamran, Eshban, Ithran, and Cheran.
42 The sons of Ezer: Bilhan, Zaavan, and
Jaakan.[e] The sons of Dishan:[f] Uz and
Aran.
43 These are the kings who reigned
in the land of Edom before any king
reigned over the Israelites: Bela son of
Beor, whose city was called Dinhabah.
44 When Bela died, Jobab son of Zerah
of Bozrah succeeded him. 45 When Jobab
died, Husham of the land of the Temanites succeeded him. 46 When Husham
died, Hadad son of Bedad, who defeated
Midian in the country of Moab, succeeded him; and the name of his city
was Avith. 47 When Hadad died, Samlah of Masrekah succeeded him. 48 When
Samlah died, Shaul[g] of Rehoboth on
the Euphrates succeeded him. 49 When
Shaul[h] died, Baal-hanan son of Achbor
succeeded him. 50 When Baal-hanan
died, Hadad succeeded him; the name
of his city was Pai, and his wife's name
Mehetabel daughter of Matred, daughter of Me-zahab. 51 And Hadad died.
The clans[i] of Edom were: clans[j]
Timna, Aliah,[k] Jetheth, 52 Oholibamah,
Elah, Pinon, 53 Kenaz, Teman, Mibzar, 54 Magdiel, and Iram; these are the
clans[l] of Edom.

THE SONS OF ISRAEL AND THE DESCENDANTS OF JUDAH

2 These are the sons of Israel: Reuben,
Simeon, Levi, Judah, Issachar, Zebulun, 2 Dan, Joseph, Benjamin, Naphtali, Gad, and Asher. 3 The sons of Judah: Er, Onan, and Shelah; these three
the Canaanite woman Bath-shua bore
to him. Now Er, Judah's firstborn, was
wicked in the sight of the LORD, and he
put him to death. 4 His daughter-in-law
Tamar also bore him Perez and Zerah.
Judah had five sons in all.
5 The sons of Perez: Hezron and Hamul. 6 The sons of Zerah: Zimri, Ethan,
Heman, Calcol, and Dara,[m] five in all.
7 The sons of Carmi: Achar, the troubler
of Israel, who transgressed in the matter of the devoted thing; 8 and Ethan's
son was Azariah.
9 The sons of Hezron, who were born
to him: Jerahmeel, Ram, and Chelubai.
10 Ram became the father of Amminadab, and Amminadab became the father of Nahshon, prince of the sons of
Judah. 11 Nahshon became the father of
Salma, Salma of Boaz, 12 Boaz of Obed,
Obed of Jesse. 13 Jesse became the father
of Eliab his firstborn, Abinadab the second, Shimea the third, 14 Nethanel the
fourth, Raddai the fifth, 15 Ozem the
sixth, David the seventh; 16 and their
sisters were Zeruiah and Abigail. The
sons of Zeruiah: Abishai, Joab, and Asahel, three. 17 Abigail bore Amasa, and
the father of Amasa was Jether the Ishmaelite.
18 Caleb son of Hezron had children
by his wife Azubah, and by Jerioth;
these were her sons: Jesher, Shobab,
and Ardon. 19 When Azubah died, Caleb
married Ephrath, who bore him Hur.
20 Hur became the father of Uri, and Uri
became the father of Bezalel.
21 Afterwards Hezron went in to
the daughter of Machir father of Gilead, whom he married when he was
sixty years old; and she bore him Segub; 22 and Segub became the father of

[e] **1.42** Or *and Akan*; See Gen 36.27 [f] **1.42** See 1.38: Heb *Dishon* [g] **1.48** Or *Saul* [h] **1.49** Or *Saul* [i] **1.51** Or *chiefs* [j] **1.51** Or *chiefs* [k] **1.51** Or *Alvah*; See Gen 36.40 [l] **1.54** Or *chiefs* [m] **2.6** Or *Darda*; Compare Syr Tg some Gk Mss; See 1 Kings 4.31

Jair, who had twenty-three towns in the
land of Gilead. 23 But Geshur and Aram
took from them Havvoth-jair, Kenath
and its villages, sixty towns. All these
were descendants of Machir, father of
Gilead. 24 After the death of Hezron, in
Caleb-ephrathah, Abijah wife of Hezron
bore him Ashhur, father of Tekoa.

25 The sons of Jerahmeel, the firstborn
of Hezron: Ram his firstborn, Bunah,
Oren, Ozem, and Ahijah. 26 Jerahmeel
also had another wife, whose name was
Atarah; she was the mother of Onam.
27 The sons of Ram, the firstborn of Jerahmeel: Maaz, Jamin, and Eker. 28 The
sons of Onam: Shammai and Jada. The
sons of Shammai: Nadab and Abishur.
29 The name of Abishur's wife was Abihail, and she bore him Ahban and Molid.
30 The sons of Nadab: Seled and Appaim;
and Seled died childless. 31 The son[n] of
Appaim: Ishi. The son[o] of Ishi: Sheshan. The son[p] of Sheshan: Ahlai. 32 The
sons of Jada, Shammai's brother: Jether
and Jonathan; and Jether died childless.
33 The sons of Jonathan: Peleth and Zaza.
These were the descendants of Jerahmeel. 34 Now Sheshan had no sons, only
daughters; but Sheshan had an Egyptian
slave, whose name was Jarha. 35 So Sheshan gave his daughter in marriage to his
slave Jarha; and she bore him Attai. 36 Attai became the father of Nathan, and Nathan of Zabad. 37 Zabad became the father
of Ephlal, and Ephlal of Obed. 38 Obed
became the father of Jehu, and Jehu of
Azariah. 39 Azariah became the father of
Helez, and Helez of Eleasah. 40 Eleasah
became the father of Sismai, and Sismai
of Shallum. 41 Shallum became the father
of Jekamiah, and Jekamiah of Elishama.

42 The sons of Caleb brother of Jerahmeel: Mesha[q] his firstborn, who was father of Ziph. The sons of Mareshah father
of Hebron. 43 The sons of Hebron: Korah,
Tappuah, Rekem, and Shema. 44 Shema
became father of Raham, father of Jor-
keam; and Rekem became the father of
Shammai. 45 The son of Shammai: Maon;
and Maon was the father of Beth-zur.
46 Ephah also, Caleb's concubine, bore
Haran, Moza, and Gazez; and Haran became the father of Gazez. 47 The sons of
Jahdai: Regem, Jotham, Geshan, Pelet,
Ephah, and Shaaph. 48 Maacah, Caleb's
concubine, bore Sheber and Tirhanah.
49 She also bore Shaaph father of Madmannah, Sheva father of Machbenah
and father of Gibea; and the daughter of
Caleb was Achsah. 50 These were the descendants of Caleb.

The sons[r] of Hur the firstborn of Ephrathah: Shobal father of Kiriath-jearim,
51 Salma father of Bethlehem, and Ha-
reph father of Beth-gader. 52 Shobal father of Kiriath-jearim had other sons:
Haroeh, half of the Menuhoth. 53 And
the families of Kiriath-jearim: the Ith-
rites, the Puthites, the Shumathites,
and the Mishraites; from these came the
Zorathites and the Eshtaolites. 54 The
sons of Salma: Bethlehem, the Netophathites, Atroth-beth-joab, and half of
the Manahathites, the Zorites. 55 The
families also of the scribes that lived at
Jabez: the Tirathites, the Shimeathites,
and the Sucathites. These are the Kenites who came from Hammath, father
of the house of Rechab.

DESCENDANTS OF DAVID AND SOLOMON

3 These are the sons of David who
were born to him in Hebron: the
firstborn Amnon, by Ahinoam the Jezreelite; the second Daniel, by Abigail
the Carmelite; 2 the third Absalom, son
of Maacah, daughter of King Talmai
of Geshur; the fourth Adonijah, son
of Haggith; 3 the fifth Shephatiah, by
Abital; the sixth Ithream, by his wife
Eglah; 4 six were born to him in Hebron,
where he reigned for seven years and six
months. And he reigned for thirty-three
years in Jerusalem. 5 These were born
to him in Jerusalem: Shimea, Shobab,
Nathan, and Solomon, four by Bath-
shua, daughter of Ammiel; 6 then Ibhar,
Elishama, Eliphelet, 7 Nogah, Nepheg,
Japhia, 8 Elishama, Eliada, and Eliphelet, nine. 9 All these were David's sons,
besides the sons of the concubines; and
Tamar was their sister.

10 The descendants of Solomon: Rehoboam, Abijah his son, Asa his son,
Jehoshaphat his son, 11 Joram his son,
Ahaziah his son, Joash his son, 12 Amaziah his son, Azariah his son, Jotham
his son, 13 Ahaz his son, Hezekiah his
son, Manasseh his son, 14 Amon his son,
Josiah his son. 15 The sons of Josiah: Johanan the firstborn, the second Jehoiakim, the third Zedekiah, the fourth
Shallum. 16 The descendants of Jehoiakim: Jeconiah his son, Zedekiah his son;
17 and the sons of Jeconiah, the captive:
Shealtiel his son, 18 Malchiram, Pedaiah, Shenazzar, Jekamiah, Hoshama,
and Nedabiah; 19 The sons of Pedaiah:

[n] **2.31** Heb *sons* [o] **2.31** Heb *sons* [p] **2.31** Heb *sons* [q] **2.42** Gk reads *Mareshah* [r] **2.50** Gk Vg: Heb *son*

Zerubbabel and Shimei; and the sons of Zerubbabel: Meshullam and Hananiah, and Shelomith was their sister; 20 and Hashubah, Ohel, Berechiah, Hasadiah, and Jushab-hesed, five. 21 The sons of Hananiah: Pelatiah and Jeshaiah, his son[s] Rephaiah, his son[t] Arnan, his son[u] Obadiah, his son[v] Shecaniah. 22 The son[w] of Shecaniah: Shemaiah. And the sons of Shemaiah: Hattush, Igal, Bariah, Neariah, and Shaphat, six. 23 The sons of Neariah: Elioenai, Hizkiah, and Azrikam, three. 24 The sons of Elioenai: Hodaviah, Eliashib, Pelaiah, Akkub, Johanan, Delaiah, and Anani, seven.

DESCENDANTS OF JUDAH

4 The sons of Judah: Perez, Hezron, Carmi, Hur, and Shobal. 2 Reaiah son of Shobal became the father of Jahath, and Jahath became the father of Ahumai and Lahad. These were the families of the Zorathites. 3 These were the sons[x] of Etam: Jezreel, Ishma, and Idbash; and the name of their sister was Hazzelelponi, 4 and Penuel was the father of Gedor, and Ezer the father of Hushah. These were the sons of Hur, the firstborn of Ephrathah, the father of Bethlehem. 5 Ashhur father of Tekoa had two wives, Helah and Naarah; 6 Naarah bore him Ahuzzam, Hepher, Temeni, and Haahashtari.[y] These were the sons of Naarah. 7 The sons of Helah: Zereth, Izhar,[z] and Ethnan. 8 Koz became the father of Anub, Zobebah, and the families of Aharhel son of Harum. 9 Jabez was honoured more than his brothers; and his mother named him Jabez, saying, 'Because I bore him in pain.' 10 Jabez called on the God of Israel, saying, 'Oh that you would bless me and enlarge my border, and that your hand might be with me, and that you would keep me from hurt and harm!' And God granted what he asked. 11 Chelub the brother of Shuhah became the father of Mehir, who was the father of Eshton. 12 Eshton became the father of Beth-rapha, Paseah, and Tehinnah the father of Ir-nahash. These are the men of Recah. 13 The sons of Kenaz: Othniel and Seraiah; and the sons of Othniel: Hathath and Meonothai.[a] 14 Meonothai became the father of Ophrah; and Seraiah became the father of Joab father of Ge-harashim,[b] so-called because they were artisans. 15 The sons of Caleb son of Jephunneh: Iru, Elah, and Naam; and the son[c] of Elah: Kenaz. 16 The sons of Jehallelel: Ziph, Ziphah, Tiria, and Asarel. 17 The sons of Ezrah: Jether, Mered, Epher, and Jalon. These are the sons of Bithiah, daughter of Pharaoh, whom Mered married;[d] and she conceived and bore[e] Miriam, Shammai, and Ishbah father of Eshtemoa. 18 And his Judean wife bore Jered father of Gedor, Heber father of Soco, and Jekuthiel father of Zanoah. 19 The sons of the wife of Hodiah, the sister of Naham, were the fathers of Keilah the Garmite and Eshtemoa the Maacathite. 20 The sons of Shimon: Amnon, Rinnah, Ben-hanan, and Tilon. The sons of Ishi: Zoheth and Ben-zoheth. 21 The sons of Shelah son of Judah: Er father of Lecah, Laadah father of Mareshah, and the families of the guild of linen workers at Beth-ashbea; 22 and Jokim, and the men of Cozeba, and Joash, and Saraph, who married into Moab but returned to Lehem[f] (now the records[g] are ancient). 23 These were the potters and inhabitants of Netaim and Gederah; they lived there with the king in his service.

DESCENDANTS OF SIMEON

24 The sons of Simeon: Nemuel, Jamin, Jarib, Zerah, Shaul;[h] 25 Shallum was his son, Mibsam his son, Mishma his son. 26 The sons of Mishma: Hammuel his son, Zaccur his son, Shimei his son. 27 Shimei had sixteen sons and six daughters; but his brothers did not have many children, nor did all their family multiply like the Judeans. 28 They lived in Beer-sheba, Moladah, Hazar-shual, 29 Bilhah, Ezem, Tolad, 30 Bethuel, Hormah, Ziklag, 31 Beth-marcaboth, Hazar-susim, Beth-biri, and Shaaraim. These were their towns until David became king. 32 And their villages were Etam, Ain, Rimmon, Tochen, and Ashan, five towns, 33 along with all their villages that were around these towns as far as Baal. These were their settlements. And they kept a genealogical record.

34 Meshobab, Jamlech, Joshah son of Amaziah, 35 Joel, Jehu son of Joshibiah son of Seraiah son of Asiel, 36 Elioenai, Jaakobah, Jeshohaiah, Asaiah, Adiel, Jesimiel, Benaiah, 37 Ziza son of

[s] 3.21 Gk Compare Syr Vg: Heb *sons of* [t] 3.21 Gk Compare Syr Vg: Heb *sons of* [u] 3.21 Gk Compare Syr Vg: Heb *sons of* [v] 3.21 Gk Compare Syr Vg: Heb *sons of* [w] 3.22 Heb *sons* [x] 4.3 Gk Compare Vg: Heb *the father* [y] 4.6 Or *Ahashtari* [z] 4.7 Another reading is *Zohar* [a] 4.13 Gk Vg: Heb lacks *and Meonothai* [b] 4.14 That is *Valley of artisans* [c] 4.15 Heb *sons* [d] 4.17 The clause: *These are . . . married* is transposed from verse 18 [e] 4.17 Heb lacks *and bore* [f] 4.22 Vg Compare Gk: Heb *and Jashubi-lahem* [g] 4.22 Or *matters* [h] 4.24 Or *Saul*

Shiphi son of Allon son of Jedaiah son
of Shimri son of Shemaiah— 38 these
mentioned by name were leaders in
their families, and their clans increased
greatly. 39 They journeyed to the entrance of Gedor, to the east side of the
valley, to seek pasture for their flocks,
40 where they found rich, good pasture,
and the land was very broad, quiet, and
peaceful; for the former inhabitants
there belonged to Ham. 41 These, registered by name, came in the days of King
Hezekiah of Judah, and attacked their
tents and the Meunim who were found
there, and exterminated them to this
day, and settled in their place, because
there was pasture there for their flocks.
42 And some of them, five hundred men
of the Simeonites, went to Mount Seir,
having as their leaders Pelatiah, Neariah, Rephaiah, and Uzziel, sons of Ishi;
43 they destroyed the remnant of the
Amalekites that had escaped, and they
have lived there to this day.

DESCENDANTS OF REUBEN

5 The sons of Reuben the firstborn
of Israel. (He was the firstborn,
but because he defiled his father's bed
his birthright was given to the sons of
Joseph son of Israel, so that he is not
enrolled in the genealogy according to
the birthright; 2 though Judah became
prominent among his brothers and a
ruler came from him, yet the birthright
belonged to Joseph.) 3 The sons of Reuben, the firstborn of Israel: Hanoch,
Pallu, Hezron, and Carmi. 4 The sons
of Joel: Shemaiah his son, Gog his son,
Shimei his son, 5 Micah his son, Reaiah
his son, Baal his son, 6 Beerah his son,
whom King Tilgath-pilneser of Assyria
carried away into exile; he was a chief-
tain of the Reubenites. 7 And his kindred
by their families, when the genealogy
of their generations was reckoned: the
chief, Jeiel, and Zechariah, 8 and Bela
son of Azaz, son of Shema, son of Joel,
who lived in Aroer, as far as Nebo and
Baal-meon. 9 He also lived to the east as
far as the beginning of the desert this
side of the Euphrates, because their cattle had multiplied in the land of Gilead.
10 And in the days of Saul they made war
on the Hagrites, who fell by their hand;
and they lived in their tents throughout
all the region east of Gilead.

DESCENDANTS OF GAD

11 The sons of Gad lived beside them
in the land of Bashan as far as Salecah:
12 Joel the chief, Shapham the second,
Janai, and Shaphat in Bashan. 13 And
their kindred according to their clans:
Michael, Meshullam, Sheba, Jorai, Ja-
can, Zia, and Eber, seven. 14 These were
the sons of Abihail son of Huri, son of
Jaroah, son of Gilead, son of Michael,
son of Jeshishai, son of Jahdo, son of
Buz; 15 Ahi son of Abdiel, son of Guni,
was chief in their clan; 16 and they lived
in Gilead, in Bashan and in its towns,
and in all the pasture lands of Sharon to
their limits. 17 All of these were enrolled
by genealogies in the days of King Jotham of Judah, and in the days of King
Jeroboam of Israel.

18 The Reubenites, the Gadites, and
the half-tribe of Manasseh had valiant
warriors, who carried shield and sword,
and drew the bow, expert in war, forty-
four thousand seven hundred and sixty,
ready for service. 19 They made war on
the Hagrites, Jetur, Naphish, and No-
dab; 20 and when they received help
against them, the Hagrites and all who
were with them were given into their
hands, for they cried to God in the battle, and he granted their entreaty because they trusted in him. 21 They captured their livestock: fifty thousand
of their camels, two hundred and fifty
thousand sheep, two thousand donkeys,
and one hundred thousand captives.
22 Many fell slain, because the war was
of God. And they lived in their territory
until the exile.

THE HALF-TRIBE OF MANASSEH

23 The members of the half-tribe
of Manasseh lived in the land; they
were very numerous from Bashan to
Baal-hermon, Senir, and Mount Hermon. 24 These were the heads of their
clans: Epher,[i] Ishi, Eliel, Azriel, Jeremiah, Hodaviah, and Jahdiel, mighty
warriors, famous men, heads of their
clans. 25 But they transgressed against
the God of their ancestors, and prostituted themselves to the gods of the
peoples of the land, whom God had destroyed before them. 26 So the God of
Israel stirred up the spirit of King Pul
of Assyria, the spirit of King Tilgath-
pilneser of Assyria, and he carried them
away, namely, the Reubenites, the Gadites, and the half-tribe of Manasseh, and
brought them to Halah, Habor, Hara,
and the river Gozan, to this day.

[i] 5.24 Gk Vg: Heb *and Epher*

DESCENDANTS OF LEVI

6[i] The sons of Levi: Gershom,[k] Kohath, and Merari. 2 The sons of Kohath: Amram, Izhar, Hebron, and Uzziel. 3 The children of Amram: Aaron, Moses, and Miriam. The sons of Aaron: Nadab, Abihu, Eleazar, and Ithamar. 4 Eleazar became the father of Phinehas, Phinehas of Abishua, 5 Abishua of Bukki, Bukki of Uzzi, 6 Uzzi of Zerahiah, Zerahiah of Meraioth, 7 Meraioth of Amariah, Amariah of Ahitub, 8 Ahitub of Zadok, Zadok of Ahimaaz, 9 Ahimaaz of Azariah, Azariah of Johanan, 10 and Johanan of Azariah (it was he who served as priest in the house that Solomon built in Jerusalem). 11 Azariah became the father of Amariah, Amariah of Ahitub, 12 Ahitub of Zadok, Zadok of Shallum, 13 Shallum of Hilkiah, Hilkiah of Azariah, 14 Azariah of Seraiah, Seraiah of Jehozadak; 15 and Jehozadak went into exile when the LORD sent Judah and Jerusalem into exile by the hand of Nebuchadnezzar.

16[l] The sons of Levi: Gershom, Kohath, and Merari. 17 These are the names of the sons of Gershom: Libni and Shimei. 18 The sons of Kohath: Amram, Izhar, Hebron, and Uzziel. 19 The sons of Merari: Mahli and Mushi. These are the clans of the Levites according to their ancestry. 20 Of Gershom: Libni his son, Jahath his son, Zimmah his son, 21 Joah his son, Iddo his son, Zerah his son, Jeatherai his son. 22 The sons of Kohath: Amminadab his son, Korah his son, Assir his son, 23 Elkanah his son, Ebiasaph his son, Assir his son, 24 Tahath his son, Uriel his son, Uzziah his son, and Shaul his son. 25 The sons of Elkanah: Amasai and Ahimoth, 26 Elkanah his son, Zophai his son, Nahath his son, 27 Eliab his son, Jeroham his son, Elkanah his son. 28 The sons of Samuel: Joel[m] his firstborn, the second Abijah.[n] 29 The sons of Merari: Mahli, Libni his son, Shimei his son, Uzzah his son, 30 Shimea his son, Haggiah his son, and Asaiah his son.

MUSICIANS APPOINTED BY DAVID

31 These are the men whom David put in charge of the service of song in the house of the LORD, after the ark came to rest there. 32 They ministered with song before the tabernacle of the tent of meeting, until Solomon had built the house of the LORD in Jerusalem; and they performed their service in due order. 33 These are the men who served; and their sons were: Of the Kohathites: Heman, the singer, son of Joel, son of Samuel, 34 son of Elkanah, son of Jeroham, son of Eliel, son of Toah, 35 son of Zuph, son of Elkanah, son of Mahath, son of Amasai, 36 son of Elkanah, son of Joel, son of Azariah, son of Zephaniah, 37 son of Tahath, son of Assir, son of Ebiasaph, son of Korah, 38 son of Izhar, son of Kohath, son of Levi, son of Israel; 39 and his brother Asaph, who stood on his right, namely, Asaph son of Berechiah, son of Shimea, 40 son of Michael, son of Baaseiah, son of Malchijah, 41 son of Ethni, son of Zerah, son of Adaiah, 42 son of Ethan, son of Zimmah, son of Shimei, 43 son of Jahath, son of Gershom, son of Levi. 44 On the left were their kindred the sons of Merari: Ethan son of Kishi, son of Abdi, son of Malluch, 45 son of Hashabiah, son of Amaziah, son of Hilkiah, 46 son of Amzi, son of Bani, son of Shemer, 47 son of Mahli, son of Mushi, son of Merari, son of Levi; 48 and their kindred the Levites were appointed for all the service of the tabernacle of the house of God.

49 But Aaron and his sons made offerings on the altar of burnt-offering and on the altar of incense, doing all the work of the most holy place, to make atonement for Israel, according to all that Moses the servant of God had commanded. 50 These are the sons of Aaron: Eleazar his son, Phinehas his son, Abishua his son, 51 Bukki his son, Uzzi his son, Zerahiah his son, 52 Meraioth his son, Amariah his son, Ahitub his son, 53 Zadok his son, Ahimaaz his son.

SETTLEMENTS OF THE LEVITES

54 These are their dwelling-places according to their settlements within their borders: to the sons of Aaron of the families of Kohathites—for the lot fell to them first— 55 to them they gave Hebron in the land of Judah and its surrounding pasture lands, 56 but the fields of the city and its villages they gave to Caleb son of Jephunneh. 57 To the sons of Aaron they gave the cities of refuge: Hebron, Libnah with its pasture lands, Jattir, Eshtemoa with its pasture lands, 58 Hilen[o] with its pasture lands, Debir with its pasture lands, 59 Ashan with its

[i] **6.1** Ch 5.27 in Heb [k] **6.1** Heb *Gershon*, variant of *Gershom*; See 6.16 [l] **6.16** Ch 6.1 in Heb [m] **6.28** Gk Syr Compare verse 33 and 1 Sam 8.2: Heb lacks *Joel* [n] **6.28** Heb reads *Vashni, and Abijah* for *the second Abijah*, taking *the second* as a proper name [o] **6.58** Other readings *Hilez, Holon*; See Josh 21.15

pasture lands, and Beth-shemesh with its pasture lands. 60 From the tribe of Benjamin, Geba with its pasture lands, Alemeth with its pasture lands, and Anathoth with its pasture lands. All their towns throughout their families were thirteen.

61 To the rest of the Kohathites were given by lot out of the family of the tribe, out of the half-tribe, the half of Manasseh, ten towns. 62 To the Gershomites according to their families were allotted thirteen towns out of the tribes of Issachar, Asher, Naphtali, and Manasseh in Bashan. 63 To the Merarites according to their families were allotted twelve towns out of the tribes of Reuben, Gad, and Zebulun. 64 So the people of Israel gave the Levites the towns with their pasture lands. 65 They also gave them by lot out of the tribes of Judah, Simeon, and Benjamin these towns that are mentioned by name.

66 And some of the families of the sons of Kohath had towns of their territory out of the tribe of Ephraim. 67 They were given the cities of refuge: Shechem with its pasture lands in the hill country of Ephraim, Gezer with its pasture lands, 68 Jokmeam with its pasture lands, Beth-horon with its pasture lands, 69 Aijalon with its pasture lands, Gath-rimmon with its pasture lands; 70 and out of the half-tribe of Manasseh, Aner with its pasture lands, and Bileam with its pasture lands, for the rest of the families of the Kohathites.

71 To the Gershomites: out of the half-tribe of Manasseh: Golan in Bashan with its pasture lands and Ashtaroth with its pasture lands; 72 and out of the tribe of Issachar: Kedesh with its pasture lands, Daberath[p] with its pasture lands, 73 Ramoth with its pasture lands, and Anem with its pasture lands; 74 out of the tribe of Asher: Mashal with its pasture lands, Abdon with its pasture lands, 75 Hukok with its pasture lands, and Rehob with its pasture lands; 76 and out of the tribe of Naphtali: Kedesh in Galilee with its pasture lands, Hammon with its pasture lands, and Kiriathaim with its pasture lands. 77 To the rest of the Merarites out of the tribe of Zebulun: Rimmono with its pasture lands, Tabor with its pasture lands, 78 and across the Jordan from Jericho, on the east side of the Jordan, out of the tribe of Reuben: Bezer in the steppe with its pasture lands, Jahzah with its pasture lands, 79 Kedemoth with its pasture lands, and Mephaath with its pasture lands; 80 and out of the tribe of Gad: Ramoth in Gilead with its pasture lands, Mahanaim with its pasture lands, 81 Heshbon with its pasture lands, and Jazer with its pasture lands.

DESCENDANTS OF ISSACHAR

7 The sons[q] of Issachar: Tola, Puah, Jashub, and Shimron, four. 2 The sons of Tola: Uzzi, Rephaiah, Jeriel, Jahmai, Ibsam, and Shemuel, heads of their ancestral houses, namely of Tola, mighty warriors of their generations, their number in the days of David being twenty-two thousand six hundred. 3 The son[r] of Uzzi: Izrahiah. And the sons of Izrahiah: Michael, Obadiah, Joel, and Isshiah, five, all of them chiefs; 4 and along with them, by their generations, according to their ancestral houses, were units of the fighting force, thirty-six thousand, for they had many wives and sons. 5 Their kindred belonging to all the families of Issachar were in all eighty-seven thousand mighty warriors, enrolled by genealogy.

DESCENDANTS OF BENJAMIN

6 The sons of Benjamin: Bela, Becher, and Jediael, three. 7 The sons of Bela: Ezbon, Uzzi, Uzziel, Jerimoth, and Iri, five, heads of ancestral houses, mighty warriors; and their enrolment by genealogies was twenty-two thousand and thirty-four. 8 The sons of Becher: Zemirah, Joash, Eliezer, Elioenai, Omri, Jeremoth, Abijah, Anathoth, and Alemeth. All these were the sons of Becher; 9 and their enrolment by genealogies, according to their generations, as heads of their ancestral houses, mighty warriors, was twenty thousand two hundred. 10 The sons of Jediael: Bilhan. And the sons of Bilhan: Jeush, Benjamin, Ehud, Chenaanah, Zethan, Tarshish, and Ahishahar. 11 All these were the sons of Jediael according to the heads of their ancestral houses, mighty warriors, seventeen thousand two hundred, ready for service in war. 12 And Shuppim and Huppim were the sons of Ir, Hushim the son[s] of Aher.

DESCENDANTS OF NAPHTALI

13 The descendants of Naphtali: Jahziel, Guni, Jezer, and Shallum, the descendants of Bilhah.

[p] 6.72 Or *Dobrath* [q] 7.1 Syr Compare Vg: Heb *And to the sons* [r] 7.3 Heb *sons*
[s] 7.12 Heb *sons*

DESCENDANTS OF MANASSEH

14 The sons of Manasseh: Asriel,
whom his Aramean concubine bore; she
bore Machir the father of Gilead. 15 And
Machir took a wife for Huppim and for
Shuppim. The name of his sister was
Maacah. And the name of the second
was Zelophehad; and Zelophehad had
daughters. 16 Maacah the wife of Machir
bore a son, and she named him Peresh;
the name of his brother was Sheresh;
and his sons were Ulam and Rekem.
17 The son[t] of Ulam: Bedan. These were
the sons of Gilead son of Machir, son
of Manasseh. 18 And his sister Ham-
molecheth bore Ishhod, Abiezer, and
Mahlah. 19 The sons of Shemida were
Ahian, Shechem, Likhi, and Aniam.

DESCENDANTS OF EPHRAIM

20 The sons of Ephraim: Shuthelah,
and Bered his son, Tahath his son, Elea-
dah his son, Tahath his son, 21 Zabad his
son, Shuthelah his son, and Ezer and El-
ead. Now the people of Gath, who were
born in the land, killed them, because
they came down to raid their cattle.
22 And their father Ephraim mourned
for many days, and his brothers came
to comfort him. 23 Ephraim[u] went in to
his wife, and she conceived and bore
a son; and he named him Beriah, because disaster[v] had befallen his house.
24 His daughter was Sheerah, who built
both Lower and Upper Beth-horon, and
Uzzen-sheerah. 25 Rephah was his son,
Resheph his son, Telah his son, Tahan
his son, 26 Ladan his son, Ammihud his
son, Elishama his son, 27 Nun[w] his son,
Joshua his son. 28 Their possessions and
settlements were Bethel and its towns,
and eastwards Naaran, and westwards
Gezer and its towns, Shechem and its
towns, as far as Ayyah and its towns;
29 also along the borders of the Manassites, Beth-shean and its towns, Taanach and its towns, Megiddo and its
towns, Dor and its towns. In these lived
the sons of Joseph son of Israel.

DESCENDANTS OF ASHER

30 The sons of Asher: Imnah, Ishvah,
Ishvi, Beriah, and their sister Serah.
31 The sons of Beriah: Heber and Malchiel, who was the father of Birzaith.
32 Heber became the father of Japhlet,
Shomer, Hotham, and their sister Shua.
33 The sons of Japhlet: Pasach, Bimhal,
and Ashvath. These are the sons of Japhlet. 34 The sons of Shemer: Ahi, Rohgah,
Hubbah, and Aram. 35 The sons of Helem[x] his brother: Zophah, Imna, She-
lesh, and Amal. 36 The sons of Zophah:
Suah, Harnepher, Shual, Beri, Imrah,
37 Bezer, Hod, Shamma, Shilshah, Ithran, and Beera. 38 The sons of Jether: Jephunneh, Pispa, and Ara. 39 The sons of
Ulla: Arah, Hanniel, and Rizia. 40 All of
these were men of Asher, heads of ancestral houses, select mighty warriors,
chief of the princes. Their number enrolled by genealogies, for service in war,
was twenty-six thousand men.

DESCENDANTS OF BENJAMIN

8 Benjamin became the father of Bela
his firstborn, Ashbel the second,
Aharah the third, 2 Nohah the fourth,
and Rapha the fifth. 3 And Bela had
sons: Addar, Gera, Abihud,[y] 4 Abishua,
Naaman, Ahoah, 5 Gera, Shephuphan,
and Huram. 6 These are the sons of Ehud
(they were heads of ancestral houses
of the inhabitants of Geba, and they
were carried into exile to Manahath):
7 Naaman,[z] Ahijah, and Gera, that is,
Heglam,[a] who became the father of
Uzza and Ahihud. 8 And Shaharaim had
sons in the country of Moab after he had
sent away his wives Hushim and Baara.
9 He had sons by his wife Hodesh: Jobab,
Zibia, Mesha, Malcam, 10 Jeuz, Sachia,
and Mirmah. These were his sons, heads
of ancestral houses. 11 He also had sons by
Hushim: Abitub and Elpaal. 12 The sons
of Elpaal: Eber, Misham, and Shemed,
who built Ono and Lod with its towns,
13 and Beriah and Shema (they were
heads of ancestral houses of the inhabitants of Aijalon, who put to flight the
inhabitants of Gath); 14 and Ahio, Shashak, and Jeremoth. 15 Zebadiah, Arad,
Eder, 16 Michael, Ishpah, and Joha were
sons of Beriah. 17 Zebadiah, Meshullam,
Hizki, Heber, 18 Ishmerai, Izliah, and
Jobab were the sons of Elpaal. 19 Jakim,
Zichri, Zabdi, 20 Elienai, Zillethai, Eliel,
21 Adaiah, Beraiah, and Shimrath were
the sons of Shimei. 22 Ishpan, Eber,
Eliel, 23 Abdon, Zichri, Hanan, 24 Hananiah, Elam, Anthothijah, 25 Iphdeiah,
and Penuel were the sons of Shashak.
26 Shamsherai, Shehariah, Athaliah,
27 Jaareshiah, Elijah, and Zichri were
the sons of Jeroham. 28 These were the
heads of ancestral houses, according to

[t] **7.17** Heb *sons* [u] **7.23** Heb *He* [v] **7.23** Heb *beraah* [w] **7.27** Here spelled *Non*; see Ex 33.11 [x] **7.35** Or *Hotham*; see 7.32 [y] **8.3** Or *father of Ehud*; see 8.6 [z] **8.7** Heb *and Naaman* [a] **8.7** Or *he carried them into exile*

their generations, chiefs. These lived in
Jerusalem.
29 Jeiel[b] the father of Gibeon lived in
Gibeon, and the name of his wife was
Maacah. 30His firstborn son: Abdon,
then Zur, Kish, Baal,[c] Nadab, 31Gedor,
Ahio, Zecher, 32and Mikloth, who became the father of Shimeah. Now these
also lived opposite their kindred in Jerusalem, with their kindred. 33Ner became
the father of Kish, Kish of Saul,[d] Saul[e] of
Jonathan, Malchishua, Abinadab, and
Esh-baal; 34and the son of Jonathan was
Merib-baal; and Merib-baal became the
father of Micah. 35The sons of Micah: Pithon, Melech, Tarea, and Ahaz. 36Ahaz
became the father of Jehoaddah; and Jehoaddah became the father of Alemeth,
Azmaveth, and Zimri; Zimri became
the father of Moza. 37Moza became the
father of Binea; Raphah was his son, Eleasah his son, Azel his son. 38Azel had
six sons, and these are their names:
Azrikam, Bocheru, Ishmael, Sheariah,
Obadiah, and Hanan; all these were the
sons of Azel. 39The sons of his brother
Eshek: Ulam his firstborn, Jeush the
second, and Eliphelet the third. 40The
sons of Ulam were mighty warriors, archers, having many children and grandchildren, one hundred and fifty. All
these were Benjaminites.

9 So all Israel was enrolled by genealogies; and these are written in the
Book of the Kings of Israel. And Judah
was taken into exile in Babylon because
of their unfaithfulness. 2Now the first
to live again in their possessions in their
towns were Israelites, priests, Levites,
and temple servants.

INHABITANTS OF JERUSALEM AFTER THE EXILE

3 And some of the people of Judah,
Benjamin, Ephraim, and Manasseh
lived in Jerusalem: 4Uthai son of Ammihud, son of Omri, son of Imri, son of
Bani, from the sons of Perez son of Judah. 5And of the Shilonites: Asaiah the
firstborn, and his sons. 6Of the sons of
Zerah: Jeuel and their kin, six hundred
and ninety. 7Of the Benjaminites: Sallu
son of Meshullam, son of Hodaviah, son
of Hassenuah, 8Ibneiah son of Jeroham,
Elah son of Uzzi, son of Michri, and Meshullam son of Shephatiah, son of Reuel,
son of Ibnijah; 9and their kindred according to their generations, nine hundred and fifty-six. All these were heads
of families according to their ancestral
houses.

PRIESTLY FAMILIES

10 Of the priests: Jedaiah, Jehoiarib,
Jachin, 11and Azariah son of Hilkiah,
son of Meshullam, son of Zadok, son of
Meraioth, son of Ahitub, the chief officer of the house of God; 12and Adaiah
son of Jeroham, son of Pashhur, son of
Malchijah, and Maasai son of Adiel, son
of Jahzerah, son of Meshullam, son of
Meshillemith, son of Immer; 13besides
their kindred, heads of their ancestral
houses, one thousand seven hundred
and sixty, qualified for the work of the
service of the house of God.

LEVITICAL FAMILIES

14 Of the Levites: Shemaiah son of
Hasshub, son of Azrikam, son of Hashabiah, of the sons of Merari; 15and Bak-
bakkar, Heresh, Galal, and Mattaniah
son of Mica, son of Zichri, son of Asaph;
16and Obadiah son of Shemaiah, son of
Galal, son of Jeduthun, and Berechiah
son of Asa, son of Elkanah, who lived in
the villages of the Netophathites.
17 The gatekeepers were: Shallum,
Akkub, Talmon, Ahiman; and their
kinsman Shallum was the chief, 18sta-
tioned previously in the king's gate on
the east side. These were the gatekeepers
of the camp of the Levites. 19Shallum
son of Kore, son of Ebiasaph, son of
Korah, and his kindred of his ancestral
house, the Korahites, were in charge of
the work of the service, guardians of the
thresholds of the tent, as their ancestors
had been in charge of the camp of the
LORD, guardians of the entrance. 20And
Phinehas son of Eleazar was chief over
them in former times; the LORD was
with him. 21Zechariah son of Meshelemiah was gatekeeper at the entrance
of the tent of meeting. 22All these,
who were chosen as gatekeepers at
the thresholds, were two hundred and
twelve. They were enrolled by genealogies in their villages. David and the seer
Samuel established them in their office
of trust. 23So they and their descendants
were in charge of the gates of the house
of the LORD, that is, the house of the
tent, as guards. 24The gatekeepers were
on the four sides, east, west, north, and
south; 25and their kindred who were in
their villages were obliged to come in
every seven days, in turn, to be with
them; 26for the four chief gatekeepers,
who were Levites, were in charge of

[b] **8.29** Compare 9.35: Heb lacks *Jeiel* [c] **8.30** Gk Ms adds *Ner*; Compare 8.33 and 9.36 [d] **8.33** Or *Shaul* [e] **8.33** Or *Shaul*

the chambers and the treasures of the
house of God. 27And they would spend
the night near the house of God; for on
them lay the duty of watching, and they
had charge of opening it every morning.
28 Some of them had charge of the
utensils of service, for they were required to count them when they were
brought in and taken out. 29Others of
them were appointed over the furniture, and over all the holy utensils, also
over the choice flour, the wine, the oil,
the incense, and the spices. 30Others,
of the sons of the priests, prepared the
mixing of the spices, 31and Mattithiah,
one of the Levites, the firstborn of Shallum the Korahite, was in charge of making the flat cakes. 32Also some of their
kindred of the Kohathites had charge of
the rows of bread, to prepare them for
each sabbath.
33 Now these are the singers, the
heads of ancestral houses of the Levites,
living in the chambers of the temple
free from other service, for they were on
duty day and night. 34These were heads
of ancestral houses of the Levites, according to their generations; these leaders lived in Jerusalem.

THE FAMILY OF KING SAUL

35 In Gibeon lived the father of Gibeon, Jeiel, and the name of his wife was
Maacah. 36His firstborn son was Abdon, then Zur, Kish, Baal, Ner, Nadab,
37Gedor, Ahio, Zechariah, and Mikloth;
38and Mikloth became the father of
Shimeam; and these also lived opposite their kindred in Jerusalem, with
their kindred. 39Ner became the father
of Kish, Kish of Saul, Saul of Jonathan,
Malchishua, Abinadab, and Esh-baal;
40and the son of Jonathan was Merib-
baal; and Merib-baal became the father
of Micah. 41The sons of Micah: Pithon,
Melech, Tahrea, and Ahaz;[f] 42and Ahaz
became the father of Jarah, and Jarah of Alemeth, Azmaveth, and Zimri;
and Zimri became the father of Moza.
43Moza became the father of Binea; and
Rephaiah was his son, Eleasah his son,
Azel his son. 44Azel had six sons, and
these are their names: Azrikam, Bocheru, Ishmael, Sheariah, Obadiah, and
Hanan; these were the sons of Azel.

DEATH OF SAUL AND HIS SONS

10 Now the Philistines fought
against Israel; and the men of
Israel fled before the Philistines, and fell
slain on Mount Gilboa. 2The Philistines
overtook Saul and his sons; and the Philistines killed Jonathan and Abinadab
and Malchishua, sons of Saul. 3The battle pressed hard on Saul; and the archers
found him, and he was wounded by the
archers. 4Then Saul said to his armour-
bearer, 'Draw your sword, and thrust
me through with it, so that these uncircumcised may not come and make sport
of me.' But his armour-bearer was unwilling, for he was terrified. So Saul took
his own sword and fell on it. 5When his
armour-bearer saw that Saul was dead,
he also fell on his sword and died. 6Thus
Saul died; he and his three sons and all
his house died together. 7When all the
men of Israel who were in the valley saw
that the army[g] had fled and that Saul
and his sons were dead, they abandoned
their towns and fled; and the Philistines
came and occupied them.
8 The next day when the Philistines
came to strip the dead, they found Saul
and his sons fallen on Mount Gilboa.
9They stripped him and took his head
and his armour, and sent messengers
throughout the land of the Philistines
to carry the good news to their idols and
to the people. 10They put his armour in
the temple of their gods, and fastened
his head in the temple of Dagon. 11But
when all Jabesh-gilead heard everything that the Philistines had done to
Saul, 12all the valiant warriors got up
and took away the body of Saul and the
bodies of his sons, and brought them
to Jabesh. Then they buried their bones
under the oak in Jabesh, and fasted for
seven days.
13 So Saul died for his unfaithfulness;
he was unfaithful to the LORD in that he
did not keep the command of the LORD;
moreover, he had consulted a medium,
seeking guidance, 14and did not seek
guidance from the LORD. Therefore the
LORD[h] put him to death and turned the
kingdom over to David son of Jesse.

DAVID ANOINTED KING OF ALL ISRAEL

11 Then all Israel gathered together
to David at Hebron and said,
'See, we are your bone and flesh. 2For
some time now, even while Saul was
king, it was you who commanded the
army of Israel. The LORD your God said
to you: It is you who shall be shepherd of
my people Israel, you who shall be ruler

[f] **9.41** Compare 8.35: Heb lacks *and Ahaz*
[g] **10.7** Heb *they* [h] **10.14** Heb *he*

over my people Israel.' 3 So all the elders
of Israel came to the king at Hebron,
and David made a covenant with them
at Hebron before the LORD. And they
anointed David king over Israel, according to the word of the LORD by Samuel.

JERUSALEM CAPTURED

4 David and all Israel marched to Jerusalem, that is, Jebus where the Jebusites were, the inhabitants of the land.
5 The inhabitants of Jebus said to David,
'You will not come in here.' Nevertheless, David took the stronghold of Zion,
now the city of David. 6 David had said,
'Whoever attacks the Jebusites first shall
be chief and commander.' And Joab son
of Zeruiah went up first, so he became
chief. 7 David resided in the stronghold;
therefore it was called the city of David. 8 He built the city all round, from
the Millo in a complete circuit; and Joab
repaired the rest of the city. 9 And David became greater and greater, for the
LORD of hosts was with him.

DAVID'S MIGHTY MEN AND THEIR EXPLOITS

10 Now these are the chiefs of David's warriors, who gave him strong
support in his kingdom, together with
all Israel, to make him king, according
to the word of the LORD concerning
Israel. 11 This is an account of David's
mighty warriors: Jashobeam, son of
Hachmoni,[i] was chief of the Three;[j] he
wielded his spear against three hundred
whom he killed at one time.

12 And next to him among the three
warriors was Eleazar son of Dodo, the
Ahohite. 13 He was with David at Pas-
dammim when the Philistines were
gathered there for battle. There was a
plot of ground full of barley. Now the
people had fled from the Philistines,
14 but he and David took their stand in
the middle of the plot, defended it, and
killed the Philistines; and the LORD
saved them by a great victory.

15 Three of the thirty chiefs went
down to the rock to David at the cave of
Adullam, while the army of Philistines
was encamped in the valley of Rephaim.
16 David was then in the stronghold; and
the garrison of the Philistines was then
at Bethlehem. 17 David said longingly,
'O that someone would give me water to
drink from the well of Bethlehem that
is by the gate!' 18 Then the Three broke
through the camp of the Philistines,
and drew water from the well of Bethlehem that was by the gate, and they
brought it to David. But David would
not drink of it; he poured it out to the
LORD, 19 and said, 'My God forbid that I
should do this. Can I drink the blood of
these men? For at the risk of their lives
they brought it.' Therefore he would not
drink it. The three warriors did these
things.

20 Now Abishai,[k] the brother of Joab,
was chief of the Thirty.[l] With his spear
he fought against three hundred and
killed them, and won a name beside the
Three. 21 He was the most renowned[m]
of the Thirty,[n] and became their commander; but he did not attain to the
Three.

22 Benaiah son of Jehoiada was a
valiant man[o] of Kabzeel, a doer of great
deeds; he struck down two sons of[p]
Ariel of Moab. He also went down and
killed a lion in a pit on a day when snow
had fallen. 23 And he killed an Egyptian,
a man of great stature, five cubits tall.
The Egyptian had in his hand a spear
like a weaver's beam; but Benaiah went
against him with a staff, snatched the
spear out of the Egyptian's hand, and
killed him with his own spear. 24 Such
were the things Benaiah son of Jehoiada
did, and he won a name beside the three
warriors. 25 He was renowned among
the Thirty, but he did not attain to the
Three. And David put him in charge of
his bodyguard.

26 The warriors of the armies were
Asahel brother of Joab, Elhanan son
of Dodo of Bethlehem, 27 Shammoth of
Harod,[q] Helez the Pelonite, 28 Ira son of
Ikkesh of Tekoa, Abiezer of Anathoth,
29 Sibbecai the Hushathite, Ilai the Ahohite, 30 Maharai of Netophah, Heled son
of Baanah of Netophah, 31 Ithai son of
Ribai of Gibeah of the Benjaminites, Benaiah of Pirathon, 32 Hurai of the wadis
of Gaash, Abiel the Arbathite, 33 Azmaveth of Baharum, Eliahba of Shaalbon,
34 Hashem[r] the Gizonite, Jonathan son
of Shagee the Hararite, 35 Ahiam son
of Sachar the Hararite, Eliphal son of
Ur, 36 Hepher the Mecherathite, Ahijah
the Pelonite, 37 Hezro of Carmel, Naarai

[i] 11.11 Or *a Hachmonite* [j] 11.11 Compare 2 Sam 23.8: Heb *Thirty* or *captains* [k] 11.20 Gk Vg Tg Compare 2 Sam 23.18: Heb *Abshai* [l] 11.20 Syr: Heb *Three* [m] 11.21 Compare 2 Sam 23.19: Heb *more renowned among the two* [n] 11.21 Syr: Heb *Three* [o] 11.22 Syr: Heb *the son of a valiant man* [p] 11.22 See 2 Sam 23.20: Heb lacks *sons of* [q] 11.27 Compare 2 Sam 23.25: Heb *the Harorite* [r] 11.34 Compare Gk and 2 Sam 23.32: Heb *the sons of Hashem*

son of Ezbai, 38Joel the brother of Nathan, Mibhar son of Hagri, 39Zelek the Ammonite, Naharai of Beeroth, the armour-bearer of Joab son of Zeruiah, 40Ira the Ithrite, Gareb the Ithrite, 41Uriah the Hittite, Zabad son of Ahlai, 42Adina son of Shiza the Reubenite, a leader of the Reubenites, and thirty with him, 43Hanan son of Maacah, and Joshaphat the Mithnite, 44Uzzia the Ashterathite, Shama and Jeiel sons of Hotham the Aroerite, 45Jediael son of Shimri, and his brother Joha the Tizite, 46Eliel the Mahavite, and Jeribai and Joshaviah sons of Elnaam, and Ithmah the Moabite, 47Eliel, and Obed, and Jaasiel the Mezobaite.

DAVID'S FOLLOWERS IN THE WILDERNESS

12 The following are those who came to David at Ziklag, while he could not move about freely because of Saul son of Kish; they were among the mighty warriors who helped him in war. 2They were archers, and could shoot arrows and sling stones with either the right hand or the left; they were Benjaminites, Saul's kindred. 3The chief was Ahiezer, then Joash, both sons of Shemaah of Gibeah; also Jeziel and Pelet sons of Azmaveth; Beracah, Jehu of Anathoth, 4Ishmaiah of Gibeon, a warrior among the Thirty and a leader over the Thirty; Jeremiah,[s] Jahaziel, Johanan, Jozabad of Gederah, 5Eluzai,[t] Jerimoth, Bealiah, Shemariah, Shephatiah the Haruphite; 6Elkanah, Isshiah, Azarel, Joezer, and Jashobeam, the Korahites; 7and Joelah and Zebadiah, sons of Jeroham of Gedor.

8 From the Gadites there went over to David at the stronghold in the wilderness mighty and experienced warriors, expert with shield and spear, whose faces were like the faces of lions, and who were swift as gazelles on the mountains: 9Ezer the chief, Obadiah second, Eliab third, 10Mishmannah fourth, Jeremiah fifth, 11Attai sixth, Eliel seventh, 12Johanan eighth, Elzabad ninth, 13Jeremiah tenth, Machbannai eleventh. 14These Gadites were officers of the army, the least equal to a hundred and the greatest to a thousand. 15These are the men who crossed the Jordan in the first month, when it was overflowing all its banks, and put to flight all those in the valleys, to the east and to the west.

16 Some Benjaminites and Judahites came to the stronghold to David. 17David went out to meet them and said to them, 'If you have come to me in friendship, to help me, then my heart will be bound to you; but if you have come to betray me to my adversaries, though my hands have done no wrong, then may the God of our ancestors see and give judgement.' 18Then the spirit came upon Amasai, chief of the Thirty, and he said,

'We are yours, O David;
    and with you, O son of Jesse!
Peace, peace to you,
    and peace to the one
        who helps you!
    For your God is the one
        who helps you.'

Then David received them, and made them officers of his troops.

19 Some of the Manassites deserted to David when he came with the Philistines for the battle against Saul. (Yet he did not help them, for the rulers of the Philistines took counsel and sent him away, saying, 'He will desert to his master Saul at the cost of our heads.') 20As he went to Ziklag these Manassites deserted to him: Adnah, Jozabad, Jediael, Michael, Jozabad, Elihu, and Zillethai, chiefs of the thousands in Manasseh. 21They helped David against the band of raiders,[u] for they were all warriors and commanders in the army. 22Indeed from day to day people kept coming to David to help him, until there was a great army, like an army of God.

DAVID'S ARMY AT HEBRON

23 These are the numbers of the divisions of the armed troops who came to David in Hebron to turn the kingdom of Saul over to him, according to the word of the LORD. 24The people of Judah bearing shield and spear numbered six thousand eight hundred armed troops. 25Of the Simeonites, mighty warriors, seven thousand one hundred. 26Of the Levites four thousand six hundred. 27Jehoiada, leader of the house of Aaron, and with him three thousand seven hundred. 28Zadok, a young warrior, and twenty-two commanders from his own ancestral house. 29Of the Benjaminites, the kindred of Saul, three thousand, of whom the majority had continued to keep their allegiance to the house of Saul. 30Of the Ephraimites, twenty

[s] **12.4** Heb verse 5 [t] **12.5** Heb verse 6
[u] **12.21** Or *as officers of his troops*

thousand eight hundred, mighty warriors, notables in their ancestral houses.
31 Of the half-tribe of Manasseh, eighteen thousand, who were expressly
named to come and make David king.
32 Of Issachar, those who had understanding of the times, to know what
Israel ought to do, two hundred chiefs,
and all their kindred under their command. 33 Of Zebulun, fifty thousand seasoned troops, equipped for battle with
all the weapons of war, to help David[v]
with singleness of purpose. 34 Of Naphtali, a thousand commanders, with
whom there were thirty-seven thousand armed with shield and spear. 35 Of
the Danites, twenty-eight thousand
six hundred equipped for battle. 36 Of
Asher, forty thousand seasoned troops
ready for battle. 37 Of the Reubenites and
Gadites and the half-tribe of Manasseh
from beyond the Jordan, one hundred
and twenty thousand armed with all
the weapons of war.

38 All these, warriors arrayed in
battle order, came to Hebron with full
intent to make David king over all Israel; likewise all the rest of Israel were
of a single mind to make David king.
39 They were there with David for three
days, eating and drinking, for their
kindred had provided for them. 40 And
also their neighbours, from as far away
as Issachar and Zebulun and Naphtali,
came bringing food on donkeys, camels,
mules, and oxen—abundant provisions
of meal, cakes of figs, clusters of raisins,
wine, oil, oxen, and sheep, for there was
joy in Israel.

THE ARK BROUGHT FROM KIRIATH-JEARIM

13 David consulted with the commanders of the thousands and
of the hundreds, with every leader. 2 David said to the whole assembly of Israel,
'If it seems good to you, and if it is the
will of the LORD our God, let us send
abroad to our kindred who remain in all
the land of Israel, including the priests
and Levites in the cities that have pasture lands, that they may come together
to us. 3 Then let us bring again the ark of
our God to us; for we did not turn to it in
the days of Saul.' 4 The whole assembly
agreed to do so, for the thing pleased all
the people.

5 So David assembled all Israel from
the Shihor of Egypt to Lebo-hamath,
to bring the ark of God from Kiriath-
jearim. 6 And David and all Israel went
up to Baalah, that is, to Kiriath-jearim,
which belongs to Judah, to bring up
from there the ark of God, the LORD,
who is enthroned on the cherubim,
which is called by his[w] name. 7 They carried the ark of God on a new cart, from
the house of Abinadab, and Uzzah and
Ahio[x] were driving the cart. 8 David and
all Israel were dancing before God with
all their might, with song and lyres and
harps and tambourines and cymbals
and trumpets.

9 When they came to the threshing-
floor of Chidon, Uzzah put out his hand
to hold the ark, for the oxen shook it.
10 The anger of the LORD was kindled
against Uzzah; he struck him down because he put out his hand to the ark;
and he died there before God. 11 David
was angry because the LORD had burst
out against Uzzah; so that place is called
Perez-uzzah[y] to this day. 12 David was
afraid of God that day; he said, 'How can
I bring the ark of God into my care?' 13 So
David did not take the ark into his care
into the city of David; he took it instead
to the house of Obed-edom the Gittite.
14 The ark of God remained with the
household of Obed-edom in his house
for three months, and the LORD blessed
the household of Obed-edom and all
that he had.

DAVID ESTABLISHED AT JERUSALEM

14 King Hiram of Tyre sent messengers to David, along with cedar logs, and masons and carpenters to
build a house for him. 2 David then perceived that the LORD had established
him as king over Israel, and that his
kingdom was highly exalted for the sake
of his people Israel.

3 David took more wives in Jerusalem, and David became the father of
more sons and daughters. 4 These are
the names of the children whom he had
in Jerusalem: Shammua, Shobab, and
Nathan; Solomon, 5 Ibhar, Elishua, and
Elpelet; 6 Nogah, Nepheg, and Japhia;
7 Elishama, Beeliada, and Eliphelet.

DEFEAT OF THE PHILISTINES

8 When the Philistines heard that David had been anointed king over all Israel, all the Philistines went up in search
of David; and David heard of it and went
out against them. 9 Now the Philistines
had come and made a raid in the valley

[v] **12.33** Gk: Heb lacks *David* [w] **13.6** Heb lacks *his* [x] **13.7** Or *and his brother* [y] **13.11** That is *Bursting Out Against Uzzah*

of Rephaim. 10David inquired of God,
'Shall I go up against the Philistines?
Will you give them into my hand?' The
LORD said to him, 'Go up, and I will give
them into your hand.' 11So he went up to
Baal-perazim, and David defeated them
there. David said, 'God has burst out[z]
against my enemies by my hand, like a
bursting flood.' Therefore that place is
called Baal-perazim.[a] 12They abandoned
their gods there, and at David's command they were burned.

13 Once again the Philistines made a
raid in the valley. 14When David again
inquired of God, God said to him, 'You
shall not go up after them; go around
and come on them opposite the balsam trees. 15When you hear the sound
of marching in the tops of the balsam
trees, then go out to battle; for God has
gone out before you to strike down the
army of the Philistines.' 16David did as
God had commanded him, and they
struck down the Philistine army from
Gibeon to Gezer. 17The fame of David
went out into all lands, and the LORD
brought the fear of him on all nations.

THE ARK BROUGHT TO JERUSALEM

15 David[b] built houses for himself in the city of David, and he
prepared a place for the ark of God and
pitched a tent for it. 2Then David commanded that no one but the Levites were
to carry the ark of God, for the LORD had
chosen them to carry the ark of the LORD
and to minister to him for ever. 3David
assembled all Israel in Jerusalem to bring
up the ark of the LORD to its place, which
he had prepared for it. 4Then David gathered together the descendants of Aaron
and the Levites: 5of the sons of Kohath,
Uriel the chief, with one hundred and
twenty of his kindred; 6of the sons of Merari, Asaiah the chief, with two hundred
and twenty of his kindred; 7of the sons
of Gershom, Joel the chief, with one hundred and thirty of his kindred; 8of the
sons of Elizaphan, Shemaiah the chief,
with two hundred of his kindred; 9of
the sons of Hebron, Eliel the chief, with
eighty of his kindred; 10of the sons of
Uzziel, Amminadab the chief, with one
hundred and twelve of his kindred.

11 David summoned the priests Zadok and Abiathar, and the Levites Uriel,
Asaiah, Joel, Shemaiah, Eliel, and Amminadab. 12He said to them, 'You are the
heads of families of the Levites; sanctify
yourselves, you and your kindred, so
that you may bring up the ark of the
LORD, the God of Israel, to the place that
I have prepared for it. 13Because you did
not carry it the first time,[c] the LORD our
God burst out against us, because we did
not give it proper care.' 14So the priests
and the Levites sanctified themselves to
bring up the ark of the LORD, the God
of Israel. 15And the Levites carried the
ark of God on their shoulders with the
poles, as Moses had commanded according to the word of the LORD.

16 David also commanded the chiefs
of the Levites to appoint their kindred
as the singers to play on musical instruments, on harps and lyres and cymbals, to
raise loud sounds of joy. 17So the Levites
appointed Heman son of Joel; and of his
kindred Asaph son of Berechiah; and of
the sons of Merari, their kindred, Ethan
son of Kushaiah; 18and with them their
kindred of the second order, Zechariah,
Jaaziel, Shemiramoth, Jehiel, Unni, Eliab,
Benaiah, Maaseiah, Mattithiah, Eliphelehu, and Mikneiah, and the gatekeepers
Obed-edom and Jeiel. 19The singers Heman, Asaph, and Ethan were to sound
bronze cymbals; 20Zechariah, Aziel, Shemiramoth, Jehiel, Unni, Eliab, Maaseiah,
and Benaiah were to play harps according
to Alamoth; 21but Mattithiah, Eliphelehu,
Mikneiah, Obed-edom, Jeiel, and Azaziah
were to lead with lyres according to the
Sheminith. 22Chenaniah, leader of the
Levites in music, was to direct the music, for he understood it. 23Berechiah and
Elkanah were to be gatekeepers for the
ark. 24Shebaniah, Joshaphat, Nethanel,
Amasai, Zechariah, Benaiah, and Eliezer,
the priests, were to blow the trumpets
before the ark of God. Obed-edom and Je-
hiah also were to be gatekeepers for the
ark.

25 So David and the elders of Israel,
and the commanders of the thousands,
went to bring up the ark of the covenant
of the LORD from the house of Obed-
edom with rejoicing. 26And because
God helped the Levites who were carrying the ark of the covenant of the LORD,
they sacrificed seven bulls and seven
rams. 27David was clothed with a robe
of fine linen, as also were all the Levites
who were carrying the ark, and the
singers, and Chenaniah the leader of the
music of the singers; and David wore a
linen ephod. 28So all Israel brought up
the ark of the covenant of the LORD
with shouting, to the sound of the horn,

[z] 14.11 Heb *paraz* [a] 14.11 That is *Lord of Bursting Out* [b] 15.1 Heb *He* [c] 15.13 Meaning of Heb uncertain

trumpets, and cymbals, and made loud music on harps and lyres.

29 As the ark of the covenant of the LORD came to the city of David, Michal daughter of Saul looked out of the window, and saw King David leaping and dancing; and she despised him in her heart.

THE ARK PLACED IN THE TENT

16 They brought in the ark of God, and set it inside the tent that David had pitched for it; and they offered burnt-offerings and offerings of well-being before God.
2 When David had finished offering the burnt-offerings and the offerings of well-being, he blessed the people in the name of the LORD;
3 and he distributed to every person in Israel—man and woman alike—to each a loaf of bread, a portion of meat,[d] and a cake of raisins.

4 He appointed certain of the Levites as ministers before the ark of the LORD, to invoke, to thank, and to praise the LORD, the God of Israel.
5 Asaph was the chief, and second to him Zechariah, Jeiel, Shemiramoth, Jehiel, Mattithiah, Eliab, Benaiah, Obed-edom, and Jeiel, with harps and lyres; Asaph was to sound the cymbals,
6 and the priests Benaiah and Jahaziel were to blow trumpets regularly, before the ark of the covenant of God.

DAVID'S PSALM OF THANKSGIVING

7 Then on that day David first appointed the singing of praises to the LORD by Asaph and his kindred.

8 O give thanks to the LORD,
call on his name,
make known his deeds
among the peoples.
9 Sing to him, sing praises to him,
tell of all his wonderful works.
10 Glory in his holy name;
let the hearts of those who
seek the LORD rejoice.
11 Seek the LORD and his strength,
seek his presence continually.
12 Remember the wonderful
works he has done,
his miracles, and the
judgements he uttered,
13 O offspring of his servant Israel,[e]
children of Jacob, his chosen ones.

14 He is the LORD our God;
his judgements are in
all the earth.
15 Remember his covenant for ever,
the word that he commanded for
a thousand generations,
16 the covenant that he made
with Abraham,
his sworn promise to Isaac,
17 which he confirmed to Jacob
as a statute,
to Israel as an everlasting
covenant,
18 saying, 'To you I will give the
land of Canaan
as your portion for an inheritance.'

19 When they were few in number,
of little account, and strangers
in the land,[f]
20 wandering from nation to nation,
from one kingdom to
another people,
21 he allowed no one to oppress them;
he rebuked kings on their account,
22 saying, 'Do not touch my
anointed ones;
do my prophets no harm.'

23 Sing to the LORD, all the earth.
Tell of his salvation from
day to day.
24 Declare his glory among the nations,
his marvellous works among
all the peoples.
25 For great is the LORD, and
greatly to be praised;
he is to be revered above all gods.
26 For all the gods of the
peoples are idols,
but the LORD made the heavens.
27 Honour and majesty are before him;
strength and joy are in his place.

28 Ascribe to the LORD, O families
of the peoples,
ascribe to the LORD glory
and strength.
29 Ascribe to the LORD the glory
due his name;
bring an offering, and
come before him.
Worship the LORD in holy splendour;
30 tremble before him, all the earth.
The world is firmly established;
it shall never be moved.
31 Let the heavens be glad, and
let the earth rejoice,
and let them say among the
nations, 'The LORD is king!'

[d] **16.3** Compare Gk Syr Vg: Meaning of Heb uncertain [e] **16.13** Another reading is *Abraham* (compare Ps 105.6) [f] **16.19** Heb *in it*

32 Let the sea roar, and all that fills it;
let the field exult, and
everything in it.
33 Then shall the trees of the
forest sing for joy
before the LORD, for he comes
to judge the earth.
34 O give thanks to the LORD,
for he is good;
for his steadfast love
endures for ever.

35 Say also:
'Save us, O God of our salvation,
and gather and rescue us from
among the nations,
that we may give thanks to
your holy name,
and glory in your praise.
36 Blessed be the LORD, the
God of Israel,
from everlasting to everlasting.'
Then all the people said 'Amen!' and
praised the LORD.

REGULAR WORSHIP MAINTAINED

37 David left Asaph and his kinsfolk
there before the ark of the covenant of
the LORD to minister regularly before
the ark as each day required, 38and also
Obed-edom and his[g] sixty-eight kinsfolk;
while Obed-edom son of Jeduthun and
Hosah were to be gatekeepers. 39And he
left the priest Zadok and his kindred the
priests before the tabernacle of the LORD
in the high place that was at Gibeon,
40to offer burnt-offerings to the LORD
on the altar of burnt-offering regularly,
morning and evening, according to all
that is written in the law of the LORD
that he commanded Israel. 41With them
were Heman and Jeduthun, and the rest
of those chosen and expressly named to
render thanks to the LORD, for his steadfast love endures for ever. 42Heman and
Jeduthun had with them trumpets and
cymbals for the music, and instruments
for sacred song. The sons of Jeduthun
were appointed to the gate.

43 Then all the people departed to
their homes, and David went home to
bless his household.

GOD'S COVENANT WITH DAVID

17 Now when David settled in his
house, David said to the prophet
Nathan, 'I am living in a house of cedar,
but the ark of the covenant of the LORD
is under a tent.' 2Nathan said to David,
'Do all that you have in mind, for God is
with you.'

3 But that same night the word of
the LORD came to Nathan, saying: 4Go
and tell my servant David: Thus says the
LORD: You shall not build me a house to
live in. 5For I have not lived in a house
since the day I brought out Israel to this
very day, but I have lived in a tent and
a tabernacle.[h] 6Wherever I have moved
about among all Israel, did I ever speak
a word with any of the judges of Israel,
whom I commanded to shepherd my
people, saying, Why have you not built
me a house of cedar? 7Now therefore,
thus you shall say to my servant David:
Thus says the LORD of hosts: I took you
from the pasture, from following the
sheep, to be ruler over my people Israel;
8and I have been with you wherever you
went, and have cut off all your enemies
before you; and I will make for you a
name, like the name of the great ones
of the earth. 9I will appoint a place for
my people Israel, and will plant them,
so that they may live in their own place,
and be disturbed no more; and evildoers
shall wear them down no more, as they
did formerly, 10from the time that I appointed judges over my people Israel;
and I will subdue all your enemies.

Moreover, I declare to you that the
LORD will build you a house. 11When
your days are fulfilled to go to be with
your ancestors, I will raise up your offspring after you, one of your own sons,
and I will establish his kingdom. 12He
shall build a house for me, and I will establish his throne for ever. 13I will be a
father to him, and he shall be a son to
me. I will not take my steadfast love
from him, as I took it from him who
was before you, 14but I will confirm him
in my house and in my kingdom for
ever, and his throne shall be established
for ever. 15In accordance with all these
words and all this vision, Nathan spoke
to David.

DAVID'S PRAYER

16 Then King David went in and sat
before the LORD, and said, 'Who am I,
O LORD God, and what is my house,
that you have brought me thus far?
17And even this was a small thing in
your sight, O God; you have also spoken
of your servant's house for a great while
to come. You regard me as someone of
high rank,[i] O LORD God! 18And what
more can David say to you for honour-

[g] **16.38** Gk Syr Vg: Heb *their* [h] **17.5** Gk 2 Sam 7.6: Heb *but I have been from tent to tent and from tabernacle* [i] **17.17** Meaning of Heb uncertain

ing your servant? You know your servant. 19For your servant's sake, O LORD, and according to your own heart, you have done all these great deeds, making known all these great things. 20There is no one like you, O LORD, and there is no God besides you, according to all that we have heard with our ears. 21Who is like your people Israel, one nation on the earth whom God went to redeem to be his people, making for yourself a name for great and terrible things, in driving out nations before your people whom you redeemed from Egypt? 22And you made your people Israel to be your people for ever; and you, O LORD, became their God.

23 'And now, O LORD, as for the word that you have spoken concerning your servant and concerning his house, let it be established for ever, and do as you have promised. 24Thus your name will be established and magnified for ever in the saying, "The LORD of hosts, the God of Israel, is Israel's God"; and the house of your servant David will be established in your presence. 25For you, my God, have revealed to your servant that you will build a house for him; therefore your servant has found it possible to pray before you. 26And now, O LORD, you are God, and you have promised this good thing to your servant; 27therefore may it please you to bless the house of your servant, that it may continue for ever before you. For you, O LORD, have blessed and are blessed[j] for ever.'

DAVID'S KINGDOM ESTABLISHED AND EXTENDED

18 Some time afterwards, David attacked the Philistines and subdued them; he took Gath and its villages from the Philistines.

2 He defeated Moab, and the Moabites became subject to David and brought tribute.

3 David also struck down King Hadadezer of Zobah, towards Hamath,[k] as he went to set up a monument at the river Euphrates. 4David took from him one thousand chariots, seven thousand cavalry, and twenty thousand foot-soldiers. David hamstrung all the chariot horses, but left one hundred of them. 5When the Arameans of Damascus came to help King Hadadezer of Zobah, David killed twenty-two thousand Arameans. 6Then David put garrisons[l] in Aram of Damascus; and the Arameans became subject to David, and brought tribute. The LORD gave victory to David wherever he went. 7David took the gold shields that were carried by the servants of Hadadezer, and brought them to Jerusalem. 8From Tibhath and from Cun, cities of Hadadezer, David took a vast quantity of bronze; with it Solomon made the bronze sea and the pillars and the vessels of bronze.

9 When King Tou of Hamath heard that David had defeated the whole army of King Hadadezer of Zobah, 10he sent his son Hadoram to King David, to greet him and to congratulate him, because he had fought against Hadadezer and defeated him. Now Hadadezer had often been at war with Tou. He sent all sorts of articles of gold, of silver, and of bronze; 11these also King David dedicated to the LORD, together with the silver and gold that he had carried off from all the nations, from Edom, Moab, the Ammonites, the Philistines, and Amalek.

12 Abishai son of Zeruiah killed eighteen thousand Edomites in the Valley of Salt. 13He put garrisons in Edom; and all the Edomites became subject to David. And the LORD gave victory to David wherever he went.

DAVID'S ADMINISTRATION

14 So David reigned over all Israel; and he administered justice and equity to all his people. 15Joab son of Zeruiah was over the army; Jehoshaphat son of Ahilud was recorder; 16Zadok son of Ahitub and Ahimelech son of Abiathar were priests; Shavsha was secretary; 17Benaiah son of Jehoiada was over the Cherethites and the Pelethites; and David's sons were the chief officials in the service of the king.

DEFEAT OF THE AMMONITES AND ARAMEANS

19 Some time afterwards, King Nahash of the Ammonites died, and his son succeeded him. 2David said, 'I will deal loyally with Hanun son of Nahash, for his father dealt loyally with me.' So David sent messengers to console him concerning his father. When David's servants came to Hanun in the land of the Ammonites, to console him, 3the officials of the Ammonites said to Hanun, 'Do you think, because David has sent people to console you, that he

[j] 17.27 Or *and it is blessed* [k] 18.3 Meaning of Heb uncertain [l] 18.6 Gk Vg 2 Sam 8.6 Compare Syr: Heb lacks *garrisons*

is honouring your father? Have not his
servants come to you to search and to
overthrow and to spy out the land?' 4So
Hanun seized David's servants, shaved
them, cut off their garments in the middle at their hips, and sent them away;
5and they departed. When David was
told about the men, he sent messengers
to them, for they felt greatly humiliated.
The king said, 'Remain at Jericho until
your beards have grown, and then return.'

6 When the Ammonites saw that
they had made themselves odious to
David, Hanun and the Ammonites
sent a thousand talents of silver to hire
chariots and cavalry from Mesopotamia, from Aram-maacah and from Zobah. 7They hired thirty-two thousand
chariots and the king of Maacah with
his army, who came and camped before Medeba. And the Ammonites were
mustered from their cities and came to
battle. 8When David heard of it, he sent
Joab and all the army of the warriors.
9The Ammonites came out and drew
up in battle array at the entrance of the
city, and the kings who had come were
by themselves in the open country.

10 When Joab saw that the line of
battle was set against him both in front
and in the rear, he chose some of the
picked men of Israel and arrayed them
against the Arameans; 11the rest of his
troops he put in charge of his brother
Abishai, and they were arrayed against
the Ammonites. 12He said, 'If the Arameans are too strong for me, then you
shall help me; but if the Ammonites are
too strong for you, then I will help you.
13Be strong, and let us be courageous
for our people and for the cities of our
God; and may the LORD do what seems
good to him.' 14So Joab and the troops
who were with him advanced towards
the Arameans for battle; and they fled
before him. 15When the Ammonites
saw that the Arameans fled, they likewise fled before Abishai, Joab's brother,
and entered the city. Then Joab came to
Jerusalem.

16 But when the Arameans saw that
they had been defeated by Israel, they
sent messengers and brought out the
Arameans who were beyond the Euphrates, with Shophach the commander
of the army of Hadadezer at their head.
17When David was informed, he gathered all Israel together, crossed the Jordan, came to them, and drew up his
forces against them. When David set the
battle in array against the Arameans,
they fought with him. 18The Arameans fled before Israel; and David killed
seven thousand Aramean charioteers
and forty thousand foot-soldiers, and
also killed Shophach the commander of
their army. 19When the servants of Hadadezer saw that they had been defeated
by Israel, they made peace with David,
and became subject to him. So the Arameans were not willing to help the Ammonites any more.

SIEGE AND CAPTURE OF RABBAH

20 In the spring of the year, the
time when kings go out to battle, Joab led out the army, ravaged the
country of the Ammonites, and came
and besieged Rabbah. But David remained at Jerusalem. Joab attacked
Rabbah, and overthrew it. 2David took
the crown of Milcom[m] from his head;
he found that it weighed a talent of
gold, and in it was a precious stone;
and it was placed on David's head. He
also brought out the booty of the city,
a very great amount. 3He brought out
the people who were in it, and set them
to work[n] with saws and iron picks and
axes.[o] Thus David did to all the cities of
the Ammonites. Then David and all the
people returned to Jerusalem.

EXPLOITS AGAINST THE PHILISTINES

4 After this, war broke out with the
Philistines at Gezer; then Sibbecai the
Hushathite killed Sippai, who was one
of the descendants of the giants; and the
Philistines were subdued. 5Again there
was war with the Philistines; and Elhanan son of Jair killed Lahmi the brother
of Goliath the Gittite, the shaft of whose
spear was like a weaver's beam. 6Again
there was war at Gath, where there was
a man of great size, who had six fingers
on each hand, and six toes on each foot,
twenty-four in number; he also was
descended from the giants. 7When he
taunted Israel, Jonathan son of Shimea,
David's brother, killed him. 8These were
descended from the giants in Gath; they
fell by the hand of David and his servants.

THE CENSUS AND PLAGUE

21 Satan stood up against Israel,
and incited David to count the
people of Israel. 2So David said to Joab

[m] 20.2 Gk Vg See 1 Kings 11.5, 33: MT *of their king*
[n] 20.3 Compare 2 Sam 12.31: Heb *and he sawed*
[o] 20.3 Compare 2 Sam 12.31: Heb *saws*

and the commanders of the army, 'Go,
number Israel, from Beer-sheba to Dan,
and bring me a report, so that I may
know their number.' 3But Joab said,
'May the LORD increase the number of
his people a hundredfold! Are they not,
my lord the king, all of them my lord's
servants? Why then should my lord require this? Why should he bring guilt on
Israel?' 4But the king's word prevailed
against Joab. So Joab departed and went
throughout all Israel, and came back to
Jerusalem. 5Joab gave the total count of
the people to David. In all Israel there
were one million one hundred thousand men who drew the sword, and in
Judah four hundred and seventy thousand who drew the sword. 6But he did
not include Levi and Benjamin in the
numbering, for the king's command
was abhorrent to Joab.

7 But God was displeased with this
thing, and he struck Israel. 8David said
to God, 'I have sinned greatly in that I
have done this thing. But now, I pray
you, take away the guilt of your servant; for I have done very foolishly.' 9The
LORD spoke to Gad, David's seer, saying,
10'Go and say to David, "Thus says the
LORD: Three things I offer you; choose
one of them, so that I may do it to you." '
11So Gad came to David and said to him,
'Thus says the LORD, "Take your choice:
12either three years of famine; or three
months of devastation by your foes,
while the sword of your enemies overtakes you; or three days of the sword
of the LORD, pestilence on the land,
and the angel of the LORD destroying
throughout all the territory of Israel."
Now decide what answer I shall return
to the one who sent me.' 13Then David
said to Gad, 'I am in great distress; let
me fall into the hand of the LORD, for
his mercy is very great; but let me not
fall into human hands.'

14 So the LORD sent a pestilence on
Israel; and seventy thousand persons
fell in Israel. 15And God sent an angel
to Jerusalem to destroy it; but when
he was about to destroy it, the LORD
took note and relented concerning the
calamity; he said to the destroying angel, 'Enough! Stay your hand.' The angel
of the LORD was then standing by the
threshing-floor of Ornan the Jebusite.
16David looked up and saw the angel of
the LORD standing between earth and
heaven, and in his hand a drawn sword
stretched out over Jerusalem. Then David and the elders, clothed in sackcloth,
fell on their faces. 17And David said to
God, 'Was it not I who gave the command to count the people? It is I who
have sinned and done very wickedly.
But these sheep, what have they done?
Let your hand, I pray, O LORD my God,
be against me and against my father's
house; but do not let your people be
plagued!'

DAVID'S ALTAR AND SACRIFICE

18 Then the angel of the LORD commanded Gad to tell David that he should
go up and erect an altar to the LORD on
the threshing-floor of Ornan the Jebusite. 19So David went up following
Gad's instructions, which he had spoken in the name of the LORD. 20Ornan
turned and saw the angel; and while
his four sons who were with him hid
themselves, Ornan continued to thresh
wheat. 21As David came to Ornan, Ornan looked and saw David; he went
out from the threshing-floor, and did
obeisance to David with his face to the
ground. 22David said to Ornan, 'Give
me the site of the threshing-floor that I
may build on it an altar to the LORD—
give it to me at its full price—so that the
plague may be averted from the people.'
23Then Ornan said to David, 'Take it;
and let my lord the king do what seems
good to him; see, I present the oxen
for burnt-offerings, and the threshing-
sledges for the wood, and the wheat for
a grain-offering. I give it all.' 24But King
David said to Ornan, 'No; I will buy
them for the full price. I will not take for
the LORD what is yours, nor offer burnt-
offerings that cost me nothing.' 25So
David paid Ornan six hundred shekels
of gold by weight for the site. 26David
built there an altar to the LORD and presented burnt-offerings and offerings of
well-being. He called upon the LORD,
and he answered him with fire from
heaven on the altar of burnt-offering.
27Then the LORD commanded the angel, and he put his sword back into its
sheath.

THE PLACE CHOSEN FOR THE TEMPLE

28 At that time, when David saw
that the LORD had answered him at the
threshing-floor of Ornan the Jebusite,
he made his sacrifices there. 29For the
tabernacle of the LORD, which Moses
had made in the wilderness, and the altar of burnt-offering were at that time
in the high place at Gibeon; 30but David

could not go before it to inquire of God, for he was afraid of the sword of the angel of the LORD.

22 1 Then David said, 'Here shall be the house of the LORD God and here the altar of burnt-offering for Israel.'

DAVID PREPARES TO BUILD THE TEMPLE

2 David gave orders to gather together the aliens who were residing in the land of Israel, and he set stonecutters to prepare dressed stones for building the house of God. 3 David also provided great stores of iron for nails for the doors of the gates and for clamps, as well as bronze in quantities beyond weighing, 4 and cedar logs without number—for the Sidonians and Tyrians brought great quantities of cedar to David. 5 For David said, 'My son Solomon is young and inexperienced, and the house that is to be built for the LORD must be exceedingly magnificent, famous and glorified throughout all lands; I will therefore make preparation for it.' So David provided materials in great quantity before his death.

DAVID'S CHARGE TO SOLOMON AND THE LEADERS

6 Then he called for his son Solomon and charged him to build a house for the LORD, the God of Israel. 7 David said to Solomon, 'My son, I had planned to build a house to the name of the LORD my God. 8 But the word of the LORD came to me, saying, "You have shed much blood and have waged great wars; you shall not build a house to my name, because you have shed so much blood in my sight on the earth. 9 See, a son shall be born to you; he shall be a man of peace. I will give him peace from all his enemies on every side; for his name shall be Solomon,[p] and I will give peace[q] and quiet to Israel in his days. 10 He shall build a house for my name. He shall be a son to me, and I will be a father to him, and I will establish his royal throne in Israel for ever." 11 Now, my son, the LORD be with you, so that you may succeed in building the house of the LORD your God, as he has spoken concerning you. 12 Only, may the LORD grant you discretion and understanding, so that when he gives you charge over Israel you may keep the law of the LORD your God. 13 Then you will prosper if you are careful to observe the statutes and the ordinances that the LORD commanded Moses for Israel. Be strong and of good courage. Do not be afraid or dismayed. 14 With great pains I have provided for the house of the LORD one hundred thousand talents of gold, one million talents of silver, and bronze and iron beyond weighing, for there is so much of it; timber and stone too I have provided. To these you must add more. 15 You have an abundance of workers: stonecutters, masons, carpenters, and all kinds of artisans without number, skilled in working 16 gold, silver, bronze, and iron. Now begin the work, and the LORD be with you.'

17 David also commanded all the leaders of Israel to help his son Solomon, saying, 18 'Is not the LORD your God with you? Has he not given you peace on every side? For he has delivered the inhabitants of the land into my hand; and the land is subdued before the LORD and his people. 19 Now set your mind and heart to seek the LORD your God. Go and build the sanctuary of the LORD God so that the ark of the covenant of the LORD and the holy vessels of God may be brought into a house built for the name of the LORD.'

FAMILIES OF THE LEVITES AND THEIR FUNCTIONS

23 When David was old and full of days, he made his son Solomon king over Israel.

2 David assembled all the leaders of Israel and the priests and the Levites. 3 The Levites, thirty years old and upwards, were counted, and the total was thirty-eight thousand. 4 'Twenty-four thousand of these', David said, 'shall have charge of the work in the house of the LORD, six thousand shall be officers and judges, 5 four thousand gatekeepers, and four thousand shall offer praises to the LORD with the instruments that I have made for praise.' 6 And David organized them in divisions corresponding to the sons of Levi: Gershon,[r] Kohath, and Merari.

7 The sons of Gershon[s] were Ladan and Shimei. 8 The sons of Ladan: Jehiel the chief, Zetham, and Joel, three. 9 The sons of Shimei: Shelomoth, Haziel, and Haran, three. These were the heads of families of Ladan. 10 And the sons of Shimei: Jahath, Zina, Jeush, and Beriah. These four were the sons of Shimei. 11 Ja-

[p] 22.9 Heb *Shelomoh* [q] 22.9 Heb *shalom*
[r] 23.6 Or *Gershom*; See 1 Chr 6.1, note, and 23.15
[s] 23.7 Vg Compare Gk Syr: Heb *to the Gershonite*

hath was the chief, and Zizah the second; but Jeush and Beriah did not have
many sons, so they were enrolled as a
single family.

12 The sons of Kohath: Amram, Izhar, Hebron, and Uzziel, four. 13The sons
of Amram: Aaron and Moses. Aaron was
set apart to consecrate the most holy
things, so that he and his sons for ever
should make offerings before the LORD,
and minister to him and pronounce
blessings in his name for ever; 14but as
for Moses the man of God, his sons were
to be reckoned among the tribe of Levi.
15The sons of Moses: Gershom and Eliezer. 16The sons of Gershom: Shebuel the
chief. 17The sons of Eliezer: Rehabiah
the chief; Eliezer had no other sons, but
the sons of Rehabiah were very numerous. 18The sons of Izhar: Shelomith the
chief. 19The sons of Hebron: Jeriah the
chief, Amariah the second, Jahaziel the
third, and Jekameam the fourth. 20The
sons of Uzziel: Micah the chief and Isshiah the second.

21 The sons of Merari: Mahli and Mushi. The sons of Mahli: Eleazar and Kish.
22Eleazar died having no sons, but only
daughters; their kindred, the sons of
Kish, married them. 23The sons of Mushi: Mahli, Eder, and Jeremoth, three.

24 These were the sons of Levi by
their ancestral houses, the heads of
families as they were enrolled according to the number of the names of the
individuals from twenty years old and
upwards who were to do the work for
the service of the house of the LORD.
25For David said, 'The LORD, the God of
Israel, has given rest to his people; and
he resides in Jerusalem for ever. 26And
so the Levites no longer need to carry
the tabernacle or any of the things for
its service'— 27for according to the last
words of David these were the number of the Levites from twenty years
old and upwards— 28'but their duty
shall be to assist the descendants of
Aaron for the service of the house of
the LORD, having the care of the courts
and the chambers, the cleansing of all
that is holy, and any work for the service of the house of God; 29to assist also
with the rows of bread, the choice flour
for the grain-offering, the wafers of unleavened bread, the baked-offering, the
offering mixed with oil, and all measures of quantity or size. 30And they
shall stand every morning, thanking
and praising the LORD, and likewise
at evening, 31and whenever burnt-
offerings are offered to the LORD on
sabbaths, new moons, and appointed
festivals, according to the number required of them, regularly before the
LORD. 32Thus they shall keep charge
of the tent of meeting and the sanctuary, and shall attend the descendants of
Aaron, their kindred, for the service of
the house of the LORD.'

DIVISIONS OF THE PRIESTS

24 The divisions of the descendants
of Aaron were these. The sons
of Aaron: Nadab, Abihu, Eleazar, and
Ithamar. 2But Nadab and Abihu died
before their father, and had no sons; so
Eleazar and Ithamar became the priests.
3Along with Zadok of the sons of Eleazar, and Ahimelech of the sons of Ithamar, David organized them according
to the appointed duties in their service. 4Since more chief men were found
among the sons of Eleazar than among
the sons of Ithamar, they organized
them under sixteen heads of ancestral
houses of the sons of Eleazar, and eight
of the sons of Ithamar. 5They organized
them by lot, all alike, for there were officers of the sanctuary and officers of
God among both the sons of Eleazar and
the sons of Ithamar. 6The scribe Shemaiah son of Nethanel, a Levite, recorded
them in the presence of the king, and
the officers, and Zadok the priest, and
Ahimelech son of Abiathar, and the
heads of ancestral houses of the priests
and of the Levites; one ancestral house
being chosen for Eleazar and one chosen
for Ithamar.

7 The first lot fell to Jehoiarib, the second to Jedaiah, 8the third to Harim, the
fourth to Seorim, 9the fifth to Malchijah, the sixth to Mijamin, 10the seventh
to Hakkoz, the eighth to Abijah, 11the
ninth to Jeshua, the tenth to Shecaniah,
12the eleventh to Eliashib, the twelfth to
Jakim, 13the thirteenth to Huppah, the
fourteenth to Jeshebeab, 14the fifteenth
to Bilgah, the sixteenth to Immer, 15the
seventeenth to Hezir, the eighteenth to
Happizzez, 16the nineteenth to Pethahiah, the twentieth to Jehezkel, 17the
twenty-first to Jachin, the twenty-
second to Gamul, 18the twenty-third to
Delaiah, the twenty-fourth to Maaziah.
19These had as their appointed duty in
their service to enter the house of the
LORD according to the procedure established for them by their ancestor Aaron,
as the LORD God of Israel had commanded him.

OTHER LEVITES

20 And of the rest of the sons of Levi:
of the sons of Amram, Shubael; of the
sons of Shubael, Jehdeiah. 21 Of Rehabiah: of the sons of Rehabiah, Isshiah
the chief. 22 Of the Izharites, Shelomoth;
of the sons of Shelomoth, Jahath. 23 The
sons of Hebron:[t] Jeriah the chief,[u] Amariah the second, Jahaziel the third, Jekameam the fourth. 24 The sons of Uzziel,
Micah; of the sons of Micah, Shamir.
25 The brother of Micah, Isshiah; of the
sons of Isshiah, Zechariah. 26 The sons
of Merari: Mahli and Mushi. The sons
of Jaaziah: Beno.[v] 27 The sons of Merari:
of Jaaziah, Beno,[w] Shoham, Zaccur,
and Ibri. 28 Of Mahli: Eleazar, who had
no sons. 29 Of Kish, the sons of Kish: Jerahmeel. 30 The sons of Mushi: Mahli,
Eder, and Jerimoth. These were the
sons of the Levites according to their
ancestral houses. 31 These also cast lots
corresponding to their kindred, the descendants of Aaron, in the presence of
King David, Zadok, Ahimelech, and the
heads of ancestral houses of the priests
and of the Levites, the chief as well as
the youngest brother.

THE TEMPLE MUSICIANS

25 David and the officers of the
army also set apart for the service the sons of Asaph, and of Heman,
and of Jeduthun, who were to prophesy
with lyres, harps, and cymbals. The list
of those who did the work and of their
duties was: 2 Of the sons of Asaph: Zaccur, Joseph, Nethaniah, and Asarelah,
sons of Asaph, under the direction of
Asaph, who prophesied under the direction of the king. 3 Of Jeduthun, the sons
of Jeduthun: Gedaliah, Zeri, Jeshaiah,
Shimei,[x] Hashabiah, and Mattithiah,
six, under the direction of their father
Jeduthun, who prophesied with the lyre
in thanksgiving and praise to the LORD.
4 Of Heman, the sons of Heman: Bukkiah, Mattaniah, Uzziel, Shebuel, and
Jerimoth, Hananiah, Hanani, Eliathah,
Giddalti, and Romamti-ezer, Joshbekashah, Mallothi, Hothir, Mahazioth.
5 All these were the sons of Heman the
king's seer, according to the promise
of God to exalt him; for God had given
Heman fourteen sons and three daughters. 6 They were all under the direction of their father for the music in the
house of the LORD with cymbals, harps,
and lyres for the service of the house
of God. Asaph, Jeduthun, and Heman
were under the order of the king. 7 They
and their kindred, who were trained in
singing to the LORD, all of whom were
skilful, numbered two hundred and
eighty-eight. 8 And they cast lots for
their duties, small and great, teacher
and pupil alike.

9 The first lot fell for Asaph to Joseph; the second to Gedaliah, to him
and his brothers and his sons, twelve;
10 the third to Zaccur, his sons and his
brothers, twelve; 11 the fourth to Izri, his
sons and his brothers, twelve; 12 the fifth
to Nethaniah, his sons and his brothers,
twelve; 13 the sixth to Bukkiah, his sons
and his brothers, twelve; 14 the seventh
to Jesarelah,[y] his sons and his brothers,
twelve; 15 the eighth to Jeshaiah, his
sons and his brothers, twelve; 16 the
ninth to Mattaniah, his sons and his
brothers, twelve; 17 the tenth to Shimei,
his sons and his brothers, twelve; 18 the
eleventh to Azarel, his sons and his
brothers, twelve; 19 the twelfth to Hashabiah, his sons and his brothers, twelve;
20 to the thirteenth, Shubael, his sons
and his brothers, twelve; 21 to the fourteenth, Mattithiah, his sons and his
brothers, twelve; 22 to the fifteenth, to
Jeremoth, his sons and his brothers,
twelve; 23 to the sixteenth, to Hananiah,
his sons and his brothers, twelve; 24 to
the seventeenth, to Joshbekashah, his
sons and his brothers, twelve; 25 to the
eighteenth, to Hanani, his sons and his
brothers, twelve; 26 to the nineteenth,
to Mallothi, his sons and his brothers,
twelve; 27 to the twentieth, to Eliathah, his sons and his brothers, twelve;
28 to the twenty-first, to Hothir, his
sons and his brothers, twelve; 29 to the
twenty-second, to Giddalti, his sons and
his brothers, twelve; 30 to the twenty-
third, to Mahazioth, his sons and his
brothers, twelve; 31 to the twenty-
fourth, to Romamti-ezer, his sons and
his brothers, twelve.

THE GATEKEEPERS

26 As for the divisions of the gatekeepers: of the Korahites, Meshelemiah son of Kore, of the sons of
Asaph. 2 Meshelemiah had sons: Zechariah the firstborn, Jediael the second,
Zebadiah the third, Jathniel the fourth,
3 Elam the fifth, Jehohanan the sixth,
Eliehoenai the seventh. 4 Obed-edom

[t] **24.23** See 23.19: Heb lacks *Hebron* [u] **24.23** See 23.19: Heb lacks *the chief* [v] **24.26** Or *his son*: Meaning of Heb uncertain [w] **24.27** Or *his son*: Meaning of Heb uncertain [x] **25.3** One Ms: Gk: MT lacks *Shimei* [y] **25.14** Or *Asarelah*; see 25.2

had sons: Shemaiah the firstborn, Jehozabad the second, Joah the third,
Sachar the fourth, Nethanel the fifth,
5 Ammiel the sixth, Issachar the seventh, Peullethai the eighth; for God
blessed him. 6 Also to his son Shemaiah
sons were born who exercised authority in their ancestral houses, for they
were men of great ability. 7 The sons
of Shemaiah: Othni, Rephael, Obed,
and Elzabad, whose brothers were able
men, Elihu and Semachiah. 8 All these,
sons of Obed-edom with their sons and
brothers, were able men qualified for
the service; sixty-two of Obed-edom.
9 Meshelemiah had sons and brothers,
able men, eighteen. 10 Hosah, of the sons
of Merari, had sons: Shimri the chief
(for though he was not the firstborn, his
father made him chief), 11 Hilkiah the
second, Tebaliah the third, Zechariah
the fourth: all the sons and brothers of
Hosah totalled thirteen.

12 These divisions of the gatekeepers,
corresponding to their leaders, had duties, just as their kindred did, ministering in the house of the LORD; 13 and
they cast lots by ancestral houses, small
and great alike, for their gates. 14 The lot
for the east fell to Shelemiah. They cast
lots also for his son Zechariah, a prudent counsellor, and his lot came out for
the north. 15 Obed-edom's came out for
the south, and to his sons was allotted
the storehouse. 16 For Shuppim and Hosah it came out for the west, at the gate
of Shallecheth on the ascending road.
Guard corresponded to guard. 17 On the
east there were six Levites each day,[z] on
the north four each day, on the south
four each day, as well as two and two at
the storehouse; 18 and for the colonnade[a]
on the west there were four at the road
and two at the colonnade.[b] 19 These were
the divisions of the gatekeepers among
the Korahites and the sons of Merari.

THE TREASURERS, OFFICERS, AND JUDGES

20 And of the Levites, Ahijah had
charge of the treasuries of the house of
God and the treasuries of the dedicated
gifts. 21 The sons of Ladan, the sons of
the Gershonites belonging to Ladan,
the heads of families belonging to Ladan the Gershonite: Jehieli.[c]

22 The sons of Jehieli, Zetham and
his brother Joel, were in charge of the
treasuries of the house of the LORD. 23 Of
the Amramites, the Izharites, the Hebronites, and the Uzzielites: 24 Shebuel
son of Gershom, son of Moses, was chief
officer in charge of the treasuries. 25 His
brothers: from Eliezer were his son Rehabiah, his son Jeshaiah, his son Joram,
his son Zichri, and his son Shelomoth.
26 This Shelomoth and his brothers were
in charge of all the treasuries of the dedicated gifts that King David, and the
heads of families, and the officers of
the thousands and the hundreds, and
the commanders of the army, had dedicated. 27 From booty won in battles they
dedicated gifts for the maintenance of
the house of the LORD. 28 Also all that
Samuel the seer, and Saul son of Kish,
and Abner son of Ner, and Joab son of
Zeruiah had dedicated—all dedicated
gifts were in the care of Shelomoth[d] and
his brothers.

29 Of the Izharites, Chenaniah and
his sons were appointed to outside duties for Israel, as officers and judges.
30 Of the Hebronites, Hashabiah and his
brothers, one thousand seven hundred
men of ability, had the oversight of Israel west of the Jordan for all the work
of the LORD and for the service of the
king. 31 Of the Hebronites, Jerijah was
chief of the Hebronites. (In the fortieth
year of David's reign search was made,
of whatever genealogy or family, and
men of great ability among them were
found at Jazer in Gilead.) 32 King David
appointed him and his brothers, two
thousand seven hundred men of ability,
heads of families, to have the oversight
of the Reubenites, the Gadites, and the
half-tribe of the Manassites for everything pertaining to God and for the affairs of the king.

THE MILITARY DIVISIONS

27 This is the list of the people of
Israel, the heads of families, the
commanders of the thousands and the
hundreds, and their officers who served
the king in all matters concerning the
divisions that came and went, month
after month throughout the year, each
division numbering twenty-four thousand:

2 Jashobeam son of Zabdiel was in
charge of the first division in the first
month; in his division were twenty-four
thousand. 3 He was a descendant of Perez, and was chief of all the commanders

[z] **26.17** Gk: Heb lacks *each day* [a] **26.18** Heb *parbar*: meaning uncertain [b] **26.18** Heb *parbar*: meaning uncertain [c] **26.21** The Hebrew text of verse 21 is confused [d] **26.28** Gk Compare 26.28: Heb *Shelomith*

of the army for the first month. 4 Dodai
the Ahohite was in charge of the division of the second month; Mikloth was
the chief officer of his division. In his
division were twenty-four thousand.
5 The third commander, for the third
month, was Benaiah son of the priest
Jehoiada, as chief; in his division were
twenty-four thousand. 6 This is the Benaiah who was a mighty man of the
Thirty and in command of the Thirty;
his son Ammizabad was in charge of his
division.[e] 7 Asahel brother of Joab was
fourth, for the fourth month, and his
son Zebadiah after him; in his division
were twenty-four thousand. 8 The fifth
commander, for the fifth month, was
Shamhuth, the Izrahite; in his division
were twenty-four thousand. 9 Sixth,
for the sixth month, was Ira son of Ikkesh the Tekoite; in his division were
twenty-four thousand. 10 Seventh, for
the seventh month, was Helez the Pelonite, of the Ephraimites; in his division
were twenty-four thousand. 11 Eighth,
for the eighth month, was Sibbecai the
Hushathite, of the Zerahites; in his division were twenty-four thousand.
12 Ninth, for the ninth month, was Abiezer of Anathoth, a Benjaminite; in his
division were twenty-four thousand.
13 Tenth, for the tenth month, was Maharai of Netophah, of the Zerahites; in
his division were twenty-four thousand.
14 Eleventh, for the eleventh month, was
Benaiah of Pirathon, of the Ephraimites; in his division were twenty-four
thousand. 15 Twelfth, for the twelfth
month, was Heldai the Netophathite,
of Othniel; in his division were twenty-
four thousand.

LEADERS OF TRIBES

16 Over the tribes of Israel, for the
Reubenites, Eliezer son of Zichri was
chief officer; for the Simeonites, Shephatiah son of Maacah; 17 for Levi, Hashabiah son of Kemuel; for Aaron, Zadok; 18 for Judah, Elihu, one of David's
brothers; for Issachar, Omri son of Michael; 19 for Zebulun, Ishmaiah son of
Obadiah; for Naphtali, Jerimoth son of
Azriel; 20 for the Ephraimites, Hoshea
son of Azaziah; for the half-tribe of Manasseh, Joel son of Pedaiah; 21 for the
half-tribe of Manasseh in Gilead, Iddo
son of Zechariah; for Benjamin, Jaasiel
son of Abner; 22 for Dan, Azarel son of
Jeroham. These were the leaders of the
tribes of Israel. 23 David did not count
those below twenty years of age, for the
LORD had promised to make Israel as
numerous as the stars of heaven. 24 Joab
son of Zeruiah began to count them, but
did not finish; yet wrath came upon Israel for this, and the number was not
entered into the account of the Annals
of King David.

OTHER CIVIC OFFICIALS

25 Over the king's treasuries was Azmaveth son of Adiel. Over the treasuries in the country, in the cities, in the
villages, and in the towers, was Jonathan son of Uzziah. 26 Over those who
did the work of the field, tilling the
soil, was Ezri son of Chelub. 27 Over the
vineyards was Shimei the Ramathite.
Over the produce of the vineyards for
the wine cellars was Zabdi the Shiph-
mite. 28 Over the olive and sycomore
trees in the Shephelah was Baal-hanan
the Gederite. Over the stores of oil was
Joash. 29 Over the herds that pastured
in Sharon was Shitrai the Sharonite.
Over the herds in the valleys was Shaphat son of Adlai. 30 Over the camels was
Obil the Ishmaelite. Over the donkeys
was Jehdeiah the Meronothite. Over the
flocks was Jaziz the Hagrite. 31 All these
were stewards of King David's property.
32 Jonathan, David's uncle, was a
counsellor, being a man of understanding and a scribe; Jehiel son of Hachmoni
attended the king's sons. 33 Ahithophel
was the king's counsellor, and Hushai
the Archite was the king's friend. 34 After Ahithophel came Jehoiada son of
Benaiah, and Abiathar. Joab was commander of the king's army.

SOLOMON INSTRUCTED TO BUILD THE TEMPLE

28 David assembled at Jerusalem
all the officials of Israel, the officials of the tribes, the officers of the
divisions that served the king, the commanders of the thousands, the commanders of the hundreds, the stewards
of all the property and cattle of the king
and his sons, together with the palace
officials, the mighty warriors, and all
the warriors. 2 Then King David rose to
his feet and said: 'Hear me, my brothers
and my people. I had planned to build
a house of rest for the ark of the covenant of the LORD, for the footstool of
our God; and I made preparations for
building. 3 But God said to me, "You
shall not build a house for my name, for

[e] 27.6 Gk Vg: Heb *Ammizabad was his division*

you are a warrior and have shed blood." 4Yet the LORD God of Israel chose me from all my ancestral house to be king over Israel for ever; for he chose Judah as leader, and in the house of Judah my father's house, and among my father's sons he took delight in making me king over all Israel. 5And of all my sons, for the LORD has given me many, he has chosen my son Solomon to sit upon the throne of the kingdom of the LORD over Israel. 6He said to me, "It is your son Solomon who shall build my house and my courts, for I have chosen him to be a son to me, and I will be a father to him. 7I will establish his kingdom for ever if he continues resolute in keeping my commandments and my ordinances, as he is today." 8Now therefore in the sight of all Israel, the assembly of the LORD, and in the hearing of our God, observe and search out all the commandments of the LORD your God; that you may possess this good land, and leave it for an inheritance to your children after you for ever.

9 'And you, my son Solomon, know the God of your father, and serve him with single mind and willing heart; for the LORD searches every mind, and understands every plan and thought. If you seek him, he will be found by you; but if you forsake him, he will abandon you for ever. 10Take heed now, for the LORD has chosen you to build a house as the sanctuary; be strong, and act.'

11 Then David gave his son Solomon the plan of the vestibule of the temple, and of its houses, its treasuries, its upper rooms, and its inner chambers, and of the room for the mercy-seat;[f] 12and the plan of all that he had in mind: for the courts of the house of the LORD, all the surrounding chambers, the treasuries of the house of God, and the treasuries for dedicated gifts; 13for the divisions of the priests and of the Levites, and all the work of the service in the house of the LORD; for all the vessels for the service in the house of the LORD, 14the weight of gold for all golden vessels for each service, the weight of silver vessels for each service, 15the weight of the golden lampstands and their lamps, the weight of gold for each lampstand and its lamps, the weight of silver for a lampstand and its lamps, according to the use of each in the service, 16the weight of gold for each table for the rows of bread, the silver for the silver tables, 17and pure gold for the forks, the basins, and the cups; for the golden bowls and the weight of each; for the silver bowls and the weight of each; 18for the altar of incense made of refined gold, and its weight; also his plan for the golden chariot of the cherubim that spread their wings and covered the ark of the covenant of the LORD.

19 'All this, in writing at the LORD's direction, he made clear to me—the plan of all the works.'

20 David said further to his son Solomon, 'Be strong and of good courage, and act. Do not be afraid or dismayed; for the LORD God, my God, is with you. He will not fail you or forsake you, until all the work for the service of the house of the LORD is finished. 21Here are the divisions of the priests and the Levites for all the service of the house of God; and with you in all the work will be every volunteer who has skill for any kind of service; also the officers and all the people will be wholly at your command.'

OFFERINGS FOR BUILDING THE TEMPLE

29 King David said to the whole assembly, 'My son Solomon, whom alone God has chosen, is young and inexperienced, and the work is great; for the temple[g] will not be for mortals but for the LORD God. 2So I have provided for the house of my God, so far as I was able, the gold for the things of gold, the silver for the things of silver, and the bronze for the things of bronze, the iron for the things of iron, and wood for the things of wood, besides great quantities of onyx and stones for setting, antimony, coloured stones, all sorts of precious stones, and marble in abundance. 3Moreover, in addition to all that I have provided for the holy house, I have a treasure of my own of gold and silver, and because of my devotion to the house of my God I give it to the house of my God: 4three thousand talents of gold, of the gold of Ophir, and seven thousand talents of refined silver, for overlaying the walls of the house, 5and for all the work to be done by artisans, gold for the things of gold and silver for the things of silver. Who then will offer willingly, consecrating themselves today to the LORD?'

6 Then the leaders of ancestral houses made their freewill-offerings, as did also the leaders of the tribes, the commanders of the thousands and of the hundreds,

[f] **28.11** Or *the cover* [g] **29.1** Heb *fortress*

and the officers over the king's work.
7They gave for the service of the house
of God five thousand talents and ten
thousand darics of gold, ten thousand
talents of silver, eighteen thousand talents of bronze, and one hundred thousand talents of iron. 8Whoever had precious stones gave them to the treasury
of the house of the LORD, into the care
of Jehiel the Gershonite. 9Then the people rejoiced because these had given
willingly, for with single mind they had
offered freely to the LORD; King David
also rejoiced greatly.

DAVID'S PRAISE TO GOD

10 Then David blessed the LORD in
the presence of all the assembly; David
said: 'Blessed are you, O LORD, the God
of our ancestor Israel, for ever and ever.
11Yours, O LORD, are the greatness, the
power, the glory, the victory, and the
majesty; for all that is in the heavens
and on the earth is yours; yours is the
kingdom, O LORD, and you are exalted
as head above all. 12Riches and honour
come from you, and you rule over all.
In your hand are power and might; and
it is in your hand to make great and to
give strength to all. 13And now, our God,
we give thanks to you and praise your
glorious name.

14 'But who am I, and what is my
people, that we should be able to make
this freewill-offering? For all things
come from you, and of your own have
we given you. 15For we are aliens and
transients before you, as were all our ancestors; our days on the earth are like a
shadow, and there is no hope. 16O LORD
our God, all this abundance that we
have provided for building you a house
for your holy name comes from your
hand and is all your own. 17I know, my
God, that you search the heart, and take
pleasure in uprightness; in the uprightness of my heart I have freely offered all
these things, and now I have seen your
people, who are present here, offering
freely and joyously to you. 18O LORD,
the God of Abraham, Isaac, and Israel,
our ancestors, keep for ever such purposes and thoughts in the hearts of your
people, and direct their hearts towards
you. 19Grant to my son Solomon that
with single mind he may keep your
commandments, your decrees, and your
statutes, performing all of them, and
that he may build the temple[h] for which
I have made provision.'

20 Then David said to the whole assembly, 'Bless the LORD your God.' And
all the assembly blessed the LORD, the
God of their ancestors, and bowed their
heads and prostrated themselves before
the LORD and the king. 21On the next
day they offered sacrifices and burnt-
offerings to the LORD, a thousand
bulls, a thousand rams, and a thousand
lambs, with their libations, and sacrifices in abundance for all Israel; 22and
they ate and drank before the LORD on
that day with great joy.

SOLOMON ANOINTED KING

They made David's son Solomon king
a second time; they anointed him as
the LORD's prince, and Zadok as priest.
23Then Solomon sat on the throne of the
LORD, succeeding his father David as
king; he prospered, and all Israel obeyed
him. 24All the leaders and the mighty
warriors, and also all the sons of King
David, pledged their allegiance to King
Solomon. 25The LORD highly exalted
Solomon in the sight of all Israel, and
bestowed upon him such royal majesty
as had not been on any king before him
in Israel.

SUMMARY OF DAVID'S REIGN

26 Thus David son of Jesse reigned
over all Israel. 27The period that he
reigned over Israel was forty years; he
reigned for seven years in Hebron and
thirty-three years in Jerusalem. 28He
died at a good old age, full of days, riches,
and honour; and his son Solomon succeeded him. 29Now the acts of King David, from first to last, are written in the
records of the seer Samuel, and in the
records of the prophet Nathan, and in
the records of the seer Gad, 30with accounts of all his rule and his might and
of the events that befell him and Israel
and all the kingdoms of the earth.

h 29.19 Heb *fortress*

2 CHRONICLES

Second Chronicles is a continuation of the history that looks back from the fifth century BCE to an idealized past of the united monarchy under Solomon and to the former grandeur of worship in the newly constructed temple in Jerusalem. The first nine chapters of 2 Chronicles contain the history of the reign of King Solomon. The remaining chapters of the second book contain the history of the separated kingdom of Judah to the time of the return from the Babylonian exile.

A passage from 2 Chronicles is provided in the Roman Missal at the liturgical celebration of the Dedication of a Church. The passage describes the placement of the ark in the new temple built by Solomon in Jerusalem (5.6–10, 13; 6.2). Also, the final verses of 2 Chronicles are read on the Fourth Sunday of Lent during Year B (36.14–17, 19–23), giving the Chronicler's interpretation of the exile followed by the proclamation of King Cyrus that anticipates the hope of a coming restoration.

SOLOMON REQUESTS WISDOM

1 Solomon son of David established
himself in his kingdom; the LORD
his God was with him and made him
exceedingly great.
2 Solomon summoned all Israel, the
commanders of the thousands and of
the hundreds, the judges, and all the
leaders of all Israel, the heads of families. 3Then Solomon, and the whole
assembly with him, went to the high
place that was at Gibeon; for God's tent
of meeting, which Moses the servant of
the LORD had made in the wilderness,
was there. 4(But David had brought the
ark of God up from Kiriath-jearim to the
place that David had prepared for it; for
he had pitched a tent for it in Jerusalem.)
5Moreover, the bronze altar that Bezalel
son of Uri, son of Hur, had made was
there in front of the tabernacle of the
LORD. And Solomon and the assembly
inquired at it. 6Solomon went up there
to the bronze altar before the LORD,
which was at the tent of meeting, and
offered a thousand burnt-offerings on it.
7 That night God appeared to Solomon, and said to him, 'Ask what I
should give you.' 8Solomon said to God,
'You have shown great and steadfast
love to my father David, and have made
me succeed him as king. 9O LORD God,
let your promise to my father David now
be fulfilled, for you have made me king
over a people as numerous as the dust
of the earth. 10Give me now wisdom and
knowledge to go out and come in before
this people, for who can rule this great
people of yours?' 11God answered Solomon, 'Because this was in your heart,
and you have not asked for possessions,
wealth, honour, or the life of those who
hate you, and have not even asked for
long life, but have asked for wisdom and
knowledge for yourself that you may
rule my people over whom I have made
you king, 12wisdom and knowledge
are granted to you. I will also give you
riches, possessions, and honour, such as
none of the kings had who were before
you, and none after you shall have the
like.' 13So Solomon came from[a] the high
place at Gibeon, from the tent of meeting, to Jerusalem. And he reigned over
Israel.

SOLOMON'S MILITARY AND COMMERCIAL ACTIVITY

14 Solomon gathered together chariots and horses; he had fourteen hundred

[a] 1.13 Gk Vg: Heb *to*

chariots and twelve thousand horses, which he stationed in the chariot cities and with the king in Jerusalem. 15 The king made silver and gold as common in Jerusalem as stone, and he made cedar as plentiful as the sycomore of the Shephelah. 16 Solomon's horses were imported from Egypt and Kue; the king's traders received them from Kue at the prevailing price. 17 They imported from Egypt, and then exported, a chariot for six hundred shekels of silver, and a horse for one hundred and fifty; so through them these were exported to all the kings of the Hittites and the kings of Aram.

PREPARATIONS FOR BUILDING THE TEMPLE

2[b] Solomon decided to build a temple for the name of the LORD, and a royal palace for himself. 2[c] Solomon conscripted seventy thousand labourers and eighty thousand stonecutters in the hill country, with three thousand six hundred to oversee them.

ALLIANCE WITH HURAM OF TYRE

3 Solomon sent word to King Huram of Tyre: 'Once you dealt with my father David and sent him cedar to build himself a house to live in. 4 I am now about to build a house for the name of the LORD my God and dedicate it to him for offering fragrant incense before him, and for the regular offering of the rows of bread, and for burnt-offerings morning and evening, on the sabbaths and the new moons and the appointed festivals of the LORD our God, as ordained for ever for Israel. 5 The house that I am about to build will be great, for our God is greater than other gods. 6 But who is able to build him a house, since heaven, even highest heaven, cannot contain him? Who am I to build a house for him, except as a place to make offerings before him? 7 So now send me an artisan skilled to work in gold, silver, bronze, and iron, and in purple, crimson, and blue fabrics, trained also in engraving, to join the skilled workers who are with me in Judah and Jerusalem, whom my father David provided. 8 Send me also cedar, cypress, and algum timber from Lebanon, for I know that your servants are skilled in cutting Lebanon timber. My servants will work with your servants 9 to prepare timber for me in abundance, for the house I am about to build will be great and wonderful. 10 I will provide for your servants, those who cut the timber, twenty thousand cors of crushed wheat, twenty thousand cors of barley, twenty thousand baths[d] of wine, and twenty thousand baths of oil.'

11 Then King Huram of Tyre answered in a letter that he sent to Solomon, 'Because the LORD loves his people he has made you king over them.' 12 Huram also said, 'Blessed be the LORD God of Israel, who made heaven and earth, who has given King David a wise son, endowed with discretion and understanding, who will build a temple for the LORD, and a royal palace for himself.

13 'I have dispatched Huram-abi, a skilled artisan, endowed with understanding, 14 the son of one of the Danite women, his father a Tyrian. He is trained to work in gold, silver, bronze, iron, stone, and wood, and in purple, blue, and crimson fabrics and fine linen, and to do all sorts of engraving and execute any design that may be assigned him, with your artisans, the artisans of my lord, your father David. 15 Now, as for the wheat, barley, oil, and wine, of which my lord has spoken, let him send them to his servants. 16 We will cut whatever timber you need from Lebanon, and bring it to you as rafts by sea to Joppa; you will take it up to Jerusalem.'

17 Then Solomon took a census of all the aliens who were residing in the land of Israel, after the census that his father David had taken; and there were found to be one hundred and fifty-three thousand six hundred. 18 Seventy thousand of them he assigned as labourers, eighty thousand as stonecutters in the hill country, and three thousand six hundred as overseers to make the people work.

SOLOMON BUILDS THE TEMPLE

3 Solomon began to build the house of the LORD in Jerusalem on Mount Moriah, where the LORD had appeared to his father David, at the place that David had designated, on the threshing-floor of Ornan the Jebusite. 2 He began to build on the second day of the second month of the fourth year of his reign. 3 These are Solomon's measurements[e] for building the house of God: the length, in cubits of the old standard, was sixty cubits, and the width

[b] 2.1 Ch 1.18 in Heb [c] 2.2 Ch 2.1 in Heb
[d] 2.10 A Hebrew measure of volume [e] 3.3 Syr: Heb *foundations*

twenty cubits. 4The vestibule in front
of the nave of the house was twenty cubits long, across the width of the house;[f]
and its height was one hundred and
twenty cubits. He overlaid it on the inside with pure gold. 5The nave he lined
with cypress, covered it with fine gold,
and made palms and chains on it. 6He
adorned the house with settings of precious stones. The gold was gold from
Parvaim. 7So he lined the house with
gold—its beams, its thresholds, its
walls, and its doors; and he carved cherubim on the walls.

8 He made the most holy place; its
length, corresponding to the width of
the house, was twenty cubits, and its
width was twenty cubits; he overlaid
it with six hundred talents of fine gold.
9The weight of the nails was fifty shekels of gold. He overlaid the upper chambers with gold.

10 In the most holy place he made
two carved cherubim and overlaid[g]
them with gold. 11The wings of the
cherubim together extended twenty cubits: one wing of one, five cubits long,
touched the wall of the house, and its
other wing, five cubits long, touched
the wing of the other cherub; 12and of
this cherub, one wing, five cubits long,
touched the wall of the house, and the
other wing, also five cubits long, was
joined to the wing of the first cherub.
13The wings of these cherubim extended
twenty cubits; the cherubim[h] stood on
their feet, facing the nave. 14And Solomon[i] made the curtain of blue and
purple and crimson fabrics and fine
linen, and worked cherubim into it.

15 In front of the house he made two
pillars thirty-five cubits high, with a
capital of five cubits on the top of each.
16He made encircling[j] chains and put
them on the tops of the pillars; and he
made one hundred pomegranates, and
put them on the chains. 17He set up the
pillars in front of the temple, one on the
right, the other on the left; the one on
the right he called Jachin, and the one
on the left, Boaz.

FURNISHINGS OF THE TEMPLE

4 He made an altar of bronze, twenty
cubits long, twenty cubits wide,
and ten cubits high. 2Then he made the
cast sea; it was round, ten cubits from
rim to rim, and five cubits high. A line
of thirty cubits would encircle it completely. 3Under it were panels all round,
each of ten cubits, surrounding the sea;
there were two rows of panels, cast
when it was cast. 4It stood on twelve
oxen, three facing north, three facing
west, three facing south, and three facing east; the sea was set on them. The
hindquarters of each were towards
the inside. 5Its thickness was a handbreadth; its rim was made like the rim
of a cup, like the flower of a lily; it held
three thousand baths.[k] 6He also made
ten basins in which to wash, and set five
on the right-hand side, and five on the
left. In these they were to rinse what
was used for the burnt-offering. The sea
was for the priests to wash in.

7 He made ten golden lampstands
as prescribed, and set them in the temple, five on the south side and five on
the north. 8He also made ten tables and
placed them in the temple, five on the
right-hand side and five on the left. And
he made one hundred basins of gold.
9He made the court of the priests, and
the great court, and doors for the court;
he overlaid their doors with bronze.
10He set the sea at the south-east corner
of the house.

11 And Huram made the pots, the
shovels, and the basins. Thus Huram
finished the work that he did for King
Solomon on the house of God: 12the two
pillars, the bowls, and the two capitals
on the top of the pillars; and the two
lattice-works to cover the two bowls of
the capitals that were on the top of the
pillars; 13the four hundred pomegranates for the two lattice-works, two rows
of pomegranates for each lattice-work,
to cover the two bowls of the capitals
that were on the pillars. 14He made the
stands, the basins on the stands, 15the
one sea, and the twelve oxen underneath it. 16The pots, the shovels, the
forks, and all the equipment for these
Huram-abi made of burnished bronze
for King Solomon for the house of the
LORD. 17In the plain of the Jordan the
king cast them, in the clay ground between Succoth and Zeredah. 18Solomon
made all these things in great quantities, so that the weight of the bronze
was not determined.

19 So Solomon made all the things
that were in the house of God: the
golden altar, the tables for the bread
of the Presence, 20the lampstands and

[f] 3.4 Compare 1 Kings 6.3: Meaning of Heb uncertain [g] 3.10 Heb *they overlaid* [h] 3.13 Heb *they* [i] 3.14 Heb *he* [j] 3.16 Cn: Heb *in the inner sanctuary* [k] 4.5 A Hebrew measure of volume

their lamps of pure gold to burn before the inner sanctuary, as prescribed; 21 the flowers, the lamps, and the tongs, of purest gold; 22 the snuffers, basins, ladles, and firepans, of pure gold. As for the entrance to the temple: the inner doors to the most holy place and the doors of the nave of the temple were of gold.

5 Thus all the work that Solomon did for the house of the LORD was finished. Solomon brought in the things that his father David had dedicated, and stored the silver, the gold, and all the vessels in the treasuries of the house of God.

THE ARK BROUGHT INTO THE TEMPLE

2 Then Solomon assembled the elders of Israel and all the heads of the tribes, the leaders of the ancestral houses of the people of Israel, in Jerusalem, to bring up the ark of the covenant of the LORD out of the city of David, which is Zion. 3 And all the Israelites assembled before the king at the festival that is in the seventh month. 4 And all the elders of Israel came, and the Levites carried the ark. 5 So they brought up the ark, the tent of meeting, and all the holy vessels that were in the tent; the priests and the Levites brought them up. 6 King Solomon and all the congregation of Israel, who had assembled before him, were before the ark, sacrificing so many sheep and oxen that they could not be numbered or counted. 7 Then the priests brought the ark of the covenant of the LORD to its place, in the inner sanctuary of the house, in the most holy place, underneath the wings of the cherubim. 8 For the cherubim spread out their wings over the place of the ark, so that the cherubim made a covering above the ark and its poles. 9 The poles were so long that the ends of the poles were seen from the holy place in front of the inner sanctuary; but they could not be seen from outside; they are there to this day. 10 There was nothing in the ark except the two tablets that Moses put there at Horeb, where the LORD made a covenant[1] with the people of Israel after they came out of Egypt.

11 Now when the priests came out of the holy place (for all the priests who were present had sanctified themselves, without regard to their divisions), 12 all the levitical singers, Asaph, Heman, and Jeduthun, their sons and kindred, arrayed in fine linen, with cymbals, harps, and lyres, stood east of the altar with one hundred and twenty priests who were trumpeters, 13 it was the duty of the trumpeters and singers to make themselves heard in unison in praise and thanksgiving to the LORD, and when the song was raised, with trumpets and cymbals and other musical instruments, in praise to the LORD,

'For he is good,
  for his steadfast love
    endures for ever',

the house, the house of the LORD, was filled with a cloud, 14 so that the priests could not stand to minister because of the cloud; for the glory of the LORD filled the house of God.

DEDICATION OF THE TEMPLE

6 Then Solomon said, 'The LORD has said that he would reside in thick darkness. 2 I have built you an exalted house, a place for you to reside in for ever.'

3 Then the king turned round and blessed all the assembly of Israel, while all the assembly of Israel stood. 4 And he said, 'Blessed be the LORD, the God of Israel, who with his hand has fulfilled what he promised with his mouth to my father David, saying, 5 "Since the day that I brought my people out of the land of Egypt, I have not chosen a city from any of the tribes of Israel in which to build a house, so that my name might be there, and I chose no one as ruler over my people Israel; 6 but I have chosen Jerusalem in order that my name may be there, and I have chosen David to be over my people Israel." 7 My father David had it in mind to build a house for the name of the LORD, the God of Israel. 8 But the LORD said to my father David, "You did well to consider building a house for my name; 9 nevertheless, you shall not build the house, but your son who shall be born to you shall build the house for my name." 10 Now the LORD has fulfilled his promise that he made; for I have succeeded my father David, and sit on the throne of Israel, as the LORD promised, and have built the house for the name of the LORD, the God of Israel. 11 There I have set the ark, in which is the covenant of the LORD that he made with the people of Israel.'

[1] **5.10** Heb lacks *a covenant*

SOLOMON'S PRAYER OF DEDICATION

12 Then Solomon[m] stood before the
altar of the LORD in the presence of the
whole assembly of Israel, and spread
out his hands. 13 Solomon had made a
bronze platform five cubits long, five
cubits wide, and three cubits high, and
had set it in the court; and he stood on
it. Then he knelt on his knees in the
presence of the whole assembly of Israel, and spread out his hands towards
heaven. 14 He said, 'O LORD, God of Israel, there is no God like you, in heaven
or on earth, keeping covenant in steadfast love with your servants who walk
before you with all their heart— 15 you
who have kept for your servant, my father David, what you promised to him.
Indeed, you promised with your mouth
and this day have fulfilled with your
hand. 16 Therefore, O LORD, God of Israel, keep for your servant, my father
David, that which you promised him,
saying, "There shall never fail you a successor before me to sit on the throne
of Israel, if only your children keep to
their way, to walk in my law as you
have walked before me." 17 Therefore,
O LORD, God of Israel, let your word be
confirmed, which you promised to your
servant David.

18 'But will God indeed reside with
mortals on earth? Even heaven and
the highest heaven cannot contain you,
how much less this house that I have
built! 19 Have regard to your servant's
prayer and his plea, O LORD my God,
heeding the cry and the prayer that
your servant prays to you. 20 May your
eyes be open day and night towards this
house, the place where you promised to
set your name, and may you heed the
prayer that your servant prays towards
this place. 21 And hear the plea of your
servant and of your people Israel, when
they pray towards this place; may you
hear from heaven your dwelling-place;
hear and forgive.

22 'If someone sins against another and is required to take an oath
and comes and swears before your altar in this house, 23 may you hear from
heaven, and act, and judge your servants, repaying the guilty by bringing
their conduct on their own head, and
vindicating those who are in the right
by rewarding them in accordance with
their righteousness.

24 'When your people Israel, having
sinned against you, are defeated before
an enemy but turn again to you, confess your name, pray and plead with
you in this house, 25 may you hear from
heaven, and forgive the sin of your people Israel, and bring them again to the
land that you gave to them and to their
ancestors.

26 'When heaven is shut up and there
is no rain because they have sinned
against you, and then they pray towards
this place, confess your name, and turn
from their sin, because you punish
them, 27 may you hear in heaven, forgive
the sin of your servants, your people Israel, when you teach them the good way
in which they should walk; and send
down rain upon your land, which you
have given to your people as an inheritance.

28 'If there is famine in the land, if
there is plague, blight, mildew, locust,
or caterpillar; if their enemies besiege
them in any of the settlements of the
lands; whatever suffering, whatever
sickness there is; 29 whatever prayer,
whatever plea from any individual or
from all your people Israel, all knowing their own suffering and their own
sorrows so that they stretch out their
hands towards this house; 30 may you
hear from heaven your dwelling-place,
forgive, and render to all whose heart
you know, according to all their ways,
for only you know the human heart.
31 Thus may they fear you and walk in
your ways all the days that they live in
the land that you gave to our ancestors.

32 'Likewise when foreigners, who
are not of your people Israel, come from
a distant land because of your great
name, and your mighty hand, and your
outstretched arm, when they come and
pray towards this house, 33 may you hear
from heaven your dwelling-place, and
do whatever the foreigners ask of you,
in order that all the peoples of the earth
may know your name and fear you, as
do your people Israel, and that they may
know that your name has been invoked
on this house that I have built.

34 'If your people go out to battle
against their enemies, by whatever way
you shall send them, and they pray to
you towards this city that you have chosen and the house that I have built for
your name, 35 then hear from heaven
their prayer and their plea, and maintain their cause.

36 'If they sin against you—for there
is no one who does not sin—and you

[m] 6.12 Heb *he*

are angry with them and give them to
an enemy, so that they are carried away
captive to a land far or near; 37 then if
they come to their senses in the land
to which they have been taken captive,
and repent, and plead with you in the
land of their captivity, saying, "We have
sinned, and have done wrong; we have
acted wickedly"; 38 if they repent with all
their heart and soul in the land of their
captivity, to which they were taken captive, and pray towards their land, which
you gave to their ancestors, the city that
you have chosen, and the house that I
have built for your name, 39 then hear
from heaven your dwelling-place their
prayer and their pleas, maintain their
cause and forgive your people who have
sinned against you. 40 Now, O my God,
let your eyes be open and your ears attentive to prayer from this place.

41 'Now rise up, O LORD God, and
go to your resting-place,
you and the ark of your might.
Let your priests, O LORD God, be
clothed with salvation,
and let your faithful rejoice
in your goodness.
42 O LORD God, do not reject your
anointed one.
Remember your steadfast love
for your servant David.'

SOLOMON DEDICATES THE TEMPLE

7 When Solomon had ended his
prayer, fire came down from heaven
and consumed the burnt-offering and
the sacrifices; and the glory of the LORD
filled the temple. 2 The priests could not
enter the house of the LORD, because
the glory of the LORD filled the LORD's
house. 3 When all the people of Israel
saw the fire come down and the glory
of the LORD on the temple, they bowed
down on the pavement with their faces
to the ground, and worshipped and gave
thanks to the LORD, saying,

'For he is good,
for his steadfast love
endures for ever.'

4 Then the king and all the people offered sacrifice before the LORD. 5 King
Solomon offered as a sacrifice twenty-
two thousand oxen and one hundred
and twenty thousand sheep. So the king
and all the people dedicated the house
of God. 6 The priests stood at their posts;
the Levites also, with the instruments
for music to the LORD that King David had made for giving thanks to the
LORD—for his steadfast love endures for
ever—whenever David offered praises
by their ministry. Opposite them the
priests sounded trumpets; and all Israel
stood.

7 Solomon consecrated the middle of
the court that was in front of the house
of the LORD; for there he offered the
burnt-offerings and the fat of the offerings of well-being because the bronze
altar Solomon had made could not
hold the burnt-offering and the grain-
offering and the fat parts.

8 At that time Solomon held the festival for seven days, and all Israel with
him, a very great congregation, from
Lebo-hamath to the Wadi of Egypt. 9 On
the eighth day they held a solemn assembly; for they had observed the dedication of the altar for seven days and
the festival for seven days. 10 On the
twenty-third day of the seventh month
he sent the people away to their homes,
joyful and in good spirits because of the
goodness that the LORD had shown to
David and to Solomon and to his people Israel.

11 Thus Solomon finished the house
of the LORD and the king's house; all
that Solomon had planned to do in the
house of the LORD and in his own house
he successfully accomplished.

GOD'S SECOND APPEARANCE TO SOLOMON

12 Then the LORD appeared to Solomon in the night and said to him: 'I
have heard your prayer, and have chosen this place for myself as a house of
sacrifice. 13 When I shut up the heavens
so that there is no rain, or command the
locust to devour the land, or send pestilence among my people, 14 if my people who are called by my name humble
themselves, pray, seek my face, and turn
from their wicked ways, then I will hear
from heaven, and will forgive their sin
and heal their land. 15 Now my eyes will
be open and my ears attentive to the
prayer that is made in this place. 16 For
now I have chosen and consecrated this
house so that my name may be there for
ever; my eyes and my heart will be there
for all time. 17 As for you, if you walk before me, as your father David walked,
doing according to all that I have commanded you and keeping my statutes
and my ordinances, 18 then I will establish your royal throne, as I made covenant with your father David saying,
"You shall never lack a successor to rule
over Israel."

19 'But if you[n] turn aside and forsake
my statutes and my commandments
that I have set before you, and go and
serve other gods and worship them,
20then I will pluck you[o] up from the
land that I have given you;[p] and this
house, which I have consecrated for my
name, I will cast out of my sight, and
will make it a proverb and a byword
among all peoples. 21And regarding this
house, now exalted, everyone passing
by will be astonished, and say, "Why has
the LORD done such a thing to this land
and to this house?" 22Then they will
say, "Because they abandoned the LORD
the God of their ancestors who brought
them out of the land of Egypt, and they
adopted other gods, and worshipped
them and served them; therefore he has
brought all this calamity upon them."'

VARIOUS ACTIVITIES OF SOLOMON

8 At the end of twenty years, during
which Solomon had built the house
of the LORD and his own house, 2Sol-
omon rebuilt the cities that Huram had
given to him, and settled the people of
Israel in them.

3 Solomon went to Hamath-zobah,
and captured it. 4He built Tadmor
in the wilderness and all the storage
towns that he built in Hamath. 5He
also built Upper Beth-horon and Lower
Beth-horon, fortified cities, with walls,
gates, and bars, 6and Baalath, as well as
all Solomon's storage towns, and all the
towns for his chariots, the towns for his
cavalry, and whatever Solomon desired
to build, in Jerusalem, in Lebanon, and
in all the land of his dominion. 7All the
people who were left of the Hittites, the
Amorites, the Perizzites, the Hivites,
and the Jebusites, who were not of Israel, 8from their descendants who were
still left in the land, whom the people
of Israel had not destroyed—these Solomon conscripted for forced labour, as
is still the case today. 9But of the people
of Israel Solomon made no slaves for his
work; they were soldiers, and his officers, the commanders of his chariotry
and cavalry. 10These were the chief officers of King Solomon, two hundred and
fifty of them, who exercised authority
over the people.

11 Solomon brought Pharaoh's daughter from the city of David to the house
that he had built for her, for he said, 'My
wife shall not live in the house of King
David of Israel, for the places to which the
ark of the LORD has come are holy.'

12 Then Solomon offered up burnt-
offerings to the LORD on the altar of the
LORD that he had built in front of the
vestibule, 13as the duty of each day required, offering according to the commandment of Moses for the sabbaths,
the new moons, and the three annual
festivals—the festival of unleavened
bread, the festival of weeks, and the festival of booths. 14According to the ordinance of his father David, he appointed
the divisions of the priests for their
service, and the Levites for their offices of praise and ministry alongside the
priests as the duty of each day required,
and the gatekeepers in their divisions
for the several gates; for so David the
man of God had commanded. 15They
did not turn away from what the king
had commanded the priests and Levites
regarding anything at all, or regarding
the treasuries.

16 Thus all the work of Solomon was
accomplished from[q] the day the foundation of the house of the LORD was laid
until the house of the LORD was finished completely.

17 Then Solomon went to Ezion-
geber and Eloth on the shore of the sea,
in the land of Edom. 18Huram sent him,
in the care of his servants, ships and servants familiar with the sea. They went
to Ophir, together with the servants of
Solomon, and imported from there four
hundred and fifty talents of gold and
brought it to King Solomon.

VISIT OF THE QUEEN OF SHEBA

9 When the queen of Sheba heard of
the fame of Solomon, she came to Jerusalem to test him with hard questions,
having a very great retinue and camels
bearing spices and very much gold and
precious stones. When she came to Solomon, she discussed with him all that
was on her mind. 2Solomon answered
all her questions; there was nothing hidden from Solomon that he could not explain to her. 3When the queen of Sheba
had observed the wisdom of Solomon,
the house that he had built, 4the food of
his table, the seating of his officials, and
the attendance of his servants, and their
clothing, his valets and their clothing,
and his burnt-offerings[r] that he offered
at the house of the LORD, there was no
more spirit left in her.

[n] 7.19 The word *you* in this verse is plural
[o] 7.20 Heb *them* [p] 7.20 Heb *them* [q] 8.16 Gk
Syr Vg: Heb *to* [r] 9.4 Gk Syr Vg 1 Kings 10.5: Heb
ascent

5 So she said to the king, 'The report
was true that I heard in my own land
of your accomplishments and of your
wisdom, 6but I did not believe the[s] reports until I came and my own eyes saw
it. Not even half of the greatness of your
wisdom had been told to me; you far surpass the report that I had heard. 7Happy
are your people! Happy are these your
servants, who continually attend you
and hear your wisdom! 8Blessed be the
LORD your God, who has delighted in
you and set you on his throne as king
for the LORD your God. Because your
God loved Israel and wished to establish
them for ever, he has made you king
over them, so that you may execute justice and righteousness.' 9Then she gave
the king one hundred and twenty talents of gold, a very great quantity of
spices, and precious stones: there were
no spices such as those that the queen of
Sheba gave to King Solomon.

10 Moreover, the servants of Huram and the servants of Solomon who
brought gold from Ophir brought algum wood and precious stones. 11From
the algum wood, the king made steps[t]
for the house of the LORD and for the
king's house, lyres also and harps for the
singers; there never was seen the like of
them before in the land of Judah.

12 Meanwhile, King Solomon
granted the queen of Sheba every desire
that she expressed, well beyond what
she had brought to the king. Then she
returned to her own land, with her servants.

SOLOMON'S GREAT WEALTH

13 The weight of gold that came to
Solomon in one year was six hundred
and sixty-six talents of gold, 14besides
that which the traders and merchants
brought; and all the kings of Arabia
and the governors of the land brought
gold and silver to Solomon. 15King Solomon made two hundred large shields
of beaten gold; six hundred shekels of
beaten gold went into each large shield.
16He made three hundred shields of
beaten gold; three hundred shekels of
gold went into each shield; and the king
put them in the House of the Forest of
Lebanon. 17The king also made a great
ivory throne, and overlaid it with pure
gold. 18The throne had six steps and a
footstool of gold, which were attached
to the throne, and on each side of the
seat were arm rests and two lions standing beside the arm rests, 19while twelve
lions were standing, one on each end
of a step on the six steps. The like of it
was never made in any kingdom. 20All
King Solomon's drinking vessels were
of gold, and all the vessels of the House
of the Forest of Lebanon were of pure
gold; silver was not considered as anything in the days of Solomon. 21For the
king's ships went to Tarshish with the
servants of Huram; once every three
years the ships of Tarshish used to come
bringing gold, silver, ivory, apes, and
peacocks.[u]

22 Thus King Solomon excelled all the
kings of the earth in riches and in wisdom. 23All the kings of the earth sought
the presence of Solomon to hear his wisdom, which God had put into his mind.
24Every one of them brought a present,
objects of silver and gold, garments,
weaponry, spices, horses, and mules,
so much year after year. 25Solomon had
four thousand stalls for horses and chariots, and twelve thousand horses, which
he stationed in the chariot cities and
with the king in Jerusalem. 26He ruled
over all the kings from the Euphrates
to the land of the Philistines, and to the
border of Egypt. 27The king made silver
as common in Jerusalem as stone, and
cedar as plentiful as the sycomore of the
Shephelah. 28Horses were imported for
Solomon from Egypt and from all lands.

DEATH OF SOLOMON

29 Now the rest of the acts of Solomon, from first to last, are they not
written in the history of the prophet
Nathan, and in the prophecy of Ahijah
the Shilonite, and in the visions of the
seer Iddo concerning Jeroboam son of
Nebat? 30Solomon reigned in Jerusalem
over all Israel for forty years. 31Solomon
slept with his ancestors and was buried
in the city of his father David; and his
son Rehoboam succeeded him.

THE REVOLT AGAINST REHOBOAM

10 Rehoboam went to Shechem, for
all Israel had come to Shechem
to make him king. 2When Jeroboam
son of Nebat heard of it (for he was in
Egypt, where he had fled from King Solomon), then Jeroboam returned from
Egypt. 3They sent and called him; and
Jeroboam and all Israel came and said to
Rehoboam, 4'Your father made our yoke
heavy. Now therefore lighten the hard

[s] 9.6 Heb *their* [t] 9.11 Gk Vg: Meaning of Heb uncertain [u] 9.21 Or *baboons*

service of your father and his heavy
yoke that he placed on us, and we will
serve you.' 5He said to them, 'Come to
me again in three days.' So the people
went away.

6 Then King Rehoboam took counsel
with the older men who had attended
his father Solomon while he was still
alive, saying, 'How do you advise me
to answer this people?' 7They answered
him, 'If you will be kind to this people
and please them, and speak good words
to them, then they will be your servants
for ever.' 8But he rejected the advice that
the older men gave him, and consulted
the young men who had grown up with
him and now attended him. 9He said
to them, 'What do you advise that we
answer this people who have said to
me, "Lighten the yoke that your father
put on us"?' 10The young men who had
grown up with him said to him, 'Thus
should you speak to the people who
said to you, "Your father made our yoke
heavy, but you must lighten it for us";
tell them, "My little finger is thicker
than my father's loins. 11Now, whereas
my father laid on you a heavy yoke, I
will add to your yoke. My father disciplined you with whips, but I will discipline you with scorpions."'

12 So Jeroboam and all the people
came to Rehoboam the third day, as the
king had said, 'Come to me again the
third day.' 13The king answered them
harshly. King Rehoboam rejected the
advice of the older men; 14he spoke to
them in accordance with the advice of
the young men, 'My father made your
yoke heavy, but I will add to it; my father disciplined you with whips, but I
will discipline you with scorpions.' 15So
the king did not listen to the people, because it was a turn of affairs brought
about by God so that the LORD might
fulfil his word, which he had spoken by
Ahijah the Shilonite to Jeroboam son of
Nebat.

16 When all Israel saw that the king
would not listen to them, the people answered the king,

'What share do we have in David?
We have no inheritance in
the son of Jesse.
Each of you to your tents, O Israel!
Look now to your own
house, O David.'

So all Israel departed to their tents.
17But Rehoboam reigned over the people of Israel who were living in the cities
of Judah. 18When King Rehoboam sent
Hadoram, who was taskmaster over
the forced labour, the people of Israel
stoned him to death. King Rehoboam
hurriedly mounted his chariot to flee to
Jerusalem. 19So Israel has been in rebellion against the house of David to this
day.

JUDAH AND BENJAMIN FORTIFIED

11 When Rehoboam came to Jerusalem, he assembled one hundred and eighty thousand chosen troops
of the house of Judah and Benjamin to
fight against Israel, to restore the kingdom to Rehoboam. 2But the word of
the LORD came to Shemaiah the man
of God: 3Say to King Rehoboam of Judah, son of Solomon, and to all Israel
in Judah and Benjamin, 4'Thus says
the LORD: You shall not go up or fight
against your kindred. Let everyone return home, for this thing is from me.'
So they heeded the word of the LORD
and turned back from the expedition
against Jeroboam.

5 Rehoboam resided in Jerusalem,
and he built cities for defence in Judah.
6He built up Bethlehem, Etam, Tekoa,
7Beth-zur, Soco, Adullam, 8Gath, Mareshah, Ziph, 9Adoraim, Lachish, Azekah,
10Zorah, Aijalon, and Hebron, fortified
cities that are in Judah and in Benjamin. 11He made the fortresses strong,
and put commanders in them, and
stores of food, oil, and wine. 12He also
put large shields and spears in all the
cities, and made them very strong. So
he held Judah and Benjamin.

PRIESTS AND LEVITES SUPPORT REHOBOAM

13 The priests and the Levites who
were in all Israel presented themselves
to him from all their territories. 14The
Levites had left their common lands
and their holdings and had come to Judah and Jerusalem, because Jeroboam
and his sons had prevented them from
serving as priests of the LORD, 15and
had appointed his own priests for the
high places, and for the goat-demons,
and for the calves that he had made.
16Those who had set their hearts to seek
the LORD God of Israel came after them
from all the tribes of Israel to Jerusalem to sacrifice to the LORD, the God of
their ancestors. 17They strengthened the
kingdom of Judah, and for three years
they made Rehoboam son of Solomon
secure, for they walked for three years
in the way of David and Solomon.

REHOBOAM'S MARRIAGES

18 Rehoboam took as his wife Mahalath daughter of Jerimoth son of David, and of Abihail daughter of Eliab son of Jesse. 19 She bore him sons: Jeush, Shemariah, and Zaham. 20 After her he took Maacah daughter of Absalom, who bore him Abijah, Attai, Ziza, and Shelomith. 21 Rehoboam loved Maacah daughter of Absalom more than all his other wives and concubines (he took eighteen wives and sixty concubines, and became the father of twenty-eight sons and sixty daughters). 22 Rehoboam appointed Abijah son of Maacah as chief prince among his brothers, for he intended to make him king. 23 He dealt wisely, and distributed some of his sons through all the districts of Judah and Benjamin, in all the fortified cities; he gave them abundant provisions, and found many wives for them.

EGYPT ATTACKS JUDAH

12 When the rule of Rehoboam was established and he grew strong, he abandoned the law of the LORD, he and all Israel with him. 2 In the fifth year of King Rehoboam, because they had been unfaithful to the LORD, King Shishak of Egypt came up against Jerusalem 3 with twelve hundred chariots and sixty thousand cavalry. A countless army came with him from Egypt—Libyans, Sukkiim, and Ethiopians.[v] 4 He took the fortified cities of Judah and came as far as Jerusalem. 5 Then the prophet Shemaiah came to Rehoboam and to the officers of Judah, who had gathered at Jerusalem because of Shishak, and said to them, 'Thus says the LORD: You abandoned me, so I have abandoned you to the hand of Shishak.' 6 Then the officers of Israel and the king humbled themselves and said, 'The LORD is in the right.' 7 When the LORD saw that they humbled themselves, the word of the LORD came to Shemaiah, saying: 'They have humbled themselves; I will not destroy them, but I will grant them some deliverance, and my wrath shall not be poured out on Jerusalem by the hand of Shishak. 8 Nevertheless they shall be his servants, so that they may know the difference between serving me and serving the kingdoms of other lands.'

9 So King Shishak of Egypt came up against Jerusalem; he took away the treasures of the house of the LORD and the treasures of the king's house; he took everything. He also took away the shields of gold that Solomon had made; 10 but King Rehoboam made in place of them shields of bronze, and committed them to the hands of the officers of the guard, who kept the door of the king's house. 11 Whenever the king went into the house of the LORD, the guard would come along bearing them, and would then bring them back to the guardroom. 12 Because he humbled himself the wrath of the LORD turned from him, so as not to destroy them completely; moreover, conditions were good in Judah.

DEATH OF REHOBOAM

13 So King Rehoboam established himself in Jerusalem and reigned. Rehoboam was forty-one years old when he began to reign; he reigned for seventeen years in Jerusalem, the city that the LORD had chosen out of all the tribes of Israel to put his name there. His mother's name was Naamah the Ammonite. 14 He did evil, for he did not set his heart to seek the LORD.

15 Now the acts of Rehoboam, from first to last, are they not written in the records of the prophet Shemaiah and of the seer Iddo, recorded by genealogy? There were continual wars between Rehoboam and Jeroboam. 16 Rehoboam slept with his ancestors and was buried in the city of David; and his son Abijah succeeded him.

ABIJAH REIGNS OVER JUDAH

13 In the eighteenth year of King Jeroboam, Abijah began to reign over Judah. 2 He reigned for three years in Jerusalem. His mother's name was Micaiah daughter of Uriel of Gibeah.

Now there was war between Abijah and Jeroboam. 3 Abijah engaged in battle, having an army of valiant warriors, four hundred thousand picked men; and Jeroboam drew up his line of battle against him with eight hundred thousand picked mighty warriors. 4 Then Abijah stood on the slope of Mount Zemaraim that is in the hill country of Ephraim, and said, 'Listen to me, Jeroboam and all Israel! 5 Do you not know that the LORD God of Israel gave the kingship over Israel for ever to David and his sons by a covenant of salt? 6 Yet Jeroboam son of Nebat, a servant of Solomon son of David, rose up and rebelled

[v] 12.3 Or *Nubians*; Heb *Cushites*

against his lord; 7and certain worthless
scoundrels gathered round him and defied Rehoboam son of Solomon, when
Rehoboam was young and irresolute
and could not withstand them.
8 'And now you think that you can
withstand the kingdom of the LORD in
the hand of the sons of David, because
you are a great multitude and have with
you the golden calves that Jeroboam
made as gods for you. 9Have you not
driven out the priests of the LORD, the
descendants of Aaron, and the Levites,
and made priests for yourselves like the
peoples of other lands? Whoever comes
to be consecrated with a young bull or
seven rams becomes a priest of what are
no gods. 10But as for us, the LORD is our
God, and we have not abandoned him. We
have priests ministering to the LORD who
are descendants of Aaron, and Levites for
their service. 11They offer to the LORD every morning and every evening burnt-
offerings and fragrant incense, set out the
rows of bread on the table of pure gold,
and care for the golden lampstand so that
its lamps may burn every evening; for we
keep the charge of the LORD our God, but
you have abandoned him. 12See, God is
with us at our head, and his priests have
their battle trumpets to sound the call to
battle against you. O Israelites, do not
fight against the LORD, the God of your
ancestors; for you cannot succeed.'
13 Jeroboam had sent an ambush
around to come on them from behind;
thus his troops[w] were in front of Judah, and the ambush was behind them.
14When Judah turned, the battle was in
front of them and behind them. They
cried out to the LORD, and the priests
blew the trumpets. 15Then the people
of Judah raised the battle shout. And
when the people of Judah shouted, God
defeated Jeroboam and all Israel before
Abijah and Judah. 16The Israelites fled
before Judah, and God gave them into
their hands. 17Abijah and his army defeated them with great slaughter; five
hundred thousand picked men of Israel fell slain. 18Thus the Israelites were
subdued at that time, and the people
of Judah prevailed, because they relied
on the LORD, the God of their ancestors. 19Abijah pursued Jeroboam, and
took cities from him: Bethel with its villages and Jeshanah with its villages and
Ephron[x] with its villages. 20Jeroboam
did not recover his power in the days
of Abijah; the LORD struck him down,
and he died. 21But Abijah grew strong.
He took fourteen wives, and became
the father of twenty-two sons and sixteen daughters. 22The rest of the acts of
Abijah, his behaviour and his deeds, are
written in the story of the prophet Iddo.

ASA REIGNS

14 [y] So Abijah slept with his ancestors, and they buried him in the
city of David. His son Asa succeeded
him. In his days the land had rest for
ten years. 2[z]Asa did what was good and
right in the sight of the LORD his God.
3He took away the foreign altars and
the high places, broke down the pillars,
hewed down the sacred poles,[a] 4and
commanded Judah to seek the LORD,
the God of their ancestors, and to keep
the law and the commandment. 5He
also removed from all the cities of Judah the high places and the incense altars. And the kingdom had rest under
him. 6He built fortified cities in Judah
while the land had rest. He had no war
in those years, for the LORD gave him
peace. 7He said to Judah, 'Let us build
these cities, and surround them with
walls and towers, gates and bars; the
land is still ours because we have sought
the LORD our God; we have sought him,
and he has given us peace on every side.'
So they built and prospered. 8Asa had
an army of three hundred thousand
from Judah, armed with large shields
and spears, and two hundred and eighty
thousand troops from Benjamin who
carried shields and drew bows; all these
were mighty warriors.

ETHIOPIAN INVASION REPULSED

9 Zerah the Ethiopian[b] came out
against them with an army of a million
men and three hundred chariots, and
came as far as Mareshah. 10Asa went
out to meet him, and they drew up their
lines of battle in the valley of Zephathah
at Mareshah. 11Asa cried to the LORD his
God, 'O LORD, there is no difference for
you between helping the mighty and
the weak. Help us, O LORD our God,
for we rely on you, and in your name
we have come against this multitude.
O LORD, you are our God; let no mortal
prevail against you.' 12So the LORD defeated the Ethiopians[c] before Asa and
before Judah, and the Ethiopians[d] fled.

[w] 13.13 Heb *they* [x] 13.19 Another reading is *Ephrain* [y] 14.1 Ch 13.23 in Heb [z] 14.2 Ch 14.1 in Heb [a] 14.3 Heb *Asherim* [b] 14.9 Or *Nubian*; Heb *Cushite* [c] 14.12 Or *Nubians*; Heb *Cushites* [d] 14.12 Or *Nubians*; Heb *Cushites*

13 Asa and the army with him pursued them as far as Gerar, and the Ethiopians[e] fell until no one remained alive; for they were broken before the LORD and his army. The people of Judah[f] carried away a great quantity of booty. 14 They defeated all the cities around Gerar, for the fear of the LORD was on them. They plundered all the cities; for there was much plunder in them. 15 They also attacked the tents of those who had livestock,[g] and carried away sheep and goats in abundance, and camels. Then they returned to Jerusalem.

15 The spirit of God came upon Azariah son of Oded. 2 He went out to meet Asa and said to him, 'Hear me, Asa, and all Judah and Benjamin: The LORD is with you, while you are with him. If you seek him, he will be found by you, but if you abandon him, he will abandon you. 3 For a long time Israel was without the true God, and without a teaching priest, and without law; 4 but when in their distress they turned to the LORD, the God of Israel, and sought him, he was found by them. 5 In those times it was not safe for anyone to go or come, for great disturbances afflicted all the inhabitants of the lands. 6 They were broken in pieces, nation against nation and city against city, for God troubled them with every sort of distress. 7 But you, take courage! Do not let your hands be weak, for your work shall be rewarded.'

8 When Asa heard these words, the prophecy of Azariah son of Oded,[h] he took courage, and put away the abominable idols from all the land of Judah and Benjamin and from the towns that he had taken in the hill country of Ephraim. He repaired the altar of the LORD that was in front of the vestibule of the house of the LORD.[i] 9 He gathered all Judah and Benjamin, and those from Ephraim, Manasseh, and Simeon who were residing as aliens with them, for great numbers had deserted to him from Israel when they saw that the LORD his God was with him. 10 They were gathered at Jerusalem in the third month of the fifteenth year of the reign of Asa. 11 They sacrificed to the LORD on that day, from the booty that they had brought, seven hundred oxen and seven thousand sheep. 12 They entered into a covenant to seek the LORD, the God of their ancestors, with all their heart and with all their soul. 13 Whoever would not seek the LORD, the God of Israel, should be put to death, whether young or old, man or woman. 14 They took an oath to the LORD with a loud voice, and with shouting, and with trumpets, and with horns. 15 All Judah rejoiced over the oath; for they had sworn with all their heart, and had sought him with their whole desire, and he was found by them, and the LORD gave them rest all around.

16 King Asa even removed his mother Maacah from being queen mother because she had made an abominable image for Asherah. Asa cut down her image, crushed it, and burned it at the Wadi Kidron. 17 But the high places were not taken out of Israel. Nevertheless, the heart of Asa was true all his days. 18 He brought into the house of God the votive gifts of his father and his own votive gifts—silver, gold, and utensils. 19 And there was no more war until the thirty-fifth year of the reign of Asa.

ALLIANCE WITH ARAM CONDEMNED

16 In the thirty-sixth year of the reign of Asa, King Baasha of Israel went up against Judah, and built Ramah, to prevent anyone from going out or coming into the territory of[j] King Asa of Judah. 2 Then Asa took silver and gold from the treasures of the house of the LORD and the king's house, and sent them to King Ben-hadad of Aram, who resided in Damascus, saying, 3 'Let there be an alliance between me and you, like that between my father and your father; I am sending to you silver and gold; go, break your alliance with King Baasha of Israel, so that he may withdraw from me.' 4 Ben-hadad listened to King Asa, and sent the commanders of his armies against the cities of Israel. They conquered Ijon, Dan, Abel-maim, and all the store-cities of Naphtali. 5 When Baasha heard of it, he stopped building Ramah, and let his work cease. 6 Then King Asa brought all Judah, and they carried away the stones of Ramah and its timber, with which Baasha had been building, and with them he built up Geba and Mizpah.

7 At that time the seer Hanani came to King Asa of Judah, and said to him, 'Because you relied on the king of Aram, and did not rely on the LORD your God,

[e] 14.13 Or *Nubians*; Heb *Cushites* [f] 14.13 Heb *They* [g] 14.15 Meaning of Heb uncertain [h] 15.8 Compare Syr Vg: Heb *the prophecy, the prophet Obed* [i] 15.8 Heb *the vestibule of the* LORD [j] 16.1 Heb lacks *the territory of*

the army of the king of Aram has escaped you. [8]Were not the Ethiopians[k] and the Libyans a huge army with exceedingly many chariots and cavalry? Yet because you relied on the LORD, he gave them into your hand. [9]For the eyes of the LORD range throughout the entire earth, to strengthen those whose heart is true to him. You have done foolishly in this; for from now on you will have wars.' [10]Then Asa was angry with the seer, and put him in the stocks, in prison, for he was in a rage with him because of this. And Asa inflicted cruelties on some of the people at the same time.

ASA'S DISEASE AND DEATH

11 The acts of Asa, from first to last, are written in the Book of the Kings of Judah and Israel. [12]In the thirty-ninth year of his reign Asa was diseased in his feet, and his disease became severe; yet even in his disease he did not seek the LORD, but sought help from physicians. [13]Then Asa slept with his ancestors, dying in the forty-first year of his reign. [14]They buried him in the tomb that he had hewn out for himself in the city of David. They laid him on a bier that had been filled with various kinds of spices prepared by the perfumer's art; and they made a very great fire in his honour.

JEHOSHAPHAT'S REIGN

17 His son Jehoshaphat succeeded him, and strengthened himself against Israel. [2]He placed forces in all the fortified cities of Judah, and set garrisons in the land of Judah, and in the cities of Ephraim that his father Asa had taken. [3]The LORD was with Jehoshaphat, because he walked in the earlier ways of his father;[l] he did not seek the Baals, [4]but sought the God of his father and walked in his commandments, and not according to the ways of Israel. [5]Therefore the LORD established the kingdom in his hand. All Judah brought tribute to Jehoshaphat, and he had great riches and honour. [6]His heart was courageous in the ways of the LORD; and furthermore he removed the high places and the sacred poles[m] from Judah.

7 In the third year of his reign he sent his officials, Ben-hail, Obadiah, Zechariah, Nethanel, and Micaiah, to teach in the cities of Judah. [8]With them were the Levites, Shemaiah, Nethaniah, Zebadiah, Asahel, Shemiramoth, Jehonathan, Adonijah, Tobijah, and Tobadonijah; and with these Levites, the priests Elishama and Jehoram. [9]They taught in Judah, having the book of the law of the LORD with them; they went around through all the cities of Judah and taught among the people.

10 The fear of the LORD fell on all the kingdoms of the lands around Judah, and they did not make war against Jehoshaphat. [11]Some of the Philistines brought Jehoshaphat presents, and silver for tribute; and the Arabs also brought him seven thousand seven hundred rams and seven thousand seven hundred male goats. [12]Jehoshaphat grew steadily greater. He built fortresses and storage cities in Judah. [13]He carried out great works in the cities of Judah. He had soldiers, mighty warriors, in Jerusalem. [14]This was the muster of them by ancestral houses: Of Judah, the commanders of the thousands: Adnah the commander, with three hundred thousand mighty warriors, [15]and next to him Jehohanan the commander, with two hundred and eighty thousand, [16]and next to him Amasiah son of Zichri, a volunteer for the service of the LORD, with two hundred thousand mighty warriors. [17]Of Benjamin: Eliada, a mighty warrior, with two hundred thousand armed with bow and shield, [18]and next to him Jehozabad with one hundred and eighty thousand armed for war. [19]These were in the service of the king, besides those whom the king had placed in the fortified cities throughout all Judah.

MICAIAH PREDICTS FAILURE

18 Now Jehoshaphat had great riches and honour; and he made a marriage alliance with Ahab. [2]After some years he went down to Ahab in Samaria. Ahab slaughtered an abundance of sheep and oxen for him and for the people who were with him, and induced him to go up against Ramoth-gilead. [3]King Ahab of Israel said to King Jehoshaphat of Judah, 'Will you go with me to Ramoth-gilead?' He answered him, 'I am with you, my people are your people. We will be with you in the war.'

4 But Jehoshaphat also said to the king of Israel, 'Inquire first for the word of the LORD.' [5]Then the king of Israel gathered the prophets together, four hundred of them, and said to them, 'Shall we go to battle against Ramoth-gilead,

[k] 16.8 Or *Nubians*; Heb *Cushites* [l] 17.3 Another reading is *his father David* [m] 17.6 Heb *Asherim*

or shall I refrain?' They said, 'Go up; for God will give it into the hand of the king.' 6But Jehoshaphat said, 'Is there no other prophet of the LORD here of whom we may inquire?' 7The king of Israel said to Jehoshaphat, 'There is still one other by whom we may inquire of the LORD, Micaiah son of Imlah; but I hate him, for he never prophesies anything favourable about me, but only disaster.' Jehoshaphat said, 'Let the king not say such a thing.' 8Then the king of Israel summoned an officer and said, 'Bring quickly Micaiah son of Imlah.' 9Now the king of Israel and King Jehoshaphat of Judah were sitting on their thrones, arrayed in their robes; and they were sitting at the threshing-floor at the entrance of the gate of Samaria; and all the prophets were prophesying before them. 10Zedekiah son of Chenaanah made for himself horns of iron, and he said, 'Thus says the LORD: With these you shall gore the Arameans until they are destroyed.' 11All the prophets were prophesying the same and saying, 'Go up to Ramoth-gilead and triumph; the LORD will give it into the hand of the king.'

12 The messenger who had gone to summon Micaiah said to him, 'Look, the words of the prophets with one accord are favourable to the king; let your word be like the word of one of them, and speak favourably.' 13But Micaiah said, 'As the LORD lives, whatever my God says, that I will speak.'

14 When he had come to the king, the king said to him, 'Micaiah, shall we go to Ramoth-gilead to battle, or shall I refrain?' He answered, 'Go up and triumph; they will be given into your hand.' 15But the king said to him, 'How many times must I make you swear to tell me nothing but the truth in the name of the LORD?' 16Then Micaiah[n] said, 'I saw all Israel scattered on the mountains, like sheep without a shepherd; and the LORD said, "These have no master; let each one go home in peace."' 17The king of Israel said to Jehoshaphat, 'Did I not tell you that he would not prophesy anything favourable about me, but only disaster?'

18 Then Micaiah[o] said, 'Therefore hear the word of the LORD: I saw the LORD sitting on his throne, with all the host of heaven standing to the right and to the left of him. 19And the LORD said, "Who will entice King Ahab of Israel, so that he may go up and fall at Ramoth-gilead?" Then one said one thing, and another said another, 20until a spirit came forward and stood before the LORD, saying, "I will entice him." The LORD asked him, "How?" 21He replied, "I will go out and be a lying spirit in the mouth of all his prophets." Then the LORD[p] said, "You are to entice him, and you shall succeed; go out and do it." 22So you see, the LORD has put a lying spirit in the mouth of these your prophets; the LORD has decreed disaster for you.'

23 Then Zedekiah son of Chenaanah came up to Micaiah, slapped him on the cheek, and said, 'Which way did the spirit of the LORD pass from me to speak to you?' 24Micaiah replied, 'You will find out on that day when you go in to hide in an inner chamber.' 25The king of Israel then ordered, 'Take Micaiah, and return him to Amon the governor of the city and to Joash the king's son; 26and say, "Thus says the king: Put this fellow in prison, and feed him on reduced rations of bread and water until I return in peace."' 27Micaiah said, 'If you return in peace, the LORD has not spoken by me.' And he said, 'Hear, you peoples, all of you!'

DEFEAT AND DEATH OF AHAB

28 So the king of Israel and King Jehoshaphat of Judah went up to Ramoth-gilead. 29The king of Israel said to Jehoshaphat, 'I will disguise myself and go into battle, but you wear your robes.' So the king of Israel disguised himself, and they went into battle. 30Now the king of Aram had commanded the captains of his chariots, 'Fight with no one small or great, but only with the king of Israel.' 31When the captains of the chariots saw Jehoshaphat, they said, 'It is the king of Israel.' So they turned to fight against him; and Jehoshaphat cried out, and the LORD helped him. God drew them away from him, 32for when the captains of the chariots saw that it was not the king of Israel, they turned back from pursuing him. 33But a certain man drew his bow and unknowingly struck the king of Israel between the scale armour and the breastplate; so he said to the driver of his chariot, 'Turn around, and carry me out of the battle, for I am wounded.' 34The battle grew hot that day, and the king of Israel propped himself up in his chariot facing the Arameans until evening; then at sunset he died.

[n] 18.16 Heb *he* [o] 18.18 Heb *he*
[p] 18.21 Heb *he*

19 King Jehoshaphat of Judah returned in safety to his house in Jerusalem. 2Jehu son of Hanani the seer went out to meet him and said to King Jehoshaphat, 'Should you help the wicked and love those who hate the LORD? Because of this, wrath has gone out against you from the LORD. 3Nevertheless, some good is found in you, for you destroyed the sacred poles[q] out of the land, and have set your heart to seek God.'

THE REFORMS OF JEHOSHAPHAT

4 Jehoshaphat resided at Jerusalem; then he went out again among the people, from Beer-sheba to the hill country of Ephraim, and brought them back to the LORD, the God of their ancestors. 5He appointed judges in the land in all the fortified cities of Judah, city by city, 6and said to the judges, 'Consider what you are doing, for you judge not on behalf of human beings but on the LORD's behalf; he is with you in giving judgement. 7Now, let the fear of the LORD be upon you; take care what you do, for there is no perversion of justice with the LORD our God, or partiality, or taking of bribes.'

8 Moreover, in Jerusalem Jehoshaphat appointed certain Levites and priests and heads of families of Israel, to give judgement for the LORD and to decide disputed cases. They had their seat at Jerusalem. 9He charged them: 'This is how you shall act: in the fear of the LORD, in faithfulness, and with your whole heart; 10whenever a case comes to you from your kindred who live in their cities, concerning bloodshed, law or commandment, statutes or ordinances, then you shall instruct them, so that they may not incur guilt before the LORD and wrath may not come on you and your kindred. Do so, and you will not incur guilt. 11See, Amariah the chief priest is over you in all matters of the LORD; and Zebadiah son of Ishmael, the governor of the house of Judah, in all the king's matters; and the Levites will serve you as officers. Deal courageously, and may the LORD be with the good!'

INVASION FROM THE EAST

20 After this the Moabites and Ammonites, and with them some of the Meunites,[r] came against Jehoshaphat for battle. 2Messengers[s] came and told Jehoshaphat, 'A great multitude is coming against you from Edom,[t] from beyond the sea; already they are at Hazazon-tamar' (that is, En-gedi). 3Jehoshaphat was afraid; he set himself to seek the LORD, and proclaimed a fast throughout all Judah. 4Judah assembled to seek help from the LORD; from all the towns of Judah they came to seek the LORD.

JEHOSHAPHAT'S PRAYER AND VICTORY

5 Jehoshaphat stood in the assembly of Judah and Jerusalem, in the house of the LORD, before the new court, 6and said, 'O LORD, God of our ancestors, are you not God in heaven? Do you not rule over all the kingdoms of the nations? In your hand are power and might, so that no one is able to withstand you. 7Did you not, O our God, drive out the inhabitants of this land before your people Israel, and give it for ever to the descendants of your friend Abraham? 8They have lived in it, and in it have built you a sanctuary for your name, saying, 9"If disaster comes upon us, the sword, judgement,[u] or pestilence, or famine, we will stand before this house, and before you, for your name is in this house, and cry to you in our distress, and you will hear and save." 10See now, the people of Ammon, Moab, and Mount Seir, whom you would not let Israel invade when they came from the land of Egypt, and whom they avoided and did not destroy— 11they reward us by coming to drive us out of your possession that you have given us to inherit. 12O our God, will you not execute judgement upon them? For we are powerless against this great multitude that is coming against us. We do not know what to do, but our eyes are on you.'

13 Meanwhile all Judah stood before the LORD, with their little ones, their wives, and their children. 14Then the spirit of the LORD came upon Jahaziel son of Zechariah, son of Benaiah, son of Jeiel, son of Mattaniah, a Levite of the sons of Asaph, in the middle of the assembly. 15He said, 'Listen, all Judah and inhabitants of Jerusalem, and King Jehoshaphat: Thus says the LORD to you: "Do not fear or be dismayed at this great multitude; for the battle is not yours but God's. 16Tomorrow go down against them; they will come up by the ascent of Ziz; you will find them at the end of

q 19.3 Heb *Asheroth* r 20.1 Compare 26.7: Heb *Ammonites* s 20.2 Heb *They* t 20.2 One Ms: MT *Aram* u 20.9 Or *the sword of judgement*

the valley, before the wilderness of Je-
ruel. [17]This battle is not for you to fight;
take your position, stand still, and see
the victory of the LORD on your behalf,
O Judah and Jerusalem." Do not fear or
be dismayed; tomorrow go out against
them, and the LORD will be with you.'

18 Then Jehoshaphat bowed down
with his face to the ground, and all Judah and the inhabitants of Jerusalem
fell down before the LORD, worshipping
the LORD. [19]And the Levites, of the Kohathites and the Korahites, stood up to
praise the LORD, the God of Israel, with
a very loud voice.

20 They rose early in the morning
and went out into the wilderness of Tekoa; and as they went out, Jehoshaphat
stood and said, 'Listen to me, O Judah
and inhabitants of Jerusalem! Believe in
the LORD your God and you will be established; believe his prophets.' [21]When
he had taken counsel with the people,
he appointed those who were to sing to
the LORD and praise him in holy splendour, as they went before the army, saying,

'Give thanks to the LORD,
for his steadfast love
endures for ever.'

[22]As they began to sing and praise, the
LORD set an ambush against the Ammonites, Moab, and Mount Seir, who
had come against Judah, so that they
were routed. [23]For the Ammonites
and Moab attacked the inhabitants of
Mount Seir, destroying them utterly;
and when they had made an end of the
inhabitants of Seir, they all helped to destroy one another.

24 When Judah came to the watch-
tower of the wilderness, they looked towards the multitude; they were corpses
lying on the ground; no one had escaped. [25]When Jehoshaphat and his people came to take the booty from them,
they found livestock[v] in great numbers,
goods, clothing, and precious things,
which they took for themselves until
they could carry no more. They spent
three days taking the booty, because of
its abundance. [26]On the fourth day they
assembled in the Valley of Beracah, for
there they blessed the LORD; therefore
that place has been called the Valley
of Beracah[w] to this day. [27]Then all the
people of Judah and Jerusalem, with Jehoshaphat at their head, returned to Jerusalem with joy, for the LORD had enabled them to rejoice over their enemies.
[28]They came to Jerusalem, with harps
and lyres and trumpets, to the house
of the LORD. [29]The fear of God came on
all the kingdoms of the countries when
they heard that the LORD had fought
against the enemies of Israel. [30]And the
realm of Jehoshaphat was quiet, for his
God gave him rest all around.

THE END OF JEHOSHAPHAT'S REIGN

31 So Jehoshaphat reigned over
Judah. He was thirty-five years old
when he began to reign; he reigned
for twenty-five years in Jerusalem. His
mother's name was Azubah daughter of
Shilhi. [32]He walked in the way of his father Asa and did not turn aside from it,
doing what was right in the sight of the
LORD. [33]Yet the high places were not removed; the people had not yet set their
hearts upon the God of their ancestors.

34 Now the rest of the acts of Jehoshaphat, from first to last, are written
in the Annals of Jehu son of Hanani,
which are recorded in the Book of the
Kings of Israel.

35 After this King Jehoshaphat of
Judah joined with King Ahaziah of Israel, who did wickedly. [36]He joined him
in building ships to go to Tarshish; they
built the ships in Ezion-geber. [37]Then
Eliezer son of Dodavahu of Mareshah
prophesied against Jehoshaphat, saying, 'Because you have joined with Ahaziah, the LORD will destroy what you
have made.' And the ships were wrecked
and were not able to go to Tarshish.

JEHORAM'S REIGN

21 Jehoshaphat slept with his ancestors and was buried with his
ancestors in the city of David; his son Jehoram succeeded him. [2]He had brothers,
the sons of Jehoshaphat: Azariah, Jehiel, Zechariah, Azariah, Michael, and
Shephatiah; all these were the sons of
King Jehoshaphat of Judah.[x] [3]Their father gave them many gifts, of silver,
gold, and valuable possessions, together
with fortified cities in Judah; but he gave
the kingdom to Jehoram, because he
was the firstborn. [4]When Jehoram had
ascended the throne of his father and
was established, he put all his brothers
to the sword, and also some of the officials of Israel. [5]Jehoram was thirty-two
years old when he began to reign; he
reigned for eight years in Jerusalem. [6]He
walked in the way of the kings of Israel,

[v] 20.25 Gk: Heb *among them* [w] 20.26 That is *Blessing* [x] 21.2 Gk Syr: Heb *Israel*

as the house of Ahab had done; for the
daughter of Ahab was his wife. He did
what was evil in the sight of the LORD.
7Yet the LORD would not destroy the
house of David because of the covenant
that he had made with David, and since
he had promised to give a lamp to him
and to his descendants for ever.

REVOLT OF EDOM

8 In his days Edom revolted against
the rule of Judah and set up a king of
their own. 9Then Jehoram crossed over
with his commanders and all his chariots. He set out by night and attacked
the Edomites, who had surrounded
him and his chariot commanders. 10So
Edom has been in revolt against the rule
of Judah to this day. At that time Libnah
also revolted against his rule, because he
had forsaken the LORD, the God of his
ancestors.

ELIJAH'S LETTER

11 Moreover, he made high places in
the hill country of Judah, and led the
inhabitants of Jerusalem into unfaithfulness, and made Judah go astray. 12A
letter came to him from the prophet
Elijah, saying: 'Thus says the LORD, the
God of your father David: Because you
have not walked in the ways of your father Jehoshaphat or in the ways of King
Asa of Judah, 13but have walked in the
way of the kings of Israel, and have led
Judah and the inhabitants of Jerusalem into unfaithfulness, as the house
of Ahab led Israel into unfaithfulness,
and because you also have killed your
brothers, members of your father's
house, who were better than yourself,
14see, the LORD will bring a great plague
on your people, your children, your
wives, and all your possessions, 15and
you yourself will have a severe sickness
with a disease of your bowels, until your
bowels come out, day after day, because
of the disease.'

16 The LORD aroused against Jehoram the anger of the Philistines and of
the Arabs who are near the Ethiopians.[y]
17They came up against Judah, invaded
it, and carried away all the possessions
they found that belonged to the king's
house, along with his sons and his
wives, so that no son was left to him except Jehoahaz, his youngest son.

DISEASE AND DEATH OF JEHORAM

18 After all this the LORD struck him
in his bowels with an incurable disease.
19In course of time, at the end of two
years, his bowels came out because of
the disease, and he died in great agony.
His people made no fire in his honour,
like the fires made for his ancestors.
20He was thirty-two years old when
he began to reign; he reigned for eight
years in Jerusalem. He departed with
no one's regret. They buried him in the
city of David, but not in the tombs of
the kings.

AHAZIAH'S REIGN

22 The inhabitants of Jerusalem
made his youngest son Aha-
ziah king as his successor; for the troops
who came with the Arabs to the camp
had killed all the older sons. So Ahaziah son of Jehoram reigned as king of
Judah. 2Ahaziah was forty-two years
old when he began to reign; he reigned
for one year in Jerusalem. His mother's
name was Athaliah, a granddaughter
of Omri. 3He also walked in the ways of
the house of Ahab, for his mother was
his counsellor in doing wickedly. 4He
did what was evil in the sight of the
LORD, as the house of Ahab had done;
for after the death of his father they
were his counsellors, to his ruin. 5He
even followed their advice, and went
with Jehoram son of King Ahab of Israel to make war against King Hazael of
Aram at Ramoth-gilead. The Arameans
wounded Joram, 6and he returned to be
healed in Jezreel of the wounds that he
had received at Ramah, when he fought
King Hazael of Aram. And Ahaziah son
of King Jehoram of Judah went down
to see Joram son of Ahab in Jezreel, because he was sick.

7 But it was ordained by God that the
downfall of Ahaziah should come about
through his going to visit Joram. For
when he came there he went out with
Jehoram to meet Jehu son of Nimshi,
whom the LORD had anointed to destroy
the house of Ahab. 8When Jehu was executing judgement on the house of Ahab,
he met the officials of Judah and the sons
of Ahaziah's brothers, who attended Ahaziah, and he killed them. 9He searched for
Ahaziah, who was captured while hiding
in Samaria and was brought to Jehu, and
put to death. They buried him, for they
said, 'He is the grandson of Jehoshaphat,
who sought the LORD with all his heart.'
And the house of Ahaziah had no one
able to rule the kingdom.

[y] **21.16** Or *Nubians*; Heb *Cushites*

ATHALIAH SEIZES THE THRONE

10 Now when Athaliah, Ahaziah's
mother, saw that her son was dead,
she set about to destroy all the royal
family of the house of Judah. 11But Jehoshabeath, the king's daughter, took
Joash son of Ahaziah, and stole him
away from among the king's children
who were about to be killed; she put
him and his nurse in a bedroom. Thus
Jehoshabeath, daughter of King Jehoram and wife of the priest Jehoiada—
because she was a sister of Ahaziah—
hid him from Athaliah, so that she did
not kill him; 12he remained with them
for six years, hidden in the house of God,
while Athaliah reigned over the land.

23 But in the seventh year Jehoiada took courage, and entered
into a compact with the commanders of
the hundreds, Azariah son of Jeroham,
Ishmael son of Jehohanan, Azariah son
of Obed, Maaseiah son of Adaiah, and
Elishaphat son of Zichri. 2They went
about through Judah and gathered the
Levites from all the towns of Judah, and
the heads of families of Israel, and they
came to Jerusalem. 3Then the whole assembly made a covenant with the king
in the house of God. Jehoiada[z] said to
them, 'Here is the king's son! Let him
reign, as the LORD promised concerning
the sons of David. 4This is what you are
to do: one-third of you, priests and Levites, who come on duty on the sabbath,
shall be gatekeepers, 5one-third shall be
at the king's house, and one-third at the
Gate of the Foundation; and all the people shall be in the courts of the house
of the LORD. 6Do not let anyone enter
the house of the LORD except the priests
and ministering Levites; they may enter, for they are holy, but all the other[a]
people shall observe the instructions of
the LORD. 7The Levites shall surround
the king, each with his weapons in his
hand; and whoever enters the house
shall be killed. Stay with the king in his
comings and goings.'

JOASH CROWNED KING

8 The Levites and all Judah did according to all that the priest Jehoiada
commanded; each brought his men,
who were to come on duty on the sabbath, with those who were to go off
duty on the sabbath; for the priest Jehoiada did not dismiss the divisions. 9The
priest Jehoiada delivered to the captains the spears and the large and small
shields that had been King David's,
which were in the house of God; 10and
he set all the people as a guard for the
king, everyone with weapon in hand,
from the south side of the house to the
north side of the house, around the altar and the house. 11Then he brought out
the king's son, put the crown on him,
and gave him the covenant;[b] they proclaimed him king, and Jehoiada and his
sons anointed him; and they shouted,
'Long live the king!'

ATHALIAH DEPOSED

12 When Athaliah heard the noise
of the people running and praising the
king, she went into the house of the
LORD to the people; 13and when she
looked, there was the king standing by
his pillar at the entrance, and the captains and the trumpeters beside the
king, and all the people of the land rejoicing and blowing trumpets, and the
singers with their musical instruments
leading in the celebration. Athaliah tore
her clothes, and cried, 'Treason! Treason!' 14Then the priest Jehoiada brought
out the captains who were set over the
army, saying to them, 'Bring her out between the ranks; anyone who follows
her is to be put to the sword.' For the
priest said, 'Do not put her to death in
the house of the LORD.' 15So they laid
hands on her; she went into the entrance of the Horse Gate of the king's
house, and there they put her to death.

16 Jehoiada made a covenant between himself and all the people and
the king that they should be the LORD's
people. 17Then all the people went to the
house of Baal, and tore it down; his altars and his images they broke in pieces,
and they killed Mattan, the priest of
Baal, in front of the altars. 18Jehoiada assigned the care of the house of the LORD
to the levitical priests whom David had
organized to be in charge of the house
of the LORD, to offer burnt-offerings to
the LORD, as it is written in the law of
Moses, with rejoicing and with singing,
according to the order of David. 19He
stationed the gatekeepers at the gates
of the house of the LORD so that no one
should enter who was in any way unclean. 20And he took the captains, the
nobles, the governors of the people,
and all the people of the land, and they
brought the king down from the house
of the LORD, marching through the upper gate to the king's house. They set the

[z] 23.3 Heb *He* [a] 23.6 Heb lacks *other*
[b] 23.11 Or *treaty*, or *testimony*; Heb *eduth*

king on the royal throne. 21So all the
people of the land rejoiced, and the city
was quiet after Athaliah had been killed
with the sword.

JOASH REPAIRS THE TEMPLE

24 Joash was seven years old when
he began to reign; he reigned for
forty years in Jerusalem; his mother's
name was Zibiah of Beer-sheba. 2Joash
did what was right in the sight of the
LORD all the days of the priest Jehoiada.
3Jehoiada got two wives for him, and he
became the father of sons and daughters.

4 Some time afterwards Joash decided to restore the house of the LORD.
5He assembled the priests and the Levites and said to them, 'Go out to the
cities of Judah and gather money from
all Israel to repair the house of your
God, year by year; and see that you act
quickly.' But the Levites did not act
quickly. 6So the king summoned Jehoiada the chief, and said to him, 'Why
have you not required the Levites to
bring in from Judah and Jerusalem the
tax levied by Moses, the servant of the
LORD, on[c] the congregation of Israel for
the tent of the covenant?'[d] 7For the children of Athaliah, that wicked woman,
had broken into the house of God, and
had even used all the dedicated things
of the house of the LORD for the Baals.

8 So the king gave command, and
they made a chest, and set it outside the
gate of the house of the LORD. 9A proclamation was made throughout Judah
and Jerusalem to bring in for the LORD
the tax that Moses the servant of God
laid on Israel in the wilderness. 10All
the leaders and all the people rejoiced,
and brought their tax and dropped it
into the chest until it was full. 11When-
ever the chest was brought to the king's
officers by the Levites, when they saw
that there was a large amount of money
in it, the king's secretary and the officer of the chief priest would come and
empty the chest and take it and return it to its place. So they did day after day, and collected money in abundance. 12The king and Jehoiada gave it
to those who had charge of the work of
the house of the LORD, and they hired
masons and carpenters to restore the
house of the LORD, and also workers in
iron and bronze to repair the house of
the LORD. 13So those who were engaged
in the work laboured, and the repairs
went forward at their hands, and they
restored the house of God to its proper
condition and strengthened it. 14When
they had finished, they brought the rest
of the money to the king and Jehoiada,
and with it were made utensils for the
house of the LORD, utensils for the service and for the burnt-offerings, and ladles, and vessels of gold and silver. They
offered burnt-offerings in the house of
the LORD regularly all the days of Jehoiada.

APOSTASY OF JOASH

15 But Jehoiada grew old and full of
days, and died; he was one hundred and
thirty years old at his death. 16And they
buried him in the city of David among
the kings, because he had done good in
Israel, and for God and his house.

17 Now after the death of Jehoiada
the officials of Judah came and did obeisance to the king; then the king listened
to them. 18They abandoned the house
of the LORD, the God of their ancestors,
and served the sacred poles[e] and the
idols. And wrath came upon Judah and
Jerusalem for this guilt of theirs. 19Yet
he sent prophets among them to bring
them back to the LORD; they testified
against them, but they would not listen.

20 Then the spirit of God took possession of[f] Zechariah son of the priest Jehoiada; he stood above the people and
said to them, 'Thus says God: Why do
you transgress the commandments of
the LORD, so that you cannot prosper?
Because you have forsaken the LORD, he
has also forsaken you.' 21But they conspired against him, and by command of
the king they stoned him to death in the
court of the house of the LORD. 22King
Joash did not remember the kindness
that Jehoiada, Zechariah's father, had
shown him, but killed his son. As he
was dying, he said, 'May the LORD see
and avenge!'

DEATH OF JOASH

23 At the end of the year the army
of Aram came up against Joash. They
came to Judah and Jerusalem, and destroyed all the officials of the people
from among them, and sent all the
booty they took to the king of Damascus. 24Although the army of Aram had
come with few men, the LORD delivered
into their hand a very great army, because they had abandoned the LORD,

[c] 24.6 Compare Vg: Heb *and* [d] 24.6 Or *treaty, or testimony*; Heb *eduth* [e] 24.18 Heb *Asherim* [f] 24.20 Heb *clothed itself with*

the God of their ancestors. Thus they executed judgement on Joash.
25 When they had withdrawn, leaving him severely wounded, his servants
conspired against him because of the
blood of the son[g] of the priest Jehoiada, and they killed him on his bed. So
he died; and they buried him in the city
of David, but they did not bury him in
the tombs of the kings. 26 Those who
conspired against him were Zabad son
of Shimeath the Ammonite, and Jehozabad son of Shimrith the Moabite. 27 Accounts of his sons, and of the many oracles against him, and of the rebuilding[h]
of the house of God are written in the
Commentary on the Book of the Kings.
And his son Amaziah succeeded him.

REIGN OF AMAZIAH

25 Amaziah was twenty-five years
old when he began to reign,
and he reigned for twenty-nine years
in Jerusalem. His mother's name was
Jehoaddan of Jerusalem. 2 He did what
was right in the sight of the LORD, yet
not with a true heart. 3 As soon as the
royal power was firmly in his hand he
killed his servants who had murdered
his father the king. 4 But he did not put
their children to death, according to
what is written in the law, in the book
of Moses, where the LORD commanded,
'The parents shall not be put to death
for the children, or the children be put
to death for the parents; but all shall be
put to death for their own sins.'

SLAUGHTER OF THE EDOMITES

5 Amaziah assembled the people of
Judah, and set them by ancestral houses
under commanders of the thousands
and of the hundreds for all Judah and
Benjamin. He mustered those twenty
years old and upwards, and found that
they were three hundred thousand
picked troops fit for war, able to handle spear and shield. 6 He also hired one
hundred thousand mighty warriors
from Israel for one hundred talents of
silver. 7 But a man of God came to him
and said, 'O king, do not let the army
of Israel go with you, for the LORD is
not with Israel—all these Ephraimites. 8 Rather, go by yourself and act; be
strong in battle, or God will fling you
down before the enemy; for God has
power to help or to overthrow.' 9 Amaziah said to the man of God, 'But what
shall we do about the hundred talents
that I have given to the army of Israel?'
The man of God answered, 'The LORD is
able to give you much more than this.'
10 Then Amaziah discharged the army
that had come to him from Ephraim,
letting them go home again. But they
became very angry with Judah, and returned home in fierce anger.
11 Amaziah took courage, and led out
his people; he went to the Valley of Salt,
and struck down ten thousand men of
Seir. 12 The people of Judah captured another ten thousand alive, took them to
the top of Sela, and threw them down
from the top of Sela, so that all of them
were dashed to pieces. 13 But the men of
the army whom Amaziah sent back, not
letting them go with him to battle, fell
on the cities of Judah from Samaria to
Beth-horon; they killed three thousand
people in them, and took much booty.
14 Now after Amaziah came from
the slaughter of the Edomites, he
brought the gods of the people of Seir,
set them up as his gods, and worshipped
them, making offerings to them. 15 The
LORD was angry with Amaziah and
sent to him a prophet, who said to him,
'Why have you resorted to a people's
gods who could not deliver their own
people from your hand?' 16 But as he was
speaking the king[i] said to him, 'Have
we made you a royal counsellor? Stop!
Why should you be put to death?' So the
prophet stopped, but said, 'I know that
God has determined to destroy you, because you have done this and have not
listened to my advice.'

ISRAEL DEFEATS JUDAH

17 Then King Amaziah of Judah took
counsel and sent to King Joash son of
Jehoahaz son of Jehu of Israel, saying,
'Come, let us look one another in the
face.' 18 King Joash of Israel sent word to
King Amaziah of Judah, 'A thornbush
on Lebanon sent to a cedar on Lebanon,
saying, "Give your daughter to my son
for a wife"; but a wild animal of Lebanon passed by and trampled down the
thornbush. 19 You say, "See, I have defeated Edom", and your heart has lifted
you up in boastfulness. Now stay at
home; why should you provoke trouble so that you fall, you and Judah with
you?'
20 But Amaziah would not listen—it
was God's doing, in order to hand them
over, because they had sought the gods

[g] 24.25 Gk Vg: Heb *sons* [h] 24.27 Heb *founding*
[i] 25.16 Heb *he*

of Edom. 21So King Joash of Israel went up; he and King Amaziah of Judah faced one another in battle at Beth-shemesh, which belongs to Judah. 22Judah was defeated by Israel; everyone fled home. 23King Joash of Israel captured King Amaziah of Judah, son of Joash, son of Ahaziah, at Beth-shemesh; he brought him to Jerusalem, and broke down the wall of Jerusalem from the Ephraim Gate to the Corner Gate, a distance of four hundred cubits. 24He seized all the gold and silver, and all the vessels that were found in the house of God, and Obed-edom with them; he seized also the treasuries of the king's house, also hostages; then he returned to Samaria.

DEATH OF AMAZIAH

25 King Amaziah son of Joash of Judah, lived fifteen years after the death of King Joash son of Jehoahaz of Israel. 26Now the rest of the deeds of Amaziah, from first to last, are they not written in the Book of the Kings of Judah and Israel? 27From the time that Amaziah turned away from the LORD they made a conspiracy against him in Jerusalem, and he fled to Lachish. But they sent after him to Lachish, and killed him there. 28They brought him back on horses; he was buried with his ancestors in the city of David.

REIGN OF UZZIAH

26 Then all the people of Judah took Uzziah, who was sixteen years old, and made him king to succeed his father Amaziah. 2He rebuilt Eloth and restored it to Judah, after the king slept with his ancestors. 3Uzziah was sixteen years old when he began to reign, and he reigned for fifty-two years in Jerusalem. His mother's name was Jecoliah of Jerusalem. 4He did what was right in the sight of the LORD, just as his father Amaziah had done. 5He set himself to seek God in the days of Zechariah, who instructed him in the fear of God; and as long as he sought the LORD, God made him prosper.

6 He went out and made war against the Philistines, and broke down the wall of Gath and the wall of Jabneh and the wall of Ashdod; he built cities in the territory of Ashdod and elsewhere among the Philistines. 7God helped him against the Philistines, against the Arabs who lived in Gur-baal, and against the Meunites. 8The Ammonites paid tribute to Uzziah, and his fame spread even to the border of Egypt, for he became very strong. 9Moreover, Uzziah built towers in Jerusalem at the Corner Gate, at the Valley Gate, and at the Angle, and fortified them. 10He built towers in the wilderness and hewed out many cisterns, for he had large herds, both in the Shephelah and in the plain, and he had farmers and vine-dressers in the hills and in the fertile lands, for he loved the soil. 11Moreover, Uzziah had an army of soldiers, fit for war, in divisions according to the numbers in the muster made by the secretary Jeiel and the officer Maaseiah, under the direction of Hananiah, one of the king's commanders. 12The whole number of the heads of ancestral houses of mighty warriors was two thousand six hundred. 13Under their command was an army of three hundred and seven thousand five hundred, who could make war with mighty power, to help the king against the enemy. 14Uzziah provided for all the army the shields, spears, helmets, coats of mail, bows, and stones for slinging. 15In Jerusalem he set up machines, invented by skilled workers, on the towers and the corners for shooting arrows and large stones. And his fame spread far, for he was marvellously helped until he became strong.

PRIDE AND APOSTASY

16 But when he had become strong he grew proud, to his destruction. For he was false to the LORD his God, and entered the temple of the LORD to make offering on the altar of incense. 17But the priest Azariah went in after him, with eighty priests of the LORD who were men of valour; 18they withstood King Uzziah, and said to him, 'It is not for you, Uzziah, to make offering to the LORD, but for the priests the descendants of Aaron, who are consecrated to make offering. Go out of the sanctuary; for you have done wrong, and it will bring you no honour from the LORD God.' 19Then Uzziah was angry. Now he had a censer in his hand to make offering, and when he became angry with the priests a leprous[j] disease broke out on his forehead, in the presence of the priests in the house of the LORD, by the altar of incense. 20When the chief priest Azariah, and all the priests, looked at him, he was leprous[k] in his forehead.

[j] **26.19** A term for several skin diseases; precise meaning uncertain [k] **26.20** A term for several skin diseases; precise meaning uncertain

They hurried him out, and he himself hurried to get out, because the LORD had struck him. 21King Uzziah was leprous[l] to the day of his death, and being leprous[m] lived in a separate house, for he was excluded from the house of the LORD. His son Jotham was in charge of the palace of the king, governing the people of the land.

22 Now the rest of the acts of Uzziah, from first to last, the prophet Isaiah son of Amoz wrote. 23Uzziah slept with his ancestors; they buried him near his ancestors in the burial field that belonged to the kings, for they said, 'He is leprous.'[n] His son Jotham succeeded him.

REIGN OF JOTHAM

27 Jotham was twenty-five years old when he began to reign; he reigned for sixteen years in Jerusalem. His mother's name was Jerushah daughter of Zadok. 2He did what was right in the sight of the LORD just as his father Uzziah had done—only he did not invade the temple of the LORD. But the people still followed corrupt practices. 3He built the upper gate of the house of the LORD, and did extensive building on the wall of Ophel. 4Moreover, he built cities in the hill country of Judah, and forts and towers on the wooded hills. 5He fought with the king of the Ammonites and prevailed against them. The Ammonites gave him that year one hundred talents of silver, ten thousand cors of wheat and ten thousand of barley. The Ammonites paid him the same amount in the second and the third years. 6So Jotham became strong because he ordered his ways before the LORD his God. 7Now the rest of the acts of Jotham, and all his wars and his ways, are written in the Book of the Kings of Israel and Judah. 8He was twenty-five years old when he began to reign; he reigned for sixteen years in Jerusalem. 9Jotham slept with his ancestors, and they buried him in the city of David; and his son Ahaz succeeded him.

REIGN OF AHAZ

28 Ahaz was twenty years old when he began to reign; he reigned for sixteen years in Jerusalem. He did not do what was right in the sight of the LORD, as his ancestor David had done, 2but he walked in the ways of the kings of Israel. He even made cast images for the Baals; 3and he made offerings in the valley of the son of Hinnom, and made his sons pass through fire, according to the abominable practices of the nations whom the LORD drove out before the people of Israel. 4He sacrificed and made offerings on the high places, on the hills, and under every green tree.

ARAM AND ISRAEL DEFEAT JUDAH

5 Therefore the LORD his God gave him into the hand of the king of Aram, who defeated him and took captive a great number of his people and brought them to Damascus. He was also given into the hand of the king of Israel, who defeated him with great slaughter. 6Pekah son of Remaliah killed one hundred and twenty thousand in Judah in one day, all of them valiant warriors, because they had abandoned the LORD, the God of their ancestors. 7And Zichri, a mighty warrior of Ephraim, killed the king's son Maaseiah, Azrikam the commander of the palace, and Elkanah the next in authority to the king.

INTERVENTION OF ODED

8 The people of Israel took captive two hundred thousand of their kin, women, sons, and daughters; they also took much booty from them and brought the booty to Samaria. 9But a prophet of the LORD was there, whose name was Oded; he went out to meet the army that came to Samaria, and said to them, 'Because the LORD, the God of your ancestors, was angry with Judah, he gave them into your hand, but you have killed them in a rage that has reached up to heaven. 10Now you intend to subjugate the people of Judah and Jerusalem, male and female, as your slaves. But what have you except sins against the LORD your God? 11Now hear me, and send back the captives whom you have taken from your kindred, for the fierce wrath of the LORD is upon you.' 12Moreover, certain chiefs of the Ephraimites, Azariah son of Johanan, Berechiah son of Meshillemoth, Jehizkiah son of Shallum, and Amasa son of Hadlai, stood up against those who were coming from the war, 13and said to them, 'You shall not bring the captives in here, for you propose to bring on us guilt against the LORD in addition to our present sins and guilt. For our guilt is already great,

[l] **26.21** A term for several skin diseases; precise meaning uncertain [m] **26.21** A term for several skin diseases; precise meaning uncertain
[n] **26.23** A term for several skin diseases; precise meaning uncertain

and there is fierce wrath against Israel.'
14 So the warriors left the captives and
the booty before the officials and all the
assembly. 15 Then those who were mentioned by name got up and took the captives, and with the booty they clothed
all that were naked among them; they
clothed them, gave them sandals, provided them with food and drink, and
anointed them; and carrying all the
feeble among them on donkeys, they
brought them to their kindred at Jericho, the city of palm trees. Then they
returned to Samaria.

ASSYRIA REFUSES TO HELP JUDAH

16 At that time King Ahaz sent to
the king[o] of Assyria for help. 17 For the
Edomites had again invaded and defeated Judah, and carried away captives.
18 And the Philistines had made raids
on the cities in the Shephelah and the
Negeb of Judah, and had taken Beth-
shemesh, Aijalon, Gederoth, Soco with
its villages, Timnah with its villages,
and Gimzo with its villages; and they
settled there. 19 For the LORD brought
Judah low because of King Ahaz of Israel, for he had behaved without restraint in Judah and had been faithless
to the LORD. 20 So King Tilgath-pilneser
of Assyria came against him, and oppressed him instead of strengthening
him. 21 For Ahaz plundered the house
of the LORD and the houses of the king
and of the officials, and gave tribute to
the king of Assyria; but it did not help
him.

APOSTASY AND DEATH OF AHAZ

22 In the time of his distress he became yet more faithless to the LORD—
this same King Ahaz. 23 For he sacrificed
to the gods of Damascus, which had defeated him, and said, 'Because the gods
of the kings of Aram helped them, I will
sacrifice to them so that they may help
me.' But they were the ruin of him, and
of all Israel. 24 Ahaz gathered together
the utensils of the house of God, and
cut in pieces the utensils of the house of
God. He shut up the doors of the house
of the LORD and made himself altars in
every corner of Jerusalem. 25 In every
city of Judah he made high places to
make offerings to other gods, provoking
to anger the LORD, the God of his ancestors. 26 Now the rest of his acts and all
his ways, from first to last, are written
in the Book of the Kings of Judah and
Israel. 27 Ahaz slept with his ancestors,
and they buried him in the city, in Jerusalem; but they did not bring him into
the tombs of the kings of Israel. His son
Hezekiah succeeded him.

REIGN OF HEZEKIAH

29 Hezekiah began to reign when
he was twenty-five years old; he
reigned for twenty-nine years in Jerusalem. His mother's name was Abijah
daughter of Zechariah. 2 He did what
was right in the sight of the LORD, just
as his ancestor David had done.

THE TEMPLE CLEANSED

3 In the first year of his reign, in the
first month, he opened the doors of the
house of the LORD and repaired them.
4 He brought in the priests and the Levites and assembled them in the square
on the east. 5 He said to them, 'Listen to
me, Levites! Sanctify yourselves, and
sanctify the house of the LORD, the God
of your ancestors, and carry out the filth
from the holy place. 6 For our ancestors
have been unfaithful and have done
what was evil in the sight of the LORD
our God; they have forsaken him, and
have turned away their faces from the
dwelling of the LORD, and turned their
backs. 7 They also shut the doors of the
vestibule and put out the lamps, and
have not offered incense or made burnt-
offerings in the holy place to the God of
Israel. 8 Therefore the wrath of the LORD
came upon Judah and Jerusalem, and he
has made them an object of horror, of
astonishment, and of hissing, as you see
with your own eyes. 9 Our fathers have
fallen by the sword and our sons and our
daughters and our wives are in captivity
for this. 10 Now it is in my heart to make
a covenant with the LORD, the God of Israel, so that his fierce anger may turn
away from us. 11 My sons, do not now be
negligent, for the LORD has chosen you
to stand in his presence to minister to
him, and to be his ministers and make
offerings to him.'

12 Then the Levites arose, Mahath
son of Amasai, and Joel son of Azariah,
of the sons of the Kohathites; and of the
sons of Merari, Kish son of Abdi, and
Azariah son of Jehallelel; and of the Gershonites, Joah son of Zimmah, and Eden
son of Joah; 13 and of the sons of Elizaphan, Shimri and Jeuel; and of the sons
of Asaph, Zechariah and Mattaniah;
14 and of the sons of Heman, Jehuel and

o 28.16 Gk Syr Vg Compare 2 Kings 16.7: Heb *kings*

Shimei; and of the sons of Jeduthun,
Shemaiah and Uzziel. [15]They gathered
their brothers, sanctified themselves,
and went in as the king had commanded,
by the words of the LORD, to cleanse the
house of the LORD. [16]The priests went
into the inner part of the house of the
LORD to cleanse it, and they brought out
all the unclean things that they found in
the temple of the LORD into the court of
the house of the LORD; and the Levites
took them and carried them out to the
Wadi Kidron. [17]They began to sanctify
on the first day of the first month, and
on the eighth day of the month they
came to the vestibule of the LORD; then
for eight days they sanctified the house
of the LORD, and on the sixteenth day
of the first month they finished. [18]Then
they went inside to King Hezekiah and
said, 'We have cleansed all the house of
the LORD, the altar of burnt-offering
and all its utensils, and the table for the
rows of bread and all its utensils. [19]All
the utensils that King Ahaz repudiated
during his reign when he was faithless,
we have made ready and sanctified;
see, they are in front of the altar of the
LORD.'

TEMPLE WORSHIP RESTORED

20 Then King Hezekiah rose early,
assembled the officials of the city, and
went up to the house of the LORD.
[21]They brought seven bulls, seven rams,
seven lambs, and seven male goats for
a sin-offering for the kingdom and for
the sanctuary and for Judah. He commanded the priests the descendants
of Aaron to offer them on the altar of
the LORD. [22]So they slaughtered the
bulls, and the priests received the blood
and dashed it against the altar; they
slaughtered the rams and their blood
was dashed against the altar; they also
slaughtered the lambs and their blood
was dashed against the altar. [23]Then
the male goats for the sin-offering were
brought to the king and the assembly;
they laid their hands on them, [24]and
the priests slaughtered them and made
a sin-offering with their blood at the altar, to make atonement for all Israel. For
the king commanded that the burnt-
offering and the sin-offering should be
made for all Israel.

25 He stationed the Levites in the
house of the LORD with cymbals, harps,
and lyres, according to the commandment of David and of Gad the king's seer
and of the prophet Nathan, for the commandment was from the LORD through
his prophets. [26]The Levites stood
with the instruments of David, and
the priests with the trumpets. [27]Then
Hezekiah commanded that the burnt-
offering be offered on the altar. When
the burnt-offering began, the song to
the LORD began also, and the trumpets, accompanied by the instruments
of King David of Israel. [28]The whole assembly worshipped, the singers sang,
and the trumpeters sounded; all this
continued until the burnt-offering was
finished. [29]When the offering was finished, the king and all who were present
with him bowed down and worshipped.
[30]King Hezekiah and the officials commanded the Levites to sing praises to
the LORD with the words of David and
of the seer Asaph. They sang praises
with gladness, and they bowed down
and worshipped.

31 Then Hezekiah said, 'You have
now consecrated yourselves to the
LORD; come near, bring sacrifices and
thank-offerings to the house of the
LORD.' The assembly brought sacrifices and thank-offerings; and all who
were of a willing heart brought burnt-
offerings. [32]The number of the burnt-
offerings that the assembly brought
was seventy bulls, one hundred rams,
and two hundred lambs; all these were
for a burnt-offering to the LORD. [33]The
consecrated offerings were six hundred
bulls and three thousand sheep. [34]But
the priests were too few and could not
skin all the burnt-offerings, so, until
other priests had sanctified themselves,
their kindred, the Levites, helped them
until the work was finished—for the
Levites were more conscientious[p] than
the priests in sanctifying themselves.
[35]Besides the great number of burnt-
offerings there was the fat of the offerings of well-being, and there were the
drink-offerings for the burnt-offerings.
Thus the service of the house of the
LORD was restored. [36]And Hezekiah
and all the people rejoiced because of
what God had done for the people; for
the thing had come about suddenly.

THE GREAT PASSOVER

30 Hezekiah sent word to all Israel
and Judah, and wrote letters
also to Ephraim and Manasseh, that
they should come to the house of the
LORD at Jerusalem, to keep the passover

[p] 29.34 Heb *upright in heart*

to the LORD the God of Israel. 2For the
king and his officials and all the assembly in Jerusalem had taken counsel to
keep the passover in the second month
3(for they could not keep it at its proper
time because the priests had not sanctified themselves in sufficient number,
nor had the people assembled in Jerusalem). 4The plan seemed right to the king
and all the assembly. 5So they decreed
the making of a proclamation throughout all Israel, from Beer-sheba to Dan,
that the people should come and keep
the passover to the LORD the God of Israel, at Jerusalem; for they had not kept
it in great numbers as prescribed. 6So
couriers went throughout all Israel and
Judah with letters from the king and his
officials, as the king had commanded,
saying, 'O people of Israel, return to
the LORD, the God of Abraham, Isaac,
and Israel, so that he may turn again to
the remnant of you who have escaped
from the hand of the kings of Assyria.
7Do not be like your ancestors and your
kindred, who were faithless to the LORD
God of their ancestors, so that he made
them a desolation, as you see. 8Do not
now be stiff-necked as your ancestors
were, but yield yourselves to the LORD
and come to his sanctuary, which he has
sanctified for ever, and serve the LORD
your God, so that his fierce anger may
turn away from you. 9For as you return
to the LORD, your kindred and your children will find compassion with their
captors, and return to this land. For the
LORD your God is gracious and merciful, and will not turn away his face from
you, if you return to him.'

10 So the couriers went from city to
city through the country of Ephraim
and Manasseh, and as far as Zebulun;
but they laughed them to scorn, and
mocked them. 11Only a few from Asher,
Manasseh, and Zebulun humbled themselves and came to Jerusalem. 12The
hand of God was also on Judah to give
them one heart to do what the king and
the officials commanded by the word of
the LORD.

13 Many people came together in Jerusalem to keep the festival of unleavened bread in the second month, a very
large assembly. 14They set to work and
removed the altars that were in Jerusalem, and all the altars for offering incense
they took away and threw into the Wadi
Kidron. 15They slaughtered the passover lamb on the fourteenth day of the
second month. The priests and the Levites were ashamed, and they sanctified
themselves and brought burnt-offerings
into the house of the LORD. 16They took
their accustomed posts according to the
law of Moses the man of God; the priests
dashed the blood that they received[q]
from the hands of the Levites. 17For
there were many in the assembly who
had not sanctified themselves; therefore
the Levites had to slaughter the passover lamb for everyone who was not
clean, to make it holy to the LORD. 18For
a multitude of the people, many of them
from Ephraim, Manasseh, Issachar, and
Zebulun, had not cleansed themselves,
yet they ate the passover otherwise than
as prescribed. But Hezekiah prayed for
them, saying, 'The good LORD pardon
all 19who set their hearts to seek God,
the LORD the God of their ancestors,
even though not in accordance with the
sanctuary's rules of cleanness.' 20The
LORD heard Hezekiah, and healed the
people. 21The people of Israel who were
present at Jerusalem kept the festival of
unleavened bread for seven days with
great gladness; and the Levites and the
priests praised the LORD day by day, accompanied by loud instruments for the
LORD. 22Hezekiah spoke encouragingly
to all the Levites who showed good skill
in the service of the LORD. So the people ate the food of the festival for seven
days, sacrificing offerings of well-being
and giving thanks to the LORD the God
of their ancestors.

23 Then the whole assembly agreed
together to keep the festival for another
seven days; so they kept it for another
seven days with gladness. 24For King
Hezekiah of Judah gave the assembly
a thousand bulls and seven thousand
sheep for offerings, and the officials
gave the assembly a thousand bulls and
ten thousand sheep. The priests sanctified themselves in great numbers. 25The
whole assembly of Judah, the priests
and the Levites, and the whole assembly that came out of Israel, and the resident aliens who came out of the land of
Israel, and the resident aliens who lived
in Judah, rejoiced. 26There was great joy
in Jerusalem, for since the time of Solomon son of King David of Israel there
had been nothing like this in Jerusalem.
27Then the priests and the Levites stood
up and blessed the people, and their
voice was heard; their prayer came to
his holy dwelling in heaven.

[q] 30.16 Heb lacks *that they received*

PAGAN SHRINES DESTROYED

31 Now when all this was finished,
all Israel who were present went
out to the cities of Judah and broke
down the pillars, hewed down the sacred poles,[r] and pulled down the high
places and the altars throughout all
Judah and Benjamin, and in Ephraim
and Manasseh, until they had destroyed
them all. Then all the people of Israel
returned to their cities, all to their individual properties.

2 Hezekiah appointed the divisions
of the priests and of the Levites, division by division, everyone according
to his service, the priests and the Levites, for burnt-offerings and offerings
of well-being, to minister in the gates
of the camp of the LORD and to give
thanks and praise. 3The contribution
of the king from his own possessions
was for the burnt-offerings: the burnt-
offerings of morning and evening, and
the burnt-offerings for the sabbaths, the
new moons, and the appointed festivals,
as it is written in the law of the LORD.
4He commanded the people who lived
in Jerusalem to give the portion due to
the priests and the Levites, so that they
might devote themselves to the law of
the LORD. 5As soon as the word spread,
the people of Israel gave in abundance
the first fruits of grain, wine, oil, honey,
and of all the produce of the field; and
they brought in abundantly the tithe of
everything. 6The people of Israel and Judah who lived in the cities of Judah also
brought in the tithe of cattle and sheep,
and the tithe of the dedicated things
that had been consecrated to the LORD
their God, and laid them in heaps. 7In
the third month they began to pile up
the heaps, and finished them in the seventh month. 8When Hezekiah and the
officials came and saw the heaps, they
blessed the LORD and his people Israel.
9Hezekiah questioned the priests and
the Levites about the heaps. 10The chief
priest Azariah, who was of the house of
Zadok, answered him, 'Since they began to bring the contributions into the
house of the LORD, we have had enough
to eat and have plenty to spare; for the
LORD has blessed his people, so that we
have this great supply left over.'

REORGANIZATION OF PRIESTS AND LEVITES

11 Then Hezekiah commanded them
to prepare store-chambers in the house
of the LORD; and they prepared them.
12Faithfully they brought in the contributions, the tithes and the dedicated
things. The chief officer in charge of
them was Conaniah the Levite, with his
brother Shimei as second; 13while Jehiel,
Azaziah, Nahath, Asahel, Jerimoth, Jozabad, Eliel, Ismachiah, Mahath, and
Benaiah were overseers assisting Conaniah and his brother Shimei, by the appointment of King Hezekiah and of Azariah the chief officer of the house of God.
14Kore son of Imnah the Levite, keeper
of the east gate, was in charge of the
freewill-offerings to God, to apportion
the contribution reserved for the LORD
and the most holy offerings. 15Eden,
Miniamin, Jeshua, Shemaiah, Amariah, and Shecaniah were faithfully assisting him in the cities of the priests, to
distribute the portions to their kindred,
old and young alike, by divisions, 16ex-
cept those enrolled by genealogy, males
from three years old and upwards, all
who entered the house of the LORD as
the duty of each day required, for their
service according to their offices, by
their divisions. 17The enrolment of the
priests was according to their ancestral
houses; that of the Levites from twenty
years old and upwards was according to
their offices, by their divisions. 18The
priests were enrolled with all their little children, their wives, their sons,
and their daughters, the whole multitude; for they were faithful in keeping
themselves holy. 19And for the descendants of Aaron, the priests, who were in
the fields of common land belonging to
their towns, town by town, the people
designated by name were to distribute portions to every male among the
priests and to everyone among the Levites who was enrolled.

20 Hezekiah did this throughout all
Judah; he did what was good and right
and faithful before the LORD his God.
21And every work that he undertook in
the service of the house of God, and in
accordance with the law and the commandments, to seek his God, he did
with all his heart; and he prospered.

SENNACHERIB'S INVASION

32 After these things and these acts
of faithfulness, King Sennacherib of Assyria came and invaded Judah
and encamped against the fortified cities, thinking to win them for himself.
2When Hezekiah saw that Sennacherib

[r] 31.1 Heb *Asherim*

had come and intended to fight against
Jerusalem, 3he planned with his officers
and his warriors to stop the flow of the
springs that were outside the city; and
they helped him. 4A great many people were gathered, and they stopped all
the springs and the wadi that flowed
through the land, saying, 'Why should
the Assyrian kings come and find water
in abundance?' 5Hezekiah[s] set to work
resolutely and built up the entire wall
that was broken down, and raised towers on it,[t] and outside it he built another
wall; he also strengthened the Millo
in the city of David, and made weapons and shields in abundance. 6He appointed combat commanders over the
people, and gathered them together to
him in the square at the gate of the city
and spoke encouragingly to them, saying, 7'Be strong and of good courage.
Do not be afraid or dismayed before the
king of Assyria and all the horde that is
with him; for there is one greater with
us than with him. 8With him is an arm
of flesh; but with us is the LORD our
God, to help us and to fight our battles.' The people were encouraged by the
words of King Hezekiah of Judah.

9 After this, while King Sennacherib
of Assyria was at Lachish with all his
forces, he sent his servants to Jerusalem
to King Hezekiah of Judah and to all the
people of Judah that were in Jerusalem,
saying, 10'Thus says King Sennacherib
of Assyria: On what are you relying,
that you undergo the siege of Jerusalem? 11Is not Hezekiah misleading you,
handing you over to die by famine and
by thirst, when he tells you, "The LORD
our God will save us from the hand of
the king of Assyria"? 12Was it not this
same Hezekiah who took away his high
places and his altars and commanded
Judah and Jerusalem, saying, "Before
one altar you shall worship, and upon
it you shall make your offerings"? 13Do
you not know what I and my ancestors
have done to all the peoples of other
lands? Were the gods of the nations of
those lands at all able to save their lands
out of my hand? 14Who among all the
gods of those nations that my ancestors utterly destroyed was able to save
his people from my hand, that your
God should be able to save you from my
hand? 15Now therefore do not let Hezekiah deceive you or mislead you in this
fashion, and do not believe him, for no
god of any nation or kingdom has been
able to save his people from my hand
or from the hand of my ancestors. How
much less will your God save you out of
my hand!'

16 His servants said still more
against the Lord GOD and against his
servant Hezekiah. 17He also wrote letters to throw contempt on the LORD
the God of Israel and to speak against
him, saying, 'Just as the gods of the
nations in other lands did not rescue
their people from my hands, so the God
of Hezekiah will not rescue his people
from my hand.' 18They shouted it with
a loud voice in the language of Judah to
the people of Jerusalem who were on
the wall, to frighten and terrify them,
in order that they might take the city.
19They spoke of the God of Jerusalem as
if he were like the gods of the peoples of
the earth, which are the work of human
hands.

SENNACHERIB'S DEFEAT AND DEATH

20 Then King Hezekiah and the
prophet Isaiah son of Amoz prayed because of this and cried to heaven. 21And
the LORD sent an angel who cut off all
the mighty warriors and commanders
and officers in the camp of the king of
Assyria. So he returned in disgrace to
his own land. When he came into the
house of his god, some of his own sons
struck him down there with the sword.
22So the LORD saved Hezekiah and the
inhabitants of Jerusalem from the hand
of King Sennacherib of Assyria and
from the hand of all his enemies; he
gave them rest[u] on every side. 23Many
brought gifts to the LORD in Jerusalem
and precious things to King Hezekiah
of Judah, so that he was exalted in the
sight of all nations from that time onwards.

HEZEKIAH'S SICKNESS

24 In those days Hezekiah became
sick and was at the point of death. He
prayed to the LORD, and he answered
him and gave him a sign. 25But Hezekiah did not respond according to the
benefit done to him, for his heart was
proud. Therefore wrath came upon him
and upon Judah and Jerusalem. 26Then
Hezekiah humbled himself for the pride
of his heart, both he and the inhabitants
of Jerusalem, so that the wrath of the
LORD did not come upon them in the
days of Hezekiah.

[s] **32.5** Heb *He* [t] **32.5** Vg: Heb *and raised on the towers* [u] **32.22** Gk Vg: Heb *guided them*

HEZEKIAH'S PROSPERITY AND ACHIEVEMENTS

27 Hezekiah had very great riches
and honour; and he made for himself
treasuries for silver, for gold, for precious stones, for spices, for shields, and
for all kinds of costly objects; 28storehouses
houses also for the yield of grain, wine,
and oil; and stalls for all kinds of cattle,
and sheepfolds.[v] 29He likewise provided
cities for himself, and flocks and herds in
abundance; for God had given him very
great possessions. 30This same Hezekiah
closed the upper outlet of the waters of
Gihon and directed them down to the
west side of the city of David. Hezekiah
prospered in all his works. 31So also in
the matter of the envoys of the officials
of Babylon, who had been sent to him
to inquire about the sign that had been
done in the land, God left him to himself, in order to test him and to know all
that was in his heart.

32 Now the rest of the acts of Hezekiah, and his good deeds, are written in
the vision of the prophet Isaiah son of
Amoz in the Book of the Kings of Judah
and Israel. 33Hezekiah slept with his
ancestors, and they buried him on the
ascent to the tombs of the descendants
of David; and all Judah and the inhabitants of Jerusalem did him honour at
his death. His son Manasseh succeeded
him.

REIGN OF MANASSEH

33 Manasseh was twelve years
old when he began to reign; he
reigned for fifty-five years in Jerusalem. 2He did what was evil in the sight
of the LORD, according to the abominable practices of the nations whom the
LORD drove out before the people of Israel. 3For he rebuilt the high places that
his father Hezekiah had pulled down,
and erected altars to the Baals, made sacred poles,[w] worshipped all the host of
heaven, and served them. 4He built altars in the house of the LORD, of which
the LORD had said, 'In Jerusalem shall
my name be for ever.' 5He built altars for
all the host of heaven in the two courts
of the house of the LORD. 6He made his
son pass through fire in the valley of the
son of Hinnom, practised soothsaying
and augury and sorcery, and dealt with
mediums and with wizards. He did
much evil in the sight of the LORD, provoking him to anger. 7The carved image
of the idol that he had made he set in
the house of God, of which God said to
David and to his son Solomon, 'In this
house, and in Jerusalem, which I have
chosen out of all the tribes of Israel, I
will put my name for ever; 8I will never
again remove the feet of Israel from the
land that I appointed for your ancestors,
if only they will be careful to do all that
I have commanded them, all the law,
the statutes, and the ordinances given
through Moses.' 9Manasseh misled Judah and the inhabitants of Jerusalem,
so that they did more evil than the nations whom the LORD had destroyed before the people of Israel.

MANASSEH RESTORED AFTER REPENTANCE

10 The LORD spoke to Manasseh and
to his people, but they gave no heed.
11Therefore the LORD brought against
them the commanders of the army of
the king of Assyria, who took Manasseh captive in manacles, bound him
with fetters, and brought him to Babylon. 12While he was in distress he entreated the favour of the LORD his God
and humbled himself greatly before
the God of his ancestors. 13He prayed
to him, and God received his entreaty,
heard his plea, and restored him again
to Jerusalem and to his kingdom. Then
Manasseh knew that the LORD indeed
was God.

14 Afterwards he built an outer wall
for the city of David west of Gihon, in
the valley, reaching the entrance at the
Fish Gate; he carried it around Ophel,
and raised it to a very great height. He
also put commanders of the army in all
the fortified cities in Judah. 15He took
away the foreign gods and the idol from
the house of the LORD, and all the altars
that he had built on the mountain of
the house of the LORD and in Jerusalem,
and he threw them out of the city. 16He
also restored the altar of the LORD and
offered on it sacrifices of well-being and
of thanksgiving; and he commanded Judah to serve the LORD the God of Israel.
17The people, however, still sacrificed at
the high places, but only to the LORD
their God.

DEATH OF MANASSEH

18 Now the rest of the acts of Manasseh, his prayer to his God, and the words
of the seers who spoke to him in the
name of the LORD God of Israel, these

v 32.28 Gk Vg: Heb *flocks for folds* w 33.3 Heb *Asheroth*

are in the Annals of the Kings of Israel.
19His prayer, and how God received his
entreaty, all his sin and his faithlessness, the sites on which he built high
places and set up the sacred poles[x] and
the images, before he humbled himself,
these are written in the records of the
seers.[y] 20So Manasseh slept with his
ancestors, and they buried him in his
house. His son Amon succeeded him.

AMON'S REIGN AND DEATH

21 Amon was twenty-two years old
when he began to reign; he reigned for
two years in Jerusalem. 22He did what
was evil in the sight of the LORD, as his
father Manasseh had done. Amon sacrificed to all the images that his father
Manasseh had made, and served them.
23He did not humble himself before the
LORD, as his father Manasseh had humbled himself, but this Amon incurred
more and more guilt. 24His servants
conspired against him and killed him
in his house. 25But the people of the
land killed all those who had conspired
against King Amon; and the people of
the land made his son Josiah king to
succeed him.

REIGN OF JOSIAH

34 Josiah was eight years old when
he began to reign; he reigned for
thirty-one years in Jerusalem. 2He did
what was right in the sight of the LORD,
and walked in the ways of his ancestor
David; he did not turn aside to the right
or to the left. 3For in the eighth year of
his reign, while he was still a boy, he began to seek the God of his ancestor David, and in the twelfth year he began to
purge Judah and Jerusalem of the high
places, the sacred poles,[z] and the carved
and the cast images. 4In his presence
they pulled down the altars of the Baals; he demolished the incense altars
that stood above them. He broke down
the sacred poles[a] and the carved and the
cast images; he made dust of them and
scattered it over the graves of those who
had sacrificed to them. 5He also burned
the bones of the priests on their altars,
and purged Judah and Jerusalem. 6In
the towns of Manasseh, Ephraim, and
Simeon, and as far as Naphtali, in their
ruins[b] all around, 7he broke down the
altars, beat the sacred poles[c] and the
images into powder, and demolished
all the incense altars throughout all the
land of Israel. Then he returned to Jerusalem.

DISCOVERY OF THE BOOK OF THE LAW

8 In the eighteenth year of his reign,
when he had purged the land and the
house, he sent Shaphan son of Azaliah,
Maaseiah the governor of the city, and
Joah son of Joahaz, the recorder, to repair the house of the LORD his God.
9They came to the high priest Hilkiah
and delivered the money that had been
brought into the house of God, which
the Levites, the keepers of the threshold, had collected from Manasseh and
Ephraim and from all the remnant of
Israel and from all Judah and Benjamin and from the inhabitants of Jerusalem. 10They delivered it to the workers
who had the oversight of the house of
the LORD, and the workers who were
working in the house of the LORD gave
it for repairing and restoring the house.
11They gave it to the carpenters and the
builders to buy quarried stone, and timber for tie-beams and joists for the buildings that the kings of Judah had let go
to ruin. 12The people did the work faithfully. Over them were appointed the Levites Jahath and Obadiah, of the sons of
Merari, along with Zechariah and Meshullam, of the sons of the Kohathites,
to have oversight. Other Levites, all skilful with instruments of music, 13were
over the burden-bearers and directed all
who did work in every kind of service;
and some of the Levites were scribes,
and officials, and gatekeepers.

14 While they were bringing out the
money that had been brought into the
house of the LORD, the priest Hilkiah
found the book of the law of the LORD
given through Moses. 15Hilkiah said to
the secretary Shaphan, 'I have found
the book of the law in the house of the
LORD'; and Hilkiah gave the book to
Shaphan. 16Shaphan brought the book
to the king, and further reported to the
king, 'All that was committed to your
servants they are doing. 17They have
emptied out the money that was found
in the house of the LORD and have delivered it into the hand of the overseers
and the workers.' 18The secretary Shaphan informed the king, 'The priest
Hilkiah has given me a book.' Shaphan
then read it aloud to the king.

19 When the king heard the words of
the law he tore his clothes. 20Then the

[x] 33.19 Heb *Asherim* [y] 33.19 One Ms Gk: MT *of Hozai* [z] 34.3 Heb *Asherim* [a] 34.4 Heb *Asherim* [b] 34.6 Meaning of Heb uncertain [c] 34.7 Heb *Asherim*

king commanded Hilkiah, Ahikam son
of Shaphan, Abdon son of Micah, the
secretary Shaphan, and the king's servant Asaiah: 21'Go, inquire of the LORD
for me and for those who are left in Israel and in Judah, concerning the words
of the book that has been found; for the
wrath of the LORD that is poured out
on us is great, because our ancestors did
not keep the word of the LORD, to act in
accordance with all that is written in
this book.'

THE PROPHET HULDAH CONSULTED

22 So Hilkiah and those whom the
king had sent went to the prophet Huldah, the wife of Shallum son of Tokhath
son of Hasrah, keeper of the wardrobe
(who lived in Jerusalem in the Second
Quarter) and spoke to her to that effect.
23She declared to them, 'Thus says the
LORD, the God of Israel: Tell the man
who sent you to me, 24Thus says the
LORD: I will indeed bring disaster upon
this place and upon its inhabitants, all
the curses that are written in the book
that was read before the king of Judah.
25Because they have forsaken me and
have made offerings to other gods, so
that they have provoked me to anger
with all the works of their hands, my
wrath will be poured out on this place
and will not be quenched. 26But as to
the king of Judah, who sent you to inquire of the LORD, thus shall you say to
him: Thus says the LORD, the God of Israel: Regarding the words that you have
heard, 27because your heart was penitent and you humbled yourself before
God when you heard his words against
this place and its inhabitants, and you
have humbled yourself before me, and
have torn your clothes and wept before me, I also have heard you, says the
LORD. 28I will gather you to your ancestors and you shall be gathered to your
grave in peace; your eyes shall not see
all the disaster that I will bring on this
place and its inhabitants.' They took the
message back to the king.

THE COVENANT RENEWED

29 Then the king sent word and gathered together all the elders of Judah and
Jerusalem. 30The king went up to the
house of the LORD, with all the people of Judah, the inhabitants of Jerusalem, the priests and the Levites, all the
people both great and small; he read in
their hearing all the words of the book
of the covenant that had been found in
the house of the LORD. 31The king stood
in his place and made a covenant before
the LORD, to follow the LORD, keeping
his commandments, his decrees, and
his statutes, with all his heart and all
his soul, to perform the words of the
covenant that were written in this book.
32Then he made all who were present
in Jerusalem and in Benjamin pledge
themselves to it. And the inhabitants
of Jerusalem acted according to the covenant of God, the God of their ancestors.
33Josiah took away all the abominations
from all the territory that belonged to
the people of Israel, and made all who
were in Israel worship the LORD their
God. All his days they did not turn away
from following the LORD the God of
their ancestors.

CELEBRATION OF THE PASSOVER

35 Josiah kept a passover to the
LORD in Jerusalem; they slaughtered the passover lamb on the fourteenth day of the first month. 2He appointed the priests to their offices and
encouraged them in the service of the
house of the LORD. 3He said to the Levites who taught all Israel and who
were holy to the LORD, 'Put the holy
ark in the house that Solomon son of
David, king of Israel, built; you need no
longer carry it on your shoulders. Now
serve the LORD your God and his people
Israel. 4Make preparations by your ancestral houses by your divisions, following the written directions of King David
of Israel and the written directions of
his son Solomon. 5Take position in the
holy place according to the groupings
of the ancestral houses of your kindred
the people, and let there be Levites for
each division of an ancestral house.[d]
6Slaughter the passover lamb, sanctify
yourselves, and on behalf of your kindred make preparations, acting according to the word of the LORD by Moses.'

7 Then Josiah contributed to the people, as passover offerings for all that were
present, lambs and kids from the flock
to the number of thirty thousand, and
three thousand bulls; these were from
the king's possessions. 8His officials
contributed willingly to the people, to
the priests, and to the Levites. Hilkiah,
Zechariah, and Jehiel, the chief officers
of the house of God, gave to the priests
for the passover offerings two thousand
six hundred lambs and kids and three

[d] 35.5 Meaning of Heb uncertain

hundred bulls. 9 Conaniah also, and his brothers Shemaiah and Nethanel, and Hashabiah and Jeiel and Jozabad, the chiefs of the Levites, gave to the Levites for the passover offerings five thousand lambs and kids and five hundred bulls.

10 When the service had been prepared for, the priests stood in their place, and the Levites in their divisions according to the king's command. 11 They slaughtered the passover lamb, and the priests dashed the blood that they received[e] from them, while the Levites did the skinning. 12 They set aside the burnt-offerings so that they might distribute them according to the groupings of the ancestral houses of the people, to offer to the LORD, as it is written in the book of Moses. And they did the same with the bulls. 13 They roasted the passover lamb with fire according to the ordinance; and they boiled the holy offerings in pots, in cauldrons, and in pans, and carried them quickly to all the people. 14 Afterwards they made preparations for themselves and for the priests, because the priests the descendants of Aaron were occupied in offering the burnt-offerings and the fat parts until night; so the Levites made preparations for themselves and for the priests, the descendants of Aaron. 15 The singers, the descendants of Asaph, were in their place according to the command of David, and Asaph, and Heman, and the king's seer Jeduthun. The gatekeepers were at each gate; they did not need to interrupt their service, for their kindred the Levites made preparations for them.

16 So all the service of the LORD was prepared that day, to keep the passover and to offer burnt-offerings on the altar of the LORD, according to the command of King Josiah. 17 The people of Israel who were present kept the passover at that time, and the festival of unleavened bread for seven days. 18 No passover like it had been kept in Israel since the days of the prophet Samuel; none of the kings of Israel had kept such a passover as was kept by Josiah, by the priests and the Levites, by all Judah and Israel who were present, and by the inhabitants of Jerusalem. 19 In the eighteenth year of the reign of Josiah this passover was kept.

DEFEAT BY PHARAOH NECO AND DEATH OF JOSIAH

20 After all this, when Josiah had set the temple in order, King Neco of Egypt went up to fight at Carchemish on the Euphrates, and Josiah went out against him. 21 But Neco[f] sent envoys to him, saying, 'What have I to do with you, king of Judah? I am not coming against you today, but against the house with which I am at war; and God has commanded me to hurry. Cease opposing God, who is with me, so that he will not destroy you.' 22 But Josiah would not turn away from him, but disguised himself in order to fight with him. He did not listen to the words of Neco from the mouth of God, but joined battle in the plain of Megiddo. 23 The archers shot King Josiah; and the king said to his servants, 'Take me away, for I am badly wounded.' 24 So his servants took him out of the chariot and carried him in his second chariot[g] and brought him to Jerusalem. There he died, and was buried in the tombs of his ancestors. All Judah and Jerusalem mourned for Josiah. 25 Jeremiah also uttered a lament for Josiah, and all the singing-men and singing-women have spoken of Josiah in their laments to this day. They made these a custom in Israel; they are recorded in the Laments. 26 Now the rest of the acts of Josiah and his faithful deeds in accordance with what is written in the law of the LORD, 27 and his acts, first and last, are written in the Book of the Kings of Israel and Judah.

REIGN OF JEHOAHAZ

36 The people of the land took Jehoahaz son of Josiah and made him king to succeed his father in Jerusalem. 2 Jehoahaz was twenty-three years old when he began to reign; he reigned for three months in Jerusalem. 3 Then the king of Egypt deposed him in Jerusalem and laid on the land a tribute of one hundred talents of silver and one talent of gold. 4 The king of Egypt made his brother Eliakim king over Judah and Jerusalem, and changed his name to Jehoiakim; but Neco took his brother Jehoahaz and carried him to Egypt.

REIGN AND CAPTIVITY OF JEHOIAKIM

5 Jehoiakim was twenty-five years old when he began to reign; he reigned for eleven years in Jerusalem. He did what was evil in the sight of the LORD his God. 6 Against him King Nebuchadnezzar

e 35.11 Heb lacks *that they received*
f 35.21 Heb *he* g 35.24 Or *the chariot of his deputy*

of Babylon came up, and bound him
with fetters to take him to Babylon.
7 Nebuchadnezzar also carried some of
the vessels of the house of the LORD to
Babylon and put them in his palace in
Babylon. 8 Now the rest of the acts of Jehoiakim, and the abominations that he
did, and what was found against him,
are written in the Book of the Kings of
Israel and Judah; and his son Jehoiachin
succeeded him.

REIGN AND CAPTIVITY OF JEHOIACHIN

9 Jehoiachin was eight years old
when he began to reign; he reigned for
three months and ten days in Jerusalem. He did what was evil in the sight
of the LORD. 10 In the spring of the year
King Nebuchadnezzar sent and brought
him to Babylon, along with the precious
vessels of the house of the LORD, and
made his brother Zedekiah king over
Judah and Jerusalem.

REIGN OF ZEDEKIAH

11 Zedekiah was twenty-one years
old when he began to reign; he reigned
for eleven years in Jerusalem. 12 He did
what was evil in the sight of the LORD
his God. He did not humble himself before the prophet Jeremiah who spoke
from the mouth of the LORD. 13 He also
rebelled against King Nebuchadnezzar, who had made him swear by God;
he stiffened his neck and hardened his
heart against turning to the LORD, the
God of Israel. 14 All the leading priests
and the people also were exceedingly
unfaithful, following all the abominations of the nations; and they polluted
the house of the LORD that he had consecrated in Jerusalem.

THE FALL OF JERUSALEM

15 The LORD, the God of their ancestors, sent persistently to them by his
messengers, because he had compassion on his people and on his dwelling-
place; 16 but they kept mocking the messengers of God, despising his words, and
scoffing at his prophets, until the wrath
of the LORD against his people became
so great that there was no remedy.

17 Therefore he brought up against
them the king of the Chaldeans, who
killed their youths with the sword in
the house of their sanctuary, and had
no compassion on young man or young
woman, the aged or the feeble; he gave
them all into his hand. 18 All the vessels
of the house of God, large and small, and
the treasures of the house of the LORD,
and the treasures of the king and of his
officials, all these he brought to Babylon.
19 They burned the house of God, broke
down the wall of Jerusalem, burned all
its palaces with fire, and destroyed all its
precious vessels. 20 He took into exile in
Babylon those who had escaped from the
sword, and they became servants to him
and to his sons until the establishment
of the kingdom of Persia, 21 to fulfil the
word of the LORD by the mouth of Jeremiah, until the land had made up for its
sabbaths. All the days that it lay desolate
it kept sabbath, to fulfil seventy years.

CYRUS PROCLAIMS LIBERTY FOR THE EXILES

22 In the first year of King Cyrus of
Persia, in fulfilment of the word of the
LORD spoken by Jeremiah, the LORD
stirred up the spirit of King Cyrus of
Persia so that he sent a herald throughout all his kingdom and also declared in
a written edict: 23 'Thus says King Cyrus
of Persia: The LORD, the God of heaven,
has given me all the kingdoms of the
earth, and he has charged me to build
him a house at Jerusalem, which is in
Judah. Whoever is among you of all his
people, may the LORD his God be with
him! Let him go up.'

EZRA

The book of Ezra is an account of events occurring from the return of the exiles during the first year of King Cyrus in 538 BCE until the completion of the new temple in Jerusalem in the sixth year of King Darius in 515 (chs. 1–6). The second half of the book is the history of the return under Ezra and of the events that took place at Jerusalem after Ezra's arrival there (chs. 7–10). The returning exiles were the remnant of Israel who were challenged by the author to rebuild Jerusalem and the temple and to live according to the law, separating themselves from foreign influences.

The books of Ezra and Nehemiah together are the only account of the time after the Babylonian exile (587–539 BCE) preserved in the Old Testament. These books focus on the religious dimension of the restored life of Judah.

Portions of the book of Ezra are read as the First Reading on Monday through Wednesday of the Twenty-Fifth Week of Year I. These texts memorialize the dramatic return from exile of the remnant to rebuild the temple in Jerusalem and the affirmation by Ezra that God has not abandoned his people.

END OF THE BABYLONIAN CAPTIVITY

1 In the first year of King Cyrus of
Persia, in order that the word of the
LORD by the mouth of Jeremiah might
be accomplished, the LORD stirred up
the spirit of King Cyrus of Persia so
that he sent a herald throughout all his
kingdom, and also in a written edict declared:
2 'Thus says King Cyrus of Persia:
The LORD, the God of heaven, has given
me all the kingdoms of the earth, and
he has charged me to build him a house
at Jerusalem in Judah. 3Any of those
among you who are of his people—may
their God be with them!—are now permitted to go up to Jerusalem in Judah,
and rebuild the house of the LORD, the
God of Israel—he is the God who is in
Jerusalem; 4and let all survivors, in
whatever place they reside, be assisted
by the people of their place with silver
and gold, with goods and with animals,
besides freewill-offerings for the house
of God in Jerusalem.'
5 The heads of the families of Judah
and Benjamin, and the priests and the
Levites—everyone whose spirit God had
stirred—got ready to go up and rebuild
the house of the LORD in Jerusalem. 6All
their neighbours aided them with silver
vessels, with gold, with goods, with animals, and with valuable gifts, besides
all that was freely offered. 7King Cyrus
himself brought out the vessels of the
house of the LORD that Nebuchadnezzar
had carried away from Jerusalem and
placed in the house of his gods. 8King
Cyrus of Persia had them released into
the charge of Mithredath the treasurer,
who counted them out to Sheshbazzar
the prince of Judah. 9And this was the
inventory: gold basins, thirty; silver
basins, one thousand; knives,[a] twenty-
nine; 10gold bowls, thirty; other silver
bowls, four hundred and ten; other vessels, one thousand; 11the total of the gold
and silver vessels was five thousand four
hundred. All these Sheshbazzar brought
up, when the exiles were brought up
from Babylonia to Jerusalem.

[a] 1.9 Vg: Meaning of Heb uncertain

LIST OF THE RETURNED EXILES

2 Now these were the people of the
province who came from those captive exiles whom King Nebuchadnezzar
of Babylon had carried captive to Babylonia; they returned to Jerusalem and
Judah, all to their own towns. 2They
came with Zerubbabel, Jeshua, Nehemiah, Seraiah, Reelaiah, Mordecai, Bil-
shan, Mispar, Bigvai, Rehum, and Baanah.

The number of the Israelite people:
3the descendants of Parosh, two thousand one hundred and seventy-two. 4Of
Shephatiah, three hundred and seventy-
two. 5Of Arah, seven hundred and
seventy-five. 6Of Pahath-moab, namely
the descendants of Jeshua and Joab, two
thousand eight hundred and twelve. 7Of
Elam, one thousand two hundred and
fifty-four. 8Of Zattu, nine hundred and
forty-five. 9Of Zaccai, seven hundred
and sixty. 10Of Bani, six hundred and
forty-two. 11Of Bebai, six hundred and
twenty-three. 12Of Azgad, one thousand two hundred and twenty-two. 13Of
Adonikam, six hundred and sixty-six.
14Of Bigvai, two thousand and fifty-six.
15Of Adin, four hundred and fifty-four.
16Of Ater, namely of Hezekiah, ninety-
eight. 17Of Bezai, three hundred and
twenty-three. 18Of Jorah, one hundred
and twelve. 19Of Hashum, two hundred and twenty-three. 20Of Gibbar,
ninety-five. 21Of Bethlehem, one hundred and twenty-three. 22The people of
Netophah, fifty-six. 23Of Anathoth, one
hundred and twenty-eight. 24The descendants of Azmaveth, forty-two. 25Of
Kiriatharim, Chephirah, and Beeroth,
seven hundred and forty-three. 26Of Ramah and Geba, six hundred and twenty-
one. 27The people of Michmas, one hundred and twenty-two. 28Of Bethel and
Ai, two hundred and twenty-three.
29The descendants of Nebo, fifty-two.
30Of Magbish, one hundred and fifty-
six. 31Of the other Elam, one thousand
two hundred and fifty-four. 32Of Harim,
three hundred and twenty. 33Of Lod,
Hadid, and Ono, seven hundred and
twenty-five. 34Of Jericho, three hundred
and forty-five. 35Of Senaah, three thousand six hundred and thirty.

36 The priests: the descendants of Jedaiah, of the house of Jeshua, nine hundred and seventy-three. 37Of Immer,
one thousand and fifty-two. 38Of Pashhur, one thousand two hundred and
forty-seven. 39Of Harim, one thousand
and seventeen.

40 The Levites: the descendants of
Jeshua and Kadmiel, of the descendants
of Hodaviah, seventy-four. 41The singers: the descendants of Asaph, one hundred and twenty-eight. 42The descendants of the gatekeepers: of Shallum, of
Ater, of Talmon, of Akkub, of Hatita,
and of Shobai, in all one hundred and
thirty-nine.

43 The temple servants: the descendants of Ziha, Hasupha, Tabbaoth,
44Keros, Siaha, Padon, 45Lebanah, Hag-
abah, Akkub, 46Hagab, Shamlai, Hanan, 47Giddel, Gahar, Reaiah, 48Rezin,
Nekoda, Gazzam, 49Uzza, Paseah, Besai,
50Asnah, Meunim, Nephisim, 51Bak-
buk, Hakupha, Harhur, 52Bazluth, Mehida, Harsha, 53Barkos, Sisera, Temah,
54Neziah, and Hatipha.

55 The descendants of Solomon's
servants: Sotai, Hassophereth, Peruda,
56Jaalah, Darkon, Giddel, 57Shephatiah,
Hattil, Pochereth-hazzebaim, and Ami.

58 All the temple servants and the
descendants of Solomon's servants were
three hundred and ninety-two.

59 The following were those who
came up from Tel-melah, Tel-harsha,
Cherub, Addan, and Immer, though
they could not prove their families or
their descent, whether they belonged
to Israel: 60the descendants of Delaiah,
Tobiah, and Nekoda, six hundred and
fifty-two. 61Also, of the descendants of
the priests: the descendants of Habaiah,
Hakkoz, and Barzillai (who had married
one of the daughters of Barzillai the Gileadite, and was called by their name).
62These looked for their entries in the
genealogical records, but they were not
found there, and so they were excluded
from the priesthood as unclean; 63the
governor told them that they were not
to partake of the most holy food, until
there should be a priest to consult Urim
and Thummim.

64 The whole assembly together was
forty-two thousand three hundred and
sixty, 65besides their male and female
servants, of whom there were seven
thousand three hundred and thirty-
seven; and they had two hundred male
and female singers. 66They had seven
hundred and thirty-six horses, two
hundred and forty-five mules, 67four
hundred and thirty-five camels, and six
thousand seven hundred and twenty
donkeys.

68 As soon as they came to the
house of the LORD in Jerusalem, some
of the heads of families made freewill-

offerings for the house of God, to erect
it on its site. 69According to their resources they gave to the building fund
sixty-one thousand darics of gold, five
thousand minas of silver, and one hundred priestly robes.
70 The priests, the Levites, and some
of the people lived in Jerusalem and
its vicinity;[b] and the singers, the gatekeepers, and the temple servants lived
in their towns, and all Israel in their
towns.

WORSHIP RESTORED AT JERUSALEM

3 When the seventh month came,
and the Israelites were in the
towns, the people gathered together in
Jerusalem. 2Then Jeshua son of Jozadak,
with his fellow priests, and Zerubbabel
son of Shealtiel with his kin set out to
build the altar of the God of Israel, to offer burnt-offerings on it, as prescribed
in the law of Moses the man of God.
3They set up the altar on its foundation, because they were in dread of the
neighbouring peoples, and they offered
burnt-offerings upon it to the LORD,
morning and evening. 4And they kept
the festival of booths,[c] as prescribed,
and offered the daily burnt-offerings by
number according to the ordinance, as
required for each day, 5and after that the
regular burnt-offerings, the offerings at
the new moon and at all the sacred festivals of the LORD, and the offerings of
everyone who made a freewill-offering
to the LORD. 6From the first day of
the seventh month they began to offer
burnt-offerings to the LORD. But the
foundation of the temple of the LORD
was not yet laid. 7So they gave money
to the masons and the carpenters, and
food, drink, and oil to the Sidonians and
the Tyrians to bring cedar trees from
Lebanon to the sea, to Joppa, according
to the grant that they had from King
Cyrus of Persia.

FOUNDATIONS LAID FOR THE TEMPLE

8 In the second year after their arrival at the house of God at Jerusalem,
in the second month, Zerubbabel son
of Shealtiel and Jeshua son of Jozadak
made a beginning, together with the
rest of their people, the priests and the
Levites and all who had come to Jerusalem from the captivity. They appointed
the Levites, from twenty years old and
upwards, to have the oversight of the
work on the house of the LORD. 9And
Jeshua with his sons and his kin, and
Kadmiel and his sons, Binnui and Hodaviah[d] along with the sons of Henadad,
the Levites, their sons and kin, together
took charge of the workers in the house
of God.
10 When the builders laid the foundation of the temple of the LORD, the
priests in their vestments were stationed to praise the LORD with trumpets, and the Levites, the sons of Asaph,
with cymbals, according to the directions of King David of Israel; 11and they
sang responsively, praising and giving
thanks to the LORD,

'For he is good,
for his steadfast love endures for
ever towards Israel.'

And all the people responded with
a great shout when they praised the
LORD, because the foundation of the
house of the LORD was laid. 12But many
of the priests and Levites and heads of
families, old people who had seen the
first house on its foundations, wept
with a loud voice when they saw this
house, though many shouted aloud for
joy, 13so that the people could not distinguish the sound of the joyful shout
from the sound of the people's weeping,
for the people shouted so loudly that the
sound was heard far away.

RESISTANCE TO REBUILDING THE TEMPLE

4 When the adversaries of Judah
and Benjamin heard that the returned exiles were building a temple to
the LORD, the God of Israel, 2they approached Zerubbabel and the heads of
families and said to them, 'Let us build
with you, for we worship your God as
you do, and we have been sacrificing to
him ever since the days of King Esar-
haddon of Assyria who brought us here.'
3But Zerubbabel, Jeshua, and the rest of
the heads of families in Israel said to
them, 'You shall have no part with us
in building a house to our God; but we
alone will build to the LORD, the God of
Israel, as King Cyrus of Persia has commanded us.'
4 Then the people of the land discouraged the people of Judah, and made
them afraid to build, 5and they bribed
officials to frustrate their plan throughout the reign of King Cyrus of Persia

[b] **2.70** 1 Esdras 5.46: Heb lacks *lived in Jerusalem and its vicinity* [c] **3.4** Or *tabernacles*; Heb *succoth* [d] **3.9** Compare 2.40; Neh 7.43; 1 Esdras 5.58: Heb *sons of Judah*

and until the reign of King Darius of
Persia.

REBUILDING OF JERUSALEM OPPOSED

6 In the reign of Ahasuerus, in his
accession year, they wrote an accusation
against the inhabitants of Judah and Jerusalem.

7 And in the days of Artaxerxes,
Bishlam and Mithredath and Tabeel
and the rest of their associates wrote
to King Artaxerxes of Persia; the letter
was written in Aramaic and translated.[e]
8Rehum the royal deputy and Shimshai
the scribe wrote a letter against Jerusalem to King Artaxerxes as follows 9(then
Rehum the royal deputy, Shimshai the
scribe, and the rest of their associates,
the judges, the envoys, the officials, the
Persians, the people of Erech, the Babylonians, the people of Susa, that is, the
Elamites, 10and the rest of the nations
whom the great and noble Osnappar
deported and settled in the cities of Samaria and in the rest of the province Beyond the River wrote—and now 11this is
a copy of the letter that they sent):

'To King Artaxerxes: Your servants,
the people of the province Beyond the
River, send greeting. And now 12may it
be known to the king that the Jews who
came up from you to us have gone to Jerusalem. They are rebuilding that rebellious and wicked city; they are finishing
the walls and repairing the foundations.
13Now may it be known to the king that,
if this city is rebuilt and the walls finished, they will not pay tribute, custom,
or toll, and the royal revenue will be reduced. 14Now because we share the salt
of the palace and it is not fitting for us to
witness the king's dishonour, therefore
we send and inform the king, 15so that
a search may be made in the annals of
your ancestors. You will discover in the
annals that this is a rebellious city, hurtful to kings and provinces, and that sedition was stirred up in it from long ago.
On that account this city was laid waste.
16We make known to the king that, if
this city is rebuilt and its walls finished,
you will then have no possession in the
province Beyond the River.'

17 The king sent an answer: 'To Rehum the royal deputy and Shimshai the
scribe and the rest of their associates
who live in Samaria and in the rest of
the province Beyond the River, greeting. And now 18the letter that you sent
to us has been read in translation before
me. 19So I made a decree, and someone
searched and discovered that this city
has risen against kings from long ago,
and that rebellion and sedition have
been made in it. 20Jerusalem has had
mighty kings who ruled over the whole
province Beyond the River, to whom
tribute, custom, and toll were paid.
21Therefore issue an order that these
people be made to cease, and that this
city be not rebuilt, until I make a decree.
22Moreover, take care not to be slack in
this matter; why should damage grow
to the hurt of the king?'

23 Then when the copy of King Artaxerxes' letter was read before Rehum
and the scribe Shimshai and their associates, they hurried to the Jews in Jerusalem and by force and power made
them cease. 24At that time the work on
the house of God in Jerusalem stopped
and was discontinued until the second year of the reign of King Darius of
Persia.

RESTORATION OF THE TEMPLE RESUMED

5 Now the prophets, Haggai[f] and
Zechariah son of Iddo, prophesied
to the Jews who were in Judah and Jerusalem, in the name of the God of Israel
who was over them. 2Then Zerubbabel
son of Shealtiel and Jeshua son of Jozadak set out to rebuild the house of God
in Jerusalem; and with them were the
prophets of God, helping them.

3 At the same time Tattenai the governor of the province Beyond the River
and Shethar-bozenai and their associates came to them and spoke to them
thus, 'Who gave you a decree to build
this house and to finish this structure?'
4They[g] also asked them this: 'What are
the names of the men who are building
this building?' 5But the eye of their God
was upon the elders of the Jews, and
they did not stop them until a report
reached Darius and then answer was returned by letter in reply to it.

6 The copy of the letter that Tattenai
the governor of the province Beyond the
River and Shethar-bozenai and his associates the envoys who were in the province Beyond the River sent to King Darius; 7they sent him a report, in which
was written as follows: 'To Darius the

[e] **4.7** Heb adds *in Aramaic,* indicating that 4.8–6.18 is in Aramaic. Another interpretation is *The letter was written in the Aramaic script and set forth in the Aramaic language* [f] **5.1** Aram adds *the prophet* [g] **5.4** Gk Syr: Aram *We*

king, all peace! 8May it be known to the
king that we went to the province of Judah, to the house of the great God. It is
being built of hewn stone, and timber
is laid in the walls; this work is being
done diligently and prospers in their
hands. 9Then we spoke to those elders
and asked them, "Who gave you a decree
to build this house and to finish this
structure?" 10We also asked them their
names, for your information, so that
we might write down the names of the
men at their head. 11This was their reply
to us: "We are the servants of the God of
heaven and earth, and we are rebuilding the house that was built many years
ago, which a great king of Israel built
and finished. 12But because our ancestors had angered the God of heaven, he
gave them into the hand of King Nebuchadnezzar of Babylon, the Chaldean,
who destroyed this house and carried
away the people to Babylonia. 13How-
ever, King Cyrus of Babylon, in the first
year of his reign, made a decree that this
house of God should be rebuilt. 14More-
over, the gold and silver vessels of the
house of God, which Nebuchadnezzar
had taken out of the temple in Jerusalem and had brought into the temple of
Babylon, these King Cyrus took out of
the temple of Babylon, and they were
delivered to a man named Sheshbazzar,
whom he had made governor. 15He said
to him, 'Take these vessels; go and put
them in the temple in Jerusalem, and
let the house of God be rebuilt on its
site.' 16Then this Sheshbazzar came and
laid the foundations of the house of God
in Jerusalem; and from that time until now it has been under construction,
and it is not yet finished." 17And now, if
it seems good to the king, have a search
made in the royal archives there in Babylon, to see whether a decree was issued
by King Cyrus for the rebuilding of this
house of God in Jerusalem. Let the king
send us his pleasure in this matter.'

THE DECREE OF DARIUS

6 Then King Darius made a decree,
and they searched the archives
where the documents were stored in
Babylon. 2But it was in Ecbatana, the
capital in the province of Media, that
a scroll was found on which this was
written: 'A record. 3In the first year of
his reign, King Cyrus issued a decree:
Concerning the house of God at Jerusalem, let the house be rebuilt, the place
where sacrifices are offered and burnt-
offerings are brought;[h] its height shall
be sixty cubits and its width sixty cubits, 4with three courses of hewn stones
and one course of timber; let the cost
be paid from the royal treasury. 5More-
over, let the gold and silver vessels of
the house of God, which Nebuchadnezzar took out of the temple in Jerusalem
and brought to Babylon, be restored and
brought back to the temple in Jerusalem, each to its place; you shall put them
in the house of God.'

6 'Now you, Tattenai, governor of the
province Beyond the River, Shethar-
bozenai, and you, their associates, the
envoys in the province Beyond the
River, keep away; 7let the work on this
house of God alone; let the governor
of the Jews and the elders of the Jews
rebuild this house of God on its site.
8Moreover, I make a decree regarding
what you shall do for these elders of the
Jews for the rebuilding of this house of
God: the cost is to be paid to these people, in full and without delay, from the
royal revenue, the tribute of the province Beyond the River. 9Whatever is
needed—young bulls, rams, or sheep for
burnt-offerings to the God of heaven,
wheat, salt, wine, or oil, as the priests
in Jerusalem require—let that be given
to them day by day without fail, 10so
that they may offer pleasing sacrifices
to the God of heaven, and pray for the
life of the king and his children. 11Fur-
thermore, I decree that if anyone alters
this edict, a beam shall be pulled out of
the house of the perpetrator, who then
shall be impaled on it. The house shall
be made a dunghill. 12May the God who
has established his name there overthrow any king or people that shall put
forth a hand to alter this, or to destroy
this house of God in Jerusalem. I, Darius, make a decree; let it be done with
all diligence.'

COMPLETION AND DEDICATION OF THE TEMPLE

13 Then, according to the word sent
by King Darius, Tattenai, the governor of the province Beyond the River,
Shethar-bozenai, and their associates
did with all diligence what King Darius
had ordered. 14So the elders of the Jews
built and prospered, through the prophesying of the prophet Haggai and Zechariah son of Iddo. They finished their
building by command of the God of Israel

[h] 6.3 Meaning of Aram uncertain

and by decree of Cyrus, Darius, and
King Artaxerxes of Persia; 15and this
house was finished on the third day of
the month of Adar, in the sixth year of
the reign of King Darius.

16 The people of Israel, the priests
and the Levites, and the rest of the returned exiles, celebrated the dedication
of this house of God with joy. 17They offered at the dedication of this house of
God one hundred bulls, two hundred
rams, four hundred lambs, and as a sin-
offering for all Israel twelve male goats,
according to the number of the tribes
of Israel. 18Then they set the priests in
their divisions and the Levites in their
courses for the service of God at Jerusalem, as it is written in the book of
Moses.

THE PASSOVER CELEBRATED

19 On the fourteenth day of the first
month the returned exiles kept the
passover. 20For both the priests and the
Levites had purified themselves; all of
them were clean. So they killed the passover lamb for all the returned exiles, for
their fellow-priests, and for themselves.
21It was eaten by the people of Israel
who had returned from exile, and also
by all who had joined them and separated themselves from the pollutions of
the nations of the land to worship the
LORD, the God of Israel. 22With joy they
celebrated the festival of unleavened
bread for seven days; for the LORD had
made them joyful, and had turned the
heart of the king of Assyria to them, so
that he aided them in the work on the
house of God, the God of Israel.

THE COMING AND WORK OF EZRA

7 After this, in the reign of King Artaxerxes of Persia, Ezra son of Seraiah, son of Azariah, son of Hilkiah, 2son
of Shallum, son of Zadok, son of Ahitub,
3son of Amariah, son of Azariah, son of
Meraioth, 4son of Zerahiah, son of Uzzi,
son of Bukki, 5son of Abishua, son of
Phinehas, son of Eleazar, son of the chief
priest Aaron— 6this Ezra went up from
Babylonia. He was a scribe skilled in the
law of Moses that the LORD the God of
Israel had given; and the king granted
him all that he asked, for the hand of the
LORD his God was upon him.

7 Some of the people of Israel, and
some of the priests and Levites, the
singers and gatekeepers, and the temple servants also went up to Jerusalem,
in the seventh year of King Artaxerxes.
8They came to Jerusalem in the fifth
month, which was in the seventh year
of the king. 9On the first day of the first
month the journey up from Babylon
was begun, and on the first day of the
fifth month he came to Jerusalem, for
the gracious hand of his God was upon
him. 10For Ezra had set his heart to
study the law of the LORD, and to do it,
and to teach the statutes and ordinances
in Israel.

THE LETTER OF ARTAXERXES TO EZRA

11 This is a copy of the letter that
King Artaxerxes gave to the priest Ezra,
the scribe, a scholar of the text of the
commandments of the LORD and his
statutes for Israel: 12'Artaxerxes, king
of kings, to the priest Ezra, the scribe
of the law of the God of heaven: Peace.[i]
And now 13I decree that any of the people of Israel or their priests or Levites
in my kingdom who freely offers to go
to Jerusalem may go with you. 14For
you are sent by the king and his seven
counsellors to make inquiries about
Judah and Jerusalem according to the
law of your God, which is in your hand,
15and also to convey the silver and gold
that the king and his counsellors have
freely offered to the God of Israel, whose
dwelling is in Jerusalem, 16with all the
silver and gold that you shall find in
the whole province of Babylonia, and
with the freewill-offerings of the people
and the priests, given willingly for the
house of their God in Jerusalem. 17With
this money, then, you shall with all diligence buy bulls, rams, and lambs, and
their grain-offerings and their drink-
offerings, and you shall offer them on
the altar of the house of your God in
Jerusalem. 18Whatever seems good to
you and your colleagues to do with the
rest of the silver and gold, you may do,
according to the will of your God. 19The
vessels that have been given you for the
service of the house of your God, you
shall deliver before the God of Jerusalem. 20And whatever else is required for
the house of your God, which you are
responsible for providing, you may provide out of the king's treasury.

21 'I, King Artaxerxes, decree to all
the treasurers in the province Beyond
the River: Whatever the priest Ezra, the
scribe of the law of the God of heaven,
requires of you, let it be done with all

[i] 7.12 Syr Vg 1 Esdras 8.9: Aram *Perfect*

diligence, 22up to one hundred talents
of silver, one hundred cors of wheat,
one hundred baths[j] of wine, one hundred baths[k] of oil, and unlimited salt.
23Whatever is commanded by the God of
heaven, let it be done with zeal for the
house of the God of heaven, or wrath
will come upon the realm of the king
and his heirs. 24We also notify you that
it shall not be lawful to impose tribute,
custom, or toll on any of the priests, the
Levites, the singers, the doorkeepers,
the temple servants, or other servants
of this house of God.

25 'And you, Ezra, according to the
God-given wisdom you possess, appoint magistrates and judges who may
judge all the people in the province Beyond the River who know the laws of
your God; and you shall teach those who
do not know them. 26All who will not
obey the law of your God and the law of
the king, let judgement be strictly executed on them, whether for death or for
banishment or for confiscation of their
goods or for imprisonment.'

27 Blessed be the LORD, the God of
our ancestors, who put such a thing as
this into the heart of the king to glorify
the house of the LORD in Jerusalem,
28and who extended to me steadfast
love before the king and his counsellors,
and before all the king's mighty officers.
I took courage, for the hand of the LORD
my God was upon me, and I gathered
leaders from Israel to go up with me.

HEADS OF FAMILIES WHO RETURNED WITH EZRA

8 These are their family heads, and
this is the genealogy of those who
went up with me from Babylonia, in
the reign of King Artaxerxes: 2Of the
descendants of Phinehas, Gershom. Of
Ithamar, Daniel. Of David, Hattush, 3of
the descendants of Shecaniah. Of Parosh, Zechariah, with whom were registered one hundred and fifty males. 4Of
the descendants of Pahath-moab, Eliehoenai son of Zerahiah, and with him
two hundred males. 5Of the descendants of Zattu,[l] Shecaniah son of Jahaziel, and with him three hundred males.
6Of the descendants of Adin, Ebed son
of Jonathan, and with him fifty males.
7Of the descendants of Elam, Jeshaiah
son of Athaliah, and with him seventy
males. 8Of the descendants of Shephatiah, Zebadiah son of Michael, and with
him eighty males. 9Of the descendants
of Joab, Obadiah son of Jehiel, and with
him two hundred and eighteen males.
10Of the descendants of Bani,[m] Shelomith son of Josiphiah, and with him
one hundred and sixty males. 11Of the
descendants of Bebai, Zechariah son
of Bebai, and with him twenty-eight
males. 12Of the descendants of Azgad,
Johanan son of Hakkatan, and with him
one hundred and ten males. 13Of the
descendants of Adonikam, those who
came later, their names being Eliphelet,
Jeuel, and Shemaiah, and with them
sixty males. 14Of the descendants of Bigvai, Uthai and Zaccur, and with them
seventy males.

SERVANTS FOR THE TEMPLE

15 I gathered them by the river that
runs to Ahava, and there we camped for
three days. As I reviewed the people and
the priests, I found there none of the descendants of Levi. 16Then I sent for Eliezer, Ariel, Shemaiah, Elnathan, Jarib,
Elnathan, Nathan, Zechariah, and Meshullam, who were leaders, and for Joiarib and Elnathan, who were wise, 17and
sent them to Iddo, the leader at the place
called Casiphia, telling them what to say
to Iddo and his colleagues the temple
servants at Casiphia, namely, to send
us ministers for the house of our God.
18Since the gracious hand of our God
was upon us, they brought us a man of
discretion, of the descendants of Mahli
son of Levi son of Israel, namely Sherebiah, with his sons and kin, eighteen;
19also Hashabiah and with him Jeshaiah of the descendants of Merari, with
his kin and their sons, twenty; 20besides
two hundred and twenty of the temple
servants, whom David and his officials
had set apart to attend the Levites.
These were all mentioned by name.

FASTING AND PRAYER FOR PROTECTION

21 Then I proclaimed a fast there, at
the river Ahava, that we might deny
ourselves[n] before our God, to seek from
him a safe journey for ourselves, our
children, and all our possessions. 22For I
was ashamed to ask the king for a band
of soldiers and cavalry to protect us
against the enemy on our way, since we
had told the king that the hand of our
God is gracious to all who seek him, but
his power and his wrath are against all

[j] **7.22** A Heb measure of volume [k] **7.22** A Heb measure of volume [l] **8.5** Gk 1 Esdras 8.32: Heb lacks *of Zattu* [m] **8.10** Gk 1 Esdras 8.36: Heb lacks *Bani* [n] **8.21** Or *might fast*

who forsake him. 23So we fasted and pe-
titioned our God for this, and he listened
to our entreaty.

GIFTS FOR THE TEMPLE

24 Then I set apart twelve of the
leading priests: Sherebiah, Hashabiah,
and ten of their kin with them. 25And I
weighed out to them the silver and the
gold and the vessels, the offering for the
house of our God that the king, his counsellors, his lords, and all Israel there
present had offered; 26I weighed out into
their hand six hundred and fifty talents
of silver, and one hundred silver vessels
worth ... talents,[o] and one hundred talents of gold, 27twenty gold bowls worth
a thousand darics, and two vessels of
fine polished bronze as precious as gold.
28And I said to them, 'You are holy to
the LORD, and the vessels are holy; and
the silver and the gold are a freewill-
offering to the LORD, the God of your
ancestors. 29Guard them and keep them
until you weigh them before the chief
priests and the Levites and the heads of
families in Israel at Jerusalem, within
the chambers of the house of the LORD.'
30So the priests and the Levites took
over the silver, the gold, and the vessels
as they were weighed out, to bring them
to Jerusalem, to the house of our God.

THE RETURN TO JERUSALEM

31 Then we left the river Ahava on
the twelfth day of the first month, to go
to Jerusalem; the hand of our God was
upon us, and he delivered us from the
hand of the enemy and from ambushes
along the way. 32We came to Jerusalem and remained there for three days.
33On the fourth day, within the house
of our God, the silver, the gold, and the
vessels were weighed into the hands of
the priest Meremoth son of Uriah, and
with him was Eleazar son of Phinehas,
and with them were the Levites, Jozabad son of Jeshua and Noadiah son of
Binnui. 34The total was counted and
weighed, and the weight of everything
was recorded.

35 At that time those who had come
from captivity, the returned exiles, offered burnt-offerings to the God of Israel, twelve bulls for all Israel, ninety-
six rams, seventy-seven lambs, and
as a sin-offering twelve male goats; all
this was a burnt-offering to the LORD.
36They also delivered the king's com-
missions to the king's satraps and to the
governors of the province Beyond the
River; and they supported the people
and the house of God.

DENUNCIATION OF MIXED MARRIAGES

9 After these things had been done,
the officials approached me and
said, 'The people of Israel, the priests,
and the Levites have not separated
themselves from the peoples of the
lands with their abominations, from
the Canaanites, the Hittites, the Perizzites, the Jebusites, the Ammonites,
the Moabites, the Egyptians, and the
Amorites. 2For they have taken some
of their daughters as wives for themselves and for their sons. Thus the holy
seed has mixed itself with the peoples of
the lands, and in this faithlessness the
officials and leaders have led the way.'
3When I heard this, I tore my garment
and my mantle, and pulled hair from
my head and beard, and sat appalled.
4Then all who trembled at the words of
the God of Israel, because of the faithlessness of the returned exiles, gathered
around me while I sat appalled until the
evening sacrifice.

EZRA'S PRAYER

5 At the evening sacrifice I got up
from my fasting, with my garments and
my mantle torn, and fell on my knees,
spread out my hands to the LORD my
God, 6and said,

'O my God, I am too ashamed and
embarrassed to lift my face to you,
my God, for our iniquities have risen
higher than our heads, and our guilt has
mounted up to the heavens. 7From the
days of our ancestors to this day we have
been deep in guilt, and for our iniquities
we, our kings, and our priests have been
handed over to the kings of the lands, to
the sword, to captivity, to plundering,
and to utter shame, as is now the case.
8But now for a brief moment favour has
been shown by the LORD our God, who
has left us a remnant, and given us a
stake in his holy place, in order that he[p]
may brighten our eyes and grant us a
little sustenance in our slavery. 9For we
are slaves; yet our God has not forsaken
us in our slavery, but has extended to
us his steadfast love before the kings of
Persia, to give us new life to set up the
house of our God, to repair its ruins, and
to give us a wall in Judea and Jerusalem.

[o] 8.26 The number of talents is lacking
[p] 9.8 Heb *our God*

10 'And now, our God, what shall
we say after this? For we have forsaken
your commandments, 11which you commanded by your servants the prophets,
saying, "The land that you are entering
to possess is a land unclean with the pollutions of the peoples of the lands, with
their abominations. They have filled it
from end to end with their uncleanness.
12Therefore do not give your daughters
to their sons, neither take their daughters for your sons, and never seek their
peace or prosperity, so that you may be
strong and eat the good of the land and
leave it for an inheritance to your children for ever." 13After all that has come
upon us for our evil deeds and for our
great guilt, seeing that you, our God,
have punished us less than our iniquities deserved and have given us such a
remnant as this, 14shall we break your
commandments again and intermarry
with the peoples who practise these
abominations? Would you not be angry
with us until you destroy us without
remnant or survivor? 15O LORD, God of
Israel, you are just, but we have escaped
as a remnant, as is now the case. Here
we are before you in our guilt, though
no one can face you because of this.'

THE PEOPLE'S RESPONSE

10 While Ezra prayed and made
confession, weeping and throwing himself down before the house of
God, a very great assembly of men,
women, and children gathered to him
out of Israel; the people also wept bitterly. 2Shecaniah son of Jehiel, of the
descendants of Elam, addressed Ezra,
saying, 'We have broken faith with our
God and have married foreign women
from the peoples of the land, but even
now there is hope for Israel in spite of
this. 3So now let us make a covenant
with our God to send away all these
wives and their children, according to
the counsel of my lord and of those who
tremble at the commandment of our
God; and let it be done according to the
law. 4Take action, for it is your duty, and
we are with you; be strong, and do it.'
5Then Ezra stood up and made the leading priests, the Levites, and all Israel
swear that they would do as had been
said. So they swore.

FOREIGN WIVES AND THEIR CHILDREN REJECTED

6 Then Ezra withdrew from before
the house of God, and went to the chamber of Jehohanan son of Eliashib, where
he spent the night.[q] He did not eat
bread or drink water, for he was mourning over the faithlessness of the exiles.
7They made a proclamation throughout
Judah and Jerusalem to all the returned
exiles that they should assemble at Jerusalem, 8and that if any did not come
within three days, by order of the officials and the elders all their property
should be forfeited, and they themselves
banned from the congregation of the
exiles.

9 Then all the people of Judah and
Benjamin assembled at Jerusalem
within the three days; it was the ninth
month, on the twentieth day of the
month. All the people sat in the open
square before the house of God, trembling because of this matter and because
of the heavy rain. 10Then Ezra the priest
stood up and said to them, 'You have
trespassed and married foreign women,
and so increased the guilt of Israel.
11Now make confession to the LORD the
God of your ancestors, and do his will;
separate yourselves from the peoples of
the land and from the foreign wives.'
12Then all the assembly answered with
a loud voice, 'It is so; we must do as you
have said. 13But the people are many,
and it is a time of heavy rain; we cannot
stand in the open. Nor is this a task for
one day or for two, for many of us have
transgressed in this matter. 14Let our
officials represent the whole assembly,
and let all in our towns who have taken
foreign wives come at appointed times,
and with them the elders and judges of
every town, until the fierce wrath of our
God on this account is averted from us.'
15Only Jonathan son of Asahel and Jah-
zeiah son of Tikvah opposed this, and
Meshullam and Shabbethai the Levites
supported them.

16 Then the returned exiles did so.
Ezra the priest selected men,[r] heads of
families, according to their families,
each of them designated by name. On
the first day of the tenth month they
sat down to examine the matter. 17By
the first day of the first month they had
come to the end of all the men who had
married foreign women.

18 There were found of the descendants of the priests who had married
foreign women, of the descendants of
Jeshua son of Jozadak and his brothers:

[q] **10.6** 1 Esdras 9.2: Heb *where he went*
[r] **10.16** 1 Esdras 9.16: Syr: Heb *And there were selected Ezra,*

Maaseiah, Eliezer, Jarib, and Gedaliah.
19They pledged themselves to send away
their wives, and their guilt-offering was
a ram of the flock for their guilt. 20Of the
descendants of Immer: Hanani and Zebadiah. 21Of the descendants of Harim:
Maaseiah, Elijah, Shemaiah, Jehiel, and
Uzziah. 22Of the descendants of Pashhur: Elioenai, Maaseiah, Ishmael, Nethanel, Jozabad, and Elasah.

23 Of the Levites: Jozabad, Shimei,
Kelaiah (that is, Kelita), Pethahiah, Judah, and Eliezer. 24Of the singers: Eliashib. Of the gatekeepers: Shallum, Telem, and Uri.

25 And of Israel: of the descendants
of Parosh: Ramiah, Izziah, Malchijah,
Mijamin, Eleazar, Hashabiah,[s] and Benaiah. 26Of the descendants of Elam:
Mattaniah, Zechariah, Jehiel, Abdi, Jeremoth, and Elijah. 27Of the descendants
of Zattu: Elioenai, Eliashib, Mattaniah,
Jeremoth, Zabad, and Aziza. 28Of the
descendants of Bebai: Jehohanan, Hananiah, Zabbai, and Athlai. 29Of the descendants of Bani: Meshullam, Malluch,
Adaiah, Jashub, Sheal, and Jeremoth.
30Of the descendants of Pahath-moab:
Adna, Chelal, Benaiah, Maaseiah, Mattaniah, Bezalel, Binnui, and Manasseh.
31Of the descendants of Harim: Eliezer,
Isshijah, Malchijah, Shemaiah, Shim-
eon, 32Benjamin, Malluch, and Shemariah. 33Of the descendants of Hashum:
Mattenai, Mattattah, Zabad, Eliphelet,
Jeremai, Manasseh, and Shimei. 34Of
the descendants of Bani: Maadai, Amram, Uel, 35Benaiah, Bedeiah, Cheluhi,
36Vaniah, Meremoth, Eliashib, 37Matta-
niah, Mattenai, and Jaasu. 38Of the descendants of Binnui:[t] Shimei, 39Shele-
miah, Nathan, Adaiah, 40Machnadebai,
Shashai, Sharai, 41Azarel, Shelemiah,
Shemariah, 42Shallum, Amariah, and
Joseph. 43Of the descendants of Nebo:
Jeiel, Mattithiah, Zabad, Zebina, Jad-
dai, Joel, and Benaiah. 44All these had
married foreign women, and they sent
them away with their children.[u]

[s] **10.25** 1 Esdras 9.26 Gk: Heb *Malchijah*
[t] **10.38** Gk: Heb *Bani, Binnui* [u] **10.44** 1 Esdras 9.36; meaning of Heb uncertain

NEHEMIAH

The last part of the Chronicler's history is presented as the book of Nehemiah. The layman Nehemiah was responsible for administrative affairs and for rebuilding the walls of Jerusalem in the period of the restoration. The first portion of the text narrates the deeds of Nehemiah (chs. 1–7). The second half describes the formal promulgation of the law (chs. 8–13).

A passage from Nehemiah is read on the Third Sunday of the Year in Cycle C. It is the text that describes Ezra the priest reading from the law before the people as they rededicate themselves to God before the newly constructed city walls.

NEHEMIAH PRAYS FOR HIS PEOPLE

1 The words of Nehemiah son of Hacaliah. In the month of Chislev, in
the twentieth year, while I was in Susa
the capital, 2one of my brothers, Hanani, came with certain men from Judah; and I asked them about the Jews
that survived, those who had escaped
the captivity, and about Jerusalem.
3They replied, 'The survivors there in
the province who escaped captivity are
in great trouble and shame; the wall of
Jerusalem is broken down, and its gates
have been destroyed by fire.'
4 When I heard these words I sat
down and wept, and mourned for days,
fasting and praying before the God of
heaven. 5I said, 'O LORD God of heaven,
the great and awesome God who keeps
covenant and steadfast love with those
who love him and keep his commandments; 6let your ear be attentive and
your eyes open to hear the prayer of
your servant that I now pray before you
day and night for your servants the people of Israel, confessing the sins of the
people of Israel, which we have sinned
against you. Both I and my family have
sinned. 7We have offended you deeply,
failing to keep the commandments, the
statutes, and the ordinances that you
commanded your servant Moses. 8Re-
member the word that you commanded
your servant Moses, "If you are unfaithful, I will scatter you among the peoples;
9but if you return to me and keep my
commandments and do them, though
your outcasts are under the farthest
skies, I will gather them from there
and bring them to the place at which
I have chosen to establish my name."
10They are your servants and your people, whom you redeemed by your great
power and your strong hand. 11O Lord,
let your ear be attentive to the prayer of
your servant, and to the prayer of your
servants who delight in revering your
name. Give success to your servant today, and grant him mercy in the sight
of this man!'
At the time, I was cupbearer to the
king.

NEHEMIAH SENT TO JUDAH

2 In the month of Nisan, in the twentieth year of King Artaxerxes, when
wine was served to him, I carried the
wine and gave it to the king. Now, I had
never been sad in his presence before.
2So the king said to me, 'Why is your
face sad, since you are not sick? This can
only be sadness of the heart.' Then I was
very much afraid. 3I said to the king,
'May the king live for ever! Why should
my face not be sad, when the city, the
place of my ancestors' graves, lies waste,
and its gates have been destroyed by
fire?' 4Then the king said to me, 'What
do you request?' So I prayed to the God
of heaven. 5Then I said to the king, 'If

it pleases the king, and if your servant has found favour with you, I ask that you send me to Judah, to the city of my ancestors' graves, so that I may rebuild it.' 6The king said to me (the queen also was sitting beside him), 'How long will you be gone, and when will you return?' So it pleased the king to send me, and I set him a date. 7Then I said to the king, 'If it pleases the king, let letters be given me to the governors of the province Beyond the River, that they may grant me passage until I arrive in Judah; 8and a letter to Asaph, the keeper of the king's forest, directing him to give me timber to make beams for the gates of the temple fortress, and for the wall of the city, and for the house that I shall occupy.' And the king granted me what I asked, for the gracious hand of my God was upon me.

9 Then I came to the governors of the province Beyond the River, and gave them the king's letters. Now the king had sent officers of the army and cavalry with me. 10When Sanballat the Horonite and Tobiah the Ammonite official heard this, it displeased them greatly that someone had come to seek the welfare of the people of Israel.

NEHEMIAH'S INSPECTION OF THE WALLS

11 So I came to Jerusalem and was there for three days. 12Then I got up during the night, I and a few men with me; I told no one what my God had put into my heart to do for Jerusalem. The only animal I took was the animal I rode. 13I went out by night by the Valley Gate past the Dragon's Spring and to the Dung Gate, and I inspected the walls of Jerusalem that had been broken down and its gates that had been destroyed by fire. 14Then I went on to the Fountain Gate and to the King's Pool; but there was no place for the animal I was riding to continue. 15So I went up by way of the valley by night and inspected the wall. Then I turned back and entered by the Valley Gate, and so returned. 16The officials did not know where I had gone or what I was doing; I had not yet told the Jews, the priests, the nobles, the officials, and the rest that were to do the work.

DECISION TO RESTORE THE WALLS

17 Then I said to them, 'You see the trouble we are in, how Jerusalem lies in ruins with its gates burnt. Come, let us rebuild the wall of Jerusalem, so that we may no longer suffer disgrace.' 18I told them that the hand of my God had been gracious upon me, and also the words that the king had spoken to me. Then they said, 'Let us start building!' So they committed themselves to the common good. 19But when Sanballat the Horonite and Tobiah the Ammonite official, and Geshem the Arab heard of it, they mocked and ridiculed us, saying, 'What is this that you are doing? Are you rebelling against the king?' 20Then I replied to them, 'The God of heaven is the one who will give us success, and we his servants are going to start building; but you have no share or claim or historic right in Jerusalem.'

ORGANIZATION OF THE WORK

3 Then the high priest Eliashib set to work with his fellow-priests and rebuilt the Sheep Gate. They consecrated it and set up its doors; they consecrated it as far as the Tower of the Hundred and as far as the Tower of Hananel. 2And the men of Jericho built next to him. And next to them[a] Zaccur son of Imri built.

3 The sons of Hassenaah built the Fish Gate; they laid its beams and set up its doors, its bolts, and its bars. 4Next to them Meremoth son of Uriah son of Hakkoz made repairs. Next to them Meshullam son of Berechiah son of Meshezabel made repairs. Next to them Zadok son of Baana made repairs. 5Next to them the Tekoites made repairs; but their nobles would not put their shoulders to the work of their Lord.[b]

6 Joiada son of Paseah and Meshullam son of Besodeiah repaired the Old Gate; they laid its beams and set up its doors, its bolts, and its bars. 7Next to them repairs were made by Melatiah the Gibeonite and Jadon the Meronothite—the men of Gibeon and of Mizpah—who were under the jurisdiction of[c] the governor of the province Beyond the River. 8Next to them Uzziel son of Harhaiah, one of the goldsmiths, made repairs. Next to him Hananiah, one of the perfumers, made repairs; and they restored Jerusalem as far as the Broad Wall. 9Next to them Rephaiah son of Hur, ruler of half the district of[d] Jerusalem, made repairs. 10Next to them Jedaiah son of Harumaph made repairs opposite his house; and next to him Hattush son

[a] 3.2 Heb *him* [b] 3.5 Or *lords* [c] 3.7 Meaning of Heb uncertain [d] 3.9 Or *supervisor of half the portion assigned to*

of Hashabneiah made repairs. 11Malchi-
jah son of Harim and Hasshub son of
Pahath-moab repaired another section
and the Tower of the Ovens. 12Next to
him Shallum son of Hallohesh, ruler of
half the district of[e] Jerusalem, made repairs, he and his daughters.

13 Hanun and the inhabitants of Zanoah repaired the Valley Gate; they rebuilt it and set up its doors, its bolts, and
its bars, and repaired a thousand cubits
of the wall, as far as the Dung Gate.

14 Malchijah son of Rechab, ruler
of the district of[f] Beth-haccherem, repaired the Dung Gate; he rebuilt it and
set up its doors, its bolts, and its bars.

15 And Shallum son of Col-hozeh,
ruler of the district of[g] Mizpah, repaired
the Fountain Gate; he rebuilt it and covered it and set up its doors, its bolts, and
its bars; and he built the wall of the Pool
of Shelah of the king's garden, as far as
the stairs that go down from the City
of David. 16After him Nehemiah son of
Azbuk, ruler of half the district of[h] Beth-
zur, repaired from a point opposite the
graves of David, as far as the artificial
pool and the house of the warriors. 17Af-
ter him the Levites made repairs: Rehum
son of Bani; next to him Hashabiah,
ruler of half the district of[i] Keilah, made
repairs for his district. 18After him their
kin made repairs: Binnui,[j] son of Henadad, ruler of half the district of[k] Keilah;
19next to him Ezer son of Jeshua, ruler[l]
of Mizpah, repaired another section opposite the ascent to the armoury at the
Angle. 20After him Baruch son of Zabbai
repaired another section from the Angle to the door of the house of the high
priest Eliashib. 21After him Meremoth
son of Uriah son of Hakkoz repaired another section from the door of the house
of Eliashib to the end of the house of Eliashib. 22After him the priests, the men
of the surrounding area, made repairs.
23After them Benjamin and Hasshub
made repairs opposite their house. After them Azariah son of Maaseiah son
of Ananiah made repairs beside his own
house. 24After him Binnui son of Henadad repaired another section, from the
house of Azariah to the Angle and to the
corner. 25Palal son of Uzai repaired opposite the Angle and the tower projecting from the upper house of the king at
the court of the guard. After him Pedaiah son of Parosh 26and the temple servants living[m] on Ophel made repairs up
to a point opposite the Water Gate on the
east and the projecting tower. 27After
him the Tekoites repaired another section opposite the great projecting tower
as far as the wall of Ophel.

28 Above the Horse Gate the priests
made repairs, each one opposite his
own house. 29After them Zadok son of
Immer made repairs opposite his own
house. After him Shemaiah son of Shecaniah, the keeper of the East Gate, made
repairs. 30After him Hananiah son of
Shelemiah and Hanun sixth son of Za-
laph repaired another section. After
him Meshullam son of Berechiah made
repairs opposite his living quarters.
31After him Malchijah, one of the goldsmiths, made repairs as far as the house
of the temple servants and of the merchants, opposite the Muster Gate,[n] and
to the upper room of the corner. 32And
between the upper room of the corner
and the Sheep Gate the goldsmiths and
the merchants made repairs.

HOSTILE PLOTS THWARTED

4[o] Now when Sanballat heard that we
were building the wall, he was angry and greatly enraged, and he mocked
the Jews. 2He said in the presence of his
associates and of the army of Samaria,
'What are these feeble Jews doing? Will
they restore things? Will they sacrifice?
Will they finish it in a day? Will they
revive the stones out of the heaps of
rubbish—and burnt ones at that?' 3To-
biah the Ammonite was beside him,
and he said, 'That stone wall they are
building—any fox going up on it would
break it down!' 4Hear, O our God, for we
are despised; turn their taunt back on
their own heads, and give them over as
plunder in a land of captivity. 5Do not
cover their guilt, and do not let their sin
be blotted out from your sight; for they
have hurled insults in the face of the
builders.

6 So we rebuilt the wall, and all the
wall was joined together to half its
height; for the people had a mind to
work.

7[p] But when Sanballat and Tobiah
and the Arabs and the Ammonites and

[e] 3.12 Or *supervisor of half the portion assigned to*
[f] 3.14 Or *supervisor of the portion assigned to*
[g] 3.15 Or *supervisor of the portion assigned to*
[h] 3.16 Or *supervisor of half the portion assigned to*
[i] 3.17 Or *supervisor of half the portion assigned to*
[j] 3.18 Gk Syr Compare verse 24, 10.9: Heb *Bavvai*
[k] 3.18 Or *supervisor of half the portion assigned to*
[l] 3.19 Or *supervisor*
[m] 3.26 Cn: Heb *were living*
[n] 3.31 Or *Hammiphkad Gate*
[o] 4.1 Ch 3.33 in Heb
[p] 4.7 Ch 4.1 in Heb

the Ashdodites heard that the repairing
of the walls of Jerusalem was going forward and the gaps were beginning to
be closed, they were very angry, 8and
all plotted together to come and fight
against Jerusalem and to cause confusion in it. 9So we prayed to our God, and
set a guard as a protection against them
day and night.

10 But Judah said, 'The strength
of the burden-bearers is failing, and
there is too much rubbish, so that we
are unable to work on the wall.' 11And
our enemies said, 'They will not know
or see anything before we come upon
them and kill them and stop the work.'
12When the Jews who lived near them
came, they said to us ten times, 'From
all the places where they live[q] they will
come up against us.'[r] 13So in the lowest parts of the space behind the wall,
in open places, I stationed the people
according to their families,[s] with their
swords, their spears, and their bows.
14After I looked these things over, I
stood up and said to the nobles and
the officials and the rest of the people,
'Do not be afraid of them. Remember
the LORD, who is great and awesome,
and fight for your kin, your sons, your
daughters, your wives, and your homes.'

15 When our enemies heard that
their plot was known to us, and that
God had frustrated it, we all returned to
the wall, each to his work. 16From that
day on, half of my servants worked on
construction, and half held the spears,
shields, bows, and body-armour; and
the leaders posted themselves behind
the whole house of Judah, 17who were
building the wall. The burden-bearers
carried their loads in such a way that
each laboured on the work with one
hand and with the other held a weapon.
18And each of the builders had his sword
strapped at his side while he built. The
man who sounded the trumpet was beside me. 19And I said to the nobles, the
officials, and the rest of the people, 'The
work is great and widely spread out, and
we are separated far from one another
on the wall. 20Rally to us wherever you
hear the sound of the trumpet. Our God
will fight for us.'

21 So we laboured at the work, and
half of them held the spears from break
of dawn until the stars came out. 22I also
said to the people at that time, 'Let every man and his servant pass the night
inside Jerusalem, so that they may be a
guard for us by night and may labour
by day.' 23So neither I nor my brothers
nor my servants nor the men of the
guard who followed me ever took off
our clothes; each kept his weapon in his
right hand.[t]

NEHEMIAH DEALS WITH OPPRESSION

5 Now there was a great outcry of the
people and of their wives against
their Jewish kin. 2For there were those
who said, 'With our sons and our daughters, we are many; we must get grain, so
that we may eat and stay alive.' 3There
were also those who said, 'We are having
to pledge our fields, our vineyards, and
our houses in order to get grain during
the famine.' 4And there were those who
said, 'We are having to borrow money
on our fields and vineyards to pay the
king's tax. 5Now our flesh is the same
as that of our kindred; our children are
the same as their children; and yet we
are forcing our sons and daughters to be
slaves, and some of our daughters have
been ravished; we are powerless, and
our fields and vineyards now belong to
others.'

6 I was very angry when I heard
their outcry and these complaints. 7Af-
ter thinking it over, I brought charges
against the nobles and the officials; I
said to them, 'You are all taking interest from your own people.' And I called a
great assembly to deal with them, 8and
said to them, 'As far as we were able, we
have bought back our Jewish kindred
who had been sold to other nations; but
now you are selling your own kin, who
must then be bought back by us!' They
were silent, and could not find a word
to say. 9So I said, 'The thing that you
are doing is not good. Should you not
walk in the fear of our God, to prevent
the taunts of the nations our enemies?
10Moreover, I and my brothers and my
servants are lending them money and
grain. Let us stop this taking of interest. 11Restore to them, this very day,
their fields, their vineyards, their olive orchards, and their houses, and the
interest on money, grain, wine, and
oil that you have been exacting from
them.' 12Then they said, 'We will restore
everything and demand nothing more
from them. We will do as you say.' And
I called the priests, and made them take

[q] 4.12 Cn: Heb *you return* [r] 4.12 Compare Gk Syr: Meaning of Heb uncertain [s] 4.13 Meaning of Heb uncertain [t] 4.23 Cn: Heb *each his weapon the water*

an oath to do as they had promised. 13 I
also shook out the fold of my garment
and said, 'So may God shake out everyone from house and from property who
does not perform this promise. Thus
may they be shaken out and emptied.'
And all the assembly said, 'Amen', and
praised the LORD. And the people did as
they had promised.

THE GENEROSITY OF NEHEMIAH

14 Moreover, from the time that I
was appointed to be their governor in
the land of Judah, from the twentieth
year to the thirty-second year of King
Artaxerxes, twelve years, neither I nor
my brothers ate the food allowance of
the governor. 15 The former governors
who were before me laid heavy burdens
on the people, and took food and wine
from them, besides forty shekels of silver. Even their servants lorded it over
the people. But I did not do so, because
of the fear of God. 16 Indeed, I devoted
myself to the work on this wall, and acquired no land; and all my servants were
gathered there for the work. 17 Moreover,
there were at my table one hundred and
fifty people, Jews and officials, besides
those who came to us from the nations
around us. 18 Now that which was prepared for one day was one ox and six
choice sheep; also fowls were prepared
for me, and every ten days skins of wine
in abundance; yet with all this I did not
demand the food allowance of the governor, because of the heavy burden of
labour on the people. 19 Remember for
my good, O my God, all that I have done
for this people.

INTRIGUES OF ENEMIES FOILED

6 Now when it was reported to Sanballat and Tobiah and to Geshem
the Arab and to the rest of our enemies that I had built the wall and that
there was no gap left in it (though up
to that time I had not set up the doors
in the gates), 2 Sanballat and Geshem
sent to me, saying, 'Come and let us
meet together in one of the villages in
the plain of Ono.' But they intended to
do me harm. 3 So I sent messengers to
them, saying, 'I am doing a great work
and I cannot come down. Why should
the work stop while I leave it to come
down to you?' 4 They sent to me four
times in this way, and I answered them
in the same manner. 5 In the same way
Sanballat for the fifth time sent his servant to me with an open letter in his
hand. 6 In it was written, 'It is reported
among the nations—and Geshem[u] also
says it—that you and the Jews intend to
rebel; that is why you are building the
wall; and according to this report you
wish to become their king. 7 You have
also set up prophets to proclaim in Jerusalem concerning you, "There is a king
in Judah!" And now it will be reported
to the king according to these words.
So come, therefore, and let us confer together.' 8 Then I sent to him, saying, 'No
such things as you say have been done;
you are inventing them out of your own
mind' 9—for they all wanted to frighten
us, thinking, 'Their hands will drop
from the work, and it will not be done.'
But now, O God, strengthen my hands.

10 One day when I went into the
house of Shemaiah son of Delaiah son
of Mehetabel, who was confined to his
house, he said, 'Let us meet together in
the house of God, within the temple,
and let us close the doors of the temple, for they are coming to kill you; indeed, tonight they are coming to kill
you.' 11 But I said, 'Should a man like me
run away? Would a man like me go into
the temple to save his life? I will not go
in!' 12 Then I perceived and saw that God
had not sent him at all, but he had pronounced the prophecy against me because Tobiah and Sanballat had hired
him. 13 He was hired for this purpose,
to intimidate me and make me sin by
acting in this way, and so they could
give me a bad name, in order to taunt
me. 14 Remember Tobiah and Sanballat, O my God, according to these things
that they did, and also the prophetess
Noadiah and the rest of the prophets
who wanted to make me afraid.

THE WALL COMPLETED

15 So the wall was finished on the
twenty-fifth day of the month Elul, in
fifty-two days. 16 And when all our enemies heard of it, all the nations around
us were afraid[v] and fell greatly in their
own esteem; for they perceived that this
work had been accomplished with the
help of our God. 17 Moreover, in those
days the nobles of Judah sent many letters to Tobiah, and Tobiah's letters came
to them. 18 For many in Judah were
bound by oath to him, because he was
the son-in-law of Shecaniah son of Arah:
and his son Jehohanan had married

[u] **6.6** Heb *Gashmu* [v] **6.16** Another reading is *saw*

the daughter of Meshullam son of Berechiah. 19Also they spoke of his good
deeds in my presence, and reported my
words to him. And Tobiah sent letters to
intimidate me.

7 Now when the wall had been built
and I had set up the doors, and the
gatekeepers, the singers, and the Levites had been appointed, 2I gave my
brother Hanani charge over Jerusalem,
along with Hananiah the commander
of the citadel—for he was a faithful man
and feared God more than many. 3And
I said to them, 'The gates of Jerusalem
are not to be opened until the sun is hot;
while the gatekeepers[w] are still standing guard, let them shut and bar the
doors. Appoint guards from among the
inhabitants of Jerusalem, some at their
watch-posts, and others before their
own houses.' 4The city was wide and
large, but the people within it were few
and no houses had been built.

LISTS OF THE RETURNED EXILES

5 Then my God put it into my mind
to assemble the nobles and the officials
and the people, to be enrolled by genealogy. And I found the book of the genealogy of those who were the first to come
back, and I found the following written
in it:

6 These are the people of the province who came up out of the captivity
of those exiles whom King Nebuchadnezzar of Babylon had carried into exile;
they returned to Jerusalem and Judah,
each to his town. 7They came with Zerubbabel, Jeshua, Nehemiah, Azariah,
Raamiah, Nahamani, Mordecai, Bil-
shan, Mispereth, Bigvai, Nehum, Baanah.

The number of the Israelite people:
8the descendants of Parosh, two thousand one hundred and seventy-two. 9Of
Shephatiah, three hundred and seventy-
two. 10Of Arah, six hundred and fifty-
two. 11Of Pahath-moab, namely the
descendants of Jeshua and Joab, two
thousand eight hundred and eighteen.
12Of Elam, one thousand two hundred
and fifty-four. 13Of Zattu, eight hundred
and forty-five. 14Of Zaccai, seven hundred and sixty. 15Of Binnui, six hundred
and forty-eight. 16Of Bebai, six hundred and twenty-eight. 17Of Azgad, two
thousand three hundred and twenty-
two. 18Of Adonikam, six hundred and
sixty-seven. 19Of Bigvai, two thousand
and sixty-seven. 20Of Adin, six hundred and fifty-five. 21Of Ater, namely of
Hezekiah, ninety-eight. 22Of Hashum,
three hundred and twenty-eight. 23Of
Bezai, three hundred and twenty-four.
24Of Hariph, one hundred and twelve.
25Of Gibeon, ninety-five. 26The people of Bethlehem and Netophah, one
hundred and eighty-eight. 27Of Anathoth, one hundred and twenty-eight.
28Of Beth-azmaveth, forty-two. 29Of
Kiriath-jearim, Chephirah, and Beeroth, seven hundred and forty-three.
30Of Ramah and Geba, six hundred and
twenty-one. 31Of Michmas, one hundred and twenty-two. 32Of Bethel and
Ai, one hundred and twenty-three. 33Of
the other Nebo, fifty-two. 34The descendants of the other Elam, one thousand
two hundred and fifty-four. 35Of Harim,
three hundred and twenty. 36Of Jericho,
three hundred and forty-five. 37Of Lod,
Hadid, and Ono, seven hundred and
twenty-one. 38Of Senaah, three thousand nine hundred and thirty.

39 The priests: the descendants of Jedaiah, namely the house of Jeshua, nine
hundred and seventy-three. 40Of Immer, one thousand and fifty-two. 41Of
Pashhur, one thousand two hundred
and forty-seven. 42Of Harim, one thousand and seventeen.

43 The Levites: the descendants of
Jeshua, namely of Kadmiel of the descendants of Hodevah, seventy-four.
44The singers: the descendants of
Asaph, one hundred and forty-eight.
45The gatekeepers: the descendants of
Shallum, of Ater, of Talmon, of Akkub,
of Hatita, of Shobai, one hundred and
thirty-eight.

46 The temple servants: the descendants of Ziha, of Hasupha, of Tabbaoth,
47of Keros, of Sia, of Padon, 48of Lebana,
of Hagaba, of Shalmai, 49of Hanan, of
Giddel, of Gahar, 50of Reaiah, of Rezin, of Nekoda, 51of Gazzam, of Uzza, of
Paseah, 52of Besai, of Meunim, of Ne-
phushesim, 53of Bakbuk, of Hakupha, of
Harhur, 54of Bazlith, of Mehida, of Harsha, 55of Barkos, of Sisera, of Temah,
56of Neziah, of Hatipha.

57 The descendants of Solomon's
servants: of Sotai, of Sophereth, of Pe-
rida, 58of Jaala, of Darkon, of Giddel,
59of Shephatiah, of Hattil, of Pochereth-
hazzebaim, of Amon.

60 All the temple servants and the
descendants of Solomon's servants were
three hundred and ninety-two.

[w] 7.3 Heb *while they*

61 The following were those who came
up from Tel-melah, Tel-harsha, Cherub,
Addon, and Immer, but they could not
prove their ancestral houses or their descent, whether they belonged to Israel:
62the descendants of Delaiah, of Tobiah,
of Nekoda, six hundred and forty-two.
63Also, of the priests: the descendants
of Hobaiah, of Hakkoz, of Barzillai (who
had married one of the daughters of
Barzillai the Gileadite and was called by
their name). 64These sought their registration among those enrolled in the genealogies, but it was not found there, so
they were excluded from the priesthood
as unclean; 65the governor told them
that they were not to partake of the most
holy food, until a priest with Urim and
Thummim should come.

66 The whole assembly together
was forty-two thousand three hundred
and sixty, 67besides their male and female slaves, of whom there were seven
thousand three hundred and thirty-
seven; and they had two hundred and
forty-five singers, male and female.
68They had seven hundred and thirty-
six horses, two hundred and forty-five
mules,[x] 69four hundred and thirty-five
camels, and six thousand seven hundred and twenty donkeys.

70 Now some of the heads of ancestral houses contributed to the work.
The governor gave to the treasury one
thousand darics of gold, fifty basins,
and five hundred and thirty priestly
robes. 71And some of the heads of ancestral houses gave into the building fund
twenty thousand darics of gold and two
thousand two hundred minas of silver.
72And what the rest of the people gave
was twenty thousand darics of gold,
two thousand minas of silver, and sixty-
seven priestly robes.

73 So the priests, the Levites, the
gatekeepers, the singers, some of the
people, the temple servants, and all Israel settled in their towns.

EZRA SUMMONS THE PEOPLE TO OBEY THE LAW

When the seventh month came—the
people of Israel being settled in their
8 towns— 1all the people gathered
together into the square before the
Water Gate. They told the scribe Ezra
to bring the book of the law of Moses,
which the LORD had given to Israel.
2Accordingly, the priest Ezra brought
the law before the assembly, both men
and women and all who could hear with
understanding. This was on the first day
of the seventh month. 3He read from it
facing the square before the Water Gate
from early morning until midday, in
the presence of the men and the women
and those who could understand; and
the ears of all the people were attentive to the book of the law. 4The scribe
Ezra stood on a wooden platform that
had been made for the purpose; and
beside him stood Mattithiah, Shema,
Anaiah, Uriah, Hilkiah, and Maaseiah on his right hand; and Pedaiah,
Mishael, Malchijah, Hashum, Hash-
baddanah, Zechariah, and Meshullam
on his left hand. 5And Ezra opened the
book in the sight of all the people, for he
was standing above all the people; and
when he opened it, all the people stood
up. 6Then Ezra blessed the LORD, the
great God, and all the people answered,
'Amen, Amen', lifting up their hands.
Then they bowed their heads and worshipped the LORD with their faces to the
ground. 7Also Jeshua, Bani, Sherebiah,
Jamin, Akkub, Shabbethai, Hodiah, Maaseiah, Kelita, Azariah, Jozabad, Hanan,
Pelaiah, the Levites,[y] helped the people
to understand the law, while the people
remained in their places. 8So they read
from the book, from the law of God, with
interpretation. They gave the sense, so
that the people understood the reading.

9 And Nehemiah, who was the governor, and Ezra the priest and scribe,
and the Levites who taught the people
said to all the people, 'This day is holy
to the LORD your God; do not mourn
or weep.' For all the people wept when
they heard the words of the law. 10Then
he said to them, 'Go your way, eat the
fat and drink sweet wine and send portions of them to those for whom nothing is prepared, for this day is holy to
our LORD; and do not be grieved, for the
joy of the LORD is your strength.' 11So
the Levites stilled all the people, saying,
'Be quiet, for this day is holy; do not be
grieved.' 12And all the people went their
way to eat and drink and to send portions and to make great rejoicing, because they had understood the words
that were declared to them.

THE FESTIVAL OF BOOTHS CELEBRATED

13 On the second day the heads of ancestral houses of all the people, with the

[x] **7.68** Ezra 2.66 and the margins of some Hebrew Mss: MT lacks *They had . . . forty-five mules*

[y] **8.7** 1 Esdras 9.48 Vg: Heb *and the Levites*

priests and the Levites, came together
to the scribe Ezra in order to study the
words of the law. 14And they found it
written in the law, which the LORD had
commanded by Moses, that the people
of Israel should live in booths[z] during
the festival of the seventh month, 15and
that they should publish and proclaim
in all their towns and in Jerusalem as
follows, 'Go out to the hills and bring
branches of olive, wild olive, myrtle,
palm, and other leafy trees to make
booths,[a] as it is written.' 16So the people
went out and brought them, and made
booths[b] for themselves, each on the
roofs of their houses, and in their courts
and in the courts of the house of God,
and in the square at the Water Gate and
in the square at the Gate of Ephraim.
17And all the assembly of those who
had returned from the captivity made
booths[c] and lived in them; for from
the days of Jeshua son of Nun to that
day the people of Israel had not done
so. And there was very great rejoicing.
18And day by day, from the first day to
the last day, he read from the book of
the law of God. They kept the festival for
seven days; and on the eighth day there
was a solemn assembly, according to the
ordinance.

NATIONAL CONFESSION

9 Now on the twenty-fourth day
of this month the people of Israel were assembled with fasting and
in sackcloth, and with dust on their
heads.[d] 2Then those of Israelite descent
separated themselves from all foreigners, and stood and confessed their sins
and the iniquities of their ancestors.
3They stood up in their place and read
from the book of the law of the LORD
their God for a fourth part of the day,
and for another fourth they made confession and worshipped the LORD their
God. 4Then Jeshua, Bani, Kadmiel,
Shebaniah, Bunni, Sherebiah, Bani,
and Chenani stood on the stairs of the
Levites and cried out with a loud voice
to the LORD their God. 5Then the Levites, Jeshua, Kadmiel, Bani, Hashabneiah, Sherebiah, Hodiah, Shebaniah,
and Pethahiah, said, 'Stand up and bless
the LORD your God from everlasting to
everlasting. Blessed be your glorious
name, which is exalted above all blessing and praise.'

6 And Ezra said:[e] 'You are the LORD,
you alone; you have made heaven, the
heaven of heavens, with all their host,
the earth and all that is on it, the seas
and all that is in them. To all of them
you give life, and the host of heaven
worships you. 7You are the LORD, the
God who chose Abram and brought him
out of Ur of the Chaldeans and gave him
the name Abraham; 8and you found
his heart faithful before you, and made
with him a covenant to give to his descendants the land of the Canaanite, the
Hittite, the Amorite, the Perizzite, the
Jebusite, and the Girgashite; and you
have fulfilled your promise, for you are
righteous.

9 'And you saw the distress of our ancestors in Egypt and heard their cry at
the Red Sea.[f] 10You performed signs and
wonders against Pharaoh and all his
servants and all the people of his land,
for you knew that they acted insolently
against our ancestors. You made a name
for yourself, which remains to this day.
11And you divided the sea before them,
so that they passed through the sea on
dry land, but you threw their pursuers
into the depths, like a stone into mighty
waters. 12Moreover, you led them by day
with a pillar of cloud, and by night with
a pillar of fire, to give them light on the
way in which they should go. 13You
came down also upon Mount Sinai, and
spoke with them from heaven, and gave
them right ordinances and true laws,
good statutes and commandments,
14and you made known your holy sabbath to them and gave them commandments and statutes and a law through
your servant Moses. 15For their hunger
you gave them bread from heaven, and
for their thirst you brought water for
them out of the rock, and you told them
to go in to possess the land that you
swore to give them.

16 'But they and our ancestors acted
presumptuously and stiffened their
necks and did not obey your commandments; 17they refused to obey, and were
not mindful of the wonders that you
performed among them; but they stiffened their necks and determined to return to their slavery in Egypt. But you
are a God ready to forgive, gracious and
merciful, slow to anger and abounding
in steadfast love, and you did not forsake them. 18Even when they had cast
an image of a calf for themselves and

[z] **8.14** Or *tabernacles*; Heb *succoth* [a] **8.15** Or *tabernacles*; Heb *succoth* [b] **8.16** Or *tabernacles*; Heb *succoth* [c] **8.17** Or *tabernacles*; Heb *succoth* [d] **9.1** Heb *on them* [e] **9.6** Gk: Heb lacks *And Ezra said* [f] **9.9** Or *Sea of Reeds*

said, "This is your God who brought you
up out of Egypt", and had committed
great blasphemies, 19 you in your great
mercies did not forsake them in the wilderness; the pillar of cloud that led them
in the way did not leave them by day,
nor the pillar of fire by night that gave
them light on the way by which they
should go. 20 You gave your good spirit
to instruct them, and did not withhold
your manna from their mouths, and
gave them water for their thirst. 21 For
forty years you sustained them in the
wilderness so that they lacked nothing;
their clothes did not wear out and their
feet did not swell. 22 And you gave them
kingdoms and peoples, and allotted to
them every corner,[g] so they took possession of the land of King Sihon of Heshbon and the land of King Og of Bashan.
23 You multiplied their descendants like
the stars of heaven, and brought them
into the land that you had told their ancestors to enter and possess. 24 So the
descendants went in and possessed the
land, and you subdued before them the
inhabitants of the land, the Canaanites,
and gave them into their hands, with
their kings and the peoples of the land,
to do with them as they pleased. 25 And
they captured fortress cities and a rich
land, and took possession of houses
filled with all sorts of goods, hewn cisterns, vineyards, olive orchards, and
fruit trees in abundance; so they ate,
and were filled and became fat, and delighted in your great goodness.

26 'Nevertheless they were disobedient and rebelled against you and cast
your law behind their backs and killed
your prophets, who had warned them in
order to turn them back to you, and they
committed great blasphemies. 27 Therefore you gave them into the hands of
their enemies, who made them suffer.
Then in the time of their suffering they
cried out to you and you heard them
from heaven, and according to your
great mercies you gave them saviours
who saved them from the hands of their
enemies. 28 But after they had rest, they
again did evil before you, and you abandoned them to the hands of their enemies, so that they had dominion over
them; yet when they turned and cried
to you, you heard from heaven, and
many times you rescued them according to your mercies. 29 And you warned
them in order to turn them back to your
law. Yet they acted presumptuously and
did not obey your commandments, but
sinned against your ordinances, by the
observance of which a person shall live.
They turned a stubborn shoulder and
stiffened their neck and would not obey.
30 For many years you were patient with
them, and warned them by your spirit
through your prophets; yet they would
not listen. Therefore you handed them
over to the peoples of the lands. 31 Nevertheless, in your great mercies you
did not make an end of them or forsake
them, for you are a gracious and merciful God.

32 'Now therefore, our God—the
great and mighty and awesome God,
keeping covenant and steadfast love—
do not treat lightly all the hardship that
has come upon us, upon our kings, our
officials, our priests, our prophets, our
ancestors, and all your people, since the
time of the kings of Assyria until today. 33 You have been just in all that has
come upon us, for you have dealt faithfully and we have acted wickedly; 34 our
kings, our officials, our priests, and
our ancestors have not kept your law
or heeded the commandments and the
warnings that you gave them. 35 Even
in their own kingdom, and in the great
goodness you bestowed on them, and
in the large and rich land that you set
before them, they did not serve you and
did not turn from their wicked works.
36 Here we are, slaves to this day—slaves
in the land that you gave to our ancestors to enjoy its fruit and its good gifts.
37 Its rich yield goes to the kings whom
you have set over us because of our sins;
they have power also over our bodies
and over our livestock at their pleasure,
and we are in great distress.'

THOSE WHO SIGNED THE COVENANT

38[h] Because of all this we make a
firm agreement in writing, and on
that sealed document are inscribed the
names of our officials, our Levites, and
our priests.

10[i] Upon the sealed document are
the names of Nehemiah the governor, son of Hacaliah, and Zedekiah;
2 Seraiah, Azariah, Jeremiah, 3 Pashhur,
Amariah, Malchijah, 4 Hattush, Shebaniah, Malluch, 5 Harim, Meremoth,
Obadiah, 6 Daniel, Ginnethon, Baruch,
7 Meshullam, Abijah, Mijamin, 8 Maaziah, Bilgai, Shemaiah; these are the
priests. 9 And the Levites: Jeshua son

[g] 9.22 Meaning of Heb uncertain [h] 9.38 Ch 10.1 in Heb [i] 10.1 Ch 10.2 in Heb

of Azaniah, Binnui of the sons of Henadad, Kadmiel; 10 and their associates, Shebaniah, Hodiah, Kelita, Pelaiah, Hanan, 11 Mica, Rehob, Hashabiah, 12 Zaccur, Sherebiah, Shebaniah, 13 Hodiah, Bani, Beninu. 14 The leaders of the people: Parosh, Pahath-moab, Elam, Zattu, Bani, 15 Bunni, Azgad, Bebai, 16 Adonijah, Bigvai, Adin, 17 Ater, Hezekiah, Azzur, 18 Hodiah, Hashum, Bezai, 19 Hariph, Anathoth, Nebai, 20 Magpiash, Meshullam, Hezir, 21 Meshezabel, Zadok, Jaddua, 22 Pelatiah, Hanan, Anaiah, 23 Hoshea, Hananiah, Hasshub, 24 Hallohesh, Pilha, Shobek, 25 Rehum, Hashabnah, Maaseiah, 26 Ahiah, Hanan, Anan, 27 Malluch, Harim, and Baanah.

SUMMARY OF THE COVENANT

28 The rest of the people, the priests, the Levites, the gatekeepers, the singers, the temple servants, and all who have separated themselves from the peoples of the lands to adhere to the law of God, their wives, their sons, their daughters, all who have knowledge and understanding, 29 join with their kin, their nobles, and enter into a curse and an oath to walk in God's law, which was given by Moses the servant of God, and to observe and do all the commandments of the LORD our Lord and his ordinances and his statutes. 30 We will not give our daughters to the peoples of the land or take their daughters for our sons; 31 and if the peoples of the land bring in merchandise or any grain on the sabbath day to sell, we will not buy it from them on the sabbath or on a holy day; and we will forego the crops of the seventh year and the exaction of every debt.

32 We also lay on ourselves the obligation to charge ourselves yearly one-third of a shekel for the service of the house of our God: 33 for the rows of bread, the regular grain-offering, the regular burnt-offering, the sabbaths, the new moons, the appointed festivals, the sacred donations, and the sin-offerings to make atonement for Israel, and for all the work of the house of our God. 34 We have also cast lots among the priests, the Levites, and the people, for the wood-offering, to bring it into the house of our God, by ancestral houses, at appointed times, year by year, to burn on the altar of the LORD our God, as it is written in the law. 35 We obligate ourselves to bring the first fruits of our soil and the first fruits of all fruit of every tree, year by year, to the house of the LORD; 36 also to bring to the house of our God, to the priests who minister in the house of our God, the firstborn of our sons and of our livestock, as it is written in the law, and the firstlings of our herds and of our flocks; 37 and to bring the first of our dough, and our contributions, the fruit of every tree, the wine and the oil, to the priests, to the chambers of the house of our God; and to bring to the Levites the tithes from our soil, for it is the Levites who collect the tithes in all our rural towns. 38 And the priest, the descendant of Aaron, shall be with the Levites when the Levites receive the tithes; and the Levites shall bring up a tithe of the tithes to the house of our God, to the chambers of the storehouse. 39 For the people of Israel and the sons of Levi shall bring the contribution of grain, wine, and oil to the storerooms where the vessels of the sanctuary are, and where the priests that minister, and the gatekeepers and the singers are. We will not neglect the house of our God.

POPULATION OF THE CITY INCREASED

11 Now the leaders of the people lived in Jerusalem; and the rest of the people cast lots to bring one out of ten to live in the holy city Jerusalem, while nine-tenths remained in the other towns. 2 And the people blessed all those who willingly offered to live in Jerusalem.

3 These are the leaders of the province who lived in Jerusalem; but in the towns of Judah all lived on their property in their towns: Israel, the priests, the Levites, the temple servants, and the descendants of Solomon's servants. 4 And in Jerusalem lived some of the Judahites and of the Benjaminites. Of the Judahites: Athaiah son of Uzziah son of Zechariah son of Amariah son of Shephatiah son of Mahalalel, of the descendants of Perez; 5 and Maaseiah son of Baruch son of Col-hozeh son of Hazaiah son of Adaiah son of Joiarib son of Zechariah son of the Shilonite. 6 All the descendants of Perez who lived in Jerusalem were four hundred and sixty-eight valiant warriors.

7 And these are the Benjaminites: Sallu son of Meshullam son of Joed son of Pedaiah son of Kolaiah son of Maaseiah son of Ithiel son of Jeshaiah. 8 And his brothers[j] Gabbai, Sallai: nine hun-

[j] **11.8** Gk Mss: Heb *And after him*

dred and twenty-eight. [9]Joel son of
Zichri was their overseer; and Judah son
of Hassenuah was second in charge of
the city.
10 Of the priests: Jedaiah son of Joiarib, Jachin, [11]Seraiah son of Hilkiah
son of Meshullam son of Zadok son of
Meraioth son of Ahitub, officer of the
house of God, [12]and their associates who
did the work of the house, eight hundred and twenty-two; and Adaiah son
of Jeroham son of Pelaliah son of Amzi
son of Zechariah son of Pashhur son of
Malchijah, [13]and his associates, heads
of ancestral houses, two hundred and
forty-two; and Amashsai son of Azarel
son of Ahzai son of Meshillemoth son
of Immer, [14]and their associates, valiant warriors, one hundred and twenty-
eight; their overseer was Zabdiel son of
Haggedolim.
15 And of the Levites: Shemaiah son
of Hasshub son of Azrikam son of Hashabiah son of Bunni; [16]and Shabbethai
and Jozabad, of the leaders of the Levites, who were over the outside work of
the house of God; [17]and Mattaniah son
of Mica son of Zabdi son of Asaph, who
was the leader to begin the thanksgiving in prayer, and Bakbukiah, the second among his associates; and Abda son
of Shammua son of Galal son of Jeduthun. [18]All the Levites in the holy city
were two hundred and eighty-four.
19 The gatekeepers, Akkub, Talmon
and their associates, who kept watch
at the gates, were one hundred and
seventy-two. [20]And the rest of Israel,
and of the priests and the Levites, were
in all the towns of Judah, all of them
in their inheritance. [21]But the temple
servants lived on Ophel; and Ziha and
Gishpa were over the temple servants.
22 The overseer of the Levites in Jerusalem was Uzzi son of Bani son of Hashabiah son of Mattaniah son of Mica, of
the descendants of Asaph, the singers,
in charge of the work of the house of
God. [23]For there was a command from
the king concerning them, and a settled provision for the singers, as was required every day. [24]And Pethahiah son
of Meshezabel, of the descendants of Zerah son of Judah, was at the king's hand
in all matters concerning the people.

VILLAGES OUTSIDE JERUSALEM

25 And as for the villages, with their
fields, some of the people of Judah lived
in Kiriath-arba and its villages, and in
Dibon and its villages, and in Jekabzeel
and its villages, [26]and in Jeshua and in
Moladah and Beth-pelet, [27]in Hazar-
shual, in Beer-sheba and its villages,
[28]in Ziklag, in Meconah and its villages,
[29]in En-rimmon, in Zorah, in Jarmuth,
[30]Zanoah, Adullam, and their villages,
Lachish and its fields, and Azekah and
its villages. So they camped from Beer-
sheba to the valley of Hinnom. [31]The
people of Benjamin also lived from Geba
onwards, at Michmash, Aija, Bethel and
its villages, [32]Anathoth, Nob, Ananiah,
[33]Hazor, Ramah, Gittaim, [34]Hadid, Zeboim, Neballat, [35]Lod, and Ono, the valley of artisans. [36]And certain divisions
of the Levites in Judah were joined to
Benjamin.

A LIST OF PRIESTS AND LEVITES

12 These are the priests and the
Levites who came up with Zerubbabel son of Shealtiel, and Jeshua:
Seraiah, Jeremiah, Ezra, [2]Amariah,
Malluch, Hattush, [3]Shecaniah, Rehum,
Meremoth, [4]Iddo, Ginnethoi, Abijah,
[5]Mijamin, Maadiah, Bilgah, [6]Shema-
iah, Joiarib, Jedaiah, [7]Sallu, Amok, Hilkiah, Jedaiah. These were the leaders of
the priests and of their associates in the
days of Jeshua.
8 And the Levites: Jeshua, Binnui,
Kadmiel, Sherebiah, Judah, and Mattaniah, who with his associates was in
charge of the songs of thanksgiving.
[9]And Bakbukiah and Unno their associates stood opposite them in the service. [10]Jeshua was the father of Joiakim,
Joiakim the father of Eliashib, Eliashib
the father of Joiada, [11]Joiada the father
of Jonathan, and Jonathan the father of
Jaddua.
12 In the days of Joiakim the priests,
heads of ancestral houses, were: of Seraiah, Meraiah; of Jeremiah, Hananiah;
[13]of Ezra, Meshullam; of Amariah, Jehohanan; [14]of Malluchi, Jonathan; of
Shebaniah, Joseph; [15]of Harim, Adna; of
Meraioth, Helkai; [16]of Iddo, Zechariah;
of Ginnethon, Meshullam; [17]of Abijah,
Zichri; of Miniamin, of Moadiah, Piltai;
[18]of Bilgah, Shammua; of Shemaiah, Jehonathan; [19]of Joiarib, Mattenai; of Jedaiah, Uzzi; [20]of Sallai, Kallai; of Amok,
Eber; [21]of Hilkiah, Hashabiah; of Jedaiah, Nethanel.
22 As for the Levites, in the days of
Eliashib, Joiada, Johanan, and Jaddua,
there were recorded the heads of ancestral houses; also the priests until the
reign of Darius the Persian. [23]The Levites, heads of ancestral houses, were

recorded in the Book of the Annals until the days of Johanan son of Eliashib. 24 And the leaders of the Levites: Hashabiah, Sherebiah, and Jeshua son of Kadmiel, with their associates over against them, to praise and to give thanks, according to the commandment of David the man of God, section opposite to section. 25 Mattaniah, Bakbukiah, Obadiah, Meshullam, Talmon, and Akkub were gatekeepers standing guard at the storehouses of the gates. 26 These were in the days of Joiakim son of Jeshua son of Jozadak, and in the days of the governor Nehemiah and of the priest Ezra, the scribe.

DEDICATION OF THE CITY WALL

27 Now at the dedication of the wall of Jerusalem they sought out the Levites in all their places, to bring them to Jerusalem to celebrate the dedication with rejoicing, with thanksgivings and with singing, with cymbals, harps, and lyres. 28 The companies of the singers gathered together from the circuit around Jerusalem and from the villages of the Netophathites; 29 also from Beth-gilgal and from the region of Geba and Azmaveth; for the singers had built for themselves villages around Jerusalem. 30 And the priests and the Levites purified themselves; and they purified the people and the gates and the wall.

31 Then I brought the leaders of Judah up on to the wall, and appointed two great companies that gave thanks and went in procession. One went to the right on the wall to the Dung Gate; 32 and after them went Hoshaiah and half the officials of Judah, 33 and Azariah, Ezra, Meshullam, 34 Judah, Benjamin, Shemaiah, and Jeremiah, 35 and some of the young priests with trumpets: Zechariah son of Jonathan son of Shemaiah son of Mattaniah son of Micaiah son of Zaccur son of Asaph; 36 and his kindred, Shemaiah, Azarel, Milalai, Gilalai, Maai, Nethanel, Judah, and Hanani, with the musical instruments of David the man of God; and the scribe Ezra went in front of them. 37 At the Fountain Gate, in front of them, they went straight up by the stairs of the city of David, at the ascent of the wall, above the house of David, to the Water Gate on the east.

38 The other company of those who gave thanks went to the left,[k] and I followed them with half of the people on the wall, above the Tower of the Ovens, to the Broad Wall, 39 and above the Gate of Ephraim, and by the Old Gate, and by the Fish Gate and the Tower of Hananel and the Tower of the Hundred, to the Sheep Gate; and they came to a halt at the Gate of the Guard. 40 So both companies of those who gave thanks stood in the house of God, and I and half of the officials with me; 41 and the priests Eliakim, Maaseiah, Miniamin, Micaiah, Elioenai, Zechariah, and Hananiah, with trumpets; 42 and Maaseiah, Shemaiah, Eleazar, Uzzi, Jehohanan, Malchijah, Elam, and Ezer. And the singers sang with Jezrahiah as their leader. 43 They offered great sacrifices that day and rejoiced, for God had made them rejoice with great joy; the women and children also rejoiced. The joy of Jerusalem was heard far away.

TEMPLE RESPONSIBILITIES

44 On that day men were appointed over the chambers for the stores, the contributions, the first fruits, and the tithes, to gather into them the portions required by the law for the priests and for the Levites from the fields belonging to the towns; for Judah rejoiced over the priests and the Levites who ministered. 45 They performed the service of their God and the service of purification, as did the singers and the gatekeepers, according to the command of David and his son Solomon. 46 For in the days of David and Asaph long ago there was a leader of the singers, and there were songs of praise and thanksgiving to God. 47 In the days of Zerubbabel and in the days of Nehemiah all Israel gave the daily portions for the singers and the gatekeepers. They set apart that which was for the Levites; and the Levites set apart that which was for the descendants of Aaron.

FOREIGNERS SEPARATED FROM ISRAEL

13 On that day they read from the book of Moses in the hearing of the people; and in it was found written that no Ammonite or Moabite should ever enter the assembly of God, 2 because they did not meet the Israelites with bread and water, but hired Balaam against them to curse them—yet our God turned the curse into a blessing. 3 When the people heard the law, they separated from Israel all those of foreign descent.

[k] **12.38** Cn: Heb *opposite*

THE REFORMS OF NEHEMIAH

4 Now before this, the priest Eliashib, who was appointed over the chambers of the house of our God, and who was related to Tobiah, [5]prepared for Tobiah a large room where they had previously put the grain-offering, the frankincense, the vessels, and the tithes of grain, wine, and oil, which were given by commandment to the Levites, singers, and gatekeepers, and the contributions for the priests. [6]While this was taking place I was not in Jerusalem, for in the thirty-second year of King Artaxerxes of Babylon I went to the king. After some time I asked leave of the king [7]and returned to Jerusalem. I then discovered the wrong that Eliashib had done on behalf of Tobiah, preparing a room for him in the courts of the house of God. [8]And I was very angry, and I threw all the household furniture of Tobiah out of the room. [9]Then I gave orders and they cleansed the chambers, and I brought back the vessels of the house of God, with the grain-offering and the frankincense.

10 I also found out that the portions of the Levites had not been given to them; so that the Levites and the singers, who had conducted the service, had gone back to their fields. [11]So I remonstrated with the officials and said, 'Why is the house of God forsaken?' And I gathered them together and set them in their stations. [12]Then all Judah brought the tithe of the grain, wine, and oil into the storehouses. [13]And I appointed as treasurers over the storehouses the priest Shelemiah, the scribe Zadok, and Pedaiah of the Levites, and as their assistant Hanan son of Zaccur son of Mattaniah, for they were considered faithful; and their duty was to distribute to their associates. [14]Remember me, O my God, concerning this, and do not wipe out my good deeds that I have done for the house of my God and for his service.

SABBATH REFORMS BEGUN

15 In those days I saw in Judah people treading wine presses on the sabbath, and bringing in heaps of grain and loading them on donkeys; and also wine, grapes, figs, and all kinds of burdens, which they brought into Jerusalem on the sabbath day; and I warned them at that time against selling food. [16]Tyrians also, who lived in the city, brought in fish and all kinds of merchandise and sold them on the sabbath to the people of Judah, and in Jerusalem. [17]Then I remonstrated with the nobles of Judah and said to them, 'What is this evil thing that you are doing, profaning the sabbath day? [18]Did not your ancestors act in this way, and did not our God bring all this disaster on us and on this city? Yet you bring more wrath on Israel by profaning the sabbath.'

19 When it began to be dark at the gates of Jerusalem before the sabbath, I commanded that the doors should be shut and gave orders that they should not be opened until after the sabbath. And I set some of my servants over the gates, to prevent any burden from being brought in on the sabbath day. [20]Then the merchants and sellers of all kinds of merchandise spent the night outside Jerusalem once or twice. [21]But I warned them and said to them, 'Why do you spend the night in front of the wall? If you do so again, I will lay hands on you.' From that time on they did not come on the sabbath. [22]And I commanded the Levites that they should purify themselves and come and guard the gates, to keep the sabbath day holy. Remember this also in my favour, O my God, and spare me according to the greatness of your steadfast love.

MIXED MARRIAGES CONDEMNED

23 In those days also I saw Jews who had married women of Ashdod, Ammon, and Moab; [24]and half of their children spoke the language of Ashdod, and they could not speak the language of Judah, but spoke the language of various peoples. [25]And I contended with them and cursed them and beat some of them and pulled out their hair; and I made them take an oath in the name of God, saying, 'You shall not give your daughters to their sons, or take their daughters for your sons or for yourselves. [26]Did not King Solomon of Israel sin on account of such women? Among the many nations there was no king like him, and he was beloved by his God, and God made him king over all Israel; nevertheless, foreign women made even him to sin. [27]Shall we then listen to you and do all this great evil and act treacherously against our God by marrying foreign women?'

28 And one of the sons of Jehoiada, son of the high priest Eliashib, was the son-in-law of Sanballat the Horonite; I chased him away from me. [29]Remember them, O my God, because they have

defiled the priesthood, the covenant of
the priests and the Levites.
30 Thus I cleansed them from everything foreign, and I established the duties of the priests and Levites, each in
his work; 31 and I provided for the wood-
offering, at appointed times, and for the
first fruits. Remember me, O my God,
for good.

TOBIT

The book of Tobit is more closely related to Jewish wisdom literature than to the historical narrative of the Old Testament. It probably was written in the early second century BCE. Its story line, however, is set in the context of eighth-century Nineveh, where Tobit lived among the captives brought there after the fall of the Northern Kingdom, Israel, in 721 BCE. The narrative depicts the intertwined stories of Tobit and a far-off maiden named Sarah. The main plot is dedicated to Tobit's son, Tobias, who is sent by his father to collect a sum of money that Tobit had deposited some time previously in the far-off land of Media, where Sarah also happened to live. The angel Rafael accompanies Tobias and enables good fortune and blessing to come upon the main characters of the story.

The book of Tobit underscores the value of prayer, fasting, and almsgiving. It is recognized for its teaching on the intercession of angels, filial piety, and reverence for the dead. Passages from Tobit are read on Monday through Saturday of the Ninth Week of Year I in the weekday liturgical calendar. Moreover, passages from Tobit are also offered as choices for readings during the celebration of marriage.

1 This book tells the story of Tobit son of Tobiel son of Hananiel son of Aduel son of Gabael son of Raphael of the descendants[a] of Asiel, of the tribe of Naphtali, 2 who in the days of King Shalmaneser[b] of the Assyrians was taken into captivity from Thisbe, which is to the south of Kedesh Naphtali in Upper Galilee, above Asher towards the west, and north of Phogor.

TOBIT'S YOUTH AND VIRTUOUS LIFE

3 I, Tobit, walked in the ways of truth and righteousness all the days of my life. I performed many acts of charity for my kindred and my people who had gone with me in exile to Nineveh in the land of the Assyrians. 4 When I was in my own country, in the land of Israel, while I was still a young man, the whole tribe of my ancestor Naphtali deserted the house of David and Jerusalem. This city had been chosen from among all the tribes of Israel, where all the tribes of Israel should offer sacrifice and where the temple, the dwelling of God, had been consecrated and established for all generations for ever.

5 All my kindred and our ancestral house of Naphtali sacrificed to the calf[c] that King Jeroboam of Israel had erected in Dan and on all the mountains of Galilee. 6 But I alone went often to Jerusalem for the festivals, as it is prescribed for all Israel by an everlasting decree. I would hurry off to Jerusalem with the first fruits of the crops and the firstlings of the flock, the tithes of the cattle, and the first shearings of the sheep. 7 I would give these to the priests, the sons of Aaron, at the altar; likewise the tenth of the grain, wine, olive oil, pomegranates, figs, and the rest of the fruits to the sons of Levi who ministered at Jerusalem. Also, for six years I would save up a second tenth in money and go and distribute it in Jerusalem. 8 A third tenth[d] I would give to the orphans and widows and to the converts who had attached themselves to Israel. I would bring it and give it to them in the third year, and we would eat it according

[a] **1.1** Other ancient authorities lack *of Raphael son of Raguel of the descendants* [b] **1.2** Gk *Enemessaros* [c] **1.5** Other ancient authorities read *heifer* [d] **1.8** *A third tenth* added from other ancient authorities

to the ordinance decreed concerning it in the law of Moses and according to the instructions of Deborah, the mother of my father Tobiel,[e] for my father had died and left me an orphan. 9 When I became a man I married a woman,[f] a member of our own family, and by her I became the father of a son whom I named Tobias.

TAKEN CAPTIVE TO NINEVEH

10 After I was carried away captive to Assyria and came as a captive to Nineveh, everyone of my kindred and my people ate the food of the Gentiles, 11 but I kept myself from eating the food of the Gentiles. 12 Because I was mindful of God with all my heart, 13 the Most High gave me favour and good standing with Shalmaneser,[g] and I used to buy everything he needed. 14 Until his death I used to go into Media, and buy for him there. While in the country of Media I left bags of silver worth ten talents in trust with Gabael, the brother of Gabri. 15 But when Shalmaneser[h] died, and his son Sennacherib reigned in his place, the highways into Media became unsafe and I could no longer go there.

COURAGE IN BURYING THE DEAD

16 In the days of Shalmaneser[i] I performed many acts of charity to my kindred, those of my tribe. 17 I would give my food to the hungry and my clothing to the naked; and if I saw the dead body of any of my people thrown out behind the wall of Nineveh, I would bury it. 18 I also buried any whom King Sennacherib put to death when he came fleeing from Judea in those days of judgement that the king of heaven executed upon him because of his blasphemies. For in his anger he put to death many Israelites; but I would secretly remove the bodies and bury them. So when Sennacherib looked for them he could not find them. 19 Then one of the Ninevites went and informed the king about me, that I was burying them; so I hid myself. But when I realized that the king knew about me and that I was being searched for to be put to death, I was afraid and ran away. 20 Then all my property was confiscated; nothing was left to me that was not taken into the royal treasury, except my wife Anna and my son Tobias.

21 But not forty[j] days passed before two of Sennacherib's[k] sons killed him, and they fled to the mountains of Ararat, and his son Esar-haddon[l] reigned after him. He appointed Ahikar, the son of my brother Hanael[m] over all the accounts of his kingdom, and he had authority over the entire administration. 22 Ahikar interceded for me, and I returned to Nineveh. Now Ahikar was chief cupbearer, keeper of the signet, and in charge of administration of the accounts under King Sennacherib of Assyria; so Esar-haddon[n] reappointed him. He was my nephew and so a close relative.

2 Then during the reign of Esar-haddon[o] I returned home, and my wife Anna and my son Tobias were restored to me. At our festival of Pentecost, which is the sacred festival of weeks, a good dinner was prepared for me and I reclined to eat. 2 When the table was set for me and an abundance of food placed before me, I said to my son Tobias, 'Go, my child, and bring whatever poor person you may find of our people among the exiles in Nineveh, who is wholeheartedly mindful of God,[p] and he shall eat together with me. I will wait for you, until you come back.' 3 So Tobias went to look for some poor person of our people. When he had returned he said, 'Father!' And I replied, 'Here I am, my child.' Then he went on to say, 'Look, father, one of our own people has been murdered and thrown into the marketplace, and now he lies there strangled.' 4 Then I sprang up, left the dinner before even tasting it, and removed the body[q] from the square[r] and laid it[s] in one of the rooms until sunset when I might bury it.[t] 5 When I returned, I washed myself and ate my food in sorrow. 6 Then I remembered the prophecy of Amos, how he said against Bethel,[u]

> 'Your festivals shall be turned
> into mourning,
> and all your songs into
> lamentation.'

And I wept.

TOBIT BECOMES BLIND

7 When the sun had set, I went and dug a grave and buried him. 8 And my

[e] **1.8** Lat: Gk *Hananiel* [f] **1.9** Other ancient authorities add *Anna* [g] **1.13** Gk *Enemessaros* [h] **1.15** Gk *Enemessaros* [i] **1.16** Gk *Enemessaros* [j] **1.21** Other ancient authorities read either *forty-five* or *fifty* [k] **1.21** Gk *his* [l] **1.21** Gk *Sacherdonos* [m] **1.21** Other authorities read *Hananael* [n] **1.22** Gk *Sacherdonos* [o] **2.1** Gk *Sacherdonos* [p] **2.2** Lat: Gk *wholeheartedly mindful* [q] **2.4** Gk *him* [r] **2.4** Other ancient authorities lack *from the square* [s] **2.4** Gk *him* [t] **2.4** Gk *him* [u] **2.6** Other ancient authorities read *against Bethlehem*

neighbours laughed and said, 'Is he
still not afraid? He has already been
hunted down to be put to death for doing this, and he ran away; yet here he
is again burying the dead!' 9That same
night I washed myself and went into
my courtyard and slept by the wall of
the courtyard; and my face was uncovered because of the heat. 10I did not
know that there were sparrows on the
wall; their fresh droppings fell into my
eyes and produced white films. I went
to physicians to be healed, but the
more they treated me with ointments
the more my vision was obscured
by the white films, until I became
completely blind. For four years I remained unable to see. All my kindred
were sorry for me, and Ahikar took
care of me for two years before he went
to Elymais.

TOBIT'S WIFE EARNS THEIR LIVELIHOOD

11 At that time, also, my wife Anna
earned money at women's work. 12She
used to send what she made to the owners and they would pay wages to her.
One day, the seventh of Dystrus, when
she cut off a piece she had woven and
sent it to the owners, they paid her
full wages and also gave her a kid for a
meal. 13When she returned to me, the
kid began to bleat. So I called her and
said, 'Where did you get this kid? It is
surely not stolen, is it? Return it to the
owners; for we have no right to eat anything stolen.' 14But she said to me, 'It
was given to me as a gift in addition
to my wages.' But I did not believe her,
and told her to return it to the owners.
I became flushed with anger against
her over this. Then she replied to me,
'Where are your acts of charity? Where
are your righteous deeds? These things
are known about you!'[v]

TOBIT'S PRAYER

3 Then with much grief and anguish
of heart I wept, and with groaning
began to pray:

2 'You are righteous, O Lord,
and all your deeds are just;
all your ways are mercy and truth;
you judge the world.[w]
3 And now, O Lord, remember me
and look favourably upon me.
Do not punish me for my sins
and for my unwitting offences
and those that my ancestors
committed before you.
They sinned against you,
4 and disobeyed your
commandments.
So you gave us over to plunder,
exile, and death,
to become the talk, the byword,
and an object of reproach,
among all the nations among
whom you have dispersed us.
5 And now your many
judgements are true
in exacting penalty from
me for my sins.
For we have not kept your
commandments
and have not walked in accordance
with truth before you.
6 So now deal with me as you will;
command my spirit to be
taken from me,
so that I may be released from
the face of the earth
and become dust.
For it is better for me to die
than to live,
because I have had to listen
to undeserved insults,
and great is the sorrow
within me.
Command, O Lord, that I be
released from this distress;
release me to go to the
eternal home,
and do not, O Lord, turn your
face away from me.
For it is better for me to die
than to see so much
distress in my life
and to listen to insults.'

SARAH FALSELY ACCUSED

7 On the same day, at Ecbatana in
Media, it also happened that Sarah, the
daughter of Raguel, was reproached by
one of her father's maids. 8For she had
been married to seven husbands, and
the wicked demon Asmodeus had killed
each of them before they had been with
her as is customary for wives. So the
maid said to her, 'You are the one who
kills[x] your husbands! See, you have already been married to seven husbands
and have not borne the name of[y] a single one of them. 9Why do you beat us?
Because your husbands are dead? Go

[v] **2.14** Or *to you*; Gk *with you* [w] **3.2** Other ancient authorities read *you render true and righteous judgement for ever* [x] **3.8** Other ancient authorities read *strangles* [y] **3.8** Other ancient authorities read *have had no benefit from*

with them! May we never see a son or
daughter of yours!'

SARAH'S PRAYER FOR DEATH

10 On that day she was grieved in
spirit and wept. When she had gone up
to her father's upper room, she intended
to hang herself. But she thought it over
and said, 'Never shall they reproach my
father, saying to him, "You had only one
beloved daughter but she hanged herself because of her distress." And I shall
bring my father in his old age down in
sorrow to Hades. It is better for me not
to hang myself, but to pray the Lord
that I may die and not listen to these
reproaches any more.' 11At that same
time, with hands outstretched towards
the window, she prayed and said,

'Blessed are you, merciful God!
Blessed is your name for ever;
let all your works praise
you for ever.
12 And now, Lord,[z] I turn my
face to you,
and raise my eyes towards you.
13 Command that I be released
from the earth
and not listen to such
reproaches any more.
14 You know, O Master, that
I am innocent
of any defilement with a man,
15 and that I have not disgraced
my name
or the name of my father in
the land of my exile.
I am my father's only child;
he has no other child to
be his heir;
and he has no close relative
or other kindred
for whom I should keep
myself as wife.
Already seven husbands of
mine have died.
Why should I still live?
But if it is not pleasing to you,
O Lord, to take my life,
hear me in my disgrace.'

AN ANSWER TO PRAYER

16 At that very moment, the prayers
of both of them were heard in the glorious presence of God. 17So Raphael was
sent to heal both of them: Tobit, by removing the white films from his eyes,
so that he might see God's light with his
eyes; and Sarah daughter of Raguel, by
giving her in marriage to Tobias son of
Tobit, and by setting her free from the
wicked demon Asmodeus. For Tobias
was entitled to have her before all others who had desired to marry her. At the
same time that Tobit returned from the
courtyard into his house, Sarah daughter of Raguel came down from her upper
room.

TOBIT GIVES INSTRUCTIONS TO HIS SON

4 That same day Tobit remembered
the money that he had left in trust
with Gabael at Rages in Media, 2and he
said to himself, 'Now I have asked for
death. Why do I not call my son Tobias
and explain to him about the money before I die?' 3Then he called his son Tobias, and when he came to him he said,
'My son, when I die,[a] give me a proper
burial. Honour your mother and do not
abandon her all the days of her life. Do
whatever pleases her, and do not grieve
her in anything. 4Remember her, my
son, because she faced many dangers for
you while you were in her womb. And
when she dies, bury her beside me in
the same grave.

5 'Revere the Lord all your days, my
son, and refuse to sin or to transgress
his commandments. Live uprightly all
the days of your life, and do not walk in
the ways of wrongdoing; 6for those who
act in accordance with truth will prosper in all their activities. To all those
who practise righteousness[b] 7give alms
from your possessions, and do not let
your eye begrudge the gift when you
make it. Do not turn your face away
from anyone who is poor, and the face of
God will not be turned away from you.
8If you have many possessions, make
your gift from them in proportion; if
few, do not be afraid to give according
to the little you have. 9So you will be
laying up a good treasure for yourself
against the day of necessity. 10For almsgiving delivers from death and keeps
you from going into the Darkness. 11In-
deed, almsgiving, for all who practise it,
is an excellent offering in the presence
of the Most High.

12 'Beware, my son, of every kind of
fornication. First of all, marry a woman
from among the descendants of your ancestors; do not marry a foreign woman,

[z] 3.12 Other ancient authorities lack *Lord*
[a] 4.3 Lat [b] 4.6 The text of codex Sinaiticus goes directly from verse 6 to verse 19, reading *To those who practise righteousness* [19]*the Lord will give good counsel.* In order to fill the lacuna, verses 7 to 18 are derived from other ancient authorities

who is not of your father's tribe; for we are the descendants of the prophets. Remember, my son, that Noah, Abraham, Isaac, and Jacob, our ancestors of old, all took wives from among their kindred. They were blessed in their children, and their posterity will inherit the land. 13 So now, my son, love your kindred, and in your heart do not disdain your kindred, the sons and daughters of your people, by refusing to take a wife for yourself from among them. For in pride there is ruin and great confusion. And in idleness there is loss and dire poverty, because idleness is the mother of famine.

14 'Do not keep over until the next day the wages of those who work for you, but pay them at once. If you serve God you will receive payment. Watch yourself, my son, in everything you do, and discipline yourself in all your conduct. 15 And what you hate, do not do to anyone. Do not drink wine to excess or let drunkenness go with you on your way. 16 Give some of your food to the hungry, and some of your clothing to the naked. Give all your surplus as alms, and do not let your eye begrudge your giving of alms. 17 Place your bread on the grave of the righteous, but give none to sinners. 18 Seek advice from every wise person and do not despise any useful counsel. 19 At all times bless the Lord God, and ask him that your ways may be made straight and that all your paths and plans may prosper. For none of the nations has understanding, but the Lord himself will give them good counsel; but if he chooses otherwise, he casts down to deepest Hades. So now, my child, remember these commandments, and do not let them be erased from your heart.

MONEY LEFT IN TRUST WITH GABAEL

20 'And now, my son, let me explain to you that I left ten talents of silver in trust with Gabael son of Gabrias, at Rages in Media. 21 Do not be afraid, my son, because we have become poor. You have great wealth if you fear God and flee from every sin and do what is good in the sight of the Lord your God.'

THE ANGEL RAPHAEL

5 Then Tobias answered his father Tobit, 'I will do everything that you have commanded me, father; 2 but how can I obtain the money[c] from him, since he does not know me and I do not know him? What evidence[d] am I to give him so that he will recognize and trust me, and give me the money? Also, I do not know the roads to Media, or how to get there.' 3 Then Tobit answered his son Tobias, 'He gave me his bond and I gave him my bond. I[e] divided his in two; we each took one part, and I put one with the money. And now twenty years have passed since I left this money in trust. So now, my son, find yourself a trustworthy man to go with you, and we will pay him wages until you return. But get back the money from Gabael.'[f]

4 So Tobias went out to look for a man to go with him to Media, someone who was acquainted with the way. He went out and found the angel Raphael standing in front of him; but he did not perceive that he was an angel of God. 5 Tobias[g] said to him, 'Where do you come from, young man?' 'From your kindred, the Israelites,' he replied, 'and I have come here to work.' Then Tobias[h] said to him, 'Do you know the way to go to Media?' 6 'Yes,' he replied, 'I have been there many times; I am acquainted with it and know all the roads. I have often travelled to Media, and stayed with our kinsman Gabael who lives in Rages of Media. It is a journey of two days from Ecbatana to Rages; for it lies in a mountainous area, while Ecbatana is in the middle of the plain.' 7 Then Tobias said to him, 'Wait for me, young man, until I go in and tell my father; for I do need you to travel with me, and I will pay you your wages.' 8 He replied, 'All right, I will wait; but do not take too long.'

9 So Tobias[i] went in to tell his father Tobit and said to him, 'I have just found a man who is one of our own Israelite kindred!' He replied, 'Call the man in, my son, so that I may learn about his family and to what tribe he belongs, and whether he is trustworthy enough to go with you.'

10 Then Tobias went out and called him, and said, 'Young man, my father is calling for you.' So he went in to him, and Tobit greeted him first. He replied, 'Joyous greetings to you!' But Tobit retorted, 'What joy is left for me any more? I am a man without eyesight; I cannot see the light of heaven, but I lie in darkness like the dead who no longer see the light. Although still alive, I am among the dead. I hear people but I cannot see them.' But the young man[j]

[c] 5.2 Gk *it* [d] 5.2 Gk *sign* [e] 5.3 Other authorities read *He* [f] 5.3 Gk *from him* [g] 5.5 Gk *He* [h] 5.5 Gk *he* [i] 5.9 Gk *he* [j] 5.10 Gk *he*

said, 'Take courage; the time is near for
God to heal you; take courage.' Then Tobit said to him, 'My son Tobias wishes
to go to Media. Can you accompany him
and guide him? I will pay your wages,
brother.' He answered, 'I can go with
him and I know all the roads, for I have
often gone to Media and have crossed
all its plains, and I am familiar with its
mountains and all of its roads.'
11 Then Tobit[k] said to him, 'Brother,
of what family are you and from what
tribe? Tell me, brother.' 12He replied,
'Why do you need to know my tribe?' But
Tobit[l] said, 'I want to be sure, brother,
whose son you are and what your name
is.' 13He replied, 'I am Azariah, the son
of the great Hananiah, one of your relatives.' 14Then Tobit said to him, 'Welcome! God save you, brother. Do not feel
bitter towards me, brother, because I
wanted to be sure about your ancestry.
It turns out that you are a kinsman, and
of good and noble lineage. For I knew
Hananiah and Nathan,[m] the two sons
of Shemeliah,[n] and they used to go with
me to Jerusalem and worshipped with
me there, and were not led astray. Your
kindred are good people; you come of
good stock. Hearty welcome!'
15 Then he added, 'I will pay you a
drachma a day as wages, as well as expenses for yourself and my son. So go
with my son, 16and[o] I will add something to your wages.' Raphael[p] answered, 'I will go with him; so do not
fear. We shall leave in good health and
return to you in good health, because
the way is safe.' 17So Tobit[q] said to him,
'Blessings be upon you, brother.'
Then he called his son and said to
him, 'Son, prepare supplies for the journey and set out with your brother. May
God in heaven bring you safely there
and return you in good health to me;
and may his angel, my son, accompany
you both for your safety.'
Before he went out to start his journey, he kissed his father and mother. Tobit then said to him, 'Have a safe journey.'
18 But his mother[r] began to weep,
and said to Tobit, 'Why is it that you
have sent my child away? Is he not the
staff of our hand as he goes in and out
before us? 19Do not heap money upon
money, but let it be a ransom for our
child. 20For the life that is given to us
by the Lord is enough for us.' 21Tobit[s]
said to her, 'Do not worry; our child will
leave in good health and return to us
in good health. Your eyes will see him
on the day when he returns to you in
good health. Say no more! Do not fear
for them, my sister. 22For a good angel
will accompany him; his journey will
be successful, and he will come back in
6 good health.' 1So she stopped weeping.

JOURNEY TO RAGES

The young man went out and the angel went with him; 2and the dog came
out with him and went along with
them. So they both journeyed along,
and when the first night overtook them
they camped by the Tigris river. 3Then
the young man went down to wash
his feet in the Tigris river. Suddenly a
large fish leapt up from the water and
tried to swallow the young man's foot,
and he cried out. 4But the angel said to
the young man, 'Catch hold of the fish
and hang on to it!' So the young man
grasped the fish and drew it up on the
land. 5Then the angel said to him, 'Cut
open the fish and take out its gall, heart,
and liver. Keep them with you, but
throw away the intestines. For its gall,
heart, and liver are useful as medicine.'
6So after cutting open the fish the young
man gathered together the gall, heart,
and liver; then he roasted and ate some
of the fish, and kept some to be salted.
The two continued on their way together until they were near Media.[t]
7Then the young man questioned the
angel and said to him, 'Brother Azariah, what medicinal value is there
in the fish's heart and liver, and in
the gall?' 8He replied, 'As for the fish's
heart and liver, you must burn them to
make a smoke in the presence of a man
or woman afflicted by a demon or evil
spirit, and every affliction will flee away
and never remain with that person any
longer. 9And as for the gall, anoint a
person's eyes where white films have
appeared on them; blow upon them,
upon the white films, and the eyes[u] will
be healed.'

RAPHAEL'S INSTRUCTIONS

10 When he entered Media and already was approaching Ecbatana,[v]

[k] **5.11** Gk *he* [l] **5.12** Gk *he* [m] **5.14** Other ancient authorities read *Jathan* or *Nathaniah* [n] **5.14** Other ancient authorities read *Shemaiah* [o] **5.16** Other ancient authorities add *when you return safely* [p] **5.16** Gk *He* [q] **5.17** Gk *he* [r] **5.18** Other ancient authorities add *Anna* [s] **5.21** Gk *He* [t] **6.6** Other ancient authorities read *Ecbatana* [u] **6.9** Gk *they* [v] **6.10** Other ancient authorities read *Rages*

11 Raphael said to the young man,
'Brother Tobias.' 'Here I am,' he answered. Then Raphael[w] said to him,
'We must stay this night in the home of
Raguel. He is your relative, and he has
a daughter named Sarah. 12 He has no
male heir and no daughter except Sarah
only, and you, as next of kin to her, have
before all other men a hereditary claim
on her. Also it is right for you to inherit
her father's possessions. Moreover, the
girl is sensible, brave, and very beautiful, and her father is a good man.' 13 He
continued, 'You have every right to
take her in marriage. So listen to me,
brother; tonight I will speak to her father about the girl, so that we may take
her to be your bride. When we return
from Rages we will celebrate her marriage. For I know that Raguel can by no
means keep her from you or promise her
to another man without incurring the
penalty of death according to the decree
of the book of Moses. Indeed he knows
that you, rather than any other man,
are entitled to marry his daughter. So
now listen to me, brother, and tonight
we shall speak concerning the girl and
arrange her engagement to you. And
when we return from Rages we will take
her and bring her back with us to your
house.'

14 Then Tobias said in answer to Raphael, 'Brother Azariah, I have heard that
she already has been married to seven
husbands and that they died in the
bridal chamber. On the night when
they went in to her, they would die. I
have heard people saying that it was a
demon that killed them. 15 It does not
harm her, but it kills anyone who desires to approach her. So now, since I am
the only son my father has, I am afraid
that I may die and bring my father's and
mother's life down to their grave, grieving for me—and they have no other son
to bury them.'

16 But Raphael[x] said to him, 'Do
you not remember your father's orders
when he commanded you to take a wife
from your father's house? Now listen
to me, brother, and say no more about
this demon. Take her. I know that this
very night she will be given to you in
marriage. 17 When you enter the bridal
chamber, take some of the fish's liver
and heart, and put them on the embers
of the incense. An odour will be given
off; 18 the demon will smell it and flee,
and will never be seen near her any
more. Now when you are about to go
to bed with her, both of you must first
stand up and pray, imploring the Lord
of heaven that mercy and safety may be
granted to you. Do not be afraid, for she
was set apart for you before the world
was made. You will save her, and she
will go with you. I presume that you
will have children by her, and they will
be as brothers to you. Now say no more!'
When Tobias heard the words of Raphael and learned that she was his kinswoman,[y] related through his father's
lineage, he loved her very much, and his
heart was drawn to her.

ARRIVAL AT THE HOME OF RAGUEL

7 Now when they[z] entered Ecbatana,
Tobias[a] said to him, 'Brother Azariah, take me straight to our brother
Raguel.' So he took him to Raguel's
house, where they found him sitting
beside the courtyard door. They greeted
him first, and he replied, 'Joyous greetings, brothers; welcome and good
health!' Then he brought them into his
house. 2 He said to his wife Edna, 'How
much the young man resembles my
kinsman Tobit!' 3 Then Edna questioned
them, saying, 'Where are you from,
brothers?' They answered, 'We belong
to the descendants of Naphtali who are
exiles in Nineveh.' 4 She said to them,
'Do you know our kinsman Tobit?' And
they replied, 'Yes, we know him.' Then
she asked them, 'Is he[b] in good health?'
5 They replied, 'He is alive and in good
health.' And Tobias added, 'He is my father!' 6 At that Raguel jumped up and
kissed him and wept. 7 He also spoke to
him as follows, 'Blessings on you, my
child, son of a good and noble father![c]
O most miserable of calamities that
such an upright and beneficent man
has become blind!' He then embraced
his kinsman Tobias and wept. 8 His
wife Edna also wept for him, and their
daughter Sarah likewise wept. 9 Then
Raguel[d] slaughtered a ram from the
flock and received them very warmly.

MARRIAGE OF TOBIAS AND SARAH

When they had bathed and washed
themselves and had reclined to dine,
Tobias said to Raphael, 'Brother Azariah, ask Raguel to give me my

[w] 6.11 Gk *he* [x] 6.16 Gk *he* [y] 6.18 Gk *sister*
[z] 7.1 Other ancient authorities read *he* [a] 7.1 Gk
he [b] 7.4 Other ancient authorities add *alive and*
[c] 7.7 Other ancient authorities add *When he heard
that Tobit had lost his sight, he was stricken with
grief and wept. Then he said,* [d] 7.9 Gk *he*

kinswoman[e] Sarah.' 10But Raguel overheard it and said to the lad, 'Eat and
drink, and be merry tonight. For no
one except you, brother, has the right
to marry my daughter Sarah. Likewise I am not at liberty to give her to
any other man than yourself, because
you are my nearest relative. But let me
explain to you the true situation more
fully, my child. 11I have given her to
seven men of our kinsmen, and all died
on the night when they went in to her.
But now, my child, eat and drink, and
the Lord will act on behalf of you both.'
But Tobias said, 'I will neither eat nor
drink anything until you settle the
things that pertain to me.' So Raguel
said, 'I will do so. She is given to you in
accordance with the decree in the book
of Moses, and it has been decreed from
heaven that she should be given to you.
Take your kinswoman;[f] from now on
you are her brother and she is your sister. She is given to you from today and
for ever. May the Lord of heaven, my
child, guide and prosper you both this
night and grant you mercy and peace.'
12Then Raguel summoned his daughter
Sarah. When she came to him he took
her by the hand and gave her to Tobias,[g]
saying, 'Take her to be your wife in accordance with the law and decree written in the book of Moses. Take her and
bring her safely to your father. And may
the God of heaven prosper your journey with his peace.' 13Then he called her
mother and told her to bring writing
material; and he wrote out a copy of a
marriage contract, to the effect that he
gave her to him as wife according to the
decree of the law of Moses. 14Then they
began to eat and drink.

15 Raguel called his wife Edna and
said to her, 'Sister, get the other room
ready, and take her there.' 16So she
went and made the bed in the room
as he had told her, and brought Sarah[h]
there. She wept for her daughter.[i] Then,
wiping away the tears,[j] she said to her,
'Take courage, my daughter; the Lord of
heaven grant you joy[k] in place of your
sorrow. Take courage, my daughter.'
Then she went out.

TOBIAS ROUTS THE DEMON

8 When they had finished eating and
drinking they wanted to retire; so
they took the young man and brought
him into the bedroom. 2Then Tobias remembered the words of Raphael, and
he took the fish's liver and heart out
of the bag where he had them and put
them on the embers of the incense. 3The
odour of the fish so repelled the demon
that he fled to the remotest parts[l] of
Egypt. But Raphael followed him, and
at once bound him there hand and foot.

4 When the parents[m] had gone out
and shut the door of the room, Tobias
got out of bed and said to Sarah,[n] 'Sister,
get up, and let us pray and implore our
Lord that he grant us mercy and safety.'
5So she got up, and they began to pray
and implore that they might be kept
safe. Tobias[o] began by saying,

'Blessed are you, O God of
 our ancestors,
and blessed is your name in all
 generations for ever.
Let the heavens and the whole
 creation bless you for ever.
6 You made Adam, and for him
 you made his wife Eve
 as a helper and support.
From the two of them the
 human race has sprung.
You said, "It is not good that the
 man should be alone;
 let us make a helper for
 him like himself."
7 I now am taking this
 kinswoman of mine,
 not because of lust,
 but with sincerity.
Grant that she and I may find mercy
 and that we may grow
 old together.'

8And they both said, 'Amen, Amen.'
9Then they went to sleep for the night.

But Raguel arose and called his servants to him, and they went and dug a
grave, 10for he said, 'It is possible that he
will die and we will become an object of
ridicule and derision.' 11When they had
finished digging the grave, Raguel went
into his house and called his wife, 12say-
ing, 'Send one of the maids and have
her go in to see if he is alive. But if he
is dead, let us bury him without anyone
knowing it.' 13So they sent the maid, lit
a lamp, and opened the door; and she
went in and found them sound asleep
together. 14Then the maid came out
and informed them that he was alive
and that nothing was wrong. 15So they

[e] **7.9** Gk *sister* [f] **7.11** Gk *sister* [g] **7.12** Gk *him*
[h] **7.16** Gk *her* [i] **7.16** Gk *her* [j] **7.16** Other ancient authorities read *the tears of her daughter*
[k] **7.16** Other ancient authorities read *favour*
[l] **8.3** Or *fled through the air to the parts*
[m] **8.4** Gk *they* [n] **8.4** Gk *her* [o] **8.5** Gk *He*

blessed the God of heaven, and Raguel[p]
said,

'Blessed are you, O God, with
every pure blessing;
let all your chosen ones bless you.[q]
Let them bless you for ever.

16 Blessed are you because you
have made me glad.
It has not turned out
as I expected,
but you have dealt with
us according to your
great mercy.

17 Blessed are you because you
had compassion
on two only children.
Be merciful to them, O Master,
and keep them safe;
bring their lives to fulfilment
in happiness and mercy.'

18 Then he ordered his servants to fill in
the grave before daybreak.

WEDDING FEAST

19 After this he asked his wife to
bake many loaves of bread; and he went
out to the herd and brought two steers
and four rams and ordered them to be
slaughtered. So they began to make
preparations. 20 Then he called for Tobias and swore on oath to him in these
words:[r] 'You shall not leave here for
fourteen days, but shall stay here eating and drinking with me; and you shall
cheer up my daughter, who has been
depressed. 21 Take at once half of what
I own and return in safety to your father; the other half will be yours when
my wife and I die. Take courage, my
child. I am your father and Edna is your
mother, and we belong to you as well
as to your wife[s] now and for ever. Take
courage, my child.'

THE MONEY RECOVERED

9 Then Tobias called Raphael and said
to him, 2 'Brother Azariah, take four
servants and two camels with you and
travel to Rages. Go to the home of Gabael, give him the bond, get the money,
and then bring him with you to the
wedding celebration. 4 For you know
that my father must be counting the
days, and if I delay even one day I will
upset him very much. 3 You are witness
to the oath Raguel has sworn, and I cannot violate his oath.'[t] 5 So Raphael with
the four servants and two camels went
to Rages in Media and stayed with Gabael. Raphael[u] gave him the bond and informed him that Tobit's son Tobias had
married and was inviting him to the
wedding celebration. So Gabael[v] got up
and counted out to him the money bags,
with their seals intact; then they loaded
them on the camels.[w] 6 In the morning
they both got up early and went to the
wedding celebration. When they came
into Raguel's house they found Tobias reclining at table. He sprang up and
greeted Gabael,[x] who wept and blessed
him with the words, 'Good and noble
son of a father good and noble, upright
and generous! May the Lord grant the
blessing of heaven to you and your wife,
and to your wife's father and mother.
Blessed be God, for I see in Tobias the
very image of my cousin Tobit.'

ANXIETY OF THE PARENTS

10 Now, day by day, Tobit kept
counting how many days To-
bias[y] would need for going and for returning. And when the days had passed
and his son did not appear, 2 he said, 'Is
it possible that he has been detained? Or
that Gabael has died, and there is no one
to give him the money?' 3 And he began
to worry. 4 His wife Anna said, 'My child
has perished and is no longer among
the living.' And she began to weep and
mourn for her son, saying, 5 'Woe is me,
my child, the light of my eyes, that I let
you make the journey.' 6 But Tobit kept
saying to her, 'Be quiet and stop worrying, my dear;[z] he is all right. Probably
something unexpected has happened
there. The man who went with him is
trustworthy and is one of our own kin.
Do not grieve for him, my dear;[a] he will
soon be here.' 7 She answered him, 'Be
quiet yourself! Stop trying to deceive
me! My child has perished.' She would
rush out every day and watch the road
her son had taken, and would heed no
one.[b] When the sun had set she would
go in and mourn and weep all night
long, getting no sleep at all.

TOBIAS AND SARAH START FOR HOME

Now when the fourteen days of the
wedding celebration had ended that
Raguel had sworn to observe for his

[p] 8.15 Gk *they* [q] 8.15 Other ancient authorities lack this line [r] 8.20 Other ancient authorities read *Tobias and said to him* [s] 8.21 Gk *sister* [t] 9.3 In other ancient authorities verse 3 precedes verse 4 [u] 9.5 Gk *He* [v] 9.5 Gk *he* [w] 9.5 Other ancient authorities lack *on the camels* [x] 9.6 Gk *him* [y] 10.1 Gk *he* [z] 10.6 Gk *sister* [a] 10.6 Gk *sister* [b] 10.7 Other ancient authorities read *and she would eat nothing*

daughter, Tobias came to him and said,
'Send me back, for I know that my father and mother do not believe that
they will see me again. So I beg of you,
father, to let me go so that I may return to my own father. I have already
explained to you how I left him.' 8 But
Raguel said to Tobias, 'Stay, my child,
stay with me; I will send messengers to
your father Tobit and they will inform
him about you.' 9 But he said, 'No! I beg
you to send me back to my father.' 10 So
Raguel promptly gave Tobias his wife
Sarah, as well as half of all his property: male and female slaves, oxen and
sheep, donkeys and camels, clothing,
money, and household goods. 11 Then he
saw them safely off; he embraced Tobias[c] and said, 'Farewell, my child; have a
safe journey. The Lord of heaven prosper
you and your wife Sarah, and may I see
children of yours before I die.' 12 Then he
kissed his daughter Sarah and said to
her, 'My daughter, honour your father-
in-law and your mother-in-law,[d] since
from now on they are as much your parents as those who gave you birth. Go in
peace, daughter, and may I hear a good
report about you as long as I live.' Then
he bade them farewell and let them go.
Then Edna said to Tobias, 'My child and
dear brother, the Lord of heaven bring
you back safely, and may I live long
enough to see children of you and of my
daughter Sarah before I die. In the sight
of the Lord I entrust my daughter to you;
do nothing to grieve her all the days of
your life. Go in peace, my child. From
now on I am your mother and Sarah is
your beloved wife.[e] May we all prosper
together all the days of our lives.' Then
she kissed them both and saw them
safely off. 13 Tobias parted from Raguel
with happiness and joy, praising the
Lord of heaven and earth, King over all,
because he had made his journey a success. Finally, he blessed Raguel and his
wife Edna, and said, 'I have been commanded by the Lord to honour you all
the days of my life.'[f]

HOMEWARD JOURNEY

11 When they came near to Kaser-
in, which is opposite Nineveh,
Raphael said, 2 'You are aware of how
we left your father. 3 Let us run ahead of
your wife and prepare the house while
they are still on the way.' 4 As they went
on together Raphael[g] said to him, 'Have
the gall ready.' And the dog[h] went along
behind them.

5 Meanwhile, Anna sat looking intently down the road by which her son
would come. 6 When she caught sight
of him coming, she said to his father,
'Look, your son is coming, and the man
who went with him!'

TOBIT'S SIGHT RESTORED

7 Raphael said to Tobias, before he
had approached his father, 'I know that
his eyes will be opened. 8 Smear the gall
of the fish on his eyes; the medicine will
make the white films shrink and peel
off from his eyes, and your father will
regain his sight and see the light.'

9 Then Anna ran up to her son and
threw her arms around him, saying,
'Now that I have seen you, my child, I
am ready to die.' And she wept. 10 Then
Tobit got up and came stumbling out
through the courtyard door. Tobias went up to him, 11 with the gall of
the fish in his hand, and holding him
firmly, he blew into his eyes, saying,
'Take courage, father.' With this he applied the medicine on his eyes, 12 and it
made them smart.[i] 13 Next, with both
his hands he peeled off the white films
from the corners of his eyes. Then Tobit[j]
saw his son and[k] threw his arms around
him, 14 and he wept and said to him, 'I
see you, my son, the light of my eyes!'
Then he said,

'Blessed be God,
  and blessed be his great name,
  and blessed be all his holy angels.
May his holy name be blessed[l]
  throughout all the ages.
15 Though he afflicted me,
  he has had mercy upon me.[m]
  Now I see my son Tobias!'

So Tobit went in rejoicing and praising
God at the top of his voice. Tobias reported to his father that his journey had
been successful, that he had brought the
money, that he had married Raguel's
daughter Sarah, and that she was, indeed, on her way there, very near to the
gate of Nineveh.

16 Then Tobit, rejoicing and praising
God, went out to meet his daughter-in-
law at the gate of Nineveh. When the

[c] 10.11 Gk *him* [d] 10.12 Other ancient authorities lack parts of *Then . . . mother-in-law* [e] 10.12 Gk *sister* [f] 10.13 Lat: Meaning of Gk uncertain [g] 11.4 Gk *he* [h] 11.4 Codex Sinaiticus reads *And the Lord* [i] 11.12 Lat: Meaning of Gk uncertain [j] 11.13 Gk *he* [k] 11.13 Other ancient authorities lack *saw his son and* [l] 11.14 Codex Sinaiticus reads *May his great name be upon us and blessed be all the angels* [m] 11.15 Lat: Gk lacks this line

people of Nineveh saw him coming,
walking along in full vigour and with
no one leading him, they were amazed.
17Before them all, Tobit acknowledged
that God had been merciful to him and
had restored his sight. When Tobit met
Sarah the wife of his son Tobias, he
blessed her saying, 'Come in, my daughter, and welcome. Blessed be your God
who has brought you to us, my daughter. Blessed be your father and your
mother, blessed be my son Tobias, and
blessed be you, my daughter. Come in
now to your home, and welcome, with
blessing and joy. Come in, my daughter.' So on that day there was rejoicing
among all the Jews who were in Nineveh. 18Ahikar and his nephew Nadab
were also present to share Tobit's joy.
With merriment they celebrated Tobias's wedding feast for seven days, and
many gifts were given to him.[n]

RAPHAEL'S WAGES

12 When the wedding celebration
was ended, Tobit called his son
Tobias and said to him, 'My child, see to
paying the wages of the man who went
with you, and give him a bonus as well.'
2He replied, 'Father, how much shall I
pay him? It would do no harm to give
him half of the possessions brought
back with me. 3For he has led me back to
you safely, he cured my wife, he brought
the money back with me, and he healed
you. How much extra shall I give him
as a bonus?' 4Tobit said, 'He deserves,
my child, to receive half of all that he
brought back.' 5So Tobias[o] called him
and said, 'Take for your wages half of all
that you brought back, and farewell.'

RAPHAEL'S EXHORTATION

6 Then Raphael[p] called the two of
them privately and said to them, 'Bless
God and acknowledge him in the presence of all the living for the good things
he has done for you. Bless and sing praise
to his name. With fitting honour declare
to all people the deeds[q] of God. Do not
be slow to acknowledge him. 7It is good
to conceal the secret of a king, but to acknowledge and reveal the works of God,
and with fitting honour to acknowledge
him. Do good, and evil will not overtake you. 8Prayer with fasting[r] is good,
but better than both is almsgiving with
righteousness. A little with righteousness is better than wealth with wrongdoing.[s] It is better to give alms than to
lay up gold. 9For almsgiving saves from
death and purges away every sin. Those
who give alms will enjoy a full life, 10but
those who commit sin and do wrong are
their own worst enemies.

RAPHAEL DISCLOSES HIS IDENTITY

11 'I will now declare the whole truth
to you and will conceal nothing from
you. Already I have declared it to you
when I said, "It is good to conceal the
secret of a king, but to reveal with due
honour the works of God." 12So now,
when you and Sarah prayed, it was I
who brought and read[t] the record of
your prayer before the glory of the Lord,
and likewise whenever you buried the
dead. 13And that time when you did not
hesitate to get up and leave your dinner
to go and bury the dead, 14I was sent to
you to test you. And at the same time
God sent me to heal you and Sarah your
daughter-in-law. 15I am Raphael, one of
the seven angels who stand ready and
enter before the glory of the Lord.'

16 The two of them were shaken;
they fell face down, for they were afraid.
17But he said to them, 'Do not be afraid;
peace be with you. Bless God for evermore. 18As for me, when I was with you,
I was not acting on my own will, but by
the will of God. Bless him each and every day; sing his praises. 19Although
you were watching me, I really did not
eat or drink anything—but what you
saw was a vision. 20So now get up from
the ground,[u] and acknowledge God. See,
I am ascending to him who sent me.
Write down all these things that have
happened to you.' And he ascended.
21Then they stood up, and could see him
no more. 22They kept blessing God and
singing his praises, and they acknowledged God for these marvellous deeds of
his, when an angel of God had appeared
to them.

TOBIT'S THANKSGIVING TO GOD

13 Then Tobit[v] said:
'Blessed be God who
lives for ever,
because his kingdom[w] lasts
throughout all ages.

[n] 11.18 Other ancient authorities lack parts of this sentence [o] 12.5 Gk *he* [p] 12.6 Gk *he* [q] 12.6 Gk *words*; other ancient authorities read *words of the deeds* [r] 12.8 Codex Sinaiticus *with sincerity* [s] 12.8 Lat [t] 12.12 Lat: Gk lacks *and read* [u] 12.20 Other ancient authorities read *now bless the Lord on earth* [v] 13.1 Gk *he* [w] 13.1 Other ancient authorities read *for ever, and his kingdom*

2 For he afflicts, and he shows mercy;
he leads down to Hades in the
lowest regions of the earth,
and he brings up from the
great abyss,[x]
and there is nothing that
can escape his hand.
3 Acknowledge him before the nations,
O children of Israel;
for he has scattered you
among them.
4 He has shown you his
greatness even there.
Exalt him in the presence of
every living being,
because he is our Lord and
he is our God;
he is our Father and he
is God for ever.
5 He will afflict[y] you for your iniquities,
but he will again show
mercy on all of you.
He will gather you from all
the nations
among whom you have
been scattered.
6 If you turn to him with all your heart
and with all your soul,
to do what is true before him,
then he will turn to you
and will no longer hide his
face from you.
So now see what he has done for you;
acknowledge him at the
top of your voice.
Bless the Lord of righteousness,
and exalt the King of the ages.[z]
In the land of my exile I
acknowledge him,
and show his power and majesty
to a nation of sinners:
"Turn back, you sinners, and do
what is right before him;
perhaps he may look with
favour upon you and
show you mercy."
7 As for me, I exalt my God,
and my soul rejoices in the
King of heaven.
8 Let all people speak of his majesty,
and acknowledge him in Jerusalem.
9 O Jerusalem, the holy city,
he afflicted[a] you for the deeds
of your hands,[b]
but will again have mercy on the
children of the righteous.
10 Acknowledge the Lord, for
he is good,[c]
and bless the King of the ages,
so that his tent[d] may be
rebuilt in you in joy.
May he cheer all those within
you who are captives,
and love all those within you
who are distressed,
to all generations for ever.
11 A bright light will shine to all
the ends of the earth;
many nations will come to
you from far away,
the inhabitants of the remotest
parts of the earth to
your holy name,
bearing gifts in their hands for
the King of heaven.
Generation after generation will
give joyful praise in you;
the name of the chosen city
will endure for ever.
12 Cursed are all who speak a harsh
word against you;
cursed are all who conquer you
and pull down your walls,
all who overthrow your towers
and set your homes on fire.
But blessed for ever will be
all who revere you.[e]
13 Go, then, and rejoice over the
children of the righteous,
for they will be gathered together
and will praise the Lord of the ages.
14 Happy are those who love you,
and happy are those who rejoice
in your prosperity.
Happy also are all people who
grieve with you
because of your afflictions;
for they will rejoice with you
and witness all your glory for ever.
15 My soul blesses[f] the Lord,
the great King!
16 For Jerusalem will be built[g] as
his house for all ages.
How happy I will be if a remnant
of my descendants
should survive
to see your glory and acknowledge
the King of heaven.
The gates of Jerusalem will be built
with sapphire and emerald,
and all your walls with
precious stones.

[x] 13.2 Gk *from destruction* [y] 13.5 Other ancient authorities read *He afflicted* [z] 13.6 The lacuna in codex Sinaiticus, verses 6b to 10a, is filled in from other ancient authorities [a] 13.9 Other ancient authorities read *will afflict* [b] 13.9 Other ancient authorities read *your children* [c] 13.10 Other ancient authorities read *Lord worthily* [d] 13.10 Or *tabernacle* [e] 13.12 Other ancient authorities read *who build you up* [f] 13.15 Or *O my soul, bless* [g] 13.16 Other ancient authorities add *for a city*

The towers of Jerusalem will
be built with gold,
and their battlements
with pure gold.
The streets of Jerusalem
will be paved
with ruby and with
stones of Ophir.
17 The gates of Jerusalem will
sing hymns of joy,
and all her houses will
cry, "Hallelujah!
Blessed be the God of Israel!"
and the blessed will bless the holy
name for ever and ever.'

TOBIT'S FINAL COUNSEL

14 So ended Tobit's words of praise.
2 Tobit[h] died in peace when he
was one hundred and twelve years old,
and was buried with great honour in
Nineveh. He was sixty-two[i] years old
when he lost his eyesight, and after re-
gaining it he lived in prosperity, giving
alms and continually blessing God and
acknowledging God's majesty.
3 When he was about to die, he called
his son Tobias and the seven sons of
Tobias[j] and gave this command: 'My
son, take your children
4 and hurry off
to Media, for I believe the word of God
that Nahum spoke about Nineveh, that
all these things will take place and overtake Assyria and Nineveh. Indeed, everything that was spoken by the prophets of Israel, whom God sent, will occur.
None of all their words will fail, but all
will come true at their appointed times.
So it will be safer in Media than in Assyria and Babylon. For I know and believe that whatever God has said will be
fulfilled and will come true; not a single word of the prophecies will fail. All
of our kindred, inhabitants of the land
of Israel, will be scattered and taken as
captives from the good land; and the
whole land of Israel will be desolate,
even Samaria and Jerusalem will be desolate. And the temple of God in it will
be burned to the ground, and it will be
desolate for a while.[k]
5 'But God will again have mercy on
them, and God will bring them back
into the land of Israel; and they will
rebuild the temple of God, but not like
the first one until the period when the
times of fulfilment shall come. After
this they all will return from their exile
and will rebuild Jerusalem in splendour;
and in it the temple of God will be rebuilt, just as the prophets of Israel have
said concerning it.
6 Then the nations in
the whole world will all be converted
and worship God in truth. They will all
abandon their idols, which deceitfully
have led them into their error;
7 and in
righteousness they will praise the eternal God. All the Israelites who are saved
in those days and are truly mindful of
God will be gathered together; they will
go to Jerusalem and live in safety for
ever in the land of Abraham, and it will
be given over to them. Those who sincerely love God will rejoice, but those
who commit sin and injustice will vanish from all the earth.
8,9 So now, my
children, I command you, serve God
faithfully and do what is pleasing in his
sight. Your children are also to be commanded to do what is right and to give
alms, and to be mindful of God and to
bless his name at all times with sincerity and with all their strength. So now,
my son, leave Nineveh; do not remain
here.
10 On whatever day you bury your
mother beside me, do not stay overnight
within the confines of the city. For I see
that there is much wickedness within
it, and that much deceit is practised
within it, while the people are without
shame. See, my son, what Nadab did to
Ahikar who had reared him. Was he not,
while still alive, brought down into the
earth? For God repaid him to his face for
this shameful treatment. Ahikar came
out into the light, but Nadab went into
the eternal darkness, because he tried
to kill Ahikar. Because he gave alms,
Ahikar[l] escaped the fatal trap that Nadab had set for him, but Nadab fell into
it himself, and was destroyed.
11 So now,
my children, see what almsgiving accomplishes, and what injustice does—it
brings death! But now my breath fails
me.'

DEATH OF TOBIT AND ANNA

Then they laid him on his bed, and
he died; and he received an honourable
funeral.
12 When Tobias's mother died,
he buried her beside his father. Then
he and his wife and children[m] returned
to Media and settled in Ecbatana with
Raguel his father-in-law.
13 He treated
his parents-in-law[n] with great respect

[h] 14.2 Gk *He* [i] 14.2 Other ancient authorities read *fifty-eight* [j] 14.3 Lat: Gk lacks *and the seven sons of Tobias* [k] 14.4 Lat: Other ancient authorities read *of God will be in distress and will be burned for a while* [l] 14.10 Gk *he*; other ancient authorities read *Manasses*
[m] 14.12 Codex Sinaiticus lacks *and children*
[n] 14.13 Gk *them*

in their old age, and buried them in Ecbatana of Media. He inherited both the property of Raguel and that of his father Tobit. [14]He died highly respected at the age of one hundred and seventeen[o] years. [15]Before he died he heard[p] of the destruction of Nineveh, and he saw its prisoners being led into Media, those whom King Cyaxares[q] of Media had taken captive. Tobias[r] praised God for all he had done to the people of Nineveh and Assyria; before he died he rejoiced over Nineveh, and he blessed the Lord God for ever and ever. Amen.[s]

[o] **14.14** Other authorities read other numbers
[p] **14.15** Codex Sinaiticus reads *saw and heard*
[q] **14.15** Cn: Codex Sinaiticus *Ahikar*; other ancient authorities read *Nebuchadnezzar and Ahasuerus*
[r] **14.15** Gk *He* [s] **14.15** Other ancient authorities lack *Amen*

JUDITH

Written sometime at the end of the second century or the beginning of the first century BCE, the book of Judith is a dramatic short story about how God intervened on behalf of his people through the heroism of a pious widow named Judith. The story tells about how the commander of the armies of Nebuchadnezzar, Holofernes, is defeated by Judith's faith and resourcefulness. This story is inspired by the exodus narrative and was written as a reflection on the meaning of Passover. It teaches how God is committed to the survival of Israel in the midst of the great adversarial powers of the day.

A passage from Judith is provided in the Common of Saints describing her faith and beauty even as she mourned the death of her husband, Manasseh (8.2–8). Also, a passage from Judith is offered in the Roman Missal for the Common of the Blessed Virgin Mary as a Responsorial (13.18–20). It is the blessing of Uzziah upon Judith for her saving deed.

ARPHAXAD FORTIFIES ECBATANA

1 It was the twelfth year of the reign
of Nebuchadnezzar, who ruled over
the Assyrians in the great city of Nineveh. In those days Arphaxad ruled over
the Medes in Ecbatana. 2He built walls
around Ecbatana with hewn stones
three cubits thick and six cubits long; he
made the walls seventy cubits high and
fifty cubits wide. 3At its gates he raised
towers one hundred cubits high and
sixty cubits wide at the foundations.
4He made its gates seventy cubits high
and forty cubits wide to allow his armies
to march out in force and his infantry
to form their ranks. 5Then King Nebuchadnezzar made war against King Arphaxad in the great plain that is on the
borders of Ragau. 6There rallied to him
all the people of the hill country and all
those who lived along the Euphrates,
the Tigris, and the Hydaspes, and, on
the plain, Arioch, king of the Elymeans.
Thus, many nations joined the forces of
the Chaldeans.[a]

NEBUCHADNEZZAR ISSUES AN ULTIMATUM

7 Then Nebuchadnezzar, king of the
Assyrians, sent messengers to all who
lived in Persia and to all who lived in the
west, those who lived in Cilicia and Damascus, Lebanon and Antilebanon, and
all who lived along the sea coast, 8and
those among the nations of Carmel and
Gilead, and Upper Galilee and the great
plain of Esdraelon, 9and all who were in
Samaria and its towns, and beyond the
Jordan as far as Jerusalem and Bethany
and Chelous and Kadesh and the river
of Egypt, and Tahpanhes and Raamses
and the whole land of Goshen, 10even
beyond Tanis and Memphis, and all
who lived in Egypt as far as the borders of Ethiopia. 11But all who lived in
the whole region disregarded the summons of Nebuchadnezzar, king of the
Assyrians, and refused to join him in
the war; for they were not afraid of him,
but regarded him as only one man.[b] So
they sent back his messengers empty-
handed and in disgrace.

12 Then Nebuchadnezzar became
very angry with this whole region, and
swore by his throne and kingdom that
he would take revenge on the whole
territory of Cilicia and Damascus and
Syria, that he would kill with his sword
also all the inhabitants of the land of
Moab, and the people of Ammon, and

[a] 1.6 Syr: Gk *Cheleoudites* [b] 1.11 Or *a man*

all Judea, and everyone in Egypt, as far
as the coasts of the two seas.

ARPHAXAD IS DEFEATED

13 In the seventeenth year he led his
forces against King Arphaxad and defeated him in battle, overthrowing the
whole army of Arphaxad and all his cavalry and all his chariots. 14 Thus he took
possession of his towns and came to Ecbatana, captured its towers, plundered
its markets, and turned its glory into
disgrace. 15 He captured Arphaxad in
the mountains of Ragau and struck him
down with his spears, thus destroying
him once and for all. 16 Then he returned
to Nineveh, he and all his combined
forces, a vast body of troops; and there
he and his forces rested and feasted for
one hundred and twenty days.

THE EXPEDITION AGAINST THE WEST

2 In the eighteenth year, on the
twenty-second day of the first
month, there was talk in the palace of
Nebuchadnezzar, king of the Assyrians,
about carrying out his revenge on the
whole region, just as he had said. 2 He
summoned all his ministers and all his
nobles and set before them his secret
plan and recounted fully, with his own
lips, all the wickedness of the region.[c]
3 They decided that everyone who had
not obeyed his command should be destroyed.

4 When he had completed his plan,
Nebuchadnezzar, king of the Assyrians,
called Holofernes, the chief general of
his army, second only to himself, and
said to him, 5 'Thus says the Great King,
the lord of the whole earth: Leave my
presence and take with you men confident in their strength, one hundred
and twenty thousand foot-soldiers and
twelve thousand cavalry. 6 March out
against all the land to the west, because
they disobeyed my orders. 7 Tell them to
prepare earth and water, for I am coming against them in my anger, and will
cover the whole face of the earth with
the feet of my troops, to whom I will
hand them over to be plundered. 8 Their
wounded shall fill their ravines and
gullies, and the swelling river shall be
filled with their dead. 9 I will lead them
away captive to the ends of the whole
earth. 10 You shall go and seize all their
territory for me in advance. They must
yield themselves to you, and you shall
hold them for me until the day of their
punishment. 11 But to those who resist
show no mercy, but hand them over to
slaughter and plunder throughout your
whole region. 12 For as I live, and by the
power of my kingdom, what I have spoken I will accomplish by my own hand.
13 And you—take care not to transgress
any of your lord's commands, but carry
them out exactly as I have ordered you;
do it without delay.'

CAMPAIGN OF HOLOFERNES

14 So Holofernes left the presence of
his lord, and summoned all the commanders, generals, and officers of the
Assyrian army. 15 He mustered the
picked troops by divisions as his lord
had ordered him to do, one hundred
and twenty thousand of them, together
with twelve thousand archers on horseback, 16 and he organized them as a great
army is marshalled for a campaign. 17 He
took along a vast number of camels and
donkeys and mules for transport, and
innumerable sheep and oxen and goats
for food; 18 also ample rations for everyone, and a huge amount of gold and silver from the royal palace.

19 Then he set out with his whole
army, to go ahead of King Nebuchadnezzar and to cover the whole face of
the earth to the west with their chariots and cavalry and picked foot-soldiers.
20 Along with them went a mixed crowd
like a swarm of locusts, like the dust[d] of
the earth—a multitude that could not
be counted.

21 They marched for three days from
Nineveh to the plain of Bectileth, and
camped opposite Bectileth near the
mountain that is to the north of Upper
Cilicia. 22 From there Holofernes[e] took
his whole army, the infantry, cavalry,
and chariots, and went up into the hill
country. 23 He ravaged Put and Lud, and
plundered all the Rassisites and the Ishmaelites on the border of the desert,
south of the country of the Chelleans.
24 Then he followed[f] the Euphrates and
passed through Mesopotamia and destroyed all the fortified towns along
the brook Abron, as far as the sea. 25 He
also seized the territory of Cilicia, and
killed everyone who resisted him. Then
he came to the southern borders of Japheth, facing Arabia. 26 He surrounded
all the Midianites, and burned their
tents and plundered their sheepfolds.
27 Then he went down into the plain of

[c] 2.2 Meaning of Gk uncertain [d] 2.20 Gk *sand*
[e] 2.22 Gk *he* [f] 2.24 Or *crossed*

Damascus during the wheat harvest,
and burned all their fields and destroyed
their flocks and herds and sacked their
towns and ravaged their lands and put
all their young men to the sword.
28 So fear and dread of him fell upon
all the people who lived along the sea
coast, at Sidon and Tyre, and those who
lived in Sur and Ocina and all who lived
in Jamnia. Those who lived in Azotus
and Ascalon feared him greatly.

ENTREATIES FOR PEACE

3 They therefore sent messengers to
him to sue for peace in these words:
2 'We, the servants of Nebuchadnezzar,
the Great King, lie prostrate before you.
Do with us whatever you will. 3 See, our
buildings and all our land and all our
wheat fields and our flocks and herds
and all our encampments[g] lie before
you; do with them as you please. 4 Our
towns and their inhabitants are also
your slaves; come and deal with them as
you see fit.'
5 The men came to Holofernes and
told him all this. 6 Then he went down
to the sea coast with his army and stationed garrisons in the fortified towns
and took picked men from them as
auxiliaries. 7 These people and all in
the countryside welcomed him with
garlands and dances and tambourines.
8 Yet he demolished all their shrines[h]
and cut down their sacred groves; for he
had been commissioned to destroy all
the gods of the land, so that all nations
should worship Nebuchadnezzar alone,
and that all their dialects and tribes
should call upon him as a god.
9 Then he came towards Esdraelon,
near Dothan, facing the great ridge of
Judea; 10 he camped between Geba and
Scythopolis, and remained for a whole
month in order to collect all the supplies
for his army.

JUDEA ON THE ALERT

4 When the Israelites living in Judea heard of everything that Holofernes, the general of Nebuchadnezzar,
the king of the Assyrians, had done to
the nations, and how he had plundered
and destroyed all their temples, 2 they
were therefore greatly terrified at his
approach; they were alarmed both for
Jerusalem and for the temple of the
Lord their God. 3 For they had only recently returned from exile, and all the
people of Judea had just now gathered
together, and the sacred vessels and the
altar and the temple had been consecrated after their profanation. 4 So they
sent word to every district of Samaria,
and to Kona, Beth-horon, Belmain, and
Jericho, and to Choba and Aesora, and
the valley of Salem. 5 They immediately
seized all the high hilltops and fortified the villages on them and stored up
food in preparation for war—since their
fields had recently been harvested.
6 The high priest, Joakim, who was
in Jerusalem at the time, wrote to the
people of Bethulia and Betomesthaim,
which faces Esdraelon opposite the plain
near Dothan, 7 ordering them to seize
the mountain passes, since by them Judea could be invaded; and it would be
easy to stop any who tried to enter, for
the approach was narrow, wide enough
for only two at a time to pass.

PRAYER AND PENANCE

8 So the Israelites did as they had
been ordered by the high priest Joakim
and the senate of the whole people of Israel, in session at Jerusalem. 9 And every man of Israel cried out to God with
great fervour, and they humbled themselves with much fasting. 10 They and
their wives and their children and their
cattle and every resident alien and hired
labourer and purchased slave—they
all put sackcloth around their waists.
11 And all the Israelite men, women, and
children living at Jerusalem prostrated
themselves before the temple and put
ashes on their heads and spread out
their sackcloth before the Lord. 12 They
even draped the altar with sackcloth and
cried out in unison, praying fervently to
the God of Israel not to allow their infants to be carried off and their wives to
be taken as booty, and the towns they
had inherited to be destroyed, and the
sanctuary to be profaned and desecrated
to the malicious joy of the Gentiles.
13 The Lord heard their prayers and
had regard for their distress; for the people fasted for many days throughout
Judea and in Jerusalem before the sanctuary of the Lord Almighty. 14 The high
priest Joakim and all the priests who
stood before the Lord and ministered to
the Lord, with sackcloth around their
loins, offered the daily burnt-offerings,
the votive offerings, and freewill-
offerings of the people. 15 With ashes on
their turbans, they cried out to the Lord

[g] 3.3 Gk *all the sheepfolds of our tents* [h] 3.8 Syr: Gk *borders*

with all their might to look with favour
on the whole house of Israel.

COUNCIL AGAINST THE ISRAELITES

5 It was reported to Holofernes, the
general of the Assyrian army, that
the people of Israel had prepared for war
and had closed the mountain passes and
fortified all the high hilltops and set up
barricades in the plains. 2 In great anger he called together all the princes of
Moab and the commanders of Ammon
and all the governors of the coastland,
3 and said to them, 'Tell me, you Canaanites, what people is this that lives
in the hill country? What towns do they
inhabit? How large is their army, and
in what does their power and strength
consist? Who rules over them as king
and leads their army? 4 And why have
they alone, of all who live in the west,
refused to come out and meet me?'

ACHIOR'S REPORT

5 Then Achior, the leader of all the
Ammonites, said to him, 'May my lord
please listen to a report from the mouth
of your servant, and I will tell you the
truth about this people that lives in the
mountain district near you. No falsehood shall come from your servant's
mouth. 6 These people are descended
from the Chaldeans. 7 At one time they
lived in Mesopotamia, because they
did not wish to follow the gods of their
ancestors who were in Chaldea. 8 Since
they had abandoned the ways of their
ancestors, and worshipped the God of
heaven, the God they had come to know,
their ancestors[i] drove them out from
the presence of their gods. So they fled
to Mesopotamia, and lived there for a
long time. 9 Then their God commanded
them to leave the place where they were
living and go to the land of Canaan.
There they settled, and grew very prosperous in gold and silver and very much
livestock. 10 When a famine spread over
the land of Canaan they went down to
Egypt and lived there as long as they
had food. There they became so great
a multitude that their race could not
be counted. 11 So the king of Egypt became hostile to them; he exploited them
and forced them to make bricks. 12 They
cried out to their God, and he afflicted
the whole land of Egypt with incurable
plagues. So the Egyptians drove them
out of their sight. 13 Then God dried up
the Red Sea before them, 14 and he led
them by the way of Sinai and Kadesh-
barnea. They drove out all the people of
the desert, 15 and took up residence in
the land of the Amorites, and by their
might destroyed all the inhabitants of
Heshbon; and crossing over the Jordan they took possession of all the hill
country. 16 They drove out before them
the Canaanites, the Perizzites, the Jebusites, the Shechemites, and all the Ger-
gesites, and lived there a long time.

17 'As long as they did not sin against
their God they prospered, for the God
who hates iniquity is with them. 18 But
when they departed from the way he
had prescribed for them, they were utterly defeated in many battles and were
led away captive to a foreign land. The
temple of their God was razed to the
ground, and their towns were occupied
by their enemies. 19 But now they have
returned to their God, and have come
back from the places where they were
scattered, and have occupied Jerusalem,
where their sanctuary is, and have settled in the hill country, because it was
uninhabited.

20 'So now, my master and lord, if
there is any oversight in this people and
they sin against their God and we find
out their offence, then we can go up
and defeat them. 21 But if they are not
a guilty nation, then let my lord pass
them by; for their Lord and God will
defend them, and we shall become the
laughing-stock of the whole world.'

22 When Achior had finished saying
these things, all the people standing
around the tent began to complain; Holofernes' officers and all the inhabitants
of the sea coast and Moab insisted that
he should be cut to pieces. 23 They said,
'We are not afraid of the Israelites; they
are a people with no strength or power
for making war. 24 Therefore let us go
ahead, Lord Holofernes, and your vast
army will swallow them up.'

ACHIOR HANDED OVER TO THE ISRAELITES

6 When the disturbance made by the
people outside the council had died
down, Holofernes, the commander of
the Assyrian army, said to Achior[j] in
the presence of all the foreign contin-
gents:

2 'Who are you, Achior and you
mercenaries of Ephraim, to prophesy
among us as you have done today and

[i] **5.8** Gk *they* [j] **6.1** Other ancient authorities add *and to all the Moabites*

tell us not to make war against the
people of Israel because their God will
defend them? What god is there except Nebuchadnezzar? He will send his
forces and destroy them from the face of
the earth. Their God will not save them;
3we the king's[k] servants will destroy
them as one man. They cannot resist
the might of our cavalry. 4We will overwhelm them;[l] their mountains will be
drunk with their blood, and their fields
will be full of their dead. Not even their
footprints will survive our attack; they
will utterly perish. So says King Nebuchadnezzar, lord of the whole earth. For
he has spoken; none of his words shall
be in vain.
5 'As for you, Achior, you Ammonite
mercenary, you have said these words
in a moment of perversity; you shall not
see my face again from this day until I
take revenge on this race that came out
of Egypt. 6Then at my return the sword
of my army and the spear[m] of my servants shall pierce your sides, and you
shall fall among their wounded. 7Now
my slaves are going to take you back
into the hill country and put you in one
of the towns beside the passes. 8You
will not die until you perish along with
them. 9If you really hope in your heart
that they will not be taken, then do not
look downcast! I have spoken, and none
of my words shall fail to come true.'
10 Then Holofernes ordered his
slaves, who waited on him in his tent,
to seize Achior and take him away to
Bethulia and hand him over to the Israelites. 11So the slaves took him and led
him out of the camp into the plain, and
from the plain they went up into the hill
country and came to the springs below
Bethulia. 12When the men of the town
saw them,[n] they seized their weapons
and ran out of the town to the top of the
hill, and all the slingers kept them from
coming up by throwing stones at them.
13So having taken shelter below the hill,
they bound Achior and left him lying at
the foot of the hill, and returned to their
master.
14 Then the Israelites came down
from their town and found him; they
untied him and brought him into
Bethulia and placed him before the
magistrates of their town, 15who in
those days were Uzziah son of Micah, of
the tribe of Simeon, and Chabris son of
Gothoniel, and Charmis son of Melchi-
el. 16They called together all the elders
of the town, and all their young men
and women ran to the assembly. They
set Achior in the midst of all their people, and Uzziah questioned him about
what had happened. 17He answered and
told them what had taken place at the
council of Holofernes, and all that he
had said in the presence of the Assyrian leaders, and all that Holofernes had
boasted he would do against the house
of Israel. 18Then the people fell down
and worshipped God, and cried out:
19 'O Lord God of heaven, see their
arrogance, and have pity on our people
in their humiliation, and look kindly today on the faces of those who are consecrated to you.'
20 Then they reassured Achior, and
praised him highly. 21Uzziah took him
from the assembly to his own house
and gave a banquet for the elders; and
all that night they called on the God of
Israel for help.

THE CAMPAIGN AGAINST BETHULIA

7 The next day Holofernes ordered
his whole army, and all the allies
who had joined him, to break camp and
move against Bethulia, and to seize the
passes up into the hill country and make
war on the Israelites. 2So all their warriors marched off that day; their fighting forces numbered one hundred and
seventy thousand infantry and twelve
thousand cavalry, not counting the baggage and the foot-soldiers handling it, a
very great multitude. 3They encamped
in the valley near Bethulia, beside the
spring, and they spread out in breadth
over Dothan as far as Balbaim and in
length from Bethulia to Cyamon, which
faces Esdraelon.
4 When the Israelites saw their vast
numbers, they were greatly terrified
and said to one another, 'They will now
strip clean the whole land; neither the
high mountains nor the valleys nor the
hills will bear their weight.' 5Yet they all
seized their weapons, and when they
had kindled fires on their towers, they
remained on guard all that night.
6 On the second day Holofernes led
out all his cavalry in full view of the Israelites in Bethulia. 7He reconnoitred
the approaches to their town, and visited the springs that supplied their water; he seized them and set guards of
soldiers over them, and then returned
to his army.

[k] **6.3** Gk *his* [l] **6.4** Other ancient authorities add *with it* [m] **6.6** Lat Syr: Gk *people* [n] **6.12** Other ancient authorities add *on the top of the hill*

8 Then all the chieftains of the Edomites and all the leaders of the Moabites and the commanders of the coastland came to him and said, 9'Listen to what we have to say, my lord, and your army will suffer no losses. 10This people, the Israelites, do not rely on their spears but on the height of the mountains where they live, for it is not easy to reach the tops of their mountains. 11Therefore, my lord, do not fight against them in regular formation, and not a man of your army will fall. 12Remain in your camp, and keep all the men in your forces with you; let your servants take possession of the spring of water that flows from the foot of the mountain, 13for this is where all the people of Bethulia get their water. So thirst will destroy them, and they will surrender their town. Meanwhile, we and our people will go up to the tops of the nearby mountains and camp there to keep watch to see that no one gets out of the town. 14They and their wives and children will waste away with famine, and before the sword reaches them they will be strewn about in the streets where they live. 15Thus you will pay them back with evil, because they rebelled and did not receive you peaceably.'

16 These words pleased Holofernes and all his attendants, and he gave orders to do as they had said. 17So the army of the Ammonites moved forward, together with five thousand Assyrians, and they encamped in the valley and seized the water supply and the springs of the Israelites. 18And the Edomites and Ammonites went up and encamped in the hill country opposite Dothan; and they sent some of their men towards the south and the east, towards Egrebeh, which is near Chusi beside the Wadi Mochmur. The rest of the Assyrian army encamped in the plain, and covered the whole face of the land. Their tents and supply trains spread out in great number, and they formed a vast multitude.

THE DISTRESS OF THE ISRAELITES

19 The Israelites then cried out to the Lord their God, for their courage failed, because all their enemies had surrounded them, and there was no way of escape from them. 20The whole Assyrian army, their infantry, chariots, and cavalry, surrounded them for thirty-four days, until all the water containers of every inhabitant of Bethulia were empty; 21their cisterns were going dry, and on no day did they have enough water to drink, for their drinking water was rationed. 22Their children were listless, and the women and young men fainted from thirst and were collapsing in the streets of the town and in the gateways; they no longer had any strength.

23 Then all the people, the young men, the women, and the children, gathered around Uzziah and the rulers of the town and cried out with a loud voice, and said before all the elders, 24'Let God judge between you and us! You have done us a great injury in not making peace with the Assyrians. 25For now we have no one to help us; God has sold us into their hands, to be strewn before them in thirst and exhaustion. 26Now summon them and surrender the whole town as booty to the army of Holofernes and to all his forces. 27For it would be better for us to be captured by them.[o] We shall indeed become slaves, but our lives will be spared, and we shall not witness our little ones dying before our eyes, and our wives and children drawing their last breath. 28We call to witness against you heaven and earth and our God, the Lord of our ancestors, who punishes us for our sins and the sins of our ancestors; do today the things that we have described!'

29 Then great and general lamentation arose throughout the assembly, and they cried out to the Lord God with a loud voice. 30But Uzziah said to them, 'Courage, my brothers and sisters![p] Let us hold out for five days more; by that time the Lord our God will turn his mercy to us again, for he will not forsake us utterly. 31But if these days pass by, and no help comes for us, I will do as you say.'

32 Then he dismissed the people to their various posts, and they went up on the walls and towers of their town. The women and children he sent home. In the town they were in great misery.

THE CHARACTER OF JUDITH

8 Now in those days Judith heard about these things: she was the daughter of Merari son of Ox son of Joseph son of Oziel son of Elkiah son of Ananias son of Gideon son of Raphain son of Ahitub son of Elijah son of Hilkiah son of Eliab son of Nathanael son

o 7.27 Other ancient authorities add *than to die of thirst* p 7.30 Gk *Courage, brothers*

of Salamiel son of Sarasadai son of Israel. [2]Her husband Manasseh, who belonged to her tribe and family, had died
during the barley harvest. [3]For as he
stood overseeing those who were binding sheaves in the field, he was overcome by the burning heat, and took to
his bed and died in his town Bethulia.
So they buried him with his ancestors
in the field between Dothan and Bala-
mon. [4]Judith remained as a widow for
three years and four months [5]at home
where she set up a tent for herself on
the roof of her house. She put sackcloth
around her waist and dressed in widow's clothing. [6]She fasted all the days of
her widowhood, except the day before
the sabbath and the sabbath itself, the
day before the new moon and the day
of the new moon, and the festivals and
days of rejoicing of the house of Israel.
[7]She was beautiful in appearance, and
was very lovely to behold. Her husband
Manasseh had left her gold and silver,
men and women slaves, livestock, and
fields; and she maintained this estate.
[8]No one spoke ill of her, for she feared
God with great devotion.

JUDITH AND THE ELDERS

9 When Judith heard the harsh words
spoken by the people against the ruler,
because they were faint for lack of water, and when she heard all that Uzziah
said to them, and how he promised
them under oath to surrender the town
to the Assyrians after five days, [10]she
sent her maid, who was in charge of all
she possessed, to summon Uzziah and[q]
Chabris and Charmis, the elders of her
town. [11]They came to her, and she said
to them:

'Listen to me, rulers of the people
of Bethulia! What you have said to the
people today is not right; you have even
sworn and pronounced this oath between God and you, promising to surrender the town to our enemies unless
the Lord turns and helps us within so
many days. [12]Who are you to put God to
the test today, and to set yourselves up
in the place of[r] God in human affairs?
[13]You are putting the Lord Almighty to
the test, but you will never learn anything! [14]You cannot plumb the depths
of the human heart or understand the
workings of the human mind; how do
you expect to search out God, who made
all these things, and find out his mind
or comprehend his thought? No, my
brothers, do not anger the Lord our
God. [15]For if he does not choose to help
us within these five days, he has power
to protect us within any time he pleases,
or even to destroy us in the presence of
our enemies. [16]Do not try to bind the
purposes of the Lord our God; for God
is not like a human being, to be threatened, or like a mere mortal, to be won
over by pleading. [17]Therefore, while we
wait for his deliverance, let us call upon
him to help us, and he will hear our
voice if it pleases him.

18 'For never in our generation,
nor in these present days, has there
been any tribe or family or people or
town of ours that worships gods made
with hands, as was done in days gone
by. [19]That was why our ancestors were
handed over to the sword and to pillage,
and so they suffered a great catastrophe
before our enemies. [20]But we know no
other god but him, and so we hope that
he will not disdain us or any of our nation. [21]For if we are captured, all Judea
will be captured and our sanctuary will
be plundered; and he will make us pay
for its desecration with our blood. [22]The
slaughter of our kindred and the captivity of the land and the desolation of
our inheritance—all this he will bring
on our heads among the Gentiles, wherever we serve as slaves; and we shall be
an offence and a disgrace in the eyes of
those who acquire us. [23]For our slavery
will not bring us into favour, but the
Lord our God will turn it to dishonour.

24 'Therefore, my brothers, let us set
an example to our kindred, for their lives
depend upon us, and the sanctuary—
both the temple and the altar—rests
upon us. [25]In spite of everything let us
give thanks to the Lord our God, who is
putting us to the test as he did our ancestors. [26]Remember what he did with
Abraham, and how he tested Isaac, and
what happened to Jacob in Syrian Mesopotamia, while he was tending the
sheep of Laban, his mother's brother.
[27]For he has not tried us with fire, as he
did them, to search their hearts, nor has
he taken vengeance on us; but the Lord
scourges those who are close to him in
order to admonish them.'

28 Then Uzziah said to her, 'All that
you have said was spoken out of a true
heart, and there is no one who can deny
your words. [29]Today is not the first time
your wisdom has been shown, but from

[q] **8.10** Other ancient authorities lack *Uzziah and* (see verses 28 and 35) [r] **8.12** Or *above*

the beginning of your life all the people have recognized your understanding, for your heart's disposition is right. 30 But the people were so thirsty that they compelled us to do for them what we have promised, and made us take an oath that we cannot break. 31 Now since you are a God-fearing woman, pray for us, so that the Lord may send us rain to fill our cisterns. Then we will no longer feel faint from thirst.'

32 Then Judith said to them, 'Listen to me. I am about to do something that will go down through all generations of our descendants. 33 Stand at the town gate tonight so that I may go out with my maid; and within the days after which you have promised to surrender the town to our enemies, the Lord will deliver Israel by my hand. 34 Only, do not try to find out what I am doing; for I will not tell you until I have finished what I am about to do.'

35 Uzziah and the rulers said to her, 'Go in peace, and may the Lord God go before you, to take vengeance on our enemies.' 36 So they returned from the tent and went to their posts.

THE PRAYER OF JUDITH

9 Then Judith prostrated herself, put ashes on her head, and uncovered the sackcloth she was wearing. At the very time when the evening incense was being offered in the house of God in Jerusalem, Judith cried out to the Lord with a loud voice, and said:

2 'O Lord God of my ancestor Simeon, to whom you gave a sword to take revenge on those strangers who had torn off a virgin's clothing[s] to defile her, and exposed her thighs to put her to shame, and polluted her womb to disgrace her; for you said, "It shall not be done"—yet they did it; 3 so you gave up their rulers to be killed, and their bed, which was ashamed of the deceit they had practised, was stained with blood, and you struck down slaves along with princes, and princes on their thrones. 4 You gave up their wives for booty and their daughters to captivity, and all their booty to be divided among your beloved children who burned with zeal for you and abhorred the pollution of their blood and called on you for help. O God, my God, hear me also, a widow.

5 'For you have done these things and those that went before and those that followed. You have designed the things that are now, and those that are to come. What you had in mind has happened; 6 the things you decided on presented themselves and said, "Here we are!" For all your ways are prepared in advance, and your judgement is with foreknowledge.

7 'Here now are the Assyrians, a greatly increased force, priding themselves on their horses and riders, boasting in the strength of their foot-soldiers, and trusting in shield and spear, in bow and sling. They do not know that you are the Lord who crushes wars; the Lord is your name. 8 Break their strength by your might, and bring down their power in your anger; for they intend to defile your sanctuary, and to pollute the tabernacle where your glorious name resides, and to break off the horns[t] of your altar with the sword. 9 Look at their pride, and send your wrath upon their heads. Give to me, a widow, the strong hand to do what I plan. 10 By the deceit of my lips strike down the slave with the prince and the prince with his servant; crush their arrogance by the hand of a woman.

11 'For your strength does not depend on numbers, nor your might on the powerful. But you are the God of the lowly, helper of the oppressed, upholder of the weak, protector of the forsaken, saviour of those without hope. 12 Please, please, God of my father, God of the heritage of Israel, Lord of heaven and earth, Creator of the waters, King of all your creation, hear my prayer! 13 Make my deceitful words bring wound and bruise on those who have planned cruel things against your covenant, and against your sacred house, and against Mount Zion, and against the house your children possess. 14 Let your whole nation and every tribe know and understand that you are God, the God of all power and might, and that there is no other who protects the people of Israel but you alone!'

JUDITH PREPARES TO GO TO HOLOFERNES

10 When Judith[u] had stopped crying out to the God of Israel, and had ended all these words, 2 she rose from where she lay prostrate. She called her maid and went down into the house where she lived on sabbaths and on her festal days. 3 She removed the sackcloth she had been wearing, took off her wid-

[s] **9.2** Cn: Gk *loosed her womb* [t] **9.8** Syr: Gk *horn*
[u] **10.1** Gk *she*

ow's garments, bathed her body with
water, and anointed herself with precious ointment. She combed her hair,
put on a tiara, and dressed herself in the
festive attire that she used to wear while
her husband Manasseh was living. 4 She
put sandals on her feet, and put on her
anklets, bracelets, rings, ear-rings, and
all her other jewellery. Thus she made
herself very beautiful, to entice the
eyes of all the men who might see her.
5 She gave her maid a skin of wine and a
flask of oil, and filled a bag with roasted
grain, dried fig cakes, and fine bread;[v]
then she wrapped up all her dishes and
gave them to her to carry.
6 Then they went out to the town gate
of Bethulia and found Uzziah standing
there with the elders of the town, Chabris and Charmis. 7 When they saw her
transformed in appearance and dressed
differently, they were very greatly astounded at her beauty and said to her,
8 'May the God of our ancestors grant you
favour and fulfil your plans, so that the
people of Israel may glory and Jerusalem
may be exalted.' She bowed down to God.
9 Then she said to them, 'Order the
gate of the town to be opened for me so
that I may go out and accomplish the
things you have just said to me.' So they
ordered the young men to open the gate
for her, as she requested. 10 When they
had done this, Judith went out, accompanied by her maid. The men of the
town watched her until she had gone
down the mountain and passed through
the valley, where they lost sight of her.

JUDITH IS CAPTURED

11 As the women[w] were going
straight on through the valley, an Assyrian patrol met her 12 and took her
into custody. They asked her, 'To what
people do you belong, and where are
you coming from, and where are you
going?' She replied, 'I am a daughter
of the Hebrews, but I am fleeing from
them, for they are about to be handed
over to you to be devoured. 13 I am on my
way to see Holofernes the commander
of your army, to give him a true report; I
will show him a way by which he can go
and capture all the hill country without
losing one of his men, captured or slain.'
14 When the men heard her words,
and observed her face—she was in their
eyes marvellously beautiful—they said
to her, 15 'You have saved your life by
hurrying down to see our lord. Go at
once to his tent; some of us will escort
you and hand you over to him. 16 When
you stand before him, have no fear in
your heart, but tell him what you have
just said, and he will treat you well.'
17 They chose from their number a
hundred men to accompany her and her
maid, and they brought them to the tent
of Holofernes. 18 There was great excite-
ment in the whole camp, for her arrival
was reported from tent to tent. They came
and gathered around her as she stood
outside the tent of Holofernes, waiting
until they told him about her. 19 They
marvelled at her beauty and admired the
Israelites, judging them by her. They said
to one another, 'Who can despise these
people, who have women like this among
them? It is not wise to leave one of their
men alive, for if we let them go they will
be able to beguile the whole world!'

JUDITH IS BROUGHT BEFORE HOLOFERNES

20 Then the guards of Holofernes and
all his servants came out and led her
into the tent. 21 Holofernes was resting
on his bed under a canopy that was woven with purple and gold, emeralds and
other precious stones. 22 When they told
him of her, he came to the front of the
tent, with silver lamps carried before
him. 23 When Judith came into the presence of Holofernes[x] and his servants,
they all marvelled at the beauty of her
face. She prostrated herself and did
obeisance to him, but his slaves raised
her up.

11 Then Holofernes said to her,
'Take courage, woman, and do
not be afraid in your heart, for I have
never hurt anyone who chose to serve
Nebuchadnezzar, king of all the earth.
2 Even now, if your people who live in
the hill country had not slighted me,
I would never have lifted my spear
against them. They have brought this
on themselves. 3 But now tell me why
you have fled from them and have come
over to us. In any event, you have come
to safety. Take courage! You will live tonight and ever after. 4 No one will hurt
you. Rather, all will treat you well, as
they do the servants of my lord King
Nebuchadnezzar.'

JUDITH EXPLAINS HER PRESENCE

5 Judith answered him, 'Accept the
words of your slave, and let your servant

[v] **10.5** Other ancient authorities add *and cheese*
[w] **10.11** Gk *they* [x] **10.23** Gk *him*

speak in your presence. I will say nothing false to my lord this night. [6]If you
follow out the words of your servant,
God will accomplish something through
you, and my lord will not fail to achieve
his purposes. [7]By the life of Nebuchadnezzar, king of the whole earth, and by
the power of him who has sent you to
direct every living being! Not only do
human beings serve him because of
you, but also the animals of the field
and the cattle and the birds of the air
will live, because of your power, under
Nebuchadnezzar and all his house. [8]For
we have heard of your wisdom and skill,
and it is reported throughout the whole
world that you alone are the best in the
whole kingdom, the most informed and
the most astounding in military strategy.

9 'Now as for Achior's speech in your
council, we have heard his words, for
the people of Bethulia spared him and
he told them all he had said to you.
[10]Therefore, lord and master, do not disregard what he said, but keep it in your
mind, for it is true. Indeed our nation
cannot be punished, nor can the sword
prevail against them, unless they sin
against their God.

11 'But now, in order that my lord
may not be defeated and his purpose
frustrated, death will fall upon them, for
a sin has overtaken them by which they
are about to provoke their God to anger
when they do what is wrong. [12]Since
their food supply is exhausted and their
water has almost given out, they have
planned to kill their livestock and have
determined to use all that God by his
laws has forbidden them to eat. [13]They
have decided to consume the first fruits
of the grain and the tithes of the wine
and oil, which they had consecrated and
set aside for the priests who minister in
the presence of our God in Jerusalem—
things it is not lawful for any of the
people even to touch with their hands.
[14]Since even the people in Jerusalem
have been doing this, they have sent
messengers there in order to bring back
permission from the council of the elders. [15]When the response reaches them
and they act upon it, on that very day
they will be handed over to you to be destroyed.

16 'So when I, your slave, learned all
this, I fled from them. God has sent me
to accomplish with you things that will
astonish the whole world wherever people shall hear about them. [17]Your servant is indeed God-fearing and serves
the God of heaven night and day. So,
my lord, I will remain with you; but every night your servant will go out into
the valley and pray to God. He will tell
me when they have committed their
sins. [18]Then I will come and tell you, so
that you may go out with your whole
army, and not one of them will be able
to withstand you. [19]Then I will lead you
through Judea, until you come to Jerusalem; there I will set your throne.[y] You
will drive them like sheep that have
no shepherd, and no dog will so much
as growl at you. For this was told me
to give me foreknowledge; it was announced to me, and I was sent to tell
you.'

20 Her words pleased Holofernes and
all his servants. They marvelled at her
wisdom and said, [21]'No other woman
from one end of the earth to the other
looks so beautiful or speaks so wisely!'
[22]Then Holofernes said to her, 'God has
done well to send you ahead of the people, to strengthen our hands and bring
destruction on those who have despised
my lord. [23]You are not only beautiful in
appearance, but wise in speech. If you
do as you have said, your God shall be
my God, and you shall live in the palace of King Nebuchadnezzar and be renowned throughout the whole world.'

JUDITH AS A GUEST OF HOLOFERNES

12 Then he commanded them to
bring her in where his silver dinnerware was kept, and ordered them to
set a table for her with some of his own
delicacies, and with some of his own
wine to drink. [2]But Judith said, 'I cannot partake of them, or it will be an offence; but I will have enough with the
things I brought with me.' [3]Holofernes
said to her, 'If your supply runs out,
where can we get you more of the same?
For none of your people are here with
us.' [4]Judith replied, 'As surely as you
live, my lord, your servant will not use
up the supplies I have with me before
the Lord carries out by my hand what
he has determined.'

5 Then the servants of Holofernes
brought her into the tent, and she slept
until midnight. Towards the morning
watch she got up [6]and sent this message
to Holofernes: 'Let my lord now give orders to allow your servant to go out and
pray.' [7]So Holofernes commanded his

[y] 11.19 Or *chariot*

guards not to hinder her. She remained
in the camp for three days. She went out
each night to the valley of Bethulia, and
bathed at the spring in the camp.[z] 8 After bathing, she prayed the Lord God of
Israel to direct her way for the triumph
of his[a] people. 9 Then she returned purified and stayed in the tent until she ate
her food towards evening.

JUDITH ATTENDS HOLOFERNES' BANQUET

10 On the fourth day Holofernes held
a banquet for his personal attendants
only, and did not invite any of his officers. 11 He said to Bagoas, the eunuch
who had charge of his personal affairs,
'Go and persuade the Hebrew woman
who is in your care to join us and to
eat and drink with us. 12 For it would
be a disgrace if we let such a woman go
without having intercourse with her.
If we do not seduce her, she will laugh
at us.'

13 So Bagoas left the presence of Holofernes, and approached her and said,
'Let this pretty girl not hesitate to come
to my lord to be honoured in his presence, and to enjoy drinking wine with
us, and to become today like one of the
Assyrian women who serve in the palace of Nebuchadnezzar.' 14 Judith replied,
'Who am I to refuse my lord? Whatever
pleases him I will do at once, and it will
be a joy to me until the day of my death.'
15 So she proceeded to dress herself in
all her woman's finery. Her maid went
ahead and spread for her on the ground
before Holofernes the lambskins she
had received from Bagoas for her daily
use in reclining.

16 Then Judith came in and lay
down. Holofernes' heart was ravished
with her and his passion was aroused,
for he had been waiting for an opportunity to seduce her from the day he first
saw her. 17 So Holofernes said to her,
'Have a drink and be merry with us!'
18 Judith said, 'I will gladly drink, my
lord, because today is the greatest day in
my whole life.' 19 Then she took what her
maid had prepared and ate and drank
before him. 20 Holofernes was greatly
pleased with her, and drank a great
quantity of wine, much more than he
had ever drunk in any one day since he
was born.

JUDITH BEHEADS HOLOFERNES

13 When evening came, his slaves
quickly withdrew. Bagoas closed
the tent from outside and shut out the
attendants from his master's presence.
They went to bed, for they all were
weary because the banquet had lasted
so long. 2 But Judith was left alone in the
tent, with Holofernes stretched out on
his bed, for he was dead drunk.

3 Now Judith had told her maid to
stand outside the bedchamber and to
wait for her to come out, as she did on
the other days; for she said she would be
going out for her prayers. She had said
the same thing to Bagoas. 4 So everyone
went out, and no one, either small or
great, was left in the bedchamber. Then
Judith, standing beside his bed, said in
her heart, 'O Lord God of all might, look
in this hour on the work of my hands
for the exaltation of Jerusalem. 5 Now
indeed is the time to help your heritage and to carry out my design to destroy the enemies who have risen up
against us.'

6 She went up to the bedpost near
Holofernes' head, and took down his
sword that hung there. 7 She came close
to his bed, took hold of the hair of his
head, and said, 'Give me strength today,
O Lord God of Israel!' 8 Then she struck
his neck twice with all her might, and
cut off his head. 9 Next she rolled his
body off the bed and pulled down the
canopy from the posts. Soon afterwards
she went out and gave Holofernes' head
to her maid, 10 who placed it in her food
bag.

JUDITH RETURNS TO BETHULIA

Then the two of them went out together, as they were accustomed to do
for prayer. They passed through the
camp, circled around the valley, and
went up the mountain to Bethulia, and
came to its gates. 11 From a distance Judith called out to the sentries at the
gates, 'Open, open the gate! God, our
God, is with us, still showing his power
in Israel and his strength against our
enemies, as he has done today!'

12 When the people of her town
heard her voice, they hurried down to
the town gate and summoned the elders of the town. 13 They all ran together,
both small and great, for it seemed un-
believable that she had returned. They
opened the gate and welcomed them.
Then they lit a fire to give light, and
gathered around them. 14 Then she said

[z] 12.7 Other ancient authorities lack *in the camp*
[a] 12.8 Other ancient authorities read *her*

to them with a loud voice, 'Praise God,
O praise him! Praise God, who has not
withdrawn his mercy from the house of
Israel, but has destroyed our enemies by
my hand this very night!'
15 Then she pulled the head out of
the bag and showed it to them, and
said, 'See here, the head of Holofernes,
the commander of the Assyrian army,
and here is the canopy beneath which
he lay in his drunken stupor. The Lord
has struck him down by the hand of a
woman. 16 As the Lord lives, who has
protected me on the way I went, I swear
that it was my face that seduced him to
his destruction, and that he committed
no sin with me, to defile and shame me.'
17 All the people were greatly astonished. They bowed down and worshipped God, and said with one accord,
'Blessed are you our God, who have this
day humiliated the enemies of your people.'
18 Then Uzziah said to her, 'O daughter, you are blessed by the Most High
God above all other women on earth;
and blessed be the Lord God, who created the heavens and the earth, who
has guided you to cut off the head of the
leader of our enemies. 19 Your praise[b]
will never depart from the hearts of
those who remember the power of God.
20 May God grant this to be a perpetual
honour to you, and may he reward you
with blessings, because you risked your
own life when our nation was brought
low, and you averted our ruin, walking
in the straight path before our God.' And
all the people said, 'Amen. Amen.'

JUDITH'S COUNSEL

14 Then Judith said to them, 'Listen to me, my friends. Take this
head and hang it upon the parapet of
your wall. 2 As soon as day breaks and
the sun rises on the earth, each of you
take up your weapons, and let every
able-bodied man go out of the town; set
a captain over them, as if you were going down to the plain against the Assyrian outpost; only do not go down. 3 Then
they will seize their arms and go into
the camp and rouse the officers of the
Assyrian army. They will rush into the
tent of Holofernes and will not find him.
Then panic will come over them, and
they will flee before you. 4 Then you and
all who live within the borders of Israel
will pursue them and cut them down in
their tracks. 5 But before you do all this,
bring Achior the Ammonite to me so
that he may see and recognize the man
who despised the house of Israel and
sent him to us as if to his death.'
6 So they summoned Achior from
the house of Uzziah. When he came
and saw the head of Holofernes in the
hand of one of the men in the assembly
of the people, he fell down on his face
in a faint. 7 When they raised him up he
threw himself at Judith's feet, and did
obeisance to her, and said, 'Blessed are
you in every tent of Judah! In every nation those who hear your name will be
alarmed. 8 Now tell me what you have
done during these days.'
So Judith told him in the presence of
the people all that she had done, from
the day she left until the moment she
began speaking to them. 9 When she had
finished, the people raised a great shout
and made a joyful noise in their town.
10 When Achior saw all that the God of
Israel had done, he believed firmly in
God. So he was circumcised, and joined
the house of Israel, remaining so to this
day.

HOLOFERNES' DEATH IS DISCOVERED

11 As soon as it was dawn they hung
the head of Holofernes on the wall. Then
they all took their weapons, and they
went out in companies to the mountain
passes. 12 When the Assyrians saw them
they sent word to their commanders,
who then went to the generals and the
captains and to all their other officers.
13 They came to Holofernes' tent and
said to the steward in charge of all his
personal affairs, 'Wake up our lord, for
the slaves have been so bold as to come
down against us to give battle, to their
utter destruction.'
14 So Bagoas went in and knocked
at the entry of the tent, for he supposed
that he was sleeping with Judith. 15 But
when no one answered, he opened it
and went into the bedchamber and
found him sprawled on the floor dead,
with his head missing. 16 He cried out
with a loud voice and wept and groaned
and shouted, and tore his clothes.
17 Then he went to the tent where Judith
had stayed, and when he did not find
her, he rushed out to the people and
shouted, 18 'The slaves have tricked us!
One Hebrew woman has brought disgrace on the house of King Nebuchadnezzar. Look, Holofernes is lying on the
ground, and his head is missing!'

[b] **13.19** Other ancient authorities read *hope*

19 When the leaders of the Assyrian
army heard this, they tore their tunics
and were greatly dismayed, and their
loud cries and shouts rose up throughout the camp.

THE ASSYRIANS FLEE IN PANIC

15 When the men in the tents
heard it, they were amazed at
what had happened. 2Overcome with
fear and trembling, they did not wait
for one another, but with one impulse
all rushed out and fled by every path
across the plain and through the hill
country. 3Those who had camped in the
hills around Bethulia also took to flight.
Then the Israelites, everyone that was a
soldier, rushed out upon them. 4Uzziah
sent men to Betomasthaim[c] and Choba
and Kola, and to all the frontiers of Israel, to tell what had taken place and
to urge all to rush out upon the enemy
to destroy them. 5When the Israelites
heard it, with one accord they fell upon
the enemy,[d] and cut them down as far
as Choba. Those in Jerusalem and all the
hill country also came, for they were told
what had happened in the camp of the
enemy. The men in Gilead and in Galilee
outflanked them with great slaughter,
even beyond Damascus and its borders.
6The rest of the people of Bethulia fell
upon the Assyrian camp and plundered
it, acquiring great riches. 7And the Israelites, when they returned from the
slaughter, took possession of what remained. Even the villages and towns in
the hill country and in the plain got a
great amount of booty, since there was
a vast quantity of it.

THE ISRAELITES CELEBRATE THEIR VICTORY

8 Then the high priest Joakim and
the elders of the Israelites who lived
in Jerusalem came to witness the good
things that the Lord had done for Israel,
and to see Judith and to wish her well.
9When they met her, they all blessed her
with one accord and said to her, 'You are
the glory of Jerusalem, you are the great
boast of Israel, you are the great pride
of our nation! 10You have done all this
with your own hand; you have done
great good to Israel, and God is well
pleased with it. May the Almighty Lord
bless you for ever!' And all the people
said, 'Amen.'

11 All the people plundered the
camp for thirty days. They gave Judith
the tent of Holofernes and all his silver
dinnerware, his beds, his bowls, and all
his furniture. She took them and loaded
her mules and hitched up her carts and
piled the things on them.

12 All the women of Israel gathered
to see her, and blessed her, and some
of them performed a dance in her honour. She took ivy-wreathed wands in
her hands and distributed them to the
women who were with her; 13and she
and those who were with her crowned
themselves with olive wreaths. She
went before all the people in the dance,
leading all the women, while all the
men of Israel followed, bearing their
arms and wearing garlands and singing
hymns.

JUDITH OFFERS HER HYMN OF PRAISE

14 Judith began this thanksgiving before all Israel, and all the people
loudly sang this song of praise.

16 1And Judith said,

Begin a song to my God with
tambourines,
sing to my Lord with cymbals.
Raise to him a new psalm;[e]
exalt him, and call upon his name.
2 For the Lord is a God who
crushes wars;
he sets up his camp among
his people;
he delivered me from the
hands of my pursuers.
3 The Assyrian came down from the
mountains of the north;
he came with myriads
of his warriors;
their numbers blocked up the wadis,
and their cavalry covered the hills.
4 He boasted that he would burn
up my territory,
and kill my young men
with the sword,
and dash my infants to the ground,
and seize my children as booty,
and take my virgins as spoil.

5 But the Lord Almighty has
foiled them
by the hand of a woman.[f]
6 For their mighty one did not fall by
the hands of the young men,
nor did the sons of the Titans
strike him down,
nor did tall giants set upon him;

[c] **15.4** Other ancient authorities add *and Bebai*
[d] **15.5** Gk *them*
[e] **16.1** Other ancient authorities read *a psalm and praise*
[f] **16.5** Other ancient authorities add *he has confounded them*

but Judith daughter of Merari
with the beauty of her
countenance undid him.

7 For she put away her
widow's clothing
to exalt the oppressed in Israel.
She anointed her face with perfume;
8 she fastened her hair with a tiara
and put on a linen gown
to beguile him.
9 Her sandal ravished his eyes,
her beauty captivated his mind,
and the sword severed his neck!
10 The Persians trembled at
her boldness,
the Medes were daunted
at her daring.

11 Then my oppressed people shouted;
my weak people cried out,[g] and
the enemy[h] trembled;
they lifted up their voices, and the
enemy[i] were turned back.
12 Sons of slave-girls pierced
them through
and wounded them like the
children of fugitives;
they perished before the
army of my Lord.

13 I will sing to my God a new song:
O Lord, you are great and glorious,
wonderful in strength,
invincible.
14 Let all your creatures serve you,
for you spoke, and they
were made.
You sent forth your spirit,[j] and
it formed them;[k]
there is none that can
resist your voice.
15 For the mountains shall be shaken
to their foundations
with the waters;
before your glance the rocks
shall melt like wax.
But to those who fear you
you show mercy.
16 For every sacrifice as a fragrant
offering is a small thing,
and the fat of all whole
burnt-offerings to you
is a very little thing;
but whoever fears the Lord
is great for ever.

17 Woe to the nations that rise up
against my people!
The Lord Almighty will take
vengeance on them in
the day of judgement;
he will send fire and worms
into their flesh;
they shall weep in pain for ever.

18 When they arrived at Jerusalem,
they worshipped God. As soon as the
people were purified, they offered their
burnt-offerings, their freewill-offerings,
and their gifts. 19 Judith also dedicated
to God all the possessions of Holofernes,
which the people had given her; and
the canopy that she had taken for herself from his bedchamber she gave as a
votive offering. 20 For three months the
people continued feasting in Jerusalem
before the sanctuary, and Judith remained with them.

THE RENOWN AND DEATH OF JUDITH

21 After this they all returned home
to their own inheritances. Judith went
to Bethulia, and remained on her estate.
For the rest of her life she was honoured
throughout the whole country. 22 Many
desired to marry her, but she gave herself
to no man all the days of her life after her
husband Manasseh died and was gathered to his people. 23 She became more
and more famous, and grew old in her
husband's house, reaching the age of one
hundred and five. She set her maid free.
She died in Bethulia, and they buried
her in the cave of her husband Manasseh; 24 and the house of Israel mourned
her for seven days. Before she died she
distributed her property to all those who
were next of kin to her husband Manasseh, and to her own nearest kindred.
25 No one ever again spread terror among
the Israelites during the lifetime of Judith, or for a long time after her death.

g **16.11** Other ancient authorities read *feared*
h **16.11** Gk *they* i **16.11** Gk *they* j **16.14** Or *breath* k **16.14** Other ancient authorities read *they were created*

ESTHER

Esther is the story of how the Jewish Queen Esther and her uncle, Mordecai, are able to thwart the wicked Haman, who conspires to destroy the Jews living in the Persian Empire at the time of King Artaxerxes (Ahasuerus) between 485 and 464 BCE. The book itself was probably written at the end of the fourth century BCE. The purpose of the book is to remind the people of Israel of God's providence on their behalf. It is a story that marks the origin and significance of the Jewish feast of Purim.

Originally written in Hebrew, the book of Esther is preserved in its Greek form by the Orthodox and Roman Catholic canons. As in the other deuterocanonical writings (Tobit and Judith), the characters in this story are exemplary role models.

A passage from the book of Esther is read in Years I and II on Thursday of the First Week of Lent. The text is the desperate prayer of Queen Esther addressed to the Lord God of Israel to intervene at a critical time to turn the fate of her people.

Note: The deuterocanonical portions of the book of Esther are translated from the Greek version (Septuagint) and comprise one hundred and seven additional verses that have been inserted at the appropriate places in the translation of the Hebrew form of the book. The disordered chapter numbers come from the displacement of the additions to the end of the Hebrew form of the book of Esther by St. Jerome in his Latin Vulgate translation and from the subsequent division of the Bible into chapters by Stephen Langton, who numbered the additions consecutively as though they formed a direct continuation of the Hebrew text. The deuterocanonical portions are given in the order found in the Greek text so that they may be read in their proper context, but the chapter and verse numbers conform to those of the King James or Authorized Version. Proper names are given according to their Hebrew rather than their Greek form; for example, Ahasuerus and Mordecai instead of Artaxerxes and Mardocheus. The additions, conveniently indicated by the letters A–F, are located as follows: A, before 1.1; B, after 3.13; C and D, after 4.17; E, after 8.12; F, after 10.3.

ADDITION A

MORDECAI'S DREAM

11[a] 2In the second year of the reign
of Ahasuerus the Great, on the
first day of Nisan, Mordecai son of Jair
son of Shimei[b] son of Kish, of the tribe
of Benjamin, had a dream. 3He was a
Jew living in the city of Susa, a great
man, serving in the court of the king.
4He was one of the captives whom
King Nebuchadnezzar of Babylon had
brought from Jerusalem with King
Jeconiah of Judah. And this was his
dream: 5Noises[c] and confusion, thunders and earthquake, tumult on the
earth! 6Then two great dragons came
forward, both ready to fight, and they
roared terribly. 7At their roaring every
nation prepared for war, to fight against
the righteous nation. 8It was a day of

[a] 11.1 Chapters 11.2—12.6 correspond to chapter A 1–17 in some translations. [b] 11.2 Gk *Semeios* [c] 11.5 Or *Voices*

darkness and gloom, of tribulation and
distress, affliction and great tumult on
the earth! 9 And the whole righteous nation was troubled; they feared the evils
that threatened them,[d] and were ready
to perish. 10 Then they cried out to God;
and at their outcry, as though from a
tiny spring, there came a great river,
with abundant water; 11 light came, and
the sun rose, and the lowly were exalted
and devoured those held in honour.

12 Mordecai saw in this dream what
God had determined to do, and after he
awoke he had it on his mind, seeking all
day to understand it in every detail.

A PLOT AGAINST THE KING

12 Now Mordecai took his rest in
the courtyard with Bigthan and
Teresh, the two eunuchs of the king
who kept watch in the courtyard. 2 He
overheard their conversation and inquired into their purposes, and learned
that they were preparing to lay hands
on King Ahasuerus; and he informed
the king concerning them. 3 Then the
king examined the two eunuchs, and
after they had confessed it, they were
led away to execution. 4 The king made
a permanent record of these things, and
Mordecai wrote an account of them.
5 And the king ordered Mordecai to
serve in the court, and rewarded him for
these things. 6 But Haman son of Hammedatha, the Agagite, who was held in
great honour by the king, determined to
injure Mordecai and his people because
of the two eunuchs of the king.

END OF ADDITION A

KING AHASUERUS DEPOSES QUEEN VASHTI

1 This happened in the days of Ahasuerus, the same Ahasuerus who
ruled over one hundred and twenty-
seven provinces from India to Ethiopia.[e]
2 In those days when King Ahasuerus
sat on his royal throne in the citadel of
Susa, 3 in the third year of his reign, he
gave a banquet for all his officials and
ministers. The army of Persia and Media and the nobles and governors of the
provinces were present, 4 while he displayed the great wealth of his kingdom
and the splendour and pomp of his majesty for many days, one hundred and
eighty days in all.

5 When these days were completed,
the king gave for all the people present in the citadel of Susa, both great
and small, a banquet lasting for seven
days, in the court of the garden of the
king's palace. 6 There were white cotton
curtains and blue hangings tied with
cords of fine linen and purple to silver
rings[f] and marble pillars. There were
couches of gold and silver on a mosaic
pavement of porphyry, marble, mother-
of-pearl, and coloured stones. 7 Drinks
were served in golden goblets, goblets
of different kinds, and the royal wine
was lavished in accordance with the
bounty of the king. 8 Drinking was by
flagons, without restraint; for the king
had given orders to all the officials of his
palace to do as each one desired. 9 Furthermore, Queen Vashti gave a banquet
for the women in the palace of King
Ahasuerus.

10 On the seventh day, when the
king was merry with wine, he commanded Mehuman, Biztha, Harbona,
Bigtha and Abagtha, Zethar and Car-
kas, the seven eunuchs who attended
him, 11 to bring Queen Vashti before the
king, wearing the royal crown, in order
to show the peoples and the officials
her beauty; for she was fair to behold.
12 But Queen Vashti refused to come at
the king's command conveyed by the
eunuchs. At this the king was enraged,
and his anger burned within him.

13 Then the king consulted the sages
who knew the laws[g] (for this was the
king's procedure towards all who were
versed in law and custom, 14 and those
next to him were Carshena, Shethar,
Admatha, Tarshish, Meres, Marsena,
and Memucan, the seven officials of
Persia and Media, who had access to
the king, and sat first in the kingdom):
15 'According to the law, what is to be
done to Queen Vashti because she has
not performed the command of King
Ahasuerus conveyed by the eunuchs?'
16 Then Memucan said in the presence
of the king and the officials, 'Not only
has Queen Vashti done wrong to the
king, but also to all the officials and
all the peoples who are in all the provinces of King Ahasuerus. 17 For this deed
of the queen will be made known to all
women, causing them to look with contempt on their husbands, since they
will say, "King Ahasuerus commanded
Queen Vashti to be brought before
him, and she did not come." 18 This very

[d] **11.9** Gk *their own evils* [e] **1.1** Or *Nubia*; Heb *Cush* [f] **1.6** Or *rods* [g] **1.13** Cn: Heb *times*

day the noble ladies of Persia and Media who have heard of the queen's behaviour will rebel against[h] the king's
officials, and there will be no end of
contempt and wrath! 19 If it pleases the
king, let a royal order go out from him,
and let it be written among the laws of
the Persians and the Medes so that it
may not be altered, that Vashti is never
again to come before King Ahasuerus;
and let the king give her royal position
to another who is better than she. 20 So
when the decree made by the king is
proclaimed throughout all his kingdom,
vast as it is, all women will give honour
to their husbands, high and low alike.'

21 This advice pleased the king and
the officials, and the king did as Memucan proposed; 22 he sent letters to all
the royal provinces, to every province
in its own script and to every people
in its own language, declaring that every man should be master in his own
house.[i]

ESTHER BECOMES QUEEN

2 After these things, when the anger
of King Ahasuerus had abated, he
remembered Vashti and what she had
done and what had been decreed against
her. 2 Then the king's servants who attended him said, 'Let beautiful young
virgins be sought out for the king. 3 And
let the king appoint commissioners
in all the provinces of his kingdom to
gather all the beautiful young virgins to
the harem in the citadel of Susa under
the custody of Hegai, the king's eunuch,
who is in charge of the women; let their
cosmetic treatments be given them.
4 And let the girl who pleases the king
be queen instead of Vashti.' This pleased
the king, and he did so.

5 Now there was a Jew in the citadel of Susa whose name was Mordecai
son of Jair son of Shimei son of Kish, a
Benjaminite. 6 Kish[j] had been carried
away from Jerusalem among the captives carried away with King Jeconiah
of Judah, whom King Nebuchadnezzar
of Babylon had carried away. 7 Mordecai[k] had brought up Hadassah, that is
Esther, his cousin, for she had neither
father nor mother; the girl was fair and
beautiful, and when her father and her
mother died, Mordecai adopted her as
his own daughter. 8 So when the king's
order and his edict were proclaimed,
and when many young women were
gathered in the citadel of Susa in the
custody of Hegai, Esther also was taken
into the king's palace and put in the
custody of Hegai, who had charge of the
women. 9 The girl pleased him and won
his favour, and he quickly provided her
with her cosmetic treatments and her
portion of food, and with seven chosen
maids from the king's palace, and advanced her and her maids to the best
place in the harem. 10 Esther did not reveal her people or kindred, for Mordecai
had charged her not to tell. 11 Every day
Mordecai would walk around in front of
the court of the harem, to learn how Esther was and how she fared.

12 The turn came for each girl to
go in to King Ahasuerus, after being
twelve months under the regulations
for the women, since this was the regular period of their cosmetic treatment,
six months with oil of myrrh and six
months with perfumes and cosmet-
ics for women. 13 When the girl went
in to the king she was given whatever
she asked for to take with her from the
harem to the king's palace. 14 In the evening she went in; then in the morning
she came back to the second harem in
the custody of Shaashgaz, the king's
eunuch, who was in charge of the concubines; she did not go in to the king
again, unless the king delighted in her
and she was summoned by name.

15 When the turn came for Esther
daughter of Abihail the uncle of Mordecai, who had adopted her as his own
daughter, to go in to the king, she asked
for nothing except what Hegai the king's
eunuch, who had charge of the women,
advised. Now Esther was admired by all
who saw her. 16 When Esther was taken
to King Ahasuerus in his royal palace in
the tenth month, which is the month of
Tebeth, in the seventh year of his reign,
17 the king loved Esther more than all the
other women; of all the virgins she won
his favour and devotion, so that he set
the royal crown on her head and made
her queen instead of Vashti. 18 Then the
king gave a great banquet to all his officials and ministers—'Esther's banquet.'
He also granted a holiday[l] to the provinces, and gave gifts with royal liberality.

MORDECAI DISCOVERS A PLOT

19 When the virgins were being gathered together,[m] Mordecai was sitting

[h] **1.18** Cn: Heb *will tell* [i] **1.22** Heb adds *and speak in accordance with the language of his people* [j] **2.6** Heb *a Benjaminite 6who*
[k] **2.7** Heb *He* [l] **2.18** Or *an amnesty*
[m] **2.19** Heb adds *a second time*

at the king's gate. 20 Now Esther had
not revealed her kindred or her people, as Mordecai had charged her; for
Esther obeyed Mordecai just as when
she was brought up by him. 21 In those
days, while Mordecai was sitting at the
king's gate, Bigthan and Teresh, two of
the king's eunuchs, who guarded the
threshold, became angry and conspired
to assassinate[n] King Ahasuerus. 22 But
the matter came to the knowledge of
Mordecai, and he told it to Queen Esther, and Esther told the king in the
name of Mordecai. 23 When the affair
was investigated and found to be so,
both the men were hanged on the gallows. It was recorded in the book of the
annals in the presence of the king.

HAMAN UNDERTAKES TO DESTROY THE JEWS

3 After these things King Ahasuerus
promoted Haman son of Hammedatha the Agagite, and advanced him
and set his seat above all the officials
who were with him. 2 And all the king's
servants who were at the king's gate
bowed down and did obeisance to Haman; for the king had so commanded
concerning him. But Mordecai did not
bow down or do obeisance. 3 Then the
king's servants who were at the king's
gate said to Mordecai, 'Why do you
disobey the king's command?' 4 When
they spoke to him day after day and
he would not listen to them, they told
Haman, in order to see whether Mordecai's words would avail; for he had
told them that he was a Jew. 5 When
Haman saw that Mordecai did not bow
down or do obeisance to him, Haman
was infuriated. 6 But he thought it beneath him to lay hands on Mordecai
alone. So, having been told who Mordecai's people were, Haman plotted to
destroy all the Jews, the people of Mordecai, throughout the whole kingdom
of Ahasuerus.

7 In the first month, which is the
month of Nisan, in the twelfth year of
King Ahasuerus, they cast Pur—which
means 'the lot'—before Haman for the
day and for the month, and the lot fell
on the thirteenth day[o] of the twelfth
month, which is the month of Adar.
8 Then Haman said to King Ahasuerus,
'There is a certain people scattered and
separated among the peoples in all the
provinces of your kingdom; their laws
are different from those of every other
people, and they do not keep the king's
laws, so that it is not appropriate for the
king to tolerate them. 9 If it pleases the
king, let a decree be issued for their destruction, and I will pay ten thousand
talents of silver into the hands of those
who have charge of the king's business,
so that they may put it into the king's
treasuries.' 10 So the king took his signet
ring from his hand and gave it to Haman son of Hammedatha the Agagite,
the enemy of the Jews. 11 The king said to
Haman, 'The money is given to you, and
the people as well, to do with them as it
seems good to you.'

12 Then the king's secretaries were
summoned on the thirteenth day of the
first month, and an edict, according to
all that Haman commanded, was written to the king's satraps and to the governors over all the provinces and to the
officials of all the peoples, to every province in its own script and every people
in its own language; it was written in
the name of King Ahasuerus and sealed
with the king's ring. 13 Letters were sent
by couriers to all the king's provinces,
giving orders to destroy, to kill, and
to annihilate all Jews, young and old,
women and children, in one day, the
thirteenth day of the twelfth month,
which is the month of Adar, and to
plunder their goods.

ADDITION B

THE KING'S LETTER

13 [p] This is a copy of the letter: 'The
Great King, Ahasuerus, writes
the following to the governors of the
hundred and twenty-seven provinces
from India to Ethiopia and to the officials under them:

2 'Having become ruler of many nations and master of the whole world
(not elated with presumption of authority but always acting reasonably and
with kindness), I have determined to
settle the lives of my subjects in lasting
tranquillity and, in order to make my
kingdom peaceable and open to travel
throughout all its extent, to restore the
peace desired by all people.

3 'When I asked my counsellors how
this might be accomplished, Haman—
who excels among us in sound judgement, and is distinguished for his

[n] **2.21** Heb *to lay hands on* [o] **3.7** Cn Compare Gk and verse 13 below: Heb *the twelfth month*
[p] **13.1** Chapter 13.1–7 corresponds to chapter B 1–7 in some translations.

unchanging goodwill and steadfast
fidelity, and has attained the second
place in the kingdom— 4pointed out
to us that among all the nations in the
world there is scattered a certain hostile people, who have laws contrary
to those of every nation and continually disregard the ordinances of kings,
so that the unifying of the kingdom
that we honourably intend cannot be
brought about. 5We understand that
this people, and it alone, stands constantly in opposition to every nation,
perversely following a strange manner of life and laws, and is ill-disposed
to our government, doing all the harm
they can so that our kingdom may not
attain stability.

6 'Therefore we have decreed that
those indicated to you in the letters
written by Haman, who is in charge of
affairs and is our second father, shall
all—wives and children included—be
utterly destroyed by the swords of their
enemies, without pity or restraint,
on the fourteenth day of the twelfth
month, Adar, of this present year, 7so
that those who have long been hostile
and remain so may in a single day go
down in violence to Hades, and leave
our government completely secure and
untroubled hereafter.'

END OF ADDITION B

---

3 14A copy of the document was to
be issued as a decree in every province by proclamation, calling on all the
peoples to be ready for that day. 15The
couriers went quickly by order of the
king, and the decree was issued in the
citadel of Susa. The king and Haman sat
down to drink; but the city of Susa was
thrown into confusion.

ESTHER AGREES TO HELP THE JEWS

4 When Mordecai learned all that
had been done, Mordecai tore his
clothes and put on sackcloth and ashes,
and went through the city, wailing with
a loud and bitter cry; 2he went up to the
entrance of the king's gate, for no one
might enter the king's gate clothed with
sackcloth. 3In every province, wherever the king's command and his decree
came, there was great mourning among
the Jews, with fasting and weeping and
lamenting, and most of them lay in
sackcloth and ashes.

4 When Esther's maids and her eunuchs came and told her, the queen
was deeply distressed; she sent garments to clothe Mordecai, so that he
might take off his sackcloth; but he
would not accept them. 5Then Esther
called for Hathach, one of the king's
eunuchs, who had been appointed to
attend her, and ordered him to go to
Mordecai to learn what was happening
and why. 6Hathach went out to Mordecai in the open square of the city in
front of the king's gate, 7and Mordecai told him all that had happened to
him, and the exact sum of money that
Haman had promised to pay into the
king's treasuries for the destruction
of the Jews. 8Mordecai also gave him
a copy of the written decree issued
in Susa for their destruction, that he
might show it to Esther, explain it to
her, and charge her to go to the king to
make supplication to him and entreat
him for her people.

9 Hathach went and told Esther
what Mordecai had said. 10Then Esther spoke to Hathach and gave him
a message for Mordecai, saying, 11'All
the king's servants and the people of
the king's provinces know that if any
man or woman goes to the king inside
the inner court without being called,
there is but one law—all alike are to be
put to death. Only if the king holds out
the golden sceptre to someone, may
that person live. I myself have not been
called to come in to the king for thirty
days.' 12When they told Mordecai what
Esther had said, 13Mordecai told them
to reply to Esther, 'Do not think that
in the king's palace you will escape any
more than all the other Jews. 14For if
you keep silence at such a time as this,
relief and deliverance will rise for the
Jews from another quarter, but you
and your father's family will perish.
Who knows? Perhaps you have come
to royal dignity for just such a time
as this.' 15Then Esther said in reply to
Mordecai, 16'Go, gather all the Jews to
be found in Susa, and hold a fast on
my behalf, and neither eat nor drink
for three days, night or day. I and my
maids will also fast as you do. After
that I will go to the king, though it is
against the law; and if I perish, I perish.' 17Mordecai then went away and
did everything as Esther had ordered
him.

ADDITION C

MORDECAI'S PRAYER

13 8[q] Then Mordecai[r] prayed to the
Lord, calling to remembrance all
the works of the Lord.
9 He said, 'O Lord, Lord, you rule as
King over all things, for the universe is
in your power and there is no one who
can oppose you when it is your will to
save Israel, 10 for you have made heaven
and earth and every wonderful thing
under heaven. 11 You are Lord of all, and
there is no one who can resist you, the
Lord. 12 You know all things; you know,
O Lord, that it was not in insolence or
pride or for any love of glory that I did
this, and refused to bow down to this
proud Haman; 13 for I would have been
willing to kiss the soles of his feet to save
Israel! 14 But I did this so that I might not
set human glory above the glory of God,
and I will not bow down to anyone but
you, who are my Lord; and I will not do
these things in pride. 15 And now, O Lord
God and King, God of Abraham, spare
your people; for the eyes of our foes are
upon us[s] to annihilate us, and they desire to destroy the inheritance that has
been yours from the beginning. 16 Do
not neglect your portion, which you redeemed for yourself out of the land of
Egypt. 17 Hear my prayer, and have mercy
upon your inheritance; turn our mourning into feasting, that we may live and
sing praise to your name, O Lord; do not
destroy the lips[t] of those who praise you.'
18 And all Israel cried out mightily,
for their death was before their eyes.

ESTHER'S PRAYER

14 Then Queen Esther, seized with
deadly anxiety, fled to the Lord.
2 She took off her splendid apparel and put
on the garments of distress and mourning, and instead of costly perfumes she
covered her head with ashes and dung,
and she utterly humbled her body; every
part that she loved to adorn she covered
with her tangled hair. 3 She prayed to the
Lord God of Israel, and said: 'O my Lord,
you only are our king; help me, who am
alone and have no helper but you, 4 for
my danger is in my hand. 5 Ever since I
was born I have heard in the tribe of my
family that you, O Lord, took Israel out
of all the nations, and our ancestors from
among all their forebears, for an everlasting inheritance, and that you did for
them all that you promised. 6 And now
we have sinned before you, and you have
handed us over to our enemies 7 because
we glorified their gods. You are righteous, O Lord! 8 And now they are not
satisfied that we are in bitter slavery, but
they have covenanted with their idols 9 to
abolish what your mouth has ordained,
and to destroy your inheritance, to stop
the mouths of those who praise you and
to quench your altar and the glory of your
house, 10 to open the mouths of the nations for the praise of vain idols, and to
magnify for ever a mortal king.
11 'O Lord, do not surrender your
sceptre to what has no being; and do not
let them laugh at our downfall; but turn
their plan against them, and make an
example of him who began this against
us. 12 Remember, O Lord; make yourself
known in this time of our affliction, and
give me courage, O King of the gods and
Master of all dominion! 13 Put eloquent
speech in my mouth before the lion, and
turn his heart to hate the man who is
fighting against us, so that there may be
an end of him and those who agree with
him. 14 But save us by your hand, and help
me, who am alone and have no helper
but you, O Lord. 15 You have knowledge of
all things, and you know that I hate the
splendour of the wicked and abhor the
bed of the uncircumcised and of any alien.
16 You know my necessity—that I abhor
the sign of my proud position, which is
upon my head on days when I appear in
public. I abhor it like a filthy rag, and I
do not wear it on the days when I am at
leisure. 17 And your servant has not eaten
at Haman's table, and I have not honoured the king's feast or drunk the wine
of libations. 18 Your servant has had no
joy since the day that I was brought here
until now, except in you, O Lord God of
Abraham. 19 O God, whose might is over
all, hear the voice of the despairing, and
save us from the hands of evildoers. And
save me from my fear!'

END OF ADDITION C

ADDITION D

ESTHER IS RECEIVED BY THE KING

15 On the third day, when she
ended her prayer, she took off
the garments in which she had wor-

[q] **13.8** Chapters 13.8—15.16 correspond to chapters C 1–30 and D 1–16 in some translations.
[r] **13.8** Gk *he* [s] **13.15** Gk *for they are eyeing us*
[t] **13.17** Gk *mouth*

shipped, and arrayed herself in splendid attire. 2Then, majestically adorned,
after invoking the aid of the all-seeing
God and Saviour, she took two maids
with her; 3on one she leaned gently for
support, 4while the other followed, carrying her train. 5She was radiant with
perfect beauty, and she looked happy, as
if beloved, but her heart was frozen with
fear. 6When she had gone through all
the doors, she stood before the king. He
was seated on his royal throne, clothed
in the full array of his majesty, all covered with gold and precious stones. He
was most terrifying.

7 Lifting his face, flushed with splendour, he looked at her in fierce anger.
The queen faltered, and turned pale and
faint, and collapsed on the head of the
maid who went in front of her. 8Then
God changed the spirit of the king to
gentleness, and in alarm he sprang from
his throne and took her in his arms until she came to herself. He comforted
her with soothing words, and said to
her, 9'What is it, Esther? I am your husband.[u] Take courage; 10You shall not
die, for our law applies only to our subjects.[v] Come near.'

11 Then he raised the golden sceptre and touched her neck with it; 12he
embraced her, and said, 'Speak to me.'
13She said to him, 'I saw you, my lord,
like an angel of God, and my heart was
shaken with fear at your glory. 14For you
are wonderful, my lord, and your countenance is full of grace.' 15And while
she was speaking, she fainted and fell.
16Then the king was agitated, and all his
servants tried to comfort her.

END OF ADDITION D

ESTHER'S BANQUET

5[w] 3The king said to her, 'What is it,
Queen Esther? What is your re-
quest? It shall be given you, even to the
half of my kingdom.' 4Then Esther said,
'If it pleases the king, let the king and
Haman come today to a banquet that I
have prepared for the king.' 5Then the
king said, 'Bring Haman quickly, so that
we may do as Esther desires.' So the
king and Haman came to the banquet
that Esther had prepared. 6While they
were drinking wine, the king said to Esther, 'What is your petition? It shall be
granted you. And what is your request?
Even to the half of my kingdom, it shall
be fulfilled.' 7Then Esther said, 'This is
my petition and request: 8If I have won
the king's favour, and if it pleases the
king to grant my petition and fulfil my
request, let the king and Haman come
tomorrow to the banquet that I will prepare for them, and then I will do as the
king has said.'

HAMAN PLANS TO HAVE MORDECAI HANGED

9 Haman went out that day happy
and in good spirits. But when Haman
saw Mordecai in the king's gate, and
observed that he neither rose nor trembled before him, he was infuriated with
Mordecai; 10nevertheless, Haman restrained himself and went home. Then
he sent and called for his friends and his
wife Zeresh, 11and Haman recounted to
them the splendour of his riches, the
number of his sons, all the promotions
with which the king had honoured him,
and how he had advanced him above the
officials and the ministers of the king.
12Haman added, 'Even Queen Esther let
no one but myself come with the king to
the banquet that she prepared. Tomorrow also I am invited by her, together
with the king. 13Yet all this does me
no good so long as I see the Jew Mordecai sitting at the king's gate.' 14Then
his wife Zeresh and all his friends said to
him, 'Let a gallows fifty cubits high be
made, and in the morning tell the king
to have Mordecai hanged on it; then go
with the king to the banquet in good
spirits.' This advice pleased Haman, and
he had the gallows made.

THE KING HONOURS MORDECAI

6 That night the king could not sleep,
and he gave orders to bring the
book of records, the annals, and they
were read to the king. 2It was found
written how Mordecai had told about
Bigthana and Teresh, two of the king's
eunuchs, who guarded the threshold,
and who had conspired to assassinate[x]
King Ahasuerus. 3Then the king said,
'What honour or distinction has been
bestowed on Mordecai for this?' The
king's servants who attended him said,
'Nothing has been done for him.' 4The
king said, 'Who is in the court?' Now
Haman had just entered the outer court
of the king's palace to speak to the king
about having Mordecai hanged on the

[u] **15.9** Gk *brother* [v] **15.10** Meaning of Gk uncertain [w] **5.1** In Greek, Chapter D replaces verses 1 and 2 in Hebrew. [x] **6.2** Heb *to lay hands on*

gallows that he had prepared for him.
5So the king's servants told him, 'Haman is there, standing in the court.' The
king said, 'Let him come in.' 6So Haman
came in, and the king said to him, 'What
shall be done for the man whom the
king wishes to honour?' Haman said to
himself, 'Whom would the king wish to
honour more than me?' 7So Haman said
to the king, 'For the man whom the king
wishes to honour, 8let royal robes be
brought, which the king has worn, and
a horse that the king has ridden, with a
royal crown on its head. 9Let the robes
and the horse be handed over to one of
the king's most noble officials; let him[y]
robe the man whom the king wishes to
honour, and let him[z] conduct the man
on horseback through the open square
of the city, proclaiming before him:
"Thus shall it be done for the man whom
the king wishes to honour." ' 10Then the
king said to Haman, 'Quickly, take the
robes and the horse, as you have said,
and do so to the Jew Mordecai who sits
at the king's gate. Leave out nothing
that you have mentioned.' 11So Haman
took the robes and the horse and robed
Mordecai and led him riding through
the open square of the city, proclaiming,
'Thus shall it be done for the man whom
the king wishes to honour.'

12 Then Mordecai returned to the
king's gate, but Haman hurried to his
house, mourning and with his head
covered. 13When Haman told his wife
Zeresh and all his friends everything
that had happened to him, his advisers
and his wife Zeresh said to him, 'If Mordecai, before whom your downfall has
begun, is of the Jewish people, you will
not prevail against him, but will surely
fall before him.'

HAMAN'S DOWNFALL AND MORDECAI'S ADVANCEMENT

14 While they were still talking with
him, the king's eunuchs arrived and
hurried Haman off to the banquet that
7 Esther had prepared. 1So the king
and Haman went in to feast with
Queen Esther. 2On the second day, as they
were drinking wine, the king again said
to Esther, 'What is your petition, Queen
Esther? It shall be granted you. And
what is your request? Even to the half of
my kingdom, it shall be fulfilled.' 3Then
Queen Esther answered, 'If I have won
your favour, O king, and if it pleases the
king, let my life be given me—that is my
petition—and the lives of my people—
that is my request. 4For we have been
sold, I and my people, to be destroyed,
to be killed, and to be annihilated. If we
had been sold merely as slaves, men and
women, I would have held my peace; but
no enemy can compensate for this damage to the king.'[a] 5Then King Ahasuerus
said to Queen Esther, 'Who is he, and
where is he, who has presumed to do
this?' 6Esther said, 'A foe and enemy, this
wicked Haman!' Then Haman was terrified before the king and the queen. 7The
king rose from the feast in wrath and
went into the palace garden, but Haman
stayed to beg his life from Queen Esther,
for he saw that the king had determined
to destroy him. 8When the king returned
from the palace garden to the banquet
hall, Haman had thrown himself on the
couch where Esther was reclining; and
the king said, 'Will he even assault the
queen in my presence, in my own house?'
As the words left the mouth of the king,
they covered Haman's face. 9Then Harbona, one of the eunuchs in attendance
on the king, said, 'Look, the very gallows
that Haman has prepared for Mordecai,
whose word saved the king, stands at
Haman's house, fifty cubits high.' And
the king said, 'Hang him on that.' 10So
they hanged Haman on the gallows that
he had prepared for Mordecai. Then the
8 anger of the king abated. 1On that
day King Ahasuerus gave to Queen
Esther the house of Haman, the enemy
of the Jews; and Mordecai came before
the king, for Esther had told what he
was to her. 2Then the king took off his
signet ring, which he had taken from
Haman, and gave it to Mordecai. So Esther set Mordecai over the house of Haman.

ESTHER SAVES THE JEWS

3 Then Esther spoke again to the
king; she fell at his feet, weeping and
pleading with him to avert the evil design of Haman the Agagite and the plot
that he had devised against the Jews.
4The king held out the golden sceptre to
Esther, 5and Esther rose and stood before the king. She said, 'If it pleases the
king, and if I have won his favour, and
if the thing seems right before the king,
and I have his approval, let an order be
written to revoke the letters devised by
Haman son of Hammedatha the Agagite, which he wrote giving orders to

[y] **6.9** Heb *them* [z] **6.9** Heb *them*
[a] **7.4** Meaning of Heb uncertain

destroy the Jews who are in all the provinces of the king. 6For how can I bear to
see the calamity that is coming on my
people? Or how can I bear to see the destruction of my kindred?' 7Then King
Ahasuerus said to Queen Esther and to
the Jew Mordecai, 'See, I have given Esther the house of Haman, and they have
hanged him on the gallows, because he
plotted to lay hands on the Jews. 8You
may write as you please with regard to
the Jews, in the name of the king, and
seal it with the king's ring; for an edict
written in the name of the king and
sealed with the king's ring cannot be revoked.'
9 The king's secretaries were summoned at that time, in the third month,
which is the month of Sivan, on the
twenty-third day; and an edict was written, according to all that Mordecai commanded, to the Jews and to the satraps
and the governors and the officials of
the provinces from India to Ethiopia,[b]
one hundred and twenty-seven provinces, to every province in its own script
and to every people in its own language,
and also to the Jews in their script and
their language. 10He wrote letters in the
name of King Ahasuerus, sealed them
with the king's ring, and sent them by
mounted couriers riding on fast steeds
bred from the royal herd.[c] 11By these
letters the king allowed the Jews who
were in every city to assemble and defend their lives, to destroy, to kill, and to
annihilate any armed force of any people or province that might attack them,
with their children and women, and to
plunder their goods 12on a single day
throughout all the provinces of King
Ahasuerus, on the thirteenth day of the
twelfth month, which is the month of
Adar.

ADDITION E

THE DECREE OF AHASUERUS

16 [d]The following is a copy of this
letter:
'The Great King, Ahasuerus, to the
governors of the provinces from India
to Ethiopia, one hundred and twenty-
seven provinces, and to those who are
loyal to our government, greetings.
2 'Many people, the more they are
honoured with the most generous
kindness of their benefactors, the more
proud do they become, 3and not only
seek to injure our subjects, but in their
inability to stand prosperity, they even
undertake to scheme against their own
benefactors. 4They not only take away
thankfulness from others, but, carried
away by the boasts of those who know
nothing of goodness, they even assume
that they will escape the evil-hating justice of God, who always sees everything.
5And often many of those who are set
in places of authority have been made in
part responsible for the shedding of innocent blood, and have been involved in
irremediable calamities, by the persuasion of friends who have been entrusted
with the administration of public affairs, 6when these persons by the false
trickery of their evil natures beguile the
sincere goodwill of their sovereigns.
7 'What has been wickedly accomplished through the pestilent behaviour
of those who exercise authority unwor-
thily can be seen, not so much from the
more ancient records that we hand on,
as from investigation of matters close at
hand.[e] 8In the future we will take care
to render our kingdom quiet and peaceable for all, 9by changing our methods
and always judging what comes before
our eyes with more equitable consideration. 10For Haman son of Hammedatha, a Macedonian (really an alien to the
Persian blood, and quite devoid of our
kindliness), having become our guest,
11enjoyed so fully the goodwill that we
have for every nation that he was called
our father and was continually bowed
down to by all as the person second to
the royal throne. 12But, unable to restrain his arrogance, he undertook to
deprive us of our kingdom and our life,[f]
13and with intricate craft and deceit
asked for the destruction of Mordecai,
our saviour and perpetual benefactor,
and of Esther, the blameless partner of
our kingdom, together with their whole
nation. 14He thought that by these
methods he would catch us undefended
and would transfer the kingdom of the
Persians to the Macedonians.
15 'But we find that the Jews, who
were consigned to annihilation by this
thrice-accursed man, are not evildoers,
but are governed by most righteous
laws 16and are children of the living
God, most high, most mighty,[g] who has
directed the kingdom both for us and

[b] **8.9** Or *Nubia*; Heb *Cush* [c] **8.10** Meaning of Heb uncertain [d] **16.1** Chapter 16.1–24 corresponds to chapter E 1–24 in some translations. [e] **16.7** Gk *matters beside* (your) *feet* [f] **16.12** Gk *our spirit* [g] **16.16** Gk *greatest*

for our ancestors in the most excellent
order.
17 'You will therefore do well not to
put in execution the letters sent by Haman son of Hammedatha, 18 since he,
the one who did these things, has been
hanged at the gate of Susa with all his
household—for God, who rules over all
things, has speedily inflicted on him the
punishment that he deserved.
19 'Therefore post a copy of this letter publicly in every place, and permit the Jews to live under their own
laws. 20 And give them reinforcements,
so that on the thirteenth day of the
twelfth month, Adar, on that very day,
they may defend themselves against
those who attack them at the time of
oppression. 21 For God, who rules over
all things, has made this day to be a joy
for his chosen people instead of a day of
destruction for them.
22 'Therefore you shall observe this
with all good cheer as a notable day
among your commemorative festivals,
23 so that both now and hereafter it may
represent deliverance for you[h] and the
loyal Persians, but that it may be a reminder of destruction for those who
plot against us.
24 'Every city and country, without
exception, that does not act accordingly shall be destroyed in wrath with
spear and fire. It shall be made not only
impassable for human beings, but also
most hateful to wild animals and birds
for all time.'

END OF ADDITION E

---

8 13 A copy of the writ was to be issued as a decree in every province
and published to all peoples, and the
Jews were to be ready on that day to
take revenge on their enemies. 14 So the
couriers, mounted on their swift royal
steeds, hurried out, urged by the king's
command. The decree was issued in the
citadel of Susa.
15 Then Mordecai went out from
the presence of the king, wearing royal
robes of blue and white, with a great
golden crown and a mantle of fine
linen and purple, while the city of Susa
shouted and rejoiced. 16 For the Jews
there was light and gladness, joy and
honour. 17 In every province and in every city, wherever the king's command
and his edict came, there was gladness
and joy among the Jews, a festival and a
holiday. Furthermore, many of the peoples of the country professed to be Jews,
because the fear of the Jews had fallen
upon them.

DESTRUCTION OF THE ENEMIES OF THE JEWS

9 Now in the twelfth month, which
is the month of Adar, on the thirteenth day, when the king's command
and edict were about to be executed, on
the very day when the enemies of the
Jews hoped to gain power over them,
but which had been changed to a day
when the Jews would gain power over
their foes, 2 the Jews gathered in their
cities throughout all the provinces of
King Ahasuerus to lay hands on those
who had sought their ruin; and no one
could withstand them, because the fear
of them had fallen upon all peoples. 3 All
the officials of the provinces, the satraps
and the governors, and the royal officials were supporting the Jews, because
the fear of Mordecai had fallen upon
them. 4 For Mordecai was powerful in
the king's house, and his fame spread
throughout all the provinces as the man
Mordecai grew more and more powerful. 5 So the Jews struck down all their
enemies with the sword, slaughtering,
and destroying them, and did as they
pleased to those who hated them. 6 In
the citadel of Susa the Jews killed and
destroyed five hundred people. 7 They
killed Parshandatha, Dalphon, Aspa-
tha, 8 Poratha, Adalia, Aridatha, 9 Par-
mashta, Arisai, Aridai, Vaizatha, 10 the
ten sons of Haman son of Hammedatha, the enemy of the Jews; but they did
not touch the plunder.
11 That very day the number of those
killed in the citadel of Susa was reported
to the king. 12 The king said to Queen
Esther, 'In the citadel of Susa the Jews
have killed five hundred people and also
the ten sons of Haman. What have they
done in the rest of the king's provinces?
Now what is your petition? It shall be
granted you. And what further is your
request? It shall be fulfilled.' 13 Esther
said, 'If it pleases the king, let the Jews
who are in Susa be allowed tomorrow
also to do according to this day's edict,
and let the ten sons of Haman be hanged
on the gallows.' 14 So the king commanded this to be done; a decree was
issued in Susa, and the ten sons of Haman were hanged. 15 The Jews who were

h 16.23 Other ancient authorities read *for us*

in Susa gathered also on the fourteenth
day of the month of Adar and they killed
three hundred people in Susa; but they
did not touch the plunder.
16 Now the other Jews who were in
the king's provinces also gathered to defend their lives, and gained relief from
their enemies, and killed seventy-five
thousand of those who hated them;
but they laid no hands on the plunder.
17 This was on the thirteenth day of the
month of Adar, and on the fourteenth
day they rested and made that a day of
feasting and gladness.

THE FEAST OF PURIM INAUGURATED

18 But the Jews who were in Susa
gathered on the thirteenth day and on
the fourteenth, and rested on the fifteenth day, making that a day of feasting and gladness. 19 Therefore the Jews
of the villages, who live in the open
towns, hold the fourteenth day of the
month of Adar as a day for gladness and
feasting, a holiday on which they send
gifts of food to one another.
20 Mordecai recorded these things,
and sent letters to all the Jews who were
in all the provinces of King Ahasuerus,
both near and far, 21 enjoining them
that they should keep the fourteenth
day of the month Adar and also the fifteenth day of the same month, year by
year, 22 as the days on which the Jews
gained relief from their enemies, and
as the month that had been turned for
them from sorrow into gladness and
from mourning into a holiday; that they
should make them days of feasting and
gladness, days for sending gifts of food
to one another and presents to the poor.
23 So the Jews adopted as a custom what
they had begun to do, as Mordecai had
written to them.
24 Haman son of Hammedatha the
Agagite, the enemy of all the Jews,
had plotted against the Jews to destroy
them, and had cast Pur—that is, 'the
lot'—to crush and destroy them; 25 but
when Esther came before the king, he
gave orders in writing that the wicked
plot that he had devised against the Jews
should come upon his own head, and
that he and his sons should be hanged
on the gallows. 26 Therefore these days
are called Purim, from the word Pur.
Thus because of all that was written in
this letter, and of what they had faced in
this matter, and of what had happened
to them, 27 the Jews established and accepted as a custom for themselves and
their descendants and all who joined
them, that without fail they would continue to observe these two days every
year, as it was written and at the time
appointed. 28 These days should be remembered and kept throughout every
generation, in every family, province,
and city; and these days of Purim should
never fall into disuse among the Jews,
nor should the commemoration of these
days cease among their descendants.
29 Queen Esther daughter of Abihail, along with the Jew Mordecai, gave
full written authority, confirming this
second letter about Purim. 30 Letters
were sent wishing peace and security
to all the Jews, to the one hundred and
twenty-seven provinces of the kingdom
of Ahasuerus, 31 and giving orders that
these days of Purim should be observed
at their appointed seasons, as the Jew
Mordecai and Queen Esther enjoined on
the Jews, just as they had laid down for
themselves and for their descendants
regulations concerning their fasts and
their lamentations. 32 The command of
Queen Esther fixed these practices of
Purim, and it was recorded in writing.

10 King Ahasuerus laid tribute on
the land and on the islands of
the sea. 2 All the acts of his power and
might, and the full account of the high
honour of Mordecai, to which the king
advanced him, are they not written in
the annals of the kings of Media and
Persia? 3 For Mordecai the Jew was next
in rank to King Ahasuerus, and he was
powerful among the Jews and popular
with his many kindred, for he sought
the good of his people and interceded for
the welfare of all his descendants.

ADDITION F

MORDECAI'S DREAM FULFILLED

4[i] And Mordecai said, 'These things
have come from God; 5 for I remember
the dream that I had concerning these
matters, and none of them has failed to
be fulfilled. 6 There was the little spring
that became a river, and there was light
and sun and abundant water—the river
is Esther, whom the king married and
made queen. 7 The two dragons are Haman and myself. 8 The nations are those
that gathered to destroy the name of
the Jews. 9 And my nation, this is Israel,

[i] **10.4** Chapter 10.4–13 and 11.1 correspond to chapter F 1–11 in some translations.

who cried out to God and was saved. The
Lord has saved his people; the Lord has
rescued us from all these evils; God has
done great signs and wonders, wonders that have never happened among
the nations. 10 For this purpose he made
two lots, one for the people of God and
one for all the nations, 11 and these two
lots came to the hour and moment and
day of decision before God and among
all the nations. 12 And God remembered
his people and vindicated his inheritance. 13 So they will observe these days
in the month of Adar, on the fourteenth
and fifteenth[j] of that month, with an
assembly and joy and gladness before
God, from generation to generation for
ever among his people Israel.'

POSTSCRIPT

11 1 In the fourth year of the reign
of Ptolemy and Cleopatra,
Dositheus, who said that he was a priest
and a Levite,[k] and his son Ptolemy
brought to Egypt[l] the foregoing Letter about Purim, which they said was
authentic and had been translated by
Lysimachus son of Ptolemy, one of the
residents of Jerusalem.

END OF ADDITION F

---

[j] 10.13 Other ancient authorities lack *and fifteenth* [k] 11.1 Or *priest, and Levitas*
[l] 11.1 Cn: Gk *brought in*

1 MACCABEES

The historical setting of 1 Maccabees is about a century after the conquest of Judea by the Greeks under Alexander the Great. Alexander's empire was divided at this point, and Judea was part of the Greek Seleucid Empire. First Maccabees narrates how the Greek ruler Antiochus IV Epiphanes attempted to suppress the practice of the Jewish law, resulting in a Jewish revolt against Seleucid rule. The book covers the revolt beginning in 167 BCE and underscores how the salvation of the Jewish people in this crisis came from God through Mattathias's family, particularly his sons Judas, Jonathan, and Simon. The book teaches that fidelity to God's law leads to continued divine support and action on behalf of the people of Israel.

Selected passages from 1 Maccabees are read at the liturgy on Monday through Saturday of the Thirty-Third Week of Year I. Also, the passage from 1 Maccabees on the occasion of the rededication of the altar is offered as a choice in the Roman Missal to be read at the Mass of the Dedication of a Church (4.52–59). The Jewish feast of Hanukkah is established with this text as well.

ALEXANDER THE GREAT

1 After Alexander son of Philip, the
Macedonian, who came from the
land of Kittim, had defeated[a] King Darius of the Persians and the Medes, he
succeeded him as king. (He had previously become king of Greece.) 2 He fought
many battles, conquered strongholds,
and put to death the kings of the earth.
3 He advanced to the ends of the earth,
and plundered many nations. When the
earth became quiet before him, he was
exalted, and his heart was lifted up. 4 He
gathered a very strong army and ruled
over countries, nations, and princes,
and they became tributary to him.
5 After this he fell sick and perceived
that he was dying. 6 So he summoned
his most honoured officers, who had
been brought up with him from youth,
and divided his kingdom among them
while he was still alive. 7 And after Alexander had reigned for twelve years, he
died.
8 Then his officers began to rule, each
in his own place. 9 They all put on crowns
after his death, and so did their descendants after them for many years; and
they caused many evils on the earth.

ANTIOCHUS EPIPHANES AND RENEGADE JEWS

10 From them came forth a sinful root, Antiochus Epiphanes, son of
King Antiochus; he had been a hostage
in Rome. He began to reign in the one
hundred and thirty-seventh year of the
kingdom of the Greeks.[b]
11 In those days certain renegades
came out from Israel and misled many,
saying, 'Let us go and make a covenant
with the Gentiles around us, for since
we separated from them many disasters have come upon us.' 12 This proposal
pleased them, 13 and some of the people
eagerly went to the king, who authorized them to observe the ordinances of
the Gentiles. 14 So they built a gymnasium in Jerusalem, according to Gentile
custom, 15 and removed the marks of
circumcision, and abandoned the holy
covenant. They joined with the Gentiles
and sold themselves to do evil.

ANTIOCHUS IN EGYPT

16 When Antiochus saw that his kingdom was established, he determined

[a] 1.1 Gk adds *and he defeated* [b] 1.10 175 BC

to become king of the land of Egypt,
in order that he might reign over both
kingdoms. 17So he invaded Egypt with
a strong force, with chariots and elephants and cavalry and with a large
fleet. 18He engaged King Ptolemy of
Egypt in battle, and Ptolemy turned
and fled before him, and many were
wounded and fell. 19They captured the
fortified cities in the land of Egypt, and
he plundered the land of Egypt.

PERSECUTION OF THE JEWS

20 After subduing Egypt, Antiochus returned in the one hundred and
forty-third year.[c] He went up against
Israel and came to Jerusalem with a
strong force. 21He arrogantly entered
the sanctuary and took the golden altar, the lampstand for the light, and all
its utensils. 22He took also the table for
the bread of the Presence, the cups for
drink-offerings, the bowls, the golden
censers, the curtain, the crowns, and
the gold decoration on the front of the
temple; he stripped it all off. 23He took
the silver and the gold, and the costly
vessels; he took also the hidden treasures that he found. 24Taking them all,
he went into his own land.

He shed much blood,
and spoke with great arrogance.
25 Israel mourned deeply in
every community,
26 rulers and elders groaned,
young women and young
men became faint,
the beauty of the women faded.
27 Every bridegroom took up
the lament;
she who sat in the bridal
chamber was mourning.
28 Even the land trembled for
its inhabitants,
and all the house of Jacob was
clothed with shame.

THE OCCUPATION OF JERUSALEM

29 Two years later the king sent to
the cities of Judah a chief collector of
tribute, and he came to Jerusalem with
a large force. 30Deceitfully he spoke
peaceable words to them, and they believed him; but he suddenly fell upon
the city, dealt it a severe blow, and destroyed many people of Israel. 31He
plundered the city, burned it with fire,
and tore down its houses and its surrounding walls. 32They took captive
the women and children, and seized
the livestock. 33Then they fortified the
city of David with a great strong wall
and strong towers, and it became their
citadel. 34They stationed there a sinful
people, men who were renegades. These
strengthened their position; 35they
stored up arms and food, and collecting
the spoils of Jerusalem they stored them
there, and became a great menace,
36 for the citadel[d] became an ambush
against the sanctuary,
an evil adversary of Israel
at all times.
37 On every side of the sanctuary
they shed innocent blood;
they even defiled the sanctuary.
38 Because of them the residents
of Jerusalem fled;
she became a dwelling
of strangers;
she became strange to her offspring,
and her children forsook her.
39 Her sanctuary became desolate
like a desert;
her feasts were turned
into mourning,
her sabbaths into a reproach,
her honour into contempt.
40 Her dishonour now grew as
great as her glory;
her exaltation was turned
into mourning.

INSTALLATION OF GENTILE CULTS

41 Then the king wrote to his whole
kingdom that all should be one people,
42and that all should give up their particular customs. 43All the Gentiles accepted the command of the king. Many
even from Israel gladly adopted his religion; they sacrificed to idols and profaned the sabbath. 44And the king sent
letters by messengers to Jerusalem and
the towns of Judah; he directed them to
follow customs strange to the land, 45to
forbid burnt-offerings and sacrifices
and drink-offerings in the sanctuary, to
profane sabbaths and festivals, 46to defile the sanctuary and the priests, 47to
build altars and sacred precincts and
shrines for idols, to sacrifice swine and
other unclean animals, 48and to leave
their sons uncircumcised. They were
to make themselves abominable by everything unclean and profane, 49so that
they would forget the law and change all
the ordinances. 50He added,[e] 'And whoever does not obey the command of the
king shall die.'

[c] **1.20** 169 BC [d] **1.36** Gk *it* [e] **1.50** Gk lacks *He added*

51 In such words he wrote to his
whole kingdom. He appointed inspec-
tors over all the people and commanded
the towns of Judah to offer sacrifice,
town by town. 52Many of the people,
everyone who forsook the law, joined
them, and they did evil in the land;
53they drove Israel into hiding in every
place of refuge they had.

54 Now on the fifteenth day of Chislev, in the one hundred and forty-fifth
year,[f] they erected a desolating sacrilege
on the altar of burnt-offering. They also
built altars in the surrounding towns
of Judah, 55and offered incense at the
doors of the houses and in the streets.
56The books of the law that they found
they tore to pieces and burned with fire.
57Anyone found possessing the book of
the covenant, or anyone who adhered
to the law, was condemned to death by
decree of the king. 58They kept using violence against Israel, against those who
were found month after month in the
towns. 59On the twenty-fifth day of the
month they offered sacrifice on the altar that was on top of the altar of burnt-
offering. 60In accordance with the decree, they put to death the women who
had their children circumcised, 61and
their families and those who circumcised them; and they hung the infants
from their mothers' necks.

62 But many in Israel stood firm and
were resolved in their hearts not to eat
unclean food. 63They chose to die rather
than to be defiled by food or to profane
the holy covenant; and they did die.
64Very great wrath came upon Israel.

MATTATHIAS AND HIS SONS

2 In those days Mattathias son of
John son of Simeon, a priest of the
family of Joarib, moved from Jerusalem and settled in Modein. 2He had five
sons, John surnamed Gaddi, 3Simon
called Thassi, 4Judas called Maccabeus,
5Eleazar called Avaran, and Jonathan
called Apphus. 6He saw the blasphemies being committed in Judah and Jerusalem, 7and said,

'Alas! Why was I born to see this,
the ruin of my people, the
ruin of the holy city,
and to live there when it was
given over to the enemy,
the sanctuary given over to aliens?
8 Her temple has become like a
person without honour;[g]
9 her glorious vessels have been
carried into exile.
Her infants have been killed
in her streets,
her youths by the sword of the foe.
10 What nation has not inherited
her palaces[h]
and has not seized her spoils?
11 All her adornment has been
taken away;
no longer free, she has
become a slave.
12 And see, our holy place, our beauty,
and our glory have been
laid waste;
the Gentiles have profaned them.
13 Why should we live any longer?'

14 Then Mattathias and his sons
tore their clothes, put on sackcloth, and
mourned greatly.

PAGAN WORSHIP REFUSED

15 The king's officers who were en-
forcing the apostasy came to the town
of Modein to make them offer sacrifice.
16Many from Israel came to them; and
Mattathias and his sons were assembled. 17Then the king's officers spoke to
Mattathias as follows: 'You are a leader,
honoured and great in this town, and
supported by sons and brothers. 18Now
be the first to come and do what the
king commands, as all the Gentiles and
the people of Judah and those that are
left in Jerusalem have done. Then you
and your sons will be numbered among
the Friends of the king, and you and
your sons will be honoured with silver
and gold and many gifts.'

19 But Mattathias answered and
said in a loud voice: 'Even if all the nations that live under the rule of the king
obey him, and have chosen to obey his
commandments, every one of them
abandoning the religion of their ancestors, 20I and my sons and my brothers
will continue to live by the covenant of
our ancestors. 21Far be it from us to desert the law and the ordinances. 22We
will not obey the king's words by turning aside from our religion to the right
hand or to the left.'

23 When he had finished speaking
these words, a Jew came forward in the
sight of all to offer sacrifice on the altar in Modein, according to the king's
command. 24When Mattathias saw it,
he burned with zeal and his heart was
stirred. He gave vent to righteous anger; he ran and killed him on the altar.

[f] **1.54** 167 BC [g] **2.8** Meaning of Gk uncertain
[h] **2.10** Other ancient authorities read *has not had a part in her kingdom*

25 At the same time he killed the king's
officer who was forcing them to sacrifice, and he tore down the altar. 26 Thus
he burned with zeal for the law, just as
Phinehas did against Zimri son of Salu.
27 Then Mattathias cried out in the
town with a loud voice, saying: 'Let everyone who is zealous for the law and
supports the covenant come out with
me!' 28 Then he and his sons fled to the
hills and left all that they had in the
town.
29 At that time many who were seeking righteousness and justice went down
to the wilderness to live there, 30 they,
their sons, their wives, and their livestock, because troubles pressed heavily
upon them. 31 And it was reported to the
king's officers, and to the troops in Jerusalem the city of David, that those who
had rejected the king's command had
gone down to the hiding-places in the
wilderness. 32 Many pursued them, and
overtook them; they encamped opposite
them and prepared for battle against
them on the sabbath day. 33 They said
to them, 'Enough of this! Come out and
do what the king commands, and you
will live.' 34 But they said, 'We will not
come out, nor will we do what the king
commands and so profane the sabbath
day.' 35 Then the enemy[i] quickly attacked
them. 36 But they did not answer them
or hurl a stone at them or block up their
hiding-places, 37 for they said, 'Let us all
die in our innocence; heaven and earth
testify for us that you are killing us unjustly.' 38 So they attacked them on the
sabbath, and they died, with their wives
and children and livestock, to the number of a thousand people.
39 When Mattathias and his friends
learned of it, they mourned for them
deeply. 40 And all said to their neighbours: 'If we all do as our kindred have
done and refuse to fight with the Gentiles for our lives and for our ordinances,
they will quickly destroy us from the
earth.' 41 So they made this decision that
day: 'Let us fight against anyone who
comes to attack us on the sabbath day;
let us not all die as our kindred died in
their hiding-places.'

COUNTER-ATTACK

42 Then there united with them a
company of Hasideans, mighty warriors
of Israel, all who offered themselves
willingly for the law. 43 And all who
became fugitives to escape their troubles joined them and reinforced them.
44 They organized an army, and struck
down sinners in their anger and renegades in their wrath; the survivors fled
to the Gentiles for safety. 45 And Mattathias and his friends went around and
tore down the altars; 46 they forcibly
circumcised all the uncircumcised boys
that they found within the borders of Israel. 47 They hunted down the arrogant,
and the work prospered in their hands.
48 They rescued the law out of the hands
of the Gentiles and kings, and they never
let the sinner gain the upper hand.

THE LAST WORDS OF MATTATHIAS

49 Now the days drew near for Mattathias to die, and he said to his sons:
'Arrogance and scorn have now become
strong; it is a time of ruin and furious
anger. 50 Now, my children, show zeal
for the law, and give your lives for the
covenant of our ancestors.
51 'Remember the deeds of the ancestors, which they did in their generations; and you will receive great honour and an everlasting name. 52 Was not
Abraham found faithful when tested,
and it was reckoned to him as righteousness? 53 Joseph in the time of his distress
kept the commandment, and became
lord of Egypt. 54 Phinehas our ancestor,
because he was deeply zealous, received
the covenant of everlasting priesthood.
55 Joshua, because he fulfilled the command, became a judge in Israel. 56 Caleb,
because he testified in the assembly, received an inheritance in the land. 57 David, because he was merciful, inherited
the throne of the kingdom for ever.
58 Elijah, because of great zeal for the
law, was taken up into heaven. 59 Hananiah, Azariah, and Mishael believed and
were saved from the flame. 60 Daniel,
because of his innocence, was delivered
from the mouth of the lions.
61 'And so observe, from generation
to generation, that none of those who
put their trust in him will lack strength.
62 Do not fear the words of sinners, for
their splendour will turn into dung and
worms. 63 Today they will be exalted,
but tomorrow they will not be found,
because they will have returned to the
dust, and their plans will have perished.
64 My children, be courageous and grow
strong in the law, for by it you will gain
honour.
65 'Here is your brother Simeon who,
I know, is wise in counsel; always listen

[i] **2.35** Gk *they*

to him; he shall be your father. 66Judas
Maccabeus has been a mighty warrior from his youth; he shall command
the army for you and fight the battle
against the peoples.[j] 67You shall rally
around you all who observe the law, and
avenge the wrong done to your people.
68Pay back the Gentiles in full, and obey
the commands of the law.'

69 Then he blessed them, and was
gathered to his ancestors. 70He died in
the one hundred and forty-sixth year[k]
and was buried in the tomb of his ancestors at Modein. And all Israel mourned
for him with great lamentation.

THE EARLY VICTORIES OF JUDAS

3 Then his son Judas, who was called
Maccabeus, took command in his
place. 2All his brothers and all who had
joined his father helped him; they gladly
fought for Israel.

3 He extended the glory of his people.
Like a giant he put on
his breastplate;
he bound on his armour of war
and waged battles,
protecting the camp by his sword.
4 He was like a lion in his deeds,
like a lion's cub roaring for prey.
5 He searched out and pursued
those who broke the law;
he burned those who
troubled his people.
6 Lawbreakers shrank back
for fear of him;
all the evildoers were confounded;
and deliverance prospered
by his hand.
7 He embittered many kings,
but he made Jacob glad
by his deeds,
and his memory is
blessed for ever.
8 He went through the cities of Judah;
he destroyed the ungodly
out of the land;[l]
thus he turned away wrath
from Israel.
9 He was renowned to the
ends of the earth;
he gathered in those who
were perishing.

10 Apollonius now gathered together
Gentiles and a large force from Samaria
to fight against Israel. 11When Judas
learned of it, he went out to meet him,
and he defeated and killed him. Many
were wounded and fell, and the rest
fled. 12Then they seized their spoils; and
Judas took the sword of Apollonius, and
used it in battle for the rest of his life.

13 When Seron, the commander of
the Syrian army, heard that Judas had
gathered a large company, including
a body of faithful soldiers who stayed
with him and went out to battle, 14he
said, 'I will make a name for myself
and win honour in the kingdom. I will
make war on Judas and his companions,
who scorn the king's command.' 15Once
again a strong army of godless men
went up with him to help him, to take
vengeance on the Israelites.

16 When he approached the ascent
of Beth-horon, Judas went out to meet
him with a small company. 17But when
they saw the army coming to meet
them, they said to Judas, 'How can we,
few as we are, fight against so great and
so strong a multitude? And we are faint,
for we have eaten nothing today.' 18Ju-
das replied, 'It is easy for many to be
hemmed in by few, for in the sight of
Heaven there is no difference between
saving by many or by few. 19It is not on
the size of the army that victory in battle depends, but strength comes from
Heaven. 20They come against us in great
insolence and lawlessness to destroy us
and our wives and our children, and to
despoil us; 21but we fight for our lives
and our laws. 22He himself will crush
them before us; as for you, do not be
afraid of them.'

23 When he finished speaking, he
rushed suddenly against Seron and
his army, and they were crushed before him. 24They pursued them[m] down
the descent of Beth-horon to the plain;
eight hundred of them fell, and the rest
fled into the land of the Philistines.
25Then Judas and his brothers began to
be feared, and terror fell on the Gentiles
all around them. 26His fame reached the
king, and the Gentiles talked of the battles of Judas.

THE POLICY OF ANTIOCHUS

27 When King Antiochus heard these
reports, he was greatly angered; and he
sent and gathered all the forces of his
kingdom, a very strong army. 28He
opened his coffers and gave a year's
pay to his forces, and ordered them to
be ready for any need. 29Then he saw
that the money in the treasury was exhausted, and that the revenues from the

j **2.66** Or *of the people* k **2.70** 166 BC l **3.8** Gk
it m **3.24** Other ancient authorities read *him*

country were small because of the dissension and disaster that he had caused
in the land by abolishing the laws that
had existed from the earliest days. 30 He
feared that he might not have such
funds as he had before for his expenses
and for the gifts that he used to give
more lavishly than preceding kings.
31 He was greatly perplexed in mind;
then he determined to go to Persia and
collect the revenues from those regions
and raise a large fund.

32 He left Lysias, a distinguished
man of royal lineage, in charge of the
king's affairs from the river Euphrates
to the borders of Egypt. 33 Lysias was
also to take care of his son Antiochus
until he returned. 34 And he turned over
to Lysias[n] half of his forces and the elephants, and gave him orders about all
that he wanted done. As for the residents of Judea and Jerusalem, 35 Lysias
was to send a force against them to wipe
out and destroy the strength of Israel
and the remnant of Jerusalem; he was
to banish the memory of them from
the place, 36 settle aliens in all their territory, and distribute their land by lot.
37 Then the king took the remaining half
of his forces and left Antioch his capital
in the one hundred and forty-seventh
year.[o] He crossed the Euphrates river
and went through the upper provinces.

PREPARATIONS FOR BATTLE

38 Lysias chose Ptolemy son of Dorymenes, and Nicanor and Gorgias, able
men among the Friends of the king,
39 and sent with them forty thousand
infantry and seven thousand cavalry to
go into the land of Judah and destroy it,
as the king had commanded. 40 So they
set out with their entire force, and when
they arrived they encamped near Emmaus in the plain. 41 When the traders of
the region heard what was said to them,
they took silver and gold in immense
amounts, and fetters,[p] and went to the
camp to get the Israelites for slaves. And
forces from Syria and the land of the
Philistines joined with them.

42 Now Judas and his brothers saw
that misfortunes had increased and
that the forces were encamped in their
territory. They also learned what the
king had commanded to be done to the
people to cause their final destruction.
43 But they said to one another, 'Let us
restore the ruins of our people, and fight
for our people and the sanctuary.' 44 So
the congregation assembled to be ready
for battle, and to pray and ask for mercy
and compassion.

45 Jerusalem was uninhabited
like a wilderness;
not one of her children
went in or out.
The sanctuary was trampled down,
and aliens held the citadel;
it was a lodging-place for
the Gentiles.
Joy was taken from Jacob;
the flute and the harp
ceased to play.

46 Then they gathered together and
went to Mizpah, opposite Jerusalem,
because Israel formerly had a place of
prayer in Mizpah. 47 They fasted that
day, put on sackcloth and sprinkled
ashes on their heads, and tore their
clothes. 48 And they opened the book
of the law to inquire into those matters about which the Gentiles consulted
the images of their gods. 49 They also
brought the vestments of the priesthood and the first fruits and the tithes,
and they stirred up the nazirites[q] who
had completed their days; 50 and they
cried aloud to Heaven, saying,

'What shall we do with these?
Where shall we take them?
51 Your sanctuary is trampled down
and profaned,
and your priests mourn
in humiliation.
52 Here the Gentiles are assembled
against us to destroy us;
you know what they plot
against us.
53 How will we be able to
withstand them,
if you do not help us?'

54 Then they sounded the trumpets
and gave a loud shout. 55 After this Judas appointed leaders of the people, in
charge of thousands and hundreds and
fifties and tens. 56 Those who were building houses, or were about to be married,
or were planting a vineyard, or were
faint-hearted, he told to go home again,
in accordance with the law. 57 Then the
army marched out and encamped to the
south of Emmaus.

58 And Judas said, 'Arm yourselves
and be courageous. Be ready early in
the morning to fight with these Gentiles who have assembled against us
to destroy us and our sanctuary. 59 It is
better for us to die in battle than to see

[n] **3.34** Gk *him* [o] **3.37** 165 BC [p] **3.41** Syr: Gk Mss, Vg *slaves* [q] **3.49** That is *those separated* or *those consecrated*

the misfortunes of our nation and of the
sanctuary. 60But as his will in heaven
may be, so shall he do.'

THE BATTLE AT EMMAUS

4 Now Gorgias took five thousand
infantry and one thousand picked
cavalry, and this division moved out by
night 2to fall upon the camp of the Jews
and attack them suddenly. Men from
the citadel were his guides. 3But Judas heard of it, and he and his warriors
moved out to attack the king's force in
Emmaus 4while the division was still
absent from the camp. 5When Gorgias
entered the camp of Judas by night, he
found no one there, so he looked for
them in the hills, because he said, 'These
men are running away from us.'

6 At daybreak Judas appeared in the
plain with three thousand men, but they
did not have armour and swords such as
they desired. 7And they saw the camp of
the Gentiles, strong and fortified, with
cavalry all around it; and these men
were trained in war. 8But Judas said to
those who were with him, 'Do not fear
their numbers or be afraid when they
charge. 9Remember how our ancestors were saved at the Red Sea, when
Pharaoh with his forces pursued them.
10And now, let us cry to Heaven, to see
whether he will favour us and remember his covenant with our ancestors and
crush this army before us today. 11Then
all the Gentiles will know that there is
one who redeems and saves Israel.'

12 When the foreigners looked up
and saw them coming against them,
13they went out from their camp to
battle. Then the men with Judas blew
their trumpets 14and engaged in battle. The Gentiles were crushed, and fled
into the plain, 15and all those in the rear
fell by the sword. They pursued them to
Gazara, and to the plains of Idumea, and
to Azotus and Jamnia; and three thousand of them fell. 16Then Judas and his
force turned back from pursuing them,
17and he said to the people, 'Do not be
greedy for plunder, for there is a battle before us; 18Gorgias and his force
are near us in the hills. But stand now
against our enemies and fight them,
and afterwards seize the plunder boldly.'

19 Just as Judas was finishing this
speech, a detachment appeared, coming
out of the hills. 20They saw that their
army[r] had been put to flight, and that
the Jews[s] were burning the camp, for
the smoke that was seen showed what
had happened. 21When they perceived
this, they were greatly frightened, and
when they also saw the army of Judas
drawn up in the plain for battle, 22they
all fled into the land of the Philistines.
23Then Judas returned to plunder the
camp, and they seized a great amount of
gold and silver, and cloth dyed blue and
sea purple, and great riches. 24On their
return they sang hymns and praises to
Heaven—'For he is good, for his mercy
endures for ever.' 25Thus Israel had a
great deliverance that day.

FIRST CAMPAIGN OF LYSIAS

26 Those of the foreigners who escaped went and reported to Lysias all
that had happened. 27When he heard it,
he was perplexed and discouraged, for
things had not happened to Israel as he
had intended, nor had they turned out
as the king had ordered. 28But the next
year he mustered sixty thousand picked
infantry and five thousand cavalry to
subdue them. 29They came into Idumea
and encamped at Beth-zur, and Judas
met them with ten thousand men.

30 When he saw that their army was
strong, he prayed, saying, 'Blessed are
you, O Saviour of Israel, who crushed the
attack of the mighty warrior by the hand
of your servant David, and gave the camp
of the Philistines into the hands of Jonathan son of Saul, and of the man who
carried his armour. 31Hem in this army
by the hand of your people Israel, and
let them be ashamed of their troops and
their cavalry. 32Fill them with cowardice; melt the boldness of their strength;
let them tremble in their destruction.
33Strike them down with the sword of
those who love you, and let all who know
your name praise you with hymns.'

34 Then both sides attacked, and
there fell of the army of Lysias five thousand men; they fell in action.[t] 35When
Lysias saw the rout of his troops and observed the boldness that inspired those
of Judas, and how ready they were either to live or to die nobly, he withdrew
to Antioch and enlisted mercenaries
in order to invade Judea again with an
even larger army.

CLEANSING AND DEDICATION OF THE TEMPLE

36 Then Judas and his brothers said,
'See, our enemies are crushed; let us go

[r] **4.20** Gk *they* [s] **4.20** Gk *they* [t] **4.34** Or *and some fell on the opposite side*

up to cleanse the sanctuary and dedicate
it.' 37So all the army assembled and went
up to Mount Zion. 38There they saw the
sanctuary desolate, the altar profaned,
and the gates burned. In the courts they
saw bushes sprung up as in a thicket, or
as on one of the mountains. They saw
also the chambers of the priests in ruins. 39Then they tore their clothes and
mourned with great lamentation; they
sprinkled themselves with ashes 40and
fell face down on the ground. And when
the signal was given with the trumpets,
they cried out to Heaven.

41 Then Judas detailed men to fight
against those in the citadel until he
had cleansed the sanctuary. 42He chose
blameless priests devoted to the law,
43and they cleansed the sanctuary and
removed the defiled stones to an unclean place. 44They deliberated what
to do about the altar of burnt-offering,
which had been profaned. 45And they
thought it best to tear it down, so that
it would not be a lasting shame to them
that the Gentiles had defiled it. So they
tore down the altar, 46and stored the
stones in a convenient place on the temple hill until a prophet should come to
tell what to do with them. 47Then they
took unhewn[u] stones, as the law directs,
and built a new altar like the former
one. 48They also rebuilt the sanctuary
and the interior of the temple, and consecrated the courts. 49They made new
holy vessels, and brought the lampstand, the altar of incense, and the table into the temple. 50Then they offered
incense on the altar and lit the lamps
on the lampstand, and these gave light
in the temple. 51They placed the bread
on the table and hung up the curtains.
Thus they finished all the work they had
undertaken.

52 Early in the morning on the
twenty-fifth day of the ninth month,
which is the month of Chislev, in the
one hundred and forty-eighth year,[v]
53they rose and offered sacrifice, as the
law directs, on the new altar of burnt-
offering that they had built. 54At the
very season and on the very day that
the Gentiles had profaned it, it was dedicated with songs and harps and lutes
and cymbals. 55All the people fell on
their faces and worshipped and blessed
Heaven, who had prospered them. 56So
they celebrated the dedication of the altar for eight days, and joyfully offered
burnt-offerings; they offered a sacrifice of well-being and a thanksgiving-
offering. 57They decorated the front
of the temple with golden crowns and
small shields; they restored the gates
and the chambers for the priests, and
fitted them with doors. 58There was
very great joy among the people, and
the disgrace brought by the Gentiles
was removed.

59 Then Judas and his brothers and
all the assembly of Israel determined
that every year at that season the days
of dedication of the altar should be observed with joy and gladness for eight
days, beginning with the twenty-fifth
day of the month of Chislev.

60 At that time they fortified Mount
Zion with high walls and strong towers all round, to keep the Gentiles from
coming and trampling them down as
they had done before. 61Judas[w] stationed a garrison there to guard it; he
also fortified Beth-zur to guard it, so
that the people might have a stronghold
that faced Idumea.

WARS WITH NEIGHBOURING PEOPLES

5 When the Gentiles all around heard
that the altar had been rebuilt and
the sanctuary dedicated as it was before, they became very angry, 2and they
determined to destroy the descendants
of Jacob who lived among them. So
they began to kill and destroy among
the people. 3But Judas made war on
the descendants of Esau in Idumea, at
Akrabattene, because they kept lying in
wait for Israel. He dealt them a heavy
blow and humbled them and despoiled
them. 4He also remembered the wickedness of the sons of Baean, who were a
trap and a snare to the people and am-
bushed them on the highways. 5They
were shut up by him in their[x] towers;
and he encamped against them, vowed
their complete destruction, and burned
with fire their towers and all who were
in them. 6Then he crossed over to attack the Ammonites, where he found
a strong band and many people, with
Timothy as their leader. 7He engaged in
many battles with them, and they were
crushed before him; he struck them
down. 8He also took Jazer and its villages; then he returned to Judea.

LIBERATION OF GALILEAN JEWS

9 Now the Gentiles in Gilead gathered
together against the Israelites who lived

[u] 4.47 Gk *whole* [v] 4.52 164 BC [w] 4.61 Gk *He*
[x] 5.5 Gk *her*

in their territory, and planned to destroy
them. But they fled to the stronghold of
Dathema, 10 and sent to Judas and his
brothers a letter that said, 'The Gentiles
around us have gathered together to destroy us. 11 They are preparing to come
and capture the stronghold to which we
have fled, and Timothy is leading their
forces. 12 Now then, come and rescue us
from their hands, for many of us have
fallen, 13 and all our kindred who were
in the land of Tob have been killed; the
enemy[y] have captured their wives and
children and goods, and have destroyed
about a thousand people there.'

14 While the letter was still being
read, other messengers, with their
garments torn, came from Galilee and
made a similar report; 15 they said that
the people of Ptolemais and Tyre and
Sidon, and all Galilee of the Gentiles,[z]
had gathered together against them 'to
annihilate us.' 16 When Judas and the
people heard these messages, a great
assembly was called to determine what
they should do for their kindred who
were in distress and were being attacked by enemies.[a] 17 Then Judas said
to his brother Simon, 'Choose your men
and go and rescue your kindred in Galilee; Jonathan my brother and I will go
to Gilead.' 18 But he left Joseph, son of
Zechariah, and Azariah, a leader of the
people, with the rest of the forces, in Judea to guard it; 19 and he gave them this
command, 'Take charge of this people,
but do not engage in battle with the
Gentiles until we return.' 20 Then three
thousand men were assigned to Simon
to go to Galilee, and eight thousand to
Judas for Gilead.

21 So Simon went to Galilee and
fought many battles against the Gentiles, and the Gentiles were crushed before him. 22 He pursued them to the gate
of Ptolemais; as many as three thousand
of the Gentiles fell, and he despoiled
them. 23 Then he took the Jews[b] of Galilee and Arbatta, with their wives and
children, and all they possessed, and led
them to Judea with great rejoicing.

JUDAS AND JONATHAN IN GILEAD

24 Judas Maccabeus and his brother
Jonathan crossed the Jordan and made
three days' journey into the wilderness.
25 They encountered the Nabateans, who
met them peaceably and told them all
that had happened to their kindred in
Gilead: 26 'Many of them have been shut
up in Bozrah and Bosor, in Alema and
Chaspho, Maked and Carnaim'—all
these towns were strong and large—
27 'and some have been shut up in the
other towns of Gilead; the enemy[c] are
getting ready to attack the strongholds
tomorrow and capture and destroy all
these people in a single day.'

28 Then Judas and his army quickly
turned back by the wilderness road to
Bozrah; and he took the town, and killed
every male by the edge of the sword;
then he seized all its spoils and burned
it with fire. 29 He left the place at night,
and they went all the way to the stronghold of Dathema.[d] 30 At dawn they
looked out and saw a large company,
which could not be counted, carrying
ladders and engines of war to capture
the stronghold, and attacking the Jews
within.[e] 31 So Judas saw that the battle
had begun and that the cry of the town
went up to Heaven, with trumpets and
loud shouts, 32 and he said to the men
of his forces, 'Fight today for your kindred!' 33 Then he came up behind them
in three companies, who sounded their
trumpets and cried aloud in prayer.
34 And when the army of Timothy realized that it was Maccabeus, they fled
before him, and he dealt them a heavy
blow. As many as eight thousand of
them fell that day.

35 Next he turned aside to Maapha,[f]
and fought against it and took it; and
he killed every male in it, plundered it,
and burned it with fire. 36 From there he
marched on and took Chaspho, Maked,
and Bosor, and the other towns of Gilead.

37 After these things Timothy gathered another army and encamped opposite Raphon, on the other side of the
stream. 38 Judas sent men to spy out the
camp, and they reported to him, 'All the
Gentiles around us have gathered to
him; it is a very large force. 39 They also
have hired Arabs to help them, and they
are encamped across the stream, ready
to come and fight against you.' And Judas went to meet them.

40 Now as Judas and his army drew
near to the stream of water, Timothy said to the officers of his forces, 'If
he crosses over to us first, we will not
be able to resist him, for he will surely
defeat us. 41 But if he shows fear and

[y] 5.13 Gk *they* [z] 5.15 Gk *aliens* [a] 5.16 Gk *them* [b] 5.23 Gk *those* [c] 5.27 Gk *they*
[d] 5.29 Gk lacks *of Dathema*. See verse 9
[e] 5.30 Gk *and they were attacking them*
[f] 5.35 Other ancient authorities read *Alema*

camps on the other side of the river, we
will cross over to him and defeat him.'
42When Judas approached the stream
of water, he stationed the officers[g] of
the army at the stream and gave them
this command, 'Permit no one to encamp, but make them all enter the battle.' 43Then he crossed over against them
first, and the whole army followed him.
All the Gentiles were defeated before
him, and they threw away their arms
and fled into the sacred precincts at
Carnaim. 44But he took the town and
burned the sacred precincts with fire,
together with all who were in them.
Thus Carnaim was conquered; they
could stand before Judas no longer.

THE RETURN TO JERUSALEM

45 Then Judas gathered together all
the Israelites in Gilead, the small and
the great, with their wives and children
and goods, a very large company, to go
to the land of Judah. 46So they came
to Ephron. This was a large and very
strong town on the road, and they could
not go around it to the right or to the
left; they had to go through it. 47But the
people of the town shut them out and
blocked up the gates with stones.

48 Judas sent them this friendly
message, 'Let us pass through your land
to get to our land. No one will do you
harm; we will simply pass by on foot.'
But they refused to open to him. 49Then
Judas ordered proclamation to be made
to the army that all should encamp
where they were. 50So the men of the
forces encamped, and he fought against
the town all that day and all the night,
and the town was delivered into his
hands. 51He destroyed every male by the
edge of the sword, and razed and plundered the town. Then he passed through
the town over the bodies of the dead.

52 Then they crossed the Jordan into
the large plain before Beth-shan. 53Ju-
das kept rallying the laggards and encouraging the people all the way until
he came to the land of Judah. 54So they
went up to Mount Zion with joy and
gladness, and offered burnt-offerings,
because they had returned in safety; not
one of them had fallen.

JOSEPH AND AZARIAH DEFEATED

55 Now while Judas and Jonathan
were in Gilead and their[h] brother Simon was in Galilee before Ptolemais,
56Joseph son of Zechariah, and Azariah,
the commanders of the forces, heard of
their brave deeds and of the heroic war
they had fought. 57So they said, 'Let us
also make a name for ourselves; let us go
and make war on the Gentiles around
us.' 58So they issued orders to the men
of the forces that were with them and
marched against Jamnia. 59Gorgias and
his men came out of the town to meet
them in battle. 60Then Joseph and Azariah were routed, and were pursued
to the borders of Judea; as many as two
thousand of the people of Israel fell that
day. 61Thus the people suffered a great
rout because, thinking to do a brave
deed, they did not listen to Judas and his
brothers. 62But they did not belong to
the family of those men through whom
deliverance was given to Israel.

63 The man Judas and his brothers
were greatly honoured in all Israel and
among all the Gentiles, wherever their
name was heard. 64People gathered to
them and praised them.

SUCCESS AT HEBRON AND PHILISTIA

65 Then Judas and his brothers went
out and fought the descendants of Esau
in the land to the south. He struck Hebron and its villages and tore down its
strongholds and burned its towers on all
sides. 66Then he marched off to go into
the land of the Philistines, and passed
through Marisa.[i] 67On that day some
priests, who wished to do a brave deed,
fell in battle, for they went out to battle
unwisely. 68But Judas turned aside to
Azotus in the land of the Philistines; he
tore down their altars, and the carved
images of their gods he burned with
fire; he plundered the towns and returned to the land of Judah.

THE LAST DAYS OF ANTIOCHUS EPIPHANES

6 King Antiochus was going through
the upper provinces when he heard
that Elymais in Persia was a city famed
for its wealth in silver and gold. 2Its temple was very rich, containing golden
shields, breastplates, and weapons left
there by Alexander son of Philip, the
Macedonian king who first reigned over
the Greeks. 3So he came and tried to take
the city and plunder it, but he could not
because his plan had become known to
the citizens 4and they withstood him in
battle. So he fled and in great disappointment left there to return to Babylon.

[g] 5.42 Or *scribes* [h] 5.55 Gk *his* [i] 5.66 Other ancient authorities read *Samaria*

5 Then someone came to him in Persia and reported that the armies that
had gone into the land of Judah had
been routed; 6 that Lysias had gone first
with a strong force, but had turned and
fled before the Jews;[j] that the Jews[k] had
grown strong from the arms, supplies,
and abundant spoils that they had taken
from the armies they had cut down;
7 that they had torn down the abomination that he had erected on the altar
in Jerusalem; and that they had surrounded the sanctuary with high walls
as before, and also Beth-zur, his town.

8 When the king heard this news,
he was astounded and badly shaken.
He took to his bed and became sick
from disappointment, because things
had not turned out for him as he had
planned. 9 He lay there for many days,
because deep disappointment continually gripped him, and he realized that he
was dying. 10 So he called all his Friends
and said to them, 'Sleep has departed
from my eyes and I am downhearted
with worry. 11 I said to myself, "To what
distress I have come! And into what a
great flood I now am plunged! For I was
kind and beloved in my power." 12 But
now I remember the wrong I did in
Jerusalem. I seized all its vessels of silver and gold, and I sent to destroy the
inhabitants of Judah without good reason. 13 I know that it is because of this
that these misfortunes have come upon
me; here I am, perishing of bitter disappointment in a strange land.'

14 Then he called for Philip, one of
his Friends, and made him ruler over
all his kingdom. 15 He gave him the
crown and his robe and the signet, so
that he might guide his son Antiochus
and bring him up to be king. 16 Thus
King Antiochus died there in the one
hundred and forty-ninth year.[l] 17 When
Lysias learned that the king was dead,
he set up Antiochus the king's[m] son to
reign. Lysias[n] had brought him up from
boyhood; he named him Eupator.

RENEWED ATTACKS FROM SYRIA

18 Meanwhile the garrison in the
citadel kept hemming Israel in around
the sanctuary. They were trying in every way to harm them and strengthen
the Gentiles. 19 Judas therefore resolved
to destroy them, and assembled all the
people to besiege them. 20 They gathered
together and besieged the citadel[o] in the
one hundred and fiftieth year;[p] and he
built siege-towers and other engines of
war. 21 But some of the garrison escaped
from the siege and some of the ungodly
Israelites joined them. 22 They went to
the king and said, 'How long will you
fail to do justice and to avenge our kindred? 23 We were happy to serve your
father, to live by what he said, and to
follow his commands. 24 For this reason
the sons of our people besieged the citadel[q] and became hostile to us; moreover,
they have put to death as many of us as
they have caught, and they have seized
our inheritances. 25 It is not against us
alone that they have stretched out their
hands; they have also attacked all the
lands on their borders. 26 And see, today
they have encamped against the citadel
in Jerusalem to take it; they have fortified both the sanctuary and Beth-zur;
27 unless you quickly prevent them, they
will do still greater things, and you will
not be able to stop them.'

28 The king was enraged when he
heard this. He assembled all his Friends,
the commanders of his forces and those
in authority.[r] 29 Mercenary forces also
came to him from other kingdoms and
from islands of the seas. 30 The number
of his forces was one hundred thousand
foot-soldiers, twenty thousand horsemen, and thirty-two elephants accustomed to war. 31 They came through Idumea and encamped against Beth-zur,
and for many days they fought and built
engines of war; but the Jews[s] sallied out
and burned these with fire, and fought
courageously.

THE BATTLE AT BETH-ZECHARIAH

32 Then Judas marched away from
the citadel and encamped at Beth-
zechariah, opposite the camp of the
king. 33 Early in the morning the king
set out and took his army by a forced
march along the road to Beth-zechariah,
and his troops made ready for battle and
sounded their trumpets. 34 They offered
the elephants the juice of grapes and
mulberries, to arouse them for battle.
35 They distributed the animals among
the phalanxes; with each elephant they
stationed a thousand men armed with
coats of mail, and with brass helmets
on their heads; and five hundred picked
horsemen were assigned to each beast.
36 These took their position beforehand
wherever the animal was; wherever it

[j] **6.6** Gk *them* [k] **6.6** Gk *they* [l] **6.16** 163 BC
[m] **6.17** Gk *his* [n] **6.17** Gk *He* [o] **6.20** Gk *it*
[p] **6.20** 162 BC [q] **6.24** Meaning of Gk uncertain
[r] **6.28** Gk *those over the reins* [s] **6.31** Gk *they*

went, they went with it, and they never
left it. 37On the elephants[t] were wooden
towers, strong and covered; they were
fastened on each animal by special harness, and on each were four[u] armed
men who fought from there, and also its
Indian driver. 38The rest of the cavalry
were stationed on either side, on the
two flanks of the army, to harass the enemy while being themselves protected
by the phalanxes. 39When the sun shone
on the shields of gold and brass, the hills
were ablaze with them and gleamed like
flaming torches.

40 Now a part of the king's army was
spread out on the high hills, and some
troops were on the plain, and they advanced steadily and in good order. 41All
who heard the noise made by their multitude, by the marching of the multitude and the clanking of their arms,
trembled, for the army was very large
and strong. 42But Judas and his army
advanced to the battle, and six hundred
of the king's army fell. 43Now Eleazar,
called Avaran, saw that one of the animals was equipped with royal armour.
It was taller than all the others, and he
supposed that the king was on it. 44So
he gave his life to save his people and
to win for himself an everlasting name.
45He courageously ran into the midst of
the phalanx to reach it; he killed men
right and left, and they parted before
him on both sides. 46He got under the
elephant, stabbed it from beneath, and
killed it; but it fell to the ground upon
him and he died. 47When the Jews[v] saw
the royal might and the fierce attack of
the forces, they turned away in flight.

THE SIEGE OF THE TEMPLE

48 The soldiers of the king's army
went up to Jerusalem against them,
and the king encamped in Judea and at
Mount Zion. 49He made peace with the
people of Beth-zur, and they evacuated
the town because they had no provisions there to withstand a siege, since it
was a sabbatical year for the land. 50So
the king took Beth-zur and stationed
a guard there to hold it. 51Then he encamped before the sanctuary for many
days. He set up siege-towers, engines
of war to throw fire and stones, machines to shoot arrows, and catapults.
52The Jews[w] also made engines of war to
match theirs, and fought for many days.
53But they had no food in storage,[x] because it was the seventh year; those who
had found safety in Judea from the Gentiles had consumed the last of the stores.
54Only a few men were left in the sanctuary; the rest scattered to their own
homes, for the famine proved too much
for them.

SYRIA OFFERS TERMS

55 Then Lysias heard that Philip,
whom King Antiochus while still living had appointed to bring up his son
Antiochus to be king, 56had returned
from Persia and Media with the forces
that had gone with the king, and that
he was trying to seize control of the government. 57So he quickly gave orders to
withdraw, and said to the king, to the
commanders of the forces, and to the
troops, 'Daily we grow weaker, our food
supply is scant, the place against which
we are fighting is strong, and the affairs of the kingdom press urgently on
us. 58Now then, let us come to terms
with these people, and make peace with
them and with all their nation. 59Let us
agree to let them live by their laws as
they did before; for it was on account of
their laws that we abolished that they
became angry and did all these things.'

60 The speech pleased the king and
the commanders, and he sent to the
Jews[y] an offer of peace, and they accepted it. 61So the king and the commanders gave them their oath. On
these conditions the Jews[z] evacuated
the stronghold. 62But when the king
entered Mount Zion and saw what a
strong fortress the place was, he broke
the oath he had sworn and gave orders
to tear down the wall all round. 63Then
he set off in haste and returned to Antioch. He found Philip in control of the
city, but he fought against him, and
took the city by force.

EXPEDITION OF BACCHIDES AND ALCIMUS

7 In the one hundred and fifty-first
year[a] Demetrius son of Seleucus set
out from Rome, sailed with a few men
to a town by the sea, and there began
to reign. 2As he was entering the royal
palace of his ancestors, the army seized
Antiochus and Lysias to bring them to
him. 3But when this act became known
to him, he said, 'Do not let me see their
faces!' 4So the army killed them, and

[t] **6.37** Gk *them* [u] **6.37** Cn: Some authorities read *thirty*; others *thirty-two* [v] **6.47** Gk *they* [w] **6.52** Gk *they* [x] **6.53** Other ancient authorities read *in the sanctuary* [y] **6.60** Gk *them* [z] **6.61** Gk *they* [a] **7.1** 161 BC

Demetrius took his seat on the throne of his kingdom.

5 Then there came to him all the renegade and godless men of Israel; they were led by Alcimus, who wanted to be high priest. 6They brought to the king this accusation against the people: 'Judas and his brothers have destroyed all your Friends, and have driven us out of our land. 7Now then, send a man whom you trust; let him go and see all the ruin that Judas[b] has brought on us and on the land of the king, and let him punish them and all who help them.'

8 So the king chose Bacchides, one of the king's Friends, governor of the province Beyond the River; he was a great man in the kingdom and was faithful to the king. 9He sent him, and with him he sent the ungodly Alcimus, whom he made high priest; and he commanded him to take vengeance on the Israelites. 10So they marched away and came with a large force into the land of Judah; and he sent messengers to Judas and his brothers with peaceable but treacherous words. 11But they paid no attention to their words, for they saw that they had come with a large force.

12 Then a group of scribes appeared in a body before Alcimus and Bacchides to ask for just terms. 13The Hasideans were first among the Israelites to seek peace from them, 14for they said, 'A priest of the line of Aaron has come with the army, and he will not harm us.' 15Alcimus[c] spoke peaceable words to them and swore this oath to them, 'We will not seek to injure you or your friends.' 16So they trusted him; but he seized sixty of them and killed them in one day, in accordance with the word that was written,

17 'The flesh of your faithful ones
and their blood
they poured out all around
Jerusalem,
and there was no one to
bury them.'

18Then the fear and dread of them fell on all the people, for they said, 'There is no truth or justice in them, for they have violated the agreement and the oath that they swore.'

19 Then Bacchides withdrew from Jerusalem and encamped in Beth-zaith. And he sent and seized many of the men who had deserted to him,[d] and some of the people, and killed them and threw them into a great pit. 20He placed Alcimus in charge of the country and left with him a force to help him; then Bacchides went back to the king.

21 Alcimus struggled to maintain his high-priesthood, 22and all who were troubling their people joined him. They gained control of the land of Judah and did great damage in Israel. 23And Judas saw all the wrongs that Alcimus and those with him had done among the Israelites; it was more than the Gentiles had done. 24So Judas[e] went out into all the surrounding parts of Judea, taking vengeance on those who had deserted and preventing those in the city[f] from going out into the country. 25When Alcimus saw that Judas and those with him had grown strong, and realized that he could not withstand them, he returned to the king and brought malicious charges against them.

NICANOR IN JUDEA

26 Then the king sent Nicanor, one of his honoured princes, who hated and detested Israel, and he commanded him to destroy the people. 27So Nicanor came to Jerusalem with a large force, and treacherously sent to Judas and his brothers this peaceable message, 28'Let there be no fighting between you and me; I shall come with a few men to see you face to face in peace.'

29 So he came to Judas, and they greeted one another peaceably; but the enemy were preparing to kidnap Judas. 30It became known to Judas that Nicanor[g] had come to him with treacherous intent, and he was afraid of him and would not meet him again. 31When Nicanor learned that his plan had been disclosed, he went out to meet Judas in battle near Caphar-salama. 32About five hundred of the army of Nicanor fell, and the rest[h] fled into the city of David.

NICANOR THREATENS THE TEMPLE

33 After these events Nicanor went up to Mount Zion. Some of the priests from the sanctuary and some of the elders of the people came out to greet him peaceably and to show him the burnt-offering that was being offered for the king. 34But he mocked them and derided them and defiled them and spoke arrogantly, 35and in anger he swore this oath, 'Unless Judas and his army are

[b] 7.7 Gk *he* [c] 7.15 Gk *He* [d] 7.19 Or *many of his men who had deserted* [e] 7.24 Gk *he* [f] 7.24 Gk *and they were prevented* [g] 7.30 Gk *he* [h] 7.32 Gk *they*

delivered into my hands this time, then
if I return safely I will burn up this
house.' And he went out in great anger.
36 At this the priests went in and stood
before the altar and the temple; they
wept and said,
37 'You chose this house to be called
by your name,
and to be for your people a house
of prayer and supplication.
38 Take vengeance on this man
and on his army,
and let them fall by the sword;
remember their blasphemies,
and let them live no longer.'

THE DEATH OF NICANOR

39 Now Nicanor went out from Jerusalem and encamped in Beth-horon,
and the Syrian army joined him. 40 Judas encamped in Adasa with three
thousand men. Then Judas prayed and
said, 41 'When the messengers from the
king spoke blasphemy, your angel went
out and struck down one hundred and
eighty-five thousand of the Assyrians.[i]
42 So also crush this army before us today; let the rest learn that Nicanor[j] has
spoken wickedly against the sanctuary,
and judge him according to this wickedness.'

43 So the armies met in battle on the
thirteenth day of the month of Adar.
The army of Nicanor was crushed, and
he himself was the first to fall in the battle. 44 When his army saw that Nicanor
had fallen, they threw down their arms
and fled. 45 The Jews[k] pursued them
a day's journey, from Adasa as far as
Gazara, and as they followed they kept
sounding the battle-call on the trumpets. 46 People came out of all the surrounding villages of Judea, and they
outflanked the enemy[l] and drove them
back to their pursuers,[m] so that they
all fell by the sword; not even one of
them was left. 47 Then the Jews[n] seized
the spoils and the plunder; they cut off
Nicanor's head and the right hand that
he had so arrogantly stretched out, and
brought them and displayed them just
outside Jerusalem. 48 The people rejoiced
greatly and celebrated that day as a day
of great gladness. 49 They decreed that
this day should be celebrated each year
on the thirteenth day of Adar. 50 So the
land of Judah had rest for a few days.

A EULOGY OF THE ROMANS

8 Now Judas heard of the fame of
the Romans, that they were very
strong and were well disposed towards
all who made an alliance with them,
that they pledged friendship to those
who came to them, 2 and that they were
very strong. He had been told of their
wars and of the brave deeds that they
were doing among the Gauls, how they
had defeated them and forced them to
pay tribute, 3 and what they had done
in the land of Spain to get control of
the silver and gold mines there, 4 and
how they had gained control of the
whole region by their planning and
patience, even though the place was
far distant from them. They also subdued the kings who came against them
from the ends of the earth, until they
crushed them and inflicted great disaster on them; the rest paid them tribute
every year. 5 They had crushed in battle
and conquered Philip, and King Per-
seus of the Macedonians,[o] and the others who rose up against them. 6 They
also had defeated Antiochus the Great,
king of Asia, who went to fight against
them with one hundred and twenty elephants and with cavalry and chariots
and a very large army. He was crushed
by them; 7 they took him alive and decreed that he and those who would
reign after him should pay a heavy
tribute and give hostages and surrender some of their best provinces, 8 the
countries of India, Media, and Lydia.
These they took from him and gave to
King Eumenes. 9 The Greeks planned
to come and destroy them, 10 but this
became known to them, and they sent
a general against the Greeks[p] and attacked them. Many of them were
wounded and fell, and the Romans[q]
took captive their wives and children;
they plundered them, conquered the
land, tore down their strongholds,
and enslaved them to this day. 11 The
remaining kingdoms and islands, as
many as ever opposed them, they destroyed and enslaved; 12 but with their
friends and those who rely on them
they have kept friendship. They have
subdued kings far and near, and as
many as have heard of their fame have
feared them. 13 Those whom they wish
to help and to make kings, they make
kings, and those whom they wish they
depose; and they have been greatly exalted. 14 Yet for all this not one of them

[i] 7.41 Gk *of them* [j] 7.42 Gk *he* [k] 7.45 Gk *they* [l] 7.46 Gk *them* [m] 7.46 Gk *these* [n] 7.47 Gk *they* [o] 8.5 Or *Kittim* [p] 8.10 Gk *them* [q] 8.10 Gk *they*

has put on a crown or worn purple as a
mark of pride, 15but they have built for
themselves a senate chamber, and every day three hundred and twenty sen-
ators constantly deliberate concerning
the people, to govern them well. 16They
trust one man each year to rule over
them and to control all their land; they
all heed the one man, and there is no
envy or jealousy among them.

AN ALLIANCE WITH ROME

17 So Judas chose Eupolemus son of
John son of Accos, and Jason son of Eleazar, and sent them to Rome to establish
friendship and alliance, 18and to free
themselves from the yoke; for they saw
that the kingdom of the Greeks was enslaving Israel completely. 19They went
to Rome, a very long journey; and they
entered the senate chamber and spoke
as follows: 20'Judas, who is also called
Maccabeus, and his brothers and the
people of the Jews have sent us to you
to establish alliance and peace with you,
so that we may be enrolled as your allies and friends.' 21The proposal pleased
them, 22and this is a copy of the letter
that they wrote in reply, on bronze tablets, and sent to Jerusalem to remain
with them there as a memorial of peace
and alliance:

23 'May all go well with the Romans
and with the nation of the Jews at sea
and on land for ever, and may sword
and enemy be far from them. 24If war
comes first to Rome or to any of their
allies in all their dominion, 25the nation of the Jews shall act as their allies
wholeheartedly, as the occasion may
indicate to them. 26To the enemy that
makes war they shall not give or supply grain, arms, money, or ships, just as
Rome has decided; and they shall keep
their obligations without receiving any
return. 27In the same way, if war comes
first to the nation of the Jews, the Romans shall willingly act as their allies,
as the occasion may indicate to them.
28And to their enemies there shall not
be given grain, arms, money, or ships,
just as Rome has decided; and they shall
keep these obligations and do so without deceit. 29Thus on these terms the
Romans make a treaty with the Jewish
people. 30If after these terms are in effect both parties shall determine to add
or delete anything, they shall do so at
their discretion, and any addition or
deletion that they may make shall be
valid.

31 'Concerning the wrongs that
King Demetrius is doing to them, we
have written to him as follows, "Why
have you made your yoke heavy on our
friends and allies the Jews? 32If now
they appeal again for help against you,
we will defend their rights and fight you
on sea and on land." '

BACCHIDES RETURNS TO JUDEA

9 When Demetrius heard that Nicanor and his army had fallen in battle, he sent Bacchides and Alcimus into
the land of Judah a second time, and
with them the right wing of the army.
2They went by the road that leads to Gilgal and encamped against Mesaloth in
Arbela, and they took it and killed many
people. 3In the first month of the one
hundred and fifty-second year[r] they encamped against Jerusalem; 4then they
marched off and went to Berea with
twenty thousand foot-soldiers and two
thousand cavalry.

5 Now Judas was encamped in Ela-
sa, and with him were three thousand
picked men. 6When they saw the huge
number of the enemy forces, they
were greatly frightened, and many
slipped away from the camp, until
no more than eight hundred of them
were left.

7 When Judas saw that his army had
slipped away and the battle was imminent, he was crushed in spirit, for
he had no time to assemble them. 8He
became faint, but he said to those who
were left, 'Let us get up and go against
our enemies. We may have the strength
to fight them.' 9But they tried to dissuade him, saying, 'We do not have the
strength. Let us rather save our own
lives now, and let us come back with our
kindred and fight them; we are too few.'
10But Judas said, 'Far be it from us to do
such a thing as to flee from them. If our
time has come, let us die bravely for our
kindred, and leave no cause to question
our honour.'

THE LAST BATTLE OF JUDAS

11 Then the army of Bacchides[s]
marched out from the camp and took
its stand for the encounter. The cavalry was divided into two companies,
and the slingers and the archers went
ahead of the army, as did all the chief
warriors. 12Bacchides was on the right
wing. Flanked by the two companies,

[r] **9.3** 160 BC [s] **9.11** Gk lacks *of Bacchides*

the phalanx advanced to the sound of
the trumpets; and the men with Judas
also blew their trumpets. 13 The earth
was shaken by the noise of the armies,
and the battle raged from morning until evening.
14 Judas saw that Bacchides and
the strength of his army were on the
right; then all the stout-hearted men
went with him, 15 and they crushed the
right wing, and he pursued them as far
as Mount Azotus. 16 When those on the
left wing saw that the right wing was
crushed, they turned and followed close
behind Judas and his men. 17 The battle
became desperate, and many on both
sides were wounded and fell. 18 Judas
also fell, and the rest fled.
19 Then Jonathan and Simon took
their brother Judas and buried him
in the tomb of their ancestors at Modein, 20 and wept for him. All Israel
made great lamentation for him; they
mourned for many days and said,
21 'How is the mighty fallen,
the saviour of Israel!'
22 Now the rest of the acts of Judas, and
his wars and the brave deeds that he
did, and his greatness, have not been recorded, but they were very many.

JONATHAN SUCCEEDS JUDAS

23 After the death of Judas, the renegades emerged in all parts of Israel; all
the wrongdoers reappeared. 24 In those
days a very great famine occurred, and
the country went over to their side.
25 Bacchides chose the godless and put
them in charge of the country. 26 They
made inquiry and searched for the
friends of Judas, and brought them to
Bacchides, who took vengeance on them
and made sport of them. 27 So there was
great distress in Israel, such as had
not been since the time that prophets
ceased to appear among them.
28 Then all the friends of Judas assembled and said to Jonathan, 29 'Since
the death of your brother Judas there
has been no one like him to go against
our enemies and Bacchides, and to deal
with those of our nation who hate us.
30 Now therefore we have chosen you
today to take his place as our ruler and
leader, to fight our battle.' 31 So Jonathan
accepted the leadership at that time in
place of his brother Judas.

THE CAMPAIGNS OF JONATHAN

32 When Bacchides learned of this, he
tried to kill him. 33 But Jonathan and his
brother Simon and all who were with
him heard of it, and they fled into the
wilderness of Tekoa and camped by the
water of the pool of Asphar. 34 Bacchides
found this out on the sabbath day, and
he with all his army crossed the Jordan.
35 So Jonathan[t] sent his brother as
leader of the multitude and begged the
Nabateans, who were his friends, for
permission to store with them the great
amount of baggage that they had. 36 But
the family of Jambri from Medeba came
out and seized John and all that he had,
and left with it.
37 After these things it was reported
to Jonathan and his brother Simon, 'The
family of Jambri are celebrating a great
wedding, and are conducting the bride,
a daughter of one of the great nobles of
Canaan, from Nadabath with a large escort.' 38 Remembering how their brother
John had been killed, they went up and
hid under cover of the mountain. 39 They
looked out and saw a tumultuous procession with a great amount of baggage;
and the bridegroom came out with his
friends and his brothers to meet them
with tambourines and musicians and
many weapons. 40 Then they rushed on
them from the ambush and began killing them. Many were wounded and fell,
and the rest fled to the mountain; and
the Jews[u] took all their goods. 41 So the
wedding was turned into mourning
and the voice of their musicians into
a funeral dirge. 42 After they had fully
avenged the blood of their brother, they
returned to the marshes of the Jordan.
43 When Bacchides heard of this, he
came with a large force on the sabbath
day to the banks of the Jordan. 44 And
Jonathan said to those with him, 'Let us
get up now and fight for our lives, for today things are not as they were before.
45 For look! the battle is in front of us
and behind us; the water of the Jordan
is on this side and on that, with marsh
and thicket; there is no place to turn.
46 Cry out now to Heaven that you may
be delivered from the hands of our enemies.' 47 So the battle began, and Jonathan stretched out his hand to strike
Bacchides, but he eluded him and went
to the rear. 48 Then Jonathan and the
men with him leapt into the Jordan and
swam across to the other side, and the
enemy[v] did not cross the Jordan to attack them. 49 And about one thousand
of Bacchides' men fell that day.

[t] 9.35 Gk *he* [u] 9.40 Gk *they* [v] 9.48 Gk *they*

BACCHIDES BUILDS FORTIFICATIONS

50 Then Bacchides[w] returned to Jerusalem and built strong cities in Judea:
the fortress in Jericho, and Emmaus,
and Beth-horon, and Bethel, and Tim-
nath, and[x] Pharathon, and Tephon,
with high walls and gates and bars.
51And he placed garrisons in them to
harass Israel. 52He also fortified the
town of Beth-zur, and Gazara, and the
citadel, and in them he put troops and
stores of food. 53And he took the sons of
the leading men of the land as hostages
and put them under guard in the citadel
at Jerusalem.

54 In the one hundred and fifty-third
year,[y] in the second month, Alcimus
gave orders to tear down the wall of the
inner court of the sanctuary. He tore
down the work of the prophets! 55But
he only began to tear it down, for at that
time Alcimus was stricken and his work
was hindered; his mouth was stopped
and he was paralysed, so that he could
no longer say a word or give commands
concerning his house. 56And Alcimus
died at that time in great agony. 57When
Bacchides saw that Alcimus was dead,
he returned to the king, and the land of
Judah had rest for two years.

THE END OF THE WAR

58 Then all the lawless plotted and
said, 'See! Jonathan and his men are
living in quiet and confidence. So now
let us bring Bacchides back, and he will
capture them all in one night.' 59And
they went and consulted with him.
60He started to come with a large force,
and secretly sent letters to all his allies
in Judea, telling them to seize Jonathan and his men; but they were unable to do it, because their plan became
known. 61And Jonathan's men[z] seized
about fifty of the men of the country
who were leaders in this treachery, and
killed them.

62 Then Jonathan with his men, and
Simon, withdrew to Bethbasi in the
wilderness; he rebuilt the parts of it that
had been demolished, and they fortified
it. 63When Bacchides learned of this,
he assembled all his forces, and sent
orders to the men of Judea. 64Then he
came and encamped against Bethbasi;
he fought against it for many days and
made machines of war.

65 But Jonathan left his brother Simon in the town, while he went out
into the country; and he went with only
a few men. 66He struck down Odomera
and his kindred and the people of Phas-
iron in their tents. 67Then he[a] began
to attack and went into battle with his
forces; and Simon and his men sallied
out from the town and set fire to the
machines of war. 68They fought with
Bacchides, and he was crushed by them.
They pressed him very hard, for his plan
and his expedition had been in vain.
69So he was very angry at the renegades who had counselled him to come
into the country, and he killed many of
them. Then he decided to go back to his
own land.

70 When Jonathan learned of this,
he sent ambassadors to him to make
peace with him and obtain release of
the captives. 71He agreed, and did as he
said; and he swore to Jonathan[b] that he
would not try to harm him as long as he
lived. 72He restored to him the captives
whom he had taken previously from
the land of Judah; then he turned and
went back to his own land, and did not
come again into their territory. 73Thus
the sword ceased from Israel. Jonathan
settled in Michmash and began to judge
the people; and he destroyed the godless
out of Israel.

REVOLT OF ALEXANDER EPIPHANES

10 In the one hundred and sixtieth
year[c] Alexander Epiphanes, son
of Antiochus, landed and occupied Ptolemais. They welcomed him, and there
he began to reign. 2When King Demetrius heard of it, he assembled a very
large army and marched out to meet
him in battle. 3Demetrius sent Jonathan a letter in peaceable words to honour him; 4for he said to himself, 'Let us
act first to make peace with him[d] before
he makes peace with Alexander against
us, 5for he will remember all the wrongs
that we did to him and to his brothers
and his nation.' 6So Demetrius[e] gave
him authority to recruit troops, to equip
them with arms, and to become his ally;
and he commanded that the hostages in
the citadel should be released to him.

7 Then Jonathan came to Jerusalem
and read the letter in the hearing of all
the people and of those in the citadel.
8They were greatly alarmed when they
heard that the king had given him authority to recruit troops. 9But those
in the citadel released the hostages to

[w] 9.50 Gk *he* [x] 9.50 Some authorities omit *and*
[y] 9.54 159 BC [z] 9.61 Gk *they* [a] 9.67 Other
ancient authorities read *they* [b] 9.71 Gk *him*
[c] 10.1 152 BC [d] 10.4 Gk *them* [e] 10.6 Gk *he*

Jonathan, and he returned them to
their parents.
10 And Jonathan took up residence
in Jerusalem and began to rebuild and
restore the city. 11He directed those who
were doing the work to build the walls
and encircle Mount Zion with squared
stones, for better fortification; and they
did so.
12 Then the foreigners who were in
the strongholds that Bacchides had built
fled; 13all of them left their places and
went back to their own lands. 14Only in
Beth-zur did some remain who had forsaken the law and the commandments,
for it served as a place of refuge.
15 Now King Alexander heard of all
the promises that Demetrius had sent
to Jonathan, and he heard of the battles that Jonathan[f] and his brothers
had fought, of the brave deeds that they
had done, and of the troubles that they
had endured. 16So he said, 'Shall we find
another such man? Come now, we will
make him our friend and ally.' 17And he
wrote a letter and sent it to him, in the
following words:

JONATHAN BECOMES HIGH PRIEST

18 'King Alexander to his brother
Jonathan, greetings. 19We have heard
about you, that you are a mighty warrior and worthy to be our friend. 20And
so we have appointed you today to be
the high priest of your nation; you are
to be called the king's Friend and you
are to take our side and keep friendship
with us.' He also sent him a purple robe
and a golden crown.
21 So Jonathan put on the sacred
vestments in the seventh month of the
one hundred and sixtieth year,[g] at the
festival of booths,[h] and he recruited
troops and equipped them with arms in
abundance. 22When Demetrius heard of
these things he was distressed and said,
23'What is this that we have done? Alexander has overtaken us in forming a
friendship with the Jews to strengthen
himself. 24I also will write them words
of encouragement and promise them
honour and gifts, so that I may have
their help.' 25So he sent a message to
them in the following words:

A LETTER FROM DEMETRIUS TO JONATHAN

'King Demetrius to the nation of the
Jews, greetings. 26Since you have kept
your agreement with us and have continued your friendship with us, and
have not sided with our enemies, we
have heard of it and rejoiced. 27Now
continue still to keep faith with us, and
we will repay you with good for what
you do for us. 28We will grant you many
immunities and give you gifts.
29 'I now free you and exempt all the
Jews from payment of tribute and salt
tax and crown levies, 30and instead of
collecting the third of the grain and the
half of the fruit of the trees that I should
receive, I release them from this day
and henceforth. I will not collect them
from the land of Judah or from the three
districts added to it from Samaria and
Galilee, from this day and for all time.
31Jerusalem and its environs, its tithes
and its revenues, shall be holy and free
from tax. 32I release also my control of
the citadel in Jerusalem and give it to
the high priest, so that he may station
in it men of his own choice to guard it.
33And everyone of the Jews taken as a
captive from the land of Judah into any
part of my kingdom, I set free without
payment; and let all officials cancel also
the taxes on their livestock.
34 'All the festivals and sabbaths and
new moons and appointed days, and the
three days before a festival and the three
after a festival—let them all be days of
immunity and release for all the Jews
who are in my kingdom. 35No one shall
have authority to exact anything from
them or annoy any of them about any
matter.
36 'Let Jews be enrolled in the king's
forces to the number of thirty thousand
men, and let the maintenance be given
them that is due to all the forces of the
king. 37Let some of them be stationed in
the great strongholds of the king, and
let some of them be put in positions of
trust in the kingdom. Let their officers
and leaders be of their own number, and
let them live by their own laws, just as
the king has commanded in the land of
Judah.
38 'As for the three districts that have
been added to Judea from the country
of Samaria, let them be annexed to Judea so that they may be considered to
be under one ruler and obey no other
authority than the high priest. 39Ptol-
emais and the land adjoining it I have
given as a gift to the sanctuary in Jerusalem, to meet the necessary expenses
of the sanctuary. 40I also grant fifteen

[f] **10.15** Gk *he* [g] **10.21** 152 BC [h] **10.21** Or *tabernacles*

thousand shekels of silver yearly out of
the king's revenues from appropriate
places. 41And all the additional funds
that the government officials have not
paid as they did in the first years,[i] they
shall give from now on for the service of
the temple.[j] 42Moreover, the five thousand shekels of silver that my officials[k]
have received every year from the income of the services of the temple, this
too is cancelled, because it belongs to
the priests who minister there. 43And
all who take refuge at the temple in Jerusalem, or in any of its precincts, because they owe money to the king or are
in debt, let them be released and receive
back all their property in my kingdom.

44 'Let the cost of rebuilding and restoring the structures of the sanctuary
be paid from the revenues of the king.
45And let the cost of rebuilding the walls
of Jerusalem and fortifying it all round,
and the cost of rebuilding the walls in
Judea, also be paid from the revenues of
the king.'

DEATH OF DEMETRIUS

46 When Jonathan and the people
heard these words, they did not believe
or accept them, because they remembered the great wrongs that Demetrius[l]
had done in Israel and how much he
had oppressed them. 47They favoured
Alexander, because he had been the
first to speak peaceable words to them,
and they remained his allies all his days.

48 Now King Alexander assembled
large forces and encamped opposite Demetrius. 49The two kings met in battle,
and the army of Demetrius fled, and
Alexander[m] pursued him and defeated
them. 50He pressed the battle strongly
until the sun set, and on that day Demetrius fell.

TREATY OF PTOLEMY AND ALEXANDER

51 Then Alexander sent ambassadors to Ptolemy king of Egypt with the
following message: 52'Since I have returned to my kingdom and have taken
my seat on the throne of my ancestors,
and established my rule—for I crushed
Demetrius and gained control of our
country; 53I met him in battle, and he
and his army were crushed by us, and
we have taken our seat on the throne of
his kingdom— 54now therefore let us
establish friendship with one another;
give me now your daughter as my wife,
and I will become your son-in-law, and
will make gifts to you and to her in
keeping with your position.'

55 Ptolemy the king replied and said,
'Happy was the day on which you returned to the land of your ancestors and
took your seat on the throne of their
kingdom. 56And now I will do for you
as you wrote, but meet me at Ptolemais,
so that we may see one another, and I
will become your father-in-law, as you
have said.'

57 So Ptolemy set out from Egypt, he
and his daughter Cleopatra, and came
to Ptolemais in the one hundred and
sixty-second year.[n] 58King Alexander
met him, and Ptolemy[o] gave him his
daughter Cleopatra in marriage, and
celebrated her wedding at Ptolemais
with great pomp, as kings do.

59 Then King Alexander wrote to
Jonathan to come and meet him. 60So he
went with pomp to Ptolemais and met
the two kings; he gave them and their
Friends silver and gold and many gifts,
and found favour with them. 61A group
of malcontents from Israel, renegades,
gathered together against him to accuse
him; but the king paid no attention to
them. 62The king gave orders to take off
Jonathan's garments and to clothe him
in purple, and they did so. 63The king
also seated him at his side; and he said
to his officers, 'Go out with him into
the middle of the city and proclaim that
no one is to bring charges against him
about any matter, and let no one annoy
him for any reason.' 64When his accusers saw the honour that was paid him,
in accordance with the proclamation,
and saw him clothed in purple, they all
fled. 65Thus the king honoured him and
enrolled him among his chief[p] Friends,
and made him general and governor of
the province. 66And Jonathan returned
to Jerusalem in peace and gladness.

APOLLONIUS IS DEFEATED BY JONATHAN

67 In the one hundred and sixty-fifth
year[q] Demetrius son of Demetrius came
from Crete to the land of his ancestors.
68When King Alexander heard of it, he
was greatly distressed and returned to
Antioch. 69And Demetrius appointed
Apollonius the governor of Coelesyria, and he assembled a large force and

[i] 10.41 Meaning of Gk uncertain [j] 10.41 Gk *house* [k] 10.42 Gk *they* [l] 10.46 Gk *he* [m] 10.49 Other ancient authorities read *Alexander fled, and Demetrius* [n] 10.57 150 BC [o] 10.58 Gk *he* [p] 10.65 Gk *first* [q] 10.67 147 BC

encamped against Jamnia. Then he sent
the following message to the high priest
Jonathan:

70 'You are the only one to rise up
against us, and I have fallen into ridicule and disgrace because of you. Why
do you assume authority against us in
the hill country? 71 If you now have confidence in your forces, come down to
the plain to meet us, and let us match
strength with each other there, for I
have with me the power of the cities.
72 Ask and learn who I am and who the
others are that are helping us. People
will tell you that you cannot stand before us, for your ancestors were twice
put to flight in their own land. 73 And
now you will not be able to withstand
my cavalry and such an army in the
plain, where there is no stone or pebble,
or place to flee.'

74 When Jonathan heard the words
of Apollonius, his spirit was aroused.
He chose ten thousand men and set out
from Jerusalem, and his brother Simon
met him to help him. 75 He encamped
before Joppa, but the people of the city
closed its gates, for Apollonius had a
garrison in Joppa. 76 So they fought
against it, and the people of the city became afraid and opened the gates, and
Jonathan gained possession of Joppa.

77 When Apollonius heard of it, he
mustered three thousand cavalry and
a large army, and went to Azotus as
though he were going farther. At the
same time he advanced into the plain,
for he had a large troop of cavalry and
put confidence in it. 78 Jonathan[r] pursued him to Azotus, and the armies engaged in battle. 79 Now Apollonius had
secretly left a thousand cavalry behind
them. 80 Jonathan learned that there
was an ambush behind him, for they
surrounded his army and shot arrows at
his men from early morning until late
afternoon. 81 But his men stood fast, as
Jonathan had commanded, and the enemy's[s] horses grew tired.

82 Then Simon brought forward his
force and engaged the phalanx in battle (for the cavalry was exhausted); they
were overwhelmed by him and fled,
83 and the cavalry was dispersed in the
plain. They fled to Azotus and entered
Beth-dagon, the temple of their idol, for
safety. 84 But Jonathan burned Azotus
and the surrounding towns and plundered them; and the temple of Dagon,
and those who had taken refuge in it,
he burned with fire. 85 The number of
those who fell by the sword, with those
burned alive, came to eight thousand.

86 Then Jonathan left there and encamped against Askalon, and the people
of the city came out to meet him with
great pomp.

87 He and those with him then
returned to Jerusalem with a large
amount of booty. 88 When King Alexander heard of these things, he honoured
Jonathan still more; 89 and he sent to
him a golden buckle, such as it is the
custom to give to the King's Kinsmen.
He also gave him Ekron and all its environs as his possession.

PTOLEMY INVADES SYRIA

11 Then the king of Egypt gathered
great forces, like the sand by the
seashore, and many ships; and he tried
to get possession of Alexander's kingdom by trickery and add it to his own
kingdom. 2 He set out for Syria with
peaceable words, and the people of the
towns opened their gates to him and
went to meet him, for King Alexander
had commanded them to meet him,
since he was Alexander's[t] father-in-law.
3 But when Ptolemy entered the towns
he stationed forces as a garrison in each
town.

4 When he[u] approached Azotus, they
showed him the burnt-out temple of
Dagon, and Azotus and its suburbs destroyed, and the corpses lying about,
and the charred bodies of those whom
Jonathan[v] had burned in the war, for
they had piled them in heaps along his
route. 5 They also told the king what
Jonathan had done, to throw blame on
him; but the king kept silent. 6 Jonathan
met the king at Joppa with pomp, and
they greeted one another and spent the
night there. 7 And Jonathan went with
the king as far as the river called Eleutherus; then he returned to Jerusalem.

8 So King Ptolemy gained control of
the coastal cities as far as Seleucia by
the sea, and he kept devising wicked
designs against Alexander. 9 He sent envoys to King Demetrius, saying, 'Come,
let us make a covenant with each other,
and I will give you in marriage my
daughter who was Alexander's wife,
and you shall reign over your father's
kingdom. 10 I now regret that I gave
him my daughter, for he has tried to kill
me.' 11 He threw blame on Alexander[w]

[r] **10.78** Gk *he* [s] **10.81** Gk *their* [t] **11.2** Gk *his*
[u] **11.4** Other ancient authorities read *they*
[v] **11.4** Gk *he* [w] **11.11** Gk *him*

because he coveted his kingdom. 12So he took his daughter away from him and gave her to Demetrius. He was estranged from Alexander, and their enmity became manifest.

13 Then Ptolemy entered Antioch and put on the crown of Asia. Thus he put two crowns on his head, the crown of Egypt and that of Asia. 14Now King Alexander was in Cilicia at that time, because the people of that region were in revolt. 15When Alexander heard of it, he came against him in battle. Ptolemy marched out and met him with a strong force, and put him to flight. 16So Alexander fled into Arabia to find protection there, and King Ptolemy was triumphant. 17Zabdiel the Arab cut off the head of Alexander and sent it to Ptolemy. 18But King Ptolemy died three days later, and his troops in the strongholds were killed by the inhabitants of the strongholds. 19So Demetrius became king in the one hundred and sixty-seventh year.[x]

JONATHAN'S DIPLOMACY

20 In those days Jonathan assembled the Judeans to attack the citadel in Jerusalem, and he built many engines of war to use against it. 21But certain renegades who hated their nation went to the king and reported to him that Jonathan was besieging the citadel. 22When he heard this he was angry, and as soon as he heard it he set out and came to Ptolemais; and he wrote to order Jonathan not to continue the siege, but to meet him for a conference at Ptolemais as quickly as possible.

23 When Jonathan heard this, he gave orders to continue the siege. He chose some of the elders of Israel and some of the priests, and put himself in danger, 24for he went to the king at Ptolemais, taking silver and gold and clothing and numerous other gifts. And he won his favour. 25Although certain renegades of his nation kept making complaints against him, 26the king treated him as his predecessors had treated him; he exalted him in the presence of all his Friends. 27He confirmed him in the high-priesthood and in as many other honours as he had formerly had, and caused him to be reckoned among his chief[y] Friends. 28Then Jonathan asked the king to free Judea and the three districts of Samaria[z] from tribute, and promised him three hundred talents. 29The king consented, and wrote a letter to Jonathan about all these things; its contents were as follows:

30 'King Demetrius to his brother Jonathan and to the nation of the Jews, greetings. 31This copy of the letter that we wrote concerning you to our kinsman Lasthenes we have written to you also, so that you may know what it says. 32"King Demetrius to his father Lasthenes, greetings. 33We have determined to do good to the nation of the Jews, who are our friends and fulfil their obligations to us, because of the goodwill they show towards us. 34We have confirmed as their possession both the territory of Judea and the three districts of Aphairema and Lydda and Rathamin; the latter, with all the region bordering them, were added to Judea from Samaria. To all those who offer sacrifice in Jerusalem we have granted release from[a] the royal taxes that the king formerly received from them each year, from the crops of the land and the fruit of the trees. 35And the other payments henceforth due to us of the tithes, and the taxes due to us, and the salt pits and the crown taxes due to us—from all these we shall grant them release. 36And not one of these grants shall be cancelled from this time on for ever. 37Now therefore take care to make a copy of this, and let it be given to Jonathan and put up in a conspicuous place on the holy mountain." '

THE INTRIGUE OF TRYPHO

38 When King Demetrius saw that the land was quiet before him and that there was no opposition to him, he dismissed all his troops, all of them to their own homes, except the foreign troops that he had recruited from the islands of the nations. So all the troops who had served under his predecessors hated him. 39A certain Trypho had formerly been one of Alexander's supporters; he saw that all the troops were grumbling against Demetrius. So he went to Imalkue the Arab, who was bringing up Antiochus, the young son of Alexander, 40and insistently urged him to hand Antiochus[b] over to him, to become king in place of his father. He also reported to Imalkue[c] what Demetrius had done and told of the hatred that the troops of Demetrius[d] had for him; and he stayed there for many days.

[x] 11.19 145 BC [y] 11.27 Gk *first* [z] 11.28 Cn: Gk *the three districts and Samaria* [a] 11.34 Or *Samaria, for all those who offer sacrifice in Jerusalem, in place of* [b] 11.40 Gk *him* [c] 11.40 Gk *him* [d] 11.40 Gk *his troops*

41 Now Jonathan sent to King Demetrius the request that he remove the
troops of the citadel from Jerusalem, and
the troops in the strongholds; for they
kept fighting against Israel. 42And Demetrius sent this message back to Jonathan: 'Not only will I do these things for
you and your nation, but I will confer
great honour on you and your nation, if
I find an opportunity. 43Now then, you
will do well to send me men who will
help me, for all my troops have revolted.'
44So Jonathan sent three thousand stalwart men to him at Antioch, and when
they came to the king, the king rejoiced
at their arrival.

45 Then the people of the city assembled within the city, to the number of
a hundred and twenty thousand, and
they wanted to kill the king. 46But the
king fled into the palace. Then the people of the city seized the main streets
of the city and began to fight. 47So the
king called the Jews to his aid, and they
all rallied around him and then spread
out through the city; and they killed on
that day about one hundred thousand.
48They set fire to the city and seized a
large amount of spoil on that day, and
saved the king. 49When the people of
the city saw that the Jews had gained
control of the city as they pleased, their
courage failed and they cried out to the
king with this entreaty: 50'Grant us
peace, and make the Jews stop fighting against us and our city.' 51And they
threw down their arms and made peace.
So the Jews gained glory in the sight
of the king and of all the people in his
kingdom, and they returned to Jerusalem with a large amount of spoil.

52 So King Demetrius sat on the
throne of his kingdom, and the land
was quiet before him. 53But he broke his
word about all that he had promised;
he became estranged from Jonathan
and did not repay the favours that Jonathan[e] had done him, but treated him
very harshly.

TRYPHO SEIZES POWER

54 After this Trypho returned, and
with him the young boy Antiochus who
began to reign and put on the crown.
55All the troops that Demetrius had
discharged gathered around him; they
fought against Demetrius,[f] and he fled
and was routed. 56Trypho captured the
elephants[g] and gained control of Antioch. 57Then the young Antiochus wrote
to Jonathan, saying, 'I confirm you in
the high-priesthood and set you over
the four districts and make you one of
the king's Friends.' 58He also sent him
gold plates and a table service, and
granted him the right to drink from
gold cups and dress in purple and wear a
gold buckle. 59He appointed Jonathan's[h]
brother Simon governor from the Ladder of Tyre to the borders of Egypt.

CAMPAIGNS OF JONATHAN AND SIMON

60 Then Jonathan set out and travelled beyond the river and among the
towns, and all the army of Syria gathered to him as allies. When he came to
Askalon, the people of the city met him
and paid him honour. 61From there he
went to Gaza, but the people of Gaza
shut him out. So he besieged it and
burned its suburbs with fire and plundered them. 62Then the people of Gaza
pleaded with Jonathan, and he made
peace with them, and took the sons of
their rulers as hostages and sent them
to Jerusalem. And he passed through
the country as far as Damascus.

63 Then Jonathan heard that the officers of Demetrius had come to Kadesh
in Galilee with a large army, intending
to remove him from office. 64He went to
meet them, but left his brother Simon
in the country. 65Simon encamped before Beth-zur and fought against it for
many days and hemmed it in. 66Then
they asked him to grant them terms of
peace, and he did so. He removed them
from there, took possession of the town,
and set a garrison over it.

67 Jonathan and his army encamped
by the waters of Gennesaret. Early in
the morning they marched to the plain
of Hazor, 68and there in the plain the
army of the foreigners met him; they
had set an ambush against him in the
mountains, but they themselves met
him face to face. 69Then the men in ambush emerged from their places and
joined battle. 70All the men with Jonathan fled; not one of them was left
except Mattathias son of Absalom and
Judas son of Chalphi, commanders of
the forces of the army. 71Jonathan tore
his clothes, put dust on his head, and
prayed. 72Then he turned back to the
battle against the enemy[i] and routed
them, and they fled. 73When his men
who were fleeing saw this, they re-

[e] **11.53** Gk *he* [f] **11.55** Gk *him* [g] **11.56** Gk *animals* [h] **11.59** Gk *his* [i] **11.72** Gk *them*

turned to him and joined him in the pursuit as far as Kadesh, to their camp, and there they encamped. 74As many as three thousand of the foreigners fell that day. And Jonathan returned to Jerusalem.

ALLIANCES WITH ROME AND SPARTA

12 Now when Jonathan saw that the time was favourable for him, he chose men and sent them to Rome to confirm and renew the friendship with them. 2He also sent letters to the same effect to the Spartans and to other places. 3So they went to Rome and entered the senate chamber and said, 'The high priest Jonathan and the Jewish nation have sent us to renew the former friendship and alliance with them.' 4And the Romans[j] gave them letters to the people in every place, asking them to provide for the envoys[k] safe conduct to the land of Judah.

5 This is a copy of the letter that Jonathan wrote to the Spartans: 6'The high priest Jonathan, the senate of the nation, the priests, and the rest of the Jewish people to their brothers the Spartans, greetings. 7Already in time past a letter was sent to the high priest Onias from Arius,[l] who was king among you, stating that you are our brothers, as the appended copy shows. 8Onias welcomed the envoy with honour, and received the letter, which contained a clear declaration of alliance and friendship. 9Therefore, though we have no need of these things, since we have as encouragement the holy books that are in our hands, 10we have undertaken to send to renew our family ties and friendship with you, so that we may not become estranged from you, for considerable time has passed since you sent your letter to us. 11We therefore remember you constantly on every occasion, both at our festivals and on other appropriate days, at the sacrifices that we offer and in our prayers, as it is right and proper to remember brothers. 12And we rejoice in your glory. 13But as for ourselves, many trials and many wars have encircled us; the kings around us have waged war against us. 14We were unwilling to annoy you and our other allies and friends with these wars, 15for we have the help that comes from Heaven for our aid, and so we were delivered from our enemies, and our enemies were humbled. 16We therefore have chosen Numenius son of Antiochus and Antipater son of Jason, and have sent them to Rome to renew our former friendship and alliance with them. 17We have commanded them to go also to you and greet you and deliver to you this letter from us concerning the renewal of our family ties. 18And now please send us a reply to this.'

19 This is a copy of the letter that they sent to Onias: 20'King Arius of the Spartans, to the high priest Onias, greetings. 21It has been found in writing concerning the Spartans and the Jews that they are brothers and are of the family of Abraham. 22And now that we have learned this, please write us concerning your welfare; 23we on our part write to you that your livestock and your property belong to us, and ours belong to you. We therefore command that our envoys[m] report to you accordingly.'

FURTHER CAMPAIGNS OF JONATHAN AND SIMON

24 Now Jonathan heard that the commanders of Demetrius had returned, with a larger force than before, to wage war against him. 25So he marched away from Jerusalem and met them in the region of Hamath, for he gave them no opportunity to invade his own country. 26He sent spies to their camp, and they returned and reported to him that the enemy[n] were being drawn up in formation to attack the Jews[o] by night. 27So when the sun had set, Jonathan commanded his troops to be alert and to keep their arms at hand so as to be ready all night for battle, and he stationed outposts around the camp. 28When the enemy heard that Jonathan and his troops were prepared for battle, they were afraid and were terrified at heart; so they kindled fires in their camp and withdrew.[p] 29But Jonathan and his troops did not know it until morning, for they saw the fires burning. 30Then Jonathan pursued them, but he did not overtake them, for they had crossed the Eleutherus river. 31So Jonathan turned aside against the Arabs who are called Zabadeans, and he crushed them and plundered them. 32Then he broke camp and went to Damascus, and marched through all that region.

33 Simon also went out and marched through the country as far as Askalon

[j] 12.4 Gk *they* [k] 12.4 Gk *them* [l] 12.7 Vg Compare verse 20: Gk *Darius* [m] 12.23 Gk *they* [n] 12.26 Gk *they* [o] 12.26 Gk *them* [p] 12.28 Other ancient authorities omit *and withdrew*

and the neighbouring strongholds. He
turned aside to Joppa and took it by
surprise, 34for he had heard that they
were ready to hand over the stronghold
to those whom Demetrius had sent.
And he stationed a garrison there to
guard it.

35 When Jonathan returned he convened the elders of the people and
planned with them to build strongholds
in Judea, 36to build the walls of Jerusalem still higher, and to erect a high
barrier between the citadel and the city
to separate it from the city, in order
to isolate it so that its garrison[q] could
neither buy nor sell. 37So they gathered together to rebuild the city; part
of the wall on the valley to the east had
fallen, and he repaired the section called
Chaphenatha. 38Simon also built Adida
in the Shephelah; he fortified it and installed gates with bolts.

TRYPHO CAPTURES JONATHAN

39 Then Trypho attempted to become king in Asia and put on the
crown, and to raise his hand against
King Antiochus. 40He feared that Jonathan might not permit him to do so,
but might make war on him, so he kept
seeking to seize and kill him, and he
marched out and came to Beth-shan.
41Jonathan went out to meet him with
forty thousand picked warriors, and he
came to Beth-shan. 42When Trypho saw
that he had come with a large army,
he was afraid to raise his hand against
him. 43So he received him with honour
and commended him to all his Friends,
and he gave him gifts and commanded
his Friends and his troops to obey him
as they would himself. 44Then he said to
Jonathan, 'Why have you put all these
people to so much trouble when we
are not at war? 45Dismiss them now
to their homes and choose for yourself
a few men to stay with you, and come
with me to Ptolemais. I will hand it over
to you as well as the other strongholds
and the remaining troops and all the
officials, and will turn around and go
home. For that is why I am here.'

46 Jonathan[r] trusted him and did
as he said; he sent away the troops,
and they returned to the land of Judah.
47He kept with himself three thousand
men, two thousand of whom he left
in Galilee, while one thousand accompanied him. 48But when Jonathan entered Ptolemais, the people of Ptolemais
closed the gates and seized him, and
they killed with the sword all who had
entered with him.

49 Then Trypho sent troops and cavalry into Galilee and the Great Plain to
destroy all Jonathan's soldiers. 50But
they realized that Jonathan had been
seized and had perished along with his
men, and they encouraged one another
and kept marching in close formation,
ready for battle. 51When their pursuers
saw that they would fight for their lives,
they turned back. 52So they all reached
the land of Judah safely, and they
mourned for Jonathan and his companions and were in great fear; and all Israel mourned deeply. 53All the nations
around them tried to destroy them, for
they said, 'They have no leader or helper.
Now therefore let us make war on them
and blot out the memory of them from
humankind.'

SIMON TAKES COMMAND

13 Simon heard that Trypho had
assembled a large army to invade the land of Judah and destroy it,
2and he saw that the people were trembling with fear. So he went up to Jerusalem, and gathering the people together
3he encouraged them, saying to them,
'You yourselves know what great things
my brothers and I and the house of my
father have done for the laws and the
sanctuary; you know also the wars and
the difficulties that my brothers and
I have seen. 4By reason of this all my
brothers have perished for the sake of
Israel, and I alone am left. 5And now,
far be it from me to spare my life in any
time of distress, for I am not better than
my brothers. 6But I will avenge my nation and the sanctuary and your wives
and children, for all the nations have
gathered together out of hatred to destroy us.'

7 The spirit of the people was rekindled when they heard these words,
8and they answered in a loud voice,
'You are our leader in place of Judas and
your brother Jonathan. 9Fight our battles, and all that you say to us we will
do.' 10So he assembled all the warriors
and hurried to complete the walls of
Jerusalem, and he fortified it on every
side. 11He sent Jonathan son of Absalom
to Joppa, and with him a considerable
army; he drove out its occupants and remained there.

[q] 12.36 Gk *they* [r] 12.46 Gk *he*

Where you go, I will go.

RUTH 1:16

He heals the broken-hearted,
and binds up their wounds.

PSALM 147:3

Look, the young woman is with child and shall bear a son, and shall name him Immanuel.

ISAIAH 7:14

I have loved you with an everlasting love.

JEREMIAH 31:3

DECEIT AND TREACHERY OF TRYPHO

12 Then Trypho left Ptolemais with
a large army to invade the land of Judah, and Jonathan was with him under
guard. 13 Simon encamped in Adida, facing the plain. 14 Trypho learned that Simon had risen up in place of his brother
Jonathan, and that he was about to join
battle with him, so he sent envoys to
him and said, 15 'It is for the money that
your brother Jonathan owed the royal
treasury, in connection with the offices he held, that we are detaining him.
16 Send now one hundred talents of silver and two of his sons as hostages, so
that when released he will not revolt
against us, and we will release him.'

17 Simon knew that they were
speaking deceitfully to him, but he sent
to get the money and the sons, so that
he would not arouse great hostility
among the people, who might say, 18 'It
was because Simon[s] did not send him
the money and the sons, that Jonathan[t]
perished.' 19 So he sent the sons and the
hundred talents, but Trypho[u] broke his
word and did not release Jonathan.

20 After this Trypho came to invade
the country and destroy it, and he circled around by the way to Adora. But
Simon and his army kept marching
along opposite him to every place he
went. 21 Now the men in the citadel kept
sending envoys to Trypho urging him
to come to them by way of the wilderness and to send them food. 22 So Trypho got all his cavalry ready to go, but
that night a very heavy snow fell, and
he did not go because of the snow. He
marched off and went into the land of
Gilead. 23 When he approached Baska-
ma, he killed Jonathan, and he was buried there. 24 Then Trypho turned and
went back to his own land.

JONATHAN'S TOMB

25 Simon sent and took the bones
of his brother Jonathan, and buried
him in Modein, the city of his ancestors. 26 All Israel bewailed him with
great lamentation, and mourned for
him for many days. 27 And Simon built
a monument over the tomb of his father and his brothers; he made it high
so that it might be seen, with polished
stone at the front and back. 28 He also
erected seven pyramids, opposite one
another, for his father and mother and
four brothers. 29 For the pyramids[v] he
devised an elaborate setting, erecting
about them great columns, and on the
columns he put suits of armour for a
permanent memorial, and beside the
suits of armour he carved ships, so that
they could be seen by all who sail the
sea. 30 This is the tomb that he built in
Modein; it remains to this day.

JUDEA GAINS INDEPENDENCE

31 Trypho dealt treacherously with
the young King Antiochus; he killed
him 32 and became king in his place,
putting on the crown of Asia; and he
brought great calamity on the land.
33 But Simon built up the strongholds
of Judea and walled them all round,
with high towers and great walls and
gates and bolts, and he stored food in
the strongholds. 34 Simon also chose
emissaries and sent them to King Demetrius with a request to grant relief to
the country, for all that Trypho did was
to plunder. 35 King Demetrius sent him
a favourable reply to this request, and
wrote him a letter as follows, 36 'King
Demetrius to Simon, the high priest
and friend of kings, and to the elders and
nation of the Jews, greetings. 37 We have
received the gold crown and the palm
branch that you[w] sent, and we are ready
to make a general peace with you and
to write to our officials to grant you release from tribute. 38 All the grants that
we have made to you remain valid, and
let the strongholds that you have built
be your possession. 39 We pardon any
errors and offences committed to this
day, and cancel the crown tax that you
owe; and whatever other tax has been
collected in Jerusalem shall be collected
no longer. 40 And if any of you are qualified to be enrolled in our bodyguard,[x] let
them be enrolled, and let there be peace
between us.'

41 In the one hundred and seventi-
eth year[y] the yoke of the Gentiles was
removed from Israel, 42 and the people
began to write in their documents and
contracts, 'In the first year of Simon the
great high priest and commander and
leader of the Jews.'

THE CAPTURE OF GAZARA BY SIMON

43 In those days Simon[z] encamped
against Gazara[a] and surrounded it
with troops. He made a siege-engine,
brought it up to the city, and battered

[s] 13.18 Gk *I* [t] 13.18 Gk *he* [u] 13.19 Gk *he*
[v] 13.29 Gk *For these* [w] 13.37 The word *you* in verses 37–40 is plural [x] 13.40 Or *court*
[y] 13.41 142 BC [z] 13.43 Gk *he* [a] 13.43 Cn: Gk *Gaza*

and captured one tower. 44 The men
in the siege-engine leapt out into the
city, and a great tumult arose in the
city. 45 The men in the city, with their
wives and children, went up on the wall
with their clothes torn, and they cried
out with a loud voice, asking Simon to
make peace with them; 46 they said, 'Do
not treat us according to our wicked acts
but according to your mercy.' 47 So Simon reached an agreement with them
and stopped fighting against them.
But he expelled them from the city and
cleansed the houses in which the idols
were located, and then entered it with
hymns and praise. 48 He removed all uncleanness from it, and settled in it those
who observed the law. He also strengthened its fortifications and built in it a
house for himself.

SIMON REGAINS THE CITADEL AT JERUSALEM

49 Those who were in the citadel at
Jerusalem were prevented from going in
and out to buy and sell in the country.
So they were very hungry, and many of
them perished from famine. 50 Then they
cried to Simon to make peace with them,
and he did so. But he expelled them from
there and cleansed the citadel from its
pollutions. 51 On the twenty-third day of
the second month, in the one hundred
and seventy-first year,[b] the Jews[c] entered it with praise and palm branches,
and with harps and cymbals and
stringed instruments, and with hymns
and songs, because a great enemy had
been crushed and removed from Israel.
52 Simon[d] decreed that every year they
should celebrate this day with rejoicing.
He strengthened the fortifications of the
temple hill alongside the citadel, and he
and his men lived there. 53 Simon saw
that his son John had reached manhood,
and so he made him commander of all
the forces; and he lived at Gazara.

CAPTURE OF DEMETRIUS

14 In the one hundred and seventy-
second year[e] King Demetrius
assembled his forces and marched into
Media to obtain help, so that he could
make war against Trypho. 2 When King
Arsaces of Persia and Media heard that
Demetrius had invaded his territory,
he sent one of his generals to take him
alive. 3 The general[f] went and defeated
the army of Demetrius, and seized him
and took him to Arsaces, who put him
under guard.

EULOGY OF SIMON

4 The land[g] had rest all the days
of Simon.
He sought the good of his nation;
his rule was pleasing to them,
as was the honour shown
him, all his days.
5 To crown all his honours he took
Joppa for a harbour,
and opened a way to the
isles of the sea.
6 He extended the borders
of his nation,
and gained full control
of the country.
7 He gathered a host of captives;
he ruled over Gazara and Beth-zur
and the citadel,
and he removed its uncleanness
from it;
and there was none to oppose him.
8 They tilled their land in peace;
the ground gave its increase,
and the trees of the plains
their fruit.
9 Old men sat in the streets;
they all talked together
of good things,
and the youths put on splendid
military attire.
10 He supplied the towns with food,
and furnished them with the
means of defence,
until his renown spread to
the ends of the earth.
11 He established peace in the land,
and Israel rejoiced with great joy.
12 All the people sat under their
own vines and fig trees,
and there was none to
make them afraid.
13 No one was left in the land
to fight them,
and the kings were crushed
in those days.
14 He gave help to all the humble
among his people;
he sought out the law,
and did away with all the
renegades and outlaws.
15 He made the sanctuary glorious,
and added to the vessels
of the sanctuary.

DIPLOMACY WITH ROME AND SPARTA

16 It was heard in Rome, and as far
away as Sparta, that Jonathan had died,

b 13.51 141 BC c 13.51 Gk *they* d 13.52 Gk *He* e 14.1 140 BC f 14.3 Gk *He* g 14.4 Other ancient authorities add *of Judah*

and they were deeply grieved. 17When they heard that his brother Simon had become high priest in his stead, and that he was ruling over the country and the towns in it, 18they wrote to him on bronze tablets to renew with him the friendship and alliance that they had established with his brothers Judas and Jonathan. 19And these were read before the assembly in Jerusalem.

20 This is a copy of the letter that the Spartans sent:

'The rulers and the city of the Spartans to the high priest Simon and to the elders and the priests and the rest of the Jewish people, our brothers, greetings. 21The envoys who were sent to our people have told us about your glory and honour, and we rejoiced at their coming. 22We have recorded what they said in our public decrees, as follows, "Numenius son of Antiochus and Antipater son of Jason, envoys of the Jews, have come to us to renew their friendship with us. 23It has pleased our people to receive these men with honour and to put a copy of their words in the public archives, so that the people of the Spartans may have a record of them. And they have sent a copy of this to the high priest Simon." '

24 After this Simon sent Numenius to Rome with a large gold shield weighing one thousand minas, to confirm the alliance with the Romans.[h]

OFFICIAL HONOURS FOR SIMON

25 When the people heard these things they said, 'How shall we thank Simon and his sons? 26For he and his brothers and the house of his father have stood firm; they have fought and repulsed Israel's enemies and established its freedom.' 27So they made a record on bronze tablets and put it on pillars on Mount Zion.

This is a copy of what they wrote: 'On the eighteenth day of Elul, in the one hundred and seventy-second year,[i] which is the third year of the great high priest Simon, 28in Asaramel,[j] in the great assembly of the priests and the people and the rulers of the nation and the elders of the country, the following was proclaimed to us:

29 'Since wars often occurred in the country, Simon son of Mattathias, a priest of the sons[k] of Joarib, and his brothers, exposed themselves to danger and resisted the enemies of their nation, in order that their sanctuary and the law might be preserved; and they brought great glory to their nation. 30Jonathan rallied the[l] nation, became their high priest, and was gathered to his people. 31When their enemies decided to invade their country and lay hands on their sanctuary, 32then Simon rose up and fought for his nation. He spent great sums of his own money; he armed the soldiers of his nation and paid them wages. 33He fortified the towns of Judea, and Beth-zur on the borders of Judea, where formerly the arms of the enemy had been stored, and he placed there a garrison of Jews. 34He also fortified Joppa, which is by the sea, and Gazara, which is on the borders of Azotus, where the enemy formerly lived. He settled Jews there, and provided in those towns[m] whatever was necessary for their restoration.

35 'The people saw Simon's faithfulness[n] and the glory that he had resolved to win for his nation, and they made him their leader and high priest, because he had done all these things and because of the justice and loyalty that he had maintained towards his nation. He sought in every way to exalt his people. 36In his days things prospered in his hands, so that the Gentiles were put out of the[o] country, as were also those in the city of David in Jerusalem, who had built themselves a citadel from which they used to sally forth and defile the environs of the sanctuary, doing great damage to its purity. 37He settled Jews in it and fortified it for the safety of the country and of the city, and built the walls of Jerusalem higher.

38 'In view of these things King Demetrius confirmed him in the high-priesthood, 39made him one of his Friends, and paid him high honours. 40For he had heard that the Jews were addressed by the Romans as friends and allies and brothers, and that the Romans[p] had received the envoys of Simon with honour.

41 'The Jews and their priests have resolved that Simon should be their leader and high priest for ever, until a trustworthy prophet should arise, 42and that he should be governor over them and

[h] 14.24 Gk *them* [i] 14.27 140 BC [j] 14.28 This word resembles the Hebrew words for *the court of the people of God* or *the prince of the people of God* [k] 14.29 Meaning of Gk uncertain
[l] 14.30 Gk *their* [m] 14.34 Gk *them*
[n] 14.35 Other ancient authorities read *conduct*
[o] 14.36 Gk *their* [p] 14.40 Gk *they*

that he should take charge of the sanctuary and appoint officials over its tasks and over the country and the weapons and the strongholds, and that he should take charge of the sanctuary, 43 and that he should be obeyed by all, and that all contracts in the country should be written in his name, and that he should be clothed in purple and wear gold.

44 'None of the people or priests shall be permitted to nullify any of these decisions or to oppose what he says, or to convene an assembly in the country without his permission, or to be clothed in purple or put on a gold buckle. 45 Whoever acts contrary to these decisions or rejects any of them shall be liable to punishment.'

46 All the people agreed to grant Simon the right to act in accordance with these decisions. 47 So Simon accepted and agreed to be high priest, to be commander and ethnarch of the Jews and priests, and to be protector of them all.[q] 48 And they gave orders to inscribe this decree on bronze tablets, to put them up in a conspicuous place in the precincts of the sanctuary, 49 and to deposit copies of them in the treasury, so that Simon and his sons might have them.

LETTER OF ANTIOCHUS VII

15 Antiochus, son of King Demetrius, sent a letter from the islands of the sea to Simon, the priest and ethnarch of the Jews, and to all the nation; 2 its contents were as follows: 'King Antiochus to Simon the high priest and ethnarch and to the nation of the Jews, greetings. 3 Whereas certain scoundrels have gained control of the kingdom of our ancestors, and I intend to lay claim to the kingdom so that I may restore it as it formerly was, and have recruited a host of mercenary troops and have equipped warships, 4 and intend to make a landing in the country so that I may proceed against those who have destroyed our country and those who have devastated many cities in my kingdom, 5 now therefore I confirm to you all the tax remissions that the kings before me have granted you, and a release from all the other payments from which they have released you. 6 I permit you to mint your own coinage as money for your country, 7 and I grant freedom to Jerusalem and the sanctuary. All the weapons that you have prepared and the strongholds that you have built and now hold shall remain yours. 8 Every debt you owe to the royal treasury and any such future debts shall be cancelled for you from henceforth and for all time. 9 When we gain control of our kingdom, we will bestow great honour on you and your nation and the temple, so that your glory will become manifest in all the earth.'

10 In the one hundred and seventy-fourth year[r] Antiochus set out and invaded the land of his ancestors. All the troops rallied to him, so that there were only a few with Trypho. 11 Antiochus pursued him, and Trypho[s] came in his flight to Dor, which is by the sea; 12 for he knew that troubles had converged on him, and his troops had deserted him. 13 So Antiochus encamped against Dor, and with him were one hundred and twenty thousand warriors and eight thousand cavalry. 14 He surrounded the town, and the ships joined battle from the sea; he pressed the town hard from land and sea, and permitted no one to leave or enter it.

ROME SUPPORTS THE JEWS

15 Then Numenius and his companions arrived from Rome, with letters to the kings and countries, in which the following was written: 16 'Lucius, consul of the Romans, to King Ptolemy, greetings. 17 The envoys of the Jews have come to us as our friends and allies to renew our ancient friendship and alliance. They had been sent by the high priest Simon and by the Jewish people 18 and have brought a gold shield weighing one thousand minas. 19 We therefore have decided to write to the kings and countries that they should not seek their harm or make war against them and their cities and their country, or make alliance with those who war against them. 20 And it has seemed good to us to accept the shield from them. 21 Therefore if any scoundrels have fled to you from their country, hand them over to the high priest Simon, so that he may punish them according to their law.'

22 The consul[t] wrote the same thing to King Demetrius and to Attalus and Ariarathes and Arsaces, 23 and to all the countries, and to Sampsames,[u] and to the Spartans, and to Delos, and to Myndos, and to Sicyon, and to Caria, and to Samos, and to Pamphylia, and to Lycia, and to Halicarnassus, and to Rhodes,

[q] **14.47** *Or to preside over them all* [r] **15.10** 138 BC [s] **15.11** Gk *he* [t] **15.22** Gk *He* [u] **15.23** The name is uncertain

and to Phaselis, and to Cos, and to Side,
and to Aradus and Gortyna and Cnidus
and Cyprus and Cyrene. 24They also sent
a copy of these things to the high priest
Simon.

ANTIOCHUS VII THREATENS SIMON

25 King Antiochus besieged Dor for
the second time, continually throwing
his forces against it and making engines
of war; and he shut Trypho up and kept
him from going out or in. 26And Simon sent to Antiochus[v] two thousand
picked troops, to fight for him, and silver and gold and a large amount of military equipment. 27But he refused to
receive them, and broke all the agree-
ments he formerly had made with Simon, and became estranged from him.
28He sent to him Athenobius, one of
his Friends, to confer with him, saying,
'You hold control of Joppa and Gazara
and the citadel in Jerusalem; they are
cities of my kingdom. 29You have devastated their territory, you have done
great damage in the land, and you have
taken possession of many places in my
kingdom. 30Now then, hand over the
cities that you have seized and the tribute money of the places that you have
conquered outside the borders of Judea;
31or else pay me five hundred talents of
silver for the destruction that you have
caused and five hundred talents more
for the tribute money of the cities. Otherwise we will come and make war on
you.'

32 So Athenobius, the king's Friend,
came to Jerusalem, and when he saw
the splendour of Simon, and the side-
board with its gold and silver plate, and
his great magnificence, he was amazed.
When he reported to him the king's
message, 33Simon said to him in reply:
'We have neither taken foreign land nor
seized foreign property, but only the inheritance of our ancestors, which at one
time had been unjustly taken by our enemies. 34Now that we have the opportunity, we are firmly holding the inheritance of our ancestors. 35As for Joppa
and Gazara, which you demand, they
were causing great damage among the
people and to our land; for them we will
give you one hundred talents.'

Athenobius[w] did not answer him a
word, 36but returned in wrath to the
king and reported to him these words,
and also the splendour of Simon and all
that he had seen. And the king was very
angry.

VICTORY OVER CENDEBEUS

37 Meanwhile Trypho embarked on
a ship and escaped to Orthosia. 38Then
the king made Cendebeus commander-
in-chief of the coastal country, and gave
him troops of infantry and cavalry. 39He
commanded him to encamp against
Judea, to build up Kedron and fortify
its gates, and to make war on the people; but the king pursued Trypho. 40So
Cendebeus came to Jamnia and began
to provoke the people and invade Judea and take the people captive and kill
them. 41He built up Kedron and stationed horsemen and troops there, so
that they might go out and make raids
along the highways of Judea, as the king
had ordered him.

16 John went up from Gazara and
reported to his father Simon
what Cendebeus had done. 2And Simon
called in his two eldest sons Judas and
John, and said to them: 'My brothers
and I and my father's house have fought
the wars of Israel from our youth until
this day, and things have prospered in
our hands so that we have delivered Israel many times. 3But now I have grown
old, and you by Heaven's[x] mercy are
mature in years. Take my place and my
brother's, and go out and fight for our
nation, and may the help that comes
from Heaven be with you.'

4 So John[y] chose out of the country
twenty thousand warriors and cavalry,
and they marched against Cendebeus
and camped for the night in Modein.
5Early in the morning they started out
and marched into the plain, where a large
force of infantry and cavalry was coming
to meet them; and a stream lay between
them. 6Then he and his army lined up
against them. He saw that the soldiers
were afraid to cross the stream, so he
crossed over first; and when his troops
saw him, they crossed over after him.
7Then he divided the army and placed
the cavalry in the centre of the infantry,
for the cavalry of the enemy were very
numerous. 8They sounded the trumpets, and Cendebeus and his army were
put to flight; many of them fell wounded
and the rest fled into the stronghold. 9At
that time Judas the brother of John was
wounded, but John pursued them until
Cendebeus[z] reached Kedron, which he
had built. 10They also fled into the towers that were in the fields of Azotus, and

[v] 15.26 Gk *him* [w] 15.35 Gk *He* [x] 16.3 Gk *his*
[y] 16.4 Other ancient authorities read *he*
[z] 16.9 Gk *he*

John[a] burned it with fire, and about two
thousand of them fell. He then returned
to Judea safely.

MURDER OF SIMON AND HIS SONS

11 Now Ptolemy son of Abubus had
been appointed governor over the plain
of Jericho; he had a large store of silver
and gold, 12 for he was son-in-law of the
high priest. 13 His heart was lifted up; he
determined to get control of the country, and made treacherous plans against
Simon and his sons, to do away with
them. 14 Now Simon was visiting the
towns of the country and attending to
their needs, and he went down to Jericho with his sons Mattathias and Judas, in the one hundred and seventy-
seventh year,[b] in the eleventh month,
which is the month of Shebat. 15 The
son of Abubus received them treacherously in the little stronghold called
Dok, which he had built; he gave them
a great banquet, and hid men there.
16 When Simon and his sons were drunk,
Ptolemy and his men rose up, took their
weapons, rushed in against Simon in
the banqueting-hall and killed him and
his two sons, as well as some of his servants. 17 So he committed an act of great
treachery and returned evil for good.

JOHN SUCCEEDS SIMON

18 Then Ptolemy wrote a report
about these things and sent it to the
king, asking him to send troops to aid
him and to turn over to him the towns
and the country. 19 He sent other troops
to Gazara to do away with John; he sent
letters to the captains asking them to
come to him so that he might give
them silver and gold and gifts; 20 and
he sent other troops to take possession of Jerusalem and the temple hill.
21 But someone ran ahead and reported
to John at Gazara that his father and
brothers had perished, and that 'he
has sent men to kill you also.' 22 When
he heard this, he was greatly shocked;
he seized the men who came to destroy
him and killed them, for he had found
out that they were seeking to destroy
him.

23 The rest of the acts of John and
his wars, and the brave deeds that he
did, and the building of the walls that
he completed, and his achievements,
24 are written in the annals of his high-
priesthood, from the time that he became high priest after his father.

[a] 16.10 Gk *he* [b] 16.14 134 BC

2 MACCABEES

Second Maccabees is not a continuation of 1 Maccabees but a supplement to it. Second Maccabees concentrates on the events of the persecution of the Jews by Antiochus IV Epiphanes and the resulting revolt between 180 and 161 BCE. It was a writing that encouraged the Jews to celebrate the festival of Hanukkah.

According to the narrative, the heroic efforts of Judas Maccabeus and the sacrificial deaths of the martyrs enabled the people of Israel to overcome the tyranny and persecution of Antiochus IV Epiphanes. In this book, there is notable theological support for belief in the resurrection of the just (7.9, 11, 14, 23; 14.46), intercession of the saints for the living (15.11–16), and prayers for the dead (12.39–46). A critical issue raised by this narrative is the justification of violence, martyrdom, and even suicide in pursuit of ultimate religious values.

The passage about the persecution of the seven brothers is read on the Thirty-Second Sunday of the Year in Cycle C of the liturgical calendar. Texts from 2 Maccabees are also offered as choices for Readings in the Common of Martyrs of the Roman Missal.

A LETTER TO THE JEWS IN EGYPT

1 The Jews in Jerusalem and those in
the land of Judea,
To their Jewish kindred in Egypt,
Greetings and true peace.
2 May God do good to you, and may
he remember his covenant with Abraham and Isaac and Jacob, his faithful
servants. 3May he give you all a heart to
worship him and to do his will with a
strong heart and a willing spirit. 4May
he open your heart to his law and his
commandments, and may he bring
peace. 5May he hear your prayers and be
reconciled to you, and may he not forsake you in time of evil. 6We are now
praying for you here.
7 In the reign of Demetrius, in the
one hundred and sixty-ninth year,[a] we
Jews wrote to you, in the critical distress that came upon us in those years
after Jason and his company revolted
from the holy land and the kingdom
8and burned the gate and shed innocent blood. We prayed to the Lord and
were heard, and we offered sacrifice and
grain-offering, and we lit the lamps and
set out the loaves. 9And now see that
you keep the festival of booths in the
month of Chislev, in the one hundred
and eighty-eighth year.[b]

A LETTER TO ARISTOBULUS

10 The people of Jerusalem and of Judea and the senate and Judas,
To Aristobulus, who is of the family
of the anointed priests, teacher of King
Ptolemy, and to the Jews in Egypt,
Greetings and good health.
11 Having been saved by God out of
grave dangers we thank him greatly for
taking our side against the king,[c] 12for
he drove out those who fought against
the holy city. 13When the leader reached
Persia with a force that seemed irresistible, they were cut to pieces in the temple of Nanea by a deception employed by
the priests of the goddess[d] Nanea. 14On
the pretext of intending to marry her,
Antiochus came to the place together
with his Friends, to secure most of its

[a] 1.7 143 BC [b] 1.9 124 BC [c] 1.11 Cn: Gk *as those who array themselves against a king*
[d] 1.13 Gk lacks *the goddess*

treasures as a dowry. 15When the priests of the temple of Nanea had set out the treasures and Antiochus had come with a few men inside the wall of the sacred precinct, they closed the temple as soon as he entered it. 16Opening a secret door in the ceiling, they threw stones and struck down the leader and his men; they dismembered them and cut off their heads and threw them to the people outside. 17Blessed in every way be our God, who has brought judgement on those who have behaved impiously.

FIRE CONSUMES NEHEMIAH'S SACRIFICE

18 Since on the twenty-fifth day of Chislev we shall celebrate the purification of the temple, we thought it necessary to notify you, in order that you also may celebrate the festival of booths and the festival of the fire given when Nehemiah, who built the temple and the altar, offered sacrifices.

19 For when our ancestors were being led captive to Persia, the pious priests of that time took some of the fire of the altar and secretly hid it in the hollow of a dry cistern, where they took such precautions that the place was unknown to anyone. 20But after many years had passed, when it pleased God, Nehemiah, having been commissioned by the king of Persia, sent the descendants of the priests who had hidden the fire to get it. And when they reported to us that they had not found fire but only a thick liquid, he ordered them to dip it out and bring it. 21When the materials for the sacrifices were presented, Nehemiah ordered the priests to sprinkle the liquid on the wood and on the things laid upon it. 22When this had been done and some time had passed, and when the sun, which had been clouded over, shone out, a great fire blazed up, so that all marvelled. 23And while the sacrifice was being consumed, the priests offered prayer—the priests and everyone. Jonathan led, and the rest responded, as did Nehemiah. 24The prayer was to this effect:

'O Lord, Lord God, Creator of all things, you are awe-inspiring and strong and just and merciful, you alone are king and are kind, 25you alone are bountiful, you alone are just and almighty and eternal. You rescue Israel from every evil; you chose the ancestors and consecrated them. 26Accept this sacrifice on behalf of all your people Israel and preserve your portion and make it holy. 27Gather together our scattered people, set free those who are slaves among the Gentiles, look on those who are rejected and despised, and let the Gentiles know that you are our God. 28Punish those who oppress and are insolent with pride. 29Plant your people in your holy place, as Moses promised.'

30 Then the priests sang the hymns. 31After the materials of the sacrifice had been consumed, Nehemiah ordered that the liquid that was left should be poured on large stones. 32When this was done, a flame blazed up; but when the light from the altar shone back, it went out. 33When this matter became known, and it was reported to the king of the Persians that, in the place where the exiled priests had hidden the fire, the liquid had appeared with which Nehemiah and his associates had burned the materials of the sacrifice, 34the king investigated the matter, and enclosed the place and made it sacred. 35And with those persons whom the king favoured he exchanged many excellent gifts. 36Nehemiah and his associates called this 'nephthar', which means purification, but by most people it is called naphtha.[e]

JEREMIAH HIDES THE TENT, ARK, AND ALTAR

2 One finds in the records that the prophet Jeremiah ordered those who were being deported to take some of the fire, as has been mentioned, 2and that the prophet, after giving them the law, instructed those who were being deported not to forget the commandments of the Lord, or to be led astray in their thoughts on seeing the gold and silver statues and their adornment. 3And with other similar words he exhorted them that the law should not depart from their hearts.

4 It was also in the same document that the prophet, having received an oracle, ordered that the tent and the ark should follow with him, and that he went out to the mountain where Moses had gone up and had seen the inheritance of God. 5Jeremiah came and found a cave-dwelling, and he brought there the tent and the ark and the altar of incense; then he sealed up the entrance. 6Some of those who followed him came up intending to mark the way, but could

[e] 1.36 Gk *nephthai*

not find it. 7When Jeremiah learned of
it, he rebuked them and declared: 'The
place shall remain unknown until God
gathers his people together again and
shows his mercy. 8Then the Lord will
disclose these things, and the glory of
the Lord and the cloud will appear, as
they were shown in the case of Moses,
and as Solomon asked that the place
should be specially consecrated.'

9 It was also made clear that being
possessed of wisdom Solomon[f] offered
sacrifice for the dedication and completion of the temple. 10Just as Moses prayed to the Lord, and fire came
down from heaven and consumed the
sacrifices, so also Solomon prayed, and
the fire came down and consumed the
whole burnt-offerings. 11And Moses
said, 'They were consumed because the
sin-offering had not been eaten.' 12Like-
wise, Solomon also kept the eight days.

13 The same things are reported in
the records and in the memoirs of Nehemiah, and also that he founded a library and collected the books about the
kings and prophets, and the writings of
David, and letters of kings about votive
offerings. 14In the same way Judas also
collected all the books that had been lost
on account of the war that had come
upon us, and they are in our possession.
15So if you have need of them, send people to get them for you.

16 Since, therefore, we are about to
celebrate the purification, we write to
you. Will you therefore please keep the
days? 17It is God who has saved all his
people, and has returned the inheritance to all, and the kingship and the
priesthood and the consecration, 18as
he promised through the law. We have
hope in God that he will soon have
mercy on us and will gather us from
everywhere under heaven into his holy
place, for he has rescued us from great
evils and has purified the place.

THE COMPILER'S PREFACE

19 The story of Judas Maccabeus and
his brothers, and the purification of the
great temple, and the dedication of the
altar, 20and further the wars against Antiochus Epiphanes and his son Eupator,
21and the appearances that came from
heaven to those who fought bravely for
Judaism, so that though few in number they seized the whole land and pursued the barbarian hordes, 22and regained possession of the temple famous
throughout the world, and liberated the
city, and re-established the laws that
were about to be abolished, while the
Lord with great kindness became gracious to them— 23all this, which has
been set forth by Jason of Cyrene in five
volumes, we shall attempt to condense
into a single book. 24For considering
the flood of statistics involved and the
difficulty there is for those who wish
to enter upon the narratives of history
because of the mass of material, 25we
have aimed to please those who wish to
read, to make it easy for those who are
inclined to memorize, and to profit all
readers. 26For us who have undertaken
the toil of abbreviating, it is no light
matter but calls for sweat and loss of
sleep, 27just as it is not easy for one who
prepares a banquet and seeks the benefit of others. Nevertheless, to secure the
gratitude of many we will gladly endure
the uncomfortable toil, 28leaving the
responsibility for exact details to the
compiler, while devoting our effort to
arriving at the outlines of the conden-
sation. 29For as the master builder of a
new house must be concerned with the
whole construction, while the one who
undertakes its painting and decoration
has to consider only what is suitable for
its adornment, such in my judgement is
the case with us. 30It is the duty of the
original historian to occupy the ground,
to discuss matters from every side, and
to take trouble with details, 31but the
one who recasts the narrative should be
allowed to strive for brevity of expression and to forego exhaustive treatment.
32At this point therefore let us begin our
narrative, without adding any more to
what has already been said; for it would
be foolish to lengthen the preface while
cutting short the history itself.

ARRIVAL OF HELIODORUS IN JERUSALEM

3 While the holy city was inhabited in
unbroken peace and the laws were
strictly observed because of the piety
of the high priest Onias and his hatred
of wickedness, 2it came about that the
kings themselves honoured the place
and glorified the temple with the finest
presents, 3even to the extent that King
Seleucus of Asia defrayed from his own
revenues all the expenses connected
with the service of the sacrifices.

4 But a man named Simon, of the
tribe of Benjamin, who had been made

f 2.9 Gk *he*

captain of the temple, had a disagreement
with the high priest about the administration of the city market. 5 Since he could
not prevail over Onias, he went to Apollonius of Tarsus,[g] who at that time was
governor of Coelesyria and Phoenicia,
6 and reported to him that the treasury
in Jerusalem was full of untold sums of
money, so that the amount of the funds
could not be reckoned, and that they did
not belong to the account of the sacrifices, but that it was possible for them to
fall under the control of the king. 7 When
Apollonius met the king, he told him of
the money about which he had been informed. The king[h] chose Heliodorus, who
was in charge of his affairs, and sent him
with commands to effect the removal of
the reported wealth. 8 Heliodorus at once
set out on his journey, ostensibly to make
a tour of inspection of the cities of Coelesyria and Phoenicia, but in fact to carry
out the king's purpose.

9 When he had arrived at Jerusalem
and had been kindly welcomed by the
high priest of[i] the city, he told about
the disclosure that had been made and
stated why he had come, and he inquired whether this really was the situation. 10 The high priest explained that
there were some deposits belonging to
widows and orphans, 11 and also some
money of Hyrcanus son of Tobias, a man
of very prominent position, and that it
totalled in all four hundred talents of
silver and two hundred of gold. To such
an extent the impious Simon had mis-
represented the facts. 12 And he said that
it was utterly impossible that wrong
should be done to those people who had
trusted in the holiness of the place and
in the sanctity and inviolability of the
temple that is honoured throughout the
whole world.

HELIODORUS PLANS TO ROB THE TEMPLE

13 But Heliodorus, because of the orders he had from the king, said that this
money must in any case be confiscated
for the king's treasury. 14 So he set a day
and went in to direct the inspection of
these funds.

There was no little distress throughout the whole city. 15 The priests prostrated themselves before the altar in
their priestly vestments and called towards heaven upon him who had given
the law about deposits, that he should
keep them safe for those who had deposited them. 16 To see the appearance
of the high priest was to be wounded
at heart, for his face and the change in
his colour disclosed the anguish of his
soul. 17 For terror and bodily trembling
had come over the man, which plainly
showed to those who looked at him the
pain lodged in his heart. 18 People also
hurried out of their houses in crowds to
make a general supplication because the
holy place was about to be brought into
dishonour. 19 Women, girded with sackcloth under their breasts, thronged the
streets. Some of the young women who
were kept indoors ran together to the
gates, and some to the walls, while others peered out of the windows. 20 And
holding up their hands to heaven, they
all made supplication. 21 There was
something pitiable in the prostration of
the whole populace and the anxiety of
the high priest in his great anguish.

THE LORD PROTECTS HIS TEMPLE

22 While they were calling upon the
Almighty Lord that he would keep what
had been entrusted safe and secure for
those who had entrusted it, 23 Heliodorus
went on with what had been decided.
24 But when he arrived at the treasury
with his bodyguard, then and there the
Sovereign of spirits and of all authority
caused so great a manifestation that all
who had been so bold as to accompany
him were astounded by the power of
God, and became faint with terror. 25 For
there appeared to them a magnificently
caparisoned horse, with a rider of frightening mien; it rushed furiously at Heliodorus and struck at him with its front
hoofs. Its rider was seen to have armour
and weapons of gold. 26 Two young men
also appeared to him, remarkably strong,
gloriously beautiful and splendidly
dressed, who stood on either side of him
and flogged him continuously, inflicting
many blows on him. 27 When he suddenly fell to the ground and deep darkness came over him, his men took him
up, put him on a stretcher, 28 and carried
him away—this man who had just entered the aforesaid treasury with a great
retinue and all his bodyguard but was
now unable to help himself. They recognized clearly the sovereign power of God.

ONIAS PRAYS FOR HELIODORUS

29 While he lay prostrate, speechless because of the divine intervention

[g] 3.5 Gk *Apollonius son of Tharseas* [h] 3.7 Gk *He*
[i] 3.9 Other ancient authorities read *and*

and deprived of any hope of recovery,
30they praised the Lord who had acted
marvellously for his own place. And the
temple, which a little while before was
full of fear and disturbance, was filled
with joy and gladness, now that the Almighty Lord had appeared.
31 Some of Heliodorus's friends
quickly begged Onias to call upon the
Most High to grant life to one who was
lying quite at his last breath. 32So the
high priest, fearing that the king might
get the notion that some foul play had
been perpetrated by the Jews with regard to Heliodorus, offered sacrifice for
the man's recovery. 33While the high
priest was making an atonement, the
same young men appeared again to Heliodorus dressed in the same clothing,
and they stood and said, 'Be very grateful to the high priest Onias, since for
his sake the Lord has granted you your
life. 34And see that you, who have been
flogged by heaven, report to all people
the majestic power of God.' Having said
this they vanished.

THE CONVERSION OF HELIODORUS

35 Then Heliodorus offered sacrifice
to the Lord and made very great vows to
the Saviour of his life, and having bidden Onias farewell, he marched off with
his forces to the king. 36He bore testimony to all concerning the deeds of the
supreme God, which he had seen with
his own eyes. 37When the king asked
Heliodorus what sort of person would be
suitable to send on another mission to
Jerusalem, he replied, 38'If you have any
enemy or plotter against your government, send him there, for you will get
him back thoroughly flogged, if he survives at all; for there is certainly some
power of God about the place. 39For he
who has his dwelling in heaven watches
over that place himself and brings it aid,
and he strikes and destroys those who
come to do it injury.' 40This was the outcome of the episode of Heliodorus and
the protection of the treasury.

SIMON ACCUSES ONIAS

4 The previously mentioned Simon, who had informed about the
money against[j] his own country, slandered Onias, saying that it was he who
had incited Heliodorus and had been
the real cause of the misfortune. 2He
dared to designate as a plotter against
the government the man who was the
benefactor of the city, the protector of
his compatriots, and a zealot for the
laws. 3When his hatred progressed to
such a degree that even murders were
committed by one of Simon's approved
agents, 4Onias recognized that the rivalry was serious and that Apollonius
son of Menestheus,[k] and governor of
Coelesyria and Phoenicia, was inten-
sifying the malice of Simon. 5So he
appealed to the king, not accusing his
compatriots but having in view the welfare, both public and private, of all the
people. 6For he saw that without the
king's attention public affairs could not
again reach a peaceful settlement, and
that Simon would not stop his folly.

JASON'S REFORMS

7 When Seleucus died and Antiochus,
who was called Epiphanes, succeeded
to the kingdom, Jason the brother of
Onias obtained the high-priesthood by
corruption, 8promising the king at an
interview[l] three hundred and sixty talents of silver, and from another source
of revenue eighty talents. 9In addition
to this he promised to pay one hundred
and fifty more if permission were given
to establish by his authority a gymnasium and a body of youth for it, and to enrol the people of Jerusalem as citizens of
Antioch. 10When the king assented and
Jason[m] came to office, he at once shifted
his compatriots over to the Greek way of
life.
11 He set aside the existing royal
concessions to the Jews, secured
through John the father of Eupolemus,
who went on the mission to establish
friendship and alliance with the Romans; and he destroyed the lawful ways
of living and introduced new customs
contrary to the law. 12He took delight in
establishing a gymnasium right under
the citadel, and he induced the noblest
of the young men to wear the Greek hat.
13There was such an extreme of Helle-
nization and increase in the adoption
of foreign ways because of the surpassing wickedness of Jason, who was ungodly and no true[n] high priest, 14that
the priests were no longer intent upon
their service at the altar. Despising the
sanctuary and neglecting the sacrifices,
they hurried to take part in the unlawful proceedings in the wrestling arena
after the signal for the discus-throwing,
15disdaining the honours prized by their

[j] 4.1 Gk *and* [k] 4.4 Vg Compare verse 21: Meaning of Gk uncertain [l] 4.8 Or *by a petition* [m] 4.10 Gk *he* [n] 4.13 Gk lacks *true*

ancestors and putting the highest value
upon Greek forms of prestige. 16 For this
reason heavy disaster overtook them,
and those whose ways of living they admired and wished to imitate completely
became their enemies and punished
them. 17 It is no light thing to show ir-
reverence to the divine laws—a fact that
later events will make clear.

JASON INTRODUCES GREEK CUSTOMS

18 When the quadrennial games were
being held at Tyre and the king was present, 19 the vile Jason sent envoys, chosen
as being Antiochian citizens from Jerusalem, to carry three hundred silver
drachmas for the sacrifice to Hercules.
Those who carried the money, however,
thought best not to use it for sacrifice,
because that was inappropriate, but to
expend it for another purpose. 20 So this
money was intended by the sender for
the sacrifice to Hercules, but by the decision of its carriers it was applied to the
construction of triremes.

21 When Apollonius son of Menestheus was sent to Egypt for the corona-
tion[o] of Philometor as king, Antiochus
learned that Philometor[p] had become
hostile to his government, and he took
measures for his own security. Therefore
upon arriving at Joppa he proceeded to
Jerusalem. 22 He was welcomed magnificently by Jason and the city, and ush-
ered in with a blaze of torches and with
shouts. Then he marched his army into
Phoenicia.

MENELAUS BECOMES HIGH PRIEST

23 After a period of three years Jason
sent Menelaus, the brother of the previously mentioned Simon, to carry the
money to the king and to complete the
records of essential business. 24 But he,
when presented to the king, extolled
him with an air of authority, and secured the high-priesthood for himself,
outbidding Jason by three hundred
talents of silver. 25 After receiving the
king's orders he returned, possessing no
qualification for the high-priesthood,
but having the hot temper of a cruel tyrant and the rage of a savage wild beast.
26 So Jason, who after supplanting his
own brother was supplanted by another
man, was driven as a fugitive into the
land of Ammon. 27 Although Menelaus
continued to hold the office, he did not
pay regularly any of the money promised to the king. 28 When Sostratus the
captain of the citadel kept requesting
payment—for the collection of the revenue was his responsibility—the two of
them were summoned by the king on
account of this issue. 29 Menelaus left
his own brother Lysimachus as deputy
in the high-priesthood, while Sostratus
left Crates, the commander of the Cypri-
ot troops.

THE MURDER OF ONIAS

30 While such was the state of affairs, it happened that the people of
Tarsus and of Mallus revolted because
their cities had been given as a present
to Antiochis, the king's concubine. 31 So
the king went hurriedly to settle the
trouble, leaving Andronicus, a man of
high rank, to act as his deputy. 32 But
Menelaus, thinking he had obtained
a suitable opportunity, stole some of
the gold vessels of the temple and gave
them to Andronicus; other vessels, as it
happened, he had sold to Tyre and the
neighbouring cities. 33 When Onias became fully aware of these acts, he publicly exposed them, having first withdrawn to a place of sanctuary at Daphne
near Antioch. 34 Therefore Menelaus,
taking Andronicus aside, urged him to
kill Onias. Andronicus[q] came to Onias,
and resorting to treachery, offered him
sworn pledges and gave him his right
hand; he persuaded him, though still
suspicious, to come out from the place
of sanctuary; then, with no regard for
justice, he immediately put him out of
the way.

ANDRONICUS IS PUNISHED

35 For this reason not only Jews,
but many also of other nations, were
grieved and displeased at the unjust
murder of the man. 36 When the king
returned from the region of Cilicia, the
Jews in the city[r] appealed to him with
regard to the unreasonable murder of
Onias, and the Greeks shared their hatred of the crime. 37 Therefore Antiochus
was grieved at heart and filled with
pity, and wept because of the moderation and good conduct of the deceased.
38 Inflamed with anger, he immediately stripped off the purple robe from
Andronicus, tore off his clothes, and
led him around the whole city to that
very place where he had committed
the outrage against Onias, and there he
dispatched the bloodthirsty fellow. The

[o] **4.21** Meaning of Gk uncertain [p] **4.21** Gk *he*
[q] **4.34** Gk *He* [r] **4.36** Or *in each city*

Lord thus repaid him with the punishment he deserved.

UNPOPULARITY OF LYSIMACHUS AND MENELAUS

39 When many acts of sacrilege had
been committed in the city by Lysimachus with the connivance of Menelaus,
and when report of them had spread
abroad, the populace gathered against
Lysimachus, because many of the gold
vessels had already been stolen. 40 Since
the crowds were becoming aroused
and filled with anger, Lysimachus
armed about three thousand men and
launched an unjust attack, under the
leadership of a certain Auranus, a man
advanced in years and no less advanced
in folly. 41 But when the Jews[s] became
aware that Lysimachus was attacking
them, some picked up stones, some
blocks of wood, and others took handfuls of the ashes that were lying around,
and threw them in wild confusion at
Lysimachus and his men. 42 As a result,
they wounded many of them, and killed
some, and put all the rest to flight; the
temple robber himself they killed close
by the treasury.

43 Charges were brought against
Menelaus about this incident. 44 When
the king came to Tyre, three men sent
by the senate presented the case before
him. 45 But Menelaus, already as good
as beaten, promised a substantial bribe
to Ptolemy son of Dorymenes to win
over the king. 46 Therefore Ptolemy, taking the king aside into a colonnade as
if for refreshment, induced the king to
change his mind. 47 Menelaus, the cause
of all the trouble, he acquitted of the
charges against him, while he sentenced
to death those unfortunate men, who
would have been freed uncondemned if
they had pleaded even before Scythians.
48 And so those who had spoken for the
city and the villages[t] and the holy vessels quickly suffered the unjust penalty.
49 Therefore even the Tyrians, showing their hatred of the crime, provided
magnificently for their funeral. 50 But
Menelaus, because of the greed of those
in power, remained in office, growing
in wickedness, having become the chief
plotter against his compatriots.

JASON TRIES TO REGAIN CONTROL

5 About this time Antiochus made
his second invasion of Egypt. 2 And
it happened that, for almost forty days,
there appeared over all the city golden-
clad cavalry charging through the air,
in companies fully armed with lances
and drawn swords— 3 troops of cavalry
drawn up, attacks and counter-attacks
made on this side and on that, bran-
dishing of shields, massing of spears,
hurling of missiles, the flash of golden
trappings, and armour of all kinds.
4 Therefore everyone prayed that the
apparition might prove to have been a
good omen.

5 When a false rumour arose that
Antiochus was dead, Jason took no fewer than a thousand men and suddenly
made an assault on the city. When the
troops on the wall had been forced back
and at last the city was being taken, Menelaus took refuge in the citadel. 6 But Jason kept relentlessly slaughtering his
compatriots, not realizing that success
at the cost of one's kindred is the greatest misfortune, but imagining that he
was setting up trophies of victory over
enemies and not over compatriots. 7 He
did not, however, gain control of the
government; in the end he got only
disgrace from his conspiracy, and fled
again into the country of the Ammonites. 8 Finally he met a miserable end.
Accused[u] before Aretas the ruler of the
Arabs, fleeing from city to city, pursued
by everyone, hated as a rebel against the
laws, and abhorred as the executioner of
his country and his compatriots, he was
cast ashore in Egypt. 9 There he who had
driven many from their own country
into exile died in exile, having embarked
to go to the Lacedaemonians in hope of
finding protection because of their kinship. 10 He who had cast out many to lie
unburied had no one to mourn for him;
he had no funeral of any sort and no
place in the tomb of his ancestors.

11 When news of what had happened
reached the king, he took it to mean
that Judea was in revolt. So, raging inwardly, he left Egypt and took the city
by storm. 12 He commanded his soldiers
to cut down relentlessly everyone they
met and to kill those who went into
their houses. 13 Then there was massacre
of young and old, destruction of boys,
women, and children, and slaughter of
young girls and infants. 14 Within the total of three days eighty thousand were
destroyed, forty thousand in hand-to-
hand fighting, and as many were sold
into slavery as were killed.

[s] **4.41** Gk *they* [t] **4.48** Other ancient authorities read *the people* [u] **5.8** Cn: Gk *Imprisoned*

PILLAGE OF THE TEMPLE

15 Not content with this, Antiochus[v]
dared to enter the most holy temple in
all the world, guided by Menelaus, who
had become a traitor both to the laws
and to his country. 16 He took the holy
vessels with his polluted hands, and
swept away with profane hands the votive offerings that other kings had made
to enhance the glory and honour of the
place. 17 Antiochus was elated in spirit,
and did not perceive that the Lord was
angered for a little while because of the
sins of those who lived in the city, and
that this was the reason he was disregarding the holy place. 18 But if it had
not happened that they were involved
in many sins, this man would have
been flogged and turned back from his
rash act as soon as he came forward,
just as Heliodorus had been, whom
King Seleucus sent to inspect the treasury. 19 But the Lord did not choose the
nation for the sake of the holy place,
but the place for the sake of the nation.
20 Therefore the place itself shared in the
misfortunes that befell the nation and
afterwards participated in its benefits;
and what was forsaken in the wrath of
the Almighty was restored again in all
its glory when the great Lord became
reconciled.

21 So Antiochus carried off eighteen hundred talents from the temple,
and hurried away to Antioch, thinking
in his arrogance that he could sail on
the land and walk on the sea, because
his mind was elated. 22 He left governors to oppress the people: at Jerusalem, Philip, by birth a Phrygian and
in character more barbarous than the
man who appointed him; 23 and at Gerizim, Andronicus; and besides these
Menelaus, who lorded it over his compatriots worse than the others did.
In his malice towards the Jewish citizens,[w] 24 Antiochus[x] sent Apollonius,
the captain of the Mysians, with an
army of twenty-two thousand, and
commanded him to kill all the grown
men and to sell the women and boys as
slaves. 25 When this man arrived in Jerusalem, he pretended to be peaceably
disposed and waited until the holy sabbath day; then, finding the Jews not at
work, he ordered his troops to parade
under arms. 26 He put to the sword all
those who came out to see them, then
rushed into the city with his armed
warriors and killed great numbers of
people.

27 But Judas Maccabeus, with about
nine others, got away to the wilderness,
and kept himself and his companions
alive in the mountains as wild animals
do; they continued to live on what grew
wild, so that they might not share in
the defilement.

THE SUPPRESSION OF JUDAISM

6 Not long after this, the king sent an
Athenian[y] senator[z] to compel the
Jews to forsake the laws of their ances-
tors and no longer to live by the laws
of God; 2 also to pollute the temple in
Jerusalem and to call it the temple of
Olympian Zeus, and to call the one in
Gerizim the temple of Zeus-the-Friend-
of-Strangers, as did the people who
lived in that place.

3 Harsh and utterly grievous was the
onslaught of evil. 4 For the temple was
filled with debauchery and revelling by
the Gentiles, who dallied with prostitutes and had intercourse with women
within the sacred precincts, and besides brought in things for sacrifice that
were unfit. 5 The altar was covered with
abominable offerings that were forbidden by the laws. 6 People could neither
keep the sabbath, nor observe the festivals of their ancestors, nor so much as
confess themselves to be Jews.

7 On the monthly celebration of the
king's birthday, the Jews[a] were taken,
under bitter constraint, to partake of
the sacrifices; and when a festival of Dionysus was celebrated, they were compelled to wear wreaths of ivy and to
walk in the procession in honour of Dionysus. 8 At the suggestion of the people of Ptolemais[b] a decree was issued to
the neighbouring Greek cities that they
should adopt the same policy towards
the Jews and make them partake of the
sacrifices, 9 and should kill those who
did not choose to change over to Greek
customs. One could see, therefore, the
misery that had come upon them. 10 For
example, two women were brought in
for having circumcised their children.
They publicly paraded them around the
city, with their babies hanging at their
breasts, and then hurled them down
headlong from the wall. 11 Others who
had assembled in the caves nearby, in

[v] **5.15** Gk *he* [w] **5.23** Or *worse than the others did in his malice towards the Jewish citizens* [x] **5.24** Gk *he* [y] **6.1** Other ancient authorities read *Antiochian* [z] **6.1** Or *Geron an Athenian* [a] **6.7** Gk *they* [b] **6.8** Cn: Gk *suggestion of the Ptolemies* (or *of Ptolemy*)

order to observe the seventh day secretly, were betrayed to Philip and were all burned together, because their piety kept them from defending themselves, in view of their regard for that most holy day.

PROVIDENTIAL SIGNIFICANCE OF THE PERSECUTION

12 Now I urge those who read this
book not to be depressed by such calamities, but to recognize that these punishments were designed not to destroy but
to discipline our people. 13In fact, it is a
sign of great kindness not to let the impious alone for long, but to punish them
immediately. 14For in the case of the
other nations the Lord waits patiently to
punish them until they have reached the
full measure of their sins; but he does
not deal in this way with us, 15in order
that he should not take vengeance on us
afterwards when our sins have reached
their height. 16Therefore he never withdraws his mercy from us. Although he
disciplines us with calamities, he does
not forsake his own people. 17Let what
we have said serve as a reminder; we
must go on briefly with the story.

THE MARTYRDOM OF ELEAZAR

18 Eleazar, one of the scribes in high
position, a man now advanced in age
and of noble presence, was being forced
to open his mouth to eat swine's flesh.
19But he, welcoming death with honour
rather than life with pollution, went up
to the rack of his own accord, spitting
out the flesh, 20as all ought to go who
have the courage to refuse things that it
is not right to taste, even for the natural
love of life.

21 Those who were in charge of that
unlawful sacrifice took the man aside
because of their long acquaintance with
him, and privately urged him to bring
meat of his own providing, proper for
him to use, and to pretend that he was
eating the flesh of the sacrificial meal
that had been commanded by the king,
22so that by doing this he might be saved
from death, and be treated kindly on account of his old friendship with them.
23But making a high resolve, worthy of
his years and the dignity of his old age
and the grey hairs that he had reached
with distinction and his excellent life
even from childhood, and moreover according to the holy God-given law, he
declared himself quickly, telling them to
send him to Hades.

24 'Such pretence is not worthy of
our time of life,' he said, 'for many of the
young might suppose that Eleazar in his
ninetieth year had gone over to an alien
religion, 25and through my pretence, for
the sake of living a brief moment longer,
they would be led astray because of me,
while I defile and disgrace my old age.
26Even if for the present I would avoid
the punishment of mortals, yet whether
I live or die I will not escape the hands
of the Almighty. 27Therefore, by bravely
giving up my life now, I will show myself worthy of my old age 28and leave to
the young a noble example of how to die
a good death willingly and nobly for the
revered and holy laws.'

When he had said this, he went[c]
at once to the rack. 29Those who a little before had acted towards him with
goodwill now changed to ill will, because the words he had uttered were in
their opinion sheer madness.[d] 30When
he was about to die under the blows,
he groaned aloud and said: 'It is clear
to the Lord in his holy knowledge that,
though I might have been saved from
death, I am enduring terrible sufferings
in my body under this beating, but in
my soul I am glad to suffer these things
because I fear him.'

31 So in this way he died, leaving in
his death an example of nobility and a
memorial of courage, not only to the
young but to the great body of his nation.

THE MARTYRDOM OF SEVEN BROTHERS

7 It happened also that seven
brothers and their mother were
arrested and were being compelled by
the king, under torture with whips and
thongs, to partake of unlawful swine's
flesh. 2One of them, acting as their
spokesman, said, 'What do you intend to
ask and learn from us? For we are ready
to die rather than transgress the laws of
our ancestors.'

3 The king fell into a rage, and gave orders to have pans and cauldrons heated.
4These were heated immediately, and
he commanded that the tongue of their
spokesman be cut out and that they
scalp him and cut off his hands and feet,
while the rest of the brothers and the
mother looked on. 5When he was utterly helpless, the king[e] ordered them to

[c] 6.28 Other ancient authorities read *was dragged*
[d] 6.29 Meaning of Gk uncertain [e] 7.5 Gk *he*

take him to the fire, still breathing, and
to fry him in a pan. The smoke from the
pan spread widely, but the brothers[f] and
their mother encouraged one another
to die nobly, saying, 6 'The Lord God is
watching over us and in truth has compassion on us, as Moses declared in his
song that bore witness against the people to their faces, when he said, "And he
will have compassion on his servants." '[g]

7 After the first brother had died in
this way, they brought forward the second for their sport. They tore off the skin
of his head with the hair, and asked him,
'Will you eat rather than have your body
punished limb by limb?' 8 He replied in
the language of his ancestors and said
to them, 'No.' Therefore he in turn un-
derwent tortures as the first brother
had done. 9 And when he was at his last
breath, he said, 'You accursed wretch,
you dismiss us from this present life,
but the King of the universe will raise
us up to an everlasting renewal of life,
because we have died for his laws.'

10 After him, the third was the
victim of their sport. When it was demanded, he quickly put out his tongue
and courageously stretched forth his
hands, 11 and said nobly, 'I got these
from Heaven, and because of his laws I
disdain them, and from him I hope to
get them back again.' 12 As a result the
king himself and those with him were
astonished at the young man's spirit, for
he regarded his sufferings as nothing.

13 After he too had died, they maltreated and tortured the fourth in the
same way. 14 When he was near death,
he said, 'One cannot but choose to die at
the hands of mortals and to cherish the
hope God gives of being raised again by
him. But for you there will be no resurrection to life!'

15 Next they brought forward the
fifth and maltreated him. 16 But he
looked at the king,[h] and said, 'Because
you have authority among mortals,
though you also are mortal, you do what
you please. But do not think that God
has forsaken our people. 17 Keep on, and
see how his mighty power will torture
you and your descendants!'

18 After him they brought forward
the sixth. And when he was about to
die, he said, 'Do not deceive yourself in
vain. For we are suffering these things
on our own account, because of our sins
against our own God. Therefore[i] astounding things have happened. 19 But
do not think that you will go unpunished for having tried to fight against
God!'

20 The mother was especially admi-
rable and worthy of honourable memory. Although she saw her seven sons
perish within a single day, she bore it
with good courage because of her hope
in the Lord. 21 She encouraged each of
them in the language of their ancestors.
Filled with a noble spirit, she reinforced
her woman's reasoning with a man's
courage, and said to them, 22 'I do not
know how you came into being in my
womb. It was not I who gave you life
and breath, nor I who set in order the elements within each of you. 23 Therefore
the Creator of the world, who shaped
the beginning of humankind and devised the origin of all things, will in his
mercy give life and breath back to you
again, since you now forget yourselves
for the sake of his laws.'

24 Antiochus felt that he was being treated with contempt, and he was
suspicious of her reproachful tone. The
youngest brother being still alive, Antiochus[j] not only appealed to him in
words, but promised with oaths that he
would make him rich and enviable if he
would turn from the ways of his ancestors, and that he would take him for his
Friend and entrust him with public affairs. 25 Since the young man would not
listen to him at all, the king called the
mother to him and urged her to advise
the youth to save himself. 26 After much
urging on his part, she undertook to
persuade her son. 27 But, leaning close to
him, she spoke in their native language
as follows, deriding the cruel tyrant: 'My
son, have pity on me. I carried you for
nine months in my womb, and nursed
you for three years, and have reared you
and brought you up to this point in your
life, and have taken care of you.[k] 28 I beg
you, my child, to look at the heaven
and the earth and see everything that
is in them, and recognize that God
did not make them out of things that
existed.[l] And in the same way the human race came into being. 29 Do not fear
this butcher, but prove worthy of your
brothers. Accept death, so that in God's
mercy I may get you back again along
with your brothers.'

[f] 7.5 Gk *they* [g] 7.6 Gk *slaves* [h] 7.16 Gk *at him*
[i] 7.18 Lat: Other ancient authorities lack *Therefore*
[j] 7.24 Gk *he* [k] 7.27 Or *have borne the burden of your education* [l] 7.28 Or *God made them out of things that did not exist*

30 While she was still speaking, the
young man said, 'What are you[m] waiting for? I will not obey the king's command, but I obey the command of the
law that was given to our ancestors
through Moses. 31But you,[n] who have
contrived all sorts of evil against the
Hebrews, will certainly not escape the
hands of God. 32For we are suffering because of our own sins. 33And if our living Lord is angry for a little while, to
rebuke and discipline us, he will again
be reconciled with his own servants.[o]
34But you, unholy wretch, you most defiled of all mortals, do not be elated in
vain and puffed up by uncertain hopes,
when you raise your hand against the
children of heaven. 35You have not yet
escaped the judgement of the almighty,
all-seeing God. 36For our brothers after
enduring a brief suffering have drunk[p]
of ever-flowing life, under God's covenant; but you, by the judgement of
God, will receive just punishment for
your arrogance. 37I, like my brothers,
give up body and life for the laws of our
ancestors, appealing to God to show
mercy soon to our nation and by trials
and plagues to make you confess that he
alone is God, 38and through me and my
brothers to bring to an end the wrath of
the Almighty that has justly fallen on
our whole nation.'

39 The king fell into a rage, and han-
dled him worse than the others, being
exasperated at his scorn. 40So he died in
his integrity, putting his whole trust in
the Lord.

41 Last of all, the mother died, after
her sons.

42 Let this be enough, then, about
the eating of sacrifices and the extreme
tortures.

THE REVOLT OF JUDAS MACCABEUS

8 Meanwhile Judas, who was also
called Maccabeus, and his companions secretly entered the villages and
summoned their kindred and enlisted
those who had continued in the Jewish faith, and so they gathered about
six thousand. 2They implored the Lord
to look upon the people who were oppressed by all; and to have pity on the
temple that had been profaned by the
godless; 3to have mercy on the city that
was being destroyed and about to be
levelled to the ground; to hearken to the
blood that cried out to him; 4to remember also the lawless destruction of the
innocent babies and the blasphemies
committed against his name; and to
show his hatred of evil.

5 As soon as Maccabeus got his army
organized, the Gentiles could not withstand him, for the wrath of the Lord
had turned to mercy. 6Coming without
warning, he would set fire to towns and
villages. He captured strategic positions
and put to flight not a few of the enemy.
7He found the nights most advanta-
geous for such attacks. And talk of his
valour spread everywhere.

8 When Philip saw that the man was
gaining ground little by little, and that
he was pushing ahead with more frequent successes, he wrote to Ptolemy,
the governor of Coelesyria and Phoenicia, to come to the aid of the king's
government. 9Then Ptolemy[q] promptly appointed Nicanor son of Patroclus,
one of the king's chief[r] Friends, and
sent him, in command of no fewer than
twenty thousand Gentiles of all nations,
to wipe out the whole race of Judea. He
associated with him Gorgias, a general
and a man of experience in military service. 10Nicanor determined to make up
for the king the tribute due to the Romans, two thousand talents, by selling
the captured Jews into slavery. 11So he
immediately sent to the towns on the
sea coast, inviting them to buy Jewish slaves and promising to hand over
ninety slaves for a talent, not expecting
the judgement from the Almighty that
was about to overtake him.

PREPARATION FOR BATTLE

12 Word came to Judas concerning
Nicanor's invasion; and when he told
his companions of the arrival of the
army, 13those who were cowardly and
distrustful of God's justice ran off and
got away. 14Others sold all their remaining property, and at the same time implored the Lord to rescue those who had
been sold by the ungodly Nicanor before
he ever met them, 15if not for their own
sake, then for the sake of the covenants
made with their ancestors, and because
he had called them by his holy and glorious name. 16But Maccabeus gathered
his forces together, to the number of six
thousand, and exhorted them not to
be frightened by the enemy and not to
fear the great multitude of Gentiles who
were wickedly coming against them,

[m] 7.30 The Gk here for *you* is plural [n] 7.31 The Gk here for *you* is singular [o] 7.33 Gk *slaves* [p] 7.36 Cn: Gk *fallen* [q] 8.9 Gk *he* [r] 8.9 Gk *one of the first*

but to fight nobly, 17keeping before their eyes the lawless outrage that the Gentiles[s] had committed against the holy place, and the torture of the derided city, and besides, the overthrow of their ancestral way of life. 18'For they trust to arms and acts of daring', he said, 'but we trust in the Almighty God, who is able with a single nod to strike down those who are coming against us, and even, if necessary, the whole world.'

19 Moreover, he told them of the occasions when help came to their ancestors; how, in the time of Sennacherib, when one hundred and eighty-five thousand perished, 20and the time of the battle against the Galatians that took place in Babylonia, when eight thousand Jews[t] fought along with four thousand Macedonians; yet when the Macedonians were hard pressed, the eight thousand, by the help that came to them from heaven, destroyed one hundred and twenty thousand Galatians[u] and took a great amount of booty.

JUDAS DEFEATS NICANOR

21 With these words he filled them with courage and made them ready to die for their laws and their country; then he divided his army into four parts. 22He appointed his brothers also, Simon and Joseph and Jonathan, each to command a division, putting fifteen hundred men under each. 23Besides, he appointed Eleazar to read aloud[v] from the holy book, and gave the watchword, 'The help of God'; then, leading the first division himself, he joined battle with Nicanor.

24 With the Almighty as their ally, they killed more than nine thousand of the enemy, and wounded and disabled most of Nicanor's army, and forced them all to flee. 25They captured the money of those who had come to buy them as slaves. After pursuing them for some distance, they were obliged to return because the hour was late. 26It was the day before the sabbath, and for that reason they did not continue their pursuit. 27When they had collected the arms of the enemy and stripped them of their spoils, they kept the sabbath, giving great praise and thanks to the Lord, who had preserved them for that day and allotted it to them as the beginning of mercy. 28After the sabbath they gave some of the spoils to those who had been tortured and to the widows and orphans, and distributed the rest among themselves and their children. 29When they had done this, they made common supplication and implored the merciful Lord to be wholly reconciled with his servants.[w]

JUDAS DEFEATS TIMOTHY AND BACCHIDES

30 In encounters with the forces of Timothy and Bacchides they killed more than twenty thousand of them and got possession of some exceedingly high strongholds, and they divided a very large amount of plunder, giving to those who had been tortured and to the orphans and widows, and also to the aged, shares equal to their own. 31They collected the arms of the enemy,[x] and carefully stored all of them in strategic places; the rest of the spoils they carried to Jerusalem. 32They killed the commander of Timothy's forces, a most wicked man, and one who had greatly troubled the Jews. 33While they were celebrating the victory in the city of their ancestors, they burned those who had set fire to the sacred gates, Callisthenes and some others, who had fled into one little house; so these received the proper reward for their impiety.[y]

34 The thrice-accursed Nicanor, who had brought the thousand merchants to buy the Jews, 35having been humbled with the help of the Lord by opponents whom he regarded as of the least account, took off his splendid uniform and made his way alone like a runaway slave across the country until he reached Antioch, having succeeded chiefly in the destruction of his own army! 36So he who had undertaken to secure tribute for the Romans by the capture of the people of Jerusalem proclaimed that the Jews had a Defender, and that therefore the Jews were invulnerable, because they followed the laws ordained by him.

THE LAST CAMPAIGN OF ANTIOCHUS EPIPHANES

9 About that time, as it happened, Antiochus had retreated in disorder from the region of Persia. 2He had entered the city called Persepolis and attempted to rob the temples and control the city. Therefore the people rushed to the rescue with arms, and Antiochus and his army were defeated,[z]

[s] 8.17 Gk *they* [t] 8.20 Gk lacks *Jews* [u] 8.20 Gk lacks *Galatians* [v] 8.23 Meaning of Gk uncertain [w] 8.29 Gk *slaves* [x] 8.31 Gk *their arms* [y] 8.33 Meaning of Gk uncertain [z] 9.2 Gk *they were defeated*

with the result that Antiochus was put
to flight by the inhabitants and beat a
shameful retreat. [3]While he was in Ecbatana, news came to him of what had
happened to Nicanor and the forces of
Timothy. [4]Transported with rage, he
conceived the idea of turning upon
the Jews the injury done by those who
had put him to flight; so he ordered his
charioteer to drive without stopping
until he completed the journey. But the
judgement of heaven rode with him!
For in his arrogance he said, 'When I get
there I will make Jerusalem a cemetery
of Jews.'

5 But the all-seeing Lord, the God of
Israel, struck him with an incurable and
invisible blow. As soon as he stopped
speaking he was seized with a pain in
his bowels, for which there was no relief,
and with sharp internal tortures— [6]and
that very justly, for he had tortured the
bowels of others with many and strange
inflictions. [7]Yet he did not in any way
stop his insolence, but was even more
filled with arrogance, breathing fire in
his rage against the Jews, and giving orders to drive even faster. And so it came
about that he fell out of his chariot as
it was rushing along, and the fall was
so hard as to torture every limb of his
body. [8]Thus he who only a little while
before had thought in his superhuman
arrogance that he could command the
waves of the sea, and had imagined that
he could weigh the high mountains in a
balance, was brought down to earth and
carried in a litter, making the power of
God manifest to all. [9]And so the ungodly
man's body swarmed with worms, and
while he was still living in anguish and
pain, his flesh rotted away, and because
of the stench the whole army felt revul-
sion at his decay. [10]Because of his intol-
erable stench no one was able to carry
the man who a little while before had
thought that he could touch the stars
of heaven. [11]Then it was that, broken in
spirit, he began to lose much of his arrogance and to come to his senses under
the scourge of God, for he was tortured
with pain at every moment. [12]And when
he could not endure his own stench, he
uttered these words, 'It is right to be
subject to God; mortals should not think
that they are equal to God.'[a]

ANTIOCHUS MAKES A PROMISE TO GOD

13 Then the abominable fellow made
a vow to the Lord, who would no longer have mercy on him, stating [14]that
the holy city, which he was hurrying to
level to the ground and to make a cemetery, he was now declaring to be free;
[15]and the Jews, whom he had not considered worth burying but had planned
to throw out with their children for the
wild animals and for the birds to eat, he
would make, all of them, equal to citizens of Athens; [16]and the holy sanctuary, which he had formerly plundered,
he would adorn with the finest offerings; and all the holy vessels he would
give back, many times over; and the
expenses incurred for the sacrifices he
would provide from his own revenues;
[17]and in addition to all this he also would
become a Jew and would visit every inhabited place to proclaim the power of
God. [18]But when his sufferings did not
in any way abate, for the judgement of
God had justly come upon him, he gave
up all hope for himself and wrote to the
Jews the following letter, in the form of
a supplication. This was its content:

ANTIOCHUS'S LETTER AND DEATH

19 'To his worthy Jewish citizens,
Antiochus their king and general sends
hearty greetings and good wishes for
their health and prosperity. [20]If you
and your children are well and your
affairs are as you wish, I am glad. As
my hope is in heaven, [21]I remember
with affection your esteem and goodwill. On my way back from the region
of Persia I suffered an annoying illness,
and I have deemed it necessary to take
thought for the general security of all.
[22]I do not despair of my condition, for
I have good hope of recovering from my
illness, [23]but I observed that my father,
on the occasions when he made expedi-
tions into the upper country, appointed
his successor, [24]so that, if anything unexpected happened or any unwelcome
news came, the people throughout the
realm would not be troubled, for they
would know to whom the government
was left. [25]Moreover, I understand how
the princes along the borders and the
neighbours of my kingdom keep watching for opportunities and waiting to see
what will happen. So I have appointed
my son Antiochus to be king, whom I
have often entrusted and commended
to most of you when I hurried off to the
upper provinces; and I have written to
him what is written here. [26]I therefore

[a] 9.12 Or *not think thoughts proper only to God*

urge and beg you to remember the public and private services rendered to you
and to maintain your present goodwill,
each of you, towards me and my son.
27For I am sure that he will follow my
policy and will treat you with moderation and kindness.'

28 So the murderer and blasphemer, having endured the more
intense suffering, such as he had inflicted on others, came to the end of
his life by a most pitiable fate, among
the mountains in a strange land.
29And Philip, one of his courtiers, took
his body home; then, fearing the son
of Antiochus, he withdrew to Ptolemy
Philometor in Egypt.

PURIFICATION OF THE TEMPLE

10 Now Maccabeus and his followers, the Lord leading them
on, recovered the temple and the city;
2they tore down the altars that had
been built in the public square by the
foreigners, and also destroyed the sacred precincts. 3They purified the sanctuary, and made another altar of sacrifice; then, striking fire out of flint, they
offered sacrifices, after a lapse of two
years, and they offered incense and
lighted lamps and set out the bread
of the Presence. 4When they had done
this, they fell prostrate and implored
the Lord that they might never again
fall into such misfortunes, but that,
if they should ever sin, they might be
disciplined by him with forbearance
and not be handed over to blasphemous and barbarous nations. 5It happened that on the same day on which
the sanctuary had been profaned by
the foreigners, the purification of the
sanctuary took place, that is, on the
twenty-fifth day of the same month,
which was Chislev. 6They celebrated
it for eight days with rejoicing, in the
manner of the festival of booths, remembering how not long before, during the festival of booths, they had been
wandering in the mountains and caves
like wild animals. 7Therefore, carrying ivy-wreathed wands and beautiful
branches and also fronds of palm, they
offered hymns of thanksgiving to him
who had given success to the purifying
of his own holy place. 8They decreed by
public edict, ratified by vote, that the
whole nation of the Jews should observe these days every year.

9 Such then was the end of Antiochus, who was called Epiphanes.

ACCESSION OF ANTIOCHUS EUPATOR

10 Now we will tell what took place
under Antiochus Eupator, who was the
son of that ungodly man, and will give
a brief summary of the principal calamities of the wars. 11This man, when he
succeeded to the kingdom, appointed
one Lysias to have charge of the government and to be chief governor of
Coelesyria and Phoenicia. 12Ptolemy,
who was called Macron, took the lead in
showing justice to the Jews because of
the wrong that had been done to them,
and attempted to maintain peaceful relations with them. 13As a result he was
accused before Eupator by the king's
Friends. He heard himself called a traitor at every turn, because he had abandoned Cyprus, which Philometor had
entrusted to him, and had gone over to
Antiochus Epiphanes. Unable to command the respect due to his office,[b] he
took poison and ended his life.

CAMPAIGN IN IDUMEA

14 When Gorgias became governor
of the region, he maintained a force of
mercenaries, and at every turn kept attacking the Jews. 15Besides this, the Idumeans, who had control of important
strongholds, were harassing the Jews;
they received those who were banished
from Jerusalem, and endeavoured to
keep up the war. 16But Maccabeus and
his forces, after making solemn supplication and imploring God to fight on
their side, rushed to the strongholds of
the Idumeans. 17Attacking them vigorously, they gained possession of the
places, and beat off all who fought upon
the wall, and slaughtered those whom
they encountered, killing no fewer than
twenty thousand.

18 When at least nine thousand took
refuge in two very strong towers well
equipped to withstand a siege, 19Mac-
cabeus left Simon and Joseph, and also
Zacchaeus and his troops, a force sufficient to besiege them; and he himself
set off for places where he was more
urgently needed. 20But those with Simon, who were money-hungry, were
bribed by some of those who were in the
towers, and on receiving seventy thousand drachmas let some of them slip
away. 21When word of what had happened came to Maccabeus, he gathered
the leaders of the people, and accused
these men of having sold their kindred

[b] 10.13 Cn: Meaning of Gk uncertain

for money by setting their enemies free
to fight against them. 22 Then he killed
these men who had turned traitor, and
immediately captured the two towers.
23 Having success at arms in everything
he undertook, he destroyed more than
twenty thousand in the two strongholds.

JUDAS DEFEATS TIMOTHY

24 Now Timothy, who had been defeated by the Jews before, gathered a tre-
mendous force of mercenaries and collected the cavalry from Asia in no small
number. He came on, intending to take
Judea by storm. 25 As he drew near, Maccabeus and his men sprinkled dust on
their heads and girded their loins with
sackcloth, in supplication to God. 26 Falling upon the steps before the altar, they
implored him to be gracious to them
and to be an enemy to their enemies
and an adversary to their adversaries,
as the law declares. 27 And rising from
their prayer they took up their arms and
advanced a considerable distance from
the city; and when they came near the
enemy they halted. 28 Just as dawn was
breaking, the two armies joined battle,
one having as pledge of success and victory not only their valour but also their
reliance on the Lord, while the other
made rage their leader in the fight.

29 When the battle became fierce,
there appeared to the enemy from
heaven five resplendent men on horses
with golden bridles, and they were leading the Jews. 30 Two of them took Maccabeus between them, and shielding
him with their own armour and weapons, they kept him from being wounded.
They showered arrows and thunderbolts on the enemy, so that, confused
and blinded, they were thrown into disorder and cut to pieces. 31 Twenty thousand five hundred were slaughtered, besides six hundred cavalry.

32 Timothy himself fled to a stronghold called Gazara, especially well
garrisoned, where Chaereas was commander. 33 Then Maccabeus and his men
were glad, and they besieged the fort
for four days. 34 The men within, relying
on the strength of the place, kept blaspheming terribly and uttering wicked
words. 35 But at dawn on the fifth day,
twenty young men in the army of Maccabeus, fired with anger because of the
blasphemies, bravely stormed the wall
and with savage fury cut down everyone they met. 36 Others who came up in
the same way wheeled around against
the defenders and set fire to the towers; they kindled fires and burned the
blasphemers alive. Others broke open
the gates and let in the rest of the force,
and they occupied the city. 37 They killed
Timothy, who was hiding in a cistern,
and his brother Chaereas, and Apollo-
phanes. 38 When they had accomplished
these things, with hymns and thanksgivings they blessed the Lord who
shows great kindness to Israel and gives
them the victory.

LYSIAS BESIEGES BETH-ZUR

11 Very soon after this, Lysias, the
king's guardian and kinsman,
who was in charge of the government,
being vexed at what had happened,
2 gathered about eighty thousand infantry and all his cavalry and came against
the Jews. He intended to make the city a
home for Greeks, 3 and to levy tribute on
the temple as he did on the sacred places
of the other nations, and to put the
high-priesthood up for sale every year.
4 He took no account whatever of the
power of God, but was elated with his
tens of thousands of infantry, and his
thousands of cavalry, and his eighty elephants. 5 Invading Judea, he approached
Beth-zur, which was a fortified place
about five stadia[c] from Jerusalem, and
pressed it hard.

6 When Maccabeus and his men got
word that Lysias[d] was besieging the
strongholds, they and all the people,
with lamentations and tears, prayed
the Lord to send a good angel to save Israel. 7 Maccabeus himself was the first to
take up arms, and he urged the others to
risk their lives with him to aid their kindred. Then they eagerly rushed off together. 8 And there, while they were still
near Jerusalem, a horseman appeared at
their head, clothed in white and bran-
dishing weapons of gold. 9 And together
they all praised the merciful God, and
were strengthened in heart, ready to assail not only humans but the wildest animals or walls of iron. 10 They advanced
in battle order, having their heavenly
ally, for the Lord had mercy on them.
11 They hurled themselves like lions
against the enemy, and laid low eleven
thousand of them and sixteen hundred
cavalry, and forced all the rest to flee.
12 Most of them got away stripped and

[c] 11.5 Meaning of Gk uncertain [d] 11.6 Gk *he*

wounded, and Lysias himself escaped
by disgraceful flight.

LYSIAS MAKES PEACE WITH THE JEWS

13 As he was not without intelligence, he pondered over the defeat that
had befallen him, and realized that the
Hebrews were invincible because the
mighty God fought on their side. So he
sent to them 14 and persuaded them to
settle everything on just terms, promising that he would persuade the king,
constraining him to be their friend.[e]
15 Maccabeus, having regard for the
common good, agreed to all that Lysias
urged. For the king granted every request in behalf of the Jews which Maccabeus delivered to Lysias in writing.

16 The letter written to the Jews by
Lysias was to this effect:

'Lysias to the people of the Jews,
greetings. 17 John and Absalom, who
were sent by you, have delivered your
signed communication and have asked
about the matters indicated in it. 18 I
have informed the king of everything
that needed to be brought before him,
and he has agreed to what was possible. 19 If you will maintain your goodwill
towards the government, I will endeav-
our in the future to help promote your
welfare. 20 And concerning such matters
and their details, I have ordered these
men and my representatives to confer
with you. 21 Farewell. The one hundred
and forty-eighth year,[f] the twenty-
fourth of Dioscorinthius.'

22 The king's letter ran thus:

'King Antiochus to his brother Lysias, greetings. 23 Now that our father
has gone on to the gods, we desire that
the subjects of the kingdom be undis-
turbed in caring for their own affairs.
24 We have heard that the Jews do not
consent to our father's change to Greek
customs, but prefer their own way of
living and ask that their own customs
be allowed them. 25 Accordingly, since
we choose that this nation also should
be free from disturbance, our decision
is that their temple be restored to them
and that they shall live according to the
customs of their ancestors. 26 You will
do well, therefore, to send word to them
and give them pledges of friendship, so
that they may know our policy and be
of good cheer and go on happily in the
conduct of their own affairs.'

27 To the nation the king's letter was
as follows:

'King Antiochus to the senate of the
Jews and to the other Jews, greetings.
28 If you are well, it is as we desire. We
also are in good health. 29 Menelaus has
informed us that you wish to return
home and look after your own affairs.
30 Therefore those who go home by the
thirtieth of Xanthicus will have our
pledge of friendship and full permission
31 for the Jews to enjoy their own food
and laws, just as formerly, and none
of them shall be molested in any way
for what may have been done in ignorance. 32 And I have also sent Menelaus
to encourage you. 33 Farewell. The one
hundred and forty-eighth year,[g] the fifteenth of Xanthicus.'

34 The Romans also sent them a letter, which read thus:

'Quintus Memmius and Titus Mani-
us, envoys of the Romans, to the
people of the Jews, greetings. 35 With
regard to what Lysias the kinsman of
the king has granted you, we also give
consent. 36 But as to the matters that he
decided are to be referred to the king,
as soon as you have considered them,
send someone promptly so that we may
make proposals appropriate for you. For
we are on our way to Antioch. 37 Therefore make haste and send messengers
so that we may have your judgement.
38 Farewell. The one hundred and forty-
eighth year,[h] the fifteenth of Xanthicus.'

INCIDENTS AT JOPPA AND JAMNIA

12 When this agreement had been
reached, Lysias returned to the
king, and the Jews went about their
farming.

2 But some of the governors in various places, Timothy and Apollonius son
of Gennaeus, as well as Hieronymus and
Demophon, and in addition to these Nicanor the governor of Cyprus, would
not let them live quietly and in peace.
3 And the people of Joppa did so ungodly
a deed as this: they invited the Jews who
lived among them to embark, with their
wives and children, on boats that they
had provided, as though there were no
ill will to the Jews;[i] 4 and this was done
by public vote of the city. When they
accepted, because they wished to live
peaceably and suspected nothing, the
people of Joppa[j] took them out to sea
and drowned them, at least two hundred. 5 When Judas heard of the cruelty

[e] **11.14** Meaning of Gk uncertain [f] **11.21** 164 BC [g] **11.33** 164 BC [h] **11.38** 164 BC [i] **12.3** Gk *to them* [j] **12.4** Gk *they*

visited on his compatriots, he gave orders to his men 6and, calling upon God, the righteous judge, attacked the murderers of his kindred. He set fire to the harbour by night, burned the boats, and massacred those who had taken refuge there. 7Then, because the city's gates were closed, he withdrew, intending to come again and root out the whole community of Joppa. 8But learning that the people in Jamnia meant in the same way to wipe out the Jews who were living among them, 9he attacked the Jamnites by night and set fire to the harbour and the fleet, so that the glow of the light was seen in Jerusalem, thirty miles[k] distant.

THE CAMPAIGN IN GILEAD

10 When they had gone more than a mile[l] from there, on their march against Timothy, at least five thousand Arabs with five hundred cavalry attacked them. 11After a hard fight, Judas and his companions, with God's help, were victorious. The defeated nomads begged Judas to grant them pledges of friendship, promising to give him livestock and to help his people[m] in all other ways. 12Judas, realizing that they might indeed be useful in many ways, agreed to make peace with them; and after receiving his pledges they went back to their tents.

13 He also attacked a certain town that was strongly fortified with earthworks[n] and walls, and inhabited by all sorts of Gentiles. Its name was Caspin. 14Those who were within, relying on the strength of the walls and on their supply of provisions, behaved most insolently towards Judas and his men, railing at them and even blaspheming and saying unholy things. 15But Judas and his men, calling upon the great Sovereign of the world, who without battering-rams or engines of war overthrew Jericho in the days of Joshua, rushed furiously upon the walls. 16They took the town by the will of God, and slaughtered untold numbers, so that the adjoining lake, a quarter of a mile[o] wide, appeared to be running over with blood.

JUDAS DEFEATS TIMOTHY'S ARMY

17 When they had gone ninety-five miles[p] from there, they came to Charax, to the Jews who are called Toubiani. 18They did not find Timothy in that region, for he had by then left there without accomplishing anything, though in one place he had left a very strong garrison. 19Dositheus and Sosipater, who were captains under Maccabeus, marched out and destroyed those whom Timothy had left in the stronghold, more than ten thousand men. 20But Maccabeus arranged his army in divisions, set men[q] in command of the divisions, and hurried after Timothy, who had with him one hundred and twenty thousand infantry and two thousand five hundred cavalry. 21When Timothy learned of the approach of Judas, he sent off the women and the children and also the baggage to a place called Carnaim; for that place was hard to besiege and difficult of access because of the narrowness of all the approaches. 22But when Judas's first division appeared, terror and fear came over the enemy at the manifestation to them of him who sees all things. In their flight they rushed headlong in every direction, so that often they were injured by their own men and pierced by the points of their own swords. 23Judas pressed the pursuit with the utmost vigour, putting the sinners to the sword, and destroyed as many as thirty thousand.

24 Timothy himself fell into the hands of Dositheus and Sosipater and their men. With great guile he begged them to let him go in safety, because he held the parents of most of them, and the brothers of some, to whom no consideration would be shown. 25And when with many words he had confirmed his solemn promise to restore them unharmed, they let him go, for the sake of saving their kindred.

JUDAS WINS OTHER VICTORIES

26 Then Judas[r] marched against Carnaim and the temple of Atargatis, and slaughtered twenty-five thousand people. 27After the rout and destruction of these, he marched also against Ephron, a fortified town where Lysias lived with multitudes of people of all nationalities.[s] Stalwart young men took their stand before the walls and made a vigorous defence; and great stores of war engines and missiles were there. 28But the Jews[t] called upon the Sovereign who with

[k] 12.9 Gk *two hundred and forty stadia*
[l] 12.10 Gk *nine stadia* [m] 12.11 Gk *them*
[n] 12.13 Meaning of Gk uncertain [o] 12.16 Gk *two stadia* [p] 12.17 Gk *seven hundred and fifty stadia* [q] 12.20 Gk *them* [r] 12.26 Gk *he*
[s] 12.27 Meaning of Gk uncertain
[t] 12.28 Gk *they*

power shatters the might of his enemies, and they got the town into their
hands, and killed as many as twenty-
five thousand of those who were in it.
29 Setting out from there, they hastened to Scythopolis, which is seventy-
five miles[u] from Jerusalem. 30 But when
the Jews who lived there bore witness to the goodwill that the people of
Scythopolis had shown them and their
kind treatment of them in times of misfortune, 31 they thanked them and exhorted them to be well disposed to their
race in the future also. Then they went
up to Jerusalem, as the festival of weeks
was close at hand.

JUDAS DEFEATS GORGIAS

32 After the festival called Pentecost,
they hurried against Gorgias, the governor of Idumea, 33 who came out with
three thousand infantry and four hundred cavalry. 34 When they joined battle,
it happened that a few of the Jews fell.
35 But a certain Dositheus, one of Ba-
cenor's men, who was on horseback and
was a strong man, caught hold of Gorgias, and grasping his cloak was dragging him off by main strength, wishing
to take the accursed man alive, when
one of the Thracian cavalry bore down
on him and cut off his arm; so Gorgias
escaped and reached Marisa.
36 As Esdris and his men had been
fighting for a long time and were weary,
Judas called upon the Lord to show himself their ally and leader in the battle.
37 In the language of their ancestors he
raised the battle-cry, with hymns; then
he charged against Gorgias's troops
when they were not expecting it, and
put them to flight.

PRAYERS FOR THOSE KILLED IN BATTLE

38 Then Judas assembled his army
and went to the city of Adullam. As the
seventh day was coming on, they purified themselves according to the custom, and kept the sabbath there.
39 On the next day, as had now become necessary, Judas and his men
went to take up the bodies of the fallen
and to bring them back to lie with their
kindred in the sepulchres of their ancestors. 40 Then under the tunic of each
one of the dead they found sacred to-
kens of the idols of Jamnia, which the
law forbids the Jews to wear. And it became clear to all that this was the reason these men had fallen. 41 So they all
blessed the ways of the Lord, the righteous judge, who reveals the things that
are hidden; 42 and they turned to supplication, praying that the sin that had
been committed might be wholly blotted out. The noble Judas exhorted the
people to keep themselves free from sin,
for they had seen with their own eyes
what had happened as the result of the
sin of those who had fallen. 43 He also
took up a collection, man by man, to the
amount of two thousand drachmas of
silver, and sent it to Jerusalem to provide for a sin-offering. In doing this he
acted very well and honourably, taking
account of the resurrection. 44 For if he
were not expecting that those who had
fallen would rise again, it would have
been superfluous and foolish to pray
for the dead. 45 But if he was looking to
the splendid reward that is laid up for
those who fall asleep in godliness, it was
a holy and pious thought. Therefore he
made atonement for the dead, so that
they might be delivered from their sin.

MENELAUS IS PUT TO DEATH

13 In the one hundred and forty-
ninth year[v] word came to Judas
and his men that Antiochus Eupator
was coming with a great army against
Judea, 2 and with him Lysias, his guardian, who had charge of the government.
Each of them had a Greek force of one
hundred and ten thousand infantry,
five thousand three hundred cavalry,
twenty-two elephants, and three hundred chariots armed with scythes.
3 Menelaus also joined them and
with utter hypocrisy urged Antiochus
on, not for the sake of his country's
welfare, but because he thought that
he would be established in office. 4 But
the King of kings aroused the anger of
Antiochus against the scoundrel; and
when Lysias informed him that this
man was to blame for all the trouble, he
ordered them to take him to Beroea and
to put him to death by the method that
is customary in that place. 5 For there is
a tower there, fifty cubits high, full of
ashes, and it has a rim running round
it that on all sides inclines precipitously
into the ashes. 6 There they all push to
destruction anyone guilty of sacrilege
or notorious for other crimes. 7 By such
a fate it came about that Menelaus the
lawbreaker died, without even burial in
the earth. 8 And this was eminently just;

[u] **12.29** Gk *six hundred stadia* [v] **13.1** 163 BC

because he had committed many sins
against the altar whose fire and ashes
were holy, he met his death in ashes.

A BATTLE NEAR THE CITY OF MODEIN

9 The king with barbarous arrogance
was coming to show the Jews things far
worse than those that had been done[w]
in his father's time. 10But when Judas
heard of this, he ordered the people to
call upon the Lord day and night, now
more than ever to help those who were
on the point of being deprived of the law
and their country and the holy temple,
11and not to let the people who had just
begun to revive fall into the hands of the
blasphemous Gentiles. 12When they had
all joined in the same petition and had
implored the merciful Lord with weeping and fasting and lying prostrate for
three days without ceasing, Judas exhorted them and ordered them to stand
ready.

13 After consulting privately with
the elders, he determined to march out
and decide the matter by the help of God
before the king's army could enter Judea and get possession of the city. 14So,
committing the decision to the Creator
of the world and exhorting his troops to
fight bravely to the death for the laws,
temple, city, country, and commonwealth, he pitched his camp near Modein. 15He gave his troops the watchword, 'God's victory', and with a picked
force of the bravest young men, he attacked the king's pavilion at night and
killed as many as two thousand men in
the camp. He stabbed[x] the leading elephant and its rider. 16In the end they
filled the camp with terror and confusion and withdrew in triumph. 17This
happened, just as day was dawning, because the Lord's help protected him.

ANTIOCHUS MAKES A TREATY WITH THE JEWS

18 The king, having had a taste of the
daring of the Jews, tried strategy in attacking their positions. 19He advanced
against Beth-zur, a strong fortress of the
Jews, was turned back, attacked again,[y]
and was defeated. 20Judas sent in to the
garrison whatever was necessary. 21But
Rhodocus, a man from the ranks of the
Jews, gave secret information to the enemy; he was sought for, caught, and put
in prison. 22The king negotiated a second time with the people in Beth-zur,
gave pledges, received theirs, withdrew,
attacked Judas and his men, and was
defeated; 23he got word that Philip, who
had been left in charge of the government, had revolted in Antioch; he was
dismayed, called in the Jews, yielded
and swore to observe all their rights,
settled with them and offered sacrifice,
honoured the sanctuary, and showed
generosity to the holy place. 24He received Maccabeus, left Hegemonides
as governor from Ptolemais to Gerar,
25and went to Ptolemais. The people
of Ptolemais were indignant over the
treaty; in fact they were so angry that
they wanted to annul its terms.[z] 26Lys-
ias took the public platform, made the
best possible defence, convinced them,
appeased them, gained their goodwill,
and set out for Antioch. This is how the
king's attack and withdrawal turned
out.

ALCIMUS SPEAKS AGAINST JUDAS

14 Three years later, word came to
Judas and his men that Deme-
trius son of Seleucus had sailed into the
harbour of Tripolis with a strong army
and a fleet, 2and had taken possession
of the country, having made away with
Antiochus and his guardian Lysias.

3 Now a certain Alcimus, who had
formerly been high priest but had wilfully defiled himself in the times of
separation,[a] realized that there was no
way for him to be safe or to have access
again to the holy altar, 4and went to
King Demetrius in about the one hundred and fifty-first year,[b] presenting to
him a crown of gold and a palm, and
besides these some of the customary olive branches from the temple. During
that day he kept quiet. 5But he found
an opportunity that furthered his mad
purpose when he was invited by Demetrius to a meeting of the council and was
asked about the attitude and intentions
of the Jews. He answered:

6 'Those of the Jews who are called
Hasideans, whose leader is Judas Maccabeus, are keeping up war and stirring
up sedition, and will not let the kingdom attain tranquillity. 7Therefore I
have laid aside my ancestral glory—I
mean the high-priesthood—and have
now come here, 8first because I am
genuinely concerned for the interests

[w] 13.9 Or *the worst of the things that had been done* [x] 13.15 Meaning of Gk uncertain [y] 13.19 Or *faltered* [z] 13.25 Meaning of Gk uncertain [a] 14.3 Other ancient authorities read *of mixing* [b] 14.4 161 BC

of the king, and second because I have
regard also for my compatriots. For
through the folly of those whom I have
mentioned our whole nation is now in
no small misfortune. 9 Since you are
acquainted, O king, with the details
of this matter, may it please you to
take thought for our country and our
hard-pressed nation with the gracious
kindness that you show to all. 10 For as
long as Judas lives, it is impossible for
the government to find peace.' 11 When
he had said this, the rest of the king's
Friends,[c] who were hostile to Judas,
quickly inflamed Demetrius still more.
12 He immediately chose Nicanor, who
had been in command of the elephants,
appointed him governor of Judea, and
sent him off 13 with orders to kill Judas
and scatter his troops, and to instal Alcimus as high priest of the great[d] temple.
14 And the Gentiles throughout Judea,
who had fled before[e] Judas, flocked to
join Nicanor, thinking that the misfortunes and calamities of the Jews would
mean prosperity for themselves.

NICANOR MAKES FRIENDS WITH JUDAS

15 When the Jews[f] heard of Nicanor's
coming and the gathering of the Gentiles, they sprinkled dust on their heads
and prayed to him who established his
own people for ever and always upholds
his own heritage by manifesting himself. 16 At the command of the leader,
they[g] set out from there immediately
and engaged them in battle at a village
called Dessau.[h] 17 Simon, the brother of
Judas, had encountered Nicanor, but
had been temporarily[i] checked because
of the sudden consternation created by
the enemy.

18 Nevertheless Nicanor, hearing of
the valour of Judas and his troops and
their courage in battle for their country,
shrank from deciding the issue by bloodshed. 19 Therefore he sent Posidonius,
Theodotus, and Mattathias to give and
receive pledges of friendship. 20 When
the terms had been fully considered,
and the leader had informed the people,
and it had appeared that they were of
one mind, they agreed to the covenant.
21 The leaders[j] set a day on which to meet
by themselves. A chariot came forward
from each army; seats of honour were
set in place; 22 Judas posted armed men
in readiness at key places to prevent sudden treachery on the part of the enemy;
so they duly held the consultation.

23 Nicanor stayed on in Jerusalem
and did nothing out of the way, but
dismissed the flocks of people that had
gathered. 24 And he kept Judas always in
his presence; he was warmly attached to
the man. 25 He urged him to marry and
have children; so Judas[k] married, settled
down, and shared the common life.

NICANOR TURNS AGAINST JUDAS

26 But when Alcimus noticed their
goodwill for one another, he took the
covenant that had been made and went
to Demetrius. He told him that Nicanor was disloyal to the government,
since he had appointed that conspirator
against the kingdom, Judas, to be his
successor. 27 The king became excited
and, provoked by the false accusations
of that depraved man, wrote to Nicanor,
stating that he was displeased with the
covenant and commanding him to send
Maccabeus to Antioch as a prisoner
without delay.

28 When this message came to Nicanor, he was troubled and grieved that
he had to annul their agreement when
the man had done no wrong. 29 Since
it was not possible to oppose the king,
he watched for an opportunity to accomplish this by a stratagem. 30 But
Maccabeus, noticing that Nicanor was
more austere in his dealings with him
and was meeting him more rudely
than had been his custom, concluded
that this austerity did not spring from
the best motives. So he gathered not a
few of his men, and went into hiding
from Nicanor. 31 When the latter became aware that he had been cleverly
outwitted by the man, he went to the
great[l] and holy temple while the priests
were offering the customary sacrifices,
and commanded them to hand the man
over. 32 When they declared on oath that
they did not know where the man was
whom he wanted, 33 he stretched out his
right hand towards the sanctuary, and
swore this oath: 'If you do not hand Judas over to me as a prisoner, I will level
this shrine of God to the ground and
tear down the altar, and build here a
splendid temple to Dionysus.'

34 Having said this, he went away.
Then the priests stretched out their

[c] **14.11** Gk *of the Friends* [d] **14.13** Gk *greatest* [e] **14.14** Meaning of Gk uncertain [f] **14.15** Gk *they* [g] **14.16** Gk *he* [h] **14.16** Meaning of Gk uncertain [i] **14.17** Other ancient authorities read *slowly* [j] **14.21** Gk *They* [k] **14.25** Gk *he* [l] **14.31** Gk *greatest*

hands towards heaven and called upon
the constant Defender of our nation, in
these words: 35‘O Lord of all, though you
have need of nothing, you were pleased
that there should be a temple for your
habitation among us; 36so now, O holy
One, Lord of all holiness, keep undefiled
for ever this house that has been so recently purified.’

RAZIS DIES FOR HIS COUNTRY

37 A certain Razis, one of the elders
of Jerusalem, was denounced to Nicanor as a man who loved his compatriots
and was very well thought of and for his
goodwill was called father of the Jews.
38In former times, when there was no
mingling with the Gentiles, he had been
accused of Judaism, and he had most
zealously risked body and life for Judaism. 39Nicanor, wishing to exhibit the
enmity that he had for the Jews, sent
more than five hundred soldiers to arrest him; 40for he thought that by arrest-
ing[m] him he would do them an injury.
41When the troops were about to capture the tower and were forcing the door
of the courtyard, they ordered that fire
be brought and the doors burned. Being
surrounded, Razis[n] fell upon his own
sword, 42preferring to die nobly rather
than to fall into the hands of sinners
and suffer outrages unworthy of his noble birth. 43But in the heat of the struggle he did not hit exactly, and the crowd
was now rushing in through the doors.
He courageously ran up on the wall,
and bravely threw himself down into
the crowd. 44But as they quickly drew
back, a space opened and he fell in the
middle of the empty space. 45Still alive
and aflame with anger, he rose, and
though his blood gushed forth and his
wounds were severe he ran through
the crowd; and standing upon a steep
rock, 46with his blood now completely
drained from him, he tore out his entrails, took them in both hands, and
hurled them at the crowd, calling upon
the Lord of life and spirit to give them
back to him again. This was the manner
of his death.

NICANOR'S ARROGANCE

15 When Nicanor heard that Judas and his troops were in the
region of Samaria, he made plans to attack them with complete safety on the
day of rest. 2When the Jews who were
compelled to follow him said, ‘Do not
destroy so savagely and barbarously,
but show respect for the day that he
who sees all things has honoured and
hallowed above other days’, 3the thrice-
accursed wretch asked if there were
a sovereign in heaven who had commanded the keeping of the sabbath day.
4When they declared, ‘It is the living
Lord himself, the Sovereign in heaven,
who ordered us to observe the seventh
day,’ 5he replied, ‘But I am a sovereign
also, on earth, and I command you to
take up arms and finish the king's business.’ Nevertheless, he did not succeed
in carrying out his abominable design.

JUDAS PREPARES THE JEWS FOR BATTLE

6 This Nicanor in his utter boastfulness and arrogance had determined to
erect a public monument of victory over
Judas and his forces. 7But Maccabeus
did not cease to trust with all confidence
that he would get help from the Lord.
8He exhorted his troops not to fear the
attack of the Gentiles, but to keep in
mind the former times when help had
come to them from heaven, and so to
look for the victory that the Almighty
would give them. 9Encouraging them
from the law and the prophets, and reminding them also of the struggles they
had won, he made them the more eager.
10When he had aroused their courage,
he issued his orders, at the same time
pointing out the perfidy of the Gentiles and their violation of oaths. 11He
armed each of them not so much with
confidence in shields and spears as with
the inspiration of brave words, and he
cheered them all by relating a dream, a
sort of vision,[o] which was worthy of belief.

12 What he saw was this: Onias,
who had been high priest, a noble and
good man, of modest bearing and gentle manner, one who spoke fittingly and
had been trained from childhood in all
that belongs to excellence, was praying with outstretched hands for the
whole body of the Jews. 13Then in the
same fashion another appeared, distinguished by his grey hair and dignity,
and of marvellous majesty and authority. 14And Onias spoke, saying, ‘This is a
man who loves the family of Israel and
prays much for the people and the holy
city—Jeremiah, the prophet of God.’
15Jeremiah stretched out his right hand

[m] 14.40 Meaning of Gk uncertain [n] 14.41 Gk *he*
[o] 15.11 Meaning of Gk uncertain

and gave to Judas a golden sword, and
as he gave it he addressed him thus:
16‘Take this holy sword, a gift from God,
with which you will strike down your
adversaries.’

17 Encouraged by the words of Judas, so noble and so effective in arous-
ing valour and awaking courage in the
souls of the young, they determined
not to carry on a campaign[p] but to attack bravely, and to decide the matter by
fighting hand to hand with all courage,
because the city and the sanctuary and
the temple were in danger. 18Their concern for wives and children, and also for
brothers and sisters[q] and relatives, lay
upon them less heavily; their greatest
and first fear was for the consecrated
sanctuary. 19And those who had to remain in the city were in no little distress, being anxious over the encounter
in the open country.

THE DEFEAT AND DEATH OF NICANOR

20 When all were now looking forward to the coming issue, and the enemy was already close at hand with
their army drawn up for battle, the elephants[r] strategically stationed and the
cavalry deployed on the flanks, 21Mac-
cabeus, observing the masses that were
in front of him and the varied supply of
arms and the savagery of the elephants,
stretched out his hands towards heaven
and called upon the Lord who works
wonders; for he knew that it is not by
arms, but as the Lord[s] decides, that he
gains the victory for those who deserve
it. 22He called upon him in these words:
‘O Lord, you sent your angel in the
time of King Hezekiah of Judea, and he
killed fully one hundred and eighty-five
thousand in the camp of Sennacherib.
23So now, O Sovereign of the heavens,
send a good angel to spread terror and
trembling before us. 24By the might of
your arm may these blasphemers who
come against your holy people be struck
down.’ With these words he ended his
prayer.

25 Nicanor and his troops advanced
with trumpets and battle-songs, 26but
Judas and his troops met the enemy
in battle with invocations to God and
prayers. 27So, fighting with their hands
and praying to God in their hearts, they
laid low at least thirty-five thousand,
and were greatly gladdened by God’s
manifestation.

28 When the action was over and
they were returning with joy, they recognized Nicanor, lying dead, in full armour. 29Then there was shouting and
tumult, and they blessed the Sovereign
Lord in the language of their ancestors.
30Then the man who was ever in body
and soul the defender of his people, the
man who maintained his youthful goodwill towards his compatriots, ordered
them to cut off Nicanor’s head and arm
and carry them to Jerusalem. 31When he
arrived there and had called his compatriots together and stationed the priests
before the altar, he sent for those who
were in the citadel. 32He showed them
the vile Nicanor’s head and that profane
man’s arm, which had been boastfully
stretched out against the holy house of
the Almighty. 33He cut out the tongue
of the ungodly Nicanor and said that he
would feed it piecemeal to the birds and
would hang up these rewards of his folly
opposite the sanctuary. 34And they all,
looking to heaven, blessed the Lord who
had manifested himself, saying, ‘Blessed
is he who has kept his own place undefiled!’ 35Judas[t] hung Nicanor’s head
from the citadel, a clear and conspicuous sign to everyone of the help of the
Lord. 36And they all decreed by public
vote never to let this day go unobserved,
but to celebrate the thirteenth day of the
twelfth month—which is called Adar in
the Aramaic language—the day before
Mordecai’s day.

37 This, then, is how matters turned
out with Nicanor, and from that time
the city has been in the possession of
the Hebrews. So I will here end my
story.

THE COMPILER’S EPILOGUE

38 If it is well told and to the point,
that is what I myself desired; if it is
poorly done and mediocre, that was the
best I could do. 39For just as it is harmful
to drink wine alone, or, again, to drink
water alone, while wine mixed with water is sweet and delicious and enhances
one’s enjoyment, so also the style of the
story delights the ears of those who read
the work. And here will be the end.

[p] **15.17** Or *to remain in camp* [q] **15.18** Gk *for brothers* [r] **15.20** Gk *animals* [s] **15.21** Gk *he* [t] **15.35** Gk *He*

JOB

The righteous Job suffers severe affliction leading to one of the most studied and debated questions in ancient wisdom literature: What is the meaning and purpose of the suffering of a just person? After Job argues his innocence before his friends in this poetic narrative, he finally hears from the Lord, whose response challenges Job and leads to the conclusion that the meaning of suffering is beyond human comprehension. The book was probably written between the sixth and fourth centuries BCE. The setting of the story, however, is the patriarchal period in Uz or Edom, the legendary home of wisdom.

Passages from Job are read in the liturgy on Monday through Saturday of the Twenty-Sixth Week of Year II. Texts from Job are also read during Cycle B of the Fifth and Twelfth Sundays of the Year. Also, a passage from Job is offered as a First Reading at Masses for the Dead where Job asserts, "For I know that my Redeemer lives" (19.25).

JOB AND HIS FAMILY

1 There was once a man in the land of
Uz whose name was Job. That man
was blameless and upright, one who
feared God and turned away from evil.
2There were born to him seven sons and
three daughters. 3He had seven thousand sheep, three thousand camels,
five hundred yoke of oxen, five hundred
donkeys, and very many servants; so
that this man was the greatest of all the
people of the east. 4His sons used to go
and hold feasts in one another's houses
in turn; and they would send and invite
their three sisters to eat and drink with
them. 5And when the feast days had run
their course, Job would send and sanctify them, and he would rise early in
the morning and offer burnt-offerings
according to the number of them all;
for Job said, 'It may be that my children
have sinned, and cursed God in their
hearts.' This is what Job always did.

ATTACK ON JOB'S CHARACTER

6 One day the heavenly beings[a] came
to present themselves before the LORD,
and Satan[b] also came among them.
7The LORD said to Satan,[c] 'Where have
you come from?' Satan[d] answered the
LORD, 'From going to and fro on the
earth, and from walking up and down
on it.' 8The LORD said to Satan,[e] 'Have
you considered my servant Job? There is
no one like him on the earth, a blameless and upright man who fears God
and turns away from evil.' 9Then Satan[f] answered the LORD, 'Does Job fear
God for nothing? 10Have you not put
a fence around him and his house and
all that he has, on every side? You have
blessed the work of his hands, and his
possessions have increased in the land.
11But stretch out your hand now, and
touch all that he has, and he will curse
you to your face.' 12The LORD said to
Satan,[g] 'Very well, all that he has is in
your power; only do not stretch out your
hand against him!' So Satan[h] went out
from the presence of the LORD.

JOB LOSES PROPERTY AND CHILDREN

13 One day when his sons and
daughters were eating and drinking
wine in the eldest brother's house, 14a
messenger came to Job and said, 'The

[a] 1.6 Heb *sons of God* [b] 1.6 Or *the Accuser*; Heb *ha-satan* [c] 1.7 Or *the Accuser*; Heb *ha-satan* [d] 1.7 Or *the Accuser*; Heb *ha-satan* [e] 1.8 Or *the Accuser*; Heb *ha-satan* [f] 1.9 Or *the Accuser*; Heb *ha-satan* [g] 1.12 Or *the Accuser*; Heb *ha-satan* [h] 1.12 Or *the Accuser*; Heb *ha-satan*

oxen were ploughing and the donkeys
were feeding beside them, 15 and the Sabeans fell on them and carried them off,
and killed the servants with the edge of
the sword; I alone have escaped to tell
you.' 16 While he was still speaking, another came and said, 'The fire of God fell
from heaven and burned up the sheep
and the servants, and consumed them;
I alone have escaped to tell you.' 17 While
he was still speaking, another came and
said, 'The Chaldeans formed three columns, made a raid on the camels and
carried them off, and killed the servants
with the edge of the sword; I alone have
escaped to tell you.' 18 While he was still
speaking, another came and said, 'Your
sons and daughters were eating and
drinking wine in their eldest brother's house, 19 and suddenly a great wind
came across the desert, struck the four
corners of the house, and it fell on the
young people, and they are dead; I alone
have escaped to tell you.'

20 Then Job arose, tore his robe,
shaved his head, and fell on the ground
and worshipped. 21 He said, 'Naked I
came from my mother's womb, and naked shall I return there; the LORD gave,
and the LORD has taken away; blessed
be the name of the LORD.'

22 In all this Job did not sin or charge
God with wrongdoing.

ATTACK ON JOB'S HEALTH

2 One day the heavenly beings[i] came
to present themselves before the
LORD, and Satan[j] also came among
them to present himself before the
LORD. 2 The LORD said to Satan,[k] 'Where
have you come from?' Satan[l] answered
the LORD, 'From going to and fro on the
earth, and from walking up and down
on it.' 3 The LORD said to Satan,[m] 'Have
you considered my servant Job? There is
no one like him on the earth, a blameless and upright man who fears God and
turns away from evil. He still persists in
his integrity, although you incited me
against him, to destroy him for no reason.' 4 Then Satan[n] answered the LORD,
'Skin for skin! All that people have they
will give to save their lives.[o] 5 But stretch
out your hand now and touch his bone
and his flesh, and he will curse you to
your face.' 6 The LORD said to Satan,[p]
'Very well, he is in your power; only
spare his life.'

7 So Satan[q] went out from the presence of the LORD, and inflicted loathsome sores on Job from the sole of his
foot to the crown of his head. 8 Job[r] took
a potsherd with which to scrape himself, and sat among the ashes.

9 Then his wife said to him, 'Do you
still persist in your integrity? Curse[s]
God, and die.' 10 But he said to her, 'You
speak as any foolish woman would
speak. Shall we receive the good at the
hand of God, and not receive the bad?'
In all this Job did not sin with his lips.

JOB'S THREE FRIENDS

11 Now when Job's three friends
heard of all these troubles that had
come upon him, each of them set out
from his home—Eliphaz the Temanite,
Bildad the Shuhite, and Zophar the Naamathite. They met together to go and
console and comfort him. 12 When they
saw him from a distance, they did not
recognize him, and they raised their
voices and wept aloud; they tore their
robes and threw dust in the air upon
their heads. 13 They sat with him on the
ground for seven days and seven nights,
and no one spoke a word to him, for they
saw that his suffering was very great.

JOB CURSES THE DAY HE WAS BORN

3 After this Job opened his mouth
and cursed the day of his birth. 2 Job
said:

3 'Let the day perish on which
I was born,
and the night that said,
"A man-child is conceived."
4 Let that day be darkness!
May God above not seek it,
or light shine on it.
5 Let gloom and deep darkness
claim it.
Let clouds settle upon it;
let the blackness of the
day terrify it.
6 That night—let thick
darkness seize it!
let it not rejoice among the
days of the year;
let it not come into the
number of the months.
7 Yes, let that night be barren;
let no joyful cry be heard[t] in it.

[i] 2.1 Heb *sons of God* [j] 2.1 Or *the Accuser*; Heb *ha-satan* [k] 2.2 Or *the Accuser*; Heb *ha-satan* [l] 2.2 Or *The Accuser*; Heb *ha-satan* [m] 2.3 Or *the Accuser*; Heb *ha-satan* [n] 2.4 Or *the Accuser*; Heb *ha-satan* [o] 2.4 Or *All that the man has he will give for his life* [p] 2.6 Or *the Accuser*; Heb *ha-satan* [q] 2.7 Or *the Accuser*; Heb *ha-satan* [r] 2.8 Heb *He* [s] 2.9 Heb *Bless* [t] 3.7 Heb *come*

8 Let those curse it who curse the Sea,[u]
those who are skilled to
rouse up Leviathan.
9 Let the stars of its dawn be dark;
let it hope for light, but have none;
may it not see the eyelids
of the morning—
10 because it did not shut the doors
of my mother's womb,
and hide trouble from my eyes.

11 'Why did I not die at birth,
come forth from the womb
and expire?
12 Why were there knees to receive me,
or breasts for me to suck?
13 Now I would be lying down
and quiet;
I would be asleep; then I
would be at rest
14 with kings and counsellors
of the earth
who rebuild ruins for themselves,
15 or with princes who have gold,
who fill their houses with silver.
16 Or why was I not buried like
a stillborn child,
like an infant that never
sees the light?
17 There the wicked cease
from troubling,
and there the weary are at rest.
18 There the prisoners are at
ease together;
they do not hear the voice
of the taskmaster.
19 The small and the great are there,
and the slaves are free from
their masters.

20 'Why is light given to one in misery,
and life to the bitter in soul,
21 who long for death, but it
does not come,
and dig for it more than for
hidden treasures;
22 who rejoice exceedingly,
and are glad when they
find the grave?
23 Why is light given to one who
cannot see the way,
whom God has fenced in?
24 For my sighing comes like[v]
my bread,
and my groanings are poured
out like water.
25 Truly the thing that I fear
comes upon me,
and what I dread befalls me.
26 I am not at ease, nor am I quiet;
I have no rest; but trouble comes.'

ELIPHAZ SPEAKS: JOB HAS SINNED

4 Then Eliphaz the Temanite answered:
2 'If one ventures a word with you,
will you be offended?
But who can keep from speaking?
3 See, you have instructed many;
you have strengthened
the weak hands.
4 Your words have supported those
who were stumbling,
and you have made firm
the feeble knees.
5 But now it has come to you, and
you are impatient;
it touches you, and you
are dismayed.
6 Is not your fear of God your confidence,
and the integrity of your
ways your hope?

7 'Think now, who that was
innocent ever perished?
Or where were the upright cut off?
8 As I have seen, those who
plough iniquity
and sow trouble reap the same.
9 By the breath of God they perish,
and by the blast of his anger
they are consumed.
10 The roar of the lion, the voice
of the fierce lion,
and the teeth of the young
lions are broken.
11 The strong lion perishes for
lack of prey,
and the whelps of the lioness
are scattered.

12 'Now a word came stealing to me,
my ear received the whisper of it.
13 Amid thoughts from visions
of the night,
when deep sleep falls on mortals,
14 dread came upon me, and trembling,
which made all my bones shake.
15 A spirit glided past my face;
the hair of my flesh bristled.
16 It stood still,
but I could not discern
its appearance.
A form was before my eyes;
there was silence, then I
heard a voice:
17 "Can mortals be righteous
before[w] God?
Can human beings be pure
before[x] their Maker?

[u] 3.8 Cn: Heb *day* [v] 3.24 Heb *before*
[w] 4.17 *Or more than* [x] 4.17 *Or more than*

18 Even in his servants he
puts no trust,
and his angels he charges
with error;
19 how much more those who live
in houses of clay,
whose foundation is in the dust,
who are crushed like a moth.
20 Between morning and evening
they are destroyed;
they perish for ever without
any regarding it.
21 Their tent-cord is plucked up
within them,
and they die devoid
of wisdom.'

JOB IS CORRECTED BY GOD

5 'Call now; is there anyone who
will answer you?
To which of the holy ones
will you turn?
2 Surely vexation kills the fool,
and jealousy slays the simple.
3 I have seen fools taking root,
but suddenly I cursed
their dwelling.
4 Their children are far from safety,
they are crushed in the gate,
and there is no one to
deliver them.
5 The hungry eat their harvest,
and they take it even out
of the thorns;[y]
and the thirsty[z] pant after
their wealth.
6 For misery does not come
from the earth,
nor does trouble sprout
from the ground;
7 but human beings are born
to trouble
just as sparks[a] fly upward.

8 'As for me, I would seek God,
and to God I would commit
my cause.
9 He does great things and
unsearchable,
marvellous things without
number.
10 He gives rain on the earth
and sends waters on the fields;
11 he sets on high those
who are lowly,
and those who mourn are
lifted to safety.
12 He frustrates the devices
of the crafty,
so that their hands achieve
no success.
13 He takes the wise in their
own craftiness;
and the schemes of the wily are
brought to a quick end.
14 They meet with darkness
in the daytime,
and grope at noonday as
in the night.
15 But he saves the needy from the
sword of their mouth,
from the hand of the mighty.
16 So the poor have hope,
and injustice shuts its mouth.

17 'How happy is the one whom
God reproves;
therefore do not despise the
discipline of the Almighty.[b]
18 For he wounds, but he binds up;
he strikes, but his hands heal.
19 He will deliver you from
six troubles;
in seven no harm
shall touch you.
20 In famine he will redeem
you from death,
and in war from the power
of the sword.
21 You shall be hidden from the
scourge of the tongue,
and shall not fear destruction
when it comes.
22 At destruction and famine
you shall laugh,
and shall not fear the wild
animals of the earth.
23 For you shall be in league with
the stones of the field,
and the wild animals shall
be at peace with you.
24 You shall know that
your tent is safe,
you shall inspect your fold
and miss nothing.
25 You shall know that your
descendants will be many,
and your offspring like the
grass of the earth.
26 You shall come to your grave
in ripe old age,
as a shock of grain comes up to the
threshing-floor in its season.
27 See, we have searched this
out; it is true.
Hear, and know it for yourself.'

[y] **5.5** Meaning of Heb uncertain [z] **5.5** Aquila Symmachus Syr Vg: Heb *snare* [a] **5.7** Or *birds*; Heb *sons of Resheph* [b] **5.17** Traditional rendering of Heb *Shaddai*

JOB REPLIES: MY COMPLAINT IS JUST

6 Then Job answered:
2 'O that my vexation were weighed,
and all my calamity laid
in the balances!
3 For then it would be heavier than
the sand of the sea;
therefore my words have
been rash.
4 For the arrows of the Almighty[c]
are in me;
my spirit drinks their poison;
the terrors of God are
arrayed against me.
5 Does the wild ass bray over its grass,
or the ox low over its fodder?
6 Can that which is tasteless be
eaten without salt,
or is there any flavour in the
juice of mallows?[d]
7 My appetite refuses to touch them;
they are like food that is
loathsome to me.[e]

8 'O that I might have my request,
and that God would grant
my desire;
9 that it would please God to crush me,
that he would let loose his
hand and cut me off!
10 This would be my consolation;
I would even exult[f] in
unrelenting pain;
for I have not denied the
words of the Holy One.
11 What is my strength, that
I should wait?
And what is my end, that I
should be patient?
12 Is my strength the strength
of stones,
or is my flesh bronze?
13 In truth I have no help in me,
and any resource is driven
from me.

14 'Those who withhold[g] kindness
from a friend
forsake the fear of the Almighty.[h]
15 My companions are treacherous
like a torrent-bed,
like freshets that pass away,
16 that run dark with ice,
turbid with melting snow.
17 In time of heat they disappear;
when it is hot, they vanish
from their place.
18 The caravans turn aside from
their course;
they go up into the waste,
and perish.
19 The caravans of Tema look,
the travellers of Sheba hope.
20 They are disappointed because
they were confident;
they come there and are
confounded.
21 Such you have now become to me;[i]
you see my calamity,
and are afraid.
22 Have I said, "Make me a gift"?
Or, "From your wealth offer
a bribe for me"?
23 Or, "Save me from an
opponent's hand"?
Or, "Ransom me from the
hand of oppressors"?

24 'Teach me, and I will be silent;
make me understand how
I have gone wrong.
25 How forceful are honest words!
But your reproof, what
does it reprove?
26 Do you think that you can
reprove words,
as if the speech of the
desperate were wind?
27 You would even cast lots
over the orphan,
and bargain over your friend.

28 'But now, be pleased to look at me;
for I will not lie to your face.
29 Turn, I pray, let no wrong be done.
Turn now, my vindication
is at stake.
30 Is there any wrong on my tongue?
Cannot my taste discern calamity?

JOB: MY SUFFERING IS WITHOUT END

7 'Do not human beings have a
hard service on earth,
and are not their days like the
days of a labourer?
2 Like a slave who longs for
the shadow,
and like labourers who look
for their wages,
3 so I am allotted months
of emptiness,
and nights of misery are
apportioned to me.

[c] 6.4 Traditional rendering of Heb *Shaddai* [d] 6.6 Meaning of Heb uncertain [e] 6.7 Meaning of Heb uncertain [f] 6.10 Meaning of Heb uncertain [g] 6.14 Syr Vg Compare Tg: Meaning of Heb uncertain [h] 6.14 Traditional rendering of Heb *Shaddai* [i] 6.21 Cn Compare Gk Syr: Meaning of Heb uncertain

4 When I lie down I say, "When
shall I rise?"
But the night is long,
and I am full of tossing
until dawn.
5 My flesh is clothed with
worms and dirt;
my skin hardens, then
breaks out again.
6 My days are swifter than a
weaver's shuttle,
and come to their end
without hope.[j]

7 'Remember that my life is a breath;
my eye will never again see good.
8 The eye that beholds me will
see me no more;
while your eyes are upon
me, I shall be gone.
9 As the cloud fades and vanishes,
so those who go down to
Sheol do not come up;
10 they return no more to their houses,
nor do their places know
them any more.

11 'Therefore I will not restrain
my mouth;
I will speak in the anguish
of my spirit;
I will complain in the
bitterness of my soul.
12 Am I the Sea, or the Dragon,
that you set a guard over me?
13 When I say, "My bed will
comfort me,
my couch will ease my complaint",
14 then you scare me with dreams
and terrify me with visions,
15 so that I would choose strangling
and death rather than this body.
16 I loathe my life; I would not
live for ever.
Let me alone, for my days
are a breath.
17 What are human beings, that you
make so much of them,
that you set your mind on them,
18 visit them every morning,
test them every moment?
19 Will you not look away from
me for a while,
let me alone until I swallow
my spittle?
20 If I sin, what do I do to you, you
watcher of humanity?
Why have you made me
your target?
Why have I become a
burden to you?
21 Why do you not pardon my
transgression
and take away my iniquity?
For now I shall lie in the earth;
you will seek me, but I
shall not be.'

BILDAD SPEAKS: JOB SHOULD REPENT

8 Then Bildad the Shuhite answered:
2 'How long will you say
these things,
and the words of your mouth
be a great wind?
3 Does God pervert justice?
Or does the Almighty[k]
pervert the right?
4 If your children sinned against him,
he delivered them into the power
of their transgression.
5 If you will seek God
and make supplication to
the Almighty,[l]
6 if you are pure and upright,
surely then he will rouse
himself for you
and restore to you your
rightful place.
7 Though your beginning was small,
your latter days will be very great.

8 'For inquire now of bygone
generations,
and consider what their
ancestors have found;
9 for we are but of yesterday, and
we know nothing,
for our days on earth are
but a shadow.
10 Will they not teach you and tell you
and utter words out of their
understanding?

11 'Can papyrus grow where
there is no marsh?
Can reeds flourish where
there is no water?
12 While yet in flower and
not cut down,
they wither before any
other plant.
13 Such are the paths of all
who forget God;
the hope of the godless
shall perish.
14 Their confidence is gossamer,
a spider's house their trust.

[j] 7.6 *Or as the thread runs out* [k] 8.3 Traditional rendering of Heb *Shaddai* [l] 8.5 Traditional rendering of Heb *Shaddai*

15 If one leans against its house,
it will not stand;
if one lays hold of it, it
will not endure.
16 The wicked thrive[m] before the sun,
and their shoots spread
over the garden.
17 Their roots twine around
the stoneheap;
they live among the rocks.[n]
18 If they are destroyed from
their place,
then it will deny them, saying,
"I have never seen you."
19 See, these are their happy ways,[o]
and out of the earth still
others will spring.

20 'See, God will not reject a
blameless person,
nor take the hand of evildoers.
21 He will yet fill your mouth
with laughter,
and your lips with shouts of joy.
22 Those who hate you will be
clothed with shame,
and the tent of the wicked
will be no more.'

JOB REPLIES: THERE IS NO MEDIATOR

9 Then Job answered:
2 'Indeed I know that this is so;
but how can a mortal be
just before God?
3 If one wished to contend with him,
one could not answer him
once in a thousand.
4 He is wise in heart, and
mighty in strength
—who has resisted him, and
succeeded?—
5 he who removes mountains, and
they do not know it,
when he overturns them
in his anger;
6 who shakes the earth out of its place,
and its pillars tremble;
7 who commands the sun, and
it does not rise;
who seals up the stars;
8 who alone stretched out the heavens
and trampled the waves
of the Sea;[p]
9 who made the Bear and Orion,
the Pleiades and the chambers
of the south;
10 who does great things beyond
understanding,
and marvellous things
without number.
11 Look, he passes by me, and
I do not see him;
he moves on, but I do not
perceive him.
12 He snatches away; who
can stop him?
Who will say to him, "What
are you doing?"
13 'God will not turn back his anger;
the helpers of Rahab bowed
beneath him.
14 How then can I answer him,
choosing my words with him?
15 Though I am innocent, I
cannot answer him;
I must appeal for mercy
to my accuser.[q]
16 If I summoned him and he
answered me,
I do not believe that he would
listen to my voice.
17 For he crushes me with a tempest,
and multiplies my wounds
without cause;
18 he will not let me get my breath,
but fills me with bitterness.
19 If it is a contest of strength, he
is the strong one!
If it is a matter of justice, who
can summon him?[r]
20 Though I am innocent, my own
mouth would condemn me;
though I am blameless, he
would prove me perverse.
21 I am blameless; I do not
know myself;
I loathe my life.
22 It is all one; therefore I say,
he destroys both the blameless
and the wicked.
23 When disaster brings sudden death,
he mocks at the calamity[s]
of the innocent.
24 The earth is given into the
hand of the wicked;
he covers the eyes of its judges—
if it is not he, who then is it?

25 'My days are swifter than a runner;
they flee away, they see no good.
26 They go by like skiffs of reed,
like an eagle swooping
on the prey.

[m] 8.16 Heb *He thrives* [n] 8.17 Gk Vg: Meaning of Heb uncertain [o] 8.19 Meaning of Heb uncertain
[p] 9.8 Or *trampled the back of the sea dragon*
[q] 9.15 Or *for my right* [r] 9.19 Compare Gk: Heb *me* [s] 9.23 Meaning of Heb uncertain

27 If I say, "I will forget my complaint;
I will put off my sad countenance
and be of good cheer",
28 I become afraid of all my suffering,
for I know you will not
hold me innocent.
29 I shall be condemned;
why then do I labour in vain?
30 If I wash myself with soap
and cleanse my hands with lye,
31 yet you will plunge me into filth,
and my own clothes
will abhor me.
32 For he is not a mortal, as I am,
that I might answer him,
that we should come to
trial together.
33 There is no umpire[t] between us,
who might lay his hand
on us both.
34 If he would take his rod
away from me,
and not let dread of him
terrify me,
35 then I would speak without
fear of him,
for I know I am not what I
am thought to be.[u]

JOB: I LOATHE MY LIFE

10 'I loathe my life;
I will give free utterance
to my complaint;
I will speak in the bitterness
of my soul.
2 I will say to God, Do not
condemn me;
let me know why you
contend against me.
3 Does it seem good to you to oppress,
to despise the work of your hands
and favour the schemes
of the wicked?
4 Do you have eyes of flesh?
Do you see as humans see?
5 Are your days like the days
of mortals,
or your years like human years,
6 that you seek out my iniquity
and search for my sin,
7 although you know that I
am not guilty,
and there is no one to deliver
out of your hand?
8 Your hands fashioned and made me;
and now you turn and
destroy me.[v]
9 Remember that you fashioned
me like clay;
and will you turn me to
dust again?
10 Did you not pour me out like milk
and curdle me like cheese?
11 You clothed me with skin and flesh,
and knit me together with
bones and sinews.
12 You have granted me life and
steadfast love,
and your care has preserved
my spirit.
13 Yet these things you hid
in your heart;
I know that this was
your purpose.
14 If I sin, you watch me,
and do not acquit me of
my iniquity.
15 If I am wicked, woe to me!
If I am righteous, I cannot
lift up my head,
for I am filled with disgrace
and look upon my affliction.
16 Bold as a lion you hunt me;
you repeat your exploits
against me.
17 You renew your witnesses
against me,
and increase your vexation
towards me;
you bring fresh troops
against me.[w]

18 'Why did you bring me forth
from the womb?
Would that I had died before
any eye had seen me,
19 and were as though I had not been,
carried from the womb
to the grave.
20 Are not the days of my life few?[x]
Let me alone, that I may
find a little comfort[y]
21 before I go, never to return,
to the land of gloom and
deep darkness,
22 the land of gloom[z] and chaos,
where light is like darkness.'

ZOPHAR SPEAKS: JOB'S GUILT DESERVES PUNISHMENT

11 Then Zophar the Naamathite answered:

[t] 9.33 Another reading is *Would that there were an umpire* [u] 9.35 Cn: Heb *for I am not so in myself* [v] 10.8 Cn Compare Gk Syr: Heb *made me together all around, and you destroy me* [w] 10.17 Cn Compare Gk: Heb *towards me; changes and a troop are with me* [x] 10.20 Cn Compare Gk Syr: Heb *Are not my days few? Let him cease!* [y] 10.20 Heb *that I may brighten up a little* [z] 10.22 Heb *gloom as darkness, deep darkness*

2 'Should a multitude of words
go unanswered,
and should one full of talk
be vindicated?
3 Should your babble put
others to silence,
and when you mock, shall
no one shame you?
4 For you say, "My conduct[a] is pure,
and I am clean in God's[b] sight."
5 But O that God would speak,
and open his lips to you,
6 and that he would tell you the
secrets of wisdom!
For wisdom is many-sided.[c]
Know then that God exacts of you
less than your guilt deserves.

7 'Can you find out the deep
things of God?
Can you find out the limit
of the Almighty?[d]
8 It is higher than heaven[e]—what
can you do?
Deeper than Sheol—what
can you know?
9 Its measure is longer than the earth,
and broader than the sea.
10 If he passes through, and imprisons,
and assembles for judgement,
who can hinder him?
11 For he knows those who
are worthless;
when he sees iniquity, will
he not consider it?
12 But a stupid person will get
understanding,
when a wild ass is born human.[f]

13 'If you direct your heart rightly,
you will stretch out your
hands towards him.
14 If iniquity is in your hand,
put it far away,
and do not let wickedness
reside in your tents.
15 Surely then you will lift up your
face without blemish;
you will be secure, and
will not fear.
16 You will forget your misery;
you will remember it as waters
that have passed away.
17 And your life will be brighter
than the noonday;
its darkness will be like
the morning.
18 And you will have confidence,
because there is hope;
you will be protected[g] and
take your rest in safety.
19 You will lie down, and no one
will make you afraid;
many will entreat your favour.
20 But the eyes of the wicked will fail;
all way of escape will be
lost to them,
and their hope is to
breathe their last.'

JOB REPLIES: I AM A LAUGHING-STOCK

12 Then Job answered:
2 'No doubt you are the people,
and wisdom will die with you.
3 But I have understanding
as well as you;
I am not inferior to you.
Who does not know such
things as these?
4 I am a laughing-stock to my friends;
I, who called upon God and
he answered me,
a just and blameless man, I
am a laughing-stock.
5 Those at ease have contempt
for misfortune,[h]
but it is ready for those whose
feet are unstable.
6 The tents of robbers are at peace,
and those who provoke
God are secure,
who bring their god in
their hands.[i]

7 'But ask the animals, and they
will teach you;
the birds of the air, and
they will tell you;
8 ask the plants of the earth,[j] and
they will teach you;
and the fish of the sea will
declare to you.
9 Who among all these
does not know
that the hand of the LORD
has done this?
10 In his hand is the life of every
living thing
and the breath of every
human being.
11 Does not the ear test words
as the palate tastes food?

[a] 11.4 Gk: Heb *teaching* [b] 11.4 Heb *your*
[c] 11.6 Meaning of Heb uncertain
[d] 11.7 Traditional rendering of Heb *Shaddai*
[e] 11.8 Heb *The heights of heaven*
[f] 11.12 Meaning of Heb uncertain [g] 11.18 Or *you will look around* [h] 12.5 Meaning of Heb uncertain [i] 12.6 Or *whom God brought forth by his hand*; Meaning of Heb uncertain [j] 12.8 Or *speak to the earth*

12 Is wisdom with the aged,
and understanding in
length of days?
13 'With God[k] are wisdom and strength;
he has counsel and
understanding.
14 If he tears down, no one can rebuild;
if he shuts someone in, no
one can open up.
15 If he withholds the waters,
they dry up;
if he sends them out, they
overwhelm the land.
16 With him are strength and wisdom;
the deceived and the
deceiver are his.
17 He leads counsellors away stripped,
and makes fools of judges.
18 He looses the sash of kings,
and binds a waistcloth
on their loins.
19 He leads priests away stripped,
and overthrows the mighty.
20 He deprives of speech those
who are trusted,
and takes away the discernment
of the elders.
21 He pours contempt on princes,
and looses the belt of the strong.
22 He uncovers the deeps out
of darkness,
and brings deep darkness to light.
23 He makes nations great, then
destroys them;
he enlarges nations, then
leads them away.
24 He strips understanding from the
leaders[l] of the earth,
and makes them wander in
a pathless waste.
25 They grope in the dark
without light;
he makes them stagger
like a drunkard.

13 'Look, my eye has seen all this,
my ear has heard and
understood it.
2 What you know, I also know;
I am not inferior to you.
3 But I would speak to the Almighty,[m]
and I desire to argue my
case with God.
4 As for you, you whitewash with lies;
all of you are worthless physicians.
5 If you would only keep silent,
that would be your wisdom!
6 Hear now my reasoning,
and listen to the pleadings
of my lips.
7 Will you speak falsely for God,
and speak deceitfully for him?
8 Will you show partiality
towards him,
will you plead the case for God?
9 Will it be well with you when
he searches you out?
Or can you deceive him, as one
person deceives another?
10 He will surely rebuke you
if in secret you show partiality.
11 Will not his majesty terrify you,
and the dread of him
fall upon you?
12 Your maxims are proverbs of ashes,
your defences are defences of clay.

13 'Let me have silence, and
I will speak,
and let come on me what may.
14 I will take my flesh in my teeth,
and put my life in my hand.[n]
15 See, he will kill me; I have no hope;[o]
but I will defend my
ways to his face.
16 This will be my salvation,
that the godless shall not
come before him.
17 Listen carefully to my words,
and let my declaration
be in your ears.
18 I have indeed prepared my case;
I know that I shall be vindicated.
19 Who is there that will
contend with me?
For then I would be silent and die.

JOB'S DESPONDENT PRAYER

20 Only grant two things to me,
then I will not hide myself
from your face:
21 withdraw your hand far from me,
and do not let dread of
you terrify me.
22 Then call, and I will answer;
or let me speak, and you
reply to me.
23 How many are my iniquities
and my sins?
Make me know my transgression
and my sin.
24 Why do you hide your face,
and count me as your enemy?
25 Will you frighten a windblown leaf
and pursue dry chaff?

k 12.13 Heb *him* l 12.24 Heb adds *of the people*
m 13.3 Traditional rendering of Heb *Shaddai*
n 13.14 Gk: Heb *Why should I take . . . in my hand?*
o 13.15 Or *Though he kill me, yet I will trust in him*

26 For you write bitter things
against me,
and make me reap[p] the
iniquities of my youth.
27 You put my feet in the stocks,
and watch all my paths;
you set a bound to the
soles of my feet.
28 One wastes away like a rotten thing,
like a garment that
is moth-eaten.

14 'A mortal, born of woman, few
of days and full of trouble,
2 comes up like a flower
and withers,
flees like a shadow and
does not last.
3 Do you fix your eyes on such a one?
Do you bring me into
judgement with you?
4 Who can bring a clean thing
out of an unclean?
No one can.
5 Since their days are determined,
and the number of their months
is known to you,
and you have appointed
the bounds that they
cannot pass,
6 look away from them, and desist,[q]
that they may enjoy, like
labourers, their days.

7 'For there is hope for a tree,
if it is cut down, that it
will sprout again,
and that its shoots will not cease.
8 Though its root grows old
in the earth,
and its stump dies in
the ground,
9 yet at the scent of water it will bud
and put forth branches like
a young plant.
10 But mortals die, and are laid low;
humans expire, and
where are they?
11 As waters fail from a lake,
and a river wastes away
and dries up,
12 so mortals lie down and do
not rise again;
until the heavens are no more,
they will not awake
or be roused out of their sleep.
13 O that you would hide me in Sheol,
that you would conceal me
until your wrath is past,
that you would appoint me a set
time, and remember me!
14 If mortals die, will they live again?
All the days of my service
I would wait
until my release should come.
15 You would call, and I would
answer you;
you would long for the work
of your hands.
16 For then you would not[r]
number my steps,
you would not keep watch
over my sin;
17 my transgression would be
sealed up in a bag,
and you would cover over
my iniquity.

18 'But the mountain falls and
crumbles away,
and the rock is removed
from its place;
19 the waters wear away the stones;
the torrents wash away the
soil of the earth;
so you destroy the hope
of mortals.
20 You prevail for ever against them,
and they pass away;
you change their countenance,
and send them away.
21 Their children come to honour,
and they do not know it;
they are brought low, and
it goes unnoticed.
22 They feel only the pain of
their own bodies,
and mourn only for themselves.'

ELIPHAZ SPEAKS: JOB UNDERMINES RELIGION

15 Then Eliphaz the Temanite answered:
2 'Should the wise answer with
windy knowledge,
and fill themselves with
the east wind?
3 Should they argue in
unprofitable talk,
or in words with which they
can do no good?
4 But you are doing away with
the fear of God,
and hindering meditation
before God.
5 For your iniquity teaches
your mouth,
and you choose the tongue
of the crafty.

p 13.26 Heb *inherit* q 14.6 Cn: Heb *that they may desist* r 14.16 Syr: Heb lacks *not*

6 Your own mouth condemns
you, and not I;
your own lips testify against you.
7 'Are you the firstborn of the
human race?
Were you brought forth
before the hills?
8 Have you listened in the
council of God?
And do you limit wisdom
to yourself?
9 What do you know that we
do not know?
What do you understand that
is not clear to us?
10 The grey-haired and the aged
are on our side,
those older than your father.
11 Are the consolations of God
too small for you,
or the word that deals
gently with you?
12 Why does your heart carry you away,
and why do your eyes flash,[s]
13 so that you turn your spirit
against God,
and let such words go out
of your mouth?
14 What are mortals, that they
can be clean?
Or those born of woman, that
they can be righteous?
15 God puts no trust even in
his holy ones,
and the heavens are not
clean in his sight;
16 how much less one who is
abominable and corrupt,
one who drinks iniquity
like water!

17 'I will show you; listen to me;
what I have seen I will declare—
18 what sages have told,
and their ancestors have
not hidden,
19 to whom alone the land was given,
and no stranger passed
among them.
20 The wicked writhe in pain
all their days,
through all the years that are
laid up for the ruthless.
21 Terrifying sounds are in their ears;
in prosperity the destroyer
will come upon them.
22 They despair of returning
from darkness,
and they are destined
for the sword.
23 They wander abroad for bread,
saying, "Where is it?"
They know that a day of darkness
is ready at hand;
24 distress and anguish terrify them;
they prevail against them, like a
king prepared for battle.
25 Because they stretched out their
hands against God,
and bid defiance to the Almighty,[t]
26 running stubbornly against him
with a thick-bossed shield;
27 because they have covered their
faces with their fat,
and gathered fat upon their loins,
28 they will live in desolate cities,
in houses that no one
should inhabit,
houses destined to become
heaps of ruins;
29 they will not be rich, and their
wealth will not endure,
nor will they strike root
in the earth;[u]
30 they will not escape from darkness;
the flame will dry up their shoots,
and their blossom[v] will be swept
away[w] by the wind.
31 Let them not trust in emptiness,
deceiving themselves;
for emptiness will be their
recompense.
32 It will be paid in full before
their time,
and their branch will
not be green.
33 They will shake off their unripe
grape, like the vine,
and cast off their blossoms,
like the olive tree.
34 For the company of the
godless is barren,
and fire consumes the
tents of bribery.
35 They conceive mischief and
bring forth evil
and their heart prepares deceit.'

JOB REAFFIRMS HIS INNOCENCE

16 Then Job answered:
2 'I have heard many
such things;
miserable comforters are you all.
3 Have windy words no limit?
Or what provokes you that
you keep on talking?

[s] 15.12 Meaning of Heb uncertain
[t] 15.25 Traditional rendering of Heb *Shaddai*
[u] 15.29 Vg: Meaning of Heb uncertain
[v] 15.30 Gk: Heb *mouth* [w] 15.30 Cn: Heb *will depart*

4 I also could talk as you do,
if you were in my place;
I could join words together
against you,
and shake my head at you.
5 I could encourage you with
my mouth,
and the solace of my lips would
assuage your pain.

6 'If I speak, my pain is not assuaged,
and if I forbear, how much
of it leaves me?
7 Surely now God has worn me out;
he has[x] made desolate all
my company.
8 And he has[y] shrivelled me up,
which is a witness against me;
my leanness has risen
up against me,
and it testifies to my face.
9 He has torn me in his wrath,
and hated me;
he has gnashed his teeth at me;
my adversary sharpens his
eyes against me.
10 They have gaped at me with
their mouths;
they have struck me insolently
on the cheek;
they mass themselves
together against me.
11 God gives me up to the ungodly,
and casts me into the hands
of the wicked.
12 I was at ease, and he broke
me in two;
he seized me by the neck and
dashed me to pieces;
he set me up as his target;
13 his archers surround me.
He slashes open my kidneys,
and shows no mercy;
he pours out my gall on
the ground.
14 He bursts upon me again and again;
he rushes at me like a warrior.
15 I have sewed sackcloth
upon my skin,
and have laid my strength
in the dust.
16 My face is red with weeping,
and deep darkness is on
my eyelids,
17 though there is no violence
in my hands,
and my prayer is pure.

18 'O earth, do not cover my blood;
let my outcry find no
resting-place.
19 Even now, in fact, my witness
is in heaven,
and he that vouches for
me is on high.
20 My friends scorn me;
my eye pours out tears to God,
21 that he would maintain the right
of a mortal with God,
as[z] one does for a neighbour.
22 For when a few years have come,
I shall go the way from which
I shall not return.

JOB PRAYS FOR RELIEF

17 My spirit is broken, my
days are extinct,
the grave is ready for me.
2 Surely there are mockers around me,
and my eye dwells on their
provocation.

3 'Lay down a pledge for me
with yourself;
who is there that will give
surety for me?
4 Since you have closed their minds
to understanding,
therefore you will not let
them triumph.
5 Those who denounce friends
for reward—
the eyes of their children will fail.

6 'He has made me a byword
of the peoples,
and I am one before whom
people spit.
7 My eye has grown dim from grief,
and all my members are
like a shadow.
8 The upright are appalled at this,
and the innocent stir themselves
up against the godless.
9 Yet the righteous hold to their way,
and they that have clean hands
grow stronger and stronger.
10 But you, come back now, all of you,
and I shall not find a sensible
person among you.
11 My days are past, my plans
are broken off,
the desires of my heart.
12 They make night into day;
"The light", they say, "is near
to the darkness."[a]
13 If I look for Sheol as my house,
if I spread my couch in darkness,

[x] 16.7 Heb *you have* [y] 16.8 Heb *you have*
[z] 16.21 Syr Vg Tg: Heb *and* [a] 17.12 Meaning of Heb uncertain

14 if I say to the Pit, "You are
my father",
and to the worm, "My mother",
or "My sister",
15 where then is my hope?
Who will see my hope?
16 Will it go down to the bars of Sheol?
Shall we descend together
into the dust?'

BILDAD SPEAKS: GOD PUNISHES THE WICKED

18 Then Bildad the Shuhite answered:
2 'How long will you hunt for words?
Consider, and then we shall speak.
3 Why are we counted as cattle?
Why are we stupid in your sight?
4 You who tear yourself in
your anger—
shall the earth be forsaken
because of you,
or the rock be removed
out of its place?

5 'Surely the light of the
wicked is put out,
and the flame of their fire
does not shine.
6 The light is dark in their tent,
and the lamp above them
is put out.
7 Their strong steps are shortened,
and their own schemes
throw them down.
8 For they are thrust into a net
by their own feet,
and they walk into a pitfall.
9 A trap seizes them by the heel;
a snare lays hold of them.
10 A rope is hid for them
in the ground,
a trap for them in the path.
11 Terrors frighten them on every side,
and chase them at their heels.
12 Their strength is consumed
by hunger,[b]
and calamity is ready for
their stumbling.
13 By disease their skin is consumed,[c]
the firstborn of Death
consumes their limbs.
14 They are torn from the tent in
which they trusted,
and are brought to the
king of terrors.
15 In their tents nothing remains;
sulphur is scattered upon
their habitations.
16 Their roots dry up beneath,
and their branches wither above.
17 Their memory perishes
from the earth,
and they have no name
in the street.
18 They are thrust from light
into darkness,
and driven out of the world.
19 They have no offspring or descendant
among their people,
and no survivor where
they used to live.
20 They of the west are appalled
at their fate,
and horror seizes those of the east.
21 Surely such are the dwellings
of the ungodly,
such is the place of those who
do not know God.'

JOB REPLIES: I KNOW THAT MY REDEEMER LIVES

19 Then Job answered:
2 'How long will you
torment me,
and break me in pieces
with words?
3 These ten times you have cast
reproach upon me;
are you not ashamed to
wrong me?
4 And even if it is true that
I have erred,
my error remains with me.
5 If indeed you magnify yourselves
against me,
and make my humiliation an
argument against me,
6 know then that God has put
me in the wrong,
and closed his net around me.
7 Even when I cry out, "Violence!"
I am not answered;
I call aloud, but there is no justice.
8 He has walled up my way so
that I cannot pass,
and he has set darkness
upon my paths.
9 He has stripped my glory from me,
and taken the crown
from my head.
10 He breaks me down on every
side, and I am gone,
he has uprooted my hope
like a tree.
11 He has kindled his wrath
against me,
and counts me as his adversary.

[b] **18.12** Or *Disaster is hungry for them*
[c] **18.13** Cn: Heb *It consumes the limbs of his skin*

12 His troops come on together;
they have thrown up
siege-works[d] against me,
and encamp around my tent.

13 'He has put my family far from me,
and my acquaintances are wholly
estranged from me.
14 My relatives and my close friends
have failed me;
15 the guests in my house
have forgotten me;
my serving-girls count me
as a stranger;
I have become an alien
in their eyes.
16 I call to my servant, but he
gives me no answer;
I must myself plead with him.
17 My breath is repulsive to my wife;
I am loathsome to
my own family.
18 Even young children despise me;
when I rise, they talk against me.
19 All my intimate friends abhor me,
and those whom I loved have
turned against me.
20 My bones cling to my skin
and to my flesh,
and I have escaped by the
skin of my teeth.
21 Have pity on me, have pity on
me, O you my friends,
for the hand of God has
touched me!
22 Why do you, like God, pursue me,
never satisfied with my flesh?

23 'O that my words were
written down!
O that they were inscribed
in a book!
24 O that with an iron pen
and with lead
they were engraved on
a rock for ever!
25 For I know that my
Redeemer[e] lives,
and that at the last he[f] will
stand upon the earth;[g]
26 and after my skin has been
thus destroyed,
then in[h] my flesh I shall see God,[i]
27 whom I shall see on my side,[j]
and my eyes shall behold,
and not another.
My heart faints within me!
28 If you say, "How we will
persecute him!"
and, "The root of the matter
is found in him";
29 be afraid of the sword,
for wrath brings the punishment
of the sword,
so that you may know there
is a judgement.'

ZOPHAR SPEAKS: WICKEDNESS RECEIVES JUST RETRIBUTION

20 Then Zophar the Naamathite
answered:
2 'Pay attention! My thoughts
urge me to answer,
because of the agitation within me.
3 I hear censure that insults me,
and a spirit beyond my
understanding answers me.
4 Do you not know this from of old,
ever since mortals were
placed on earth,
5 that the exulting of the
wicked is short,
and the joy of the godless is
but for a moment?
6 Even though they mount up
high as the heavens,
and their head reaches
to the clouds,
7 they will perish for ever like
their own dung;
those who have seen them will
say, "Where are they?"
8 They will fly away like a dream,
and not be found;
they will be chased away like
a vision of the night.
9 The eye that saw them will
see them no more,
nor will their place behold
them any longer.
10 Their children will seek the
favour of the poor,
and their hands will give
back their wealth.
11 Their bodies, once full of youth,
will lie down in the dust
with them.

12 'Though wickedness is sweet
in their mouth,
though they hide it under
their tongues,
13 though they are loath to let it go,
and hold it in their mouths,
14 yet their food is turned in
their stomachs;
it is the venom of asps
within them.

[d] 19.12 Cn: Heb *their way* [e] 19.25 Or *Vindicator*
[f] 19.25 Or *that he the Last* [g] 19.25 Heb *dust*
[h] 19.26 Or *without* [i] 19.26 Meaning of Heb of
this verse uncertain [j] 19.27 Or *for myself*

15 They swallow down riches and
vomit them up again;
God casts them out of their bellies.
16 They will suck the poison of asps;
the tongue of a viper
will kill them.
17 They will not look on the rivers,
the streams flowing with
honey and curds.
18 They will give back the fruit
of their toil,
and will not swallow it down;
from the profit of their trading
they will get no enjoyment.
19 For they have crushed and
abandoned the poor,
they have seized a house that
they did not build.

20 'They knew no quiet in their bellies;
in their greed they let
nothing escape.
21 There was nothing left after
they had eaten;
therefore their prosperity
will not endure.
22 In full sufficiency they will
be in distress;
all the force of misery will
come upon them.
23 To fill their belly to the full
God[k] will send his fierce
anger into them,
and rain it upon them
as their food.[l]
24 They will flee from an iron weapon;
a bronze arrow will strike
them through.
25 It is drawn forth and comes
out of their body,
and the glittering point comes
out of their gall;
terrors come upon them.
26 Utter darkness is laid up for
their treasures;
a fire fanned by no one
will devour them;
what is left in their tent
will be consumed.
27 The heavens will reveal
their iniquity,
and the earth will rise up
against them.
28 The possessions of their house
will be carried away,
dragged off on the day of
God's[m] wrath.
29 This is the portion of the
wicked from God,
the heritage decreed for
them by God.'

JOB REPLIES: THE WICKED OFTEN GO UNPUNISHED

21 Then Job answered:
2 'Listen carefully to my words,
and let this be your consolation.
3 Bear with me, and I will speak;
then after I have spoken, mock on.
4 As for me, is my complaint
addressed to mortals?
Why should I not be impatient?
5 Look at me, and be appalled,
and lay your hand upon
your mouth.
6 When I think of it I am dismayed,
and shuddering seizes my flesh.
7 Why do the wicked live on,
reach old age, and grow
mighty in power?
8 Their children are established
in their presence,
and their offspring before
their eyes.
9 Their houses are safe from fear,
and no rod of God is upon them.
10 Their bull breeds without fail;
their cow calves and never
miscarries.
11 They send out their little
ones like a flock,
and their children dance around.
12 They sing to the tambourine
and the lyre,
and rejoice to the sound
of the pipe.
13 They spend their days in prosperity,
and in peace they go
down to Sheol.
14 They say to God, "Leave us alone!
We do not desire to know
your ways.
15 What is the Almighty,[n] that we
should serve him?
And what profit do we get
if we pray to him?"
16 Is not their prosperity indeed their
own achievement?[o]
The plans of the wicked are
repugnant to me.

17 'How often is the lamp of the
wicked put out?
How often does calamity
come upon them?
How often does God[p] distribute
pains in his anger?

[k] 20.23 Heb *he* [l] 20.23 Cn: Meaning of Heb uncertain [m] 20.28 Heb *his* [n] 21.15 Traditional rendering of Heb *Shaddai* [o] 21.16 Heb *in their hand* [p] 21.17 Heb *he*

18 How often are they like straw
before the wind,
and like chaff that the storm
carries away?
19 You say, "God stores up their
iniquity for their children."
Let it be paid back to them, so
that they may know it.
20 Let their own eyes see their
destruction,
and let them drink of the wrath
of the Almighty.[q]
21 For what do they care for their
household after them,
when the number of their
months is cut off?
22 Will any teach God knowledge,
seeing that he judges those
that are on high?
23 One dies in full prosperity,
being wholly at ease and secure,
24 his loins full of milk
and the marrow of his bones moist.
25 Another dies in bitterness of soul,
never having tasted of good.
26 They lie down alike in the dust,
and the worms cover them.

27 'Oh, I know your thoughts,
and your schemes to wrong me.
28 For you say, "Where is the
house of the prince?
Where is the tent in which
the wicked lived?"
29 Have you not asked those who
travel the roads,
and do you not accept
their testimony,
30 that the wicked are spared on
the day of calamity,
and are rescued on the
day of wrath?
31 Who declares their way to their face,
and who repays them for
what they have done?
32 When they are carried to the grave,
a watch is kept over their tomb.
33 The clods of the valley are
sweet to them;
everyone will follow after,
and those who went before
are innumerable.
34 How then will you comfort me
with empty nothings?
There is nothing left of your
answers but falsehood.'

ELIPHAZ SPEAKS: JOB'S WICKEDNESS IS GREAT

22 Then Eliphaz the Temanite answered:

2 'Can a mortal be of use to God?
Can even the wisest be of
service to him?
3 Is it any pleasure to the Almighty[r]
if you are righteous,
or is it gain to him if you make
your ways blameless?
4 Is it for your piety that he
reproves you,
and enters into judgement
with you?
5 Is not your wickedness great?
There is no end to
your iniquities.
6 For you have exacted pledges from
your family for no reason,
and stripped the naked of
their clothing.
7 You have given no water to
the weary to drink,
and you have withheld bread
from the hungry.
8 The powerful possess the land,
and the favoured live in it.
9 You have sent widows away
empty-handed,
and the arms of the orphans
you have crushed.[s]
10 Therefore snares are around you,
and sudden terror
overwhelms you,
11 or darkness so that
you cannot see;
a flood of water covers you.

12 'Is not God high in the heavens?
See the highest stars, how
lofty they are!
13 Therefore you say, "What
does God know?
Can he judge through the
deep darkness?
14 Thick clouds enwrap him, so
that he does not see,
and he walks on the dome
of heaven."
15 Will you keep to the old way
that the wicked have trod?
16 They were snatched away
before their time;
their foundation was washed
away by a flood.
17 They said to God, "Leave us alone",
and "What can the Almighty[t]
do to us?"[u]

[q] **21.20** Traditional rendering of Heb *Shaddai*
[r] **22.3** Traditional rendering of Heb *Shaddai*
[s] **22.9** Gk Syr Tg Vg: Heb *were crushed*
[t] **22.17** Traditional rendering of Heb *Shaddai*
[u] **22.17** Gk Syr: Heb *them*

18 Yet he filled their houses with
good things—
but the plans of the wicked
are repugnant to me.
19 The righteous see it and are glad;
the innocent laugh
them to scorn,
20 saying, "Surely our adversaries
are cut off,
and what they left, the fire
has consumed."

21 'Agree with God,[v] and be at peace;
in this way good will come to you.
22 Receive instruction from his mouth,
and lay up his words
in your heart.
23 If you return to the Almighty,[w]
you will be restored,
if you remove unrighteousness
from your tents,
24 if you treat gold like dust,
and gold of Ophir like the stones
of the torrent-bed,
25 and if the Almighty[x] is your gold
and your precious silver,
26 then you will delight in the
Almighty,[y]
and lift up your face to God.
27 You will pray to him, and he
will hear you,
and you will pay your vows.
28 You will decide on a matter, and it
will be established for you,
and light will shine on your ways.
29 When others are humiliated,
you say it is pride;
for he saves the humble.
30 He will deliver even those
who are guilty;
they will escape because of the
cleanness of your hands.'[z]

JOB REPLIES: MY COMPLAINT IS BITTER

23 Then Job answered:
2 'Today also my complaint
is bitter;[a]
his[b] hand is heavy despite
my groaning.
3 O that I knew where I
might find him,
that I might come even
to his dwelling!
4 I would lay my case before him,
and fill my mouth with
arguments.
5 I would learn what he would
answer me,
and understand what he
would say to me.
6 Would he contend with me in the
greatness of his power?
No; but he would give heed to me.
7 There an upright person could
reason with him,
and I should be acquitted for
ever by my judge.

8 'If I go forward, he is not there;
or backward, I cannot
perceive him;
9 on the left he hides, and I
cannot behold him;
I turn[c] to the right, but I
cannot see him.
10 But he knows the way that I take;
when he has tested me, I shall
come out like gold.
11 My foot has held fast to his steps;
I have kept his way and have
not turned aside.
12 I have not departed from the
commandment of his lips;
I have treasured in[d] my bosom
the words of his mouth.
13 But he stands alone and who
can dissuade him?
What he desires, that he does.
14 For he will complete what he
appoints for me;
and many such things
are in his mind.
15 Therefore I am terrified at
his presence;
when I consider, I am in
dread of him.
16 God has made my heart faint;
the Almighty[e] has terrified me;
17 If only I could vanish in darkness,
and thick darkness would
cover my face![f]

JOB COMPLAINS OF VIOLENCE ON THE EARTH

24 'Why are times not kept
by the Almighty,[g]
and why do those who know
him never see his days?
2 The wicked[h] remove landmarks;
they seize flocks and
pasture them.

[v] 22.21 Heb *him* [w] 22.23 Traditional rendering of Heb *Shaddai* [x] 22.25 Traditional rendering of Heb *Shaddai* [y] 22.26 Traditional rendering of Heb *Shaddai* [z] 22.30 Meaning of Heb uncertain [a] 23.2 Syr Vg Tg: Heb *rebellious* [b] 23.2 Gk Syr: Heb *my* [c] 23.9 Syr Vg: Heb *he turns* [d] 23.12 Gk Vg: Heb *from* [e] 23.16 Traditional rendering of Heb *Shaddai* [f] 23.17 Or *But I am not destroyed by the darkness; he has concealed the thick darkness from me* [g] 24.1 Traditional rendering of Heb *Shaddai* [h] 24.2 Gk: Heb *they*

3 They drive away the donkey
of the orphan;
they take the widow's
ox for a pledge.
4 They thrust the needy off the road;
the poor of the earth all
hide themselves.
5 Like wild asses in the desert
they go out to their toil,
scavenging in the waste-land
food for their young.
6 They reap in a field not their own
and they glean in the vineyard
of the wicked.
7 They lie all night naked,
without clothing,
and have no covering
in the cold.
8 They are wet with the rain of
the mountains,
and cling to the rock for
want of shelter.

9 'There are those who snatch the
orphan child from the breast,
and take as a pledge the
infant of the poor.
10 They go about naked,
without clothing;
though hungry, they carry
the sheaves;
11 between their terraces[i] they
press out oil;
they tread the wine presses,
but suffer thirst.
12 From the city the dying groan,
and the throat of the wounded
cries for help;
yet God pays no attention
to their prayer.

13 'There are those who rebel
against the light,
who are not acquainted
with its ways,
and do not stay in its paths.
14 The murderer rises at dusk
to kill the poor and needy,
and in the night is like a thief.
15 The eye of the adulterer also
waits for the twilight,
saying, "No eye will see me";
and he disguises his face.
16 In the dark they dig
through houses;
by day they shut themselves up;
they do not know the light.
17 For deep darkness is morning
to all of them;
for they are friends with the
terrors of deep darkness.

18 'Swift are they on the face
of the waters;
their portion in the land is cursed;
no treader turns towards
their vineyards.
19 Drought and heat snatch away
the snow-waters;
so does Sheol those who
have sinned.
20 The womb forgets them;
the worm finds them sweet;
they are no longer remembered;
so wickedness is broken like a tree.

21 'They harm[j] the childless woman,
and do no good to the widow.
22 Yet God[k] prolongs the life of the
mighty by his power;
they rise up when they
despair of life.
23 He gives them security, and
they are supported;
his eyes are upon their ways.
24 They are exalted a little while,
and then are gone;
they wither and fade like
the mallow;[l]
they are cut off like the
heads of grain.
25 If it is not so, who will
prove me a liar,
and show that there is nothing
in what I say?'

BILDAD SPEAKS: HOW CAN A MORTAL BE RIGHTEOUS BEFORE GOD?

25 Then Bildad the Shuhite answered:
2 'Dominion and fear are with God;[m]
he makes peace in his
high heaven.
3 Is there any number to his armies?
Upon whom does his
light not arise?
4 How then can a mortal be
righteous before God?
How can one born of
woman be pure?
5 If even the moon is not bright
and the stars are not pure
in his sight,
6 how much less a mortal,
who is a maggot,
and a human being, who
is a worm!'

[i] 24.11 Meaning of Heb uncertain [j] 24.21 Gk Tg: Heb *feed on* or *associate with* [k] 24.22 Heb *he* [l] 24.24 Gk: Heb *like all others* [m] 25.2 Heb *him*

JOB REPLIES: GOD'S MAJESTY IS UNSEARCHABLE

26 Then Job answered:
2 'How you have helped one
who has no power!
How you have assisted the arm
that has no strength!
3 How you have counselled one
who has no wisdom,
and given much good advice!
4 With whose help have you
uttered words,
and whose spirit has come
forth from you?
5 The shades below tremble,
the waters and their inhabitants.
6 Sheol is naked before God,
and Abaddon has no covering.
7 He stretches out Zaphon[n]
over the void,
and hangs the earth
upon nothing.
8 He binds up the waters in
his thick clouds,
and the cloud is not torn
open by them.
9 He covers the face of the full moon,
and spreads over it his cloud.
10 He has described a circle on the
face of the waters,
at the boundary between
light and darkness.
11 The pillars of heaven tremble,
and are astounded at his rebuke.
12 By his power he stilled the Sea;
by his understanding he
struck down Rahab.
13 By his wind the heavens
were made fair;
his hand pierced the
fleeing serpent.
14 These are indeed but the
outskirts of his ways;
and how small a whisper
do we hear of him!
But the thunder of his power
who can understand?'

JOB MAINTAINS HIS INTEGRITY

27 Job again took up his discourse
and said:
2 'As God lives, who has taken
away my right,
and the Almighty,[o] who has
made my soul bitter,
3 as long as my breath is in me
and the spirit of God is
in my nostrils,
4 my lips will not speak falsehood,
and my tongue will not
utter deceit.
5 Far be it from me to say that
you are right;
until I die I will not put away
my integrity from me.
6 I hold fast my righteousness,
and will not let it go;
my heart does not reproach
me for any of my days.

7 'May my enemy be like the wicked,
and may my opponent be
like the unrighteous.
8 For what is the hope of the godless
when God cuts them off,
when God takes away their lives?
9 Will God hear their cry
when trouble comes upon them?
10 Will they take delight in the
Almighty?[p]
Will they call upon God
at all times?
11 I will teach you concerning
the hand of God;
that which is with the Almighty[q]
I will not conceal.
12 All of you have seen it yourselves;
why then have you become
altogether vain?

13 'This is the portion of the
wicked with God,
and the heritage that oppressors
receive from the Almighty:[r]
14 If their children are multiplied,
it is for the sword;
and their offspring have
not enough to eat.
15 Those who survive them the
pestilence buries,
and their widows make
no lamentation.
16 Though they heap up
silver like dust,
and pile up clothing like clay—
17 they may pile it up, but the
just will wear it,
and the innocent will
divide the silver.
18 They build their houses like nests,
like booths made by sentinels
of the vineyard.
19 They go to bed with wealth, but
will do so no more;
they open their eyes,
and it is gone.

[n] **26.7** Or *the north* [o] **27.2** Traditional rendering of Heb *Shaddai* [p] **27.10** Traditional rendering of Heb *Shaddai* [q] **27.11** Traditional rendering of Heb *Shaddai* [r] **27.13** Traditional rendering of Heb *Shaddai*

20 Terrors overtake them like a flood;
in the night a whirlwind
carries them off.
21 The east wind lifts them up
and they are gone;
it sweeps them out of their place.
22 It[s] hurls at them without pity;
they flee from its[t] power in
headlong flight.
23 It[u] claps its[v] hands at them,
and hisses at them from
its[w] place.

INTERLUDE: WHERE WISDOM IS FOUND

28 'Surely there is a mine for silver,
and a place for gold
to be refined.
2 Iron is taken out of the earth,
and copper is smelted from ore.
3 Miners put[x] an end to darkness,
and search out to the
farthest bound
the ore in gloom and
deep darkness.
4 They open shafts in a valley away
from human habitation;
they are forgotten by travellers,
they sway suspended,
remote from people.
5 As for the earth, out of it
comes bread;
but underneath it is turned
up as by fire.
6 Its stones are the place of sapphires,[y]
and its dust contains gold.

7 'That path no bird of prey knows,
and the falcon's eye has
not seen it.
8 The proud wild animals have
not trodden it;
the lion has not passed over it.

9 'They put their hand to the
flinty rock,
and overturn mountains
by the roots.
10 They cut out channels in the rocks,
and their eyes see every
precious thing.
11 The sources of the rivers
they probe;[z]
hidden things they bring to light.

12 'But where shall wisdom be found?
And where is the place of
understanding?
13 Mortals do not know the way to it,[a]
and it is not found in the
land of the living.
14 The deep says, "It is not in me",
and the sea says, "It is
not with me."
15 It cannot be bought for gold,
and silver cannot be weighed
out as its price.
16 It cannot be valued in the
gold of Ophir,
in precious onyx or sapphire.[b]
17 Gold and glass cannot equal it,
nor can it be exchanged for
jewels of fine gold.
18 No mention shall be made of
coral or of crystal;
the price of wisdom is above pearls.
19 The chrysolite of Ethiopia[c] cannot
compare with it,
nor can it be valued in pure gold.

20 'Where then does wisdom come from?
And where is the place of
understanding?
21 It is hidden from the eyes of all living,
and concealed from the
birds of the air.
22 Abaddon and Death say,
"We have heard a rumour
of it with our ears."

23 'God understands the way to it,
and he knows its place.
24 For he looks to the ends of the earth,
and sees everything under
the heavens.
25 When he gave to the wind its weight,
and apportioned out the
waters by measure;
26 when he made a decree for the rain,
and a way for the thunderbolt;
27 then he saw it and declared it;
he established it, and
searched it out.
28 And he said to humankind,
"Truly, the fear of the Lord,
that is wisdom;
and to depart from evil is
understanding."'

JOB FINISHES HIS DEFENCE

29 Job again took up his discourse
and said:
2 'O that I were as in the
months of old,
as in the days when God
watched over me;

s 27.22 Or *He* (that is God) t 27.22 Or *his*
u 27.23 Or *He* (that is God) v 27.23 Or *his*
w 27.23 Or *his* x 28.3 Heb *He puts* y 28.6 Or *lapis lazuli* z 28.11 Gk Vg: Heb *bind*
a 28.13 Gk: Heb *its price* b 28.16 Or *lapis lazuli*
c 28.19 Or *Nubia*; Heb *Cush*

3 when his lamp shone over my head,
and by his light I walked
through darkness;
4 when I was in my prime,
when the friendship of God
was upon my tent;
5 when the Almighty[d] was
still with me,
when my children were
around me;
6 when my steps were washed
with milk,
and the rock poured out for
me streams of oil!
7 When I went out to the
gate of the city,
when I took my seat in the square,
8 the young men saw me
and withdrew,
and the aged rose up and stood;
9 the nobles refrained from talking,
and laid their hands on
their mouths;
10 the voices of princes were hushed,
and their tongues stuck to the
roof of their mouths.
11 When the ear heard, it
commended me,
and when the eye saw,
it approved;
12 because I delivered the poor
who cried,
and the orphan who
had no helper.
13 The blessing of the wretched
came upon me,
and I caused the widow's
heart to sing for joy.
14 I put on righteousness, and
it clothed me;
my justice was like a robe
and a turban.
15 I was eyes to the blind,
and feet to the lame.
16 I was a father to the needy,
and I championed the cause
of the stranger.
17 I broke the fangs of
the unrighteous,
and made them drop their
prey from their teeth.
18 Then I thought, "I shall die
in my nest,
and I shall multiply my days
like the phoenix;[e]
19 my roots spread out to the waters,
with the dew all night on
my branches;
20 my glory was fresh with me,
and my bow ever new
in my hand."
21 'They listened to me, and waited,
and kept silence for my counsel.
22 After I spoke they did not
speak again,
and my word dropped upon
them like dew.[f]
23 They waited for me as for the rain;
they opened their mouths as
for the spring rain.
24 I smiled on them when they
had no confidence;
and the light of my countenance
they did not extinguish.[g]
25 I chose their way, and sat as chief,
and I lived like a king
among his troops,
like one who comforts mourners.

30 'But now they make
sport of me,
those who are younger than I,
whose fathers I would have
disdained
to set with the dogs of my flock.
2 What could I gain from the
strength of their hands?
All their vigour is gone.
3 Through want and hard hunger
they gnaw the dry and
desolate ground,
4 they pick mallow and the
leaves of bushes,
and to warm themselves
the roots of broom.
5 They are driven out from society;
people shout after them
as after a thief.
6 In the gullies of wadis they
must live,
in holes in the ground,
and in the rocks.
7 Among the bushes they bray;
under the nettles they
huddle together.
8 A senseless, disreputable brood,
they have been whipped
out of the land.

9 'And now they mock me in song;
I am a byword to them.
10 They abhor me, they keep
aloof from me;
they do not hesitate to spit
at the sight of me.
11 Because God has loosed my
bowstring and humbled me,
they have cast off restraint
in my presence.

[d] 29.5 Traditional rendering of Heb *Shaddai*
[e] 29.18 Or *like sand* [f] 29.22 Heb lacks *like dew*
[g] 29.24 Meaning of Heb uncertain

12 On my right hand the rabble rise up;
they send me sprawling,
and build roads for my ruin.
13 They break up my path,
they promote my calamity;
no one restrains[h] them.
14 As through a wide breach they come;
amid the crash they roll on.
15 Terrors are turned upon me;
my honour is pursued as
by the wind,
and my prosperity has passed
away like a cloud.

16 'And now my soul is poured
out within me;
days of affliction have
taken hold of me.
17 The night racks my bones,
and the pain that gnaws
me takes no rest.
18 With violence he seizes my garment;[i]
he grasps me by[j] the collar
of my tunic.
19 He has cast me into the mire,
and I have become like
dust and ashes.
20 I cry to you and you do not
answer me;
I stand, and you merely
look at me.
21 You have turned cruel to me;
with the might of your hand
you persecute me.
22 You lift me up on the wind, you
make me ride on it,
and you toss me about in the
roar of the storm.
23 I know that you will bring
me to death,
and to the house appointed
for all living.

24 'Surely one does not turn
against the needy,[k]
when in disaster they cry for help.[l]
25 Did I not weep for those whose
day was hard?
Was not my soul grieved
for the poor?
26 But when I looked for good,
evil came;
and when I waited for light,
darkness came.
27 My inward parts are in turmoil,
and are never still;
days of affliction come
to meet me.
28 I go about in sunless gloom;
I stand up in the assembly
and cry for help.
29 I am a brother of jackals,
and a companion of ostriches.
30 My skin turns black and
falls from me,
and my bones burn with heat.
31 My lyre is turned to mourning,
and my pipe to the voice of
those who weep.

31

'I have made a covenant
with my eyes;
how then could I look
upon a virgin?
2 What would be my portion
from God above,
and my heritage from the
Almighty[m] on high?
3 Does not calamity befall the
unrighteous,
and disaster the workers
of iniquity?
4 Does he not see my ways,
and number all my steps?

5 'If I have walked with falsehood,
and my foot has hurried
to deceit—
6 let me be weighed in a just balance,
and let God know my integrity!—
7 if my step has turned aside
from the way,
and my heart has followed
my eyes,
and if any spot has clung
to my hands;
8 then let me sow, and another eat;
and let what grows for me
be rooted out.

9 'If my heart has been enticed
by a woman,
and I have lain in wait at my
neighbour's door;
10 then let my wife grind for another,
and let other men kneel over her.
11 For that would be a heinous crime;
that would be a criminal offence;
12 for that would be a fire consuming
down to Abaddon,
and it would burn to the
root all my harvest.

13 'If I have rejected the cause of my
male or female slaves,
when they brought a
complaint against me;

[h] 30.13 Cn: Heb *helps* [i] 30.18 Gk: Heb *my garment is disfigured* [j] 30.18 Heb *like* [k] 30.24 Heb *ruin* [l] 30.24 Cn: Meaning of Heb uncertain [m] 31.2 Traditional rendering of Heb *Shaddai*

14 what then shall I do when
God rises up?
When he makes inquiry, what
shall I answer him?
15 Did not he who made me in the
womb make them?
And did not one fashion
us in the womb?

16 'If I have withheld anything
that the poor desired,
or have caused the eyes of
the widow to fail,
17 or have eaten my morsel alone,
and the orphan has not
eaten from it—
18 for from my youth I reared the
orphan[n] like a father,
and from my mother's womb
I guided the widow[o]—
19 if I have seen anyone perish
for lack of clothing,
or a poor person without covering,
20 whose loins have not blessed me,
and who was not warmed with
the fleece of my sheep;
21 if I have raised my hand
against the orphan,
because I saw I had supporters
at the gate;
22 then let my shoulder blade fall
from my shoulder,
and let my arm be broken
from its socket.
23 For I was in terror of calamity
from God,
and I could not have faced
his majesty.

24 'If I have made gold my trust,
or called fine gold my confidence;
25 if I have rejoiced because my
wealth was great,
or because my hand had
acquired much;
26 if I have looked at the sun[p]
when it shone,
or the moon moving in splendour,
27 and my heart has been
secretly enticed,
and my mouth has kissed
my hand;
28 this also would be an iniquity to be
punished by the judges,
for I should have been false
to God above.

29 'If I have rejoiced at the ruin of
those who hated me,
or exulted when evil
overtook them—
30 I have not let my mouth sin
by asking for their lives
with a curse—
31 if those of my tent ever said,
"O that we might be sated
with his flesh!"[q]—
32 the stranger has not lodged
in the street;
I have opened my doors
to the traveller—
33 if I have concealed my transgressions
as others do,[r]
by hiding my iniquity
in my bosom,
34 because I stood in great fear
of the multitude,
and the contempt of families
terrified me,
so that I kept silence, and did
not go out of doors—
35 O that I had one to hear me!
(Here is my signature! Let the
Almighty[s] answer me!)
O that I had the indictment
written by my adversary!
36 Surely I would carry it on
my shoulder;
I would bind it on me
like a crown;
37 I would give him an account
of all my steps;
like a prince I would
approach him.

38 'If my land has cried out
against me,
and its furrows have
wept together;
39 if I have eaten its yield
without payment,
and caused the death
of its owners;
40 let thorns grow instead of wheat,
and foul weeds instead of barley.'

The words of Job are ended.

ELIHU REBUKES JOB'S FRIENDS

32 So these three men ceased to answer Job, because he was righteous in his own eyes. 2Then Elihu son
of Barachel the Buzite, of the family of
Ram, became angry. He was angry at
Job because he justified himself rather
than God; 3he was angry also at Job's
three friends because they had found
no answer, though they had declared

[n] **31.18** Heb *him* [o] **31.18** Heb *her*
[p] **31.26** Heb *the light* [q] **31.31** Meaning of Heb
uncertain [r] **31.33** Or *as Adam did*
[s] **31.35** Traditional rendering of Heb *Shaddai*

Job to be in the wrong.[t] 4Now Elihu
had waited to speak to Job, because they
were older than he. 5But when Elihu saw
that there was no answer in the mouths
of these three men, he became angry.

6 Elihu son of Barachel the Buzite answered:

'I am young in years,
and you are aged;
therefore I was timid and afraid
to declare my opinion to you.
7 I said, "Let days speak,
and many years teach wisdom."
8 But truly it is the spirit in a mortal,
the breath of the Almighty,[u] that
makes for understanding.
9 It is not the old[v] that are wise,
nor the aged that understand
what is right.
10 Therefore I say, "Listen to me;
let me also declare my opinion."

11 'See, I waited for your words,
I listened for your wise sayings,
while you searched out
what to say.
12 I gave you my attention,
but there was in fact no one
that confuted Job,
no one among you that
answered his words.
13 Yet do not say, "We have
found wisdom;
God may vanquish him,
not a human."
14 He has not directed his words
against me,
and I will not answer him
with your speeches.

15 'They are dismayed, they
answer no more;
they have not a word to say.
16 And am I to wait, because
they do not speak,
because they stand there, and
answer no more?
17 I also will give my answer;
I also will declare my opinion.
18 For I am full of words;
the spirit within me
constrains me.
19 My heart is indeed like wine
that has no vent;
like new wineskins, it is
ready to burst.
20 I must speak, so that I may find relief;
I must open my lips and answer.
21 I will not show partiality
to any person
or use flattery towards anyone.
22 For I do not know how to flatter—
or my Maker would soon
put an end to me!

ELIHU REBUKES JOB

33 'But now, hear my
speech, O Job,
and listen to all my words.
2 See, I open my mouth;
the tongue in my mouth speaks.
3 My words declare the uprightness
of my heart,
and what my lips know they
speak sincerely.
4 The spirit of God has made me,
and the breath of the Almighty[w]
gives me life.
5 Answer me, if you can;
set your words in order before
me; take your stand.
6 See, before God I am as you are;
I too was formed from
a piece of clay.
7 No fear of me need terrify you;
my pressure will not be
heavy on you.

8 'Surely, you have spoken in
my hearing,
and I have heard the sound
of your words.
9 You say, "I am clean, without
transgression;
I am pure, and there is no
iniquity in me.
10 Look, he finds occasions against me,
he counts me as his enemy;
11 he puts my feet in the stocks,
and watches all my paths."

12 'But in this you are not right.
I will answer you:
God is greater than any mortal.
13 Why do you contend against him,
saying, "He will answer none
of my[x] words"?
14 For God speaks in one way,
and in two, though people
do not perceive it.
15 In a dream, in a vision of the night,
when deep sleep falls on mortals,
while they slumber on their beds,
16 then he opens their ears,
and terrifies them
with warnings,

[t] **32.3** Another ancient tradition reads *answer, and had put God in the wrong* [u] **32.8** Traditional rendering of Heb *Shaddai* [v] **32.9** Gk Syr Vg: Heb *many* [w] **33.4** Traditional rendering of Heb *Shaddai* [x] **33.13** Compare Gk: Heb *his*

17 that he may turn them aside
from their deeds,
and keep them from pride,
18 to spare their souls from the Pit,
their lives from traversing
the River.
19 They are also chastened with
pain upon their beds,
and with continual strife
in their bones,
20 so that their lives loathe bread,
and their appetites
dainty food.
21 Their flesh is so wasted away
that it cannot be seen;
and their bones, once invisible,
now stick out.
22 Their souls draw near the Pit,
and their lives to those
who bring death.
23 Then, if there should be for one
of them an angel,
a mediator, one of a thousand,
one who declares a
person upright,
24 and he is gracious to that
person, and says,
"Deliver him from going
down into the Pit;
I have found a ransom;
25 let his flesh become fresh
with youth;
let him return to the days of
his youthful vigour";
26 then he prays to God, and is
accepted by him,
he comes into his presence
with joy,
and God[y] repays him for his
righteousness.
27 That person sings to
others and says,
"I sinned, and perverted
what was right,
and it was not paid back to me.
28 He has redeemed my soul from
going down to the Pit,
and my life shall see the light."

29 'God indeed does all these things,
twice, three times,
with mortals,
30 to bring back their souls
from the Pit,
so that they may see the
light of life.[z]
31 Pay heed, Job, listen to me;
be silent, and I will speak.
32 If you have anything to say,
answer me;
speak, for I desire to justify you.
33 If not, listen to me;
be silent, and I will teach
you wisdom.'

ELIHU PROCLAIMS GOD'S JUSTICE

34 Then Elihu continued and said:
2 'Hear my words, you
wise men,
and give ear to me, you
who know;
3 for the ear tests words
as the palate tastes food.
4 Let us choose what is right;
let us determine among
ourselves what is good.
5 For Job has said, "I am innocent,
and God has taken away my right;
6 in spite of being right I am
counted a liar;
my wound is incurable, though I
am without transgression."
7 Who is there like Job,
who drinks up scoffing like water,
8 who goes in company with evildoers
and walks with the wicked?
9 For he has said, "It profits
one nothing
to take delight in God."

10 'Therefore, hear me, you
who have sense,
far be it from God that he
should do wickedness,
and from the Almighty[a] that
he should do wrong.
11 For according to their deeds
he will repay them,
and according to their ways he
will make it befall them.
12 Of a truth, God will not do wickedly,
and the Almighty[b] will not
pervert justice.
13 Who gave him charge over the earth
and who laid on him[c] the
whole world?
14 If he should take back his
spirit[d] to himself,
and gather to himself his breath,
15 all flesh would perish together,
and all mortals return to dust.

16 'If you have understanding,
hear this;
listen to what I say.

[y] **33.26** Heb *he* [z] **33.30** Syr: Heb *to be lighted with the light of life* [a] **34.10** Traditional rendering of Heb *Shaddai* [b] **34.12** Traditional rendering of Heb *Shaddai* [c] **34.13** Heb lacks *on him* [d] **34.14** Heb *his heart his spirit*

17 Shall one who hates justice govern?
Will you condemn one who is
righteous and mighty,
18 who says to a king, "You scoundrel!"
and to princes, "You
wicked men!";
19 who shows no partiality to nobles,
nor regards the rich more
than the poor,
for they are all the work
of his hands?
20 In a moment they die;
at midnight the people are
shaken and pass away,
and the mighty are taken away
by no human hand.

21 'For his eyes are upon the
ways of mortals,
and he sees all their steps.
22 There is no gloom or deep darkness
where evildoers may hide
themselves.
23 For he has not appointed a
time[e] for anyone
to go before God in judgement.
24 He shatters the mighty without
investigation,
and sets others in their place.
25 Thus, knowing their works,
he overturns them in the night,
and they are crushed.
26 He strikes them for their wickedness
while others look on,
27 because they turned aside from
following him,
and had no regard for
any of his ways,
28 so that they caused the cry of the
poor to come to him,
and he heard the cry of
the afflicted—
29 When he is quiet, who can condemn?
When he hides his face, who
can behold him,
whether it be a nation or
an individual?—
30 so that the godless should
not reign,
or those who ensnare the people.

31 'For has anyone said to God,
"I have endured punishment; I
will not offend any more;
32 teach me what I do not see;
if I have done iniquity, I
will do it no more"?
33 Will he then pay back to suit you,
because you reject it?
For you must choose, and not I;
therefore declare what you know.[f]
34 Those who have sense will say to me,
and the wise who hear me will say,
35 "Job speaks without knowledge,
his words are without insight."
36 Would that Job were tried
to the limit,
because his answers are
those of the wicked.
37 For he adds rebellion to his sin;
he claps his hands among us,
and multiplies his words
against God.'

ELIHU CONDEMNS SELF-RIGHTEOUSNESS

35 Elihu continued and said:
2 'Do you think this to be just?
You say, "I am in the right
before God."
3 If you ask, "What advantage have I?
How am I better off than
if I had sinned?"
4 I will answer you
and your friends with you.
5 Look at the heavens and see;
observe the clouds, which
are higher than you.
6 If you have sinned, what do you
accomplish against him?
And if your transgressions
are multiplied, what
do you do to him?
7 If you are righteous, what do
you give to him;
or what does he receive
from your hand?
8 Your wickedness affects
others like you,
and your righteousness, other
human beings.

9 'Because of the multitude of
oppressions people cry out;
they call for help because of
the arm of the mighty.
10 But no one says, "Where is
God my Maker,
who gives strength in the night,
11 who teaches us more than the
animals of the earth,
and makes us wiser than the
birds of the air?"
12 There they cry out, but he
does not answer,
because of the pride of evildoers.
13 Surely God does not hear an empty cry,
nor does the Almighty[g] regard it.

[e] 34.23 Cn: Heb *yet* [f] 34.33 Meaning of Heb of verses 29–33 uncertain [g] 35.13 Traditional rendering of Heb *Shaddai*

14 How much less when you say that
you do not see him,
that the case is before him, and
you are waiting for him!
15 And now, because his anger
does not punish,
and he does not greatly heed
transgression,[h]
16 Job opens his mouth in empty talk,
he multiplies words without
knowledge.'

ELIHU EXALTS GOD'S GOODNESS

36 Elihu continued and said:
2 'Bear with me a little,
and I will show you,
for I have yet something to
say on God's behalf.
3 I will bring my knowledge
from far away,
and ascribe righteousness
to my Maker.
4 For truly my words are not false;
one who is perfect in
knowledge is with you.

5 'Surely God is mighty and does
not despise any;
he is mighty in strength
of understanding.
6 He does not keep the wicked alive,
but gives the afflicted
their right.
7 He does not withdraw his eyes
from the righteous,
but with kings on the throne
he sets them for ever, and
they are exalted.
8 And if they are bound in fetters
and caught in the cords
of affliction,
9 then he declares to them their work
and their transgressions,
that they are behaving
arrogantly.
10 He opens their ears to instruction,
and commands that they
return from iniquity.
11 If they listen, and serve him,
they complete their days
in prosperity,
and their years in pleasantness.
12 But if they do not listen, they shall
perish by the sword,
and die without knowledge.

13 'The godless in heart cherish anger;
they do not cry for help when
he binds them.
14 They die in their youth,
and their life ends in shame.[i]
15 He delivers the afflicted by
their affliction,
and opens their ear by adversity.
16 He also allured you out of distress
into a broad place where there
was no constraint,
and what was set on your table
was full of fatness.

17 'But you are obsessed with the
case of the wicked;
judgement and justice seize you.
18 Beware that wrath does not
entice you into scoffing,
and do not let the greatness of
the ransom turn you aside.
19 Will your cry avail to keep
you from distress,
or will all the force of
your strength?
20 Do not long for the night,
when peoples are cut off
in their place.
21 Beware! Do not turn to iniquity;
because of that you have been
tried by affliction.
22 See, God is exalted in his power;
who is a teacher like him?
23 Who has prescribed for him his way,
or who can say, "You have
done wrong"?

ELIHU PROCLAIMS GOD'S MAJESTY

24 'Remember to extol his work,
of which mortals have sung.
25 All people have looked on it;
everyone watches it
from far away.
26 Surely God is great, and we
do not know him;
the number of his years
is unsearchable.
27 For he draws up the drops of water;
he distils[j] his mist in rain,
28 which the skies pour down
and drop upon mortals
abundantly.
29 Can anyone understand the
spreading of the clouds,
the thunderings of his pavilion?
30 See, he scatters his lightning
around him
and covers the roots of the sea.
31 For by these he governs peoples;
he gives food in abundance.

[h] **35.15** Theodotion Symmachus Compare Vg: Meaning of Heb uncertain [i] **36.14** Heb *ends among the temple prostitutes* [j] **36.27** Cn: Heb *they distil*

32 He covers his hands with
the lightning,
and commands it to
strike the mark.
33 Its crashing[k] tells about him;
he is jealous[l] with anger
against iniquity.

37 'At this also my
heart trembles,
and leaps out of its place.
2 Listen, listen to the thunder
of his voice
and the rumbling that comes
from his mouth.
3 Under the whole heaven
he lets it loose,
and his lightning to the
corners of the earth.
4 After it his voice roars;
he thunders with his
majestic voice
and he does not restrain
the lightnings[m] when
his voice is heard.
5 God thunders wondrously
with his voice;
he does great things that we
cannot comprehend.
6 For to the snow he says, "Fall
on the earth";
and the shower of rain, his
heavy shower of rain,
7 serves as a sign on everyone's hand,
so that all whom he has
made may know it.[n]
8 Then the animals go
into their lairs
and remain in their dens.
9 From its chamber comes
the whirlwind,
and cold from the
scattering winds.
10 By the breath of God ice is given,
and the broad waters
are frozen fast.
11 He loads the thick cloud
with moisture;
the clouds scatter his lightning.
12 They turn round and round
by his guidance,
to accomplish all that he
commands them
on the face of the habitable world.
13 Whether for correction, or
for his land,
or for love, he causes it to happen.

14 'Hear this, O Job;
stop and consider the wondrous
works of God.
15 Do you know how God lays his
command upon them,
and causes the lightning of
his cloud to shine?
16 Do you know the balancings
of the clouds,
the wondrous works of the one
whose knowledge is perfect,
17 you whose garments are hot
when the earth is still because
of the south wind?
18 Can you, like him, spread
out the skies,
unyielding as a cast mirror?
19 Teach us what we shall say to him;
we cannot draw up our case
because of darkness.
20 Should he be told that I
want to speak?
Did anyone ever wish to
be swallowed up?
21 Now, no one can look on the light
when it is bright in the skies,
when the wind has passed
and cleared them.
22 Out of the north comes
golden splendour;
around God is awesome majesty.
23 The Almighty[o]—we cannot
find him;
he is great in power and justice,
and abundant righteousness
he will not violate.
24 Therefore mortals fear him;
he does not regard any who are
wise in their own conceit.'

THE LORD ANSWERS JOB

38 Then the LORD answered Job
out of the whirlwind:
2 'Who is this that darkens counsel by
words without knowledge?
3 Gird up your loins like a man,
I will question you, and you
shall declare to me.

4 'Where were you when I laid the
foundation of the earth?
Tell me, if you have
understanding.
5 Who determined its
measurements—
surely you know!
Or who stretched the line upon it?
6 On what were its bases sunk,
or who laid its cornerstone

[k] 36.33 Meaning of Heb uncertain
[l] 36.33 Meaning of Heb uncertain [m] 37.4 Heb *them* [n] 37.7 Meaning of Heb of verse 7 uncertain [o] 37.23 Traditional rendering of Heb *Shaddai*

7 when the morning stars
sang together
and all the heavenly beings[p]
shouted for joy?

8 'Or who shut in the sea with doors
when it burst out from
the womb?—
9 when I made the clouds its garment,
and thick darkness its
swaddling band,
10 and prescribed bounds for it,
and set bars and doors,
11 and said, "Thus far shall you
come, and no farther,
and here shall your proud
waves be stopped"?

12 'Have you commanded the morning
since your days began,
and caused the dawn to
know its place,
13 so that it might take hold of the
skirts of the earth,
and the wicked be shaken
out of it?
14 It is changed like clay under the seal,
and it is dyed[q] like a garment.
15 Light is withheld from the wicked,
and their uplifted arm is broken.

16 'Have you entered into the
springs of the sea,
or walked in the recesses
of the deep?
17 Have the gates of death been
revealed to you,
or have you seen the gates
of deep darkness?
18 Have you comprehended the
expanse of the earth?
Declare, if you know all this.

19 'Where is the way to the
dwelling of light,
and where is the place of darkness,
20 that you may take it to its territory
and that you may discern the
paths to its home?
21 Surely you know, for you
were born then,
and the number of your
days is great!

22 'Have you entered the storehouses
of the snow,
or have you seen the
storehouses of the hail,
23 which I have reserved for the
time of trouble,
for the day of battle and war?
24 What is the way to the place where
the light is distributed,
or where the east wind is
scattered upon the earth?

25 'Who has cut a channel for the
torrents of rain,
and a way for the thunderbolt,
26 to bring rain on a land where
no one lives,
on the desert, which is
empty of human life,
27 to satisfy the waste and
desolate land,
and to make the ground
put forth grass?

28 'Has the rain a father,
or who has begotten the
drops of dew?
29 From whose womb did the
ice come forth,
and who has given birth to the
hoar-frost of heaven?
30 The waters become hard like stone,
and the face of the
deep is frozen.

31 'Can you bind the chains of
the Pleiades,
or loose the cords of Orion?
32 Can you lead forth the Mazzaroth
in their season,
or can you guide the Bear
with its children?
33 Do you know the ordinances
of the heavens?
Can you establish their
rule on the earth?

34 'Can you lift up your voice
to the clouds,
so that a flood of waters
may cover you?
35 Can you send forth lightnings,
so that they may go
and say to you, "Here we are"?
36 Who has put wisdom in the
inward parts,[r]
or given understanding
to the mind?[s]
37 Who has the wisdom to
number the clouds?
Or who can tilt the waterskins
of the heavens,
38 when the dust runs into a mass
and the clods cling together?

[p] **38.7** Heb *sons of God* [q] **38.14** Cn: Heb *and they stand forth* [r] **38.36** Meaning of Heb uncertain [s] **38.36** Meaning of Heb uncertain

39 'Can you hunt the prey for the lion,
or satisfy the appetite of
the young lions,
40 when they crouch in their dens,
or lie in wait in their covert?
41 Who provides for the raven its prey,
when its young ones cry to God,
and wander about for lack of food?

39 'Do you know when the
mountain goats give birth?
Do you observe the calving
of the deer?
2 Can you number the months
that they fulfil,
and do you know the time
when they give birth,
3 when they crouch to give birth
to their offspring,
and are delivered of their young?
4 Their young ones become strong,
they grow up in the open;
they go forth, and do not
return to them.

5 'Who has let the wild ass go free?
Who has loosed the bonds
of the swift ass,
6 to which I have given the
steppe for its home,
the salt land for its
dwelling-place?
7 It scorns the tumult of the city;
it does not hear the shouts
of the driver.
8 It ranges the mountains
as its pasture,
and it searches after every
green thing.

9 'Is the wild ox willing to serve you?
Will it spend the night
at your crib?
10 Can you tie it in the furrow
with ropes,
or will it harrow the
valleys after you?
11 Will you depend on it because
its strength is great,
and will you hand over
your labour to it?
12 Do you have faith in it that
it will return,
and bring your grain to your
threshing-floor?[t]

13 'The ostrich's wings flap wildly,
though its pinions lack plumage.[u]
14 For it leaves its eggs to the earth,
and lets them be warmed
on the ground,
15 forgetting that a foot may crush them,
and that a wild animal may
trample them.
16 It deals cruelly with its young, as
if they were not its own;
though its labour should be in
vain, yet it has no fear;
17 because God has made it
forget wisdom,
and given it no share in
understanding.
18 When it spreads its plumes aloft,[v]
it laughs at the horse and its rider.

19 'Do you give the horse its might?
Do you clothe its neck with mane?
20 Do you make it leap like the locust?
Its majestic snorting is terrible.
21 It paws[w] violently, exults mightily;
it goes out to meet the weapons.
22 It laughs at fear, and is not dismayed;
it does not turn back from
the sword.
23 Upon it rattle the quiver,
the flashing spear, and the javelin.
24 With fierceness and rage it
swallows the ground;
it cannot stand still at the
sound of the trumpet.
25 When the trumpet sounds,
it says "Aha!"
From a distance it smells the battle,
the thunder of the captains,
and the shouting.

26 'Is it by your wisdom that
the hawk soars,
and spreads its wings
towards the south?
27 Is it at your command that the
eagle mounts up
and makes its nest on high?
28 It lives on the rock and
makes its home
in the fastness of the rocky crag.
29 From there it spies the prey;
its eyes see it from far away.
30 Its young ones suck up blood;
and where the slain are, there it is.'

40 And the LORD said to Job:
2 'Shall a fault-finder contend
with the Almighty?[x]
Anyone who argues with
God must respond.'

[t] 39.12 Heb *your grain and your threshing-floor*
[u] 39.13 Meaning of Heb uncertain
[v] 39.18 Meaning of Heb uncertain [w] 39.21 Gk Syr Vg: Heb *they dig* [x] 40.2 Traditional rendering of Heb *Shaddai*

JOB'S RESPONSE TO GOD

3 Then Job answered the LORD:
4 'See, I am of small account; what
shall I answer you?
I lay my hand on my mouth.
5 I have spoken once, and I
will not answer;
twice, but will proceed
no further.'

GOD'S CHALLENGE TO JOB

6 Then the LORD answered Job out of
the whirlwind:
7 'Gird up your loins like a man;
I will question you, and
you declare to me.
8 Will you even put me in the wrong?
Will you condemn me that
you may be justified?
9 Have you an arm like God,
and can you thunder with
a voice like his?

10 'Deck yourself with majesty
and dignity;
clothe yourself with glory
and splendour.
11 Pour out the overflowings
of your anger,
and look on all who are proud,
and abase them.
12 Look on all who are proud, and
bring them low;
tread down the wicked
where they stand.
13 Hide them all in the dust together;
bind their faces in the
world below.[y]
14 Then I will also acknowledge to you
that your own right hand
can give you victory.

15 'Look at Behemoth,
which I made just as
I made you;
it eats grass like an ox.
16 Its strength is in its loins,
and its power in the
muscles of its belly.
17 It makes its tail stiff like a cedar;
the sinews of its thighs
are knit together.
18 Its bones are tubes of bronze,
its limbs like bars of iron.

19 'It is the first of the great
acts of God—
only its Maker can approach
it with the sword.
20 For the mountains yield food for it
where all the wild animals play.
21 Under the lotus plants it lies,
in the covert of the reeds
and in the marsh.
22 The lotus trees cover it for shade;
the willows of the wadi
surround it.
23 Even if the river is turbulent,
it is not frightened;
it is confident though Jordan
rushes against its mouth.
24 Can one take it with hooks[z]
or pierce its nose with a snare?

41[a] 'Can you draw out Leviathan[b]
with a fish-hook,
or press down its tongue
with a cord?
2 Can you put a rope in its nose,
or pierce its jaw with a hook?
3 Will it make many supplications
to you?
Will it speak soft words to you?
4 Will it make a covenant with you
to be taken as your
servant for ever?
5 Will you play with it as with a bird,
or will you put it on a leash
for your girls?
6 Will traders bargain over it?
Will they divide it up among
the merchants?
7 Can you fill its skin with harpoons,
or its head with fishing-spears?
8 Lay hands on it;
think of the battle; you will
not do it again!
9[c] Any hope of capturing it[d] will
be disappointed;
were not even the gods[e]
overwhelmed at
the sight of it?
10 No one is so fierce as to dare
to stir it up.
Who can stand before it?[f]
11 Who can confront it[g] and be safe?[h]
—under the whole heaven, who?[i]

12 'I will not keep silence
concerning its limbs,
or its mighty strength, or
its splendid frame.
13 Who can strip off its outer garment?
Who can penetrate its double
coat of mail?[j]

[y] 40.13 Heb *the hidden place* [z] 40.24 Cn: Heb *in his eyes* [a] 41.1 Ch 40.25 in Heb [b] 41.1 Or *the crocodile* [c] 41.9 Ch 41.1 in Heb [d] 41.9 Heb *of it* [e] 41.9 Cn Compare Symmachus Syr: Heb *one is* [f] 41.10 Heb *me* [g] 41.11 Heb *me* [h] 41.11 Gk: Heb *that I shall repay* [i] 41.11 Heb *to me* [j] 41.13 Gk: Heb *bridle*

14 Who can open the doors of its face?
There is terror all around its teeth.
15 Its back[k] is made of shields in rows,
shut up closely as with a seal.
16 One is so near to another
that no air can come between them.
17 They are joined one to another;
they clasp each other and
cannot be separated.
18 Its sneezes flash forth light,
and its eyes are like the
eyelids of the dawn.
19 From its mouth go flaming torches;
sparks of fire leap out.
20 Out of its nostrils comes smoke,
as from a boiling pot and
burning rushes.
21 Its breath kindles coals,
and a flame comes out of its mouth.
22 In its neck abides strength,
and terror dances before it.
23 The folds of its flesh cling together;
it is firmly cast and immovable.
24 Its heart is as hard as stone,
as hard as the lower millstone.
25 When it raises itself up the
gods are afraid;
at the crashing they are
beside themselves.
26 Though the sword reaches it,
it does not avail,
nor does the spear, the dart,
or the javelin.
27 It counts iron as straw,
and bronze as rotten wood.
28 The arrow cannot make it flee;
slingstones, for it, are
turned to chaff.
29 Clubs are counted as chaff;
it laughs at the rattle of javelins.
30 Its underparts are like sharp
potsherds;
it spreads itself like a
threshing-sledge on the mire.
31 It makes the deep boil like a pot;
it makes the sea like a pot
of ointment.
32 It leaves a shining wake behind it;
one would think the deep
to be white-haired.
33 On earth it has no equal,
a creature without fear.
34 It surveys everything that is lofty;
it is king over all that are proud.'

JOB IS HUMBLED AND SATISFIED

42 Then Job answered the LORD:
2 'I know that you can
do all things,
and that no purpose of yours
can be thwarted.
3 "Who is this that hides counsel
without knowledge?"
Therefore I have uttered what I
did not understand,
things too wonderful for me,
which I did not know.
4 "Hear, and I will speak;
I will question you, and
you declare to me."
5 I had heard of you by the
hearing of the ear,
but now my eye sees you;
6 therefore I despise myself,
and repent in dust and ashes.'

JOB'S FRIENDS ARE HUMILIATED

7 After the LORD had spoken these
words to Job, the LORD said to Eliphaz the Temanite: 'My wrath is kindled against you and against your two
friends; for you have not spoken of me
what is right, as my servant Job has.
8 Now therefore take seven bulls and
seven rams, and go to my servant Job,
and offer up for yourselves a burnt-offering; and my servant Job shall pray for
you, for I will accept his prayer not to
deal with you according to your folly; for
you have not spoken of me what is right,
as my servant Job has done.' 9 So Eliphaz
the Temanite and Bildad the Shuhite
and Zophar the Naamathite went and
did what the LORD had told them; and
the LORD accepted Job's prayer.

JOB'S FORTUNES ARE RESTORED TWOFOLD

10 And the LORD restored the fortunes of Job when he had prayed for his
friends; and the LORD gave Job twice
as much as he had before. 11 Then there
came to him all his brothers and sisters and all who had known him before, and they ate bread with him in his
house; they showed him sympathy and
comforted him for all the evil that the
LORD had brought upon him; and each
of them gave him a piece of money[l] and
a gold ring. 12 The LORD blessed the latter days of Job more than his beginning;
and he had fourteen thousand sheep,
six thousand camels, a thousand yoke of
oxen, and a thousand donkeys. 13 He also
had seven sons and three daughters.
14 He named the first Jemimah, the second Keziah, and the third Keren-hap-
puch. 15 In all the land there were no
women so beautiful as Job's daughters;

[k] 41.15 Cn Compare Gk Vg: Heb *pride*
[l] 42.11 Heb *a qesitah*

and their father gave them an inheritance along with their brothers. 16 After
this Job lived for one hundred and forty
years, and saw his children, and his children's children, four generations. 17 And
Job died, old and full of days.

The

PSALMS

The Psalms are a collection of 150 poetical songs associated with temple worship in Israel. The date of composition of the psalms varies over five centuries, but most were written during the monarchical period before the Babylonian exile. There is a long tradition that attributes the Psalms to David. In the final redaction of the Psalter, the collection is divided like the Pentateuch, into five books.

The Psalms can be read as inspirational readings or sung as hymns of praise and supplication to God. The Psalms are a treasury of prayers for communal and private devotion. Generally, the Psalms provide a daily sung or spoken responsorial to the First Reading at the Sunday and Weekday liturgies of the Roman Missal. All 150 Psalms are utilized throughout the Sunday and weekday liturgical calendar over a three-year cycle.

Book I (Psalms 1–41)

PSALM 1

THE TWO WAYS

1 Happy are those
who do not follow the advice
of the wicked,
or take the path that sinners tread,
or sit in the seat of scoffers;
2 but their delight is in the
law of the LORD,
and on his law they meditate
day and night.
3 They are like trees
planted by streams of water,
which yield their fruit in its season,
and their leaves do not wither.
In all that they do, they prosper.

4 The wicked are not so,
but are like chaff that the
wind drives away.
5 Therefore the wicked will not
stand in the judgement,
nor sinners in the congregation
of the righteous;
6 for the LORD watches over the
way of the righteous,
but the way of the wicked
will perish.

PSALM 2

GOD'S PROMISE TO HIS ANOINTED

1 Why do the nations conspire,
and the peoples plot in vain?
2 The kings of the earth set themselves,
and the rulers take counsel
together,
against the LORD and his
anointed, saying,
3 'Let us burst their bonds asunder,
and cast their cords from us.'

4 He who sits in the heavens laughs;
the LORD has them in derision.
5 Then he will speak to them
in his wrath,
and terrify them in his
fury, saying,
6 'I have set my king on Zion,
my holy hill.'

7 I will tell of the decree of the LORD:
He said to me, 'You are my son;
today I have begotten you.
8 Ask of me, and I will make the
nations your heritage,
and the ends of the earth
your possession.
9 You shall break them with
a rod of iron,
and dash them in pieces like
a potter's vessel.'

10 Now therefore, O kings, be wise;
be warned, O rulers of the earth.
11 Serve the LORD with fear,
with trembling 12kiss his feet,[a]
or he will be angry, and you will perish in the way;
for his wrath is quickly kindled.

Happy are all who take refuge in him.

PSALM 3

TRUST IN GOD UNDER ADVERSITY

A Psalm of David, when he fled from his son Absalom.

1 O LORD, how many are my foes!
Many are rising against me;
2 many are saying to me,
'There is no help for you[b] in God.' *Selah*

3 But you, O LORD, are a shield around me,
my glory, and the one who lifts up my head.
4 I cry aloud to the LORD,
and he answers me from his holy hill. *Selah*

5 I lie down and sleep;
I wake again, for the LORD sustains me.
6 I am not afraid of tens of thousands of people
who have set themselves against me all around.

7 Rise up, O LORD!
Deliver me, O my God!
For you strike all my enemies on the cheek;
you break the teeth of the wicked.

8 Deliverance belongs to the LORD;
may your blessing be on your people! *Selah*

PSALM 4

CONFIDENT PLEA FOR DELIVERANCE FROM ENEMIES

To the leader: with stringed instruments. A Psalm of David.

1 Answer me when I call,
O God of my right!
You gave me room when I was in distress.
Be gracious to me, and hear my prayer.

2 How long, you people, shall my honour suffer shame?
How long will you love vain words, and seek after lies? *Selah*
3 But know that the LORD has set apart the faithful for himself;
the LORD hears when I call to him.

4 When you are disturbed,[c] do not sin;
ponder it on your beds, and be silent. *Selah*
5 Offer right sacrifices,
and put your trust in the LORD.

6 There are many who say, 'O that we might see some good!
Let the light of your face shine on us, O LORD!'
7 You have put gladness in my heart
more than when their grain and wine abound.

8 I will both lie down and sleep in peace;
for you alone, O LORD, make me lie down in safety.

PSALM 5

TRUST IN GOD FOR DELIVERANCE FROM ENEMIES

To the leader: for the flutes. A Psalm of David.

1 Give ear to my words, O LORD;
give heed to my sighing.
2 Listen to the sound of my cry,
my King and my God,
for to you I pray.
3 O LORD, in the morning you hear my voice;
in the morning I plead my case to you, and watch.

4 For you are not a God who delights in wickedness;
evil will not sojourn with you.
5 The boastful will not stand before your eyes;
you hate all evildoers.
6 You destroy those who speak lies;
the LORD abhors the bloodthirsty and deceitful.

7 But I, through the abundance of your steadfast love,
will enter your house,

[a] **2.12** Cn: Meaning of Heb of verses 11b and 12a is uncertain [b] **3.2** Syr: Heb *him* [c] **4.4** Or *are angry*

I will bow down towards
your holy temple
in awe of you.
8 Lead me, O LORD, in your
righteousness
because of my enemies;
make your way straight before me.

9 For there is no truth in
their mouths;
their hearts are destruction;
their throats are open graves;
they flatter with their tongues.
10 Make them bear their guilt, O God;
let them fall by their
own counsels;
because of their many transgressions
cast them out,
for they have rebelled against you.

11 But let all who take refuge
in you rejoice;
let them ever sing for joy.
Spread your protection over them,
so that those who love your
name may exult in you.
12 For you bless the righteous, O LORD;
you cover them with favour
as with a shield.

PSALM 6

PRAYER FOR RECOVERY FROM GRAVE ILLNESS

To the leader: with stringed instruments; according to The Sheminith. A Psalm of David.

1 O LORD, do not rebuke me
in your anger,
or discipline me in your wrath.
2 Be gracious to me, O LORD, for
I am languishing;
O LORD, heal me, for my bones
are shaking with terror.
3 My soul also is struck with terror,
while you, O LORD—how long?

4 Turn, O LORD, save my life;
deliver me for the sake of
your steadfast love.
5 For in death there is no
remembrance of you;
in Sheol who can
give you praise?

6 I am weary with my moaning;
every night I flood my
bed with tears;
I drench my couch with
my weeping.
7 My eyes waste away because of grief;
they grow weak because
of all my foes.

8 Depart from me, all you
workers of evil,
for the LORD has heard the
sound of my weeping.
9 The LORD has heard my supplication;
the LORD accepts my prayer.
10 All my enemies shall be ashamed
and struck with terror;
they shall turn back, and in a
moment be put to shame.

PSALM 7

PLEA FOR HELP AGAINST PERSECUTORS

A Shiggaion of David, which he sang to the LORD concerning Cush, a Benjaminite.

1 O LORD my God, in you I take refuge;
save me from all my pursuers,
and deliver me,
2 or like a lion they will tear me apart;
they will drag me away, with
no one to rescue.

3 O LORD my God, if I have done this,
if there is wrong in my hands,
4 if I have repaid my ally with harm
or plundered my foe
without cause,
5 then let the enemy pursue
and overtake me,
trample my life to the ground,
and lay my soul in the dust. *Selah*

6 Rise up, O LORD, in your anger;
lift yourself up against the
fury of my enemies;
awake, O my God;[d] you have
appointed a judgement.
7 Let the assembly of the peoples
be gathered around you,
and over it take your
seat[e] on high.
8 The LORD judges the peoples;
judge me, O LORD, according
to my righteousness
and according to the integrity
that is in me.

9 O let the evil of the wicked
come to an end,
but establish the righteous,

[d] 7.6 Or *awake for me* [e] 7.7 Cn: Heb *return*

you who test the minds and hearts,
O righteous God.
10 God is my shield,
who saves the upright in heart.
11 God is a righteous judge,
and a God who has indignation
every day.

12 If one does not repent, God[f]
will whet his sword;
he has bent and strung his bow;
13 he has prepared his deadly weapons,
making his arrows fiery shafts.
14 See how they conceive evil,
and are pregnant with mischief,
and bring forth lies.
15 They make a pit, digging it out,
and fall into the hole that
they have made.
16 Their mischief returns upon
their own heads,
and on their own heads their
violence descends.

17 I will give to the LORD the thanks
due to his righteousness,
and sing praise to the name of
the LORD, the Most High.

PSALM 8

DIVINE MAJESTY AND HUMAN DIGNITY

To the leader: according to The Gittith. A Psalm of David.

1 O LORD, our Sovereign,
how majestic is your name
in all the earth!

You have set your glory above
the heavens.
2 Out of the mouths of
babes and infants
you have founded a bulwark
because of your foes,
to silence the enemy and
the avenger.

3 When I look at your heavens, the
work of your fingers,
the moon and the stars that
you have established;
4 what are human beings that you
are mindful of them,
mortals[g] that you care for them?

5 Yet you have made them a little
lower than God,[h]
and crowned them with
glory and honour.
6 You have given them dominion over
the works of your hands;
you have put all things
under their feet,
7 all sheep and oxen,
and also the beasts of the field,
8 the birds of the air, and the
fish of the sea,
whatever passes along the
paths of the seas.

9 O LORD, our Sovereign,
how majestic is your name
in all the earth!

PSALM 9

GOD'S POWER AND JUSTICE

To the leader: according to Muth-labben. A Psalm of David.

1 I will give thanks to the LORD
with my whole heart;
I will tell of all your
wonderful deeds.
2 I will be glad and exult in you;
I will sing praise to your
name, O Most High.

3 When my enemies turned back,
they stumbled and perished
before you.
4 For you have maintained
my just cause;
you have sat on the throne giving
righteous judgement.

5 You have rebuked the nations, you
have destroyed the wicked;
you have blotted out their
name for ever and ever.
6 The enemies have vanished in
everlasting ruins;
their cities you have rooted out;
the very memory of them
has perished.

7 But the LORD sits enthroned for ever,
he has established his throne
for judgement.
8 He judges the world with
righteousness;
he judges the peoples with equity.

9 The LORD is a stronghold for
the oppressed,
a stronghold in times of trouble.

[f] **7.12** Heb *he* [g] **8.4** Heb *ben adam*, lit. *son of man* [h] **8.5** *Or than the divine beings or angels*: Heb *elohim*

10 And those who know your name
put their trust in you,
for you, O LORD, have not forsaken
those who seek you.

11 Sing praises to the LORD, who
dwells in Zion.
Declare his deeds among
the peoples.
12 For he who avenges blood is
mindful of them;
he does not forget the cry
of the afflicted.

13 Be gracious to me, O LORD.
See what I suffer from those
who hate me;
you are the one who lifts me up
from the gates of death,
14 so that I may recount all your praises,
and, in the gates of daughter Zion,
rejoice in your deliverance.

15 The nations have sunk in the
pit that they made;
in the net that they hid has their
own foot been caught.
16 The LORD has made himself known,
he has executed judgement;
the wicked are snared in the
work of their own hands.
Higgaion. Selah

17 The wicked shall depart to Sheol,
all the nations that forget God.

18 For the needy shall not always
be forgotten,
nor the hope of the poor
perish for ever.

19 Rise up, O LORD! Do not let
mortals prevail;
let the nations be judged
before you.
20 Put them in fear, O LORD;
let the nations know that they are
only human. *Selah*

PSALM 10

PRAYER FOR DELIVERANCE FROM ENEMIES

1 Why, O LORD, do you stand far off?
Why do you hide yourself
in times of trouble?
2 In arrogance the wicked
persecute the poor—
let them be caught in the schemes
they have devised.

3 For the wicked boast of the
desires of their heart,
those greedy for gain curse and
renounce the LORD.
4 In the pride of their countenance
the wicked say, 'God
will not seek it out';
all their thoughts are,
'There is no God.'

5 Their ways prosper at all times;
your judgements are on high,
out of their sight;
as for their foes, they
scoff at them.
6 They think in their heart, 'We
shall not be moved;
throughout all generations we
shall not meet adversity.'

7 Their mouths are filled with cursing
and deceit and oppression;
under their tongues are
mischief and iniquity.
8 They sit in ambush in
the villages;
in hiding-places they murder
the innocent.

Their eyes stealthily watch
for the helpless;
9 they lurk in secret like a
lion in its covert;
they lurk that they may
seize the poor;
they seize the poor and drag
them off in their net.

10 They stoop, they crouch,
and the helpless fall by
their might.
11 They think in their heart,
'God has forgotten,
he has hidden his face, he
will never see it.'

12 Rise up, O LORD; O God, lift
up your hand;
do not forget the oppressed.
13 Why do the wicked renounce God,
and say in their hearts, 'You will
not call us to account'?

14 But you do see! Indeed you note
trouble and grief,
that you may take it into
your hands;
the helpless commit
themselves to you;
you have been the helper
of the orphan.

15 Break the arm of the wicked
and evildoers;
seek out their wickedness
until you find none.
16 The LORD is king for
ever and ever;
the nations shall perish
from his land.

17 O LORD, you will hear the
desire of the meek;
you will strengthen their heart,
you will incline your ear
18 to do justice for the orphan
and the oppressed,
so that those from earth may
strike terror no more.[i]

PSALM 11

SONG OF TRUST IN GOD

To the leader. Of David.

1 In the LORD I take refuge; how
can you say to me,
'Flee like a bird to the
mountains;[j]
2 for look, the wicked bend the bow,
they have fitted their arrow
to the string,
to shoot in the dark at the
upright in heart.
3 If the foundations are destroyed,
what can the righteous do?'

4 The LORD is in his holy temple;
the LORD's throne is in heaven.
His eyes behold, his gaze
examines humankind.
5 The LORD tests the righteous
and the wicked,
and his soul hates the
lover of violence.
6 On the wicked he will rain coals
of fire and sulphur;
a scorching wind shall be the
portion of their cup.
7 For the LORD is righteous;
he loves righteous deeds;
the upright shall behold his face.

PSALM 12

PLEA FOR HELP IN EVIL TIMES

To the leader: according to The Sheminith. A Psalm of David.

1 Help, O LORD, for there is no longer
anyone who is godly;
the faithful have disappeared
from humankind.
2 They utter lies to each other;
with flattering lips and a
double heart they speak.

3 May the LORD cut off all
flattering lips,
the tongue that makes
great boasts,
4 those who say, 'With our tongues
we will prevail;
our lips are our own—who
is our master?'

5 'Because the poor are despoiled,
because the needy groan,
I will now rise up,'
says the LORD;
'I will place them in the safety
for which they long.'
6 The promises of the LORD are
promises that are pure,
silver refined in a furnace
on the ground,
purified seven times.

7 You, O LORD, will protect us;
you will guard us from this
generation for ever.
8 On every side the wicked prowl,
as vileness is exalted among
humankind.

PSALM 13

PRAYER FOR DELIVERANCE FROM ENEMIES

To the leader. A Psalm of David.

1 How long, O LORD? Will you
forget me for ever?
How long will you hide
your face from me?
2 How long must I bear pain[k]
in my soul,
and have sorrow in my
heart all day long?
How long shall my enemy be
exalted over me?

3 Consider and answer me,
O LORD my God!
Give light to my eyes, or I will
sleep the sleep of death,
4 and my enemy will say, 'I
have prevailed';
my foes will rejoice because
I am shaken.

[i] 10.18 Meaning of Heb uncertain [j] 11.1 Gk Syr Jerome Tg: Heb *flee to your mountain, O bird*
[k] 13.2 Syr: Heb *hold counsels*

5 But I trusted in your steadfast love;
my heart shall rejoice in
your salvation.
6 I will sing to the LORD,
because he has dealt
bountifully with me.

PSALM 14

DENUNCIATION OF GODLESSNESS

To the leader. Of David.

1 Fools say in their hearts,
'There is no God.'
They are corrupt, they do
abominable deeds;
there is no one who does good.

2 The LORD looks down from
heaven on humankind
to see if there are any who are wise,
who seek after God.

3 They have all gone astray, they
are all alike perverse;
there is no one who does good,
no, not one.

4 Have they no knowledge, all
the evildoers
who eat up my people as
they eat bread,
and do not call upon the LORD?

5 There they shall be in great terror,
for God is with the company
of the righteous.
6 You would confound the
plans of the poor,
but the LORD is their refuge.

7 O that deliverance for Israel
would come from Zion!
When the LORD restores the
fortunes of his people,
Jacob will rejoice; Israel will be glad.

PSALM 15

WHO SHALL ABIDE IN GOD'S SANCTUARY?

A Psalm of David.

1 O LORD, who may abide
in your tent?
Who may dwell on your holy hill?

2 Those who walk blamelessly,
and do what is right,
and speak the truth from
their heart;
3 who do not slander with
their tongue,
and do no evil to their friends,
nor take up a reproach against
their neighbours;
4 in whose eyes the wicked
are despised,
but who honour those who
fear the LORD;
who stand by their oath even
to their hurt;
5 who do not lend money at interest,
and do not take a bribe
against the innocent.

Those who do these things shall
never be moved.

PSALM 16

SONG OF TRUST AND SECURITY IN GOD

A Miktam of David.

1 Protect me, O God, for in you
I take refuge.
2 I say to the LORD, 'You are my Lord;
I have no good apart from you.'[l]

3 As for the holy ones in the land,
they are the noble,
in whom is all my delight.

4 Those who choose another god
multiply their sorrows;[m]
their drink-offerings of blood
I will not pour out
or take their names upon my lips.

5 The LORD is my chosen portion
and my cup;
you hold my lot.
6 The boundary lines have fallen for
me in pleasant places;
I have a goodly heritage.

7 I bless the LORD who gives
me counsel;
in the night also my heart
instructs me.
8 I keep the LORD always before me;
because he is at my right hand,
I shall not be moved.

9 Therefore my heart is glad, and
my soul rejoices;
my body also rests secure.

[l] **16.2** Jerome Tg: Meaning of Heb uncertain
[m] **16.4** Cn: Meaning of Heb uncertain

10 For you do not give me up to Sheol,
or let your faithful one see the Pit.

11 You show me the path of life.
In your presence there is
fullness of joy;
in your right hand are
pleasures for evermore.

PSALM 17

PRAYER FOR DELIVERANCE FROM PERSECUTORS

A Prayer of David.

1 Hear a just cause, O LORD;
attend to my cry;
give ear to my prayer from
lips free of deceit.
2 From you let my vindication come;
let your eyes see the right.

3 If you try my heart, if you
visit me by night,
if you test me, you will find
no wickedness in me;
my mouth does not transgress.
4 As for what others do, by the
word of your lips
I have avoided the ways
of the violent.
5 My steps have held fast to your paths;
my feet have not slipped.

6 I call upon you, for you will
answer me, O God;
incline your ear to me,
hear my words.
7 Wondrously show your
steadfast love,
O saviour of those who
seek refuge
from their adversaries at
your right hand.

8 Guard me as the apple of the eye;
hide me in the shadow
of your wings,
9 from the wicked who despoil me,
my deadly enemies who
surround me.
10 They close their hearts to pity;
with their mouths they
speak arrogantly.
11 They track me down;[n] now
they surround me;
they set their eyes to cast
me to the ground.
12 They are like a lion eager to tear,
like a young lion lurking
in ambush.

13 Rise up, O LORD, confront them,
overthrow them!
By your sword deliver my
life from the wicked,
14 from mortals—by your
hand, O LORD—
from mortals whose portion
in life is in this world.
May their bellies be filled with what
you have stored up for them;
may their children have
more than enough;
may they leave something
over to their little ones.

15 As for me, I shall behold your
face in righteousness;
when I awake I shall be satisfied,
beholding your likeness.

PSALM 18

ROYAL THANKSGIVING FOR VICTORY

To the leader. A Psalm of David the servant of the LORD, who addressed the words of this song to the LORD on the day when the LORD delivered him from the hand of all his enemies, and from the hand of Saul. He said:

1 I love you, O LORD, my strength.
2 The LORD is my rock, my fortress,
and my deliverer,
my God, my rock in whom
I take refuge,
my shield, and the horn of my
salvation, my stronghold.
3 I call upon the LORD, who is
worthy to be praised;
so I shall be saved from
my enemies.

4 The cords of death encompassed me;
the torrents of perdition
assailed me;
5 the cords of Sheol entangled me;
the snares of death confronted me.

6 In my distress I called upon the LORD;
to my God I cried for help.
From his temple he heard my voice,
and my cry to him reached his ears.

7 Then the earth reeled and rocked;
the foundations also of the
mountains trembled
and quaked, because he
was angry.

[n] 17.11 One Ms Compare Syr: MT *Our steps*

8 Smoke went up from his nostrils,
and devouring fire from
his mouth;
glowing coals flamed
forth from him.
9 He bowed the heavens, and
came down;
thick darkness was under his feet.
10 He rode on a cherub, and flew;
he came swiftly upon the
wings of the wind.
11 He made darkness his covering
around him,
his canopy thick clouds
dark with water.
12 Out of the brightness before him
there broke through his clouds
hailstones and coals of fire.
13 The LORD also thundered
in the heavens,
and the Most High uttered
his voice.[o]
14 And he sent out his arrows,
and scattered them;
he flashed forth lightnings,
and routed them.
15 Then the channels of the
sea were seen,
and the foundations of the
world were laid bare
at your rebuke, O LORD,
at the blast of the breath
of your nostrils.

16 He reached down from on
high, he took me;
he drew me out of mighty waters.
17 He delivered me from my
strong enemy,
and from those who hated me;
for they were too mighty for me.
18 They confronted me in the day
of my calamity;
but the LORD was my support.
19 He brought me out into a
broad place;
he delivered me, because
he delighted in me.

20 The LORD rewarded me according
to my righteousness;
according to the cleanness of my
hands he recompensed me.
21 For I have kept the ways
of the LORD,
and have not wickedly
departed from my God.
22 For all his ordinances were
before me,
and his statutes I did not
put away from me.
23 I was blameless before him,
and I kept myself from guilt.
24 Therefore the LORD has
recompensed me according
to my righteousness,
according to the cleanness of
my hands in his sight.

25 With the loyal you show
yourself loyal;
with the blameless you show
yourself blameless;
26 with the pure you show
yourself pure;
and with the crooked you
show yourself perverse.
27 For you deliver a humble people,
but the haughty eyes you
bring down.
28 It is you who light my lamp;
the LORD, my God, lights
up my darkness.
29 By you I can crush a troop,
and by my God I can leap
over a wall.
30 This God—his way is perfect;
the promise of the LORD
proves true;
he is a shield for all who
take refuge in him.

31 For who is God except the LORD?
And who is a rock besides
our God?—
32 the God who girded me
with strength,
and made my way safe.
33 He made my feet like the
feet of a deer,
and set me secure on the heights.
34 He trains my hands for war,
so that my arms can bend
a bow of bronze.
35 You have given me the shield
of your salvation,
and your right hand has
supported me;
your help[p] has made me great.
36 You gave me a wide place for
my steps under me,
and my feet did not slip.
37 I pursued my enemies and
overtook them;
and did not turn back until
they were consumed.
38 I struck them down, so that they
were not able to rise;
they fell under my feet.

o **18.13** Gk See 2 Sam 22.14: Heb adds *hailstones and coals of fire* p **18.35** Or *gentleness*

39 For you girded me with strength
for the battle;
you made my assailants
sink under me.
40 You made my enemies turn
their backs to me,
and those who hated me
I destroyed.
41 They cried for help, but there was
no one to save them;
they cried to the LORD, but he
did not answer them.
42 I beat them fine, like dust
before the wind;
I cast them out like the
mire of the streets.

43 You delivered me from strife
with the peoples;[q]
you made me head of the nations;
people whom I had not
known served me.
44 As soon as they heard of me
they obeyed me;
foreigners came cringing to me.
45 Foreigners lost heart,
and came trembling out of
their strongholds.

46 The LORD lives! Blessed be my rock,
and exalted be the God of
my salvation,
47 the God who gave me vengeance
and subdued peoples under me;
48 who delivered me from my enemies;
indeed, you exalted me above
my adversaries;
you delivered me from the violent.

49 For this I will extol you, O LORD,
among the nations,
and sing praises to your name.
50 Great triumphs he gives to his king,
and shows steadfast love
to his anointed,
to David and his descendants
for ever.

PSALM 19

GOD'S GLORY IN CREATION AND THE LAW

To the leader. A Psalm of David.

1 The heavens are telling the
glory of God;
and the firmament[r] proclaims
his handiwork.
2 Day to day pours forth speech,
and night to night declares
knowledge.
3 There is no speech, nor are
there words;
their voice is not heard;
4 yet their voice[s] goes out through
all the earth,
and their words to the
end of the world.

In the heavens[t] he has set a
tent for the sun,
5 which comes out like a bridegroom
from his wedding canopy,
and like a strong man runs
its course with joy.
6 Its rising is from the end of
the heavens,
and its circuit to the end of them;
and nothing is hidden
from its heat.

7 The law of the LORD is perfect,
reviving the soul;
the decrees of the LORD are sure,
making wise the simple;
8 the precepts of the LORD are right,
rejoicing the heart;
the commandment of the
LORD is clear,
enlightening the eyes;
9 the fear of the LORD is pure,
enduring for ever;
the ordinances of the LORD are true
and righteous altogether.
10 More to be desired are they than gold,
even much fine gold;
sweeter also than honey,
and drippings of the honeycomb.

11 Moreover by them is your
servant warned;
in keeping them there is
great reward.
12 But who can detect their errors?
Clear me from hidden faults.
13 Keep back your servant also
from the insolent;[u]
do not let them have
dominion over me.
Then I shall be blameless,
and innocent of great
transgression.

14 Let the words of my mouth and the
meditation of my heart
be acceptable to you,
O LORD, my rock and
my redeemer.

[q] 18.43 Gk Tg: Heb *people* [r] 19.1 Or *dome*
[s] 19.4 Gk Jerome Compare Syr: Heb *line*
[t] 19.4 Heb *In them* [u] 19.13 Or *from proud thoughts*

PSALM 20

PRAYER FOR VICTORY

To the leader. A Psalm of David.

1 The LORD answer you in the
day of trouble!
The name of the God of
Jacob protect you!
2 May he send you help from
the sanctuary,
and give you support from Zion.
3 May he remember all your offerings,
and regard with favour your burnt
sacrifices. *Selah*

4 May he grant you your
heart's desire,
and fulfil all your plans.
5 May we shout for joy over
your victory,
and in the name of our God
set up our banners.
May the LORD fulfil all
your petitions.

6 Now I know that the LORD will
help his anointed;
he will answer him from
his holy heaven
with mighty victories by
his right hand.
7 Some take pride in chariots,
and some in horses,
but our pride is in the name
of the LORD our God.
8 They will collapse and fall,
but we shall rise and
stand upright.

9 Give victory to the king, O LORD;
answer us when we call.[v]

PSALM 21

THANKSGIVING FOR VICTORY

To the leader. A Psalm of David.

1 In your strength the king
rejoices, O LORD,
and in your help how
greatly he exults!
2 You have given him his
heart's desire,
and have not withheld the request
of his lips. *Selah*
3 For you meet him with
rich blessings;
you set a crown of fine
gold on his head.
4 He asked you for life; you
gave it to him—
length of days for ever and ever.
5 His glory is great through your help;
splendour and majesty you
bestow on him.
6 You bestow on him blessings for ever;
you make him glad with the
joy of your presence.
7 For the king trusts in the LORD,
and through the steadfast
love of the Most High he
shall not be moved.

8 Your hand will find out all
your enemies;
your right hand will find out
those who hate you.
9 You will make them like a fiery furnace
when you appear.
The LORD will swallow them
up in his wrath,
and fire will consume them.
10 You will destroy their offspring
from the earth,
and their children from
among humankind.
11 If they plan evil against you,
if they devise mischief, they
will not succeed.
12 For you will put them to flight;
you will aim at their faces
with your bows.

13 Be exalted, O LORD, in your strength!
We will sing and praise your power.

PSALM 22

PLEA FOR DELIVERANCE FROM SUFFERING AND HOSTILITY

To the leader: according to The Deer of the Dawn. A Psalm of David.

1 My God, my God, why have
you forsaken me?
Why are you so far from
helping me, from the
words of my groaning?
2 O my God, I cry by day, but
you do not answer;
and by night, but find no rest.

3 Yet you are holy,
enthroned on the praises of Israel.
4 In you our ancestors trusted;
they trusted, and you
delivered them.
5 To you they cried, and were saved;
in you they trusted, and were
not put to shame.

[v] **20.9** Gk: Heb *give victory, O LORD; let the King answer us when we call*

6 But I am a worm, and not human;
scorned by others, and
despised by the people.
7 All who see me mock at me;
they make mouths at me, they
shake their heads;
8 'Commit your cause to the LORD;
let him deliver—
let him rescue the one in
whom he delights!'

9 Yet it was you who took me
from the womb;
you kept me safe on my
mother's breast.
10 On you I was cast from my birth,
and since my mother bore me
you have been my God.
11 Do not be far from me,
for trouble is near
and there is no one to help.

12 Many bulls encircle me,
strong bulls of Bashan
surround me;
13 they open wide their
mouths at me,
like a ravening and roaring lion.

14 I am poured out like water,
and all my bones are out of joint;
my heart is like wax;
it is melted within my breast;
15 my mouth[w] is dried up like
a potsherd,
and my tongue sticks to my jaws;
you lay me in the dust of death.

16 For dogs are all around me;
a company of evildoers
encircles me.
My hands and feet have shrivelled;[x]
17 I can count all my bones.
They stare and gloat over me;
18 they divide my clothes among
themselves,
and for my clothing they cast lots.

19 But you, O LORD, do not be far away!
O my help, come quickly to my aid!
20 Deliver my soul from the sword,
my life[y] from the power of the dog!
21 Save me from the mouth
of the lion!

From the horns of the wild oxen
you have rescued[z] me.
22 I will tell of your name to my
brothers and sisters;[a]
in the midst of the congregation
I will praise you:

23 You who fear the LORD, praise him!
All you offspring of Jacob,
glorify him;
stand in awe of him, all you
offspring of Israel!
24 For he did not despise or abhor
the affliction of the afflicted;
he did not hide his face from me,[b]
but heard when I[c] cried to him.

25 From you comes my praise in
the great congregation;
my vows I will pay before
those who fear him.
26 The poor[d] shall eat and be satisfied;
those who seek him shall
praise the LORD.
May your hearts live for ever!

27 All the ends of the earth
shall remember
and turn to the LORD;
and all the families of the nations
shall worship before him.[e]
28 For dominion belongs to the LORD,
and he rules over the nations.

29 To him,[f] indeed, shall all who sleep
in[g] the earth bow down;
before him shall bow all who
go down to the dust,
and I shall live for him.[h]
30 Posterity will serve him;
future generations will be
told about the Lord,
31 and[i] proclaim his deliverance to
a people yet unborn,
saying that he has done it.

PSALM 23

THE DIVINE SHEPHERD

A Psalm of David.

1 The LORD is my shepherd, I
shall not want.
2 He makes me lie down in
green pastures;
he leads me beside still waters;[j]
3 he restores my soul.[k]

[w] 22.15 Cn: Heb *strength* [x] 22.16 Meaning of Heb uncertain [y] 22.20 Heb *my only one* [z] 22.21 Heb *answered* [a] 22.22 Or *kindred* [b] 22.24 Heb *him* [c] 22.24 Heb *he* [d] 22.26 Or *afflicted* [e] 22.27 Gk Syr Jerome: Heb *you* [f] 22.29 Cn: Heb *They have eaten and* [g] 22.29 Cn: Heb *all the fat ones* [h] 22.29 Compare Gk Syr Vg: Heb *and he who cannot keep himself alive* [i] 22.31 Compare Gk: Heb *it will be told about the Lord to the generation, 31they will come and* [j] 23.2 Heb *waters of rest* [k] 23.3 Or *life*

He leads me in right paths[l]
for his name's sake.

4 Even though I walk through
the darkest valley,[m]
I fear no evil;
for you are with me;
your rod and your staff—
they comfort me.

5 You prepare a table before me
in the presence of my enemies;
you anoint my head with oil;
my cup overflows.
6 Surely[n] goodness and mercy[o]
shall follow me
all the days of my life,
and I shall dwell in the house
of the LORD
my whole life long.[p]

PSALM 24

ENTRANCE INTO THE TEMPLE

Of David. A Psalm.

1 The earth is the LORD's and
all that is in it,
the world, and those who live in it;
2 for he has founded it on the seas,
and established it on the rivers.

3 Who shall ascend the hill
of the LORD?
And who shall stand in
his holy place?
4 Those who have clean hands
and pure hearts,
who do not lift up their souls
to what is false,
and do not swear deceitfully.
5 They will receive blessing
from the LORD,
and vindication from the God
of their salvation.
6 Such is the company of those
who seek him,
who seek the face of the God of
Jacob.[q] *Selah*

7 Lift up your heads, O gates!
and be lifted up, O ancient doors!
that the King of glory
may come in.
8 Who is the King of glory?
The LORD, strong and mighty,
the LORD, mighty in battle.
9 Lift up your heads, O gates!
and be lifted up, O ancient doors!
that the King of glory
may come in.
10 Who is this King of glory?
The LORD of hosts,
he is the King of glory. *Selah*

PSALM 25

PRAYER FOR GUIDANCE AND FOR DELIVERANCE

Of David.

1 To you, O LORD, I lift up my soul.
2 O my God, in you I trust;
do not let me be put to shame;
do not let my enemies
exult over me.
3 Do not let those who wait for
you be put to shame;
let them be ashamed who are
wantonly treacherous.

4 Make me to know your
ways, O LORD;
teach me your paths.
5 Lead me in your truth, and teach me,
for you are the God of
my salvation;
for you I wait all day long.

6 Be mindful of your mercy, O LORD,
and of your steadfast love,
for they have been from of old.
7 Do not remember the sins of my
youth or my transgressions;
according to your steadfast
love remember me,
for your goodness' sake, O LORD!

8 Good and upright is the LORD;
therefore he instructs
sinners in the way.
9 He leads the humble in what is right,
and teaches the humble his way.
10 All the paths of the LORD
are steadfast love
and faithfulness,
for those who keep his covenant
and his decrees.

11 For your name's sake, O LORD,
pardon my guilt, for it is great.
12 Who are they that fear the LORD?
He will teach them the way
that they should choose.

13 They will abide in prosperity,
and their children shall
possess the land.

[l] 23.3 Or *paths of righteousness* [m] 23.4 Or *the valley of the shadow of death* [n] 23.6 Or *Only* [o] 23.6 Or *kindness* [p] 23.6 Heb *for length of days* [q] 24.6 Gk Syr: Heb *your face, O Jacob*

14 The friendship of the LORD is for
those who fear him,
and he makes his covenant
known to them.
15 My eyes are ever towards the LORD,
for he will pluck my feet
out of the net.

16 Turn to me and be gracious to me,
for I am lonely and afflicted.
17 Relieve the troubles of my heart,
and bring me[r] out of my distress.
18 Consider my affliction and
my trouble,
and forgive all my sins.

19 Consider how many are my foes,
and with what violent
hatred they hate me.
20 O guard my life, and deliver me;
do not let me be put to shame,
for I take refuge in you.
21 May integrity and uprightness
preserve me,
for I wait for you.

22 Redeem Israel, O God,
out of all its troubles.

PSALM 26

PLEA FOR JUSTICE AND DECLARATION OF RIGHTEOUSNESS

Of David.

1 Vindicate me, O LORD,
for I have walked in my integrity,
and I have trusted in the LORD
without wavering.
2 Prove me, O LORD, and try me;
test my heart and mind.
3 For your steadfast love is
before my eyes,
and I walk in faithfulness to you.[s]

4 I do not sit with the worthless,
nor do I consort with hypocrites;
5 I hate the company of evildoers,
and will not sit with the wicked.

6 I wash my hands in innocence,
and go around your altar, O LORD,
7 singing aloud a song of
thanksgiving,
and telling all your
wondrous deeds.

8 O LORD, I love the house in
which you dwell,
and the place where your
glory abides.

9 Do not sweep me away with sinners,
nor my life with the bloodthirsty,
10 those in whose hands are
evil devices,
and whose right hands
are full of bribes.

11 But as for me, I walk in my integrity;
redeem me, and be
gracious to me.
12 My foot stands on level ground;
in the great congregation I
will bless the LORD.

PSALM 27

TRIUMPHANT SONG OF CONFIDENCE

Of David.

1 The LORD is my light and
my salvation;
whom shall I fear?
The LORD is the stronghold[t]
of my life;
of whom shall I be afraid?

2 When evildoers assail me
to devour my flesh—
my adversaries and foes—
they shall stumble and fall.

3 Though an army encamp against me,
my heart shall not fear;
though war rise up against me,
yet I will be confident.

4 One thing I asked of the LORD,
that will I seek after:
to live in the house of the LORD
all the days of my life,
to behold the beauty of the LORD,
and to inquire in his temple.

5 For he will hide me in his shelter
in the day of trouble;
he will conceal me under the
cover of his tent;
he will set me high on a rock.

6 Now my head is lifted up
above my enemies all around me,
and I will offer in his tent
sacrifices with shouts of joy;
I will sing and make melody
to the LORD.

7 Hear, O LORD, when I cry aloud,
be gracious to me and answer me!

[r] **25.17** Or *The troubles of my heart are enlarged; bring me* [s] **26.3** Or *in your faithfulness*
[t] **27.1** Or *refuge*

8 'Come,' my heart says, 'seek his face!'
Your face, LORD, do I seek.
9 Do not hide your face from me.

Do not turn your servant
away in anger,
you who have been my help.
Do not cast me off, do not
forsake me,
O God of my salvation!
10 If my father and mother forsake me,
the LORD will take me up.

11 Teach me your way, O LORD,
and lead me on a level path
because of my enemies.
12 Do not give me up to the will
of my adversaries,
for false witnesses have
risen against me,
and they are breathing
out violence.

13 I believe that I shall see the
goodness of the LORD
in the land of the living.
14 Wait for the LORD;
be strong, and let your
heart take courage;
wait for the LORD!

PSALM 28

PRAYER FOR HELP AND THANKSGIVING FOR IT

Of David.

1 To you, O LORD, I call;
my rock, do not refuse to hear me,
for if you are silent to me,
I shall be like those who go
down to the Pit.
2 Hear the voice of my supplication,
as I cry to you for help,
as I lift up my hands
towards your most holy
sanctuary.[u]

3 Do not drag me away with
the wicked,
with those who are
workers of evil,
who speak peace with their
neighbours,
while mischief is in their hearts.
4 Repay them according to their work,
and according to the evil
of their deeds;
repay them according to the
work of their hands;
render them their due reward.
5 Because they do not regard the
works of the LORD,
or the work of his hands,
he will break them down and
build them up no more.

6 Blessed be the LORD,
for he has heard the sound
of my pleadings.
7 The LORD is my strength
and my shield;
in him my heart trusts;
so I am helped, and my heart exults,
and with my song I give
thanks to him.

8 The LORD is the strength
of his people;
he is the saving refuge
of his anointed.
9 O save your people, and bless
your heritage;
be their shepherd, and carry
them for ever.

PSALM 29

THE VOICE OF GOD IN A GREAT STORM

A Psalm of David.

1 Ascribe to the LORD,
O heavenly beings,[v]
ascribe to the LORD glory
and strength.
2 Ascribe to the LORD the
glory of his name;
worship the LORD in
holy splendour.

3 The voice of the LORD is
over the waters;
the God of glory thunders,
the LORD, over mighty waters.
4 The voice of the LORD is powerful;
the voice of the LORD is
full of majesty.

5 The voice of the LORD breaks
the cedars;
the LORD breaks the cedars
of Lebanon.
6 He makes Lebanon skip like a calf,
and Sirion like a young wild ox.

7 The voice of the LORD flashes
forth flames of fire.

u **28.2** Heb *your innermost sanctuary*
v **29.1** Heb *sons of gods*

8 The voice of the LORD shakes
the wilderness;
the LORD shakes the
wilderness of Kadesh.

9 The voice of the LORD causes
the oaks to whirl,[w]
and strips the forest bare;
and in his temple all say, 'Glory!'

10 The LORD sits enthroned
over the flood;
the LORD sits enthroned
as king for ever.
11 May the LORD give strength
to his people!
May the LORD bless his
people with peace!

PSALM 30

THANKSGIVING FOR RECOVERY FROM GRAVE ILLNESS

A Psalm. A Song at the dedication of the temple. Of David.

1 I will extol you, O LORD, for you
have drawn me up,
and did not let my foes
rejoice over me.
2 O LORD my God, I cried to
you for help,
and you have healed me.
3 O LORD, you brought up my
soul from Sheol,
restored me to life from among
those gone down to the Pit.[x]

4 Sing praises to the LORD, O you
his faithful ones,
and give thanks to his holy name.
5 For his anger is but for a moment;
his favour is for a lifetime.
Weeping may linger for the night,
but joy comes with the morning.

6 As for me, I said in my prosperity,
'I shall never be moved.'
7 By your favour, O LORD,
you had established me as
a strong mountain;
you hid your face;
I was dismayed.

8 To you, O LORD, I cried,
and to the LORD I made
supplication:
9 'What profit is there in my death,
if I go down to the Pit?
Will the dust praise you?
Will it tell of your faithfulness?
10 Hear, O LORD, and be gracious to me!
O LORD, be my helper!'
11 You have turned my mourning
into dancing;
you have taken off my sackcloth
and clothed me with joy,
12 so that my soul[y] may praise you
and not be silent.
O LORD my God, I will give
thanks to you for ever.

PSALM 31

PRAYER AND PRAISE FOR DELIVERANCE FROM ENEMIES

To the leader. A Psalm of David.

1 In you, O LORD, I seek refuge;
do not let me ever be
put to shame;
in your righteousness deliver me.
2 Incline your ear to me;
rescue me speedily.
Be a rock of refuge for me,
a strong fortress to save me.

3 You are indeed my rock and
my fortress;
for your name's sake lead
me and guide me,
4 take me out of the net that
is hidden for me,
for you are my refuge.
5 Into your hand I commit my spirit;
you have redeemed me,
O LORD, faithful God.

6 You hate[z] those who pay regard
to worthless idols,
but I trust in the LORD.
7 I will exult and rejoice in your
steadfast love,
because you have seen
my affliction;
you have taken heed of
my adversities,
8 and have not delivered me into
the hand of the enemy;
you have set my feet in
a broad place.

9 Be gracious to me, O LORD,
for I am in distress;
my eye wastes away from grief,
my soul and body also.

[w] **29.9** *Or causes the deer to calve* [x] **30.3** *Or that I should not go down to the Pit* [y] **30.12** *Heb that glory* [z] **31.6** One Heb Ms Gk Syr Jerome: MT *I hate*

10 For my life is spent with sorrow,
and my years with sighing;
my strength fails because
of my misery,[a]
and my bones waste away.

11 I am the scorn of all my adversaries,
a horror[b] to my neighbours,
an object of dread to my
acquaintances;
those who see me in the
street flee from me.
12 I have passed out of mind like
one who is dead;
I have become like a broken vessel.
13 For I hear the whispering of many—
terror all around!—
as they scheme together against me,
as they plot to take my life.

14 But I trust in you, O LORD;
I say, 'You are my God.'
15 My times are in your hand;
deliver me from the hand of my
enemies and persecutors.
16 Let your face shine upon
your servant;
save me in your steadfast love.
17 Do not let me be put to
shame, O LORD,
for I call on you;
let the wicked be put to shame;
let them go dumbfounded
to Sheol.
18 Let the lying lips be stilled
that speak insolently against
the righteous
with pride and contempt.

19 O how abundant is your goodness
that you have laid up for
those who fear you,
and accomplished for those who
take refuge in you,
in the sight of everyone!
20 In the shelter of your presence
you hide them
from human plots;
you hold them safe under
your shelter
from contentious tongues.

21 Blessed be the LORD,
for he has wondrously shown
his steadfast love to me
when I was beset as a city
under siege.
22 I had said in my alarm,
'I am driven far[c] from your sight.'
But you heard my supplications
when I cried out to you for help.

23 Love the LORD, all you his saints.
The LORD preserves the faithful,
but abundantly repays the one
who acts haughtily.
24 Be strong, and let your heart
take courage,
all you who wait for the LORD.

PSALM 32

THE JOY OF FORGIVENESS

Of David. A Maskil.

1 Happy are those whose
transgression is forgiven,
whose sin is covered.
2 Happy are those to whom the LORD
imputes no iniquity,
and in whose spirit there
is no deceit.

3 While I kept silence, my body
wasted away
through my groaning all day long.
4 For day and night your hand
was heavy upon me;
my strength was dried up[d] as by
the heat of summer. *Selah*

5 Then I acknowledged my sin to you,
and I did not hide my iniquity;
I said, 'I will confess my
transgressions to the LORD',
and you forgave the guilt of my
sin. *Selah*

6 Therefore let all who are faithful
offer prayer to you;
at a time of distress,[e] the rush
of mighty waters
shall not reach them.
7 You are a hiding-place for me;
you preserve me from trouble;
you surround me with glad cries
of deliverance. *Selah*

8 I will instruct you and teach you
the way you should go;
I will counsel you with my
eye upon you.
9 Do not be like a horse or a mule,
without understanding,
whose temper must be curbed
with bit and bridle,
else it will not stay near you.

[a] **31.10** Gk Syr: Heb *my iniquity* [b] **31.11** Cn: Heb *exceedingly* [c] **31.22** Another reading is *cut off* [d] **32.4** Meaning of Heb uncertain [e] **32.6** Cn: Heb *at a time of finding only*

10 Many are the torments of
the wicked,
but steadfast love surrounds those
who trust in the LORD.
11 Be glad in the LORD and
rejoice, O righteous,
and shout for joy, all you
upright in heart.

PSALM 33

THE GREATNESS AND GOODNESS OF GOD

1 Rejoice in the LORD, O you
righteous.
Praise befits the upright.
2 Praise the LORD with the lyre;
make melody to him with the
harp of ten strings.
3 Sing to him a new song;
play skilfully on the strings,
with loud shouts.

4 For the word of the LORD is upright,
and all his work is done
in faithfulness.
5 He loves righteousness and justice;
the earth is full of the steadfast
love of the LORD.

6 By the word of the LORD the
heavens were made,
and all their host by the
breath of his mouth.
7 He gathered the waters of the
sea as in a bottle;
he put the deeps in storehouses.

8 Let all the earth fear the LORD;
let all the inhabitants of the
world stand in awe of him.
9 For he spoke, and it came to be;
he commanded, and
it stood firm.

10 The LORD brings the counsel of
the nations to nothing;
he frustrates the plans
of the peoples.
11 The counsel of the LORD
stands for ever,
the thoughts of his heart
to all generations.
12 Happy is the nation whose
God is the LORD,
the people whom he has
chosen as his heritage.

13 The LORD looks down from heaven;
he sees all humankind.
14 From where he sits enthroned
he watches
all the inhabitants of the earth—
15 he who fashions the hearts
of them all,
and observes all their deeds.
16 A king is not saved by his
great army;
a warrior is not delivered by
his great strength.
17 The war horse is a vain hope
for victory,
and by its great might
it cannot save.

18 Truly the eye of the LORD is on
those who fear him,
on those who hope in his
steadfast love,
19 to deliver their soul from death,
and to keep them alive in famine.

20 Our soul waits for the LORD;
he is our help and shield.
21 Our heart is glad in him,
because we trust in his holy name.
22 Let your steadfast love, O LORD,
be upon us,
even as we hope in you.

PSALM 34

PRAISE FOR DELIVERANCE FROM TROUBLE

Of David, when he feigned madness before Abimelech, so that he drove him out, and he went away.

1 I will bless the LORD at all times;
his praise shall continually
be in my mouth.
2 My soul makes its boast in the LORD;
let the humble hear and be glad.
3 O magnify the LORD with me,
and let us exalt his name together.

4 I sought the LORD, and he
answered me,
and delivered me from
all my fears.
5 Look to him, and be radiant;
so your[f] faces shall never
be ashamed.
6 This poor soul cried, and was
heard by the LORD,
and was saved from every trouble.
7 The angel of the LORD encamps
around those who fear him,
and delivers them.

[f] 34.5 Gk Syr Jerome: Heb *their*

8 O taste and see that the LORD is good;
happy are those who take
refuge in him.
9 O fear the LORD, you his holy ones,
for those who fear him
have no want.
10 The young lions suffer want
and hunger,
but those who seek the LORD
lack no good thing.

11 Come, O children, listen to me;
I will teach you the fear
of the LORD.
12 Which of you desires life,
and covets many days to
enjoy good?
13 Keep your tongue from evil,
and your lips from speaking deceit.
14 Depart from evil, and do good;
seek peace, and pursue it.

15 The eyes of the LORD are on
the righteous,
and his ears are open to their cry.
16 The face of the LORD is
against evildoers,
to cut off the remembrance of
them from the earth.
17 When the righteous cry for help,
the LORD hears,
and rescues them from all
their troubles.
18 The LORD is near to the
broken-hearted,
and saves the crushed in spirit.

19 Many are the afflictions of
the righteous,
but the LORD rescues them
from them all.
20 He keeps all their bones;
not one of them will be broken.
21 Evil brings death to the wicked,
and those who hate the righteous
will be condemned.
22 The LORD redeems the life
of his servants;
none of those who take refuge in
him will be condemned.

PSALM 35

PRAYER FOR DELIVERANCE FROM ENEMIES

Of David.

1 Contend, O LORD, with those
who contend with me;
fight against those who
fight against me!
2 Take hold of shield and buckler,
and rise up to help me!
3 Draw the spear and javelin
against my pursuers;
say to my soul,
'I am your salvation.'

4 Let them be put to shame
and dishonour
who seek after my life.
Let them be turned back
and confounded
who devise evil against me.
5 Let them be like chaff before
the wind,
with the angel of the LORD
driving them on.
6 Let their way be dark and slippery,
with the angel of the LORD
pursuing them.

7 For without cause they hid
their net[g] for me;
without cause they dug a
pit[h] for my life.
8 Let ruin come on them unawares.
And let the net that they hid
ensnare them;
let them fall in it—to their ruin.

9 Then my soul shall rejoice
in the LORD,
exulting in his deliverance.
10 All my bones shall say,
'O LORD, who is like you?
You deliver the weak
from those too strong for them,
the weak and needy from those
who despoil them.'

11 Malicious witnesses rise up;
they ask me about things
I do not know.
12 They repay me evil for good;
my soul is forlorn.
13 But as for me, when they were sick,
I wore sackcloth;
I afflicted myself with fasting.
I prayed with head bowed[i]
on my bosom,
14 as though I grieved for a
friend or a brother;
I went about as one who
laments for a mother,
bowed down and in mourning.

[g] 35.7 Heb *a pit, their net* [h] 35.7 The word *pit* is transposed from the preceding line [i] 35.13 Or *My prayer turned back*

15 But at my stumbling they
gathered in glee,
they gathered together
against me;
ruffians whom I did not know
tore at me without ceasing;
16 they impiously mocked
more and more,[j]
gnashing at me with their teeth.

17 How long, O LORD, will you look on?
Rescue me from their ravages,
my life from the lions!
18 Then I will thank you in the
great congregation;
in the mighty throng I
will praise you.

19 Do not let my treacherous enemies
rejoice over me,
or those who hate me without
cause wink the eye.
20 For they do not speak peace,
but they conceive deceitful words
against those who are
quiet in the land.
21 They open wide their mouths
against me;
they say, 'Aha, Aha,
our eyes have seen it.'

22 You have seen, O LORD; do
not be silent!
O Lord, do not be far from me!
23 Wake up! Bestir yourself
for my defence,
for my cause, my God
and my Lord!
24 Vindicate me, O LORD, my God,
according to your righteousness,
and do not let them
rejoice over me.
25 Do not let them say to themselves,
'Aha, we have our heart's desire.'
Do not let them say, 'We have
swallowed you[k] up.'

26 Let all those who rejoice at
my calamity
be put to shame and confusion;
let those who exalt themselves
against me
be clothed with shame
and dishonour.

27 Let those who desire my vindication
shout for joy and be glad,
and say evermore,
'Great is the LORD,
who delights in the welfare
of his servant.'
28 Then my tongue shall tell of
your righteousness
and of your praise all day long.

PSALM 36

HUMAN WICKEDNESS AND DIVINE GOODNESS

To the leader. Of David, the servant of the LORD.

1 Transgression speaks to the wicked
deep in their hearts;
there is no fear of God
before their eyes.
2 For they flatter themselves
in their own eyes
that their iniquity cannot be
found out and hated.
3 The words of their mouths are
mischief and deceit;
they have ceased to act
wisely and do good.
4 They plot mischief while
on their beds;
they are set on a way that
is not good;
they do not reject evil.

5 Your steadfast love, O LORD,
extends to the heavens,
your faithfulness to the clouds.
6 Your righteousness is like the
mighty mountains,
your judgements are like
the great deep;
you save humans and animals
alike, O LORD.

7 How precious is your steadfast
love, O God!
All people may take refuge in
the shadow of your wings.
8 They feast on the abundance
of your house,
and you give them drink from
the river of your delights.
9 For with you is the fountain of life;
in your light we see light.

10 O continue your steadfast love to
those who know you,
and your salvation to the
upright of heart!
11 Do not let the foot of the
arrogant tread on me,
or the hand of the wicked
drive me away.

j 35.16 Cn Compare Gk: Heb *like the profanest of mockers of a cake* k 35.25 Heb *him*

12 There the evildoers lie prostrate;
they are thrust down,
unable to rise.

PSALM 37

EXHORTATION TO PATIENCE AND TRUST

Of David.

1 Do not fret because of the wicked;
do not be envious of wrongdoers,
2 for they will soon fade like the grass,
and wither like the green herb.

3 Trust in the LORD, and do good;
so you will live in the land,
and enjoy security.
4 Take delight in the LORD,
and he will give you the
desires of your heart.

5 Commit your way to the LORD;
trust in him, and he will act.
6 He will make your vindication
shine like the light,
and the justice of your cause
like the noonday.

7 Be still before the LORD, and
wait patiently for him;
do not fret over those who
prosper in their way,
over those who carry out
evil devices.

8 Refrain from anger, and
forsake wrath.
Do not fret—it leads only to evil.
9 For the wicked shall be cut off,
but those who wait for the LORD
shall inherit the land.

10 Yet a little while, and the wicked
will be no more;
though you look diligently for their
place, they will not be there.
11 But the meek shall inherit the land,
and delight in abundant
prosperity.

12 The wicked plot against
the righteous,
and gnash their teeth at them;
13 but the LORD laughs at the wicked,
for he sees that their day is coming.

14 The wicked draw the sword
and bend their bows
to bring down the poor and needy,
to kill those who walk uprightly;
15 their sword shall enter their
own heart,
and their bows shall be broken.

16 Better is a little that the
righteous person has
than the abundance of
many wicked.
17 For the arms of the wicked
shall be broken,
but the LORD upholds
the righteous.

18 The LORD knows the days of
the blameless,
and their heritage will
abide for ever;
19 they are not put to shame
in evil times,
in the days of famine they
have abundance.

20 But the wicked perish,
and the enemies of the LORD are
like the glory of the pastures;
they vanish—like smoke
they vanish away.

21 The wicked borrow, and do
not pay back,
but the righteous are generous
and keep giving;
22 for those blessed by the LORD
shall inherit the land,
but those cursed by him
shall be cut off.

23 Our steps[l] are made firm
by the LORD,
when he delights in our[m] way;
24 though we stumble,[n] we[o] shall
not fall headlong,
for the LORD holds us[p]
by the hand.

25 I have been young, and now am old,
yet I have not seen the
righteous forsaken
or their children begging bread.
26 They are ever giving liberally
and lending,
and their children become
a blessing.

27 Depart from evil, and do good;
so you shall abide for ever.

[l] 37.23 Heb *A man's steps* [m] 37.23 Heb *his*
[n] 37.24 Heb *he stumbles* [o] 37.24 Heb *he*
[p] 37.24 Heb *him*

28 For the LORD loves justice;
he will not forsake his
faithful ones.

The righteous shall be kept
safe for ever,
but the children of the wicked
shall be cut off.
29 The righteous shall inherit the land,
and live in it for ever.

30 The mouths of the righteous
utter wisdom,
and their tongues speak justice.
31 The law of their God is in
their hearts;
their steps do not slip.

32 The wicked watch for
the righteous,
and seek to kill them.
33 The LORD will not abandon
them to their power,
or let them be condemned when
they are brought to trial.

34 Wait for the LORD, and keep
to his way,
and he will exalt you to
inherit the land;
you will look on the destruction
of the wicked.

35 I have seen the wicked
oppressing,
and towering like a cedar
of Lebanon.[q]
36 Again I[r] passed by, and they
were no more;
though I sought them, they
could not be found.

37 Mark the blameless, and
behold the upright,
for there is posterity for
the peaceable.
38 But transgressors shall be
altogether destroyed;
the posterity of the wicked
shall be cut off.

39 The salvation of the righteous
is from the LORD;
he is their refuge in the
time of trouble.
40 The LORD helps them and
rescues them;
he rescues them from the
wicked, and saves them,
because they take
refuge in him.

PSALM 38

A PENITENT SUFFERER'S PLEA FOR HEALING

A Psalm of David, for the memorial offering.

1 O LORD, do not rebuke me
in your anger,
or discipline me in your wrath.
2 For your arrows have sunk into me,
and your hand has come
down on me.

3 There is no soundness in my flesh
because of your indignation;
there is no health in my bones
because of my sin.
4 For my iniquities have gone
over my head;
they weigh like a burden
too heavy for me.

5 My wounds grow foul and fester
because of my foolishness;
6 I am utterly bowed down
and prostrate;
all day long I go around
mourning.
7 For my loins are filled with burning,
and there is no soundness
in my flesh.
8 I am utterly spent and crushed;
I groan because of the
tumult of my heart.

9 O Lord, all my longing is
known to you;
my sighing is not hidden
from you.
10 My heart throbs, my strength
fails me;
as for the light of my eyes—it
also has gone from me.
11 My friends and companions stand
aloof from my affliction,
and my neighbours stand far off.

12 Those who seek my life lay
their snares;
those who seek to hurt
me speak of ruin,
and meditate treachery
all day long.

13 But I am like the deaf, I do not hear;
like the mute, who cannot speak.
14 Truly, I am like one who
does not hear,
and in whose mouth is no retort.

[q] 37.35 Gk: Meaning of Heb uncertain
[r] 37.36 Gk Syr Jerome: Heb *he*

15 But it is for you, O LORD, that I wait;
it is you, O Lord my God,
who will answer.
16 For I pray, 'Only do not let them
rejoice over me,
those who boast against me
when my foot slips.'

17 For I am ready to fall,
and my pain is ever with me.
18 I confess my iniquity;
I am sorry for my sin.
19 Those who are my foes without
cause[s] are mighty,
and many are those who
hate me wrongfully.
20 Those who render me evil for good
are my adversaries because
I follow after good.

21 Do not forsake me, O LORD;
O my God, do not be far from me;
22 make haste to help me,
O Lord, my salvation.

PSALM 39

PRAYER FOR WISDOM AND FORGIVENESS

To the leader: to Jeduthun.
A Psalm of David.

1 I said, 'I will guard my ways
that I may not sin with my tongue;
I will keep a muzzle on my mouth
as long as the wicked are
in my presence.'
2 I was silent and still;
I held my peace to no avail;
my distress grew worse,
3 my heart became hot within me.
While I mused, the fire burned;
then I spoke with my tongue:

4 'LORD, let me know my end,
and what is the measure
of my days;
let me know how fleeting
my life is.
5 You have made my days a few
handbreadths,
and my lifetime is as nothing
in your sight.
Surely everyone stands as a mere
breath. *Selah*
6 Surely everyone goes about
like a shadow.
Surely for nothing they
are in turmoil;
they heap up, and do not
know who will gather.
7 'And now, O Lord, what
do I wait for?
My hope is in you.
8 Deliver me from all my
transgressions.
Do not make me the
scorn of the fool.
9 I am silent; I do not open my mouth,
for it is you who have done it.
10 Remove your stroke from me;
I am worn down by the
blows[t] of your hand.

11 'You chastise mortals
in punishment for sin,
consuming like a moth what
is dear to them;
surely everyone is a mere breath.
Selah

12 'Hear my prayer, O LORD,
and give ear to my cry;
do not hold your peace at my tears.
For I am your passing guest,
an alien, like all my forebears.
13 Turn your gaze away from me,
that I may smile again,
before I depart and am no more.'

PSALM 40

THANKSGIVING FOR DELIVERANCE AND PRAYER FOR HELP

To the leader. Of David. A Psalm.

1 I waited patiently for the LORD;
he inclined to me and
heard my cry.
2 He drew me up from the
desolate pit,[u]
out of the miry bog,
and set my feet upon a rock,
making my steps secure.
3 He put a new song in my mouth,
a song of praise to our God.
Many will see and fear,
and put their trust in the LORD.

4 Happy are those who make
the LORD their trust,
who do not turn to the proud,
to those who go astray
after false gods.
5 You have multiplied,
O LORD my God,
your wondrous deeds and your
thoughts towards us;
none can compare with you.

[s] 38.19 Q Ms: MT *my living foes* [t] 39.10 Heb *hostility* [u] 40.2 Cn: Heb *pit of tumult*

Were I to proclaim and tell of them,
they would be more than
can be counted.

6 Sacrifice and offering you
do not desire,
but you have given me
an open ear.[v]
Burnt-offering and sin-offering
you have not required.
7 Then I said, 'Here I am;
in the scroll of the book it
is written of me.[w]
8 I delight to do your will, O my God;
your law is within my heart.'

9 I have told the glad news
of deliverance
in the great congregation;
see, I have not restrained my lips,
as you know, O LORD.
10 I have not hidden your saving
help within my heart,
I have spoken of your faithfulness
and your salvation;
I have not concealed your steadfast
love and your faithfulness
from the great congregation.

11 Do not, O LORD, withhold
your mercy from me;
let your steadfast love and
your faithfulness
keep me safe for ever.
12 For evils have encompassed me
without number;
my iniquities have overtaken me,
until I cannot see;
they are more than the hairs
of my head,
and my heart fails me.

13 Be pleased, O LORD, to deliver me;
O LORD, make haste to help me.
14 Let all those be put to shame
and confusion
who seek to snatch away my life;
let those be turned back and
brought to dishonour
who desire my hurt.
15 Let those be appalled because
of their shame
who say to me, 'Aha, Aha!'

16 But may all who seek you
rejoice and be glad in you;
may those who love your salvation
say continually, 'Great
is the LORD!'
17 As for me, I am poor and needy,
but the Lord takes thought for me.
You are my help and my deliverer;
do not delay, O my God.

PSALM 41

ASSURANCE OF GOD'S HELP AND A PLEA FOR HEALING

To the leader. A Psalm of David.

1 Happy are those who consider
the poor;[x]
the LORD delivers them in
the day of trouble.
2 The LORD protects them and
keeps them alive;
they are called happy in the land.
You do not give them up to the
will of their enemies.
3 The LORD sustains them on
their sickbed;
in their illness you heal all
their infirmities.[y]

4 As for me, I said, 'O LORD, be
gracious to me;
heal me, for I have sinned
against you.'
5 My enemies wonder in malice
when I will die, and my name perish.
6 And when they come to see me,
they utter empty words,
while their hearts gather mischief;
when they go out, they
tell it abroad.
7 All who hate me whisper
together about me;
they imagine the worst for me.

8 They think that a deadly thing
has fastened on me,
that I will not rise again
from where I lie.
9 Even my bosom friend in
whom I trusted,
who ate of my bread, has lifted
the heel against me.
10 But you, O LORD, be gracious to me,
and raise me up, that I
may repay them.

11 By this I know that you are
pleased with me;
because my enemy has not
triumphed over me.
12 But you have upheld me because
of my integrity,
and set me in your
presence for ever.

[v] **40.6** Heb *ears you have dug for me*
[w] **40.7** Meaning of Heb uncertain [x] **41.1** Or *weak* [y] **41.3** Heb *you change all his bed*

13 Blessed be the LORD, the
God of Israel,
from everlasting to everlasting.
Amen and Amen.

Book II (Psalms 42–72)

PSALM 42

LONGING FOR GOD AND HIS HELP IN DISTRESS

To the leader. A Maskil of the Korahites.

1 As a deer longs for
flowing streams,
so my soul longs for you, O God.
2 My soul thirsts for God,
for the living God.
When shall I come and behold
the face of God?
3 My tears have been my food
day and night,
while people say to me continually,
'Where is your God?'

4 These things I remember,
as I pour out my soul:
how I went with the throng,[z]
and led them in procession
to the house of God,
with glad shouts and songs
of thanksgiving,
a multitude keeping festival.
5 Why are you cast down, O my soul,
and why are you disquieted
within me?
Hope in God; for I shall again
praise him,
my help 6and my God.

My soul is cast down within me;
therefore I remember you
from the land of Jordan and
of Hermon,
from Mount Mizar.
7 Deep calls to deep
at the thunder of
your cataracts;
all your waves and your billows
have gone over me.
8 By day the LORD commands
his steadfast love,
and at night his song is with me,
a prayer to the God of my life.

9 I say to God, my rock,
'Why have you forgotten me?
Why must I walk about mournfully
because the enemy oppresses me?'
10 As with a deadly wound in my body,
my adversaries taunt me,
while they say to me continually,
'Where is your God?'

11 Why are you cast down, O my soul,
and why are you disquieted
within me?
Hope in God; for I shall again
praise him,
my help and my God.

PSALM 43

PRAYER TO GOD IN TIME OF TROUBLE

1 Vindicate me, O God, and
defend my cause
against an ungodly people;
from those who are deceitful
and unjust
deliver me!
2 For you are the God in whom
I take refuge;
why have you cast me off?
Why must I walk about mournfully
because of the oppression
of the enemy?

3 O send out your light and your truth;
let them lead me;
let them bring me to your holy hill
and to your dwelling.
4 Then I will go to the altar of God,
to God my exceeding joy;
and I will praise you with the harp,
O God, my God.

5 Why are you cast down, O my soul,
and why are you disquieted
within me?
Hope in God; for I shall again
praise him,
my help and my God.

PSALM 44

NATIONAL LAMENT AND PRAYER FOR HELP

To the leader. Of the Korahites. A Maskil.

1 We have heard with our ears, O God,
our ancestors have told us,
what deeds you performed
in their days,
in the days of old:

[z] 42.4 Meaning of Heb uncertain

2 you with your own hand drove
out the nations,
but them you planted;
you afflicted the peoples,
but them you set free;
3 for not by their own sword did
they win the land,
nor did their own arm give
them victory;
but your right hand, and your arm,
and the light of your countenance,
for you delighted in them.

4 You are my King and my God;
you command[a] victories for Jacob.
5 Through you we push down our foes;
through your name we tread
down our assailants.
6 For not in my bow do I trust,
nor can my sword save me.
7 But you have saved us from our foes,
and have put to confusion
those who hate us.
8 In God we have boasted continually,
and we will give thanks to your
name for ever. *Selah*

9 Yet you have rejected us and abased us,
and have not gone out
with our armies.
10 You made us turn back from the foe,
and our enemies have taken
spoil for themselves.
11 You have made us like sheep
for slaughter,
and have scattered us among
the nations.
12 You have sold your people for a trifle,
demanding no high price for them.

13 You have made us the taunt
of our neighbours,
the derision and scorn of
those around us.
14 You have made us a byword
among the nations,
a laughing-stock[b] among
the peoples.
15 All day long my disgrace is before me,
and shame has covered my face
16 at the words of the taunters
and revilers,
at the sight of the enemy
and the avenger.

17 All this has come upon us,
yet we have not forgotten you,
or been false to your covenant.
18 Our heart has not turned back,
nor have our steps departed
from your way,
19 yet you have broken us in the
haunt of jackals,
and covered us with deep darkness.

20 If we had forgotten the name
of our God,
or spread out our hands to
a strange god,
21 would not God discover this?
For he knows the secrets
of the heart.
22 Because of you we are being
killed all day long,
and accounted as sheep for
the slaughter.

23 Rouse yourself! Why do you
sleep, O Lord?
Awake, do not cast us off for ever!
24 Why do you hide your face?
Why do you forget our affliction
and oppression?
25 For we sink down to the dust;
our bodies cling to the ground.
26 Rise up, come to our help.
Redeem us for the sake of
your steadfast love.

PSALM 45

ODE FOR A ROYAL WEDDING

To the leader: according to Lilies. Of the Korahites. A Maskil. A love song.

1 My heart overflows with a
goodly theme;
I address my verses to the king;
my tongue is like the pen
of a ready scribe.

2 You are the most handsome of men;
grace is poured upon your lips;
therefore God has blessed
you for ever.
3 Gird your sword on your thigh,
O mighty one,
in your glory and majesty.

4 In your majesty ride on victoriously
for the cause of truth and to
defend[c] the right;
let your right hand teach
you dread deeds.
5 Your arrows are sharp
in the heart of the king's enemies;
the peoples fall under you.

[a] **44.4** Gk Syr: Heb *You are my King, O God; command* [b] **44.14** Heb *a shaking of the head*
[c] **45.4** Cn: Heb *and the meekness of*

6 Your throne, O God,[d] endures
for ever and ever.
Your royal sceptre is a
sceptre of equity;
7 you love righteousness and
hate wickedness.
Therefore God, your God, has
anointed you
with the oil of gladness beyond
your companions;
8 your robes are all fragrant with
myrrh and aloes and cassia.
From ivory palaces stringed
instruments make you glad;
9 daughters of kings are among
your ladies of honour;
at your right hand stands the
queen in gold of Ophir.

10 Hear, O daughter, consider and
incline your ear;
forget your people and your
father's house,
11 and the king will desire
your beauty.
Since he is your lord, bow to him;
12 the people[e] of Tyre will seek
your favour with gifts,
the richest of the people 13with
all kinds of wealth.

The princess is decked in
her chamber with
gold-woven robes;[f]
14 in many-coloured robes she
is led to the king;
behind her the virgins, her
companions, follow.
15 With joy and gladness they
are led along
as they enter the palace
of the king.

16 In the place of ancestors you,
O king,[g] shall have sons;
you will make them princes
in all the earth.
17 I will cause your name to be
celebrated in all generations;
therefore the peoples will praise
you for ever and ever.

PSALM 46

GOD'S DEFENCE OF HIS CITY AND PEOPLE

To the leader. Of the Korahites. According to Alamoth. A Song.

1 God is our refuge and strength,
a very present[h] help in trouble.
2 Therefore we will not fear, though
the earth should change,
though the mountains shake
in the heart of the sea;
3 though its waters roar and foam,
though the mountains tremble
with its tumult. *Selah*

4 There is a river whose streams
make glad the city of God,
the holy habitation of
the Most High.
5 God is in the midst of the city;[i]
it shall not be moved;
God will help it when the
morning dawns.
6 The nations are in an uproar,
the kingdoms totter;
he utters his voice, the
earth melts.
7 The LORD of hosts is with us;
the God of Jacob is our refuge.[j]
Selah

8 Come, behold the works of the LORD;
see what desolations he has
brought on the earth.
9 He makes wars cease to the
end of the earth;
he breaks the bow, and
shatters the spear;
he burns the shields with fire.
10 'Be still, and know that I am God!
I am exalted among the nations,
I am exalted in the earth.'
11 The LORD of hosts is with us;
the God of Jacob is our refuge.[k]
Selah

PSALM 47

GOD'S RULE OVER THE NATIONS

To the leader. Of the Korahites. A Psalm.

1 Clap your hands, all you peoples;
shout to God with loud
songs of joy.
2 For the LORD, the Most High,
is awesome,
a great king over all the earth.
3 He subdued peoples under us,
and nations under our feet.

[d] **45.6** Or *Your throne is a throne of God, it*
[e] **45.12** Heb *daughter* [f] **45.13** Or *people.* 13*All glorious is the princess within, gold embroidery is her clothing* [g] **45.16** Heb lacks *O king*
[h] **46.1** Or *well proved* [i] **46.5** Heb *of it*
[j] **46.7** Or *fortress* [k] **46.11** Or *fortress*

4 He chose our heritage for us,
the pride of Jacob whom he loves.
Selah

5 God has gone up with a shout,
the LORD with the sound
of a trumpet.
6 Sing praises to God, sing praises;
sing praises to our King,
sing praises.
7 For God is the king of all the earth;
sing praises with a psalm.[l]

8 God is king over the nations;
God sits on his holy throne.
9 The princes of the peoples gather
as the people of the God
of Abraham.
For the shields of the earth
belong to God;
he is highly exalted.

PSALM 48

THE GLORY AND STRENGTH OF ZION

A Song. A Psalm of the Korahites.

1 Great is the LORD and greatly
to be praised
in the city of our God.
His holy mountain, 2beautiful
in elevation,
is the joy of all the earth,
Mount Zion, in the far north,
the city of the great King.
3 Within its citadels God
has shown himself a
sure defence.

4 Then the kings assembled,
they came on together.
5 As soon as they saw it, they
were astounded;
they were in panic, they
took to flight;
6 trembling took hold of them there,
pains as of a woman in labour,
7 as when an east wind shatters
the ships of Tarshish.
8 As we have heard, so have we seen
in the city of the LORD of hosts,
in the city of our God,
which God establishes for ever.
Selah

9 We ponder your steadfast
love, O God,
in the midst of your temple.
10 Your name, O God, like your praise,
reaches to the ends of the earth.
Your right hand is filled
with victory.
11 Let Mount Zion be glad,
let the towns[m] of Judah rejoice
because of your judgements.

12 Walk about Zion, go all around it,
count its towers,
13 consider well its ramparts;
go through its citadels,
that you may tell the next
generation
14 that this is God,
our God for ever and ever.
He will be our guide for ever.

PSALM 49

THE FOLLY OF TRUST IN RICHES

To the leader. Of the Korahites. A Psalm.

1 Hear this, all you peoples;
give ear, all inhabitants
of the world,
2 both low and high,
rich and poor together.
3 My mouth shall speak wisdom;
the meditation of my heart
shall be understanding.
4 I will incline my ear to a proverb;
I will solve my riddle to the
music of the harp.

5 Why should I fear in times of trouble,
when the iniquity of my
persecutors surrounds me,
6 those who trust in their wealth
and boast of the abundance
of their riches?
7 Truly, no ransom avails for one's life,[n]
there is no price one can
give to God for it.
8 For the ransom of life is costly,
and can never suffice,
9 that one should live on for ever
and never see the grave.[o]

10 When we look at the wise, they die;
fool and dolt perish together
and leave their wealth to others.
11 Their graves[p] are their
homes for ever,
their dwelling-places to
all generations,
though they named lands
their own.

[l] **47.7** Heb *Maskil* [m] **48.11** Heb *daughters*
[n] **49.7** Another reading is *no one can ransom a brother* [o] **49.9** Heb *the pit* [p] **49.11** Gk Syr Compare Tg: Heb *their inward* (thought)

12 Mortals cannot abide in their pomp;
they are like the animals
that perish.

13 Such is the fate of the foolhardy,
the end of those[q] who are pleased
with their lot. *Selah*
14 Like sheep they are appointed
for Sheol;
Death shall be their shepherd;
straight to the grave they descend,[r]
and their form shall waste away;
Sheol shall be their home.[s]
15 But God will ransom my soul from
the power of Sheol,
for he will receive me. *Selah*

16 Do not be afraid when some
become rich,
when the wealth of their
houses increases.
17 For when they die they will
carry nothing away;
their wealth will not go
down after them.
18 Though in their lifetime they
count themselves happy
—for you are praised when you
do well for yourself—
19 they[t] will go to the company
of their ancestors,
who will never again
see the light.
20 Mortals cannot abide in
their pomp;
they are like the animals
that perish.

PSALM 50

THE ACCEPTABLE SACRIFICE

A Psalm of Asaph.

1 The mighty one, God the LORD,
speaks and summons the earth
from the rising of the sun
to its setting.
2 Out of Zion, the perfection of beauty,
God shines forth.

3 Our God comes and does not
keep silence,
before him is a devouring fire,
and a mighty tempest all
around him.
4 He calls to the heavens above
and to the earth, that he may
judge his people:
5 'Gather to me my faithful ones,
who made a covenant with
me by sacrifice!'
6 The heavens declare his
righteousness,
for God himself is judge. *Selah*

7 'Hear, O my people, and I will speak,
O Israel, I will testify against you.
I am God, your God.
8 Not for your sacrifices do
I rebuke you;
your burnt-offerings are
continually before me.
9 I will not accept a bull from
your house,
or goats from your folds.
10 For every wild animal of the
forest is mine,
the cattle on a thousand hills.
11 I know all the birds of the air,[u]
and all that moves in the
field is mine.

12 'If I were hungry, I would
not tell you,
for the world and all that
is in it is mine.
13 Do I eat the flesh of bulls,
or drink the blood of goats?
14 Offer to God a sacrifice of
thanksgiving,[v]
and pay your vows to
the Most High.
15 Call on me in the day of trouble;
I will deliver you, and you
shall glorify me.'

16 But to the wicked God says:
'What right have you to
recite my statutes,
or take my covenant on your lips?
17 For you hate discipline,
and you cast my words
behind you.
18 You make friends with a thief
when you see one,
and you keep company
with adulterers.

19 'You give your mouth free
rein for evil,
and your tongue frames deceit.
20 You sit and speak against your kin;
you slander your own
mother's child.

[q] 49.13 Tg: Heb *after them* [r] 49.14 Cn: Heb *the upright shall have dominion over them in the morning* [s] 49.14 Meaning of Heb uncertain [t] 49.19 Cn: Heb *you* [u] 50.11 Gk Syr Tg: Heb *mountains* [v] 50.14 Or *make thanksgiving your sacrifice to God*

21 These things you have done and
I have been silent;
you thought that I was one
just like yourself.
But now I rebuke you, and lay
the charge before you.

22 'Mark this, then, you who
forget God,
or I will tear you apart, and there
will be no one to deliver.
23 Those who bring thanksgiving as
their sacrifice honour me;
to those who go the right way[w]
I will show the
salvation of God.'

PSALM 51

PRAYER FOR CLEANSING AND PARDON

To the leader. A Psalm of David, when the prophet Nathan came to him, after he had gone in to Bathsheba.

1 Have mercy on me, O God,
according to your steadfast love;
according to your abundant mercy
blot out my transgressions.
2 Wash me thoroughly from
my iniquity,
and cleanse me from my sin.

3 For I know my transgressions,
and my sin is ever before me.
4 Against you, you alone,
have I sinned,
and done what is evil
in your sight,
so that you are justified in
your sentence
and blameless when you
pass judgement.
5 Indeed, I was born guilty,
a sinner when my mother
conceived me.

6 You desire truth in the
inward being;[x]
therefore teach me wisdom
in my secret heart.
7 Purge me with hyssop, and
I shall be clean;
wash me, and I shall be
whiter than snow.
8 Let me hear joy and gladness;
let the bones that you have
crushed rejoice.
9 Hide your face from my sins,
and blot out all my iniquities.

10 Create in me a clean heart, O God,
and put a new and right[y]
spirit within me.
11 Do not cast me away from
your presence,
and do not take your holy
spirit from me.
12 Restore to me the joy of
your salvation,
and sustain in me a willing[z] spirit.

13 Then I will teach transgressors
your ways,
and sinners will return to you.
14 Deliver me from bloodshed, O God,
O God of my salvation,
and my tongue will sing aloud
of your deliverance.

15 O Lord, open my lips,
and my mouth will declare
your praise.
16 For you have no delight in sacrifice;
if I were to give a burnt-offering,
you would not be pleased.
17 The sacrifice acceptable to God[a]
is a broken spirit;
a broken and contrite heart,
O God, you will not despise.

18 Do good to Zion in your
good pleasure;
rebuild the walls of Jerusalem,
19 then you will delight in
right sacrifices,
in burnt-offerings and whole
burnt-offerings;
then bulls will be offered
on your altar.

PSALM 52

JUDGEMENT ON THE DECEITFUL

To the leader. A Maskil of David, when Doeg the Edomite came to Saul and said to him, 'David has come to the house of Ahimelech.'

1 Why do you boast, O mighty one,
of mischief done against
the godly?[b]
All day long 2you are
plotting destruction.
Your tongue is like a sharp razor,
you worker of treachery.

[w] 50.23 Heb *who set a way* [x] 51.6 Meaning of Heb uncertain [y] 51.10 Or *steadfast* [z] 51.12 Or *generous* [a] 51.17 Or *My sacrifice, O God,* [b] 52.1 Cn Compare Syr: Heb *the kindness of God*

3 You love evil more than good,
and lying more than speaking the truth. *Selah*
4 You love all words that devour,
O deceitful tongue.
5 But God will break you down for ever;
he will snatch and tear you from your tent;
he will uproot you from the land of the living. *Selah*
6 The righteous will see, and fear,
and will laugh at the evildoer,[c] saying,
7 'See the one who would not take refuge in God,
but trusted in abundant riches,
and sought refuge in wealth!'[d]

8 But I am like a green olive tree
in the house of God.
I trust in the steadfast love of God
for ever and ever.
9 I will thank you for ever,
because of what you have done.
In the presence of the faithful
I will proclaim[e] your name,
for it is good.

PSALM 53
DENUNCIATION OF GODLESSNESS
To the leader: according to Mahalath. A Maskil of David.

1 Fools say in their hearts,
'There is no God.'
They are corrupt, they commit abominable acts;
there is no one who does good.

2 God looks down from heaven on humankind
to see if there are any who are wise,
who seek after God.

3 They have all fallen away, they are all alike perverse;
there is no one who does good,
no, not one.

4 Have they no knowledge, those evildoers,
who eat up my people as they eat bread,
and do not call upon God?

5 There they shall be in great terror,
in terror such as has not been.
For God will scatter the bones of the ungodly;[f]
they will be put to shame,[g] for God has rejected them.

6 O that deliverance for Israel would come from Zion!
When God restores the fortunes of his people,
Jacob will rejoice; Israel will be glad.

PSALM 54
PRAYER FOR VINDICATION
To the leader: with stringed instruments. A Maskil of David, when the Ziphites went and told Saul, 'David is in hiding among us.'

1 Save me, O God, by your name,
and vindicate me by your might.
2 Hear my prayer, O God;
give ear to the words of my mouth.

3 For the insolent have risen against me,
the ruthless seek my life;
they do not set God before them. *Selah*

4 But surely, God is my helper;
the Lord is the upholder of[h] my life.
5 He will repay my enemies for their evil.
In your faithfulness, put an end to them.

6 With a freewill-offering I will sacrifice to you;
I will give thanks to your name,
O LORD, for it is good.
7 For he has delivered me from every trouble,
and my eye has looked in triumph on my enemies.

PSALM 55
COMPLAINT ABOUT A FRIEND'S TREACHERY
To the leader: with stringed instruments. A Maskil of David.

1 Give ear to my prayer, O God;
do not hide yourself from my supplication.

[c] 52.6 Heb *him* [d] 52.7 Syr Tg: Heb *in his destruction* [e] 52.9 Cn: Heb *wait for* [f] 53.5 Cn Compare Gk Syr: Heb *him who encamps against you* [g] 53.5 Gk: Heb *you will put to shame* [h] 54.4 Gk Syr Jerome: Heb *is of those who uphold* or *is with those who uphold*

2 Attend to me, and answer me;
I am troubled in my complaint.
I am distraught 3by the noise
of the enemy,
because of the clamour
of the wicked.
For they bring[i] trouble upon me,
and in anger they cherish
enmity against me.

4 My heart is in anguish within me,
the terrors of death have
fallen upon me.
5 Fear and trembling come upon me,
and horror overwhelms me.
6 And I say, 'O that I had
wings like a dove!
I would fly away and be at rest;
7 truly, I would flee far away;
I would lodge in the wilderness;
Selah
8 I would hurry to find a
shelter for myself
from the raging wind
and tempest.'

9 Confuse, O Lord, confound
their speech;
for I see violence and
strife in the city.
10 Day and night they go around it
on its walls,
and iniquity and trouble
are within it;
11 ruin is in its midst;
oppression and fraud
do not depart from its
market-place.

12 It is not enemies who taunt me—
I could bear that;
it is not adversaries who deal
insolently with me—
I could hide from them.
13 But it is you, my equal,
my companion, my
familiar friend,
14 with whom I kept
pleasant company;
we walked in the house of
God with the throng.
15 Let death come upon them;
let them go down alive to Sheol;
for evil is in their homes
and in their hearts.

16 But I call upon God,
and the LORD will save me.
17 Evening and morning and at noon
I utter my complaint and moan,
and he will hear my voice.
18 He will redeem me unharmed
from the battle that I wage,
for many are arrayed against me.
19 God, who is enthroned from old,
Selah
will hear, and will humble them—
because they do not change,
and do not fear God.

20 My companion laid hands
on a friend
and violated a covenant with me[j]
21 with speech smoother than butter,
but with a heart set on war;
with words that were softer than oil,
but in fact were drawn swords.

22 Cast your burden[k] on the LORD,
and he will sustain you;
he will never permit
the righteous to be moved.

23 But you, O God, will cast them down
into the lowest pit;
the bloodthirsty and treacherous
shall not live out half their days.
But I will trust in you.

PSALM 56

TRUST IN GOD UNDER PERSECUTION

To the leader: according to The Dove on Far-off Terebinths. Of David. A Miktam, when the Philistines seized him in Gath.

1 Be gracious to me, O God, for
people trample on me;
all day long foes oppress me;
2 my enemies trample on me
all day long,
for many fight against me.
O Most High, 3when I am afraid,
I put my trust in you.
4 In God, whose word I praise,
in God I trust; I am not afraid;
what can flesh do to me?

5 All day long they seek to
injure my cause;
all their thoughts are
against me for evil.
6 They stir up strife, they lurk,
they watch my steps.
As they hoped to have my life,
7 so repay[l] them for their crime;
in wrath cast down the
peoples, O God!

[i] 55.3 Cn Compare Gk: Heb *they cause to totter*
[j] 55.20 Heb lacks *with me* [k] 55.22 Or *Cast what he has given you* [l] 56.7 Cn: Heb *rescue*

8 You have kept count of my tossings;
put my tears in your bottle.
Are they not in your record?
9 Then my enemies will retreat
on the day when I call.
This I know, that[m] God is for me.
10 In God, whose word I praise,
in the LORD, whose word I praise,
11 in God I trust; I am not afraid.
What can a mere mortal do to me?

12 My vows to you I must
perform, O God;
I will render thank-offerings
to you.
13 For you have delivered my
soul from death,
and my feet from falling,
so that I may walk before God
in the light of life.

PSALM 57

PRAISE AND ASSURANCE UNDER PERSECUTION

To the leader: Do Not Destroy. Of David. A Miktam, when he fled from Saul, in the cave.

1 Be merciful to me, O God, be
merciful to me,
for in you my soul takes refuge;
in the shadow of your wings
I will take refuge,
until the destroying
storms pass by.
2 I cry to God Most High,
to God who fulfils his
purpose for me.
3 He will send from heaven
and save me,
he will put to shame those who
trample on me. *Selah*
God will send forth his steadfast
love and his faithfulness.

4 I lie down among lions
that greedily devour[n] human prey;
their teeth are spears and arrows,
their tongues sharp swords.

5 Be exalted, O God, above
the heavens.
Let your glory be over
all the earth.

6 They set a net for my steps;
my soul was bowed down.
They dug a pit in my path,
but they have fallen into it
themselves. *Selah*

7 My heart is steadfast, O God,
my heart is steadfast.
I will sing and make melody.
8 Awake, my soul!
Awake, O harp and lyre!
I will awake the dawn.
9 I will give thanks to you, O Lord,
among the peoples;
I will sing praises to you
among the nations.
10 For your steadfast love is as
high as the heavens;
your faithfulness extends
to the clouds.

11 Be exalted, O God, above
the heavens.
Let your glory be over
all the earth.

PSALM 58

PRAYER FOR VENGEANCE

To the leader: Do Not Destroy. Of David. A Miktam.

1 Do you indeed decree what is
right, you gods?[o]
Do you judge people fairly?
2 No, in your hearts you
devise wrongs;
your hands deal out
violence on earth.

3 The wicked go astray from
the womb;
they err from their birth,
speaking lies.
4 They have venom like the
venom of a serpent,
like the deaf adder that
stops its ear,
5 so that it does not hear the
voice of charmers
or of the cunning enchanter.

6 O God, break the teeth in
their mouths;
tear out the fangs of the
young lions, O LORD!
7 Let them vanish like water
that runs away;
like grass let them be trodden
down[p] and wither.
8 Let them be like the snail that
dissolves into slime;
like the untimely birth that
never sees the sun.

[m] 56.9 Or *because* [n] 57.4 Cn: Heb *are aflame for* [o] 58.1 Or *mighty lords* [p] 58.7 Cn: Meaning of Heb uncertain

9 Sooner than your pots can feel
the heat of thorns,
whether green or ablaze, may
he sweep them away!

10 The righteous will rejoice when
they see vengeance done;
they will bathe their feet in
the blood of the wicked.
11 People will say, 'Surely there is a
reward for the righteous;
surely there is a God who
judges on earth.'

PSALM 59

PRAYER FOR DELIVERANCE FROM ENEMIES

To the leader: Do Not Destroy. Of David. A Miktam, when Saul ordered his house to be watched in order to kill him.

1 Deliver me from my enemies,
O my God;
protect me from those who
rise up against me.
2 Deliver me from those who
work evil;
from the bloodthirsty save me.

3 Even now they lie in wait for my life;
the mighty stir up strife
against me.
For no transgression or sin
of mine, O LORD,
4 for no fault of mine, they
run and make ready.

Rouse yourself, come to my
help and see!
5 You, LORD God of hosts,
are God of Israel.
Awake to punish all the nations;
spare none of those who
treacherously plot evil. *Selah*

6 Each evening they come back,
howling like dogs
and prowling about the city.
7 There they are, bellowing
with their mouths,
with sharp words[q] on their lips—
for 'Who', they think,[r]
'will hear us?'

8 But you laugh at them, O LORD;
you hold all the nations
in derision.
9 O my strength, I will watch for you;
for you, O God, are my fortress.
10 My God in his steadfast love
will meet me;
my God will let me look in
triumph on my enemies.

11 Do not kill them, or my
people may forget;
make them totter by your power,
and bring them down,
O Lord, our shield.
12 For the sin of their mouths, the
words of their lips,
let them be trapped in their pride.
For the cursing and lies
that they utter,
13 consume them in wrath;
consume them until they
are no more.
Then it will be known to the
ends of the earth
that God rules over Jacob. *Selah*

14 Each evening they come back,
howling like dogs
and prowling about the city.
15 They roam about for food,
and growl if they do not
get their fill.

16 But I will sing of your might;
I will sing aloud of your steadfast
love in the morning.
For you have been a fortress for me
and a refuge on the day
of my distress.
17 O my strength, I will sing
praises to you,
for you, O God, are my fortress,
the God who shows me
steadfast love.

PSALM 60

PRAYER FOR NATIONAL VICTORY AFTER DEFEAT

To the leader: according to The Lily of the Covenant. A Miktam of David; for instruction; when he struggled with Aram-naharaim and with Aram-zobah, and when Joab on his return killed twelve thousand Edomites in the Valley of Salt.

1 O God, you have rejected us,
broken our defences;
you have been angry;
now restore us!

[q] 59.7 Heb *with swords* [r] 59.7 Heb lacks *they think*

2 You have caused the land to quake;
you have torn it open;
repair the cracks in it, for
it is tottering.
3 You have made your people
suffer hard things;
you have given us wine to
drink that made us reel.

4 You have set up a banner for
those who fear you,
to rally to it out of bowshot.[s] *Selah*
5 Give victory with your right
hand, and answer us,[t]
so that those whom you love
may be rescued.

6 God has promised in his sanctuary:[u]
'With exultation I will divide
up Shechem,
and portion out the Vale
of Succoth.
7 Gilead is mine, and Manasseh is mine;
Ephraim is my helmet;
Judah is my sceptre.
8 Moab is my wash-basin;
on Edom I hurl my shoe;
over Philistia I shout in triumph.'

9 Who will bring me to the
fortified city?
Who will lead me to Edom?
10 Have you not rejected us, O God?
You do not go out, O God,
with our armies.
11 O grant us help against the foe,
for human help is worthless.
12 With God we shall do valiantly;
it is he who will tread
down our foes.

PSALM 61

ASSURANCE OF GOD'S PROTECTION

To the leader: with stringed instruments. Of David.

1 Hear my cry, O God;
listen to my prayer.
2 From the end of the earth
I call to you,
when my heart is faint.

Lead me to the rock
that is higher than I;
3 for you are my refuge,
a strong tower against the enemy.

4 Let me abide in your tent for ever,
find refuge under the shelter of
your wings. *Selah*

5 For you, O God, have heard my vows;
you have given me the heritage of
those who fear your name.

6 Prolong the life of the king;
may his years endure to
all generations!
7 May he be enthroned for
ever before God;
appoint steadfast love
and faithfulness to
watch over him!

8 So I will always sing praises
to your name,
as I pay my vows day after day.

PSALM 62

SONG OF TRUST IN GOD ALONE

To the leader: according to Jeduthun. A Psalm of David.

1 For God alone my soul waits
in silence;
from him comes my salvation.
2 He alone is my rock and
my salvation,
my fortress; I shall never
be shaken.

3 How long will you assail a person,
will you batter your
victim, all of you,
as you would a leaning wall,
a tottering fence?
4 Their only plan is to bring down
a person of prominence.
They take pleasure in falsehood;
they bless with their mouths,
but inwardly they curse. *Selah*

5 For God alone my soul waits
in silence,
for my hope is from him.
6 He alone is my rock and
my salvation,
my fortress; I shall not be shaken.
7 On God rests my deliverance
and my honour;
my mighty rock, my
refuge is in God.

8 Trust in him at all times, O people;
pour out your heart before him;
God is a refuge for us. *Selah*

s **60.4** Gk Syr Jerome: Heb *because of the truth*
t **60.5** Another reading is *me* u **60.6** Or *by his holiness*

9 Those of low estate are but a breath,
those of high estate
are a delusion;
in the balances they go up;
they are together lighter
than a breath.
10 Put no confidence in extortion,
and set no vain
hopes on robbery;
if riches increase, do not set
your heart on them.

11 Once God has spoken;
twice have I heard this:
that power belongs to God,
12 and steadfast love belongs
to you, O Lord.
For you repay to all
according to their work.

PSALM 63

COMFORT AND ASSURANCE IN GOD'S PRESENCE

A Psalm of David, when he was in the Wilderness of Judah.

1 O God, you are my God, I seek you,
my soul thirsts for you;
my flesh faints for you,
as in a dry and weary land
where there is no water.
2 So I have looked upon you
in the sanctuary,
beholding your power and glory.
3 Because your steadfast love
is better than life,
my lips will praise you.
4 So I will bless you as long as I live;
I will lift up my hands and
call on your name.

5 My soul is satisfied as with
a rich feast,[v]
and my mouth praises you
with joyful lips
6 when I think of you on my bed,
and meditate on you in the
watches of the night;
7 for you have been my help,
and in the shadow of your
wings I sing for joy.
8 My soul clings to you;
your right hand upholds me.

9 But those who seek to destroy my life
shall go down into the
depths of the earth;
10 they shall be given over to the
power of the sword,
they shall be prey for jackals.
11 But the king shall rejoice in God;
all who swear by him shall exult,
for the mouths of liars
will be stopped.

PSALM 64

PRAYER FOR PROTECTION FROM ENEMIES

To the leader. A Psalm of David.

1 Hear my voice, O God, in
my complaint;
preserve my life from the
dread enemy.
2 Hide me from the secret plots
of the wicked,
from the scheming of evildoers,
3 who whet their tongues like swords,
who aim bitter words like arrows,
4 shooting from ambush at
the blameless;
they shoot suddenly and
without fear.
5 They hold fast to their evil purpose;
they talk of laying snares secretly,
thinking, 'Who can see us?[w]
6 Who can search out our crimes?[x]
We have thought out a cunningly
conceived plot.'
For the human heart and
mind are deep.

7 But God will shoot his arrow at them;
they will be wounded suddenly.
8 Because of their tongue he will
bring them to ruin;[y]
all who see them will shake
with horror.
9 Then everyone will fear;
they will tell what God has
brought about,
and ponder what he has done.

10 Let the righteous rejoice in the LORD
and take refuge in him.
Let all the upright in heart glory.

PSALM 65

THANKSGIVING FOR EARTH'S BOUNTY

To the leader. A Psalm of David. A Song.

1 Praise is due to you,
O God, in Zion;

[v] 63.5 Heb *with fat and fatness* [w] 64.5 Syr: Heb *them* [x] 64.6 Cn: Heb *They search out crimes* [y] 64.8 Cn: Heb *They will bring him to ruin, their tongue being against them*

and to you shall vows be performed,
2 O you who answer prayer!
To you all flesh shall come.
3 When deeds of iniquity overwhelm us,
you forgive our transgressions.
4 Happy are those whom you
choose and bring near
to live in your courts.
We shall be satisfied with the
goodness of your house,
your holy temple.

5 By awesome deeds you answer
us with deliverance,
O God of our salvation;
you are the hope of all the
ends of the earth
and of the farthest seas.
6 By your[z] strength you established
the mountains;
you are girded with might.
7 You silence the roaring of the seas,
the roaring of their waves,
the tumult of the peoples.
8 Those who live at earth's
farthest bounds are
awed by your signs;
you make the gateways of the morning
and the evening shout for joy.

9 You visit the earth and water it,
you greatly enrich it;
the river of God is full of water;
you provide the people with grain,
for so you have prepared it.
10 You water its furrows abundantly,
settling its ridges,
softening it with showers,
and blessing its growth.
11 You crown the year with your bounty;
your wagon tracks overflow
with richness.
12 The pastures of the wilderness
overflow,
the hills gird themselves with joy,
13 the meadows clothe themselves
with flocks,
the valleys deck themselves
with grain,
they shout and sing together for joy.

PSALM 66

PRAISE FOR GOD'S GOODNESS TO ISRAEL

To the leader. A Song. A Psalm.

1 Make a joyful noise to God,
all the earth;
2 sing the glory of his name;
give to him glorious praise.
3 Say to God, 'How awesome
are your deeds!
Because of your great power, your
enemies cringe before you.
4 All the earth worships you;
they sing praises to you,
sing praises to your name.' *Selah*

5 Come and see what God has done:
he is awesome in his deeds
among mortals.
6 He turned the sea into dry land;
they passed through the
river on foot.
There we rejoiced in him,
7 who rules by his might for ever,
whose eyes keep watch on
the nations—
let the rebellious not exalt
themselves. *Selah*

8 Bless our God, O peoples,
let the sound of his praise
be heard,
9 who has kept us among the living,
and has not let our feet slip.
10 For you, O God, have tested us;
you have tried us as silver is tried.
11 You brought us into the net;
you laid burdens on our backs;
12 you let people ride over our heads;
we went through fire and
through water;
yet you have brought us out to
a spacious place.[a]

13 I will come into your house
with burnt-offerings;
I will pay you my vows,
14 those that my lips uttered
and my mouth promised
when I was in trouble.
15 I will offer to you burnt-offerings
of fatlings,
with the smoke of the
sacrifice of rams;
I will make an offering of bulls and
goats. *Selah*

16 Come and hear, all you who fear God,
and I will tell what he has
done for me.
17 I cried aloud to him,
and he was extolled with
my tongue.
18 If I had cherished iniquity
in my heart,
the Lord would not have listened.

[z] 65.6 Gk Jerome: Heb *his* [a] 66.12 Cn Compare Gk Syr Jerome Tg: Heb *to a saturation*

19 But truly God has listened;
he has given heed to the words of my prayer.

20 Blessed be God,
because he has not rejected my prayer
or removed his steadfast love from me.

PSALM 67

THE NATIONS CALLED TO PRAISE GOD

To the leader: with stringed instruments. A Psalm. A Song.

1 May God be gracious to us and bless us
and make his face to shine upon us, *Selah*
2 that your way may be known upon earth,
your saving power among all nations.
3 Let the peoples praise you, O God;
let all the peoples praise you.
4 Let the nations be glad and sing for joy,
for you judge the peoples with equity
and guide the nations upon earth. *Selah*
5 Let the peoples praise you, O God;
let all the peoples praise you.
6 The earth has yielded its increase;
God, our God, has blessed us.
7 May God continue to bless us;
let all the ends of the earth revere him.

PSALM 68

PRAISE AND THANKSGIVING

To the leader. Of David. A Psalm. A Song.

1 Let God rise up, let his enemies be scattered;
let those who hate him flee before him.
2 As smoke is driven away, so drive them away;
as wax melts before the fire,
let the wicked perish before God.
3 But let the righteous be joyful;
let them exult before God;
let them be jubilant with joy.

4 Sing to God, sing praises to his name;
lift up a song to him who rides upon the clouds[b]—
his name is the LORD—
be exultant before him.

5 Father of orphans and protector of widows
is God in his holy habitation.
6 God gives the desolate a home to live in;
he leads out the prisoners to prosperity,
but the rebellious live in a parched land.

7 O God, when you went out before your people,
when you marched through the wilderness, *Selah*
8 the earth quaked, the heavens poured down rain
at the presence of God, the God of Sinai,
at the presence of God, the God of Israel.
9 Rain in abundance, O God, you showered abroad;
you restored your heritage when it languished;
10 your flock found a dwelling in it;
in your goodness, O God, you provided for the needy.

11 The Lord gives the command;
great is the company of those[c] who bore the tidings:
12 'The kings of the armies, they flee, they flee!'
The women at home divide the spoil,
13 though they stay among the sheepfolds—
the wings of a dove covered with silver,
its pinions with green gold.
14 When the Almighty[d] scattered kings there,
snow fell on Zalmon.

15 O mighty mountain, mountain of Bashan;
O many-peaked mountain, mountain of Bashan!
16 Why do you look with envy,
O many-peaked mountain,
at the mount that God desired for his abode,
where the LORD will reside for ever?

[b] 68.4 Or *cast up a highway for him who rides through the deserts* [c] 68.11 Or *company of the women* [d] 68.14 Traditional rendering of Heb *Shaddai*

17 With mighty chariotry, twice
ten thousand,
thousands upon thousands,
the Lord came from Sinai
into the holy place.[e]
18 You ascended the high mount,
leading captives in your train
and receiving gifts from people,
even from those who rebel against the
LORD God's abiding there.
19 Blessed be the Lord,
who daily bears us up;
God is our salvation. *Selah*
20 Our God is a God of salvation,
and to GOD, the Lord, belongs
escape from death.

21 But God will shatter the heads
of his enemies,
the hairy crown of those who
walk in their guilty ways.
22 The Lord said,
'I will bring them back
from Bashan,
I will bring them back from the
depths of the sea,
23 so that you may bathe[f] your
feet in blood,
so that the tongues of your
dogs may have their
share from the foe.'

24 Your solemn processions are
seen,[g] O God,
the processions of my God, my
King, into the sanctuary—
25 the singers in front, the musicians last,
between them girls playing
tambourines:
26 'Bless God in the great congregation,
the LORD, O you who are of
Israel's fountain!'
27 There is Benjamin, the least of
them, in the lead,
the princes of Judah in a body,
the princes of Zebulun, the
princes of Naphtali.

28 Summon your might, O God;
show your strength, O God, as you
have done for us before.
29 Because of your temple at Jerusalem
kings bear gifts to you.
30 Rebuke the wild animals that
live among the reeds,
the herd of bulls with the
calves of the peoples.
Trample[h] under foot those who
lust after tribute;
scatter the peoples who
delight in war.[i]
31 Let bronze be brought from Egypt;
let Ethiopia[j] hasten to stretch
out its hands to God.

32 Sing to God, O kingdoms
of the earth;
sing praises to the Lord, *Selah*
33 O rider in the heavens, the
ancient heavens;
listen, he sends out his voice,
his mighty voice.
34 Ascribe power to God,
whose majesty is over Israel;
and whose power is in the skies.
35 Awesome is God in his[k] sanctuary,
the God of Israel;
he gives power and strength
to his people.

Blessed be God!

PSALM 69

PRAYER FOR DELIVERANCE FROM PERSECUTION

To the leader: according to Lilies. Of David.

1 Save me, O God,
for the waters have come
up to my neck.
2 I sink in deep mire,
where there is no foothold;
I have come into deep waters,
and the flood sweeps over me.
3 I am weary with my crying;
my throat is parched.
My eyes grow dim
with waiting for my God.

4 More in number than the
hairs of my head
are those who hate me
without cause;
many are those who would
destroy me,
my enemies who accuse
me falsely.
What I did not steal
must I now restore?
5 O God, you know my folly;
the wrongs I have done are
not hidden from you.

[e] 68.17 Cn: Heb *The Lord among them Sinai in the holy* (place) [f] 68.23 Gk Syr Tg: Heb *shatter* [g] 68.24 Or *have been seen* [h] 68.30 Cn: Heb *Trampling* [i] 68.30 Meaning of Heb of verse 30 is uncertain [j] 68.31 Or *Nubia*; Heb *Cush* [k] 68.35 Gk: Heb *from your*

6 Do not let those who hope in you be
put to shame because of me,
O Lord GOD of hosts;
do not let those who seek you be
dishonoured because of me,
O God of Israel.
7 It is for your sake that I have
borne reproach,
that shame has covered my face.
8 I have become a stranger to
my kindred,
an alien to my mother's children.
9 It is zeal for your house that
has consumed me;
the insults of those who insult
you have fallen on me.
10 When I humbled my soul with fasting,[l]
they insulted me for doing so.
11 When I made sackcloth my clothing,
I became a byword to them.
12 I am the subject of gossip for those
who sit in the gate,
and the drunkards make
songs about me.

13 But as for me, my prayer is
to you, O LORD.
At an acceptable time, O God,
in the abundance of your
steadfast love, answer me.
With your faithful help 14rescue me
from sinking in the mire;
let me be delivered from my enemies
and from the deep waters.
15 Do not let the flood sweep over me,
or the deep swallow me up,
or the Pit close its mouth over me.

16 Answer me, O LORD, for your
steadfast love is good;
according to your abundant
mercy, turn to me.
17 Do not hide your face from
your servant,
for I am in distress—make
haste to answer me.
18 Draw near to me, redeem me,
set me free because of my enemies.

19 You know the insults I receive,
and my shame and dishonour;
my foes are all known to you.
20 Insults have broken my heart,
so that I am in despair.
I looked for pity, but there was none;
and for comforters, but
I found none.
21 They gave me poison for food,
and for my thirst they gave
me vinegar to drink.

22 Let their table be a
trap for them,
a snare for their allies.
23 Let their eyes be darkened so
that they cannot see,
and make their loins tremble
continually.
24 Pour out your indignation
upon them,
and let your burning anger
overtake them.
25 May their camp be a desolation;
let no one live in their tents.
26 For they persecute those whom
you have struck down,
and those whom you have
wounded, they attack
still more.[m]
27 Add guilt to their guilt;
may they have no acquittal
from you.
28 Let them be blotted out of the
book of the living;
let them not be enrolled
among the righteous.
29 But I am lowly and in pain;
let your salvation, O God,
protect me.

30 I will praise the name of God
with a song;
I will magnify him with
thanksgiving.
31 This will please the LORD
more than an ox
or a bull with horns and hoofs.
32 Let the oppressed see
it and be glad;
you who seek God, let your
hearts revive.
33 For the LORD hears the needy,
and does not despise his own
that are in bonds.

34 Let heaven and earth praise him,
the seas and everything that
moves in them.
35 For God will save Zion
and rebuild the cities of Judah;
and his servants shall live[n]
there and possess it;
36 the children of his servants
shall inherit it,
and those who love his
name shall live in it.

[l] **69.10** Gk Syr: Heb *I wept, with fasting my soul*, or *I made my soul mourn with fasting* [m] **69.26** Gk Syr: Heb *recount the pain of* [n] **69.35** Syr: Heb *and they shall live*

PSALM 70

PRAYER FOR DELIVERANCE FROM ENEMIES

To the leader. Of David, for the memorial offering.

1 Be pleased, O God, to deliver me.
O LORD, make haste to help me!
2 Let those be put to shame
and confusion
who seek my life.
Let those be turned back and
brought to dishonour
who desire to hurt me.
3 Let those who say, 'Aha, Aha!'
turn back because of their shame.

4 Let all who seek you
rejoice and be glad in you.
Let those who love your salvation
say evermore, 'God is great!'
5 But I am poor and needy;
hasten to me, O God!
You are my help and my deliverer;
O LORD, do not delay!

PSALM 71

PRAYER FOR LIFELONG PROTECTION AND HELP

1 In you, O LORD, I take refuge;
let me never be put to shame.
2 In your righteousness deliver
me and rescue me;
incline your ear to me
and save me.
3 Be to me a rock of refuge,
a strong fortress,[o] to save me,
for you are my rock and
my fortress.

4 Rescue me, O my God, from the
hand of the wicked,
from the grasp of the
unjust and cruel.
5 For you, O Lord, are my hope,
my trust, O LORD, from my youth.
6 Upon you I have leaned
from my birth;
it was you who took me from
my mother's womb.
My praise is continually of you.

7 I have been like a portent to many,
but you are my strong refuge.
8 My mouth is filled with your praise,
and with your glory all day long.
9 Do not cast me off in the
time of old age;
do not forsake me when my
strength is spent.
10 For my enemies speak
concerning me,
and those who watch for my
life consult together.
11 They say, 'Pursue and seize
that person
whom God has forsaken,
for there is no one to deliver.'

12 O God, do not be far from me;
O my God, make haste to help me!
13 Let my accusers be put to shame
and consumed;
let those who seek to hurt me
be covered with scorn
and disgrace.
14 But I will hope continually,
and will praise you yet
more and more.
15 My mouth will tell of your
righteous acts,
of your deeds of salvation
all day long,
though their number is past
my knowledge.
16 I will come praising the mighty
deeds of the Lord GOD,
I will praise your righteousness,
yours alone.

17 O God, from my youth you
have taught me,
and I still proclaim your
wondrous deeds.
18 So even to old age and grey hairs,
O God, do not forsake me,
until I proclaim your might
to all the generations to come.[p]
Your power 19and your
righteousness, O God,
reach the high heavens.

You who have done great things,
O God, who is like you?
20 You who have made me see many
troubles and calamities
will revive me again;
from the depths of the earth
you will bring me up again.
21 You will increase my honour,
and comfort me once again.

22 I will also praise you with the harp
for your faithfulness, O my God;
I will sing praises to you
with the lyre,
O Holy One of Israel.

[o] **71.3** Gk Compare 31.3: Heb *to come continually you have commanded* [p] **71.18** Gk Compare Syr: Heb *to a generation, to all that come*

23 My lips will shout for joy
when I sing praises to you;
my soul also, which you
have rescued.
24 All day long my tongue will talk
of your righteous help,
for those who tried to do me harm
have been put to shame,
and disgraced.

PSALM 72

PRAYER FOR GUIDANCE AND SUPPORT FOR THE KING

Of Solomon.

1 Give the king your justice, O God,
and your righteousness
to a king's son.
2 May he judge your people with
righteousness,
and your poor with justice.
3 May the mountains yield prosperity
for the people,
and the hills, in righteousness.
4 May he defend the cause of the
poor of the people,
give deliverance to the needy,
and crush the oppressor.

5 May he live[q] while the sun endures,
and as long as the moon,
throughout all generations.
6 May he be like rain that falls on
the mown grass,
like showers that water the earth.
7 In his days may righteousness flourish
and peace abound, until the
moon is no more.

8 May he have dominion
from sea to sea,
and from the River to the
ends of the earth.
9 May his foes[r] bow down before him,
and his enemies lick the dust.
10 May the kings of Tarshish
and of the isles
render him tribute,
may the kings of Sheba and Seba
bring gifts.
11 May all kings fall down before him,
all nations give him service.

12 For he delivers the needy
when they call,
the poor and those who
have no helper.
13 He has pity on the weak
and the needy,
and saves the lives of the needy.
14 From oppression and violence
he redeems their life;
and precious is their blood
in his sight.

15 Long may he live!
May gold of Sheba be
given to him.
May prayer be made for him
continually,
and blessings invoked for
him all day long.
16 May there be abundance of
grain in the land;
may it wave on the tops of
the mountains;
may its fruit be like Lebanon;
and may people blossom in the cities
like the grass of the field.
17 May his name endure for ever,
his fame continue as
long as the sun.
May all nations be blessed in him;[s]
may they pronounce him happy.

18 Blessed be the LORD, the
God of Israel,
who alone does wondrous things.
19 Blessed be his glorious name for ever;
may his glory fill the whole earth.
Amen and Amen.

20 The prayers of David son of
Jesse are ended.

Book III (Psalms 73–89)

PSALM 73

PLEA FOR RELIEF FROM OPPRESSORS

A Psalm of Asaph.

1 Truly God is good to the upright,[t]
to those who are pure in heart.
2 But as for me, my feet had
almost stumbled;
my steps had nearly slipped.
3 For I was envious of the arrogant;
I saw the prosperity of the wicked.

4 For they have no pain;
their bodies are sound and sleek.
5 They are not in trouble as others are;
they are not plagued like
other people.

[q] **72.5** Gk: Heb *may they fear you* [r] **72.9** Cn: Heb *those who live in the wilderness* [s] **72.17** Or *bless themselves by him* [t] **73.1** Or *good to Israel*

6 Therefore pride is their necklace;
violence covers them like
a garment.
7 Their eyes swell out with fatness;
their hearts overflow with follies.
8 They scoff and speak with malice;
loftily they threaten oppression.
9 They set their mouths against heaven,
and their tongues range
over the earth.

10 Therefore the people turn and
praise them,[u]
and find no fault in them.[v]
11 And they say, 'How can God know?
Is there knowledge in the
Most High?'
12 Such are the wicked;
always at ease, they
increase in riches.
13 All in vain I have kept my heart clean
and washed my hands
in innocence.
14 For all day long I have been plagued,
and am punished every morning.

15 If I had said, 'I will talk on in this way',
I would have been untrue to the
circle of your children.
16 But when I thought how to
understand this,
it seemed to me a
wearisome task,
17 until I went into the sanctuary of God;
then I perceived their end.
18 Truly you set them in slippery places;
you make them fall to ruin.
19 How they are destroyed in a moment,
swept away utterly by terrors!
20 They are[w] like a dream when
one awakes;
on awaking you despise
their phantoms.

21 When my soul was embittered,
when I was pricked in heart,
22 I was stupid and ignorant;
I was like a brute beast towards you.
23 Nevertheless I am continually
with you;
you hold my right hand.
24 You guide me with your counsel,
and afterwards you will receive
me with honour.[x]
25 Whom have I in heaven but you?
And there is nothing on earth
that I desire other than you.
26 My flesh and my heart may fail,
but God is the strength[y]
of my heart and my
portion for ever.

27 Indeed, those who are far from
you will perish;
you put an end to those who
are false to you.
28 But for me it is good to be near God;
I have made the Lord
GOD my refuge,
to tell of all your works.

PSALM 74

PLEA FOR HELP IN TIME OF NATIONAL HUMILIATION

A Maskil of Asaph.

1 O God, why do you cast us
off for ever?
Why does your anger smoke
against the sheep of
your pasture?
2 Remember your congregation,
which you acquired long ago,
which you redeemed to be the
tribe of your heritage.
Remember Mount Zion, where
you came to dwell.
3 Direct your steps to the
perpetual ruins;
the enemy has destroyed
everything in the sanctuary.

4 Your foes have roared within
your holy place;
they set up their emblems there.
5 At the upper entrance they hacked
the wooden trellis with axes.[z]
6 And then, with hatchets
and hammers,
they smashed all its carved work.
7 They set your sanctuary on fire;
they desecrated the dwelling-place
of your name,
bringing it to the ground.
8 They said to themselves, 'We will
utterly subdue them';
they burned all the meeting-places
of God in the land.

9 We do not see our emblems;
there is no longer any prophet,
and there is no one among us
who knows how long.
10 How long, O God, is the foe to scoff?
Is the enemy to revile your
name for ever?

[u] 73.10 Cn: Heb *his people return here*
[v] 73.10 Cn: Heb *abundant waters are drained by them* [w] 73.20 Cn: Heb *Lord* [x] 73.24 Or *to glory* [y] 73.26 Heb *rock* [z] 74.5 Cn Compare Gk Syr: Meaning of Heb uncertain

11 Why do you hold back your hand;
why do you keep your hand
in[a] your bosom?

12 Yet God my King is from of old,
working salvation in the earth.
13 You divided the sea
by your might;
you broke the heads of the
dragons in the waters.
14 You crushed the heads
of Leviathan;
you gave him as food[b] for the
creatures of the wilderness.
15 You cut openings for springs
and torrents;
you dried up ever-flowing
streams.
16 Yours is the day, yours
also the night;
you established the luminaries[c]
and the sun.
17 You have fixed all the bounds
of the earth;
you made summer and winter.

18 Remember this, O LORD, how
the enemy scoffs,
and an impious people
reviles your name.
19 Do not deliver the soul of your
dove to the wild animals;
do not forget the life of
your poor for ever.

20 Have regard for your[d] covenant,
for the dark places of the land are
full of the haunts of violence.
21 Do not let the downtrodden
be put to shame;
let the poor and needy
praise your name.
22 Rise up, O God, plead your cause;
remember how the impious
scoff at you all day long.
23 Do not forget the clamour
of your foes,
the uproar of your adversaries
that goes up continually.

PSALM 75

THANKSGIVING FOR GOD'S WONDROUS DEEDS

To the leader: Do Not Destroy. A Psalm of Asaph. A Song.

1 We give thanks to you, O God;
we give thanks; your
name is near.
People tell of your wondrous deeds.

2 At the set time that I appoint
I will judge with equity.
3 When the earth totters, with
all its inhabitants,
it is I who keep its pillars steady.
Selah
4 I say to the boastful, 'Do not boast',
and to the wicked, 'Do not
lift up your horn;
5 do not lift up your horn on high,
or speak with insolent neck.'

6 For not from the east or
from the west
and not from the wilderness
comes lifting up;
7 but it is God who executes
judgement,
putting down one and
lifting up another.
8 For in the hand of the LORD
there is a cup
with foaming wine, well mixed;
he will pour a draught from it,
and all the wicked of the earth
shall drain it down to the dregs.
9 But I will rejoice[e] for ever;
I will sing praises to the
God of Jacob.

10 All the horns of the wicked
I will cut off,
but the horns of the righteous
shall be exalted.

PSALM 76

ISRAEL'S GOD—JUDGE OF ALL THE EARTH

To the leader: with stringed instruments. A Psalm of Asaph. A Song.

1 In Judah God is known,
his name is great in Israel.
2 His abode has been established
in Salem,
his dwelling-place in Zion.
3 There he broke the flashing arrows,
the shield, the sword, and the
weapons of war. *Selah*

4 Glorious are you, more majestic
than the everlasting mountains.[f]

[a] 74.11 Cn: Heb *do you consume your right hand from* [b] 74.14 Heb *food for the people* [c] 74.16 Or *moon*; Heb *light* [d] 74.20 Gk Syr: Heb *the* [e] 75.9 Gk: Heb *declare* [f] 76.4 Gk: Heb *the mountains of prey*

5 The stout-hearted were stripped
of their spoil;
they sank into sleep;
none of the troops
was able to lift a hand.
6 At your rebuke, O God of Jacob,
both rider and horse lay stunned.

7 But you indeed are awesome!
Who can stand before you
when once your anger is roused?
8 From the heavens you uttered
judgement;
the earth feared and was still
9 when God rose up to establish
judgement,
to save all the oppressed of the
earth. *Selah*

10 Human wrath serves only
to praise you,
when you bind the last bit of
your[g] wrath around you.
11 Make vows to the LORD your God,
and perform them;
let all who are around
him bring gifts
to the one who is awesome,
12 who cuts off the spirit of princes,
who inspires fear in the
kings of the earth.

PSALM 77

GOD'S MIGHTY DEEDS RECALLED

To the leader: according to Jeduthun. Of Asaph. A Psalm.

1 I cry aloud to God,
aloud to God, that he
may hear me.
2 In the day of my trouble I
seek the Lord;
in the night my hand is stretched
out without wearying;
my soul refuses to be comforted.
3 I think of God, and I moan;
I meditate, and my spirit faints.
Selah

4 You keep my eyelids from closing;
I am so troubled that I
cannot speak.
5 I consider the days of old,
and remember the years
of long ago.
6 I commune[h] with my heart
in the night;
I meditate and search my spirit:[i]
7 'Will the Lord spurn for ever,
and never again be favourable?
8 Has his steadfast love
ceased for ever?
Are his promises at an
end for all time?
9 Has God forgotten to be gracious?
Has he in anger shut up his
compassion?' *Selah*
10 And I say, 'It is my grief
that the right hand of the Most
High has changed.'

11 I will call to mind the deeds
of the LORD;
I will remember your
wonders of old.
12 I will meditate on all your work,
and muse on your mighty deeds.
13 Your way, O God, is holy.
What god is so great as our God?
14 You are the God who works wonders;
you have displayed your might
among the peoples.
15 With your strong arm you
redeemed your people,
the descendants of Jacob and
Joseph. *Selah*

16 When the waters saw you, O God,
when the waters saw you,
they were afraid;
the very deep trembled.
17 The clouds poured out water;
the skies thundered;
your arrows flashed on every side.
18 The crash of your thunder was
in the whirlwind;
your lightnings lit up the world;
the earth trembled and shook.
19 Your way was through the sea,
your path, through the
mighty waters;
yet your footprints were unseen.
20 You led your people like a flock
by the hand of Moses and Aaron.

PSALM 78

GOD'S GOODNESS AND ISRAEL'S INGRATITUDE

A Maskil of Asaph.

1 Give ear, O my people, to
my teaching;
incline your ears to the
words of my mouth.
2 I will open my mouth in a parable;
I will utter dark sayings
from of old,

[g] 76.10 Heb lacks *your* [h] 77.6 Gk Syr: Heb *My music* [i] 77.6 Syr Jerome: Heb *my spirit searches*

3 things that we have heard
and known,
that our ancestors have told us.
4 We will not hide them from
their children;
we will tell to the coming
generation
the glorious deeds of the LORD,
and his might,
and the wonders that he has done.

5 He established a decree in Jacob,
and appointed a law in Israel,
which he commanded our ancestors
to teach to their children;
6 that the next generation
might know them,
the children yet unborn,
and rise up and tell them to
their children,
7 so that they should set
their hope in God,
and not forget the works of God,
but keep his commandments;
8 and that they should not be
like their ancestors,
a stubborn and rebellious
generation,
a generation whose heart
was not steadfast,
whose spirit was not
faithful to God.

9 The Ephraimites, armed
with[j] the bow,
turned back on the day of battle.
10 They did not keep God's covenant,
but refused to walk according
to his law.
11 They forgot what he had done,
and the miracles that he
had shown them.
12 In the sight of their ancestors
he worked marvels
in the land of Egypt, in
the fields of Zoan.
13 He divided the sea and let them
pass through it,
and made the waters
stand like a heap.
14 In the daytime he led them
with a cloud,
and all night long with
a fiery light.
15 He split rocks open in the wilderness,
and gave them drink abundantly
as from the deep.
16 He made streams come out
of the rock,
and caused waters to flow
down like rivers.

17 Yet they sinned still more
against him,
rebelling against the Most
High in the desert.
18 They tested God in their heart
by demanding the food
they craved.
19 They spoke against God, saying,
'Can God spread a table in
the wilderness?
20 Even though he struck the rock so
that water gushed out
and torrents overflowed,
can he also give bread,
or provide meat for his people?'

21 Therefore, when the LORD heard,
he was full of rage;
a fire was kindled against Jacob,
his anger mounted against Israel,
22 because they had no faith in God,
and did not trust his
saving power.
23 Yet he commanded the skies above,
and opened the doors of heaven;
24 he rained down on them
manna to eat,
and gave them the grain
of heaven.
25 Mortals ate of the bread of angels;
he sent them food in abundance.
26 He caused the east wind to
blow in the heavens,
and by his power he led out
the south wind;
27 he rained flesh upon them like dust,
winged birds like the
sand of the seas;
28 he let them fall within their camp,
all around their dwellings.
29 And they ate and were well filled,
for he gave them what
they craved.
30 But before they had satisfied
their craving,
while the food was still in
their mouths,
31 the anger of God rose against them
and he killed the strongest
of them,
and laid low the flower of Israel.

32 In spite of all this they still sinned;
they did not believe in
his wonders.
33 So he made their days vanish
like a breath,
and their years in terror.

j 78.9 Heb *armed with shooting*

34 When he killed them, they
sought for him;
they repented and sought
God earnestly.
35 They remembered that God
was their rock,
the Most High God their
redeemer.
36 But they flattered him with
their mouths;
they lied to him with
their tongues.
37 Their heart was not steadfast
towards him;
they were not true to
his covenant.
38 Yet he, being compassionate,
forgave their iniquity,
and did not destroy them;
often he restrained his anger,
and did not stir up all his wrath.
39 He remembered that they
were but flesh,
a wind that passes and does
not come again.
40 How often they rebelled against
him in the wilderness
and grieved him in the desert!
41 They tested God again and again,
and provoked the Holy
One of Israel.
42 They did not keep in mind his power,
or the day when he redeemed
them from the foe;
43 when he displayed his
signs in Egypt,
and his miracles in the
fields of Zoan.
44 He turned their rivers to blood,
so that they could not drink
of their streams.
45 He sent among them swarms of
flies, which devoured them,
and frogs, which destroyed them.
46 He gave their crops to the caterpillar,
and the fruit of their labour
to the locust.
47 He destroyed their vines with hail,
and their sycomores with frost.
48 He gave over their cattle to the hail,
and their flocks to thunderbolts.
49 He let loose on them his fierce anger,
wrath, indignation, and distress,
a company of destroying angels.
50 He made a path for his anger;
he did not spare them from death,
but gave their lives over
to the plague.
51 He struck all the firstborn in Egypt,
the first issue of their strength
in the tents of Ham.
52 Then he led out his people like sheep,
and guided them in the
wilderness like a flock.
53 He led them in safety, so that
they were not afraid;
but the sea overwhelmed
their enemies.
54 And he brought them to his holy hill,
to the mountain that his
right hand had won.
55 He drove out nations before them;
he apportioned them for
a possession
and settled the tribes of
Israel in their tents.

56 Yet they tested the Most High God,
and rebelled against him.
They did not observe his decrees,
57 but turned away and were faithless
like their ancestors;
they twisted like a
treacherous bow.
58 For they provoked him to anger
with their high places;
they moved him to jealousy
with their idols.
59 When God heard, he was
full of wrath,
and he utterly rejected Israel.
60 He abandoned his dwelling
at Shiloh,
the tent where he dwelt
among mortals,
61 and delivered his power to captivity,
his glory to the hand of the foe.
62 He gave his people to the sword,
and vented his wrath on
his heritage.
63 Fire devoured their young men,
and their girls had no
marriage song.
64 Their priests fell by the sword,
and their widows made
no lamentation.
65 Then the Lord awoke as from sleep,
like a warrior shouting
because of wine.
66 He put his adversaries to rout;
he put them to everlasting
disgrace.

67 He rejected the tent of Joseph,
he did not choose the
tribe of Ephraim;
68 but he chose the tribe of Judah,
Mount Zion, which he loves.
69 He built his sanctuary like
the high heavens,
like the earth, which he has
founded for ever.

70 He chose his servant David,
and took him from the sheepfolds;
71 from tending the nursing ewes
he brought him
to be the shepherd of his
people Jacob,
of Israel, his inheritance.
72 With upright heart he tended them,
and guided them with
skilful hand.

PSALM 79

PLEA FOR MERCY FOR JERUSALEM

A Psalm of Asaph.

1 O God, the nations have come
into your inheritance;
they have defiled your holy temple;
they have laid Jerusalem in ruins.
2 They have given the bodies
of your servants
to the birds of the air for food,
the flesh of your faithful to the
wild animals of the earth.
3 They have poured out their
blood like water
all around Jerusalem,
and there was no one
to bury them.
4 We have become a taunt to
our neighbours,
mocked and derided by
those around us.

5 How long, O LORD? Will you
be angry for ever?
Will your jealous wrath
burn like fire?
6 Pour out your anger on the nations
that do not know you,
and on the kingdoms
that do not call on your name.
7 For they have devoured Jacob
and laid waste his habitation.

8 Do not remember against us the
iniquities of our ancestors;
let your compassion come
speedily to meet us,
for we are brought very low.
9 Help us, O God of our salvation,
for the glory of your name;
deliver us, and forgive our sins,
for your name's sake.
10 Why should the nations say,
'Where is their God?'
Let the avenging of the outpoured
blood of your servants
be known among the nations
before our eyes.
11 Let the groans of the prisoners
come before you;
according to your great
power preserve those
doomed to die.
12 Return sevenfold into the bosom
of our neighbours
the taunts with which they
taunted you, O Lord!
13 Then we your people, the flock
of your pasture,
will give thanks to you for ever;
from generation to generation we
will recount your praise.

PSALM 80

PRAYER FOR ISRAEL'S RESTORATION

To the leader: on Lilies, a Covenant. Of Asaph. A Psalm.

1 Give ear, O Shepherd of Israel,
you who lead Joseph like a flock!
You who are enthroned upon the
cherubim, shine forth
2 before Ephraim and Benjamin
and Manasseh.
Stir up your might,
and come to save us!

3 Restore us, O God;
let your face shine, that
we may be saved.

4 O LORD God of hosts,
how long will you be angry with
your people's prayers?
5 You have fed them with the
bread of tears,
and given them tears to drink
in full measure.
6 You make us the scorn[k] of
our neighbours;
our enemies laugh among
themselves.

7 Restore us, O God of hosts;
let your face shine, that
we may be saved.

8 You brought a vine out of Egypt;
you drove out the nations
and planted it.
9 You cleared the ground for it;
it took deep root and
filled the land.

[k] 80.6 Syr: Heb *strife*

10 The mountains were covered
with its shade,
the mighty cedars with
its branches;
11 it sent out its branches to the sea,
and its shoots to the River.
12 Why then have you broken
down its walls,
so that all who pass along the
way pluck its fruit?
13 The boar from the forest ravages it,
and all that move in the
field feed on it.

14 Turn again, O God of hosts;
look down from heaven, and see;
have regard for this vine,
15 the stock that your right
hand planted.[l]
16 They have burned it with fire,
they have cut it down;[m]
may they perish at the rebuke
of your countenance.
17 But let your hand be upon the
one at your right hand,
the one whom you made
strong for yourself.
18 Then we will never turn
back from you;
give us life, and we will call
on your name.

19 Restore us, O LORD God of hosts;
let your face shine, that
we may be saved.

PSALM 81

GOD'S APPEAL TO STUBBORN ISRAEL

To the leader: according to The Gittith. Of Asaph.

1 Sing aloud to God our strength;
shout for joy to the God of Jacob.
2 Raise a song, sound the
tambourine,
the sweet lyre with the harp.
3 Blow the trumpet at the new moon,
at the full moon, on
our festal day.
4 For it is a statute for Israel,
an ordinance of the God of Jacob.
5 He made it a decree in Joseph,
when he went out over[n]
the land of Egypt.

I hear a voice I had not known:
6 'I relieved your[o] shoulder
of the burden;
your[p] hands were freed
from the basket.
7 In distress you called, and
I rescued you;
I answered you in the secret
place of thunder;
I tested you at the waters of
Meribah. *Selah*
8 Hear, O my people, while I
admonish you;
O Israel, if you would but
listen to me!
9 There shall be no strange
god among you;
you shall not bow down
to a foreign god.
10 I am the LORD your God,
who brought you up out of
the land of Egypt.
Open your mouth wide
and I will fill it.

11 'But my people did not listen
to my voice;
Israel would not submit to me.
12 So I gave them over to their
stubborn hearts,
to follow their own counsels.
13 O that my people would
listen to me,
that Israel would walk
in my ways!
14 Then I would quickly subdue
their enemies,
and turn my hand against
their foes.
15 Those who hate the LORD would
cringe before him,
and their doom would
last for ever.
16 I would feed you[q] with the
finest of the wheat,
and with honey from the rock
I would satisfy you.'

PSALM 82

A PLEA FOR JUSTICE

A Psalm of Asaph.

1 God has taken his place in the
divine council;
in the midst of the gods he
holds judgement:
2 'How long will you judge unjustly
and show partiality to the wicked?
Selah

[l] **80.15** Heb adds from verse 17 *and upon the one whom you made strong for yourself* [m] **80.16** Cn: Heb *it is cut down* [n] **81.5** Or *against* [o] **81.6** Heb *his* [p] **81.6** Heb *his* [q] **81.16** Cn Compare verse 16b: Heb *he would feed him*

3 Give justice to the weak and
the orphan;
maintain the right of the lowly
and the destitute.
4 Rescue the weak and the needy;
deliver them from the hand
of the wicked.'

5 They have neither knowledge
nor understanding,
they walk around in darkness;
all the foundations of the
earth are shaken.

6 I say, 'You are gods,
children of the Most
High, all of you;
7 nevertheless, you shall die
like mortals,
and fall like any prince.'[r]

8 Rise up, O God, judge the earth;
for all the nations belong to you!

PSALM 83

PRAYER FOR JUDGEMENT ON ISRAEL'S FOES

A Song. A Psalm of Asaph.

1 O God, do not keep silence;
do not hold your peace or
be still, O God!
2 Even now your enemies
are in tumult;
those who hate you have
raised their heads.
3 They lay crafty plans against
your people;
they consult together against
those you protect.
4 They say, 'Come, let us wipe
them out as a nation;
let the name of Israel be
remembered no more.'
5 They conspire with one accord;
against you they make
a covenant—
6 the tents of Edom and the
Ishmaelites,
Moab and the Hagrites,
7 Gebal and Ammon and Amalek,
Philistia with the
inhabitants of Tyre;
8 Assyria also has joined them;
they are the strong arm of the
children of Lot. *Selah*

9 Do to them as you did to Midian,
as to Sisera and Jabin at
the Wadi Kishon,
10 who were destroyed at En-dor,
who became dung for the ground.
11 Make their nobles like Oreb
and Zeeb,
all their princes like Zebah
and Zalmunna,
12 who said, 'Let us take the
pastures of God
for our own possession.'

13 O my God, make them like
whirling dust,[s]
like chaff before the wind.
14 As fire consumes the forest,
as the flame sets the
mountains ablaze,
15 so pursue them with your tempest
and terrify them with
your hurricane.
16 Fill their faces with shame,
so that they may seek your
name, O LORD.
17 Let them be put to shame and
dismayed for ever;
let them perish in disgrace.
18 Let them know that you alone,
whose name is the LORD,
are the Most High over
all the earth.

PSALM 84

THE JOY OF WORSHIP IN THE TEMPLE

To the leader: according to The Gittith. Of the Korahites. A Psalm.

1 How lovely is your dwelling place,
O LORD of hosts!
2 My soul longs, indeed it faints
for the courts of the LORD;
my heart and my flesh sing for joy
to the living God.

3 Even the sparrow finds a home,
and the swallow a nest for herself,
where she may lay her young,
at your altars, O LORD of hosts,
my King and my God.
4 Happy are those who live
in your house,
ever singing your praise. *Selah*

5 Happy are those whose
strength is in you,
in whose heart are the
highways to Zion.[t]

[r] 82.7 *Or fall as one man, O princes* [s] 83.13 *Or a tumbleweed* [t] 84.5 *Heb lacks to Zion*

6 As they go through the
valley of Baca
they make it a place of springs;
the early rain also covers
it with pools.
7 They go from strength to strength;
the God of gods will be
seen in Zion.

8 O LORD God of hosts, hear
my prayer;
give ear, O God of Jacob! *Selah*
9 Behold our shield, O God;
look on the face of your anointed.

10 For a day in your courts is better
than a thousand elsewhere.
I would rather be a doorkeeper
in the house of my God
than live in the tents of
wickedness.
11 For the LORD God is a sun and shield;
he bestows favour and honour.
No good thing does the
LORD withhold
from those who walk uprightly.
12 O LORD of hosts,
happy is everyone who
trusts in you.

PSALM 85

PRAYER FOR THE RESTORATION OF GOD'S FAVOUR

To the leader. Of the Korahites. A Psalm.

1 LORD, you were favourable
to your land;
you restored the fortunes
of Jacob.
2 You forgave the iniquity of
your people;
you pardoned all their
sin. *Selah*
3 You withdrew all your wrath;
you turned from your hot anger.

4 Restore us again, O God of
our salvation,
and put away your indignation
towards us.
5 Will you be angry with us for ever?
Will you prolong your anger
to all generations?
6 Will you not revive us again,
so that your people may
rejoice in you?
7 Show us your steadfast
love, O LORD,
and grant us your salvation.

8 Let me hear what God the
LORD will speak,
for he will speak peace
to his people,
to his faithful, to those who turn
to him in their hearts.[u]
9 Surely his salvation is at hand
for those who fear him,
that his glory may dwell
in our land.

10 Steadfast love and faithfulness
will meet;
righteousness and peace
will kiss each other.
11 Faithfulness will spring up
from the ground,
and righteousness will look
down from the sky.
12 The LORD will give what is good,
and our land will yield
its increase.
13 Righteousness will go before him,
and will make a path for his steps.

PSALM 86

SUPPLICATION FOR HELP AGAINST ENEMIES

A Prayer of David.

1 Incline your ear, O LORD,
and answer me,
for I am poor and needy.
2 Preserve my life, for I am
devoted to you;
save your servant who
trusts in you.
You are my God; 3be gracious
to me, O Lord,
for to you do I cry all day long.
4 Gladden the soul of your servant,
for to you, O Lord, I lift
up my soul.
5 For you, O Lord, are good
and forgiving,
abounding in steadfast love
to all who call on you.
6 Give ear, O LORD, to my prayer;
listen to my cry of supplication.
7 In the day of my trouble
I call on you,
for you will answer me.

8 There is none like you among
the gods, O Lord,
nor are there any works like yours.

[u] **85.8** Gk: Heb *but let them not turn back to folly*

9 All the nations you have
made shall come
and bow down before
you, O Lord,
and shall glorify your name.
10 For you are great and do
wondrous things;
you alone are God.
11 Teach me your way, O LORD,
that I may walk in your truth;
give me an undivided heart
to revere your name.
12 I give thanks to you, O Lord my
God, with my whole heart,
and I will glorify your
name for ever.
13 For great is your steadfast
love towards me;
you have delivered my soul
from the depths of Sheol.

14 O God, the insolent rise up
against me;
a band of ruffians seeks my life,
and they do not set you
before them.
15 But you, O Lord, are a God
merciful and gracious,
slow to anger and abounding
in steadfast love and
faithfulness.
16 Turn to me and be gracious to me;
give your strength to
your servant;
save the child of your
serving-maid.
17 Show me a sign of your favour,
so that those who hate me may
see it and be put to shame,
because you, LORD, have helped
me and comforted me.

PSALM 87

THE JOY OF LIVING IN ZION

Of the Korahites. A Psalm. A Song.

1 On the holy mount stands the
city he founded;
2 the LORD loves the gates of Zion
more than all the dwellings
of Jacob.
3 Glorious things are spoken of you,
O city of God. *Selah*

4 Among those who know me I
mention Rahab and Babylon;
Philistia too, and Tyre,
with Ethiopia[v]—
'This one was born there,'
they say.
5 And of Zion it shall be said,
'This one and that one
were born in it';
for the Most High himself
will establish it.
6 The LORD records, as he
registers the peoples,
'This one was born there.' *Selah*

7 Singers and dancers alike say,
'All my springs are in you.'

PSALM 88

PRAYER FOR HELP IN DESPONDENCY

A Song. A Psalm of the Korahites. To the leader: according to Mahalath Leannoth. A Maskil of Heman the Ezrahite.

1 O LORD, God of my salvation,
when, at night, I cry out
in your presence,
2 let my prayer come before you;
incline your ear to my cry.

3 For my soul is full of troubles,
and my life draws near to Sheol.
4 I am counted among those who
go down to the Pit;
I am like those who have no help,
5 like those forsaken among the dead,
like the slain that lie in the grave,
like those whom you remember
no more,
for they are cut off from
your hand.
6 You have put me in the
depths of the Pit,
in the regions dark and deep.
7 Your wrath lies heavy upon me,
and you overwhelm me with all
your waves. *Selah*

8 You have caused my companions
to shun me;
you have made me a thing
of horror to them.
I am shut in so that I cannot escape;
9 my eye grows dim
through sorrow.
Every day I call on you, O LORD;
I spread out my hands to you.
10 Do you work wonders for the dead?
Do the shades rise up to praise
you? *Selah*
11 Is your steadfast love declared
in the grave,
or your faithfulness in Abaddon?

[v] 87.4 Or *Nubia*; Heb *Cush*

12 Are your wonders known
in the darkness,
or your saving help in the
land of forgetfulness?
13 But I, O LORD, cry out to you;
in the morning my prayer
comes before you.
14 O LORD, why do you cast me off?
Why do you hide your
face from me?
15 Wretched and close to death
from my youth up,
I suffer your terrors; I
am desperate.[w]
16 Your wrath has swept over me;
your dread assaults destroy me.
17 They surround me like a
flood all day long;
from all sides they close
in on me.
18 You have caused friend and
neighbour to shun me;
my companions are in darkness.

PSALM 89

GOD'S COVENANT WITH DAVID

A Maskil of Ethan the Ezrahite.

1 I will sing of your steadfast love,
O LORD,[x] for ever;
with my mouth I will proclaim
your faithfulness to
all generations.
2 I declare that your steadfast love
is established for ever;
your faithfulness is as firm
as the heavens.

3 You said, 'I have made a covenant
with my chosen one,
I have sworn to my
servant David:
4 "I will establish your
descendants for ever,
and build your throne for all
generations."' *Selah*

5 Let the heavens praise your
wonders, O LORD,
your faithfulness in the assembly
of the holy ones.
6 For who in the skies can be
compared to the LORD?
Who among the heavenly
beings is like the LORD,
7 a God feared in the council
of the holy ones,
great and awesome[y] above all
that are around him?
8 O LORD God of hosts,
who is as mighty as you, O LORD?
Your faithfulness surrounds you.
9 You rule the raging of the sea;
when its waves rise, you still them.
10 You crushed Rahab like a carcass;
you scattered your enemies
with your mighty arm.
11 The heavens are yours, the
earth also is yours;
the world and all that is in it—
you have founded them.
12 The north and the south[z]—you
created them;
Tabor and Hermon joyously
praise your name.
13 You have a mighty arm;
strong is your hand, high
your right hand.
14 Righteousness and justice are the
foundation of your throne;
steadfast love and faithfulness
go before you.
15 Happy are the people who know
the festal shout,
who walk, O LORD, in the light
of your countenance;
16 they exult in your name all day long,
and extol[a] your righteousness.
17 For you are the glory of
their strength;
by your favour our horn is exalted.
18 For our shield belongs to the LORD,
our king to the Holy One of Israel.

19 Then you spoke in a vision to your
faithful one, and said:
'I have set the crown[b] on
one who is mighty,
I have exalted one chosen
from the people.
20 I have found my servant David;
with my holy oil I have
anointed him;
21 my hand shall always remain
with him;
my arm also shall strengthen him.
22 The enemy shall not outwit him,
the wicked shall not humble him.
23 I will crush his foes before him
and strike down those
who hate him.
24 My faithfulness and steadfast
love shall be with him;
and in my name his horn
shall be exalted.

[w] **88.15** Meaning of Heb uncertain [x] **89.1** Gk: Heb *the steadfast love of the LORD* [y] **89.7** Gk Syr: Heb *greatly awesome* [z] **89.12** Or *Zaphon and Yamin* [a] **89.16** Cn: Heb *are exalted in* [b] **89.19** Cn: Heb *help*

25 I will set his hand on the sea
and his right hand on the rivers.
26 He shall cry to me, "You
are my Father,
my God, and the Rock of
my salvation!"
27 I will make him the firstborn,
the highest of the kings
of the earth.
28 For ever I will keep my steadfast
love for him,
and my covenant with him
will stand firm.
29 I will establish his line for ever,
and his throne as long as
the heavens endure.
30 If his children forsake my law
and do not walk according
to my ordinances,
31 if they violate my statutes
and do not keep my
commandments,
32 then I will punish their
transgression with the rod
and their iniquity with scourges;
33 but I will not remove from him
my steadfast love,
or be false to my faithfulness.
34 I will not violate my covenant,
or alter the word that went
forth from my lips.
35 Once and for all I have sworn
by my holiness;
I will not lie to David.
36 His line shall continue for ever,
and his throne endure before
me like the sun.
37 It shall be established for ever
like the moon,
an enduring witness in the skies.'
Selah

38 But now you have spurned
and rejected him;
you are full of wrath against
your anointed.
39 You have renounced the covenant
with your servant;
you have defiled his crown
in the dust.
40 You have broken through
all his walls;
you have laid his strongholds
in ruins.
41 All who pass by plunder him;
he has become the scorn
of his neighbours.
42 You have exalted the right
hand of his foes;
you have made all his
enemies rejoice.
43 Moreover, you have turned back
the edge of his sword,
and you have not supported
him in battle.
44 You have removed the sceptre
from his hand,[c]
and hurled his throne to the ground.
45 You have cut short the days
of his youth;
you have covered him with shame.
Selah

46 How long, O LORD? Will you hide
yourself for ever?
How long will your wrath
burn like fire?
47 Remember how short my time is—[d]
for what vanity you have
created all mortals!
48 Who can live and never see death?
Who can escape the power of Sheol?
Selah

49 Lord, where is your steadfast
love of old,
which by your faithfulness
you swore to David?
50 Remember, O Lord, how your
servant is taunted;
how I bear in my bosom the
insults of the peoples,[e]
51 with which your enemies
taunt, O LORD,
with which they taunted the
footsteps of your anointed.

52 Blessed be the LORD for ever.
Amen and Amen.

Book IV (Psalms 90–106)

PSALM 90

GOD'S ETERNITY AND HUMAN FRAILTY

A Prayer of Moses, the man of God.

1 Lord, you have been our
dwelling-place[f]
in all generations.
2 Before the mountains were
brought forth,
or ever you had formed the
earth and the world,
from everlasting to everlasting
you are God.

[c] 89.44 Cn: Heb *removed his cleanness*
[d] 89.47 Meaning of Heb uncertain [e] 89.50 Cn: Heb *bosom all of many peoples* [f] 90.1 Another reading is *our refuge*

3 You turn us[g] back to dust,
and say, 'Turn back, you mortals.'
4 For a thousand years in your sight
are like yesterday when it is past,
or like a watch in the night.

5 You sweep them away; they
are like a dream,
like grass that is renewed
in the morning;
6 in the morning it flourishes
and is renewed;
in the evening it fades
and withers.

7 For we are consumed by your anger;
by your wrath we are
overwhelmed.
8 You have set our iniquities
before you,
our secret sins in the light of
your countenance.

9 For all our days pass away
under your wrath;
our years come to an
end[h] like a sigh.
10 The days of our life are seventy years,
or perhaps eighty, if we are strong;
even then their span[i] is only
toil and trouble;
they are soon gone, and
we fly away.

11 Who considers the power
of your anger?
Your wrath is as great as the
fear that is due to you.
12 So teach us to count our days
that we may gain a wise heart.

13 Turn, O LORD! How long?
Have compassion on
your servants!
14 Satisfy us in the morning with
your steadfast love,
so that we may rejoice and
be glad all our days.
15 Make us glad for as many days as
you have afflicted us,
and for as many years as
we have seen evil.
16 Let your work be manifest
to your servants,
and your glorious power
to their children.
17 Let the favour of the Lord our
God be upon us,
and prosper for us the work
of our hands—
O prosper the work of our hands!

PSALM 91

ASSURANCE OF GOD'S PROTECTION

1 You who live in the shelter
of the Most High,
who abide in the shadow
of the Almighty,[j]
2 will say to the LORD, 'My refuge
and my fortress;
my God, in whom I trust.'
3 For he will deliver you from the
snare of the fowler
and from the deadly pestilence;
4 he will cover you with his pinions,
and under his wings you
will find refuge;
his faithfulness is a shield
and buckler.
5 You will not fear the terror
of the night,
or the arrow that flies by day,
6 or the pestilence that stalks
in darkness,
or the destruction that
wastes at noonday.

7 A thousand may fall at your side,
ten thousand at your right hand,
but it will not come near you.
8 You will only look with your eyes
and see the punishment
of the wicked.

9 Because you have made the
LORD your refuge,[k]
the Most High your
dwelling-place,
10 no evil shall befall you,
no scourge come near your tent.

11 For he will command his angels
concerning you
to guard you in all your ways.
12 On their hands they will bear you up,
so that you will not dash your
foot against a stone.
13 You will tread on the lion
and the adder,
the young lion and the serpent
you will trample under foot.

14 Those who love me, I will deliver;
I will protect those who
know my name.

[g] 90.3 Heb *humankind* [h] 90.9 Syr: Heb *we bring our years to an end* [i] 90.10 Cn Compare Gk Syr Jerome Tg: Heb *pride* [j] 91.1 Traditional rendering of Heb *Shaddai* [k] 91.9 Cn: Heb *Because you, LORD, are my refuge; you have made*

15 When they call to me, I will
answer them;
I will be with them in trouble,
I will rescue them and
honour them.
16 With long life I will satisfy them,
and show them my salvation.

PSALM 92

THANKSGIVING FOR VINDICATION

*A Psalm. A Song for
the Sabbath Day.*

1 It is good to give thanks to the LORD,
to sing praises to your name,
O Most High;
2 to declare your steadfast love
in the morning,
and your faithfulness by night,
3 to the music of the lute and the harp,
to the melody of the lyre.
4 For you, O LORD, have made me
glad by your work;
at the works of your hands
I sing for joy.

5 How great are your works, O LORD!
Your thoughts are very deep!
6 The dullard cannot know,
the stupid cannot
understand this:
7 though the wicked sprout like grass
and all evildoers flourish,
they are doomed to destruction
for ever,
8 but you, O LORD, are on
high for ever.
9 For your enemies, O LORD,
for your enemies shall perish;
all evildoers shall be scattered.

10 But you have exalted my horn
like that of the wild ox;
you have poured over
me[l] fresh oil.
11 My eyes have seen the downfall
of my enemies;
my ears have heard the doom
of my evil assailants.

12 The righteous flourish like
the palm tree,
and grow like a cedar in Lebanon.
13 They are planted in the house
of the LORD;
they flourish in the courts
of our God.
14 In old age they still produce fruit;
they are always green
and full of sap,
15 showing that the LORD is upright;
he is my rock, and there is no
unrighteousness in him.

PSALM 93

THE MAJESTY OF GOD'S RULE

1 The LORD is king, he is robed
in majesty;
the LORD is robed, he is
girded with strength.
He has established the world; it
shall never be moved;
2 your throne is established
from of old;
you are from everlasting.

3 The floods have lifted up, O LORD,
the floods have lifted up
their voice;
the floods lift up their roaring.
4 More majestic than the thunders
of mighty waters,
more majestic than the
waves[m] of the sea,
majestic on high is the LORD!

5 Your decrees are very sure;
holiness befits your house,
O LORD, for evermore.

PSALM 94

GOD THE AVENGER OF THE RIGHTEOUS

1 O LORD, you God of vengeance,
you God of vengeance, shine forth!
2 Rise up, O judge of the earth;
give to the proud what
they deserve!
3 O LORD, how long shall the wicked,
how long shall the wicked exult?
4 They pour out their arrogant words;
all the evildoers boast.
5 They crush your people, O LORD,
and afflict your heritage.
6 They kill the widow and the stranger,
they murder the orphan,
7 and they say, 'The LORD does not see;
the God of Jacob does not perceive.'

8 Understand, O dullest of the people;
fools, when will you be wise?
9 He who planted the ear, does
he not hear?

[l] 92.10 Syr: Meaning of Heb uncertain
[m] 93.4 Cn: Heb *majestic are the waves*

He who formed the eye,
does he not see?
10 He who disciplines the nations,
he who teaches knowledge
to humankind,
does he not chastise?
11 The LORD knows our thoughts,[n]
that they are but an empty breath.

12 Happy are those whom you
discipline, O LORD,
and whom you teach out
of your law,
13 giving them respite from
days of trouble,
until a pit is dug for the wicked.
14 For the LORD will not forsake
his people;
he will not abandon his heritage;
15 for justice will return to
the righteous,
and all the upright in heart
will follow it.

16 Who rises up for me against
the wicked?
Who stands up for me
against evildoers?
17 If the LORD had not been my help,
my soul would soon have lived
in the land of silence.
18 When I thought, 'My foot is slipping',
your steadfast love, O LORD,
held me up.
19 When the cares of my heart
are many,
your consolations cheer my soul.
20 Can wicked rulers be allied with you,
those who contrive mischief
by statute?
21 They band together against the
life of the righteous,
and condemn the innocent
to death.
22 But the LORD has become
my stronghold,
and my God the rock
of my refuge.
23 He will repay them for their iniquity
and wipe them out for
their wickedness;
the LORD our God will
wipe them out.

PSALM 95

A CALL TO WORSHIP AND OBEDIENCE

1 O come, let us sing to the LORD;
let us make a joyful noise to the
rock of our salvation!
2 Let us come into his presence
with thanksgiving;
let us make a joyful noise to
him with songs of praise!
3 For the LORD is a great God,
and a great King above all gods.
4 In his hand are the depths
of the earth;
the heights of the mountains
are his also.
5 The sea is his, for he made it,
and the dry land, which his
hands have formed.

6 O come, let us worship and
bow down,
let us kneel before the
LORD, our Maker!
7 For he is our God,
and we are the people
of his pasture,
and the sheep of his hand.

O that today you would listen
to his voice!
8 Do not harden your hearts,
as at Meribah,
as on the day at Massah in
the wilderness,
9 when your ancestors tested me,
and put me to the proof, though
they had seen my work.
10 For forty years I loathed
that generation
and said, 'They are a people
whose hearts go astray,
and they do not regard my ways.'
11 Therefore in my anger I swore,
'They shall not enter my rest.'

PSALM 96

PRAISE TO GOD WHO COMES IN JUDGEMENT

1 O sing to the LORD a new song;
sing to the LORD, all the earth.
2 Sing to the LORD, bless his name;
tell of his salvation from
day to day.
3 Declare his glory among the nations,
his marvellous works among
all the peoples.
4 For great is the LORD, and
greatly to be praised;
he is to be revered above all gods.
5 For all the gods of the
peoples are idols,
but the LORD made the heavens.

[n] 94.11 Heb *the thoughts of humankind*

6 Honour and majesty are before him;
strength and beauty are
in his sanctuary.

7 Ascribe to the LORD, O families
of the peoples,
ascribe to the LORD glory
and strength.
8 Ascribe to the LORD the glory
due his name;
bring an offering, and come
into his courts.
9 Worship the LORD in
holy splendour;
tremble before him, all the earth.

10 Say among the nations, 'The
LORD is king!
The world is firmly established;
it shall never be moved.
He will judge the peoples
with equity.'
11 Let the heavens be glad, and
let the earth rejoice;
let the sea roar, and all that fills it;
12 let the field exult, and
everything in it.
Then shall all the trees of the
forest sing for joy
13 before the LORD;
for he is coming,
for he is coming to judge
the earth.
He will judge the world with
righteousness,
and the peoples with his truth.

PSALM 97

THE GLORY OF GOD'S REIGN

1 The LORD is king! Let the
earth rejoice;
let the many coastlands be glad!
2 Clouds and thick darkness are
all around him;
righteousness and justice are the
foundation of his throne.
3 Fire goes before him,
and consumes his adversaries
on every side.
4 His lightnings light up the world;
the earth sees and trembles.
5 The mountains melt like wax
before the LORD,
before the Lord of all the earth.

6 The heavens proclaim his
righteousness;
and all the peoples behold
his glory.
7 All worshippers of images
are put to shame,
those who make their boast
in worthless idols;
all gods bow down before him.
8 Zion hears and is glad,
and the towns[o] of Judah rejoice,
because of your judgements,
O God.
9 For you, O LORD, are most high
over all the earth;
you are exalted far above all gods.

10 The LORD loves those who hate[p] evil;
he guards the lives of his faithful;
he rescues them from the
hand of the wicked.
11 Light dawns[q] for the righteous,
and joy for the upright in heart.
12 Rejoice in the LORD, O you
righteous,
and give thanks to his holy name!

PSALM 98

PRAISE THE JUDGE OF THE WORLD

A Psalm.

1 O sing to the LORD a new song,
for he has done marvellous things.
His right hand and his holy arm
have gained him victory.
2 The LORD has made known
his victory;
he has revealed his vindication
in the sight of the nations.
3 He has remembered his steadfast
love and faithfulness
to the house of Israel.
All the ends of the earth have seen
the victory of our God.

4 Make a joyful noise to the
LORD, all the earth;
break forth into joyous song
and sing praises.
5 Sing praises to the LORD
with the lyre,
with the lyre and the
sound of melody.
6 With trumpets and the sound
of the horn
make a joyful noise before
the King, the LORD.

7 Let the sea roar, and all that fills it;
the world and those who live in it.

[o] 97.8 Heb *daughters* [p] 97.10 Cn: Heb *You who love the LORD hate* [q] 97.11 Gk Syr Jerome: Heb *is sown*

8 Let the floods clap their hands;
let the hills sing together for joy
9 at the presence of the LORD,
for he is coming
to judge the earth.
He will judge the world with
righteousness,
and the peoples with equity.

PSALM 99

PRAISE TO GOD FOR HIS HOLINESS

1 The LORD is king; let the
peoples tremble!
He sits enthroned upon
the cherubim; let
the earth quake!
2 The LORD is great in Zion;
he is exalted over all the peoples.
3 Let them praise your great and
awesome name.
Holy is he!
4 Mighty King,[r] lover of justice,
you have established equity;
you have executed justice
and righteousness in Jacob.
5 Extol the LORD our God;
worship at his footstool.
Holy is he!

6 Moses and Aaron were among
his priests,
Samuel also was among those
who called on his name.
They cried to the LORD, and
he answered them.
7 He spoke to them in the
pillar of cloud;
they kept his decrees,
and the statutes that he gave them.

8 O LORD our God, you answered them;
you were a forgiving God to them,
but an avenger of their
wrongdoings.
9 Extol the LORD our God,
and worship at his holy mountain;
for the LORD our God is holy.

PSALM 100

ALL LANDS SUMMONED TO PRAISE GOD

A Psalm of thanksgiving.

1 Make a joyful noise to the
LORD, all the earth.
2 Worship the LORD with gladness;
come into his presence
with singing.
3 Know that the LORD is God.
It is he that made us, and
we are his;[s]
we are his people, and the
sheep of his pasture.

4 Enter his gates with thanksgiving,
and his courts with praise.
Give thanks to him, bless
his name.
5 For the LORD is good;
his steadfast love endures for ever,
and his faithfulness to
all generations.

PSALM 101

A SOVEREIGN'S PLEDGE OF INTEGRITY AND JUSTICE

Of David. A Psalm.

1 I will sing of loyalty and of justice;
to you, O LORD, I will sing.
2 I will study the way that
is blameless.
When shall I attain it?

I will walk with integrity of heart
within my house;
3 I will not set before my eyes
anything that is base.

I hate the work of those
who fall away;
it shall not cling to me.
4 Perverseness of heart shall
be far from me;
I will know nothing of evil.

5 One who secretly slanders
a neighbour
I will destroy.
A haughty look and an
arrogant heart
I will not tolerate.

6 I will look with favour on the
faithful in the land,
so that they may live with me;
whoever walks in the way
that is blameless
shall minister to me.

7 No one who practises deceit
shall remain in my house;
no one who utters lies
shall continue in my presence.

r 99.4 Cn: Heb *And a king's strength*
s 100.3 Another reading is *and not we ourselves*

8 Morning by morning I will destroy
all the wicked in the land,
cutting off all evildoers
from the city of the LORD.

PSALM 102

PRAYER TO THE ETERNAL KING FOR HELP

A prayer of one afflicted, when faint and pleading before the LORD.

1 Hear my prayer, O LORD;
let my cry come to you.
2 Do not hide your face from me
on the day of my distress.
Incline your ear to me;
answer me speedily on the
day when I call.

3 For my days pass away like smoke,
and my bones burn like a furnace.
4 My heart is stricken and
withered like grass;
I am too wasted to eat my bread.
5 Because of my loud groaning
my bones cling to my skin.
6 I am like an owl of the wilderness,
like a little owl of the waste places.
7 I lie awake;
I am like a lonely bird on
the housetop.
8 All day long my enemies taunt me;
those who deride me use my
name for a curse.
9 For I eat ashes like bread,
and mingle tears with my drink,
10 because of your indignation
and anger;
for you have lifted me up and
thrown me aside.
11 My days are like an evening shadow;
I wither away like grass.

12 But you, O LORD, are
enthroned for ever;
your name endures to all
generations.
13 You will rise up and have
compassion on Zion,
for it is time to favour it;
the appointed time has come.
14 For your servants hold its
stones dear,
and have pity on its dust.
15 The nations will fear the
name of the LORD,
and all the kings of the
earth your glory.
16 For the LORD will build up Zion;
he will appear in his glory.
17 He will regard the prayer of
the destitute,
and will not despise their prayer.

18 Let this be recorded for a
generation to come,
so that a people yet unborn
may praise the LORD:
19 that he looked down from
his holy height,
from heaven the LORD
looked at the earth,
20 to hear the groans of the prisoners,
to set free those who were
doomed to die;
21 so that the name of the LORD may
be declared in Zion,
and his praise in Jerusalem,
22 when peoples gather together,
and kingdoms, to worship
the LORD.

23 He has broken my strength
in mid-course;
he has shortened my days.
24 'O my God,' I say, 'do not
take me away
at the mid-point of my life,
you whose years endure
throughout all generations.'

25 Long ago you laid the foundation
of the earth,
and the heavens are the
work of your hands.
26 They will perish, but you endure;
they will all wear out
like a garment.
You change them like clothing,
and they pass away;
27 but you are the same, and your
years have no end.
28 The children of your servants
shall live secure;
their offspring shall be established
in your presence.

PSALM 103

THANKSGIVING FOR GOD'S GOODNESS

Of David.

1 Bless the LORD, O my soul,
and all that is within me,
bless his holy name.
2 Bless the LORD, O my soul,
and do not forget all
his benefits—
3 who forgives all your iniquity,
who heals all your diseases,

4 who redeems your life from the Pit,
who crowns you with steadfast
love and mercy,
5 who satisfies you with good
as long as you live[t]
so that your youth is renewed
like the eagle's.

6 The LORD works vindication
and justice for all who
are oppressed.
7 He made known his ways to Moses,
his acts to the people of Israel.
8 The LORD is merciful and gracious,
slow to anger and abounding
in steadfast love.
9 He will not always accuse,
nor will he keep his
anger for ever.
10 He does not deal with us
according to our sins,
nor repay us according to
our iniquities.
11 For as the heavens are high
above the earth,
so great is his steadfast love
towards those who fear him;
12 as far as the east is from the west,
so far he removes our
transgressions from us.
13 As a father has compassion
for his children,
so the LORD has compassion
for those who fear him.
14 For he knows how we were made;
he remembers that we are dust.

15 As for mortals, their days
are like grass;
they flourish like a flower
of the field;
16 for the wind passes over it,
and it is gone,
and its place knows it no more.
17 But the steadfast love of the
LORD is from everlasting
to everlasting
on those who fear him,
and his righteousness to
children's children,
18 to those who keep his covenant
and remember to do his
commandments.

19 The LORD has established his
throne in the heavens,
and his kingdom rules over all.
20 Bless the LORD, O you his angels,
you mighty ones who
do his bidding,
obedient to his spoken word.
21 Bless the LORD, all his hosts,
his ministers that do his will.
22 Bless the LORD, all his works,
in all places of his dominion.
Bless the LORD, O my soul.

PSALM 104

GOD THE CREATOR AND PROVIDER

1 Bless the LORD, O my soul.
O LORD my God, you
are very great.
You are clothed with honour
and majesty,
2 wrapped in light as with
a garment.
You stretch out the heavens
like a tent,
3 you set the beams of your[u]
chambers on the waters,
you make the clouds your[v] chariot,
you ride on the wings of the wind,
4 you make the winds your[w]
messengers,
fire and flame your[x] ministers.

5 You set the earth on its foundations,
so that it shall never be shaken.
6 You cover it with the deep as
with a garment;
the waters stood above
the mountains.
7 At your rebuke they flee;
at the sound of your thunder
they take to flight.
8 They rose up to the mountains,
ran down to the valleys
to the place that you
appointed for them.
9 You set a boundary that they
may not pass,
so that they might not again
cover the earth.

10 You make springs gush forth
in the valleys;
they flow between the hills,
11 giving drink to every wild animal;
the wild asses quench their thirst.
12 By the streams[y] the birds of the
air have their habitation;
they sing among the branches.
13 From your lofty abode you
water the mountains;
the earth is satisfied with the
fruit of your work.

[t] **103.5** Meaning of Heb uncertain [u] **104.3** Heb *his* [v] **104.3** Heb *his* [w] **104.4** Heb *his* [x] **104.4** Heb *his* [y] **104.12** Heb *By them*

14 You cause the grass to grow
for the cattle,
and plants for people to use,[z]
to bring forth food from the earth,
15 and wine to gladden the
human heart,
oil to make the face shine,
and bread to strengthen
the human heart.
16 The trees of the LORD are
watered abundantly,
the cedars of Lebanon
that he planted.
17 In them the birds build their nests;
the stork has its home
in the fir trees.
18 The high mountains are for
the wild goats;
the rocks are a refuge
for the coneys.
19 You have made the moon to
mark the seasons;
the sun knows its
time for setting.
20 You make darkness, and it is night,
when all the animals of the
forest come creeping out.
21 The young lions roar for their prey,
seeking their food from God.
22 When the sun rises, they withdraw
and lie down in their dens.
23 People go out to their work
and to their labour until
the evening.

24 O LORD, how manifold are
your works!
In wisdom you have
made them all;
the earth is full of your creatures.
25 Yonder is the sea, great and wide,
creeping things innumerable
are there,
living things both
small and great.
26 There go the ships,
and Leviathan that you
formed to sport in it.

27 These all look to you
to give them their food
in due season;
28 when you give to them, they
gather it up;
when you open your hand, they
are filled with good things.
29 When you hide your face, they
are dismayed;
when you take away their
breath, they die
and return to their dust.
30 When you send forth your spirit,[a]
they are created;
and you renew the face
of the ground.

31 May the glory of the LORD
endure for ever;
may the LORD rejoice in
his works—
32 who looks on the earth and
it trembles,
who touches the mountains
and they smoke.
33 I will sing to the LORD as
long as I live;
I will sing praise to my God
while I have being.
34 May my meditation be
pleasing to him,
for I rejoice in the LORD.
35 Let sinners be consumed
from the earth,
and let the wicked be no more.
Bless the LORD, O my soul.
Praise the LORD!

PSALM 105

GOD'S FAITHFULNESS TO ISRAEL

1 O give thanks to the LORD,
call on his name,
make known his deeds
among the peoples.
2 Sing to him, sing praises to him;
tell of all his wonderful works.
3 Glory in his holy name;
let the hearts of those who
seek the LORD rejoice.
4 Seek the LORD and his strength;
seek his presence continually.
5 Remember the wonderful
works he has done,
his miracles, and the judgements
he has uttered,
6 O offspring of his servant Abraham,[b]
children of Jacob, his chosen ones.

7 He is the LORD our God;
his judgements are in
all the earth.
8 He is mindful of his covenant
for ever,
of the word that he commanded,
for a thousand generations,
9 the covenant that he made
with Abraham,
his sworn promise to Isaac,

[z] 104.14 Or *to cultivate* [a] 104.30 Or *your breath* [b] 105.6 Another reading is *Israel* (compare 1 Chr 16.13)

10 which he confirmed to Jacob
as a statute,
to Israel as an everlasting
covenant,
11 saying, 'To you I will give the
land of Canaan
as your portion for an inheritance.'

12 When they were few in number,
of little account, and
strangers in it,
13 wandering from nation to nation,
from one kingdom to
another people,
14 he allowed no one to oppress them;
he rebuked kings on their account,
15 saying, 'Do not touch my
anointed ones;
do my prophets no harm.'

16 When he summoned famine
against the land,
and broke every staff of bread,
17 he had sent a man ahead of them,
Joseph, who was sold as a slave.
18 His feet were hurt with fetters,
his neck was put in
a collar of iron;
19 until what he had said came to pass,
the word of the LORD kept
testing him.
20 The king sent and released him;
the ruler of the peoples
set him free.
21 He made him lord of his house,
and ruler of all his possessions,
22 to instruct[c] his officials at
his pleasure,
and to teach his elders wisdom.

23 Then Israel came to Egypt;
Jacob lived as an alien in
the land of Ham.
24 And the LORD made his people
very fruitful,
and made them stronger
than their foes,
25 whose hearts he then turned
to hate his people,
to deal craftily with his servants.

26 He sent his servant Moses,
and Aaron whom he had chosen.
27 They performed his signs
among them,
and miracles in the land of Ham.
28 He sent darkness, and made
the land dark;
they rebelled[d] against his words.
29 He turned their waters into blood,
and caused their fish to die.
30 Their land swarmed with frogs,
even in the chambers of their kings.
31 He spoke, and there came
swarms of flies,
and gnats throughout
their country.
32 He gave them hail for rain,
and lightning that flashed
through their land.
33 He struck their vines and fig trees,
and shattered the trees of
their country.
34 He spoke, and the locusts came,
and young locusts without number;
35 they devoured all the vegetation
in their land,
and ate up the fruit of their ground.
36 He struck down all the firstborn
in their land,
the first issue of all their strength.

37 Then he brought Israel[e] out
with silver and gold,
and there was no one among
their tribes who stumbled.
38 Egypt was glad when they departed,
for dread of them had
fallen upon it.
39 He spread a cloud for a covering,
and fire to give light by night.
40 They asked, and he brought quails,
and gave them food from
heaven in abundance.
41 He opened the rock, and
water gushed out;
it flowed through the
desert like a river.
42 For he remembered his holy promise,
and Abraham, his servant.

43 So he brought his people out with joy,
his chosen ones with singing.
44 He gave them the lands of the nations,
and they took possession of the
wealth of the peoples,
45 that they might keep his statutes
and observe his laws.
Praise the LORD!

PSALM 106

A CONFESSION OF ISRAEL'S SINS

1 Praise the LORD!
O give thanks to the LORD,
for he is good;
for his steadfast love
endures for ever.

[c] 105.22 Gk Syr Jerome: Heb *to bind*
[d] 105.28 Cn Compare Gk Syr: Heb *they did not rebel*
[e] 105.37 Heb *them*

2 Who can utter the mighty
doings of the LORD,
or declare all his praise?
3 Happy are those who
observe justice,
who do righteousness at all times.

4 Remember me, O LORD, when you
show favour to your people;
help me when you deliver them;
5 that I may see the prosperity
of your chosen ones,
that I may rejoice in the
gladness of your nation,
that I may glory in your heritage.

6 Both we and our ancestors
have sinned;
we have committed iniquity,
have done wickedly.
7 Our ancestors, when they
were in Egypt,
did not consider your
wonderful works;
they did not remember the
abundance of your
steadfast love,
but rebelled against the Most
High[f] at the Red Sea.[g]
8 Yet he saved them for his
name's sake,
so that he might make known
his mighty power.
9 He rebuked the Red Sea,[h] and
it became dry;
he led them through the deep
as through a desert.
10 So he saved them from the
hand of the foe,
and delivered them from the
hand of the enemy.
11 The waters covered
their adversaries;
not one of them was left.
12 Then they believed his words;
they sang his praise.

13 But they soon forgot his works;
they did not wait for his counsel.
14 But they had a wanton craving
in the wilderness,
and put God to the test
in the desert;
15 he gave them what they asked,
but sent a wasting disease
among them.

16 They were jealous of Moses
in the camp,
and of Aaron, the holy
one of the LORD.
17 The earth opened and swallowed
up Dathan,
and covered the faction of Abiram.
18 Fire also broke out in their company;
the flame burned up the wicked.

19 They made a calf at Horeb
and worshipped a cast image.
20 They exchanged the glory of God[i]
for the image of an ox
that eats grass.
21 They forgot God, their Saviour,
who had done great
things in Egypt,
22 wondrous works in the land of Ham,
and awesome deeds by
the Red Sea.[j]
23 Therefore he said he would
destroy them—
had not Moses, his chosen one,
stood in the breach before him,
to turn away his wrath from
destroying them.

24 Then they despised the
pleasant land,
having no faith in his promise.
25 They grumbled in their tents,
and did not obey the voice
of the LORD.
26 Therefore he raised his hand
and swore to them
that he would make them
fall in the wilderness,
27 and would disperse[k] their
descendants among
the nations,
scattering them over the lands.

28 Then they attached themselves
to the Baal of Peor,
and ate sacrifices offered
to the dead;
29 they provoked the LORD to anger
with their deeds,
and a plague broke out
among them.
30 Then Phinehas stood up
and interceded,
and the plague was stopped.
31 And that has been reckoned to
him as righteousness
from generation to
generation for ever.

[f] **106.7** Cn Compare 78.17, 56: Heb *rebelled at the sea* [g] **106.7** Or *Sea of Reeds* [h] **106.9** Or *Sea of Reeds* [i] **106.20** Compare Gk Mss: Heb *exchanged their glory* [j] **106.22** Or *Sea of Reeds* [k] **106.27** Syr Compare Ezek 20.23: Heb *cause to fall*

32 They angered the LORD[l] at the
waters of Meribah,
and it went ill with Moses
on their account;
33 for they made his spirit bitter,
and he spoke words that
were rash.

34 They did not destroy the peoples
as the LORD commanded them,
35 but they mingled with the nations
and learned to do as they did.
36 They served their idols,
which became a snare to them.
37 They sacrificed their sons
and their daughters to
the demons;
38 they poured out innocent blood,
the blood of their sons
and daughters,
whom they sacrificed to the
idols of Canaan;
and the land was polluted
with blood.
39 Thus they became unclean
by their acts,
and prostituted themselves
in their doings.

40 Then the anger of the LORD was
kindled against his people,
and he abhorred his heritage;
41 he gave them into the hand
of the nations,
so that those who hated them
ruled over them.
42 Their enemies oppressed them,
and they were brought into
subjection under their power.
43 Many times he delivered them,
but they were rebellious
in their purposes,
and were brought low through
their iniquity.
44 Nevertheless, he regarded
their distress
when he heard their cry.
45 For their sake he remembered
his covenant,
and showed compassion
according to the abundance
of his steadfast love.
46 He caused them to be pitied
by all who held them captive.

47 Save us, O LORD our God,
and gather us from among
the nations,
that we may give thanks to
your holy name
and glory in your praise.

48 Blessed be the LORD, the
God of Israel,
from everlasting to everlasting.
And let all the people say, 'Amen.'
Praise the LORD!

Book V (Psalms 107–150)

PSALM 107

THANKSGIVING FOR DELIVERANCE FROM MANY TROUBLES

1 O give thanks to the LORD,
for he is good;
for his steadfast love
endures for ever.
2 Let the redeemed of the LORD say so,
those he redeemed from trouble
3 and gathered in from the lands,
from the east and from the west,
from the north and from
the south.[m]

4 Some wandered in desert wastes,
finding no way to an
inhabited town;
5 hungry and thirsty,
their soul fainted within them.
6 Then they cried to the LORD
in their trouble,
and he delivered them from
their distress;
7 he led them by a straight way,
until they reached an
inhabited town.
8 Let them thank the LORD for
his steadfast love,
for his wonderful works
to humankind.
9 For he satisfies the thirsty,
and the hungry he fills
with good things.

10 Some sat in darkness and in gloom,
prisoners in misery and in irons,
11 for they had rebelled against
the words of God,
and spurned the counsel
of the Most High.
12 Their hearts were bowed down
with hard labour;
they fell down, with no
one to help.
13 Then they cried to the LORD
in their trouble,
and he saved them from
their distress;

[l] **106.32** Heb *him* [m] **107.3** Cn: Heb *sea*

14 he brought them out of
darkness and gloom,
and broke their bonds asunder.
15 Let them thank the LORD for
his steadfast love,
for his wonderful works
to humankind.
16 For he shatters the doors of bronze,
and cuts in two the bars of iron.

17 Some were sick[n] through
their sinful ways,
and because of their iniquities
endured affliction;
18 they loathed any kind of food,
and they drew near to the
gates of death.
19 Then they cried to the LORD
in their trouble,
and he saved them from
their distress;
20 he sent out his word and
healed them,
and delivered them from
destruction.
21 Let them thank the LORD for
his steadfast love,
for his wonderful works
to humankind.
22 And let them offer thanksgiving
sacrifices,
and tell of his deeds with
songs of joy.

23 Some went down to the sea in ships,
doing business on the
mighty waters;
24 they saw the deeds of the LORD,
his wondrous works in the deep.
25 For he commanded and raised
the stormy wind,
which lifted up the waves
of the sea.
26 They mounted up to heaven, they
went down to the depths;
their courage melted away
in their calamity;
27 they reeled and staggered
like drunkards,
and were at their wits' end.
28 Then they cried to the LORD
in their trouble,
and he brought them out
from their distress;
29 he made the storm be still,
and the waves of the sea
were hushed.
30 Then they were glad because
they had quiet,
and he brought them to
their desired haven.
31 Let them thank the LORD for
his steadfast love,
for his wonderful works
to humankind.
32 Let them extol him in the
congregation of the people,
and praise him in the
assembly of the elders.

33 He turns rivers into a desert,
springs of water into
thirsty ground,
34 a fruitful land into a salty waste,
because of the wickedness
of its inhabitants.
35 He turns a desert into pools of water,
a parched land into
springs of water.
36 And there he lets the hungry live,
and they establish a
town to live in;
37 they sow fields, and plant vineyards,
and get a fruitful yield.
38 By his blessing they multiply greatly,
and he does not let their
cattle decrease.

39 When they are diminished
and brought low
through oppression, trouble,
and sorrow,
40 he pours contempt on princes
and makes them wander in
trackless wastes;
41 but he raises up the needy
out of distress,
and makes their families
like flocks.
42 The upright see it and are glad;
and all wickedness stops
its mouth.
43 Let those who are wise give
heed to these things,
and consider the steadfast
love of the LORD.

PSALM 108

PRAISE AND PRAYER FOR VICTORY

A Song. A Psalm of David.

1 My heart is steadfast, O God, my
heart is steadfast;[o]
I will sing and make melody.
Awake, my soul![p]
2 Awake, O harp and lyre!
I will awake the dawn.

[n] **107.17** Cn: Heb *fools* [o] **108.1** Heb Mss Gk Syr: MT lacks *my heart is steadfast* [p] **108.1** Compare 57.8: Heb *also my soul*

3 I will give thanks to you, O LORD,
among the peoples,
and I will sing praises to you
among the nations.
4 For your steadfast love is higher
than the heavens,
and your faithfulness reaches
to the clouds.

5 Be exalted, O God, above the heavens,
and let your glory be over
all the earth.
6 Give victory with your right
hand, and answer me,
so that those whom you love
may be rescued.

7 God has promised in his sanctuary:[q]
'With exultation I will divide
up Shechem,
and portion out the Vale of Succoth.
8 Gilead is mine; Manasseh is mine;
Ephraim is my helmet;
Judah is my sceptre.
9 Moab is my wash-basin;
on Edom I hurl my shoe;
over Philistia I shout in triumph.'

10 Who will bring me to the fortified city?
Who will lead me to Edom?
11 Have you not rejected us, O God?
You do not go out, O God,
with our armies.
12 O grant us help against the foe,
for human help is worthless.
13 With God we shall do valiantly;
it is he who will tread
down our foes.

PSALM 109

PRAYER FOR VINDICATION AND VENGEANCE

To the leader. Of David. A Psalm.

1 Do not be silent, O God of my praise.
2 For wicked and deceitful mouths
are opened against me,
speaking against me with
lying tongues.
3 They beset me with words of hate,
and attack me without cause.
4 In return for my love they accuse me,
even while I make prayer
for them.[r]
5 So they reward me evil for good,
and hatred for my love.

6 They say,[s] 'Appoint a wicked
man against him;
let an accuser stand on his right.
7 When he is tried, let him be
found guilty;
let his prayer be counted as sin.
8 May his days be few;
may another seize his position.
9 May his children be orphans,
and his wife a widow.
10 May his children wander
about and beg;
may they be driven out of[t] the
ruins they inhabit.
11 May the creditor seize all that he has;
may strangers plunder the
fruits of his toil.
12 May there be no one to do
him a kindness,
nor anyone to pity his
orphaned children.
13 May his posterity be cut off;
may his name be blotted out in
the second generation.
14 May the iniquity of his father[u]
be remembered
before the LORD,
and do not let the sin of his
mother be blotted out.
15 Let them be before the LORD
continually,
and may his[v] memory be cut
off from the earth.
16 For he did not remember to
show kindness,
but pursued the poor and needy
and the broken-hearted
to their death.
17 He loved to curse; let curses
come on him.
He did not like blessing; may
it be far from him.
18 He clothed himself with
cursing as his coat,
may it soak into his body
like water,
like oil into his bones.
19 May it be like a garment that he
wraps around himself,
like a belt that he wears every day.'

20 May that be the reward of my
accusers from the LORD,
of those who speak evil
against my life.
21 But you, O LORD my Lord,
act on my behalf for your
name's sake;
because your steadfast love
is good, deliver me.

[q] **108.7** *Or by his holiness* [r] **109.4** Syr: Heb *I prayer* [s] **109.6** Heb lacks *They say* [t] **109.10** Gk: Heb *and seek* [u] **109.14** Cn: Heb *fathers* [v] **109.15** Gk: Heb *their*

22 For I am poor and needy,
and my heart is pierced
within me.
23 I am gone like a shadow at evening;
I am shaken off like a locust.
24 My knees are weak through fasting;
my body has become gaunt.
25 I am an object of scorn to
my accusers;
when they see me, they
shake their heads.

26 Help me, O LORD my God!
Save me according to your
steadfast love.
27 Let them know that this
is your hand;
you, O LORD, have done it.
28 Let them curse, but you will bless.
Let my assailants be put
to shame;[w] may your
servant be glad.
29 May my accusers be clothed
with dishonour;
may they be wrapped in their
own shame as in a mantle.
30 With my mouth I will give great
thanks to the LORD;
I will praise him in the
midst of the throng.
31 For he stands at the right
hand of the needy,
to save them from those
who would condemn
them to death.

PSALM 110

ASSURANCE OF VICTORY FOR GOD'S PRIEST-KING

Of David. A Psalm.

1 The LORD says to my lord,
'Sit at my right hand
until I make your enemies
your footstool.'

2 The LORD sends out from Zion
your mighty sceptre.
Rule in the midst of your foes.
3 Your people will offer
themselves willingly
on the day you lead your forces
on the holy mountains.[x]
From the womb of the morning,
like dew, your youth[y] will
come to you.
4 The LORD has sworn and will
not change his mind,
'You are a priest for ever according
to the order of Melchizedek.'[z]

5 The Lord is at your right hand;
he will shatter kings on the
day of his wrath.
6 He will execute judgement
among the nations,
filling them with corpses;
he will shatter heads
over the wide earth.
7 He will drink from the stream
by the path;
therefore he will lift up his head.

PSALM 111

PRAISE FOR GOD'S WONDERFUL WORKS

1 Praise the LORD!
I will give thanks to the LORD
with my whole heart,
in the company of the upright,
in the congregation.
2 Great are the works of the LORD,
studied by all who delight
in them.
3 Full of honour and majesty
is his work,
and his righteousness
endures for ever.
4 He has gained renown by his
wonderful deeds;
the LORD is gracious and merciful.
5 He provides food for those
who fear him;
he is ever mindful of his covenant.
6 He has shown his people the
power of his works,
in giving them the heritage
of the nations.
7 The works of his hands are
faithful and just;
all his precepts are trustworthy.
8 They are established for
ever and ever,
to be performed with faithfulness
and uprightness.
9 He sent redemption to his people;
he has commanded his
covenant for ever.
Holy and awesome is his name.
10 The fear of the LORD is the
beginning of wisdom;
all those who practise it[a] have
a good understanding.
His praise endures for ever.

[w] **109.28** Gk: Heb *They have risen up and have been put to shame* [x] **110.3** Another reading is *in holy splendour* [y] **110.3** Cn: Heb *the dew of your youth* [z] **110.4** Or *for ever, a rightful king by my edict* [a] **111.10** Gk Syr: Heb *them*

PSALM 112

BLESSINGS OF THE RIGHTEOUS

1 Praise the LORD!
Happy are those who
fear the LORD,
who greatly delight in his
commandments.
2 Their descendants will be
mighty in the land;
the generation of the upright
will be blessed.
3 Wealth and riches are in
their houses,
and their righteousness
endures for ever.
4 They rise in the darkness as a
light for the upright;
they are gracious, merciful,
and righteous.
5 It is well with those who deal
generously and lend,
who conduct their affairs
with justice.
6 For the righteous will never
be moved;
they will be remembered for ever.
7 They are not afraid of evil tidings;
their hearts are firm, secure
in the LORD.
8 Their hearts are steady, they
will not be afraid;
in the end they will look in
triumph on their foes.
9 They have distributed freely, they
have given to the poor;
their righteousness
endures for ever;
their horn is exalted in honour.
10 The wicked see it and are angry;
they gnash their teeth
and melt away;
the desire of the wicked
comes to nothing.

PSALM 113

GOD THE HELPER OF THE NEEDY

1 Praise the LORD!
Praise, O servants of the LORD;
praise the name of the LORD.

2 Blessed be the name of the LORD
from this time on and
for evermore.
3 From the rising of the sun
to its setting
the name of the LORD is
to be praised.
4 The LORD is high above all nations,
and his glory above the heavens.
5 Who is like the LORD our God,
who is seated on high,
6 who looks far down
on the heavens and the earth?
7 He raises the poor from the dust,
and lifts the needy from
the ash heap,
8 to make them sit with princes,
with the princes of his people.
9 He gives the barren woman a home,
making her the joyous
mother of children.
Praise the LORD!

PSALM 114

GOD'S WONDERS AT THE EXODUS

1 When Israel went out from Egypt,
the house of Jacob from a people
of strange language,
2 Judah became God's[b] sanctuary,
Israel his dominion.

3 The sea looked and fled;
Jordan turned back.
4 The mountains skipped like rams,
the hills like lambs.

5 Why is it, O sea, that you flee?
O Jordan, that you turn back?
6 O mountains, that you skip
like rams?
O hills, like lambs?

7 Tremble, O earth, at the
presence of the LORD,
at the presence of the God of Jacob,
8 who turns the rock into a
pool of water,
the flint into a spring of water.

PSALM 115

THE IMPOTENCE OF IDOLS AND THE GREATNESS OF GOD

1 Not to us, O LORD, not to us, but
to your name give glory,
for the sake of your steadfast love
and your faithfulness.
2 Why should the nations say,
'Where is their God?'

3 Our God is in the heavens;
he does whatever he pleases.
4 Their idols are silver and gold,
the work of human hands.

[b] 114.2 Heb *his*

5 They have mouths, but do not speak;
eyes, but do not see.
6 They have ears, but do not hear;
noses, but do not smell.
7 They have hands, but do not feel;
feet, but do not walk;
they make no sound in
their throats.
8 Those who make them are like them;
so are all who trust in them.

9 O Israel, trust in the LORD!
He is their help and their shield.
10 O house of Aaron, trust in the LORD!
He is their help and their shield.
11 You who fear the LORD, trust
in the LORD!
He is their help and their shield.

12 The LORD has been mindful of
us; he will bless us;
he will bless the house of Israel;
he will bless the house of Aaron;
13 he will bless those who
fear the LORD,
both small and great.

14 May the LORD give you increase,
both you and your children.
15 May you be blessed by the LORD,
who made heaven and earth.

16 The heavens are the LORD's heavens,
but the earth he has given
to human beings.
17 The dead do not praise the LORD,
nor do any that go down
into silence.
18 But we will bless the LORD
from this time on and
for evermore.
Praise the LORD!

PSALM 116

THANKSGIVING FOR RECOVERY FROM ILLNESS

1 I love the LORD, because
he has heard
my voice and my supplications.
2 Because he inclined his ear to me,
therefore I will call on him
as long as I live.
3 The snares of death encompassed me;
the pangs of Sheol laid
hold on me;
I suffered distress and anguish.
4 Then I called on the name
of the LORD:
'O LORD, I pray, save my life!'

5 Gracious is the LORD, and righteous;
our God is merciful.
6 The LORD protects the simple;
when I was brought low,
he saved me.
7 Return, O my soul, to your rest,
for the LORD has dealt
bountifully with you.

8 For you have delivered my
soul from death,
my eyes from tears,
my feet from stumbling.
9 I walk before the LORD
in the land of the living.
10 I kept my faith, even when I said,
'I am greatly afflicted';
11 I said in my consternation,
'Everyone is a liar.'

12 What shall I return to the LORD
for all his bounty to me?
13 I will lift up the cup of salvation
and call on the name of the LORD,
14 I will pay my vows to the LORD
in the presence of all his people.
15 Precious in the sight of the LORD
is the death of his faithful ones.
16 O LORD, I am your servant;
I am your servant, the child
of your serving-maid.
You have loosed my bonds.
17 I will offer to you a thanksgiving
sacrifice
and call on the name of the LORD.
18 I will pay my vows to the LORD
in the presence of all his people,
19 in the courts of the house
of the LORD,
in your midst, O Jerusalem.
Praise the LORD!

PSALM 117

UNIVERSAL CALL TO WORSHIP

1 Praise the LORD, all you nations!
Extol him, all you peoples!
2 For great is his steadfast
love towards us,
and the faithfulness of the
LORD endures for ever.
Praise the LORD!

PSALM 118

A SONG OF VICTORY

1 O give thanks to the LORD,
for he is good;
his steadfast love endures for ever!

2 Let Israel say,
'His steadfast love endures
for ever.'
3 Let the house of Aaron say,
'His steadfast love endures
for ever.'
4 Let those who fear the LORD say,
'His steadfast love endures
for ever.'

5 Out of my distress I called
on the LORD;
the LORD answered me and
set me in a broad place.
6 With the LORD on my side
I do not fear.
What can mortals do to me?
7 The LORD is on my side to help me;
I shall look in triumph on
those who hate me.
8 It is better to take refuge in the LORD
than to put confidence in mortals.
9 It is better to take refuge in the LORD
than to put confidence in princes.

10 All nations surrounded me;
in the name of the LORD
I cut them off!
11 They surrounded me, surrounded
me on every side;
in the name of the LORD
I cut them off!
12 They surrounded me like bees;
they blazed[c] like a fire of thorns;
in the name of the LORD
I cut them off!
13 I was pushed hard,[d] so that
I was falling,
but the LORD helped me.
14 The LORD is my strength
and my might;
he has become my salvation.

15 There are glad songs of victory in
the tents of the righteous:
'The right hand of the LORD
does valiantly;
16 the right hand of the
LORD is exalted;
the right hand of the LORD
does valiantly.'
17 I shall not die, but I shall live,
and recount the deeds of the LORD.
18 The LORD has punished me severely,
but he did not give me
over to death.

19 Open to me the gates of
righteousness,
that I may enter through them
and give thanks to the LORD.
20 This is the gate of the LORD;
the righteous shall enter
through it.

21 I thank you that you have
answered me
and have become my salvation.
22 The stone that the builders rejected
has become the chief cornerstone.
23 This is the LORD's doing;
it is marvellous in our eyes.
24 This is the day that the
LORD has made;
let us rejoice and be glad in it.[e]
25 Save us, we beseech you, O LORD!
O LORD, we beseech you,
give us success!

26 Blessed is the one who comes in
the name of the LORD.[f]
We bless you from the
house of the LORD.
27 The LORD is God,
and he has given us light.
Bind the festal procession
with branches,
up to the horns of the altar.[g]

28 You are my God, and I will
give thanks to you;
you are my God, I will extol you.

29 O give thanks to the LORD,
for he is good,
for his steadfast love
endures for ever.

PSALM 119

THE GLORIES OF GOD'S LAW

1 Happy are those whose way
is blameless,
who walk in the law of the LORD.
2 Happy are those who keep
his decrees,
who seek him with their
whole heart,
3 who also do no wrong,
but walk in his ways.
4 You have commanded your precepts
to be kept diligently.
5 O that my ways may be steadfast
in keeping your statutes!

[c] **118.12** Gk: Heb *were extinguished*
[d] **118.13** Gk Syr Jerome: Heb *You pushed me hard*
[e] **118.24** Or *in him* [f] **118.26** Or *Blessed in the name of the LORD is the one who comes*
[g] **118.27** Meaning of Heb uncertain

6 Then I shall not be put to shame,
having my eyes fixed on all
your commandments.
7 I will praise you with an
upright heart,
when I learn your righteous
ordinances.
8 I will observe your statutes;
do not utterly forsake me.

9 How can young people keep
their way pure?
By guarding it according
to your word.
10 With my whole heart I seek you;
do not let me stray from your
commandments.
11 I treasure your word in my heart,
so that I may not sin against you.
12 Blessed are you, O LORD;
teach me your statutes.
13 With my lips I declare
all the ordinances of
your mouth.
14 I delight in the way of your decrees
as much as in all riches.
15 I will meditate on your precepts,
and fix my eyes on your ways.
16 I will delight in your statutes;
I will not forget your word.

17 Deal bountifully with your servant,
so that I may live and
observe your word.
18 Open my eyes, so that I may behold
wondrous things
out of your law.
19 I live as an alien in the land;
do not hide your commandments
from me.
20 My soul is consumed with longing
for your ordinances at all times.
21 You rebuke the insolent,
accursed ones,
who wander from your
commandments;
22 take away from me their scorn
and contempt,
for I have kept your decrees.
23 Even though princes sit
plotting against me,
your servant will meditate
on your statutes.
24 Your decrees are my delight,
they are my counsellors.

25 My soul clings to the dust;
revive me according to your word.
26 When I told of my ways, you
answered me;
teach me your statutes.
27 Make me understand the way
of your precepts,
and I will meditate on your
wondrous works.
28 My soul melts away for sorrow;
strengthen me according
to your word.
29 Put false ways far from me;
and graciously teach me your law.
30 I have chosen the way of
faithfulness;
I set your ordinances before me.
31 I cling to your decrees, O LORD;
let me not be put to shame.
32 I run the way of your
commandments,
for you enlarge my understanding.

33 Teach me, O LORD, the way
of your statutes,
and I will observe it to the end.
34 Give me understanding, that I
may keep your law
and observe it with my
whole heart.
35 Lead me in the path of your
commandments,
for I delight in it.
36 Turn my heart to your decrees,
and not to selfish gain.
37 Turn my eyes from looking
at vanities;
give me life in your ways.
38 Confirm to your servant
your promise,
which is for those who fear you.
39 Turn away the disgrace that I dread,
for your ordinances are good.
40 See, I have longed for your precepts;
in your righteousness give me life.

41 Let your steadfast love come
to me, O LORD,
your salvation according
to your promise.
42 Then I shall have an answer for
those who taunt me,
for I trust in your word.
43 Do not take the word of truth
utterly out of my mouth,
for my hope is in your ordinances.
44 I will keep your law continually,
for ever and ever.
45 I shall walk at liberty,
for I have sought your precepts.
46 I will also speak of your decrees
before kings,
and shall not be put to shame;
47 I find my delight in your
commandments,
because I love them.

48 I revere your commandments,
which I love,
and I will meditate on
your statutes.

49 Remember your word to
your servant,
in which you have made me hope.
50 This is my comfort in my distress,
that your promise gives me life.
51 The arrogant utterly deride me,
but I do not turn away
from your law.
52 When I think of your ordinances
from of old,
I take comfort, O LORD.
53 Hot indignation seizes me
because of the wicked,
those who forsake your law.
54 Your statutes have been my songs
wherever I make my home.
55 I remember your name in the
night, O LORD,
and keep your law.
56 This blessing has fallen to me,
for I have kept your precepts.

57 The LORD is my portion;
I promise to keep your words.
58 I implore your favour with
all my heart;
be gracious to me according
to your promise.
59 When I think of your ways,
I turn my feet to your decrees;
60 I hurry and do not delay
to keep your commandments.
61 Though the cords of the wicked
ensnare me,
I do not forget your law.
62 At midnight I rise to praise you,
because of your righteous
ordinances.
63 I am a companion of all
who fear you,
of those who keep your precepts.
64 The earth, O LORD, is full of
your steadfast love;
teach me your statutes.

65 You have dealt well with
your servant,
O LORD, according to your word.
66 Teach me good judgement
and knowledge,
for I believe in your
commandments.
67 Before I was humbled I went astray,
but now I keep your word.
68 You are good and do good;
teach me your statutes.
69 The arrogant smear me with lies,
but with my whole heart I
keep your precepts.
70 Their hearts are fat and gross,
but I delight in your law.
71 It is good for me that I was humbled,
so that I might learn
your statutes.
72 The law of your mouth is
better to me
than thousands of gold
and silver pieces.

73 Your hands have made and
fashioned me;
give me understanding that I may
learn your commandments.
74 Those who fear you shall see
me and rejoice,
because I have hoped
in your word.
75 I know, O LORD, that your
judgements are right,
and that in faithfulness you
have humbled me.
76 Let your steadfast love become
my comfort
according to your promise
to your servant.
77 Let your mercy come to me,
that I may live;
for your law is my delight.
78 Let the arrogant be put to shame,
because they have subverted
me with guile;
as for me, I will meditate
on your precepts.
79 Let those who fear you turn to me,
so that they may know
your decrees.
80 May my heart be blameless
in your statutes,
so that I may not be put to shame.

81 My soul languishes for
your salvation;
I hope in your word.
82 My eyes fail with watching
for your promise;
I ask, 'When will you comfort me?'
83 For I have become like a wineskin
in the smoke,
yet I have not forgotten
your statutes.
84 How long must your
servant endure?
When will you judge those
who persecute me?
85 The arrogant have dug
pitfalls for me;
they flout your law.

86 All your commandments
are enduring;
I am persecuted without
cause; help me!
87 They have almost made an
end of me on earth;
but I have not forsaken
your precepts.
88 In your steadfast love
spare my life,
so that I may keep the decrees
of your mouth.

89 The LORD exists for ever;
your word is firmly fixed
in heaven.
90 Your faithfulness endures to
all generations;
you have established the earth,
and it stands fast.
91 By your appointment they
stand today,
for all things are your servants.
92 If your law had not
been my delight,
I would have perished
in my misery.
93 I will never forget your precepts,
for by them you have
given me life.
94 I am yours; save me,
for I have sought your precepts.
95 The wicked lie in wait to destroy me,
but I consider your decrees.
96 I have seen a limit to all perfection,
but your commandment is
exceedingly broad.

97 Oh, how I love your law!
It is my meditation all day long.
98 Your commandment makes me
wiser than my enemies,
for it is always with me.
99 I have more understanding
than all my teachers,
for your decrees are my
meditation.
100 I understand more than the aged,
for I keep your precepts.
101 I hold back my feet from
every evil way,
in order to keep your word.
102 I do not turn away from
your ordinances,
for you have taught me.
103 How sweet are your words
to my taste,
sweeter than honey to my mouth!
104 Through your precepts I get
understanding;
therefore I hate every false way.

105 Your word is a lamp to my feet
and a light to my path.
106 I have sworn an oath and
confirmed it,
to observe your righteous
ordinances.
107 I am severely afflicted;
give me life, O LORD, according
to your word.
108 Accept my offerings of
praise, O LORD,
and teach me your ordinances.
109 I hold my life in my hand
continually,
but I do not forget your law.
110 The wicked have laid a snare for me,
but I do not stray from
your precepts.
111 Your decrees are my
heritage for ever;
they are the joy of my heart.
112 I incline my heart to perform
your statutes
for ever, to the end.

113 I hate the double-minded,
but I love your law.
114 You are my hiding-place
and my shield;
I hope in your word.
115 Go away from me, you evildoers,
that I may keep the
commandments of my God.
116 Uphold me according to your
promise, that I may live,
and let me not be put to
shame in my hope.
117 Hold me up, that I may be safe
and have regard for your
statutes continually.
118 You spurn all who go astray
from your statutes;
for their cunning is in vain.
119 All the wicked of the earth
you count as dross;
therefore I love your decrees.
120 My flesh trembles for fear of you,
and I am afraid of your
judgements.

121 I have done what is just and right;
do not leave me to my oppressors.
122 Guarantee your servant's well-being;
do not let the godless oppress me.
123 My eyes fail from watching
for your salvation,
and for the fulfilment of your
righteous promise.
124 Deal with your servant according
to your steadfast love,
and teach me your statutes.

125 I am your servant; give me
understanding,
so that I may know your decrees.
126 It is time for the LORD to act,
for your law has been broken.
127 Truly I love your commandments
more than gold, more
than fine gold.
128 Truly I direct my steps by all
your precepts;[h]
I hate every false way.

129 Your decrees are wonderful;
therefore my soul keeps them.
130 The unfolding of your words
gives light;
it imparts understanding
to the simple.
131 With open mouth I pant,
because I long for your
commandments.
132 Turn to me and be
gracious to me,
as is your custom towards those
who love your name.
133 Keep my steps steady according
to your promise,
and never let iniquity have
dominion over me.
134 Redeem me from human
oppression,
that I may keep your precepts.
135 Make your face shine upon
your servant,
and teach me your statutes.
136 My eyes shed streams of tears
because your law is not kept.

137 You are righteous, O LORD,
and your judgements are right.
138 You have appointed your decrees
in righteousness
and in all faithfulness.
139 My zeal consumes me
because my foes forget
your words.
140 Your promise is well tried,
and your servant loves it.
141 I am small and despised,
yet I do not forget your precepts.
142 Your righteousness is an
everlasting righteousness,
and your law is the truth.
143 Trouble and anguish have
come upon me,
but your commandments
are my delight.
144 Your decrees are righteous
for ever;
give me understanding
that I may live.

145 With my whole heart I cry;
answer me, O LORD.
I will keep your statutes.
146 I cry to you; save me,
that I may observe your decrees.
147 I rise before dawn and cry for help;
I put my hope in your words.
148 My eyes are awake before each
watch of the night,
that I may meditate on
your promise.
149 In your steadfast love hear my voice;
O LORD, in your justice
preserve my life.
150 Those who persecute me with
evil purpose draw near;
they are far from your law.
151 Yet you are near, O LORD,
and all your commandments
are true.
152 Long ago I learned from
your decrees
that you have established
them for ever.

153 Look on my misery and rescue me,
for I do not forget your law.
154 Plead my cause and redeem me;
give me life according to
your promise.
155 Salvation is far from the wicked,
for they do not seek your statutes.
156 Great is your mercy, O LORD;
give me life according to
your justice.
157 Many are my persecutors and
my adversaries,
yet I do not swerve from
your decrees.
158 I look at the faithless with disgust,
because they do not keep
your commands.
159 Consider how I love your precepts;
preserve my life according to
your steadfast love.
160 The sum of your word is truth;
and every one of your righteous
ordinances endures for ever.

161 Princes persecute me without cause,
but my heart stands in awe
of your words.
162 I rejoice at your word
like one who finds great spoil.
163 I hate and abhor falsehood,
but I love your law.
164 Seven times a day I praise you
for your righteous ordinances.

[h] **119.128** Gk Jerome: Meaning of Heb uncertain

165 Great peace have those who
love your law;
nothing can make them stumble.
166 I hope for your salvation, O LORD,
and I fulfil your commandments.
167 My soul keeps your decrees;
I love them exceedingly.
168 I keep your precepts and decrees,
for all my ways are before you.

169 Let my cry come before
you, O LORD;
give me understanding
according to your word.
170 Let my supplication come
before you;
deliver me according to
your promise.
171 My lips will pour forth praise,
because you teach me
your statutes.
172 My tongue will sing of your promise,
for all your commandments
are right.
173 Let your hand be ready to help me,
for I have chosen your precepts.
174 I long for your salvation, O LORD,
and your law is my delight.
175 Let me live that I may praise you,
and let your ordinances help me.
176 I have gone astray like a lost sheep;
seek out your servant,
for I do not forget your
commandments.

PSALM 120

PRAYER FOR DELIVERANCE FROM SLANDERERS

A Song of Ascents.

1 In my distress I cry to the LORD,
that he may answer me:
2 'Deliver me, O LORD,
from lying lips,
from a deceitful tongue.'

3 What shall be given to you?
And what more shall be
done to you,
you deceitful tongue?
4 A warrior's sharp arrows,
with glowing coals of
the broom tree!

5 Woe is me, that I am an
alien in Meshech,
that I must live among the
tents of Kedar.
6 Too long have I had my dwelling
among those who hate peace.
7 I am for peace;
but when I speak,
they are for war.

PSALM 121

ASSURANCE OF GOD'S PROTECTION

A Song of Ascents.

1 I lift up my eyes to the hills—
from where will my help come?
2 My help comes from the LORD,
who made heaven and earth.

3 He will not let your foot be moved;
he who keeps you will
not slumber.
4 He who keeps Israel
will neither slumber nor sleep.

5 The LORD is your keeper;
the LORD is your shade at
your right hand.
6 The sun shall not strike you by day,
nor the moon by night.

7 The LORD will keep you from all evil;
he will keep your life.
8 The LORD will keep
your going out and your
coming in
from this time on and
for evermore.

PSALM 122

SONG OF PRAISE AND PRAYER FOR JERUSALEM

A Song of Ascents. Of David.

1 I was glad when they said to me,
'Let us go to the house
of the LORD!'
2 Our feet are standing
within your gates, O Jerusalem.

3 Jerusalem—built as a city
that is bound firmly together.
4 To it the tribes go up,
the tribes of the LORD,
as was decreed for Israel,
to give thanks to the name
of the LORD.
5 For there the thrones for
judgement were set up,
the thrones of the house of David.

6 Pray for the peace of Jerusalem:
'May they prosper who love you.
7 Peace be within your walls,
and security within your towers.'

8 For the sake of my relatives
and friends
I will say, 'Peace be within you.'
9 For the sake of the house of
the LORD our God,
I will seek your good.

PSALM 123

SUPPLICATION FOR MERCY

A Song of Ascents.

1 To you I lift up my eyes,
O you who are enthroned
in the heavens!
2 As the eyes of servants
look to the hand of their master,
as the eyes of a maid
to the hand of her mistress,
so our eyes look to the LORD our God,
until he has mercy upon us.

3 Have mercy upon us, O LORD,
have mercy upon us,
for we have had more than
enough of contempt.
4 Our soul has had more than its fill
of the scorn of those who
are at ease,
of the contempt of the proud.

PSALM 124

THANKSGIVING FOR ISRAEL'S DELIVERANCE

A Song of Ascents. Of David.

1 If it had not been the LORD
who was on our side
—let Israel now say—
2 if it had not been the LORD
who was on our side,
when our enemies attacked us,
3 then they would have swallowed
us up alive,
when their anger was
kindled against us;
4 then the flood would have
swept us away,
the torrent would have
gone over us;
5 then over us would have gone
the raging waters.

6 Blessed be the LORD,
who has not given us
as prey to their teeth.
7 We have escaped like a bird
from the snare of the fowlers;
the snare is broken,
and we have escaped.
8 Our help is in the name of the LORD,
who made heaven and earth.

PSALM 125

THE SECURITY OF GOD'S PEOPLE

A Song of Ascents.

1 Those who trust in the LORD
are like Mount Zion,
which cannot be moved,
but abides for ever.
2 As the mountains surround
Jerusalem,
so the LORD surrounds his people,
from this time on and
for evermore.
3 For the sceptre of wickedness
shall not rest
on the land allotted to
the righteous,
so that the righteous may
not stretch out
their hands to do wrong.
4 Do good, O LORD, to those
who are good,
and to those who are upright
in their hearts.
5 But those who turn aside to their
own crooked ways
the LORD will lead away
with evildoers.
Peace be upon Israel!

PSALM 126

A HARVEST OF JOY

A Song of Ascents.

1 When the LORD restored the
fortunes of Zion,[i]
we were like those who dream.
2 Then our mouth was filled
with laughter,
and our tongue with shouts of joy;
then it was said among the nations,
'The LORD has done great
things for them.'
3 The LORD has done great
things for us,
and we rejoiced.

4 Restore our fortunes, O LORD,
like the watercourses
in the Negeb.
5 May those who sow in tears
reap with shouts of joy.

[i] **126.1** *Or brought back those who returned to Zion*

6 Those who go out weeping,
bearing the seed for sowing,
shall come home with shouts of joy,
carrying their sheaves.

PSALM 127

GOD'S BLESSINGS IN THE HOME

A Song of Ascents. Of Solomon.

1 Unless the LORD builds the house,
those who build it
labour in vain.
Unless the LORD guards the city,
the guard keeps watch in vain.
2 It is in vain that you rise up early
and go late to rest,
eating the bread of anxious toil;
for he gives sleep to his beloved.[j]

3 Sons are indeed a heritage
from the LORD,
the fruit of the womb a reward.
4 Like arrows in the
hand of a warrior
are the sons of one's youth.
5 Happy is the man who has
his quiver full of them.
He shall not be put to shame
when he speaks with his
enemies in the gate.

PSALM 128

THE HAPPY HOME OF THE FAITHFUL

A Song of Ascents.

1 Happy is everyone who
fears the LORD,
who walks in his ways.
2 You shall eat the fruit of the
labour of your hands;
you shall be happy, and it
shall go well with you.

3 Your wife will be like a fruitful vine
within your house;
your children will be
like olive shoots
around your table.
4 Thus shall the man be blessed
who fears the LORD.

5 The LORD bless you from Zion.
May you see the prosperity
of Jerusalem
all the days of your life.
6 May you see your children's
children.
Peace be upon Israel!

PSALM 129

PRAYER FOR THE DOWNFALL OF ISRAEL'S ENEMIES

A Song of Ascents.

1 'Often have they attacked me
from my youth'
—let Israel now say—
2 'often have they attacked me
from my youth,
yet they have not prevailed
against me.
3 Those who plough ploughed
on my back;
they made their furrows long.'
4 The LORD is righteous;
he has cut the cords
of the wicked.
5 May all who hate Zion
be put to shame and turned back.
6 Let them be like the grass
on the housetops
that withers before it grows up,
7 with which reapers do not
fill their hands
or binders of sheaves their arms,
8 while those who pass by do not say,
'The blessing of the LORD
be upon you!
We bless you in the name
of the LORD!'

PSALM 130

WAITING FOR DIVINE REDEMPTION

A Song of Ascents.

1 Out of the depths I cry to
you, O LORD.
2 Lord, hear my voice!
Let your ears be attentive
to the voice of my
supplications!

3 If you, O LORD, should mark
iniquities,
Lord, who could stand?
4 But there is forgiveness with you,
so that you may be revered.

5 I wait for the LORD,
my soul waits,
and in his word I hope;
6 my soul waits for the Lord
more than those who watch
for the morning,
more than those who watch
for the morning.

j **127.2** *Or for he provides for his beloved during sleep*

7 O Israel, hope in the LORD!
For with the LORD there
is steadfast love,
and with him is great
power to redeem.
8 It is he who will redeem Israel
from all its iniquities.

PSALM 131

SONG OF QUIET TRUST

A Song of Ascents. Of David.

1 O LORD, my heart is not lifted up,
my eyes are not raised too high;
I do not occupy myself
with things
too great and too
marvellous for me.
2 But I have calmed and
quieted my soul,
like a weaned child with
its mother;
my soul is like the weaned
child that is with me.[k]

3 O Israel, hope in the LORD
from this time on and
for evermore.

PSALM 132

THE ETERNAL DWELLING OF GOD IN ZION

A Song of Ascents.

1 O LORD, remember in
David's favour
all the hardships he endured;
2 how he swore to the LORD
and vowed to the Mighty
One of Jacob,
3 'I will not enter my house
or get into my bed;
4 I will not give sleep to my eyes
or slumber to my eyelids,
5 until I find a place for the LORD,
a dwelling-place for the
Mighty One of Jacob.'

6 We heard of it in Ephrathah;
we found it in the fields of Jaar.
7 'Let us go to his dwelling-place;
let us worship at his footstool.'

8 Rise up, O LORD, and go to
your resting-place,
you and the ark of your might.
9 Let your priests be clothed
with righteousness,
and let your faithful shout for joy.
10 For your servant David's sake
do not turn away the face of
your anointed one.

11 The LORD swore to David a sure oath
from which he will not turn back:
'One of the sons of your body
I will set on your throne.
12 If your sons keep my covenant
and my decrees that I
shall teach them,
their sons also, for evermore,
shall sit on your throne.'

13 For the LORD has chosen Zion;
he has desired it for
his habitation:
14 'This is my resting-place for ever;
here I will reside, for I
have desired it.
15 I will abundantly bless
its provisions;
I will satisfy its poor with bread.
16 Its priests I will clothe
with salvation,
and its faithful will shout for joy.
17 There I will cause a horn to
sprout up for David;
I have prepared a lamp for
my anointed one.
18 His enemies I will clothe
with disgrace,
but on him, his crown
will gleam.'

PSALM 133

THE BLESSEDNESS OF UNITY

A Song of Ascents.

1 How very good and pleasant it is
when kindred live together
in unity!
2 It is like the precious
oil on the head,
running down upon the beard,
on the beard of Aaron,
running down over the
collar of his robes.
3 It is like the dew of Hermon,
which falls on the
mountains of Zion.
For there the LORD ordained
his blessing,
life for evermore.

[k] 131.2 Or *my soul within me is like a weaned child*

PSALM 134

PRAISE IN THE NIGHT

A Song of Ascents.

1 Come, bless the LORD, all you
servants of the LORD,
who stand by night in the
house of the LORD!
2 Lift up your hands to the holy place,
and bless the LORD.

3 May the LORD, maker of
heaven and earth,
bless you from Zion.

PSALM 135

PRAISE FOR GOD'S GOODNESS AND MIGHT

1 Praise the LORD!
Praise the name of the LORD;
give praise, O servants
of the LORD,
2 you that stand in the house
of the LORD,
in the courts of the house
of our God.
3 Praise the LORD, for the
LORD is good;
sing to his name, for he
is gracious.
4 For the LORD has chosen
Jacob for himself,
Israel as his own possession.

5 For I know that the LORD is great;
our Lord is above all gods.
6 Whatever the LORD pleases he does,
in heaven and on earth,
in the seas and all deeps.
7 He it is who makes the clouds rise
at the end of the earth;
he makes lightnings for the rain
and brings out the wind
from his storehouses.

8 He it was who struck down the
firstborn of Egypt,
both human beings and animals;
9 he sent signs and wonders
into your midst, O Egypt,
against Pharaoh and all
his servants.
10 He struck down many nations
and killed mighty kings—
11 Sihon, king of the Amorites,
and Og, king of Bashan,
and all the kingdoms of Canaan—
12 and gave their land as a heritage,
a heritage to his people Israel.

13 Your name, O LORD,
endures for ever,
your renown, O LORD,
throughout all ages.
14 For the LORD will vindicate
his people,
and have compassion on
his servants.

15 The idols of the nations are
silver and gold,
the work of human hands.
16 They have mouths, but they
do not speak;
they have eyes, but they
do not see;
17 they have ears, but they do not hear,
and there is no breath in
their mouths.
18 Those who make them
and all who trust them
shall become like them.

19 O house of Israel, bless the LORD!
O house of Aaron,
bless the LORD!
20 O house of Levi, bless the LORD!
You that fear the LORD,
bless the LORD!
21 Blessed be the LORD from Zion,
he who resides in Jerusalem.
Praise the LORD!

PSALM 136

GOD'S WORK IN CREATION AND IN HISTORY

1 O give thanks to the LORD,
for he is good,
for his steadfast love
endures for ever.
2 O give thanks to the God of gods,
for his steadfast love
endures for ever.
3 O give thanks to the
Lord of lords,
for his steadfast love
endures for ever;

4 who alone does great wonders,
for his steadfast love
endures for ever;
5 who by understanding made
the heavens,
for his steadfast love
endures for ever;
6 who spread out the earth
on the waters,
for his steadfast love
endures for ever;

7 who made the great lights,
for his steadfast love
endures for ever;
8 the sun to rule over the day,
for his steadfast love
endures for ever;
9 the moon and stars to rule
over the night,
for his steadfast love
endures for ever;

10 who struck Egypt through
their firstborn,
for his steadfast love
endures for ever;
11 and brought Israel out from
among them,
for his steadfast love
endures for ever;
12 with a strong hand and an
outstretched arm,
for his steadfast love
endures for ever;
13 who divided the Red Sea[l] in two,
for his steadfast love
endures for ever;
14 and made Israel pass through
the midst of it,
for his steadfast love
endures for ever;
15 but overthrew Pharaoh and his
army in the Red Sea,[m]
for his steadfast love
endures for ever;
16 who led his people through
the wilderness,
for his steadfast love
endures for ever;
17 who struck down great kings,
for his steadfast love
endures for ever;
18 and killed famous kings,
for his steadfast love
endures for ever;
19 Sihon, king of the Amorites,
for his steadfast love
endures for ever;
20 and Og, king of Bashan,
for his steadfast love
endures for ever;
21 and gave their land as a heritage,
for his steadfast love
endures for ever;
22 a heritage to his servant Israel,
for his steadfast love
endures for ever.

23 It is he who remembered us
in our low estate,
for his steadfast love
endures for ever;
24 and rescued us from our foes,
for his steadfast love
endures for ever;
25 who gives food to all flesh,
for his steadfast love
endures for ever.

26 O give thanks to the God of heaven,
for his steadfast love
endures for ever.

PSALM 137

LAMENT OVER THE DESTRUCTION OF JERUSALEM

1 By the rivers of Babylon—
there we sat down and
there we wept
when we remembered Zion.
2 On the willows[n] there
we hung up our harps.
3 For there our captors
asked us for songs,
and our tormentors asked for
mirth, saying,
'Sing us one of the
songs of Zion!'

4 How could we sing
the LORD's song
in a foreign land?
5 If I forget you, O Jerusalem,
let my right hand wither!
6 Let my tongue cling to the
roof of my mouth,
if I do not remember you,
if I do not set Jerusalem
above my highest joy.

7 Remember, O LORD, against
the Edomites
the day of Jerusalem's fall,
how they said, 'Tear it down!
Tear it down!
Down to its foundations!'
8 O daughter Babylon, you
devastator![o]
Happy shall they be who
pay you back
what you have done to us!
9 Happy shall they be who take
your little ones
and dash them against the rock!

[l] 136.13 Or *Sea of Reeds* [m] 136.15 Or *Sea of Reeds* [n] 137.2 Or *poplars* [o] 137.8 Or *you who are devastated*

PSALM 138

THANKSGIVING AND PRAISE

Of David.

1 I give you thanks, O LORD, with
my whole heart;
before the gods I sing your praise;
2 I bow down towards your
holy temple
and give thanks to your name
for your steadfast love
and your faithfulness;
for you have exalted your
name and your word
above everything.[p]
3 On the day I called, you
answered me,
you increased my strength
of soul.[q]

4 All the kings of the earth shall
praise you, O LORD,
for they have heard the words
of your mouth.
5 They shall sing of the ways
of the LORD,
for great is the glory
of the LORD.
6 For though the LORD is high,
he regards the lowly;
but the haughty he perceives
from far away.

7 Though I walk in the midst
of trouble,
you preserve me against the
wrath of my enemies;
you stretch out your hand,
and your right hand delivers me.
8 The LORD will fulfil his
purpose for me;
your steadfast love, O LORD,
endures for ever.
Do not forsake the work
of your hands.

PSALM 139

THE INESCAPABLE GOD

To the leader. Of David. A Psalm.

1 O LORD, you have searched
me and known me.
2 You know when I sit down
and when I rise up;
you discern my thoughts
from far away.
3 You search out my path and
my lying down,
and are acquainted with
all my ways.
4 Even before a word is on my tongue,
O LORD, you know it completely.
5 You hem me in, behind and before,
and lay your hand upon me.
6 Such knowledge is too
wonderful for me;
it is so high that I cannot attain it.

7 Where can I go from your spirit?
Or where can I flee from
your presence?
8 If I ascend to heaven, you are there;
if I make my bed in Sheol,
you are there.
9 If I take the wings of the morning
and settle at the farthest
limits of the sea,
10 even there your hand shall lead me,
and your right hand shall
hold me fast.
11 If I say, 'Surely the darkness
shall cover me,
and the light around me
become night',
12 even the darkness is not
dark to you;
the night is as bright as the day,
for darkness is as light to you.

13 For it was you who formed
my inward parts;
you knit me together in my
mother's womb.
14 I praise you, for I am fearfully
and wonderfully made.
Wonderful are your works;
that I know very well.
15 My frame was not hidden
from you,
when I was being made in secret,
intricately woven in the
depths of the earth.
16 Your eyes beheld my unformed
substance.
In your book were written
all the days that were
formed for me,
when none of them as
yet existed.
17 How weighty to me are your
thoughts, O God!
How vast is the sum of them!
18 I try to count them—they are
more than the sand;
I come to the end[r]—I am
still with you.

[p] 138.2 Cn: Heb *you have exalted your word above all your name* [q] 138.3 Syr Compare Gk Tg: Heb *you made me arrogant in my soul with strength* [r] 139.18 Or *I awake*

19 O that you would kill the
wicked, O God,
and that the bloodthirsty would
depart from me—
20 those who speak of you
maliciously,
and lift themselves up
against you for evil![s]
21 Do I not hate those who hate
you, O LORD?
And do I not loathe those who
rise up against you?
22 I hate them with perfect hatred;
I count them my enemies.
23 Search me, O God, and
know my heart;
test me and know my thoughts.
24 See if there is any wicked[t]
way in me,
and lead me in the way
everlasting.[u]

PSALM 140

PRAYER FOR DELIVERANCE FROM ENEMIES

To the leader. A Psalm of David.

1 Deliver me, O LORD, from evildoers;
protect me from those
who are violent,
2 who plan evil things in
their minds
and stir up wars continually.
3 They make their tongue
sharp as a snake's,
and under their lips is the venom
of vipers. *Selah*

4 Guard me, O LORD, from the
hands of the wicked;
protect me from the violent
who have planned my downfall.
5 The arrogant have hidden
a trap for me,
and with cords they have
spread a net;[v]
along the road they have set
snares for me. *Selah*

6 I say to the LORD, 'You are my God;
give ear, O LORD, to the voice
of my supplications.'
7 O LORD, my Lord, my strong
deliverer,
you have covered my head
in the day of battle.
8 Do not grant, O LORD, the
desires of the wicked;
do not further their evil plot.[w]
Selah

9 Those who surround me lift
up their heads;[x]
let the mischief of their lips
overwhelm them!
10 Let burning coals fall on them!
Let them be flung into pits,
no more to rise!
11 Do not let the slanderer be
established in the land;
let evil speedily hunt down
the violent!

12 I know that the LORD maintains
the cause of the needy,
and executes justice for the poor.
13 Surely the righteous shall give
thanks to your name;
the upright shall live in
your presence.

PSALM 141

PRAYER FOR PRESERVATION FROM EVIL

A Psalm of David.

1 I call upon you, O LORD; come
quickly to me;
give ear to my voice when
I call to you.
2 Let my prayer be counted as
incense before you,
and the lifting up of my hands
as an evening sacrifice.

3 Set a guard over my
mouth, O LORD;
keep watch over the door
of my lips.
4 Do not turn my heart to any evil,
to busy myself with wicked deeds
in company with those who
work iniquity;
do not let me eat of their
delicacies.

5 Let the righteous strike me;
let the faithful correct me.
Never let the oil of the wicked
anoint my head,[y]
for my prayer is continually[z]
against their wicked deeds.

[s] **139.20** Cn: Meaning of Heb uncertain
[t] **139.24** Heb *hurtful* [u] **139.24** Or *the ancient way.* Compare Jer 6.16 [v] **140.5** Or *they have spread cords as a net* [w] **140.8** Heb adds *they are exalted* [x] **140.9** Cn Compare Gk: Heb *those who surround me are uplifted in head;* Heb divides verses 8 and 9 differently [y] **141.5** Gk: Meaning of Heb uncertain [z] **141.5** Cn: Heb *for continually and my prayer*

6 When they are given over to those
who shall condemn them,
then they shall learn that my
words were pleasant.
7 Like a rock that one breaks apart
and shatters on the land,
so shall their bones be strewn
at the mouth of Sheol.[a]

8 But my eyes are turned towards
you, O GOD, my Lord;
in you I seek refuge; do not
leave me defenceless.
9 Keep me from the trap that
they have laid for me,
and from the snares
of evildoers.
10 Let the wicked fall into
their own nets,
while I alone escape.

PSALM 142

PRAYER FOR DELIVERANCE FROM PERSECUTORS

A Maskil of David. When he was in the cave. A Prayer.

1 With my voice I cry to the LORD;
with my voice I make
supplication to the LORD.
2 I pour out my complaint
before him;
I tell my trouble before him.
3 When my spirit is faint,
you know my way.

In the path where I walk
they have hidden a
trap for me.
4 Look on my right hand and see—
there is no one who takes
notice of me;
no refuge remains to me;
no one cares for me.

5 I cry to you, O LORD;
I say, 'You are my refuge,
my portion in the land
of the living.'
6 Give heed to my cry,
for I am brought very low.

Save me from my persecutors,
for they are too strong for me.
7 Bring me out of prison,
so that I may give thanks
to your name.
The righteous will surround me,
for you will deal bountifully
with me.

PSALM 143

PRAYER FOR DELIVERANCE FROM ENEMIES

A Psalm of David.

1 Hear my prayer, O LORD;
give ear to my supplications
in your faithfulness;
answer me in your
righteousness.
2 Do not enter into judgement
with your servant,
for no one living is righteous
before you.

3 For the enemy has pursued me,
crushing my life to the ground,
making me sit in darkness
like those long dead.
4 Therefore my spirit faints
within me;
my heart within me is appalled.

5 I remember the days of old,
I think about all your deeds,
I meditate on the works
of your hands.
6 I stretch out my hands to you;
my soul thirsts for you like a
parched land. *Selah*

7 Answer me quickly, O LORD;
my spirit fails.
Do not hide your face from me,
or I shall be like those who
go down to the Pit.
8 Let me hear of your steadfast
love in the morning,
for in you I put my trust.
Teach me the way I should go,
for to you I lift up my soul.

9 Save me, O LORD, from
my enemies;
I have fled to you for refuge.[b]
10 Teach me to do your will,
for you are my God.
Let your good spirit lead me
on a level path.

11 For your name's sake, O LORD,
preserve my life.
In your righteousness bring
me out of trouble.
12 In your steadfast love cut
off my enemies,
and destroy all my adversaries,
for I am your servant.

[a] **141.7** Meaning of Heb of verses 5–7 is uncertain
[b] **143.9** One Heb Ms Gk: MT *to you I have hidden*

PSALM 144

PRAYER FOR NATIONAL DELIVERANCE AND SECURITY

Of David.

1 Blessed be the LORD, my rock,
who trains my hands for war,
and my fingers for battle;
2 my rock[c] and my fortress,
my stronghold and my deliverer,
my shield, in whom I take refuge,
who subdues the peoples[d]
under me.

3 O LORD, what are human beings
that you regard them,
or mortals that you
think of them?
4 They are like a breath;
their days are like a
passing shadow.

5 Bow your heavens, O LORD,
and come down;
touch the mountains so
that they smoke.
6 Make the lightning flash and
scatter them;
send out your arrows
and rout them.
7 Stretch out your hand
from on high;
set me free and rescue me from
the mighty waters,
from the hand of aliens,
8 whose mouths speak lies,
and whose right hands are false.

9 I will sing a new song
to you, O God;
upon a ten-stringed harp
I will play to you,
10 the one who gives victory to kings,
who rescues his servant David.
11 Rescue me from the cruel sword,
and deliver me from the
hand of aliens,
whose mouths speak lies,
and whose right hands are false.

12 May our sons in their youth
be like plants full grown,
our daughters like corner pillars,
cut for the building of a palace.
13 May our barns be filled
with produce of every kind;
may our sheep increase by
thousands,
by tens of thousands
in our fields,
14 and may our cattle be
heavy with young.
May there be no breach in the
walls,[e] no exile,
and no cry of distress
in our streets.

15 Happy are the people to whom
such blessings fall;
happy are the people whose
God is the LORD.

PSALM 145

THE GREATNESS AND THE GOODNESS OF GOD

Praise. Of David.

1 I will extol you, my God and King,
and bless your name for
ever and ever.
2 Every day I will bless you,
and praise your name for
ever and ever.
3 Great is the LORD, and greatly
to be praised;
his greatness is unsearchable.

4 One generation shall laud your
works to another,
and shall declare your mighty acts.
5 On the glorious splendour
of your majesty,
and on your wondrous works,
I will meditate.
6 The might of your awesome deeds
shall be proclaimed,
and I will declare your greatness.
7 They shall celebrate the fame of
your abundant goodness,
and shall sing aloud of your
righteousness.

8 The LORD is gracious and merciful,
slow to anger and abounding
in steadfast love.
9 The LORD is good to all,
and his compassion is over
all that he has made.

10 All your works shall give thanks
to you, O LORD,
and all your faithful
shall bless you.
11 They shall speak of the glory
of your kingdom,
and tell of your power,

[c] 144.2 With 18.2 and 2 Sam 22.2: Heb *my steadfast love* [d] 144.2 Heb Mss Syr Aquila Jerome: MT *my people* [e] 144.14 Heb lacks *in the walls*

12 to make known to all people
your[f] mighty deeds,
and the glorious splendour
of your[g] kingdom.
13 Your kingdom is an everlasting
kingdom,
and your dominion endures
throughout all generations.

The LORD is faithful in all his words,
and gracious in all his deeds.[h]
14 The LORD upholds all who are falling,
and raises up all who are
bowed down.
15 The eyes of all look to you,
and you give them their
food in due season.
16 You open your hand,
satisfying the desire of
every living thing.
17 The LORD is just in all his ways,
and kind in all his doings.
18 The LORD is near to all who
call on him,
to all who call on him in truth.
19 He fulfils the desire of all
who fear him;
he also hears their cry,
and saves them.
20 The LORD watches over all
who love him,
but all the wicked he will destroy.

21 My mouth will speak the
praise of the LORD,
and all flesh will bless his holy
name for ever and ever.

PSALM 146

PRAISE FOR GOD'S HELP

1 Praise the LORD!
Praise the LORD, O my soul!
2 I will praise the LORD as
long as I live;
I will sing praises to my
God all my life long.

3 Do not put your trust in princes,
in mortals, in whom
there is no help.
4 When their breath departs, they
return to the earth;
on that very day their
plans perish.

5 Happy are those whose help
is the God of Jacob,
whose hope is in the
LORD their God,
6 who made heaven and earth,
the sea, and all that is in them;
who keeps faith for ever;
7 who executes justice for
the oppressed;
who gives food to the hungry.

The LORD sets the prisoners free;
8 the LORD opens the eyes
of the blind.
The LORD lifts up those who
are bowed down;
the LORD loves the righteous.
9 The LORD watches over
the strangers;
he upholds the orphan
and the widow,
but the way of the wicked
he brings to ruin.

10 The LORD will reign for ever,
your God, O Zion, for all
generations.
Praise the LORD!

PSALM 147

PRAISE FOR GOD'S CARE FOR JERUSALEM

1 Praise the LORD!
How good it is to sing praises
to our God;
for he is gracious, and a song
of praise is fitting.
2 The LORD builds up Jerusalem;
he gathers the outcasts of Israel.
3 He heals the broken-hearted,
and binds up their wounds.
4 He determines the number
of the stars;
he gives to all of them
their names.
5 Great is our Lord, and
abundant in power;
his understanding is
beyond measure.
6 The LORD lifts up the downtrodden;
he casts the wicked to the ground.

7 Sing to the LORD with thanksgiving;
make melody to our God
on the lyre.
8 He covers the heavens with clouds,
prepares rain for the earth,
makes grass grow on the hills.

[f] 145.12 Gk Jerome Syr: Heb *his* [g] 145.12 Heb *his* [h] 145.13 These two lines supplied by Q Ms Gk Syr

9 He gives to the animals their food,
and to the young ravens
when they cry.
10 His delight is not in the
strength of the horse,
nor his pleasure in the
speed of a runner;[i]
11 but the LORD takes pleasure in
those who fear him,
in those who hope in his
steadfast love.

12 Praise the LORD, O Jerusalem!
Praise your God, O Zion!
13 For he strengthens the bars
of your gates;
he blesses your children
within you.
14 He grants peace[j] within
your borders;
he fills you with the
finest of wheat.
15 He sends out his command
to the earth;
his word runs swiftly.
16 He gives snow like wool;
he scatters frost like ashes.
17 He hurls down hail like crumbs—
who can stand before his cold?
18 He sends out his word, and
melts them;
he makes his wind blow,
and the waters flow.
19 He declares his word to Jacob,
his statutes and ordinances
to Israel.
20 He has not dealt thus with
any other nation;
they do not know his ordinances.
Praise the LORD!

PSALM 148

PRAISE FOR GOD'S UNIVERSAL GLORY

1 Praise the LORD!
Praise the LORD from the heavens;
praise him in the heights!
2 Praise him, all his angels;
praise him, all his host!

3 Praise him, sun and moon;
praise him, all you shining stars!
4 Praise him, you highest heavens,
and you waters above the heavens!

5 Let them praise the name
of the LORD,
for he commanded and
they were created.
6 He established them for
ever and ever;
he fixed their bounds, which
cannot be passed.[k]

7 Praise the LORD from the earth,
you sea monsters and all deeps,
8 fire and hail, snow and frost,
stormy wind fulfilling
his command!

9 Mountains and all hills,
fruit trees and all cedars!
10 Wild animals and all cattle,
creeping things and flying birds!

11 Kings of the earth and all peoples,
princes and all rulers of the earth!
12 Young men and women alike,
old and young together!

13 Let them praise the name
of the LORD,
for his name alone is exalted;
his glory is above earth
and heaven.
14 He has raised up a horn
for his people,
praise for all his faithful,
for the people of Israel who
are close to him.
Praise the LORD!

PSALM 149

PRAISE FOR GOD'S GOODNESS TO ISRAEL

1 Praise the LORD!
Sing to the LORD a new song,
his praise in the assembly
of the faithful.
2 Let Israel be glad in its Maker;
let the children of Zion
rejoice in their King.
3 Let them praise his name
with dancing,
making melody to him with
tambourine and lyre.
4 For the LORD takes pleasure
in his people;
he adorns the humble
with victory.
5 Let the faithful exult in glory;
let them sing for joy on
their couches.

[i] **147.10** Heb *legs of a person* [j] **147.14** Or *prosperity* [k] **148.6** Or *he set a law that cannot pass away*

6 Let the high praises of God be
in their throats
and two-edged swords
in their hands,
7 to execute vengeance on the nations
and punishment on the peoples,
8 to bind their kings with fetters
and their nobles with
chains of iron,
9 to execute on them the
judgement decreed.
This is glory for all his faithful ones.
Praise the LORD!

PSALM 150

PRAISE FOR GOD'S SURPASSING GREATNESS

1 Praise the LORD!
Praise God in his sanctuary;
praise him in his mighty
firmament![1]
2 Praise him for his mighty deeds;
praise him according to his
surpassing greatness!

3 Praise him with trumpet sound;
praise him with lute and harp!
4 Praise him with tambourine
and dance;
praise him with
strings and pipe!
5 Praise him with clanging cymbals;
praise him with loud
clashing cymbals!
6 Let everything that breathes
praise the LORD!
Praise the LORD!

[1] **150.1** Or *dome*

PROVERBS

Proverbs is a collection of wise sayings, instructions, and poems that date to the preexilic period, but they were edited after the exile probably in the early part of the fifth century BCE. The sayings are attributed to Solomon because of his legendary wisdom. The purpose of the writing is to provide moral teaching to young people based on the experience of the elders. The underlying insight is that "the fear of the LORD is the beginning of wisdom" (9.10; see also 1.7; 15.33). Also, the book contains a characteristic contrast between good and evil, rich and poor, wisdom and folly.

Passages from the book of Proverbs are presented in the liturgy as the First Reading on Monday through Wednesday of the Twenty-Fifth Week of Year II. Also, selections from Proverbs are read on the Twentieth Sunday of Year B and the Thirty-Third Sunday of Year A in the Roman Missal. Selections from Proverbs are offered as choices for the Old Testament reading in the Ritual Mass for the Blessing of Abbots and Abbesses and at the Common of the Blessed Virgin Mary (8.22–31).

1 The proverbs of Solomon son of David, king of Israel:

PROLOGUE

2 For learning about wisdom
and instruction,
for understanding words of insight,
3 for gaining instruction in
wise dealing,
righteousness, justice, and equity;
4 to teach shrewdness to the simple,
knowledge and prudence
to the young—
5 let the wise also hear and
gain in learning,
and the discerning acquire skill,
6 to understand a proverb and a figure,
the words of the wise and
their riddles.

7 The fear of the LORD is the
beginning of knowledge;
fools despise wisdom and
instruction.

WARNINGS AGAINST EVIL COMPANIONS

8 Hear, my child, your father's
instruction,
and do not reject your
mother's teaching;
9 for they are a fair garland
for your head,
and pendants for your neck.
10 My child, if sinners entice you,
do not consent.
11 If they say, 'Come with us, let us
lie in wait for blood;
let us wantonly ambush
the innocent;
12 like Sheol let us swallow them alive
and whole, like those who
go down to the Pit.
13 We shall find all kinds of costly things;
we shall fill our houses with booty.
14 Throw in your lot among us;
we will all have one purse'—
15 my child, do not walk in their way,
keep your foot from their paths;
16 for their feet run to evil,
and they hurry to shed blood.
17 For in vain is the net baited
while the bird is looking on;
18 yet they lie in wait—to kill themselves!
and set an ambush—for
their own lives!
19 Such is the end[a] of all who are
greedy for gain;
it takes away the life of
its possessors.

[a] 1.19 Gk: Heb *are the ways*

THE CALL OF WISDOM

20 Wisdom cries out in the street;
in the squares she raises her voice.
21 At the busiest corner she cries out;
at the entrance of the city
gates she speaks:
22 'How long, O simple ones, will
you love being simple?
How long will scoffers delight
in their scoffing
and fools hate knowledge?
23 Give heed to my reproof;
I will pour out my thoughts to you;
I will make my words
known to you.
24 Because I have called and you refused,
have stretched out my hand
and no one heeded,
25 and because you have ignored
all my counsel
and would have none of
my reproof,
26 I also will laugh at your calamity;
I will mock when panic
strikes you,
27 when panic strikes you like a storm,
and your calamity comes
like a whirlwind,
when distress and anguish
come upon you.
28 Then they will call upon me, but
I will not answer;
they will seek me diligently,
but will not find me.
29 Because they hated knowledge
and did not choose the
fear of the LORD,
30 would have none of my counsel,
and despised all my reproof,
31 therefore they shall eat the
fruit of their way
and be sated with their
own devices.
32 For waywardness kills the simple,
and the complacency of fools
destroys them;
33 but those who listen to me
will be secure
and will live at ease, without
dread of disaster.'

THE VALUE OF WISDOM

2 My child, if you accept my words
and treasure up my
commandments within you,
2 making your ear attentive to wisdom
and inclining your heart
to understanding;
3 if you indeed cry out for insight,
and raise your voice for
understanding;
4 if you seek it like silver,
and search for it as for
hidden treasures—
5 then you will understand the
fear of the LORD
and find the knowledge of God.
6 For the LORD gives wisdom;
from his mouth come knowledge
and understanding;
7 he stores up sound wisdom
for the upright;
he is a shield to those who
walk blamelessly,
8 guarding the paths of justice
and preserving the way of
his faithful ones.
9 Then you will understand
righteousness and justice
and equity, every good path;
10 for wisdom will come into
your heart,
and knowledge will be
pleasant to your soul;
11 prudence will watch over you;
and understanding will guard you.
12 It will save you from the way of evil,
from those who speak perversely,
13 who forsake the paths of uprightness
to walk in the ways of darkness,
14 who rejoice in doing evil
and delight in the
perverseness of evil;
15 those whose paths are crooked,
and who are devious in
their ways.

16 You will be saved from the
loose[b] woman,
from the adulteress with
her smooth words,
17 who forsakes the partner
of her youth
and forgets her sacred covenant;
18 for her way[c] leads down to death,
and her paths to the shades;
19 those who go to her never come back,
nor do they regain the
paths of life.

20 Therefore walk in the way
of the good,
and keep to the paths of the just.
21 For the upright will abide
in the land,
and the innocent will remain in it;
22 but the wicked will be cut off
from the land,
and the treacherous will
be rooted out of it.

[b] 2.16 Heb *strange* [c] 2.18 Cn: Heb *house*

ADMONITION TO TRUST AND HONOUR GOD

3 My child, do not forget
my teaching,
but let your heart keep my
commandments;
2 for length of days and years of life
and abundant welfare they
will give you.

3 Do not let loyalty and faithfulness
forsake you;
bind them round your neck,
write them on the tablet
of your heart.
4 So you will find favour and
good repute
in the sight of God and of people.

5 Trust in the LORD with all
your heart,
and do not rely on your
own insight.
6 In all your ways acknowledge him,
and he will make straight
your paths.
7 Do not be wise in your own eyes;
fear the LORD, and turn
away from evil.
8 It will be a healing for your flesh
and a refreshment for your body.

9 Honour the LORD with
your substance
and with the first fruits of
all your produce;
10 then your barns will be filled
with plenty,
and your vats will be
bursting with wine.

11 My child, do not despise the
LORD's discipline
or be weary of his reproof,
12 for the LORD reproves the
one he loves,
as a father the son in
whom he delights.

THE TRUE WEALTH

13 Happy are those who find wisdom,
and those who get understanding,
14 for her income is better than silver,
and her revenue
better than gold.
15 She is more precious than jewels,
and nothing you desire can
compare with her.
16 Long life is in her right hand;
in her left hand are riches
and honour.
17 Her ways are ways of pleasantness,
and all her paths are peace.
18 She is a tree of life to those
who lay hold of her;
those who hold her fast
are called happy.

GOD'S WISDOM IN CREATION

19 The LORD by wisdom founded
the earth;
by understanding he established
the heavens;
20 by his knowledge the deeps
broke open,
and the clouds drop
down the dew.

THE TRUE SECURITY

21 My child, do not let these escape
from your sight:
keep sound wisdom and prudence,
22 and they will be life for your soul
and adornment for your neck.
23 Then you will walk on your
way securely
and your foot will not stumble.
24 If you sit down,[d] you will
not be afraid;
when you lie down, your
sleep will be sweet.
25 Do not be afraid of sudden panic,
or of the storm that strikes
the wicked;
26 for the LORD will be your confidence
and will keep your foot
from being caught.

27 Do not withhold good from those
to whom it is due,[e]
when it is in your power to do it.
28 Do not say to your neighbour,
'Go, and come again;
tomorrow I will give it'—when
you have it with you.
29 Do not plan harm against
your neighbour
who lives trustingly beside you.
30 Do not quarrel with anyone
without cause,
when no harm has been
done to you.
31 Do not envy the violent
and do not choose any
of their ways;
32 for the perverse are an abomination
to the LORD,
but the upright are in
his confidence.

[d] **3.24** Gk: Heb *lie down* [e] **3.27** Heb *from its owners*

33 The LORD's curse is on the house of the wicked,
but he blesses the abode of the righteous.
34 Towards the scorners he is scornful,
but to the humble he shows favour.
35 The wise will inherit honour,
but stubborn fools, disgrace.

PARENTAL ADVICE

4 Listen, children, to a father's instruction,
and be attentive, that you may gain[f] insight;
2 for I give you good precepts:
do not forsake my teaching.
3 When I was a son with my father,
tender, and my mother's favourite,
4 he taught me, and said to me,
'Let your heart hold fast my words;
keep my commandments, and live.
5 Get wisdom; get insight: do not forget, nor turn away
from the words of my mouth.
6 Do not forsake her, and she will keep you;
love her, and she will guard you.
7 The beginning of wisdom is this: Get wisdom,
and whatever else you get, get insight.
8 Prize her highly, and she will exalt you;
she will honour you if you embrace her.
9 She will place on your head a fair garland;
she will bestow on you a beautiful crown.'

ADMONITION TO KEEP TO THE RIGHT PATH

10 Hear, my child, and accept my words,
that the years of your life may be many.
11 I have taught you the way of wisdom;
I have led you in the paths of uprightness.
12 When you walk, your step will not be hampered;
and if you run, you will not stumble.
13 Keep hold of instruction; do not let go;
guard her, for she is your life.
14 Do not enter the path of the wicked,
and do not walk in the way of evildoers.
15 Avoid it; do not go on it;
turn away from it and pass on.
16 For they cannot sleep unless they have done wrong;
they are robbed of sleep unless they have made someone stumble.
17 For they eat the bread of wickedness
and drink the wine of violence.
18 But the path of the righteous is like the light of dawn,
which shines brighter and brighter until full day.
19 The way of the wicked is like deep darkness;
they do not know what they stumble over.
20 My child, be attentive to my words;
incline your ear to my sayings.
21 Do not let them escape from your sight;
keep them within your heart.
22 For they are life to those who find them,
and healing to all their flesh.
23 Keep your heart with all vigilance,
for from it flow the springs of life.
24 Put away from you crooked speech,
and put devious talk far from you.
25 Let your eyes look directly forwards,
and your gaze be straight before you.
26 Keep straight the path of your feet,
and all your ways will be sure.
27 Do not swerve to the right or to the left;
turn your foot away from evil.

WARNING AGAINST IMPURITY AND INFIDELITY

5 My child, be attentive to my wisdom;
incline your ear to my understanding,
2 so that you may hold on to prudence,
and your lips may guard knowledge.
3 For the lips of a loose[g] woman drip honey,
and her speech is smoother than oil;
4 but in the end she is bitter as wormwood,
sharp as a two-edged sword.
5 Her feet go down to death;
her steps follow the path to Sheol.
6 She does not keep straight to the path of life;
her ways wander, and she does not know it.

[f] 4.1 Heb *know* [g] 5.3 Heb *strange*

7 And now, my child,[h] listen to me,
and do not depart from the
words of my mouth.
8 Keep your way far from her,
and do not go near the
door of her house;
9 or you will give your honour
to others,
and your years to the merciless,
10 and strangers will take their
fill of your wealth,
and your labours will go to
the house of an alien;
11 and at the end of your life
you will groan,
when your flesh and body
are consumed,
12 and you say, 'Oh, how I
hated discipline,
and my heart despised reproof!
13 I did not listen to the voice
of my teachers
or incline my ear to my instructors.
14 Now I am at the point of utter ruin
in the public assembly.'

15 Drink water from your own cistern,
flowing water from your own well.
16 Should your springs be
scattered abroad,
streams of water in the streets?
17 Let them be for yourself alone,
and not for sharing with strangers.
18 Let your fountain be blessed,
and rejoice in the wife
of your youth,
19 a lovely deer, a graceful doe.
May her breasts satisfy you
at all times;
may you be intoxicated
always by her love.
20 Why should you be intoxicated, my
son, by another woman
and embrace the bosom
of an adulteress?
21 For human ways are under the
eyes of the LORD,
and he examines all their paths.
22 The iniquities of the wicked
ensnare them,
and they are caught in the
toils of their sin.
23 They die for lack of discipline,
and because of their great
folly they are lost.

PRACTICAL ADMONITIONS

6 My child, if you have given your
pledge to your neighbour,
if you have bound yourself
to another,[i]
2 you are snared by the utterance
of your lips,[j]
caught by the words of
your mouth.
3 So do this, my child, and
save yourself,
for you have come into your
neighbour's power:
go, hurry,[k] and plead with
your neighbour.
4 Give your eyes no sleep
and your eyelids no slumber;
5 save yourself like a gazelle
from the hunter,[l]
like a bird from the hand
of the fowler.

6 Go to the ant, you lazybones;
consider its ways, and be wise.
7 Without having any chief
or officer or ruler,
8 it prepares its food in summer,
and gathers its sustenance
in harvest.
9 How long will you lie there,
O lazybones?
When will you rise from
your sleep?
10 A little sleep, a little slumber,
a little folding of the hands to rest,
11 and poverty will come upon
you like a robber,
and want, like an armed warrior.

12 A scoundrel and a villain
goes around with crooked speech,
13 winking the eyes, shuffling the feet,
pointing the fingers,
14 with perverted mind devising evil,
continually sowing discord;
15 on such a one calamity will
descend suddenly;
in a moment, damage
beyond repair.

16 There are six things that
the LORD hates,
seven that are an
abomination to him:
17 haughty eyes, a lying tongue,
and hands that shed
innocent blood,
18 a heart that devises wicked plans,
feet that hurry to run to evil,
19 a lying witness who testifies falsely,
and one who sows discord
in a family.

[h] 5.7 Gk Vg: Heb *children* [i] 6.1 Or *a stranger* [j] 6.2 Cn Compare Gk Syr: Heb *the words of your mouth* [k] 6.3 Or *humble yourself* [l] 6.5 Cn: Heb *from the hand*

20 My child, keep your father's
commandment,
and do not forsake your
mother's teaching.
21 Bind them upon your heart always;
tie them around your neck.
22 When you walk, they[m] will lead you;
when you lie down, they[n]
will watch over you;
and when you awake, they[o]
will talk with you.
23 For the commandment is a lamp
and the teaching a light,
and the reproofs of discipline
are the way of life,
24 to preserve you from the
wife of another,[p]
from the smooth tongue
of the adulteress.
25 Do not desire her beauty
in your heart,
and do not let her capture you
with her eyelashes;
26 for a prostitute's fee is only
a loaf of bread,[q]
but the wife of another stalks
a man's very life.
27 Can fire be carried in the bosom
without burning one's clothes?
28 Or can one walk on hot coals
without scorching the feet?
29 So is he who sleeps with his
neighbour's wife;
no one who touches her will
go unpunished.
30 Thieves are not despised
who steal only
to satisfy their appetite when
they are hungry.
31 Yet if they are caught, they
will pay sevenfold;
they will forfeit all the goods
of their house.
32 But he who commits adultery
has no sense;
he who does it destroys himself.
33 He will get wounds and dishonour,
and his disgrace will not
be wiped away.
34 For jealousy arouses a husband's fury,
and he shows no restraint
when he takes revenge.
35 He will accept no compensation,
and refuses a bribe no
matter how great.

THE FALSE ATTRACTIONS OF ADULTERY

7 My child, keep my words
and store up my commandments
with you;
2 keep my commandments and live,
keep my teachings as the
apple of your eye;
3 bind them on your fingers,
write them on the tablet
of your heart.
4 Say to wisdom, 'You are my sister',
and call insight your
intimate friend,
5 that they may keep you from
the loose[r] woman,
from the adulteress with
her smooth words.

6 For at the window of my house
I looked out through my lattice,
7 and I saw among the simple ones,
I observed among the youths,
a young man without sense,
8 passing along the street
near her corner,
taking the road to her house
9 in the twilight, in the evening,
at the time of night and darkness.

10 Then a woman comes towards him,
decked out like a prostitute,
wily of heart.[s]
11 She is loud and wayward;
her feet do not stay at home;
12 now in the street, now in
the squares,
and at every corner she
lies in wait.
13 She seizes him and kisses him,
and with impudent face
she says to him:
14 'I had to offer sacrifices,
and today I have paid my vows;
15 so now I have come out to meet you,
to seek you eagerly, and I
have found you!
16 I have decked my couch
with coverings,
coloured spreads of
Egyptian linen;
17 I have perfumed my bed with myrrh,
aloes, and cinnamon.
18 Come, let us take our fill of
love until morning;
let us delight ourselves with love.
19 For my husband is not at home;
he has gone on a long journey.
20 He took a bag of money with him;
he will not come home
until full moon.'

[m] 6.22 Heb *it* [n] 6.22 Heb *it* [o] 6.22 Heb *it*
[p] 6.24 Gk: MT *the evil woman* [q] 6.26 Cn
Compare Gk Syr Vg Tg: Heb *for because of a harlot to a piece of bread* [r] 7.5 Heb *strange*
[s] 7.10 Meaning of Heb uncertain

21 With much seductive speech
she persuades him;
with her smooth talk she
compels him.
22 Right away he follows her,
and goes like an ox to
the slaughter,
or bounds like a stag towards
the trap[t]
23 until an arrow pierces its entrails.
He is like a bird rushing into a snare,
not knowing that it will
cost him his life.

24 And now, my children, listen to me,
and be attentive to the
words of my mouth.
25 Do not let your hearts turn
aside to her ways;
do not stray into her paths.
26 For many are those she has laid low,
and numerous are her victims.
27 Her house is the way to Sheol,
going down to the
chambers of death.

THE GIFTS OF WISDOM

8 Does not wisdom call,
and does not understanding
raise her voice?
2 On the heights, beside the way,
at the crossroads she
takes her stand;
3 beside the gates in front of the town,
at the entrance of the portals
she cries out:
4 'To you, O people, I call,
and my cry is to all that live.
5 O simple ones, learn prudence;
acquire intelligence, you
who lack it.
6 Hear, for I will speak noble things,
and from my lips will come
what is right;
7 for my mouth will utter truth;
wickedness is an abomination
to my lips.
8 All the words of my mouth
are righteous;
there is nothing twisted or
crooked in them.
9 They are all straight to one
who understands
and right to those who
find knowledge.
10 Take my instruction instead of silver,
and knowledge rather
than choice gold;
11 for wisdom is better than jewels,
and all that you may desire
cannot compare with her.
12 I, wisdom, live with prudence,[u]
and I attain knowledge
and discretion.
13 The fear of the LORD is hatred of evil.
Pride and arrogance and
the way of evil
and perverted speech I hate.
14 I have good advice and
sound wisdom;
I have insight, I have strength.
15 By me kings reign,
and rulers decree what is just;
16 by me rulers rule,
and nobles, all who govern rightly.
17 I love those who love me,
and those who seek me
diligently find me.
18 Riches and honour are with me,
enduring wealth and prosperity.
19 My fruit is better than gold,
even fine gold,
and my yield than choice silver.
20 I walk in the way of righteousness,
along the paths of justice,
21 endowing with wealth those
who love me,
and filling their treasuries.

WISDOM'S PART IN CREATION

22 The LORD created me at the
beginning[v] of his work,[w]
the first of his acts of long ago.
23 Ages ago I was set up,
at the first, before the
beginning of the earth.
24 When there were no depths I
was brought forth,
when there were no springs
abounding with water.
25 Before the mountains had
been shaped,
before the hills, I was
brought forth—
26 when he had not yet made
earth and fields,[x]
or the world's first bits of soil.
27 When he established the
heavens, I was there,
when he drew a circle on
the face of the deep,
28 when he made firm the skies above,
when he established the
fountains of the deep,
29 when he assigned to the sea its limit,
so that the waters might not
transgress his command,

[t] 7.22 Cn Compare Gk: Meaning of Heb uncertain
[u] 8.12 Meaning of Heb uncertain [v] 8.22 Or *me as the beginning* [w] 8.22 Heb *way*
[x] 8.26 Meaning of Heb uncertain

when he marked out the
foundations of the earth,
30 then I was beside him, like
a master worker;[y]
and I was daily his[z] delight,
rejoicing before him always,
31 rejoicing in his inhabited world
and delighting in the human race.

32 'And now, my children, listen to me:
happy are those who keep my ways.
33 Hear instruction and be wise,
and do not neglect it.
34 Happy is the one who listens to me,
watching daily at my gates,
waiting beside my doors.
35 For whoever finds me finds life
and obtains favour from the LORD;
36 but those who miss me injure
themselves;
all who hate me love death.'

WISDOM'S FEAST

9 Wisdom has built her house,
she has hewn her seven pillars.
2 She has slaughtered her animals,
she has mixed her wine,
she has also set her table.
3 She has sent out her
servant-girls, she calls
from the highest places
in the town,
4 'You that are simple, turn in here!'
To those without sense she says,
5 'Come, eat of my bread
and drink of the wine I
have mixed.
6 Lay aside immaturity,[a] and live,
and walk in the way of insight.'

GENERAL MAXIMS

7 Whoever corrects a scoffer
wins abuse;
whoever rebukes the
wicked gets hurt.
8 A scoffer who is rebuked will
only hate you;
the wise, when rebuked,
will love you.
9 Give instruction[b] to the wise, and
they will become wiser still;
teach the righteous and they
will gain in learning.
10 The fear of the LORD is the
beginning of wisdom,
and the knowledge of the
Holy One is insight.
11 For by me your days will
be multiplied,
and years will be added
to your life.
12 If you are wise, you are wise
for yourself;
if you scoff, you alone will bear it.

FOLLY'S INVITATION AND PROMISE

13 The foolish woman is loud;
she is ignorant and
knows nothing.
14 She sits at the door of her house,
on a seat at the high places
of the town,
15 calling to those who pass by,
who are going straight
on their way,
16 'You who are simple, turn in here!'
And to those without
sense she says,
17 'Stolen water is sweet,
and bread eaten in secret
is pleasant.'
18 But they do not know that the
dead[c] are there,
that her guests are in the
depths of Sheol.

WISE SAYINGS OF SOLOMON

10 The proverbs of Solomon.

A wise child makes a glad father,
but a foolish child is a
mother's grief.
2 Treasures gained by wickedness
do not profit,
but righteousness delivers
from death.
3 The LORD does not let the
righteous go hungry,
but he thwarts the craving
of the wicked.
4 A slack hand causes poverty,
but the hand of the diligent
makes rich.
5 A child who gathers in
summer is prudent,
but a child who sleeps in
harvest brings shame.
6 Blessings are on the head of
the righteous,
but the mouth of the wicked
conceals violence.
7 The memory of the righteous
is a blessing,
but the name of the
wicked will rot.
8 The wise of heart will heed
commandments,
but a babbling fool will
come to ruin.

[y] 8.30 Another reading is *little child* [z] 8.30 Gk: Heb lacks *his* [a] 9.6 Or *simpleness* [b] 9.9 Heb lacks *instruction* [c] 9.18 Heb *shades*

9 Whoever walks in integrity
walks securely,
but whoever follows perverse
ways will be found out.
10 Whoever winks the eye
causes trouble,
but the one who rebukes
boldly makes peace.[d]
11 The mouth of the righteous is
a fountain of life,
but the mouth of the wicked
conceals violence.
12 Hatred stirs up strife,
but love covers all offences.
13 On the lips of one who has
understanding
wisdom is found,
but a rod is for the back of
one who lacks sense.
14 The wise lay up knowledge,
but the babbling of a fool
brings ruin near.
15 The wealth of the rich is their fortress;
the poverty of the poor
is their ruin.
16 The wage of the righteous
leads to life,
the gain of the wicked to sin.
17 Whoever heeds instruction is
on the path to life,
but one who rejects a
rebuke goes astray.
18 Lying lips conceal hatred,
and whoever utters
slander is a fool.
19 When words are many, transgression
is not lacking,
but the prudent are
restrained in speech.
20 The tongue of the righteous
is choice silver;
the mind of the wicked is
of little worth.
21 The lips of the righteous feed many,
but fools die for lack of sense.
22 The blessing of the LORD makes rich,
and he adds no sorrow with it.[e]
23 Doing wrong is like sport to a fool,
but wise conduct is pleasure to a
person of understanding.
24 What the wicked dread will
come upon them,
but the desire of the righteous
will be granted.
25 When the tempest passes, the
wicked are no more,
but the righteous are
established for ever.
26 Like vinegar to the teeth, and
smoke to the eyes,
so are the lazy to their employers.
27 The fear of the LORD prolongs life,
but the years of the wicked
will be short.
28 The hope of the righteous
ends in gladness,
but the expectation of the
wicked comes to nothing.
29 The way of the LORD is a stronghold
for the upright,
but destruction for evildoers.
30 The righteous will never
be removed,
but the wicked will not
remain in the land.
31 The mouth of the righteous
brings forth wisdom,
but the perverse tongue
will be cut off.
32 The lips of the righteous know
what is acceptable,
but the mouth of the wicked
what is perverse.

11 A false balance is an
abomination to the LORD,
but an accurate weight
is his delight.
2 When pride comes, then
comes disgrace;
but wisdom is with the humble.
3 The integrity of the upright
guides them,
but the crookedness of the
treacherous destroys them.
4 Riches do not profit in the
day of wrath,
but righteousness delivers
from death.
5 The righteousness of the blameless
keeps their ways straight,
but the wicked fall by their
own wickedness.
6 The righteousness of the
upright saves them,
but the treacherous are taken
captive by their schemes.
7 When the wicked die, their
hope perishes,
and the expectation of the
godless comes to nothing.
8 The righteous are delivered
from trouble,
and the wicked get
into it instead.
9 With their mouths the godless would
destroy their neighbours,
but by knowledge the righteous
are delivered.

[d] **10.10** Gk: Heb *but a babbling fool will come to ruin* [e] **10.22** *Or and toil adds nothing to it*

10 When it goes well with the righteous,
the city rejoices;
and when the wicked perish,
there is jubilation.
11 By the blessing of the upright
a city is exalted,
but it is overthrown by the
mouth of the wicked.
12 Whoever belittles another lacks sense,
but an intelligent person
remains silent.
13 A gossip goes about telling secrets,
but one who is trustworthy in
spirit keeps a confidence.
14 Where there is no guidance,
a nation[f] falls,
but in an abundance of
counsellors there is safety.
15 To guarantee loans for a stranger
brings trouble,
but there is safety in
refusing to do so.
16 A gracious woman gets honour,
but she who hates virtue is
covered with shame.[g]
The timid become destitute,[h]
but the aggressive gain riches.
17 Those who are kind reward themselves,
but the cruel do themselves harm.
18 The wicked earn no real gain,
but those who sow righteousness
get a true reward.
19 Whoever is steadfast in
righteousness will live,
but whoever pursues evil will die.
20 Crooked minds are an abomination
to the LORD,
but those of blameless ways
are his delight.
21 Be assured, the wicked will not
go unpunished,
but those who are righteous
will escape.
22 Like a gold ring in a pig's snout
is a beautiful woman without
good sense.
23 The desire of the righteous
ends only in good;
the expectation of the
wicked in wrath.
24 Some give freely, yet grow
all the richer;
others withhold what is due,
and only suffer want.
25 A generous person will be enriched,
and one who gives water
will get water.
26 The people curse those who
hold back grain,
but a blessing is on the head
of those who sell it.
27 Whoever diligently seeks
good seeks favour,
but evil comes to the one
who searches for it.
28 Those who trust in their
riches will wither,[i]
but the righteous will flourish
like green leaves.
29 Those who trouble their households
will inherit wind,
and the fool will be servant
to the wise.
30 The fruit of the righteous
is a tree of life,
but violence[j] takes lives away.
31 If the righteous are repaid on earth,
how much more the wicked
and the sinner!

12 Whoever loves discipline
loves knowledge,
but those who hate to be
rebuked are stupid.
2 The good obtain favour
from the LORD,
but those who devise evil
he condemns.
3 No one finds security by
wickedness,
but the root of the righteous
will never be moved.
4 A good wife is the crown of
her husband,
but she who brings shame is like
rottenness in his bones.
5 The thoughts of the righteous
are just;
the advice of the wicked
is treacherous.
6 The words of the wicked are
a deadly ambush,
but the speech of the upright
delivers them.
7 The wicked are overthrown
and are no more,
but the house of the
righteous will stand.
8 One is commended for good sense,
but a perverse mind is despised.
9 Better to be despised and
have a servant,
than to be self-important
and lack food.
10 The righteous know the needs
of their animals,
but the mercy of the
wicked is cruel.

[f] **11.14** Or *an army* [g] **11.16** Compare Gk Syr: Heb lacks *but she . . . shame* [h] **11.16** Gk: Heb lacks *The timid . . . destitute* [i] **11.28** Cn: Heb *fall* [j] **11.30** Cn Compare Gk Syr: Heb *a wise man*

11 Those who till their land will
have plenty of food,
but those who follow worthless
pursuits have no sense.
12 The wicked covet the proceeds
of wickedness,[k]
but the root of the righteous
bears fruit.
13 The evil are ensnared by the
transgression of their lips,
but the righteous escape
from trouble.
14 From the fruit of the mouth one is
filled with good things,
and manual labour has its reward.
15 Fools think their own way is right,
but the wise listen to advice.
16 Fools show their anger at once,
but the prudent ignore an insult.
17 Whoever speaks the truth gives
honest evidence,
but a false witness speaks
deceitfully.
18 Rash words are like sword thrusts,
but the tongue of the wise
brings healing.
19 Truthful lips endure for ever,
but a lying tongue lasts
only a moment.
20 Deceit is in the mind of those
who plan evil,
but those who counsel
peace have joy.
21 No harm happens to the righteous,
but the wicked are filled
with trouble.
22 Lying lips are an abomination
to the LORD,
but those who act faithfully
are his delight.
23 One who is clever conceals
knowledge,
but the mind of a fool[l]
broadcasts folly.
24 The hand of the diligent will rule,
while the lazy will be put
to forced labour.
25 Anxiety weighs down the
human heart,
but a good word cheers it up.
26 The righteous gives good
advice to friends,[m]
but the way of the wicked
leads astray.
27 The lazy do not roast[n] their game,
but the diligent obtain
precious wealth.[o]
28 In the path of righteousness
there is life,
in walking its path there
is no death.

13 A wise child loves discipline,[p]
but a scoffer does not
listen to rebuke.
2 From the fruit of their words good
people eat good things,
but the desire of the treacherous
is for wrongdoing.
3 Those who guard their mouths
preserve their lives;
those who open wide their
lips come to ruin.
4 The appetite of the lazy craves,
and gets nothing,
while the appetite of the diligent
is richly supplied.
5 The righteous hate falsehood,
but the wicked act shamefully
and disgracefully.
6 Righteousness guards one
whose way is upright,
but sin overthrows the wicked.
7 Some pretend to be rich, yet
have nothing;
others pretend to be poor, yet
have great wealth.
8 Wealth is a ransom for a person's life,
but the poor get no threats.
9 The light of the righteous rejoices,
but the lamp of the
wicked goes out.
10 By insolence the heedless
make strife,
but wisdom is with those
who take advice.
11 Wealth hastily gained[q] will dwindle,
but those who gather little by
little will increase it.
12 Hope deferred makes the heart sick,
but a desire fulfilled is
a tree of life.
13 Those who despise the word bring
destruction on themselves,
but those who respect the
commandment will
be rewarded.
14 The teaching of the wise is a
fountain of life,
so that one may avoid the
snares of death.
15 Good sense wins favour,
but the way of the faithless
is their ruin.[r]
16 The clever do all things intelligently,
but the fool displays folly.

[k] **12.12** Or *covet the catch of the wicked*
[l] **12.23** Heb *the heart of fools* [m] **12.26** Syr: Meaning of Heb uncertain [n] **12.27** Meaning of Heb uncertain [o] **12.27** Meaning of Heb uncertain [p] **13.1** Cn: Heb *A wise child the discipline of his father* [q] **13.11** Gk Vg: Heb *from vanity* [r] **13.15** Cn Compare Gk Syr Vg Tg: Heb *is enduring*

17 A bad messenger brings trouble,
but a faithful envoy, healing.
18 Poverty and disgrace are for the one
who ignores instruction,
but one who heeds reproof
is honoured.
19 A desire realized is sweet to the soul,
but to turn away from evil is an
abomination to fools.
20 Whoever walks with the wise
becomes wise,
but the companion of fools
suffers harm.
21 Misfortune pursues sinners,
but prosperity rewards
the righteous.
22 The good leave an inheritance to
their children's children,
but the sinner's wealth is laid
up for the righteous.
23 The field of the poor may
yield much food,
but it is swept away
through injustice.
24 Those who spare the rod hate
their children,
but those who love them are
diligent to discipline them.
25 The righteous have enough to
satisfy their appetite,
but the belly of the wicked is empty.

14 The wise woman[s] builds
her house,
but the foolish tears it down
with her own hands.
2 Those who walk uprightly
fear the LORD,
but one who is devious in
conduct despises him.
3 The talk of fools is a rod for
their backs,[t]
but the lips of the wise
preserve them.
4 Where there are no oxen,
there is no grain;
abundant crops come by the
strength of the ox.
5 A faithful witness does not lie,
but a false witness
breathes out lies.
6 A scoffer seeks wisdom in vain,
but knowledge is easy for one
who understands.
7 Leave the presence of a fool,
for there you do not find
words of knowledge.
8 It is the wisdom of the clever to
understand where they go,
but the folly of fools misleads.
9 Fools mock at the guilt-offering,[u]
but the upright enjoy God's favour.
10 The heart knows its own bitterness,
and no stranger shares its joy.
11 The house of the wicked is destroyed,
but the tent of the upright
flourishes.
12 There is a way that seems
right to a person,
but its end is the way to death.[v]
13 Even in laughter the heart is sad,
and the end of joy is grief.
14 The perverse get what their
ways deserve,
and the good, what their
deeds deserve.[w]
15 The simple believe everything,
but the clever consider their steps.
16 The wise are cautious and turn
away from evil,
but the fool throws off restraint
and is careless.
17 One who is quick-tempered
acts foolishly,
and the schemer is hated.
18 The simple are adorned with[x] folly,
but the clever are crowned
with knowledge.
19 The evil bow down before the good,
the wicked at the gates of
the righteous.
20 The poor are disliked even by
their neighbours,
but the rich have many friends.
21 Those who despise their
neighbours are sinners,
but happy are those who are
kind to the poor.
22 Do they not err that plan evil?
Those who plan good find
loyalty and faithfulness.
23 In all toil there is profit,
but mere talk leads only to poverty.
24 The crown of the wise is
their wisdom,[y]
but folly is the garland[z] of fools.
25 A truthful witness saves lives,
but one who utters lies
is a betrayer.
26 In the fear of the LORD one has
strong confidence,
and one's children will
have a refuge.
27 The fear of the LORD is a
fountain of life,
so that one may avoid the
snares of death.

[s] 14.1 Heb *Wisdom of women* [t] 14.3 Cn: Heb *a rod of pride* [u] 14.9 Meaning of Heb uncertain [v] 14.12 Heb *ways of death* [w] 14.14 Cn: Heb *from upon him* [x] 14.18 Or *inherit* [y] 14.24 Cn Compare Gk: Heb *riches* [z] 14.24 Cn: Heb *is the folly*

28 The glory of a king is a
multitude of people;
without people a prince is ruined.
29 Whoever is slow to anger has
great understanding,
but one who has a hasty
temper exalts folly.
30 A tranquil mind gives life
to the flesh,
but passion makes the
bones rot.
31 Those who oppress the poor
insult their Maker,
but those who are kind to the
needy honour him.
32 The wicked are overthrown
by their evildoing,
but the righteous find a refuge
in their integrity.[a]
33 Wisdom is at home in the mind of
one who has understanding,
but it is not[b] known in
the heart of fools.
34 Righteousness exalts a nation,
but sin is a reproach to any people.
35 A servant who deals wisely has
the king's favour,
but his wrath falls on one
who acts shamefully.

15 A soft answer turns
away wrath,
but a harsh word stirs up anger.
2 The tongue of the wise dispenses
knowledge,[c]
but the mouths of fools
pour out folly.
3 The eyes of the LORD are
in every place,
keeping watch on the evil
and the good.
4 A gentle tongue is a tree of life,
but perverseness in it
breaks the spirit.
5 A fool despises a parent's instruction,
but the one who heeds
admonition is prudent.
6 In the house of the righteous
there is much treasure,
but trouble befalls the income
of the wicked.
7 The lips of the wise spread
knowledge;
not so the minds of fools.
8 The sacrifice of the wicked is an
abomination to the LORD,
but the prayer of the upright
is his delight.
9 The way of the wicked is an
abomination to the LORD,
but he loves the one who
pursues righteousness.
10 There is severe discipline for one
who forsakes the way,
but one who hates a
rebuke will die.
11 Sheol and Abaddon lie open
before the LORD,
how much more human hearts!
12 Scoffers do not like to be rebuked;
they will not go to the wise.
13 A glad heart makes a cheerful
countenance,
but by sorrow of heart the
spirit is broken.
14 The mind of one who has
understanding seeks
knowledge,
but the mouths of fools
feed on folly.
15 All the days of the poor are hard,
but a cheerful heart has a
continual feast.
16 Better is a little with the
fear of the LORD
than great treasure and
trouble with it.
17 Better is a dinner of vegetables
where love is
than a fatted ox and
hatred with it.
18 Those who are hot-tempered
stir up strife,
but those who are slow to
anger calm contention.
19 The way of the lazy is overgrown
with thorns,
but the path of the upright
is a level highway.
20 A wise child makes a glad father,
but the foolish despise
their mothers.
21 Folly is a joy to one who
has no sense,
but a person of understanding
walks straight ahead.
22 Without counsel, plans go wrong,
but with many advisers
they succeed.
23 To make an apt answer is a
joy to anyone,
and a word in season,
how good it is!
24 For the wise the path of life
leads upwards,
in order to avoid Sheol below.
25 The LORD tears down the
house of the proud,
but maintains the widow's
boundaries.

[a] **14.32** Gk Syr: Heb *in their death* [b] **14.33** Gk Syr: Heb lacks *not* [c] **15.2** Cn: Heb *makes knowledge good*

26 Evil plans are an abomination
to the LORD,
but gracious words are pure.
27 Those who are greedy for unjust
gain make trouble for
their households,
but those who hate bribes will live.
28 The mind of the righteous
ponders how to answer,
but the mouth of the wicked
pours out evil.
29 The LORD is far from the wicked,
but he hears the prayer of
the righteous.
30 The light of the eyes rejoices
the heart,
and good news refreshes the body.
31 The ear that heeds wholesome
admonition
will lodge among the wise.
32 Those who ignore instruction
despise themselves,
but those who heed admonition
gain understanding.
33 The fear of the LORD is instruction
in wisdom,
and humility goes before honour.

16 The plans of the mind
belong to mortals,
but the answer of the tongue
is from the LORD.
2 All one's ways may be pure
in one's own eyes,
but the LORD weighs the spirit.
3 Commit your work to the LORD,
and your plans will be established.
4 The LORD has made everything
for its purpose,
even the wicked for the
day of trouble.
5 All those who are arrogant are an
abomination to the LORD;
be assured, they will not
go unpunished.
6 By loyalty and faithfulness
iniquity is atoned for,
and by the fear of the LORD
one avoids evil.
7 When the ways of people
please the LORD,
he causes even their enemies to
be at peace with them.
8 Better is a little with righteousness
than large income with injustice.
9 The human mind plans the way,
but the LORD directs the steps.
10 Inspired decisions are on the
lips of a king;
his mouth does not sin
in judgement.
11 Honest balances and scales
are the LORD's;
all the weights in the bag
are his work.
12 It is an abomination to
kings to do evil,
for the throne is established
by righteousness.
13 Righteous lips are the
delight of a king,
and he loves those who
speak what is right.
14 A king's wrath is a messenger
of death,
and whoever is wise will
appease it.
15 In the light of a king's face
there is life,
and his favour is like the clouds
that bring the spring rain.
16 How much better to get
wisdom than gold!
To get understanding is to be
chosen rather than silver.
17 The highway of the upright
avoids evil;
those who guard their way
preserve their lives.
18 Pride goes before destruction,
and a haughty spirit before a fall.
19 It is better to be of a lowly spirit
among the poor
than to divide the spoil
with the proud.
20 Those who are attentive to a
matter will prosper,
and happy are those who
trust in the LORD.
21 The wise of heart is called
perceptive,
and pleasant speech increases
persuasiveness.
22 Wisdom is a fountain of life
to one who has it,
but folly is the punishment
of fools.
23 The mind of the wise makes
their speech judicious,
and adds persuasiveness
to their lips.
24 Pleasant words are like a
honeycomb,
sweetness to the soul and
health to the body.
25 Sometimes there is a way that
seems to be right,
but in the end it is the
way to death.
26 The appetite of workers
works for them;
their hunger urges them on.

27 Scoundrels concoct evil,
and their speech is like a
scorching fire.
28 A perverse person spreads strife,
and a whisperer separates
close friends.
29 The violent entice their neighbours,
and lead them in a way
that is not good.
30 One who winks the eyes plans[d]
perverse things;
one who compresses the lips
brings evil to pass.
31 Grey hair is a crown of glory;
it is gained in a righteous life.
32 One who is slow to anger is better
than the mighty,
and one whose temper is
controlled than one
who captures a city.
33 The lot is cast into the lap,
but the decision is the
LORD's alone.

17 Better is a dry morsel with quiet
than a house full of
feasting with strife.
2 A slave who deals wisely will
rule over a child who
acts shamefully,
and will share the inheritance
as one of the family.
3 The crucible is for silver, and the
furnace is for gold,
but the LORD tests the heart.
4 An evildoer listens to wicked lips;
and a liar gives heed to a
mischievous tongue.
5 Those who mock the poor
insult their Maker;
those who are glad at calamity
will not go unpunished.
6 Grandchildren are the crown
of the aged,
and the glory of children
is their parents.
7 Fine speech is not becoming
to a fool;
still less is false speech to a ruler.[e]
8 A bribe is like a magic stone in the
eyes of those who give it;
wherever they turn they prosper.
9 One who forgives an affront
fosters friendship,
but one who dwells on disputes
will alienate a friend.
10 A rebuke strikes deeper into a
discerning person
than a hundred blows into a fool.
11 Evil people seek only rebellion,
but a cruel messenger will be
sent against them.
12 Better to meet a she-bear
robbed of its cubs
than to confront a fool
immersed in folly.
13 Evil will not depart from the house
of one who returns evil for good.
14 The beginning of strife is like
letting out water;
so stop before the quarrel
breaks out.
15 One who justifies the wicked and one
who condemns the righteous
are both alike an abomination
to the LORD.
16 Why should fools have a
price in hand
to buy wisdom, when they
have no mind to learn?
17 A friend loves at all times,
and kinsfolk are born to
share adversity.
18 It is senseless to give a pledge,
to become surety for a neighbour.
19 One who loves transgression
loves strife;
one who builds a high threshold
invites broken bones.
20 The crooked of mind do not prosper,
and the perverse of tongue
fall into calamity.
21 The one who begets a fool
gets trouble;
the parent of a fool has no joy.
22 A cheerful heart is a good medicine,
but a downcast spirit dries
up the bones.
23 The wicked accept a concealed bribe
to pervert the ways of justice.
24 The discerning person looks
to wisdom,
but the eyes of a fool to the
ends of the earth.
25 Foolish children are a grief
to their father
and bitterness to her
who bore them.
26 To impose a fine on the
innocent is not right,
or to flog the noble for
their integrity.
27 One who spares words is
knowledgeable;
one who is cool in spirit has
understanding.
28 Even fools who keep silent are
considered wise;
when they close their lips, they
are deemed intelligent.

[d] 16.30 Gk Syr Vg Tg: Heb *to plan* [e] 17.7 Or *a noble person*

18

The one who lives alone
is self-indulgent,
showing contempt for all who
have sound judgement.[f]
2 A fool takes no pleasure in
understanding,
but only in expressing
personal opinion.
3 When wickedness comes,
contempt comes also;
and with dishonour
comes disgrace.
4 The words of the mouth are
deep waters;
the fountain of wisdom is
a gushing stream.
5 It is not right to be partial
to the guilty,
or to subvert the innocent
in judgement.
6 A fool's lips bring strife,
and a fool's mouth invites
a flogging.
7 The mouths of fools are their ruin,
and their lips a snare to
themselves.
8 The words of a whisperer are
like delicious morsels;
they go down into the inner
parts of the body.
9 One who is slack in work
is close kin to a vandal.
10 The name of the LORD is a
strong tower;
the righteous run into
it and are safe.
11 The wealth of the rich is
their strong city;
in their imagination it is
like a high wall.
12 Before destruction one's
heart is haughty,
but humility goes
before honour.
13 If one gives answer
before hearing,
it is folly and shame.
14 The human spirit will
endure sickness;
but a broken spirit—
who can bear?
15 An intelligent mind acquires
knowledge,
and the ear of the wise
seeks knowledge.
16 A gift opens doors;
it gives access to the great.
17 The one who first states a
case seems right,
until the other comes and
cross-examines.
18 Casting the lot puts an end
to disputes
and decides between
powerful contenders.
19 An ally offended is stronger
than a city;[g]
such quarrelling is like the
bars of a castle.
20 From the fruit of the mouth one's
stomach is satisfied;
the yield of the lips brings
satisfaction.
21 Death and life are in the power
of the tongue,
and those who love it will
eat its fruits.
22 He who finds a wife finds
a good thing,
and obtains favour from the LORD.
23 The poor use entreaties,
but the rich answer roughly.
24 Some[h] friends play at friendship[i]
but a true friend sticks closer
than one's nearest kin.

19

Better the poor walking
in integrity
than one perverse of speech
who is a fool.
2 Desire without knowledge
is not good,
and one who moves too
hurriedly misses the way.
3 One's own folly leads to ruin,
yet the heart rages against
the LORD.
4 Wealth brings many friends,
but the poor are left friendless.
5 A false witness will not go
unpunished,
and a liar will not escape.
6 Many seek the favour of
the generous,
and everyone is a friend
to a giver of gifts.
7 If the poor are hated even
by their kin,
how much more are they
shunned by their friends!
When they call after them,
they are not there.[j]
8 To get wisdom is to love oneself;
to keep understanding
is to prosper.
9 A false witness will not go
unpunished,
and the liar will perish.

[f] **18.1** Meaning of Heb uncertain [g] **18.19** Gk Syr Vg Tg: Meaning of Heb uncertain [h] **18.24** Syr Tg: Heb *A man of* [i] **18.24** Cn Compare Syr Vg Tg: Meaning of Heb uncertain [j] **19.7** Meaning of Heb uncertain

10 It is not fitting for a fool to
live in luxury,
much less for a slave to
rule over princes.
11 Those with good sense are
slow to anger,
and it is their glory to
overlook an offence.
12 A king's anger is like the
growling of a lion,
but his favour is like dew
on the grass.
13 A stupid child is ruin to a father,
and a wife's quarrelling is a
continual dripping of rain.
14 House and wealth are inherited
from parents,
but a prudent wife is
from the LORD.
15 Laziness brings on deep sleep;
an idle person will suffer hunger.
16 Those who keep the commandment
will live;
those who are heedless of
their ways will die.
17 Whoever is kind to the poor
lends to the LORD,
and will be repaid in full.
18 Discipline your children while
there is hope;
do not set your heart on
their destruction.
19 A violent-tempered person will
pay the penalty;
if you effect a rescue, you will
only have to do it again.[k]
20 Listen to advice and accept
instruction,
that you may gain wisdom
for the future.
21 The human mind may devise
many plans,
but it is the purpose of the LORD
that will be established.
22 What is desirable in a person is loyalty,
and it is better to be poor than a liar.
23 The fear of the LORD is life indeed;
filled with it one rests secure
and suffers no harm.
24 The lazy person buries a hand
in the dish,
and will not even bring it
back to the mouth.
25 Strike a scoffer, and the simple
will learn prudence;
reprove the intelligent, and they
will gain knowledge.
26 Those who do violence to their father
and chase away their mother
are children who cause shame
and bring reproach.
27 Cease straying, my child, from the
words of knowledge,
in order that you may
hear instruction.
28 A worthless witness mocks at justice,
and the mouth of the wicked
devours iniquity.
29 Condemnation is ready for scoffers,
and flogging for the backs of fools.

20 Wine is a mocker, strong
drink a brawler,
and whoever is led astray
by it is not wise.
2 The dread anger of a king is like
the growling of a lion;
anyone who provokes him to
anger forfeits life itself.
3 It is honourable to refrain
from strife,
but every fool is quick
to quarrel.
4 The lazy person does not
plough in season;
harvest comes, and there is
nothing to be found.
5 The purposes in the human mind
are like deep water,
but the intelligent will
draw them out.
6 Many proclaim themselves loyal,
but who can find one
worthy of trust?
7 The righteous walk in integrity—
happy are the children
who follow them!
8 A king who sits on the throne
of judgement
winnows all evil with his eyes.
9 Who can say, 'I have made
my heart clean;
I am pure from my sin'?
10 Diverse weights and diverse
measures
are both alike an abomination
to the LORD.
11 Even children make themselves
known by their acts,
by whether what they do
is pure and right.
12 The hearing ear and the
seeing eye—
the LORD has made them both.
13 Do not love sleep, or else you
will come to poverty;
open your eyes, and you will
have plenty of bread.
14 'Bad, bad', says the buyer,
then goes away and boasts.

[k] 19.19 Meaning of Heb uncertain

15 There is gold, and abundance
of costly stones;
but the lips informed by
knowledge are a
precious jewel.
16 Take the garment of one who has
given surety for a stranger;
seize the pledge given as
surety for foreigners.
17 Bread gained by deceit is sweet,
but afterwards the mouth
will be full of gravel.
18 Plans are established by
taking advice;
wage war by following
wise guidance.
19 A gossip reveals secrets;
therefore do not associate
with a babbler.
20 If you curse father or mother,
your lamp will go out in
utter darkness.
21 An estate quickly acquired
in the beginning
will not be blessed in the end.
22 Do not say, 'I will repay evil';
wait for the LORD, and he
will help you.
23 Differing weights are an
abomination to the LORD,
and false scales are not good.
24 All our steps are ordered
by the LORD;
how then can we understand
our own ways?
25 It is a snare for one to say
rashly, 'It is holy',
and begin to reflect only
after making a vow.
26 A wise king winnows the wicked,
and drives the wheel over them.
27 The human spirit is the lamp
of the LORD,
searching every inmost part.
28 Loyalty and faithfulness
preserve the king,
and his throne is upheld
by righteousness.[l]
29 The glory of youths is their strength,
but the beauty of the aged
is their grey hair.
30 Blows that wound cleanse away evil;
beatings make clean the
innermost parts.

21 The king's heart is a
stream of water in the
hand of the LORD;
he turns it wherever he will.
2 All deeds are right in the
sight of the doer,
but the LORD weighs the heart.
3 To do righteousness and justice
is more acceptable to the
LORD than sacrifice.
4 Haughty eyes and a proud heart—
the lamp of the wicked—are sin.
5 The plans of the diligent lead
surely to abundance,
but everyone who is hasty
comes only to want.
6 The getting of treasures by
a lying tongue
is a fleeting vapour and a
snare[m] of death.
7 The violence of the wicked will
sweep them away,
because they refuse to
do what is just.
8 The way of the guilty is crooked,
but the conduct of the
pure is right.
9 It is better to live in a corner
of the housetop
than in a house shared with
a contentious wife.
10 The souls of the wicked desire evil;
their neighbours find no
mercy in their eyes.
11 When a scoffer is punished, the
simple become wiser;
when the wise are instructed,
they increase in knowledge.
12 The Righteous One observes the
house of the wicked;
he casts the wicked down to ruin.
13 If you close your ear to the
cry of the poor,
you will cry out and not be heard.
14 A gift in secret averts anger;
and a concealed bribe in the
bosom, strong wrath.
15 When justice is done, it is a joy
to the righteous,
but dismay to evildoers.
16 Whoever wanders from the way
of understanding
will rest in the assembly
of the dead.
17 Whoever loves pleasure will
suffer want;
whoever loves wine and oil
will not be rich.
18 The wicked is a ransom for
the righteous,
and the faithless for the upright.
19 It is better to live in a desert land
than with a contentious
and fretful wife.

[l] **20.28** Gk: Heb *loyalty* [m] **21.6** Gk: Heb *seekers*

20 Precious treasure remains[n] in
the house of the wise,
but the fool devours it.
21 Whoever pursues righteousness
and kindness
will find life[o] and honour.
22 One wise person went up against
a city of warriors
and brought down the stronghold
in which they trusted.
23 To watch over mouth and tongue
is to keep out of trouble.
24 The proud, haughty person,
named 'Scoffer',
acts with arrogant pride.
25 The craving of the lazy
person is fatal,
for lazy hands refuse to labour.
26 All day long the wicked covet,[p]
but the righteous give and
do not hold back.
27 The sacrifice of the wicked is
an abomination;
how much more when brought
with evil intent.
28 A false witness will perish,
but a good listener will
testify successfully.
29 The wicked put on a bold face,
but the upright give thought
to[q] their ways.
30 No wisdom, no understanding,
no counsel,
can avail against the LORD.
31 The horse is made ready for
the day of battle,
but the victory belongs
to the LORD.

22 A good name is to be chosen
rather than great riches,
and favour is better than
silver or gold.
2 The rich and the poor have
this in common:
the LORD is the maker
of them all.
3 The clever see danger and hide;
but the simple go on,
and suffer for it.
4 The reward for humility and
fear of the LORD
is riches and honour and life.
5 Thorns and snares are in the
way of the perverse;
the cautious will keep
far from them.
6 Train children in the right way,
and when old, they will not stray.
7 The rich rules over the poor,
and the borrower is the
slave of the lender.
8 Whoever sows injustice will
reap calamity,
and the rod of anger will fail.
9 Those who are generous are blessed,
for they share their bread
with the poor.
10 Drive out a scoffer, and
strife goes out;
quarrelling and abuse will cease.
11 Those who love a pure heart and
are gracious in speech
will have the king as a friend.
12 The eyes of the LORD keep watch
over knowledge,
but he overthrows the words
of the faithless.
13 The lazy person says, 'There
is a lion outside!
I shall be killed in the streets!'
14 The mouth of a loose[r] woman
is a deep pit;
he with whom the LORD is
angry falls into it.
15 Folly is bound up in the
heart of a boy,
but the rod of discipline
drives it far away.
16 Oppressing the poor in order
to enrich oneself,
and giving to the rich, will
lead only to loss.

SAYINGS OF THE WISE

17 The words of the wise:

Incline your ear and hear
my words,[s]
and apply your mind to
my teaching;
18 for it will be pleasant if you keep
them within you,
if all of them are ready
on your lips.
19 So that your trust may be
in the LORD,
I have made them known to
you today—yes, to you.
20 Have I not written for you
thirty sayings
of admonition and knowledge,
21 to show you what is right and true,
so that you may give a
true answer to those
who sent you?

[n] 21.20 Gk: Heb *and oil* [o] 21.21 Gk: Heb *life and righteousness* [p] 21.26 Gk: Heb *all day long one covets covetously* [q] 21.29 Another reading is *establish* [r] 22.14 Heb *strange* [s] 22.17 Cn Compare Gk: Heb *Incline your ear, and hear the words of the wise*

22 Do not rob the poor because
they are poor,
or crush the afflicted at the gate;
23 for the LORD pleads their cause
and despoils of life those
who despoil them.
24 Make no friends with those
given to anger,
and do not associate
with hotheads,
25 or you may learn their ways
and entangle yourself in a snare.
26 Do not be one of those who
give pledges,
who become surety for debts.
27 If you have nothing with
which to pay,
why should your bed be taken
from under you?
28 Do not remove the ancient landmark
that your ancestors set up.
29 Do you see those who are skilful
in their work?
They will serve kings;
they will not serve
common people.

23

When you sit down to
eat with a ruler,
observe carefully what[t]
is before you,
2 and put a knife to your throat
if you have a big appetite.
3 Do not desire the ruler's[u] delicacies,
for they are deceptive food.
4 Do not wear yourself out to get rich;
be wise enough to desist.
5 When your eyes light upon
it, it is gone;
for suddenly it takes
wings to itself,
flying like an eagle
towards heaven.
6 Do not eat the bread of the stingy;
do not desire their delicacies;
7 for like a hair in the throat,
so are they.[v]
'Eat and drink!' they say to you;
but they do not mean it.
8 You will vomit up the little
you have eaten,
and you will waste your
pleasant words.
9 Do not speak in the
hearing of a fool,
who will only despise the
wisdom of your words.
10 Do not remove an
ancient landmark
or encroach on the fields
of orphans,
11 for their redeemer is strong;
he will plead their cause
against you.
12 Apply your mind to instruction
and your ear to words
of knowledge.
13 Do not withhold discipline
from your children;
if you beat them with a rod,
they will not die.
14 If you beat them with the rod,
you will save their lives
from Sheol.
15 My child, if your heart is wise,
my heart too will be glad.
16 My soul will rejoice
when your lips speak
what is right.
17 Do not let your heart envy sinners,
but always continue in the
fear of the LORD.
18 Surely there is a future,
and your hope will not be cut off.
19 Hear, my child, and be wise,
and direct your mind in the way.
20 Do not be among winebibbers,
or among gluttonous
eaters of meat;
21 for the drunkard and the glutton
will come to poverty,
and drowsiness will clothe
them with rags.
22 Listen to your father who begot you,
and do not despise your mother
when she is old.
23 Buy truth, and do not sell it;
buy wisdom, instruction,
and understanding.
24 The father of the righteous
will greatly rejoice;
he who begets a wise son
will be glad in him.
25 Let your father and mother be glad;
let her who bore you rejoice.
26 My child, give me your heart,
and let your eyes observe[w]
my ways.
27 For a prostitute is a deep pit;
an adulteress[x] is a narrow well.
28 She lies in wait like a robber
and increases the number
of the faithless.

[t] 23.1 Or *who* [u] 23.3 Heb *his* [v] 23.7 Meaning of Heb uncertain [w] 23.26 Another reading is *delight in* [x] 23.27 Heb *an alien woman*

29 Who has woe? Who has sorrow?
Who has strife? Who has
complaining?
Who has wounds without cause?
Who has redness of eyes?
30 Those who linger late over wine,
those who keep trying
mixed wines.
31 Do not look at wine when it is red,
when it sparkles in the cup
and goes down smoothly.
32 At the last it bites like a serpent,
and stings like an adder.
33 Your eyes will see strange things,
and your mind utter
perverse things.
34 You will be like one who lies down
in the midst of the sea,
like one who lies on the
top of a mast.[y]
35 'They struck me', you will say,[z]
'but I was not hurt;
they beat me, but I did not feel it.
When shall I awake?
I will seek another drink.'

24 Do not envy the wicked,
nor desire to be with them;
2 for their minds devise violence,
and their lips talk of mischief.

3 By wisdom a house is built,
and by understanding it
is established;
4 by knowledge the rooms are filled
with all precious and
pleasant riches.
5 Wise warriors are mightier
than strong ones,[a]
and those who have
knowledge than those
who have strength;
6 for by wise guidance you can
wage your war,
and in abundance of counsellors
there is victory.
7 Wisdom is too high for fools;
in the gate they do not
open their mouths.

8 Whoever plans to do evil
will be called a mischief-maker.
9 The devising of folly is sin,
and the scoffer is an
abomination to all.

10 If you faint in the day of adversity,
your strength being small;
11 if you hold back from rescuing
those taken away to death,
those who go staggering
to the slaughter;
12 if you say, 'Look, we did not
know this'—
does not he who weighs the
heart perceive it?
Does not he who keeps watch
over your soul know it?
And will he not repay all
according to their deeds?

13 My child, eat honey, for it is good,
and the drippings of the
honeycomb are sweet
to your taste.
14 Know that wisdom is such
to your soul;
if you find it, you will
find a future,
and your hope will not be cut off.

15 Do not lie in wait like an outlaw
against the home of
the righteous;
do no violence to the place
where the righteous live;
16 for though they fall seven times,
they will rise again;
but the wicked are overthrown
by calamity.

17 Do not rejoice when your
enemies fall,
and do not let your heart be
glad when they stumble,
18 or else the LORD will see it
and be displeased,
and turn away his anger
from them.

19 Do not fret because of evildoers.
Do not envy the wicked;
20 for the evil have no future;
the lamp of the wicked will go out.

21 My child, fear the LORD
and the king,
and do not disobey either
of them;[b]
22 for disaster comes from
them suddenly,
and who knows the ruin
that both can bring?

FURTHER SAYINGS OF THE WISE

23 These also are sayings of the wise:

Partiality in judging is not good.

[y] **23.34** Meaning of Heb uncertain [z] **23.35** Gk Syr Vg Tg: Heb lacks *you will say* [a] **24.5** Gk Compare Syr Tg: Heb *A wise man is strength* [b] **24.21** Gk: Heb *do not associate with those who change*

24 Whoever says to the wicked,
'You are innocent',
will be cursed by peoples,
abhorred by nations;
25 but those who rebuke the wicked
will have delight,
and a good blessing will
come upon them.
26 One who gives an honest answer
gives a kiss on the lips.

27 Prepare your work outside,
get everything ready for
you in the field;
and after that build your house.

28 Do not be a witness against your
neighbour without cause,
and do not deceive with your lips.
29 Do not say, 'I will do to others as
they have done to me;
I will pay them back for what
they have done.'

30 I passed by the field of one
who was lazy,
by the vineyard of a stupid person;
31 and see, it was all overgrown
with thorns;
the ground was covered
with nettles,
and its stone wall was broken down.
32 Then I saw and considered it;
I looked and received instruction.
33 A little sleep, a little slumber,
a little folding of the hands to rest,
34 and poverty will come upon
you like a robber,
and want, like an armed warrior.

FURTHER WISE SAYINGS OF SOLOMON

25 These are other proverbs of Solomon that the officials of King Hezekiah of Judah copied.

2 It is the glory of God to
conceal things,
but the glory of kings is to
search things out.
3 Like the heavens for height, like
the earth for depth,
so the mind of kings is
unsearchable.
4 Take away the dross from the silver,
and the smith has material
for a vessel;
5 take away the wicked from the
presence of the king,
and his throne will be established
in righteousness.
6 Do not put yourself forward in
the king's presence
or stand in the place of the great;
7 for it is better to be told,
'Come up here',
than to be put lower in the
presence of a noble.

What your eyes have seen
8 do not hastily bring into court;
for[c] what will you do in the end,
when your neighbour puts
you to shame?
9 Argue your case with your
neighbour directly,
and do not disclose another's secret;
10 or else someone who hears you will
bring shame upon you,
and your ill repute will
have no end.

11 A word fitly spoken
is like apples of gold in a
setting of silver.
12 Like a gold ring or an
ornament of gold
is a wise rebuke to a listening ear.
13 Like the cold of snow in the
time of harvest
are faithful messengers to
those who send them;
they refresh the spirit of
their masters.
14 Like clouds and wind without rain
is one who boasts of a gift
never given.
15 With patience a ruler may
be persuaded,
and a soft tongue can break bones.
16 If you have found honey, eat
only enough for you,
or else, having too much,
you will vomit it.
17 Let your foot be seldom in your
neighbour's house,
otherwise the neighbour
will become weary of
you and hate you.
18 Like a war club, a sword, or
a sharp arrow
is one who bears false witness
against a neighbour.
19 Like a bad tooth or a lame foot
is trust in a faithless person
in time of trouble.
20 Like vinegar on a wound[d]
is one who sings songs to
a heavy heart.

[c] 25.8 Cn: Heb *or else* [d] 25.20 Gk: Heb *Like one who takes off a garment on a cold day, like vinegar on lye*

Like a moth in clothing or a
worm in wood,
sorrow gnaws at the
human heart.[e]
21 If your enemies are hungry, give
them bread to eat;
and if they are thirsty, give
them water to drink;
22 for you will heap coals of fire
on their heads,
and the LORD will reward you.
23 The north wind produces rain,
and a backbiting tongue,
angry looks.
24 It is better to live in a corner
of the housetop
than in a house shared with
a contentious wife.
25 Like cold water to a thirsty soul,
so is good news from a far country.
26 Like a muddied spring or a
polluted fountain
are the righteous who give
way before the wicked.
27 It is not good to eat much honey,
or to seek honour on
top of honour.
28 Like a city breached, without walls,
is one who lacks self-control.

26 Like snow in summer or
rain in harvest,
so honour is not fitting for a fool.
2 Like a sparrow in its flitting, like
a swallow in its flying,
an undeserved curse
goes nowhere.
3 A whip for the horse, a bridle
for the donkey,
and a rod for the back of fools.
4 Do not answer fools according
to their folly,
or you will be a fool yourself.
5 Answer fools according to their folly,
or they will be wise in
their own eyes.
6 It is like cutting off one's foot and
drinking down violence,
to send a message by a fool.
7 The legs of a disabled person
hang limp;
so does a proverb in the
mouth of a fool.
8 It is like binding a stone in a sling
to give honour to a fool.
9 Like a thornbush brandished by
the hand of a drunkard
is a proverb in the mouth of a fool.
10 Like an archer who wounds
everybody
is one who hires a passing
fool or drunkard.[f]
11 Like a dog that returns to its vomit
is a fool who reverts to his folly.
12 Do you see persons wise in
their own eyes?
There is more hope for fools
than for them.
13 The lazy person says, 'There is
a lion in the road!
There is a lion in the streets!'
14 As a door turns on its hinges,
so does a lazy person in bed.
15 The lazy person buries a
hand in the dish,
and is too tired to bring it
back to the mouth.
16 The lazy person is wiser in
self-esteem
than seven who can
answer discreetly.
17 Like somebody who takes a
passing dog by the ears
is one who meddles in the
quarrel of another.
18 Like a maniac who shoots deadly
firebrands and arrows,
19 so is one who deceives a neighbour
and says, 'I am only joking!'
20 For lack of wood the fire goes out,
and where there is no whisperer,
quarrelling ceases.
21 As charcoal is to hot embers
and wood to fire,
so is a quarrelsome person
for kindling strife.
22 The words of a whisperer are
like delicious morsels;
they go down into the inner
parts of the body.
23 Like the glaze[g] covering an
earthen vessel
are smooth[h] lips with
an evil heart.
24 An enemy dissembles in speaking
while harbouring deceit within;
25 when an enemy speaks graciously,
do not believe it,
for there are seven abominations
concealed within;
26 though hatred is covered with guile,
the enemy's wickedness will be
exposed in the assembly.
27 Whoever digs a pit will fall into it,
and a stone will come back on the
one who starts it rolling.
28 A lying tongue hates its victims,
and a flattering mouth
works ruin.

[e] **25.20** Gk Syr Tg: Heb lacks *Like a moth . . . human heart* [f] **26.10** Meaning of Heb uncertain
[g] **26.23** Cn: Heb *silver of dross* [h] **26.23** Gk: Heb *burning*

27 Do not boast about tomorrow,
for you do not know what
a day may bring.
2 Let another praise you, and not
your own mouth—
a stranger, and not your own lips.
3 A stone is heavy, and sand
is weighty,
but a fool's provocation is
heavier than both.
4 Wrath is cruel, anger is
overwhelming,
but who is able to stand
before jealousy?
5 Better is open rebuke
than hidden love.
6 Well meant are the wounds
a friend inflicts,
but profuse are the kisses
of an enemy.
7 The sated appetite spurns honey,
but to a ravenous appetite
even the bitter is sweet.
8 Like a bird that strays from its nest
is one who strays from home.
9 Perfume and incense make
the heart glad,
but the soul is torn by trouble.[i]
10 Do not forsake your friend or the
friend of your parent;
do not go to the house of
your kindred on the
day of your calamity.
Better is a neighbour who is nearby
than kindred who are far away.
11 Be wise, my child, and make
my heart glad,
so that I may answer whoever
reproaches me.
12 The clever see danger and hide;
but the simple go on,
and suffer for it.
13 Take the garment of one who has
given surety for a stranger;
seize the pledge given as
surety for foreigners.[j]
14 Whoever blesses a neighbour
with a loud voice,
rising early in the morning,
will be counted as cursing.
15 A continual dripping on a rainy day
and a contentious wife are alike;
16 to restrain her is to restrain the wind
or to grasp oil in the right hand.[k]
17 Iron sharpens iron,
and one person sharpens
the wits[l] of another.
18 Anyone who tends a fig tree
will eat its fruit,
and anyone who takes care of a
master will be honoured.
19 Just as water reflects the face,
so one human heart
reflects another.
20 Sheol and Abaddon are
never satisfied,
and human eyes are
never satisfied.
21 The crucible is for silver, and the
furnace is for gold,
so a person is tested[m] by
being praised.
22 Crush a fool in a mortar with a pestle
along with crushed grain,
but the folly will not be
driven out.

23 Know well the condition
of your flocks,
and give attention to your herds;
24 for riches do not last for ever,
nor a crown for all generations.
25 When the grass is gone, and
new growth appears,
and the herbage of the
mountains is gathered,
26 the lambs will provide
your clothing,
and the goats the price of a field;
27 there will be enough goats'
milk for your food,
for the food of your household
and nourishment for your
servant-girls.

28 The wicked flee when
no one pursues,
but the righteous are as
bold as a lion.
2 When a land rebels
it has many rulers;
but with an intelligent ruler
there is lasting order.[n]
3 A ruler[o] who oppresses the poor
is a beating rain that
leaves no food.
4 Those who forsake the law
praise the wicked,
but those who keep the law
struggle against them.
5 The evil do not understand justice,
but those who seek the LORD
understand it completely.
6 Better to be poor and walk
in integrity
than to be crooked in one's
ways even though rich.

[i] 27.9 Gk: Heb *the sweetness of a friend is better than one's own counsel* [j] 27.13 Vg and 20.16: Heb *for a foreign woman* [k] 27.16 Meaning of Heb uncertain [l] 27.17 Heb *face* [m] 27.21 Heb lacks *is tested* [n] 28.2 Meaning of Heb uncertain [o] 28.3 Cn: Heb *A poor person*

7 Those who keep the law are
wise children,
but companions of gluttons
shame their parents.
8 One who augments wealth by
exorbitant interest
gathers it for another who
is kind to the poor.
9 When one will not listen to the law,
even one's prayers are an
abomination.
10 Those who mislead the upright
into evil ways
will fall into pits of their
own making,
but the blameless will have a
goodly inheritance.
11 The rich is wise in self-esteem,
but an intelligent poor person
sees through the pose.
12 When the righteous triumph,
there is great glory,
but when the wicked prevail,
people go into hiding.
13 No one who conceals transgressions
will prosper,
but one who confesses and
forsakes them will
obtain mercy.
14 Happy is the one who is never
without fear,
but one who is hard-hearted
will fall into calamity.
15 Like a roaring lion or a charging bear
is a wicked ruler over a
poor people.
16 A ruler who lacks understanding
is a cruel oppressor;
but one who hates unjust gain
will enjoy a long life.
17 If someone is burdened with
the blood of another,
let that killer be a fugitive
until death;
let no one offer assistance.
18 One who walks in integrity
will be safe,
but whoever follows crooked
ways will fall into the Pit.[p]
19 Anyone who tills the land will
have plenty of bread,
but one who follows worthless
pursuits will have
plenty of poverty.
20 The faithful will abound
with blessings,
but one who is in a hurry to be
rich will not go unpunished.
21 To show partiality is not good—
yet for a piece of bread a
person may do wrong.
22 The miser is in a hurry to get rich
and does not know that loss
is sure to come.
23 Whoever rebukes a person will
afterwards find more favour
than one who flatters
with the tongue.
24 Anyone who robs father or mother
and says, 'That is no crime',
is partner to a thug.
25 The greedy person stirs up strife,
but whoever trusts in the
LORD will be enriched.
26 Those who trust in their own
wits are fools;
but those who walk in wisdom
come through safely.
27 Whoever gives to the poor
will lack nothing,
but one who turns a blind eye
will get many a curse.
28 When the wicked prevail, people
go into hiding;
but when they perish, the
righteous increase.

29

One who is often reproved,
yet remains stubborn,
will suddenly be broken
beyond healing.
2 When the righteous are
in authority, the
people rejoice;
but when the wicked rule,
the people groan.
3 A child who loves wisdom
makes a parent glad,
but to keep company with
prostitutes is to squander
one's substance.
4 By justice a king gives stability
to the land,
but one who makes heavy
exactions ruins it.
5 Whoever flatters a neighbour
is spreading a net for the
neighbour's feet.
6 In the transgression of the evil
there is a snare,
but the righteous sing and rejoice.
7 The righteous know the
rights of the poor;
the wicked have no such
understanding.
8 Scoffers set a city aflame,
but the wise turn away wrath.
9 If the wise go to law with fools,
there is ranting and ridicule
without relief.

p **28.18** Syr: Heb *fall all at once*

10 The bloodthirsty hate the blameless,
and they seek the life of
the upright.
11 A fool gives full vent to anger,
but the wise quietly holds it back.
12 If a ruler listens to falsehood,
all his officials will be wicked.
13 The poor and the oppressor have
this in common:
the LORD gives light to
the eyes of both.
14 If a king judges the poor
with equity,
his throne will be established
for ever.
15 The rod and reproof give wisdom,
but a mother is disgraced by
a neglected child.
16 When the wicked are in authority,
transgression increases,
but the righteous will look
upon their downfall.
17 Discipline your children, and
they will give you rest;
they will give delight to
your heart.
18 Where there is no prophecy, the
people cast off restraint,
but happy are those who
keep the law.
19 By mere words servants are
not disciplined,
for though they understand,
they will not give heed.
20 Do you see someone who is
hasty in speech?
There is more hope for a fool
than for anyone like that.
21 A slave pampered from childhood
will come to a bad end.[q]
22 One given to anger stirs up strife,
and the hothead causes
much transgression.
23 A person's pride will bring
humiliation,
but one who is lowly in spirit
will obtain honour.
24 To be a partner of a thief is to
hate one's own life;
one hears the victim's curse,
but discloses nothing.[r]
25 The fear of others[s] lays a snare,
but one who trusts in the
LORD is secure.
26 Many seek the favour of a ruler,
but it is from the LORD that
one gets justice.
27 The unjust are an abomination
to the righteous,
but the upright are an
abomination to the wicked.

SAYINGS OF AGUR

30 The words of Agur son of Jakeh.
An oracle.

Thus says the man: I am
weary, O God,
I am weary, O God. How
can I prevail?[t]
2 Surely I am too stupid to be human;
I do not have human
understanding.
3 I have not learned wisdom,
nor have I knowledge of
the holy ones.[u]
4 Who has ascended to heaven
and come down?
Who has gathered the wind in
the hollow of the hand?
Who has wrapped up the waters
in a garment?
Who has established all the
ends of the earth?
What is the person's name?
And what is the name of
the person's child?
Surely you know!

5 Every word of God proves true;
he is a shield to those who
take refuge in him.
6 Do not add to his words,
or else he will rebuke you, and
you will be found a liar.

7 Two things I ask of you;
do not deny them to me
before I die:
8 Remove far from me falsehood
and lying;
give me neither poverty nor riches;
feed me with the food that I need,
9 or I shall be full, and deny you,
and say, 'Who is the LORD?'
or I shall be poor, and steal,
and profane the name of my God.

10 Do not slander a servant to a master,
or the servant will curse you, and
you will be held guilty.

11 There are those who curse
their fathers
and do not bless their mothers.
12 There are those who are pure
in their own eyes
yet are not cleansed of
their filthiness.

[q] **29.21** Vg: Meaning of Heb uncertain
[r] **29.24** Meaning of Heb uncertain [s] **29.25** Or *human fear* [t] **30.1** Or *I am spent.* Meaning of Heb uncertain [u] **30.3** Or *Holy One*

13 There are those—how lofty
are their eyes,
how high their eyelids lift!—
14 there are those whose teeth
are swords,
whose teeth are knives,
to devour the poor from
off the earth,
the needy from among mortals.

15 The leech[v] has two daughters;
'Give, give,' they cry.
Three things are never satisfied;
four never say, 'Enough':
16 Sheol, the barren womb,
the earth ever thirsty for water,
and the fire that never
says, 'Enough.'[w]

17 The eye that mocks a father
and scorns to obey a mother
will be pecked out by the
ravens of the valley
and eaten by the vultures.

18 Three things are too
wonderful for me;
four I do not understand:
19 the way of an eagle in the sky,
the way of a snake on a rock,
the way of a ship on the high seas,
and the way of a man
with a girl.

20 This is the way of an adulteress:
she eats, and wipes her mouth,
and says, 'I have done no wrong.'

21 Under three things the
earth trembles;
under four it cannot bear up:
22 a slave when he becomes king,
and a fool when glutted
with food;
23 an unloved woman when she
gets a husband,
and a maid when she succeeds
her mistress.

24 Four things on earth are small,
yet they are exceedingly wise:
25 the ants are a people without
strength,
yet they provide their food
in the summer;
26 the badgers are a people
without power,
yet they make their homes
in the rocks;
27 the locusts have no king,
yet all of them march in rank;
28 the lizard[x] can be grasped
in the hand,
yet it is found in kings' palaces.

29 Three things are stately in
their stride;
four are stately in their gait:
30 the lion, which is mightiest
among wild animals
and does not turn back before any;
31 the strutting rooster,[y] the he-goat,
and a king striding before[z]
his people.

32 If you have been foolish,
exalting yourself,
or if you have been devising evil,
put your hand on your mouth.
33 For as pressing milk produces curds,
and pressing the nose
produces blood,
so pressing anger produces strife.

THE TEACHING OF KING LEMUEL'S MOTHER

31 The words of King Lemuel. An
oracle that his mother taught
him:

2 No, my son! No, son of my womb!
No, son of my vows!
3 Do not give your strength
to women,
your ways to those who
destroy kings.
4 It is not for kings, O Lemuel,
it is not for kings to drink wine,
or for rulers to desire[a]
strong drink;
5 or else they will drink and forget
what has been decreed,
and will pervert the rights
of all the afflicted.
6 Give strong drink to one
who is perishing,
and wine to those in
bitter distress;
7 let them drink and forget
their poverty,
and remember their
misery no more.
8 Speak out for those who
cannot speak,
for the rights of all the destitute.[b]

[v] 30.15 Meaning of Heb uncertain
[w] 30.16 Meaning of Heb uncertain [x] 30.28 Or *spider* [y] 30.31 Gk Syr Tg Compare Vg: Meaning of Heb uncertain [z] 30.31 Meaning of Heb uncertain [a] 31.4 Cn: Heb *where* [b] 31.8 Heb *all children of passing away*

9 Speak out, judge righteously,
defend the rights of the
poor and needy.

ODE TO A CAPABLE WIFE

10 A capable wife who can find?
She is far more precious
than jewels.
11 The heart of her husband trusts in her,
and he will have no lack of gain.
12 She does him good, and not harm,
all the days of her life.
13 She seeks wool and flax,
and works with willing hands.
14 She is like the ships of the merchant,
she brings her food from far away.
15 She rises while it is still night
and provides food for her household
and tasks for her servant-girls.
16 She considers a field and buys it;
with the fruit of her hands
she plants a vineyard.
17 She girds herself with strength,
and makes her arms strong.
18 She perceives that her merchandise
is profitable.
Her lamp does not go out at night.
19 She puts her hands to the distaff,
and her hands hold the spindle.
20 She opens her hand to the poor,
and reaches out her hands
to the needy.
21 She is not afraid for her household
when it snows,
for all her household are
clothed in crimson.
22 She makes herself coverings;
her clothing is fine linen
and purple.
23 Her husband is known in
the city gates,
taking his seat among the
elders of the land.
24 She makes linen garments
and sells them;
she supplies the merchant
with sashes.
25 Strength and dignity are
her clothing,
and she laughs at the
time to come.
26 She opens her mouth with wisdom,
and the teaching of kindness
is on her tongue.
27 She looks well to the ways of
her household,
and does not eat the bread
of idleness.
28 Her children rise up and
call her happy;
her husband too, and he
praises her:
29 'Many women have done excellently,
but you surpass them all.'
30 Charm is deceitful, and
beauty is vain,
but a woman who fears the
LORD is to be praised.
31 Give her a share in the fruit
of her hands,
and let her works praise her
in the city gates.

ECCLESIASTES

Ecclesiastes is the Latin name for the Hebrew *Qoheleth*, traditionally known as the "Teacher" and in whose name the writing is presented. The book is dated by some scholars between 450 and 330 BCE and by others a century or two later. The hard observation of the book is that the world is indifferent, life is monotonous, and one's fate is inevitable. Wisdom means accepting the fact that human beings do not have control of their lives: "All is vanity" (1.2). It means that the purpose of life can only be found in God, who alone can determine life's course: "For God will bring every deed into judgement, including every secret thing, whether good or evil" (12.14).

Texts from Ecclesiastes are read on Thursday through Saturday of the Twenty-Fifth Week of Year II. The opening verses of Ecclesiastes are also read at the Mass of the Eighteenth Sunday of the Year in Cycle C.

REFLECTIONS OF A ROYAL PHILOSOPHER

1 The words of the Teacher,[a] the son of David, king in Jerusalem.

2 Vanity of vanities, says the Teacher,[b]
vanity of vanities! All is vanity.
3 What do people gain from all the toil
at which they toil under the sun?
4 A generation goes, and a
generation comes,
but the earth remains for ever.
5 The sun rises and the sun
goes down,
and hurries to the place
where it rises.
6 The wind blows to the south,
and goes round to the north;
round and round goes the wind,
and on its circuits the
wind returns.
7 All streams run to the sea,
but the sea is not full;
to the place where the streams flow,
there they continue to flow.
8 All things[c] are wearisome;
more than one can express;
the eye is not satisfied with seeing,
or the ear filled with hearing.
9 What has been is what will be,
and what has been done is
what will be done;
there is nothing new
under the sun.
10 Is there a thing of which it is said,
'See, this is new'?
It has already been,
in the ages before us.
11 The people of long ago are
not remembered,
nor will there be any
remembrance
of people yet to come
by those who come after them.

THE FUTILITY OF SEEKING WISDOM

12 I, the Teacher,[d] when king over
Israel in Jerusalem, 13 applied my mind
to seek and to search out by wisdom all
that is done under heaven; it is an unhappy business that God has given to
human beings to be busy with. 14 I saw
all the deeds that are done under the
sun; and see, all is vanity and a chasing
after wind.[e]
15 What is crooked cannot be
made straight,
and what is lacking cannot
be counted.
16 I said to myself, 'I have acquired
great wisdom, surpassing all who were
over Jerusalem before me; and my mind

[a] 1.1 Heb *Qoheleth*, traditionally rendered *Preacher* [b] 1.2 Heb *Qoheleth*, traditionally rendered *Preacher* [c] 1.8 Or *words* [d] 1.12 Heb *Qoheleth*, traditionally rendered *Preacher* [e] 1.14 Or *a feeding on wind*. See Hos 12.1

has had great experience of wisdom and
knowledge.' 17 And I applied my mind
to know wisdom and to know madness
and folly. I perceived that this also is but
a chasing after wind.[f]

18 For in much wisdom is
much vexation,
and those who increase knowledge
increase sorrow.

THE FUTILITY OF SELF-INDULGENCE

2 I said to myself, 'Come now, I will
make a test of pleasure; enjoy yourself.' But again, this also was vanity. 2 I
said of laughter, 'It is mad', and of pleasure, 'What use is it?' 3 I searched with my
mind how to cheer my body with wine—
my mind still guiding me with wisdom—
and how to lay hold on folly, until I might
see what was good for mortals to do under heaven during the few days of their
life. 4 I made great works; I built houses
and planted vineyards for myself; 5 I
made myself gardens and parks, and
planted in them all kinds of fruit trees.
6 I made myself pools from which to water the forest of growing trees. 7 I bought
male and female slaves, and had slaves
who were born in my house; I also had
great possessions of herds and flocks,
more than any who had been before me
in Jerusalem. 8 I also gathered for myself
silver and gold and the treasure of kings
and of the provinces; I got singers, both
men and women, and delights of the
flesh, and many concubines.[g]

9 So I became great and surpassed all
who were before me in Jerusalem; also
my wisdom remained with me. 10 Whatever my eyes desired I did not keep from
them; I kept my heart from no pleasure, for my heart found pleasure in all
my toil, and this was my reward for all
my toil. 11 Then I considered all that my
hands had done and the toil I had spent
in doing it, and again, all was vanity
and a chasing after wind,[h] and there
was nothing to be gained under the sun.

WISDOM AND JOY GIVEN TO ONE WHO PLEASES GOD

12 So I turned to consider wisdom
and madness and folly; for what can the
one do who comes after the king? Only
what has already been done. 13 Then I
saw that wisdom excels folly as light excels darkness.

14 The wise have eyes in their head,
but fools walk in darkness.

Yet I perceived that the same fate befalls all of them. 15 Then I said to myself,
'What happens to the fool will happen
to me also; why then have I been so very
wise?' And I said to myself that this also
is vanity. 16 For there is no enduring remembrance of the wise or of fools, seeing that in the days to come all will have
been long forgotten. How can the wise
die just like fools? 17 So I hated life, because what is done under the sun was
grievous to me; for all is vanity and a
chasing after wind.[i]

18 I hated all my toil in which I had
toiled under the sun, seeing that I must
leave it to those who come after me
19 —and who knows whether they will
be wise or foolish? Yet they will be master of all for which I toiled and used my
wisdom under the sun. This also is vanity. 20 So I turned and gave my heart up
to despair concerning all the toil of my
labours under the sun, 21 because sometimes one who has toiled with wisdom
and knowledge and skill must leave all
to be enjoyed by another who did not
toil for it. This also is vanity and a great
evil. 22 What do mortals get from all the
toil and strain with which they toil under the sun? 23 For all their days are full
of pain, and their work is a vexation;
even at night their minds do not rest.
This also is vanity.

24 There is nothing better for mortals than to eat and drink, and find enjoyment in their toil. This also, I saw, is
from the hand of God; 25 for apart from
him[j] who can eat or who can have enjoyment? 26 For to the one who pleases
him God gives wisdom and knowledge
and joy; but to the sinner he gives the
work of gathering and heaping, only to
give to one who pleases God. This also is
vanity and a chasing after wind.[k]

EVERYTHING HAS ITS TIME

3 For everything there is a season,
and a time for every matter under
heaven:

2 a time to be born, and a time to die;
a time to plant, and a time to
pluck up what is planted;
3 a time to kill, and a time to heal;
a time to break down, and a
time to build up;
4 a time to weep, and a time to laugh;
a time to mourn, and a
time to dance;

[f] **1.17** Or *a feeding on wind.* See Hos 12.1
[g] **2.8** Meaning of Heb uncertain [h] **2.11** Or *a feeding on wind.* See Hos 12.1 [i] **2.17** Or *a feeding on wind.* See Hos 12.1 [j] **2.25** Gk Syr: Heb *apart from me* [k] **2.26** Or *a feeding on wind.* See Hos 12.1

5 a time to throw away stones,
and a time to gather
stones together;
a time to embrace, and a time to
refrain from embracing;
6 a time to seek, and a time to lose;
a time to keep, and a time
to throw away;
7 a time to tear, and a time to sew;
a time to keep silence, and
a time to speak;
8 a time to love, and a time to hate;
a time for war, and a time for peace.

THE GOD-GIVEN TASK

9 What gain have the workers from
their toil? 10 I have seen the business
that God has given to everyone to be
busy with. 11 He has made everything
suitable for its time; moreover, he has
put a sense of past and future into their
minds, yet they cannot find out what
God has done from the beginning to
the end. 12 I know that there is nothing better for them than to be happy
and enjoy themselves as long as they
live; 13 moreover, it is God's gift that all
should eat and drink and take pleasure
in all their toil. 14 I know that whatever
God does endures for ever; nothing can
be added to it, nor anything taken from
it; God has done this, so that all should
stand in awe before him. 15 That which
is, already has been; that which is to be,
already is; and God seeks out what has
gone by.[l]

JUDGEMENT AND THE FUTURE BELONG TO GOD

16 Moreover, I saw under the sun
that in the place of justice, wickedness
was there, and in the place of righteousness, wickedness was there as well. 17 I
said in my heart, God will judge the
righteous and the wicked, for he has appointed a time for every matter, and for
every work. 18 I said in my heart with
regard to human beings that God is
testing them to show that they are but
animals. 19 For the fate of humans and
the fate of animals is the same; as one
dies, so dies the other. They all have the
same breath, and humans have no advantage over the animals; for all is vanity. 20 All go to one place; all are from the
dust, and all turn to dust again. 21 Who
knows whether the human spirit goes
upwards and the spirit of animals goes
downwards to the earth? 22 So I saw that
there is nothing better than that all
should enjoy their work, for that is their
lot; who can bring them to see what will
be after them?

4 Again I saw all the oppressions that
are practised under the sun. Look,
the tears of the oppressed—with no one
to comfort them! On the side of their
oppressors there was power—with no
one to comfort them. 2 And I thought
the dead, who have already died, more
fortunate than the living, who are still
alive; 3 but better than both is the one
who has not yet been, and has not seen
the evil deeds that are done under the
sun.

4 Then I saw that all toil and all skill
in work come from one person's envy of
another. This also is vanity and a chasing after wind.[m]

5 Fools fold their hands
and consume their own flesh.
6 Better is a handful with quiet
than two handfuls with toil,
and a chasing after wind.[n]

7 Again, I saw vanity under the sun:
8 the case of solitary individuals, without sons or brothers; yet there is no end
to all their toil, and their eyes are never
satisfied with riches. 'For whom am I
toiling', they ask, 'and depriving myself
of pleasure?' This also is vanity and an
unhappy business.

THE VALUE OF A FRIEND

9 Two are better than one, because
they have a good reward for their toil.
10 For if they fall, one will lift up the
other; but woe to one who is alone and
falls and does not have another to help.
11 Again, if two lie together, they keep
warm; but how can one keep warm
alone? 12 And though one might prevail
against another, two will withstand
one. A threefold cord is not quickly broken.

13 Better is a poor but wise youth
than an old but foolish king, who will
no longer take advice. 14 One can indeed come out of prison to reign, even
though born poor in the kingdom. 15 I
saw all the living who, moving about
under the sun, follow that[o] youth who
replaced the king;[p] 16 there was no end
to all those people whom he led. Yet
those who come later will not rejoice
in him. Surely this also is vanity and a
chasing after wind.[q]

[l] 3.15 Heb *what is pursued* [m] 4.4 Or *a feeding on wind.* See Hos 12.1 [n] 4.6 Or *a feeding on wind.* See Hos 12.1 [o] 4.15 Heb *the second* [p] 4.15 Heb *him* [q] 4.16 Or *a feeding on wind.* See Hos 12.1

REVERENCE, HUMILITY, AND CONTENTMENT

5 [r]Guard your steps when you go to
the house of God; to draw near to listen is better than the sacrifice offered by
fools; for they do not know how to keep
from doing evil.[s] 2 [t]Never be rash with
your mouth, nor let your heart be quick
to utter a word before God, for God is in
heaven, and you upon earth; therefore
let your words be few.
3 For dreams come with many cares,
and a fool's voice with many words.
4 When you make a vow to God, do
not delay fulfilling it; for he has no pleasure in fools. Fulfil what you vow. 5 It is
better that you should not vow than that
you should vow and not fulfil it. 6 Do not
let your mouth lead you into sin, and do
not say before the messenger that it was
a mistake; why should God be angry at
your words, and destroy the work of your
hands?
7 With many dreams come vanities
and a multitude of words;[u] but fear God.
8 If you see in a province the oppression of the poor and the violation of justice and right, do not be amazed at the
matter; for the high official is watched by
a higher, and there are yet higher ones
over them. 9 But all things considered,
this is an advantage for a land: a king for
a ploughed field.[v]
10 The lover of money will not be
satisfied with money; nor the lover of
wealth, with gain. This also is vanity.
11 When goods increase, those who
eat them increase; and what gain has
their owner but to see them with his
eyes?
12 Sweet is the sleep of labourers,
whether they eat little or much; but the
surfeit of the rich will not let them sleep.
13 There is a grievous ill that I have
seen under the sun: riches were kept by
their owners to their hurt, 14 and those
riches were lost in a bad venture; though
they are parents of children, they have
nothing in their hands. 15 As they came
from their mother's womb, so they shall
go again, naked as they came; they shall
take nothing for their toil, which they
may carry away with their hands. 16 This
also is a grievous ill: just as they came, so
shall they go; and what gain do they have
from toiling for the wind? 17 Besides, all
their days they eat in darkness, in much
vexation and sickness and resentment.
18 This is what I have seen to be good:
it is fitting to eat and drink and find enjoyment in all the toil with which one toils
under the sun the few days of the life God
gives us; for this is our lot. 19 Likewise all to
whom God gives wealth and possessions
and whom he enables to enjoy them, and
to accept their lot and find enjoyment in
their toil—this is the gift of God. 20 For
they will scarcely brood over the days of
their lives, because God keeps them occupied with the joy of their hearts.

THE FRUSTRATION OF DESIRES

6 There is an evil that I have seen under the sun, and it lies heavy upon
humankind: 2 those to whom God gives
wealth, possessions, and honour, so that
they lack nothing of all that they desire,
yet God does not enable them to enjoy
these things, but a stranger enjoys them.
This is vanity; it is a grievous ill. 3 A man
may beget a hundred children, and live
for many years; but however many are
the days of his years, if he does not enjoy
life's good things, or has no burial, I say
that a stillborn child is better off than
he. 4 For it comes into vanity and goes
into darkness, and in darkness its name
is covered; 5 moreover, it has not seen the
sun or known anything; yet it finds rest
rather than he. 6 Even though he should
live a thousand years twice over, yet enjoy no good—do not all go to one place?
7 All human toil is for the mouth, yet
the appetite is not satisfied. 8 For what
advantage have the wise over fools?
And what do the poor have who know
how to conduct themselves before the
living? 9 Better is the sight of the eyes
than the wandering of desire; this also
is vanity and a chasing after wind.[w]
10 Whatever has come to be has already been named, and it is known
what human beings are, and that they
are not able to dispute with those who
are stronger. 11 The more words, the
more vanity, so how is one the better?
12 For who knows what is good for mortals while they live the few days of their
vain life, which they pass like a shadow?
For who can tell them what will be after
them under the sun?

A DISILLUSIONED VIEW OF LIFE

7 A good name is better than
precious ointment,
and the day of death, than
the day of birth.

[r] **5.1** Ch 4.17 in Heb [s] **5.1** Cn: Heb *they do not know how to do evil* [t] **5.2** Ch 5.1 in Heb [u] **5.7** Meaning of Heb uncertain [v] **5.9** Meaning of Heb uncertain [w] **6.9** Or *a feeding on wind.* See Hos 12.1

2 It is better to go to the house
of mourning
than to go to the house of feasting;
for this is the end of everyone,
and the living will lay it to heart.
3 Sorrow is better than laughter,
for by sadness of countenance
the heart is made glad.
4 The heart of the wise is in the
house of mourning;
but the heart of fools is in
the house of mirth.
5 It is better to hear the rebuke
of the wise
than to hear the song of fools.
6 For like the crackling of thorns
under a pot,
so is the laughter of fools;
this also is vanity.
7 Surely oppression makes
the wise foolish,
and a bribe corrupts the heart.
8 Better is the end of a thing
than its beginning;
the patient in spirit are better
than the proud in spirit.
9 Do not be quick to anger,
for anger lodges in the
bosom of fools.
10 Do not say, 'Why were the former
days better than these?'
For it is not from wisdom
that you ask this.
11 Wisdom is as good as an inheritance,
an advantage to those
who see the sun.
12 For the protection of wisdom is like
the protection of money,
and the advantage of knowledge
is that wisdom gives life to
the one who possesses it.
13 Consider the work of God;
who can make straight what
he has made crooked?

14 On the day of prosperity be joyful,
and on the day of adversity consider;
God has made the one as well as the
other, so that mortals may not find out
anything that will come after them.

THE RIDDLES OF LIFE

15 In my vain life I have seen everything; there are righteous people
who perish in their righteousness, and
there are wicked people who prolong
their life in their evildoing. 16 Do not be
too righteous, and do not act too wise;
why should you destroy yourself? 17 Do
not be too wicked, and do not be a fool;
why should you die before your time?
18 It is good that you should take hold of
the one, without letting go of the other;
for the one who fears God shall succeed
with both.

19 Wisdom gives strength to the wise
more than ten rulers that are in a city.

20 Surely there is no one on earth
so righteous as to do good without ever
sinning.

21 Do not give heed to everything
that people say, or you may hear your
servant cursing you; 22 your heart knows
that many times you have yourself
cursed others.

23 All this I have tested by wisdom; I
said, 'I will be wise', but it was far from
me. 24 That which is, is far off, and deep,
very deep; who can find it out? 25 I turned
my mind to know and to search out and
to seek wisdom and the sum of things,
and to know that wickedness is folly and
that foolishness is madness. 26 I found
more bitter than death the woman who
is a trap, whose heart is snares and nets,
whose hands are fetters; one who pleases
God escapes her, but the sinner is taken
by her. 27 See, this is what I found, says the
Teacher,[x] adding one thing to another
to find the sum, 28 which my mind has
sought repeatedly, but I have not found.
One man among a thousand I found,
but a woman among all these I have not
found. 29 See, this alone I found, that God
made human beings straightforward, but
they have devised many schemes.

OBEY THE KING AND ENJOY YOURSELF

8 Who is like the wise man?
And who knows the
interpretation of a thing?
Wisdom makes one's face shine,
and the hardness of one's
countenance is changed.

2 Keep[y] the king's command because
of your sacred oath. 3 Do not be terrified;
go from his presence, do not delay when
the matter is unpleasant, for he does
whatever he pleases. 4 For the word of
the king is powerful, and who can say
to him, 'What are you doing?' 5 Whoever
obeys a command will meet no harm,
and the wise mind will know the time
and way. 6 For every matter has its time
and way, although the troubles of mortals lie heavy upon them. 7 Indeed, they
do not know what is to be, for who can
tell them how it will be? 8 No one has
power over the wind[z] to restrain the

[x] 7.27 *Qoheleth*, traditionally rendered *Preacher*
[y] 8.2 Heb *I keep* [z] 8.8 Or *breath*

wind,[a] or power over the day of death;
there is no discharge from the battle,
nor does wickedness deliver those who
practise it. 9 All this I observed, applying my mind to all that is done under
the sun, while one person exercises authority over another to the other's hurt.

GOD'S WAYS ARE INSCRUTABLE

10 Then I saw the wicked buried;
they used to go in and out of the holy
place, and were praised in the city
where they had done such things.[b]
This also is vanity. 11 Because sentence
against an evil deed is not executed
speedily, the human heart is fully set to
do evil. 12 Though sinners do evil a hundred times and prolong their lives, yet I
know that it will be well with those who
fear God, because they stand in fear before him, 13 but it will not be well with
the wicked, neither will they prolong
their days like a shadow, because they
do not stand in fear before God.

14 There is a vanity that takes place
on earth, that there are righteous people who are treated according to the
conduct of the wicked, and there are
wicked people who are treated according to the conduct of the righteous. I
said that this also is vanity. 15 So I commend enjoyment, for there is nothing
better for people under the sun than to
eat, and drink, and enjoy themselves,
for this will go with them in their toil
through the days of life that God gives
them under the sun.

16 When I applied my mind to know
wisdom, and to see the business that is
done on earth, how one's eyes see sleep
neither day nor night, 17 then I saw all
the work of God, that no one can find
out what is happening under the sun.
However much they may toil in seeking,
they will not find it out; even though
those who are wise claim to know, they
cannot find it out.

TAKE LIFE AS IT COMES

9 All this I laid to heart, examining it
all, how the righteous and the wise
and their deeds are in the hand of God;
whether it is love or hate one does not
know. Everything that confronts them
2 is vanity,[c] since the same fate comes
to all, to the righteous and the wicked,
to the good and the evil,[d] to the clean
and the unclean, to those who sacrifice
and those who do not sacrifice. As are
the good, so are the sinners; those who
swear are like those who shun an oath.
3 This is an evil in all that happens under
the sun, that the same fate comes to everyone. Moreover, the hearts of all are
full of evil; madness is in their hearts
while they live, and after that they go
to the dead. 4 But whoever is joined with
all the living has hope, for a living dog
is better than a dead lion. 5 The living
know that they will die, but the dead
know nothing; they have no more reward, and even the memory of them is
lost. 6 Their love and their hate and their
envy have already perished; never again
will they have any share in all that happens under the sun.

7 Go, eat your bread with enjoyment,
and drink your wine with a merry
heart; for God has long ago approved
what you do. 8 Let your garments always be white; do not let oil be lacking
on your head. 9 Enjoy life with the wife
whom you love, all the days of your vain
life that are given you under the sun,
because that is your portion in life and
in your toil at which you toil under the
sun. 10 Whatever your hand finds to do,
do with your might; for there is no work
or thought or knowledge or wisdom in
Sheol, to which you are going.

11 Again I saw that under the sun the
race is not to the swift, nor the battle to
the strong, nor bread to the wise, nor
riches to the intelligent, nor favour to the
skilful; but time and chance happen to
them all. 12 For no one can anticipate the
time of disaster. Like fish taken in a cruel
net, and like birds caught in a snare, so
mortals are snared at a time of calamity,
when it suddenly falls upon them.

WISDOM SUPERIOR TO FOLLY

13 I have also seen this example of
wisdom under the sun, and it seemed
important to me. 14 There was a little city
with few people in it. A great king came
against it and besieged it, building great
siege-works against it. 15 Now there was
found in it a poor, wise man, and he by
his wisdom delivered the city. Yet no
one remembered that poor man. 16 So I
said, 'Wisdom is better than might; yet
the poor man's wisdom is despised, and
his words are not heeded.'

17 The quiet words of the wise are
more to be heeded
than the shouting of a
ruler among fools.

[a] **8.8** Or *breath* [b] **8.10** Meaning of Heb uncertain [c] **9.2** Syr Compare Gk: Heb *Everything that confronts them* 2*is everything* [d] **9.2** Gk Syr Vg: Heb lacks *and the evil*

18 Wisdom is better than weapons
of war,
but one bungler destroys
much good.

MISCELLANEOUS OBSERVATIONS

10 Dead flies make the
perfumer's ointment
give off a foul odour;
so a little folly outweighs
wisdom and honour.
2 The heart of the wise inclines
to the right,
but the heart of a fool to the left.
3 Even when fools walk on the
road, they lack sense,
and show to everyone that
they are fools.
4 If the anger of the ruler rises against
you, do not leave your post,
for calmness will undo
great offences.

5 There is an evil that I have seen
under the sun, as great an error as if it
proceeded from the ruler: 6folly is set in
many high places, and the rich sit in a
low place. 7I have seen slaves on horseback, and princes walking on foot like
slaves.

8 Whoever digs a pit will fall into it;
and whoever breaks through a
wall will be bitten by a snake.
9 Whoever quarries stones will
be hurt by them;
and whoever splits logs will be
endangered by them.
10 If the iron is blunt, and one does
not whet the edge,
then more strength must
be exerted;
but wisdom helps one to succeed.
11 If the snake bites before it
is charmed,
there is no advantage
in a charmer.

12 Words spoken by the wise
bring them favour,
but the lips of fools
consume them.
13 The words of their mouths
begin in foolishness,
and their talk ends in
wicked madness;
14 yet fools talk on and on.
No one knows what is to happen,
and who can tell anyone what
the future holds?
15 The toil of fools wears them out,
for they do not even know
the way to town.

16 Alas for you, O land, when your
king is a servant,[e]
and your princes feast in
the morning!
17 Happy are you, O land, when your
king is a nobleman,
and your princes feast at
the proper time—
for strength, and not for
drunkenness!
18 Through sloth the roof sinks in,
and through indolence
the house leaks.
19 Feasts are made for laughter;
wine gladdens life,
and money meets every need.
20 Do not curse the king, even
in your thoughts,
or curse the rich, even in
your bedroom;
for a bird of the air may
carry your voice,
or some winged creature
tell the matter.

THE VALUE OF DILIGENCE

11 Send out your bread upon
the waters,
for after many days you
will get it back.
2 Divide your means seven
ways, or even eight,
for you do not know what disaster
may happen on earth.
3 When clouds are full,
they empty rain on the earth;
whether a tree falls to the south
or to the north,
in the place where the tree
falls, there it will lie.
4 Whoever observes the wind
will not sow;
and whoever regards the
clouds will not reap.

5 Just as you do not know how the
breath comes to the bones in the mother's womb, so you do not know the work
of God, who makes everything.

6 In the morning sow your seed, and
at evening do not let your hands be idle;
for you do not know which will prosper,
this or that, or whether both alike will
be good.

YOUTH AND OLD AGE

7 Light is sweet, and it is pleasant for
the eyes to see the sun.

8 Even those who live for many years
should rejoice in them all; yet let them

[e] **10.16** Or *a child*

remember that the days of darkness will
be many. All that comes is vanity.
9 Rejoice, young man, while you are
young, and let your heart cheer you in
the days of your youth. Follow the inclination of your heart and the desire
of your eyes, but know that for all these
things God will bring you into judgement.
10 Banish anxiety from your mind,
and put away pain from your body; for
youth and the dawn of life are vanity.

12 Remember your creator in the
days of your youth, before the
days of trouble come, and the years
draw near when you will say, 'I have no
pleasure in them'; 2before the sun and
the light and the moon and the stars are
darkened and the clouds return with[f]
the rain; 3on the day when the guards
of the house tremble, and the strong
men are bent, and the women who
grind cease working because they are
few, and those who look through the
windows see dimly; 4when the doors
on the street are shut, and the sound of
the grinding is low, and one rises up at
the sound of a bird, and all the daughters of song are brought low; 5when
one is afraid of heights, and terrors are
in the road; the almond tree blossoms,
the grasshopper drags itself along[g] and
desire fails; because all must go to their
eternal home, and the mourners will
go about the streets; 6before the silver
cord is snapped,[h] and the golden bowl
is broken, and the pitcher is broken at
the fountain, and the wheel broken at
the cistern, 7and the dust returns to the
earth as it was, and the breath[i] returns
to God who gave it. 8Vanity of vanities,
says the Teacher;[j] all is vanity.

EPILOGUE

9 Besides being wise, the Teacher[k]
also taught the people knowledge,
weighing and studying and arranging
many proverbs. 10The Teacher[l] sought
to find pleasing words, and he wrote
words of truth plainly.
11 The sayings of the wise are like
goads, and like nails firmly fixed are the
collected sayings that are given by one
shepherd.[m] 12Of anything beyond these,
my child, beware. Of making many
books there is no end, and much study
is a weariness of the flesh.
13 The end of the matter; all has been
heard. Fear God, and keep his commandments; for that is the whole duty
of everyone. 14For God will bring every
deed into judgement, including[n] every
secret thing, whether good or evil.

[f] **12.2** Or *after*; Heb *'ahar* [g] **12.5** Or *is a burden*
[h] **12.6** Syr Vg Compare Gk: Heb *is removed*
[i] **12.7** Or *the spirit* [j] **12.8** *Qoheleth*, traditionally rendered *Preacher*
[k] **12.9** *Qoheleth*, traditionally rendered *Preacher*
[l] **12.10** *Qoheleth*, traditionally rendered *Preacher* [m] **12.11** Meaning of Heb uncertain
[n] **12.14** Or *into the judgement on*

The
SONG OF SOLOMON

The Song of Solomon was composed by an unknown author sometime after the end of the Babylonian exile and maybe as late as the third or second century BCE. It is a collection of poems presented as a dialogue between two lovers. The poems are about the erotic love of a bridal couple, but they are also understood allegorically as a depiction of God's love for the people of Israel. In the Christian tradition, the Song of Solomon is interpreted as an allegory about the relationship between Christ and the church.

A selection from the Song of Solomon is offered as a choice for the First Reading during the liturgy every year on December 21 before Christmas. A passage from the Song of Solomon also is read at the Memorial Feast of Mary Magdalene on July 22. Finally, other passages are offered as choices for Readings at the Mass of the Common of Virgins, at the Celebration of Marriage, and at the Consecration of Virgins and Religious Profession.

1 The Song of Songs, which is Solomon's.

COLLOQUY OF BRIDE AND FRIENDS

2 Let him kiss me with the
kisses of his mouth!
For your love is better than wine,
3 your anointing oils are fragrant,
your name is perfume poured out;
therefore the maidens love you.
4 Draw me after you, let us
make haste.
The king has brought me
into his chambers.
We will exult and rejoice in you;
we will extol your love
more than wine;
rightly do they love you.

5 I am black and beautiful,
O daughters of Jerusalem,
like the tents of Kedar,
like the curtains of Solomon.
6 Do not gaze at me because
I am dark,
because the sun has gazed on me.
My mother's sons were
angry with me;
they made me keeper of
the vineyards,
but my own vineyard I
have not kept!
7 Tell me, you whom my soul loves,
where you pasture your flock,
where you make it lie
down at noon;
for why should I be like one
who is veiled
beside the flocks of your
companions?

8 If you do not know,
O fairest among women,
follow the tracks of the flock,
and pasture your kids
beside the shepherds' tents.

COLLOQUY OF BRIDEGROOM, FRIENDS, AND BRIDE

9 I compare you, my love,
to a mare among Pharaoh's
chariots.
10 Your cheeks are comely with
ornaments,
your neck with strings
of jewels.
11 We will make you ornaments of gold,
studded with silver.

12 While the king was on his couch,
my nard gave forth
its fragrance.
13 My beloved is to me a bag of myrrh
that lies between my breasts.

14 My beloved is to me a cluster
of henna blossoms
in the vineyards of En-gedi.

15 Ah, you are beautiful, my love;
ah, you are beautiful;
your eyes are doves.
16 Ah, you are beautiful, my beloved,
truly lovely.
Our couch is green;
17 the beams of our house are cedar,
our rafters[a] are pine.

2 I am a rose[b] of Sharon,
a lily of the valleys.

2 As a lily among brambles,
so is my love among maidens.

3 As an apple tree among the
trees of the wood,
so is my beloved among
young men.
With great delight I sat in
his shadow,
and his fruit was sweet to my taste.
4 He brought me to the
banqueting house,
and his intention towards
me was love.
5 Sustain me with raisins,
refresh me with apples;
for I am faint with love.
6 O that his left hand were
under my head,
and that his right hand
embraced me!
7 I adjure you, O daughters
of Jerusalem,
by the gazelles or the wild does:
do not stir up or awaken love
until it is ready!

SPRINGTIME RHAPSODY

8 The voice of my beloved!
Look, he comes,
leaping upon the mountains,
bounding over the hills.
9 My beloved is like a gazelle
or a young stag.
Look, there he stands
behind our wall,
gazing in at the windows,
looking through the lattice.
10 My beloved speaks and says to me:
'Arise, my love, my fair one,
and come away;
11 for now the winter is past,
the rain is over and gone.
12 The flowers appear on the earth;
the time of singing has come,
and the voice of the turtle-dove
is heard in our land.
13 The fig tree puts forth its figs,
and the vines are in blossom;
they give forth fragrance.
Arise, my love, my fair one,
and come away.
14 O my dove, in the clefts of the rock,
in the covert of the cliff,
let me see your face,
let me hear your voice;
for your voice is sweet,
and your face is lovely.
15 Catch us the foxes,
the little foxes,
that ruin the vineyards—
for our vineyards are in blossom.'

16 My beloved is mine and I am his;
he pastures his flock
among the lilies.
17 Until the day breathes
and the shadows flee,
turn, my beloved, be like a gazelle
or a young stag on the
cleft mountains.[c]

A DREAM OF LOVE

3 Upon my bed at night
I sought him whom
my soul loves;
I sought him, but found him not;
I called him, but he gave
no answer.[d]
2 'I will rise now and go
about the city,
in the streets and in the squares;
I will seek him whom my soul loves.'
I sought him, but found him not.
3 The sentinels found me,
as they went about in the city.
'Have you seen him whom
my soul loves?'
4 Scarcely had I passed them,
when I found him whom
my soul loves.
I held him, and would not let him go
until I brought him into my
mother's house,
and into the chamber of her
that conceived me.
5 I adjure you, O daughters
of Jerusalem,
by the gazelles or the wild does:
do not stir up or awaken love
until it is ready!

[a] 1.17 Meaning of Heb uncertain [b] 2.1 Heb *crocus* [c] 2.17 Or *on the mountains of Bether*; meaning of Heb uncertain [d] 3.1 Gk: Heb lacks this line

THE GROOM AND HIS PARTY APPROACH

6 What is that coming up from
the wilderness,
like a column of smoke,
perfumed with myrrh and
frankincense,
with all the fragrant powders
of the merchant?
7 Look, it is the litter of Solomon!
Around it are sixty mighty men
of the mighty men of Israel,
8 all equipped with swords
and expert in war,
each with his sword at his thigh
because of alarms by night.
9 King Solomon made himself
a palanquin
from the wood of Lebanon.
10 He made its posts of silver,
its back of gold, its seat of purple;
its interior was inlaid with love.[e]
Daughters of Jerusalem,
11 come out.
Look, O daughters of Zion,
at King Solomon,
at the crown with which his
mother crowned him
on the day of his wedding,
on the day of the gladness
of his heart.

THE BRIDE'S BEAUTY EXTOLLED

4 How beautiful you are, my love,
how very beautiful!
Your eyes are doves
behind your veil.
Your hair is like a flock of goats,
moving down the slopes of Gilead.
2 Your teeth are like a flock
of shorn ewes
that have come up from
the washing,
all of which bear twins,
and not one among them
is bereaved.
3 Your lips are like a crimson thread,
and your mouth is lovely.
Your cheeks are like halves
of a pomegranate
behind your veil.
4 Your neck is like the
tower of David,
built in courses;
on it hang a thousand bucklers,
all of them shields of warriors.
5 Your two breasts are like two fawns,
twins of a gazelle,
that feed among the lilies.
6 Until the day breathes
and the shadows flee,
I will hasten to the mountain
of myrrh
and the hill of frankincense.
7 You are altogether beautiful,
my love;
there is no flaw in you.
8 Come with me from Lebanon,
my bride;
come with me from Lebanon.
Depart[f] from the peak of Amana,
from the peak of Senir
and Hermon,
from the dens of lions,
from the mountains of leopards.

9 You have ravished my heart,
my sister, my bride,
you have ravished my heart with
a glance of your eyes,
with one jewel of your necklace.
10 How sweet is your love, my
sister, my bride!
how much better is your
love than wine,
and the fragrance of your
oils than any spice!
11 Your lips distil nectar, my bride;
honey and milk are under
your tongue;
the scent of your garments is
like the scent of Lebanon.
12 A garden locked is my sister,
my bride,
a garden locked, a
fountain sealed.
13 Your channel[g] is an orchard
of pomegranates
with all choicest fruits,
henna with nard,
14 nard and saffron, calamus
and cinnamon,
with all trees of frankincense,
myrrh and aloes,
with all chief spices—
15 a garden fountain, a well
of living water,
and flowing streams
from Lebanon.

16 Awake, O north wind,
and come, O south wind!
Blow upon my garden
that its fragrance may be
wafted abroad.
Let my beloved come to his garden,
and eat its choicest fruits.

[e] 3.10 Meaning of Heb uncertain [f] 4.8 Or *Look*
[g] 4.13 Meaning of Heb uncertain

5 I come to my garden, my
sister, my bride;
I gather my myrrh with my spice,
I eat my honeycomb
with my honey,
I drink my wine with my milk.

Eat, friends, drink,
and be drunk with love.

ANOTHER DREAM

2 I slept, but my heart was awake.
Listen! my beloved is knocking.
'Open to me, my sister, my love,
my dove, my perfect one;
for my head is wet with dew,
my locks with the drops
of the night.'
3 I had put off my garment;
how could I put it on again?
I had bathed my feet;
how could I soil them?
4 My beloved thrust his hand
into the opening,
and my inmost being
yearned for him.
5 I arose to open to my beloved,
and my hands dripped
with myrrh,
my fingers with liquid myrrh,
upon the handles of the bolt.
6 I opened to my beloved,
but my beloved had turned
and was gone.
My soul failed me when he spoke.
I sought him, but did
not find him;
I called him, but he gave
no answer.
7 Making their rounds in the city
the sentinels found me;
they beat me, they wounded me,
they took away my mantle,
those sentinels of the walls.
8 I adjure you, O daughters
of Jerusalem,
if you find my beloved,
tell him this:
I am faint with love.

COLLOQUY OF FRIENDS AND BRIDE

9 What is your beloved more than
another beloved,
O fairest among women?
What is your beloved more than
another beloved,
that you thus adjure us?

10 My beloved is all radiant and ruddy,
distinguished among
ten thousand.
11 His head is the finest gold;
his locks are wavy,
black as a raven.
12 His eyes are like doves
beside springs of water,
bathed in milk,
fitly set.[h]
13 His cheeks are like beds of spices,
yielding fragrance.
His lips are lilies,
distilling liquid myrrh.
14 His arms are rounded gold,
set with jewels.
His body is ivory work,[i]
encrusted with sapphires.[j]
15 His legs are alabaster columns,
set upon bases of gold.
His appearance is like Lebanon,
choice as the cedars.
16 His speech is most sweet,
and he is altogether desirable.
This is my beloved and this
is my friend,
O daughters of Jerusalem.

6 Where has your beloved gone,
O fairest among women?
Which way has your beloved turned,
that we may seek him with you?

2 My beloved has gone down
to his garden,
to the beds of spices,
to pasture his flock in the gardens,
and to gather lilies.
3 I am my beloved's and my
beloved is mine;
he pastures his flock
among the lilies.

THE BRIDE'S MATCHLESS BEAUTY

4 You are beautiful as Tirzah, my love,
comely as Jerusalem,
terrible as an army with banners.
5 Turn away your eyes from me,
for they overwhelm me!
Your hair is like a flock of goats,
moving down the slopes of Gilead.
6 Your teeth are like a flock of ewes,
that have come up from
the washing;
all of them bear twins,
and not one among them
is bereaved.
7 Your cheeks are like halves
of a pomegranate
behind your veil.

[h] 5.12 Meaning of Heb uncertain
[i] 5.14 Meaning of Heb uncertain [j] 5.14 Heb *lapis lazuli*

8 There are sixty queens and
eighty concubines,
and maidens without number.
9 My dove, my perfect one, is
the only one,
the darling of her mother,
flawless to her that bore her.
The maidens saw her and
called her happy;
the queens and concubines also,
and they praised her.
10 'Who is this that looks forth
like the dawn,
fair as the moon, bright
as the sun,
terrible as an army with banners?'

11 I went down to the nut orchard,
to look at the blossoms
of the valley,
to see whether the vines had budded,
whether the pomegranates
were in bloom.
12 Before I was aware, my fancy set me
in a chariot beside my prince.[k]

13 [l]Return, return, O Shulammite!
Return, return, that we
may look upon you.

Why should you look upon
the Shulammite,
as upon a dance before
two armies?[m]

EXPRESSIONS OF PRAISE

7 How graceful are your
feet in sandals,
O queenly maiden!
Your rounded thighs are like jewels,
the work of a master hand.
2 Your navel is a rounded bowl
that never lacks mixed wine.
Your belly is a heap of wheat,
encircled with lilies.
3 Your two breasts are like two fawns,
twins of a gazelle.
4 Your neck is like an ivory tower.
Your eyes are pools in Heshbon,
by the gate of Bath-rabbim.
Your nose is like a
tower of Lebanon,
overlooking Damascus.
5 Your head crowns you like Carmel,
and your flowing locks
are like purple;
a king is held captive in
the tresses.[n]

6 How fair and pleasant you are,
O loved one, delectable maiden![o]
7 You are stately[p] as a palm tree,
and your breasts are like
its clusters.
8 I say I will climb the palm tree
and lay hold of its branches.
O may your breasts be like
clusters of the vine,
and the scent of your
breath like apples,
9 and your kisses[q] like the best wine
that goes down[r] smoothly,
gliding over lips and teeth.[s]

10 I am my beloved's,
and his desire is for me.
11 Come, my beloved,
let us go forth into the fields,
and lodge in the villages;
12 let us go out early to the vineyards,
and see whether the vines
have budded,
whether the grape blossoms
have opened
and the pomegranates
are in bloom.
There I will give you my love.
13 The mandrakes give forth fragrance,
and over our doors are
all choice fruits,
new as well as old,
which I have laid up for
you, O my beloved.

8 O that you were like a
brother to me,
who nursed at my
mother's breast!
If I met you outside, I
would kiss you,
and no one would despise me.
2 I would lead you and bring you
into the house of my mother,
and into the chamber of the
one who bore me.[t]
I would give you spiced
wine to drink,
the juice of my pomegranates.
3 O that his left hand were
under my head,
and that his right hand
embraced me!
4 I adjure you, O daughters
of Jerusalem,
do not stir up or awaken love
until it is ready!

[k] 6.12 Cn: Meaning of Heb uncertain [l] 6.13 Ch 7.1 in Heb [m] 6.13 Or *dance of Mahanaim* [n] 7.5 Meaning of Heb uncertain [o] 7.6 Syr: Heb *in delights* [p] 7.7 Heb *This your stature is* [q] 7.9 Heb *palate* [r] 7.9 Heb *down for my lover* [s] 7.9 Gk Syr Vg: Heb *lips of sleepers* [t] 8.2 Gk Syr: Heb *my mother; she (or you) will teach me*

HOMECOMING

5 Who is that coming up from
the wilderness,
leaning upon her beloved?

Under the apple tree I awakened you.
There your mother was in
labour with you;
there she who bore you
was in labour.

6 Set me as a seal upon your heart,
as a seal upon your arm;
for love is strong as death,
passion fierce as the grave.
Its flashes are flashes of fire,
a raging flame.
7 Many waters cannot quench love,
neither can floods drown it.
If one offered for love
all the wealth of one's house,
it would be utterly scorned.

8 We have a little sister,
and she has no breasts.
What shall we do for our sister,
on the day when she is
spoken for?
9 If she is a wall,
we will build upon her a
battlement of silver;
but if she is a door,
we will enclose her with
boards of cedar.
10 I was a wall,
and my breasts were like towers;
then I was in his eyes
as one who brings[u] peace.
11 Solomon had a vineyard at
Baal-hamon;
he entrusted the vineyard
to keepers;
each one was to bring for its fruit
a thousand pieces of silver.
12 My vineyard, my very own,
is for myself;
you, O Solomon, may have
the thousand,
and the keepers of the fruit
two hundred!

13 O you who dwell in the gardens,
my companions are listening
for your voice;
let me hear it.

14 Make haste, my beloved,
and be like a gazelle
or a young stag
upon the mountains of spices!

[u] **8.10** Or *finds*

THE WISDOM OF SOLOMON

The Wisdom of Solomon was not written by Solomon himself, but by a learned Alexandrine author sometime within the second to first century BCE. The purpose of the text seems to be a sympathetic defense of the traditional Jewish faith. Wisdom is personified and emanates from God's power and glory (7.25–26, 29–30). Various themes are addressed in the book including the immortality of the soul and the danger of idolatry. The Christian tradition sees the focus on the "word" (9.1) and the Holy Spirit (1.5–7; 7.22–23; 9.17) as a prefiguring of the revelation of the Trinity in the New Testament.

Wisdom is read at various times throughout the liturgical calendar. Passages are read during Cycle A on the Sixteenth and Thirty-Second Sunday of the Year; they are read during Cycle B on the Thirteenth, Twenty-Fifth, and Twenty-Eighth Sundays of the Year. Also, passages from Wisdom are read at Mass on weekdays of Year I on Monday through Saturday of the Thirty-Second Week in Ordinary Time. The text about the suffering of the righteous man is read every year on Friday of the Fourth Week of Lent. This text, like the Servant Song in Isaiah (52.13—53.12), was interpreted by early church fathers as a prediction of Jesus' crucifixion.

EXHORTATION TO UPRIGHTNESS

1 Love righteousness, you
rulers of the earth,
think of the Lord in goodness
and seek him with
sincerity of heart;
2 because he is found by those who
do not put him to the test,
and manifests himself to those
who do not distrust him.
3 For perverse thoughts separate
people from God,
and when his power is tested, it
exposes the foolish;
4 because wisdom will not enter
a deceitful soul,
or dwell in a body enslaved to sin.
5 For a holy and disciplined spirit
will flee from deceit,
and will leave foolish
thoughts behind,
and will be ashamed at the approach
of unrighteousness.
6 For wisdom is a kindly spirit,
but will not free blasphemers from
the guilt of their words;
because God is witness of their
inmost feelings,
and a true observer of their hearts,
and a hearer of their tongues.
7 Because the spirit of the Lord
has filled the world,
and that which holds all things
together knows what is said,
8 therefore those who utter
unrighteous things will
not escape notice,
and justice, when it punishes,
will not pass them by.
9 For inquiry will be made into the
counsels of the ungodly,
and a report of their words will
come to the Lord,
to convict them of their
lawless deeds;
10 because a jealous ear hears all things,

and the sound of grumbling
does not go unheard.
11 Beware then of useless grumbling,
and keep your tongue from slander;
because no secret word is
without result,[a]
and a lying mouth destroys the soul.

12 Do not invite death by the
error of your life,
or bring on destruction by the
works of your hands;
13 because God did not make death,
and he does not delight in the
death of the living.
14 For he created all things so that
they might exist;
the generative forces[b] of the
world are wholesome,
and there is no destructive
poison in them,
and the dominion[c] of Hades
is not on earth.
15 For righteousness is immortal.

LIFE AS THE UNGODLY SEE IT

16 But the ungodly by their words and
deeds summoned death;[d]
considering him a friend,
they pined away
and made a covenant with him,
because they are fit to belong
to his company.

2 For they reasoned unsoundly,
saying to themselves,
'Short and sorrowful is our life,
and there is no remedy when a
life comes to its end,
and no one has been known to
return from Hades.
2 For we were born by mere chance,
and hereafter we shall be as though
we had never been,
for the breath in our nostrils
is smoke,
and reason is a spark kindled by
the beating of our hearts;
3 when it is extinguished, the body
will turn to ashes,
and the spirit will dissolve
like empty air.
4 Our name will be forgotten in time,
and no one will remember
our works;
our life will pass away like the
traces of a cloud,
and be scattered like mist
that is chased by the rays of the sun
and overcome by its heat.
5 For our allotted time is the
passing of a shadow,
and there is no return from
our death,
because it is sealed up and no
one turns back.

6 'Come, therefore, let us enjoy the
good things that exist,
and make use of the creation to
the full as in youth.
7 Let us take our fill of costly
wine and perfumes,
and let no flower of spring
pass us by.
8 Let us crown ourselves with
rosebuds before they wither.
9 Let none of us fail to share
in our revelry;
everywhere let us leave signs
of enjoyment,
because this is our portion,
and this our lot.
10 Let us oppress the righteous
poor man;
let us not spare the widow
or regard the grey hairs of the aged.
11 But let our might be our law of right,
for what is weak proves itself
to be useless.

12 'Let us lie in wait for the
righteous man,
because he is inconvenient to us
and opposes our actions;
he reproaches us for sins
against the law,
and accuses us of sins against
our training.
13 He professes to have
knowledge of God,
and calls himself a child[e] of the Lord.
14 He became to us a reproof
of our thoughts;
15 the very sight of him is a
burden to us,
because his manner of life is
unlike that of others,
and his ways are strange.
16 We are considered by him as
something base,
and he avoids our ways as unclean;
he calls the last end of the
righteous happy,
and boasts that God is his father.
17 Let us see if his words are true,
and let us test what will happen
at the end of his life;
18 for if the righteous man is God's
child, he will help him,

[a] 1.11 Or *will go unpunished* [b] 1.14 Or *the creatures* [c] 1.14 Or *palace* [d] 1.16 Gk *him* [e] 2.13 Or *servant*

and will deliver him from the
hand of his adversaries.
19 Let us test him with insult
and torture,
so that we may find out how
gentle he is,
and make trial of his forbearance.
20 Let us condemn him to a
shameful death,
for, according to what he says,
he will be protected.'

ERROR OF THE WICKED

21 Thus they reasoned, but they
were led astray,
for their wickedness blinded them,
22 and they did not know the secret
purposes of God,
nor hoped for the wages
of holiness,
nor discerned the prize for
blameless souls;
23 for God created us for incorruption,
and made us in the image of
his own eternity,[f]
24 but through the devil's envy death
entered the world,
and those who belong to his
company experience it.

THE DESTINY OF THE RIGHTEOUS

3 But the souls of the righteous
are in the hand of God,
and no torment will ever
touch them.
2 In the eyes of the foolish they
seemed to have died,
and their departure was thought
to be a disaster,
3 and their going from us to be
their destruction;
but they are at peace.
4 For though in the sight of others
they were punished,
their hope is full of immortality.
5 Having been disciplined a little, they
will receive great good,
because God tested them and found
them worthy of himself;
6 like gold in the furnace he
tried them,
and like a sacrificial burnt-offering
he accepted them.
7 In the time of their visitation
they will shine forth,
and will run like sparks
through the stubble.
8 They will govern nations and
rule over peoples,
and the Lord will reign over
them for ever.
9 Those who trust in him will
understand truth,
and the faithful will abide
with him in love,
because grace and mercy are
upon his holy ones,
and he watches over his elect.[g]

THE DESTINY OF THE UNGODLY

10 But the ungodly will be punished as
their reasoning deserves,
those who disregarded the
righteous[h]
and rebelled against the Lord;
11 for those who despise wisdom and
instruction are miserable.
Their hope is vain, their labours
are unprofitable,
and their works are useless.
12 Their wives are foolish, and
their children evil;
13 their offspring are accursed.

ON CHILDLESSNESS

For blessed is the barren woman
who is undefiled,
who has not entered into
a sinful union;
she will have fruit when God
examines souls.
14 Blessed also is the eunuch
whose hands have done
no lawless deed,
and who has not devised wicked
things against the Lord;
for special favour will be shown
him for his faithfulness,
and a place of great delight in
the temple of the Lord.
15 For the fruit of good labours
is renowned,
and the root of understanding
does not fail.
16 But children of adulterers will
not come to maturity,
and the offspring of an unlawful
union will perish.
17 Even if they live long they will
be held of no account,
and finally their old age will
be without honour.
18 If they die young, they will
have no hope
and no consolation on the
day of judgement.
19 For the end of an unrighteous
generation is grievous.

[f] **2.23** Other ancient authorities read *nature*
[g] **3.9** Text of this line uncertain; omitted by some ancient authorities. Compare 4.15 [h] **3.10** Or *what is right*

4 Better than this is childlessness
with virtue,
for in the memory of virtue[i]
is immortality,
because it is known both by
God and by mortals.
2 When it is present, people imitate[j] it,
and they long for it when it has gone;
throughout all time it marches,
crowned in triumph,
victor in the contest for prizes
that are undefiled.
3 But the prolific brood of the
ungodly will be of no use,
and none of their illegitimate
seedlings will strike
a deep root
or take a firm hold.
4 For even if they put forth
boughs for a while,
standing insecurely they will be
shaken by the wind,
and by the violence of the winds
they will be uprooted.
5 The branches will be broken
off before they come
to maturity,
and their fruit will be useless,
not ripe enough to eat, and
good for nothing.
6 For children born of unlawful unions
are witnesses of evil against
their parents when God
examines them.[k]
7 But the righteous, though they
die early, will be at rest.
8 For old age is not honoured
for length of time,
or measured by number of years;
9 but understanding is grey
hair for anyone,
and a blameless life is ripe old age.

10 There were some who pleased God
and were loved by him,
and while living among sinners
were taken up.
11 They were caught up so that
evil might not change
their understanding
or guile deceive their souls.
12 For the fascination of wickedness
obscures what is good,
and roving desire perverts the
innocent mind.
13 Being perfected in a short time,
they fulfilled long years;
14 for their souls were pleasing
to the Lord,
therefore he took them quickly from
the midst of wickedness.
15 Yet the peoples saw and did
not understand,
or take such a thing to heart,
that God's grace and mercy
are with his elect,
and that he watches over
his holy ones.

THE TRIUMPH OF THE RIGHTEOUS

16 The righteous who have died will
condemn the ungodly
who are living,
and youth that is quickly perfected[l]
will condemn the prolonged
old age of the unrighteous.
17 For they will see the end of the wise,
and will not understand what the
Lord purposed for them,
and for what he kept them safe.
18 The unrighteous[m] will see, and will
have contempt for them,
but the Lord will laugh
them to scorn.
After this they will become
dishonoured corpses,
and an outrage among the
dead for ever;
19 because he will dash them
speechless to the ground,
and shake them from the
foundations;
they will be left utterly dry
and barren,
and they will suffer anguish,
and the memory of them will perish.

THE FINAL JUDGEMENT

20 They will come with dread when
their sins are reckoned up,
and their lawless deeds will convict
them to their face.

5 Then the righteous will stand
with great confidence
in the presence of those who
have oppressed them
and those who make light
of their labours.
2 When the unrighteous[n] see
them, they will be shaken
with dreadful fear,
and they will be amazed at the
unexpected salvation
of the righteous.
3 They will speak to one another
in repentance,
and in anguish of spirit they
will groan, and say,

[i] 4.1 Gk *it* [j] 4.2 Other ancient authorities read *honour* [k] 4.6 Gk *at their examination* [l] 4.16 Or *ended* [m] 4.18 Gk *They* [n] 5.2 Gk *they*

4 'These are persons whom we
once held in derision
and made a byword of reproach—
fools that we were!
We thought that their lives
were madness
and that their end was
without honour.
5 Why have they been numbered
among the children of God?
And why is their lot among
the saints?
6 So it was we who strayed from
the way of truth,
and the light of righteousness
did not shine on us,
and the sun did not rise upon us.
7 We took our fill of the paths of
lawlessness and destruction,
and we journeyed through
trackless deserts,
but the way of the Lord we
have not known.
8 What has our arrogance profited us?
And what good has our boasted
wealth brought us?

9 'All those things have vanished
like a shadow,
and like a rumour that passes by;
10 like a ship that sails through
the billowy water,
and when it has passed no
trace can be found,
no track of its keel in the waves;
11 or as, when a bird flies
through the air,
no evidence of its passage is found;
the light air, lashed by the
beat of its pinions
and pierced by the force of
its rushing flight,
is traversed by the movement
of its wings,
and afterwards no sign of its
coming is found there;
12 or as, when an arrow is
shot at a target,
the air, thus divided, comes
together at once,
so that no one knows its pathway.
13 So we also, as soon as we were
born, ceased to be,
and we had no sign of virtue to show,
but were consumed in our
wickedness.'
14 Because the hope of the ungodly
is like thistledown[o]
carried by the wind,
and like a light frost[p] driven
away by a storm;
it is dispersed like smoke
before the wind,
and it passes like the
remembrance of a guest
who stays but a day.

THE REWARD OF THE RIGHTEOUS

15 But the righteous live for ever,
and their reward is with the Lord;
the Most High takes care of them.
16 Therefore they will receive a
glorious crown
and a beautiful diadem from
the hand of the Lord,
because with his right hand
he will cover them,
and with his arm he will
shield them.
17 The Lord[q] will take his zeal as
his whole armour,
and will arm all creation to
repel[r] his enemies;
18 he will put on righteousness
as a breastplate,
and wear impartial justice
as a helmet;
19 he will take holiness as an
invincible shield,
20 and sharpen stern wrath for a sword,
and creation will join with
him to fight against
his frenzied foes.
21 Shafts of lightning will fly
with true aim,
and will leap from the clouds
to the target, as from
a well-drawn bow,
22 and hailstones full of wrath will be
hurled as from a catapult;
the water of the sea will rage
against them,
and rivers will relentlessly
overwhelm them;
23 a mighty wind will rise
against them,
and like a tempest it will
winnow them away.
Lawlessness will lay waste
the whole earth,
and evildoing will overturn the
thrones of rulers.

KINGS SHOULD SEEK WISDOM

6 Listen therefore, O kings,
and understand;
learn, O judges of the ends
of the earth.

[o] 5.14 Other ancient authorities read *dust*
[p] 5.14 Other ancient authorities read *spider's web*
[q] 5.17 Gk *He* [r] 5.17 Or *punish*

2 Give ear, you that rule over
multitudes,
and boast of many nations.
3 For your dominion was given
you from the Lord,
and your sovereignty from
the Most High;
he will search out your works and
inquire into your plans.
4 Because as servants of his kingdom
you did not rule rightly,
or keep the law,
or walk according to the
purpose of God,
5 he will come upon you terribly
and swiftly,
because severe judgement falls
on those in high places.
6 For the lowliest may be
pardoned in mercy,
but the mighty will be
mightily tested.
7 For the Lord of all will not stand
in awe of anyone,
or show deference to greatness;
because he himself made both
small and great,
and he takes thought
for all alike.
8 But a strict inquiry is in store
for the mighty.
9 To you then, O monarchs, my
words are directed,
so that you may learn wisdom
and not transgress.
10 For they will be made holy
who observe holy
things in holiness,
and those who have been taught
them will find a defence.
11 Therefore set your desire
on my words;
long for them, and you will
be instructed.

DESCRIPTION OF WISDOM

12 Wisdom is radiant and unfading,
and she is easily discerned by
those who love her,
and is found by those who seek her.
13 She hastens to make herself known
to those who desire her.
14 One who rises early to seek her
will have no difficulty,
for she will be found sitting
at the gate.
15 To fix one's thought on her is
perfect understanding,
and one who is vigilant on
her account will soon
be free from care,
16 because she goes about seeking
those worthy of her,
and she graciously appears to
them in their paths,
and meets them in every thought.

17 The beginning of wisdom[s] is
the most sincere desire
for instruction,
and concern for instruction
is love of her,
18 and love of her is the keeping
of her laws,
and giving heed to her laws is
assurance of immortality,
19 and immortality brings one
near to God;
20 so the desire for wisdom leads
to a kingdom.

21 Therefore if you delight in thrones
and sceptres, O monarchs
over the peoples,
honour wisdom, so that you
may reign for ever.
22 I will tell you what wisdom is and
how she came to be,
and I will hide no secrets from you,
but I will trace her course from the
beginning of creation,
and make knowledge of her clear,
and I will not pass by the truth;
23 nor will I travel in the company
of sickly envy,
for envy[t] does not associate
with wisdom.
24 The multitude of the wise is the
salvation of the world,
and a sensible king is the
stability of any people.
25 Therefore be instructed by my
words, and you will profit.

SOLOMON LIKE OTHER MORTALS

7 I also am mortal, like
everyone else,
a descendant of the first-formed
child of earth;
and in the womb of a mother I
was moulded into flesh,
2 within the period of ten months,
compacted with blood,
from the seed of a man and the
pleasure of marriage.
3 And when I was born, I began to
breathe the common air,
and fell upon the kindred earth;
my first sound was a cry,
as is true of all.

[s] 6.17 Gk *Her beginning* [t] 6.23 Gk *this*

4 I was nursed with care in
swaddling cloths.
5 For no king has had a different
beginning of existence;
6 there is for all one entrance into
life, and one way out.

SOLOMON'S RESPECT FOR WISDOM

7 Therefore I prayed, and
understanding
was given me;
I called on God, and the spirit of
wisdom came to me.
8 I preferred her to sceptres
and thrones,
and I accounted wealth as nothing
in comparison with her.
9 Neither did I liken to her any
priceless gem,
because all gold is but a little
sand in her sight,
and silver will be accounted
as clay before her.
10 I loved her more than health
and beauty,
and I chose to have her
rather than light,
because her radiance never ceases.
11 All good things came to me
along with her,
and in her hands uncounted wealth.
12 I rejoiced in them all, because
wisdom leads them;
but I did not know that she
was their mother.
13 I learned without guile and I
impart without grudging;
I do not hide her wealth,
14 for it is an unfailing treasure
for mortals;
those who get it obtain
friendship with God,
commended for the gifts that
come from instruction.

SOLOMON PRAYS FOR WISDOM

15 May God grant me to speak
with judgement,
and to have thoughts worthy of
what I have received;
for he is the guide even of wisdom
and the corrector of the wise.
16 For both we and our words
are in his hand,
as are all understanding and
skill in crafts.
17 For it is he who gave me unerring
knowledge of what exists,
to know the structure of the
world and the activity
of the elements;
18 the beginning and end and
middle of times,
the alternations of the solstices and
the changes of the seasons,
19 the cycles of the year and the
constellations of the stars,
20 the natures of animals and the
tempers of wild animals,
the powers of spirits[u] and the
thoughts of human beings,
the varieties of plants and the
virtues of roots;
21 I learned both what is secret
and what is manifest,
22 for wisdom, the fashioner of all
things, taught me.

THE NATURE OF WISDOM

There is in her a spirit that is
intelligent, holy,
unique, manifold, subtle,
mobile, clear, unpolluted,
distinct, invulnerable, loving
the good, keen,
irresistible, 23 beneficent, humane,
steadfast, sure, free from anxiety,
all-powerful, overseeing all,
and penetrating through all spirits
that are intelligent, pure, and
altogether subtle.
24 For wisdom is more mobile
than any motion;
because of her pureness she pervades
and penetrates all things.
25 For she is a breath of the
power of God,
and a pure emanation of the
glory of the Almighty;
therefore nothing defiled gains
entrance into her.
26 For she is a reflection of
eternal light,
a spotless mirror of the
working of God,
and an image of his goodness.
27 Although she is but one, she
can do all things,
and while remaining in herself,
she renews all things;
in every generation she passes
into holy souls
and makes them friends of
God, and prophets;
28 for God loves nothing so much
as the person who
lives with wisdom.
29 She is more beautiful than the sun,
and excels every constellation
of the stars.

u 7.20 Or *winds*

Compared with the light she is
found to be superior,
30 for it is succeeded by the night,
but against wisdom evil
does not prevail.

8 She reaches mightily from one end
of the earth to the other,
and she orders all things well.

SOLOMON'S LOVE FOR WISDOM

2 I loved her and sought her
from my youth;
I desired to take her for my bride,
and became enamoured
of her beauty.
3 She glorifies her noble birth
by living with God,
and the Lord of all loves her.
4 For she is an initiate in the
knowledge of God,
and an associate in his works.
5 If riches are a desirable
possession in life,
what is richer than wisdom, the
active cause of all things?
6 And if understanding is effective,
who more than she is fashioner
of what exists?
7 And if anyone loves righteousness,
her labours are virtues;
for she teaches self-control
and prudence,
justice and courage;
nothing in life is more profitable
for mortals than these.
8 And if anyone longs for
wide experience,
she knows the things of old, and
infers the things to come;
she understands turns of speech and
the solutions of riddles;
she has foreknowledge of
signs and wonders
and of the outcome of seasons
and times.

WISDOM INDISPENSABLE TO RULERS

9 Therefore I determined to take
her to live with me,
knowing that she would give
me good counsel
and encouragement in
cares and grief.
10 Because of her I shall have glory
among the multitudes
and honour in the presence of the
elders, though I am young.
11 I shall be found keen in judgement,
and in the sight of rulers I
shall be admired.
12 When I am silent they will
wait for me,
and when I speak they
will give heed;
if I speak at greater length,
they will put their hands on
their mouths.
13 Because of her I shall have
immortality,
and leave an everlasting
remembrance to those
who come after me.
14 I shall govern peoples,
and nations will be subject to me;
15 dread monarchs will be afraid of
me when they hear of me;
among the people I shall show
myself capable, and
courageous in war.
16 When I enter my house, I shall
find rest with her;
for companionship with her
has no bitterness,
and life with her has no pain,
but gladness and joy.
17 When I considered these
things inwardly,
and pondered in my heart
that in kinship with wisdom
there is immortality,
18 and in friendship with her,
pure delight,
and in the labours of her hands,
unfailing wealth,
and in the experience of her
company, understanding,
and renown in sharing her words,
I went about seeking how to
get her for myself.
19 As a child I was naturally gifted,
and a good soul fell to my lot;
20 or rather, being good, I entered
an undefiled body.
21 But I perceived that I would not
possess wisdom unless
God gave her to me—
and it was a mark of insight to
know whose gift she was—
so I appealed to the Lord and
implored him,
and with my whole heart I said:

SOLOMON'S PRAYER FOR WISDOM

9 'O God of my ancestors and
Lord of mercy,
who have made all things
by your word,
2 and by your wisdom have
formed humankind
to have dominion over the
creatures you have made,

3 and rule the world in holiness
and righteousness,
and pronounce judgement in
uprightness of soul,
4 give me the wisdom that sits
by your throne,
and do not reject me from
among your servants.
5 For I am your servant,[v] the son
of your servant-girl,
a man who is weak and short-lived,
with little understanding of
judgement and laws;
6 for even one who is perfect
among human beings
will be regarded as nothing
without the wisdom
that comes from you.
7 You have chosen me to be
king of your people
and to be judge over your sons
and daughters.
8 You have given command to
build a temple on your
holy mountain,
and an altar in the city of
your habitation,
a copy of the holy tent that
you prepared from
the beginning.
9 With you is wisdom, she who
knows your works
and was present when you
made the world;
she understands what is
pleasing in your sight
and what is right according to
your commandments.
10 Send her forth from the
holy heavens,
and from the throne of your
glory send her,
that she may labour at my side,
and that I may learn what is
pleasing to you.
11 For she knows and understands
all things,
and she will guide me wisely
in my actions
and guard me with her glory.
12 Then my works will be acceptable,
and I shall judge your people justly,
and shall be worthy of the
throne[w] of my father.
13 For who can learn the
counsel of God?
Or who can discern what
the Lord wills?
14 For the reasoning of mortals
is worthless,
and our designs are likely to fail;
15 for a perishable body weighs
down the soul,
and this earthy tent burdens the
thoughtful[x] mind.
16 We can hardly guess at what
is on earth,
and what is at hand we find
with labour;
but who has traced out what
is in the heavens?
17 Who has learned your counsel,
unless you have given wisdom
and sent your holy spirit
from on high?
18 And thus the paths of those on
earth were set right,
and people were taught what
pleases you,
and were saved by wisdom.'

THE WORK OF WISDOM FROM ADAM TO MOSES

10 Wisdom[y] protected the
first-formed father of the
world, when he alone
had been created;
she delivered him from his
transgression,
2 and gave him strength to
rule all things.
3 But when an unrighteous
man departed from
her in his anger,
he perished because in rage he
killed his brother.
4 When the earth was flooded
because of him, wisdom
again saved it,
steering the righteous man by a
paltry piece of wood.

5 Wisdom[z] also, when the nations
in wicked agreement had
been put to confusion,
recognized the righteous man
and preserved him
blameless before God,
and kept him strong in the face of
his compassion for his child.

6 Wisdom[a] rescued a righteous
man when the ungodly
were perishing;
he escaped the fire that descended
on the Five Cities.[b]
7 Evidence of their wickedness
still remains:
a continually smoking waste-land,

[v] **9.5** Gk *slave* [w] **9.12** Gk *thrones* [x] **9.15** Or *anxious* [y] **10.1** Gk *She* [z] **10.5** Gk *She* [a] **10.6** Gk *She* [b] **10.6** Or *on Pentapolis*

plants bearing fruit that
does not ripen,
and a pillar of salt standing
as a monument to an
unbelieving soul.
8 For because they passed wisdom by,
they not only were hindered from
recognizing the good,
but also left for humankind a
reminder of their folly,
so that their failures could
never go unnoticed.

9 Wisdom rescued from troubles
those who served her.
10 When a righteous man fled from
his brother's wrath,
she guided him on straight paths;
she showed him the kingdom of God,
and gave him knowledge
of holy things;
she prospered him in his labours,
and increased the fruit of his toil.
11 When his oppressors were covetous,
she stood by him and made him rich.
12 She protected him from
his enemies,
and kept him safe from those
who lay in wait for him;
in his arduous contest she gave
him the victory,
so that he might learn that
godliness is more powerful
than anything else.

13 When a righteous man was sold,
wisdom[c] did not desert him,
but delivered him from sin.
She descended with him into
the dungeon,
14 and when he was in prison she
did not leave him,
until she brought him the
sceptre of a kingdom
and authority over his masters.
Those who accused him she
showed to be false,
and she gave him everlasting
honour.

WISDOM LED THE ISRAELITES OUT OF EGYPT

15 A holy people and blameless race
wisdom delivered from a nation
of oppressors.
16 She entered the soul of a
servant of the Lord,
and withstood dread kings with
wonders and signs.
17 She gave to holy people the
reward of their labours;
she guided them along a
marvellous way,
and became a shelter to them by day,
and a starry flame through
the night.
18 She brought them over the Red Sea,
and led them through deep waters;
19 but she drowned their enemies,
and cast them up from the
depths of the sea.
20 Therefore the righteous plundered
the ungodly;
they sang hymns, O Lord, to
your holy name,
and praised with one accord
your defending hand;
21 for wisdom opened the mouths of
those who were mute,
and made the tongues of
infants speak clearly.

WISDOM LED THE ISRAELITES THROUGH THE DESERT

11 Wisdom[d] prospered their
works by the hand of
a holy prophet.
2 They journeyed through an
uninhabited wilderness,
and pitched their tents in
untrodden places.
3 They withstood their enemies and
fought off their foes.
4 When they were thirsty, they
called upon you,
and water was given them
out of flinty rock,
and from hard stone a remedy
for their thirst.
5 For through the very things by
which their enemies
were punished,
they themselves received
benefit in their need.
6 Instead of the fountain of an
ever-flowing river,
stirred up and defiled with blood
7 in rebuke for the decree to
kill the infants,
you gave them abundant water
unexpectedly,
8 showing by their thirst at that time
how you punished their enemies.
9 For when they were tried,
though they were being
disciplined in mercy,
they learned how the ungodly
were tormented when
judged in wrath.

[c] 10.13 Gk *she* [d] 11.1 Gk *She*

10 For you tested them as a parent[e]
does in warning,
but you examined the ungodly[f]
as a stern king does
in condemnation.
11 Whether absent or present, they
were equally distressed,
12 for a twofold grief possessed them,
and a groaning at the memory
of what had occurred.
13 For when they heard that through
their own punishments
the righteous[g] had received
benefit, they perceived it
was the Lord's doing.
14 For though they had mockingly
rejected him who long
before had been cast
out and exposed,
at the end of the events they
marvelled at him,
when they felt thirst in a different
way from the righteous.

PUNISHMENT OF THE WICKED

15 In return for their foolish and
wicked thoughts,
which led them astray to worship
irrational serpents and
worthless animals,
you sent upon them a multitude
of irrational creatures
to punish them,
16 so that they might learn that one
is punished by the very
things by which one sins.
17 For your all-powerful hand,
which created the world out
of formless matter,
did not lack the means to send
upon them a multitude
of bears, or bold lions,
18 or newly-created unknown
beasts full of rage,
or such as breathe out
fiery breath,
or belch forth a thick pall of smoke,
or flash terrible sparks from
their eyes;
19 not only could the harm they
did destroy people,[h]
but the mere sight of them
could kill by fright.
20 Even apart from these, people[i]
could fall at a single breath
when pursued by justice
and scattered by the breath
of your power.
But you have arranged all
things by measure and
number and weight.

GOD IS POWERFUL AND MERCIFUL

21 For it is always in your power to
show great strength,
and who can withstand the
might of your arm?
22 Because the whole world before you is
like a speck that tips the scales,
and like a drop of morning dew
that falls on the ground.
23 But you are merciful to all, for
you can do all things,
and you overlook people's sins, so
that they may repent.
24 For you love all things that exist,
and detest none of the things
that you have made,
for you would not have made
anything if you had hated it.
25 How would anything have endured
if you had not willed it?
Or how would anything not
called forth by you have
been preserved?
26 You spare all things, for they
are yours, O Lord, you
who love the living.

12 For your immortal spirit
is in all things.
2 Therefore you correct little by little
those who trespass,
and you remind and warn them
of the things through
which they sin,
so that they may be freed from
wickedness and put their
trust in you, O Lord.

THE SINS OF THE CANAANITES

3 Those who lived long ago in
your holy land
4 you hated for their detestable
practices,
their works of sorcery and
unholy rites,
5 their merciless slaughter[j] of children,
and their sacrificial feasting on
human flesh and blood.
These initiates from the midst
of a heathen cult,[k]
6 these parents who murder
helpless lives,
you willed to destroy by the
hands of our ancestors,
7 so that the land most precious
of all to you
might receive a worthy colony of
the servants[l] of God.

e 11.10 Gk *a father* f 11.10 Gk *those* g 11.13 Gk *they* h 11.19 Gk *them* i 11.20 Gk *they* j 12.5 Gk *slaughterers* k 12.5 Meaning of Gk uncertain l 12.7 Or *children*

8 But even these you spared, since
they were but mortals,
and sent wasps[m] as forerunners
of your army
to destroy them little by little,
9 though you were not unable to give
the ungodly into the hands
of the righteous in battle,
or to destroy them at one blow
by dread wild animals
or your stern word.
10 But judging them little by
little you gave them an
opportunity to repent,
though you were not unaware that
their origin[n] was evil
and their wickedness inborn,
and that their way of thinking
would never change.
11 For they were an accursed race
from the beginning,
and it was not through fear of
anyone that you left them
unpunished for their sins.

GOD IS SOVEREIGN

12 For who will say, 'What
have you done?'
or will resist your judgement?
Who will accuse you for the
destruction of nations
that you made?
Or who will come before you
to plead as an advocate
for the unrighteous?
13 For neither is there any god
besides you, whose care
is for all people,[o]
to whom you should prove that you
have not judged unjustly;
14 nor can any king or monarch
confront you about those
whom you have punished.
15 You are righteous and you rule
all things righteously,
deeming it alien to
your power
to condemn anyone who does not
deserve to be punished.
16 For your strength is the source
of righteousness,
and your sovereignty over all
causes you to spare all.
17 For you show your strength
when people doubt the
completeness of your power,
and you rebuke any insolence
among those who know it.[p]
18 Although you are sovereign
in strength, you judge
with mildness,
and with great forbearance
you govern us;
for you have power to act
whenever you choose.

GOD'S LESSONS FOR ISRAEL

19 Through such works you have
taught your people
that the righteous must be kind,
and you have filled your children
with good hope,
because you give repentance for sins.
20 For if you punished with such great
care and indulgence[q]
the enemies of your servants[r] and
those deserving of death,
granting them time and opportunity
to give up their wickedness,
21 with what strictness you have
judged your children,
to whose ancestors you gave
oaths and covenants
full of good promises!
22 So while chastening us you
scourge our enemies ten
thousand times more,
so that, when we judge, we
may meditate upon
your goodness,
and when we are judged, we
may expect mercy.

THE PUNISHMENT OF THE EGYPTIANS

23 Therefore those who lived
unrighteously, in
a life of folly,
you tormented through their
own abominations.
24 For they went far astray on
the paths of error,
accepting as gods those animals that
even their enemies[s] despised;
they were deceived like
foolish infants.
25 Therefore, as though to children
who cannot reason,
you sent your judgement
to mock them.
26 But those who have not heeded the
warning of mild rebukes
will experience the deserved
judgement of God.
27 For when in their suffering they
became incensed

[m] 12.8 Or *hornets* [n] 12.10 Or *nature*
[o] 12.13 Or *all things* [p] 12.17 Meaning of Gk uncertain [q] 12.20 Other ancient authorities lack *and indulgence*; others read *and entreaty*
[r] 12.20 Or *children* [s] 12.24 Gk *they*

at those creatures that they had
thought to be gods, being
punished by means
of them,
they saw and recognized as the true
God the one whom they had
before refused to know.
Therefore the utmost condemnation
came upon them.

THE FOOLISHNESS OF NATURE WORSHIP

13 For all people who were
ignorant of God were
foolish by nature;
and they were unable from the
good things that are seen to
know the one who exists,
nor did they recognize the
artisan while paying
heed to his works;
2 but they supposed that either fire
or wind or swift air,
or the circle of the stars, or
turbulent water,
or the luminaries of heaven were the
gods that rule the world.
3 If through delight in the beauty
of these things people
assumed them to be gods,
let them know how much better
than these is their Lord,
for the author of beauty
created them.
4 And if people[t] were amazed at
their power and working,
let them perceive from them
how much more powerful is the
one who formed them.
5 For from the greatness and
beauty of created things
comes a corresponding perception
of their Creator.
6 Yet these people are little
to be blamed,
for perhaps they go astray
while seeking God and desiring
to find him.
7 For while they live among his works,
they keep searching,
and they trust in what they see,
because the things that
are seen are beautiful.
8 Yet again, not even they are
to be excused;
9 for if they had the power to
know so much
that they could investigate
the world,
how did they fail to find sooner
the Lord of these things?

THE FOOLISHNESS OF IDOLATRY

10 But miserable, with their hopes set
on dead things, are those
who give the name 'gods' to the
works of human hands,
gold and silver fashioned with skill,
and likenesses of animals,
or a useless stone, the work of
an ancient hand.
11 A skilled woodcutter may saw down
a tree easy to handle
and skilfully strip off all its bark,
and then with pleasing
workmanship
make a useful vessel that
serves life's needs,
12 and burn the cast-off pieces
of his work
to prepare his food, and eat his fill.
13 But a cast-off piece from among
them, useful for nothing,
a stick crooked and full of knots,
he takes and carves with care
in his leisure,
and shapes it with skill gained
in idleness;[u]
he forms it in the likeness of
a human being,
14 or makes it like some
worthless animal,
giving it a coat of red paint and
colouring its surface red
and covering every blemish
in it with paint;
15 then he makes a suitable niche for it,
and sets it in the wall, and fastens
it there with iron.
16 He takes thought for it, so
that it may not fall,
because he knows that it
cannot help itself,
for it is only an image and
has need of help.
17 When he prays about possessions
and his marriage
and children,
he is not ashamed to address
a lifeless thing.
18 For health he appeals to a
thing that is weak;
for life he prays to a thing
that is dead;
for aid he entreats a thing that is
utterly inexperienced;
for a prosperous journey, a thing
that cannot take a step;
19 for money-making and work and
success with his hands

[t] **13.4** Gk *they* [u] **13.13** Other ancient authorities read *with intelligent skill*

he asks strength of a thing whose
hands have no strength.

FOLLY OF A NAVIGATOR PRAYING TO AN IDOL

14 Again, one preparing to
sail and about to voyage
over raging waves
calls upon a piece of wood more
fragile than the ship
that carries him.
2 For it was desire for gain that
planned that vessel,
and wisdom was the artisan
who built it;
3 but it is your providence, O Father,
that steers its course,
because you have given it a
path in the sea,
and a safe way through the waves,
4 showing that you can save
from every danger,
so that even a person who lacks
skill may put to sea.
5 It is your will that works of
your wisdom should
not be without effect;
therefore people trust their lives even
to the smallest piece of wood,
and passing through the billows on a
raft they come safely to land.
6 For even in the beginning,
when arrogant giants
were perishing,
the hope of the world took
refuge on a raft,
and guided by your hand left
to the world the seed
of a new generation.
7 For blessed is the wood by which
righteousness comes.

8 But the idol made with hands is
accursed, and so is the
one who made it—
he for having made it, and the
perishable thing because
it was named a god.
9 For equally hateful to God
are the ungodly and
their ungodliness;
10 for what was done will be
punished together with
the one who did it.
11 Therefore there will be a visitation
also upon the heathen idols,
because, though part of what
God created, they became
an abomination,
snares for human souls
and a trap for the feet of the foolish.

THE ORIGIN AND EVILS OF IDOLATRY

12 For the idea of making idols was the
beginning of fornication,
and the invention of them was
the corruption of life;
13 for they did not exist from
the beginning,
nor will they last for ever.
14 For through human vanity they
entered the world,
and therefore their speedy end
has been planned.

15 For a father, consumed with grief at
an untimely bereavement,
made an image of his child,
who had been suddenly
taken from him;
he now honoured as a god what was
once a dead human being,
and handed on to his dependants
secret rites and initiations.
16 Then the ungodly custom,
grown strong with time,
was kept as a law,
and at the command of monarchs
carved images were
worshipped.
17 When people could not honour
monarchs[v] in their presence,
since they lived at a distance,
they imagined their appearance
far away,
and made a visible image of the
king whom they honoured,
so that by their zeal they might
flatter the absent one
as though present.

18 Then the ambition of the
artisan impelled
even those who did not know
the king to intensify
their worship.
19 For he, perhaps wishing to
please his ruler,
skilfully forced the likeness to take
more beautiful form,
20 and the multitude, attracted by
the charm of his work,
now regarded as an object of worship
the one whom shortly
before they had honoured
as a human being.
21 And this became a hidden trap
for humankind,

[v] 14.17 Gk *them*

because people, in bondage
to misfortune or to
royal authority,
bestowed on objects of stone
or wood the name that
ought not to be shared.
22 Then it was not enough for
them to err about the
knowledge of God,
but though living in great strife
due to ignorance,
they call such great evils peace.
23 For whether they kill children
in their initiations, or
celebrate secret mysteries,
or hold frenzied revels with
strange customs,
24 they no longer keep either their lives
or their marriages pure,
but they either treacherously kill
one another, or grieve one
another by adultery,
25 and all is a raging riot of blood and
murder, theft and deceit,
corruption, faithlessness,
tumult, perjury,
26 confusion over what is good,
forgetfulness of favours,
defiling of souls, sexual
perversion,
disorder in marriages, adultery,
and debauchery.
27 For the worship of idols not
to be named
is the beginning and cause and
end of every evil.
28 For their worshippers[w] either
rave in exultation,
or prophesy lies, or live
unrighteously, or readily
commit perjury;
29 for because they trust in
lifeless idols
they swear wicked oaths and
expect to suffer no harm.
30 But just penalties will overtake
them on two counts:
because they thought wrongly
about God in devoting
themselves to idols,
and because in deceit they swore
unrighteously through
contempt for holiness.
31 For it is not the power of the things
by which people swear,[x]
but the just penalty for
those who sin,
that always pursues the
transgression of the
unrighteous.

BENEFITS OF WORSHIPPING THE TRUE GOD

15 But you, our God, are
kind and true,
patient, and ruling all
things[y] in mercy.
2 For even if we sin we are yours,
knowing your power;
but we will not sin, because
we know that you
acknowledge us as yours.
3 For to know you is complete
righteousness,
and to know your power is the
root of immortality.
4 For neither has the evil intent of
human art misled us,
nor the fruitless toil of painters,
a figure stained with varied colours,
5 whose appearance arouses
yearning in fools,
so that they desire[z] the lifeless
form of a dead image.
6 Lovers of evil things and fit for
such objects of hope[a]
are those who either make or
desire or worship them.

THE FOOLISHNESS OF WORSHIPPING CLAY IDOLS

7 A potter kneads the soft earth
and laboriously moulds each
vessel for our service,
fashioning out of the same clay
both the vessels that serve clean uses
and those for contrary uses,
making all alike;
but which shall be the use
of each of them
the worker in clay decides.
8 With misspent toil, these workers
form a futile god from
the same clay—
these mortals who were made of
earth a short time before
and after a little while go to the
earth from which all
mortals are taken,
when the time comes to return the
souls that were borrowed.
9 But the workers are not
concerned that mortals
are destined to die
or that their life is brief,
but they compete with workers
in gold and silver,
and imitate workers in copper;

[w] 14.28 Gk *they* [x] 14.31 Or *of the oaths people swear* [y] 15.1 Or *ruling the universe* [z] 15.5 Gk *and he desires* [a] 15.6 Gk *such hopes*

and they count it a glorious thing
to mould counterfeit gods.
10 Their heart is ashes, their hope
is cheaper than dirt,
and their lives are of less
worth than clay,
11 because they failed to know the
one who formed them
and inspired them with active souls
and breathed a living spirit into them.
12 But they considered our existence
an idle game,
and life a festival held for profit,
for they say one must get money
however one can, even
by base means.
13 For these people, more than all
others, know that they sin
when they make from earthy
matter fragile vessels
and carved images.

14 But most foolish, and more
miserable than an infant,
are all the enemies who oppressed
your people.
15 For they thought that all their
heathen idols were gods,
though these have neither the use
of their eyes to see with,
nor nostrils with which to
draw breath,
nor ears with which to hear,
nor fingers to feel with,
and their feet are of no use
for walking.
16 For a human being made them,
and one whose spirit is borrowed
formed them;
for none can form gods that
are like themselves.
17 People are mortal, and what
they make with lawless
hands is dead;
for they are better than the
objects they worship,
since[b] they have life, but the
idols[c] never had.

SERPENTS IN THE DESERT

18 Moreover, they worship even the
most hateful animals,
which are worse than all others
when judged by their
lack of intelligence;
19 and even as animals they are not so
beautiful in appearance that
one would desire them,
but they have escaped both
the praise of God
and his blessing.

16 Therefore those people[d] were
deservedly punished
through such creatures,
and were tormented by a
multitude of animals.
2 Instead of this punishment
you showed kindness
to your people,
and you prepared quails to eat,
a delicacy to satisfy the desire
of appetite;
3 in order that those people, when
they desired food,
might lose the least remnant
of appetite[e]
because of the odious creatures
sent to them,
while your people,[f] after suffering
want a short time,
might partake of delicacies.
4 For it was necessary that upon those
oppressors inescapable
want should come,
while to these others it was merely
shown how their enemies
were being tormented.

5 For when the terrible rage of
wild animals came
upon your people[g]
and they were being destroyed
by the bites of
writhing serpents,
your wrath did not continue
to the end;
6 they were troubled for a little
while as a warning,
and received a symbol of deliverance
to remind them of your
law's command.

7 For the one who turned towards
it was saved, not by the
thing that was beheld,
but by you, the Saviour of all.
8 And by this also you convinced
our enemies
that it is you who deliver
from every evil.
9 For they were killed by the bites
of locusts and flies,
and no healing was found for them,
because they deserved to be
punished by such things.
10 But your children were not
conquered even by the fangs
of venomous serpents,

[b] 15.17 Other ancient authorities read *of which* [c] 15.17 Gk *but they* [d] 16.1 Gk *they* [e] 16.3 Gk *loathed the necessary appetite* [f] 16.3 Gk *they* [g] 16.5 Gk *them*

for your mercy came to their
help and healed them.
11 To remind them of your oracles
they were bitten,
and then were quickly delivered,
so that they would not fall into
deep forgetfulness
and become unresponsive[h]
to your kindness.
12 For neither herb nor poultice
cured them,
but it was your word, O Lord,
that heals all people.
13 For you have power over
life and death;
you lead mortals down to the gates
of Hades and back again.
14 A person in wickedness kills another,
but cannot bring back the
departed spirit,
or set free the imprisoned soul.

DISASTROUS STORMS STRIKE EGYPT

15 To escape from your hand
is impossible;
16 for the ungodly, refusing
to know you,
were flogged by the strength
of your arm,
pursued by unusual rains and hail
and relentless storms,
and utterly consumed by fire.
17 For—most incredible of
all—in water, which
quenches all things,
the fire had still greater effect,
for the universe defends
the righteous.
18 At one time the flame was
restrained,
so that it might not consume
the creatures sent
against the ungodly,
but that seeing this they
might know
that they were being pursued by
the judgement of God;
19 and at another time even in the
midst of water it burned
more intensely than fire,
to destroy the crops of the
unrighteous land.

THE ISRAELITES RECEIVE MANNA

20 Instead of these things you gave
your people food of angels,
and without their toil you supplied
them from heaven with
bread ready to eat,
providing every pleasure and
suited to every taste.
21 For your sustenance manifested
your sweetness towards
your children;
and the bread, ministering[i] to the
desire of the one who took it,
was changed to suit
everyone's liking.
22 Snow and ice withstood fire
without melting,
so that they might know that the
crops of their enemies
were being destroyed by the fire
that blazed in the hail
and flashed in the showers of rain;
23 whereas the fire,[j] in order that the
righteous might be fed,
even forgot its native power.

24 For creation, serving you
who made it,
exerts itself to punish the
unrighteous,
and in kindness relaxes on behalf
of those who trust in you.
25 Therefore at that time also,
changed into all forms,
it served your all-nourishing bounty,
according to the desire of those
who had need,[k]
26 so that your children, whom you
loved, O Lord, might learn
that it is not the production of crops
that feeds humankind
but that your word sustains
those who trust in you.
27 For what was not destroyed by fire
was melted when simply warmed
by a fleeting ray of the sun,
28 to make it known that one must
rise before the sun to
give you thanks,
and must pray to you at the
dawning of the light;
29 for the hope of an ungrateful person
will melt like wintry frost,
and flow away like waste water.

TERROR STRIKES THE EGYPTIANS AT NIGHT

17 Great are your judgements
and hard to describe;
therefore uninstructed souls
have gone astray.
2 For when lawless people supposed
that they held the holy
nation in their power,

[h] **16.11** Meaning of Gk uncertain [i] **16.21** Gk *and it, ministering* [j] **16.23** Gk *this* [k] **16.25** Or *who made supplication*

they themselves lay as captives of
darkness and prisoners
of long night,
shut in under their roofs, exiles
from eternal providence.
3 For thinking that in their secret
sins they were unobserved
behind a dark curtain of
forgetfulness,
they were scattered, terribly[l]
alarmed,
and appalled by spectres.
4 For not even the inner chamber
that held them protected
them from fear,
but terrifying sounds rang
out around them,
and dismal phantoms with
gloomy faces appeared.
5 And no power of fire was
able to give light,
nor did the brilliant flames
of the stars
avail to illumine that
hateful night.
6 Nothing was shining
through to them
except a dreadful, self-kindled fire,
and in terror they deemed the
things that they saw
to be worse than that unseen
appearance.
7 The delusions of their magic
art lay humbled,
and their boasted wisdom was
scornfully rebuked.
8 For those who promised to
drive off the fears and
disorders of a sick soul
were sick themselves with
ridiculous fear.
9 For even if nothing disturbing
frightened them,
yet, scared by the passing of
wild animals and the
hissing of snakes
10 they perished in trembling fear,
refusing to look even at the
air, though it nowhere
could be avoided.
11 For wickedness is a cowardly
thing, condemned by
its own testimony;[m]
distressed by conscience, it has
always exaggerated[n]
the difficulties.
12 For fear is nothing but a giving
up of the helps that
come from reason;
13 and hope, defeated by this
inward weakness,
prefers ignorance of what
causes the torment.
14 But throughout the night, which
was really powerless
and which came upon them from the
recesses of powerless Hades,
they all slept the same sleep,
15 and now were driven by
monstrous spectres,
and now were paralysed by their
souls' surrender;
for sudden and unexpected fear
overwhelmed them.
16 And whoever was there fell down,
and thus was kept shut up in a
prison not made of iron;
17 for whether they were farmers
or shepherds
or workers who toiled in
the wilderness,
they were seized, and endured
the inescapable fate;
for with one chain of darkness
they all were bound.
18 Whether there came a
whistling wind,
or a melodious sound of birds in
wide-spreading branches,
or the rhythm of violently
rushing water,
19 or the harsh crash of rocks
hurled down,
or the unseen running of
leaping animals,
or the sound of the most savage
roaring beasts,
or an echo thrown back from a
hollow of the mountains,
it paralysed them with terror.
20 For the whole world was illumined
with brilliant light,
and went about its work unhindered,
21 while over those people alone
heavy night was spread,
an image of the darkness that was
destined to receive them;
but still heavier than darkness
were they to themselves.

LIGHT SHINES ON THE ISRAELITES

18 But for your holy ones there
was very great light.
Their enemies[o] heard their voices
but did not see their forms,
and counted them happy for
not having suffered,

[l] 17.3 Other ancient authorities read *unobserved, they were darkened behind a dark curtain of forgetfulness, terribly* [m] 17.11 Meaning of Gk uncertain [n] 17.11 Other ancient authorities read *anticipated* [o] 18.1 Gk *They*

2 and were thankful that your holy
ones,[p] though previously
wronged, were doing
them no injury;
and they begged their pardon
for having been at
variance with them.[q]
3 Therefore you provided a
flaming pillar of fire
as a guide for your people's[r]
unknown journey,
and a harmless sun for their
glorious wandering.
4 For their enemies[s] deserved to
be deprived of light and
imprisoned in darkness,
those who had kept your
children imprisoned,
through whom the imperishable
light of the law was to
be given to the world.

THE DEATH OF THE EGYPTIAN FIRSTBORN

5 When they had resolved to kill the
infants of your holy ones,
and one child had been abandoned
and rescued,
you in punishment took away a
multitude of their children;
and you destroyed them all together
by a mighty flood.
6 That night was made known
beforehand to our ancestors,
so that they might rejoice in sure
knowledge of the oaths
in which they trusted.
7 The deliverance of the righteous
and the destruction
of their enemies
were expected by your people.
8 For by the same means by which
you punished our enemies
you called us to yourself and
glorified us.
9 For in secret the holy children
of good people
offered sacrifices,
and with one accord agreed
to the divine law,
so that the saints would share
alike the same things,
both blessings and dangers;
and already they were singing the
praises of the ancestors.[t]
10 But the discordant cry of their
enemies echoed back,
and their piteous lament for their
children was spread abroad.
11 The slave was punished with the
same penalty as the master,
and the commoner suffered the
same loss as the king;
12 and they all together, by one
form[u] of death,
had corpses too many to count.
For the living were not sufficient
even to bury them,
since in one instant their most
valued children had
been destroyed.
13 For though they had disbelieved
everything because of
their magic arts,
yet, when their firstborn
were destroyed, they
acknowledged your
people to be God's child.
14 For while gentle silence
enveloped all things,
and night in its swift course
was now half gone,
15 your all-powerful word leapt
from heaven, from
the royal throne,
into the midst of the land
that was doomed,
a stern warrior
16 carrying the sharp sword of your
authentic command,
and stood and filled all things
with death,
and touched heaven while
standing on the earth.
17 Then at once apparitions in
dreadful dreams greatly
troubled them,
and unexpected fears assailed them;
18 and one here and another there,
hurled down half dead,
made known why they were dying;
19 for the dreams that disturbed them
forewarned them of this,
so that they might not perish
without knowing
why they suffered.

THREAT OF ANNIHILATION IN THE DESERT

20 The experience of death touched
also the righteous,
and a plague came upon the
multitude in the desert,
but the wrath did not long continue.
21 For a blameless man was quick to
act as their champion;

[p] 18.2 Meaning of Gk uncertain [q] 18.2 Meaning of Gk uncertain [r] 18.3 Gk *their* [s] 18.4 Gk *those persons* [t] 18.9 Other ancient authorities read *dangers, the ancestors already leading the songs of praise* [u] 18.12 Gk *name*

he brought forward the shield
of his ministry,
prayer and propitiation
by incense;
he withstood the anger and put
an end to the disaster,
showing that he was your servant.
22 He conquered the wrath[v] not
by strength of body,
not by force of arms,
but by his word he subdued
the avenger,
appealing to the oaths and covenants
given to our ancestors.
23 For when the dead had already fallen
on one another in heaps,
he intervened and held
back the wrath,
and cut off its way to the living.
24 For on his long robe the whole
world was depicted,
and the glories of the ancestors
were engraved on the
four rows of stones,
and your majesty was on the
diadem upon his head.
25 To these the destroyer yielded,
these he[w] feared;
for merely to test the wrath
was enough.

THE RED SEA

19 But the ungodly were assailed
to the end by pitiless anger,
for God[x] knew in advance even
their future actions:
2 how, though they themselves
had permitted[y] your
people to depart
and hastily sent them out,
they would change their minds
and pursue them.
3 For while they were still engaged
in mourning,
and were lamenting at the
graves of their dead,
they reached another foolish
decision,
and pursued as fugitives those
whom they had begged
and compelled to leave.
4 For the fate they deserved drew
them on to this end,
and made them forget what
had happened,
in order that they might fill up
the punishment that their
torments still lacked,
5 and that your people might
experience[z] an
incredible journey,
but they themselves might
meet a strange death.

GOD GUIDES AND PROTECTS HIS PEOPLE

6 For the whole creation in its nature
was fashioned anew,
complying with your commands,
so that your children[a] might
be kept unharmed.
7 The cloud was seen overshadowing
the camp,
and dry land emerging where
water had stood before,
an unhindered way out of
the Red Sea,
and a grassy plain out of the
raging waves,
8 where those protected by your
hand passed through
as one nation,
after gazing on marvellous wonders.
9 For they ranged like horses,
and leapt like lambs,
praising you, O Lord, who
delivered them.
10 For they still recalled the events
of their sojourn,
how instead of producing
animals the earth
brought forth gnats,
and instead of fish the river spewed
out vast numbers of frogs.
11 Afterwards they saw also a
new kind[b] of birds,
when desire led them to ask
for luxurious food;
12 for, to give them relief, quails
came up from the sea.

THE PUNISHMENT OF THE EGYPTIANS

13 The punishments did not come
upon the sinners
without prior signs in the
violence of thunder,
for they justly suffered because
of their wicked acts;
for they practised a more bitter
hatred of strangers.
14 Others had refused to receive
strangers when they
came to them,
but these made slaves of guests who
were their benefactors.

[v] 18.22 Cn: Gk *multitude* [w] 18.25 Other ancient authorities read *they* [x] 19.1 Gk *he* [y] 19.2 Other ancient authorities read *had changed their minds to permit* [z] 19.5 Other ancient authorities read *accomplish* [a] 19.6 Or *servants* [b] 19.11 Or *production*

15 And not only so—but, while
punishment of some sort
will come upon the former
for having received strangers
with hostility,
16 the latter, having first received them
with festal celebrations,
afterwards afflicted with
terrible sufferings
those who had already shared
the same rights.
17 They were stricken also with
loss of sight—
just as were those at the door of
the righteous man—
when, surrounded by yawning
darkness,
all of them tried to find the way
through their own doors.

A NEW HARMONY IN NATURE

18 For the elements changed[c] places
with one another,
as on a harp the notes vary the
nature of the rhythm,
while each note remains the same.[d]
This may be clearly inferred from
the sight of what took place.
19 For land animals were transformed
into water creatures,
and creatures that swim moved
over to the land.
20 Fire even in water retained
its normal power,
and water forgot its
fire-quenching nature.
21 Flames, on the contrary,
failed to consume
the flesh of perishable creatures
that walked among them,
nor did they melt[e] the crystalline,
quick-melting kind
of heavenly food.

CONCLUSION

22 For in everything, O Lord,
you have exalted and
glorified your people,
and you have not neglected to
help them at all times
and in all places.

[c] 19.18 Gk *changing* [d] 19.18 Meaning of Gk uncertain [e] 19.21 Cn: Gk *nor could be melted*

Ecclesiasticus, or the Wisdom of Jesus Son of

SIRACH

Sirach is a collection of Jewish wisdom sayings and poems written around 180 BCE. Joshua Ben Sira was a teacher in the wisdom tradition. The context of the writing was Hellenistic Judaism with a strong influence of Greek culture. Sirach is not negative to Greek culture, but seeks to merge Jewish beliefs, practical advice, and Greek perspectives about moral living. Sirach draws readily from the Jewish scriptures. Wisdom, in the author's view, is synonymous with fear of the Lord and sometimes identified with adherence to Mosaic law.

The passage from Sirach that speaks of honor of one's parents is read during the liturgy every year on the Feast of the Holy Family (3.2–6, 12–14). On the Second Sunday of the Year, a passage about Wisdom coming from God's mouth is read each year (24.1–4, 8–12). Also, passages from Sirach are read consecutively on Monday of the Seventh Week through Saturday of the Eighth Week of Year I.

THE PROLOGUE

Many great teachings have been given to us through the Law and the Prophets and the others[a] that followed them, and for these we should praise Israel for instruction and wisdom. Now, those who read the scriptures must not only themselves understand them, but must also as lovers of learning be able through the spoken and written word to help the outsiders. So my grandfather Jesus, who had devoted himself especially to the reading of the Law and the Prophets and the other books of our ancestors, and had acquired considerable proficiency in them, was himself also led to write something pertaining to instruction and wisdom, so that by becoming familiar also with his book[b] those who love learning might make even greater progress in living according to the law.

You are invited therefore to read it with goodwill and attention, and to be indulgent in cases where, despite our diligent labour in translating, we may seem to have rendered some phrases imperfectly. For what was originally expressed in Hebrew does not have exactly the same sense when translated into another language. Not only this book, but even the Law itself, the Prophecies, and the rest of the books differ not a little when read in the original.

When I came to Egypt in the thirty-eighth year of the reign of Euergetes and stayed for some time, I found opportunity for no little instruction.[c] It seemed highly necessary that I should myself devote some diligence and labour to the translation of this book. During that time I have applied my skill day and night to complete and publish the book for those living abroad who wished to gain learning and are disposed to live according to the law.

IN PRAISE OF WISDOM

1 All wisdom is from the Lord,
and with him it remains for ever.
2 The sand of the sea, the drops of rain,
and the days of eternity—
who can count them?
3 The height of heaven, the
breadth of the earth,
the abyss, and wisdom[d]—who
can search them out?

[a] **Prologue** Or *other books* [b] **Prologue** Gk *with these things* [c] **Prologue** Other ancient authorities read *I found a copy affording no little instruction* [d] **1.3** Other ancient authorities read *the depth of the abyss*

4 Wisdom was created before
all other things,
and prudent understanding
from eternity.[e]
6 The root of wisdom—to whom
has it been revealed?
Her subtleties—who
knows them?[f]
8 There is but one who is wise,
greatly to be feared,
seated upon his throne—the Lord.
9 It is he who created her;
he saw her and took her measure;
he poured her out upon
all his works,
10 upon all the living according
to his gift;
he lavished her upon those
who love him.[g]

FEAR OF THE LORD IS TRUE WISDOM

11 The fear of the Lord is glory
and exultation,
and gladness and a crown
of rejoicing.
12 The fear of the Lord delights
the heart,
and gives gladness and joy
and long life.[h]
13 Those who fear the Lord will
have a happy end;
on the day of their death
they will be blessed.

14 To fear the Lord is the beginning
of wisdom;
she is created with the
faithful in the womb.
15 She made[i] among human beings
an eternal foundation,
and among their descendants
she will abide faithfully.
16 To fear the Lord is fullness
of wisdom;
she inebriates mortals
with her fruits;
17 she fills their[j] whole house with
desirable goods,
and their[k] storehouses
with her produce.
18 The fear of the Lord is the
crown of wisdom,
making peace and perfect
health to flourish.[l]
19 She rained down knowledge and
discerning comprehension,
and she heightened the glory of
those who held her fast.
20 To fear the Lord is the root
of wisdom,
and her branches are long life.[m]

22 Unjust anger cannot be justified,
for anger tips the scale
to one's ruin.
23 Those who are patient stay calm
until the right moment,
and then cheerfulness comes
back to them.
24 They hold back their words until
the right moment;
then the lips of many tell of
their good sense.

25 In the treasuries of wisdom
are wise sayings,
but godliness is an abomination
to a sinner.
26 If you desire wisdom, keep the
commandments,
and the Lord will lavish
her upon you.
27 For the fear of the Lord is wisdom
and discipline,
fidelity and humility are
his delight.

28 Do not disobey the fear of the Lord;
do not approach him with
a divided mind.
29 Do not be a hypocrite before others,
and keep watch over your lips.
30 Do not exalt yourself, or you may fall
and bring dishonour upon yourself.
The Lord will reveal your secrets
and overthrow you before the
whole congregation,
because you did not come in
the fear of the Lord,
and your heart was full of deceit.

DUTIES TOWARDS GOD

2 My child, when you come
to serve the Lord,
prepare yourself for testing.[n]

[e] 1.4 Other ancient authorities add as verse 5, *The source of wisdom is God's word in the highest heaven, and her ways are the eternal commandments.* [f] 1.6 Other ancient authorities add as verse 7, *The knowledge of wisdom—to whom was it manifested? And her abundant experience—who has understood it?*
[g] 1.10 Other ancient authorities add *Love of the Lord is glorious wisdom; to those to whom he appears he apportions her, that they may see him.*
[h] 1.12 Other ancient authorities add *The fear of the Lord is a gift from the Lord; also for love he makes firm paths.* [i] 1.15 Gk *made as a nest*
[j] 1.17 Other ancient authorities read *her*
[k] 1.17 Other ancient authorities read *her*
[l] 1.18 Other ancient authorities add *Both are gifts of God for peace; glory opens out for those who love him. He saw her and took her measure.*
[m] 1.20 Other ancient authorities add as verse 21, *The fear of the Lord drives away sins; and where it abides, it will turn away all anger.* [n] 2.1 Or *trials*

2 Set your heart right and be steadfast,
and do not be impetuous in
time of calamity.
3 Cling to him and do not depart,
so that your last days may
be prosperous.
4 Accept whatever befalls you,
and in times of humiliation
be patient.
5 For gold is tested in the fire,
and those found acceptable, in the
furnace of humiliation.[o]
6 Trust in him, and he will help you;
make your ways straight,
and hope in him.

7 You who fear the Lord, wait
for his mercy;
do not stray, or else you may fall.
8 You who fear the Lord, trust in him,
and your reward will not be lost.
9 You who fear the Lord, hope
for good things,
for lasting joy and mercy.[p]
10 Consider the generations
of old and see:
has anyone trusted in the Lord
and been disappointed?
Or has anyone persevered in
the fear of the Lord[q]
and been forsaken?
Or has anyone called upon him
and been neglected?
11 For the Lord is compassionate
and merciful;
he forgives sins and saves
in time of distress.

12 Woe to timid hearts and to
slack hands,
and to the sinner who walks
a double path!
13 Woe to the faint-hearted who
have no trust!
Therefore they will have no shelter.
14 Woe to you who have lost your nerve!
What will you do when the
Lord's reckoning comes?

15 Those who fear the Lord do not
disobey his words,
and those who love him
keep his ways.
16 Those who fear the Lord seek
to please him,
and those who love him are
filled with his law.
17 Those who fear the Lord
prepare their hearts,
and humble themselves
before him.
18 Let us fall into the hands
of the Lord,
but not into the hands of mortals;
for equal to his majesty is his mercy,
and equal to his name
are his works.[r]

DUTIES TOWARDS PARENTS

3 Listen to me your father,
O children;
act accordingly, that you may
be kept in safety.
2 For the Lord honours a father
above his children,
and he confirms a mother's
right over her children.
3 Those who honour their father
atone for sins,
4 and those who respect their
mother are like those
who lay up treasure.
5 Those who honour their father
will have joy in their
own children,
and when they pray they
will be heard.
6 Those who respect their father
will have long life,
and those who honour[s] their
mother obey the Lord;
7 they will serve their parents
as their masters.[t]
8 Honour your father by
word and deed,
that his blessing may
come upon you.
9 For a father's blessing strengthens
the houses of the children,
but a mother's curse uproots
their foundations.
10 Do not glorify yourself by
dishonouring your father,
for your father's dishonour
is no glory to you.
11 The glory of one's father is
one's own glory,
and it is a disgrace for children
not to respect their mother.

12 My child, help your father
in his old age,
and do not grieve him as
long as he lives;

[o] **2.5** Other ancient authorities add *in sickness and poverty put your trust in him* [p] **2.9** Other ancient authorities add *For his reward is an everlasting gift with joy.* [q] **2.10** Gk *of him* [r] **2.18** Syr: Gk lacks this line [s] **3.6** Heb: Other ancient authorities read *comfort* [t] **3.7** In other ancient authorities this line is preceded by *Those who fear the Lord honour their father,*

13 even if his mind fails, be
patient with him;
because you have all your faculties
do not despise him.
14 For kindness to a father will
not be forgotten,
and will be credited to you
against your sins;
15 in the day of your distress it will be
remembered in your favour;
like frost in fair weather, your
sins will melt away.
16 Whoever forsakes a father is
like a blasphemer,
and whoever angers a mother
is cursed by the Lord.

HUMILITY

17 My child, perform your tasks
with humility;[u]
then you will be loved by those
whom God accepts.
18 The greater you are, the more you
must humble yourself;
so you will find favour in the
sight of the Lord.[v]
20 For great is the might
of the Lord;
but by the humble
he is glorified.
21 Neither seek what is too
difficult for you,
nor investigate what is
beyond your power.
22 Reflect upon what you have
been commanded,
for what is hidden is not
your concern.
23 Do not meddle in matters that
are beyond you,
for more than you can understand
has been shown to you.
24 For their conceit has led
many astray,
and wrong opinion has impaired
their judgement.

25 Without eyes there is no light;
without knowledge there
is no wisdom.[w]
26 A stubborn mind will fare
badly at the end,
and whoever loves danger
will perish in it.
27 A stubborn mind will be
burdened by troubles,
and the sinner adds sin to sins.
28 When calamity befalls the proud,
there is no healing,
for an evil plant has taken
root in him.
29 The mind of the intelligent
appreciates proverbs,
and an attentive ear is the
desire of the wise.

ALMS FOR THE POOR

30 As water extinguishes a blazing fire,
so almsgiving atones for sin.
31 Those who repay favours give
thought to the future;
when they fall they will
find support.

DUTIES TOWARDS THE POOR AND THE OPPRESSED

4 My child, do not cheat the
poor of their living,
and do not keep needy
eyes waiting.
2 Do not grieve the hungry,
or anger one in need.
3 Do not add to the troubles
of the desperate,
or delay giving to the needy.
4 Do not reject a suppliant in distress,
or turn your face away
from the poor.
5 Do not avert your eye from
the needy,
and give no one reason
to curse you;
6 for if in bitterness of soul some
should curse you,
their Creator will hear
their prayer.

7 Endear yourself to the congregation;
bow your head low to the great.
8 Give a hearing to the poor,
and return their greeting politely.
9 Rescue the oppressed from
the oppressor;
and do not be hesitant in
giving a verdict.
10 Be a father to orphans,
and be like a husband to
their mother;
you will then be like a son of
the Most High,
and he will love you more than
does your mother.

THE REWARDS OF WISDOM

11 Wisdom teaches[x] her children
and gives help to those
who seek her.

[u] **3.17** Heb: Gk *meekness* [v] **3.18** Other ancient authorities add as verse 19, *Many are lofty and renowned, but to the humble he reveals his secrets.* [w] **3.25** Heb: Other ancient authorities lack verse 25 [x] **4.11** Heb Syr: Gk *exalts*

12 Whoever loves her loves life,
and those who seek her from early
morning are filled with joy.
13 Whoever holds her fast
inherits glory,
and the Lord blesses the
place she[y] enters.
14 Those who serve her minister
to the Holy One;
the Lord loves those who love her.
15 Those who obey her will
judge the nations,
and all who listen to her
will live secure.
16 If they remain faithful, they
will inherit her;
their descendants will
also obtain her.
17 For at first she will walk with
them on tortuous paths;
she will bring fear and
dread upon them,
and will torment them by
her discipline
until she trusts them,[z]
and she will test them with
her ordinances.
18 Then she will come straight
back to them again
and gladden them,
and will reveal her secrets
to them.
19 If they go astray she will
forsake them,
and hand them over to their ruin.

20 Watch for the opportune time,
and beware of evil,
and do not be ashamed
to be yourself.
21 For there is a shame that leads to sin,
and there is a shame that is
glory and favour.
22 Do not show partiality, to
your own harm,
or deference, to your downfall.
23 Do not refrain from speaking at
the proper moment,[a]
and do not hide your wisdom.[b]
24 For wisdom becomes known
through speech,
and education through the
words of the tongue.
25 Never speak against the truth,
but be ashamed of your ignorance.
26 Do not be ashamed to confess
your sins,
and do not try to stop the
current of a river.
27 Do not subject yourself to a fool,
or show partiality to a ruler.
28 Fight to the death for truth,
and the Lord God will
fight for you.

29 Do not be reckless in your speech,
or sluggish and remiss
in your deeds.
30 Do not be like a lion in your home,
or suspicious of your servants.
31 Do not let your hand be stretched
out to receive
and closed when it is time to give.

PRECEPTS FOR EVERYDAY LIVING

5 Do not rely on your wealth,
or say, 'I have enough.'
2 Do not follow your inclination
and strength
in pursuing the desires
of your heart.
3 Do not say, 'Who can have
power over me?'
for the Lord will surely
punish you.

4 Do not say, 'I sinned, yet what
has happened to me?'
for the Lord is slow to anger.
5 Do not be so confident of
forgiveness[c]
that you add sin to sin.
6 Do not say, 'His mercy is great,
he will forgive[d] the multitude
of my sins',
for both mercy and wrath
are with him,
and his anger will rest on sinners.
7 Do not delay to turn back
to the Lord,
and do not postpone it
from day to day;
for suddenly the wrath of the Lord
will come upon you,
and at the time of punishment
you will perish.
8 Do not depend on dishonest wealth,
for it will not benefit you on
the day of calamity.

9 Do not winnow in every wind,
or follow every path.[e]
10 Stand firm for what you know,
and let your speech be consistent.

[y] 4.13 Or *he* [z] 4.17 Or *until they remain faithful in their heart* [a] 4.23 Heb: Gk *at a time of salvation* [b] 4.23 So some Gk Mss and Heb Syr Lat: Other Gk Mss lack *and do not hide your wisdom* [c] 5.5 Heb: Gk *atonement* [d] 5.6 Heb: Gk *he* (or *it*) *will atone for* [e] 5.9 Gk adds *so it is with the double-tongued sinner* (see 6.1)

11 Be quick to hear,
but deliberate in answering.
12 If you know what to say, answer
your neighbour;
but if not, put your hand
over your mouth.

13 Honour and dishonour come
from speaking,
and the tongue of mortals
may be their downfall.
14 Do not be called
double-tongued[f]
and do not lay traps with
your tongue;
for shame comes to the thief,
and severe condemnation to
the double-tongued.
15 In great and small matters
cause no harm,[g]
6 1and do not become an enemy
instead of a friend;
for a bad name incurs shame
and reproach;
so it is with the double-tongued
sinner.

2 Do not fall into the
grip of passion,[h]
or you may be torn apart
as by a bull.[i]
3 Your leaves will be devoured and
your fruit destroyed,
and you will be left like a
withered tree.
4 Evil passion destroys those
who have it,
and makes them the
laughing-stock of
their enemies.

FRIENDSHIP, FALSE AND TRUE

5 Pleasant speech multiplies
friends,
and a gracious tongue
multiplies courtesies.
6 Let those who are friendly
with you be many,
but let your advisers be one
in a thousand.
7 When you gain friends, gain
them through testing,
and do not trust them hastily.
8 For there are friends who are such
when it suits them,
but they will not stand by you
in time of trouble.
9 And there are friends who
change into enemies,
and tell of the quarrel to
your disgrace.
10 And there are friends who
sit at your table,
but they will not stand by you
in time of trouble.
11 When you are prosperous, they
become your second self,
and lord it over your servants;
12 but if you are brought low, they
turn against you,
and hide themselves from you.
13 Keep away from your enemies,
and be on guard with your friends.

14 Faithful friends are a sturdy shelter:
whoever finds one has
found a treasure.
15 Faithful friends are beyond price;
no amount can balance
their worth.
16 Faithful friends are life-saving
medicine;
and those who fear the Lord
will find them.
17 Those who fear the Lord direct
their friendship aright,
for as they are, so are their
neighbours also.

BLESSINGS OF WISDOM

18 My child, from your youth
choose discipline,
and when you have grey hair
you will still find wisdom.
19 Come to her like one who
ploughs and sows,
and wait for her good harvest.
For when you cultivate her you
will toil but little,
and soon you will eat of
her produce.
20 She seems very harsh to the
undisciplined;
fools cannot remain with her.
21 She will be like a heavy stone
to test them,
and they will not delay in
casting her aside.
22 For wisdom is like her name;
she is not readily perceived
by many.

23 Listen, my child, and accept
my judgement;
do not reject my counsel.
24 Put your feet into her fetters,
and your neck into her collar.
25 Bend your shoulders and carry her,
and do not fret under her bonds.

f 5.14 Heb: Gk *a slanderer* g 5.15 Heb Syr: Gk *be ignorant* h 6.2 Heb: Meaning of Gk uncertain
i 6.2 Meaning of Gk uncertain

26 Come to her with all your soul,
and keep her ways with
all your might.
27 Search out and seek, and she will
become known to you;
and when you get hold of
her, do not let her go.
28 For at last you will find the
rest she gives,
and she will be changed
into joy for you.
29 Then her fetters will become for
you a strong defence,
and her collar a glorious robe.
30 Her yoke[j] is a golden ornament,
and her bonds a purple cord.
31 You will wear her like a
glorious robe,
and put her on like a
splendid crown.[k]

32 If you are willing, my child, you
can be disciplined,
and if you apply yourself you
will become clever.
33 If you love to listen you will
gain knowledge,
and if you pay attention you
will become wise.
34 Stand in the company of the elders.
Who is wise? Attach yourself
to such a one.
35 Be ready to listen to every
godly discourse,
and let no wise proverbs
escape you.
36 If you see an intelligent person,
rise early to visit him;
let your foot wear out his doorstep.
37 Reflect on the statutes of the Lord,
and meditate at all times on
his commandments.
It is he who will give insight
to[l] your mind,
and your desire for wisdom
will be granted.

MISCELLANEOUS ADVICE

7 Do no evil, and evil will
never overtake you.
2 Stay away from wrong, and it will
turn away from you.
3 Do[m] not sow in the furrows
of injustice,
and you will not reap a
sevenfold crop.

4 Do not seek from the Lord
high office,
or the seat of honour
from the king.
5 Do not assert your righteousness
before the Lord,
or display your wisdom
before the king.
6 Do not seek to become a judge,
or you may be unable to
root out injustice;
you may be partial to the powerful,
and so mar your integrity.
7 Commit no offence against the public,
and do not disgrace yourself
among the people.

8 Do not commit a sin twice;
not even for one will you
go unpunished.
9 Do not say, 'He will consider the
great number of my gifts,
and when I make an offering
to the Most High God,
he will accept it.'
10 Do not grow weary when you pray;
do not neglect to give alms.
11 Do not ridicule a person who is
embittered in spirit,
for there is One who
humbles and exalts.
12 Do not devise[n] a lie against
your brother,
or do the same to a friend.
13 Refuse to utter any lie,
for it is a habit that results
in no good.
14 Do not babble in the assembly
of the elders,
and do not repeat yourself
when you pray.

15 Do not hate hard labour
or farm work, which was created
by the Most High.
16 Do not enrol in the ranks of sinners;
remember that retribution
does not delay.
17 Humble yourself to the utmost,
for the punishment of the ungodly
is fire and worms.[o]

RELATIONS WITH OTHERS

18 Do not exchange a friend for money,
or a real brother for the
gold of Ophir.
19 Do not dismiss[p] a wise and
good wife,
for her charm is worth
more than gold.

[j] 6.30 Heb: Gk *Upon her* [k] 6.31 Heb: Gk *crown of gladness* [l] 6.37 Heb: Gk *will confirm*
[m] 7.3 Gk *My child, do* [n] 7.12 Heb: Gk *plough*
[o] 7.17 Heb *for the expectation of mortals is worms*
[p] 7.19 Heb: Gk *deprive yourself of*

20 Do not abuse slaves who
work faithfully,
or hired labourers who devote
themselves to their task.
21 Let your soul love intelligent slaves;[q]
do not withhold from them
their freedom.

22 Do you have cattle? Look after them;
if they are profitable to
you, keep them.
23 Do you have children?
Discipline them,
and make them obedient[r]
from their youth.
24 Do you have daughters? Be
concerned for their chastity,[s]
and do not show yourself too
indulgent with them.
25 Give a daughter in marriage, and
you complete a great task;
but give her to a sensible man.
26 Do you have a wife who pleases
you?[t] Do not divorce her;
but do not trust yourself to
one whom you detest.

27 With all your heart honour
your father,
and do not forget the birth
pangs of your mother.
28 Remember that it was of your
parents[u] you were born;
how can you repay what they
have given to you?

29 With all your soul fear the Lord,
and revere his priests.
30 With all your might love your Maker,
and do not neglect his ministers.
31 Fear the Lord and honour the priest,
and give him his portion, as you
have been commanded:
the first fruits, the guilt-offering,
the gift of the shoulders,
the sacrifice of sanctification,
and the first fruits of
the holy things.

32 Stretch out your hand to the poor,
so that your blessing may
be complete.
33 Give graciously to all the living;
do not withhold kindness
even from the dead.
34 Do not avoid those who weep,
but mourn with those
who mourn.
35 Do not hesitate to visit the sick,
because for such deeds
you will be loved.
36 In all you do, remember the
end of your life,
and then you will never sin.

PRUDENCE AND COMMON SENSE

8 Do not contend with the powerful,
or you may fall into their hands.
2 Do not quarrel with the rich,
in case their resources
outweigh yours;
for gold has ruined many,
and has perverted the
minds of kings.
3 Do not argue with the loud of mouth,
and do not heap wood
on their fire.

4 Do not make fun of one
who is ill-bred,
or your ancestors may be insulted.
5 Do not reproach one who is
turning away from sin;
remember that we all deserve
punishment.
6 Do not disdain one who is old,
for some of us are also
growing old.
7 Do not rejoice over anyone's death;
remember that we must all die.

8 Do not slight the discourse
of the sages,
but busy yourself with
their maxims;
because from them you will
learn discipline
and how to serve princes.
9 Do not ignore the discourse
of the aged,
for they themselves learned
from their parents;[v]
from them you learn how
to understand
and to give an answer when
the need arises.

10 Do not kindle the coals of sinners,
or you may be burned in
their flaming fire.
11 Do not let the insolent bring
you to your feet,
or they may lie in ambush
against your words.
12 Do not lend to one who is
stronger than you;
but if you do lend anything,
count it as a loss.

[q] **7.21** Heb *Love a wise slave as yourself*
[r] **7.23** Gk *bend their necks* [s] **7.24** Gk *body*
[t] **7.26** Heb Syr lack *who pleases you* [u] **7.28** Gk *them* [v] **8.9** Or *ancestors*

13 Do not give surety beyond your means;
but if you give surety, be
prepared to pay.

14 Do not go to law against a judge,
for the decision will favour him
because of his standing.
15 Do not go travelling with the reckless,
or they will be burdensome to you;
for they will act as they please,
and through their folly you
will perish with them.
16 Do not pick a fight with the
quick-tempered,
and do not journey with them
through lonely country,
because bloodshed means
nothing to them,
and where no help is at hand
they will strike you down.
17 Do not consult with fools,
for they cannot keep a secret.
18 In the presence of strangers
do nothing that is to
be kept secret,
for you do not know what
they will divulge.[w]
19 Do not reveal your thoughts
to anyone,
or you may drive away
your happiness.[x]

ADVICE CONCERNING WOMEN

9 Do not be jealous of the wife
of your bosom,
or you will teach her an evil
lesson to your own hurt.
2 Do not give yourself to a woman
and let her trample down
your strength.
3 Do not go near a loose woman,
or you will fall into her snares.
4 Do not dally with a singing-girl,
or you will be caught by her tricks.
5 Do not look intently at a virgin,
or you may stumble and incur
penalties for her.
6 Do not give yourself to prostitutes,
or you may lose your inheritance.
7 Do not look around in the
streets of a city,
or wander about in its
deserted sections.
8 Turn away your eyes from a
shapely woman,
and do not gaze at beauty
belonging to another;
many have been seduced by a
woman's beauty,
and by it passion is kindled
like a fire.
9 Never dine with another man's wife,
or revel with her at wine;
or your heart may turn aside to her,
and in blood[y] you may be
plunged into destruction.

CHOICE OF FRIENDS

10 Do not abandon old friends,
for new ones cannot equal them.
A new friend is like new wine;
when it has aged, you can
drink it with pleasure.

11 Do not envy the success of sinners,
for you do not know what
their end will be like.
12 Do not delight in what pleases
the ungodly;
remember that they will not be
held guiltless all their lives.

13 Keep far from those who have
power to kill,
and you will not be haunted
by the fear of death.
But if you approach them,
take no false step,
or they may rob you of your life.
Know that you are stepping
among snares,
and that you are walking on
the city battlements.

14 As much as you can, aim to know
your neighbours,
and consult with the wise.
15 Let your conversation be with
intelligent people,
and let all your discussion be about
the law of the Most High.
16 Let the righteous be your
dinner companions,
and let your glory be in the
fear of the Lord.

CONCERNING RULERS

17 A work is praised for the skill
of the artisan;
so a people's leader is proved
wise by his words.
18 The loud of mouth are feared
in their city,
and the one who is reckless
in speech is hated.

10 A wise magistrate
educates his people,
and the rule of an intelligent
person is well ordered.

[w] **8.18** *Or it will bring forth* [x] **8.19** Heb: Gk *and let him not return a favour to you* [y] **9.9** Heb: Gk *by your spirit*

2 As the people's judge is, so
are his officials;
as the ruler of the city is, so
are all its inhabitants.
3 An undisciplined king ruins
his people,
but a city becomes fit to
live in through the
understanding of its rulers.
4 The government of the earth is in
the hand of the Lord,
and over it he will raise up the
right leader for the time.
5 Human success is in the
hand of the Lord,
and it is he who confers honour
upon the lawgiver.[z]

THE SIN OF PRIDE

6 Do not get angry with your
neighbour for every injury,
and do not resort to acts
of insolence.
7 Arrogance is hateful to the
Lord and to mortals,
and injustice is outrageous to both.
8 Sovereignty passes from
nation to nation
on account of injustice and
insolence and wealth.[a]
9 How can dust and ashes be proud?
Even in life the human
body decays.[b]
10 A long illness baffles the physician;[c]
the king of today will
die tomorrow.
11 For when one is dead
he inherits maggots and
vermin[d] and worms.
12 The beginning of human pride
is to forsake the Lord;
the heart has withdrawn
from its Maker.
13 For the beginning of pride is sin,
and the one who clings to it
pours out abominations.
Therefore the Lord brings upon them
unheard-of calamities,
and destroys them completely.
14 The Lord overthrows the
thrones of rulers,
and enthrones the lowly
in their place.
15 The Lord plucks up the roots
of the nations,[e]
and plants the humble
in their place.
16 The Lord lays waste the lands
of the nations,
and destroys them to the
foundations of the earth.
17 He removes some of them and
destroys them,
and erases the memory of
them from the earth.
18 Pride was not created for
human beings,
or violent anger for those
born of women.

PERSONS DESERVING HONOUR

19 Whose offspring are worthy
of honour?
Human offspring.
Whose offspring are worthy
of honour?
Those who fear the Lord.
Whose offspring are unworthy
of honour?
Human offspring.
Whose offspring are unworthy
of honour?
Those who break the
commandments.
20 Among family members their leader
is worthy of honour,
but those who fear the Lord are
worthy of honour in his eyes.[f]
22 The rich, and the eminent,
and the poor—
their glory is the fear of the Lord.
23 It is not right to despise one who
is intelligent but poor,
and it is not proper to honour
one who is sinful.
24 The prince and the judge and the
ruler are honoured,
but none of them is greater than
one who fears the Lord.
25 Free citizens will serve a wise servant,
and an intelligent person
will not complain.

CONCERNING HUMILITY

26 Do not make a display of your
wisdom when you
do your work,
and do not boast when
you are in need.
27 Better is the worker who has
goods in plenty
than the boaster who lacks bread.

[z] 10.5 Heb: Gk *scribe* [a] 10.8 Other ancient authorities add here or after verse 9a, *Nothing is more wicked than one who loves money, for such a person puts his own soul up for sale.* [b] 10.9 Heb: Meaning of Gk uncertain [c] 10.10 Heb Lat: Meaning of Gk uncertain [d] 10.11 Heb: Gk *wild animals* [e] 10.15 Other ancient authorities read *proud nations* [f] 10.20 Other ancient authorities add as verse 21, *The fear of the Lord is the beginning of acceptance; obduracy and pride are the beginning of rejection.*

28 My child, honour yourself
with humility,
and give yourself the esteem
you deserve.
29 Who will acquit those who
condemn[g] themselves?
And who will honour those who
dishonour themselves?[h]
30 The poor are honoured for
their knowledge,
while the rich are honoured
for their wealth.
31 One who is honoured in poverty,
how much more in wealth!
And one dishonoured in wealth,
how much more in poverty!

THE DECEPTIVENESS OF APPEARANCES

11 The wisdom of the humble
lifts their heads high,
and seats them among
the great.
2 Do not praise individuals for
their good looks,
or loathe anyone because of
appearance alone.
3 The bee is small among
flying creatures,
but what it produces is the
best of sweet things.
4 Do not boast about wearing
fine clothes,
and do not exalt yourself when
you are honoured;
for the works of the Lord
are wonderful,
and his works are concealed
from humankind.
5 Many kings have had to sit
on the ground,
but one who was never thought
of has worn a crown.
6 Many rulers have been
utterly disgraced,
and the honoured have been
handed over to others.

DELIBERATION AND CAUTION

7 Do not find fault before you
investigate;
examine first, and
then criticize.
8 Do not answer before you listen,
and do not interrupt when
another is speaking.
9 Do not argue about a
matter that does not
concern you,
and do not sit with sinners
when they judge a case.

10 My child, do not busy yourself
with many matters;
if you multiply activities, you
will not be held blameless.
If you pursue, you will not overtake,
and by fleeing you will not escape.
11 There are those who work and
struggle and hurry,
but are so much the more in want.
12 There are others who are slow
and need help,
who lack strength and
abound in poverty;
but the eyes of the Lord look
kindly upon them;
he lifts them out of their
lowly condition
13 and raises up their heads
to the amazement of many.

14 Good things and bad, life and death,
poverty and wealth, come
from the Lord.[i]
17 The Lord's gift remains with
the devout,
and his favour brings
lasting success.
18 One becomes rich through
diligence and self-denial,
and the reward allotted
to him is this:
19 when he says, 'I have found rest,
and now I shall feast on
my goods!'
he does not know how long it will be
until he leaves them to
others and dies.

20 Stand by your agreement
and attend to it,
and grow old in your work.
21 Do not wonder at the works
of a sinner,
but trust in the Lord and
keep at your job;
for it is easy in the sight of the Lord
to make the poor rich suddenly,
in an instant.
22 The blessing of the Lord is[j] the
reward of the pious,
and quickly God causes his
blessing to flourish.

[g] **10.29** Heb: Gk *sin against* [h] **10.29** Heb Lat: Gk *their own life* [i] **11.14** Other ancient authorities add as verses 15 and 16, [15]*Wisdom, understanding, and knowledge of the law come from the Lord; affection and the ways of good works come from him.* [16]*Error and darkness were created with sinners; evil grows old with those who take pride in malice.* [j] **11.22** Heb: Gk *is in*

23 Do not say, 'What do I need,
and what further benefit
can be mine?'
24 Do not say, 'I have enough,
and what harm can come
to me now?'
25 In the day of prosperity,
adversity is forgotten,
and in the day of adversity,
prosperity is not
remembered.
26 For it is easy for the Lord on
the day of death
to reward individuals according
to their conduct.
27 An hour's misery makes one
forget past delights,
and at the close of one's life
one's deeds are revealed.
28 Call no one happy before his death;
by how he ends, a person
becomes known.[k]

CARE IN CHOOSING FRIENDS

29 Do not invite everyone into
your home,
for many are the tricks
of the crafty.
30 Like a decoy partridge in a cage, so
is the mind of the proud,
and like spies they observe
your weakness;[l]
31 for they lie in wait, turning
good into evil,
and to worthy actions they
attach blame.
32 From a spark many coals
are kindled,
and a sinner lies in wait
to shed blood.
33 Beware of scoundrels, for
they devise evil,
and they may ruin your
reputation for ever.
34 Receive strangers into your
home and they will stir
up trouble for you,
and will make you a stranger
to your own family.

12 If you do good, know to
whom you do it,
and you will be thanked for
your good deeds.
2 Do good to the devout, and
you will be repaid—
if not by them, certainly
by the Most High.
3 No good comes to one who
persists in evil
or to one who does not give alms.
4 Give to the devout, but do not
help the sinner.
5 Do good to the humble, but do
not give to the ungodly;
hold back their bread, and do
not give it to them,
for by means of it they
might subdue you;
then you will receive twice
as much evil
for all the good you have
done to them.
6 For the Most High also hates sinners
and will inflict punishment
on the ungodly.[m]
7 Give to one who is good, but do
not help the sinner.
8 A friend is not known[n]
in prosperity,
nor is an enemy hidden
in adversity.
9 One's enemies are friendly[o]
when one prospers,
but in adversity even one's
friend disappears.
10 Never trust your enemy,
for like corrosion in copper,
so is his wickedness.
11 Even if he humbles himself and
walks bowed down,
take care to be on your
guard against him.
Be to him like one who
polishes a mirror,
to be sure it does not become
completely tarnished.
12 Do not put him next to you,
or he may overthrow you
and take your place.
Do not let him sit at your right hand,
or else he may try to take
your own seat,
and at last you will realize the
truth of my words,
and be stung by what I have said.

13 Who pities a snake-charmer
when he is bitten,
or all those who go near
wild animals?
14 So no one pities a person who
associates with a sinner
and becomes involved in
the other's sins.

[k] 11.28 Heb: Gk *and through his children a person becomes known* [l] 11.30 Heb: Gk *downfall*
[m] 12.6 Other ancient authorities add *and he is keeping them for the day of their punishment*
[n] 12.8 Other ancient authorities read *punished*
[o] 12.9 Heb: Gk *grieved*

15 He stands by you for a while,
but if you falter, he will
not be there.
16 An enemy speaks sweetly
with his lips,
but in his heart he plans to
throw you into a pit;
an enemy may have tears
in his eyes,
but if he finds an opportunity
he will never have
enough of your blood.
17 If evil comes upon you, you will find
him there ahead of you;
pretending to help, he
will trip you up.
18 Then he will shake his head,
and clap his hands,
and whisper much, and
show his true face.

CAUTION REGARDING ASSOCIATES

13 Whoever touches pitch
gets dirty,
and whoever associates
with a proud person
becomes like him.
2 Do not lift a weight too
heavy for you,
or associate with one mightier
and richer than you.
How can the clay pot associate
with the iron kettle?
The pot will strike against
it and be smashed.
3 A rich person does wrong, and
even adds insults;
a poor person suffers wrong,
and must add apologies.
4 A rich person[p] will exploit you if
you can be of use to him,
but if you are in need he
will abandon you.
5 If you own something, he
will live with you;
he will drain your resources
without a qualm.
6 When he needs you he will
deceive you,
and will smile at you and
encourage you;
he will speak to you kindly and
say, 'What do you need?'
7 He will embarrass you with
his delicacies,
until he has drained you
two or three times,
and finally he will laugh at you.
Should he see you afterwards,
he will pass you by
and shake his head at you.
8 Take care not to be led astray
and humiliated when you are
enjoying yourself.[q]
9 When an influential person
invites you, be reserved,
and he will invite you
more insistently.
10 Do not be forward, or you
may be rebuffed;
do not stand aloof, or you
will be forgotten.
11 Do not try to treat him as an equal,
or trust his lengthy conversations;
for he will test you by prolonged talk,
and while he smiles he will
be examining you.
12 Cruel are those who do not
keep your secrets;
they will not spare you harm
or imprisonment.
13 Be on your guard and very careful,
for you are walking about with
your own downfall.[r]

15 Every creature loves its like,
and every person a neighbour.
16 All living beings associate with
their own kind,
and people stick close to those
like themselves.
17 What does a wolf have in
common with a lamb?
No more has a sinner
with the devout.
18 What peace is there between
a hyena and a dog?
And what peace between the
rich and the poor?
19 Wild asses in the wilderness
are the prey of lions;
likewise the poor are
feeding-grounds for the rich.
20 Humility is an abomination
to the proud;
likewise the poor are an
abomination to the rich.
21 When the rich person totters, he
is supported by friends,
but when the humble[s] falls, he is
pushed away even by friends.
22 If the rich person slips, many
come to the rescue;
he speaks unseemly words,
but they justify him.

[p] 13.4 Gk *He* [q] 13.8 Other ancient authorities read *in your folly* [r] 13.13 Other ancient authorities add as verse 14, *When you hear these things in your sleep, wake up! During all your life love the Lord, and call on him for your salvation.* [s] 13.21 Other ancient authorities read *poor*

If the humble person slips, they
even criticize him;
he talks sense, but is not
given a hearing.
23 The rich person speaks and
all are silent;
they extol to the clouds
what he says.
The poor person speaks and they
say, 'Who is this fellow?'
And should he stumble, they
even push him down.
24 Riches are good if they are
free from sin;
poverty is evil only in the
opinion of the ungodly.

25 The heart changes the
countenance,
either for good or for evil.[t]
26 The sign of a happy heart is
a cheerful face,
but to devise proverbs requires
painful thinking.

14 Happy are those who do not
blunder with their lips,
and need not suffer
remorse for sin.
2 Happy are those whose hearts
do not condemn them,
and who have not given
up their hope.

RESPONSIBLE USE OF WEALTH

3 Riches are inappropriate for a
small-minded person;
and of what use is wealth
to a miser?
4 What he denies himself he
collects for others;
and others will live in luxury
on his goods.
5 If one is mean to himself, to whom
will he be generous?
He will not enjoy his own riches.
6 No one is worse than one who is
grudging to himself;
this is the punishment for
his meanness.
7 If ever he does good, it is by mistake;
and in the end he reveals
his meanness.
8 The miser is an evil person;
he turns away and
disregards people.
9 The eye of the greedy person is not
satisfied with his share;
greedy injustice withers
the soul.
10 A miser begrudges bread,
and it is lacking at his table.

11 My child, treat yourself well,
according to your means,
and present worthy offerings
to the Lord.
12 Remember that death does not tarry,
and the decree[u] of Hades has
not been shown to you.
13 Do good to friends before you die,
and reach out and give to them
as much as you can.
14 Do not deprive yourself of a
day's enjoyment;
do not let your share of desired
good pass by you.
15 Will you not leave the fruit of
your labours to another,
and what you acquired by toil
to be divided by lot?
16 Give, and take, and indulge yourself,
because in Hades one cannot
look for luxury.
17 All living beings become old
like a garment,
for the decree[v] from of old
is, 'You must die!'
18 Like abundant leaves on a
spreading tree
that sheds some and puts
forth others,
so are the generations of
flesh and blood:
one dies and another is born.
19 Every work decays and
ceases to exist,
and the one who made it will
pass away with it.

THE HAPPINESS OF SEEKING WISDOM

20 Happy is the person who
meditates on[w] wisdom
and reasons intelligently,
21 who[x] reflects in his heart
on her ways
and ponders her secrets,
22 pursuing her like a hunter,
and lying in wait on her paths;
23 who peers through her windows
and listens at her doors;
24 who camps near her house
and fastens his tent-peg
to her walls;
25 who pitches his tent near her,
and so occupies an excellent
lodging-place;

[t] **13.25** Other ancient authorities add *and a glad heart makes a cheerful countenance*
[u] **14.12** Heb Syr: Gk *covenant* [v] **14.17** Heb: Gk *covenant* [w] **14.20** Other ancient authorities read *dies in* [x] **14.21** The structure adopted in verses 21–27 follows the Heb

26 who places his children
under her shelter,
and lodges under her boughs;
27 who is sheltered by her
from the heat,
and dwells in the midst
of her glory.

15 Whoever fears the Lord
will do this,
and whoever holds to the law
will obtain wisdom.[y]
2 She will come to meet him
like a mother,
and like a young bride she
will welcome him.
3 She will feed him with the
bread of learning,
and give him the water of
wisdom to drink.
4 He will lean on her and not fall,
and he will rely on her and
not be put to shame.
5 She will exalt him above
his neighbours,
and will open his mouth in the
midst of the assembly.
6 He will find gladness and a
crown of rejoicing,
and will inherit an
everlasting name.
7 The foolish will not obtain her,
and sinners will not see her.
8 She is far from arrogance,
and liars will never think of her.
9 Praise is unseemly on the
lips of a sinner,
for it has not been sent
from the Lord.
10 For in wisdom must praise
be uttered,
and the Lord will make it prosper.

FREEDOM OF CHOICE

11 Do not say, 'It was the Lord's
doing that I fell away';
for he does not do[z] what he hates.
12 Do not say, 'It was he who
led me astray';
for he has no need of the sinful.
13 The Lord hates all abominations;
such things are not loved by
those who fear him.
14 It was he who created humankind
in the beginning,
and he left them in the power
of their own free choice.
15 If you choose, you can keep the
commandments,
and to act faithfully is a matter
of your own choice.
16 He has placed before you
fire and water;
stretch out your hand for
whichever you choose.
17 Before each person are life and death,
and whichever one chooses
will be given.
18 For great is the wisdom of the Lord;
he is mighty in power and
sees everything;
19 his eyes are on those who fear him,
and he knows every human action.
20 He has not commanded anyone
to be wicked,
and he has not given anyone
permission to sin.

GOD'S PUNISHMENT OF SINNERS

16 Do not desire a multitude
of worthless[a] children,
and do not rejoice in
ungodly offspring.
2 If they multiply, do not
rejoice in them,
unless the fear of the
Lord is in them.
3 Do not trust in their survival,
or rely on their numbers;[b]
for one can be better than a thousand,
and to die childless is better than
to have ungodly children.
4 For through one intelligent person a
city can be filled with people,
but through a clan of outlaws
it becomes desolate.
5 Many such things my eye has seen,
and my ear has heard things
more striking than these.
6 In an assembly of sinners a
fire is kindled,
and in a disobedient nation
wrath blazes up.
7 He did not forgive the ancient giants
who revolted in their might.
8 He did not spare the
neighbours of Lot,
whom he loathed on account
of their arrogance.
9 He showed no pity on the
doomed nation,
on those dispossessed because
of their sins;[c]

[y] **15.1** Gk *her* [z] **15.11** Heb: Gk *you ought not to do* [a] **16.1** Heb: Gk *unprofitable* [b] **16.3** Other ancient authorities add *For you will groan in untimely mourning, and will know of their sudden end.* [c] **16.9** Other ancient authorities add *All these things he did to the hard-hearted nations, and by the multitude of his holy ones he was not appeased.*

10 or on the six hundred thousand
foot-soldiers
who assembled in their
stubbornness.[d]
11 Even if there were only one
stiff-necked person,
it would be a wonder if he
remained unpunished.
For mercy and wrath are
with the Lord;[e]
he is mighty to forgive—but
he also pours out wrath.
12 Great as is his mercy, so also is
his chastisement;
he judges a person according
to his or her deeds.
13 The sinner will not escape
with plunder,
and the patience of the godly
will not be frustrated.
14 He makes room for every
act of mercy;
everyone receives in accordance
with his or her deeds.[f]

17 Do not say, 'I am hidden
from the Lord,
and who from on high
has me in mind?
Among so many people I
am unknown,
for what am I in a boundless
creation?
18 Lo, heaven and the
highest heaven,
the abyss and the earth, tremble
at his visitation![g]
19 The very mountains and the
foundations of the earth
quiver and quake when he
looks upon them.
20 But no human mind can grasp this,
and who can comprehend
his ways?
21 Like a tempest that no one can see,
so most of his works are
concealed.[h]
22 Who is to announce his
acts of justice?
Or who can await them? For
his decree[i] is far off.'[j]
23 Such are the thoughts of one
devoid of understanding;
a senseless and misguided
person thinks foolishly.

GOD'S WISDOM SEEN IN CREATION

24 Listen to me, my child, and
acquire knowledge,
and pay close attention
to my words.
25 I will impart discipline precisely[k]
and declare knowledge accurately.
26 When the Lord created[l] his works
from the beginning,
and, in making them, determined
their boundaries,
27 he arranged his works in an
eternal order,
and their dominion[m] for
all generations.
They neither hunger nor
grow weary,
and they do not abandon
their tasks.
28 They do not crowd one another,
and they never disobey his word.
29 Then the Lord looked upon the earth,
and filled it with his good things.
30 With all kinds of living beings
he covered its surface,
and into it they must return.

17 The Lord created human
beings out of earth,
and makes them return
to it again.
2 He gave them a fixed
number of days,
but granted them authority over
everything on the earth.[n]
3 He endowed them with strength
like his own,[o]
and made them in his own image.
4 He put the fear of them[p] in
all living beings,
and gave them dominion over
beasts and birds.[q]
6 Discretion and tongue and eyes,
ears and a mind for thinking
he gave them.

[d] **16.10** Other ancient authorities add *Chastising, showing mercy, striking, healing, the Lord persisted in mercy and discipline.* [e] **16.11** Gk *him*
[f] **16.14** Other ancient authorities add [15]*The Lord hardened Pharaoh so that he did not recognize him, in order that his works might be known under heaven.* [16]*His mercy is manifest to the whole of creation, and he divided his light and darkness with a plumb-line.* [g] **16.18** Other ancient authorities add *The whole world past and present is in his will.* [h] **16.21** Meaning of Gk uncertain: Heb Syr *If I sin, no eye can see me, and if I am disloyal all in secret, who is to know?*
[i] **16.22** Heb *the decree*: Gk *the covenant*
[j] **16.22** Other ancient authorities add *and a scrutiny for all comes at the end* [k] **16.25** Gk *by weight* [l] **16.26** Heb: Gk *judged* [m] **16.27** Or *elements* [n] **17.2** Lat: Gk *it* [o] **17.3** Lat: Gk *proper to them* [p] **17.4** Syr: Gk *him*
[q] **17.4** Other ancient authorities add as verse 5, *They obtained the use of the five faculties of the Lord; as sixth he distributed to them the gift of mind, and as seventh, reason, the interpreter of one's faculties.*

7 He filled them with knowledge
and understanding,
and showed them good and evil.
8 He put the fear of him into[r]
their hearts
to show them the majesty
of his works.[s]
10 And they will praise his holy name,
9 to proclaim the grandeur
of his works.
11 He bestowed knowledge upon them,
and allotted to them the
law of life.[t]
12 He established with them an
eternal covenant,
and revealed to them his decrees.
13 Their eyes saw his glorious majesty,
and their ears heard the
glory of his voice.
14 He said to them, 'Beware of all evil.'
And he gave commandment to
each of them concerning
a neighbour.
15 Their ways are always known to him;
they will not be hid
from his eyes.[u]
17 He appointed a ruler for
every nation,
but Israel is the Lord's
own portion.[v]
19 All their works are as clear as
the sun before him,
and his eyes are ever upon
their ways.
20 Their iniquities are not
hidden from him,
and all their sins are
before the Lord.[w]
22 One's almsgiving is like a signet
ring with the Lord,[x]
and he will keep a person's
kindness like the
apple of his eye.[y]
23 Afterwards he will rise up
and repay them,
and he will bring their
recompense on their heads.
24 Yet to those who repent he
grants a return,
and he encourages those
who are losing hope.

A CALL TO REPENTANCE

25 Turn back to the Lord and
forsake your sins;
pray in his presence and
lessen your offence.
26 Return to the Most High and turn
away from iniquity,[z]
and hate intensely what
he abhors.
27 Who will sing praises to the
Most High in Hades
in place of the living who
give thanks?
28 From the dead, as from one
who does not exist,
thanksgiving has ceased;
those who are alive and well
sing the Lord's praises.
29 How great is the
mercy of the Lord,
and his forgiveness for those
who return to him!
30 For not everything is within
human capability,
since human beings are
not immortal.
31 What is brighter than the sun?
Yet it can be eclipsed.
So flesh and blood devise evil.
32 He marshals the host of the
height of heaven;
but all human beings are
dust and ashes.

THE MAJESTY OF GOD

18 He who lives for ever created
the whole universe;
2 the Lord alone is just.[a]
4 To none has he given power to
proclaim his works;
and who can search out
his mighty deeds?
5 Who can measure his
majestic power?
And who can fully recount
his mercies?

[r] 17.8 Other ancient authorities read *He set his eye upon* [s] 17.8 Other ancient authorities add *and he gave them to boast of his marvels for ever* [t] 17.11 Other ancient authorities add *so that they may know that they who are alive now are mortal* [u] 17.15 Other ancient authorities add [16]*Their ways from youth tend towards evil, and they are unable to make for themselves hearts of flesh in place of their stony hearts.* [17]*For in the division of the nations of the whole earth, he appointed* [v] 17.17 Other ancient authorities add as verse 18, *whom, being his firstborn, he brings up with discipline, and allotting to him the light of his love, he does not neglect him.* [w] 17.20 Other ancient authorities add as verse 21, *But the Lord, who is gracious and knows how they are formed, has neither left them nor abandoned them, but has spared them.* [x] 17.22 Gk *him* [y] 17.22 Other ancient authorities add *apportioning repentance to his sons and daughters* [z] 17.26 Other ancient authorities add *for he will lead you out of darkness to the light of health.* [a] 18.2 Other ancient authorities add *and there is no other beside him;* [3]*he steers the world with the span of his hand, and all things obey his will; for he is king of all things by his power, separating among them the holy things from the profane.*

6 It is not possible to diminish
or increase them,
nor is it possible to fathom the
wonders of the Lord.
7 When human beings have finished,
they are just beginning,
and when they stop, they
are still perplexed.
8 What are human beings, and of
what use are they?
What is good in them,
and what is evil?
9 The number of days in their life
is great if they reach
one hundred years.[b]
10 Like a drop of water from the sea
and a grain of sand,
so are a few years among
the days of eternity.
11 That is why the Lord is
patient with them
and pours out his mercy
upon them.
12 He sees and recognizes that
their end is miserable;
therefore he grants them
forgiveness all the more.
13 The compassion of human beings
is for their neighbours,
but the compassion of the Lord
is for every living thing.
He rebukes and trains and
teaches them,
and turns them back, as a
shepherd his flock.
14 He has compassion on those who
accept his discipline
and who are eager for
his precepts.

THE RIGHT SPIRIT IN GIVING ALMS

15 My child, do not mix reproach
with your good deeds,
or spoil your gift by
harsh words.
16 Does not the dew give relief from
the scorching heat?
So a word is better than a gift.
17 Indeed, does not a word
surpass a good gift?
Both are to be found in a
gracious person.
18 A fool is ungracious and abusive,
and the gift of a grudging giver
makes the eyes dim.

THE NEED FOR REFLECTION AND SELF-CONTROL

19 Before you speak, learn;
and before you fall ill, take
care of your health.
20 Before judgement comes,
examine yourself;
and at the time of scrutiny you
will find forgiveness.
21 Before falling ill, humble yourself;
and when you have
sinned, repent.
22 Let nothing hinder you from
paying a vow promptly,
and do not wait until death
to be released from it.
23 Before making a vow,
prepare yourself;
do not be like one who puts
the Lord to the test.
24 Think of his wrath on the
day of death,
and of the moment of vengeance
when he turns away his face.
25 In the time of plenty think of
the time of hunger;
in days of wealth think of
poverty and need.
26 From morning to evening
conditions change;
all things move swiftly
before the Lord.

27 One who is wise is cautious
in everything;
when sin is all around, one guards
against wrongdoing.
28 Every intelligent person
knows wisdom,
and praises one who finds her.
29 Those who are skilled in words
become wise themselves,
and pour forth apt proverbs.[c]

SELF-CONTROL[d]

30 Do not follow your base desires,
but restrain your appetites.
31 If you allow your soul to take
pleasure in base desire,
it will make you the
laughing-stock of
your enemies.
32 Do not revel in great luxury,
or you may become impoverished
by its expense.

[b] **18.9** Other ancient authorities add *but the death of each one is beyond the calculation of all*
[c] **18.29** Other ancient authorities add *Better is confidence in the one Lord than clinging with a dead heart to a dead one.* [d] **18.30** This heading is included in the Gk text.

33 Do not become a beggar by feasting
with borrowed money
when you have nothing
in your purse.[e]

19 One who does this[f] will
not become rich;
one who despises small things
will fail little by little.
2 Wine and women lead intelligent
men astray,
and the man who consorts with
prostitutes is reckless.
3 Decay and worms will take
possession of him,
and the reckless person will
be snatched away.

AGAINST LOOSE TALK

4 One who trusts others too quickly
has a shallow mind,
and one who sins does
wrong to himself.
5 One who rejoices in wickedness[g]
will be condemned,[h]
6 but one who hates gossip
has less evil.
7 Never repeat a conversation,
and you will lose nothing at all.
8 With friend or foe do not report it,
and unless it would be a sin for
you, do not reveal it;
9 for someone may have heard
you and watched you,
and in time will hate you.
10 Have you heard something?
Let it die with you.
Be brave, it will not make
you burst!
11 Having heard something, the fool
suffers birth-pangs
like a woman in labour with a child.
12 Like an arrow stuck in a
person's thigh,
so is gossip inside a fool.

13 Question a friend; perhaps
he did not do it;
or if he did, so that he may
not do it again.
14 Question a neighbour; perhaps
he did not say it;
or if he said it, so that he
may not repeat it.
15 Question a friend, for often
it is slander;
so do not believe everything
you hear.
16 A person may make a slip
without intending it.
Who has not sinned with
his tongue?
17 Question your neighbour before
you threaten him;
and let the law of the Most
High take its course.[i]

TRUE AND FALSE WISDOM

20 The whole of wisdom is fear
of the Lord,
and in all wisdom there is the
fulfilment of the law.[j]
22 The knowledge of wickedness
is not wisdom,
nor is there prudence in the
counsel of sinners.
23 There is a cleverness that
is detestable,
and there is a fool who
merely lacks wisdom.
24 Better are the God-fearing who
lack understanding
than the highly intelligent
who transgress the law.
25 There is a cleverness that is
exact but unjust,
and there are people who abuse
favours to gain a verdict.
26 There is the villain bowed
down in mourning,
but inwardly he is full of deceit.
27 He hides his face and pretends
not to hear,
but when no one notices, he will
take advantage of you.
28 Even if lack of strength keeps
him from sinning,
he will nevertheless do evil when
he finds the opportunity.
29 A person is known by his
appearance,
and a sensible person is known
when first met face to face.
30 A person's attire and
hearty laughter,
and the way he walks,
show what he is.

[e] **18.33** Other ancient authorities add *for you will be plotting against your own life* [f] **19.1** Heb: Gk *A worker who is a drunkard* [g] **19.5** Other ancient authorities read *heart* [h] **19.5** Other ancient authorities add *but one who withstands pleasures crowns his life.* [6]*One who controls the tongue will live without strife,* [i] **19.17** Other ancient authorities add *and do not be angry.* [18]*The fear of the Lord is the beginning of acceptance, and wisdom obtains his love.* [19]*The knowledge of the Lord's commandments is life-giving discipline; and those who do what is pleasing to him enjoy the fruit of the tree of immortality.* [j] **19.20** Other ancient authorities add *and the knowledge of his omnipotence.* [21]*When a slave says to his master, 'I will not act as you wish', even if later he does it, he angers the one who supports him.*

SILENCE AND SPEECH

20 There is a rebuke that
is untimely,
and there is the person who is
wise enough to keep silent.
2 How much better it is to rebuke
than to fume!
3 And one who admits his fault will
be kept from failure.
4 Like a eunuch lusting to violate a girl
is the person who does right
under compulsion.
5 Some people keep silent and are
thought to be wise,
while others are detested
for being talkative.
6 Some people keep silent because
they have nothing to say,
while others keep silent because
they know when to speak.
7 The wise remain silent until
the right moment,
but a boasting fool misses
the right moment.
8 Whoever talks too much is detested,
and whoever pretends to
authority is hated.[k]

PARADOXES

9 There may be good fortune for
a person in adversity,
but a windfall may result in a loss.
10 There is the gift that profits
you nothing,
and the gift to be paid
back double.
11 There are losses for the sake of glory,
and there are some who have
raised their heads from
humble circumstances.
12 Some buy much for little,
but pay for it seven times over.
13 The wise make themselves beloved
by only few words,[l]
but the courtesies of fools
are wasted.
14 A fool's gift will profit you nothing,[m]
for he looks for recompense
sevenfold.[n]
15 He gives little and upbraids much;
he opens his mouth like
a town crier.
Today he lends and tomorrow
he asks for it back;
such a one is hateful to God
and humans.[o]
16 The fool says, 'I have no friends,
and I get no thanks for
my good deeds.
Those who eat my bread
are evil-tongued.'
17 How many will ridicule him,
and how often![p]

INAPPROPRIATE SPEECH

18 A slip on the pavement is better
than a slip of the tongue;
the downfall of the wicked will
occur just as speedily.
19 A coarse person is like an
inappropriate story
continually on the lips of
the ignorant.
20 A proverb from a fool's lips
will be rejected,
for he does not tell it at
the proper time.

21 One may be prevented from
sinning by poverty;
so when he rests he feels
no remorse.
22 One may lose his life through shame,
or lose it because of
human respect.[q]
23 Another out of shame makes
promises to a friend,
and so makes an enemy
for nothing.

LYING

24 A lie is an ugly blot on a person;
it is continually on the lips
of the ignorant.
25 A thief is preferable to a habitual liar,
but the lot of both is ruin.
26 A liar's way leads to disgrace,
and his shame is ever with him.

PROVERBIAL SAYINGS[r]

27 The wise person advances
himself by his words,
and one who is sensible
pleases the great.
28 Those who cultivate the soil
heap up their harvest,
and those who please the great
atone for injustice.

[k] **20.8** Other ancient authorities add *How good it is to show repentance when you are reproved, for so you will escape deliberate sin!* [l] **20.13** Heb: Gk *by words* [m] **20.14** Other ancient authorities add *so it is with the envious who give under compulsion* [n] **20.14** Syr: Gk *he has many eyes instead of one* [o] **20.15** Other ancient authorities lack *to God and humans* [p] **20.17** Other ancient authorities add *for he has not honestly received what he has, and what he does not have is unimportant to him* [q] **20.22** Other ancient authorities read *his foolish look* [r] **20.27** This heading is included in the Gk text.

29 Favours and gifts blind the
eyes of the wise;
like a muzzle on the mouth
they stop reproofs.
30 Hidden wisdom and unseen treasure,
of what value is either?
31 Better are those who hide their folly
than those who hide
their wisdom.[s]

VARIOUS SINS

21 Have you sinned, my
child? Do so no more,
but ask forgiveness for
your past sins.
2 Flee from sin as from a snake;
for if you approach sin,
it will bite you.
Its teeth are lion's teeth,
and can destroy human lives.
3 All lawlessness is like a
two-edged sword;
there is no healing for the
wound it inflicts.

4 Panic and insolence will
waste away riches;
thus the house of the proud
will be laid waste.[t]
5 The prayer of the poor goes from
their lips to the ears of God,[u]
and his judgement comes speedily.
6 Those who hate reproof walk
in the sinner's steps,
but those who fear the Lord
repent in their heart.
7 The mighty in speech are
widely known;
when they slip, the sensible
person knows it.

8 Whoever builds his house with
other people's money
is like one who gathers stones
for his burial mound.[v]
9 An assembly of the wicked is
like a bundle of tow,
and their end is a blazing fire.
10 The way of sinners is paved
with smooth stones,
but at its end is the pit of Hades.

WISDOM AND FOOLISHNESS

11 Whoever keeps the law controls
his thoughts,
and the fulfilment of the fear
of the Lord is wisdom.
12 One who is not clever cannot
be taught,
but there is a cleverness that
increases bitterness.
13 The knowledge of the wise will
increase like a flood,
and their counsel like a
life-giving spring.
14 The mind[w] of a fool is like
a broken jar;
it can hold no knowledge.

15 When an intelligent person
hears a wise saying,
he praises it and adds to it;
when a fool[x] hears it, he laughs at[y] it
and throws it behind his back.
16 A fool's chatter is like a burden
on a journey,
but delight is found in the
speech of the intelligent.
17 The utterance of a sensible person
is sought in the assembly,
and they ponder his words
in their minds.

18 Like a house in ruins is
wisdom to a fool,
and to the ignorant, knowledge is
talk that has no meaning.
19 To a senseless person education
is fetters on his feet,
and like manacles on his
right hand.
20 A fool raises his voice when he laughs,
but the wise[z] smile quietly.
21 To the sensible person education is
like a golden ornament,
and like a bracelet on
the right arm.

22 The foot of a fool rushes into a house,
but an experienced person waits
respectfully outside.
23 A boor peers into the house
from the door,
but a cultivated person
remains outside.
24 It is ill-mannered for a person
to listen at a door;
the discreet would be grieved
by the disgrace.

25 The lips of babblers speak of what
is not their concern,[a]

[s] **20.31** Other ancient authorities add [32]*Unwearied endurance in seeking the Lord is better than a masterless charioteer of one's own life.*
[t] **21.4** Other ancient authorities read *uprooted*
[u] **21.5** Gk *his ears* [v] **21.8** Other ancient authorities read *for the winter* [w] **21.14** Syr Lat: Gk *entrails* [x] **21.15** Syr: Gk *reveller*
[y] **21.15** Syr: Gk *dislikes* [z] **21.20** Syr Lat: Gk *clever* [a] **21.25** Other ancient authorities read *of strangers speak of these things*

but the words of the prudent are
weighed in the balance.
26 The mind of fools is in their mouth,
but the mouth of the wise
is in[b] their mind.
27 When an ungodly person curses
an adversary,[c]
he curses himself.
28 A whisperer degrades himself
and is hated in his
neighbourhood.

THE IDLER

22 The idler is like a filthy stone,
and everyone hisses
at his disgrace.
2 The idler is like the filth
of dunghills;
anyone that picks it up will
shake it off his hand.

DEGENERATE CHILDREN

3 It is a disgrace to be the father of
an undisciplined son,
and the birth of a daughter
is a loss.
4 A sensible daughter obtains a
husband of her own,
but one who acts shamefully
is a grief to her father.
5 An impudent daughter disgraces
father and husband,
and is despised by both.
6 Like music in time of mourning is
ill-timed conversation,
but a thrashing and discipline
are at all times wisdom.[d]

WISDOM AND FOLLY

9 Whoever teaches a fool is
like one who glues
potsherds together,
or who rouses a sleeper
from deep slumber.
10 Whoever tells a story to a fool
tells it to a drowsy man;
and at the end he will
say, 'What is it?'
11 Weep for the dead, for he has
left the light behind;
and weep for the fool, for he has
left intelligence behind.
Weep less bitterly for the dead,
for he is at rest;
but the life of the fool is
worse than death.
12 Mourning for the dead lasts
seven days,
but for the foolish or the
ungodly it lasts all the
days of their lives.
13 Do not talk much with a
senseless person
or visit an unintelligent person.[e]
Stay clear of him, or you may
have trouble,
and be spattered when he
shakes himself.
Avoid him and you will find rest,
and you will never be wearied
by his lack of sense.
14 What is heavier than lead?
And what is its name
except 'Fool'?
15 Sand, salt, and a piece of iron
are easier to bear than a
stupid person.
16 A wooden beam firmly bonded
into a building
is not loosened by an earthquake;
so the mind firmly resolved
after due reflection
will not be afraid in a crisis.
17 A mind settled on an
intelligent thought
is like stucco decoration that
makes a wall smooth.
18 Fences[f] set on a high place
will not stand firm against
the wind;
so a timid mind with a fool's resolve
will not stand firm
against any fear.

THE PRESERVATION
OF FRIENDSHIP

19 One who pricks the eye brings tears,
and one who pricks the heart
makes clear its feelings.
20 One who throws a stone at birds
scares them away,
and one who reviles a friend
destroys a friendship.
21 Even if you draw your sword
against a friend,
do not despair, for there
is a way back.
22 If you open your mouth
against your friend,
do not worry, for reconciliation
is possible.

[b] 21.26 Other ancient authorities omit *in*
[c] 21.27 Or *curses Satan* [d] 22.6 Other ancient authorities add [7]*Children who are brought up in a good life conceal the lowly birth of their parents.* [8]*Children who are disdainfully and boorishly haughty stain the nobility of their kindred.*
[e] 22.13 Other ancient authorities add *For being without sense he will despise everything about you*
[f] 22.18 Other ancient authorities read *Pebbles*

But as for reviling, arrogance,
disclosure of secrets, or
a treacherous blow—
in these cases any friend
will take to flight.

23 Gain the trust of your neighbour
in his poverty,
so that you may rejoice with
him in his prosperity.
Stand by him in time of distress,
so that you may share with
him in his inheritance.[g]
24 The vapour and smoke of the
furnace precede the fire;
so insults precede bloodshed.
25 I am not ashamed to shelter a friend,
and I will not hide from him.
26 But if harm should come to
me because of him,
whoever hears of it will
beware of him.

A PRAYER FOR HELP AGAINST SINNING

27 Who will set a guard over my mouth,
and an effective seal upon my lips,
so that I may not fall because
of them,
and my tongue may not
destroy me?

23 O Lord, Father and
Master of my life,
do not abandon me to their designs,
and do not let me fall
because of them!
2 Who will set whips over my thoughts,
and the discipline of wisdom
over my mind,
so as not to spare me in my errors,
and not overlook my[h] sins?
3 Otherwise my mistakes may
be multiplied,
and my sins may abound,
and I may fall before my adversaries,
and my enemy may rejoice over me.[i]
4 O Lord, Father and God of my life,
do not give me haughty eyes,
5 and remove evil desire from me.
6 Let neither gluttony nor lust
overcome me,
and do not give me over to
shameless passion.

DISCIPLINE OF THE TONGUE[j]

7 Listen, my children, to instruction
concerning the mouth;
one who observes it will
never be caught.
8 Sinners are overtaken
through their lips;
by them the reviler and the
arrogant are tripped up.
9 Do not accustom your
mouth to oaths,
nor habitually utter the name
of the Holy One;
10 for as a servant who is constantly
under scrutiny
will not lack bruises,
so also the person who always
swears and utters the Name
will never be cleansed[k] from sin.
11 One who swears many oaths
is full of iniquity,
and the scourge will not
leave his house.
If he swears in error, his sin
remains on him,
and if he disregards it,
he sins doubly;
if he swears a false oath, he
will not be justified,
for his house will be filled
with calamities.

FOUL LANGUAGE

12 There is a manner of speaking
comparable to death;[l]
may it never be found in the
inheritance of Jacob!
Such conduct will be far
from the godly,
and they will not wallow in sins.
13 Do not accustom your mouth to
coarse, foul language,
for it involves sinful speech.
14 Remember your father and mother
when you sit among the great,
or you may forget yourself in
their presence,
and behave like a fool
through bad habit;
then you will wish that you had
never been born,
and you will curse the day
of your birth.
15 Those who are accustomed to
using abusive language
will never become disciplined
as long as they live.

[g] 22.23 Other ancient authorities add *For one should not always despise restricted circumstances, or admire a rich person who is stupid.* [h] 23.2 Gk *their* [i] 23.3 Other ancient authorities add *From them the hope of your mercy is remote* [j] 23.7 This heading is included in the Gk text. [k] 23.10 Syr *be free* [l] 23.12 Other ancient authorities read *clothed about with death*

CONCERNING SEXUAL SINS

16 Two kinds of individuals
multiply sins,
and a third incurs wrath.
Hot passion that blazes like a fire
will not be quenched until
it burns itself out;
one who commits fornication
with his near of kin
will never cease until the
fire burns him up.
17 To a fornicator all bread is sweet;
he will never weary until he dies.
18 One who sins against his
marriage bed
says to himself, 'Who can see me?
Darkness surrounds me, the
walls hide me,
and no one sees me. Why
should I worry?
The Most High will not
remember sins.'
19 His fear is confined to human eyes
and he does not realize that
the eyes of the Lord
are ten thousand times
brighter than the sun;
they look upon every aspect of
human behaviour
and see into hidden corners.
20 Before the universe was created,
it was known to him,
and so it is since its completion.
21 This man will be punished in
the streets of the city,
and where he least suspects
it, he will be seized.

22 So it is with a woman who
leaves her husband
and presents him with an
heir by another man.
23 For first of all, she has disobeyed
the law of the Most High;
second, she has committed an
offence against her husband;
and third, through her fornication
she has committed adultery
and brought forth children
by another man.
24 She herself will be brought
before the assembly,
and her punishment will
extend to her children.
25 Her children will not take root,
and her branches will
not bear fruit.
26 She will leave behind an
accursed memory
and her disgrace will never
be blotted out.
27 Those who survive her will recognize
that nothing is better than
the fear of the Lord,
and nothing sweeter than to
heed the commandments
of the Lord.[m]

THE PRAISE OF WISDOM[n]

24 Wisdom praises herself,
and tells of her glory in the
midst of her people.
2 In the assembly of the Most High
she opens her mouth,
and in the presence of his hosts
she tells of her glory:
3 'I came forth from the mouth
of the Most High,
and covered the earth like a mist.
4 I dwelt in the highest heavens,
and my throne was in a
pillar of cloud.
5 Alone I compassed the
vault of heaven
and traversed the depths
of the abyss.
6 Over waves of the sea, over
all the earth,
and over every people and
nation I have held sway.[o]
7 Among all these I sought a
resting-place;
in whose territory should I abide?

8 'Then the Creator of all things
gave me a command,
and my Creator chose the
place for my tent.
He said, "Make your dwelling
in Jacob,
and in Israel receive your
inheritance."
9 Before the ages, in the beginning,
he created me,
and for all the ages I shall
not cease to be.
10 In the holy tent I ministered
before him,
and so I was established in Zion.
11 Thus in the beloved city he gave
me a resting-place,
and in Jerusalem was my domain.
12 I took root in an honoured people,
in the portion of the Lord,
his heritage.

m **23.27** Other ancient authorities add as verse 28, *It is a great honour to follow God, and to be received by him is long life.* n **24.1** This heading is included in the Gk text. o **24.6** Other ancient authorities read *I have acquired a possession*

13 'I grew tall like a cedar in Lebanon,
and like a cypress on the
heights of Hermon.
14 I grew tall like a palm tree
in En-gedi,[p]
and like rose-bushes in Jericho;
like a fair olive tree in the field,
and like a plane tree beside
water[q] I grew tall.
15 Like cassia and camel's thorn I
gave forth perfume,
and like choice myrrh I
spread my fragrance,
like galbanum, onycha, and stacte,
and like the odour of
incense in the tent.
16 Like a terebinth I spread out
my branches,
and my branches are glorious
and graceful.
17 Like the vine I bud forth delights,
and my blossoms become glorious
and abundant fruit.[r]

19 'Come to me, you who desire me,
and eat your fill of my fruits.
20 For the memory of me is
sweeter than honey,
and the possession of me sweeter
than the honeycomb.
21 Those who eat of me will
hunger for more,
and those who drink of me
will thirst for more.
22 Whoever obeys me will not
be put to shame,
and those who work with
me will not sin.'

WISDOM AND THE LAW

23 All this is the book of the covenant
of the Most High God,
the law that Moses
commanded us
as an inheritance for the
congregations of Jacob.[s]
25 It overflows, like the Pishon,
with wisdom,
and like the Tigris at the time
of the first fruits.
26 It runs over, like the Euphrates,
with understanding,
and like the Jordan at
harvest time.
27 It pours forth instruction
like the Nile,[t]
like the Gihon at the
time of vintage.
28 The first man did not know
wisdom[u] fully,
nor will the last one fathom her.
29 For her thoughts are more
abundant than the sea,
and her counsel deeper than
the great abyss.
30 As for me, I was like a canal
from a river,
like a water channel into a garden.
31 I said, 'I will water my garden
and drench my flower-beds.'
And lo, my canal became a river,
and my river a sea.
32 I will again make instruction shine
forth like the dawn,
and I will make it clear
from far away.
33 I will again pour out teaching
like prophecy,
and leave it to all future
generations.
34 Observe that I have not laboured
for myself alone,
but for all who seek wisdom.[v]

THOSE WHO ARE WORTHY OF PRAISE

25 I take pleasure in three things,
and they are beautiful in the
sight of God and of mortals:[w]
agreement among brothers
and sisters, friendship
among neighbours,
and a wife and husband who
live in harmony.
2 I hate three kinds of people,
and I loathe their manner of life:
a pauper who boasts, a rich
person who lies,
and an old fool who
commits adultery.

3 If you gathered nothing in
your youth,
how can you find anything
in your old age?
4 How attractive is sound judgement
in the grey-haired,
and for the aged to possess
good counsel!

[p] **24.14** Other ancient authorities read *on the beaches* [q] **24.14** Other ancient authorities omit *beside water* [r] **24.17** Other ancient authorities add as verse 18, *I am the mother of beautiful love, of fear, of knowledge, and of holy hope; being eternal, I am given to all my children, to those who are named by him.* [s] **24.23** Other ancient authorities add as verse 24, *'Do not cease to be strong in the Lord, cling to him so that he may strengthen you; the Lord Almighty alone is God, and besides him there is no saviour.'* [t] **24.27** Syr: Gk *It makes instruction shine forth like light* [u] **24.28** Gk *her* [v] **24.34** Gk *her* [w] **25.1** Syr Lat: Gk *In three things I was beautiful and I stood in beauty before the Lord and mortals.*

5 How attractive is wisdom
in the aged,
and understanding and counsel
in the venerable!
6 Rich experience is the crown
of the aged,
and their boast is the fear
of the Lord.

7 I can think of nine whom I
would call blessed,
and a tenth my tongue proclaims:
a man who can rejoice in
his children;
a man who lives to see the
downfall of his foes.
8 Happy the man who lives with
a sensible wife,
and one who does not plough
with ox and ass together.[x]
Happy is one who does not sin
with the tongue,
and one who has not
served an inferior.
9 Happy is one who finds a friend,[y]
and one who speaks to
attentive listeners.
10 How great is one who finds wisdom!
But none is superior to one
who fears the Lord.
11 Fear of the Lord surpasses
everything;
to whom can we compare
one who has it?[z]

SOME EXTREME FORMS OF EVIL

13 Any wound, but not a wound
of the heart!
Any wickedness, but not the
wickedness of a woman!
14 Any suffering, but not suffering
from those who hate!
And any vengeance, but not the
vengeance of enemies!
15 There is no venom[a] worse than
a snake's venom,[b]
and no anger worse than a
woman's[c] wrath.

THE EVIL OF A WICKED WOMAN

16 I would rather live with a
lion and a dragon
than live with an evil woman.
17 A woman's wickedness changes
her appearance,
and darkens her face like
that of a bear.
18 Her husband sits[d] among
the neighbours,
and he cannot help
sighing[e] bitterly.
19 Any iniquity is small compared
to a woman's iniquity;
may a sinner's lot befall her!
20 A sandy ascent for the feet
of the aged—
such is a garrulous wife to
a quiet husband.
21 Do not be ensnared by a
woman's beauty,
and do not desire a woman
for her possessions.[f]
22 There is wrath and impudence
and great disgrace
when a wife supports
her husband.
23 Dejected mind, gloomy face,
and wounded heart come
from an evil wife.
Drooping hands and
weak knees
come from the wife who does not
make her husband happy.
24 From a woman sin had its
beginning,
and because of her we all die.
25 Allow no outlet to water,
and no boldness of speech
to an evil wife.
26 If she does not go as you direct,
separate her from yourself.

THE JOY OF A GOOD WIFE

26 Happy is the husband
of a good wife;
the number of his days
will be doubled.
2 A loyal wife brings joy to
her husband,
and he will complete his
years in peace.
3 A good wife is a great blessing;
she will be granted among
the blessings of the man
who fears the Lord.
4 Whether rich or poor, his
heart is content,
and at all times his face
is cheerful.

[x] **25.8** Heb Syr: Gk lacks *and one who does not plough with ox and ass together* [y] **25.9** Lat Syr: Gk *good sense* [z] **25.11** Other ancient authorities add as verse 12, *The fear of the Lord is the beginning of love for him, and faith is the beginning of clinging to him.* [a] **25.15** Syr: Gk *head* [b] **25.15** Syr: Gk *head* [c] **25.15** Other ancient authorities read *an enemy's* [d] **25.18** Heb Syr: Gk *loses heart* [e] **25.18** Other ancient authorities read *and listening he sighs* [f] **25.21** Heb Syr: Other Gk authorities read *for her beauty*

THE WORST OF EVILS: A WICKED WIFE

5 Of three things my heart
is frightened,
and of a fourth I am in great fear:[g]
Slander in the city, the
gathering of a mob,
and false accusation—all these
are worse than death.
6 But it is heartache and sorrow when
a wife is jealous of a rival,
and a tongue-lashing makes
it known to all.
7 A bad wife is a chafing yoke;
taking hold of her is like
grasping a scorpion.
8 A drunken wife arouses
great anger;
she cannot hide her shame.
9 The haughty stare betrays an
unchaste wife;
her eyelids give her away.

10 Keep strict watch over a
headstrong daughter,
or else, when she finds liberty,
she will make use of it.
11 Be on guard against her
impudent eye,
and do not be surprised if
she sins against you.
12 As a thirsty traveller opens
his mouth
and drinks from any
water near him,
so she will sit in front of
every tent-peg
and open her quiver to the arrow.

THE BLESSING OF A GOOD WIFE

13 A wife's charm delights
her husband,
and her skill puts flesh
on his bones.
14 A silent wife is a gift from the Lord,
and nothing is so precious
as her self-discipline.
15 A modest wife adds charm to charm,
and no scales can weigh the
value of her chastity.
16 Like the sun rising in the
heights of the Lord,
so is the beauty of a good wife
in her well-ordered home.
17 Like the shining lamp on the
holy lampstand,
so is a beautiful face on
a stately figure.
18 Like golden pillars on silver bases,
so are shapely legs and
steadfast feet.

Other ancient authorities
add verses 19–27:

19 *My child, keep sound the bloom*
of your youth,
and do not give your strength
to strangers.
20 *Seek a fertile field within*
the whole plain,
and sow it with your own seed,
trusting in your fine stock.
21 *So your offspring will prosper,*
and, having confidence in
their good descent,
will grow great.
22 *A prostitute is regarded as spittle,*
and a married woman as a tower
of death to her lovers.
23 *A godless wife is given as a portion*
to a lawless man,
but a pious wife is given to the
man who fears the Lord.
24 *A shameless woman constantly*
acts disgracefully,
but a modest daughter will
even be embarrassed
before her husband.
25 *A headstrong wife is regarded*
as a dog,
but one who has a sense of
shame will fear the Lord.
26 *A wife honouring her husband*
will seem wise to all,
but if she dishonours him
in her pride she will be
known to all as ungodly.
Happy is the husband
of a good wife,
for the number of his years
will be doubled.
27 *A loud-voiced and garrulous*
wife is like a trumpet
sounding the charge,
and every person like this lives
in the anarchy of war.

THREE DEPRESSING THINGS

28 At two things my heart is grieved,
and because of a third anger
comes over me:
a warrior in want through poverty,
intelligent men who are treated
contemptuously,
and a man who turns back from
righteousness to sin—
the Lord will prepare him
for the sword!

g 26.5 Syr: Meaning of Gk uncertain

THE TEMPTATIONS OF COMMERCE

29 A merchant can hardly keep
from wrongdoing,
nor is a tradesman
innocent of sin.

27 Many have committed
sin for gain,[h]
and those who seek to get rich
will avert their eyes.
2 As a stake is driven firmly into a
fissure between stones,
so sin is wedged in between
selling and buying.
3 If a person is not steadfast in
the fear of the Lord,
his house will be quickly
overthrown.

TESTS IN LIFE

4 When a sieve is shaken, the
refuse appears;
so do a person's faults
when he speaks.
5 The kiln tests the potter's vessels;
so the test of a person is in
his conversation.
6 Its fruit discloses the
cultivation of a tree;
so a person's speech discloses the
cultivation of his mind.
7 Do not praise anyone before
he speaks,
for this is the way people
are tested.

REWARD AND RETRIBUTION

8 If you pursue justice, you
will attain it
and wear it like a glorious robe.
9 Birds roost with their own kind,
so honesty comes home to
those who practise it.
10 A lion lies in wait for prey;
so does sin for evildoers.

VARIETIES OF SPEECH

11 The conversation of the godly
is always wise,
but the fool changes like
the moon.
12 Among stupid people limit
your time,
but among thoughtful
people linger on.
13 The talk of fools is offensive,
and their laughter is
wantonly sinful.
14 Their cursing and swearing make
one's hair stand on end,
and their quarrels make
others stop their ears.
15 The strife of the proud leads
to bloodshed,
and their abuse is
grievous to hear.

BETRAYING SECRETS

16 Whoever betrays secrets
destroys confidence,
and will never find a
congenial friend.
17 Love your friend and keep
faith with him;
but if you betray his secrets,
do not follow after him.
18 For as a person destroys
his enemy,
so you have destroyed the
friendship of your neighbour.
19 And as you allow a bird to escape
from your hand,
so you have let your neighbour go,
and will not catch him again.
20 Do not go after him, for he
is too far off,
and has escaped like a gazelle
from a snare.
21 For a wound may be bandaged,
and there is reconciliation
after abuse,
but whoever has betrayed
secrets is without hope.

HYPOCRISY AND RETRIBUTION

22 Whoever winks the eye
plots mischief,
and those who know him will
keep their distance.
23 In your presence his mouth
is all sweetness,
and he admires your words;
but later he will twist his speech
and with your own words
he will trip you up.
24 I have hated many things,
but him above all;
even the Lord hates him.
25 Whoever throws a stone straight up
throws it on his own head,
and a treacherous blow opens
up many wounds.
26 Whoever digs a pit will
fall into it,
and whoever sets a snare
will be caught in it.
27 If a person does evil, it will
roll back upon him,
and he will not know where
it came from.

h 27.1 Other ancient authorities read *a trifle*

28 Mockery and abuse issue
from the proud,
but vengeance lies in wait
for them like a lion.
29 Those who rejoice in the fall
of the godly will be
caught in a snare,
and pain will consume them
before their death.

ANGER AND VENGEANCE

30 Anger and wrath, these also
are abominations,
yet a sinner holds on to them.

28 The vengeful will face the
Lord's vengeance,
for he keeps a strict account
of[i] their sins.
2 Forgive your neighbour the
wrong he has done,
and then your sins will be
pardoned when you pray.
3 Does anyone harbour anger
against another,
and expect healing from the Lord?
4 If someone has no mercy towards
another like himself,
can he then seek pardon
for his own sins?
5 If a mere mortal harbours wrath,
who will make an atoning
sacrifice for his sins?
6 Remember the end of your life,
and set enmity aside;
remember corruption and
death, and be true to
the commandments.
7 Remember the commandments,
and do not be angry
with your neighbour;
remember the covenant of
the Most High, and
overlook faults.

8 Refrain from strife, and your
sins will be fewer;
for the hot-tempered kindle strife,
9 and the sinner disrupts friendships
and sows discord among those
who are at peace.
10 In proportion to the fuel, so
will the fire burn,
and in proportion to the
obstinacy, so will
strife increase;[j]
in proportion to a person's strength
will be his anger,
and in proportion to his wealth
he will increase his wrath.
11 A hasty quarrel kindles a fire,
and a hasty dispute sheds blood.

THE EVIL TONGUE

12 If you blow on a spark, it will glow;
if you spit on it, it will be put out;
yet both come out of your mouth.

13 Curse the gossips and the
double-tongued,
for they destroy the
peace of many.
14 Slander[k] has shaken many,
and scattered them from
nation to nation;
it has destroyed strong cities,
and overturned the houses
of the great.
15 Slander[l] has driven virtuous
women from their homes,
and deprived them of the
fruit of their toil.
16 Those who pay heed to slander[m]
will not find rest,
nor will they settle down in peace.
17 The blow of a whip raises a welt,
but a blow of the tongue
crushes the bones.
18 Many have fallen by the edge
of the sword,
but not as many as have fallen
because of the tongue.
19 Happy is one who is
protected from it,
who has not been exposed
to its anger,
who has not borne its yoke,
and has not been bound
with its fetters.
20 For its yoke is a yoke of iron,
and its fetters are fetters of bronze;
21 its death is an evil death,
and Hades is preferable to it.
22 It has no power over the godly;
they will not be burned
in its flame.
23 Those who forsake the Lord will
fall into its power;
it will burn among them and
will not be put out.
It will be sent out against
them like a lion;
like a leopard it will mangle them.
24a As you fence in your property
with thorns,
25b so make a door and a bolt
for your mouth.
24b As you lock up your silver and gold,
25a so make balances and scales
for your words.

[i] **28.1** Other ancient authorities read *for he firmly establishes* [j] **28.10** Other ancient authorities read *burn* [k] **28.14** Gk *A third tongue* [l] **28.15** Gk *A third tongue* [m] **28.16** Gk *it*

26 Take care not to err with
your tongue,[n]
and fall victim to one
lying in wait.

ON LENDING AND BORROWING

29 The merciful lend to
their neighbours;
by holding out a helping
hand they keep the
commandments.
2 Lend to your neighbour in
his time of need;
repay your neighbour when
a loan falls due.
3 Keep your promise and be
honest with him,
and on every occasion you will
find what you need.
4 Many regard a loan as a windfall,
and cause trouble to those
who help them.
5 One kisses another's hands
until he gets a loan,
and is deferential in speaking of
his neighbour's money;
but at the time for repayment
he delays,
and pays back with empty
promises,
and finds fault with the time.
6 If he can pay, his creditor[o] will
hardly get back half,
and will regard that as a windfall.
If he cannot pay, the borrower[p]
has robbed the other
of his money,
and he has needlessly made
him an enemy;
he will repay him with curses
and reproaches,
and instead of glory will repay
him with dishonour.
7 Many refuse to lend, not
because of meanness,
but from fear[q] of being
defrauded needlessly.

8 Nevertheless, be patient with
someone in humble
circumstances,
and do not keep him waiting
for your alms.
9 Help the poor for the
commandment's sake,
and in their need do not send
them away empty-handed.
10 Lose your silver for the sake of
a brother or a friend,
and do not let it rust under
a stone and be lost.
11 Lay up your treasure according
to the commandments
of the Most High,
and it will profit you
more than gold.
12 Store up almsgiving in
your treasury,
and it will rescue you from
every disaster;
13 better than a stout shield and
a sturdy spear,
it will fight for you against
the enemy.

ON GUARANTEEING DEBTS

14 A good person will be surety
for his neighbour,
but one who has lost all sense
of shame will fail him.
15 Do not forget the kindness of
your guarantor,
for he has given his life for you.
16 A sinner wastes the property
of his guarantor,
17 and the ungrateful person
abandons his rescuer.
18 Being surety has ruined many
who were prosperous,
and has tossed them about
like waves of the sea;
it has driven the influential
into exile,
and they have wandered
among foreign nations.
19 The sinner comes to grief
through surety;
his pursuit of gain involves
him in lawsuits.
20 Assist your neighbour to the
best of your ability,
but be careful not to
fall yourself.

HOME AND HOSPITALITY

21 The necessities of life are water,
bread, and clothing,
and also a house to
assure privacy.
22 Better is the life of the poor under
their own crude roof
than sumptuous food in the
house of others.
23 Be content with little or much,
and you will hear no reproach
for being a guest.[r]

[n] 28.26 Gk *with it* [o] 29.6 Gk *he* [p] 29.6 Gk *he*
[q] 29.7 Other ancient authorities read *many refuse to lend, therefore, because of such meanness; they are afraid* [r] 29.23 Lat: Gk *reproach from your family*; other ancient authorities lack this line

24 It is a miserable life to go from
house to house;
as a guest you should not
open your mouth;
25 you will play the host and
provide drink without
being thanked,
and besides this you will hear
rude words like these:
26 'Come here, stranger, prepare
the table;
let me eat what you
have there.'
27 'Be off, stranger, for an honoured
guest is here;
my brother has come for a visit,
and I need the guest-room.'
28 It is hard for a sensitive
person to bear
scolding about lodging[s] and the
insults of the moneylender.

CONCERNING CHILDREN[t]

30 He who loves his son will
whip him often,
so that he may rejoice at the
way he turns out.
2 He who disciplines his son
will profit by him,
and will boast of him among
acquaintances.
3 He who teaches his son will make
his enemies envious,
and will glory in him
among his friends.
4 When the father dies he will
not seem to be dead,
for he has left behind him
one like himself,
5 whom in his life he looked
upon with joy
and at death, without grief.
6 He has left behind him an avenger
against his enemies,
and one to repay the kindness
of his friends.

7 Whoever spoils his son will
bind up his wounds,
and will suffer heartache
at every cry.
8 An unbroken horse turns
out stubborn,
and an unchecked son turns
out headstrong.
9 Pamper a child, and he will
terrorize you;
play with him, and he
will grieve you.
10 Do not laugh with him, or you will
have sorrow with him,
and in the end you will
gnash your teeth.
11 Give him no freedom in his youth,
and do not ignore his errors.
12 Bow down his neck in his youth,[u]
and beat his sides while
he is young,
or else he will become stubborn
and disobey you,
and you will have sorrow
of soul from him.[v]
13 Discipline your son and make
his yoke heavy,[w]
so that you may not be offended
by his shamelessness.

14 Better off poor, healthy, and fit
than rich and afflicted in body.
15 Health and fitness are better
than any gold,
and a robust body than
countless riches.
16 There is no wealth better than
health of body,
and no gladness above
joy of heart.
17 Death is better than
a life of misery,
and eternal sleep[x] than
chronic sickness.

CONCERNING FOODS[y]

18 Good things poured out upon a
mouth that is closed
are like offerings of food
placed upon a grave.
19 Of what use to an idol is a sacrifice?
For it can neither eat nor smell.
So is one punished by the Lord;
20 he sees with his eyes and groans
as a eunuch groans when
embracing a girl.[z]

21 Do not give yourself over to sorrow,
and do not distress yourself
deliberately.

[s] 29.28 Or *scolding from the household*
[t] 30.1 This heading is included in the Gk text.
[u] 30.12 Other ancient authorities lack this line and the preceding line [v] 30.12 Other ancient authorities lack this line [w] 30.13 Heb: Gk *take pains with him* [x] 30.17 Other ancient authorities lack *eternal sleep* [y] 30.18 This heading is included in the Gk text; other ancient authorities place the heading before verse 16
[z] 30.20 Other ancient authorities add *So is the person who does right under compulsion*

22 A joyful heart is life itself,
and rejoicing lengthens
one's life span.
23 Indulge yourself[a] and take comfort,
and remove sorrow far from you,
for sorrow has destroyed many,
and no advantage ever
comes from it.
24 Jealousy and anger shorten life,
and anxiety brings on
premature old age.
25 Those who are cheerful and
merry at table
will benefit from their food.

RIGHT ATTITUDE TOWARDS RICHES

31 Wakefulness over wealth
wastes away one's flesh,
and anxiety about it drives
away sleep.
2 Wakeful anxiety prevents slumber,
and a severe illness carries
off sleep.[b]
3 The rich person toils to
amass a fortune,
and when he rests he fills
himself with his dainties.
4 The poor person toils to make
a meagre living,
and if ever he rests he
becomes needy.

5 One who loves gold will not
be justified;
one who pursues money will
be led astray[c] by it.
6 Many have come to ruin
because of gold,
and their destruction has met
them face to face.
7 It is a stumbling-block to those
who are avid for it,
and every fool will be taken
captive by it.
8 Blessed is the rich person who
is found blameless,
and who does not go after gold.
9 Who is he, that we may
praise him?
For he has done wonders
among his people.
10 Who has been tested by it and
been found perfect?
Let it be for him a ground
for boasting.
Who has had the power to transgress
and did not transgress,
and to do evil and did not do it?
11 His prosperity will be established,[d]
and the assembly will proclaim
his acts of charity.

TABLE ETIQUETTE

12 Are you seated at the table
of the great?[e]
Do not be greedy at it,
and do not say, 'How much
food there is here!'
13 Remember that a greedy eye
is a bad thing.
What has been created more
greedy than the eye?
Therefore it sheds tears
for any reason.
14 Do not reach out your hand for
everything you see,
and do not crowd your
neighbour[f] at the dish.
15 Judge your neighbour's feelings
by your own,
and in every matter
be thoughtful.
16 Eat what is set before you like
a well-bred person,[g]
and do not chew greedily, or
you will give offence.
17 Be the first to stop, as befits
good manners,
and do not be insatiable, or
you will give offence.
18 If you are seated among
many others,
do not help yourself[h]
before they do.
19 How ample a little is for a
well-disciplined person!
He does not breathe heavily
when in bed.
20 Healthy sleep depends on
moderate eating;
he rises early, and feels fit.
The distress of sleeplessness
and of nausea
and colic are with the glutton.
21 If you are overstuffed with food,
get up to vomit, and you
will have relief.
22 Listen to me, my child, and do
not disregard me,
and in the end you will
appreciate my words.
In everything you do be moderate,[i]
and no sickness will overtake you.

[a] **30.23** Other ancient authorities read *Beguile yourself* [b] **31.2** Other ancient authorities read *sleep carries off a severe illness* [c] **31.5** Heb Syr: Gk *pursues destruction will be filled*
[d] **31.11** Other ancient authorities add *because of this* [e] **31.12** Heb Syr: Gk *at a great table*
[f] **31.14** Gk *him* [g] **31.16** Heb: Gk *like a human being* [h] **31.18** Gk *reach out your hand*
[i] **31.22** Heb Syr: Gk *industrious*

23 People bless someone who is
liberal with food,
and their testimony to his
generosity is trustworthy.
24 The city complains of someone
who is stingy with food,
and their testimony to his
stinginess is accurate.

TEMPERANCE IN DRINKING WINE

25 Do not try to prove your strength
by wine-drinking,
for wine has destroyed many.
26 As the furnace tests the work
of the smith,[j]
so wine tests hearts when
the insolent quarrel.
27 Wine is very life to
human beings
if taken in moderation.
What is life to one who is
without wine?
It has been created to make
people happy.
28 Wine drunk at the proper time
and in moderation
is rejoicing of heart and
gladness of soul.
29 Wine drunk to excess leads to
bitterness of spirit,
to quarrels and stumbling.
30 Drunkenness increases the anger
of a fool to his own hurt,
reducing his strength and
adding wounds.
31 Do not reprove your neighbour
at a banquet of wine,
and do not despise him in
his merrymaking;
speak no word of reproach to him,
and do not distress him by
making demands of him.

ETIQUETTE AT A BANQUET

32 If they make you master of the
feast, do not exalt yourself;
be among them as one of
their number.
Take care of them first and
then sit down;
2 when you have fulfilled all your
duties, take your place,
so that you may be merry
along with them
and receive a garland for your
excellent leadership.

3 Speak, you who are older, for
it is your right,
but with accurate knowledge, and
do not interrupt the music.
4 Where there is entertainment,
do not pour out talk;
do not display your cleverness
at the wrong time.
5 A ruby seal in a setting of gold
is a concert of music at a
banquet of wine.
6 A seal of emerald in a rich
setting of gold
is the melody of music
with good wine.

7 Speak, you who are young, if
you are obliged to,
but no more than twice,
and only if asked.
8 Be brief; say much in few words;
be as one who knows and can
still hold his tongue.
9 Among the great do not act
as their equal;
and when another is speaking,
do not babble.

10 Lightning travels ahead of
the thunder,
and approval goes before
one who is modest.
11 Leave in good time and do
not be the last;
go home quickly and
do not linger.
12 Amuse yourself there to your
heart's content,
but do not sin through
proud speech.
13 But above all bless your Maker,
who fills you with
his good gifts.

THE PROVIDENCE OF GOD

14 One who seeks God[k] will accept
his discipline,
and those who rise early to seek
him[l] will find favour.
15 One who seeks the law will
be filled with it,
but the hypocrite will
stumble at it.
16 Those who fear the Lord will
form true judgements,
and they will kindle righteous
deeds like a light.
17 The sinner will shun reproof,
and will find a decision
according to his liking.

[j] **31.26** Heb: Gk *tests the hardening of steel by dipping* [k] **32.14** Heb: Gk *who fears the Lord*
[l] **32.14** Other ancient authorities lack *to seek him*

18 A sensible person will not overlook
a thoughtful suggestion;
an insolent[m] and proud person
will not be deterred by fear.[n]
19 Do nothing without deliberation,
but when you have acted,
do not regret it.
20 Do not go on a path full of hazards,
and do not stumble at an
obstacle twice.[o]
21 Do not be overconfident on
a smooth[p] road,
22 and give good heed to your paths.[q]
23 Guard[r] yourself in every act,
for this is the keeping of the
commandments.

24 One who keeps the law
preserves himself,[s]
and one who trusts the Lord
will not suffer loss.

33 No evil will befall someone
who fears the Lord,
but in trials such a one will be
rescued again and again.
2 The wise will not hate the law,
but someone who is
hypocritical about it is
like a boat in a storm.
3 The sensible person will
trust in the law;
for such a one the law is as
dependable as a divine oracle.

4 Prepare what to say, and then
you will be listened to;
draw upon your training, and
give your answer.
5 The heart of a fool is like a cartwheel,
and his thoughts like a
turning axle.
6 A mocking friend is like a stallion
that neighs no matter
who the rider is.

DIFFERENCES IN NATURE AND IN HUMANKIND

7 Why is one day more important
than another,
when all the daylight in the
year is from the sun?
8 By the Lord's wisdom they
were distinguished,
and he appointed the different
seasons and festivals.
9 Some days he exalted and hallowed,
and some he made ordinary days.
10 All human beings come
from the ground,
and humankind[t] was created
out of the dust.
11 In the fullness of his knowledge the
Lord distinguished them
and appointed their
different ways.
12 Some he blessed and exalted,
and some he made holy and
brought near to himself;
but some he cursed and brought low,
and turned them out of
their place.
13 Like clay in the hand of the potter,
to be moulded as he pleases,
so all are in the hand of their Maker,
to be given whatever he decides.

14 Good is the opposite of evil,
and life the opposite of death;
so the sinner is the opposite
of the godly.
15 Look at all the works of the
Most High;
they come in pairs, one the
opposite of the other.

16 Now I was the last to keep vigil;
I was like a gleaner following
the grape-pickers;
17 by the blessing of the Lord
I arrived first,
and like a grape-picker I
filled my wine press.
18 Consider that I have not laboured
for myself alone,
but for all who seek instruction.
19 Hear me, you who are great
among the people,
and you leaders of the
congregation, pay heed!

THE ADVANTAGE OF INDEPENDENCE

20 To son or wife, to brother or friend,
do not give power over yourself,
as long as you live;
and do not give your property
to another,
in case you change your mind
and must ask for it.
21 While you are still alive and
have breath in you,
do not let anyone take your place.

[m] **32.18** Heb: Gk *alien* [n] **32.18** Meaning of Gk uncertain. Other ancient authorities add *and after acting, with him, without deliberation*
[o] **32.20** Heb: Gk *stumble on stony ground*
[p] **32.21** Or *an unexplored* [q] **32.22** Heb Syr: Gk *and beware of your children* [r] **32.23** Heb Syr: Gk *Trust* [s] **32.24** Heb: Gk *who believes the law heeds the commandments* [t] **33.10** Heb: Gk *Adam*

22 For it is better that your children
should ask from you
than that you should look to the
hand of your children.
23 Excel in all that you do;
bring no stain upon
your honour.
24 At the time when you end the
days of your life,
in the hour of death, distribute
your inheritance.

THE TREATMENT OF SLAVES

25 Fodder and a stick and burdens
for a donkey;
bread and discipline and
work for a slave.
26 Set your slave to work, and
you will find rest;
leave his hands idle, and he
will seek liberty.
27 Yoke and thong will
bow the neck,
and for a wicked slave there
are racks and tortures.
28 Put him to work, in order that
he may not be idle,
29 for idleness teaches much evil.
30 Set him to work, as is
fitting for him,
and if he does not obey, make
his fetters heavy.
Do not be overbearing
towards anyone,
and do nothing unjust.

31 If you have but one slave, treat
him like yourself,
because you have bought
him with blood.
If you have but one slave, treat
him like a brother,
for you will need him as
you need your life.
32 If you ill-treat him, and he leaves
you and runs away,
33 which way will you go
to seek him?

DREAMS MEAN NOTHING

34 The senseless have vain
and false hopes,
and dreams give wings to fools.
2 As one who catches at a shadow
and pursues the wind,
so is anyone who believes
in[u] dreams.
3 What is seen in dreams is
but a reflection,
the likeness of a face
looking at itself.
4 From an unclean thing what
can be clean?
And from something false
what can be true?
5 Divinations and omens and
dreams are unreal,
and like a woman in labour,
the mind has fantasies.
6 Unless they are sent by intervention
from the Most High,
pay no attention to them.
7 For dreams have deceived many,
and those who put their hope
in them have perished.
8 Without such deceptions the
law will be fulfilled,
and wisdom is complete in the
mouth of the faithful.

EXPERIENCE AS A TEACHER

9 An educated[v] person knows
many things,
and one with much experience
knows what he is
talking about.
10 An inexperienced person
knows few things,
11 but he that has travelled acquires
much cleverness.
12 I have seen many things
in my travels,
and I understand more
than I can express.
13 I have often been in danger of death,
but have escaped because of
these experiences.

FEAR THE LORD

14 The spirit of those who fear
the Lord will live,
15 for their hope is in him
who saves them.
16 Those who fear the Lord will
not be timid,
or play the coward, for he
is their hope.
17 Happy is the soul that fears the Lord!
18 To whom does he look? And
who is his support?
19 The eyes of the Lord are on
those who love him,
a mighty shield and
strong support,
a shelter from scorching wind and
a shade from noonday sun,
a guard against stumbling and
a help against falling.

[u] 34.2 Syr: Gk *pays heed to* [v] 34.9 Other ancient authorities read *A travelled*

20 He lifts up the soul and makes
the eyes sparkle;
he gives health and life
and blessing.

OFFERING SACRIFICES

21 If one sacrifices ill-gotten goods,
the offering is blemished;[w]
22 the gifts[x] of the lawless are
not acceptable.
23 The Most High is not pleased with
the offerings of the ungodly,
nor for a multitude of sacrifices
does he forgive sins.
24 Like one who kills a son before
his father's eyes
is the person who offers
a sacrifice from the
property of the poor.
25 The bread of the needy is the
life of the poor;
whoever deprives them of
it is a murderer.
26 To take away a neighbour's living
is to commit murder;
27 to deprive an employee of
wages is to shed blood.

28 When one builds and another
tears down,
what do they gain
but hard work?
29 When one prays and
another curses,
to whose voice will the
Lord listen?
30 If one washes after touching a
corpse, and touches it again,
what has been gained
by washing?
31 So if someone fasts for his sins,
and goes again and does
the same things,
who will listen to his prayer?
And what has he gained by
humbling himself?

THE LAW AND SACRIFICES

35 One who keeps the law
makes many offerings;
2 one who heeds the
commandments makes an
offering of well-being.
3 One who returns a kindness
offers choice flour,
4 and one who gives alms sacrifices
a thank-offering.
5 To keep from wickedness is
pleasing to the Lord,
and to forsake unrighteousness
is an atonement.
6 Do not appear before the Lord
empty-handed,
7 for all that you offer is
in fulfilment of the
commandment.
8 The offering of the righteous
enriches the altar,
and its pleasing odour rises
before the Most High.
9 The sacrifice of the righteous
is acceptable,
and it will never be forgotten.
10 Be generous when you
worship the Lord,
and do not stint the first
fruits of your hands.
11 With every gift show a cheerful face,
and dedicate your tithe
with gladness.
12 Give to the Most High as he
has given to you,
and as generously as
you can afford.
13 For the Lord is the one who repays,
and he will repay you sevenfold.

DIVINE JUSTICE

14 Do not offer him a bribe, for he
will not accept it;
15 and do not rely on a
dishonest sacrifice;
for the Lord is the judge,
and with him there is
no partiality.
16 He will not show partiality
to the poor;
but he will listen to the prayer
of one who is wronged.
17 He will not ignore the supplication
of the orphan,
or the widow when she pours
out her complaint.
18 Do not the tears of the widow
run down her cheek
19 as she cries out against the one
who causes them to fall?
20 One whose service is pleasing to
the Lord will be accepted,
and his prayer will reach
to the clouds.
21 The prayer of the humble
pierces the clouds,
and it will not rest until it
reaches its goal;
it will not desist until the Most
High responds
22 and does justice to the righteous,
and executes judgement.

[w] **34.21** Other ancient authorities read *is made in mockery* [x] **34.22** Other ancient authorities read *mockeries*

Indeed, the Lord will not delay,
and like a warrior[y] will
not be patient
until he crushes the loins of
the unmerciful
23 and repays vengeance
on the nations;
until he destroys the multitude
of the insolent,
and breaks the sceptres of
the unrighteous;
24 until he repays mortals according
to their deeds,
and the works of all according
to their thoughts;
25 until he judges the case of his people
and makes them rejoice
in his mercy.
26 His mercy is as welcome in
time of distress
as clouds of rain in time
of drought.

A PRAYER FOR GOD'S PEOPLE

36 Have mercy upon us,
O God[z] of all,
2 and put all the nations
in fear of you.
3 Lift up your hand against
foreign nations
and let them see your might.
4 As you have used us to show
your holiness to them,
so use them to show your
glory to us.
5 Then they will know,[a] as we
have known,
that there is no God but
you, O Lord.
6 Give new signs, and work
other wonders;
7 make your hand and right
arm glorious.
8 Rouse your anger and pour
out your wrath;
9 destroy the adversary and
wipe out the enemy.
10 Hasten the day, and remember
the appointed time,[b]
and let people recount your
mighty deeds.
11 Let survivors be consumed in
the fiery wrath,
and may those who harm your
people meet destruction.
12 Crush the heads of hostile rulers
who say, 'There is no one
but ourselves.'
13 Gather all the tribes of Jacob,[c]
16 and give them their inheritance,
as at the beginning.
17 Have mercy, O Lord, on the people
called by your name,
on Israel, whom you have
named[d] your firstborn,
18 Have pity on the city of
your sanctuary,[e]
Jerusalem, the place of
your dwelling.[f]
19 Fill Zion with your majesty,[g]
and your temple[h] with your glory.
20 Bear witness to those whom you
created in the beginning,
and fulfil the prophecies
spoken in your name.
21 Reward those who wait for you
and let your prophets be
found trustworthy.
22 Hear, O Lord, the prayer of your
servants, according to
your goodwill towards[i]
your people,
and all who are on the earth
will know
that you are the Lord, the
God of the ages.

CONCERNING DISCRIMINATION

23 The stomach will take any food,
yet one food is better
than another.
24 As the palate tastes the
kinds of game,
so an intelligent mind
detects false words.
25 A perverse mind will cause grief,
but a person with experience
will pay him back.
26 A woman will accept any
man as a husband,
but one girl is preferable
to another.
27 A woman's beauty lights
up a man's face,
and there is nothing he
desires more.
28 If kindness and humility
mark her speech,
her husband is more fortunate
than other men.

[y] 35.22 Heb: Gk *and with them* [z] 36.1 Heb: Gk *O Master, the God* [a] 36.5 Heb: Gk *And let them know you* [b] 36.10 Other ancient authorities read *remember your oath* [c] 36.13 Owing to a dislocation in the Greek Mss of Sirach, the verse numbers 14 and 15 are not used in chapter 36, though no text is missing. [d] 36.17 Other ancient authorities read *you have likened to* [e] 36.18 Or *on your holy city* [f] 36.18 Heb: Gk *your rest* [g] 36.19 Heb Syr: Gk *the celebration of your wondrous deeds* [h] 36.19 Heb Syr: Gk Lat *people* [i] 36.22 Heb and two Gk witnesses: Lat and most Gk witnesses read *according to the blessing of Aaron for*

29 He who acquires a wife gets
his best possession,[j]
a helper fit for him and a
pillar of support.[k]
30 Where there is no fence, the
property will be plundered;
and where there is no wife,
a man will become a
fugitive and a wanderer.[l]
31 For who will trust a nimble robber
that skips from city to city?
So who will trust a man that
has no nest,
but lodges wherever night
overtakes him?

FALSE FRIENDS

37 Every friend says, 'I
too am a friend';
but some friends are friends
only in name.
2 Is it not a sorrow like that
for death itself
when a dear friend turns
into an enemy?
3 O inclination to evil, why
were you formed
to cover the land with deceit?
4 Some companions rejoice in the
happiness of a friend,
but in time of trouble they
are against him.
5 Some companions help a friend
for their stomachs' sake,
yet in battle they will
carry his shield.
6 Do not forget a friend during
the battle,[m]
and do not be unmindful
of him when you
distribute your spoils.[n]

CAUTION IN TAKING ADVICE

7 All counsellors praise the
counsel they give,
but some give counsel in
their own interest.
8 Be wary of a counsellor,
and learn first what is his interest,
for he will take thought for himself.
He may cast the lot against you
9 and tell you, 'Your way is good',
and then stand aside to see
what happens to you.
10 Do not consult one who regards
you with suspicion;
hide your intentions from those
who are jealous of you.
11 Do not consult with a woman
about her rival
or with a coward about war,
with a merchant about business
or with a buyer about selling,
with a miser about generosity[o]
or with the merciless
about kindness,
with an idler about any work
or with a seasonal labourer about
completing his work,
with a lazy servant about
a big task—
pay no attention to any
advice they give.
12 But associate with a godly person
whom you know to be a keeper
of the commandments,
who is like-minded with yourself,
and who will grieve with
you if you fail.
13 And heed[p] the counsel of
your own heart,
for no one is more faithful
to you than it is.
14 For our own mind sometimes
keeps us better informed
than seven sentinels sitting
high on a watch-tower.
15 But above all pray to the Most High
that he may direct your
way in truth.

TRUE AND FALSE WISDOM

16 Discussion is the beginning
of every work,
and counsel precedes every
undertaking.
17 The mind is the root of all conduct;
18 it sprouts four branches,[q]
good and evil, life and death;
and it is the tongue that
continually rules them.
19 Some people may be clever
enough to teach many,
and yet be useless to themselves.
20 A skilful speaker may be hated;
he will be destitute of all food,
21 for the Lord has withheld
the gift of charm,
since he is lacking in all wisdom.
22 If a person is wise to his
own advantage,
the fruits of his good sense
will be praiseworthy.[r]

[j] 36.29 Heb: Gk *enters upon a possession*
[k] 36.29 Heb: Gk *rest* [l] 36.30 Heb: Gk *wander about and sigh* [m] 37.6 Heb: Gk *in your heart*
[n] 37.6 Heb: Gk *him in your wealth* [o] 37.11 Heb: Gk *gratitude* [p] 37.13 Heb: Gk *establish*
[q] 37.18 Heb: Gk *As a clue to changes of heart four kinds of destiny appear* [r] 37.22 Other ancient witnesses read *trustworthy*

23 A wise person instructs his
own people,
and the fruits of his good
sense will endure.
24 A wise person will have praise
heaped upon him,
and all who see him will
call him happy.
25 The days of a person's life
are numbered,
but the days of Israel are
without number.
26 One who is wise among his people
will inherit honour,[s]
and his name will live for ever.

CONCERNING MODERATION

27 My child, test yourself while you live;
see what is bad for you and
do not give in to it.
28 For not everything is good
for everyone,
and no one enjoys everything.
29 Do not be greedy for every delicacy,
and do not eat without restraint;
30 for overeating brings sickness,
and gluttony leads to nausea.
31 Many have died of gluttony,
but one who guards against
it prolongs his life.

CONCERNING PHYSICIANS AND HEALTH

38 Honour physicians for
their services,
for the Lord created them;
2 for their gift of healing comes
from the Most High,
and they are rewarded by the king.
3 The skill of physicians makes
them distinguished,
and in the presence of the
great they are admired.
4 The Lord created medicines
out of the earth,
and the sensible will not
despise them.
5 Was not water made sweet
with a tree
in order that its[t] power
might be known?
6 And he gave skill to human beings
that he[u] might be glorified in
his marvellous works.
7 By them the physician[v] heals
and takes away pain;
8 the pharmacist makes a
mixture from them.
God's[w] works will never be finished;
and from him health[x] spreads
over all the earth.

9 My child, when you are ill,
do not delay,
but pray to the Lord, and
he will heal you.
10 Give up your faults and direct
your hands rightly,
and cleanse your heart
from all sin.
11 Offer a sweet-smelling sacrifice,
and a memorial portion
of choice flour,
and pour oil on your offering, as
much as you can afford.[y]
12 Then give the physician his place,
for the Lord created him;
do not let him leave you,
for you need him.
13 There may come a time when
recovery lies in the
hands of physicians,[z]
14 for they too pray to the Lord
that he will grant them success
in diagnosis[a]
and in healing, for the sake
of preserving life.
15 He who sins against his Maker
will be defiant towards
the physician.[b]

ON MOURNING FOR THE DEAD

16 My child, let your tears fall
for the dead,
and as one in great pain
begin the lament.
Lay out the body with due ceremony,
and do not neglect the burial.
17 Let your weeping be bitter and
your wailing fervent;
make your mourning worthy
of the departed,
for one day, or two, to avoid
criticism;
then be comforted for your grief.
18 For grief may result in death,
and a sorrowful heart saps
one's strength.
19 When a person is taken away,
sorrow is over;
but the life of the poor weighs
down the heart.
20 Do not give your heart to grief;
drive it away, and remember
your own end.

[s] **37.26** Other ancient authorities read *confidence* [t] **38.5** Or *his* [u] **38.6** Or *they* [v] **38.7** Heb: Gk *he* [w] **38.8** Gk *His* [x] **38.8** Or *peace* [y] **38.11** Heb: Lat lacks *as much as you can afford*; Meaning of Gk uncertain [z] **38.13** Gk *in their hands* [a] **38.14** Heb: Gk *rest* [b] **38.15** Heb: Gk *may he fall into the hands of the physician*

21 Do not forget, there is no
coming back;
you do the dead[c] no good, and
you injure yourself.
22 Remember his[d] fate, for
yours is like it;
yesterday it was his,[e] and
today it is yours.
23 When the dead is at rest, let his
remembrance rest too,
and be comforted for him when
his spirit has departed.

TRADES AND CRAFTS

24 The wisdom of the scribe depends on
the opportunity of leisure;
only the one who has little
business can become wise.
25 How can one become wise who
handles the plough,
and who glories in the
shaft of a goad,
who drives oxen and is occupied
with their work,
and whose talk is about bulls?
26 He sets his heart on ploughing
furrows,
and he is careful about fodder
for the heifers.
27 So it is with every artisan and
master artisan
who labours by night as
well as by day;
those who cut the signets of seals,
each is diligent in making
a great variety;
they set their heart on painting
a lifelike image,
and they are careful to
finish their work.
28 So it is with the smith, sitting
by the anvil,
intent on his ironwork;
the breath of the fire melts his flesh,
and he struggles with the
heat of the furnace;
the sound of the hammer
deafens his ears,[f]
and his eyes are on the
pattern of the object.
He sets his heart on finishing
his handiwork,
and he is careful to complete
its decoration.
29 So it is with is the potter
sitting at his work
and turning the wheel
with his feet;
he is always deeply concerned
over his products,
and he produces them in quantity.
30 He moulds the clay with his arm
and makes it pliable with his feet;
he sets his heart on finishing
the glazing,
and he takes care in
firing[g] the kiln.

31 All these rely on their hands,
and all are skilful in their
own work.
32 Without them no city can
be inhabited,
and wherever they live, they
will not go hungry.[h]
Yet they are not sought out for the
council of the people,[i]
33 nor do they attain eminence
in the public assembly.
They do not sit in the judge's seat,
nor do they understand the
decisions of the courts;
they cannot expound discipline
or judgement,
and they are not found
among the rulers.[j]
34 But they maintain the fabric
of the world,
and their concern is for[k] the
exercise of their trade.

THE ACTIVITY OF THE SCRIBE

How different the one who
devotes himself
to the study of the law of
the Most High!
39 He seeks out the wisdom
of all the ancients,
and is concerned with prophecies;
2 he preserves the sayings
of the famous
and penetrates the subtleties
of parables;
3 he seeks out the hidden
meanings of proverbs
and is at home with the
obscurities of parables.
4 He serves among the great
and appears before rulers;
he travels in foreign lands
and learns what is good and
evil in the human lot.
5 He sets his heart on rising early
to seek the Lord who made him,
and to petition the Most High;

[c] 38.21 Gk *him* [d] 38.22 Heb: Gk *my*
[e] 38.22 Heb: Gk *mine* [f] 38.28 Cn: Gk *renews his ear* [g] 38.30 Cn: Gk *cleaning* [h] 38.32 Syr: Gk *and people can neither live nor walk there*
[i] 38.32 Most ancient authorities lack this line
[j] 38.33 Cn: Gk *among parables* [k] 38.34 Syr: Gk *prayer is in*

he opens his mouth in prayer
and asks pardon for his sins.
6 If the great Lord is willing,
he will be filled with the spirit
of understanding;
he will pour forth words of
wisdom of his own
and give thanks to the
Lord in prayer.
7 The Lord[l] will direct his counsel
and knowledge,
as he meditates on his mysteries.
8 He will show the wisdom of
what he has learned,
and will glory in the law of
the Lord's covenant.
9 Many will praise his understanding;
it will never be blotted out.
His memory will not disappear,
and his name will live through
all generations.
10 Nations will speak of his wisdom,
and the congregation will
proclaim his praise.
11 If he lives long, he will leave a name
greater than a thousand,
and if he goes to rest, it is
enough[m] for him.

A HYMN OF PRAISE TO GOD

12 I have more on my mind to express;
I am full like the full moon.
13 Listen to me, my faithful
children, and blossom
like a rose growing by a
stream of water.
14 Send out fragrance like incense,
and put forth blossoms like a lily.
Scatter the fragrance, and sing
a hymn of praise;
bless the Lord for all his works.
15 Ascribe majesty to his name
and give thanks to him with praise,
with songs on your lips, and
with harps;
this is what you shall say
in thanksgiving:

16 'All the works of the Lord
are very good,
and whatever he commands will be
done at the appointed time.
17 No one can say, "What is this?"
or "Why is that?"—
for at the appointed time all such
questions will be answered.
At his word the waters
stood in a heap,
and the reservoirs of water at
the word of his mouth.
18 When he commands, his every
purpose is fulfilled,
and none can limit his
saving power.
19 The works of all are before him,
and nothing can be hidden
from his eyes.
20 From the beginning to the end of
time he can see everything,
and nothing is too
marvellous for him.
21 No one can say, "What is this?"
or "Why is that?"—
for everything has been created
for its own purpose.

22 'His blessing covers the dry
land like a river,
and drenches it like a flood.
23 But his wrath drives out the nations,
as when he turned a watered
land into salt.
24 To the faithful his ways are straight,
but full of pitfalls for the wicked.
25 From the beginning good things
were created for the good,
but for sinners good
things and bad.[n]
26 The basic necessities of human life
are water and fire and
iron and salt
and wheat flour and milk and honey,
the blood of the grape and
oil and clothing.
27 All these are good for the godly,
but for sinners they turn into evils.

28 'There are winds created
for vengeance,
and in their anger they can
dislodge mountains;[o]
on the day of reckoning they will
pour out their strength
and calm the anger of their Maker.
29 Fire and hail and famine
and pestilence,
all these have been created
for vengeance;
30 the fangs of wild animals and
scorpions and vipers,
and the sword that punishes the
ungodly with destruction.
31 They take delight in doing
his bidding,
always ready for his
service on earth;
and when their time comes they
never disobey his command.'

[l] 39.7 Gk *He himself* [m] 39.11 Cn: Meaning of Gk uncertain [n] 39.25 Heb Lat: Gk *sinners bad things* [o] 39.28 Heb Syr: Gk *can scourge mightily*

32 So from the beginning I have been
convinced of all this
and have thought it out and
left it in writing:
33 All the works of the Lord are good,
and he will supply every
need in its time.
34 No one can say, 'This is not
as good as that',
for everything proves good
in its appointed time.
35 So now sing praise with all
your heart and voice,
and bless the name of the Lord.

HUMAN WRETCHEDNESS

40 Hard work was created
for everyone,
and a heavy yoke is laid on
the children of Adam,
from the day they come forth from
their mother's womb
until the day they return to[p] the
mother of all the living.[q]
2 Perplexities and fear of
heart are theirs,
and anxious thought of the
day of their death.
3 From the one who sits on a
splendid throne
to the one who grovels in
dust and ashes,
4 from the one who wears
purple and a crown
to the one who is clothed
in sackcloth,
5 there is anger and envy and
trouble and unrest,
and fear of death, and
fury and strife.
And when one rests upon his bed,
his sleep at night confuses
his mind.
6 He gets little or no rest;
he struggles in his sleep
as he did by day.[r]
He is troubled by the visions
of his mind
like one who has escaped
from the battlefield.
7 At the moment he reaches
safety he wakes up,
astonished that his fears
were groundless.
8 To all creatures, human
and animal,
but to sinners seven times more,
9 come death and bloodshed and
strife and sword,
calamities and famine and
ruin and plague.
10 All these were created for
the wicked,
and on their account the
flood came.
11 All that is of earth returns to earth,
and what is from above
returns above.[s]

INJUSTICE WILL NOT PROSPER

12 All bribery and injustice will
be blotted out,
but good faith will last for ever.
13 The wealth of the unjust will
dry up like a river,
and crash like a loud clap of
thunder in a storm.
14 As a generous person has
cause to rejoice,
so lawbreakers will utterly fail.
15 The children of the ungodly put
out few branches;
they are unhealthy roots
on sheer rock.
16 The reeds by any water
or river bank
are plucked up before any grass;
17 but kindness is like a garden
of blessings,
and almsgiving endures for ever.

THE JOYS OF LIFE

18 Wealth and wages
make life sweet,[t]
but better than either is
finding a treasure.
19 Children and the building of a city
establish one's name,
but better than either is one
who finds wisdom.
Cattle and orchards make
one prosperous;[u]
but a blameless wife is accounted
better than either.
20 Wine and music gladden the heart,
but the love of friends[v] is
better than either.
21 The flute and the harp make
sweet melody,
but a pleasant voice is
better than either.
22 The eye desires grace and beauty,
but the green shoots of grain
more than either.

[p] **40.1** Other Gk and Lat authorities read *are buried in* [q] **40.1** Heb: Gk *of all* [r] **40.6** Arm: Meaning of Gk uncertain [s] **40.11** Heb Syr: Gk Lat *from the waters returns to the sea* [t] **40.18** Heb: Gk *Life is sweet for the self-reliant worker* [u] **40.19** Heb Syr: Gk lacks *but better . . . prosperous* [v] **40.20** Heb: Gk *wisdom*

23 A friend or companion is
always welcome,
but a sensible wife[w] is
better than either.
24 Kindred and helpers are for a
time of trouble,
but almsgiving rescues
better than either.
25 Gold and silver make one stand firm,
but good counsel is esteemed
more than either.
26 Riches and strength build
up confidence,
but the fear of the Lord is
better than either.
There is no want in the fear
of the Lord,
and with it there is no need
to seek for help.
27 The fear of the Lord is like a
garden of blessing,
and covers a person better
than any glory.

THE DISGRACE OF BEGGING

28 My child, do not lead the
life of a beggar;
it is better to die than to beg.
29 When one looks to the table
of another,
one's way of life cannot be
considered a life.
One loses self-respect with
another person's food,
but one who is intelligent and well
instructed guards against that.
30 In the mouth of the shameless
begging is sweet,
but it kindles a fire inside him.

CONCERNING DEATH

41 O death, how bitter is
the thought of you
to one at peace among
possessions,
who has nothing to worry about and
is prosperous in everything,
and still is vigorous enough
to enjoy food!
2 O death, how welcome is
your sentence
to one who is needy and
failing in strength,
worn down by age and anxious
about everything;
to one who is contrary, and
has lost all patience!
3 Do not fear death's decree for you;
remember those who went
before you and those
who will come after.
4 This is the Lord's decree for all flesh;
why then should you reject the
will of the Most High?
Whether life lasts for ten years or
a hundred or a thousand,
there are no questions
asked in Hades.

THE FATE OF THE WICKED

5 The children of sinners are
abominable children,
and they frequent the haunts
of the ungodly.
6 The inheritance of the children
of sinners will perish,
and on their offspring will be
a perpetual disgrace.
7 Children will blame an ungodly father,
for they suffer disgrace
because of him.
8 Woe to you, the ungodly,
who have forsaken the law of
the Most High God!
9 If you have children, calamity
will be theirs;
you will beget them only
for groaning.
When you stumble, there
is lasting joy;[x]
and when you die, a curse
is your lot.
10 Whatever comes from earth
returns to earth;
so the ungodly go from curse
to destruction.

11 The human body is a fleeting thing,
but a virtuous name will
never be blotted out.[y]
12 Have regard for your name, since
it will outlive you
longer than a thousand
hoards of gold.
13 The days of a good life are numbered,
but a good name lasts for ever.

14 My children, be true to your
training and be at peace;
hidden wisdom and unseen
treasure—
of what value is either?

A SERIES OF CONTRASTS

15 Better are those who hide their folly
than those who hide
their wisdom.

[w] 40.23 Heb Compare Syr: Gk *wife with her husband* [x] 41.9 Heb: Meaning of Gk uncertain [y] 41.11 Heb: Gk *People grieve over the death of the body, but the bad name of sinners will be blotted out*

16 Therefore show respect for my words;
for it is not good to feel shame in
every circumstance,
nor is every kind of abashment
to be approved.[z]

17 Be ashamed of sexual immorality,
before your father or mother;
and of a lie, before a prince
or a ruler;
18 of a crime, before a judge or magistrate;
and of a breach of the law, before the
congregation and the people;
of unjust dealing, before your
partner or your friend;
19 and of theft, in the place
where you live.
Be ashamed of breaking an
oath or agreement,[a]
and of leaning on your
elbow at meals;
of surliness in receiving or giving,
20 and of silence, before those
who greet you;
of looking at a prostitute,
21 and of rejecting the appeal
of a relative;
of taking away someone's
portion or gift,
and of gazing at another man's wife;
22 of meddling with his servant-girl—
and do not approach her bed;
of abusive words, before friends—
and do not be insulting after
making a gift.

42 Be ashamed of repeating
what you hear,
and of betraying secrets.
Then you will show proper shame,
and will find favour
with everyone.

Of the following things do
not be ashamed,
and do not sin to save face:
2 Do not be ashamed of the law of the
Most High and his covenant,
and of rendering judgement
to acquit the ungodly;
3 of keeping accounts with a partner or
with travelling-companions,
and of dividing the
inheritance of friends;
4 of accuracy with scales and weights,
and of acquiring much or little;
5 of profit from dealing with
merchants,
and of frequent disciplining
of children,
and of drawing blood from the
back of a wicked slave.
6 Where there is an untrustworthy
wife, a seal is a good thing;
and where there are many
hands, lock things up.
7 When you make a deposit, be sure
it is counted and weighed,
and when you give or receive,
put it all in writing.
8 Do not be ashamed to correct
the stupid or foolish
or the aged who are guilty of
sexual immorality.
Then you will show your
sound training,
and will be approved by all.

DAUGHTERS AND FATHERS

9 A daughter is a secret anxiety
to her father,
and worry over her robs
him of sleep:
when she is young, for fear
she may not marry,
or if married, for fear she
may be disliked;
10 while a virgin, for fear she
may be seduced
and become pregnant in
her father's house;
or having a husband, for fear
she may go astray,
or, though married, for fear
she may be barren.
11 Keep strict watch over a
headstrong daughter,
or she may make you a
laughing-stock to
your enemies,
a byword in the city and the
assembly of[b] the people,
and put you to shame in
public gatherings.[c]
See that there is no lattice
in her room,
no spot that overlooks the
approaches to the house.[d]
12 Do not let her parade her beauty
before any man,
or spend her time among
married women;[e]
13 for from garments comes the moth,
and from a woman comes
woman's wickedness.

[z] **41.16** Heb: Gk *and not everything is confidently esteemed by everyone* [a] **41.19** Heb: Gk *before the truth of God and the covenant* [b] **42.11** Heb: Meaning of Gk uncertain [c] **42.11** Heb: Gk *to shame before the great multitude* [d] **42.11** Heb: Gk lacks *See . . . house* [e] **42.12** Heb: Meaning of Gk uncertain

14 Better is the wickedness of a
man than a woman
who does good;
it is woman who brings
shame and disgrace.

THE WORKS OF GOD IN NATURE

15 I will now call to mind the
works of the Lord,
and will declare what I have seen.
By the word of the Lord his
works are made;
and all his creatures do his will.[f]
16 The sun looks down on everything
with its light,
and the work of the Lord
is full of his glory.
17 The Lord has not empowered
even his holy ones
to recount all his
marvellous works,
which the Lord the Almighty
has established
so that the universe may
stand firm in his glory.
18 He searches out the abyss and
the human heart;
he understands their
innermost secrets.
For the Most High knows all
that may be known;
he sees from of old the things
that are to come.[g]
19 He discloses what has been
and what is to be,
and he reveals the traces
of hidden things.
20 No thought escapes him,
and nothing is hidden from him.
21 He has set in order the splendours
of his wisdom;
he is from all eternity one
and the same.
Nothing can be added or taken away,
and he needs no one to be
his counsellor.
22 How desirable are all his works,
and how sparkling they
are to see![h]
23 All these things live and
remain for ever;
each creature is preserved to
meet a particular need.[i]
24 All things come in pairs, one
opposite to the other,
and he has made nothing
incomplete.
25 Each supplements the virtues
of the other.
Who could ever tire of
seeing his glory?

THE SPLENDOUR OF THE SUN

43 The pride of the higher realms
is the clear vault of the sky,
as glorious to behold as the
sight of the heavens.
2 The sun, when it appears,
proclaims as it rises
what a marvellous instrument
it is, the work of
the Most High.
3 At noon it parches the land,
and who can withstand
its burning heat?
4 A man tending[j] a furnace works
in burning heat,
but three times as hot is the sun
scorching the mountains;
it breathes out fiery vapours,
and its bright rays blind the eyes.
5 Great is the Lord who made it;
at his orders it hurries
on its course.

THE SPLENDOUR OF THE MOON

6 It is the moon that marks the
changing seasons,[k]
governing the times, their
everlasting sign.
7 From the moon comes the
sign for festal days,
a light that wanes when it
completes its course.
8 The new moon, as its name
suggests, renews itself;[l]
how marvellous it is in
this change,
a beacon to the hosts on high,
shining in the vault of
the heavens!

THE GLORY OF THE STARS AND THE RAINBOW

9 The glory of the stars is the
beauty of heaven,
a glittering array in the
heights of the Lord.
10 On the orders of the Holy One
they stand in their
appointed places;
they never relax in their watches.
11 Look at the rainbow, and praise
him who made it;
it is exceedingly beautiful
in its brightness.

[f] **42.15** Syr Compare Heb: most Gk witnesses lack *and all . . . will* [g] **42.18** Heb: Gk *he sees the sign(s) of the age* [h] **42.22** Meaning of Gk uncertain [i] **42.23** Heb: Gk *for ever for every need, and all are obedient* [j] **43.4** Other ancient authorities read *blowing upon* [k] **43.6** Heb: Meaning of Gk uncertain [l] **43.8** Heb: Gk *The month is named after the moon*

12 It encircles the sky with its
glorious arc;
the hands of the Most High
have stretched it out.

THE MARVELS OF NATURE

13 By his command he sends
the driving snow
and speeds the lightnings
of his judgement.
14 Therefore the storehouses
are opened,
and the clouds fly out like birds.
15 In his majesty he gives the
clouds their strength,
and the hailstones are
broken in pieces.
17a The voice of his thunder
rebukes the earth;
16 when he appears, the
mountains shake.
At his will the south wind blows;
17b so do the storm from the north
and the whirlwind.
He scatters the snow like
birds flying down,
and its descent is like
locusts alighting.
18 The eye is dazzled by the beauty
of its whiteness,
and the mind is amazed as it falls.
19 He pours frost over the
earth like salt,
and icicles form like
pointed thorns.
20 The cold north wind blows,
and ice freezes on the water;
it settles on every pool of water,
and the water puts it on
like a breastplate.
21 He consumes the mountains and
burns up the wilderness,
and withers the tender
grass like fire.
22 A mist quickly heals all things;
the falling dew gives refreshment
from the heat.

23 By his plan he stilled the deep
and planted islands in it.
24 Those who sail the sea tell
of its dangers,
and we marvel at what we hear.
25 In it are strange and marvellous
creatures,
all kinds of living things, and
huge sea-monsters.
26 Because of him each of his
messengers succeeds,
and by his word all things
hold together.

27 We could say more but could
never say enough;
let the final word be: 'He is the all.'
28 Where can we find the strength
to praise him?
For he is greater than
all his works.
29 Awesome is the Lord and very great,
and marvellous is his power.
30 Glorify the Lord and exalt him
as much as you can,
for he surpasses even that.
When you exalt him, summon
all your strength,
and do not grow weary, for you
cannot praise him enough.
31 Who has seen him and can
describe him?
Or who can extol him as he is?
32 Many things greater than
these lie hidden,
for I[m] have seen but few
of his works.
33 For the Lord has made all things,
and to the godly he has
given wisdom.

HYMN IN HONOUR OF OUR ANCESTORS[n]

44 Let us now sing the praises
of famous men,
our ancestors in their generations.
2 The Lord apportioned to
them[o] great glory,
his majesty from the beginning.
3 There were those who ruled
in their kingdoms,
and made a name for themselves
by their valour;
those who gave counsel because
they were intelligent;
those who spoke in
prophetic oracles;
4 those who led the people by
their counsels
and by their knowledge of
the people's lore;
they were wise in their
words of instruction;
5 those who composed musical tunes,
or put verses in writing;
6 rich men endowed with resources,
living peacefully in their homes—
7 all these were honoured in
their generations,
and were the pride of their times.

m 43.32 Heb: Gk *we* n 44.1 This title is included in the Gk text. o 44.2 Heb: Gk *created*

8 Some of them have left
behind a name,
so that others declare their praise.
9 But of others there is no memory;
they have perished as though
they had never existed;
they have become as though they
had never been born,
they and their children
after them.
10 But these also were godly men,
whose righteous deeds have
not been forgotten;
11 their wealth will remain with
their descendants,
and their inheritance with their
children's children.[p]
12 Their descendants stand by
the covenants;
their children also, for their sake.
13 Their offspring will continue for ever,
and their glory will never
be blotted out.
14 Their bodies are buried in peace,
but their name lives on
generation after generation.
15 The assembly declares[q]
their wisdom,
and the congregation
proclaims their praise.

ENOCH

16 Enoch pleased the Lord and
was taken up,
an example of repentance
to all generations.

NOAH

17 Noah was found perfect
and righteous;
in the time of wrath he
kept the race alive;[r]
therefore a remnant was
left on the earth
when the flood came.
18 Everlasting covenants were
made with him
that all flesh should never again
be blotted out by a flood.

ABRAHAM

19 Abraham was the great father of
a multitude of nations,
and no one has been found
like him in glory.
20 He kept the law of the Most High,
and entered into a covenant
with him;
he certified the covenant in his flesh,
and when he was tested he
proved faithful.
21 Therefore the Lord[s] assured
him with an oath
that the nations would be blessed
through his offspring;
that he would make him
as numerous as the
dust of the earth,
and exalt his offspring
like the stars,
and give them an inheritance
from sea to sea
and from the Euphrates[t] to
the ends of the earth.

ISAAC AND JACOB

22 To Isaac also he gave the
same assurance
for the sake of his father
Abraham.
The blessing of all people and
the covenant
23 he made to rest on the
head of Jacob;
he acknowledged him with
his blessings,
and gave him his inheritance;
he divided his portions,
and distributed them among
twelve tribes.

MOSES

From his descendants the Lord[u]
brought forth a godly man,
who found favour in
the sight of all
45 1and was beloved by
God and people,
Moses, whose memory is blessed.
2 He made him equal in glory
to the holy ones,
and made him great, to the
terror of his enemies.
3 By his words he performed
swift miracles;[v]
the Lord[w] glorified him in
the presence of kings.
He gave him commandments
for his people,
and revealed to him his glory.
4 For his faithfulness and meekness
he consecrated him,
choosing him out of all
humankind.
5 He allowed him to hear his voice,
and led him into the dark cloud,

p 44.11 Heb Compare Lat Syr: Meaning of Gk uncertain q 44.15 Heb: Gk *Peoples declare*
r 44.17 Heb: Gk *was taken in exchange*
s 44.21 Gk *he* t 44.21 Syr: Heb Gk *River*
u 44.23 Gk *he* v 45.3 Heb: Gk *caused signs to cease* w 45.3 Gk *he*

and gave him the commandments
face to face,
the law of life and knowledge,
so that he might teach Jacob
the covenant,
and Israel his decrees.

AARON

6 He exalted Aaron, a holy
man like Moses[x]
who was his brother, of
the tribe of Levi.
7 He made an everlasting
covenant with him,
and gave him the priesthood
of the people.
He blessed him with stateliness,
and put a glorious robe on him.
8 He clothed him in perfect splendour,
and strengthened him with the
symbols of authority,
the linen undergarments, the
long robe, and the ephod.
9 And he encircled him with
pomegranates,
with many golden bells all round,
to send forth a sound as he walked,
to make their ringing heard
in the temple
as a reminder to his people;
10 with the sacred vestment, of
gold and violet
and purple, the work of
an embroiderer;
with the oracle of judgement,
Urim and Thummim;
11 with twisted crimson, the
work of an artisan;
with precious stones engraved
like seals,
in a setting of gold, the
work of a jeweller,
to commemorate in engraved letters
each of the tribes of Israel;
12 with a gold crown upon his turban,
inscribed like a seal with
'Holiness',
a distinction to be prized, the
work of an expert,
a delight to the eyes,
richly adorned.
13 Before him such beautiful
things did not exist.
No outsider ever put them on,
but only his sons
and his descendants
in perpetuity.
14 His sacrifices shall be wholly burned
twice every day continually.
15 Moses ordained him,
and anointed him with holy oil;
it was an everlasting
covenant for him
and for his descendants as long
as the heavens endure,
to minister to the Lord[y] and
serve as priest
and bless his people in his name.
16 He chose him out of all the living
to offer sacrifice to the Lord,
incense and a pleasing odour as
a memorial portion,
to make atonement for
the[z] people.
17 In his commandments he gave him
authority and statutes
and[a] judgements,
to teach Jacob the testimonies,
and to enlighten Israel
with his law.
18 Outsiders conspired against him,
and envied him in the wilderness,
Dathan and Abiram and
their followers
and the company of Korah,
in wrath and anger.
19 The Lord saw it and was not pleased,
and in the heat of his anger
they were destroyed;
he performed wonders against them
to consume them in flaming fire.
20 He added glory to Aaron
and gave him a heritage;
he allotted to him the best of
the first fruits,
and prepared bread of first
fruits in abundance;
21 for they eat the sacrifices
of the Lord,
which he gave to him and
his descendants.
22 But in the land of the people he
has no inheritance,
and he has no portion
among the people;
for the Lord[b] himself is his[c]
portion and inheritance.

PHINEHAS

23 Phinehas son of Eleazar ranks
third in glory
for being zealous in the
fear of the Lord,
and standing firm, when the
people turned away,
in the noble courage of his soul;
and he made atonement for Israel.

[x] **45.6** Gk *him* [y] **45.15** Gk *him* [z] **45.16** Other ancient authorities read *his* or *your* [a] **45.17** Heb: Gk *authority in covenants of* [b] **45.22** Gk *he* [c] **45.22** Other ancient authorities read *your*

24 Therefore a covenant of friendship
was established with him,
that he should be leader of the
sanctuary and of his people,
that he and his descendants
should have
the dignity of the priesthood
for ever.
25 Just as a covenant was established
with David
son of Jesse of the tribe of Judah,
that the king's heritage passes
only from son to son,
so the heritage of Aaron is for
his descendants alone.

26 And now bless the Lord
who has crowned you
with glory.[d]
May the Lord[e] grant you
wisdom of mind
to judge his people with justice,
so that their prosperity may
not vanish,
and that their glory may
endure through all
their generations.

JOSHUA AND CALEB

46 Joshua son of Nun was
mighty in war,
and was the successor of Moses
in the prophetic office.
He became, as his name implies,
a great saviour of God's[f] elect,
to take vengeance on the enemies
that rose against them,
so that he might give Israel
its inheritance.
2 How glorious he was when
he lifted his hands
and brandished his sword
against the cities!
3 Who before him ever
stood so firm?
For he waged the wars
of the Lord.
4 Was it not through him that
the sun stood still
and one day became as
long as two?
5 He called upon the Most High,
the Mighty One,
when enemies pressed him
on every side,
and the great Lord answered him
with hailstones of mighty power.
6 He overwhelmed that
nation in battle,
and on the slope he destroyed
his opponents,
so that the nations might know
his armament,
that he was fighting in the
sight of the Lord;
for he was a devoted follower
of the Mighty One.
7 And in the days of Moses he
proved his loyalty,
he and Caleb son of Jephunneh:
they opposed the congregation,[g]
restrained the people from sin,
and stilled their wicked
grumbling.
8 And these two alone were spared
out of six hundred thousand
infantry,
to lead the people[h] into their
inheritance,
the land flowing with
milk and honey.
9 The Lord gave Caleb strength,
which remained with him
in his old age,
so that he went up to the
hill country,
and his children obtained it
for an inheritance,
10 so that all the Israelites might see
how good it is to follow the Lord.

THE JUDGES

11 The judges also, with their
respective names,
whose hearts did not fall
into idolatry
and who did not turn away
from the Lord—
may their memory be blessed!
12 May their bones send forth new
life from where they lie,
and may the names of those
who have been honoured
live again in their children!

13 Samuel was beloved by his Lord;
a prophet of the Lord, he
established the kingdom
and anointed rulers over
his people.
14 By the law of the Lord he judged
the congregation,
and the Lord watched over Jacob.
15 By his faithfulness he was proved
to be a prophet,
and by his words he became
known as a trustworthy seer.

[d] 45.26 Heb: Gk lacks *And . . . glory* [e] 45.26 Gk *he* [f] 46.1 Gk *his* [g] 46.7 Other ancient authorities read *the enemy* [h] 46.8 Gk *them*

16 He called upon the Lord, the
Mighty One,
when his enemies pressed
him on every side,
and he offered in sacrifice
a sucking-lamb.
17 Then the Lord thundered
from heaven,
and made his voice heard
with a mighty sound;
18 he subdued the leaders of the enemy[i]
and all the rulers of the Philistines.
19 Before the time of his eternal sleep,
Samuel[j] bore witness before the
Lord and his anointed:
'No property, not so much as
a pair of shoes,
have I taken from anyone!'
And no one accused him.
20 Even after he had fallen asleep,
he prophesied
and made known to the
king his death,
and lifted up his voice from the ground
in prophecy, to blot out the
wickedness of the people.

NATHAN

47 After him Nathan rose up
to prophesy in the
days of David.

DAVID

2 As the fat is set apart from the
offering of well-being,
so David was set apart from
the Israelites.
3 He played with lions as though
they were young goats,
and with bears as though they
were lambs of the flock.
4 In his youth did he not kill a giant,
and take away the people's
disgrace,
when he whirled the stone
in the sling
and struck down the
boasting Goliath?
5 For he called on the Lord,
the Most High,
and he gave strength to
his right arm
to strike down a mighty warrior,
and to exalt the power[k]
of his people.
6 So they glorified him for the tens of
thousands he conquered,
and praised him for the blessings
bestowed by the Lord,
when the glorious diadem
was given to him.
7 For he wiped out his enemies
on every side,
and annihilated his adversaries
the Philistines;
he crushed their power[l]
to our own day.
8 In all that he did he gave thanks
to the Holy One, the Most High,
proclaiming his glory;
he sang praise with all his heart,
and he loved his Maker.
9 He placed singers before the altar,
to make sweet melody with
their voices.[m]
10 He gave beauty to the festivals,
and arranged their times
throughout the year,[n]
while they praised God's[o] holy name,
and the sanctuary resounded
from early morning.
11 The Lord took away his sins,
and exalted his power[p] for ever;
he gave him a covenant of kingship
and a glorious throne in Israel.

SOLOMON

12 After him a wise son rose up
who because of him lived
in security:[q]
13 Solomon reigned in an age of peace,
because God made all his
borders tranquil,
so that he might build a
house in his name
and provide a sanctuary
to stand for ever.
14 How wise you were when
you were young!
You overflowed like the Nile[r]
with understanding.
15 Your influence spread
throughout the earth,
and you filled it with proverbs
having deep meaning.
16 Your fame reached to far-off islands,
and you were loved for your
peaceful reign.
17 Your songs, proverbs, and parables,
and the answers you gave
astounded the nations.
18 In the name of the Lord God,
who is called the God of Israel,
you gathered gold like tin
and amassed silver like lead.

[i] 46.18 Heb: Gk *leaders of the people of Tyre*
[j] 46.19 Gk *he* [k] 47.5 Gk *horn* [l] 47.7 Gk *horn*
[m] 47.9 Other ancient authorities add *and daily they sing his praises* [n] 47.10 Gk *to completion*
[o] 47.10 Gk *his* [p] 47.11 Gk *horn* [q] 47.12 Heb: Gk *in a broad place* [r] 47.14 Heb: Gk *a river*

19 But you brought in women
to lie at your side,
and through your body you were
brought into subjection.
20 You stained your honour
and defiled your family line,
so that you brought wrath
upon your children,
and they were grieved[s]
at your folly,
21 because the sovereignty was divided
and a rebel kingdom arose
out of Ephraim.
22 But the Lord will never give
up his mercy,
or cause any of his works
to perish;
he will never blot out the
descendants of his
chosen one,
or destroy the family line of
him who loved him.
So he gave a remnant to Jacob,
and to David a root from
his own family.

REHOBOAM AND JEROBOAM

23 Solomon rested with his ancestors,
and left behind him one
of his sons,
broad in[t] folly and lacking in sense,
Rehoboam, whose policy drove
the people to revolt.
Then Jeroboam son of Nebat
led Israel into sin
and started Ephraim on
its sinful ways.
24 Their sins increased more and more,
until they were exiled
from their land.
25 For they sought out every
kind of wickedness,
until vengeance came upon them.

ELIJAH

48 Then Elijah arose, a
prophet like fire,
and his word burned like a torch.
2 He brought a famine upon them,
and by his zeal he made
them few in number.
3 By the word of the Lord he
shut up the heavens,
and also three times
brought down fire.
4 How glorious you were, Elijah, in
your wondrous deeds!
Whose glory is equal to yours?
5 You raised a corpse from death
and from Hades, by the word
of the Most High.
6 You sent kings down to destruction,
and famous men, from
their sickbeds.
7 You heard rebuke at Sinai
and judgements of
vengeance at Horeb.
8 You anointed kings to inflict
retribution,
and prophets to succeed you.[u]
9 You were taken up by a
whirlwind of fire,
in a chariot with horses of fire.
10 At the appointed time, it is written,
you are destined[v]
to calm the wrath of God before
it breaks out in fury,
to turn the hearts of parents
to their children,
and to restore the tribes of Jacob.
11 Happy are those who saw you
and were adorned[w] with
your love!
For we also shall surely live.[x]

ELISHA

12 When Elijah was enveloped
in the whirlwind,
Elisha was filled with his spirit.
He performed twice as many signs,
and marvels with every
utterance of his mouth.[y]
Never in his lifetime did he
tremble before any ruler,
nor could anyone intimidate
him at all.
13 Nothing was too hard for him,
and when he was dead, his
body prophesied.
14 In his life he did wonders,
and in death his deeds
were marvellous.

15 Despite all this the people
did not repent,
nor did they forsake their sins,
until they were carried off as
plunder from their land,
and were scattered over
all the earth.
The people were left very
few in number,
but with a ruler from the
house of David.

[s] **47.20** Other ancient authorities read *I was grieved* [t] **47.23** Heb (with a play on the name Rehoboam) Syr: Gk *the people's* [u] **48.8** Heb: Gk *him* [v] **48.10** Heb: Gk *are for reproofs* [w] **48.11** Other ancient authorities read *and have died* [x] **48.11** Text and meaning of Gk uncertain [y] **48.12** Heb: Gk lacks *He performed . . . mouth*

16 Some of them did what was right,
but others sinned more and more.

HEZEKIAH

17 Hezekiah fortified his city,
and brought water into its midst;
he tunnelled the rock with iron tools,
and built cisterns for the water.
18 In his days Sennacherib invaded
the country;
he sent his commander[z]
and departed;
he shook his fist against Zion,
and made great boasts in
his arrogance.
19 Then their hearts were shaken and
their hands trembled,
and they were in anguish,
like women in labour.
20 But they called upon the Lord
who is merciful,
spreading out their hands
towards him.
The Holy One quickly heard
them from heaven,
and delivered them through Isaiah.
21 The Lord[a] struck down the camp
of the Assyrians,
and his angel wiped them out.
22 For Hezekiah did what was
pleasing to the Lord,
and he kept firmly to the ways
of his ancestor David,
as he was commanded by the
prophet Isaiah,
who was great and trustworthy
in his visions.

ISAIAH

23 In Isaiah's[b] days the sun
went backwards,
and he prolonged the life
of the king.
24 By his dauntless spirit he
saw the future,
and comforted the
mourners in Zion.
25 He revealed what was to occur
to the end of time,
and the hidden things before
they happened.

JOSIAH AND OTHER WORTHIES

49 The name[c] of Josiah is
like blended incense
prepared by the skill of
the perfumer;
his memory[d] is as sweet as
honey to every mouth,
and like music at a
banquet of wine.
2 He did what was right by
reforming the people,
and removing the wicked
abominations.
3 He kept his heart fixed on the Lord;
in lawless times he made
godliness prevail.

4 Except for David and Hezekiah
and Josiah,
all of them were great sinners,
for they abandoned the law
of the Most High;
the kings of Judah came to an end.
5 They[e] gave their power to others,
and their glory to a
foreign nation,
6 who set fire to the chosen city
of the sanctuary,
and made its streets desolate,
as Jeremiah had foretold.[f]
7 For they had maltreated him,
who even in the womb had been
consecrated a prophet,
to pluck up and ruin and destroy,
and likewise to build and to plant.

8 It was Ezekiel who saw the
vision of glory,
which God[g] showed him above
the chariot of the cherubim.
9 For God[h] also mentioned Job
who held fast to all the
ways of justice.[i]
10 May the bones of the Twelve
Prophets
send forth new life from
where they lie,
for they comforted the
people of Jacob
and delivered them with
confident hope.

11 How shall we magnify Zerubbabel?
He was like a signet ring
on the right hand,
12 and so was Jeshua son of Jozadak;
in their days they built the house
and raised a temple[j] holy
to the Lord,
destined for everlasting glory.
13 The memory of Nehemiah
also is lasting;
he raised our fallen walls,

[z] 48.18 Other ancient authorities add *from Lachish* [a] 48.21 Gk *He* [b] 48.23 Gk *his* [c] 49.1 Heb: Gk *memory* [d] 49.1 Heb: Gk *it* [e] 49.5 Heb *He* [f] 49.6 Gk *by the hand of Jeremiah* [g] 49.8 Gk *He* [h] 49.9 Gk *he* [i] 49.9 Heb Compare Syr: Meaning of Gk uncertain [j] 49.12 Other ancient authorities read *people*

and set up gates and bars,
and rebuilt our ruined houses.

RETROSPECT

14 Few have[k] ever been created
on earth like Enoch,
for he was taken up from
the earth.
15 Nor was anyone ever born
like Joseph;[l]
even his bones were cared for.
16 Shem and Seth and Enosh
were honoured,[m]
but above every other created
living being was Adam.

SIMON SON OF ONIAS

50 The leader of his brothers and
the pride of his people[n]
was the high priest, Simon
son of Onias,
who in his life repaired the house,
and in his time fortified
the temple.
2 He laid the foundations for the
high double walls,
the high retaining walls for
the temple enclosure.
3 In his days a water cistern was dug,[o]
a reservoir like the sea in
circumference.
4 He considered how to save his
people from ruin,
and fortified the city
against siege.
5 How glorious he was, surrounded
by the people,
as he came out of the house
of the curtain.
6 Like the morning star among
the clouds,
like the full moon at the
festal season;[p]
7 like the sun shining on the temple
of the Most High,
like the rainbow gleaming
in splendid clouds;
8 like roses in the days of first fruits,
like lilies by a spring of water,
like a green shoot on Lebanon
on a summer day;
9 like fire and incense in the censer,
like a vessel of hammered gold
studded with all kinds of
precious stones;
10 like an olive tree laden with fruit,
and like a cypress towering
in the clouds.
11 When he put on his glorious robe
and clothed himself in
perfect splendour,
when he went up to the holy altar,
he made the court of the
sanctuary glorious.
12 When he received the portions from
the hands of the priests,
as he stood by the hearth
of the altar
with a garland of brothers
around him,
he was like a young cedar
on Lebanon
surrounded by the trunks
of palm trees.
13 All the sons of Aaron in
their splendour
held the Lord's offering
in their hands
before the whole congregation
of Israel.
14 Finishing the service at the altars,[q]
and arranging the offering to the
Most High, the Almighty,
15 he held out his hand for the cup
and poured a drink-offering of
the blood of the grape;
he poured it out at the foot
of the altar,
a pleasing odour to the Most
High, the king of all.
16 Then the sons of Aaron shouted;
they blew their trumpets of
hammered metal;
they sounded a mighty fanfare
as a reminder before the
Most High.
17 Then all the people together quickly
fell to the ground on their faces
to worship their Lord,
the Almighty, God Most High.

18 Then the singers praised him
with their voices
in sweet and full-toned melody.[r]
19 And the people of the Lord
Most High offered
their prayers before the
Merciful One,
until the order of worship of
the Lord was ended,
and they completed his ritual.

[k] 49.14 Heb Syr: Gk *No one has* [l] 49.15 Heb Syr: Gk adds *the leader of his brothers, the support of the people* [m] 49.16 Heb: Gk *Shem and Seth were honoured by people* [n] 50.1 Heb Syr: Gk lacks this line. Compare 49.15 [o] 50.3 Heb: Meaning of Gk uncertain [p] 50.6 Heb: Meaning of Gk uncertain [q] 50.14 Other ancient authorities read *altar* [r] 50.18 Other ancient authorities read *in sweet melody throughout the house*

20 Then Simon[s] came down and
raised his hands
over the whole congregation
of Israelites,
to pronounce the blessing of the
Lord with his lips,
and to glory in his name;
21 and they bowed down in worship
a second time,
to receive the blessing from
the Most High.

A BENEDICTION

22 And now bless the God of all,
who everywhere works
great wonders,
who fosters our growth from birth,
and deals with us according
to his mercy.
23 May he give us[t] gladness of heart,
and may there be peace
in our[u] days
in Israel, as in the days of old.
24 May he entrust to us his mercy,
and may he deliver us
in our[v] days!

EPILOGUE

25 Two nations my soul detests,
and the third is not
even a people:
26 Those who live in Seir,[w] and
the Philistines,
and the foolish people that
live in Shechem.

27 Instruction in understanding
and knowledge
I have written in this book,
Jesus son of Eleazar son of
Sirach[x] of Jerusalem,
whose mind poured
forth wisdom.
28 Happy are those who concern
themselves with
these things,
and those who lay them to
heart will become wise.
29 For if they put them into
practice, they will be
equal to anything,
for the fear[y] of the Lord
is their path.

PRAYER OF JESUS SON OF SIRACH[z]

51 I give you thanks,
O Lord and King,
and praise you, O God my Saviour.
I give thanks to your name,
2 for you have been my
protector and helper
and have delivered me from
destruction
and from the trap laid by a
slanderous tongue,
from lips that fabricate lies.
In the face of my adversaries
you have been my helper
3 and delivered me,
in the greatness of your mercy
and of your name,
from grinding teeth about
to devour me,
from the hand of those
seeking my life,
from the many troubles I endured,
4 from choking fire on every side,
and from the midst of fire
that I had not kindled,
5 from the deep belly of Hades,
from an unclean tongue
and lying words—
6 the slander of an unrighteous
tongue to the king.
My soul drew near to death,
and my life was on the brink
of Hades below.
7 They surrounded me on every side,
and there was no one to help me;
I looked for human assistance,
and there was none.
8 Then I remembered your
mercy, O Lord,
and your kindness[a] from of old,
for you rescue those who wait for you
and save them from the hand
of their enemies.
9 And I sent up my prayer
from the earth,
and begged for rescue from death.
10 I cried out, 'Lord, you are
my Father;[b]
do not forsake me in the
days of trouble,
when there is no help
against the proud.
11 I will praise your name continually,
and will sing hymns of
thanksgiving.'

[s] **50.20** Gk *he* [t] **50.23** Other ancient authorities read *you* [u] **50.23** Other ancient authorities read *your* [v] **50.24** Other ancient authorities read *his* [w] **50.26** Heb Compare Lat: Gk *on the mountain of Samaria* [x] **50.27** Heb: Meaning of Gk uncertain [y] **50.29** Heb: Other ancient authorities read *light* [z] **51.1** This title is included in the Gk text. [a] **51.8** Other ancient authorities read *work* [b] **51.10** Heb: Gk *the Father of my lord*

My prayer was heard,
12 for you saved me from destruction
and rescued me in
time of trouble.
For this reason I thank you
and praise you,
and I bless the name of the Lord.

Hebrew adds:

Give thanks to the LORD,
for he is good,
for his steadfast love
endures for ever;

Give thanks to the God of praises,
for his steadfast love
endures for ever;

Give thanks to the guardian
of Israel,
for his steadfast love
endures for ever;

Give thanks to him who
formed all things,
for his steadfast love
endures for ever;

Give thanks to the redeemer
of Israel,
for his steadfast love
endures for ever;

Give thanks to him who gathers
the dispersed of Israel,
for his steadfast love
endures for ever;

Give thanks to him who rebuilt his
city and his sanctuary,
for his steadfast love
endures for ever;

Give thanks to him who makes
a horn to sprout for
the house of David,
for his steadfast love
endures for ever;

Give thanks to him who has
chosen the sons of
Zadok to be priests,
for his steadfast love
endures for ever;

Give thanks to the shield
of Abraham,
for his steadfast love
endures for ever;

Give thanks to the rock of Isaac,
for his steadfast love
endures for ever;

Give thanks to the mighty
one of Jacob,
for his steadfast love
endures for ever;

Give thanks to him who has
chosen Zion,
for his steadfast love
endures for ever;

Give thanks to the King of
the kings of kings,
for his steadfast love
endures for ever;

He has raised up a horn
for his people,
praise for all his loyal ones.

For the children of Israel, the
people close to him.
Praise the LORD!

AUTOBIOGRAPHICAL POEM ON WISDOM

13 While I was still young, before I
went on my travels,
I sought wisdom openly
in my prayer.
14 Before the temple I asked for her,
and I will search for her
until the end.

15 From the first blossom to the
ripening grape
my heart delighted in her;
my foot walked on the straight path;
from my youth I followed her steps.

16 I inclined my ear a little and
received her,
and I found for myself
much instruction.
17 I made progress in her;
to him who gives wisdom
I will give glory.

18 For I resolved to live according
to wisdom,[c]
and I was zealous for the good,
and I shall never be disappointed.
19 My soul grappled with wisdom,[d]
and in my conduct I was strict;[e]

[c] 51.18 Gk *her* [d] 51.19 Gk *her*
[e] 51.19 Meaning of Gk uncertain

I spread out my hands to
the heavens,
and lamented my
ignorance of her.
20 I directed my soul to her,
and in purity I found her.

With her I gained understanding
from the first;
therefore I will never be forsaken.
21 My heart was stirred to seek her;
therefore I have gained a
prize possession.
22 The Lord gave me my tongue
as a reward,
and I will praise him with it.

23 Draw near to me, you who
are uneducated,
and lodge in the house
of instruction.
24 Why do you say you are lacking
in these things,[f]
and why do you endure
such great thirst?
25 I opened my mouth and said,
Acquire wisdom[g] for yourselves
without money.
26 Put your neck under her[h] yoke,
and let your souls receive
instruction;
it is to be found close by.

27 See with your own eyes that I
have laboured but little
and found for myself
much serenity.
28 Hear but a little of my instruction,
and through me you will
acquire silver and gold.[i]

29 May your soul rejoice in
God's[j] mercy,
and may you never be ashamed
to praise him.
30 Do your work in good time,
and in his own time God[k] will
give you your reward.

[f] 51.24 Cn Compare Heb Syr: Meaning of Gk uncertain [g] 51.25 Heb: Gk lacks *wisdom* [h] 51.26 Heb: other ancient authorities read *the* [i] 51.28 Syr Compare Heb: Gk *Get instruction with a large sum of silver, and you will gain by it much gold.* [j] 51.29 Gk *his* [k] 51.30 Gk *he*

ISAIAH

Isaiah the prophet lived and preached between the time of the death of King Uzziah of Judah (ca. 738 BCE) and the end of the century through the administrations of the Judean kings Jotham, Ahaz, and Hezekiah. The book of Isaiah is usually divided into three distinct sections: chapters 1–39 (First Isaiah), attributed to the eighth-century prophet who witnessed the fall of the northern kingdom, Israel, and the moral breakdown of Judah; chapters 40–55 (Second Isaiah or Deutero-Isaiah), attributed to an unknown prophet during the Babylonian exile; and chapters 56–66 (Third Isaiah or Trito-Isaiah), attributed to prophets who lived following the exile after 539 BCE. There is a consistency and literary unity of the whole book of Isaiah despite evidence of additions and editing over three centuries.

The prophecies in the book of Isaiah require an understanding of the historical events that establish their context. Major themes, however, dominate the writing. Isaiah underscores that the God of Israel and Judah is the God of all nations and that the whole world is subject to the providence and will of the "Holy One of Israel." The people of Israel have a special destiny and a responsibility to live up to their call. The spiritual center of the people is the city of Jerusalem, and the Davidic dynasty is important for upholding the covenant. Isaiah prophesied "messianic oracles" known as the Four Servant Songs (chs. 40–55), which seem to refer to the role of Israel but are interpreted by Christians as fulfilled in the person of Christ.

Isaiah is the most widely quoted prophet in the New Testament. The book of Isaiah is also the most widely read of the prophetic books in the liturgical calendar of the Roman Missal. Passages from Isaiah are read in all three Sunday Cycles at various Feasts: the Christmas Vigil (62.1–5), Christmas Mass at Midnight (9.1–6), Christmas Mass at Dawn (62.11–12), Christmas Mass During the Day (52.7–10), the Epiphany (60.1–6), the Baptism of the Lord (42.1–4, 6–7), Palm Sunday (50.4–7), Holy Thursday (61.1–3, 6, 8–9), Good Friday (52.13—53.12), and as Reading IV (54.5–14) and Reading V (55.1–11) of the Easter Vigil.

1 The vision of Isaiah son of Amoz, which he saw concerning Judah and Jerusalem in the days of Uzziah, Jotham, Ahaz, and Hezekiah, kings of Judah.

THE WICKEDNESS OF JUDAH

2 Hear, O heavens, and listen, O earth;
for the LORD has spoken:
I reared children and brought
them up,
but they have rebelled against me.
3 The ox knows its owner,
and the donkey its master's crib;
but Israel does not know,
my people do not understand.

4 Ah, sinful nation,
people laden with iniquity,
offspring who do evil,
children who deal corruptly,
who have forsaken the LORD,
who have despised the
Holy One of Israel,
who are utterly estranged!

5 Why do you seek further beatings?
Why do you continue to rebel?

The whole head is sick,
and the whole heart faint.
6 From the sole of the foot
even to the head,
there is no soundness in it,
but bruises and sores
and bleeding wounds;
they have not been drained,
or bound up,
or softened with oil.

7 Your country lies desolate,
your cities are burned with fire;
in your very presence
aliens devour your land;
it is desolate, as overthrown
by foreigners.
8 And daughter Zion is left
like a booth in a vineyard,
like a shelter in a cucumber field,
like a besieged city.
9 If the LORD of hosts
had not left us a few survivors,
we would have been like Sodom,
and become like Gomorrah.

10 Hear the word of the LORD,
you rulers of Sodom!
Listen to the teaching of our God,
you people of Gomorrah!
11 What to me is the multitude
of your sacrifices?
says the LORD;
I have had enough of burnt-offerings
of rams
and the fat of fed beasts;
I do not delight in the
blood of bulls,
or of lambs, or of goats.

12 When you come to appear
before me,[a]
who asked this from your hand?
Trample my courts no more;
13 bringing offerings is futile;
incense is an abomination to me.
New moon and sabbath and
calling of convocation—
I cannot endure solemn
assemblies with iniquity.
14 Your new moons and your
appointed festivals
my soul hates;
they have become a burden to me,
I am weary of bearing them.
15 When you stretch out your hands,
I will hide my eyes from you;
even though you make
many prayers,
I will not listen;
your hands are full of blood.
16 Wash yourselves; make
yourselves clean;
remove the evil of your doings
from before my eyes;
cease to do evil,
17 learn to do good;
seek justice,
rescue the oppressed,
defend the orphan,
plead for the widow.

18 Come now, let us argue it out,
says the LORD:
though your sins are like scarlet,
they shall be like snow;
though they are red like crimson,
they shall become like wool.
19 If you are willing and obedient,
you shall eat the good of the land;
20 but if you refuse and rebel,
you shall be devoured
by the sword;
for the mouth of the LORD
has spoken.

THE DEGENERATE CITY

21 How the faithful city
has become a whore!
She that was full of justice,
righteousness lodged in her—
but now murderers!
22 Your silver has become dross,
your wine is mixed with water.
23 Your princes are rebels
and companions of thieves.
Everyone loves a bribe
and runs after gifts.
They do not defend the orphan,
and the widow's cause does
not come before them.

24 Therefore says the Sovereign,
the LORD of hosts, the
Mighty One of Israel:
Ah, I will pour out my wrath
on my enemies,
and avenge myself on my foes!
25 I will turn my hand against you;
I will smelt away your
dross as with lye
and remove all your alloy.
26 And I will restore your judges
as at the first,
and your counsellors as at
the beginning.
Afterwards you shall be called the
city of righteousness,
the faithful city.

[a] 1.12 Or *see my face*

27 Zion shall be redeemed by justice,
and those in her who repent,
by righteousness.
28 But rebels and sinners shall be
destroyed together,
and those who forsake the
LORD shall be consumed.
29 For you shall be ashamed of the oaks
in which you delighted;
and you shall blush for the gardens
that you have chosen.
30 For you shall be like an oak
whose leaf withers,
and like a garden without water.
31 The strong shall become like tinder,
and their work[b] like a spark;
they and their work shall
burn together,
with no one to quench them.

THE FUTURE HOUSE OF GOD

2 The word that Isaiah son of Amoz saw concerning Judah and Jerusalem.

2 In days to come
the mountain of the
LORD's house
shall be established as the highest
of the mountains,
and shall be raised above the hills;
all the nations shall stream to it.
3 Many peoples shall come and say,
'Come, let us go up to the
mountain of the LORD,
to the house of the God of Jacob;
that he may teach us his ways
and that we may walk
in his paths.'
For out of Zion shall go forth
instruction,
and the word of the LORD
from Jerusalem.
4 He shall judge between
the nations,
and shall arbitrate for
many peoples;
they shall beat their swords
into ploughshares,
and their spears into
pruning-hooks;
nation shall not lift up sword
against nation,
neither shall they learn
war any more.

JUDGEMENT PRONOUNCED ON ARROGANCE

5 O house of Jacob,
come, let us walk
in the light of the LORD!
6 For you have forsaken the ways
of[c] your people,
O house of Jacob.
Indeed they are full of diviners[d]
from the east
and of soothsayers like
the Philistines,
and they clasp hands
with foreigners.
7 Their land is filled with
silver and gold,
and there is no end to
their treasures;
their land is filled with horses,
and there is no end to
their chariots.
8 Their land is filled with idols;
they bow down to the work
of their hands,
to what their own fingers
have made.
9 And so people are humbled,
and everyone is brought low—
do not forgive them!
10 Enter into the rock,
and hide in the dust
from the terror of the LORD,
and from the glory of his majesty.
11 The haughty eyes of people
shall be brought low,
and the pride of everyone
shall be humbled;
and the LORD alone will be
exalted on that day.
12 For the LORD of hosts has a day
against all that is proud and lofty,
against all that is lifted
up and high;[e]
13 against all the cedars of Lebanon,
lofty and lifted up;
and against all the oaks of Bashan;
14 against all the high mountains,
and against all the lofty hills;
15 against every high tower,
and against every fortified wall;
16 against all the ships of Tarshish,
and against all the beautiful craft.[f]
17 The haughtiness of people
shall be humbled,
and the pride of everyone
shall be brought low;
and the LORD alone will be
exalted on that day.
18 The idols shall utterly pass away.
19 Enter the caves of the rocks
and the holes of the ground,

[b] **1.31** Or *its makers* [c] **2.6** Heb lacks *the ways of* [d] **2.6** Cn: Heb lacks *of diviners* [e] **2.12** Cn Compare Gk: Heb *low* [f] **2.16** Compare Gk: Meaning of Heb uncertain

from the terror of the LORD,
and from the glory of his majesty,
when he rises to terrify the earth.
20 On that day people will throw away
to the moles and to the bats
their idols of silver and their
idols of gold,
which they made for
themselves to worship,
21 to enter the caverns of the rocks
and the clefts in the crags,
from the terror of the LORD,
and from the glory of
his majesty,
when he rises to terrify the earth.
22 Turn away from mortals,
who have only breath in
their nostrils,
for of what account are they?

3 For now the Sovereign, the
LORD of hosts,
is taking away from Jerusalem
and from Judah
support and staff—
all support of bread,
and all support of water—
2 warrior and soldier,
judge and prophet,
diviner and elder,
3 captain of fifty
and dignitary,
counsellor and skilful magician
and expert enchanter.
4 And I will make boys
their princes,
and babes shall rule over them.
5 The people will be oppressed,
everyone by another
and everyone by a neighbour;
the youth will be insolent
to the elder,
and the base to the honourable.

6 Someone will even seize a relative,
a member of the clan, saying,
'You have a cloak;
you shall be our leader,
and this heap of ruins
shall be under your rule.'
7 But the other will cry out on
that day, saying,
'I will not be a healer;
in my house there is neither
bread nor cloak;
you shall not make me
leader of the people.'
8 For Jerusalem has stumbled
and Judah has fallen,
because their speech and their deeds
are against the LORD,
defying his glorious presence.
9 The look on their faces bears
witness against them;
they proclaim their sin
like Sodom,
they do not hide it.
Woe to them!
For they have brought evil
on themselves.
10 Tell the innocent how
fortunate they are,
for they shall eat the fruit
of their labours.
11 Woe to the guilty! How
unfortunate they are,
for what their hands have done
shall be done to them.
12 My people—children are
their oppressors,
and women rule over them.
O my people, your leaders
mislead you,
and confuse the course
of your paths.

13 The LORD rises to argue his case;
he stands to judge the peoples.
14 The LORD enters into judgement
with the elders and princes
of his people:
It is you who have devoured
the vineyard;
the spoil of the poor is in
your houses.
15 What do you mean by crushing
my people,
by grinding the face of the poor?
says the Lord GOD of hosts.

16 The LORD said:
Because the daughters of
Zion are haughty
and walk with outstretched necks,
glancing wantonly with their eyes,
mincing along as they go,
tinkling with their feet;
17 the Lord will afflict with scabs
the heads of the daughters of Zion,
and the LORD will lay bare
their secret parts.

18 On that day the Lord will take
away the finery of the anklets, the head-
bands, and the crescents; 19the pendants, the bracelets, and the scarves;
20the head-dresses, the armlets, the
sashes, the perfume boxes, and the
amulets; 21the signet rings and nose-
rings; 22the festal robes, the mantles,
the cloaks, and the handbags; 23the garments of gauze, the linen garments, the
turbans, and the veils.

24 Instead of perfume there
will be a stench;
and instead of a sash, a rope;
and instead of well-arranged
hair, baldness;
and instead of a rich robe, a
binding of sackcloth;
instead of beauty, shame.[g]
25 Your men shall fall by the sword
and your warriors in battle.
26 And her gates shall lament
and mourn;
ravaged, she shall sit upon
the ground.

4 Seven women shall take hold of one
man on that day, saying,
'We will eat our own bread and
wear our own clothes;
just let us be called by your name;
take away our disgrace.'

THE FUTURE GLORY OF THE SURVIVORS IN ZION

2 On that day the branch of the LORD
shall be beautiful and glorious, and the
fruit of the land shall be the pride and
glory of the survivors of Israel. 3Who-
ever is left in Zion and remains in Jerusalem will be called holy, everyone
who has been recorded for life in Jerusalem, 4once the Lord has washed away
the filth of the daughters of Zion and
cleansed the bloodstains of Jerusalem
from its midst by a spirit of judgement
and by a spirit of burning. 5Then the
LORD will create over the whole site of
Mount Zion and over its places of assembly a cloud by day and smoke and
the shining of a flaming fire by night.
Indeed, over all the glory there will be
a canopy. 6It will serve as a pavilion, a
shade by day from the heat, and a refuge
and a shelter from the storm and rain.

THE SONG OF THE UNFRUITFUL VINEYARD

5 Let me sing for my beloved
my love-song concerning
his vineyard:
My beloved had a vineyard
on a very fertile hill.
2 He dug it and cleared it of stones,
and planted it with choice vines;
he built a watch-tower in
the midst of it,
and hewed out a wine vat in it;
he expected it to yield grapes,
but it yielded wild grapes.

3 And now, inhabitants of Jerusalem
and people of Judah,
judge between me
and my vineyard.
4 What more was there to do
for my vineyard
that I have not done in it?
When I expected it to yield grapes,
why did it yield wild grapes?

5 And now I will tell you
what I will do to my vineyard.
I will remove its hedge,
and it shall be devoured;
I will break down its wall,
and it shall be trampled down.
6 I will make it a waste;
it shall not be pruned or hoed,
and it shall be overgrown with
briers and thorns;
I will also command the clouds
that they rain no rain upon it.

7 For the vineyard of the LORD of hosts
is the house of Israel,
and the people of Judah
are his pleasant planting;
he expected justice,
but saw bloodshed;
righteousness,
but heard a cry!

SOCIAL INJUSTICE DENOUNCED

8 Ah, you who join house to house,
who add field to field,
until there is room for no
one but you,
and you are left to live alone
in the midst of the land!
9 The LORD of hosts has sworn
in my hearing:
Surely many houses shall
be desolate,
large and beautiful houses,
without inhabitant.
10 For ten acres of vineyard shall
yield but one bath,
and a homer of seed shall
yield a mere ephah.[h]

11 Ah, you who rise early in
the morning
in pursuit of strong drink,
who linger in the evening
to be inflamed by wine,
12 whose feasts consist of lyre and harp,
tambourine and flute and wine,
but who do not regard the
deeds of the LORD,
or see the work of his hands!

[g] **3.24** Q Ms: MT lacks *shame* [h] **5.10** The Heb *bath*, *homer*, and *ephah* are measures of quantity

13 Therefore my people go into exile
without knowledge;
their nobles are dying of hunger,
and their multitude is
parched with thirst.
14 Therefore Sheol has enlarged
its appetite
and opened its mouth
beyond measure;
the nobility of Jerusalem[i] and her
multitude go down,
her throng and all who
exult in her.
15 People are bowed down, everyone
is brought low,
and the eyes of the haughty
are humbled.
16 But the LORD of hosts is
exalted by justice,
and the Holy God shows himself
holy by righteousness.
17 Then the lambs shall graze as
in their pasture,
fatlings and kids[j] shall feed
among the ruins.

18 Ah, you who drag iniquity along
with cords of falsehood,
who drag sin along as
with cart-ropes,
19 who say, 'Let him make haste,
let him speed his work
that we may see it;
let the plan of the Holy One of
Israel hasten to fulfilment,
that we may know it!'
20 Ah, you who call evil good
and good evil,
who put darkness for light
and light for darkness,
who put bitter for sweet
and sweet for bitter!
21 Ah, you who are wise in
your own eyes,
and shrewd in your own sight!
22 Ah, you who are heroes in
drinking wine
and valiant at mixing drink,
23 who acquit the guilty for a bribe,
and deprive the innocent
of their rights!

FOREIGN INVASION PREDICTED

24 Therefore, as the tongue of fire
devours the stubble,
and as dry grass sinks
down in the flame,
so their root will become rotten,
and their blossom go
up like dust;
for they have rejected the instruction
of the LORD of hosts,
and have despised the word of
the Holy One of Israel.

25 Therefore the anger of the LORD was
kindled against his people,
and he stretched out his
hand against them
and struck them;
the mountains quaked,
and their corpses were like refuse
in the streets.
For all this his anger has not
turned away,
and his hand is stretched out still.

26 He will raise a signal for a
nation far away,
and whistle for a people at
the ends of the earth;
Here they come, swiftly, speedily!
27 None of them is weary,
none stumbles,
none slumbers or sleeps,
not a loincloth is loose,
not a sandal-thong broken;
28 their arrows are sharp,
all their bows bent,
their horses' hoofs seem like flint,
and their wheels like the
whirlwind.
29 Their roaring is like a lion,
like young lions they roar;
they growl and seize their prey,
they carry it off, and no
one can rescue.
30 They will roar over it on that day,
like the roaring of the sea.
And if one looks to the land—
only darkness and distress;
and the light grows dark
with clouds.

A VISION OF GOD IN THE TEMPLE

6 In the year that King Uzziah died,
I saw the Lord sitting on a throne,
high and lofty; and the hem of his robe
filled the temple. 2Seraphs were in attendance above him; each had six wings:
with two they covered their faces, and
with two they covered their feet, and
with two they flew. 3And one called to
another and said:
'Holy, holy, holy is the LORD of hosts;
the whole earth is full of his glory.'
4The pivots[k] on the thresholds shook at
the voices of those who called, and the

[i] 5.14 Heb *her nobility* [j] 5.17 Cn Compare Gk: Heb *aliens* [k] 6.4 Meaning of Heb uncertain

house filled with smoke. 5And I said:
'Woe is me! I am lost, for I am a man of
unclean lips, and I live among a people
of unclean lips; yet my eyes have seen
the King, the LORD of hosts!'

6 Then one of the seraphs flew to me,
holding a live coal that had been taken
from the altar with a pair of tongs. 7The
seraph[l] touched my mouth with it and
said: 'Now that this has touched your
lips, your guilt has departed and your
sin is blotted out.' 8Then I heard the
voice of the Lord saying, 'Whom shall
I send, and who will go for us?' And I
said, 'Here am I; send me!' 9And he said,
'Go and say to this people:

"Keep listening, but do not
comprehend;
keep looking, but do not
understand."
10 Make the mind of this people dull,
and stop their ears,
and shut their eyes,
so that they may not look
with their eyes,
and listen with their ears,
and comprehend with their minds,
and turn and be healed.'
11 Then I said, 'How long, O Lord?'
And he said:
'Until cities lie waste
without inhabitant,
and houses without people,
and the land is utterly desolate;
12 until the LORD sends everyone
far away,
and vast is the emptiness in
the midst of the land.
13 Even if a tenth part remains in it,
it will be burned again,
like a terebinth or an oak
whose stump remains standing
when it is felled.'[m]
The holy seed is its stump.

ISAIAH REASSURES KING AHAZ

7 In the days of Ahaz son of Jotham
son of Uzziah, king of Judah, King
Rezin of Aram and King Pekah son of
Remaliah of Israel went up to attack Jerusalem, but could not mount an attack
against it. 2When the house of David
heard that Aram had allied itself with
Ephraim, the heart of Ahaz[n] and the
heart of his people shook as the trees of
the forest shake before the wind.

3 Then the LORD said to Isaiah, Go
out to meet Ahaz, you and your son
Shear-jashub,[o] at the end of the conduit of the upper pool on the highway
to the Fuller's Field, 4and say to him,
Take heed, be quiet, do not fear, and do
not let your heart be faint because of
these two smouldering stumps of firebrands, because of the fierce anger of
Rezin and Aram and the son of Remaliah. 5Because Aram—with Ephraim
and the son of Remaliah—has plotted
evil against you, saying, 6Let us go up
against Judah and cut off Jerusalem[p]
and conquer it for ourselves and make
the son of Tabeel king in it; 7therefore
thus says the Lord GOD:

It shall not stand,
and it shall not come to pass.
8 For the head of Aram is Damascus,
and the head of Damascus
is Rezin.
(Within sixty-five years Ephraim will
be shattered, no longer a people.)
9 The head of Ephraim is Samaria,
and the head of Samaria is
the son of Remaliah.
If you do not stand firm in faith,
you shall not stand at all.

ISAIAH GIVES AHAZ THE SIGN OF IMMANUEL

10 Again the LORD spoke to Ahaz,
saying, 11Ask a sign of the LORD your
God; let it be deep as Sheol or high as
heaven. 12But Ahaz said, I will not ask,
and I will not put the LORD to the test.
13Then Isaiah[q] said: 'Hear then, O house
of David! Is it too little for you to weary
mortals, that you weary my God also?
14Therefore the Lord himself will give
you a sign. Look, the young woman[r] is
with child and shall bear a son, and shall
name him Immanuel.[s] 15He shall eat
curds and honey by the time he knows
how to refuse the evil and choose the
good. 16For before the child knows how
to refuse the evil and choose the good,
the land before whose two kings you are
in dread will be deserted. 17The LORD will
bring on you and on your people and on
your ancestral house such days as have
not come since the day that Ephraim departed from Judah—the king of Assyria.'

18 On that day the LORD will whistle
for the fly that is at the sources of the
streams of Egypt, and for the bee that is
in the land of Assyria. 19And they will
all come and settle in the steep ravines,
and in the clefts of the rocks, and on all
the thorn bushes, and on all the pastures.

[l] 6.7 Heb *He* [m] 6.13 Meaning of Heb uncertain
[n] 7.2 Heb *his heart* [o] 7.3 That is *A remnant shall return* [p] 7.6 Heb *cut it off* [q] 7.13 Heb *he*
[r] 7.14 Gk *the virgin* [s] 7.14 That is *God is with us*

20 On that day the Lord will shave
with a razor hired beyond the River—
with the king of Assyria—the head and
the hair of the feet, and it will take off
the beard as well.
21 On that day one will keep alive a
young cow and two sheep, 22 and will eat
curds because of the abundance of milk
that they give; for everyone that is left
in the land shall eat curds and honey.
23 On that day every place where
there used to be a thousand vines,
worth a thousand shekels of silver, will
become briers and thorns. 24 With bow
and arrows one will go there, for all the
land will be briers and thorns; 25 and as
for all the hills that used to be hoed with
a hoe, you will not go there for fear of
briers and thorns; but they will become
a place where cattle are let loose and
where sheep tread.

ISAIAH'S SON A SIGN OF THE ASSYRIAN INVASION

8 Then the LORD said to me, Take a
large tablet and write on it in common characters, 'Belonging to Maher-
shalal-hash-baz',[t] 2 and have it attested[u]
for me by reliable witnesses, the priest
Uriah and Zechariah son of Jeberechi-
ah. 3 And I went to the prophetess, and
she conceived and bore a son. Then the
LORD said to me, Name him Maher-
shalal-hash-baz; 4 for before the child
knows how to call 'My father' or 'My
mother', the wealth of Damascus and
the spoil of Samaria will be carried away
by the king of Assyria.
5 The LORD spoke to me again: 6 Because this people has refused the waters
of Shiloah that flow gently, and melt in
fear before[v] Rezin and the son of Remaliah; 7 therefore, the Lord is bringing
up against it the mighty flood waters of
the River, the king of Assyria and all his
glory; it will rise above all its channels
and overflow all its banks; 8 it will sweep
on into Judah as a flood, and, pouring
over, it will reach up to the neck; and its
outspread wings will fill the breadth of
your land, O Immanuel.

9 Band together, you peoples,
and be dismayed;
listen, all you far countries;
gird yourselves and be dismayed;
gird yourselves and be dismayed!
10 Take counsel together, but it shall
be brought to naught;
speak a word, but it will not stand,
for God is with us.[w]

11 For the LORD spoke thus to me
while his hand was strong upon me,
and warned me not to walk in the way
of this people, saying: 12 Do not call conspiracy all that this people calls conspiracy, and do not fear what it fears, or be
in dread. 13 But the LORD of hosts, him
you shall regard as holy; let him be your
fear, and let him be your dread. 14 He will
become a sanctuary, a stone one strikes
against; for both houses of Israel he will
become a rock one stumbles over—a
trap and a snare for the inhabitants of
Jerusalem. 15 And many among them
shall stumble; they shall fall and be broken; they shall be snared and taken.

DISCIPLES OF ISAIAH

16 Bind up the testimony, seal the
teaching among my disciples. 17 I will
wait for the LORD, who is hiding his
face from the house of Jacob, and I will
hope in him. 18 See, I and the children
whom the LORD has given me are signs
and portents in Israel from the LORD
of hosts, who dwells on Mount Zion.
19 Now if people say to you, 'Consult the
ghosts and the familiar spirits that chirp
and mutter; should not a people consult
their gods, the dead on behalf of the living, 20 for teaching and for instruction?'
surely, those who speak like this will
have no dawn! 21 They will pass through
the land,[x] greatly distressed and hungry; when they are hungry, they will be
enraged and will curse[y] their king and
their gods. They will turn their faces upwards, 22 or they will look to the earth,
but will see only distress and darkness,
the gloom of anguish; and they will be
thrust into thick darkness.[z]

THE RIGHTEOUS REIGN OF THE COMING KING

9 [a] But there will be no gloom for those
who were in anguish. In the former
time he brought into contempt the land
of Zebulun and the land of Naphtali, but
in the latter time he will make glorious
the way of the sea, the land beyond the
Jordan, Galilee of the nations.
2[b] The people who walked in darkness
have seen a great light;

[t] 8.1 That is *The spoil speeds, the prey hastens*
[u] 8.2 Q Ms Gk Syr: MT *and I caused to be attested*
[v] 8.6 Cn: Meaning of Heb uncertain
[w] 8.10 Heb *immanu el*
[x] 8.21 Heb *it*
[y] 8.21 *Or curse by*
[z] 8.22 Meaning of Heb uncertain
[a] 9.1 Ch 8.23 in Heb
[b] 9.2 Ch 9.1 in Heb

those who lived in a land of
deep darkness—
on them light has shined.
3 You have multiplied the nation,
you have increased its joy;
they rejoice before you
as with joy at the harvest,
as people exult when
dividing plunder.
4 For the yoke of their burden,
and the bar across their shoulders,
the rod of their oppressor,
you have broken as on the
day of Midian.
5 For all the boots of the
tramping warriors
and all the garments
rolled in blood
shall be burned as fuel for the fire.
6 For a child has been born for us,
a son given to us;
authority rests upon his shoulders;
and he is named
Wonderful Counsellor, Mighty God,
Everlasting Father, Prince of Peace.
7 His authority shall grow continually,
and there shall be endless peace
for the throne of David and
his kingdom.
He will establish and uphold it
with justice and with righteousness
from this time onwards
and for evermore.
The zeal of the LORD of hosts
will do this.

JUDGEMENT ON ARROGANCE AND OPPRESSION

8 The Lord sent a word against Jacob,
and it fell on Israel;
9 and all the people knew it—
Ephraim and the inhabitants
of Samaria—
but in pride and arrogance
of heart they said:
10 'The bricks have fallen,
but we will build with
dressed stones;
the sycomores have been cut down,
but we will put cedars
in their place.'
11 So the LORD raised adversaries[c]
against them,
and stirred up their enemies,
12 the Arameans in the east and the
Philistines in the west,
and they devoured Israel
with open mouth.
For all this, his anger has
not turned away;
his hand is stretched out still.
13 The people did not turn to him
who struck them,
or seek the LORD of hosts.
14 So the LORD cut off from Israel
head and tail,
palm branch and reed in one day—
15 elders and dignitaries are the head,
and prophets who teach
lies are the tail;
16 for those who led this people
led them astray,
and those who were led by them
were left in confusion.
17 That is why the Lord did not have
pity on[d] their young people,
or compassion on their
orphans and widows;
for everyone was godless
and an evildoer,
and every mouth spoke folly.
For all this, his anger has not
turned away;
his hand is stretched out still.

18 For wickedness burned like a fire,
consuming briers and thorns;
it kindled the thickets of the forest,
and they swirled upwards in
a column of smoke.
19 Through the wrath of the
LORD of hosts
the land was burned,
and the people became like
fuel for the fire;
no one spared another.
20 They gorged on the right, but
still were hungry,
and they devoured on the left,
but were not satisfied;
they devoured the flesh of
their own kindred;[e]
21 Manasseh devoured Ephraim, and
Ephraim Manasseh,
and together they were
against Judah.
For all this, his anger has not
turned away;
his hand is stretched out still.

10 Ah, you who make
iniquitous decrees,
who write oppressive statutes,
2 to turn aside the needy from justice
and to rob the poor of my
people of their right,
that widows may be your spoil,
and that you may make the
orphans your prey!

[c] 9.11 Cn: Heb *the adversaries of Rezin* [d] 9.17 Q Ms: MT *rejoice over* [e] 9.20 Or *arm*

3 What will you do on the day
of punishment,
in the calamity that will
come from far away?
To whom will you flee for help,
and where will you leave
your wealth,
4 so as not to crouch among
the prisoners
or fall among the slain?
For all this, his anger has
not turned away;
his hand is stretched out still.

ARROGANT ASSYRIA ALSO JUDGED

5 Ah, Assyria, the rod of my anger—
the club in their hands
is my fury!
6 Against a godless nation I send him,
and against the people of my
wrath I command him,
to take spoil and seize plunder,
and to tread them down like
the mire of the streets.
7 But this is not what he intends,
nor does he have this in mind;
but it is in his heart to destroy,
and to cut off nations not a few.
8 For he says:
'Are not my commanders all kings?
9 Is not Calno like Carchemish?
Is not Hamath like Arpad?
Is not Samaria like Damascus?
10 As my hand has reached to the
kingdoms of the idols
whose images were greater
than those of Jerusalem
and Samaria,
11 shall I not do to Jerusalem
and her idols
what I have done to Samaria
and her images?'

12 When the Lord has finished all his
work on Mount Zion and on Jerusalem,
he[f] will punish the arrogant boasting
of the king of Assyria and his haughty
pride. 13For he says:
'By the strength of my hand
I have done it,
and by my wisdom, for I
have understanding;
I have removed the boundaries
of peoples,
and have plundered
their treasures;
like a bull I have brought down
those who sat on thrones.
14 My hand has found, like a nest,
the wealth of the peoples;
and as one gathers eggs that
have been forsaken,
so I have gathered all the earth;
and there was none that
moved a wing,
or opened its mouth, or chirped.'

15 Shall the axe vaunt itself over
the one who wields it,
or the saw magnify itself against
the one who handles it?
As if a rod should raise the
one who lifts it up,
or as if a staff should lift the
one who is not wood!
16 Therefore the Sovereign, the
LORD of hosts,
will send wasting sickness
among his stout warriors,
and under his glory a burning
will be kindled,
like the burning of fire.
17 The light of Israel will become a fire,
and his Holy One a flame;
and it will burn and devour
his thorns and briers in one day.
18 The glory of his forest and
his fruitful land
the LORD will destroy, both
soul and body,
and it will be as when an
invalid wastes away.
19 The remnant of the trees of his
forest will be so few
that a child can write them down.

THE REPENTANT REMNANT OF ISRAEL

20 On that day the remnant of Israel
and the survivors of the house of Jacob
will no more lean on the one who struck
them, but will lean on the LORD, the
Holy One of Israel, in truth. 21A remnant will return, the remnant of Jacob,
to the mighty God. 22For though your
people Israel were like the sand of the
sea, only a remnant of them will return.
Destruction is decreed, overflowing
with righteousness. 23For the Lord GOD
of hosts will make a full end, as decreed,
in all the earth.[g]

24 Therefore thus says the Lord GOD
of hosts: O my people, who live in Zion,
do not be afraid of the Assyrians when
they beat you with a rod and lift up their
staff against you as the Egyptians did.
25For in a very little while my indignation will come to an end, and my anger
will be directed to their destruction.

[f] 10.12 Heb *I* [g] 10.23 Or *land*

26 The LORD of hosts will wield a whip
against them, as when he struck Midian at the rock of Oreb; his staff will be
over the sea, and he will lift it as he did
in Egypt. 27 On that day his burden will
be removed from your shoulder, and his
yoke will be destroyed from your neck.

He has gone up from Rimmon,[h]
28 he has come to Aiath;
he has passed through Migron,
at Michmash he stores
his baggage;
29 they have crossed over the pass,
at Geba they lodge for the night;
Ramah trembles,
Gibeah of Saul has fled.
30 Cry aloud, O daughter Gallim!
Listen, O Laishah!
Answer her, O Anathoth!
31 Madmenah is in flight,
the inhabitants of Gebim
flee for safety.
32 This very day he will halt at Nob,
he will shake his fist
at the mount of daughter Zion,
the hill of Jerusalem.

33 Look, the Sovereign, the
LORD of hosts,
will lop the boughs with
terrifying power;
the tallest trees will be cut down,
and the lofty will be brought low.
34 He will hack down the thickets of
the forest with an axe,
and Lebanon with its majestic
trees[i] will fall.

THE PEACEFUL KINGDOM

11 A shoot shall come out from
the stock of Jesse,
and a branch shall grow
out of his roots.
2 The spirit of the LORD shall
rest on him,
the spirit of wisdom and
understanding,
the spirit of counsel and might,
the spirit of knowledge and
the fear of the LORD.
3 His delight shall be in the
fear of the LORD.

He shall not judge by what
his eyes see,
or decide by what his ears hear;
4 but with righteousness he
shall judge the poor,
and decide with equity for
the meek of the earth;
he shall strike the earth with
the rod of his mouth,
and with the breath of his lips
he shall kill the wicked.
5 Righteousness shall be the belt
around his waist,
and faithfulness the belt
around his loins.

6 The wolf shall live with the lamb,
the leopard shall lie down
with the kid,
the calf and the lion and the
fatling together,
and a little child shall
lead them.
7 The cow and the bear shall graze,
their young shall lie
down together;
and the lion shall eat
straw like the ox.
8 The nursing child shall play over
the hole of the asp,
and the weaned child shall put its
hand on the adder's den.
9 They will not hurt or destroy
on all my holy mountain;
for the earth will be full of the
knowledge of the LORD
as the waters cover the sea.

RETURN OF THE REMNANT OF ISRAEL AND JUDAH

10 On that day the root of Jesse shall
stand as a signal to the peoples; the nations shall inquire of him, and his dwelling shall be glorious.
11 On that day the Lord will extend
his hand yet a second time to recover
the remnant that is left of his people,
from Assyria, from Egypt, from Pathros, from Ethiopia,[j] from Elam, from
Shinar, from Hamath, and from the
coastlands of the sea.
12 He will raise a signal for the nations,
and will assemble the
outcasts of Israel,
and gather the dispersed of Judah
from the four corners of the earth.
13 The jealousy of Ephraim shall depart,
the hostility of Judah
shall be cut off;
Ephraim shall not be jealous
of Judah,
and Judah shall not be hostile
towards Ephraim.

[h] **10.27** Cn: Heb *and his yoke from your neck, and a yoke will be destroyed because of fatness*
[i] **10.34** Cn Compare Gk Vg: Heb *with a majestic one*
[j] **11.11** Or *Nubia*; Heb *Cush*

14 But they shall swoop down
on the backs of the
Philistines in the west;
together they shall plunder
the people of the east.
They shall put forth their hand
against Edom and Moab,
and the Ammonites shall
obey them.
15 And the LORD will utterly destroy
the tongue of the sea of Egypt;
and will wave his hand over the River
with his scorching wind;
and will split it into seven channels,
and make a way to cross on foot;
16 so there shall be a highway
from Assyria
for the remnant that is
left of his people,
as there was for Israel
when they came up from
the land of Egypt.

THANKSGIVING AND PRAISE

12 You will say on that day:
I will give thanks to
you, O LORD,
for though you were
angry with me,
your anger turned away,
and you comforted me.

2 Surely God is my salvation;
I will trust, and will not be afraid,
for the LORD GOD[k] is my strength
and my might;
he has become my salvation.

3 With joy you will draw water from
the wells of salvation. 4 And you will say
on that day:
Give thanks to the LORD,
call on his name;
make known his deeds among
the nations;
proclaim that his name is exalted.

5 Sing praises to the LORD, for he
has done gloriously;
let this be known[l] in all the earth.
6 Shout aloud and sing for joy,
O royal[m] Zion,
for great in your midst is the
Holy One of Israel.

PROCLAMATION AGAINST BABYLON

13 The oracle concerning Babylon
that Isaiah son of Amoz saw.

2 On a bare hill raise a signal,
cry aloud to them;
wave the hand for them to enter
the gates of the nobles.
3 I myself have commanded my
consecrated ones,
have summoned my warriors,
my proudly exulting ones,
to execute my anger.

4 Listen, a tumult on the mountains
as of a great multitude!
Listen, an uproar of kingdoms,
of nations gathering together!
The LORD of hosts is mustering
an army for battle.
5 They come from a distant land,
from the end of the heavens,
the LORD and the weapons of
his indignation,
to destroy the whole earth.

6 Wail, for the day of the LORD is near;
it will come like destruction
from the Almighty![n]
7 Therefore all hands will be feeble,
and every human heart will fail,
8 and they will be dismayed.
Pangs and agony will seize them;
they will be in anguish like
a woman in labour.
They will look aghast at one another;
their faces will be aflame.
9 See, the day of the LORD comes,
cruel, with wrath and fierce anger,
to make the earth a desolation,
and to destroy its sinners from it.
10 For the stars of the heavens and
their constellations
will not give their light;
the sun will be dark at its rising,
and the moon will not
shed its light.
11 I will punish the world for its evil,
and the wicked for their iniquity;
I will put an end to the pride
of the arrogant,
and lay low the insolence
of tyrants.
12 I will make mortals more rare
than fine gold,
and humans than the
gold of Ophir.
13 Therefore I will make the
heavens tremble,
and the earth will be shaken
out of its place,
at the wrath of the LORD of hosts
on the day of his fierce anger.

[k] 12.2 Heb *for Yah, the LORD* [l] 12.5 Or *this is made known* [m] 12.6 Or *O inhabitant of* [n] 13.6 Traditional rendering of Heb *Shaddai*

14 Like a hunted gazelle,
or like sheep with no one
to gather them,
all will turn to their own people,
and all will flee to their own lands.
15 Whoever is found will be
thrust through,
and whoever is caught will
fall by the sword.
16 Their infants will be dashed to pieces
before their eyes;
their houses will be plundered,
and their wives ravished.
17 See, I am stirring up the Medes
against them,
who have no regard for silver
and do not delight in gold.
18 Their bows will slaughter
the young men;
they will have no mercy on
the fruit of the womb;
their eyes will not pity children.
19 And Babylon, the glory of kingdoms,
the splendour and pride
of the Chaldeans,
will be like Sodom and Gomorrah
when God overthrew them.
20 It will never be inhabited
or lived in for all generations;
Arabs will not pitch their
tents there,
shepherds will not make their
flocks lie down there.
21 But wild animals will lie down there,
and its houses will be full of
howling creatures;
there ostriches will live,
and there goat-demons will dance.
22 Hyenas will cry in its towers,
and jackals in the pleasant palaces;
its time is close at hand,
and its days will not be prolonged.

RESTORATION OF JUDAH

14 But the LORD will have compassion on Jacob and will again
choose Israel, and will set them in their
own land; and aliens will join them and
attach themselves to the house of Jacob. 2 And the nations will take them
and bring them to their place, and the
house of Israel will possess the nations[o]
as male and female slaves in the LORD's
land; they will take captive those who
were their captors, and rule over those
who oppressed them.

DOWNFALL OF THE KING OF BABYLON

3 When the LORD has given you rest
from your pain and turmoil and the
hard service with which you were made
to serve, 4 you will take up this taunt
against the king of Babylon:
How the oppressor has ceased!
How his insolence[p] has ceased!
5 The LORD has broken the staff
of the wicked,
the sceptre of rulers,
6 that struck down the peoples
in wrath
with unceasing blows,
that ruled the nations in anger
with unrelenting persecution.
7 The whole earth is at rest and quiet;
they break forth into singing.
8 The cypresses exult over you,
the cedars of Lebanon, saying,
'Since you were laid low,
no one comes to cut us down.'
9 Sheol beneath is stirred up
to meet you when you come;
it rouses the shades to greet you,
all who were leaders of the earth;
it raises from their thrones
all who were kings of the nations.
10 All of them will speak
and say to you:
'You too have become as
weak as we are!
You have become like us!'
11 Your pomp is brought
down to Sheol,
and the sound of your harps;
maggots are the bed beneath you,
and worms are your covering.

12 How you are fallen from heaven,
O Day Star, son of Dawn!
How you are cut down to
the ground,
you who laid the nations low!
13 You said in your heart,
'I will ascend to heaven;
I will raise my throne
above the stars of God;
I will sit on the mount of assembly
on the heights of Zaphon;[q]
14 I will ascend to the tops
of the clouds,
I will make myself like
the Most High.'
15 But you are brought down to Sheol,
to the depths of the Pit.
16 Those who see you will stare at you,
and ponder over you:
'Is this the man who made
the earth tremble,
who shook kingdoms,

[o] 14.2 Heb *them* [p] 14.4 Q Ms Compare Gk Syr Vg: Meaning of MT uncertain [q] 14.13 Or *assembly in the far north*

17 who made the world like a desert
and overthrew its cities,
who would not let his
prisoners go home?'
18 All the kings of the nations
lie in glory,
each in his own tomb;
19 but you are cast out, away
from your grave,
like loathsome carrion,[r]
clothed with the dead, those
pierced by the sword,
who go down to the
stones of the Pit,
like a corpse trampled underfoot.
20 You will not be joined with
them in burial,
because you have destroyed
your land,
you have killed your people.

May the descendants of evildoers
nevermore be named!
21 Prepare slaughter for his sons
because of the guilt of their father.[s]
Let them never rise to
possess the earth
or cover the face of the
world with cities.

22 I will rise up against them, says
the LORD of hosts, and will cut off from
Babylon name and remnant, offspring
and posterity, says the LORD. 23 And I
will make it a possession of the hedgehog, and pools of water, and I will sweep
it with the broom of destruction, says
the LORD of hosts.

AN ORACLE CONCERNING ASSYRIA

24 The LORD of hosts has sworn:
As I have designed,
so shall it be;
and as I have planned,
so shall it come to pass:
25 I will break the Assyrian in my land,
and on my mountains trample
him under foot;
his yoke shall be removed
from them,
and his burden from
their shoulders.
26 This is the plan that is planned
concerning the whole earth;
and this is the hand that is
stretched out
over all the nations.
27 For the LORD of hosts has planned,
and who will annul it?
His hand is stretched out,
and who will turn it back?

AN ORACLE CONCERNING PHILISTIA

28 In the year that King Ahaz died this
oracle came:

29 Do not rejoice, all you Philistines,
that the rod that struck
you is broken,
for from the root of the snake will
come forth an adder,
and its fruit will be a flying
fiery serpent.
30 The firstborn of the poor will graze,
and the needy lie down in safety;
but I will make your root
die of famine,
and your remnant I[t] will kill.
31 Wail, O gate; cry, O city;
melt in fear, O Philistia, all of you!
For smoke comes out of the north,
and there is no straggler
in its ranks.

32 What will one answer the
messengers of the nation?
'The LORD has founded Zion,
and the needy among his people
will find refuge in her.'

AN ORACLE CONCERNING MOAB

15 An oracle concerning Moab.

Because Ar is laid waste in a night,
Moab is undone;
because Kir is laid waste in a night,
Moab is undone.
2 Dibon[u] has gone up to the temple,
to the high places to weep;
over Nebo and over Medeba
Moab wails.
On every head is baldness,
every beard is shorn;
3 in the streets they bind on sackcloth;
on the housetops and
in the squares
everyone wails and melts in tears.
4 Heshbon and Elealeh cry out,
their voices are heard as
far as Jahaz;
therefore the loins of Moab quiver;[v]
his soul trembles.
5 My heart cries out for Moab;
his fugitives flee to Zoar,
to Eglath-shelishiyah.
For at the ascent of Luhith
they go up weeping;

[r] 14.19 Cn Compare Gk: Heb *like a loathed branch*
[s] 14.21 Syr Compare Gk: Heb *fathers* [t] 14.30 Q Ms Vg: MT *he* [u] 15.2 Cn: Heb *the house and Dibon* [v] 15.4 Cn Compare Gk Syr: Heb *the armed men of Moab cry aloud*

on the road to Horonaim
they raise a cry of destruction;
6 the waters of Nimrim
are a desolation;
the grass is withered, the
new growth fails,
the verdure is no more.
7 Therefore the abundance
they have gained
and what they have laid up
they carry away
over the Wadi of the Willows.
8 For a cry has gone
around the land of Moab;
the wailing reaches to Eglaim,
the wailing reaches to Beer-elim.
9 For the waters of Dibon[w]
are full of blood;
yet I will bring upon Dibon[x]
even more—
a lion for those of Moab who escape,
for the remnant of the land.

16 Send lambs
to the ruler of the land,
from Sela, by way of the desert,
to the mount of daughter Zion.
2 Like fluttering birds,
like scattered nestlings,
so are the daughters of Moab
at the fords of the Arnon.
3 'Give counsel,
grant justice;
make your shade like night
at the height of noon;
hide the outcasts,
do not betray the fugitive;
4 let the outcasts of Moab
settle among you;
be a refuge to them
from the destroyer.'

When the oppressor is no more,
and destruction has ceased,
and marauders have vanished
from the land,
5 then a throne shall be established
in steadfast love
in the tent of David,
and on it shall sit
in faithfulness
a ruler who seeks justice
and is swift to do what is right.

6 We have heard of the
pride of Moab
—how proud he is!—
of his arrogance, his pride,
and his insolence;
his boasts are false.
7 Therefore let Moab wail,
let everyone wail for Moab.
Mourn, utterly stricken,
for the raisin cakes of
Kir-hareseth.
8 For the fields of Heshbon languish,
and the vines of Sibmah,
whose clusters once made drunk
the lords of the nations,
reached to Jazer
and strayed to the desert;
their shoots once spread abroad
and crossed over the sea.
9 Therefore I weep with the
weeping of Jazer
for the vines of Sibmah;
I drench you with my tears,
O Heshbon and Elealeh;
for the shout over your fruit harvest
and your grain harvest has ceased.
10 Joy and gladness are taken away
from the fruitful field;
and in the vineyards no
songs are sung,
no shouts are raised;
no treader treads out wine
in the presses;
the vintage-shout is hushed.[y]
11 Therefore my heart throbs like
a harp for Moab,
and my very soul for Kir-heres.
12 When Moab presents himself,
when he wearies himself upon the high
place, when he comes to his sanctuary
to pray, he will not prevail.
13 This was the word that the LORD
spoke concerning Moab in the past.
14 But now the LORD says, In three
years, like the years of a hired worker,
the glory of Moab will be brought into
contempt, in spite of all its great multitude; and those who survive will be very
few and feeble.

AN ORACLE CONCERNING DAMASCUS

17 An oracle concerning Damascus.

See, Damascus will cease to be a city,
and will become a heap of ruins.
2 Her towns will be deserted for ever;[z]
they will be places for flocks,
which will lie down, and no one
will make them afraid.
3 The fortress will disappear
from Ephraim,
and the kingdom from Damascus;

[w] 15.9 Q Ms Vg Compare Syr: MT *Dimon*
[x] 15.9 Q Ms Vg Compare Syr: MT *Dimon*
[y] 16.10 Gk: Heb *I have hushed* [z] 17.2 Cn Compare Gk: Heb *the cities of Aroer are deserted*

and the remnant of Aram will be
like the glory of the
children of Israel,
says the LORD of hosts.

4 On that day
the glory of Jacob will be
brought low,
and the fat of his flesh
will grow lean.
5 And it shall be as when reapers
gather standing grain
and their arms harvest the ears,
and as when one gleans the
ears of grain
in the Valley of Rephaim.
6 Gleanings will be left in it,
as when an olive tree is beaten—
two or three berries
in the top of the highest bough,
four or five
on the branches of a fruit tree,
says the LORD God of Israel.

7 On that day people will regard their
Maker, and their eyes will look to the
Holy One of Israel; 8they will not have
regard for the altars, the work of their
hands, and they will not look to what
their own fingers have made, either the
sacred poles[a] or the altars of incense.
9 On that day their strong cities will
be like the deserted places of the Hivites
and the Amorites,[b] which they deserted
because of the children of Israel, and
there will be desolation.

10 For you have forgotten the God
of your salvation,
and have not remembered the
Rock of your refuge;
therefore, though you plant
pleasant plants
and set out slips of an alien god,
11 though you make them grow on the
day that you plant them,
and make them blossom in the
morning that you sow;
yet the harvest will flee away
on a day of grief and incurable pain.

12 Ah, the thunder of many peoples,
they thunder like the
thundering of the sea!
Ah, the roar of nations,
they roar like the roaring
of mighty waters!
13 The nations roar like the roaring
of many waters,
but he will rebuke them, and
they will flee far away,
chased like chaff on the mountains
before the wind
and whirling dust before
the storm.
14 At evening time, lo, terror!
Before morning, they are no more.
This is the fate of those
who despoil us,
and the lot of those who
plunder us.

AN ORACLE CONCERNING ETHIOPIA

18 Ah, land of whirring wings
beyond the rivers of Ethiopia,[c]
2 sending ambassadors by the Nile
in vessels of papyrus on
the waters!
Go, you swift messengers,
to a nation tall and smooth,
to a people feared near and far,
a nation mighty and conquering,
whose land the rivers divide.

3 All you inhabitants of the world,
you who live on the earth,
when a signal is raised on the
mountains, look!
When a trumpet is blown, listen!
4 For thus the LORD said to me:
I will quietly look from my dwelling
like clear heat in sunshine,
like a cloud of dew in the
heat of harvest.
5 For before the harvest, when
the blossom is over
and the flower becomes a
ripening grape,
he will cut off the shoots with
pruning-hooks,
and the spreading branches
he will hew away.
6 They shall all be left
to the birds of prey of
the mountains
and to the animals of the earth.
And the birds of prey will
summer on them,
and all the animals of the earth
will winter on them.

7 At that time gifts will be brought
to the LORD of hosts from[d] a people tall
and smooth, from a people feared near
and far, a nation mighty and conquering, whose land the rivers divide, to
Mount Zion, the place of the name of
the LORD of hosts.

[a] 17.8 Heb *Asherim* [b] 17.9 Cn Compare Gk: Heb *places of the wood and the highest bough*
[c] 18.1 Or *Nubia*; Heb *Cush* [d] 18.7 Q Ms Gk Vg: MT *of*

AN ORACLE CONCERNING EGYPT

19 An oracle concerning Egypt.
See, the LORD is riding on
a swift cloud
and comes to Egypt;
the idols of Egypt will tremble
at his presence,
and the heart of the Egyptians
will melt within them.
2 I will stir up Egyptians against
Egyptians,
and they will fight, one
against the other,
neighbour against neighbour,
city against city, kingdom
against kingdom;
3 the spirit of the Egyptians within
them will be emptied out,
and I will confound their plans;
they will consult the idols and
the spirits of the dead
and the ghosts and the
familiar spirits;
4 I will deliver the Egyptians
into the hand of a hard master;
a fierce king will rule over them,
says the Sovereign, the
LORD of hosts.

5 The waters of the Nile will
be dried up,
and the river will be
parched and dry;
6 its canals will become foul,
and the branches of Egypt's Nile
will diminish and dry up;
reeds and rushes will rot away.
7 There will be bare places by the Nile,
on the brink of the Nile;
and all that is sown by the
Nile will dry up,
be driven away, and be no more.
8 Those who fish will mourn;
all who cast hooks in the
Nile will lament,
and those who spread nets on
the water will languish.
9 The workers in flax will be in despair,
and the carders and those at
the loom will grow pale.
10 Its weavers will be dismayed,
and all who work for wages
will be grieved.

11 The princes of Zoan are utterly foolish;
the wise counsellors of Pharaoh
give stupid counsel.
How can you say to Pharaoh,
'I am one of the sages,
a descendant of ancient kings'?
12 Where now are your sages?
Let them tell you and
make known
what the LORD of hosts has
planned against Egypt.
13 The princes of Zoan have
become fools,
and the princes of Memphis
are deluded;
those who are the cornerstones
of its tribes
have led Egypt astray.
14 The LORD has poured into them[e]
a spirit of confusion;
and they have made Egypt
stagger in all its doings
as a drunkard staggers
around in vomit.
15 Neither head nor tail, palm
branch nor reed,
will be able to do anything
for Egypt.

16 On that day the Egyptians will be
like women, and tremble with fear before the hand that the LORD of hosts
raises against them. 17 And the land of
Judah will become a terror to the Egyptians; everyone to whom it is mentioned
will fear because of the plan that the
LORD of hosts is planning against them.

EGYPT, ASSYRIA, AND ISRAEL BLESSED

18 On that day there will be five cities
in the land of Egypt that speak the language of Canaan and swear allegiance to
the LORD of hosts. One of these will be
called the City of the Sun.
19 On that day there will be an altar
to the LORD in the centre of the land of
Egypt, and a pillar to the LORD at its border. 20 It will be a sign and a witness to
the LORD of hosts in the land of Egypt;
when they cry to the LORD because of
oppressors, he will send them a saviour,
and will defend and deliver them. 21 The
LORD will make himself known to the
Egyptians; and the Egyptians will know
the LORD on that day, and will worship
with sacrifice and burnt-offering, and
they will make vows to the LORD and
perform them. 22 The LORD will strike
Egypt, striking and healing; they will
return to the LORD, and he will listen to
their supplications and heal them.
23 On that day there will be a highway from Egypt to Assyria, and the
Assyrian will come into Egypt, and the

[e] 19.14 Gk Compare Tg: Heb *it*

Egyptian into Assyria, and the Egyptians will worship with the Assyrians.

24 On that day Israel will be the
third with Egypt and Assyria, a blessing in the midst of the earth, 25whom
the LORD of hosts has blessed, saying,
'Blessed be Egypt my people, and Assyria the work of my hands, and Israel my heritage.'

ISAIAH DRAMATIZES THE CONQUEST OF EGYPT AND ETHIOPIA

20 In the year that the commander-in-chief, who was sent by King Sargon of Assyria, came to Ashdod and
fought against it and took it— 2at that
time the LORD had spoken to Isaiah son of Amoz, saying, 'Go, and loose the sackcloth from your loins and take your sandals off your feet', and he had done
so, walking naked and barefoot. 3Then
the LORD said, 'Just as my servant Isaiah has walked naked and barefoot for three years as a sign and a portent
against Egypt and Ethiopia,[f] 4so shall
the king of Assyria lead away the Egyptians as captives and the Ethiopians[g] as exiles, both the young and the old, naked and barefoot, with buttocks uncovered, to the shame of Egypt. 5And
they shall be dismayed and confounded because of Ethiopia[h] their hope and
of Egypt their boast. 6On that day the
inhabitants of this coastland will say, "See, this is what has happened to those in whom we hoped and to whom we fled for help and deliverance from the king of Assyria! And we, how shall we escape?"'

ORACLES CONCERNING BABYLON, EDOM, AND ARABIA

21 The oracle concerning the wilderness of the sea.

As whirlwinds in the Negeb
sweep on,
it comes from the desert,
from a terrible land.
2 A stern vision is told to me;
the betrayer betrays,
and the destroyer destroys.
Go up, O Elam,
lay siege, O Media;
all the sighing she has caused
I bring to an end.
3 Therefore my loins are filled
with anguish;
pangs have seized me,
like the pangs of a woman
in labour;
I am bowed down so that
I cannot hear,
I am dismayed so that
I cannot see.
4 My mind reels, horror has
appalled me;
the twilight I longed for
has been turned for me
into trembling.
5 They prepare the table,
they spread the rugs,
they eat, they drink.
Rise up, commanders,
oil the shield!
6 For thus the Lord said to me:
'Go, post a lookout,
let him announce what he sees.
7 When he sees riders,
horsemen in pairs,
riders on donkeys, riders
on camels,
let him listen diligently,
very diligently.'
8 Then the watcher[i] called out:
'Upon a watch-tower I stand, O Lord,
continually by day,
and at my post I am stationed
throughout the night.
9 Look, there they come, riders,
horsemen in pairs!'
Then he responded,
'Fallen, fallen is Babylon;
and all the images of her gods
lie shattered on the ground.'
10 O my threshed and winnowed one,
what I have heard from
the LORD of hosts,
the God of Israel, I
announce to you.

11 The oracle concerning Dumah.

One is calling to me from Seir,
'Sentinel, what of the night?
Sentinel, what of the night?'
12 The sentinel says:
'Morning comes, and also the night.
If you will inquire, inquire;
come back again.'

13 The oracle concerning the desert plain.

In the scrub of the desert plain
you will lodge,
O caravans of Dedanites.

[f] 20.3 Or *Nubia*; Heb *Cush* [g] 20.4 Or *Nubians*; Heb *Cushites* [h] 20.5 Or *Nubia*; Heb *Cush*
[i] 21.8 Q Ms: MT *a lion*

14 Bring water to the thirsty,
meet the fugitive with bread,
O inhabitants of the land of Tema.
15 For they have fled from the swords,
from the drawn sword,
from the bent bow,
and from the stress of battle.

16 For thus the Lord said to me:
Within a year, according to the years
of a hired worker, all the glory of Kedar
will come to an end; 17and the remaining bows of Kedar's warriors will be few;
for the LORD, the God of Israel, has spoken.

A WARNING OF THE DESTRUCTION OF JERUSALEM

22 The oracle concerning the valley of vision.

What do you mean that you
have gone up,
all of you, to the housetops,
2 you that are full of shoutings,
tumultuous city, exultant town?
Your slain are not slain by the sword,
nor are they dead in battle.
3 Your rulers have all fled together;
they were captured without
the use of a bow.[j]
All of you who were found
were captured,
though they had fled far away.[k]
4 Therefore I said:
Look away from me,
let me weep bitter tears;
do not try to comfort me
for the destruction of my
beloved people.

5 For the Lord GOD of hosts has a day
of tumult and trampling
and confusion
in the valley of vision,
a battering down of walls
and a cry for help to the
mountains.
6 Elam bore the quiver
with chariots and cavalry,[l]
and Kir uncovered the shield.
7 Your choicest valleys were
full of chariots,
and the cavalry took their
stand at the gates.
8 He has taken away the
covering of Judah.

On that day you looked to the weapons of the House of the Forest, 9and you
saw that there were many breaches in
the city of David, and you collected the
waters of the lower pool. 10You counted
the houses of Jerusalem, and you broke
down the houses to fortify the wall.
11You made a reservoir between the two
walls for the water of the old pool. But
you did not look to him who did it, or
have regard for him who planned it long
ago.

12 On that day the Lord GOD of hosts
called to weeping and mourning,
to baldness and putting
on sackcloth;
13 but instead there was joy
and festivity,
killing oxen and
slaughtering sheep,
eating meat and drinking wine.
'Let us eat and drink,
for tomorrow we die.'
14 The LORD of hosts has revealed
himself in my ears:
Surely this iniquity will not be
forgiven you until you die,
says the Lord GOD of hosts.

DENUNCIATION OF SELF-SEEKING OFFICIALS

15 Thus says the Lord GOD of hosts:
Come, go to this steward, to Shebna,
who is master of the household, and
say to him: 16What right do you have
here? Who are your relatives here, that
you have cut out a tomb here for yourself, cutting a tomb on the height, and
carving a habitation for yourself in the
rock? 17The LORD is about to hurl you
away violently, my man. He will seize
firm hold of you, 18whirl you round and
round, and throw you like a ball into a
wide land; there you shall die, and there
your splendid chariots shall lie, O you
disgrace to your master's house! 19I will
thrust you from your office, and you
will be pulled down from your post.

20 On that day I will call my servant
Eliakim son of Hilkiah, 21and will clothe
him with your robe and bind your sash
on him. I will commit your authority to his hand, and he shall be a father
to the inhabitants of Jerusalem and to
the house of Judah. 22I will place on his
shoulder the key of the house of David;
he shall open, and no one shall shut; he
shall shut, and no one shall open. 23I will
fasten him like a peg in a secure place,
and he will become a throne of honour
to his ancestral house. 24And they will

[j] 22.3 Or *without their bows* [k] 22.3 Gk Syr Vg: Heb *fled from far away* [l] 22.6 Meaning of Heb uncertain

hang on him the whole weight of his ancestral house, the offspring and issue, every small vessel, from the cups to all the
flagons. 25On that day, says the LORD
of hosts, the peg that was fastened in a
secure place will give way; it will be cut
down and fall, and the load that was on
it will perish, for the LORD has spoken.

AN ORACLE CONCERNING TYRE

23 The oracle concerning Tyre.

Wail, O ships of Tarshish,
for your fortress is destroyed.[m]
When they came in from Cyprus
they learned of it.
2 Be still, O inhabitants of the coast,
O merchants of Sidon;
your messengers crossed
over the sea[n]
3 and were on the mighty waters;
your revenue was the grain
of Shihor,
the harvest of the Nile;
you were the merchant
of the nations.
4 Be ashamed, O Sidon, for the
sea has spoken,
the fortress of the sea, saying:
'I have neither laboured nor
given birth,
I have neither reared young men
nor brought up young women.'
5 When the report comes to Egypt,
they will be in anguish over
the report about Tyre.
6 Cross over to Tarshish—
wail, O inhabitants of the coast!
7 Is this your exultant city
whose origin is from days of old,
whose feet carried her
to settle far away?
8 Who has planned this
against Tyre, the bestower
of crowns,
whose merchants were princes,
whose traders were the honoured
ones of the earth?
9 The LORD of hosts has planned it—
to defile the pride of all glory,
to shame all the honoured
ones of the earth.
10 Cross over to your own land,
O ships of[o] Tarshish;
this is a harbour[p] no more.
11 He has stretched out his hand
over the sea,
he has shaken the kingdoms;
the LORD has given command
concerning Canaan
to destroy its fortresses.
12 He said:
You will exult no longer,
O oppressed virgin
daughter Sidon;
rise, cross over to Cyprus—
even there you will have no rest.

13 Look at the land of the Chaldeans!
This is the people; it was not Assyria.
They destined Tyre for wild animals.
They erected their siege-towers, they tore
down her palaces, they made her a ruin.[q]
14 Wail, O ships of Tarshish,
for your fortress is destroyed.
15From that day Tyre will be forgotten
for seventy years, the lifetime of one
king. At the end of seventy years, it will
happen to Tyre as in the song about the
prostitute:
16 Take a harp,
go about the city,
you forgotten prostitute!
Make sweet melody,
sing many songs,
that you may be remembered.
17At the end of seventy years, the LORD
will visit Tyre, and she will return to her
trade, and will prostitute herself with all
the kingdoms of the world on the face
of the earth. 18Her merchandise and her
wages will be dedicated to the LORD; her
profits[r] will not be stored or hoarded,
but her merchandise will supply abundant food and fine clothing for those
who live in the presence of the LORD.

IMPENDING JUDGEMENT ON THE EARTH

24 Now the LORD is about
to lay waste the earth
and make it desolate,
and he will twist its surface and
scatter its inhabitants.
2 And it shall be, as with the people,
so with the priest;
as with the slave, so with
his master;
as with the maid, so with
her mistress;
as with the buyer, so with the seller;
as with the lender, so with
the borrower;
as with the creditor, so
with the debtor.

m 23.1 Cn Compare verse 14: Heb *for it is destroyed, without houses* n 23.2 Q Ms: MT *crossing over the sea, they replenished you*
o 23.10 Cn Compare Gk: Heb *like the Nile, daughter* p 23.10 Cn: Heb *restraint*
q 23.13 Meaning of Heb uncertain
r 23.18 Heb *it*

3 The earth shall be utterly laid waste
and utterly despoiled;
for the LORD has spoken
this word.

4 The earth dries up and withers,
the world languishes and withers;
the heavens languish together
with the earth.
5 The earth lies polluted
under its inhabitants;
for they have transgressed laws,
violated the statutes,
broken the everlasting covenant.
6 Therefore a curse devours the earth,
and its inhabitants suffer
for their guilt;
therefore the inhabitants of
the earth dwindled,
and few people are left.
7 The wine dries up,
the vine languishes,
all the merry-hearted sigh.
8 The mirth of the timbrels is stilled,
the noise of the jubilant
has ceased,
the mirth of the lyre is stilled.
9 No longer do they drink wine
with singing;
strong drink is bitter to
those who drink it.
10 The city of chaos is broken down,
every house is shut up so that
no one can enter.
11 There is an outcry in the streets
for lack of wine;
all joy has reached its eventide;
the gladness of the earth
is banished.
12 Desolation is left in the city,
the gates are battered into ruins.
13 For thus it shall be on the earth
and among the nations,
as when an olive tree is beaten,
as at the gleaning when the
grape harvest is ended.

14 They lift up their voices,
they sing for joy;
they shout from the west over
the majesty of the LORD.
15 Therefore in the east give
glory to the LORD;
in the coastlands of the sea
glorify the name of the
LORD, the God of Israel.
16 From the ends of the earth we
hear songs of praise,
of glory to the Righteous One.
But I say, I pine away,
I pine away. Woe is me!
For the treacherous deal treacherously,
the treacherous deal very
treacherously.

17 Terror, and the pit, and the snare
are upon you, O inhabitant
of the earth!
18 Whoever flees at the sound
of the terror
shall fall into the pit,
and whoever climbs out of the pit
shall be caught in the snare.
For the windows of heaven
are opened,
and the foundations of the
earth tremble.
19 The earth is utterly broken,
the earth is torn asunder,
the earth is violently shaken.
20 The earth staggers like a drunkard,
it sways like a hut;
its transgression lies heavy upon it,
and it falls, and will not rise again.

21 On that day the LORD will punish
the host of heaven in heaven,
and on earth the kings of the earth.
22 They will be gathered together
like prisoners in a pit;
they will be shut up in a prison,
and after many days they
will be punished.
23 Then the moon will be abashed,
and the sun ashamed;
for the LORD of hosts will reign
on Mount Zion and in Jerusalem,
and before his elders he will
manifest his glory.

PRAISE FOR DELIVERANCE FROM OPPRESSION

25 O LORD, you are my God;
I will exalt you, I will
praise your name;
for you have done wonderful things,
plans formed of old,
faithful and sure.
2 For you have made the city a heap,
the fortified city a ruin;
the palace of aliens is a city no more,
it will never be rebuilt.
3 Therefore strong peoples
will glorify you;
cities of ruthless nations
will fear you.
4 For you have been a refuge
to the poor,
a refuge to the needy in
their distress,
a shelter from the rainstorm and
a shade from the heat.

When the blast of the ruthless was
like a winter rainstorm,
5 the noise of aliens like heat
in a dry place,
you subdued the heat with
the shade of clouds;
the song of the ruthless
was stilled.

6 On this mountain the LORD of hosts
will make for all peoples
a feast of rich food, a feast of
well-matured wines,
of rich food filled with
marrow, of well-matured
wines strained clear.
7 And he will destroy on
this mountain
the shroud that is cast
over all peoples,
the sheet that is spread
over all nations;
8 he will swallow up death for ever.
Then the Lord GOD will wipe away
the tears from all faces,
and the disgrace of his people
he will take away
from all the earth,
for the LORD has spoken.
9 It will be said on that day,
Lo, this is our God; we have
waited for him, so that
he might save us.
This is the LORD for whom
we have waited;
let us be glad and rejoice
in his salvation.
10 For the hand of the LORD will
rest on this mountain.

The Moabites shall be trodden
down in their place
as straw is trodden down
in a dung-pit.
11 Though they spread out their
hands in the midst of it,
as swimmers spread out
their hands to swim,
their pride will be laid low despite
the struggle[s] of their hands.
12 The high fortifications of his walls
will be brought down,
laid low, cast to the ground,
even to the dust.

JUDAH'S SONG OF VICTORY

26 On that day this song will be
sung in the land of Judah:
We have a strong city;
he sets up victory
like walls and bulwarks.
2 Open the gates,
so that the righteous nation
that keeps faith
may enter in.
3 Those of steadfast mind you
keep in peace—
in peace because they trust in you.
4 Trust in the LORD for ever,
for in the LORD GOD[t]
you have an everlasting rock.
5 For he has brought low
the inhabitants of the height;
the lofty city he lays low.
He lays it low to the ground,
casts it to the dust.
6 The foot tramples it,
the feet of the poor,
the steps of the needy.

7 The way of the righteous is level;
O Just One, you make smooth
the path of the righteous.
8 In the path of your judgements,
O LORD, we wait for you;
your name and your renown
are the soul's desire.
9 My soul yearns for you
in the night,
my spirit within me
earnestly seeks you.
For when your judgements
are in the earth,
the inhabitants of the world
learn righteousness.
10 If favour is shown to the wicked,
they do not learn righteousness;
in the land of uprightness they
deal perversely
and do not see the majesty
of the LORD.
11 O LORD, your hand is lifted up,
but they do not see it.
Let them see your zeal for your
people, and be ashamed.
Let the fire for your adversaries
consume them.
12 O LORD, you will ordain
peace for us,
for indeed, all that we have done,
you have done for us.
13 O LORD our God,
other lords besides you
have ruled over us,
but we acknowledge your
name alone.
14 The dead do not live;
shades do not rise—

[s] **25.11** Meaning of Heb uncertain [t] **26.4** Heb *in Yah, the LORD*

because you have punished and
destroyed them,
and wiped out all memory
of them.
15 But you have increased the
nation, O LORD,
you have increased the nation;
you are glorified;
you have enlarged all the
borders of the land.

16 O LORD, in distress they sought you,
they poured out a prayer[u]
when your chastening
was on them.
17 Like a woman with child,
who writhes and cries
out in her pangs
when she is near her time,
so were we because of you, O LORD;
18 we were with child, we writhed,
but we gave birth only to wind.
We have won no victories on earth,
and no one is born to
inhabit the world.
19 Your dead shall live, their
corpses[v] shall rise.
O dwellers in the dust, awake
and sing for joy!
For your dew is a radiant dew,
and the earth will give birth
to those long dead.[w]

20 Come, my people, enter
your chambers,
and shut your doors behind you;
hide yourselves for a little while
until the wrath is past.
21 For the LORD comes out
from his place
to punish the inhabitants of the
earth for their iniquity;
the earth will disclose the
blood shed on it,
and will no longer cover its slain.

ISRAEL'S REDEMPTION

27 On that day the LORD with
his cruel and great and strong
sword will punish Leviathan the fleeing serpent, Leviathan the twisting serpent, and he will kill the dragon that is
in the sea.

2 On that day:
A pleasant vineyard, sing about it!
3 I, the LORD, am its keeper;
every moment I water it.
I guard it night and day
so that no one can harm it;
4 I have no wrath.
If it gives me thorns and briers,
I will march to battle against it.
I will burn it up.
5 Or else let it cling to me
for protection,
let it make peace with me,
let it make peace with me.

6 In days to come[x] Jacob
shall take root,
Israel shall blossom and
put forth shoots,
and fill the whole world
with fruit.

7 Has he struck them down as
he struck down those
who struck them?
Or have they been killed as
their killers were killed?
8 By expulsion,[y] by exile you
struggled against them;
with his fierce blast he
removed them on the
day of the east wind.
9 Therefore by this the guilt of
Jacob will be expiated,
and this will be the full fruit of
the removal of his sin:
when he makes all the stones
of the altars
like chalkstones crushed to pieces,
no sacred poles[z] or incense altars
will remain standing.
10 For the fortified city is solitary,
a habitation deserted and
forsaken, like the wilderness;
the calves graze there,
there they lie down, and
strip its branches.
11 When its boughs are dry,
they are broken;
women come and make
a fire of them.
For this is a people without
understanding;
therefore he that made
them will not have
compassion on them,
he that formed them will
show them no favour.

12 On that day the LORD will thresh
from the channel of the Euphrates to the
Wadi of Egypt, and you will be gathered
one by one, O people of Israel. 13 And on

[u] 26.16 Meaning of Heb uncertain [v] 26.19 Cn Compare Syr Tg: Heb *my corpse* [w] 26.19 Heb *to the shades* [x] 27.6 Heb *Those to come* [y] 27.8 Meaning of Heb uncertain [z] 27.9 Heb *Asherim*

that day a great trumpet will be blown, and those who were lost in the land of Assyria and those who were driven out to the land of Egypt will come and worship the LORD on the holy mountain at Jerusalem.

JUDGEMENT ON CORRUPT RULERS, PRIESTS, AND PROPHETS

28 Ah, the proud garland of the drunkards of Ephraim,
and the fading flower of its glorious beauty,
which is on the head of those bloated with rich food, of those overcome with wine!
2 See, the Lord has one who is mighty and strong;
like a storm of hail, a destroying tempest,
like a storm of mighty, overflowing waters;
with his hand he will hurl them down to the earth.
3 Trampled under foot will be the proud garland of the drunkards of Ephraim.
4 And the fading flower of its glorious beauty,
which is on the head of those bloated with rich food,
will be like a first-ripe fig before the summer;
whoever sees it, eats it up as soon as it comes to hand.

5 On that day the LORD of hosts will be a garland of glory,
and a diadem of beauty, to the remnant of his people;
6 and a spirit of justice to the one who sits in judgement,
and strength to those who turn back the battle at the gate.

7 These also reel with wine
and stagger with strong drink;
the priest and the prophet reel with strong drink,
they are confused with wine,
they stagger with strong drink;
they err in vision,
they stumble in giving judgement.
8 All tables are covered with filthy vomit;
no place is clean.

9 'Whom will he teach knowledge,
and to whom will he explain the message?
Those who are weaned from milk,
those taken from the breast?
10 For it is precept upon precept,
precept upon precept,
line upon line, line upon line,
here a little, there a little.'[a]

11 Truly, with stammering lip
and with alien tongue
he will speak to this people,
12 to whom he has said,
'This is rest;
give rest to the weary;
and this is repose';
yet they would not hear.
13 Therefore the word of the LORD will be to them,
'Precept upon precept, precept upon precept,
line upon line, line upon line,
here a little, there a little';[b]
in order that they may go, and fall backwards,
and be broken, and snared, and taken.

14 Therefore hear the word of the LORD, you scoffers
who rule this people in Jerusalem.
15 Because you have said, 'We have made a covenant with death,
and with Sheol we have an agreement;
when the overwhelming scourge passes through
it will not come to us;
for we have made lies our refuge,
and in falsehood we have taken shelter';
16 therefore thus says the Lord GOD,
See, I am laying in Zion a foundation stone,
a tested stone,
a precious cornerstone, a sure foundation:
'One who trusts will not panic.'
17 And I will make justice the line,
and righteousness the plummet;
hail will sweep away the refuge of lies,
and waters will overwhelm the shelter.
18 Then your covenant with death will be annulled,
and your agreement with Sheol will not stand;
when the overwhelming scourge passes through
you will be beaten down by it.

[a] 28.10 Meaning of Heb of this verse uncertain
[b] 28.13 Meaning of Heb of this verse uncertain

19 As often as it passes through,
it will take you;
for morning by morning it
will pass through,
by day and by night;
and it will be sheer terror to
understand the message.
20 For the bed is too short to
stretch oneself on it,
and the covering too narrow
to wrap oneself in it.
21 For the LORD will rise up as
on Mount Perazim,
he will rage as in the
valley of Gibeon
to do his deed—strange is his deed!—
and to work his work—
alien is his work!
22 Now therefore do not scoff,
or your bonds will be
made stronger;
for I have heard a decree
of destruction
from the Lord GOD of hosts
upon the whole land.

23 Listen, and hear my voice;
Pay attention, and hear
my speech.
24 Do those who plough for sowing
plough continually?
Do they continually open and
harrow their ground?
25 When they have levelled its surface,
do they not scatter dill,
sow cummin,
and plant wheat in rows
and barley in its proper place,
and spelt as the border?
26 For they are well instructed;
their God teaches them.

27 Dill is not threshed with a
threshing-sledge,
nor is a cartwheel rolled
over cummin;
but dill is beaten out with a stick,
and cummin with a rod.
28 Grain is crushed for bread,
but one does not thresh it for ever;
one drives the cartwheel and
horses over it,
but does not pulverize it.
29 This also comes from the
LORD of hosts;
he is wonderful in counsel,
and excellent in wisdom.

THE SIEGE OF JERUSALEM

29 Ah, Ariel, Ariel,
the city where David encamped!
Add year to year;
let the festivals run their round.
2 Yet I will distress Ariel,
and there shall be moaning
and lamentation,
and Jerusalem[c] shall be to
me like an Ariel.[d]
3 And like David[e] I will encamp
against you;
I will besiege you with towers
and raise siege-works against you.
4 Then deep from the earth
you shall speak,
from low in the dust your
words shall come;
your voice shall come from
the ground like the
voice of a ghost,
and your speech shall whisper
out of the dust.

5 But the multitude of your foes[f]
shall be like fine dust,
and the multitude of tyrants
like flying chaff.
And in an instant, suddenly,
6 you will be visited by the
LORD of hosts
with thunder and earthquake
and great noise,
with whirlwind and tempest, and
the flame of a devouring fire.
7 And the multitude of all the nations
that fight against Ariel,
all that fight against her and
her stronghold, and
who distress her,
shall be like a dream, a
vision of the night.
8 Just as when a hungry person
dreams of eating
and wakes up still hungry,
or a thirsty person dreams
of drinking
and wakes up faint, still thirsty,
so shall the multitude of all
the nations be
that fight against Mount Zion.

9 Stupefy yourselves and be
in a stupor,
blind yourselves and be blind!
Be drunk, but not from wine;
stagger, but not from
strong drink!
10 For the LORD has poured
out upon you
a spirit of deep sleep;

c 29.2 Heb *she* d 29.2 Probable meaning, *altar hearth*; compare Ezek 43.15 e 29.3 Gk: Meaning of Heb uncertain f 29.5 Cn: Heb *strangers*

he has closed your eyes,
you prophets,
and covered your heads, you seers.
11 The vision of all this has become
for you like the words of a sealed document. If it is given to those who can
read, with the command, 'Read this',
they say, 'We cannot, for it is sealed.'
12 And if it is given to those who cannot
read, saying, 'Read this', they say, 'We
cannot read.'

13 The Lord said:
Because these people draw near
with their mouths
and honour me with their lips,
while their hearts are far from me,
and their worship of me is a
human commandment
learned by rote;
14 so I will again do
amazing things with this people,
shocking and amazing.
The wisdom of their wise
shall perish,
and the discernment of the
discerning shall be hidden.

15 Ha! You who hide a plan too
deep for the LORD,
whose deeds are in the dark,
and who say, 'Who sees us?
Who knows us?'
16 You turn things upside down!
Shall the potter be regarded
as the clay?
Shall the thing made say
of its maker,
'He did not make me';
or the thing formed say of the
one who formed it,
'He has no understanding'?

HOPE FOR THE FUTURE

17 Shall not Lebanon in a very
little while
become a fruitful field,
and the fruitful field be
regarded as a forest?
18 On that day the deaf shall hear
the words of a scroll,
and out of their gloom and darkness
the eyes of the blind shall see.
19 The meek shall obtain fresh
joy in the LORD,
and the neediest people shall exult
in the Holy One of Israel.
20 For the tyrant shall be no more,
and the scoffer shall cease to be;
all those alert to do evil
shall be cut off—
21 those who cause a person to
lose a lawsuit,
who set a trap for the
arbiter in the gate,
and without grounds deny justice
to the one in the right.

22 Therefore thus says the LORD,
who redeemed Abraham, concerning
the house of Jacob:
No longer shall Jacob be ashamed,
no longer shall his face grow pale.
23 For when he sees his children,
the work of my hands,
in his midst,
they will sanctify my name;
they will sanctify the Holy
One of Jacob,
and will stand in awe of
the God of Israel.
24 And those who err in spirit will
come to understanding,
and those who grumble will
accept instruction.

THE FUTILITY OF RELIANCE ON EGYPT

30 Oh, rebellious children,
says the LORD,
who carry out a plan, but not mine;
who make an alliance, but
against my will,
adding sin to sin;
2 who set out to go down to Egypt
without asking for my counsel,
to take refuge in the protection
of Pharaoh,
and to seek shelter in the
shadow of Egypt;
3 Therefore the protection of Pharaoh
shall become your shame,
and the shelter in the shadow of
Egypt your humiliation.
4 For though his officials are at Zoan
and his envoys reach Hanes,
5 everyone comes to shame
through a people that
cannot profit them,
that brings neither help nor profit,
but shame and disgrace.

6 An oracle concerning the animals
of the Negeb.
Through a land of trouble
and distress,
of lioness and roaring[g] lion,
of viper and flying serpent,

g 30.6 Cn: Heb *from them*

they carry their riches on the
backs of donkeys,
and their treasures on the
humps of camels,
to a people that cannot
profit them.
7 For Egypt's help is worthless
and empty,
therefore I have called her,
'Rahab who sits still.'[h]

A REBELLIOUS PEOPLE

8 Go now, write it before them
on a tablet,
and inscribe it in a book,
so that it may be for the
time to come
as a witness for ever.
9 For they are a rebellious people,
faithless children,
children who will not hear
the instruction of the LORD;
10 who say to the seers, 'Do not see';
and to the prophets, 'Do not
prophesy to us what is right;
speak to us smooth things,
prophesy illusions,
11 leave the way, turn aside
from the path,
let us hear no more about the
Holy One of Israel.'
12 Therefore thus says the Holy
One of Israel:
Because you reject this word,
and put your trust in
oppression and deceit,
and rely on them;
13 therefore this iniquity shall
become for you
like a break in a high wall, bulging
out, and about to collapse,
whose crash comes suddenly,
in an instant;
14 its breaking is like that of a
potter's vessel
that is smashed so ruthlessly
that among its fragments not
a sherd is found
for taking fire from the hearth,
or dipping water out of
the cistern.

15 For thus said the Lord GOD, the
Holy One of Israel:
In returning and rest you
shall be saved;
in quietness and in trust shall
be your strength.
But you refused 16and said,
'No! We will flee upon horses'—
therefore you shall flee!
and, 'We will ride upon
swift steeds'—
therefore your pursuers
shall be swift!
17 A thousand shall flee at the
threat of one,
at the threat of five
you shall flee,
until you are left
like a flagstaff on the top
of a mountain,
like a signal on a hill.

GOD'S PROMISE TO ZION

18 Therefore the LORD waits to
be gracious to you;
therefore he will rise up to
show mercy to you.
For the LORD is a God of justice;
blessed are all those who
wait for him.

19 Truly, O people in Zion, inhabitants of Jerusalem, you shall weep
no more. He will surely be gracious to
you at the sound of your cry; when he
hears it, he will answer you. 20Though
the Lord may give you the bread of
adversity and the water of affliction,
yet your Teacher will not hide himself any more, but your eyes shall see
your Teacher. 21And when you turn to
the right or when you turn to the left,
your ears shall hear a word behind
you, saying, 'This is the way; walk in
it.' 22Then you will defile your silver-
covered idols and your gold-plated images. You will scatter them like filthy
rags; you will say to them, 'Away with
you!'

23 He will give rain for the seed
with which you sow the ground, and
grain, the produce of the ground,
which will be rich and plenteous. On
that day your cattle will graze in broad
pastures; 24and the oxen and donkeys
that till the ground will eat silage,
which has been winnowed with shovel
and fork. 25On every lofty mountain
and every high hill there will be brooks
running with water—on a day of the
great slaughter, when the towers fall.
26Moreover, the light of the moon
will be like the light of the sun, and
the light of the sun will be sevenfold,
like the light of seven days, on the day
when the LORD binds up the injuries
of his people, and heals the wounds inflicted by his blow.

h 30.7 Meaning of Heb uncertain

JUDGEMENT ON ASSYRIA

27 See, the name of the LORD
comes from far away,
burning with his anger, and
in thick rising smoke;[i]
his lips are full of indignation,
and his tongue is like a
devouring fire;
28 his breath is like an overflowing stream
that reaches up to the neck—
to sift the nations with the
sieve of destruction,
and to place on the jaws of
the peoples a bridle that
leads them astray.

29 You shall have a song as in the
night when a holy festival is kept; and
gladness of heart, as when one sets out to
the sound of the flute to go to the mountain of the LORD, to the Rock of Israel.
30 And the LORD will cause his majestic
voice to be heard and the descending
blow of his arm to be seen, in furious anger and a flame of devouring fire, with
a cloudburst and tempest and hailstones.
31 The Assyrian will be terror-stricken at
the voice of the LORD, when he strikes
with his rod. 32 And every stroke of the
staff of punishment that the LORD lays
upon him will be to the sound of timbrels and lyres; battling with brandished
arm he will fight with him. 33 For his
burning-place[j] has long been prepared;
truly it is made ready for the king,[k] its
pyre made deep and wide, with fire and
wood in abundance; the breath of the
LORD, like a stream of sulphur, kindles it.

ALLIANCE WITH EGYPT IS FUTILE

31 Alas for those who go down
to Egypt for help
and who rely on horses,
who trust in chariots because
they are many
and in horsemen because
they are very strong,
but do not look to the Holy
One of Israel
or consult the LORD!
2 Yet he too is wise and
brings disaster;
he does not call back his words,
but will rise against the house
of the evildoers,
and against the helpers of those
who work iniquity.
3 The Egyptians are human,
and not God;
their horses are flesh,
and not spirit.
When the LORD stretches
out his hand,
the helper will stumble, and
the one helped will fall,
and they will all perish together.

4 For thus the LORD said to me,
As a lion or a young lion
growls over its prey,
and—when a band of shepherds
is called out against it—
is not terrified by their shouting
or daunted at their noise,
so the LORD of hosts will come down
to fight upon Mount Zion
and upon its hill.
5 Like birds hovering overhead,
so the LORD of hosts
will protect Jerusalem;
he will protect and deliver it,
he will spare and rescue it.

6 Turn back to him whom you[l] have
deeply betrayed, O people of Israel. 7 For
on that day all of you shall throw away
your idols of silver and idols of gold,
which your hands have sinfully made
for you.
8 'Then the Assyrian shall fall by a
sword, not of mortals;
and a sword, not of humans,
shall devour him;
he shall flee from the sword,
and his young men shall be
put to forced labour.
9 His rock shall pass away in terror,
and his officers desert the
standard in panic,'
says the LORD, whose fire is in Zion,
and whose furnace is
in Jerusalem.

GOVERNMENT WITH JUSTICE PREDICTED

32 See, a king will reign in
righteousness,
and princes will rule with justice.
2 Each will be like a hiding-place
from the wind,
a covert from the tempest,
like streams of water in a dry place,
like the shade of a great rock
in a weary land.
3 Then the eyes of those who have
sight will not be closed,
and the ears of those who have
hearing will listen.

[i] 30.27 Meaning of Heb uncertain [j] 30.33 Or *Topheth* [k] 30.33 Or *Molech* [l] 31.6 Heb *they*

4 The minds of the rash will have
good judgement,
and the tongues of stammerers
will speak readily
and distinctly.
5 A fool will no longer be called noble,
nor a villain be said to
be honourable.
6 For fools speak folly,
and their minds plot iniquity:
to practise ungodliness,
to utter error concerning
the LORD,
to leave the craving of the
hungry unsatisfied,
and to deprive the thirsty of drink.
7 The villainies of villains are evil;
they devise wicked devices
to ruin the poor with lying words,
even when the plea of the
needy is right.
8 But those who are noble plan
noble things,
and by noble things they stand.

COMPLACENT WOMEN WARNED OF DISASTER

9 Rise up, you women who are at
ease, hear my voice;
you complacent daughters,
listen to my speech.
10 In little more than a year
you will shudder, you
complacent ones;
for the vintage will fail,
the fruit harvest will not come.
11 Tremble, you women who
are at ease,
shudder, you complacent ones;
strip, and make yourselves bare,
and put sackcloth on your loins.
12 Beat your breasts for the
pleasant fields,
for the fruitful vine,
13 for the soil of my people
growing up in thorns
and briers;
yes, for all the joyous houses
in the jubilant city.
14 For the palace will be forsaken,
the populous city deserted;
the hill and the watch-tower
will become dens for ever,
the joy of wild asses,
a pasture for flocks;
15 until a spirit from on high is
poured out on us,
and the wilderness becomes
a fruitful field,
and the fruitful field is
deemed a forest.

THE PEACE OF GOD'S REIGN

16 Then justice will dwell in
the wilderness,
and righteousness abide in
the fruitful field.
17 The effect of righteousness
will be peace,
and the result of righteousness,
quietness and trust for ever.
18 My people will abide in a
peaceful habitation,
in secure dwellings, and in
quiet resting-places.
19 The forest will disappear
completely,[m]
and the city will be
utterly laid low.
20 Happy will you be who sow
beside every stream,
who let the ox and the
donkey range freely.

A PROPHECY OF DELIVERANCE FROM FOES

33 Ah, you destroyer,
who yourself have not
been destroyed;
you treacherous one,
with whom no one has
dealt treacherously!
When you have ceased to destroy,
you will be destroyed;
and when you have stopped
dealing treacherously,
you will be dealt with
treacherously.

2 O LORD, be gracious to us;
we wait for you.
Be our arm every morning,
our salvation in the time
of trouble.
3 At the sound of tumult, peoples fled;
before your majesty,
nations scattered.
4 Spoil was gathered as the
caterpillar gathers;
as locusts leap, they leapt[n] upon it.
5 The LORD is exalted, he
dwells on high;
he filled Zion with justice
and righteousness;
6 he will be the stability of your times,
abundance of salvation,
wisdom, and knowledge;
the fear of the LORD is
Zion's treasure.[o]

m 32.19 Cn: Heb *And it will hail when the forest comes down* n 33.4 Meaning of Heb uncertain
o 33.6 Heb *his treasure*; meaning of Heb uncertain

7 Listen! the valiant[p] cry
in the streets;
the envoys of peace
weep bitterly.
8 The highways are deserted,
travellers have left the road.
The treaty is broken,
its oaths[q] are despised,
its obligation[r] is disregarded.
9 The land mourns and languishes;
Lebanon is confounded
and withers away;
Sharon is like a desert;
and Bashan and Carmel
shake off their leaves.

10 'Now I will arise,' says the LORD,
'now I will lift myself up;
now I will be exalted.
11 You conceive chaff, you bring
forth stubble;
your breath is a fire that
will consume you.
12 And the peoples will be as if
burned to lime,
like thorns cut down, that are
burned in the fire.'

13 Hear, you who are far away,
what I have done;
and you who are near,
acknowledge my might.
14 The sinners in Zion are afraid;
trembling has seized
the godless:
'Who among us can live with
the devouring fire?
Who among us can live with
everlasting flames?'
15 Those who walk righteously
and speak uprightly,
who despise the gain of
oppression,
who wave away a bribe instead
of accepting it,
who stop their ears from
hearing of bloodshed
and shut their eyes from
looking on evil,
16 they will live on the heights;
their refuge will be the
fortresses of rocks;
their food will be supplied,
their water assured.

THE LAND OF THE MAJESTIC KING

17 Your eyes will see the king
in his beauty;
they will behold a land that
stretches far away.
18 Your mind will muse on the terror:
'Where is the one who counted?
Where is the one who
weighed the tribute?
Where is the one who
counted the towers?'
19 No longer will you see the
insolent people,
the people of an obscure speech
that you cannot comprehend,
stammering in a language that
you cannot understand.
20 Look on Zion, the city of our
appointed festivals!
Your eyes will see Jerusalem,
a quiet habitation, an
immovable tent,
whose stakes will never be pulled up,
and none of whose ropes
will be broken.
21 But there the LORD in majesty
will be for us
a place of broad rivers
and streams,
where no galley with oars can go,
nor stately ship can pass.
22 For the LORD is our judge, the
LORD is our ruler,
the LORD is our king; he
will save us.

23 Your rigging hangs loose;
it cannot hold the mast
firm in its place,
or keep the sail spread out.

Then prey and spoil in abundance
will be divided;
even the lame will fall
to plundering.
24 And no inhabitant will say,
'I am sick';
the people who live there will be
forgiven their iniquity.

JUDGEMENT ON THE NATIONS

34 Draw near, O nations, to hear;
O peoples, give heed!
Let the earth hear, and all
that fills it;
the world, and all that
comes from it.
2 For the LORD is enraged against
all the nations,
and furious against all
their hordes;
he has doomed them, has given
them over for slaughter.

[p] 33.7 Meaning of Heb uncertain [q] 33.8 Q Ms: MT *cities* [r] 33.8 Or *everyone*

3 Their slain shall be cast out,
and the stench of their
corpses shall rise;
the mountains shall flow
with their blood.
4 All the host of heaven
shall rot away,
and the skies roll up like a scroll.
All their host shall wither
like a leaf withering on a vine,
or fruit withering on a fig tree.

5 When my sword has drunk its
fill in the heavens,
lo, it will descend upon Edom,
upon the people I have
doomed to judgement.
6 The LORD has a sword; it is
sated with blood,
it is gorged with fat,
with the blood of lambs and goats,
with the fat of the
kidneys of rams.
For the LORD has a sacrifice
in Bozrah,
a great slaughter in the
land of Edom.
7 Wild oxen shall fall with them,
and young steers with the
mighty bulls.
Their land shall be soaked
with blood,
and their soil made rich with fat.

8 For the LORD has a day of vengeance,
a year of vindication by
Zion's cause.[s]
9 And the streams of Edom[t] shall
be turned into pitch,
and her soil into sulphur;
her land shall become
burning pitch.
10 Night and day it shall not
be quenched;
its smoke shall go up for ever.
From generation to generation
it shall lie waste;
no one shall pass through
it for ever and ever.
11 But the hawk[u] and the hedgehog[v]
shall possess it;
the owl[w] and the raven
shall live in it.
He shall stretch the line of
confusion over it,
and the plummet of chaos
over[x] its nobles.
12 They shall name it No
Kingdom There,
and all its princes shall
be nothing.
13 Thorns shall grow over its
strongholds,
nettles and thistles in
its fortresses.
It shall be the haunt of jackals,
an abode for ostriches.
14 Wildcats shall meet with hyenas,
goat-demons shall call
to each other;
there too Lilith shall repose,
and find a place to rest.
15 There shall the owl nest
and lay and hatch and brood
in its shadow;
there too the buzzards shall gather,
each one with its mate.
16 Seek and read from the book
of the LORD:
Not one of these shall be missing;
none shall be without its mate.
For the mouth of the LORD
has commanded,
and his spirit has gathered them.
17 He has cast the lot for them,
his hand has portioned it out
to them with the line;
they shall possess it for ever,
from generation to generation
they shall live in it.

THE RETURN OF THE REDEEMED TO ZION

35 The wilderness and the dry
land shall be glad,
the desert shall rejoice
and blossom;
like the crocus 2it shall blossom
abundantly,
and rejoice with joy and singing.
The glory of Lebanon shall
be given to it,
the majesty of Carmel
and Sharon.
They shall see the glory of the LORD,
the majesty of our God.

3 Strengthen the weak hands,
and make firm the feeble knees.
4 Say to those who are of a
fearful heart,
'Be strong, do not fear!
Here is your God.
He will come with vengeance,
with terrible recompense.
He will come and save you.'

[s] 34.8 Or *of recompense by Zion's defender*
[t] 34.9 Heb *her streams* [u] 34.11 Identification uncertain [v] 34.11 Identification uncertain
[w] 34.11 Identification uncertain [x] 34.11 Heb lacks *over*

5 Then the eyes of the blind
shall be opened,
and the ears of the deaf
unstopped;
6 then the lame shall leap like a deer,
and the tongue of the
speechless sing for joy.
For waters shall break forth
in the wilderness,
and streams in the desert;
7 the burning sand shall
become a pool,
and the thirsty ground
springs of water;
the haunt of jackals shall
become a swamp,[y]
the grass shall become
reeds and rushes.

8 A highway shall be there,
and it shall be called the Holy Way;
the unclean shall not travel on it,[z]
but it shall be for God's people;[a]
no traveller, not even fools,
shall go astray.
9 No lion shall be there,
nor shall any ravenous beast
come up on it;
they shall not be found there,
but the redeemed shall walk there.
10 And the ransomed of the
LORD shall return,
and come to Zion with singing;
everlasting joy shall be upon
their heads;
they shall obtain joy and gladness,
and sorrow and sighing
shall flee away.

SENNACHERIB THREATENS JERUSALEM

36 In the fourteenth year of King
Hezekiah, King Sennacherib of
Assyria came up against all the fortified cities of Judah and captured them.
2The king of Assyria sent the Rabshakeh
from Lachish to King Hezekiah at Jerusalem, with a great army. He stood by
the conduit of the upper pool on the
highway to the Fuller's Field. 3And
there came out to him Eliakim son of
Hilkiah, who was in charge of the palace, and Shebna the secretary, and Joah
son of Asaph, the recorder.

4 The Rabshakeh said to them, 'Say to
Hezekiah: Thus says the great king, the
king of Assyria: On what do you base
this confidence of yours? 5Do you think
that mere words are strategy and power
for war? On whom do you now rely, that
you have rebelled against me? 6See, you
are relying on Egypt, that broken reed
of a staff, which will pierce the hand of
anyone who leans on it. Such is Pharaoh
king of Egypt to all who rely on him.
7But if you say to me, "We rely on the
LORD our God", is it not he whose high
places and altars Hezekiah has removed,
saying to Judah and to Jerusalem, "You
shall worship before this altar"? 8Come
now, make a wager with my master
the king of Assyria: I will give you two
thousand horses, if you are able on your
part to set riders on them. 9How then
can you repulse a single captain among
the least of my master's servants, when
you rely on Egypt for chariots and for
horsemen? 10Moreover, is it without the
LORD that I have come up against this
land to destroy it? The LORD said to me,
Go up against this land, and destroy it.'

11 Then Eliakim, Shebna, and Joah
said to the Rabshakeh, 'Please speak to
your servants in Aramaic, for we understand it; do not speak to us in the language of Judah within the hearing of
the people who are on the wall.' 12But
the Rabshakeh said, 'Has my master
sent me to speak these words to your
master and to you, and not to the people sitting on the wall, who are doomed
with you to eat their own dung and
drink their own urine?'

13 Then the Rabshakeh stood and
called out in a loud voice in the language of Judah, 'Hear the words of the
great king, the king of Assyria! 14Thus
says the king: "Do not let Hezekiah deceive you, for he will not be able to deliver you. 15Do not let Hezekiah make
you rely on the LORD by saying, The
LORD will surely deliver us; this city will
not be given into the hand of the king
of Assyria." 16Do not listen to Hezekiah;
for thus says the king of Assyria: "Make
your peace with me and come out to
me; then every one of you will eat from
your own vine and your own fig tree
and drink water from your own cistern,
17until I come and take you away to a
land like your own land, a land of grain
and wine, a land of bread and vineyards.
18Do not let Hezekiah mislead you by
saying, The LORD will save us. Has any
of the gods of the nations saved their
land out of the hand of the king of Assyria? 19Where are the gods of Hamath
and Arpad? Where are the gods of Sepharvaim? Have they delivered Samaria

[y] **35.7** Cn: Heb *in the haunt of jackals is her resting-place* [z] **35.8** *Or pass it by* [a] **35.8** Cn: Heb *for them*

out of my hand? 20Who among all the
gods of these countries have saved their
countries out of my hand, that the
LORD should save Jerusalem out of my
hand?"'

21 But they were silent and answered him not a word, for the king's
command was, 'Do not answer him.'
22Then Eliakim son of Hilkiah, who was
in charge of the palace, and Shebna the
secretary, and Joah son of Asaph, the
recorder, came to Hezekiah with their
clothes torn, and told him the words of
the Rabshakeh.

HEZEKIAH CONSULTS ISAIAH

37 When King Hezekiah heard it,
he tore his clothes, covered himself with sackcloth, and went into the
house of the LORD. 2And he sent Eliakim, who was in charge of the palace,
and Shebna the secretary, and the senior priests, covered with sackcloth, to
the prophet Isaiah son of Amoz. 3They
said to him, 'Thus says Hezekiah, This
day is a day of distress, of rebuke, and
of disgrace; children have come to birth,
and there is no strength to bring them
forth. 4It may be that the LORD your
God heard the words of the Rabshakeh,
whom his master the king of Assyria
has sent to mock the living God, and
will rebuke the words that the LORD
your God has heard; therefore lift up
your prayer for the remnant that is left.'

5 When the servants of King Hezekiah came to Isaiah, 6Isaiah said to
them, 'Say to your master, "Thus says
the LORD: Do not be afraid because of
the words that you have heard, with
which the servants of the king of Assyria have reviled me. 7I myself will put
a spirit in him, so that he shall hear a
rumour, and return to his own land; I
will cause him to fall by the sword in his
own land."'

8 The Rabshakeh returned, and found
the king of Assyria fighting against Libnah; for he had heard that the king had
left Lachish. 9Now the king[b] heard concerning King Tirhakah of Ethiopia,[c] 'He
has set out to fight against you.' When
he heard it, he sent messengers to Hezekiah, saying, 10'Thus shall you speak to
King Hezekiah of Judah: Do not let your
God on whom you rely deceive you by
promising that Jerusalem will not be
given into the hand of the king of Assyria. 11See, you have heard what the
kings of Assyria have done to all lands,
destroying them utterly. Shall you be
delivered? 12Have the gods of the nations delivered them, the nations that
my predecessors destroyed, Gozan, Haran, Rezeph, and the people of Eden
who were in Telassar? 13Where is the
king of Hamath, the king of Arpad, the
king of the city of Sepharvaim, the king
of Hena, or the king of Ivvah?'

HEZEKIAH'S PRAYER

14 Hezekiah received the letter from
the hand of the messengers and read
it; then Hezekiah went up to the house
of the LORD and spread it before the
LORD. 15And Hezekiah prayed to the
LORD, saying: 16'O LORD of hosts, God
of Israel, who are enthroned above the
cherubim, you are God, you alone, of
all the kingdoms of the earth; you have
made heaven and earth. 17Incline your
ear, O LORD, and hear; open your eyes,
O LORD, and see; hear all the words
of Sennacherib, which he has sent to
mock the living God. 18Truly, O LORD,
the kings of Assyria have laid waste all
the nations and their lands, 19and have
hurled their gods into the fire, though
they were no gods, but the work of human hands—wood and stone—and so
they were destroyed. 20So now, O LORD
our God, save us from his hand, so that
all the kingdoms of the earth may know
that you alone are the LORD.'

21 Then Isaiah son of Amoz sent to
Hezekiah, saying: 'Thus says the LORD,
the God of Israel: Because you have
prayed to me concerning King Sennacherib of Assyria, 22this is the word that
the LORD has spoken concerning him:

She despises you, she scorns you—
virgin daughter Zion;
she tosses her head—behind
your back,
daughter Jerusalem.

23 'Whom have you mocked
and reviled?
Against whom have you
raised your voice
and haughtily lifted your eyes?
Against the Holy One of Israel!
24 By your servants you have
mocked the Lord,
and you have said, "With
my many chariots
I have gone up the heights of
the mountains,
to the far recesses of Lebanon;

[b] 37.9 Heb *he* [c] 37.9 Or *Nubia*; Heb *Cush*

I felled its tallest cedars,
its choicest cypresses;
I came to its remotest height,
its densest forest.
25 I dug wells
and drank waters,
I dried up with the sole of my foot
all the streams of Egypt."

26 'Have you not heard
that I determined it long ago?
I planned from days of old
what now I bring to pass,
that you should make fortified cities
crash into heaps of ruins,
27 while their inhabitants,
shorn of strength,
are dismayed and confounded;
they have become like plants
of the field
and like tender grass,
like grass on the housetops,
blighted[d] before it is grown.

28 'I know your rising up[e] and
your sitting down,
your going out and coming in,
and your raging against me.
29 Because you have raged against me
and your arrogance has
come to my ears,
I will put my hook in your nose
and my bit in your mouth;
I will turn you back on the way
by which you came.

30 'And this shall be the sign for you:
This year eat what grows of itself, and in
the second year what springs from that;
then in the third year sow, reap, plant
vineyards, and eat their fruit. 31 The surviving remnant of the house of Judah
shall again take root downwards, and
bear fruit upwards; 32 for from Jerusalem
a remnant shall go out, and from Mount
Zion a band of survivors. The zeal of the
LORD of hosts will do this.

33 'Therefore thus says the LORD
concerning the king of Assyria: He shall
not come into this city, shoot an arrow
there, come before it with a shield, or
cast up a siege-ramp against it. 34 By the
way that he came, by the same he shall
return; he shall not come into this city,
says the LORD. 35 For I will defend this
city to save it, for my own sake and for
the sake of my servant David.'

SENNACHERIB'S DEFEAT AND DEATH

36 Then the angel of the LORD set
out and struck down one hundred and
eighty-five thousand in the camp of
the Assyrians; when morning dawned,
they were all dead bodies. 37 Then King
Sennacherib of Assyria left, went home,
and lived at Nineveh. 38 As he was worshipping in the house of his god Nisroch, his sons Adrammelech and Sharezer killed him with the sword, and they
escaped into the land of Ararat. His son
Esar-haddon succeeded him.

HEZEKIAH'S ILLNESS

38 In those days Hezekiah became
sick and was at the point of
death. The prophet Isaiah son of Amoz
came to him, and said to him, 'Thus
says the LORD: Set your house in order,
for you shall die; you shall not recover.'
2 Then Hezekiah turned his face to the
wall, and prayed to the LORD: 3 'Remember now, O LORD, I implore you, how I
have walked before you in faithfulness
with a whole heart, and have done what
is good in your sight.' And Hezekiah
wept bitterly.

4 Then the word of the LORD came to
Isaiah: 5 'Go and say to Hezekiah, Thus
says the LORD, the God of your ancestor
David: I have heard your prayer, I have
seen your tears; I will add fifteen years
to your life. 6 I will deliver you and this
city out of the hand of the king of Assyria, and defend this city.

7 'This is the sign to you from the
LORD, that the LORD will do this thing
that he has promised: 8 See, I will make
the shadow cast by the declining sun on
the dial of Ahaz turn back ten steps.' So
the sun turned back on the dial the ten
steps by which it had declined.[f]

9 A writing of King Hezekiah of Judah, after he had been sick and had recovered from his sickness:
10 I said: In the noontide of my days
I must depart;
I am consigned to the gates of Sheol
for the rest of my years.
11 I said, I shall not see the LORD
in the land of the living;
I shall look upon mortals no more
among the inhabitants
of the world.
12 My dwelling is plucked up and
removed from me
like a shepherd's tent;
like a weaver I have rolled up my life;
he cuts me off from the loom;

[d] 37.27 With 2 Kings 19.26: Heb *field* [e] 37.28 Q Ms Gk: MT lacks *your rising up* [f] 38.8 Meaning of Heb uncertain

from day to night you bring
me to an end;[g]
13 I cry for help[h] until morning;
like a lion he breaks all my bones;
from day to night you bring
me to an end.[i]

14 Like a swallow or a crane[j] I clamour,
I moan like a dove.
My eyes are weary with
looking upwards.
O Lord, I am oppressed;
be my security!
15 But what can I say? For he
has spoken to me,
and he himself has done it.
All my sleep has fled[k]
because of the bitterness
of my soul.

16 O Lord, by these things people live,
and in all these is the life
of my spirit.[l]
O restore me to health and
make me live!
17 Surely it was for my welfare
that I had great bitterness;
but you have held back[m] my life
from the pit of destruction,
for you have cast all my sins
behind your back.
18 For Sheol cannot thank you,
death cannot praise you;
those who go down to the
Pit cannot hope
for your faithfulness.
19 The living, the living, they
thank you,
as I do this day;
fathers make known to children
your faithfulness.

20 The LORD will save me,
and we will sing to stringed
instruments[n]
all the days of our lives,
at the house of the LORD.

21 Now Isaiah had said, 'Let them
take a lump of figs, and apply it to the
boil, so that he may recover.' 22Hezekiah
also had said, 'What is the sign that I
shall go up to the house of the LORD?'

ENVOYS FROM BABYLON WELCOMED

39 At that time King Merodach-
baladan son of Baladan of Babylon sent envoys with letters and a present to Hezekiah, for he heard that he
had been sick and had recovered. 2Hez-
ekiah welcomed them; he showed them
his treasure-house, the silver, the gold,
the spices, the precious oil, his whole
armoury, all that was found in his storehouses. There was nothing in his house
or in all his realm that Hezekiah did
not show them. 3Then the prophet Isaiah came to King Hezekiah and said to
him, 'What did these men say? From
where did they come to you?' Hezekiah
answered, 'They have come to me from
a far country, from Babylon.' 4He said,
'What have they seen in your house?'
Hezekiah answered, 'They have seen all
that is in my house; there is nothing
in my storehouses that I did not show
them.'

5 Then Isaiah said to Hezekiah, 'Hear
the word of the LORD of hosts: 6Days are
coming when all that is in your house,
and that which your ancestors have
stored up until this day, shall be carried
to Babylon; nothing shall be left, says
the LORD. 7Some of your own sons who
are born to you shall be taken away;
they shall be eunuchs in the palace of
the king of Babylon.' 8Then Hezekiah
said to Isaiah, 'The word of the LORD
that you have spoken is good.' For he
thought, 'There will be peace and security in my days.'

GOD'S PEOPLE ARE COMFORTED

40 Comfort, O comfort my people,
says your God.
2 Speak tenderly to Jerusalem,
and cry to her
that she has served her term,
that her penalty is paid,
that she has received from
the LORD's hand
double for all her sins.

3 A voice cries out:
'In the wilderness prepare the
way of the LORD,
make straight in the desert a
highway for our God.
4 Every valley shall be lifted up,
and every mountain and
hill be made low;
the uneven ground shall
become level,
and the rough places a plain.

[g] 38.12 Meaning of Heb uncertain [h] 38.13 Cn: Meaning of Heb uncertain [i] 38.13 Meaning of Heb uncertain [j] 38.14 Meaning of Heb uncertain [k] 38.15 Cn Compare Syr: Heb *I will walk slowly all my years* [l] 38.16 Meaning of Heb uncertain [m] 38.17 Cn Compare Gk Vg: Heb *loved* [n] 38.20 Heb *my stringed instruments*

5 Then the glory of the LORD
shall be revealed,
and all people shall see it together,
for the mouth of the LORD
has spoken.'

6 A voice says, 'Cry out!'
And I said, 'What shall I cry?'
All people are grass,
their constancy is like the
flower of the field.
7 The grass withers, the flower fades,
when the breath of the LORD
blows upon it;
surely the people are grass.
8 The grass withers, the flower fades;
but the word of our God
will stand for ever.
9 Get you up to a high mountain,
O Zion, herald of good tidings;[o]
lift up your voice with strength,
O Jerusalem, herald of good tidings,[p]
lift it up, do not fear;
say to the cities of Judah,
'Here is your God!'
10 See, the Lord GOD comes with might,
and his arm rules for him;
his reward is with him,
and his recompense before him.
11 He will feed his flock like a shepherd;
he will gather the lambs
in his arms,
and carry them in his bosom,
and gently lead the mother sheep.

12 Who has measured the waters in
the hollow of his hand
and marked off the heavens
with a span,
enclosed the dust of the earth
in a measure,
and weighed the mountains
in scales
and the hills in a balance?
13 Who has directed the spirit
of the LORD,
or as his counsellor has
instructed him?
14 Whom did he consult for his
enlightenment,
and who taught him the
path of justice?
Who taught him knowledge,
and showed him the way of
understanding?
15 Even the nations are like a
drop from a bucket,
and are accounted as dust
on the scales;
see, he takes up the isles
like fine dust.
16 Lebanon would not provide
fuel enough,
nor are its animals enough
for a burnt-offering.
17 All the nations are as nothing
before him;
they are accounted by him as less
than nothing and emptiness.

18 To whom then will you liken God,
or what likeness compare
with him?
19 An idol? —A workman casts it,
and a goldsmith overlays
it with gold,
and casts for it silver chains.
20 As a gift one chooses
mulberry wood[q]
—wood that will not rot—
then seeks out a skilled artisan
to set up an image that
will not topple.

21 Have you not known? Have
you not heard?
Has it not been told you
from the beginning?
Have you not understood from
the foundations of the earth?
22 It is he who sits above the
circle of the earth,
and its inhabitants are like
grasshoppers;
who stretches out the heavens
like a curtain,
and spreads them like a
tent to live in;
23 who brings princes to naught,
and makes the rulers of the
earth as nothing.

24 Scarcely are they planted,
scarcely sown,
scarcely has their stem taken
root in the earth,
when he blows upon them,
and they wither,
and the tempest carries them
off like stubble.

25 To whom then will you compare me,
or who is my equal? says
the Holy One.
26 Lift up your eyes on high and see:
Who created these?
He who brings out their host
and numbers them,
calling them all by name;

o 40.9 Or *O herald of good tidings to Zion*
p 40.9 Or *O herald of good tidings to Jerusalem*
q 40.20 Meaning of Heb uncertain

because he is great in strength,
mighty in power,
not one is missing.

27 Why do you say, O Jacob,
and speak, O Israel,
'My way is hidden from the LORD,
and my right is disregarded
by my God'?
28 Have you not known? Have
you not heard?
The LORD is the everlasting God,
the Creator of the ends
of the earth.
He does not faint or grow weary;
his understanding is unsearchable.
29 He gives power to the faint,
and strengthens the powerless.
30 Even youths will faint and be weary,
and the young will fall exhausted;
31 but those who wait for the LORD
shall renew their strength,
they shall mount up with
wings like eagles,
they shall run and not be weary,
they shall walk and not faint.

ISRAEL ASSURED OF GOD'S HELP

41 Listen to me in silence,
O coastlands;
let the peoples renew
their strength;
let them approach, then let
them speak;
let us together draw near
for judgement.

2 Who has roused a victor
from the east,
summoned him to his service?
He delivers up nations to him,
and tramples kings under foot;
he makes them like dust
with his sword,
like driven stubble with his bow.
3 He pursues them and passes
on safely,
scarcely touching the path
with his feet.
4 Who has performed and done this,
calling the generations from
the beginning?
I, the LORD, am first,
and will be with the last.
5 The coastlands have seen
and are afraid,
the ends of the earth tremble;
they have drawn near and come.
6 Each one helps the other,
saying to one another,
'Take courage!'
7 The artisan encourages the
goldsmith,
and the one who smooths with
the hammer encourages the
one who strikes the anvil,
saying of the soldering, 'It is good';
and they fasten it with nails so
that it cannot be moved.
8 But you, Israel, my servant,
Jacob, whom I have chosen,
the offspring of Abraham,
my friend;
9 you whom I took from the
ends of the earth,
and called from its
farthest corners,
saying to you, 'You are my servant,
I have chosen you and
not cast you off';
10 do not fear, for I am with you,
do not be afraid, for I
am your God;
I will strengthen you, I will help you,
I will uphold you with my
victorious right hand.

11 Yes, all who are incensed
against you
shall be ashamed and disgraced;
those who strive against you
shall be as nothing and
shall perish.
12 You shall seek those who
contend with you,
but you shall not find them;
those who war against you
shall be as nothing at all.
13 For I, the LORD your God,
hold your right hand;
it is I who say to you, 'Do not fear,
I will help you.'

14 Do not fear, you worm Jacob,
you insect[r] Israel!
I will help you, says the LORD;
your Redeemer is the Holy
One of Israel.
15 Now, I will make of you a
threshing-sledge,
sharp, new, and having teeth;
you shall thresh the mountains
and crush them,
and you shall make the
hills like chaff.
16 You shall winnow them and the
wind shall carry them away,
and the tempest shall
scatter them.

[r] **41.14** Syr: Heb *men of*

Then you shall rejoice in the LORD;
in the Holy One of Israel
you shall glory.

17 When the poor and needy seek water,
and there is none,
and their tongue is parched
with thirst,
I the LORD will answer them,
I the God of Israel will not
forsake them.
18 I will open rivers on the
bare heights,[s]
and fountains in the midst
of the valleys;
I will make the wilderness
a pool of water,
and the dry land springs of water.
19 I will put in the wilderness the cedar,
the acacia, the myrtle,
and the olive;
I will set in the desert the cypress,
the plane and the pine together,
20 so that all may see and know,
all may consider and understand,
that the hand of the LORD
has done this,
the Holy One of Israel
has created it.

THE FUTILITY OF IDOLS

21 Set forth your case, says the LORD;
bring your proofs, says the
King of Jacob.
22 Let them bring them, and tell us
what is to happen.
Tell us the former things,
what they are,
so that we may consider them,
and that we may know
their outcome;
or declare to us the
things to come.
23 Tell us what is to come hereafter,
that we may know that
you are gods;
do good, or do harm,
that we may be afraid
and terrified.
24 You, indeed, are nothing
and your work is nothing at all;
whoever chooses you is
an abomination.

25 I stirred up one from the north,
and he has come,
from the rising of the sun he
was summoned by name.[t]
He shall trample[u] on rulers
as on mortar,
as the potter treads clay.
26 Who declared it from the beginning,
so that we might know,
and beforehand, so that we
might say, 'He is right'?
There was no one who declared it,
none who proclaimed,
none who heard your words.
27 I first have declared it to Zion,[v]
and I give to Jerusalem a
herald of good tidings.
28 But when I look there is no one;
among these there is
no counsellor
who, when I ask, gives an answer.
29 No, they are all a delusion;
their works are nothing;
their images are empty wind.

THE SERVANT, A LIGHT TO THE NATIONS

42 Here is my servant,
whom I uphold,
my chosen, in whom my
soul delights;
I have put my spirit upon him;
he will bring forth justice
to the nations.
2 He will not cry or lift up his voice,
or make it heard in the street;
3 a bruised reed he will not break,
and a dimly burning wick
he will not quench;
he will faithfully bring
forth justice.
4 He will not grow faint or be crushed
until he has established
justice in the earth;
and the coastlands wait
for his teaching.

5 Thus says God, the LORD,
who created the heavens and
stretched them out,
who spread out the earth and
what comes from it,
who gives breath to the
people upon it
and spirit to those who walk in it:
6 I am the LORD, I have called
you in righteousness,
I have taken you by the
hand and kept you;
I have given you as a covenant
to the people,[w]
a light to the nations,
7 to open the eyes that are blind,

[s] 41.18 Or *trails* [t] 41.25 Cn Compare Q Ms Gk: MT *and he shall call on my name* [u] 41.25 Cn: Heb *come* [v] 41.27 Cn: Heb *First to Zion—Behold, behold them* [w] 42.6 Meaning of Heb uncertain

to bring out the prisoners
from the dungeon,
from the prison those who
sit in darkness.
8 I am the LORD, that is my name;
my glory I give to no other,
nor my praise to idols.
9 See, the former things have
come to pass,
and new things I now declare;
before they spring forth,
I tell you of them.

A HYMN OF PRAISE

10 Sing to the LORD a new song,
his praise from the end
of the earth!
Let the sea roar[x] and all that fills it,
the coastlands and their
inhabitants.
11 Let the desert and its towns
lift up their voice,
the villages that Kedar inhabits;
let the inhabitants of Sela
sing for joy,
let them shout from the tops
of the mountains.
12 Let them give glory to the LORD,
and declare his praise in
the coastlands.
13 The LORD goes forth like a soldier,
like a warrior he stirs up his fury;
he cries out, he shouts aloud,
he shows himself mighty
against his foes.

14 For a long time I have
held my peace,
I have kept still and
restrained myself;
now I will cry out like a
woman in labour,
I will gasp and pant.
15 I will lay waste mountains and hills,
and dry up all their herbage;
I will turn the rivers into islands,
and dry up the pools.
16 I will lead the blind
by a road they do not know,
by paths they have not known
I will guide them.
I will turn the darkness before
them into light,
the rough places into level ground.
These are the things I will do,
and I will not forsake them.
17 They shall be turned back and
utterly put to shame—
those who trust in carved images,
who say to cast images,
'You are our gods.'

18 Listen, you that are deaf;
and you that are blind,
look up and see!
19 Who is blind but my servant,
or deaf like my messenger
whom I send?
Who is blind like my dedicated one,
or blind like the servant
of the LORD?
20 He sees many things, but does[y]
not observe them;
his ears are open, but he
does not hear.

ISRAEL'S DISOBEDIENCE

21 The LORD was pleased, for the sake
of his righteousness,
to magnify his teaching and
make it glorious.
22 But this is a people robbed
and plundered,
all of them are trapped in holes
and hidden in prisons;
they have become a prey with
no one to rescue,
a spoil with no one to
say, 'Restore!'
23 Who among you will give
heed to this,
who will attend and listen
for the time to come?
24 Who gave up Jacob to the spoiler,
and Israel to the robbers?
Was it not the LORD, against
whom we have sinned,
in whose ways they
would not walk,
and whose law they
would not obey?
25 So he poured upon him the
heat of his anger
and the fury of war;
it set him on fire all around, but
he did not understand;
it burned him, but he did
not take it to heart.

RESTORATION AND PROTECTION PROMISED

43 But now thus says the LORD,
he who created you, O Jacob,
he who formed you, O Israel:
Do not fear, for I have redeemed you;
I have called you by name,
you are mine.

[x] **42.10** Cn Compare Ps 96.11; 98.7: Heb *Those who go down to the sea* [y] **42.20** Heb *You see many things but do*

2 When you pass through the waters,
I will be with you;
and through the rivers, they
shall not overwhelm you;
when you walk through fire you
shall not be burned,
and the flame shall not
consume you.
3 For I am the LORD your God,
the Holy One of Israel,
your Saviour.
I give Egypt as your ransom,
Ethiopia[z] and Seba in
exchange for you.
4 Because you are precious in my sight,
and honoured, and I love you,
I give people in return for you,
nations in exchange for your life.
5 Do not fear, for I am with you;
I will bring your offspring
from the east,
and from the west I will
gather you;
6 I will say to the north, 'Give them up',
and to the south, 'Do
not withhold;
bring my sons from far away
and my daughters from the
end of the earth—
7 everyone who is called by my name,
whom I created for my glory,
whom I formed and made.'

8 Bring forth the people who are
blind, yet have eyes,
who are deaf, yet have ears!
9 Let all the nations gather together,
and let the peoples assemble.
Who among them declared this,
and foretold to us the
former things?
Let them bring their witnesses
to justify them,
and let them hear and
say, 'It is true.'
10 You are my witnesses, says
the LORD,
and my servant whom
I have chosen,
so that you may know and
believe me
and understand that I am he.
Before me no god was formed,
nor shall there be any after me.
11 I, I am the LORD,
and besides me there is no saviour.
12 I declared and saved and proclaimed,
when there was no strange
god among you;
and you are my witnesses,
says the LORD.
13 I am God, and also henceforth
I am He;
there is no one who can
deliver from my hand;
I work and who can hinder it?

14 Thus says the LORD,
your Redeemer, the Holy
One of Israel:
For your sake I will send to Babylon
and break down all the bars,
and the shouting of the
Chaldeans will be turned
to lamentation.[a]
15 I am the LORD, your Holy One,
the Creator of Israel, your King.
16 Thus says the LORD,
who makes a way in the sea,
a path in the mighty waters,
17 who brings out chariot and horse,
army and warrior;
they lie down, they cannot rise,
they are extinguished,
quenched like a wick:
18 Do not remember the former things,
or consider the things of old.
19 I am about to do a new thing;
now it springs forth, do you
not perceive it?
I will make a way in the wilderness
and rivers in the desert.
20 The wild animals will honour me,
the jackals and the ostriches;
for I give water in the wilderness,
rivers in the desert,
to give drink to my chosen people,
21 the people whom I formed
for myself
so that they might declare
my praise.

22 Yet you did not call upon
me, O Jacob;
but you have been weary
of me, O Israel!
23 You have not brought me your
sheep for burnt-offerings,
or honoured me with
your sacrifices.
I have not burdened you
with offerings,
or wearied you with
frankincense.
24 You have not bought me sweet
cane with money,
or satisfied me with the fat
of your sacrifices.

[z] 43.3 Or *Nubia*; Heb *Cush* [a] 43.14 Meaning of Heb uncertain

But you have burdened me
with your sins;
you have wearied me with
your iniquities.

25 I, I am He
who blots out your transgressions
for my own sake,
and I will not remember
your sins.
26 Accuse me, let us go to trial;
set forth your case, so that you
may be proved right.
27 Your first ancestor sinned,
and your interpreters
transgressed against me.
28 Therefore I profaned the princes
of the sanctuary,
I delivered Jacob to utter
destruction,
and Israel to reviling.

GOD'S BLESSING ON ISRAEL

44 But now hear, O Jacob
my servant,
Israel whom I have chosen!
2 Thus says the LORD who made you,
who formed you in the womb
and will help you:
Do not fear, O Jacob my servant,
Jeshurun whom I have chosen.
3 For I will pour water on the
thirsty land,
and streams on the dry ground;
I will pour my spirit upon
your descendants,
and my blessing on
your offspring.
4 They shall spring up like a
green tamarisk,
like willows by flowing streams.
5 This one will say, 'I am the LORD's',
another will be called by
the name of Jacob,
yet another will write on the
hand, 'The LORD's',
and adopt the name of Israel.

6 Thus says the LORD, the
King of Israel
and his Redeemer, the
LORD of hosts:
I am the first and I am the last;
besides me there is no god.
7 Who is like me? Let them
proclaim it,
let them declare and set it
forth before me.
Who has announced from of old
the things to come?[b]
Let them tell us[c] what is yet to be.
8 Do not fear, or be afraid;
have I not told you from of
old and declared it?
You are my witnesses!
Is there any god besides me?
There is no other rock; I
know not one.

THE ABSURDITY OF IDOL-WORSHIP

9 All who make idols are nothing,
and the things they delight in do not
profit; their witnesses neither see nor
know. And so they will be put to shame.
10 Who would fashion a god or cast an
image that can do no good? 11 Look, all
its devotees shall be put to shame; the
artisans too are merely human. Let
them all assemble, let them stand up;
they shall be terrified, they shall all be
put to shame.

12 The blacksmith fashions it[d] and
works it over the coals, shaping it
with hammers, and forging it with his
strong arm; he becomes hungry and his
strength fails, he drinks no water and is
faint. 13 The carpenter stretches a line,
marks it out with a stylus, fashions it
with planes, and marks it with a com-
pass; he makes it in human form, with
human beauty, to be set up in a shrine.
14 He cuts down cedars or chooses a holm
tree or an oak and lets it grow strong
among the trees of the forest. He plants
a cedar and the rain nourishes it. 15 Then
it can be used as fuel. Part of it he takes
and warms himself; he kindles a fire
and bakes bread. Then he makes a god
and worships it, makes it a carved image and bows down before it. 16 Half of
it he burns in the fire; over this half he
roasts meat, eats it, and is satisfied. He
also warms himself and says, 'Ah, I am
warm, I can feel the fire!' 17 The rest of
it he makes into a god, his idol, bows
down to it, and worships it; he prays
to it and says, 'Save me, for you are my
god!'

18 They do not know, nor do they
comprehend; for their eyes are shut, so
that they cannot see, and their minds
as well, so that they cannot understand.
19 No one considers, nor is there knowledge or discernment to say, 'Half of it I
burned in the fire; I also baked bread on
its coals, I roasted meat and have eaten.
Now shall I make the rest of it an abomination? Shall I fall down before a block
of wood?' 20 He feeds on ashes; a deluded

[b] **44.7** Cn: Heb *from my placing an eternal people and things to come* [c] **44.7** Tg: Heb *them*
[d] **44.12** Cn: Heb *an axe*

mind has led him astray, and he cannot save himself or say, 'Is not this thing in my right hand a fraud?'

ISRAEL IS NOT FORGOTTEN

21 Remember these things, O Jacob,
and Israel, for you are my servant;
I formed you, you are my servant;
O Israel, you will not be
forgotten by me.
22 I have swept away your
transgressions like a cloud,
and your sins like mist;
return to me, for I have
redeemed you.

23 Sing, O heavens, for the
LORD has done it;
shout, O depths of the earth;
break forth into singing,
O mountains,
O forest, and every tree in it!
For the LORD has redeemed Jacob,
and will be glorified in Israel.

24 Thus says the LORD, your Redeemer,
who formed you in the womb:
I am the LORD, who made all things,
who alone stretched out
the heavens,
who by myself spread
out the earth;
25 who frustrates the omens of liars,
and makes fools of diviners;
who turns back the wise,
and makes their knowledge
foolish;
26 who confirms the word of
his servant,
and fulfils the prediction
of his messengers;
who says of Jerusalem, 'It
shall be inhabited',
and of the cities of Judah,
'They shall be rebuilt,
and I will raise up their ruins';
27 who says to the deep, 'Be dry—
I will dry up your rivers';
28 who says of Cyrus, 'He is
my shepherd,
and he shall carry out all
my purpose';
and who says of Jerusalem,
'It shall be rebuilt',
and of the temple, 'Your
foundation shall be laid.'

CYRUS, GOD'S INSTRUMENT

45 Thus says the LORD to his
anointed, to Cyrus,
whose right hand I have grasped
to subdue nations before him
and strip kings of their robes,
to open doors before him—
and the gates shall not be closed:
2 I will go before you
and level the mountains,[e]
I will break in pieces the
doors of bronze
and cut through the bars of iron,
3 I will give you the treasures
of darkness
and riches hidden in secret places,
so that you may know that
it is I, the LORD,
the God of Israel, who call
you by your name.
4 For the sake of my servant Jacob,
and Israel my chosen,
I call you by your name,
I surname you, though you
do not know me.
5 I am the LORD, and there is no other;
besides me there is no god.
I arm you, though you do
not know me,
6 so that they may know, from
the rising of the sun
and from the west, that there
is no one besides me;
I am the LORD, and there
is no other.
7 I form light and create darkness,
I make weal and create woe;
I the LORD do all these things.

8 Shower, O heavens, from above,
and let the skies rain down
righteousness;
let the earth open, that salvation
may spring up,[f]
and let it cause righteousness
to sprout up also;
I the LORD have created it.

9 Woe to you who strive with
your Maker,
earthen vessels with the potter![g]
Does the clay say to the one
who fashions it, 'What
are you making?'
or 'Your work has no handles'?
10 Woe to anyone who says to a father,
'What are you begetting?'
or to a woman, 'With what
are you in labour?'

[e] **45.2** Q Ms Gk: MT *the swellings* [f] **45.8** Q Ms: MT *that they may bring forth salvation*
[g] **45.9** Cn: Heb *with the potsherds, or with the potters*

11 Thus says the LORD,
the Holy One of Israel,
and its Maker:
Will you question me[h] about
my children,
or command me concerning
the work of my hands?
12 I made the earth,
and created humankind upon it;
it was my hands that stretched
out the heavens,
and I commanded all their host.
13 I have aroused Cyrus[i] in
righteousness,
and I will make all his
paths straight;
he shall build my city
and set my exiles free,
not for price or reward,
says the LORD of hosts.
14 Thus says the LORD:
The wealth of Egypt and the
merchandise of Ethiopia,[j]
and the Sabeans, tall of stature,
shall come over to you and be yours,
they shall follow you;
they shall come over in chains
and bow down to you.
They will make supplication
to you, saying,
'God is with you alone, and
there is no other;
there is no god besides him.'
15 Truly, you are a God who
hides himself,
O God of Israel, the Saviour.
16 All of them are put to shame
and confounded,
the makers of idols go in
confusion together.
17 But Israel is saved by the LORD
with everlasting salvation;
you shall not be put to shame
or confounded
to all eternity.

18 For thus says the LORD,
who created the heavens
(he is God!),
who formed the earth and made it
(he established it;
he did not create it a chaos,
he formed it to be inhabited!):
I am the LORD, and there
is no other.
19 I did not speak in secret,
in a land of darkness;
I did not say to the offspring of Jacob,
'Seek me in chaos.'
I the LORD speak the truth,
I declare what is right.

IDOLS CANNOT SAVE BABYLON

20 Assemble yourselves and
come together,
draw near, you survivors
of the nations!
They have no knowledge—
those who carry about their
wooden idols,
and keep on praying to a god
that cannot save.
21 Declare and present your case;
let them take counsel together!
Who told this long ago?
Who declared it of old?
Was it not I, the LORD?
There is no other god besides me,
a righteous God and a Saviour;
there is no one besides me.

22 Turn to me and be saved,
all the ends of the earth!
For I am God, and there
is no other.
23 By myself I have sworn,
from my mouth has gone
forth in righteousness
a word that shall not return:
'To me every knee shall bow,
every tongue shall swear.'

24 Only in the LORD, it shall
be said of me,
are righteousness and strength;
all who were incensed against him
shall come to him and
be ashamed.
25 In the LORD all the offspring of Israel
shall triumph and glory.

46 Bel bows down, Nebo stoops,
their idols are on beasts
and cattle;
these things you carry are loaded
as burdens on weary animals.
2 They stoop, they bow down together;
they cannot save the burden,
but themselves go into captivity.

3 Listen to me, O house of Jacob,
all the remnant of the
house of Israel,
who have been borne by me
from your birth,
carried from the womb;
4 even to your old age I am he,
even when you turn grey
I will carry you.

[h] 45.11 Cn: Heb *Ask me of things to come*
[i] 45.13 Heb *him* [j] 45.14 Or *Nubia*; Heb *Cush*

I have made, and I will bear;
I will carry and will save.

5 To whom will you liken me
and make me equal,
and compare me, as though
we were alike?
6 Those who lavish gold from
the purse,
and weigh out silver in
the scales—
they hire a goldsmith, who
makes it into a god;
then they fall down and worship!
7 They lift it to their shoulders,
they carry it,
they set it in its place, and
it stands there;
it cannot move from its place.
If one cries out to it, it does
not answer
or save anyone from trouble.

8 Remember this and consider,[k]
recall it to mind, you
transgressors,
9 remember the former
things of old;
for I am God, and there is no other;
I am God, and there is
no one like me,
10 declaring the end from the
beginning
and from ancient times
things not yet done,
saying, 'My purpose shall stand,
and I will fulfil my intention',
11 calling a bird of prey from the east,
the man for my purpose
from a far country.
I have spoken, and I will
bring it to pass;
I have planned, and I will do it.

12 Listen to me, you stubborn of heart,
you who are far from deliverance:
13 I bring near my deliverance,
it is not far off,
and my salvation will not tarry;
I will put salvation in Zion,
for Israel my glory.

THE HUMILIATION OF BABYLON

47 Come down and sit in the dust,
virgin daughter Babylon!
Sit on the ground without a throne,
daughter Chaldea!
For you shall no more be called
tender and delicate.
2 Take the millstones and grind meal,
remove your veil,
strip off your robe, uncover your legs,
pass through the rivers.
3 Your nakedness shall be uncovered,
and your shame shall be seen.
I will take vengeance,
and I will spare no one.
4 Our Redeemer—the LORD of
hosts is his name—
is the Holy One of Israel.

5 Sit in silence, and go into darkness,
daughter Chaldea!
For you shall no more be called
the mistress of kingdoms.
6 I was angry with my people,
I profaned my heritage;
I gave them into your hand,
you showed them no mercy;
on the aged you made your yoke
exceedingly heavy.
7 You said, 'I shall be mistress for ever',
so that you did not lay these
things to heart
or remember their end.

8 Now therefore hear this, you
lover of pleasures,
who sit securely,
who say in your heart,
'I am, and there is no
one besides me;
I shall not sit as a widow
or know the loss of children'—
9 both these things shall
come upon you
in a moment, in one day:
the loss of children and widowhood
shall come upon you in
full measure,
in spite of your many sorceries
and the great power of your
enchantments.

10 You felt secure in your wickedness;
you said, 'No one sees me.'
Your wisdom and your knowledge
led you astray,
and you said in your heart,
'I am, and there is no one
besides me.'
11 But evil shall come upon you,
which you cannot charm away;
disaster shall fall upon you,
which you will not be
able to ward off;
and ruin shall come on
you suddenly,
of which you know nothing.

[k] 46.8 Meaning of Heb uncertain

12 Stand fast in your enchantments
and your many sorceries,
with which you have laboured
from your youth;
perhaps you may be able to succeed,
perhaps you may inspire terror.
13 You are wearied with your
many consultations;
let those who study[l] the heavens
stand up and save you,
those who gaze at the stars
and at each new moon predict
what[m] shall befall you.

14 See, they are like stubble,
the fire consumes them;
they cannot deliver themselves
from the power of the flame.
No coal for warming oneself is this,
no fire to sit before!
15 Such to you are those with whom
you have laboured,
who have trafficked with
you from your youth;
they all wander about in
their own paths;
there is no one to save you.

GOD THE CREATOR AND REDEEMER

48 Hear this, O house of Jacob,
who are called by the
name of Israel,
and who came forth from
the loins[n] of Judah;
who swear by the name
of the LORD,
and invoke the God of Israel,
but not in truth or right.
2 For they call themselves after
the holy city,
and lean on the God of Israel;
the LORD of hosts is his name.

3 The former things I declared
long ago,
they went out from my mouth
and I made them known;
then suddenly I did them and
they came to pass.
4 Because I know that you
are obstinate,
and your neck is an iron sinew
and your forehead brass,
5 I declared them to you
from long ago,
before they came to pass I
announced them to you,
so that you would not say,
'My idol did them,
my carved image and my cast
image commanded them.'
6 You have heard; now see all this;
and will you not declare it?
From this time forward I make
you hear new things,
hidden things that you
have not known.
7 They are created now, not long ago;
before today you have never
heard of them,
so that you could not say, 'I
already knew them.'
8 You have never heard, you
have never known,
from of old your ear has
not been opened.
For I knew that you would deal
very treacherously,
and that from birth you
were called a rebel.

9 For my name's sake I defer my anger,
for the sake of my praise I
restrain it for you,
so that I may not cut you off.
10 See, I have refined you, but
not like[o] silver;
I have tested you in the
furnace of adversity.
11 For my own sake, for my
own sake, I do it,
for why should my name[p]
be profaned?
My glory I will not give to another.

12 Listen to me, O Jacob,
and Israel, whom I called:
I am He; I am the first,
and I am the last.
13 My hand laid the foundation
of the earth,
and my right hand spread
out the heavens;
when I summon them,
they stand at attention.

14 Assemble, all of you, and hear!
Who among them has
declared these things?
The LORD loves him;
he shall perform his purpose
on Babylon,
and his arm shall be against
the Chaldeans.
15 I, even I, have spoken and
called him,
I have brought him, and he
will prosper in his way.

[l] **47.13** Meaning of Heb uncertain [m] **47.13** Gk Syr Compare Vg: Heb *from what* [n] **48.1** Cn: Heb *waters* [o] **48.10** Cn: Heb *with* [p] **48.11** Gk Old Latin: Heb *for why should it*

16 Draw near to me, hear this!
From the beginning I have
not spoken in secret,
from the time it came to be
I have been there.
And now the Lord GOD has sent
me and his spirit.

17 Thus says the LORD,
your Redeemer, the Holy
One of Israel:
I am the LORD your God,
who teaches you for your
own good,
who leads you in the way
you should go.
18 O that you had paid attention to
my commandments!
Then your prosperity would
have been like a river,
and your success like the
waves of the sea;
19 your offspring would have
been like the sand,
and your descendants
like its grains;
their name would never be cut off
or destroyed from before me.

20 Go out from Babylon, flee
from Chaldea,
declare this with a shout
of joy, proclaim it,
send it forth to the end
of the earth;
say, 'The LORD has redeemed
his servant Jacob!'
21 They did not thirst when he led
them through the deserts;
he made water flow for
them from the rock;
he split open the rock and the
water gushed out.

22 'There is no peace', says the
LORD, 'for the wicked.'

THE SERVANT'S MISSION

49 Listen to me, O coastlands,
pay attention, you peoples
from far away!
The LORD called me before
I was born,
while I was in my mother's
womb he named me.
2 He made my mouth like a
sharp sword,
in the shadow of his hand
he hid me;
he made me a polished arrow,
in his quiver he hid me away.
3 And he said to me, 'You are
my servant,
Israel, in whom I will be glorified.'
4 But I said, 'I have laboured in vain,
I have spent my strength for
nothing and vanity;
yet surely my cause is with
the LORD,
and my reward with my God.'

5 And now the LORD says,
who formed me in the womb
to be his servant,
to bring Jacob back to him,
and that Israel might be
gathered to him,
for I am honoured in the
sight of the LORD,
and my God has become
my strength—
6 he says,
'It is too light a thing that you
should be my servant
to raise up the tribes of Jacob
and to restore the survivors
of Israel;
I will give you as a light to
the nations,
that my salvation may reach
to the end of the earth.'

7 Thus says the LORD,
the Redeemer of Israel
and his Holy One,
to one deeply despised, abhorred
by the nations,
the slave of rulers,
'Kings shall see and stand up,
princes, and they shall
prostrate themselves,
because of the LORD, who is faithful,
the Holy One of Israel, who
has chosen you.'

ZION'S CHILDREN TO BE BROUGHT HOME

8 Thus says the LORD:
In a time of favour I have
answered you,
on a day of salvation I
have helped you;
I have kept you and given you
as a covenant to the people,[q]
to establish the land,
to apportion the desolate
heritages;
9 saying to the prisoners, 'Come out',
to those who are in darkness,
'Show yourselves.'

[q] 49.8 Meaning of Heb uncertain

They shall feed along the ways,
on all the bare heights[r] shall
be their pasture;
10 they shall not hunger or thirst,
neither scorching wind nor sun
shall strike them down,
for he who has pity on them
will lead them,
and by springs of water
will guide them.
11 And I will turn all my mountains
into a road,
and my highways shall be raised up.
12 Lo, these shall come from far away,
and lo, these from the north
and from the west,
and these from the land of Syene.[s]

13 Sing for joy, O heavens, and
exult, O earth;
break forth, O mountains,
into singing!
For the LORD has comforted
his people,
and will have compassion on
his suffering ones.

14 But Zion said, 'The LORD has
forsaken me,
my Lord has forgotten me.'
15 Can a woman forget her
nursing-child,
or show no compassion for the
child of her womb?
Even these may forget,
yet I will not forget you.
16 See, I have inscribed you on the
palms of my hands;
your walls are continually
before me.
17 Your builders outdo your destroyers,[t]
and those who laid you waste
go away from you.
18 Lift up your eyes all around and see;
they all gather, they come to you.
As I live, says the LORD,
you shall put all of them on
like an ornament,
and like a bride you shall
bind them on.

19 Surely your waste and your
desolate places
and your devastated land—
surely now you will be too crowded
for your inhabitants,
and those who swallowed you
up will be far away.
20 The children born in the time
of your bereavement
will yet say in your hearing:
'The place is too crowded for me;
make room for me to settle.'
21 Then you will say in your heart,
'Who has borne me these?
I was bereaved and barren,
exiled and put away—
so who has reared these?
I was left all alone—
where then have these
come from?'

22 Thus says the Lord GOD:
I will soon lift up my hand
to the nations,
and raise my signal to the peoples;
and they shall bring your sons
in their bosom,
and your daughters shall be
carried on their shoulders.
23 Kings shall be your foster-fathers,
and their queens your
nursing-mothers.
With their faces to the ground they
shall bow down to you,
and lick the dust of your feet.
Then you will know that I
am the LORD;
those who wait for me shall
not be put to shame.

24 Can the prey be taken from
the mighty,
or the captives of a tyrant[u]
be rescued?
25 But thus says the LORD:
Even the captives of the mighty
shall be taken,
and the prey of the tyrant
be rescued;
for I will contend with those
who contend with you,
and I will save your children.
26 I will make your oppressors
eat their own flesh,
and they shall be drunk with their
own blood as with wine.
Then all flesh shall know
that I am the LORD your Saviour,
and your Redeemer, the
Mighty One of Jacob.

50 Thus says the LORD:
Where is your mother's
bill of divorce
with which I put her away?
Or which of my creditors is it
to whom I have sold you?

[r] 49.9 *Or the trails* [s] 49.12 Q Ms: MT *Sinim*
[t] 49.17 Or *Your children come swiftly; your destroyers* [u] 49.24 Q Ms Syr Vg: MT *of a righteous person*

No, because of your sins
you were sold,
and for your transgressions your
mother was put away.
2 Why was no one there when I came?
Why did no one answer
when I called?
Is my hand shortened, that
it cannot redeem?
Or have I no power to deliver?
By my rebuke I dry up the sea,
I make the rivers a desert;
their fish stink for lack of water,
and die of thirst.[v]
3 I clothe the heavens with blackness,
and make sackcloth
their covering.

THE SERVANT'S HUMILIATION AND VINDICATION

4 The Lord GOD has given me
the tongue of a teacher,[w]
that I may know how to sustain
the weary with a word.
Morning by morning he wakens—
wakens my ear
to listen as those who are taught.
5 The Lord GOD has opened my ear,
and I was not rebellious,
I did not turn backwards.
6 I gave my back to those
who struck me,
and my cheeks to those who
pulled out the beard;
I did not hide my face
from insult and spitting.

7 The Lord GOD helps me;
therefore I have not been
disgraced;
therefore I have set my
face like flint,
and I know that I shall not
be put to shame;
8 he who vindicates me is near.
Who will contend with me?
Let us stand up together.
Who are my adversaries?
Let them confront me.
9 It is the Lord GOD who helps me;
who will declare me guilty?
All of them will wear out
like a garment;
the moth will eat them up.

10 Who among you fears the LORD
and obeys the voice of his servant,
who walks in darkness
and has no light,
yet trusts in the name of the LORD
and relies upon his God?
11 But all of you are kindlers of fire,
lighters of firebrands.[x]
Walk in the flame of your fire,
and among the brands that
you have kindled!
This is what you shall have
from my hand:
you shall lie down in torment.

BLESSINGS IN STORE FOR GOD'S PEOPLE

51 Listen to me, you that
pursue righteousness,
you that seek the LORD.
Look to the rock from which
you were hewn,
and to the quarry from
which you were dug.
2 Look to Abraham your father
and to Sarah who bore you;
for he was but one when
I called him,
but I blessed him and
made him many.
3 For the LORD will comfort Zion;
he will comfort all her
waste places,
and will make her wilderness
like Eden,
her desert like the garden
of the LORD;
joy and gladness will be found in her,
thanksgiving and the
voice of song.

4 Listen to me, my people,
and give heed to me, my nation;
for a teaching will go out from me,
and my justice for a light
to the peoples.
5 I will bring near my
deliverance swiftly,
my salvation has gone out
and my arms will rule the peoples;
the coastlands wait for me,
and for my arm they hope.
6 Lift up your eyes to the heavens,
and look at the earth beneath;
for the heavens will vanish
like smoke,
the earth will wear out
like a garment,
and those who live on it
will die like gnats;[y]
but my salvation will be for ever,
and my deliverance will
never be ended.

[v] 50.2 *Or die on the thirsty ground* [w] 50.4 Cn: Heb *of those who are taught* [x] 50.11 Syr: Heb *you gird yourselves with firebrands* [y] 51.6 *Or in like manner*

7 Listen to me, you who know
righteousness,
you people who have my
teaching in your hearts;
do not fear the reproach of others,
and do not be dismayed
when they revile you.
8 For the moth will eat them
up like a garment,
and the worm will eat
them like wool;
but my deliverance will be for ever,
and my salvation to all
generations.

9 Awake, awake, put on strength,
O arm of the LORD!
Awake, as in days of old,
the generations of long ago!
Was it not you who cut
Rahab in pieces,
who pierced the dragon?
10 Was it not you who dried up the sea,
the waters of the great deep;
who made the depths of
the sea a way
for the redeemed to cross over?
11 So the ransomed of the LORD
shall return,
and come to Zion with singing;
everlasting joy shall be upon
their heads;
they shall obtain joy and gladness,
and sorrow and sighing
shall flee away.

12 I, I am he who comforts you;
why then are you afraid of a mere
mortal who must die,
a human being who fades
like grass?
13 You have forgotten the LORD,
your Maker,
who stretched out the heavens
and laid the foundations
of the earth.
You fear continually all day long
because of the fury of
the oppressor,
who is bent on destruction.
But where is the fury of
the oppressor?
14 The oppressed shall speedily
be released;
they shall not die and go
down to the Pit,
nor shall they lack bread.
15 For I am the LORD your God,
who stirs up the sea so that
its waves roar—
the LORD of hosts is his name.
16 I have put my words in your mouth,
and hidden you in the
shadow of my hand,
stretching out[z] the heavens
and laying the foundations
of the earth,
and saying to Zion, 'You
are my people.'

17 Rouse yourself, rouse yourself!
Stand up, O Jerusalem,
you who have drunk at the
hand of the LORD
the cup of his wrath,
who have drunk to the dregs
the bowl of staggering.
18 There is no one to guide her
among all the children
she has borne;
there is no one to take her
by the hand
among all the children she
has brought up.
19 These two things have befallen you
—who will grieve with you?—
devastation and destruction,
famine and sword—
who will comfort you?[a]
20 Your children have fainted,
they lie at the head of every street
like an antelope in a net;
they are full of the wrath
of the LORD,
the rebuke of your God.

21 Therefore hear this, you who
are wounded,[b]
who are drunk, but not with wine:
22 Thus says your Sovereign, the LORD,
your God who pleads the
cause of his people:
See, I have taken from your hand
the cup of staggering;
you shall drink no more
from the bowl of my wrath.
23 And I will put it into the hand
of your tormentors,
who have said to you,
'Bow down, that we may
walk on you';
and you have made your back
like the ground
and like the street for
them to walk on.

LET ZION REJOICE

52 Awake, awake,
put on your strength, O Zion!

[z] 51.16 Syr: Heb *planting* [a] 51.19 Q Ms Gk Syr Vg: MT *how may I comfort you?* [b] 51.21 Or *humbled*

Put on your beautiful garments,
O Jerusalem, the holy city;
for the uncircumcised and the unclean
shall enter you no more.
2 Shake yourself from the dust, rise up,
O captive[c] Jerusalem;
loose the bonds from your neck,
O captive daughter Zion!

3 For thus says the LORD: You were
sold for nothing, and you shall be redeemed without money. 4For thus says
the Lord GOD: Long ago, my people
went down into Egypt to reside there as
aliens; the Assyrian, too, has oppressed
them without cause. 5Now therefore,
what am I doing here, says the LORD,
seeing that my people are taken away
without cause? Their rulers howl, says
the LORD, and continually, all day long,
my name is despised. 6Therefore my
people shall know my name; therefore
on that day they shall know that it is I
who speak; here am I.

7 How beautiful upon the mountains
are the feet of the messenger
who announces peace,
who brings good news,
who announces salvation,
who says to Zion, 'Your God reigns.'
8 Listen! Your sentinels lift
up their voices,
together they sing for joy;
for in plain sight they see
the return of the LORD to Zion.
9 Break forth together into singing,
you ruins of Jerusalem;
for the LORD has comforted his people,
he has redeemed Jerusalem.
10 The LORD has bared his holy arm
before the eyes of all the nations;
and all the ends of the earth shall see
the salvation of our God.

11 Depart, depart, go out from there!
Touch no unclean thing;
go out from the midst of it,
purify yourselves,
you who carry the vessels
of the LORD.
12 For you shall not go out in haste,
and you shall not go in flight;
for the LORD will go before you,
and the God of Israel will be
your rearguard.

THE SUFFERING SERVANT

13 See, my servant shall prosper;
he shall be exalted and lifted up,
and shall be very high.
14 Just as there were many who were
astonished at him[d]
—so marred was his appearance,
beyond human semblance,
and his form beyond that
of mortals—
15 so he shall startle[e] many nations;
kings shall shut their mouths
because of him;
for that which had not been told
them they shall see,
and that which they had not heard
they shall contemplate.

53 Who has believed what
we have heard?
And to whom has the arm of
the LORD been revealed?
2 For he grew up before him
like a young plant,
and like a root out of dry ground;
he had no form or majesty that
we should look at him,
nothing in his appearance that
we should desire him.
3 He was despised and rejected
by others;
a man of suffering[f] and
acquainted with infirmity;
and as one from whom others
hide their faces[g]
he was despised, and we held
him of no account.

4 Surely he has borne our infirmities
and carried our diseases;
yet we accounted him stricken,
struck down by God, and afflicted.
5 But he was wounded for our
transgressions,
crushed for our iniquities;
upon him was the punishment
that made us whole,
and by his bruises we are healed.
6 All we like sheep have gone astray;
we have all turned to
our own way,
and the LORD has laid on him
the iniquity of us all.

7 He was oppressed, and he
was afflicted,
yet he did not open his mouth;
like a lamb that is led to
the slaughter,
and like a sheep that before
its shearers is silent,
so he did not open his mouth.

[c] 52.2 Cn: Heb *rise up, sit* [d] 52.14 Syr Tg: Heb *you* [e] 52.15 Meaning of Heb uncertain [f] 53.3 Or *a man of sorrows* [g] 53.3 Or *as one who hides his face from us*

8 By a perversion of justice he
was taken away.
Who could have imagined
his future?
For he was cut off from the
land of the living,
stricken for the transgression
of my people.
9 They made his grave with the wicked
and his tomb[h] with the rich,[i]
although he had done no violence,
and there was no deceit
in his mouth.

10 Yet it was the will of the LORD to
crush him with pain.[j]
When you make his life an
offering for sin,[k]
he shall see his offspring, and
shall prolong his days;
through him the will of the
LORD shall prosper.
11 Out of his anguish he
shall see light;[l]
he shall find satisfaction through
his knowledge.
The righteous one,[m] my servant,
shall make many righteous,
and he shall bear their iniquities.
12 Therefore I will allot him a
portion with the great,
and he shall divide the spoil
with the strong;
because he poured out
himself to death,
and was numbered with
the transgressors;
yet he bore the sin of many,
and made intercession for
the transgressors.

THE ETERNAL COVENANT OF PEACE

54 Sing, O barren one who
did not bear;
burst into song and shout,
you who have not been in labour!
For the children of the desolate
woman will be more
than the children of her that is
married, says the LORD.
2 Enlarge the site of your tent,
and let the curtains of your
habitations be stretched out;
do not hold back; lengthen
your cords
and strengthen your stakes.
3 For you will spread out to the
right and to the left,
and your descendants will
possess the nations
and will settle the desolate towns.
4 Do not fear, for you will not
be ashamed;
do not be discouraged, for you
will not suffer disgrace;
for you will forget the shame
of your youth,
and the disgrace of your
widowhood you will
remember no more.
5 For your Maker is your husband,
the LORD of hosts is his name;
the Holy One of Israel is
your Redeemer,
the God of the whole earth
he is called.
6 For the LORD has called you
like a wife forsaken and
grieved in spirit,
like the wife of a man's youth
when she is cast off,
says your God.
7 For a brief moment I abandoned you,
but with great compassion
I will gather you.
8 In overflowing wrath for a moment
I hid my face from you,
but with everlasting love I will
have compassion on you,
says the LORD, your Redeemer.

9 This is like the days of Noah to me:
Just as I swore that the
waters of Noah
would never again go
over the earth,
so I have sworn that I will not
be angry with you
and will not rebuke you.
10 For the mountains may depart
and the hills be removed,
but my steadfast love shall not
depart from you,
and my covenant of peace
shall not be removed,
says the LORD, who has
compassion on you.

11 O afflicted one, storm-tossed,
and not comforted,
I am about to set your
stones in antimony,
and lay your foundations
with sapphires.[n]

[h] **53.9** Q Ms: MT *and in his death* [i] **53.9** Cn: Heb *with a rich person* [j] **53.10** Or *by disease*; meaning of Heb uncertain [k] **53.10** Meaning of Heb uncertain [l] **53.11** Q Mss: MT lacks *light* [m] **53.11** Or *and he shall find satisfaction. Through his knowledge, the righteous one* [n] **54.11** Or *lapis lazuli*

Great is your faithfulness.

LAMENTATIONS 3:23

The LORD is good, a stronghold on a day of trouble.

NAHUM 1:7

He will renew you in his love.

ZEPHANIAH 3:17

Mary's Song of Praise

My soul magnifies the Lord,
    and my spirit rejoices in God my Saviour,
for he has looked with favour on the lowliness
        of his servant.
    Surely, from now on all generations will call me
        blessed;
for the Mighty One has done great things for me,
    and holy is his name.
His mercy is for those who fear him
    from generation to generation.

Luke 1:46-50

12 I will make your pinnacles of rubies,
your gates of jewels,
and all your wall of precious stones.
13 All your children shall be
taught by the LORD,
and great shall be the prosperity
of your children.
14 In righteousness you shall
be established;
you shall be far from oppression,
for you shall not fear;
and from terror, for it shall
not come near you.
15 If anyone stirs up strife,
it is not from me;
whoever stirs up strife with you
shall fall because of you.
16 See, it is I who have created the smith
who blows the fire of coals,
and produces a weapon fit
for its purpose;
I have also created the ravager
to destroy.
17 No weapon that is fashioned
against you shall prosper,
and you shall confute every
tongue that rises against
you in judgement.
This is the heritage of the
servants of the LORD
and their vindication from
me, says the LORD.

AN INVITATION TO ABUNDANT LIFE

55 Ho, everyone who thirsts,
come to the waters;
and you that have no money,
come, buy and eat!
Come, buy wine and milk
without money and without price.
2 Why do you spend your money for
that which is not bread,
and your labour for that which
does not satisfy?
Listen carefully to me, and
eat what is good,
and delight yourselves
in rich food.
3 Incline your ear, and come to me;
listen, so that you may live.
I will make with you an
everlasting covenant,
my steadfast, sure love for David.
4 See, I made him a witness
to the peoples,
a leader and commander
for the peoples.
5 See, you shall call nations that
you do not know,
and nations that do not know
you shall run to you,
because of the LORD your God,
the Holy One of Israel,
for he has glorified you.

6 Seek the LORD while he
may be found,
call upon him while he is near;
7 let the wicked forsake their way,
and the unrighteous
their thoughts;
let them return to the LORD, that he
may have mercy on them,
and to our God, for he will
abundantly pardon.
8 For my thoughts are not
your thoughts,
nor are your ways my ways,
says the LORD.
9 For as the heavens are higher
than the earth,
so are my ways higher
than your ways
and my thoughts than
your thoughts.

10 For as the rain and the snow come
down from heaven,
and do not return there until they
have watered the earth,
making it bring forth and sprout,
giving seed to the sower and
bread to the eater,
11 so shall my word be that goes
out from my mouth;
it shall not return to me empty,
but it shall accomplish that
which I purpose,
and succeed in the thing
for which I sent it.

12 For you shall go out in joy,
and be led back in peace;
the mountains and the
hills before you
shall burst into song,
and all the trees of the field
shall clap their hands.
13 Instead of the thorn shall come
up the cypress;
instead of the brier shall
come up the myrtle;
and it shall be to the LORD
for a memorial,
for an everlasting sign that
shall not be cut off.

THE COVENANT EXTENDED TO ALL WHO OBEY

56 Thus says the LORD:
Maintain justice, and
do what is right,

for soon my salvation will come,
and my deliverance be revealed.

2 Happy is the mortal who does this,
the one who holds it fast,
who keeps the sabbath, not
profaning it,
and refrains from doing any evil.

3 Do not let the foreigner joined
to the LORD say,
'The LORD will surely separate
me from his people';
and do not let the eunuch say,
'I am just a dry tree.'
4 For thus says the LORD:
To the eunuchs who keep
my sabbaths,
who choose the things
that please me
and hold fast my covenant,
5 I will give, in my house and
within my walls,
a monument and a name
better than sons and daughters;
I will give them an
everlasting name
that shall not be cut off.

6 And the foreigners who join
themselves to the LORD,
to minister to him, to love the
name of the LORD,
and to be his servants,
all who keep the sabbath, and
do not profane it,
and hold fast my covenant—
7 these I will bring to my
holy mountain,
and make them joyful in
my house of prayer;
their burnt-offerings and
their sacrifices
will be accepted on my altar;
for my house shall be called
a house of prayer
for all peoples.
8 Thus says the Lord GOD,
who gathers the outcasts of Israel,
I will gather others to them
besides those already gathered.[o]

THE CORRUPTION OF ISRAEL'S RULERS

9 All you wild animals,
all you wild animals in the
forest, come to devour!
10 Israel's[p] sentinels are blind,
they are all without knowledge;
they are all silent dogs
that cannot bark;
dreaming, lying down,
loving to slumber.
11 The dogs have a mighty appetite;
they never have enough.
The shepherds also have no
understanding;
they have all turned to
their own way,
to their own gain, one and all.
12 'Come,' they say, 'let us[q] get wine;
let us fill ourselves with
strong drink.
And tomorrow will be like today,
great beyond measure.'

ISRAEL'S FUTILE IDOLATRY

57 The righteous perish,
and no one takes it to heart;
the devout are taken away,
while no one understands.
For the righteous are taken
away from calamity,
2 and they enter into peace;
those who walk uprightly
will rest on their couches.
3 But as for you, come here,
you children of a sorceress,
you offspring of an adulterer
and a whore.[r]
4 Whom are you mocking?
Against whom do you open
your mouth wide
and stick out your tongue?
Are you not children of
transgression,
the offspring of deceit—
5 you that burn with lust
among the oaks,
under every green tree;
you that slaughter your children
in the valleys,
under the clefts of the rocks?
6 Among the smooth stones of the
valley is your portion;
they, they, are your lot;
to them you have poured out
a drink-offering,
you have brought a grain-offering.
Shall I be appeased for
these things?
7 Upon a high and lofty mountain
you have set your bed,
and there you went up to
offer sacrifice.
8 Behind the door and the doorpost
you have set up your symbol;

[o] 56.8 Heb *besides his gathered ones*
[p] 56.10 Heb *His* [q] 56.12 Q Ms Syr Vg Tg: MT *me*
[r] 57.3 Heb *an adulterer and she plays the whore*

for, in deserting me,[s] you have
uncovered your bed,
you have gone up to it,
you have made it wide;
and you have made a bargain for
yourself with them,
you have loved their bed,
you have gazed on their nakedness.[t]
9 You journeyed to Molech[u] with oil,
and multiplied your perfumes;
you sent your envoys far away,
and sent down even to Sheol.
10 You grew weary from your
many wanderings,
but you did not say, 'It is useless.'
You found your desire rekindled,
and so you did not weaken.

11 Whom did you dread and fear
so that you lied,
and did not remember me
or give me a thought?
Have I not kept silent and
closed my eyes,[v]
and so you do not fear me?
12 I will concede your righteousness
and your works,
but they will not help you.
13 When you cry out, let your collection
of idols deliver you!
The wind will carry them off,
a breath will take them away.
But whoever takes refuge in me
shall possess the land
and inherit my holy mountain.

A PROMISE OF HELP AND HEALING

14 It shall be said,
'Build up, build up, prepare the way,
remove every obstruction
from my people's way.'
15 For thus says the high and lofty one
who inhabits eternity, whose
name is Holy:
I dwell in the high and holy place,
and also with those who are
contrite and humble in spirit,
to revive the spirit of the humble,
and to revive the heart
of the contrite.
16 For I will not continually accuse,
nor will I always be angry;
for then the spirits would grow
faint before me,
even the souls that I have made.
17 Because of their wicked
covetousness I was angry;
I struck them, I hid and
was angry;
but they kept turning back
to their own ways.
18 I have seen their ways, but I
will heal them;
I will lead them and repay
them with comfort,
creating for their mourners
the fruit of the lips.[w]
19 Peace, peace, to the far and the
near, says the LORD;
and I will heal them.
20 But the wicked are like the
tossing sea
that cannot keep still;
its waters toss up mire and mud.
21 There is no peace, says my
God, for the wicked.

FALSE AND TRUE WORSHIP

58 Shout out, do not hold back!
Lift up your voice like
a trumpet!
Announce to my people
their rebellion,
to the house of Jacob their sins.
2 Yet day after day they seek me
and delight to know my ways,
as if they were a nation that
practised righteousness
and did not forsake the
ordinance of their God;
they ask of me righteous
judgements,
they delight to draw near to God.
3 'Why do we fast, but you do not see?
Why humble ourselves, but
you do not notice?'
Look, you serve your own interest
on your fast-day,
and oppress all your workers.
4 Look, you fast only to quarrel
and to fight
and to strike with a wicked fist.
Such fasting as you do today
will not make your voice
heard on high.
5 Is such the fast that I choose,
a day to humble oneself?
Is it to bow down the head
like a bulrush,
and to lie in sackcloth and ashes?
Will you call this a fast,
a day acceptable to the LORD?

6 Is not this the fast that I choose:
to loose the bonds of injustice,
to undo the thongs of the yoke,
to let the oppressed go free,
and to break every yoke?

s 57.8 Meaning of Heb uncertain t 57.8 Or *their phallus*; Heb *the hand* u 57.9 Or *the king*
v 57.11 Gk Vg: Heb *silent even for a long time*
w 57.18 Meaning of Heb uncertain

7 Is it not to share your bread
with the hungry,
and bring the homeless poor
into your house;
when you see the naked,
to cover them,
and not to hide yourself
from your own kin?
8 Then your light shall break
forth like the dawn,
and your healing shall
spring up quickly;
your vindicator[x] shall go before you,
the glory of the LORD shall
be your rearguard.
9 Then you shall call, and the
LORD will answer;
you shall cry for help, and he
will say, Here I am.

If you remove the yoke from
among you,
the pointing of the finger,
the speaking of evil,
10 if you offer your food to the hungry
and satisfy the needs of
the afflicted,
then your light shall rise in
the darkness
and your gloom be like
the noonday.
11 The LORD will guide you continually,
and satisfy your needs in
parched places,
and make your bones strong;
and you shall be like a
watered garden,
like a spring of water,
whose waters never fail.
12 Your ancient ruins shall be rebuilt;
you shall raise up the foundations
of many generations;
you shall be called the repairer
of the breach,
the restorer of streets to live in.

13 If you refrain from trampling
the sabbath,
from pursuing your own
interests on my holy day;
if you call the sabbath a delight
and the holy day of the
LORD honourable;
if you honour it, not going
your own ways,
serving your own interests, or
pursuing your own affairs;[y]
14 then you shall take delight
in the LORD,
and I will make you ride upon
the heights of the earth;
I will feed you with the heritage
of your ancestor Jacob,
for the mouth of the LORD
has spoken.

INJUSTICE AND OPPRESSION TO BE PUNISHED

59 See, the LORD's hand is
not too short to save,
nor his ear too dull to hear.
2 Rather, your iniquities have
been barriers
between you and your God,
and your sins have hidden
his face from you
so that he does not hear.
3 For your hands are defiled with blood,
and your fingers with iniquity;
your lips have spoken lies,
your tongue mutters wickedness.
4 No one brings suit justly,
no one goes to law honestly;
they rely on empty pleas,
they speak lies,
conceiving mischief and
begetting iniquity.
5 They hatch adders' eggs,
and weave the spider's web;
whoever eats their eggs dies,
and the crushed egg hatches
out a viper.
6 Their webs cannot serve as clothing;
they cannot cover themselves
with what they make.
Their works are works of iniquity,
and deeds of violence are
in their hands.
7 Their feet run to evil,
and they rush to shed
innocent blood;
their thoughts are thoughts
of iniquity,
desolation and destruction
are in their highways.
8 The way of peace they do not know,
and there is no justice
in their paths.
Their roads they have made crooked;
no one who walks in them
knows peace.

9 Therefore justice is far from us,
and righteousness does
not reach us;
we wait for light, and lo!
there is darkness;
and for brightness, but we
walk in gloom.

x 58.8 Or *vindication* y 58.13 Heb *or speaking words*

10 We grope like the blind along a wall,
groping like those who
have no eyes;
we stumble at noon as in
the twilight,
among the vigorous[z] as
though we were dead.
11 We all growl like bears;
like doves we moan mournfully.
We wait for justice, but there is none;
for salvation, but it is far from us.
12 For our transgressions before
you are many,
and our sins testify against us.
Our transgressions indeed
are with us,
and we know our iniquities:
13 transgressing, and denying
the LORD,
and turning away from
following our God,
talking oppression and revolt,
conceiving lying words
and uttering them
from the heart.
14 Justice is turned back,
and righteousness stands
at a distance;
for truth stumbles in the
public square,
and uprightness cannot enter.
15 Truth is lacking,
and whoever turns from
evil is despoiled.

The LORD saw it, and it
displeased him
that there was no justice.
16 He saw that there was no one,
and was appalled that there
was no one to intervene;
so his own arm brought
him victory,
and his righteousness upheld him.
17 He put on righteousness like
a breastplate,
and a helmet of salvation
on his head;
he put on garments of vengeance
for clothing,
and wrapped himself in
fury as in a mantle.
18 According to their deeds, so
will he repay;
wrath to his adversaries,
requital to his enemies;
to the coastlands he will
render requital.
19 So those in the west shall fear
the name of the LORD,
and those in the east, his glory;
for he will come like a pent-up
stream
that the wind of the
LORD drives on.

20 And he will come to Zion
as Redeemer,
to those in Jacob who turn
from transgression,
says the LORD.
21 And as for me, this is my covenant
with them, says the LORD: my spirit
that is upon you, and my words that I
have put in your mouth, shall not depart out of your mouth, or out of the
mouths of your children, or out of the
mouths of your children's children, says
the LORD, from now on and for ever.

THE INGATHERING OF THE DISPERSED

60 Arise, shine; for your
light has come,
and the glory of the LORD
has risen upon you.
2 For darkness shall cover the earth,
and thick darkness the peoples;
but the LORD will arise upon you,
and his glory will appear over you.
3 Nations shall come to your light,
and kings to the brightness
of your dawn.

4 Lift up your eyes and look around;
they all gather together,
they come to you;
your sons shall come from far away,
and your daughters shall be
carried on their nurses' arms.
5 Then you shall see and be radiant;
your heart shall thrill and rejoice,[a]
because the abundance of the sea
shall be brought to you,
the wealth of the nations
shall come to you.
6 A multitude of camels shall
cover you,
the young camels of Midian
and Ephah;
all those from Sheba shall come.
They shall bring gold and
frankincense,
and shall proclaim the
praise of the LORD.
7 All the flocks of Kedar shall be
gathered to you,
the rams of Nebaioth shall
minister to you;

[z] 59.10 Meaning of Heb uncertain [a] 60.5 Heb *be enlarged*

they shall be acceptable on my altar,
and I will glorify my
glorious house.

8 Who are these that fly like a cloud,
and like doves to their windows?
9 For the coastlands shall wait for me,
the ships of Tarshish first,
to bring your children from far away,
their silver and gold with them,
for the name of the LORD your God,
and for the Holy One of Israel,
because he has glorified you.
10 Foreigners shall build up your walls,
and their kings shall
minister to you;
for in my wrath I struck you down,
but in my favour I have
had mercy on you.
11 Your gates shall always be open;
day and night they shall
not be shut,
so that nations shall bring
you their wealth,
with their kings led in procession.
12 For the nation and kingdom
that will not serve you
shall perish;
those nations shall be
utterly laid waste.
13 The glory of Lebanon shall
come to you,
the cypress, the plane,
and the pine,
to beautify the place of my sanctuary;
and I will glorify where
my feet rest.
14 The descendants of those who
oppressed you
shall come bending low to you,
and all who despised you
shall bow down at your feet;
they shall call you the City
of the LORD,
the Zion of the Holy One of Israel.
15 Whereas you have been
forsaken and hated,
with no one passing through,
I will make you majestic for ever,
a joy from age to age.
16 You shall suck the milk of nations,
you shall suck the breasts of kings;
and you shall know that I, the
LORD, am your Saviour
and your Redeemer, the
Mighty One of Jacob.

17 Instead of bronze I will bring gold,
instead of iron I will bring silver;
instead of wood, bronze,
instead of stones, iron.
I will appoint Peace as your overseer
and Righteousness as
your taskmaster.
18 Violence shall no more be
heard in your land,
devastation or destruction
within your borders;
you shall call your walls Salvation,
and your gates Praise.

GOD THE GLORY OF ZION

19 The sun shall no longer be
your light by day,
nor for brightness shall the moon
give light to you by night;[b]
but the LORD will be your
everlasting light,
and your God will be your glory.
20 Your sun shall no more go down,
or your moon withdraw itself;
for the LORD will be your
everlasting light,
and your days of mourning
shall be ended.
21 Your people shall all be righteous;
they shall possess the land for ever.
They are the shoot that I planted,
the work of my hands,
so that I might be glorified.
22 The least of them shall become a clan,
and the smallest one a
mighty nation;
I am the LORD;
in its time I will accomplish
it quickly.

THE GOOD NEWS OF DELIVERANCE

61 The spirit of the Lord
GOD is upon me,
because the LORD has
anointed me;
he has sent me to bring good
news to the oppressed,
to bind up the broken-hearted,
to proclaim liberty to the captives,
and release to the prisoners;
2 to proclaim the year of the
LORD's favour,
and the day of vengeance
of our God;
to comfort all who mourn;
3 to provide for those who
mourn in Zion—
to give them a garland
instead of ashes,
the oil of gladness instead
of mourning,
the mantle of praise instead
of a faint spirit.

[b] 60.19 Q Ms Gk Old Latin Tg: MT lacks *by night*

They will be called oaks of
righteousness,
the planting of the LORD,
to display his glory.
4 They shall build up the ancient ruins,
they shall raise up the
former devastations;
they shall repair the ruined cities,
the devastations of many
generations.

5 Strangers shall stand and
feed your flocks,
foreigners shall till your land
and dress your vines;
6 but you shall be called priests
of the LORD,
you shall be named ministers
of our God;
you shall enjoy the wealth
of the nations,
and in their riches you
shall glory.
7 Because their[c] shame was double,
and dishonour was proclaimed
as their lot,
therefore they shall possess
a double portion;
everlasting joy shall be theirs.

8 For I the LORD love justice,
I hate robbery and wrongdoing;[d]
I will faithfully give them
their recompense,
and I will make an everlasting
covenant with them.
9 Their descendants shall be known
among the nations,
and their offspring among
the peoples;
all who see them shall acknowledge
that they are a people whom
the LORD has blessed.
10 I will greatly rejoice in the LORD,
my whole being shall
exult in my God;
for he has clothed me with the
garments of salvation,
he has covered me with the
robe of righteousness,
as a bridegroom decks himself
with a garland,
and as a bride adorns herself
with her jewels.
11 For as the earth brings
forth its shoots,
and as a garden causes what is
sown in it to spring up,
so the Lord GOD will cause
righteousness and praise
to spring up before all the nations.

THE VINDICATION AND SALVATION OF ZION

62 For Zion's sake I will
not keep silent,
and for Jerusalem's sake
I will not rest,
until her vindication shines
out like the dawn,
and her salvation like a
burning torch.
2 The nations shall see your
vindication,
and all the kings your glory;
and you shall be called by
a new name
that the mouth of the
LORD will give.
3 You shall be a crown of beauty in
the hand of the LORD,
and a royal diadem in the
hand of your God.
4 You shall no more be termed
Forsaken,[e]
and your land shall no more
be termed Desolate;[f]
but you shall be called My
Delight Is in Her,[g]
and your land Married;[h]
for the LORD delights in you,
and your land shall be married.
5 For as a young man marries
a young woman,
so shall your builder[i] marry you,
and as the bridegroom rejoices
over the bride,
so shall your God rejoice over you.
6 Upon your walls, O Jerusalem,
I have posted sentinels;
all day and all night
they shall never be silent.
You who remind the LORD,
take no rest,
7 and give him no rest
until he establishes Jerusalem
and makes it renowned
throughout the earth.
8 The LORD has sworn by
his right hand
and by his mighty arm:
I will not again give your grain
to be food for your enemies,
and foreigners shall not
drink the wine
for which you have laboured;
9 but those who garner it shall eat it
and praise the LORD,

[c] 61.7 Heb *your* [d] 61.8 *Or robbery with a burnt-offering* [e] 62.4 Heb *Azubah* [f] 62.4 Heb *Shemamah* [g] 62.4 Heb *Hephzibah* [h] 62.4 Heb *Beulah* [i] 62.5 Cn: Heb *your sons*

and those who gather it shall drink it
in my holy courts.

10 Go through, go through the gates,
prepare the way for the people;
build up, build up the highway,
clear it of stones,
lift up an ensign over the peoples.
11 The LORD has proclaimed
to the end of the earth:
Say to daughter Zion,
'See, your salvation comes;
his reward is with him,
and his recompense before him.'
12 They shall be called, 'The Holy People,
The Redeemed of the LORD';
and you shall be called, 'Sought Out,
A City Not Forsaken.'

VENGEANCE ON EDOM

63 'Who is this that comes
from Edom,
from Bozrah in garments
stained crimson?
Who is this so splendidly robed,
marching in his great might?'

'It is I, announcing vindication,
mighty to save.'

2 'Why are your robes red,
and your garments like theirs
who tread the wine press?'

3 'I have trodden the wine press alone,
and from the peoples no
one was with me;
I trod them in my anger
and trampled them in my wrath;
their juice spattered on
my garments,
and stained all my robes.
4 For the day of vengeance
was in my heart,
and the year for my redeeming
work had come.
5 I looked, but there was no helper;
I stared, but there was no
one to sustain me;
so my own arm brought me victory,
and my wrath sustained me.
6 I trampled down peoples
in my anger,
I crushed them in my wrath,
and I poured out their
lifeblood on the earth.'

GOD'S MERCY REMEMBERED

7 I will recount the gracious
deeds of the LORD,
the praiseworthy acts of the LORD,
because of all that the LORD
has done for us,
and the great favour to the
house of Israel
that he has shown them
according to his mercy,
according to the abundance
of his steadfast love.
8 For he said, 'Surely they
are my people,
children who will not deal falsely';
and he became their saviour
9 in all their distress.
It was no messenger[j] or angel
but his presence that saved them;[k]
in his love and in his pity he
redeemed them;
he lifted them up and carried
them all the days of old.

10 But they rebelled
and grieved his holy spirit;
therefore he became their enemy;
he himself fought against them.
11 Then they[l] remembered
the days of old,
of Moses his servant.[m]
Where is the one who brought
them up out of the sea
with the shepherds of his flock?
Where is the one who put
within them
his holy spirit,
12 who caused his glorious arm
to march at the right
hand of Moses,
who divided the waters before them
to make for himself an
everlasting name,
13 who led them through
the depths?
Like a horse in the desert,
they did not stumble.
14 Like cattle that go down
into the valley,
the spirit of the LORD
gave them rest.
Thus you led your people,
to make for yourself a
glorious name.

A PRAYER OF PENITENCE

15 Look down from heaven and see,
from your holy and glorious
habitation.

[j] **63.9** Gk: Heb *anguish* [k] **63.9** Or *saviour. In all their distress he was distressed; the angel of his presence saved them;* [l] **63.11** Heb *he* [m] **63.11** Cn: Heb *his people*

Where are your zeal and your might?
The yearning of your heart
and your compassion?
They are withheld from me.
16 For you are our father,
though Abraham does
not know us
and Israel does not
acknowledge us;
you, O LORD, are our father;
our Redeemer from of old
is your name.
17 Why, O LORD, do you make us
stray from your ways
and harden our heart, so that
we do not fear you?
Turn back for the sake of
your servants,
for the sake of the tribes that
are your heritage.
18 Your holy people took possession
for a little while;
but now our adversaries
have trampled down
your sanctuary.
19 We have long been like those
whom you do not rule,
like those not called by your name.

64 O that you would tear open the
heavens and come down,
so that the mountains would
quake at your presence—
2[n] as when fire kindles brushwood
and the fire causes water to boil—
to make your name known to
your adversaries,
so that the nations might
tremble at your presence!
3 When you did awesome deeds
that we did not expect,
you came down, the mountains
quaked at your presence.
4 From ages past no one has heard,
no ear has perceived,
no eye has seen any God besides you,
who works for those who
wait for him.
5 You meet those who gladly do right,
those who remember you
in your ways.
But you were angry, and we sinned;
because you hid yourself
we transgressed.[o]
6 We have all become like one
who is unclean,
and all our righteous deeds
are like a filthy cloth.
We all fade like a leaf,
and our iniquities, like the
wind, take us away.
7 There is no one who calls
on your name,
or attempts to take hold of you;
for you have hidden your
face from us,
and have delivered[p] us into the
hand of our iniquity.
8 Yet, O LORD, you are our Father;
we are the clay, and you
are our potter;
we are all the work of your hand.
9 Do not be exceedingly
angry, O LORD,
and do not remember
iniquity for ever.
Now consider, we are all
your people.
10 Your holy cities have become
a wilderness,
Zion has become a wilderness,
Jerusalem a desolation.
11 Our holy and beautiful house,
where our ancestors praised you,
has been burned by fire,
and all our pleasant places
have become ruins.
12 After all this, will you restrain
yourself, O LORD?
Will you keep silent, and
punish us so severely?

THE RIGHTEOUSNESS OF GOD'S JUDGEMENT

65 I was ready to be sought out
by those who did not ask,
to be found by those who
did not seek me.
I said, 'Here I am, here I am',
to a nation that did not
call on my name.
2 I held out my hands all day long
to a rebellious people,
who walk in a way that is not good,
following their own devices;
3 a people who provoke me
to my face continually,
sacrificing in gardens
and offering incense on bricks;
4 who sit inside tombs,
and spend the night in
secret places;
who eat swine's flesh,
with broth of abominable
things in their vessels;
5 who say, 'Keep to yourself,
do not come near me, for I
am too holy for you.'

[n] 64.2 Ch 64.1 in Heb [o] 64.5 Meaning of Heb uncertain [p] 64.7 Gk Syr Old Latin Tg: Heb *melted*

These are a smoke in my nostrils,
a fire that burns all day long.
6 See, it is written before me:
I will not keep silent, but
I will repay;
I will indeed repay into their laps
7 their[q] iniquities and their[r]
ancestors' iniquities
together,
says the LORD;
because they offered incense
on the mountains
and reviled me on the hills,
I will measure into their laps
full payment for their actions.
8 Thus says the LORD:
As the wine is found in the cluster,
and they say, 'Do not destroy it,
for there is a blessing in it',
so I will do for my servants' sake,
and not destroy them all.
9 I will bring forth descendants[s]
from Jacob,
and from Judah inheritors[t]
of my mountains;
my chosen shall inherit it,
and my servants
shall settle there.
10 Sharon shall become a
pasture for flocks,
and the Valley of Achor a place
for herds to lie down,
for my people who have
sought me.
11 But you who forsake the LORD,
who forget my holy mountain,
who set a table for Fortune
and fill cups of mixed
wine for Destiny,
12 I will destine you to the sword,
and all of you shall bow down
to the slaughter;
because, when I called, you
did not answer,
when I spoke, you did not listen,
but you did what was evil
in my sight,
and chose what I did
not delight in.
13 Therefore thus says the Lord GOD:
My servants shall eat,
but you shall be hungry;
my servants shall drink,
but you shall be thirsty;
my servants shall rejoice,
but you shall be put to shame;
14 my servants shall sing for
gladness of heart,
but you shall cry out for
pain of heart,
and shall wail for anguish of spirit.
15 You shall leave your name to my
chosen to use as a curse,
and the Lord GOD will put
you to death;
but to his servants he will
give a different name.
16 Then whoever invokes a
blessing in the land
shall bless by the God of
faithfulness,
and whoever takes an oath
in the land
shall swear by the God
of faithfulness;
because the former troubles
are forgotten
and are hidden from my sight.

THE GLORIOUS NEW CREATION

17 For I am about to create new heavens
and a new earth;
the former things shall not
be remembered
or come to mind.
18 But be glad and rejoice for ever
in what I am creating;
for I am about to create
Jerusalem as a joy,
and its people as a delight.
19 I will rejoice in Jerusalem,
and delight in my people;
no more shall the sound of
weeping be heard in it,
or the cry of distress.
20 No more shall there be in it
an infant that lives but a few days,
or an old person who does
not live out a lifetime;
for one who dies at a hundred years
will be considered a youth,
and one who falls short
of a hundred will be
considered accursed.
21 They shall build houses and
inhabit them;
they shall plant vineyards
and eat their fruit.
22 They shall not build and
another inhabit;
they shall not plant and
another eat;
for like the days of a tree shall the
days of my people be,
and my chosen shall long enjoy
the work of their hands.
23 They shall not labour in vain,
or bear children for calamity;[u]

[q] 65.7 Gk Syr: Heb *your* [r] 65.7 Gk Syr: Heb *your*
[s] 65.9 Or *a descendant* [t] 65.9 Or *an inheritor*
[u] 65.23 Or *sudden terror*

for they shall be offspring blessed
by the LORD—
and their descendants as well.
24 Before they call I will answer,
while they are yet speaking
I will hear.
25 The wolf and the lamb shall
feed together,
the lion shall eat straw like the ox;
but the serpent—its food
shall be dust!
They shall not hurt or destroy
on all my holy mountain,
says the LORD.

THE WORSHIP GOD DEMANDS

66 Thus says the LORD:
Heaven is my throne
and the earth is my footstool;
what is the house that you
would build for me,
and what is my resting-place?
2 All these things my hand has made,
and so all these things are mine,[v]
says the LORD.
But this is the one to whom
I will look,
to the humble and contrite in spirit,
who trembles at my word.

3 Whoever slaughters an ox is like one
who kills a human being;
whoever sacrifices a lamb, like one
who breaks a dog's neck;
whoever presents a grain-offering, like
one who offers swine's blood;[w]
whoever makes a memorial
offering of frankincense, like
one who blesses an idol.
These have chosen their own ways,
and in their abominations
they take delight;
4 I also will choose to mock[x] them,
and bring upon them
what they fear;
because, when I called, no
one answered,
when I spoke, they did not listen;
but they did what was evil
in my sight,
and chose what did not please me.

THE LORD VINDICATES ZION

5 Hear the word of the LORD,
you who tremble at his word:
Your own people who hate you
and reject you for my name's sake
have said, 'Let the LORD be glorified,
so that we may see your joy';
but it is they who shall be
put to shame.

6 Listen, an uproar from the city!
A voice from the temple!
The voice of the LORD,
dealing retribution to his enemies!

7 Before she was in labour
she gave birth;
before her pain came upon her
she delivered a son.
8 Who has heard of such a thing?
Who has seen such things?
Shall a land be born in one day?
Shall a nation be delivered
in one moment?
Yet as soon as Zion was in labour
she delivered her children.
9 Shall I open the womb and
not deliver?
says the LORD;
shall I, the one who delivers,
shut the womb?
says your God.

10 Rejoice with Jerusalem, and
be glad for her,
all you who love her;
rejoice with her in joy,
all you who mourn over her—
11 that you may nurse and be satisfied
from her consoling breast;
that you may drink deeply
with delight
from her glorious bosom.

12 For thus says the LORD:
I will extend prosperity to
her like a river,
and the wealth of the nations like
an overflowing stream;
and you shall nurse and be
carried on her arm,
and dandled on her knees.
13 As a mother comforts her child,
so I will comfort you;
you shall be comforted
in Jerusalem.

THE REIGN AND INDIGNATION OF GOD

14 You shall see, and your heart
shall rejoice;
your bodies[y] shall flourish
like the grass;
and it shall be known that the
hand of the LORD is
with his servants,
and his indignation is
against his enemies.

[v] **66.2** Gk Syr: Heb *these things came to be*
[w] **66.3** Meaning of Heb uncertain [x] **66.4** Or *to punish* [y] **66.14** Heb *bones*

15 For the LORD will come in fire,
and his chariots like the whirlwind,
to pay back his anger in fury,
and his rebuke in flames of fire.
16 For by fire will the LORD execute judgement,
and by his sword, on all flesh;
and those slain by the LORD shall be many.

17 Those who sanctify and purify themselves to go into the gardens, following the one in the centre, eating the flesh of pigs, vermin, and rodents, shall come to an end together, says the LORD.

18 For I know[z] their works and
their thoughts, and I am[a] coming to
gather all nations and tongues; and
they shall come and shall see my glory,
19and I will set a sign among them.
From them I will send survivors to the
nations, to Tarshish, Put,[b] and Lud—
which draw the bow—to Tubal and
Javan, to the coastlands far away that
have not heard of my fame or seen my
glory; and they shall declare my glory
among the nations. 20They shall bring
all your kindred from all the nations
as an offering to the LORD, on horses,
and in chariots, and in litters, and on
mules, and on dromedaries, to my holy
mountain Jerusalem, says the LORD,
just as the Israelites bring a grain-
offering in a clean vessel to the house
of the LORD. 21And I will also take
some of them as priests and as Levites,
says the LORD.

22 For as the new heavens and the new earth,
which I will make,
shall remain before me,
says the LORD,
so shall your descendants and your name remain.
23 From new moon to new moon,
and from sabbath to sabbath,
all flesh shall come to worship before me,
says the LORD.

24 And they shall go out and look at the dead bodies of the people who have rebelled against me; for their worm shall not die, their fire shall not be quenched, and they shall be an abhorrence to all flesh.

[z] 66.18 Gk Syr: Heb lacks *know* [a] 66.18 Gk Syr Vg Tg: Heb *it is* [b] 66.19 Gk: Heb *Pul*

JEREMIAH

The book of Jeremiah presents prophecy at a time of national tragedy for the kingdom of Judah before, during, and after the Babylonian exile in 587 BCE. At that time Babylon invaded Judah, laid siege to Jerusalem, and destroyed the great temple. Anguish and grief as well as hope and promise for a new future mark the prophecy of Jeremiah as he struggles to make sense of all the chaos and destruction. He looks forward to a day when a new covenant would be made by God with the house of Israel and the house of Judah (31.31–34). Christians later will interpret this prophecy as fulfilled in the gospel of the New Testament.

Readings from the prophet Jeremiah occur consecutively from Wednesday of the Sixteenth Week of Year II through Thursday of the Eighteenth Week. Also, the famous prophecy from Jeremiah about the coming of a new covenant is read on the Fifth Sunday of Lent during Cycle B. Other texts from Jeremiah are selected for reading from time to time throughout the Sunday and weekday liturgical calendar and at occasions from the Proper of Saints and Commons and from the Ritual, Various and Votive Masses.

1 The words of Jeremiah son of Hilkiah, of the priests who were in
Anathoth in the land of Benjamin, 2to
whom the word of the LORD came in
the days of King Josiah son of Amon
of Judah, in the thirteenth year of his
reign. 3It came also in the days of King
Jehoiakim son of Josiah of Judah, and
until the end of the eleventh year of
King Zedekiah son of Josiah of Judah,
until the captivity of Jerusalem in the
fifth month.

JEREMIAH'S CALL AND COMMISSION

4 Now the word of the LORD came to
me saying,

5 'Before I formed you in the
womb I knew you,
and before you were born I
consecrated you;
I appointed you a prophet
to the nations.'

6Then I said, 'Ah, Lord GOD! Truly I do
not know how to speak, for I am only a
boy.' 7But the LORD said to me,

'Do not say, "I am only a boy";
for you shall go to all to
whom I send you,
and you shall speak whatever
I command you.

8 Do not be afraid of them,
for I am with you to deliver you,
says the LORD.'

9Then the LORD put out his hand and
touched my mouth; and the LORD said
to me,

'Now I have put my words
in your mouth.

10 See, today I appoint you over nations
and over kingdoms,
to pluck up and to pull down,
to destroy and to overthrow,
to build and to plant.'

11 The word of the LORD came to me,
saying, 'Jeremiah, what do you see?'
And I said, 'I see a branch of an almond
tree.'[a] 12Then the LORD said to me, 'You
have seen well, for I am watching[b] over
my word to perform it.' 13The word of
the LORD came to me a second time,
saying, 'What do you see?' And I said, 'I
see a boiling pot, tilted away from the
north.'

14 Then the LORD said to me: Out of
the north disaster shall break out on all
the inhabitants of the land. 15For now I
am calling all the tribes of the kingdoms
of the north, says the LORD; and they

[a] 1.11 Heb *shaqed* [b] 1.12 Heb *shoqed*

shall come and all of them shall set their
thrones at the entrance of the gates of
Jerusalem, against all its surrounding
walls and against all the cities of Judah. 16 And I will utter my judgements
against them, for all their wickedness
in forsaking me; they have made offerings to other gods, and worshipped the
works of their own hands. 17 But you,
gird up your loins; stand up and tell
them everything that I command you.
Do not break down before them, or I
will break you before them. 18 And I for
my part have made you today a fortified
city, an iron pillar, and a bronze wall,
against the whole land—against the
kings of Judah, its princes, its priests,
and the people of the land. 19 They will
fight against you; but they shall not prevail against you, for I am with you, says
the LORD, to deliver you.

GOD PLEADS WITH ISRAEL TO REPENT

2 The word of the LORD came to me,
saying: 2 Go and proclaim in the
hearing of Jerusalem, Thus says the
LORD:

I remember the devotion
of your youth,
your love as a bride,
how you followed me in
the wilderness,
in a land not sown.
3 Israel was holy to the LORD,
the first fruits of his harvest.
All who ate of it were
held guilty;
disaster came upon them,
says the LORD.

4 Hear the word of the LORD, O house
of Jacob, and all the families of the house
of Israel. 5 Thus says the LORD:

What wrong did your ancestors
find in me
that they went far from me,
and went after worthless
things, and became
worthless themselves?
6 They did not say, 'Where
is the LORD
who brought us up from
the land of Egypt,
who led us in the wilderness,
in a land of deserts and pits,
in a land of drought and
deep darkness,
in a land that no one
passes through,
where no one lives?'
7 I brought you into a plentiful land
to eat its fruits and its
good things.
But when you entered you
defiled my land,
and made my heritage an
abomination.
8 The priests did not say, 'Where
is the LORD?'
Those who handle the law
did not know me;
the rulers[c] transgressed against me;
the prophets prophesied by Baal,
and went after things that
do not profit.

9 Therefore once more I accuse you,
says the LORD,
and I accuse your children's
children.
10 Cross to the coasts of Cyprus
and look,
send to Kedar and examine
with care;
see if there has ever been
such a thing.
11 Has a nation changed its gods,
even though they are no gods?
But my people have changed
their glory
for something that does not profit.
12 Be appalled, O heavens, at this,
be shocked, be utterly desolate,
says the LORD,
13 for my people have committed
two evils:
they have forsaken me,
the fountain of living water,
and dug out cisterns for
themselves,
cracked cisterns
that can hold no water.

14 Is Israel a slave? Is he a home-
born servant?
Why then has he become plunder?
15 The lions have roared against him,
they have roared loudly.
They have made his land a waste;
his cities are in ruins,
without inhabitant.
16 Moreover, the people of Memphis
and Tahpanhes
have broken the crown
of your head.
17 Have you not brought this
upon yourself
by forsaking the LORD your God,
while he led you in the way?

[c] 2.8 Heb *shepherds*

18 What then do you gain by
going to Egypt,
to drink the waters of the Nile?
Or what do you gain by
going to Assyria,
to drink the waters of
the Euphrates?
19 Your wickedness will punish you,
and your apostasies will
convict you.
Know and see that it is
evil and bitter
for you to forsake the
LORD your God;
the fear of me is not in you,
says the Lord GOD of hosts.

20 For long ago you broke your yoke
and burst your bonds,
and you said, 'I will not serve!'
On every high hill
and under every green tree
you sprawled and played
the whore.
21 Yet I planted you as a choice vine,
from the purest stock.
How then did you turn degenerate
and become a wild vine?
22 Though you wash
yourself with lye
and use much soap,
the stain of your guilt is
still before me,
says the Lord GOD.
23 How can you say, 'I am not defiled,
I have not gone after the Baals'?
Look at your way in the valley;
know what you have done—
a restive young camel interlacing
her tracks,
24 a wild ass at home in the
wilderness,
in her heat sniffing the wind!
Who can restrain her lust?
None who seek her need
weary themselves;
in her month they will find her.
25 Keep your feet from going unshod
and your throat from thirst.
But you said, 'It is hopeless,
for I have loved strangers,
and after them I will go.'

26 As a thief is shamed when caught,
so the house of Israel shall
be shamed—
they, their kings, their officials,
their priests, and their prophets,
27 who say to a tree, 'You are my father',
and to a stone, 'You gave
me birth.'
For they have turned their
backs to me,
and not their faces.
But in the time of their
trouble they say,
'Come and save us!'
28 But where are your gods
that you made for yourself?
Let them come, if they can save you,
in your time of trouble;
for you have as many gods
as you have towns, O Judah.

29 Why do you complain against me?
You have all rebelled against me,
says the LORD.
30 In vain I have struck down
your children;
they accepted no correction.
Your own sword devoured
your prophets
like a ravening lion.
31 And you, O generation, behold
the word of the LORD![d]
Have I been a wilderness to Israel,
or a land of thick darkness?
Why then do my people say,
'We are free,
we will come to you no more'?
32 Can a girl forget her ornaments,
or a bride her attire?
Yet my people have forgotten me,
days without number.

33 How well you direct your course
to seek lovers!
So that even to wicked women
you have taught your ways.
34 Also on your skirts is found
the lifeblood of the innocent poor,
though you did not catch
them breaking in.
Yet in spite of all these things[e]
35 you say, 'I am innocent;
surely his anger has
turned from me.'
Now I am bringing you to
judgement
for saying, 'I have not sinned.'
36 How lightly you gad about,
changing your ways!
You shall be put to shame by Egypt
as you were put to shame
by Assyria.
37 From there also you will come away
with your hands on your head;

[d] 2.31 Meaning of Heb uncertain [e] 2.34 Meaning of Heb uncertain

for the LORD has rejected those
in whom you trust,
and you will not prosper
through them.

UNFAITHFUL ISRAEL

3 If[f] a man divorces his wife
and she goes from him
and becomes another man's wife,
will he return to her?
Would not such a land be
greatly polluted?
You have played the whore
with many lovers;
and would you return to me?
says the LORD.
2 Look up to the bare heights,[g]
and see!
Where have you not
been lain with?
By the waysides you have sat
waiting for lovers,
like a nomad in the wilderness.
You have polluted the land
with your whoring and
wickedness.
3 Therefore the showers have
been withheld,
and the spring rain has not come;
yet you have the forehead of a whore,
you refuse to be ashamed.
4 Have you not just now called to me,
'My Father, you are the
friend of my youth—
5 will he be angry for ever,
will he be indignant to the end?'
This is how you have spoken,
but you have done all the
evil that you could.

A CALL TO REPENTANCE

6 The LORD said to me in the days of
King Josiah: Have you seen what she
did, that faithless one, Israel, how she
went up on every high hill and under
every green tree, and played the whore
there? 7 And I thought, 'After she has
done all this she will return to me'; but
she did not return, and her false sister
Judah saw it. 8 She[h] saw that for all the
adulteries of that faithless one, Israel, I
had sent her away with a decree of divorce; yet her false sister Judah did not
fear, but she too went and played the
whore. 9 Because she took her whoredom so lightly, she polluted the land,
committing adultery with stone and
tree. 10 Yet for all this her false sister
Judah did not return to me with her
whole heart, but only in pretence, says
the LORD.

11 Then the LORD said to me: Faithless Israel has shown herself less guilty
than false Judah. 12 Go, and proclaim
these words towards the north, and
say:
Return, faithless Israel,
says the LORD.
I will not look on you in anger,
for I am merciful,
says the LORD;
I will not be angry for ever.
13 Only acknowledge your guilt,
that you have rebelled against
the LORD your God,
and scattered your favours
among strangers under
every green tree,
and have not obeyed my voice,
says the LORD.
14 Return, O faithless children,
says the LORD,
for I am your master;
I will take you, one from a city
and two from a family,
and I will bring you to Zion.

15 I will give you shepherds after my own heart, who will feed you
with knowledge and understanding.
16 And when you have multiplied and
increased in the land, in those days,
says the LORD, they shall no longer say,
'The ark of the covenant of the LORD.' It
shall not come to mind, or be remembered, or missed; nor shall another
one be made. 17 At that time Jerusalem
shall be called the throne of the LORD,
and all nations shall gather to it, to the
presence of the LORD in Jerusalem, and
they shall no longer stubbornly follow
their own evil will. 18 In those days the
house of Judah shall join the house of
Israel, and together they shall come
from the land of the north to the land
that I gave your ancestors for a heritage.

19 I thought
how I would set you among
my children,
and give you a pleasant land,
the most beautiful heritage
of all the nations.
And I thought you would call
me, My Father,
and would not turn from
following me.

[f] 3.1 Q Ms Gk Syr: MT *Saying, If* [g] 3.2 Or *the trails* [h] 3.8 Q Ms Gk Mss Syr: MT *I*

20 Instead, as a faithless wife
leaves her husband,
so you have been faithless to
me, O house of Israel,
says the LORD.

21 A voice on the bare heights[i]
is heard,
the plaintive weeping of
Israel's children,
because they have perverted
their way,
they have forgotten the
LORD their God:
22 Return, O faithless children,
I will heal your faithlessness.

'Here we come to you;
for you are the LORD our God.
23 Truly the hills are[j] a delusion,
the orgies on the mountains.
Truly in the LORD our God
is the salvation of Israel.

24 'But from our youth the shameful thing has devoured all for which our
ancestors had laboured, their flocks and
their herds, their sons and their daughters. 25 Let us lie down in our shame, and
let our dishonour cover us; for we have
sinned against the LORD our God, we
and our ancestors, from our youth even
to this day; and we have not obeyed the
voice of the LORD our God.'

4 If you return, O Israel,
says the LORD,
if you return to me,
if you remove your abominations
from my presence,
and do not waver,
2 and if you swear, 'As the LORD lives!'
in truth, in justice, and
in uprightness,
then nations shall be
blessed[k] by him,
and by him they shall boast.

3 For thus says the LORD to the people of Judah and to the inhabitants of
Jerusalem:
Break up your fallow ground,
and do not sow among thorns.
4 Circumcise yourselves to the LORD,
remove the foreskin of
your hearts,
O people of Judah and
inhabitants of Jerusalem,
or else my wrath will go
forth like fire,
and burn with no one
to quench it,
because of the evil of your doings.

INVASION AND DESOLATION OF JUDAH THREATENED

5 Declare in Judah, and proclaim in
Jerusalem, and say:
Blow the trumpet through the land;
shout aloud[l] and say,
'Gather together, and let us go
into the fortified cities!'
6 Raise a standard towards Zion,
flee for safety, do not delay,
for I am bringing evil from
the north,
and a great destruction.
7 A lion has gone up from its thicket,
a destroyer of nations has set out;
he has gone out from his place
to make your land a waste;
your cities will be ruins
without inhabitant.
8 Because of this put on sackcloth,
lament and wail:
'The fierce anger of the LORD
has not turned away from us.'

9 On that day, says the LORD, courage
shall fail the king and the officials; the
priests shall be appalled and the prophets astounded. 10 Then I said, 'Ah, Lord
GOD, how utterly you have deceived this
people and Jerusalem, saying, "It shall
be well with you", even while the sword
is at the throat!'

11 At that time it will be said to this
people and to Jerusalem: A hot wind
comes from me out of the bare heights[m]
in the desert towards my poor people,
not to winnow or cleanse— 12 a wind too
strong for that. Now it is I who speak in
judgement against them.
13 Look! He comes up like clouds,
his chariots like the whirlwind;
his horses are swifter than eagles—
woe to us, for we are ruined!
14 O Jerusalem, wash your heart
clean of wickedness
so that you may be saved.
How long shall your evil schemes
lodge within you?
15 For a voice declares from Dan
and proclaims disaster from
Mount Ephraim.
16 Tell the nations, 'Here they are!'
Proclaim against Jerusalem,
'Besiegers come from a distant land;
they shout against the
cities of Judah.

[i] **3.21** Or *the trails* [j] **3.23** Gk Syr Vg: Heb *Truly from the hills is* [k] **4.2** Or *shall bless themselves* [l] **4.5** Or *shout, take your weapons*: Heb *shout, fill (your hand)* [m] **4.11** Or *the trails*

17 They have closed in around her
like watchers of a field,
because she has rebelled
against me,
says the LORD.
18 Your ways and your doings
have brought this upon you.
This is your doom; how bitter it is!
It has reached your very heart.'

SORROW FOR A DOOMED NATION

19 My anguish, my anguish! I
writhe in pain!
Oh, the walls of my heart!
My heart is beating wildly;
I cannot keep silent;
for I[n] hear the sound of
the trumpet,
the alarm of war.
20 Disaster overtakes disaster,
the whole land is laid waste.
Suddenly my tents are destroyed,
my curtains in a moment.
21 How long must I see the standard,
and hear the sound of
the trumpet?
22 'For my people are foolish,
they do not know me;
they are stupid children,
they have no understanding.
They are skilled in doing evil,
but do not know how to do good.'

23 I looked on the earth, and lo, it
was waste and void;
and to the heavens, and
they had no light.
24 I looked on the mountains, and
lo, they were quaking,
and all the hills moved to and fro.
25 I looked, and lo, there was
no one at all,
and all the birds of the
air had fled.
26 I looked, and lo, the fruitful
land was a desert,
and all its cities were laid in ruins
before the LORD, before
his fierce anger.

27 For thus says the LORD: The whole
land shall be a desolation; yet I will not
make a full end.

28 Because of this the earth
shall mourn,
and the heavens above grow black;
for I have spoken, I have purposed;
I have not relented nor
will I turn back.

29 At the noise of horseman and archer
every town takes to flight;
they enter thickets; they climb
among rocks;
all the towns are forsaken,
and no one lives in them.
30 And you, O desolate one,
what do you mean that you
dress in crimson,
that you deck yourself with
ornaments of gold,
that you enlarge your
eyes with paint?
In vain you beautify yourself.
Your lovers despise you;
they seek your life.
31 For I heard a cry as of a
woman in labour,
anguish as of one bringing
forth her first child,
the cry of daughter Zion
gasping for breath,
stretching out her hands,
'Woe is me! I am fainting
before killers!'

THE UTTER CORRUPTION OF GOD'S PEOPLE

5 Run to and fro through the
streets of Jerusalem,
look around and take note!
Search its squares and see
if you can find one person
who acts justly
and seeks truth—
so that I may pardon Jerusalem.[o]
2 Although they say, 'As the
LORD lives',
yet they swear falsely.
3 O LORD, do your eyes not
look for truth?
You have struck them,
but they felt no anguish;
you have consumed them,
but they refused to take
correction.
They have made their faces
harder than rock;
they have refused to turn back.

4 Then I said, 'These are only the poor,
they have no sense;
for they do not know the
way of the LORD,
the law of their God.
5 Let me go to the rich[p]
and speak to them;
surely they know the way
of the LORD,
the law of their God.'

[n] **4.19** Another reading is *for you, O my soul,*
[o] **5.1** Heb *it* [p] **5.5** Or *the great*

But they all alike had broken
the yoke,
they had burst the bonds.
6 Therefore a lion from the forest
shall kill them,
a wolf from the desert shall
destroy them.
A leopard is watching against
their cities;
everyone who goes out of them
shall be torn in pieces—
because their transgressions
are many,
their apostasies are great.

7 How can I pardon you?
Your children have forsaken me,
and have sworn by those
who are no gods.
When I fed them to the full,
they committed adultery
and trooped to the houses
of prostitutes.
8 They were well-fed lusty stallions,
each neighing for his
neighbour's wife.
9 Shall I not punish them for
these things?
says the LORD;
and shall I not bring retribution
on a nation such as this?

10 Go up through her vine-
rows and destroy,
but do not make a full end;
strip away her branches,
for they are not the LORD's.
11 For the house of Israel and
the house of Judah
have been utterly faithless to me,
says the LORD.
12 They have spoken falsely
of the LORD,
and have said, 'He will
do nothing.
No evil will come upon us,
and we shall not see sword
or famine.'
13 The prophets are nothing but wind,
for the word is not in them.
Thus shall it be done to them!

14 Therefore thus says the LORD,
the God of hosts:
Because they[q] have spoken
this word,
I am now making my words in
your mouth a fire,
and this people wood, and the
fire shall devour them.
15 I am going to bring upon you
a nation from far away,
O house of Israel,
says the LORD.
It is an enduring nation,
it is an ancient nation,
a nation whose language
you do not know,
nor can you understand
what they say.
16 Their quiver is like an open tomb;
all of them are mighty warriors.
17 They shall eat up your harvest
and your food;
they shall eat up your sons
and your daughters;
they shall eat up your flocks
and your herds;
they shall eat up your vines
and your fig trees;
they shall destroy with the sword
your fortified cities in
which you trust.

18 But even in those days, says the
LORD, I will not make a full end of you.
19 And when your people say, 'Why has
the LORD our God done all these things
to us?' you shall say to them, 'As you
have forsaken me and served foreign
gods in your land, so you shall serve
strangers in a land that is not yours.'

20 Declare this in the house of Jacob,
proclaim it in Judah:
21 Hear this, O foolish and
senseless people,
who have eyes, but do not see,
who have ears, but do not hear.
22 Do you not fear me? says the LORD;
Do you not tremble before me?
I placed the sand as a boundary
for the sea,
a perpetual barrier that
it cannot pass;
though the waves toss, they
cannot prevail,
though they roar, they
cannot pass over it.
23 But this people has a stubborn
and rebellious heart;
they have turned aside
and gone away.
24 They do not say in their hearts,
'Let us fear the LORD our God,
who gives the rain in its season,
the autumn rain and the
spring rain,

[q] 5.14 Heb *you*

and keeps for us
the weeks appointed for the harvest.'
25 Your iniquities have turned
these away,
and your sins have deprived
you of good.
26 For scoundrels are found
among my people;
they take over the goods of others.
Like fowlers they set a trap;[r]
they catch human beings.
27 Like a cage full of birds,
their houses are full of treachery;
therefore they have become
great and rich,
28 they have grown fat and sleek.
They know no limits in deeds
of wickedness;
they do not judge with justice
the cause of the orphan, to
make it prosper,
and they do not defend the
rights of the needy.
29 Shall I not punish them for
these things?
says the LORD,
and shall I not bring retribution
on a nation such as this?

30 An appalling and horrible thing
has happened in the land:
31 the prophets prophesy falsely,
and the priests rule as the
prophets direct;[s]
my people love to have it so,
but what will you do when
the end comes?

THE IMMINENCE AND HORROR OF THE INVASION

6 Flee for safety, O children
of Benjamin,
from the midst of Jerusalem!
Blow the trumpet in Tekoa,
and raise a signal on Beth-haccherem;
for evil looms out of the north,
and great destruction.
2 I have likened daughter Zion
to the loveliest pasture.[t]
3 Shepherds with their flocks shall
come against her.
They shall pitch their
tents around her;
they shall pasture, all in
their places.
4 'Prepare war against her;
up, and let us attack at noon!'
'Woe to us, for the day declines,
the shadows of evening lengthen!'
5 'Up, and let us attack by night,
and destroy her palaces!'
6 For thus says the LORD of hosts:
Cut down her trees;
cast up a siege-ramp
against Jerusalem.
This is the city that must
be punished;[u]
there is nothing but
oppression within her.
7 As a well keeps its water fresh,
so she keeps fresh her wickedness;
violence and destruction are
heard within her;
sickness and wounds are
ever before me.
8 Take warning, O Jerusalem,
or I shall turn from you in disgust,
and make you a desolation,
an uninhabited land.

9 Thus says the LORD of hosts:
Glean[v] thoroughly as a vine
the remnant of Israel;
like a grape-gatherer, pass
your hand again
over its branches.

10 To whom shall I speak and
give warning,
that they may hear?
See, their ears are closed,[w]
they cannot listen.
The word of the LORD is to them
an object of scorn;
they take no pleasure in it.
11 But I am full of the wrath
of the LORD;
I am weary of holding it in.

Pour it out on the children
in the street,
and on the gatherings of
young men as well;
both husband and wife
shall be taken,
the old folk and the very aged.
12 Their houses shall be turned
over to others,
their fields and wives together;
for I will stretch out my hand
against the inhabitants
of the land,
says the LORD.

13 For from the least to the
greatest of them,
everyone is greedy for unjust gain;

[r] **5.26** Meaning of Heb uncertain [s] **5.31** Or *rule by their own authority* [t] **6.2** Or *I will destroy daughter Zion, the loveliest pasture* [u] **6.6** Or *the city of licence* [v] **6.9** Cn: Heb *They shall glean* [w] **6.10** Heb *are uncircumcised*

and from prophet to priest,
everyone deals falsely.
14 They have treated the wound of
my people carelessly,
saying, 'Peace, peace',
when there is no peace.
15 They acted shamefully, they
committed abomination;
yet they were not ashamed,
they did not know how to blush.
Therefore they shall fall among
those who fall;
at the time that I punish them,
they shall be overthrown,
says the LORD.
16 Thus says the LORD:
Stand at the crossroads, and look,
and ask for the ancient paths,
where the good way lies;
and walk in it,
and find rest for your souls.
But they said, 'We will not walk in it.'
17 Also I raised up sentinels for you:
'Give heed to the sound
of the trumpet!'
But they said, 'We will not give heed.'
18 Therefore hear, O nations,
and know, O congregation, what
will happen to them.
19 Hear, O earth; I am going to bring
disaster on this people,
the fruit of their schemes,
because they have not given
heed to my words;
and as for my teaching, they
have rejected it.
20 Of what use to me is frankincense
that comes from Sheba,
or sweet cane from a distant land?
Your burnt-offerings are
not acceptable,
nor are your sacrifices
pleasing to me.
21 Therefore thus says the LORD:
See, I am laying before this people
stumbling-blocks against which
they shall stumble;
parents and children together,
neighbour and friend shall perish.

22 Thus says the LORD:
See, a people is coming from
the land of the north,
a great nation is stirring from the
farthest parts of the earth.
23 They grasp the bow and the javelin,
they are cruel and have no mercy,
their sound is like the roaring sea;
they ride on horses,
equipped like a warrior for battle,
against you, O daughter Zion!

24 'We have heard news of them,
our hands fall helpless;
anguish has taken hold of us,
pain as of a woman in labour.
25 Do not go out into the field,
or walk on the road;
for the enemy has a sword,
terror is on every side.'

26 O my poor people, put on sackcloth,
and roll in ashes;
make mourning as for an only child,
most bitter lamentation:
for suddenly the destroyer
will come upon us.

27 I have made you a tester and a
refiner[x] among my people
so that you may know and
test their ways.
28 They are all stubbornly rebellious,
going about with slanders;
they are bronze and iron,
all of them act corruptly.
29 The bellows blow fiercely,
the lead is consumed by the fire;
in vain the refining goes on,
for the wicked are not removed.
30 They are called 'rejected silver',
for the LORD has rejected them.

JEREMIAH PROCLAIMS GOD'S JUDGEMENT ON THE NATION

7 The word that came to Jeremiah
from the LORD: 2Stand in the gate
of the LORD's house, and proclaim there
this word, and say, Hear the word of the
LORD, all you people of Judah, you that
enter these gates to worship the LORD.
3Thus says the LORD of hosts, the God of
Israel: Amend your ways and your doings, and let me dwell with you[y] in this
place. 4Do not trust in these deceptive
words: 'This is[z] the temple of the LORD,
the temple of the LORD, the temple of
the LORD.'
5 For if you truly amend your ways
and your doings, if you truly act justly
one with another, 6if you do not oppress
the alien, the orphan, and the widow, or
shed innocent blood in this place, and if
you do not go after other gods to your
own hurt, 7then I will dwell with you in
this place, in the land that I gave of old
to your ancestors for ever and ever.
8 Here you are, trusting in deceptive words to no avail. 9Will you steal,
murder, commit adultery, swear falsely,

[x] 6.27 *Or a fortress* [y] 7.3 *Or and I will let you dwell* [z] 7.4 Heb *They are*

make offerings to Baal, and go after
other gods that you have not known,
10and then come and stand before me
in this house, which is called by my
name, and say, 'We are safe!'—only to go
on doing all these abominations? 11Has
this house, which is called by my name,
become a den of robbers in your sight?
You know, I too am watching, says the
LORD. 12Go now to my place that was in
Shiloh, where I made my name dwell
at first, and see what I did to it for the
wickedness of my people Israel. 13And
now, because you have done all these
things, says the LORD, and when I spoke
to you persistently, you did not listen,
and when I called you, you did not answer, 14therefore I will do to the house
that is called by my name, in which you
trust, and to the place that I gave to you
and to your ancestors, just what I did to
Shiloh. 15And I will cast you out of my
sight, just as I cast out all your kinsfolk,
all the offspring of Ephraim.

THE PEOPLE'S DISOBEDIENCE

16 As for you, do not pray for this
people, do not raise a cry or prayer on
their behalf, and do not intercede with
me, for I will not hear you. 17Do you not
see what they are doing in the towns of
Judah and in the streets of Jerusalem?
18The children gather wood, the fathers kindle fire, and the women knead
dough, to make cakes for the queen
of heaven; and they pour out drink-
offerings to other gods, to provoke me
to anger. 19Is it I whom they provoke?
says the LORD. Is it not themselves, to
their own hurt? 20Therefore thus says
the Lord GOD: My anger and my wrath
shall be poured out on this place, on human beings and animals, on the trees of
the field and the fruit of the ground; it
will burn and not be quenched.

21 Thus says the LORD of hosts, the
God of Israel: Add your burnt-offerings
to your sacrifices, and eat the flesh. 22For
on the day that I brought your ancestors
out of the land of Egypt, I did not speak
to them or command them concerning
burnt-offerings and sacrifices. 23But this
command I gave them, 'Obey my voice,
and I will be your God, and you shall be
my people; and walk only in the way
that I command you, so that it may be
well with you.' 24Yet they did not obey
or incline their ear, but, in the stubbornness of their evil will, they walked
in their own counsels, and looked backwards rather than forwards. 25From the
day that your ancestors came out of the
land of Egypt until this day, I have persistently sent all my servants the prophets to them, day after day; 26yet they
did not listen to me, or pay attention,
but they stiffened their necks. They did
worse than their ancestors did.

27 So you shall speak all these words
to them, but they will not listen to you.
You shall call to them, but they will not
answer you. 28You shall say to them:
This is the nation that did not obey the
voice of the LORD their God, and did not
accept discipline; truth has perished; it
is cut off from their lips.

29 Cut off your hair and throw it away;
raise a lamentation on the
bare heights,[a]
for the LORD has rejected
and forsaken
the generation that
provoked his wrath.

30 For the people of Judah have done
evil in my sight, says the LORD; they
have set their abominations in the
house that is called by my name, defiling it. 31And they go on building the
high place[b] of Topheth, which is in the
valley of the son of Hinnom, to burn
their sons and their daughters in the
fire—which I did not command, nor did
it come into my mind. 32Therefore, the
days are surely coming, says the LORD,
when it will no more be called Topheth,
or the valley of the son of Hinnom, but
the valley of Slaughter: for they will
bury in Topheth until there is no more
room. 33The corpses of this people will
be food for the birds of the air, and for
the animals of the earth; and no one will
frighten them away. 34And I will bring
to an end the sound of mirth and gladness, the voice of the bride and bridegroom in the cities of Judah and in the
streets of Jerusalem; for the land shall
become a waste.

8 At that time, says the LORD, the
bones of the kings of Judah, the
bones of its officials, the bones of the
priests, the bones of the prophets, and
the bones of the inhabitants of Jerusalem shall be brought out of their
tombs; 2and they shall be spread before
the sun and the moon and all the host
of heaven, which they have loved and
served, which they have followed, and
which they have inquired of and worshipped; and they shall not be gathered

[a] 7.29 Or *the trails* [b] 7.31 Gk Tg: Heb *high places*

or buried; they shall be like dung on
the surface of the ground. 3 Death shall
be preferred to life by all the remnant
that remains of this evil family in all the
places where I have driven them, says
the LORD of hosts.

THE BLIND PERVERSITY OF THE WHOLE NATION

4 You shall say to them, Thus
says the LORD:
When people fall, do they
not get up again?
If they go astray, do they
not turn back?
5 Why then has this people[c]
turned away
in perpetual backsliding?
They have held fast to deceit,
they have refused to return.
6 I have given heed and listened,
but they do not speak honestly;
no one repents of wickedness,
saying, 'What have I done!'
All of them turn to their own course,
like a horse plunging
headlong into battle.
7 Even the stork in the heavens
knows its times;
and the turtle-dove, swallow,
and crane[d]
observe the time of their coming;
but my people do not know
the ordinance of the LORD.

8 How can you say, 'We are wise,
and the law of the LORD
is with us',
when, in fact, the false pen
of the scribes
has made it into a lie?
9 The wise shall be put to shame,
they shall be dismayed and taken;
since they have rejected the
word of the LORD,
what wisdom is in them?
10 Therefore I will give their
wives to others
and their fields to conquerors,
because from the least to the greatest
everyone is greedy for unjust gain;
from prophet to priest
everyone deals falsely.
11 They have treated the wound of
my people carelessly,
saying, 'Peace, peace',
when there is no peace.
12 They acted shamefully, they
committed abomination;
yet they were not at all ashamed,
they did not know how to blush.
Therefore they shall fall among
those who fall;
at the time when I punish them,
they shall be overthrown,
says the LORD.
13 When I wanted to gather them,
says the LORD,
there are[e] no grapes on the vine,
nor figs on the fig tree;
even the leaves are withered,
and what I gave them has
passed away from them.[f]
14 Why do we sit still?
Gather together, let us go into
the fortified cities
and perish there;
for the LORD our God has
doomed us to perish,
and has given us poisoned
water to drink,
because we have sinned
against the LORD.
15 We look for peace, but
find no good,
for a time of healing, but
there is terror instead.

16 The snorting of their horses
is heard from Dan;
at the sound of the neighing
of their stallions
the whole land quakes.
They come and devour the land
and all that fills it,
the city and those who live in it.
17 See, I am letting snakes loose
among you,
adders that cannot be charmed,
and they shall bite you,
says the LORD.

THE PROPHET MOURNS FOR THE PEOPLE

18 My joy is gone, grief is upon me,
my heart is sick.
19 Hark, the cry of my poor people
from far and wide in the land:
'Is the LORD not in Zion?
Is her King not in her?'
('Why have they provoked me to
anger with their images,
with their foreign idols?')
20 'The harvest is past, the
summer is ended,
and we are not saved.'

[c] 8.5 One Ms Gk: MT *this people, Jerusalem,*
[d] 8.7 Meaning of Heb uncertain [e] 8.13 Or *I will make an end of them, says the LORD. There are*
[f] 8.13 Meaning of Heb uncertain

21 For the hurt of my poor
people I am hurt,
I mourn, and dismay has
taken hold of me.

22 Is there no balm in Gilead?
Is there no physician there?
Why then has the health of
my poor people
not been restored?

9 [g] O that my head were a
spring of water,
and my eyes a fountain of tears,
so that I might weep day and night
for the slain of my poor people!
2[h] O that I had in the desert
a traveller's lodging-place,
that I might leave my people
and go away from them!
For they are all adulterers,
a band of traitors.
3 They bend their tongues like bows;
they have grown strong in
the land for falsehood,
and not for truth;
for they proceed from evil to evil,
and they do not know me,
says the LORD.

4 Beware of your neighbours,
and put no trust in any of your kin;[i]
for all your kin[j] are supplanters,
and every neighbour goes
around like a slanderer.
5 They all deceive their neighbours,
and no one speaks the truth;
they have taught their tongues
to speak lies;
they commit iniquity and are
too weary to repent.[k]
6 Oppression upon oppression,
deceit[l] upon deceit!
They refuse to know me,
says the LORD.

7 Therefore, thus says the
LORD of hosts:
I will now refine and test them,
for what else can I do with
my sinful people?[m]
8 Their tongue is a deadly arrow;
it speaks deceit through
the mouth.
They all speak friendly words
to their neighbours,
but inwardly are planning
to lay an ambush.
9 Shall I not punish them for these
things? says the LORD;
and shall I not bring retribution
on a nation such as this?

10 Take up[n] weeping and wailing
for the mountains,
and a lamentation for the
pastures of the wilderness,
because they are laid waste so that
no one passes through,
and the lowing of cattle
is not heard;
both the birds of the air and
the animals
have fled and are gone.
11 I will make Jerusalem a
heap of ruins,
a lair of jackals;
and I will make the towns of
Judah a desolation
without inhabitant.

12 Who is wise enough to understand this? To whom has the mouth of
the LORD spoken, so that they may declare it? Why is the land ruined and laid
waste like a wilderness, so that no one
passes through? 13 And the LORD says:
Because they have forsaken my law that
I set before them, and have not obeyed
my voice, or walked in accordance with
it, 14 but have stubbornly followed their
own hearts and have gone after the
Baals, as their ancestors taught them.
15 Therefore, thus says the LORD of hosts,
the God of Israel: I am feeding this people with wormwood, and giving them
poisonous water to drink. 16 I will scatter
them among nations that neither they
nor their ancestors have known; and I
will send the sword after them, until I
have consumed them.

THE PEOPLE MOURN IN JUDGEMENT

17 Thus says the LORD of hosts:
Consider, and call for the
mourning-women to come;
send for the skilled
women to come;
18 let them quickly raise a dirge over us,
so that our eyes may run
down with tears,
and our eyelids flow with water.
19 For a sound of wailing is
heard from Zion:
'How we are ruined!
We are utterly shamed,

[g] **9.1** Ch 8.23 in Heb [h] **9.2** Ch 9.1 in Heb [i] **9.4** Heb *in a brother* [j] **9.4** Heb *for every brother* [k] **9.5** Cn Compare Gk: Heb *they weary themselves with iniquity.* [6]*Your dwelling* [l] **9.6** Cn: Heb *Your dwelling in the midst of deceit* [m] **9.7** Or *my poor people* [n] **9.10** Gk Syr: Heb *I will take up*

because we have left the land,
because they have cast down
our dwellings.'

20 Hear, O women, the word
of the LORD,
and let your ears receive the
word of his mouth;
teach to your daughters a dirge,
and each to her neighbour
a lament.
21 'Death has come up into our windows,
it has entered our palaces,
to cut off the children from the streets
and the young men from
the squares.'
22 Speak! Thus says the LORD:
'Human corpses shall fall
like dung upon the open field,
like sheaves behind the reaper,
and no one shall gather them.'

23 Thus says the LORD: Do not let the
wise boast in their wisdom, do not let
the mighty boast in their might, do not
let the wealthy boast in their wealth;
24but let those who boast boast in this,
that they understand and know me,
that I am the LORD; I act with steadfast
love, justice, and righteousness in the
earth, for in these things I delight, says
the LORD.
25 The days are surely coming, says
the LORD, when I will attend to all
those who are circumcised only in the
foreskin: 26Egypt, Judah, Edom, the
Ammonites, Moab, and all those with
shaven temples who live in the desert.
For all these nations are uncircumcised,
and all the house of Israel is uncircumcised in heart.

IDOLATRY HAS BROUGHT RUIN ON ISRAEL

10 Hear the word that the LORD speaks to you, O house of Israel.
2Thus says the LORD:
Do not learn the way of the nations,
or be dismayed at the signs
of the heavens;
for the nations are
dismayed at them.
3 For the customs of the
peoples are false:
a tree from the forest is cut down,
and worked with an axe by the
hands of an artisan;
4 people deck it with silver and gold;
they fasten it with hammer
and nails
so that it cannot move.
5 Their idols[o] are like scarecrows
in a cucumber field,
and they cannot speak;
they have to be carried,
for they cannot walk.
Do not be afraid of them,
for they cannot do evil,
nor is it in them to do good.

6 There is none like you, O LORD;
you are great, and your name
is great in might.
7 Who would not fear you, O King
of the nations?
For that is your due;
among all the wise ones
of the nations
and in all their kingdoms
there is no one like you.
8 They are both stupid and foolish;
the instruction given by idols
is no better than wood![p]
9 Beaten silver is brought
from Tarshish,
and gold from Uphaz.
They are the work of the artisan
and of the hands of
the goldsmith;
their clothing is blue and purple;
they are all the product of
skilled workers.
10 But the LORD is the true God;
he is the living God and the
everlasting King.
At his wrath the earth quakes,
and the nations cannot endure
his indignation.

11 Thus shall you say to them: The
gods who did not make the heavens and
the earth shall perish from the earth
and from under the heavens.[q]

12 It is he who made the earth
by his power,
who established the world
by his wisdom,
and by his understanding
stretched out the heavens.
13 When he utters his voice, there
is a tumult of waters
in the heavens,
and he makes the mist rise from
the ends of the earth.
He makes lightnings for the rain,
and he brings out the wind
from his storehouses.

[o] 10.5 Heb *They* [p] 10.8 Meaning of Heb uncertain [q] 10.11 This verse is in Aramaic

14 Everyone is stupid and without
knowledge;
goldsmiths are all put to
shame by their idols;
for their images are false,
and there is no breath in them.
15 They are worthless, a work of delusion;
at the time of their punishment
they shall perish.
16 Not like these is the LORD,[r] the
portion of Jacob,
for he is the one who
formed all things,
and Israel is the tribe of his
inheritance;
the LORD of hosts is his name.

THE COMING EXILE

17 Gather up your bundle from
the ground,
O you who live under siege!
18 For thus says the LORD:
I am going to fling away the
inhabitants of the land
at this time,
and I will bring distress on them,
so that they shall feel it.

19 Woe is me because of my hurt!
My wound is severe.
But I said, 'Truly this is my
punishment,
and I must bear it.'
20 My tent is destroyed,
and all my cords are broken;
my children have gone from me,
and they are no more;
there is no one to spread
my tent again,
and to set up my curtains.
21 For the shepherds are stupid,
and do not inquire of the LORD;
therefore they have not prospered,
and all their flock is scattered.

22 Hear, a noise! Listen, it is coming—
a great commotion from the
land of the north
to make the cities of Judah
a desolation,
a lair of jackals.

23 I know, O LORD, that the way
of human beings is not
in their control,
that mortals as they walk
cannot direct their steps.
24 Correct me, O LORD, but in
just measure;
not in your anger, or you will
bring me to nothing.
25 Pour out your wrath on the nations
that do not know you,
and on the peoples that do
not call on your name;
for they have devoured Jacob;
they have devoured him
and consumed him,
and have laid waste his
habitation.

ISRAEL AND JUDAH HAVE BROKEN THE COVENANT

11 The word that came to Jeremiah
from the LORD: 2 Hear the words
of this covenant, and speak to the people of Judah and the inhabitants of Jerusalem. 3 You shall say to them, Thus
says the LORD, the God of Israel: Cursed
be anyone who does not heed the words
of this covenant, 4 which I commanded
your ancestors when I brought them
out of the land of Egypt, from the iron-
smelter, saying, Listen to my voice, and
do all that I command you. So shall you
be my people, and I will be your God,
5 that I may perform the oath that I
swore to your ancestors, to give them
a land flowing with milk and honey, as
at this day. Then I answered, 'So be it,
LORD.'
6 And the LORD said to me: Proclaim
all these words in the cities of Judah,
and in the streets of Jerusalem: Hear
the words of this covenant and do them.
7 For I solemnly warned your ancestors
when I brought them up out of the land
of Egypt, warning them persistently,
even to this day, saying, Obey my voice.
8 Yet they did not obey or incline their
ear, but everyone walked in the stubbornness of an evil will. So I brought
upon them all the words of this covenant, which I commanded them to do,
but they did not.
9 And the LORD said to me: Conspiracy exists among the people of Judah and the inhabitants of Jerusalem.
10 They have turned back to the iniquities of their ancestors of old, who
refused to heed my words; they have
gone after other gods to serve them; the
house of Israel and the house of Judah
have broken the covenant that I made
with their ancestors. 11 Therefore, thus
says the LORD, assuredly I am going to
bring disaster upon them that they cannot escape; though they cry out to me,
I will not listen to them. 12 Then the cities of Judah and the inhabitants of Je-

r 10.16 Heb lacks *the LORD*

rusalem will go and cry out to the gods
to whom they make offerings, but they
will never save them in the time of their
trouble. 13 For your gods have become as
many as your towns, O Judah; and as
many as the streets of Jerusalem are the
altars to shame that you have set up, altars to make offerings to Baal.
14 As for you, do not pray for this
people, or lift up a cry or prayer on their
behalf, for I will not listen when they call
to me in the time of their trouble. 15 What
right has my beloved in my house, when
she has done vile deeds? Can vows[s] and
sacrificial flesh avert your doom? Can
you then exult? 16 The LORD once called
you, 'A green olive tree, fair with goodly
fruit'; but with the roar of a great tempest he will set fire to it, and its branches
will be consumed. 17 The LORD of hosts,
who planted you, has pronounced evil
against you, because of the evil that the
house of Israel and the house of Judah
have done, provoking me to anger by
making offerings to Baal.

JEREMIAH'S LIFE THREATENED

18 It was the LORD who made it
known to me, and I knew;
then you showed me
their evil deeds.
19 But I was like a gentle lamb
led to the slaughter.
And I did not know it was
against me
that they devised schemes, saying,
'Let us destroy the tree with its fruit,
let us cut him off from the
land of the living,
so that his name will no longer
be remembered!'
20 But you, O LORD of hosts, who
judge righteously,
who try the heart and the mind,
let me see your retribution
upon them,
for to you I have committed
my cause.

21 Therefore thus says the LORD concerning the people of Anathoth, who
seek your life, and say, 'You shall not
prophesy in the name of the LORD, or
you will die by our hand'— 22 therefore
thus says the LORD of hosts: I am going
to punish them; the young men shall
die by the sword; their sons and their
daughters shall die by famine; 23 and not
even a remnant shall be left of them.
For I will bring disaster upon the people of Anathoth, the year of their punishment.

JEREMIAH COMPLAINS TO GOD

12 You will be in the
right, O LORD,
when I lay charges against you;
but let me put my case to you.
Why does the way of the
guilty prosper?
Why do all who are
treacherous thrive?
2 You plant them, and they take root;
they grow and bring forth fruit;
you are near in their mouths
yet far from their hearts.
3 But you, O LORD, know me;
You see me and test me—my
heart is with you.
Pull them out like sheep for
the slaughter,
and set them apart for the
day of slaughter.
4 How long will the land mourn,
and the grass of every
field wither?
For the wickedness of those
who live in it
the animals and the birds
are swept away,
and because people said, 'He
is blind to our ways.'[t]

GOD REPLIES TO JEREMIAH

5 If you have raced with foot-runners
and they have wearied you,
how will you compete
with horses?
And if in a safe land you fall down,
how will you fare in the
thickets of the Jordan?
6 For even your kinsfolk and
your own family,
even they have dealt
treacherously with you;
they are in full cry after you;
do not believe them,
though they speak friendly
words to you.

7 I have forsaken my house,
I have abandoned my heritage;
I have given the beloved
of my heart
into the hands of her enemies.
8 My heritage has become to me
like a lion in the forest;
she has lifted up her voice
against me—
therefore I hate her.

[s] 11.15 Gk: Heb *Can many* [t] 12.4 Gk: Heb *to our future*

9 Is the hyena greedy[u] for my
heritage at my command?
Are the birds of prey all
around her?
Go, assemble all the wild animals;
bring them to devour her.
10 Many shepherds have destroyed
my vineyard,
they have trampled down
my portion,
they have made my pleasant portion
a desolate wilderness.
11 They have made it a desolation;
desolate, it mourns to me.
The whole land is made desolate,
but no one lays it to heart.
12 Upon all the bare heights[v]
in the desert
spoilers have come;
for the sword of the LORD devours
from one end of the land
to the other;
no one shall be safe.
13 They have sown wheat and
have reaped thorns,
they have tired themselves
out but profit nothing.
They shall be ashamed of
their[w] harvests
because of the fierce anger
of the LORD.

14 Thus says the LORD concerning all
my evil neighbours who touch the heritage that I have given my people Israel
to inherit: I am about to pluck them
up from their land, and I will pluck up
the house of Judah from among them.
15 And after I have plucked them up, I
will again have compassion on them,
and I will bring them again to their
heritage and to their land, every one of
them. 16 And then, if they will diligently
learn the ways of my people, to swear
by my name, 'As the LORD lives', as they
taught my people to swear by Baal, then
they shall be built up in the midst of my
people. 17 But if any nation will not listen, then I will completely uproot it and
destroy it, says the LORD.

THE LINEN LOINCLOTH

13 Thus said the LORD to me, 'Go
and buy yourself a linen loin-
cloth, and put it on your loins, but do not
dip it in water.' 2 So I bought a loincloth
according to the word of the LORD, and
put it on my loins. 3 And the word of the
LORD came to me a second time, saying,
4 'Take the loincloth that you bought
and are wearing, and go now to the Euphrates,[x] and hide it there in a cleft of
the rock.' 5 So I went, and hid it by the
Euphrates,[y] as the LORD commanded
me. 6 And after many days the LORD
said to me, 'Go now to the Euphrates,[z]
and take from there the loincloth that I
commanded you to hide there.' 7 Then I
went to the Euphrates,[a] and dug, and I
took the loincloth from the place where
I had hidden it. But now the loincloth
was ruined; it was good for nothing.
8 Then the word of the LORD came to
me: 9 Thus says the LORD: Just so I will
ruin the pride of Judah and the great
pride of Jerusalem. 10 This evil people,
who refuse to hear my words, who stubbornly follow their own will and have
gone after other gods to serve them and
worship them, shall be like this loincloth, which is good for nothing. 11 For
as the loincloth clings to one's loins, so I
made the whole house of Israel and the
whole house of Judah cling to me, says
the LORD, in order that they might be
for me a people, a name, a praise, and a
glory. But they would not listen.

SYMBOL OF THE WINE-JARS

12 You shall speak to them this word:
Thus says the LORD, the God of Israel: Every wine-jar should be filled with wine.
And they will say to you, 'Do you think
we do not know that every wine-jar
should be filled with wine?' 13 Then you
shall say to them: Thus says the LORD:
I am about to fill all the inhabitants of
this land—the kings who sit on David's
throne, the priests, the prophets, and
all the inhabitants of Jerusalem—with
drunkenness. 14 And I will dash them
one against another, parents and children together, says the LORD. I will not
pity or spare or have compassion when
I destroy them.

EXILE THREATENED

15 Hear and give ear; do not
be haughty,
for the LORD has spoken.
16 Give glory to the LORD your God
before he brings darkness,
and before your feet stumble
on the mountains at twilight;
while you look for light,
he turns it into gloom
and makes it deep darkness.

[u] 12.9 Cn: Heb *Is the hyena, the bird of prey*
[v] 12.12 Or *the trails* [w] 12.13 Heb *your*
[x] 13.4 Or *to Parah*; Heb *perath* [y] 13.5 Or *by Parah*; Heb *perath* [z] 13.6 Or *to Parah*; Heb *perath* [a] 13.7 Or *to Parah*; Heb *perath*

17 But if you will not listen,
my soul will weep in secret
for your pride;
my eyes will weep bitterly and
run down with tears,
because the LORD's flock has
been taken captive.

18 Say to the king and the
queen mother:
'Take a lowly seat,
for your beautiful crown
has come down from your head.'[b]
19 The towns of the Negeb are shut up
with no one to open them;
all Judah is taken into exile,
wholly taken into exile.

20 Lift up your eyes and see
those who come from the north.
Where is the flock that was given you,
your beautiful flock?
21 What will you say when they
set as head over you
those whom you have trained
to be your allies?
Will not pangs take hold of you,
like those of a woman in labour?
22 And if you say in your heart,
'Why have these things
come upon me?'
it is for the greatness of your iniquity
that your skirts are lifted up,
and you are violated.
23 Can Ethiopians[c] change their skin
or leopards their spots?
Then also you can do good
who are accustomed to do evil.
24 I will scatter you[d] like chaff
driven by the wind from
the desert.
25 This is your lot,
the portion I have measured out
to you, says the LORD,
because you have forgotten me
and trusted in lies.
26 I myself will lift up your skirts
over your face,
and your shame will be seen.
27 I have seen your abominations,
your adulteries and neighings,
your shameless prostitutions
on the hills of the countryside.
Woe to you, O Jerusalem!
How long will it be
before you are made clean?

THE GREAT DROUGHT

14 The word of the LORD that came to Jeremiah concerning the drought:

2 Judah mourns
and her gates languish;
they lie in gloom on the ground,
and the cry of Jerusalem goes up.
3 Her nobles send their servants
for water;
they come to the cisterns,
they find no water,
they return with their
vessels empty.
They are ashamed and dismayed
and cover their heads,
4 because the ground is cracked.
Because there has been no
rain on the land
the farmers are dismayed;
they cover their heads.
5 Even the doe in the field forsakes
her newborn fawn
because there is no grass.
6 The wild asses stand on the
bare heights,[e]
they pant for air like jackals;
their eyes fail
because there is no herbage.

7 Although our iniquities
testify against us,
act, O LORD, for your name's sake;
our apostasies indeed are many,
and we have sinned against you.
8 O hope of Israel,
its saviour in time of trouble,
why should you be like a
stranger in the land,
like a traveller turning aside
for the night?
9 Why should you be like
someone confused,
like a mighty warrior who
cannot give help?
Yet you, O LORD, are in the
midst of us,
and we are called by your name;
do not forsake us!

10 Thus says the LORD concerning
this people:
Truly they have loved to wander,
they have not restrained their feet;
therefore the LORD does not
accept them,
now he will remember
their iniquity
and punish their sins.

11 The LORD said to me: Do not pray
for the welfare of this people. 12 Although

[b] 13.18 Gk Syr Vg: Meaning of Heb uncertain
[c] 13.23 Or *Nubians*; Heb *Cushites* [d] 13.24 Heb *them* [e] 14.6 Or *the trails*

they fast, I do not hear their cry, and
although they offer burnt-offering and
grain-offering, I do not accept them; but
by the sword, by famine, and by pestilence I consume them.

DENUNCIATION OF LYING PROPHETS

13 Then I said: 'Ah, Lord GOD! Here
are the prophets saying to them, "You
shall not see the sword, nor shall you
have famine, but I will give you true
peace in this place." ' 14 And the LORD
said to me: The prophets are prophesying lies in my name; I did not send
them, nor did I command them or
speak to them. They are prophesying
to you a lying vision, worthless divination, and the deceit of their own
minds. 15 Therefore thus says the LORD
concerning the prophets who prophesy in my name though I did not send
them, and who say, 'Sword and famine
shall not come on this land': By sword
and famine those prophets shall be consumed. 16 And the people to whom they
prophesy shall be thrown out into the
streets of Jerusalem, victims of famine
and sword. There shall be no one to bury
them—themselves, their wives, their
sons, and their daughters. For I will
pour out their wickedness upon them.

17 You shall say to them this word:
Let my eyes run down with
tears night and day,
and let them not cease,
for the virgin daughter—my
people—is struck down
with a crushing blow,
with a very grievous wound.
18 If I go out into the field,
look—those killed by the sword!
And if I enter the city,
look—those sick with[f] famine!
For both prophet and priest ply their
trade throughout the land,
and have no knowledge.

THE PEOPLE PLEAD FOR MERCY

19 Have you completely
rejected Judah?
Does your heart loathe Zion?
Why have you struck us down
so that there is no healing for us?
We look for peace, but find no good;
for a time of healing, but
there is terror instead.
20 We acknowledge our
wickedness, O LORD,
the iniquity of our ancestors,
for we have sinned against you.
21 Do not spurn us, for your
name's sake;
do not dishonour your
glorious throne;
remember and do not break
your covenant with us.
22 Can any idols of the nations
bring rain?
Or can the heavens give showers?
Is it not you, O LORD our God?
We set our hope on you,
for it is you who do all this.

PUNISHMENT IS INEVITABLE

15 Then the LORD said to me:
Though Moses and Samuel stood
before me, yet my heart would not turn
towards this people. Send them out of
my sight, and let them go! 2 And when
they say to you, 'Where shall we go?' you
shall say to them: Thus says the LORD:
Those destined for pestilence,
to pestilence,
and those destined for the
sword, to the sword;
those destined for famine, to famine,
and those destined for
captivity, to captivity.
3 And I will appoint over them four
kinds of destroyers, says the LORD: the
sword to kill, the dogs to drag away, and
the birds of the air and the wild animals
of the earth to devour and destroy. 4 I
will make them a horror to all the kingdoms of the earth because of what King
Manasseh son of Hezekiah of Judah did
in Jerusalem.

5 Who will have pity on you,
O Jerusalem,
or who will bemoan you?
Who will turn aside
to ask about your welfare?
6 You have rejected me,
says the LORD,
you are going backwards;
so I have stretched out my
hand against you and
destroyed you—
I am weary of relenting.
7 I have winnowed them with
a winnowing-fork
in the gates of the land;
I have bereaved them, I have
destroyed my people;
they did not turn from their ways.
8 Their widows became more
numerous
than the sand of the seas;

[f] **14.18** Heb *look—the sicknesses of*

I have brought against the
mothers of youths
a destroyer at noonday;
I have made anguish and terror
fall upon her suddenly.
9 She who bore seven has
languished;
she has swooned away;
her sun went down while
it was yet day;
she has been shamed
and disgraced.
And the rest of them I will
give to the sword
before their enemies,
says the LORD.

JEREMIAH COMPLAINS AGAIN AND IS REASSURED

10 Woe is me, my mother, that you
ever bore me, a man of strife and contention to the whole land! I have not
lent, nor have I borrowed, yet all of
them curse me. 11The LORD said: Surely
I have intervened in your life[g] for good,
surely I have imposed enemies on you
in a time of trouble and in a time of distress.[h] 12Can iron and bronze break iron
from the north?
13 Your wealth and your treasures I
will give as plunder, without price, for
all your sins, throughout all your territory. 14I will make you serve your enemies in a land that you do not know, for
in my anger a fire is kindled that shall
burn for ever.
15 O LORD, you know;
remember me and visit me,
and bring down retribution for
me on my persecutors.
In your forbearance do not
take me away;
know that on your account
I suffer insult.
16 Your words were found,
and I ate them,
and your words became
to me a joy
and the delight of my heart;
for I am called by your name,
O LORD, God of hosts.
17 I did not sit in the company
of merrymakers,
nor did I rejoice;
under the weight of your
hand I sat alone,
for you had filled me with
indignation.
18 Why is my pain unceasing,
my wound incurable,
refusing to be healed?
Truly, you are to me like a
deceitful brook,
like waters that fail.
19 Therefore, thus says the LORD:
If you turn back, I will take you back,
and you shall stand before me.
If you utter what is precious, and
not what is worthless,
you shall serve as my mouth.
It is they who will turn to you,
not you who will turn to them.
20 And I will make you to this people
a fortified wall of bronze;
they will fight against you,
but they shall not prevail over you,
for I am with you
to save you and deliver you,
says the LORD.
21 I will deliver you out of the
hand of the wicked,
and redeem you from the
grasp of the ruthless.

JEREMIAH'S CELIBACY AND MESSAGE

16 The word of the LORD came to
me: 2You shall not take a wife,
nor shall you have sons or daughters in
this place. 3For thus says the LORD concerning the sons and daughters who are
born in this place, and concerning the
mothers who bear them and the fathers
who beget them in this land: 4They shall
die of deadly diseases. They shall not be
lamented, nor shall they be buried; they
shall become like dung on the surface
of the ground. They shall perish by the
sword and by famine, and their dead
bodies shall become food for the birds of
the air and for the wild animals of the
earth.
5 For thus says the LORD: Do not enter the house of mourning, or go to lament, or bemoan them; for I have taken
away my peace from this people, says
the LORD, my steadfast love and mercy.
6Both great and small shall die in this
land; they shall not be buried, and no
one shall lament for them; there shall be
no gashing, no shaving of the head for
them. 7No one shall break bread[i] for the
mourner, to offer comfort for the dead;
nor shall anyone give them the cup of
consolation to drink for their fathers or
their mothers. 8You shall not go into
the house of feasting to sit with them, to
eat and drink. 9For thus says the LORD
of hosts, the God of Israel: I am going to

g 15.11 Heb *intervened with you*
h 15.11 Meaning of Heb uncertain i 16.7 Two Mss Gk: MT *break for them*

banish from this place, in your days and
before your eyes, the voice of mirth and
the voice of gladness, the voice of the
bridegroom and the voice of the bride.
10 And when you tell this people all
these words, and they say to you, 'Why
has the LORD pronounced all this great
evil against us? What is our iniquity?
What is the sin that we have committed against the LORD our God?' 11then
you shall say to them: It is because
your ancestors have forsaken me, says
the LORD, and have gone after other
gods and have served and worshipped
them, and have forsaken me and have
not kept my law; 12and because you have
behaved worse than your ancestors, for
here you are, every one of you, following your stubborn, evil will, refusing to
listen to me. 13Therefore I will hurl you
out of this land into a land that neither
you nor your ancestors have known,
and there you shall serve other gods day
and night, for I will show you no favour.

GOD WILL RESTORE ISRAEL

14 Therefore, the days are surely
coming, says the LORD, when it shall no
longer be said, 'As the LORD lives who
brought the people of Israel up out of the
land of Egypt', 15but 'As the LORD lives
who brought the people of Israel up out
of the land of the north and out of all the
lands where he had driven them.' For I
will bring them back to their own land
that I gave to their ancestors.
16 I am now sending for many fishermen, says the LORD, and they shall
catch them; and afterwards I will send
for many hunters, and they shall hunt
them from every mountain and every
hill, and out of the clefts of the rocks.
17For my eyes are on all their ways; they
are not hidden from my presence, nor is
their iniquity concealed from my sight.
18And[j] I will doubly repay their iniquity and their sin, because they have
polluted my land with the carcasses of
their detestable idols, and have filled my
inheritance with their abominations.

19 O LORD, my strength and
my stronghold,
my refuge on the day of trouble,
to you shall the nations come
from the ends of the
earth and say:
Our ancestors have inherited
nothing but lies,
worthless things in which
there is no profit.
20 Can mortals make for
themselves gods?
Such are no gods!

21 'Therefore I am surely going to
teach them, this time I am going to
teach them my power and my might,
and they shall know that my name is
the LORD.'

JUDAH'S SIN AND PUNISHMENT

17 The sin of Judah is written with
an iron pen; with a diamond
point it is engraved on the tablet of their
hearts, and on the horns of their altars,
2while their children remember their
altars and their sacred poles,[k] beside
every green tree, and on the high hills,
3on the mountains in the open country.
Your wealth and all your treasures I will
give for spoil as the price of your sin[l]
throughout all your territory. 4By your
own act you shall lose the heritage that
I gave you, and I will make you serve
your enemies in a land that you do not
know, for in my anger a fire is kindled[m]
that shall burn for ever.

5 Thus says the LORD:
Cursed are those who trust
in mere mortals
and make mere flesh
their strength,
whose hearts turn away
from the LORD.
6 They shall be like a shrub
in the desert,
and shall not see when
relief comes.
They shall live in the parched
places of the wilderness,
in an uninhabited salt land.

7 Blessed are those who trust
in the LORD,
whose trust is the LORD.
8 They shall be like a tree
planted by water,
sending out its roots by the stream.
It shall not fear when heat comes,
and its leaves shall stay green;
in the year of drought it is
not anxious,
and it does not cease to bear fruit.

9 The heart is devious above all else;
it is perverse—
who can understand it?

[j] **16.18** Gk: Heb *And first* [k] **17.2** Heb *Asherim*
[l] **17.3** Cn: Heb *spoil your high places for sin*
[m] **17.4** Two Mss Theodotion: *you kindled*

10 I the LORD test the mind
and search the heart,
to give to all according to their ways,
according to the fruit of
their doings.

11 Like the partridge hatching
what it did not lay,
so are all who amass
wealth unjustly;
in mid-life it will leave them,
and at their end they will
prove to be fools.

12 O glorious throne, exalted
from the beginning,
shrine of our sanctuary!
13 O hope of Israel! O LORD!
All who forsake you shall
be put to shame;
those who turn away from
you[n] shall be recorded
in the underworld,[o]
for they have forsaken the
fountain of living
water, the LORD.

JEREMIAH PRAYS FOR VINDICATION

14 Heal me, O LORD, and I
shall be healed;
save me, and I shall be saved;
for you are my praise.
15 See how they say to me,
'Where is the word of the LORD?
Let it come!'
16 But I have not run away from being
a shepherd[p] in your service,
nor have I desired the fatal day.
You know what came from my lips;
it was before your face.
17 Do not become a terror to me;
you are my refuge on the
day of disaster;
18 Let my persecutors be shamed,
but do not let me be shamed;
let them be dismayed,
but do not let me be dismayed;
bring on them the day of disaster;
destroy them with double
destruction!

HALLOW THE SABBATH DAY

19 Thus said the LORD to me: Go and
stand in the People's Gate, by which
the kings of Judah enter and by which
they go out, and in all the gates of Jerusalem, 20 and say to them: Hear the
word of the LORD, you kings of Judah,
and all Judah, and all the inhabitants
of Jerusalem, who enter by these gates.
21 Thus says the LORD: For the sake of
your lives, take care that you do not bear
a burden on the sabbath day or bring it
in by the gates of Jerusalem. 22 And do
not carry a burden out of your houses
on the sabbath or do any work, but keep
the sabbath day holy, as I commanded
your ancestors. 23 Yet they did not listen
or incline their ear; they stiffened their
necks and would not hear or receive instruction.

24 But if you listen to me, says the
LORD, and bring in no burden by the
gates of this city on the sabbath day,
but keep the sabbath day holy and do
no work on it, 25 then there shall enter
by the gates of this city kings[q] who sit
on the throne of David, riding in chariots and on horses, they and their officials, the people of Judah and the inhabitants of Jerusalem; and this city shall
be inhabited for ever. 26 And people shall
come from the towns of Judah and the
places around Jerusalem, from the land
of Benjamin, from the Shephelah, from
the hill country, and from the Negeb,
bringing burnt-offerings and sacrifices,
grain-offerings and frankincense, and
bringing thank-offerings to the house
of the LORD. 27 But if you do not listen
to me, to keep the sabbath day holy, and
to carry in no burden through the gates
of Jerusalem on the sabbath day, then I
will kindle a fire in its gates; it shall devour the palaces of Jerusalem and shall
not be quenched.

THE POTTER AND THE CLAY

18 The word that came to Jeremiah from the LORD: 2 'Come, go
down to the potter's house, and there I
will let you hear my words.' 3 So I went
down to the potter's house, and there he
was working at his wheel. 4 The vessel he
was making of clay was spoiled in the
potter's hand, and he reworked it into
another vessel, as seemed good to him.

5 Then the word of the LORD came
to me: 6 Can I not do with you, O house
of Israel, just as this potter has done?
says the LORD. Just like the clay in the
potter's hand, so are you in my hand,
O house of Israel. 7 At one moment I
may declare concerning a nation or a
kingdom, that I will pluck up and break
down and destroy it, 8 but if that nation,
concerning which I have spoken, turns
from its evil, I will change my mind
about the disaster that I intended to

[n] 17.13 Heb *me* [o] 17.13 Or *in the earth*
[p] 17.16 Meaning of Heb uncertain [q] 17.25 Cn:
Heb *kings and officials*

bring on it. 9And at another moment
I may declare concerning a nation or a
kingdom that I will build and plant it,
10but if it does evil in my sight, not listening to my voice, then I will change
my mind about the good that I had intended to do to it. 11Now, therefore, say
to the people of Judah and the inhabitants of Jerusalem: Thus says the LORD:
Look, I am a potter shaping evil against
you and devising a plan against you.
Turn now, all of you from your evil way,
and amend your ways and your doings.

ISRAEL'S STUBBORN IDOLATRY

12 But they say, 'It is no use! We will
follow our own plans, and each of us will
act according to the stubbornness of our
evil will.'

13 Therefore, thus says the LORD:
Ask among the nations:
Who has heard the like of this?
The virgin Israel has done
a most horrible thing.
14 Does the snow of Lebanon leave
the crags of Sirion?[r]
Do the mountain[s] waters run dry,[t]
the cold flowing streams?
15 But my people have forgotten me,
they burn offerings
to a delusion;
they have stumbled[u] in their ways,
in the ancient roads,
and have gone into bypaths,
not the highway,
16 making their land a horror,
a thing to be hissed at for ever.
All who pass by it are horrified
and shake their heads.
17 Like the wind from the east,
I will scatter them before
the enemy.
I will show them my back,
not my face,
on the day of their calamity.

A PLOT AGAINST JEREMIAH

18 Then they said, 'Come, let us make
plots against Jeremiah—for instruction
shall not perish from the priest, nor
counsel from the wise, nor the word
from the prophet. Come, let us bring
charges against him,[v] and let us not
heed any of his words.'

19 Give heed to me, O LORD,
and listen to what my
adversaries say!
20 Is evil a recompense for good?
Yet they have dug a pit for my life.
Remember how I stood before you
to speak good for them,
to turn away your wrath
from them.
21 Therefore give their children
over to famine;
hurl them out to the power
of the sword,
let their wives become childless
and widowed.
May their men meet death
by pestilence,
their youths be slain by the
sword in battle.
22 May a cry be heard from
their houses,
when you bring the marauder
suddenly upon them!
For they have dug a pit to catch me,
and laid snares for my feet.
23 Yet you, O LORD, know
all their plotting to kill me.
Do not forgive their iniquity,
do not blot out their sin
from your sight.
Let them be tripped up before you;
deal with them while
you are angry.

THE BROKEN EARTHENWARE JUG

19 Thus said the LORD: Go and buy
a potter's earthenware jug. Take
with you[w] some of the elders of the people and some of the senior priests, 2and
go out to the valley of the son of Hinnom at the entry of the Potsherd Gate,
and proclaim there the words that I tell
you. 3You shall say: Hear the word of
the LORD, O kings of Judah and inhabitants of Jerusalem. Thus says the LORD
of hosts, the God of Israel: I am going to
bring such disaster upon this place that
the ears of everyone who hears of it will
tingle. 4Because the people have forsaken me, and have profaned this place
by making offerings in it to other gods
whom neither they nor their ancestors
nor the kings of Judah have known,
and because they have filled this place
with the blood of the innocent, 5and
gone on building the high places of
Baal to burn their children in the fire
as burnt-offerings to Baal, which I did
not command or decree, nor did it enter
my mind; 6therefore the days are surely

[r] 18.14 Cn: Heb *of the field* [s] 18.14 Cn: Heb *foreign* [t] 18.14 Cn: Heb *Are . . . plucked up?*
[u] 18.15 Gk Syr Vg: Heb *they made them stumble*
[v] 18.18 Heb *strike him with the tongue*
[w] 19.1 Syr Tg Compare Gk: Heb lacks *take with you*

coming, says the LORD, when this place
shall no more be called Topheth, or the
valley of the son of Hinnom, but the
valley of Slaughter. 7And in this place I
will make void the plans of Judah and
Jerusalem, and will make them fall by
the sword before their enemies, and by
the hand of those who seek their life. I
will give their dead bodies for food to
the birds of the air and to the wild animals of the earth. 8And I will make
this city a horror, a thing to be hissed
at; everyone who passes by it will be
horrified and will hiss because of all its
disasters. 9And I will make them eat the
flesh of their sons and the flesh of their
daughters, and all shall eat the flesh of
their neighbours in the siege, and in the
distress with which their enemies and
those who seek their life afflict them.

10 Then you shall break the jug in the
sight of those who go with you, 11and
shall say to them: Thus says the LORD of
hosts: So will I break this people and this
city, as one breaks a potter's vessel, so
that it can never be mended. In Topheth
they shall bury until there is no more
room to bury. 12Thus will I do to this
place, says the LORD, and to its inhabitants, making this city like Topheth.
13And the houses of Jerusalem and the
houses of the kings of Judah shall be defiled like the place of Topheth—all the
houses upon whose roofs offerings have
been made to the whole host of heaven,
and libations have been poured out to
other gods.

14 When Jeremiah came from Topheth, where the LORD had sent him
to prophesy, he stood in the court of the
LORD's house and said to all the people:
15Thus says the LORD of hosts, the God
of Israel: I am now bringing upon this
city and upon all its towns all the disaster that I have pronounced against it,
because they have stiffened their necks,
refusing to hear my words.

JEREMIAH PERSECUTED BY PASHHUR

20 Now the priest Pashhur son of
Immer, who was chief officer
in the house of the LORD, heard Jeremiah prophesying these things. 2Then
Pashhur struck the prophet Jeremiah,
and put him in the stocks that were in
the upper Benjamin Gate of the house
of the LORD. 3The next morning when
Pashhur released Jeremiah from the
stocks, Jeremiah said to him, The LORD
has named you not Pashhur but 'Terror-
all-around.' 4For thus says the LORD: I
am making you a terror to yourself and
to all your friends; and they shall fall by
the sword of their enemies while you
look on. And I will give all Judah into
the hand of the king of Babylon; he shall
carry them captive to Babylon, and shall
kill them with the sword. 5I will give all
the wealth of this city, all its gains, all its
prized belongings, and all the treasures
of the kings of Judah into the hand of
their enemies, who shall plunder them,
and seize them, and carry them to Babylon. 6And you, Pashhur, and all who
live in your house, shall go into captivity, and to Babylon you shall go; there
you shall die, and there you shall be buried, you and all your friends, to whom
you have prophesied falsely.

JEREMIAH DENOUNCES HIS PERSECUTORS

7 O LORD, you have enticed me,
and I was enticed;
you have overpowered me,
and you have prevailed.
I have become a laughing-stock
all day long;
everyone mocks me.
8 For whenever I speak, I must cry out,
I must shout, 'Violence
and destruction!'
For the word of the LORD has
become for me
a reproach and derision
all day long.
9 If I say, 'I will not mention him,
or speak any more in his name',
then within me there is something
like a burning fire
shut up in my bones;
I am weary with holding it in,
and I cannot.
10 For I hear many whispering:
'Terror is all around!
Denounce him! Let us
denounce him!'
All my close friends
are watching for me to stumble.
'Perhaps he can be enticed,
and we can prevail against him,
and take our revenge on him.'
11 But the LORD is with me like
a dread warrior;
therefore my persecutors
will stumble,
and they will not prevail.
They will be greatly shamed,
for they will not succeed.
Their eternal dishonour
will never be forgotten.

12 O LORD of hosts, you test
the righteous,
you see the heart and the mind;
let me see your retribution
upon them,
for to you I have committed
my cause.

13 Sing to the LORD;
praise the LORD!
For he has delivered the life
of the needy
from the hands of evildoers.

14 Cursed be the day
on which I was born!
The day when my mother
bore me,
let it not be blessed!
15 Cursed be the man
who brought the news to
my father, saying,
'A child is born to you, a son',
making him very glad.
16 Let that man be like the cities
that the LORD overthrew
without pity;
let him hear a cry in the morning
and an alarm at noon,
17 because he did not kill me
in the womb;
so my mother would have
been my grave,
and her womb for ever great.
18 Why did I come forth from
the womb
to see toil and sorrow,
and spend my days in shame?

JERUSALEM WILL FALL TO NEBUCHADREZZAR

21 This is the word that came to
Jeremiah from the LORD, when
King Zedekiah sent to him Pashhur
son of Malchiah and the priest Zephaniah son of Maaseiah, saying, 2 'Please
inquire of the LORD on our behalf, for
King Nebuchadrezzar of Babylon is
making war against us; perhaps the
LORD will perform a wonderful deed for
us, as he has often done, and will make
him withdraw from us.'

3 Then Jeremiah said to them: 4 Thus
you shall say to Zedekiah: Thus says the
LORD, the God of Israel: I am going to
turn back the weapons of war that are
in your hands and with which you are
fighting against the king of Babylon
and against the Chaldeans who are besieging you outside the walls; and I will
bring them together into the centre of
this city. 5 I myself will fight against you
with outstretched hand and mighty
arm, in anger, in fury, and in great
wrath. 6 And I will strike down the
inhabitants of this city, both human
beings and animals; they shall die of a
great pestilence. 7 Afterwards, says the
LORD, I will give King Zedekiah of Judah, and his servants, and the people in
this city—those who survive the pestilence, sword, and famine—into the
hands of King Nebuchadrezzar of Babylon, into the hands of their enemies,
into the hands of those who seek their
lives. He shall strike them down with
the edge of the sword; he shall not pity
them, or spare them, or have compassion.

8 And to this people you shall say:
Thus says the LORD: See, I am setting
before you the way of life and the way of
death. 9 Those who stay in this city shall
die by the sword, by famine, and by pestilence; but those who go out and surrender to the Chaldeans who are besieging you shall live and shall have their
lives as a prize of war. 10 For I have set
my face against this city for evil and not
for good, says the LORD: it shall be given
into the hands of the king of Babylon,
and he shall burn it with fire.

MESSAGE TO THE HOUSE OF DAVID

11 To the house of the king of Judah say: Hear the word of the LORD,
12 O house of David! Thus says the LORD:
Execute justice in the morning,
and deliver from the hand
of the oppressor
anyone who has been robbed,
or else my wrath will go
forth like fire,
and burn, with no one
to quench it,
because of your evil doings.

13 See, I am against you, O inhabitant
of the valley,
O rock of the plain,
says the LORD;
you who say, 'Who can come
down against us,
or who can enter our
places of refuge?'
14 I will punish you according to the
fruit of your doings,
says the LORD;
I will kindle a fire in its forest,
and it shall devour all
that is around it.

EXHORTATION TO REPENT

22 Thus says the LORD: Go down to
the house of the king of Judah,
and speak there this word, 2and say:
Hear the word of the LORD, O King of
Judah sitting on the throne of David—
you, and your servants, and your people
who enter these gates. 3Thus says the
LORD: Act with justice and righteousness, and deliver from the hand of the
oppressor anyone who has been robbed.
And do no wrong or violence to the
alien, the orphan, and the widow, nor
shed innocent blood in this place. 4For
if you will indeed obey this word, then
through the gates of this house shall enter kings who sit on the throne of David,
riding in chariots and on horses, they,
and their servants, and their people.
5But if you will not heed these words,
I swear by myself, says the LORD, that
this house shall become a desolation.
6For thus says the LORD concerning the
house of the king of Judah:

You are like Gilead to me,
like the summit of Lebanon;
but I swear that I will make
you a desert,
an uninhabited city.[x]
7 I will prepare destroyers against you,
all with their weapons;
they shall cut down your
choicest cedars
and cast them into the fire.

8 And many nations will pass by this
city, and all of them will say one to another, 'Why has the LORD dealt in this
way with that great city?' 9And they
will answer, 'Because they abandoned
the covenant of the LORD their God, and
worshipped other gods and served them.'

10 Do not weep for him who is dead,
nor bemoan him;
weep rather for him who goes away,
for he shall return no more
to see his native land.

MESSAGE TO THE SONS OF JOSIAH

11 For thus says the LORD concerning Shallum son of King Josiah of Judah, who succeeded his father Josiah,
and who went away from this place: He
shall return here no more, 12but in the
place where they have carried him captive he shall die, and he shall never see
this land again.

13 Woe to him who builds his house
by unrighteousness,
and his upper rooms by injustice;
who makes his neighbours
work for nothing,
and does not give them
their wages;
14 who says, 'I will build myself
a spacious house
with large upper rooms',
and who cuts out windows for it,
panelling it with cedar,
and painting it with vermilion.
15 Are you a king
because you compete in cedar?
Did not your father eat and drink
and do justice and righteousness?
Then it was well with him.
16 He judged the cause of the
poor and needy;
then it was well.
Is not this to know me?
says the LORD.
17 But your eyes and heart
are only on your dishonest gain,
for shedding innocent blood,
and for practising oppression
and violence.

18 Therefore thus says the LORD concerning King Jehoiakim son of Josiah of
Judah:

They shall not lament for him, saying,
'Alas, my brother!' or 'Alas, sister!'
They shall not lament for him, saying,
'Alas, lord!' or 'Alas, his majesty!'
19 With the burial of a donkey he
shall be buried—
dragged off and thrown out beyond
the gates of Jerusalem.

20 Go up to Lebanon, and cry out,
and lift up your voice in Bashan;
cry out from Abarim,
for all your lovers are crushed.
21 I spoke to you in your prosperity,
but you said, 'I will not listen.'
This has been your way from
your youth,
for you have not obeyed my voice.
22 The wind shall shepherd all
your shepherds,
and your lovers shall go
into captivity;
then you will be ashamed
and dismayed
because of all your wickedness.
23 O inhabitant of Lebanon,
nested among the cedars,
how you will groan[y] when pangs
come upon you,
pain as of a woman in labour!

[x] 22.6 Cn: Heb *uninhabited cities* [y] 22.23 Gk Vg Syr: Heb *will be pitied*

JUDGEMENT ON CONIAH (JEHOIACHIN)

24 As I live, says the LORD, even if
King Coniah son of Jehoiakim of Judah
were the signet ring on my right hand,
even from there I would tear you off
25 and give you into the hands of those
who seek your life, into the hands of
those of whom you are afraid, even into
the hands of King Nebuchadrezzar of
Babylon and into the hands of the Chaldeans. 26 I will hurl you and the mother
who bore you into another country,
where you were not born, and there you
shall die. 27 But they shall not return to
the land to which they long to return.

28 Is this man Coniah a despised
broken pot,
a vessel no one wants?
Why are he and his offspring
hurled out
and cast away in a land that
they do not know?
29 O land, land, land,
hear the word of the LORD!
30 Thus says the LORD:
Record this man as childless,
a man who shall not
succeed in his days;
for none of his offspring
shall succeed
in sitting on the throne of David,
and ruling again in Judah.

RESTORATION AFTER EXILE

23 Woe to the shepherds who destroy and scatter the sheep of my
pasture! says the LORD. 2 Therefore, thus
says the LORD, the God of Israel, concerning the shepherds who shepherd
my people: It is you who have scattered
my flock, and have driven them away,
and you have not attended to them.
So I will attend to you for your evil doings, says the LORD. 3 Then I myself will
gather the remnant of my flock out of
all the lands where I have driven them,
and I will bring them back to their fold,
and they shall be fruitful and multiply.
4 I will raise up shepherds over them
who will shepherd them, and they shall
not fear any longer, or be dismayed, nor
shall any be missing, says the LORD.

THE RIGHTEOUS BRANCH OF DAVID

5 The days are surely coming, says
the LORD, when I will raise up for David
a righteous Branch, and he shall reign
as king and deal wisely, and shall execute justice and righteousness in the
land. 6 In his days Judah will be saved
and Israel will live in safety. And this
is the name by which he will be called:
'The LORD is our righteousness.'
7 Therefore, the days are surely coming, says the LORD, when it shall no
longer be said, 'As the LORD lives who
brought the people of Israel up out of
the land of Egypt', 8 but 'As the LORD
lives who brought out and led the offspring of the house of Israel out of the
land of the north and out of all the lands
where he[z] had driven them.' Then they
shall live in their own land.

FALSE PROPHETS OF HOPE DENOUNCED

9 Concerning the prophets:
My heart is crushed within me,
all my bones shake;
I have become like a drunkard,
like one overcome by wine,
because of the LORD
and because of his holy words.
10 For the land is full of adulterers;
because of the curse the
land mourns,
and the pastures of the
wilderness are dried up.
Their course has been evil,
and their might is not right.
11 Both prophet and priest
are ungodly;
even in my house I have found
their wickedness,
says the LORD.
12 Therefore their way shall be to them
like slippery paths in
the darkness,
into which they shall be
driven and fall;
for I will bring disaster upon them
in the year of their punishment,
says the LORD.
13 In the prophets of Samaria
I saw a disgusting thing:
they prophesied by Baal
and led my people Israel astray.
14 But in the prophets of Jerusalem
I have seen a more
shocking thing:
they commit adultery and
walk in lies;
they strengthen the hands
of evildoers,
so that no one turns from
wickedness;
all of them have become like
Sodom to me,
and its inhabitants like Gomorrah.

[z] 23.8 Gk: Heb *I*

15 Therefore thus says the LORD
of hosts concerning
the prophets:
'I am going to make them
eat wormwood,
and give them poisoned
water to drink;
for from the prophets of Jerusalem
ungodliness has spread
throughout the land.'

16 Thus says the LORD of hosts: Do
not listen to the words of the prophets
who prophesy to you; they are deluding
you. They speak visions of their own
minds, not from the mouth of the LORD.
17They keep saying to those who despise
the word of the LORD, 'It shall be well
with you'; and to all who stubbornly follow their own stubborn hearts, they say,
'No calamity shall come upon you.'

18 For who has stood in the
council of the LORD
so as to see and to hear his word?
Who has given heed to his word
so as to proclaim it?
19 Look, the storm of the LORD!
Wrath has gone forth,
a whirling tempest;
it will burst upon the head
of the wicked.
20 The anger of the LORD will
not turn back
until he has executed and
accomplished
the intents of his mind.
In the latter days you will
understand it clearly.

21 I did not send the prophets,
yet they ran;
I did not speak to them,
yet they prophesied.
22 But if they had stood in my council,
then they would have proclaimed
my words to my people,
and they would have turned them
from their evil way,
and from the evil of their doings.

23 Am I a God near by, says the
LORD, and not a God far off? 24Who
can hide in secret places so that I cannot see them? says the LORD. Do I not
fill heaven and earth? says the LORD.
25I have heard what the prophets have
said who prophesy lies in my name, saying, 'I have dreamed, I have dreamed!'
26How long? Will the hearts of the
prophets ever turn back—those who
prophesy lies, and who prophesy the
deceit of their own heart? 27They plan
to make my people forget my name by
their dreams that they tell one another,
just as their ancestors forgot my name
for Baal. 28Let the prophet who has a
dream tell the dream, but let the one
who has my word speak my word faithfully. What has straw in common with
wheat? says the LORD. 29Is not my word
like fire, says the LORD, and like a hammer that breaks a rock in pieces? 30See,
therefore, I am against the prophets,
says the LORD, who steal my words
from one another. 31See, I am against
the prophets, says the LORD, who use
their own tongues and say, 'Says the
LORD.' 32See, I am against those who
prophesy lying dreams, says the LORD,
and who tell them, and who lead my
people astray by their lies and their
recklessness, when I did not send them
or appoint them; so they do not profit
this people at all, says the LORD.

33 When this people, or a prophet, or
a priest asks you, 'What is the burden of
the LORD?' you shall say to them, 'You
are the burden,[a] and I will cast you off,
says the LORD.' 34And as for the prophet,
priest, or the people who say, 'The burden of the LORD', I will punish them and
their households. 35Thus shall you say to
one another, among yourselves, 'What
has the LORD answered?' or 'What has
the LORD spoken?' 36But 'the burden of
the LORD' you shall mention no more,
for the burden is everyone's own word,
and so you pervert the words of the living God, the LORD of hosts, our God.
37Thus you shall ask the prophet, 'What
has the LORD answered you?' or 'What
has the LORD spoken?' 38But if you say,
'the burden of the LORD', thus says the
LORD: Because you have said these
words, 'the burden of the LORD', when
I sent to you, saying, You shall not say,
'the burden of the LORD', 39therefore,
I will surely lift you up[b] and cast you
away from my presence, you and the
city that I gave to you and your ancestors. 40And I will bring upon you everlasting disgrace and perpetual shame,
which shall not be forgotten.

THE GOOD AND THE BAD FIGS

24 The LORD showed me two baskets of figs placed before the
temple of the LORD. This was after King
Nebuchadrezzar of Babylon had taken

[a] 23.33 Gk Vg: Heb *What burden* [b] 23.39 Heb Mss Gk Vg: MT *forget you*

into exile from Jerusalem King Jeconiah son of Jehoiakim of Judah, together with the officials of Judah, the artisans, and the smiths, and had brought them to Babylon. 2One basket had very good figs, like first-ripe figs, but the other basket had very bad figs, so bad that they could not be eaten. 3And the LORD said to me, 'What do you see, Jeremiah?' I said, 'Figs, the good figs very good, and the bad figs very bad, so bad that they cannot be eaten.'

4 Then the word of the LORD came to me: 5Thus says the LORD, the God of Israel: Like these good figs, so I will regard as good the exiles from Judah, whom I have sent away from this place to the land of the Chaldeans. 6I will set my eyes upon them for good, and I will bring them back to this land. I will build them up, and not tear them down; I will plant them, and not pluck them up. 7I will give them a heart to know that I am the LORD; and they shall be my people and I will be their God, for they shall return to me with their whole heart.

8 But thus says the LORD: Like the bad figs that are so bad they cannot be eaten, so will I treat King Zedekiah of Judah, his officials, the remnant of Jerusalem who remain in this land, and those who live in the land of Egypt. 9I will make them a horror, an evil thing, to all the kingdoms of the earth—a disgrace, a byword, a taunt, and a curse in all the places where I shall drive them. 10And I will send sword, famine, and pestilence upon them, until they are utterly destroyed from the land that I gave to them and their ancestors.

THE BABYLONIAN CAPTIVITY FORETOLD

25 The word that came to Jeremiah concerning all the people of Judah, in the fourth year of King Jehoiakim son of Josiah of Judah (that was the first year of King Nebuchadrezzar of Babylon), 2which the prophet Jeremiah spoke to all the people of Judah and all the inhabitants of Jerusalem: 3For twenty-three years, from the thirteenth year of King Josiah son of Amon of Judah to this day, the word of the LORD has come to me, and I have spoken persistently to you, but you have not listened. 4And though the LORD persistently sent you all his servants the prophets, you have neither listened nor inclined your ears to hear 5when they said, 'Turn now, every one of you, from your evil way and wicked doings, and you will remain upon the land that the LORD has given to you and your ancestors from of old and for ever; 6do not go after other gods to serve and worship them, and do not provoke me to anger with the work of your hands. Then I will do you no harm.' 7Yet you did not listen to me, says the LORD, and so you have provoked me to anger with the work of your hands to your own harm.

8 Therefore thus says the LORD of hosts: Because you have not obeyed my words, 9I am going to send for all the tribes of the north, says the LORD, even for King Nebuchadrezzar of Babylon, my servant, and I will bring them against this land and its inhabitants, and against all these nations around; I will utterly destroy them, and make them an object of horror and of hissing, and an everlasting disgrace.[c] 10And I will banish from them the sound of mirth and the sound of gladness, the voice of the bridegroom and the voice of the bride, the sound of the millstones and the light of the lamp. 11This whole land shall become a ruin and a waste, and these nations shall serve the king of Babylon for seventy years. 12Then after seventy years are completed, I will punish the king of Babylon and that nation, the land of the Chaldeans, for their iniquity, says the LORD, making the land an everlasting waste. 13I will bring upon that land all the words that I have uttered against it, everything written in this book, which Jeremiah prophesied against all the nations. 14For many nations and great kings shall make slaves of them also; and I will repay them according to their deeds and the work of their hands.

THE CUP OF GOD'S WRATH

15 For thus the LORD, the God of Israel, said to me: Take from my hand this cup of the wine of wrath, and make all the nations to whom I send you drink it. 16They shall drink and stagger and go out of their minds because of the sword that I am sending among them.

17 So I took the cup from the LORD's hand, and made all the nations to whom the LORD sent me drink it: 18Jerusalem and the towns of Judah, its kings and officials, to make them a desolation and a waste, an object of hissing and of curs-

[c] 25.9 Gk Compare Syr: Heb *and everlasting desolations*

ing, as they are today; 19 Pharaoh king
of Egypt, his servants, his officials, and
all his people; 20 all the mixed people;[d]
all the kings of the land of Uz; all the
kings of the land of the Philistines—
Ashkelon, Gaza, Ekron, and the remnant of Ashdod; 21 Edom, Moab, and
the Ammonites; 22 all the kings of Tyre,
all the kings of Sidon, and the kings of
the coastland across the sea; 23 Dedan,
Tema, Buz, and all who have shaven
temples; 24 all the kings of Arabia and all
the kings of the mixed peoples[e] that live
in the desert; 25 all the kings of Zimri, all
the kings of Elam, and all the kings of
Media; 26 all the kings of the north, far
and near, one after another, and all the
kingdoms of the world that are on the
face of the earth. And after them the
king of Sheshach[f] shall drink.

27 Then you shall say to them, Thus
says the LORD of hosts, the God of Israel:
Drink, get drunk and vomit, fall and rise
no more, because of the sword that I am
sending among you.

28 And if they refuse to accept the
cup from your hand to drink, then you
shall say to them: Thus says the LORD
of hosts: You must drink! 29 See, I am
beginning to bring disaster on the city
that is called by my name, and how can
you possibly avoid punishment? You
shall not go unpunished, for I am summoning a sword against all the inhabitants of the earth, says the LORD of
hosts.

30 You, therefore, shall prophesy
against them all these words, and say
to them:

The LORD will roar from on high,
and from his holy habitation
utter his voice;
he will roar mightily against
his fold,
and shout, like those who
tread grapes,
against all the inhabitants
of the earth.
31 The clamour will resound to the
ends of the earth,
for the LORD has an indictment
against the nations;
he is entering into judgement
with all flesh,
and the guilty he will put
to the sword,
says the LORD.

32 Thus says the LORD of hosts:
See, disaster is spreading
from nation to nation,
and a great tempest is stirring
from the farthest parts
of the earth!

33 Those slain by the LORD on that
day shall extend from one end of the
earth to the other. They shall not be lamented, or gathered, or buried; they
shall become dung on the surface of the
ground.

34 Wail, you shepherds, and cry out;
roll in ashes, you lords of the flock,
for the days of your slaughter
have come—and
your dispersions,[g]
and you shall fall like a
choice vessel.
35 Flight shall fail the shepherds,
and there shall be no escape for
the lords of the flock.
36 Hark! the cry of the shepherds,
and the wail of the lords
of the flock!
For the LORD is despoiling
their pasture,
37 and the peaceful folds
are devastated,
because of the fierce anger
of the LORD.
38 Like a lion he has left his covert;
for their land has become a waste
because of the cruel sword,
and because of his fierce anger.

JEREMIAH'S PROPHECIES IN THE TEMPLE

26 At the beginning of the reign of
King Jehoiakim son of Josiah of
Judah, this word came from the LORD:
2 Thus says the LORD: Stand in the court
of the LORD's house, and speak to all the
cities of Judah that come to worship in
the house of the LORD; speak to them all
the words that I command you; do not
hold back a word. 3 It may be that they
will listen, all of them, and will turn
from their evil way, that I may change
my mind about the disaster that I intend to bring on them because of their
evil doings. 4 You shall say to them: Thus
says the LORD: If you will not listen to
me, to walk in my law that I have set
before you, 5 and to heed the words of
my servants the prophets whom I send
to you urgently—though you have not
heeded— 6 then I will make this house
like Shiloh, and I will make this city a
curse for all the nations of the earth.

[d] 25.20 Meaning of Heb uncertain
[e] 25.24 Meaning of Heb uncertain
[f] 25.26 *Sheshach* is a cryptogram for *Babel*, Babylon [g] 25.34 Meaning of Heb uncertain

7 The priests and the prophets and
all the people heard Jeremiah speaking
these words in the house of the LORD.
8 And when Jeremiah had finished
speaking all that the LORD had commanded him to speak to all the people,
then the priests and the prophets and all
the people laid hold of him, saying, 'You
shall die! 9 Why have you prophesied
in the name of the LORD, saying, "This
house shall be like Shiloh, and this city
shall be desolate, without inhabitant"?'
And all the people gathered around Jeremiah in the house of the LORD.

10 When the officials of Judah heard
these things, they came up from the
king's house to the house of the LORD
and took their seat in the entry of the
New Gate of the house of the LORD.
11 Then the priests and the prophets said
to the officials and to all the people, 'This
man deserves the sentence of death because he has prophesied against this
city, as you have heard with your own
ears.'

12 Then Jeremiah spoke to all the
officials and all the people, saying, 'It
is the LORD who sent me to prophesy
against this house and this city all the
words you have heard. 13 Now therefore
amend your ways and your doings, and
obey the voice of the LORD your God,
and the LORD will change his mind
about the disaster that he has pronounced against you. 14 But as for me,
here I am in your hands. Do with me
as seems good and right to you. 15 Only
know for certain that if you put me to
death, you will be bringing innocent
blood upon yourselves and upon this
city and its inhabitants, for in truth the
LORD sent me to you to speak all these
words in your ears.'

16 Then the officials and all the people said to the priests and the prophets,
'This man does not deserve the sentence
of death, for he has spoken to us in the
name of the LORD our God.' 17 And some
of the elders of the land arose and said
to all the assembled people, 18 'Micah of
Moresheth, who prophesied during the
days of King Hezekiah of Judah, said to
all the people of Judah: "Thus says the
LORD of hosts,

Zion shall be ploughed as a field;
  Jerusalem shall become
    a heap of ruins,
  and the mountain of the house
    a wooded height."

19 Did King Hezekiah of Judah and all
Judah actually put him to death? Did
he not fear the LORD and entreat the favour of the LORD, and did not the LORD
change his mind about the disaster that
he had pronounced against them? But
we are about to bring great disaster on
ourselves!'

20 There was another man prophesying in the name of the LORD, Uriah son
of Shemaiah from Kiriath-jearim. He
prophesied against this city and against
this land in words exactly like those of
Jeremiah. 21 And when King Jehoiakim,
with all his warriors and all the officials,
heard his words, the king sought to put
him to death; but when Uriah heard of
it, he was afraid and fled and escaped
to Egypt. 22 Then King Jehoiakim sent[h]
Elnathan son of Achbor and men with
him to Egypt, 23 and they took Uriah
from Egypt and brought him to King
Jehoiakim, who struck him down with
the sword and threw his dead body into
the burial place of the common people.

24 But the hand of Ahikam son of
Shaphan was with Jeremiah so that he
was not given over into the hands of the
people to be put to death.

THE SIGN OF THE YOKE

27 In the beginning of the reign of
King Zedekiah[i] son of Josiah of
Judah, this word came to Jeremiah from
the LORD. 2 Thus the LORD said to me:
Make yourself a yoke of straps and bars,
and put them on your neck. 3 Send word[j]
to the king of Edom, the king of Moab,
the king of the Ammonites, the king of
Tyre, and the king of Sidon by the hand
of the envoys who have come to Jerusalem to King Zedekiah of Judah. 4 Give
them this charge for their masters: Thus
says the LORD of hosts, the God of Israel: This is what you shall say to your
masters: 5 It is I who by my great power
and my outstretched arm have made the
earth, with the people and animals that
are on the earth, and I give it to whomsoever I please. 6 Now I have given all
these lands into the hand of King Nebuchadnezzar of Babylon, my servant, and
I have given him even the wild animals
of the field to serve him. 7 All the nations shall serve him and his son and his
grandson, until the time of his own land
comes; then many nations and great
kings shall make him their slave.

8 But if any nation or kingdom will
not serve this king, Nebuchadnezzar

h 26.22 Heb adds *men to Egypt* i 27.1 Another reading is *Jehoiakim* j 27.3 Cn: Heb *send them*

of Babylon, and put its neck under the
yoke of the king of Babylon, then I will
punish that nation with the sword,
with famine, and with pestilence, says
the LORD, until I have completed its[k]
destruction by his hand. 9You, therefore, must not listen to your prophets,
your diviners, your dreamers,[l] your
soothsayers, or your sorcerers, who are
saying to you, 'You shall not serve the
king of Babylon.' 10For they are prophesying a lie to you, with the result that
you will be removed far from your land;
I will drive you out, and you will perish.
11But any nation that will bring its neck
under the yoke of the king of Babylon
and serve him, I will leave on its own
land, says the LORD, to till it and live
there.

12 I spoke to King Zedekiah of Judah in the same way: Bring your necks
under the yoke of the king of Babylon,
and serve him and his people, and live.
13Why should you and your people die
by the sword, by famine, and by pestilence, as the LORD has spoken concerning any nation that will not serve the
king of Babylon? 14Do not listen to the
words of the prophets who are telling
you not to serve the king of Babylon,
for they are prophesying a lie to you.
15I have not sent them, says the LORD,
but they are prophesying falsely in my
name, with the result that I will drive
you out and you will perish, you and the
prophets who are prophesying to you.

16 Then I spoke to the priests and
to all this people, saying, Thus says the
LORD: Do not listen to the words of your
prophets who are prophesying to you,
saying, 'The vessels of the LORD's house
will soon be brought back from Babylon', for they are prophesying a lie to
you. 17Do not listen to them; serve the
king of Babylon and live. Why should
this city become a desolation? 18If indeed they are prophets, and if the word
of the LORD is with them, then let them
intercede with the LORD of hosts, that
the vessels left in the house of the LORD,
in the house of the king of Judah, and
in Jerusalem may not go to Babylon.
19For thus says the LORD of hosts concerning the pillars, the sea, the stands,
and the rest of the vessels that are left in
this city, 20which King Nebuchadnezzar
of Babylon did not take away when he
took into exile from Jerusalem to Babylon King Jeconiah son of Jehoiakim of
Judah, and all the nobles of Judah and
Jerusalem— 21thus says the LORD of
hosts, the God of Israel, concerning the
vessels left in the house of the LORD,
in the house of the king of Judah, and
in Jerusalem: 22They shall be carried to
Babylon, and there they shall stay, until
the day when I give attention to them,
says the LORD. Then I will bring them
up and restore them to this place.

HANANIAH OPPOSES JEREMIAH AND DIES

28 In that same year, at the beginning of the reign of King Zedekiah of Judah, in the fifth month of the
fourth year, the prophet Hananiah son
of Azzur, from Gibeon, spoke to me in
the house of the LORD, in the presence
of the priests and all the people, saying,
2'Thus says the LORD of hosts, the God
of Israel: I have broken the yoke of the
king of Babylon. 3Within two years I
will bring back to this place all the vessels of the LORD's house, which King
Nebuchadnezzar of Babylon took away
from this place and carried to Babylon.
4I will also bring back to this place King
Jeconiah son of Jehoiakim of Judah, and
all the exiles from Judah who went to
Babylon, says the LORD, for I will break
the yoke of the king of Babylon.'

5 Then the prophet Jeremiah spoke to
the prophet Hananiah in the presence
of the priests and all the people who
were standing in the house of the LORD;
6and the prophet Jeremiah said, 'Amen!
May the LORD do so; may the LORD
fulfil the words that you have prophesied, and bring back to this place from
Babylon the vessels of the house of the
LORD, and all the exiles. 7But listen now
to this word that I speak in your hearing and in the hearing of all the people.
8The prophets who preceded you and
me from ancient times prophesied war,
famine, and pestilence against many
countries and great kingdoms. 9As
for the prophet who prophesies peace,
when the word of that prophet comes
true, then it will be known that the
LORD has truly sent the prophet.'

10 Then the prophet Hananiah took
the yoke from the neck of the prophet
Jeremiah, and broke it. 11And Hananiah
spoke in the presence of all the people,
saying, 'Thus says the LORD: This is how
I will break the yoke of King Nebuchadnezzar of Babylon from the neck of all
the nations within two years.' At this,
the prophet Jeremiah went his way.

[k] 27.8 Heb *their* [l] 27.9 Gk Syr Vg: Heb *dreams*

12 Some time after the prophet Hananiah had broken the yoke from the
neck of the prophet Jeremiah, the word
of the LORD came to Jeremiah: 13 Go, tell
Hananiah, Thus says the LORD: You
have broken wooden bars only to forge
iron bars in place of them! 14 For thus
says the LORD of hosts, the God of Israel:
I have put an iron yoke on the neck of
all these nations so that they may serve
King Nebuchadnezzar of Babylon, and
they shall indeed serve him; I have even
given him the wild animals. 15 And the
prophet Jeremiah said to the prophet
Hananiah, 'Listen, Hananiah, the LORD
has not sent you, and you made this
people trust in a lie. 16 Therefore thus
says the LORD: I am going to send you
off the face of the earth. Within this year
you will be dead, because you have spoken rebellion against the LORD.'

17 In that same year, in the seventh
month, the prophet Hananiah died.

JEREMIAH'S LETTER TO THE EXILES IN BABYLON

29 These are the words of the letter that the prophet Jeremiah
sent from Jerusalem to the remaining
elders among the exiles, and to the
priests, the prophets, and all the people,
whom Nebuchadnezzar had taken into
exile from Jerusalem to Babylon. 2 This
was after King Jeconiah, and the queen
mother, the court officials, the leaders
of Judah and Jerusalem, the artisans,
and the smiths had departed from Jerusalem. 3 The letter was sent by the hand
of Elasah son of Shaphan and Gemariah
son of Hilkiah, whom King Zedekiah
of Judah sent to Babylon to King Nebuchadnezzar of Babylon. It said: 4 Thus
says the LORD of hosts, the God of Israel, to all the exiles whom I have sent
into exile from Jerusalem to Babylon:
5 Build houses and live in them; plant
gardens and eat what they produce.
6 Take wives and have sons and daughters; take wives for your sons, and give
your daughters in marriage, that they
may bear sons and daughters; multiply
there, and do not decrease. 7 But seek
the welfare of the city where I have sent
you into exile, and pray to the LORD on
its behalf, for in its welfare you will find
your welfare. 8 For thus says the LORD
of hosts, the God of Israel: Do not let
the prophets and the diviners who are
among you deceive you, and do not listen to the dreams that they dream,[m]
9 for it is a lie that they are prophesying
to you in my name; I did not send them,
says the LORD.

10 For thus says the LORD: Only
when Babylon's seventy years are completed will I visit you, and I will fulfil to
you my promise and bring you back to
this place. 11 For surely I know the plans
I have for you, says the LORD, plans for
your welfare and not for harm, to give
you a future with hope. 12 Then when
you call upon me and come and pray to
me, I will hear you. 13 When you search
for me, you will find me; if you seek me
with all your heart, 14 I will let you find
me, says the LORD, and I will restore
your fortunes and gather you from all
the nations and all the places where I
have driven you, says the LORD, and I
will bring you back to the place from
which I sent you into exile.

15 Because you have said, 'The LORD
has raised up prophets for us in Babylon'— 16 thus says the LORD concerning
the king who sits on the throne of David, and concerning all the people who
live in this city, your kinsfolk who did
not go out with you into exile: 17 Thus
says the LORD of hosts, I am going to let
loose on them sword, famine, and pestilence, and I will make them like rotten
figs that are so bad they cannot be eaten.
18 I will pursue them with the sword,
with famine, and with pestilence, and
will make them a horror to all the kingdoms of the earth, to be an object of
cursing, and horror, and hissing, and a
derision among all the nations where
I have driven them, 19 because they did
not heed my words, says the LORD,
when I persistently sent to you my servants the prophets, but they[n] would not
listen, says the LORD. 20 But now, all you
exiles whom I sent away from Jerusalem to Babylon, hear the word of the
LORD: 21 Thus says the LORD of hosts,
the God of Israel, concerning Ahab son
of Kolaiah and Zedekiah son of Maaseiah, who are prophesying a lie to you in
my name: I am going to deliver them
into the hand of King Nebuchadrezzar
of Babylon, and he shall kill them before
your eyes. 22 And on account of them
this curse shall be used by all the exiles
from Judah in Babylon: 'The LORD make
you like Zedekiah and Ahab, whom the
king of Babylon roasted in the fire', 23 because they have perpetrated outrage in
Israel and have committed adultery

[m] 29.8 Cn: Heb *your dreams that you cause to dream* [n] 29.19 Syr: Heb *you*

with their neighbours' wives, and have
spoken in my name lying words that I
did not command them; I am the one
who knows and bears witness, says the
LORD.

THE LETTER OF SHEMAIAH

24 To Shemaiah of Nehelam you
shall say: 25 Thus says the LORD of hosts,
the God of Israel: In your own name you
sent a letter to all the people who are in
Jerusalem, and to the priest Zephaniah
son of Maaseiah, and to all the priests,
saying, 26 The LORD himself has made
you priest instead of the priest Jehoiada, so that there may be officers in the
house of the LORD to control any madman who plays the prophet, to put him
in the stocks and the collar. 27 So now
why have you not rebuked Jeremiah of
Anathoth who plays the prophet for
you? 28 For he has actually sent to us in
Babylon, saying, 'It will be a long time;
build houses and live in them, and plant
gardens and eat what they produce.'

29 The priest Zephaniah read this
letter in the hearing of the prophet Jeremiah. 30 Then the word of the LORD
came to Jeremiah: 31 Send to all the exiles, saying, Thus says the LORD concerning Shemaiah of Nehelam: Because Shemaiah has prophesied to you,
though I did not send him, and has led
you to trust in a lie, 32 therefore thus
says the LORD: I am going to punish
Shemaiah of Nehelam and his descendants; he shall not have anyone living
among this people to see[o] the good that
I am going to do to my people, says
the LORD, for he has spoken rebellion
against the LORD.

RESTORATION PROMISED FOR ISRAEL AND JUDAH

30 The word that came to Jeremiah
from the LORD: 2 Thus says the
LORD, the God of Israel: Write in a book
all the words that I have spoken to you.
3 For the days are surely coming, says the
LORD, when I will restore the fortunes
of my people, Israel and Judah, says the
LORD, and I will bring them back to the
land that I gave to their ancestors and
they shall take possession of it.

4 These are the words that the LORD
spoke concerning Israel and Judah:

5 Thus says the LORD:
We have heard a cry of panic,
of terror, and no peace.
6 Ask now, and see,
can a man bear a child?
Why then do I see every man
with his hands on his loins like
a woman in labour?
Why has every face turned pale?
7 Alas! that day is so great
there is none like it;
it is a time of distress for Jacob;
yet he shall be rescued from it.

8 On that day, says the LORD of hosts,
I will break the yoke from off his[p] neck,
and I will burst his[q] bonds, and strangers shall no more make a servant of
him. 9 But they shall serve the LORD
their God and David their king, whom
I will raise up for them.

10 But as for you, have no fear, my
servant Jacob, says the LORD,
and do not be dismayed, O Israel;
for I am going to save you
from far away,
and your offspring from the
land of their captivity.
Jacob shall return and have
quiet and ease,
and no one shall make him afraid.
11 For I am with you, says the
LORD, to save you;
I will make an end of all the nations
among which I scattered you,
but of you I will not make an end.
I will chastise you in just measure,
and I will by no means leave
you unpunished.

12 For thus says the LORD:
Your hurt is incurable,
your wound is grievous.
13 There is no one to uphold your cause,
no medicine for your wound,
no healing for you.
14 All your lovers have forgotten you;
they care nothing for you;
for I have dealt you the blow
of an enemy,
the punishment of a merciless foe,
because your guilt is great,
because your sins are so numerous.
15 Why do you cry out over your hurt?
Your pain is incurable.
Because your guilt is great,
because your sins are so numerous,
I have done these things to you.
16 Therefore all who devour you
shall be devoured,
and all your foes, every one of
them, shall go into captivity;

[o] **29.32** Gk: Heb *and he shall not see* [p] **30.8** Cn: Heb *your* [q] **30.8** Cn: Heb *your*

those who plunder you shall
be plundered,
and all who prey on you I
will make a prey.
17 For I will restore health to you,
and your wounds I will heal,
says the LORD,
because they have called
you an outcast:
'It is Zion; no one cares for her!'

18 Thus says the LORD:
I am going to restore the fortunes
of the tents of Jacob,
and have compassion on
his dwellings;
the city shall be rebuilt upon
its mound,
and the citadel set on its
rightful site.
19 Out of them shall come
thanksgiving,
and the sound of merrymakers.
I will make them many, and
they shall not be few;
I will make them honoured, and
they shall not be disdained.
20 Their children shall be as of old,
their congregation shall be
established before me;
and I will punish all who
oppress them.
21 Their prince shall be one
of their own,
their ruler shall come
from their midst;
I will bring him near, and he
shall approach me,
for who would otherwise
dare to approach me?
says the LORD.
22 And you shall be my people,
and I will be your God.

23 Look, the storm of the LORD!
Wrath has gone forth,
a whirling[r] tempest;
it will burst upon the head
of the wicked.
24 The fierce anger of the LORD
will not turn back
until he has executed and
accomplished
the intents of his mind.
In the latter days you will
understand this.

THE JOYFUL RETURN OF THE EXILES

31 At that time, says the LORD, I
will be the God of all the families
of Israel, and they shall be my people.

2 Thus says the LORD:
The people who survived the sword
found grace in the wilderness;
when Israel sought for rest,
3 the LORD appeared to him[s]
from far away.[t]
I have loved you with an
everlasting love;
therefore I have continued my
faithfulness to you.
4 Again I will build you, and
you shall be built,
O virgin Israel!
Again you shall take[u] your
tambourines,
and go forth in the dance of
the merrymakers.
5 Again you shall plant vineyards
on the mountains of Samaria;
the planters shall plant,
and shall enjoy the fruit.
6 For there shall be a day when
sentinels will call
in the hill country of Ephraim:
'Come, let us go up to Zion,
to the LORD our God.'

7 For thus says the LORD:
Sing aloud with gladness for Jacob,
and raise shouts for the
chief of the nations;
proclaim, give praise, and say,
'Save, O LORD, your people,
the remnant of Israel.'
8 See, I am going to bring them from
the land of the north,
and gather them from the
farthest parts of the earth,
among them the blind and the lame,
those with child and those
in labour, together;
a great company, they
shall return here.
9 With weeping they shall come,
and with consolations[v] I
will lead them back,
I will let them walk by
brooks of water,
in a straight path in which
they shall not stumble;
for I have become a father to Israel,
and Ephraim is my firstborn.

10 Hear the word of the LORD,
O nations,
and declare it in the
coastlands far away;

[r] 30.23 One Ms: Meaning of MT uncertain
[s] 31.3 Gk: Heb *me* [t] 31.3 Or *to him long ago*
[u] 31.4 Or *adorn yourself with* [v] 31.9 Gk
Compare Vg Tg: Heb *supplications*

say, 'He who scattered Israel
will gather him,
and will keep him as a
shepherd a flock.'
11 For the LORD has ransomed Jacob,
and has redeemed him from
hands too strong for him.
12 They shall come and sing aloud
on the height of Zion,
and they shall be radiant over
the goodness of the LORD,
over the grain, the wine, and the oil,
and over the young of the
flock and the herd;
their life shall become like a
watered garden,
and they shall never
languish again.
13 Then shall the young women
rejoice in the dance,
and the young men and the
old shall be merry.
I will turn their mourning
into joy,
I will comfort them, and give
them gladness for sorrow.
14 I will give the priests their
fill of fatness,
and my people shall be satisfied
with my bounty,
says the LORD.

15 Thus says the LORD:
A voice is heard in Ramah,
lamentation and bitter weeping.
Rachel is weeping for her children;
she refuses to be comforted
for her children,
because they are no more.
16 Thus says the LORD:
Keep your voice from weeping,
and your eyes from tears;
for there is a reward for your work,
says the LORD:
they shall come back from the
land of the enemy;
17 there is hope for your future,
says the LORD:
your children shall come back
to their own country.

18 Indeed I heard Ephraim pleading:
'You disciplined me, and I
took the discipline;
I was like a calf untrained.
Bring me back, let me come back,
for you are the LORD my God.
19 For after I had turned away
I repented;
and after I was discovered,
I struck my thigh;
I was ashamed, and I was dismayed
because I bore the disgrace
of my youth.'
20 Is Ephraim my dear son?
Is he the child I delight in?
As often as I speak against him,
I still remember him.
Therefore I am deeply
moved for him;
I will surely have mercy on him,
says the LORD.

21 Set up road markers for yourself,
make yourself signposts;
consider well the highway,
the road by which you went.
Return, O virgin Israel,
return to these your cities.
22 How long will you waver,
O faithless daughter?
For the LORD has created a new
thing on the earth:
a woman encompasses[w] a man.

23 Thus says the LORD of hosts, the
God of Israel: Once more they shall use
these words in the land of Judah and in
its towns when I restore their fortunes:
'The LORD bless you, O abode
of righteousness,
O holy hill!'
24 And Judah and all its towns shall live
there together, and the farmers and
those who wander[x] with their flocks.
25 I will satisfy the weary,
and all who are faint I
will replenish.
26 Thereupon I awoke and looked,
and my sleep was pleasant to me.

INDIVIDUAL RETRIBUTION

27 The days are surely coming, says
the LORD, when I will sow the house of
Israel and the house of Judah with the
seed of humans and the seed of animals.
28 And just as I have watched over them
to pluck up and break down, to overthrow, destroy, and bring evil, so I will
watch over them to build and to plant,
says the LORD. 29 In those days they
shall no longer say:
'The parents have eaten sour grapes,
and the children's teeth
are set on edge.'
30 But all shall die for their own sins; the
teeth of everyone who eats sour grapes
shall be set on edge.

w 31.22 Meaning of Heb uncertain x 31.24 Cn
Compare Syr Vg Tg: Heb *and they shall wander*

A NEW COVENANT

31 The days are surely coming, says
the LORD, when I will make a new covenant with the house of Israel and the
house of Judah. [32]It will not be like the
covenant that I made with their ancestors when I took them by the hand to
bring them out of the land of Egypt—a
covenant that they broke, though I was
their husband,[y] says the LORD. [33]But
this is the covenant that I will make
with the house of Israel after those
days, says the LORD: I will put my law
within them, and I will write it on their
hearts; and I will be their God, and they
shall be my people. [34]No longer shall
they teach one another, or say to each
other, 'Know the LORD', for they shall all
know me, from the least of them to the
greatest, says the LORD; for I will forgive
their iniquity, and remember their sin
no more.

[35] Thus says the LORD,
who gives the sun for light by day
and the fixed order of the
moon and the stars
for light by night,
who stirs up the sea so that
its waves roar—
the LORD of hosts is his name:
[36] If this fixed order were
ever to cease
from my presence, says the LORD,
then also the offspring of
Israel would cease
to be a nation before me for ever.

[37] Thus says the LORD:
If the heavens above can
be measured,
and the foundations of the earth
below can be explored,
then I will reject all the
offspring of Israel
because of all they have done,
says the LORD.

JERUSALEM TO BE ENLARGED

38 The days are surely coming, says
the LORD, when the city shall be rebuilt
for the LORD from the tower of Hananel to the Corner Gate. [39]And the measuring line shall go out farther, straight
to the hill Gareb, and shall then turn
to Goah. [40]The whole valley of the dead
bodies and the ashes, and all the fields
as far as the Wadi Kidron, to the corner
of the Horse Gate towards the east, shall
be sacred to the LORD. It shall never
again be uprooted or overthrown.

JEREMIAH BUYS A FIELD DURING THE SIEGE

32 The word that came to Jeremiah
from the LORD in the tenth year
of King Zedekiah of Judah, which was
the eighteenth year of Nebuchadrezzar.
[2]At that time the army of the king of
Babylon was besieging Jerusalem, and
the prophet Jeremiah was confined in
the court of the guard that was in the
palace of the king of Judah, [3]where King
Zedekiah of Judah had confined him.
Zedekiah had said, 'Why do you prophesy and say: Thus says the LORD: I am
going to give this city into the hand of
the king of Babylon, and he shall take
it; [4]King Zedekiah of Judah shall not escape out of the hands of the Chaldeans,
but shall surely be given into the hands
of the king of Babylon, and shall speak
with him face to face and see him eye to
eye; [5]and he shall take Zedekiah to Babylon, and there he shall remain until I
attend to him, says the LORD; though
you fight against the Chaldeans, you
shall not succeed?'

6 Jeremiah said, The word of the
LORD came to me: [7]Hanamel son of
your uncle Shallum is going to come
to you and say, 'Buy my field that is at
Anathoth, for the right of redemption
by purchase is yours.' [8]Then my cousin
Hanamel came to me in the court of the
guard, in accordance with the word of
the LORD, and said to me, 'Buy my field
that is at Anathoth in the land of Benjamin, for the right of possession and
redemption is yours; buy it for yourself.'
Then I knew that this was the word of
the LORD.

9 And I bought the field at Anathoth
from my cousin Hanamel, and weighed
out the money to him, seventeen shekels of silver. [10]I signed the deed, sealed it,
got witnesses, and weighed the money
on scales. [11]Then I took the sealed deed
of purchase, containing the terms and
conditions, and the open copy; [12]and I
gave the deed of purchase to Baruch son
of Neriah son of Mahseiah, in the presence of my cousin Hanamel, in the presence of the witnesses who signed the
deed of purchase, and in the presence of
all the Judeans who were sitting in the
court of the guard. [13]In their presence I
charged Baruch, saying, [14]Thus says the
LORD of hosts, the God of Israel: Take
these deeds, both this sealed deed of
purchase and this open deed, and put

[y] **31.32** Or *master*

them in an earthenware jar, in order that they may last for a long time. 15 For thus says the LORD of hosts, the God of Israel: Houses and fields and vineyards shall again be bought in this land.

JEREMIAH PRAYS FOR UNDERSTANDING

16 After I had given the deed of purchase to Baruch son of Neriah, I prayed to the LORD, saying: 17 Ah Lord GOD! It is you who made the heavens and the earth by your great power and by your outstretched arm! Nothing is too hard for you. 18 You show steadfast love to the thousandth generation,[z] but repay the guilt of parents into the laps of their children after them, O great and mighty God whose name is the LORD of hosts, 19 great in counsel and mighty in deed; whose eyes are open to all the ways of mortals, rewarding all according to their ways and according to the fruit of their doings. 20 You showed signs and wonders in the land of Egypt, and to this day in Israel and among all humankind, and have made yourself a name that continues to this very day. 21 You brought your people Israel out of the land of Egypt with signs and wonders, with a strong hand and outstretched arm, and with great terror; 22 and you gave them this land, which you swore to their ancestors to give them, a land flowing with milk and honey; 23 and they entered and took possession of it. But they did not obey your voice or follow your law; of all you commanded them to do, they did nothing. Therefore you have made all these disasters come upon them. 24 See, the siege-ramps have been cast up against the city to take it, and the city, faced with sword, famine, and pestilence, has been given into the hands of the Chaldeans who are fighting against it. What you spoke has happened, as you yourself can see. 25 Yet you, O Lord GOD, have said to me, 'Buy the field for money and get witnesses'—though the city has been given into the hands of the Chaldeans.

GOD'S ASSURANCE OF THE PEOPLE'S RETURN

26 The word of the LORD came to Jeremiah: 27 See, I am the LORD, the God of all flesh; is anything too hard for me? 28 Therefore, thus says the LORD: I am going to give this city into the hands of the Chaldeans and into the hand of King Nebuchadrezzar of Babylon, and he shall take it. 29 The Chaldeans who are fighting against this city shall come, set it on fire, and burn it, with the houses on whose roofs offerings have been made to Baal and libations have been poured out to other gods, to provoke me to anger. 30 For the people of Israel and the people of Judah have done nothing but evil in my sight from their youth; the people of Israel have done nothing but provoke me to anger by the work of their hands, says the LORD. 31 This city has aroused my anger and wrath, from the day it was built until this day, so that I will remove it from my sight 32 because of all the evil of the people of Israel and the people of Judah that they did to provoke me to anger—they, their kings and their officials, their priests and their prophets, the citizens of Judah and the inhabitants of Jerusalem. 33 They have turned their backs to me, not their faces; though I have taught them persistently, they would not listen and accept correction. 34 They set up their abominations in the house that bears my name, and defiled it. 35 They built the high places of Baal in the valley of the son of Hinnom, to offer up their sons and daughters to Molech, though I did not command them, nor did it enter my mind that they should do this abomination, causing Judah to sin.

36 Now therefore, thus says the LORD, the God of Israel, concerning this city of which you say, 'It is being given into the hand of the king of Babylon by the sword, by famine, and by pestilence': 37 See, I am going to gather them from all the lands to which I drove them in my anger and my wrath and in great indignation; I will bring them back to this place, and I will settle them in safety. 38 They shall be my people, and I will be their God. 39 I will give them one heart and one way, that they may fear me for all time, for their own good and the good of their children after them. 40 I will make an everlasting covenant with them, never to draw back from doing good to them; and I will put the fear of me in their hearts, so that they may not turn from me. 41 I will rejoice in doing good to them, and I will plant them in this land in faithfulness, with all my heart and all my soul.

42 For thus says the LORD: Just as I have brought all this great disaster upon this people, so I will bring upon

[z] **32.18** Or *to thousands*

them all the good fortune that I now
promise them. 43Fields shall be bought
in this land of which you are saying, It
is a desolation, without human beings
or animals; it has been given into the
hands of the Chaldeans. 44Fields shall
be bought for money, and deeds shall be
signed and sealed and witnessed, in the
land of Benjamin, in the places around
Jerusalem, and in the cities of Judah, of
the hill country, of the Shephelah, and
of the Negeb; for I will restore their fortunes, says the LORD.

HEALING AFTER PUNISHMENT

33 The word of the LORD came to
Jeremiah a second time, while
he was still confined in the court of the
guard: 2Thus says the LORD who made
the earth,[a] the LORD who formed it to
establish it—the LORD is his name:
3Call to me and I will answer you, and
will tell you great and hidden things
that you have not known. 4For thus
says the LORD, the God of Israel, concerning the houses of this city and the
houses of the kings of Judah that were
torn down to make a defence against
the siege-ramps and before the sword:[b]
5The Chaldeans are coming in to fight[c]
and to fill them with the dead bodies of those whom I shall strike down
in my anger and my wrath, for I have
hidden my face from this city because
of all their wickedness. 6I am going to
bring it recovery and healing; I will heal
them and reveal to them abundance[d] of
prosperity and security. 7I will restore
the fortunes of Judah and the fortunes
of Israel, and rebuild them as they were
at first. 8I will cleanse them from all the
guilt of their sin against me, and I will
forgive all the guilt of their sin and rebellion against me. 9And this city[e] shall
be to me a name of joy, a praise and a
glory before all the nations of the earth
who shall hear of all the good that I do
for them; they shall fear and tremble because of all the good and all the prosperity I provide for it.

10 Thus says the LORD: In this place of
which you say, 'It is a waste without human beings or animals', in the towns of
Judah and the streets of Jerusalem that
are desolate, without inhabitants, human or animal, there shall once more be
heard 11the voice of mirth and the voice
of gladness, the voice of the bridegroom
and the voice of the bride, the voices of
those who sing, as they bring thank-
offerings to the house of the LORD:

'Give thanks to the LORD of hosts,
for the LORD is good,
for his steadfast love
endures for ever!'

For I will restore the fortunes of the land
as at first, says the LORD.

12 Thus says the LORD of hosts: In
this place that is waste, without human beings or animals, and in all its
towns there shall again be pasture for
shepherds resting their flocks. 13In the
towns of the hill country, of the Shephelah, and of the Negeb, in the land of
Benjamin, the places around Jerusalem,
and in the towns of Judah, flocks shall
again pass under the hands of the one
who counts them, says the LORD.

THE RIGHTEOUS BRANCH AND THE COVENANT WITH DAVID

14 The days are surely coming, says
the LORD, when I will fulfil the promise I made to the house of Israel and
the house of Judah. 15In those days and
at that time I will cause a righteous
Branch to spring up for David; and he
shall execute justice and righteousness
in the land. 16In those days Judah will be
saved and Jerusalem will live in safety.
And this is the name by which it will be
called: 'The LORD is our righteousness.'

17 For thus says the LORD: David
shall never lack a man to sit on the
throne of the house of Israel, 18and the
levitical priests shall never lack a man in
my presence to offer burnt-offerings, to
make grain-offerings, and to make sacrifices for all time.

19 The word of the LORD came to Jeremiah: 20Thus says the LORD: If any of
you could break my covenant with the
day and my covenant with the night, so
that day and night would not come at
their appointed time, 21only then could
my covenant with my servant David be
broken, so that he would not have a son
to reign on his throne, and my covenant
with my ministers the Levites. 22Just as
the host of heaven cannot be numbered
and the sands of the sea cannot be measured, so I will increase the offspring of
my servant David, and the Levites who
minister to me.

23 The word of the LORD came to Jeremiah: 24Have you not observed how
these people say, 'The two families that
the LORD chose have been rejected by

[a] 33.2 Gk: Heb *it* [b] 33.4 Meaning of Heb uncertain [c] 33.5 Cn: Heb *They are coming in to fight against the Chaldeans* [d] 33.6 Meaning of Heb uncertain [e] 33.9 Heb *And it*

him', and how they hold my people in
such contempt that they no longer regard them as a nation? 25Thus says the
LORD: Only if I had not established my
covenant with day and night and the ordinances of heaven and earth, 26would I
reject the offspring of Jacob and of my
servant David and not choose any of his
descendants as rulers over the offspring
of Abraham, Isaac, and Jacob. For I will
restore their fortunes, and will have
mercy upon them.

DEATH IN CAPTIVITY PREDICTED FOR ZEDEKIAH

34 The word that came to Jeremiah
from the LORD, when King Nebuchadrezzar of Babylon and all his army
and all the kingdoms of the earth and
all the peoples under his dominion were
fighting against Jerusalem and all its
cities: 2Thus says the LORD, the God of
Israel: Go and speak to King Zedekiah
of Judah and say to him: Thus says the
LORD: I am going to give this city into
the hand of the king of Babylon, and he
shall burn it with fire. 3And you yourself shall not escape from his hand, but
shall surely be captured and handed
over to him; you shall see the king of
Babylon eye to eye and speak with him
face to face; and you shall go to Babylon.
4Yet hear the word of the LORD, O King
Zedekiah of Judah! Thus says the LORD
concerning you: You shall not die by the
sword; 5you shall die in peace. And as
spices were burned[f] for your ancestors,
the earlier kings who preceded you, so
they shall burn spices[g] for you and lament for you, saying, 'Alas, lord!' For I
have spoken the word, says the LORD.
6 Then the prophet Jeremiah spoke all
these words to Zedekiah king of Judah,
in Jerusalem, 7when the army of the
king of Babylon was fighting against Jerusalem and against all the cities of Judah that were left, Lachish and Azekah;
for these were the only fortified cities of
Judah that remained.

TREACHEROUS TREATMENT OF SLAVES

8 The word that came to Jeremiah
from the LORD, after King Zedekiah had
made a covenant with all the people in
Jerusalem to make a proclamation of liberty to them— 9that all should set free
their Hebrew slaves, male and female,
so that no one should hold another Judean in slavery. 10And they obeyed, all
the officials and all the people who had
entered into the covenant that all would
set free their slaves, male or female, so
that they would not be enslaved again;
they obeyed and set them free. 11But
afterwards they turned about and took
back the male and female slaves they
had set free, and brought them again
into subjection as slaves. 12The word of
the LORD came to Jeremiah from the
LORD: 13Thus says the LORD, the God of
Israel: I myself made a covenant with
your ancestors when I brought them
out of the land of Egypt, out of the house
of slavery, saying, 14'Every seventh year
each of you must set free any Hebrews
who have been sold to you and have
served you for six years; you must set
them free from your service.' But your
ancestors did not listen to me or incline
their ears to me. 15You yourselves recently repented and did what was right
in my sight by proclaiming liberty to
one another, and you made a covenant
before me in the house that is called by
my name; 16but then you turned about
and profaned my name when each of
you took back your male and female
slaves, whom you had set free according
to their desire, and you brought them
again into subjection to be your slaves.
17Therefore, thus says the LORD: You
have not obeyed me by granting a release to your neighbours and friends; I
am going to grant a release to you, says
the LORD—a release to the sword, to
pestilence, and to famine. I will make
you a horror to all the kingdoms of the
earth. 18And those who transgressed
my covenant and did not keep the terms
of the covenant that they made before
me, I will make like[h] the calf when
they cut it in two and passed between
its parts: 19the officials of Judah, the officials of Jerusalem, the eunuchs, the
priests, and all the people of the land
who passed between the parts of the
calf 20shall be handed over to their enemies and to those who seek their lives.
Their corpses shall become food for the
birds of the air and the wild animals of
the earth. 21And as for King Zedekiah of
Judah and his officials, I will hand them
over to their enemies and to those who
seek their lives, to the army of the king
of Babylon, which has withdrawn from
you. 22I am going to command, says the
LORD, and will bring them back to this
city; and they will fight against it, and

[f] 34.5 Heb *as there was burning* [g] 34.5 Heb *shall burn* [h] 34.18 Cn: Heb lacks *like*

take it, and burn it with fire. The towns of Judah I will make a desolation without inhabitant.

THE RECHABITES COMMENDED

35 The word that came to Jeremiah from the LORD in the days of King Jehoiakim son of Josiah of Judah: 2Go to the house of the Rechabites, and speak with them, and bring them to the house of the LORD, into one of the chambers; then offer them wine to drink. 3So I took Jaazaniah son of Jeremiah son of Habazziniah, and his brothers, and all his sons, and the whole house of the Rechabites. 4I brought them to the house of the LORD into the chamber of the sons of Hanan son of Igdaliah, the man of God, which was near the chamber of the officials, above the chamber of Maaseiah son of Shallum, keeper of the threshold. 5Then I set before the Rechabites pitchers full of wine, and cups; and I said to them, 'Have some wine.' 6But they answered, 'We will drink no wine, for our ancestor Jonadab son of Rechab commanded us, "You shall never drink wine, neither you nor your children; 7nor shall you ever build a house, or sow seed; nor shall you plant a vineyard, or even own one; but you shall live in tents all your days, that you may live many days in the land where you reside." 8We have obeyed the charge of our ancestor Jonadab son of Rechab in all that he commanded us, to drink no wine all our days, ourselves, our wives, our sons, and our daughters, 9and not to build houses to live in. We have no vineyard or field or seed; 10but we have lived in tents, and have obeyed and done all that our ancestor Jonadab commanded us. 11But when King Nebuchadrezzar of Babylon came up against the land, we said, "Come, and let us go to Jerusalem for fear of the army of the Chaldeans and the army of the Arameans." That is why we are living in Jerusalem.'

12 Then the word of the LORD came to Jeremiah: 13Thus says the LORD of hosts, the God of Israel: Go and say to the people of Judah and the inhabitants of Jerusalem, Can you not learn a lesson and obey my words? says the LORD. 14The command has been carried out that Jonadab son of Rechab gave to his descendants to drink no wine; and they drink none to this day, for they have obeyed their ancestor's command. But I myself have spoken to you persistently, and you have not obeyed me. 15I have sent to you all my servants the prophets, sending them persistently, saying, 'Turn now every one of you from your evil way, and amend your doings, and do not go after other gods to serve them, and then you shall live in the land that I gave to you and your ancestors.' But you did not incline your ear or obey me. 16The descendants of Jonadab son of Rechab have carried out the command that their ancestor gave them, but this people has not obeyed me. 17Therefore, thus says the LORD, the God of hosts, the God of Israel: I am going to bring on Judah and on all the inhabitants of Jerusalem every disaster that I have pronounced against them; because I have spoken to them and they have not listened, I have called to them and they have not answered.

18 But to the house of the Rechabites Jeremiah said: Thus says the LORD of hosts, the God of Israel: Because you have obeyed the command of your ancestor Jonadab, and kept all his precepts, and done all that he commanded you, 19therefore thus says the LORD of hosts, the God of Israel: Jonadab son of Rechab shall not lack a descendant to stand before me for all time.

THE SCROLL READ IN THE TEMPLE

36 In the fourth year of King Jehoiakim son of Josiah of Judah, this word came to Jeremiah from the LORD: 2Take a scroll and write on it all the words that I have spoken to you against Israel and Judah and all the nations, from the day I spoke to you, from the days of Josiah until today. 3It may be that when the house of Judah hears of all the disasters that I intend to do to them, all of them may turn from their evil ways, so that I may forgive their iniquity and their sin.

4 Then Jeremiah called Baruch son of Neriah, and Baruch wrote on a scroll at Jeremiah's dictation all the words of the LORD that he had spoken to him. 5And Jeremiah ordered Baruch, saying, 'I am prevented from entering the house of the LORD; 6so you go yourself, and on a fast day in the hearing of the people in the LORD's house you shall read the words of the LORD from the scroll that you have written at my dictation. You shall read them also in the hearing of all the people of Judah who come up from their towns. 7It may be that their plea will come before the LORD, and that all of them will turn from their evil ways,

for great is the anger and wrath that the
LORD has pronounced against this people.' 8 And Baruch son of Neriah did all
that the prophet Jeremiah ordered him
about reading from the scroll the words
of the LORD in the LORD's house.
9 In the fifth year of King Jehoiakim son of Josiah of Judah, in the ninth
month, all the people in Jerusalem and
all the people who came from the towns
of Judah to Jerusalem proclaimed a fast
before the LORD. 10 Then, in the hearing of all the people, Baruch read the
words of Jeremiah from the scroll, in
the house of the LORD, in the chamber
of Gemariah son of Shaphan the secretary, which was in the upper court, at
the entry of the New Gate of the LORD's
house.

THE SCROLL READ IN THE PALACE

11 When Micaiah son of Gemariah
son of Shaphan heard all the words of
the LORD from the scroll, 12 he went
down to the king's house, into the secretary's chamber; and all the officials
were sitting there: Elishama the secretary, Delaiah son of Shemaiah, Elnathan son of Achbor, Gemariah son of
Shaphan, Zedekiah son of Hananiah,
and all the officials. 13 And Micaiah told
them all the words that he had heard,
when Baruch read the scroll in the
hearing of the people. 14 Then all the officials sent Jehudi son of Nethaniah son
of Shelemiah son of Cushi to say to Baruch, 'Bring the scroll that you read in
the hearing of the people, and come.' So
Baruch son of Neriah took the scroll in
his hand and came to them. 15 And they
said to him, 'Sit down and read it to
us.' So Baruch read it to them. 16 When
they heard all the words, they turned to
one another in alarm, and said to Baruch, 'We certainly must report all these
words to the king.' 17 Then they questioned Baruch, 'Tell us now, how did
you write all these words? Was it at his
dictation?' 18 Baruch answered them,
'He dictated all these words to me, and
I wrote them with ink on the scroll.'
19 Then the officials said to Baruch, 'Go
and hide, you and Jeremiah, and let no
one know where you are.'

JEHOIAKIM BURNS THE SCROLL

20 Leaving the scroll in the chamber
of Elishama the secretary, they went to
the court of the king; and they reported
all the words to the king. 21 Then the
king sent Jehudi to get the scroll, and
he took it from the chamber of Elishama the secretary; and Jehudi read
it to the king and all the officials who
stood beside the king. 22 Now the king
was sitting in his winter apartment (it
was the ninth month), and there was a
fire burning in the brazier before him.
23 As Jehudi read three or four columns,
the king[i] would cut them off with a
penknife and throw them into the fire
in the brazier, until the entire scroll
was consumed in the fire that was in
the brazier. 24 Yet neither the king, nor
any of his servants who heard all these
words, was alarmed, nor did they tear
their garments. 25 Even when Elnathan
and Delaiah and Gemariah urged the
king not to burn the scroll, he would
not listen to them. 26 And the king commanded Jerahmeel the king's son and
Seraiah son of Azriel and Shelemiah
son of Abdeel to arrest the secretary
Baruch and the prophet Jeremiah. But
the LORD hid them.

JEREMIAH DICTATES ANOTHER

27 Now, after the king had burned
the scroll with the words that Baruch
wrote at Jeremiah's dictation, the word
of the LORD came to Jeremiah: 28 Take
another scroll and write on it all the former words that were in the first scroll,
which King Jehoiakim of Judah has
burned. 29 And concerning King Jehoiakim of Judah you shall say: Thus says
the LORD, You have dared to burn this
scroll, saying, Why have you written in
it that the king of Babylon will certainly
come and destroy this land, and will cut
off from it human beings and animals?
30 Therefore thus says the LORD concerning King Jehoiakim of Judah: He
shall have no one to sit upon the throne
of David, and his dead body shall be cast
out to the heat by day and the frost by
night. 31 And I will punish him and his
offspring and his servants for their iniquity; I will bring on them, and on the
inhabitants of Jerusalem, and on the
people of Judah, all the disasters with
which I have threatened them—but
they would not listen.
32 Then Jeremiah took another scroll
and gave it to the secretary Baruch son
of Neriah, who wrote on it at Jeremiah's
dictation all the words of the scroll that
King Jehoiakim of Judah had burned in
the fire; and many similar words were
added to them.

i 36.23 Heb *he*

ZEDEKIAH'S VAIN HOPE

37 Zedekiah son of Josiah, whom
King Nebuchadrezzar of Babylon made king in the land of Judah,
succeeded Coniah son of Jehoiakim.
2 But neither he nor his servants nor the
people of the land listened to the words
of the LORD that he spoke through the
prophet Jeremiah.

3 King Zedekiah sent Jehucal son of
Shelemiah and the priest Zephaniah
son of Maaseiah to the prophet Jeremiah saying, 'Please pray for us to the
LORD our God.' 4 Now Jeremiah was still
going in and out among the people,
for he had not yet been put in prison.
5 Meanwhile, the army of Pharaoh had
come out of Egypt; and when the Chaldeans who were besieging Jerusalem
heard news of them, they withdrew
from Jerusalem.

6 Then the word of the LORD came
to the prophet Jeremiah: 7 Thus says the
LORD, God of Israel: This is what the
two of you shall say to the king of Judah, who sent you to me to inquire of
me: Pharaoh's army, which set out to
help you, is going to return to its own
land, to Egypt. 8 And the Chaldeans
shall return and fight against this city;
they shall take it and burn it with fire.
9 Thus says the LORD: Do not deceive
yourselves, saying, 'The Chaldeans will
surely go away from us', for they will
not go away. 10 Even if you defeated the
whole army of Chaldeans who are fighting against you, and there remained of
them only wounded men in their tents,
they would rise up and burn this city
with fire.

JEREMIAH IS IMPRISONED

11 Now when the Chaldean army
had withdrawn from Jerusalem at the
approach of Pharaoh's army, 12 Jeremiah set out from Jerusalem to go to
the land of Benjamin to receive his
share of property[j] among the people
there. 13 When he reached the Benjamin
Gate, a sentinel there named Irijah son
of Shelemiah son of Hananiah arrested
the prophet Jeremiah, saying, 'You are
deserting to the Chaldeans.' 14 And Jeremiah said, 'That is a lie; I am not deserting to the Chaldeans.' But Irijah would
not listen to him, and arrested Jeremiah
and brought him to the officials. 15 The
officials were enraged at Jeremiah, and
they beat him and imprisoned him in
the house of the secretary Jonathan, for
it had been made a prison. 16 Thus Jeremiah was put in the cistern house, in
the cells, and remained there for many
days.

17 Then King Zedekiah sent for him,
and received him. The king questioned
him secretly in his house, and said, 'Is
there any word from the LORD?' Jeremiah said, 'There is!' Then he said, 'You
shall be handed over to the king of Babylon.' 18 Jeremiah also said to King Zedekiah, 'What wrong have I done to you
or your servants or this people, that
you have put me in prison? 19 Where
are your prophets who prophesied to
you, saying, "The king of Babylon will
not come against you and against this
land"? 20 Now please hear me, my lord
king: be good enough to listen to my
plea, and do not send me back to the
house of the secretary Jonathan to die
there.' 21 So King Zedekiah gave orders,
and they committed Jeremiah to the
court of the guard; and a loaf of bread
was given him daily from the bakers'
street, until all the bread of the city
was gone. So Jeremiah remained in the
court of the guard.

JEREMIAH IN THE CISTERN

38 Now Shephatiah son of Mattan, Gedaliah son of Pashhur,
Jucal son of Shelemiah, and Pashhur
son of Malchiah heard the words that
Jeremiah was saying to all the people,
2 Thus says the LORD, Those who stay in
this city shall die by the sword, by famine, and by pestilence; but those who
go out to the Chaldeans shall live; they
shall have their lives as a prize of war,
and live. 3 Thus says the LORD, This city
shall surely be handed over to the army
of the king of Babylon and be taken.
4 Then the officials said to the king, 'This
man ought to be put to death, because
he is discouraging the soldiers who are
left in this city, and all the people, by
speaking such words to them. For this
man is not seeking the welfare of this
people, but their harm.' 5 King Zedekiah
said, 'Here he is; he is in your hands; for
the king is powerless against you.' 6 So
they took Jeremiah and threw him into
the cistern of Malchiah, the king's son,
which was in the court of the guard,
letting Jeremiah down by ropes. Now
there was no water in the cistern, but
only mud, and Jeremiah sank in the
mud.

[j] 37.12 Meaning of Heb uncertain

JEREMIAH IS RESCUED BY EBED-MELECH

7 Ebed-melech the Ethiopian,[k] a eunuch in the king's house, heard that
they had put Jeremiah into the cistern.
The king happened to be sitting at the
Benjamin Gate, 8So Ebed-melech left
the king's house and spoke to the king,
9'My lord king, these men have acted
wickedly in all they did to the prophet
Jeremiah by throwing him into the cistern to die there of hunger, for there
is no bread left in the city.' 10Then the
king commanded Ebed-melech the
Ethiopian,[l] 'Take three men with you
from here, and pull the prophet Jeremiah up from the cistern before he dies.'
11So Ebed-melech took the men with
him and went to the house of the king,
to a wardrobe of[m] the storehouse, and
took from there old rags and worn-out
clothes, which he let down to Jeremiah
in the cistern by ropes. 12Then Ebed-
melech the Ethiopian[n] said to Jeremiah,
'Just put the rags and clothes between
your armpits and the ropes.' Jeremiah
did so. 13Then they drew Jeremiah up
by the ropes and pulled him out of the
cistern. And Jeremiah remained in the
court of the guard.

ZEDEKIAH CONSULTS JEREMIAH AGAIN

14 King Zedekiah sent for the prophet
Jeremiah and received him at the third
entrance of the temple of the LORD. The
king said to Jeremiah, 'I have something to ask you; do not hide anything
from me.' 15Jeremiah said to Zedekiah,
'If I tell you, you will put me to death,
will you not? And if I give you advice,
you will not listen to me.' 16So King Zedekiah swore an oath in secret to Jeremiah, 'As the LORD lives, who gave us
our lives, I will not put you to death or
hand you over to these men who seek
your life.'

17 Then Jeremiah said to Zedekiah,
'Thus says the LORD, the God of hosts,
the God of Israel, If you will only surrender to the officials of the king of
Babylon, then your life shall be spared,
and this city shall not be burned with
fire, and you and your house shall live.
18But if you do not surrender to the officials of the king of Babylon, then this
city shall be handed over to the Chaldeans, and they shall burn it with fire, and
you yourself shall not escape from their
hand.' 19King Zedekiah said to Jeremiah,
'I am afraid of the Judeans who have deserted to the Chaldeans, for I might be
handed over to them and they would
abuse me.' 20Jeremiah said, 'That will
not happen. Just obey the voice of the
LORD in what I say to you, and it shall
go well with you, and your life shall be
spared. 21But if you are determined not
to surrender, this is what the LORD has
shown me— 22a vision of all the women
remaining in the house of the king of
Judah being led out to the officials of the
king of Babylon and saying,

"Your trusted friends have
seduced you
and have overcome you;
Now that your feet are stuck
in the mud,
they desert you."

23All your wives and your children shall
be led out to the Chaldeans, and you
yourself shall not escape from their
hand, but shall be seized by the king of
Babylon; and this city shall be burned
with fire.'

24 Then Zedekiah said to Jeremiah,
'Do not let anyone else know of this
conversation, or you will die. 25If the
officials should hear that I have spoken
with you, and they should come and
say to you, "Just tell us what you said
to the king; do not conceal it from us,
or we will put you to death. What did
the king say to you?" 26then you shall
say to them, "I was presenting my plea
to the king not to send me back to the
house of Jonathan to die there."' 27All
the officials did come to Jeremiah and
questioned him; and he answered them
in the very words the king had commanded. So they stopped questioning
him, for the conversation had not been
overheard. 28And Jeremiah remained in
the court of the guard until the day that
Jerusalem was taken.

THE FALL OF JERUSALEM

39 In the ninth year of King Zedekiah of Judah, in the tenth
month, King Nebuchadrezzar of Babylon and all his army came against Jerusalem and besieged it; 2in the eleventh
year of Zedekiah, in the fourth month,
on the ninth day of the month, a breach
was made in the city. 3When Jerusalem
was taken,[o] all the officials of the king
of Babylon came and sat in the middle
gate: Nergal-sharezer, Samgar-nebo,

[k] 38.7 Or *Nubian*; Heb *Cushite* [l] 38.10 Or *Nubian*; Heb *Cushite* [m] 38.11 Cn: Heb *to under* [n] 38.12 Or *Nubian*; Heb *Cushite* [o] 39.3 This clause has been transposed from 38.28

Sarsechim the Rabsaris, Nergal-sharezer
the Rabmag, with all the rest of the officials of the king of Babylon. [4]When
King Zedekiah of Judah and all the soldiers saw them, they fled, going out of
the city at night by way of the king's
garden through the gate between the
two walls; and they went towards the
Arabah. [5]But the army of the Chaldeans pursued them, and overtook Zedekiah in the plains of Jericho; and when
they had taken him, they brought him
up to King Nebuchadrezzar of Babylon,
at Riblah, in the land of Hamath; and
he passed sentence on him. [6]The king
of Babylon slaughtered the sons of Zedekiah at Riblah before his eyes; also the
king of Babylon slaughtered all the nobles of Judah. [7]He put out the eyes of
Zedekiah, and bound him in fetters to
take him to Babylon. [8]The Chaldeans
burned the king's house and the houses
of the people, and broke down the walls
of Jerusalem. [9]Then Nebuzaradan the
captain of the guard exiled to Babylon
the rest of the people who were left in
the city, those who had deserted to him,
and the people who remained. [10]Nebu-
zaradan the captain of the guard left in
the land of Judah some of the poor people who owned nothing, and gave them
vineyards and fields at the same time.

JEREMIAH, SET FREE, REMEMBERS EBED-MELECH

11 King Nebuchadrezzar of Babylon
gave command concerning Jeremiah
through Nebuzaradan, the captain of
the guard, saying, [12]'Take him, look after him well and do him no harm, but
deal with him as he may ask you.' [13]So
Nebuzaradan the captain of the guard,
Nebushazban the Rabsaris, Nergal-
sharezer the Rabmag, and all the chief
officers of the king of Babylon sent
[14]and took Jeremiah from the court of
the guard. They entrusted him to Gedaliah son of Ahikam son of Shaphan to
be brought home. So he stayed with his
own people.

15 The word of the LORD came to
Jeremiah while he was confined in the
court of the guard: [16]Go and say to Ebed-
melech the Ethiopian:[p] Thus says the
LORD of hosts, the God of Israel: I am
going to fulfil my words against this
city for evil and not for good, and they
shall be accomplished in your presence
on that day. [17]But I will save you on that
day, says the LORD, and you shall not be
handed over to those whom you dread.
[18]For I will surely save you, and you
shall not fall by the sword; but you shall
have your life as a prize of war, because
you have trusted in me, says the LORD.

JEREMIAH WITH GEDALIAH THE GOVERNOR

40 The word that came to Jeremiah
from the LORD after Nebuzaradan the captain of the guard had let
him go from Ramah, when he took him
bound in fetters along with all the captives of Jerusalem and Judah who were
being exiled to Babylon. [2]The captain
of the guard took Jeremiah and said to
him, 'The LORD your God threatened
this place with this disaster; [3]and now
the LORD has brought it about, and
has done as he said, because all of you
sinned against the LORD and did not
obey his voice. Therefore this thing has
come upon you. [4]Now look, I have just
released you today from the fetters on
your hands. If you wish to come with
me to Babylon, come, and I will take
good care of you; but if you do not wish
to come with me to Babylon, you need
not come. See, the whole land is before
you; go wherever you think it good and
right to go. [5]If you remain,[q] then return to Gedaliah son of Ahikam son of
Shaphan, whom the king of Babylon
appointed governor of the towns of Judah, and stay with him among the people; or go wherever you think it right
to go.' So the captain of the guard gave
him an allowance of food and a present,
and let him go. [6]Then Jeremiah went to
Gedaliah son of Ahikam at Mizpah, and
stayed with him among the people who
were left in the land.

7 When all the leaders of the forces in
the open country and their troops heard
that the king of Babylon had appointed
Gedaliah son of Ahikam governor in the
land, and had committed to him men,
women, and children, those of the poorest of the land who had not been taken
into exile to Babylon, [8]they went to Gedaliah at Mizpah—Ishmael son of Nethaniah, Johanan son of Kareah, Seraiah
son of Tanhumeth, the sons of Ephai the
Netophathite, Jezaniah son of the Maacathite, they and their troops. [9]Gedaliah
son of Ahikam son of Shaphan swore to
them and their troops, saying, 'Do not
be afraid to serve the Chaldeans. Stay in
the land and serve the king of Babylon,

[p] 39.16 Or *Nubian*; Heb *Cushite* [q] 40.5 Syr: Meaning of Heb uncertain

and it shall go well with you. 10As for
me, I am staying at Mizpah to represent
you before the Chaldeans who come to
us; but as for you, gather wine and summer fruits and oil, and store them in
your vessels, and live in the towns that
you have taken over.' 11Likewise, when
all the Judeans who were in Moab and
among the Ammonites and in Edom
and in other lands heard that the king
of Babylon had left a remnant in Judah
and had appointed Gedaliah son of Ahikam son of Shaphan as governor over
them, 12then all the Judeans returned
from all the places to which they had
been scattered and came to the land of
Judah, to Gedaliah at Mizpah; and they
gathered wine and summer fruits in
great abundance.

13 Now Johanan son of Kareah and
all the leaders of the forces in the open
country came to Gedaliah at Mizpah
14and said to him, 'Are you at all aware
that Baalis king of the Ammonites has
sent Ishmael son of Nethaniah to take
your life?' But Gedaliah son of Ahikam
would not believe them. 15Then Johanan
son of Kareah spoke secretly to Gedaliah
at Mizpah, 'Please let me go and kill Ishmael son of Nethaniah, and no one else
will know. Why should he take your life,
so that all the Judeans who are gathered
around you would be scattered, and the
remnant of Judah would perish?' 16But
Gedaliah son of Ahikam said to Johanan
son of Kareah, 'Do not do such a thing,
for you are telling a lie about Ishmael.'

INSURRECTION AGAINST GEDALIAH

41 In the seventh month, Ishmael
son of Nethaniah son of Elish-
ama, of the royal family, one of the chief
officers of the king, came with ten men
to Gedaliah son of Ahikam, at Mizpah.
As they ate bread together there at Mizpah, 2Ishmael son of Nethaniah and the
ten men with him got up and struck
down Gedaliah son of Ahikam son of
Shaphan with the sword and killed him,
because the king of Babylon had appointed him governor in the land. 3Ish-
mael also killed all the Judeans who were
with Gedaliah at Mizpah, and the Chaldean soldiers who happened to be there.

4 On the day after the murder of Gedaliah, before anyone knew of it, 5eighty
men arrived from Shechem and Shiloh
and Samaria, with their beards shaved
and their clothes torn, and their bodies
gashed, bringing grain-offerings and
incense to present at the temple of the
LORD. 6And Ishmael son of Nethaniah
came out from Mizpah to meet them,
weeping as he came. As he met them,
he said to them, 'Come to Gedaliah son
of Ahikam.' 7When they reached the
middle of the city, Ishmael son of Nethaniah and the men with him slaughtered them, and threw them[r] into a cistern. 8But there were ten men among
them who said to Ishmael, 'Do not kill
us, for we have stores of wheat, barley, oil, and honey hidden in the fields.'
So he refrained, and did not kill them
along with their companions.

9 Now the cistern into which Ishmael had thrown all the bodies of the
men whom he had struck down was the
large cistern[s] that King Asa had made
for defence against King Baasha of Israel; Ishmael son of Nethaniah filled
that cistern with those whom he had
killed. 10Then Ishmael took captive all
the rest of the people who were in Mizpah, the king's daughters and all the
people who were left at Mizpah, whom
Nebuzaradan, the captain of the guard,
had committed to Gedaliah son of Ahikam. Ishmael son of Nethaniah took
them captive and set out to cross over to
the Ammonites.

11 But when Johanan son of Kareah
and all the leaders of the forces with
him heard of all the crimes that Ishmael
son of Nethaniah had done, 12they took
all their men and went to fight against
Ishmael son of Nethaniah. They came
upon him at the great pool that is in
Gibeon. 13And when all the people who
were with Ishmael saw Johanan son of
Kareah and all the leaders of the forces
with him, they were glad. 14So all the
people whom Ishmael had carried away
captive from Mizpah turned and came
back, and went to Johanan son of Kareah. 15But Ishmael son of Nethaniah
escaped from Johanan with eight men,
and went to the Ammonites. 16Then Johanan son of Kareah and all the leaders
of the forces with him took all the rest of
the people whom Ishmael son of Nethaniah had carried away captive[t] from
Mizpah after he had slain Gedaliah son
of Ahikam—soldiers, women, children,
and eunuchs, whom Johanan brought
back from Gibeon.[u] 17And they set out,
and stopped at Geruth Chimham near

[r] **41.7** Syr: Heb lacks *and threw them*; compare verse 9 [s] **41.9** Gk: Heb *whom he had killed by the hand of Gedaliah* [t] **41.16** Cn: Heb *whom he recovered from Ishmael son of Nethaniah*
[u] **41.16** Meaning of Heb uncertain

Bethlehem, intending to go to Egypt
18because of the Chaldeans; for they
were afraid of them, because Ishmael
son of Nethaniah had killed Gedaliah
son of Ahikam, whom the king of Babylon had made governor over the land.

JEREMIAH ADVISES SURVIVORS NOT TO MIGRATE

42 Then all the commanders of the
forces, and Johanan son of Kareah and Azariah[v] son of Hoshaiah, and
all the people from the least to the greatest, approached 2the prophet Jeremiah
and said, 'Be good enough to listen to
our plea, and pray to the LORD your God
for us—for all this remnant. For there
are only a few of us left out of many, as
your eyes can see. 3Let the LORD your
God show us where we should go and
what we should do.' 4The prophet Jeremiah said to them, 'Very well: I am
going to pray to the LORD your God as
you request, and whatever the LORD
answers you I will tell you; I will keep
nothing back from you.' 5They in their
turn said to Jeremiah, 'May the LORD
be a true and faithful witness against
us if we do not act according to everything that the LORD your God sends us
through you. 6Whether it is good or bad,
we will obey the voice of the LORD our
God to whom we are sending you, in order that it may go well with us when we
obey the voice of the LORD our God.'

7 At the end of ten days the word
of the LORD came to Jeremiah. 8Then
he summoned Johanan son of Kareah
and all the commanders of the forces
who were with him, and all the people
from the least to the greatest, 9and said
to them, 'Thus says the LORD, the God
of Israel, to whom you sent me to present your plea before him: 10If you will
only remain in this land, then I will
build you up and not pull you down; I
will plant you, and not pluck you up; for
I am sorry for the disaster that I have
brought upon you. 11Do not be afraid of
the king of Babylon, as you have been;
do not be afraid of him, says the LORD,
for I am with you, to save you and to rescue you from his hand. 12I will grant you
mercy, and he will have mercy on you
and restore you to your native soil. 13But
if you continue to say, "We will not stay
in this land", thus disobeying the voice
of the LORD your God 14and saying, "No,
we will go to the land of Egypt, where
we shall not see war, or hear the sound
of the trumpet, or be hungry for bread,
and there we will stay", 15then hear the
word of the LORD, O remnant of Judah.
Thus says the LORD of hosts, the God
of Israel: If you are determined to enter Egypt and go to settle there, 16then
the sword that you fear shall overtake
you there, in the land of Egypt; and
the famine that you dread shall follow
close after you into Egypt; and there you
shall die. 17All the people who have determined to go to Egypt to settle there
shall die by the sword, by famine, and
by pestilence; they shall have no remnant or survivor from the disaster that
I am bringing upon them.

18 'For thus says the LORD of hosts,
the God of Israel: Just as my anger
and my wrath were poured out on the
inhabitants of Jerusalem, so my wrath
will be poured out on you when you
go to Egypt. You shall become an object of execration and horror, of cursing and ridicule. You shall see this
place no more. 19The LORD has said to
you, O remnant of Judah, Do not go to
Egypt. Be well aware that I have warned
you today 20that you have made a fatal
mistake. For you yourselves sent me to
the LORD your God, saying, "Pray for us
to the LORD our God, and whatever the
LORD our God says, tell us and we will
do it." 21So I have told you today, but you
have not obeyed the voice of the LORD
your God in anything that he sent me
to tell you. 22Be well aware, then, that
you shall die by the sword, by famine,
and by pestilence in the place where you
desire to go and settle.'

TAKEN TO EGYPT, JEREMIAH WARNS OF JUDGEMENT

43 When Jeremiah finished speaking to all the people all these
words of the LORD their God, with
which the LORD their God had sent him
to them, 2Azariah son of Hoshaiah and
Johanan son of Kareah and all the other
insolent men said to Jeremiah, 'You are
telling a lie. The LORD our God did not
send you to say, "Do not go to Egypt to
settle there"; 3but Baruch son of Neriah
is inciting you against us, to hand us
over to the Chaldeans, in order that they
may kill us or take us into exile in Babylon.' 4So Johanan son of Kareah and all
the commanders of the forces and all
the people did not obey the voice of the
LORD, to stay in the land of Judah. 5But
Johanan son of Kareah and all the com-

[v] 42.1 Gk: Heb *Jezaniah*

manders of the forces took all the remnant of Judah who had returned to settle
in the land of Judah from all the nations
to which they had been driven— 6the
men, the women, the children, the
princesses, and everyone whom Nebuzaradan the captain of the guard had
left with Gedaliah son of Ahikam son of
Shaphan; also the prophet Jeremiah and
Baruch son of Neriah. 7And they came
into the land of Egypt, for they did not
obey the voice of the LORD. And they arrived at Tahpanhes.
8 Then the word of the LORD came
to Jeremiah in Tahpanhes: 9Take some
large stones in your hands, and bury
them in the clay pavement[w] that is at
the entrance to Pharaoh's palace in Tahpanhes. Let the Judeans see you do it,
10and say to them, Thus says the LORD
of hosts, the God of Israel: I am going
to send and take my servant King Nebuchadrezzar of Babylon, and he[x] will
set his throne above these stones that I
have buried, and he will spread his royal
canopy over them. 11He shall come and
ravage the land of Egypt, giving

those who are destined for
pestilence, to pestilence,
and those who are destined for
captivity, to captivity,
and those who are destined for
the sword, to the sword.

12He[y] shall kindle a fire in the temples
of the gods of Egypt; and he shall burn
them and carry them away captive; and
he shall pick clean the land of Egypt,
as a shepherd picks his cloak clean of
vermin; and he shall depart from there
safely. 13He shall break the obelisks of
Heliopolis, which is in the land of Egypt;
and the temples of the gods of Egypt he
shall burn with fire.

DENUNCIATION OF PERSISTENT IDOLATRY

44 The word that came to Jeremiah
for all the Judeans living in the
land of Egypt, at Migdol, at Tahpanhes,
at Memphis, and in the land of Pathros,
2Thus says the LORD of hosts, the God
of Israel: You yourselves have seen all
the disaster that I have brought on Jerusalem and on all the towns of Judah.
Look at them; today they are a desolation, without an inhabitant in them,
3because of the wickedness that they
committed, provoking me to anger, in
that they went to make offerings and
serve other gods that they had not
known, neither they, nor you, nor your
ancestors. 4Yet I persistently sent to
you all my servants the prophets, saying, 'I beg you not to do this abominable thing that I hate!' 5But they did not
listen or incline their ear, to turn from
their wickedness and make no offerings to other gods. 6So my wrath and
my anger were poured out and kindled
in the towns of Judah and in the streets
of Jerusalem; and they became a waste
and a desolation, as they still are today.
7And now, thus says the LORD God of
hosts, the God of Israel: Why are you
doing such great harm to yourselves, to
cut off man and woman, child and infant, from the midst of Judah, leaving
yourselves without a remnant? 8Why
do you provoke me to anger with the
works of your hands, making offerings to other gods in the land of Egypt
where you have come to settle? Will you
be cut off and become an object of cursing and ridicule among all the nations
of the earth? 9Have you forgotten the
crimes of your ancestors, of the kings of
Judah, of their[z] wives, your own crimes
and those of your wives, which they
committed in the land of Judah and in
the streets of Jerusalem? 10They have
shown no contrition or fear to this day,
nor have they walked in my law and my
statutes that I set before you and before
your ancestors.
11 Therefore, thus says the LORD
of hosts, the God of Israel: I am determined to bring disaster on you, to bring
all Judah to an end. 12I will take the remnant of Judah who are determined to
come to the land of Egypt to settle, and
they shall perish, everyone; in the land
of Egypt they shall fall; by the sword and
by famine they shall perish; from the
least to the greatest, they shall die by
the sword and by famine; and they shall
become an object of execration and horror, of cursing and ridicule. 13I will punish those who live in the land of Egypt,
as I have punished Jerusalem, with the
sword, with famine, and with pestilence, 14so that none of the remnant of
Judah who have come to settle in the
land of Egypt shall escape or survive or
return to the land of Judah. Although
they long to go back to live there, they
shall not go back, except some fugitives.
15 Then all the men who were aware
that their wives had been making offerings to other gods, and all the women

[w] 43.9 Meaning of Heb uncertain [x] 43.10 Gk Syr: Heb *I* [y] 43.12 Gk Syr Vg: Heb *I* [z] 44.9 Heb *his*

who stood by, a great assembly, all the
people who lived in Pathros in the land
of Egypt, answered Jeremiah: 16 'As for
the word that you have spoken to us in
the name of the LORD, we are not going
to listen to you. 17 Instead, we will do everything that we have vowed, make offerings to the queen of heaven and pour
out libations to her, just as we and our
ancestors, our kings and our officials,
used to do in the towns of Judah and in
the streets of Jerusalem. We used to have
plenty of food, and prospered, and saw
no misfortune. 18 But from the time we
stopped making offerings to the queen
of heaven and pouring out libations
to her, we have lacked everything and
have perished by the sword and by famine.' 19 And the women said,[a] 'Indeed
we will go on making offerings to the
queen of heaven and pouring out libations to her; do you think that we made
cakes for her, marked with her image,
and poured out libations to her without
our husbands being involved?'

20 Then Jeremiah said to all the
people, men and women, all the people who were giving him this answer:
21 'As for the offerings that you made in
the towns of Judah and in the streets
of Jerusalem, you and your ancestors,
your kings and your officials, and the
people of the land, did not the LORD
remember them? Did it not come into
his mind? 22 The LORD could no longer bear the sight of your evil doings,
the abominations that you committed;
therefore your land became a desolation
and a waste and a curse, without inhabitant, as it is to this day. 23 It is because
you burned offerings, and because you
sinned against the LORD and did not
obey the voice of the LORD or walk in
his law and in his statutes and in his decrees, that this disaster has befallen you,
as is still evident today.'

24 Jeremiah said to all the people and
all the women, 'Hear the word of the
LORD, all you Judeans who are in the
land of Egypt, 25 Thus says the LORD of
hosts, the God of Israel: You and your
wives have accomplished in deeds what
you declared in words, saying, "We are
determined to perform the vows that
we have made, to make offerings to the
queen of heaven and to pour out libations to her." By all means, keep your
vows and make your libations! 26 Therefore hear the word of the LORD, all you
Judeans who live in the land of Egypt:
Lo, I swear by my great name, says the
LORD, that my name shall no longer be
pronounced on the lips of any of the
people of Judah in all the land of Egypt,
saying, "As the Lord GOD lives." 27 I am
going to watch over them for harm and
not for good; all the people of Judah
who are in the land of Egypt shall perish by the sword and by famine, until
not one is left. 28 And those who escape
the sword shall return from the land of
Egypt to the land of Judah, few in number; and all the remnant of Judah, who
have come to the land of Egypt to settle, shall know whose words will stand,
mine or theirs! 29 This shall be the sign
to you, says the LORD, that I am going
to punish you in this place, in order that
you may know that my words against
you will surely be carried out: 30 Thus
says the LORD, I am going to give Pharaoh Hophra, king of Egypt, into the
hands of his enemies, those who seek
his life, just as I gave King Zedekiah
of Judah into the hand of King Nebuchadrezzar of Babylon, his enemy who
sought his life.'

A WORD OF COMFORT TO BARUCH

45 The word that the prophet Jeremiah spoke to Baruch son of
Neriah, when he wrote these words in
a scroll at the dictation of Jeremiah, in
the fourth year of King Jehoiakim son
of Josiah of Judah: 2 Thus says the LORD,
the God of Israel, to you, O Baruch: 3 You
said, 'Woe is me! The LORD has added
sorrow to my pain; I am weary with
my groaning, and I find no rest.' 4 Thus
you shall say to him, 'Thus says the
LORD: I am going to break down what
I have built, and pluck up what I have
planted—that is, the whole land. 5 And
you, do you seek great things for yourself? Do not seek them; for I am going
to bring disaster upon all flesh, says the
LORD; but I will give you your life as a
prize of war in every place to which you
may go.'

JUDGEMENT ON EGYPT

46 The word of the LORD that came
to the prophet Jeremiah concerning the nations.

2 Concerning Egypt, about the army
of Pharaoh Neco, king of Egypt, which
was by the river Euphrates at Carchemish and which King Nebuchadrezzar

[a] 44.19 Compare Syr: Heb lacks *And the women said*

of Babylon defeated in the fourth year of King Jehoiakim son of Josiah of Judah:

3 Prepare buckler and shield,
and advance for battle!
4 Harness the horses;
mount the steeds!
Take your stations with
your helmets,
whet your lances,
put on your coats of mail!
5 Why do I see them terrified?
They have fallen back;
their warriors are beaten down,
and have fled in haste.
They do not look back—
terror is all around!
says the LORD.
6 The swift cannot flee away,
nor can the warrior escape;
in the north by the river Euphrates
they have stumbled and fallen.

7 Who is this, rising like the Nile,
like rivers whose waters surge?
8 Egypt rises like the Nile,
like rivers whose waters surge.
It said, Let me rise, let me
cover the earth,
let me destroy cities and
their inhabitants.
9 Advance, O horses,
and dash madly, O chariots!
Let the warriors go forth:
Ethiopia[b] and Put who
carry the shield,
the Ludim, who draw[c] the bow.
10 That day is the day of the
Lord GOD of hosts,
a day of retribution,
to gain vindication from his foes.
The sword shall devour and be sated,
and drink its fill of their blood.
For the Lord GOD of hosts
holds a sacrifice
in the land of the north by
the river Euphrates.
11 Go up to Gilead, and take balm,
O virgin daughter Egypt!
In vain you have used many
medicines;
there is no healing for you.
12 The nations have heard of
your shame,
and the earth is full of your cry;
for warrior has stumbled
against warrior;
both have fallen together.

BABYLONIA WILL STRIKE EGYPT

13 The word that the LORD spoke to the prophet Jeremiah about the coming of King Nebuchadrezzar of Babylon to attack the land of Egypt:

14 Declare in Egypt, and proclaim
in Migdol;
proclaim in Memphis
and Tahpanhes;
Say, 'Take your stations and be ready,
for the sword shall devour
those around you.'
15 Why has Apis fled?[d]
Why did your bull not stand?
—because the LORD thrust
him down.
16 Your multitude stumbled[e] and fell,
and one said to another,[f]
'Come, let us go back to our
own people
and to the land of our birth,
because of the destroying sword.'
17 Give Pharaoh, king of Egypt,
the name
'Braggart who missed his chance.'

18 As I live, says the King,
whose name is the LORD of hosts,
one is coming
like Tabor among the mountains,
and like Carmel by the sea.
19 Pack your bags for exile,
sheltered daughter Egypt!
For Memphis shall become a waste,
a ruin, without inhabitant.

20 A beautiful heifer is Egypt—
a gadfly from the north
lights upon her.
21 Even her mercenaries in her midst
are like fatted calves;
they too have turned and
fled together,
they did not stand;
for the day of their calamity has
come upon them,
the time of their punishment.
22 She makes a sound like a snake
gliding away;
for her enemies march in force,
and come against her with axes,
like those who fell trees.
23 They shall cut down her forest,
says the LORD,
though it is impenetrable,
because they are more numerous
than locusts;
they are without number.

[b] 46.9 Or *Nubia*; Heb *Cush* [c] 46.9 Cn: Heb *who grasp, who draw* [d] 46.15 Gk: Heb *Why was it swept away* [e] 46.16 Gk: Meaning of Heb uncertain [f] 46.16 Gk: Heb *and fell one to another and they said*

24 Daughter Egypt shall be
put to shame;
she shall be handed over to a
people from the north.

25 The LORD of hosts, the God of Israel, said: See, I am bringing punishment upon Amon of Thebes, and Pharaoh, and Egypt and her gods and her
kings, upon Pharaoh and those who
trust in him. 26 I will hand them over to
those who seek their life, to King Nebuchadrezzar of Babylon and his officers.
Afterwards Egypt shall be inhabited as
in the days of old, says the LORD.

GOD WILL SAVE ISRAEL

27 But as for you, have no fear,
my servant Jacob,
and do not be dismayed, O Israel;
for I am going to save you
from far away,
and your offspring from the
land of their captivity.
Jacob shall return and have
quiet and ease,
and no one shall make
him afraid.
28 As for you, have no fear, my
servant Jacob,
says the LORD,
for I am with you.
I will make an end of
all the nations
among which I have
banished you,
but I will not make an end of you!
I will chastise you in just measure,
and I will by no means leave
you unpunished.

JUDGEMENT ON THE PHILISTINES

47 The word of the LORD that came
to the prophet Jeremiah concerning the Philistines, before Pharaoh
attacked Gaza:
2 Thus says the LORD:
See, waters are rising out
of the north
and shall become an
overflowing torrent;
they shall overflow the land
and all that fills it,
the city and those who live in it.
People shall cry out,
and all the inhabitants of
the land shall wail.
3 At the noise of the stamping of
the hoofs of his stallions,
at the clatter of his chariots, at the
rumbling of their wheels,
parents do not turn back
for children,
so feeble are their hands,
4 because of the day that is coming
to destroy all the Philistines,
to cut off from Tyre and Sidon
every helper that remains.
For the LORD is destroying
the Philistines,
the remnant of the coastland
of Caphtor.
5 Baldness has come upon Gaza,
Ashkelon is silenced.
O remnant of their power![g]
How long will you gash
yourselves?
6 Ah, sword of the LORD!
How long until you are quiet?
Put yourself into your scabbard,
rest and be still!
7 How can it[h] be quiet,
when the LORD has given
it an order?
Against Ashkelon and against
the seashore—
there he has appointed it.

JUDGEMENT ON MOAB

48 Concerning Moab.
Thus says the LORD of hosts, the God of
Israel:
Alas for Nebo, it is laid waste!
Kiriathaim is put to
shame, it is taken;
the fortress is put to shame
and broken down;
2 the renown of Moab is no more.
In Heshbon they planned
evil against her:
'Come, let us cut her off from
being a nation!'
You also, O Madmen, shall be
brought to silence;[i]
the sword shall pursue you.

3 Hark! a cry from Horonaim,
'Desolation and great destruction!'
4 'Moab is destroyed!'
her little ones cry out.
5 For at the ascent of Luhith
they go[j] up weeping bitterly;
for at the descent of Horonaim
they have heard the distressing
cry of anguish.
6 Flee! Save yourselves!
Be like a wild ass[k] in the desert!

[g] **47.5** Gk: Heb *their valley* [h] **47.7** Gk Vg: Heb *you* [i] **48.2** The place-name *Madmen* sounds like the Hebrew verb *to be silent* [j] **48.5** Cn: Heb *he goes* [k] **48.6** Gk Aquila: Heb *like Aroer*

7 Surely, because you trusted
in your strongholds[l]
and your treasures,
you also shall be taken;
Chemosh shall go out into exile,
with his priests and his
attendants.
8 The destroyer shall come
upon every town,
and no town shall escape;
the valley shall perish,
and the plain shall be destroyed,
as the LORD has spoken.

9 Set aside salt for Moab,
for she will surely fall;
her towns shall become a desolation,
with no inhabitant in them.

10 Accursed is the one who is slack in doing the work of the LORD; and accursed is the one who keeps back the sword from bloodshed.

11 Moab has been at ease from
his youth,
settled like wine[m] on its dregs;
he has not been emptied from
vessel to vessel,
nor has he gone into exile;
therefore his flavour has remained
and his aroma is unspoiled.

12 Therefore, the time is surely coming, says the LORD, when I shall send
to him decanters to decant him, and
empty his vessels, and break his[n] jars in
pieces. 13 Then Moab shall be ashamed
of Chemosh, as the house of Israel was
ashamed of Bethel, their confidence.

14 How can you say, 'We are heroes
and mighty warriors'?
15 The destroyer of Moab and his
towns has come up,
and the choicest of his young men
have gone down to slaughter,
says the King, whose name
is the LORD of hosts.
16 The calamity of Moab is
near at hand
and his doom approaches swiftly.
17 Mourn over him, all you
his neighbours,
and all who know his name;
say, 'How the mighty sceptre
is broken,
the glorious staff!'

18 Come down from glory,
and sit on the parched ground,
enthroned daughter Dibon!
For the destroyer of Moab has
come up against you;
he has destroyed your
strongholds.
19 Stand by the road and watch,
you inhabitant of Aroer!
Ask the man fleeing and the
woman escaping;
say, 'What has happened?'
20 Moab is put to shame, for it
is broken down;
wail and cry!
Tell it by the Arnon,
that Moab is laid waste.

21 Judgement has come upon the tableland, upon Holon, and Jahzah, and
Mephaath, 22 and Dibon, and Nebo, and
Beth-diblathaim, 23 and Kiriathaim,
and Beth-gamul, and Beth-meon, 24 and
Kerioth, and Bozrah, and all the towns
of the land of Moab, far and near. 25 The
horn of Moab is cut off, and his arm is
broken, says the LORD.
26 Make him drunk, because he
magnified himself against the LORD; let
Moab wallow in his vomit; he too shall
become a laughing-stock. 27 Israel was a
laughing-stock for you, though he was
not caught among thieves; but whenever you spoke of him you shook your
head!

28 Leave the towns, and live
on the rock,
O inhabitants of Moab!
Be like the dove that nests
on the sides of the mouth
of a gorge.
29 We have heard of the pride
of Moab—
he is very proud—
of his loftiness, his pride, and
his arrogance,
and the haughtiness of his heart.
30 I myself know his insolence,
says the LORD;
his boasts are false,
his deeds are false.
31 Therefore I wail for Moab;
I cry out for all Moab;
for the people of Kir-
heres I mourn.
32 More than for Jazer I weep for you,
O vine of Sibmah!
Your branches crossed over the sea,
reached as far as Jazer;[o]

[l] **48.7** Gk: Heb *works* [m] **48.11** Heb lacks *like wine* [n] **48.12** Gk Aquila: Heb *their*
[o] **48.32** Two Mss and Isa 16.8: MT *the sea of Jazer*

upon your summer fruits
and your vintage
the destroyer has fallen.
33 Gladness and joy have been
taken away
from the fruitful land of Moab;
I have stopped the wine from
the wine presses;
no one treads them with
shouts of joy;
the shouting is not the
shout of joy.

34 Heshbon and Elealeh cry out;[p]
as far as Jahaz they utter their voice,
from Zoar to Horonaim and Eglath-
shelishiyah. For even the waters of
Nimrim have become desolate. 35 And I
will bring to an end in Moab, says the
LORD, those who offer sacrifice at a high
place and make offerings to their gods.
36 Therefore my heart moans for Moab
like a flute, and my heart moans like a
flute for the people of Kir-heres; for the
riches they gained have perished.
37 For every head is shaved and every beard cut off; on all the hands there
are gashes, and on the loins sackcloth.
38 On all the housetops of Moab and in
the squares there is nothing but lamentation; for I have broken Moab like a
vessel that no one wants, says the LORD.
39 How it is broken! How they wail! How
Moab has turned his back in shame! So
Moab has become a derision and a horror to all his neighbours.
40 For thus says the LORD:
Look, he shall swoop down
like an eagle,
and spread his wings
against Moab;
41 the towns[q] shall be taken
and the strongholds seized.
The hearts of the warriors of
Moab, on that day,
shall be like the heart of a
woman in labour.
42 Moab shall be destroyed
as a people,
because he magnified himself
against the LORD.
43 Terror, pit, and trap
are before you, O inhabitants
of Moab!
says the LORD.
44 Everyone who flees from
the terror
shall fall into the pit,
and everyone who climbs
out of the pit
shall be caught in the trap.
For I will bring these things[r]
upon Moab
in the year of their punishment,
says the LORD.
45 In the shadow of Heshbon
fugitives stop exhausted;
for a fire has gone out from Heshbon,
a flame from the house of Sihon;
it has destroyed the forehead
of Moab,
the scalp of the people of tumult.[s]
46 Woe to you, O Moab!
The people of Chemosh
have perished,
for your sons have been
taken captive,
and your daughters into captivity.
47 Yet I will restore the fortunes
of Moab
in the latter days, says the LORD.
Thus far is the judgement on Moab.

JUDGEMENT ON THE AMMONITES

49 Concerning the Ammonites.
Thus says the LORD:
Has Israel no sons?
Has he no heir?
Why then has Milcom
dispossessed Gad,
and his people settled
in its towns?
2 Therefore, the time is surely coming,
says the LORD,
when I will sound the battle alarm
against Rabbah of the
Ammonites;
it shall become a desolate mound,
and its villages shall be
burned with fire;
then Israel shall dispossess those
who dispossessed him,
says the LORD.

3 Wail, O Heshbon, for Ai is laid waste!
Cry out, O daughters[t] of Rabbah!
Put on sackcloth,
lament, and slash yourselves
with whips![u]
For Milcom shall go into exile,
with his priests and his
attendants.
4 Why do you boast in your strength?
Your strength is ebbing,

[p] 48.34 Cn: Heb *From the cry of Heshbon to Elealeh* [q] 48.41 Or *Kerioth* [r] 48.44 Gk Syr: Heb *bring upon it* [s] 48.45 Or *of Shaon* [t] 49.3 Or *villages* [u] 49.3 Cn: Meaning of Heb uncertain

O faithless daughter.
You trusted in your
treasures, saying,
'Who will attack me?'
5 I am going to bring terror upon you,
says the Lord GOD of hosts,
from all your neighbours,
and you will be scattered,
each headlong,
with no one to gather
the fugitives.

6 But afterwards I will restore the
fortunes of the Ammonites, says the
LORD.

JUDGEMENT ON EDOM

7 Concerning Edom.

Thus says the LORD of hosts:
Is there no longer wisdom in Teman?
Has counsel perished from
the prudent?
Has their wisdom vanished?
8 Flee, turn back, get down low,
inhabitants of Dedan!
For I will bring the calamity
of Esau upon him,
at the time when I punish him.
9 If grape-gatherers came to you,
would they not leave gleanings?
If thieves came by night,
even they would pillage only
what they wanted.
10 But as for me, I have stripped
Esau bare,
I have uncovered his hiding-places,
and he is not able to
conceal himself.
His offspring are destroyed,
his kinsfolk
and his neighbours; and
he is no more.
11 Leave your orphans, I will
keep them alive;
and let your widows trust in me.

12 For thus says the LORD: If those
who do not deserve to drink the cup
still have to drink it, shall you be the
one to go unpunished? You shall not go
unpunished; you must drink it. 13 For
by myself I have sworn, says the LORD,
that Bozrah shall become an object of
horror and ridicule, a waste, and an object of cursing; and all her towns shall be
perpetual wastes.

14 I have heard tidings from the LORD,
and a messenger has been sent
among the nations:
'Gather yourselves together and
come against her,
and rise up for battle!'
15 For I will make you least
among the nations,
despised by humankind.
16 The terror you inspire
and the pride of your heart
have deceived you,
you who live in the clefts
of the rock,[v]
who hold the height of the hill.
Although you make your nest
as high as the eagle's,
from there I will bring you down,
says the LORD.

17 Edom shall become an object of
horror; everyone who passes by it will
be horrified and will hiss because of
all its disasters. 18 As when Sodom and
Gomorrah and their neighbours were
overthrown, says the LORD, no one
shall live there, nor shall anyone settle in it. 19 Like a lion coming up from
the thickets of the Jordan against a pe-
rennial pasture, I will suddenly chase
Edom[w] away from it; and I will appoint
over it whomsoever I choose.[x] For who
is like me? Who can summon me? Who
is the shepherd who can stand before
me? 20 Therefore hear the plan that the
LORD has made against Edom and the
purposes that he has formed against
the inhabitants of Teman: Surely the
little ones of the flock shall be dragged
away; surely their fold shall be appalled
at their fate. 21 At the sound of their fall
the earth shall tremble; the sound of
their cry shall be heard at the Red Sea.[y]
22 Look, he shall mount up and swoop
down like an eagle, and spread his
wings against Bozrah, and the heart of
the warriors of Edom on that day shall
be like the heart of a woman in labour.

JUDGEMENT ON DAMASCUS

23 Concerning Damascus.

Hamath and Arpad are confounded,
for they have heard bad news;
they melt in fear, they are
troubled like the sea[z]
that cannot be quiet.
24 Damascus has become feeble,
she turned to flee,
and panic seized her;
anguish and sorrows have
taken hold of her,
as of a woman in labour.

[v] 49.16 Or *of Sela* [w] 49.19 Heb *him*
[x] 49.19 Or *and I will single out the choicest of his rams*: Meaning of Heb uncertain [y] 49.21 Or *Sea of Reeds* [z] 49.23 Cn: Heb *there is trouble in the sea*

25 How the famous city is forsaken,[a]
the joyful town![b]
26 Therefore her young men shall
fall in her squares,
and all her soldiers shall be
destroyed on that day,
says the LORD of hosts.
27 And I will kindle a fire at the
wall of Damascus,
and it shall devour the
strongholds of Ben-hadad.

JUDGEMENT ON KEDAR AND HAZOR

28 Concerning Kedar and the kingdoms of Hazor that King Nebuchadrezzar of Babylon defeated.

Thus says the LORD:
Rise up, advance against Kedar!
Destroy the people of the east!
29 Take their tents and their flocks,
their curtains and all their goods;
carry off their camels for yourselves,
and a cry shall go up: 'Terror
is all around!'
30 Flee, wander far away, hide
in deep places,
O inhabitants of Hazor!
says the LORD.
For King Nebuchadrezzar of Babylon
has made a plan against you
and formed a purpose against you.

31 Rise up, advance against a
nation at ease,
that lives secure,
says the LORD,
that has no gates or bars,
that lives alone.
32 Their camels shall become booty,
their herds of cattle a spoil.
I will scatter to every wind
those who have shaven temples,
and I will bring calamity
against them from every side,
says the LORD.
33 Hazor shall become a lair of jackals,
an everlasting waste;
no one shall live there,
nor shall anyone settle in it.

JUDGEMENT ON ELAM

34 The word of the LORD that came to
the prophet Jeremiah concerning Elam,
at the beginning of the reign of King
Zedekiah of Judah.
35 Thus says the LORD of hosts: I am
going to break the bow of Elam, the
mainstay of their might; 36and I will
bring upon Elam the four winds from
the four quarters of heaven; and I will
scatter them to all these winds, and
there shall be no nation to which the
exiles from Elam shall not come. 37I will
terrify Elam before their enemies, and
before those who seek their life; I will
bring disaster upon them, my fierce anger, says the LORD. I will send the sword
after them, until I have consumed them;
38and I will set my throne in Elam, and
destroy their king and officials, says the
LORD.
39 But in the latter days I will restore
the fortunes of Elam, says the LORD.

JUDGEMENT ON BABYLON

50 The word that the LORD spoke
concerning Babylon, concerning the land of the Chaldeans, by the
prophet Jeremiah:
2 Declare among the nations
and proclaim,
set up a banner and proclaim,
do not conceal it, say:
Babylon is taken,
Bel is put to shame,
Merodach is dismayed.
Her images are put to shame,
her idols are dismayed.
3 For out of the north a nation has
come up against her; it shall make her
land a desolation, and no one shall live
in it; both human beings and animals
shall flee away.

4 In those days and at that time,
says the LORD, the people of Israel shall
come, they and the people of Judah together; they shall come weeping as they
seek the LORD their God. 5They shall ask
the way to Zion, with faces turned towards it, and they shall come and join[c]
themselves to the LORD by an everlasting covenant that will never be forgotten.

6 My people have been lost sheep;
their shepherds have led them astray,
turning them away on the mountains;
from mountain to hill they have gone,
they have forgotten their fold. 7All who
found them have devoured them, and
their enemies have said, 'We are not
guilty, because they have sinned against
the LORD, the true pasture, the LORD,
the hope of their ancestors.'

8 Flee from Babylon, and go out of
the land of the Chaldeans, and be like

[a] 49.25 Vg: Heb *is not forsaken* [b] 49.25 Syr Vg Tg: Heb *the town of my joy* [c] 50.5 Gk: Heb *towards it. Come! They shall join*

male goats leading the flock. [9]For I am
going to stir up and bring against Babylon a company of great nations from
the land of the north; and they shall array themselves against her; from there
she shall be taken. Their arrows are like
the arrows of a skilled warrior who does
not return empty-handed. [10]Chaldea
shall be plundered; all who plunder her
shall be sated, says the LORD.

11 Though you rejoice, though
you exult,
O plunderers of my heritage,
though you frisk about like a
heifer on the grass,
and neigh like stallions,
12 your mother shall be utterly shamed,
and she who bore you shall
be disgraced.
Lo, she shall be the last of
the nations,
a wilderness, dry land,
and a desert.
13 Because of the wrath of the LORD
she shall not be inhabited,
but shall be an utter desolation;
everyone who passes by Babylon
shall be appalled
and hiss because of all
her wounds.
14 Take up your positions
around Babylon,
all you that bend the bow;
shoot at her, spare no arrows,
for she has sinned against
the LORD.
15 Raise a shout against her
from all sides,
'She has surrendered;
her bulwarks have fallen,
her walls are thrown down.'
For this is the vengeance
of the LORD:
take vengeance on her,
do to her as she has done.
16 Cut off from Babylon the sower,
and the wielder of the sickle
in time of harvest;
because of the destroying sword
all of them shall return to
their own people,
and all of them shall flee
to their own land.

17 Israel is a hunted sheep driven
away by lions. First the king of Assyria devoured it, and now at the end King Nebuchadrezzar of Babylon has gnawed its
bones. [18]Therefore, thus says the LORD
of hosts, the God of Israel: I am going
to punish the king of Babylon and his
land, as I punished the king of Assyria.
[19]I will restore Israel to its pasture, and it
shall feed on Carmel and in Bashan, and
on the hills of Ephraim and in Gilead its
hunger shall be satisfied. [20]In those days
and at that time, says the LORD, the iniquity of Israel shall be sought, and there
shall be none; and the sins of Judah, and
none shall be found; for I will pardon the
remnant that I have spared.

21 Go up to the land of Merathaim;[d]
go up against her,
and attack the inhabitants of Pekod[e]
and utterly destroy the
last of them,[f]
says the LORD;
do all that I have commanded you.
22 The noise of battle is in the land,
and great destruction!
23 How the hammer of the whole earth
is cut down and broken!
How Babylon has become
a horror among the nations!
24 You set a snare for yourself and you
were caught, O Babylon,
but you did not know it;
you were discovered and seized,
because you challenged the LORD.
25 The LORD has opened his armoury,
and brought out the weapons
of his wrath,
for the Lord GOD of hosts
has a task to do
in the land of the Chaldeans.
26 Come against her from
every quarter;
open her granaries;
pile her up like heaps of grain,
and destroy her utterly;
let nothing be left of her.
27 Kill all her bulls,
let them go down to the slaughter.
Alas for them, their day has come,
the time of their punishment!

28 Listen! Fugitives and refugees
from the land of Babylon are coming
to declare in Zion the vengeance of the
LORD our God, vengeance for his temple.

29 Summon archers against Babylon, all who bend the bow. Encamp all
around her; let no one escape. Repay her
according to her deeds; just as she has
done, do to her—for she has arrogantly
defied the LORD, the Holy One of Israel.

[d] **50.21** Or *of Double Rebellion* [e] **50.21** Or *of Punishment* [f] **50.21** Tg: Heb *destroy after them*

30 Therefore her young men shall fall in
her squares, and all her soldiers shall be
destroyed on that day, says the LORD.

31 I am against you, O arrogant one,
says the Lord GOD of hosts;
for your day has come,
the time when I will punish you.
32 The arrogant one shall
stumble and fall,
with no one to raise him up,
and I will kindle a fire in his cities,
and it will devour everything
around him.

33 Thus says the LORD of hosts: The
people of Israel are oppressed, and so
too are the people of Judah; all their captors have held them fast and refuse to
let them go. 34 Their Redeemer is strong;
the LORD of hosts is his name. He will
surely plead their cause, that he may
give rest to the earth, but unrest to the
inhabitants of Babylon.

35 A sword against the Chaldeans,
says the LORD,
and against the inhabitants
of Babylon,
and against her officials
and her sages!
36 A sword against the diviners,
so that they may become fools!
A sword against her warriors,
so that they may be destroyed!
37 A sword against her[g] horses and
against her[h] chariots,
and against all the foreign
troops in her midst,
so that they may become women!
A sword against all her treasures,
that they may be plundered!
38 A drought[i] against her waters,
that they may be dried up!
For it is a land of images,
and they go mad over idols.

39 Therefore wild animals shall live
with hyenas in Babylon,[j] and ostriches
shall inhabit her; she shall never again
be peopled, or inhabited for all generations. 40 As when God overthrew Sodom
and Gomorrah and their neighbours,
says the LORD, so no one shall live there,
nor shall anyone settle in her.

41 Look, a people is coming
from the north;
a mighty nation and many kings
are stirring from the farthest
parts of the earth.
42 They wield bow and spear,
they are cruel and have no mercy.
The sound of them is like
the roaring sea;
they ride upon horses,
set in array as a warrior for battle,
against you, O daughter Babylon!
43 The king of Babylon heard
news of them,
and his hands fell helpless;
anguish seized him,
pain like that of a woman
in labour.

44 Like a lion coming up from the
thickets of the Jordan against a peren-
nial pasture, I will suddenly chase them
away from her; and I will appoint over
her whomsoever I choose.[k] For who is
like me? Who can summon me? Who
is the shepherd who can stand before
me? 45 Therefore hear the plan that the
LORD has made against Babylon, and
the purposes that he has formed against
the land of the Chaldeans: Surely the
little ones of the flock shall be dragged
away; surely their[l] fold shall be appalled
at their fate. 46 At the sound of the capture of Babylon the earth shall tremble,
and her cry shall be heard among the
nations.

51 Thus says the LORD:
I am going to stir up a
destructive wind[m]
against Babylon
and against the inhabitants
of Leb-qamai;[n]
2 and I will send winnowers
to Babylon,
and they shall winnow her.
They shall empty her land
when they come against
her from every side
on the day of trouble.
3 Let not the archer bend his bow,
and let him not array himself
in his coat of mail.
Do not spare her young men;
utterly destroy her entire army.
4 They shall fall down slain in the
land of the Chaldeans,
and wounded in her streets.

[g] **50.37** Cn: Heb *his* [h] **50.37** Cn: Heb *his*
[i] **50.38** Another reading is *A sword* [j] **50.39** Heb
lacks *in Babylon* [k] **50.44** Or *and I will single out
the choicest of her rams*: Meaning of Heb uncertain
[l] **50.45** Syr Gk Tg Compare 49.20: Heb lacks *their*
[m] **51.1** Or *stir up the spirit of a destroyer*
[n] **51.1** *Leb-qamai* is a cryptogram for *Kasdim*,
Chaldea

5 Israel and Judah have not
been forsaken
by their God, the LORD of hosts,
though their land is full of guilt
before the Holy One of Israel.

6 Flee from the midst of Babylon,
save your lives, each of you!
Do not perish because of her guilt,
for this is the time of the
LORD's vengeance;
he is repaying her what is due.
7 Babylon was a golden cup in
the LORD's hand,
making all the earth drunken;
the nations drank of her wine,
and so the nations went mad.
8 Suddenly Babylon has fallen
and is shattered;
wail for her!
Bring balm for her wound;
perhaps she may be healed.
9 We tried to heal Babylon,
but she could not be healed.
Forsake her, and let each of us go
to our own country;
for her judgement has reached
up to heaven
and has been lifted up
even to the skies.
10 The LORD has brought forth
our vindication;
come, let us declare in Zion
the work of the LORD our God.

11 Sharpen the arrows!
Fill the quivers!
The LORD has stirred up the spirit of the
kings of the Medes, because his purpose
concerning Babylon is to destroy it, for
that is the vengeance of the LORD, vengeance for his temple.
12 Raise a standard against the
walls of Babylon;
make the watch strong;
post sentinels;
prepare the ambushes;
for the LORD has both
planned and done
what he spoke concerning the
inhabitants of Babylon.
13 You who live by mighty waters,
rich in treasures,
your end has come,
the thread of your life is cut.
14 The LORD of hosts has sworn
by himself:
Surely I will fill you with troops
like a swarm of locusts,
and they shall raise a shout
of victory over you.

15 It is he who made the earth
by his power,
who established the world
by his wisdom,
and by his understanding stretched
out the heavens.
16 When he utters his voice there
is a tumult of waters
in the heavens,
and he makes the mist rise from
the ends of the earth.
He makes lightnings for the rain,
and he brings out the wind
from his storehouses.
17 Everyone is stupid and without
knowledge;
goldsmiths are all put to
shame by their idols;
for their images are false,
and there is no breath in them.
18 They are worthless, a work
of delusion;
at the time of their punishment
they shall perish.
19 Not like these is the LORD,[o]
the portion of Jacob,
for he is the one who
formed all things,
and Israel is the tribe of his
inheritance;
the LORD of hosts is his name.

ISRAEL THE CREATOR'S INSTRUMENT

20 You are my war-club, my
weapon of battle:
with you I smash nations;
with you I destroy kingdoms;
21 with you I smash the horse
and its rider;
with you I smash the chariot
and the charioteer;
22 with you I smash man and woman;
with you I smash the old
man and the boy;
with you I smash the young
man and the girl;
23 with you I smash shepherds
and their flocks;
with you I smash farmers
and their teams;
with you I smash governors
and deputies.

THE DOOM OF BABYLON

24 I will repay Babylon and all the
inhabitants of Chaldea before your very
eyes for all the wrong that they have
done in Zion, says the LORD.

o **51.19** Heb lacks *the LORD*

25 I am against you, O destroying
mountain,
says the LORD,
that destroys the whole earth;
I will stretch out my hand
against you,
and roll you down from the crags,
and make you a burned-out
mountain.
26 No stone shall be taken from
you for a corner
and no stone for a foundation,
but you shall be a perpetual waste,
says the LORD.

27 Raise a standard in the land,
blow the trumpet among
the nations;
prepare the nations for war
against her,
summon against her
the kingdoms,
Ararat, Minni, and Ashkenaz;
appoint a marshal against her,
bring up horses like
bristling locusts.
28 Prepare the nations for war
against her,
the kings of the Medes, with their
governors and deputies,
and every land under
their dominion.
29 The land trembles and writhes,
for the LORD's purposes
against Babylon stand,
to make the land of Babylon
a desolation,
without inhabitant.
30 The warriors of Babylon have
given up fighting,
they remain in their
strongholds;
their strength has failed,
they have become women;
her buildings are set on fire,
her bars are broken.
31 One runner runs to meet another,
and one messenger to
meet another,
to tell the king of Babylon
that his city is taken from
end to end:
32 the fords have been seized,
the marshes have been
burned with fire,
and the soldiers are in panic.
33 For thus says the LORD of hosts,
the God of Israel:
Daughter Babylon is like a
threshing-floor
at the time when it is trodden;
yet a little while
and the time of her harvest
will come.
34 'King Nebuchadrezzar of Babylon
has devoured me,
he has crushed me;
he has made me an empty vessel,
he has swallowed me
like a monster;
he has filled his belly with
my delicacies,
he has spewed me out.
35 May my torn flesh be avenged
on Babylon,'
the inhabitants of Zion shall say.
'May my blood be avenged on the
inhabitants of Chaldea,'
Jerusalem shall say.
36 Therefore thus says the LORD:
I am going to defend your cause
and take vengeance for you.
I will dry up her sea
and make her fountain dry;
37 and Babylon shall become
a heap of ruins,
a den of jackals,
an object of horror and of hissing,
without inhabitant.

38 Like lions they shall roar together;
they shall growl like
lions' whelps.
39 When they are inflamed, I will
set out their drink
and make them drunk, until
they become merry
and then sleep a perpetual sleep
and never wake, says the LORD.
40 I will bring them down like
lambs to the slaughter,
like rams and goats.

41 How Sheshach[p] is taken,
the pride of the whole
earth seized!
How Babylon has become
an object of horror among
the nations!
42 The sea has risen over Babylon;
she has been covered by its
tumultuous waves.
43 Her cities have become an
object of horror,
a land of drought and a desert,
a land in which no one lives,
and through which no
mortal passes.

[p] 51.41 *Sheshach* is a cryptogram for *Babel*, Babylon

44 I will punish Bel in Babylon,
and make him disgorge what
he has swallowed.
The nations shall no longer
stream to him;
the wall of Babylon has fallen.

45 Come out of her, my people!
Save your lives, each of you,
from the fierce anger of the LORD!
46 Do not be faint-hearted or fearful
at the rumours heard
in the land—
one year one rumour comes,
the next year another,
rumours of violence in the land
and of ruler against ruler.

47 Assuredly, the days are coming
when I will punish the
images of Babylon;
her whole land shall be put to shame,
and all her slain shall fall
in her midst.
48 Then the heavens and the earth,
and all that is in them,
shall shout for joy over Babylon;
for the destroyers shall
come against them
out of the north,
says the LORD.
49 Babylon must fall for the
slain of Israel,
as the slain of all the earth have
fallen because of Babylon.

50 You survivors of the sword,
go, do not linger!
Remember the LORD in a
distant land,
and let Jerusalem come
into your mind:
51 We are put to shame, for we
have heard insults;
dishonour has covered our face,
for aliens have come
into the holy places of the
LORD's house.

52 Therefore the time is surely
coming, says the LORD,
when I will punish her idols,
and through all her land
the wounded shall groan.
53 Though Babylon should mount
up to heaven,
and though she should fortify
her strong height,
from me destroyers would
come upon her,
says the LORD.

54 Listen!—a cry from Babylon!
A great crashing from the
land of the Chaldeans!
55 For the LORD is laying
Babylon waste,
and stilling her loud clamour.
Their waves roar like mighty waters,
the sound of their clamour
resounds;
56 for a destroyer has come against her,
against Babylon;
her warriors are taken,
their bows are broken;
for the LORD is a God of recompense,
he will repay in full.
57 I will make her officials and
her sages drunk,
also her governors, her deputies,
and her warriors;
they shall sleep a perpetual
sleep and never wake,
says the King, whose name
is the LORD of hosts.

58 Thus says the LORD of hosts:
The broad wall of Babylon
shall be levelled to the ground,
and her high gates
shall be burned with fire.
The peoples exhaust themselves
for nothing,
and the nations weary
themselves only for fire.[q]

JEREMIAH'S COMMAND TO SERAIAH

59 The word that the prophet Jeremiah commanded Seraiah son of Neriah
son of Mahseiah, when he went with
King Zedekiah of Judah to Babylon, in
the fourth year of his reign. Seraiah was
the quartermaster. 60 Jeremiah wrote
in a[r] scroll all the disasters that would
come on Babylon, all these words that
are written concerning Babylon. 61 And
Jeremiah said to Seraiah: 'When you
come to Babylon, see that you read all
these words, 62 and say, "O LORD, you
yourself threatened to destroy this place
so that neither human beings nor animals shall live in it, and it shall be desolate for ever." 63 When you finish reading
this scroll, tie a stone to it, and throw it
into the middle of the Euphrates, 64 and
say, "Thus shall Babylon sink, to rise no
more, because of the disasters that I am
bringing on her."'[s]

q 51.58 Gk Syr Compare Hab 2.13: Heb *and the nations for fire, and they are weary* r 51.60 Or *one* s 51.64 Gk: Heb *on her. And they shall weary themselves*

Thus far are the words of Jeremiah.

THE DESTRUCTION OF JERUSALEM RECALLED

52 Zedekiah was twenty-one years old when he began to reign; he reigned for eleven years in Jerusalem. His mother's name was Hamutal daughter of Jeremiah of Libnah. 2 He did what was evil in the sight of the LORD, just as Jehoiakim had done. 3 Indeed, Jerusalem and Judah so angered the LORD that he expelled them from his presence.

Zedekiah rebelled against the king of Babylon. 4 And in the ninth year of his reign, in the tenth month, on the tenth day of the month, King Nebuchadrezzar of Babylon came with all his army against Jerusalem, and they laid siege to it; they built siege-works against it all round. 5 So the city was besieged until the eleventh year of King Zedekiah. 6 On the ninth day of the fourth month the famine became so severe in the city that there was no food for the people of the land. 7 Then a breach was made in the city wall;[t] and all the soldiers fled and went out from the city by night by the way of the gate between the two walls, by the king's garden, though the Chaldeans were all round the city. They went in the direction of the Arabah. 8 But the army of the Chaldeans pursued the king, and overtook Zedekiah in the plains of Jericho; and all his army was scattered, deserting him. 9 Then they captured the king, and brought him up to the king of Babylon at Riblah in the land of Hamath, and he passed sentence on him. 10 The king of Babylon killed the sons of Zedekiah before his eyes, and also killed all the officers of Judah at Riblah. 11 He put out the eyes of Zedekiah, and bound him in fetters, and the king of Babylon took him to Babylon, and put him in prison until the day of his death.

12 In the fifth month, on the tenth day of the month—which was the nineteenth year of King Nebuchadrezzar, king of Babylon—Nebuzaradan the captain of the bodyguard who served the king of Babylon, entered Jerusalem. 13 He burned the house of the LORD, the king's house, and all the houses of Jerusalem; every great house he burned down. 14 All the army of the Chaldeans, who were with the captain of the guard, broke down all the walls around Jerusalem. 15 Nebuzaradan the captain of the guard carried into exile some of the poorest of the people and the rest of the people who were left in the city and the deserters who had defected to the king of Babylon, together with the rest of the artisans. 16 But Nebuzaradan the captain of the guard left some of the poorest people of the land to be vine-dressers and tillers of the soil.

17 The pillars of bronze that were in the house of the LORD, and the stands and the bronze sea that were in the house of the LORD, the Chaldeans broke in pieces, and carried all the bronze to Babylon. 18 They took away the pots, the shovels, the snuffers, the basins, the ladles, and all the vessels of bronze used in the temple service. 19 The captain of the guard took away the small bowls also, the firepans, the basins, the pots, the lampstands, the ladles, and the bowls for libation, both those of gold and those of silver. 20 As for the two pillars, the one sea, the twelve bronze bulls that were under the sea, and the stands,[u] which King Solomon had made for the house of the LORD, the bronze of all these vessels was beyond weighing. 21 As for the pillars, the height of one pillar was eighteen cubits, its circumference was twelve cubits; it was hollow and its thickness was four fingers. 22 Upon it was a capital of bronze; the height of the capital was five cubits; lattice-work and pomegranates, all of bronze, encircled the top of the capital. And the second pillar had the same, with pomegranates. 23 There were ninety-six pomegranates on the sides; all the pomegranates encircling the lattice-work numbered one hundred.

24 The captain of the guard took the chief priest Seraiah, the second priest Zephaniah, and the three guardians of the threshold; 25 and from the city he took an officer who had been in command of the soldiers, and seven men of the king's council who were found in the city; the secretary of the commander of the army who mustered the people of the land; and sixty men of the people of the land who were found inside the city. 26 Then Nebuzaradan the captain of the guard took them, and brought them to the king of Babylon at Riblah. 27 And the king of Babylon struck them down, and put them to death at Riblah in the land of Hamath. So Judah went into exile out of its land.

28 This is the number of the people whom Nebuchadrezzar took into exile:

[t] **52.7** Heb lacks *wall* [u] **52.20** Cn: Heb *that were under the stands*

in the seventh year, three thousand and
twenty-three Judeans; 29in the eighteenth year of Nebuchadrezzar he took
into exile from Jerusalem eight hundred and thirty-two persons; 30in the
twenty-third year of Nebuchadrezzar,
Nebuzaradan the captain of the guard
took into exile of the Judeans seven
hundred and forty-five persons; all the
people were four thousand six hundred.

JEHOIACHIN FAVOURED IN CAPTIVITY

31 In the thirty-seventh year of the
exile of King Jehoiachin of Judah, in the
twelfth month, on the twenty-fifth day
of the month, King Evil-merodach of
Babylon, in the year he began to reign,
showed favour to King Jehoiachin of
Judah and brought him out of prison;
32he spoke kindly to him, and gave him
a seat above the seats of the other kings
who were with him in Babylon. 33So
Jehoiachin put aside his prison clothes,
and every day of his life he dined regularly at the king's table. 34For his allowance, a regular daily allowance was
given him by the king of Babylon, as
long as he lived, up to the day of his
death.

LAMENTATIONS

Tradition assigns authorship of Lamentations to Jeremiah, as the writing expresses profound grief over the destruction of Jerusalem by the Babylonians in 587 BCE. The book is carefully constructed as a five-part poem. The first four poems (chapters) are acrostics, like some of the Psalms (25; 34; 37; 119), i.e., each verse starting with a letter of the Hebrew alphabet taken in order. The poetry wails against the disgrace and calamity that befell Jerusalem and assigns responsibility to the sinfulness and infidelity of the nation. The misery and sorrow expressed in the book are tempered by the enduring hope that the present chastisement will yield to God's steadfast love and never-ending mercy (3.22–33).

The same passage from Lamentations is offered as a choice for the first reading at Masses for the Dead, for the Burial of Children, and at Masses for Any Need (3.17–26). This passage focuses on the expression of hope in the midst of sorrow, a key message at the heart of the book.

THE DESERTED CITY

1 How lonely sits the city
that once was full of people!
How like a widow she has become,
she that was great among
the nations!
She that was a princess among
the provinces
has become a vassal.

2 She weeps bitterly in the night,
with tears on her cheeks;
among all her lovers
she has no one to comfort her;
all her friends have dealt
treacherously with her,
they have become her enemies.

3 Judah has gone into exile
with suffering
and hard servitude;
she lives now among the nations,
and finds no resting-place;
her pursuers have all
overtaken her
in the midst of her distress.

4 The roads to Zion mourn,
for no one comes to the festivals;
all her gates are desolate,
her priests groan;
her young girls grieve,[a]
and her lot is bitter.

5 Her foes have become the masters,
her enemies prosper,
because the LORD has made
her suffer
for the multitude of her
transgressions;
her children have gone away,
captives before the foe.

6 From daughter Zion has departed
all her majesty.
Her princes have become like stags
that find no pasture;
they fled without strength
before the pursuer.

7 Jerusalem remembers,
in the days of her affliction
and wandering,
all the precious things
that were hers in days of old.
When her people fell into the
hand of the foe,
and there was no one to help her,
the foe looked on mocking
over her downfall.

[a] 1.4 Meaning of Heb uncertain

8 Jerusalem sinned grievously,
so she has become a mockery;
all who honoured her despise her,
for they have seen her nakedness;
she herself groans,
and turns her face away.

9 Her uncleanness was in her skirts;
she took no thought of her future;
her downfall was appalling,
with none to comfort her.
'O LORD, look at my affliction,
for the enemy has triumphed!'

10 Enemies have stretched out
their hands
over all her precious things;
she has even seen the nations
invade her sanctuary,
those whom you forbade
to enter your congregation.

11 All her people groan
as they search for bread;
they trade their treasures for food
to revive their strength.
Look, O LORD, and see
how worthless I have become.

12 Is it nothing to you,[b] all you
who pass by?
Look and see
if there is any sorrow like my sorrow,
which was brought upon me,
which the LORD inflicted
on the day of his fierce anger.

13 From on high he sent fire;
it went deep into my bones;
he spread a net for my feet;
he turned me back;
he has left me stunned,
faint all day long.

14 My transgressions were
bound[c] into a yoke;
by his hand they were
fastened together;
they weigh on my neck,
sapping my strength;
the Lord handed me over
to those whom I cannot
withstand.

15 The LORD has rejected
all my warriors in the midst of me;
he proclaimed a time against me
to crush my young men;
the Lord has trodden as in
a wine press
the virgin daughter Judah.

16 For these things I weep;
my eyes flow with tears;
for a comforter is far from me,
one to revive my courage;
my children are desolate,
for the enemy has prevailed.

17 Zion stretches out her hands,
but there is no one
to comfort her;
the LORD has commanded
against Jacob
that his neighbours should
become his foes;
Jerusalem has become
a filthy thing among them.

18 The LORD is in the right,
for I have rebelled against
his word;
but hear, all you peoples,
and behold my suffering;
my young women and young men
have gone into captivity.

19 I called to my lovers
but they deceived me;
my priests and elders
perished in the city
while seeking food
to revive their strength.

20 See, O LORD, how distressed I am;
my stomach churns,
my heart is wrung within me,
because I have been very
rebellious.
In the street the sword bereaves;
in the house it is like death.

21 They heard how I was groaning,
with no one to comfort me.
All my enemies heard
of my trouble;
they are glad that you
have done it.
Bring on the day you have
announced,
and let them be as I am.

22 Let all their evildoing come
before you;
and deal with them
as you have dealt with me
because of all my transgressions;
for my groans are many
and my heart is faint.

[b] 1.12 Meaning of Heb uncertain [c] 1.14 Meaning of Heb uncertain

GOD'S WARNINGS FULFILLED

2 How the Lord in his anger
has humiliated[d] daughter Zion!
He has thrown down from
heaven to earth
the splendour of Israel;
he has not remembered his footstool
on the day of his anger.

2 The Lord has destroyed
without mercy
all the dwellings of Jacob;
in his wrath he has broken down
the strongholds of
daughter Judah;
he has brought down to the
ground in dishonour
the kingdom and its rulers.

3 He has cut down in fierce anger
all the might of Israel;
he has withdrawn his right
hand from them
in the face of the enemy;
he has burned like a flaming
fire in Jacob,
consuming all around.

4 He has bent his bow like an enemy,
with his right hand
set like a foe;
he has killed all in whom
we took pride
in the tent of daughter Zion;
he has poured out his fury like fire.

5 The Lord has become
like an enemy;
he has destroyed Israel.
He has destroyed all its palaces,
laid in ruins its strongholds,
and multiplied in daughter Judah
mourning and lamentation.

6 He has broken down his booth
like a garden,
he has destroyed his tabernacle;
the LORD has abolished in Zion
festival and sabbath,
and in his fierce indignation
has spurned
king and priest.

7 The Lord has scorned his altar,
disowned his sanctuary;
he has delivered into the hand
of the enemy
the walls of her palaces;
a clamour was raised in the
house of the LORD
as on a day of festival.

8 The LORD determined to lay in ruins
the wall of daughter Zion;
he stretched the line;
he did not withhold his hand
from destroying;
he caused rampart and
wall to lament;
they languish together.

9 Her gates have sunk into the ground;
he has ruined and broken her bars;
her king and princes are
among the nations;
guidance is no more,
and her prophets obtain
no vision from the LORD.

10 The elders of daughter Zion
sit on the ground in silence;
they have thrown dust on
their heads
and put on sackcloth;
the young girls of Jerusalem
have bowed their heads
to the ground.

11 My eyes are spent with weeping;
my stomach churns;
my bile is poured out on the ground
because of the destruction
of my people,
because infants and babes faint
in the streets of the city.

12 They cry to their mothers,
'Where is bread and wine?'
as they faint like the wounded
in the streets of the city,
as their life is poured out
on their mothers' bosom.

13 What can I say for you, to
what compare you,
O daughter Jerusalem?
To what can I liken you, that
I may comfort you,
O virgin daughter Zion?
For vast as the sea is your ruin;
who can heal you?

14 Your prophets have seen for you
false and deceptive visions;
they have not exposed your iniquity
to restore your fortunes,
but have seen oracles for you
that are false and misleading.

15 All who pass along the way
clap their hands at you;

[d] 2.1 Meaning of Heb uncertain

they hiss and wag their heads
at daughter Jerusalem;
'Is this the city that was called
the perfection of beauty,
the joy of all the earth?'

16 All your enemies
open their mouths against you;
they hiss, they gnash their teeth,
they cry: 'We have devoured her!
Ah, this is the day we longed for;
at last we have seen it!'

17 The LORD has done what
he purposed,
he has carried out his threat;
as he ordained long ago,
he has demolished without pity;
he has made the enemy
rejoice over you,
and exalted the might of your foes.

18 Cry aloud[e] to the Lord!
O wall of daughter Zion!
Let tears stream down
like a torrent
day and night!
Give yourself no rest,
your eyes no respite!

19 Arise, cry out in the night,
at the beginning of the watches!
Pour out your heart like water
before the presence of the Lord!
Lift your hands to him
for the lives of your children,
who faint for hunger
at the head of every street.

20 Look, O LORD, and consider!
To whom have you done this?
Should women eat their offspring,
the children they have borne?
Should priest and prophet be killed
in the sanctuary of the Lord?

21 The young and the old are lying
on the ground in the streets;
my young women and my
young men
have fallen by the sword;
on the day of your anger you
have killed them,
slaughtering without mercy.

22 You invited my enemies
from all around
as if for a day of festival;
and on the day of the anger
of the LORD
no one escaped or survived;
those whom I bore and reared
my enemy has destroyed.

GOD'S STEADFAST LOVE ENDURES

3 I am one who has seen affliction
under the rod of God's[f] wrath;
2 he has driven and brought me
into darkness without any light;
3 against me alone he turns his hand,
again and again, all day long.

4 He has made my flesh and my
skin waste away,
and broken my bones;
5 he has besieged and enveloped me
with bitterness and tribulation;
6 he has made me sit in darkness
like the dead of long ago.

7 He has walled me about so that
I cannot escape;
he has put heavy chains on me;
8 though I call and cry for help,
he shuts out my prayer;
9 he has blocked my ways with
hewn stones,
he has made my paths crooked.

10 He is a bear lying in wait for me,
a lion in hiding;
11 he led me off my way and
tore me to pieces;
he has made me desolate;
12 he bent his bow and set me
as a mark for his arrow.

13 He shot into my vitals
the arrows of his quiver;
14 I have become the laughing-stock
of all my people,
the object of their taunt-songs
all day long.
15 He has filled me with bitterness,
he has glutted me with
wormwood.

16 He has made my teeth
grind on gravel,
and made me cower in ashes;
17 my soul is bereft of peace;
I have forgotten what
happiness is;
18 so I say, 'Gone is my glory,
and all that I had hoped for
from the LORD.'

19 The thought of my affliction
and my homelessness
is wormwood and gall!

[e] **2.18** Cn: Heb *Their heart cried* [f] **3.1** Heb *his*

20 My soul continually thinks of it
and is bowed down within me.
21 But this I call to mind,
and therefore I have hope:

22 The steadfast love of the LORD
never ceases,[g]
his mercies never come to an end;
23 they are new every morning;
great is your faithfulness.
24 'The LORD is my portion,'
says my soul,
'therefore I will hope in him.'

25 The LORD is good to those
who wait for him,
to the soul that seeks him.
26 It is good that one should
wait quietly
for the salvation of the LORD.
27 It is good for one to bear
the yoke in youth,
28 to sit alone in silence
when the Lord has imposed it,
29 to put one's mouth to the dust
(there may yet be hope),
30 to give one's cheek to the smiter,
and be filled with insults.

31 For the Lord will not
reject for ever.
32 Although he causes grief, he
will have compassion
according to the abundance
of his steadfast love;
33 for he does not willingly afflict
or grieve anyone.

34 When all the prisoners of the land
are crushed under foot,
35 when human rights are perverted
in the presence of the Most High,
36 when one's case is subverted
—does the Lord not see it?

37 Who can command and
have it done,
if the Lord has not ordained it?
38 Is it not from the mouth of
the Most High
that good and bad come?
39 Why should any who draw
breath complain
about the punishment
of their sins?

40 Let us test and examine our ways,
and return to the LORD.
41 Let us lift up our hearts as
well as our hands
to God in heaven.
42 We have transgressed and rebelled,
and you have not forgiven.

43 You have wrapped yourself with
anger and pursued us,
killing without pity;
44 you have wrapped yourself
with a cloud
so that no prayer can
pass through.
45 You have made us filth and rubbish
among the peoples.

46 All our enemies
have opened their mouths
against us;
47 panic and pitfall have come upon us,
devastation and destruction.
48 My eyes flow with rivers of tears
because of the destruction
of my people.

49 My eyes will flow without ceasing,
without respite,
50 until the LORD from heaven
looks down and sees.
51 My eyes cause me grief
at the fate of all the young
women in my city.

52 Those who were my enemies
without cause
have hunted me like a bird;
53 they flung me alive into a pit
and hurled stones on me;
54 water closed over my head;
I said, 'I am lost.'

55 I called on your name, O LORD,
from the depths of the pit;
56 you heard my plea, 'Do not
close your ear
to my cry for help, but
give me relief!'
57 You came near when I called on you;
you said, 'Do not fear!'

58 You have taken up my cause, O Lord,
you have redeemed my life.
59 You have seen the wrong done
to me, O LORD;
judge my cause.
60 You have seen all their malice,
all their plots against me.

61 You have heard their
taunts, O LORD,
all their plots against me.

g 3.22 Syr Tg: Heb *LORD, we are not cut off*

62 The whispers and murmurs
of my assailants
are against me all day long.
63 Whether they sit or rise—see,
I am the object of their
taunt-songs.

64 Pay them back for their
deeds, O LORD,
according to the work of
their hands!
65 Give them anguish of heart;
your curse be on them!
66 Pursue them in anger and
destroy them
from under the LORD's heavens.

THE PUNISHMENT OF ZION

4 How the gold has grown dim,
how the pure gold is changed!
The sacred stones lie scattered
at the head of every street.

2 The precious children of Zion,
worth their weight in fine gold—
how they are reckoned as
earthen pots,
the work of a potter's hands!

3 Even the jackals offer the breast
and nurse their young,
but my people has become cruel,
like the ostriches in the
wilderness.

4 The tongue of the infant sticks
to the roof of its mouth for thirst;
the children beg for food,
but no one gives them anything.

5 Those who feasted on delicacies
perish in the streets;
those who were brought up in purple
cling to ash heaps.

6 For the chastisement[h] of my
people has been greater
than the punishment[i] of Sodom,
which was overthrown in a moment,
though no hand was laid on it.[j]

7 Her princes were purer than snow,
whiter than milk;
their bodies were more
ruddy than coral,
their hair[k] like sapphire.[l]

8 Now their visage is blacker
than soot;
they are not recognized
in the streets.
Their skin has shrivelled
on their bones;
it has become as dry as wood.

9 Happier were those pierced
by the sword
than those pierced by hunger,
whose life drains away, deprived
of the produce of the field.

10 The hands of compassionate women
have boiled their own children;
they became their food
in the destruction of my people.

11 The LORD gave full vent to his wrath;
he poured out his hot anger,
and kindled a fire in Zion
that consumed its foundations.

12 The kings of the earth did
not believe,
nor did any of the inhabitants
of the world,
that foe or enemy could enter
the gates of Jerusalem.

13 It was for the sins of her prophets
and the iniquities of her priests,
who shed the blood of
the righteous
in the midst of her.

14 Blindly they wandered through
the streets,
so defiled with blood
that no one was able
to touch their garments.

15 'Away! Unclean!' people
shouted at them;
'Away! Away! Do not touch!'
So they became fugitives
and wanderers;
it was said among the nations,
'They shall stay here no longer.'

16 The LORD himself has
scattered them,
he will regard them no more;
no honour was shown to the priests,
no favour to the elders.

17 Our eyes failed, ever watching
vainly for help;
we were watching eagerly
for a nation that could not save.

[h] 4.6 Or *iniquity* [i] 4.6 Or *sin* [j] 4.6 Meaning of Heb uncertain [k] 4.7 Meaning of Heb uncertain [l] 4.7 Or *lapis lazuli*

18 They dogged our steps
so that we could not walk
in our streets;
our end drew near; our days
were numbered;
for our end had come.

19 Our pursuers were swifter
than the eagles in the heavens;
they chased us on the mountains,
they lay in wait for us in
the wilderness.

20 The LORD's anointed, the
breath of our life,
was taken in their pits—
the one of whom we said,
'Under his shadow
we shall live among the nations.'

21 Rejoice and be glad,
O daughter Edom,
you that live in the land of Uz;
but to you also the cup shall pass;
you shall become drunk and
strip yourself bare.

22 The punishment of your iniquity,
O daughter Zion, is
accomplished,
he will keep you in exile no longer;
but your iniquity, O daughter
Edom, he will punish,
he will uncover your sins.

A PLEA FOR MERCY

5 Remember, O LORD, what
has befallen us;
look, and see our disgrace!
2 Our inheritance has been turned
over to strangers,
our homes to aliens.
3 We have become orphans, fatherless;
our mothers are like widows.
4 We must pay for the
water we drink;
the wood we get must be bought.
5 With a yoke[m] on our necks we
are hard driven;
we are weary, we are
given no rest.
6 We have made a pact with[n]
Egypt and Assyria,
to get enough bread.
7 Our ancestors sinned; they
are no more,
and we bear their iniquities.
8 Slaves rule over us;
there is no one to deliver us
from their hand.
9 We get our bread at the peril
of our lives,
because of the sword in
the wilderness.
10 Our skin is black as an oven
from the scorching heat of famine.
11 Women are raped in Zion,
virgins in the towns of Judah.
12 Princes are hung up by their hands;
no respect is shown to the elders.
13 Young men are compelled to grind,
and boys stagger under
loads of wood.
14 The old men have left the city gate,
the young men their music.
15 The joy of our hearts has ceased;
our dancing has been turned
to mourning.
16 The crown has fallen from our head;
woe to us, for we have sinned!
17 Because of this our hearts are sick,
because of these things our
eyes have grown dim:
18 because of Mount Zion, which
lies desolate;
jackals prowl over it.

19 But you, O LORD, reign for ever;
your throne endures to
all generations.
20 Why have you forgotten us completely?
Why have you forsaken us
these many days?
21 Restore us to yourself, O LORD,
that we may be restored;
renew our days as of old—
22 unless you have utterly rejected us,
and are angry with us
beyond measure.

m 5.5 Symmachus: Heb lacks *With a yoke*
n 5.6 Heb *have given the hand to*

BARUCH

The book of Baruch was probably written as late as 200 to 60 BCE. Its context, however, is the Babylonian exile. Baruch seems to be the secretary or scribe of the prophet Jeremiah. The writing is a collection of prayers and hymns that are a reflection upon the circumstances of the exiles in Babylon. Repentance is expected and observance of the law of Moses is presented as the way to life and peace. Jerusalem is represented as the mother of all exiles and is assured that all her children will be restored to her (4.30—5.9).

The passage from Baruch that speaks of walking in the way of God leading to lasting peace is presented as Reading VI at the Easter Vigil every year. In this passage, wisdom is identified with "the book of the commandments of God" (4.1) that has been given to Israel. This truth leads to the assertion: "Happy are we, O Israel, for we know what is pleasing to God" (4.4).

BARUCH AND THE JEWS IN BABYLON

1 These are the words of the book that
Baruch son of Neriah son of Mahseiah son of Zedekiah son of Hasadiah
son of Hilkiah wrote in Babylon, 2in
the fifth year, on the seventh day of the
month, at the time when the Chaldeans
took Jerusalem and burned it with fire.
3 Baruch read the words of this book
to Jeconiah son of Jehoiakim, king of Judah, and to all the people who came to
hear the book, 4and to the nobles and
the princes, and to the elders, and to
all the people, small and great, all who
lived in Babylon by the river Sud.
5 Then they wept, and fasted, and
prayed before the Lord; 6they collected
as much money as each could give, 7and
sent it to Jerusalem to the high priest[a]
Jehoiakim son of Hilkiah son of Shallum, and to the priests, and to all the
people who were present with him in
Jerusalem. 8At the same time, on the
tenth day of Sivan, Baruch[b] took the
vessels of the house of the Lord, which
had been carried away from the temple,
to return them to the land of Judah—
the silver vessels that Zedekiah son of
Josiah, king of Judah, had made, 9after
King Nebuchadnezzar of Babylon had
carried away from Jerusalem Jeconiah
and the princes and the prisoners and
the nobles and the people of the land,
and brought them to Babylon.

A LETTER TO JERUSALEM

10 They said: Here we send you
money; so buy with the money burnt-
offerings and sin-offerings and incense,
and prepare a grain-offering, and offer
them on the altar of the Lord our God;
11and pray for the life of King Nebuchadnezzar of Babylon, and for the life
of his son Belshazzar, so that their days
on earth may be like the days of heaven.
12The Lord will give us strength, and
light to our eyes; we shall live under the
protection[c] of King Nebuchadnezzar of
Babylon, and under the protection of
his son Belshazzar, and we shall serve
them for many days and find favour in
their sight. 13Pray also for us to the Lord
our God, for we have sinned against the
Lord our God, and to this day the anger of the Lord and his wrath have not
turned away from us. 14And you shall
read aloud this scroll that we are sending you, to make your confession in the

[a] 1.7 Gk *the priest* [b] 1.8 Gk *he* [c] 1.12 Gk *in the shadow*

house of the Lord on the days of the festivals and at appointed seasons.

CONFESSION OF SINS

15 And you shall say: The Lord our God is in the right, but there is open shame on us today, on the people of Judah, on the inhabitants of Jerusalem, 16 and on our kings, our rulers, our priests, our prophets, and our ancestors, 17 because we have sinned before the Lord. 18 We have disobeyed him, and have not heeded the voice of the Lord our God, to walk in the statutes of the Lord that he set before us. 19 From the time when the Lord brought our ancestors out of the land of Egypt until today, we have been disobedient to the Lord our God, and we have been negligent, in not heeding his voice. 20 So to this day there have clung to us the calamities and the curse that the Lord declared through his servant Moses at the time when he brought our ancestors out of the land of Egypt to give to us a land flowing with milk and honey. 21 We did not listen to the voice of the Lord our God in all the words of the prophets whom he sent to us, 22 but all of us followed the intent of our own wicked hearts by serving other gods and doing what is evil in the sight of the Lord our God.

2 So the Lord carried out the threat he spoke against us: against our judges who ruled Israel, and against our kings and our rulers and the people of Israel and Judah. 2 Under the whole heaven there has not been done the like of what he has done in Jerusalem, in accordance with the threats that were[d] written in the law of Moses. 3 Some of us ate the flesh of their sons and others the flesh of their daughters. 4 He made them subject to all the kingdoms around us, to be an object of scorn and a desolation among all the surrounding peoples, where the Lord has scattered them. 5 They were brought down and not raised up, because our nation[e] sinned against the Lord our God, in not heeding his voice.

6 The Lord our God is in the right, but there is open shame on us and our ancestors this very day. 7 All those calamities with which the Lord threatened us have come upon us. 8 Yet we have not entreated the favour of the Lord by turning away, each of us, from the thoughts of our wicked hearts. 9 And the Lord has kept the calamities ready, and the Lord has brought them upon us, for the Lord is just in all the works that he has commanded us to do. 10 Yet we have not obeyed his voice, to walk in the statutes of the Lord that he set before us.

PRAYER FOR DELIVERANCE

11 And now, O Lord God of Israel, who brought your people out of the land of Egypt with a mighty hand and with signs and wonders and with great power and outstretched arm, and made yourself a name that continues to this day, 12 we have sinned, we have been ungodly, we have done wrong, O Lord our God, against all your ordinances. 13 Let your anger turn away from us, for we are left, few in number, among the nations where you have scattered us. 14 Hear, O Lord, our prayer and our supplication, and for your own sake deliver us, and grant us favour in the sight of those who have carried us into exile; 15 so that all the earth may know that you are the Lord our God, for Israel and his descendants are called by your name.

16 O Lord, look down from your holy dwelling, and consider us. Incline your ear, O Lord, and hear; 17 open your eyes, O Lord, and see, for the dead who are in Hades, whose spirit has been taken from their bodies, will not ascribe glory or justice to the Lord; 18 but the person who is deeply grieved, who walks bowed and feeble, with failing eyes and famished soul, will declare your glory and righteousness, O Lord.

19 For it is not because of any righteous deeds of our ancestors or our kings that we bring before you our prayer for mercy, O Lord our God. 20 For you have sent your anger and your wrath upon us, as you declared by your servants the prophets, saying: 21 Thus says the Lord: Bend your shoulders and serve the king of Babylon, and you will remain in the land that I gave to your ancestors. 22 But if you will not obey the voice of the Lord and will not serve the king of Babylon, 23 I will make to cease from the towns of Judah and from the region around Jerusalem the voice of mirth and the voice of gladness, the voice of the bridegroom and the voice of the bride, and the whole land will be a desolation without inhabitants.

24 But we did not obey your voice, to serve the king of Babylon; and you have carried out your threats, which

[d] 2.2 Gk *in accordance with what is* [e] 2.5 Gk *because we*

you spoke by your servants the prophets, that the bones of our kings and the
bones of our ancestors would be brought
out of their resting-place; 25and indeed
they have been thrown out to the heat
of day and the frost of night. They perished in great misery, by famine and
sword and pestilence. 26And the house
that is called by your name you have
made as it is today, because of the wickedness of the house of Israel and the
house of Judah.

GOD'S PROMISE RECALLED

27 Yet you have dealt with us, O Lord
our God, in all your kindness and in all
your great compassion, 28as you spoke
by your servant Moses on the day when
you commanded him to write your law
in the presence of the people of Israel,
saying, 29'If you will not obey my voice,
this very great multitude will surely
turn into a small number among the
nations, where I will scatter them. 30For
I know that they will not obey me, for
they are a stiff-necked people. But in
the land of their exile they will come to
themselves 31and know that I am the
Lord their God. I will give them a heart
that obeys and ears that hear; 32they
will praise me in the land of their exile, and will remember my name 33and
turn from their stubbornness and their
wicked deeds; for they will remember
the ways of their ancestors, who sinned
before the Lord. 34I will bring them
again into the land that I swore to give
to their ancestors, to Abraham, Isaac,
and Jacob, and they will rule over it; and
I will increase them, and they will not be
diminished. 35I will make an everlasting
covenant with them to be their God and
they shall be my people; and I will never
again remove my people Israel from the
land that I have given them.'

3 O Lord Almighty, God of Israel, the
soul in anguish and the wearied
spirit cry out to you. 2Hear, O Lord, and
have mercy, for we have sinned before
you. 3For you are enthroned for ever,
and we are perishing for ever. 4O Lord
Almighty, God of Israel, hear now the
prayer of the people[f] of Israel, the children of those who sinned before you,
who did not heed the voice of the Lord
their God, so that calamities have clung
to us. 5Do not remember the iniquities
of our ancestors, but in this crisis remember your power and your name.
6For you are the Lord our God, and it
is you, O Lord, whom we will praise.
7For you have put the fear of you in our
hearts so that we call upon your name;
and we will praise you in our exile, for
we have put away from our hearts all
the iniquity of our ancestors who sinned
against you. 8See, we are today in our
exile where you have scattered us, to be
reproached and cursed and punished for
all the iniquities of our ancestors, who
forsook the Lord our God.

IN PRAISE OF WISDOM

9 Hear the commandments
of life, O Israel;
give ear, and learn wisdom!
10 Why is it, O Israel, why is it
that you are in the land
of your enemies,
that you are growing old in
a foreign country,
that you are defiled with the dead,
11 that you are counted among
those in Hades?
12 You have forsaken the fountain
of wisdom.
13 If you had walked in the way of God,
you would be living in
peace for ever.
14 Learn where there is wisdom,
where there is strength,
where there is understanding,
so that you may at the same
time discern
where there is length of
days, and life,
where there is light for the
eyes, and peace.

15 Who has found her place?
And who has entered her
storehouses?
16 Where are the rulers of the nations,
and those who lorded it over
the animals on earth;
17 those who made sport of the
birds of the air,
and who hoarded up
silver and gold
in which people trust,
and there is no end to
their getting;
18 those who schemed to get silver,
and were anxious,
but there is no trace of
their works?
19 They have vanished and gone
down to Hades,
and others have arisen
in their place.

f 3.4 Gk *dead*

20 Later generations have seen
the light of day,
and have lived upon the earth;
but they have not learned the
way to knowledge,
nor understood her paths,
nor laid hold of her.
21 Their descendants have strayed
far from her[g] way.
22 She has not been heard of in Canaan,
or seen in Teman;
23 the descendants of Hagar, who seek for
understanding on the earth,
the merchants of Merran
and Teman,
the story-tellers and the seekers
for understanding,
have not learned the way to wisdom,
or given thought to her paths.

24 O Israel, how great is the
house of God,
how vast the territory that
he possesses!
25 It is great and has no bounds;
it is high and immeasurable.
26 The giants were born there, who
were famous of old,
great in stature, expert in war.
27 God did not choose them,
or give them the way to knowledge;
28 so they perished because they
had no wisdom,
they perished through their folly.

29 Who has gone up into heaven,
and taken her,
and brought her down
from the clouds?
30 Who has gone over the sea,
and found her,
and will buy her for pure gold?
31 No one knows the way to her,
or is concerned about the
path to her.
32 But the one who knows all
things knows her,
he found her by his understanding.
The one who prepared the
earth for all time
filled it with four-footed creatures;
33 the one who sends forth the
light, and it goes;
he called it, and it obeyed
him, trembling;
34 the stars shone in their watches,
and were glad;
he called them, and they
said, 'Here we are!'
They shone with gladness for
him who made them.
35 This is our God;
no other can be compared to him.
36 He found the whole way
to knowledge,
and gave her to his servant Jacob
and to Israel, whom he loved.
37 Afterwards she appeared on earth
and lived with humankind.

4 She is the book of the
commandments of God,
the law that endures for ever.
All who hold her fast will live,
and those who forsake her will die.
2 Turn, O Jacob, and take her;
walk towards the shining
of her light.
3 Do not give your glory to another,
or your advantages to an
alien people.
4 Happy are we, O Israel,
for we know what is
pleasing to God.

ENCOURAGEMENT FOR ISRAEL

5 Take courage, my people,
who perpetuate Israel's name!
6 It was not for destruction
that you were sold to the nations,
but you were handed over
to your enemies
because you angered God.
7 For you provoked the one
who made you
by sacrificing to demons
and not to God.
8 You forgot the everlasting God,
who brought you up,
and you grieved Jerusalem,
who reared you.
9 For she saw the wrath that came
upon you from God,
and she said:
Listen, you neighbours of Zion,
God has brought great
sorrow upon me;
10 for I have seen the exile of my
sons and daughters,
which the Everlasting
brought upon them.
11 With joy I nurtured them,
but I sent them away with
weeping and sorrow.
12 Let no one rejoice over me, a widow
and bereaved of many;
I was left desolate because of the
sins of my children,
because they turned away
from the law of God.

g 3.21 Other ancient authorities read *their*

13 They had no regard for
his statutes;
they did not walk in the ways
of God's commandments,
or tread the paths his
righteousness showed them.
14 Let the neighbours of Zion come;
remember the capture of my
sons and daughters,
which the Everlasting
brought upon them.
15 For he brought a distant nation
against them,
a nation ruthless and of a
strange language,
which had no respect
for the aged
and no pity for a child.
16 They led away the widow's
beloved sons,
and bereaved the lonely woman
of her daughters.

17 But I, how can I help you?
18 For he who brought these
calamities upon you
will deliver you from the
hand of your enemies.
19 Go, my children, go;
for I have been left desolate.
20 I have taken off the robe of peace
and put on sackcloth for
my supplication;
I will cry to the Everlasting
all my days.

21 Take courage, my children,
cry to God,
and he will deliver you
from the power and
hand of the enemy.
22 For I have put my hope in the
Everlasting to save you,
and joy has come to me
from the Holy One,
because of the mercy that will
soon come to you
from your everlasting saviour.[h]
23 For I sent you out with sorrow
and weeping,
but God will give you back
to me with joy and
gladness for ever.
24 For as the neighbours of Zion have
now seen your capture,
so they soon will see your
salvation by God,
which will come to you
with great glory
and with the splendour of
the Everlasting.
25 My children, endure with patience
the wrath that has come
upon you from God.
Your enemy has overtaken you,
but you will soon see their
destruction
and will tread upon their necks.
26 My pampered children have
travelled rough roads;
they were taken away like a flock
carried off by the enemy.

27 Take courage, my children,
and cry to God,
for you will be remembered
by the one who brought
this upon you.
28 For just as you were disposed to
go astray from God,
return with tenfold zeal
to seek him.
29 For the one who brought these
calamities upon you
will bring you everlasting joy
with your salvation.

JERUSALEM IS ASSURED OF HELP

30 Take courage, O Jerusalem,
for the one who named you
will comfort you.
31 Wretched will be those who
mistreated you
and who rejoiced at your fall.
32 Wretched will be the cities that your
children served as slaves;
wretched will be the city that
received your offspring.
33 For just as she rejoiced at your fall
and was glad at your ruin,
so she will be grieved at her
own desolation.
34 I will take away her pride in
her great population,
and her insolence will be
turned to grief.
35 For fire will come upon her from the
Everlasting for many days,
and for a long time she will be
inhabited by demons.

36 Look towards the east, O Jerusalem,
and see the joy that is coming
to you from God.
37 Look, your children are coming,
whom you sent away;
they are coming, gathered
from east and west,
at the word of the Holy One,
rejoicing in the glory of God.

[h] 4.22 *Or from the Everlasting, your saviour*

5 Take off the garment of your
sorrow and affliction,
O Jerusalem,
and put on for ever the beauty
of the glory from God.
2 Put on the robe of the righteousness
that comes from God;
put on your head the diadem of
the glory of the Everlasting;
3 for God will show your splendour
everywhere under heaven.
4 For God will give you evermore
the name,
'Righteous Peace, Godly Glory'.

5 Arise, O Jerusalem, stand
upon the height;
look towards the east,
and see your children gathered
from west and east
at the word of the Holy One,
rejoicing that God has
remembered them.
6 For they went out from you on foot,
led away by their enemies;
but God will bring them back to you,
carried in glory, as on a
royal throne.
7 For God has ordered that every
high mountain and the
everlasting hills be made low
and the valleys filled up, to
make level ground,
so that Israel may walk safely
in the glory of God.
8 The woods and every fragrant tree
have shaded Israel at
God's command.
9 For God will lead Israel with joy,
in the light of his glory,
with the mercy and righteousness
that come from him.

THE LETTER OF JEREMIAH

6[i] A copy of a letter that Jeremiah
sent to those who were to be taken
to Babylon as exiles by the king of the
Babylonians, to give them the message
that God had commanded him.

THE PEOPLE FACE A LONG CAPTIVITY

2 Because of the sins that you have
committed before God, you will be taken
to Babylon as exiles by Nebuchadnezzar, king of the Babylonians. 3 Therefore,
when you have come to Babylon you
will remain there for many years, for a
long time, up to seven generations; after that I will bring you away from there
in peace. 4 Now in Babylon you will see
gods made of silver and gold and wood,
which people carry on their shoulders,
and which cause the heathen to fear. 5 So
beware of becoming at all like the foreigners or of letting fear for these gods[j]
possess you 6 when you see the multitude before and behind them worshipping them. But say in your heart, 'It is
you, O Lord, whom we must worship.'
7 For my angel is with you, and he is
watching over your lives.

THE HELPLESSNESS OF IDOLS

8 Their tongues are smoothed by
the carpenter, and they themselves
are overlaid with gold and silver; but
they are false and cannot speak. 9 People[k] take gold and make crowns for the
heads of their gods, as they might for a
girl who loves ornaments. 10 Sometimes
the priests secretly take gold and silver
from their gods and spend it on themselves, 11 or even give some of it to the
prostitutes on the terrace. They deck
their gods[l] out with garments like human beings—these gods of silver and
gold and wood 12 that cannot save themselves from rust and corrosion. When
they have been dressed in purple robes,
13 their faces are wiped because of the
dust from the temple, which is thick
upon them. 14 One of them holds a sceptre, like a district judge, but is unable
to destroy anyone who offends it. 15 Another has a dagger in its right hand, and
an axe, but cannot defend itself from
war and robbers. 16 From this it is evident that they are not gods; so do not
fear them.

17 For just as someone's dish is useless when it is broken, 18 so are their
gods when they have been set up in the
temples. Their eyes are full of the dust
raised by the feet of those who enter.
And just as the gates are shut on every
side against anyone who has offended
a king, as though under sentence of
death, so the priests make their temples
secure with doors and locks and bars, in
order that they may not be plundered
by robbers. 19 They light more lamps for
them than they light for themselves,
though their gods[m] can see none of
them. 20 They are[n] just like a beam of
the temple, but their hearts, it is said,

[i] **6.1** The King James Version (like the Latin Vulgate) prints The Letter of Jeremiah as Chapter 6 of the Book of Baruch, and the chapter and verse numbers are here retained. In the Greek Septuagint, the Letter is separated from Baruch by the Book of Lamentations. [j] **6.5** Gk *for them* [k] **6.9** Gk *They* [l] **6.11** Gk *them* [m] **6.19** Gk *they* [n] **6.20** Gk *It is*

are eaten away when crawling creatures from the earth devour them and their robes. They do not notice 21 when their faces have been blackened by the smoke of the temple. 22 Bats, swallows, and birds alight on their bodies and heads; and so do cats. 23 From this you will know that they are not gods; so do not fear them.

24 As for the gold that they wear for beauty—it[o] will not shine unless someone wipes off the tarnish; for even when they were being cast, they did not feel it. 25 They are bought without regard to cost, but there is no breath in them. 26 Having no feet, they are carried on the shoulders of others, revealing to humankind their worthlessness. And those who serve them are put to shame 27 because, if any of these gods falls[p] to the ground, they themselves must pick it up. If anyone sets it upright, it cannot move itself; and if it is tipped over, it cannot straighten itself. Gifts are placed before them just as before the dead. 28 The priests sell the sacrifices that are offered to these gods[q] and use the money themselves. Likewise their wives preserve some of the meat[r] with salt, but give none to the poor or helpless. 29 Sacrifices to them may even be touched by women in their periods or at childbirth. Since you know by these things that they are not gods, do not fear them.

30 For how can they be called gods? Women serve meals for gods of silver and gold and wood; 31 and in their temples the priests sit with their clothes torn, their heads and beards shaved, and their heads uncovered. 32 They howl and shout before their gods as some do at a funeral banquet. 33 The priests take some of the clothing of their gods[s] to clothe their wives and children. 34 Whether one does evil to them or good, they will not be able to repay it. They cannot set up a king or depose one. 35 Likewise they are not able to give either wealth or money; if one makes a vow to them and does not keep it, they will not require it. 36 They cannot save anyone from death or rescue the weak from the strong. 37 They cannot restore sight to the blind; they cannot rescue one who is in distress. 38 They cannot take pity on a widow or do good to an orphan. 39 These things that are made of wood and overlaid with gold and silver are like stones from the mountain, and those who serve them will be put to shame. 40 Why then must anyone think that they are gods, or call them gods?

THE FOOLISHNESS OF WORSHIPPING IDOLS

Besides, even the Chaldeans themselves dishonour them; for when they see someone who cannot speak, they bring Bel and pray that the mute may speak, as though Bel[t] were able to understand! 41 Yet they themselves cannot perceive this and abandon them, for they have no sense. 42 And the women, with cords around them, sit along the passageways, burning bran for incense. 43 When one of them is led off by one of the passers-by and is taken to bed by him, she derides the woman next to her, because she was not as attractive as herself and her cord was not broken. 44 Whatever is done for these idols[u] is false. Why then must anyone think that they are gods, or call them gods?

45 They are made by carpenters and goldsmiths; they can be nothing but what the artisans wish them to be. 46 Those who make them will certainly not live very long themselves; 47 how then can the things that are made by them be gods? They have left only lies and reproach for those who come after. 48 For when war or calamity comes upon them, the priests consult together as to where they can hide themselves and their gods.[v] 49 How then can one fail to see that these are not gods, for they cannot save themselves from war or calamity? 50 Since they are made of wood and overlaid with gold and silver, it will afterwards be known that they are false. 51 It will be manifest to all the nations and kings that they are not gods but the work of human hands, and that there is no work of God in them. 52 Who then can fail to know that they are not gods?[w]

53 For they cannot set up a king over a country or give rain to people. 54 They cannot judge their own cause or deliver one who is wronged, for they have no power; 55 they are like crows between heaven and earth. When fire breaks out in a temple of wooden gods overlaid with gold or silver, their priests will flee and escape, but the gods[x] will be burned up like timbers. 56 Besides, they can offer no resistance to king or enemy. Why

[o] **6.24** Lat Syr: Gk *they* [p] **6.27** Gk *if they fall*
[q] **6.28** Gk *to them* [r] **6.28** Gk *of them*
[s] **6.33** Gk *some of their clothing* [t] **6.40** Gk *he*
[u] **6.44** Gk *them* [v] **6.48** Gk *them*
[w] **6.52** Meaning of Gk uncertain [x] **6.55** Gk *they*

then must anyone admit or think that
they are gods?

57 Gods made of wood and overlaid
with silver and gold are unable to save
themselves from thieves or robbers.
58Anyone who can will strip them of
their gold and silver and of the robes
they wear, and go off with this booty,
and they will not be able to help themselves. 59So it is better to be a king who
shows his courage, or a household uten-
sil that serves its owner's need, than
to be these false gods; better even the
door of a house that protects its contents, than these false gods; better also
a wooden pillar in a palace, than these
false gods.

60 For sun and moon and stars are
bright, and when sent to do a service,
they are obedient. 61So also the lightning, when it flashes, is widely seen;
and the wind likewise blows in every
land. 62When God commands the clouds
to go over the whole world, they carry
out his command. 63And the fire sent
from above to consume mountains and
woods does what it is ordered. But these
idols[y] are not to be compared with them
in appearance or power. 64Therefore one
must not think that they are gods, nor
call them gods, for they are not able
either to decide a case or to do good to
anyone. 65Since you know then that
they are not gods, do not fear them.

66 They can neither curse nor bless
kings; 67they cannot show signs in the
heavens for the nations, or shine like
the sun or give light like the moon.
68The wild animals are better than they
are, for they can flee to shelter and help
themselves. 69So we have no evidence
whatever that they are gods; therefore
do not fear them.

70 Like a scarecrow in a cucumber
bed, which guards nothing, so are their
gods of wood, overlaid with gold and
silver. 71In the same way, their gods
of wood, overlaid with gold and silver, are like a thornbush in a garden
on which every bird perches; or like
a corpse thrown out in the darkness.
72From the purple and linen[z] that rot
upon them you will know that they are
not gods; and they will finally be consumed themselves, and be a reproach in
the land. 73Better, therefore, is someone
upright who has no idols; such a person
will be far above reproach.

[y] **6.63** Gk *these things* [z] **6.72** Cn: Gk *marble*, Syr *silk*

EZEKIEL

The book of Ezekiel contains the oracles, visions, allegories, and symbolic actions of the priest/prophet Ezekiel, who lived during the time of the Babylonian exile. Ezekiel received his inaugurating vision while living in Babylon by the river Chebar (1.3) during the reign of King Jehoiachin of Judah. Ezekiel lived among and prophesied for the Judahites living in exile in Babylon. Now that the people had lost their city and its temple, Ezekiel had to make sense of the events and point the way to a new future even as they began to settle into their new circumstances in exile.

Ezekiel's prophecy is marked by visions and ecstasy and various forms of severe maladies, i.e., paralysis of limb and tongue (3.22ff.). He, more than any other prophet, uses symbolic actions to annouce judgments and interpret events. He would perform dramatic actions to make his point or get the attention of his hearers, for example, by taking a sword to his own hair (5.1–4) or by refusing to grieve at the death of his wife (24.15–27). After the exile was accomplished, Ezekiel's famous vision of dry bones (37.1–14) announces the coming of a future restoration for Israel rising up out of the ashes of Babylon.

Ezekiel's prophecy that the Lord will purify his people and give them a new heart and a new spirit is read every year at the Easter Vigil (36.16–28). The same passage from Ezekiel about a new heart and a new spirit is also provided at certain Ritual Masses for Christian Initiation (36.24–28), Baptism of Children (36.24–28), and Confirmation (36.24–28). Additionally, Ezekiel's famous vision of the dry bones is offered as a choice for the first reading on the Vigil of Pentecost.

THE VISION OF THE CHARIOT

1 In the thirtieth year, in the fourth month, on the fifth day of the
month, as I was among the exiles by the
river Chebar, the heavens were opened,
and I saw visions of God. 2On the fifth
day of the month (it was the fifth year of
the exile of King Jehoiachin), 3the word
of the LORD came to the priest Ezekiel
son of Buzi, in the land of the Chaldeans
by the river Chebar; and the hand of the
LORD was on him there.

4 As I looked, a stormy wind came
out of the north: a great cloud with
brightness around it and fire flashing
forth continually, and in the middle
of the fire, something like gleaming
amber. 5In the middle of it was something like four living creatures. This was
their appearance: they were of human
form. 6Each had four faces, and each of
them had four wings. 7Their legs were
straight, and the soles of their feet were
like the sole of a calf's foot; and they
sparkled like burnished bronze. 8Under
their wings on their four sides they had
human hands. And the four had their
faces and their wings thus: 9their wings
touched one another; each of them
moved straight ahead, without turning
as they moved. 10As for the appearance
of their faces: the four had the face of a
human being, the face of a lion on the
right side, the face of an ox on the left
side, and the face of an eagle; 11such were
their faces. Their wings were spread out
above; each creature had two wings,
each of which touched the wing of another, while two covered their bodies.
12Each moved straight ahead; wherever

the spirit would go, they went, without
turning as they went. 13 In the middle
of[a] the living creatures there was something that looked like burning coals
of fire, like torches moving to and fro
among the living creatures; the fire was
bright, and lightning issued from the
fire. 14 The living creatures darted to and
fro, like a flash of lightning.

15 As I looked at the living creatures,
I saw a wheel on the earth beside the
living creatures, one for each of the four
of them.[b] 16 As for the appearance of the
wheels and their construction: their
appearance was like the gleaming of
beryl; and the four had the same form,
their construction being something like
a wheel within a wheel. 17 When they
moved, they moved in any of the four directions without veering as they moved.
18 Their rims were tall and awesome, for
the rims of all four were full of eyes all
round. 19 When the living creatures
moved, the wheels moved beside them;
and when the living creatures rose from
the earth, the wheels rose. 20 Wherever
the spirit would go, they went, and the
wheels rose along with them; for the
spirit of the living creatures was in the
wheels. 21 When they moved, the others
moved; when they stopped, the others
stopped; and when they rose from the
earth, the wheels rose along with them;
for the spirit of the living creatures was
in the wheels.

22 Over the heads of the living creatures there was something like a dome,
shining like crystal,[c] spread out above
their heads. 23 Under the dome their
wings were stretched out straight,
one towards another; and each of the
creatures had two wings covering its
body. 24 When they moved, I heard the
sound of their wings like the sound of
mighty waters, like the thunder of the
Almighty,[d] a sound of tumult like the
sound of an army; when they stopped,
they let down their wings. 25 And there
came a voice from above the dome over
their heads; when they stopped, they let
down their wings.

26 And above the dome over their
heads there was something like a
throne, in appearance like sapphire;[e]
and seated above the likeness of a
throne was something that seemed like
a human form. 27 Upwards from what
appeared like the loins I saw something like gleaming amber, something
that looked like fire enclosed all round;
and downwards from what looked like
the loins I saw something that looked
like fire, and there was a splendour all
round. 28 Like the bow in a cloud on a
rainy day, such was the appearance of
the splendour all round. This was the
appearance of the likeness of the glory
of the LORD.

When I saw it, I fell on my face, and
I heard the voice of someone speaking.

THE VISION OF THE SCROLL

2 He said to me: O mortal,[f] stand up
on your feet, and I will speak with
you. 2 And when he spoke to me, a spirit
entered into me and set me on my feet;
and I heard him speaking to me. 3 He
said to me, Mortal, I am sending you
to the people of Israel, to a nation[g] of
rebels who have rebelled against me;
they and their ancestors have transgressed against me to this very day.
4 The descendants are impudent and
stubborn. I am sending you to them,
and you shall say to them, 'Thus says
the Lord GOD.' 5 Whether they hear or
refuse to hear (for they are a rebellious
house), they shall know that there has
been a prophet among them. 6 And you,
O mortal, do not be afraid of them, and
do not be afraid of their words, though
briers and thorns surround you and you
live among scorpions; do not be afraid
of their words, and do not be dismayed
at their looks, for they are a rebellious
house. 7 You shall speak my words to
them, whether they hear or refuse to
hear; for they are a rebellious house.

8 But you, mortal, hear what I say to
you; do not be rebellious like that rebellious house; open your mouth and eat
what I give you. 9 I looked, and a hand
was stretched out to me, and a written
scroll was in it. 10 He spread it before me;
it had writing on the front and on the
back, and written on it were words of
lamentation and mourning and woe.

3 He said to me, O mortal, eat what
is offered to you; eat this scroll, and
go, speak to the house of Israel. 2 So I
opened my mouth, and he gave me the
scroll to eat. 3 He said to me, Mortal, eat
this scroll that I give you and fill your
stomach with it. Then I ate it; and in my
mouth it was as sweet as honey.

[a] 1.13 Gk OL: Heb *And the appearance of*
[b] 1.15 Heb *of their faces* [c] 1.22 Gk: Heb *like the awesome crystal* [d] 1.24 Traditional rendering of Heb *Shaddai* [e] 1.26 Or *lapis lazuli* [f] 2.1 Or *son of man*; Heb *ben adam* (and so throughout the book when Ezekiel is addressed) [g] 2.3 Syr: Heb *to nations*

4 He said to me: Mortal, go to the
house of Israel and speak my very words
to them. 5For you are not sent to a people of obscure speech and difficult language, but to the house of Israel— 6not
to many peoples of obscure speech and
difficult language, whose words you
cannot understand. Surely, if I sent
you to them, they would listen to you.
7But the house of Israel will not listen
to you, for they are not willing to listen
to me; because all the house of Israel
have a hard forehead and a stubborn
heart. 8See, I have made your face hard
against their faces, and your forehead
hard against their foreheads. 9Like the
hardest stone, harder than flint, I have
made your forehead; do not fear them or
be dismayed at their looks, for they are a
rebellious house. 10He said to me: Mortal, all my words that I shall speak to
you receive in your heart and hear with
your ears; 11then go to the exiles, to your
people, and speak to them. Say to them,
'Thus says the Lord GOD'; whether they
hear or refuse to hear.

EZEKIEL AT THE RIVER CHEBAR

12 Then the spirit lifted me up, and
as the glory of the LORD rose[h] from its
place, I heard behind me the sound of
loud rumbling; 13it was the sound of the
wings of the living creatures brushing
against one another, and the sound of
the wheels beside them, that sounded
like a loud rumbling. 14The spirit lifted
me up and bore me away; I went in
bitterness in the heat of my spirit, the
hand of the LORD being strong upon
me. 15I came to the exiles at Tel-abib,
who lived by the river Chebar.[i] And I sat
there among them, stunned, for seven
days.

16 At the end of seven days, the word
of the LORD came to me: 17Mortal, I have
made you a sentinel for the house of Israel; whenever you hear a word from
my mouth, you shall give them warning from me. 18If I say to the wicked,
'You shall surely die', and you give them
no warning, and do not speak to warn
the wicked from their wicked way, in
order to save their life, those wicked
persons shall die for their iniquity; but
their blood I will require at your hand.
19But if you warn the wicked, and they
do not turn from their wickedness, or
from their wicked way, they shall die for
their iniquity; but you will have saved
your life. 20Again, if the righteous turn
from their righteousness and commit
iniquity, and I lay a stumbling-block
before them, they shall die; because you
have not warned them, they shall die
for their sin, and their righteous deeds
that they have done shall not be remembered; but their blood I will require at
your hand. 21If, however, you warn the
righteous not to sin, and they do not
sin, they shall surely live, because they
took warning; and you will have saved
your life.

EZEKIEL ISOLATED AND SILENCED

22 Then the hand of the LORD was
upon me there; and he said to me, Rise
up, go out into the valley, and there I
will speak with you. 23So I rose up and
went out into the valley; and the glory
of the LORD stood there, like the glory
that I had seen by the river Chebar; and
I fell on my face. 24The spirit entered
into me, and set me on my feet; and he
spoke with me and said to me: Go, shut
yourself inside your house. 25As for you,
mortal, cords shall be placed on you, and
you shall be bound with them, so that
you cannot go out among the people;
26and I will make your tongue cling to
the roof of your mouth, so that you shall
be speechless and unable to reprove
them; for they are a rebellious house.
27But when I speak with you, I will open
your mouth, and you shall say to them,
'Thus says the Lord GOD'; let those who
will hear, hear; and let those who refuse
to hear, refuse; for they are a rebellious
house.

THE SIEGE OF JERUSALEM PORTRAYED

4 And you, O mortal, take a brick and
set it before you. On it portray a city,
Jerusalem; 2and put siege-works against
it, and build a siege-wall against it, and
cast up a ramp against it; set camps also
against it, and plant battering-rams
against it all round. 3Then take an iron
plate and place it as an iron wall between you and the city; set your face towards it, and let it be in a state of siege,
and press the siege against it. This is a
sign for the house of Israel.

4 Then lie on your left side, and place
the punishment of the house of Israel
upon it; you shall bear their punishment
for the number of the days that you lie
there. 5For I assign to you a number of

[h] 3.12 Cn: Heb *and blessed be the glory of the LORD* [i] 3.15 Two Mss Syr: Heb *Chebar, and to where they lived*. Another reading is *Chebar, and I sat where they sat*

days, three hundred and ninety days,
equal to the number of the years of
their punishment; and so you shall bear
the punishment of the house of Israel.
6When you have completed these, you
shall lie down a second time, but on
your right side, and bear the punishment of the house of Judah; forty days I
assign you, one day for each year. 7You
shall set your face towards the siege of
Jerusalem, and with your arm bared
you shall prophesy against it. 8See, I am
putting cords on you so that you cannot
turn from one side to the other until you
have completed the days of your siege.

9 And you, take wheat and barley,
beans and lentils, millet and spelt; put
them into one vessel, and make bread
for yourself. During the number of days
that you lie on your side, three hundred
and ninety days, you shall eat it. 10The
food that you eat shall be twenty shekels a day by weight; at fixed times you
shall eat it. 11And you shall drink water
by measure, one-sixth of a hin; at fixed
times you shall drink. 12You shall eat it
as a barley-cake, baking it in their sight
on human dung. 13The LORD said, 'Thus
shall the people of Israel eat their bread,
unclean, among the nations to which I
will drive them.' 14Then I said, 'Ah Lord
GOD! I have never defiled myself; from
my youth up until now I have never
eaten what died of itself or was torn by
animals, nor has carrion flesh come into
my mouth.' 15Then he said to me, 'See, I
will let you have cow's dung instead of
human dung, on which you may prepare your bread.'

16 Then he said to me, Mortal, I am
going to break the staff of bread in Jerusalem; they shall eat bread by weight
and with fearfulness; and they shall
drink water by measure and in dismay. 17Lacking bread and water, they
will look at one another in dismay, and
waste away under their punishment.

A SWORD AGAINST JERUSALEM

5 And you, O mortal, take a sharp
sword; use it as a barber's razor
and run it over your head and your
beard; then take balances for weighing, and divide the hair. 2One-third of
the hair you shall burn in the fire inside the city, when the days of the siege
are completed; one-third you shall take
and strike with the sword all around
the city;[j] and one-third you shall scatter
to the wind, and I will unsheathe the
sword after them. 3Then you shall take
from these a small number, and bind
them in the skirts of your robe. 4From
these, again, you shall take some, throw
them into the fire, and burn them up;
from there a fire will come out against
all the house of Israel.

5 Thus says the Lord GOD: This is Jerusalem; I have set her in the centre of
the nations, with countries all around
her. 6But she has rebelled against my
ordinances and my statutes, becoming more wicked than the nations and
the countries all around her, rejecting
my ordinances and not following my
statutes. 7Therefore thus says the Lord
GOD: Because you are more turbulent
than the nations that are all around
you, and have not followed my statutes
or kept my ordinances, but have acted
according to the ordinances of the nations that are all around you; 8there-
fore thus says the Lord GOD: I, I myself,
am coming against you; I will execute
judgements among you in the sight of
the nations. 9And because of all your
abominations, I will do to you what
I have never yet done, and the like of
which I will never do again. 10Surely,
parents shall eat their children in your
midst, and children shall eat their parents; I will execute judgements on you,
and any of you who survive I will scatter to every wind. 11Therefore, as I live,
says the Lord GOD, surely, because you
have defiled my sanctuary with all your
detestable things and with all your
abominations—therefore I will cut you
down;[k] my eye will not spare, and I will
have no pity. 12One-third of you shall die
of pestilence or be consumed by famine among you; one-third shall fall by
the sword around you; and one-third I
will scatter to every wind and will unsheathe the sword after them.

13 My anger shall spend itself, and I
will vent my fury on them and satisfy
myself; and they shall know that I, the
LORD, have spoken in my jealousy, when
I spend my fury on them. 14Moreover, I
will make you a desolation and an object
of mocking among the nations around
you, in the sight of all that pass by.
15You shall be[l] a mockery and a taunt,
a warning and a horror, to the nations
around you, when I execute judgements
on you in anger and fury, and with furious punishments—I, the LORD, have
spoken— 16when I loose against you[m]

[j] **5.2** Heb *it* [k] **5.11** Another reading is *I will withdraw* [l] **5.15** Gk Syr Vg Tg: Heb *It shall be* [m] **5.16** Heb *them*

my deadly arrows of famine, arrows for
destruction, which I will let loose to destroy you, and when I bring more and
more famine upon you, and break your
staff of bread. 17 I will send famine and
wild animals against you, and they will
rob you of your children; pestilence and
bloodshed shall pass through you; and
I will bring the sword upon you. I, the
LORD, have spoken.

JUDGEMENT ON IDOLATROUS ISRAEL

6 The word of the LORD came to me:
2 O mortal, set your face towards
the mountains of Israel, and prophesy
against them, 3 and say, You mountains of Israel, hear the word of the Lord
GOD! Thus says the Lord GOD to the
mountains and the hills, to the ravines
and the valleys: I, I myself will bring a
sword upon you, and I will destroy your
high places. 4 Your altars shall become
desolate, and your incense-stands shall
be broken; and I will throw down your
slain in front of your idols. 5 I will lay the
corpses of the people of Israel in front of
their idols; and I will scatter your bones
around your altars. 6 Wherever you live,
your towns shall be waste and your high
places ruined, so that your altars will be
waste and ruined,[n] your idols broken
and destroyed, your incense-stands cut
down, and your works wiped out. 7 The
slain shall fall in your midst; then you
shall know that I am the LORD.

8 But I will spare some. Some of
you shall escape the sword among the
nations and be scattered through the
countries. 9 Those of you who escape
shall remember me among the nations
where they are carried captive, how I
was crushed by their wanton heart that
turned away from me, and their wanton eyes that turned after their idols.
Then they will be loathsome in their
own sight for the evils that they have
committed, for all their abominations.
10 And they shall know that I am the
LORD; I did not threaten in vain to bring
this disaster upon them.

11 Thus says the Lord GOD: Clap your
hands and stamp your foot, and say,
Alas for all the vile abominations of the
house of Israel! For they shall fall by the
sword, by famine, and by pestilence.
12 Those far off shall die of pestilence;
those nearby shall fall by the sword;
and any who are left and are spared
shall die of famine. Thus I will spend my
fury upon them. 13 And you shall know
that I am the LORD, when their slain lie
among their idols around their altars,
on every high hill, on all the mountain
tops, under every green tree, and under every leafy oak, wherever they offered pleasing odour to all their idols. 14 I
will stretch out my hand against them,
and make the land desolate and waste,
throughout all their settlements, from
the wilderness to Riblah.[o] Then they
shall know that I am the LORD.

IMPENDING DISASTER

7 The word of the LORD came to me:
2 You, O mortal, thus says the Lord
GOD to the land of Israel:

An end! The end has come
upon the four corners of the land.
3 Now the end is upon you,
I will let loose my anger upon you;
I will judge you according
to your ways,
I will punish you for all
your abominations.
4 My eye will not spare you, I
will have no pity.
I will punish you for your ways,
while your abominations
are among you.

Then you shall know that I am the
LORD.

5 Thus says the Lord GOD:

Disaster after disaster! See, it comes.
6 An end has come, the
end has come.
It has awakened against you;
see, it comes!
7 Your doom[p] has come to you,
O inhabitant of the land.
The time has come, the day is near—
of tumult, not of revelling
on the mountains.
8 Soon now I will pour out my
wrath upon you;
I will spend my anger against you.
I will judge you according
to your ways,
and punish you for all your
abominations.
9 My eye will not spare; I will
have no pity.
I will punish you according
to your ways,
while your abominations
are among you.

Then you shall know that it is I the
LORD who strike.

10 See, the day! See, it comes!
Your doom[q] has gone out.

[n] **6.6** Syr Vg Tg: Heb *and be made guilty*
[o] **6.14** Another reading is *Diblah* [p] **7.7** Meaning of Heb uncertain [q] **7.10** Meaning of Heb uncertain

The rod has blossomed, pride
has budded.
11 Violence has grown into a
rod of wickedness.
None of them shall remain,
not their abundance, not
their wealth;
no pre-eminence among them.[r]
12 The time has come, the day
draws near;
let not the buyer rejoice, nor
the seller mourn,
for wrath is upon all their
multitude.
13For the sellers shall not return to
what has been sold as long as they remain alive. For the vision concerns all
their multitude; it shall not be revoked.
Because of their iniquity, they cannot
maintain their lives.[s]
14 They have blown the horn and
made everything ready;
but no one goes to battle,
for my wrath is upon all
their multitude.
15 The sword is outside, pestilence
and famine are inside;
those in the field die by the sword;
those in the city—famine and
pestilence devour them.
16 If any survivors escape,
they shall be found on
the mountains
like doves of the valleys,
all of them moaning over
their iniquity.
17 All hands shall grow feeble,
all knees turn to water.
18 They shall put on sackcloth,
horror shall cover them.
Shame shall be on all faces,
baldness on all their heads.
19 They shall fling their silver
into the streets,
their gold shall be treated
as unclean.
Their silver and gold cannot save them
on the day of the wrath of the LORD.
They shall not satisfy their hunger or
fill their stomachs with it. For it was
the stumbling-block of their iniquity.
20From their[t] beautiful ornament, in
which they took pride, they made their
abominable images, their detestable
things; therefore I will make of it an unclean thing to them.
21 I will hand it over to strangers
as booty,
to the wicked of the earth
as plunder;
they shall profane it.
22 I will avert my face from them,
so that they may profane
my treasured[u] place;
the violent shall enter it,
they shall profane it.
23 Make a chain![v]
For the land is full of bloody crimes;
the city is full of violence.
24 I will bring the worst of the nations
to take possession of their houses.
I will put an end to the arrogance
of the strong,
and their holy places shall
be profaned.
25 When anguish comes, they
will seek peace,
but there shall be none.
26 Disaster comes upon disaster,
rumour follows rumour;
they shall keep seeking a vision
from the prophet;
instruction shall perish
from the priest,
and counsel from the elders.
27 The king shall mourn,
the prince shall be wrapped
in despair,
and the hands of the people of
the land shall tremble.
According to their way I will
deal with them;
according to their own
judgements I will
judge them.
And they shall know that I am the
LORD.

ABOMINATIONS IN THE TEMPLE

8 In the sixth year, in the sixth
month, on the fifth day of the
month, as I sat in my house, with the
elders of Judah sitting before me, the
hand of the Lord GOD fell upon me
there. 2I looked, and there was a figure
that looked like a human being;[w] below
what appeared to be its loins it was fire,
and above the loins it was like the appearance of brightness, like gleaming
amber. 3It stretched out the form of a
hand, and took me by a lock of my head;
and the spirit lifted me up between
earth and heaven, and brought me in
visions of God to Jerusalem, to the entrance of the gateway of the inner court
that faces north, to the seat of the image
of jealousy, which provokes to jealousy.

[r] 7.11 Meaning of Heb uncertain
[s] 7.13 Meaning of Heb uncertain [t] 7.20 Syr Symmachus: Heb *its* [u] 7.22 Or *secret*
[v] 7.23 Meaning of Heb uncertain [w] 8.2 Gk: Heb *like fire*

4 And the glory of the God of Israel was there, like the vision that I had seen in the valley.

5 Then God[x] said to me, 'O mortal, lift up your eyes now in the direction of the north.' So I lifted up my eyes towards the north, and there, north of the altar gate, in the entrance, was this image of jealousy. 6 He said to me, 'Mortal, do you see what they are doing, the great abominations that the house of Israel are committing here, to drive me far from my sanctuary? Yet you will see still greater abominations.'

7 And he brought me to the entrance of the court; I looked, and there was a hole in the wall. 8 Then he said to me, 'Mortal, dig through the wall'; and when I dug through the wall, there was an entrance. 9 He said to me, 'Go in, and see the vile abominations that they are committing here.' 10 So I went in and looked; there, portrayed on the wall all round, were all kinds of creeping things, and loathsome animals, and all the idols of the house of Israel. 11 Before them stood seventy of the elders of the house of Israel, with Jaazaniah son of Shaphan standing among them. Each had his censer in his hand, and the fragrant cloud of incense was ascending. 12 Then he said to me, 'Mortal, have you seen what the elders of the house of Israel are doing in the dark, each in his room of images? For they say, "The LORD does not see us, the LORD has forsaken the land."' 13 He said also to me, 'You will see still greater abominations that they are committing.'

14 Then he brought me to the entrance of the north gate of the house of the LORD; women were sitting there weeping for Tammuz. 15 Then he said to me, 'Have you seen this, O mortal? You will see still greater abominations than these.'

16 And he brought me into the inner court of the house of the LORD; there, at the entrance of the temple of the LORD, between the porch and the altar, were about twenty-five men, with their backs to the temple of the LORD, and their faces towards the east, prostrating themselves to the sun towards the east. 17 Then he said to me, 'Have you seen this, O mortal? Is it not bad enough that the house of Judah commits the abominations done here? Must they fill the land with violence, and provoke my anger still further? See, they are putting the branch to their nose! 18 Therefore I will act in wrath; my eye will not spare, nor will I have pity; and though they cry in my hearing with a loud voice, I will not listen to them.'

THE SLAUGHTER OF THE IDOLATERS

9 Then he cried in my hearing with a loud voice, saying, 'Draw near, you executioners of the city, each with his destroying weapon in his hand.' 2 And six men came from the direction of the upper gate, which faces north, each with his weapon for slaughter in his hand; among them was a man clothed in linen, with a writing-case at his side. They went in and stood beside the bronze altar.

3 Now the glory of the God of Israel had gone up, from the cherub on which it rested, to the threshold of the house. The LORD called to the man clothed in linen, who had the writing-case at his side, 4 and said to him, 'Go through the city, through Jerusalem, and put a mark on the foreheads of those who sigh and groan over all the abominations that are committed in it.' 5 To the others he said in my hearing, 'Pass through the city after him, and kill; your eye shall not spare, and you shall show no pity. 6 Cut down old men, young men and young women, little children and women, but touch no one who has the mark. And begin at my sanctuary.' So they began with the elders who were in front of the house. 7 Then he said to them, 'Defile the house, and fill the courts with the slain. Go!' So they went out and killed in the city. 8 While they were killing, and I was left alone, I fell prostrate on my face and cried out, 'Ah Lord GOD! will you destroy all who remain of Israel as you pour out your wrath upon Jerusalem?' 9 He said to me, 'The guilt of the house of Israel and Judah is exceedingly great; the land is full of bloodshed and the city full of perversity; for they say, "The LORD has forsaken the land, and the LORD does not see." 10 As for me, my eye will not spare, nor will I have pity, but I will bring down their deeds upon their heads.'

11 Then the man clothed in linen, with the writing-case at his side, brought back word, saying, 'I have done as you commanded me.'

[x] **8.5** Heb *he*

GOD'S GLORY LEAVES JERUSALEM

10 Then I looked, and above the
dome that was over the heads
of the cherubim there appeared above
them something like a sapphire,[y] in
form resembling a throne. 2He said to
the man clothed in linen, 'Go within the
wheel-work underneath the cherubim;
fill your hands with burning coals from
among the cherubim, and scatter them
over the city.' He went in as I looked on.
3Now the cherubim were standing on
the south side of the house when the
man went in; and a cloud filled the inner court. 4Then the glory of the LORD
rose up from the cherub to the threshold of the house; the house was filled
with the cloud, and the court was full of
the brightness of the glory of the LORD.
5The sound of the wings of the cherubim was heard as far as the outer court,
like the voice of God Almighty[z] when he
speaks.

6 When he commanded the man
clothed in linen, 'Take fire from within
the wheel-work, from among the cherubim', he went in and stood beside a
wheel. 7And a cherub stretched out his
hand from among the cherubim to the
fire that was among the cherubim, took
some of it, and put it into the hands of
the man clothed in linen, who took it
and went out. 8The cherubim appeared
to have the form of a human hand under
their wings.

9 I looked, and there were four
wheels beside the cherubim, one beside
each cherub; and the appearance of the
wheels was like gleaming beryl. 10And
as for their appearance, the four looked
alike, something like a wheel within a
wheel. 11When they moved, they moved
in any of the four directions without
veering as they moved; but in whatever direction the front wheel faced,
the others followed without veering as
they moved. 12Their entire body, their
rims, their spokes, their wings, and
the wheels—the wheels of the four of
them—were full of eyes all round. 13As
for the wheels, they were called in my
hearing 'the wheel-work'. 14Each one
had four faces: the first face was that of
the cherub, the second face was that of
a human being, the third that of a lion,
and the fourth that of an eagle.

15 The cherubim rose up. These were
the living creatures that I saw by the
river Chebar. 16When the cherubim
moved, the wheels moved beside them;
and when the cherubim lifted up their
wings to rise up from the earth, the
wheels at their side did not veer. 17When
they stopped, the others stopped, and
when they rose up, the others rose up
with them; for the spirit of the living
creatures was in them.

18 Then the glory of the LORD went
out from the threshold of the house and
stopped above the cherubim. 19The cherubim lifted up their wings and rose up
from the earth in my sight as they went
out with the wheels beside them. They
stopped at the entrance of the east gate
of the house of the LORD; and the glory
of the God of Israel was above them.

20 These were the living creatures
that I saw underneath the God of Israel
by the river Chebar; and I knew that
they were cherubim. 21Each had four
faces, each four wings, and underneath
their wings something like human
hands. 22As for what their faces were
like, they were the same faces whose appearance I had seen by the river Chebar.
Each one moved straight ahead.

JUDGEMENT ON WICKED COUNSELLORS

11 The spirit lifted me up and
brought me to the east gate of
the house of the LORD, which faces east.
There, at the entrance of the gateway,
were twenty-five men; among them
I saw Jaazaniah son of Azzur, and Pelatiah son of Benaiah, officials of the
people. 2He said to me, 'Mortal, these
are the men who devise iniquity and
who give wicked counsel in this city;
3they say, "The time is not near to build
houses; this city is the pot, and we are
the meat." 4Therefore prophesy against
them; prophesy, O mortal.'

5 Then the spirit of the LORD fell
upon me, and he said to me, 'Say, Thus
says the LORD: This is what you think,
O house of Israel; I know the things that
come into your mind. 6You have killed
many in this city, and have filled its
streets with the slain. 7Therefore thus
says the Lord GOD: The slain whom
you have placed within it are the meat,
and this city is the pot; but you shall be
taken out of it. 8You have feared the
sword; and I will bring the sword upon
you, says the Lord GOD. 9I will take you
out of it and give you over to the hands
of foreigners, and execute judgements
upon you. 10You shall fall by the sword;

[y] **10.1** Or *lapis lazuli* [z] **10.5** Traditional rendering of Heb *El Shaddai*

I will judge you at the border of Israel. And you shall know that I am the
LORD. 11This city shall not be your pot,
and you shall not be the meat inside it;
I will judge you at the border of Israel.
12Then you shall know that I am the
LORD, whose statutes you have not followed, and whose ordinances you have
not kept, but you have acted according
to the ordinances of the nations that are
around you.'

13 Now, while I was prophesying,
Pelatiah son of Benaiah died. Then I
fell down on my face, cried with a loud
voice, and said, 'Ah Lord GOD! will you
make a full end of the remnant of Israel?'

GOD WILL RESTORE ISRAEL

14 Then the word of the LORD came
to me: 15Mortal, your kinsfolk, your own
kin, your fellow exiles,[a] the whole house
of Israel, all of them, are those of whom
the inhabitants of Jerusalem have said,
'They have gone far from the LORD; to
us this land is given for a possession.'
16Therefore say: Thus says the Lord
GOD: Though I removed them far away
among the nations, and though I scattered them among the countries, yet I
have been a sanctuary to them for a little while[b] in the countries where they
have gone. 17Therefore say: Thus says
the Lord GOD: I will gather you from
the peoples, and assemble you out of
the countries where you have been scattered, and I will give you the land of Israel. 18When they come there, they will
remove from it all its detestable things
and all its abominations. 19I will give
them one[c] heart, and put a new spirit
within them; I will remove the heart of
stone from their flesh and give them a
heart of flesh, 20so that they may follow
my statutes and keep my ordinances
and obey them. Then they shall be my
people, and I will be their God. 21But as
for those whose heart goes after their
detestable things and their abominations,[d] I will bring their deeds upon
their own heads, says the Lord GOD.

22 Then the cherubim lifted up their
wings, with the wheels beside them;
and the glory of the God of Israel was
above them. 23And the glory of the
LORD ascended from the middle of the
city, and stopped on the mountain east
of the city. 24The spirit lifted me up and
brought me in a vision by the spirit of
God into Chaldea, to the exiles. Then the
vision that I had seen left me. 25And I
told the exiles all the things that the
LORD had shown me.

JUDAH'S CAPTIVITY PORTRAYED

12 The word of the LORD came to
me: 2Mortal, you are living in
the midst of a rebellious house, who
have eyes to see but do not see, who
have ears to hear but do not hear; 3for
they are a rebellious house. Therefore,
mortal, prepare for yourself an exile's
baggage, and go into exile by day in
their sight; you shall go like an exile
from your place to another place in their
sight. Perhaps they will understand,
though they are a rebellious house.
4You shall bring out your baggage by
day in their sight, as baggage for exile;
and you shall go out yourself at evening
in their sight, as those do who go into
exile. 5Dig through the wall in their
sight, and carry the baggage through
it. 6In their sight you shall lift the baggage on your shoulder, and carry it out
in the dark; you shall cover your face, so
that you may not see the land; for I have
made you a sign for the house of Israel.

7 I did just as I was commanded. I
brought out my baggage by day, as baggage for exile, and in the evening I dug
through the wall with my own hands; I
brought it out in the dark, carrying it on
my shoulder in their sight.

8 In the morning the word of the
LORD came to me: 9Mortal, has not the
house of Israel, the rebellious house,
said to you, 'What are you doing?' 10Say
to them, 'Thus says the Lord GOD: This
oracle concerns the prince in Jerusalem
and all the house of Israel in it.' 11Say,
'I am a sign for you: as I have done, so
shall it be done to them; they shall go
into exile, into captivity.' 12And the
prince who is among them shall lift his
baggage on his shoulder in the dark,
and shall go out; he[e] shall dig through
the wall and carry it through; he shall
cover his face, so that he may not see the
land with his eyes. 13I will spread my net
over him, and he shall be caught in my
snare; and I will bring him to Babylon,
the land of the Chaldeans, yet he shall
not see it; and he shall die there. 14I will
scatter to every wind all who are around
him, his helpers and all his troops; and I

[a] **11.15** Gk Syr: Heb *people of your kindred*
[b] **11.16** Or *to some extent* [c] **11.19** Another reading is *a new* [d] **11.21** Cn: Heb *And to the heart of their detestable things and their abominations their heart goes* [e] **12.12** Gk Syr: Heb *they*

will unsheathe the sword behind them.
15 And they shall know that I am the
LORD, when I disperse them among
the nations and scatter them through
the countries. 16 But I will let a few of
them escape from the sword, from famine and pestilence, so that they may tell
of all their abominations among the
nations where they go; then they shall
know that I am the LORD.

JUDGEMENT NOT POSTPONED

17 The word of the LORD came to me:
18 Mortal, eat your bread with quaking,
and drink your water with trembling
and with fearfulness; 19 and say to the
people of the land, Thus says the Lord
GOD concerning the inhabitants of Jerusalem in the land of Israel: They shall
eat their bread with fearfulness, and
drink their water in dismay, because
their land shall be stripped of all it contains, on account of the violence of all
those who live in it. 20 The inhabited
cities shall be laid waste, and the land
shall become a desolation; and you shall
know that I am the LORD.

21 The word of the LORD came to me:
22 Mortal, what is this proverb of yours
about the land of Israel, which says, 'The
days are prolonged, and every vision
comes to nothing'? 23 Tell them therefore, 'Thus says the Lord GOD: I will put
an end to this proverb, and they shall
use it no more as a proverb in Israel.'
But say to them, The days are near, and
the fulfilment of every vision. 24 For
there shall no longer be any false vision or flattering divination within the
house of Israel. 25 But I the LORD will
speak the word that I speak, and it will
be fulfilled. It will no longer be delayed;
but in your days, O rebellious house, I
will speak the word and fulfil it, says the
Lord GOD.

26 The word of the LORD came to me:
27 Mortal, the house of Israel is saying,
'The vision that he sees is for many years
ahead; he prophesies for distant times.'
28 Therefore say to them, Thus says the
Lord GOD: None of my words will be
delayed any longer, but the word that
I speak will be fulfilled, says the Lord
GOD.

FALSE PROPHETS CONDEMNED

13 The word of the LORD came to
me: 2 Mortal, prophesy against
the prophets of Israel who are prophesying; say to those who prophesy out of
their own imagination: 'Hear the word
of the LORD!' 3 Thus says the Lord GOD,
Alas for the senseless prophets who
follow their own spirit, and have seen
nothing! 4 Your prophets have been
like jackals among ruins, O Israel. 5 You
have not gone up into the breaches, or
repaired a wall for the house of Israel,
so that it might stand in battle on the
day of the LORD. 6 They have prophesied
falsehood and lying divination; they
say, 'Says the LORD', when the LORD has
not sent them, and yet they wait for the
fulfilment of their word! 7 Have you not
seen a false vision or uttered a lying divination, when you have said, 'Says the
LORD', even though I did not speak?

8 Therefore thus says the Lord GOD:
Because you have uttered falsehood and
prophesied lies, I am against you, says
the Lord GOD. 9 My hand will be against
the prophets who see false visions and
utter lying divinations; they shall not
be in the council of my people, nor be
enrolled in the register of the house of
Israel, nor shall they enter the land of
Israel; and you shall know that I am
the Lord GOD. 10 Because, in truth, because they have misled my people, saying, 'Peace', when there is no peace; and
because, when the people build a wall,
these prophets[f] smear whitewash on it.
11 Say to those who smear whitewash on
it that it shall fall. There will be a deluge
of rain,[g] great hailstones will fall, and
a stormy wind will break out. 12 When
the wall falls, will it not be said to you,
'Where is the whitewash you smeared
on it?' 13 Therefore thus says the Lord
GOD: In my wrath I will make a stormy
wind break out, and in my anger there
shall be a deluge of rain, and hailstones
in wrath to destroy it. 14 I will break
down the wall that you have smeared
with whitewash, and bring it to the
ground, so that its foundation will be
laid bare; when it falls, you shall perish
within it; and you shall know that I am
the LORD. 15 Thus I will spend my wrath
upon the wall, and upon those who
have smeared it with whitewash; and I
will say to you, The wall is no more, nor
those who smeared it— 16 the prophets
of Israel who prophesied concerning Jerusalem and saw visions of peace for it,
when there was no peace, says the Lord
GOD.

17 As for you, mortal, set your face
against the daughters of your people,
who prophesy out of their own imag-

[f] 13.10 Heb *they* [g] 13.11 Heb *rain and you*

ination; prophesy against them 18 and say, Thus says the Lord GOD: Woe to the women who sew bands on all wrists, and make veils for the heads of people of every height, in the hunt for human lives! Will you hunt down lives among my people, and maintain your own lives? 19 You have profaned me among my people for handfuls of barley and for pieces of bread, putting to death those who should not die and keeping alive those who should not live, by your lies to my people, who listen to lies.

20 Therefore thus says the Lord GOD: I am against your bands with which you hunt lives;[h] I will tear them from your arms, and let the lives go free, the lives that you hunt down like birds. 21 I will tear off your veils, and save my people from your hands; they shall no longer be prey in your hands; and you shall know that I am the LORD. 22 Because you have disheartened the righteous falsely, although I have not disheartened them, and you have encouraged the wicked not to turn from their wicked way and save their lives; 23 therefore you shall no longer see false visions nor practise divination; I will save my people from your hand. Then you will know that I am the LORD.

GOD'S JUDGEMENTS JUSTIFIED

14 Certain elders of Israel came to me and sat down before me. 2 And the word of the LORD came to me: 3 Mortal, these men have taken their idols into their hearts, and placed their iniquity as a stumbling-block before them; shall I let myself be consulted by them? 4 Therefore speak to them, and say to them, Thus says the Lord GOD: Any of those of the house of Israel who take their idols into their hearts and place their iniquity as a stumbling-block before them, and yet come to the prophet—I the LORD will answer those who come with the multitude of their idols, 5 in order that I may take hold of the hearts of the house of Israel, all of whom are estranged from me through their idols.

6 Therefore say to the house of Israel, Thus says the Lord GOD: Repent and turn away from your idols; and turn away your faces from all your abominations. 7 For any of those of the house of Israel, or of the aliens who reside in Israel, who separate themselves from me, taking their idols into their hearts and placing their iniquity as a stumbling-block before them, and yet come to a prophet to inquire of me by him, I the LORD will answer them myself. 8 I will set my face against them; I will make them a sign and a byword and cut them off from the midst of my people; and you shall know that I am the LORD.

9 If a prophet is deceived and speaks a word, I, the LORD, have deceived that prophet, and I will stretch out my hand against him, and will destroy him from the midst of my people Israel. 10 And they shall bear their punishment—the punishment of the inquirer and the punishment of the prophet shall be the same— 11 so that the house of Israel may no longer go astray from me, nor defile themselves any more with all their transgressions. Then they shall be my people, and I will be their God, says the Lord GOD.

12 The word of the LORD came to me: 13 Mortal, when a land sins against me by acting faithlessly, and I stretch out my hand against it, and break its staff of bread and send famine upon it, and cut off from it human beings and animals, 14 even if Noah, Daniel,[i] and Job, these three, were in it, they would save only their own lives by their righteousness, says the Lord GOD. 15 If I send wild animals through the land to ravage it, so that it is made desolate, and no one may pass through because of the animals; 16 even if these three men were in it, as I live, says the Lord GOD, they would save neither sons nor daughters; they alone would be saved, but the land would be desolate. 17 Or if I bring a sword upon that land and say, 'Let a sword pass through the land', and I cut off human beings and animals from it; 18 though these three men were in it, as I live, says the Lord GOD, they would save neither sons nor daughters, but they alone would be saved. 19 Or if I send a pestilence into that land, and pour out my wrath upon it with blood, to cut off humans and animals from it; 20 even if Noah, Daniel,[j] and Job were in it, as I live, says the Lord GOD, they would save neither son nor daughter; they would save only their own lives by their righteousness.

21 For thus says the Lord GOD: How much more when I send upon Jerusalem my four deadly acts of judgement, sword, famine, wild animals, and pestilence,

[h] **13.20** Gk Syr: Heb *lives for birds* [i] **14.14** Or, as otherwise read, *Danel* [j] **14.20** Or, as otherwise read, *Danel*

to cut off humans and animals from it!
22 Yet, survivors shall be left in it, sons
and daughters who will be brought
out; they will come out to you. When
you see their ways and their deeds, you
will be consoled for the evil that I have
brought upon Jerusalem, for all that I
have brought upon it. 23 They shall console you, when you see their ways and
their deeds; and you shall know that
it was not without cause that I did all
that I have done in it, says the Lord
God.

THE USELESS VINE

15 The word of the LORD came to
me:

2 O mortal, how does the wood
of the vine surpass
all other wood—
the vine branch that is among
the trees of the forest?
3 Is wood taken from it to
make anything?
Does one take a peg from it on
which to hang any object?
4 It is put in the fire for fuel;
when the fire has consumed
both ends of it
and the middle of it is charred,
is it useful for anything?
5 When it was whole it was
used for nothing;
how much less—when the
fire has consumed it,
and it is charred—
can it ever be used for anything!

6 Therefore thus says the Lord GOD:
Like the wood of the vine among the
trees of the forest, which I have given
to the fire for fuel, so I will give up the
inhabitants of Jerusalem. 7 I will set my
face against them; although they escape
from the fire, the fire shall still consume
them; and you shall know that I am the
LORD, when I set my face against them.
8 And I will make the land desolate, because they have acted faithlessly, says
the Lord GOD.

GOD'S FAITHLESS BRIDE

16 The word of the LORD came to
me: 2 Mortal, make known to
Jerusalem her abominations, 3 and say,
Thus says the Lord GOD to Jerusalem:
Your origin and your birth were in the
land of the Canaanites; your father was
an Amorite, and your mother a Hittite.
4 As for your birth, on the day you were
born your navel cord was not cut, nor
were you washed with water to cleanse
you, nor rubbed with salt, nor wrapped
in cloths. 5 No eye pitied you, to do any
of these things for you out of compassion for you; but you were thrown out
in the open field, for you were abhorred
on the day you were born.

6 I passed by you, and saw you flailing about in your blood. As you lay in
your blood, I said to you, 'Live! 7 and
grow up[k] like a plant of the field.' You
grew up and became tall and arrived
at full womanhood;[l] your breasts were
formed, and your hair had grown; yet
you were naked and bare.

8 I passed by you again and looked
on you; you were at the age for love. I
spread the edge of my cloak over you,
and covered your nakedness: I pledged
myself to you and entered into a covenant with you, says the Lord GOD, and
you became mine. 9 Then I bathed you
with water and washed off the blood
from you, and anointed you with oil. 10 I
clothed you with embroidered cloth and
with sandals of fine leather; I bound
you in fine linen and covered you with
rich fabric.[m] 11 I adorned you with ornaments: I put bracelets on your arms,
a chain on your neck, 12 a ring on your
nose, ear-rings in your ears, and a beautiful crown upon your head. 13 You were
adorned with gold and silver, while
your clothing was of fine linen, rich
fabric,[n] and embroidered cloth. You had
choice flour and honey and oil for food.
You grew exceedingly beautiful, fit to
be a queen. 14 Your fame spread among
the nations on account of your beauty,
for it was perfect because of my splendour that I had bestowed on you, says
the Lord GOD.

15 But you trusted in your beauty,
and played the whore because of your
fame, and lavished your whorings on
any passer-by.[o] 16 You took some of your
garments, and made for yourself col-
ourful shrines, and on them played the
whore; nothing like this has ever been
or ever shall be.[p] 17 You also took your
beautiful jewels of my gold and my silver that I had given you, and made for
yourself male images, and with them
played the whore; 18 and you took your
embroidered garments to cover them,
and set my oil and my incense be-

[k] 16.7 Gk Syr: Heb *Live! I made you a myriad*
[l] 16.7 Cn: Heb *ornament of ornaments*
[m] 16.10 Meaning of Heb uncertain
[n] 16.13 Meaning of Heb uncertain [o] 16.15 Heb adds *let it be his* [p] 16.16 Meaning of Heb uncertain

fore them. 19 Also my bread that I gave
you—I fed you with choice flour and oil
and honey—you set it before them as a
pleasing odour; and so it was, says the
Lord GOD. 20 You took your sons and
your daughters, whom you had borne to
me, and these you sacrificed to them to
be devoured. As if your whorings were
not enough! 21 You slaughtered my children and delivered them up as an offering to them. 22 And in all your abominations and your whorings you did not
remember the days of your youth, when
you were naked and bare, flailing about
in your blood.

23 After all your wickedness (woe,
woe to you! says the Lord GOD), 24 you
built yourself a platform and made yourself a lofty place in every square; 25 at
the head of every street you built your
lofty place and prostituted your beauty,
offering yourself to every passer-by,
and multiplying your whoring. 26 You
played the whore with the Egyptians,
your lustful neighbours, multiplying
your whoring, to provoke me to anger.
27 Therefore I stretched out my hand
against you, reduced your rations, and
gave you up to the will of your enemies,
the daughters of the Philistines, who
were ashamed of your lewd behaviour.
28 You played the whore with the Assyrians, because you were insatiable; you
played the whore with them, and still
you were not satisfied. 29 You multiplied
your whoring with Chaldea, the land of
merchants; and even with this you were
not satisfied.

30 How sick is your heart, says the
Lord GOD, that you did all these things,
the deeds of a brazen whore; 31 building your platform at the head of every
street, and making your lofty place in
every square! Yet you were not like a
whore, because you scorned payment.
32 Adulterous wife, who receives strangers instead of her husband! 33 Gifts are
given to all whores; but you gave your
gifts to all your lovers, bribing them to
come to you from all around for your
whorings. 34 So you were different from
other women in your whorings: no one
solicited you to play the whore; and you
gave payment, while no payment was
given to you; you were different.

35 Therefore, O whore, hear the
word of the LORD: 36 Thus says the Lord
GOD, Because your lust was poured out
and your nakedness uncovered in your
whoring with your lovers, and because of all your abominable idols, and
because of the blood of your children
that you gave to them, 37 therefore, I
will gather all your lovers, with whom
you took pleasure, all those you loved
and all those you hated; I will gather
them against you from all around, and
will uncover your nakedness to them,
so that they may see all your nakedness. 38 I will judge you as women who
commit adultery and shed blood are
judged, and bring blood upon you in
wrath and jealousy. 39 I will deliver you
into their hands, and they shall throw
down your platform and break down
your lofty places; they shall strip you
of your clothes and take your beautiful
objects and leave you naked and bare.
40 They shall bring up a mob against
you, and they shall stone you and cut
you to pieces with their swords. 41 They
shall burn your houses and execute
judgements on you in the sight of many
women; I will stop you from playing the
whore, and you shall also make no more
payments. 42 So I will satisfy my fury on
you, and my jealousy shall turn away
from you; I will be calm, and will be angry no longer. 43 Because you have not
remembered the days of your youth, but
have enraged me with all these things;
therefore, I have returned your deeds
upon your head, says the Lord GOD.

Have you not committed lewdness
beyond all your abominations? 44 See,
everyone who uses proverbs will use
this proverb about you, 'Like mother,
like daughter.' 45 You are the daughter of
your mother, who loathed her husband
and her children; and you are the sister
of your sisters, who loathed their husbands and their children. Your mother
was a Hittite and your father an Amorite. 46 Your elder sister is Samaria,
who lived with her daughters to the
north of you; and your younger sister,
who lived to the south of you, is Sodom
with her daughters. 47 You not only followed their ways, and acted according
to their abominations; within a very
little time you were more corrupt than
they in all your ways. 48 As I live, says
the Lord GOD, your sister Sodom and
her daughters have not done as you and
your daughters have done. 49 This was
the guilt of your sister Sodom: she and
her daughters had pride, excess of food,
and prosperous ease, but did not aid the
poor and needy. 50 They were haughty,
and did abominable things before me;
therefore I removed them when I saw it.
51 Samaria has not committed half your

sins; you have committed more abominations than they, and have made
your sisters appear righteous by all the
abominations that you have committed. 52 Bear your disgrace, you also, for
you have brought about for your sisters
a more favourable judgement; because
of your sins in which you acted more
abominably than they, they are more
in the right than you. So be ashamed,
you also, and bear your disgrace, for you
have made your sisters appear righteous.

53 I will restore their fortunes, the
fortunes of Sodom and her daughters
and the fortunes of Samaria and her
daughters, and I will restore your own
fortunes along with theirs, 54 in order
that you may bear your disgrace and be
ashamed of all that you have done, becoming a consolation to them. 55 As for
your sisters, Sodom and her daughters
shall return to their former state, Samaria and her daughters shall return
to their former state, and you and your
daughters shall return to your former
state. 56 Was not your sister Sodom a byword in your mouth in the day of your
pride, 57 before your wickedness was uncovered? Now you are a mockery to the
daughters of Aram[q] and all her neighbours, and to the daughters of the Philistines, those all around who despise
you. 58 You must bear the penalty of
your lewdness and your abominations,
says the LORD.

AN EVERLASTING COVENANT

59 Yes, thus says the Lord GOD: I will
deal with you as you have done, you
who have despised the oath, breaking
the covenant; 60 yet I will remember my
covenant with you in the days of your
youth, and I will establish with you an
everlasting covenant. 61 Then you will
remember your ways, and be ashamed
when I[r] take your sisters, both your elder and your younger, and give them to
you as daughters, but not on account of
my[s] covenant with you. 62 I will establish my covenant with you, and you
shall know that I am the LORD, 63 in order that you may remember and be confounded, and never open your mouth
again because of your shame, when I
forgive you all that you have done, says
the Lord GOD.

THE TWO EAGLES AND THE VINE

17 The word of the LORD came to
me: 2 O mortal, propound a riddle, and speak an allegory to the house
of Israel. 3 Say: Thus says the Lord GOD:

A great eagle, with great wings
and long pinions,
rich in plumage of many colours,
came to the Lebanon.
He took the top of the cedar,
4 broke off its topmost shoot;
he carried it to a land of trade,
set it in a city of merchants.
5 Then he took a seed from the land,
placed it in fertile soil;
a plant[t] by abundant waters,
he set it like a willow twig.
6 It sprouted and became a vine,
spreading out, but low;
its branches turned towards him,
its roots remained where it stood.
So it became a vine;
it brought forth branches,
put forth foliage.

7 There was another great eagle,
with great wings and
much plumage.
And see! This vine stretched out
its roots towards him;
it shot out its branches towards him,
so that he might water it.
From the bed where it was planted
8 it was transplanted
to good soil by abundant waters,
so that it might produce branches
and bear fruit
and become a noble vine.

9 Say: Thus says the Lord GOD:
Will it prosper?
Will he not pull up its roots,
cause its fruit to rot[u] and wither,
its fresh sprouting leaves to fade?
No strong arm or mighty army
will be needed
to pull it from its roots.
10 When it is transplanted,
will it thrive?
When the east wind strikes it,
will it not utterly wither,
wither on the bed where it grew?

11 Then the word of the LORD came
to me: 12 Say now to the rebellious house:
Do you not know what these things
mean? Tell them: The king of Babylon
came to Jerusalem, took its king and its
officials, and brought them back with
him to Babylon. 13 He took one of the
royal offspring and made a covenant
with him, putting him under oath (he

q 16.57 Another reading is *Edom* r 16.61 Syr: Heb *you* s 16.61 Heb lacks *my* t 17.5 Meaning of Heb uncertain u 17.9 Meaning of Heb uncertain

had taken away the chief men of the
land), [14]so that the kingdom might be
humble and not lift itself up, and that
by keeping his covenant it might stand.
[15]But he rebelled against him by sending ambassadors to Egypt, in order that
they might give him horses and a large
army. Will he succeed? Can one escape
who does such things? Can he break
the covenant and yet escape? [16]As I
live, says the Lord GOD, surely in the
place where the king resides who made
him king, whose oath he despised, and
whose covenant with him he broke—in
Babylon he shall die. [17]Pharaoh with
his mighty army and great company
will not help him in war, when ramps
are cast up and siege-walls built to cut
off many lives. [18]Because he despised
the oath and broke the covenant, because he gave his hand and yet did
all these things, he shall not escape.
[19]Therefore, thus says the Lord GOD: As
I live, I will surely return upon his head
my oath that he despised, and my covenant that he broke. [20]I will spread my
net over him, and he shall be caught in
my snare; I will bring him to Babylon
and enter into judgement with him
there for the treason he has committed
against me. [21]All the pick[v] of his troops
shall fall by the sword, and the survivors shall be scattered to every wind;
and you shall know that I, the LORD,
have spoken.

ISRAEL EXALTED AT LAST

22 Thus says the Lord GOD:
I myself will take a sprig
from the lofty top of a cedar;
I will set it out.
I will break off a tender one
from the topmost of its
young twigs;
I myself will plant it
on a high and lofty mountain.
23 On the mountain height of Israel
I will plant it,
in order that it may produce
boughs and bear fruit,
and become a noble cedar.
Under it every kind of bird will live;
in the shade of its branches
will nest
winged creatures of every kind.
24 All the trees of the field shall know
that I am the LORD.
I bring low the high tree,
I make high the low tree;
I dry up the green tree
and make the dry tree flourish.
I the LORD have spoken;
I will accomplish it.

INDIVIDUAL RETRIBUTION

18 The word of the LORD came to
me: [2]What do you mean by repeating this proverb concerning the
land of Israel, 'The parents have eaten
sour grapes, and the children's teeth are
set on edge'? [3]As I live, says the Lord
GOD, this proverb shall no more be used
by you in Israel. [4]Know that all lives are
mine; the life of the parent as well as
the life of the child is mine: it is only the
person who sins that shall die.

5 If a man is righteous and does what
is lawful and right— [6]if he does not eat
upon the mountains or lift up his eyes to
the idols of the house of Israel, does not
defile his neighbour's wife or approach
a woman during her menstrual period,
[7]does not oppress anyone, but restores
to the debtor his pledge, commits no
robbery, gives his bread to the hungry
and covers the naked with a garment,
[8]does not take advance or accrued interest, withholds his hand from iniquity,
executes true justice between contend-
ing parties, [9]follows my statutes, and is
careful to observe my ordinances, acting
faithfully—such a one is righteous; he
shall surely live, says the Lord GOD.

10 If he has a son who is violent, a
shedder of blood, [11]who does any of these
things (though his father[w] does none of
them), who eats upon the mountains,
defiles his neighbour's wife, [12]oppresses
the poor and needy, commits robbery,
does not restore the pledge, lifts up his
eyes to the idols, commits abomination,
[13]takes advance or accrued interest; shall
he then live? He shall not. He has done
all these abominable things; he shall
surely die; his blood shall be upon himself.

14 But if this man has a son who sees
all the sins that his father has done, considers, and does not do likewise, [15]who
does not eat upon the mountains or lift
up his eyes to the idols of the house of
Israel, does not defile his neighbour's
wife, [16]does not wrong anyone, exacts
no pledge, commits no robbery, but
gives his bread to the hungry and covers the naked with a garment, [17]with-
holds his hand from iniquity,[x] takes no
advance or accrued interest, observes
my ordinances, and follows my statutes;

[v] 17.21 Another reading is *fugitives*
[w] 18.11 Heb *he* [x] 18.17 Gk: Heb *the poor*

he shall not die for his father's iniquity;
he shall surely live. 18 As for his father,
because he practised extortion, robbed
his brother, and did what is not good
among his people, he dies for his iniquity.

19 Yet you say, 'Why should not the
son suffer for the iniquity of the father?'
When the son has done what is lawful
and right, and has been careful to observe all my statutes, he shall surely live.
20 The person who sins shall die. A child
shall not suffer for the iniquity of a parent, nor a parent suffer for the iniquity
of a child; the righteousness of the righteous shall be his own, and the wickedness of the wicked shall be his own.

21 But if the wicked turn away from
all their sins that they have committed
and keep all my statutes and do what is
lawful and right, they shall surely live;
they shall not die. 22 None of the transgressions that they have committed
shall be remembered against them; for
the righteousness that they have done
they shall live. 23 Have I any pleasure in
the death of the wicked, says the Lord
GOD, and not rather that they should
turn from their ways and live? 24 But
when the righteous turn away from
their righteousness and commit iniquity and do the same abominable
things that the wicked do, shall they
live? None of the righteous deeds that
they have done shall be remembered;
for the treachery of which they are
guilty and the sin they have committed,
they shall die.

25 Yet you say, 'The way of the Lord
is unfair.' Hear now, O house of Israel:
Is my way unfair? Is it not your ways
that are unfair? 26 When the righteous
turn away from their righteousness
and commit iniquity, they shall die for
it; for the iniquity that they have committed they shall die. 27 Again, when
the wicked turn away from the wickedness they have committed and do
what is lawful and right, they shall save
their life. 28 Because they considered and
turned away from all the transgressions
that they had committed, they shall
surely live; they shall not die. 29 Yet the
house of Israel says, 'The way of the Lord
is unfair.' O house of Israel, are my ways
unfair? Is it not your ways that are unfair?

30 Therefore I will judge you,
O house of Israel, all of you according to
your ways, says the Lord GOD. Repent
and turn from all your transgressions;
otherwise iniquity will be your ruin.[y]
31 Cast away from you all the transgressions that you have committed against
me, and get yourselves a new heart and
a new spirit! Why will you die, O house
of Israel? 32 For I have no pleasure in
the death of anyone, says the Lord GOD.
Turn, then, and live.

ISRAEL DEGRADED

19 As for you, raise up a lamentation for the princes of Israel,
2 and say:

What a lioness was your mother
among lions!
She lay down among young lions,
rearing her cubs.
3 She raised up one of her cubs;
he became a young lion,
and he learned to catch prey;
he devoured humans.
4 The nations sounded an alarm
against him;
he was caught in their pit;
and they brought him with hooks
to the land of Egypt.
5 When she saw that she
was thwarted,
that her hope was lost,
she took another of her cubs
and made him a young lion.
6 He prowled among the lions;
he became a young lion,
and he learned to catch prey;
he devoured people.
7 And he ravaged their strongholds,[z]
and laid waste their towns;
the land was appalled, and all in it,
at the sound of his roaring.
8 The nations set upon him
from the provinces all around;
they spread their net over him;
he was caught in their pit.
9 With hooks they put him in a cage,
and brought him to the
king of Babylon;
they brought him into custody,
so that his voice should be
heard no more
on the mountains of Israel.
10 Your mother was like a vine
in a vineyard[a]
transplanted by the water,
fruitful and full of branches
from abundant water.
11 Its strongest stem became
a ruler's sceptre;[b]

[y] **18.30** *Or so that they shall not be a stumbling-block of iniquity to you* [z] **19.7** Heb *his widows* [a] **19.10** Cn: Heb *in your blood* [b] **19.11** Heb *Its strongest stems became rulers' sceptres*

it towered aloft
among the thick boughs;
it stood out in its height
with its mass of branches.
12 But it was plucked up in fury,
cast down to the ground;
the east wind dried it up;
its fruit was stripped off,
its strong stem was withered;
the fire consumed it.
13 Now it is transplanted into
the wilderness,
into a dry and thirsty land.
14 And fire has gone out from its stem,
has consumed its branches
and fruit,
so that there remains in it
no strong stem,
no sceptre for ruling.

This is a lamentation, and it is used as a lamentation.

ISRAEL'S CONTINUING REBELLION

20 In the seventh year, in the fifth
month, on the tenth day of the
month, certain elders of Israel came to
consult the LORD, and sat down before
me. 2 And the word of the LORD came
to me: 3 Mortal, speak to the elders of
Israel, and say to them: Thus says the
Lord GOD: Why are you coming? To consult me? As I live, says the Lord GOD, I
will not be consulted by you. 4 Will you
judge them, mortal, will you judge
them? Then let them know the abominations of their ancestors, 5 and say
to them: Thus says the Lord GOD: On
the day when I chose Israel, I swore to
the offspring of the house of Jacob—
making myself known to them in the
land of Egypt—I swore to them, saying,
I am the LORD your God. 6 On that day I
swore to them that I would bring them
out of the land of Egypt into a land that
I had searched out for them, a land flowing with milk and honey, the most glorious of all lands. 7 And I said to them,
Cast away the detestable things your
eyes feast on, every one of you, and do
not defile yourselves with the idols of
Egypt; I am the LORD your God. 8 But
they rebelled against me and would not
listen to me; not one of them cast away
the detestable things their eyes feasted
on, nor did they forsake the idols of
Egypt.

Then I thought I would pour out my
wrath upon them and spend my anger
against them in the midst of the land
of Egypt. 9 But I acted for the sake of my
name, that it should not be profaned in
the sight of the nations among whom
they lived, in whose sight I made myself known to them in bringing them
out of the land of Egypt. 10 So I led them
out of the land of Egypt and brought
them into the wilderness. 11 I gave them
my statutes and showed them my ordinances, by whose observance everyone
shall live. 12 Moreover, I gave them my
sabbaths, as a sign between me and
them, so that they might know that
I the LORD sanctify them. 13 But the
house of Israel rebelled against me in
the wilderness; they did not observe my
statutes but rejected my ordinances, by
whose observance everyone shall live;
and my sabbaths they greatly profaned.

Then I thought I would pour out my
wrath upon them in the wilderness, to
make an end of them. 14 But I acted for
the sake of my name, so that it should
not be profaned in the sight of the nations, in whose sight I had brought
them out. 15 Moreover, I swore to them
in the wilderness that I would not bring
them into the land that I had given
them, a land flowing with milk and
honey, the most glorious of all lands,
16 because they rejected my ordinances
and did not observe my statutes, and
profaned my sabbaths; for their heart
went after their idols. 17 Nevertheless,
my eye spared them, and I did not destroy them or make an end of them in
the wilderness.

18 I said to their children in the wilderness, Do not follow the statutes of
your parents, nor observe their ordinances, nor defile yourselves with their
idols. 19 I the LORD am your God; follow
my statutes, and be careful to observe
my ordinances, 20 and hallow my sabbaths that they may be a sign between
me and you, so that you may know that
I the LORD am your God. 21 But the children rebelled against me; they did not
follow my statutes, and were not careful
to observe my ordinances, by whose observance everyone shall live; they profaned my sabbaths.

Then I thought I would pour out my
wrath upon them and spend my anger
against them in the wilderness. 22 But
I withheld my hand, and acted for the
sake of my name, so that it should not
be profaned in the sight of the nations,
in whose sight I had brought them out.
23 Moreover, I swore to them in the
wilderness that I would scatter them
among the nations and disperse them

through the countries, [24]because they
had not executed my ordinances, but
had rejected my statutes and profaned
my sabbaths, and their eyes were set
on their ancestors' idols. [25]Moreover, I
gave them statutes that were not good
and ordinances by which they could
not live. [26]I defiled them through their
very gifts, in their offering up all their
firstborn, in order that I might horrify
them, so that they might know that I
am the LORD.

27 Therefore, mortal, speak to the
house of Israel and say to them, Thus
says the Lord GOD: In this again your
ancestors blasphemed me, by dealing
treacherously with me. [28]For when I
had brought them into the land that
I swore to give them, then wherever
they saw any high hill or any leafy tree,
there they offered their sacrifices and
presented the provocation of their offering; there they sent up their pleasing
odours, and there they poured out their
drink-offerings. [29](I said to them, What
is the high place to which you go? So it
is called Bamah[c] to this day.) [30]There-
fore say to the house of Israel, Thus says
the Lord GOD: Will you defile yourselves
after the manner of your ancestors and
go astray after their detestable things?
[31]When you offer your gifts and make
your children pass through the fire,
you defile yourselves with all your idols
to this day. And shall I be consulted by
you, O house of Israel? As I live, says the
Lord GOD, I will not be consulted by you.

32 What is in your mind shall never
happen—the thought, 'Let us be like the
nations, like the tribes of the countries,
and worship wood and stone.'

GOD WILL RESTORE ISRAEL

33 As I live, says the Lord GOD, surely
with a mighty hand and an outstretched
arm, and with wrath poured out, I will
be king over you. [34]I will bring you out
from the peoples and gather you out of
the countries where you are scattered,
with a mighty hand and an outstretched
arm, and with wrath poured out; [35]and
I will bring you into the wilderness of
the peoples, and there I will enter into
judgement with you face to face. [36]As I
entered into judgement with your ancestors in the wilderness of the land of
Egypt, so I will enter into judgement
with you, says the Lord GOD. [37]I will
make you pass under the staff, and will
bring you within the bond of the covenant. [38]I will purge out the rebels
among you, and those who transgress
against me; I will bring them out of the
land where they reside as aliens, but
they shall not enter the land of Israel.
Then you shall know that I am the LORD.

39 As for you, O house of Israel, thus
says the Lord GOD: Go, serve your idols,
every one of you now and hereafter, if
you will not listen to me; but my holy
name you shall no more profane with
your gifts and your idols.

40 For on my holy mountain, the
mountain height of Israel, says the Lord
GOD, there all the house of Israel, all of
them, shall serve me in the land; there
I will accept them, and there I will require your contributions and the choicest of your gifts, with all your sacred
things. [41]As a pleasing odour I will accept you, when I bring you out from the
peoples, and gather you out of the countries where you have been scattered; and
I will manifest my holiness among you
in the sight of the nations. [42]You shall
know that I am the LORD, when I bring
you into the land of Israel, the country
that I swore to give to your ancestors.
[43]There you shall remember your ways
and all the deeds by which you have polluted yourselves; and you shall loathe
yourselves for all the evils that you have
committed. [44]And you shall know that I
am the LORD, when I deal with you for
my name's sake, not according to your
evil ways or corrupt deeds, O house of
Israel, says the Lord GOD.

A PROPHECY AGAINST THE NEGEB

45[d] The word of the LORD came to
me: [46]Mortal, set your face towards
the south, preach against the south,
and prophesy against the forest land
in the Negeb; [47]say to the forest of the
Negeb, Hear the word of the LORD: Thus
says the Lord GOD, I will kindle a fire
in you, and it shall devour every green
tree in you and every dry tree; the blazing flame shall not be quenched, and
all faces from south to north shall be
scorched by it. [48]All flesh shall see that I
the LORD have kindled it; it shall not be
quenched. [49]Then I said, 'Ah Lord GOD!
they are saying of me, "Is he not a maker
of allegories?" '

THE DRAWN SWORD OF GOD

21[e] The word of the LORD came
to me: [2]Mortal, set your face

[c] 20.29 That is *High Place* [d] 20.45 Ch 21.1 in Heb
[e] 21.1 Ch 21.6 in Heb

towards Jerusalem and preach against
the sanctuaries; prophesy against the
land of Israel 3and say to the land of Israel, Thus says the LORD: I am coming
against you, and will draw my sword out
of its sheath, and will cut off from you
both righteous and wicked. 4Because I
will cut off from you both righteous and
wicked, therefore my sword shall go out
of its sheath against all flesh from south
to north; 5and all flesh shall know that I
the LORD have drawn my sword out of
its sheath; it shall not be sheathed again.
6Moan therefore, mortal; moan with
breaking heart and bitter grief before
their eyes. 7And when they say to you,
'Why do you moan?' you shall say, 'Because of the news that has come. Every
heart will fail and all hands will be feeble, every spirit will faint and all knees
will turn to water. See, it comes and it
will be fulfilled,' says the Lord GOD.

8 And the word of the LORD came
to me: 9Mortal, prophesy and say: Thus
says the Lord; Say:

A sword, a sword is sharpened,
 it is also polished;
10 it is sharpened for slaughter,
 honed to flash like lightning!
How can we make merry?
 You have despised the rod
 and all discipline.[f]
11 The sword[g] is given to be polished,
 to be grasped in the hand;
it is sharpened, the sword
 is polished,
 to be placed in the slayer's hand.
12 Cry and wail, O mortal,
 for it is against my people;
it is against all Israel's princes;
 they are thrown to the sword,
 together with my people.
 Ah! Strike the thigh!
13For consider: What! If you despise the
rod, will it not happen?[h] says the Lord
GOD.
14 And you, mortal, prophesy;
 strike hand to hand.
Let the sword fall twice, thrice;
 it is a sword for killing.
A sword for great slaughter—
 it surrounds them;
15 therefore hearts fail
 and many stumble.
At all their gates I have set
 the point[i] of the sword.
Ah! It is made for flashing,
 it is polished[j] for slaughter.
16 Attack to the right!
 Engage to the left!—wherever
 your edge is directed.
17 I too will strike hand to hand,
 I will satisfy my fury;
 I the LORD have spoken.

18 The word of the LORD came to me:
19Mortal, mark out two roads for the
sword of the king of Babylon to come;
both of them shall issue from the same
land. And make a signpost, make it for a
fork in the road leading to a city; 20mark
out the road for the sword to come to
Rabbah of the Ammonites or to Judah
and to[k] Jerusalem the fortified. 21For the
king of Babylon stands at the parting of
the way, at the fork in the two roads, to
use divination; he shakes the arrows, he
consults the teraphim,[l] he inspects the
liver. 22Into his right hand comes the
lot for Jerusalem, to set battering-rams,
to call out for slaughter, for raising the
battle cry, to set battering-rams against
the gates, to cast up ramps, to build
siege-towers. 23But to them it will seem
like a false divination; they have sworn
solemn oaths; but he brings their guilt
to remembrance, bringing about their
capture.

24 Therefore, thus says the Lord GOD:
Because you have brought your guilt to
remembrance, in that your transgressions are uncovered, so that in all your
deeds your sins appear—because you
have come to remembrance, you shall
be taken in hand.[m]
25 As for you, vile, wicked
 prince of Israel,
 you whose day has come,
 the time of final punishment,
26 thus says the Lord GOD:
Remove the turban, take
 off the crown;
 things shall not remain
 as they are.
Exalt that which is low,
 abase that which is high.
27 A ruin, a ruin, a ruin—
 I will make it!
 (Such has never occurred.)
Until he comes whose right it is;
 to him I will give it.

28 As for you, mortal, prophesy, and
say, Thus says the Lord GOD concerning
the Ammonites, and concerning their
reproach; say:

[f] **21.10** Meaning of Heb uncertain [g] **21.11** Heb *It* [h] **21.13** Meaning of Heb uncertain [i] **21.15** Meaning of Heb uncertain [j] **21.15** Tg: Heb *wrapped up* [k] **21.20** Gk Syr: Heb *Judah in* [l] **21.21** Or *the household gods* [m] **21.24** Or *be taken captive*

A sword, a sword! Drawn
for slaughter,
polished to consume,[n] to
flash like lightning.
29 Offering false visions for you,
divining lies for you,
they place you over the necks
of the vile, wicked ones—
those whose day has come,
the time of final punishment.
30 Return it to its sheath!
In the place where you were created,
in the land of your origin,
I will judge you.
31 I will pour out my indignation
upon you,
with the fire of my wrath
I will blow upon you.
I will deliver you into brutish hands,
those skilful to destroy.
32 You shall be fuel for the fire,
your blood shall enter the earth;
you shall be remembered no more,
for I the LORD have spoken.

THE BLOODY CITY

22 The word of the LORD came
to me: 2 You, mortal, will you
judge, will you judge the bloody city?
Then declare to it all its abominable
deeds. 3 You shall say, Thus says the Lord
GOD: A city! Shedding blood within itself; its time has come; making its idols,
defiling itself. 4 You have become guilty
by the blood that you have shed, and defiled by the idols that you have made;
you have brought your day near, the
appointed time of your years has come.
Therefore I have made you a disgrace
before the nations, and a mockery to all
the countries. 5 Those who are near and
those who are far from you will mock
you, you infamous one, full of tumult.

6 The princes of Israel in you, every one according to his power, have
been bent on shedding blood. 7 Father
and mother are treated with contempt
in you; the alien residing within you
suffers extortion; the orphan and the
widow are wronged in you. 8 You have
despised my holy things, and profaned
my sabbaths. 9 In you are those who
slander to shed blood, those in you who
eat upon the mountains, who commit
lewdness in your midst. 10 In you they
uncover their fathers' nakedness; in
you they violate women in their menstrual periods. 11 One commits abomination with his neighbour's wife; another
lewdly defiles his daughter-in-law; another in you defiles his sister, his father's daughter. 12 In you, they take
bribes to shed blood; you take both advance interest and accrued interest, and
make gain of your neighbours by extortion; and you have forgotten me, says
the Lord GOD.

13 See, I strike my hands together
at the dishonest gain you have made,
and at the blood that has been shed
within you. 14 Can your courage endure,
or can your hands remain strong in the
days when I shall deal with you? I the
LORD have spoken, and I will do it. 15 I
will scatter you among the nations and
disperse you through the countries, and
I will purge your filthiness out of you.
16 And I[o] shall be profaned through you
in the sight of the nations; and you shall
know that I am the LORD.

17 The word of the LORD came to me:
18 Mortal, the house of Israel has become
dross to me; all of them, silver,[p] bronze,
tin, iron, and lead. In the smelter they
have become dross. 19 Therefore thus
says the Lord GOD: Because you have
all become dross, I will gather you into
the midst of Jerusalem. 20 As one gathers silver, bronze, iron, lead, and tin into
a smelter, to blow the fire upon them
in order to melt them; so I will gather
you in my anger and in my wrath, and
I will put you in and melt you. 21 I will
gather you and blow upon you with
the fire of my wrath, and you shall be
melted within it. 22 As silver is melted
in a smelter, so you shall be melted in
it; and you shall know that I the LORD
have poured out my wrath upon you.

23 The word of the LORD came to me:
24 Mortal, say to it: You are a land that is
not cleansed, not rained upon in the day
of indignation. 25 Its princes[q] within it
are like a roaring lion tearing the prey;
they have devoured human lives; they
have taken treasure and precious things;
they have made many widows within
it. 26 Its priests have done violence to
my teaching and have profaned my holy
things; they have made no distinction
between the holy and the common,
neither have they taught the difference
between the unclean and the clean, and
they have disregarded my sabbaths, so
that I am profaned among them. 27 Its
officials within it are like wolves tearing
the prey, shedding blood, destroying
lives to get dishonest gain. 28 Its proph-

[n] **21.28** Cn: Heb *to contain* [o] **22.16** Gk Syr Vg: Heb *you* [p] **22.18** Transposed from the end of the verse; compare verse 20 [q] **22.25** Gk: Heb *indignation.* *25 A conspiracy of its prophets*

ets have smeared whitewash on their
behalf, seeing false visions and divining
lies for them, saying, 'Thus says the Lord
GOD', when the LORD has not spoken.
29The people of the land have practised
extortion and committed robbery; they
have oppressed the poor and needy, and
have extorted from the alien without re-
dress. 30And I sought for anyone among
them who would repair the wall and
stand in the breach before me on behalf
of the land, so that I would not destroy
it; but I found no one. 31Therefore I have
poured out my indignation upon them;
I have consumed them with the fire of
my wrath; I have returned their conduct
upon their heads, says the Lord GOD.

OHOLAH AND OHOLIBAH

23 The word of the LORD came to
me: 2Mortal, there were two
women, the daughters of one mother;
3they played the whore in Egypt; they
played the whore in their youth; their
breasts were caressed there, and their
virgin bosoms were fondled. 4Oholah
was the name of the elder and Oholibah the name of her sister. They became
mine, and they bore sons and daughters. As for their names, Oholah is Samaria, and Oholibah is Jerusalem.

5 Oholah played the whore while
she was mine; she lusted after her lovers the Assyrians, warriors[r] 6clothed in
blue, governors and commanders, all of
them handsome young men, mounted
horsemen. 7She bestowed her favours
upon them, the choicest men of Assyria
all of them; and she defiled herself with
all the idols of everyone for whom she
lusted. 8She did not give up her whorings that she had practised since Egypt;
for in her youth men had lain with
her and fondled her virgin bosom and
poured out their lust upon her. 9There-
fore I delivered her into the hands of her
lovers, into the hands of the Assyrians,
for whom she lusted. 10These uncovered
her nakedness; they seized her sons and
her daughters; and they killed her with
the sword. Judgement was executed
upon her, and she became a byword
among women.

11 Her sister Oholibah saw this, yet
she was more corrupt than her sister in her lusting and in her whorings,
which were worse than those of her
sister. 12She lusted after the Assyrians,
governors and commanders, warriors[s]
clothed in full armour, mounted horsemen, all of them handsome young men.
13And I saw that she was defiled; they
both took the same way. 14But she carried her whorings further; she saw male
figures carved on the wall, images of
the Chaldeans portrayed in vermilion,
15with belts around their waists, with
flowing turbans on their heads, all of
them looking like officers—a picture
of Babylonians whose native land was
Chaldea. 16When she saw them she
lusted after them, and sent messengers
to them in Chaldea. 17And the Babylonians came to her into the bed of love,
and they defiled her with their lust; and
after she defiled herself with them, she
turned from them in disgust. 18When
she carried on her whorings so openly
and flaunted her nakedness, I turned
in disgust from her, as I had turned
from her sister. 19Yet she increased her
whorings, remembering the days of her
youth, when she played the whore in
the land of Egypt 20and lusted after her
paramours there, whose members were
like those of donkeys, and whose emission was like that of stallions. 21Thus
you longed for the lewdness of your
youth, when the Egyptians[t] fondled
your bosom and caressed[u] your young
breasts.

22 Therefore, O Oholibah, thus says
the Lord GOD: I will arouse against you
your lovers from whom you turned in
disgust, and I will bring them against
you from every side: 23the Babylonians
and all the Chaldeans, Pekod and Shoa
and Koa, and all the Assyrians with
them, handsome young men, governors and commanders all of them, officers and warriors,[v] all of them riding
on horses. 24They shall come against
you from the north[w] with chariots and
wagons and a host of peoples; they shall
set themselves against you on every
side with buckler, shield, and helmet,
and I will commit the judgement to
them, and they shall judge you according to their ordinances. 25I will direct
my indignation against you, in order
that they may deal with you in fury.
They shall cut off your nose and your
ears, and your survivors shall fall by
the sword. They shall seize your sons
and your daughters, and your survivors
shall be devoured by fire. 26They shall

[r] 23.5 Meaning of Heb uncertain
[s] 23.12 Meaning of Heb uncertain [t] 23.21 Two Mss: MT *from Egypt* [u] 23.21 Cn: Heb *for the sake of* [v] 23.23 Compare verses 6 and 12: Heb *officers and called ones* [w] 23.24 Gk: Meaning of Heb uncertain

also strip you of your clothes and take
away your fine jewels. 27So I will put an
end to your lewdness and your whoring
brought from the land of Egypt; you
shall not long for them, or remember
Egypt any more. 28For thus says the
Lord GOD: I will deliver you into the
hands of those whom you hate, into the
hands of those from whom you turned
in disgust; 29and they shall deal with
you in hatred, and take away all the
fruit of your labour, and leave you naked and bare, and the nakedness of your
whorings shall be exposed. Your lewdness and your whorings 30have brought
this upon you, because you played the
whore with the nations, and polluted
yourself with their idols. 31You have
gone the way of your sister; therefore I
will give her cup into your hand. 32Thus
says the Lord GOD:

You shall drink your sister's cup,
  deep and wide;
you shall be scorned and derided,
  it holds so much.
33 You shall be filled with
    drunkenness and sorrow.
A cup of horror and desolation
  is the cup of your sister Samaria;
34 you shall drink it and drain it out,
  and gnaw its sherds,
  and tear out your breasts;

for I have spoken, says the Lord GOD.
35Therefore thus says the Lord GOD: Because you have forgotten me and cast
me behind your back, therefore bear
the consequences of your lewdness and
whorings.

36 The LORD said to me: Mortal, will
you judge Oholah and Oholibah? Then
declare to them their abominable deeds.
37For they have committed adultery,
and blood is on their hands; with their
idols they have committed adultery;
and they have even offered up to them
for food the children whom they had
borne to me. 38Moreover, this they have
done to me: they have defiled my sanctuary on the same day and profaned my
sabbaths. 39For when they had slaughtered their children for their idols, on
the same day they came into my sanctuary to profane it. This is what they did
in my house.

40 They even sent for men to come
from far away, to whom a messenger
was sent, and they came. For them you
bathed yourself, painted your eyes, and
decked yourself with ornaments; 41you
sat on a stately couch, with a table
spread before it on which you had placed
my incense and my oil. 42The sound of a
raucous multitude was around her, with
many of the rabble brought in drunken
from the wilderness; and they put
bracelets on the arms[x] of the women,
and beautiful crowns upon their heads.

43 Then I said, Ah, she is worn out
with adulteries, but they carry on their
sexual acts with her. 44For they have
gone in to her, as one goes in to a whore.
Thus they went in to Oholah and to Oholibah, wanton women. 45But righteous
judges shall declare them guilty of adultery and of bloodshed; because they are
adulteresses, and blood is on their hands.

46 For thus says the Lord GOD: Bring
up an assembly against them, and make
them an object of terror and of plunder. 47The assembly shall stone them
and with their swords they shall cut
them down; they shall kill their sons
and their daughters, and burn up their
houses. 48Thus will I put an end to lewdness in the land, so that all women may
take warning and not commit lewdness
as you have done. 49They shall repay you
for your lewdness, and you shall bear
the penalty for your sinful idolatry; and
you shall know that I am the Lord GOD.

THE BOILING POT

24 In the ninth year, in the tenth
month, on the tenth day of the
month, the word of the LORD came to
me: 2Mortal, write down the name of
this day, this very day. The king of Babylon has laid siege to Jerusalem this
very day. 3And utter an allegory to the
rebellious house and say to them, Thus
says the Lord GOD:

Set on the pot, set it on,
  pour in water also;
4 put in it the pieces,
  all the good pieces, the thigh
    and the shoulder;
  fill it with choice bones.
5 Take the choicest one of the flock,
  pile the logs[y] under it;
boil its pieces,[z]
  seethe[a] also its bones in it.

6 Therefore, thus says the Lord GOD:
Woe to the bloody city,
  the pot whose rust is in it,
  whose rust has not gone out of it!
Empty it piece by piece,
  making no choice at all.[b]

[x] 23.42 Heb *hands* [y] 24.5 Compare verse 10: Heb *the bones* [z] 24.5 Two Mss: Heb *its boilings* [a] 24.5 Cn: Heb *its bones seethe* [b] 24.6 Heb *piece, no lot has fallen on it*

7 For the blood she shed is inside it;
she placed it on a bare rock;
she did not pour it out on
the ground,
to cover it with earth.
8 To rouse my wrath, to take
vengeance,
I have placed the blood she shed
on a bare rock,
so that it may not be covered.
9Therefore thus says the Lord GOD:
Woe to the bloody city!
I will even make the pile great.
10 Heap up the logs, kindle the fire;
boil the meat well, mix
in the spices,
let the bones be burned.
11 Stand it empty upon the coals,
so that it may become hot,
its copper glow,
its filth melt in it, its rust
be consumed.
12 In vain I have wearied myself;[c]
its thick rust does not depart.
To the fire with its rust![d]
13 Yet, when I cleansed you in
your filthy lewdness,
you did not become clean
from your filth;
you shall not again be cleansed
until I have satisfied my
fury upon you.
14I the LORD have spoken; the time is
coming, I will act. I will not refrain, I
will not spare, I will not relent. According to your ways and your doings I will
judge you, says the Lord GOD.

EZEKIEL'S BEREAVEMENT

15 The word of the LORD came to me:
16Mortal, with one blow I am about to
take away from you the delight of your
eyes; yet you shall not mourn or weep,
nor shall your tears run down. 17Sigh,
but not aloud; make no mourning for
the dead. Bind on your turban, and
put your sandals on your feet; do not
cover your upper lip or eat the bread of
mourners.[e] 18So I spoke to the people in
the morning, and at evening my wife
died. And on the next morning I did as
I was commanded.
19 Then the people said to me, 'Will
you not tell us what these things mean
for us, that you are acting in this way?'
20Then I said to them: The word of the
LORD came to me: 21Say to the house
of Israel, Thus says the Lord GOD: I will
profane my sanctuary, the pride of your
power, the delight of your eyes, and your
heart's desire; and your sons and your
daughters whom you left behind shall
fall by the sword. 22And you shall do
as I have done; you shall not cover your
upper lip or eat the bread of mourners.[f]
23Your turbans shall be on your heads
and your sandals on your feet; you shall
not mourn or weep, but you shall pine
away in your iniquities and groan to
one another. 24Thus Ezekiel shall be a
sign to you; you shall do just as he has
done. When this comes, then you shall
know that I am the Lord GOD.
25 And you, mortal, on the day when
I take from them their stronghold, their
joy and glory, the delight of their eyes
and their heart's affection, and also[g]
their sons and their daughters, 26on
that day, one who has escaped will come
to you to report to you the news. 27On
that day your mouth shall be opened to
the one who has escaped, and you shall
speak and no longer be silent. So you
shall be a sign to them; and they shall
know that I am the LORD.

PROCLAMATION AGAINST AMMON

25 The word of the LORD came to
me: 2Mortal, set your face towards the Ammonites and prophesy
against them. 3Say to the Ammonites, Hear the word of the Lord GOD:
Thus says the Lord GOD, Because you
said, 'Aha!' over my sanctuary when it
was profaned, and over the land of Israel when it was made desolate, and
over the house of Judah when it went
into exile; 4therefore I am handing you
over to the people of the east for a possession. They shall set their encampments among you and pitch their tents
in your midst; they shall eat your fruit,
and they shall drink your milk. 5I will
make Rabbah a pasture for camels and
Ammon a fold for flocks. Then you shall
know that I am the LORD. 6For thus
says the Lord GOD: Because you have
clapped your hands and stamped your
feet and rejoiced with all the malice
within you against the land of Israel,
7therefore I have stretched out my hand
against you, and will hand you over as
plunder to the nations. I will cut you
off from the peoples and will make you
perish out of the countries; I will destroy you. Then you shall know that I
am the LORD.

[c] 24.12 Cn: Meaning of Heb uncertain
[d] 24.12 Meaning of Heb uncertain [e] 24.17 Vg
Tg: Heb *of men* [f] 24.22 Vg Tg: Heb *of men*
[g] 24.25 Heb lacks *and also*

PROCLAMATION AGAINST MOAB

8 Thus says the Lord GOD: Because
Moab[h] said, The house of Judah is like
all the other nations, 9therefore I will
lay open the flank of Moab from the
towns[i] on its frontier, the glory of the
country, Beth-jeshimoth, Baal-meon,
and Kiriathaim. 10I will give it along
with Ammon to the people of the east
as a possession. Thus Ammon shall be
remembered no more among the nations, 11and I will execute judgements
upon Moab. Then they shall know that
I am the LORD.

PROCLAMATION AGAINST EDOM

12 Thus says the Lord GOD: Because
Edom acted vengefully against the
house of Judah and has grievously offended in taking vengeance upon them,
13therefore thus says the Lord GOD, I
will stretch out my hand against Edom,
and cut off from it humans and animals,
and I will make it desolate; from Teman
even to Dedan they shall fall by the
sword. 14I will lay my vengeance upon
Edom by the hand of my people Israel;
and they shall act in Edom according to
my anger and according to my wrath;
and they shall know my vengeance, says
the Lord GOD.

PROCLAMATION AGAINST PHILISTIA

15 Thus says the Lord GOD: Because
with unending hostilities the Philistines acted in vengeance, and with malice of heart took revenge in destruction;
16therefore thus says the Lord GOD, I
will stretch out my hand against the
Philistines, cut off the Cherethites, and
destroy the rest of the sea coast. 17I will
execute great vengeance on them with
wrathful punishments. Then they shall
know that I am the LORD, when I lay
my vengeance on them.

PROCLAMATION AGAINST TYRE

26 In the eleventh year, on the first
day of the month, the word of
the LORD came to me: 2Mortal, because
Tyre said concerning Jerusalem,
'Aha, broken is the gateway
of the peoples;
it has swung open to me;
I shall be replenished,
now that it is wasted',
3therefore, thus says the Lord GOD:
See, I am against you, O Tyre!
I will hurl many nations
against you,
as the sea hurls its waves.
4 They shall destroy the walls of Tyre
and break down its towers.
I will scrape its soil from it
and make it a bare rock.
5 It shall become, in the midst
of the sea,
a place for spreading nets.
I have spoken, says the Lord GOD.
It shall become plunder for
the nations,
6 and its daughter-towns
in the country
shall be killed by the sword.
Then they shall know that I am the
LORD.

7 For thus says the Lord GOD: I will
bring against Tyre from the north King
Nebuchadrezzar of Babylon, king of
kings, together with horses, chariots,
cavalry, and a great and powerful army.
8 Your daughter-towns in the country
he shall put to the sword.
He shall set up a siege-wall
against you,
cast up a ramp against you,
and raise a roof of shields
against you.
9 He shall direct the shock of
his battering-rams
against your walls
and break down your towers
with his axes.
10 His horses shall be so many
that their dust shall cover you.
At the noise of cavalry, wheels,
and chariots
your very walls shall shake,
when he enters your gates
like those entering a breached city.
11 With the hoofs of his horses
he shall trample all your streets.
He shall put your people
to the sword,
and your strong pillars shall
fall to the ground.
12 They will plunder your riches
and loot your merchandise;
they shall break down your walls
and destroy your fine houses.
Your stones and timber and soil
they shall cast into the water.
13 I will silence the music of your songs;
the sound of your lyres shall
be heard no more.
14 I will make you a bare rock;
you shall be a place for
spreading nets.

[h] 25.8 Gk Old Latin: Heb *Moab and Seir*
[i] 25.9 Heb *towns from its towns*

You shall never again be rebuilt,
for I the LORD have spoken,
says the Lord GOD.

15 Thus says the Lord GOD to Tyre:
Shall not the coastlands shake at the
sound of your fall, when the wounded
groan, when slaughter goes on within
you? 16Then all the princes of the sea
shall step down from their thrones;
they shall remove their robes and strip
off their embroidered garments. They
shall clothe themselves with trembling,
and shall sit on the ground; they shall
tremble every moment, and be appalled
at you. 17And they shall raise a lamentation over you, and say to you:

How you have vanished[j]
from the seas,
O city renowned,
once mighty on the sea,
you and your inhabitants,[k]
who imposed your[l] terror
on all the mainland![m]
18 Now the coastlands tremble
on the day of your fall;
the coastlands by the sea
are dismayed at your passing.

19 For thus says the Lord GOD: When I
make you a city laid waste, like cities that
are not inhabited, when I bring up the
deep over you, and the great waters cover
you, 20then I will thrust you down with
those who descend into the Pit, to the
people of long ago, and I will make you
live in the world below, among primeval
ruins, with those who go down to the Pit,
so that you will not be inhabited or have
a place[n] in the land of the living. 21I will
bring you to a dreadful end, and you shall
be no more; though sought for, you will
never be found again, says the Lord GOD.

LAMENTATION OVER TYRE

27 The word of the LORD came to
me: 2Now you, mortal, raise
a lamentation over Tyre, 3and say to
Tyre, which sits at the entrance to the
sea, merchant of the peoples on many
coastlands, Thus says the Lord GOD:

O Tyre, you have said,
'I am perfect in beauty.'
4 Your borders are in the
heart of the seas;
your builders made perfect
your beauty.
5 They made all your planks
of fir trees from Senir;
they took a cedar from Lebanon
to make a mast for you.
6 From oaks of Bashan
they made your oars;
they made your deck of pines[o]
from the coasts of Cyprus,
inlaid with ivory.
7 Of fine embroidered linen from Egypt
was your sail,
serving as your ensign;
blue and purple from the
coasts of Elishah
was your awning.
8 The inhabitants of Sidon and Arvad
were your rowers;
skilled men of Zemer[p] were
within you,
they were your pilots.
9 The elders of Gebal and its artisans
were within you,
caulking your seams;
all the ships of the sea with their
mariners were within you,
to barter for your wares.
10 Paras[q] and Lud and Put
were in your army,
your mighty warriors;
they hung shield and helmet in you;
they gave you splendour.
11 Men of Arvad and Helech[r]
were on your walls all round;
men of Gamad were at
your towers.
They hung their quivers all
round your walls;
they made perfect your beauty.

12 Tarshish did business with you
out of the abundance of your great
wealth; silver, iron, tin, and lead they
exchanged for your wares. 13Javan, Tubal, and Meshech traded with you; they
exchanged human beings and vessels of
bronze for your merchandise. 14Beth-
togarmah exchanged for your wares
horses, war-horses, and mules. 15The
Rhodians[s] traded with you; many coastlands were your own special markets;
they brought you in payment ivory
tusks and ebony. 16Edom[t] did business
with you because of your abundant
goods; they exchanged for your wares
turquoise, purple, embroidered work,
fine linen, coral, and rubies. 17Judah and
the land of Israel traded with you; they
exchanged for your merchandise wheat
from Minnith, millet,[u] honey, oil, and

[j] 26.17 Gk OL Aquila: Heb *have vanished, O inhabited one,* [k] 26.17 Heb *it and its inhabitants* [l] 26.17 Heb *their* [m] 26.17 Cn: Heb *its inhabitants* [n] 26.20 Gk: Heb *I will give beauty* [o] 27.6 Or *boxwood* [p] 27.8 Cn Compare Gen 10.18: Heb *your skilled men, O Tyre* [q] 27.10 Or *Persia* [r] 27.11 Or *and your army* [s] 27.15 Gk: Heb *The Dedanites* [t] 27.16 Another reading is *Aram* [u] 27.17 Meaning of Heb uncertain

balm. 18Damascus traded with you for
your abundant goods—because of your
great wealth of every kind—wine of
Helbon, and white wool. 19Vedan and
Javan from Uzal[v] entered into trade for
your wares; wrought iron, cassia, and
sweet cane were bartered for your merchandise. 20Dedan traded with you in
saddlecloths for riding. 21Arabia and all
the princes of Kedar were your favoured
dealers in lambs, rams, and goats; in
these they did business with you. 22The
merchants of Sheba and Raamah traded
with you; they exchanged for your
wares the best of all kinds of spices, and
all precious stones, and gold. 23Haran,
Canneh, Eden, the merchants of Sheba,
Asshur, and Chilmad traded with you.
24These traded with you in choice garments, in clothes of blue and embroidered work, and in carpets of coloured
material, bound with cords and made
secure; in these they traded with you.[w]
25The ships of Tarshish travelled for you
in your trade.

So you were filled and heavily laden
in the heart of the seas.
26 Your rowers have brought you
into the high seas.
The east wind has wrecked you
in the heart of the seas.
27 Your riches, your wares, your
merchandise,
your mariners and your pilots,
your caulkers, your dealers
in merchandise,
and all your warriors within you,
with all the company
that is with you,
sink into the heart of the seas
on the day of your ruin.
28 At the sound of the
cry of your pilots
the countryside shakes,
29 and down from their ships
come all that handle the oar.
The mariners and all the
pilots of the sea
stand on the shore
30 and wail aloud over you,
and cry bitterly.
They throw dust on their heads
and wallow in ashes;
31 they make themselves bald for you,
and put on sackcloth,
and they weep over you in
bitterness of soul,
with bitter mourning.
32 In their wailing they raise a
lamentation for you,
and lament over you:
'Who was ever destroyed[x] like Tyre
in the midst of the sea?
33 When your wares came
from the seas,
you satisfied many peoples;
with your abundant wealth
and merchandise
you enriched the kings
of the earth.
34 Now you are wrecked by the seas,
in the depths of the waters;
your merchandise and all your crew
have sunk with you.
35 All the inhabitants of
the coastlands
are appalled at you;
and their kings are horribly afraid,
their faces are convulsed.
36 The merchants among the
peoples hiss at you;
you have come to a dreadful end
and shall be no more for ever.'

PROCLAMATION AGAINST THE KING OF TYRE

28 The word of the LORD came to
me: 2Mortal, say to the prince of
Tyre, Thus says the Lord GOD:
Because your heart is proud
and you have said, 'I am a god;
I sit in the seat of the gods,
in the heart of the seas',
yet you are but a mortal,
and no god,
though you compare your mind
with the mind of a god.
3 You are indeed wiser than Daniel;[y]
no secret is hidden from you;
4 by your wisdom and your
understanding
you have amassed wealth
for yourself,
and have gathered gold and silver
into your treasuries.
5 By your great wisdom in trade
you have increased your wealth,
and your heart has become
proud in your wealth.
6 Therefore, thus says the Lord GOD:
Because you compare your mind
with the mind of a god,
7 therefore, I will bring strangers
against you,
the most terrible of the nations;
they shall draw their swords against
the beauty of your wisdom
and defile your splendour.

[v] 27.19 Meaning of Heb uncertain [w] 27.24 Cn: Heb *in your market* [x] 27.32 Tg Vg: Heb *like silence* [y] 28.3 Or, as otherwise read, *Danel*

8 They shall thrust you down
to the Pit,
and you shall die a violent death
in the heart of the seas.
9 Will you still say, 'I am a god',
in the presence of those
who kill you,
though you are but a mortal,
and no god,
in the hands of those who
wound you?
10 You shall die the death of the
uncircumcised
by the hand of foreigners;
for I have spoken, says
the Lord GOD.

LAMENTATION OVER THE KING OF TYRE

11 Moreover, the word of the LORD
came to me: 12Mortal, raise a lamentation over the king of Tyre, and say to
him, Thus says the Lord GOD:
You were the signet of perfection,[z]
full of wisdom and perfect
in beauty.
13 You were in Eden, the
garden of God;
every precious stone was
your covering,
carnelian, chrysolite, and
moonstone,
beryl, onyx, and jasper,
sapphire,[a] turquoise, and emerald;
and worked in gold were
your settings
and your engravings.[b]
On the day that you were created
they were prepared.
14 With an anointed cherub as
guardian I placed you;[c]
you were on the holy
mountain of God;
you walked among the
stones of fire.
15 You were blameless in your ways
from the day that you
were created,
until iniquity was found in you.
16 In the abundance of your trade
you were filled with violence,
and you sinned;
so I cast you as a profane thing
from the mountain of God,
and the guardian cherub
drove you out
from among the stones of fire.
17 Your heart was proud because
of your beauty;
you corrupted your wisdom for
the sake of your splendour.
I cast you to the ground;
I exposed you before kings,
to feast their eyes on you.
18 By the multitude of your iniquities,
in the unrighteousness
of your trade,
you profaned your sanctuaries.
So I brought out fire from
within you;
it consumed you,
and I turned you to ashes
on the earth
in the sight of all who saw you.
19 All who know you among
the peoples
are appalled at you;
you have come to a dreadful end
and shall be no more for ever.

PROCLAMATION AGAINST SIDON

20 The word of the LORD came to me:
21Mortal, set your face towards Sidon,
and prophesy against it, 22and say, Thus
says the Lord GOD:
I am against you, O Sidon,
and I will gain glory in
your midst.
They shall know that I am the LORD
when I execute judgements in it,
and manifest my holiness in it;
23 for I will send pestilence into it,
and bloodshed into its streets;
and the dead shall fall in its midst,
by the sword that is against
it on every side.
And they shall know that I
am the LORD.

24 The house of Israel shall no longer
find a pricking brier or a piercing thorn
among all their neighbours who have
treated them with contempt. And they
shall know that I am the Lord GOD.

FUTURE BLESSING FOR ISRAEL

25 Thus says the Lord GOD: When I
gather the house of Israel from the peoples among whom they are scattered,
and manifest my holiness in them in
the sight of the nations, then they shall
settle on their own soil that I gave to
my servant Jacob. 26They shall live in
safety in it, and shall build houses and
plant vineyards. They shall live in safety,
when I execute judgements upon all
their neighbours who have treated
them with contempt. And they shall
know that I am the LORD their God.

z 28.12 Meaning of Heb uncertain a 28.13 Or *lapis lazuli* b 28.13 Meaning of Heb uncertain c 28.14 Meaning of Heb uncertain

PROCLAMATION AGAINST EGYPT

29 In the tenth year, in the tenth
month, on the twelfth day of the
month, the word of the LORD came to
me: 2 Mortal, set your face against Pharaoh king of Egypt, and prophesy against
him and against all Egypt; 3 speak, and
say, Thus says the Lord GOD:

I am against you,
Pharaoh king of Egypt,
the great dragon sprawling
in the midst of its channels,
saying, 'My Nile is my own;
I made it for myself.'
4 I will put hooks in your jaws,
and make the fish of your
channels stick to your scales.
I will draw you up from
your channels,
with all the fish of your channels
sticking to your scales.
5 I will fling you into the wilderness,
you and all the fish of
your channels;
you shall fall in the open field,
and not be gathered and buried.
To the animals of the earth and
to the birds of the air
I have given you as food.
6 Then all the inhabitants of
Egypt shall know
that I am the LORD
because you[d] were a staff of reed
to the house of Israel;
7 when they grasped you with
the hand, you broke,
and tore all their shoulders;
and when they leaned on
you, you broke,
and made all their legs unsteady.[e]

8 Therefore, thus says the Lord GOD:
I will bring a sword upon you, and will
cut off from you human being and animal; 9 and the land of Egypt shall be a
desolation and a waste. Then they shall
know that I am the LORD.

Because you[f] said, 'The Nile is mine,
and I made it', 10 therefore, I am against
you, and against your channels, and
I will make the land of Egypt an utter
waste and desolation, from Migdol to
Syene, as far as the border of Ethiopia.[g]
11 No human foot shall pass through it,
and no animal foot shall pass through
it; it shall be uninhabited for forty years.
12 I will make the land of Egypt a desolation among desolated countries; and
her cities shall be a desolation for forty
years among cities that are laid waste.
I will scatter the Egyptians among the
nations, and disperse them among the
countries.

13 Further, thus says the Lord GOD:
At the end of forty years I will gather
the Egyptians from the peoples among
whom they were scattered; 14 and I will
restore the fortunes of Egypt, and bring
them back to the land of Pathros, the
land of their origin; and there they shall
be a lowly kingdom. 15 It shall be the
most lowly of the kingdoms, and never
again exalt itself above the nations; and
I will make them so small that they will
never again rule over the nations. 16 The
Egyptians[h] shall never again be the reliance of the house of Israel; they will recall their iniquity, when they turned to
them for aid. Then they shall know that
I am the Lord GOD.

BABYLONIA WILL PLUNDER EGYPT

17 In the twenty-seventh year, in
the first month, on the first day of the
month, the word of the LORD came to
me: 18 Mortal, King Nebuchadrezzar of
Babylon made his army labour hard
against Tyre; every head was made bald
and every shoulder was rubbed bare; yet
neither he nor his army got anything
from Tyre to pay for the labour that he
had expended against it. 19 Therefore,
thus says the Lord GOD: I will give the
land of Egypt to King Nebuchadrezzar
of Babylon; and he shall carry off its
wealth and despoil it and plunder it;
and it shall be the wages for his army.
20 I have given him the land of Egypt as
his payment for which he laboured, because they worked for me, says the Lord
GOD.

21 On that day I will cause a horn to
sprout up for the house of Israel, and I
will open your lips among them. Then
they shall know that I am the LORD.

LAMENTATION FOR EGYPT

30 The word of the LORD came to
me: 2 Mortal, prophesy, and say,
Thus says the Lord GOD:

Wail, 'Alas for the day!'
3 For a day is near,
the day of the LORD is near;
it will be a day of clouds,
a time of doom[i] for the nations.
4 A sword shall come upon Egypt,
and anguish shall be in Ethiopia,[j]

[d] 29.6 Gk Syr Vg: Heb *they* [e] 29.7 Syr: Heb *stand* [f] 29.9 Gk Syr Vg: Heb *he* [g] 29.10 Or *Nubia*; Heb *Cush* [h] 29.16 Heb *It* [i] 30.3 Heb lacks *of doom* [j] 30.4 Or *Nubia*; Heb *Cush*

when the slain fall in Egypt,
and its wealth is carried away,
and its foundations are torn down.
5 Ethiopia,[k] and Put, and Lud, and all
Arabia, and Libya,[l] and the people of
the allied land[m] shall fall with them by
the sword.

6 Thus says the LORD:
Those who support Egypt shall fall,
and its proud might shall
come down;
from Migdol to Syene
they shall fall within it by the sword,
says the Lord GOD.
7 They shall be desolated among other
desolated countries,
and their cities shall lie among
cities laid waste.
8 Then they shall know that I
am the LORD,
when I have set fire to Egypt,
and all who help it are broken.

9 On that day, messengers shall go
out from me in ships to terrify the unsuspecting Ethiopians;[n] and anguish
shall come upon them on the day of
Egypt's doom;[o] for it is coming!

10 Thus says the Lord GOD:
I will put an end to the
hordes of Egypt,
by the hand of King
Nebuchadrezzar of Babylon.
11 He and his people with him, the
most terrible of the nations,
shall be brought in to
destroy the land;
and they shall draw their swords
against Egypt,
and fill the land with the slain.
12 I will dry up the channels,
and will sell the land into the
hand of evildoers;
I will bring desolation upon the
land and everything in it
by the hand of foreigners;
I the LORD have spoken.

13 Thus says the Lord GOD:
I will destroy the idols
and put an end to the
images in Memphis;
there shall no longer be a prince
in the land of Egypt;
so I will put fear in the
land of Egypt.
14 I will make Pathros a desolation,
and will set fire to Zoan,
and will execute acts of
judgement on Thebes.
15 I will pour my wrath upon Pelusium,
the stronghold of Egypt,
and cut off the hordes of Thebes.
16 I will set fire to Egypt;
Pelusium shall be in great agony;
Thebes shall be breached,
and Memphis face
adversaries by day.
17 The young men of On and of Pi-beseth
shall fall by the sword;
and the cities themselves[p]
shall go into captivity.
18 At Tehaphnehes the day
shall be dark,
when I break there the
dominion of Egypt,
and its proud might shall
come to an end;
the city[q] shall be covered
by a cloud,
and its daughter-towns shall
go into captivity.
19 Thus I will execute acts of
judgement on Egypt.
Then they shall know that
I am the LORD.

PROCLAMATION AGAINST PHARAOH

20 In the eleventh year, in the first
month, on the seventh day of the
month, the word of the LORD came to
me: 21 Mortal, I have broken the arm of
Pharaoh king of Egypt; it has not been
bound up for healing or wrapped with a
bandage, so that it may become strong
to wield the sword. 22 Therefore, thus
says the Lord GOD: I am against Pharaoh king of Egypt, and will break his
arms, both the strong arm and the one
that was broken; and I will make the
sword fall from his hand. 23 I will scatter
the Egyptians among the nations, and
disperse them throughout the lands. 24 I
will strengthen the arms of the king of
Babylon, and put my sword in his hand;
but I will break the arms of Pharaoh,
and he will groan before him with the
groans of one mortally wounded. 25 I will
strengthen the arms of the king of Babylon, but the arms of Pharaoh shall fall.
And they shall know that I am the LORD,
when I put my sword into the hand of
the king of Babylon. He shall stretch it
out against the land of Egypt, 26 and I
will scatter the Egyptians among the
nations and disperse them throughout

[k] 30.5 Or *Nubia*; Heb *Cush* [l] 30.5 Compare Gk Syr Vg: Heb *Cub* [m] 30.5 Meaning of Heb uncertain [n] 30.9 Or *Nubians*; Heb *Cush* [o] 30.9 Heb *the day of Egypt* [p] 30.17 Heb *and they* [q] 30.18 Heb *she*

the countries. Then they shall know that
I am the LORD.

THE LOFTY CEDAR

31 In the eleventh year, in the
third month, on the first day of
the month, the word of the LORD came
to me: 2Mortal, say to Pharaoh king of
Egypt and to his hordes:

Whom are you like in your greatness?
3 Consider Assyria, a cedar
of Lebanon,
with fair branches and forest shade,
and of great height,
its top among the clouds.[r]
4 The waters nourished it,
the deep made it grow tall,
making its rivers flow[s]
around the place where
it was planted,
sending forth its streams
to all the trees of the field.
5 So it towered high
above all the trees of the field;
its boughs grew large
and its branches long,
from abundant water in its shoots.
6 All the birds of the air
made their nests in its boughs;
under its branches all the
animals of the field
gave birth to their young;
and in its shade
all great nations lived.
7 It was beautiful in its greatness,
in the length of its branches;
for its roots went down
to abundant water.
8 The cedars in the garden of God
could not rival it,
nor the fir trees equal its boughs;
the plane trees were as nothing
compared with its branches;
no tree in the garden of God
was like it in beauty.
9 I made it beautiful
with its mass of branches,
the envy of all the trees of Eden
that were in the garden of God.

10 Therefore, thus says the Lord GOD:
Because it[t] towered high and set its top
among the clouds,[u] and its heart was
proud of its height, 11I gave it into the
hand of the prince of the nations; he has
dealt with it as its wickedness deserves.
I have cast it out. 12Foreigners from the
most terrible of the nations have cut
it down and left it. On the mountains
and in all the valleys its branches have
fallen, and its boughs lie broken in all
the watercourses of the land; and all the
peoples of the earth went away from its
shade and left it.

13 On its fallen trunk settle
all the birds of the air,
and among its boughs lodge
all the wild animals.

14All this is in order that no trees by the
waters may grow to lofty height or set
their tops among the clouds,[v] and that
no trees that drink water may reach up
to them in height.

For all of them are handed
over to death,
to the world below;
along with all mortals,
with those who go down to the Pit.

15 Thus says the Lord GOD: On the
day it went down to Sheol I closed the
deep over it and covered it; I restrained
its rivers, and its mighty waters were
checked. I clothed Lebanon in gloom for
it, and all the trees of the field fainted
because of it. 16I made the nations quake
at the sound of its fall, when I cast it
down to Sheol with those who go down
to the Pit; and all the trees of Eden, the
choice and best of Lebanon, all that
were well watered, were consoled in
the world below. 17They also went down
to Sheol with it, to those killed by the
sword, along with its allies,[w] those who
lived in its shade among the nations.

18 Which among the trees of Eden
was like you in glory and in greatness?
Now you shall be brought down with
the trees of Eden to the world below;
you shall lie among the uncircumcised,
with those who are killed by the sword.
This is Pharaoh and all his horde, says
the Lord GOD.

LAMENTATION OVER PHARAOH AND EGYPT

32 In the twelfth year, in the
twelfth month, on the first day
of the month, the word of the LORD
came to me: 2Mortal, raise a lamentation over Pharaoh king of Egypt, and
say to him:

You consider yourself a lion
among the nations,
but you are like a dragon
in the seas;
you thrash about in your streams,
trouble the water with your feet,
and foul your[x] streams.

[r] 31.3 Gk: Heb *thick boughs* [s] 31.4 Gk: Heb *rivers going* [t] 31.10 Syr Vg: Heb *you* [u] 31.10 Gk: Heb *thick boughs* [v] 31.14 Gk: Heb *thick boughs* [w] 31.17 Heb *its arms* [x] 32.2 Heb *their*

3 Thus says the Lord GOD:
In an assembly of many peoples
I will throw my net over you;
and I[y] will haul you up
in my dragnet.
4 I will throw you on the ground,
on the open field I will fling you,
and will cause all the birds of the
air to settle on you,
and I will let the wild animals
of the whole earth gorge
themselves on you.
5 I will strew your flesh on
the mountains,
and fill the valleys with
your carcass.[z]
6 I will drench the land with
your flowing blood
up to the mountains,
and the watercourses will
be filled with you.
7 When I blot you out, I will
cover the heavens,
and make their stars dark;
I will cover the sun with a cloud,
and the moon shall not
give its light.
8 All the shining lights of the heavens
I will darken above you,
and put darkness on your land,
says the Lord GOD.
9 I will trouble the hearts of
many peoples,
as I carry you captive[a]
among the nations,
into countries you have not known.
10 I will make many peoples
appalled at you;
their kings shall shudder
because of you.
When I brandish my sword
before them,
they shall tremble at every moment
for their lives, each one of them,
on the day of your downfall.
11 For thus says the Lord GOD:
The sword of the king of Babylon
shall come against you.
12 I will cause your hordes to fall
by the swords of mighty ones,
all of them most terrible
among the nations.
They shall bring to ruin the
pride of Egypt,
and all its hordes shall perish.
13 I will destroy all its livestock
from beside abundant waters;
and no human foot shall trouble
them any more,
nor shall the hoofs of cattle
trouble them.
14 Then I will make their waters clear,
and cause their streams to run
like oil, says the Lord GOD.
15 When I make the land of
Egypt desolate
and when the land is stripped
of all that fills it,
when I strike down all who live in it,
then they shall know that
I am the LORD.
16 This is a lamentation; it
shall be chanted.
The women of the nations
shall chant it.
Over Egypt and all its hordes
they shall chant it,
says the Lord GOD.

DIRGE OVER EGYPT

17 In the twelfth year, in the first
month,[b] on the fifteenth day of the
month, the word of the LORD came to
me:
18 Mortal, wail over the hordes
of Egypt,
and send them down,
with Egypt[c] and the daughters
of majestic nations,
to the world below,
with those who go down
to the Pit.
19 'Whom do you surpass in beauty?
Go down! Be laid to rest with
the uncircumcised!'
20 They shall fall among those who are
killed by the sword. Egypt[d] has been
handed over to the sword; carry away
both it and its hordes. 21 The mighty
chiefs shall speak of them, with their
helpers, out of the midst of Sheol: 'They
have come down, they lie still, the uncircumcised, killed by the sword.'
22 Assyria is there, and all its company, their graves all around it, all of
them killed, fallen by the sword. 23 Their
graves are set in the uttermost parts of
the Pit. Its company is all around its
grave, all of them killed, fallen by the
sword, who spread terror in the land of
the living.
24 Elam is there, and all its hordes
around its grave; all of them killed,
fallen by the sword, who went down uncircumcised into the world below, who
spread terror in the land of the living.
They bear their shame with those who
go down to the Pit. 25 They have made

[y] 32.3 Gk Vg: Heb *they* [z] 32.5 Symmachus Syr Vg: Heb *your height* [a] 32.9 Gk: Heb *bring your destruction* [b] 32.17 Gk: Heb lacks *in the first month* [c] 32.18 Heb *it* [d] 32.20 Heb *It*

Elam[e] a bed among the slain with all its hordes, their graves all around it, all of them uncircumcised, killed by the sword; for terror of them was spread in the land of the living, and they bear their shame with those who go down to the Pit; they are placed among the slain.

26 Meshech and Tubal are there, and all their multitude, their graves all around them, all of them uncircumcised, killed by the sword; for they spread terror in the land of the living. 27 And they do not lie with the fallen warriors of long ago[f] who went down to Sheol with their weapons of war, whose swords were laid under their heads, and whose shields[g] are upon their bones; for the terror of the warriors was in the land of the living. 28 So you shall be broken and lie among the uncircumcised, with those who are killed by the sword.

29 Edom is there, its kings and all its princes, who for all their might are laid with those who are killed by the sword; they lie with the uncircumcised, with those who go down to the Pit.

30 The princes of the north are there, all of them, and all the Sidonians, who have gone down in shame with the slain, for all the terror that they caused by their might; they lie uncircumcised with those who are killed by the sword, and bear their shame with those who go down to the Pit.

31 When Pharaoh sees them, he will be consoled for all his hordes—Pharaoh and all his army, killed by the sword, says the Lord GOD. 32 For he[h] spread terror in the land of the living; therefore he shall be laid to rest among the uncircumcised, with those who are slain by the sword—Pharaoh and all his multitude, says the Lord GOD.

EZEKIEL ISRAEL'S SENTINEL

33 The word of the LORD came to me: 2 O Mortal, speak to your people and say to them, If I bring the sword upon a land, and the people of the land take one of their number as their sentinel; 3 and if the sentinel sees the sword coming upon the land and blows the trumpet and warns the people; 4 then if any who hear the sound of the trumpet do not take warning, and the sword comes and takes them away, their blood shall be upon their own heads. 5 They heard the sound of the trumpet and did not take warning; their blood shall be upon themselves. But if they had taken warning, they would have saved their lives. 6 But if the sentinel sees the sword coming and does not blow the trumpet, so that the people are not warned, and the sword comes and takes any of them, they are taken away in their iniquity, but their blood I will require at the sentinel's hand.

7 So you, mortal, I have made a sentinel for the house of Israel; whenever you hear a word from my mouth, you shall give them warning from me. 8 If I say to the wicked, 'O wicked ones, you shall surely die', and you do not speak to warn the wicked to turn from their ways, the wicked shall die in their iniquity, but their blood I will require at your hand. 9 But if you warn the wicked to turn from their ways, and they do not turn from their ways, the wicked shall die in their iniquity, but you will have saved your life.

GOD'S JUSTICE AND MERCY

10 Now you, mortal, say to the house of Israel, Thus you have said: 'Our transgressions and our sins weigh upon us, and we waste away because of them; how then can we live?' 11 Say to them, As I live, says the Lord GOD, I have no pleasure in the death of the wicked, but that the wicked turn from their ways and live; turn back, turn back from your evil ways; for why will you die, O house of Israel? 12 And you, mortal, say to your people, The righteousness of the righteous shall not save them when they transgress; and as for the wickedness of the wicked, it shall not make them stumble when they turn from their wickedness; and the righteous shall not be able to live by their righteousness[i] when they sin. 13 Though I say to the righteous that they shall surely live, yet if they trust in their righteousness and commit iniquity, none of their righteous deeds shall be remembered; but in the iniquity that they have committed they shall die. 14 Again, though I say to the wicked, 'You shall surely die', yet if they turn from their sin and do what is lawful and right— 15 if the wicked restore the pledge, give back what they have taken by robbery, and walk in the statutes of life, committing no iniquity—they shall surely live, they shall not die. 16 None of the sins that they have committed shall be remembered against them; they have

[e] 32.25 Heb *it* [f] 32.27 Gk Old Latin: Heb *of the uncircumcised* [g] 32.27 Cn: Heb *iniquities* [h] 32.32 Cn: Heb *I* [i] 33.12 Heb *by it*

done what is lawful and right, they shall surely live.

17 Yet your people say, 'The way of the Lord is not just', when it is their own way that is not just. 18When the righteous turn from their righteousness, and commit iniquity, they shall die for it.[j] 19And when the wicked turn from their wickedness, and do what is lawful and right, they shall live by it.[k] 20Yet you say, 'The way of the Lord is not just.' O house of Israel, I will judge all of you according to your ways!

THE FALL OF JERUSALEM

21 In the twelfth year of our exile, in the tenth month, on the fifth day of the month, someone who had escaped from Jerusalem came to me and said, 'The city has fallen.' 22Now the hand of the LORD had been upon me the evening before the fugitive came; but he had opened my mouth by the time the fugitive came to me in the morning; so my mouth was opened, and I was no longer unable to speak.

THE SURVIVORS IN JUDAH

23 The word of the LORD came to me: 24Mortal, the inhabitants of these waste places in the land of Israel keep saying, 'Abraham was only one man, yet he got possession of the land; but we are many; the land is surely given to us to possess.' 25Therefore say to them, Thus says the Lord GOD: You eat flesh with the blood, and lift up your eyes to your idols, and shed blood; shall you then possess the land? 26You depend on your swords, you commit abominations, and each of you defiles his neighbour's wife; shall you then possess the land? 27Say this to them, Thus says the Lord GOD: As I live, surely those who are in the waste places shall fall by the sword; and those who are in the open field I will give to the wild animals to be devoured; and those who are in strongholds and in caves shall die by pestilence. 28I will make the land a desolation and a waste, and its proud might shall come to an end; and the mountains of Israel shall be so desolate that no one will pass through. 29Then they shall know that I am the LORD, when I have made the land a desolation and a waste because of all their abominations that they have committed.

30 As for you, mortal, your people who talk together about you by the walls, and at the doors of the houses, say to one another, each to a neighbour, 'Come and hear what the word is that comes from the LORD.' 31They come to you as people come, and they sit before you as my people, and they hear your words, but they will not obey them. For flattery is on their lips, but their heart is set on their gain. 32To them you are like a singer of love songs,[l] one who has a beautiful voice and plays well on an instrument; they hear what you say, but they will not do it. 33When this comes—and come it will!—then they shall know that a prophet has been among them.

ISRAEL'S FALSE SHEPHERDS

34 The word of the LORD came to me: 2Mortal, prophesy against the shepherds of Israel: prophesy, and say to them—to the shepherds: Thus says the Lord GOD: Ah, you shepherds of Israel who have been feeding yourselves! Should not shepherds feed the sheep? 3You eat the fat, you clothe yourselves with the wool, you slaughter the fatlings; but you do not feed the sheep. 4You have not strengthened the weak, you have not healed the sick, you have not bound up the injured, you have not brought back the strayed, you have not sought the lost, but with force and harshness you have ruled them. 5So they were scattered, because there was no shepherd; and scattered, they became food for all the wild animals. 6My sheep were scattered, they wandered over all the mountains and on every high hill; my sheep were scattered over all the face of the earth, with no one to search or seek for them.

7 Therefore, you shepherds, hear the word of the LORD: 8As I live, says the Lord GOD, because my sheep have become a prey, and my sheep have become food for all the wild animals, since there was no shepherd; and because my shepherds have not searched for my sheep, but the shepherds have fed themselves, and have not fed my sheep; 9therefore, you shepherds, hear the word of the LORD: 10Thus says the Lord GOD, I am against the shepherds; and I will demand my sheep at their hand, and put a stop to their feeding the sheep; no longer shall the shepherds feed themselves. I will rescue my sheep from their mouths, so that they may not be food for them.

[j] 33.18 Heb *them* [k] 33.19 Heb *them*
[l] 33.32 Cn: Heb *like a love song*

GOD THE TRUE SHEPHERD

11 For thus says the Lord GOD: I myself will search for my sheep, and will
seek them out. 12 As shepherds seek out
their flocks when they are among their
scattered sheep, so I will seek out my
sheep. I will rescue them from all the
places to which they have been scattered
on a day of clouds and thick darkness.
13 I will bring them out from the peoples
and gather them from the countries,
and will bring them into their own
land; and I will feed them on the mountains of Israel, by the watercourses, and
in all the inhabited parts of the land. 14 I
will feed them with good pasture, and
the mountain heights of Israel shall be
their pasture; there they shall lie down
in good grazing land, and they shall
feed on rich pasture on the mountains
of Israel. 15 I myself will be the shepherd of my sheep, and I will make them
lie down, says the Lord GOD. 16 I will
seek the lost, and I will bring back the
strayed, and I will bind up the injured,
and I will strengthen the weak, but the
fat and the strong I will destroy. I will
feed them with justice.

17 As for you, my flock, thus says the
Lord GOD: I shall judge between sheep
and sheep, between rams and goats: 18 Is
it not enough for you to feed on the good
pasture, but you must tread down with
your feet the rest of your pasture? When
you drink of clear water, must you foul
the rest with your feet? 19 And must my
sheep eat what you have trodden with
your feet, and drink what you have
fouled with your feet?

20 Therefore, thus says the Lord GOD
to them: I myself will judge between the
fat sheep and the lean sheep. 21 Because
you pushed with flank and shoulder,
and butted at all the weak animals with
your horns until you scattered them far
and wide, 22 I will save my flock, and
they shall no longer be ravaged; and I
will judge between sheep and sheep.

23 I will set up over them one shepherd, my servant David, and he shall
feed them: he shall feed them and be
their shepherd. 24 And I, the LORD,
will be their God, and my servant David shall be prince among them; I, the
LORD, have spoken.

25 I will make with them a covenant
of peace and banish wild animals from
the land, so that they may live in the
wild and sleep in the woods securely. 26 I
will make them and the region around
my hill a blessing; and I will send down
the showers in their season; they shall
be showers of blessing. 27 The trees of
the field shall yield their fruit, and the
earth shall yield its increase. They shall
be secure on their soil; and they shall
know that I am the LORD, when I break
the bars of their yoke, and save them
from the hands of those who enslaved
them. 28 They shall no more be plunder
for the nations, nor shall the animals
of the land devour them; they shall live
in safety, and no one shall make them
afraid. 29 I will provide for them splendid vegetation, so that they shall no
more be consumed with hunger in the
land, and no longer suffer the insults of
the nations. 30 They shall know that I,
the LORD their God, am with them, and
that they, the house of Israel, are my
people, says the Lord GOD. 31 You are my
sheep, the sheep of my pasture,[m] and I
am your God, says the Lord GOD.

JUDGEMENT ON MOUNT SEIR

35 The word of the LORD came
to me: 2 Mortal, set your face
against Mount Seir, and prophesy
against it, 3 and say to it, Thus says the
Lord GOD:

I am against you, Mount Seir;
I stretch out my hand against you
to make you a desolation
and a waste.
4 I lay your towns in ruins;
you shall become a desolation,
and you shall know that
I am the LORD.

5 Because you cherished an ancient enmity, and gave over the people of Israel
to the power of the sword at the time
of their calamity, at the time of their
final punishment; 6 therefore, as I live,
says the Lord GOD, I will prepare you for
blood, and blood shall pursue you; since
you did not hate bloodshed, bloodshed
shall pursue you. 7 I will make Mount
Seir a waste and a desolation; and I will
cut off from it all who come and go. 8 I
will fill its mountains with the slain; on
your hills and in your valleys and in all
your watercourses those killed with the
sword shall fall. 9 I will make you a perpetual desolation, and your cities shall
never be inhabited. Then you shall know
that I am the LORD.

10 Because you said, 'These two nations and these two countries shall be
mine, and we will take possession of
them'—although the LORD was there—

[m] 34.31 Gk OL: Heb *pasture, you are people*

11therefore, as I live, says the Lord GOD,
I will deal with you according to the anger and envy that you showed because
of your hatred against them; and I will
make myself known among you,[n] when
I judge you. 12You shall know that I, the
LORD, have heard all the abusive speech
that you uttered against the mountains
of Israel, saying, 'They are laid desolate,
they are given to us to devour.' 13And
you magnified yourselves against me
with your mouth, and multiplied your
words against me; I heard it. 14Thus
says the Lord GOD: As the whole earth
rejoices, I will make you desolate. 15As
you rejoiced over the inheritance of the
house of Israel, because it was desolate,
so I will deal with you; you shall be desolate, Mount Seir, and all Edom, all of
it. Then they shall know that I am the
LORD.

BLESSING ON ISRAEL

36 And you, mortal, prophesy to
the mountains of Israel, and say:
O mountains of Israel, hear the word of
the LORD. 2Thus says the Lord GOD: Because the enemy said of you, 'Aha!' and,
'The ancient heights have become our
possession', 3therefore prophesy, and say:
Thus says the Lord GOD: Because they
made you desolate indeed, and crushed
you from all sides, so that you became
the possession of the rest of the nations,
and you became an object of gossip and
slander among the people; 4therefore,
O mountains of Israel, hear the word of
the Lord GOD: Thus says the Lord GOD
to the mountains and the hills, the watercourses and the valleys, the desolate
wastes and the deserted towns, which
have become a source of plunder and an
object of derision to the rest of the nations all around; 5therefore thus says
the Lord GOD: I am speaking in my hot
jealousy against the rest of the nations,
and against all Edom, who, with whole-
hearted joy and utter contempt, took my
land as their possession, because of its
pasture, to plunder it. 6Therefore prophesy concerning the land of Israel, and
say to the mountains and hills, to the
watercourses and valleys, Thus says the
Lord GOD: I am speaking in my jealous
wrath, because you have suffered the insults of the nations; 7therefore thus says
the Lord GOD: I swear that the nations
that are all around you shall themselves
suffer insults.

8 But you, O mountains of Israel,
shall shoot out your branches, and yield
your fruit to my people Israel; for they
shall soon come home. 9See now, I am
for you; I will turn to you, and you shall
be tilled and sown; 10and I will multiply
your population, the whole house of Israel, all of it; the towns shall be inhabited and the waste places rebuilt; 11and
I will multiply human beings and animals upon you. They shall increase and
be fruitful; and I will cause you to be
inhabited as in your former times, and
will do more good to you than ever before. Then you shall know that I am the
LORD. 12I will lead people upon you—
my people Israel—and they shall possess you, and you shall be their inheritance. No longer shall you bereave them
of children.

13 Thus says the Lord GOD: Because
they say to you, 'You devour people, and
you bereave your nation of children',
14therefore you shall no longer devour
people and no longer bereave your nation of children, says the Lord GOD;
15and no longer will I let you hear the
insults of the nations, no longer shall
you bear the disgrace of the peoples; and
no longer shall you cause your nation to
stumble, says the Lord GOD.

THE RENEWAL OF ISRAEL

16 The word of the LORD came to me:
17Mortal, when the house of Israel lived
on their own soil, they defiled it with
their ways and their deeds; their conduct in my sight was like the uncleanness of a woman in her menstrual period. 18So I poured out my wrath upon
them for the blood that they had shed
upon the land, and for the idols with
which they had defiled it. 19I scattered
them among the nations, and they were
dispersed through the countries; in accordance with their conduct and their
deeds I judged them. 20But when they
came to the nations, wherever they
came, they profaned my holy name, in
that it was said of them, 'These are the
people of the LORD, and yet they had to
go out of his land.' 21But I had concern
for my holy name, which the house of
Israel had profaned among the nations
to which they came.

22 Therefore say to the house of Israel, Thus says the Lord GOD: It is not for
your sake, O house of Israel, that I am
about to act, but for the sake of my holy
name, which you have profaned among
the nations to which you came. 23I will

[n] **35.11** Gk: Heb *them*

sanctify my great name, which has been profaned among the nations, and which you have profaned among them; and the nations shall know that I am the LORD, says the Lord GOD, when through you I display my holiness before their eyes. 24 I will take you from the nations, and gather you from all the countries, and bring you into your own land. 25 I will sprinkle clean water upon you, and you shall be clean from all your uncleannesses, and from all your idols I will cleanse you. 26 A new heart I will give you, and a new spirit I will put within you; and I will remove from your body the heart of stone and give you a heart of flesh. 27 I will put my spirit within you, and make you follow my statutes and be careful to observe my ordinances. 28 Then you shall live in the land that I gave to your ancestors; and you shall be my people, and I will be your God. 29 I will save you from all your uncleannesses, and I will summon the grain and make it abundant and lay no famine upon you. 30 I will make the fruit of the tree and the produce of the field abundant, so that you may never again suffer the disgrace of famine among the nations. 31 Then you shall remember your evil ways, and your dealings that were not good; and you shall loathe yourselves for your iniquities and your abominable deeds. 32 It is not for your sake that I will act, says the Lord GOD; let that be known to you. Be ashamed and dismayed for your ways, O house of Israel.

33 Thus says the Lord GOD: On the day that I cleanse you from all your iniquities, I will cause the towns to be inhabited, and the waste places shall be rebuilt. 34 The land that was desolate shall be tilled, instead of being the desolation that it was in the sight of all who passed by. 35 And they will say, 'This land that was desolate has become like the garden of Eden; and the waste and desolate and ruined towns are now inhabited and fortified.' 36 Then the nations that are left all around you shall know that I, the LORD, have rebuilt the ruined places, and replanted that which was desolate; I, the LORD, have spoken, and I will do it.

37 Thus says the Lord GOD: I will also let the house of Israel ask me to do this for them: to increase their population like a flock. 38 Like the flock for sacrifices,[o] like the flock at Jerusalem during her appointed festivals, so shall the ruined towns be filled with flocks of people. Then they shall know that I am the LORD.

THE VALLEY OF DRY BONES

37 The hand of the LORD came upon me, and he brought me out by the spirit of the LORD and set me down in the middle of a valley; it was full of bones. 2 He led me all round them; there were very many lying in the valley, and they were very dry. 3 He said to me, 'Mortal, can these bones live?' I answered, 'O Lord GOD, you know.' 4 Then he said to me, 'Prophesy to these bones, and say to them: O dry bones, hear the word of the LORD. 5 Thus says the Lord GOD to these bones: I will cause breath[p] to enter you, and you shall live. 6 I will lay sinews on you, and will cause flesh to come upon you, and cover you with skin, and put breath[q] in you, and you shall live; and you shall know that I am the LORD.'

7 So I prophesied as I had been commanded; and as I prophesied, suddenly there was a noise, a rattling, and the bones came together, bone to its bone. 8 I looked, and there were sinews on them, and flesh had come upon them, and skin had covered them; but there was no breath in them. 9 Then he said to me, 'Prophesy to the breath, prophesy, mortal, and say to the breath:[r] Thus says the Lord GOD: Come from the four winds, O breath,[s] and breathe upon these slain, that they may live.' 10 I prophesied as he commanded me, and the breath came into them, and they lived, and stood on their feet, a vast multitude.

11 Then he said to me, 'Mortal, these bones are the whole house of Israel. They say, "Our bones are dried up, and our hope is lost; we are cut off completely." 12 Therefore prophesy, and say to them, Thus says the Lord GOD: I am going to open your graves, and bring you up from your graves, O my people; and I will bring you back to the land of Israel. 13 And you shall know that I am the LORD, when I open your graves, and bring you up from your graves, O my people. 14 I will put my spirit within you, and you shall live, and I will place you on your own soil; then you shall know that I, the LORD, have spoken and will act, says the LORD.'

[o] **36.38** Heb *flock of holy things* [p] **37.5** Or *spirit* [q] **37.6** Or *spirit* [r] **37.9** Or *wind or spirit* [s] **37.9** Or *wind or spirit*

THE TWO STICKS

15 The word of the LORD came to me:
16 Mortal, take a stick and write on it, 'For
Judah, and the Israelites associated with
it'; then take another stick and write
on it, 'For Joseph (the stick of Ephraim)
and all the house of Israel associated
with it'; 17 and join them together into
one stick, so that they may become one
in your hand. 18 And when your people
say to you, 'Will you not show us what
you mean by these?' 19 say to them, Thus
says the Lord GOD: I am about to take the
stick of Joseph (which is in the hand of
Ephraim) and the tribes of Israel associated with it; and I will put the stick of Judah upon it,[t] and make them one stick, in
order that they may be one in my hand.
20 When the sticks on which you write are
in your hand before their eyes, 21 then say
to them, Thus says the Lord GOD: I will
take the people of Israel from the nations among which they have gone, and
will gather them from every quarter, and
bring them to their own land. 22 I will
make them one nation in the land, on the
mountains of Israel; and one king shall
be king over them all. Never again shall
they be two nations, and never again
shall they be divided into two kingdoms.
23 They shall never again defile themselves with their idols and their detestable things, or with any of their transgressions. I will save them from all the
apostasies into which they have fallen,[u]
and will cleanse them. Then they shall be
my people, and I will be their God.

24 My servant David shall be king
over them; and they shall all have one
shepherd. They shall follow my ordinances and be careful to observe my
statutes. 25 They shall live in the land
that I gave to my servant Jacob, in which
your ancestors lived; they and their
children and their children's children
shall live there for ever; and my servant David shall be their prince for ever.
26 I will make a covenant of peace with
them; it shall be an everlasting covenant
with them; and I will bless[v] them and
multiply them, and will set my sanctuary among them for evermore. 27 My
dwelling-place shall be with them; and
I will be their God, and they shall be my
people. 28 Then the nations shall know
that I the LORD sanctify Israel, when my
sanctuary is among them for evermore.

INVASION BY GOG

38 The word of the LORD came to
me: 2 Mortal, set your face towards Gog, of the land of Magog, the
chief prince of Meshech and Tubal.
Prophesy against him 3 and say: Thus
says the Lord GOD: I am against you,
O Gog, chief prince of Meshech and Tubal; 4 I will turn you round and put hooks
into your jaws, and I will lead you out
with all your army, horses and horsemen, all of them clothed in full armour,
a great company, all of them with shield
and buckler, wielding swords. 5 Persia,
Ethiopia,[w] and Put are with them, all of
them with buckler and helmet; 6 Gomer
and all its troops; Beth-togarmah from
the remotest parts of the north with all
its troops—many peoples are with you.

7 Be ready and keep ready, you and
all the companies that are assembled
around you, and hold yourselves in reserve for them. 8 After many days you
shall be mustered; in the latter years you
shall go against a land restored from
war, a land where people were gathered
from many nations on the mountains
of Israel, which had long lain waste; its
people were brought out from the nations and now are living in safety, all
of them. 9 You shall advance, coming
on like a storm; you shall be like a cloud
covering the land, you and all your
troops, and many peoples with you.

10 Thus says the Lord GOD: On that
day thoughts will come into your mind,
and you will devise an evil scheme.
11 You will say, 'I will go up against the
land of unwalled villages; I will fall upon
the quiet people who live in safety, all
of them living without walls, and having no bars or gates'; 12 to seize spoil and
carry off plunder; to assail the waste
places that are now inhabited, and the
people who were gathered from the
nations, who are acquiring cattle and
goods, who live at the centre[x] of the
earth. 13 Sheba and Dedan and the merchants of Tarshish and all its young
warriors[y] will say to you, 'Have you
come to seize spoil? Have you assembled your horde to carry off plunder, to
carry away silver and gold, to take away
cattle and goods, to seize a great amount
of booty?'

14 Therefore, mortal, prophesy, and
say to Gog: Thus says the Lord GOD: On
that day when my people Israel are living

[t] 37.19 Heb *I will put them upon it*
[u] 37.23 Another reading is *from all the settlements in which they have sinned*
[v] 37.26 Tg: Heb *give* [w] 38.5 Or *Nubia*; Heb *Cush*
[x] 38.12 Heb *navel* [y] 38.13 Heb *young lions*

securely, you will rouse yourself[z] 15and
come from your place out of the remotest parts of the north, you and many
peoples with you, all of them riding on
horses, a great horde, a mighty army;
16you will come up against my people
Israel, like a cloud covering the earth. In
the latter days I will bring you against
my land, so that the nations may know
me, when through you, O Gog, I display
my holiness before their eyes.

JUDGEMENT ON GOG

17 Thus says the Lord GOD: Are you
he of whom I spoke in former days by
my servants the prophets of Israel, who
in those days prophesied for years that
I would bring you against them? 18On
that day, when Gog comes against the
land of Israel, says the Lord GOD, my
wrath shall be aroused. 19For in my
jealousy and in my blazing wrath I declare: On that day there shall be a great
shaking in the land of Israel; 20the fish
of the sea, and the birds of the air, and
the animals of the field, and all creeping
things that creep on the ground, and all
human beings that are on the face of
the earth, shall quake at my presence,
and the mountains shall be thrown
down, and the cliffs shall fall, and every
wall shall tumble to the ground. 21I will
summon the sword against Gog[a] in[b] all
my mountains, says the Lord GOD; the
swords of all will be against their comrades. 22With pestilence and bloodshed
I will enter into judgement with him;
and I will pour down torrential rains
and hailstones, fire and sulphur, upon
him and his troops and the many peoples that are with him. 23So I will display my greatness and my holiness and
make myself known in the eyes of many
nations. Then they shall know that I am
the LORD.

GOG'S ARMIES DESTROYED

39 And you, mortal, prophesy
against Gog, and say: Thus says
the Lord GOD: I am against you, O Gog,
chief prince of Meshech and Tubal! 2I
will turn you round and drive you forwards, and bring you up from the remotest parts of the north, and lead you
against the mountains of Israel. 3I will
strike your bow from your left hand, and
will make your arrows drop out of your
right hand. 4You shall fall on the mountains of Israel, you and all your troops
and the peoples that are with you; I will
give you to birds of prey of every kind
and to the wild animals to be devoured.
5You shall fall in the open field; for I
have spoken, says the Lord GOD. 6I will
send fire on Magog and on those who
live securely in the coastlands; and they
shall know that I am the LORD.

7 My holy name I will make known
among my people Israel; and I will not
let my holy name be profaned any more;
and the nations shall know that I am
the LORD, the Holy One in Israel. 8It has
come! It has happened, says the Lord GOD.
This is the day of which I have spoken.

9 Then those who live in the towns of
Israel will go out and make fires of the
weapons and burn them—bucklers and
shields, bows and arrows, hand-pikes
and spears—and they will make fires
of them for seven years. 10They will not
need to take wood out of the field or cut
down any trees in the forests, for they
will make their fires of the weapons;
they will despoil those who despoiled
them, and plunder those who plundered them, says the Lord GOD.

THE BURIAL OF GOG

11 On that day I will give to Gog a
place for burial in Israel, the Valley of
the Travellers[c] east of the sea; it shall
block the path of the travellers, for there
Gog and all his horde will be buried; it
shall be called the Valley of Hamon-gog.[d]
12Seven months the house of Israel shall
spend burying them, in order to cleanse
the land. 13All the people of the land
shall bury them; and it will bring them
honour on the day that I show my glory,
says the Lord GOD. 14They will set apart
men to pass through the land regularly
and bury any invaders[e] who remain on
the face of the land, so as to cleanse it;
for seven months they shall make their
search. 15As the searchers[f] pass through
the land, anyone who sees a human bone
shall set up a sign by it, until the buriers
have buried it in the Valley of Hamon-
gog.[g] 16(A city Hamonah[h] is there also.)
Thus they shall cleanse the land.

17 As for you, mortal, thus says the
Lord GOD: Speak to the birds of every
kind and to all the wild animals: Assemble and come, gather from all around to
the sacrificial feast that I am preparing
for you, a great sacrificial feast on the

[z] **38.14** Gk: Heb *will you not know?* [a] **38.21** Heb *him* [b] **38.21** Heb *to* or *for* [c] **39.11** Or *of the Abarim* [d] **39.11** That is, *the Horde of Gog* [e] **39.14** Heb *travellers* [f] **39.15** Heb *travellers* [g] **39.15** That is, *the Horde of Gog* [h] **39.16** That is *The Horde*

mountains of Israel, and you shall eat flesh and drink blood. 18You shall eat the flesh of the mighty, and drink the blood of the princes of the earth—of rams, of lambs, and of goats, of bulls, all of them fatlings of Bashan. 19You shall eat fat until you are filled, and drink blood until you are drunk, at the sacrificial feast that I am preparing for you. 20And you shall be filled at my table with horses and charioteers,[i] with warriors and all kinds of soldiers, says the Lord GOD.

ISRAEL RESTORED TO THE LAND

21 I will display my glory among the nations; and all the nations shall see my judgement that I have executed, and my hand that I have laid on them. 22The house of Israel shall know that I am the LORD their God, from that day forward. 23And the nations shall know that the house of Israel went into captivity for their iniquity, because they dealt treacherously with me. So I hid my face from them and gave them into the hand of their adversaries, and they all fell by the sword. 24I dealt with them according to their uncleanness and their transgressions, and hid my face from them.

25 Therefore, thus says the Lord GOD: Now I will restore the fortunes of Jacob, and have mercy on the whole house of Israel; and I will be jealous for my holy name. 26They shall forget[j] their shame, and all the treachery they have practised against me, when they live securely in their land with no one to make them afraid, 27when I have brought them back from the peoples and gathered them from their enemies' lands, and through them have displayed my holiness in the sight of many nations. 28Then they shall know that I am the LORD their God because I sent them into exile among the nations, and then gathered them into their own land. I will leave none of them behind; 29and I will never again hide my face from them, when I pour out my spirit upon the house of Israel, says the Lord GOD.

THE VISION OF THE NEW TEMPLE

40 In the twenty-fifth year of our exile, at the beginning of the year, on the tenth day of the month, in the fourteenth year after the city was struck down, on that very day, the hand of the LORD was upon me, and he brought me there. 2He brought me, in visions of God, to the land of Israel, and set me down upon a very high mountain, on which was a structure like a city to the south. 3When he brought me there, a man was there, whose appearance shone like bronze, with a linen cord and a measuring reed in his hand; and he was standing in the gateway. 4The man said to me, 'Mortal, look closely and listen attentively, and set your mind upon all that I shall show you, for you were brought here in order that I might show it to you; declare all that you see to the house of Israel.'

5 Now there was a wall all round the outside of the temple area. The length of the measuring reed in the man's hand was six long cubits, each being a cubit and a handbreadth in length; so he measured the thickness of the wall, one reed; and the height, one reed. 6Then he went into the gateway facing east, going up its steps, and measured the threshold of the gate, one reed deep.[k] There were 7recesses, and each recess was one reed wide and one reed deep; and the space between the recesses, five cubits; and the threshold of the gate by the vestibule of the gate at the inner end was one reed deep. 8Then he measured the inner vestibule of the gateway, one cubit. 9Then he measured the vestibule of the gateway, eight cubits; and its pilasters, two cubits; and the vestibule of the gate was at the inner end. 10There were three recesses on either side of the east gate; the three were of the same size; and the pilasters on either side were of the same size. 11Then he measured the width of the opening of the gateway, ten cubits; and the width of the gateway, thirteen cubits. 12There was a barrier before the recesses, one cubit on either side; and the recesses were six cubits on either side. 13Then he measured the gate from the back[l] of one recess to the back[m] of the other, a width of twenty-five cubits, from wall to wall.[n] 14He measured[o] also the vestibule, twenty cubits; and the gate next to the pilaster on every side of the court.[p] 15From the front of the gate at the entrance to the end of the inner vestibule of the gate was fifty cubits. 16The recesses and their pilasters had windows, with shutters[q] on the inside of the gateway all round, and the

[i] 39.20 Heb *chariots* [j] 39.26 Another reading is *They shall bear* [k] 40.6 Heb *deep, and one threshold, one reed deep* [l] 40.13 Gk: Heb *roof* [m] 40.13 Gk: Heb *roof* [n] 40.13 Heb *opening facing opening* [o] 40.14 Heb *made* [p] 40.14 Meaning of Heb uncertain [q] 40.16 Meaning of Heb uncertain

vestibules also had windows on the inside all round; and on the pilasters were
palm trees.
17 Then he brought me into the outer
court; there were chambers there, and a
pavement, all round the court; thirty
chambers fronted on the pavement.
18 The pavement ran along the side of
the gates, corresponding to the length
of the gates; this was the lower pavement. 19 Then he measured the distance
from the inner front of[r] the lower gate
to the outer front of the inner court, one
hundred cubits.[s]
20 Then he measured the gate of the
outer court that faced north—its depth
and width. 21 Its recesses, three on either
side, and its pilasters and its vestibule
were of the same size as those of the
first gate; its depth was fifty cubits, and
its width twenty-five cubits. 22 Its windows, its vestibule, and its palm trees
were of the same size as those of the
gate that faced towards the east. Seven
steps led up to it; and its vestibule was
on the inside.[t] 23 Opposite the gate on
the north, as on the east, was a gate to
the inner court; he measured from gate
to gate, one hundred cubits.
24 Then he led me towards the south,
and there was a gate on the south; and
he measured its pilasters and its vestibule; they had the same dimensions as
the others. 25 There were windows all
round in it and in its vestibule, like the
windows of the others; its depth was
fifty cubits, and its width twenty-five
cubits. 26 There were seven steps leading up to it; its vestibule was on the inside.[u] It had palm trees on its pilasters,
one on either side. 27 There was a gate
on the south of the inner court; and he
measured from gate to gate towards the
south, one hundred cubits.
28 Then he brought me to the inner
court by the south gate, and he measured the south gate; it was of the same
dimensions as the others. 29 Its recesses,
its pilasters, and its vestibule were of the
same size as the others; and there were
windows all round in it and in its vestibule; its depth was fifty cubits, and its
width twenty-five cubits. 30 There were
vestibules all round, twenty-five cubits
deep and five cubits wide. 31 Its vestibule
faced the outer court, and palm trees
were on its pilasters, and its stairway
had eight steps.
32 Then he brought me to the inner
court on the east side, and he measured
the gate; it was of the same size as the
others. 33 Its recesses, its pilasters, and
its vestibule were of the same dimensions as the others; and there were windows all round in it and in its vestibule;
its depth was fifty cubits, and its width
twenty-five cubits. 34 Its vestibule faced
the outer court, and it had palm trees on
its pilasters, on either side; and its stairway had eight steps.
35 Then he brought me to the north
gate, and he measured it; it had the
same dimensions as the others. 36 Its
recesses, its pilasters, and its vestibule
were of the same size as the others;[v] and
it had windows all round. Its depth was
fifty cubits, and its width twenty-five
cubits. 37 Its vestibule[w] faced the outer
court, and it had palm trees on its pilasters, on either side; and its stairway had
eight steps.
38 There was a chamber with its
door in the vestibule of the gate,[x] where
the burnt-offering was to be washed.
39 And in the vestibule of the gate were
two tables on either side, on which the
burnt-offering and the sin-offering and
the guilt-offering were to be slaughtered. 40 On the outside of the vestibule[y]
at the entrance of the north gate were
two tables; and on the other side of the
vestibule of the gate were two tables.
41 Four tables were on the inside, and
four tables on the outside of the side of
the gate, eight tables, on which the sacrifices were to be slaughtered. 42 There
were also four tables of hewn stone for
the burnt-offering, a cubit and a half
long, and one cubit and a half wide, and
one cubit high, on which the instruments were to be laid with which the
burnt-offerings and the sacrifices were
slaughtered. 43 There were pegs, one
handbreadth long, fastened all round
the inside. And on the tables the flesh of
the offering was to be laid.
44 On the outside of the inner gateway there were chambers for the singers in the inner court, one[z] at the side
of the north gate facing south, the other
at the side of the east gate facing north.
45 He said to me, 'This chamber that faces
south is for the priests who have charge
of the temple, 46 and the chamber that

[r] **40.19** Compare Gk: Heb *from before*
[s] **40.19** Heb adds *the east and the north*
[t] **40.22** Gk: Heb *before them* [u] **40.26** Gk: Heb *before them* [v] **40.36** One Ms: Compare verses 29 and 33: MT lacks *were of the same size as the others* [w] **40.37** Gk Vg Compare verses 26, 31, 34: Heb *pilasters* [x] **40.38** Cn: Heb *at the pilasters of the gates* [y] **40.40** Cn: Heb *to him who goes up*
[z] **40.44** Heb lacks *one*

faces north is for the priests who have
charge of the altar; these are the descendants of Zadok, who alone among the descendants of Levi may come near to the
LORD to minister to him.' 47He measured
the court, one hundred cubits deep, and
one hundred cubits wide, a square; and
the altar was in front of the temple.

THE TEMPLE

48 Then he brought me to the vestibule of the temple and measured the pilasters of the vestibule, five cubits on either side; and the width of the gate was
fourteen cubits; and the side walls of the
gate were three cubits[a] on either side.
49The depth of the vestibule was twenty
cubits, and the width twelve[b] cubits; ten
steps led up[c] to it; and there were pillars
beside the pilasters on either side.

41 Then he brought me to the nave,
and measured the pilasters; on
each side six cubits was the width of the
pilasters.[d] 2The width of the entrance
was ten cubits; and the side walls of the
entrance were five cubits on either side.
He measured the length of the nave,
forty cubits, and its width, twenty cubits. 3Then he went into the inner room
and measured the pilasters of the entrance, two cubits; and the width of the
entrance, six cubits; and the side walls[e]
of the entrance, seven cubits. 4He measured the depth of the room, twenty
cubits, and its width, twenty cubits, beyond the nave. And he said to me, This
is the most holy place.

5 Then he measured the wall of the
temple, six cubits thick; and the width
of the side chambers, four cubits, all
round the temple. 6The side chambers
were in three stories, one over another,
thirty in each story. There were offsets[f]
all round the wall of the temple to serve
as supports for the side chambers, so
that they should not be supported by
the wall of the temple. 7The passage-
way[g] of the side chambers widened
from story to story; for the structure
was supplied with a stairway all round
the temple. For this reason the structure became wider from story to story.
One ascended from the bottom story to
the uppermost story by way of the middle one. 8I saw also that the temple had
a raised platform all around; the foundations of the side chambers measured
a full reed of six long cubits. 9The thickness of the outer wall of the side chambers was five cubits; and the free space
between the side chambers of the temple 10and the chambers of the court was
a width of twenty cubits all round the
temple on every side. 11The side chambers opened on to the area left free, one
door towards the north, and another
door towards the south; and the width
of the part that was left free was five cubits all round.

12 The building that was facing the
temple yard on the west side was seventy cubits wide; and the wall of the
building was five cubits thick all round,
and its depth ninety cubits.

13 Then he measured the temple, one
hundred cubits deep; and the yard and
the building with its walls, one hundred
cubits deep; 14also the width of the east
front of the temple and the yard, one
hundred cubits.

15 Then he measured the depth of
the building facing the yard at the west,
together with its galleries[h] on either
side, one hundred cubits.

The nave of the temple and the inner
room and the outer[i] vestibule 16were
panelled,[j] and, all round, all three had
windows with recessed[k] frames. Facing
the threshold the temple was panelled
with wood all round, from the floor up
to the windows (now the windows were
covered), 17to the space above the door,
even to the inner room, and on the outside. And on all the walls all round in
the inner room and the nave there was
a pattern.[l] 18It was formed of cherubim
and palm trees, a palm tree between
cherub and cherub. Each cherub had
two faces: 19a human face turned towards the palm tree on one side, and the
face of a young lion turned towards the
palm tree on the other side. They were
carved on the whole temple all round;
20from the floor to the area above the
door, cherubim and palm trees were
carved on the wall.[m]

21 The doorposts of the nave were
square. In front of the holy place was
something resembling 22an altar of
wood, three cubits high, two cubits
long, and two cubits wide;[n] its corners,

[a] **40.48** Gk: Heb *and the width of the gate was three cubits* [b] **40.49** Gk: Heb *eleven*
[c] **40.49** Gk: Heb *and by steps that went up*
[d] **41.1** Compare Gk: Heb *tent* [e] **41.3** Gk: Heb *width* [f] **41.6** Gk Compare 1 Kings 6.6: Heb *they entered* [g] **41.7** Cn: Heb *it was surrounded*
[h] **41.15** Cn: Meaning of Heb uncertain
[i] **41.15** Gk: Heb *of the court* [j] **41.16** Gk: Heb *the thresholds* [k] **41.16** Cn Compare Gk 1 Kings 6.4: Meaning of Heb uncertain [l] **41.17** Heb *measures*
[m] **41.20** Cn Compare verse 25: Heb *and the wall*
[n] **41.22** Gk: Heb lacks *two cubits wide*

its base,[o] and its walls were of wood. He
said to me, 'This is the table that stands
before the LORD.' 23 The nave and the
holy place had each a double door. 24 The
doors had two leaves apiece, two swing-
ing leaves for each door. 25 On the doors
of the nave were carved cherubim and
palm trees, such as were carved on the
walls; and there was a canopy of wood
in front of the vestibule outside. 26 And
there were recessed windows and palm
trees on either side, on the side walls of
the vestibule.[p]

THE HOLY CHAMBERS AND THE OUTER WALL

42 Then he led me out into the
outer court, towards the north,
and he brought me to the chambers that
were opposite the temple yard and opposite the building on the north. 2 The
length of the building that was on the
north side[q] was[r] one hundred cubits,
and the width fifty cubits. 3 Across the
twenty cubits that belonged to the inner court, and facing the pavement that
belonged to the outer court, the chambers rose[s] gallery[t] by gallery[u] in three
stories. 4 In front of the chambers was
a passage on the inner side, ten cubits
wide and one hundred cubits deep,[v] and
its[w] entrances were on the north. 5 Now
the upper chambers were narrower,
for the galleries[x] took more away from
them than from the lower and middle
chambers in the building. 6 For they
were in three stories, and they had no
pillars like the pillars of the outer[y] court;
for this reason the upper chambers were
set back from the ground more than the
lower and the middle ones. 7 There was
a wall outside parallel to the chambers,
towards the outer court, opposite the
chambers, fifty cubits long. 8 For the
chambers on the outer court were fifty
cubits long, while those opposite the
temple were one hundred cubits long.
9 At the foot of these chambers ran a
passage that one entered from the east
in order to enter them from the outer
court. 10 The width of the passage[z] was
fixed by the wall of the court.

On the south[a] also, opposite the vacant area and opposite the building,
there were chambers 11 with a passage
in front of them; they were similar to
the chambers on the north, of the same
length and width, with the same exits[b]
and arrangements and doors. 12 So the
entrances of the chambers to the south
were entered through the entrance at
the head of the corresponding passage,
from the east, along the matching wall.[c]

13 Then he said to me, 'The north
chambers and the south chambers opposite the vacant area are the holy chambers, where the priests who approach
the LORD shall eat the most holy offerings; there they shall deposit the most
holy offerings—the grain-offering, the
sin-offering, and the guilt-offering—for
the place is holy. 14 When the priests enter the holy place, they shall not go out
of it into the outer court without laying
there the vestments in which they minister, for these are holy; they shall put
on other garments before they go near
to the area open to the people.'

15 When he had finished measuring
the interior of the temple area, he led
me out by the gate that faces east, and
measured the temple area all round.
16 He measured the east side with the
measuring reed, five hundred cubits by
the measuring reed. 17 Then he turned
and measured[d] the north side, five
hundred cubits by the measuring reed.
18 Then he turned and measured[e] the
south side, five hundred cubits by the
measuring reed. 19 Then he turned to
the west side and measured, five hundred cubits by the measuring reed. 20 He
measured it on the four sides. It had a
wall around it, five hundred cubits long
and five hundred cubits wide, to make
a separation between the holy and the
common.

THE DIVINE GLORY RETURNS TO THE TEMPLE

43 Then he brought me to the gate,
the gate facing east. 2 And there,
the glory of the God of Israel was coming from the east; the sound was like the
sound of mighty waters; and the earth
shone with his glory. 3 The[f] vision I saw
was like the vision that I had seen when
he came to destroy the city, and[g] like
the vision that I had seen by the river

[o] 41.22 Gk: Heb *length* [p] 41.26 Cn: Heb *vestibule. And the side chambers of the temple and the canopies* [q] 42.2 Gk: Heb *door* [r] 42.2 Gk: Heb *before the length* [s] 42.3 Heb lacks *the chambers rose* [t] 42.3 Meaning of Heb uncertain [u] 42.3 Meaning of Heb uncertain [v] 42.4 Gk Syr: Heb *a way of one cubit* [w] 42.4 Heb *their* [x] 42.5 Meaning of Heb uncertain [y] 42.6 Gk: Heb lacks *outer* [z] 42.10 Heb lacks *of the passage* [a] 42.10 Gk: Heb *east* [b] 42.11 Heb *and all their exits* [c] 42.12 Meaning of Heb uncertain [d] 42.17 Gk: Heb *measuring reed all round. He measured* [e] 42.18 Gk: Heb *measuring reed all round. He measured* [f] 43.3 Gk: Heb *Like the vision* [g] 43.3 Syr: Heb *and the visions*

Chebar; and I fell upon my face. 4As the
glory of the LORD entered the temple
by the gate facing east, 5the spirit lifted
me up, and brought me into the inner
court; and the glory of the LORD filled
the temple.

6 While the man was standing beside me, I heard someone speaking to
me out of the temple. 7He said to me:
Mortal, this is the place of my throne
and the place for the soles of my feet,
where I will reside among the people of
Israel for ever. The house of Israel shall
no more defile my holy name, neither
they nor their kings, by their whoring,
and by the corpses of their kings at their
death.[h] 8When they placed their threshold by my threshold and their doorposts beside my doorposts, with only a
wall between me and them, they were
defiling my holy name by their abominations that they committed; therefore
I have consumed them in my anger.
9Now let them put away their idolatry
and the corpses of their kings far from
me, and I will reside among them for
ever.

10 As for you, mortal, describe the
temple to the house of Israel, and let
them measure the pattern; and let them
be ashamed of their iniquities. 11When
they are ashamed of all that they have
done, make known to them the plan of
the temple, its arrangement, its exits
and its entrances, and its whole form—
all its ordinances and its entire plan and
all its laws; and write it down in their
sight, so that they may observe and
follow the entire plan and all its ordinances. 12This is the law of the temple:
the whole territory on the top of the
mountain all around shall be most holy.
This is the law of the temple.

THE ALTAR

13 These are the dimensions of the
altar by cubits (the cubit being one cubit
and a handbreadth): its base shall be one
cubit high,[i] and one cubit wide, with a
rim of one span round its edge. This
shall be the height of the altar: 14From
the base on the ground to the lower
ledge, two cubits, with a width of one
cubit; and from the smaller ledge to the
larger ledge, four cubits, with a width
of one cubit; 15and the altar hearth, four
cubits; and from the altar hearth projecting upwards, four horns. 16The altar
hearth shall be square, twelve cubits
long by twelve wide. 17The ledge also
shall be square, fourteen cubits long by
fourteen wide, with a rim round it half
a cubit wide, and its surrounding base,
one cubit. Its steps shall face east.

18 Then he said to me: Mortal, thus
says the Lord GOD: These are the ordinances for the altar: On the day when
it is erected for offering burnt-offerings
upon it and for dashing blood against it,
19you shall give to the levitical priests
of the family of Zadok, who draw near
to me to minister to me, says the Lord
GOD, a bull for a sin-offering. 20And you
shall take some of its blood, and put it
on the four horns of the altar, and on the
four corners of the ledge, and upon the
rim all round; thus you shall purify it
and make atonement for it. 21You shall
also take the bull of the sin-offering, and
it shall be burnt in the appointed place
belonging to the temple, outside the sacred area.

22 On the second day you shall offer
a male goat without blemish for a sin-
offering; and the altar shall be purified,
as it was purified with the bull. 23When
you have finished purifying it, you shall
offer a bull without blemish and a ram
from the flock without blemish. 24You
shall present them before the LORD, and
the priests shall throw salt on them and
offer them up as a burnt-offering to the
LORD. 25For seven days you shall provide daily a goat for a sin-offering; also
a bull and a ram from the flock, without
blemish, shall be provided. 26For seven
days shall they make atonement for the
altar and cleanse it, and so consecrate it.
27When these days are over, then from
the eighth day onwards the priests shall
offer upon the altar your burnt-offerings
and your offerings of well-being; and I
will accept you, says the Lord GOD.

THE CLOSED GATE

44 Then he brought me back to
the outer gate of the sanctuary,
which faces east; and it was shut. 2The
LORD said to me: This gate shall remain
shut; it shall not be opened, and no one
shall enter by it; for the LORD, the God
of Israel, has entered by it; therefore it
shall remain shut. 3Only the prince,
because he is a prince, may sit in it to
eat food before the LORD; he shall enter
by way of the vestibule of the gate, and
shall go out by the same way.

h 43.7 Or *on their high places* i 43.13 Gk: Heb lacks *high*

ADMISSION TO THE TEMPLE

4 Then he brought me by way of the
north gate to the front of the temple;
and I looked, and lo! the glory of the
LORD filled the temple of the LORD; and
I fell upon my face. 5 The LORD said to
me: Mortal, mark well, look closely, and
listen attentively to all that I shall tell
you concerning all the ordinances of the
temple of the LORD and all its laws; and
mark well those who may be admitted
to[j] the temple and all those who are to
be excluded from the sanctuary. 6 Say
to the rebellious house,[k] to the house of
Israel, Thus says the Lord GOD: O house
of Israel, let there be an end to all your
abominations 7 in admitting foreigners,
uncircumcised in heart and flesh, to be
in my sanctuary, profaning my temple
when you offer to me my food, the fat
and the blood. You[l] have broken my
covenant with all your abominations.
8 And you have not kept charge of my sacred offerings; but you have appointed
foreigners[m] to act for you in keeping my
charge in my sanctuary.

9 Thus says the Lord GOD: No foreigner, uncircumcised in heart and
flesh, of all the foreigners who are
among the people of Israel, shall enter
my sanctuary. 10 But the Levites who
went far from me, going astray from
me after their idols when Israel went
astray, shall bear their punishment.
11 They shall be ministers in my sanctuary, having oversight at the gates of the
temple, and serving in the temple; they
shall slaughter the burnt-offering and
the sacrifice for the people, and they
shall attend on them and serve them.
12 Because they ministered to them before their idols and made the house of
Israel stumble into iniquity, therefore I
have sworn concerning them, says the
Lord GOD, that they shall bear their
punishment. 13 They shall not come near
to me, to serve me as priest, nor come
near any of my sacred offerings, the
things that are most sacred; but they
shall bear their shame, and the consequences of the abominations that they
have committed. 14 Yet I will appoint
them to keep charge of the temple, to do
all its chores, all that is to be done in it.

THE LEVITICAL PRIESTS

15 But the levitical priests, the descendants of Zadok, who kept the
charge of my sanctuary when the people of Israel went astray from me, shall
come near to me to minister to me; and
they shall attend me to offer me the fat
and the blood, says the Lord GOD. 16 It
is they who shall enter my sanctuary,
it is they who shall approach my table, to minister to me, and they shall
keep my charge. 17 When they enter
the gates of the inner court, they shall
wear linen vestments; they shall have
nothing of wool on them, while they
minister at the gates of the inner court,
and within. 18 They shall have linen turbans on their heads, and linen undergarments on their loins; they shall not
bind themselves with anything that
causes sweat. 19 When they go out into
the outer court to the people, they shall
remove the vestments in which they
have been ministering, and lay them in
the holy chambers; and they shall put
on other garments, so that they may
not communicate holiness to the people
with their vestments. 20 They shall not
shave their heads or let their locks grow
long; they shall only trim the hair of
their heads. 21 No priest shall drink wine
when he enters the inner court. 22 They
shall not marry a widow, or a divorced
woman, but only a virgin of the stock of
the house of Israel, or a widow who is
the widow of a priest. 23 They shall teach
my people the difference between the
holy and the common, and show them
how to distinguish between the unclean and the clean. 24 In a controversy
they shall act as judges, and they shall
decide it according to my judgements.
They shall keep my laws and my statutes regarding all my appointed festivals, and they shall keep my sabbaths
holy. 25 They shall not defile themselves
by going near to a dead person; for father or mother, however, and for son
or daughter, and for brother or unmarried sister they may defile themselves.
26 After he has become clean, they shall
count seven days for him. 27 On the day
that he goes into the holy place, into
the inner court, to minister in the holy
place, he shall offer his sin-offering, says
the Lord GOD.

28 This shall be their inheritance: I
am their inheritance; and you shall give
them no holding in Israel; I am their
holding. 29 They shall eat the grain-offering, the sin-offering, and the guilt-offering; and every devoted thing in Israel shall be theirs. 30 The first of all the
first fruits of all kinds, and every offer-

[j] 44.5 Cn: Heb *the entrance of* [k] 44.6 Gk: Heb lacks *house* [l] 44.7 Gk Syr Vg: Heb *They* [m] 44.8 Heb lacks *foreigners*

ing of all kinds from all your offerings, shall belong to the priests; you shall also give to the priests the first of your dough, in order that a blessing may rest on your house. 31The priests shall not eat of anything, whether bird or animal, that died of itself or was torn by animals.

THE HOLY DISTRICT

45 When you allot the land as an inheritance, you shall set aside for the LORD a portion of the land as a holy district, twenty-five thousand cubits long and twenty[n] thousand cubits wide; it shall be holy throughout its entire extent. 2Of this, a square plot of five hundred by five hundred cubits shall be for the sanctuary, with fifty cubits for an open space around it. 3In the holy district you shall measure off a section twenty-five thousand cubits long and ten thousand wide, in which shall be the sanctuary, the most holy place. 4It shall be a holy portion of the land; it shall be for the priests, who minister in the sanctuary and approach the LORD to minister to him; and it shall be both a place for their houses and a holy place for the sanctuary. 5Another section, twenty-five thousand cubits long and ten thousand cubits wide, shall be for the Levites who minister at the temple, as their holding for cities to live in.[o]

6 Alongside the portion set apart as the holy district you shall assign as a holding for the city an area five thousand cubits wide, and twenty-five thousand cubits long; it shall belong to the whole house of Israel.

7 And to the prince shall belong the land on both sides of the holy district and the holding of the city, alongside the holy district and the holding of the city, on the west and on the east, corresponding in length to one of the tribal portions, and extending from the western to the eastern boundary 8of the land. It is to be his property in Israel. And my princes shall no longer oppress my people; but they shall let the house of Israel have the land according to their tribes.

9 Thus says the Lord GOD: Enough, O princes of Israel! Put away violence and oppression, and do what is just and right. Cease your evictions of my people, says the Lord GOD.

WEIGHTS AND MEASURES

10 You shall have honest balances, an honest ephah, and an honest bath.[p] 11The ephah and the bath shall be of the same measure, the bath containing one-tenth of a homer, and the ephah one-tenth of a homer; the homer shall be the standard measure. 12The shekel shall be twenty gerahs. Twenty shekels, twenty-five shekels, and fifteen shekels shall make a mina for you.

OFFERINGS

13 This is the offering that you shall make: one-sixth of an ephah from each homer of wheat, and one-sixth of an ephah from each homer of barley, 14and as the fixed portion of oil,[q] one-tenth of a bath from each cor (the cor,[r] like the homer, contains ten baths); 15and one sheep from every flock of two hundred, from the pastures of Israel. This is the offering for grain-offerings, burnt-offerings, and offerings of well-being, to make atonement for them, says the Lord GOD. 16All the people of the land shall join with the prince in Israel in making this offering. 17But this shall be the obligation of the prince regarding the burnt-offerings, grain-offerings, and drink-offerings at the festivals, the new moons, and the sabbaths, all the appointed festivals of the house of Israel: he shall provide the sin-offerings, grain-offerings, the burnt-offerings, and the offerings of well-being, to make atonement for the house of Israel.

FESTIVALS

18 Thus says the Lord GOD: In the first month, on the first day of the month, you shall take a young bull without blemish, and purify the sanctuary. 19The priest shall take some of the blood of the sin-offering and put it on the doorposts of the temple, the four corners of the ledge of the altar, and the posts of the gate of the inner court. 20You shall do the same on the seventh day of the month for anyone who has sinned through error or ignorance; so you shall make atonement for the temple.

21 In the first month, on the fourteenth day of the month, you shall celebrate the festival of the passover, and for seven days unleavened bread shall be eaten. 22On that day the prince shall provide for himself and all the people of the land a young bull for a sin-offering.

[n] 45.1 Gk: Heb *ten* [o] 45.5 Gk: Heb *as their holding, twenty chambers* [p] 45.10 A Heb measure of volume [q] 45.14 Cn: Heb *oil, the bath the oil* [r] 45.14 Vg: Heb *homer*

23 And during the seven days of the festival he shall provide as a burnt-offering
to the LORD seven young bulls and
seven rams without blemish, on each
of the seven days; and a male goat daily
for a sin-offering. 24 He shall provide as
a grain-offering an ephah for each bull,
an ephah for each ram, and a hin of oil
to each ephah. 25 In the seventh month,
on the fifteenth day of the month and
for the seven days of the festival, he
shall make the same provision for sin-
offerings, burnt-offerings, and grain-
offerings, and for the oil.

MISCELLANEOUS REGULATIONS

46 Thus says the Lord GOD: The
gate of the inner court that faces
east shall remain closed on the six working days; but on the sabbath day it shall
be opened and on the day of the new
moon it shall be opened. 2 The prince
shall enter by the vestibule of the gate
from outside, and shall take his stand by
the post of the gate. The priests shall offer his burnt-offering and his offerings
of well-being, and he shall bow down at
the threshold of the gate. Then he shall
go out, but the gate shall not be closed
until evening. 3 The people of the land
shall bow down at the entrance of that
gate before the LORD on the sabbaths
and on the new moons. 4 The burnt-
offering that the prince offers to the
LORD on the sabbath day shall be six
lambs without blemish and a ram without blemish; 5 and the grain-offering
with the ram shall be an ephah, and the
grain-offering with the lambs shall be
as much as he wishes to give, together
with a hin of oil to each ephah. 6 On
the day of the new moon he shall offer
a young bull without blemish, and six
lambs and a ram, which shall be without blemish; 7 as a grain-offering he
shall provide an ephah with the bull and
an ephah with the ram, and with the
lambs as much as he wishes, together
with a hin of oil to each ephah. 8 When
the prince enters, he shall come in by
the vestibule of the gate, and he shall go
out by the same way.

9 When the people of the land come
before the LORD at the appointed festivals, whoever enters by the north gate
to worship shall go out by the south
gate; and whoever enters by the south
gate shall go out by the north gate: they
shall not return by way of the gate by
which they entered, but shall go out
straight ahead. 10 When they come in,
the prince shall come in with them; and
when they go out, he shall go out.

11 At the festivals and the appointed
seasons the grain-offering with a young
bull shall be an ephah, and with a ram
an ephah, and with the lambs as much
as one wishes to give, together with a
hin of oil to an ephah. 12 When the prince
provides a freewill-offering, either a
burnt-offering or offerings of well-being
as a freewill-offering to the LORD, the
gate facing east shall be opened for him;
and he shall offer his burnt-offering or
his offerings of well-being as he does on
the sabbath day. Then he shall go out,
and after he has gone out the gate shall
be closed.

13 He shall provide a lamb, a yearling
without blemish, for a burnt-offering
to the LORD daily; morning by morning he shall provide it. 14 And he shall
provide a grain-offering with it morning by morning regularly, one-sixth of
an ephah, and one-third of a hin of oil
to moisten the choice flour, as a grain-
offering to the LORD; this is the ordinance for all time. 15 Thus the lamb and
the grain-offering and the oil shall be
provided, morning by morning, as a
regular burnt-offering.

16 Thus says the Lord GOD: If the
prince makes a gift to any of his sons out
of his inheritance,[s] it shall belong to his
sons, it is their holding by inheritance.
17 But if he makes a gift out of his inheritance to one of his servants, it shall be
his to the year of liberty; then it shall
revert to the prince; only his sons may
keep a gift from his inheritance. 18 The
prince shall not take any of the inheritance of the people, thrusting them out
of their holding; he shall give his sons
their inheritance out of his own holding, so that none of my people shall be
dispossessed of their holding.

19 Then he brought me through the
entrance, which was at the side of the
gate, to the north row of the holy chambers for the priests; and there I saw a
place at the extreme western end of
them. 20 He said to me, 'This is the place
where the priests shall boil the guilt-
offering and the sin-offering, and where
they shall bake the grain-offering, in order not to bring them out into the outer
court and so communicate holiness to
the people.'

21 Then he brought me out to the
outer court, and led me past the four

[s] **46.16** Gk: Heb *it is his inheritance*

corners of the court; and in each corner of the court there was a court—
22in the four corners of the court were
small[t] courts, forty cubits long and
thirty wide; the four were of the same
size. 23On the inside, round each of the
four courts[u] was a row of masonry, with
hearths made at the bottom of the rows
all round. 24Then he said to me, 'These
are the kitchens where those who serve
at the temple shall boil the sacrifices of
the people.'

WATER FLOWING FROM THE TEMPLE

47 Then he brought me back to the
entrance of the temple; there,
water was flowing from below the
threshold of the temple towards the east
(for the temple faced east); and the water was flowing down from below the
south end of the threshold of the temple, south of the altar. 2Then he brought
me out by way of the north gate, and led
me round on the outside to the outer
gate that faces towards the east;[v] and
the water was coming out on the south
side.

3 Going on eastwards with a cord in
his hand, the man measured one thousand cubits, and then led me through
the water; and it was ankle-deep.
4Again he measured one thousand,
and led me through the water; and it
was knee-deep. Again he measured one
thousand, and led me through the water; and it was up to the waist. 5Again
he measured one thousand, and it was a
river that I could not cross, for the water
had risen; it was deep enough to swim
in, a river that could not be crossed. 6He
said to me, 'Mortal, have you seen this?'

Then he led me back along the bank
of the river. 7As I came back, I saw on
the bank of the river a great many trees
on one side and on the other. 8He said to
me, 'This water flows towards the eastern region and goes down into the Arabah; and when it enters the sea, the sea
of stagnant waters, the water will become fresh. 9Wherever the river goes,[w]
every living creature that swarms will
live, and there will be very many fish,
once these waters reach there. It will
become fresh; and everything will live
where the river goes. 10People will
stand fishing beside the sea[x] from En-
gedi to En-eglaim; it will be a place
for the spreading of nets; its fish will
be of a great many kinds, like the fish
of the Great Sea. 11But its swamps and
marshes will not become fresh; they
are to be left for salt. 12On the banks, on
both sides of the river, there will grow
all kinds of trees for food. Their leaves
will not wither nor their fruit fail, but
they will bear fresh fruit every month,
because the water for them flows from
the sanctuary. Their fruit will be for
food, and their leaves for healing.'

THE NEW BOUNDARIES OF THE LAND

13 Thus says the Lord GOD: These
are the boundaries by which you shall
divide the land for inheritance among
the twelve tribes of Israel. Joseph shall
have two portions. 14You shall divide
it equally; I swore to give it to your ancestors, and this land shall fall to you as
your inheritance.

15 This shall be the boundary of the
land: On the north side, from the Great
Sea by way of Hethlon to Lebo-hamath,
and on to Zedad,[y] 16Berothah, Sibraim
(which lies between the border of Damascus and the border of Hamath), as
far as Hazer-hatticon, which is on the
border of Hauran. 17So the boundary
shall run from the sea to Hazar-enon,
which is north of the border of Damascus, with the border of Hamath to the
north.[z] This shall be the north side.

18 On the east side, between Hauran and Damascus; along the Jordan
between Gilead and the land of Israel;
to the eastern sea and as far as Tamar.[a]
This shall be the east side.

19 On the south side, it shall run
from Tamar as far as the waters of
Meribath-kadesh, from there along the
Wadi of Egypt[b] to the Great Sea. This
shall be the south side.

20 On the west side, the Great Sea
shall be the boundary to a point opposite Lebo-hamath. This shall be the west
side.

21 So you shall divide this land
among you according to the tribes of
Israel. 22You shall allot it as an inheritance for yourselves and for the aliens
who reside among you and have begotten children among you. They shall be to
you as citizens of Israel; with you they
shall be allotted an inheritance among
the tribes of Israel. 23In whatever tribe
aliens reside, there you shall assign

[t] **46.22** Gk Syr Vg: Meaning of Heb uncertain [u] **46.23** Heb *the four of them* [v] **47.2** Meaning of Heb uncertain [w] **47.9** Gk Syr Vg Tg: Heb *the two rivers go* [x] **47.10** Heb *it* [y] **47.15** Gk: Heb *Lebo-zedad, 16Hamath* [z] **47.17** Meaning of Heb uncertain [a] **47.18** Compare Syr: Heb *you shall measure* [b] **47.19** Heb lacks *of Egypt*

them their inheritance, says the Lord
GOD.

THE TRIBAL PORTIONS

48 These are the names of the
tribes: Beginning at the northern border, on the Hethlon road,[c] from
Lebo-hamath, as far as Hazar-enon
(which is on the border of Damascus,
with Hamath to the north), and[d] extending from the east side to the west,[e]
Dan, one portion. 2 Adjoining the territory of Dan, from the east side to the
west, Asher, one portion. 3 Adjoining
the territory of Asher, from the east side
to the west, Naphtali, one portion. 4 Adjoining the territory of Naphtali, from
the east side to the west, Manasseh, one
portion. 5 Adjoining the territory of Manasseh, from the east side to the west,
Ephraim, one portion. 6 Adjoining the
territory of Ephraim, from the east side
to the west, Reuben, one portion. 7 Adjoining the territory of Reuben, from
the east side to the west, Judah, one
portion.

8 Adjoining the territory of Judah,
from the east side to the west, shall be
the portion that you shall set apart,
twenty-five thousand cubits in width,
and in length equal to one of the tribal
portions, from the east side to the
west, with the sanctuary in the middle of it. 9 The portion that you shall set
apart for the LORD shall be twenty-five
thousand cubits in length, and twenty[f]
thousand in width. 10 These shall be
the allotments of the holy portion: the
priests shall have an allotment measuring twenty-five thousand cubits on
the northern side, ten thousand cubits
in width on the western side, ten thousand in width on the eastern side, and
twenty-five thousand in length on the
southern side, with the sanctuary of the
LORD in the middle of it. 11 This shall be
for the consecrated priests, the descendants[g] of Zadok, who kept my charge,
who did not go astray when the people
of Israel went astray, as the Levites did.
12 It shall belong to them as a special portion from the holy portion of the land, a
most holy place, adjoining the territory
of the Levites. 13 Alongside the territory
of the priests, the Levites shall have an
allotment twenty-five thousand cubits
in length and ten thousand in width.
The whole length shall be twenty-five
thousand cubits and the width twenty[h]
thousand. 14 They shall not sell or exchange any of it; they shall not transfer
this choice portion of the land, for it is
holy to the LORD.

15 The remainder, five thousand
cubits in width and twenty-five thousand in length, shall be for ordinary
use for the city, for dwellings and for
open country. In the middle of it shall
be the city; 16 and these shall be its dimensions: the north side four thousand
five hundred cubits, the south side four
thousand five hundred, the east side
four thousand five hundred, and the
west side four thousand five hundred.
17 The city shall have open land: on the
north two hundred and fifty cubits, on
the south two hundred and fifty, on the
east two hundred and fifty, on the west
two hundred and fifty. 18 The remainder
of the length alongside the holy portion
shall be ten thousand cubits to the east,
and ten thousand to the west, and it
shall be alongside the holy portion. Its
produce shall be food for the workers of
the city. 19 The workers of the city, from
all the tribes of Israel, shall cultivate it.
20 The whole portion that you shall set
apart shall be twenty-five thousand cubits square, that is, the holy portion together with the property of the city.

21 What remains on both sides of
the holy portion and of the property
of the city shall belong to the prince.
Extending from the twenty-five thousand cubits of the holy portion to the
east border, and westwards from the
twenty-five thousand cubits to the west
border, parallel to the tribal portions, it
shall belong to the prince. The holy portion with the sanctuary of the temple
in the middle of it, 22 and the property
of the Levites and of the city, shall be in
the middle of that which belongs to the
prince. The portion of the prince shall lie
between the territory of Judah and the
territory of Benjamin.

23 As for the rest of the tribes: from
the east side to the west, Benjamin,
one portion. 24 Adjoining the territory
of Benjamin, from the east side to the
west, Simeon, one portion. 25 Adjoining
the territory of Simeon, from the east
side to the west, Issachar, one portion.
26 Adjoining the territory of Issachar,
from the east side to the west, Zebulun,
one portion. 27 Adjoining the territory
of Zebulun, from the east side to the

[c] **48.1** Compare 47.15: Heb *by the side of the way*
[d] **48.1** Cn: Heb *and they shall be his* [e] **48.1** Gk
Compare verses 2–8: Heb *the east side the west*
[f] **48.9** Compare 45.1: Heb *ten* [g] **48.11** One Ms
Gk: Heb *of the descendants* [h] **48.13** Gk: Heb *ten*

west, Gad, one portion. 28And adjoining the territory of Gad to the south, the
boundary shall run from Tamar to the
waters of Meribath-kadesh, from there
along the Wadi of Egypt[i] to the Great
Sea. 29This is the land that you shall allot as an inheritance among the tribes
of Israel, and these are their portions,
says the Lord GOD.

30 These shall be the exits of the city:
On the north side, which is to be four
thousand five hundred cubits by measure, 31three gates, the gate of Reuben,
the gate of Judah, and the gate of Levi,
the gates of the city being named after
the tribes of Israel. 32On the east side,
which is to be four thousand five hundred cubits, three gates, the gate of Joseph, the gate of Benjamin, and the gate
of Dan. 33On the south side, which is to
be four thousand five hundred cubits by
measure, three gates, the gate of Simeon, the gate of Issachar, and the gate
of Zebulun. 34On the west side, which is
to be four thousand five hundred cubits,
three gates,[j] the gate of Gad, the gate of
Asher, and the gate of Naphtali. 35The
circumference of the city shall be eighteen thousand cubits. And the name of
the city from that time on shall be, The
LORD is There.

i 48.28 Heb lacks *of Egypt* j 48.34 One Ms Gk Syr: MT *their gates three*

DANIEL

The book of Daniel seems to come from the time of the persecution of the Jews by Antiochus IV Epiphanes (167–164 BCE). The writing introduces the apocalyptic genre by its vision of the last days and by its use of otherworldly images and divine figures. The story line is about a legendary youth named Daniel who remains faithful to the God of Israel and, thereby, is able to overcome adversity and torment in the days of the Babylonian exile. Daniel interprets the king's dreams and offers counsel to him about the future. The message of the book would have been immediately evident to the persecuted Jews of the second century BCE.

Several sections of the book of Daniel that were preserved in the Greek or Septuagint version of the Scriptures are considered Apocrypha in Protestant Bibles. These sections include the Prayer of Azariah, the Song of the Three Jews, Susanna, and Bel and the Dragon. These sections provide material for Catholic and Orthodox prayer at the Liturgy of the Hours.

Passages from Daniel are read in the liturgy during Monday through Saturday of the Thirty-Fourth or Last Week of Year I. Also, the apocalyptic vision from Daniel about one like a son of man coming to rule the world (7.9–10, 13–14) is read on several occasions during the liturgical year: on the Feast of Christ the King; the Feast of the Transfiguration; and the Feast of the Archangels Michael, Gabriel, and Raphael.

FOUR YOUNG ISRAELITES AT THE BABYLONIAN COURT

1 In the third year of the reign of
King Jehoiakim of Judah, King
Nebuchadnezzar of Babylon came to Jerusalem and besieged it. 2The Lord let
King Jehoiakim of Judah fall into his
power, as well as some of the vessels of
the house of God. These he brought to
the land of Shinar,[a] and placed the vessels in the treasury of his gods.
3 Then the king commanded his palace master Ashpenaz to bring some of
the Israelites of the royal family and of
the nobility, 4young men without physical defect and handsome, versed in every branch of wisdom, endowed with
knowledge and insight, and competent
to serve in the king's palace; they were
to be taught the literature and language
of the Chaldeans. 5The king assigned
them a daily portion of the royal rations
of food and wine. They were to be educated for three years, so that at the end
of that time they could be stationed in
the king's court. 6Among them were
Daniel, Hananiah, Mishael, and Azariah, from the tribe of Judah. 7The palace
master gave them other names: Daniel
he called Belteshazzar, Hananiah he
called Shadrach, Mishael he called Meshach, and Azariah he called Abednego.
8 But Daniel resolved that he would
not defile himself with the royal rations
of food and wine; so he asked the palace
master to allow him not to defile himself. 9Now God allowed Daniel to receive
favour and compassion from the palace
master. 10The palace master said to Daniel, 'I am afraid of my lord the king; he
has appointed your food and your drink.
If he should see you in poorer condition
than the other young men of your own

[a] 1.2 Gk Theodotion: Heb adds *to the house of his own gods*

age, you would endanger my head with
the king.' 11Then Daniel asked the guard
whom the palace master had appointed
over Daniel, Hananiah, Mishael, and
Azariah: 12'Please test your servants for
ten days. Let us be given vegetables to
eat and water to drink. 13You can then
compare our appearance with the appearance of the young men who eat the
royal rations, and deal with your servants according to what you observe.'
14So he agreed to this proposal and
tested them for ten days. 15At the end
of ten days it was observed that they
appeared better and fatter than all the
young men who had been eating the
royal rations. 16So the guard continued
to withdraw their royal rations and the
wine they were to drink, and gave them
vegetables. 17To these four young men
God gave knowledge and skill in every
aspect of literature and wisdom; Daniel also had insight into all visions and
dreams.

18 At the end of the time that the
king had set for them to be brought in,
the palace master brought them into
the presence of Nebuchadnezzar, 19and
the king spoke with them. And among
them all, no one was found to compare
with Daniel, Hananiah, Mishael, and
Azariah; therefore they were stationed
in the king's court. 20In every matter of
wisdom and understanding concerning
which the king inquired of them, he
found them ten times better than all the
magicians and enchanters in his whole
kingdom. 21And Daniel continued there
until the first year of King Cyrus.

NEBUCHADNEZZAR'S DREAM

2 In the second year of Nebuchadnezzar's reign, Nebuchadnezzar
dreamed such dreams that his spirit
was troubled and his sleep left him.
2So the king commanded that the magicians, the enchanters, the sorcerers,
and the Chaldeans be summoned to tell
the king his dreams. When they came
in and stood before the king, 3he said
to them, 'I have had such a dream that
my spirit is troubled by the desire to
understand it.' 4The Chaldeans said to
the king (in Aramaic),[b] 'O king, live for
ever! Tell your servants the dream, and
we will reveal the interpretation.' 5The
king answered the Chaldeans, 'This is a
public decree: if you do not tell me both
the dream and its interpretation, you
shall be torn limb from limb, and your
houses shall be laid in ruins. 6But if you
do tell me the dream and its interpretation, you shall receive from me gifts and
rewards and great honour. Therefore tell
me the dream and its interpretation.'
7They answered a second time, 'Let the
king first tell his servants the dream,
then we can give its interpretation.'
8The king answered, 'I know with certainty that you are trying to gain time,
because you see I have firmly decreed:
9if you do not tell me the dream, there is
but one verdict for you. You have agreed
to speak lying and misleading words to
me until things take a turn. Therefore,
tell me the dream, and I shall know
that you can give me its interpretation.'
10The Chaldeans answered the king,
'There is no one on earth who can reveal
what the king demands! In fact no king,
however great and powerful, has ever
asked such a thing of any magician or
enchanter or Chaldean. 11The thing that
the king is asking is too difficult, and no
one can reveal it to the king except the
gods, whose dwelling is not with mortals.'

12 Because of this the king flew into
a violent rage and commanded that all
the wise men of Babylon be destroyed.
13The decree was issued, and the wise
men were about to be executed; and
they looked for Daniel and his companions, to execute them. 14Then Daniel responded with prudence and discretion
to Arioch, the king's chief executioner,
who had gone out to execute the wise
men of Babylon; 15he asked Arioch, the
royal official, 'Why is the decree of the
king so urgent?' Arioch then explained
the matter to Daniel. 16So Daniel went
in and requested that the king give him
time and he would tell the king the interpretation.

GOD REVEALS NEBUCHADNEZZAR'S DREAM

17 Then Daniel went to his home and
informed his companions, Hananiah,
Mishael, and Azariah, 18and told them
to seek mercy from the God of heaven
concerning this mystery, so that Daniel and his companions with the rest of
the wise men of Babylon might not perish. 19Then the mystery was revealed to
Daniel in a vision of the night, and Daniel blessed the God of heaven.
20 Daniel said:

[b] **2.4** The text from this point to the end of chapter 7 is in Aramaic, except for 3.24–91a, the text of which is in Greek

'Blessed be the name of God
from age to age,
for wisdom and power are his.
21 He changes times and seasons,
deposes kings and sets up kings;
he gives wisdom to the wise
and knowledge to those who
have understanding.
22 He reveals deep and hidden things;
he knows what is in the darkness,
and light dwells with him.
23 To you, O God of my ancestors,
I give thanks and praise,
for you have given me wisdom
and power,
and have now revealed to me
what we asked of you,
for you have revealed to us
what the king ordered.'

DANIEL INTERPRETS THE DREAM

24 Therefore Daniel went to Arioch,
whom the king had appointed to destroy the wise men of Babylon, and said
to him, 'Do not destroy the wise men of
Babylon; bring me in before the king,
and I will give the king the interpretation.'

25 Then Arioch quickly brought Daniel before the king and said to him: 'I
have found among the exiles from Judah a man who can tell the king the interpretation.'
26 The king said to Daniel,
whose name was Belteshazzar, 'Are you
able to tell me the dream that I have
seen and its interpretation?'
27 Daniel
answered the king, 'No wise men, enchanters, magicians, or diviners can
show to the king the mystery that the
king is asking,
28 but there is a God in
heaven who reveals mysteries, and he
has disclosed to King Nebuchadnezzar
what will happen at the end of days.
Your dream and the visions of your
head as you lay in bed were these:
29 To
you, O king, as you lay in bed, came
thoughts of what would be hereafter,
and the revealer of mysteries disclosed
to you what is to be.
30 But as for me,
this mystery has not been revealed to
me because of any wisdom that I have
more than any other living being, but
in order that the interpretation may be
known to the king and that you may
understand the thoughts of your mind.

31 'You were looking, O king, and
lo! there was a great statue. This statue
was huge, its brilliance extraordinary; it
was standing before you, and its appearance was frightening.
32 The head of that
statue was of fine gold, its chest and
arms of silver, its middle and thighs of
bronze,
33 its legs of iron, its feet partly of
iron and partly of clay.
34 As you looked
on, a stone was cut out, not by human
hands, and it struck the statue on its
feet of iron and clay and broke them
in pieces.
35 Then the iron, the clay, the
bronze, the silver, and the gold, were
all broken in pieces and became like the
chaff of the summer threshing-floors;
and the wind carried them away, so
that not a trace of them could be found.
But the stone that struck the statue became a great mountain and filled the
whole earth.

36 'This was the dream; now we will
tell the king its interpretation.
37 You,
O king, the king of kings—to whom the
God of heaven has given the kingdom,
the power, the might, and the glory,
38 into whose hand he has given human
beings, wherever they live, the wild animals of the field, and the birds of the air,
and whom he has established as ruler
over them all—you are the head of gold.
39 After you shall arise another kingdom
inferior to yours, and yet a third kingdom of bronze, which shall rule over
the whole earth.
40 And there shall be a
fourth kingdom, strong as iron; just as
iron crushes and smashes everything,[c]
it shall crush and shatter all these.
41 As
you saw the feet and toes partly of potter's clay and partly of iron, it shall be
a divided kingdom; but some of the
strength of iron shall be in it, as you
saw the iron mixed with the clay.
42 As
the toes of the feet were part iron and
part clay, so the kingdom shall be partly
strong and partly brittle.
43 As you saw
the iron mixed with clay, so will they
mix with one another in marriage,[d] but
they will not hold together, just as iron
does not mix with clay.
44 And in the
days of those kings the God of heaven
will set up a kingdom that shall never
be destroyed, nor shall this kingdom be
left to another people. It shall crush all
these kingdoms and bring them to an
end, and it shall stand for ever;
45 just
as you saw that a stone was cut from
the mountain not by hands, and that it
crushed the iron, the bronze, the clay,
the silver, and the gold. The great God
has informed the king what shall be
hereafter. The dream is certain, and its
interpretation trustworthy.'

[c] 2.40 Gk Theodotion Syr Vg: Aram adds *and like iron that crushes* [d] 2.43 Aram *by human seed*

DANIEL AND HIS FRIENDS PROMOTED

46 Then King Nebuchadnezzar fell on
his face, worshipped Daniel, and commanded that a grain-offering and incense be offered to him. 47 The king said
to Daniel, 'Truly, your God is God of gods
and Lord of kings and a revealer of mysteries, for you have been able to reveal
this mystery!' 48 Then the king promoted
Daniel, gave him many great gifts, and
made him ruler over the whole province
of Babylon and chief prefect over all the
wise men of Babylon. 49 Daniel made a
request of the king, and he appointed
Shadrach, Meshach, and Abednego over
the affairs of the province of Babylon.
But Daniel remained at the king's court.

THE GOLDEN IMAGE

3 King Nebuchadnezzar made a
golden statue whose height was
sixty cubits and whose width was six
cubits; he set it up on the plain of Dura
in the province of Babylon. 2 Then King
Nebuchadnezzar sent for the satraps,
the prefects, and the governors, the
counsellors, the treasurers, the justices,
the magistrates, and all the officials of
the provinces, to assemble and come
to the dedication of the statue that
King Nebuchadnezzar had set up. 3 So
the satraps, the prefects, and the governors, the counsellors, the treasurers,
the justices, the magistrates, and all the
officials of the provinces, assembled for
the dedication of the statue that King
Nebuchadnezzar had set up. When they
were standing before the statue that
Nebuchadnezzar had set up, 4 the herald
proclaimed aloud, 'You are commanded,
O peoples, nations, and languages, 5 that
when you hear the sound of the horn,
pipe, lyre, trigon, harp, drum, and entire musical ensemble, you are to fall
down and worship the golden statue
that King Nebuchadnezzar has set up.
6 Whoever does not fall down and worship shall immediately be thrown into
a furnace of blazing fire.' 7 Therefore, as
soon as all the peoples heard the sound
of the horn, pipe, lyre, trigon, harp,
drum, and entire musical ensemble, all
the peoples, nations, and languages fell
down and worshipped the golden statue
that King Nebuchadnezzar had set up.

8 Accordingly, at this time certain Chaldeans came forward and denounced the Jews. 9 They said to King
Nebuchadnezzar, 'O king, live for ever!
10 You, O king, have made a decree, that
everyone who hears the sound of the
horn, pipe, lyre, trigon, harp, drum,
and entire musical ensemble, shall fall
down and worship the golden statue,
11 and whoever does not fall down and
worship shall be thrown into a furnace
of blazing fire. 12 There are certain Jews
whom you have appointed over the affairs of the province of Babylon: Shadrach, Meshach, and Abednego. These
pay no heed to you, O king. They do not
serve your gods and they do not worship
the golden statue that you have set up.'

13 Then Nebuchadnezzar in furious
rage commanded that Shadrach, Meshach, and Abednego be brought in;
so they brought those men before the
king. 14 Nebuchadnezzar said to them,
'Is it true, O Shadrach, Meshach, and
Abednego, that you do not serve my
gods and you do not worship the golden
statue that I have set up? 15 Now if you
are ready when you hear the sound
of the horn, pipe, lyre, trigon, harp,
drum, and entire musical ensemble to
fall down and worship the statue that
I have made, well and good.[e] But if you
do not worship, you shall immediately
be thrown into a furnace of blazing fire,
and who is the god that will deliver you
out of my hands?'

16 Shadrach, Meshach, and Abednego answered the king, 'O Nebuchadnezzar, we have no need to present a
defence to you in this matter. 17 If our
God whom we serve is able to deliver us
from the furnace of blazing fire and out
of your hand, O king, let him deliver us.[f]
18 But if not, be it known to you, O king,
that we will not serve your gods and we
will not worship the golden statue that
you have set up.'

THE FIERY FURNACE

19 Then Nebuchadnezzar was so
filled with rage against Shadrach, Meshach, and Abednego that his face was
distorted. He ordered the furnace to be
heated up seven times more than was
customary, 20 and ordered some of the
strongest guards in his army to bind
Shadrach, Meshach, and Abednego and
to throw them into the furnace of blazing fire. 21 So the men were bound, still
wearing their tunics,[g] their trousers,[h]

[e] 3.15 Aram lacks *well and good* [f] 3.17 Or *If our God whom we serve is able to deliver us, he will deliver us from the furnace of blazing fire and out of your hand, O king.* [g] 3.21 Meaning of Aram word uncertain [h] 3.21 Meaning of Aram word uncertain

their hats, and their other garments,
and they were thrown into the furnace
of blazing fire. 22Because the king's
command was urgent and the furnace
was so overheated, the raging flames
killed the men who lifted Shadrach, Meshach, and Abednego. 23But the three
men, Shadrach, Meshach, and Abednego, fell down, bound, into the furnace
of blazing fire.

THE PRAYER OF AZARIAH IN THE FURNACE

24 They walked around in the midst
of the flames, singing hymns to God and
blessing the Lord. 25Then Azariah stood
still in the fire and prayed aloud:

26 'Blessed are you, O Lord, God
of our ancestors, and
worthy of praise;
and glorious is your name for ever!
27 For you are just in all you have done;
all your works are true and
your ways right,
and all your judgements are true.
28 You have executed true judgements in
all you have brought upon us
and upon Jerusalem, the holy
city of our ancestors;
by a true judgement you have
brought all this upon us
because of our sins.
29 For we have sinned and broken
your law in turning
away from you;
in all matters we have
sinned grievously.
30 We have not obeyed your
commandments,
we have not kept them or done
what you have commanded
us for our own good.
31 So all that you have brought upon us,
and all that you have done to us,
you have done by a true
judgement.
32 You have handed us over to
our enemies, lawless
and hateful rebels,
and to an unjust king, the most
wicked in all the world.
33 And now we cannot open
our mouths;
we, your servants who worship
you, have become a
shame and a reproach.
34 For your name's sake do not
give us up for ever,
and do not annul your covenant.
35 Do not withdraw your
mercy from us,
for the sake of Abraham your beloved
and for the sake of your
servant Isaac
and Israel your holy one,
36 to whom you promised
to multiply their descendants
like the stars of heaven
and like the sand on the
shore of the sea.
37 For we, O Lord, have become fewer
than any other nation,
and are brought low this day in all
the world because of our sins.
38 In our day we have no ruler, or
prophet, or leader,
no burnt-offering, or sacrifice,
or oblation, or incense,
no place to make an offering
before you and to find mercy.
39 Yet with a contrite heart and
a humble spirit may
we be accepted,
40 as though it were with
burnt-offerings of
rams and bulls,
or with tens of thousands
of fat lambs;
such may our sacrifice be in
your sight today,
and may we unreservedly
follow you,[i]
for no shame will come to
those who trust in you.
41 And now with all our heart
we follow you;
we fear you and seek
your presence.
42 Do not put us to shame,
but deal with us in your patience
and in your abundant mercy.
43 Deliver us in accordance with
your marvellous works,
and bring glory to your
name, O Lord.
44 Let all who do harm to your
servants be put to shame;
let them be disgraced and
deprived of all power,
and let their strength be broken.
45 Let them know that you alone
are the Lord God,
glorious over the whole world.'

THE SONG OF THE THREE JEWS

46 Now the king's servants who
threw them in kept stoking the furnace with naphtha, pitch, tow, and
brushwood. 47And the flames poured
out above the furnace forty-nine cu-

[i] 3.40 Meaning of Gk uncertain

bits, 48and spread out and burned those
Chaldeans who were caught near the
furnace. 49But the angel of the Lord
came down into the furnace to be with
Azariah and his companions, and drove
the fiery flame out of the furnace, 50and
made the inside of the furnace as though
a moist wind were whistling through it.
The fire did not touch them at all and
caused them no pain or distress.

51 Then the three with one voice
praised and glorified and blessed God in
the furnace:

52 'Blessed are you, O Lord, God
of our ancestors,
and to be praised and highly
exalted for ever;
And blessed is your glorious,
holy name,
and to be highly praised and
highly exalted for ever.
53 Blessed are you in the temple
of your holy glory,
and to be extolled and highly
glorified for ever.
54 Blessed are you who look into
the depths from your
throne on the cherubim,
and to be praised and highly
exalted for ever.
55 Blessed are you on the throne
of your kingdom,
and to be extolled and highly
exalted for ever.
56 Blessed are you in the firmament
of heaven,
and to be sung and
glorified for ever.

57 'Bless the Lord, all you works
of the Lord;
sing praise to him and highly
exalt him for ever.
58 Bless the Lord, you heavens;
sing praise to him and highly
exalt him for ever.
59 Bless the Lord, you angels
of the Lord;
sing praise to him and highly
exalt him for ever.
60 Bless the Lord, all you waters
above the heavens;
sing praise to him and highly
exalt him for ever.
61 Bless the Lord, all you powers
of the Lord;
sing praise to him and highly
exalt him for ever.
62 Bless the Lord, sun and moon;
sing praise to him and highly
exalt him for ever.
63 Bless the Lord, stars of heaven;
sing praise to him and highly
exalt him for ever.

64 'Bless the Lord, all rain and dew;
sing praise to him and highly
exalt him for ever.
65 Bless the Lord, all you winds;
sing praise to him and highly
exalt him for ever.
66 Bless the Lord, fire and heat;
sing praise to him and highly
exalt him for ever.
67 Bless the Lord, winter cold
and summer heat;
sing praise to him and highly
exalt him for ever.
68 Bless the Lord, dews and
falling snow;
sing praise to him and highly
exalt him for ever.
69 Bless the Lord, ice and cold;
sing praise to him and highly
exalt him for ever.
70 Bless the Lord, frosts and snows;
sing praise to him and highly
exalt him for ever.
71 Bless the Lord, nights and days;
sing praise to him and highly
exalt him for ever.
72 Bless the Lord, light and darkness;
sing praise to him and highly
exalt him for ever.
73 Bless the Lord, lightnings
and clouds;
sing praise to him and highly
exalt him for ever.

74 'Let the earth bless the Lord;
let it sing praise to him and
highly exalt him for ever.
75 Bless the Lord, mountains and hills;
sing praise to him and highly
exalt him for ever.
76 Bless the Lord, all that grows
in the ground;
sing praise to him and highly
exalt him for ever.
77 Bless the Lord, you springs;
sing praise to him and highly
exalt him for ever.
78 Bless the Lord, seas and rivers;
sing praise to him and highly
exalt him for ever.
79 Bless the Lord, you whales and all
that swim in the waters;
sing praise to him and highly
exalt him for ever.
80 Bless the Lord, all birds of the air;
sing praise to him and highly
exalt him for ever.

81 Bless the Lord, all wild
animals and cattle;
sing praise to him and highly
exalt him for ever.

82 'Bless the Lord, all people on earth;
sing praise to him and highly
exalt him for ever.
83 Bless the Lord, O Israel;
sing praise to him and highly
exalt him for ever.
84 Bless the Lord, you priests
of the Lord;
sing praise to him and highly
exalt him for ever.
85 Bless the Lord, you servants
of the Lord;
sing praise to him and highly
exalt him for ever.
86 Bless the Lord, spirits and souls
of the righteous;
sing praise to him and highly
exalt him for ever.
87 Bless the Lord, you who are holy
and humble in heart;
sing praise to him and highly
exalt him for ever.

88 'Bless the Lord, Hananiah,
Azariah, and Mishael;
sing praise to him and highly
exalt him for ever.
For he has rescued us from
Hades and saved us from
the power[j] of death,
and delivered us from the midst
of the burning fiery furnace;
from the midst of the fire
he has delivered us.
89 Give thanks to the Lord,
for he is good,
for his mercy endures for ever.
90 All who worship the Lord, bless
the God of gods,
sing praise to him and give
thanks to him,
for his mercy endures for ever.'

91 Hearing them sing, and amazed
at seeing them alive, King Nebuchadnezzar was astonished and rose up
quickly. He said to his counsellors, 'Was
it not three men that we threw bound
into the fire?' They answered the king,
'True, O king.' 92He replied, 'But I see
four men unbound, walking in the middle of the fire, and they are not hurt; and
the fourth has the appearance of a god.'[k]
93Nebuchadnezzar then approached the
door of the furnace of blazing fire and
said, 'Shadrach, Meshach, and Abednego, servants of the Most High God,
come out! Come here!' So Shadrach, Meshach, and Abednego came out from the
fire. 94And the satraps, the prefects, the
governors, and the king's counsellors
gathered together and saw that the fire
had not had any power over the bodies
of those men; the hair of their heads
was not singed, their tunics[l] were not
harmed, and not even the smell of fire
came from them. 95Nebuchadnezzar
said, 'Blessed be the God of Shadrach,
Meshach, and Abednego, who has sent
his angel and delivered his servants
who trusted in him. They disobeyed the
king's command and yielded up their
bodies rather than serve and worship
any god except their own God. 96There-
fore I make a decree: Any people, nation, or language that utters blasphemy
against the God of Shadrach, Meshach,
and Abednego shall be torn limb from
limb, and their houses laid in ruins; for
there is no other god who is able to deliver in this way.' 97Then the king promoted Shadrach, Meshach, and Abednego in the province of Babylon.

NEBUCHADNEZZAR'S SECOND DREAM

4 [m]King Nebuchadnezzar to all peoples, nations, and languages that
live throughout the earth: May you
have abundant prosperity! 2The signs
and wonders that the Most High God
has worked for me I am pleased to recount.

3 How great are his signs,
how mighty his wonders!
His kingdom is an everlasting
kingdom,
and his sovereignty is from
generation to generation.

4[n] I, Nebuchadnezzar, was living at
ease in my home and prospering in my
palace. 5I saw a dream that frightened
me; my fantasies in bed and the visions
of my head terrified me. 6So I made a
decree that all the wise men of Babylon
should be brought before me, in order
that they might tell me the interpretation of the dream. 7Then the magicians,
the enchanters, the Chaldeans, and the
diviners came in, and I told them the
dream, but they could not tell me its
interpretation. 8At last Daniel came in
before me—he who was named Belteshazzar after the name of my god, and
who is endowed with a spirit of the

[j] **3.88** Gk *hand* [k] **3.92** Aram *a son of the gods*
[l] **3.94** Meaning of Aram word uncertain
[m] **4.1** Ch 3.31 in Aram [n] **4.4** Ch 4.1 in Aram

holy gods[o]—and I told him the dream:
[9]'O Belteshazzar, chief of the magicians,
I know that you are endowed with a
spirit of the holy gods[p] and that no mystery is too difficult for you. Hear[q] the
dream that I saw; tell me its interpretation.

[10][r]Upon my bed this is what I saw;
there was a tree at the
centre of the earth,
and its height was great.
11 The tree grew great and strong,
its top reached to heaven,
and it was visible to the ends
of the whole earth.
12 Its foliage was beautiful,
its fruit abundant,
and it provided food for all.
The animals of the field found
shade under it,
the birds of the air nested
in its branches,
and from it all living
beings were fed.

13 'I continued looking, in the visions of my head as I lay in bed, and
there was a holy watcher, coming down
from heaven. [14]He cried aloud and said:
"Cut down the tree and chop
off its branches,
strip off its foliage and
scatter its fruit.
Let the animals flee from beneath it
and the birds from its branches.
15 But leave its stump and roots
in the ground,
with a band of iron and bronze,
in the tender grass of the field.
Let him be bathed with the
dew of heaven,
and let his lot be with the
animals of the field
in the grass of the earth.
16 Let his mind be changed from
that of a human,
and let the mind of an animal
be given to him.
And let seven times
pass over him.
17 The sentence is rendered by
decree of the watchers,
the decision is given by order
of the holy ones,
in order that all who
live may know
that the Most High is sovereign
over the kingdom of mortals;
he gives it to whom he will
and sets over it the lowliest
of human beings."

18 'This is the dream that I, King
Nebuchadnezzar, saw. Now you, Belteshazzar, declare the interpretation,
since all the wise men of my kingdom
are unable to tell me the interpretation.
You are able, however, for you are endowed with a spirit of the holy gods.'[s]

DANIEL INTERPRETS THE SECOND DREAM

19 Then Daniel, who was called Belteshazzar, was severely distressed for
a while. His thoughts terrified him.
The king said, 'Belteshazzar, do not let
the dream or the interpretation terrify
you.' Belteshazzar answered, 'My lord,
may the dream be for those who hate
you, and its interpretation for your enemies! [20]The tree that you saw, which
grew great and strong, so that its top
reached to heaven and was visible to the
end of the whole earth, [21]whose foliage
was beautiful and its fruit abundant,
and which provided food for all, under
which animals of the field lived, and
in whose branches the birds of the air
had nests— [22]it is you, O king! You have
grown great and strong. Your greatness
has increased and reaches to heaven,
and your sovereignty to the ends of the
earth. [23]And whereas the king saw a
holy watcher coming down from heaven
and saying, "Cut down the tree and destroy it, but leave its stump and roots
in the ground, with a band of iron and
bronze, in the grass of the field; and let
him be bathed with the dew of heaven,
and let his lot be with the animals of the
field, until seven times pass over him"—
[24]this is the interpretation, O king, and
it is a decree of the Most High that has
come upon my lord the king: [25]You shall
be driven away from human society,
and your dwelling shall be with the wild
animals. You shall be made to eat grass
like oxen, you shall be bathed with the
dew of heaven, and seven times shall
pass over you, until you have learned
that the Most High has sovereignty over
the kingdom of mortals, and gives it to
whom he will. [26]As it was commanded
to leave the stump and roots of the tree,
your kingdom shall be re-established
for you from the time that you learn
that Heaven is sovereign. [27]Therefore,
O king, may my counsel be acceptable to

[o] **4.8** Or *a holy, divine spirit* [p] **4.9** Or *a holy, divine spirit* [q] **4.9** Theodotion: Aram *The visions of* [r] **4.10** Theodotion Syr Compare Gk: Aram adds *The visions of my head* [s] **4.18** Or *a holy, divine spirit*

you: atone for[t] your sins with righteousness, and your iniquities with mercy to
the oppressed, so that your prosperity
may be prolonged.'

NEBUCHADNEZZAR'S HUMILIATION

28 All this came upon King Nebuchadnezzar. 29At the end of twelve
months he was walking on the roof of
the royal palace of Babylon, 30and the
king said, 'Is this not magnificent Babylon, which I have built as a royal capital by my mighty power and for my glorious majesty?' 31While the words were
still in the king's mouth, a voice came
from heaven: 'O King Nebuchadnezzar, to you it is declared: The kingdom
has departed from you! 32You shall be
driven away from human society, and
your dwelling shall be with the animals
of the field. You shall be made to eat
grass like oxen, and seven times shall
pass over you, until you have learned
that the Most High has sovereignty
over the kingdom of mortals and gives
it to whom he will.' 33Immediately the
sentence was fulfilled against Nebuchadnezzar. He was driven away from
human society, ate grass like oxen, and
his body was bathed with the dew of
heaven, until his hair grew as long as
eagles' feathers and his nails became
like birds' claws.

NEBUCHADNEZZAR PRAISES GOD

34 When that period was over, I, Nebuchadnezzar, lifted my eyes to heaven,
and my reason returned to me.

I blessed the Most High,
and praised and honoured the
one who lives for ever.
For his sovereignty is an
everlasting sovereignty,
and his kingdom endures from
generation to generation.
35 All the inhabitants of the earth are
accounted as nothing,
and he does what he wills with
the host of heaven
and the inhabitants of the earth.
There is no one who can
stay his hand
or say to him, 'What are
you doing?'

36At that time my reason returned to
me; and my majesty and splendour
were restored to me for the glory of my
kingdom. My counsellors and my lords
sought me out, I was re-established over
my kingdom, and still more greatness
was added to me. 37Now I, Nebuchadnezzar, praise and extol and honour the
King of heaven,

for all his works are truth,
and his ways are justice;
and he is able to bring low
those who walk in pride.

BELSHAZZAR'S FEAST

5 King Belshazzar made a great festival for a thousand of his lords, and
he was drinking wine in the presence of
the thousand.
2 Under the influence of the wine,
Belshazzar commanded that they bring
in the vessels of gold and silver that his
father Nebuchadnezzar had taken out
of the temple in Jerusalem, so that the
king and his lords, his wives, and his
concubines might drink from them. 3So
they brought in the vessels of gold and
silver[u] that had been taken out of the
temple, the house of God in Jerusalem,
and the king and his lords, his wives,
and his concubines drank from them.
4They drank the wine and praised the
gods of gold and silver, bronze, iron,
wood, and stone.

THE WRITING ON THE WALL

5 Immediately the fingers of a human hand appeared and began writing
on the plaster of the wall of the royal
palace, next to the lampstand. The king
was watching the hand as it wrote.
6Then the king's face turned pale, and
his thoughts terrified him. His limbs
gave way, and his knees knocked together. 7The king cried aloud to bring
in the enchanters, the Chaldeans, and
the diviners; and the king said to the
wise men of Babylon, 'Whoever can
read this writing and tell me its interpretation shall be clothed in purple,
have a chain of gold around his neck,
and rank third in the kingdom.' 8Then
all the king's wise men came in, but
they could not read the writing or tell
the king the interpretation. 9Then King
Belshazzar became greatly terrified and
his face turned pale, and his lords were
perplexed.
10 The queen, when she heard the
discussion of the king and his lords,
came into the banqueting-hall. The
queen said, 'O king, live for ever! Do not
let your thoughts terrify you or your
face grow pale. 11There is a man in your
kingdom who is endowed with a spirit

[t] **4.27** Aram *break off* [u] **5.3** Theodotion Vg: Aram lacks *and silver*

of the holy gods.[v] In the days of your
father he was found to have enlightenment, understanding, and wisdom like
the wisdom of the gods. Your father,
King Nebuchadnezzar, made him chief
of the magicians, enchanters, Chaldeans, and diviners,[w] 12because an excellent spirit, knowledge, and understanding to interpret dreams, explain riddles,
and solve problems were found in this
Daniel, whom the king named Belteshazzar. Now let Daniel be called, and
he will give the interpretation.'

THE WRITING ON THE WALL INTERPRETED

13 Then Daniel was brought in before
the king. The king said to Daniel, 'So
you are Daniel, one of the exiles of Judah, whom my father the king brought
from Judah? 14I have heard of you that
a spirit of the gods[x] is in you, and that
enlightenment, understanding, and excellent wisdom are found in you. 15Now
the wise men, the enchanters, have
been brought in before me to read this
writing and tell me its interpretation,
but they were not able to give the interpretation of the matter. 16But I have
heard that you can give interpretations
and solve problems. Now if you are able
to read the writing and tell me its interpretation, you shall be clothed in purple, have a chain of gold around your
neck, and rank third in the kingdom.'

17 Then Daniel answered in the presence of the king, 'Let your gifts be for
yourself, or give your rewards to someone else! Nevertheless, I will read the
writing to the king and let him know
the interpretation. 18O king, the Most
High God gave your father Nebuchadnezzar kingship, greatness, glory, and
majesty. 19And because of the greatness
that he gave him, all peoples, nations,
and languages trembled and feared before him. He killed those he wanted to
kill, kept alive those he wanted to keep
alive, honoured those he wanted to
honour, and degraded those he wanted
to degrade. 20But when his heart was
lifted up and his spirit was hardened so
that he acted proudly, he was deposed
from his kingly throne, and his glory
was stripped from him. 21He was driven
from human society, and his mind was
made like that of an animal. His dwelling was with the wild asses, he was fed
grass like oxen, and his body was bathed
with the dew of heaven, until he learned
that the Most High God has sovereignty
over the kingdom of mortals, and sets
over it whomsoever he will. 22And you,
Belshazzar his son, have not humbled
your heart, even though you knew all
this! 23You have exalted yourself against
the Lord of heaven! The vessels of his
temple have been brought in before
you, and you and your lords, your wives
and your concubines have been drinking wine from them. You have praised
the gods of silver and gold, of bronze,
iron, wood, and stone, which do not see
or hear or know; but the God in whose
power is your very breath, and to whom
belong all your ways, you have not honoured.

24 'So from his presence the hand
was sent and this writing was inscribed.
25And this is the writing that was inscribed: MENE, MENE, TEKEL, and PAR-
SIN. 26This is the interpretation of the
matter: MENE, God has numbered the
days of[y] your kingdom and brought
it to an end; 27TEKEL, you have been
weighed on the scales and found wanting; 28PERES,[z] your kingdom is divided
and given to the Medes and Persians.'

29 Then Belshazzar gave the command, and Daniel was clothed in purple, a chain of gold was put around his
neck, and a proclamation was made
concerning him that he should rank
third in the kingdom.

30 That very night Belshazzar, the
Chaldean king, was killed. 31[a]And Darius the Mede received the kingdom,
being about sixty-two years old.

THE PLOT AGAINST DANIEL

6 It pleased Darius to set over the
kingdom one hundred and twenty
satraps, stationed throughout the
whole kingdom, 2and over them three
presidents, including Daniel; to these
the satraps gave account, so that the
king might suffer no loss. 3Soon Daniel distinguished himself above all the
other presidents and satraps because
an excellent spirit was in him, and the
king planned to appoint him over the
whole kingdom. 4So the presidents and
the satraps tried to find grounds for
complaint against Daniel in connection
with the kingdom. But they could find
no grounds for complaint or any corruption, because he was faithful, and no
negligence or corruption could be found

[v] 5.11 Or *a holy, divine spirit* [w] 5.11 Aram adds *the king your father* [x] 5.14 Or *a divine spirit* [y] 5.26 Aram lacks *the days of* [z] 5.28 The singular of *Parsin* [a] 5.31 Ch 6.1 in Aram

in him. 5The men said, 'We shall not find
any ground for complaint against this
Daniel unless we find it in connection
with the law of his God.'
6 So the presidents and satraps conspired and came to the king and said to
him, 'O King Darius, live for ever! 7All
the presidents of the kingdom, the prefects and the satraps, the counsellors
and the governors, are agreed that the
king should establish an ordinance
and enforce an interdict, that whoever prays to anyone, divine or human,
for thirty days, except to you, O king,
shall be thrown into a den of lions.
8Now, O king, establish the interdict
and sign the document, so that it cannot be changed, according to the law of
the Medes and the Persians, which cannot be revoked.' 9Therefore King Darius
signed the document and interdict.

DANIEL IN THE LIONS' DEN

10 Although Daniel knew that the
document had been signed, he continued to go to his house, which had windows in its upper room open towards
Jerusalem, and to get down on his
knees three times a day to pray to his
God and praise him, just as he had done
previously. 11The conspirators came
and found Daniel praying and seeking
mercy before his God. 12Then they approached the king and said concerning
the interdict, 'O king! Did you not sign
an interdict, that anyone who prays
to anyone, divine or human, within
thirty days except to you, O king, shall
be thrown into a den of lions?' The king
answered, 'The thing stands fast, according to the law of the Medes and Persians, which cannot be revoked.' 13Then
they responded to the king, 'Daniel, one
of the exiles from Judah, pays no attention to you, O king, or to the interdict
you have signed, but he is saying his
prayers three times a day.'
14 When the king heard the charge,
he was very much distressed. He was
determined to save Daniel, and until
the sun went down he made every effort to rescue him. 15Then the conspirators came to the king and said to him,
'Know, O king, that it is a law of the
Medes and Persians that no interdict or
ordinance that the king establishes can
be changed.'
16 Then the king gave the command,
and Daniel was brought and thrown
into the den of lions. The king said to
Daniel, 'May your God, whom you faithfully serve, deliver you!' 17A stone was
brought and laid on the mouth of the
den, and the king sealed it with his own
signet and with the signet of his lords,
so that nothing might be changed concerning Daniel. 18Then the king went to
his palace and spent the night fasting;
no food was brought to him, and sleep
fled from him.

DANIEL SAVED FROM THE LIONS

19 Then, at break of day, the king
got up and hurried to the den of lions.
20When he came near the den where
Daniel was, he cried out anxiously to
Daniel, 'O Daniel, servant of the living
God, has your God whom you faithfully
serve been able to deliver you from the
lions?' 21Daniel then said to the king,
'O king, live for ever! 22My God sent
his angel and shut the lions' mouths so
that they would not hurt me, because
I was found blameless before him; and
also before you, O king, I have done no
wrong.' 23Then the king was exceedingly
glad and commanded that Daniel be
taken up out of the den. So Daniel was
taken up out of the den, and no kind
of harm was found on him, because he
had trusted in his God. 24The king gave
a command, and those who had accused
Daniel were brought and thrown into
the den of lions—they, their children,
and their wives. Before they reached
the bottom of the den the lions overpowered them and broke all their bones
in pieces.
25 Then King Darius wrote to all
peoples and nations of every language
throughout the whole world: 'May you
have abundant prosperity! 26I make a
decree, that in all my royal dominion
people should tremble and fear before
the God of Daniel:

For he is the living God,
 enduring for ever.
His kingdom shall never
  be destroyed,
 and his dominion has no end.
27 He delivers and rescues,
 he works signs and wonders in
  heaven and on earth;
for he has saved Daniel
 from the power of the lions.'

28So this Daniel prospered during the
reign of Darius and the reign of Cyrus
the Persian.

VISIONS OF THE FOUR BEASTS

7 In the first year of King Belshazzar of Babylon, Daniel had a dream

and visions of his head as he lay in bed.
Then he wrote down the dream:[b] 2I,[c]
Daniel, saw in my vision by night the
four winds of heaven stirring up the
great sea, 3and four great beasts came
up out of the sea, different from one
another. 4The first was like a lion and
had eagles' wings. Then, as I watched,
its wings were plucked off, and it was
lifted up from the ground and made to
stand on two feet like a human being;
and a human mind was given to it. 5An-
other beast appeared, a second one, that
looked like a bear. It was raised up on
one side, had three tusks[d] in its mouth
among its teeth and was told, 'Arise,
devour many bodies!' 6After this, as I
watched, another appeared, like a leopard. The beast had four wings of a bird
on its back and four heads; and dominion was given to it. 7After this I saw
in the visions by night a fourth beast,
terrifying and dreadful and exceedingly strong. It had great iron teeth and
was devouring, breaking in pieces, and
stamping what was left with its feet. It
was different from all the beasts that
preceded it, and it had ten horns. 8I was
considering the horns, when another
horn appeared, a little one coming up
among them; to make room for it, three
of the earlier horns were plucked up by
the roots. There were eyes like human
eyes in this horn, and a mouth speaking
arrogantly.

JUDGEMENT BEFORE THE ANCIENT ONE

9 As I watched,
thrones were set in place,
and an Ancient One[e]
took his throne;
his clothing was white as snow,
and the hair of his head
like pure wool;
his throne was fiery flames,
and its wheels were burning fire.
10 A stream of fire issued
and flowed out from his presence.
A thousand thousand served him,
and ten thousand times
ten thousand stood
attending him.
The court sat in judgement,
and the books were opened.

11I watched then because of the noise of
the arrogant words that the horn was
speaking. And as I watched, the beast
was put to death, and its body destroyed
and given over to be burned with fire.
12As for the rest of the beasts, their dominion was taken away, but their lives
were prolonged for a season and a time.
13As I watched in the night visions,
I saw one like a human being[f]
coming with the clouds of heaven.
And he came to the Ancient One[g]
and was presented before him.
14 To him was given dominion
and glory and kingship,
that all peoples, nations,
and languages
should serve him.
His dominion is an everlasting
dominion
that shall not pass away,
and his kingship is one
that shall never be destroyed.

DANIEL'S VISIONS INTERPRETED

15 As for me, Daniel, my spirit was
troubled within me,[h] and the visions
of my head terrified me. 16I approached
one of the attendants to ask him the
truth concerning all this. So he said that
he would disclose to me the interpretation of the matter: 17'As for these four
great beasts, four kings shall arise out
of the earth. 18But the holy ones of the
Most High shall receive the kingdom
and possess the kingdom for ever—for
ever and ever.'

19 Then I desired to know the truth
concerning the fourth beast, which was
different from all the rest, exceedingly
terrifying, with its teeth of iron and
claws of bronze, and which devoured
and broke in pieces, and stamped what
was left with its feet; 20and concerning
the ten horns that were on its head, and
concerning the other horn that came
up, and to make room for which three
of them fell out—the horn that had eyes
and a mouth that spoke arrogantly, and
that seemed greater than the others.
21As I looked, this horn made war with
the holy ones and was prevailing over
them, 22until the Ancient One[i] came;
then judgement was given for the holy
ones of the Most High, and the time arrived when the holy ones gained possession of the kingdom.

23 This is what he said: 'As for the
fourth beast,

[b] 7.1 Q Ms Theodotion: MT adds *the beginning of the words; he said* [c] 7.2 Theodotion: Aram *Daniel answered and said, 'I* [d] 7.5 Or *ribs* [e] 7.9 Aram *an Ancient of Days* [f] 7.13 Aram *one like a son of man* [g] 7.13 Aram *the Ancient of Days* [h] 7.15 Aram *troubled in its sheath* [i] 7.22 Aram *the Ancient of Days*

there shall be a fourth
kingdom on earth
that shall be different from all
the other kingdoms;
it shall devour the whole earth,
and trample it down, and
break it to pieces.
24 As for the ten horns,
out of this kingdom ten
kings shall arise,
and another shall arise after them.
This one shall be different from
the former ones,
and shall put down three kings.
25 He shall speak words against
the Most High,
shall wear out the holy ones
of the Most High,
and shall attempt to change the
sacred seasons and the law;
and they shall be given
into his power
for a time, two times,[j]
and half a time.
26 Then the court shall sit in
judgement,
and his dominion shall
be taken away,
to be consumed and
totally destroyed.
27 The kingship and dominion
and the greatness of the kingdoms
under the whole heaven
shall be given to the people of the
holy ones of the Most High;
their kingdom shall be an
everlasting kingdom,
and all dominions shall serve
and obey them.'

28 Here the account ends. As for me,
Daniel, my thoughts greatly terrified
me, and my face turned pale; but I kept
the matter in my mind.

VISION OF A RAM AND A GOAT

8 In the third year of the reign of
King Belshazzar a vision appeared
to me, Daniel, after the one that had
appeared to me at first. 2In the vision I
was looking and saw myself in Susa the
capital, in the province of Elam,[k] and I
was by the river Ulai.[l] 3I looked up and
saw a ram standing beside the river.[m] It
had two horns. Both horns were long,
but one was longer than the other, and
the longer one came up second. 4I saw
the ram charging westwards and northwards and southwards. All beasts were
powerless to withstand it, and no one
could rescue from its power; it did as it
pleased and became strong.

5 As I was watching, a male goat appeared from the west, coming across the
face of the whole earth without touching the ground. The goat had a horn[n]
between its eyes. 6It came towards the
ram with the two horns that I had seen
standing beside the river,[o] and it ran at
it with savage force. 7I saw it approaching the ram. It was enraged against it
and struck the ram, breaking its two
horns. The ram did not have power to
withstand it; it threw the ram down to
the ground and trampled upon it, and
there was no one who could rescue the
ram from its power. 8Then the male
goat grew exceedingly great; but at the
height of its power, the great horn was
broken, and in its place there came up
four prominent horns towards the four
winds of heaven.

9 Out of one of them came another[p]
horn, a little one, which grew exceedingly great towards the south, towards
the east, and towards the beautiful land.
10It grew as high as the host of heaven.
It threw down to the earth some of the
host and some of the stars, and trampled on them. 11Even against the prince
of the host it acted arrogantly; it took
the regular burnt-offering away from
him and overthrew the place of his
sanctuary. 12Because of wickedness, the
host was given over to it together with
the regular burnt-offering;[q] it cast truth
to the ground, and kept prospering in
what it did. 13Then I heard a holy one
speaking, and another holy one said
to the one that spoke, 'For how long
is this vision concerning the regular
burnt-offering, the transgression that
makes desolate, and the giving over
of the sanctuary and host to be trampled?'[r] 14And he answered him,[s] 'For
two thousand three hundred evenings
and mornings; then the sanctuary shall
be restored to its rightful state.'

GABRIEL INTERPRETS THE VISION

15 When I, Daniel, had seen the vision, I tried to understand it. Then
someone appeared standing before me,
having the appearance of a man, 16and
I heard a human voice by the Ulai, calling, 'Gabriel, help this man understand

[j] **7.25** Aram *a time, times* [k] **8.2** Gk Theodotion: MT Q Ms repeat *in the vision I was looking*
[l] **8.2** Or *the Ulai Gate* [m] **8.3** Or *gate*
[n] **8.5** Theodotion: Gk *one horn*; Heb *a horn of vision* [o] **8.6** Or *gate* [p] **8.9** Cn Compare 7.8: Heb *one* [q] **8.12** Meaning of Heb uncertain
[r] **8.13** Meaning of Heb uncertain [s] **8.14** Gk Theodotion Syr Vg: Heb *me*

the vision.' 17 So he came near where
I stood; and when he came, I became
frightened and fell prostrate. But he said
to me, 'Understand, O mortal,[t] that the
vision is for the time of the end.'

18 As he was speaking to me, I fell
into a trance, face to the ground; then
he touched me and set me on my feet.
19 He said, 'Listen, and I will tell you
what will take place later in the period
of wrath; for it refers to the appointed
time of the end. 20 As for the ram that
you saw with the two horns, these are
the kings of Media and Persia. 21 The
male goat[u] is the king of Greece, and the
great horn between its eyes is the first
king. 22 As for the horn that was broken,
in place of which four others arose, four
kingdoms shall arise from his[v] nation,
but not with his power.

23 At the end of their rule,
when the transgressions have
reached their full measure,
a king of bold countenance
shall arise,
skilled in intrigue.
24 He shall grow strong in power,[w]
shall cause fearful destruction,
and shall succeed in
what he does.
He shall destroy the powerful
and the people of the holy ones.
25 By his cunning
he shall make deceit prosper
under his hand,
and in his own mind he
shall be great.
Without warning he shall
destroy many
and shall even rise up against
the Prince of princes.
But he shall be broken, and not
by human hands.

26 The vision of the evenings and the
mornings that has been told is true. As
for you, seal up the vision, for it refers to
many days from now.'

27 So I, Daniel, was overcome and
lay sick for some days; then I arose and
went about the king's business. But I
was dismayed by the vision and did not
understand it.

DANIEL'S PRAYER FOR THE PEOPLE

9 In the first year of Darius son of
Ahasuerus, by birth a Mede, who
became king over the realm of the Chaldeans— 2 in the first year of his reign, I,
Daniel, perceived in the books the number of years that, according to the word
of the LORD to the prophet Jeremiah,
must be fulfilled for the devastation of
Jerusalem, namely, seventy years.

3 Then I turned to the Lord God, to
seek an answer by prayer and supplication with fasting and sackcloth and
ashes. 4 I prayed to the LORD my God
and made confession, saying,

'Ah, Lord, great and awesome God,
keeping covenant and steadfast love
with those who love you and keep your
commandments, 5 we have sinned and
done wrong, acted wickedly and rebelled, turning aside from your commandments and ordinances. 6 We have
not listened to your servants the prophets, who spoke in your name to our
kings, our princes, and our ancestors,
and to all the people of the land.

7 'Righteousness is on your side,
O Lord, but open shame, as at this day,
falls on us, the people of Judah, the
inhabitants of Jerusalem, and all Israel,
those who are near and those who are far
away, in all the lands to which you have
driven them, because of the treachery
that they have committed against you.
8 Open shame, O LORD, falls on us, our
kings, our officials, and our ancestors,
because we have sinned against you.
9 To the Lord our God belong mercy and
forgiveness, for we have rebelled against
him, 10 and have not obeyed the voice of
the LORD our God by following his laws,
which he set before us by his servants
the prophets.

11 'All Israel has transgressed your
law and turned aside, refusing to obey
your voice. So the curse and the oath
written in the law of Moses, the servant
of God, have been poured out upon us,
because we have sinned against you.
12 He has confirmed his words, which he
spoke against us and against our rulers,
by bringing upon us a calamity so great
that what has been done against Jerusalem has never before been done under
the whole heaven. 13 Just as it is written
in the law of Moses, all this calamity has
come upon us. We did not entreat the favour of the LORD our God, turning from
our iniquities and reflecting on his[x] fidelity. 14 So the LORD kept watch over
this calamity until he brought it upon
us. Indeed, the LORD our God is right
in all that he has done; for we have disobeyed his voice.

[t] 8.17 Heb *son of man* [u] 8.21 Or *shaggy male goat* [v] 8.22 Gk Theodotion Vg: Heb *the* [w] 8.24 Theodotion and one Gk Ms: Heb repeats (from 8.22) *but not with his power* [x] 9.13 Heb *your*

15 'And now, O Lord our God, who
brought your people out of the land of
Egypt with a mighty hand and made
your name renowned even to this day—
we have sinned, we have done wickedly.
16 O Lord, in view of all your righteous
acts, let your anger and wrath, we pray,
turn away from your city Jerusalem,
your holy mountain; because of our sins
and the iniquities of our ancestors, Jerusalem and your people have become
a disgrace among all our neighbours.
17 Now therefore, O our God, listen to
the prayer of your servant and to his
supplication, and for your own sake,
Lord,[y] let your face shine upon your
desolated sanctuary. 18 Incline your ear,
O my God, and hear. Open your eyes
and look at our desolation and the city
that bears your name. We do not present our supplication before you on the
ground of our righteousness, but on the
ground of your great mercies. 19 O Lord,
hear; O Lord, forgive; O Lord, listen and
act and do not delay! For your own sake,
O my God, because your city and your
people bear your name!'

THE SEVENTY WEEKS

20 While I was speaking, and was
praying and confessing my sin and the
sin of my people Israel, and presenting
my supplication before the LORD my
God on behalf of the holy mountain of
my God— 21 while I was speaking in
prayer, the man Gabriel, whom I had
seen before in a vision, came to me in
swift flight at the time of the evening
sacrifice. 22 He came[z] and said to me,
'Daniel, I have now come out to give you
wisdom and understanding. 23 At the
beginning of your supplications a word
went out, and I have come to declare it,
for you are greatly beloved. So consider
the word and understand the vision:

24 'Seventy weeks are decreed for your
people and your holy city: to finish the
transgression, to put an end to sin, and
to atone for iniquity, to bring in everlasting righteousness, to seal both vision
and prophet, and to anoint a most holy
place.[a] 25 Know therefore and understand: from the time that the word went
out to restore and rebuild Jerusalem until the time of an anointed prince, there
shall be seven weeks; and for sixty-two
weeks it shall be built again with streets
and moat, but in a troubled time. 26 After the sixty-two weeks, an anointed one
shall be cut off and shall have nothing,
and the troops of the prince who is to
come shall destroy the city and the sanctuary. Its[b] end shall come with a flood,
and to the end there shall be war. Desolations are decreed. 27 He shall make
a strong covenant with many for one
week, and for half of the week he shall
make sacrifice and offering cease; and
in their place[c] shall be an abomination
that desolates, until the decreed end is
poured out upon the desolator.'

CONFLICT OF NATIONS AND HEAVENLY POWERS

10 In the third year of King Cyrus
of Persia a word was revealed to
Daniel, who was named Belteshazzar.
The word was true, and it concerned a
great conflict. He understood the word,
having received understanding in the
vision.

2 At that time I, Daniel, had been
mourning for three weeks. 3 I had eaten
no rich food, no meat or wine had entered my mouth, and I had not anointed
myself at all, for the full three weeks.
4 On the twenty-fourth day of the first
month, as I was standing on the bank
of the great river (that is, the Tigris),
5 I looked up and saw a man clothed in
linen, with a belt of gold from Uphaz
around his waist. 6 His body was like
beryl, his face like lightning, his eyes
like flaming torches, his arms and legs
like the gleam of burnished bronze, and
the sound of his words like the roar of a
multitude. 7 I, Daniel, alone saw the vision; the people who were with me did
not see the vision, though a great trembling fell upon them, and they fled and
hid themselves. 8 So I was left alone to
see this great vision. My strength left
me, and my complexion grew deathly
pale, and I retained no strength. 9 Then I
heard the sound of his words; and when
I heard the sound of his words, I fell into
a trance, face to the ground.

10 But then a hand touched me and
roused me to my hands and knees. 11 He
said to me, 'Daniel, greatly beloved, pay
attention to the words that I am going
to speak to you. Stand on your feet, for I
have now been sent to you.' So while he
was speaking this word to me, I stood up
trembling. 12 He said to me, 'Do not fear,
Daniel, for from the first day that you set
your mind to gain understanding and to
humble yourself before your God, your

[y] **9.17** Theodotion Vg Compare Syr: Heb *for the Lord's sake* [z] **9.22** Gk Syr: Heb *He made to understand* [a] **9.24** Or *thing* or *one* [b] **9.26** Or *His* [c] **9.27** Cn: Meaning of Heb uncertain

words have been heard, and I have come because of your words. 13 But the prince of the kingdom of Persia opposed me for twenty-one days. So Michael, one of the chief princes, came to help me, and I left him there with the prince of the kingdom of Persia,[d] 14 and have come to help you understand what is to happen to your people at the end of days. For there is a further vision for those days.'

15 While he was speaking these words to me, I turned my face towards the ground and was speechless. 16 Then one in human form touched my lips, and I opened my mouth to speak, and said to the one who stood before me, 'My lord, because of the vision such pains have come upon me that I retain no strength. 17 How can my lord's servant talk with my lord? For I am shaking,[e] no strength remains in me, and no breath is left in me.'

18 Again one in human form touched me and strengthened me. 19 He said, 'Do not fear, greatly beloved, you are safe. Be strong and courageous!' When he spoke to me, I was strengthened and said, 'Let my lord speak, for you have strengthened me.' 20 Then he said, 'Do you know why I have come to you? Now I must return to fight against the prince of Persia, and when I am through with him, the prince of Greece will come. 21 But I am to tell you what is inscribed in the book of truth. There is no one with me who contends against these princes except Michael, your prince.

11 1 As for me, in the first year of Darius the Mede, I stood up to support and strengthen him.

2 'Now I will announce the truth to you. Three more kings shall arise in Persia. The fourth shall be far richer than all of them, and when he has become strong through his riches, he shall stir up all against the kingdom of Greece. 3 Then a warrior king shall arise, who shall rule with great dominion and take action as he pleases. 4 And while still rising in power, his kingdom shall be broken and divided towards the four winds of heaven, but not to his posterity, nor according to the dominion with which he ruled; for his kingdom shall be uprooted and go to others besides these.

5 'Then the king of the south shall grow strong, but one of his officers shall grow stronger than he and shall rule a realm greater than his own realm. 6 After some years they shall make an alliance, and the daughter of the king of the south shall come to the king of the north to ratify the agreement. But she shall not retain her power, and his offspring shall not endure. She shall be given up, she and her attendants and her child and the one who supported her.

'In those times 7 a branch from her roots shall rise up in his place. He shall come against the army and enter the fortress of the king of the north, and he shall take action against them and prevail. 8 Even their gods, with their idols and with their precious vessels of silver and gold, he shall carry off to Egypt as spoils of war. For some years he shall refrain from attacking the king of the north; 9 then the latter shall invade the realm of the king of the south, but will return to his own land.

10 'His sons shall wage war and assemble a multitude of great forces, which shall advance like a flood and pass through, and again shall carry the war as far as his fortress. 11 Moved with rage, the king of the south shall go out and do battle against the king of the north, who shall muster a great multitude, which shall, however, be defeated by his enemy. 12 When the multitude has been carried off, his heart shall be exalted, and he shall overthrow tens of thousands, but he shall not prevail. 13 For the king of the north shall again raise a multitude, larger than the former, and after some years[f] he shall advance with a great army and abundant supplies.

14 'In those times many shall rise against the king of the south. The lawless among your own people shall lift themselves up in order to fulfil the vision, but they shall fail. 15 Then the king of the north shall come and throw up siege-works, and take a well-fortified city. And the forces of the south shall not stand, not even his picked troops, for there shall be no strength to resist. 16 But he who comes against him shall take the actions he pleases, and no one shall withstand him. He shall take a position in the beautiful land, and all of it shall be in his power. 17 He shall set his mind to come with the strength of his whole kingdom, and he shall bring terms of peace[g] and perform them. In order to destroy the kingdom,[h] he shall

[d] **10.13** Gk Theodotion: Heb *I was left there with the kings of Persia* [e] **10.17** Gk: Heb *from now*
[f] **11.13** Heb *and at the end of the times years*
[g] **11.17** Gk: Heb *kingdom, and upright ones with him* [h] **11.17** Heb *it*

give him a woman in marriage; but it
shall not succeed or be to his advantage. 18 Afterwards he shall turn to the
coastlands, and shall capture many. But
a commander shall put an end to his
insolence; indeed,[i] he shall turn his insolence back upon him. 19 Then he shall
turn back towards the fortresses of his
own land, but he shall stumble and fall,
and shall not be found.

20 'Then shall arise in his place one
who shall send an official for the glory
of the kingdom; but within a few days
he shall be broken, though not in anger or in battle. 21 In his place shall arise
a contemptible person on whom royal
majesty had not been conferred; he shall
come in without warning and obtain
the kingdom through intrigue. 22 Armies shall be utterly swept away and
broken before him, and the prince of the
covenant as well. 23 And after an alliance
is made with him, he shall act deceitfully
and become strong with a small party.
24 Without warning he shall come into
the richest parts[j] of the province and
do what none of his predecessors had
ever done, lavishing plunder, spoil, and
wealth on them. He shall devise plans
against strongholds, but only for a time.
25 He shall stir up his power and determi-
nation against the king of the south with
a great army, and the king of the south
shall wage war with a much greater and
stronger army. But he shall not succeed,
for plots shall be devised against him
26 by those who eat of the royal rations.
They shall break him, his army shall be
swept away, and many shall fall slain.
27 The two kings, their minds bent on
evil, shall sit at one table and exchange
lies. But it shall not succeed, for there
remains an end at the time appointed.
28 He shall return to his land with great
wealth, but his heart shall be set against
the holy covenant. He shall work his
will, and return to his own land.

29 'At the time appointed he shall return and come into the south, but this
time it shall not be as it was before. 30 For
ships of Kittim shall come against him,
and he shall lose heart and withdraw.
He shall be enraged and take action
against the holy covenant. He shall turn
back and pay heed to those who forsake
the holy covenant. 31 Forces sent by him
shall occupy and profane the temple and
fortress. They shall abolish the regular
burnt-offering and set up the abomination that makes desolate. 32 He shall
seduce with intrigue those who violate
the covenant; but the people who are
loyal to their God shall stand firm and
take action. 33 The wise among the people shall give understanding to many;
for some days, however, they shall fall
by sword and flame, and suffer captivity
and plunder. 34 When they fall victim,
they shall receive a little help, and many
shall join them insincerely. 35 Some of
the wise shall fall, so that they may be
refined, purified, and cleansed,[k] until
the time of the end, for there is still an
interval until the time appointed.

36 'The king shall act as he pleases.
He shall exalt himself and consider
himself greater than any god, and shall
speak horrendous things against the
God of gods. He shall prosper until the
period of wrath is completed, for what is
determined shall be done. 37 He shall pay
no respect to the gods of his ancestors,
or to the one beloved by women; he shall
pay no respect to any other god, for he
shall consider himself greater than all.
38 He shall honour the god of fortresses
instead of these; a god whom his ancestors did not know he shall honour with
gold and silver, with precious stones
and costly gifts. 39 He shall deal with the
strongest fortresses by the help of a foreign god. Those who acknowledge him
he shall make more wealthy, and shall
appoint them as rulers over many, and
shall distribute the land for a price.

THE TIME OF THE END

40 'At the time of the end the king
of the south shall attack him. But the
king of the north shall rush upon him
like a whirlwind, with chariots and
horsemen, and with many ships. He
shall advance against countries and
pass through like a flood. 41 He shall
come into the beautiful land, and tens
of thousands shall fall victim, but Edom
and Moab and the main part of the Ammonites shall escape from his power.
42 He shall stretch out his hand against
the countries, and the land of Egypt
shall not escape. 43 He shall become ruler
of the treasures of gold and of silver, and
all the riches of Egypt; and the Libyans
and the Ethiopians[l] shall follow in his
train. 44 But reports from the east and
the north shall alarm him, and he shall
go out with great fury to bring ruin and
complete destruction to many. 45 He
shall pitch his palatial tents between

[i] **11.18** Meaning of Heb uncertain [j] **11.24** Or *among the richest men* [k] **11.35** Heb *made them white* [l] **11.43** Or *Nubians*; Heb *Cushites*

the sea and the beautiful holy mountain. Yet he shall come to his end, with no one to help him.

THE RESURRECTION OF THE DEAD

12 'At that time Michael, the great prince, the protector of your people, shall arise. There shall be a time of anguish, such as has never occurred since nations first came into existence. But at that time your people shall be delivered, everyone who is found written in the book. 2 Many of those who sleep in the dust of the earth[m] shall awake, some to everlasting life, and some to shame and everlasting contempt. 3 Those who are wise shall shine like the brightness of the sky,[n] and those who lead many to righteousness, like the stars for ever and ever. 4 But you, Daniel, keep the words secret and the book sealed until the time of the end. Many shall be running back and forth, and evil[o] shall increase.'

5 Then I, Daniel, looked, and two others appeared, one standing on this bank of the stream and one on the other. 6 One of them said to the man clothed in linen, who was upstream, 'How long shall it be until the end of these wonders?' 7 The man clothed in linen, who was upstream, raised his right hand and his left hand towards heaven. And I heard him swear by the one who lives for ever that it would be for a time, two times, and half a time,[p] and that when the shattering of the power of the holy people comes to an end, all these things would be accomplished. 8 I heard but could not understand; so I said, 'My lord, what shall be the outcome of these things?' 9 He said, 'Go your way, Daniel, for the words are to remain secret and sealed until the time of the end. 10 Many shall be purified, cleansed, and refined, but the wicked shall continue to act wickedly. None of the wicked shall understand, but those who are wise shall understand. 11 From the time that the regular burnt-offering is taken away and the abomination that desolates is set up, there shall be one thousand two hundred and ninety days. 12 Happy are those who persevere and attain the thousand three hundred and thirty-five days. 13 But you, go your way,[q] and rest; you shall rise for your reward at the end of the days.'

SUSANNA'S BEAUTY ATTRACTS TWO ELDERS

13 There was a man living in Babylon whose name was Joakim. 2 He married the daughter of Hilkiah, named Susanna, a very beautiful woman and one who feared the Lord. 3 Her parents were righteous, and had trained their daughter according to the law of Moses. 4 Joakim was very rich, and had a fine garden adjoining his house; the Jews used to come to him because he was the most honoured of them all.

5 That year two elders from the people were appointed as judges. Concerning them the Lord had said: 'Wickedness came forth from Babylon, from elders who were judges, who were supposed to govern the people.' 6 These men were frequently at Joakim's house, and all who had a case to be tried came to them there.

7 When the people left at noon, Susanna would go into her husband's garden to walk. 8 Every day the two elders used to see her, going in and walking about, and they began to lust for her. 9 They suppressed their consciences and turned away their eyes from looking to Heaven or remembering their duty to administer justice. 10 Both were overwhelmed with passion for her, but they did not tell each other of their distress, 11 for they were ashamed to disclose their lustful desire to seduce her. 12 Day after day they watched eagerly to see her.

13 One day they said to each other, 'Let us go home, for it is time for lunch.' So they both left and parted from each other. 14 But turning back, they met again; and when each pressed the other for the reason, they confessed their lust. Then together they arranged for a time when they could find her alone.

THE ELDERS ATTEMPT TO SEDUCE SUSANNA

15 Once, while they were watching for an opportune day, she went in as before with only two maids, and wished to bathe in the garden, for it was a hot day. 16 No one was there except the two elders, who had hidden themselves and were watching her. 17 She said to her maids, 'Bring me olive oil and ointments, and shut the garden doors so that I can bathe.' 18 They did as she told them: they shut the doors of the garden and went out by the side doors to bring what they had been commanded; they

m 12.2 Or *the land of dust* n 12.3 Or *dome*
o 12.4 Cn Compare Gk: Heb *knowledge*
p 12.7 Heb *a time, times, and a half* q 12.13 Gk Theodotion: Heb adds *to the end*

did not see the elders, because they were
hiding.
19 When the maids had gone out, the
two elders got up and ran to her. 20 They
said, 'Look, the garden doors are shut,
and no one can see us. We are burning
with desire for you; so give your consent, and lie with us. 21 If you refuse,
we will testify against you that a young
man was with you, and this was why
you sent your maids away.'
22 Susanna groaned and said, 'I am
completely trapped. For if I do this, it
will mean death for me; if I do not, I
cannot escape your hands. 23 I choose
not to do it; I will fall into your hands,
rather than sin in the sight of the Lord.'
24 Then Susanna cried out with a
loud voice, and the two elders shouted
against her. 25 And one of them ran and
opened the garden doors. 26 When the
people in the house heard the shouting
in the garden, they rushed in at the side
door to see what had happened to her.
27 And when the elders told their story,
the servants felt very much ashamed,
for nothing like this had ever been said
about Susanna.

THE ELDERS TESTIFY AGAINST SUSANNA

28 The next day, when the people
gathered at the house of her husband
Joakim, the two elders came, full of
their wicked plot to have Susanna put
to death. In the presence of the people
they said, 29 'Send for Susanna daughter
of Hilkiah, the wife of Joakim.' 30 So they
sent for her. And she came with her parents, her children, and all her relatives.
31 Now Susanna was a woman of
great refinement and beautiful in appearance. 32 As she was veiled, the
scoundrels ordered her to be unveiled,
so that they might feast their eyes on
her beauty. 33 Those who were with her
and all who saw her were weeping.
34 Then the two elders stood up before the people and laid their hands
on her head. 35 Through her tears she
looked up towards Heaven, for her heart
trusted in the Lord. 36 The elders said,
'While we were walking in the garden
alone, this woman came in with two
maids, shut the garden doors, and dismissed the maids. 37 Then a young man,
who was hiding there, came to her and
lay with her. 38 We were in a corner of
the garden, and when we saw this wickedness we ran to them. 39 Although we
saw them embracing, we could not hold
the man, because he was stronger than
we are, and he opened the doors and
got away. 40 We did, however, seize this
woman and asked who the young man
was, 41 but she would not tell us. These
things we testify.'
Because they were elders of the people and judges, the assembly believed
them and condemned her to death.
42 Then Susanna cried out with a
loud voice, and said, 'O eternal God, you
know what is secret and are aware of
all things before they come to be; 43 you
know that these men have given false
evidence against me. And now I am
to die, though I have done none of the
wicked things that they have charged
against me!'
44 The Lord heard her cry. 45 Just as
she was being led off to execution, God
stirred up the holy spirit of a young lad
named Daniel, 46 and he shouted with a
loud voice, 'I want no part in shedding
this woman's blood!'

DANIEL RESCUES SUSANNA

47 All the people turned to him and
asked, 'What is this you are saying?'
48 Taking his stand among them he
said, 'Are you such fools, O Israelites, as
to condemn a daughter of Israel without
examination and without learning the
facts? 49 Return to court, for these men
have given false evidence against her.'
50 So all the people hurried back.
And the rest of the[r] elders said to him,
'Come, sit among us and inform us, for
God has given you the standing of an
elder.' 51 Daniel said to them, 'Separate
them far from each other, and I will examine them.'
52 When they were separated from
each other, he summoned one of them
and said to him, 'You old relic of wicked
days, your sins have now come home,
which you have committed in the past,
53 pronouncing unjust judgements, condemning the innocent and acquitting
the guilty, though the Lord said, "You
shall not put an innocent and righteous person to death." 54 Now then, if
you really saw this woman, tell me this:
Under what tree did you see them being intimate with each other?' He answered, 'Under a mastic tree.'[s] 55 And
Daniel said, 'Very well! This lie has cost
you your head, for the angel of God has

[r] **13.50** Gk lacks *rest of the* [s] **13.54** The Greek words for *mastic tree* and *cut* are similar, thus forming an ironic wordplay

received the sentence from God and will
immediately cut[t] you in two.'

56 Then, putting him to one side, he
ordered them to bring the other. And
he said to him, 'You offspring of Canaan
and not of Judah, beauty has beguiled
you and lust has perverted your heart.
57 This is how you have been treating
the daughters of Israel, and they were
intimate with you through fear; but a
daughter of Judah would not tolerate
your wickedness. 58 Now then, tell me:
Under what tree did you catch them
being intimate with each other?' He
answered, 'Under an evergreen oak.'[u]
59 Daniel said to him, 'Very well! This
lie has cost you also your head, for the
angel of God is waiting with his sword
to split[v] you in two, so as to destroy you
both.'

60 Then the whole assembly raised a
great shout and blessed God, who saves
those who hope in him. 61 And they took
action against the two elders, because
out of their own mouths Daniel had
convicted them of bearing false witness;
they did to them as they had wickedly
planned to do to their neighbour. 62 Acting in accordance with the law of Moses,
they put them to death. Thus innocent
blood was spared that day.

63 Hilkiah and his wife praised God
for their daughter Susanna, and so did
her husband Joakim and all her relatives, because she was found innocent of
a shameful deed. 64 And from that day
onwards Daniel had a great reputation
among the people.

DANIEL AND THE PRIESTS OF BEL

14 When King Astyages was laid
to rest with his ancestors, Cyrus
the Persian succeeded to his kingdom.
2 Daniel was a companion of the king,
and was the most honoured of all his
friends.

3 Now the Babylonians had an idol
called Bel, and every day they provided
for it twelve bushels of choice flour and
forty sheep and six measures[w] of wine.
4 The king revered it and went every day
to worship it. But Daniel worshipped
his own God.

So the king said to him, 'Why do you
not worship Bel?' 5 He answered, 'Because I do not revere idols made with
hands, but the living God, who created
heaven and earth and has dominion
over all living creatures.'

6 The king said to him, 'Do you not
think that Bel is a living god? Do you
not see how much he eats and drinks
every day?' 7 And Daniel laughed, and
said, 'Do not be deceived, O king, for this
thing is only clay inside and bronze outside, and it never ate or drank anything.'

8 Then the king was angry and called
the priests of Bel[x] and said to them, 'If
you do not tell me who is eating these
provisions, you shall die. 9 But if you
prove that Bel is eating them, Daniel
shall die, because he has spoken blasphemy against Bel.' Daniel said to the
king, 'Let it be done as you have said.'

10 Now there were seventy priests
of Bel, besides their wives and children.
So the king went with Daniel into the
temple of Bel. 11 The priests of Bel said,
'See, we are now going outside; you
yourself, O king, set out the food and
prepare the wine, and shut the door and
seal it with your signet. 12 When you return in the morning, if you do not find
that Bel has eaten it all, we will die; otherwise Daniel will, who is telling lies
about us.' 13 They were unconcerned, for
beneath the table they had made a hidden entrance, through which they used
to go in regularly and consume the provisions. 14 After they had gone out, the
king set out the food for Bel. Then Daniel ordered his servants to bring ashes,
and they scattered them throughout
the whole temple in the presence of the
king alone. Then they went out, shut the
door and sealed it with the king's signet,
and departed. 15 During the night the
priests came as usual, with their wives
and children, and they ate and drank everything.

16 Early in the morning the king
rose and came, and Daniel with him.
17 The king said, 'Are the seals unbroken,
Daniel?' He answered, 'They are unbroken, O king.' 18 As soon as the doors
were opened, the king looked at the table, and shouted in a loud voice, 'You are
great, O Bel, and in you there is no deceit at all!'

19 But Daniel laughed and restrained
the king from going in. 'Look at the
floor', he said, 'and notice whose footprints these are.' 20 The king said, 'I see
the footprints of men and women and
children.'

[t] **13.55** The Greek words for *mastic tree* and *cut* are similar, thus forming an ironic wordplay
[u] **13.58** The Greek words for *evergreen oak* and *split* are similar, thus forming an ironic wordplay
[v] **13.59** The Greek words for *evergreen oak* and *split* are similar, thus forming an ironic wordplay
[w] **14.3** A little more than fifty gallons [x] **14.8** Gk *his priests*

21 Then the king was enraged, and
he arrested the priests and their wives
and children. They showed him the secret doors through which they used to
enter to consume what was on the table. 22 Therefore the king put them to
death, and gave Bel over to Daniel, who
destroyed it and its temple.

DANIEL KILLS THE DRAGON

23 Now in that place[y] there was a
great dragon, which the Babylonians
revered. 24 The king said to Daniel, 'You
cannot deny that this is a living god; so
worship him.' 25 Daniel said, 'I worship
the Lord my God, for he is the living
God. 26 But give me permission, O king,
and I will kill the dragon without sword
or club.' The king said, 'I give you permission.'

27 Then Daniel took pitch, fat, and
hair, and boiled them together and
made cakes, which he fed to the dragon.
The dragon ate them, and burst open.
Then Daniel said, 'See what you have
been worshipping!'

28 When the Babylonians heard
about it, they were very indignant and
conspired against the king, saying, 'The
king has become a Jew; he has destroyed
Bel, and killed the dragon, and slaughtered the priests.' 29 Going to the king,
they said, 'Hand Daniel over to us, or
else we will kill you and your household.'
30 The king saw that they were pressing
him hard, and under compulsion he
handed Daniel over to them.

DANIEL IN THE LIONS' DEN

31 They threw Daniel into the lions' den, and he was there for six days.
32 There were seven lions in the den, and
every day they had been given two human bodies and two sheep; but now
they were given nothing, so that they
would devour Daniel.

33 Now the prophet Habakkuk was
in Judea; he had made a stew and had
broken bread into a bowl, and was going into the field to take it to the reapers. 34 But the angel of the Lord said to
Habakkuk, 'Take the food that you have
to Babylon, to Daniel, in the lions' den.'
35 Habakkuk said, 'Sir, I have never seen
Babylon, and I know nothing about the
den.' 36 Then the angel of the Lord took
him by the crown of his head and carried him by his hair; with the speed of
the wind[z] he set him down in Babylon,
right over the den.

37 Then Habakkuk shouted, 'Daniel,
Daniel! Take the food that God has sent
you.' 38 Daniel said, 'You have remembered me, O God, and have not forsaken
those who love you.' 39 So Daniel got up
and ate. And the angel of God immediately returned Habakkuk to his own
place.

40 On the seventh day the king came
to mourn for Daniel. When he came to
the den he looked in, and there sat Daniel! 41 The king shouted with a loud voice,
'You are great, O Lord, the God of Daniel, and there is no other besides you!'
42 Then he pulled Daniel[a] out, and threw
into the den those who had attempted
his destruction, and they were instantly
eaten before his eyes.

[y] **14.23** Other ancient authorities lack *in that place* [z] **14.36** Or *by the power of his spirit*
[a] **14.42** Gk *him*

HOSEA

The book of Hosea is first in order of the works known as the Twelve Minor Prophets. Hosea lived and prophesied in the northern kingdom during the eighth century BCE (ca. 780–710). He was a contemporary of Isaiah, who preached in the south. It was a difficult and devastating time for the northern kingdom as the Assyrians were about to overtake Samaria and carry the people off into captivity.

The image used by Hosea to communicate his message to Israel came from his own life circumstance, his marriage to Gomer. Despite the prophet's love for his wife, she was not faithful to him. So it is with God and Israel. Israel had fallen into idolatry, becoming a prostitute like Gomer. Hosea's prophecy is a declaration of God's steadfast love for Israel despite her infidelities. Hosea pleads for the repentance of Israel and foretells the impending destruction of the kingdom at the hands of the Assyrians as punishment for its idolatries. Hosea is the first to use the metaphor of marriage in describing God's covenant with his people. This metaphor influenced later prophets including Jeremiah.

Hosea's teaching that steadfast love and loyalty are more important to God than empty ritual is read during the liturgy on Saturday of the Third Week of Lent (6.1–6). The same text is read on the Tenth Sunday of the Year of Cycle A. The passage from Hosea about the Lord taking Israel for his wife forever (2.14–15, 19–20) is read on various occasions: on the Eighth Sunday of Year B, on Monday of the Fourteenth Week of Year II, at the Common of Virgins, and at the Celebration of Religious Profession.

1 The word of the LORD that came to
Hosea son of Beeri, in the days of
Kings Uzziah, Jotham, Ahaz, and Hez-
ekiah of Judah, and in the days of King
Jeroboam son of Joash of Israel.

THE FAMILY OF HOSEA

2 When the LORD first spoke through
Hosea, the LORD said to Hosea, 'Go, take
for yourself a wife of whoredom and
have children of whoredom, for the land
commits great whoredom by forsaking
the LORD.' 3 So he went and took Gomer
daughter of Diblaim, and she conceived
and bore him a son.
4 And the LORD said to him, 'Name
him Jezreel;[a] for in a little while I will
punish the house of Jehu for the blood
of Jezreel, and I will put an end to the
kingdom of the house of Israel. 5 On that
day I will break the bow of Israel in the
valley of Jezreel.'
6 She conceived again and bore a
daughter. Then the LORD said to him,
'Name her Lo-ruhamah,[b] for I will no
longer have pity on the house of Israel
or forgive them. 7 But I will have pity on
the house of Judah, and I will save them
by the LORD their God; I will not save
them by bow, or by sword, or by war, or
by horses, or by horsemen.'
8 When she had weaned Lo-ruhamah,
she conceived and bore a son. 9 Then the
LORD said, 'Name him Lo-ammi,[c] for
you are not my people and I am not your
God.'[d]

THE RESTORATION OF ISRAEL

10[e] Yet the number of the people of
Israel shall be like the sand of the sea,
which can be neither measured nor

[a] 1.4 That is *God sows* [b] 1.6 That is *Not pitied* [c] 1.9 That is *Not my people* [d] 1.9 Heb *I am not yours* [e] 1.10 Ch 2.1 in Heb

numbered; and in the place where it was said to them, 'You are not my people', it shall be said to them, 'Children of the living God.' 11The people of Judah and the people of Israel shall be gathered together, and they shall appoint for themselves one head; and they shall take possession of[f] the land, for great shall be the day of Jezreel.

2 [g] Say to your brother,[h] Ammi,[i] and to your sister,[j] Ruhamah.[k]

ISRAEL'S INFIDELITY, PUNISHMENT, AND REDEMPTION

2 Plead with your mother, plead—
for she is not my wife,
and I am not her husband—
that she put away her whoring
from her face,
and her adultery from
between her breasts,
3 or I will strip her naked
and expose her as in the
day she was born,
and make her like a wilderness,
and turn her into a parched land,
and kill her with thirst.
4 Upon her children also I will
have no pity,
because they are children
of whoredom.
5 For their mother has played
the whore;
she who conceived them has
acted shamefully.
For she said, 'I will go after
my lovers;
they give me my bread
and my water,
my wool and my flax, my
oil and my drink.'
6 Therefore I will hedge her[l]
way with thorns;
and I will build a wall against her,
so that she cannot find her paths.
7 She shall pursue her lovers,
but not overtake them;
and she shall seek them,
but shall not find them.
Then she shall say, 'I will go
and return to my first husband,
for it was better with me
then than now.'
8 She did not know
that it was I who gave her
the grain, the wine, and the oil,
and who lavished upon her silver
and gold that they used for Baal.
9 Therefore I will take back
my grain in its time,
and my wine in its season;
and I will take away my wool
and my flax,
which were to cover her
nakedness.
10 Now I will uncover her shame
in the sight of her lovers,
and no one shall rescue her
out of my hand.
11 I will put an end to all her mirth,
her festivals, her new moons,
her sabbaths,
and all her appointed festivals.
12 I will lay waste her vines
and her fig trees,
of which she said,
'These are my pay,
which my lovers have given me.'
I will make them a forest,
and the wild animals shall
devour them.
13 I will punish her for the festival
days of the Baals,
when she offered incense to them
and decked herself with her
ring and jewellery,
and went after her lovers,
and forgot me, says the LORD.

14 Therefore, I will now persuade her,
and bring her into the wilderness,
and speak tenderly to her.
15 From there I will give her
her vineyards,
and make the Valley of Achor
a door of hope.
There she shall respond as in
the days of her youth,
as at the time when she came
out of the land of Egypt.

16On that day, says the LORD, you will
call me, 'My husband', and no longer
will you call me, 'My Baal'.[m] 17For I will
remove the names of the Baals from her
mouth, and they shall be mentioned
by name no more. 18I will make for
you[n] a covenant on that day with the
wild animals, the birds of the air, and
the creeping things of the ground; and
I will abolish[o] the bow, the sword, and
war from the land; and I will make you
lie down in safety. 19And I will take you
for my wife for ever; I will take you for
my wife in righteousness and in justice,
in steadfast love, and in mercy. 20I will
take you for my wife in faithfulness; and
you shall know the LORD.

[f] 1.11 Heb *rise up from* [g] 2.1 Ch 2.3 in Heb [h] 2.1 Gk: Heb *brothers* [i] 2.1 That is *My people* [j] 2.1 Gk Vg: Heb *sisters* [k] 2.1 That is *Pitied* [l] 2.6 Gk Syr: Heb *your* [m] 2.16 That is, '*My master*' [n] 2.18 Heb *them* [o] 2.18 Heb *break*

21 On that day I will answer,
says the LORD,
I will answer the heavens
and they shall answer the earth;
22 and the earth shall answer the grain,
the wine, and the oil,
and they shall answer Jezreel;[p]
23 and I will sow him[q] for
myself in the land.
And I will have pity on
Lo-ruhamah,[r]
and I will say to Lo-ammi,[s]
'You are my people';
and he shall say, 'You are my God.'

FURTHER ASSURANCES OF GOD'S REDEEMING LOVE

3 The LORD said to me again, 'Go,
love a woman who has a lover and
is an adulteress, just as the LORD loves
the people of Israel, though they turn
to other gods and love raisin cakes.' 2So
I bought her for fifteen shekels of silver
and a homer of barley and a measure of
wine.[t] 3And I said to her, 'You must remain as mine for many days; you shall
not play the whore, you shall not have
intercourse with a man, nor I with you.'
4For the Israelites shall remain many
days without king or prince, without
sacrifice or pillar, without ephod or teraphim. 5Afterwards the Israelites shall
return and seek the LORD their God, and
David their king; they shall come in awe
to the LORD and to his goodness in the
latter days.

GOD ACCUSES ISRAEL

4 Hear the word of the LORD,
O people of Israel;
for the LORD has an indictment
against the inhabitants
of the land.
There is no faithfulness or loyalty,
and no knowledge of God
in the land.
2 Swearing, lying, and murder,
and stealing and adultery
break out;
bloodshed follows bloodshed.
3 Therefore the land mourns,
and all who live in it languish;
together with the wild animals
and the birds of the air,
even the fish of the sea
are perishing.

4 Yet let no one contend,
and let none accuse,
for with you is my contention,
O priest.[u]
5 You shall stumble by day;
the prophet also shall stumble
with you by night,
and I will destroy your mother.
6 My people are destroyed for
lack of knowledge;
because you have rejected
knowledge,
I reject you from being
a priest to me.
And since you have forgotten
the law of your God,
I also will forget your children.

7 The more they increased,
the more they sinned against me;
they changed[v] their glory
into shame.
8 They feed on the sin of my people;
they are greedy for their iniquity.
9 And it shall be like people, like priest;
I will punish them for their ways,
and repay them for their deeds.
10 They shall eat, but not be satisfied;
they shall play the whore,
but not multiply;
because they have forsaken the LORD
to devote themselves to
11whoredom.

THE IDOLATRY OF ISRAEL

Wine and new wine
take away the understanding.
12 My people consult a piece of wood,
and their divining-rod
gives them oracles.
For a spirit of whoredom has
led them astray,
and they have played the whore,
forsaking their God.
13 They sacrifice on the tops of
the mountains,
and make offerings upon the hills,
under oak, poplar, and terebinth,
because their shade is good.

Therefore your daughters
play the whore,
and your daughters-in-law
commit adultery.
14 I will not punish your daughters
when they play the whore,
nor your daughters-in-law when
they commit adultery;

p 2.22 That is *God sows* q 2.23 Cn: Heb *her* r 2.23 That is *Not pitied* s 2.23 That is *Not my people* t 3.2 Gk: Heb *a homer of barley and a lethech of barley* u 4.4 Cn: Meaning of Heb uncertain v 4.7 Ancient Heb tradition: MT *I will change*

for the men themselves go
aside with whores,
and sacrifice with temple
prostitutes;
thus a people without understanding
comes to ruin.

15 Though you play the whore, O Israel,
do not let Judah become guilty.
Do not enter into Gilgal,
or go up to Beth-aven,
and do not swear, 'As the
LORD lives.'
16 Like a stubborn heifer,
Israel is stubborn;
can the LORD now feed them
like a lamb in a broad pasture?

17 Ephraim is joined to idols—
let him alone.
18 When their drinking is ended, they
indulge in sexual orgies;
they love lewdness more
than their glory.[w]
19 A wind has wrapped them[x]
in its wings,
and they shall be ashamed
because of their altars.[y]

IMPENDING JUDGEMENT ON ISRAEL AND JUDAH

5 Hear this, O priests!
Give heed, O house of Israel!
Listen, O house of the king!
For the judgement
pertains to you;
for you have been a
snare at Mizpah,
and a net spread upon Tabor,
2 and a pit dug deep in Shittim;[z]
but I will punish all of them.

3 I know Ephraim,
and Israel is not hidden from me;
for now, O Ephraim, you have
played the whore;
Israel is defiled.
4 Their deeds do not permit them
to return to their God.
For the spirit of whoredom
is within them,
and they do not know the LORD.

5 Israel's pride testifies against him;
Ephraim[a] stumbles in his guilt;
Judah also stumbles with them.
6 With their flocks and herds
they shall go
to seek the LORD,
but they will not find him;
he has withdrawn from them.
7 They have dealt faithlessly
with the LORD;
for they have borne
illegitimate children.
Now the new moon shall devour
them along with their fields.

8 Blow the horn in Gibeah,
the trumpet in Ramah.
Sound the alarm at Beth-aven;
look behind you, Benjamin!
9 Ephraim shall become
a desolation
on the day of punishment;
among the tribes of Israel
I declare what is sure.
10 The princes of Judah have become
like those who remove
the landmark;
on them I will pour out
my wrath like water.
11 Ephraim is oppressed, crushed
in judgement,
because he was determined
to go after vanity.[b]
12 Therefore I am like maggots
to Ephraim,
and like rottenness to the
house of Judah.
13 When Ephraim saw his sickness,
and Judah his wound,
then Ephraim went to Assyria,
and sent to the great king.[c]
But he is not able to cure you
or heal your wound.
14 For I will be like a lion
to Ephraim,
and like a young lion to the
house of Judah.
I myself will tear and go away;
I will carry off, and no
one shall rescue.
15 I will return again to my place
until they acknowledge their
guilt and seek my face.
In their distress they will
beg my favour:

A CALL TO REPENTANCE

6 'Come, let us return to the LORD;
for it is he who has torn,
and he will heal us;
he has struck down, and
he will bind us up.

[w] 4.18 Cn Compare Gk: Meaning of Heb uncertain
[x] 4.19 Heb *her* [y] 4.19 Gk Syr: Heb *sacrifices*
[z] 5.2 Cn: Meaning of Heb uncertain [a] 5.5 Heb *Israel and Ephraim* [b] 5.11 Gk: Meaning of Heb uncertain [c] 5.13 Cn: Heb *to a king who will contend*

2 After two days he will revive us;
on the third day he will
raise us up,
that we may live before him.
3 Let us know, let us press on
to know the LORD;
his appearing is as sure
as the dawn;
he will come to us like the showers,
like the spring rains that
water the earth.'

IMPENITENCE OF ISRAEL AND JUDAH

4 What shall I do with you,
O Ephraim?
What shall I do with you, O Judah?
Your love is like a morning cloud,
like the dew that goes away early.
5 Therefore I have hewn them
by the prophets,
I have killed them by the
words of my mouth,
and my[d] judgement goes
forth as the light.
6 For I desire steadfast love
and not sacrifice,
the knowledge of God rather
than burnt-offerings.

7 But at[e] Adam they transgressed
the covenant;
there they dealt faithlessly
with me.
8 Gilead is a city of evildoers,
tracked with blood.
9 As robbers lie in wait[f] for someone,
so the priests are banded
together;[g]
they murder on the road
to Shechem,
they commit a monstrous crime.
10 In the house of Israel I have
seen a horrible thing;
Ephraim's whoredom is there,
Israel is defiled.

11 For you also, O Judah, a harvest
is appointed.

When I would restore the
fortunes of my people,
7 1when I would heal Israel,
the corruption of Ephraim
is revealed,
and the wicked deeds of Samaria;
for they deal falsely,
the thief breaks in,
and the bandits raid outside.
2 But they do not consider
that I remember all their
wickedness.
Now their deeds surround them,
they are before my face.
3 By their wickedness they make
the king glad,
and the officials by their
treachery.
4 They are all adulterers;
they are like a heated oven,
whose baker does not need
to stir the fire,
from the kneading of the dough
until it is leavened.
5 On the day of our king the officials
became sick with the heat of wine;
he stretched out his hand
with mockers.
6 For they are kindled[h] like
an oven, their heart
burns within them;
all night their anger smoulders;
in the morning it blazes
like a flaming fire.
7 All of them are hot as an oven,
and they devour their rulers.
All their kings have fallen;
none of them calls upon me.

8 Ephraim mixes himself with
the peoples;
Ephraim is a cake not turned.
9 Foreigners devour his strength,
but he does not know it;
grey hairs are sprinkled upon him,
but he does not know it.
10 Israel's pride testifies against[i] him;
yet they do not return to
the LORD their God,
or seek him, for all this.

FUTILE RELIANCE ON THE NATIONS

11 Ephraim has become like a dove,
silly and without sense;
they call upon Egypt, they
go to Assyria.
12 As they go, I will cast my
net over them;
I will bring them down like
birds of the air;
I will discipline them according
to the report made to
their assembly.[j]
13 Woe to them, for they have
strayed from me!
Destruction to them, for they
have rebelled against me!

[d] 6.5 Gk Syr: Heb *your* [e] 6.7 Cn: Heb *like* [f] 6.9 Cn: Meaning of Heb uncertain [g] 6.9 Syr: Heb *are a company* [h] 7.6 Gk Syr: Heb *brought near* [i] 7.10 Or *humbles* [j] 7.12 Meaning of Heb uncertain

I would redeem them,
but they speak lies against me.
14 They do not cry to me from the heart,
but they wail upon their beds;
they gash themselves for grain and wine;
they rebel against me.
15 It was I who trained and strengthened their arms,
yet they plot evil against me.
16 They turn to that which does not profit;[k]
they have become like a defective bow;
their officials shall fall by the sword
because of the rage of their tongue.
So much for their babbling in the land of Egypt.

ISRAEL'S APOSTASY

8 Set the trumpet to your lips!
One like a vulture[l] is over the house of the LORD,
because they have broken my covenant,
and transgressed my law.
2 Israel cries to me,
'My God, we—Israel—know you!'
3 Israel has spurned the good;
the enemy shall pursue him.

4 They made kings, but not through me;
they set up princes, but without my knowledge.
With their silver and gold
they made idols
for their own destruction.
5 Your calf is rejected, O Samaria.
My anger burns against them.
How long will they be incapable of innocence?
6 For it is from Israel,
an artisan made it;
it is not God.
The calf of Samaria
shall be broken to pieces.[m]

7 For they sow the wind,
and they shall reap the whirlwind.
The standing grain has no heads,
it shall yield no meal;
if it were to yield,
foreigners would devour it.
8 Israel is swallowed up;
now they are among the nations
as a useless vessel.
9 For they have gone up to Assyria,
a wild ass wandering alone;
Ephraim has bargained for lovers.
10 Though they bargain with the nations,
I will now gather them up.
They shall soon writhe
under the burden of kings and princes.

11 When Ephraim multiplied altars to expiate sin,
they became to him altars for sinning.
12 Though I write for him the multitude of my instructions,
they are regarded as a strange thing.
13 Though they offer choice sacrifices,[n]
though they eat flesh,
the LORD does not accept them.
Now he will remember their iniquity,
and punish their sins;
they shall return to Egypt.
14 Israel has forgotten his Maker,
and built palaces;
and Judah has multiplied fortified cities;
but I will send a fire upon his cities,
and it shall devour his strongholds.

PUNISHMENT FOR ISRAEL'S SIN

9 Do not rejoice, O Israel!
Do not exult[o] as other nations do;
for you have played the whore,
departing from your God.
You have loved a prostitute's pay
on all threshing-floors.
2 Threshing-floor and wine vat
shall not feed them,
and the new wine shall fail them.
3 They shall not remain in the land of the LORD;
but Ephraim shall return to Egypt,
and in Assyria they shall eat unclean food.

4 They shall not pour drink-offerings of wine to the LORD,
and their sacrifices shall not please him.

[k] 7.16 Cn: Meaning of Heb uncertain
[l] 8.1 Meaning of Heb uncertain [m] 8.6 Or *shall go up in flames* [n] 8.13 Cn: Meaning of Heb uncertain [o] 9.1 Gk: Heb *To exultation*

Such sacrifices shall be like
mourners' bread;
all who eat of it shall be defiled;
for their bread shall be for
their hunger only;
it shall not come to the
house of the LORD.

5 What will you do on the day of
appointed festival,
and on the day of the festival
of the LORD?
6 For even if they escape destruction,
Egypt shall gather them,
Memphis shall bury them.
Nettles shall possess their precious
things of silver;[p]
thorns shall be in their tents.

7 The days of punishment have come,
the days of recompense
have come;
Israel cries,[q]
'The prophet is a fool,
the man of the spirit is mad!'
Because of your great iniquity,
your hostility is great.
8 The prophet is a sentinel for my
God over Ephraim,
yet a fowler's snare is on all his ways,
and hostility in the house
of his God.
9 They have deeply corrupted
themselves
as in the days of Gibeah;
he will remember their iniquity,
he will punish their sins.

10 Like grapes in the wilderness,
I found Israel.
Like the first fruit on the fig tree,
in its first season,
I saw your ancestors.
But they came to Baal-peor,
and consecrated themselves
to a thing of shame,
and became detestable like
the thing they loved.
11 Ephraim's glory shall fly
away like a bird—
no birth, no pregnancy,
no conception!
12 Even if they bring up children,
I will bereave them until
no one is left.
Woe to them indeed
when I depart from them!
13 Once I saw Ephraim as a young palm
planted in a lovely meadow,[r]
but now Ephraim must lead out
his children for slaughter.

14 Give them, O LORD—
what will you give?
Give them a miscarrying womb
and dry breasts.

15 Every evil of theirs began at Gilgal;
there I came to hate them.
Because of the wickedness
of their deeds
I will drive them out of my house.
I will love them no more;
all their officials are rebels.

16 Ephraim is stricken,
their root is dried up,
they shall bear no fruit.
Even though they give birth,
I will kill the cherished
offspring of their womb.
17 Because they have not
listened to him,
my God will reject them;
they shall become wanderers
among the nations.

ISRAEL'S SIN AND CAPTIVITY

10 Israel is a luxuriant vine
that yields its fruit.
The more his fruit increased
the more altars he built;
as his country improved,
he improved his pillars.
2 Their heart is false;
now they must bear their guilt.
The LORD[s] will break down
their altars,
and destroy their pillars.

3 For now they will say:
'We have no king,
for we do not fear the LORD,
and a king—what could
he do for us?'
4 They utter mere words;
with empty oaths they
make covenants;
so litigation springs up like
poisonous weeds
in the furrows of the field.
5 The inhabitants of Samaria tremble
for the calf[t] of Beth-aven.
Its people shall mourn for it,
and its idolatrous priests
shall wail[u] over it,
over its glory that has
departed from it.

[p] 9.6 Meaning of Heb uncertain [q] 9.7 Cn Compare Gk: Heb *shall know* [r] 9.13 Meaning of Heb uncertain [s] 10.2 Heb *he* [t] 10.5 Gk Syr: Heb *calves* [u] 10.5 Cn: Heb *exult*

6 The thing itself shall be
carried to Assyria
as tribute to the great king.[v]
Ephraim shall be put to shame,
and Israel shall be ashamed
of his idol.[w]

7 Samaria's king shall perish
like a splinter on the face
of the waters.
8 The high places of Aven, the
sin of Israel,
shall be destroyed.
Thorn and thistle shall grow up
on their altars.
They shall say to the mountains,
Cover us,
and to the hills, Fall on us.

9 Since the days of Gibeah you
have sinned, O Israel;
there they have continued.
Shall not war overtake
them in Gibeah?
10 I will come[x] against the wayward
people to punish them;
and nations shall be gathered
against them
when they are punished[y] for
their double iniquity.

11 Ephraim was a trained heifer
that loved to thresh,
and I spared her fair neck;
but I will make Ephraim
break the ground;
Judah must plough;
Jacob must harrow for himself.
12 Sow for yourselves
righteousness;
reap steadfast love;
break up your fallow ground;
for it is time to seek the LORD,
that he may come and rain
righteousness upon you.

13 You have ploughed wickedness,
you have reaped injustice,
you have eaten the fruit of lies.
Because you have trusted
in your power
and in the multitude of
your warriors,
14 therefore the tumult of war shall
rise against your people,
and all your fortresses shall
be destroyed,
as Shalman destroyed Beth-arbel
on the day of battle
when mothers were dashed in
pieces with their children.
15 Thus it shall be done to
you, O Bethel,
because of your great wickedness.
At dawn the king of Israel
shall be utterly cut off.

GOD'S COMPASSION DESPITE ISRAEL'S INGRATITUDE

11 When Israel was a child,
I loved him,
and out of Egypt I called my son.
2 The more I[z] called them,
the more they went from me;[a]
they kept sacrificing to the Baals,
and offering incense to idols.

3 Yet it was I who taught
Ephraim to walk,
I took them up in my[b] arms;
but they did not know that
I healed them.
4 I led them with cords of
human kindness,
with bands of love.
I was to them like those
who lift infants to their cheeks.[c]
I bent down to them
and fed them.

5 They shall return to the
land of Egypt,
and Assyria shall be their king,
because they have refused
to return to me.
6 The sword rages in their cities,
it consumes their oracle-priests,
and devours because of
their schemes.
7 My people are bent on turning
away from me.
To the Most High they call,
but he does not raise
them up at all.[d]

8 How can I give you up, Ephraim?
How can I hand you
over, O Israel?
How can I make you like Admah?
How can I treat you like Zeboiim?
My heart recoils within me;
my compassion grows
warm and tender.
9 I will not execute my fierce anger;
I will not again destroy Ephraim;

[v] 10.6 Cn: Heb *to a king who will contend*
[w] 10.6 Cn: Heb *counsel* [x] 10.10 Cn Compare Gk: Heb *In my desire* [y] 10.10 Gk: Heb *bound*
[z] 11.2 Gk: Heb *they* [a] 11.2 Gk: Heb *them*
[b] 11.3 Gk Syr Vg: Heb *his* [c] 11.4 Or *who ease the yoke on their jaws* [d] 11.7 Meaning of Heb uncertain

for I am God and no mortal,
the Holy One in your midst,
and I will not come in wrath.[e]

10 They shall go after the LORD,
who roars like a lion;
when he roars,
his children shall come
trembling from the west.
11 They shall come trembling like
birds from Egypt,
and like doves from the
land of Assyria;
and I will return them to their
homes, says the LORD.

12[f] Ephraim has surrounded
me with lies,
and the house of Israel
with deceit;
but Judah still walks[g] with God,
and is faithful to the Holy One.

12 Ephraim herds the wind,
and pursues the east
wind all day long;
they multiply falsehood and violence;
they make a treaty with Assyria,
and oil is carried to Egypt.

THE LONG HISTORY OF REBELLION

2 The LORD has an indictment
against Judah,
and will punish Jacob
according to his ways,
and repay him according
to his deeds.
3 In the womb he tried to
supplant his brother,
and in his manhood he
strove with God.
4 He strove with the angel
and prevailed,
he wept and sought his favour;
he met him at Bethel,
and there he spoke with him.[h]
5 The LORD the God of hosts,
the LORD is his name!
6 But as for you, return to your God,
hold fast to love and justice,
and wait continually for your God.

7 A trader, in whose hands are
false balances,
he loves to oppress.
8 Ephraim has said, 'Ah, I am rich,
I have gained wealth for myself;
in all of my gain
no offence has been found in me
that would be sin.'[i]
9 I am the LORD your God
from the land of Egypt;
I will make you live in tents again,
as on the days of the
appointed festival.

10 I spoke to the prophets;
it was I who multiplied visions,
and through the prophets I
will bring destruction.
11 In Gilead[j] there is iniquity,
they shall surely come to nothing.
In Gilgal they sacrifice bulls,
so their altars shall be
like stone heaps
on the furrows of the field.
12 Jacob fled to the land of Aram;
there Israel served for a wife,
and for a wife he guarded sheep.[k]
13 By a prophet the LORD brought
Israel up from Egypt,
and by a prophet he was guarded.
14 Ephraim has given bitter offence,
so his Lord will bring his
crimes down on him
and pay him back for his insults.

RELENTLESS JUDGEMENT ON ISRAEL

13 When Ephraim spoke,
there was trembling;
he was exalted in Israel;
but he incurred guilt through
Baal and died.
2 And now they keep on sinning
and make a cast image
for themselves,
idols of silver made according to
their understanding,
all of them the work of artisans.
'Sacrifice to these', they say.[l]
People are kissing calves!
3 Therefore they shall be like
the morning mist
or like the dew that goes
away early,
like chaff that swirls from the
threshing-floor
or like smoke from a window.

4 Yet I have been the LORD your God
ever since the land of Egypt;
you know no God but me,
and besides me there is no saviour.
5 It was I who fed[m] you in
the wilderness,
in the land of drought.

[e] 11.9 Meaning of Heb uncertain [f] 11.12 Ch 12.1 in Heb [g] 11.12 Heb *roams* or *rules* [h] 12.4 Gk Syr: Heb *us* [i] 12.8 Meaning of Heb uncertain [j] 12.11 Compare Syr: Heb *Gilead* [k] 12.12 Heb lacks *sheep* [l] 13.2 Cn Compare Gk: Heb *To these they say sacrifices of people* [m] 13.5 Gk Syr: Heb *knew*

6 When I fed[n] them, they
were satisfied;
they were satisfied, and their
heart was proud;
therefore they forgot me.
7 So I will become like a lion to them,
like a leopard I will lurk
beside the way.
8 I will fall upon them like a bear
robbed of her cubs,
and will tear open the covering
of their heart;
there I will devour them like a lion,
as a wild animal would
mangle them.

9 I will destroy you, O Israel;
who can help you?[o]
10 Where now is[p] your king, that
he may save you?
Where in all your cities
are your rulers,
of whom you said,
'Give me a king and rulers'?
11 I gave you a king in my anger,
and I took him away in my wrath.

12 Ephraim's iniquity is bound up;
his sin is kept in store.
13 The pangs of childbirth come for him,
but he is an unwise son;
for at the proper time he does
not present himself
at the mouth of the womb.

14 Shall I ransom them from the
power of Sheol?
Shall I redeem them from Death?
O Death, where are[q] your plagues?
O Sheol, where is[r] your
destruction?
Compassion is hidden
from my eyes.

15 Although he may flourish
among rushes,[s]
the east wind shall come, a
blast from the LORD,
rising from the wilderness;
and his fountain shall dry up,
his spring shall be parched.
It shall strip his treasury
of every precious thing.
16[t] Samaria shall bear her guilt,
because she has rebelled
against her God;
they shall fall by the sword,
their little ones shall be
dashed in pieces,
and their pregnant women
ripped open.

A PLEA FOR REPENTANCE

14 Return, O Israel, to the
LORD your God,
for you have stumbled because
of your iniquity.
2 Take words with you
and return to the LORD;
say to him,
'Take away all guilt;
accept that which is good,
and we will offer
the fruit[u] of our lips.
3 Assyria shall not save us;
we will not ride upon horses;
we will say no more, "Our God",
to the work of our hands.
In you the orphan finds mercy.'

ASSURANCE OF FORGIVENESS

4 I will heal their disloyalty;
I will love them freely,
for my anger has turned
from them.
5 I will be like the dew to Israel;
he shall blossom like the lily,
he shall strike root like the
forests of Lebanon.[v]
6 His shoots shall spread out;
his beauty shall be like
the olive tree,
and his fragrance like
that of Lebanon.
7 They shall again live beneath
my[w] shadow,
they shall flourish as a garden;[x]
they shall blossom like the vine,
their fragrance shall be like
the wine of Lebanon.

8 O Ephraim, what have I[y] to
do with idols?
It is I who answer and
look after you.[z]
I am like an evergreen cypress;
your faithfulness[a] comes from me.
9 Those who are wise understand
these things;
those who are discerning
know them.
For the ways of the LORD are right,
and the upright walk in them,
but transgressors stumble
in them.

[n] 13.6 Cn: Heb *according to their pasture* [o] 13.9 Gk Syr: Heb *for in me is your help* [p] 13.10 Gk Syr Vg: Heb *I will be* [q] 13.14 Gk Syr: Heb *I will be* [r] 13.14 Gk Syr: Heb *I will be* [s] 13.15 Or *among brothers* [t] 13.16 Ch 14.1 in Heb [u] 14.2 Gk Syr: Heb *bulls* [v] 14.5 Cn: Heb *like Lebanon* [w] 14.7 Heb *his* [x] 14.7 Cn: Heb *they shall grow grain* [y] 14.8 Or *What more has Ephraim* [z] 14.8 Heb *him* [a] 14.8 Heb *your fruit*

JOEL

The book of Joel starts with a description of a terrible and unparalleled infestation of locusts on the land inhabited by the people of Israel. The prophet Joel interprets the infestation to be the equivalent of an invading army and the result of the sinfulness of God's people. Joel calls for repentance before the day of the Lord and predicts judgment and divine action. Joel's day of the Lord also anticipates a restoration or renewal of Israel by God (2.18–27). There is no clear historical connection of the plague of locusts to a particular time in Israel's history. Many scholars believe the writing of this book to be sometime after the destruction of Jerusalem, perhaps as late as the fifth or fourth century BCE.

The passage in Joel that describes the outpouring of the Spirit (2.28–30) is taken up in the Acts of the Apostles in the New Testament. St. Peter in his first words at Pentecost (Acts 2.16–21) interprets the coming of the Holy Spirit to be the fulfillment of Joel's prophecy. This same text from Joel is offered as a Reading at the Vigil of Pentecost. It is also offered as a choice for the First Reading in the Confirmation liturgy.

1 The word of the LORD that came to Joel son of Pethuel:

LAMENT OVER THE RUIN OF THE COUNTRY

2 Hear this, O elders,
give ear, all inhabitants
of the land!
Has such a thing happened
in your days,
or in the days of your ancestors?
3 Tell your children of it,
and let your children tell
their children,
and their children another
generation.

4 What the cutting locust left,
the swarming locust has eaten.
What the swarming locust left,
the hopping locust has eaten,
and what the hopping locust left,
the destroying locust has eaten.

5 Wake up, you drunkards, and weep;
and wail, all you wine-drinkers,
over the sweet wine,
for it is cut off from your mouth.
6 For a nation has invaded my land,
powerful and innumerable;
its teeth are lions' teeth,
and it has the fangs of a lioness.
7 It has laid waste my vines,
and splintered my fig trees;
it has stripped off their bark
and thrown it down;
their branches have
turned white.

8 Lament like a virgin dressed
in sackcloth
for the husband of her youth.
9 The grain-offering and the
drink-offering are cut off
from the house of the LORD.
The priests mourn,
the ministers of the LORD.
10 The fields are devastated,
the ground mourns;
for the grain is destroyed,
the wine dries up,
the oil fails.

11 Be dismayed, you farmers,
wail, you vine-dressers,
over the wheat and the barley;
for the crops of the field
are ruined.
12 The vine withers,
the fig tree droops.

Pomegranate, palm, and apple—
all the trees of the field
are dried up;
surely, joy withers away
among the people.

A CALL TO REPENTANCE AND PRAYER

13 Put on sackcloth and lament,
you priests;
wail, you ministers of the altar.
Come, pass the night in sackcloth,
you ministers of my God!
Grain-offering and drink-offering
are withheld from the
house of your God.

14 Sanctify a fast,
call a solemn assembly.
Gather the elders
and all the inhabitants of the land
to the house of the LORD your God,
and cry out to the LORD.

15 Alas for the day!
For the day of the LORD is near,
and as destruction from the
Almighty[a] it comes.
16 Is not the food cut off
before our eyes,
joy and gladness
from the house of our God?

17 The seed shrivels under the clods,[b]
the storehouses are desolate;
the granaries are ruined
because the grain has failed.
18 How the animals groan!
The herds of cattle wander about
because there is no pasture for them;
even the flocks of sheep are dazed.[c]

19 To you, O LORD, I cry.
For fire has devoured
the pastures of the wilderness,
and flames have burned
all the trees of the field.
20 Even the wild animals cry to you
because the watercourses
are dried up,
and fire has devoured
the pastures of the wilderness.

2 Blow the trumpet in Zion;
sound the alarm on my
holy mountain!
Let all the inhabitants of the
land tremble,
for the day of the LORD is
coming, it is near—
2 a day of darkness and gloom,
a day of clouds and thick darkness!
Like blackness spread upon
the mountains
a great and powerful army comes;
their like has never been from of old,
nor will be again after them
in ages to come.

3 Fire devours in front of them,
and behind them a flame burns.
Before them the land is like
the garden of Eden,
but after them a desolate
wilderness,
and nothing escapes them.

4 They have the appearance of horses,
and like warhorses they charge.
5 As with the rumbling of chariots,
they leap on the tops of
the mountains,
like the crackling of a flame of fire
devouring the stubble,
like a powerful army
drawn up for battle.

6 Before them peoples are in anguish,
all faces grow pale.[d]
7 Like warriors they charge,
like soldiers they scale the wall.
Each keeps to its own course,
they do not swerve from[e]
their paths.
8 They do not jostle one another,
each keeps to its own track;
they burst through the weapons
and are not halted.
9 They leap upon the city,
they run upon the walls;
they climb up into the houses,
they enter through the
windows like a thief.

10 The earth quakes before them,
the heavens tremble.
The sun and the moon are darkened,
and the stars withdraw
their shining.
11 The LORD utters his voice
at the head of his army;
how vast is his host!
Numberless are those who
obey his command.
Truly the day of the LORD is great;
terrible indeed—who
can endure it?

[a] 1.15 Traditional rendering of Heb *Shaddai*
[b] 1.17 Meaning of Heb uncertain
[c] 1.18 Compare Gk Syr Vg: Meaning of Heb uncertain
[d] 2.6 Meaning of Heb uncertain
[e] 2.7 Gk Syr Vg: Heb *they do not take a pledge along*

12 Yet even now, says the LORD,
return to me with all your heart,
with fasting, with weeping,
and with mourning;
13 rend your hearts and not
your clothing.
Return to the LORD, your God,
for he is gracious and merciful,
slow to anger, and abounding
in steadfast love,
and relents from punishing.
14 Who knows whether he will
not turn and relent,
and leave a blessing behind him,
a grain-offering and a drink-offering
for the LORD, your God?

15 Blow the trumpet in Zion;
sanctify a fast;
call a solemn assembly;
16 gather the people.
Sanctify the congregation;
assemble the aged;
gather the children,
even infants at the breast.
Let the bridegroom leave his room,
and the bride her canopy.

17 Between the vestibule and the altar
let the priests, the ministers
of the LORD, weep.
Let them say, 'Spare your
people, O LORD,
and do not make your
heritage a mockery,
a byword among the nations.
Why should it be said among
the peoples,
"Where is their God?"'

GOD'S RESPONSE AND PROMISE

18 Then the LORD became jealous
for his land,
and had pity on his people.
19 In response to his people
the LORD said:
I am sending you
grain, wine, and oil,
and you will be satisfied;
and I will no more make you
a mockery among the nations.

20 I will remove the northern
army far from you,
and drive it into a parched
and desolate land,
its front into the eastern sea,
and its rear into the western sea;
its stench and foul smell
will rise up.
Surely he has done great things!

21 Do not fear, O soil;
be glad and rejoice,
for the LORD has done great things!
22 Do not fear, you animals of the field,
for the pastures of the
wilderness are green;
the tree bears its fruit,
the fig tree and vine give
their full yield.

23 O children of Zion, be glad
and rejoice in the LORD your God;
for he has given the early rain[f]
for your vindication,
he has poured down for you
abundant rain,
the early and the later
rain, as before.
24 The threshing-floors shall
be full of grain,
the vats shall overflow
with wine and oil.

25 I will repay you for the years
that the swarming locust
has eaten,
the hopper, the destroyer,
and the cutter,
my great army, which I
sent against you.

26 You shall eat in plenty and
be satisfied,
and praise the name of the
LORD your God,
who has dealt wondrously
with you.
And my people shall never again
be put to shame.
27 You shall know that I am in
the midst of Israel,
and that I, the LORD, am your
God and there is no other.
And my people shall never again
be put to shame.

GOD'S SPIRIT POURED OUT

28[g] Then afterwards
I will pour out my spirit
on all flesh;
your sons and your daughters
shall prophesy,
your old men shall dream dreams,
and your young men shall
see visions.
29 Even on the male and female slaves,
in those days, I will pour
out my spirit.

[f] 2.23 Meaning of Heb uncertain [g] 2.28 Ch 3.1 in Heb

30 I will show portents in the heavens and on the earth, blood and fire
and columns of smoke. 31The sun shall
be turned to darkness, and the moon
to blood, before the great and terrible
day of the LORD comes. 32Then everyone who calls on the name of the LORD
shall be saved; for in Mount Zion and in
Jerusalem there shall be those who escape, as the LORD has said, and among
the survivors shall be those whom the
LORD calls.

3[h] For then, in those days and at that
time, when I restore the fortunes of
Judah and Jerusalem, 2I will gather all
the nations and bring them down to
the valley of Jehoshaphat, and I will enter into judgement with them there, on
account of my people and my heritage
Israel, because they have scattered them
among the nations. They have divided
my land, 3and cast lots for my people,
and traded boys for prostitutes, and sold
girls for wine, and drunk it down.

4 What are you to me, O Tyre and Sidon, and all the regions of Philistia? Are
you paying me back for something? If
you are paying me back, I will turn your
deeds back upon your own heads swiftly
and speedily. 5For you have taken my
silver and my gold, and have carried my
rich treasures into your temples.[i] 6You
have sold the people of Judah and Jerusalem to the Greeks, removing them far
from their own border. 7But now I will
rouse them to leave the places to which
you have sold them, and I will turn your
deeds back upon your own heads. 8I will
sell your sons and your daughters into
the hand of the people of Judah, and
they will sell them to the Sabeans, to a
nation far away; for the LORD has spoken.

JUDGEMENT IN THE VALLEY OF JEHOSHAPHAT

9 Proclaim this among the nations:
Prepare war,[j]
stir up the warriors.
Let all the soldiers draw near,
let them come up.
10 Beat your ploughshares into swords,
and your pruning-hooks
into spears;
let the weakling say, 'I
am a warrior.'

11 Come quickly,[k]
all you nations all around,
gather yourselves there.
Bring down your warriors, O LORD.
12 Let the nations rouse themselves,
and come up to the valley
of Jehoshaphat;
for there I will sit to judge
all the neighbouring nations.

13 Put in the sickle,
for the harvest is ripe.
Go in, tread,
for the wine press is full.
The vats overflow,
for their wickedness is great.

14 Multitudes, multitudes,
in the valley of decision!
For the day of the LORD is near
in the valley of decision.
15 The sun and the moon are darkened,
and the stars withdraw
their shining.

16 The LORD roars from Zion,
and utters his voice from Jerusalem,
and the heavens and the
earth shake.
But the LORD is a refuge
for his people,
a stronghold for the people of Israel.

THE GLORIOUS FUTURE OF JUDAH

17 So you shall know that I, the
LORD your God,
dwell in Zion, my holy mountain.
And Jerusalem shall be holy,
and strangers shall never
again pass through it.

18 On that day
the mountains shall drip sweet wine,
the hills shall flow with milk,
and all the stream beds of Judah
shall flow with water;
a fountain shall come forth from
the house of the LORD
and water the Wadi Shittim.

19 Egypt shall become a desolation
and Edom a desolate wilderness,
because of the violence done to
the people of Judah,
in whose land they have shed
innocent blood.
20 But Judah shall be inhabited for ever,
and Jerusalem to all generations.
21 I will avenge their blood, and I
will not clear the guilty,[l]
for the LORD dwells in Zion.

[h] 3.1 Ch 4.1 in Heb [i] 3.5 Or *palaces* [j] 3.9 Heb *sanctify war* [k] 3.11 Meaning of Heb uncertain [l] 3.21 Gk Syr: Heb *I will hold innocent their blood that I have not held innocent*

AMOS

Amos was a shepherd and farmer who prophesied against the northern kingdom, Israel, at the cult center of Bethel during the reign of Jeroboam II (786–746 BCE). This was a prosperous time for Israel, but also a time of corruption, injustice, and moral decadence. Amos delivers a scathing rebuke denouncing the social inequities and moral corruption. He prophesied that Israel would be overthrown and its people taken into captivity. Amos announced that the coming "day of the LORD" (5.18, 20) would not be a time of celebration, but a day of divine judgment against Israel for its own iniquity. His preaching so offended the leadership that he was expelled from Bethel by the priest Amaziah, who was in charge of the royal sanctuary at the time.

Passages from Amos are read at the liturgy on the Fifteenth Sunday of Year B and the Twenty-Fifth and Twenty-Sixth Sundays of Year C. Also, Amos is read during the Thirteenth Week of Ordinary Time in Year II. His prophecy is one of the most vindictive in expression of all the prophets. However, the final passage in Amos (9.8b–15) gives a positive spin on the future of Israel, leading some scholars to believe that it was an addition to the book at a later time.

1 The words of Amos, who was among the shepherds of Tekoa, which he saw concerning Israel in the days of King Uzziah of Judah and in the days of King Jeroboam son of Joash of Israel, two years[a] before the earthquake.

JUDGEMENT ON ISRAEL'S NEIGHBOURS

2 And he said:
The LORD roars from Zion,
and utters his voice from Jerusalem;
the pastures of the shepherds wither,
and the top of Carmel dries up.

3 Thus says the LORD:
For three transgressions of Damascus,
and for four, I will not revoke the punishment;[b]
because they have threshed Gilead
with threshing-sledges of iron.
4 So I will send a fire on the house of Hazael,
and it shall devour the strongholds of Ben-hadad.
5 I will break the gate-bars of Damascus,
and cut off the inhabitants from the Valley of Aven,
and the one who holds the sceptre from Beth-eden;
and the people of Aram shall go into exile to Kir,
says the LORD.

6 Thus says the LORD:
For three transgressions of Gaza,
and for four, I will not revoke the punishment;[c]
because they carried into exile entire communities,
to hand them over to Edom.
7 So I will send a fire on the wall of Gaza,
fire that shall devour its strongholds.
8 I will cut off the inhabitants from Ashdod,
and the one who holds the sceptre from Ashkelon;

[a] 1.1 Or *during two years* [b] 1.3 Heb *cause it to return* [c] 1.6 Heb *cause it to return*

I will turn my hand against Ekron,
and the remnant of the
Philistines shall perish,
says the Lord GOD.

9 Thus says the LORD:
For three transgressions of Tyre,
and for four, I will not revoke
the punishment;[d]
because they delivered entire
communities over to Edom,
and did not remember the
covenant of kinship.
10 So I will send a fire on the wall of Tyre,
fire that shall devour its
strongholds.

11 Thus says the LORD:
For three transgressions of Edom,
and for four, I will not revoke
the punishment;[e]
because he pursued his brother
with the sword
and cast off all pity;
he maintained his anger perpetually,[f]
and kept his wrath[g] for ever.
12 So I will send a fire on Teman,
and it shall devour the
strongholds of Bozrah.

13 Thus says the LORD:
For three transgressions of
the Ammonites,
and for four, I will not revoke
the punishment;[h]
because they have ripped open
pregnant women in Gilead
in order to enlarge their territory.
14 So I will kindle a fire against
the wall of Rabbah,
fire that shall devour its
strongholds,
with shouting on the day of battle,
with a storm on the day of
the whirlwind;
15 then their king shall go into exile,
he and his officials together,
says the LORD.

2 Thus says the LORD:
For three transgressions of Moab,
and for four, I will not revoke
the punishment;[i]
because he burned to lime
the bones of the king of Edom.
2 So I will send a fire on Moab,
and it shall devour the
strongholds of Kerioth,
and Moab shall die amid uproar,
amid shouting and the sound
of the trumpet;
3 I will cut off the ruler from its midst,
and will kill all its officials
with him,
says the LORD.

JUDGEMENT ON JUDAH

4 Thus says the LORD:
For three transgressions of Judah,
and for four, I will not revoke
the punishment;[j]
because they have rejected the
law of the LORD,
and have not kept his statutes,
but they have been led astray
by the same lies
after which their ancestors walked.
5 So I will send a fire on Judah,
and it shall devour the
strongholds of Jerusalem.

JUDGEMENT ON ISRAEL

6 Thus says the LORD:
For three transgressions of Israel,
and for four, I will not revoke
the punishment;[k]
because they sell the righteous
for silver,
and the needy for a pair
of sandals—
7 they who trample the head of the poor
into the dust of the earth,
and push the afflicted
out of the way;
father and son go in to the same girl,
so that my holy name is profaned;
8 they lay themselves down
beside every altar
on garments taken in pledge;
and in the house of their
God they drink
wine bought with fines
they imposed.

9 Yet I destroyed the Amorite
before them,
whose height was like the
height of cedars,
and who was as strong as oaks;
I destroyed his fruit above,
and his roots beneath.
10 Also I brought you up out of
the land of Egypt,
and led you for forty years
in the wilderness,
to possess the land of the Amorite.

[d] 1.9 Heb *cause it to return* [e] 1.11 Heb *cause it to return* [f] 1.11 Syr Vg: Heb *and his anger tore perpetually* [g] 1.11 Gk Syr Vg: Heb *and his wrath kept* [h] 1.13 Heb *cause it to return* [i] 2.1 Heb *cause it to return* [j] 2.4 Heb *cause it to return* [k] 2.6 Heb *cause it to return*

11 And I raised up some of your
children to be prophets
and some of your youths
to be nazirites.[l]
Is it not indeed so, O people
of Israel?
says the LORD.

12 But you made the nazirites[m]
drink wine,
and commanded the prophets,
saying, 'You shall not prophesy.'

13 So, I will press you down
in your place,
just as a cart presses down
when it is full of sheaves.[n]
14 Flight shall perish from the swift,
and the strong shall not
retain their strength,
nor shall the mighty
save their lives;
15 those who handle the bow
shall not stand,
and those who are swift of foot
shall not save themselves,
nor shall those who ride
horses save their lives;
16 and those who are stout of heart
among the mighty
shall flee away naked on that day,
says the LORD.

ISRAEL'S GUILT AND PUNISHMENT

3 Hear this word that the LORD has
spoken against you, O people of Israel, against the whole family that I
brought up out of the land of Egypt:
2 You only have I known
of all the families of the earth;
therefore I will punish you
for all your iniquities.

3 Do two walk together
unless they have made an
appointment?
4 Does a lion roar in the forest,
when it has no prey?
Does a young lion cry out
from its den,
if it has caught nothing?
5 Does a bird fall into a snare
on the earth,
when there is no trap for it?
Does a snare spring up from
the ground,
when it has taken nothing?
6 Is a trumpet blown in a city,
and the people are not afraid?
Does disaster befall a city,
unless the LORD has done it?
7 Surely the Lord GOD does nothing,
without revealing his secret
to his servants the prophets.
8 The lion has roared;
who will not fear?
The Lord GOD has spoken;
who can but prophesy?

9 Proclaim to the strongholds
in Ashdod,
and to the strongholds in
the land of Egypt,
and say, 'Assemble yourselves
on Mount[o] Samaria,
and see what great tumults
are within it,
and what oppressions
are in its midst.'
10 They do not know how to do
right, says the LORD,
those who store up violence and
robbery in their strongholds.
11 Therefore, thus says the Lord GOD:
An adversary shall surround
the land,
and strip you of your defence;
and your strongholds shall
be plundered.

12 Thus says the LORD: As the shepherd rescues from the mouth of the lion
two legs, or a piece of an ear, so shall the
people of Israel who live in Samaria be
rescued, with the corner of a couch and
part[p] of a bed.

13 Hear, and testify against the
house of Jacob,
says the Lord GOD, the
God of hosts:
14 On the day I punish Israel for
its transgressions,
I will punish the altars of Bethel,
and the horns of the altar
shall be cut off
and fall to the ground.
15 I will tear down the winter house as
well as the summer house;
and the houses of ivory
shall perish,
and the great houses[q] shall
come to an end,
says the LORD.

[l] **2.11** That is, *those separated* or *those consecrated* [m] **2.12** That is, *those separated* or *those consecrated* [n] **2.13** Meaning of Heb uncertain [o] **3.9** Gk Syr: Heb *the mountains of* [p] **3.12** Meaning of Heb uncertain [q] **3.15** Or *many houses*

4 Hear this word, you cows of Bashan
who are on Mount Samaria,
who oppress the poor, who
crush the needy,
who say to their husbands, 'Bring
something to drink!'
2 The Lord GOD has sworn by
his holiness:
The time is surely coming
upon you,
when they shall take you
away with hooks,
even the last of you with
fish-hooks.
3 Through breaches in the wall
you shall leave,
each one straight ahead;
and you shall be flung out
into Harmon,[r]
says the LORD.
4 Come to Bethel—and transgress;
to Gilgal—and multiply
transgression;
bring your sacrifices every morning,
your tithes every three days;
5 bring a thank-offering of
leavened bread,
and proclaim freewill-offerings,
publish them;
for so you love to do,
O people of Israel!
says the Lord GOD.

ISRAEL REJECTS CORRECTION

6 I gave you cleanness of teeth
in all your cities,
and lack of bread in all your places,
yet you did not return to me,
says the LORD.

7 And I also withheld the
rain from you
when there were still three
months to the harvest;
I would send rain on one city,
and send no rain on another city;
one field would be rained upon,
and the field on which it did
not rain withered;
8 so two or three towns wandered
to one town
to drink water, and were
not satisfied;
yet you did not return to me,
says the LORD.

9 I struck you with blight and mildew;
I laid waste[s] your gardens
and your vineyards;
the locust devoured your fig
trees and your olive trees;
yet you did not return to me,
says the LORD.
10 I sent among you a pestilence after
the manner of Egypt;
I killed your young men
with the sword;
I carried away your horses;[t]
and I made the stench of
your camp go up into
your nostrils;
yet you did not return to me,
says the LORD.

11 I overthrew some of you,
as when God overthrew
Sodom and Gomorrah,
and you were like a brand
snatched from the fire;
yet you did not return to me,
says the LORD.

12 Therefore, thus I will do to
you, O Israel;
because I will do this to you,
prepare to meet your
God, O Israel!

13 For lo, the one who forms the
mountains, creates the wind,
reveals his thoughts to mortals,
makes the morning darkness,
and treads on the heights
of the earth—
the LORD, the God of hosts,
is his name!

A LAMENT FOR ISRAEL'S SIN

5 Hear this word that I take up over
you in lamentation, O house of Israel:
2 Fallen, no more to rise,
is maiden Israel;
forsaken on her land,
with no one to raise her up.

3 For thus says the Lord GOD:
The city that marched out
a thousand
shall have a hundred left,
and that which marched
out a hundred
shall have ten left.[u]

4 For thus says the LORD to the
house of Israel:
Seek me and live;
5 but do not seek Bethel,

[r] 4.3 Meaning of Heb uncertain [s] 4.9 Cn: Heb *the multitude of* [t] 4.10 Heb *with the captivity of your horses* [u] 5.3 Heb adds *to the house of Israel*

and do not enter into Gilgal
or cross over to Beer-sheba;
for Gilgal shall surely go into exile,
and Bethel shall come to nothing.

6 Seek the LORD and live,
or he will break out against the house of Joseph like fire,
and it will devour Bethel, with no one to quench it.
7 Ah, you that turn justice to wormwood,
and bring righteousness to the ground!
8 The one who made the Pleiades and Orion,
and turns deep darkness into the morning,
and darkens the day into night,
who calls for the waters of the sea,
and pours them out on the surface of the earth,
the LORD is his name,
9 who makes destruction flash out against the strong,
so that destruction comes upon the fortress.
10 They hate the one who reproves in the gate,
and they abhor the one who speaks the truth.
11 Therefore, because you trample on the poor
and take from them levies of grain,
you have built houses of hewn stone,
but you shall not live in them;
you have planted pleasant vineyards,
but you shall not drink their wine.
12 For I know how many are your transgressions,
and how great are your sins—
you who afflict the righteous, who take a bribe,
and push aside the needy in the gate.
13 Therefore the prudent will keep silent in such a time;
for it is an evil time.

14 Seek good and not evil,
that you may live;
and so the LORD, the God of hosts, will be with you,
just as you have said.
15 Hate evil and love good,
and establish justice in the gate;
it may be that the LORD, the God of hosts,
will be gracious to the remnant of Joseph.

16 Therefore thus says the LORD, the God of hosts, the Lord:
In all the squares there shall be wailing;
and in all the streets they shall say, 'Alas! alas!'
They shall call the farmers to mourning,
and those skilled in lamentation, to wailing;
17 in all the vineyards there shall be wailing,
for I will pass through the midst of you,
says the LORD.

THE DAY OF THE LORD A DARK DAY

18 Alas for you who desire the day of the LORD!
Why do you want the day of the LORD?
It is darkness, not light;
19 as if someone fled from a lion,
and was met by a bear;
or went into the house and rested a hand against the wall,
and was bitten by a snake.
20 Is not the day of the LORD darkness, not light,
and gloom with no brightness in it?

21 I hate, I despise your festivals,
and I take no delight in your solemn assemblies.
22 Even though you offer me your burnt-offerings and grain-offerings,
I will not accept them;
and the offerings of well-being of your fatted animals
I will not look upon.
23 Take away from me the noise of your songs;
I will not listen to the melody of your harps.
24 But let justice roll down like waters,
and righteousness like an ever-flowing stream.

25 Did you bring to me sacrifices and
offerings the forty years in the wilderness, O house of Israel? 26 You shall take
up Sakkuth your king, and Kaiwan your
star-god, your images[v] that you made

[v] 5.26 Heb *your images, your star-god*

for yourselves; 27therefore I will take you into exile beyond Damascus, says the LORD, whose name is the God of hosts.

COMPLACENT SELF-INDULGENCE WILL BE PUNISHED

6 Alas for those who are at
ease in Zion,
and for those who feel secure
on Mount Samaria,
the notables of the first of
the nations,
to whom the house of
Israel resorts!
2 Cross over to Calneh, and see;
from there go to Hamath
the great;
then go down to Gath of
the Philistines.
Are you better[w] than these
kingdoms?
Or is your[x] territory greater
than their[y] territory,
3 O you that put far away the evil day,
and bring near a reign of violence?

4 Alas for those who lie on
beds of ivory,
and lounge on their couches,
and eat lambs from the flock,
and calves from the stall;
5 who sing idle songs to the
sound of the harp,
and like David improvise on
instruments of music;
6 who drink wine from bowls,
and anoint themselves with
the finest oils,
but are not grieved over
the ruin of Joseph!
7 Therefore they shall now be the
first to go into exile,
and the revelry of the loungers
shall pass away.

8 The Lord GOD has sworn by himself
(says the LORD, the God of hosts):
I abhor the pride of Jacob
and hate his strongholds;
and I will deliver up the city
and all that is in it.

9 If ten people remain in one house,
they shall die. 10And if a relative, one
who burns the dead,[z] shall take up the
body to bring it out of the house, and
shall say to someone in the innermost
parts of the house, 'Is anyone else with
you?' the answer will come, 'No.' Then
the relative[a] shall say, 'Hush! We must
not mention the name of the LORD.'

11 See, the LORD commands,
and the great house shall be
shattered to bits,
and the little house to pieces.
12 Do horses run on rocks?
Does one plough the sea
with oxen?[b]
But you have turned justice
into poison
and the fruit of righteousness
into wormwood—
13 you who rejoice in Lo-debar,[c]
who say, 'Have we not by
our own strength
taken Karnaim[d] for ourselves?'
14 Indeed, I am raising up against
you a nation,
O house of Israel, says the
LORD, the God of hosts,
and they shall oppress you
from Lebo-hamath
to the Wadi Arabah.

LOCUSTS, FIRE, AND A PLUMB-LINE

7 This is what the Lord GOD showed
me: he was forming locusts at the
time the latter growth began to sprout
(it was the latter growth after the king's
mowings). 2When they had finished
eating the grass of the land, I said,
'O Lord GOD, forgive, I beg you!
How can Jacob stand?
He is so small!'
3 The LORD relented concerning this;
'It shall not be,' said the LORD.

4 This is what the Lord GOD showed
me: the Lord GOD was calling for a
shower of fire,[e] and it devoured the
great deep and was eating up the land.
5Then I said,
'O Lord GOD, cease, I beg you!
How can Jacob stand?
He is so small!'
6 The LORD relented concerning this;
'This also shall not be,' said
the Lord GOD.

7 This is what he showed me: the
Lord was standing beside a wall built
with a plumb-line, with a plumb-line
in his hand. 8And the LORD said to me,
'Amos, what do you see?' And I said, 'A
plumb-line.' Then the Lord said,

[w] 6.2 Or *Are they better* [x] 6.2 Heb *their* [y] 6.2 Heb *your* [z] 6.10 Or *who makes a burning for him* [a] 6.10 Heb *he* [b] 6.12 Or *Does one plough them with oxen* [c] 6.13 Or *in a thing of nothingness* [d] 6.13 Or *horns* [e] 7.4 Or *for a judgement by fire*

'See, I am setting a plumb-line
in the midst of my people Israel;
I will never again pass them by;
9 the high places of Isaac shall
be made desolate,
and the sanctuaries of Israel
shall be laid waste,
and I will rise against the house of
Jeroboam with the sword.'

AMAZIAH COMPLAINS TO THE KING

10 Then Amaziah, the priest of
Bethel, sent to King Jeroboam of Israel,
saying, 'Amos has conspired against you
in the very centre of the house of Israel;
the land is not able to bear all his words.
11 For thus Amos has said,
"Jeroboam shall die by the sword,
and Israel must go into exile
away from his land." '
12 And Amaziah said to Amos, 'O seer,
go, flee away to the land of Judah, earn
your bread there, and prophesy there;
13 but never again prophesy at Bethel,
for it is the king's sanctuary, and it is a
temple of the kingdom.'
14 Then Amos answered Amaziah,
'I am[f] no prophet, nor a prophet's son;
but I am[g] a herdsman, and a dresser of
sycomore trees, 15 and the LORD took me
from following the flock, and the LORD
said to me, "Go, prophesy to my people
Israel."
16 'Now therefore hear the word
of the LORD.
You say, "Do not prophesy
against Israel,
and do not preach against
the house of Isaac."
17 Therefore, thus says the LORD:
"Your wife shall become a
prostitute in the city,
and your sons and your daughters
shall fall by the sword,
and your land shall be
parcelled out by line;
you yourself shall die in an
unclean land,
and Israel shall surely go into
exile away from its land." '

THE BASKET OF FRUIT

8 This is what the Lord GOD showed
me—a basket of summer fruit.[h]
2 He said, 'Amos, what do you see?' And
I said, 'A basket of summer fruit.'[i] Then
the LORD said to me,
'The end[j] has come upon my
people Israel;
I will never again pass them by.
3 The songs of the temple[k] shall
become wailings on that day,'
says the Lord GOD;
'the dead bodies shall be many,
cast out in every place. Be silent!'

4 Hear this, you that trample
on the needy,
and bring to ruin the
poor of the land,
5 saying, 'When will the new
moon be over
so that we may sell grain;
and the sabbath,
so that we may offer
wheat for sale?
We will make the ephah small
and the shekel great,
and practise deceit with
false balances,
6 buying the poor for silver
and the needy for a pair of sandals,
and selling the sweepings
of the wheat.'

7 The LORD has sworn by the
pride of Jacob:
Surely I will never forget any
of their deeds.
8 Shall not the land tremble
on this account,
and everyone mourn
who lives in it,
and all of it rise like the Nile,
and be tossed about and sink
again, like the Nile of Egypt?

9 On that day, says the Lord GOD,
I will make the sun go
down at noon,
and darken the earth in
broad daylight.
10 I will turn your feasts into
mourning,
and all your songs into
lamentation;
I will bring sackcloth on all loins,
and baldness on every head;
I will make it like the mourning
for an only son,
and the end of it like a bitter day.

11 The time is surely coming,
says the Lord GOD,
when I will send a famine
on the land;

[f] 7.14 Or *was* [g] 7.14 Or *was* [h] 8.1 Heb *qayits* [i] 8.2 Heb *qayits* [j] 8.2 Heb *qets* [k] 8.3 Or *palace*

not a famine of bread, or a
thirst for water,
but of hearing the words
of the LORD.
12 They shall wander from sea to sea,
and from north to east;
they shall run to and fro, seeking
the word of the LORD,
but they shall not find it.

13 In that day the beautiful young
women and the young men
shall faint for thirst.
14 Those who swear by Ashimah
of Samaria,
and say, 'As your god lives, O Dan',
and, 'As the way of Beer-sheba
lives'—
they shall fall, and never rise again.

THE DESTRUCTION OF ISRAEL

9 I saw the LORD standing beside[l]
the altar, and he said:
Strike the capitals until the
thresholds shake,
and shatter them on the heads
of all the people;[m]
and those who are left I will
kill with the sword;
not one of them shall flee away,
not one of them shall escape.

2 Though they dig into Sheol,
from there shall my hand
take them;
though they climb up to heaven,
from there I will bring
them down.
3 Though they hide themselves
on the top of Carmel,
from there I will search out
and take them;
and though they hide from my sight
at the bottom of the sea,
there I will command the
sea-serpent, and it
shall bite them.
4 And though they go into captivity
in front of their enemies,
there I will command the sword,
and it shall kill them;
and I will fix my eyes on them
for harm and not for good.

5 The Lord, GOD of hosts,
he who touches the earth
and it melts,
and all who live in it mourn,
and all of it rises like the Nile,
and sinks again, like the
Nile of Egypt;
6 who builds his upper chambers
in the heavens,
and founds his vault
upon the earth;
who calls for the waters of the sea,
and pours them out upon the
surface of the earth—
the LORD is his name.

7 Are you not like the
Ethiopians[n] to me,
O people of Israel? says the LORD.
Did I not bring Israel up from
the land of Egypt,
and the Philistines from Caphtor
and the Arameans from Kir?
8 The eyes of the Lord GOD are upon
the sinful kingdom,
and I will destroy it from
the face of the earth
—except that I will not utterly
destroy the house of Jacob,
says the LORD.

9 For lo, I will command,
and shake the house of Israel
among all the nations
as one shakes with a sieve,
but no pebble shall fall
to the ground.
10 All the sinners of my people
shall die by the sword,
who say, 'Evil shall not
overtake or meet us.'

THE RESTORATION OF DAVID'S KINGDOM

11 On that day I will raise up
the booth of David that is fallen,
and repair its[o] breaches,
and raise up its[p] ruins,
and rebuild it as in the days of old;
12 in order that they may possess
the remnant of Edom
and all the nations who are
called by my name,
says the LORD who does this.

13 The time is surely coming,
says the LORD,
when the one who ploughs shall
overtake the one who reaps,
and the treader of grapes the
one who sows the seed;
the mountains shall drip sweet wine,
and all the hills shall flow with it.

[l] **9.1** Or *on* [m] **9.1** Heb *all of them* [n] **9.7** Or *Nubians*; Heb *Cushites* [o] **9.11** Gk: Heb *their* [p] **9.11** Gk: Heb *his*

14 I will restore the fortunes of
my people Israel,
and they shall rebuild the ruined
cities and inhabit them;
they shall plant vineyards and
drink their wine,
and they shall make gardens
and eat their fruit.
15 I will plant them upon their land,
and they shall never again
be plucked up
out of the land that I have
given them,
says the LORD your God.

OBADIAH

Obadiah is the shortest book of the Old Testament. It contains only 21 verses, which preserve Obadiah's bitter prophecy against Edom. The date of composition of the book of Obadiah is thought by many scholars to be sometime in the sixth or fifth century BCE following the Babylonian exile in 587. Obadiah's call for vengeance against Edom (Esau) draws from the historical enmity between the twin brothers Jacob and Esau and probably was provoked by the fact of the Edomites' complicity in the Babylonian destruction of Jerusalem. Obadiah calls for the vindication of Israel on the day of the Lord when Israel's enemies will be punished, the house of Esau destroyed, and the house of Jacob restored.

There are no verses from the book of Obadiah quoted in the New Testament, nor are there passages taken up by the Roman Missal. However, Obadiah's judgment against Edom is not without parallel oracles elsewhere in the Old Testament (e.g., Jer 49.7–22).

PROUD EDOM WILL BE BROUGHT LOW

1 The vision of Obadiah.

Thus says the Lord GOD
concerning Edom:
We have heard a report from the LORD,
and a messenger has been sent
among the nations:
'Rise up! Let us rise against it for battle!'
2 I will surely make you least
among the nations;
you shall be utterly despised.
3 Your proud heart has deceived you,
you that live in the clefts
of the rock,[a]
whose dwelling is in the heights.
You say in your heart,
'Who will bring me down
to the ground?'
4 Though you soar aloft like the eagle,
though your nest is set
among the stars,
from there I will bring you down,
says the LORD.

PILLAGE AND SLAUGHTER WILL REPAY EDOM'S CRUELTY

5 If thieves came to you,
if plunderers by night
—how you have been destroyed!—
would they not steal only
what they wanted?
If grape-gatherers came to you,
would they not leave gleanings?
6 How Esau has been pillaged,
his treasures searched out!
7 All your allies have deceived you,
they have driven you to the border;
your confederates have prevailed
against you;
those who ate[b] your bread have
set a trap for you—
there is no understanding of it.
8 On that day, says the LORD,
I will destroy the wise
out of Edom,
and understanding out
of Mount Esau.
9 Your warriors shall be
shattered, O Teman,
so that everyone from Mount
Esau will be cut off.

EDOM WRONGED HIS BROTHER

10 For the slaughter and violence done
to your brother Jacob,
shame shall cover you,
and you shall be cut off for ever.
11 On the day that you stood aside,
on the day that strangers
carried off his wealth,

[a] **3** Or *clefts of Sela* [b] **7** Cn: Heb lacks *those who ate*

and foreigners entered his gates
and cast lots for Jerusalem,
you too were like one of them.
12 But you should not have gloated[c]
over[d] your brother
on the day of his misfortune;
you should not have rejoiced over
the people of Judah
on the day of their ruin;
you should not have boasted
on the day of distress.
13 You should not have entered
the gate of my people
on the day of their calamity;
you should not have joined
in the gloating over
Judah's[e] disaster
on the day of his calamity;
you should not have
looted his goods
on the day of his calamity.
14 You should not have stood
at the crossings
to cut off his fugitives;
you should not have handed
over his survivors
on the day of distress.

15 For the day of the LORD is near
against all the nations.
As you have done, it shall
be done to you;
your deeds shall return on
your own head.
16 For as you have drunk on my
holy mountain,
all the nations around
you shall drink;
they shall drink and gulp down,[f]
and shall be as though they
had never been.

ISRAEL'S FINAL TRIUMPH

17 But on Mount Zion there shall
be those that escape,
and it shall be holy;
and the house of Jacob shall take
possession of those who
dispossessed them.
18 The house of Jacob shall be a fire,
the house of Joseph a flame,
and the house of Esau stubble;
they shall burn them and
consume them,
and there shall be no survivor
of the house of Esau;
for the LORD has spoken.
19 Those of the Negeb shall
possess Mount Esau,
and those of the Shephelah the
land of the Philistines;
they shall possess the land
of Ephraim and the
land of Samaria,
and Benjamin shall possess Gilead.
20 The exiles of the Israelites
who are in Halah[g]
shall possess[h] Phoenicia as
far as Zarephath;
and the exiles of Jerusalem
who are in Sepharad
shall possess the towns
of the Negeb.
21 Those who have been saved[i] shall
go up to Mount Zion
to rule Mount Esau;
and the kingdom shall
be the LORD's.

[c] 12 Heb *But do not gloat* (and similarly up to and including verse 14) [d] 12 Heb *on the day of* [e] 13 Heb *his* [f] 16 Meaning of Heb uncertain [g] 20 Cn: Heb *in this army* [h] 20 Cn: Meaning of Heb uncertain [i] 21 Or *Saviours*

JONAH

Written sometime after the Babylonian exile, the book of Jonah is a story about a reluctant prophet who is called by God to preach repentance to the inhabitants of Nineveh, the capital city of Assyria and Israel's traditional enemy in the eighth century BCE. This popular story reveals, to the surprise and disappointment of Jonah, how God actively intends the salvation of all people, including the enemies of Israel. There is much humor and irony in the story of Jonah, who is saved from drowning by being swallowed by a great fish and sent by God on an unwelcome mission to Nineveh.

Texts from Jonah are read during the liturgy on the first three days of the Twenty-Seventh Week of Year I. A passage from Jonah is also the first reading on Wednesday of the First Week of Lent. Also, a passage is read on the Third Sunday of Year B in the liturgical calendar. In the New Testament both Matthew and Luke record Jesus' interpretation that Jonah is a sign and a prefiguring of his mission and burial.

JONAH TRIES TO RUN AWAY FROM GOD

1 Now the word of the LORD came to
Jonah son of Amittai, saying, 2'Go
at once to Nineveh, that great city, and
cry out against it; for their wickedness
has come up before me.' 3But Jonah set
out to flee to Tarshish from the presence
of the LORD. He went down to Joppa
and found a ship going to Tarshish; so
he paid his fare and went on board, to go
with them to Tarshish, away from the
presence of the LORD.
4 But the LORD hurled a great wind
upon the sea, and such a mighty storm
came upon the sea that the ship threatened to break up. 5Then the mariners
were afraid, and each cried to his god.
They threw the cargo that was in the
ship into the sea, to lighten it for them.
Jonah, meanwhile, had gone down into
the hold of the ship and had lain down,
and was fast asleep. 6The captain came
and said to him, 'What are you doing
sound asleep? Get up, call on your god!
Perhaps the god will spare us a thought
so that we do not perish.'
7 The sailors[a] said to one another,
'Come, let us cast lots, so that we may
know on whose account this calamity
has come upon us.' So they cast lots, and
the lot fell on Jonah. 8Then they said
to him, 'Tell us why this calamity has
come upon us. What is your occupation?
Where do you come from? What is your
country? And of what people are you?'
9'I am a Hebrew,' he replied. 'I worship
the LORD, the God of heaven, who made
the sea and the dry land.' 10Then the
men were even more afraid, and said to
him, 'What is this that you have done!'
For the men knew that he was fleeing
from the presence of the LORD, because
he had told them so.
11 Then they said to him, 'What shall
we do to you, that the sea may quieten
down for us?' For the sea was growing
more and more tempestuous. 12He said
to them, 'Pick me up and throw me into
the sea; then the sea will quieten down
for you; for I know it is because of me
that this great storm has come upon
you.' 13Nevertheless, the men rowed
hard to bring the ship back to land, but
they could not, for the sea grew more
and more stormy against them. 14Then
they cried out to the LORD, 'Please,
O LORD, we pray, do not let us perish on

[a] 1.7 Heb *They*

account of this man's life. Do not make us guilty of innocent blood; for you, O LORD, have done as it pleased you.'
15So they picked Jonah up and threw him into the sea; and the sea ceased from its raging.
16Then the men feared the LORD even more, and they offered a sacrifice to the LORD and made vows.

17[b] But the LORD provided a large fish to swallow up Jonah; and Jonah was in the belly of the fish for three days and three nights.

A PSALM OF THANKSGIVING

2 Then Jonah prayed to the LORD his God from the belly of the fish,
2saying,

'I called to the LORD out of
my distress,
and he answered me;
out of the belly of Sheol I cried,
and you heard my voice.
3 You cast me into the deep,
into the heart of the seas,
and the flood surrounded me;
all your waves and your billows
passed over me.
4 Then I said, "I am driven away
from your sight;
how[c] shall I look again
upon your holy temple?"
5 The waters closed in over me;
the deep surrounded me;
weeds were wrapped around
my head
6 at the roots of the mountains.
I went down to the land
whose bars closed upon
me for ever;
yet you brought up my life
from the Pit,
O LORD my God.
7 As my life was ebbing away,
I remembered the LORD;
and my prayer came to you,
into your holy temple.
8 Those who worship vain idols
forsake their true loyalty.
9 But I with the voice of thanksgiving
will sacrifice to you;
what I have vowed I will pay.
Deliverance belongs to the LORD!'

10Then the LORD spoke to the fish, and it spewed Jonah out upon the dry land.

CONVERSION OF NINEVEH

3 The word of the LORD came to Jonah a second time, saying,
2'Get up, go to Nineveh, that great city, and proclaim to it the message that I tell you.'
3So Jonah set out and went to Nineveh, according to the word of the LORD. Now Nineveh was an exceedingly large city, a three days' walk across.
4Jonah began to go into the city, going a day's walk. And he cried out, 'Forty days more, and Nineveh shall be overthrown!'
5And the people of Nineveh believed God; they proclaimed a fast, and everyone, great and small, put on sackcloth.

6 When the news reached the king of Nineveh, he rose from his throne, removed his robe, covered himself with sackcloth, and sat in ashes.
7Then he had a proclamation made in Nineveh: 'By the decree of the king and his nobles: No human being or animal, no herd or flock, shall taste anything. They shall not feed, nor shall they drink water.
8Human beings and animals shall be covered with sackcloth, and they shall cry mightily to God. All shall turn from their evil ways and from the violence that is in their hands.
9Who knows? God may relent and change his mind; he may turn from his fierce anger, so that we do not perish.'

10 When God saw what they did, how they turned from their evil ways, God changed his mind about the calamity that he had said he would bring upon them; and he did not do it.

JONAH'S ANGER

4 But this was very displeasing to Jonah, and he became angry.
2He prayed to the LORD and said, 'O LORD! Is not this what I said while I was still in my own country? That is why I fled to Tarshish at the beginning; for I knew that you are a gracious God and merciful, slow to anger, and abounding in steadfast love, and ready to relent from punishing.
3And now, O LORD, please take my life from me, for it is better for me to die than to live.'
4And the LORD said, 'Is it right for you to be angry?'
5Then Jonah went out of the city and sat down east of the city, and made a booth for himself there. He sat under it in the shade, waiting to see what would become of the city.

6 The LORD God appointed a bush,[d] and made it come up over Jonah, to give shade over his head, to save him from his discomfort; so Jonah was very happy about the bush.
7But when dawn came up the next day, God appointed a worm that attacked the bush, so that it withered.

[b] **1.17** Ch 2.1 in Heb [c] **2.4** Theodotion: Heb *surely* [d] **4.6** Heb *qiqayon*, possibly *the castor bean plant*

8 When the sun rose, God prepared a sul-
try east wind, and the sun beat down on
the head of Jonah so that he was faint
and asked that he might die. He said, 'It
is better for me to die than to live.'

JONAH IS REPROVED

9 But God said to Jonah, 'Is it right for
you to be angry about the bush?' And he
said, 'Yes, angry enough to die.' 10 Then
the LORD said, 'You are concerned about
the bush, for which you did not labour
and which you did not grow; it came
into being in a night and perished in a
night. 11 And should I not be concerned
about Nineveh, that great city, in which
there are more than a hundred and
twenty thousand people who do not
know their right hand from their left,
and also many animals?'

MICAH

Along with Isaiah, Hosea, and Amos, Micah was a prophet of the eighth century BCE. Micah prophesied at a time when the Assyrians under the leadership of Sennacherib were attacking Judah in 701 BCE. Micah warned that the iniquity of Judah would lead to inevitable punishment at the hands of the Assyrians. Micah condemned the corruption of the political and religious officials of his day. Despite the condemnation of his prophecy, Micah's preaching also delivers a message of divine forgiveness. His prophecy ends with hope in a future restoration (7.7–20).

A well-quoted passage from Micah is read during the liturgy on Monday of the Sixteenth Week of Year II and as a choice for the first reading for the Common of Saints. There it is written: "What does the LORD require of you but to do justice, and to love kindness, and to walk humbly with your God?" (6.8).

1 The word of the LORD that came
to Micah of Moresheth in the days
of Kings Jotham, Ahaz, and Hezekiah
of Judah, which he saw concerning Samaria and Jerusalem.

JUDGEMENT PRONOUNCED AGAINST SAMARIA

2 Hear, you peoples, all of you;
listen, O earth, and all that is in it;
and let the Lord GOD be a witness against you,
the Lord from his holy temple.
3 For lo, the LORD is coming out of his place,
and will come down and tread upon the high places of the earth.
4 Then the mountains will melt under him
and the valleys will burst open,
like wax near the fire,
like waters poured down a steep place.
5 All this is for the transgression of Jacob
and for the sins of the house of Israel.
What is the transgression of Jacob?
Is it not Samaria?
And what is the high place[a] of Judah?
Is it not Jerusalem?
6 Therefore I will make Samaria a heap in the open country,
a place for planting vineyards.
I will pour down her stones into the valley,
and uncover her foundations.
7 All her images shall be beaten to pieces,
all her wages shall be burned with fire,
and all her idols I will lay waste;
for as the wages of a prostitute she gathered them,
and as the wages of a prostitute they shall again be used.

THE DOOM OF THE CITIES OF JUDAH

8 For this I will lament and wail;
I will go barefoot and naked;
I will make lamentation like the jackals,
and mourning like the ostriches.
9 For her wound[b] is incurable.
It has come to Judah;
it has reached to the gate of my people,
to Jerusalem.

10 Tell it not in Gath,
weep not at all;

[a] 1.5 Heb *what are the high places* [b] 1.9 Gk Syr Vg: Heb *wounds*

in Beth-leaphrah
roll yourselves in the dust.
11 Pass on your way,
inhabitants of Shaphir,
in nakedness and shame;
the inhabitants of Zaanan
do not come forth;
Beth-ezel is wailing
and shall remove its
support from you.
12 For the inhabitants of Maroth
wait anxiously for good,
yet disaster has come down
from the LORD
to the gate of Jerusalem.
13 Harness the steeds to the chariots,
inhabitants of Lachish;
it was the beginning of sin
to daughter Zion,
for in you were found
the transgressions of Israel.
14 Therefore you shall give
parting gifts
to Moresheth-gath;
the houses of Achzib shall
be a deception
to the kings of Israel.
15 I will again bring a conqueror
upon you,
inhabitants of Mareshah;
the glory of Israel
shall come to Adullam.
16 Make yourselves bald and
cut off your hair
for your pampered children;
make yourselves as bald as the eagle,
for they have gone from
you into exile.

SOCIAL EVILS DENOUNCED

2 Alas for those who devise
wickedness
and evil deeds[c] on their beds!
When the morning dawns,
they perform it,
because it is in their power.
2 They covet fields, and seize them;
houses, and take them away;
they oppress householder
and house,
people and their inheritance.
3 Therefore, thus says the LORD:
Now, I am devising against
this family an evil
from which you cannot
remove your necks;
and you shall not walk haughtily,
for it will be an evil time.
4 On that day they shall take up a
taunt-song against you,
and wail with bitter lamentation,
and say, 'We are utterly ruined;
the LORD[d] alters the inheritance
of my people;
how he removes it from me!
Among our captors[e] he
parcels out our fields.'
5 Therefore you will have no one
to cast the line by lot
in the assembly of the LORD.

6 'Do not preach'—thus they preach—
'one should not preach
of such things;
disgrace will not overtake us.'
7 Should this be said, O house of Jacob?
Is the LORD's patience exhausted?
Are these his doings?
Do not my words do good
to one who walks uprightly?
8 But you rise up against my
people[f] as an enemy;
you strip the robe from
the peaceful,[g]
from those who pass by trustingly
with no thought of war.
9 The women of my people
you drive out
from their pleasant houses;
from their young children
you take away
my glory for ever.
10 Arise and go;
for this is no place to rest,
because of uncleanness that destroys
with a grievous destruction.[h]
11 If someone were to go about
uttering empty falsehoods,
saying, 'I will preach to you of
wine and strong drink',
such a one would be the
preacher for this people!

A PROMISE FOR THE REMNANT OF ISRAEL

12 I will surely gather all of
you, O Jacob,
I will gather the survivors
of Israel;
I will set them together
like sheep in a fold,
like a flock in its pasture;
it will resound with people.
13 The one who breaks out will
go up before them;
they will break through
and pass the gate,
going out by it.

[c] 2.1 Cn: Heb *work evil* [d] 2.4 Heb *he* [e] 2.4 Cn: Heb *the rebellious* [f] 2.8 Cn: Heb *But yesterday my people rose* [g] 2.8 Cn: Heb *from before a garment* [h] 2.10 Meaning of Heb uncertain

Their king will pass on before them,
the LORD at their head.

WICKED RULERS AND PROPHETS

3 And I said:
Listen, you heads of Jacob
and rulers of the house of Israel!
Should you not know justice?—
2 you who hate the good
and love the evil,
who tear the skin off my people,[i]
and the flesh off their bones;
3 who eat the flesh of my people,
flay their skin off them,
break their bones in pieces,
and chop them up like
meat[j] in a kettle,
like flesh in a cauldron.

4 Then they will cry to the LORD,
but he will not answer them;
he will hide his face from
them at that time,
because they have acted wickedly.

5 Thus says the LORD concerning
the prophets
who lead my people astray,
who cry 'Peace'
when they have something to eat,
but declare war against those
who put nothing into their mouths.
6 Therefore it shall be night to
you, without vision,
and darkness to you,
without revelation.
The sun shall go down upon
the prophets,
and the day shall be black
over them;
7 the seers shall be disgraced,
and the diviners put to shame;
they shall all cover their lips,
for there is no answer from God.
8 But as for me, I am filled with power,
with the spirit of the LORD,
and with justice and might,
to declare to Jacob his transgression
and to Israel his sin.

9 Hear this, you rulers of the
house of Jacob
and chiefs of the house of Israel,
who abhor justice
and pervert all equity,
10 who build Zion with blood
and Jerusalem with wrong!
11 Its rulers give judgement for a bribe,
its priests teach for a price,
its prophets give oracles
for money;
yet they lean upon the LORD and say,
'Surely the LORD is with us!
No harm shall come upon us.'
12 Therefore because of you
Zion shall be ploughed as a field;
Jerusalem shall become a
heap of ruins,
and the mountain of the house
a wooded height.

PEACE AND SECURITY THROUGH OBEDIENCE

4 In days to come
the mountain of the LORD's house
shall be established as the highest
of the mountains,
and shall be raised up
above the hills.
Peoples shall stream to it,
2 and many nations shall
come and say:
'Come, let us go up to the
mountain of the LORD,
to the house of the God of Jacob;
that he may teach us his ways
and that we may walk in his paths.'
For out of Zion shall go forth
instruction,
and the word of the LORD
from Jerusalem.
3 He shall judge between
many peoples,
and shall arbitrate between
strong nations far away;
they shall beat their swords
into ploughshares,
and their spears into
pruning-hooks;
nation shall not lift up sword
against nation,
neither shall they learn
war any more;
4 but they shall all sit under their
own vines and under
their own fig trees,
and no one shall make them afraid;
for the mouth of the LORD
of hosts has spoken.

5 For all the peoples walk,
each in the name of its god,
but we will walk in the name
of the LORD our God
for ever and ever.

RESTORATION PROMISED AFTER EXILE

6 On that day, says the LORD,
I will assemble the lame

[i] 3.2 Heb *from them* [j] 3.3 Gk: Heb *as*

and gather those who have
been driven away,
and those whom I have afflicted.
7 The lame I will make
the remnant,
and those who were cast
off, a strong nation;
and the LORD will reign over
them in Mount Zion
now and for evermore.

8 And you, O tower of the flock,
hill of daughter Zion,
to you it shall come,
the former dominion shall come,
the sovereignty of daughter
Jerusalem.

9 Now why do you cry aloud?
Is there no king in you?
Has your counsellor perished,
that pangs have seized you like
a woman in labour?
10 Writhe and groan,[k]
O daughter Zion,
like a woman in labour;
for now you shall go forth
from the city
and camp in the open country;
you shall go to Babylon.
There you shall be rescued,
there the LORD will redeem you
from the hands of your enemies.

11 Now many nations
are assembled against you,
saying, 'Let her be profaned,
and let our eyes gaze upon Zion.'
12 But they do not know
the thoughts of the LORD;
they do not understand his plan,
that he has gathered them
as sheaves to the
threshing-floor.
13 Arise and thresh,
O daughter Zion,
for I will make your horn iron
and your hoofs bronze;
you shall beat in pieces
many peoples,
and shall[l] devote their
gain to the LORD,
their wealth to the Lord of
the whole earth.

5[m] Now you are walled around
with a wall;[n]
siege is laid against us;
with a rod they strike the
ruler of Israel
upon the cheek.

THE RULER FROM BETHLEHEM

2[o] But you, O Bethlehem of
Ephrathah,
who are one of the little
clans of Judah,
from you shall come forth for me
one who is to rule in Israel,
whose origin is from of old,
from ancient days.
3 Therefore he shall give them
up until the time
when she who is in labour
has brought forth;
then the rest of his kindred
shall return
to the people of Israel.
4 And he shall stand and feed his flock
in the strength of the LORD,
in the majesty of the name
of the LORD his God.
And they shall live secure, for
now he shall be great
to the ends of the earth;
5 and he shall be the one of peace.

If the Assyrians come
into our land
and tread upon our soil,[p]
we will raise against them
seven shepherds
and eight installed as rulers.
6 They shall rule the land of Assyria
with the sword,
and the land of Nimrod with
the drawn sword;[q]
they[r] shall rescue us from
the Assyrians
if they come into our land
or tread within our border.

THE FUTURE ROLE OF THE REMNANT

7 Then the remnant of Jacob,
surrounded by many peoples,
shall be like dew from the LORD,
like showers on the grass,
which do not depend upon people
or wait for any mortal.
8 And among the nations the
remnant of Jacob,
surrounded by many peoples,
shall be like a lion among the
animals of the forest,
like a young lion among
the flocks of sheep,

[k] **4.10** Meaning of Heb uncertain [l] **4.13** Gk Syr Tg: Heb *and I will* [m] **5.1** Ch 4.14 in Heb
[n] **5.1** Cn Compare Gk: Meaning of Heb uncertain
[o] **5.2** Ch 5.1 in Heb [p] **5.5** Gk: Heb *in our palaces*
[q] **5.6** Cn: Heb *in its entrances* [r] **5.6** Heb *he*

which, when it goes through,
treads down
and tears in pieces, with
no one to deliver.
9 Your hand shall be lifted up over
your adversaries,
and all your enemies shall be cut off.

10 On that day, says the LORD,
I will cut off your horses
from among you
and will destroy your chariots;
11 and I will cut off the cities of your land
and throw down all your
strongholds;
12 and I will cut off sorceries
from your hand,
and you shall have no more
soothsayers;
13 and I will cut off your images
and your pillars from among you,
and you shall bow down no more
to the work of your hands;
14 and I will uproot your sacred
poles[s] from among you
and destroy your towns.
15 And in anger and wrath I will
execute vengeance
on the nations that did not obey.

GOD CHALLENGES ISRAEL

6 Hear what the LORD says:
Rise, plead your case before
the mountains,
and let the hills hear your voice.
2 Hear, you mountains, the
controversy of the LORD,
and you enduring foundations
of the earth;
for the LORD has a controversy
with his people,
and he will contend with Israel.

3 'O my people, what have I
done to you?
In what have I wearied
you? Answer me!
4 For I brought you up from
the land of Egypt,
and redeemed you from the
house of slavery;
and I sent before you Moses,
Aaron, and Miriam.
5 O my people, remember now what
King Balak of Moab devised,
what Balaam son of Beor
answered him,
and what happened from
Shittim to Gilgal,
that you may know the saving
acts of the LORD.'

WHAT GOD REQUIRES

6 'With what shall I come
before the LORD,
and bow myself before
God on high?
Shall I come before him with
burnt-offerings,
with calves a year old?
7 Will the LORD be pleased with
thousands of rams,
with tens of thousands
of rivers of oil?
Shall I give my firstborn for
my transgression,
the fruit of my body for the
sin of my soul?'
8 He has told you, O mortal,
what is good;
and what does the LORD
require of you
but to do justice, and to
love kindness,
and to walk humbly
with your God?

CHEATING AND VIOLENCE TO BE PUNISHED

9 The voice of the LORD cries
to the city
(it is sound wisdom to
fear your name):
Hear, O tribe and assembly
of the city![t]
10 Can I forget[u] the treasures
of wickedness in the
house of the wicked,
and the scant measure
that is accursed?
11 Can I tolerate wicked scales
and a bag of dishonest weights?
12 Your[v] wealthy are full of violence;
your[w] inhabitants speak lies,
with tongues of deceit in
their mouths.
13 Therefore I have begun[x] to
strike you down,
making you desolate because
of your sins.
14 You shall eat, but not be satisfied,
and there shall be a gnawing
hunger within you;
you shall put away, but not save,
and what you save, I will hand
over to the sword.

[s] **5.14** Heb *Asherim* [t] **6.9** Cn Compare Gk: Heb *tribe, and who has appointed it yet?* [u] **6.10** Cn: Meaning of Heb uncertain [v] **6.12** Heb *Whose* [w] **6.12** Heb *whose* [x] **6.13** Gk Syr Vg: Heb *have made sick*

15 You shall sow, but not reap;
you shall tread olives, but not
anoint yourselves with oil;
you shall tread grapes, but
not drink wine.
16 For you have kept the
statutes of Omri[y]
and all the works of the
house of Ahab,
and you have followed
their counsels.
Therefore I will make you
a desolation, and
your[z] inhabitants an
object of hissing;
so you shall bear the scorn
of my people.

THE TOTAL CORRUPTION OF THE PEOPLE

7 Woe is me! For I have become
like one who,
after the summer fruit has
been gathered,
after the vintage has
been gleaned,
finds no cluster to eat;
there is no first-ripe fig for
which I hunger.
2 The faithful have disappeared
from the land,
and there is no one left
who is upright;
they all lie in wait for blood,
and they hunt each other
with nets.
3 Their hands are skilled to do evil;
the official and the judge
ask for a bribe,
and the powerful dictate
what they desire;
thus they pervert justice.[a]
4 The best of them is like a brier,
the most upright of them
a thorn hedge.
The day of their[b] sentinels, of their[c]
punishment, has come;
now their confusion is at hand.
5 Put no trust in a friend,
have no confidence in a loved one;
guard the doors of your mouth
from her who lies in
your embrace;
6 for the son treats the father
with contempt,
the daughter rises up
against her mother,
the daughter-in-law against
her mother-in-law;
your enemies are members of
your own household.

7 But as for me, I will look
to the LORD,
I will wait for the God of
my salvation;
my God will hear me.

PENITENCE AND TRUST IN GOD

8 Do not rejoice over me, O my enemy;
when I fall, I shall rise;
when I sit in darkness,
the LORD will be a light to me.
9 I must bear the indignation
of the LORD,
because I have sinned
against him,
until he takes my side
and executes judgement for me.
He will bring me out to the light;
I shall see his vindication.
10 Then my enemy will see,
and shame will cover her
who said to me,
'Where is the LORD your God?'
My eyes will see her downfall;[d]
now she will be trodden down
like the mire of the streets.

A PROPHECY OF RESTORATION

11 A day for the building of your walls!
In that day the boundary
shall be far extended.
12 In that day they will come to you
from Assyria to[e] Egypt,
and from Egypt to the River,
from sea to sea and from
mountain to mountain.
13 But the earth will be desolate
because of its inhabitants,
for the fruit of their doings.

14 Shepherd your people with
your staff,
the flock that belongs to you,
which lives alone in a forest
in the midst of a garden land;
let them feed in Bashan and Gilead
as in the days of old.
15 As in the days when you came
out of the land of Egypt,
show us[f] marvellous things.
16 The nations shall see and be ashamed
of all their might;
they shall lay their hands on
their mouths;
their ears shall be deaf;

[y] **6.16** Gk Syr Vg Tg: Heb *the statutes of Omri are kept* [z] **6.16** Heb *its* [a] **7.3** Cn: Heb *they weave it* [b] **7.4** Heb *your* [c] **7.4** Heb *your* [d] **7.10** Heb lacks *downfall* [e] **7.12** One Ms: MT *Assyria and cities of* [f] **7.15** Cn: Heb *I will show him*

17 they shall lick dust like a snake,
like the crawling things
of the earth;
they shall come trembling out
of their fortresses;
they shall turn in dread to
the LORD our God,
and they shall stand in fear of you.

GOD'S COMPASSION AND STEADFAST LOVE

18 Who is a God like you,
pardoning iniquity
and passing over the
transgression
of the remnant of your[g]
possession?
He does not retain his anger for ever,
because he delights in
showing clemency.
19 He will again have compassion
upon us;
he will tread our iniquities
under foot.
You will cast all our[h] sins
into the depths of the sea.
20 You will show faithfulness to Jacob
and unswerving loyalty
to Abraham,
as you have sworn to our ancestors
from the days of old.

g 7.18 Heb *his* h 7.19 Gk Syr Vg Tg: Heb *their*

NAHUM

Nahum prophesied at the time just before the fall of Nineveh to the Babylonians, about 612 BCE. Nahum did not know that a few decades later the Babylonians would attack Judah in 587. However, he attributes the fall of Assyria to the vengeance of the Lord God of Israel. For Nahum, Nineveh receives what it deserves, and Judah is spared further threat. The main part of Nahum's prophecy is a vivid poem (2.3–9; 3.1–3) celebrating Nineveh's destruction.

A text from Nahum is read at the liturgy on Friday of the Eighteenth Week of Year II (1.15–16; 2.2; 3.1–3, 6–7). In this passage, Nineveh receives divine punishment for its crimes against neighboring peoples. The obvious parallel lesson in the New Testament is that everyone will be repaid according to what each has done when the Son of Man comes in the last days (Mt 16.27).

1 An oracle concerning Nineveh. The book of the vision of Nahum of Elkosh.

THE CONSUMING WRATH OF GOD

2 A jealous and avenging God
is the LORD,
the LORD is avenging and wrathful;
the LORD takes vengeance on
his adversaries
and rages against his enemies.
3 The LORD is slow to anger but
great in power,
and the LORD will by no
means clear the guilty.

His way is in whirlwind and storm,
and the clouds are the
dust of his feet.
4 He rebukes the sea and makes it dry,
and he dries up all the rivers;
Bashan and Carmel wither,
and the bloom of Lebanon fades.
5 The mountains quake before him,
and the hills melt;
the earth heaves before him,
the world and all who live in it.

6 Who can stand before his indignation?
Who can endure the heat
of his anger?
His wrath is poured out like fire,
and by him the rocks are
broken in pieces.
7 The LORD is good,
a stronghold on a day of trouble;
he protects those who take
refuge in him,
8 even in a rushing flood.
He will make a full end of
his adversaries,[a]
and will pursue his enemies
into darkness.
9 Why do you plot against the LORD?
He will make an end;
no adversary will rise up twice.
10 Like thorns they are entangled,
like drunkards they are drunk;
they are consumed
like dry straw.
11 From you one has gone out
who plots evil against the LORD,
one who counsels wickedness.

GOOD NEWS FOR JUDAH

12 Thus says the LORD,
'Though they are at full
strength and many,[b]
they will be cut off and pass away.
Though I have afflicted you,
I will afflict you no more.
13 And now I will break off his
yoke from you
and snap the bonds that bind you.'

[a] **1.8** Gk: Heb *of her place* [b] **1.12** Meaning of Heb uncertain

14 The LORD has commanded
concerning you:
'Your name shall be
perpetuated no longer;
from the house of your gods
I will cut off
the carved image and
the cast image.
I will make your grave, for
you are worthless.'

15[c] Look! On the mountains
the feet of one
who brings good tidings,
who proclaims peace!
Celebrate your festivals, O Judah,
fulfil your vows,
for never again shall the
wicked invade you;
they are utterly cut off.

THE DESTRUCTION OF THE WICKED CITY

2 A shatterer[d] has come up
against you.
Guard the ramparts;
watch the road;
gird your loins;
collect all your strength.

2 (For the LORD is restoring the
majesty of Jacob,
as well as the majesty of Israel,
though ravagers have
ravaged them
and ruined their branches.)

3 The shields of his warriors are red;
his soldiers are clothed
in crimson.
The metal on the chariots flashes
on the day when he
musters them;
the chargers[e] prance.
4 The chariots race madly
through the streets,
they rush to and fro through
the squares;
their appearance is like torches,
they dart like lightning.
5 He calls his officers;
they stumble as they
come forward;
they hasten to the wall,
and the mantelet[f] is set up.
6 The river gates are opened,
the palace trembles.
7 It is decreed[g] that the city[h] be exiled,
its slave-women led away,
moaning like doves
and beating their breasts.
8 Nineveh is like a pool
whose waters[i] run away.
'Halt! Halt!'—
but no one turns back.
9 'Plunder the silver,
plunder the gold!
There is no end of treasure!
An abundance of every
precious thing!'

10 Devastation, desolation, and
destruction!
Hearts faint and knees tremble,
all loins quake,
all faces grow pale!
11 What became of the lions' den,
the cave[j] of the young lions,
where the lion goes,
and the lion's cubs, with no
one to disturb them?
12 The lion has torn enough
for his whelps
and strangled prey for his lionesses;
he has filled his caves with prey
and his dens with torn flesh.

13 See, I am against you, says the
LORD of hosts, and I will burn your[k]
chariots in smoke, and the sword shall
devour your young lions; I will cut off
your prey from the earth, and the voice
of your messengers shall be heard no
more.

RUIN IMMINENT AND INEVITABLE

3 Ah! City of bloodshed,
utterly deceitful, full of booty—
no end to the plunder!
2 The crack of whip and
rumble of wheel,
galloping horse and
bounding chariot!
3 Horsemen charging,
flashing sword and
glittering spear,
piles of dead,
heaps of corpses,
dead bodies without end—
they stumble over the bodies!
4 Because of the countless
debaucheries of
the prostitute,
gracefully alluring, mistress
of sorcery,

[c] 1.15 Ch 2.1 in Heb [d] 2.1 Cn: Heb *scatterer* [e] 2.3 Cn Compare Gk Syr: Heb *cypresses* [f] 2.5 Meaning of Heb uncertain [g] 2.7 Meaning of Heb uncertain [h] 2.7 Heb *it* [i] 2.8 Cn Compare Gk: Heb *a pool, from the days that she has become, and they* [j] 2.11 Cn: Heb *pasture* [k] 2.13 Heb *her*

who enslaves[l] nations through
her debaucheries,
and peoples through her sorcery,
5 I am against you,
says the LORD of hosts,
and will lift up your skirts
over your face;
and I will let nations look on
your nakedness
and kingdoms on your shame.
6 I will throw filth at you
and treat you with contempt,
and make you a spectacle.
7 Then all who see you will shrink
from you and say,
'Nineveh is devastated; who
will bemoan her?'
Where shall I seek
comforters for you?

8 Are you better than Thebes[m]
that sat by the Nile,
with water around her,
her rampart a sea,
water her wall?
9 Ethiopia[n] was her strength,
Egypt too, and that without limit;
Put and the Libyans were
her[o] helpers.
10 Yet she became an exile,
she went into captivity;
even her infants were
dashed in pieces
at the head of every street;
lots were cast for her nobles,
all her dignitaries were
bound in fetters.
11 You also will be drunken,
you will go into hiding;[p]
you will seek
a refuge from the enemy.
12 All your fortresses are like fig trees
with first-ripe figs—
if shaken they fall
into the mouth of the eater.
13 Look at your troops:
they are women in your midst.
The gates of your land
are wide open to your foes;
fire has devoured the bars
of your gates.

14 Draw water for the siege,
strengthen your forts;
trample the clay,
tread the mortar,
take hold of the brick-mould!
15 There the fire will devour you,
the sword will cut you off.
It will devour you like the locust.

Multiply yourselves like the locust,
multiply like the grasshopper!
16 You increased your merchants
more than the stars of
the heavens.
The locust sheds its skin
and flies away.
17 Your guards are like grasshoppers,
your scribes like swarms[q]
of locusts
settling on the fences
on a cold day—
when the sun rises,
they fly away;
no one knows where
they have gone.

18 Your shepherds are asleep,
O king of Assyria;
your nobles slumber.
Your people are scattered on
the mountains
with no one to gather them.
19 There is no assuaging your hurt,
your wound is mortal.
All who hear the news about you
clap their hands over you.
For who has ever escaped
your endless cruelty?

[l] 3.4 Heb *sells* [m] 3.8 Heb *No-amon* [n] 3.9 Or *Nubia*; Heb *Cush* [o] 3.9 Gk: Heb *your*
[p] 3.11 Meaning of Heb uncertain
[q] 3.17 Meaning of Heb uncertain

HABAKKUK

The prophecy of Habakkuk dates from 605–597 BCE. Habakkuk was a contemporary of Jeremiah and contended similarly that the invading Babylon was a divine instrument sent to chastise Judah. Habakkuk, however, was the first to question God with his famous opening oracle: "O LORD, how long shall I cry for help, and you will not listen? Or cry to you 'Violence!' and you will not save?" (1.2). God's response is provided as a vision to be written down that Babylon is a chastising rod, and that the just will not perish but will live by their faith (2.4).

This text in which Habakkuk complains to God and receives a vision in response comes from the first two chapters of Habakkuk and is read at the liturgy on the Twenty-Seventh Sunday of Year C and on Saturday of the Eighteenth Week of Year II.

1 The oracle that the prophet Habakkuk saw.

THE PROPHET'S COMPLAINT

2 O LORD, how long shall I cry for help,
and you will not listen?
Or cry to you 'Violence!'
and you will not save?
3 Why do you make me see
wrongdoing
and look at trouble?
Destruction and violence
are before me;
strife and contention arise.
4 So the law becomes slack
and justice never prevails.
The wicked surround the
righteous—
therefore judgement comes
forth perverted.

5 Look at the nations, and see!
Be astonished! Be astounded!
For a work is being done in your days
that you would not believe
if you were told.
6 For I am rousing the Chaldeans,
that fierce and impetuous nation,
who march through the
breadth of the earth
to seize dwellings not their own.
7 Dread and fearsome are they;
their justice and dignity proceed
from themselves.
8 Their horses are swifter
than leopards,
more menacing than
wolves at dusk;
their horses charge.
Their horsemen come from far away;
they fly like an eagle
swift to devour.
9 They all come for violence,
with faces pressing[a] forward;
they gather captives like sand.
10 At kings they scoff,
and of rulers they make sport.
They laugh at every fortress,
and heap up earth to take it.
11 Then they sweep by like the wind;
they transgress and
become guilty;
their own might is their god!

12 Are you not from of old,
O LORD my God, my Holy One?
You[b] shall not die.
O LORD, you have marked
them for judgement;
and you, O Rock, have established
them for punishment.
13 Your eyes are too pure to behold evil,
and you cannot look on
wrongdoing;

[a] 1.9 Meaning of Heb uncertain [b] 1.12 Ancient Heb tradition: MT *We*

why do you look on the treacherous,
and are silent when the
wicked swallow
those more righteous than they?
14 You have made people like
the fish of the sea,
like crawling things that
have no ruler.

15 The enemy[c] brings all of them
up with a hook;
he drags them out with his net,
he gathers them in his seine;
so he rejoices and exults.
16 Therefore he sacrifices to his net
and makes offerings to his seine;
for by them his portion is lavish,
and his food is rich.
17 Is he then to keep on
emptying his net,
and destroying nations
without mercy?

GOD'S REPLY TO THE PROPHET'S COMPLAINT

2 I will stand at my watch-post,
and station myself on the rampart;
I will keep watch to see what
he will say to me,
and what he[d] will answer
concerning my complaint.
2 Then the LORD answered
me and said:
Write the vision;
make it plain on tablets,
so that a runner may read it.
3 For there is still a vision for
the appointed time;
it speaks of the end, and
does not lie.
If it seems to tarry, wait for it;
it will surely come, it
will not delay.
4 Look at the proud!
Their spirit is not right in them,
but the righteous live by
their faith.[e]
5 Moreover, wealth[f] is treacherous;
the arrogant do not endure.
They open their throats
wide as Sheol;
like Death they never
have enough.
They gather all nations for
themselves,
and collect all peoples as their own.

THE WOES OF THE WICKED

6 Shall not everyone taunt such
people and, with mocking riddles, say
about them,
'Alas for you who heap up what
is not your own!'
How long will you load yourselves
with goods taken in pledge?
7 Will not your own creditors
suddenly rise,
and those who make you
tremble wake up?
Then you will be booty for them.
8 Because you have plundered
many nations,
all that survive of the peoples
shall plunder you—
because of human bloodshed, and
violence to the earth,
to cities and all who live in them.
9 'Alas for you who get evil gain
for your house,
setting your nest on high
to be safe from the reach of harm!'
10 You have devised shame
for your house
by cutting off many peoples;
you have forfeited your life.
11 The very stones will cry out
from the wall,
and the plaster[g] will respond
from the woodwork.

12 'Alas for you who build a town
by bloodshed,
and found a city on iniquity!'
13 Is it not from the LORD of hosts
that peoples labour only to
feed the flames,
and nations weary themselves
for nothing?
14 But the earth will be filled
with the knowledge of the
glory of the LORD,
as the waters cover the sea.

15 'Alas for you who make your
neighbours drink,
pouring out your wrath[h]
until they are drunk,
in order to gaze on their
nakedness!'
16 You will be sated with contempt
instead of glory.
Drink, you yourself, and stagger![i]
The cup in the LORD's right hand
will come around to you,
and shame will come
upon your glory!

[c] 1.15 Heb *He* [d] 2.1 Syr: Heb *I* [e] 2.4 Or *faithfulness* [f] 2.5 Other Heb Mss read *wine* [g] 2.11 Or *beam* [h] 2.15 Or *poison* [i] 2.16 Q Ms Gk: MT *be uncircumcised*

17 For the violence done to Lebanon
will overwhelm you;
the destruction of the animals
will terrify you—[j]
because of human bloodshed and
violence to the earth,
to cities and all who live in them.

18 What use is an idol
once its maker has shaped it—
a cast image, a teacher of lies?
For its maker trusts in what
has been made,
though the product is only an
idol that cannot speak!
19 Alas for you who say to the
wood, 'Wake up!'
to silent stone, 'Rouse yourself!'
Can it teach?
See, it is plated with
gold and silver,
and there is no breath in it at all.

20 But the LORD is in his holy temple;
let all the earth keep silence
before him!

3 A prayer of the prophet Habakkuk according to Shigionoth.

THE PROPHET'S PRAYER

2 O LORD, I have heard of
your renown,
and I stand in awe, O LORD,
of your work.
In our own time revive it;
in our own time make it known;
in wrath may you
remember mercy.
3 God came from Teman,
the Holy One from Mount Paran.
Selah
His glory covered the heavens,
and the earth was full
of his praise.
4 The brightness was like the sun;
rays came forth from his hand,
where his power lay hidden.
5 Before him went pestilence,
and plague followed close behind.
6 He stopped and shook the earth;
he looked and made the
nations tremble.
The eternal mountains
were shattered;
along his ancient pathways
the everlasting hills sank low.
7 I saw the tents of Cushan
under affliction;
the tent-curtains of the land
of Midian trembled.
8 Was your wrath against the
rivers,[k] O LORD?
Or your anger against the rivers,[l]
or your rage against the sea,[m]
when you drove your horses,
your chariots to victory?
9 You brandished your naked bow,
sated[n] were the arrows at your
command.[o] *Selah*
You split the earth with rivers.
10 The mountains saw you,
and writhed;
a torrent of water swept by;
the deep gave forth its voice.
The sun[p] raised high its hands;
11 the moon[q] stood still in its
exalted place,
at the light of your arrows
speeding by,
at the gleam of your
flashing spear.
12 In fury you trod the earth,
in anger you trampled nations.
13 You came forth to save your people,
to save your anointed.
You crushed the head of the
wicked house,
laying it bare from foundation to
roof.[r] *Selah*
14 You pierced with their[s] own arrows
the head[t] of his warriors,[u]
who came like a whirlwind
to scatter us,[v]
gloating as if ready to devour the
poor who were in hiding.
15 You trampled the sea with
your horses,
churning the mighty waters.

16 I hear, and I tremble within;
my lips quiver at the sound.
Rottenness enters into my bones,
and my steps tremble[w]
beneath me.
I wait quietly for the day of calamity
to come upon the people
who attack us.

TRUST AND JOY IN THE MIDST OF TROUBLE

17 Though the fig tree does
not blossom,
and no fruit is on the vines;

[j] **2.17** Gk Syr: Meaning of Heb uncertain
[k] **3.8** Or *against River* [l] **3.8** Or *against River*
[m] **3.8** Or *against Sea* [n] **3.9** Cn: Heb *oaths*
[o] **3.9** Meaning of Heb uncertain [p] **3.10** Heb *It*
[q] **3.11** Heb *sun, moon* [r] **3.13** Meaning of Heb uncertain [s] **3.14** Heb *his* [t] **3.14** Or *leader*
[u] **3.14** Vg Compare Gk Syr: Meaning of Heb uncertain [v] **3.14** Heb *me* [w] **3.16** Cn Compare Gk: Meaning of Heb uncertain

though the produce of
the olive fails
and the fields yield no food;
though the flock is cut off
from the fold
and there is no herd
in the stalls,
18 yet I will rejoice in the LORD;
I will exult in the God of
my salvation.
19 GOD, the Lord, is my strength;
he makes my feet like the
feet of a deer,
and makes me tread upon
the heights.[x]

To the leader: with stringed[y]
instruments.

[x] 3.19 Heb *my heights* [y] 3.19 Heb *my stringed*

ZEPHANIAH

Zephaniah was active as a prophet during the reign of Josiah (640–609 BCE). He preached about the coming day of the Lord as a day of doom and disaster. The Christian hymn "Dies Irae" is based upon a passage from Zephaniah (1.2–18). However, that day of judgment will also be a time when a remnant finally will enjoy peace. The prophecy closes with a hymn of joy over the restored city of Zion (3.14–20).

Zephaniah's prophecy about the preservation of a remnant of Israel is read on the Fourth Sunday of Year A in the liturgical calendar. The concluding hymn of joy proclaimed by Zephaniah over the restoration of Zion is read on the Third Sunday of Advent in Year C as well as on December 21 in anticipation of Christmas.

1 The word of the LORD that came to Zephaniah son of Cushi son of Gedaliah son of Amariah son of Hezekiah, in the days of King Josiah son of Amon of Judah.

THE COMING JUDGEMENT ON JUDAH

2 I will utterly sweep away everything
from the face of the earth,
says the LORD.
3 I will sweep away humans and animals;
I will sweep away the birds of the air
and the fish of the sea.
I will make the wicked stumble.[a]
I will cut off humanity
from the face of the earth,
says the LORD.
4 I will stretch out my hand against Judah,
and against all the inhabitants of Jerusalem;
and I will cut off from this place
every remnant of Baal
and the name of the idolatrous priests;[b]
5 those who bow down on the roofs
to the host of the heavens;
those who bow down and swear to the LORD,
but also swear by Milcom;[c]
6 those who have turned back from following the LORD,
who have not sought the LORD or inquired of him.

7 Be silent before the Lord GOD!
For the day of the LORD is at hand;
the LORD has prepared a sacrifice,
he has consecrated his guests.
8 And on the day of the LORD's sacrifice
I will punish the officials and the king's sons
and all who dress themselves in foreign attire.
9 On that day I will punish
all who leap over the threshold,
who fill their master's house
with violence and fraud.

10 On that day, says the LORD,
a cry will be heard from the Fish Gate,
a wail from the Second Quarter,
a loud crash from the hills.
11 The inhabitants of the Mortar wail,
for all the traders have perished;
all who weigh out silver are cut off.

[a] 1.3 Cn: Heb *sea, and those who cause the wicked to stumble* [b] 1.4 Compare Gk: Heb *the idolatrous priests with the priests* [c] 1.5 Gk Mss Syr Vg: Heb *Malcam* (or, *their king*)

12 At that time I will search
Jerusalem with lamps,
and I will punish the people
who rest complacently[d] on
their dregs,
those who say in their hearts,
'The LORD will not do good,
nor will he do harm.'
13 Their wealth shall be plundered,
and their houses laid waste.
Though they build houses,
they shall not inhabit them;
though they plant vineyards,
they shall not drink wine
from them.

THE GREAT DAY OF THE LORD

14 The great day of the LORD is near,
near and hastening fast;
the sound of the day of the
LORD is bitter,
the warrior cries aloud there.
15 That day will be a day of wrath,
a day of distress and anguish,
a day of ruin and devastation,
a day of darkness and gloom,
a day of clouds and thick darkness,
16 a day of trumpet blast
and battle cry
against the fortified cities
and against the lofty battlements.

17 I will bring such distress upon people
that they shall walk like the blind;
because they have sinned
against the LORD,
their blood shall be poured
out like dust,
and their flesh like dung.
18 Neither their silver nor their gold
will be able to save them
on the day of the LORD's wrath;
in the fire of his passion
the whole earth shall
be consumed;
for a full, a terrible end
he will make of all the
inhabitants of the earth.

JUDGEMENT ON ISRAEL'S ENEMIES

2 Gather together, gather,
O shameless nation,
2 before you are driven away
like the drifting chaff,[e]
before there comes upon you
the fierce anger of the LORD,
before there comes upon you
the day of the LORD's wrath.
3 Seek the LORD, all you humble
of the land,
who do his commands;
seek righteousness, seek humility;
perhaps you may be hidden
on the day of the LORD's wrath.
4 For Gaza shall be deserted,
and Ashkelon shall become
a desolation;
Ashdod's people shall be driven
out at noon,
and Ekron shall be uprooted.

5 Ah, inhabitants of the sea coast,
you nation of the Cherethites!
The word of the LORD is against you,
O Canaan, land of the Philistines;
and I will destroy you until
no inhabitant is left.
6 And you, O sea coast, shall
be pastures,
meadows for shepherds
and folds for flocks.
7 The sea coast shall become
the possession
of the remnant of the
house of Judah,
on which they shall pasture,
and in the houses of Ashkelon
they shall lie down at evening.
For the LORD their God will be
mindful of them
and restore their fortunes.

8 I have heard the taunts of Moab
and the revilings of the
Ammonites,
how they have taunted my people
and made boasts against
their territory.
9 Therefore, as I live, says the
LORD of hosts,
the God of Israel,
Moab shall become like Sodom
and the Ammonites like Gomorrah,
a land possessed by nettles
and salt-pits,
and a waste for ever.
The remnant of my people
shall plunder them,
and the survivors of my nation
shall possess them.
10 This shall be their lot in return
for their pride,
because they scoffed and boasted
against the people of the
LORD of hosts.
11 The LORD will be terrible
against them;
he will shrivel all the gods
of the earth,

[d] 1.12 Heb *who thicken* [e] 2.2 Cn Compare Gk Syr: Heb *before a decree is born; like chaff a day has passed away*

and to him shall bow down,
each in its place,
all the coasts and islands
of the nations.

12 You also, O Ethiopians,[f]
shall be killed by my sword.

13 And he will stretch out his hand
against the north,
and destroy Assyria;
and he will make Nineveh
a desolation,
a dry waste like the desert.
14 Herds shall lie down in it,
every wild animal;[g]
the desert-owl[h] and
the screech-owl[i]
shall lodge on its capitals;
the owl[j] shall hoot at the window,
the raven[k] croak on the threshold;
for its cedar-work will be laid bare.
15 Is this the exultant city
that lived secure,
that said to itself,
'I am, and there is no one else'?
What a desolation it has become,
a lair for wild animals!
Everyone who passes by it
hisses and shakes the fist.

THE WICKEDNESS OF JERUSALEM

3 Ah, soiled, defiled,
oppressing city!
2 It has listened to no voice;
it has accepted no correction.
It has not trusted in the LORD;
it has not drawn near to its God.

3 The officials within it
are roaring lions;
its judges are evening wolves
that leave nothing until
the morning.
4 Its prophets are reckless,
faithless persons;
its priests have profaned
what is sacred,
they have done violence
to the law.
5 The LORD within it is righteous;
he does no wrong.
Every morning he renders
his judgement,
each dawn without fail;
but the unjust knows no shame.

6 I have cut off nations;
their battlements are in ruins;
I have laid waste their streets
so that no one walks in them;
their cities have been made desolate,
without people, without
inhabitants.
7 I said, 'Surely the city[l] will fear me,
it will accept correction;
it will not lose sight[m]
of all that I have brought upon it.'
But they were the more eager
to make all their deeds corrupt.

PUNISHMENT AND CONVERSION OF THE NATIONS

8 Therefore wait for me, says
the LORD,
for the day when I arise
as a witness.
For my decision is to gather nations,
to assemble kingdoms,
to pour out upon them my
indignation,
all the heat of my anger;
for in the fire of my passion
all the earth shall be consumed.

9 At that time I will change the
speech of the peoples
to a pure speech,
that all of them may call on the
name of the LORD
and serve him with one accord.
10 From beyond the rivers of Ethiopia[n]
my suppliants, my scattered ones,
shall bring my offering.

11 On that day you shall not
be put to shame
because of all the deeds
by which you have
rebelled against me;
for then I will remove from
your midst
your proudly exultant ones,
and you shall no longer be haughty
in my holy mountain.
12 For I will leave in the midst of you
a people humble and lowly.
They shall seek refuge in the
name of the LORD—
13 the remnant of Israel;
they shall do no wrong
and utter no lies,
nor shall a deceitful tongue
be found in their mouths.

[f] **2.12** Or *Nubians*; Heb *Cushites* [g] **2.14** Tg Compare Gk: Heb *nation* [h] **2.14** Meaning of Heb uncertain [i] **2.14** Meaning of Heb uncertain [j] **2.14** Cn: Heb *a voice* [k] **2.14** Gk Vg: Heb *desolation* [l] **3.7** Heb *it* [m] **3.7** Gk Syr: Heb *its dwelling will not be cut off* [n] **3.10** Or *Nubia*; Heb *Cush*

Then they will pasture and lie down,
and no one shall make
them afraid.

A SONG OF JOY

14 Sing aloud, O daughter Zion;
shout, O Israel!
Rejoice and exult with all your heart,
O daughter Jerusalem!
15 The LORD has taken away the
judgements against you,
he has turned away your enemies.
The king of Israel, the LORD,
is in your midst;
you shall fear disaster no more.
16 On that day it shall be said
to Jerusalem:
Do not fear, O Zion;
do not let your hands grow weak.
17 The LORD, your God, is in
your midst,
a warrior who gives victory;
he will rejoice over you
with gladness,
he will renew you[o] in his love;
he will exult over you with
loud singing
18 as on a day of festival.[p]
I will remove disaster from you,[q]
so that you will not bear
reproach for it.
19 I will deal with all your oppressors
at that time.
And I will save the lame
and gather the outcast,
and I will change their shame
into praise
and renown in all the earth.
20 At that time I will bring you home,
at the time when I gather you;
for I will make you renowned
and praised
among all the peoples
of the earth,
when I restore your fortunes
before your eyes, says the LORD.

[o] 3.17 Gk Syr: Heb *he will be silent* [p] 3.18 Gk Syr: Meaning of Heb uncertain [q] 3.18 Cn: Heb *I will remove from you; they were*

HAGGAI

Haggai was a prophet of the restoration who challenged the returning exiles to rebuild the temple in Jerusalem. King Cyrus had issued his decree in 537 BCE to allow the Judeans to return from Babylon to Jerusalem. By the year 520, in the second year of the reign of Darius, Haggai was calling for the building of the temple as a condition for the eventual prosperity of the nation. Haggai promoted not only the rebuilding of the temple, but also the restoration of the Davidic dynasty by supporting the emerging authority of Zerubbabel, governor of Judah, as bearer of the messianic hopes (2.20–23).

Haggai is read at the liturgy on Thursday and Friday of the Twenty-Fifth Week of Year I. These passages recall the prophet's words challenging the people to make room for the Lord's glory by having the courage to rebuild his house.

THE COMMAND TO REBUILD THE TEMPLE

1 In the second year of King Darius, in
the sixth month, on the first day of
the month, the word of the LORD came
by the prophet Haggai to Zerubbabel son
of Shealtiel, governor of Judah, and to
Joshua son of Jehozadak, the high priest:
2 Thus says the LORD of hosts: These people say the time has not yet come to rebuild the LORD's house. 3 Then the word
of the LORD came by the prophet Haggai, saying: 4 Is it a time for you yourselves to live in your panelled houses,
while this house lies in ruins? 5 Now
therefore, thus says the LORD of hosts:
Consider how you have fared. 6 You have
sown much, and harvested little; you
eat, but you never have enough; you
drink, but you never have your fill; you
clothe yourselves, but no one is warm;
and you that earn wages earn wages to
put them into a bag with holes.
7 Thus says the LORD of hosts: Consider how you have fared. 8 Go up to
the hills and bring wood and build the
house, so that I may take pleasure in it
and be honoured, says the LORD. 9 You
have looked for much, and, lo, it came
to little; and when you brought it home,
I blew it away. Why? says the LORD of
hosts. Because my house lies in ruins,
while all of you hurry off to your own
houses. 10 Therefore the heavens above
you have withheld the dew, and the
earth has withheld its produce. 11 And
I have called for a drought on the land
and the hills, on the grain, the new
wine, the oil, on what the soil produces,
on human beings and animals, and on
all their labours.
12 Then Zerubbabel son of Shealtiel,
and Joshua son of Jehozadak, the high
priest, with all the remnant of the people, obeyed the voice of the LORD their
God, and the words of the prophet Haggai, as the LORD their God had sent him;
and the people feared the LORD. 13 Then
Haggai, the messenger of the LORD,
spoke to the people with the LORD's
message, saying, I am with you, says
the LORD. 14 And the LORD stirred up
the spirit of Zerubbabel son of Shealtiel, governor of Judah, and the spirit of
Joshua son of Jehozadak, the high priest,
and the spirit of all the remnant of the
people; and they came and worked on
the house of the LORD of hosts, their
God, 15 on the twenty-fourth day of the
month, in the sixth month.

THE FUTURE GLORY OF THE TEMPLE

2 In the second year of King Darius,
1 in the seventh month, on the

twenty-first day of the month, the word of the LORD came by the prophet Haggai, saying: [2]Speak now to Zerubbabel son of Shealtiel, governor of Judah, and to Joshua son of Jehozadak, the high priest, and to the remnant of the people, and say, [3]Who is left among you that saw this house in its former glory? How does it look to you now? Is it not in your sight as nothing? [4]Yet now take courage, O Zerubbabel, says the LORD; take courage, O Joshua, son of Jehozadak, the high priest; take courage, all you people of the land, says the LORD; work, for I am with you, says the LORD of hosts, [5]according to the promise that I made you when you came out of Egypt. My spirit abides among you; do not fear. [6]For thus says the LORD of hosts: Once again, in a little while, I will shake the heavens and the earth and the sea and the dry land; [7]and I will shake all the nations, so that the treasure of all nations shall come, and I will fill this house with splendour, says the LORD of hosts. [8]The silver is mine, and the gold is mine, says the LORD of hosts. [9]The latter splendour of this house shall be greater than the former, says the LORD of hosts; and in this place I will give prosperity, says the LORD of hosts.

A REBUKE AND A PROMISE

10 On the twenty-fourth day of the ninth month, in the second year of Darius, the word of the LORD came by the prophet Haggai, saying: [11]Thus says the LORD of hosts: Ask the priests for a ruling: [12]If one carries consecrated meat in the fold of one's garment, and with the fold touches bread, or stew, or wine, or oil, or any kind of food, does it become holy? The priests answered, 'No.' [13]Then Haggai said, 'If one who is unclean by contact with a dead body touches any of these, does it become unclean?' The priests answered, 'Yes, it becomes unclean.' [14]Haggai then said, So is it with this people, and with this nation before me, says the LORD; and so with every work of their hands; and what they offer there is unclean. [15]But now, consider what will come to pass from this day on. Before a stone was placed upon a stone in the LORD's temple, [16]how did you fare?[a] When one came to a heap of twenty measures, there were but ten; when one came to the wine vat to draw fifty measures, there were but twenty. [17]I struck you and all the products of your toil with blight and mildew and hail; yet you did not return to me, says the LORD. [18]Consider from this day on, from the twenty-fourth day of the ninth month. Since the day that the foundation of the LORD's temple was laid, consider: [19]Is there any seed left in the barn? Do the vine, the fig tree, the pomegranate, and the olive tree still yield nothing? From this day on I will bless you.

GOD'S PROMISE TO ZERUBBABEL

20 The word of the LORD came a second time to Haggai on the twenty-fourth day of the month: [21]Speak to Zerubbabel, governor of Judah, saying, I am about to shake the heavens and the earth, [22]and to overthrow the throne of kingdoms; I am about to destroy the strength of the kingdoms of the nations, and overthrow the chariots and their riders; and the horses and their riders shall fall, every one by the sword of a comrade. [23]On that day, says the LORD of hosts, I will take you, O Zerubbabel my servant, son of Shealtiel, says the LORD, and make you like a signet ring; for I have chosen you, says the LORD of hosts.

[a] 2.16 Gk: Heb *since they were*

ZECHARIAH

Zechariah was a contemporary of Haggai and, like him, promoted the rebuilding of the temple in Jerusalem following the return of the exiles from Babylon. The first eight chapters of Zechariah are from the prophet himself, while the remaining part (chs. 9–14) is from other editors and sources more difficult to identify and from a much later period. The first eight chapters of the book present oracles and symbolic visions about the restoration and purification of Jerusalem. The second part of Zechariah presents oracles concluding with a messianic vision of the coming of the Prince of Peace.

The passage about the messianic vision of the coming of the humble king riding on a donkey is referenced in the four Gospels of the New Testament to describe the entry of Jesus into Jerusalem on Palm Sunday. Also, the text from Zechariah that speaks of "the one whom they have pierced" (12.10–11; 13.6–7), which is interpreted by John's Gospel as fulfilled in the piercing of Christ's side (Jn 19.37), is offered as a choice for the first reading at the Votive Mass of the Triumph of the Cross and at the liturgy on the Twelfth Sunday of Year C.

ISRAEL URGED TO REPENT

1 In the eighth month, in the second year of Darius, the word of the
LORD came to the prophet Zechariah
son of Berechiah son of Iddo, saying:
2The LORD was very angry with your
ancestors. 3Therefore say to them, Thus
says the LORD of hosts: Return to me,
says the LORD of hosts, and I will return to you, says the LORD of hosts. 4Do
not be like your ancestors, to whom the
former prophets proclaimed, 'Thus says
the LORD of hosts, Return from your
evil ways and from your evil deeds.' But
they did not hear or heed me, says the
LORD. 5Your ancestors, where are they?
And the prophets, do they live for ever?
6But my words and my statutes, which I
commanded my servants the prophets,
did they not overtake your ancestors?
So they repented and said, 'The LORD
of hosts has dealt with us according to
our ways and deeds, just as he planned
to do.'

FIRST VISION: THE HORSEMEN

7 On the twenty-fourth day of the
eleventh month, the month of Shebat,
in the second year of Darius, the word of
the LORD came to the prophet Zechariah
son of Berechiah son of Iddo; and Zechariah[a] said, 8In the night I saw a man
riding on a red horse! He was standing
among the myrtle trees in the glen; and
behind him were red, sorrel, and white
horses. 9Then I said, 'What are these,
my lord?' The angel who talked with me
said to me, 'I will show you what they
are.' 10So the man who was standing
among the myrtle trees answered, 'They
are those whom the LORD has sent to
patrol the earth.' 11Then they spoke to
the angel of the LORD who was standing among the myrtle trees, 'We have
patrolled the earth, and lo, the whole
earth remains at peace.' 12Then the angel of the LORD said, 'O LORD of hosts,
how long will you withhold mercy from
Jerusalem and the cities of Judah, with
which you have been angry these seventy years?' 13Then the LORD replied
with gracious and comforting words
to the angel who talked with me. 14So
the angel who talked with me said to

[a] 1.7 Heb *and he*

me, Proclaim this message: Thus says
the LORD of hosts; I am very jealous
for Jerusalem and for Zion. 15And I am
extremely angry with the nations that
are at ease; for while I was only a little
angry, they made the disaster worse.
16Therefore, thus says the LORD, I have
returned to Jerusalem with compassion;
my house shall be built in it, says the
LORD of hosts, and the measuring line
shall be stretched out over Jerusalem.
17Proclaim further: Thus says the LORD
of hosts: My cities shall again overflow
with prosperity; the LORD will again
comfort Zion and again choose Jerusalem.

SECOND VISION: THE HORNS AND THE SMITHS

18[b] And I looked up and saw four
horns. 19I asked the angel who talked
with me, 'What are these?' And he answered me, 'These are the horns that
have scattered Judah, Israel, and Jerusalem.' 20Then the LORD showed me
four blacksmiths. 21And I asked, 'What
are they coming to do?' He answered,
'These are the horns that scattered Judah, so that no head could be raised;
but these have come to terrify them,
to strike down the horns of the nations
that lifted up their horns against the
land of Judah to scatter its people.'[c]

THIRD VISION: THE MAN WITH A MEASURING LINE

2[d] I looked up and saw a man with a
measuring line in his hand. 2Then
I asked, 'Where are you going?' He answered me, 'To measure Jerusalem, to
see what is its width and what is its
length.' 3Then the angel who talked
with me came forward, and another angel came forward to meet him, 4and said
to him, 'Run, say to that young man: Jerusalem shall be inhabited like villages
without walls, because of the multitude
of people and animals in it. 5For I will be
a wall of fire all round it, says the LORD,
and I will be the glory within it.'

INTERLUDE: AN APPEAL TO THE EXILES

6 Up, up! Flee from the land of the
north, says the LORD; for I have spread
you abroad like the four winds of
heaven, says the LORD. 7Up! Escape to
Zion, you that live with daughter Babylon. 8For thus said the LORD of hosts
(after his glory[e] sent me) regarding the
nations that plundered you: Truly, one
who touches you touches the apple of
my eye.[f] 9See now, I am going to raise[g]
my hand against them, and they shall
become plunder for their own slaves.
Then you will know that the LORD of
hosts has sent me. 10Sing and rejoice,
O daughter Zion! For lo, I will come
and dwell in your midst, says the LORD.
11Many nations shall join themselves to
the LORD on that day, and shall be my
people; and I will dwell in your midst.
And you shall know that the LORD of
hosts has sent me to you. 12The LORD
will inherit Judah as his portion in the
holy land, and will again choose Jerusalem.

13 Be silent, all people, before the
LORD; for he has roused himself from
his holy dwelling.

FOURTH VISION: JOSHUA AND SATAN

3 Then he showed me the high priest
Joshua standing before the angel
of the LORD, and Satan[h] standing at
his right hand to accuse him. 2And the
LORD said to Satan,[i] 'The LORD rebuke
you, O Satan![j] The LORD who has chosen
Jerusalem rebuke you! Is not this man
a brand plucked from the fire?' 3Now
Joshua was dressed in filthy clothes as
he stood before the angel. 4The angel
said to those who were standing before
him, 'Take off his filthy clothes.' And
to him he said, 'See, I have taken your
guilt away from you, and I will clothe
you in festal apparel.' 5And I said, 'Let
them put a clean turban on his head.' So
they put a clean turban on his head and
clothed him in the apparel; and the angel of the LORD was standing by.

6 Then the angel of the LORD assured
Joshua, saying 7'Thus says the LORD of
hosts: If you will walk in my ways and
keep my requirements, then you shall
rule my house and have charge of my
courts, and I will give you the right of
access among those who are standing
here. 8Now listen, Joshua, high priest,
you and your colleagues who sit before
you! For they are an omen of things to
come: I am going to bring my servant
the Branch. 9For on the stone that I
have set before Joshua, on a single stone
with seven facets, I will engrave its inscription, says the LORD of hosts, and

[b] 1.18 Ch 2.1 in Heb [c] 1.21 Heb *it* [d] 2.1 Ch 2.5 in Heb [e] 2.8 Cn: Heb *after glory he* [f] 2.8 Heb *his eye* [g] 2.9 Or *wave* [h] 3.1 Or *the Accuser*; Heb *the Adversary* [i] 3.2 Or *the Accuser*; Heb *the Adversary* [j] 3.2 Or *the Accuser*; Heb *the Adversary*

I will remove the guilt of this land in a single day. 10On that day, says the LORD of hosts, you shall invite each other to come under your vine and fig tree.'

FIFTH VISION: THE LAMPSTAND AND OLIVE TREES

4 The angel who talked with me came again, and wakened me, as one is wakened from sleep. 2He said to me, 'What do you see?' And I said, 'I see a lampstand all of gold, with a bowl on the top of it; there are seven lamps on it, with seven lips on each of the lamps that are on the top of it. 3And by it there are two olive trees, one on the right of the bowl and the other on its left.' 4I said to the angel who talked with me, 'What are these, my lord?' 5Then the angel who talked with me answered me, 'Do you not know what these are?' I said, 'No, my lord.' 6He said to me, 'This is the word of the LORD to Zerubbabel: Not by might, nor by power, but by my spirit, says the LORD of hosts. 7What are you, O great mountain? Before Zerubbabel you shall become a plain; and he shall bring out the top stone amid shouts of "Grace, grace to it!" '

8 Moreover, the word of the LORD came to me, saying, 9'The hands of Zerubbabel have laid the foundation of this house; his hands shall also complete it. Then you will know that the LORD of hosts has sent me to you. 10For whoever has despised the day of small things shall rejoice, and shall see the plummet in the hand of Zerubbabel.

'These seven are the eyes of the LORD, which range through the whole earth.' 11Then I said to him, 'What are these two olive trees on the right and the left of the lampstand?' 12And a second time I said to him, 'What are these two branches of the olive trees, which pour out the oil[k] through the two golden pipes?' 13He said to me, 'Do you not know what these are?' I said, 'No, my lord.' 14Then he said, 'These are the two anointed ones who stand by the Lord of the whole earth.'

SIXTH VISION: THE FLYING SCROLL

5 Again I looked up and saw a flying scroll. 2And he said to me, 'What do you see?' I answered, 'I see a flying scroll; its length is twenty cubits, and its width ten cubits.' 3Then he said to me, 'This is the curse that goes out over the face of the whole land; for everyone who steals shall be cut off according to the writing on one side, and everyone who swears falsely[l] shall be cut off according to the writing on the other side. 4I have sent it out, says the LORD of hosts, and it shall enter the house of the thief, and the house of anyone who swears falsely by my name; and it shall abide in that house and consume it, both timber and stones.'

SEVENTH VISION: THE WOMAN IN A BASKET

5 Then the angel who talked with me came forward and said to me, 'Look up and see what this is that is coming out.' 6I said, 'What is it?' He said, 'This is a basket[m] coming out.' And he said, 'This is their iniquity[n] in all the land.' 7Then a leaden cover was lifted, and there was a woman sitting in the basket![o] 8And he said, 'This is Wickedness.' So he thrust her back into the basket,[p] and pressed the leaden weight down on its mouth. 9Then I looked up and saw two women coming forward. The wind was in their wings; they had wings like the wings of a stork, and they lifted up the basket[q] between earth and sky. 10Then I said to the angel who talked with me, 'Where are they taking the basket?'[r] 11He said to me, 'To the land of Shinar, to build a house for it; and when this is prepared, they will set the basket[s] down there on its base.'

EIGHTH VISION: FOUR CHARIOTS

6 And again I looked up and saw four chariots coming out from between two mountains—mountains of bronze. 2The first chariot had red horses, the second chariot black horses, 3the third chariot white horses, and the fourth chariot dappled grey[t] horses. 4Then I said to the angel who talked with me, 'What are these, my lord?' 5The angel answered me, 'These are the four winds[u] of heaven going out, after presenting themselves before the Lord of all the earth. 6The chariot with the black horses goes towards the north country, the white ones go towards the west country,[v] and the dappled ones go towards the south country.' 7When the steeds came out, they were impatient to get off and patrol the earth. And he

[k] **4.12** Cn: Heb *gold* [l] **5.3** The word *falsely* added from verse 4 [m] **5.6** Heb *ephah* [n] **5.6** Gk Compare Syr: Heb *their eye* [o] **5.7** Heb *ephah* [p] **5.8** Heb *ephah* [q] **5.9** Heb *ephah* [r] **5.10** Heb *ephah* [s] **5.11** Heb *ephah* [t] **6.3** Compare Gk: Meaning of Heb uncertain [u] **6.5** Or *spirits* [v] **6.6** Cn: Heb *go after them*

said, 'Go, patrol the earth.' So they patrolled the earth. 8Then he cried out to me, 'Lo, those who go towards the north country have set my spirit at rest in the north country.'

THE CORONATION OF THE BRANCH

9 The word of the LORD came to me: 10Collect silver and gold[w] from the exiles—from Heldai, Tobijah, and Jedaiah—who have arrived from Babylon; and go the same day to the house of Josiah son of Zephaniah. 11Take the silver and gold and make a crown,[x] and set it on the head of the high priest Joshua son of Jehozadak; 12say to him: Thus says the LORD of hosts: Here is a man whose name is Branch: for he shall branch out in his place, and he shall build the temple of the LORD. 13It is he that shall build the temple of the LORD; he shall bear royal honour, and shall sit and rule on his throne. There shall be a priest by his throne, with peaceful understanding between the two of them. 14And the crown[y] shall be in the care of Heldai,[z] Tobijah, Jedaiah, and Josiah[a] son of Zephaniah, as a memorial in the temple of the LORD.

15 Those who are far off shall come and help to build the temple of the LORD; and you shall know that the LORD of hosts has sent me to you. This will happen if you diligently obey the voice of the LORD your God.

HYPOCRITICAL FASTING CONDEMNED

7 In the fourth year of King Darius, the word of the LORD came to Zechariah on the fourth day of the ninth month, which is Chislev. 2Now the people of Bethel had sent Sharezer and Regem-melech and their men, to entreat the favour of the LORD, 3and to ask the priests of the house of the LORD of hosts and the prophets, 'Should I mourn and practise abstinence in the fifth month, as I have done for so many years?' 4Then the word of the LORD of hosts came to me: 5Say to all the people of the land and the priests: When you fasted and lamented in the fifth month and in the seventh, for these seventy years, was it for me that you fasted? 6And when you eat and when you drink, do you not eat and drink only for yourselves? 7Were not these the words that the LORD proclaimed by the former prophets, when Jerusalem was inhabited and in prosperity, along with the towns around it, and when the Negeb and the Shephelah were inhabited?

PUNISHMENT FOR REJECTING GOD'S DEMANDS

8 The word of the LORD came to Zechariah, saying: 9Thus says the LORD of hosts: Render true judgements, show kindness and mercy to one another; 10do not oppress the widow, the orphan, the alien, or the poor; and do not devise evil in your hearts against one another. 11But they refused to listen, and turned a stubborn shoulder, and stopped their ears in order not to hear. 12They made their hearts adamant in order not to hear the law and the words that the LORD of hosts had sent by his spirit through the former prophets. Therefore great wrath came from the LORD of hosts. 13Just as, when I[b] called, they would not hear, so, when they called, I would not hear, says the LORD of hosts, 14and I scattered them with a whirlwind among all the nations that they had not known. Thus the land they left was desolate, so that no one went to and fro, and a pleasant land was made desolate.

GOD'S PROMISES TO ZION

8 The word of the LORD of hosts came to me, saying: 2Thus says the LORD of hosts: I am jealous for Zion with great jealousy, and I am jealous for her with great wrath. 3Thus says the LORD: I will return to Zion, and will dwell in the midst of Jerusalem; Jerusalem shall be called the faithful city, and the mountain of the LORD of hosts shall be called the holy mountain. 4Thus says the LORD of hosts: Old men and old women shall again sit in the streets of Jerusalem, each with staff in hand because of their great age. 5And the streets of the city shall be full of boys and girls playing in its streets. 6Thus says the LORD of hosts: Even though it seems impossible to the remnant of this people in these days, should it also seem impossible to me, says the LORD of hosts? 7Thus says the LORD of hosts: I will save my people from the east country and from the west country; 8and I will bring them to live in Jerusalem. They shall be my people

[w] **6.10** Cn Compare verse 11: Heb lacks *silver and gold* [x] **6.11** Gk Mss Syr Tg: Heb *crowns* [y] **6.14** Gk Syr: Heb *crowns* [z] **6.14** Syr Compare verse 10: Heb *Helem* [a] **6.14** Syr Compare verse 10: Heb *Hen* [b] **7.13** Heb *he*

and I will be their God, in faithfulness
and in righteousness.
9 Thus says the LORD of hosts: Let
your hands be strong—you that have
recently been hearing these words from
the mouths of the prophets who were
present when the foundation was laid
for the rebuilding of the temple, the
house of the LORD of hosts. 10For before those days there were no wages for
people or for animals, nor was there any
safety from the foe for those who went
out or came in, and I set them all against
one another. 11But now I will not deal
with the remnant of this people as in
the former days, says the LORD of hosts.
12For there shall be a sowing of peace;
the vine shall yield its fruit, the ground
shall give its produce, and the skies shall
give their dew; and I will cause the remnant of this people to possess all these
things. 13Just as you have been a cursing
among the nations, O house of Judah
and house of Israel, so I will save you
and you shall be a blessing. Do not be
afraid, but let your hands be strong.
14 For thus says the LORD of hosts:
Just as I purposed to bring disaster upon
you, when your ancestors provoked me
to wrath, and I did not relent, says the
LORD of hosts, 15so again I have purposed in these days to do good to Jerusalem and to the house of Judah; do not
be afraid. 16These are the things that
you shall do: Speak the truth to one another, render in your gates judgements
that are true and make for peace, 17do
not devise evil in your hearts against
one another, and love no false oath; for
all these are things that I hate, says the
LORD.

JOYFUL FASTING

18 The word of the LORD of hosts
came to me, saying: 19Thus says the
LORD of hosts: The fast of the fourth
month, and the fast of the fifth, and the
fast of the seventh, and the fast of the
tenth, shall be seasons of joy and gladness, and cheerful festivals for the house
of Judah: therefore love truth and peace.

MANY PEOPLES DRAWN TO JERUSALEM

20 Thus says the LORD of hosts: Peoples shall yet come, the inhabitants of
many cities; 21the inhabitants of one
city shall go to another, saying, 'Come,
let us go to entreat the favour of the
LORD, and to seek the LORD of hosts; I
myself am going.' 22Many peoples and
strong nations shall come to seek the
LORD of hosts in Jerusalem, and to entreat the favour of the LORD. 23Thus says
the LORD of hosts: In those days ten men
from nations of every language shall
take hold of a Jew, grasping his garment
and saying, 'Let us go with you, for we
have heard that God is with you.'

JUDGEMENT ON ISRAEL'S ENEMIES

9 An Oracle.

The word of the LORD is against
the land of Hadrach
and will rest upon Damascus.
For to the LORD belongs the
capital[c] of Aram,[d]
as do all the tribes of Israel;
2 Hamath also, which borders on it,
Tyre and Sidon, though
they are very wise.
3 Tyre has built itself a rampart,
and heaped up silver like dust,
and gold like the dirt of
the streets.
4 But now, the Lord will strip it
of its possessions
and hurl its wealth into the sea,
and it shall be devoured by fire.

5 Ashkelon shall see it and be afraid;
Gaza too, and shall writhe
in anguish;
Ekron also, because its
hopes are withered.
The king shall perish from Gaza;
Ashkelon shall be uninhabited;
6 a mongrel people shall settle
in Ashdod,
and I will make an end of the
pride of Philistia.
7 I will take away its blood
from its mouth,
and its abominations from
between its teeth;
it too shall be a remnant for our God;
it shall be like a clan in Judah,
and Ekron shall be like
the Jebusites.
8 Then I will encamp at my
house as a guard,
so that no one shall march
to and fro;
no oppressor shall again
overrun them,
for now I have seen with
my own eyes.

[c] 9.1 Heb *eye* [d] 9.1 Cn: Heb *of Adam* (or *of humankind*)

THE COMING RULER OF GOD'S PEOPLE

9 Rejoice greatly, O daughter Zion!
Shout aloud, O daughter Jerusalem!
Lo, your king comes to you;
triumphant and victorious is he,
humble and riding on a donkey,
on a colt, the foal of a donkey.
10 He[e] will cut off the chariot from Ephraim
and the warhorse from Jerusalem;
and the battle-bow shall be cut off,
and he shall command peace to the nations;
his dominion shall be from sea to sea,
and from the River to the ends of the earth.

11 As for you also, because of the blood of my covenant with you,
I will set your prisoners free from the waterless pit.
12 Return to your stronghold, O prisoners of hope;
today I declare that I will restore to you double.
13 For I have bent Judah as my bow;
I have made Ephraim its arrow.
I will arouse your sons, O Zion,
against your sons, O Greece,
and wield you like a warrior's sword.

14 Then the LORD will appear over them,
and his arrow go forth like lightning;
the Lord GOD will sound the trumpet
and march forth in the whirlwinds of the south.
15 The LORD of hosts will protect them,
and they shall devour and tread down the slingers;[f]
they shall drink their blood[g] like wine,
and be full like a bowl,
drenched like the corners of the altar.

16 On that day the LORD their God will save them,
for they are the flock of his people;
for like the jewels of a crown
they shall shine on his land.
17 For what goodness and beauty are his!
Grain shall make the young men flourish,
and new wine the young women.

RESTORATION OF JUDAH AND ISRAEL

10 Ask rain from the LORD
in the season of the spring rain,
from the LORD who makes the storm-clouds,
who gives showers of rain to you,[h]
the vegetation in the field to everyone.
2 For the teraphim[i] utter nonsense,
and the diviners see lies;
the dreamers tell false dreams,
and give empty consolation.
Therefore the people wander like sheep;
they suffer for lack of a shepherd.

3 My anger is hot against the shepherds,
and I will punish the leaders;[j]
for the LORD of hosts cares for his flock, the house of Judah,
and will make them like his proud warhorse.
4 Out of them shall come the cornerstone,
out of them the tent-peg,
out of them the battle-bow,
out of them every commander.
5 Together they shall be like warriors in battle,
trampling the foe in the mud of the streets;
they shall fight, for the LORD is with them,
and they shall put to shame the riders on horses.

6 I will strengthen the house of Judah,
and I will save the house of Joseph.
I will bring them back because I have compassion on them,
and they shall be as though I had not rejected them;
for I am the LORD their God and I will answer them.
7 Then the people of Ephraim shall become like warriors,
and their hearts shall be glad as with wine.
Their children shall see it and rejoice,
their hearts shall exult in the LORD.

[e] 9.10 Gk: Heb *I* [f] 9.15 Cn: Heb *the slingstones*
[g] 9.15 Gk: Heb *shall drink* [h] 10.1 Heb *them*
[i] 10.2 Or *household gods* [j] 10.3 Or *male goats*

8 I will signal for them and
gather them in,
for I have redeemed them,
and they shall be as numerous
as they were before.
9 Though I scattered them
among the nations,
yet in far countries they
shall remember me,
and they shall rear their
children and return.
10 I will bring them home from
the land of Egypt,
and gather them from Assyria;
I will bring them to the land of
Gilead and to Lebanon,
until there is no room for them.
11 They[k] shall pass through the
sea of distress,
and the waves of the sea
shall be struck down,
and all the depths of the
Nile dried up.
The pride of Assyria shall be laid low,
and the sceptre of Egypt
shall depart.
12 I will make them strong in the LORD,
and they shall walk in his name,
says the LORD.

11 Open your doors, O Lebanon,
so that fire may devour
your cedars!
2 Wail, O cypress, for the
cedar has fallen,
for the glorious trees are ruined!
Wail, oaks of Bashan,
for the thick forest has been felled!
3 Listen, the wail of the shepherds,
for their glory is despoiled!
Listen, the roar of the lions,
for the thickets of the Jordan
are destroyed!

TWO KINDS OF SHEPHERDS

4 Thus said the LORD my God: Be a
shepherd of the flock doomed to slaughter. 5Those who buy them kill them
and go unpunished; and those who sell
them say, 'Blessed be the LORD, for I
have become rich'; and their own shepherds have no pity on them. 6For I will
no longer have pity on the inhabitants
of the earth, says the LORD. I will cause
them, every one, to fall each into the
hand of a neighbour, and each into the
hand of the king; and they shall devas-
tate the earth, and I will deliver no one
from their hand.
7 So, on behalf of the sheep dealers, I became the shepherd of the flock
doomed to slaughter. I took two staffs;
one I named Favour, the other I named
Unity, and I tended the sheep. 8In one
month I disposed of the three shepherds, for I had become impatient
with them, and they also detested me.
9So I said, 'I will not be your shepherd.
What is to die, let it die; what is to be
destroyed, let it be destroyed; and let
those that are left devour the flesh of
one another!' 10I took my staff Favour
and broke it, annulling the covenant
that I had made with all the peoples.
11So it was annulled on that day, and
the sheep dealers, who were watching
me, knew that it was the word of the
LORD. 12I then said to them, 'If it seems
right to you, give me my wages; but if
not, keep them.' So they weighed out as
my wages thirty shekels of silver. 13Then
the LORD said to me, 'Throw it into the
treasury'[l]—this lordly price at which I
was valued by them. So I took the thirty
shekels of silver and threw them into
the treasury[m] in the house of the LORD.
14Then I broke my second staff Unity,
annulling the family ties between Judah and Israel.
15 Then the LORD said to me: Take
once more the implements of a worthless shepherd. 16For I am now raising
up in the land a shepherd who does not
care for the perishing, or seek the wandering,[n] or heal the maimed, or nourish
the healthy,[o] but devours the flesh of
the fat ones, tearing off even their hoofs.
17 Oh, my worthless shepherd,
who deserts the flock!
May the sword strike his arm
and his right eye!
Let his arm be completely withered,
his right eye utterly blinded!

JERUSALEM'S VICTORY

12 An Oracle.
The word of the LORD concerning Israel: Thus says the LORD, who stretched
out the heavens and founded the earth
and formed the human spirit within:
2See, I am about to make Jerusalem a
cup of reeling for all the surrounding
peoples; it will be against Judah also in
the siege against Jerusalem. 3On that
day I will make Jerusalem a heavy stone
for all the peoples; all who lift it shall
grievously hurt themselves. And all the

[k] 10.11 Gk: Heb *He* [l] 11.13 Syr: Heb *it to the potter* [m] 11.13 Syr: Heb *it to the potter*
[n] 11.16 Syr Compare Gk Vg: Heb *the youth*
[o] 11.16 Meaning of Heb uncertain

nations of the earth shall come together against it. 4 On that day, says the LORD, I will strike every horse with panic, and its rider with madness. But on the house of Judah I will keep a watchful eye, when I strike every horse of the peoples with blindness. 5 Then the clans of Judah shall say to themselves, 'The inhabitants of Jerusalem have strength through the LORD of hosts, their God.'

6 On that day I will make the clans of Judah like a blazing pot on a pile of wood, like a flaming torch among sheaves; and they shall devour to the right and to the left all the surrounding peoples, while Jerusalem shall again be inhabited in its place, in Jerusalem.

7 And the LORD will give victory to the tents of Judah first, so that the glory of the house of David and the glory of the inhabitants of Jerusalem may not be exalted over that of Judah. 8 On that day the LORD will shield the inhabitants of Jerusalem, so that the feeblest among them on that day shall be like David, and the house of David shall be like God, like the angel of the LORD, at their head. 9 And on that day I will seek to destroy all the nations that come against Jerusalem.

MOURNING FOR THE PIERCED ONE

10 And I will pour out a spirit of compassion and supplication on the house of David and the inhabitants of Jerusalem, so that, when they look on the one[p] whom they have pierced, they shall mourn for him, as one mourns for an only child, and weep bitterly over him, as one weeps over a firstborn. 11 On that day the mourning in Jerusalem will be as great as the mourning for Hadad-rimmon in the plain of Megiddo. 12 The land shall mourn, each family by itself; the family of the house of David by itself, and their wives by themselves; the family of the house of Nathan by itself, and their wives by themselves; 13 the family of the house of Levi by itself, and their wives by themselves; the family of the Shimeites by itself, and their wives by themselves; 14 and all the families that are left, each by itself, and their wives by themselves.

13 On that day a fountain shall be opened for the house of David and the inhabitants of Jerusalem, to cleanse them from sin and impurity.

IDOLATRY CUT OFF

2 On that day, says the LORD of hosts, I will cut off the names of the idols from the land, so that they shall be remembered no more; and also I will remove from the land the prophets and the unclean spirit. 3 And if any prophets appear again, their fathers and mothers who bore them will say to them, 'You shall not live, for you speak lies in the name of the LORD'; and their fathers and their mothers who bore them shall pierce them through when they prophesy. 4 On that day the prophets will be ashamed, every one, of their visions when they prophesy; they will not put on a hairy mantle in order to deceive, 5 but each of them will say, 'I am no prophet, I am a tiller of the soil; for the land has been my possession[q] since my youth.' 6 And if anyone asks them, 'What are these wounds on your chest?'[r] the answer will be 'The wounds I received in the house of my friends.'

THE SHEPHERD STRUCK, THE FLOCK SCATTERED

7 'Awake, O sword, against
my shepherd,
against the man who is
my associate,'
says the LORD of hosts.
Strike the shepherd, that the
sheep may be scattered;
I will turn my hand against
the little ones.
8 In the whole land, says the LORD,
two-thirds shall be cut
off and perish,
and one-third shall be left alive.
9 And I will put this third into the fire,
refine them as one refines silver,
and test them as gold is tested.
They will call on my name,
and I will answer them.
I will say, 'They are my people';
and they will say, 'The
LORD is our God.'

FUTURE WARFARE AND FINAL VICTORY

14 See, a day is coming for the LORD, when the plunder taken from you will be divided in your midst. 2 For I will gather all the nations against Jerusalem to battle, and the city shall be taken and the houses looted and the women raped; half the city shall go into exile, but the rest of the people shall not be cut off from the city. 3 Then the LORD will go forth and fight against those na-

[p] 12.10 Heb *on me* [q] 13.5 Cn: Heb *for humankind has caused me to possess* [r] 13.6 Heb *wounds between your hands*

tions as when he fights on a day of battle. 4 On that day his feet shall stand on
the Mount of Olives, which lies before
Jerusalem on the east; and the Mount of
Olives shall be split in two from east to
west by a very wide valley; so that half of
the Mount shall withdraw northwards,
and the other half southwards. 5 And
you shall flee by the valley of the LORD's
mountain,[s] for the valley between the
mountains shall reach to Azal;[t] and you
shall flee as you fled from the earthquake in the days of King Uzziah of Judah. Then the LORD my God will come,
and all the holy ones with him.

6 On that day there shall not be[u] either cold or frost.[v] 7 And there shall
be continuous day (it is known to the
LORD), not day and not night, for at evening time there shall be light.

8 On that day living waters shall flow
out from Jerusalem, half of them to the
eastern sea and half of them to the western sea; it shall continue in summer as
in winter.

9 And the LORD will become king
over all the earth; on that day the LORD
will be one and his name one.

10 The whole land shall be turned
into a plain from Geba to Rimmon
south of Jerusalem. But Jerusalem shall
remain aloft on its site from the Gate
of Benjamin to the place of the former
gate, to the Corner Gate, and from the
Tower of Hananel to the king's wine
presses. 11 And it shall be inhabited, for
never again shall it be doomed to destruction; Jerusalem shall abide in security.

12 This shall be the plague with
which the LORD will strike all the peoples that wage war against Jerusalem:
their flesh shall rot while they are still
on their feet; their eyes shall rot in
their sockets, and their tongues shall
rot in their mouths. 13 On that day a
great panic from the LORD shall fall on
them, so that each will seize the hand
of a neighbour, and the hand of one will
be raised against the hand of the other;
14 even Judah will fight at Jerusalem.
And the wealth of all the surrounding
nations shall be collected—gold, silver, and garments in great abundance.
15 And a plague like this plague shall fall
on the horses, the mules, the camels,
the donkeys, and whatever animals may
be in those camps.

16 Then all who survive of the nations that have come against Jerusalem
shall go up year by year to worship the
King, the LORD of hosts, and to keep the
festival of booths.[w] 17 If any of the families of the earth do not go up to Jerusalem to worship the King, the LORD of
hosts, there will be no rain upon them.
18 And if the family of Egypt do not go
up and present themselves, then on
them shall[x] come the plague that the
LORD inflicts on the nations that do
not go up to keep the festival of booths.[y]
19 Such shall be the punishment of Egypt
and the punishment of all the nations
that do not go up to keep the festival of
booths.[z]

20 On that day there shall be inscribed on the bells of the horses, 'Holy
to the LORD.' And the cooking-pots in
the house of the LORD shall be as holy
as[a] the bowls in front of the altar; 21 and
every cooking-pot in Jerusalem and Judah shall be sacred to the LORD of hosts,
so that all who sacrifice may come and
use them to boil the flesh of the sacrifice. And there shall no longer be traders[b] in the house of the LORD of hosts
on that day.

[s] 14.5 Heb *my mountains* [t] 14.5 Meaning of Heb uncertain [u] 14.6 Cn: Heb *there shall not be light* [v] 14.6 Compare Gk Syr Vg Tg: Meaning of Heb uncertain [w] 14.16 Or *tabernacles*; Heb *succoth* [x] 14.18 Gk Syr: Heb *shall not* [y] 14.18 Or *tabernacles*; Heb *succoth* [z] 14.19 Or *tabernacles*; Heb *succoth* [a] 14.20 Heb *shall be like* [b] 14.21 Or *Canaanites*

MALACHI

The book of Malachi is by an anonymous author at the time of Nehemiah's arrival in Jerusalem (455 BCE). The name Malachi comes from the Hebrew meaning "My Messenger" and was intentionally used to disguise the actual author of the harsh criticism leveled against the leadership at the time. Malachi prophesies about the coming of a day when a forerunner will bring the message of repentance and true worship (3.1–4). Jesus quotes this text as being fulfilled in John the Baptist (Mt 11.10). Also, Malachi is the final book of the Old Testament and, for Christians, it anticipates the New Testament with its ending passage about the coming of Elijah "before the great and terrible day of the LORD" (4.5). This is understood to refer to the time of Christ.

1 An oracle. The word of the LORD to
Israel by Malachi.[a]

ISRAEL PREFERRED TO EDOM

2 I have loved you, says the LORD.
But you say, 'How have you loved us?'
Is not Esau Jacob's brother? says the
LORD. Yet I have loved Jacob 3but I have
hated Esau; I have made his hill country
a desolation and his heritage a desert for
jackals. 4If Edom says, 'We are shattered
but we will rebuild the ruins,' the LORD
of hosts says: They may build, but I will
tear down, until they are called the
wicked country, the people with whom
the LORD is angry for ever. 5Your own
eyes shall see this, and you shall say,
'Great is the LORD beyond the borders
of Israel!'

CORRUPTION OF THE PRIESTHOOD

6 A son honours his father, and servants their master. If then I am a father,
where is the honour due to me? And if
I am a master, where is the respect due
to me? says the LORD of hosts to you,
O priests, who despise my name. You
say, 'How have we despised your name?'
7By offering polluted food on my altar.
And you say, 'How have we polluted
it?'[b] By thinking that the LORD's table
may be despised. 8When you offer blind
animals in sacrifice, is that not wrong?
And when you offer those that are lame
or sick, is that not wrong? Try presenting that to your governor; will he be
pleased with you or show you favour?
says the LORD of hosts. 9And now implore the favour of God, that he may be
gracious to us. The fault is yours. Will
he show favour to any of you? says the
LORD of hosts. 10O that someone among
you would shut the temple[c] doors, so
that you would not kindle fire on my
altar in vain! I have no pleasure in you,
says the LORD of hosts, and I will not accept an offering from your hands. 11For
from the rising of the sun to its setting
my name is great among the nations,
and in every place incense is offered to
my name, and a pure offering; for my
name is great among the nations, says
the LORD of hosts. 12But you profane
it when you say that the Lord's table is
polluted, and the food for it[d] may be despised. 13'What a weariness this is', you
say, and you sniff at me,[e] says the LORD
of hosts. You bring what has been taken
by violence or is lame or sick, and this
you bring as your offering! Shall I accept
that from your hand? says the LORD.
14Cursed be the cheat who has a male
in the flock and vows to give it, and yet
sacrifices to the Lord what is blemished;
for I am a great King, says the LORD
of hosts, and my name is reverenced
among the nations.

2 And now, O priests, this command
is for you. 2If you will not listen, if
you will not lay it to heart to give glory

[a] 1.1 Or *by my messenger* [b] 1.7 Gk: Heb *you* [c] 1.10 Heb lacks *temple* [d] 1.12 Compare Syr Tg: Heb *its fruit, its food* [e] 1.13 Another reading is *at it*

to my name, says the LORD of hosts,
then I will send the curse on you and I
will curse your blessings; indeed I have
already cursed them,[f] because you do
not lay it to heart. 3I will rebuke your
offspring, and spread dung on your
faces, the dung of your offerings, and I
will put you out of my presence.[g]
4 Know, then, that I have sent this
command to you, so that my covenant
with Levi may hold, says the LORD of
hosts. 5My covenant with him was a
covenant of life and well-being, which
I gave him; this called for reverence,
and he revered me and stood in awe of
my name. 6True instruction was in his
mouth, and no wrong was found on his
lips. He walked with me in integrity and
uprightness, and he turned many from
iniquity. 7For the lips of a priest should
guard knowledge, and people should
seek instruction from his mouth, for he
is the messenger of the LORD of hosts.
8But you have turned aside from the
way; you have caused many to stumble
by your instruction; you have corrupted
the covenant of Levi, says the LORD of
hosts, 9and so I make you despised and
abased before all the people, inasmuch
as you have not kept my ways but have
shown partiality in your instruction.

THE COVENANT PROFANED BY JUDAH

10 Have we not all one father? Has
not one God created us? Why then are
we faithless to one another, profaning
the covenant of our ancestors? 11Judah
has been faithless, and abomination has
been committed in Israel and in Jerusalem; for Judah has profaned the sanctuary of the LORD, which he loves, and has
married the daughter of a foreign god.
12May the LORD cut off from the tents
of Jacob anyone who does this—any to
witness[h] or answer, or to bring an offering to the LORD of hosts.
13 And this you do as well: You cover
the LORD's altar with tears, with weeping and groaning because he no longer
regards the offering or accepts it with
favour at your hand. 14You ask, 'Why
does he not?' Because the LORD was a
witness between you and the wife of
your youth, to whom you have been
faithless, though she is your companion and your wife by covenant. 15Did
not one God make her?[i] Both flesh and
spirit are his.[j] And what does the one
God[k] desire? Godly offspring. So look
to yourselves, and do not let anyone be
faithless to the wife of his youth. 16For I
hate[l] divorce, says the LORD, the God of
Israel, and covering one's garment with
violence, says the LORD of hosts. So take
heed to yourselves and do not be faithless.
17 You have wearied the LORD with
your words. Yet you say, 'How have we
wearied him?' By saying, 'All who do
evil are good in the sight of the LORD,
and he delights in them.' Or by asking,
'Where is the God of justice?'

THE COMING MESSENGER

3 See, I am sending my messenger
to prepare the way before me, and
the Lord whom you seek will suddenly
come to his temple. The messenger of
the covenant in whom you delight—
indeed, he is coming, says the LORD of
hosts. 2But who can endure the day of
his coming, and who can stand when he
appears?
For he is like a refiner's fire and like
fullers' soap; 3he will sit as a refiner and
purifier of silver, and he will purify the
descendants of Levi and refine them like
gold and silver, until they present offerings to the LORD in righteousness.[m]
4Then the offering of Judah and Jerusalem will be pleasing to the LORD as in
the days of old and as in former years.
5 Then I will draw near to you for
judgement; I will be swift to bear witness against the sorcerers, against the
adulterers, against those who swear
falsely, against those who oppress
the hired workers in their wages, the
widow, and the orphan, against those
who thrust aside the alien, and do not
fear me, says the LORD of hosts.
6 For I the LORD do not change;
therefore you, O children of Jacob, have
not perished. 7Ever since the days of
your ancestors you have turned aside
from my statutes and have not kept
them. Return to me, and I will return to
you, says the LORD of hosts. But you say,
'How shall we return?'

DO NOT ROB GOD

8 Will anyone rob God? Yet you are
robbing me! But you say, 'How are we
robbing you?' In your tithes and offerings! 9You are cursed with a curse, for

[f] 2.2 Heb *it* [g] 2.3 Cn Compare Gk Syr: Heb *and he shall bear you to it* [h] 2.12 Cn Compare Gk: Heb *arouse* [i] 2.15 Or *Has he not made one?* [j] 2.15 Cn: Heb *and a remnant of spirit was his* [k] 2.15 Heb *he* [l] 2.16 Cn: Heb *he hates* [m] 3.3 Or *right offerings to the LORD*

you are robbing me—the whole nation
of you! 10Bring the full tithe into the
storehouse, so that there may be food in
my house, and thus put me to the test,
says the LORD of hosts; see if I will not
open the windows of heaven for you and
pour down for you an overflowing blessing. 11I will rebuke the locust[n] for you,
so that it will not destroy the produce of
your soil; and your vine in the field shall
not be barren, says the LORD of hosts.
12Then all nations will count you happy,
for you will be a land of delight, says the
LORD of hosts.

13 You have spoken harsh words
against me, says the LORD. Yet you
say, 'How have we spoken against you?'
14You have said, 'It is vain to serve God.
What do we profit by keeping his command or by going about as mourners
before the LORD of hosts? 15Now we
count the arrogant happy; evildoers not
only prosper, but when they put God to
the test they escape.'

THE REWARD OF THE FAITHFUL

16 Then those who revered the LORD
spoke with one another. The LORD took
note and listened, and a book of remembrance was written before him of those
who revered the LORD and thought on
his name. 17They shall be mine, says the
LORD of hosts, my special possession on
the day when I act, and I will spare them
as parents spare their children who
serve them. 18Then once more you shall
see the difference between the righteous
and the wicked, between one who serves
God and one who does not serve him.

THE GREAT DAY OF THE LORD

4 [o] See, the day is coming, burning
like an oven, when all the arrogant
and all evildoers will be stubble; the day
that comes shall burn them up, says
the LORD of hosts, so that it will leave
them neither root nor branch. 2But for
you who revere my name the sun of
righteousness shall rise, with healing
in its wings. You shall go out leaping
like calves from the stall. 3And you shall
tread down the wicked, for they will be
ashes under the soles of your feet, on the
day when I act, says the LORD of hosts.

4 Remember the teaching of my servant Moses, the statutes and ordinances
that I commanded him at Horeb for all
Israel.

5 Lo, I will send you the prophet Elijah before the great and terrible day
of the LORD comes. 6He will turn the
hearts of parents to their children and
the hearts of children to their parents,
so that I will not come and strike the
land with a curse.[p]

[n] 3.11 Heb *devourer* [o] 4.1 Ch 4.1–6 are Ch 3.19–24 in Heb [p] 4.6 Or *a ban of utter destruction*

THE NEW TESTAMENT

The Gospel According to

MATTHEW

Every year at the Christmas Vigil Mass, the opening narrative (1.1–25) from the Gospel According to Matthew is read in Catholic churches throughout the world. This narrative about the birth of Jesus begins with a genealogy that shows Jesus to be "the son of David, the son of Abraham" (1.1). It is appropriate that this first proclamation at Christmas comes from the Gospel of Matthew, itself positioned first among the sacred books of the New Testament. The Gospel intentionally is written to show how all that has gone before in the Old Testament is fulfilled in the person of Jesus, the Messiah. Matthew's Gospel presents Jesus as the one who fulfills the law of Moses and who teaches his followers to observe the law in a way that surpasses the expectations of the scribes and Pharisees of his day.

Matthew's Gospel responds to the tensions that existed among Greek-speaking Gentiles and Jews living together in Antioch sometime after the destruction of the Jerusalem temple in 70 CE. It appears that the actual author of this Gospel (not the disciple of Jesus known to be the tax-collector) was a Greek-speaking Christian scribe writing between 80 and 90 CE. The writer of this Gospel emphasizes more than the other Gospel writers how Jesus was the Jewish Messiah descended from King David and how Jesus opposed the Pharisees as "hypocrites" and emphasized a "righteousness" that goes beyond that of the Jewish leaders of the day. The tensions experienced between Christian Jews and non-Christian Jews of Antioch in their respective attempt to live faithfully the law of Moses come through the narrative of this Gospel in a pointed way.

Besides the infancy narrative at the beginning and the final commissioning scene at the end (28.9–20), the content of Matthew's Gospel is striking in its five major discourses: (5.1—7.27; 10.5–42; 13.1–52; 18.1–35; 24.3—25.46). These discourses seem to recall the five books of the Torah and suggest Jesus as the new Moses offering a new law that fulfills and supercedes the old. Matthew's Gospel portrays Jesus as the one who fulfills the Law and the Prophets and who calls on his followers to spread the good news not only among the Jews, but also to Gentiles of all nations (28.16–20).

Portions of Matthew's Gospel are read on Sundays throughout Year A of the liturgical cycle. Also, Matthew's account of the Visit of the Wise Men is read every year at the Feast of the Epiphany (2.1–12).

THE GENEALOGY OF JESUS THE MESSIAH

1 An account of the genealogy[a] of
Jesus the Messiah,[b] the son of David, the son of Abraham.
2 Abraham was the father of Isaac,
and Isaac the father of Jacob, and Jacob
the father of Judah and his brothers,
3 and Judah the father of Perez and Zerah by Tamar, and Perez the father of
Hezron, and Hezron the father of Aram,
4 and Aram the father of Aminadab,
and Aminadab the father of Nahshon,
and Nahshon the father of Salmon,

[a] 1.1 Or *birth* [b] 1.1 Or *Jesus Christ*

5and Salmon the father of Boaz by Rahab, and Boaz the father of Obed by
Ruth, and Obed the father of Jesse, 6and
Jesse the father of King David.
And David was the father of Solomon
by the wife of Uriah, 7and Solomon
the father of Rehoboam, and Rehoboam the father of Abijah, and Abijah
the father of Asaph,[c] 8and Asaph[d]
the father of Jehoshaphat, and Jehoshaphat the father of Joram, and Joram
the father of Uzziah, 9and Uzziah the
father of Jotham, and Jotham the father of Ahaz, and Ahaz the father of
Hezekiah, 10and Hezekiah the father
of Manasseh, and Manasseh the father
of Amos,[e] and Amos[f] the father of Josiah, 11and Josiah the father of Jechoniah and his brothers, at the time of the
deportation to Babylon.
12 And after the deportation to Babylon: Jechoniah was the father of Salathiel, and Salathiel the father of Zerubbabel, 13and Zerubbabel the father of
Abiud, and Abiud the father of Eliakim,
and Eliakim the father of Azor, 14and
Azor the father of Zadok, and Zadok the
father of Achim, and Achim the father
of Eliud, 15and Eliud the father of Eleazar, and Eleazar the father of Matthan,
and Matthan the father of Jacob, 16and
Jacob the father of Joseph the husband
of Mary, of whom Jesus was born, who
is called the Messiah.[g]
17 So all the generations from Abraham to David are fourteen generations;
and from David to the deportation to
Babylon, fourteen generations; and
from the deportation to Babylon to the
Messiah,[h] fourteen generations.

THE BIRTH OF JESUS THE MESSIAH

18 Now the birth of Jesus the Messiah[i] took place in this way. When his
mother Mary had been engaged to Joseph, but before they lived together,
she was found to be with child from the
Holy Spirit. 19Her husband Joseph, being a righteous man and unwilling to
expose her to public disgrace, planned
to dismiss her quietly. 20But just when
he had resolved to do this, an angel of
the Lord appeared to him in a dream
and said, 'Joseph, son of David, do not be
afraid to take Mary as your wife, for the
child conceived in her is from the Holy
Spirit. 21She will bear a son, and you are
to name him Jesus, for he will save his
people from their sins.' 22All this took
place to fulfil what had been spoken by
the Lord through the prophet:
23 'Look, the virgin shall conceive
and bear a son,
and they shall name him
Emmanuel',
which means, 'God is with us.' 24When
Joseph awoke from sleep, he did as the
angel of the Lord commanded him; he
took her as his wife, 25but had no marital relations with her until she had
borne a son;[j] and he named him Jesus.

THE VISIT OF THE WISE MEN

2 In the time of King Herod, after
Jesus was born in Bethlehem of Judea, wise men[k] from the East came to
Jerusalem, 2asking, 'Where is the child
who has been born king of the Jews? For
we observed his star at its rising,[l] and
have come to pay him homage.' 3When
King Herod heard this, he was frightened, and all Jerusalem with him; 4and
calling together all the chief priests and
scribes of the people, he inquired of
them where the Messiah[m] was to be
born. 5They told him, 'In Bethlehem of
Judea; for so it has been written by the
prophet:
6 "And you, Bethlehem, in the
land of Judah,
are by no means least among
the rulers of Judah;
for from you shall come a ruler
who is to shepherd[n] my
people Israel." '
7 Then Herod secretly called for the
wise men[o] and learned from them
the exact time when the star had appeared. 8Then he sent them to Bethlehem, saying, 'Go and search diligently
for the child; and when you have found
him, bring me word so that I may also
go and pay him homage.' 9When they
had heard the king, they set out; and
there, ahead of them, went the star
that they had seen at its rising,[p] until it
stopped over the place where the child
was. 10When they saw that the star had
stopped,[q] they were overwhelmed with
joy. 11On entering the house, they saw
the child with Mary his mother; and
they knelt down and paid him homage.

[c] 1.7 Other ancient authorities read *Asa* [d] 1.8 Other ancient authorities read *Asa* [e] 1.10 Other ancient authorities read *Amon* [f] 1.10 Other ancient authorities read *Amon* [g] 1.16 Or *the Christ* [h] 1.17 Or *the Christ* [i] 1.18 Or *Jesus Christ* [j] 1.25 Other ancient authorities read *her firstborn son* [k] 2.1 Or *astrologers*; Gk *magi* [l] 2.2 Or *in the East* [m] 2.4 Or *the Christ* [n] 2.6 Or *rule* [o] 2.7 Or *astrologers*; Gk *magi* [p] 2.9 Or *in the East* [q] 2.10 Gk *saw the star*

Then, opening their treasure-chests,
they offered him gifts of gold, frankincense, and myrrh. 12 And having been
warned in a dream not to return to
Herod, they left for their own country
by another road.

THE ESCAPE TO EGYPT

13 Now after they had left, an angel of the Lord appeared to Joseph in a
dream and said, 'Get up, take the child
and his mother, and flee to Egypt, and
remain there until I tell you; for Herod
is about to search for the child, to destroy him.' 14 Then Joseph[r] got up, took
the child and his mother by night, and
went to Egypt, 15 and remained there
until the death of Herod. This was to
fulfil what had been spoken by the Lord
through the prophet, 'Out of Egypt I
have called my son.'

THE MASSACRE OF THE INFANTS

16 When Herod saw that he had been
tricked by the wise men,[s] he was infuriated, and he sent and killed all the
children in and around Bethlehem who
were two years old or under, according
to the time that he had learned from
the wise men.[t] 17 Then was fulfilled what
had been spoken through the prophet
Jeremiah:
18 'A voice was heard in Ramah,
  wailing and loud lamentation,
Rachel weeping for her children;
  she refused to be consoled,
    because they are no more.'

THE RETURN FROM EGYPT

19 When Herod died, an angel of the
Lord suddenly appeared in a dream to
Joseph in Egypt and said, 20 'Get up, take
the child and his mother, and go to the
land of Israel, for those who were seeking the child's life are dead.' 21 Then Joseph[u] got up, took the child and his
mother, and went to the land of Israel.
22 But when he heard that Archelaus
was ruling over Judea in place of his father Herod, he was afraid to go there.
And after being warned in a dream,
he went away to the district of Galilee.
23 There he made his home in a town
called Nazareth, so that what had been
spoken through the prophets might be
fulfilled, 'He will be called a Nazorean.'

THE PROCLAMATION OF JOHN THE BAPTIST

3 In those days John the Baptist appeared in the wilderness of Judea,
proclaiming, 2 'Repent, for the kingdom
of heaven has come near.'[v] 3 This is the
one of whom the prophet Isaiah spoke
when he said,
  'The voice of one crying out
    in the wilderness:
  "Prepare the way of the Lord,
    make his paths straight." '
4 Now John wore clothing of camel's hair
with a leather belt around his waist,
and his food was locusts and wild honey.
5 Then the people of Jerusalem and all
Judea were going out to him, and all the
region along the Jordan, 6 and they were
baptized by him in the river Jordan,
confessing their sins.

7 But when he saw many Pharisees
and Sadducees coming for baptism, he
said to them, 'You brood of vipers! Who
warned you to flee from the wrath to
come? 8 Bear fruit worthy of repentance.
9 Do not presume to say to yourselves,
"We have Abraham as our ancestor"; for
I tell you, God is able from these stones
to raise up children to Abraham. 10 Even
now the axe is lying at the root of the
trees; every tree therefore that does not
bear good fruit is cut down and thrown
into the fire.

11 'I baptize you with[w] water for repentance, but one who is more powerful
than I is coming after me; I am not worthy to carry his sandals. He will baptize
you with[x] the Holy Spirit and fire. 12 His
winnowing-fork is in his hand, and he
will clear his threshing-floor and will
gather his wheat into the granary; but
the chaff he will burn with unquenchable fire.'

THE BAPTISM OF JESUS

13 Then Jesus came from Galilee to
John at the Jordan, to be baptized by
him. 14 John would have prevented him,
saying, 'I need to be baptized by you,
and do you come to me?' 15 But Jesus
answered him, 'Let it be so now; for it
is proper for us in this way to fulfil all
righteousness.' Then he consented.
16 And when Jesus had been baptized,
just as he came up from the water, suddenly the heavens were opened to him
and he saw the Spirit of God descending like a dove and alighting on him.
17 And a voice from heaven said, 'This is
my Son, the Beloved,[y] with whom I am
well pleased.'

[r] 2.14 Gk *he* [s] 2.16 Or *astrologers*; Gk *magi*
[t] 2.16 Or *astrologers*; Gk *magi* [u] 2.21 Gk *he*
[v] 3.2 Or *is at hand* [w] 3.11 Or *in* [x] 3.11 Or *in*
[y] 3.17 Or *my beloved Son*

THE TEMPTATION OF JESUS

4 Then Jesus was led up by the Spirit into the wilderness to be tempted by the devil. 2He fasted for forty days and forty nights, and afterwards he was famished. 3The tempter came and said to him, 'If you are the Son of God, command these stones to become loaves of bread.' 4But he answered, 'It is written,

"One does not live by bread alone,
but by every word that comes
from the mouth of God."'

5 Then the devil took him to the holy city and placed him on the pinnacle of the temple, 6saying to him, 'If you are the Son of God, throw yourself down; for it is written,

"He will command his angels
concerning you",
and "On their hands they
will bear you up,
so that you will not dash your
foot against a stone."'

7Jesus said to him, 'Again it is written, "Do not put the Lord your God to the test."'

8 Again, the devil took him to a very high mountain and showed him all the kingdoms of the world and their splendour; 9and he said to him, 'All these I will give you, if you will fall down and worship me.' 10Jesus said to him, 'Away with you, Satan! for it is written,

"Worship the Lord your God,
and serve only him."'

11Then the devil left him, and suddenly angels came and waited on him.

JESUS BEGINS HIS MINISTRY IN GALILEE

12 Now when Jesus[z] heard that John had been arrested, he withdrew to Galilee. 13He left Nazareth and made his home in Capernaum by the lake, in the territory of Zebulun and Naphtali, 14so that what had been spoken through the prophet Isaiah might be fulfilled:

15 'Land of Zebulun, land of Naphtali,
on the road by the sea, across
the Jordan, Galilee
of the Gentiles—
16 the people who sat in darkness
have seen a great light,
and for those who sat in the region
and shadow of death
light has dawned.'

17From that time Jesus began to proclaim, 'Repent, for the kingdom of heaven has come near.'[a]

JESUS CALLS THE FIRST DISCIPLES

18 As he walked by the Sea of Galilee, he saw two brothers, Simon, who is called Peter, and Andrew his brother, casting a net into the lake—for they were fishermen. 19And he said to them, 'Follow me, and I will make you fish for people.' 20Immediately they left their nets and followed him. 21As he went from there, he saw two other brothers, James son of Zebedee and his brother John, in the boat with their father Zebedee, mending their nets, and he called them. 22Immediately they left the boat and their father, and followed him.

JESUS MINISTERS TO CROWDS OF PEOPLE

23 Jesus[b] went throughout Galilee, teaching in their synagogues and proclaiming the good news[c] of the kingdom and curing every disease and every sickness among the people. 24So his fame spread throughout all Syria, and they brought to him all the sick, those who were afflicted with various diseases and pains, demoniacs, epileptics, and paralytics, and he cured them. 25And great crowds followed him from Galilee, the Decapolis, Jerusalem, Judea, and from beyond the Jordan.

THE BEATITUDES

5 When Jesus[d] saw the crowds, he went up the mountain; and after he sat down, his disciples came to him. 2Then he began to speak, and taught them, saying:

3 'Blessed are the poor in spirit, for theirs is the kingdom of heaven.

4 'Blessed are those who mourn, for they will be comforted.

5 'Blessed are the meek, for they will inherit the earth.

6 'Blessed are those who hunger and thirst for righteousness, for they will be filled.

7 'Blessed are the merciful, for they will receive mercy.

8 'Blessed are the pure in heart, for they will see God.

9 'Blessed are the peacemakers, for they will be called children of God.

10 'Blessed are those who are persecuted for righteousness' sake, for theirs is the kingdom of heaven.

11 'Blessed are you when people revile you and persecute you and utter all

[z] 4.12 Gk *he* [a] 4.17 Or *is at hand* [b] 4.23 Gk *He* [c] 4.23 Gk *gospel* [d] 5.1 Gk *he*

kinds of evil against you falsely[e] on my
account. 12 Rejoice and be glad, for your
reward is great in heaven, for in the
same way they persecuted the prophets
who were before you.

SALT AND LIGHT

13 'You are the salt of the earth; but
if salt has lost its taste, how can its saltiness be restored? It is no longer good for
anything, but is thrown out and trampled under foot.

14 'You are the light of the world.
A city built on a hill cannot be hidden.
15 No one after lighting a lamp puts it
under the bushel basket, but on the
lampstand, and it gives light to all in
the house. 16 In the same way, let your
light shine before others, so that they
may see your good works and give glory
to your Father in heaven.

THE LAW AND THE PROPHETS

17 'Do not think that I have come to
abolish the law or the prophets; I have
come not to abolish but to fulfil. 18 For
truly I tell you, until heaven and earth
pass away, not one letter,[f] not one stroke
of a letter, will pass from the law until
all is accomplished. 19 Therefore, whoever breaks[g] one of the least of these
commandments, and teaches others to
do the same, will be called least in the
kingdom of heaven; but whoever does
them and teaches them will be called
great in the kingdom of heaven. 20 For
I tell you, unless your righteousness
exceeds that of the scribes and Pharisees, you will never enter the kingdom
of heaven.

CONCERNING ANGER

21 'You have heard that it was said
to those of ancient times, "You shall
not murder"; and "whoever murders
shall be liable to judgement." 22 But I
say to you that if you are angry with a
brother or sister,[h] you will be liable to
judgement; and if you insult[i] a brother
or sister,[j] you will be liable to the council; and if you say, "You fool", you will
be liable to the hell[k] of fire. 23 So when
you are offering your gift at the altar, if
you remember that your brother or sister[l] has something against you, 24 leave
your gift there before the altar and go;
first be reconciled to your brother or sister,[m] and then come and offer your gift.
25 Come to terms quickly with your accuser while you are on the way to court[n]
with him, or your accuser may hand
you over to the judge, and the judge to
the guard, and you will be thrown into
prison. 26 Truly I tell you, you will never
get out until you have paid the last
penny.

CONCERNING ADULTERY

27 'You have heard that it was said,
"You shall not commit adultery." 28 But
I say to you that everyone who looks at
a woman with lust has already committed adultery with her in his heart. 29 If
your right eye causes you to sin, tear it
out and throw it away; it is better for
you to lose one of your members than
for your whole body to be thrown into
hell.[o] 30 And if your right hand causes
you to sin, cut it off and throw it away;
it is better for you to lose one of your
members than for your whole body to
go into hell.[p]

CONCERNING DIVORCE

31 'It was also said, "Whoever divorces his wife, let him give her a certificate of divorce." 32 But I say to you that
anyone who divorces his wife, except
on the ground of unchastity, causes her
to commit adultery; and whoever marries a divorced woman commits adultery.

CONCERNING OATHS

33 'Again, you have heard that it was
said to those of ancient times, "You shall
not swear falsely, but carry out the vows
you have made to the Lord." 34 But I say
to you, Do not swear at all, either by
heaven, for it is the throne of God, 35 or
by the earth, for it is his footstool, or by
Jerusalem, for it is the city of the great
King. 36 And do not swear by your head,
for you cannot make one hair white or
black. 37 Let your word be "Yes, Yes"
or "No, No"; anything more than this
comes from the evil one.[q]

CONCERNING RETALIATION

38 'You have heard that it was said,
"An eye for an eye and a tooth for a
tooth." 39 But I say to you, Do not resist
an evildoer. But if anyone strikes you
on the right cheek, turn the other also;
40 and if anyone wants to sue you and

[e] **5.11** Other ancient authorities lack *falsely*
[f] **5.18** Gk *one iota* [g] **5.19** Or *annuls* [h] **5.22** Gk *a brother*; other ancient authorities add *without cause* [i] **5.22** Gk *say Raca to* (an obscure term of abuse) [j] **5.22** Gk *a brother* [k] **5.22** Gk *Gehenna*
[l] **5.23** Gk *your brother* [m] **5.24** Gk *your brother*
[n] **5.25** Gk lacks *to court* [o] **5.29** Gk *Gehenna*
[p] **5.30** Gk *Gehenna* [q] **5.37** Or *evil*

take your coat, give your cloak as well;
41and if anyone forces you to go one
mile, go also the second mile. 42Give to
everyone who begs from you, and do
not refuse anyone who wants to borrow
from you.

LOVE FOR ENEMIES

43 'You have heard that it was said,
"You shall love your neighbour and hate
your enemy." 44But I say to you, Love
your enemies and pray for those who
persecute you, 45so that you may be
children of your Father in heaven; for
he makes his sun rise on the evil and on
the good, and sends rain on the righteous and on the unrighteous. 46For if
you love those who love you, what reward do you have? Do not even the
tax-collectors do the same? 47And if you
greet only your brothers and sisters,[r]
what more are you doing than others?
Do not even the Gentiles do the same?
48Be perfect, therefore, as your heavenly
Father is perfect.

CONCERNING ALMSGIVING

6 'Beware of practising your piety before others in order to be seen by
them; for then you have no reward from
your Father in heaven.

2 'So whenever you give alms, do not
sound a trumpet before you, as the hypocrites do in the synagogues and in the
streets, so that they may be praised by
others. Truly I tell you, they have received their reward. 3But when you give
alms, do not let your left hand know
what your right hand is doing, 4so that
your alms may be done in secret; and
your Father who sees in secret will reward you.[s]

CONCERNING PRAYER

5 'And whenever you pray, do not be
like the hypocrites; for they love to stand
and pray in the synagogues and at the
street corners, so that they may be seen
by others. Truly I tell you, they have received their reward. 6But whenever you
pray, go into your room and shut the
door and pray to your Father who is in
secret; and your Father who sees in secret will reward you.[t]

7 'When you are praying, do not heap
up empty phrases as the Gentiles do; for
they think that they will be heard because of their many words. 8Do not be
like them, for your Father knows what
you need before you ask him.

9 'Pray then in this way:

Our Father in heaven,
hallowed be your name.
10 Your kingdom come.
Your will be done,
on earth as it is in heaven.
11 Give us this day our daily bread.[u]
12 And forgive us our debts,
as we also have forgiven
our debtors.
13 And do not bring us to
the time of trial,[v]
but rescue us from
the evil one.[w]

14For if you forgive others their trespasses, your heavenly Father will also
forgive you; 15but if you do not forgive
others, neither will your Father forgive
your trespasses.

CONCERNING FASTING

16 'And whenever you fast, do not
look dismal, like the hypocrites, for they
disfigure their faces so as to show others that they are fasting. Truly I tell you,
they have received their reward. 17But
when you fast, put oil on your head and
wash your face, 18so that your fasting
may be seen not by others but by your
Father who is in secret; and your Father
who sees in secret will reward you.[x]

CONCERNING TREASURES

19 'Do not store up for yourselves
treasures on earth, where moth and
rust[y] consume and where thieves break
in and steal; 20but store up for yourselves treasures in heaven, where neither moth nor rust[z] consumes and
where thieves do not break in and steal.
21For where your treasure is, there your
heart will be also.

THE SOUND EYE

22 'The eye is the lamp of the body.
So, if your eye is healthy, your whole
body will be full of light; 23but if your eye
is unhealthy, your whole body will be
full of darkness. If then the light in you
is darkness, how great is the darkness!

SERVING TWO MASTERS

24 'No one can serve two masters; for
a slave will either hate the one and love

[r] **5.47** Gk *your brothers* [s] **6.4** Other ancient authorities add *openly* [t] **6.6** Other ancient authorities add *openly* [u] **6.11** Or *our bread for tomorrow* [v] **6.13** Or *us into temptation* [w] **6.13** Or *from evil.* Other ancient authorities add, in some form, *For the kingdom and the power and the glory are yours for ever. Amen.* [x] **6.18** Other ancient authorities add *openly* [y] **6.19** Gk *eating* [z] **6.20** Gk *eating*

the other, or be devoted to the one and
despise the other. You cannot serve God
and wealth.[a]

DO NOT WORRY

25 'Therefore I tell you, do not worry
about your life, what you will eat or
what you will drink,[b] or about your
body, what you will wear. Is not life
more than food, and the body more
than clothing? 26 Look at the birds of
the air; they neither sow nor reap nor
gather into barns, and yet your heavenly Father feeds them. Are you not of
more value than they? 27 And can any
of you by worrying add a single hour
to your span of life?[c] 28 And why do you
worry about clothing? Consider the lilies of the field, how they grow; they neither toil nor spin, 29 yet I tell you, even
Solomon in all his glory was not clothed
like one of these. 30 But if God so clothes
the grass of the field, which is alive today and tomorrow is thrown into the
oven, will he not much more clothe
you—you of little faith? 31 Therefore do
not worry, saying, "What will we eat?"
or "What will we drink?" or "What will
we wear?" 32 For it is the Gentiles who
strive for all these things; and indeed
your heavenly Father knows that you
need all these things. 33 But strive first
for the kingdom of God[d] and his[e] righteousness, and all these things will be
given to you as well.

34 'So do not worry about tomorrow,
for tomorrow will bring worries of its
own. Today's trouble is enough for today.

JUDGING OTHERS

7 'Do not judge, so that you may not
be judged. 2 For with the judgement you make you will be judged,
and the measure you give will be the
measure you get. 3 Why do you see the
speck in your neighbour's[f] eye, but do
not notice the log in your own eye? 4 Or
how can you say to your neighbour,[g]
"Let me take the speck out of your eye",
while the log is in your own eye? 5 You
hypocrite, first take the log out of your
own eye, and then you will see clearly
to take the speck out of your neighbour's[h] eye.

PROFANING THE HOLY

6 'Do not give what is holy to dogs;
and do not throw your pearls before
swine, or they will trample them under
foot and turn and maul you.

ASK, SEARCH, KNOCK

7 'Ask, and it will be given to you;
search, and you will find; knock, and
the door will be opened for you. 8 For everyone who asks receives, and everyone
who searches finds, and for everyone
who knocks, the door will be opened.
9 Is there anyone among you who, if
your child asks for bread, will give a
stone? 10 Or if the child asks for a fish,
will give a snake? 11 If you then, who are
evil, know how to give good gifts to your
children, how much more will your Father in heaven give good things to those
who ask him!

THE GOLDEN RULE

12 'In everything do to others as you
would have them do to you; for this is
the law and the prophets.

THE NARROW GATE

13 'Enter through the narrow gate;
for the gate is wide and the road is easy[i]
that leads to destruction, and there are
many who take it. 14 For the gate is narrow and the road is hard that leads to
life, and there are few who find it.

A TREE AND ITS FRUIT

15 'Beware of false prophets, who come
to you in sheep's clothing but inwardly
are ravenous wolves. 16 You will know
them by their fruits. Are grapes gathered
from thorns, or figs from thistles? 17 In
the same way, every good tree bears good
fruit, but the bad tree bears bad fruit. 18 A
good tree cannot bear bad fruit, nor can
a bad tree bear good fruit. 19 Every tree
that does not bear good fruit is cut down
and thrown into the fire. 20 Thus you will
know them by their fruits.

CONCERNING SELF-DECEPTION

21 'Not everyone who says to me,
"Lord, Lord", will enter the kingdom of
heaven, but only one who does the will
of my Father in heaven. 22 On that day
many will say to me, "Lord, Lord, did
we not prophesy in your name, and cast
out demons in your name, and do many
deeds of power in your name?" 23 Then I
will declare to them, "I never knew you;
go away from me, you evildoers."

[a] 6.24 Gk *mammon* [b] 6.25 Other ancient authorities lack *or what you will drink* [c] 6.27 Or *add one cubit to your height* [d] 6.33 Other ancient authorities lack *of God* [e] 6.33 Or *its* [f] 7.3 Gk *brother's* [g] 7.4 Gk *brother* [h] 7.5 Gk *brother's* [i] 7.13 Other ancient authorities read *for the road is wide and easy*

HEARERS AND DOERS

24 'Everyone then who hears these words of mine and acts on them will be like a wise man who built his house on rock. 25 The rain fell, the floods came, and the winds blew and beat on that house, but it did not fall, because it had been founded on rock. 26 And everyone who hears these words of mine and does not act on them will be like a foolish man who built his house on sand. 27 The rain fell, and the floods came, and the winds blew and beat against that house, and it fell—and great was its fall!'

28 Now when Jesus had finished saying these things, the crowds were astounded at his teaching, 29 for he taught them as one having authority, and not as their scribes.

JESUS CLEANSES A LEPER

8 When Jesus[j] had come down from the mountain, great crowds followed him; 2 and there was a leper[k] who came to him and knelt before him, saying, 'Lord, if you choose, you can make me clean.' 3 He stretched out his hand and touched him, saying, 'I do choose. Be made clean!' Immediately his leprosy[l] was cleansed. 4 Then Jesus said to him, 'See that you say nothing to anyone; but go, show yourself to the priest, and offer the gift that Moses commanded, as a testimony to them.'

JESUS HEALS A CENTURION'S SERVANT

5 When he entered Capernaum, a centurion came to him, appealing to him 6 and saying, 'Lord, my servant is lying at home paralysed, in terrible distress.' 7 And he said to him, 'I will come and cure him.' 8 The centurion answered, 'Lord, I am not worthy to have you come under my roof; but only speak the word, and my servant will be healed. 9 For I also am a man under authority, with soldiers under me; and I say to one, "Go", and he goes, and to another, "Come", and he comes, and to my slave, "Do this", and the slave does it.' 10 When Jesus heard him, he was amazed and said to those who followed him, 'Truly I tell you, in no one[m] in Israel have I found such faith. 11 I tell you, many will come from east and west and will eat with Abraham and Isaac and Jacob in the kingdom of heaven, 12 while the heirs of the kingdom will be thrown into the outer darkness, where there will be weeping and gnashing of teeth.' 13 And to the centurion Jesus said, 'Go; let it be done for you according to your faith.' And the servant was healed in that hour.

JESUS HEALS MANY AT PETER'S HOUSE

14 When Jesus entered Peter's house, he saw his mother-in-law lying in bed with a fever; 15 he touched her hand, and the fever left her, and she got up and began to serve him. 16 That evening they brought to him many who were possessed by demons; and he cast out the spirits with a word, and cured all who were sick. 17 This was to fulfil what had been spoken through the prophet Isaiah, 'He took our infirmities and bore our diseases.'

WOULD-BE FOLLOWERS OF JESUS

18 Now when Jesus saw great crowds around him, he gave orders to go over to the other side. 19 A scribe then approached and said, 'Teacher, I will follow you wherever you go.' 20 And Jesus said to him, 'Foxes have holes, and birds of the air have nests; but the Son of Man has nowhere to lay his head.' 21 Another of his disciples said to him, 'Lord, first let me go and bury my father.' 22 But Jesus said to him, 'Follow me, and let the dead bury their own dead.'

JESUS STILLS THE STORM

23 And when he got into the boat, his disciples followed him. 24 A gale arose on the lake, so great that the boat was being swamped by the waves; but he was asleep. 25 And they went and woke him up, saying, 'Lord, save us! We are perishing!' 26 And he said to them, 'Why are you afraid, you of little faith?' Then he got up and rebuked the winds and the sea; and there was a dead calm. 27 They were amazed, saying, 'What sort of man is this, that even the winds and the sea obey him?'

JESUS HEALS THE GADARENE DEMONIACS

28 When he came to the other side, to the country of the Gadarenes,[n] two demoniacs coming out of the tombs met him. They were so fierce that no one

[j] 8.1 Gk *he* [k] 8.2 The terms *leper* and *leprosy* can refer to several diseases [l] 8.3 The terms *leper* and *leprosy* can refer to several diseases [m] 8.10 Other ancient authorities read *Truly I tell you, not even* [n] 8.28 Other ancient authorities read *Gergesenes*; others, *Gerasenes*

could pass that way. 29Suddenly they
shouted, 'What have you to do with us,
Son of God? Have you come here to torment us before the time?' 30Now a large
herd of swine was feeding at some distance from them. 31The demons begged
him, 'If you cast us out, send us into the
herd of swine.' 32And he said to them,
'Go!' So they came out and entered the
swine; and suddenly, the whole herd
rushed down the steep bank into the
lake and perished in the water. 33The
swineherds ran off, and on going into
the town, they told the whole story
about what had happened to the demoniacs. 34Then the whole town came
out to meet Jesus; and when they saw
him, they begged him to leave their
9 neighbourhood. 1And after getting
into a boat he crossed the water and
came to his own town.

JESUS HEALS A PARALYTIC

2 And just then some people were
carrying a paralysed man lying on a
bed. When Jesus saw their faith, he said
to the paralytic, 'Take heart, son; your
sins are forgiven.' 3Then some of the
scribes said to themselves, 'This man
is blaspheming.' 4But Jesus, perceiving
their thoughts, said, 'Why do you think
evil in your hearts? 5For which is easier, to say, "Your sins are forgiven", or to
say, "Stand up and walk"? 6But so that
you may know that the Son of Man has
authority on earth to forgive sins'—he
then said to the paralytic—'Stand up,
take your bed and go to your home.'
7And he stood up and went to his home.
8When the crowds saw it, they were
filled with awe, and they glorified God,
who had given such authority to human
beings.

THE CALLING OF MATTHEW

9 As Jesus was walking along, he saw
a man called Matthew sitting at the tax
booth; and he said to him, 'Follow me.'
And he got up and followed him.

10 And as he sat at dinner[o] in the
house, many tax-collectors and sinners
came and were sitting[p] with him and
his disciples. 11When the Pharisees saw
this, they said to his disciples, 'Why does
your teacher eat with tax-collectors and
sinners?' 12But when he heard this, he
said, 'Those who are well have no need of
a physician, but those who are sick. 13Go
and learn what this means, "I desire
mercy, not sacrifice." For I have come to
call not the righteous but sinners.'

THE QUESTION ABOUT FASTING

14 Then the disciples of John came
to him, saying, 'Why do we and the
Pharisees fast often,[q] but your disciples
do not fast?' 15And Jesus said to them,
'The wedding-guests cannot mourn as
long as the bridegroom is with them,
can they? The days will come when the
bridegroom is taken away from them,
and then they will fast. 16No one sews a
piece of unshrunk cloth on an old cloak,
for the patch pulls away from the cloak,
and a worse tear is made. 17Neither is
new wine put into old wineskins; otherwise, the skins burst, and the wine is
spilled, and the skins are destroyed; but
new wine is put into fresh wineskins,
and so both are preserved.'

A GIRL RESTORED TO LIFE AND A WOMAN HEALED

18 While he was saying these things
to them, suddenly a leader of the synagogue[r] came in and knelt before him,
saying, 'My daughter has just died; but
come and lay your hand on her, and she
will live.' 19And Jesus got up and followed him, with his disciples. 20Then
suddenly a woman who had been suffering from haemorrhages for twelve years
came up behind him and touched the
fringe of his cloak, 21for she said to herself, 'If I only touch his cloak, I will be
made well.' 22Jesus turned, and seeing
her he said, 'Take heart, daughter; your
faith has made you well.' And instantly
the woman was made well. 23When
Jesus came to the leader's house and saw
the flute-players and the crowd making
a commotion, 24he said, 'Go away; for
the girl is not dead but sleeping.' And
they laughed at him. 25But when the
crowd had been put outside, he went in
and took her by the hand, and the girl
got up. 26And the report of this spread
throughout that district.

JESUS HEALS TWO BLIND MEN

27 As Jesus went on from there,
two blind men followed him, crying
loudly, 'Have mercy on us, Son of David!' 28When he entered the house, the
blind men came to him; and Jesus said
to them, 'Do you believe that I am able
to do this?' They said to him, 'Yes, Lord.'
29Then he touched their eyes and said,
'According to your faith let it be done
to you.' 30And their eyes were opened.

[o] 9.10 Gk *reclined* [p] 9.10 Gk *were reclining*
[q] 9.14 Other ancient authorities lack *often*
[r] 9.18 Gk lacks *of the synagogue*

Then Jesus sternly ordered them, 'See that no one knows of this.' 31 But they went away and spread the news about him throughout that district.

JESUS HEALS ONE WHO WAS MUTE

32 After they had gone away, a demoniac who was mute was brought to him. 33 And when the demon had been cast out, the one who had been mute spoke; and the crowds were amazed and said, 'Never has anything like this been seen in Israel.' 34 But the Pharisees said, 'By the ruler of the demons he casts out the demons.'[s]

THE HARVEST IS GREAT, THE LABOURERS FEW

35 Then Jesus went about all the cities and villages, teaching in their synagogues, and proclaiming the good news of the kingdom, and curing every disease and every sickness. 36 When he saw the crowds, he had compassion for them, because they were harassed and helpless, like sheep without a shepherd. 37 Then he said to his disciples, 'The harvest is plentiful, but the labourers are few; 38 therefore ask the Lord of the harvest to send out labourers into his harvest.'

THE TWELVE APOSTLES

10 Then Jesus[t] summoned his twelve disciples and gave them authority over unclean spirits, to cast them out, and to cure every disease and every sickness. 2 These are the names of the twelve apostles: first, Simon, also known as Peter, and his brother Andrew; James son of Zebedee, and his brother John; 3 Philip and Bartholomew; Thomas and Matthew the tax-collector; James son of Alphaeus, and Thaddaeus;[u] 4 Simon the Cananaean, and Judas Iscariot, the one who betrayed him.

THE MISSION OF THE TWELVE

5 These twelve Jesus sent out with the following instructions: 'Go nowhere among the Gentiles, and enter no town of the Samaritans, 6 but go rather to the lost sheep of the house of Israel. 7 As you go, proclaim the good news, "The kingdom of heaven has come near."[v] 8 Cure the sick, raise the dead, cleanse the lepers,[w] cast out demons. You received without payment; give without payment. 9 Take no gold, or silver, or copper in your belts, 10 no bag for your journey, or two tunics, or sandals, or a staff; for labourers deserve their food. 11 Whatever town or village you enter, find out who in it is worthy, and stay there until you leave. 12 As you enter the house, greet it. 13 If the house is worthy, let your peace come upon it; but if it is not worthy, let your peace return to you. 14 If anyone will not welcome you or listen to your words, shake off the dust from your feet as you leave that house or town. 15 Truly I tell you, it will be more tolerable for the land of Sodom and Gomorrah on the day of judgement than for that town.

COMING PERSECUTIONS

16 'See, I am sending you out like sheep into the midst of wolves; so be wise as serpents and innocent as doves. 17 Beware of them, for they will hand you over to councils and flog you in their synagogues; 18 and you will be dragged before governors and kings because of me, as a testimony to them and the Gentiles. 19 When they hand you over, do not worry about how you are to speak or what you are to say; for what you are to say will be given to you at that time; 20 for it is not you who speak, but the Spirit of your Father speaking through you. 21 Brother will betray brother to death, and a father his child, and children will rise against parents and have them put to death; 22 and you will be hated by all because of my name. But the one who endures to the end will be saved. 23 When they persecute you in one town, flee to the next; for truly I tell you, you will not have gone through all the towns of Israel before the Son of Man comes.

24 'A disciple is not above the teacher, nor a slave above the master; 25 it is enough for the disciple to be like the teacher, and the slave like the master. If they have called the master of the house Beelzebul, how much more will they malign those of his household!

WHOM TO FEAR

26 'So have no fear of them; for nothing is covered up that will not be uncovered, and nothing secret that will not become known. 27 What I say to you in the dark, tell in the light; and what you hear whispered, proclaim from the housetops. 28 Do not fear those who kill the

[s] **9.34** Other ancient authorities lack this verse
[t] **10.1** Gk *he* [u] **10.3** Other ancient authorities read *Lebbaeus*, or *Lebbaeus called Thaddaeus*
[v] **10.7** Or *is at hand* [w] **10.8** The terms *leper* and *leprosy* can refer to several diseases

body but cannot kill the soul; rather fear
him who can destroy both soul and body
in hell.[x] 29Are not two sparrows sold for
a penny? Yet not one of them will fall to
the ground unperceived by your Father.
30And even the hairs of your head are all
counted. 31So do not be afraid; you are of
more value than many sparrows.

32 'Everyone therefore who acknowledges me before others, I also will acknowledge before my Father in heaven;
33but whoever denies me before others,
I also will deny before my Father in
heaven.

NOT PEACE, BUT A SWORD

34 'Do not think that I have come
to bring peace to the earth; I have not
come to bring peace, but a sword.

35 For I have come to set a man
against his father,
and a daughter against her mother,
and a daughter-in-law against
her mother-in-law;
36 and one's foes will be members of
one's own household.

37Whoever loves father or mother more
than me is not worthy of me; and whoever loves son or daughter more than
me is not worthy of me; 38and whoever
does not take up the cross and follow me
is not worthy of me. 39Those who find
their life will lose it, and those who lose
their life for my sake will find it.

REWARDS

40 'Whoever welcomes you welcomes
me, and whoever welcomes me welcomes the one who sent me. 41Whoever
welcomes a prophet in the name of a
prophet will receive a prophet's reward;
and whoever welcomes a righteous person in the name of a righteous person
will receive the reward of the righteous;
42and whoever gives even a cup of cold
water to one of these little ones in the
name of a disciple—truly I tell you,
none of these will lose their reward.'

11 Now when Jesus had finished
instructing his twelve disciples,
he went on from there to teach and proclaim his message in their cities.

MESSENGERS FROM JOHN THE BAPTIST

2 When John heard in prison what
the Messiah[y] was doing, he sent word
by his[z] disciples 3and said to him, 'Are
you the one who is to come, or are we
to wait for another?' 4Jesus answered
them, 'Go and tell John what you hear
and see: 5the blind receive their sight,
the lame walk, the lepers[a] are cleansed,
the deaf hear, the dead are raised, and
the poor have good news brought to
them. 6And blessed is anyone who takes
no offence at me.'

JESUS PRAISES JOHN THE BAPTIST

7 As they went away, Jesus began to
speak to the crowds about John: 'What
did you go out into the wilderness to
look at? A reed shaken by the wind?
8What then did you go out to see?
Someone[b] dressed in soft robes? Look,
those who wear soft robes are in royal
palaces. 9What then did you go out to
see? A prophet?[c] Yes, I tell you, and
more than a prophet. 10This is the one
about whom it is written,

"See, I am sending my messenger
ahead of you,
who will prepare your
way before you."

11Truly I tell you, among those born of
women no one has arisen greater than
John the Baptist; yet the least in the
kingdom of heaven is greater than he.
12From the days of John the Baptist until now the kingdom of heaven has suffered violence,[d] and the violent take it
by force. 13For all the prophets and the
law prophesied until John came; 14and
if you are willing to accept it, he is Elijah who is to come. 15Let anyone with
ears[e] listen!

16 'But to what will I compare this
generation? It is like children sitting in
the market-places and calling to one another,

17 "We played the flute for you, and
you did not dance;
we wailed, and you did
not mourn."

18For John came neither eating nor
drinking, and they say, "He has a demon"; 19the Son of Man came eating
and drinking, and they say, "Look, a
glutton and a drunkard, a friend of tax-
collectors and sinners!" Yet wisdom is
vindicated by her deeds.'[f]

[x] **10.28** Gk *Gehenna* [y] **11.2** Or *the Christ*
[z] **11.2** Other ancient authorities read *two of his*
[a] **11.5** The terms *leper* and *leprosy* can refer to several diseases [b] **11.8** Or *Why then did you go out? To see someone* [c] **11.9** Other ancient authorities read *Why then did you go out? To see a prophet?* [d] **11.12** Or *has been coming violently*
[e] **11.15** Other ancient authorities add *to hear*
[f] **11.19** Other ancient authorities read *children*

WOES TO UNREPENTANT CITIES

20 Then he began to reproach the cities in which most of his deeds of power
had been done, because they did not repent. 21 'Woe to you, Chorazin! Woe to
you, Bethsaida! For if the deeds of power
done in you had been done in Tyre and
Sidon, they would have repented long
ago in sackcloth and ashes. 22 But I tell
you, on the day of judgement it will be
more tolerable for Tyre and Sidon than
for you. 23 And you, Capernaum,
will you be exalted to heaven?
No, you will be brought
down to Hades.
For if the deeds of power done in you
had been done in Sodom, it would have
remained until this day. 24 But I tell you
that on the day of judgement it will be
more tolerable for the land of Sodom
than for you.'

JESUS THANKS HIS FATHER

25 At that time Jesus said, 'I thank[g]
you, Father, Lord of heaven and earth,
because you have hidden these things
from the wise and the intelligent and
have revealed them to infants; 26 yes,
Father, for such was your gracious will.[h]
27 All things have been handed over to
me by my Father; and no one knows
the Son except the Father, and no one
knows the Father except the Son and
anyone to whom the Son chooses to reveal him.

28 'Come to me, all you that are
weary and are carrying heavy burdens,
and I will give you rest. 29 Take my yoke
upon you, and learn from me; for I am
gentle and humble in heart, and you
will find rest for your souls. 30 For my
yoke is easy, and my burden is light.'

PLUCKING GRAIN ON THE SABBATH

12 At that time Jesus went through
the cornfields on the sabbath;
his disciples were hungry, and they began to pluck heads of grain and to eat.
2 When the Pharisees saw it, they said
to him, 'Look, your disciples are doing
what is not lawful to do on the sabbath.'
3 He said to them, 'Have you not read
what David did when he and his companions were hungry? 4 He entered the
house of God and ate the bread of the
Presence, which it was not lawful for
him or his companions to eat, but only
for the priests. 5 Or have you not read in
the law that on the sabbath the priests
in the temple break the sabbath and
yet are guiltless? 6 I tell you, something
greater than the temple is here. 7 But if
you had known what this means, "I desire mercy and not sacrifice", you would
not have condemned the guiltless. 8 For
the Son of Man is lord of the sabbath.'

THE MAN WITH A WITHERED HAND

9 He left that place and entered their
synagogue; 10 a man was there with a
withered hand, and they asked him,
'Is it lawful to cure on the sabbath?' so
that they might accuse him. 11 He said to
them, 'Suppose one of you has only one
sheep and it falls into a pit on the sabbath; will you not lay hold of it and lift
it out? 12 How much more valuable is a
human being than a sheep! So it is lawful to do good on the sabbath.' 13 Then he
said to the man, 'Stretch out your hand.'
He stretched it out, and it was restored,
as sound as the other. 14 But the Pharisees went out and conspired against
him, how to destroy him.

GOD'S CHOSEN SERVANT

15 When Jesus became aware of this,
he departed. Many crowds[i] followed
him, and he cured all of them, 16 and he
ordered them not to make him known.
17 This was to fulfil what had been spoken through the prophet Isaiah:
18 'Here is my servant, whom
I have chosen,
my beloved, with whom my
soul is well pleased.
I will put my Spirit upon him,
and he will proclaim justice
to the Gentiles.
19 He will not wrangle or cry aloud,
nor will anyone hear his
voice in the streets.
20 He will not break a bruised reed
or quench a smouldering wick
until he brings justice to victory.
21 And in his name the
Gentiles will hope.'

JESUS AND BEELZEBUL

22 Then they brought to him a demoniac who was blind and mute; and
he cured him, so that the one who had
been mute could speak and see. 23 All the
crowds were amazed and said, 'Can this
be the Son of David?' 24 But when the
Pharisees heard it, they said, 'It is only
by Beelzebul, the ruler of the demons,
that this fellow casts out the demons.'
25 He knew what they were thinking and

g 11.25 Or *praise* h 11.26 Or *for so it was well-pleasing in your sight* i 12.15 Other ancient authorities lack *crowds*

said to them, 'Every kingdom divided against itself is laid waste, and no city or house divided against itself will stand. 26 If Satan casts out Satan, he is divided against himself; how then will his kingdom stand? 27 If I cast out demons by Beelzebul, by whom do your own exorcists[j] cast them out? Therefore they will be your judges. 28 But if it is by the Spirit of God that I cast out demons, then the kingdom of God has come to you. 29 Or how can one enter a strong man's house and plunder his property, without first tying up the strong man? Then indeed the house can be plundered. 30 Whoever is not with me is against me, and whoever does not gather with me scatters. 31 Therefore I tell you, people will be forgiven for every sin and blasphemy, but blasphemy against the Spirit will not be forgiven. 32 Whoever speaks a word against the Son of Man will be forgiven, but whoever speaks against the Holy Spirit will not be forgiven, either in this age or in the age to come.

A TREE AND ITS FRUIT

33 'Either make the tree good, and its fruit good; or make the tree bad, and its fruit bad; for the tree is known by its fruit. 34 You brood of vipers! How can you speak good things, when you are evil? For out of the abundance of the heart the mouth speaks. 35 The good person brings good things out of a good treasure, and the evil person brings evil things out of an evil treasure. 36 I tell you, on the day of judgement you will have to give an account for every careless word you utter; 37 for by your words you will be justified, and by your words you will be condemned.'

THE SIGN OF JONAH

38 Then some of the scribes and Pharisees said to him, 'Teacher, we wish to see a sign from you.' 39 But he answered them, 'An evil and adulterous generation asks for a sign, but no sign will be given to it except the sign of the prophet Jonah. 40 For just as Jonah was for three days and three nights in the belly of the sea monster, so for three days and three nights the Son of Man will be in the heart of the earth. 41 The people of Nineveh will rise up at the judgement with this generation and condemn it, because they repented at the proclamation of Jonah, and see, something greater than Jonah is here! 42 The queen of the South will rise up at the judgement with this generation and condemn it, because she came from the ends of the earth to listen to the wisdom of Solomon, and see, something greater than Solomon is here!

THE RETURN OF THE UNCLEAN SPIRIT

43 'When the unclean spirit has gone out of a person, it wanders through waterless regions looking for a resting-place, but it finds none. 44 Then it says, "I will return to my house from which I came." When it comes, it finds it empty, swept, and put in order. 45 Then it goes and brings along seven other spirits more evil than itself, and they enter and live there; and the last state of that person is worse than the first. So will it be also with this evil generation.'

THE TRUE KINDRED OF JESUS

46 While he was still speaking to the crowds, his mother and his brothers were standing outside, wanting to speak to him. 47 Someone told him, 'Look, your mother and your brothers are standing outside, wanting to speak to you.'[k] 48 But to the one who had told him this, Jesus[l] replied, 'Who is my mother, and who are my brothers?' 49 And pointing to his disciples, he said, 'Here are my mother and my brothers! 50 For whoever does the will of my Father in heaven is my brother and sister and mother.'

THE PARABLE OF THE SOWER

13 That same day Jesus went out of the house and sat beside the lake. 2 Such great crowds gathered around him that he got into a boat and sat there, while the whole crowd stood on the beach. 3 And he told them many things in parables, saying: 'Listen! A sower went out to sow. 4 And as he sowed, some seeds fell on the path, and the birds came and ate them up. 5 Other seeds fell on rocky ground, where they did not have much soil, and they sprang up quickly, since they had no depth of soil. 6 But when the sun rose, they were scorched; and since they had no root, they withered away. 7 Other seeds fell among thorns, and the thorns grew up and choked them. 8 Other seeds fell on good soil and brought forth grain, some a hundredfold, some sixty, some thirty. 9 Let anyone with ears[m] listen!'

j **12.27** Gk *sons* k **12.47** Other ancient authorities lack verse 47 l **12.48** Gk *he*
m **13.9** Other ancient authorities add *to hear*

THE PURPOSE OF THE PARABLES

10 Then the disciples came and
asked him, 'Why do you speak to them
in parables?' 11 He answered, 'To you it
has been given to know the secrets[n] of
the kingdom of heaven, but to them it
has not been given. 12 For to those who
have, more will be given, and they will
have an abundance; but from those who
have nothing, even what they have will
be taken away. 13 The reason I speak to
them in parables is that "seeing they do
not perceive, and hearing they do not
listen, nor do they understand." 14 With
them indeed is fulfilled the prophecy of
Isaiah that says:

"You will indeed listen, but
 never understand,
and you will indeed look,
 but never perceive.
15 For this people's heart has
 grown dull,
and their ears are hard of hearing,
 and they have shut their eyes;
 so that they might not
 look with their eyes,
and listen with their ears,
and understand with their
 heart and turn—
and I would heal them."

16 But blessed are your eyes, for they see,
and your ears, for they hear. 17 Truly I
tell you, many prophets and righteous
people longed to see what you see, but
did not see it, and to hear what you
hear, but did not hear it.

THE PARABLE OF THE SOWER EXPLAINED

18 'Hear then the parable of the
sower. 19 When anyone hears the word of
the kingdom and does not understand
it, the evil one comes and snatches away
what is sown in the heart; this is what
was sown on the path. 20 As for what
was sown on rocky ground, this is the
one who hears the word and immediately receives it with joy; 21 yet such a
person has no root, but endures only for
a while, and when trouble or persecution arises on account of the word, that
person immediately falls away.[o] 22 As
for what was sown among thorns, this
is the one who hears the word, but the
cares of the world and the lure of wealth
choke the word, and it yields nothing.
23 But as for what was sown on good soil,
this is the one who hears the word and
understands it, who indeed bears fruit
and yields, in one case a hundredfold, in
another sixty, and in another thirty.'

THE PARABLE OF WEEDS AMONG THE WHEAT

24 He put before them another
parable: 'The kingdom of heaven may
be compared to someone who sowed
good seed in his field; 25 but while everybody was asleep, an enemy came
and sowed weeds among the wheat,
and then went away. 26 So when the
plants came up and bore grain, then
the weeds appeared as well. 27 And the
slaves of the householder came and
said to him, "Master, did you not sow
good seed in your field? Where, then,
did these weeds come from?" 28 He answered, "An enemy has done this." The
slaves said to him, "Then do you want
us to go and gather them?" 29 But he replied, "No; for in gathering the weeds
you would uproot the wheat along
with them. 30 Let both of them grow together until the harvest; and at harvest
time I will tell the reapers, Collect the
weeds first and bind them in bundles
to be burned, but gather the wheat into
my barn." '

THE PARABLE OF THE MUSTARD SEED

31 He put before them another parable: 'The kingdom of heaven is like a
mustard seed that someone took and
sowed in his field; 32 it is the smallest of
all the seeds, but when it has grown it
is the greatest of shrubs and becomes
a tree, so that the birds of the air come
and make nests in its branches.'

THE PARABLE OF THE YEAST

33 He told them another parable:
'The kingdom of heaven is like yeast
that a woman took and mixed in with[p]
three measures of flour until all of it was
leavened.'

THE USE OF PARABLES

34 Jesus told the crowds all these
things in parables; without a parable
he told them nothing. 35 This was to fulfil what had been spoken through the
prophet:[q]

'I will open my mouth to
 speak in parables;
I will proclaim what has
 been hidden from the
 foundation of the world.'[r]

[n] 13.11 Or *mysteries* [o] 13.21 Gk *stumbles*
[p] 13.33 Gk *hid in* [q] 13.35 Other ancient
authorities read *the prophet Isaiah*
[r] 13.35 Other ancient authorities lack *of the world*

JESUS EXPLAINS THE PARABLE OF THE WEEDS

36 Then he left the crowds and went
into the house. And his disciples approached him, saying, 'Explain to us the
parable of the weeds of the field.' 37He
answered, 'The one who sows the good
seed is the Son of Man; 38the field is the
world, and the good seed are the children of the kingdom; the weeds are the
children of the evil one, 39and the enemy
who sowed them is the devil; the harvest
is the end of the age, and the reapers are
angels. 40Just as the weeds are collected
and burned up with fire, so will it be at
the end of the age. 41The Son of Man will
send his angels, and they will collect out
of his kingdom all causes of sin and all
evildoers, 42and they will throw them
into the furnace of fire, where there
will be weeping and gnashing of teeth.
43Then the righteous will shine like the
sun in the kingdom of their Father. Let
anyone with ears[s] listen!

THREE PARABLES

44 'The kingdom of heaven is like treasure hidden in a field, which someone
found and hid; then in his joy he goes and
sells all that he has and buys that field.

45 'Again, the kingdom of heaven is
like a merchant in search of fine pearls;
46on finding one pearl of great value,
he went and sold all that he had and
bought it.

47 'Again, the kingdom of heaven is
like a net that was thrown into the sea
and caught fish of every kind; 48when it
was full, they drew it ashore, sat down,
and put the good into baskets but threw
out the bad. 49So it will be at the end of
the age. The angels will come out and
separate the evil from the righteous
50and throw them into the furnace of
fire, where there will be weeping and
gnashing of teeth.

TREASURES NEW AND OLD

51 'Have you understood all this?'
They answered, 'Yes.' 52And he said to
them, 'Therefore every scribe who has
been trained for the kingdom of heaven
is like the master of a household who
brings out of his treasure what is new
and what is old.' 53When Jesus had finished these parables, he left that place.

THE REJECTION OF JESUS AT NAZARETH

54 He came to his home town and
began to teach the people[t] in their synagogue, so that they were astounded
and said, 'Where did this man get this
wisdom and these deeds of power? 55Is
not this the carpenter's son? Is not his
mother called Mary? And are not his
brothers James and Joseph and Simon
and Judas? 56And are not all his sisters
with us? Where then did this man get
all this?' 57And they took offence at him.
But Jesus said to them, 'Prophets are
not without honour except in their own
country and in their own house.' 58And
he did not do many deeds of power
there, because of their unbelief.

THE DEATH OF JOHN THE BAPTIST

14 At that time Herod the ruler[u]
heard reports about Jesus; 2and
he said to his servants, 'This is John the
Baptist; he has been raised from the
dead, and for this reason these powers
are at work in him.' 3For Herod had arrested John, bound him, and put him
in prison on account of Herodias, his
brother Philip's wife,[v] 4because John
had been telling him, 'It is not lawful
for you to have her.' 5Though Herod[w]
wanted to put him to death, he feared
the crowd, because they regarded him
as a prophet. 6But when Herod's birthday came, the daughter of Herodias
danced before the company, and she
pleased Herod 7so much that he promised on oath to grant her whatever she
might ask. 8Prompted by her mother,
she said, 'Give me the head of John the
Baptist here on a platter.' 9The king was
grieved, yet out of regard for his oaths
and for the guests, he commanded it
to be given; 10he sent and had John beheaded in the prison. 11The head was
brought on a platter and given to the
girl, who brought it to her mother. 12His
disciples came and took the body and
buried it; then they went and told Jesus.

FEEDING THE FIVE THOUSAND

13 Now when Jesus heard this, he
withdrew from there in a boat to a deserted place by himself. But when the
crowds heard it, they followed him on
foot from the towns. 14When he went
ashore, he saw a great crowd; and he
had compassion for them and cured
their sick. 15When it was evening, the
disciples came to him and said, 'This is a
deserted place, and the hour is now late;

[s] **13.43** Other ancient authorities add *to hear*
[t] **13.54** Gk *them* [u] **14.1** Gk *tetrarch*
[v] **14.3** Other ancient authorities read *his brother's wife* [w] **14.5** Gk *he*

send the crowds away so that they may go into the villages and buy food for themselves.' 16Jesus said to them, 'They need not go away; you give them something to eat.' 17They replied, 'We have nothing here but five loaves and two fish.' 18And he said, 'Bring them here to me.' 19Then he ordered the crowds to sit down on the grass. Taking the five loaves and the two fish, he looked up to heaven, and blessed and broke the loaves, and gave them to the disciples, and the disciples gave them to the crowds. 20And all ate and were filled; and they took up what was left over of the broken pieces, twelve baskets full. 21And those who ate were about five thousand men, besides women and children.

JESUS WALKS ON THE WATER

22 Immediately he made the disciples get into the boat and go on ahead to the other side, while he dismissed the crowds. 23And after he had dismissed the crowds, he went up the mountain by himself to pray. When evening came, he was there alone, 24but by this time the boat, battered by the waves, was far from the land,[x] for the wind was against them. 25And early in the morning he came walking towards them on the lake. 26But when the disciples saw him walking on the lake, they were terrified, saying, 'It is a ghost!' And they cried out in fear. 27But immediately Jesus spoke to them and said, 'Take heart, it is I; do not be afraid.'

28 Peter answered him, 'Lord, if it is you, command me to come to you on the water.' 29He said, 'Come.' So Peter got out of the boat, started walking on the water, and came towards Jesus. 30But when he noticed the strong wind,[y] he became frightened, and beginning to sink, he cried out, 'Lord, save me!' 31Jesus immediately reached out his hand and caught him, saying to him, 'You of little faith, why did you doubt?' 32When they got into the boat, the wind ceased. 33And those in the boat worshipped him, saying, 'Truly you are the Son of God.'

JESUS HEALS THE SICK IN GENNESARET

34 When they had crossed over, they came to land at Gennesaret. 35After the people of that place recognized him, they sent word throughout the region and brought all who were sick to him, 36and begged him that they might touch even the fringe of his cloak; and all who touched it were healed.

THE TRADITION OF THE ELDERS

15 Then Pharisees and scribes came to Jesus from Jerusalem and said, 2'Why do your disciples break the tradition of the elders? For they do not wash their hands before they eat.' 3He answered them, 'And why do you break the commandment of God for the sake of your tradition? 4For God said,[z] "Honour your father and your mother," and, "Whoever speaks evil of father or mother must surely die." 5But you say that whoever tells father or mother, "Whatever support you might have had from me is given to God",[a] then that person need not honour the father.[b] 6So, for the sake of your tradition, you make void the word[c] of God. 7You hypocrites! Isaiah prophesied rightly about you when he said:

8 "This people honours me
with their lips,
but their hearts are far from me;
9 in vain do they worship me,
teaching human precepts
as doctrines." '

THINGS THAT DEFILE

10 Then he called the crowd to him and said to them, 'Listen and understand: 11it is not what goes into the mouth that defiles a person, but it is what comes out of the mouth that defiles.' 12Then the disciples approached and said to him, 'Do you know that the Pharisees took offence when they heard what you said?' 13He answered, 'Every plant that my heavenly Father has not planted will be uprooted. 14Let them alone; they are blind guides of the blind.[d] And if one blind person guides another, both will fall into a pit.' 15But Peter said to him, 'Explain this parable to us.' 16Then he said, 'Are you also still without understanding? 17Do you not see that whatever goes into the mouth enters the stomach, and goes out into the sewer? 18But what comes out of the mouth proceeds from the heart, and this is what defiles. 19For out of

x **14.24** Other ancient authorities read *was out on the lake* y **14.30** Other ancient authorities read *the wind* z **15.4** Other ancient authorities read *commanded, saying* a **15.5** Or *is an offering* b **15.5** Other ancient authorities add *or the mother* c **15.6** Other ancient authorities read *law*; others, *commandment* d **15.14** Other ancient authorities lack *of the blind*

the heart come evil intentions, murder, adultery, fornication, theft, false witness, slander. 20 These are what defile a person, but to eat with unwashed hands does not defile.'

THE CANAANITE WOMAN'S FAITH

21 Jesus left that place and went away to the district of Tyre and Sidon. 22 Just then a Canaanite woman from that region came out and started shouting, 'Have mercy on me, Lord, Son of David; my daughter is tormented by a demon.' 23 But he did not answer her at all. And his disciples came and urged him, saying, 'Send her away, for she keeps shouting after us.' 24 He answered, 'I was sent only to the lost sheep of the house of Israel.' 25 But she came and knelt before him, saying, 'Lord, help me.' 26 He answered, 'It is not fair to take the children's food and throw it to the dogs.' 27 She said, 'Yes, Lord, yet even the dogs eat the crumbs that fall from their masters' table.' 28 Then Jesus answered her, 'Woman, great is your faith! Let it be done for you as you wish.' And her daughter was healed instantly.

JESUS CURES MANY PEOPLE

29 After Jesus had left that place, he passed along the Sea of Galilee, and he went up the mountain, where he sat down. 30 Great crowds came to him, bringing with them the lame, the maimed, the blind, the mute, and many others. They put them at his feet, and he cured them, 31 so that the crowd was amazed when they saw the mute speaking, the maimed whole, the lame walking, and the blind seeing. And they praised the God of Israel.

FEEDING THE FOUR THOUSAND

32 Then Jesus called his disciples to him and said, 'I have compassion for the crowd, because they have been with me now for three days and have nothing to eat; and I do not want to send them away hungry, for they might faint on the way.' 33 The disciples said to him, 'Where are we to get enough bread in the desert to feed so great a crowd?' 34 Jesus asked them, 'How many loaves have you?' They said, 'Seven, and a few small fish.' 35 Then ordering the crowd to sit down on the ground, 36 he took the seven loaves and the fish; and after giving thanks he broke them and gave them to the disciples, and the disciples gave them to the crowds. 37 And all of them ate and were filled; and they took up the broken pieces left over, seven baskets full. 38 Those who had eaten were four thousand men, besides women and children. 39 After sending away the crowds, he got into the boat and went to the region of Magadan.[e]

THE DEMAND FOR A SIGN

16 The Pharisees and Sadducees came, and to test Jesus[f] they asked him to show them a sign from heaven. 2 He answered them, 'When it is evening, you say, "It will be fair weather, for the sky is red." 3 And in the morning, "It will be stormy today, for the sky is red and threatening." You know how to interpret the appearance of the sky, but you cannot interpret the signs of the times.[g] 4 An evil and adulterous generation asks for a sign, but no sign will be given to it except the sign of Jonah.' Then he left them and went away.

THE YEAST OF THE PHARISEES AND SADDUCEES

5 When the disciples reached the other side, they had forgotten to bring any bread. 6 Jesus said to them, 'Watch out, and beware of the yeast of the Pharisees and Sadducees.' 7 They said to one another, 'It is because we have brought no bread.' 8 And becoming aware of it, Jesus said, 'You of little faith, why are you talking about having no bread? 9 Do you still not perceive? Do you not remember the five loaves for the five thousand, and how many baskets you gathered? 10 Or the seven loaves for the four thousand, and how many baskets you gathered? 11 How could you fail to perceive that I was not speaking about bread? Beware of the yeast of the Pharisees and Sadducees!' 12 Then they understood that he had not told them to beware of the yeast of bread, but of the teaching of the Pharisees and Sadducees.

PETER'S DECLARATION ABOUT JESUS

13 Now when Jesus came into the district of Caesarea Philippi, he asked his disciples, 'Who do people say that the Son of Man is?' 14 And they said, 'Some say John the Baptist, but others Elijah, and still others Jeremiah or one of the prophets.' 15 He said to them, 'But who do you say that I am?' 16 Simon Peter

[e] 15.39 Other ancient authorities read *Magdala* or *Magdalan* [f] 16.1 Gk *him* [g] 16.3 Other ancient authorities lack *2When it is . . . of the times*

answered, 'You are the Messiah,[h] the
Son of the living God.' 17 And Jesus answered him, 'Blessed are you, Simon
son of Jonah! For flesh and blood has not
revealed this to you, but my Father in
heaven. 18 And I tell you, you are Peter,[i]
and on this rock[j] I will build my church,
and the gates of Hades will not prevail
against it. 19 I will give you the keys
of the kingdom of heaven, and whatever you bind on earth will be bound
in heaven, and whatever you loose on
earth will be loosed in heaven.' 20 Then
he sternly ordered the disciples not to
tell anyone that he was[k] the Messiah.[l]

JESUS FORETELLS HIS DEATH AND RESURRECTION

21 From that time on, Jesus began to
show his disciples that he must go to Jerusalem and undergo great suffering at
the hands of the elders and chief priests
and scribes, and be killed, and on the
third day be raised. 22 And Peter took
him aside and began to rebuke him, saying, 'God forbid it, Lord! This must never
happen to you.' 23 But he turned and said
to Peter, 'Get behind me, Satan! You are
a stumbling-block to me; for you are setting your mind not on divine things but
on human things.'

THE CROSS AND SELF-DENIAL

24 Then Jesus told his disciples, 'If
any want to become my followers, let
them deny themselves and take up their
cross and follow me. 25 For those who
want to save their life will lose it, and
those who lose their life for my sake will
find it. 26 For what will it profit them if
they gain the whole world but forfeit
their life? Or what will they give in return for their life?

27 'For the Son of Man is to come
with his angels in the glory of his Father, and then he will repay everyone
for what has been done. 28 Truly I tell
you, there are some standing here who
will not taste death before they see the
Son of Man coming in his kingdom.'

THE TRANSFIGURATION

17 Six days later, Jesus took with
him Peter and James and his
brother John and led them up a high
mountain, by themselves. 2 And he was
transfigured before them, and his face
shone like the sun, and his clothes became dazzling white. 3 Suddenly there
appeared to them Moses and Elijah,
talking with him. 4 Then Peter said to
Jesus, 'Lord, it is good for us to be here; if
you wish, I[m] will make three dwellings[n]
here, one for you, one for Moses, and one
for Elijah.' 5 While he was still speaking,
suddenly a bright cloud overshadowed
them, and from the cloud a voice said,
'This is my Son, the Beloved;[o] with him
I am well pleased; listen to him!' 6 When
the disciples heard this, they fell to the
ground and were overcome by fear. 7 But
Jesus came and touched them, saying,
'Get up and do not be afraid.' 8 And when
they looked up, they saw no one except
Jesus himself alone.

9 As they were coming down the
mountain, Jesus ordered them, 'Tell
no one about the vision until after the
Son of Man has been raised from the
dead.' 10 And the disciples asked him,
'Why, then, do the scribes say that Elijah must come first?' 11 He replied, 'Elijah is indeed coming and will restore all
things; 12 but I tell you that Elijah has already come, and they did not recognize
him, but they did to him whatever they
pleased. So also the Son of Man is about
to suffer at their hands.' 13 Then the disciples understood that he was speaking
to them about John the Baptist.

JESUS CURES A BOY WITH A DEMON

14 When they came to the crowd,
a man came to him, knelt before him,
15 and said, 'Lord, have mercy on my son,
for he is an epileptic and he suffers terribly; he often falls into the fire and often
into the water. 16 And I brought him to
your disciples, but they could not cure
him.' 17 Jesus answered, 'You faithless
and perverse generation, how much
longer must I be with you? How much
longer must I put up with you? Bring
him here to me.' 18 And Jesus rebuked
the demon,[p] and it[q] came out of him,
and the boy was cured instantly. 19 Then
the disciples came to Jesus privately
and said, 'Why could we not cast it out?'
20 He said to them, 'Because of your little faith. For truly I tell you, if you have
faith the size of a[r] mustard seed, you
will say to this mountain, "Move from
here to there", and it will move; and
nothing will be impossible for you.'[s]

[h] 16.16 Or *the Christ* [i] 16.18 Gk *Petros*
[j] 16.18 Gk *petra* [k] 16.20 Other ancient authorities add *Jesus* [l] 16.20 Or *the Christ*
[m] 17.4 Other ancient authorities read *we*
[n] 17.4 Or *tents* [o] 17.5 Or *my beloved Son*
[p] 17.18 Gk *it* or *him* [q] 17.18 Gk *the demon*
[r] 17.20 Gk *faith as a grain of* [s] 17.20 Other ancient authorities add verse 21, *But this kind does not come out except by prayer and fasting*

JESUS AGAIN FORETELLS HIS DEATH AND RESURRECTION

22 As they were gathering[t] in Galilee, Jesus said to them, 'The Son of Man
is going to be betrayed into human
hands, 23 and they will kill him, and on
the third day he will be raised.' And they
were greatly distressed.

JESUS AND THE TEMPLE TAX

24 When they reached Capernaum,
the collectors of the temple tax[u] came
to Peter and said, 'Does your teacher not
pay the temple tax?'[v] 25 He said, 'Yes, he
does.' And when he came home, Jesus
spoke of it first, asking, 'What do you
think, Simon? From whom do kings of
the earth take toll or tribute? From their
children or from others?' 26 When Peter[w]
said, 'From others', Jesus said to him,
'Then the children are free. 27 However, so
that we do not give offence to them, go
to the lake and cast a hook; take the first
fish that comes up; and when you open
its mouth, you will find a coin;[x] take that
and give it to them for you and me.'

TRUE GREATNESS

18 At that time the disciples came
to Jesus and asked, 'Who is the
greatest in the kingdom of heaven?'
2 He called a child, whom he put among
them, 3 and said, 'Truly I tell you, unless
you change and become like children,
you will never enter the kingdom of
heaven. 4 Whoever becomes humble like
this child is the greatest in the kingdom
of heaven. 5 Whoever welcomes one such
child in my name welcomes me.

TEMPTATIONS TO SIN

6 'If any of you put a stumbling-block
before one of these little ones who believe in me, it would be better for you if
a great millstone were fastened around
your neck and you were drowned in the
depth of the sea. 7 Woe to the world because of stumbling-blocks! Occasions
for stumbling are bound to come, but
woe to the one by whom the stumbling-
block comes!

8 'If your hand or your foot causes you
to stumble, cut it off and throw it away;
it is better for you to enter life maimed or
lame than to have two hands or two feet
and to be thrown into the eternal fire.
9 And if your eye causes you to stumble,
tear it out and throw it away; it is better
for you to enter life with one eye than to
have two eyes and to be thrown into the
hell[y] of fire.

THE PARABLE OF THE LOST SHEEP

10 'Take care that you do not despise
one of these little ones; for, I tell you, in
heaven their angels continually see the
face of my Father in heaven.[z] 12 What do
you think? If a shepherd has a hundred
sheep, and one of them has gone astray,
does he not leave the ninety-nine on the
mountains and go in search of the one
that went astray? 13 And if he finds it,
truly I tell you, he rejoices over it more
than over the ninety-nine that never
went astray. 14 So it is not the will of
your[a] Father in heaven that one of these
little ones should be lost.

REPROVING ANOTHER WHO SINS

15 'If another member of the church[b]
sins against you,[c] go and point out the
fault when the two of you are alone. If the
member listens to you, you have regained
that one.[d] 16 But if you are not listened to,
take one or two others along with you,
so that every word may be confirmed by
the evidence of two or three witnesses.
17 If the member refuses to listen to them,
tell it to the church; and if the offender refuses to listen even to the church, let such
a one be to you as a Gentile and a tax-
collector. 18 Truly I tell you, whatever you
bind on earth will be bound in heaven,
and whatever you loose on earth will be
loosed in heaven. 19 Again, truly I tell you,
if two of you agree on earth about anything you ask, it will be done for you by
my Father in heaven. 20 For where two
or three are gathered in my name, I am
there among them.'

FORGIVENESS

21 Then Peter came and said to him,
'Lord, if another member of the church[e]
sins against me, how often should I forgive? As many as seven times?' 22 Jesus
said to him, 'Not seven times, but, I tell
you, seventy-seven[f] times.

THE PARABLE OF THE UNFORGIVING SERVANT

23 'For this reason the kingdom of
heaven may be compared to a king who

[t] **17.22** Other ancient authorities read *living*
[u] **17.24** Gk *didrachma* [v] **17.24** Gk *didrachma*
[w] **17.26** Gk *he* [x] **17.27** Gk *stater*; the stater was worth two didrachmas [y] **18.9** Gk *Gehenna*
[z] **18.10** Other ancient authorities add verse 11, *For the Son of Man came to save the lost*
[a] **18.14** Other ancient authorities read *my*
[b] **18.15** Gk *If your brother* [c] **18.15** Other ancient authorities lack *against you* [d] **18.15** Gk *the brother* [e] **18.21** Gk *if my brother* [f] **18.22** Or *seventy times seven*

wished to settle accounts with his
slaves. 24When he began the reckoning, one who owed him ten thousand
talents[g] was brought to him; 25and, as
he could not pay, his lord ordered him
to be sold, together with his wife and
children and all his possessions, and
payment to be made. 26So the slave fell
on his knees before him, saying, "Have
patience with me, and I will pay you
everything." 27And out of pity for him,
the lord of that slave released him and
forgave him the debt. 28But that same
slave, as he went out, came upon one
of his fellow-slaves who owed him a
hundred denarii;[h] and seizing him
by the throat, he said, "Pay what you
owe." 29Then his fellow-slave fell down
and pleaded with him, "Have patience
with me, and I will pay you." 30But he
refused; then he went and threw him
into prison until he should pay the debt.
31When his fellow-slaves saw what had
happened, they were greatly distressed,
and they went and reported to their lord
all that had taken place. 32Then his lord
summoned him and said to him, "You
wicked slave! I forgave you all that debt
because you pleaded with me. 33Should
you not have had mercy on your fellow-
slave, as I had mercy on you?" 34And in
anger his lord handed him over to be
tortured until he should pay his entire
debt. 35So my heavenly Father will also
do to every one of you, if you do not forgive your brother or sister[i] from your
heart.'

TEACHING ABOUT DIVORCE

19 When Jesus had finished saying
these things, he left Galilee and
went to the region of Judea beyond the
Jordan. 2Large crowds followed him,
and he cured them there.

3 Some Pharisees came to him, and
to test him they asked, 'Is it lawful for a
man to divorce his wife for any cause?'
4He answered, 'Have you not read that
the one who made them at the beginning "made them male and female",
5and said, "For this reason a man shall
leave his father and mother and be
joined to his wife, and the two shall become one flesh"? 6So they are no longer
two, but one flesh. Therefore what God
has joined together, let no one separate.'
7They said to him, 'Why then did Moses command us to give a certificate of
dismissal and to divorce her?' 8He said
to them, 'It was because you were so
hard-hearted that Moses allowed you to
divorce your wives, but at the beginning
it was not so. 9And I say to you, whoever divorces his wife, except for unchastity, and marries another commits
adultery.'[j]

10 His disciples said to him, 'If such
is the case of a man with his wife, it is
better not to marry.' 11But he said to
them, 'Not everyone can accept this
teaching, but only those to whom it is
given. 12For there are eunuchs who have
been so from birth, and there are eunuchs who have been made eunuchs by
others, and there are eunuchs who have
made themselves eunuchs for the sake
of the kingdom of heaven. Let anyone
accept this who can.'

JESUS BLESSES LITTLE CHILDREN

13 Then little children were being
brought to him in order that he might
lay his hands on them and pray. The
disciples spoke sternly to those who
brought them; 14but Jesus said, 'Let the
little children come to me, and do not
stop them; for it is to such as these that
the kingdom of heaven belongs.' 15And
he laid his hands on them and went on
his way.

THE RICH YOUNG MAN

16 Then someone came to him and
said, 'Teacher, what good deed must I
do to have eternal life?' 17And he said
to him, 'Why do you ask me about what
is good? There is only one who is good.
If you wish to enter into life, keep the
commandments.' 18He said to him,
'Which ones?' And Jesus said, 'You shall
not murder; You shall not commit adultery; You shall not steal; You shall not
bear false witness; 19Honour your father
and mother; also, You shall love your
neighbour as yourself.' 20The young
man said to him, 'I have kept all these;[k]
what do I still lack?' 21Jesus said to him,
'If you wish to be perfect, go, sell your
possessions, and give the money[l] to
the poor, and you will have treasure in
heaven; then come, follow me.' 22When
the young man heard this word, he

[g] **18.24** A talent was worth more than fifteen years' wages of a labourer [h] **18.28** The denarius was the usual day's wage for a labourer [i] **18.35** Gk *brother* [j] **19.9** Other ancient authorities read *except on the ground of unchastity, causes her to commit adultery*; others add at the end of the verse *and he who marries a divorced woman commits adultery* [k] **19.20** Other ancient authorities add *from my youth* [l] **19.21** Gk lacks *the money*

went away grieving, for he had many
possessions.
23 Then Jesus said to his disciples,
'Truly I tell you, it will be hard for a rich
person to enter the kingdom of heaven.
24 Again I tell you, it is easier for a camel
to go through the eye of a needle than
for someone who is rich to enter the
kingdom of God.' 25 When the disciples
heard this, they were greatly astounded
and said, 'Then who can be saved?' 26 But
Jesus looked at them and said, 'For
mortals it is impossible, but for God all
things are possible.'
27 Then Peter said in reply, 'Look,
we have left everything and followed
you. What then will we have?' 28 Jesus
said to them, 'Truly I tell you, at the
renewal of all things, when the Son of
Man is seated on the throne of his glory,
you who have followed me will also sit
on twelve thrones, judging the twelve
tribes of Israel. 29 And everyone who has
left houses or brothers or sisters or father or mother or children or fields, for
my name's sake, will receive a hundredfold,[m] and will inherit eternal life. 30 But
many who are first will be last, and the
last will be first.

THE LABOURERS IN THE VINEYARD

20 'For the kingdom of heaven is
like a landowner who went out
early in the morning to hire labourers
for his vineyard. 2 After agreeing with
the labourers for the usual daily wage,[n]
he sent them into his vineyard. 3 When
he went out about nine o'clock, he saw
others standing idle in the market-
place; 4 and he said to them, "You also
go into the vineyard, and I will pay
you whatever is right." So they went.
5 When he went out again about noon
and about three o'clock, he did the same.
6 And about five o'clock he went out and
found others standing around; and he
said to them, "Why are you standing
here idle all day?" 7 They said to him,
"Because no one has hired us." He said
to them, "You also go into the vineyard."
8 When evening came, the owner of the
vineyard said to his manager, "Call the
labourers and give them their pay, beginning with the last and then going to
the first." 9 When those hired about five
o'clock came, each of them received the
usual daily wage.[o] 10 Now when the first
came, they thought they would receive
more; but each of them also received
the usual daily wage.[p] 11 And when they
received it, they grumbled against the
landowner, 12 saying, "These last worked
only one hour, and you have made them
equal to us who have borne the burden
of the day and the scorching heat." 13 But
he replied to one of them, "Friend, I am
doing you no wrong; did you not agree
with me for the usual daily wage?[q]
14 Take what belongs to you and go; I
choose to give to this last the same as
I give to you. 15 Am I not allowed to do
what I choose with what belongs to me?
Or are you envious because I am generous?"[r] 16 So the last will be first, and the
first will be last.'[s]

A THIRD TIME JESUS FORETELLS HIS DEATH AND RESURRECTION

17 While Jesus was going up to Jerusalem, he took the twelve disciples aside
by themselves, and said to them on the
way, 18 'See, we are going up to Jerusalem, and the Son of Man will be handed
over to the chief priests and scribes, and
they will condemn him to death; 19 then
they will hand him over to the Gentiles
to be mocked and flogged and crucified;
and on the third day he will be raised.'

THE REQUEST OF THE MOTHER OF JAMES AND JOHN

20 Then the mother of the sons of
Zebedee came to him with her sons, and
kneeling before him, she asked a favour
of him. 21 And he said to her, 'What do
you want?' She said to him, 'Declare
that these two sons of mine will sit, one
at your right hand and one at your left,
in your kingdom.' 22 But Jesus answered,
'You do not know what you are asking.
Are you able to drink the cup that I am
about to drink?'[t] They said to him, 'We
are able.' 23 He said to them, 'You will indeed drink my cup, but to sit at my right
hand and at my left, this is not mine to
grant, but it is for those for whom it has
been prepared by my Father.'
24 When the ten heard it, they were
angry with the two brothers. 25 But
Jesus called them to him and said, 'You
know that the rulers of the Gentiles lord
it over them, and their great ones are
tyrants over them. 26 It will not be so
among you; but whoever wishes to be
great among you must be your servant,

[m] 19.29 Other ancient authorities read *manifold*
[n] 20.2 Gk *a denarius* [o] 20.9 Gk *a denarius*
[p] 20.10 Gk *a denarius* [q] 20.13 Gk *a denarius*
[r] 20.15 Gk *is your eye evil because I am good?*
[s] 20.16 Other ancient authorities add *for many are called but few are chosen* [t] 20.22 Other ancient authorities add *or to be baptized with the baptism that I am baptized with?*

27 and whoever wishes to be first among you must be your slave; 28 just as the Son of Man came not to be served but to serve, and to give his life a ransom for many.'

JESUS HEALS TWO BLIND MEN

29 As they were leaving Jericho, a large crowd followed him. 30 There were two blind men sitting by the roadside. When they heard that Jesus was passing by, they shouted, 'Lord,[u] have mercy on us, Son of David!' 31 The crowd sternly ordered them to be quiet; but they shouted even more loudly, 'Have mercy on us, Lord, Son of David!' 32 Jesus stood still and called them, saying, 'What do you want me to do for you?' 33 They said to him, 'Lord, let our eyes be opened.' 34 Moved with compassion, Jesus touched their eyes. Immediately they regained their sight and followed him.

JESUS' TRIUMPHAL ENTRY INTO JERUSALEM

21 When they had come near Jerusalem and had reached Bethphage, at the Mount of Olives, Jesus sent two disciples, 2 saying to them, 'Go into the village ahead of you, and immediately you will find a donkey tied, and a colt with her; untie them and bring them to me. 3 If anyone says anything to you, just say this, "The Lord needs them." And he will send them immediately.'[v] 4 This took place to fulfil what had been spoken through the prophet, saying,

5 'Tell the daughter of Zion,
Look, your king is coming to you,
humble, and mounted
on a donkey,
and on a colt, the foal
of a donkey.'

6 The disciples went and did as Jesus had directed them; 7 they brought the donkey and the colt, and put their cloaks on them, and he sat on them. 8 A very large crowd[w] spread their cloaks on the road, and others cut branches from the trees and spread them on the road. 9 The crowds that went ahead of him and that followed were shouting,

'Hosanna to the Son of David!
Blessed is the one who comes
in the name of the Lord!
Hosanna in the highest heaven!'

10 When he entered Jerusalem, the whole city was in turmoil, asking, 'Who is this?' 11 The crowds were saying, 'This is the prophet Jesus from Nazareth in Galilee.'

JESUS CLEANSES THE TEMPLE

12 Then Jesus entered the temple[x] and drove out all who were selling and buying in the temple, and he overturned the tables of the money-changers and the seats of those who sold doves. 13 He said to them, 'It is written,

"My house shall be called a
house of prayer";
but you are making it a
den of robbers.'

14 The blind and the lame came to him in the temple, and he cured them. 15 But when the chief priests and the scribes saw the amazing things that he did, and heard[y] the children crying out in the temple, 'Hosanna to the Son of David', they became angry 16 and said to him, 'Do you hear what these are saying?' Jesus said to them, 'Yes; have you never read,

"Out of the mouths of infants
and nursing babies
you have prepared praise
for yourself"?'

17 He left them, went out of the city to Bethany, and spent the night there.

JESUS CURSES THE FIG TREE

18 In the morning, when he returned to the city, he was hungry. 19 And seeing a fig tree by the side of the road, he went to it and found nothing at all on it but leaves. Then he said to it, 'May no fruit ever come from you again!' And the fig tree withered at once. 20 When the disciples saw it, they were amazed, saying, 'How did the fig tree wither at once?' 21 Jesus answered them, 'Truly I tell you, if you have faith and do not doubt, not only will you do what has been done to the fig tree, but even if you say to this mountain, "Be lifted up and thrown into the sea", it will be done. 22 Whatever you ask for in prayer with faith, you will receive.'

THE AUTHORITY OF JESUS QUESTIONED

23 When he entered the temple, the chief priests and the elders of the people came to him as he was teaching, and said, 'By what authority are you doing these things, and who gave you this authority?' 24 Jesus said to them, 'I will also ask you one question; if you tell me

[u] **20.30** Other ancient authorities lack *Lord*
[v] **21.3** Or *"The Lord needs them and will send them back immediately."* [w] **21.8** Or *Most of the crowd* [x] **21.12** Other ancient authorities add *of God* [y] **21.15** Gk lacks *heard*

the answer, then I will also tell you by
what authority I do these things. 25 Did
the baptism of John come from heaven,
or was it of human origin?' And they
argued with one another, 'If we say,
"From heaven", he will say to us, "Why
then did you not believe him?" 26 But if
we say, "Of human origin", we are afraid
of the crowd; for all regard John as a
prophet.' 27 So they answered Jesus, 'We
do not know.' And he said to them, 'Neither will I tell you by what authority I
am doing these things.

THE PARABLE OF THE TWO SONS

28 'What do you think? A man had
two sons; he went to the first and said,
"Son, go and work in the vineyard today." 29 He answered, "I will not"; but
later he changed his mind and went.
30 The father[z] went to the second and
said the same; and he answered, "I go,
sir"; but he did not go. 31 Which of the
two did the will of his father?' They said,
'The first.' Jesus said to them, 'Truly I
tell you, the tax-collectors and the prostitutes are going into the kingdom of
God ahead of you. 32 For John came to
you in the way of righteousness and
you did not believe him, but the tax-
collectors and the prostitutes believed
him; and even after you saw it, you did
not change your minds and believe him.

THE PARABLE OF THE WICKED TENANTS

33 'Listen to another parable. There
was a landowner who planted a vineyard,
put a fence around it, dug a wine press
in it, and built a watch-tower. Then he
leased it to tenants and went to another
country. 34 When the harvest time had
come, he sent his slaves to the tenants
to collect his produce. 35 But the tenants
seized his slaves and beat one, killed another, and stoned another. 36 Again he
sent other slaves, more than the first;
and they treated them in the same way.
37 Finally he sent his son to them, saying, "They will respect my son." 38 But
when the tenants saw the son, they said
to themselves, "This is the heir; come, let
us kill him and get his inheritance." 39 So
they seized him, threw him out of the
vineyard, and killed him. 40 Now when
the owner of the vineyard comes, what
will he do to those tenants?' 41 They said
to him, 'He will put those wretches to a
miserable death, and lease the vineyard
to other tenants who will give him the
produce at the harvest time.'

42 Jesus said to them, 'Have you
never read in the scriptures:

"The stone that the builders rejected
has become the cornerstone;[a]
this was the Lord's doing,
and it is amazing in our eyes"?

43 Therefore I tell you, the kingdom of
God will be taken away from you and
given to a people that produces the fruits
of the kingdom.[b] 44 The one who falls on
this stone will be broken to pieces; and
it will crush anyone on whom it falls.'[c]

45 When the chief priests and the
Pharisees heard his parables, they realized that he was speaking about them.
46 They wanted to arrest him, but they
feared the crowds, because they regarded him as a prophet.

THE PARABLE OF THE WEDDING BANQUET

22 Once more Jesus spoke to them
in parables, saying: 2 'The kingdom of heaven may be compared to a
king who gave a wedding banquet for
his son. 3 He sent his slaves to call those
who had been invited to the wedding
banquet, but they would not come.
4 Again he sent other slaves, saying,
"Tell those who have been invited: Look,
I have prepared my dinner, my oxen and
my fat calves have been slaughtered,
and everything is ready; come to the
wedding banquet." 5 But they made light
of it and went away, one to his farm, another to his business, 6 while the rest
seized his slaves, maltreated them, and
killed them. 7 The king was enraged. He
sent his troops, destroyed those murderers, and burned their city. 8 Then he
said to his slaves, "The wedding is ready,
but those invited were not worthy. 9 Go
therefore into the main streets, and invite everyone you find to the wedding
banquet." 10 Those slaves went out into
the streets and gathered all whom they
found, both good and bad; so the wedding hall was filled with guests.

11 'But when the king came in to see
the guests, he noticed a man there who
was not wearing a wedding robe, 12 and
he said to him, "Friend, how did you
get in here without a wedding robe?"
And he was speechless. 13 Then the king
said to the attendants, "Bind him hand
and foot, and throw him into the outer
darkness, where there will be weeping

[z] 21.30 Gk *He* [a] 21.42 Or *keystone*
[b] 21.43 Gk *the fruits of it* [c] 21.44 Other ancient
authorities lack verse 44

and gnashing of teeth.' 14For many are called, but few are chosen.'

THE QUESTION ABOUT PAYING TAXES

15 Then the Pharisees went and plotted to entrap him in what he said. 16So they sent their disciples to him, along with the Herodians, saying, 'Teacher, we know that you are sincere, and teach the way of God in accordance with truth, and show deference to no one; for you do not regard people with partiality. 17Tell us, then, what you think. Is it lawful to pay taxes to the emperor, or not?' 18But Jesus, aware of their malice, said, 'Why are you putting me to the test, you hypocrites? 19Show me the coin used for the tax.' And they brought him a denarius. 20Then he said to them, 'Whose head is this, and whose title?' 21They answered, 'The emperor's.' Then he said to them, 'Give therefore to the emperor the things that are the emperor's, and to God the things that are God's.' 22When they heard this, they were amazed; and they left him and went away.

THE QUESTION ABOUT THE RESURRECTION

23 The same day some Sadducees came to him, saying there is no resurrection;[d] and they asked him a question, saying, 24'Teacher, Moses said, "If a man dies childless, his brother shall marry the widow, and raise up children for his brother." 25Now there were seven brothers among us; the first married, and died childless, leaving the widow to his brother. 26The second did the same, so also the third, down to the seventh. 27Last of all, the woman herself died. 28In the resurrection, then, whose wife of the seven will she be? For all of them had married her.'

29 Jesus answered them, 'You are wrong, because you know neither the scriptures nor the power of God. 30For in the resurrection they neither marry nor are given in marriage, but are like angels[e] in heaven. 31And as for the resurrection of the dead, have you not read what was said to you by God, 32"I am the God of Abraham, the God of Isaac, and the God of Jacob"? He is God not of the dead, but of the living.' 33And when the crowd heard it, they were astounded at his teaching.

THE GREATEST COMMANDMENT

34 When the Pharisees heard that he had silenced the Sadducees, they gathered together, 35and one of them, a lawyer, asked him a question to test him. 36'Teacher, which commandment in the law is the greatest?' 37He said to him, '"You shall love the Lord your God with all your heart, and with all your soul, and with all your mind." 38This is the greatest and first commandment. 39And a second is like it: "You shall love your neighbour as yourself." 40On these two commandments hang all the law and the prophets.'

THE QUESTION ABOUT DAVID'S SON

41 Now while the Pharisees were gathered together, Jesus asked them this question: 42'What do you think of the Messiah?[f] Whose son is he?' They said to him, 'The son of David.' 43He said to them, 'How is it then that David by the Spirit[g] calls him Lord, saying,

44 "The Lord said to my Lord,
'Sit at my right hand,
until I put your enemies
under your feet'"?

45If David thus calls him Lord, how can he be his son?' 46No one was able to give him an answer, nor from that day did anyone dare to ask him any more questions.

JESUS DENOUNCES SCRIBES AND PHARISEES

23 Then Jesus said to the crowds and to his disciples, 2'The scribes and the Pharisees sit on Moses' seat; 3therefore, do whatever they teach you and follow it; but do not do as they do, for they do not practise what they teach. 4They tie up heavy burdens, hard to bear,[h] and lay them on the shoulders of others; but they themselves are unwilling to lift a finger to move them. 5They do all their deeds to be seen by others; for they make their phylacteries broad and their fringes long. 6They love to have the place of honour at banquets and the best seats in the synagogues, 7and to be greeted with respect in the market-places, and to have people call them rabbi. 8But you are not to be called rabbi, for you have one teacher, and you are all students.[i] 9And call no one your father on earth, for you have one Father—the one in heaven. 10Nor are you to be called instructors, for you

[d] **22.23** Other ancient authorities read *who say that there is no resurrection* [e] **22.30** Other ancient authorities add *of God* [f] **22.42** Or *Christ* [g] **22.43** Gk *in spirit* [h] **23.4** Other ancient authorities lack *hard to bear* [i] **23.8** Gk *brothers*

have one instructor, the Messiah.[j] 11The greatest among you will be your servant. 12All who exalt themselves will be humbled, and all who humble themselves will be exalted.

13 'But woe to you, scribes and Pharisees, hypocrites! For you lock people out of the kingdom of heaven. For you do not go in yourselves, and when others are going in, you stop them.[k] 15Woe to you, scribes and Pharisees, hypocrites! For you cross sea and land to make a single convert, and you make the new convert twice as much a child of hell[l] as yourselves.

16 'Woe to you, blind guides, who say, "Whoever swears by the sanctuary is bound by nothing, but whoever swears by the gold of the sanctuary is bound by the oath." 17You blind fools! For which is greater, the gold or the sanctuary that has made the gold sacred? 18And you say, "Whoever swears by the altar is bound by nothing, but whoever swears by the gift that is on the altar is bound by the oath." 19How blind you are! For which is greater, the gift or the altar that makes the gift sacred? 20So whoever swears by the altar, swears by it and by everything on it; 21and whoever swears by the sanctuary, swears by it and by the one who dwells in it; 22and whoever swears by heaven, swears by the throne of God and by the one who is seated upon it.

23 'Woe to you, scribes and Pharisees, hypocrites! For you tithe mint, dill, and cummin, and have neglected the weightier matters of the law: justice and mercy and faith. It is these you ought to have practised without neglecting the others. 24You blind guides! You strain out a gnat but swallow a camel!

25 'Woe to you, scribes and Pharisees, hypocrites! For you clean the outside of the cup and of the plate, but inside they are full of greed and self-indulgence. 26You blind Pharisee! First clean the inside of the cup,[m] so that the outside also may become clean.

27 'Woe to you, scribes and Pharisees, hypocrites! For you are like whitewashed tombs, which on the outside look beautiful, but inside they are full of the bones of the dead and of all kinds of filth. 28So you also on the outside look righteous to others, but inside you are full of hypocrisy and lawlessness.

29 'Woe to you, scribes and Pharisees, hypocrites! For you build the tombs of the prophets and decorate the graves of the righteous, 30and you say, "If we had lived in the days of our ancestors, we would not have taken part with them in shedding the blood of the prophets." 31Thus you testify against yourselves that you are descendants of those who murdered the prophets. 32Fill up, then, the measure of your ancestors. 33You snakes, you brood of vipers! How can you escape being sentenced to hell?[n] 34Therefore I send you prophets, sages, and scribes, some of whom you will kill and crucify, and some you will flog in your synagogues and pursue from town to town, 35so that upon you may come all the righteous blood shed on earth, from the blood of righteous Abel to the blood of Zechariah son of Barachiah, whom you murdered between the sanctuary and the altar. 36Truly I tell you, all this will come upon this generation.

THE LAMENT OVER JERUSALEM

37 'Jerusalem, Jerusalem, the city that kills the prophets and stones those who are sent to it! How often have I desired to gather your children together as a hen gathers her brood under her wings, and you were not willing! 38See, your house is left to you, desolate.[o] 39For I tell you, you will not see me again until you say, "Blessed is the one who comes in the name of the Lord."'

THE DESTRUCTION OF THE TEMPLE FORETOLD

24 As Jesus came out of the temple and was going away, his disciples came to point out to him the buildings of the temple. 2Then he asked them, 'You see all these, do you not? Truly I tell you, not one stone will be left here upon another; all will be thrown down.'

SIGNS OF THE END OF THE AGE

3 When he was sitting on the Mount of Olives, the disciples came to him privately, saying, 'Tell us, when will this be, and what will be the sign of your coming and of the end of the age?' 4Jesus answered them, 'Beware that no one leads you astray. 5For many will come in my

[j] 23.10 Or *the Christ* [k] 23.13 Other authorities add here (or after verse 12) verse 14, *Woe to you, scribes and Pharisees, hypocrites! For you devour widows' houses and for the sake of appearance you make long prayers; therefore you will receive the greater condemnation* [l] 23.15 Gk *Gehenna* [m] 23.26 Other ancient authorities add *and of the plate* [n] 23.33 Gk *Gehenna* [o] 23.38 Other ancient authorities lack *desolate*

name, saying, "I am the Messiah!"[p] and
they will lead many astray. 6And you
will hear of wars and rumours of wars;
see that you are not alarmed; for this
must take place, but the end is not yet.
7For nation will rise against nation, and
kingdom against kingdom, and there
will be famines[q] and earthquakes in
various places: 8all this is but the beginning of the birth pangs.

PERSECUTIONS FORETOLD

9 'Then they will hand you over to
be tortured and will put you to death,
and you will be hated by all nations because of my name. 10Then many will
fall away,[r] and they will betray one
another and hate one another. 11And
many false prophets will arise and lead
many astray. 12And because of the increase of lawlessness, the love of many
will grow cold. 13But anyone who endures to the end will be saved. 14And
this good news[s] of the kingdom will be
proclaimed throughout the world, as a
testimony to all the nations; and then
the end will come.

THE DESOLATING SACRILEGE

15 'So when you see the desolating
sacrilege standing in the holy place, as
was spoken of by the prophet Daniel (let
the reader understand), 16then those
in Judea must flee to the mountains;
17someone on the housetop must not
go down to take what is in the house;
18someone in the field must not turn
back to get a coat. 19Woe to those who
are pregnant and to those who are nursing infants in those days! 20Pray that
your flight may not be in winter or on
a sabbath. 21For at that time there will
be great suffering, such as has not been
from the beginning of the world until now, no, and never will be. 22And if
those days had not been cut short, no
one would be saved; but for the sake of
the elect those days will be cut short.
23Then if anyone says to you, "Look!
Here is the Messiah!"[t] or "There he
is!"—do not believe it. 24For false messiahs[u] and false prophets will appear and
produce great signs and omens, to lead
astray, if possible, even the elect. 25Take
note, I have told you beforehand. 26So,
if they say to you, "Look! He is in the
wilderness", do not go out. If they say,
"Look! He is in the inner rooms", do not
believe it. 27For as the lightning comes
from the east and flashes as far as the
west, so will be the coming of the Son
of Man. 28Wherever the corpse is, there
the vultures will gather.

THE COMING OF THE SON OF MAN

29 'Immediately after the suffering of
those days

the sun will be darkened,
and the moon will not
give its light;
the stars will fall from heaven,
and the powers of heaven
will be shaken.

30Then the sign of the Son of Man will
appear in heaven, and then all the tribes
of the earth will mourn, and they will
see "the Son of Man coming on the
clouds of heaven" with power and great
glory. 31And he will send out his angels
with a loud trumpet call, and they will
gather his elect from the four winds,
from one end of heaven to the other.

THE LESSON OF THE FIG TREE

32 'From the fig tree learn its lesson:
as soon as its branch becomes tender
and puts forth its leaves, you know that
summer is near. 33So also, when you
see all these things, you know that he[v]
is near, at the very gates. 34Truly I tell
you, this generation will not pass away
until all these things have taken place.
35Heaven and earth will pass away, but
my words will not pass away.

THE NECESSITY FOR WATCHFULNESS

36 'But about that day and hour
no one knows, neither the angels of
heaven, nor the Son,[w] but only the Father. 37For as the days of Noah were, so
will be the coming of the Son of Man.
38For as in those days before the flood
they were eating and drinking, marrying and giving in marriage, until the
day Noah entered the ark, 39and they
knew nothing until the flood came and
swept them all away, so too will be the
coming of the Son of Man. 40Then two
will be in the field; one will be taken
and one will be left. 41Two women will
be grinding meal together; one will be
taken and one will be left. 42Keep awake
therefore, for you do not know on what
day[x] your Lord is coming. 43But understand this: if the owner of the house

[p] **24.5** Or *the Christ* [q] **24.7** Other ancient authorities add *and pestilences* [r] **24.10** Or *stumble* [s] **24.14** Or *gospel* [t] **24.23** Or *the Christ* [u] **24.24** Or *christs* [v] **24.33** Or *it* [w] **24.36** Other ancient authorities lack *nor the Son* [x] **24.42** Other ancient authorities read *at what hour*

had known in what part of the night the thief was coming, he would have stayed awake and would not have let his house be broken into. 44Therefore you also must be ready, for the Son of Man is coming at an unexpected hour.

THE FAITHFUL OR THE UNFAITHFUL SLAVE

45 'Who then is the faithful and wise slave, whom his master has put in charge of his household, to give the other slaves[y] their allowance of food at the proper time? 46Blessed is that slave whom his master will find at work when he arrives. 47Truly I tell you, he will put that one in charge of all his possessions. 48But if that wicked slave says to himself, "My master is delayed", 49and he begins to beat his fellow-slaves, and eats and drinks with drunkards, 50the master of that slave will come on a day when he does not expect him and at an hour that he does not know. 51He will cut him in pieces[z] and put him with the hypocrites, where there will be weeping and gnashing of teeth.

THE PARABLE OF THE TEN BRIDESMAIDS

25 'Then the kingdom of heaven will be like this. Ten bridesmaids[a] took their lamps and went to meet the bridegroom.[b] 2Five of them were foolish, and five were wise. 3When the foolish took their lamps, they took no oil with them; 4but the wise took flasks of oil with their lamps. 5As the bridegroom was delayed, all of them became drowsy and slept. 6But at midnight there was a shout, "Look! Here is the bridegroom! Come out to meet him." 7Then all those bridesmaids[c] got up and trimmed their lamps. 8The foolish said to the wise, "Give us some of your oil, for our lamps are going out." 9But the wise replied, "No! there will not be enough for you and for us; you had better go to the dealers and buy some for yourselves." 10And while they went to buy it, the bridegroom came, and those who were ready went with him into the wedding banquet; and the door was shut. 11Later the other bridesmaids[d] came also, saying, "Lord, lord, open to us." 12But he replied, "Truly I tell you, I do not know you." 13Keep awake therefore, for you know neither the day nor the hour.[e]

THE PARABLE OF THE TALENTS

14 'For it is as if a man, going on a journey, summoned his slaves and entrusted his property to them; 15to one he gave five talents,[f] to another two, to another one, to each according to his ability. Then he went away. 16The one who had received the five talents went off at once and traded with them, and made five more talents. 17In the same way, the one who had the two talents made two more talents. 18But the one who had received the one talent went off and dug a hole in the ground and hid his master's money. 19After a long time the master of those slaves came and settled accounts with them. 20Then the one who had received the five talents came forward, bringing five more talents, saying, "Master, you handed over to me five talents; see, I have made five more talents." 21His master said to him, "Well done, good and trustworthy slave; you have been trustworthy in a few things, I will put you in charge of many things; enter into the joy of your master." 22And the one with the two talents also came forward, saying, "Master, you handed over to me two talents; see, I have made two more talents." 23His master said to him, "Well done, good and trustworthy slave; you have been trustworthy in a few things, I will put you in charge of many things; enter into the joy of your master." 24Then the one who had received the one talent also came forward, saying, "Master, I knew that you were a harsh man, reaping where you did not sow, and gathering where you did not scatter seed; 25so I was afraid, and I went and hid your talent in the ground. Here you have what is yours." 26But his master replied, "You wicked and lazy slave! You knew, did you, that I reap where I did not sow, and gather where I did not scatter? 27Then you ought to have invested my money with the bankers, and on my return I would have received what was my own with interest. 28So take the talent from him, and give it to the one with the ten talents. 29For to all those who have, more will be given, and they will have an abundance; but from those who have nothing, even what they have will be taken away. 30As for this worthless slave, throw him into the outer darkness, where there will be weeping and gnashing of teeth."

[y] 24.45 Gk *to give them* [z] 24.51 Or *cut him off*
[a] 25.1 Gk *virgins* [b] 25.1 Other ancient authorities add *and the bride* [c] 25.7 Gk *virgins*
[d] 25.11 Gk *virgins* [e] 25.13 Other ancient authorities add *in which the Son of Man is coming*
[f] 25.15 A talent was worth more than fifteen years' wages of a labourer

THE JUDGEMENT OF THE NATIONS

31 'When the Son of Man comes in
his glory, and all the angels with him,
then he will sit on the throne of his
glory. 32All the nations will be gathered
before him, and he will separate people
one from another as a shepherd separates the sheep from the goats, 33and he
will put the sheep at his right hand and
the goats at the left. 34Then the king will
say to those at his right hand, "Come,
you that are blessed by my Father, inherit the kingdom prepared for you
from the foundation of the world; 35for
I was hungry and you gave me food, I
was thirsty and you gave me something to drink, I was a stranger and
you welcomed me, 36I was naked and
you gave me clothing, I was sick and you
took care of me, I was in prison and you
visited me." 37Then the righteous will
answer him, "Lord, when was it that
we saw you hungry and gave you food,
or thirsty and gave you something to
drink? 38And when was it that we saw
you a stranger and welcomed you, or
naked and gave you clothing? 39And
when was it that we saw you sick or in
prison and visited you?" 40And the king
will answer them, "Truly I tell you, just
as you did it to one of the least of these
who are members of my family,[g] you
did it to me." 41Then he will say to those
at his left hand, "You that are accursed,
depart from me into the eternal fire prepared for the devil and his angels; 42for
I was hungry and you gave me no food,
I was thirsty and you gave me nothing
to drink, 43I was a stranger and you did
not welcome me, naked and you did not
give me clothing, sick and in prison and
you did not visit me." 44Then they also
will answer, "Lord, when was it that we
saw you hungry or thirsty or a stranger
or naked or sick or in prison, and did not
take care of you?" 45Then he will answer
them, "Truly I tell you, just as you did
not do it to one of the least of these, you
did not do it to me." 46And these will go
away into eternal punishment, but the
righteous into eternal life.'

THE PLOT TO KILL JESUS

26 When Jesus had finished saying all these things, he said to
his disciples, 2'You know that after two
days the Passover is coming, and the
Son of Man will be handed over to be
crucified.'

3 Then the chief priests and the elders of the people gathered in the palace
of the high priest, who was called Caiaphas, 4and they conspired to arrest
Jesus by stealth and kill him. 5But they
said, 'Not during the festival, or there
may be a riot among the people.'

THE ANOINTING AT BETHANY

6 Now while Jesus was at Bethany
in the house of Simon the leper,[h] 7a
woman came to him with an alabaster jar of very costly ointment, and she
poured it on his head as he sat at the table. 8But when the disciples saw it, they
were angry and said, 'Why this waste?
9For this ointment could have been sold
for a large sum, and the money given
to the poor.' 10But Jesus, aware of this,
said to them, 'Why do you trouble the
woman? She has performed a good service for me. 11For you always have the
poor with you, but you will not always
have me. 12By pouring this ointment
on my body she has prepared me for
burial. 13Truly I tell you, wherever this
good news[i] is proclaimed in the whole
world, what she has done will be told in
remembrance of her.'

JUDAS AGREES TO BETRAY JESUS

14 Then one of the twelve, who was
called Judas Iscariot, went to the chief
priests 15and said, 'What will you give
me if I betray him to you?' They paid
him thirty pieces of silver. 16And from
that moment he began to look for an opportunity to betray him.

THE PASSOVER WITH THE DISCIPLES

17 On the first day of Unleavened
Bread the disciples came to Jesus, saying, 'Where do you want us to make
the preparations for you to eat the
Passover?' 18He said, 'Go into the city
to a certain man, and say to him, "The
Teacher says, My time is near; I will
keep the Passover at your house with
my disciples." ' 19So the disciples did as
Jesus had directed them, and they prepared the Passover meal.

20 When it was evening, he took his
place with the twelve;[j] 21and while they
were eating, he said, 'Truly I tell you,
one of you will betray me.' 22And they
became greatly distressed and began to
say to him one after another, 'Surely not
I, Lord?' 23He answered, 'The one who
has dipped his hand into the bowl with

[g] **25.40** Gk *these my brothers* [h] **26.6** The terms *leper* and *leprosy* can refer to several diseases [i] **26.13** Or *gospel* [j] **26.20** Other ancient authorities add *disciples*

me will betray me. 24The Son of Man
goes as it is written of him, but woe to
that one by whom the Son of Man is
betrayed! It would have been better for
that one not to have been born.' 25Judas,
who betrayed him, said, 'Surely not I,
Rabbi?' He replied, 'You have said so.'

THE INSTITUTION OF THE LORD'S SUPPER

26 While they were eating, Jesus took
a loaf of bread, and after blessing it he
broke it, gave it to the disciples, and
said, 'Take, eat; this is my body.' 27Then
he took a cup, and after giving thanks
he gave it to them, saying, 'Drink from
it, all of you; 28for this is my blood of
the[k] covenant, which is poured out for
many for the forgiveness of sins. 29I tell
you, I will never again drink of this fruit
of the vine until that day when I drink it
new with you in my Father's kingdom.'

30 When they had sung the hymn,
they went out to the Mount of Olives.

PETER'S DENIAL FORETOLD

31 Then Jesus said to them, 'You will
all become deserters because of me this
night; for it is written,

"I will strike the shepherd,
and the sheep of the flock
will be scattered."

32But after I am raised up, I will go
ahead of you to Galilee.' 33Peter said to
him, 'Though all become deserters because of you, I will never desert you.'
34Jesus said to him, 'Truly I tell you, this
very night, before the cock crows, you
will deny me three times.' 35Peter said
to him, 'Even though I must die with
you, I will not deny you.' And so said all
the disciples.

JESUS PRAYS IN GETHSEMANE

36 Then Jesus went with them to a
place called Gethsemane; and he said
to his disciples, 'Sit here while I go over
there and pray.' 37He took with him Peter and the two sons of Zebedee, and began to be grieved and agitated. 38Then
he said to them, 'I am deeply grieved,
even to death; remain here, and stay
awake with me.' 39And going a little farther, he threw himself on the ground
and prayed, 'My Father, if it is possible,
let this cup pass from me; yet not what
I want but what you want.' 40Then he
came to the disciples and found them
sleeping; and he said to Peter, 'So, could
you not stay awake with me one hour?
41Stay awake and pray that you may not
come into the time of trial;[l] the spirit
indeed is willing, but the flesh is weak.'
42Again he went away for the second
time and prayed, 'My Father, if this cannot pass unless I drink it, your will be
done.' 43Again he came and found them
sleeping, for their eyes were heavy. 44So
leaving them again, he went away and
prayed for the third time, saying the
same words. 45Then he came to the disciples and said to them, 'Are you still
sleeping and taking your rest? See, the
hour is at hand, and the Son of Man
is betrayed into the hands of sinners.
46Get up, let us be going. See, my betrayer is at hand.'

THE BETRAYAL AND ARREST OF JESUS

47 While he was still speaking, Judas,
one of the twelve, arrived; with him was
a large crowd with swords and clubs,
from the chief priests and the elders
of the people. 48Now the betrayer had
given them a sign, saying, 'The one I will
kiss is the man; arrest him.' 49At once
he came up to Jesus and said, 'Greetings,
Rabbi!' and kissed him. 50Jesus said to
him, 'Friend, do what you are here to
do.' Then they came and laid hands on
Jesus and arrested him. 51Suddenly,
one of those with Jesus put his hand
on his sword, drew it, and struck the
slave of the high priest, cutting off his
ear. 52Then Jesus said to him, 'Put your
sword back into its place; for all who
take the sword will perish by the sword.
53Do you think that I cannot appeal to
my Father, and he will at once send me
more than twelve legions of angels?
54But how then would the scriptures
be fulfilled, which say it must happen
in this way?' 55At that hour Jesus said
to the crowds, 'Have you come out with
swords and clubs to arrest me as though
I were a bandit? Day after day I sat in
the temple teaching, and you did not arrest me. 56But all this has taken place,
so that the scriptures of the prophets
may be fulfilled.' Then all the disciples
deserted him and fled.

JESUS BEFORE THE HIGH PRIEST

57 Those who had arrested Jesus
took him to Caiaphas the high priest, in
whose house the scribes and the elders
had gathered. 58But Peter was following
him at a distance, as far as the courtyard

[k] **26.28** Other ancient authorities add *new*
[l] **26.41** Or *into temptation*

of the high priest; and going inside, he
sat with the guards in order to see how
this would end. 59 Now the chief priests
and the whole council were looking for
false testimony against Jesus so that
they might put him to death, 60 but they
found none, though many false witnesses came forward. At last two came
forward 61 and said, 'This fellow said, "I
am able to destroy the temple of God
and to build it in three days." ' 62 The
high priest stood up and said, 'Have you
no answer? What is it that they testify
against you?' 63 But Jesus was silent.
Then the high priest said to him, 'I put
you under oath before the living God,
tell us if you are the Messiah,[m] the Son
of God.' 64 Jesus said to him, 'You have
said so. But I tell you,

From now on you will see
 the Son of Man
 seated at the right hand of Power
 and coming on the clouds
 of heaven.'

65 Then the high priest tore his clothes
and said, 'He has blasphemed! Why do
we still need witnesses? You have now
heard his blasphemy. 66 What is your
verdict?' They answered, 'He deserves
death.' 67 Then they spat in his face and
struck him; and some slapped him,
68 saying, 'Prophesy to us, you Messiah![n]
Who is it that struck you?'

PETER'S DENIAL OF JESUS

69 Now Peter was sitting outside in
the courtyard. A servant-girl came to
him and said, 'You also were with Jesus
the Galilean.' 70 But he denied it before all
of them, saying, 'I do not know what you
are talking about.' 71 When he went out to
the porch, another servant-girl saw him,
and she said to the bystanders, 'This man
was with Jesus of Nazareth.'[o] 72 Again he
denied it with an oath, 'I do not know the
man.' 73 After a little while the bystanders came up and said to Peter, 'Certainly
you are also one of them, for your accent
betrays you.' 74 Then he began to curse,
and he swore an oath, 'I do not know the
man!' At that moment the cock crowed.
75 Then Peter remembered what Jesus
had said: 'Before the cock crows, you will
deny me three times.' And he went out
and wept bitterly.

JESUS BROUGHT BEFORE PILATE

27 When morning came, all the
chief priests and the elders of
the people conferred together against
Jesus in order to bring about his death.
2 They bound him, led him away, and
handed him over to Pilate the governor.

THE SUICIDE OF JUDAS

3 When Judas, his betrayer, saw that
Jesus[p] was condemned, he repented and
brought back the thirty pieces of silver
to the chief priests and the elders. 4 He
said, 'I have sinned by betraying innocent[q] blood.' But they said, 'What is
that to us? See to it yourself.' 5 Throwing
down the pieces of silver in the temple,
he departed; and he went and hanged
himself. 6 But the chief priests, taking
the pieces of silver, said, 'It is not lawful to put them into the treasury, since
they are blood money.' 7 After confer-
ring together, they used them to buy
the potter's field as a place to bury foreigners. 8 For this reason that field has
been called the Field of Blood to this
day. 9 Then was fulfilled what had been
spoken through the prophet Jeremi-
ah,[r] 'And they took[s] the thirty pieces of
silver, the price of the one on whom a
price had been set,[t] on whom some of
the people of Israel had set a price, 10 and
they gave[u] them for the potter's field, as
the Lord commanded me.'

PILATE QUESTIONS JESUS

11 Now Jesus stood before the governor; and the governor asked him, 'Are
you the King of the Jews?' Jesus said,
'You say so.' 12 But when he was accused
by the chief priests and elders, he did
not answer. 13 Then Pilate said to him,
'Do you not hear how many accusations
they make against you?' 14 But he gave
him no answer, not even to a single
charge, so that the governor was greatly
amazed.

BARABBAS OR JESUS?

15 Now at the festival the governor
was accustomed to release a prisoner for
the crowd, anyone whom they wanted.
16 At that time they had a notorious
prisoner, called Jesus[v] Barabbas. 17 So
after they had gathered, Pilate said to
them, 'Whom do you want me to release
for you, Jesus[w] Barabbas or Jesus who is
called the Messiah?'[x] 18 For he realized

[m] 26.63 Or *Christ* [n] 26.68 Or *Christ*
[o] 26.71 Gk *the Nazorean* [p] 27.3 Gk *he*
[q] 27.4 Other ancient authorities read *righteous*
[r] 27.9 Other ancient authorities read *Zechariah* or *Isaiah* [s] 27.9 Or *I took* [t] 27.9 Or *the price of the precious One* [u] 27.10 Other ancient authorities read *I gave* [v] 27.16 Other ancient authorities lack *Jesus* [w] 27.17 Other ancient authorities lack *Jesus* [x] 27.17 Or *the Christ*

that it was out of jealousy that they had
handed him over. 19 While he was sitting
on the judgement seat, his wife sent
word to him, 'Have nothing to do with
that innocent man, for today I have suffered a great deal because of a dream
about him.' 20 Now the chief priests and
the elders persuaded the crowds to ask
for Barabbas and to have Jesus killed.
21 The governor again said to them,
'Which of the two do you want me to release for you?' And they said, 'Barabbas.'
22 Pilate said to them, 'Then what should
I do with Jesus who is called the Messiah?'[y] All of them said, 'Let him be crucified!' 23 Then he asked, 'Why, what evil
has he done?' But they shouted all the
more, 'Let him be crucified!'

PILATE HANDS JESUS OVER TO BE CRUCIFIED

24 So when Pilate saw that he could
do nothing, but rather that a riot was
beginning, he took some water and
washed his hands before the crowd, saying, 'I am innocent of this man's blood;[z]
see to it yourselves.' 25 Then the people as
a whole answered, 'His blood be on us
and on our children!' 26 So he released
Barabbas for them; and after flogging
Jesus, he handed him over to be crucified.

THE SOLDIERS MOCK JESUS

27 Then the soldiers of the governor
took Jesus into the governor's headquarters,[a] and they gathered the whole
cohort around him. 28 They stripped him
and put a scarlet robe on him, 29 and after twisting some thorns into a crown,
they put it on his head. They put a reed
in his right hand and knelt before him
and mocked him, saying, 'Hail, King of
the Jews!' 30 They spat on him, and took
the reed and struck him on the head.
31 After mocking him, they stripped him
of the robe and put his own clothes on
him. Then they led him away to crucify
him.

THE CRUCIFIXION OF JESUS

32 As they went out, they came upon
a man from Cyrene named Simon;
they compelled this man to carry his
cross. 33 And when they came to a place
called Golgotha (which means Place of a
Skull), 34 they offered him wine to drink,
mixed with gall; but when he tasted
it, he would not drink it. 35 And when
they had crucified him, they divided his
clothes among themselves by casting
lots;[b] 36 then they sat down there and
kept watch over him. 37 Over his head
they put the charge against him, which
read, 'This is Jesus, the King of the Jews.'

38 Then two bandits were crucified
with him, one on his right and one on
his left. 39 Those who passed by derided[c]
him, shaking their heads 40 and saying,
'You who would destroy the temple and
build it in three days, save yourself!
If you are the Son of God, come down
from the cross.' 41 In the same way the
chief priests also, along with the scribes
and elders, were mocking him, saying,
42 'He saved others; he cannot save himself.[d] He is the King of Israel; let him
come down from the cross now, and we
will believe in him. 43 He trusts in God;
let God deliver him now, if he wants to;
for he said, "I am God's Son." ' 44 The bandits who were crucified with him also
taunted him in the same way.

THE DEATH OF JESUS

45 From noon on, darkness came
over the whole land[e] until three in the
afternoon. 46 And about three o'clock
Jesus cried with a loud voice, 'Eli, Eli,
lema sabachthani?' that is, 'My God,
my God, why have you forsaken me?'
47 When some of the bystanders heard
it, they said, 'This man is calling for
Elijah.' 48 At once one of them ran and
got a sponge, filled it with sour wine,
put it on a stick, and gave it to him to
drink. 49 But the others said, 'Wait, let
us see whether Elijah will come to save
him.'[f] 50 Then Jesus cried again with a
loud voice and breathed his last.[g] 51 At
that moment the curtain of the temple
was torn in two, from top to bottom.
The earth shook, and the rocks were
split. 52 The tombs also were opened,
and many bodies of the saints who had
fallen asleep were raised. 53 After his resurrection they came out of the tombs
and entered the holy city and appeared
to many. 54 Now when the centurion
and those with him, who were keeping
watch over Jesus, saw the earthquake

[y] **27.22** Or *the Christ* [z] **27.24** Other ancient authorities read *this righteous blood, or this righteous man's blood* [a] **27.27** Gk *the praetorium* [b] **27.35** Other ancient authorities add *in order that what had been spoken through the prophet might be fulfilled, 'They divided my clothes among themselves, and for my clothing they cast lots.'* [c] **27.39** Or *blasphemed* [d] **27.42** Or *is he unable to save himself?* [e] **27.45** Or *earth* [f] **27.49** Other ancient authorities add *And another took a spear and pierced his side, and out came water and blood* [g] **27.50** Or *gave up his spirit*

and what took place, they were terrified and said, 'Truly this man was God's
Son!'[h]
55 Many women were also there,
looking on from a distance; they had
followed Jesus from Galilee and had
provided for him. 56 Among them were
Mary Magdalene, and Mary the mother
of James and Joseph, and the mother of
the sons of Zebedee.

THE BURIAL OF JESUS

57 When it was evening, there came
a rich man from Arimathea, named Joseph, who was also a disciple of Jesus.
58 He went to Pilate and asked for the
body of Jesus; then Pilate ordered it to
be given to him. 59 So Joseph took the
body and wrapped it in a clean linen
cloth 60 and laid it in his own new tomb,
which he had hewn in the rock. He then
rolled a great stone to the door of the
tomb and went away. 61 Mary Magdalene and the other Mary were there, sitting opposite the tomb.

THE GUARD AT THE TOMB

62 The next day, that is, after the
day of Preparation, the chief priests
and the Pharisees gathered before Pilate 63 and said, 'Sir, we remember what
that impostor said while he was still
alive, "After three days I will rise again."
64 Therefore command that the tomb be
made secure until the third day; otherwise his disciples may go and steal him
away, and tell the people, "He has been
raised from the dead", and the last deception would be worse than the first.'
65 Pilate said to them, 'You have a guard[i]
of soldiers; go, make it as secure as you
can.'[j] 66 So they went with the guard
and made the tomb secure by sealing
the stone.

THE RESURRECTION OF JESUS

28 After the sabbath, as the first
day of the week was dawning,
Mary Magdalene and the other Mary
went to see the tomb. 2 And suddenly
there was a great earthquake; for an
angel of the Lord, descending from
heaven, came and rolled back the stone
and sat on it. 3 His appearance was like
lightning, and his clothing white as
snow. 4 For fear of him the guards shook
and became like dead men. 5 But the angel said to the women, 'Do not be afraid;
I know that you are looking for Jesus
who was crucified. 6 He is not here; for
he has been raised, as he said. Come,
see the place where he[k] lay. 7 Then go
quickly and tell his disciples, "He has
been raised from the dead,[l] and indeed
he is going ahead of you to Galilee; there
you will see him." This is my message for
you.' 8 So they left the tomb quickly with
fear and great joy, and ran to tell his disciples. 9 Suddenly Jesus met them and
said, 'Greetings!' And they came to him,
took hold of his feet, and worshipped
him. 10 Then Jesus said to them, 'Do not
be afraid; go and tell my brothers to go
to Galilee; there they will see me.'

THE REPORT OF THE GUARD

11 While they were going, some of
the guard went into the city and told
the chief priests everything that had
happened. 12 After the priests[m] had assembled with the elders, they devised
a plan to give a large sum of money to
the soldiers, 13 telling them, 'You must
say, "His disciples came by night and
stole him away while we were asleep."
14 If this comes to the governor's ears,
we will satisfy him and keep you out of
trouble.' 15 So they took the money and
did as they were directed. And this story
is still told among the Jews to this day.

THE COMMISSIONING OF THE DISCIPLES

16 Now the eleven disciples went to
Galilee, to the mountain to which Jesus
had directed them. 17 When they saw
him, they worshipped him; but some
doubted. 18 And Jesus came and said to
them, 'All authority in heaven and on
earth has been given to me. 19 Go therefore and make disciples of all nations,
baptizing them in the name of the Father and of the Son and of the Holy
Spirit, 20 and teaching them to obey everything that I have commanded you.
And remember, I am with you always,
to the end of the age.'[n]

[h] **27.54** Or *a son of God* [i] **27.65** Or *Take a guard*
[j] **27.65** Gk *you know how* [k] **28.6** Other ancient
authorities read *the Lord* [l] **28.7** Other ancient
authorities lack *from the dead* [m] **28.12** Gk *they*
[n] **28.20** Other ancient authorities add *Amen*

The Gospel According to

MARK

Even though the Gospel of Mark is the earliest and shortest account of Jesus' life and death, this narrative should not be underestimated for the sophistication of its literary development. Written sometime in the late 60s by a Greek-speaking Christian, the Gospel contains stories about Jesus' teachings and miracles that are also taken up in Matthew and Luke a decade or two later. Mark's Gospel is more than a brief collection of the words and deeds of Jesus. It is a carefully developed account that responds to Jesus' question, "Who do people say that I am?" (8.27). The Gospel of Mark is the first known attempt by an evangelist to present in writing a testimony about the true meaning and purpose of Jesus' life.

Mark's Gospel has a distinctive emphasis that seeks to explain how Jesus is the Messiah, the Son of God (1.1). The Gospel narrates how Jesus performs unusual and miraculous works and how his teachings are received with wonder and amazement by his disciples. But the more spectacular his words and deeds, the more curious is the question about the identity of Jesus. Even after Peter answers Jesus' question by declaring, "You are the Messiah" (8.29), the literary suspense about Jesus continues, and Peter and the other disciples still misunderstand what it means to be the Messiah. The disciples seem to expect the Messiah to be a person of worldly power and glory, rather than one who must suffer and give up his life as a ransom for others.

The second half of Mark's Gospel goes on to show that the Messiah must suffer and die in order to be the true Son of God. In fact, it is at the climactic moment toward the end of the Gospel when Jesus literally dies on the cross that the centurion declares, "Truly this man was God's Son!" (15.39). This finally reveals the mystery surrounding the true identity of Jesus developed in Mark's Gospel. For Mark, Jesus really is the true Messiah, Son of God, especially because of his passion and sacrifice. The proper response for the followers of Jesus is to "take up their cross and follow" him (8.34).

The Gospel of Mark has special significance for readers who lived during the time of Nero's persecution of Christians (64 CE) or during the crushing of the Jewish revolt against imperial Rome (67–70). The threat of persecution of the followers of Jesus seems to be the background of the writing of Mark's Gospel.

Today Mark's Gospel is read during the liturgy on Sundays of Year B of the liturgical calendar. Also, Mark's passion narrative is read on Palm Sunday in the same liturgical Year B. His account is especially noteworthy because of its depiction of Jesus' expressed emotion and very human reaction to the events (14.33–34; 14.48–49; 15.34, 37).

THE PROCLAMATION OF JOHN THE BAPTIST

1 The beginning of the good news[a] of
Jesus Christ, the Son of God.[b]
2 As it is written in the prophet Isaiah,[c]

'See, I am sending my messenger
ahead of you,[d]
who will prepare your way;
3 the voice of one crying out in
the wilderness:
"Prepare the way of the Lord,
make his paths straight"',

4John the baptizer appeared[e] in the
wilderness, proclaiming a baptism of
repentance for the forgiveness of sins.
5And people from the whole Judean
countryside and all the people of Jerusalem were going out to him, and were
baptized by him in the river Jordan,
confessing their sins. 6Now John was
clothed with camel's hair, with a leather
belt around his waist, and he ate locusts
and wild honey. 7He proclaimed, 'The
one who is more powerful than I is coming after me; I am not worthy to stoop
down and untie the thong of his sandals. 8I have baptized you with[f] water;
but he will baptize you with[g] the Holy
Spirit.'

THE BAPTISM OF JESUS

9 In those days Jesus came from
Nazareth of Galilee and was baptized
by John in the Jordan. 10And just as he
was coming up out of the water, he saw
the heavens torn apart and the Spirit
descending like a dove on him. 11And
a voice came from heaven, 'You are my
Son, the Beloved;[h] with you I am well
pleased.'

THE TEMPTATION OF JESUS

12 And the Spirit immediately drove
him out into the wilderness. 13He was in
the wilderness for forty days, tempted
by Satan; and he was with the wild
beasts; and the angels waited on him.

THE BEGINNING OF THE GALILEAN MINISTRY

14 Now after John was arrested,
Jesus came to Galilee, proclaiming the
good news[i] of God,[j] 15and saying, 'The
time is fulfilled, and the kingdom of God
has come near;[k] repent, and believe in
the good news.'[l]

JESUS CALLS THE FIRST DISCIPLES

16 As Jesus passed along the Sea of
Galilee, he saw Simon and his brother
Andrew casting a net into the lake—for
they were fishermen. 17And Jesus said
to them, 'Follow me and I will make you
fish for people.' 18And immediately they
left their nets and followed him. 19As he
went a little farther, he saw James son of
Zebedee and his brother John, who were
in their boat mending the nets. 20Im-
mediately he called them; and they left
their father Zebedee in the boat with
the hired men, and followed him.

THE MAN WITH AN UNCLEAN SPIRIT

21 They went to Capernaum; and
when the sabbath came, he entered the
synagogue and taught. 22They were astounded at his teaching, for he taught
them as one having authority, and not
as the scribes. 23Just then there was in
their synagogue a man with an unclean
spirit, 24and he cried out, 'What have
you to do with us, Jesus of Nazareth?
Have you come to destroy us? I know
who you are, the Holy One of God.' 25But
Jesus rebuked him, saying, 'Be silent,
and come out of him!' 26And the unclean spirit, throwing him into convulsions and crying with a loud voice, came
out of him. 27They were all amazed, and
they kept on asking one another, 'What
is this? A new teaching—with authority! He[m] commands even the unclean
spirits, and they obey him.' 28At once
his fame began to spread throughout
the surrounding region of Galilee.

JESUS HEALS MANY AT SIMON'S HOUSE

29 As soon as they[n] left the synagogue, they entered the house of Simon
and Andrew, with James and John.
30Now Simon's mother-in-law was
in bed with a fever, and they told him
about her at once. 31He came and took
her by the hand and lifted her up. Then
the fever left her, and she began to serve
them.

32 That evening, at sunset, they
brought to him all who were sick or
possessed with demons. 33And the
whole city was gathered around the
door. 34And he cured many who were

[a] 1.1 Or *gospel* [b] 1.1 Other ancient authorities lack *the Son of God* [c] 1.2 Other ancient authorities read *in the prophets* [d] 1.2 Gk *before your face* [e] 1.4 Other ancient authorities read *John was baptizing* [f] 1.8 Or *in* [g] 1.8 Or *in* [h] 1.11 Or *my beloved Son* [i] 1.14 Or *gospel* [j] 1.14 Other ancient authorities read *of the kingdom* [k] 1.15 Or *is at hand* [l] 1.15 Or *gospel* [m] 1.27 Or *A new teaching! With authority he* [n] 1.29 Other ancient authorities read *he*

sick with various diseases, and cast out
many demons; and he would not permit the demons to speak, because they
knew him.

A PREACHING TOUR IN GALILEE

35 In the morning, while it was still
very dark, he got up and went out to a
deserted place, and there he prayed.
36And Simon and his companions
hunted for him. 37When they found
him, they said to him, 'Everyone is
searching for you.' 38He answered, 'Let
us go on to the neighbouring towns, so
that I may proclaim the message there
also; for that is what I came out to do.'
39And he went throughout Galilee, proclaiming the message in their synagogues and casting out demons.

JESUS CLEANSES A LEPER

40 A leper[o] came to him begging
him, and kneeling[p] he said to him, 'If
you choose, you can make me clean.'
41Moved with pity,[q] Jesus[r] stretched out
his hand and touched him, and said to
him, 'I do choose. Be made clean!' 42Im-
mediately the leprosy[s] left him, and he
was made clean. 43After sternly warning
him he sent him away at once, 44saying
to him, 'See that you say nothing to anyone; but go, show yourself to the priest,
and offer for your cleansing what Moses
commanded, as a testimony to them.'
45But he went out and began to proclaim it freely, and to spread the word,
so that Jesus[t] could no longer go into a
town openly, but stayed out in the country; and people came to him from every
quarter.

JESUS HEALS A PARALYTIC

2 When he returned to Capernaum
after some days, it was reported
that he was at home. 2So many gathered around that there was no longer
room for them, not even in front of the
door; and he was speaking the word to
them. 3Then some people[u] came, bringing to him a paralysed man, carried by
four of them. 4And when they could
not bring him to Jesus because of the
crowd, they removed the roof above
him; and after having dug through it,
they let down the mat on which the paralytic lay. 5When Jesus saw their faith,
he said to the paralytic, 'Son, your sins
are forgiven.' 6Now some of the scribes
were sitting there, questioning in their
hearts, 7'Why does this fellow speak
in this way? It is blasphemy! Who can
forgive sins but God alone?' 8At once
Jesus perceived in his spirit that they
were discussing these questions among
themselves; and he said to them, 'Why
do you raise such questions in your
hearts? 9Which is easier, to say to the
paralytic, "Your sins are forgiven", or to
say, "Stand up and take your mat and
walk"? 10But so that you may know that
the Son of Man has authority on earth
to forgive sins'—he said to the paralytic— 11'I say to you, stand up, take your
mat and go to your home.' 12And he
stood up, and immediately took the mat
and went out before all of them; so that
they were all amazed and glorified God,
saying, 'We have never seen anything
like this!'

JESUS CALLS LEVI

13 Jesus[v] went out again beside the
lake; the whole crowd gathered around
him, and he taught them. 14As he was
walking along, he saw Levi son of Alphaeus sitting at the tax booth, and he
said to him, 'Follow me.' And he got up
and followed him.

15 And as he sat at dinner[w] in Levi's[x]
house, many tax-collectors and sinners
were also sitting[y] with Jesus and his
disciples—for there were many who followed him. 16When the scribes of[z] the
Pharisees saw that he was eating with
sinners and tax-collectors, they said to
his disciples, 'Why does he eat[a] with tax-
collectors and sinners?' 17When Jesus
heard this, he said to them, 'Those who
are well have no need of a physician, but
those who are sick; I have come to call
not the righteous but sinners.'

THE QUESTION ABOUT FASTING

18 Now John's disciples and the Pharisees were fasting; and people[b] came
and said to him, 'Why do John's disciples
and the disciples of the Pharisees fast,
but your disciples do not fast?' 19Jesus
said to them, 'The wedding-guests cannot fast while the bridegroom is with
them, can they? As long as they have
the bridegroom with them, they cannot fast. 20The days will come when the

[o] **1.40** The terms *leper* and *leprosy* can refer to several diseases [p] **1.40** Other ancient authorities lack *kneeling* [q] **1.41** Other ancient authorities read *anger* [r] **1.41** Gk *he* [s] **1.42** The terms *leper* and *leprosy* can refer to several diseases [t] **1.45** Gk *he* [u] **2.3** Gk *they* [v] **2.13** Gk *He* [w] **2.15** Gk *reclined* [x] **2.15** Gk *his* [y] **2.15** Gk *reclining* [z] **2.16** Other ancient authorities read *and* [a] **2.16** Other ancient authorities add *and drink* [b] **2.18** Gk *they*

bridegroom is taken away from them,
and then they will fast on that day.
21 'No one sews a piece of unshrunk
cloth on an old cloak; otherwise, the
patch pulls away from it, the new from
the old, and a worse tear is made. 22And
no one puts new wine into old wineskins; otherwise, the wine will burst
the skins, and the wine is lost, and so
are the skins; but one puts new wine
into fresh wineskins.'[c]

PRONOUNCEMENT ABOUT THE SABBATH

23 One sabbath he was going through
the cornfields; and as they made their
way his disciples began to pluck heads
of grain. 24The Pharisees said to him,
'Look, why are they doing what is not
lawful on the sabbath?' 25And he said to
them, 'Have you never read what David
did when he and his companions were
hungry and in need of food? 26He entered the house of God, when Abiathar
was high priest, and ate the bread of
the Presence, which it is not lawful for
any but the priests to eat, and he gave
some to his companions.' 27Then he said
to them, 'The sabbath was made for humankind, and not humankind for the
sabbath; 28so the Son of Man is lord
even of the sabbath.'

THE MAN WITH A WITHERED HAND

3 Again he entered the synagogue,
and a man was there who had a
withered hand. 2They watched him to
see whether he would cure him on the
sabbath, so that they might accuse him.
3And he said to the man who had the
withered hand, 'Come forward.' 4Then
he said to them, 'Is it lawful to do good
or to do harm on the sabbath, to save
life or to kill?' But they were silent. 5He
looked around at them with anger; he
was grieved at their hardness of heart
and said to the man, 'Stretch out your
hand.' He stretched it out, and his hand
was restored. 6The Pharisees went out
and immediately conspired with the
Herodians against him, how to destroy
him.

A MULTITUDE AT THE LAKESIDE

7 Jesus departed with his disciples
to the lake, and a great multitude from
Galilee followed him; 8hearing all that
he was doing, they came to him in great
numbers from Judea, Jerusalem, Idumea, beyond the Jordan, and the region
around Tyre and Sidon. 9He told his disciples to have a boat ready for him because of the crowd, so that they would
not crush him; 10for he had cured many,
so that all who had diseases pressed
upon him to touch him. 11Whenever the
unclean spirits saw him, they fell down
before him and shouted, 'You are the
Son of God!' 12But he sternly ordered
them not to make him known.

JESUS APPOINTS THE TWELVE

13 He went up the mountain and
called to him those whom he wanted,
and they came to him. 14And he appointed twelve, whom he also named
apostles,[d] to be with him, and to be sent
out to proclaim the message, 15and to
have authority to cast out demons. 16So
he appointed the twelve:[e] Simon (to
whom he gave the name Peter); 17James
son of Zebedee and John the brother of
James (to whom he gave the name Boa-
nerges, that is, Sons of Thunder); 18and
Andrew, and Philip, and Bartholomew,
and Matthew, and Thomas, and James
son of Alphaeus, and Thaddaeus, and Simon the Cananaean, 19and Judas Iscariot, who betrayed him.

JESUS AND BEELZEBUL

Then he went home; 20and the crowd
came together again, so that they could
not even eat. 21When his family heard
it, they went out to restrain him, for
people were saying, 'He has gone out of
his mind.' 22And the scribes who came
down from Jerusalem said, 'He has Beelzebul, and by the ruler of the demons he
casts out demons.' 23And he called them
to him, and spoke to them in parables,
'How can Satan cast out Satan? 24If a
kingdom is divided against itself, that
kingdom cannot stand. 25And if a house
is divided against itself, that house will
not be able to stand. 26And if Satan has
risen up against himself and is divided,
he cannot stand, but his end has come.
27But no one can enter a strong man's
house and plunder his property without
first tying up the strong man; then indeed the house can be plundered.
28 'Truly I tell you, people will be
forgiven for their sins and whatever
blasphemies they utter; 29but whoever
blasphemes against the Holy Spirit can
never have forgiveness, but is guilty of

[c] **2.22** Other ancient authorities lack *but one puts new wine into fresh wineskins* [d] **3.14** Other ancient authorities lack *whom he also named apostles* [e] **3.16** Other ancient authorities lack *So he appointed the twelve*

Our Father

Our Father in heaven,
hallowed be your name.
Your kingdom come.
Your will be done,
on earth as it is in heaven.
Give us this day our daily bread.
And forgive us our debts,
as we also have forgiven our debtors.
And do not bring us to the time of trial,
but rescue us from the evil one.

Matthew 6:9–13

Knock, and the door will be opened for you.

MATTHEW 7:7

The Son of Man came to seek out and to save the lost.

LUKE 19:10

For God so loved the world
that he gave his only Son.

JOHN 3:16

shrubs, and puts forth large branches,
so that the birds of the air can make
nests in its shade.'

THE USE OF PARABLES

33 With many such parables he spoke
the word to them, as they were able to
hear it; 34he did not speak to them except in parables, but he explained everything in private to his disciples.

JESUS STILLS A STORM

35 On that day, when evening had
come, he said to them, 'Let us go across
to the other side.' 36And leaving the
crowd behind, they took him with them
in the boat, just as he was. Other boats
were with him. 37A great gale arose, and
the waves beat into the boat, so that the
boat was already being swamped. 38But
he was in the stern, asleep on the cush-
ion; and they woke him up and said to
him, 'Teacher, do you not care that we
are perishing?' 39He woke up and rebuked the wind, and said to the sea,
'Peace! Be still!' Then the wind ceased,
and there was a dead calm. 40He said
to them, 'Why are you afraid? Have you
still no faith?' 41And they were filled
with great awe and said to one another,
'Who then is this, that even the wind
and the sea obey him?'

JESUS HEALS THE GERASENE DEMONIAC

5 They came to the other side of the
lake, to the country of the Gerasenes.[i] 2And when he had stepped out
of the boat, immediately a man out of
the tombs with an unclean spirit met
him. 3He lived among the tombs; and no
one could restrain him any more, even
with a chain; 4for he had often been restrained with shackles and chains, but
the chains he wrenched apart, and the
shackles he broke in pieces; and no one
had the strength to subdue him. 5Night
and day among the tombs and on the
mountains he was always howling and
bruising himself with stones. 6When
he saw Jesus from a distance, he ran
and bowed down before him; 7and he
shouted at the top of his voice, 'What
have you to do with me, Jesus, Son of
the Most High God? I adjure you by God,
do not torment me.' 8For he had said to
him, 'Come out of the man, you unclean
spirit!' 9Then Jesus[j] asked him, 'What
is your name?' He replied, 'My name is
Legion; for we are many.' 10He begged
him earnestly not to send them out of
the country. 11Now there on the hillside
a great herd of swine was feeding; 12and
the unclean spirits[k] begged him, 'Send
us into the swine; let us enter them.'
13So he gave them permission. And
the unclean spirits came out and entered the swine; and the herd, numbering about two thousand, rushed down
the steep bank into the lake, and were
drowned in the lake.

14 The swineherds ran off and told
it in the city and in the country. Then
people came to see what it was that had
happened. 15They came to Jesus and
saw the demoniac sitting there, clothed
and in his right mind, the very man
who had had the legion; and they were
afraid. 16Those who had seen what had
happened to the demoniac and to the
swine reported it. 17Then they began to
beg Jesus[l] to leave their neighbourhood.
18As he was getting into the boat, the
man who had been possessed by demons begged him that he might be with
him. 19But Jesus[m] refused, and said to
him, 'Go home to your friends, and tell
them how much the Lord has done for
you, and what mercy he has shown you.'
20And he went away and began to proclaim in the Decapolis how much Jesus
had done for him; and everyone was
amazed.

A GIRL RESTORED TO LIFE AND A WOMAN HEALED

21 When Jesus had crossed again
in the boat[n] to the other side, a great
crowd gathered round him; and he was
by the lake. 22Then one of the leaders of
the synagogue named Jairus came and,
when he saw him, fell at his feet 23and
begged him repeatedly, 'My little daughter is at the point of death. Come and lay
your hands on her, so that she may be
made well, and live.' 24So he went with
him.

And a large crowd followed him and
pressed in on him. 25Now there was a
woman who had been suffering from
haemorrhages for twelve years. 26She
had endured much under many physicians, and had spent all that she had;
and she was no better, but rather grew
worse. 27She had heard about Jesus,
and came up behind him in the crowd
and touched his cloak, 28for she said, 'If
I but touch his clothes, I will be made

[i] 5.1 Other ancient authorities read *Gergesenes*; others, *Gadarenes* [j] 5.9 Gk *he* [k] 5.12 Gk *they* [l] 5.17 Gk *him* [m] 5.19 Gk *he* [n] 5.21 Other ancient authorities lack *in the boat*

an eternal sin'— 30for they had said, 'He
has an unclean spirit.'

THE TRUE KINDRED OF JESUS

31 Then his mother and his brothers
came; and standing outside, they sent to
him and called him. 32A crowd was sitting around him; and they said to him,
'Your mother and your brothers and sisters[f] are outside, asking for you.' 33And
he replied, 'Who are my mother and my
brothers?' 34And looking at those who
sat around him, he said, 'Here are my
mother and my brothers! 35Whoever
does the will of God is my brother and
sister and mother.'

THE PARABLE OF THE SOWER

4 Again he began to teach beside
the lake. Such a very large crowd
gathered around him that he got into
a boat on the lake and sat there, while
the whole crowd was beside the lake on
the land. 2He began to teach them many
things in parables, and in his teaching
he said to them: 3'Listen! A sower went
out to sow. 4And as he sowed, some
seed fell on the path, and the birds came
and ate it up. 5Other seed fell on rocky
ground, where it did not have much
soil, and it sprang up quickly, since it
had no depth of soil. 6And when the
sun rose, it was scorched; and since it
had no root, it withered away. 7Other
seed fell among thorns, and the thorns
grew up and choked it, and it yielded no
grain. 8Other seed fell into good soil and
brought forth grain, growing up and increasing and yielding thirty and sixty
and a hundredfold.' 9And he said, 'Let
anyone with ears to hear listen!'

THE PURPOSE OF THE PARABLES

10 When he was alone, those who
were around him along with the twelve
asked him about the parables. 11And he
said to them, 'To you has been given the
secret[g] of the kingdom of God, but for
those outside, everything comes in parables; 12in order that
"they may indeed look, but
not perceive,
and may indeed listen, but
not understand;
so that they may not turn again
and be forgiven."'
13 And he said to them, 'Do you not
understand this parable? Then how
will you understand all the parables?
14The sower sows the word. 15These are
the ones on the path where the word
is sown: when they hear, Satan immediately comes and takes away the word
that is sown in them. 16And these are
the ones sown on rocky ground: when
they hear the word, they immediately
receive it with joy. 17But they have no
root, and endure only for a while; then,
when trouble or persecution arises on
account of the word, immediately they
fall away.[h] 18And others are those sown
among the thorns: these are the ones
who hear the word, 19but the cares of
the world, and the lure of wealth, and
the desire for other things come in and
choke the word, and it yields nothing.
20And these are the ones sown on the
good soil: they hear the word and accept
it and bear fruit, thirty and sixty and a
hundredfold.'

A LAMP UNDER A BUSHEL BASKET

21 He said to them, 'Is a lamp brought
in to be put under the bushel basket, or
under the bed, and not on the lampstand? 22For there is nothing hidden,
except to be disclosed; nor is anything
secret, except to come to light. 23Let
anyone with ears to hear listen!' 24And
he said to them, 'Pay attention to what
you hear; the measure you give will be
the measure you get, and still more will
be given you. 25For to those who have,
more will be given; and from those who
have nothing, even what they have will
be taken away.'

THE PARABLE OF THE GROWING SEED

26 He also said, 'The kingdom of God
is as if someone would scatter seed on
the ground, 27and would sleep and
rise night and day, and the seed would
sprout and grow, he does not know how.
28The earth produces of itself, first the
stalk, then the head, then the full grain
in the head. 29But when the grain is
ripe, at once he goes in with his sickle,
because the harvest has come.'

THE PARABLE OF THE MUSTARD SEED

30 He also said, 'With what can we
compare the kingdom of God, or what
parable will we use for it? 31It is like a
mustard seed, which, when sown upon
the ground, is the smallest of all the
seeds on earth; 32yet when it is sown it
grows up and becomes the greatest of all

[f] **3.32** Other ancient authorities lack *and sisters*
[g] **4.11** Or *mystery* [h] **4.17** Or *stumble*

well.' 29Immediately her haemorrhage stopped; and she felt in her body that she was healed of her disease. 30Immediately aware that power had gone forth from him, Jesus turned about in the crowd and said, 'Who touched my clothes?' 31And his disciples said to him, 'You see the crowd pressing in on you; how can you say, "Who touched me?"' 32He looked all round to see who had done it. 33But the woman, knowing what had happened to her, came in fear and trembling, fell down before him, and told him the whole truth. 34He said to her, 'Daughter, your faith has made you well; go in peace, and be healed of your disease.'

35 While he was still speaking, some people came from the leader's house to say, 'Your daughter is dead. Why trouble the teacher any further?' 36But overhearing[o] what they said, Jesus said to the leader of the synagogue, 'Do not fear, only believe.' 37He allowed no one to follow him except Peter, James, and John, the brother of James. 38When they came to the house of the leader of the synagogue, he saw a commotion, people weeping and wailing loudly. 39When he had entered, he said to them, 'Why do you make a commotion and weep? The child is not dead but sleeping.' 40And they laughed at him. Then he put them all outside, and took the child's father and mother and those who were with him, and went in where the child was. 41He took her by the hand and said to her, 'Talitha cum', which means, 'Little girl, get up!' 42And immediately the girl got up and began to walk about (she was twelve years of age). At this they were overcome with amazement. 43He strictly ordered them that no one should know this, and told them to give her something to eat.

THE REJECTION OF JESUS AT NAZARETH

6 He left that place and came to his home town, and his disciples followed him. 2On the sabbath he began to teach in the synagogue, and many who heard him were astounded. They said, 'Where did this man get all this? What is this wisdom that has been given to him? What deeds of power are being done by his hands! 3Is not this the carpenter, the son of Mary[p] and brother of James and Joses and Judas and Simon, and are not his sisters here with us?' And they took offence[q] at him. 4Then Jesus said to them, 'Prophets are not without honour, except in their home town, and among their own kin, and in their own house.' 5And he could do no deed of power there, except that he laid his hands on a few sick people and cured them. 6And he was amazed at their unbelief.

THE MISSION OF THE TWELVE

Then he went about among the villages teaching. 7He called the twelve and began to send them out two by two, and gave them authority over the unclean spirits. 8He ordered them to take nothing for their journey except a staff; no bread, no bag, no money in their belts; 9but to wear sandals and not to put on two tunics. 10He said to them, 'Wherever you enter a house, stay there until you leave the place. 11If any place will not welcome you and they refuse to hear you, as you leave, shake off the dust that is on your feet as a testimony against them.' 12So they went out and proclaimed that all should repent. 13They cast out many demons, and anointed with oil many who were sick and cured them.

THE DEATH OF JOHN THE BAPTIST

14 King Herod heard of it, for Jesus'[r] name had become known. Some were[s] saying, 'John the baptizer has been raised from the dead; and for this reason these powers are at work in him.' 15But others said, 'It is Elijah.' And others said, 'It is a prophet, like one of the prophets of old.' 16But when Herod heard of it, he said, 'John, whom I beheaded, has been raised.'

17 For Herod himself had sent men who arrested John, bound him, and put him in prison on account of Herodias, his brother Philip's wife, because Herod[t] had married her. 18For John had been telling Herod, 'It is not lawful for you to have your brother's wife.' 19And Herodias had a grudge against him, and wanted to kill him. But she could not, 20for Herod feared John, knowing that he was a righteous and holy man, and he protected him. When he heard him, he was greatly perplexed;[u] and yet he liked to listen to him. 21But an opportunity

[o] **5.36** Or *ignoring*; other ancient authorities read *hearing* [p] **6.3** Other ancient authorities read *son of the carpenter and of Mary* [q] **6.3** Or *stumbled* [r] **6.14** Gk *his* [s] **6.14** Other ancient authorities read *He was* [t] **6.17** Gk *he* [u] **6.20** Other ancient authorities read *he did many things*

came when Herod on his birthday gave a banquet for his courtiers and officers and for the leaders of Galilee. 22When his daughter Herodias[v] came in and danced, she pleased Herod and his guests; and the king said to the girl, 'Ask me for whatever you wish, and I will give it.' 23And he solemnly swore to her, 'Whatever you ask me, I will give you, even half of my kingdom.' 24She went out and said to her mother, 'What should I ask for?' She replied, 'The head of John the baptizer.' 25Immediately she rushed back to the king and requested, 'I want you to give me at once the head of John the Baptist on a platter.' 26The king was deeply grieved; yet out of regard for his oaths and for the guests, he did not want to refuse her. 27Immediately the king sent a soldier of the guard with orders to bring John's[w] head. He went and beheaded him in the prison, 28brought his head on a platter, and gave it to the girl. Then the girl gave it to her mother. 29When his disciples heard about it, they came and took his body, and laid it in a tomb.

FEEDING THE FIVE THOUSAND

30 The apostles gathered around Jesus, and told him all that they had done and taught. 31He said to them, 'Come away to a deserted place all by yourselves and rest a while.' For many were coming and going, and they had no leisure even to eat. 32And they went away in the boat to a deserted place by themselves. 33Now many saw them going and recognized them, and they hurried there on foot from all the towns and arrived ahead of them. 34As he went ashore, he saw a great crowd; and he had compassion for them, because they were like sheep without a shepherd; and he began to teach them many things. 35When it grew late, his disciples came to him and said, 'This is a deserted place, and the hour is now very late; 36send them away so that they may go into the surrounding country and villages and buy something for themselves to eat.' 37But he answered them, 'You give them something to eat.' They said to him, 'Are we to go and buy two hundred denarii[x] worth of bread, and give it to them to eat?' 38And he said to them, 'How many loaves have you? Go and see.' When they had found out, they said, 'Five, and two fish.' 39Then he ordered them to get all the people to sit down in groups on the green grass. 40So they sat down in groups of hundreds and of fifties. 41Taking the five loaves and the two fish, he looked up to heaven, and blessed and broke the loaves, and gave them to his disciples to set before the people; and he divided the two fish among them all. 42And all ate and were filled; 43and they took up twelve baskets full of broken pieces and of the fish. 44Those who had eaten the loaves numbered five thousand men.

JESUS WALKS ON THE WATER

45 Immediately he made his disciples get into the boat and go on ahead to the other side, to Bethsaida, while he dismissed the crowd. 46After saying farewell to them, he went up on the mountain to pray.

47 When evening came, the boat was out on the lake, and he was alone on the land. 48When he saw that they were straining at the oars against an adverse wind, he came towards them early in the morning, walking on the lake. He intended to pass them by. 49But when they saw him walking on the lake, they thought it was a ghost and cried out; 50for they all saw him and were terrified. But immediately he spoke to them and said, 'Take heart, it is I; do not be afraid.' 51Then he got into the boat with them and the wind ceased. And they were utterly astounded, 52for they did not understand about the loaves, but their hearts were hardened.

HEALING THE SICK IN GENNESARET

53 When they had crossed over, they came to land at Gennesaret and moored the boat. 54When they got out of the boat, people at once recognized him, 55and rushed about that whole region and began to bring the sick on mats to wherever they heard he was. 56And wherever he went, into villages or cities or farms, they laid the sick in the market-places, and begged him that they might touch even the fringe of his cloak; and all who touched it were healed.

THE TRADITION OF THE ELDERS

7 Now when the Pharisees and some of the scribes who had come from Jerusalem gathered around him, 2they noticed that some of his disciples were eating with defiled hands, that is, with-

[v] 6.22 Other ancient authorities read *the daughter of Herodias herself* [w] 6.27 Gk *his* [x] 6.37 The denarius was the usual day's wage for a labourer

out washing them. 3(For the Pharisees,
and all the Jews, do not eat unless they
thoroughly wash their hands,[y] thus observing the tradition of the elders; 4and
they do not eat anything from the market unless they wash it;[z] and there are
also many other traditions that they
observe, the washing of cups, pots, and
bronze kettles.[a]) 5So the Pharisees and
the scribes asked him, 'Why do your disciples not live[b] according to the tradition of the elders, but eat with defiled
hands?' 6He said to them, 'Isaiah prophesied rightly about you hypocrites, as it
is written,

"This people honours me
with their lips,
but their hearts are far from me;
7 in vain do they worship me,
teaching human precepts
as doctrines."

8You abandon the commandment of
God and hold to human tradition.'

9 Then he said to them, 'You have
a fine way of rejecting the commandment of God in order to keep your tradition! 10For Moses said, "Honour your
father and your mother"; and, "Whoever
speaks evil of father or mother must
surely die." 11But you say that if anyone
tells father or mother, "Whatever support you might have had from me is
Corban" (that is, an offering to God[c])—
12then you no longer permit doing anything for a father or mother, 13thus
making void the word of God through
your tradition that you have handed on.
And you do many things like this.'

14 Then he called the crowd again
and said to them, 'Listen to me, all of
you, and understand: 15there is nothing
outside a person that by going in can
defile, but the things that come out are
what defile.'[d]

17 When he had left the crowd and
entered the house, his disciples asked
him about the parable. 18He said to
them, 'Then do you also fail to understand? Do you not see that whatever
goes into a person from outside cannot
defile, 19since it enters, not the heart but
the stomach, and goes out into the sewer?' (Thus he declared all foods clean.)
20And he said, 'It is what comes out of
a person that defiles. 21For it is from
within, from the human heart, that
evil intentions come: fornication, theft,
murder, 22adultery, avarice, wickedness,
deceit, licentiousness, envy, slander,
pride, folly. 23All these evil things come
from within, and they defile a person.'

THE SYROPHOENICIAN WOMAN'S FAITH

24 From there he set out and went
away to the region of Tyre.[e] He entered
a house and did not want anyone to
know he was there. Yet he could not escape notice, 25but a woman whose little
daughter had an unclean spirit immediately heard about him, and she came
and bowed down at his feet. 26Now the
woman was a Gentile, of Syrophoeni-
cian origin. She begged him to cast the
demon out of her daughter. 27He said
to her, 'Let the children be fed first, for
it is not fair to take the children's food
and throw it to the dogs.' 28But she
answered him, 'Sir,[f] even the dogs under the table eat the children's crumbs.'
29Then he said to her, 'For saying that,
you may go—the demon has left your
daughter.' 30So she went home, found
the child lying on the bed, and the demon gone.

JESUS CURES A DEAF MAN

31 Then he returned from the region
of Tyre, and went by way of Sidon towards the Sea of Galilee, in the region
of the Decapolis. 32They brought to him
a deaf man who had an impediment in
his speech; and they begged him to lay
his hand on him. 33He took him aside in
private, away from the crowd, and put
his fingers into his ears, and he spat and
touched his tongue. 34Then looking up
to heaven, he sighed and said to him,
'Ephphatha', that is, 'Be opened.' 35And
immediately his ears were opened,
his tongue was released, and he spoke
plainly. 36Then Jesus[g] ordered them to
tell no one; but the more he ordered
them, the more zealously they proclaimed it. 37They were astounded beyond measure, saying, 'He has done everything well; he even makes the deaf to
hear and the mute to speak.'

FEEDING THE FOUR THOUSAND

8 In those days when there was
again a great crowd without anything to eat, he called his disciples and
said to them, 2'I have compassion for

[y] **7.3** Meaning of Gk uncertain [z] **7.4** Other ancient authorities read *and when they come from the market-place, they do not eat unless they purify themselves* [a] **7.4** Other ancient authorities add *and beds* [b] **7.5** Gk *walk* [c] **7.11** Gk lacks *to God* [d] **7.15** Other ancient authorities add verse 16, *'Let anyone with ears to hear listen'* [e] **7.24** Other ancient authorities add *and Sidon* [f] **7.28** Or *Lord*; other ancient authorities prefix *Yes* [g] **7.36** Gk *he*

the crowd, because they have been with me now for three days and have nothing to eat. 3 If I send them away hungry to their homes, they will faint on the way—and some of them have come from a great distance.' 4 His disciples replied, 'How can one feed these people with bread here in the desert?' 5 He asked them, 'How many loaves do you have?' They said, 'Seven.' 6 Then he ordered the crowd to sit down on the ground; and he took the seven loaves, and after giving thanks he broke them and gave them to his disciples to distribute; and they distributed them to the crowd. 7 They had also a few small fish; and after blessing them, he ordered that these too should be distributed. 8 They ate and were filled; and they took up the broken pieces left over, seven baskets full. 9 Now there were about four thousand people. And he sent them away. 10 And immediately he got into the boat with his disciples and went to the district of Dalmanutha.[h]

THE DEMAND FOR A SIGN

11 The Pharisees came and began to argue with him, asking him for a sign from heaven, to test him. 12 And he sighed deeply in his spirit and said, 'Why does this generation ask for a sign? Truly I tell you, no sign will be given to this generation.' 13 And he left them, and getting into the boat again, he went across to the other side.

THE YEAST OF THE PHARISEES AND OF HEROD

14 Now the disciples[i] had forgotten to bring any bread; and they had only one loaf with them in the boat. 15 And he cautioned them, saying, 'Watch out—beware of the yeast of the Pharisees and the yeast of Herod.'[j] 16 They said to one another, 'It is because we have no bread.' 17 And becoming aware of it, Jesus said to them, 'Why are you talking about having no bread? Do you still not perceive or understand? Are your hearts hardened? 18 Do you have eyes, and fail to see? Do you have ears, and fail to hear? And do you not remember? 19 When I broke the five loaves for the five thousand, how many baskets full of broken pieces did you collect?' They said to him, 'Twelve.' 20 'And the seven for the four thousand, how many baskets full of broken pieces did you collect?' And they said to him, 'Seven.' 21 Then he said to them, 'Do you not yet understand?'

JESUS CURES A BLIND MAN AT BETHSAIDA

22 They came to Bethsaida. Some people[k] brought a blind man to him and begged him to touch him. 23 He took the blind man by the hand and led him out of the village; and when he had put saliva on his eyes and laid his hands on him, he asked him, 'Can you see anything?' 24 And the man[l] looked up and said, 'I can see people, but they look like trees, walking.' 25 Then Jesus[m] laid his hands on his eyes again; and he looked intently and his sight was restored, and he saw everything clearly. 26 Then he sent him away to his home, saying, 'Do not even go into the village.'[n]

PETER'S DECLARATION ABOUT JESUS

27 Jesus went on with his disciples to the villages of Caesarea Philippi; and on the way he asked his disciples, 'Who do people say that I am?' 28 And they answered him, 'John the Baptist; and others, Elijah; and still others, one of the prophets.' 29 He asked them, 'But who do you say that I am?' Peter answered him, 'You are the Messiah.'[o] 30 And he sternly ordered them not to tell anyone about him.

JESUS FORETELLS HIS DEATH AND RESURRECTION

31 Then he began to teach them that the Son of Man must undergo great suffering, and be rejected by the elders, the chief priests, and the scribes, and be killed, and after three days rise again. 32 He said all this quite openly. And Peter took him aside and began to rebuke him. 33 But turning and looking at his disciples, he rebuked Peter and said, 'Get behind me, Satan! For you are setting your mind not on divine things but on human things.'

34 He called the crowd with his disciples, and said to them, 'If any want to become my followers, let them deny themselves and take up their cross and follow me. 35 For those who want to save their life will lose it, and those who lose their life for my sake, and for the sake of the gospel,[p] will save it. 36 For what will it profit them to gain the whole world

[h] **8.10** Other ancient authorities read *Mageda* or *Magdala* [i] **8.14** Gk *they* [j] **8.15** Other ancient authorities read *the Herodians* [k] **8.22** Gk *They* [l] **8.24** Gk *he* [m] **8.25** Gk *he* [n] **8.26** Other ancient authorities add *or tell anyone in the village* [o] **8.29** Or *the Christ* [p] **8.35** Other ancient authorities read *lose their life for the sake of the gospel*

and forfeit their life? 37 Indeed, what can they give in return for their life? 38 Those who are ashamed of me and of my words[q] in this adulterous and sinful generation, of them the Son of Man will also be ashamed when he comes in the glory of his Father with the holy angels.'

9 1 And he said to them, 'Truly I tell you, there are some standing here who will not taste death until they see that the kingdom of God has come with[r] power.'

THE TRANSFIGURATION

2 Six days later, Jesus took with him Peter and James and John, and led them up a high mountain apart, by themselves. And he was transfigured before them, 3 and his clothes became dazzling white, such as no one[s] on earth could bleach them. 4 And there appeared to them Elijah with Moses, who were talking with Jesus. 5 Then Peter said to Jesus, 'Rabbi, it is good for us to be here; let us make three dwellings,[t] one for you, one for Moses, and one for Elijah.' 6 He did not know what to say, for they were terrified. 7 Then a cloud overshadowed them, and from the cloud there came a voice, 'This is my Son, the Beloved;[u] listen to him!' 8 Suddenly when they looked around, they saw no one with them any more, but only Jesus.

THE COMING OF ELIJAH

9 As they were coming down the mountain, he ordered them to tell no one about what they had seen, until after the Son of Man had risen from the dead. 10 So they kept the matter to themselves, questioning what this rising from the dead could mean. 11 Then they asked him, 'Why do the scribes say that Elijah must come first?' 12 He said to them, 'Elijah is indeed coming first to restore all things. How then is it written about the Son of Man, that he is to go through many sufferings and be treated with contempt? 13 But I tell you that Elijah has come, and they did to him whatever they pleased, as it is written about him.'

THE HEALING OF A BOY WITH A SPIRIT

14 When they came to the disciples, they saw a great crowd around them, and some scribes arguing with them. 15 When the whole crowd saw him, they were immediately overcome with awe, and they ran forward to greet him. 16 He asked them, 'What are you arguing about with them?' 17 Someone from the crowd answered him, 'Teacher, I brought you my son; he has a spirit that makes him unable to speak; 18 and whenever it seizes him, it dashes him down; and he foams and grinds his teeth and becomes rigid; and I asked your disciples to cast it out, but they could not do so.' 19 He answered them, 'You faithless generation, how much longer must I be among you? How much longer must I put up with you? Bring him to me.' 20 And they brought the boy[v] to him. When the spirit saw him, immediately it threw the boy[w] into convulsions, and he fell on the ground and rolled about, foaming at the mouth. 21 Jesus[x] asked the father, 'How long has this been happening to him?' And he said, 'From childhood. 22 It has often cast him into the fire and into the water, to destroy him; but if you are able to do anything, have pity on us and help us.' 23 Jesus said to him, 'If you are able!—All things can be done for the one who believes.' 24 Immediately the father of the child cried out,[y] 'I believe; help my unbelief!' 25 When Jesus saw that a crowd came running together, he rebuked the unclean spirit, saying to it, 'You spirit that keep this boy from speaking and hearing, I command you, come out of him, and never enter him again!' 26 After crying out and convulsing him terribly, it came out, and the boy was like a corpse, so that most of them said, 'He is dead.' 27 But Jesus took him by the hand and lifted him up, and he was able to stand. 28 When he had entered the house, his disciples asked him privately, 'Why could we not cast it out?' 29 He said to them, 'This kind can come out only through prayer.'[z]

JESUS AGAIN FORETELLS HIS DEATH AND RESURRECTION

30 They went on from there and passed through Galilee. He did not want anyone to know it; 31 for he was teaching his disciples, saying to them, 'The Son of Man is to be betrayed into human hands, and they will kill him, and three days after being killed, he will rise again.' 32 But they did not understand what he was saying and were afraid to ask him.

[q] **8.38** Other ancient authorities read *and of mine*
[r] **9.1** Or *in* [s] **9.3** Gk *no fuller* [t] **9.5** Or *tents*
[u] **9.7** Or *my beloved Son* [v] **9.20** Gk *him*
[w] **9.20** Gk *him* [x] **9.21** Gk *He* [y] **9.24** Other ancient authorities add *with tears* [z] **9.29** Other ancient authorities add *and fasting*

WHO IS THE GREATEST?

33 Then they came to Capernaum;
and when he was in the house he asked
them, 'What were you arguing about on
the way?' 34 But they were silent, for on
the way they had argued with one another about who was the greatest. 35 He
sat down, called the twelve, and said to
them, 'Whoever wants to be first must
be last of all and servant of all.' 36 Then
he took a little child and put it among
them; and taking it in his arms, he said
to them, 37 'Whoever welcomes one such
child in my name welcomes me, and
whoever welcomes me welcomes not
me but the one who sent me.'

ANOTHER EXORCIST

38 John said to him, 'Teacher, we saw
someone[a] casting out demons in your
name, and we tried to stop him, because
he was not following us.' 39 But Jesus
said, 'Do not stop him; for no one who
does a deed of power in my name will be
able soon afterwards to speak evil of me.
40 Whoever is not against us is for us.
41 For truly I tell you, whoever gives you
a cup of water to drink because you bear
the name of Christ will by no means lose
the reward.

TEMPTATIONS TO SIN

42 'If any of you put a stumbling-
block before one of these little ones who
believe in me,[b] it would be better for you
if a great millstone were hung around
your neck and you were thrown into the
sea. 43 If your hand causes you to stumble, cut it off; it is better for you to enter
life maimed than to have two hands and
to go to hell,[c] to the unquenchable fire.[d]
45 And if your foot causes you to stumble, cut it off; it is better for you to enter life lame than to have two feet and
to be thrown into hell.[e,f] 47 And if your
eye causes you to stumble, tear it out; it
is better for you to enter the kingdom of
God with one eye than to have two eyes
and to be thrown into hell,[g] 48 where
their worm never dies, and the fire is
never quenched.

49 'For everyone will be salted with
fire.[h] 50 Salt is good; but if salt has lost its
saltiness, how can you season it?[i] Have
salt in yourselves, and be at peace with
one another.'

TEACHING ABOUT DIVORCE

10 He left that place and went to
the region of Judea and[j] beyond
the Jordan. And crowds again gathered
around him; and, as was his custom, he
again taught them.

2 Some Pharisees came, and to test
him they asked, 'Is it lawful for a man to
divorce his wife?' 3 He answered them,
'What did Moses command you?' 4 They
said, 'Moses allowed a man to write a certificate of dismissal and to divorce her.'
5 But Jesus said to them, 'Because of your
hardness of heart he wrote this commandment for you. 6 But from the beginning of creation, "God made them male
and female." 7 "For this reason a man
shall leave his father and mother and be
joined to his wife,[k] 8 and the two shall
become one flesh." So they are no longer
two, but one flesh. 9 Therefore what God
has joined together, let no one separate.'

10 Then in the house the disciples
asked him again about this matter. 11 He
said to them, 'Whoever divorces his wife
and marries another commits adultery
against her; 12 and if she divorces her
husband and marries another, she commits adultery.'

JESUS BLESSES LITTLE CHILDREN

13 People were bringing little children to him in order that he might
touch them; and the disciples spoke
sternly to them. 14 But when Jesus saw
this, he was indignant and said to
them, 'Let the little children come to
me; do not stop them; for it is to such as
these that the kingdom of God belongs.
15 Truly I tell you, whoever does not receive the kingdom of God as a little child
will never enter it.' 16 And he took them
up in his arms, laid his hands on them,
and blessed them.

THE RICH MAN

17 As he was setting out on a journey,
a man ran up and knelt before him, and
asked him, 'Good Teacher, what must I
do to inherit eternal life?' 18 Jesus said to
him, 'Why do you call me good? No one
is good but God alone. 19 You know the
commandments: "You shall not murder; You shall not commit adultery; You

[a] **9.38** Other ancient authorities add *who does not follow us* [b] **9.42** Other ancient authorities lack *in me* [c] **9.43** Gk *Gehenna* [d] **9.43** Verses 44 and 46 (which are identical with verse 48) are lacking in the best ancient authorities [e] **9.45** Gk *Gehenna* [f] **9.45** Verses 44 and 46 (which are identical with verse 48) are lacking in the best ancient authorities [g] **9.47** Gk *Gehenna* [h] **9.49** Other ancient authorities either add or substitute *and every sacrifice will be salted with salt* [i] **9.50** Or *how can you restore its saltiness?* [j] **10.1** Other ancient authorities lack *and* [k] **10.7** Other ancient authorities lack *and be joined to his wife*

shall not steal; You shall not bear false
witness; You shall not defraud; Honour
your father and mother."' 20He said to
him, 'Teacher, I have kept all these since
my youth.' 21Jesus, looking at him, loved
him and said, 'You lack one thing; go,
sell what you own, and give the money[l]
to the poor, and you will have treasure in heaven; then come, follow me.'
22When he heard this, he was shocked
and went away grieving, for he had
many possessions.

23 Then Jesus looked around and
said to his disciples, 'How hard it will
be for those who have wealth to enter
the kingdom of God!' 24And the disciples were perplexed at these words. But
Jesus said to them again, 'Children, how
hard it is[m] to enter the kingdom of God!
25It is easier for a camel to go through
the eye of a needle than for someone
who is rich to enter the kingdom of
God.' 26They were greatly astounded and
said to one another,[n] 'Then who can be
saved?' 27Jesus looked at them and said,
'For mortals it is impossible, but not for
God; for God all things are possible.'

28 Peter began to say to him, 'Look,
we have left everything and followed
you.' 29Jesus said, 'Truly I tell you, there
is no one who has left house or brothers
or sisters or mother or father or children
or fields, for my sake and for the sake of
the good news,[o] 30who will not receive
a hundredfold now in this age—houses,
brothers and sisters, mothers and children, and fields, with persecutions—
and in the age to come eternal life. 31But
many who are first will be last, and the
last will be first.'

A THIRD TIME JESUS FORETELLS HIS DEATH AND RESURRECTION

32 They were on the road, going up
to Jerusalem, and Jesus was walking
ahead of them; they were amazed, and
those who followed were afraid. He took
the twelve aside again and began to tell
them what was to happen to him, 33say-
ing, 'See, we are going up to Jerusalem,
and the Son of Man will be handed over
to the chief priests and the scribes, and
they will condemn him to death; then
they will hand him over to the Gentiles;
34they will mock him, and spit upon
him, and flog him, and kill him; and after three days he will rise again.'

THE REQUEST OF JAMES AND JOHN

35 James and John, the sons of Zebedee, came forward to him and said to
him, 'Teacher, we want you to do for us
whatever we ask of you.' 36And he said
to them, 'What is it you want me to do
for you?' 37And they said to him, 'Grant
us to sit, one at your right hand and one
at your left, in your glory.' 38But Jesus
said to them, 'You do not know what
you are asking. Are you able to drink
the cup that I drink, or be baptized with
the baptism that I am baptized with?'
39They replied, 'We are able.' Then Jesus
said to them, 'The cup that I drink you
will drink; and with the baptism with
which I am baptized, you will be baptized; 40but to sit at my right hand or at
my left is not mine to grant, but it is for
those for whom it has been prepared.'

41 When the ten heard this, they began to be angry with James and John.
42So Jesus called them and said to them,
'You know that among the Gentiles
those whom they recognize as their rulers lord it over them, and their great
ones are tyrants over them. 43But it is
not so among you; but whoever wishes
to become great among you must be
your servant, 44and whoever wishes to
be first among you must be slave of all.
45For the Son of Man came not to be
served but to serve, and to give his life a
ransom for many.'

THE HEALING OF BLIND BARTIMAEUS

46 They came to Jericho. As he and
his disciples and a large crowd were
leaving Jericho, Bartimaeus son of Ti-
maeus, a blind beggar, was sitting by
the roadside. 47When he heard that
it was Jesus of Nazareth, he began to
shout out and say, 'Jesus, Son of David,
have mercy on me!' 48Many sternly ordered him to be quiet, but he cried out
even more loudly, 'Son of David, have
mercy on me!' 49Jesus stood still and
said, 'Call him here.' And they called the
blind man, saying to him, 'Take heart;
get up, he is calling you.' 50So throwing
off his cloak, he sprang up and came to
Jesus. 51Then Jesus said to him, 'What do
you want me to do for you?' The blind
man said to him, 'My teacher,[p] let me
see again.' 52Jesus said to him, 'Go; your
faith has made you well.' Immediately
he regained his sight and followed him
on the way.

[l] **10.21** Gk lacks *the money* [m] **10.24** Other ancient authorities add *for those who trust in riches* [n] **10.26** Other ancient authorities read *to him* [o] **10.29** Or *gospel* [p] **10.51** Aramaic *Rabbouni*

JESUS' TRIUMPHAL ENTRY INTO JERUSALEM

11 When they were approaching Jerusalem, at Bethphage and Bethany, near the Mount of Olives, he sent two of his disciples 2and said to them, 'Go into the village ahead of you, and immediately as you enter it, you will find tied there a colt that has never been ridden; untie it and bring it. 3If anyone says to you, "Why are you doing this?" just say this, "The Lord needs it and will send it back here immediately."' 4They went away and found a colt tied near a door, outside in the street. As they were untying it, 5some of the bystanders said to them, 'What are you doing, untying the colt?' 6They told them what Jesus had said; and they allowed them to take it. 7Then they brought the colt to Jesus and threw their cloaks on it; and he sat on it. 8Many people spread their cloaks on the road, and others spread leafy branches that they had cut in the fields. 9Then those who went ahead and those who followed were shouting,

'Hosanna!
Blessed is the one who comes
in the name of the Lord!
10 Blessed is the coming kingdom
of our ancestor David!
Hosanna in the highest heaven!'

11 Then he entered Jerusalem and went into the temple; and when he had looked around at everything, as it was already late, he went out to Bethany with the twelve.

JESUS CURSES THE FIG TREE

12 On the following day, when they came from Bethany, he was hungry. 13Seeing in the distance a fig tree in leaf, he went to see whether perhaps he would find anything on it. When he came to it, he found nothing but leaves, for it was not the season for figs. 14He said to it, 'May no one ever eat fruit from you again.' And his disciples heard it.

JESUS CLEANSES THE TEMPLE

15 Then they came to Jerusalem. And he entered the temple and began to drive out those who were selling and those who were buying in the temple, and he overturned the tables of the money-changers and the seats of those who sold doves; 16and he would not allow anyone to carry anything through the temple. 17He was teaching and saying, 'Is it not written,

"My house shall be called a house of
prayer for all the nations"?
But you have made it a
den of robbers.'

18And when the chief priests and the scribes heard it, they kept looking for a way to kill him; for they were afraid of him, because the whole crowd was spellbound by his teaching. 19And when evening came, Jesus and his disciples[q] went out of the city.

THE LESSON FROM THE WITHERED FIG TREE

20 In the morning as they passed by, they saw the fig tree withered away to its roots. 21Then Peter remembered and said to him, 'Rabbi, look! The fig tree that you cursed has withered.' 22Jesus answered them, 'Have[r] faith in God. 23Truly I tell you, if you say to this mountain, "Be taken up and thrown into the sea", and if you do not doubt in your heart, but believe that what you say will come to pass, it will be done for you. 24So I tell you, whatever you ask for in prayer, believe that you have received[s] it, and it will be yours.

25 'Whenever you stand praying, forgive, if you have anything against anyone; so that your Father in heaven may also forgive you your trespasses.'[t]

JESUS' AUTHORITY IS QUESTIONED

27 Again they came to Jerusalem. As he was walking in the temple, the chief priests, the scribes, and the elders came to him 28and said, 'By what authority are you doing these things? Who gave you this authority to do them?' 29Jesus said to them, 'I will ask you one question; answer me, and I will tell you by what authority I do these things. 30Did the baptism of John come from heaven, or was it of human origin? Answer me.' 31They argued with one another, 'If we say, "From heaven", he will say, "Why then did you not believe him?" 32But shall we say, "Of human origin"?'—they were afraid of the crowd, for all regarded John as truly a prophet. 33So they answered Jesus, 'We do not know.' And Jesus said to them, 'Neither will I tell you by what authority I am doing these things.'

[q] 11.19 Gk *they*: other ancient authorities read *he*
[r] 11.22 Other ancient authorities read *'If you have*
[s] 11.24 Other ancient authorities read *are receiving*
[t] 11.25 Other ancient authorities add verse 26, *'But if you do not forgive, neither will your Father in heaven forgive your trespasses.'*

THE PARABLE OF THE WICKED TENANTS

12 Then he began to speak to them in parables. 'A man planted a vineyard, put a fence around it, dug a pit for the wine press, and built a watchtower; then he leased it to tenants and went to another country. 2 When the season came, he sent a slave to the tenants to collect from them his share of the produce of the vineyard. 3 But they seized him, and beat him, and sent him away empty-handed. 4 And again he sent another slave to them; this one they beat over the head and insulted. 5 Then he sent another, and that one they killed. And so it was with many others; some they beat, and others they killed. 6 He had still one other, a beloved son. Finally he sent him to them, saying, "They will respect my son." 7 But those tenants said to one another, "This is the heir; come, let us kill him, and the inheritance will be ours." 8 So they seized him, killed him, and threw him out of the vineyard. 9 What then will the owner of the vineyard do? He will come and destroy the tenants and give the vineyard to others. 10 Have you not read this scripture:

"The stone that the builders rejected
 has become the cornerstone;[u]
11 this was the Lord's doing,
 and it is amazing in our eyes"?'

12 When they realized that he had told this parable against them, they wanted to arrest him, but they feared the crowd. So they left him and went away.

THE QUESTION ABOUT PAYING TAXES

13 Then they sent to him some Pharisees and some Herodians to trap him in what he said. 14 And they came and said to him, 'Teacher, we know that you are sincere, and show deference to no one; for you do not regard people with partiality, but teach the way of God in accordance with truth. Is it lawful to pay taxes to the emperor, or not? 15 Should we pay them, or should we not?' But knowing their hypocrisy, he said to them, 'Why are you putting me to the test? Bring me a denarius and let me see it.' 16 And they brought one. Then he said to them, 'Whose head is this, and whose title?' They answered, 'The emperor's.' 17 Jesus said to them, 'Give to the emperor the things that are the emperor's, and to God the things that are God's.' And they were utterly amazed at him.

THE QUESTION ABOUT THE RESURRECTION

18 Some Sadducees, who say there is no resurrection, came to him and asked him a question, saying, 19 'Teacher, Moses wrote for us that if a man's brother dies, leaving a wife but no child, the man[v] shall marry the widow and raise up children for his brother. 20 There were seven brothers; the first married and, when he died, left no children; 21 and the second married the widow[w] and died, leaving no children; and the third likewise; 22 none of the seven left children. Last of all the woman herself died. 23 In the resurrection[x] whose wife will she be? For the seven had married her.'

24 Jesus said to them, 'Is not this the reason you are wrong, that you know neither the scriptures nor the power of God? 25 For when they rise from the dead, they neither marry nor are given in marriage, but are like angels in heaven. 26 And as for the dead being raised, have you not read in the book of Moses, in the story about the bush, how God said to him, "I am the God of Abraham, the God of Isaac, and the God of Jacob"? 27 He is God not of the dead, but of the living; you are quite wrong.'

THE FIRST COMMANDMENT

28 One of the scribes came near and heard them disputing with one another, and seeing that he answered them well, he asked him, 'Which commandment is the first of all?' 29 Jesus answered, 'The first is, "Hear, O Israel: the Lord our God, the Lord is one; 30 you shall love the Lord your God with all your heart, and with all your soul, and with all your mind, and with all your strength." 31 The second is this, "You shall love your neighbour as yourself." There is no other commandment greater than these.' 32 Then the scribe said to him, 'You are right, Teacher; you have truly said that "he is one, and besides him there is no other"; 33 and "to love him with all the heart, and with all the understanding, and with all the strength", and "to love one's neighbour as oneself",—this is much more important than all whole burnt-offerings and sacrifices.' 34 When Jesus saw that he answered wisely, he said to him, 'You are not far from the kingdom of God.' After that no one dared to ask him any question.

[u] 12.10 Or *keystone* [v] 12.19 Gk *his brother* [w] 12.21 Gk *her* [x] 12.23 Other ancient authorities add *when they rise*

THE QUESTION ABOUT DAVID'S SON

35 While Jesus was teaching in the
temple, he said, 'How can the scribes
say that the Messiah[y] is the son of David? 36 David himself, by the Holy Spirit,
declared,

"The Lord said to my Lord,
'Sit at my right hand,
until I put your enemies
under your feet.'"

37 David himself calls him Lord; so how
can he be his son?' And the large crowd
was listening to him with delight.

JESUS DENOUNCES THE SCRIBES

38 As he taught, he said, 'Beware of
the scribes, who like to walk around in
long robes, and to be greeted with respect in the market-places, 39 and to have
the best seats in the synagogues and
places of honour at banquets! 40 They devour widows' houses and for the sake of
appearance say long prayers. They will
receive the greater condemnation.'

THE WIDOW'S OFFERING

41 He sat down opposite the treasury,
and watched the crowd putting money
into the treasury. Many rich people put
in large sums. 42 A poor widow came and
put in two small copper coins, which are
worth a penny. 43 Then he called his disciples and said to them, 'Truly I tell you,
this poor widow has put in more than
all those who are contributing to the
treasury. 44 For all of them have contributed out of their abundance; but she out
of her poverty has put in everything she
had, all she had to live on.'

THE DESTRUCTION OF THE TEMPLE FORETOLD

13 As he came out of the temple,
one of his disciples said to him,
'Look, Teacher, what large stones and
what large buildings!' 2 Then Jesus asked
him, 'Do you see these great buildings?
Not one stone will be left here upon another; all will be thrown down.'

3 When he was sitting on the Mount
of Olives opposite the temple, Peter,
James, John, and Andrew asked him
privately, 4 'Tell us, when will this be,
and what will be the sign that all these
things are about to be accomplished?'
5 Then Jesus began to say to them, 'Beware that no one leads you astray.
6 Many will come in my name and say, "I
am he!"[z] and they will lead many astray.
7 When you hear of wars and rumours
of wars, do not be alarmed; this must
take place, but the end is still to come.
8 For nation will rise against nation, and
kingdom against kingdom; there will be
earthquakes in various places; there will
be famines. This is but the beginning of
the birth pangs.

PERSECUTION FORETOLD

9 'As for yourselves, beware; for they
will hand you over to councils; and you
will be beaten in synagogues; and you
will stand before governors and kings
because of me, as a testimony to them.
10 And the good news[a] must first be
proclaimed to all nations. 11 When they
bring you to trial and hand you over, do
not worry beforehand about what you
are to say; but say whatever is given you
at that time, for it is not you who speak,
but the Holy Spirit. 12 Brother will betray brother to death, and a father his
child, and children will rise against parents and have them put to death; 13 and
you will be hated by all because of my
name. But the one who endures to the
end will be saved.

THE DESOLATING SACRILEGE

14 'But when you see the desolating sacrilege set up where it ought not
to be (let the reader understand), then
those in Judea must flee to the mountains; 15 someone on the housetop must
not go down or enter the house to take
anything away; 16 someone in the field
must not turn back to get a coat. 17 Woe
to those who are pregnant and to those
who are nursing infants in those days!
18 Pray that it may not be in winter.
19 For in those days there will be suffering, such as has not been from the beginning of the creation that God created
until now, no, and never will be. 20 And
if the Lord had not cut short those days,
no one would be saved; but for the sake
of the elect, whom he chose, he has cut
short those days. 21 And if anyone says
to you at that time, "Look! Here is the
Messiah!"[b] or "Look! There he is!"—do
not believe it. 22 False messiahs[c] and
false prophets will appear and produce
signs and omens, to lead astray, if possible, the elect. 23 But be alert; I have already told you everything.

THE COMING OF THE SON OF MAN

24 'But in those days, after that suffering,

[y] 12.35 Or *the Christ* [z] 13.6 Gk *I am*
[a] 13.10 Gk *gospel* [b] 13.21 Or *the Christ*
[c] 13.22 Or *christs*

the sun will be darkened,
and the moon will not
give its light,
25 and the stars will be falling
from heaven,
and the powers in the heavens
will be shaken.
26Then they will see "the Son of Man
coming in clouds" with great power and
glory. 27Then he will send out the angels, and gather his elect from the four
winds, from the ends of the earth to the
ends of heaven.

THE LESSON OF THE FIG TREE

28 'From the fig tree learn its lesson: as soon as its branch becomes tender and puts forth its leaves, you know
that summer is near. 29So also, when
you see these things taking place, you
know that he[d] is near, at the very gates.
30Truly I tell you, this generation will
not pass away until all these things
have taken place. 31Heaven and earth
will pass away, but my words will not
pass away.

THE NECESSITY FOR WATCHFULNESS

32 'But about that day or hour no one
knows, neither the angels in heaven,
nor the Son, but only the Father. 33Be-
ware, keep alert;[e] for you do not know
when the time will come. 34It is like a
man going on a journey, when he leaves
home and puts his slaves in charge, each
with his work, and commands the doorkeeper to be on the watch. 35Therefore,
keep awake—for you do not know when
the master of the house will come, in
the evening, or at midnight, or at cock-
crow, or at dawn, 36or else he may find
you asleep when he comes suddenly.
37And what I say to you I say to all: Keep
awake.'

THE PLOT TO KILL JESUS

14 It was two days before the Passover and the festival of Unleavened Bread. The chief priests and the
scribes were looking for a way to arrest
Jesus[f] by stealth and kill him; 2for they
said, 'Not during the festival, or there
may be a riot among the people.'

THE ANOINTING AT BETHANY

3 While he was at Bethany in the
house of Simon the leper,[g] as he sat at
the table, a woman came with an alabaster jar of very costly ointment of
nard, and she broke open the jar and
poured the ointment on his head. 4But
some were there who said to one another in anger, 'Why was the ointment
wasted in this way? 5For this ointment
could have been sold for more than
three hundred denarii,[h] and the money
given to the poor.' And they scolded her.
6But Jesus said, 'Let her alone; why do
you trouble her? She has performed a
good service for me. 7For you always
have the poor with you, and you can
show kindness to them whenever you
wish; but you will not always have me.
8She has done what she could; she has
anointed my body beforehand for its
burial. 9Truly I tell you, wherever the
good news[i] is proclaimed in the whole
world, what she has done will be told in
remembrance of her.'

JUDAS AGREES TO BETRAY JESUS

10 Then Judas Iscariot, who was one
of the twelve, went to the chief priests
in order to betray him to them. 11When
they heard it, they were greatly pleased,
and promised to give him money. So he
began to look for an opportunity to betray him.

THE PASSOVER WITH THE DISCIPLES

12 On the first day of Unleavened
Bread, when the Passover lamb is sacrificed, his disciples said to him, 'Where
do you want us to go and make the preparations for you to eat the Passover?'
13So he sent two of his disciples, saying
to them, 'Go into the city, and a man
carrying a jar of water will meet you; follow him, 14and wherever he enters, say
to the owner of the house, "The Teacher
asks, Where is my guest room where I
may eat the Passover with my disciples?" 15He will show you a large room
upstairs, furnished and ready. Make
preparations for us there.' 16So the disciples set out and went to the city, and
found everything as he had told them;
and they prepared the Passover meal.
17 When it was evening, he came
with the twelve. 18And when they had
taken their places and were eating,
Jesus said, 'Truly I tell you, one of you
will betray me, one who is eating with
me.' 19They began to be distressed and
to say to him one after another, 'Surely,
not I?' 20He said to them, 'It is one of
the twelve, one who is dipping bread[j]

[d] 13.29 Or *it* [e] 13.33 Other ancient authorities add *and pray* [f] 14.1 Gk *him* [g] 14.3 The terms *leper* and *leprosy* can refer to several diseases [h] 14.5 The denarius was the usual day's wage for a labourer [i] 14.9 Or *gospel* [j] 14.20 Gk lacks *bread*

into the bowl[k] with me. 21For the Son of Man goes as it is written of him, but woe to that one by whom the Son of Man is betrayed! It would have been better for that one not to have been born.'

THE INSTITUTION OF THE LORD'S SUPPER

22 While they were eating, he took a loaf of bread, and after blessing it he broke it, gave it to them, and said, 'Take; this is my body.' 23Then he took a cup, and after giving thanks he gave it to them, and all of them drank from it. 24He said to them, 'This is my blood of the[l] covenant, which is poured out for many. 25Truly I tell you, I will never again drink of the fruit of the vine until that day when I drink it new in the kingdom of God.'

PETER'S DENIAL FORETOLD

26 When they had sung the hymn, they went out to the Mount of Olives. 27And Jesus said to them, 'You will all become deserters; for it is written,

"I will strike the shepherd,
and the sheep will be scattered."

28But after I am raised up, I will go before you to Galilee.' 29Peter said to him, 'Even though all become deserters, I will not.' 30Jesus said to him, 'Truly I tell you, this day, this very night, before the cock crows twice, you will deny me three times.' 31But he said vehemently, 'Even though I must die with you, I will not deny you.' And all of them said the same.

JESUS PRAYS IN GETHSEMANE

32 They went to a place called Gethsemane; and he said to his disciples, 'Sit here while I pray.' 33He took with him Peter and James and John, and began to be distressed and agitated. 34And he said to them, 'I am deeply grieved, even to death; remain here, and keep awake.' 35And going a little farther, he threw himself on the ground and prayed that, if it were possible, the hour might pass from him. 36He said, 'Abba,[m] Father, for you all things are possible; remove this cup from me; yet, not what I want, but what you want.' 37He came and found them sleeping; and he said to Peter, 'Simon, are you asleep? Could you not keep awake one hour? 38Keep awake and pray that you may not come into the time of trial;[n] the spirit indeed is willing, but the flesh is weak.' 39And again he went away and prayed, saying the same words. 40And once more he came and found them sleeping, for their eyes were very heavy; and they did not know what to say to him. 41He came a third time and said to them, 'Are you still sleeping and taking your rest? Enough! The hour has come; the Son of Man is betrayed into the hands of sinners. 42Get up, let us be going. See, my betrayer is at hand.'

THE BETRAYAL AND ARREST OF JESUS

43 Immediately, while he was still speaking, Judas, one of the twelve, arrived; and with him there was a crowd with swords and clubs, from the chief priests, the scribes, and the elders. 44Now the betrayer had given them a sign, saying, 'The one I will kiss is the man; arrest him and lead him away under guard.' 45So when he came, he went up to him at once and said, 'Rabbi!' and kissed him. 46Then they laid hands on him and arrested him. 47But one of those who stood near drew his sword and struck the slave of the high priest, cutting off his ear. 48Then Jesus said to them, 'Have you come out with swords and clubs to arrest me as though I were a bandit? 49Day after day I was with you in the temple teaching, and you did not arrest me. But let the scriptures be fulfilled.' 50All of them deserted him and fled.

51 A certain young man was following him, wearing nothing but a linen cloth. They caught hold of him, 52but he left the linen cloth and ran off naked.

JESUS BEFORE THE COUNCIL

53 They took Jesus to the high priest; and all the chief priests, the elders, and the scribes were assembled. 54Peter had followed him at a distance, right into the courtyard of the high priest; and he was sitting with the guards, warming himself at the fire. 55Now the chief priests and the whole council were looking for testimony against Jesus to put him to death; but they found none. 56For many gave false testimony against him, and their testimony did not agree. 57Some stood up and gave false testimony against him, saying, 58'We heard him say, "I will destroy this temple that is made with hands, and in three days

[k] 14.20 Other ancient authorities read *same bowl*
[l] 14.24 Other ancient authorities add *new*
[m] 14.36 Aramaic for *Father* [n] 14.38 Or *into temptation*

I will build another, not made with
hands." ' 59But even on this point their
testimony did not agree. 60Then the
high priest stood up before them and
asked Jesus, 'Have you no answer? What
is it that they testify against you?' 61But
he was silent and did not answer. Again
the high priest asked him, 'Are you the
Messiah,[o] the Son of the Blessed One?'
62Jesus said, 'I am; and
"you will see the Son of Man
seated at the right hand of
the Power",
and "coming with the clouds
of heaven." '
63Then the high priest tore his clothes
and said, 'Why do we still need witnesses? 64You have heard his blasphemy! What is your decision?' All of
them condemned him as deserving
death. 65Some began to spit on him, to
blindfold him, and to strike him, saying
to him, 'Prophesy!' The guards also took
him over and beat him.

PETER DENIES JESUS

66 While Peter was below in the
courtyard, one of the servant-girls of
the high priest came by. 67When she saw
Peter warming himself, she stared at
him and said, 'You also were with Jesus,
the man from Nazareth.' 68But he denied it, saying, 'I do not know or understand what you are talking about.' And
he went out into the forecourt.[p] Then
the cock crowed.[q] 69And the servant-
girl, on seeing him, began again to say
to the bystanders, 'This man is one of
them.' 70But again he denied it. Then
after a little while the bystanders again
said to Peter, 'Certainly you are one of
them; for you are a Galilean.' 71But he
began to curse, and he swore an oath,
'I do not know this man you are talking about.' 72At that moment the cock
crowed for the second time. Then Peter remembered that Jesus had said to
him, 'Before the cock crows twice, you
will deny me three times.' And he broke
down and wept.

JESUS BEFORE PILATE

15 As soon as it was morning, the
chief priests held a consultation with the elders and scribes and
the whole council. They bound Jesus,
led him away, and handed him over to
Pilate. 2Pilate asked him, 'Are you the
King of the Jews?' He answered him,
'You say so.' 3Then the chief priests accused him of many things. 4Pilate asked
him again, 'Have you no answer? See
how many charges they bring against
you.' 5But Jesus made no further reply,
so that Pilate was amazed.

PILATE HANDS JESUS OVER TO BE CRUCIFIED

6 Now at the festival he used to release a prisoner for them, anyone for
whom they asked. 7Now a man called
Barabbas was in prison with the rebels
who had committed murder during
the insurrection. 8So the crowd came
and began to ask Pilate to do for them
according to his custom. 9Then he answered them, 'Do you want me to release for you the King of the Jews?' 10For
he realized that it was out of jealousy
that the chief priests had handed him
over. 11But the chief priests stirred up
the crowd to have him release Barabbas
for them instead. 12Pilate spoke to them
again, 'Then what do you wish me to
do[r] with the man you call[s] the King of
the Jews?' 13They shouted back, 'Crucify
him!' 14Pilate asked them, 'Why, what
evil has he done?' But they shouted
all the more, 'Crucify him!' 15So Pilate,
wishing to satisfy the crowd, released
Barabbas for them; and after flogging
Jesus, he handed him over to be crucified.

THE SOLDIERS MOCK JESUS

16 Then the soldiers led him into the
courtyard of the palace (that is, the governor's headquarters[t]); and they called
together the whole cohort. 17And they
clothed him in a purple cloak; and after
twisting some thorns into a crown, they
put it on him. 18And they began salut-
ing him, 'Hail, King of the Jews!' 19They
struck his head with a reed, spat upon
him, and knelt down in homage to him.
20After mocking him, they stripped
him of the purple cloak and put his own
clothes on him. Then they led him out
to crucify him.

THE CRUCIFIXION OF JESUS

21 They compelled a passer-by, who
was coming in from the country, to
carry his cross; it was Simon of Cyrene,
the father of Alexander and Rufus.
22Then they brought Jesus[u] to the place

[o] **14.61** Or *the Christ* [p] **14.68** Or *gateway*
[q] **14.68** Other ancient authorities lack *Then the cock crowed* [r] **15.12** Other ancient authorities read *what should I do* [s] **15.12** Other ancient authorities lack *the man you call* [t] **15.16** Gk *the praetorium* [u] **15.22** Gk *him*

called Golgotha (which means the place
of a skull). 23And they offered him wine
mixed with myrrh; but he did not take
it. 24And they crucified him, and divided his clothes among them, casting
lots to decide what each should take.

25 It was nine o'clock in the morning
when they crucified him. 26The inscription of the charge against him read, 'The
King of the Jews.' 27And with him they
crucified two bandits, one on his right
and one on his left.[v] 29Those who passed
by derided[w] him, shaking their heads
and saying, 'Aha! You who would destroy the temple and build it in three
days, 30save yourself, and come down
from the cross!' 31In the same way the
chief priests, along with the scribes,
were also mocking him among themselves and saying, 'He saved others; he
cannot save himself. 32Let the Messiah,[x]
the King of Israel, come down from the
cross now, so that we may see and believe.' Those who were crucified with
him also taunted him.

THE DEATH OF JESUS

33 When it was noon, darkness came
over the whole land[y] until three in the
afternoon. 34At three o'clock Jesus cried
out with a loud voice, 'Eloi, Eloi, lema
sabachthani?' which means, 'My God,
my God, why have you forsaken me?'[z]
35When some of the bystanders heard
it, they said, 'Listen, he is calling for Elijah.' 36And someone ran, filled a sponge
with sour wine, put it on a stick, and
gave it to him to drink, saying, 'Wait, let
us see whether Elijah will come to take
him down.' 37Then Jesus gave a loud cry
and breathed his last. 38And the curtain
of the temple was torn in two, from top
to bottom. 39Now when the centurion,
who stood facing him, saw that in this
way he[a] breathed his last, he said, 'Truly
this man was God's Son!'[b]

40 There were also women looking
on from a distance; among them were
Mary Magdalene, and Mary the mother
of James the younger and of Joses, and
Salome. 41These used to follow him and
provided for him when he was in Galilee; and there were many other women
who had come up with him to Jerusalem.

THE BURIAL OF JESUS

42 When evening had come, and
since it was the day of Preparation, that
is, the day before the sabbath, 43Joseph
of Arimathea, a respected member of
the council, who was also himself waiting expectantly for the kingdom of God,
went boldly to Pilate and asked for the
body of Jesus. 44Then Pilate wondered if
he were already dead; and summoning
the centurion, he asked him whether he
had been dead for some time. 45When he
learned from the centurion that he was
dead, he granted the body to Joseph.
46Then Joseph[c] bought a linen cloth,
and taking down the body,[d] wrapped it
in the linen cloth, and laid it in a tomb
that had been hewn out of the rock. He
then rolled a stone against the door of
the tomb. 47Mary Magdalene and Mary
the mother of Joses saw where the
body[e] was laid.

THE RESURRECTION OF JESUS

16 When the sabbath was over,
Mary Magdalene, and Mary the
mother of James, and Salome bought
spices, so that they might go and anoint
him. 2And very early on the first day of
the week, when the sun had risen, they
went to the tomb. 3They had been saying to one another, 'Who will roll away
the stone for us from the entrance to
the tomb?' 4When they looked up, they
saw that the stone, which was very
large, had already been rolled back.
5As they entered the tomb, they saw
a young man, dressed in a white robe,
sitting on the right side; and they were
alarmed. 6But he said to them, 'Do not
be alarmed; you are looking for Jesus
of Nazareth, who was crucified. He has
been raised; he is not here. Look, there
is the place they laid him. 7But go, tell
his disciples and Peter that he is going
ahead of you to Galilee; there you will
see him, just as he told you.' 8So they
went out and fled from the tomb, for
terror and amazement had seized them;
and they said nothing to anyone, for
they were afraid.[f]

[v] **15.27** Other ancient authorities add verse 28, *And the scripture was fulfilled that says, 'And he was counted among the lawless.'* [w] **15.29** Or *blasphemed* [x] **15.32** Or *the Christ* [y] **15.33** Or *earth* [z] **15.34** Other ancient authorities read *made me a reproach* [a] **15.39** Other ancient authorities add *cried out and* [b] **15.39** Or *a son of God* [c] **15.46** Gk *he* [d] **15.46** Gk *it* [e] **15.47** Gk *it* [f] **16.8** Some of the most ancient authorities bring the book to a close at the end of verse 8. One authority concludes the book with the shorter ending; others include the shorter ending and then continue with verses 9–20. In most authorities verses 9–20 follow immediately after verse 8, though in some of these authorities the passage is marked as being doubtful.

The Shorter Ending of Mark

⟦And all that had been commanded
them they told briefly to those around
Peter. And afterwards Jesus himself
sent out through them, from east to
west, the sacred and imperishable proclamation of eternal salvation.[g]⟧

The Longer Ending of Mark

JESUS APPEARS TO MARY MAGDALENE

9 ⟦Now after he rose early on the
first day of the week, he appeared first
to Mary Magdalene, from whom he had
cast out seven demons. 10 She went out
and told those who had been with him,
while they were mourning and weeping. 11 But when they heard that he was
alive and had been seen by her, they
would not believe it.

JESUS APPEARS TO TWO DISCIPLES

12 After this he appeared in another
form to two of them, as they were walking into the country. 13 And they went
back and told the rest, but they did not
believe them.

JESUS COMMISSIONS THE DISCIPLES

14 Later he appeared to the eleven
themselves as they were sitting at the
table; and he upbraided them for their
lack of faith and stubbornness, because
they had not believed those who saw
him after he had risen.[h] 15 And he said
to them, 'Go into all the world and proclaim the good news[i] to the whole creation. 16 The one who believes and is
baptized will be saved; but the one who
does not believe will be condemned.
17 And these signs will accompany those
who believe: by using my name they
will cast out demons; they will speak in
new tongues; 18 they will pick up snakes
in their hands,[j] and if they drink any
deadly thing, it will not hurt them; they
will lay their hands on the sick, and
they will recover.'

THE ASCENSION OF JESUS

19 So then the Lord Jesus, after he
had spoken to them, was taken up into
heaven and sat down at the right hand
of God. 20 And they went out and proclaimed the good news everywhere,
while the Lord worked with them and
confirmed the message by the signs
that accompanied it.[k]⟧

[g] **16.8** Other ancient authorities add *Amen*
[h] **16.14** Other ancient authorities add, in whole or in part, *And they excused themselves, saying, 'This age of lawlessness and unbelief is under Satan, who does not allow the truth and power of God to prevail over the unclean things of the spirits. Therefore reveal your righteousness now'—thus they spoke to Christ. And Christ replied to them, 'The term of years of Satan's power has been fulfilled, but other terrible things draw near. And for those who have sinned I was handed over to death, that they may return to the truth and sin no more, that they may inherit the spiritual and imperishable glory of righteousness that is in heaven.'* [i] **16.15** Or *gospel* [j] **16.18** Other ancient authorities lack *in their hands*
[k] **16.20** Other ancient authorities add *Amen*

The Gospel According to

LUKE

At the Chrism Mass on Holy Thursday every year, the church proclaims a story from Luke's Gospel about the time when Jesus rolls up the scroll after reading from Isaiah the prophet at the synagogue in Nazareth and declares, "Today this scripture has been fulfilled in your hearing" (4.16–30). The scene reveals Luke's particular interest in portraying Jesus as the fulfillment of the prophecy of Israel that anticipated one who would come "to bring good news to the poor" and salvation to the whole world. Luke's Gospel develops the theme that salvation was intended not only for Israel, but also for the Gentiles. The author of the Gospel of Luke is also the writer of the Acts of the Apostles. These books go together to form a two-volume work that shows how the ministry of Jesus continues in the ministry of the apostles and how salvation is spread through the power of the Holy Spirit (Acts 4.8).

Like the two Gospels of Matthew and Mark, Luke's Gospel narrates many of the same stories about the teachings and miracles of Jesus. Unlike the other Gospels, Luke emphasizes his own particular perspective about Jesus fulfilling the Old Testament prophets (4.21; 18.31; 22.37; 24.26–27, 44) and bringing mercy and compassion to the poor, the lowly, the outcast, the sinners and the afflicted (4.18; 6.20–23; 7.36–50; 14.12–14; 15.1–32; 16.19–31; 18.9–14; 19.1–10; 21.1–4). Jesus is on a mission in the Gospel of Luke. He is on his way from Galilee to Jerusalem, bringing salvation (4.30; 9.51–56; 13.31–35). Moreover, Jesus is presented as completely in charge of the events occurring around him, as these events follow according to the will of God. Even in his passion and death, Jesus, like a prophet, remains in complete control and has full confidence in the unfolding of God's plan (22.42, 51–52, 70; 23.3, 28–31, 34, 43, 46).

The characteristics of the Gospel of Luke suggest that its author probably was a non-Jewish Christian writing to a non-Jewish audience. Luke's emphasis on the mission to the Gentiles and his shifting away from an earlier Christian emphasis on the imminent return of Christ also distinguishes his Gospel account from that of Matthew and Mark.

The Gospel of Luke is featured in Year C of the liturgical calendar. In addition to the Chrism Mass, memorable selections of this Gospel are read every year on other special feasts, i.e., the Christmas Mass at midnight (2.1–14) and at dawn (2.15–20), and the Solemnity of Mary, Mother of God (2.16–21). Luke's account of the birth of Jesus and the presentation of Jesus in the temple are very popular texts proclaimed every year during the Christmas season. Additionally, Luke's account of the appearance of the risen Jesus to the disciples on the road to Emmaus is told every year at the afternoon Mass on Easter Sunday (24.13–35). Luke is the only Gospel to preserve this special appearance narrative.

DEDICATION TO THEOPHILUS

1 Since many have undertaken to
set down an orderly account of the
events that have been fulfilled among
us, 2 just as they were handed on to us
by those who from the beginning were
eyewitnesses and servants of the word,
3 I too decided, after investigating everything carefully from the very first,[a] to
write an orderly account for you, most
excellent Theophilus, 4 so that you may
know the truth concerning the things
about which you have been instructed.

THE BIRTH OF JOHN THE BAPTIST FORETOLD

5 In the days of King Herod of Judea,
there was a priest named Zechariah,
who belonged to the priestly order of
Abijah. His wife was a descendant of
Aaron, and her name was Elizabeth.
6 Both of them were righteous before
God, living blamelessly according to all
the commandments and regulations of
the Lord. 7 But they had no children, because Elizabeth was barren, and both
were getting on in years.

8 Once when he was serving as priest
before God and his section was on duty,
9 he was chosen by lot, according to
the custom of the priesthood, to enter
the sanctuary of the Lord and offer incense. 10 Now at the time of the incense-
offering, the whole assembly of the people was praying outside. 11 Then there
appeared to him an angel of the Lord,
standing at the right side of the altar
of incense. 12 When Zechariah saw him,
he was terrified; and fear overwhelmed
him. 13 But the angel said to him, 'Do
not be afraid, Zechariah, for your prayer
has been heard. Your wife Elizabeth will
bear you a son, and you will name him
John. 14 You will have joy and gladness,
and many will rejoice at his birth, 15 for
he will be great in the sight of the Lord.
He must never drink wine or strong
drink; even before his birth he will be
filled with the Holy Spirit. 16 He will
turn many of the people of Israel to the
Lord their God. 17 With the spirit and
power of Elijah he will go before him, to
turn the hearts of parents to their children, and the disobedient to the wisdom of the righteous, to make ready a
people prepared for the Lord.' 18 Zechariah said to the angel, 'How will I know
that this is so? For I am an old man, and
my wife is getting on in years.' 19 The angel replied, 'I am Gabriel. I stand in the
presence of God, and I have been sent to
speak to you and to bring you this good
news. 20 But now, because you did not
believe my words, which will be fulfilled
in their time, you will become mute,
unable to speak, until the day these
things occur.'

21 Meanwhile, the people were waiting for Zechariah, and wondered at his
delay in the sanctuary. 22 When he did
come out, he could not speak to them,
and they realized that he had seen a vision in the sanctuary. He kept motioning to them and remained unable to
speak. 23 When his time of service was
ended, he went to his home.

24 After those days his wife Elizabeth
conceived, and for five months she remained in seclusion. She said, 25 'This is
what the Lord has done for me when he
looked favourably on me and took away
the disgrace I have endured among my
people.'

THE BIRTH OF JESUS FORETOLD

26 In the sixth month the angel
Gabriel was sent by God to a town in
Galilee called Nazareth, 27 to a virgin
engaged to a man whose name was
Joseph, of the house of David. The virgin's name was Mary. 28 And he came to
her and said, 'Greetings, favoured one!
The Lord is with you.'[b] 29 But she was
much perplexed by his words and pondered what sort of greeting this might
be. 30 The angel said to her, 'Do not be
afraid, Mary, for you have found favour
with God. 31 And now, you will conceive
in your womb and bear a son, and you
will name him Jesus. 32 He will be great,
and will be called the Son of the Most
High, and the Lord God will give to him
the throne of his ancestor David. 33 He
will reign over the house of Jacob for
ever, and of his kingdom there will be
no end.' 34 Mary said to the angel, 'How
can this be, since I am a virgin?'[c] 35 The
angel said to her, 'The Holy Spirit will
come upon you, and the power of the
Most High will overshadow you; therefore the child to be born[d] will be holy;
he will be called Son of God. 36 And now,
your relative Elizabeth in her old age
has also conceived a son; and this is the
sixth month for her who was said to be
barren. 37 For nothing will be impossible
with God.' 38 Then Mary said, 'Here am I,
the servant of the Lord; let it be with me

[a] **1.3** Or *for a long time* [b] **1.28** Other ancient authorities add *Blessed are you among women*
[c] **1.34** Gk *I do not know a man* [d] **1.35** Other ancient authorities add *of you*

according to your word.' Then the angel
departed from her.

MARY VISITS ELIZABETH

39 In those days Mary set out and
went with haste to a Judean town in
the hill country, 40 where she entered
the house of Zechariah and greeted
Elizabeth. 41 When Elizabeth heard
Mary's greeting, the child leapt in her
womb. And Elizabeth was filled with
the Holy Spirit 42 and exclaimed with
a loud cry, 'Blessed are you among
women, and blessed is the fruit of your
womb. 43 And why has this happened
to me, that the mother of my Lord
comes to me? 44 For as soon as I heard
the sound of your greeting, the child in
my womb leapt for joy. 45 And blessed is
she who believed that there would be[e]
a fulfilment of what was spoken to her
by the Lord.'

MARY'S SONG OF PRAISE

46 And Mary[f] said,
'My soul magnifies the Lord,
47 and my spirit rejoices in
God my Saviour,
48 for he has looked with favour on the
lowliness of his servant.
Surely, from now on all
generations will
call me blessed;
49 for the Mighty One has done
great things for me,
and holy is his name.
50 His mercy is for those who fear him
from generation to generation.
51 He has shown strength with his arm;
he has scattered the proud in the
thoughts of their hearts.
52 He has brought down the powerful
from their thrones,
and lifted up the lowly;
53 he has filled the hungry with
good things,
and sent the rich away empty.
54 He has helped his servant Israel,
in remembrance of his mercy,
55 according to the promise he
made to our ancestors,
to Abraham and to his
descendants for ever.'

56 And Mary remained with her for
about three months and then returned
to her home.

THE BIRTH OF JOHN THE BAPTIST

57 Now the time came for Elizabeth
to give birth, and she bore a son. 58 Her
neighbours and relatives heard that the
Lord had shown his great mercy to her,
and they rejoiced with her.

59 On the eighth day they came to
circumcise the child, and they were going to name him Zechariah after his father. 60 But his mother said, 'No; he is to
be called John.' 61 They said to her, 'None
of your relatives has this name.' 62 Then
they began motioning to his father to
find out what name he wanted to give
him. 63 He asked for a writing-tablet
and wrote, 'His name is John.' And all
of them were amazed. 64 Immediately
his mouth was opened and his tongue
freed, and he began to speak, praising
God. 65 Fear came over all their neighbours, and all these things were talked
about throughout the entire hill country of Judea. 66 All who heard them pondered them and said, 'What then will
this child become?' For, indeed, the
hand of the Lord was with him.

ZECHARIAH'S PROPHECY

67 Then his father Zechariah was
filled with the Holy Spirit and spoke
this prophecy:
68 'Blessed be the Lord God of Israel,
for he has looked favourably on his
people and redeemed them.
69 He has raised up a mighty
saviour[g] for us
in the house of his servant David,
70 as he spoke through the mouth of
his holy prophets from of old,
71 that we would be saved from
our enemies and from the
hand of all who hate us.
72 Thus he has shown the mercy
promised to our ancestors,
and has remembered his
holy covenant,
73 the oath that he swore to our
ancestor Abraham,
to grant us 74 that we, being
rescued from the hands
of our enemies,
might serve him without fear, 75 in
holiness and righteousness
before him all our days.
76 And you, child, will be called the
prophet of the Most High;
for you will go before the Lord
to prepare his ways,
77 to give knowledge of salvation
to his people
by the forgiveness of their sins.

[e] **1.45** Or *believed, for there will be* [f] **1.46** Other ancient authorities read *Elizabeth* [g] **1.69** Gk *a horn of salvation*

78 By the tender mercy of our God,
the dawn from on high will
break upon[h] us,
79 to give light to those who sit
in darkness and in the
shadow of death,
to guide our feet into the
way of peace.'
80 The child grew and became strong
in spirit, and he was in the wilderness
until the day he appeared publicly to Israel.

THE BIRTH OF JESUS

2 In those days a decree went out
from Emperor Augustus that all
the world should be registered. 2This
was the first registration and was taken
while Quirinius was governor of Syria.
3All went to their own towns to be registered. 4Joseph also went from the
town of Nazareth in Galilee to Judea,
to the city of David called Bethlehem,
because he was descended from the
house and family of David. 5He went to
be registered with Mary, to whom he
was engaged and who was expecting a
child. 6While they were there, the time
came for her to deliver her child. 7And
she gave birth to her firstborn son and
wrapped him in bands of cloth, and laid
him in a manger, because there was no
place for them in the inn.

THE SHEPHERDS AND THE ANGELS

8 In that region there were shepherds living in the fields, keeping watch
over their flock by night. 9Then an angel
of the Lord stood before them, and the
glory of the Lord shone around them,
and they were terrified. 10But the angel said to them, 'Do not be afraid; for
see—I am bringing you good news
of great joy for all the people: 11to you
is born this day in the city of David a
Saviour, who is the Messiah,[i] the Lord.
12This will be a sign for you: you will find
a child wrapped in bands of cloth and lying in a manger.' 13And suddenly there
was with the angel a multitude of the
heavenly host,[j] praising God and saying,
14 'Glory to God in the highest heaven,
and on earth peace among those
whom he favours!'[k]

15 When the angels had left them
and gone into heaven, the shepherds
said to one another, 'Let us go now to
Bethlehem and see this thing that has
taken place, which the Lord has made
known to us.' 16So they went with haste
and found Mary and Joseph, and the
child lying in the manger. 17When they
saw this, they made known what had
been told them about this child; 18and
all who heard it were amazed at what
the shepherds told them. 19But Mary
treasured all these words and pondered
them in her heart. 20The shepherds returned, glorifying and praising God for
all they had heard and seen, as it had
been told them.

JESUS IS NAMED

21 After eight days had passed, it
was time to circumcise the child; and
he was called Jesus, the name given by
the angel before he was conceived in the
womb.

JESUS IS PRESENTED IN THE TEMPLE

22 When the time came for their purification according to the law of Moses,
they brought him up to Jerusalem to
present him to the Lord 23(as it is written in the law of the Lord, 'Every firstborn male shall be designated as holy to
the Lord'), 24and they offered a sacrifice
according to what is stated in the law of
the Lord, 'a pair of turtle-doves or two
young pigeons.'

25 Now there was a man in Jerusalem whose name was Simeon;[l] this
man was righteous and devout, looking
forward to the consolation of Israel, and
the Holy Spirit rested on him. 26It had
been revealed to him by the Holy Spirit
that he would not see death before he
had seen the Lord's Messiah.[m] 27Guided
by the Spirit, Simeon[n] came into the
temple; and when the parents brought
in the child Jesus, to do for him what
was customary under the law, 28Sim-
eon[o] took him in his arms and praised
God, saying,
29 'Master, now you are dismissing
your servant[p] in peace,
according to your word;
30 for my eyes have seen your salvation,
31 which you have prepared in the
presence of all peoples,
32 a light for revelation to the Gentiles
and for glory to your people Israel.'

33 And the child's father and mother
were amazed at what was being said
about him. 34Then Simeon[q] blessed

[h] **1.78** Other ancient authorities read *has broken upon* [i] **2.11** Or *the Christ* [j] **2.13** Gk *army*
[k] **2.14** Other ancient authorities read *peace, goodwill among people* [l] **2.25** Gk *Symeon*
[m] **2.26** Or *the Lord's Christ* [n] **2.27** Gk *In the Spirit, he* [o] **2.28** Gk *he* [p] **2.29** Gk *slave*
[q] **2.34** Gk *Symeon*

them and said to his mother Mary, 'This child is destined for the falling and the rising of many in Israel, and to be a sign that will be opposed 35 so that the inner thoughts of many will be revealed—and a sword will pierce your own soul too.'

36 There was also a prophet, Anna[r] the daughter of Phanuel, of the tribe of Asher. She was of a great age, having lived with her husband for seven years after her marriage, 37 then as a widow to the age of eighty-four. She never left the temple but worshipped there with fasting and prayer night and day. 38 At that moment she came, and began to praise God and to speak about the child[s] to all who were looking for the redemption of Jerusalem.

THE RETURN TO NAZARETH

39 When they had finished everything required by the law of the Lord, they returned to Galilee, to their own town of Nazareth. 40 The child grew and became strong, filled with wisdom; and the favour of God was upon him.

THE BOY JESUS IN THE TEMPLE

41 Now every year his parents went to Jerusalem for the festival of the Passover. 42 And when he was twelve years old, they went up as usual for the festival. 43 When the festival was ended and they started to return, the boy Jesus stayed behind in Jerusalem, but his parents did not know it. 44 Assuming that he was in the group of travellers, they went a day's journey. Then they started to look for him among their relatives and friends. 45 When they did not find him, they returned to Jerusalem to search for him. 46 After three days they found him in the temple, sitting among the teachers, listening to them and asking them questions. 47 And all who heard him were amazed at his understanding and his answers. 48 When his parents[t] saw him they were astonished; and his mother said to him, 'Child, why have you treated us like this? Look, your father and I have been searching for you in great anxiety.' 49 He said to them, 'Why were you searching for me? Did you not know that I must be in my Father's house?'[u] 50 But they did not understand what he said to them. 51 Then he went down with them and came to Nazareth, and was obedient to them. His mother treasured all these things in her heart.

52 And Jesus increased in wisdom and in years,[v] and in divine and human favour.

THE PROCLAMATION OF JOHN THE BAPTIST

3 In the fifteenth year of the reign of Emperor Tiberius, when Pontius Pilate was governor of Judea, and Herod was ruler[w] of Galilee, and his brother Philip ruler[x] of the region of Ituraea and Trachonitis, and Lysanias ruler[y] of Abilene, 2 during the high-priesthood of Annas and Caiaphas, the word of God came to John son of Zechariah in the wilderness. 3 He went into all the region around the Jordan, proclaiming a baptism of repentance for the forgiveness of sins, 4 as it is written in the book of the words of the prophet Isaiah,

'The voice of one crying out
in the wilderness:
"Prepare the way of the Lord,
make his paths straight.
5 Every valley shall be filled,
and every mountain and hill
shall be made low,
and the crooked shall be
made straight,
and the rough ways made smooth;
6 and all flesh shall see the
salvation of God." '

7 John said to the crowds that came out to be baptized by him, 'You brood of vipers! Who warned you to flee from the wrath to come? 8 Bear fruits worthy of repentance. Do not begin to say to yourselves, "We have Abraham as our ancestor"; for I tell you, God is able from these stones to raise up children to Abraham. 9 Even now the axe is lying at the root of the trees; every tree therefore that does not bear good fruit is cut down and thrown into the fire.'

10 And the crowds asked him, 'What then should we do?' 11 In reply he said to them, 'Whoever has two coats must share with anyone who has none; and whoever has food must do likewise.' 12 Even tax-collectors came to be baptized, and they asked him, 'Teacher, what should we do?' 13 He said to them, 'Collect no more than the amount prescribed for you.' 14 Soldiers also asked him, 'And we, what should we do?' He said to them, 'Do not extort money from anyone by threats or false accusation, and be satisfied with your wages.'

15 As the people were filled with expectation, and all were questioning in their hearts concerning John, whether

r 2.36 Gk *Hanna* s 2.38 Gk *him* t 2.48 Gk *they*
u 2.49 Or *be about my Father's interests?*
v 2.52 Or *in stature* w 3.1 Gk *tetrarch*
x 3.1 Gk *tetrarch* y 3.1 Gk *tetrarch*

he might be the Messiah,[z] 16John answered all of them by saying, 'I baptize
you with water; but one who is more
powerful than I is coming; I am not
worthy to untie the thong of his sandals. He will baptize you with[a] the Holy
Spirit and fire. 17His winnowing-fork is
in his hand, to clear his threshing-floor
and to gather the wheat into his granary; but the chaff he will burn with unquenchable fire.'
18 So, with many other exhortations, he proclaimed the good news to
the people. 19But Herod the ruler,[b] who
had been rebuked by him because of Herodias, his brother's wife, and because of
all the evil things that Herod had done,
20added to them all by shutting up John
in prison.

THE BAPTISM OF JESUS

21 Now when all the people were
baptized, and when Jesus also had been
baptized and was praying, the heaven
was opened, 22and the Holy Spirit descended upon him in bodily form like
a dove. And a voice came from heaven,
'You are my Son, the Beloved;[c] with you
I am well pleased.'[d]

THE ANCESTORS OF JESUS

23 Jesus was about thirty years old
when he began his work. He was the
son (as was thought) of Joseph son of
Heli, 24son of Matthat, son of Levi, son
of Melchi, son of Jannai, son of Joseph,
25son of Mattathias, son of Amos, son
of Nahum, son of Esli, son of Naggai,
26son of Maath, son of Mattathias, son
of Semein, son of Josech, son of Joda,
27son of Joanan, son of Rhesa, son of Zerubbabel, son of Shealtiel,[e] son of Neri,
28son of Melchi, son of Addi, son of Co-
sam, son of Elmadam, son of Er, 29son of
Joshua, son of Eliezer, son of Jorim, son
of Matthat, son of Levi, 30son of Simeon, son of Judah, son of Joseph, son of
Jonam, son of Eliakim, 31son of Melea,
son of Menna, son of Mattatha, son of
Nathan, son of David, 32son of Jesse, son
of Obed, son of Boaz, son of Sala,[f] son
of Nahshon, 33son of Amminadab, son
of Admin, son of Arni,[g] son of Hezron,
son of Perez, son of Judah, 34son of Jacob, son of Isaac, son of Abraham, son
of Terah, son of Nahor, 35son of Serug,
son of Reu, son of Peleg, son of Eber, son
of Shelah, 36son of Cainan, son of Arphaxad, son of Shem, son of Noah, son
of Lamech, 37son of Methuselah, son of
Enoch, son of Jared, son of Mahalaleel,
son of Cainan, 38son of Enos, son of
Seth, son of Adam, son of God.

THE TEMPTATION OF JESUS

4 Jesus, full of the Holy Spirit, returned from the Jordan and was led
by the Spirit in the wilderness, 2where
for forty days he was tempted by the
devil. He ate nothing at all during those
days, and when they were over, he was
famished. 3The devil said to him, 'If you
are the Son of God, command this stone
to become a loaf of bread.' 4Jesus answered him, 'It is written, "One does not
live by bread alone." '
5 Then the devil[h] led him up and
showed him in an instant all the kingdoms of the world. 6And the devil[i] said
to him, 'To you I will give their glory
and all this authority; for it has been
given over to me, and I give it to anyone I please. 7If you, then, will worship
me, it will all be yours.' 8Jesus answered
him, 'It is written,

"Worship the Lord your God,
and serve only him." '

9 Then the devil[j] took him to Jerusalem, and placed him on the pinnacle of
the temple, saying to him, 'If you are the
Son of God, throw yourself down from
here, 10for it is written,

"He will command his angels
concerning you,
to protect you",

11and

"On their hands they will
bear you up,
so that you will not dash your
foot against a stone." '

12Jesus answered him, 'It is said, "Do
not put the Lord your God to the test." '
13When the devil had finished every
test, he departed from him until an opportune time.

THE BEGINNING OF THE GALILEAN MINISTRY

14 Then Jesus, filled with the power
of the Spirit, returned to Galilee, and
a report about him spread through all
the surrounding country. 15He began
to teach in their synagogues and was
praised by everyone.

[z] 3.15 Or *the Christ* [a] 3.16 Or *in* [b] 3.19 Gk *tetrarch* [c] 3.22 Or *my beloved Son*
[d] 3.22 Other ancient authorities read *You are my Son, today I have begotten you* [e] 3.27 Gk *Salathiel* [f] 3.32 Other ancient authorities read *Salmon* [g] 3.33 Other ancient authorities read *Amminadab, son of Aram*; others vary widely
[h] 4.5 Gk *he* [i] 4.6 Gk *he* [j] 4.9 Gk *he*

THE REJECTION OF JESUS AT NAZARETH

16 When he came to Nazareth, where
he had been brought up, he went to the
synagogue on the sabbath day, as was
his custom. He stood up to read, 17and
the scroll of the prophet Isaiah was
given to him. He unrolled the scroll and
found the place where it was written:

18 'The Spirit of the Lord is upon me,
  because he has anointed me
    to bring good news to the poor.
 He has sent me to proclaim
    release to the captives
  and recovery of sight to the blind,
    to let the oppressed go free,
19 to proclaim the year of the
    Lord's favour.'

20And he rolled up the scroll, gave it
back to the attendant, and sat down.
The eyes of all in the synagogue were
fixed on him. 21Then he began to say to
them, 'Today this scripture has been fulfilled in your hearing.' 22All spoke well
of him and were amazed at the gracious
words that came from his mouth. They
said, 'Is not this Joseph's son?' 23He said
to them, 'Doubtless you will quote to
me this proverb, "Doctor, cure yourself!"
And you will say, "Do here also in your
home town the things that we have
heard you did at Capernaum." ' 24And
he said, 'Truly I tell you, no prophet is
accepted in the prophet's home town.
25But the truth is, there were many
widows in Israel in the time of Elijah,
when the heaven was shut up for three
years and six months, and there was a
severe famine over all the land; 26yet
Elijah was sent to none of them except to a widow at Zarephath in Sidon.
27There were also many lepers[k] in Israel
in the time of the prophet Elisha, and
none of them was cleansed except Naaman the Syrian.' 28When they heard
this, all in the synagogue were filled
with rage. 29They got up, drove him out
of the town, and led him to the brow of
the hill on which their town was built,
so that they might hurl him off the cliff.
30But he passed through the midst of
them and went on his way.

THE MAN WITH AN UNCLEAN SPIRIT

31 He went down to Capernaum, a
city in Galilee, and was teaching them
on the sabbath. 32They were astounded
at his teaching, because he spoke with
authority. 33In the synagogue there was
a man who had the spirit of an unclean
demon, and he cried out with a loud
voice, 34'Let us alone! What have you to
do with us, Jesus of Nazareth? Have you
come to destroy us? I know who you are,
the Holy One of God.' 35But Jesus rebuked
him, saying, 'Be silent, and come out of
him!' When the demon had thrown him
down before them, he came out of him
without having done him any harm.
36They were all amazed and kept saying
to one another, 'What kind of utterance
is this? For with authority and power he
commands the unclean spirits, and out
they come!' 37And a report about him
began to reach every place in the region.

HEALINGS AT SIMON'S HOUSE

38 After leaving the synagogue he
entered Simon's house. Now Simon's
mother-in-law was suffering from a
high fever, and they asked him about
her. 39Then he stood over her and rebuked the fever, and it left her. Immediately she got up and began to serve
them.

40 As the sun was setting, all those
who had any who were sick with various
kinds of diseases brought them to him;
and he laid his hands on each of them
and cured them. 41Demons also came
out of many, shouting, 'You are the Son
of God!' But he rebuked them and would
not allow them to speak, because they
knew that he was the Messiah.[l]

JESUS PREACHES IN THE SYNAGOGUES

42 At daybreak he departed and went
into a deserted place. And the crowds
were looking for him; and when they
reached him, they wanted to prevent
him from leaving them. 43But he said to
them, 'I must proclaim the good news
of the kingdom of God to the other cities
also; for I was sent for this purpose.' 44So
he continued proclaiming the message
in the synagogues of Judea.[m]

JESUS CALLS THE FIRST DISCIPLES

5 Once while Jesus[n] was standing
beside the lake of Gennesaret, and
the crowd was pressing in on him to
hear the word of God, 2he saw two boats
there at the shore of the lake; the fishermen had gone out of them and were
washing their nets. 3He got into one of
the boats, the one belonging to Simon,
and asked him to put out a little way

[k] **4.27** The terms *leper* and *leprosy* can refer to several diseases [l] **4.41** Or *the Christ*
[m] **4.44** Other ancient authorities read *Galilee*
[n] **5.1** Gk *he*

from the shore. Then he sat down and taught the crowds from the boat. 4 When he had finished speaking, he said to Simon, 'Put out into the deep water and let down your nets for a catch.' 5 Simon answered, 'Master, we have worked all night long but have caught nothing. Yet if you say so, I will let down the nets.' 6 When they had done this, they caught so many fish that their nets were beginning to break. 7 So they signalled to their partners in the other boat to come and help them. And they came and filled both boats, so that they began to sink. 8 But when Simon Peter saw it, he fell down at Jesus' knees, saying, 'Go away from me, Lord, for I am a sinful man!' 9 For he and all who were with him were amazed at the catch of fish that they had taken; 10 and so also were James and John, sons of Zebedee, who were partners with Simon. Then Jesus said to Simon, 'Do not be afraid; from now on you will be catching people.' 11 When they had brought their boats to shore, they left everything and followed him.

JESUS CLEANSES A LEPER

12 Once, when he was in one of the cities, there was a man covered with leprosy.[o] When he saw Jesus, he bowed with his face to the ground and begged him, 'Lord, if you choose, you can make me clean.' 13 Then Jesus[p] stretched out his hand, touched him, and said, 'I do choose. Be made clean.' Immediately the leprosy[q] left him. 14 And he ordered him to tell no one. 'Go', he said, 'and show yourself to the priest, and, as Moses commanded, make an offering for your cleansing, for a testimony to them.' 15 But now more than ever the word about Jesus[r] spread abroad; many crowds would gather to hear him and to be cured of their diseases. 16 But he would withdraw to deserted places and pray.

JESUS HEALS A PARALYTIC

17 One day, while he was teaching, Pharisees and teachers of the law were sitting nearby (they had come from every village of Galilee and Judea and from Jerusalem); and the power of the Lord was with him to heal.[s] 18 Just then some men came, carrying a paralysed man on a bed. They were trying to bring him in and lay him before Jesus;[t] 19 but finding no way to bring him in because of the crowd, they went up on the roof and let him down with his bed through the tiles into the middle of the crowd[u] in front of Jesus. 20 When he saw their faith, he said, 'Friend,[v] your sins are forgiven you.' 21 Then the scribes and the Pharisees began to question, 'Who is this who is speaking blasphemies? Who can forgive sins but God alone?' 22 When Jesus perceived their questionings, he answered them, 'Why do you raise such questions in your hearts? 23 Which is easier, to say, "Your sins are forgiven you", or to say, "Stand up and walk"? 24 But so that you may know that the Son of Man has authority on earth to forgive sins'—he said to the one who was paralysed—'I say to you, stand up and take your bed and go to your home.' 25 Immediately he stood up before them, took what he had been lying on, and went to his home, glorifying God. 26 Amazement seized all of them, and they glorified God and were filled with awe, saying, 'We have seen strange things today.'

JESUS CALLS LEVI

27 After this he went out and saw a tax-collector named Levi, sitting at the tax booth; and he said to him, 'Follow me.' 28 And he got up, left everything, and followed him.

29 Then Levi gave a great banquet for him in his house; and there was a large crowd of tax-collectors and others sitting at the table[w] with them. 30 The Pharisees and their scribes were complaining to his disciples, saying, 'Why do you eat and drink with tax-collectors and sinners?' 31 Jesus answered, 'Those who are well have no need of a physician, but those who are sick; 32 I have come to call not the righteous but sinners to repentance.'

THE QUESTION ABOUT FASTING

33 Then they said to him, 'John's disciples, like the disciples of the Pharisees, frequently fast and pray, but your disciples eat and drink.' 34 Jesus said to them, 'You cannot make wedding-guests fast while the bridegroom is with them, can you? 35 The days will come when the bridegroom will be taken away from them, and then they will fast in those days.' 36 He also told them a parable: 'No

[o] **5.12** The terms *leper* and *leprosy* can refer to several diseases [p] **5.13** Gk *he* [q] **5.13** The terms *leper* and *leprosy* can refer to several diseases [r] **5.15** Gk *him* [s] **5.17** Other ancient authorities read *was present to heal them* [t] **5.18** Gk *him* [u] **5.19** Gk *into the midst* [v] **5.20** Gk *Man* [w] **5.29** Gk *reclining*

one tears a piece from a new garment
and sews it on an old garment; otherwise the new will be torn, and the piece
from the new will not match the old.
37 And no one puts new wine into old
wineskins; otherwise the new wine will
burst the skins and will be spilled, and
the skins will be destroyed. 38 But new
wine must be put into fresh wineskins.
39 And no one after drinking old wine
desires new wine, but says, "The old is
good." '[x]

THE QUESTION ABOUT THE SABBATH

6 One sabbath[y] while Jesus[z] was going through the cornfields, his
disciples plucked some heads of grain,
rubbed them in their hands, and ate
them. 2 But some of the Pharisees said,
'Why are you doing what is not lawful[a]
on the sabbath?' 3 Jesus answered, 'Have
you not read what David did when he
and his companions were hungry? 4 He
entered the house of God and took and
ate the bread of the Presence, which it
is not lawful for any but the priests to
eat, and gave some to his companions?'
5 Then he said to them, 'The Son of Man
is lord of the sabbath.'

THE MAN WITH A WITHERED HAND

6 On another sabbath he entered the
synagogue and taught, and there was a
man there whose right hand was withered. 7 The scribes and the Pharisees
watched him to see whether he would
cure on the sabbath, so that they might
find an accusation against him. 8 Even
though he knew what they were thinking, he said to the man who had the
withered hand, 'Come and stand here.'
He got up and stood there. 9 Then Jesus
said to them, 'I ask you, is it lawful to do
good or to do harm on the sabbath, to
save life or to destroy it?' 10 After looking
around at all of them, he said to him,
'Stretch out your hand.' He did so, and
his hand was restored. 11 But they were
filled with fury and discussed with one
another what they might do to Jesus.

JESUS CHOOSES THE TWELVE APOSTLES

12 Now during those days he went
out to the mountain to pray; and he
spent the night in prayer to God. 13 And
when day came, he called his disciples
and chose twelve of them, whom he
also named apostles: 14 Simon, whom
he named Peter, and his brother Andrew, and James, and John, and Philip,
and Bartholomew, 15 and Matthew, and
Thomas, and James son of Alphaeus,
and Simon, who was called the Zealot,
16 and Judas son of James, and Judas Iscariot, who became a traitor.

JESUS TEACHES AND HEALS

17 He came down with them and
stood on a level place, with a great
crowd of his disciples and a great multitude of people from all Judea, Jerusalem, and the coast of Tyre and Sidon.
18 They had come to hear him and to be
healed of their diseases; and those who
were troubled with unclean spirits were
cured. 19 And all in the crowd were trying to touch him, for power came out
from him and healed all of them.

BLESSINGS AND WOES

20 Then he looked up at his disciples
and said:

'Blessed are you who are poor,
  for yours is the kingdom of God.
21 'Blessed are you who are
    hungry now,
  for you will be filled.
'Blessed are you who weep now,
  for you will laugh.

22 'Blessed are you when people hate
you, and when they exclude you, revile
you, and defame you[b] on account of the
Son of Man. 23 Rejoice on that day and
leap for joy, for surely your reward is
great in heaven; for that is what their
ancestors did to the prophets.

24 'But woe to you who are rich,
  for you have received your
    consolation.
25 'Woe to you who are full now,
  for you will be hungry.
'Woe to you who are laughing now,
  for you will mourn and weep.

26 'Woe to you when all speak well of
you, for that is what their ancestors did
to the false prophets.

LOVE FOR ENEMIES

27 'But I say to you that listen, Love
your enemies, do good to those who
hate you, 28 bless those who curse you,
pray for those who abuse you. 29 If anyone strikes you on the cheek, offer the
other also; and from anyone who takes
away your coat do not withhold even
your shirt. 30 Give to everyone who begs

[x] **5.39** Other ancient authorities read *better*; others lack verse 39 [y] **6.1** Other ancient authorities read *On the second first sabbath* [z] **6.1** Gk *he* [a] **6.2** Other ancient authorities add *to do* [b] **6.22** Gk *cast out your name as evil*

from you; and if anyone takes away your
goods, do not ask for them again. 31Do
to others as you would have them do to
you.

32 'If you love those who love you,
what credit is that to you? For even sinners love those who love them. 33If you
do good to those who do good to you,
what credit is that to you? For even sinners do the same. 34If you lend to those
from whom you hope to receive, what
credit is that to you? Even sinners lend
to sinners, to receive as much again.
35But love your enemies, do good, and
lend, expecting nothing in return.[c] Your
reward will be great, and you will be
children of the Most High; for he is kind
to the ungrateful and the wicked. 36Be
merciful, just as your Father is merciful.

JUDGING OTHERS

37 'Do not judge, and you will not be
judged; do not condemn, and you will
not be condemned. Forgive, and you
will be forgiven; 38give, and it will be
given to you. A good measure, pressed
down, shaken together, running over,
will be put into your lap; for the measure you give will be the measure you
get back.'

39 He also told them a parable: 'Can
a blind person guide a blind person?
Will not both fall into a pit? 40A disciple is not above the teacher, but everyone who is fully qualified will be like the
teacher. 41Why do you see the speck in
your neighbour's[d] eye, but do not notice
the log in your own eye? 42Or how can
you say to your neighbour,[e] "Friend,[f]
let me take out the speck in your eye",
when you yourself do not see the log in
your own eye? You hypocrite, first take
the log out of your own eye, and then
you will see clearly to take the speck out
of your neighbour's[g] eye.

A TREE AND ITS FRUIT

43 'No good tree bears bad fruit, nor
again does a bad tree bear good fruit;
44for each tree is known by its own fruit.
Figs are not gathered from thorns, nor
are grapes picked from a bramble bush.
45The good person out of the good treasure of the heart produces good, and the
evil person out of evil treasure produces
evil; for it is out of the abundance of the
heart that the mouth speaks.

THE TWO FOUNDATIONS

46 'Why do you call me "Lord, Lord",
and do not do what I tell you? 47I will
show you what someone is like who
comes to me, hears my words, and acts
on them. 48That one is like a man building a house, who dug deeply and laid the
foundation on rock; when a flood arose,
the river burst against that house but
could not shake it, because it had been
well built.[h] 49But the one who hears
and does not act is like a man who built
a house on the ground without a foundation. When the river burst against it,
immediately it fell, and great was the
ruin of that house.'

JESUS HEALS A CENTURION'S SERVANT

7 After Jesus[i] had finished all his sayings in the hearing of the people, he
entered Capernaum. 2A centurion there
had a slave whom he valued highly, and
who was ill and close to death. 3When
he heard about Jesus, he sent some Jewish elders to him, asking him to come
and heal his slave. 4When they came
to Jesus, they appealed to him earnestly, saying, 'He is worthy of having
you do this for him, 5for he loves our
people, and it is he who built our synagogue for us.' 6And Jesus went with
them, but when he was not far from the
house, the centurion sent friends to say
to him, 'Lord, do not trouble yourself,
for I am not worthy to have you come
under my roof; 7therefore I did not presume to come to you. But only speak
the word, and let my servant be healed.
8For I also am a man set under authority, with soldiers under me; and I say to
one, "Go", and he goes, and to another,
"Come", and he comes, and to my slave,
"Do this", and the slave does it.' 9When
Jesus heard this he was amazed at him,
and turning to the crowd that followed
him, he said, 'I tell you, not even in Israel have I found such faith.' 10When
those who had been sent returned to
the house, they found the slave in good
health.

JESUS RAISES THE WIDOW'S SON AT NAIN

11 Soon afterwards[j] he went to a
town called Nain, and his disciples and
a large crowd went with him. 12As he
approached the gate of the town, a man

c 6.35 Other ancient authorities read *despairing of no one* d 6.41 Gk *brother's* e 6.42 Gk *brother*
f 6.42 Gk *brother* g 6.42 Gk *brother's*
h 6.48 Other ancient authorities read *founded upon the rock* i 7.1 Gk *he* j 7.11 Other ancient authorities read *Next day*

who had died was being carried out. He
was his mother's only son, and she was
a widow; and with her was a large crowd
from the town. 13When the Lord saw
her, he had compassion for her and said
to her, 'Do not weep.' 14Then he came
forward and touched the bier, and the
bearers stood still. And he said, 'Young
man, I say to you, rise!' 15The dead man
sat up and began to speak, and Jesus[k]
gave him to his mother. 16Fear seized all
of them; and they glorified God, saying,
'A great prophet has risen among us!'
and 'God has looked favourably on his
people!' 17This word about him spread
throughout Judea and all the surrounding country.

MESSENGERS FROM JOHN THE BAPTIST

18 The disciples of John reported all
these things to him. So John summoned
two of his disciples 19and sent them to
the Lord to ask, 'Are you the one who is
to come, or are we to wait for another?'
20When the men had come to him, they
said, 'John the Baptist has sent us to you
to ask, "Are you the one who is to come,
or are we to wait for another?"' 21Jesus[l]
had just then cured many people of diseases, plagues, and evil spirits, and had
given sight to many who were blind.
22And he answered them, 'Go and tell
John what you have seen and heard: the
blind receive their sight, the lame walk,
the lepers[m] are cleansed, the deaf hear,
the dead are raised, the poor have good
news brought to them. 23And blessed is
anyone who takes no offence at me.'
24 When John's messengers had
gone, Jesus[n] began to speak to the
crowds about John:[o] 'What did you go
out into the wilderness to look at? A
reed shaken by the wind? 25What then
did you go out to see? Someone[p] dressed
in soft robes? Look, those who put on
fine clothing and live in luxury are in
royal palaces. 26What then did you go
out to see? A prophet? Yes, I tell you,
and more than a prophet. 27This is the
one about whom it is written,

"See, I am sending my messenger
ahead of you,
who will prepare your
way before you."

28I tell you, among those born of women
no one is greater than John; yet the least
in the kingdom of God is greater than
he.' 29(And all the people who heard
this, including the tax-collectors, acknowledged the justice of God,[q] because
they had been baptized with John's baptism. 30But by refusing to be baptized
by him, the Pharisees and the lawyers
rejected God's purpose for themselves.)
31 'To what then will I compare the
people of this generation, and what are
they like? 32They are like children sitting in the market-place and calling to
one another,

"We played the flute for you, and
you did not dance;
we wailed, and you did not weep."

33For John the Baptist has come eating
no bread and drinking no wine, and you
say, "He has a demon"; 34the Son of Man
has come eating and drinking, and you
say, "Look, a glutton and a drunkard,
a friend of tax-collectors and sinners!"
35Nevertheless, wisdom is vindicated by
all her children.'

A SINFUL WOMAN FORGIVEN

36 One of the Pharisees asked Jesus[r]
to eat with him, and he went into the
Pharisee's house and took his place at
the table. 37And a woman in the city,
who was a sinner, having learned that
he was eating in the Pharisee's house,
brought an alabaster jar of ointment.
38She stood behind him at his feet,
weeping, and began to bathe his feet
with her tears and to dry them with her
hair. Then she continued kissing his feet
and anointing them with the ointment.
39Now when the Pharisee who had invited him saw it, he said to himself, 'If
this man were a prophet, he would have
known who and what kind of woman
this is who is touching him—that she
is a sinner.' 40Jesus spoke up and said
to him, 'Simon, I have something to
say to you.' 'Teacher,' he replied, 'speak.'
41'A certain creditor had two debtors;
one owed five hundred denarii,[s] and the
other fifty. 42When they could not pay,
he cancelled the debts for both of them.
Now which of them will love him more?'
43Simon answered, 'I suppose the one
for whom he cancelled the greater debt.'
And Jesus[t] said to him, 'You have judged
rightly.' 44Then turning towards the
woman, he said to Simon, 'Do you see
this woman? I entered your house; you
gave me no water for my feet, but she

[k] **7.15** Gk *he* [l] **7.21** Gk *He* [m] **7.22** The terms *leper* and *leprosy* can refer to several diseases [n] **7.24** Gk *he* [o] **7.24** Gk *him* [p] **7.25** Or *Why then did you go out? To see someone* [q] **7.29** Or *praised God* [r] **7.36** Gk *him* [s] **7.41** The denarius was the usual day's wage for a labourer [t] **7.43** Gk *he*

has bathed my feet with her tears and
dried them with her hair. 45You gave
me no kiss, but from the time I came
in she has not stopped kissing my feet.
46You did not anoint my head with oil,
but she has anointed my feet with ointment. 47Therefore, I tell you, her sins,
which were many, have been forgiven;
hence she has shown great love. But
the one to whom little is forgiven, loves
little.' 48Then he said to her, 'Your sins
are forgiven.' 49But those who were at
the table with him began to say among
themselves, 'Who is this who even forgives sins?' 50And he said to the woman,
'Your faith has saved you; go in peace.'

SOME WOMEN ACCOMPANY JESUS

8 Soon afterwards he went on
through cities and villages, proclaiming and bringing the good news
of the kingdom of God. The twelve were
with him, 2as well as some women who
had been cured of evil spirits and infirmities: Mary, called Magdalene, from
whom seven demons had gone out,
3and Joanna, the wife of Herod's steward Chuza, and Susanna, and many others, who provided for them[u] out of their
resources.

THE PARABLE OF THE SOWER

4 When a great crowd gathered and
people from town after town came to
him, he said in a parable: 5'A sower
went out to sow his seed; and as he
sowed, some fell on the path and was
trampled on, and the birds of the air ate
it up. 6Some fell on the rock; and as it
grew up, it withered for lack of moisture. 7Some fell among thorns, and
the thorns grew with it and choked it.
8Some fell into good soil, and when it
grew, it produced a hundredfold.' As he
said this, he called out, 'Let anyone with
ears to hear listen!'

THE PURPOSE OF THE PARABLES

9 Then his disciples asked him what
this parable meant. 10He said, 'To you
it has been given to know the secrets[v]
of the kingdom of God; but to others I
speak[w] in parables, so that

"looking they may not perceive,
and listening they may
not understand."

THE PARABLE OF THE SOWER EXPLAINED

11 'Now the parable is this: The seed
is the word of God. 12The ones on the
path are those who have heard; then the
devil comes and takes away the word
from their hearts, so that they may not
believe and be saved. 13The ones on the
rock are those who, when they hear the
word, receive it with joy. But these have
no root; they believe only for a while
and in a time of testing fall away. 14As
for what fell among the thorns, these
are the ones who hear; but as they go on
their way, they are choked by the cares
and riches and pleasures of life, and
their fruit does not mature. 15But as for
that in the good soil, these are the ones
who, when they hear the word, hold it
fast in an honest and good heart, and
bear fruit with patient endurance.

A LAMP UNDER A JAR

16 'No one after lighting a lamp hides
it under a jar, or puts it under a bed, but
puts it on a lampstand, so that those
who enter may see the light. 17For nothing is hidden that will not be disclosed,
nor is anything secret that will not become known and come to light. 18Then
pay attention to how you listen; for to
those who have, more will be given; and
from those who do not have, even what
they seem to have will be taken away.'

THE TRUE KINDRED OF JESUS

19 Then his mother and his brothers
came to him, but they could not reach
him because of the crowd. 20And he was
told, 'Your mother and your brothers
are standing outside, wanting to see
you.' 21But he said to them, 'My mother
and my brothers are those who hear the
word of God and do it.'

JESUS CALMS A STORM

22 One day he got into a boat with his
disciples, and he said to them, 'Let us go
across to the other side of the lake.' So they
put out, 23and while they were sailing
he fell asleep. A gale swept down on the
lake, and the boat was filling with water,
and they were in danger. 24They went to
him and woke him up, shouting, 'Master,
Master, we are perishing!' And he woke
up and rebuked the wind and the raging
waves; they ceased, and there was a calm.
25He said to them, 'Where is your faith?'
They were afraid and amazed, and said
to one another, 'Who then is this, that he
commands even the winds and the water, and they obey him?'

[u] 8.3 Other ancient authorities read *him*
[v] 8.10 Or *mysteries* [w] 8.10 Gk lacks *I speak*

JESUS HEALS THE GERASENE DEMONIAC

26 Then they arrived at the country
of the Gerasenes,[x] which is opposite
Galilee. 27 As he stepped out on land, a
man of the city who had demons met
him. For a long time he had worn[y] no
clothes, and he did not live in a house
but in the tombs. 28 When he saw Jesus,
he fell down before him and shouted
at the top of his voice, 'What have you
to do with me, Jesus, Son of the Most
High God? I beg you, do not torment
me'— 29 for Jesus[z] had commanded the
unclean spirit to come out of the man.
(For many times it had seized him; he
was kept under guard and bound with
chains and shackles, but he would break
the bonds and be driven by the demon
into the wilds.) 30 Jesus then asked him,
'What is your name?' He said, 'Legion';
for many demons had entered him.
31 They begged him not to order them to
go back into the abyss.

32 Now there on the hillside a large
herd of swine was feeding; and the demons[a] begged Jesus[b] to let them enter
these. So he gave them permission.
33 Then the demons came out of the man
and entered the swine, and the herd
rushed down the steep bank into the
lake and was drowned.

34 When the swineherds saw what
had happened, they ran off and told it in
the city and in the country. 35 Then people came out to see what had happened,
and when they came to Jesus, they
found the man from whom the demons
had gone sitting at the feet of Jesus,
clothed and in his right mind. And they
were afraid. 36 Those who had seen it
told them how the one who had been
possessed by demons had been healed.
37 Then all the people of the surrounding
country of the Gerasenes[c] asked Jesus[d]
to leave them; for they were seized with
great fear. So he got into the boat and
returned. 38 The man from whom the demons had gone begged that he might be
with him; but Jesus[e] sent him away, saying, 39 'Return to your home, and declare
how much God has done for you.' So he
went away, proclaiming throughout the
city how much Jesus had done for him.

A GIRL RESTORED TO LIFE AND A WOMAN HEALED

40 Now when Jesus returned, the
crowd welcomed him, for they were all
waiting for him. 41 Just then there came
a man named Jairus, a leader of the synagogue. He fell at Jesus' feet and begged
him to come to his house, 42 for he had
an only daughter, about twelve years
old, who was dying.

As he went, the crowds pressed in
on him. 43 Now there was a woman
who had been suffering from haemorrhages for twelve years; and though she
had spent all she had on physicians,[f] no
one could cure her. 44 She came up behind him and touched the fringe of his
clothes, and immediately her haemorrhage stopped. 45 Then Jesus asked, 'Who
touched me?' When all denied it, Peter[g]
said, 'Master, the crowds surround you
and press in on you.' 46 But Jesus said,
'Someone touched me; for I noticed that
power had gone out from me.' 47 When
the woman saw that she could not remain hidden, she came trembling; and
falling down before him, she declared
in the presence of all the people why
she had touched him, and how she had
been immediately healed. 48 He said to
her, 'Daughter, your faith has made you
well; go in peace.'

49 While he was still speaking, someone came from the leader's house to say,
'Your daughter is dead; do not trouble
the teacher any longer.' 50 When Jesus
heard this, he replied, 'Do not fear. Only
believe, and she will be saved.' 51 When
he came to the house, he did not allow
anyone to enter with him, except Peter,
John, and James, and the child's father
and mother. 52 They were all weeping
and wailing for her; but he said, 'Do not
weep; for she is not dead but sleeping.'
53 And they laughed at him, knowing
that she was dead. 54 But he took her by
the hand and called out, 'Child, get up!'
55 Her spirit returned, and she got up at
once. Then he directed them to give her
something to eat. 56 Her parents were
astounded; but he ordered them to tell
no one what had happened.

THE MISSION OF THE TWELVE

9 Then Jesus[h] called the twelve together and gave them power and
authority over all demons and to cure

[x] **8.26** Other ancient authorities read *Gadarenes*; others, *Gergesenes* [y] **8.27** Other ancient authorities read *a man of the city who had had demons for a long time met him. He wore* [z] **8.29** Gk *he* [a] **8.32** Gk *they* [b] **8.32** Gk *him* [c] **8.37** Other ancient authorities read *Gadarenes*; others, *Gergesenes* [d] **8.37** Gk *him* [e] **8.38** Gk *he* [f] **8.43** Other ancient authorities lack *and though she had spent all she had on physicians* [g] **8.45** Other ancient authorities add *and those who were with him* [h] **9.1** Gk *he*

diseases, 2and he sent them out to proclaim the kingdom of God and to heal.
3He said to them, 'Take nothing for your
journey, no staff, nor bag, nor bread,
nor money—not even an extra tunic.
4Whatever house you enter, stay there,
and leave from there. 5Wherever they
do not welcome you, as you are leaving
that town shake the dust off your feet
as a testimony against them.' 6They departed and went through the villages,
bringing the good news and curing diseases everywhere.

HEROD'S PERPLEXITY

7 Now Herod the ruler[i] heard about
all that had taken place, and he was perplexed, because it was said by some that
John had been raised from the dead, 8by
some that Elijah had appeared, and by
others that one of the ancient prophets had arisen. 9Herod said, 'John I beheaded; but who is this about whom I
hear such things?' And he tried to see
him.

FEEDING THE FIVE THOUSAND

10 On their return the apostles told
Jesus[j] all they had done. He took them
with him and withdrew privately to
a city called Bethsaida. 11When the
crowds found out about it, they followed
him; and he welcomed them, and spoke
to them about the kingdom of God, and
healed those who needed to be cured.

12 The day was drawing to a close,
and the twelve came to him and said,
'Send the crowd away, so that they
may go into the surrounding villages
and countryside, to lodge and get provisions; for we are here in a deserted
place.' 13But he said to them, 'You give
them something to eat.' They said, 'We
have no more than five loaves and two
fish—unless we are to go and buy food
for all these people.' 14For there were
about five thousand men. And he said
to his disciples, 'Make them sit down in
groups of about fifty each.' 15They did
so and made them all sit down. 16And
taking the five loaves and the two fish,
he looked up to heaven, and blessed and
broke them, and gave them to the disciples to set before the crowd. 17And all
ate and were filled. What was left over
was gathered up, twelve baskets of broken pieces.

PETER'S DECLARATION ABOUT JESUS

18 Once when Jesus[k] was praying
alone, with only the disciples near him,
he asked them, 'Who do the crowds say
that I am?' 19They answered, 'John the
Baptist; but others, Elijah; and still others, that one of the ancient prophets has
arisen.' 20He said to them, 'But who do
you say that I am?' Peter answered, 'The
Messiah[l] of God.'

JESUS FORETELLS HIS DEATH AND RESURRECTION

21 He sternly ordered and commanded them not to tell anyone, 22say-
ing, 'The Son of Man must undergo
great suffering, and be rejected by the
elders, chief priests, and scribes, and be
killed, and on the third day be raised.'

23 Then he said to them all, 'If any
want to become my followers, let them
deny themselves and take up their cross
daily and follow me. 24For those who
want to save their life will lose it, and
those who lose their life for my sake will
save it. 25What does it profit them if they
gain the whole world, but lose or forfeit
themselves? 26Those who are ashamed
of me and of my words, of them the Son
of Man will be ashamed when he comes
in his glory and the glory of the Father
and of the holy angels. 27But truly I tell
you, there are some standing here who
will not taste death before they see the
kingdom of God.'

THE TRANSFIGURATION

28 Now about eight days after these
sayings Jesus[m] took with him Peter
and John and James, and went up on
the mountain to pray. 29And while
he was praying, the appearance of his
face changed, and his clothes became
dazzling white. 30Suddenly they saw
two men, Moses and Elijah, talking to
him. 31They appeared in glory and were
speaking of his departure, which he
was about to accomplish at Jerusalem.
32Now Peter and his companions were
weighed down with sleep; but since
they had stayed awake,[n] they saw his
glory and the two men who stood with
him. 33Just as they were leaving him,
Peter said to Jesus, 'Master, it is good for
us to be here; let us make three dwellings,[o] one for you, one for Moses, and
one for Elijah'—not knowing what he
said. 34While he was saying this, a cloud
came and overshadowed them; and they
were terrified as they entered the cloud.
35Then from the cloud came a voice that

[i] 9.7 Gk *tetrarch* [j] 9.10 Gk *him* [k] 9.18 Gk *he* [l] 9.20 Or *The Christ* [m] 9.28 Gk *he* [n] 9.32 Or *but when they were fully awake* [o] 9.33 Or *tents*

said, 'This is my Son, my Chosen;[p] listen
to him!' 36When the voice had spoken,
Jesus was found alone. And they kept silent and in those days told no one any of
the things they had seen.

JESUS HEALS A BOY WITH A DEMON

37 On the next day, when they had
come down from the mountain, a great
crowd met him. 38Just then a man from
the crowd shouted, 'Teacher, I beg you
to look at my son; he is my only child.
39Suddenly a spirit seizes him, and
all at once he[q] shrieks. It throws him
into convulsions until he foams at the
mouth; it mauls him and will scarcely
leave him. 40I begged your disciples to
cast it out, but they could not.' 41Jesus
answered, 'You faithless and perverse
generation, how much longer must I
be with you and bear with you? Bring
your son here.' 42While he was coming,
the demon dashed him to the ground
in convulsions. But Jesus rebuked the
unclean spirit, healed the boy, and
gave him back to his father. 43And all
were astounded at the greatness of
God.

JESUS AGAIN FORETELLS HIS DEATH

While everyone was amazed at all
that he was doing, he said to his disciples, 44'Let these words sink into your
ears: The Son of Man is going to be betrayed into human hands.' 45But they
did not understand this saying; its
meaning was concealed from them, so
that they could not perceive it. And they
were afraid to ask him about this saying.

TRUE GREATNESS

46 An argument arose among them
as to which one of them was the greatest. 47But Jesus, aware of their inner
thoughts, took a little child and put it
by his side, 48and said to them, 'Whoever welcomes this child in my name
welcomes me, and whoever welcomes
me welcomes the one who sent me; for
the least among all of you is the greatest.'

ANOTHER EXORCIST

49 John answered, 'Master, we saw
someone casting out demons in your
name, and we tried to stop him, because
he does not follow with us.' 50But Jesus
said to him, 'Do not stop him; for whoever is not against you is for you.'

A SAMARITAN VILLAGE REFUSES TO RECEIVE JESUS

51 When the days drew near for him
to be taken up, he set his face to go to
Jerusalem. 52And he sent messengers
ahead of him. On their way they entered
a village of the Samaritans to make
ready for him; 53but they did not receive
him, because his face was set towards
Jerusalem. 54When his disciples James
and John saw it, they said, 'Lord, do you
want us to command fire to come down
from heaven and consume them?'[r]
55But he turned and rebuked them.
56Then[s] they went on to another village.

WOULD-BE FOLLOWERS OF JESUS

57 As they were going along the
road, someone said to him, 'I will follow
you wherever you go.' 58And Jesus said
to him, 'Foxes have holes, and birds of
the air have nests; but the Son of Man
has nowhere to lay his head.' 59To another he said, 'Follow me.' But he said,
'Lord, first let me go and bury my father.' 60But Jesus[t] said to him, 'Let the
dead bury their own dead; but as for
you, go and proclaim the kingdom of
God.' 61Another said, 'I will follow you,
Lord; but let me first say farewell to
those at my home.' 62Jesus said to him,
'No one who puts a hand to the plough
and looks back is fit for the kingdom of
God.'

THE MISSION OF THE SEVENTY

10 After this the Lord appointed
seventy[u] others and sent them
on ahead of him in pairs to every town
and place where he himself intended
to go. 2He said to them, 'The harvest
is plentiful, but the labourers are few;
therefore ask the Lord of the harvest
to send out labourers into his harvest.
3Go on your way. See, I am sending you
out like lambs into the midst of wolves.
4Carry no purse, no bag, no sandals; and
greet no one on the road. 5Whatever
house you enter, first say, "Peace to this
house!" 6And if anyone is there who
shares in peace, your peace will rest on
that person; but if not, it will return to
you. 7Remain in the same house, eating
and drinking whatever they provide,

p 9.35 Other ancient authorities read *my Beloved*
q 9.39 Or *it* r 9.54 Other ancient authorities add *as Elijah did* s 9.56 Other ancient authorities read *rebuked them, and said, 'You do not know what spirit you are of, 56for the Son of Man has not come to destroy the lives of human beings but to save them.' Then* t 9.60 Gk *he* u 10.1 Other ancient authorities read *seventy-two*

for the labourer deserves to be paid. Do
not move about from house to house.
8Whenever you enter a town and its
people welcome you, eat what is set before you; 9cure the sick who are there,
and say to them, "The kingdom of God
has come near to you."[v] 10But whenever you enter a town and they do not
welcome you, go out into its streets and
say, 11"Even the dust of your town that
clings to our feet, we wipe off in protest
against you. Yet know this: the kingdom of God has come near."[w] 12I tell you,
on that day it will be more tolerable for
Sodom than for that town.

WOES TO UNREPENTANT CITIES

13 'Woe to you, Chorazin! Woe to you,
Bethsaida! For if the deeds of power
done in you had been done in Tyre and
Sidon, they would have repented long
ago, sitting in sackcloth and ashes.
14But at the judgement it will be more
tolerable for Tyre and Sidon than for
you. 15And you, Capernaum,
  will you be exalted to heaven?
    No, you will be brought
      down to Hades.

16 'Whoever listens to you listens to
me, and whoever rejects you rejects me,
and whoever rejects me rejects the one
who sent me.'

THE RETURN OF THE SEVENTY

17 The seventy[x] returned with joy,
saying, 'Lord, in your name even the demons submit to us!' 18He said to them,
'I watched Satan fall from heaven like
a flash of lightning. 19See, I have given
you authority to tread on snakes and
scorpions, and over all the power of
the enemy; and nothing will hurt you.
20Nevertheless, do not rejoice at this,
that the spirits submit to you, but rejoice that your names are written in
heaven.'

JESUS REJOICES

21 At that same hour Jesus[y] rejoiced
in the Holy Spirit[z] and said, 'I thank[a]
you, Father, Lord of heaven and earth,
because you have hidden these things
from the wise and the intelligent and
have revealed them to infants; yes, Father, for such was your gracious will.[b]
22All things have been handed over to
me by my Father; and no one knows
who the Son is except the Father, or
who the Father is except the Son and
anyone to whom the Son chooses to reveal him.'

23 Then turning to the disciples,
Jesus[c] said to them privately, 'Blessed
are the eyes that see what you see! 24For
I tell you that many prophets and kings
desired to see what you see, but did not
see it, and to hear what you hear, but
did not hear it.'

THE PARABLE OF THE GOOD SAMARITAN

25 Just then a lawyer stood up to test
Jesus.[d] 'Teacher,' he said, 'what must I
do to inherit eternal life?' 26He said to
him, 'What is written in the law? What
do you read there?' 27He answered, 'You
shall love the Lord your God with all
your heart, and with all your soul, and
with all your strength, and with all your
mind; and your neighbour as yourself.'
28And he said to him, 'You have given
the right answer; do this, and you will
live.'

29 But wanting to justify himself,
he asked Jesus, 'And who is my neighbour?' 30Jesus replied, 'A man was going
down from Jerusalem to Jericho, and fell
into the hands of robbers, who stripped
him, beat him, and went away, leaving
him half dead. 31Now by chance a priest
was going down that road; and when
he saw him, he passed by on the other
side. 32So likewise a Levite, when he
came to the place and saw him, passed
by on the other side. 33But a Samaritan while travelling came near him;
and when he saw him, he was moved
with pity. 34He went to him and bandaged his wounds, having poured oil
and wine on them. Then he put him on
his own animal, brought him to an inn,
and took care of him. 35The next day he
took out two denarii,[e] gave them to the
innkeeper, and said, "Take care of him;
and when I come back, I will repay you
whatever more you spend." 36Which of
these three, do you think, was a neighbour to the man who fell into the hands
of the robbers?' 37He said, 'The one who
showed him mercy.' Jesus said to him,
'Go and do likewise.'

JESUS VISITS MARTHA AND MARY

38 Now as they went on their way,
he entered a certain village, where a

[v] **10.9** Or *is at hand for you* [w] **10.11** Or *is at hand* [x] **10.17** Other ancient authorities read *seventy-two* [y] **10.21** Gk *he* [z] **10.21** Other authorities read *in the spirit* [a] **10.21** Or *praise* [b] **10.21** Or *for so it was well-pleasing in your sight* [c] **10.23** Gk *he* [d] **10.25** Gk *him* [e] **10.35** The denarius was the usual day's wage for a labourer

woman named Martha welcomed him
into her home. 39She had a sister named
Mary, who sat at the Lord's feet and
listened to what he was saying. 40But
Martha was distracted by her many
tasks; so she came to him and asked,
'Lord, do you not care that my sister has
left me to do all the work by myself? Tell
her then to help me.' 41But the Lord answered her, 'Martha, Martha, you are
worried and distracted by many things;
42there is need of only one thing.[f] Mary
has chosen the better part, which will
not be taken away from her.'

THE LORD'S PRAYER

11 He was praying in a certain
place, and after he had finished,
one of his disciples said to him, 'Lord,
teach us to pray, as John taught his
disciples.' 2He said to them, 'When you
pray, say:

Father,[g] hallowed be your name.
Your kingdom come.[h]
3 Give us each day our daily bread.[i]
4 And forgive us our sins,
for we ourselves forgive
everyone indebted to us.
And do not bring us to
the time of trial.'[j]

PERSEVERANCE IN PRAYER

5 And he said to them, 'Suppose one
of you has a friend, and you go to him at
midnight and say to him, "Friend, lend
me three loaves of bread; 6for a friend of
mine has arrived, and I have nothing to
set before him." 7And he answers from
within, "Do not bother me; the door
has already been locked, and my children are with me in bed; I cannot get
up and give you anything." 8I tell you,
even though he will not get up and give
him anything because he is his friend,
at least because of his persistence he will
get up and give him whatever he needs.
9 'So I say to you, Ask, and it will be
given to you; search, and you will find;
knock, and the door will be opened for
you. 10For everyone who asks receives,
and everyone who searches finds, and
for everyone who knocks, the door will
be opened. 11Is there anyone among you
who, if your child asks for[k] a fish, will
give a snake instead of a fish? 12Or if the
child asks for an egg, will give a scorpion? 13If you then, who are evil, know
how to give good gifts to your children,
how much more will the heavenly Father give the Holy Spirit[l] to those who
ask him!'

JESUS AND BEELZEBUL

14 Now he was casting out a demon
that was mute; when the demon had
gone out, the one who had been mute
spoke, and the crowds were amazed.
15But some of them said, 'He casts out
demons by Beelzebul, the ruler of the
demons.' 16Others, to test him, kept demanding from him a sign from heaven.
17But he knew what they were thinking and said to them, 'Every kingdom
divided against itself becomes a desert,
and house falls on house. 18If Satan also
is divided against himself, how will his
kingdom stand? —for you say that I cast
out the demons by Beelzebul. 19Now if
I cast out the demons by Beelzebul, by
whom do your exorcists[m] cast them
out? Therefore they will be your judges.
20But if it is by the finger of God that I
cast out the demons, then the kingdom
of God has come to you. 21When a strong
man, fully armed, guards his castle, his
property is safe. 22But when one stronger than he attacks him and overpowers
him, he takes away his armour in which
he trusted and divides his plunder.
23Whoever is not with me is against me,
and whoever does not gather with me
scatters.

THE RETURN OF THE UNCLEAN SPIRIT

24 'When the unclean spirit has gone
out of a person, it wanders through
waterless regions looking for a resting-
place, but not finding any, it says, "I will
return to my house from which I came."
25When it comes, it finds it swept and
put in order. 26Then it goes and brings
seven other spirits more evil than itself,
and they enter and live there; and the
last state of that person is worse than
the first.'

TRUE BLESSEDNESS

27 While he was saying this, a woman
in the crowd raised her voice and said to
him, 'Blessed is the womb that bore you

[f] 10.42 Other ancient authorities read *few things are necessary, or only one* [g] 11.2 Other ancient authorities read *Our Father in heaven* [h] 11.2 A few ancient authorities read *Your Holy Spirit come upon us and cleanse us.* Other ancient authorities add *Your will be done, on earth as in heaven*
[i] 11.3 Or *our bread for tomorrow* [j] 11.4 Or *us into temptation.* Other ancient authorities add *but rescue us from the evil one* (or *from evil*)
[k] 11.11 Other ancient authorities add *bread, will give a stone; or if your child asks for*
[l] 11.13 Other ancient authorities read *the Father give the Holy Spirit from heaven*
[m] 11.19 Gk *sons*

and the breasts that nursed you!' 28 But
he said, 'Blessed rather are those who
hear the word of God and obey it!'

THE SIGN OF JONAH

29 When the crowds were increasing,
he began to say, 'This generation is an
evil generation; it asks for a sign, but no
sign will be given to it except the sign
of Jonah. 30 For just as Jonah became a
sign to the people of Nineveh, so the
Son of Man will be to this generation.
31 The queen of the South will rise at the
judgement with the people of this generation and condemn them, because
she came from the ends of the earth to
listen to the wisdom of Solomon, and
see, something greater than Solomon is
here! 32 The people of Nineveh will rise
up at the judgement with this generation and condemn it, because they repented at the proclamation of Jonah,
and see, something greater than Jonah
is here!

THE LIGHT OF THE BODY

33 'No one after lighting a lamp puts
it in a cellar,[n] but on the lampstand so
that those who enter may see the light.
34 Your eye is the lamp of your body. If
your eye is healthy, your whole body is
full of light; but if it is not healthy, your
body is full of darkness. 35 Therefore consider whether the light in you is not
darkness. 36 If then your whole body is
full of light, with no part of it in darkness, it will be as full of light as when a
lamp gives you light with its rays.'

JESUS DENOUNCES PHARISEES AND LAWYERS

37 While he was speaking, a Pharisee invited him to dine with him; so he
went in and took his place at the table.
38 The Pharisee was amazed to see that
he did not first wash before dinner.
39 Then the Lord said to him, 'Now you
Pharisees clean the outside of the cup
and of the dish, but inside you are full of
greed and wickedness. 40 You fools! Did
not the one who made the outside make
the inside also? 41 So give for alms those
things that are within; and see, everything will be clean for you.

42 'But woe to you Pharisees! For
you tithe mint and rue and herbs of all
kinds, and neglect justice and the love of
God; it is these you ought to have practised, without neglecting the others.
43 Woe to you Pharisees! For you love
to have the seat of honour in the synagogues and to be greeted with respect
in the market-places. 44 Woe to you! For
you are like unmarked graves, and people walk over them without realizing it.'

45 One of the lawyers answered him,
'Teacher, when you say these things,
you insult us too.' 46 And he said, 'Woe
also to you lawyers! For you load people with burdens hard to bear, and you
yourselves do not lift a finger to ease
them. 47 Woe to you! For you build the
tombs of the prophets whom your ancestors killed. 48 So you are witnesses
and approve of the deeds of your ancestors; for they killed them, and you
build their tombs. 49 Therefore also the
Wisdom of God said, "I will send them
prophets and apostles, some of whom
they will kill and persecute", 50 so that
this generation may be charged with
the blood of all the prophets shed since
the foundation of the world, 51 from the
blood of Abel to the blood of Zechariah,
who perished between the altar and
the sanctuary. Yes, I tell you, it will be
charged against this generation. 52 Woe
to you lawyers! For you have taken away
the key of knowledge; you did not enter
yourselves, and you hindered those who
were entering.'

53 When he went outside, the scribes
and the Pharisees began to be very hostile towards him and to cross-examine
him about many things, 54 lying in wait
for him, to catch him in something he
might say.

A WARNING AGAINST HYPOCRISY

12 Meanwhile, when the crowd
gathered in thousands, so that
they trampled on one another, he began to speak first to his disciples, 'Beware of the yeast of the Pharisees, that
is, their hypocrisy. 2 Nothing is covered
up that will not be uncovered, and nothing secret that will not become known.
3 Therefore whatever you have said in
the dark will be heard in the light, and
what you have whispered behind closed
doors will be proclaimed from the
housetops.

EXHORTATION TO FEARLESS CONFESSION

4 'I tell you, my friends, do not fear
those who kill the body, and after that
can do nothing more. 5 But I will warn
you whom to fear: fear him who, after

[n] 11.33 Other ancient authorities add *or under the bushel basket*

he has killed, has authority[o] to cast into
hell.[p] Yes, I tell you, fear him! 6 Are not
five sparrows sold for two pennies? Yet
not one of them is forgotten in God's
sight. 7 But even the hairs of your head
are all counted. Do not be afraid; you are
of more value than many sparrows.

8 'And I tell you, everyone who acknowledges me before others, the Son of
Man also will acknowledge before the angels of God; 9 but whoever denies me before others will be denied before the angels of God. 10 And everyone who speaks a
word against the Son of Man will be forgiven; but whoever blasphemes against
the Holy Spirit will not be forgiven.
11 When they bring you before the synagogues, the rulers, and the authorities,
do not worry about how[q] you are to defend yourselves or what you are to say;
12 for the Holy Spirit will teach you at that
very hour what you ought to say.'

THE PARABLE OF THE RICH FOOL

13 Someone in the crowd said to him,
'Teacher, tell my brother to divide the
family inheritance with me.' 14 But he
said to him, 'Friend, who set me to be
a judge or arbitrator over you?' 15 And
he said to them, 'Take care! Be on your
guard against all kinds of greed; for one's
life does not consist in the abundance of
possessions.' 16 Then he told them a parable: 'The land of a rich man produced
abundantly. 17 And he thought to himself,
"What should I do, for I have no place to
store my crops?" 18 Then he said, "I will do
this: I will pull down my barns and build
larger ones, and there I will store all my
grain and my goods. 19 And I will say to
my soul, Soul, you have ample goods
laid up for many years; relax, eat, drink,
be merry." 20 But God said to him, "You
fool! This very night your life is being demanded of you. And the things you have
prepared, whose will they be?" 21 So it is
with those who store up treasures for
themselves but are not rich towards God.'

DO NOT WORRY

22 He said to his disciples, 'Therefore
I tell you, do not worry about your life,
what you will eat, or about your body,
what you will wear. 23 For life is more
than food, and the body more than
clothing. 24 Consider the ravens: they
neither sow nor reap, they have neither
storehouse nor barn, and yet God feeds
them. Of how much more value are you
than the birds! 25 And can any of you by
worrying add a single hour to your span
of life?[r] 26 If then you are not able to do
so small a thing as that, why do you
worry about the rest? 27 Consider the
lilies, how they grow: they neither toil
nor spin;[s] yet I tell you, even Solomon in
all his glory was not clothed like one of
these. 28 But if God so clothes the grass
of the field, which is alive today and tomorrow is thrown into the oven, how
much more will he clothe you—you of
little faith! 29 And do not keep striving
for what you are to eat and what you
are to drink, and do not keep worrying.
30 For it is the nations of the world that
strive after all these things, and your
Father knows that you need them. 31 Instead, strive for his[t] kingdom, and these
things will be given to you as well.

32 'Do not be afraid, little flock,
for it is your Father's good pleasure to
give you the kingdom. 33 Sell your possessions, and give alms. Make purses
for yourselves that do not wear out, an
unfailing treasure in heaven, where no
thief comes near and no moth destroys.
34 For where your treasure is, there your
heart will be also.

WATCHFUL SLAVES

35 'Be dressed for action and have
your lamps lit; 36 be like those who are
waiting for their master to return from
the wedding banquet, so that they may
open the door for him as soon as he
comes and knocks. 37 Blessed are those
slaves whom the master finds alert
when he comes; truly I tell you, he will
fasten his belt and have them sit down
to eat, and he will come and serve them.
38 If he comes during the middle of the
night, or near dawn, and finds them so,
blessed are those slaves.

39 'But know this: if the owner of the
house had known at what hour the thief
was coming, he[u] would not have let his
house be broken into. 40 You also must
be ready, for the Son of Man is coming
at an unexpected hour.'

THE FAITHFUL OR THE UNFAITHFUL SLAVE

41 Peter said, 'Lord, are you telling this
parable for us or for everyone?' 42 And the
Lord said, 'Who then is the faithful and

[o] 12.5 Or *power* [p] 12.5 Gk *Gehenna*
[q] 12.11 Other ancient authorities add *or what*
[r] 12.25 Or *add a cubit to your stature*
[s] 12.27 Other ancient authorities read *Consider the lilies; they neither spin nor weave*
[t] 12.31 Other ancient authorities read *God's*
[u] 12.39 Other ancient authorities add *would have watched and*

prudent manager whom his master will
put in charge of his slaves, to give them
their allowance of food at the proper
time? 43Blessed is that slave whom his
master will find at work when he arrives.
44Truly I tell you, he will put that one
in charge of all his possessions. 45But if
that slave says to himself, "My master is
delayed in coming", and if he begins to
beat the other slaves, men and women,
and to eat and drink and get drunk, 46the
master of that slave will come on a day
when he does not expect him and at an
hour that he does not know, and will cut
him in pieces,[v] and put him with the
unfaithful. 47That slave who knew what
his master wanted, but did not prepare
himself or do what was wanted, will receive a severe beating. 48But one who did
not know and did what deserved a beating will receive a light beating. From everyone to whom much has been given,
much will be required; and from one to
whom much has been entrusted, even
more will be demanded.

JESUS THE CAUSE OF DIVISION

49 'I came to bring fire to the earth,
and how I wish it were already kindled! 50I have a baptism with which to
be baptized, and what stress I am under until it is completed! 51Do you think
that I have come to bring peace to the
earth? No, I tell you, but rather division!
52From now on, five in one household
will be divided, three against two and
two against three; 53they will be divided:
father against son
  and son against father,
mother against daughter
  and daughter against mother,
mother-in-law against her
    daughter-in-law
  and daughter-in-law against
    mother-in-law.'

INTERPRETING THE TIME

54 He also said to the crowds, 'When
you see a cloud rising in the west, you
immediately say, "It is going to rain";
and so it happens. 55And when you see
the south wind blowing, you say, "There
will be scorching heat"; and it happens.
56You hypocrites! You know how to interpret the appearance of earth and sky,
but why do you not know how to interpret the present time?

SETTLING WITH YOUR OPPONENT

57 'And why do you not judge for
yourselves what is right? 58Thus, when
you go with your accuser before a magistrate, on the way make an effort to settle the case,[w] or you may be dragged before the judge, and the judge hand you
over to the officer, and the officer throw
you in prison. 59I tell you, you will never
get out until you have paid the very last
penny.'

REPENT OR PERISH

13 At that very time there were
some present who told him
about the Galileans whose blood Pilate
had mingled with their sacrifices. 2He
asked them, 'Do you think that because
these Galileans suffered in this way they
were worse sinners than all other Galileans? 3No, I tell you; but unless you repent, you will all perish as they did. 4Or
those eighteen who were killed when
the tower of Siloam fell on them—do
you think that they were worse offenders than all the others living in Jerusalem? 5No, I tell you; but unless you repent, you will all perish just as they did.'

THE PARABLE OF THE BARREN FIG TREE

6 Then he told this parable: 'A man
had a fig tree planted in his vineyard;
and he came looking for fruit on it and
found none. 7So he said to the gardener,
"See here! For three years I have come
looking for fruit on this fig tree, and still
I find none. Cut it down! Why should it
be wasting the soil?" 8He replied, "Sir,
let it alone for one more year, until I
dig round it and put manure on it. 9If it
bears fruit next year, well and good; but
if not, you can cut it down."'

JESUS HEALS A CRIPPLED WOMAN

10 Now he was teaching in one of
the synagogues on the sabbath. 11And
just then there appeared a woman
with a spirit that had crippled her for
eighteen years. She was bent over and
was quite unable to stand up straight.
12When Jesus saw her, he called her
over and said, 'Woman, you are set free
from your ailment.' 13When he laid his
hands on her, immediately she stood
up straight and began praising God.
14But the leader of the synagogue, indignant because Jesus had cured on
the sabbath, kept saying to the crowd,
'There are six days on which work
ought to be done; come on those days

[v] **12.46** *Or cut him off* [w] **12.58** *Gk settle with him*

and be cured, and not on the sabbath
day.' 15 But the Lord answered him and
said, 'You hypocrites! Does not each of
you on the sabbath untie his ox or his
donkey from the manger, and lead it
away to give it water? 16 And ought not
this woman, a daughter of Abraham
whom Satan bound for eighteen long
years, be set free from this bondage on
the sabbath day?' 17 When he said this,
all his opponents were put to shame;
and the entire crowd was rejoicing at
all the wonderful things that he was
doing.

THE PARABLE OF THE MUSTARD SEED

18 He said therefore, 'What is the
kingdom of God like? And to what
should I compare it? 19 It is like a mustard seed that someone took and sowed
in the garden; it grew and became a
tree, and the birds of the air made nests
in its branches.'

THE PARABLE OF THE YEAST

20 And again he said, 'To what
should I compare the kingdom of God?
21 It is like yeast that a woman took and
mixed in with[x] three measures of flour
until all of it was leavened.'

THE NARROW DOOR

22 Jesus[y] went through one town
and village after another, teaching as
he made his way to Jerusalem. 23 Someone asked him, 'Lord, will only a few be
saved?' He said to them, 24 'Strive to enter through the narrow door; for many,
I tell you, will try to enter and will not
be able. 25 When once the owner of the
house has got up and shut the door,
and you begin to stand outside and to
knock at the door, saying, "Lord, open
to us", then in reply he will say to you,
"I do not know where you come from."
26 Then you will begin to say, "We ate
and drank with you, and you taught in
our streets." 27 But he will say, "I do not
know where you come from; go away
from me, all you evildoers!" 28 There
will be weeping and gnashing of teeth
when you see Abraham and Isaac
and Jacob and all the prophets in the
kingdom of God, and you yourselves
thrown out. 29 Then people will come
from east and west, from north and
south, and will eat in the kingdom of
God. 30 Indeed, some are last who will
be first, and some are first who will be
last.'

THE LAMENT OVER JERUSALEM

31 At that very hour some Pharisees
came and said to him, 'Get away from
here, for Herod wants to kill you.' 32 He
said to them, 'Go and tell that fox for
me,[z] "Listen, I am casting out demons
and performing cures today and tomorrow, and on the third day I finish my
work. 33 Yet today, tomorrow, and the
next day I must be on my way, because
it is impossible for a prophet to be killed
away from Jerusalem." 34 Jerusalem, Jerusalem, the city that kills the prophets and stones those who are sent to it!
How often have I desired to gather your
children together as a hen gathers her
brood under her wings, and you were
not willing! 35 See, your house is left to
you. And I tell you, you will not see me
until the time comes when[a] you say,
"Blessed is the one who comes in the
name of the Lord." '

JESUS HEALS THE MAN WITH DROPSY

14 On one occasion when Jesus[b]
was going to the house of a
leader of the Pharisees to eat a meal on
the sabbath, they were watching him
closely. 2 Just then, in front of him, there
was a man who had dropsy. 3 And Jesus
asked the lawyers and Pharisees, 'Is it
lawful to cure people on the sabbath,
or not?' 4 But they were silent. So Jesus[c]
took him and healed him, and sent him
away. 5 Then he said to them, 'If one of
you has a child[d] or an ox that has fallen
into a well, will you not immediately
pull it out on a sabbath day?' 6 And they
could not reply to this.

HUMILITY AND HOSPITALITY

7 When he noticed how the guests
chose the places of honour, he told them
a parable. 8 'When you are invited by
someone to a wedding banquet, do not
sit down at the place of honour, in case
someone more distinguished than you
has been invited by your host; 9 and the
host who invited both of you may come
and say to you, "Give this person your
place", and then in disgrace you would
start to take the lowest place. 10 But
when you are invited, go and sit down
at the lowest place, so that when your
host comes, he may say to you, "Friend,

[x] 13.21 Gk *hid in* [y] 13.22 Gk *He* [z] 13.32 Gk lacks *for me* [a] 13.35 Other ancient authorities lack *the time comes when* [b] 14.1 Gk *he* [c] 14.4 Gk *he* [d] 14.5 Other ancient authorities read *a donkey*

move up higher"; then you will be honoured in the presence of all who sit at the table with you. 11 For all who exalt themselves will be humbled, and those who humble themselves will be exalted.'

12 He said also to the one who had invited him, 'When you give a luncheon or a dinner, do not invite your friends or your brothers or your relatives or rich neighbours, in case they may invite you in return, and you would be repaid. 13 But when you give a banquet, invite the poor, the crippled, the lame, and the blind. 14 And you will be blessed, because they cannot repay you, for you will be repaid at the resurrection of the righteous.'

THE PARABLE OF THE GREAT DINNER

15 One of the dinner guests, on hearing this, said to him, 'Blessed is anyone who will eat bread in the kingdom of God!' 16 Then Jesus[e] said to him, 'Someone gave a great dinner and invited many. 17 At the time for the dinner he sent his slave to say to those who had been invited, "Come; for everything is ready now." 18 But they all alike began to make excuses. The first said to him, "I have bought a piece of land, and I must go out and see it; please accept my apologies." 19 Another said, "I have bought five yoke of oxen, and I am going to try them out; please accept my apologies." 20 Another said, "I have just been married, and therefore I cannot come." 21 So the slave returned and reported this to his master. Then the owner of the house became angry and said to his slave, "Go out at once into the streets and lanes of the town and bring in the poor, the crippled, the blind, and the lame." 22 And the slave said, "Sir, what you ordered has been done, and there is still room." 23 Then the master said to the slave, "Go out into the roads and lanes, and compel people to come in, so that my house may be filled. 24 For I tell you,[f] none of those who were invited will taste my dinner." '

THE COST OF DISCIPLESHIP

25 Now large crowds were travelling with him; and he turned and said to them, 26 'Whoever comes to me and does not hate father and mother, wife and children, brothers and sisters, yes, and even life itself, cannot be my disciple. 27 Whoever does not carry the cross and follow me cannot be my disciple. 28 For which of you, intending to build a tower, does not first sit down and estimate the cost, to see whether he has enough to complete it? 29 Otherwise, when he has laid a foundation and is not able to finish, all who see it will begin to ridicule him, 30 saying, "This fellow began to build and was not able to finish." 31 Or what king, going out to wage war against another king, will not sit down first and consider whether he is able with ten thousand to oppose the one who comes against him with twenty thousand? 32 If he cannot, then, while the other is still far away, he sends a delegation and asks for the terms of peace. 33 So therefore, none of you can become my disciple if you do not give up all your possessions.

ABOUT SALT

34 'Salt is good; but if salt has lost its taste, how can its saltiness be restored?[g] 35 It is fit neither for the soil nor for the manure heap; they throw it away. Let anyone with ears to hear listen!'

THE PARABLE OF THE LOST SHEEP

15 Now all the tax-collectors and sinners were coming near to listen to him. 2 And the Pharisees and the scribes were grumbling and saying, 'This fellow welcomes sinners and eats with them.'

3 So he told them this parable: 4 'Which one of you, having a hundred sheep and losing one of them, does not leave the ninety-nine in the wilderness and go after the one that is lost until he finds it? 5 When he has found it, he lays it on his shoulders and rejoices. 6 And when he comes home, he calls together his friends and neighbours, saying to them, "Rejoice with me, for I have found my sheep that was lost." 7 Just so, I tell you, there will be more joy in heaven over one sinner who repents than over ninety-nine righteous people who need no repentance.

THE PARABLE OF THE LOST COIN

8 'Or what woman having ten silver coins,[h] if she loses one of them, does not light a lamp, sweep the house, and search carefully until she finds it? 9 When she has found it, she calls together her friends and neighbours, saying,

[e] 14.16 Gk *he* [f] 14.24 The Greek word for *you* here is plural [g] 14.34 Or *how can it be used for seasoning?* [h] 15.8 Gk *drachmas*, each worth about a day's wage for a labourer

"Rejoice with me, for I have found the
coin that I had lost." 10 Just so, I tell you,
there is joy in the presence of the angels
of God over one sinner who repents.'

THE PARABLE OF THE PRODIGAL AND HIS BROTHER

11 Then Jesus[i] said, 'There was a
man who had two sons. 12 The younger
of them said to his father, "Father, give
me the share of the property that will
belong to me." So he divided his property between them. 13 A few days later
the younger son gathered all he had and
travelled to a distant country, and there
he squandered his property in dissolute
living. 14 When he had spent everything,
a severe famine took place throughout
that country, and he began to be in
need. 15 So he went and hired himself
out to one of the citizens of that country, who sent him to his fields to feed
the pigs. 16 He would gladly have filled
himself with[j] the pods that the pigs
were eating; and no one gave him anything. 17 But when he came to himself he
said, "How many of my father's hired
hands have bread enough and to spare,
but here I am dying of hunger! 18 I will
get up and go to my father, and I will say
to him, 'Father, I have sinned against
heaven and before you; 19 I am no longer
worthy to be called your son; treat me
like one of your hired hands.' " 20 So he
set off and went to his father. But while
he was still far off, his father saw him
and was filled with compassion; he
ran and put his arms around him and
kissed him. 21 Then the son said to him,
"Father, I have sinned against heaven
and before you; I am no longer worthy
to be called your son."[k] 22 But the father
said to his slaves, "Quickly, bring out a
robe—the best one—and put it on him;
put a ring on his finger and sandals on
his feet. 23 And get the fatted calf and kill
it, and let us eat and celebrate; 24 for this
son of mine was dead and is alive again;
he was lost and is found!" And they began to celebrate.

25 'Now his elder son was in the field;
and when he came and approached the
house, he heard music and dancing.
26 He called one of the slaves and asked
what was going on. 27 He replied, "Your
brother has come, and your father has
killed the fatted calf, because he has
got him back safe and sound." 28 Then
he became angry and refused to go in.
His father came out and began to plead
with him. 29 But he answered his father,
"Listen! For all these years I have been
working like a slave for you, and I have
never disobeyed your command; yet
you have never given me even a young
goat so that I might celebrate with my
friends. 30 But when this son of yours
came back, who has devoured your
property with prostitutes, you killed the
fatted calf for him!" 31 Then the father[l]
said to him, "Son, you are always with
me, and all that is mine is yours. 32 But
we had to celebrate and rejoice, because
this brother of yours was dead and has
come to life; he was lost and has been
found." '

THE PARABLE OF THE DISHONEST MANAGER

16 Then Jesus[m] said to the disciples,
'There was a rich man who had
a manager, and charges were brought
to him that this man was squandering
his property. 2 So he summoned him
and said to him, "What is this that I
hear about you? Give me an account of
your management, because you cannot
be my manager any longer." 3 Then the
manager said to himself, "What will I
do, now that my master is taking the
position away from me? I am not strong
enough to dig, and I am ashamed to
beg. 4 I have decided what to do so that,
when I am dismissed as manager, people may welcome me into their homes."
5 So, summoning his master's debtors
one by one, he asked the first, "How
much do you owe my master?" 6 He answered, "A hundred jugs of olive oil." He
said to him, "Take your bill, sit down
quickly, and make it fifty." 7 Then he
asked another, "And how much do you
owe?" He replied, "A hundred containers of wheat." He said to him, "Take your
bill and make it eighty." 8 And his master commended the dishonest manager
because he had acted shrewdly; for the
children of this age are more shrewd in
dealing with their own generation than
are the children of light. 9 And I tell you,
make friends for yourselves by means
of dishonest wealth[n] so that when it is
gone, they may welcome you into the
eternal homes.[o]

10 'Whoever is faithful in a very little is faithful also in much; and whoever is dishonest in a very little is dis-

[i] **15.11** Gk *he* [j] **15.16** Other ancient authorities read *filled his stomach with* [k] **15.21** Other ancient authorities add *Treat me as one of your hired servants* [l] **15.31** Gk *he* [m] **16.1** Gk *he* [n] **16.9** Gk *mammon* [o] **16.9** Gk *tents*

honest also in much. 11If then you have
not been faithful with the dishonest
wealth,[p] who will entrust to you the
true riches? 12And if you have not been
faithful with what belongs to another,
who will give you what is your own?
13No slave can serve two masters; for a
slave will either hate the one and love
the other, or be devoted to the one and
despise the other. You cannot serve God
and wealth.'[q]

THE LAW AND THE KINGDOM OF GOD

14 The Pharisees, who were lovers
of money, heard all this, and they ridiculed him. 15So he said to them, 'You are
those who justify yourselves in the sight
of others; but God knows your hearts;
for what is prized by human beings is an
abomination in the sight of God.

16 'The law and the prophets were in
effect until John came; since then the
good news of the kingdom of God is proclaimed, and everyone tries to enter it
by force.[r] 17But it is easier for heaven and
earth to pass away, than for one stroke
of a letter in the law to be dropped.

18 'Anyone who divorces his wife
and marries another commits adultery,
and whoever marries a woman divorced
from her husband commits adultery.

THE RICH MAN AND LAZARUS

19 'There was a rich man who was
dressed in purple and fine linen and who
feasted sumptuously every day. 20And at
his gate lay a poor man named Lazarus,
covered with sores, 21who longed to satisfy his hunger with what fell from the
rich man's table; even the dogs would
come and lick his sores. 22The poor man
died and was carried away by the angels
to be with Abraham.[s] The rich man also
died and was buried. 23In Hades, where
he was being tormented, he looked up
and saw Abraham far away with Lazarus by his side.[t] 24He called out, "Father
Abraham, have mercy on me, and send
Lazarus to dip the tip of his finger in
water and cool my tongue; for I am in
agony in these flames." 25But Abraham
said, "Child, remember that during your
lifetime you received your good things,
and Lazarus in like manner evil things;
but now he is comforted here, and you
are in agony. 26Besides all this, between
you and us a great chasm has been
fixed, so that those who might want to
pass from here to you cannot do so, and
no one can cross from there to us." 27He
said, "Then, father, I beg you to send
him to my father's house— 28for I have
five brothers—that he may warn them,
so that they will not also come into this
place of torment." 29Abraham replied,
"They have Moses and the prophets;
they should listen to them." 30He said,
"No, father Abraham; but if someone
goes to them from the dead, they will
repent." 31He said to him, "If they do
not listen to Moses and the prophets,
neither will they be convinced even if
someone rises from the dead."'

SOME SAYINGS OF JESUS

17 Jesus[u] said to his disciples, 'Occasions for stumbling are bound
to come, but woe to anyone by whom
they come! 2It would be better for you
if a millstone were hung around your
neck and you were thrown into the sea
than for you to cause one of these little
ones to stumble. 3Be on your guard! If
another disciple[v] sins, you must rebuke
the offender, and if there is repentance,
you must forgive. 4And if the same person sins against you seven times a day,
and turns back to you seven times and
says, "I repent", you must forgive.'

5 The apostles said to the Lord, 'Increase our faith!' 6The Lord replied, 'If
you had faith the size of a[w] mustard
seed, you could say to this mulberry
tree, "Be uprooted and planted in the
sea", and it would obey you.

7 'Who among you would say to your
slave who has just come in from ploughing or tending sheep in the field, "Come
here at once and take your place at the
table"? 8Would you not rather say to
him, "Prepare supper for me, put on
your apron and serve me while I eat and
drink; later you may eat and drink"? 9Do
you thank the slave for doing what was
commanded? 10So you also, when you
have done all that you were ordered to
do, say, "We are worthless slaves; we
have done only what we ought to have
done!"'

JESUS CLEANSES TEN LEPERS

11 On the way to Jerusalem Jesus[x]
was going through the region between
Samaria and Galilee. 12As he entered
a village, ten lepers[y] approached him.

[p] 16.11 Gk *mammon* [q] 16.13 Gk *mammon*
[r] 16.16 Or *everyone is strongly urged to enter it*
[s] 16.22 Gk *to Abraham's bosom* [t] 16.23 Gk *in his bosom* [u] 17.1 Gk *He* [v] 17.3 Gk *your brother* [w] 17.6 Gk *faith as a grain of*
[x] 17.11 Gk *he* [y] 17.12 The terms *leper* and *leprosy* can refer to several diseases

Keeping their distance, 13 they called
out, saying, 'Jesus, Master, have mercy
on us!' 14 When he saw them, he said to
them, 'Go and show yourselves to the
priests.' And as they went, they were
made clean. 15 Then one of them, when
he saw that he was healed, turned back,
praising God with a loud voice. 16 He
prostrated himself at Jesus'[z] feet and
thanked him. And he was a Samaritan.
17 Then Jesus asked, 'Were not ten made
clean? But the other nine, where are
they? 18 Was none of them found to return and give praise to God except this
foreigner?' 19 Then he said to him, 'Get
up and go on your way; your faith has
made you well.'

THE COMING OF THE KINGDOM

20 Once Jesus[a] was asked by the
Pharisees when the kingdom of God
was coming, and he answered, 'The
kingdom of God is not coming with
things that can be observed; 21 nor will
they say, "Look, here it is!" or "There it
is!" For, in fact, the kingdom of God is
among[b] you.'

22 Then he said to the disciples, 'The
days are coming when you will long to
see one of the days of the Son of Man,
and you will not see it. 23 They will say
to you, "Look there!" or "Look here!"
Do not go, do not set off in pursuit.
24 For as the lightning flashes and lights
up the sky from one side to the other,
so will the Son of Man be in his day.[c]
25 But first he must endure much suffering and be rejected by this generation.
26 Just as it was in the days of Noah, so
too it will be in the days of the Son of
Man. 27 They were eating and drinking,
and marrying and being given in marriage, until the day Noah entered the
ark, and the flood came and destroyed
all of them. 28 Likewise, just as it was in
the days of Lot: they were eating and
drinking, buying and selling, planting
and building, 29 but on the day that Lot
left Sodom, it rained fire and sulphur
from heaven and destroyed all of them
30 —it will be like that on the day that
the Son of Man is revealed. 31 On that
day, anyone on the housetop who has
belongings in the house must not come
down to take them away; and likewise
anyone in the field must not turn back.
32 Remember Lot's wife. 33 Those who
try to make their life secure will lose it,
but those who lose their life will keep
it. 34 I tell you, on that night there will
be two in one bed; one will be taken
and the other left. 35 There will be two
women grinding meal together; one
will be taken and the other left.'[d] 37 Then
they asked him, 'Where, Lord?' He said
to them, 'Where the corpse is, there the
vultures will gather.'

THE PARABLE OF THE WIDOW AND THE UNJUST JUDGE

18 Then Jesus[e] told them a parable
about their need to pray always
and not to lose heart. 2 He said, 'In a certain city there was a judge who neither
feared God nor had respect for people.
3 In that city there was a widow who
kept coming to him and saying, "Grant
me justice against my opponent." 4 For
a while he refused; but later he said to
himself, "Though I have no fear of God
and no respect for anyone, 5 yet because
this widow keeps bothering me, I will
grant her justice, so that she may not
wear me out by continually coming." '[f]
6 And the Lord said, 'Listen to what the
unjust judge says. 7 And will not God
grant justice to his chosen ones who
cry to him day and night? Will he delay long in helping them? 8 I tell you, he
will quickly grant justice to them. And
yet, when the Son of Man comes, will he
find faith on earth?'

THE PARABLE OF THE PHARISEE AND THE TAX-COLLECTOR

9 He also told this parable to some
who trusted in themselves that they
were righteous and regarded others
with contempt: 10 'Two men went up to
the temple to pray, one a Pharisee and
the other a tax-collector. 11 The Pharisee, standing by himself, was praying
thus, "God, I thank you that I am not
like other people: thieves, rogues, adulterers, or even like this tax-collector. 12 I
fast twice a week; I give a tenth of all my
income." 13 But the tax-collector, standing far off, would not even look up to
heaven, but was beating his breast and
saying, "God, be merciful to me, a sinner!" 14 I tell you, this man went down
to his home justified rather than the
other; for all who exalt themselves will
be humbled, but all who humble themselves will be exalted.'

[z] **17.16** Gk *his* [a] **17.20** Gk *he* [b] **17.21** Or *within* [c] **17.24** Other ancient authorities lack *in his day* [d] **17.35** Other ancient authorities add verse 36, *'Two will be in the field; one will be taken and the other left.'* [e] **18.1** Gk *he* [f] **18.5** Or *so that she may not finally come and slap me in the face*

JESUS BLESSES LITTLE CHILDREN

15 People were bringing even infants
to him that he might touch them; and
when the disciples saw it, they sternly ordered them not to do it. 16But Jesus called
for them and said, 'Let the little children
come to me, and do not stop them; for it
is to such as these that the kingdom of
God belongs. 17Truly I tell you, whoever
does not receive the kingdom of God as a
little child will never enter it.'

THE RICH RULER

18 A certain ruler asked him, 'Good
Teacher, what must I do to inherit eternal life?' 19Jesus said to him, 'Why do
you call me good? No one is good but
God alone. 20You know the commandments: "You shall not commit adultery;
You shall not murder; You shall not
steal; You shall not bear false witness;
Honour your father and mother." ' 21He
replied, 'I have kept all these since my
youth.' 22When Jesus heard this, he said
to him, 'There is still one thing lacking.
Sell all that you own and distribute the
money[g] to the poor, and you will have
treasure in heaven; then come, follow
me.' 23But when he heard this, he became sad; for he was very rich. 24Jesus
looked at him and said, 'How hard it is
for those who have wealth to enter the
kingdom of God! 25Indeed, it is easier
for a camel to go through the eye of a
needle than for someone who is rich to
enter the kingdom of God.'

26 Those who heard it said, 'Then
who can be saved?' 27He replied, 'What
is impossible for mortals is possible for
God.'

28 Then Peter said, 'Look, we have
left our homes and followed you.' 29And
he said to them, 'Truly I tell you, there
is no one who has left house or wife or
brothers or parents or children, for the
sake of the kingdom of God, 30who will
not get back very much more in this
age, and in the age to come eternal life.'

A THIRD TIME JESUS FORETELLS HIS DEATH AND RESURRECTION

31 Then he took the twelve aside and
said to them, 'See, we are going up to Jerusalem, and everything that is written
about the Son of Man by the prophets
will be accomplished. 32For he will be
handed over to the Gentiles; and he will
be mocked and insulted and spat upon.
33After they have flogged him, they will
kill him, and on the third day he will
rise again.' 34But they understood nothing about all these things; in fact, what
he said was hidden from them, and they
did not grasp what was said.

JESUS HEALS A BLIND BEGGAR NEAR JERICHO

35 As he approached Jericho, a blind
man was sitting by the roadside begging. 36When he heard a crowd going by,
he asked what was happening. 37They
told him, 'Jesus of Nazareth[h] is passing by.' 38Then he shouted, 'Jesus, Son
of David, have mercy on me!' 39Those
who were in front sternly ordered him
to be quiet; but he shouted even more
loudly, 'Son of David, have mercy on
me!' 40Jesus stood still and ordered the
man to be brought to him; and when
he came near, he asked him, 41'What
do you want me to do for you?' He said,
'Lord, let me see again.' 42Jesus said to
him, 'Receive your sight; your faith has
saved you.' 43Immediately he regained
his sight and followed him, glorifying
God; and all the people, when they saw
it, praised God.

JESUS AND ZACCHAEUS

19 He entered Jericho and was
passing through it. 2A man was
there named Zacchaeus; he was a chief
tax-collector and was rich. 3He was trying to see who Jesus was, but on account
of the crowd he could not, because he
was short in stature. 4So he ran ahead
and climbed a sycomore tree to see
him, because he was going to pass that
way. 5When Jesus came to the place, he
looked up and said to him, 'Zacchaeus,
hurry and come down; for I must stay
at your house today.' 6So he hurried
down and was happy to welcome him.
7All who saw it began to grumble and
said, 'He has gone to be the guest of
one who is a sinner.' 8Zacchaeus stood
there and said to the Lord, 'Look, half of
my possessions, Lord, I will give to the
poor; and if I have defrauded anyone of
anything, I will pay back four times as
much.' 9Then Jesus said to him, 'Today
salvation has come to this house, because he too is a son of Abraham. 10For
the Son of Man came to seek out and to
save the lost.'

THE PARABLE OF THE TEN POUNDS

11 As they were listening to this, he
went on to tell a parable, because he

[g] 18.22 Gk lacks *the money* [h] 18.37 Gk *the Nazorean*

was near Jerusalem, and because they
supposed that the kingdom of God was
to appear immediately. 12 So he said, 'A
nobleman went to a distant country to
get royal power for himself and then return. 13 He summoned ten of his slaves,
and gave them ten pounds,[i] and said
to them, "Do business with these until
I come back." 14 But the citizens of his
country hated him and sent a delegation after him, saying, "We do not want
this man to rule over us." 15 When he returned, having received royal power, he
ordered these slaves, to whom he had
given the money, to be summoned so
that he might find out what they had
gained by trading. 16 The first came forward and said, "Lord, your pound has
made ten more pounds." 17 He said to
him, "Well done, good slave! Because
you have been trustworthy in a very
small thing, take charge of ten cities."
18 Then the second came, saying, "Lord,
your pound has made five pounds." 19 He
said to him, "And you, rule over five
cities." 20 Then the other came, saying,
"Lord, here is your pound. I wrapped it
up in a piece of cloth, 21 for I was afraid of
you, because you are a harsh man; you
take what you did not deposit, and reap
what you did not sow." 22 He said to him,
"I will judge you by your own words,
you wicked slave! You knew, did you,
that I was a harsh man, taking what I
did not deposit and reaping what I did
not sow? 23 Why then did you not put
my money into the bank? Then when I
returned, I could have collected it with
interest." 24 He said to the bystanders,
"Take the pound from him and give it
to the one who has ten pounds." 25 (And
they said to him, "Lord, he has ten
pounds!") 26 "I tell you, to all those who
have, more will be given; but from those
who have nothing, even what they have
will be taken away. 27 But as for these
enemies of mine who did not want me
to be king over them—bring them here
and slaughter them in my presence." '

JESUS' TRIUMPHAL ENTRY INTO JERUSALEM

28 After he had said this, he went on
ahead, going up to Jerusalem.

29 When he had come near Bethphage and Bethany, at the place called
the Mount of Olives, he sent two of the
disciples, 30 saying, 'Go into the village
ahead of you, and as you enter it you
will find tied there a colt that has never
been ridden. Untie it and bring it here.
31 If anyone asks you, "Why are you untying it?" just say this: "The Lord needs
it." ' 32 So those who were sent departed
and found it as he had told them. 33 As
they were untying the colt, its owners asked them, 'Why are you untying
the colt?' 34 They said, 'The Lord needs
it.' 35 Then they brought it to Jesus; and
after throwing their cloaks on the colt,
they set Jesus on it. 36 As he rode along,
people kept spreading their cloaks on
the road. 37 As he was now approaching the path down from the Mount of
Olives, the whole multitude of the disciples began to praise God joyfully with a
loud voice for all the deeds of power that
they had seen, 38 saying,

'Blessed is the king
  who comes in the name
    of the Lord!
Peace in heaven,
  and glory in the highest heaven!'

39 Some of the Pharisees in the crowd
said to him, 'Teacher, order your disciples to stop.' 40 He answered, 'I tell you,
if these were silent, the stones would
shout out.'

JESUS WEEPS OVER JERUSALEM

41 As he came near and saw the city,
he wept over it, 42 saying, 'If you, even
you, had only recognized on this day
the things that make for peace! But
now they are hidden from your eyes.
43 Indeed, the days will come upon you,
when your enemies will set up ramparts
around you and surround you, and hem
you in on every side. 44 They will crush
you to the ground, you and your children within you, and they will not leave
within you one stone upon another; because you did not recognize the time of
your visitation from God.'[j]

JESUS CLEANSES THE TEMPLE

45 Then he entered the temple and
began to drive out those who were selling things there; 46 and he said, 'It is
written,

"My house shall be a house
    of prayer";
  but you have made it a
    den of robbers.'

47 Every day he was teaching in the
temple. The chief priests, the scribes,
and the leaders of the people kept looking for a way to kill him; 48 but they did
not find anything they could do, for all

[i] **19.13** The mina, rendered here by *pound*, was about three months' wages for a labourer
[j] **19.44** Gk lacks *from God*

the people were spellbound by what they heard.

THE AUTHORITY OF JESUS QUESTIONED

20 One day, as he was teaching the people in the temple and telling the good news, the chief priests and the scribes came with the elders 2and said to him, 'Tell us, by what authority are you doing these things? Who is it who gave you this authority?' 3He answered them, 'I will also ask you a question, and you tell me: 4Did the baptism of John come from heaven, or was it of human origin?' 5They discussed it with one another, saying, 'If we say, "From heaven", he will say, "Why did you not believe him?" 6But if we say, "Of human origin", all the people will stone us; for they are convinced that John was a prophet.' 7So they answered that they did not know where it came from. 8Then Jesus said to them, 'Neither will I tell you by what authority I am doing these things.'

THE PARABLE OF THE WICKED TENANTS

9 He began to tell the people this parable: 'A man planted a vineyard, and leased it to tenants, and went to another country for a long time. 10When the season came, he sent a slave to the tenants in order that they might give him his share of the produce of the vineyard; but the tenants beat him and sent him away empty-handed. 11Next he sent another slave; that one also they beat and insulted and sent away empty-handed. 12And he sent yet a third; this one also they wounded and threw out. 13Then the owner of the vineyard said, "What shall I do? I will send my beloved son; perhaps they will respect him." 14But when the tenants saw him, they discussed it among themselves and said, "This is the heir; let us kill him so that the inheritance may be ours." 15So they threw him out of the vineyard and killed him. What then will the owner of the vineyard do to them? 16He will come and destroy those tenants and give the vineyard to others.' When they heard this, they said, 'Heaven forbid!' 17But he looked at them and said, 'What then does this text mean:

"The stone that the builders rejected
has become the cornerstone"?[k]

18Everyone who falls on that stone will be broken to pieces; and it will crush anyone on whom it falls.' 19When the scribes and chief priests realized that he had told this parable against them, they wanted to lay hands on him at that very hour, but they feared the people.

THE QUESTION ABOUT PAYING TAXES

20 So they watched him and sent spies who pretended to be honest, in order to trap him by what he said, so as to hand him over to the jurisdiction and authority of the governor. 21So they asked him, 'Teacher, we know that you are right in what you say and teach, and you show deference to no one, but teach the way of God in accordance with truth. 22Is it lawful for us to pay taxes to the emperor, or not?' 23But he perceived their craftiness and said to them, 24'Show me a denarius. Whose head and whose title does it bear?' They said, 'The emperor's.' 25He said to them, 'Then give to the emperor the things that are the emperor's, and to God the things that are God's.' 26And they were not able in the presence of the people to trap him by what he said; and being amazed by his answer, they became silent.

THE QUESTION ABOUT THE RESURRECTION

27 Some Sadducees, those who say there is no resurrection, came to him 28and asked him a question, 'Teacher, Moses wrote for us that if a man's brother dies, leaving a wife but no children, the man[l] shall marry the widow and raise up children for his brother. 29Now there were seven brothers; the first married, and died childless; 30then the second 31and the third married her, and so in the same way all seven died childless. 32Finally the woman also died. 33In the resurrection, therefore, whose wife will the woman be? For the seven had married her.'

34 Jesus said to them, 'Those who belong to this age marry and are given in marriage; 35but those who are considered worthy of a place in that age and in the resurrection from the dead neither marry nor are given in marriage. 36Indeed they cannot die any more, because they are like angels and are children of God, being children of the resurrection. 37And the fact that the dead are raised Moses himself showed, in the story about the bush, where he speaks of the Lord as the God of Abraham, the God of

[k] **20.17** Or *keystone* [l] **20.28** Gk *his brother*

Isaac, and the God of Jacob. 38 Now he is
God not of the dead, but of the living;
for to him all of them are alive.' 39 Then
some of the scribes answered, 'Teacher,
you have spoken well.' 40 For they no
longer dared to ask him another question.

THE QUESTION ABOUT DAVID'S SON

41 Then he said to them, 'How can
they say that the Messiah[m] is David's
son? 42 For David himself says in the
book of Psalms,

"The Lord said to my Lord,
'Sit at my right hand,
43 until I make your enemies
your footstool.'"

44 David thus calls him Lord; so how can
he be his son?'

JESUS DENOUNCES THE SCRIBES

45 In the hearing of all the people he
said to the[n] disciples, 46 'Beware of the
scribes, who like to walk around in long
robes, and love to be greeted with respect in the market-places, and to have
the best seats in the synagogues and
places of honour at banquets. 47 They devour widows' houses and for the sake of
appearance say long prayers. They will
receive the greater condemnation.'

THE WIDOW'S OFFERING

21 He looked up and saw rich people putting their gifts into the
treasury; 2 he also saw a poor widow
put in two small copper coins. 3 He said,
'Truly I tell you, this poor widow has
put in more than all of them; 4 for all
of them have contributed out of their
abundance, but she out of her poverty
has put in all she had to live on.'

THE DESTRUCTION OF THE TEMPLE FORETOLD

5 When some were speaking about
the temple, how it was adorned with
beautiful stones and gifts dedicated to
God, he said, 6 'As for these things that
you see, the days will come when not
one stone will be left upon another; all
will be thrown down.'

SIGNS AND PERSECUTIONS

7 They asked him, 'Teacher, when
will this be, and what will be the sign
that this is about to take place?' 8 And he
said, 'Beware that you are not led astray;
for many will come in my name and say,
"I am he!"[o] and, "The time is near!"[p] Do
not go after them.

9 'When you hear of wars and insur-
rections, do not be terrified; for these
things must take place first, but the end
will not follow immediately.' 10 Then he
said to them, 'Nation will rise against
nation, and kingdom against kingdom;
11 there will be great earthquakes, and
in various places famines and plagues;
and there will be dreadful portents and
great signs from heaven.

12 'But before all this occurs, they
will arrest you and persecute you; they
will hand you over to synagogues and
prisons, and you will be brought before kings and governors because of
my name. 13 This will give you an opportunity to testify. 14 So make up your
minds not to prepare your defence in
advance; 15 for I will give you words[q] and
a wisdom that none of your opponents
will be able to withstand or contradict.
16 You will be betrayed even by parents
and brothers, by relatives and friends;
and they will put some of you to death.
17 You will be hated by all because of my
name. 18 But not a hair of your head will
perish. 19 By your endurance you will
gain your souls.

THE DESTRUCTION OF JERUSALEM FORETOLD

20 'When you see Jerusalem surrounded by armies, then know that its
desolation has come near.[r] 21 Then those
in Judea must flee to the mountains, and
those inside the city must leave it, and
those out in the country must not enter
it; 22 for these are days of vengeance, as
a fulfilment of all that is written. 23 Woe
to those who are pregnant and to those
who are nursing infants in those days!
For there will be great distress on the
earth and wrath against this people;
24 they will fall by the edge of the sword
and be taken away as captives among all
nations; and Jerusalem will be trampled
on by the Gentiles, until the times of the
Gentiles are fulfilled.

THE COMING OF THE SON OF MAN

25 'There will be signs in the sun, the
moon, and the stars, and on the earth
distress among nations confused by the
roaring of the sea and the waves. 26 People will faint from fear and forebod-
ing of what is coming upon the world,
for the powers of the heavens will be

[m] **20.41** Or *the Christ* [n] **20.45** Other ancient authorities read *his* [o] **21.8** Gk *I am* [p] **21.8** Or *at hand* [q] **21.15** Gk *a mouth* [r] **21.20** Or *is at hand*

shaken. 27 Then they will see "the Son of
Man coming in a cloud" with power and
great glory. 28 Now when these things
begin to take place, stand up and raise
your heads, because your redemption is
drawing near.'

THE LESSON OF THE FIG TREE

29 Then he told them a parable: 'Look
at the fig tree and all the trees; 30 as
soon as they sprout leaves you can see
for yourselves and know that summer
is already near. 31 So also, when you see
these things taking place, you know
that the kingdom of God is near. 32 Truly
I tell you, this generation will not pass
away until all things have taken place.
33 Heaven and earth will pass away, but
my words will not pass away.

EXHORTATION TO WATCH

34 'Be on guard so that your hearts
are not weighed down with dissipation
and drunkenness and the worries of
this life, and that day does not catch you
unexpectedly, 35 like a trap. For it will
come upon all who live on the face of
the whole earth. 36 Be alert at all times,
praying that you may have the strength
to escape all these things that will take
place, and to stand before the Son of
Man.'

37 Every day he was teaching in the
temple, and at night he would go out
and spend the night on the Mount of Olives, as it was called. 38 And all the people would get up early in the morning to
listen to him in the temple.

THE PLOT TO KILL JESUS

22 Now the festival of Unleavened
Bread, which is called the Passover, was near. 2 The chief priests and
the scribes were looking for a way to put
Jesus[s] to death, for they were afraid of
the people.

3 Then Satan entered into Judas
called Iscariot, who was one of the
twelve; 4 he went away and conferred
with the chief priests and officers of
the temple police about how he might
betray him to them. 5 They were greatly
pleased and agreed to give him money.
6 So he consented and began to look for
an opportunity to betray him to them
when no crowd was present.

THE PREPARATION OF THE PASSOVER

7 Then came the day of Unleavened
Bread, on which the Passover lamb had
to be sacrificed. 8 So Jesus[t] sent Peter
and John, saying, 'Go and prepare the
Passover meal for us that we may eat it.'
9 They asked him, 'Where do you want us
to make preparations for it?' 10 'Listen,'
he said to them, 'when you have entered
the city, a man carrying a jar of water
will meet you; follow him into the house
he enters 11 and say to the owner of the
house, "The teacher asks you, 'Where is
the guest room, where I may eat the
Passover with my disciples?' " 12 He will
show you a large room upstairs, already
furnished. Make preparations for us
there.' 13 So they went and found everything as he had told them; and they prepared the Passover meal.

THE INSTITUTION OF THE LORD'S SUPPER

14 When the hour came, he took his
place at the table, and the apostles with
him. 15 He said to them, 'I have eagerly
desired to eat this Passover with you before I suffer; 16 for I tell you, I will not eat
it[u] until it is fulfilled in the kingdom of
God.' 17 Then he took a cup, and after giving thanks he said, 'Take this and divide
it among yourselves; 18 for I tell you that
from now on I will not drink of the fruit
of the vine until the kingdom of God
comes.' 19 Then he took a loaf of bread,
and when he had given thanks, he broke
it and gave it to them, saying, 'This is
my body, which is given for you. Do this
in remembrance of me.' 20 And he did
the same with the cup after supper, saying, 'This cup that is poured out for you
is the new covenant in my blood.[v] 21 But
see, the one who betrays me is with me,
and his hand is on the table. 22 For the
Son of Man is going as it has been determined, but woe to that one by whom
he is betrayed!' 23 Then they began to ask
one another which one of them it could
be who would do this.

THE DISPUTE ABOUT GREATNESS

24 A dispute also arose among them
as to which one of them was to be regarded as the greatest. 25 But he said to
them, 'The kings of the Gentiles lord it
over them; and those in authority over
them are called benefactors. 26 But not
so with you; rather the greatest among
you must become like the youngest, and

[s] 22.2 Gk *him* [t] 22.8 Gk *he* [u] 22.16 Other ancient authorities read *never eat it again*
[v] 22.20 Other ancient authorities lack, in whole or in part, verses 19b–20 (*which is given . . . in my blood*)

the leader like one who serves. 27For
who is greater, the one who is at the table or the one who serves? Is it not the
one at the table? But I am among you as
one who serves.

28 'You are those who have stood by
me in my trials; 29and I confer on you,
just as my Father has conferred on me,
a kingdom, 30so that you may eat and
drink at my table in my kingdom, and
you will sit on thrones judging the
twelve tribes of Israel.

JESUS PREDICTS PETER'S DENIAL

31 'Simon, Simon, listen! Satan has
demanded[w] to sift all of you like wheat,
32but I have prayed for you that your
own faith may not fail; and you, when
once you have turned back, strengthen
your brothers.' 33And he said to him,
'Lord, I am ready to go with you to
prison and to death!' 34Jesus[x] said, 'I tell
you, Peter, the cock will not crow this
day, until you have denied three times
that you know me.'

PURSE, BAG, AND SWORD

35 He said to them, 'When I sent you
out without a purse, bag, or sandals, did
you lack anything?' They said, 'No, not a
thing.' 36He said to them, 'But now, the
one who has a purse must take it, and
likewise a bag. And the one who has no
sword must sell his cloak and buy one.
37For I tell you, this scripture must be
fulfilled in me, "And he was counted
among the lawless"; and indeed what
is written about me is being fulfilled.'
38They said, 'Lord, look, here are two
swords.' He replied, 'It is enough.'

JESUS PRAYS ON THE MOUNT OF OLIVES

39 He came out and went, as was
his custom, to the Mount of Olives; and
the disciples followed him. 40When he
reached the place, he said to them, 'Pray
that you may not come into the time of
trial.'[y] 41Then he withdrew from them
about a stone's throw, knelt down, and
prayed, 42'Father, if you are willing,
remove this cup from me; yet, not my
will but yours be done.' [[43Then an angel from heaven appeared to him and
gave him strength. 44In his anguish he
prayed more earnestly, and his sweat
became like great drops of blood falling
down on the ground.]][z] 45When he got
up from prayer, he came to the disciples and found them sleeping because
of grief, 46and he said to them, 'Why are
you sleeping? Get up and pray that you
may not come into the time of trial.'[a]

THE BETRAYAL AND ARREST OF JESUS

47 While he was still speaking, suddenly a crowd came, and the one called
Judas, one of the twelve, was leading
them. He approached Jesus to kiss him;
48but Jesus said to him, 'Judas, is it with
a kiss that you are betraying the Son of
Man?' 49When those who were around
him saw what was coming, they asked,
'Lord, should we strike with the sword?'
50Then one of them struck the slave
of the high priest and cut off his right
ear. 51But Jesus said, 'No more of this!'
And he touched his ear and healed him.
52Then Jesus said to the chief priests, the
officers of the temple police, and the
elders who had come for him, 'Have you
come out with swords and clubs as if I
were a bandit? 53When I was with you
day after day in the temple, you did not
lay hands on me. But this is your hour,
and the power of darkness!'

PETER DENIES JESUS

54 Then they seized him and led him
away, bringing him into the high priest's
house. But Peter was following at a distance. 55When they had kindled a fire
in the middle of the courtyard and sat
down together, Peter sat among them.
56Then a servant-girl, seeing him in the
firelight, stared at him and said, 'This
man also was with him.' 57But he denied
it, saying, 'Woman, I do not know him.'
58A little later someone else, on seeing
him, said, 'You also are one of them.' But
Peter said, 'Man, I am not!' 59Then about
an hour later yet another kept insisting,
'Surely this man also was with him; for
he is a Galilean.' 60But Peter said, 'Man, I
do not know what you are talking about!'
At that moment, while he was still speaking, the cock crowed. 61The Lord turned
and looked at Peter. Then Peter remembered the word of the Lord, how he had
said to him, 'Before the cock crows today,
you will deny me three times.' 62And he
went out and wept bitterly.

THE MOCKING AND BEATING OF JESUS

63 Now the men who were holding
Jesus began to mock him and beat him;

[w] **22.31** Or *has obtained permission* [x] **22.34** Gk *He* [y] **22.40** Or *into temptation* [z] **22.44** Other ancient authorities lack verses 43 and 44
[a] **22.46** Or *into temptation*

64they also blindfolded him and kept
asking him, 'Prophesy! Who is it that
struck you?' 65They kept heaping many
other insults on him.

JESUS BEFORE THE COUNCIL

66 When day came, the assembly
of the elders of the people, both chief
priests and scribes, gathered together,
and they brought him to their council.
67They said, 'If you are the Messiah,[b] tell
us.' He replied, 'If I tell you, you will not
believe; 68and if I question you, you will
not answer. 69But from now on the Son
of Man will be seated at the right hand
of the power of God.' 70All of them asked,
'Are you, then, the Son of God?' He said
to them, 'You say that I am.' 71Then they
said, 'What further testimony do we
need? We have heard it ourselves from
his own lips!'

JESUS BEFORE PILATE

23 Then the assembly rose as a
body and brought Jesus[c] before
Pilate. 2They began to accuse him, saying, 'We found this man perverting our
nation, forbidding us to pay taxes to the
emperor, and saying that he himself is
the Messiah, a king.'[d] 3Then Pilate asked
him, 'Are you the king of the Jews?' He
answered, 'You say so.' 4Then Pilate said
to the chief priests and the crowds, 'I
find no basis for an accusation against
this man.' 5But they were insistent and
said, 'He stirs up the people by teaching throughout all Judea, from Galilee
where he began even to this place.'

JESUS BEFORE HEROD

6 When Pilate heard this, he asked
whether the man was a Galilean. 7And
when he learned that he was under
Herod's jurisdiction, he sent him off to
Herod, who was himself in Jerusalem
at that time. 8When Herod saw Jesus,
he was very glad, for he had been
wanting to see him for a long time, because he had heard about him and was
hoping to see him perform some sign.
9He questioned him at some length,
but Jesus[e] gave him no answer. 10The
chief priests and the scribes stood
by, vehemently accusing him. 11Even
Herod with his soldiers treated him
with contempt and mocked him; then
he put an elegant robe on him, and
sent him back to Pilate. 12That same
day Herod and Pilate became friends
with each other; before this they had
been enemies.

JESUS SENTENCED TO DEATH

13 Pilate then called together the
chief priests, the leaders, and the people, 14and said to them, 'You brought me
this man as one who was perverting the
people; and here I have examined him
in your presence and have not found
this man guilty of any of your charges
against him. 15Neither has Herod, for he
sent him back to us. Indeed, he has done
nothing to deserve death. 16I will therefore have him flogged and release him.'[f]

18 Then they all shouted out together, 'Away with this fellow! Release
Barabbas for us!' 19(This was a man who
had been put in prison for an insurrection that had taken place in the city, and
for murder.) 20Pilate, wanting to release
Jesus, addressed them again; 21but they
kept shouting, 'Crucify, crucify him!' 22A
third time he said to them, 'Why, what
evil has he done? I have found in him no
ground for the sentence of death; I will
therefore have him flogged and then
release him.' 23But they kept urgently
demanding with loud shouts that he
should be crucified; and their voices prevailed. 24So Pilate gave his verdict that
their demand should be granted. 25He
released the man they asked for, the one
who had been put in prison for insurrection and murder, and he handed Jesus
over as they wished.

THE CRUCIFIXION OF JESUS

26 As they led him away, they seized
a man, Simon of Cyrene, who was coming from the country, and they laid the
cross on him, and made him carry it behind Jesus. 27A great number of the people followed him, and among them were
women who were beating their breasts
and wailing for him. 28But Jesus turned
to them and said, 'Daughters of Jerusalem, do not weep for me, but weep for
yourselves and for your children. 29For
the days are surely coming when they
will say, "Blessed are the barren, and
the wombs that never bore, and the
breasts that never nursed." 30Then they
will begin to say to the mountains, "Fall
on us"; and to the hills, "Cover us." 31For
if they do this when the wood is green,
what will happen when it is dry?'

32 Two others also, who were criminals, were led away to be put to death

[b] 22.67 *Or the Christ* [c] 23.1 Gk *him* [d] 23.2 Or *is an anointed king* [e] 23.9 Gk *he* [f] 23.16 Here, or after verse 19, other ancient authorities add verse 17, *Now he was obliged to release someone for them at the festival*

with him. 33 When they came to the place that is called The Skull, they crucified Jesus[g] there with the criminals, one on his right and one on his left. [[34 Then Jesus said, 'Father, forgive them; for they do not know what they are doing.']][h] And they cast lots to divide his clothing. 35 And the people stood by, watching; but the leaders scoffed at him, saying, 'He saved others; let him save himself if he is the Messiah[i] of God, his chosen one!' 36 The soldiers also mocked him, coming up and offering him sour wine, 37 and saying, 'If you are the King of the Jews, save yourself!' 38 There was also an inscription over him,[j] 'This is the King of the Jews.'

39 One of the criminals who were hanged there kept deriding[k] him and saying, 'Are you not the Messiah?[l] Save yourself and us!' 40 But the other rebuked him, saying, 'Do you not fear God, since you are under the same sentence of condemnation? 41 And we indeed have been condemned justly, for we are getting what we deserve for our deeds, but this man has done nothing wrong.' 42 Then he said, 'Jesus, remember me when you come into[m] your kingdom.' 43 He replied, 'Truly I tell you, today you will be with me in Paradise.'

THE DEATH OF JESUS

44 It was now about noon, and darkness came over the whole land[n] until three in the afternoon, 45 while the sun's light failed;[o] and the curtain of the temple was torn in two. 46 Then Jesus, crying with a loud voice, said, 'Father, into your hands I commend my spirit.' Having said this, he breathed his last. 47 When the centurion saw what had taken place, he praised God and said, 'Certainly this man was innocent.'[p] 48 And when all the crowds who had gathered there for this spectacle saw what had taken place, they returned home, beating their breasts. 49 But all his acquaintances, including the women who had followed him from Galilee, stood at a distance, watching these things.

THE BURIAL OF JESUS

50 Now there was a good and righteous man named Joseph, who, though a member of the council, 51 had not agreed to their plan and action. He came from the Jewish town of Arimathea, and he was waiting expectantly for the kingdom of God. 52 This man went to Pilate and asked for the body of Jesus. 53 Then he took it down, wrapped it in a linen cloth, and laid it in a rock-hewn tomb where no one had ever been laid. 54 It was the day of Preparation, and the sabbath was beginning.[q] 55 The women who had come with him from Galilee followed, and they saw the tomb and how his body was laid. 56 Then they returned, and prepared spices and ointments.

On the sabbath they rested according to the commandment.

THE RESURRECTION OF JESUS

24 But on the first day of the week, at early dawn, they came to the tomb, taking the spices that they had prepared. 2 They found the stone rolled away from the tomb, 3 but when they went in, they did not find the body.[r] 4 While they were perplexed about this, suddenly two men in dazzling clothes stood beside them. 5 The women[s] were terrified and bowed their faces to the ground, but the men[t] said to them, 'Why do you look for the living among the dead? He is not here, but has risen.[u] 6 Remember how he told you, while he was still in Galilee, 7 that the Son of Man must be handed over to sinners, and be crucified, and on the third day rise again.' 8 Then they remembered his words, 9 and returning from the tomb, they told all this to the eleven and to all the rest. 10 Now it was Mary Magdalene, Joanna, Mary the mother of James, and the other women with them who told this to the apostles. 11 But these words seemed to them an idle tale, and they did not believe them. 12 But Peter got up and ran to the tomb; stooping and looking in, he saw the linen cloths by themselves; then he went home, amazed at what had happened.[v]

THE WALK TO EMMAUS

13 Now on that same day two of them were going to a village called Emmaus, about seven miles[w] from Jerusalem,

[g] 23.33 Gk *him* [h] 23.34 Other ancient authorities lack the sentence *Then Jesus . . . what they are doing* [i] 23.35 Or *the Christ*
[j] 23.38 Other ancient authorities add *written in Greek and Latin and Hebrew* (that is, *Aramaic*)
[k] 23.39 Or *blaspheming* [l] 23.39 Or *the Christ*
[m] 23.42 Other ancient authorities read *in*
[n] 23.44 Or *earth* [o] 23.45 Or *the sun was eclipsed.* Other ancient authorities read *the sun was darkened* [p] 23.47 Or *righteous*
[q] 23.54 Gk *was dawning* [r] 24.3 Other ancient authorities add *of the Lord Jesus* [s] 24.5 Gk *They*
[t] 24.5 Gk *but they* [u] 24.5 Other ancient authorities lack *He is not here, but has risen*
[v] 24.12 Other ancient authorities lack verse 12
[w] 24.13 Gk *sixty stadia;* other ancient authorities read *a hundred and sixty stadia*

14and talking with each other about all
these things that had happened. 15While
they were talking and discussing, Jesus
himself came near and went with them,
16but their eyes were kept from recognizing him. 17And he said to them, 'What
are you discussing with each other while
you walk along?' They stood still, looking
sad.[x] 18Then one of them, whose name
was Cleopas, answered him, 'Are you the
only stranger in Jerusalem who does not
know the things that have taken place
there in these days?' 19He asked them,
'What things?' They replied, 'The things
about Jesus of Nazareth,[y] who was a
prophet mighty in deed and word before God and all the people, 20and how
our chief priests and leaders handed
him over to be condemned to death
and crucified him. 21But we had hoped
that he was the one to redeem Israel.[z]
Yes, and besides all this, it is now the
third day since these things took place.
22Moreover, some women of our group
astounded us. They were at the tomb
early this morning, 23and when they did
not find his body there, they came back
and told us that they had indeed seen
a vision of angels who said that he was
alive. 24Some of those who were with us
went to the tomb and found it just as the
women had said; but they did not see
him.' 25Then he said to them, 'Oh, how
foolish you are, and how slow of heart
to believe all that the prophets have declared! 26Was it not necessary that the
Messiah[a] should suffer these things and
then enter into his glory?' 27Then beginning with Moses and all the prophets,
he interpreted to them the things about
himself in all the scriptures.

28 As they came near the village
to which they were going, he walked
ahead as if he were going on. 29But they
urged him strongly, saying, 'Stay with
us, because it is almost evening and the
day is now nearly over.' So he went in to
stay with them. 30When he was at the
table with them, he took bread, blessed
and broke it, and gave it to them. 31Then
their eyes were opened, and they recognized him; and he vanished from their
sight. 32They said to each other, 'Were
not our hearts burning within us[b] while
he was talking to us on the road, while
he was opening the scriptures to us?'
33That same hour they got up and returned to Jerusalem; and they found the
eleven and their companions gathered
together. 34They were saying, 'The Lord
has risen indeed, and he has appeared to
Simon!' 35Then they told what had happened on the road, and how he had been
made known to them in the breaking of
the bread.

JESUS APPEARS TO HIS DISCIPLES

36 While they were talking about this,
Jesus himself stood among them and
said to them, 'Peace be with you.'[c] 37They
were startled and terrified, and thought
that they were seeing a ghost. 38He said
to them, 'Why are you frightened, and
why do doubts arise in your hearts?
39Look at my hands and my feet; see
that it is I myself. Touch me and see; for
a ghost does not have flesh and bones as
you see that I have.' 40And when he had
said this, he showed them his hands and
his feet.[d] 41While in their joy they were
disbelieving and still wondering, he said
to them, 'Have you anything here to eat?'
42They gave him a piece of broiled fish,
43and he took it and ate in their presence.

44 Then he said to them, 'These are
my words that I spoke to you while I was
still with you—that everything written about me in the law of Moses, the
prophets, and the psalms must be fulfilled.' 45Then he opened their minds to
understand the scriptures, 46and he said
to them, 'Thus it is written, that the Messiah[e] is to suffer and to rise from the dead
on the third day, 47and that repentance
and forgiveness of sins is to be proclaimed
in his name to all nations, beginning
from Jerusalem. 48You are witnesses[f] of
these things. 49And see, I am sending
upon you what my Father promised; so
stay here in the city until you have been
clothed with power from on high.'

THE ASCENSION OF JESUS

50 Then he led them out as far as
Bethany, and, lifting up his hands, he
blessed them. 51While he was blessing
them, he withdrew from them and was
carried up into heaven.[g] 52And they
worshipped him, and[h] returned to Jerusalem with great joy; 53and they were
continually in the temple blessing God.[i]

[x] **24.17** Other ancient authorities read *walk along, looking sad?'* [y] **24.19** Other ancient authorities read *Jesus the Nazorean* [z] **24.21** Or *to set Israel free* [a] **24.26** Or *the Christ* [b] **24.32** Other ancient authorities lack *within us* [c] **24.36** Other ancient authorities lack *and said to them, 'Peace be with you.'* [d] **24.40** Other ancient authorities lack verse 40 [e] **24.46** Or *the Christ* [f] **24.48** Or *nations. Beginning from Jerusalem 48you are witnesses* [g] **24.51** Other ancient authorities lack *and was carried up into heaven* [h] **24.52** Other ancient authorities lack *worshipped him, and* [i] **24.53** Other ancient authorities add *Amen*

The Gospel According to

JOHN

John's Gospel was written late in the first century and draws from a tradition independent of that used by the other three Gospels. Its author is unknown, though a late second-century tradition associates the account with John, the son of Zebedee (21.2).

The Gospel of John presents a portrayal of the ministry and life of Jesus quite different from that found in the other three Gospels. Very few stories told in Matthew, Mark, and Luke are presented in the Gospel of John. None of the parables remembered in the first three Gospels are ever mentioned in John's Gospel. Instead, John's Gospel is a unique and fresh presentation about Jesus that contains new memorable stories, such as Jesus turning water into wine (2.1–12) and raising Lazarus from the dead (11.1–44). Moreover, only John's Gospel has the teaching of Jesus to Nicodemus in which he says, "No one can see the kingdom of God without being born from above" (3.3) and the famous "I am" sayings in which Jesus states: "I am the light of the world" (8.12), "I am the bread of life" (6.48), "I am the good shepherd" (10.11), "I am the resurrection and the life" (11.25), "I am the way, and the truth, and the life" (14.6). The Gospel is not history, but testimony written so that "you may come to believe that Jesus is the Messiah, the Son of God, and that through believing you may have life in his name" (20.31).

The Gospel of John is read every year at certain solemn feasts throughout the liturgical calendar, e.g., the Mass During the Day at Christmas (1.1–18); the Second Sunday of Christmas (1.1–18); the Third (4.5–42), Fourth (9.1–41) and Fifth (11.1–45) Sundays of Lent for the preparation of the catechumens; the Mass of the Lord's Supper on Holy Thursday (13.1–15); the Passion of the Lord on Good Friday (18.1—19.42); Easter Sunday (20.1–9); the Second Sunday of Easter (20.19–31); and the Vigil (7.37–39) and Sunday of Pentecost (20.19–23). No other Gospel is featured in this way by being read at as many solemn feasts across the three years of the liturgical cycle. The selection of readings from this Gospel on these feasts highlights the importance of the Fourth Gospel in its explicit emphasis on the proclamation of the divinity of Jesus.

THE WORD BECAME FLESH

1 In the beginning was the Word,
and the Word was with God, and
the Word was God. 2 He was in the beginning with God. 3 All things came
into being through him, and without
him not one thing came into being.
What has come into being 4 in him was
life,[a] and the life was the light of all
people. 5 The light shines in the darkness, and the darkness did not overcome it.

6 There was a man sent from God,
whose name was John. 7 He came as a
witness to testify to the light, so that all
might believe through him. 8 He himself
was not the light, but he came to testify
to the light. 9 The true light, which enlightens everyone, was coming into the
world.[b]

[a] 1.4 Or *3through him. And without him not one thing came into being that has come into being. 4In him was life* [b] 1.9 Or *He was the true light that enlightens everyone coming into the world*

10 He was in the world, and the
world came into being through him; yet
the world did not know him. 11He came
to what was his own,[c] and his own people did not accept him. 12But to all who
received him, who believed in his name,
he gave power to become children of
God, 13who were born, not of blood or of
the will of the flesh or of the will of man,
but of God.

14 And the Word became flesh and
lived among us, and we have seen his
glory, the glory as of a father's only son,[d]
full of grace and truth. 15(John testified
to him and cried out, 'This was he of
whom I said, "He who comes after me
ranks ahead of me because he was before me." ') 16From his fullness we have
all received, grace upon grace. 17The law
indeed was given through Moses; grace
and truth came through Jesus Christ.
18No one has ever seen God. It is God the
only Son,[e] who is close to the Father's
heart,[f] who has made him known.

THE TESTIMONY OF JOHN THE BAPTIST

19 This is the testimony given by
John when the Jews sent priests and
Levites from Jerusalem to ask him,
'Who are you?' 20He confessed and did
not deny it, but confessed, 'I am not
the Messiah.'[g] 21And they asked him,
'What then? Are you Elijah?' He said, 'I
am not.' 'Are you the prophet?' He answered, 'No.' 22Then they said to him,
'Who are you? Let us have an answer
for those who sent us. What do you say
about yourself?' 23He said,

'I am the voice of one crying out
in the wilderness,
"Make straight the way of the Lord" ',

as the prophet Isaiah said.

24 Now they had been sent from
the Pharisees. 25They asked him, 'Why
then are you baptizing if you are neither the Messiah,[h] nor Elijah, nor the
prophet?' 26John answered them, 'I baptize with water. Among you stands one
whom you do not know, 27the one who
is coming after me; I am not worthy to
untie the thong of his sandal.' 28This
took place in Bethany across the Jordan
where John was baptizing.

THE LAMB OF GOD

29 The next day he saw Jesus coming towards him and declared, 'Here is
the Lamb of God who takes away the
sin of the world! 30This is he of whom I
said, "After me comes a man who ranks
ahead of me because he was before me."
31I myself did not know him; but I came
baptizing with water for this reason,
that he might be revealed to Israel.'
32And John testified, 'I saw the Spirit
descending from heaven like a dove,
and it remained on him. 33I myself did
not know him, but the one who sent me
to baptize with water said to me, "He on
whom you see the Spirit descend and
remain is the one who baptizes with the
Holy Spirit." 34And I myself have seen
and have testified that this is the Son of
God.'[i]

THE FIRST DISCIPLES OF JESUS

35 The next day John again was
standing with two of his disciples,
36and as he watched Jesus walk by, he
exclaimed, 'Look, here is the Lamb of
God!' 37The two disciples heard him say
this, and they followed Jesus. 38When
Jesus turned and saw them following,
he said to them, 'What are you looking
for?' They said to him, 'Rabbi' (which
translated means Teacher), 'where are
you staying?' 39He said to them, 'Come
and see.' They came and saw where he
was staying, and they remained with
him that day. It was about four o'clock
in the afternoon. 40One of the two who
heard John speak and followed him was
Andrew, Simon Peter's brother. 41He
first found his brother Simon and said
to him, 'We have found the Messiah'
(which is translated Anointed[j]). 42He
brought Simon[k] to Jesus, who looked
at him and said, 'You are Simon son
of John. You are to be called Cephas'
(which is translated Peter[l]).

JESUS CALLS PHILIP AND NATHANAEL

43 The next day Jesus decided to go to
Galilee. He found Philip and said to him,
'Follow me.' 44Now Philip was from
Bethsaida, the city of Andrew and Peter.
45Philip found Nathanael and said to
him, 'We have found him about whom
Moses in the law and also the proph-
ets wrote, Jesus son of Joseph from
Nazareth.' 46Nathanael said to him,

[c] 1.11 Or *to his own home* [d] 1.14 Or *the Father's only Son* [e] 1.18 Other ancient authorities read *It is an only Son, God,* or *It is the only Son* [f] 1.18 Gk *bosom* [g] 1.20 Or *the Christ* [h] 1.25 Or *the Christ* [i] 1.34 Other ancient authorities read *is God's chosen one* [j] 1.41 Or *Christ* [k] 1.42 Gk *him* [l] 1.42 From the word for *rock* in Aramaic (*kepha*) and Greek (*petra*), respectively

'Can anything good come out of Nazareth?' Philip said to him, 'Come and see.'
47When Jesus saw Nathanael coming towards him, he said of him, 'Here is truly
an Israelite in whom there is no deceit!'
48Nathanael asked him, 'Where did you
come to know me?' Jesus answered, 'I
saw you under the fig tree before Philip
called you.' 49Nathanael replied, 'Rabbi,
you are the Son of God! You are the King
of Israel!' 50Jesus answered, 'Do you believe because I told you that I saw you
under the fig tree? You will see greater
things than these.' 51And he said to
him, 'Very truly, I tell you,[m] you will see
heaven opened and the angels of God
ascending and descending upon the Son
of Man.'

THE WEDDING AT CANA

2 On the third day there was a wedding in Cana of Galilee, and the
mother of Jesus was there. 2Jesus and
his disciples had also been invited to
the wedding. 3When the wine gave out,
the mother of Jesus said to him, 'They
have no wine.' 4And Jesus said to her,
'Woman, what concern is that to you
and to me? My hour has not yet come.'
5His mother said to the servants, 'Do
whatever he tells you.' 6Now standing
there were six stone water-jars for the
Jewish rites of purification, each holding twenty or thirty gallons. 7Jesus
said to them, 'Fill the jars with water.'
And they filled them up to the brim.
8He said to them, 'Now draw some out,
and take it to the chief steward.' So they
took it. 9When the steward tasted the
water that had become wine, and did
not know where it came from (though
the servants who had drawn the water
knew), the steward called the bridegroom 10and said to him, 'Everyone
serves the good wine first, and then
the inferior wine after the guests have
become drunk. But you have kept the
good wine until now.' 11Jesus did this,
the first of his signs, in Cana of Galilee,
and revealed his glory; and his disciples
believed in him.

12 After this he went down to Capernaum with his mother, his brothers,
and his disciples; and they remained
there for a few days.

JESUS CLEANSES THE TEMPLE

13 The Passover of the Jews was near,
and Jesus went up to Jerusalem. 14In
the temple he found people selling cattle, sheep, and doves, and the money-
changers seated at their tables. 15Mak-
ing a whip of cords, he drove all of them
out of the temple, both the sheep and
the cattle. He also poured out the coins
of the money-changers and overturned
their tables. 16He told those who were
selling the doves, 'Take these things out
of here! Stop making my Father's house
a market-place!' 17His disciples remembered that it was written, 'Zeal for your
house will consume me.' 18The Jews then
said to him, 'What sign can you show us
for doing this?' 19Jesus answered them,
'Destroy this temple, and in three days
I will raise it up.' 20The Jews then said,
'This temple has been under construction for forty-six years, and will you
raise it up in three days?' 21But he was
speaking of the temple of his body. 22Af-
ter he was raised from the dead, his
disciples remembered that he had said
this; and they believed the scripture and
the word that Jesus had spoken.

23 When he was in Jerusalem during
the Passover festival, many believed in
his name because they saw the signs
that he was doing. 24But Jesus on his
part would not entrust himself to them,
because he knew all people 25and needed
no one to testify about anyone; for he
himself knew what was in everyone.

NICODEMUS VISITS JESUS

3 Now there was a Pharisee named
Nicodemus, a leader of the Jews.
2He came to Jesus[n] by night and said
to him, 'Rabbi, we know that you are
a teacher who has come from God; for
no one can do these signs that you do
apart from the presence of God.' 3Jesus
answered him, 'Very truly, I tell you, no
one can see the kingdom of God without being born from above.'[o] 4Nicode-
mus said to him, 'How can anyone be
born after having grown old? Can one
enter a second time into the mother's
womb and be born?' 5Jesus answered,
'Very truly, I tell you, no one can enter
the kingdom of God without being born
of water and Spirit. 6What is born of the
flesh is flesh, and what is born of the
Spirit is spirit.[p] 7Do not be astonished
that I said to you, "You[q] must be born
from above."[r] 8The wind[s] blows where
it chooses, and you hear the sound of

[m] **1.51** Both instances of the Greek word for *you* in this verse are plural [n] **3.2** Gk *him* [o] **3.3** Or *born anew* [p] **3.6** The same Greek word means both *wind* and *spirit* [q] **3.7** The Greek word for *you* here is plural [r] **3.7** Or *anew* [s] **3.8** The same Greek word means both *wind* and *spirit*

it, but you do not know where it comes from or where it goes. So it is with everyone who is born of the Spirit.' 9Nicodemus said to him, 'How can these things be?' 10Jesus answered him, 'Are you a teacher of Israel, and yet you do not understand these things?

11 'Very truly, I tell you, we speak of what we know and testify to what we have seen; yet you[t] do not receive our testimony. 12If I have told you about earthly things and you do not believe, how can you believe if I tell you about heavenly things? 13No one has ascended into heaven except the one who descended from heaven, the Son of Man.[u] 14And just as Moses lifted up the serpent in the wilderness, so must the Son of Man be lifted up, 15that whoever believes in him may have eternal life.[v]

16 'For God so loved the world that he gave his only Son, so that everyone who believes in him may not perish but may have eternal life.

17 'Indeed, God did not send the Son into the world to condemn the world, but in order that the world might be saved through him. 18Those who believe in him are not condemned; but those who do not believe are condemned already, because they have not believed in the name of the only Son of God. 19And this is the judgement, that the light has come into the world, and people loved darkness rather than light because their deeds were evil. 20For all who do evil hate the light and do not come to the light, so that their deeds may not be exposed. 21But those who do what is true come to the light, so that it may be clearly seen that their deeds have been done in God.'[w]

JESUS AND JOHN THE BAPTIST

22 After this Jesus and his disciples went into the Judean countryside, and he spent some time there with them and baptized. 23John also was baptizing at Aenon near Salim because water was abundant there; and people kept coming and were being baptized— 24John, of course, had not yet been thrown into prison.

25 Now a discussion about purification arose between John's disciples and a Jew.[x] 26They came to John and said to him, 'Rabbi, the one who was with you across the Jordan, to whom you testified, here he is baptizing, and all are going to him.' 27John answered, 'No one can receive anything except what has been given from heaven. 28You yourselves are my witnesses that I said, "I am not the Messiah,[y] but I have been sent ahead of him." 29He who has the bride is the bridegroom. The friend of the bridegroom, who stands and hears him, rejoices greatly at the bridegroom's voice. For this reason my joy has been fulfilled. 30He must increase, but I must decrease.'[z]

THE ONE WHO COMES FROM HEAVEN

31 The one who comes from above is above all; the one who is of the earth belongs to the earth and speaks about earthly things. The one who comes from heaven is above all. 32He testifies to what he has seen and heard, yet no one accepts his testimony. 33Whoever has accepted his testimony has certified[a] this, that God is true. 34He whom God has sent speaks the words of God, for he gives the Spirit without measure. 35The Father loves the Son and has placed all things in his hands. 36Whoever believes in the Son has eternal life; whoever disobeys the Son will not see life, but must endure God's wrath.

JESUS AND THE WOMAN OF SAMARIA

4 Now when Jesus[b] learned that the Pharisees had heard, 'Jesus is making and baptizing more disciples than John'— 2although it was not Jesus himself but his disciples who baptized— 3he left Judea and started back to Galilee. 4But he had to go through Samaria. 5So he came to a Samaritan city called Sychar, near the plot of ground that Jacob had given to his son Joseph. 6Jacob's well was there, and Jesus, tired out by his journey, was sitting by the well. It was about noon.

7 A Samaritan woman came to draw water, and Jesus said to her, 'Give me a drink'. 8(His disciples had gone to the city to buy food.) 9The Samaritan woman said to him, 'How is it that you, a Jew, ask a drink of me, a woman of Samaria?' (Jews do not share things in

[t] **3.11** The Greek word for *you* here and in verse 12 is plural [u] **3.13** Other ancient authorities add *who is in heaven* [v] **3.15** Some interpreters hold that the quotation concludes with verse 15 [w] **3.21** Some interpreters hold that the quotation concludes with verse 15 [x] **3.25** Other ancient authorities read *the Jews* [y] **3.28** Or *the Christ* [z] **3.30** Some interpreters hold that the quotation continues to the end of verse 36 [a] **3.33** Gk *set a seal to* [b] **4.1** Other ancient authorities read *the Lord*

common with Samaritans.)[c] 10 Jesus answered her, 'If you knew the gift of God,
and who it is that is saying to you, "Give
me a drink", you would have asked him,
and he would have given you living water.' 11 The woman said to him, 'Sir, you
have no bucket, and the well is deep.
Where do you get that living water?
12 Are you greater than our ancestor Jacob, who gave us the well, and with his
sons and his flocks drank from it?' 13 Jesus
said to her, 'Everyone who drinks of this
water will be thirsty again, 14 but those
who drink of the water that I will give
them will never be thirsty. The water that
I will give will become in them a spring
of water gushing up to eternal life.' 15 The
woman said to him, 'Sir, give me this water, so that I may never be thirsty or have
to keep coming here to draw water.'

16 Jesus said to her, 'Go, call your husband, and come back.' 17 The woman answered him, 'I have no husband.' Jesus
said to her, 'You are right in saying, "I
have no husband"; 18 for you have had
five husbands, and the one you have
now is not your husband. What you
have said is true!' 19 The woman said to
him, 'Sir, I see that you are a prophet.
20 Our ancestors worshipped on this
mountain, but you[d] say that the place
where people must worship is in Jerusalem.' 21 Jesus said to her, 'Woman, believe me, the hour is coming when you
will worship the Father neither on this
mountain nor in Jerusalem. 22 You worship what you do not know; we worship
what we know, for salvation is from the
Jews. 23 But the hour is coming, and is
now here, when the true worshippers
will worship the Father in spirit and
truth, for the Father seeks such as these
to worship him. 24 God is spirit, and
those who worship him must worship
in spirit and truth.' 25 The woman said
to him, 'I know that Messiah is coming'
(who is called Christ). 'When he comes,
he will proclaim all things to us.' 26 Jesus
said to her, 'I am he,[e] the one who is
speaking to you.'

27 Just then his disciples came. They
were astonished that he was speaking
with a woman, but no one said, 'What
do you want?' or, 'Why are you speaking with her?' 28 Then the woman left
her water-jar and went back to the city.
She said to the people, 29 'Come and see
a man who told me everything I have
ever done! He cannot be the Messiah,[f]
can he?' 30 They left the city and were on
their way to him.

31 Meanwhile the disciples were urging him, 'Rabbi, eat something.' 32 But
he said to them, 'I have food to eat that
you do not know about.' 33 So the disciples said to one another, 'Surely no one
has brought him something to eat?'
34 Jesus said to them, 'My food is to do
the will of him who sent me and to complete his work. 35 Do you not say, "Four
months more, then comes the harvest"?
But I tell you, look around you, and see
how the fields are ripe for harvesting.
36 The reaper is already receiving[g] wages
and is gathering fruit for eternal life, so
that sower and reaper may rejoice together. 37 For here the saying holds true,
"One sows and another reaps." 38 I sent
you to reap that for which you did not
labour. Others have laboured, and you
have entered into their labour.'

39 Many Samaritans from that city
believed in him because of the woman's testimony, 'He told me everything
I have ever done.' 40 So when the Samaritans came to him, they asked him
to stay with them; and he stayed there
for two days. 41 And many more believed
because of his word. 42 They said to the
woman, 'It is no longer because of what
you said that we believe, for we have
heard for ourselves, and we know that
this is truly the Saviour of the world.'

JESUS RETURNS TO GALILEE

43 When the two days were over,
he went from that place to Galilee
44 (for Jesus himself had testified that a
prophet has no honour in the prophet's
own country). 45 When he came to Galilee, the Galileans welcomed him, since
they had seen all that he had done in Jerusalem at the festival; for they too had
gone to the festival.

JESUS HEALS AN OFFICIAL'S SON

46 Then he came again to Cana in
Galilee where he had changed the water
into wine. Now there was a royal official
whose son lay ill in Capernaum. 47 When
he heard that Jesus had come from Judea to Galilee, he went and begged him
to come down and heal his son, for he
was at the point of death. 48 Then Jesus
said to him, 'Unless you[h] see signs and

[c] **4.9** Other ancient authorities lack this sentence
[d] **4.20** The Greek word for *you* here and in verses 21 and 22 is plural
[e] **4.26** Gk *I am*
[f] **4.29** Or *the Christ*
[g] **4.36** Or [35] . . . *the fields are already ripe for harvesting.* [36] *The reaper is receiving*
[h] **4.48** Both instances of the Greek word for *you* in this verse are plural

wonders you will not believe.' 49The official said to him, 'Sir, come down before
my little boy dies.' 50Jesus said to him,
'Go; your son will live.' The man believed
the word that Jesus spoke to him and
started on his way. 51As he was going
down, his slaves met him and told him
that his child was alive. 52So he asked
them the hour when he began to recover, and they said to him, 'Yesterday
at one in the afternoon the fever left
him.' 53The father realized that this was
the hour when Jesus had said to him,
'Your son will live.' So he himself believed, along with his whole household.
54Now this was the second sign that
Jesus did after coming from Judea to
Galilee.

JESUS HEALS ON THE SABBATH

5 After this there was a festival of the
Jews, and Jesus went up to Jerusalem.

2 Now in Jerusalem by the Sheep
Gate there is a pool, called in Hebrew[i]
Beth-zatha,[j] which has five porticoes.
3In these lay many invalids—blind,
lame, and paralysed.[k] 5One man was
there who had been ill for thirty-eight
years. 6When Jesus saw him lying there
and knew that he had been there a long
time, he said to him, 'Do you want to
be made well?' 7The sick man answered
him, 'Sir, I have no one to put me into
the pool when the water is stirred up;
and while I am making my way, someone else steps down ahead of me.' 8Jesus
said to him, 'Stand up, take your mat
and walk.' 9At once the man was made
well, and he took up his mat and began
to walk.

Now that day was a sabbath. 10So
the Jews said to the man who had been
cured, 'It is the sabbath; it is not lawful for you to carry your mat.' 11But he
answered them, 'The man who made
me well said to me, "Take up your mat
and walk." ' 12They asked him, 'Who is
the man who said to you, "Take it up
and walk"?' 13Now the man who had
been healed did not know who it was,
for Jesus had disappeared in[l] the crowd
that was there. 14Later Jesus found him
in the temple and said to him, 'See, you
have been made well! Do not sin any
more, so that nothing worse happens to
you.' 15The man went away and told the
Jews that it was Jesus who had made
him well. 16Therefore the Jews started
persecuting Jesus, because he was doing such things on the sabbath. 17But
Jesus answered them, 'My Father is still
working, and I also am working.' 18For
this reason the Jews were seeking all
the more to kill him, because he was
not only breaking the sabbath, but was
also calling God his own Father, thereby
making himself equal to God.

THE AUTHORITY OF THE SON

19 Jesus said to them, 'Very truly, I
tell you, the Son can do nothing on his
own, but only what he sees the Father
doing; for whatever the Father[m] does,
the Son does likewise. 20The Father
loves the Son and shows him all that he
himself is doing; and he will show him
greater works than these, so that you
will be astonished. 21Indeed, just as the
Father raises the dead and gives them
life, so also the Son gives life to whomsoever he wishes. 22The Father judges
no one but has given all judgement to
the Son, 23so that all may honour the
Son just as they honour the Father.
Anyone who does not honour the Son
does not honour the Father who sent
him. 24Very truly, I tell you, anyone
who hears my word and believes him
who sent me has eternal life, and does
not come under judgement, but has
passed from death to life.

25 'Very truly, I tell you, the hour is
coming, and is now here, when the dead
will hear the voice of the Son of God,
and those who hear will live. 26For just
as the Father has life in himself, so he
has granted the Son also to have life in
himself; 27and he has given him authority to execute judgement, because he is
the Son of Man. 28Do not be astonished
at this; for the hour is coming when all
who are in their graves will hear his
voice 29and will come out—those who
have done good, to the resurrection of
life, and those who have done evil, to
the resurrection of condemnation.

WITNESSES TO JESUS

30 'I can do nothing on my own. As I
hear, I judge; and my judgement is just,
because I seek to do not my own will but
the will of him who sent me.

[i] **5.2** That is, *Aramaic* [j] **5.2** Other ancient authorities read *Bethesda*, others *Bethsaida*
[k] **5.3** Other ancient authorities add, wholly or in part, *waiting for the stirring of the water; 4for an angel of the Lord went down at certain seasons into the pool, and stirred up the water; whoever stepped in first after the stirring of the water was made well from whatever disease that person had.*
[l] **5.13** Or *had left because of* [m] **5.19** Gk *that one*

31 'If I testify about myself, my testimony is not true. 32There is another
who testifies on my behalf, and I know
that his testimony to me is true. 33You
sent messengers to John, and he testified to the truth. 34Not that I accept
such human testimony, but I say these
things so that you may be saved. 35He
was a burning and shining lamp, and
you were willing to rejoice for a while
in his light. 36But I have a testimony
greater than John's. The works that the
Father has given me to complete, the
very works that I am doing, testify on
my behalf that the Father has sent me.
37And the Father who sent me has himself testified on my behalf. You have
never heard his voice or seen his form,
38and you do not have his word abiding
in you, because you do not believe him
whom he has sent.

39 'You search the scriptures because
you think that in them you have eternal life; and it is they that testify on
my behalf. 40Yet you refuse to come to
me to have life. 41I do not accept glory
from human beings. 42But I know that
you do not have the love of God in[n] you.
43I have come in my Father's name, and
you do not accept me; if another comes
in his own name, you will accept him.
44How can you believe when you accept
glory from one another and do not seek
the glory that comes from the one who
alone is God? 45Do not think that I will
accuse you before the Father; your accuser is Moses, on whom you have set
your hope. 46If you believed Moses, you
would believe me, for he wrote about
me. 47But if you do not believe what he
wrote, how will you believe what I say?'

FEEDING THE FIVE THOUSAND

6 After this Jesus went to the other
side of the Sea of Galilee, also called
the Sea of Tiberias.[o] 2A large crowd
kept following him, because they saw
the signs that he was doing for the sick.
3Jesus went up the mountain and sat
down there with his disciples. 4Now
the Passover, the festival of the Jews,
was near. 5When he looked up and saw
a large crowd coming towards him,
Jesus said to Philip, 'Where are we to
buy bread for these people to eat?' 6He
said this to test him, for he himself
knew what he was going to do. 7Philip
answered him, 'Six months' wages[p]
would not buy enough bread for each
of them to get a little.' 8One of his disciples, Andrew, Simon Peter's brother,
said to him, 9'There is a boy here who
has five barley loaves and two fish. But
what are they among so many people?'
10Jesus said, 'Make the people sit down.'
Now there was a great deal of grass in
the place; so they[q] sat down, about five
thousand in all. 11Then Jesus took the
loaves, and when he had given thanks,
he distributed them to those who were
seated; so also the fish, as much as they
wanted. 12When they were satisfied, he
told his disciples, 'Gather up the fragments left over, so that nothing may be
lost.' 13So they gathered them up, and
from the fragments of the five barley
loaves, left by those who had eaten, they
filled twelve baskets. 14When the people
saw the sign that he had done, they began to say, 'This is indeed the prophet
who is to come into the world.'

15 When Jesus realized that they
were about to come and take him by
force to make him king, he withdrew
again to the mountain by himself.

JESUS WALKS ON THE WATER

16 When evening came, his disciples
went down to the lake, 17got into a boat,
and started across the lake to Capernaum. It was now dark, and Jesus had
not yet come to them. 18The lake became
rough because a strong wind was blowing. 19When they had rowed about three
or four miles,[r] they saw Jesus walking
on the lake and coming near the boat,
and they were terrified. 20But he said to
them, 'It is I;[s] do not be afraid.' 21Then
they wanted to take him into the boat,
and immediately the boat reached the
land towards which they were going.

THE BREAD FROM HEAVEN

22 The next day the crowd that had
stayed on the other side of the lake
saw that there had been only one boat
there. They also saw that Jesus had not
got into the boat with his disciples, but
that his disciples had gone away alone.
23Then some boats from Tiberias came
near the place where they had eaten the
bread after the Lord had given thanks.[t]
24So when the crowd saw that neither
Jesus nor his disciples were there, they
themselves got into the boats and went
to Capernaum looking for Jesus.

[n] **5.42** Or *among* [o] **6.1** Gk *of Galilee of Tiberias*
[p] **6.7** Gk *Two hundred denarii*; the denarius was the usual day's wage for a labourer [q] **6.10** Gk *the men* [r] **6.19** Gk *about twenty-five or thirty stadia* [s] **6.20** Gk *I am* [t] **6.23** Other ancient authorities lack *after the Lord had given thanks*

25 When they found him on the other
side of the lake, they said to him, 'Rabbi,
when did you come here?' 26Jesus answered them, 'Very truly, I tell you, you
are looking for me, not because you saw
signs, but because you ate your fill of
the loaves. 27Do not work for the food
that perishes, but for the food that endures for eternal life, which the Son of
Man will give you. For it is on him that
God the Father has set his seal.' 28Then
they said to him, 'What must we do to
perform the works of God?' 29Jesus answered them, 'This is the work of God,
that you believe in him whom he has
sent.' 30So they said to him, 'What sign
are you going to give us then, so that
we may see it and believe you? What
work are you performing? 31Our ancestors ate the manna in the wilderness;
as it is written, "He gave them bread
from heaven to eat."' 32Then Jesus said
to them, 'Very truly, I tell you, it was
not Moses who gave you the bread from
heaven, but it is my Father who gives
you the true bread from heaven. 33For
the bread of God is that which[u] comes
down from heaven and gives life to the
world.' 34They said to him, 'Sir, give us
this bread always.'

35 Jesus said to them, 'I am the bread
of life. Whoever comes to me will never
be hungry, and whoever believes in me
will never be thirsty. 36But I said to you
that you have seen me and yet do not
believe. 37Everything that the Father
gives me will come to me, and anyone
who comes to me I will never drive
away; 38for I have come down from
heaven, not to do my own will, but the
will of him who sent me. 39And this
is the will of him who sent me, that I
should lose nothing of all that he has
given me, but raise it up on the last day.
40This is indeed the will of my Father,
that all who see the Son and believe in
him may have eternal life; and I will
raise them up on the last day.'

41 Then the Jews began to complain
about him because he said, 'I am the
bread that came down from heaven.'
42They were saying, 'Is not this Jesus,
the son of Joseph, whose father and
mother we know? How can he now
say, "I have come down from heaven"?'
43Jesus answered them, 'Do not complain among yourselves. 44No one can
come to me unless drawn by the Father
who sent me; and I will raise that person
up on the last day. 45It is written in the
prophets, "And they shall all be taught
by God." Everyone who has heard and
learned from the Father comes to me.
46Not that anyone has seen the Father
except the one who is from God; he has
seen the Father. 47Very truly, I tell you,
whoever believes has eternal life. 48I
am the bread of life. 49Your ancestors
ate the manna in the wilderness, and
they died. 50This is the bread that comes
down from heaven, so that one may eat
of it and not die. 51I am the living bread
that came down from heaven. Whoever
eats of this bread will live for ever; and
the bread that I will give for the life of
the world is my flesh.'

52 The Jews then disputed among
themselves, saying, 'How can this man
give us his flesh to eat?' 53So Jesus said
to them, 'Very truly, I tell you, unless
you eat the flesh of the Son of Man and
drink his blood, you have no life in you.
54Those who eat my flesh and drink my
blood have eternal life, and I will raise
them up on the last day; 55for my flesh
is true food and my blood is true drink.
56Those who eat my flesh and drink my
blood abide in me, and I in them. 57Just
as the living Father sent me, and I live
because of the Father, so whoever eats
me will live because of me. 58This is the
bread that came down from heaven, not
like that which your ancestors ate, and
they died. But the one who eats this
bread will live for ever.' 59He said these
things while he was teaching in the
synagogue at Capernaum.

THE WORDS OF ETERNAL LIFE

60 When many of his disciples heard
it, they said, 'This teaching is difficult;
who can accept it?' 61But Jesus, being
aware that his disciples were complaining about it, said to them, 'Does this offend you? 62Then what if you were to see
the Son of Man ascending to where he
was before? 63It is the spirit that gives
life; the flesh is useless. The words that
I have spoken to you are spirit and life.
64But among you there are some who
do not believe.' For Jesus knew from the
first who were the ones that did not believe, and who was the one that would
betray him. 65And he said, 'For this reason I have told you that no one can come
to me unless it is granted by the Father.'

66 Because of this many of his disciples turned back and no longer went
about with him. 67So Jesus asked the
twelve, 'Do you also wish to go away?'

u 6.33 Or *he who*

68 Simon Peter answered him, 'Lord, to
whom can we go? You have the words
of eternal life. 69 We have come to believe
and know that you are the Holy One of
God.'[v] 70 Jesus answered them, 'Did I not
choose you, the twelve? Yet one of you is
a devil.' 71 He was speaking of Judas son
of Simon Iscariot,[w] for he, though one
of the twelve, was going to betray him.

THE UNBELIEF OF JESUS' BROTHERS

7 After this Jesus went about in Galilee. He did not wish[x] to go about
in Judea because the Jews were looking
for an opportunity to kill him. 2 Now the
Jewish festival of Booths[y] was near. 3 So
his brothers said to him, 'Leave here and
go to Judea so that your disciples also
may see the works you are doing; 4 for no
one who wants[z] to be widely known acts
in secret. If you do these things, show
yourself to the world.' 5 (For not even his
brothers believed in him.) 6 Jesus said to
them, 'My time has not yet come, but
your time is always here. 7 The world
cannot hate you, but it hates me because
I testify against it that its works are evil.
8 Go to the festival yourselves. I am not[a]
going to this festival, for my time has
not yet fully come.' 9 After saying this,
he remained in Galilee.

JESUS AT THE FESTIVAL OF BOOTHS

10 But after his brothers had gone to
the festival, then he also went, not publicly but as it were[b] in secret. 11 The Jews
were looking for him at the festival and
saying, 'Where is he?' 12 And there was
considerable complaining about him
among the crowds. While some were
saying, 'He is a good man', others were
saying, 'No, he is deceiving the crowd.'
13 Yet no one would speak openly about
him for fear of the Jews.
14 About the middle of the festival
Jesus went up into the temple and began to teach. 15 The Jews were astonished
at it, saying, 'How does this man have
such learning,[c] when he has never been
taught?' 16 Then Jesus answered them,
'My teaching is not mine but his who
sent me. 17 Anyone who resolves to do
the will of God will know whether the
teaching is from God or whether I am
speaking on my own. 18 Those who speak
on their own seek their own glory; but
the one who seeks the glory of him who
sent him is true, and there is nothing
false in him.
19 'Did not Moses give you the law?
Yet none of you keeps the law. Why are
you looking for an opportunity to kill
me?' 20 The crowd answered, 'You have
a demon! Who is trying to kill you?'
21 Jesus answered them, 'I performed
one work, and all of you are astonished.
22 Moses gave you circumcision (it is, of
course, not from Moses, but from the
patriarchs), and you circumcise a man
on the sabbath. 23 If a man receives circumcision on the sabbath in order that
the law of Moses may not be broken, are
you angry with me because I healed a
man's whole body on the sabbath? 24 Do
not judge by appearances, but judge
with right judgement.'

IS THIS THE CHRIST?

25 Now some of the people of Jerusalem were saying, 'Is not this the man
whom they are trying to kill? 26 And
here he is, speaking openly, but they
say nothing to him! Can it be that the
authorities really know that this is the
Messiah?[d] 27 Yet we know where this
man is from; but when the Messiah[e]
comes, no one will know where he is
from.' 28 Then Jesus cried out as he was
teaching in the temple, 'You know me,
and you know where I am from. I have
not come on my own. But the one who
sent me is true, and you do not know
him. 29 I know him, because I am from
him, and he sent me.' 30 Then they tried
to arrest him, but no one laid hands on
him, because his hour had not yet come.
31 Yet many in the crowd believed in him
and were saying, 'When the Messiah[f]
comes, will he do more signs than this
man has done?'[g]

OFFICERS ARE SENT TO ARREST JESUS

32 The Pharisees heard the crowd
muttering such things about him, and
the chief priests and Pharisees sent temple police to arrest him. 33 Jesus then
said, 'I will be with you a little while
longer, and then I am going to him who
sent me. 34 You will search for me, but
you will not find me; and where I am,

[v] **6.69** Other ancient authorities read *the Christ, the Son of the living God* [w] **6.71** Other ancient authorities read *Judas Iscariot son of Simon;* others, *Judas son of Simon from Karyot* (Kerioth) [x] **7.1** Other ancient authorities read *was not at liberty* [y] **7.2** Or *Tabernacles* [z] **7.4** Other ancient authorities read *wants it* [a] **7.8** Other ancient authorities add *yet* [b] **7.10** Other ancient authorities lack *as it were* [c] **7.15** Or *this man know his letters* [d] **7.26** Or *the Christ* [e] **7.27** Or *the Christ* [f] **7.31** Or *the Christ* [g] **7.31** Other ancient authorities read *is doing*

you cannot come.' 35The Jews said to one
another, 'Where does this man intend to
go that we will not find him? Does he intend to go to the Dispersion among the
Greeks and teach the Greeks? 36What
does he mean by saying, "You will
search for me and you will not find me"
and, "Where I am, you cannot come"?'

RIVERS OF LIVING WATER

37 On the last day of the festival,
the great day, while Jesus was standing there, he cried out, 'Let anyone
who is thirsty come to me, 38and let the
one who believes in me drink. As[h] the
scripture has said, "Out of the believer's
heart[i] shall flow rivers of living water." '
39Now he said this about the Spirit,
which believers in him were to receive;
for as yet there was no Spirit,[j] because
Jesus was not yet glorified.

DIVISION AMONG THE PEOPLE

40 When they heard these words,
some in the crowd said, 'This is really
the prophet.' 41Others said, 'This is the
Messiah.'[k] But some asked, 'Surely the
Messiah[l] does not come from Galilee,
does he? 42Has not the scripture said
that the Messiah[m] is descended from
David and comes from Bethlehem, the
village where David lived?' 43So there
was a division in the crowd because of
him. 44Some of them wanted to arrest
him, but no one laid hands on him.

THE UNBELIEF OF THOSE IN AUTHORITY

45 Then the temple police went back
to the chief priests and Pharisees, who
asked them, 'Why did you not arrest
him?' 46The police answered, 'Never
has anyone spoken like this!' 47Then the
Pharisees replied, 'Surely you have not
been deceived too, have you? 48Has any
one of the authorities or of the Pharisees believed in him? 49But this crowd,
which does not know the law—they are
accursed.' 50Nicodemus, who had gone
to Jesus[n] before, and who was one of
them, asked, 51'Our law does not judge
people without first giving them a
hearing to find out what they are doing,
does it?' 52They replied, 'Surely you are
not also from Galilee, are you? Search
and you will see that no prophet is to
arise from Galilee.'

THE WOMAN CAUGHT IN ADULTERY

8 [[53Then each of them went home,
1while Jesus went to the Mount of
Olives. 2Early in the morning he came
again to the temple. All the people came
to him and he sat down and began to
teach them. 3The scribes and the Pharisees brought a woman who had been
caught in adultery; and making her
stand before all of them, 4they said to
him, 'Teacher, this woman was caught
in the very act of committing adultery.
5Now in the law Moses commanded us
to stone such women. Now what do you
say?' 6They said this to test him, so that
they might have some charge to bring
against him. Jesus bent down and wrote
with his finger on the ground. 7When
they kept on questioning him, he
straightened up and said to them, 'Let
anyone among you who is without sin
be the first to throw a stone at her.' 8And
once again he bent down and wrote on
the ground.[o] 9When they heard it, they
went away, one by one, beginning with
the elders; and Jesus was left alone
with the woman standing before him.
10Jesus straightened up and said to her,
'Woman, where are they? Has no one
condemned you?' 11She said, 'No one,
sir.'[p] And Jesus said, 'Neither do I condemn you. Go your way, and from now
on do not sin again.']][q]

JESUS THE LIGHT OF THE WORLD

12 Again Jesus spoke to them, saying,
'I am the light of the world. Whoever
follows me will never walk in darkness
but will have the light of life.' 13Then the
Pharisees said to him, 'You are testifying on your own behalf; your testimony
is not valid.' 14Jesus answered, 'Even
if I testify on my own behalf, my testimony is valid because I know where
I have come from and where I am going, but you do not know where I come
from or where I am going. 15You judge
by human standards;[r] I judge no one.
16Yet even if I do judge, my judgement
is valid; for it is not I alone who judge,
but I and the Father[s] who sent me. 17In
your law it is written that the testimony

[h] 7.38 Or *come to me and drink.* 38*The one who believes in me, as* [i] 7.38 Gk *out of his belly*
[j] 7.39 Other ancient authorities read *for as yet the Spirit* (others, *Holy Spirit*) *had not been given*
[k] 7.41 Or *the Christ* [l] 7.41 Or *the Christ*
[m] 7.42 Or *the Christ* [n] 7.50 Gk *him*
[o] 8.8 Other ancient authorities add *the sins of each of them* [p] 8.11 Or *Lord* [q] 8.11 The most ancient authorities lack 7.53—8.11; other authorities add the passage here or after 7.36 or after 21.25 or after Luke 21.38, with variations of text; some mark the passage as doubtful.
[r] 8.15 Gk *according to the flesh* [s] 8.16 Other ancient authorities read *he*

of two witnesses is valid. 18 I testify on
my own behalf, and the Father who
sent me testifies on my behalf.' 19 Then
they said to him, 'Where is your Father?'
Jesus answered, 'You know neither me
nor my Father. If you knew me, you
would know my Father also.' 20 He spoke
these words while he was teaching in
the treasury of the temple, but no one
arrested him, because his hour had not
yet come.

JESUS FORETELLS HIS DEATH

21 Again he said to them, 'I am going
away, and you will search for me, but
you will die in your sin. Where I am going, you cannot come.' 22 Then the Jews
said, 'Is he going to kill himself? Is that
what he means by saying, "Where I am
going, you cannot come"?' 23 He said to
them, 'You are from below, I am from
above; you are of this world, I am not of
this world. 24 I told you that you would
die in your sins, for you will die in your
sins unless you believe that I am he.'[t]
25 They said to him, 'Who are you?' Jesus
said to them, 'Why do I speak to you at
all?[u] 26 I have much to say about you and
much to condemn; but the one who sent
me is true, and I declare to the world
what I have heard from him.' 27 They
did not understand that he was speaking to them about the Father. 28 So Jesus
said, 'When you have lifted up the Son
of Man, then you will realize that I am
he,[v] and that I do nothing on my own,
but I speak these things as the Father
instructed me. 29 And the one who sent
me is with me; he has not left me alone,
for I always do what is pleasing to him.'
30 As he was saying these things, many
believed in him.

TRUE DISCIPLES

31 Then Jesus said to the Jews who
had believed in him, 'If you continue
in my word, you are truly my disciples;
32 and you will know the truth, and the
truth will make you free.' 33 They answered him, 'We are descendants of
Abraham and have never been slaves to
anyone. What do you mean by saying,
"You will be made free"?'

34 Jesus answered them, 'Very truly,
I tell you, everyone who commits sin is
a slave to sin. 35 The slave does not have
a permanent place in the household;
the son has a place there for ever. 36 So if
the Son makes you free, you will be free
indeed. 37 I know that you are descendants of Abraham; yet you look for an
opportunity to kill me, because there is
no place in you for my word. 38 I declare
what I have seen in the Father's presence; as for you, you should do what you
have heard from the Father.'[w]

JESUS AND ABRAHAM

39 They answered him, 'Abraham is
our father.' Jesus said to them, 'If you
were Abraham's children, you would be
doing[x] what Abraham did, 40 but now
you are trying to kill me, a man who
has told you the truth that I heard from
God. This is not what Abraham did.
41 You are indeed doing what your father does.' They said to him, 'We are not
illegitimate children; we have one father, God himself.' 42 Jesus said to them,
'If God were your Father, you would love
me, for I came from God and now I am
here. I did not come on my own, but he
sent me. 43 Why do you not understand
what I say? It is because you cannot
accept my word. 44 You are from your
father the devil, and you choose to do
your father's desires. He was a murderer
from the beginning and does not stand
in the truth, because there is no truth
in him. When he lies, he speaks according to his own nature, for he is a liar and
the father of lies. 45 But because I tell the
truth, you do not believe me. 46 Which of
you convicts me of sin? If I tell the truth,
why do you not believe me? 47 Whoever
is from God hears the words of God. The
reason you do not hear them is that you
are not from God.'

48 The Jews answered him, 'Are we
not right in saying that you are a Samaritan and have a demon?' 49 Jesus
answered, 'I do not have a demon; but
I honour my Father, and you dishonour
me. 50 Yet I do not seek my own glory;
there is one who seeks it and he is the
judge. 51 Very truly, I tell you, whoever
keeps my word will never see death.'
52 The Jews said to him, 'Now we know
that you have a demon. Abraham died,
and so did the prophets; yet you say,
"Whoever keeps my word will never
taste death." 53 Are you greater than our
father Abraham, who died? The prophets also died. Who do you claim to be?'
54 Jesus answered, 'If I glorify myself, my
glory is nothing. It is my Father who

[t] **8.24** Gk *I am* [u] **8.25** Or *What I have told you from the beginning* [v] **8.28** Gk *I am*
[w] **8.38** Other ancient authorities read *you do what you have heard from your father* [x] **8.39** Other ancient authorities read *If you are Abraham's children, then do*

glorifies me, he of whom you say, "He
is our God", 55though you do not know
him. But I know him; if I were to say
that I do not know him, I would be a liar
like you. But I do know him and I keep
his word. 56Your ancestor Abraham rejoiced that he would see my day; he saw
it and was glad.' 57Then the Jews said to
him, 'You are not yet fifty years old, and
have you seen Abraham?'[y] 58Jesus said
to them, 'Very truly, I tell you, before
Abraham was, I am.' 59So they picked
up stones to throw at him, but Jesus hid
himself and went out of the temple.

A MAN BORN BLIND RECEIVES SIGHT

9 As he walked along, he saw a man
blind from birth. 2His disciples
asked him, 'Rabbi, who sinned, this
man or his parents, that he was born
blind?' 3Jesus answered, 'Neither this
man nor his parents sinned; he was
born blind so that God's works might
be revealed in him. 4We[z] must work the
works of him who sent me[a] while it is
day; night is coming when no one can
work. 5As long as I am in the world, I
am the light of the world.' 6When he
had said this, he spat on the ground and
made mud with the saliva and spread
the mud on the man's eyes, 7saying to
him, 'Go, wash in the pool of Siloam'
(which means Sent). Then he went and
washed and came back able to see. 8The
neighbours and those who had seen
him before as a beggar began to ask, 'Is
this not the man who used to sit and
beg?' 9Some were saying, 'It is he.' Others were saying, 'No, but it is someone
like him.' He kept saying, 'I am the man.'
10But they kept asking him, 'Then how
were your eyes opened?' 11He answered,
'The man called Jesus made mud, spread
it on my eyes, and said to me, "Go to
Siloam and wash." Then I went and
washed and received my sight.' 12They
said to him, 'Where is he?' He said, 'I do
not know.'

THE PHARISEES INVESTIGATE THE HEALING

13 They brought to the Pharisees
the man who had formerly been blind.
14Now it was a sabbath day when Jesus
made the mud and opened his eyes.
15Then the Pharisees also began to ask
him how he had received his sight. He
said to them, 'He put mud on my eyes.
Then I washed, and now I see.' 16Some
of the Pharisees said, 'This man is not
from God, for he does not observe the
sabbath.' But others said, 'How can
a man who is a sinner perform such
signs?' And they were divided. 17So they
said again to the blind man, 'What do
you say about him? It was your eyes he
opened.' He said, 'He is a prophet.'

18 The Jews did not believe that he
had been blind and had received his
sight until they called the parents of the
man who had received his sight 19and
asked them, 'Is this your son, who you
say was born blind? How then does he
now see?' 20His parents answered, 'We
know that this is our son, and that he
was born blind; 21but we do not know
how it is that now he sees, nor do we
know who opened his eyes. Ask him;
he is of age. He will speak for himself.'
22His parents said this because they
were afraid of the Jews; for the Jews had
already agreed that anyone who confessed Jesus[b] to be the Messiah[c] would
be put out of the synagogue. 23There-
fore his parents said, 'He is of age; ask
him.'

24 So for the second time they called
the man who had been blind, and they
said to him, 'Give glory to God! We
know that this man is a sinner.' 25He
answered, 'I do not know whether he
is a sinner. One thing I do know, that
though I was blind, now I see.' 26They
said to him, 'What did he do to you?
How did he open your eyes?' 27He answered them, 'I have told you already,
and you would not listen. Why do you
want to hear it again? Do you also want
to become his disciples?' 28Then they
reviled him, saying, 'You are his disciple, but we are disciples of Moses. 29We
know that God has spoken to Moses,
but as for this man, we do not know
where he comes from.' 30The man answered, 'Here is an astonishing thing!
You do not know where he comes from,
and yet he opened my eyes. 31We know
that God does not listen to sinners, but
he does listen to one who worships him
and obeys his will. 32Never since the
world began has it been heard that anyone opened the eyes of a person born
blind. 33If this man were not from God,
he could do nothing.' 34They answered
him, 'You were born entirely in sins,
and are you trying to teach us?' And
they drove him out.

[y] **8.57** Other ancient authorities read *has Abraham seen you?* [z] **9.4** Other ancient authorities read *I* [a] **9.4** Other ancient authorities read *us* [b] **9.22** Gk *him* [c] **9.22** Or *the Christ*

SPIRITUAL BLINDNESS

35 Jesus heard that they had driven
him out, and when he found him,
he said, 'Do you believe in the Son of
Man?'[d] 36He answered, 'And who is
he, sir?[e] Tell me, so that I may believe
in him.' 37Jesus said to him, 'You have
seen him, and the one speaking with
you is he.' 38He said, 'Lord,[f] I believe.'
And he worshipped him. 39Jesus said, 'I
came into this world for judgement so
that those who do not see may see, and
those who do see may become blind.'
40Some of the Pharisees near him heard
this and said to him, 'Surely we are not
blind, are we?' 41Jesus said to them, 'If
you were blind, you would not have sin.
But now that you say, "We see", your sin
remains.

JESUS THE GOOD SHEPHERD

10 'Very truly, I tell you, anyone
who does not enter the sheep-
fold by the gate but climbs in by another way is a thief and a bandit. 2The
one who enters by the gate is the shepherd of the sheep. 3The gatekeeper
opens the gate for him, and the sheep
hear his voice. He calls his own sheep by
name and leads them out. 4When he has
brought out all his own, he goes ahead
of them, and the sheep follow him because they know his voice. 5They will
not follow a stranger, but they will run
from him because they do not know the
voice of strangers.' 6Jesus used this figure of speech with them, but they did
not understand what he was saying to
them.

7 So again Jesus said to them, 'Very
truly, I tell you, I am the gate for the
sheep. 8All who came before me are
thieves and bandits; but the sheep did
not listen to them. 9I am the gate. Whoever enters by me will be saved, and will
come in and go out and find pasture.
10The thief comes only to steal and kill
and destroy. I came that they may have
life, and have it abundantly.

11 'I am the good shepherd. The
good shepherd lays down his life for the
sheep. 12The hired hand, who is not the
shepherd and does not own the sheep,
sees the wolf coming and leaves the
sheep and runs away—and the wolf
snatches them and scatters them. 13The
hired hand runs away because a hired
hand does not care for the sheep. 14I am
the good shepherd. I know my own and
my own know me, 15just as the Father
knows me and I know the Father. And I
lay down my life for the sheep. 16I have
other sheep that do not belong to this
fold. I must bring them also, and they
will listen to my voice. So there will
be one flock, one shepherd. 17For this
reason the Father loves me, because I
lay down my life in order to take it up
again. 18No one takes[g] it from me, but
I lay it down of my own accord. I have
power to lay it down, and I have power
to take it up again. I have received this
command from my Father.'

19 Again the Jews were divided because of these words. 20Many of them
were saying, 'He has a demon and is
out of his mind. Why listen to him?'
21Others were saying, 'These are not the
words of one who has a demon. Can a
demon open the eyes of the blind?'

JESUS IS REJECTED BY THE JEWS

22 At that time the festival of the
Dedication took place in Jerusalem. It
was winter, 23and Jesus was walking in
the temple, in the portico of Solomon.
24So the Jews gathered around him and
said to him, 'How long will you keep us
in suspense? If you are the Messiah,[h]
tell us plainly.' 25Jesus answered, 'I have
told you, and you do not believe. The
works that I do in my Father's name
testify to me; 26but you do not believe,
because you do not belong to my sheep.
27My sheep hear my voice. I know them,
and they follow me. 28I give them eternal life, and they will never perish. No
one will snatch them out of my hand.
29What my Father has given me is
greater than all else, and no one can
snatch it out of the Father's hand.[i] 30The
Father and I are one.'

31 The Jews took up stones again
to stone him. 32Jesus replied, 'I have
shown you many good works from the
Father. For which of these are you going
to stone me?' 33The Jews answered, 'It is
not for a good work that we are going
to stone you, but for blasphemy, because
you, though only a human being, are
making yourself God.' 34Jesus answered,
'Is it not written in your law,[j] "I said,
you are gods"? 35If those to whom the
word of God came were called "gods"—

[d] 9.35 Other ancient authorities read *the Son of God* [e] 9.36 *Sir* and *Lord* translate the same Greek word [f] 9.38 *Sir* and *Lord* translate the same Greek word [g] 10.18 Other ancient authorities read *has taken* [h] 10.24 Or *the Christ* [i] 10.29 Other ancient authorities read *My Father who has given them to me is greater than all, and no one can snatch them out of the Father's hand* [j] 10.34 Other ancient authorities read *in the law*

and the scripture cannot be annulled—
36can you say that the one whom the
Father has sanctified and sent into the
world is blaspheming because I said, "I
am God's Son"? 37If I am not doing the
works of my Father, then do not believe
me. 38But if I do them, even though you
do not believe me, believe the works, so
that you may know and understand[k]
that the Father is in me and I am in the
Father.' 39Then they tried to arrest him
again, but he escaped from their hands.
40 He went away again across the
Jordan to the place where John had
been baptizing earlier, and he remained
there. 41Many came to him, and they
were saying, 'John performed no sign,
but everything that John said about
this man was true.' 42And many believed in him there.

THE DEATH OF LAZARUS

11 Now a certain man was ill, Lazarus of Bethany, the village of
Mary and her sister Martha. 2Mary was
the one who anointed the Lord with
perfume and wiped his feet with her
hair; her brother Lazarus was ill. 3So the
sisters sent a message to Jesus,[l] 'Lord, he
whom you love is ill.' 4But when Jesus
heard it, he said, 'This illness does not
lead to death; rather it is for God's glory,
so that the Son of God may be glorified
through it.' 5Accordingly, though Jesus
loved Martha and her sister and Lazarus, 6after having heard that Lazarus[m]
was ill, he stayed two days longer in the
place where he was.
7 Then after this he said to the disciples, 'Let us go to Judea again.' 8The
disciples said to him, 'Rabbi, the Jews
were just now trying to stone you, and
are you going there again?' 9Jesus answered, 'Are there not twelve hours of
daylight? Those who walk during the
day do not stumble, because they see
the light of this world. 10But those who
walk at night stumble, because the light
is not in them.' 11After saying this, he
told them, 'Our friend Lazarus has fallen
asleep, but I am going there to awaken
him.' 12The disciples said to him, 'Lord, if
he has fallen asleep, he will be all right.'
13Jesus, however, had been speaking
about his death, but they thought that
he was referring merely to sleep. 14Then
Jesus told them plainly, 'Lazarus is dead.
15For your sake I am glad I was not
there, so that you may believe. But let
us go to him.' 16Thomas, who was called
the Twin,[n] said to his fellow-disciples,
'Let us also go, that we may die with
him.'

JESUS THE RESURRECTION AND THE LIFE

17 When Jesus arrived, he found that
Lazarus[o] had already been in the tomb
for four days. 18Now Bethany was near
Jerusalem, some two miles[p] away, 19and
many of the Jews had come to Martha and Mary to console them about
their brother. 20When Martha heard
that Jesus was coming, she went and
met him, while Mary stayed at home.
21Martha said to Jesus, 'Lord, if you had
been here, my brother would not have
died. 22But even now I know that God
will give you whatever you ask of him.'
23Jesus said to her, 'Your brother will
rise again.' 24Martha said to him, 'I
know that he will rise again in the resurrection on the last day.' 25Jesus said to
her, 'I am the resurrection and the life.[q]
Those who believe in me, even though
they die, will live, 26and everyone who
lives and believes in me will never die.
Do you believe this?' 27She said to him,
'Yes, Lord, I believe that you are the
Messiah,[r] the Son of God, the one coming into the world.'

JESUS WEEPS

28 When she had said this, she went
back and called her sister Mary, and told
her privately, 'The Teacher is here and is
calling for you.' 29And when she heard
it, she got up quickly and went to him.
30Now Jesus had not yet come to the
village, but was still at the place where
Martha had met him. 31The Jews who
were with her in the house, consoling
her, saw Mary get up quickly and go out.
They followed her because they thought
that she was going to the tomb to weep
there. 32When Mary came where Jesus
was and saw him, she knelt at his feet
and said to him, 'Lord, if you had been
here, my brother would not have died.'
33When Jesus saw her weeping, and the
Jews who came with her also weeping,
he was greatly disturbed in spirit and
deeply moved. 34He said, 'Where have
you laid him?' They said to him, 'Lord,
come and see.' 35Jesus began to weep.
36So the Jews said, 'See how he loved

[k] **10.38** Other ancient authorities lack *and understand*; others read *and believe* [l] **11.3** Gk *him* [m] **11.6** Gk *he* [n] **11.16** Gk *Didymus* [o] **11.17** Gk *he* [p] **11.18** Gk *fifteen stadia* [q] **11.25** Other ancient authorities lack *and the life* [r] **11.27** Or *the Christ*

him!' 37 But some of them said, 'Could not he who opened the eyes of the blind man have kept this man from dying?'

JESUS RAISES LAZARUS TO LIFE

38 Then Jesus, again greatly disturbed, came to the tomb. It was a cave, and a stone was lying against it. 39 Jesus said, 'Take away the stone.' Martha, the sister of the dead man, said to him, 'Lord, already there is a stench because he has been dead for four days.' 40 Jesus said to her, 'Did I not tell you that if you believed, you would see the glory of God?' 41 So they took away the stone. And Jesus looked upwards and said, 'Father, I thank you for having heard me. 42 I knew that you always hear me, but I have said this for the sake of the crowd standing here, so that they may believe that you sent me.' 43 When he had said this, he cried with a loud voice, 'Lazarus, come out!' 44 The dead man came out, his hands and feet bound with strips of cloth, and his face wrapped in a cloth. Jesus said to them, 'Unbind him, and let him go.'

THE PLOT TO KILL JESUS

45 Many of the Jews therefore, who had come with Mary and had seen what Jesus did, believed in him. 46 But some of them went to the Pharisees and told them what he had done. 47 So the chief priests and the Pharisees called a meeting of the council, and said, 'What are we to do? This man is performing many signs. 48 If we let him go on like this, everyone will believe in him, and the Romans will come and destroy both our holy place[s] and our nation.' 49 But one of them, Caiaphas, who was high priest that year, said to them, 'You know nothing at all! 50 You do not understand that it is better for you to have one man die for the people than to have the whole nation destroyed.' 51 He did not say this on his own, but being high priest that year he prophesied that Jesus was about to die for the nation, 52 and not for the nation only, but to gather into one the dispersed children of God. 53 So from that day on they planned to put him to death.

54 Jesus therefore no longer walked about openly among the Jews, but went from there to a town called Ephraim in the region near the wilderness; and he remained there with the disciples.

55 Now the Passover of the Jews was near, and many went up from the country to Jerusalem before the Passover to purify themselves. 56 They were looking for Jesus and were asking one another as they stood in the temple, 'What do you think? Surely he will not come to the festival, will he?' 57 Now the chief priests and the Pharisees had given orders that anyone who knew where Jesus[t] was should let them know, so that they might arrest him.

MARY ANOINTS JESUS

12 Six days before the Passover Jesus came to Bethany, the home of Lazarus, whom he had raised from the dead. 2 There they gave a dinner for him. Martha served, and Lazarus was one of those at the table with him. 3 Mary took a pound of costly perfume made of pure nard, anointed Jesus' feet, and wiped them[u] with her hair. The house was filled with the fragrance of the perfume. 4 But Judas Iscariot, one of his disciples (the one who was about to betray him), said, 5 'Why was this perfume not sold for three hundred denarii[v] and the money given to the poor?' 6 (He said this not because he cared about the poor, but because he was a thief; he kept the common purse and used to steal what was put into it.) 7 Jesus said, 'Leave her alone. She bought it[w] so that she might keep it for the day of my burial. 8 You always have the poor with you, but you do not always have me.'

THE PLOT TO KILL LAZARUS

9 When the great crowd of the Jews learned that he was there, they came not only because of Jesus but also to see Lazarus, whom he had raised from the dead. 10 So the chief priests planned to put Lazarus to death as well, 11 since it was on account of him that many of the Jews were deserting and were believing in Jesus.

JESUS' TRIUMPHAL ENTRY INTO JERUSALEM

12 The next day the great crowd that had come to the festival heard that Jesus was coming to Jerusalem. 13 So they took branches of palm trees and went out to meet him, shouting,

'Hosanna!
Blessed is the one who comes in
the name of the Lord—
the King of Israel!'

[s] 11.48 Or *our temple*; Greek *our place*
[t] 11.57 Gk *he* [u] 12.3 Gk *his feet* [v] 12.5 Three hundred denarii would be nearly a year's wages for a labourer [w] 12.7 Gk lacks *She bought it*

14 Jesus found a young donkey and sat on
it; as it is written:
15 'Do not be afraid, daughter of Zion.
Look, your king is coming,
sitting on a donkey's colt!'
16 His disciples did not understand these
things at first; but when Jesus was glorified, then they remembered that these
things had been written of him and had
been done to him. 17 So the crowd that
had been with him when he called Lazarus out of the tomb and raised him from
the dead continued to testify.[x] 18 It was
also because they heard that he had performed this sign that the crowd went to
meet him. 19 The Pharisees then said to
one another, 'You see, you can do nothing. Look, the world has gone after him!'

SOME GREEKS WISH TO SEE JESUS

20 Now among those who went up
to worship at the festival were some
Greeks. 21 They came to Philip, who was
from Bethsaida in Galilee, and said to
him, 'Sir, we wish to see Jesus.' 22 Philip
went and told Andrew; then Andrew
and Philip went and told Jesus. 23 Jesus
answered them, 'The hour has come for
the Son of Man to be glorified. 24 Very
truly, I tell you, unless a grain of wheat
falls into the earth and dies, it remains
just a single grain; but if it dies, it bears
much fruit. 25 Those who love their life
lose it, and those who hate their life in
this world will keep it for eternal life.
26 Whoever serves me must follow me,
and where I am, there will my servant
be also. Whoever serves me, the Father
will honour.

JESUS SPEAKS ABOUT HIS DEATH

27 'Now my soul is troubled. And
what should I say—"Father, save me
from this hour"? No, it is for this reason that I have come to this hour. 28 Father, glorify your name.' Then a voice
came from heaven, 'I have glorified it,
and I will glorify it again.' 29 The crowd
standing there heard it and said that it
was thunder. Others said, 'An angel has
spoken to him.' 30 Jesus answered, 'This
voice has come for your sake, not for
mine. 31 Now is the judgement of this
world; now the ruler of this world will
be driven out. 32 And I, when I am lifted
up from the earth, will draw all people[y]
to myself.' 33 He said this to indicate the
kind of death he was to die. 34 The crowd
answered him, 'We have heard from the
law that the Messiah[z] remains for ever.
How can you say that the Son of Man
must be lifted up? Who is this Son of
Man?' 35 Jesus said to them, 'The light is
with you for a little longer. Walk while
you have the light, so that the darkness
may not overtake you. If you walk in the
darkness, you do not know where you
are going. 36 While you have the light,
believe in the light, so that you may become children of light.'

THE UNBELIEF OF THE PEOPLE

After Jesus had said this, he departed
and hid from them. 37 Although he had
performed so many signs in their presence, they did not believe in him. 38 This
was to fulfil the word spoken by the
prophet Isaiah:
'Lord, who has believed our message,
and to whom has the arm of
the Lord been revealed?'
39 And so they could not believe, because
Isaiah also said,
40 'He has blinded their eyes
and hardened their heart,
so that they might not look
with their eyes,
and understand with their
heart and turn—
and I would heal them.'
41 Isaiah said this because[a] he saw his
glory and spoke about him. 42 Nevertheless many, even of the authorities, believed in him. But because of the Pharisees they did not confess it, for fear that
they would be put out of the synagogue;
43 for they loved human glory more than
the glory that comes from God.

SUMMARY OF JESUS' TEACHING

44 Then Jesus cried aloud: 'Whoever
believes in me believes not in me but in
him who sent me. 45 And whoever sees
me sees him who sent me. 46 I have come
as light into the world, so that everyone
who believes in me should not remain
in the darkness. 47 I do not judge anyone
who hears my words and does not keep
them, for I came not to judge the world,
but to save the world. 48 The one who rejects me and does not receive my word
has a judge; on the last day the word
that I have spoken will serve as judge,
49 for I have not spoken on my own, but
the Father who sent me has himself
given me a commandment about what
to say and what to speak. 50 And I know

[x] **12.17** Other ancient authorities read *with him began to testify that he had called . . . from the dead* [y] **12.32** Other ancient authorities read *all things* [z] **12.34** Or *the Christ* [a] **12.41** Other ancient witnesses read *when*

that his commandment is eternal life.
What I speak, therefore, I speak just as
the Father has told me.'

JESUS WASHES THE DISCIPLES' FEET

13 Now before the festival of the
Passover, Jesus knew that his
hour had come to depart from this
world and go to the Father. Having
loved his own who were in the world,
he loved them to the end. 2The devil
had already put it into the heart of Judas son of Simon Iscariot to betray
him. And during supper 3Jesus, knowing that the Father had given all things
into his hands, and that he had come
from God and was going to God, 4got
up from the table,[b] took off his outer
robe, and tied a towel around himself.
5Then he poured water into a basin and
began to wash the disciples' feet and to
wipe them with the towel that was tied
around him. 6He came to Simon Peter,
who said to him, 'Lord, are you going to
wash my feet?' 7Jesus answered, 'You
do not know now what I am doing, but
later you will understand.' 8Peter said to
him, 'You will never wash my feet.' Jesus
answered, 'Unless I wash you, you have
no share with me.' 9Simon Peter said to
him, 'Lord, not my feet only but also my
hands and my head!' 10Jesus said to him,
'One who has bathed does not need to
wash, except for the feet,[c] but is entirely
clean. And you[d] are clean, though not
all of you.' 11For he knew who was to betray him; for this reason he said, 'Not all
of you are clean.'

12 After he had washed their feet,
had put on his robe, and had returned to
the table, he said to them, 'Do you know
what I have done to you? 13You call me
Teacher and Lord—and you are right,
for that is what I am. 14So if I, your Lord
and Teacher, have washed your feet, you
also ought to wash one another's feet.
15For I have set you an example, that
you also should do as I have done to you.
16Very truly, I tell you, servants[e] are not
greater than their master, nor are messengers greater than the one who sent
them. 17If you know these things, you
are blessed if you do them. 18I am not
speaking of all of you; I know whom I
have chosen. But it is to fulfil the scripture, "The one who ate my bread[f] has
lifted his heel against me." 19I tell you
this now, before it occurs, so that when
it does occur, you may believe that I am
he.[g] 20Very truly, I tell you, whoever
receives one whom I send receives me;
and whoever receives me receives him
who sent me.'

JESUS FORETELLS HIS BETRAYAL

21 After saying this Jesus was troubled in spirit, and declared, 'Very truly, I
tell you, one of you will betray me.' 22The
disciples looked at one another, uncertain of whom he was speaking. 23One
of his disciples—the one whom Jesus
loved—was reclining next to him; 24Si-
mon Peter therefore motioned to him
to ask Jesus of whom he was speaking.
25So while reclining next to Jesus, he
asked him, 'Lord, who is it?' 26Jesus answered, 'It is the one to whom I give this
piece of bread when I have dipped it in
the dish.'[h] So when he had dipped the
piece of bread, he gave it to Judas son
of Simon Iscariot.[i] 27After he received
the piece of bread,[j] Satan entered into
him. Jesus said to him, 'Do quickly what
you are going to do.' 28Now no one at
the table knew why he said this to him.
29Some thought that, because Judas had
the common purse, Jesus was telling
him, 'Buy what we need for the festival';
or, that he should give something to the
poor. 30So, after receiving the piece of
bread, he immediately went out. And it
was night.

THE NEW COMMANDMENT

31 When he had gone out, Jesus said,
'Now the Son of Man has been glorified,
and God has been glorified in him. 32If
God has been glorified in him,[k] God will
also glorify him in himself and will glorify him at once. 33Little children, I am
with you only a little longer. You will
look for me; and as I said to the Jews so
now I say to you, "Where I am going,
you cannot come." 34I give you a new
commandment, that you love one another. Just as I have loved you, you also
should love one another. 35By this everyone will know that you are my disciples, if you have love for one another.'

JESUS FORETELLS PETER'S DENIAL

36 Simon Peter said to him, 'Lord,
where are you going?' Jesus answered,

[b] **13.4** Gk *from supper* [c] **13.10** Other ancient authorities lack *except for the feet* [d] **13.10** The Greek word for *you* here is plural [e] **13.16** Gk *slaves* [f] **13.18** Other ancient authorities read *ate bread with me* [g] **13.19** Gk *I am* [h] **13.26** Gk *dipped it* [i] **13.26** Other ancient authorities read *Judas Iscariot son of Simon*; others, *Judas son of Simon from Karyot* (Kerioth) [j] **13.27** Gk *After the piece of bread* [k] **13.32** Other ancient authorities lack *If God has been glorified in him*

'Where I am going, you cannot follow
me now; but you will follow afterwards.'
37 Peter said to him, 'Lord, why can I
not follow you now? I will lay down my
life for you.' 38 Jesus answered, 'Will you
lay down your life for me? Very truly, I
tell you, before the cock crows, you will
have denied me three times.

JESUS THE WAY TO THE FATHER

14 'Do not let your hearts be troubled. Believe[l] in God, believe also
in me. 2 In my Father's house there are
many dwelling-places. If it were not so,
would I have told you that I go to prepare a place for you?[m] 3 And if I go and
prepare a place for you, I will come
again and will take you to myself, so
that where I am, there you may be also.
4 And you know the way to the place
where I am going.'[n] 5 Thomas said to
him, 'Lord, we do not know where you
are going. How can we know the way?'
6 Jesus said to him, 'I am the way, and
the truth, and the life. No one comes to
the Father except through me. 7 If you
know me, you will know[o] my Father
also. From now on you do know him
and have seen him.'

8 Philip said to him, 'Lord, show us
the Father, and we will be satisfied.'
9 Jesus said to him, 'Have I been with
you all this time, Philip, and you still
do not know me? Whoever has seen me
has seen the Father. How can you say,
"Show us the Father"? 10 Do you not believe that I am in the Father and the
Father is in me? The words that I say to
you I do not speak on my own; but the
Father who dwells in me does his works.
11 Believe me that I am in the Father and
the Father is in me; but if you do not,
then believe me because of the works
themselves. 12 Very truly, I tell you, the
one who believes in me will also do
the works that I do and, in fact, will do
greater works than these, because I am
going to the Father. 13 I will do whatever
you ask in my name, so that the Father
may be glorified in the Son. 14 If in my
name you ask me[p] for anything, I will
do it.

THE PROMISE OF THE HOLY SPIRIT

15 'If you love me, you will keep[q] my
commandments. 16 And I will ask the
Father, and he will give you another
Advocate,[r] to be with you for ever. 17 This
is the Spirit of truth, whom the world
cannot receive, because it neither sees
him nor knows him. You know him, because he abides with you, and he will be
in[s] you.

18 'I will not leave you orphaned;
I am coming to you. 19 In a little while
the world will no longer see me, but you
will see me; because I live, you also will
live. 20 On that day you will know that I
am in my Father, and you in me, and I
in you. 21 They who have my commandments and keep them are those who
love me; and those who love me will
be loved by my Father, and I will love
them and reveal myself to them.' 22 Judas (not Iscariot) said to him, 'Lord, how
is it that you will reveal yourself to us,
and not to the world?' 23 Jesus answered
him, 'Those who love me will keep my
word, and my Father will love them,
and we will come to them and make our
home with them. 24 Whoever does not
love me does not keep my words; and
the word that you hear is not mine, but
is from the Father who sent me.

25 'I have said these things to you
while I am still with you. 26 But the Advocate,[t] the Holy Spirit, whom the Father will send in my name, will teach
you everything, and remind you of all
that I have said to you. 27 Peace I leave
with you; my peace I give to you. I do
not give to you as the world gives. Do
not let your hearts be troubled, and do
not let them be afraid. 28 You heard me
say to you, "I am going away, and I am
coming to you." If you loved me, you
would rejoice that I am going to the Father, because the Father is greater than
I. 29 And now I have told you this before
it occurs, so that when it does occur, you
may believe. 30 I will no longer talk much
with you, for the ruler of this world is
coming. He has no power over me; 31 but
I do as the Father has commanded me,
so that the world may know that I love
the Father. Rise, let us be on our way.

JESUS THE TRUE VINE

15 'I am the true vine, and my Father is the vine-grower. 2 He removes every branch in me that bears no
fruit. Every branch that bears fruit he
prunes[u] to make it bear more fruit. 3 You

[l] 14.1 Or *You believe* [m] 14.2 Or *If it were not so, I would have told you; for I go to prepare a place for you* [n] 14.4 Other ancient authorities read *Where I am going you know, and the way you know*
[o] 14.7 Other ancient authorities read *If you had known me, you would have known* [p] 14.14 Other ancient authorities lack *me* [q] 14.15 Other ancient authorities read *me, keep* [r] 14.16 Or *Helper*
[s] 14.17 Or *among* [t] 14.26 Or *Helper* [u] 15.2 The same Greek root refers to pruning and cleansing

have already been cleansed[v] by the word
that I have spoken to you. 4Abide in me
as I abide in you. Just as the branch cannot bear fruit by itself unless it abides
in the vine, neither can you unless you
abide in me. 5I am the vine, you are the
branches. Those who abide in me and I
in them bear much fruit, because apart
from me you can do nothing. 6Whoever
does not abide in me is thrown away like
a branch and withers; such branches
are gathered, thrown into the fire, and
burned. 7If you abide in me, and my
words abide in you, ask for whatever
you wish, and it will be done for you.
8My Father is glorified by this, that you
bear much fruit and become[w] my disciples. 9As the Father has loved me, so
I have loved you; abide in my love. 10If
you keep my commandments, you will
abide in my love, just as I have kept my
Father's commandments and abide in
his love. 11I have said these things to you
so that my joy may be in you, and that
your joy may be complete.

12 'This is my commandment, that
you love one another as I have loved
you. 13No one has greater love than this,
to lay down one's life for one's friends.
14You are my friends if you do what I
command you. 15I do not call you servants[x] any longer, because the servant[y]
does not know what the master is doing;
but I have called you friends, because
I have made known to you everything
that I have heard from my Father. 16You
did not choose me but I chose you. And I
appointed you to go and bear fruit, fruit
that will last, so that the Father will give
you whatever you ask him in my name.
17I am giving you these commands so
that you may love one another.

THE WORLD'S HATRED

18 'If the world hates you, be aware
that it hated me before it hated you. 19If
you belonged to the world,[z] the world
would love you as its own. Because you
do not belong to the world, but I have
chosen you out of the world—therefore
the world hates you. 20Remember the
word that I said to you, "Servants[a] are
not greater than their master." If they
persecuted me, they will persecute you;
if they kept my word, they will keep
yours also. 21But they will do all these
things to you on account of my name,
because they do not know him who sent
me. 22If I had not come and spoken to
them, they would not have sin; but
now they have no excuse for their sin.
23Whoever hates me hates my Father
also. 24If I had not done among them
the works that no one else did, they
would not have sin. But now they have
seen and hated both me and my Father.
25It was to fulfil the word that is written
in their law, "They hated me without a
cause."

26 'When the Advocate[b] comes,
whom I will send to you from the Father, the Spirit of truth who comes from
the Father, he will testify on my behalf.
27You also are to testify because you
have been with me from the beginning.

16 'I have said these things to you to
keep you from stumbling. 2They
will put you out of the synagogues. Indeed, an hour is coming when those
who kill you will think that by doing so
they are offering worship to God. 3And
they will do this because they have not
known the Father or me. 4But I have
said these things to you so that when
their hour comes you may remember
that I told you about them.

THE WORK OF THE SPIRIT

'I did not say these things to you from
the beginning, because I was with you.
5But now I am going to him who sent
me; yet none of you asks me, "Where are
you going?" 6But because I have said
these things to you, sorrow has filled
your hearts. 7Nevertheless, I tell you the
truth: it is to your advantage that I go
away, for if I do not go away, the Advocate[c] will not come to you; but if I go,
I will send him to you. 8And when he
comes, he will prove the world wrong
about[d] sin and righteousness and
judgement: 9about sin, because they do
not believe in me; 10about righteousness, because I am going to the Father
and you will see me no longer; 11about
judgement, because the ruler of this
world has been condemned.

12 'I still have many things to say to
you, but you cannot bear them now.
13When the Spirit of truth comes, he
will guide you into all the truth; for he
will not speak on his own, but will speak
whatever he hears, and he will declare
to you the things that are to come. 14He
will glorify me, because he will take
what is mine and declare it to you. 15All

[v] **15.3** The same Greek root refers to pruning and cleansing [w] **15.8** Or *be* [x] **15.15** Gk *slaves*
[y] **15.15** Gk *slave* [z] **15.19** Gk *were of the world*
[a] **15.20** Gk *Slaves* [b] **15.26** Or *Helper* [c] **16.7** Or *Helper* [d] **16.8** Or *convict the world of*

that the Father has is mine. For this
reason I said that he will take what is
mine and declare it to you.

SORROW WILL TURN INTO JOY

16 'A little while, and you will no
longer see me, and again a little while,
and you will see me.' 17 Then some of
his disciples said to one another, 'What
does he mean by saying to us, "A little
while, and you will no longer see me,
and again a little while, and you will see
me"; and "Because I am going to the Father"?' 18 They said, 'What does he mean
by this "a little while"? We do not know
what he is talking about.' 19 Jesus knew
that they wanted to ask him, so he said
to them, 'Are you discussing among
yourselves what I meant when I said, "A
little while, and you will no longer see
me, and again a little while, and you will
see me"? 20 Very truly, I tell you, you will
weep and mourn, but the world will rejoice; you will have pain, but your pain
will turn into joy. 21 When a woman is in
labour, she has pain, because her hour
has come. But when her child is born,
she no longer remembers the anguish
because of the joy of having brought a
human being into the world. 22 So you
have pain now; but I will see you again,
and your hearts will rejoice, and no one
will take your joy from you. 23 On that
day you will ask nothing of me.[e] Very
truly, I tell you, if you ask anything of
the Father in my name, he will give it
to you.[f] 24 Until now you have not asked
for anything in my name. Ask and you
will receive, so that your joy may be
complete.

PEACE FOR THE DISCIPLES

25 'I have said these things to you in
figures of speech. The hour is coming
when I will no longer speak to you in
figures, but will tell you plainly of the
Father. 26 On that day you will ask in my
name. I do not say to you that I will ask
the Father on your behalf; 27 for the Father himself loves you, because you have
loved me and have believed that I came
from God.[g] 28 I came from the Father
and have come into the world; again, I
am leaving the world and am going to
the Father.'

29 His disciples said, 'Yes, now you
are speaking plainly, not in any figure of
speech! 30 Now we know that you know
all things, and do not need to have anyone question you; by this we believe that
you came from God.' 31 Jesus answered
them, 'Do you now believe? 32 The hour
is coming, indeed it has come, when you
will be scattered, each one to his home,
and you will leave me alone. Yet I am
not alone because the Father is with
me. 33 I have said this to you, so that in
me you may have peace. In the world
you face persecution. But take courage;
I have conquered the world!'

JESUS PRAYS FOR HIS DISCIPLES

17 After Jesus had spoken these
words, he looked up to heaven
and said, 'Father, the hour has come;
glorify your Son so that the Son may
glorify you, 2 since you have given him
authority over all people,[h] to give eternal life to all whom you have given him.
3 And this is eternal life, that they may
know you, the only true God, and Jesus
Christ whom you have sent. 4 I glorified
you on earth by finishing the work that
you gave me to do. 5 So now, Father, glorify me in your own presence with the
glory that I had in your presence before
the world existed.

6 'I have made your name known
to those whom you gave me from the
world. They were yours, and you gave
them to me, and they have kept your
word. 7 Now they know that everything
you have given me is from you; 8 for the
words that you gave to me I have given
to them, and they have received them
and know in truth that I came from
you; and they have believed that you
sent me. 9 I am asking on their behalf;
I am not asking on behalf of the world,
but on behalf of those whom you gave
me, because they are yours. 10 All mine
are yours, and yours are mine; and I
have been glorified in them. 11 And now
I am no longer in the world, but they
are in the world, and I am coming to
you. Holy Father, protect them in your
name that you have given me, so that
they may be one, as we are one. 12 While
I was with them, I protected them in
your name that[i] you have given me. I
guarded them, and not one of them was
lost except the one destined to be lost,[j]
so that the scripture might be fulfilled.
13 But now I am coming to you, and I

[e] **16.23** Or *will ask me no question*
[f] **16.23** Other ancient authorities read *Father, he will give it to you in my name* [g] **16.27** Other ancient authorities read *the Father* [h] **17.2** Gk *flesh* [i] **17.12** Other ancient authorities read *protected in your name those whom* [j] **17.12** Gk *except the son of destruction*

speak these things in the world so that
they may have my joy made complete in
themselves.[k] 14I have given them your
word, and the world has hated them because they do not belong to the world,
just as I do not belong to the world. 15I
am not asking you to take them out of
the world, but I ask you to protect them
from the evil one.[l] 16They do not belong
to the world, just as I do not belong to
the world. 17Sanctify them in the truth;
your word is truth. 18As you have sent
me into the world, so I have sent them
into the world. 19And for their sakes I
sanctify myself, so that they also may be
sanctified in truth.

20 'I ask not only on behalf of these,
but also on behalf of those who will believe in me through their word, 21that
they may all be one. As you, Father, are
in me and I am in you, may they also
be in us,[m] so that the world may believe
that you have sent me. 22The glory that
you have given me I have given them,
so that they may be one, as we are one,
23I in them and you in me, that they
may become completely one, so that the
world may know that you have sent me
and have loved them even as you have
loved me. 24Father, I desire that those
also, whom you have given me, may be
with me where I am, to see my glory,
which you have given me because you
loved me before the foundation of the
world.

25 'Righteous Father, the world does
not know you, but I know you; and
these know that you have sent me. 26I
made your name known to them, and
I will make it known, so that the love
with which you have loved me may be
in them, and I in them.'

THE BETRAYAL AND ARREST OF JESUS

18 After Jesus had spoken these
words, he went out with his disciples across the Kidron valley to a place
where there was a garden, which he and
his disciples entered. 2Now Judas, who
betrayed him, also knew the place, because Jesus often met there with his disciples. 3So Judas brought a detachment
of soldiers together with police from the
chief priests and the Pharisees, and they
came there with lanterns and torches
and weapons. 4Then Jesus, knowing all
that was to happen to him, came forward and asked them, 'For whom are
you looking?' 5They answered, 'Jesus of
Nazareth.'[n] Jesus replied, 'I am he.'[o] Judas, who betrayed him, was standing
with them. 6When Jesus[p] said to them,
'I am he',[q] they stepped back and fell to
the ground. 7Again he asked them, 'For
whom are you looking?' And they said,
'Jesus of Nazareth.'[r] 8Jesus answered, 'I
told you that I am he.[s] So if you are looking for me, let these men go.' 9This was
to fulfil the word that he had spoken, 'I
did not lose a single one of those whom
you gave me.' 10Then Simon Peter, who
had a sword, drew it, struck the high
priest's slave, and cut off his right ear.
The slave's name was Malchus. 11Jesus
said to Peter, 'Put your sword back into
its sheath. Am I not to drink the cup
that the Father has given me?'

JESUS BEFORE THE HIGH PRIEST

12 So the soldiers, their officer, and
the Jewish police arrested Jesus and
bound him. 13First they took him to Annas, who was the father-in-law of Caiaphas, the high priest that year. 14Caia-
phas was the one who had advised the
Jews that it was better to have one person die for the people.

PETER DENIES JESUS

15 Simon Peter and another disciple
followed Jesus. Since that disciple was
known to the high priest, he went with
Jesus into the courtyard of the high
priest, 16but Peter was standing outside
at the gate. So the other disciple, who
was known to the high priest, went
out, spoke to the woman who guarded
the gate, and brought Peter in. 17The
woman said to Peter, 'You are not also
one of this man's disciples, are you?' He
said, 'I am not.' 18Now the slaves and
the police had made a charcoal fire because it was cold, and they were standing round it and warming themselves.
Peter also was standing with them and
warming himself.

THE HIGH PRIEST QUESTIONS JESUS

19 Then the high priest questioned
Jesus about his disciples and about his
teaching. 20Jesus answered, 'I have spoken openly to the world; I have always
taught in synagogues and in the temple,
where all the Jews come together. I have
said nothing in secret. 21Why do you ask
me? Ask those who heard what I said to

[k] 17.13 Or *among themselves* [l] 17.15 Or *from evil* [m] 17.21 Other ancient authorities read *be one in us* [n] 18.5 Gk *the Nazorean* [o] 18.5 Gk *I am* [p] 18.6 Gk *he* [q] 18.6 Gk *I am* [r] 18.7 Gk *the Nazorean* [s] 18.8 Gk *I am*

them; they know what I said.' 22When
he had said this, one of the police standing nearby struck Jesus on the face, saying, 'Is that how you answer the high
priest?' 23Jesus answered, 'If I have spoken wrongly, testify to the wrong. But if
I have spoken rightly, why do you strike
me?' 24Then Annas sent him bound to
Caiaphas the high priest.

PETER DENIES JESUS AGAIN

25 Now Simon Peter was standing
and warming himself. They asked him,
'You are not also one of his disciples, are
you?' He denied it and said, 'I am not.'
26One of the slaves of the high priest,
a relative of the man whose ear Peter
had cut off, asked, 'Did I not see you in
the garden with him?' 27Again Peter
denied it, and at that moment the cock
crowed.

JESUS BEFORE PILATE

28 Then they took Jesus from Caiaphas to Pilate's headquarters.[t] It was
early in the morning. They themselves
did not enter the headquarters,[u] so as
to avoid ritual defilement and to be able
to eat the Passover. 29So Pilate went out
to them and said, 'What accusation do
you bring against this man?' 30They answered, 'If this man were not a criminal,
we would not have handed him over to
you.' 31Pilate said to them, 'Take him
yourselves and judge him according
to your law.' The Jews replied, 'We are
not permitted to put anyone to death.'
32(This was to fulfil what Jesus had said
when he indicated the kind of death he
was to die.)

33 Then Pilate entered the headquarters[v] again, summoned Jesus, and asked
him, 'Are you the King of the Jews?'
34Jesus answered, 'Do you ask this on
your own, or did others tell you about
me?' 35Pilate replied, 'I am not a Jew, am
I? Your own nation and the chief priests
have handed you over to me. What have
you done?' 36Jesus answered, 'My kingdom is not from this world. If my kingdom were from this world, my followers
would be fighting to keep me from being handed over to the Jews. But as it is,
my kingdom is not from here.' 37Pilate
asked him, 'So you are a king?' Jesus answered, 'You say that I am a king. For
this I was born, and for this I came into
the world, to testify to the truth. Everyone who belongs to the truth listens to
my voice.' 38Pilate asked him, 'What is
truth?'

JESUS SENTENCED TO DEATH

After he had said this, he went out to
the Jews again and told them, 'I find no
case against him. 39But you have a custom that I release someone for you at
the Passover. Do you want me to release
for you the King of the Jews?' 40They
shouted in reply, 'Not this man, but Barabbas!' Now Barabbas was a bandit.

19 Then Pilate took Jesus and had
him flogged. 2And the soldiers
wove a crown of thorns and put it on
his head, and they dressed him in a purple robe. 3They kept coming up to him,
saying, 'Hail, King of the Jews!' and
striking him on the face. 4Pilate went
out again and said to them, 'Look, I
am bringing him out to you to let you
know that I find no case against him.'
5So Jesus came out, wearing the crown
of thorns and the purple robe. Pilate
said to them, 'Here is the man!' 6When
the chief priests and the police saw
him, they shouted, 'Crucify him! Crucify him!' Pilate said to them, 'Take him
yourselves and crucify him; I find no
case against him.' 7The Jews answered
him, 'We have a law, and according to
that law he ought to die because he has
claimed to be the Son of God.'

8 Now when Pilate heard this, he was
more afraid than ever. 9He entered his
headquarters[w] again and asked Jesus,
'Where are you from?' But Jesus gave
him no answer. 10Pilate therefore said
to him, 'Do you refuse to speak to me?
Do you not know that I have power to
release you, and power to crucify you?'
11Jesus answered him, 'You would have
no power over me unless it had been
given you from above; therefore the one
who handed me over to you is guilty of a
greater sin.' 12From then on Pilate tried
to release him, but the Jews cried out, 'If
you release this man, you are no friend
of the emperor. Everyone who claims to
be a king sets himself against the emperor.'

13 When Pilate heard these words,
he brought Jesus outside and sat[x] on
the judge's bench at a place called The
Stone Pavement, or in Hebrew[y] Gabba-
tha. 14Now it was the day of Preparation
for the Passover; and it was about noon.
He said to the Jews, 'Here is your King!'
15They cried out, 'Away with him! Away
with him! Crucify him!' Pilate asked

[t] **18.28** Gk *the praetorium* [u] **18.28** Gk *the praetorium* [v] **18.33** Gk *the praetorium* [w] **19.9** Gk *the praetorium* [x] **19.13** Or *seated him* [y] **19.13** That is, *Aramaic*

them, 'Shall I crucify your King?' The
chief priests answered, 'We have no king
but the emperor.' 16 Then he handed him
over to them to be crucified.

THE CRUCIFIXION OF JESUS

So they took Jesus; 17 and carrying the
cross by himself, he went out to what
is called The Place of the Skull, which
in Hebrew[z] is called Golgotha. 18 There
they crucified him, and with him two
others, one on either side, with Jesus
between them. 19 Pilate also had an inscription written and put on the cross.
It read, 'Jesus of Nazareth,[a] the King of
the Jews.' 20 Many of the Jews read this
inscription, because the place where
Jesus was crucified was near the city;
and it was written in Hebrew,[b] in Latin,
and in Greek. 21 Then the chief priests of
the Jews said to Pilate, 'Do not write,
"The King of the Jews", but, "This man
said, I am King of the Jews."' 22 Pilate
answered, 'What I have written I have
written.' 23 When the soldiers had crucified Jesus, they took his clothes and divided them into four parts, one for each
soldier. They also took his tunic; now the
tunic was seamless, woven in one piece
from the top. 24 So they said to one another, 'Let us not tear it, but cast lots for
it to see who will get it.' This was to fulfil
what the scripture says,

'They divided my clothes
among themselves,
and for my clothing they cast lots.'

25 And that is what the soldiers did.
Meanwhile, standing near the cross
of Jesus were his mother, and his mother's sister, Mary the wife of Clopas, and
Mary Magdalene. 26 When Jesus saw
his mother and the disciple whom he
loved standing beside her, he said to
his mother, 'Woman, here is your son.'
27 Then he said to the disciple, 'Here is
your mother.' And from that hour the
disciple took her into his own home.

28 After this, when Jesus knew that
all was now finished, he said (in order
to fulfil the scripture), 'I am thirsty.' 29 A
jar full of sour wine was standing there.
So they put a sponge full of the wine
on a branch of hyssop and held it to his
mouth. 30 When Jesus had received the
wine, he said, 'It is finished.' Then he
bowed his head and gave up his spirit.

JESUS' SIDE IS PIERCED

31 Since it was the day of Preparation, the Jews did not want the bodies
left on the cross during the sabbath, especially because that sabbath was a day
of great solemnity. So they asked Pilate
to have the legs of the crucified men
broken and the bodies removed. 32 Then
the soldiers came and broke the legs of
the first and of the other who had been
crucified with him. 33 But when they
came to Jesus and saw that he was already dead, they did not break his legs.
34 Instead, one of the soldiers pierced his
side with a spear, and at once blood and
water came out. 35 (He who saw this has
testified so that you also may believe.
His testimony is true, and he knows[c]
that he tells the truth.) 36 These things
occurred so that the scripture might
be fulfilled, 'None of his bones shall be
broken.' 37 And again another passage of
scripture says, 'They will look on the one
whom they have pierced.'

THE BURIAL OF JESUS

38 After these things, Joseph of Arimathea, who was a disciple of Jesus,
though a secret one because of his fear
of the Jews, asked Pilate to let him take
away the body of Jesus. Pilate gave
him permission; so he came and removed his body. 39 Nicodemus, who
had at first come to Jesus by night, also
came, bringing a mixture of myrrh
and aloes, weighing about a hundred
pounds. 40 They took the body of Jesus
and wrapped it with the spices in linen
cloths, according to the burial custom
of the Jews. 41 Now there was a garden
in the place where he was crucified, and
in the garden there was a new tomb in
which no one had ever been laid. 42 And
so, because it was the Jewish day of
Preparation, and the tomb was nearby,
they laid Jesus there.

THE RESURRECTION OF JESUS

20 Early on the first day of the
week, while it was still dark,
Mary Magdalene came to the tomb and
saw that the stone had been removed
from the tomb. 2 So she ran and went
to Simon Peter and the other disciple,
the one whom Jesus loved, and said to
them, 'They have taken the Lord out of
the tomb, and we do not know where
they have laid him.' 3 Then Peter and
the other disciple set out and went towards the tomb. 4 The two were running
together, but the other disciple outran
Peter and reached the tomb first. 5 He

[z] **19.17** That is, *Aramaic* [a] **19.19** Gk *the Nazorean* [b] **19.20** That is, *Aramaic* [c] **19.35** Or *there is one who knows*

bent down to look in and saw the linen wrappings lying there, but he did not go in. 6 Then Simon Peter came, following him, and went into the tomb. He saw the linen wrappings lying there, 7 and the cloth that had been on Jesus' head, not lying with the linen wrappings but rolled up in a place by itself. 8 Then the other disciple, who reached the tomb first, also went in, and he saw and believed; 9 for as yet they did not understand the scripture, that he must rise from the dead. 10 Then the disciples returned to their homes.

JESUS APPEARS TO MARY MAGDALENE

11 But Mary stood weeping outside the tomb. As she wept, she bent over to look[d] into the tomb; 12 and she saw two angels in white, sitting where the body of Jesus had been lying, one at the head and the other at the feet. 13 They said to her, 'Woman, why are you weeping?' She said to them, 'They have taken away my Lord, and I do not know where they have laid him.' 14 When she had said this, she turned round and saw Jesus standing there, but she did not know that it was Jesus. 15 Jesus said to her, 'Woman, why are you weeping? For whom are you looking?' Supposing him to be the gardener, she said to him, 'Sir, if you have carried him away, tell me where you have laid him, and I will take him away.' 16 Jesus said to her, 'Mary!' She turned and said to him in Hebrew,[e] 'Rabbouni!' (which means Teacher). 17 Jesus said to her, 'Do not hold on to me, because I have not yet ascended to the Father. But go to my brothers and say to them, "I am ascending to my Father and your Father, to my God and your God."' 18 Mary Magdalene went and announced to the disciples, 'I have seen the Lord'; and she told them that he had said these things to her.

JESUS APPEARS TO THE DISCIPLES

19 When it was evening on that day, the first day of the week, and the doors of the house where the disciples had met were locked for fear of the Jews, Jesus came and stood among them and said, 'Peace be with you.' 20 After he said this, he showed them his hands and his side. Then the disciples rejoiced when they saw the Lord. 21 Jesus said to them again, 'Peace be with you. As the Father has sent me, so I send you.' 22 When he had said this, he breathed on them and said to them, 'Receive the Holy Spirit. 23 If you forgive the sins of any, they are forgiven them; if you retain the sins of any, they are retained.'

JESUS AND THOMAS

24 But Thomas (who was called the Twin[f]), one of the twelve, was not with them when Jesus came. 25 So the other disciples told him, 'We have seen the Lord.' But he said to them, 'Unless I see the mark of the nails in his hands, and put my finger in the mark of the nails and my hand in his side, I will not believe.'

26 A week later his disciples were again in the house, and Thomas was with them. Although the doors were shut, Jesus came and stood among them and said, 'Peace be with you.' 27 Then he said to Thomas, 'Put your finger here and see my hands. Reach out your hand and put it in my side. Do not doubt but believe.' 28 Thomas answered him, 'My Lord and my God!' 29 Jesus said to him, 'Have you believed because you have seen me? Blessed are those who have not seen and yet have come to believe.'

THE PURPOSE OF THIS BOOK

30 Now Jesus did many other signs in the presence of his disciples, which are not written in this book. 31 But these are written so that you may come to believe[g] that Jesus is the Messiah,[h] the Son of God, and that through believing you may have life in his name.

JESUS APPEARS TO SEVEN DISCIPLES

21 After these things Jesus showed himself again to the disciples by the Sea of Tiberias; and he showed himself in this way. 2 Gathered there together were Simon Peter, Thomas called the Twin,[i] Nathanael of Cana in Galilee, the sons of Zebedee, and two others of his disciples. 3 Simon Peter said to them, 'I am going fishing.' They said to him, 'We will go with you.' They went out and got into the boat, but that night they caught nothing.

4 Just after daybreak, Jesus stood on the beach; but the disciples did not know that it was Jesus. 5 Jesus said to them, 'Children, you have no fish, have you?' They answered him, 'No.' 6 He said to them, 'Cast the net to the right side

[d] **20.11** Gk lacks *to look* [e] **20.16** That is, *Aramaic* [f] **20.24** Gk *Didymus* [g] **20.31** Other ancient authorities read *may continue to believe* [h] **20.31** Or *the Christ* [i] **21.2** Gk *Didymus*

of the boat, and you will find some.' So
they cast it, and now they were not able
to haul it in because there were so many
fish. 7That disciple whom Jesus loved
said to Peter, 'It is the Lord!' When Simon Peter heard that it was the Lord,
he put on some clothes, for he was naked, and jumped into the lake. 8But the
other disciples came in the boat, dragging the net full of fish, for they were
not far from the land, only about a hundred yards[j] off.

9 When they had gone ashore, they
saw a charcoal fire there, with fish on it,
and bread. 10Jesus said to them, 'Bring
some of the fish that you have just
caught.' 11So Simon Peter went aboard
and hauled the net ashore, full of large
fish, a hundred and fifty-three of them;
and though there were so many, the
net was not torn. 12Jesus said to them,
'Come and have breakfast.' Now none
of the disciples dared to ask him, 'Who
are you?' because they knew it was the
Lord. 13Jesus came and took the bread
and gave it to them, and did the same
with the fish. 14This was now the third
time that Jesus appeared to the disciples
after he was raised from the dead.

JESUS AND PETER

15 When they had finished breakfast, Jesus said to Simon Peter, 'Simon
son of John, do you love me more than
these?' He said to him, 'Yes, Lord; you
know that I love you.' Jesus said to him,
'Feed my lambs.' 16A second time he
said to him, 'Simon son of John, do you
love me?' He said to him, 'Yes, Lord;
you know that I love you.' Jesus said to
him, 'Tend my sheep.' 17He said to him
the third time, 'Simon son of John, do
you love me?' Peter felt hurt because
he said to him the third time, 'Do you
love me?' And he said to him, 'Lord, you
know everything; you know that I love
you.' Jesus said to him, 'Feed my sheep.
18Very truly, I tell you, when you were
younger, you used to fasten your own
belt and to go wherever you wished.
But when you grow old, you will stretch
out your hands, and someone else will
fasten a belt around you and take you
where you do not wish to go.' 19(He said
this to indicate the kind of death by
which he would glorify God.) After this
he said to him, 'Follow me.'

JESUS AND THE BELOVED DISCIPLE

20 Peter turned and saw the disciple
whom Jesus loved following them; he
was the one who had reclined next to
Jesus at the supper and had said, 'Lord,
who is it that is going to betray you?'
21When Peter saw him, he said to Jesus,
'Lord, what about him?' 22Jesus said to
him, 'If it is my will that he remain until
I come, what is that to you? Follow me!'
23So the rumour spread in the community[k] that this disciple would not die.
Yet Jesus did not say to him that he
would not die, but, 'If it is my will that
he remain until I come, what is that to
you?'[l]

24 This is the disciple who is testifying to these things and has written
them, and we know that his testimony
is true. 25But there are also many other
things that Jesus did; if every one of
them were written down, I suppose
that the world itself could not contain
the books that would be written.

[j] **21.8** Gk *two hundred cubits* [k] **21.23** Gk *among the brothers* [l] **21.23** Other ancient authorities lack *what is that to you*

The ACTS of the Apostles

The Acts of the Apostles is the second volume attributed to Luke and the first historical account of the development of the early Christian community from the time of the ascension of Jesus until the arrival of Paul as a prisoner under house arrest in Rome. The Spirit-led growth of the early Christian community as it faced the implications of its mission to preach the gospel is the major concern of the book of Acts. The Gospels focus on the life of Jesus; the book of Acts gives an account of the life of the church as it advances under the guidance of the Holy Spirit and by the leadership of the apostles, especially that of Peter and Paul.

The Acts of the Apostles opens with the ascension of Jesus, who hands on responsibility to his disciples to be his witnesses to the ends of the earth. The purpose of Acts is to show how the preaching of the good news was made possible by the power of the Holy Spirit and how the spread of the gospel was not to be sabotaged (5.33–39). The gospel was first preached to the Jews and then, in time, to the Gentiles, leading to the spread of Christianity to diverse peoples (Jews, Samaritans, and Gentiles) throughout the Roman Empire. Ultimately, according to Acts, the divine plan was behind the growth and diffusion of the church. The important figures in the narrative are the apostles, especially Peter (chs. 1–12), and then the newly converted apostle Paul, who is largely responsible for the preaching to the Gentiles (chs. 13–28).

Every year during the liturgical celebrations of Ascension and Pentecost, the first reading is taken from the Acts of the Apostles. These selected passages highlight the important theological themes in Luke's account. In the passage read on the Feast of the Ascension, the disciples expect Israel to be restored, but Jesus asserts that the end of all things is not yet at hand. In other words, there would not be an imminent restoration as the disciples expected. Instead, Jesus hands over to the apostles the responsibility to be his witnesses and to carry on his mission to the ends of the earth (1.8).

In the text read on Pentecost, the disciples are empowered in a dramatic scene by the coming of the Holy Spirit. The Spirit empowers the apostles in their mission to preach the gospel starting in Jerusalem and eventually reaching all the world. The narrative goes on to describe the success of the apostles in converting large numbers of people despite obstacles and significant opposition. The book of Acts is instructive about a fast-growing Gentile Christian community.

THE PROMISE OF THE HOLY SPIRIT

1 In the first book, Theophilus, I
wrote about all that Jesus did and
taught from the beginning 2until the
day when he was taken up to heaven,
after giving instructions through the
Holy Spirit to the apostles whom he
had chosen. 3After his suffering he presented himself alive to them by many
convincing proofs, appearing to them

over the course of forty days and speaking about the kingdom of God. 4 While
staying[a] with them, he ordered them
not to leave Jerusalem, but to wait there
for the promise of the Father. 'This', he
said, 'is what you have heard from me;
5 for John baptized with water, but you
will be baptized with[b] the Holy Spirit
not many days from now.'

THE ASCENSION OF JESUS

6 So when they had come together,
they asked him, 'Lord, is this the time
when you will restore the kingdom to
Israel?' 7 He replied, 'It is not for you to
know the times or periods that the Father has set by his own authority. 8 But
you will receive power when the Holy
Spirit has come upon you; and you will
be my witnesses in Jerusalem, in all
Judea and Samaria, and to the ends of
the earth.' 9 When he had said this, as
they were watching, he was lifted up,
and a cloud took him out of their sight.
10 While he was going and they were
gazing up towards heaven, suddenly
two men in white robes stood by them.
11 They said, 'Men of Galilee, why do you
stand looking up towards heaven? This
Jesus, who has been taken up from you
into heaven, will come in the same way
as you saw him go into heaven.'

MATTHIAS CHOSEN TO REPLACE JUDAS

12 Then they returned to Jerusalem
from the mount called Olivet, which is
near Jerusalem, a sabbath day's journey
away. 13 When they had entered the city,
they went to the room upstairs where
they were staying, Peter, and John, and
James, and Andrew, Philip and Thomas,
Bartholomew and Matthew, James son
of Alphaeus, and Simon the Zealot,
and Judas son of[c] James. 14 All these
were constantly devoting themselves to
prayer, together with certain women,
including Mary the mother of Jesus, as
well as his brothers.

15 In those days Peter stood up
among the believers[d] (together the
crowd numbered about one hundred
and twenty people) and said, 16 'Friends,[e]
the scripture had to be fulfilled, which
the Holy Spirit through David foretold
concerning Judas, who became a guide
for those who arrested Jesus— 17 for he
was numbered among us and was allotted his share in this ministry.' 18 (Now
this man acquired a field with the reward of his wickedness; and falling
headlong,[f] he burst open in the middle
and all his bowels gushed out. 19 This
became known to all the residents of
Jerusalem, so that the field was called
in their language Hakeldama, that is,
Field of Blood.) 20 'For it is written in the
book of Psalms,

> "Let his homestead become desolate,
> and let there be no one
> to live in it";

and

> "Let another take his position
> of overseer."

21 So one of the men who have accompanied us throughout the time that
the Lord Jesus went in and out among
us, 22 beginning from the baptism of
John until the day when he was taken
up from us—one of these must become
a witness with us to his resurrection.'
23 So they proposed two, Joseph called
Barsabbas, who was also known as Justus, and Matthias. 24 Then they prayed
and said, 'Lord, you know everyone's
heart. Show us which one of these two
you have chosen 25 to take the place[g]
in this ministry and apostleship from
which Judas turned aside to go to his
own place.' 26 And they cast lots for
them, and the lot fell on Matthias; and
he was added to the eleven apostles.

THE COMING OF THE HOLY SPIRIT

2 When the day of Pentecost had
come, they were all together in
one place. 2 And suddenly from heaven
there came a sound like the rush of a
violent wind, and it filled the entire
house where they were sitting. 3 Divided
tongues, as of fire, appeared among
them, and a tongue rested on each of
them. 4 All of them were filled with the
Holy Spirit and began to speak in other
languages, as the Spirit gave them
ability.

5 Now there were devout Jews from
every nation under heaven living in Jerusalem. 6 And at this sound the crowd
gathered and was bewildered, because
each one heard them speaking in the
native language of each. 7 Amazed and
astonished, they asked, 'Are not all these
who are speaking Galileans? 8 And how
is it that we hear, each of us, in our own
native language? 9 Parthians, Medes,
Elamites, and residents of Mesopotamia, Judea and Cappadocia, Pontus and

[a] 1.4 Or *eating* [b] 1.5 Or *by* [c] 1.13 Or *the brother of* [d] 1.15 Gk *brothers* [e] 1.16 Gk *Men, brothers* [f] 1.18 Or *swelling up* [g] 1.25 Other ancient authorities read *the share*

Asia, 10Phrygia and Pamphylia, Egypt
and the parts of Libya belonging to Cyrene, and visitors from Rome, both Jews
and proselytes, 11Cretans and Arabs—in
our own languages we hear them speaking about God's deeds of power.' 12All
were amazed and perplexed, saying to
one another, 'What does this mean?'
13But others sneered and said, 'They are
filled with new wine.'

PETER ADDRESSES THE CROWD

14 But Peter, standing with the eleven,
raised his voice and addressed them: 'Men
of Judea and all who live in Jerusalem, let
this be known to you, and listen to what I
say. 15Indeed, these are not drunk, as you
suppose, for it is only nine o'clock in the
morning. 16No, this is what was spoken
through the prophet Joel:

17 "In the last days it will be,
God declares,
that I will pour out my Spirit
upon all flesh,
and your sons and your
daughters shall prophesy,
and your young men shall
see visions,
and your old men shall
dream dreams.
18 Even upon my slaves, both
men and women,
in those days I will pour
out my Spirit;
and they shall prophesy.
19 And I will show portents in
the heaven above
and signs on the earth below,
blood, and fire, and
smoky mist.
20 The sun shall be turned to darkness
and the moon to blood,
before the coming of the Lord's
great and glorious day.
21 Then everyone who calls on
the name of the Lord
shall be saved."

22 'You that are Israelites,[h] listen to
what I have to say: Jesus of Nazareth,[i] a
man attested to you by God with deeds
of power, wonders, and signs that God
did through him among you, as you
yourselves know— 23this man, handed
over to you according to the definite
plan and foreknowledge of God, you crucified and killed by the hands of those
outside the law. 24But God raised him
up, having freed him from death,[j] because it was impossible for him to be
held in its power. 25For David says concerning him,

"I saw the Lord always before me,
for he is at my right hand so
that I will not be shaken;
26 therefore my heart was glad, and
my tongue rejoiced;
moreover, my flesh will
live in hope.
27 For you will not abandon my
soul to Hades,
or let your Holy One
experience corruption.
28 You have made known to me
the ways of life;
you will make me full of gladness
with your presence."

29 'Fellow-Israelites,[k] I may say to you
confidently of our ancestor David that he
both died and was buried, and his tomb
is with us to this day. 30Since he was a
prophet, he knew that God had sworn
with an oath to him that he would put
one of his descendants on his throne.
31Foreseeing this, David[l] spoke of the
resurrection of the Messiah,[m] saying,

"He was not abandoned to Hades,
nor did his flesh experience
corruption."

32This Jesus God raised up, and of that
all of us are witnesses. 33Being therefore exalted at[n] the right hand of God,
and having received from the Father
the promise of the Holy Spirit, he has
poured out this that you both see and
hear. 34For David did not ascend into
the heavens, but he himself says,

"The Lord said to my Lord,
'Sit at my right hand,
35 until I make your enemies
your footstool.'"

36Therefore let the entire house of Israel
know with certainty that God has made
him both Lord and Messiah,[o] this Jesus
whom you crucified.'

THE FIRST CONVERTS

37 Now when they heard this, they
were cut to the heart and said to Peter
and to the other apostles, 'Brothers,[p]
what should we do?' 38Peter said to
them, 'Repent, and be baptized every
one of you in the name of Jesus Christ so
that your sins may be forgiven; and you
will receive the gift of the Holy Spirit.
39For the promise is for you, for your
children, and for all who are far away,
everyone whom the Lord our God calls

[h] 2.22 Gk *Men, Israelites* [i] 2.22 Gk *the Nazorean* [j] 2.24 Gk *the pains of death* [k] 2.29 Gk *Men, brothers* [l] 2.31 Gk *he* [m] 2.31 Or *the Christ* [n] 2.33 Or *by* [o] 2.36 Or *Christ* [p] 2.37 Gk *Men, brothers*

to him.' 40And he testified with many other arguments and exhorted them, saying, 'Save yourselves from this corrupt generation.' 41So those who welcomed his message were baptized, and that day about three thousand persons were added. 42They devoted themselves to the apostles' teaching and fellowship, to the breaking of bread and the prayers.

LIFE AMONG THE BELIEVERS

43 Awe came upon everyone, because many wonders and signs were being done by the apostles. 44All who believed were together and had all things in common; 45they would sell their possessions and goods and distribute the proceeds[q] to all, as any had need. 46Day by day, as they spent much time together in the temple, they broke bread at home[r] and ate their food with glad and generous[s] hearts, 47praising God and having the goodwill of all the people. And day by day the Lord added to their number those who were being saved.

PETER HEALS A CRIPPLED BEGGAR

3 One day Peter and John were going up to the temple at the hour of prayer, at three o'clock in the afternoon. 2And a man lame from birth was being carried in. People would lay him daily at the gate of the temple called the Beautiful Gate so that he could ask for alms from those entering the temple. 3When he saw Peter and John about to go into the temple, he asked them for alms. 4Peter looked intently at him, as did John, and said, 'Look at us.' 5And he fixed his attention on them, expecting to receive something from them. 6But Peter said, 'I have no silver or gold, but what I have I give you; in the name of Jesus Christ of Nazareth,[t] stand up and walk.' 7And he took him by the right hand and raised him up; and immediately his feet and ankles were made strong. 8Jumping up, he stood and began to walk, and he entered the temple with them, walking and leaping and praising God. 9All the people saw him walking and praising God, 10and they recognized him as the one who used to sit and ask for alms at the Beautiful Gate of the temple; and they were filled with wonder and amazement at what had happened to him.

PETER SPEAKS IN SOLOMON'S PORTICO

11 While he clung to Peter and John, all the people ran together to them in the portico called Solomon's Portico, utterly astonished. 12When Peter saw it, he addressed the people, 'You Israelites,[u] why do you wonder at this, or why do you stare at us, as though by our own power or piety we had made him walk? 13The God of Abraham, the God of Isaac, and the God of Jacob, the God of our ancestors has glorified his servant[v] Jesus, whom you handed over and rejected in the presence of Pilate, though he had decided to release him. 14But you rejected the Holy and Righteous One and asked to have a murderer given to you, 15and you killed the Author of life, whom God raised from the dead. To this we are witnesses. 16And by faith in his name, his name itself has made this man strong, whom you see and know; and the faith that is through Jesus[w] has given him this perfect health in the presence of all of you.

17 'And now, friends,[x] I know that you acted in ignorance, as did also your rulers. 18In this way God fulfilled what he had foretold through all the prophets, that his Messiah[y] would suffer. 19Repent therefore, and turn to God so that your sins may be wiped out, 20so that times of refreshing may come from the presence of the Lord, and that he may send the Messiah[z] appointed for you, that is, Jesus, 21who must remain in heaven until the time of universal restoration that God announced long ago through his holy prophets. 22Moses said, "The Lord your God will raise up for you from your own people[a] a prophet like me. You must listen to whatever he tells you. 23And it will be that everyone who does not listen to that prophet will be utterly rooted out from the people." 24And all the prophets, as many as have spoken, from Samuel and those after him, also predicted these days. 25You are the descendants of the prophets and of the covenant that God gave to your ancestors, saying to Abraham, "And in your descendants all the families of the earth shall be blessed." 26When God raised up his servant,[b] he sent him first to you, to bless you by turning each of you from your wicked ways.'

[q] 2.45 Gk *them* [r] 2.46 Or *from house to house* [s] 2.46 Or *sincere* [t] 3.6 Gk *the Nazorean* [u] 3.12 Gk *Men, Israelites* [v] 3.13 Or *child* [w] 3.16 Gk *him* [x] 3.17 Gk *brothers* [y] 3.18 Or *his Christ* [z] 3.20 Or *the Christ* [a] 3.22 Gk *brothers* [b] 3.26 Or *child*

PETER AND JOHN BEFORE THE COUNCIL

4 While Peter and John[c] were speaking to the people, the priests, the
captain of the temple, and the Sadducees came to them, 2much annoyed
because they were teaching the people
and proclaiming that in Jesus there is
the resurrection of the dead. 3So they
arrested them and put them in custody
until the next day, for it was already
evening. 4But many of those who heard
the word believed; and they numbered
about five thousand.

5 The next day their rulers, elders,
and scribes assembled in Jerusalem,
6with Annas the high priest, Caiaphas,
John,[d] and Alexander, and all who were
of the high-priestly family. 7When they
had made the prisoners[e] stand in their
midst, they inquired, 'By what power or
by what name did you do this?' 8Then
Peter, filled with the Holy Spirit, said to
them, 'Rulers of the people and elders,
9if we are questioned today because of
a good deed done to someone who was
sick and are asked how this man has
been healed, 10let it be known to all
of you, and to all the people of Israel,
that this man is standing before you in
good health by the name of Jesus Christ
of Nazareth,[f] whom you crucified,
whom God raised from the dead. 11This
Jesus[g] is

"the stone that was rejected by
you, the builders;
it has become the cornerstone."[h]

12There is salvation in no one else, for
there is no other name under heaven
given among mortals by which we must
be saved.'

13 Now when they saw the boldness of Peter and John and realized that
they were uneducated and ordinary
men, they were amazed and recognized
them as companions of Jesus. 14When
they saw the man who had been cured
standing beside them, they had nothing
to say in opposition. 15So they ordered
them to leave the council while they
discussed the matter with one another.
16They said, 'What will we do with
them? For it is obvious to all who live in
Jerusalem that a notable sign has been
done through them; we cannot deny it.
17But to keep it from spreading further
among the people, let us warn them to
speak no more to anyone in this name.'
18So they called them and ordered them
not to speak or teach at all in the name
of Jesus. 19But Peter and John answered
them, 'Whether it is right in God's sight
to listen to you rather than to God, you
must judge; 20for we cannot keep from
speaking about what we have seen and
heard.' 21After threatening them again,
they let them go, finding no way to
punish them because of the people, for
all of them praised God for what had
happened. 22For the man on whom this
sign of healing had been performed was
more than forty years old.

THE BELIEVERS PRAY FOR BOLDNESS

23 After they were released, they
went to their friends[i] and reported what
the chief priests and the elders had said
to them. 24When they heard it, they
raised their voices together to God and
said, 'Sovereign Lord, who made the
heaven and the earth, the sea, and everything in them, 25it is you who said
by the Holy Spirit through our ancestor
David, your servant:[j]

"Why did the Gentiles rage,
and the peoples imagine
vain things?
26 The kings of the earth took
their stand,
and the rulers have
gathered together
against the Lord and
against his Messiah."[k]

27For in this city, in fact, both Herod
and Pontius Pilate, with the Gentiles
and the peoples of Israel, gathered together against your holy servant[l] Jesus,
whom you anointed, 28to do whatever
your hand and your plan had predestined to take place. 29And now, Lord,
look at their threats, and grant to your
servants[m] to speak your word with all
boldness, 30while you stretch out your
hand to heal, and signs and wonders are
performed through the name of your
holy servant[n] Jesus.' 31When they had
prayed, the place in which they were
gathered together was shaken; and they
were all filled with the Holy Spirit and
spoke the word of God with boldness.

THE BELIEVERS SHARE THEIR POSSESSIONS

32 Now the whole group of those
who believed were of one heart and soul,
and no one claimed private ownership

[c] 4.1 Gk *While they* [d] 4.6 Other ancient authorities read *Jonathan* [e] 4.7 Gk *them* [f] 4.10 Gk *the Nazorean* [g] 4.11 Gk *This* [h] 4.11 Or *keystone* [i] 4.23 Gk *their own* [j] 4.25 Or *child* [k] 4.26 Or *his Christ* [l] 4.27 Or *child* [m] 4.29 Gk *slaves* [n] 4.30 Or *child*

of any possessions, but everything they
owned was held in common. 33With
great power the apostles gave their testimony to the resurrection of the Lord
Jesus, and great grace was upon them
all. 34There was not a needy person
among them, for as many as owned
lands or houses sold them and brought
the proceeds of what was sold. 35They
laid it at the apostles' feet, and it was
distributed to each as any had need.
36There was a Levite, a native of Cyprus, Joseph, to whom the apostles gave
the name Barnabas (which means 'son
of encouragement'). 37He sold a field
that belonged to him, then brought the
money, and laid it at the apostles' feet.

ANANIAS AND SAPPHIRA

5 But a man named Ananias, with
the consent of his wife Sapphira,
sold a piece of property; 2with his wife's
knowledge, he kept back some of the
proceeds, and brought only a part and
laid it at the apostles' feet. 3'Ananias,'
Peter asked, 'why has Satan filled your
heart to lie to the Holy Spirit and to
keep back part of the proceeds of the
land? 4While it remained unsold, did it
not remain your own? And after it was
sold, were not the proceeds at your disposal? How is it that you have contrived
this deed in your heart? You did not
lie to us[o] but to God!' 5Now when Ananias heard these words, he fell down
and died. And great fear seized all who
heard of it. 6The young men came and
wrapped up his body,[p] then carried him
out and buried him.

7 After an interval of about three
hours his wife came in, not knowing
what had happened. 8Peter said to her,
'Tell me whether you and your husband
sold the land for such and such a price.'
And she said, 'Yes, that was the price.'
9Then Peter said to her, 'How is it that
you have agreed together to put the
Spirit of the Lord to the test? Look, the
feet of those who have buried your husband are at the door, and they will carry
you out.' 10Immediately she fell down at
his feet and died. When the young men
came in they found her dead, so they
carried her out and buried her beside
her husband. 11And great fear seized the
whole church and all who heard of these
things.

THE APOSTLES HEAL MANY

12 Now many signs and wonders
were done among the people through
the apostles. And they were all together
in Solomon's Portico. 13None of the rest
dared to join them, but the people held
them in high esteem. 14Yet more than
ever believers were added to the Lord,
great numbers of both men and women,
15so that they even carried out the sick
into the streets, and laid them on cots
and mats, in order that Peter's shadow
might fall on some of them as he came
by. 16A great number of people would
also gather from the towns around Jerusalem, bringing the sick and those
tormented by unclean spirits, and they
were all cured.

THE APOSTLES ARE PERSECUTED

17 Then the high priest took action;
he and all who were with him (that is,
the sect of the Sadducees), being filled
with jealousy, 18arrested the apostles
and put them in the public prison. 19But
during the night an angel of the Lord
opened the prison doors, brought them
out, and said, 20'Go, stand in the temple
and tell the people the whole message
about this life.' 21When they heard this,
they entered the temple at daybreak
and went on with their teaching.

When the high priest and those with
him arrived, they called together the
council and the whole body of the elders
of Israel, and sent to the prison to have
them brought. 22But when the temple police went there, they did not find
them in the prison; so they returned
and reported, 23'We found the prison
securely locked and the guards standing at the doors, but when we opened
them, we found no one inside.' 24Now
when the captain of the temple and the
chief priests heard these words, they
were perplexed about them, wondering
what might be going on. 25Then someone arrived and announced, 'Look, the
men whom you put in prison are standing in the temple and teaching the people!' 26Then the captain went with the
temple police and brought them, but
without violence, for they were afraid of
being stoned by the people.

27 When they had brought them,
they had them stand before the council.
The high priest questioned them, 28say-
ing, 'We gave you strict orders not to
teach in this name,[q] yet here you have
filled Jerusalem with your teaching and
you are determined to bring this man's

[o] 5.4 Gk *to men* [p] 5.6 Meaning of Gk uncertain
[q] 5.28 Other ancient authorities read *Did we not give you strict orders not to teach in this name?*

blood on us.' 29 But Peter and the apostles answered, 'We must obey God rather than any human authority.[r] 30 The God of our ancestors raised up Jesus, whom you had killed by hanging him on a tree. 31 God exalted him at his right hand as Leader and Saviour, so that he might give repentance to Israel and forgiveness of sins. 32 And we are witnesses to these things, and so is the Holy Spirit whom God has given to those who obey him.'

33 When they heard this, they were enraged and wanted to kill them. 34 But a Pharisee in the council named Gamaliel, a teacher of the law, respected by all the people, stood up and ordered the men to be put outside for a short time. 35 Then he said to them, 'Fellow-Israelites,[s] consider carefully what you propose to do to these men. 36 For some time ago Theudas rose up, claiming to be somebody, and a number of men, about four hundred, joined him; but he was killed, and all who followed him were dispersed and disappeared. 37 After him Judas the Galilean rose up at the time of the census and got people to follow him; he also perished, and all who followed him were scattered. 38 So in the present case, I tell you, keep away from these men and let them alone; because if this plan or this undertaking is of human origin, it will fail; 39 but if it is of God, you will not be able to overthrow them—in that case you may even be found fighting against God!'

They were convinced by him, 40 and when they had called in the apostles, they had them flogged. Then they ordered them not to speak in the name of Jesus, and let them go. 41 As they left the council, they rejoiced that they were considered worthy to suffer dishonour for the sake of the name. 42 And every day in the temple and at home[t] they did not cease to teach and proclaim Jesus as the Messiah.[u]

SEVEN CHOSEN TO SERVE

6 Now during those days, when the disciples were increasing in number, the Hellenists complained against the Hebrews because their widows were being neglected in the daily distribution of food. 2 And the twelve called together the whole community of the disciples and said, 'It is not right that we should neglect the word of God in order to wait at tables.[v] 3 Therefore, friends,[w] select from among yourselves seven men of good standing, full of the Spirit and of wisdom, whom we may appoint to this task, 4 while we, for our part, will devote ourselves to prayer and to serving the word.' 5 What they said pleased the whole community, and they chose Stephen, a man full of faith and the Holy Spirit, together with Philip, Prochorus, Nicanor, Timon, Parmenas, and Nicolaus, a proselyte of Antioch. 6 They had these men stand before the apostles, who prayed and laid their hands on them.

7 The word of God continued to spread; the number of the disciples increased greatly in Jerusalem, and a great many of the priests became obedient to the faith.

THE ARREST OF STEPHEN

8 Stephen, full of grace and power, did great wonders and signs among the people. 9 Then some of those who belonged to the synagogue of the Freedmen (as it was called), Cyrenians, Alexandrians, and others of those from Cilicia and Asia, stood up and argued with Stephen. 10 But they could not withstand the wisdom and the Spirit[x] with which he spoke. 11 Then they secretly instigated some men to say, 'We have heard him speak blasphemous words against Moses and God.' 12 They stirred up the people as well as the elders and the scribes; then they suddenly confronted him, seized him, and brought him before the council. 13 They set up false witnesses who said, 'This man never stops saying things against this holy place and the law; 14 for we have heard him say that this Jesus of Nazareth[y] will destroy this place and will change the customs that Moses handed on to us.' 15 And all who sat in the council looked intently at him, and they saw that his face was like the face of an angel.

STEPHEN'S SPEECH TO THE COUNCIL

7 Then the high priest asked him, 'Are these things so?' 2 And Stephen replied:

'Brothers[z] and fathers, listen to me. The God of glory appeared to our ancestor Abraham when he was in Mesopotamia, before he lived in Haran, 3 and said to him, "Leave your country and your

[r] 5.29 Gk *than men* [s] 5.35 Gk *Men, Israelites* [t] 5.42 Or *from house to house* [u] 5.42 Or *the Christ* [v] 6.2 Or *keep accounts* [w] 6.3 Gk *brothers* [x] 6.10 Or *spirit* [y] 6.14 Gk *the Nazorean* [z] 7.2 Gk *Men, brothers*

relatives and go to the land that I will
show you." 4 Then he left the country of
the Chaldeans and settled in Haran. After his father died, God had him move
from there to this country in which you
are now living. 5 He did not give him
any of it as a heritage, not even a foot's
length, but promised to give it to him
as his possession and to his descendants
after him, even though he had no child.
6 And God spoke in these terms, that his
descendants would be resident aliens
in a country belonging to others, who
would enslave them and maltreat them
for four hundred years. 7 "But I will judge
the nation that they serve," said God,
"and after that they shall come out and
worship me in this place." 8 Then he gave
him the covenant of circumcision. And
so Abraham[a] became the father of Isaac
and circumcised him on the eighth day;
and Isaac became the father of Jacob,
and Jacob of the twelve patriarchs.

9 'The patriarchs, jealous of Joseph,
sold him into Egypt; but God was with
him, 10 and rescued him from all his afflictions, and enabled him to win favour
and to show wisdom when he stood
before Pharaoh, king of Egypt, who appointed him ruler over Egypt and over
all his household. 11 Now there came a
famine throughout Egypt and Canaan,
and great suffering, and our ancestors
could find no food. 12 But when Jacob
heard that there was grain in Egypt, he
sent our ancestors there on their first
visit. 13 On the second visit Joseph made
himself known to his brothers, and Joseph's family became known to Pharaoh. 14 Then Joseph sent and invited his
father Jacob and all his relatives to come
to him, seventy-five in all; 15 so Jacob
went down to Egypt. He himself died
there as well as our ancestors, 16 and
their bodies[b] were brought back to Shechem and laid in the tomb that Abraham had bought for a sum of silver from
the sons of Hamor in Shechem.

17 'But as the time drew near for the
fulfilment of the promise that God had
made to Abraham, our people in Egypt
increased and multiplied 18 until another king who had not known Joseph
ruled over Egypt. 19 He dealt craftily
with our race and forced our ancestors
to abandon their infants so that they
would die. 20 At this time Moses was
born, and he was beautiful before God.
For three months he was brought up
in his father's house; 21 and when he
was abandoned, Pharaoh's daughter
adopted him and brought him up as her
own son. 22 So Moses was instructed in
all the wisdom of the Egyptians and was
powerful in his words and deeds.

23 'When he was forty years old,
it came into his heart to visit his relatives, the Israelites.[c] 24 When he saw one
of them being wronged, he defended
the oppressed man and avenged him
by striking down the Egyptian. 25 He
supposed that his kinsfolk would understand that God through him was
rescuing them, but they did not understand. 26 The next day he came to some
of them as they were quarrelling and
tried to reconcile them, saying, "Men,
you are brothers; why do you wrong
each other?" 27 But the man who was
wronging his neighbour pushed Moses[d]
aside, saying, "Who made you a ruler
and a judge over us? 28 Do you want to
kill me as you killed the Egyptian yesterday?" 29 When he heard this, Moses
fled and became a resident alien in the
land of Midian. There he became the father of two sons.

30 'Now when forty years had passed,
an angel appeared to him in the wilderness of Mount Sinai, in the flame of a
burning bush. 31 When Moses saw it, he
was amazed at the sight; and as he approached to look, there came the voice
of the Lord: 32 "I am the God of your ancestors, the God of Abraham, Isaac, and
Jacob." Moses began to tremble and did
not dare to look. 33 Then the Lord said
to him, "Take off the sandals from your
feet, for the place where you are standing is holy ground. 34 I have surely seen
the mistreatment of my people who are
in Egypt and have heard their groaning,
and I have come down to rescue them.
Come now, I will send you to Egypt."

35 'It was this Moses whom they rejected when they said, "Who made you
a ruler and a judge?" and whom God
now sent as both ruler and liberator
through the angel who appeared to him
in the bush. 36 He led them out, having
performed wonders and signs in Egypt,
at the Red Sea, and in the wilderness
for forty years. 37 This is the Moses who
said to the Israelites, "God will raise up
a prophet for you from your own people[e] as he raised me up." 38 He is the one
who was in the congregation in the
wilderness with the angel who spoke
to him at Mount Sinai, and with our

[a] **7.8** Gk *he* [b] **7.16** Gk *they* [c] **7.23** Gk *his brothers, the sons of Israel* [d] **7.27** Gk *him* [e] **7.37** Gk *your brothers*

ancestors; and he received living oracles to give to us. 39 Our ancestors were
unwilling to obey him; instead, they
pushed him aside, and in their hearts
they turned back to Egypt, 40 saying
to Aaron, "Make gods for us who will
lead the way for us; as for this Moses
who led us out from the land of Egypt,
we do not know what has happened
to him." 41 At that time they made a
calf, offered a sacrifice to the idol, and
revelled in the works of their hands.
42 But God turned away from them and
handed them over to worship the host
of heaven, as it is written in the book of
the prophets:

"Did you offer to me slain
victims and sacrifices
for forty years in the wilderness,
O house of Israel?
43 No; you took along the tent
of Moloch,
and the star of your god Rephan,
the images that you
made to worship;
so I will remove you beyond
Babylon."

44 'Our ancestors had the tent of
testimony in the wilderness, as God[f]
directed when he spoke to Moses, ordering him to make it according to the
pattern he had seen. 45 Our ancestors in
turn brought it in with Joshua when
they dispossessed the nations that God
drove out before our ancestors. And
it was there until the time of David,
46 who found favour with God and asked
that he might find a dwelling-place for
the house of Jacob.[g] 47 But it was Solomon who built a house for him. 48 Yet
the Most High does not dwell in houses
made by human hands;[h] as the prophet
says,

49 "Heaven is my throne,
and the earth is my footstool.
What kind of house will you build
for me, says the Lord,
or what is the place of my rest?
50 Did not my hand make all
these things?"

51 'You stiff-necked people, uncircumcised in heart and ears, you are
for ever opposing the Holy Spirit, just
as your ancestors used to do. 52 Which
of the prophets did your ancestors not
persecute? They killed those who foretold the coming of the Righteous One,
and now you have become his betrayers
and murderers. 53 You are the ones that
received the law as ordained by angels,
and yet you have not kept it.'

THE STONING OF STEPHEN

54 When they heard these things,
they became enraged and ground their
teeth at Stephen.[i] 55 But filled with the
Holy Spirit, he gazed into heaven and
saw the glory of God and Jesus standing at the right hand of God. 56 'Look,' he
said, 'I see the heavens opened and the
Son of Man standing at the right hand of
God!' 57 But they covered their ears, and
with a loud shout all rushed together
against him. 58 Then they dragged him
out of the city and began to stone him;
and the witnesses laid their coats at
the feet of a young man named Saul.
59 While they were stoning Stephen, he
prayed, 'Lord Jesus, receive my spirit.'
60 Then he knelt down and cried out in
a loud voice, 'Lord, do not hold this sin
against them.'
When he had said this, he died.[j]
8 1 And Saul approved of their killing
him.

SAUL PERSECUTES THE CHURCH

That day a severe persecution began
against the church in Jerusalem, and
all except the apostles were scattered
throughout the countryside of Judea
and Samaria. 2 Devout men buried Stephen and made loud lamentation over
him. 3 But Saul was ravaging the church
by entering house after house; dragging
off both men and women, he committed them to prison.

PHILIP PREACHES IN SAMARIA

4 Now those who were scattered
went from place to place, proclaiming
the word. 5 Philip went down to the
city[k] of Samaria and proclaimed the
Messiah[l] to them. 6 The crowds with one
accord listened eagerly to what was said
by Philip, hearing and seeing the signs
that he did, 7 for unclean spirits, crying
with loud shrieks, came out of many
who were possessed; and many others
who were paralysed or lame were cured.
8 So there was great joy in that city.

9 Now a certain man named Simon
had previously practised magic in the
city and amazed the people of Samaria,
saying that he was someone great. 10 All
of them, from the least to the greatest,
listened to him eagerly, saying, 'This
man is the power of God that is called
Great.' 11 And they listened eagerly to

[f] **7.44** Gk *he* [g] **7.46** Other ancient authorities read *for the God of Jacob* [h] **7.48** Gk *with hands* [i] **7.54** Gk *him* [j] **7.60** Gk *fell asleep* [k] **8.5** Other ancient authorities read *a city* [l] **8.5** Or *the Christ*

him because for a long time he had
amazed them with his magic. 12But
when they believed Philip, who was
proclaiming the good news about the
kingdom of God and the name of Jesus
Christ, they were baptized, both men
and women. 13Even Simon himself believed. After being baptized, he stayed
constantly with Philip and was amazed
when he saw the signs and great miracles that took place.

14 Now when the apostles at Jerusalem heard that Samaria had accepted
the word of God, they sent Peter and
John to them. 15The two went down and
prayed for them that they might receive
the Holy Spirit 16(for as yet the Spirit
had not come[m] upon any of them; they
had only been baptized in the name of
the Lord Jesus). 17Then Peter and John[n]
laid their hands on them, and they received the Holy Spirit. 18Now when
Simon saw that the Spirit was given
through the laying on of the apostles'
hands, he offered them money, 19say-
ing, 'Give me also this power so that
anyone on whom I lay my hands may
receive the Holy Spirit.' 20But Peter said
to him, 'May your silver perish with
you, because you thought you could obtain God's gift with money! 21You have
no part or share in this, for your heart is
not right before God. 22Repent therefore
of this wickedness of yours, and pray to
the Lord that, if possible, the intent of
your heart may be forgiven you. 23For I
see that you are in the gall of bitterness
and the chains of wickedness.' 24Simon
answered, 'Pray for me to the Lord, that
nothing of what you[o] have said may
happen to me.'

25 Now after Peter and John[p] had
testified and spoken the word of the
Lord, they returned to Jerusalem, proclaiming the good news to many villages of the Samaritans.

PHILIP AND THE ETHIOPIAN EUNUCH

26 Then an angel of the Lord said
to Philip, 'Get up and go towards the
south[q] to the road that goes down from
Jerusalem to Gaza.' (This is a wilderness road.) 27So he got up and went.
Now there was an Ethiopian eunuch,
a court official of the Candace, queen
of the Ethiopians, in charge of her entire treasury. He had come to Jerusalem
to worship 28and was returning home;
seated in his chariot, he was reading
the prophet Isaiah. 29Then the Spirit
said to Philip, 'Go over to this chariot
and join it.' 30So Philip ran up to it and
heard him reading the prophet Isaiah.
He asked, 'Do you understand what you
are reading?' 31He replied, 'How can I,
unless someone guides me?' And he invited Philip to get in and sit beside him.
32Now the passage of the scripture that
he was reading was this:

'Like a sheep he was led to
the slaughter,
and like a lamb silent
before its shearer,
so he does not open his mouth.
33 In his humiliation justice
was denied him.
Who can describe his generation?
For his life is taken away
from the earth.'

34The eunuch asked Philip, 'About
whom, may I ask you, does the prophet
say this, about himself or about someone else?' 35Then Philip began to speak,
and starting with this scripture, he proclaimed to him the good news about
Jesus. 36As they were going along the
road, they came to some water; and
the eunuch said, 'Look, here is water!
What is to prevent me from being baptized?'[r] 38He commanded the chariot
to stop, and both of them, Philip and
the eunuch, went down into the water,
and Philip[s] baptized him. 39When they
came up out of the water, the Spirit of
the Lord snatched Philip away; the eunuch saw him no more, and went on
his way rejoicing. 40But Philip found
himself at Azotus, and as he was passing through the region, he proclaimed
the good news to all the towns until he
came to Caesarea.

THE CONVERSION OF SAUL

9 Meanwhile Saul, still breathing
threats and murder against the
disciples of the Lord, went to the high
priest 2and asked him for letters to the
synagogues at Damascus, so that if he
found any who belonged to the Way,
men or women, he might bring them
bound to Jerusalem. 3Now as he was going along and approaching Damascus,
suddenly a light from heaven flashed
around him. 4He fell to the ground

[m] **8.16** Gk *fallen* [n] **8.17** Gk *they* [o] **8.24** The Greek word for *you* and the verb *pray* are plural [p] **8.25** Gk *after they* [q] **8.26** Or *go at noon* [r] **8.36** Other ancient authorities add all or most of verse 37, *And Philip said, 'If you believe with all your heart, you may.' And he replied, 'I believe that Jesus Christ is the Son of God.'* [s] **8.38** Gk *he*

and heard a voice saying to him, 'Saul,
Saul, why do you persecute me?' 5He
asked, 'Who are you, Lord?' The reply
came, 'I am Jesus, whom you are persecuting. 6But get up and enter the city,
and you will be told what you are to do.'
7The men who were travelling with him
stood speechless because they heard the
voice but saw no one. 8Saul got up from
the ground, and though his eyes were
open, he could see nothing; so they led
him by the hand and brought him into
Damascus. 9For three days he was without sight, and neither ate nor drank.

10 Now there was a disciple in Damascus named Ananias. The Lord said
to him in a vision, 'Ananias.' He answered, 'Here I am, Lord.' 11The Lord
said to him, 'Get up and go to the street
called Straight, and at the house of Judas look for a man of Tarsus named Saul.
At this moment he is praying, 12and
he has seen in a vision[t] a man named
Ananias come in and lay his hands on
him so that he might regain his sight.'
13But Ananias answered, 'Lord, I have
heard from many about this man, how
much evil he has done to your saints in
Jerusalem; 14and here he has authority
from the chief priests to bind all who invoke your name.' 15But the Lord said to
him, 'Go, for he is an instrument whom
I have chosen to bring my name before
Gentiles and kings and before the people
of Israel; 16I myself will show him how
much he must suffer for the sake of my
name.' 17So Ananias went and entered
the house. He laid his hands on Saul[u]
and said, 'Brother Saul, the Lord Jesus,
who appeared to you on your way here,
has sent me so that you may regain your
sight and be filled with the Holy Spirit.'
18And immediately something like
scales fell from his eyes, and his sight
was restored. Then he got up and was
baptized, 19and after taking some food,
he regained his strength.

SAUL PREACHES IN DAMASCUS

For several days he was with the disciples in Damascus, 20and immediately
he began to proclaim Jesus in the synagogues, saying, 'He is the Son of God.'
21All who heard him were amazed and
said, 'Is not this the man who made
havoc in Jerusalem among those who
invoked this name? And has he not
come here for the purpose of bringing
them bound before the chief priests?'
22Saul became increasingly more powerful and confounded the Jews who lived
in Damascus by proving that Jesus[v] was
the Messiah.[w]

SAUL ESCAPES FROM THE JEWS

23 After some time had passed, the
Jews plotted to kill him, 24but their
plot became known to Saul. They were
watching the gates day and night so
that they might kill him; 25but his disciples took him by night and let him
down through an opening in the wall,[x]
lowering him in a basket.

SAUL IN JERUSALEM

26 When he had come to Jerusalem,
he attempted to join the disciples; and
they were all afraid of him, for they did
not believe that he was a disciple. 27But
Barnabas took him, brought him to the
apostles, and described for them how on
the road he had seen the Lord, who had
spoken to him, and how in Damascus he
had spoken boldly in the name of Jesus.
28So he went in and out among them in
Jerusalem, speaking boldly in the name
of the Lord. 29He spoke and argued with
the Hellenists; but they were attempt-
ing to kill him. 30When the believers[y]
learned of it, they brought him down to
Caesarea and sent him off to Tarsus.

31 Meanwhile the church throughout Judea, Galilee, and Samaria had
peace and was built up. Living in the
fear of the Lord and in the comfort of
the Holy Spirit, it increased in numbers.

THE HEALING OF AENEAS

32 Now as Peter went here and
there among all the believers,[z] he came
down also to the saints living in Lydda.
33There he found a man named Aeneas, who had been bedridden for eight
years, for he was paralysed. 34Peter said
to him, 'Aeneas, Jesus Christ heals you;
get up and make your bed!' And immediately he got up. 35And all the residents of Lydda and Sharon saw him and
turned to the Lord.

PETER IN LYDDA AND JOPPA

36 Now in Joppa there was a disciple whose name was Tabitha, which
in Greek is Dorcas.[a] She was devoted
to good works and acts of charity. 37At
that time she became ill and died. When

[t] **9.12** Other ancient authorities lack *in a vision*
[u] **9.17** Gk *him* [v] **9.22** Gk *that this* [w] **9.22** Or *the Christ* [x] **9.25** Gk *through the wall*
[y] **9.30** Gk *brothers* [z] **9.32** Gk *all of them*
[a] **9.36** The name Tabitha in Aramaic and the name Dorcas in Greek mean *a gazelle*

they had washed her, they laid her in a
room upstairs. 38Since Lydda was near
Joppa, the disciples, who heard that Peter was there, sent two men to him with
the request, 'Please come to us without
delay.' 39So Peter got up and went with
them; and when he arrived, they took
him to the room upstairs. All the widows stood beside him, weeping and
showing tunics and other clothing that
Dorcas had made while she was with
them. 40Peter put all of them outside,
and then he knelt down and prayed. He
turned to the body and said, 'Tabitha,
get up.' Then she opened her eyes, and
seeing Peter, she sat up. 41He gave her
his hand and helped her up. Then calling the saints and widows, he showed
her to be alive. 42This became known
throughout Joppa, and many believed
in the Lord. 43Meanwhile he stayed in
Joppa for some time with a certain Simon, a tanner.

PETER AND CORNELIUS

10 In Caesarea there was a man
named Cornelius, a centurion of
the Italian Cohort, as it was called. 2He
was a devout man who feared God with
all his household; he gave alms generously to the people and prayed constantly to God. 3One afternoon at about
three o'clock he had a vision in which
he clearly saw an angel of God coming
in and saying to him, 'Cornelius.' 4He
stared at him in terror and said, 'What
is it, Lord?' He answered, 'Your prayers
and your alms have ascended as a memorial before God. 5Now send men to
Joppa for a certain Simon who is called
Peter; 6he is lodging with Simon, a
tanner, whose house is by the seaside.'
7When the angel who spoke to him had
left, he called two of his slaves and a
devout soldier from the ranks of those
who served him, 8and after telling them
everything, he sent them to Joppa.

9 About noon the next day, as they
were on their journey and approaching
the city, Peter went up on the roof to
pray. 10He became hungry and wanted
something to eat; and while it was being prepared, he fell into a trance. 11He
saw the heaven opened and something
like a large sheet coming down, being
lowered to the ground by its four corners. 12In it were all kinds of four-footed
creatures and reptiles and birds of the
air. 13Then he heard a voice saying, 'Get
up, Peter; kill and eat.' 14But Peter said,
'By no means, Lord; for I have never
eaten anything that is profane or unclean.' 15The voice said to him again, a
second time, 'What God has made clean,
you must not call profane.' 16This happened three times, and the thing was
suddenly taken up to heaven.

17 Now while Peter was greatly puz-
zled about what to make of the vision
that he had seen, suddenly the men
sent by Cornelius appeared. They were
asking for Simon's house and were
standing by the gate. 18They called out
to ask whether Simon, who was called
Peter, was staying there. 19While Peter
was still thinking about the vision, the
Spirit said to him, 'Look, three[b] men
are searching for you. 20Now get up, go
down, and go with them without hes-
itation; for I have sent them.' 21So Peter went down to the men and said, 'I
am the one you are looking for; what is
the reason for your coming?' 22They answered, 'Cornelius, a centurion, an upright and God-fearing man, who is well
spoken of by the whole Jewish nation,
was directed by a holy angel to send for
you to come to his house and to hear
what you have to say.' 23So Peter[c] invited them in and gave them lodging.

The next day he got up and went with
them, and some of the believers[d] from
Joppa accompanied him. 24The following day they came to Caesarea. Cornelius was expecting them and had called
together his relatives and close friends.
25On Peter's arrival Cornelius met him,
and falling at his feet, worshipped him.
26But Peter made him get up, saying,
'Stand up; I am only a mortal.' 27And
as he talked with him, he went in and
found that many had assembled; 28and
he said to them, 'You yourselves know
that it is unlawful for a Jew to associate
with or to visit a Gentile; but God has
shown me that I should not call anyone
profane or unclean. 29So when I was
sent for, I came without objection. Now
may I ask why you sent for me?'

30 Cornelius replied, 'Four days ago
at this very hour, at three o'clock, I was
praying in my house when suddenly a
man in dazzling clothes stood before
me. 31He said, "Cornelius, your prayer
has been heard and your alms have been
remembered before God. 32Send therefore to Joppa and ask for Simon, who is
called Peter; he is staying in the home
of Simon, a tanner, by the sea." 33There-

[b] **10.19** One ancient authority reads *two*; others lack the word [c] **10.23** Gk *he* [d] **10.23** Gk *brothers*

fore I sent for you immediately, and you
have been kind enough to come. So now
all of us are here in the presence of God
to listen to all that the Lord has commanded you to say.'

GENTILES HEAR THE GOOD NEWS

34 Then Peter began to speak to
them: 'I truly understand that God
shows no partiality, 35but in every nation anyone who fears him and does
what is right is acceptable to him. 36You
know the message he sent to the people of Israel, preaching peace by Jesus
Christ—he is Lord of all. 37That message
spread throughout Judea, beginning in
Galilee after the baptism that John announced: 38how God anointed Jesus of
Nazareth with the Holy Spirit and with
power; how he went about doing good
and healing all who were oppressed by
the devil, for God was with him. 39We
are witnesses to all that he did both in
Judea and in Jerusalem. They put him
to death by hanging him on a tree;
40but God raised him on the third day
and allowed him to appear, 41not to all
the people but to us who were chosen
by God as witnesses, and who ate and
drank with him after he rose from the
dead. 42He commanded us to preach to
the people and to testify that he is the
one ordained by God as judge of the
living and the dead. 43All the prophets
testify about him that everyone who believes in him receives forgiveness of sins
through his name.'

GENTILES RECEIVE THE HOLY SPIRIT

44 While Peter was still speaking,
the Holy Spirit fell upon all who heard
the word. 45The circumcised believers who had come with Peter were astounded that the gift of the Holy Spirit
had been poured out even on the Gentiles, 46for they heard them speaking in
tongues and extolling God. Then Peter
said, 47'Can anyone withhold the water
for baptizing these people who have received the Holy Spirit just as we have?'
48So he ordered them to be baptized in
the name of Jesus Christ. Then they invited him to stay for several days.

PETER'S REPORT TO THE CHURCH AT JERUSALEM

11 Now the apostles and the believers[e] who were in Judea heard
that the Gentiles had also accepted the
word of God. 2So when Peter went up
to Jerusalem, the circumcised believers[f]
criticized him, 3saying, 'Why did you
go to uncircumcised men and eat with
them?' 4Then Peter began to explain it
to them, step by step, saying, 5'I was
in the city of Joppa praying, and in a
trance I saw a vision. There was something like a large sheet coming down
from heaven, being lowered by its four
corners; and it came close to me. 6As I
looked at it closely I saw four-footed animals, beasts of prey, reptiles, and birds
of the air. 7I also heard a voice saying to
me, "Get up, Peter; kill and eat." 8But I
replied, "By no means, Lord; for nothing
profane or unclean has ever entered my
mouth." 9But a second time the voice
answered from heaven, "What God has
made clean, you must not call profane."
10This happened three times; then everything was pulled up again to heaven.
11At that very moment three men, sent
to me from Caesarea, arrived at the
house where we were. 12The Spirit told
me to go with them and not to make
a distinction between them and us.[g]
These six brothers also accompanied
me, and we entered the man's house.
13He told us how he had seen the angel
standing in his house and saying, "Send
to Joppa and bring Simon, who is called
Peter; 14he will give you a message by
which you and your entire household
will be saved." 15And as I began to speak,
the Holy Spirit fell upon them just as it
had upon us at the beginning. 16And I
remembered the word of the Lord, how
he had said, "John baptized with water, but you will be baptized with the
Holy Spirit." 17If then God gave them
the same gift that he gave us when we
believed in the Lord Jesus Christ, who
was I that I could hinder God?' 18When
they heard this, they were silenced. And
they praised God, saying, 'Then God has
given even to the Gentiles the repentance that leads to life.'

THE CHURCH IN ANTIOCH

19 Now those who were scattered because of the persecution that took place
over Stephen travelled as far as Phoenicia, Cyprus, and Antioch, and they
spoke the word to no one except Jews.
20But among them were some men of
Cyprus and Cyrene who, on coming to
Antioch, spoke to the Hellenists[h] also,
proclaiming the Lord Jesus. 21The hand
of the Lord was with them, and a great

[e] 11.1 Gk *brothers* [f] 11.2 Gk lacks *believers*
[g] 11.12 Or *not to hesitate* [h] 11.20 Other
ancient authorities read *Greeks*

number became believers and turned to the Lord. 22 News of this came to the ears of the church in Jerusalem, and they sent Barnabas to Antioch. 23 When he came and saw the grace of God, he rejoiced, and he exhorted them all to remain faithful to the Lord with steadfast devotion; 24 for he was a good man, full of the Holy Spirit and of faith. And a great many people were brought to the Lord. 25 Then Barnabas went to Tarsus to look for Saul, 26 and when he had found him, he brought him to Antioch. So it was that for an entire year they associated with[i] the church and taught a great many people, and it was in Antioch that the disciples were first called 'Christians'.

27 At that time prophets came down from Jerusalem to Antioch. 28 One of them named Agabus stood up and predicted by the Spirit that there would be a severe famine over all the world; and this took place during the reign of Claudius. 29 The disciples determined that according to their ability, each would send relief to the believers[j] living in Judea; 30 this they did, sending it to the elders by Barnabas and Saul.

JAMES KILLED AND PETER IMPRISONED

12 About that time King Herod laid violent hands upon some who belonged to the church. 2 He had James, the brother of John, killed with the sword. 3 After he saw that it pleased the Jews, he proceeded to arrest Peter also. (This was during the festival of Unleavened Bread.) 4 When he had seized him, he put him in prison and handed him over to four squads of soldiers to guard him, intending to bring him out to the people after the Passover. 5 While Peter was kept in prison, the church prayed fervently to God for him.

PETER DELIVERED FROM PRISON

6 The very night before Herod was going to bring him out, Peter, bound with two chains, was sleeping between two soldiers, while guards in front of the door were keeping watch over the prison. 7 Suddenly an angel of the Lord appeared and a light shone in the cell. He tapped Peter on the side and woke him, saying, 'Get up quickly.' And the chains fell off his wrists. 8 The angel said to him, 'Fasten your belt and put on your sandals.' He did so. Then he said to him, 'Wrap your cloak around you and follow me.' 9 Peter[k] went out and followed him; he did not realize that what was happening with the angel's help was real; he thought he was seeing a vision. 10 After they had passed the first and the second guard, they came before the iron gate leading into the city. It opened for them of its own accord, and they went outside and walked along a lane, when suddenly the angel left him. 11 Then Peter came to himself and said, 'Now I am sure that the Lord has sent his angel and rescued me from the hands of Herod and from all that the Jewish people were expecting.'

12 As soon as he realized this, he went to the house of Mary, the mother of John whose other name was Mark, where many had gathered and were praying. 13 When he knocked at the outer gate, a maid named Rhoda came to answer. 14 On recognizing Peter's voice, she was so overjoyed that, instead of opening the gate, she ran in and announced that Peter was standing at the gate. 15 They said to her, 'You are out of your mind!' But she insisted that it was so. They said, 'It is his angel.' 16 Meanwhile, Peter continued knocking; and when they opened the gate, they saw him and were amazed. 17 He motioned to them with his hand to be silent, and described for them how the Lord had brought him out of the prison. And he added, 'Tell this to James and to the believers.'[l] Then he left and went to another place.

18 When morning came, there was no small commotion among the soldiers over what had become of Peter. 19 When Herod had searched for him and could not find him, he examined the guards and ordered them to be put to death. Then he went down from Judea to Caesarea and stayed there.

THE DEATH OF HEROD

20 Now Herod[m] was angry with the people of Tyre and Sidon. So they came to him in a body; and after winning over Blastus, the king's chamberlain, they asked for a reconciliation, because their country depended on the king's country for food. 21 On an appointed day Herod put on his royal robes, took his seat on the platform, and delivered a public address to them. 22 The people kept shouting, 'The voice of a god, and not of a mortal!' 23 And immediately, because he

[i] **11.26** Or *were guests of* [j] **11.29** Gk *brothers*
[k] **12.9** Gk *He* [l] **12.17** Gk *brothers*
[m] **12.20** Gk *he*

had not given the glory to God, an angel of the Lord struck him down, and he
was eaten by worms and died.
24 But the word of God continued to
advance and gain adherents. 25 Then after completing their mission Barnabas
and Saul returned to[n] Jerusalem and
brought with them John, whose other
name was Mark.

BARNABAS AND SAUL COMMISSIONED

13 Now in the church at Antioch
there were prophets and teachers: Barnabas, Simeon who was called
Niger, Lucius of Cyrene, Manaen a member of the court of Herod the ruler,[o] and
Saul. 2 While they were worshipping the
Lord and fasting, the Holy Spirit said,
'Set apart for me Barnabas and Saul for
the work to which I have called them.'
3 Then after fasting and praying they laid
their hands on them and sent them off.

THE APOSTLES PREACH IN CYPRUS

4 So, being sent out by the Holy
Spirit, they went down to Seleucia; and
from there they sailed to Cyprus. 5 When
they arrived at Salamis, they proclaimed
the word of God in the synagogues of the
Jews. And they had John also to assist
them. 6 When they had gone through the
whole island as far as Paphos, they met a
certain magician, a Jewish false prophet,
named Bar-Jesus. 7 He was with the proconsul, Sergius Paulus, an intelligent
man, who summoned Barnabas and
Saul and wanted to hear the word of God.
8 But the magician Elymas (for that is the
translation of his name) opposed them
and tried to turn the proconsul away
from the faith. 9 But Saul, also known as
Paul, filled with the Holy Spirit, looked
intently at him 10 and said, 'You son of
the devil, you enemy of all righteousness,
full of all deceit and villainy, will you not
stop making crooked the straight paths
of the Lord? 11 And now listen—the hand
of the Lord is against you, and you will
be blind for a while, unable to see the
sun.' Immediately mist and darkness
came over him, and he went about groping for someone to lead him by the hand.
12 When the proconsul saw what had
happened, he believed, for he was astonished at the teaching about the Lord.

PAUL AND BARNABAS IN ANTIOCH OF PISIDIA

13 Then Paul and his companions set
sail from Paphos and came to Perga in
Pamphylia. John, however, left them
and returned to Jerusalem; 14 but they
went on from Perga and came to Antioch in Pisidia. And on the sabbath day
they went into the synagogue and sat
down. 15 After the reading of the law
and the prophets, the officials of the
synagogue sent them a message, saying, 'Brothers, if you have any word of
exhortation for the people, give it.' 16 So
Paul stood up and with a gesture began
to speak:
'You Israelites,[p] and others who fear
God, listen. 17 The God of this people Israel chose our ancestors and made the
people great during their stay in the
land of Egypt, and with uplifted arm
he led them out of it. 18 For about forty
years he put up with[q] them in the wilderness. 19 After he had destroyed seven
nations in the land of Canaan, he gave
them their land as an inheritance 20 for
about four hundred and fifty years. After that he gave them judges until the
time of the prophet Samuel. 21 Then they
asked for a king; and God gave them
Saul son of Kish, a man of the tribe of
Benjamin, who reigned for forty years.
22 When he had removed him, he made
David their king. In his testimony about
him he said, "I have found David, son of
Jesse, to be a man after my heart, who
will carry out all my wishes." 23 Of this
man's posterity God has brought to Israel a Saviour, Jesus, as he promised;
24 before his coming John had already
proclaimed a baptism of repentance to
all the people of Israel. 25 And as John
was finishing his work, he said, "What
do you suppose that I am? I am not he.
No, but one is coming after me; I am not
worthy to untie the thong of the sandals[r] on his feet."
26 'My brothers, you descendants of
Abraham's family, and others who fear
God, to us[s] the message of this salvation has been sent. 27 Because the residents of Jerusalem and their leaders did
not recognize him or understand the
words of the prophets that are read every sabbath, they fulfilled those words
by condemning him. 28 Even though
they found no cause for a sentence of
death, they asked Pilate to have him
killed. 29 When they had carried out everything that was written about him,

[n] **12.25** Other ancient authorities read *from*
[o] **13.1** Gk *tetrarch* [p] **13.16** Gk *Men, Israelites*
[q] **13.18** Other ancient authorities read *cared for*
[r] **13.25** Gk *untie the sandals* [s] **13.26** Other ancient authorities read *you*

they took him down from the tree and
laid him in a tomb. 30But God raised
him from the dead; 31and for many days
he appeared to those who came up with
him from Galilee to Jerusalem, and they
are now his witnesses to the people.
32And we bring you the good news that
what God promised to our ancestors
33he has fulfilled for us, their children,
by raising Jesus; as also it is written in
the second psalm,

"You are my Son;
today I have begotten you."

34As to his raising him from the dead,
no more to return to corruption, he has
spoken in this way,

"I will give you the holy promises
made to David."

35Therefore he has also said in another
psalm,

"You will not let your Holy One
experience corruption."

36For David, after he had served the
purpose of God in his own generation,
died,[t] was laid beside his ancestors, and
experienced corruption; 37but he whom
God raised up experienced no corruption. 38Let it be known to you therefore,
my brothers, that through this man
forgiveness of sins is proclaimed to you;
39by this Jesus[u] everyone who believes is
set free from all those sins[v] from which
you could not be freed by the law of Moses. 40Beware, therefore, that what the
prophets said does not happen to you:

41 "Look, you scoffers!
Be amazed and perish,
for in your days I am doing a work,
a work that you will never believe,
even if someone tells you.""

42 As Paul and Barnabas[w] were going out, the people urged them to speak
about these things again the next sabbath. 43When the meeting of the synagogue broke up, many Jews and devout
converts to Judaism followed Paul and
Barnabas, who spoke to them and urged
them to continue in the grace of God.

44 The next sabbath almost the
whole city gathered to hear the word of
the Lord.[x] 45But when the Jews saw the
crowds, they were filled with jealousy;
and blaspheming, they contradicted
what was spoken by Paul. 46Then both
Paul and Barnabas spoke out boldly,
saying, 'It was necessary that the word
of God should be spoken first to you.
Since you reject it and judge yourselves
to be unworthy of eternal life, we are
now turning to the Gentiles. 47For so
the Lord has commanded us, saying,

"I have set you to be a light
for the Gentiles,
so that you may bring salvation
to the ends of the earth." '

48 When the Gentiles heard this, they
were glad and praised the word of the
Lord; and as many as had been destined
for eternal life became believers. 49Thus
the word of the Lord spread throughout
the region. 50But the Jews incited the
devout women of high standing and the
leading men of the city, and stirred up
persecution against Paul and Barnabas,
and drove them out of their region. 51So
they shook the dust off their feet in protest against them, and went to Iconium.
52And the disciples were filled with joy
and with the Holy Spirit.

PAUL AND BARNABAS IN ICONIUM

14 The same thing occurred in Iconium, where Paul and Barna-
bas[y] went into the Jewish synagogue
and spoke in such a way that a great
number of both Jews and Greeks became believers. 2But the unbelieving
Jews stirred up the Gentiles and poisoned their minds against the brothers.
3So they remained for a long time,
speaking boldly for the Lord, who testified to the word of his grace by granting
signs and wonders to be done through
them. 4But the residents of the city
were divided; some sided with the Jews,
and some with the apostles. 5And when
an attempt was made by both Gentiles
and Jews, with their rulers, to maltreat
them and to stone them, 6the apostles[z] learned of it and fled to Lystra and
Derbe, cities of Lycaonia, and to the surrounding country; 7and there they continued proclaiming the good news.

PAUL AND BARNABAS IN LYSTRA AND DERBE

8 In Lystra there was a man sitting
who could not use his feet and had
never walked, for he had been crippled from birth. 9He listened to Paul
as he was speaking. And Paul, looking at him intently and seeing that he
had faith to be healed, 10said in a loud
voice, 'Stand upright on your feet.' And
the man[a] sprang up and began to walk.
11When the crowds saw what Paul had
done, they shouted in the Lycaonian
language, 'The gods have come down

[t] 13.36 Gk *fell asleep* [u] 13.39 Gk *this*
[v] 13.39 Gk *all* [w] 13.42 Gk *they* [x] 13.44 Other ancient authorities read *God* [y] 14.1 Gk *they*
[z] 14.6 Gk *they* [a] 14.10 Gk *he*

to us in human form!' 12Barnabas they
called Zeus, and Paul they called Hermes, because he was the chief speaker.
13The priest of Zeus, whose temple was
just outside the city,[b] brought oxen and
garlands to the gates; he and the crowds
wanted to offer sacrifice. 14When the
apostles Barnabas and Paul heard of it,
they tore their clothes and rushed out
into the crowd, shouting, 15'Friends,[c]
why are you doing this? We are mortals just like you, and we bring you good
news, that you should turn from these
worthless things to the living God,
who made the heaven and the earth
and the sea and all that is in them. 16In
past generations he allowed all the nations to follow their own ways; 17yet he
has not left himself without a witness
in doing good—giving you rains from
heaven and fruitful seasons, and filling
you with food and your hearts with joy.'
18Even with these words, they scarcely
restrained the crowds from offering sacrifice to them.

19 But Jews came there from Antioch
and Iconium and won over the crowds.
Then they stoned Paul and dragged
him out of the city, supposing that he
was dead. 20But when the disciples surrounded him, he got up and went into
the city. The next day he went on with
Barnabas to Derbe.

THE RETURN TO ANTIOCH IN SYRIA

21 After they had proclaimed the
good news to that city and had made
many disciples, they returned to Lystra, then on to Iconium and Antioch.
22There they strengthened the souls
of the disciples and encouraged them
to continue in the faith, saying, 'It is
through many persecutions that we
must enter the kingdom of God.' 23And
after they had appointed elders for them
in each church, with prayer and fasting they entrusted them to the Lord in
whom they had come to believe.

24 Then they passed through Pisidia
and came to Pamphylia. 25When they
had spoken the word in Perga, they
went down to Attalia. 26From there
they sailed back to Antioch, where they
had been commended to the grace of
God for the work[d] that they had completed. 27When they arrived, they called
the church together and related all that
God had done with them, and how he
had opened a door of faith for the Gentiles. 28And they stayed there with the
disciples for some time.

THE COUNCIL AT JERUSALEM

15 Then certain individuals came
down from Judea and were
teaching the brothers, 'Unless you are
circumcised according to the custom
of Moses, you cannot be saved.' 2And
after Paul and Barnabas had no small
dissension and debate with them, Paul
and Barnabas and some of the others
were appointed to go up to Jerusalem
to discuss this question with the apostles and the elders. 3So they were sent
on their way by the church, and as they
passed through both Phoenicia and Samaria, they reported the conversion of
the Gentiles, and brought great joy to
all the believers.[e] 4When they came to
Jerusalem, they were welcomed by the
church and the apostles and the elders,
and they reported all that God had done
with them. 5But some believers who belonged to the sect of the Pharisees stood
up and said, 'It is necessary for them to
be circumcised and ordered to keep the
law of Moses.'

6 The apostles and the elders met
together to consider this matter. 7Af-
ter there had been much debate, Peter
stood up and said to them, 'My brothers,[f] you know that in the early days God
made a choice among you, that I should
be the one through whom the Gentiles
would hear the message of the good
news and become believers. 8And God,
who knows the human heart, testified
to them by giving them the Holy Spirit,
just as he did to us; 9and in cleansing
their hearts by faith he has made no distinction between them and us. 10Now
therefore why are you putting God to
the test by placing on the neck of the
disciples a yoke that neither our ancestors nor we have been able to bear? 11On
the contrary, we believe that we will
be saved through the grace of the Lord
Jesus, just as they will.'

12 The whole assembly kept silence,
and listened to Barnabas and Paul
as they told of all the signs and wonders that God had done through them
among the Gentiles. 13After they finished speaking, James replied, 'My
brothers,[g] listen to me. 14Simeon has related how God first looked favourably on
the Gentiles, to take from among them
a people for his name. 15This agrees with

[b] 14.13 Or *The priest of Zeus-Outside-the-City*
[c] 14.15 Gk *Men* [d] 14.26 Or *committed in the grace of God to the work* [e] 15.3 Gk *brothers*
[f] 15.7 Gk *Men, brothers* [g] 15.13 Gk *Men, brothers*

the words of the prophets, as it is written,
16 "After this I will return,
and I will rebuild the dwelling of
David, which has fallen;
from its ruins I will rebuild it,
and I will set it up,
17 so that all other peoples may
seek the Lord—
even all the Gentiles over whom
my name has been called.
Thus says the Lord, who has
been making these things
18 known from long ago."[h]
19 Therefore I have reached the decision
that we should not trouble those Gentiles who are turning to God, 20 but we
should write to them to abstain only
from things polluted by idols and from
fornication and from whatever has been
strangled[i] and from blood. 21 For in every city, for generations past, Moses has
had those who proclaim him, for he has
been read aloud every sabbath in the
synagogues.'

THE COUNCIL'S LETTER TO GENTILE BELIEVERS

22 Then the apostles and the elders,
with the consent of the whole church,
decided to choose men from among their
members[j] and to send them to Antioch
with Paul and Barnabas. They sent Judas called Barsabbas, and Silas, leaders
among the brothers, 23 with the following letter: 'The brothers, both the apostles and the elders, to the believers[k] of
Gentile origin in Antioch and Syria and
Cilicia, greetings. 24 Since we have heard
that certain persons who have gone out
from us, though with no instructions
from us, have said things to disturb you
and have unsettled your minds,[l] 25 we
have decided unanimously to choose
representatives[m] and send them to you,
along with our beloved Barnabas and
Paul, 26 who have risked their lives for
the sake of our Lord Jesus Christ. 27 We
have therefore sent Judas and Silas,
who themselves will tell you the same
things by word of mouth. 28 For it has
seemed good to the Holy Spirit and to
us to impose on you no further burden
than these essentials: 29 that you abstain
from what has been sacrificed to idols
and from blood and from what is strangled[n] and from fornication. If you keep
yourselves from these, you will do well.
Farewell.'

30 So they were sent off and went
down to Antioch. When they gathered
the congregation together, they delivered the letter. 31 When its members[o]
read it, they rejoiced at the exhortation.
32 Judas and Silas, who were themselves
prophets, said much to encourage and
strengthen the believers.[p] 33 After they
had been there for some time, they were
sent off in peace by the believers[q] to
those who had sent them.[r] 35 But Paul
and Barnabas remained in Antioch, and
there, with many others, they taught
and proclaimed the word of the Lord.

PAUL AND BARNABAS SEPARATE

36 After some days Paul said to Barnabas, 'Come, let us return and visit
the believers[s] in every city where we
proclaimed the word of the Lord and
see how they are doing.' 37 Barnabas
wanted to take with them John called
Mark. 38 But Paul decided not to take
with them one who had deserted them
in Pamphylia and had not accompanied
them in the work. 39 The disagreement
became so sharp that they parted company; Barnabas took Mark with him
and sailed away to Cyprus. 40 But Paul
chose Silas and set out, the believers[t]
commending him to the grace of the
Lord. 41 He went through Syria and Cilicia, strengthening the churches.

TIMOTHY JOINS PAUL AND SILAS

16 Paul[u] went on also to Derbe and
to Lystra, where there was a disciple named Timothy, the son of a Jewish woman who was a believer; but his
father was a Greek. 2 He was well spoken
of by the believers[v] in Lystra and Iconium. 3 Paul wanted Timothy to accompany him; and he took him and had him
circumcised because of the Jews who
were in those places, for they all knew
that his father was a Greek. 4 As they
went from town to town, they delivered
to them for observance the decisions
that had been reached by the apostles
and elders who were in Jerusalem. 5 So

[h] 15.18 Other ancient authorities read *things. 18 Known to God from of old are all his works."*
[i] 15.20 Other ancient authorities lack *and from whatever has been strangled* [j] 15.22 Gk *from among them* [k] 15.23 Gk *brothers*
[l] 15.24 Other ancient authorities add *saying, "You must be circumcised and keep the law",*
[m] 15.25 Gk *men* [n] 15.29 Other ancient authorities lack *and from what is strangled*
[o] 15.31 Gk *When they* [p] 15.32 Gk *brothers*
[q] 15.33 Gk *brothers* [r] 15.33 Other ancient authorities add verse 34, *But it seemed good to Silas to remain there* [s] 15.36 Gk *brothers*
[t] 15.40 Gk *brothers* [u] 16.1 Gk *He*
[v] 16.2 Gk *brothers*

the churches were strengthened in the
faith and increased in numbers daily.

PAUL'S VISION OF THE MAN OF MACEDONIA

6 They went through the region of
Phrygia and Galatia, having been forbidden by the Holy Spirit to speak the
word in Asia. 7 When they had come opposite Mysia, they attempted to go into
Bithynia, but the Spirit of Jesus did not
allow them; 8 so, passing by Mysia, they
went down to Troas. 9 During the night
Paul had a vision: there stood a man of
Macedonia pleading with him and saying, 'Come over to Macedonia and help
us.' 10 When he had seen the vision, we
immediately tried to cross over to Macedonia, being convinced that God had
called us to proclaim the good news to
them.

THE CONVERSION OF LYDIA

11 We set sail from Troas and took
a straight course to Samothrace, the
following day to Neapolis, 12 and from
there to Philippi, which is a leading city
of the district[w] of Macedonia and a Roman colony. We remained in this city
for some days. 13 On the sabbath day
we went outside the gate by the river,
where we supposed there was a place
of prayer; and we sat down and spoke
to the women who had gathered there.
14 A certain woman named Lydia, a
worshipper of God, was listening to us;
she was from the city of Thyatira and a
dealer in purple cloth. The Lord opened
her heart to listen eagerly to what was
said by Paul. 15 When she and her household were baptized, she urged us, saying, 'If you have judged me to be faithful
to the Lord, come and stay at my home.'
And she prevailed upon us.

PAUL AND SILAS IN PRISON

16 One day, as we were going to the
place of prayer, we met a slave-girl who
had a spirit of divination and brought
her owners a great deal of money by
fortune-telling. 17 While she followed
Paul and us, she would cry out, 'These
men are slaves of the Most High God,
who proclaim to you[x] a way of salvation.' 18 She kept doing this for many
days. But Paul, very much annoyed,
turned and said to the spirit, 'I order you
in the name of Jesus Christ to come out
of her.' And it came out that very hour.

19 But when her owners saw that
their hope of making money was gone,
they seized Paul and Silas and dragged
them into the market-place before the
authorities. 20 When they had brought
them before the magistrates, they said,
'These men are disturbing our city; they
are Jews 21 and are advocating customs
that are not lawful for us as Romans to
adopt or observe.' 22 The crowd joined
in attacking them, and the magistrates
had them stripped of their clothing and
ordered them to be beaten with rods.
23 After they had given them a severe
flogging, they threw them into prison
and ordered the jailer to keep them securely. 24 Following these instructions,
he put them in the innermost cell and
fastened their feet in the stocks.

25 About midnight Paul and Silas were praying and singing hymns
to God, and the prisoners were listening to them. 26 Suddenly there was an
earthquake, so violent that the foundations of the prison were shaken; and
immediately all the doors were opened
and everyone's chains were unfastened.
27 When the jailer woke up and saw
the prison doors wide open, he drew
his sword and was about to kill himself, since he supposed that the prisoners had escaped. 28 But Paul shouted
in a loud voice, 'Do not harm yourself,
for we are all here.' 29 The jailer[y] called
for lights, and rushing in, he fell down
trembling before Paul and Silas. 30 Then
he brought them outside and said, 'Sirs,
what must I do to be saved?' 31 They answered, 'Believe on the Lord Jesus, and
you will be saved, you and your household.' 32 They spoke the word of the Lord[z]
to him and to all who were in his house.
33 At the same hour of the night he took
them and washed their wounds; then
he and his entire family were baptized
without delay. 34 He brought them up
into the house and set food before them;
and he and his entire household rejoiced
that he had become a believer in God.

35 When morning came, the magistrates sent the police, saying, 'Let those
men go.' 36 And the jailer reported the
message to Paul, saying, 'The magistrates sent word to let you go; therefore
come out now and go in peace.' 37 But Paul
replied, 'They have beaten us in public,
uncondemned, men who are Roman citizens, and have thrown us into prison;
and now are they going to discharge

[w] **16.12** Other authorities read *a city of the first district* [x] **16.17** Other ancient authorities read *to us* [y] **16.29** Gk *He* [z] **16.32** Other ancient authorities read *word of God*

us in secret? Certainly not! Let them come and take us out themselves.' 38 The police reported these words to the magistrates, and they were afraid when they heard that they were Roman citizens; 39 so they came and apologized to them. And they took them out and asked them to leave the city. 40 After leaving the prison they went to Lydia's home; and when they had seen and encouraged the brothers and sisters[a] there, they departed.

THE UPROAR IN THESSALONICA

17 After Paul and Silas[b] had passed through Amphipolis and Apollonia, they came to Thessalonica, where there was a synagogue of the Jews. 2 And Paul went in, as was his custom, and on three sabbath days argued with them from the scriptures, 3 explaining and proving that it was necessary for the Messiah[c] to suffer and to rise from the dead, and saying, 'This is the Messiah,[d] Jesus whom I am proclaiming to you.' 4 Some of them were persuaded and joined Paul and Silas, as did a great many of the devout Greeks and not a few of the leading women. 5 But the Jews became jealous, and with the help of some ruffians in the market-places they formed a mob and set the city in an uproar. While they were searching for Paul and Silas to bring them out to the assembly, they attacked Jason's house. 6 When they could not find them, they dragged Jason and some believers[e] before the city authorities,[f] shouting, 'These people who have been turning the world upside down have come here also, 7 and Jason has entertained them as guests. They are all acting contrary to the decrees of the emperor, saying that there is another king named Jesus.' 8 The people and the city officials were disturbed when they heard this, 9 and after they had taken bail from Jason and the others, they let them go.

PAUL AND SILAS IN BEROEA

10 That very night the believers[g] sent Paul and Silas off to Beroea; and when they arrived, they went to the Jewish synagogue. 11 These Jews were more receptive than those in Thessalonica, for they welcomed the message very eagerly and examined the scriptures every day to see whether these things were so. 12 Many of them therefore believed, including not a few Greek women and men of high standing. 13 But when the Jews of Thessalonica learned that the word of God had been proclaimed by Paul in Beroea as well, they came there too, to stir up and incite the crowds. 14 Then the believers[h] immediately sent Paul away to the coast, but Silas and Timothy remained behind. 15 Those who conducted Paul brought him as far as Athens; and after receiving instructions to have Silas and Timothy join him as soon as possible, they left him.

PAUL IN ATHENS

16 While Paul was waiting for them in Athens, he was deeply distressed to see that the city was full of idols. 17 So he argued in the synagogue with the Jews and the devout persons, and also in the market-place[i] every day with those who happened to be there. 18 Also some Epicurean and Stoic philosophers debated with him. Some said, 'What does this babbler want to say?' Others said, 'He seems to be a proclaimer of foreign divinities.' (This was because he was telling the good news about Jesus and the resurrection.) 19 So they took him and brought him to the Areopagus and asked him, 'May we know what this new teaching is that you are presenting? 20 It sounds rather strange to us, so we would like to know what it means.' 21 Now all the Athenians and the foreigners living there would spend their time in nothing but telling or hearing something new.

22 Then Paul stood in front of the Areopagus and said, 'Athenians, I see how extremely religious you are in every way. 23 For as I went through the city and looked carefully at the objects of your worship, I found among them an altar with the inscription, "To an unknown god." What therefore you worship as unknown, this I proclaim to you. 24 The God who made the world and everything in it, he who is Lord of heaven and earth, does not live in shrines made by human hands, 25 nor is he served by human hands, as though he needed anything, since he himself gives to all mortals life and breath and all things. 26 From one ancestor[j] he made all nations to inhabit the whole earth, and he allotted the times of their existence and

[a] **16.40** Gk *brothers* [b] **17.1** Gk *they* [c] **17.3** Or *the Christ* [d] **17.3** Or *the Christ* [e] **17.6** Gk *brothers* [f] **17.6** Gk *politarchs* [g] **17.10** Gk *brothers* [h] **17.14** Gk *brothers* [i] **17.17** Or *civic centre*; Gk *agora* [j] **17.26** Gk *From one*; other ancient authorities read *From one blood*

the boundaries of the places where they
would live, 27so that they would search
for God[k] and perhaps grope for him and
find him—though indeed he is not far
from each one of us. 28For "In him we
live and move and have our being"; as
even some of your own poets have said,
"For we too are his offspring."
29Since we are God's offspring, we ought
not to think that the deity is like gold, or
silver, or stone, an image formed by the
art and imagination of mortals. 30While
God has overlooked the times of human
ignorance, now he commands all people
everywhere to repent, 31because he has
fixed a day on which he will have the
world judged in righteousness by a man
whom he has appointed, and of this he
has given assurance to all by raising
him from the dead.'
32 When they heard of the resurrection of the dead, some scoffed; but others said, 'We will hear you again about
this.' 33At that point Paul left them.
34But some of them joined him and became believers, including Dionysius the
Areopagite and a woman named Dama-
ris, and others with them.

PAUL IN CORINTH

18 After this Paul[l] left Athens and
went to Corinth. 2There he found
a Jew named Aquila, a native of Pontus,
who had recently come from Italy with
his wife Priscilla, because Claudius had
ordered all Jews to leave Rome. Paul[m]
went to see them, 3and, because he was
of the same trade, he stayed with them,
and they worked together—by trade
they were tentmakers. 4Every sabbath
he would argue in the synagogue and
would try to convince Jews and Greeks.
5 When Silas and Timothy arrived
from Macedonia, Paul was occupied
with proclaiming the word,[n] testifying
to the Jews that the Messiah[o] was Jesus.
6When they opposed and reviled him,
in protest he shook the dust from his
clothes[p] and said to them, 'Your blood
be on your own heads! I am innocent.
From now on I will go to the Gentiles.'
7Then he left the synagogue[q] and went
to the house of a man named Titius[r] Justus, a worshipper of God; his house was
next door to the synagogue. 8Crispus,
the official of the synagogue, became a
believer in the Lord, together with all
his household; and many of the Corinthians who heard Paul became believers
and were baptized. 9One night the Lord
said to Paul in a vision, 'Do not be afraid,
but speak and do not be silent; 10for I am
with you, and no one will lay a hand on
you to harm you, for there are many in
this city who are my people.' 11He stayed
there for a year and six months, teaching the word of God among them.
12 But when Gallio was proconsul of
Achaia, the Jews made a united attack
on Paul and brought him before the tribunal. 13They said, 'This man is persuading people to worship God in ways that
are contrary to the law.' 14Just as Paul
was about to speak, Gallio said to the
Jews, 'If it were a matter of crime or serious villainy, I would be justified in accepting the complaint of you Jews; 15but
since it is a matter of questions about
words and names and your own law,
see to it yourselves; I do not wish to be
a judge of these matters.' 16And he dismissed them from the tribunal. 17Then
all of them[s] seized Sosthenes, the official of the synagogue, and beat him in
front of the tribunal. But Gallio paid no
attention to any of these things.

PAUL'S RETURN TO ANTIOCH

18 After staying there for a considerable time, Paul said farewell to
the believers[t] and sailed for Syria, accompanied by Priscilla and Aquila. At
Cenchreae he had his hair cut, for he
was under a vow. 19When they reached
Ephesus, he left them there, but first he
himself went into the synagogue and
had a discussion with the Jews. 20When
they asked him to stay longer, he declined; 21but on taking leave of them, he
said, 'I[u] will return to you, if God wills.'
Then he set sail from Ephesus.
22 When he had landed at Caesarea,
he went up to Jerusalem[v] and greeted
the church, and then went down to Antioch. 23After spending some time there
he departed and went from place to
place through the region of Galatia[w] and
Phrygia, strengthening all the disciples.

MINISTRY OF APOLLOS

24 Now there came to Ephesus a Jew
named Apollos, a native of Alexandria.

[k] 17.27 Other ancient authorities read *the Lord*
[l] 18.1 Gk *he* [m] 18.2 Gk *He* [n] 18.5 Gk *with the word* [o] 18.5 Or *the Christ* [p] 18.6 Gk *reviled him, he shook out his clothes* [q] 18.7 Gk *left there*
[r] 18.7 Other ancient authorities read *Titus*
[s] 18.17 Other ancient authorities read *all the Greeks* [t] 18.18 Gk *brothers* [u] 18.21 Other ancient authorities read *I must at all costs keep the approaching festival in Jerusalem, but I*
[v] 18.22 Gk *went up* [w] 18.23 Gk *the Galatian region*

He was an eloquent man, well-versed in the scriptures. 25 He had been instructed in the Way of the Lord; and he spoke with burning enthusiasm and taught accurately the things concerning Jesus, though he knew only the baptism of John. 26 He began to speak boldly in the synagogue; but when Priscilla and Aquila heard him, they took him aside and explained the Way of God to him more accurately. 27 And when he wished to cross over to Achaia, the believers[x] encouraged him and wrote to the disciples to welcome him. On his arrival he greatly helped those who through grace had become believers, 28 for he powerfully refuted the Jews in public, showing by the scriptures that the Messiah[y] is Jesus.

PAUL IN EPHESUS

19 While Apollos was in Corinth, Paul passed through the inland regions and came to Ephesus, where he found some disciples. 2 He said to them, 'Did you receive the Holy Spirit when you became believers?' They replied, 'No, we have not even heard that there is a Holy Spirit.' 3 Then he said, 'Into what then were you baptized?' They answered, 'Into John's baptism.' 4 Paul said, 'John baptized with the baptism of repentance, telling the people to believe in the one who was to come after him, that is, in Jesus.' 5 On hearing this, they were baptized in the name of the Lord Jesus. 6 When Paul had laid his hands on them, the Holy Spirit came upon them, and they spoke in tongues and prophesied— 7 altogether there were about twelve of them.

8 He entered the synagogue and for three months spoke out boldly, and argued persuasively about the kingdom of God. 9 When some stubbornly refused to believe and spoke evil of the Way before the congregation, he left them, taking the disciples with him, and argued daily in the lecture hall of Tyrannus.[z] 10 This continued for two years, so that all the residents of Asia, both Jews and Greeks, heard the word of the Lord.

THE SONS OF SCEVA

11 God did extraordinary miracles through Paul, 12 so that when the handkerchiefs or aprons that had touched his skin were brought to the sick, their diseases left them, and the evil spirits came out of them. 13 Then some itinerant Jewish exorcists tried to use the name of the Lord Jesus over those who had evil spirits, saying, 'I adjure you by the Jesus whom Paul proclaims.' 14 Seven sons of a Jewish high priest named Sceva were doing this. 15 But the evil spirit said to them in reply, 'Jesus I know, and Paul I know; but who are you?' 16 Then the man with the evil spirit leapt on them, mastered them all, and so overpowered them that they fled out of the house naked and wounded. 17 When this became known to all residents of Ephesus, both Jews and Greeks, everyone was awestruck; and the name of the Lord Jesus was praised. 18 Also many of those who became believers confessed and disclosed their practices. 19 A number of those who practised magic collected their books and burned them publicly; when the value of these books[a] was calculated, it was found to come to fifty thousand silver coins. 20 So the word of the Lord grew mightily and prevailed.

THE RIOT IN EPHESUS

21 Now after these things had been accomplished, Paul resolved in the Spirit to go through Macedonia and Achaia, and then to go on to Jerusalem. He said, 'After I have gone there, I must also see Rome.' 22 So he sent two of his helpers, Timothy and Erastus, to Macedonia, while he himself stayed for some time longer in Asia.

23 About that time no little disturbance broke out concerning the Way. 24 A man named Demetrius, a silversmith who made silver shrines of Artemis, brought no little business to the artisans. 25 These he gathered together, with the workers of the same trade, and said, 'Men, you know that we get our wealth from this business. 26 You also see and hear that not only in Ephesus but in almost the whole of Asia this Paul has persuaded and drawn away a considerable number of people by saying that gods made with hands are not gods. 27 And there is danger not only that this trade of ours may come into disrepute but also that the temple of the great goddess Artemis will be scorned, and she will be deprived of her majesty that brought all Asia and the world to worship her.'

28 When they heard this, they were enraged and shouted, 'Great is Arte-

[x] **18.27** Gk *brothers* [y] **18.28** Or *the Christ*
[z] **19.9** Other ancient authorities read *of a certain Tyrannus, from eleven o'clock in the morning to four in the afternoon* [a] **19.19** Gk *them*

mis of the Ephesians!' 29 The city was filled with the confusion; and people[b] rushed together to the theatre, dragging with them Gaius and Aristarchus, Macedonians who were Paul's travelling-companions. 30 Paul wished to go into the crowd, but the disciples would not let him; 31 even some officials of the province of Asia,[c] who were friendly to him, sent him a message urging him not to venture into the theatre. 32 Meanwhile, some were shouting one thing, some another; for the assembly was in confusion, and most of them did not know why they had come together. 33 Some of the crowd gave instructions to Alexander, whom the Jews had pushed forward. And Alexander motioned for silence and tried to make a defence before the people. 34 But when they recognized that he was a Jew, for about two hours all of them shouted in unison, 'Great is Artemis of the Ephesians!' 35 But when the town clerk had quietened the crowd, he said, 'Citizens of Ephesus, who is there that does not know that the city of the Ephesians is the temple-keeper of the great Artemis and of the statue that fell from heaven?[d] 36 Since these things cannot be denied, you ought to be quiet and do nothing rash. 37 You have brought these men here who are neither temple-robbers nor blasphemers of our[e] goddess. 38 If therefore Demetrius and the artisans with him have a complaint against anyone, the courts are open, and there are proconsuls; let them bring charges there against one another. 39 If there is anything further[f] you want to know, it must be settled in the regular assembly. 40 For we are in danger of being charged with rioting today, since there is no cause that we can give to justify this commotion.' 41 When he had said this, he dismissed the assembly.

PAUL GOES TO MACEDONIA AND GREECE

20 After the uproar had ceased, Paul sent for the disciples; and after encouraging them and saying farewell, he left for Macedonia. 2 When he had gone through those regions and had given the believers[g] much encouragement, he came to Greece, 3 where he stayed for three months. He was about to set sail for Syria when a plot was made against him by the Jews, and so he decided to return through Macedonia. 4 He was accompanied by Sopater son of Pyrrhus from Beroea, by Aristarchus and Secundus from Thessalonica, by Gaius from Derbe, and by Timothy, as well as by Tychicus and Trophimus from Asia. 5 They went ahead and were waiting for us in Troas; 6 but we sailed from Philippi after the days of Unleavened Bread, and in five days we joined them in Troas, where we stayed for seven days.

PAUL'S FAREWELL VISIT TO TROAS

7 On the first day of the week, when we met to break bread, Paul was holding a discussion with them; since he intended to leave the next day, he continued speaking until midnight. 8 There were many lamps in the room upstairs where we were meeting. 9 A young man named Eutychus, who was sitting in the window, began to sink off into a deep sleep while Paul talked still longer. Overcome by sleep, he fell to the ground three floors below and was picked up dead. 10 But Paul went down, and bending over him took him in his arms, and said, 'Do not be alarmed, for his life is in him.' 11 Then Paul went upstairs, and after he had broken bread and eaten, he continued to converse with them until dawn; then he left. 12 Meanwhile they had taken the boy away alive and were not a little comforted.

THE VOYAGE FROM TROAS TO MILETUS

13 We went ahead to the ship and set sail for Assos, intending to take Paul on board there; for he had made this arrangement, intending to go by land himself. 14 When he met us in Assos, we took him on board and went to Mitylene. 15 We sailed from there, and on the following day we arrived opposite Chios. The next day we touched at Samos, and[h] the day after that we came to Miletus. 16 For Paul had decided to sail past Ephesus, so that he might not have to spend time in Asia; he was eager to be in Jerusalem, if possible, on the day of Pentecost.

PAUL SPEAKS TO THE EPHESIAN ELDERS

17 From Miletus he sent a message to Ephesus, asking the elders of the church

[b] **19.29** Gk *they* [c] **19.31** Gk *some of the Asiarchs* [d] **19.35** Meaning of Gk uncertain [e] **19.37** Other ancient authorities read *your* [f] **19.39** Other ancient authorities read *about other matters* [g] **20.2** Gk *given them* [h] **20.15** Other ancient authorities add *after remaining at Trogyllium*

to meet him. 18When they came to him, he said to them:

'You yourselves know how I lived among you the entire time from the first day that I set foot in Asia, 19serving the Lord with all humility and with tears, enduring the trials that came to me through the plots of the Jews. 20I did not shrink from doing anything helpful, proclaiming the message to you and teaching you publicly and from house to house, 21as I testified to both Jews and Greeks about repentance towards God and faith towards our Lord Jesus. 22And now, as a captive to the Spirit,[i] I am on my way to Jerusalem, not knowing what will happen to me there, 23except that the Holy Spirit testifies to me in every city that imprisonment and persecutions are waiting for me. 24But I do not count my life of any value to myself, if only I may finish my course and the ministry that I received from the Lord Jesus, to testify to the good news of God's grace.

25 'And now I know that none of you, among whom I have gone about proclaiming the kingdom, will ever see my face again. 26Therefore I declare to you this day that I am not responsible for the blood of any of you, 27for I did not shrink from declaring to you the whole purpose of God. 28Keep watch over yourselves and over all the flock, of which the Holy Spirit has made you overseers, to shepherd the church of God[j] that he obtained with the blood of his own Son.[k] 29I know that after I have gone, savage wolves will come in among you, not sparing the flock. 30Some even from your own group will come distorting the truth in order to entice the disciples to follow them. 31Therefore be alert, remembering that for three years I did not cease night or day to warn everyone with tears. 32And now I commend you to God and to the message of his grace, a message that is able to build you up and to give you the inheritance among all who are sanctified. 33I coveted no one's silver or gold or clothing. 34You know for yourselves that I worked with my own hands to support myself and my companions. 35In all this I have given you an example that by such work we must support the weak, remembering the words of the Lord Jesus, for he himself said, "It is more blessed to give than to receive." '

36 When he had finished speaking, he knelt down with them all and prayed. 37There was much weeping among them all; they embraced Paul and kissed him, 38grieving especially because of what he had said, that they would not see him again. Then they brought him to the ship.

PAUL'S JOURNEY TO JERUSALEM

21 When we had parted from them and set sail, we came by a straight course to Cos, and the next day to Rhodes, and from there to Patara.[l] 2When we found a ship bound for Phoenicia, we went on board and set sail. 3We came in sight of Cyprus; and leaving it on our left, we sailed to Syria and landed at Tyre, because the ship was to unload its cargo there. 4We looked up the disciples and stayed there for seven days. Through the Spirit they told Paul not to go on to Jerusalem. 5When our days there were ended, we left and proceeded on our journey; and all of them, with wives and children, escorted us outside the city. There we knelt down on the beach and prayed 6and said farewell to one another. Then we went on board the ship, and they returned home.

7 When we had finished[m] the voyage from Tyre, we arrived at Ptolemais; and we greeted the believers[n] and stayed with them for one day. 8The next day we left and came to Caesarea; and we went into the house of Philip the evangelist, one of the seven, and stayed with him. 9He had four unmarried daughters[o] who had the gift of prophecy. 10While we were staying there for several days, a prophet named Agabus came down from Judea. 11He came to us and took Paul's belt, bound his own feet and hands with it, and said, 'Thus says the Holy Spirit, "This is the way the Jews in Jerusalem will bind the man who owns this belt and will hand him over to the Gentiles." ' 12When we heard this, we and the people there urged him not to go up to Jerusalem. 13Then Paul answered, 'What are you doing, weeping and breaking my heart? For I am ready not only to be bound but even to die in Jerusalem for the name of the Lord Jesus.' 14Since he would not be persuaded, we remained silent except to say, 'The Lord's will be done.'

[i] 20.22 Or *And now, bound in the spirit*
[j] 20.28 Other ancient authorities read *of the Lord*
[k] 20.28 Or *with his own blood*; Gk *with the blood of his Own*
[l] 21.1 Other ancient authorities add *and Myra*
[m] 21.7 Or *continued*
[n] 21.7 Gk *brothers*
[o] 21.9 Gk *four daughters, virgins,*

15 After these days we got ready and
started to go up to Jerusalem. 16 Some of
the disciples from Caesarea also came
along and brought us to the house of
Mnason of Cyprus, an early disciple,
with whom we were to stay.

PAUL VISITS JAMES AT JERUSALEM

17 When we arrived in Jerusalem,
the brothers welcomed us warmly.
18 The next day Paul went with us to
visit James; and all the elders were present. 19 After greeting them, he related
one by one the things that God had
done among the Gentiles through his
ministry. 20 When they heard it, they
praised God. Then they said to him, 'You
see, brother, how many thousands of
believers there are among the Jews, and
they are all zealous for the law. 21 They
have been told about you that you teach
all the Jews living among the Gentiles
to forsake Moses, and that you tell them
not to circumcise their children or observe the customs. 22 What then is to
be done? They will certainly hear that
you have come. 23 So do what we tell
you. We have four men who are under
a vow. 24 Join these men, go through the
rite of purification with them, and pay
for the shaving of their heads. Thus all
will know that there is nothing in what
they have been told about you, but that
you yourself observe and guard the law.
25 But as for the Gentiles who have become believers, we have sent a letter
with our judgement that they should
abstain from what has been sacrificed to
idols and from blood and from what is
strangled[p] and from fornication.' 26 Then
Paul took the men, and the next day,
having purified himself, he entered the
temple with them, making public the
completion of the days of purification
when the sacrifice would be made for
each of them.

PAUL ARRESTED IN THE TEMPLE

27 When the seven days were almost
completed, the Jews from Asia, who had
seen him in the temple, stirred up the
whole crowd. They seized him, 28 shouting, 'Fellow-Israelites, help! This is the
man who is teaching everyone everywhere against our people, our law, and
this place; more than that, he has actually brought Greeks into the temple and
has defiled this holy place.' 29 For they
had previously seen Trophimus the
Ephesian with him in the city, and they
supposed that Paul had brought him
into the temple. 30 Then all the city was
aroused, and the people rushed together.
They seized Paul and dragged him out of
the temple, and immediately the doors
were shut. 31 While they were trying to
kill him, word came to the tribune of
the cohort that all Jerusalem was in an
uproar. 32 Immediately he took soldiers
and centurions and ran down to them.
When they saw the tribune and the soldiers, they stopped beating Paul. 33 Then
the tribune came, arrested him, and ordered him to be bound with two chains;
he inquired who he was and what he
had done. 34 Some in the crowd shouted
one thing, some another; and as he
could not learn the facts because of the
uproar, he ordered him to be brought
into the barracks. 35 When Paul[q] came to
the steps, the violence of the mob was
so great that he had to be carried by the
soldiers. 36 The crowd that followed kept
shouting, 'Away with him!'

PAUL DEFENDS HIMSELF

37 Just as Paul was about to be
brought into the barracks, he said to the
tribune, 'May I say something to you?'
The tribune[r] replied, 'Do you know
Greek? 38 Then you are not the Egyptian
who recently stirred up a revolt and led
the four thousand assassins out into the
wilderness?' 39 Paul replied, 'I am a Jew,
from Tarsus in Cilicia, a citizen of an
important city; I beg you, let me speak
to the people.' 40 When he had given him
permission, Paul stood on the steps and
motioned to the people for silence; and
when there was a great hush, he addressed them in the Hebrew[s] language,
saying:

22 'Brothers and fathers, listen to
the defence that I now make before you.'

2 When they heard him addressing
them in Hebrew,[t] they became even
more quiet. Then he said:

3 'I am a Jew, born in Tarsus in Cilicia, but brought up in this city at the
feet of Gamaliel, educated strictly according to our ancestral law, being zealous for God, just as all of you are today.
4 I persecuted this Way up to the point of
death by binding both men and women
and putting them in prison, 5 as the
high priest and the whole council of elders can testify about me. From them I
also received letters to the brothers in

p 21.25 Other ancient authorities lack *and from what is strangled* q 21.35 Gk *he* r 21.37 Gk *He* s 21.40 That is, *Aramaic* t 22.2 That is, *Aramaic*

Damascus, and I went there in order to bind those who were there and to bring them back to Jerusalem for punishment.

PAUL TELLS OF HIS CONVERSION

6 'While I was on my way and approaching Damascus, about noon a great light from heaven suddenly shone about me. 7 I fell to the ground and heard a voice saying to me, "Saul, Saul, why are you persecuting me?" 8 I answered, "Who are you, Lord?" Then he said to me, "I am Jesus of Nazareth[u] whom you are persecuting." 9 Now those who were with me saw the light but did not hear the voice of the one who was speaking to me. 10 I asked, "What am I to do, Lord?" The Lord said to me, "Get up and go to Damascus; there you will be told everything that has been assigned to you to do." 11 Since I could not see because of the brightness of that light, those who were with me took my hand and led me to Damascus.

12 'A certain Ananias, who was a devout man according to the law and well spoken of by all the Jews living there, 13 came to me; and standing beside me, he said, "Brother Saul, regain your sight!" In that very hour I regained my sight and saw him. 14 Then he said, "The God of our ancestors has chosen you to know his will, to see the Righteous One and to hear his own voice; 15 for you will be his witness to all the world of what you have seen and heard. 16 And now why do you delay? Get up, be baptized, and have your sins washed away, calling on his name."

PAUL SENT TO THE GENTILES

17 'After I had returned to Jerusalem and while I was praying in the temple, I fell into a trance 18 and saw Jesus[v] saying to me, "Hurry and get out of Jerusalem quickly, because they will not accept your testimony about me." 19 And I said, "Lord, they themselves know that in every synagogue I imprisoned and beat those who believed in you. 20 And while the blood of your witness Stephen was shed, I myself was standing by, approving and keeping the coats of those who killed him." 21 Then he said to me, "Go, for I will send you far away to the Gentiles." '

PAUL AND THE ROMAN TRIBUNE

22 Up to this point they listened to him, but then they shouted, 'Away with such a fellow from the earth! For he should not be allowed to live.' 23 And while they were shouting, throwing off their cloaks, and tossing dust into the air, 24 the tribune directed that he was to be brought into the barracks, and ordered him to be examined by flogging, to find out the reason for this outcry against him. 25 But when they had tied him up with thongs,[w] Paul said to the centurion who was standing by, 'Is it legal for you to flog a Roman citizen who is uncondemned?' 26 When the centurion heard that, he went to the tribune and said to him, 'What are you about to do? This man is a Roman citizen.' 27 The tribune came and asked Paul,[x] 'Tell me, are you a Roman citizen?' And he said, 'Yes.' 28 The tribune answered, 'It cost me a large sum of money to get my citizenship.' Paul said, 'But I was born a citizen.' 29 Immediately those who were about to examine him drew back from him; and the tribune also was afraid, for he realized that Paul was a Roman citizen and that he had bound him.

PAUL BEFORE THE COUNCIL

30 Since he wanted to find out what Paul[y] was being accused of by the Jews, the next day he released him and ordered the chief priests and the entire council to meet. He brought Paul down and had him stand before them.

23 While Paul was looking intently at the council he said, 'Brothers,[z] up to this day I have lived my life with a clear conscience before God.' 2 Then the high priest Ananias ordered those standing near him to strike him on the mouth. 3 At this Paul said to him, 'God will strike you, you whitewashed wall! Are you sitting there to judge me according to the law, and yet in violation of the law you order me to be struck?' 4 Those standing nearby said, 'Do you dare to insult God's high priest?' 5 And Paul said, 'I did not realize, brothers, that he was high priest; for it is written, "You shall not speak evil of a leader of your people." '

6 When Paul noticed that some were Sadducees and others were Pharisees, he called out in the council, 'Brothers, I am a Pharisee, a son of Pharisees. I am on trial concerning the hope of the resurrection[a] of the dead.' 7 When he said this, a dissension began between the

[u] 22.8 Gk *the Nazorean* [v] 22.18 Gk *him*
[w] 22.25 *Or up for the lashes* [x] 22.27 Gk *him*
[y] 22.30 Gk *he* [z] 23.1 Gk *Men, brothers*
[a] 23.6 Gk *concerning hope and resurrection*

Pharisees and the Sadducees, and the assembly was divided. 8(The Sadducees say that there is no resurrection, or angel, or spirit; but the Pharisees acknowledge all three.) 9The great clamour arose, and certain scribes of the Pharisees' group stood up and contended, 'We find nothing wrong with this man. What if a spirit or an angel has spoken to him?' 10When the dissension became violent, the tribune, fearing that they would tear Paul to pieces, ordered the soldiers to go down, take him by force, and bring him into the barracks.

11 That night the Lord stood near him and said, 'Keep up your courage! For just as you have testified for me in Jerusalem, so you must bear witness also in Rome.'

THE PLOT TO KILL PAUL

12 In the morning the Jews joined in a conspiracy and bound themselves by an oath neither to eat nor drink until they had killed Paul. 13There were more than forty who joined in this conspiracy. 14They went to the chief priests and elders and said, 'We have strictly bound ourselves by an oath to taste no food until we have killed Paul. 15Now then, you and the council must notify the tribune to bring him down to you, on the pretext that you want to make a more thorough examination of his case. And we are ready to do away with him before he arrives.'

16 Now the son of Paul's sister heard about the ambush; so he went and gained entrance to the barracks and told Paul. 17Paul called one of the centurions and said, 'Take this young man to the tribune, for he has something to report to him.' 18So he took him, brought him to the tribune, and said, 'The prisoner Paul called me and asked me to bring this young man to you; he has something to tell you.' 19The tribune took him by the hand, drew him aside privately, and asked, 'What is it that you have to report to me?' 20He answered, 'The Jews have agreed to ask you to bring Paul down to the council tomorrow, as though they were going to inquire more thoroughly into his case. 21But do not be persuaded by them, for more than forty of their men are lying in ambush for him. They have bound themselves by an oath neither to eat nor drink until they kill him. They are ready now and are waiting for your consent.' 22So the tribune dismissed the young man, ordering him, 'Tell no one that you have informed me of this.'

PAUL SENT TO FELIX THE GOVERNOR

23 Then he summoned two of the centurions and said, 'Get ready to leave by nine o'clock tonight for Caesarea with two hundred soldiers, seventy horsemen, and two hundred spearmen. 24Also provide mounts for Paul to ride, and take him safely to Felix the governor.' 25He wrote a letter to this effect:

26 'Claudius Lysias to his Excellency the governor Felix, greetings. 27This man was seized by the Jews and was about to be killed by them, but when I had learned that he was a Roman citizen, I came with the guard and rescued him. 28Since I wanted to know the charge for which they accused him, I had him brought to their council. 29I found that he was accused concerning questions of their law, but was charged with nothing deserving death or imprisonment. 30When I was informed that there would be a plot against the man, I sent him to you at once, ordering his accusers also to state before you what they have against him.'[b]

31 So the soldiers, according to their instructions, took Paul and brought him during the night to Antipatris. 32The next day they let the horsemen go on with him, while they returned to the barracks. 33When they came to Caesarea and delivered the letter to the governor, they presented Paul also before him. 34On reading the letter, he asked what province he belonged to, and when he learned that he was from Cilicia, 35he said, 'I will give you a hearing when your accusers arrive.' Then he ordered that he be kept under guard in Herod's headquarters.[c]

PAUL BEFORE FELIX AT CAESAREA

24 Five days later the high priest Ananias came down with some elders and an attorney, a certain Tertullus, and they reported their case against Paul to the governor. 2When Paul[d] had been summoned, Tertullus began to accuse him, saying:

'Your Excellency,[e] because of you we have long enjoyed peace, and reforms have been made for this people because of your foresight. 3We welcome this in every way and everywhere with utmost

[b] **23.30** Other ancient authorities add *Farewell*
[c] **23.35** Gk *praetorium* [d] **24.2** Gk *he* [e] **24.2** Gk lacks *Your Excellency*

gratitude. 4But, to detain you no further, I beg you to hear us briefly with your customary graciousness. 5We have, in fact, found this man a pestilent fellow, an agitator among all the Jews throughout the world, and a ringleader of the sect of the Nazarenes.[f] 6He even tried to profane the temple, and so we seized him.[g] 8By examining him yourself you will be able to learn from him concerning everything of which we accuse him.'

9 The Jews also joined in the charge by asserting that all this was true.

PAUL'S DEFENCE BEFORE FELIX

10 When the governor motioned to him to speak, Paul replied:

'I cheerfully make my defence, knowing that for many years you have been a judge over this nation. 11As you can find out, it is not more than twelve days since I went up to worship in Jerusalem. 12They did not find me disputing with anyone in the temple or stirring up a crowd either in the synagogues or throughout the city. 13Neither can they prove to you the charge that they now bring against me. 14But this I admit to you, that according to the Way, which they call a sect, I worship the God of our ancestors, believing everything laid down according to the law or written in the prophets. 15I have a hope in God—a hope that they themselves also accept—that there will be a resurrection of both[h] the righteous and the unrighteous. 16Therefore I do my best always to have a clear conscience towards God and all people. 17Now after some years I came to bring alms to my nation and to offer sacrifices. 18While I was doing this, they found me in the temple, completing the rite of purification, without any crowd or disturbance. 19But there were some Jews from Asia—they ought to be here before you to make an accusation, if they have anything against me. 20Or let these men here tell what crime they had found when I stood before the council, 21unless it was this one sentence that I called out while standing before them, "It is about the resurrection of the dead that I am on trial before you today." '

22 But Felix, who was rather well informed about the Way, adjourned the hearing with the comment, 'When Lysias the tribune comes down, I will decide your case.' 23Then he ordered the centurion to keep him in custody, but to let him have some liberty and not to prevent any of his friends from taking care of his needs.

PAUL HELD IN CUSTODY

24 Some days later when Felix came with his wife Drusilla, who was Jewish, he sent for Paul and heard him speak concerning faith in Christ Jesus. 25And as he discussed justice, self-control, and the coming judgement, Felix became frightened and said, 'Go away for the present; when I have an opportunity, I will send for you.' 26At the same time he hoped that money would be given to him by Paul, and for that reason he used to send for him very often and converse with him.

27 After two years had passed, Felix was succeeded by Porcius Festus; and since he wanted to grant the Jews a favour, Felix left Paul in prison.

PAUL APPEALS TO THE EMPEROR

25 Three days after Festus had arrived in the province, he went up from Caesarea to Jerusalem 2where the chief priests and the leaders of the Jews gave him a report against Paul. They appealed to him 3and requested, as a favour to them against Paul,[i] to have him transferred to Jerusalem. They were, in fact, planning an ambush to kill him along the way. 4Festus replied that Paul was being kept at Caesarea, and that he himself intended to go there shortly. 5'So', he said, 'let those of you who have the authority come down with me, and if there is anything wrong about the man, let them accuse him.'

6 After he had stayed among them for not more than eight or ten days, he went down to Caesarea; the next day he took his seat on the tribunal and ordered Paul to be brought. 7When he arrived, the Jews who had gone down from Jerusalem surrounded him, bringing many serious charges against him, which they could not prove. 8Paul said in his defence, 'I have in no way committed an offence against the law of the Jews, or against the temple, or against the emperor.' 9But Festus, wishing to do the Jews a favour, asked Paul, 'Do you wish to go up to Jerusalem and be

[f] **24.5** Gk *Nazoreans* [g] **24.6** Other ancient authorities add *and we would have judged him according to our law. 7But the chief captain Lysias came and with great violence took him out of our hands, 8commanding his accusers to come before you.* [h] **24.15** Other ancient authorities read *of the dead, both of* [i] **25.3** Gk *him*

tried there before me on these charges?'
10 Paul said, 'I am appealing to the emperor's tribunal; this is where I should
be tried. I have done no wrong to the
Jews, as you very well know. 11 Now if I
am in the wrong and have committed
something for which I deserve to die,
I am not trying to escape death; but if
there is nothing to their charges against
me, no one can turn me over to them.
I appeal to the emperor.' 12 Then Festus,
after he had conferred with his council,
replied, 'You have appealed to the emperor; to the emperor you will go.'

FESTUS CONSULTS KING AGRIPPA

13 After several days had passed,
King Agrippa and Bernice arrived at
Caesarea to welcome Festus. 14 Since
they were staying there for several days,
Festus laid Paul's case before the king,
saying, 'There is a man here who was
left in prison by Felix. 15 When I was in
Jerusalem, the chief priests and the elders of the Jews informed me about him
and asked for a sentence against him. 16 I
told them that it was not the custom of
the Romans to hand over anyone before
the accused had met the accusers face to
face and had been given an opportunity
to make a defence against the charge.
17 So when they met here, I lost no time,
but on the next day took my seat on
the tribunal and ordered the man to be
brought. 18 When the accusers stood up,
they did not charge him with any of the
crimes[j] that I was expecting. 19 Instead
they had certain points of disagreement
with him about their own religion and
about a certain Jesus, who had died, but
whom Paul asserted to be alive. 20 Since
I was at a loss how to investigate these
questions, I asked whether he wished
to go to Jerusalem and be tried there on
these charges.[k] 21 But when Paul had appealed to be kept in custody for the decision of his Imperial Majesty, I ordered
him to be held until I could send him to
the emperor.' 22 Agrippa said to Festus, 'I
would like to hear the man myself.' 'Tomorrow', he said, 'you will hear him.'

PAUL BROUGHT BEFORE AGRIPPA

23 So on the next day Agrippa and
Bernice came with great pomp, and
they entered the audience hall with the
military tribunes and the prominent
men of the city. Then Festus gave the
order and Paul was brought in. 24 And
Festus said, 'King Agrippa and all here
present with us, you see this man about
whom the whole Jewish community pe-
titioned me, both in Jerusalem and here,
shouting that he ought not to live any
longer. 25 But I found that he had done
nothing deserving death; and when he
appealed to his Imperial Majesty, I decided to send him. 26 But I have nothing
definite to write to our sovereign about
him. Therefore I have brought him before all of you, and especially before you,
King Agrippa, so that, after we have examined him, I may have something to
write— 27 for it seems to me unreasonable to send a prisoner without indicating the charges against him.'

PAUL DEFENDS HIMSELF BEFORE AGRIPPA

26 Agrippa said to Paul, 'You have
permission to speak for yourself.' Then Paul stretched out his hand
and began to defend himself:

2 'I consider myself fortunate that
it is before you, King Agrippa, I am to
make my defence today against all the
accusations of the Jews, 3 because you
are especially familiar with all the customs and controversies of the Jews;
therefore I beg of you to listen to me patiently.

4 'All the Jews know my way of life
from my youth, a life spent from the
beginning among my own people and
in Jerusalem. 5 They have known for a
long time, if they are willing to testify,
that I have belonged to the strictest sect
of our religion and lived as a Pharisee.
6 And now I stand here on trial on account of my hope in the promise made
by God to our ancestors, 7 a promise that
our twelve tribes hope to attain, as they
earnestly worship day and night. It is
for this hope, your Excellency,[l] that I
am accused by Jews! 8 Why is it thought
incredible by any of you that God raises
the dead?

9 'Indeed, I myself was convinced
that I ought to do many things against
the name of Jesus of Nazareth.[m] 10 And
that is what I did in Jerusalem; with authority received from the chief priests,
I not only locked up many of the saints
in prison, but I also cast my vote against
them when they were being condemned
to death. 11 By punishing them often in
all the synagogues I tried to force them to
blaspheme; and since I was so furiously

j 25.18 Other ancient authorities read *with anything* k 25.20 Gk *on them* l 26.7 Gk *O king* m 26.9 Gk *the Nazorean*

enraged at them, I pursued them even to foreign cities.

PAUL TELLS OF HIS CONVERSION

12 'With this in mind, I was travelling to Damascus with the authority and commission of the chief priests, 13 when at midday along the road, your Excellency,[n] I saw a light from heaven, brighter than the sun, shining around me and my companions. 14 When we had all fallen to the ground, I heard a voice saying to me in the Hebrew[o] language, "Saul, Saul, why are you persecuting me? It hurts you to kick against the goads." 15 I asked, "Who are you, Lord?" The Lord answered, "I am Jesus whom you are persecuting. 16 But get up and stand on your feet; for I have appeared to you for this purpose, to appoint you to serve and testify to the things in which you have seen me[p] and to those in which I will appear to you. 17 I will rescue you from your people and from the Gentiles—to whom I am sending you 18 to open their eyes so that they may turn from darkness to light and from the power of Satan to God, so that they may receive forgiveness of sins and a place among those who are sanctified by faith in me."

PAUL TELLS OF HIS PREACHING

19 'After that, King Agrippa, I was not disobedient to the heavenly vision, 20 but declared first to those in Damascus, then in Jerusalem and throughout the countryside of Judea, and also to the Gentiles, that they should repent and turn to God and do deeds consistent with repentance. 21 For this reason the Jews seized me in the temple and tried to kill me. 22 To this day I have had help from God, and so I stand here, testifying to both small and great, saying nothing but what the prophets and Moses said would take place: 23 that the Messiah[q] must suffer, and that, by being the first to rise from the dead, he would proclaim light both to our people and to the Gentiles.'

PAUL APPEALS TO AGRIPPA TO BELIEVE

24 While he was making this defence, Festus exclaimed, 'You are out of your mind, Paul! Too much learning is driving you insane!' 25 But Paul said, 'I am not out of my mind, most excellent Festus, but I am speaking the sober truth. 26 Indeed the king knows about these things, and to him I speak freely; for I am certain that none of these things has escaped his notice, for this was not done in a corner. 27 King Agrippa, do you believe the prophets? I know that you believe.' 28 Agrippa said to Paul, 'Are you so quickly persuading me to become a Christian?'[r] 29 Paul replied, 'Whether quickly or not, I pray to God that not only you but also all who are listening to me today might become such as I am—except for these chains.'

30 Then the king got up, and with him the governor and Bernice and those who had been seated with them; 31 and as they were leaving, they said to one another, 'This man is doing nothing to deserve death or imprisonment.' 32 Agrippa said to Festus, 'This man could have been set free if he had not appealed to the emperor.'

PAUL SAILS FOR ROME

27 When it was decided that we were to sail for Italy, they transferred Paul and some other prisoners to a centurion of the Augustan Cohort, named Julius. 2 Embarking on a ship of Adramyttium that was about to set sail to the ports along the coast of Asia, we put to sea, accompanied by Aristarchus, a Macedonian from Thessalonica. 3 The next day we put in at Sidon; and Julius treated Paul kindly, and allowed him to go to his friends to be cared for. 4 Putting out to sea from there, we sailed under the lee of Cyprus, because the winds were against us. 5 After we had sailed across the sea that is off Cilicia and Pamphylia, we came to Myra in Lycia. 6 There the centurion found an Alexandrian ship bound for Italy and put us on board. 7 We sailed slowly for a number of days and arrived with difficulty off Cnidus, and as the wind was against us, we sailed under the lee of Crete off Salmone. 8 Sailing past it with difficulty, we came to a place called Fair Havens, near the city of Lasea.

9 Since much time had been lost and sailing was now dangerous, because even the Fast had already gone by, Paul advised them, 10 saying, 'Sirs, I can see that the voyage will be with danger and much heavy loss, not only of the cargo and the ship, but also of our lives.' 11 But

[n] **26.13** Gk *O king* [o] **26.14** That is, *Aramaic*
[p] **26.16** Other ancient authorities read *the things that you have seen* [q] **26.23** Or *the Christ*
[r] **26.28** Or *Quickly you will persuade me to play the Christian*

the centurion paid more attention to the pilot and to the owner of the ship than to what Paul said. 12Since the harbour was not suitable for spending the winter, the majority was in favour of putting to sea from there, on the chance that somehow they could reach Phoenix, where they could spend the winter. It was a harbour of Crete, facing south-west and north-west.

THE STORM AT SEA

13 When a moderate south wind began to blow, they thought they could achieve their purpose; so they weighed anchor and began to sail past Crete, close to the shore. 14But soon a violent wind, called the northeaster, rushed down from Crete.[s] 15Since the ship was caught and could not be turned with its head to the wind, we gave way to it and were driven. 16By running under the lee of a small island called Cauda[t] we were scarcely able to get the ship's boat under control. 17After hoisting it up they took measures[u] to undergird the ship; then, fearing that they would run on the Syrtis, they lowered the sea-anchor and so were driven. 18We were being pounded by the storm so violently that on the next day they began to throw the cargo overboard, 19and on the third day with their own hands they threw the ship's tackle overboard. 20When neither sun nor stars appeared for many days, and no small tempest raged, all hope of our being saved was at last abandoned.

21 Since they had been without food for a long time, Paul then stood up among them and said, 'Men, you should have listened to me and not have set sail from Crete and thereby avoided this damage and loss. 22I urge you now to keep up your courage, for there will be no loss of life among you, but only of the ship. 23For last night there stood by me an angel of the God to whom I belong and whom I worship, 24and he said, "Do not be afraid, Paul; you must stand before the emperor; and indeed, God has granted safety to all those who are sailing with you." 25So keep up your courage, men, for I have faith in God that it will be exactly as I have been told. 26But we will have to run aground on some island.'

27 When the fourteenth night had come, as we were drifting across the sea of Adria, about midnight the sailors suspected that they were nearing land. 28So they took soundings and found twenty fathoms; a little farther on they took soundings again and found fifteen fathoms. 29Fearing that we might run on the rocks, they let down four anchors from the stern and prayed for day to come. 30But when the sailors tried to escape from the ship and had lowered the boat into the sea, on the pretext of putting out anchors from the bow, 31Paul said to the centurion and the soldiers, 'Unless these men stay in the ship, you cannot be saved.' 32Then the soldiers cut away the ropes of the boat and set it adrift.

33 Just before daybreak, Paul urged all of them to take some food, saying, 'Today is the fourteenth day that you have been in suspense and remaining without food, having eaten nothing. 34Therefore I urge you to take some food, for it will help you survive; for none of you will lose a hair from your heads.' 35After he had said this, he took bread; and giving thanks to God in the presence of all, he broke it and began to eat. 36Then all of them were encouraged and took food for themselves. 37(We were in all two hundred and seventy-six[v] persons in the ship.) 38After they had satisfied their hunger, they lightened the ship by throwing the wheat into the sea.

THE SHIPWRECK

39 In the morning they did not recognize the land, but they noticed a bay with a beach, on which they planned to run the ship ashore, if they could. 40So they cast off the anchors and left them in the sea. At the same time they loosened the ropes that tied the steering-oars; then hoisting the foresail to the wind, they made for the beach. 41But striking a reef,[w] they ran the ship aground; the bow stuck and remained immovable, but the stern was being broken up by the force of the waves. 42The soldiers' plan was to kill the prisoners, so that none might swim away and escape; 43but the centurion, wishing to save Paul, kept them from carrying out their plan. He ordered those who could swim to jump overboard first and make for the land, 44and the rest to follow, some on planks and others on pieces of the ship. And so it was that all were brought safely to land.

[s] **27.14** Gk *it* [t] **27.16** Other ancient authorities read *Clauda* [u] **27.17** Gk *helps* [v] **27.37** Other ancient authorities read *seventy-six*; others, *about seventy-six* [w] **27.41** Gk *place of two seas*

PAUL ON THE ISLAND OF MALTA

28 After we had reached safety,
we then learned that the island
was called Malta. 2 The natives showed
us unusual kindness. Since it had begun to rain and was cold, they kindled
a fire and welcomed all of us round it.
3 Paul had gathered a bundle of brushwood and was putting it on the fire,
when a viper, driven out by the heat,
fastened itself on his hand. 4 When the
natives saw the creature hanging from
his hand, they said to one another,
'This man must be a murderer; though
he has escaped from the sea, justice has
not allowed him to live.' 5 He, however,
shook off the creature into the fire
and suffered no harm. 6 They were expecting him to swell up or drop dead,
but after they had waited a long time
and saw that nothing unusual had
happened to him, they changed their
minds and began to say that he was a
god.

7 Now in the neighbourhood of that
place were lands belonging to the leading man of the island, named Publius,
who received us and entertained us hos-
pitably for three days. 8 It so happened
that the father of Publius lay sick in
bed with fever and dysentery. Paul visited him and cured him by praying and
putting his hands on him. 9 After this
happened, the rest of the people on the
island who had diseases also came and
were cured. 10 They bestowed many honours on us, and when we were about to
sail, they put on board all the provisions
we needed.

PAUL ARRIVES AT ROME

11 Three months later we set sail on
a ship that had wintered at the island,
an Alexandrian ship with the Twin
Brothers as its figurehead. 12 We put in
at Syracuse and stayed there for three
days; 13 then we weighed anchor and
came to Rhegium. After one day there
a south wind sprang up, and on the
second day we came to Puteoli. 14 There
we found believers[x] and were invited
to stay with them for seven days. And
so we came to Rome. 15 The believers[y]
from there, when they heard of us,
came as far as the Forum of Appius
and Three Taverns to meet us. On seeing them, Paul thanked God and took
courage.

16 When we came into Rome, Paul
was allowed to live by himself, with the
soldier who was guarding him.

PAUL AND JEWISH LEADERS IN ROME

17 Three days later he called together
the local leaders of the Jews. When
they had assembled, he said to them,
'Brothers, though I had done nothing against our people or the customs
of our ancestors, yet I was arrested in
Jerusalem and handed over to the Romans. 18 When they had examined me,
the Romans[z] wanted to release me, because there was no reason for the death
penalty in my case. 19 But when the
Jews objected, I was compelled to appeal to the emperor—even though I had
no charge to bring against my nation.
20 For this reason therefore I have asked
to see you and speak with you,[a] since it
is for the sake of the hope of Israel that
I am bound with this chain.' 21 They
replied, 'We have received no letters
from Judea about you, and none of the
brothers coming here has reported or
spoken anything evil about you. 22 But
we would like to hear from you what
you think, for with regard to this sect
we know that everywhere it is spoken
against.'

PAUL PREACHES IN ROME

23 After they had fixed a day to meet
him, they came to him at his lodgings
in great numbers. From morning until evening he explained the matter to
them, testifying to the kingdom of God
and trying to convince them about Jesus
both from the law of Moses and from
the prophets. 24 Some were convinced by
what he had said, while others refused
to believe. 25 So they disagreed with each
other; and as they were leaving, Paul
made one further statement: 'The Holy
Spirit was right in saying to your ancestors through the prophet Isaiah,

26 "Go to this people and say,
You will indeed listen, but
never understand,
and you will indeed look,
but never perceive.
27 For this people's heart has
grown dull,
and their ears are hard of hearing,
and they have shut their eyes;
so that they might not
look with their eyes,
and listen with their ears,
and understand with their
heart and turn—
and I would heal them."

[x] 28.14 Gk *brothers* [y] 28.15 Gk *brothers*
[z] 28.18 Gk *they* [a] 28.20 Or *I have asked you to see me and speak with me*

28Let it be known to you then that this
salvation of God has been sent to the
Gentiles; they will listen.'[b]

30 He lived there for two whole years
at his own expense[c] and welcomed all
who came to him, 31proclaiming the
kingdom of God and teaching about the
Lord Jesus Christ with all boldness and without hindrance.

[b] 28.28 Other ancient authorities add verse 29, *And when he had said these words, the Jews departed, arguing vigorously among themselves*

[c] 28.30 Or *in his own rented dwelling*

The Letter of Paul to the

ROMANS

The Letter to the Romans (56–58 CE) is unique in that it was written to a church that Paul neither founded nor previously had visited. Paul wrote the Letter to introduce himself and his message to the Christians in Rome, looking for their support as he anticipated his mission to Spain. The Letter is the longest and most systematic of his writings. It is a presentation of Paul's views on how Christ's death and resurrection bring salvation to all people—Jew and Gentile alike—and how justification comes through faith in Christ, apart from works of Mosaic law.

In Romans, Paul speaks about how everyone is guilty of sin under the law, but that God freely bestows his grace on all those who have faith in Christ. There is no distinction here between Jew and Gentile. All are justified by faith apart from works of the law (3.21–31). It is only by Christ's death and resurrection that God brings salvation.

The divine plan of salvation is to include the whole of humanity. The Letter to the Romans has a universal outlook. Although faith in Christ frees one from observance of the law, it is not a license to freedom that leads to shirking responsibility for others (12.1–2), nor is it a repudiation of God's law (3.31; 7.7–25). The law has a purpose, but one that helps to reveal sin. It does not in itself save one from sin. It is only through Christ that we are saved.

Selections from Paul's Letter to the Romans are featured as the second reading on Sundays of Year A in the liturgical calendar. Passages are also read at the Easter Vigil (6.3–11) and the Vigil of Pentecost (8.22–27) every year. In the passage on the Vigil of Pentecost, Paul urges the church to wait in hope by letting the Spirit within us intercede for us according to God's will.

SALUTATION

1 Paul, a servant[a] of Jesus Christ,
called to be an apostle, set apart for
the gospel of God, 2which he promised
beforehand through his prophets in the
holy scriptures, 3the gospel concerning
his Son, who was descended from David
according to the flesh 4and was declared
to be Son of God with power according
to the spirit[b] of holiness by resurrection
from the dead, Jesus Christ our Lord,
5through whom we have received grace
and apostleship to bring about the obedience of faith among all the Gentiles for
the sake of his name, 6including yourselves who are called to belong to Jesus
Christ,

7 To all God's beloved in Rome, who
are called to be saints:

Grace to you and peace from God our
Father and the Lord Jesus Christ.

PRAYER OF THANKSGIVING

8 First, I thank my God through
Jesus Christ for all of you, because your
faith is proclaimed throughout the
world. 9For God, whom I serve with my
spirit by announcing the gospel[c] of his
Son, is my witness that without ceasing
I remember you always in my prayers,
10asking that by God's will I may some-

[a] 1.1 Gk *slave* [b] 1.4 Or *Spirit* [c] 1.9 Gk *my spirit in the gospel*

how at last succeed in coming to you.
11For I am longing to see you so that I
may share with you some spiritual gift
to strengthen you— 12or rather so that
we may be mutually encouraged by
each other's faith, both yours and mine.
13I want you to know, brothers and
sisters,[d] that I have often intended to
come to you (but thus far have been prevented), in order that I may reap some
harvest among you as I have among the
rest of the Gentiles. 14I am a debtor both
to Greeks and to barbarians, both to the
wise and to the foolish 15—hence my
eagerness to proclaim the gospel to you
also who are in Rome.

THE POWER OF THE GOSPEL

16 For I am not ashamed of the gospel; it is the power of God for salvation
to everyone who has faith, to the Jew
first and also to the Greek. 17For in it
the righteousness of God is revealed
through faith for faith; as it is written,
'The one who is righteous will live by
faith.'[e]

THE GUILT OF HUMANKIND

18 For the wrath of God is revealed
from heaven against all ungodliness
and wickedness of those who by their
wickedness suppress the truth. 19For
what can be known about God is plain
to them, because God has shown it to
them. 20Ever since the creation of the
world his eternal power and divine nature, invisible though they are, have
been understood and seen through the
things he has made. So they are without excuse; 21for though they knew God,
they did not honour him as God or give
thanks to him, but they became futile
in their thinking, and their senseless
minds were darkened. 22Claiming to be
wise, they became fools; 23and they exchanged the glory of the immortal God
for images resembling a mortal human
being or birds or four-footed animals or
reptiles.

24 Therefore God gave them up in the
lusts of their hearts to impurity, to the
degrading of their bodies among themselves, 25because they exchanged the
truth about God for a lie and worshipped
and served the creature rather than the
Creator, who is blessed for ever! Amen.

26 For this reason God gave them
up to degrading passions. Their women
exchanged natural intercourse for unnatural, 27and in the same way also
the men, giving up natural intercourse
with women, were consumed with passion for one another. Men committed
shameless acts with men and received
in their own persons the due penalty for
their error.

28 And since they did not see fit to
acknowledge God, God gave them up
to a debased mind and to things that
should not be done. 29They were filled
with every kind of wickedness, evil,
covetousness, malice. Full of envy, murder, strife, deceit, craftiness, they are
gossips, 30slanderers, God-haters,[f] insolent, haughty, boastful, inventors of
evil, rebellious towards parents, 31fool-
ish, faithless, heartless, ruthless. 32They
know God's decree, that those who
practise such things deserve to die—yet
they not only do them but even applaud
others who practise them.

THE RIGHTEOUS JUDGEMENT OF GOD

2 Therefore you have no excuse, whoever you are, when you judge others; for in passing judgement on another you condemn yourself, because
you, the judge, are doing the very same
things. 2You say,[g] 'We know that God's
judgement on those who do such things
is in accordance with truth.' 3Do you
imagine, whoever you are, that when
you judge those who do such things and
yet do them yourself, you will escape
the judgement of God? 4Or do you despise the riches of his kindness and forbearance and patience? Do you not realize that God's kindness is meant to lead
you to repentance? 5But by your hard
and impenitent heart you are storing up
wrath for yourself on the day of wrath,
when God's righteous judgement will
be revealed. 6For he will repay according to each one's deeds: 7to those who by
patiently doing good seek for glory and
honour and immortality, he will give
eternal life; 8while for those who are
self-seeking and who obey not the truth
but wickedness, there will be wrath and
fury. 9There will be anguish and distress
for everyone who does evil, the Jew first
and also the Greek, 10but glory and honour and peace for everyone who does
good, the Jew first and also the Greek.
11For God shows no partiality.

12 All who have sinned apart from
the law will also perish apart from the
law, and all who have sinned under the
law will be judged by the law. 13For it is

[d] **1.13** Gk *brothers* [e] **1.17** Or *The one who is righteous through faith will live* [f] **1.30** Or *God-hated* [g] **2.2** Gk lacks *You say*

not the hearers of the law who are righteous in God's sight, but the doers of the
law who will be justified. 14When Gentiles, who do not possess the law, do in-
stinctively what the law requires, these,
though not having the law, are a law
to themselves. 15They show that what
the law requires is written on their
hearts, to which their own conscience
also bears witness; and their conflicting
thoughts will accuse or perhaps excuse
them 16on the day when, according to
my gospel, God, through Jesus Christ,
will judge the secret thoughts of all.

THE JEWS AND THE LAW

17 But if you call yourself a Jew and
rely on the law and boast of your rela-
tion to God 18and know his will and determine what is best because you are instructed in the law, 19and if you are sure
that you are a guide to the blind, a light
to those who are in darkness, 20a corrector of the foolish, a teacher of children,
having in the law the embodiment of
knowledge and truth, 21you, then, that
teach others, will you not teach yourself? While you preach against stealing,
do you steal? 22You that forbid adultery,
do you commit adultery? You that abhor idols, do you rob temples? 23You
that boast in the law, do you dishonour God by breaking the law? 24For, as
it is written, 'The name of God is blasphemed among the Gentiles because of
you.'

25 Circumcision indeed is of value if
you obey the law; but if you break the
law, your circumcision has become uncircumcision. 26So, if those who are uncircumcised keep the requirements of
the law, will not their uncircumcision
be regarded as circumcision? 27Then
those who are physically uncircumcised
but keep the law will condemn you that
have the written code and circumcision
but break the law. 28For a person is not
a Jew who is one outwardly, nor is true
circumcision something external and
physical. 29Rather, a person is a Jew who
is one inwardly, and real circumcision is
a matter of the heart—it is spiritual and
not literal. Such a person receives praise
not from others but from God.

3 Then what advantage has the Jew?
Or what is the value of circumcision? 2Much, in every way. For in the
first place the Jews[h] were entrusted
with the oracles of God. 3What if some
were unfaithful? Will their faithlessness
nullify the faithfulness of God? 4By no
means! Although everyone is a liar, let
God be proved true, as it is written,

'So that you may be justified
in your words,
and prevail in your judging.'[i]

5But if our injustice serves to confirm
the justice of God, what should we say?
That God is unjust to inflict wrath on
us? (I speak in a human way.) 6By no
means! For then how could God judge
the world? 7But if through my falsehood God's truthfulness abounds to his
glory, why am I still being condemned
as a sinner? 8And why not say (as some
people slander us by saying that we say),
'Let us do evil so that good may come'?
Their condemnation is deserved!

NONE IS RIGHTEOUS

9 What then? Are we any better
off?[j] No, not at all; for we have already
charged that all, both Jews and Greeks,
are under the power of sin, 10as it is
written:

'There is no one who is righteous,
not even one;
11 there is no one who has
understanding,
there is no one who seeks God.
12 All have turned aside, together they
have become worthless;
there is no one who
shows kindness,
there is not even one.'
13 'Their throats are opened graves;
they use their tongues to deceive.'
'The venom of vipers is
under their lips.'
14 'Their mouths are full of
cursing and bitterness.'
15 'Their feet are swift to shed blood;
16 ruin and misery are in their paths,
17 and the way of peace they
have not known.'
18 'There is no fear of God
before their eyes.'

19 Now we know that whatever the
law says, it speaks to those who are under the law, so that every mouth may
be silenced, and the whole world may
be held accountable to God. 20For 'no
human being will be justified in his
sight' by deeds prescribed by the law, for
through the law comes the knowledge
of sin.

RIGHTEOUSNESS THROUGH FAITH

21 But now, irrespective of law, the
righteousness of God has been disclosed,

[h] 3.2 Gk *they* [i] 3.4 Gk *when you are being judged* [j] 3.9 *Or at any disadvantage?*

and is attested by the law and the prophets, 22the righteousness of God through
faith in Jesus Christ[k] for all who believe.
For there is no distinction, 23since all
have sinned and fall short of the glory
of God; 24they are now justified by his
grace as a gift, through the redemption
that is in Christ Jesus, 25whom God put
forward as a sacrifice of atonement[l] by
his blood, effective through faith. He
did this to show his righteousness, because in his divine forbearance he had
passed over the sins previously committed; 26it was to prove at the present time
that he himself is righteous and that he
justifies the one who has faith in Jesus.[m]
27 Then what becomes of boasting?
It is excluded. By what law? By that
of works? No, but by the law of faith.
28For we hold that a person is justified
by faith apart from works prescribed
by the law. 29Or is God the God of Jews
only? Is he not the God of Gentiles also?
Yes, of Gentiles also, 30since God is one;
and he will justify the circumcised on
the ground of faith and the uncircumcised through that same faith. 31Do we
then overthrow the law by this faith?
By no means! On the contrary, we uphold the law.

THE EXAMPLE OF ABRAHAM

4 What then are we to say was gained
by[n] Abraham, our ancestor according to the flesh? 2For if Abraham was
justified by works, he has something
to boast about, but not before God. 3For
what does the scripture say? 'Abraham
believed God, and it was reckoned to
him as righteousness.' 4Now to one who
works, wages are not reckoned as a gift
but as something due. 5But to one who
without works trusts him who justifies
the ungodly, such faith is reckoned as
righteousness. 6So also David speaks of
the blessedness of those to whom God
reckons righteousness irrespective of
works:

7 'Blessed are those whose
    iniquities are forgiven,
  and whose sins are covered;
8 blessed is the one against whom the
    Lord will not reckon sin.'

9 Is this blessedness, then, pronounced only on the circumcised, or also
on the uncircumcised? We say, 'Faith
was reckoned to Abraham as righteousness.' 10How then was it reckoned to
him? Was it before or after he had been
circumcised? It was not after, but before he was circumcised. 11He received
the sign of circumcision as a seal of the
righteousness that he had by faith while
he was still uncircumcised. The purpose
was to make him the ancestor of all who
believe without being circumcised and
who thus have righteousness reckoned
to them, 12and likewise the ancestor of
the circumcised who are not only circumcised but who also follow the example of the faith that our ancestor Abraham had before he was circumcised.

GOD'S PROMISE REALIZED THROUGH FAITH

13 For the promise that he would inherit the world did not come to Abraham or to his descendants through the
law but through the righteousness of
faith. 14If it is the adherents of the law
who are to be the heirs, faith is null and
the promise is void. 15For the law brings
wrath; but where there is no law, neither is there violation.
16 For this reason it depends on
faith, in order that the promise may
rest on grace and be guaranteed to all
his descendants, not only to the adherents of the law but also to those who
share the faith of Abraham (for he is
the father of all of us, 17as it is written,
'I have made you the father of many
nations')—in the presence of the God
in whom he believed, who gives life
to the dead and calls into existence
the things that do not exist. 18Hoping
against hope, he believed that he would
become 'the father of many nations', according to what was said, 'So numerous
shall your descendants be.' 19He did not
weaken in faith when he considered his
own body, which was already[o] as good
as dead (for he was about a hundred
years old), or when he considered the
barrenness of Sarah's womb. 20No distrust made him waver concerning the
promise of God, but he grew strong in
his faith as he gave glory to God, 21be-
ing fully convinced that God was able
to do what he had promised. 22There-
fore his faith[p] 'was reckoned to him as
righteousness.' 23Now the words, 'it
was reckoned to him', were written not
for his sake alone, 24but for ours also. It
will be reckoned to us who believe in
him who raised Jesus our Lord from the

[k] **3.22** Or *through the faith of Jesus Christ*
[l] **3.25** Or *a place of atonement* [m] **3.26** Or *who has the faith of Jesus* [n] **4.1** Other ancient authorities read *say about* [o] **4.19** Other ancient authorities lack *already* [p] **4.22** Gk *Therefore it*

dead, 25who was handed over to death
for our trespasses and was raised for our
justification.

RESULTS OF JUSTIFICATION

5 Therefore, since we are justified
by faith, we[q] have peace with God
through our Lord Jesus Christ, 2through
whom we have obtained access[r] to this
grace in which we stand; and we[s] boast
in our hope of sharing the glory of God.
3And not only that, but we[t] also boast
in our sufferings, knowing that suffering produces endurance, 4and endurance produces character, and character
produces hope, 5and hope does not dis-
appoint us, because God's love has been
poured into our hearts through the Holy
Spirit that has been given to us.

6 For while we were still weak, at the
right time Christ died for the ungodly.
7Indeed, rarely will anyone die for a
righteous person—though perhaps for
a good person someone might actually
dare to die. 8But God proves his love for
us in that while we still were sinners
Christ died for us. 9Much more surely
then, now that we have been justified
by his blood, will we be saved through
him from the wrath of God.[u] 10For if
while we were enemies, we were reconciled to God through the death of his
Son, much more surely, having been
reconciled, will we be saved by his life.
11But more than that, we even boast
in God through our Lord Jesus Christ,
through whom we have now received
reconciliation.

ADAM AND CHRIST

12 Therefore, just as sin came into
the world through one man, and death
came through sin, and so death spread
to all because all have sinned— 13sin
was indeed in the world before the law,
but sin is not reckoned when there is
no law. 14Yet death exercised dominion
from Adam to Moses, even over those
whose sins were not like the transgression of Adam, who is a type of the one
who was to come.

15 But the free gift is not like the trespass. For if the many died through the
one man's trespass, much more surely
have the grace of God and the free gift in
the grace of the one man, Jesus Christ,
abounded for the many. 16And the free
gift is not like the effect of the one man's
sin. For the judgement following one
trespass brought condemnation, but
the free gift following many trespasses
brings justification. 17If, because of the
one man's trespass, death exercised dominion through that one, much more
surely will those who receive the abundance of grace and the free gift of righteousness exercise dominion in life
through the one man, Jesus Christ.

18 Therefore just as one man's trespass led to condemnation for all, so
one man's act of righteousness leads to
justification and life for all. 19For just
as by the one man's disobedience the
many were made sinners, so by the one
man's obedience the many will be made
righteous. 20But law came in, with the
result that the trespass multiplied; but
where sin increased, grace abounded
all the more, 21so that, just as sin exercised dominion in death, so grace might
also exercise dominion through justification[v] leading to eternal life through
Jesus Christ our Lord.

DYING AND RISING WITH CHRIST

6 What then are we to say? Should we
continue in sin in order that grace
may abound? 2By no means! How can
we who died to sin go on living in it?
3Do you not know that all of us who
have been baptized into Christ Jesus
were baptized into his death? 4Therefore
we have been buried with him by baptism into death, so that, just as Christ
was raised from the dead by the glory
of the Father, so we too might walk in
newness of life.

5 For if we have been united with
him in a death like his, we will certainly
be united with him in a resurrection
like his. 6We know that our old self was
crucified with him so that the body of
sin might be destroyed, and we might
no longer be enslaved to sin. 7For whoever has died is freed from sin. 8But if
we have died with Christ, we believe
that we will also live with him. 9We
know that Christ, being raised from the
dead, will never die again; death no longer has dominion over him. 10The death
he died, he died to sin, once for all; but
the life he lives, he lives to God. 11So you
also must consider yourselves dead to
sin and alive to God in Christ Jesus.

12 Therefore, do not let sin exercise
dominion in your mortal bodies, to
make you obey their passions. 13No long-

[q] 5.1 Other ancient authorities read *let us*
[r] 5.2 Other ancient authorities add *by faith*
[s] 5.2 Or *let us* [t] 5.3 Or *let us* [u] 5.9 Gk *the wrath* [v] 5.21 Or *righteousness*

er present your members to sin as instruments[w] of wickedness, but present
yourselves to God as those who have
been brought from death to life, and
present your members to God as instruments[x] of righteousness. 14For sin will
have no dominion over you, since you
are not under law but under grace.

SLAVES OF RIGHTEOUSNESS

15 What then? Should we sin because
we are not under law but under grace?
By no means! 16Do you not know that
if you present yourselves to anyone as
obedient slaves, you are slaves of the
one whom you obey, either of sin, which
leads to death, or of obedience, which
leads to righteousness? 17But thanks be
to God that you, having once been slaves
of sin, have become obedient from the
heart to the form of teaching to which
you were entrusted, 18and that you, having been set free from sin, have become
slaves of righteousness. 19I am speaking
in human terms because of your natural
limitations.[y] For just as you once presented your members as slaves to impurity and to greater and greater iniquity,
so now present your members as slaves
to righteousness for sanctification.

20 When you were slaves of sin, you
were free in regard to righteousness.
21So what advantage did you then get
from the things of which you now are
ashamed? The end of those things is
death. 22But now that you have been
freed from sin and enslaved to God, the
advantage you get is sanctification. The
end is eternal life. 23For the wages of sin
is death, but the free gift of God is eternal life in Christ Jesus our Lord.

AN ANALOGY FROM MARRIAGE

7 Do you not know, brothers and sisters[z]—for I am speaking to those
who know the law—that the law is binding on a person only during that person's lifetime? 2Thus a married woman
is bound by the law to her husband as
long as he lives; but if her husband dies,
she is discharged from the law concerning the husband. 3Accordingly, she will
be called an adulteress if she lives with
another man while her husband is alive.
But if her husband dies, she is free from
that law, and if she marries another
man, she is not an adulteress.

4 In the same way, my friends,[a] you
have died to the law through the body
of Christ, so that you may belong to another, to him who has been raised from
the dead in order that we may bear fruit
for God. 5While we were living in the
flesh, our sinful passions, aroused by
the law, were at work in our members
to bear fruit for death. 6But now we are
discharged from the law, dead to that
which held us captive, so that we are
slaves not under the old written code
but in the new life of the Spirit.

THE LAW AND SIN

7 What then should we say? That the
law is sin? By no means! Yet, if it had
not been for the law, I would not have
known sin. I would not have known
what it is to covet if the law had not said,
'You shall not covet.' 8But sin, seizing
an opportunity in the commandment,
produced in me all kinds of covetousness. Apart from the law sin lies dead.
9I was once alive apart from the law,
but when the commandment came, sin
revived 10and I died, and the very commandment that promised life proved
to be death to me. 11For sin, seizing an
opportunity in the commandment, deceived me and through it killed me. 12So
the law is holy, and the commandment
is holy and just and good.

13 Did what is good, then, bring
death to me? By no means! It was sin,
working death in me through what is
good, in order that sin might be shown
to be sin, and through the commandment might become sinful beyond measure.

THE INNER CONFLICT

14 For we know that the law is spiritual; but I am of the flesh, sold into slavery under sin.[b] 15I do not understand
my own actions. For I do not do what
I want, but I do the very thing I hate.
16Now if I do what I do not want, I agree
that the law is good. 17But in fact it is no
longer I that do it, but sin that dwells
within me. 18For I know that nothing
good dwells within me, that is, in my
flesh. I can will what is right, but I cannot do it. 19For I do not do the good I
want, but the evil I do not want is what
I do. 20Now if I do what I do not want,
it is no longer I that do it, but sin that
dwells within me.

21 So I find it to be a law that when
I want to do what is good, evil lies close
at hand. 22For I delight in the law of

[w] **6.13** Or *weapons* [x] **6.13** Or *weapons*
[y] **6.19** Gk *the weakness of your flesh* [z] **7.1** Gk
brothers [a] **7.4** Gk *brothers* [b] **7.14** Gk *sold
under sin*

God in my inmost self, 23but I see in my members another law at war with the law of my mind, making me captive to the law of sin that dwells in my members. 24Wretched man that I am! Who will rescue me from this body of death? 25Thanks be to God through Jesus Christ our Lord!

So then, with my mind I am a slave to the law of God, but with my flesh I am a slave to the law of sin.

LIFE IN THE SPIRIT

8 There is therefore now no condemnation for those who are in Christ Jesus. 2For the law of the Spirit[c] of life in Christ Jesus has set you[d] free from the law of sin and of death. 3For God has done what the law, weakened by the flesh, could not do: by sending his own Son in the likeness of sinful flesh, and to deal with sin,[e] he condemned sin in the flesh, 4so that the just requirement of the law might be fulfilled in us, who walk not according to the flesh but according to the Spirit.[f] 5For those who live according to the flesh set their minds on the things of the flesh, but those who live according to the Spirit[g] set their minds on the things of the Spirit.[h] 6To set the mind on the flesh is death, but to set the mind on the Spirit[i] is life and peace. 7For this reason the mind that is set on the flesh is hostile to God; it does not submit to God's law—indeed it cannot, 8and those who are in the flesh cannot please God.

9 But you are not in the flesh; you are in the Spirit,[j] since the Spirit of God dwells in you. Anyone who does not have the Spirit of Christ does not belong to him. 10But if Christ is in you, though the body is dead because of sin, the Spirit[k] is life because of righteousness. 11If the Spirit of him who raised Jesus from the dead dwells in you, he who raised Christ[l] from the dead will give life to your mortal bodies also through[m] his Spirit that dwells in you.

12 So then, brothers and sisters,[n] we are debtors, not to the flesh, to live according to the flesh— 13for if you live according to the flesh, you will die; but if by the Spirit you put to death the deeds of the body, you will live. 14For all who are led by the Spirit of God are children of God. 15For you did not receive a spirit of slavery to fall back into fear, but you have received a spirit of adoption. When we cry, 'Abba![o] Father!' 16it is that very Spirit bearing witness[p] with our spirit that we are children of God, 17and if children, then heirs, heirs of God and joint heirs with Christ—if, in fact, we suffer with him so that we may also be glorified with him.

FUTURE GLORY

18 I consider that the sufferings of this present time are not worth comparing with the glory about to be revealed to us. 19For the creation waits with eager longing for the revealing of the children of God; 20for the creation was subjected to futility, not of its own will but by the will of the one who subjected it, in hope 21that the creation itself will be set free from its bondage to decay and will obtain the freedom of the glory of the children of God. 22We know that the whole creation has been groaning in labour pains until now; 23and not only the creation, but we ourselves, who have the first fruits of the Spirit, groan inwardly while we wait for adoption, the redemption of our bodies. 24For in[q] hope we were saved. Now hope that is seen is not hope. For who hopes[r] for what is seen? 25But if we hope for what we do not see, we wait for it with patience.

26 Likewise the Spirit helps us in our weakness; for we do not know how to pray as we ought, but that very Spirit intercedes[s] with sighs too deep for words. 27And God,[t] who searches the heart, knows what is the mind of the Spirit, because the Spirit[u] intercedes for the saints according to the will of God.[v]

28 We know that all things work together for good[w] for those who love God, who are called according to his purpose. 29For those whom he foreknew he also predestined to be conformed to the image of his Son, in order that he might be the firstborn within a large family.[x] 30And those whom he predestined he also called; and those whom he called he

[c] **8.2** Or *spirit* [d] **8.2** Here the Greek word *you* is singular number; other ancient authorities read *me* or *us* [e] **8.3** Or *and as a sin-offering* [f] **8.4** Or *spirit* [g] **8.5** Or *spirit* [h] **8.5** Or *spirit* [i] **8.6** Or *spirit* [j] **8.9** Or *spirit* [k] **8.10** Or *spirit* [l] **8.11** Other ancient authorities read *the Christ* or *Christ Jesus* or *Jesus Christ* [m] **8.11** Other ancient authorities read *on account of* [n] **8.12** Gk *brothers* [o] **8.15** Aramaic for *Father* [p] **8.16** Or *15a spirit of adoption, by which we cry, 'Abba! Father!' 16The Spirit itself bears witness* [q] **8.24** Or *by* [r] **8.24** Other ancient authorities read *awaits* [s] **8.26** Other ancient authorities add *for us* [t] **8.27** Gk *the one* [u] **8.27** Gk *he or it* [v] **8.27** Gk *according to God* [w] **8.28** Other ancient authorities read *God makes all things work together for good,* or *in all things God works for good* [x] **8.29** Gk *among many brothers*

also justified; and those whom he justified he also glorified.

GOD'S LOVE IN CHRIST JESUS

31 What then are we to say about
these things? If God is for us, who is
against us? 32He who did not withhold
his own Son, but gave him up for all
of us, will he not with him also give us
everything else? 33Who will bring any
charge against God's elect? It is God
who justifies. 34Who is to condemn? It
is Christ Jesus, who died, yes, who was
raised, who is at the right hand of God,
who indeed intercedes for us.[y] 35Who
will separate us from the love of Christ?
Will hardship, or distress, or persecution, or famine, or nakedness, or peril,
or sword? 36As it is written,

'For your sake we are being
    killed all day long;
  we are accounted as sheep
    to be slaughtered.'

37No, in all these things we are more
than conquerors through him who
loved us. 38For I am convinced that
neither death, nor life, nor angels, nor
rulers, nor things present, nor things
to come, nor powers, 39nor height, nor
depth, nor anything else in all creation,
will be able to separate us from the love
of God in Christ Jesus our Lord.

GOD'S ELECTION OF ISRAEL

9 I am speaking the truth in
Christ—I am not lying; my conscience confirms it by the Holy Spirit— 2I have great sorrow and unceasing
anguish in my heart. 3For I could wish
that I myself were accursed and cut off
from Christ for the sake of my own people,[z] my kindred according to the flesh.
4They are Israelites, and to them belong
the adoption, the glory, the covenants,
the giving of the law, the worship, and
the promises; 5to them belong the patriarchs, and from them, according to the
flesh, comes the Messiah,[a] who is over
all, God blessed for ever.[b] Amen.

6 It is not as though the word of God
had failed. For not all Israelites truly belong to Israel, 7and not all of Abraham's
children are his true descendants; but 'It
is through Isaac that descendants shall
be named after you.' 8This means that
it is not the children of the flesh who
are the children of God, but the children
of the promise are counted as descendants. 9For this is what the promise
said, 'About this time I will return and
Sarah shall have a son.' 10Nor is that all;
something similar happened to Rebec-
ca when she had conceived children by
one husband, our ancestor Isaac. 11Even
before they had been born or had done
anything good or bad (so that God's purpose of election might continue, 12not
by works but by his call) she was told,
'The elder shall serve the younger.' 13As
it is written,

'I have loved Jacob,
  but I have hated Esau.'

14 What then are we to say? Is there
injustice on God's part? By no means!
15For he says to Moses,

'I will have mercy on whom
    I have mercy,
  and I will have compassion on
    whom I have compassion.'

16So it depends not on human will or
exertion, but on God who shows mercy.
17For the scripture says to Pharaoh,
'I have raised you up for the very purpose of showing my power in you, so
that my name may be proclaimed in
all the earth.' 18So then he has mercy
on whomsoever he chooses, and he
hardens the heart of whomsoever he
chooses.

GOD'S WRATH AND MERCY

19 You will say to me then, 'Why
then does he still find fault? For who
can resist his will?' 20But who indeed
are you, a human being, to argue with
God? Will what is moulded say to the
one who moulds it, 'Why have you made
me like this?' 21Has the potter no right
over the clay, to make out of the same
lump one object for special use and another for ordinary use? 22What if God,
desiring to show his wrath and to make
known his power, has endured with
much patience the objects of wrath that
are made for destruction; 23and what if
he has done so in order to make known
the riches of his glory for the objects of
mercy, which he has prepared beforehand for glory— 24including us whom
he has called, not from the Jews only
but also from the Gentiles? 25As indeed
he says in Hosea,

'Those who were not my people
    I will call "my people",
  and her who was not beloved
    I will call "beloved".'

[y] **8.34** *Or Is it Christ Jesus . . . for us?* [z] **9.3** *Gk my brothers* [a] **9.5** *Or the Christ* [b] **9.5** *Or Messiah, who is God over all, blessed for ever; or Messiah. May he who is God over all be blessed for ever*

26 'And in the very place where it
was said to them, "You
are not my people",
there they shall be called children
of the living God.'
27 And Isaiah cries out concerning
Israel, 'Though the number of the children of Israel were like the sand of the
sea, only a remnant of them will be
saved; 28for the Lord will execute his
sentence on the earth quickly and deci-
sively.'[c] 29And as Isaiah predicted,
'If the Lord of hosts had not
left survivors[d] to us,
we would have fared like Sodom
and been made like Gomorrah.'

ISRAEL'S UNBELIEF

30 What then are we to say? Gentiles,
who did not strive for righteousness,
have attained it, that is, righteousness
through faith; 31but Israel, who did
strive for the righteousness that is based
on the law, did not succeed in fulfilling
that law. 32Why not? Because they did
not strive for it on the basis of faith, but
as if it were based on works. They have
stumbled over the stumbling-stone, 33as
it is written,
'See, I am laying in Zion a stone
that will make people
stumble, a rock that
will make them fall,
and whoever believes in him[e]
will not be put to shame.'

10 Brothers and sisters,[f] my
heart's desire and prayer to God
for them is that they may be saved.
2I can testify that they have a zeal for
God, but it is not enlightened. 3For, being ignorant of the righteousness that
comes from God, and seeking to establish their own, they have not submit-
ted to God's righteousness. 4For Christ
is the end of the law so that there may
be righteousness for everyone who believes.

SALVATION IS FOR ALL

5 Moses writes concerning the righteousness that comes from the law, that
'the person who does these things will
live by them.' 6But the righteousness
that comes from faith says, 'Do not say
in your heart, "Who will ascend into
heaven?"' (that is, to bring Christ down)
7'or "Who will descend into the abyss?"'
(that is, to bring Christ up from the
dead). 8But what does it say?
'The word is near you,
on your lips and in your heart'
(that is, the word of faith that we proclaim); 9because[g] if you confess with
your lips that Jesus is Lord and believe
in your heart that God raised him from
the dead, you will be saved. 10For one
believes with the heart and so is justified, and one confesses with the mouth
and so is saved. 11The scripture says, 'No
one who believes in him will be put to
shame.' 12For there is no distinction between Jew and Greek; the same Lord is
Lord of all and is generous to all who
call on him. 13For, 'Everyone who calls
on the name of the Lord shall be saved.'
14 But how are they to call on one in
whom they have not believed? And how
are they to believe in one of whom they
have never heard? And how are they to
hear without someone to proclaim him?
15And how are they to proclaim him unless they are sent? As it is written, 'How
beautiful are the feet of those who bring
good news!' 16But not all have obeyed
the good news;[h] for Isaiah says, 'Lord,
who has believed our message?' 17So
faith comes from what is heard, and
what is heard comes through the word
of Christ.[i]
18 But I ask, have they not heard? Indeed they have; for
'Their voice has gone out to
all the earth,
and their words to the
ends of the world.'
19Again I ask, did Israel not understand? First Moses says,
'I will make you jealous of those
who are not a nation;
with a foolish nation I will
make you angry.'
20Then Isaiah is so bold as to say,
'I have been found by those
who did not seek me;
I have shown myself to those
who did not ask for me.'
21But of Israel he says, 'All day long I
have held out my hands to a disobedient
and contrary people.'

ISRAEL'S REJECTION IS NOT FINAL

11 I ask, then, has God rejected his
people? By no means! I myself
am an Israelite, a descendant of Abraham, a member of the tribe of Benjamin.

[c] 9.28 Other ancient authorities read *for he will finish his work and cut it short in righteousness, because the Lord will make the sentence shortened on the earth* [d] 9.29 Or *descendants*; Gk *seed* [e] 9.33 Or *trusts in it* [f] 10.1 Gk *Brothers* [g] 10.9 Or *namely, that* [h] 10.16 Or *gospel* [i] 10.17 Or *about Christ*; other ancient authorities read *of God*

2God has not rejected his people whom
he foreknew. Do you not know what the
scripture says of Elijah, how he pleads
with God against Israel? 3'Lord, they
have killed your prophets, they have
demolished your altars; I alone am left,
and they are seeking my life.' 4But what
is the divine reply to him? 'I have kept
for myself seven thousand who have not
bowed the knee to Baal.' 5So too at the
present time there is a remnant, chosen
by grace. 6But if it is by grace, it is no
longer on the basis of works, otherwise
grace would no longer be grace.[j]

7 What then? Israel failed to obtain
what it was seeking. The elect obtained
it, but the rest were hardened, 8as it is
written,

'God gave them a sluggish spirit,
eyes that would not see
and ears that would not hear,
down to this very day.'

9And David says,

'Let their table become a
snare and a trap,
a stumbling-block and a
retribution for them;
10 let their eyes be darkened so
that they cannot see,
and keep their backs for ever bent.'

THE SALVATION OF THE GENTILES

11 So I ask, have they stumbled so as
to fall? By no means! But through their
stumbling[k] salvation has come to the
Gentiles, so as to make Israel[l] jealous.
12Now if their stumbling[m] means riches
for the world, and if their defeat means
riches for Gentiles, how much more will
their full inclusion mean!

13 Now I am speaking to you Gentiles. Inasmuch then as I am an apostle
to the Gentiles, I glorify my ministry
14in order to make my own people[n] jealous, and thus save some of them. 15For
if their rejection is the reconciliation of
the world, what will their acceptance be
but life from the dead! 16If the part of
the dough offered as first fruits is holy,
then the whole batch is holy; and if the
root is holy, then the branches also are
holy.

17 But if some of the branches were
broken off, and you, a wild olive shoot,
were grafted in their place to share the
rich root[o] of the olive tree, 18do not
vaunt yourselves over the branches. If
you do vaunt yourselves, remember that
it is not you that support the root, but
the root that supports you. 19You will
say, 'Branches were broken off so that I
might be grafted in.' 20That is true. They
were broken off because of their unbelief, but you stand only through faith.
So do not become proud, but stand in
awe. 21For if God did not spare the natural branches, perhaps he will not spare
you.[p] 22Note then the kindness and the
severity of God: severity towards those
who have fallen, but God's kindness towards you, provided you continue in his
kindness; otherwise you also will be cut
off. 23And even those of Israel,[q] if they
do not persist in unbelief, will be grafted
in, for God has the power to graft them
in again. 24For if you have been cut from
what is by nature a wild olive tree and
grafted, contrary to nature, into a cultivated olive tree, how much more will
these natural branches be grafted back
into their own olive tree.

ALL ISRAEL WILL BE SAVED

25 So that you may not claim to be
wiser than you are, brothers and sisters,[r] I want you to understand this
mystery: a hardening has come upon
part of Israel, until the full number of
the Gentiles has come in. 26And so all
Israel will be saved; as it is written,

'Out of Zion will come the Deliverer;
he will banish ungodliness
from Jacob.'
27 'And this is my covenant with them,
when I take away their sins.'

28As regards the gospel they are enemies of God[s] for your sake; but as regards election they are beloved, for the
sake of their ancestors; 29for the gifts
and the calling of God are irrevocable.
30Just as you were once disobedient to
God but have now received mercy because of their disobedience, 31so they
have now been disobedient in order
that, by the mercy shown to you, they
too may now[t] receive mercy. 32For God
has imprisoned all in disobedience so
that he may be merciful to all.

33 O the depth of the riches and wisdom and knowledge of God! How unsearchable are his judgements and how
inscrutable his ways!

[j] **11.6** Other ancient authorities add *But if it is by works, it is no longer on the basis of grace, otherwise work would no longer be work*
[k] **11.11** Gk *transgression* [l] **11.11** Gk *them*
[m] **11.12** Gk *transgression* [n] **11.14** Gk *my flesh*
[o] **11.17** Other ancient authorities read *the richness* [p] **11.21** Other ancient authorities read *neither will he spare you* [q] **11.23** Gk lacks *of Israel* [r] **11.25** Gk *brothers* [s] **11.28** Gk lacks *of God* [t] **11.31** Other ancient authorities lack *now*

34 'For who has known the
mind of the Lord?
Or who has been his counsellor?'
35 'Or who has given a gift to him,
to receive a gift in return?'
36For from him and through him and to
him are all things. To him be the glory
for ever. Amen.

THE NEW LIFE IN CHRIST

12 I appeal to you therefore,
brothers and sisters,[u] by the
mercies of God, to present your bodies
as a living sacrifice, holy and acceptable
to God, which is your spiritual[v] worship.
2Do not be conformed to this world,[w]
but be transformed by the renewing of
your minds, so that you may discern
what is the will of God—what is good
and acceptable and perfect.[x]

3 For by the grace given to me I say
to everyone among you not to think of
yourself more highly than you ought to
think, but to think with sober judgement, each according to the measure
of faith that God has assigned. 4For as
in one body we have many members,
and not all the members have the same
function, 5so we, who are many, are one
body in Christ, and individually we are
members one of another. 6We have gifts
that differ according to the grace given
to us: prophecy, in proportion to faith;
7ministry, in ministering; the teacher,
in teaching; 8the exhorter, in exhortation; the giver, in generosity; the leader,
in diligence; the compassionate, in
cheerfulness.

MARKS OF THE TRUE CHRISTIAN

9 Let love be genuine; hate what is
evil, hold fast to what is good; 10love one
another with mutual affection; outdo
one another in showing honour. 11Do
not lag in zeal, be ardent in spirit, serve
the Lord.[y] 12Rejoice in hope, be patient
in suffering, persevere in prayer. 13Con-
tribute to the needs of the saints; extend
hospitality to strangers.

14 Bless those who persecute you;
bless and do not curse them. 15Rejoice
with those who rejoice, weep with those
who weep. 16Live in harmony with one
another; do not be haughty, but associate with the lowly;[z] do not claim to be
wiser than you are. 17Do not repay anyone evil for evil, but take thought for
what is noble in the sight of all. 18If it
is possible, so far as it depends on you,
live peaceably with all. 19Beloved, never
avenge yourselves, but leave room for
the wrath of God;[a] for it is written, 'Vengeance is mine, I will repay, says the Lord.'
20No, 'if your enemies are hungry, feed
them; if they are thirsty, give them
something to drink; for by doing this
you will heap burning coals on their
heads.' 21Do not be overcome by evil, but
overcome evil with good.

BEING SUBJECT TO AUTHORITIES

13 Let every person be subject to
the governing authorities; for
there is no authority except from God,
and those authorities that exist have
been instituted by God. 2Therefore whoever resists authority resists what God
has appointed, and those who resist will
incur judgement. 3For rulers are not a
terror to good conduct, but to bad. Do
you wish to have no fear of the authority? Then do what is good, and you will
receive its approval; 4for it is God's servant for your good. But if you do what
is wrong, you should be afraid, for the
authority[b] does not bear the sword in
vain! It is the servant of God to execute
wrath on the wrongdoer. 5Therefore
one must be subject, not only because
of wrath but also because of conscience.
6For the same reason you also pay taxes,
for the authorities are God's servants,
busy with this very thing. 7Pay to all
what is due to them—taxes to whom
taxes are due, revenue to whom revenue
is due, respect to whom respect is due,
honour to whom honour is due.

LOVE FOR ONE ANOTHER

8 Owe no one anything, except to
love one another; for the one who loves
another has fulfilled the law. 9The commandments, 'You shall not commit
adultery; You shall not murder; You
shall not steal; You shall not covet'; and
any other commandment, are summed
up in this word, 'Love your neighbour
as yourself.' 10Love does no wrong to a
neighbour; therefore, love is the fulfilling of the law.

AN URGENT APPEAL

11 Besides this, you know what time
it is, how it is now the moment for you
to wake from sleep. For salvation is
nearer to us now than when we became

[u] **12.1** Gk *brothers* [v] **12.1** Or *reasonable*
[w] **12.2** Gk *age* [x] **12.2** Or *what is the good and acceptable and perfect will of God* [y] **12.11** Other ancient authorities read *serve the opportune time*
[z] **12.16** Or *give yourselves to humble tasks*
[a] **12.19** Gk *the wrath* [b] **13.4** Gk *it*

believers; 12the night is far gone, the day
is near. Let us then lay aside the works
of darkness and put on the armour of
light; 13let us live honourably as in the
day, not in revelling and drunkenness,
not in debauchery and licentiousness,
not in quarrelling and jealousy. 14In-
stead, put on the Lord Jesus Christ, and
make no provision for the flesh, to gratify its desires.

DO NOT JUDGE ANOTHER

14 Welcome those who are weak in
faith,[c] but not for the purpose
of quarrelling over opinions. 2Some
believe in eating anything, while the
weak eat only vegetables. 3Those who
eat must not despise those who abstain, and those who abstain must not
pass judgement on those who eat; for
God has welcomed them. 4Who are you
to pass judgement on servants of another? It is before their own lord that
they stand or fall. And they will be upheld, for the Lord[d] is able to make them
stand.

5 Some judge one day to be better
than another, while others judge all
days to be alike. Let all be fully convinced in their own minds. 6Those who
observe the day, observe it in honour
of the Lord. Also those who eat, eat
in honour of the Lord, since they give
thanks to God; while those who abstain,
abstain in honour of the Lord and give
thanks to God.

7 We do not live to ourselves, and we
do not die to ourselves. 8If we live, we
live to the Lord, and if we die, we die to
the Lord; so then, whether we live or
whether we die, we are the Lord's. 9For
to this end Christ died and lived again,
so that he might be Lord of both the
dead and the living.

10 Why do you pass judgement on
your brother or sister?[e] Or you, why do
you despise your brother or sister?[f] For
we will all stand before the judgement
seat of God.[g] 11For it is written,

'As I live, says the Lord, every
knee shall bow to me,
and every tongue shall give
praise to[h] God.'

12So then, each of us will be accountable
to God.[i]

DO NOT MAKE ANOTHER STUMBLE

13 Let us therefore no longer pass
judgement on one another, but resolve
instead never to put a stumbling-block
or hindrance in the way of another.[j] 14I
know and am persuaded in the Lord
Jesus that nothing is unclean in itself;
but it is unclean for anyone who thinks
it unclean. 15If your brother or sister[k] is
being injured by what you eat, you are
no longer walking in love. Do not let
what you eat cause the ruin of one for
whom Christ died. 16So do not let your
good be spoken of as evil. 17For the kingdom of God is not food and drink but
righteousness and peace and joy in the
Holy Spirit. 18The one who thus serves
Christ is acceptable to God and has human approval. 19Let us then pursue
what makes for peace and for mutual
edification. 20Do not, for the sake of
food, destroy the work of God. Everything is indeed clean, but it is wrong for
you to make others fall by what you eat;
21it is good not to eat meat or drink wine
or do anything that makes your brother
or sister[l] stumble.[m] 22The faith that you
have, have as your own conviction before God. Blessed are those who have no
reason to condemn themselves because
of what they approve. 23But those who
have doubts are condemned if they eat,
because they do not act from faith;[n] for
whatever does not proceed from faith[o]
is sin.[p]

PLEASE OTHERS, NOT YOURSELVES

15 We who are strong ought to put
up with the failings of the weak,
and not to please ourselves. 2Each of us
must please our neighbour for the good
purpose of building up the neighbour.
3For Christ did not please himself; but,
as it is written, 'The insults of those
who insult you have fallen on me.' 4For
whatever was written in former days
was written for our instruction, so that
by steadfastness and by the encouragement of the scriptures we might have
hope. 5May the God of steadfastness and
encouragement grant you to live in harmony with one another, in accordance
with Christ Jesus, 6so that together you
may with one voice glorify the God and
Father of our Lord Jesus Christ.

[c] **14.1** Or *conviction* [d] **14.4** Other ancient authorities read *for God* [e] **14.10** Gk *brother* [f] **14.10** Gk *brother* [g] **14.10** Other ancient authorities read *of Christ* [h] **14.11** Or *confess* [i] **14.12** Other ancient authorities lack *to God* [j] **14.13** Gk *of a brother* [k] **14.15** Gk *brother* [l] **14.21** Gk *brother* [m] **14.21** Other ancient authorities add *or be upset or be weakened* [n] **14.23** Or *conviction* [o] **14.23** Or *conviction* [p] **14.23** Other authorities, some ancient, add here 16.25–27

THE GOSPEL FOR JEWS AND GENTILES ALIKE

7 Welcome one another, therefore,
just as Christ has welcomed you, for
the glory of God. 8For I tell you that
Christ has become a servant of the circumcised on behalf of the truth of God
in order that he might confirm the
promises given to the patriarchs, 9and
in order that the Gentiles might glorify
God for his mercy. As it is written,

'Therefore I will confess[q] you
among the Gentiles,
and sing praises to your name';

10and again he says,

'Rejoice, O Gentiles, with
his people';

11and again,

'Praise the Lord, all you Gentiles,
and let all the peoples
praise him';

12and again Isaiah says,

'The root of Jesse shall come,
the one who rises to rule
the Gentiles;
in him the Gentiles shall hope.'

13May the God of hope fill you with all
joy and peace in believing, so that you
may abound in hope by the power of
the Holy Spirit.

PAUL'S REASON FOR WRITING SO BOLDLY

14 I myself feel confident about
you, my brothers and sisters,[r] that
you yourselves are full of goodness,
filled with all knowledge, and able to
instruct one another. 15Nevertheless,
on some points I have written to you
rather boldly by way of reminder, because of the grace given me by God
16to be a minister of Christ Jesus to the
Gentiles in the priestly service of the
gospel of God, so that the offering of
the Gentiles may be acceptable, sanctified by the Holy Spirit. 17In Christ
Jesus, then, I have reason to boast of
my work for God. 18For I will not venture to speak of anything except what
Christ has accomplished[s] through me
to win obedience from the Gentiles,
by word and deed, 19by the power of
signs and wonders, by the power of the
Spirit of God,[t] so that from Jerusalem
and as far around as Illyricum I have
fully proclaimed the good news[u] of
Christ. 20Thus I make it my ambition
to proclaim the good news,[v] not where
Christ has already been named, so that
I do not build on someone else's foundation, 21but as it is written,

'Those who have never been
told of him shall see,
and those who have never heard
of him shall understand.'

PAUL'S PLAN TO VISIT ROME

22 This is the reason that I have so often been hindered from coming to you.
23But now, with no further place for me
in these regions, I desire, as I have for
many years, to come to you 24when I go
to Spain. For I do hope to see you on my
journey and to be sent on by you, once
I have enjoyed your company for a little while. 25At present, however, I am
going to Jerusalem in a ministry to the
saints; 26for Macedonia and Achaia have
been pleased to share their resources
with the poor among the saints at Jerusalem. 27They were pleased to do this,
and indeed they owe it to them; for if
the Gentiles have come to share in their
spiritual blessings, they ought also to be
of service to them in material things.
28So, when I have completed this, and
have delivered to them what has been
collected,[w] I will set out by way of you to
Spain; 29and I know that when I come
to you, I will come in the fullness of the
blessing[x] of Christ.

30 I appeal to you, brothers and sisters,[y] by our Lord Jesus Christ and by
the love of the Spirit, to join me in earnest prayer to God on my behalf, 31that
I may be rescued from the unbelievers
in Judea, and that my ministry[z] to Jerusalem may be acceptable to the saints,
32so that by God's will I may come to you
with joy and be refreshed in your company. 33The God of peace be with all of
you.[a] Amen.

PERSONAL GREETINGS

16 I commend to you our sister
Phoebe, a deacon[b] of the church
at Cenchreae, 2so that you may welcome her in the Lord as is fitting for
the saints, and help her in whatever she
may require from you, for she has been
a benefactor of many and of myself as
well.

[q] **15.9** Or *thank* [r] **15.14** Gk *brothers*
[s] **15.18** Gk *speak of those things that Christ has not accomplished* [t] **15.19** Other ancient authorities read *of the Spirit* or *of the Holy Spirit*
[u] **15.19** Or *gospel* [v] **15.20** Or *gospel*
[w] **15.28** Gk *have sealed to them this fruit*
[x] **15.29** Other ancient authorities add *of the gospel* [y] **15.30** Gk *brothers* [z] **15.31** Other ancient authorities read *my bringing of a gift*
[a] **15.33** One ancient authority adds 16.25–27 here
[b] **16.1** Or *minister*

3 Greet Prisca and Aquila, who work
with me in Christ Jesus, 4and who
risked their necks for my life, to whom
not only I give thanks, but also all the
churches of the Gentiles. 5Greet also
the church in their house. Greet my beloved Epaenetus, who was the first convert[c] in Asia for Christ. 6Greet Mary,
who has worked very hard among you.
7Greet Andronicus and Junia,[d] my relatives[e] who were in prison with me;
they are prominent among the apostles,
and they were in Christ before I was.
8Greet Ampliatus, my beloved in the
Lord. 9Greet Urbanus, our co-worker in
Christ, and my beloved Stachys. 10Greet
Apelles, who is approved in Christ.
Greet those who belong to the family of
Aristobulus. 11Greet my relative[f] Hero-
dion. Greet those in the Lord who belong to the family of Narcissus. 12Greet
those workers in the Lord, Tryphaena
and Tryphosa. Greet the beloved Per-
sis, who has worked hard in the Lord.
13Greet Rufus, chosen in the Lord; and
greet his mother—a mother to me also.
14Greet Asyncritus, Phlegon, Hermes,
Patrobas, Hermas, and the brothers
and sisters[g] who are with them. 15Greet
Philologus, Julia, Nereus and his sister,
and Olympas, and all the saints who are
with them. 16Greet one another with
a holy kiss. All the churches of Christ
greet you.

FINAL INSTRUCTIONS

17 I urge you, brothers and sisters,[h]
to keep an eye on those who cause dissensions and offences, in opposition
to the teaching that you have learned;
avoid them. 18For such people do not
serve our Lord Christ, but their own appetites,[i] and by smooth talk and flattery
they deceive the hearts of the simple-
minded. 19For while your obedience is
known to all, so that I rejoice over you,
I want you to be wise in what is good,
and guileless in what is evil. 20The God
of peace will shortly crush Satan under
your feet. The grace of our Lord Jesus
Christ be with you.[j]

21 Timothy, my co-worker, greets
you; so do Lucius and Jason and Sosipater, my relatives.[k]

22 I Tertius, the writer of this letter,
greet you in the Lord.[l]

23 Gaius, who is host to me and to
the whole church, greets you. Erastus, the city treasurer, and our brother
Quartus, greet you.[m]

FINAL DOXOLOGY

25 Now to God[n] who is able to
strengthen you according to my gospel
and the proclamation of Jesus Christ,
according to the revelation of the mystery that was kept secret for long ages
26but is now disclosed, and through the
prophetic writings is made known to all
the Gentiles, according to the command
of the eternal God, to bring about the
obedience of faith— 27to the only wise
God, through Jesus Christ, to whom[o] be
the glory for ever! Amen.[p]

[c] 16.5 Gk *first fruits* [d] 16.7 Or *Junias*; other ancient authorities read *Julia* [e] 16.7 Or *compatriots* [f] 16.11 Or *compatriot* [g] 16.14 Gk *brothers* [h] 16.17 Gk *brothers* [i] 16.18 Gk *their own belly* [j] 16.20 Other ancient authorities lack this sentence [k] 16.21 Or *compatriots*
[l] 16.22 Or *I Tertius, writing this letter in the Lord, greet you* [m] 16.23 Other ancient authorities add verse 24, *The grace of our Lord Jesus Christ be with all of you. Amen.* [n] 16.25 Gk *the one*
[o] 16.27 Other ancient authorities lack *to whom*. The verse then reads, *to the only wise God be the glory through Jesus Christ for ever. Amen.*
[p] 16.27 Other ancient authorities lack 16.25–27 or include it after 14.23 or 15.33; others put verse 24 after verse 27

The First Letter of Paul to the

CORINTHIANS

The Christian community at Corinth was founded by Paul sometime in the early 50s CE. He wrote his first Letter to that community around 54–56 in order to address disputed matters (7.1) and various disorders within the congregation, e.g., divisions and quarreling among them (1.10–11), disputes about ethical issues (chs. 7–10), immorality (chs. 5–6) and disruptive worship (chs. 11–14). The Letter is very insightful into the struggle of the early Christian community to live out the implications of its faith in Christ. The Letter calls on the community to overcome its divisions in order to manifest the unity and love that is the mark of those who belong to Christ. Paul addresses the problems one by one and, toward the end of the Letter, deals with a key doctrinal issue that underlies all the rest. That issue is the true understanding of the resurrection of Christ.

Paul deals with this in his famous passage on the resurrection (ch. 15). For Paul, Christ's resurrection was not just a spiritual one, but a physical one. It was a bodily resurrection made visible to those who had received an appearance of Christ (15.5–8). Christ's resurrection is the first fruit of what God has in store for all believers. However, the rest of us have not yet experienced the end (15.20–28). The Christian community members are not yet enjoying the full benefits of salvation that will come only when Christ returns. Therefore, all must live humbly and morally, working for unity and setting a good example for one another until Christ returns. Paul's belief in the resurrection of Christ has clear ethical implications for the Christian community at Corinth and grounds Paul's response to all the other issues that divide it.

A famous passage from 1 Corinthians is about the gift of love, which is often selected as the reading for wedding celebrations (13.1–7). This passage addresses the need for Christians to use their gifts for the sake of all members of the community out of love for others, not for elevating themselves. Although the love that Paul speaks of here is not specifically about the relationship of husband and wife, it does underscore that none of the spiritual gifts have enduring value unless rooted in the love made possible because of the death and resurrection of Christ.

SALUTATION

1 Paul, called to be an apostle of Christ Jesus by the will of God, and our brother Sosthenes,

2 To the church of God that is in Corinth, to those who are sanctified in Christ Jesus, called to be saints, together with all those who in every place call on the name of our Lord Jesus Christ, both their Lord[a] and ours:

3 Grace to you and peace from God our Father and the Lord Jesus Christ.

4 I give thanks to my[b] God always for you because of the grace of God that has been given you in Christ Jesus, 5 for in every way you have been enriched in him, in speech and knowledge of every kind— 6 just as the testimony of[c] Christ has been strengthened among you— 7 so that you are not lacking in any spiritual gift as you wait for the revealing

[a] **1.2** Gk *theirs* [b] **1.4** Other ancient authorities lack *my* [c] **1.6** Or *to*

of our Lord Jesus Christ. 8He will also strengthen you to the end, so that you may be blameless on the day of our Lord Jesus Christ. 9God is faithful; by him you were called into the fellowship of his Son, Jesus Christ our Lord.

DIVISIONS IN THE CHURCH

10 Now I appeal to you, brothers and sisters,[d] by the name of our Lord Jesus Christ, that all of you should be in agreement and that there should be no divisions among you, but that you should be united in the same mind and the same purpose. 11For it has been reported to me by Chloe's people that there are quarrels among you, my brothers and sisters.[e] 12What I mean is that each of you says, 'I belong to Paul', or 'I belong to Apollos', or 'I belong to Cephas', or 'I belong to Christ.' 13Has Christ been divided? Was Paul crucified for you? Or were you baptized in the name of Paul? 14I thank God[f] that I baptized none of you except Crispus and Gaius, 15so that no one can say that you were baptized in my name. 16(I did baptize also the household of Stephanas; beyond that, I do not know whether I baptized anyone else.) 17For Christ did not send me to baptize but to proclaim the gospel, and not with eloquent wisdom, so that the cross of Christ might not be emptied of its power.

CHRIST THE POWER AND WISDOM OF GOD

18 For the message about the cross is foolishness to those who are perishing, but to us who are being saved it is the power of God. 19For it is written,

'I will destroy the wisdom
of the wise,
and the discernment of the
discerning I will thwart.'

20Where is the one who is wise? Where is the scribe? Where is the debater of this age? Has not God made foolish the wisdom of the world? 21For since, in the wisdom of God, the world did not know God through wisdom, God decided, through the foolishness of our proclamation, to save those who believe. 22For Jews demand signs and Greeks desire wisdom, 23but we proclaim Christ crucified, a stumbling-block to Jews and foolishness to Gentiles, 24but to those who are the called, both Jews and Greeks, Christ the power of God and the wisdom of God. 25For God's foolishness is wiser than human wisdom, and God's weakness is stronger than human strength.

26 Consider your own call, brothers and sisters:[g] not many of you were wise by human standards,[h] not many were powerful, not many were of noble birth. 27But God chose what is foolish in the world to shame the wise; God chose what is weak in the world to shame the strong; 28God chose what is low and despised in the world, things that are not, to reduce to nothing things that are, 29so that no one[i] might boast in the presence of God. 30He is the source of your life in Christ Jesus, who became for us wisdom from God, and righteousness and sanctification and redemption, 31in order that, as it is written, 'Let the one who boasts, boast in[j] the Lord.'

PROCLAIMING CHRIST CRUCIFIED

2 When I came to you, brothers and sisters,[k] I did not come proclaiming the mystery[l] of God to you in lofty words or wisdom. 2For I decided to know nothing among you except Jesus Christ, and him crucified. 3And I came to you in weakness and in fear and in much trembling. 4My speech and my proclamation were not with plausible words of wisdom,[m] but with a demonstration of the Spirit and of power, 5so that your faith might rest not on human wisdom but on the power of God.

THE TRUE WISDOM OF GOD

6 Yet among the mature we do speak wisdom, though it is not a wisdom of this age or of the rulers of this age, who are doomed to perish. 7But we speak God's wisdom, secret and hidden, which God decreed before the ages for our glory. 8None of the rulers of this age understood this; for if they had, they would not have crucified the Lord of glory. 9But, as it is written,

'What no eye has seen, nor ear heard,
nor the human heart conceived,
what God has prepared for those
who love him'—

10these things God has revealed to us through the Spirit; for the Spirit searches everything, even the depths of God. 11For what human being knows what is truly human except the human spirit that is within? So also no one

[d] 1.10 Gk *brothers* [e] 1.11 Gk *my brothers* [f] 1.14 Other ancient authorities read *I am thankful* [g] 1.26 Gk *brothers* [h] 1.26 Gk *according to the flesh* [i] 1.29 Gk *no flesh* [j] 1.31 Or *of* [k] 2.1 Gk *brothers* [l] 2.1 Other ancient authorities read *testimony* [m] 2.4 Other ancient authorities read *the persuasiveness of wisdom*

comprehends what is truly God's except the Spirit of God. 12Now we have
received not the spirit of the world,
but the Spirit that is from God, so that
we may understand the gifts bestowed
on us by God. 13And we speak of these
things in words not taught by human
wisdom but taught by the Spirit, interpreting spiritual things to those who
are spiritual.[n]

14 Those who are unspiritual[o] do
not receive the gifts of God's Spirit, for
they are foolishness to them, and they
are unable to understand them because
they are discerned spiritually. 15Those
who are spiritual discern all things, and
they are themselves subject to no one
else's scrutiny.

16 'For who has known the
mind of the Lord
so as to instruct him?'

But we have the mind of Christ.

ON DIVISIONS IN THE CORINTHIAN CHURCH

3 And so, brothers and sisters,[p] I
could not speak to you as spiritual
people, but rather as people of the flesh,
as infants in Christ. 2I fed you with
milk, not solid food, for you were not
ready for solid food. Even now you are
still not ready, 3for you are still of the
flesh. For as long as there is jealousy and
quarrelling among you, are you not of
the flesh, and behaving according to human inclinations? 4For when one says,
'I belong to Paul', and another, 'I belong
to Apollos', are you not merely human?

5 What then is Apollos? What is Paul?
Servants through whom you came to
believe, as the Lord assigned to each.
6I planted, Apollos watered, but God
gave the growth. 7So neither the one
who plants nor the one who waters is
anything, but only God who gives the
growth. 8The one who plants and the
one who waters have a common purpose, and each will receive wages according to the labour of each. 9For we
are God's servants, working together;
you are God's field, God's building.

10 According to the grace of God
given to me, like a skilled master builder
I laid a foundation, and someone else is
building on it. Each builder must choose
with care how to build on it. 11For no
one can lay any foundation other than
the one that has been laid; that foundation is Jesus Christ. 12Now if anyone
builds on the foundation with gold, silver, precious stones, wood, hay, straw—
13the work of each builder will become
visible, for the Day will disclose it, because it will be revealed with fire, and
the fire will test what sort of work each
has done. 14If what has been built on the
foundation survives, the builder will receive a reward. 15If the work is burned,
the builder will suffer loss; the builder
will be saved, but only as through fire.

16 Do you not know that you are
God's temple and that God's Spirit
dwells in you?[q] 17If anyone destroys
God's temple, God will destroy that person. For God's temple is holy, and you
are that temple.

18 Do not deceive yourselves. If you
think that you are wise in this age, you
should become fools so that you may
become wise. 19For the wisdom of this
world is foolishness with God. For it is
written,

'He catches the wise in their
craftiness',

20and again,

'The Lord knows the thoughts
of the wise,
that they are futile.'

21So let no one boast about human leaders. For all things are yours, 22whether
Paul or Apollos or Cephas or the world
or life or death or the present or the
future—all belong to you, 23and you
belong to Christ, and Christ belongs to
God.

THE MINISTRY OF THE APOSTLES

4 Think of us in this way, as servants
of Christ and stewards of God's
mysteries. 2Moreover, it is required
of stewards that they should be found
trustworthy. 3But with me it is a very
small thing that I should be judged by
you or by any human court. I do not
even judge myself. 4I am not aware of
anything against myself, but I am not
thereby acquitted. It is the Lord who
judges me. 5Therefore do not pronounce
judgement before the time, before the
Lord comes, who will bring to light the
things now hidden in darkness and will
disclose the purposes of the heart. Then
each one will receive commendation
from God.

6 I have applied all this to Apollos
and myself for your benefit, brothers
and sisters,[r] so that you may learn

[n] **2.13** Or *interpreting spiritual things in spiritual language*, or *comparing spiritual things with spiritual* [o] **2.14** Or *natural* [p] **3.1** Gk *brothers* [q] **3.16** In verses 16 and 17 the Greek word for *you* is plural [r] **4.6** Gk *brothers*

through us the meaning of the saying,
'Nothing beyond what is written', so
that none of you will be puffed up in
favour of one against another. 7For who
sees anything different in you?[s] What
do you have that you did not receive?
And if you received it, why do you boast
as if it were not a gift?

8 Already you have all you want! Already you have become rich! Quite apart
from us you have become kings! Indeed,
I wish that you had become kings, so
that we might be kings with you! 9For
I think that God has exhibited us apostles as last of all, as though sentenced to
death, because we have become a spectacle to the world, to angels and to mortals. 10We are fools for the sake of Christ,
but you are wise in Christ. We are weak,
but you are strong. You are held in honour, but we in disrepute. 11To the present hour we are hungry and thirsty,
we are poorly clothed and beaten and
homeless, 12and we grow weary from
the work of our own hands. When reviled, we bless; when persecuted, we
endure; 13when slandered, we speak
kindly. We have become like the rubbish
of the world, the dregs of all things, to
this very day.

FATHERLY ADMONITION

14 I am not writing this to make
you ashamed, but to admonish you as
my beloved children. 15For though you
might have ten thousand guardians in
Christ, you do not have many fathers.
Indeed, in Christ Jesus I became your
father through the gospel. 16I appeal to
you, then, be imitators of me. 17For this
reason I sent[t] you Timothy, who is my
beloved and faithful child in the Lord,
to remind you of my ways in Christ
Jesus, as I teach them everywhere in
every church. 18But some of you, thinking that I am not coming to you, have
become arrogant. 19But I will come to
you soon, if the Lord wills, and I will
find out not the talk of these arrogant
people but their power. 20For the kingdom of God depends not on talk but on
power. 21What would you prefer? Am I
to come to you with a stick, or with love
in a spirit of gentleness?

SEXUAL IMMORALITY DEFILES THE CHURCH

5 It is actually reported that there is
sexual immorality among you, and
of a kind that is not found even among
pagans; for a man is living with his father's wife. 2And you are arrogant!
Should you not rather have mourned, so
that he who has done this would have
been removed from among you?

3 For though absent in body, I am
present in spirit; and as if present I have
already pronounced judgement 4in the
name of the Lord Jesus on the man
who has done such a thing.[u] When you
are assembled, and my spirit is present
with the power of our Lord Jesus, 5you
are to hand this man over to Satan for
the destruction of the flesh, so that his
spirit may be saved on the day of the
Lord.[v]

6 Your boasting is not a good thing.
Do you not know that a little yeast leavens the whole batch of dough? 7Clean
out the old yeast so that you may be a
new batch, as you really are unleavened.
For our paschal lamb, Christ, has been
sacrificed. 8Therefore, let us celebrate
the festival, not with the old yeast, the
yeast of malice and evil, but with the
unleavened bread of sincerity and truth.

SEXUAL IMMORALITY MUST BE JUDGED

9 I wrote to you in my letter not to
associate with sexually immoral persons— 10not at all meaning the immoral of this world, or the greedy and
robbers, or idolaters, since you would
then need to go out of the world. 11But
now I am writing to you not to associate with anyone who bears the name
of brother or sister[w] who is sexually
immoral or greedy, or is an idolater, reviler, drunkard, or robber. Do not even
eat with such a one. 12For what have I
to do with judging those outside? Is it
not those who are inside that you are
to judge? 13God will judge those outside. 'Drive out the wicked person from
among you.'

LAWSUITS AMONG BELIEVERS

6 When any of you has a grievance
against another, do you dare to take
it to court before the unrighteous, instead of taking it before the saints? 2Do
you not know that the saints will judge
the world? And if the world is to be
judged by you, are you incompetent to
try trivial cases? 3Do you not know that
we are to judge angels—to say nothing

[s] **4.7** Or *Who makes you different from another?*
[t] **4.17** Or *am sending* [u] **5.4** Or *on the man who has done such a thing in the name of the Lord Jesus*
[v] **5.5** Other ancient authorities add *Jesus*
[w] **5.11** Gk *brother*

of ordinary matters? 4If you have ordinary cases, then, do you appoint as
judges those who have no standing in
the church? 5I say this to your shame.
Can it be that there is no one among
you wise enough to decide between one
believer[x] and another, 6but a believer[y]
goes to court against a believer[z]—and
before unbelievers at that?

7 In fact, to have lawsuits at all with
one another is already a defeat for you.
Why not rather be wronged? Why not
rather be defrauded? 8But you yourselves wrong and defraud—and believers[a] at that.

9 Do you not know that wrongdoers
will not inherit the kingdom of God? Do
not be deceived! Fornicators, idolaters,
adulterers, male prostitutes, sodomites,
10thieves, the greedy, drunkards, revilers, robbers—none of these will inherit
the kingdom of God. 11And this is what
some of you used to be. But you were
washed, you were sanctified, you were
justified in the name of the Lord Jesus
Christ and in the Spirit of our God.

GLORIFY GOD IN BODY AND SPIRIT

12 'All things are lawful for me', but
not all things are beneficial. 'All things
are lawful for me', but I will not be dom-
inated by anything. 13'Food is meant for
the stomach and the stomach for food',[b]
and God will destroy both one and the
other. The body is meant not for fornication but for the Lord, and the Lord for
the body. 14And God raised the Lord and
will also raise us by his power. 15Do you
not know that your bodies are members of Christ? Should I therefore take
the members of Christ and make them
members of a prostitute? Never! 16Do
you not know that whoever is united
to a prostitute becomes one body with
her? For it is said, 'The two shall be one
flesh.' 17But anyone united to the Lord
becomes one spirit with him. 18Shun
fornication! Every sin that a person
commits is outside the body; but the
fornicator sins against the body itself.
19Or do you not know that your body
is a temple[c] of the Holy Spirit within
you, which you have from God, and that
you are not your own? 20For you were
bought with a price; therefore glorify
God in your body.

DIRECTIONS CONCERNING MARRIAGE

7 Now concerning the matters about
which you wrote: 'It is well for a
man not to touch a woman.' 2But because of cases of sexual immorality,
each man should have his own wife and
each woman her own husband. 3The
husband should give to his wife her
conjugal rights, and likewise the wife
to her husband. 4For the wife does not
have authority over her own body, but
the husband does; likewise the husband
does not have authority over his own
body, but the wife does. 5Do not deprive
one another except perhaps by agreement for a set time, to devote yourselves to prayer, and then come together
again, so that Satan may not tempt you
because of your lack of self-control. 6This
I say by way of concession, not of command. 7I wish that all were as I myself
am. But each has a particular gift from
God, one having one kind and another a
different kind.

8 To the unmarried and the widows
I say that it is well for them to remain
unmarried as I am. 9But if they are
not practising self-control, they should
marry. For it is better to marry than to
be aflame with passion.

10 To the married I give this
command—not I but the Lord—that
the wife should not separate from her
husband 11(but if she does separate, let
her remain unmarried or else be reconciled to her husband), and that the husband should not divorce his wife.

12 To the rest I say—I and not the
Lord—that if any believer[d] has a wife
who is an unbeliever, and she consents
to live with him, he should not divorce
her. 13And if any woman has a husband
who is an unbeliever, and he consents
to live with her, she should not divorce
him. 14For the unbelieving husband is
made holy through his wife, and the
unbelieving wife is made holy through
her husband. Otherwise, your children
would be unclean, but as it is, they are
holy. 15But if the unbelieving partner
separates, let it be so; in such a case the
brother or sister is not bound. It is to
peace that God has called you.[e] 16Wife,
for all you know, you might save your
husband. Husband, for all you know,
you might save your wife.

[x] **6.5** Gk *brother* [y] **6.6** Gk *brother* [z] **6.6** Gk *brother* [a] **6.8** Gk *brothers* [b] **6.13** The quotation may extend to the word *other* [c] **6.19** Or *sanctuary* [d] **7.12** Gk *brother* [e] **7.15** Other ancient authorities read *us*

THE LIFE THAT THE LORD HAS ASSIGNED

17 However that may be, let each of you lead the life that the Lord has assigned, to which God called you. This is my rule in all the churches. 18 Was anyone at the time of his call already circumcised? Let him not seek to remove the marks of circumcision. Was anyone at the time of his call uncircumcised? Let him not seek circumcision. 19 Circumcision is nothing, and uncircumcision is nothing; but obeying the commandments of God is everything. 20 Let each of you remain in the condition in which you were called.

21 Were you a slave when called? Do not be concerned about it. Even if you can gain your freedom, make use of your present condition now more than ever.[f] 22 For whoever was called in the Lord as a slave is a freed person belonging to the Lord, just as whoever was free when called is a slave of Christ. 23 You were bought with a price; do not become slaves of human masters. 24 In whatever condition you were called, brothers and sisters,[g] there remain with God.

THE UNMARRIED AND THE WIDOWS

25 Now concerning virgins, I have no command of the Lord, but I give my opinion as one who by the Lord's mercy is trustworthy. 26 I think that, in view of the impending[h] crisis, it is well for you to remain as you are. 27 Are you bound to a wife? Do not seek to be free. Are you free from a wife? Do not seek a wife. 28 But if you marry, you do not sin, and if a virgin marries, she does not sin. Yet those who marry will experience distress in this life,[i] and I would spare you that. 29 I mean, brothers and sisters,[j] the appointed time has grown short; from now on, let even those who have wives be as though they had none, 30 and those who mourn as though they were not mourning, and those who rejoice as though they were not rejoicing, and those who buy as though they had no possessions, 31 and those who deal with the world as though they had no dealings with it. For the present form of this world is passing away.

32 I want you to be free from anxieties. The unmarried man is anxious about the affairs of the Lord, how to please the Lord; 33 but the married man is anxious about the affairs of the world, how to please his wife, 34 and his interests are divided. And the unmarried woman and the virgin are anxious about the affairs of the Lord, so that they may be holy in body and spirit; but the married woman is anxious about the affairs of the world, how to please her husband. 35 I say this for your own benefit, not to put any restraint upon you, but to promote good order and unhindered devotion to the Lord.

36 If anyone thinks that he is not behaving properly towards his fiancée,[k] if his passions are strong, and so it has to be, let him marry as he wishes; it is no sin. Let them marry. 37 But if someone stands firm in his resolve, being under no necessity but having his own desire under control, and has determined in his own mind to keep her as his fiancée,[l] he will do well. 38 So then, he who marries his fiancée[m] does well; and he who refrains from marriage will do better.

39 A wife is bound as long as her husband lives. But if the husband dies,[n] she is free to marry anyone she wishes, only in the Lord. 40 But in my judgement she is more blessed if she remains as she is. And I think that I too have the Spirit of God.

FOOD OFFERED TO IDOLS

8 Now concerning food sacrificed to idols: we know that 'all of us possess knowledge.' Knowledge puffs up, but love builds up. 2 Anyone who claims to know something does not yet have the necessary knowledge; 3 but anyone who loves God is known by him.

4 Hence, as to the eating of food offered to idols, we know that 'no idol in the world really exists', and that 'there is no God but one.' 5 Indeed, even though there may be so-called gods in heaven or on earth—as in fact there are many gods and many lords— 6 yet for us there is one God, the Father, from whom are all things and for whom we exist, and one Lord, Jesus Christ, through whom are all things and through whom we exist.

7 It is not everyone, however, who has this knowledge. Since some have become so accustomed to idols until now, they still think of the food they eat as food offered to an idol; and their conscience, being weak, is defiled. 8 'Food will not bring us close to God.'[o] We are no

[f] 7.21 Or *avail yourself of the opportunity*
[g] 7.24 Gk *brothers* [h] 7.26 Or *present*
[i] 7.28 Gk *in the flesh* [j] 7.29 Gk *brothers*
[k] 7.36 Gk *virgin* [l] 7.37 Gk *virgin* [m] 7.38 Gk *virgin* [n] 7.39 Gk *falls asleep* [o] 8.8 The quotation may extend to the end of the verse

worse off if we do not eat, and no better off if we do. 9 But take care that this liberty of yours does not somehow become a stumbling-block to the weak. 10 For if others see you, who possess knowledge, eating in the temple of an idol, might they not, since their conscience is weak, be encouraged to the point of eating food sacrificed to idols? 11 So by your knowledge those weak believers for whom Christ died are destroyed.[p] 12 But when you thus sin against members of your family,[q] and wound their conscience when it is weak, you sin against Christ. 13 Therefore, if food is a cause of their falling,[r] I will never eat meat, so that I may not cause one of them[s] to fall.

THE RIGHTS OF AN APOSTLE

9 Am I not free? Am I not an apostle? Have I not seen Jesus our Lord? Are you not my work in the Lord? 2 If I am not an apostle to others, at least I am to you; for you are the seal of my apostleship in the Lord.

3 This is my defence to those who would examine me. 4 Do we not have the right to our food and drink? 5 Do we not have the right to be accompanied by a believing wife,[t] as do the other apostles and the brothers of the Lord and Cephas? 6 Or is it only Barnabas and I who have no right to refrain from working for a living? 7 Who at any time pays the expenses for doing military service? Who plants a vineyard and does not eat any of its fruit? Or who tends a flock and does not get any of its milk?

8 Do I say this on human authority? Does not the law also say the same? 9 For it is written in the law of Moses, 'You shall not muzzle an ox while it is treading out the grain.' Is it for oxen that God is concerned? 10 Or does he not speak entirely for our sake? It was indeed written for our sake, for whoever ploughs should plough in hope and whoever threshes should thresh in hope of a share in the crop. 11 If we have sown spiritual good among you, is it too much if we reap your material benefits? 12 If others share this rightful claim on you, do not we still more?

Nevertheless, we have not made use of this right, but we endure anything rather than put an obstacle in the way of the gospel of Christ. 13 Do you not know that those who are employed in the temple service get their food from the temple, and those who serve at the altar share in what is sacrificed on the altar? 14 In the same way, the Lord commanded that those who proclaim the gospel should get their living by the gospel.

15 But I have made no use of any of these rights, nor am I writing this so that they may be applied in my case. Indeed, I would rather die than that—no one will deprive me of my ground for boasting! 16 If I proclaim the gospel, this gives me no ground for boasting, for an obligation is laid on me, and woe betide me if I do not proclaim the gospel! 17 For if I do this of my own will, I have a reward; but if not of my own will, I am entrusted with a commission. 18 What then is my reward? Just this: that in my proclamation I may make the gospel free of charge, so as not to make full use of my rights in the gospel.

19 For though I am free with respect to all, I have made myself a slave to all, so that I might win more of them. 20 To the Jews I became as a Jew, in order to win Jews. To those under the law I became as one under the law (though I myself am not under the law) so that I might win those under the law. 21 To those outside the law I became as one outside the law (though I am not free from God's law but am under Christ's law) so that I might win those outside the law. 22 To the weak I became weak, so that I might win the weak. I have become all things to all people, so that I might by any means save some. 23 I do it all for the sake of the gospel, so that I may share in its blessings.

24 Do you not know that in a race the runners all compete, but only one receives the prize? Run in such a way that you may win it. 25 Athletes exercise self-control in all things; they do it to receive a perishable garland, but we an imperishable one. 26 So I do not run aimlessly, nor do I box as though beating the air; 27 but I punish my body and enslave it, so that after proclaiming to others I myself should not be disqualified.

WARNINGS FROM ISRAEL'S HISTORY

10 I do not want you to be unaware, brothers and sisters,[u] that our ancestors were all under the cloud, and all passed through the sea, 2 and all were baptized into Moses in the cloud and in the sea, 3 and all ate the

[p] **8.11** Gk *the weak brother . . . is destroyed*
[q] **8.12** Gk *against the brothers* [r] **8.13** Gk *my brother's falling* [s] **8.13** Gk *cause my brother*
[t] **9.5** Gk *a sister as wife* [u] **10.1** Gk *brothers*

same spiritual food, 4and all drank the
same spiritual drink. For they drank
from the spiritual rock that followed
them, and the rock was Christ. 5Never-
theless, God was not pleased with most
of them, and they were struck down in
the wilderness.

6 Now these things occurred as examples for us, so that we might not
desire evil as they did. 7Do not become
idolaters as some of them did; as it is
written, 'The people sat down to eat and
drink, and they rose up to play.' 8We
must not indulge in sexual immorality
as some of them did, and twenty-three
thousand fell in a single day. 9We must
not put Christ[v] to the test, as some of
them did, and were destroyed by serpents. 10And do not complain as some
of them did, and were destroyed by the
destroyer. 11These things happened to
them to serve as an example, and they
were written down to instruct us, on
whom the ends of the ages have come.
12So if you think you are standing,
watch out that you do not fall. 13No testing has overtaken you that is not common to everyone. God is faithful, and he
will not let you be tested beyond your
strength, but with the testing he will
also provide the way out so that you
may be able to endure it.

14 Therefore, my dear friends,[w] flee
from the worship of idols. 15I speak as
to sensible people; judge for yourselves
what I say. 16The cup of blessing that we
bless, is it not a sharing in the blood of
Christ? The bread that we break, is it not
a sharing in the body of Christ? 17Be-
cause there is one bread, we who are
many are one body, for we all partake of
the one bread. 18Consider the people of
Israel;[x] are not those who eat the sacrifices partners in the altar? 19What do I
imply then? That food sacrificed to idols
is anything, or that an idol is anything?
20No, I imply that what pagans sacrifice, they sacrifice to demons and not
to God. I do not want you to be partners
with demons. 21You cannot drink the
cup of the Lord and the cup of demons.
You cannot partake of the table of the
Lord and the table of demons. 22Or are
we provoking the Lord to jealousy? Are
we stronger than he?

DO ALL TO THE GLORY OF GOD

23 'All things are lawful', but not all
things are beneficial. 'All things are
lawful', but not all things build up. 24Do
not seek your own advantage, but that
of others. 25Eat whatever is sold in the
meat market without raising any question on the ground of conscience, 26for
'the earth and its fullness are the Lord's.'
27If an unbeliever invites you to a meal
and you are disposed to go, eat whatever
is set before you without raising any
question on the ground of conscience.
28But if someone says to you, 'This has
been offered in sacrifice', then do not
eat it, out of consideration for the one
who informed you, and for the sake of
conscience— 29I mean the other's conscience, not your own. For why should
my liberty be subject to the judgement
of someone else's conscience? 30If I partake with thankfulness, why should I be
denounced because of that for which I
give thanks?

31 So, whether you eat or drink, or
whatever you do, do everything for the
glory of God. 32Give no offence to Jews
or to Greeks or to the church of God,
33just as I try to please everyone in everything I do, not seeking my own
advantage, but that of many, so that
11 they may be saved. 1Be imitators
of me, as I am of Christ.

HEAD COVERINGS

2 I commend you because you remember me in everything and maintain the traditions just as I handed
them on to you. 3But I want you to understand that Christ is the head of every
man, and the husband[y] is the head of
his wife,[z] and God is the head of Christ.
4Any man who prays or prophesies
with something on his head disgraces
his head, 5but any woman who prays or
prophesies with her head unveiled disgraces her head—it is one and the same
thing as having her head shaved. 6For if
a woman will not veil herself, then she
should cut off her hair; but if it is disgraceful for a woman to have her hair
cut off or to be shaved, she should wear
a veil. 7For a man ought not to have his
head veiled, since he is the image and
reflection[a] of God; but woman is the reflection[b] of man. 8Indeed, man was not
made from woman, but woman from
man. 9Neither was man created for the
sake of woman, but woman for the sake
of man. 10For this reason a woman ought

[v] 10.9 Other ancient authorities read *the Lord*
[w] 10.14 Gk *my beloved* [x] 10.18 Gk *Israel according to the flesh* [y] 11.3 The same Greek word means *man* or *husband* [z] 11.3 Or *head of the woman* [a] 11.7 Or *glory* [b] 11.7 Or *glory*

to have a symbol of[c] authority on her head,[d] because of the angels. 11Nevertheless, in the Lord woman is not independent of man or man independent of woman. 12For just as woman came from man, so man comes through woman; but all things come from God. 13Judge for yourselves: is it proper for a woman to pray to God with her head unveiled? 14Does not nature itself teach you that if a man wears long hair, it is degrading to him, 15but if a woman has long hair, it is her glory? For her hair is given to her for a covering. 16But if anyone is disposed to be contentious—we have no such custom, nor do the churches of God.

ABUSES AT THE LORD'S SUPPER

17 Now in the following instructions I do not commend you, because when you come together it is not for the better but for the worse. 18For, to begin with, when you come together as a church, I hear that there are divisions among you; and to some extent I believe it. 19Indeed, there have to be factions among you, for only so will it become clear who among you are genuine. 20When you come together, it is not really to eat the Lord's supper. 21For when the time comes to eat, each of you goes ahead with your own supper, and one goes hungry and another becomes drunk. 22What! Do you not have homes to eat and drink in? Or do you show contempt for the church of God and humiliate those who have nothing? What should I say to you? Should I commend you? In this matter I do not commend you!

THE INSTITUTION OF THE LORD'S SUPPER

23 For I received from the Lord what I also handed on to you, that the Lord Jesus on the night when he was betrayed took a loaf of bread, 24and when he had given thanks, he broke it and said, 'This is my body that is for[e] you. Do this in remembrance of me.' 25In the same way he took the cup also, after supper, saying, 'This cup is the new covenant in my blood. Do this, as often as you drink it, in remembrance of me.' 26For as often as you eat this bread and drink the cup, you proclaim the Lord's death until he comes.

PARTAKING OF THE SUPPER UNWORTHILY

27 Whoever, therefore, eats the bread or drinks the cup of the Lord in an unworthy manner will be answerable for the body and blood of the Lord. 28Examine yourselves, and only then eat of the bread and drink of the cup. 29For all who eat and drink[f] without discerning the body,[g] eat and drink judgement against themselves. 30For this reason many of you are weak and ill, and some have died.[h] 31But if we judged ourselves, we would not be judged. 32But when we are judged by the Lord, we are disciplined[i] so that we may not be condemned along with the world.

33 So then, my brothers and sisters,[j] when you come together to eat, wait for one another. 34If you are hungry, eat at home, so that when you come together, it will not be for your condemnation. About the other things I will give instructions when I come.

SPIRITUAL GIFTS

12 Now concerning spiritual gifts,[k] brothers and sisters,[l] I do not want you to be uninformed. 2You know that when you were pagans, you were enticed and led astray to idols that could not speak. 3Therefore I want you to understand that no one speaking by the Spirit of God ever says 'Let Jesus be cursed!' and no one can say 'Jesus is Lord' except by the Holy Spirit.

4 Now there are varieties of gifts, but the same Spirit; 5and there are varieties of services, but the same Lord; 6and there are varieties of activities, but it is the same God who activates all of them in everyone. 7To each is given the manifestation of the Spirit for the common good. 8To one is given through the Spirit the utterance of wisdom, and to another the utterance of knowledge according to the same Spirit, 9to another faith by the same Spirit, to another gifts of healing by the one Spirit, 10to another the working of miracles, to another prophecy, to another the discernment of spirits, to another various kinds of tongues, to another the interpretation of tongues. 11All these are activated by one and the same Spirit, who allots to

[c] 11.10 Gk lacks *a symbol of* [d] 11.10 Or *have freedom of choice regarding her head* [e] 11.24 Other ancient authorities read *is broken for* [f] 11.29 Other ancient authorities add *in an unworthy manner,* [g] 11.29 Other ancient authorities read *the Lord's body* [h] 11.30 Gk *fallen asleep* [i] 11.32 Or *When we are judged, we are being disciplined by the Lord* [j] 11.33 Gk *brothers* [k] 12.1 Or *spiritual persons* [l] 12.1 Gk *brothers*

each one individually just as the Spirit
chooses.

ONE BODY WITH MANY MEMBERS

12 For just as the body is one and
has many members, and all the members of the body, though many, are one
body, so it is with Christ. 13For in the
one Spirit we were all baptized into one
body—Jews or Greeks, slaves or free—
and we were all made to drink of one
Spirit.
14 Indeed, the body does not consist
of one member but of many. 15If the foot
were to say, 'Because I am not a hand, I
do not belong to the body', that would
not make it any less a part of the body.
16And if the ear were to say, 'Because I
am not an eye, I do not belong to the
body', that would not make it any less
a part of the body. 17If the whole body
were an eye, where would the hearing
be? If the whole body were hearing,
where would the sense of smell be?
18But as it is, God arranged the members in the body, each one of them, as
he chose. 19If all were a single member, where would the body be? 20As it
is, there are many members, yet one
body. 21The eye cannot say to the hand,
'I have no need of you', nor again the
head to the feet, 'I have no need of you.'
22On the contrary, the members of the
body that seem to be weaker are indis-
pensable, 23and those members of the
body that we think less honourable we
clothe with greater honour, and our less
respectable members are treated with
greater respect; 24whereas our more
respectable members do not need this.
But God has so arranged the body, giving the greater honour to the inferior
member, 25that there may be no dissension within the body, but the members may have the same care for one
another. 26If one member suffers, all
suffer together with it; if one member
is honoured, all rejoice together with it.
27 Now you are the body of Christ
and individually members of it. 28And
God has appointed in the church first
apostles, second prophets, third teachers; then deeds of power, then gifts of
healing, forms of assistance, forms of
leadership, various kinds of tongues.
29Are all apostles? Are all prophets?
Are all teachers? Do all work miracles?
30Do all possess gifts of healing? Do
all speak in tongues? Do all interpret?
31But strive for the greater gifts. And I
will show you a still more excellent way.

THE GIFT OF LOVE

13 If I speak in the tongues of mortals and of angels, but do not
have love, I am a noisy gong or a clanging cymbal. 2And if I have prophetic
powers, and understand all mysteries
and all knowledge, and if I have all faith,
so as to remove mountains, but do not
have love, I am nothing. 3If I give away
all my possessions, and if I hand over
my body so that I may boast,[m] but do
not have love, I gain nothing.
4 Love is patient; love is kind; love is
not envious or boastful or arrogant 5or
rude. It does not insist on its own way;
it is not irritable or resentful; 6it does
not rejoice in wrongdoing, but rejoices
in the truth. 7It bears all things, believes
all things, hopes all things, endures all
things.
8 Love never ends. But as for prophecies, they will come to an end; as for
tongues, they will cease; as for knowledge, it will come to an end. 9For we
know only in part, and we prophesy
only in part; 10but when the complete
comes, the partial will come to an end.
11When I was a child, I spoke like a child,
I thought like a child, I reasoned like a
child; when I became an adult, I put an
end to childish ways. 12For now we see
in a mirror, dimly,[n] but then we will see
face to face. Now I know only in part;
then I will know fully, even as I have
been fully known. 13And now faith,
hope, and love abide, these three; and
the greatest of these is love.

GIFTS OF PROPHECY AND TONGUES

14 Pursue love and strive for the
spiritual gifts, and especially
that you may prophesy. 2For those who
speak in a tongue do not speak to other
people but to God; for nobody understands them, since they are speaking
mysteries in the Spirit. 3On the other
hand, those who prophesy speak to
other people for their building up and
encouragement and consolation. 4Those
who speak in a tongue build up themselves, but those who prophesy build up
the church. 5Now I would like all of you
to speak in tongues, but even more to
prophesy. One who prophesies is greater
than one who speaks in tongues, unless
someone interprets, so that the church
may be built up.

[m] 13.3 Other ancient authorities read *body to be burned* [n] 13.12 Gk *in a riddle*

6 Now, brothers and sisters,[o] if I come
to you speaking in tongues, how will I
benefit you unless I speak to you in some
revelation or knowledge or prophecy or
teaching? 7It is the same way with lifeless instruments that produce sound,
such as the flute or the harp. If they do
not give distinct notes, how will anyone
know what is being played? 8And if the
bugle gives an indistinct sound, who will
get ready for battle? 9So with yourselves;
if in a tongue you utter speech that is not
intelligible, how will anyone know what
is being said? For you will be speaking
into the air. 10There are doubtless many
different kinds of sounds in the world,
and nothing is without sound. 11If then
I do not know the meaning of a sound,
I will be a foreigner to the speaker and
the speaker a foreigner to me. 12So with
yourselves; since you are eager for spiritual gifts, strive to excel in them for
building up the church.

13 Therefore, one who speaks in a
tongue should pray for the power to interpret. 14For if I pray in a tongue, my
spirit prays but my mind is unproductive. 15What should I do then? I will
pray with the spirit, but I will pray with
the mind also; I will sing praise with
the spirit, but I will sing praise with
the mind also. 16Otherwise, if you say
a blessing with the spirit, how can anyone in the position of an outsider say
the 'Amen' to your thanksgiving, since
the outsider does not know what you
are saying? 17For you may give thanks
well enough, but the other person is not
built up. 18I thank God that I speak in
tongues more than all of you; 19never-
theless, in church I would rather speak
five words with my mind, in order to
instruct others also, than ten thousand
words in a tongue.

20 Brothers and sisters,[p] do not be
children in your thinking; rather, be infants in evil, but in thinking be adults.
21In the law it is written,

'By people of strange tongues
and by the lips of foreigners
I will speak to this people;
yet even then they will
not listen to me,'

says the Lord. 22Tongues, then, are a
sign not for believers but for unbelievers,
while prophecy is not for unbelievers but
for believers. 23If, therefore, the whole
church comes together and all speak
in tongues, and outsiders or unbelievers enter, will they not say that you are
out of your mind? 24But if all prophesy,
an unbeliever or outsider who enters is
reproved by all and called to account by
all. 25After the secrets of the unbeliever's
heart are disclosed, that person will bow
down before God and worship him, declaring, 'God is really among you.'

ORDERLY WORSHIP

26 What should be done then, my
friends?[q] When you come together, each
one has a hymn, a lesson, a revelation,
a tongue, or an interpretation. Let all
things be done for building up. 27If anyone speaks in a tongue, let there be only
two or at most three, and each in turn;
and let one interpret. 28But if there is
no one to interpret, let them be silent in
church and speak to themselves and to
God. 29Let two or three prophets speak,
and let the others weigh what is said.
30If a revelation is made to someone else
sitting nearby, let the first person be silent. 31For you can all prophesy one by
one, so that all may learn and all be encouraged. 32And the spirits of prophets
are subject to the prophets, 33for God is a
God not of disorder but of peace.

(As in all the churches of the saints,
34women should be silent in the
churches. For they are not permitted to
speak, but should be subordinate, as the
law also says. 35If there is anything they
desire to know, let them ask their husbands at home. For it is shameful for a
woman to speak in church.[r] 36Or did the
word of God originate with you? Or are
you the only ones it has reached?)

37 Anyone who claims to be a
prophet, or to have spiritual powers,
must acknowledge that what I am writing to you is a command of the Lord.
38Anyone who does not recognize this is
not to be recognized. 39So, my friends,[s]
be eager to prophesy, and do not forbid
speaking in tongues; 40but all things
should be done decently and in order.

THE RESURRECTION OF CHRIST

15 Now I should remind you,
brothers and sisters,[t] of the good
news[u] that I proclaimed to you, which
you in turn received, in which also you
stand, 2through which also you are being saved, if you hold firmly to the message that I proclaimed to you—unless
you have come to believe in vain.

[o] 14.6 Gk *brothers* [p] 14.20 Gk *brothers*
[q] 14.26 Gk *brothers* [r] 14.35 Other ancient authorities put verses 34–35 after verse 40
[s] 14.39 Gk *my brothers* [t] 15.1 Gk *brothers*
[u] 15.1 Or *gospel*

3 For I handed on to you as of first
importance what I in turn had received:
that Christ died for our sins in accordance with the scriptures, 4and that he
was buried, and that he was raised on the
third day in accordance with the scriptures, 5and that he appeared to Cephas,
then to the twelve. 6Then he appeared to
more than five hundred brothers and sisters[v] at one time, most of whom are still
alive, though some have died.[w] 7Then he
appeared to James, then to all the apostles. 8Last of all, as to someone untimely
born, he appeared also to me. 9For I am
the least of the apostles, unfit to be called
an apostle, because I persecuted the
church of God. 10But by the grace of God I
am what I am, and his grace towards me
has not been in vain. On the contrary,
I worked harder than any of them—
though it was not I, but the grace of God
that is with me. 11Whether then it was I
or they, so we proclaim and so you have
come to believe.

THE RESURRECTION OF THE DEAD

12 Now if Christ is proclaimed as
raised from the dead, how can some of
you say there is no resurrection of the
dead? 13If there is no resurrection of the
dead, then Christ has not been raised;
14and if Christ has not been raised, then
our proclamation has been in vain and
your faith has been in vain. 15We are
even found to be misrepresenting God,
because we testified of God that he raised
Christ—whom he did not raise if it is
true that the dead are not raised. 16For if
the dead are not raised, then Christ has
not been raised. 17If Christ has not been
raised, your faith is futile and you are
still in your sins. 18Then those also who
have died[x] in Christ have perished. 19If
for this life only we have hoped in Christ,
we are of all people most to be pitied.

20 But in fact Christ has been raised
from the dead, the first fruits of those
who have died.[y] 21For since death came
through a human being, the resurrection of the dead has also come through
a human being; 22for as all die in Adam,
so all will be made alive in Christ. 23But
each in his own order: Christ the first
fruits, then at his coming those who belong to Christ. 24Then comes the end,[z]
when he hands over the kingdom to God
the Father, after he has destroyed every
ruler and every authority and power.
25For he must reign until he has put all
his enemies under his feet. 26The last enemy to be destroyed is death. 27For 'God[a]
has put all things in subjection under his
feet.' But when it says, 'All things are put
in subjection', it is plain that this does
not include the one who put all things in
subjection under him. 28When all things
are subjected to him, then the Son himself will also be subjected to the one who
put all things in subjection under him,
so that God may be all in all.

29 Otherwise, what will those people
do who receive baptism on behalf of the
dead? If the dead are not raised at all,
why are people baptized on their behalf?

30 And why are we putting ourselves
in danger every hour? 31I die every day!
That is as certain, brothers and sisters,[b]
as my boasting of you—a boast that I
make in Christ Jesus our Lord. 32If with
merely human hopes I fought with wild
animals at Ephesus, what would I have
gained by it? If the dead are not raised,

'Let us eat and drink,
for tomorrow we die.'

33Do not be deceived:

'Bad company ruins good morals.'

34Come to a sober and right mind, and
sin no more; for some people have no
knowledge of God. I say this to your
shame.

THE RESURRECTION BODY

35 But someone will ask, 'How are
the dead raised? With what kind of
body do they come?' 36Fool! What you
sow does not come to life unless it dies.
37And as for what you sow, you do not
sow the body that is to be, but a bare
seed, perhaps of wheat or of some other
grain. 38But God gives it a body as he has
chosen, and to each kind of seed its own
body. 39Not all flesh is alike, but there is
one flesh for human beings, another for
animals, another for birds, and another
for fish. 40There are both heavenly bodies and earthly bodies, but the glory of
the heavenly is one thing, and that of the
earthly is another. 41There is one glory of
the sun, and another glory of the moon,
and another glory of the stars; indeed,
star differs from star in glory.

42 So it is with the resurrection of
the dead. What is sown is perishable,
what is raised is imperishable. 43It is
sown in dishonour, it is raised in glory.
It is sown in weakness, it is raised in
power. 44It is sown a physical body, it
is raised a spiritual body. If there is a

[v] 15.6 Gk *brothers* [w] 15.6 Gk *fallen asleep*
[x] 15.18 Gk *fallen asleep* [y] 15.20 Gk *fallen asleep* [z] 15.24 Or *Then come the rest*
[a] 15.27 Gk *he* [b] 15.31 Gk *brothers*

physical body, there is also a spiritual
body. 45 Thus it is written, 'The first man,
Adam, became a living being'; the last
Adam became a life-giving spirit. 46 But
it is not the spiritual that is first, but the
physical, and then the spiritual. 47 The
first man was from the earth, a man of
dust; the second man is[c] from heaven.
48 As was the man of dust, so are those
who are of the dust; and as is the man of
heaven, so are those who are of heaven.
49 Just as we have borne the image of the
man of dust, we will[d] also bear the image of the man of heaven.

50 What I am saying, brothers and
sisters,[e] is this: flesh and blood cannot
inherit the kingdom of God, nor does
the perishable inherit the imperishable. 51 Listen, I will tell you a mystery!
We will not all die,[f] but we will all be
changed, 52 in a moment, in the twin-
kling of an eye, at the last trumpet. For
the trumpet will sound, and the dead
will be raised imperishable, and we will
be changed. 53 For this perishable body
must put on imperishability, and this
mortal body must put on immortality.
54 When this perishable body puts on
imperishability, and this mortal body
puts on immortality, then the saying
that is written will be fulfilled:

'Death has been swallowed
up in victory.'
55 'Where, O death, is your victory?
Where, O death, is your sting?'

56 The sting of death is sin, and the power
of sin is the law. 57 But thanks be to God,
who gives us the victory through our
Lord Jesus Christ.

58 Therefore, my beloved,[g] be steadfast, immovable, always excelling in
the work of the Lord, because you know
that in the Lord your labour is not in
vain.

THE COLLECTION FOR THE SAINTS

16 Now concerning the collection
for the saints: you should follow
the directions I gave to the churches of
Galatia. 2 On the first day of every week,
each of you is to put aside and save whatever extra you earn, so that collections
need not be taken when I come. 3 And
when I arrive, I will send any whom you
approve with letters to take your gift to
Jerusalem. 4 If it seems advisable that I
should go also, they will accompany me.

PLANS FOR TRAVEL

5 I will visit you after passing
through Macedonia—for I intend to
pass through Macedonia— 6 and perhaps I will stay with you or even spend
the winter, so that you may send me on
my way, wherever I go. 7 I do not want to
see you now just in passing, for I hope to
spend some time with you, if the Lord
permits. 8 But I will stay in Ephesus until Pentecost, 9 for a wide door for effective work has opened to me, and there
are many adversaries.

10 If Timothy comes, see that he
has nothing to fear among you, for he
is doing the work of the Lord just as I
am; 11 therefore let no one despise him.
Send him on his way in peace, so that he
may come to me; for I am expecting him
with the brothers.

12 Now concerning our brother
Apollos, I strongly urged him to visit
you with the other brothers, but he was
not at all willing[h] to come now. He will
come when he has the opportunity.

FINAL MESSAGES AND GREETINGS

13 Keep alert, stand firm in your
faith, be courageous, be strong. 14 Let all
that you do be done in love.

15 Now, brothers and sisters,[i] you
know that members of the household
of Stephanas were the first converts in
Achaia, and they have devoted themselves to the service of the saints; 16 I
urge you to put yourselves at the service
of such people, and of everyone who
works and toils with them. 17 I rejoice
at the coming of Stephanas and Fortu-
natus and Achaicus, because they have
made up for your absence; 18 for they
refreshed my spirit as well as yours. So
give recognition to such people.

19 The churches of Asia send greetings. Aquila and Prisca, together with
the church in their house, greet you
warmly in the Lord. 20 All the brothers
and sisters[j] send greetings. Greet one
another with a holy kiss.

21 I, Paul, write this greeting with
my own hand. 22 Let anyone be accursed
who has no love for the Lord. Our Lord,
come![k] 23 The grace of the Lord Jesus be
with you. 24 My love be with all of you in
Christ Jesus.[l]

[c] **15.47** Other ancient authorities add *the Lord*
[d] **15.49** Other ancient authorities read *let us*
[e] **15.50** Gk *brothers* [f] **15.51** Gk *fall asleep*
[g] **15.58** Gk *beloved brothers* [h] **16.12** Or *it was not at all God's will for him* [i] **16.15** Gk *brothers*
[j] **16.20** Gk *brothers* [k] **16.22** Gk *Marana tha.* These Aramaic words can also be read *Maran atha,* meaning *Our Lord has come* [l] **16.24** Other ancient authorities add *Amen*

The Second Letter of Paul to the

CORINTHIANS

Paul's Second Letter to the Corinthians seems to be a compilation of writings separated by intervals and completed around 57 CE. The Letter anticipates another visit by Paul to the community. Paul has a very personal relationship to the Christian community at Corinth, and this Letter reveals both his frustrations with and affections for it. He shares in this Letter his vision of the ministry of reconciliation, underscoring his faith in Jesus' death and resurrection as the pattern of all Christian life and of Paul's purpose to be an ambassador for Christ (5.11–21).

One of the issues Paul addresses in this Letter is the challenge to his ministry. In Corinth, other missionaries had come and taught differently than Paul, creating comparisons, questions, and confusion about Paul's authority. In this Letter Paul acknowledges his shortcomings but states forcefully, "So, I will boast all the more gladly of my weaknesses, so that the power of Christ may dwell in me" (12.9). Paul turns his own weaknesses and sufferings into a matter of his integrity for preaching the gospel. He urges his readers not to receive "the grace of God in vain" (6.1), but to hold fast to what Paul had preached to them in truth (6.1–13). In one of the more memorable texts written by Paul, he describes his ministry in this way: "But we have this treasure in clay jars, so that it may be made clear that this extraordinary power belongs to God and does not come from us" (4.7).

The conclusion of this Letter is a trinitarian formula that acts as a kind of blessing upon the Corinthians. It is memorialized in the liturgy today as one of the choices for the opening greeting of the Mass. It is also read as part of the second reading on Trinity Sunday in Year A. "The grace of the Lord Jesus Christ, the love of God, and the communion of the Holy Spirit be with all of you" (13.13).

SALUTATION

1 Paul, an apostle of Christ Jesus by
the will of God, and Timothy our
brother,

To the church of God that is in Corinth, including all the saints throughout Achaia:

2 Grace to you and peace from God
our Father and the Lord Jesus Christ.

PAUL'S THANKSGIVING AFTER AFFLICTION

3 Blessed be the God and Father of our
Lord Jesus Christ, the Father of mercies
and the God of all consolation, 4who consoles us in all our affliction, so that we
may be able to console those who are in
any affliction with the consolation with
which we ourselves are consoled by God.
5For just as the sufferings of Christ are
abundant for us, so also our consolation
is abundant through Christ. 6If we are
being afflicted, it is for your consolation
and salvation; if we are being consoled,
it is for your consolation, which you experience when you patiently endure the
same sufferings that we are also suffering. 7Our hope for you is unshaken; for
we know that as you share in our sufferings, so also you share in our consolation.

8 We do not want you to be unaware,
brothers and sisters,[a] of the affliction

[a] 1.8 Gk *brothers*

we experienced in Asia; for we were so
utterly, unbearably crushed that we de-
spaired of life itself. 9Indeed, we felt that
we had received the sentence of death so
that we would rely not on ourselves but
on God who raises the dead. 10He who
rescued us from so deadly a peril will
continue to rescue us; on him we have
set our hope that he will rescue us again,
11as you also join in helping us by your
prayers, so that many will give thanks
on our[b] behalf for the blessing granted
to us through the prayers of many.

THE POSTPONEMENT OF PAUL'S VISIT

12 Indeed, this is our boast, the testimony of our conscience: we have behaved in the world with frankness[c] and
godly sincerity, not by earthly wisdom
but by the grace of God—and all the
more towards you. 13For we write to you
nothing other than what you can read
and also understand; I hope you will understand until the end— 14as you have
already understood us in part—that on
the day of the Lord Jesus we are your
boast even as you are our boast.

15 Since I was sure of this, I wanted
to come to you first, so that you might
have a double favour;[d] 16I wanted to visit
you on my way to Macedonia, and to
come back to you from Macedonia and
have you send me on to Judea. 17Was I
vacillating when I wanted to do this?
Do I make my plans according to ordinary human standards,[e] ready to say
'Yes, yes' and 'No, no' at the same time?
18As surely as God is faithful, our word
to you has not been 'Yes and No.' 19For
the Son of God, Jesus Christ, whom we
proclaimed among you, Silvanus and
Timothy and I, was not 'Yes and No'; but
in him it is always 'Yes.' 20For in him every one of God's promises is a 'Yes.' For
this reason it is through him that we
say the 'Amen', to the glory of God. 21But
it is God who establishes us with you in
Christ and has anointed us, 22by putting
his seal on us and giving us his Spirit in
our hearts as a first instalment.

23 But I call on God as witness
against me: it was to spare you that I
did not come again to Corinth. 24I do
not mean to imply that we lord it over
your faith; rather, we are workers with
you for your joy, because you stand firm

2 in the faith. 1So I made up my
mind not to make you another
painful visit. 2For if I cause you pain,
who is there to make me glad but the
one whom I have pained? 3And I wrote
as I did, so that when I came, I might
not suffer pain from those who should
have made me rejoice; for I am confident about all of you, that my joy would
be the joy of all of you. 4For I wrote to
you out of much distress and anguish of
heart and with many tears, not to cause
you pain, but to let you know the abundant love that I have for you.

FORGIVENESS FOR THE OFFENDER

5 But if anyone has caused pain, he
has caused it not to me, but to some
extent—not to exaggerate it—to all of
you. 6This punishment by the majority is enough for such a person; 7so now
instead you should forgive and console him, so that he may not be overwhelmed by excessive sorrow. 8So I
urge you to reaffirm your love for him.
9I wrote for this reason: to test you and
to know whether you are obedient in everything. 10Anyone whom you forgive,
I also forgive. What I have forgiven,
if I have forgiven anything, has been
for your sake in the presence of Christ.
11And we do this so that we may not be
outwitted by Satan; for we are not ignorant of his designs.

PAUL'S ANXIETY IN TROAS

12 When I came to Troas to proclaim
the good news of Christ, a door was
opened for me in the Lord; 13but my
mind could not rest because I did not
find my brother Titus there. So I said
farewell to them and went on to Macedonia.

14 But thanks be to God, who in
Christ always leads us in triumphal procession, and through us spreads in every place the fragrance that comes from
knowing him. 15For we are the aroma
of Christ to God among those who are
being saved and among those who
are perishing; 16to the one a fragrance
from death to death, to the other a fragrance from life to life. Who is sufficient
for these things? 17For we are not ped-
dlers of God's word like so many;[f] but in
Christ we speak as persons of sincerity,
as persons sent from God and standing
in his presence.

[b] 1.11 Other ancient authorities read *your*
[c] 1.12 Other ancient authorities read *holiness*
[d] 1.15 Other ancient authorities read *pleasure*
[e] 1.17 Gk *according to the flesh* [f] 2.17 Other ancient authorities read *like the others*

MINISTERS OF THE NEW COVENANT

3 Are we beginning to commend ourselves again? Surely we do not need,
as some do, letters of recommendation
to you or from you, do we? 2You yourselves are our letter, written on our[g]
hearts, to be known and read by all;
3and you show that you are a letter of
Christ, prepared by us, written not with
ink but with the Spirit of the living God,
not on tablets of stone but on tablets of
human hearts.

4 Such is the confidence that we have
through Christ towards God. 5Not that
we are competent of ourselves to claim
anything as coming from us; our com-
petence is from God, 6who has made us
competent to be ministers of a new covenant, not of letter but of spirit; for the
letter kills, but the Spirit gives life.

7 Now if the ministry of death, chis-
elled in letters on stone tablets,[h] came in
glory so that the people of Israel could
not gaze at Moses' face because of the
glory of his face, a glory now set aside,
8how much more will the ministry of
the Spirit come in glory? 9For if there
was glory in the ministry of condemnation, much more does the ministry of
justification abound in glory! 10Indeed,
what once had glory has lost its glory
because of the greater glory; 11for if what
was set aside came through glory, much
more has the permanent come in glory!

12 Since, then, we have such a hope,
we act with great boldness, 13not like
Moses, who put a veil over his face to
keep the people of Israel from gazing at
the end of the glory that[i] was being set
aside. 14But their minds were hardened.
Indeed, to this very day, when they
hear the reading of the old covenant,
that same veil is still there, since only
in Christ is it set aside. 15Indeed, to this
very day whenever Moses is read, a veil
lies over their minds; 16but when one
turns to the Lord, the veil is removed.
17Now the Lord is the Spirit, and where
the Spirit of the Lord is, there is freedom. 18And all of us, with unveiled
faces, seeing the glory of the Lord as
though reflected in a mirror, are being
transformed into the same image from
one degree of glory to another; for this
comes from the Lord, the Spirit.

TREASURE IN CLAY JARS

4 Therefore, since it is by God's mercy
that we are engaged in this ministry, we do not lose heart. 2We have renounced the shameful things that one
hides; we refuse to practise cunning or
to falsify God's word; but by the open
statement of the truth we commend
ourselves to the conscience of everyone
in the sight of God. 3And even if our
gospel is veiled, it is veiled to those who
are perishing. 4In their case the god of
this world has blinded the minds of the
unbelievers, to keep them from seeing
the light of the gospel of the glory of
Christ, who is the image of God. 5For
we do not proclaim ourselves; we proclaim Jesus Christ as Lord and ourselves
as your slaves for Jesus' sake. 6For it is
the God who said, 'Let light shine out of
darkness', who has shone in our hearts
to give the light of the knowledge of the
glory of God in the face of Jesus Christ.

7 But we have this treasure in clay
jars, so that it may be made clear that this
extraordinary power belongs to God and
does not come from us. 8We are afflicted
in every way, but not crushed; perplexed,
but not driven to despair; 9persecuted,
but not forsaken; struck down, but not
destroyed; 10always carrying in the body
the death of Jesus, so that the life of Jesus
may also be made visible in our bodies.
11For while we live, we are always being
given up to death for Jesus' sake, so that
the life of Jesus may be made visible in
our mortal flesh. 12So death is at work in
us, but life in you.

13 But just as we have the same
spirit of faith that is in accordance with
scripture—'I believed, and so I spoke'—
we also believe, and so we speak, 14be-
cause we know that the one who raised
the Lord Jesus will raise us also with
Jesus, and will bring us with you into
his presence. 15Yes, everything is for
your sake, so that grace, as it extends
to more and more people, may increase
thanksgiving, to the glory of God.

LIVING BY FAITH

16 So we do not lose heart. Even
though our outer nature is wasting
away, our inner nature is being renewed day by day. 17For this slight mo-
mentary affliction is preparing us for
an eternal weight of glory beyond all
measure, 18because we look not at what
can be seen but at what cannot be seen;
for what can be seen is temporary, but
what cannot be seen is eternal.

5 For we know that if the earthly tent
we live in is destroyed, we have a

[g] 3.2 Other ancient authorities read *your*
[h] 3.7 Gk *on stones* [i] 3.13 Gk *of what*

building from God, a house not made
with hands, eternal in the heavens.
2For in this tent we groan, longing to be
clothed with our heavenly dwelling—
3if indeed, when we have taken it off[j]
we will not be found naked. 4For while
we are still in this tent, we groan under
our burden, because we wish not to be
unclothed but to be further clothed, so
that what is mortal may be swallowed
up by life. 5He who has prepared us for
this very thing is God, who has given us
the Spirit as a guarantee.

6 So we are always confident; even
though we know that while we are at
home in the body we are away from
the Lord— 7for we walk by faith, not
by sight. 8Yes, we do have confidence,
and we would rather be away from the
body and at home with the Lord. 9So
whether we are at home or away, we
make it our aim to please him. 10For all
of us must appear before the judgement
seat of Christ, so that each may receive
recompense for what has been done in
the body, whether good or evil.

THE MINISTRY OF RECONCILIATION

11 Therefore, knowing the fear of the
Lord, we try to persuade others; but we
ourselves are well known to God, and I
hope that we are also well known to your
consciences. 12We are not commending
ourselves to you again, but giving you
an opportunity to boast about us, so
that you may be able to answer those
who boast in outward appearance and
not in the heart. 13For if we are beside
ourselves, it is for God; if we are in our
right mind, it is for you. 14For the love of
Christ urges us on, because we are convinced that one has died for all; therefore all have died. 15And he died for all,
so that those who live might live no longer for themselves, but for him who died
and was raised for them.

16 From now on, therefore, we regard no one from a human point of
view;[k] even though we once knew
Christ from a human point of view,[l] we
know him no longer in that way. 17So if
anyone is in Christ, there is a new creation: everything old has passed away;
see, everything has become new! 18All
this is from God, who reconciled us to
himself through Christ, and has given
us the ministry of reconciliation; 19that
is, in Christ God was reconciling the
world to himself,[m] not counting their
trespasses against them, and entrust-
ing the message of reconciliation to
us. 20So we are ambassadors for Christ,
since God is making his appeal through
us; we entreat you on behalf of Christ,
be reconciled to God. 21For our sake he
made him to be sin who knew no sin, so
that in him we might become the righteousness of God.

6 As we work together with him,[n] we
urge you also not to accept the grace
of God in vain. 2For he says,

'At an acceptable time I have
listened to you,
and on a day of salvation I
have helped you.'

See, now is the acceptable time; see,
now is the day of salvation! 3We are putting no obstacle in anyone's way, so that
no fault may be found with our ministry, 4but as servants of God we have
commended ourselves in every way:
through great endurance, in afflictions,
hardships, calamities, 5beatings, imprisonments, riots, labours, sleepless
nights, hunger; 6by purity, knowledge,
patience, kindness, holiness of spirit,
genuine love, 7truthful speech, and the
power of God; with the weapons of righteousness for the right hand and for the
left; 8in honour and dishonour, in ill
repute and good repute. We are treated
as impostors, and yet are true; 9as unknown, and yet are well known; as dying, and see—we are alive; as punished,
and yet not killed; 10as sorrowful, yet
always rejoicing; as poor, yet making
many rich; as having nothing, and yet
possessing everything.

11 We have spoken frankly to you Corinthians; our heart is wide open to you.
12There is no restriction in our affections, but only in yours. 13In return—I
speak as to children—open wide your
hearts also.

THE TEMPLE OF THE LIVING GOD

14 Do not be mismatched with unbelievers. For what partnership is there
between righteousness and lawlessness?
Or what fellowship is there between
light and darkness? 15What agreement
does Christ have with Beliar? Or what
does a believer share with an unbeliever? 16What agreement has the temple of God with idols? For we[o] are the
temple of the living God; as God said,

[j] 5.3 Other ancient authorities read *put it on*
[k] 5.16 Gk *according to the flesh* [l] 5.16 Gk *according to the flesh* [m] 5.19 Or *God was in Christ reconciling the world to himself* [n] 6.1 Gk *As we work together* [o] 6.16 Other ancient authorities read *you*

‘I will live in them and walk
among them,
and I will be their God,
and they shall be my people.
17 Therefore come out from them,
and be separate from them,
says the Lord,
and touch nothing unclean;
then I will welcome you,
18 and I will be your father,
and you shall be my sons
and daughters,
says the Lord Almighty.’

7 Since we have these promises, beloved, let us cleanse ourselves from
every defilement of body and of spirit,
making holiness perfect in the fear of
God.

PAUL’S JOY AT THE CHURCH’S REPENTANCE

2 Make room in your hearts[p] for us;
we have wronged no one, we have corrupted no one, we have taken advantage
of no one. 3 I do not say this to condemn
you, for I said before that you are in our
hearts, to die together and to live together. 4 I often boast about you; I have
great pride in you; I am filled with consolation; I am overjoyed in all our affliction.

5 For even when we came into Macedonia, our bodies had no rest, but we
were afflicted in every way—disputes
without and fears within. 6 But God,
who consoles the downcast, consoled
us by the arrival of Titus, 7 and not only
by his coming, but also by the consolation with which he was consoled about
you, as he told us of your longing, your
mourning, your zeal for me, so that I
rejoiced still more. 8 For even if I made
you sorry with my letter, I do not regret
it (though I did regret it, for I see that
I grieved you with that letter, though
only briefly). 9 Now I rejoice, not because
you were grieved, but because your grief
led to repentance; for you felt a godly
grief, so that you were not harmed in
any way by us. 10 For godly grief produces a repentance that leads to salvation and brings no regret, but worldly
grief produces death. 11 For see what earnestness this godly grief has produced
in you, what eagerness to clear yourselves, what indignation, what alarm,
what longing, what zeal, what punishment! At every point you have proved
yourselves guiltless in the matter. 12 So
although I wrote to you, it was not on
account of the one who did the wrong,
nor on account of the one who was
wronged, but in order that your zeal for
us might be made known to you before
God. 13 In this we find comfort.

In addition to our own consolation,
we rejoiced still more at the joy of Titus,
because his mind has been set at rest
by all of you. 14 For if I have been some-
what boastful about you to him, I was
not disgraced; but just as everything
we said to you was true, so our boasting
to Titus has proved true as well. 15 And
his heart goes out all the more to you,
as he remembers the obedience of all of
you, and how you welcomed him with
fear and trembling. 16 I rejoice, because I
have complete confidence in you.

ENCOURAGEMENT TO BE GENEROUS

8 We want you to know, brothers
and sisters,[q] about the grace of God
that has been granted to the churches of
Macedonia; 2 for during a severe ordeal
of affliction, their abundant joy and
their extreme poverty have overflowed
in a wealth of generosity on their part.
3 For, as I can testify, they voluntar-
ily gave according to their means, and
even beyond their means, 4 begging us
earnestly for the privilege[r] of sharing in
this ministry to the saints— 5 and this,
not merely as we expected; they gave
themselves first to the Lord and, by the
will of God, to us, 6 so that we might
urge Titus that, as he had already made
a beginning, so he should also complete
this generous undertaking[s] among you.
7 Now as you excel in everything—in
faith, in speech, in knowledge, in utmost eagerness, and in our love for
you[t]—so we want you to excel also in
this generous undertaking.[u]

8 I do not say this as a command, but
I am testing the genuineness of your
love against the earnestness of others.
9 For you know the generous act[v] of
our Lord Jesus Christ, that though he
was rich, yet for your sakes he became
poor, so that by his poverty you might
become rich. 10 And in this matter I
am giving my advice: it is appropriate
for you who began last year not only to
do something but even to desire to do
something— 11 now finish doing it, so
that your eagerness may be matched by
completing it according to your means.

[p] 7.2 Gk lacks *in your hearts* [q] 8.1 Gk *brothers*
[r] 8.4 Gk *grace* [s] 8.6 Gk *this grace* [t] 8.7 Other ancient authorities read *your love for us*
[u] 8.7 Gk *this grace* [v] 8.9 Gk *the grace*

12For if the eagerness is there, the gift is
acceptable according to what one has—
not according to what one does not
have. 13I do not mean that there should
be relief for others and pressure on you,
but it is a question of a fair balance between 14your present abundance and
their need, so that their abundance may
be for your need, in order that there
may be a fair balance. 15As it is written,

'The one who had much did
not have too much,
and the one who had little
did not have too little.'

COMMENDATION OF TITUS

16 But thanks be to God who put in
the heart of Titus the same eagerness
for you that I myself have. 17For he not
only accepted our appeal, but since he
is more eager than ever, he is going to
you of his own accord. 18With him we
are sending the brother who is famous
among all the churches for his proclaiming of the good news;[w] 19and not only
that, but he has also been appointed by
the churches to travel with us while we
are administering this generous undertaking[x] for the glory of the Lord himself[y] and to show our goodwill. 20We
intend that no one should blame us
about this generous gift that we are administering, 21for we intend to do what
is right not only in the Lord's sight but
also in the sight of others. 22And with
them we are sending our brother whom
we have often tested and found eager in
many matters, but who is now more eager than ever because of his great confidence in you. 23As for Titus, he is my
partner and co-worker in your service;
as for our brothers, they are messengers[z] of the churches, the glory of Christ.
24Therefore, openly before the churches,
show them the proof of your love and of
our reason for boasting about you.

THE COLLECTION FOR CHRISTIANS AT JERUSALEM

9 Now it is not necessary for me to
write to you about the ministry
to the saints, 2for I know your eagerness, which is the subject of my boasting about you to the people of Macedonia, saying that Achaia has been ready
since last year; and your zeal has stirred
up most of them. 3But I am sending
the brothers in order that our boasting
about you may not prove to have been
empty in this case, so that you may be
ready, as I said you would be; 4otherwise,
if some Macedonians come with me and
find that you are not ready, we would
be humiliated—to say nothing of you—
in this undertaking.[a] 5So I thought it
necessary to urge the brothers to go on
ahead to you, and arrange in advance for
this bountiful gift that you have promised, so that it may be ready as a voluntary gift and not as an extortion.

6 The point is this: the one who sows
sparingly will also reap sparingly, and
the one who sows bountifully will also
reap bountifully. 7Each of you must give
as you have made up your mind, not re-
luctantly or under compulsion, for God
loves a cheerful giver. 8And God is able
to provide you with every blessing in
abundance, so that by always having
enough of everything, you may share
abundantly in every good work. 9As it
is written,

'He scatters abroad, he gives
to the poor;
his righteousness[b]
endures for ever.'

10He who supplies seed to the sower and
bread for food will supply and multiply
your seed for sowing and increase the
harvest of your righteousness.[c] 11You
will be enriched in every way for your
great generosity, which will produce
thanksgiving to God through us; 12for
the rendering of this ministry not only
supplies the needs of the saints but also
overflows with many thanksgivings to
God. 13Through the testing of this ministry you glorify God by your obedience
to the confession of the gospel of Christ
and by the generosity of your sharing
with them and with all others, 14while
they long for you and pray for you because of the surpassing grace of God
that he has given you. 15Thanks be to
God for his indescribable gift!

PAUL DEFENDS HIS MINISTRY

10 I myself, Paul, appeal to you by
the meekness and gentleness of
Christ—I who am humble when face
to face with you, but bold towards you
when I am away!— 2I ask that when I
am present I need not show boldness
by daring to oppose those who think
we are acting according to human
standards.[d] 3Indeed, we live as human

[w] 8.18 Or *the gospel* [x] 8.19 Gk *this grace*
[y] 8.19 Other ancient authorities lack *himself*
[z] 8.23 Gk *apostles* [a] 9.4 Other ancient authorities add *of boasting* [b] 9.9 Or *benevolence*
[c] 9.10 Or *benevolence* [d] 10.2 Gk *according to the flesh*

beings,[e] but we do not wage war according to human standards;[f] 4for the
weapons of our warfare are not merely
human,[g] but they have divine power to
destroy strongholds. We destroy arguments 5and every proud obstacle raised
up against the knowledge of God, and
we take every thought captive to obey
Christ. 6We are ready to punish every
disobedience when your obedience is
complete.

7 Look at what is before your eyes.
If you are confident that you belong to
Christ, remind yourself of this, that just
as you belong to Christ, so also do we.
8Now, even if I boast a little too much of
our authority, which the Lord gave for
building you up and not for tearing you
down, I will not be ashamed of it. 9I do
not want to seem as though I am trying
to frighten you with my letters. 10For
they say, 'His letters are weighty and
strong, but his bodily presence is weak,
and his speech contemptible.' 11Let such
people understand that what we say
by letter when absent, we will also do
when present.

12 We do not dare to classify or compare ourselves with some of those who
commend themselves. But when they
measure themselves by one another,
and compare themselves with one another, they do not show good sense.
13We, however, will not boast beyond
limits, but will keep within the field
that God has assigned to us, to reach
out even as far as you. 14For we were
not overstepping our limits when we
reached you; we were the first to come
all the way to you with the good news[h]
of Christ. 15We do not boast beyond limits, that is, in the labours of others; but
our hope is that, as your faith increases,
our sphere of action among you may be
greatly enlarged, 16so that we may proclaim the good news[i] in lands beyond
you, without boasting of work already
done in someone else's sphere of action.
17'Let the one who boasts, boast in the
Lord.' 18For it is not those who commend themselves that are approved,
but those whom the Lord commends.

PAUL AND THE FALSE APOSTLES

11 I wish you would bear with me
in a little foolishness. Do bear
with me! 2I feel a divine jealousy for
you, for I promised you in marriage to
one husband, to present you as a chaste
virgin to Christ. 3But I am afraid that
as the serpent deceived Eve by its cunning, your thoughts will be led astray
from a sincere and pure[j] devotion to
Christ. 4For if someone comes and proclaims another Jesus than the one we
proclaimed, or if you receive a different
spirit from the one you received, or a
different gospel from the one you accepted, you submit to it readily enough.
5I think that I am not in the least inferior to these super-apostles. 6I may be
untrained in speech, but not in knowledge; certainly in every way and in all
things we have made this evident to
you.

7 Did I commit a sin by humbling
myself so that you might be exalted,
because I proclaimed God's good news[k]
to you free of charge? 8I robbed other
churches by accepting support from
them in order to serve you. 9And when
I was with you and was in need, I did
not burden anyone, for my needs were
supplied by the friends[l] who came from
Macedonia. So I refrained and will continue to refrain from burdening you in
any way. 10As the truth of Christ is in
me, this boast of mine will not be silenced in the regions of Achaia. 11And
why? Because I do not love you? God
knows I do!

12 And what I do I will also continue
to do, in order to deny an opportunity
to those who want an opportunity to be
recognized as our equals in what they
boast about. 13For such boasters are false
apostles, deceitful workers, disguising
themselves as apostles of Christ. 14And
no wonder! Even Satan disguises himself as an angel of light. 15So it is not
strange if his ministers also disguise
themselves as ministers of righteousness. Their end will match their deeds.

PAUL'S SUFFERINGS AS AN APOSTLE

16 I repeat, let no one think that I
am a fool; but if you do, then accept me
as a fool, so that I too may boast a little. 17What I am saying in regard to this
boastful confidence, I am saying not
with the Lord's authority, but as a fool;
18since many boast according to human
standards,[m] I will also boast. 19For you
gladly put up with fools, being wise
yourselves! 20For you put up with it
when someone makes slaves of you, or

[e] **10.3** Gk *in the flesh* [f] **10.3** Gk *according to the flesh* [g] **10.4** Gk *fleshly* [h] **10.14** Or *the gospel* [i] **10.16** Or *the gospel* [j] **11.3** Other ancient authorities lack *and pure* [k] **11.7** Gk *the gospel of God* [l] **11.9** Gk *brothers* [m] **11.18** Gk *according to the flesh*

preys upon you, or takes advantage of you, or puts on airs, or gives you a slap in the face. 21To my shame, I must say, we were too weak for that!

But whatever anyone dares to boast of—I am speaking as a fool—I also dare to boast of that. 22Are they Hebrews? So am I. Are they Israelites? So am I. Are they descendants of Abraham? So am I. 23Are they ministers of Christ? I am talking like a madman—I am a better one: with far greater labours, far more imprisonments, with countless floggings, and often near death. 24Five times I have received from the Jews the forty lashes minus one. 25Three times I was beaten with rods. Once I received a stoning. Three times I was shipwrecked; for a night and a day I was adrift at sea; 26on frequent journeys, in danger from rivers, danger from bandits, danger from my own people, danger from Gentiles, danger in the city, danger in the wilderness, danger at sea, danger from false brothers and sisters;[n] 27in toil and hardship, through many a sleepless night, hungry and thirsty, often without food, cold and naked. 28And, besides other things, I am under daily pressure because of my anxiety for all the churches. 29Who is weak, and I am not weak? Who is made to stumble, and I am not indignant?

30 If I must boast, I will boast of the things that show my weakness. 31The God and Father of the Lord Jesus (blessed be he for ever!) knows that I do not lie. 32In Damascus, the governor[o] under King Aretas set a guard on the city of Damascus in order to[p] seize me, 33but I was let down in a basket through a window in the wall,[q] and escaped from his hands.

PAUL'S VISIONS AND REVELATIONS

12 It is necessary to boast; nothing is to be gained by it, but I will go on to visions and revelations of the Lord. 2I know a person in Christ who fourteen years ago was caught up to the third heaven—whether in the body or out of the body I do not know; God knows. 3And I know that such a person—whether in the body or out of the body I do not know; God knows—4was caught up into Paradise and heard things that are not to be told, that no mortal is permitted to repeat. 5On behalf of such a one I will boast, but on my own behalf I will not boast, except of my weaknesses. 6But if I wish to boast, I will not be a fool, for I will be speaking the truth. But I refrain from it, so that no one may think better of me than what is seen in me or heard from me, 7even considering the exceptional character of the revelations. Therefore, to keep[r] me from being too elated, a thorn was given to me in the flesh, a messenger of Satan to torment me, to keep me from being too elated.[s] 8Three times I appealed to the Lord about this, that it would leave me, 9but he said to me, 'My grace is sufficient for you, for power[t] is made perfect in weakness.' So, I will boast all the more gladly of my weaknesses, so that the power of Christ may dwell in me. 10Therefore I am content with weaknesses, insults, hardships, persecutions, and calamities for the sake of Christ; for whenever I am weak, then I am strong.

PAUL'S CONCERN FOR THE CORINTHIAN CHURCH

11 I have been a fool! You forced me to it. Indeed you should have been the ones commending me, for I am not at all inferior to these super-apostles, even though I am nothing. 12The signs of a true apostle were performed among you with utmost patience, signs and wonders and mighty works. 13How have you been worse off than the other churches, except that I myself did not burden you? Forgive me this wrong!

14 Here I am, ready to come to you this third time. And I will not be a burden, because I do not want what is yours but you; for children ought not to lay up for their parents, but parents for their children. 15I will most gladly spend and be spent for you. If I love you more, am I to be loved less? 16Let it be assumed that I did not burden you. Nevertheless (you say) since I was crafty, I took you in by deceit. 17Did I take advantage of you through any of those whom I sent to you? 18I urged Titus to go, and sent the brother with him. Titus did not take advantage of you, did he? Did we not conduct ourselves with the same spirit? Did we not take the same steps?

19 Have you been thinking all along that we have been defending ourselves before you? We are speaking in Christ

[n] 11.26 Gk *brothers* [o] 11.32 Gk *ethnarch*
[p] 11.32 Other ancient authorities read *and wanted to* [q] 11.33 Gk *through the wall*
[r] 12.7 Other ancient authorities read *To keep*
[s] 12.7 Other ancient authorities lack *to keep me from being too elated* [t] 12.9 Other ancient authorities read *my power*

before God. Everything we do, beloved,
is for the sake of building you up. [20]For
I fear that when I come, I may find you
not as I wish, and that you may find me
not as you wish; I fear that there may
perhaps be quarrelling, jealousy, anger, selfishness, slander, gossip, conceit,
and disorder. [21]I fear that when I come
again, my God may humble me before
you, and that I may have to mourn over
many who previously sinned and have
not repented of the impurity, sexual immorality, and licentiousness that they
have practised.

FURTHER WARNING

13 This is the third time I am coming to you. 'Any charge must be
sustained by the evidence of two or three
witnesses.' [2]I warned those who sinned
previously and all the others, and I warn
them now while absent, as I did when
present on my second visit, that if I come
again, I will not be lenient— [3]since you
desire proof that Christ is speaking in
me. He is not weak in dealing with you,
but is powerful in you. [4]For he was crucified in weakness, but lives by the power
of God. For we are weak in him,[u] but in
dealing with you we will live with him
by the power of God.

5 Examine yourselves to see whether
you are living in the faith. Test yourselves. Do you not realize that Jesus
Christ is in you?—unless, indeed, you
fail to pass the test! [6]I hope you will find
out that we have not failed. [7]But we
pray to God that you may not do anything wrong—not that we may appear
to have passed the test, but that you
may do what is right, though we may
seem to have failed. [8]For we cannot do
anything against the truth, but only for
the truth. [9]For we rejoice when we are
weak and you are strong. This is what
we pray for, that you may become perfect. [10]So I write these things while I am
away from you, so that when I come, I
may not have to be severe in using the
authority that the Lord has given me for
building up and not for tearing down.

FINAL GREETINGS AND BENEDICTION

11 Finally, brothers and sisters,[v] farewell.[w] Put things in order, listen to my
appeal,[x] agree with one another, live in
peace; and the God of love and peace will
be with you. [12]Greet one another with a
holy kiss. All the saints greet you.

13 The grace of the Lord Jesus Christ,
the love of God, and the communion of[y]
the Holy Spirit be with all of you.

[u] **13.4** Other ancient authorities read *with him*
[v] **13.11** Gk *brothers* [w] **13.11** Or *rejoice*
[x] **13.11** Or *encourage one another* [y] **13.13** Or
and the sharing in

The Letter of Paul to the

GALATIANS

Every year on the Octave of Christmas, at the liturgical celebration of the Solemnity of Mary, the Mother of God, the church reads from Paul's Letter to the Galatians: "But when the fullness of time had come, God sent his Son, born of a woman, born under the law, in order to redeem those who were under the law, so that we might receive adoption as children" (4.4–5). The Letter of Paul to the Galatians reflects the struggle of the early Christian community as it attempted to define itself separately from those who observed Jewish law.

Paul's gentile converts in Galatia were expected by the Jewish Christians to be circumcised (5.2–12; 6.12–13) and to observe the Jewish laws and rituals such as the Sabbath and other festivals (4.10). Paul takes this interpretation as a threat to the truth of the gospel (2.5, 14). His Letter is an impassioned polemic against imposing these practices. To be adopted as children means, for Paul, that Christians are not saved by the law, but by the cross of Christ (6.14–16). To require gentile Christians to be circumcised would be to undermine the meaning of the death of Christ, which is the decisive event that ushers in the beginning of God's new creation (6.14–15).

Paul's Letter to the Galatians is a window into the difficulty faced by the early church in understanding and applying the full meaning of the gospel with respect to Judaism. Paul does not deny the legitimacy of the law for its own intended purpose. Paul insists, however, that it is only through Christ's sacrifice that all are set free. This literally means that believers enjoy a freedom from observance of the law and now live in a new creation (6.15). Paul's clarity and confidence about the implication of the gospel has a definitive part to play in the early church's self-definition and in its self-awareness of the universal scope of the Christian faith. In a well-quoted passage, Paul states: "There is no longer Jew or Greek, there is no longer slave or free, there is no longer male and female; for all of you are one in Christ Jesus" (3.28). This short Letter to the Galatians provides an excellent example of the strength and conviction of Paul's faith and the clarity of his message.

SALUTATION

1 Paul an apostle—sent neither by
human commission nor from human authorities, but through Jesus
Christ and God the Father, who raised
him from the dead— 2and all the members of God's family[a] who are with me,
To the churches of Galatia:
3 Grace to you and peace from God
our Father and the Lord Jesus Christ,
4who gave himself for our sins to set us
free from the present evil age, according to the will of our God and Father,
5to whom be the glory for ever and ever.
Amen.

THERE IS NO OTHER GOSPEL

6 I am astonished that you are so
quickly deserting the one who called you
in the grace of Christ and are turning to
a different gospel— 7not that there is
another gospel, but there are some who

[a] 1.2 Gk *all the brothers*

are confusing you and want to pervert the gospel of Christ. 8 But even if we or an angel[b] from heaven should proclaim to you a gospel contrary to what we proclaimed to you, let that one be accursed! 9 As we have said before, so now I repeat, if anyone proclaims to you a gospel contrary to what you received, let that one be accursed!

10 Am I now seeking human approval, or God's approval? Or am I trying to please people? If I were still pleasing people, I would not be a servant[c] of Christ.

PAUL'S VINDICATION OF HIS APOSTLESHIP

11 For I want you to know, brothers and sisters,[d] that the gospel that was proclaimed by me is not of human origin; 12 for I did not receive it from a human source, nor was I taught it, but I received it through a revelation of Jesus Christ.

13 You have heard, no doubt, of my earlier life in Judaism. I was violently persecuting the church of God and was trying to destroy it. 14 I advanced in Judaism beyond many among my people of the same age, for I was far more zealous for the traditions of my ancestors. 15 But when God, who had set me apart before I was born and called me through his grace, was pleased 16 to reveal his Son to me,[e] so that I might proclaim him among the Gentiles, I did not confer with any human being, 17 nor did I go up to Jerusalem to those who were already apostles before me, but I went away at once into Arabia, and afterwards I returned to Damascus.

18 Then after three years I did go up to Jerusalem to visit Cephas and stayed with him for fifteen days; 19 but I did not see any other apostle except James the Lord's brother. 20 In what I am writing to you, before God, I do not lie! 21 Then I went into the regions of Syria and Cilicia, 22 and I was still unknown by sight to the churches of Judea that are in Christ; 23 they only heard it said, 'The one who formerly was persecuting us is now proclaiming the faith he once tried to destroy.' 24 And they glorified God because of me.

PAUL AND THE OTHER APOSTLES

2 Then after fourteen years I went up again to Jerusalem with Barnabas, taking Titus along with me. 2 I went up in response to a revelation. Then I laid before them (though only in a private meeting with the acknowledged leaders) the gospel that I proclaim among the Gentiles, in order to make sure that I was not running, or had not run, in vain. 3 But even Titus, who was with me, was not compelled to be circumcised, though he was a Greek. 4 But because of false believers[f] secretly brought in, who slipped in to spy on the freedom we have in Christ Jesus, so that they might enslave us— 5 we did not submit to them even for a moment, so that the truth of the gospel might always remain with you. 6 And from those who were supposed to be acknowledged leaders (what they actually were makes no difference to me; God shows no partiality)—those leaders contributed nothing to me. 7 On the contrary, when they saw that I had been entrusted with the gospel for the uncircumcised, just as Peter had been entrusted with the gospel for the circumcised 8 (for he who worked through Peter making him an apostle to the circumcised also worked through me in sending me to the Gentiles), 9 and when James and Cephas and John, who were acknowledged pillars, recognized the grace that had been given to me, they gave to Barnabas and me the right hand of fellowship, agreeing that we should go to the Gentiles and they to the circumcised. 10 They asked only one thing, that we remember the poor, which was actually what I was[g] eager to do.

PAUL REBUKES PETER AT ANTIOCH

11 But when Cephas came to Antioch, I opposed him to his face, because he stood self-condemned; 12 for until certain people came from James, he used to eat with the Gentiles. But after they came, he drew back and kept himself separate for fear of the circumcision faction. 13 And the other Jews joined him in this hypocrisy, so that even Barnabas was led astray by their hypocrisy. 14 But when I saw that they were not acting consistently with the truth of the gospel, I said to Cephas before them all, 'If you, though a Jew, live like a Gentile and not like a Jew, how can you compel the Gentiles to live like Jews?'[h]

[b] 1.8 Or *a messenger* [c] 1.10 Gk *slave* [d] 1.11 Gk *brothers* [e] 1.16 Gk *in me* [f] 2.4 Gk *false brothers* [g] 2.10 Or *had been*
[h] 2.14 Some interpreters hold that the quotation extends into the following paragraph

JEWS AND GENTILES ARE SAVED BY FAITH

15 We ourselves are Jews by birth and not Gentile sinners; 16 yet we know that a person is justified[i] not by the works of the law but through faith in Jesus Christ.[j] And we have come to believe in Christ Jesus, so that we might be justified by faith in Christ,[k] and not by doing the works of the law, because no one will be justified by the works of the law. 17 But if, in our effort to be justified in Christ, we ourselves have been found to be sinners, is Christ then a servant of sin? Certainly not! 18 But if I build up again the very things that I once tore down, then I demonstrate that I am a transgressor. 19 For through the law I died to the law, so that I might live to God. I have been crucified with Christ; 20 and it is no longer I who live, but it is Christ who lives in me. And the life I now live in the flesh I live by faith in the Son of God,[l] who loved me and gave himself for me. 21 I do not nullify the grace of God; for if justification[m] comes through the law, then Christ died for nothing.

LAW OR FAITH

3 You foolish Galatians! Who has bewitched you? It was before your eyes that Jesus Christ was publicly exhibited as crucified! 2 The only thing I want to learn from you is this: Did you receive the Spirit by doing the works of the law or by believing what you heard? 3 Are you so foolish? Having started with the Spirit, are you now ending with the flesh? 4 Did you experience so much for nothing?—if it really was for nothing. 5 Well then, does God[n] supply you with the Spirit and work miracles among you by your doing the works of the law, or by your believing what you heard?

6 Just as Abraham 'believed God, and it was reckoned to him as righteousness', 7 so, you see, those who believe are the descendants of Abraham. 8 And the scripture, foreseeing that God would justify the Gentiles by faith, declared the gospel beforehand to Abraham, saying, 'All the Gentiles shall be blessed in you.' 9 For this reason, those who believe are blessed with Abraham who believed.

10 For all who rely on the works of the law are under a curse; for it is written, 'Cursed is everyone who does not observe and obey all the things written in the book of the law.' 11 Now it is evident that no one is justified before God by the law; for 'The one who is righteous will live by faith.'[o] 12 But the law does not rest on faith; on the contrary, 'Whoever does the works of the law[p] will live by them.' 13 Christ redeemed us from the curse of the law by becoming a curse for us—for it is written, 'Cursed is everyone who hangs on a tree'— 14 in order that in Christ Jesus the blessing of Abraham might come to the Gentiles, so that we might receive the promise of the Spirit through faith.

THE PROMISE TO ABRAHAM

15 Brothers and sisters,[q] I give an example from daily life: once a person's will[r] has been ratified, no one adds to it or annuls it. 16 Now the promises were made to Abraham and to his offspring;[s] it does not say, 'And to offsprings',[t] as of many; but it says, 'And to your offspring',[u] that is, to one person, who is Christ. 17 My point is this: the law, which came four hundred and thirty years later, does not annul a covenant previously ratified by God, so as to nullify the promise. 18 For if the inheritance comes from the law, it no longer comes from the promise; but God granted it to Abraham through the promise.

THE PURPOSE OF THE LAW

19 Why then the law? It was added because of transgressions, until the offspring[v] would come to whom the promise had been made; and it was ordained through angels by a mediator. 20 Now a mediator involves more than one party; but God is one.

21 Is the law then opposed to the promises of God? Certainly not! For if a law had been given that could make alive, then righteousness would indeed come through the law. 22 But the scripture has imprisoned all things under the power of sin, so that what was promised through faith in Jesus Christ[w] might be given to those who believe.

23 Now before faith came, we were imprisoned and guarded under the law until faith would be revealed. 24 Therefore the law was our disciplinarian until

[i] **2.16** Or *reckoned as righteous;* and so elsewhere
[j] **2.16** Or *the faith of Jesus Christ*
[k] **2.16** Or *the faith of Christ*
[l] **2.20** Or *by the faith of the Son of God*
[m] **2.21** Or *righteousness*
[n] **3.5** Gk *he*
[o] **3.11** Or *The one who is righteous through faith will live*
[p] **3.12** Gk *does them*
[q] **3.15** Gk *Brothers*
[r] **3.15** Or *covenant* (as in verse 17)
[s] **3.16** Gk *seed*
[t] **3.16** Gk *seeds*
[u] **3.16** Gk *seed*
[v] **3.19** Gk *seed*
[w] **3.22** Or *through the faith of Jesus Christ*

Christ came, so that we might be justified by faith. 25But now that faith has
come, we are no longer subject to a disciplinarian, 26for in Christ Jesus you are
all children of God through faith. 27As
many of you as were baptized into Christ
have clothed yourselves with Christ.
28There is no longer Jew or Greek, there
is no longer slave or free, there is no longer male and female; for all of you are one
in Christ Jesus. 29And if you belong to
Christ, then you are Abraham's offspring,[x] heirs according to the promise.
4 My point is this: heirs, as long as
they are minors, are no better than
slaves, though they are the owners of all
the property; 2but they remain under
guardians and trustees until the date
set by the father. 3So with us; while we
were minors, we were enslaved to the
elemental spirits[y] of the world. 4But
when the fullness of time had come,
God sent his Son, born of a woman,
born under the law, 5in order to redeem
those who were under the law, so that
we might receive adoption as children.
6And because you are children, God
has sent the Spirit of his Son into our[z]
hearts, crying, 'Abba![a] Father!' 7So you
are no longer a slave but a child, and if
a child then also an heir, through God.[b]

PAUL REPROVES THE GALATIANS

8 Formerly, when you did not know
God, you were enslaved to beings that
by nature are not gods. 9Now, however, that you have come to know God,
or rather to be known by God, how can
you turn back again to the weak and
beggarly elemental spirits?[c] How can
you want to be enslaved to them again?
10You are observing special days, and
months, and seasons, and years. 11I am
afraid that my work for you may have
been wasted.

12 Friends,[d] I beg you, become as I
am, for I also have become as you are.
You have done me no wrong. 13You
know that it was because of a physical
infirmity that I first announced the
gospel to you; 14though my condition
put you to the test, you did not scorn
or despise me, but welcomed me as an
angel of God, as Christ Jesus. 15What
has become of the goodwill you felt?
For I testify that, had it been possible,
you would have torn out your eyes and
given them to me. 16Have I now become
your enemy by telling you the truth?
17They make much of you, but for no
good purpose; they want to exclude you,
so that you may make much of them.
18It is good to be made much of for a
good purpose at all times, and not only
when I am present with you. 19My little children, for whom I am again in the
pain of childbirth until Christ is formed
in you, 20I wish I were present with you
now and could change my tone, for I am
perplexed about you.

THE ALLEGORY OF HAGAR AND SARAH

21 Tell me, you who desire to be subject to the law, will you not listen to the
law? 22For it is written that Abraham
had two sons, one by a slave woman and
the other by a free woman. 23One, the
child of the slave, was born according to
the flesh; the other, the child of the free
woman, was born through the promise.
24Now this is an allegory: these women
are two covenants. One woman, in
fact, is Hagar, from Mount Sinai, bearing children for slavery. 25Now Hagar
is Mount Sinai in Arabia[e] and corresponds to the present Jerusalem, for she
is in slavery with her children. 26But the
other woman corresponds to the Jerusalem above; she is free, and she is our
mother. 27For it is written,

'Rejoice, you childless one, you
who bear no children,
burst into song and shout, you
who endure no birth pangs;
for the children of the desolate
woman are more numerous
than the children of the one
who is married.'

28Now you,[f] my friends,[g] are children
of the promise, like Isaac. 29But just as
at that time the child who was born according to the flesh persecuted the child
who was born according to the Spirit, so
it is now also. 30But what does the scripture say? 'Drive out the slave and her
child; for the child of the slave will not
share the inheritance with the child of
the free woman.' 31So then, friends,[h] we
are children, not of the slave but of the
5 free woman. 1For freedom Christ
has set us free. Stand firm, therefore, and do not submit again to a yoke
of slavery.

[x] 3.29 Gk *seed* [y] 4.3 Or *the rudiments*
[z] 4.6 Other ancient authorities read *your*
[a] 4.6 Aramaic for *Father* [b] 4.7 Other ancient authorities read *an heir of God through Christ*
[c] 4.9 Or *beggarly rudiments* [d] 4.12 Gk *Brothers*
[e] 4.25 Other ancient authorities read *For Sinai is a mountain in Arabia* [f] 4.28 Other ancient authorities read *we* [g] 4.28 Gk *brothers*
[h] 4.31 Gk *brothers*

THE NATURE OF CHRISTIAN FREEDOM

2 Listen! I, Paul, am telling you that if
you let yourselves be circumcised, Christ
will be of no benefit to you. 3Once again
I testify to every man who lets himself
be circumcised that he is obliged to obey
the entire law. 4You who want to be
justified by the law have cut yourselves
off from Christ; you have fallen away
from grace. 5For through the Spirit, by
faith, we eagerly wait for the hope of
righteousness. 6For in Christ Jesus neither circumcision nor uncircumcision
counts for anything; the only thing that
counts is faith working[i] through love.

7 You were running well; who prevented you from obeying the truth?
8Such persuasion does not come from the
one who calls you. 9A little yeast leavens
the whole batch of dough. 10I am confident about you in the Lord that you will
not think otherwise. But whoever it is
that is confusing you will pay the penalty.
11But my friends,[j] why am I still being
persecuted if I am still preaching circumcision? In that case the offence of the cross
has been removed. 12I wish those who un-
settle you would castrate themselves!

13 For you were called to freedom,
brothers and sisters;[k] only do not use
your freedom as an opportunity for self-
indulgence,[l] but through love become
slaves to one another. 14For the whole
law is summed up in a single commandment, 'You shall love your neighbour as
yourself.' 15If, however, you bite and devour one another, take care that you are
not consumed by one another.

THE WORKS OF THE FLESH

16 Live by the Spirit, I say, and do not
gratify the desires of the flesh. 17For what
the flesh desires is opposed to the Spirit,
and what the Spirit desires is opposed to
the flesh; for these are opposed to each
other, to prevent you from doing what
you want. 18But if you are led by the Spirit,
you are not subject to the law. 19Now the
works of the flesh are obvious: fornication, impurity, licentiousness, 20idolatry,
sorcery, enmities, strife, jealousy, anger,
quarrels, dissensions, factions, 21envy,[m]
drunkenness, carousing, and things like
these. I am warning you, as I warned you
before: those who do such things will not
inherit the kingdom of God.

THE FRUIT OF THE SPIRIT

22 By contrast, the fruit of the Spirit
is love, joy, peace, patience, kindness,
generosity, faithfulness, 23gentleness,
and self-control. There is no law against
such things. 24And those who belong
to Christ Jesus have crucified the flesh
with its passions and desires. 25If we
live by the Spirit, let us also be guided
by the Spirit. 26Let us not become conceited, competing against one another,
envying one another.

BEAR ONE ANOTHER'S BURDENS

6 My friends,[n] if anyone is detected in
a transgression, you who have received the Spirit should restore such a
one in a spirit of gentleness. Take care
that you yourselves are not tempted.
2Bear one another's burdens, and in
this way you will fulfil[o] the law of
Christ. 3For if those who are nothing
think they are something, they deceive
themselves. 4All must test their own
work; then that work, rather than their
neighbour's work, will become a cause
for pride. 5For all must carry their own
loads.

6 Those who are taught the word
must share in all good things with their
teacher.

7 Do not be deceived; God is not
mocked, for you reap whatever you sow.
8If you sow to your own flesh, you will
reap corruption from the flesh; but if
you sow to the Spirit, you will reap eternal life from the Spirit. 9So let us not
grow weary in doing what is right, for
we will reap at harvest time, if we do
not give up. 10So then, whenever we
have an opportunity, let us work for the
good of all, and especially for those of
the family of faith.

FINAL ADMONITIONS AND BENEDICTION

11 See what large letters I make
when I am writing in my own hand!
12It is those who want to make a good
showing in the flesh that try to compel
you to be circumcised—only that they
may not be persecuted for the cross of
Christ. 13Even the circumcised do not
themselves obey the law, but they want
you to be circumcised so that they may
boast about your flesh. 14May I never
boast of anything except the cross of our

[i] 5.6 Or *made effective* [j] 5.11 Gk *brothers*
[k] 5.13 Gk *brothers* [l] 5.13 Gk *the flesh*
[m] 5.21 Other ancient authorities add *murder*
[n] 6.1 Gk *Brothers* [o] 6.2 Other ancient authorities read *in this way fulfil*

Lord Jesus Christ, by which[p] the world
has been crucified to me, and I to the
world. 15 For[q] neither circumcision nor
uncircumcision is anything; but a new
creation is everything! 16 As for those
who will follow this rule—peace be
upon them, and mercy, and upon the
Israel of God.

17 From now on, let no one make
trouble for me; for I carry the marks of
Jesus branded on my body.

18 May the grace of our Lord Jesus
Christ be with your spirit, brothers and
sisters.[r] Amen.

[p] 6.14 Or *through whom* [q] 6.15 Other ancient authorities add *in Christ Jesus* [r] 6.18 Gk *brothers*

The Letter of Paul to the

EPHESIANS

It is unlikely that the Letter to the Ephesians was actually written by Paul. It is generally thought to be pseudonymous (written in Paul's name after his death). The vocabulary, style, and general content of the Letter do not resonate with the same expression and viewpoint articulated in the seven unquestionably Pauline Letters: Romans, 1 and 2 Corinthians, Galatians, Philippians, 1 Thessalonians, and Philemon. The Letter to the Ephesians was written by a disciple of Paul in the last third of the first century. It is addressed to a gentile community that does not have a strong sense of being part of the heritage of Israel (2.11–18). The Letter also is written as though it comes from Paul while he was in captivity in prison.

The general purpose of the Letter to the Ephesians is to inform Gentiles that the past alienation from God and his people of Israel is now overcome by Christ's work of reconciliation. The Letter presents a vision of the church in which there is equality of social status between Jew and Gentile, slave and free, male and female. There is now a profound and real unity in the body of Christ. Gentiles are fellow heirs of the promise to Israel and members of the same body (3.6). It is left for those who are in Christ to live in such a way as to manifest their unity.

Passages from Ephesians are read every year in the liturgy on the second Sunday after Christmas, the Feast of the Epiphany, and the Feast of the Ascension. On the great Feast of the Ascension, the passage from Ephesians states boldly, "And [God] has put all things under [Christ's] feet and has made him the head over all things for the church, which is his body, the fullness of him who fills all in all" (1.22–23). The Letter to the Ephesians is about the universal church, not a particular congregation, and about its purpose to make God's plan of salvation known throughout the world (3.9–10).

SALUTATION

1 Paul, an apostle of Christ Jesus by
the will of God,
To the saints who are in Ephesus and
are faithful[a] in Christ Jesus:
2 Grace to you and peace from God
our Father and the Lord Jesus Christ.

SPIRITUAL BLESSINGS IN CHRIST

3 Blessed be the God and Father of
our Lord Jesus Christ, who has blessed
us in Christ with every spiritual blessing in the heavenly places, 4 just as he
chose us in Christ[b] before the foundation of the world to be holy and blameless before him in love. 5 He destined us
for adoption as his children through
Jesus Christ, according to the good pleasure of his will, 6 to the praise of his glorious grace that he freely bestowed on
us in the Beloved. 7 In him we have redemption through his blood, the forgiveness of our trespasses, according to
the riches of his grace 8 that he lavished
on us. With all wisdom and insight 9 he
has made known to us the mystery
of his will, according to his good pleasure that he set forth in Christ, 10 as a
plan for the fullness of time, to gather
up all things in him, things in heaven
and things on earth. 11 In Christ we have

[a] 1.1 Other ancient authorities lack *in Ephesus*, reading *saints who are also faithful* [b] 1.4 Gk *in him*

also obtained an inheritance,[c] having been destined according to the purpose of him who accomplishes all things according to his counsel and will, 12so that we, who were the first to set our hope on Christ, might live for the praise of his glory. 13In him you also, when you had heard the word of truth, the gospel of your salvation, and had believed in him, were marked with the seal of the promised Holy Spirit; 14this[d] is the pledge of our inheritance towards redemption as God's own people, to the praise of his glory.

PAUL'S PRAYER

15 I have heard of your faith in the Lord Jesus and your love[e] towards all the saints, and for this reason 16I do not cease to give thanks for you as I remember you in my prayers. 17I pray that the God of our Lord Jesus Christ, the Father of glory, may give you a spirit of wisdom and revelation as you come to know him, 18so that, with the eyes of your heart enlightened, you may know what is the hope to which he has called you, what are the riches of his glorious inheritance among the saints, 19and what is the immeasurable greatness of his power for us who believe, according to the working of his great power. 20God[f] put this power to work in Christ when he raised him from the dead and seated him at his right hand in the heavenly places, 21far above all rule and authority and power and dominion, and above every name that is named, not only in this age but also in the age to come. 22And he has put all things under his feet and has made him the head over all things for the church, 23which is his body, the fullness of him who fills all in all.

FROM DEATH TO LIFE

2 You were dead through the trespasses and sins 2in which you once lived, following the course of this world, following the ruler of the power of the air, the spirit that is now at work among those who are disobedient. 3All of us once lived among them in the passions of our flesh, following the desires of flesh and senses, and we were by nature children of wrath, like everyone else. 4But God, who is rich in mercy, out of the great love with which he loved us 5even when we were dead through our trespasses, made us alive together with Christ[g]—by grace you have been saved— 6and raised us up with him and seated us with him in the heavenly places in Christ Jesus, 7so that in the ages to come he might show the immeasurable riches of his grace in kindness towards us in Christ Jesus. 8For by grace you have been saved through faith, and this is not your own doing; it is the gift of God— 9not the result of works, so that no one may boast. 10For we are what he has made us, created in Christ Jesus for good works, which God prepared beforehand to be our way of life.

ONE IN CHRIST

11 So then, remember that at one time you Gentiles by birth,[h] called 'the uncircumcision' by those who are called 'the circumcision'—a physical circumcision made in the flesh by human hands— 12remember that you were at that time without Christ, being aliens from the commonwealth of Israel, and strangers to the covenants of promise, having no hope and without God in the world. 13But now in Christ Jesus you who once were far off have been brought near by the blood of Christ. 14For he is our peace; in his flesh he has made both groups into one and has broken down the dividing wall, that is, the hostility between us. 15He has abolished the law with its commandments and ordinances, so that he might create in himself one new humanity in place of the two, thus making peace, 16and might reconcile both groups to God in one body[i] through the cross, thus putting to death that hostility through it.[j] 17So he came and proclaimed peace to you who were far off and peace to those who were near; 18for through him both of us have access in one Spirit to the Father. 19So then you are no longer strangers and aliens, but you are citizens with the saints and also members of the household of God, 20built upon the foundation of the apostles and prophets, with Christ Jesus himself as the cornerstone.[k] 21In him the whole structure is joined together and grows into a holy temple in the Lord; 22in whom you also are built together spiritually[l] into a dwelling-place for God.

[c] **1.11** Or *been made a heritage* [d] **1.14** Other ancient authorities read *who* [e] **1.15** Other ancient authorities lack *and your love* [f] **1.20** Gk *He* [g] **2.5** Other ancient authorities read *in Christ* [h] **2.11** Gk *in the flesh* [i] **2.16** Or *reconcile both of us in one body for God* [j] **2.16** Or *in him, or in himself* [k] **2.20** Or *keystone* [l] **2.22** Gk *in the Spirit*

PAUL'S MINISTRY TO THE GENTILES

3 This is the reason that I Paul am a prisoner for[m] Christ Jesus for the sake of you Gentiles— 2 for surely you have already heard of the commission of God's grace that was given to me for you, 3 and how the mystery was made known to me by revelation, as I wrote above in a few words, 4 a reading of which will enable you to perceive my understanding of the mystery of Christ. 5 In former generations this mystery[n] was not made known to humankind, as it has now been revealed to his holy apostles and prophets by the Spirit: 6 that is, the Gentiles have become fellow-heirs, members of the same body, and sharers in the promise in Christ Jesus through the gospel.

7 Of this gospel I have become a servant according to the gift of God's grace that was given to me by the working of his power. 8 Although I am the very least of all the saints, this grace was given to me to bring to the Gentiles the news of the boundless riches of Christ, 9 and to make everyone see[o] what is the plan of the mystery hidden for ages in[p] God who created all things; 10 so that through the church the wisdom of God in its rich variety might now be made known to the rulers and authorities in the heavenly places. 11 This was in accordance with the eternal purpose that he has carried out in Christ Jesus our Lord, 12 in whom we have access to God in boldness and confidence through faith in him.[q] 13 I pray therefore that you[r] may not lose heart over my sufferings for you; they are your glory.

PRAYER FOR THE READERS

14 For this reason I bow my knees before the Father,[s] 15 from whom every family[t] in heaven and on earth takes its name. 16 I pray that, according to the riches of his glory, he may grant that you may be strengthened in your inner being with power through his Spirit, 17 and that Christ may dwell in your hearts through faith, as you are being rooted and grounded in love. 18 I pray that you may have the power to comprehend, with all the saints, what is the breadth and length and height and depth, 19 and to know the love of Christ that surpasses knowledge, so that you may be filled with all the fullness of God.

20 Now to him who by the power at work within us is able to accomplish abundantly far more than all we can ask or imagine, 21 to him be glory in the church and in Christ Jesus to all generations, for ever and ever. Amen.

UNITY IN THE BODY OF CHRIST

4 I therefore, the prisoner in the Lord, beg you to lead a life worthy of the calling to which you have been called, 2 with all humility and gentleness, with patience, bearing with one another in love, 3 making every effort to maintain the unity of the Spirit in the bond of peace. 4 There is one body and one Spirit, just as you were called to the one hope of your calling, 5 one Lord, one faith, one baptism, 6 one God and Father of all, who is above all and through all and in all.

7 But each of us was given grace according to the measure of Christ's gift. 8 Therefore it is said,

'When he ascended on high he made
captivity itself a captive;
he gave gifts to his people.'

9 (When it says, 'He ascended', what does it mean but that he had also descended[u] into the lower parts of the earth? 10 He who descended is the same one who ascended far above all the heavens, so that he might fill all things.) 11 The gifts he gave were that some would be apostles, some prophets, some evangelists, some pastors and teachers, 12 to equip the saints for the work of ministry, for building up the body of Christ, 13 until all of us come to the unity of the faith and of the knowledge of the Son of God, to maturity, to the measure of the full stature of Christ. 14 We must no longer be children, tossed to and fro and blown about by every wind of doctrine, by people's trickery, by their craftiness in deceitful scheming. 15 But speaking the truth in love, we must grow up in every way into him who is the head, into Christ, 16 from whom the whole body, joined and knitted together by every ligament with which it is equipped, as each part is working properly, promotes the body's growth in building itself up in love.

THE OLD LIFE AND THE NEW

17 Now this I affirm and insist on in the Lord: you must no longer live as

[m] 3.1 Or *of* [n] 3.5 Gk *it* [o] 3.9 Other ancient authorities read *to bring to light* [p] 3.9 Or *by* [q] 3.12 Or *the faith of him* [r] 3.13 Or *I* [s] 3.14 Other ancient authorities add *of our Lord Jesus Christ* [t] 3.15 Gk *fatherhood* [u] 4.9 Other ancient authorities add *first*

the Gentiles live, in the futility of their minds. 18They are darkened in their understanding, alienated from the life of God because of their ignorance and hardness of heart. 19They have lost all sensitivity and have abandoned themselves to licentiousness, greedy to practise every kind of impurity. 20That is not the way you learned Christ! 21For surely you have heard about him and were taught in him, as truth is in Jesus. 22You were taught to put away your former way of life, your old self, corrupt and deluded by its lusts, 23and to be renewed in the spirit of your minds, 24and to clothe yourselves with the new self, created according to the likeness of God in true righteousness and holiness.

RULES FOR THE NEW LIFE

25 So then, putting away falsehood, let all of us speak the truth to our neighbours, for we are members of one another. 26Be angry but do not sin; do not let the sun go down on your anger, 27and do not make room for the devil. 28Thieves must give up stealing; rather let them labour and work honestly with their own hands, so as to have something to share with the needy. 29Let no evil talk come out of your mouths, but only what is useful for building up,[v] as there is need, so that your words may give grace to those who hear. 30And do not grieve the Holy Spirit of God, with which you were marked with a seal for the day of redemption. 31Put away from you all bitterness and wrath and anger and wrangling and slander, together with all malice, 32and be kind to one another, tender-hearted, forgiving one another, as God in Christ has forgiven you.[w] **5** 1Therefore be imitators of God, as beloved children, 2and live in love, as Christ loved us[x] and gave himself up for us, a fragrant offering and sacrifice to God.

RENOUNCE PAGAN WAYS

3 But fornication and impurity of any kind, or greed, must not even be mentioned among you, as is proper among saints. 4Entirely out of place is obscene, silly, and vulgar talk; but instead, let there be thanksgiving. 5Be sure of this, that no fornicator or impure person, or one who is greedy (that is, an idolater), has any inheritance in the kingdom of Christ and of God.

6 Let no one deceive you with empty words, for because of these things the wrath of God comes on those who are disobedient. 7Therefore do not be associated with them. 8For once you were darkness, but now in the Lord you are light. Live as children of light— 9for the fruit of the light is found in all that is good and right and true. 10Try to find out what is pleasing to the Lord. 11Take no part in the unfruitful works of darkness, but instead expose them. 12For it is shameful even to mention what such people do secretly; 13but everything exposed by the light becomes visible, 14for everything that becomes visible is light. Therefore it says,

'Sleeper, awake!
 Rise from the dead,
and Christ will shine on you.'

15 Be careful then how you live, not as unwise people but as wise, 16making the most of the time, because the days are evil. 17So do not be foolish, but understand what the will of the Lord is. 18Do not get drunk with wine, for that is debauchery; but be filled with the Spirit, 19as you sing psalms and hymns and spiritual songs among yourselves, singing and making melody to the Lord in your hearts, 20giving thanks to God the Father at all times and for everything in the name of our Lord Jesus Christ.

THE CHRISTIAN HOUSEHOLD

21 Be subject to one another out of reverence for Christ.

22 Wives, be subject to your husbands as you are to the Lord. 23For the husband is the head of the wife just as Christ is the head of the church, the body of which he is the Saviour. 24Just as the church is subject to Christ, so also wives ought to be, in everything, to their husbands.

25 Husbands, love your wives, just as Christ loved the church and gave himself up for her, 26in order to make her holy by cleansing her with the washing of water by the word, 27so as to present the church to himself in splendour, without a spot or wrinkle or anything of the kind—yes, so that she may be holy and without blemish. 28In the same way, husbands should love their wives as they do their own bodies. He who loves his wife loves himself. 29For no one ever hates his own body, but he nourishes and tenderly cares for it, just

[v] **4.29** Other ancient authorities read *building up faith* [w] **4.32** Other ancient authorities read *us*
[x] **5.2** Other ancient authorities read *you*

as Christ does for the church, 30because
we are members of his body.[y] 31'For this
reason a man will leave his father and
mother and be joined to his wife, and
the two will become one flesh.' 32This
is a great mystery, and I am applying it
to Christ and the church. 33Each of you,
however, should love his wife as himself,
and a wife should respect her husband.

CHILDREN AND PARENTS

6 Children, obey your parents in the
Lord,[z] for this is right. 2'Honour
your father and mother'—this is the
first commandment with a promise:
3'so that it may be well with you and
you may live long on the earth.'

4 And, fathers, do not provoke your
children to anger, but bring them up
in the discipline and instruction of the
Lord.

SLAVES AND MASTERS

5 Slaves, obey your earthly masters
with fear and trembling, in singleness
of heart, as you obey Christ; 6not only
while being watched, and in order to
please them, but as slaves of Christ,
doing the will of God from the heart.
7Render service with enthusiasm, as to
the Lord and not to men and women,
8knowing that whatever good we do,
we will receive the same again from the
Lord, whether we are slaves or free.

9 And, masters, do the same to them.
Stop threatening them, for you know
that both of you have the same Master
in heaven, and with him there is no partiality.

THE WHOLE ARMOUR OF GOD

10 Finally, be strong in the Lord and
in the strength of his power. 11Put on
the whole armour of God, so that you
may be able to stand against the wiles
of the devil. 12For our[a] struggle is not
against enemies of blood and flesh,
but against the rulers, against the authorities, against the cosmic powers
of this present darkness, against the
spiritual forces of evil in the heavenly
places. 13Therefore take up the whole
armour of God, so that you may be able
to withstand on that evil day, and having done everything, to stand firm.
14Stand therefore, and fasten the belt
of truth around your waist, and put on
the breastplate of righteousness. 15As
shoes for your feet put on whatever will
make you ready to proclaim the gospel
of peace. 16With all of these,[b] take the
shield of faith, with which you will be
able to quench all the flaming arrows of
the evil one. 17Take the helmet of salvation, and the sword of the Spirit, which
is the word of God.

18 Pray in the Spirit at all times in
every prayer and supplication. To that
end keep alert and always persevere in
supplication for all the saints. 19Pray
also for me, so that when I speak, a message may be given to me to make known
with boldness the mystery of the gospel,[c] 20for which I am an ambassador in
chains. Pray that I may declare it boldly,
as I must speak.

PERSONAL MATTERS AND BENEDICTION

21 So that you also may know how I
am and what I am doing, Tychicus will
tell you everything. He is a dear brother
and a faithful minister in the Lord. 22I
am sending him to you for this very
purpose, to let you know how we are,
and to encourage your hearts.

23 Peace be to the whole community,[d] and love with faith, from God
the Father and the Lord Jesus Christ.
24Grace be with all who have an undy-
ing love for our Lord Jesus Christ.[e]

[y] 5.30 Other ancient authorities add *of his flesh and of his bones* [z] 6.1 Other ancient authorities lack *in the Lord* [a] 6.12 Other ancient authorities read *your* [b] 6.16 Or *In all circumstances*
[c] 6.19 Other ancient authorities lack *of the gospel*
[d] 6.23 Gk *to the brothers* [e] 6.24 Other ancient authorities add *Amen*

The Letter of Paul to the

PHILIPPIANS

It is told in Acts that Paul came to Philippi on his second missionary journey, ca. 49–50 CE, accompanied by Silas and Timothy (Acts 15.40; 16.3). Paul also seems to have visited Philippi on his way from Ephesus to Greece (Acts 20.1–2) and on his way to Jerusalem (20.6). He actually wrote this Letter from prison, though it's not certain where, and it may have been as late as in the early 60s. Paul expresses thankfulness for the Philippians' "sharing in the gospel" and for their "progress and joy in faith" (1.5, 25). Paul is very expressive of affection for this community (4.1) and is just as strong in warning against false teachers who threaten the gospel by imposing circumcision (3.2).

An eloquent hymn about God's salvation is read every year from Philippians during the liturgy on Palm Sunday (2.6–11). Paul exhorts the community to be humble and obedient like Christ. According to Paul, it is because of Christ's self-emptying that he is exalted by God, "so that at the name of Jesus every knee should bend" (2.10). Paul's readers are urged to be of one mind with Christ.

The Letter to the Philippians is only four chapters in length but carries the rich message and powerful persuasion of Paul through which he shares his hopes and convictions, his concerns and fears, and his abiding joy in a faith that professes Jesus Christ as Lord.

SALUTATION

1 Paul and Timothy, servants[a] of
Christ Jesus,
To all the saints in Christ Jesus who
are in Philippi, with the bishops[b] and
deacons:[c]
2 Grace to you and peace from God
our Father and the Lord Jesus Christ.

PAUL'S PRAYER FOR THE PHILIPPIANS

3 I thank my God every time I remember you, 4constantly praying with
joy in every one of my prayers for all
of you, 5because of your sharing in the
gospel from the first day until now. 6I
am confident of this, that the one who
began a good work among you will
bring it to completion by the day of
Jesus Christ. 7It is right for me to think
this way about all of you, because you
hold me in your heart,[d] for all of you
share in God's grace[e] with me, both in
my imprisonment and in the defence
and confirmation of the gospel. 8For
God is my witness, how I long for all
of you with the compassion of Christ
Jesus. 9And this is my prayer, that your
love may overflow more and more with
knowledge and full insight 10to help
you to determine what is best, so that
on the day of Christ you may be pure
and blameless, 11having produced the
harvest of righteousness that comes
through Jesus Christ for the glory and
praise of God.

PAUL'S PRESENT CIRCUMSTANCES

12 I want you to know, beloved,[f] that
what has happened to me has actually
helped to spread the gospel, 13so that
it has become known throughout the
whole imperial guard[g] and to everyone
else that my imprisonment is for Christ;

[a] 1.1 Gk *slaves* [b] 1.1 Or *overseers* [c] 1.1 Or *overseers and helpers* [d] 1.7 Or *because I hold you in my heart* [e] 1.7 Gk *in grace* [f] 1.12 Gk *brothers* [g] 1.13 Gk *whole praetorium*

14and most of the brothers and sisters,[h]
having been made confident in the Lord
by my imprisonment, dare to speak the
word[i] with greater boldness and without fear.

15 Some proclaim Christ from envy
and rivalry, but others from goodwill.
16These proclaim Christ out of love,
knowing that I have been put here for
the defence of the gospel; 17the others proclaim Christ out of selfish ambition, not sincerely but intending to
increase my suffering in my imprisonment. 18What does it matter? Just this,
that Christ is proclaimed in every way,
whether out of false motives or true;
and in that I rejoice.

Yes, and I will continue to rejoice,
19for I know that through your prayers
and the help of the Spirit of Jesus Christ
this will result in my deliverance. 20It is
my eager expectation and hope that I
will not be put to shame in any way, but
that by my speaking with all boldness,
Christ will be exalted now as always in
my body, whether by life or by death.
21For to me, living is Christ and dying
is gain. 22If I am to live in the flesh, that
means fruitful labour for me; and I do
not know which I prefer. 23I am hard
pressed between the two: my desire is
to depart and be with Christ, for that is
far better; 24but to remain in the flesh
is more necessary for you. 25Since I am
convinced of this, I know that I will remain and continue with all of you for
your progress and joy in faith, 26so that
I may share abundantly in your boasting in Christ Jesus when I come to you
again.

27 Only, live your life in a manner
worthy of the gospel of Christ, so that,
whether I come and see you or am absent and hear about you, I will know
that you are standing firm in one spirit,
striving side by side with one mind for
the faith of the gospel, 28and are in no
way intimidated by your opponents. For
them this is evidence of their destruction, but of your salvation. And this
is God's doing. 29For he has graciously
granted you the privilege not only of
believing in Christ, but of suffering for
him as well— 30since you are having
the same struggle that you saw I had
and now hear that I still have.

IMITATING CHRIST'S HUMILITY

2 If then there is any encouragement
in Christ, any consolation from
love, any sharing in the Spirit, any compassion and sympathy, 2make my joy
complete: be of the same mind, having
the same love, being in full accord and
of one mind. 3Do nothing from selfish
ambition or conceit, but in humility regard others as better than yourselves.
4Let each of you look not to your own
interests, but to the interests of others.
5Let the same mind be in you that was[j]
in Christ Jesus,

6 who, though he was in the
form of God,
did not regard equality with God
as something to be exploited,
7 but emptied himself,
taking the form of a slave,
being born in human likeness.
And being found in human form,
8 he humbled himself
and became obedient to the
point of death—
even death on a cross.

9 Therefore God also highly
exalted him
and gave him the name
that is above every name,
10 so that at the name of Jesus
every knee should bend,
in heaven and on earth and
under the earth,
11 and every tongue should confess
that Jesus Christ is Lord,
to the glory of God the Father.

SHINING AS LIGHTS IN THE WORLD

12 Therefore, my beloved, just as you
have always obeyed me, not only in my
presence, but much more now in my
absence, work out your own salvation
with fear and trembling; 13for it is God
who is at work in you, enabling you
both to will and to work for his good
pleasure.

14 Do all things without murmur-
ing and arguing, 15so that you may be
blameless and innocent, children of
God without blemish in the midst of
a crooked and perverse generation, in
which you shine like stars in the world.
16It is by your holding fast to the word of
life that I can boast on the day of Christ
that I did not run in vain or labour in
vain. 17But even if I am being poured
out as a libation over the sacrifice and
the offering of your faith, I am glad and
rejoice with all of you— 18and in the

[h] **1.14** Gk *brothers* [i] **1.14** Other ancient authorities read *word of God* [j] **2.5** Or *that you have*

same way you also must be glad and rejoice with me.

TIMOTHY AND EPAPHRODITUS

19 I hope in the Lord Jesus to send Timothy to you soon, so that I may be cheered by news of you. 20 I have no one like him who will be genuinely concerned for your welfare. 21 All of them are seeking their own interests, not those of Jesus Christ. 22 But Timothy's[k] worth you know, how like a son with a father he has served with me in the work of the gospel. 23 I hope therefore to send him as soon as I see how things go with me; 24 and I trust in the Lord that I will also come soon.

25 Still, I think it necessary to send to you Epaphroditus—my brother and co-worker and fellow-soldier, your messenger[l] and minister to my need; 26 for he has been longing for[m] all of you, and has been distressed because you heard that he was ill. 27 He was indeed so ill that he nearly died. But God had mercy on him, and not only on him but on me also, so that I would not have one sorrow after another. 28 I am the more eager to send him, therefore, in order that you may rejoice at seeing him again, and that I may be less anxious. 29 Welcome him then in the Lord with all joy, and honour such people, 30 because he came close to death for the work of Christ,[n] risking his life to make up for those services that you could not give me.

3 Finally, my brothers and sisters,[o] rejoice[p] in the Lord.

BREAKING WITH THE PAST

To write the same things to you is not troublesome to me, and for you it is a safeguard.

2 Beware of the dogs, beware of the evil workers, beware of those who mutilate the flesh![q] 3 For it is we who are the circumcision, who worship in the Spirit of God[r] and boast in Christ Jesus and have no confidence in the flesh— 4 even though I, too, have reason for confidence in the flesh.

If anyone else has reason to be confident in the flesh, I have more: 5 circumcised on the eighth day, a member of the people of Israel, of the tribe of Benjamin, a Hebrew born of Hebrews; as to the law, a Pharisee; 6 as to zeal, a persecutor of the church; as to righteousness under the law, blameless.

7 Yet whatever gains I had, these I have come to regard as loss because of Christ. 8 More than that, I regard everything as loss because of the surpassing value of knowing Christ Jesus my Lord. For his sake I have suffered the loss of all things, and I regard them as rubbish, in order that I may gain Christ 9 and be found in him, not having a righteousness of my own that comes from the law, but one that comes through faith in Christ,[s] the righteousness from God based on faith. 10 I want to know Christ[t] and the power of his resurrection and the sharing of his sufferings by becoming like him in his death, 11 if somehow I may attain the resurrection from the dead.

PRESSING TOWARDS THE GOAL

12 Not that I have already obtained this or have already reached the goal;[u] but I press on to make it my own, because Christ Jesus has made me his own. 13 Beloved,[v] I do not consider that I have made it my own;[w] but this one thing I do: forgetting what lies behind and straining forward to what lies ahead, 14 I press on towards the goal for the prize of the heavenly[x] call of God in Christ Jesus. 15 Let those of us then who are mature be of the same mind; and if you think differently about anything, this too God will reveal to you. 16 Only let us hold fast to what we have attained.

17 Brothers and sisters,[y] join in imitating me, and observe those who live according to the example you have in us. 18 For many live as enemies of the cross of Christ; I have often told you of them, and now I tell you even with tears. 19 Their end is destruction; their god is the belly; and their glory is in their shame; their minds are set on earthly things. 20 But our citizenship[z] is in heaven, and it is from there that we are expecting a Saviour, the Lord Jesus Christ. 21 He will transform the body of our humiliation[a] so that it may be conformed to the body of his glory,[b] by the power that also enables him to make all

[k] **2.22** Gk *his* [l] **2.25** Gk *apostle* [m] **2.26** Other ancient authorities read *longing to see*
[n] **2.30** Other ancient authorities read *of the Lord*
[o] **3.1** Gk *my brothers* [p] **3.1** Or *farewell*
[q] **3.2** Gk *the mutilation* [r] **3.3** Other ancient authorities read *worship God in spirit* [s] **3.9** Or *through the faith of Christ* [t] **3.10** Gk *him*
[u] **3.12** Or *have already been made perfect*
[v] **3.13** Gk *Brothers* [w] **3.13** Other ancient authorities read *my own yet* [x] **3.14** Gk *upward*
[y] **3.17** Gk *Brothers* [z] **3.20** Or *commonwealth*
[a] **3.21** Or *our humble bodies* [b] **3.21** Or *his glorious body*

4 things subject to himself. 1There-
fore, my brothers and sisters,[c]
whom I love and long for, my joy and
crown, stand firm in the Lord in this
way, my beloved.

EXHORTATIONS

2 I urge Euodia and I urge Synty-
che to be of the same mind in the Lord.
3Yes, and I ask you also, my loyal companion,[d] help these women, for they
have struggled beside me in the work of
the gospel, together with Clement and
the rest of my co-workers, whose names
are in the book of life.

4 Rejoice[e] in the Lord always; again
I will say, Rejoice.[f] 5Let your gentleness
be known to everyone. The Lord is near.
6Do not worry about anything, but in
everything by prayer and supplication
with thanksgiving let your requests be
made known to God. 7And the peace of
God, which surpasses all understanding, will guard your hearts and your
minds in Christ Jesus.

8 Finally, beloved,[g] whatever is true,
whatever is honourable, whatever is
just, whatever is pure, whatever is
pleasing, whatever is commendable, if
there is any excellence and if there is
anything worthy of praise, think about[h]
these things. 9Keep on doing the things
that you have learned and received and
heard and seen in me, and the God of
peace will be with you.

ACKNOWLEDGMENT OF THE PHILIPPIANS' GIFT

10 I rejoice[i] in the Lord greatly that
now at last you have revived your concern for me; indeed, you were concerned
for me, but had no opportunity to show
it.[j] 11Not that I am referring to being in
need; for I have learned to be content
with whatever I have. 12I know what
it is to have little, and I know what
it is to have plenty. In any and all circumstances I have learned the secret
of being well-fed and of going hungry,
of having plenty and of being in need.
13I can do all things through him who
strengthens me. 14In any case, it was
kind of you to share my distress.

15 You Philippians indeed know that
in the early days of the gospel, when I
left Macedonia, no church shared with
me in the matter of giving and receiving, except you alone. 16For even when
I was in Thessalonica, you sent me help
for my needs more than once. 17Not that
I seek the gift, but I seek the profit that
accumulates to your account. 18I have
been paid in full and have more than
enough; I am fully satisfied, now that
I have received from Epaphroditus the
gifts you sent, a fragrant offering, a sacrifice acceptable and pleasing to God.
19And my God will fully satisfy every
need of yours according to his riches in
glory in Christ Jesus. 20To our God and
Father be glory for ever and ever. Amen.

FINAL GREETINGS AND BENEDICTION

21 Greet every saint in Christ Jesus.
The friends[k] who are with me greet you.
22All the saints greet you, especially
those of the emperor's household.

23 The grace of the Lord Jesus Christ
be with your spirit.[l]

[c] 4.1 Gk *my brothers* [d] 4.3 Or *loyal Syzygus* [e] 4.4 Or *Farewell* [f] 4.4 Or *Farewell* [g] 4.8 Gk *brothers* [h] 4.8 Gk *take account of* [i] 4.10 Gk *I rejoiced* [j] 4.10 Gk lacks *to show it* [k] 4.21 Gk *brothers* [l] 4.23 Other ancient authorities add *Amen*

The Letter of Paul to the

COLOSSIANS

The Letter of Paul to the Colossians, like Ephesians, Philemon, and Philippians, was written while Paul was in prison. These writings are called the Captivity Letters. The Letter to the Colossians was written to deal with problems in the largely gentile Christian community at Colossae and uses expressions and concepts like those found in Ephesians ("fullness of [God]," Col 1.19; 2.9; Eph 1.23; 3.19, Christ's authority over rival powers, Col 2.10; Eph 1.21–22, and admonitions for family households, Col 3.18—4.1; Eph 5.21—6.9). Scholars today believe that a disciple of Paul, and not Paul himself, wrote the Letter to the Colossians.

There is a controversy in the Letter to the Colossians about whether Christ's work of redemption actually freed believers from the powers of the universe and gave them true access to God or whether they needed to turn to other sources of wisdom culturally popular at the time. The false teachers drew upon and promoted popular Greco-Roman religious ideas that offered wisdom and saving benefits. The Letter rejects the "empty deceit" and "philosophy" (2.8) that required observance of special worship of celestial powers as a means of gaining access to God. The Letter admonishes that it is only through "Christ in you" that the Colossians know and experience access to God (1.27). The Colossians are told to persevere and be steadfast while they live in a manner appropriate to their status in Christ. Christ is the way of access to true wisdom. The date of the writing of this Letter is probably sometime in the late 60s.

Passages from Colossians are read every year on the Feast of the Holy Family (3.12–21) and on Easter Sunday (3.1–4). The former passage speaks about true asceticism that is living a life of forgiveness and love in Christ. Such commitment defines relationships between husbands and wives, children and parents, slaves and masters. The latter passage speaks about the new life in Christ that calls each to focus on the things that are above and not on the things of the earth.

SALUTATION

1 Paul, an apostle of Christ Jesus by
the will of God, and Timothy our
brother,
2 To the saints and faithful brothers
and sisters[a] in Christ in Colossae:
Grace to you and peace from God our Father.

PAUL THANKS GOD FOR THE COLOSSIANS

3 In our prayers for you we always
thank God, the Father of our Lord Jesus
Christ, 4for we have heard of your faith
in Christ Jesus and of the love that you
have for all the saints, 5because of the
hope laid up for you in heaven. You
have heard of this hope before in the
word of the truth, the gospel 6that has
come to you. Just as it is bearing fruit
and growing in the whole world, so it
has been bearing fruit among yourselves from the day you heard it and
truly comprehended the grace of God.
7This you learned from Epaphras, our
beloved fellow-servant.[b] He is a faithful
minister of Christ on your[c] behalf, 8and

[a] 1.2 Gk *brothers* [b] 1.7 Gk *slave* [c] 1.7 Other ancient authorities read *our*

he has made known to us your love in
the Spirit.

9 For this reason, since the day we
heard it, we have not ceased praying for
you and asking that you may be filled
with the knowledge of God's[d] will in
all spiritual wisdom and understanding, 10 so that you may lead lives worthy of the Lord, fully pleasing to him, as
you bear fruit in every good work and
as you grow in the knowledge of God.
11 May you be made strong with all the
strength that comes from his glorious
power, and may you be prepared to endure everything with patience, while
joyfully 12 giving thanks to the Father,
who has enabled[e] you[f] to share in the
inheritance of the saints in the light.
13 He has rescued us from the power of
darkness and transferred us into the
kingdom of his beloved Son, 14 in whom
we have redemption, the forgiveness of
sins.[g]

THE SUPREMACY OF CHRIST

15 He is the image of the invisible
God, the firstborn of all creation; 16 for
in[h] him all things in heaven and on
earth were created, things visible and
invisible, whether thrones or dominions or rulers or powers—all things
have been created through him and for
him. 17 He himself is before all things,
and in[i] him all things hold together.
18 He is the head of the body, the church;
he is the beginning, the firstborn from
the dead, so that he might come to have
first place in everything. 19 For in him all
the fullness of God was pleased to dwell,
20 and through him God was pleased to
reconcile to himself all things, whether
on earth or in heaven, by making peace
through the blood of his cross.

21 And you who were once estranged
and hostile in mind, doing evil deeds,
22 he has now reconciled[j] in his fleshly
body[k] through death, so as to present
you holy and blameless and irreproach-
able before him— 23 provided that you
continue securely established and steadfast in the faith, without shifting from
the hope promised by the gospel that
you heard, which has been proclaimed
to every creature under heaven. I, Paul,
became a servant of this gospel.

PAUL'S INTEREST IN THE COLOSSIANS

24 I am now rejoicing in my sufferings for your sake, and in my flesh I am
completing what is lacking in Christ's
afflictions for the sake of his body, that
is, the church. 25 I became its servant according to God's commission that was
given to me for you, to make the word
of God fully known, 26 the mystery that
has been hidden throughout the ages
and generations but has now been revealed to his saints. 27 To them God
chose to make known how great among
the Gentiles are the riches of the glory
of this mystery, which is Christ in you,
the hope of glory. 28 It is he whom we
proclaim, warning everyone and teaching everyone in all wisdom, so that we
may present everyone mature in Christ.
29 For this I toil and struggle with all
the energy that he powerfully inspires
within me.

2 For I want you to know how much
I am struggling for you, and for
those in Laodicea, and for all who have
not seen me face to face. 2 I want their
hearts to be encouraged and united in
love, so that they may have all the riches
of assured understanding and have the
knowledge of God's mystery, that is,
Christ himself,[l] 3 in whom are hidden
all the treasures of wisdom and knowledge. 4 I am saying this so that no one
may deceive you with plausible arguments. 5 For though I am absent in body,
yet I am with you in spirit, and I rejoice
to see your morale and the firmness of
your faith in Christ.

FULLNESS OF LIFE IN CHRIST

6 As you therefore have received
Christ Jesus the Lord, continue to live
your lives[m] in him, 7 rooted and built
up in him and established in the faith,
just as you were taught, abounding in
thanksgiving.

8 See to it that no one takes you captive through philosophy and empty deceit, according to human tradition, according to the elemental spirits of the
universe,[n] and not according to Christ.
9 For in him the whole fullness of deity
dwells bodily, 10 and you have come to
fullness in him, who is the head of every
ruler and authority. 11 In him also you
were circumcised with a spiritual cir-

[d] 1.9 Gk *his* [e] 1.12 Other ancient authorities read *called* [f] 1.12 Other ancient authorities read *us* [g] 1.14 Other ancient authorities add *through his blood* [h] 1.16 Or *by* [i] 1.17 Or *by* [j] 1.22 Other ancient authorities read *you have now been reconciled* [k] 1.22 Gk *in the body of his flesh* [l] 2.2 Other ancient authorities read *of the mystery of God, both of the Father and of Christ* [m] 2.6 Gk *to walk* [n] 2.8 Or *the rudiments of the world*

cumcision,[o] by putting off the body of
the flesh in the circumcision of Christ;
12when you were buried with him in
baptism, you were also raised with him
through faith in the power of God, who
raised him from the dead. 13And when
you were dead in trespasses and the uncircumcision of your flesh, God[p] made
you[q] alive together with him, when he
forgave us all our trespasses, 14erasing
the record that stood against us with its
legal demands. He set this aside, nailing
it to the cross. 15He disarmed[r] the rulers
and authorities and made a public example of them, triumphing over them
in it.

16 Therefore do not let anyone condemn you in matters of food and drink
or of observing festivals, new moons, or
sabbaths. 17These are only a shadow of
what is to come, but the substance belongs to Christ. 18Do not let anyone dis-
qualify you, insisting on self-abasement
and worship of angels, dwelling[s] on
visions,[t] puffed up without cause by
a human way of thinking,[u] 19and not
holding fast to the head, from whom
the whole body, nourished and held
together by its ligaments and sinews,
grows with a growth that is from God.

WARNINGS AGAINST FALSE TEACHERS

20 If with Christ you died to the elemental spirits of the universe,[v] why do
you live as if you still belonged to the
world? Why do you submit to regulations, 21'Do not handle, Do not taste, Do
not touch'? 22All these regulations refer
to things that perish with use; they are
simply human commands and teachings. 23These have indeed an appearance
of wisdom in promoting self-imposed
piety, humility, and severe treatment
of the body, but they are of no value in
checking self-indulgence.[w]

THE NEW LIFE IN CHRIST

3 So if you have been raised with
Christ, seek the things that are
above, where Christ is, seated at the
right hand of God. 2Set your minds on
things that are above, not on things
that are on earth, 3for you have died,
and your life is hidden with Christ in
God. 4When Christ who is your[x] life is
revealed, then you also will be revealed
with him in glory.

5 Put to death, therefore, whatever
in you is earthly: fornication, impurity,
passion, evil desire, and greed (which
is idolatry). 6On account of these the
wrath of God is coming on those who
are disobedient.[y] 7These are the ways
you also once followed, when you were
living that life.[z] 8But now you must get
rid of all such things—anger, wrath,
malice, slander, and abusive[a] language
from your mouth. 9Do not lie to one
another, seeing that you have stripped
off the old self with its practices 10and
have clothed yourselves with the new
self, which is being renewed in knowledge according to the image of its creator. 11In that renewal[b] there is no longer
Greek and Jew, circumcised and uncircumcised, barbarian, Scythian, slave
and free; but Christ is all and in all!

12 As God's chosen ones, holy and
beloved, clothe yourselves with compassion, kindness, humility, meekness,
and patience. 13Bear with one another
and, if anyone has a complaint against
another, forgive each other; just as the
Lord[c] has forgiven you, so you also must
forgive. 14Above all, clothe yourselves
with love, which binds everything together in perfect harmony. 15And let the
peace of Christ rule in your hearts, to
which indeed you were called in the one
body. And be thankful. 16Let the word
of Christ[d] dwell in you richly; teach and
admonish one another in all wisdom;
and with gratitude in your hearts sing
psalms, hymns, and spiritual songs to
God.[e] 17And whatever you do, in word
or deed, do everything in the name of
the Lord Jesus, giving thanks to God the
Father through him.

RULES FOR CHRISTIAN HOUSEHOLDS

18 Wives, be subject to your husbands, as is fitting in the Lord. 19Hus-
bands, love your wives and never treat
them harshly.

20 Children, obey your parents in
everything, for this is your acceptable

[o] **2.11** Gk *a circumcision made without hands* [p] **2.13** Gk *he* [q] **2.13** Other ancient authorities read *made us*; others, *made* [r] **2.15** Or *divested himself of* [s] **2.18** Other ancient authorities read *not dwelling* [t] **2.18** Meaning of Gk uncertain [u] **2.18** Gk *by the mind of his flesh* [v] **2.20** Or *the rudiments of the world* [w] **2.23** Or *are of no value, serving only to indulge the flesh*
[x] **3.4** Other authorities read *our* [y] **3.6** Other ancient authorities lack *on those who are disobedient* (Gk *the children of disobedience*)
[z] **3.7** Or *living among such people* [a] **3.8** Or *filthy*
[b] **3.11** Gk *its creator, 11where* [c] **3.13** Other ancient authorities read *just as Christ*
[d] **3.16** Other ancient authorities read *of God*, or *of the Lord* [e] **3.16** Other ancient authorities read *to the Lord*

duty in the Lord. 21Fathers, do not provoke your children, or they may lose
heart. 22Slaves, obey your earthly masters[f] in everything, not only while being
watched and in order to please them,
but wholeheartedly, fearing the Lord.[g]
23Whatever your task, put yourselves
into it, as done for the Lord and not for
your masters,[h] 24since you know that
from the Lord you will receive the inheritance as your reward; you serve[i] the
Lord Christ. 25For the wrongdoer will be
paid back for whatever wrong has been
4 done, and there is no partiality.
1Masters, treat your slaves justly
and fairly, for you know that you also
have a Master in heaven.

FURTHER INSTRUCTIONS

2 Devote yourselves to prayer, keeping alert in it with thanksgiving. 3At
the same time pray for us as well that
God will open to us a door for the word,
that we may declare the mystery of
Christ, for which I am in prison, 4so
that I may reveal it clearly, as I should.
5 Conduct yourselves wisely towards
outsiders, making the most of the time.[j]
6Let your speech always be gracious,
seasoned with salt, so that you may
know how you ought to answer everyone.

FINAL GREETINGS AND BENEDICTION

7 Tychicus will tell you all the news
about me; he is a beloved brother, a
faithful minister, and a fellow-servant[k]
in the Lord. 8I have sent him to you
for this very purpose, so that you may
know how we are[l] and that he may encourage your hearts; 9he is coming with
Onesimus, the faithful and beloved
brother, who is one of you. They will tell
you about everything here.
10 Aristarchus my fellow-prisoner
greets you, as does Mark the cousin of
Barnabas, concerning whom you have
received instructions—if he comes to
you, welcome him. 11And Jesus who is
called Justus greets you. These are the
only ones of the circumcision among
my co-workers for the kingdom of God,
and they have been a comfort to me.
12Epaphras, who is one of you, a servant[m] of Christ Jesus, greets you. He is
always wrestling in his prayers on your
behalf, so that you may stand mature
and fully assured in everything that
God wills. 13For I testify for him that he
has worked hard for you and for those
in Laodicea and in Hierapolis. 14Luke,
the beloved physician, and Demas greet
you. 15Give my greetings to the brothers
and sisters[n] in Laodicea, and to Nym-
pha and the church in her house. 16And
when this letter has been read among
you, have it read also in the church of
the Laodiceans; and see that you read
also the letter from Laodicea. 17And say
to Archippus, 'See that you complete the
task that you have received in the Lord.'

18 I, Paul, write this greeting with
my own hand. Remember my chains.
Grace be with you.[o]

[f] 3.22 In Greek the same word is used for *master* and *Lord* [g] 3.22 In Greek the same word is used for *master* and *Lord* [h] 3.23 Gk *not for men* [i] 3.24 Or *you are slaves of*, or *be slaves of* [j] 4.5 Or *opportunity* [k] 4.7 Gk *slave* [l] 4.8 Other authorities read *that I may know how you are* [m] 4.12 Gk *slave* [n] 4.15 Gk *brothers* [o] 4.18 Other ancient authorities add *Amen*

The First Letter of Paul to the

THESSALONIANS

The First Letter to the Thessalonians is among the oldest writings of the New Testament, written by Paul around 51 CE. According to the Acts of the Apostles, after a difficult trip to Philippi (2.2; Acts 16.11–40), Paul, Silas, and Timothy went to Thessalonica and preached the gospel at a Jewish synagogue. They experienced opposition from the Jewish community there who forced them to leave (Acts 17.1–10). In this Letter, Paul addresses the community's expectation of the imminent return of Jesus and the beginning of the end time.

The community at Thessalonica seemed to be made up primarily of gentile Christians (1.9–10). The Letter has Paul's typical structure: greeting, thanksgiving, main body, farewell, and final blessing prayer. Paul was concerned with the community's stability and moral life. Paul was worried that the Thessalonians, who were experiencing the death of loved ones before the return of Christ, seemed to be grieving in a way that was without hope (4.13). The Thessalonians themselves were concerned for their salvation. Since some were dying before Jesus' return in triumph, the Thessalonians feared that they were missing out on God's victory. Paul reminded them of their salvation through Christ's death and resurrection (5.9–10) and that even the dead will share in God's victory (4.13–18). The end time will come suddenly and without warning (5.1–3). The appropriate response was to "keep awake" (5.6) by leading upright and moral lives.

Texts from 1 Thessalonians are read in Year A on the Twenty-Ninth through the Thirty-Third Sundays of the liturgical calendar. These passages are selected to encourage the church to remain faithful to Christ even as his second coming is delayed in time. The church must remain alert and watchful for the day of the Lord that will come "like a thief in the night" (5.1–6).

SALUTATION

1 Paul, Silvanus, and Timothy,
To the church of the Thessalonians
in God the Father and the Lord Jesus
Christ:
Grace to you and peace.

THE THESSALONIANS' FAITH AND EXAMPLE

2 We always give thanks to God for all
of you and mention you in our prayers,
constantly 3remembering before our
God and Father your work of faith and
labour of love and steadfastness of hope
in our Lord Jesus Christ. 4For we know,
brothers and sisters[a] beloved by God,
that he has chosen you, 5because our
message of the gospel came to you not
in word only, but also in power and in
the Holy Spirit and with full conviction;
just as you know what kind of people we
proved to be among you for your sake.
6And you became imitators of us and
of the Lord, for in spite of persecution
you received the word with joy inspired
by the Holy Spirit, 7so that you became
an example to all the believers in Macedonia and in Achaia. 8For the word of
the Lord has sounded forth from you
not only in Macedonia and Achaia, but
in every place where your faith in God
has become known, so that we have no

[a] 1.4 Gk *brothers*

need to speak about it. 9For the people of those regions[b] report about us what kind of welcome we had among you, and how you turned to God from idols, to serve a living and true God, 10and to wait for his Son from heaven, whom he raised from the dead—Jesus, who rescues us from the wrath that is coming.

PAUL'S MINISTRY IN THESSALONICA

2 You yourselves know, brothers and sisters,[c] that our coming to you was not in vain, 2but though we had already suffered and been shamefully maltreated at Philippi, as you know, we had courage in our God to declare to you the gospel of God in spite of great opposition. 3For our appeal does not spring from deceit or impure motives or trickery, 4but just as we have been approved by God to be entrusted with the message of the gospel, even so we speak, not to please mortals, but to please God who tests our hearts. 5As you know and as God is our witness, we never came with words of flattery or with a pretext for greed; 6nor did we seek praise from mortals, whether from you or from others, 7though we might have made demands as apostles of Christ. But we were gentle[d] among you, like a nurse tenderly caring for her own children. 8So deeply do we care for you that we are determined to share with you not only the gospel of God but also our own selves, because you have become very dear to us.

9 You remember our labour and toil, brothers and sisters;[e] we worked night and day, so that we might not burden any of you while we proclaimed to you the gospel of God. 10You are witnesses, and God also, how pure, upright, and blameless our conduct was towards you believers. 11As you know, we dealt with each one of you like a father with his children, 12urging and encouraging you and pleading that you should lead a life worthy of God, who calls you into his own kingdom and glory.

13 We also constantly give thanks to God for this, that when you received the word of God that you heard from us, you accepted it not as a human word but as what it really is, God's word, which is also at work in you believers. 14For you, brothers and sisters,[f] became imitators of the churches of God in Christ Jesus that are in Judea, for you suffered the same things from your own compatriots as they did from the Jews, 15who killed both the Lord Jesus and the prophets,[g] and drove us out; they displease God and oppose everyone 16by hindering us from speaking to the Gentiles so that they may be saved. Thus they have constantly been filling up the measure of their sins; but God's wrath has overtaken them at last.[h]

PAUL'S DESIRE TO VISIT THE THESSALONIANS AGAIN

17 As for us, brothers and sisters,[i] when, for a short time, we were made orphans by being separated from you—in person, not in heart—we longed with great eagerness to see you face to face. 18For we wanted to come to you—certainly I, Paul, wanted to again and again—but Satan blocked our way. 19For what is our hope or joy or crown of boasting before our Lord Jesus at his coming? Is it not you? 20Yes, you are our glory and joy!

3 Therefore when we could bear it no longer, we decided to be left alone in Athens; 2and we sent Timothy, our brother and co-worker for God in proclaiming[j] the gospel of Christ, to strengthen and encourage you for the sake of your faith, 3so that no one would be shaken by these persecutions. Indeed, you yourselves know that this is what we are destined for. 4In fact, when we were with you, we told you beforehand that we were to suffer persecution; so it turned out, as you know. 5For this reason, when I could bear it no longer, I sent to find out about your faith; I was afraid that somehow the tempter had tempted you and that our labour had been in vain.

TIMOTHY'S ENCOURAGING REPORT

6 But Timothy has just now come to us from you, and has brought us the good news of your faith and love. He has told us also that you always remember us kindly and long to see us—just as we long to see you. 7For this reason, brothers and sisters,[k] during all our distress and persecution we have been encouraged about you through your faith. 8For we now live, if you continue to stand firm in the Lord. 9How can we thank God enough for you in return for

[b] 1.9 Gk *For they* [c] 2.1 Gk *brothers* [d] 2.7 Other ancient authorities read *infants* [e] 2.9 Gk *brothers* [f] 2.14 Gk *brothers* [g] 2.15 Other ancient authorities read *their own prophets* [h] 2.16 Or *completely* or *for ever* [i] 2.17 Gk *brothers* [j] 3.2 Gk lacks *proclaiming* [k] 3.7 Gk *brothers*

all the joy that we feel before our God
because of you? 10 Night and day we pray
most earnestly that we may see you face
to face and restore whatever is lacking
in your faith.
11 Now may our God and Father
himself and our Lord Jesus direct our
way to you. 12 And may the Lord make
you increase and abound in love for one
another and for all, just as we abound in
love for you. 13 And may he so strengthen
your hearts in holiness that you may be
blameless before our God and Father at
the coming of our Lord Jesus with all his
saints.

A LIFE PLEASING TO GOD

4 Finally, brothers and sisters,[l] we
ask and urge you in the Lord Jesus
that, as you learned from us how you
ought to live and to please God (as, in
fact, you are doing), you should do so
more and more. 2 For you know what
instructions we gave you through the
Lord Jesus. 3 For this is the will of God,
your sanctification: that you abstain
from fornication; 4 that each one of you
knows how to control your own body[m]
in holiness and honour, 5 not with lustful passion, like the Gentiles who do
not know God; 6 that no one wrongs
or exploits a brother or sister[n] in this
matter, because the Lord is an avenger
in all these things, just as we have already told you beforehand and solemnly
warned you. 7 For God did not call us
to impurity but in holiness. 8 Therefore
whoever rejects this rejects not human
authority but God, who also gives his
Holy Spirit to you.
9 Now concerning love of the
brothers and sisters,[o] you do not need to
have anyone write to you, for you yourselves have been taught by God to love
one another; 10 and indeed you do love
all the brothers and sisters[p] throughout
Macedonia. But we urge you, beloved,[q]
to do so more and more, 11 to aspire to
live quietly, to mind your own affairs,
and to work with your hands, as we directed you, 12 so that you may behave
properly towards outsiders and be dependent on no one.

THE COMING OF THE LORD

13 But we do not want you to be uninformed, brothers and sisters,[r] about
those who have died,[s] so that you may
not grieve as others do who have no
hope. 14 For since we believe that Jesus
died and rose again, even so, through
Jesus, God will bring with him those
who have died.[t] 15 For this we declare
to you by the word of the Lord, that
we who are alive, who are left until the
coming of the Lord, will by no means
precede those who have died.[u] 16 For the
Lord himself, with a cry of command,
with the archangel's call and with the
sound of God's trumpet, will descend
from heaven, and the dead in Christ will
rise first. 17 Then we who are alive, who
are left, will be caught up in the clouds
together with them to meet the Lord in
the air; and so we will be with the Lord
for ever. 18 Therefore encourage one another with these words.

5 Now concerning the times and the
seasons, brothers and sisters,[v] you
do not need to have anything written
to you. 2 For you yourselves know very
well that the day of the Lord will come
like a thief in the night. 3 When they say,
'There is peace and security', then sudden destruction will come upon them,
as labour pains come upon a pregnant
woman, and there will be no escape!
4 But you, beloved,[w] are not in darkness, for that day to surprise you like a
thief; 5 for you are all children of light
and children of the day; we are not of
the night or of darkness. 6 So then, let
us not fall asleep as others do, but let us
keep awake and be sober; 7 for those who
sleep sleep at night, and those who are
drunk get drunk at night. 8 But since we
belong to the day, let us be sober, and
put on the breastplate of faith and love,
and for a helmet the hope of salvation.
9 For God has destined us not for wrath
but for obtaining salvation through our
Lord Jesus Christ, 10 who died for us, so
that whether we are awake or asleep
we may live with him. 11 Therefore encourage one another and build up each
other, as indeed you are doing.

FINAL EXHORTATIONS, GREETINGS, AND BENEDICTION

12 But we appeal to you, brothers
and sisters,[x] to respect those who labour
among you, and have charge of you in
the Lord and admonish you; 13 esteem
them very highly in love because of their
work. Be at peace among yourselves.

[l] **4.1** Gk *brothers* [m] **4.4** Or *how to take a wife for himself* [n] **4.6** Gk *brother* [o] **4.9** Gk *brothers* [p] **4.10** Gk *brothers* [q] **4.10** Gk *brothers* [r] **4.13** Gk *brothers* [s] **4.13** Gk *fallen asleep* [t] **4.14** Gk *fallen asleep* [u] **4.15** Gk *fallen asleep* [v] **5.1** Gk *brothers* [w] **5.4** Gk *brothers* [x] **5.12** Gk *brothers*

14 And we urge you, beloved,[y] to admonish the idlers, encourage the faint-
hearted, help the weak, be patient with
all of them. 15 See that none of you repays evil for evil, but always seek to do
good to one another and to all. 16 Rejoice
always, 17 pray without ceasing, 18 give
thanks in all circumstances; for this is
the will of God in Christ Jesus for you.
19 Do not quench the Spirit. 20 Do not despise the words of prophets,[z] 21 but test
everything; hold fast to what is good;
22 abstain from every form of evil.
23 May the God of peace himself
sanctify you entirely; and may your
spirit and soul and body be kept sound[a]
and blameless at the coming of our Lord
Jesus Christ. 24 The one who calls you is
faithful, and he will do this.
25 Beloved,[b] pray for us.
26 Greet all the brothers and sisters[c]
with a holy kiss. 27 I solemnly command
you by the Lord that this letter be read
to all of them.[d]
28 The grace of our Lord Jesus Christ
be with you.[e]

[y] 5.14 Gk *brothers* [z] 5.20 Gk *despise prophecies*
[a] 5.23 Or *complete* [b] 5.25 Gk *Brothers*
[c] 5.26 Gk *brothers* [d] 5.27 Gk *to all the brothers*
[e] 5.28 Other ancient authorities add *Amen*

The Second Letter of Paul to the

THESSALONIANS

Some scholars believe that 2 Thessalonians may not be Paul's own writing, but that of another disciple at a later time. Others consider this Letter to follow upon 1 Thessalonians and therefore to be authentically by Paul. If this latter interpretation is true, the Second Letter would be dated sometime shortly after 51 CE. If the former is true, the date of authorship would be sometime during the last two decades of the first century.

Because teaching about the second coming of the Lord was a source of confusion among the Thessalonians, Paul addresses this issue again in this Second Letter (2.1–2). Paul admonishes that the coming of the day of the Lord does not mean that people can stop working or live immoral lives (3.6–13). The day of the Lord will be anticipated by a number of events including persecution and lawlessness before the final time. The coming of the day of the Lord should not be a cause of panic or a distraction from carrying out the responsibilities of working and living according to the love of God.

Passages from 2 Thessalonians are read in Cycle C on the Thirty-First (1.11—2.2), Thirty-Second (2.16—3.5), and Thirty-Third (3.7–12) Sundays of the Year. The admonitions from Paul about anticipating the day of the Lord, keeping the faith, and earning one's daily bread are all appropriate texts for the church as it still awaits the Lord's coming by standing firm and holding fast to the traditions entrusted to it.

SALUTATION

1 Paul, Silvanus, and Timothy,
To the church of the Thessalonians
in God our Father and the Lord Jesus
Christ:
2 Grace to you and peace from God
our[a] Father and the Lord Jesus Christ.

THANKSGIVING

3 We must always give thanks to God
for you, brothers and sisters,[b] as is right,
because your faith is growing abundantly, and the love of every one of you
for one another is increasing. 4 Therefore
we ourselves boast of you among the
churches of God for your steadfastness
and faith during all your persecutions
and the afflictions that you are enduring.

THE JUDGEMENT AT CHRIST'S COMING

5 This is evidence of the righteous
judgement of God, and is intended to
make you worthy of the kingdom of
God, for which you are also suffering.
6 For it is indeed just of God to repay
with affliction those who afflict you,
7 and to give relief to the afflicted as well
as to us, when the Lord Jesus is revealed
from heaven with his mighty angels
8 in flaming fire, inflicting vengeance
on those who do not know God and on
those who do not obey the gospel of our
Lord Jesus. 9 These will suffer the punishment of eternal destruction, separated
from the presence of the Lord and from
the glory of his might, 10 when he comes
to be glorified by his saints and to be
marvelled at on that day among all who
have believed, because our testimony
to you was believed. 11 To this end we
always pray for you, asking that our
God will make you worthy of his call
and will fulfil by his power every good
resolve and work of faith, 12 so that the

[a] 1.2 Other ancient authorities read *the*
[b] 1.3 Gk *brothers*

name of our Lord Jesus may be glorified in you, and you in him, according to the grace of our God and the Lord Jesus Christ.

THE MAN OF LAWLESSNESS

2 As to the coming of our Lord Jesus Christ and our being gathered together to him, we beg you, brothers and sisters,[c] 2not to be quickly shaken in mind or alarmed, either by spirit or by word or by letter, as though from us, to the effect that the day of the Lord is already here. 3Let no one deceive you in any way; for that day will not come unless the rebellion comes first and the lawless one[d] is revealed, the one destined for destruction.[e] 4He opposes and exalts himself above every so-called god or object of worship, so that he takes his seat in the temple of God, declaring himself to be God. 5Do you not remember that I told you these things when I was still with you? 6And you know what is now restraining him, so that he may be revealed when his time comes. 7For the mystery of lawlessness is already at work, but only until the one who now restrains it is removed. 8And then the lawless one will be revealed, whom the Lord Jesus[f] will destroy[g] with the breath of his mouth, annihilating him by the manifestation of his coming. 9The coming of the lawless one is apparent in the working of Satan, who uses all power, signs, lying wonders, 10and every kind of wicked deception for those who are perishing, because they refused to love the truth and so be saved. 11For this reason God sends them a powerful delusion, leading them to believe what is false, 12so that all who have not believed the truth but took pleasure in unrighteousness will be condemned.

CHOSEN FOR SALVATION

13 But we must always give thanks to God for you, brothers and sisters[h] beloved by the Lord, because God chose you as the first fruits[i] for salvation through sanctification by the Spirit and through belief in the truth. 14For this purpose he called you through our proclamation of the good news,[j] so that you may obtain the glory of our Lord Jesus Christ. 15So then, brothers and sisters,[k] stand firm and hold fast to the traditions that you were taught by us, either by word of mouth or by our letter.

16 Now may our Lord Jesus Christ himself and God our Father, who loved us and through grace gave us eternal comfort and good hope, 17comfort your hearts and strengthen them in every good work and word.

REQUEST FOR PRAYER

3 Finally, brothers and sisters,[l] pray for us, so that the word of the Lord may spread rapidly and be glorified everywhere, just as it is among you, 2and that we may be rescued from wicked and evil people; for not all have faith. 3But the Lord is faithful; he will strengthen you and guard you from the evil one.[m] 4And we have confidence in the Lord concerning you, that you are doing and will go on doing the things that we command. 5May the Lord direct your hearts to the love of God and to the steadfastness of Christ.

WARNING AGAINST IDLENESS

6 Now we command you, beloved,[n] in the name of our Lord Jesus Christ, to keep away from believers who are[o] living in idleness and not according to the tradition that they[p] received from us. 7For you yourselves know how you ought to imitate us; we were not idle when we were with you, 8and we did not eat anyone's bread without paying for it; but with toil and labour we worked night and day, so that we might not burden any of you. 9This was not because we do not have that right, but in order to give you an example to imitate. 10For even when we were with you, we gave you this command: Anyone unwilling to work should not eat. 11For we hear that some of you are living in idleness, mere busybodies, not doing any work. 12Now such persons we command and exhort in the Lord Jesus Christ to do their work quietly and to earn their own living. 13Brothers and sisters,[q] do not be weary in doing what is right.

14 Take note of those who do not obey what we say in this letter; have

[c] 2.1 Gk *brothers* [d] 2.3 Gk *the man of lawlessness*; other ancient authorities read *the man of sin* [e] 2.3 Gk *the son of destruction*
[f] 2.8 Other ancient authorities lack *Jesus*
[g] 2.8 Other ancient authorities read *consume*
[h] 2.13 Gk *brothers* [i] 2.13 Other ancient authorities read *from the beginning* [j] 2.14 Or *through our gospel* [k] 2.15 Gk *brothers*
[l] 3.1 Gk *brothers* [m] 3.3 Or *from evil* [n] 3.6 Gk *brothers* [o] 3.6 Gk *from every brother who is*
[p] 3.6 Other ancient authorities read *you*
[q] 3.13 Gk *Brothers*

nothing to do with them, so that they may be ashamed. [15]Do not regard them as enemies, but warn them as believers.[r]

FINAL GREETINGS AND BENEDICTION

16 Now may the Lord of peace himself give you peace at all times in all ways. The Lord be with all of you.

17 I, Paul, write this greeting with my own hand. This is the mark in every letter of mine; it is the way I write. [18]The grace of our Lord Jesus Christ be with all of you.[s]

[r] 3.15 Gk *a brother* [s] 3.18 Other ancient authorities add *Amen*

The First Letter of Paul to

TIMOTHY

The Letters of 1 and 2 Timothy and Titus are called the Pastoral Letters. They all are addressed to a leader of a local church: Timothy in Ephesus and Titus on the Isle of Crete. The Letters are written to address pastoral problems in these churches due to the emergence of false teachers and disorganization. These Letters counsel the pastors on how to build up the church by appointing proper leadership.

Most scholars agree that Paul is not the actual author of the Pastoral Letters. The writing style, vocabulary, and historical circumstances of the Letters appear to date these writings to a much later time, probably as late as the beginning of the second century. Because of its preoccupation with church leadership (3.1–13), the lesser role of women (2.11–15), and the concern for the exercise of strong authority, the First Letter to Timothy seems to have been written at a time when the Christian churches were strengthening their own structures to meet the challenges of a time later than that of the apostolic period.

Relevant selections from 1 Timothy are presented in the Lectionary for reading at the ordination of deacons and bishops. Additionally, passages are read on Sundays of Year C at the latter part of the liturgical year: the Twenty-Fourth (1.12–17), Twenty-Fifth (2.1–8), and Twenty-Sixth (6.11–16) Sundays of Ordinary Time. As time moves on in the liturgical year, so in the passing of the faith from one generation to the next, the Pastoral Letters exhort the church to persevere and stay true to the gospel as it was originally preached by Paul and not to become distracted or discouraged as the church awaits the return of Christ in glory.

SALUTATION

1 Paul, an apostle of Christ Jesus by the command of God our Saviour and of Christ Jesus our hope,
2 To Timothy, my loyal child in the faith:

Grace, mercy, and peace from God the Father and Christ Jesus our Lord.

WARNING AGAINST FALSE TEACHERS

3 I urge you, as I did when I was on my way to Macedonia, to remain in Ephesus so that you may instruct certain people not to teach any different
doctrine, [4]and not to occupy themselves with myths and endless genealogies that promote speculations rather than the divine training[a] that is known by
faith. [5]But the aim of such instruction is love that comes from a pure heart, a good conscience, and sincere faith.
[6]Some people have deviated from these
and turned to meaningless talk, [7]desiring to be teachers of the law, without understanding either what they are saying or the things about which they make assertions.

8 Now we know that the law is good,
if one uses it legitimately. [9]This means understanding that the law is laid down not for the innocent but for the lawless and disobedient, for the godless and sinful, for the unholy and profane, for those who kill their father or mother, for murderers,
[10]fornicators, sodomites, slave-traders, liars, perjurers, and whatever else is contrary to the sound teaching
[11]that conforms to the glorious gospel

[a] 1.4 Or *plan*

of the blessed God, which he entrusted
to me.

GRATITUDE FOR MERCY

12 I am grateful to Christ Jesus our
Lord, who has strengthened me, because
he judged me faithful and appointed me
to his service, 13 even though I was formerly a blasphemer, a persecutor, and a
man of violence. But I received mercy because I had acted ignorantly in unbelief,
14 and the grace of our Lord overflowed
for me with the faith and love that are in
Christ Jesus. 15 The saying is sure and worthy of full acceptance, that Christ Jesus
came into the world to save sinners—of
whom I am the foremost. 16 But for that
very reason I received mercy, so that in
me, as the foremost, Jesus Christ might
display the utmost patience, making me
an example to those who would come to
believe in him for eternal life. 17 To the
King of the ages, immortal, invisible,
the only God, be honour and glory for
ever and ever.[b] Amen.

18 I am giving you these instructions, Timothy, my child, in accordance
with the prophecies made earlier about
you, so that by following them you may
fight the good fight, 19 having faith and
a good conscience. By rejecting conscience, certain persons have suffered
shipwreck in the faith; 20 among them
are Hymenaeus and Alexander, whom I
have turned over to Satan, so that they
may learn not to blaspheme.

INSTRUCTIONS CONCERNING PRAYER

2 First of all, then, I urge that supplications, prayers, intercessions,
and thanksgivings should be made for
everyone, 2 for kings and all who are in
high positions, so that we may lead a
quiet and peaceable life in all godliness
and dignity. 3 This is right and is acceptable in the sight of God our Saviour,
4 who desires everyone to be saved and
to come to the knowledge of the truth.
5 For

there is one God;
  there is also one mediator
    between God and
    humankind,
Christ Jesus, himself human,
6 who gave himself a ransom for all
—this was attested at the right time.
7 For this I was appointed a herald and
an apostle (I am telling the truth,[c] I am
not lying), a teacher of the Gentiles in
faith and truth.

8 I desire, then, that in every place
the men should pray, lifting up holy
hands without anger or argument; 9 also
that the women should dress themselves modestly and decently in suitable
clothing, not with their hair braided, or
with gold, pearls, or expensive clothes,
10 but with good works, as is proper for
women who profess reverence for God.
11 Let a woman[d] learn in silence with full
submission. 12 I permit no woman[e] to
teach or to have authority over a man;[f]
she is to keep silent. 13 For Adam was
formed first, then Eve; 14 and Adam was
not deceived, but the woman was deceived and became a transgressor. 15 Yet
she will be saved through childbearing,
provided they continue in faith and love
and holiness, with modesty.

QUALIFICATIONS OF BISHOPS

3 The saying is sure:[g] whoever aspires
to the office of bishop[h] desires a noble task. 2 Now a bishop[i] must be above
reproach, married only once,[j] temperate, sensible, respectable, hospitable, an
apt teacher, 3 not a drunkard, not violent
but gentle, not quarrelsome, and not a
lover of money. 4 He must manage his
own household well, keeping his children submissive and respectful in every
way— 5 for if someone does not know
how to manage his own household,
how can he take care of God's church?
6 He must not be a recent convert, or
he may be puffed up with conceit and
fall into the condemnation of the devil.
7 Moreover, he must be well thought of
by outsiders, so that he may not fall into
disgrace and the snare of the devil.

QUALIFICATIONS OF DEACONS

8 Deacons likewise must be serious, not double-tongued, not indulging
in much wine, not greedy for money;
9 they must hold fast to the mystery of
the faith with a clear conscience. 10 And
let them first be tested; then, if they
prove themselves blameless, let them
serve as deacons. 11 Women[k] likewise
must be serious, not slanderers, but
temperate, faithful in all things. 12 Let
deacons be married only once,[l] and let

[b] **1.17** Gk *to the ages of the ages* [c] **2.7** Other ancient authorities add *in Christ* [d] **2.11** Or *wife* [e] **2.12** Or *wife* [f] **2.12** Or *her husband* [g] **3.1** Some interpreters place these words at the end of the previous paragraph. Other ancient authorities read *The saying is commonly accepted* [h] **3.1** Or *overseer* [i] **3.2** Or *an overseer* [j] **3.2** Gk *the husband of one wife* [k] **3.11** Or *Their wives,* or *Women deacons* [l] **3.12** Gk *be husbands of one wife*

them manage their children and their
households well; 13for those who serve
well as deacons gain a good standing
for themselves and great boldness in the
faith that is in Christ Jesus.

THE MYSTERY OF OUR RELIGION

14 I hope to come to you soon, but I
am writing these instructions to you so
that, 15if I am delayed, you may know
how one ought to behave in the household of God, which is the church of the
living God, the pillar and bulwark of the
truth. 16Without any doubt, the mystery of our religion is great:

He[m] was revealed in flesh,
vindicated[n] in spirit,[o]
seen by angels,
proclaimed among Gentiles,
believed in throughout the world,
taken up in glory.

FALSE ASCETICISM

4 Now the Spirit expressly says that
in later[p] times some will renounce
the faith by paying attention to deceitful spirits and teachings of demons,
2through the hypocrisy of liars whose
consciences are seared with a hot iron.
3They forbid marriage and demand abstinence from foods, which God created
to be received with thanksgiving by
those who believe and know the truth.
4For everything created by God is good,
and nothing is to be rejected, provided it
is received with thanksgiving; 5for it is
sanctified by God's word and by prayer.

A GOOD MINISTER OF JESUS CHRIST

6 If you put these instructions before the brothers and sisters,[q] you will
be a good servant[r] of Christ Jesus, nourished on the words of the faith and of
the sound teaching that you have followed. 7Have nothing to do with profane myths and old wives' tales. Train
yourself in godliness, 8for, while physical training is of some value, godliness
is valuable in every way, holding promise for both the present life and the life
to come. 9The saying is sure and worthy
of full acceptance. 10For to this end we
toil and struggle,[s] because we have our
hope set on the living God, who is the
Saviour of all people, especially of those
who believe.

11 These are the things you must
insist on and teach. 12Let no one despise your youth, but set the believers
an example in speech and conduct, in
love, in faith, in purity. 13Until I arrive,
give attention to the public reading of
scripture,[t] to exhorting, to teaching.
14Do not neglect the gift that is in you,
which was given to you through prophecy with the laying on of hands by the
council of elders.[u] 15Put these things
into practice, devote yourself to them,
so that all may see your progress. 16Pay
close attention to yourself and to your
teaching; continue in these things, for
in doing this you will save both yourself
and your hearers.

DUTIES TOWARDS BELIEVERS

5 Do not speak harshly to an older
man,[v] but speak to him as to a father, to younger men as brothers, 2to
older women as mothers, to younger
women as sisters—with absolute purity.

3 Honour widows who are really
widows. 4If a widow has children or
grandchildren, they should first learn
their religious duty to their own family
and make some repayment to their parents; for this is pleasing in God's sight.
5The real widow, left alone, has set her
hope on God and continues in supplications and prayers night and day; 6but
the widow[w] who lives for pleasure is
dead even while she lives. 7Give these
commands as well, so that they may be
above reproach. 8And whoever does not
provide for relatives, and especially for
family members, has denied the faith
and is worse than an unbeliever.

9 Let a widow be put on the list if she
is not less than sixty years old and has
been married only once;[x] 10she must be
well attested for her good works, as one
who has brought up children, shown
hospitality, washed the saints' feet,
helped the afflicted, and devoted herself
to doing good in every way. 11But refuse to put younger widows on the list;
for when their sensual desires alienate
them from Christ, they want to marry,
12and so they incur condemnation for
having violated their first pledge. 13Be-
sides that, they learn to be idle, gadding
about from house to house; and they
are not merely idle, but also gossips and
busybodies, saying what they should

[m] 3.16 Gk *Who*; other ancient authorities read *God*; others, *Which* [n] 3.16 Or *justified* [o] 3.16 Or *by the Spirit* [p] 4.1 Or *the last* [q] 4.6 Gk *brothers* [r] 4.6 Or *deacon* [s] 4.10 Other ancient authorities read *suffer reproach* [t] 4.13 Gk *to the reading* [u] 4.14 Gk *by the presbytery* [v] 5.1 Or *an elder*, or *a presbyter* [w] 5.6 Gk *she* [x] 5.9 Gk *the wife of one husband*

not say. 14So I would have younger widows marry, bear children, and manage their households, so as to give the adversary no occasion to revile us. 15For some have already turned away to follow Satan. 16If any believing woman[y] has relatives who are really widows, let her assist them; let the church not be burdened, so that it can assist those who are real widows.

17 Let the elders who rule well be considered worthy of double honour,[z] especially those who labour in preaching and teaching; 18for the scripture says, 'You shall not muzzle an ox while it is treading out the grain', and, 'The labourer deserves to be paid.' 19Never accept any accusation against an elder except on the evidence of two or three witnesses. 20As for those who persist in sin, rebuke them in the presence of all, so that the rest also may stand in fear. 21In the presence of God and of Christ Jesus and of the elect angels, I warn you to keep these instructions without prejudice, doing nothing on the basis of partiality. 22Do not ordain[a] anyone hastily, and do not participate in the sins of others; keep yourself pure.

23 No longer drink only water, but take a little wine for the sake of your stomach and your frequent ailments.

24 The sins of some people are conspicuous and precede them to judgement, while the sins of others follow them there. 25So also good works are conspicuous; and even when they are not, they cannot remain hidden.

6 Let all who are under the yoke of slavery regard their masters as worthy of all honour, so that the name of God and the teaching may not be blasphemed. 2Those who have believing masters must not be disrespectful to them on the ground that they are members of the church;[b] rather they must serve them all the more, since those who benefit by their service are believers and beloved.[c]

FALSE TEACHING AND TRUE RICHES

Teach and urge these duties. 3Whoever teaches otherwise and does not agree with the sound words of our Lord Jesus Christ and the teaching that is in accordance with godliness, 4is conceited, understanding nothing, and has a morbid craving for controversy and for disputes about words. From these come envy, dissension, slander, base suspicions, 5and wrangling among those who are depraved in mind and bereft of the truth, imagining that godliness is a means of gain.[d] 6Of course, there is great gain in godliness combined with contentment; 7for we brought nothing into the world, so that[e] we can take nothing out of it; 8but if we have food and clothing, we will be content with these. 9But those who want to be rich fall into temptation and are trapped by many senseless and harmful desires that plunge people into ruin and destruction. 10For the love of money is a root of all kinds of evil, and in their eagerness to be rich some have wandered away from the faith and pierced themselves with many pains.

THE GOOD FIGHT OF FAITH

11 But as for you, man of God, shun all this; pursue righteousness, godliness, faith, love, endurance, gentleness. 12Fight the good fight of the faith; take hold of the eternal life, to which you were called and for which you made[f] the good confession in the presence of many witnesses. 13In the presence of God, who gives life to all things, and of Christ Jesus, who in his testimony before Pontius Pilate made the good confession, I charge you 14to keep the commandment without spot or blame until the manifestation of our Lord Jesus Christ, 15which he will bring about at the right time—he who is the blessed and only Sovereign, the King of kings and Lord of lords. 16It is he alone who has immortality and dwells in unapproachable light, whom no one has ever seen or can see; to him be honour and eternal dominion. Amen.

17 As for those who in the present age are rich, command them not to be haughty, or to set their hopes on the uncertainty of riches, but rather on God who richly provides us with everything for our enjoyment. 18They are to do good, to be rich in good works, generous, and ready to share, 19thus storing up for themselves the treasure of a good foundation for the future, so that they

[y] **5.16** Other ancient authorities read *believing man or woman*; others, *believing man* [z] **5.17** Or *compensation* [a] **5.22** Gk *Do not lay hands on* [b] **6.2** Gk *are brothers* [c] **6.2** *Or since they are believers and beloved, who devote themselves to good deeds* [d] **6.5** Other ancient authorities add *Withdraw yourself from such people* [e] **6.7** Other ancient authorities read *world—it is certain that* [f] **6.12** Gk *confessed*

may take hold of the life that really is life.

PERSONAL INSTRUCTIONS AND BENEDICTION

20 Timothy, guard what has been entrusted to you. Avoid the profane chatter and contradictions of what is falsely called knowledge; 21by professing it some have missed the mark as regards the faith.

Grace be with you.[g]

[g] 6.21 The Greek word for *you* here is plural; in other ancient authorities it is singular. Other ancient authorities add *Amen*

The Second Letter of Paul to

TIMOTHY

The Second Letter of Paul to Timothy was written to encourage and challenge the pastor of the church in Ephesus to be strong in guarding the faith despite hardship. The Letter is about persevering in passing on the faith without shame or fear and without distortion. The Letter was written in Paul's name from a time when Paul was in captivity facing the threat of death (4.6–8). Scholars today do not think that Paul himself was the actual author, but that the Letter was written in Paul's name to address problems in post-Pauline churches.

Paul's own suffering as a prisoner in chains is given as an example of what to expect in persevering for the sake of salvation in Christ. The Letter admonishes against false teaching and useless conflicts (2.14–19) and exhorts Timothy to rely on what he has received from Paul and on what he has learned through the sacred scriptures inspired by God (3.14–17). The emergence of false teaching and the infiltration of Gnostic ideas (3.7) and a spiritualized view of the resurrection (2.18) are acknowledged in this Letter. Timothy is to stand firm against these distractions and distortions.

The Letter presents Paul as though he is at the end of his ministry with his "departure" at hand (4.6), waiting for the "crown of righteousness" (4.8). Paul entrusts the responsibility for preserving and advancing the faith to Timothy. The Letter is like a last testament handing down the faith from the first to the second generation. The Letter ends with Paul expressing personal greetings and urging Timothy to come for a visit before winter (4.21).

Passages from 2 Timothy are read at the Twenty-Seventh through Thirtieth Sundays of the liturgical calendar in Year C with the author's words echoing to the church through the ages: "I have fought the good fight, I have finished the race, I have kept the faith" (4.7).

SALUTATION

1 Paul, an apostle of Christ Jesus by
the will of God, for the sake of the
promise of life that is in Christ Jesus,
2 To Timothy, my beloved child:
Grace, mercy, and peace from God the
Father and Christ Jesus our Lord.

THANKSGIVING AND ENCOURAGEMENT

3 I am grateful to God—whom I
worship with a clear conscience, as my
ancestors did—when I remember you
constantly in my prayers night and day.
4 Recalling your tears, I long to see you
so that I may be filled with joy. 5 I am reminded of your sincere faith, a faith that
lived first in your grandmother Lois and
your mother Eunice and now, I am sure,
lives in you. 6 For this reason I remind
you to rekindle the gift of God that is
within you through the laying on of my
hands; 7 for God did not give us a spirit of
cowardice, but rather a spirit of power
and of love and of self-discipline.
8 Do not be ashamed, then, of the
testimony about our Lord or of me his
prisoner, but join with me in suffering
for the gospel, relying on the power of
God, 9 who saved us and called us with
a holy calling, not according to our
works but according to his own purpose

and grace. This grace was given to us in
Christ Jesus before the ages began, 10but
it has now been revealed through the
appearing of our Saviour Christ Jesus,
who abolished death and brought life
and immortality to light through the
gospel. 11For this gospel I was appointed
a herald and an apostle and a teacher,[a]
12and for this reason I suffer as I do.
But I am not ashamed, for I know the
one in whom I have put my trust, and
I am sure that he is able to guard until
that day what I have entrusted to him.[b]
13Hold to the standard of sound teaching that you have heard from me, in the
faith and love that are in Christ Jesus.
14Guard the good treasure entrusted to
you, with the help of the Holy Spirit living in us.

15 You are aware that all who are in
Asia have turned away from me, including Phygelus and Hermogenes. 16May
the Lord grant mercy to the household
of Onesiphorus, because he often refreshed me and was not ashamed of my
chain; 17when he arrived in Rome, he
eagerly[c] searched for me and found me
18—may the Lord grant that he will find
mercy from the Lord on that day! And
you know very well how much service
he rendered in Ephesus.

A GOOD SOLDIER OF CHRIST JESUS

2 You then, my child, be strong in the
grace that is in Christ Jesus; 2and
what you have heard from me through
many witnesses entrust to faithful people who will be able to teach others as
well. 3Share in suffering like a good soldier of Christ Jesus. 4No one serving in
the army gets entangled in everyday
affairs; the soldier's aim is to please the
enlisting officer. 5And in the case of an
athlete, no one is crowned without competing according to the rules. 6It is the
farmer who does the work who ought to
have the first share of the crops. 7Think
over what I say, for the Lord will give
you understanding in all things.

8 Remember Jesus Christ, raised
from the dead, a descendant of David—
that is my gospel, 9for which I suffer
hardship, even to the point of being
chained like a criminal. But the word
of God is not chained. 10Therefore I endure everything for the sake of the elect,
so that they may also obtain the salvation that is in Christ Jesus, with eternal
glory. 11The saying is sure:

If we have died with him, we
  will also live with him;
12 if we endure, we will also
  reign with him;
if we deny him, he will also deny us;
13 if we are faithless, he remains
  faithful—
for he cannot deny himself.

A WORKER APPROVED BY GOD

14 Remind them of this, and warn
them before God[d] that they are to avoid
wrangling over words, which does no
good but only ruins those who are listening. 15Do your best to present yourself to
God as one approved by him, a worker
who has no need to be ashamed, rightly
explaining the word of truth. 16Avoid
profane chatter, for it will lead people
into more and more impiety, 17and their
talk will spread like gangrene. Among
them are Hymenaeus and Philetus,
18who have swerved from the truth by
claiming that the resurrection has already taken place. They are upsetting
the faith of some. 19But God's firm foundation stands, bearing this inscription:
'The Lord knows those who are his', and,
'Let everyone who calls on the name of
the Lord turn away from wickedness.'

20 In a large house there are utensils not only of gold and silver but also
of wood and clay, some for special use,
some for ordinary. 21All who cleanse
themselves of the things I have mentioned[e] will become special utensils,
dedicated and useful to the owner of
the house, ready for every good work.
22Shun youthful passions and pursue
righteousness, faith, love, and peace,
along with those who call on the Lord
from a pure heart. 23Have nothing to
do with stupid and senseless controversies; you know that they breed quarrels.
24And the Lord's servant[f] must not be
quarrelsome but kindly to everyone, an
apt teacher, patient, 25correcting opponents with gentleness. God may perhaps
grant that they will repent and come to
know the truth, 26and that they may escape from the snare of the devil, having
been held captive by him to do his will.[g]

GODLESSNESS IN THE LAST DAYS

3 You must understand this, that
in the last days distressing times
will come. 2For people will be lovers of

[a] **1.11** Other ancient authorities add *of the Gentiles* [b] **1.12** Or *what has been entrusted to me* [c] **1.17** Or *promptly* [d] **2.14** Other ancient authorities read *the Lord* [e] **2.21** Gk *of these things* [f] **2.24** Gk *slave* [g] **2.26** Or *by him, to do his* (that is, God's) *will*

themselves, lovers of money, boasters,
arrogant, abusive, disobedient to their
parents, ungrateful, unholy, 3inhuman,
implacable, slanderers, profligates,
brutes, haters of good, 4treacherous,
reckless, swollen with conceit, lovers
of pleasure rather than lovers of God,
5holding to the outward form of godliness but denying its power. Avoid them!
6For among them are those who make
their way into households and captivate
silly women, overwhelmed by their
sins and swayed by all kinds of desires,
7who are always being instructed and
can never arrive at a knowledge of the
truth. 8As Jannes and Jambres opposed
Moses, so these people, of corrupt mind
and counterfeit faith, also oppose the
truth. 9But they will not make much
progress, because, as in the case of those
two men,[h] their folly will become plain
to everyone.

PAUL'S CHARGE TO TIMOTHY

10 Now you have observed my teaching, my conduct, my aim in life, my
faith, my patience, my love, my steadfastness, 11my persecutions, and my suffering the things that happened to me
in Antioch, Iconium, and Lystra. What
persecutions I endured! Yet the Lord
rescued me from all of them. 12Indeed,
all who want to live a godly life in Christ
Jesus will be persecuted. 13But wicked
people and impostors will go from bad
to worse, deceiving others and being
deceived. 14But as for you, continue
in what you have learned and firmly
believed, knowing from whom you
learned it, 15and how from childhood
you have known the sacred writings
that are able to instruct you for salvation through faith in Christ Jesus. 16All
scripture is inspired by God and is[i] useful for teaching, for reproof, for correction, and for training in righteousness,
17so that everyone who belongs to God
may be proficient, equipped for every
good work.

4 In the presence of God and of Christ
Jesus, who is to judge the living and
the dead, and in view of his appearing
and his kingdom, I solemnly urge you:
2proclaim the message; be persistent
whether the time is favourable or unfavourable; convince, rebuke, and encourage, with the utmost patience in
teaching. 3For the time is coming when
people will not put up with sound doctrine, but having itching ears, they will
accumulate for themselves teachers to
suit their own desires, 4and will turn
away from listening to the truth and
wander away to myths. 5As for you, always be sober, endure suffering, do the
work of an evangelist, carry out your
ministry fully.

6 As for me, I am already being
poured out as a libation, and the time of
my departure has come. 7I have fought
the good fight, I have finished the
race, I have kept the faith. 8From now
on there is reserved for me the crown
of righteousness, which the Lord, the
righteous judge, will give to me on that
day, and not only to me but also to all
who have longed for his appearing.

PERSONAL INSTRUCTIONS

9 Do your best to come to me soon,
10for Demas, in love with this present
world, has deserted me and gone to
Thessalonica; Crescens has gone to Galatia,[j] Titus to Dalmatia. 11Only Luke is
with me. Get Mark and bring him with
you, for he is useful in my ministry. 12I
have sent Tychicus to Ephesus. 13When
you come, bring the cloak that I left
with Carpus at Troas, also the books,
and above all the parchments. 14Alexan-
der the coppersmith did me great harm;
the Lord will pay him back for his deeds.
15You also must beware of him, for he
strongly opposed our message.

16 At my first defence no one came to
my support, but all deserted me. May it
not be counted against them! 17But the
Lord stood by me and gave me strength,
so that through me the message might
be fully proclaimed and all the Gentiles
might hear it. So I was rescued from the
lion's mouth. 18The Lord will rescue me
from every evil attack and save me for
his heavenly kingdom. To him be the
glory for ever and ever. Amen.

FINAL GREETINGS AND BENEDICTION

19 Greet Prisca and Aquila, and the
household of Onesiphorus. 20Erastus remained in Corinth; Trophimus I left ill
in Miletus. 21Do your best to come before winter. Eubulus sends greetings to
you, as do Pudens and Linus and Clau-
dia and all the brothers and sisters.[k]

22 The Lord be with your spirit.
Grace be with you.[l]

[h] 3.9 Gk lacks *two men* [i] 3.16 Or *Every scripture inspired by God is also* [j] 4.10 Other ancient authorities read *Gaul* [k] 4.21 Gk *all the brothers* [l] 4.22 The Greek word for *you* here is plural. Other ancient authorities add *Amen*

The Letter of Paul to

TITUS

The Letter to Titus is the third of the Pastoral Letters, which are distinctive writings in the Pauline collection because they are concerned with the leadership and pastoral charge of the churches. This Letter is addressed to Paul's co-worker Titus, who is responsible for organizing the church on the island of Crete through the appointment of church leaders or presbyter-bishops (1.4–9).

This Letter matches up more closely in style and content with 1 Timothy. Titus is a short Letter that instructs various groups in the social order of the Christian community about proper moral conduct in living each day in light of the redemption won by Christ. It describes the qualities necessary for the appointed leaders (1.5–9); it advises what to do with rebellious and false teachers (1.10–16); it exhorts Titus to teach older men to be temperate (2.2), older women to be reverent (2.3), younger women to love their husbands and children (2.4), younger men to be self-controlled (2.6), and slaves to be submissive to their masters (2.9). These instructions are supported by a lengthy description of God's mercy (3.1–8). Finally, those who are a cause for the division of the community are to be warned as many as two times and then ignored altogether (3.9–11).

Passages from the Letter to Titus are read at Mass every year at Midnight (2.11–14) and at Dawn (3.4–7) on Christmas. These texts from Titus emphasize the grace of God that is revealed in Christ, whose sacrifice redeemed us from iniquity and enabled us to inherit the promise of eternal life.

SALUTATION

1 Paul, a servant[a] of God and an apostle of Jesus Christ, for the sake of the faith of God's elect and the knowledge of the truth that is in accordance with godliness, 2 in the hope of eternal life that God, who never lies, promised before the ages began— 3 in due time he revealed his word through the proclamation with which I have been entrusted by the command of God our Saviour,

4 To Titus, my loyal child in the faith we share:

Grace[b] and peace from God the Father and Christ Jesus our Saviour.

TITUS IN CRETE

5 I left you behind in Crete for this reason, that you should put in order what remained to be done, and should appoint elders in every town, as I directed you: 6 someone who is blameless, married only once,[c] whose children are believers, not accused of debauchery and not rebellious. 7 For a bishop,[d] as God's steward, must be blameless; he must not be arrogant or quick-tempered or addicted to wine or violent or greedy for gain; 8 but he must be hospitable, a lover of goodness, prudent, upright, devout, and self-controlled. 9 He must have a firm grasp of the word that is trustworthy in accordance with the teaching, so that he may be able both to preach with sound doctrine and to refute those who contradict it.

10 There are also many rebellious people, idle talkers and deceivers, especially those of the circumcision; 11 they must be

[a] 1.1 Gk *slave* [b] 1.4 Other ancient authorities read *Grace, mercy,* [c] 1.6 Gk *husband of one wife* [d] 1.7 Or *an overseer*

silenced, since they are upsetting whole
families by teaching for sordid gain what
it is not right to teach. 12It was one of
them, their very own prophet, who said,
'Cretans are always liars, vicious
brutes, lazy gluttons.'
13That testimony is true. For this reason rebuke them sharply, so that they
may become sound in the faith, 14not
paying attention to Jewish myths or
to commandments of those who reject
the truth. 15To the pure all things are
pure, but to the corrupt and unbelieving nothing is pure. Their very minds
and consciences are corrupted. 16They
profess to know God, but they deny him
by their actions. They are detestable,
disobedient, unfit for any good work.

TEACH SOUND DOCTRINE

2 But as for you, teach what is consistent with sound doctrine. 2Tell the
older men to be temperate, serious, prudent, and sound in faith, in love, and in
endurance.

3 Likewise, tell the older women to
be reverent in behaviour, not to be slanderers or slaves to drink; they are to
teach what is good, 4so that they may
encourage the young women to love
their husbands, to love their children,
5to be self-controlled, chaste, good man-
agers of the household, kind, being submissive to their husbands, so that the
word of God may not be discredited.

6 Likewise, urge the younger men to
be self-controlled. 7Show yourself in all
respects a model of good works, and in
your teaching show integrity, gravity,
8and sound speech that cannot be cen-
sured; then any opponent will be put to
shame, having nothing evil to say of us.

9 Tell slaves to be submissive to their
masters and to give satisfaction in every respect; they are not to answer back,
10not to pilfer, but to show complete and
perfect fidelity, so that in everything
they may be an ornament to the doctrine of God our Saviour.

11 For the grace of God has appeared,
bringing salvation to all,[e] 12training us
to renounce impiety and worldly passions, and in the present age to live lives
that are self-controlled, upright, and
godly, 13while we wait for the blessed
hope and the manifestation of the glory
of our great God and Saviour,[f] Jesus
Christ. 14He it is who gave himself for us
that he might redeem us from all iniquity and purify for himself a people of
his own who are zealous for good deeds.
15 Declare these things; exhort and
reprove with all authority.[g] Let no one
look down on you.

MAINTAIN GOOD DEEDS

3 Remind them to be subject to rulers
and authorities, to be obedient, to
be ready for every good work, 2to speak
evil of no one, to avoid quarrelling, to
be gentle, and to show every courtesy to
everyone. 3For we ourselves were once
foolish, disobedient, led astray, slaves
to various passions and pleasures, passing our days in malice and envy, despi-
cable, hating one another. 4But when
the goodness and loving-kindness of
God our Saviour appeared, 5he saved us,
not because of any works of righteousness that we had done, but according
to his mercy, through the water[h] of re-
birth and renewal by the Holy Spirit.
6This Spirit he poured out on us richly
through Jesus Christ our Saviour, 7so
that, having been justified by his grace,
we might become heirs according to the
hope of eternal life. 8The saying is sure.
I desire that you insist on these
things, so that those who have come
to believe in God may be careful to devote themselves to good works; these
things are excellent and profitable to
everyone. 9But avoid stupid controversies, genealogies, dissensions, and
quarrels about the law, for they are unprofitable and worthless. 10After a first
and second admonition, have nothing
more to do with anyone who causes
divisions, 11since you know that such
a person is perverted and sinful, being
self-condemned.

FINAL MESSAGES AND BENEDICTION

12 When I send Artemas to you, or
Tychicus, do your best to come to me
at Nicopolis, for I have decided to spend
the winter there. 13Make every effort to
send Zenas the lawyer and Apollos on
their way, and see that they lack nothing. 14And let people learn to devote
themselves to good works in order to
meet urgent needs, so that they may not
be unproductive.

15 All who are with me send greetings to you. Greet those who love us in
the faith.

Grace be with all of you.[i]

[e] **2.11** Or *has appeared to all, bringing salvation*
[f] **2.13** Or *of the great God and our Saviour*
[g] **2.15** Gk *commandment* [h] **3.5** Gk *washing*
[i] **3.15** Other ancient authorities add *Amen*

The Letter of Paul to

PHILEMON

The Letter to Philemon is the shortest in the Pauline collection and was written by Paul while imprisoned, perhaps as late as 61–63 CE, while under house arrest in Rome. The Letter is 25 verses in length and is an excellent example of Paul's skills at diplomacy as he attempts to write on behalf of the slave Onesimus to his master, Philemon. Paul's desire is to win Philemon's approval for letting Onesimus return to Paul's service. If that is not possible, Paul advocates that Onesimus be received by Philemon no longer as a slave, but as a brother.

Philemon was a Christian living in Colossae in Asia Minor. Paul seems to know him personally and appeals to his friendship as a co-worker in the church. Paul begins his Letter by thanking God for Philemon's faith and hospitality (vv. 4–7). Then Paul requests in a solicitous manner that Philemon let Onesimus return to Paul (vv. 12–14). It seems that Onesimus is a runaway slave and may have owed Philemon recompense, which Paul was willing to repay (vv. 18–19). Because Onesimus is now a Christian, Paul asserts that the relationship has now changed. Paul does not directly speak against the institution of slavery but appeals to Philemon's brotherhood in Christ as the basis of Paul's request for Onesimus's freedom (v. 20).

There is no evidence as to whether Paul's request was ever fulfilled. However, the Letter to Philemon contains a revolutionary idea for that time during the first century when Paul presented the slave Onesimus as "a beloved brother—especially to me but how much more to you" (v. 16). This passage is read during the liturgy in Year C on the Twenty-Fourth Sunday of Ordinary Time.

SALUTATION

1 Paul, a prisoner of Christ Jesus, and
Timothy our brother,[a]
To Philemon our dear friend and co-
worker, 2to Apphia our sister,[b] to Archippus our fellow-soldier, and to the
church in your house:
3 Grace to you and peace from God
our Father and the Lord Jesus Christ.

PHILEMON'S LOVE AND FAITH

4 When I remember you[c] in my
prayers, I always thank my God 5be-
cause I hear of your love for all the saints
and your faith towards the Lord Jesus.
6I pray that the sharing of your faith
may become effective when you perceive all the good that we[d] may do for
Christ. 7I have indeed received much joy
and encouragement from your love, because the hearts of the saints have been
refreshed through you, my brother.

PAUL'S PLEA FOR ONESIMUS

8 For this reason, though I am bold
enough in Christ to command you to do
your duty, 9yet I would rather appeal to
you on the basis of love—and I, Paul,
do this as an old man, and now also as
a prisoner of Christ Jesus.[e] 10I am appealing to you for my child, Onesimus,
whose father I have become during my
imprisonment. 11Formerly he was use-

[a] 1 Gk *the brother* [b] 2 Gk *the sister* [c] 4 In verses 4 to 21, *you* is singular [d] 6 Other ancient authorities read *you* (plural) [e] 9 Or *as an ambassador of Christ Jesus, and now also his prisoner*

less to you, but now he is indeed useful[f]
both to you and to me. 12I am sending
him, that is, my own heart, back to you.
13I wanted to keep him with me, so that
he might be of service to me in your
place during my imprisonment for the
gospel; 14but I preferred to do nothing
without your consent, in order that your
good deed might be voluntary and not
something forced. 15Perhaps this is the
reason he was separated from you for a
while, so that you might have him back
for ever, 16no longer as a slave but as
more than a slave, a beloved brother—
especially to me but how much more to
you, both in the flesh and in the Lord.

17 So if you consider me your partner, welcome him as you would welcome me. 18If he has wronged you in
any way, or owes you anything, charge
that to my account. 19I, Paul, am writing this with my own hand: I will repay
it. I say nothing about your owing me
even your own self. 20Yes, brother, let
me have this benefit from you in the
Lord! Refresh my heart in Christ. 21Con-
fident of your obedience, I am writing
to you, knowing that you will do even
more than I say.

22 One thing more—prepare a guest
room for me, for I am hoping through
your prayers to be restored to you.

FINAL GREETINGS AND BENEDICTION

23 Epaphras, my fellow-prisoner in
Christ Jesus, sends greetings to you,[g]
24and so do Mark, Aristarchus, Demas,
and Luke, my fellow-workers.

25 The grace of the Lord Jesus Christ
be with your spirit.[h]

[f] 11 The name Onesimus means *useful* or (compare verse 20) *beneficial* [g] 23 Here *you* is singular
[h] 25 Other ancient authorities add *Amen*

The Letter to the

HEBREWS

The Letter to the Hebrews is neither an epistle nor directed specifically to Hebrews or Jewish Christians. It actually seems to be an extended sermon ("word of exhortation") given to a formerly pagan or gentile audience sometime before 95 CE (13.22). The sermon deals with the relationship of Christianity and Judaism, showing how Jesus is superior to everything in the Hebrew faith. The book was not written by Paul as some originally thought, but by an unknown author.

The author of this sermon presents Jesus first as superior to the prophets (1.1–3), then as superior to Moses (3.1–6), and finally as superior to the Jewish priests (4.14—5.10; 7.1–29) and the ministry of the first covenant (9.1–28). Christ is presented as the fulfillment of all that was anticipated by the Jewish covenant. Borrowing from images of Platonic philosophy, the old law of the Jewish faith is likened to a shadow of the reality that is Christ, the new covenant. For the author of Hebrews, Christ is the reality foreshadowed in the Hebrew scriptures and is the one who establishes the new covenant once and for all (10.1–10).

Nowhere else in the New Testament is there such a clear statement of the supplanting of the Jewish religion by Christianity. The Letter to the Hebrews would be used by others to diminish the Jewish faith and eventually attack it. The Letter is not anti-Semitic itself but is a step in a trajectory of thought that will later be extended to become anti-Semitic. Hebrews, for its part, urges Christians who are experiencing persecution not to lose their own faith by turning to a more widely accepted Judaism at the time. The message of the writing is that Christians have direct access to God through Christ as the one mediator. Christians should live faithfully even in the face of persecution (10.32–34) and despite the delay in the arrival of the promised kingdom (10.25).

The Letter to the Hebrews is read during the liturgy throughout numerous Sundays of Years B and C of the liturgical calendar. The opening verses of the first chapter are read at Christmas Day Mass each year (1.1–6). The passage from Hebrews that speaks of Christ as a "high priest according to the order of Melchizedek" (5.10) is proclaimed on Good Friday every year calling hearers to see in Christ the source of eternal salvation (4.14–16; 5.7–9).

GOD HAS SPOKEN BY HIS SON

1 Long ago God spoke to our ancestors in many and various ways by
the prophets, 2but in these last days he
has spoken to us by a Son,[a] whom he
appointed heir of all things, through
whom he also created the worlds. 3He
is the reflection of God's glory and the
exact imprint of God's very being, and
he sustains[b] all things by his powerful
word. When he had made purification
for sins, he sat down at the right hand
of the Majesty on high, 4having become
as much superior to angels as the name
he has inherited is more excellent than
theirs.

[a] 1.2 Or *the Son* [b] 1.3 Or *bears along*

THE SON IS SUPERIOR TO ANGELS

5 For to which of the angels did God
ever say,
'You are my Son;
today I have begotten you'?
Or again,
'I will be his Father,
and he will be my Son'?
6 And again, when he brings the firstborn into the world, he says,
'Let all God's angels worship him.'
7 Of the angels he says,
'He makes his angels winds,
and his servants flames of fire.'
8 But of the Son he says,
'Your throne, O God, is[c] for
ever and ever,
and the righteous sceptre is the
sceptre of your[d] kingdom.
9 You have loved righteousness
and hated wickedness;
therefore God, your God, has
anointed you
with the oil of gladness beyond
your companions.'
10 And,
'In the beginning, Lord, you
founded the earth,
and the heavens are the
work of your hands;
11 they will perish, but you remain;
they will all wear out like clothing;
12 like a cloak you will roll them up,
and like clothing[e] they
will be changed.
But you are the same,
and your years will never end.'
13 But to which of the angels has he ever
said,
'Sit at my right hand
until I make your enemies a
footstool for your feet'?
14 Are not all angels[f] spirits in the divine service, sent to serve for the sake of
those who are to inherit salvation?

WARNING TO PAY ATTENTION

2 Therefore we must pay greater attention to what we have heard, so
that we do not drift away from it. 2 For
if the message declared through angels
was valid, and every transgression or
disobedience received a just penalty,
3 how can we escape if we neglect so
great a salvation? It was declared at first
through the Lord, and it was attested to
us by those who heard him, 4 while God
added his testimony by signs and wonders and various miracles, and by gifts
of the Holy Spirit, distributed according
to his will.

EXALTATION THROUGH ABASEMENT

5 Now God[g] did not subject the coming world, about which we are speaking, to angels. 6 But someone has testified somewhere,
'What are human beings that you
are mindful of them,[h]
or mortals, that you care
for them?[i]
7 You have made them for a little
while lower[j] than the angels;
you have crowned them with
glory and honour,[k]
8 subjecting all things
under their feet.'
Now in subjecting all things to them,
God[l] left nothing outside their control.
As it is, we do not yet see everything
in subjection to them, 9 but we do see
Jesus, who for a little while was made
lower[m] than the angels, now crowned
with glory and honour because of the
suffering of death, so that by the grace
of God[n] he might taste death for everyone.

10 It was fitting that God,[o] for whom
and through whom all things exist, in
bringing many children to glory, should
make the pioneer of their salvation perfect through sufferings. 11 For the one
who sanctifies and those who are sanctified all have one Father.[p] For this reason Jesus[q] is not ashamed to call them
brothers and sisters,[r] 12 saying,
'I will proclaim your name to my
brothers and sisters,[s]
in the midst of the congregation
I will praise you.'
13 And again,
'I will put my trust in him.'
And again,
'Here am I and the children whom
God has given me.'

14 Since, therefore, the children
share flesh and blood, he himself likewise shared the same things, so that
through death he might destroy the one
who has the power of death, that is, the

[c] **1.8** Or *God is your throne* [d] **1.8** Other ancient authorities read *his* [e] **1.12** Other ancient authorities lack *like clothing* [f] **1.14** Gk *all of them* [g] **2.5** Gk *he* [h] **2.6** Gk *What is man that you are mindful of him?* [i] **2.6** Gk *or the son of man that you care for him?* In the Hebrew of Psalm 8.4–6 both *man* and *son of man* refer to all humankind [j] **2.7** Or *them only a little lower* [k] **2.7** Other ancient authorities add *and set them over the works of your hands* [l] **2.8** Gk *he* [m] **2.9** Or *who was made a little lower* [n] **2.9** Other ancient authorities read *apart from God* [o] **2.10** Gk *he* [p] **2.11** Gk *are all of one* [q] **2.11** Gk *he* [r] **2.11** Gk *brothers* [s] **2.12** Gk *brothers*

devil, 15and free those who all their lives
were held in slavery by the fear of death.
16For it is clear that he did not come to
help angels, but the descendants of
Abraham. 17Therefore he had to become
like his brothers and sisters[t] in every
respect, so that he might be a merciful
and faithful high priest in the service of
God, to make a sacrifice of atonement
for the sins of the people. 18Because he
himself was tested by what he suffered,
he is able to help those who are being
tested.

MOSES A SERVANT, CHRIST A SON

3 Therefore, brothers and sisters,[u]
holy partners in a heavenly calling,
consider that Jesus, the apostle and high
priest of our confession, 2was faithful
to the one who appointed him, just as
Moses also 'was faithful in all[v] God's[w]
house.' 3Yet Jesus[x] is worthy of more
glory than Moses, just as the builder
of a house has more honour than the
house itself. 4(For every house is built
by someone, but the builder of all things
is God.) 5Now Moses was faithful in all
God's[y] house as a servant, to testify to
the things that would be spoken later.
6Christ, however, was faithful over
God's[z] house as a son, and we are his
house if we hold firm[a] the confidence
and the pride that belong to hope.

WARNING AGAINST UNBELIEF

7 Therefore, as the Holy Spirit says,
'Today, if you hear his voice,
8 do not harden your hearts as
in the rebellion,
as on the day of testing in
the wilderness,
9 where your ancestors put
me to the test,
though they had seen my
works 10for forty years.
Therefore I was angry with
that generation,
and I said, "They always go
astray in their hearts,
and they have not known
my ways."
11 As in my anger I swore,
"They will not enter my rest." '
12Take care, brothers and sisters,[b] that
none of you may have an evil, unbelieving heart that turns away from the living God. 13But exhort one another every
day, as long as it is called 'today', so that
none of you may be hardened by the de-
ceitfulness of sin. 14For we have become
partners of Christ, if only we hold our
first confidence firm to the end. 15As it
is said,
'Today, if you hear his voice,
do not harden your hearts as
in the rebellion.'
16Now who were they who heard and
yet were rebellious? Was it not all those
who left Egypt under the leadership of
Moses? 17But with whom was he angry
for forty years? Was it not those who
sinned, whose bodies fell in the wilderness? 18And to whom did he swear that
they would not enter his rest, if not to
those who were disobedient? 19So we
see that they were unable to enter because of unbelief.

THE REST THAT GOD PROMISED

4 Therefore, while the promise of entering his rest is still open, let us
take care that none of you should seem
to have failed to reach it. 2For indeed the
good news came to us just as to them;
but the message they heard did not benefit them, because they were not united
by faith with those who listened.[c] 3For
we who have believed enter that rest,
just as God[d] has said,
'As in my anger I swore,
"They shall not enter my rest" ',
though his works were finished at the
foundation of the world. 4For in one
place it speaks about the seventh day
as follows: 'And God rested on the seventh day from all his works.' 5And again
in this place it says, 'They shall not enter my rest.' 6Since therefore it remains
open for some to enter it, and those who
formerly received the good news failed
to enter because of disobedience, 7again
he sets a certain day—'today'—saying
through David much later, in the words
already quoted,
'Today, if you hear his voice,
do not harden your hearts.'
8For if Joshua had given them rest, God[e]
would not speak later about another day.
9So then, a sabbath rest still remains for
the people of God; 10for those who enter
God's rest also cease from their labours
as God did from his. 11Let us therefore
make every effort to enter that rest, so
that no one may fall through such disobedience as theirs.

[t] 2.17 Gk *brothers* [u] 3.1 Gk *brothers* [v] 3.2 Other ancient authorities lack *all* [w] 3.2 Gk *his* [x] 3.3 Gk *this one* [y] 3.5 Gk *his* [z] 3.6 Gk *his* [a] 3.6 Other ancient authorities add *to the end* [b] 3.12 Gk *brothers* [c] 4.2 Other ancient authorities read *it did not meet with faith in those who listened* [d] 4.3 Gk *he* [e] 4.8 Gk *he*

12 Indeed, the word of God is living
and active, sharper than any two-edged
sword, piercing until it divides soul
from spirit, joints from marrow; it is
able to judge the thoughts and intentions of the heart. 13And before him no
creature is hidden, but all are naked and
laid bare to the eyes of the one to whom
we must render an account.

JESUS THE GREAT HIGH PRIEST

14 Since, then, we have a great high
priest who has passed through the
heavens, Jesus, the Son of God, let us
hold fast to our confession. 15For we do
not have a high priest who is unable to
sympathize with our weaknesses, but
we have one who in every respect has
been tested[f] as we are, yet without sin.
16Let us therefore approach the throne
of grace with boldness, so that we may
receive mercy and find grace to help in
time of need.

5 Every high priest chosen from
among mortals is put in charge of
things pertaining to God on their behalf, to offer gifts and sacrifices for sins.
2He is able to deal gently with the ignorant and wayward, since he himself
is subject to weakness; 3and because of
this he must offer sacrifice for his own
sins as well as for those of the people.
4And one does not presume to take this
honour, but takes it only when called by
God, just as Aaron was.

5 So also Christ did not glorify himself in becoming a high priest, but was
appointed by the one who said to him,

'You are my Son,
today I have begotten you';
6as he says also in another place,
'You are a priest for ever,
according to the order of
Melchizedek.'

7 In the days of his flesh, Jesus[g] offered up prayers and supplications, with
loud cries and tears, to the one who was
able to save him from death, and he
was heard because of his reverent submission. 8Although he was a Son, he
learned obedience through what he suffered; 9and having been made perfect,
he became the source of eternal salvation for all who obey him, 10having been
designated by God a high priest according to the order of Melchizedek.

WARNING AGAINST FALLING AWAY

11 About this[h] we have much to say
that is hard to explain, since you have
become dull in understanding. 12For
though by this time you ought to be
teachers, you need someone to teach
you again the basic elements of the oracles of God. You need milk, not solid
food; 13for everyone who lives on milk,
being still an infant, is unskilled in the
word of righteousness. 14But solid food
is for the mature, for those whose faculties have been trained by practice to
distinguish good from evil.

THE PERIL OF FALLING AWAY

6 Therefore let us go on towards perfection,[i] leaving behind the basic
teaching about Christ, and not laying
again the foundation: repentance from
dead works and faith towards God, 2in-
struction about baptisms, laying on of
hands, resurrection of the dead, and
eternal judgement. 3And we will do[j]
this, if God permits. 4For it is impossible
to restore again to repentance those who
have once been enlightened, and have
tasted the heavenly gift, and have shared
in the Holy Spirit, 5and have tasted the
goodness of the word of God and the
powers of the age to come, 6and then
have fallen away, since on their own
they are crucifying again the Son of God
and are holding him up to contempt.
7Ground that drinks up the rain falling
on it repeatedly, and that produces a
crop useful to those for whom it is cultivated, receives a blessing from God.
8But if it produces thorns and thistles,
it is worthless and on the verge of being
cursed; its end is to be burned over.

9 Even though we speak in this way,
beloved, we are confident of better
things in your case, things that belong
to salvation. 10For God is not unjust; he
will not overlook your work and the love
that you showed for his sake[k] in serving
the saints, as you still do. 11And we want
each one of you to show the same diligence, so as to realize the full assurance
of hope to the very end, 12so that you
may not become sluggish, but imitators
of those who through faith and patience
inherit the promises.

THE CERTAINTY OF GOD'S PROMISE

13 When God made a promise to
Abraham, because he had no one greater
by whom to swear, he swore by himself,
14saying, 'I will surely bless you and multiply you.' 15And thus Abraham,[l] having

[f] 4.15 Or *tempted* [g] 5.7 Gk *he* [h] 5.11 Or *him*
[i] 6.1 Or *towards maturity* [j] 6.3 Other ancient
authorities read *let us do* [k] 6.10 Gk *for his name*
[l] 6.15 Gk *he*

patiently endured, obtained the promise. 16 Human beings, of course, swear
by someone greater than themselves,
and an oath given as confirmation puts
an end to all dispute. 17 In the same way,
when God desired to show even more
clearly to the heirs of the promise the
unchangeable character of his purpose,
he guaranteed it by an oath, 18 so that
through two unchangeable things, in
which it is impossible that God would
prove false, we who have taken refuge
might be strongly encouraged to seize
the hope set before us. 19 We have this
hope, a sure and steadfast anchor of the
soul, a hope that enters the inner shrine
behind the curtain, 20 where Jesus, a
forerunner on our behalf, has entered,
having become a high priest for ever according to the order of Melchizedek.

THE PRIESTLY ORDER OF MELCHIZEDEK

7 This 'King Melchizedek of Salem,
priest of the Most High God, met
Abraham as he was returning from
defeating the kings and blessed him';
2 and to him Abraham apportioned 'one-
tenth of everything'. His name, in the
first place, means 'king of righteousness'; next he is also king of Salem, that
is, 'king of peace'. 3 Without father, without mother, without genealogy, having
neither beginning of days nor end of
life, but resembling the Son of God, he
remains a priest for ever.

4 See how great he is! Even[m] Abraham the patriarch gave him a tenth of
the spoils. 5 And those descendants of
Levi who receive the priestly office have
a commandment in the law to collect
tithes[n] from the people, that is, from
their kindred,[o] though these also are
descended from Abraham. 6 But this
man, who does not belong to their ancestry, collected tithes[p] from Abraham
and blessed him who had received the
promises. 7 It is beyond dispute that
the inferior is blessed by the superior.
8 In the one case, tithes are received by
those who are mortal; in the other, by
one of whom it is testified that he lives.
9 One might even say that Levi himself,
who receives tithes, paid tithes through
Abraham, 10 for he was still in the loins of
his ancestor when Melchizedek met him.

ANOTHER PRIEST, LIKE MELCHIZEDEK

11 Now if perfection had been attain-
able through the levitical priesthood—
for the people received the law under
this priesthood—what further need
would there have been to speak of another priest arising according to the
order of Melchizedek, rather than one
according to the order of Aaron? 12 For
when there is a change in the priesthood, there is necessarily a change in
the law as well. 13 Now the one of whom
these things are spoken belonged to another tribe, from which no one has ever
served at the altar. 14 For it is evident
that our Lord was descended from Judah, and in connection with that tribe
Moses said nothing about priests.

15 It is even more obvious when another priest arises, resembling Melchizedek, 16 one who has become a priest,
not through a legal requirement concerning physical descent, but through
the power of an indestructible life. 17 For
it is attested of him,

'You are a priest for ever,
according to the order of
Melchizedek.'

18 There is, on the one hand, the abro-
gation of an earlier commandment because it was weak and ineffectual 19 (for
the law made nothing perfect); there
is, on the other hand, the introduction
of a better hope, through which we approach God.

20 This was confirmed with an oath;
for others who became priests took their
office without an oath, 21 but this one
became a priest with an oath, because
of the one who said to him,

'The Lord has sworn
and will not change his mind,
"You are a priest for ever"'—

22 accordingly Jesus has also become the
guarantee of a better covenant.

23 Furthermore, the former priests
were many in number, because they
were prevented by death from continuing in office; 24 but he holds his priesthood permanently, because he continues for ever. 25 Consequently he is able
for all time to save[q] those who approach
God through him, since he always lives
to make intercession for them.

26 For it was fitting that we should
have such a high priest, holy, blameless, undefiled, separated from sinners,
and exalted above the heavens. 27 Unlike
the other[r] high priests, he has no need
to offer sacrifices day after day, first for

[m] 7.4 Other ancient authorities lack *Even*
[n] 7.5 Or *a tenth* [o] 7.5 Gk *brothers* [p] 7.6 Or *a tenth* [q] 7.25 Or *able to save completely*
[r] 7.27 Gk lacks *other*

his own sins, and then for those of the
people; this he did once for all when he
offered himself. 28For the law appoints
as high priests those who are subject
to weakness, but the word of the oath,
which came later than the law, appoints
a Son who has been made perfect for
ever.

MEDIATOR OF A BETTER COVENANT

8 Now the main point in what we
are saying is this: we have such a
high priest, one who is seated at the
right hand of the throne of the Majesty
in the heavens, 2a minister in the sanctuary and the true tent[s] that the Lord,
and not any mortal, has set up. 3For
every high priest is appointed to offer
gifts and sacrifices; hence it is necessary
for this priest also to have something
to offer. 4Now if he were on earth, he
would not be a priest at all, since there
are priests who offer gifts according to
the law. 5They offer worship in a sanctuary that is a sketch and shadow of the
heavenly one; for Moses, when he was
about to erect the tent,[t] was warned,
'See that you make everything according to the pattern that was shown you
on the mountain.' 6But Jesus[u] has now
obtained a more excellent ministry, and
to that degree he is the mediator of a
better covenant, which has been enact-
ed through better promises. 7For if that
first covenant had been faultless, there
would have been no need to look for a
second one.
8 God[v] finds fault with them when
he says:

'The days are surely coming,
says the Lord,
when I will establish a new
covenant with the
house of Israel
and with the house of Judah;
9 not like the covenant that I made
with their ancestors,
on the day when I took them
by the hand to lead them
out of the land of Egypt;
for they did not continue in
my covenant,
and so I had no concern for
them, says the Lord.
10 This is the covenant that I will make
with the house of Israel
after those days, says the Lord:
I will put my laws in their minds,
and write them on their hearts,
and I will be their God,
and they shall be my people.
11 And they shall not teach one another
or say to each other,
"Know the Lord",
for they shall all know me,
from the least of them
to the greatest.
12 For I will be merciful towards
their iniquities,
and I will remember their
sins no more.'

13In speaking of 'a new covenant', he has
made the first one obsolete. And what is
obsolete and growing old will soon disappear.

THE EARTHLY AND THE HEAVENLY SANCTUARIES

9 Now even the first covenant had
regulations for worship and an
earthly sanctuary. 2For a tent[w] was constructed, the first one, in which were
the lampstand, the table, and the bread
of the Presence;[x] this is called the Holy
Place. 3Behind the second curtain was
a tent[y] called the Holy of Holies. 4In it
stood the golden altar of incense and the
ark of the covenant overlaid on all sides
with gold, in which there were a golden
urn holding the manna, and Aaron's
rod that budded, and the tablets of the
covenant; 5above it were the cherubim
of glory overshadowing the mercy-
seat.[z] Of these things we cannot speak
now in detail.
6 Such preparations having been
made, the priests go continually into
the first tent[a] to carry out their ritual
duties; 7but only the high priest goes
into the second, and he but once a year,
and not without taking the blood that
he offers for himself and for the sins
committed unintentionally by the people. 8By this the Holy Spirit indicates
that the way into the sanctuary has not
yet been disclosed as long as the first
tent[b] is still standing. 9This is a symbol[c]
of the present time, during which gifts
and sacrifices are offered that cannot
perfect the conscience of the worshipper, 10but deal only with food and drink
and various baptisms, regulations for
the body imposed until the time comes
to set things right.
11 But when Christ came as a high
priest of the good things that have

[s] 8.2 Or *tabernacle* [t] 8.5 Or *tabernacle*
[u] 8.6 Gk *he* [v] 8.8 Gk *He* [w] 9.2 Or *tabernacle*
[x] 9.2 Gk *the presentation of the loaves* [y] 9.3 Or
tabernacle [z] 9.5 Or *the place of atonement*
[a] 9.6 Or *tabernacle* [b] 9.8 Or *tabernacle*
[c] 9.9 Gk *parable*

come,[d] then through the greater and
perfect[e] tent[f] (not made with hands,
that is, not of this creation), 12 he entered once for all into the Holy Place,
not with the blood of goats and calves,
but with his own blood, thus obtaining
eternal redemption. 13 For if the blood
of goats and bulls, with the sprinkling
of the ashes of a heifer, sanctifies those
who have been defiled so that their
flesh is purified, 14 how much more will
the blood of Christ, who through the
eternal Spirit[g] offered himself without
blemish to God, purify our[h] conscience
from dead works to worship the living
God!

15 For this reason he is the mediator
of a new covenant, so that those who
are called may receive the promised
eternal inheritance, because a death
has occurred that redeems them from
the transgressions under the first covenant.[i] 16 Where a will[j] is involved, the
death of the one who made it must be
established. 17 For a will[k] takes effect
only at death, since it is not in force as
long as the one who made it is alive.
18 Hence not even the first covenant was
inaugurated without blood. 19 For when
every commandment had been told to
all the people by Moses in accordance
with the law, he took the blood of calves
and goats,[l] with water and scarlet wool
and hyssop, and sprinkled both the
scroll itself and all the people, 20 saying,
'This is the blood of the covenant that
God has ordained for you.' 21 And in the
same way he sprinkled with the blood
both the tent[m] and all the vessels used
in worship. 22 Indeed, under the law almost everything is purified with blood,
and without the shedding of blood there
is no forgiveness of sins.

CHRIST'S SACRIFICE TAKES AWAY SIN

23 Thus it was necessary for the
sketches of the heavenly things to be purified with these rites, but the heavenly
things themselves need better sacrifices
than these. 24 For Christ did not enter
a sanctuary made by human hands, a
mere copy of the true one, but he entered into heaven itself, now to appear
in the presence of God on our behalf.
25 Nor was it to offer himself again and
again, as the high priest enters the Holy
Place year after year with blood that is
not his own; 26 for then he would have
had to suffer again and again since the
foundation of the world. But as it is, he
has appeared once for all at the end of
the age to remove sin by the sacrifice of
himself. 27 And just as it is appointed for
mortals to die once, and after that the
judgement, 28 so Christ, having been offered once to bear the sins of many, will
appear a second time, not to deal with
sin, but to save those who are eagerly
waiting for him.

CHRIST'S SACRIFICE ONCE FOR ALL

10 Since the law has only a shadow
of the good things to come and
not the true form of these realities, it[n]
can never, by the same sacrifices that
are continually offered year after year,
make perfect those who approach.
2 Otherwise, would they not have ceased
being offered, since the worshippers,
cleansed once for all, would no longer
have any consciousness of sin? 3 But in
these sacrifices there is a reminder of
sin year after year. 4 For it is impossible
for the blood of bulls and goats to take
away sins. 5 Consequently, when Christ[o]
came into the world, he said,

'Sacrifices and offerings you
have not desired,
but a body you have
prepared for me;
6 in burnt-offerings and sin-offerings
you have taken no pleasure.
7 Then I said, "See, God, I have come
to do your will, O God"
(in the scroll of the book[p] it
is written of me).'

8 When he said above, 'You have neither
desired nor taken pleasure in sacrifices
and offerings and burnt-offerings and
sin-offerings' (these are offered according to the law), 9 then he added, 'See, I
have come to do your will.' He abolishes
the first in order to establish the second.
10 And it is by God's will[q] that we have
been sanctified through the offering of
the body of Jesus Christ once for all.

11 And every priest stands day after
day at his service, offering again and
again the same sacrifices that can never
take away sins. 12 But when Christ[r] had
offered for all time a single sacrifice for

[d] **9.11** Other ancient authorities read *good things to come* [e] **9.11** Gk *more perfect* [f] **9.11** Or *tabernacle* [g] **9.14** Other ancient authorities read *Holy Spirit* [h] **9.14** Other ancient authorities read *your* [i] **9.15** The Greek word used here means both *covenant* and *will* [j] **9.16** The Greek word used here means both *covenant* and *will* [k] **9.17** The Greek word used here means both *covenant* and *will* [l] **9.19** Other ancient authorities lack *and goats* [m] **9.21** Or *tabernacle* [n] **10.1** Other ancient authorities read *they* [o] **10.5** Gk *he* [p] **10.7** Meaning of Gk uncertain [q] **10.10** Gk *by that will* [r] **10.12** Gk *this one*

sins, 'he sat down at the right hand of
God', 13and since then has been waiting
'until his enemies would be made a footstool for his feet.' 14For by a single offering he has perfected for all time those
who are sanctified. 15And the Holy
Spirit also testifies to us, for after saying,

16 'This is the covenant that I will
make with them
after those days, says the Lord:
I will put my laws in their hearts,
and I will write them on
their minds',

17he also adds,

'I will remember[s] their sins and
their lawless deeds no more.'

18Where there is forgiveness of these,
there is no longer any offering for sin.

A CALL TO PERSEVERE

19 Therefore, my friends,[t] since we
have confidence to enter the sanctuary
by the blood of Jesus, 20by the new and
living way that he opened for us through
the curtain (that is, through his flesh),
21and since we have a great priest over
the house of God, 22let us approach with
a true heart in full assurance of faith,
with our hearts sprinkled clean from an
evil conscience and our bodies washed
with pure water. 23Let us hold fast to the
confession of our hope without wavering, for he who has promised is faithful.
24And let us consider how to provoke
one another to love and good deeds,
25not neglecting to meet together, as is
the habit of some, but encouraging one
another, and all the more as you see the
Day approaching.

26 For if we wilfully persist in sin
after having received the knowledge of
the truth, there no longer remains a
sacrifice for sins, 27but a fearful prospect
of judgement, and a fury of fire that
will consume the adversaries. 28Any-
one who has violated the law of Moses
dies without mercy 'on the testimony
of two or three witnesses.' 29How much
worse punishment do you think will be
deserved by those who have spurned
the Son of God, profaned the blood of
the covenant by which they were sanctified, and outraged the Spirit of grace?
30For we know the one who said, 'Vengeance is mine, I will repay.' And again,
'The Lord will judge his people.' 31It is a
fearful thing to fall into the hands of the
living God.

32 But recall those earlier days when,
after you had been enlightened, you endured a hard struggle with sufferings,
33sometimes being publicly exposed to
abuse and persecution, and sometimes
being partners with those so treated.
34For you had compassion for those
who were in prison, and you cheerfully
accepted the plundering of your possessions, knowing that you yourselves possessed something better and more lasting. 35Do not, therefore, abandon that
confidence of yours; it brings a great
reward. 36For you need endurance, so
that when you have done the will of
God, you may receive what was promised. 37For yet

'in a very little while,
the one who is coming will
come and will not delay;
38 but my righteous one will
live by faith.
My soul takes no pleasure in
anyone who shrinks back.'

39But we are not among those who
shrink back and so are lost, but among
those who have faith and so are saved.

THE MEANING OF FAITH

11 Now faith is the assurance of
things hoped for, the conviction
of things not seen. 2Indeed, by faith[u]
our ancestors received approval. 3By
faith we understand that the worlds
were prepared by the word of God, so
that what is seen was made from things
that are not visible.[v]

THE EXAMPLES OF ABEL, ENOCH, AND NOAH

4 By faith Abel offered to God a
more acceptable[w] sacrifice than Cain's.
Through this he received approval as
righteous, God himself giving approval
to his gifts; he died, but through his
faith[x] he still speaks. 5By faith Enoch
was taken so that he did not experience
death; and 'he was not found, because
God had taken him.' For it was attested
before he was taken away that 'he had
pleased God.' 6And without faith it is
impossible to please God, for whoever
would approach him must believe that
he exists and that he rewards those
who seek him. 7By faith Noah, warned
by God about events as yet unseen, respected the warning and built an ark
to save his household; by this he condemned the world and became an heir

[s] 10.17 Gk *on their minds and I will remember*
[t] 10.19 Gk *Therefore, brothers* [u] 11.2 Gk *by this*
[v] 11.3 Or *was not made out of visible things*
[w] 11.4 Gk *greater* [x] 11.4 Gk *through it*

to the righteousness that is in accordance with faith.

THE FAITH OF ABRAHAM

8 By faith Abraham obeyed when he
was called to set out for a place that he
was to receive as an inheritance; and
he set out, not knowing where he was
going. 9By faith he stayed for a time in
the land he had been promised, as in a
foreign land, living in tents, as did Isaac
and Jacob, who were heirs with him of
the same promise. 10For he looked forward to the city that has foundations,
whose architect and builder is God. 11By
faith he received power of procreation,
even though he was too old—and Sarah
herself was barren—because he considered him faithful who had promised.[y]
12Therefore from one person, and this
one as good as dead, descendants were
born, 'as many as the stars of heaven
and as the innumerable grains of sand
by the seashore.'

13 All of these died in faith without
having received the promises, but from
a distance they saw and greeted them.
They confessed that they were strangers and foreigners on the earth, 14for
people who speak in this way make it
clear that they are seeking a homeland.
15If they had been thinking of the land
that they had left behind, they would
have had opportunity to return. 16But
as it is, they desire a better country, that
is, a heavenly one. Therefore God is not
ashamed to be called their God; indeed,
he has prepared a city for them.

17 By faith Abraham, when put to
the test, offered up Isaac. He who had
received the promises was ready to offer up his only son, 18of whom he had
been told, 'It is through Isaac that descendants shall be named after you.'
19He considered the fact that God is
able even to raise someone from the
dead—and figuratively speaking, he did
receive him back. 20By faith Isaac invoked blessings for the future on Jacob
and Esau. 21By faith Jacob, when dying,
blessed each of the sons of Joseph, 'bowing in worship over the top of his staff.'
22By faith Joseph, at the end of his life,
made mention of the exodus of the Israelites and gave instructions about his
burial.[z]

THE FAITH OF MOSES

23 By faith Moses was hidden by his
parents for three months after his birth,
because they saw that the child was
beautiful; and they were not afraid of
the king's edict.[a] 24By faith Moses, when
he was grown up, refused to be called a
son of Pharaoh's daughter, 25choosing
rather to share ill-treatment with the
people of God than to enjoy the fleeting
pleasures of sin. 26He considered abuse
suffered for the Christ[b] to be greater
wealth than the treasures of Egypt, for
he was looking ahead to the reward.
27By faith he left Egypt, unafraid of
the king's anger; for he persevered as
though[c] he saw him who is invisible.
28By faith he kept the Passover and
the sprinkling of blood, so that the destroyer of the firstborn would not touch
the firstborn of Israel.[d]

THE FAITH OF OTHER ISRAELITE HEROES

29 By faith the people passed through
the Red Sea as if it were dry land, but
when the Egyptians attempted to do so
they were drowned. 30By faith the walls
of Jericho fell after they had been encircled for seven days. 31By faith Rahab
the prostitute did not perish with those
who were disobedient,[e] because she had
received the spies in peace.

32 And what more should I say? For
time would fail me to tell of Gideon,
Barak, Samson, Jephthah, of David
and Samuel and the prophets— 33who
through faith conquered kingdoms, administered justice, obtained promises,
shut the mouths of lions, 34quenched
raging fire, escaped the edge of the
sword, won strength out of weakness,
became mighty in war, put foreign armies to flight. 35Women received their
dead by resurrection. Others were tortured, refusing to accept release, in
order to obtain a better resurrection.
36Others suffered mocking and flogging, and even chains and imprisonment. 37They were stoned to death, they
were sawn in two,[f] they were killed by
the sword; they went about in skins of
sheep and goats, destitute, persecuted,
tormented— 38of whom the world was
not worthy. They wandered in deserts

[y] **11.11** Or *By faith Sarah herself, though barren, received power to conceive, even when she was too old, because she considered him faithful who had promised.* [z] **11.22** Gk *his bones* [a] **11.23** Other ancient authorities add *By faith Moses, when he was grown up, killed the Egyptian, because he observed the humiliation of his people* (Gk *brothers*) [b] **11.26** Or *the Messiah* [c] **11.27** Or *because* [d] **11.28** Gk *would not touch them* [e] **11.31** Or *unbelieving* [f] **11.37** Other ancient authorities add *they were tempted*

Be strong in the Lord and in the strength of his power.

EPHESIANS 6:10

I can do all things through him who strengthens me.

PHILIPPIANS 4:13

Cast all your anxiety on him,
because he cares for you.

1 PETER 5:7

Beloved, we are God's children now.

1 JOHN 3:2

and mountains, and in caves and holes
in the ground.
39 Yet all these, though they were
commended for their faith, did not receive what was promised, 40since God
had provided something better so that
they would not, without us, be made
perfect.

THE EXAMPLE OF JESUS

12 Therefore, since we are surrounded by so great a cloud of
witnesses, let us also lay aside every
weight and the sin that clings so closely,[g]
and let us run with perseverance the race
that is set before us, 2looking to Jesus the
pioneer and perfecter of our faith, who
for the sake of[h] the joy that was set before him endured the cross, disregarding
its shame, and has taken his seat at the
right hand of the throne of God.
3 Consider him who endured such
hostility against himself from sinners,[i]
so that you may not grow weary or lose
heart. 4In your struggle against sin you
have not yet resisted to the point of
shedding your blood. 5And you have forgotten the exhortation that addresses
you as children—

'My child, do not regard lightly the
discipline of the Lord,
or lose heart when you are
punished by him;
6 for the Lord disciplines those
whom he loves,
and chastises every child
whom he accepts.'

7Endure trials for the sake of discipline.
God is treating you as children; for what
child is there whom a parent does not
discipline? 8If you do not have that discipline in which all children share, then
you are illegitimate and not his children. 9Moreover, we had human parents to discipline us, and we respected
them. Should we not be even more willing to be subject to the Father of spirits
and live? 10For they disciplined us for a
short time as seemed best to them, but
he disciplines us for our good, in order
that we may share his holiness. 11Now,
discipline always seems painful rather
than pleasant at the time, but later it
yields the peaceful fruit of righteousness to those who have been trained
by it.
12 Therefore lift your drooping hands
and strengthen your weak knees, 13and
make straight paths for your feet, so
that what is lame may not be put out of
joint, but rather be healed.

WARNINGS AGAINST REJECTING GOD'S GRACE

14 Pursue peace with everyone, and
the holiness without which no one will
see the Lord. 15See to it that no one
fails to obtain the grace of God; that no
root of bitterness springs up and causes
trouble, and through it many become
defiled. 16See to it that no one becomes
like Esau, an immoral and godless person, who sold his birthright for a single
meal. 17You know that later, when he
wanted to inherit the blessing, he was
rejected, for he found no chance to repent,[j] even though he sought the blessing[k] with tears.
18 You have not come to something[l]
that can be touched, a blazing fire, and
darkness, and gloom, and a tempest,
19and the sound of a trumpet, and a
voice whose words made the hearers
beg that not another word be spoken
to them. 20(For they could not endure
the order that was given, 'If even an animal touches the mountain, it shall be
stoned to death.' 21Indeed, so terrifying
was the sight that Moses said, 'I tremble with fear.') 22But you have come to
Mount Zion and to the city of the living
God, the heavenly Jerusalem, and to innumerable angels in festal gathering,
23and to the assembly[m] of the firstborn
who are enrolled in heaven, and to God
the judge of all, and to the spirits of the
righteous made perfect, 24and to Jesus,
the mediator of a new covenant, and to
the sprinkled blood that speaks a better
word than the blood of Abel.
25 See that you do not refuse the one
who is speaking; for if they did not escape when they refused the one who
warned them on earth, how much less
will we escape if we reject the one who
warns from heaven! 26At that time his
voice shook the earth; but now he has
promised, 'Yet once more I will shake
not only the earth but also the heaven.'
27This phrase 'Yet once more' indicates
the removal of what is shaken—that is,
created things—so that what cannot be
shaken may remain. 28Therefore, since
we are receiving a kingdom that cannot
be shaken, let us give thanks, by which
we offer to God an acceptable worship

[g] 12.1 Other ancient authorities read *sin that easily distracts* [h] 12.2 Or *who instead of*
[i] 12.3 Other ancient authorities read *such hostility from sinners against themselves* [j] 12.17 Or *no chance to change his father's mind* [k] 12.17 Gk *it*
[l] 12.18 Other ancient authorities read *a mountain*
[m] 12.23 Or *angels, and to the festal gathering 23and assembly*

with reverence and awe; 29for indeed
our God is a consuming fire.

SERVICE WELL-PLEASING TO GOD

13 Let mutual love continue. 2Do
not neglect to show hospital-
ity to strangers, for by doing that some
have entertained angels without knowing it. 3Remember those who are in
prison, as though you were in prison
with them; those who are being tortured, as though you yourselves were
being tortured.[n] 4Let marriage be held
in honour by all, and let the marriage
bed be kept undefiled; for God will judge
fornicators and adulterers. 5Keep your
lives free from the love of money, and be
content with what you have; for he has
said, 'I will never leave you or forsake
you.' 6So we can say with confidence,

'The Lord is my helper;
    I will not be afraid.
What can anyone do to me?'

7 Remember your leaders, those who
spoke the word of God to you; consider
the outcome of their way of life, and
imitate their faith. 8Jesus Christ is the
same yesterday and today and for ever.
9Do not be carried away by all kinds of
strange teachings; for it is well for the
heart to be strengthened by grace, not
by regulations about food,[o] which have
not benefited those who observe them.
10We have an altar from which those
who officiate in the tent[p] have no right
to eat. 11For the bodies of those animals
whose blood is brought into the sanctuary by the high priest as a sacrifice
for sin are burned outside the camp.
12Therefore Jesus also suffered outside
the city gate in order to sanctify the
people by his own blood. 13Let us then
go to him outside the camp and bear the
abuse he endured. 14For here we have no
lasting city, but we are looking for the
city that is to come. 15Through him,
then, let us continually offer a sacrifice
of praise to God, that is, the fruit of lips
that confess his name. 16Do not neglect
to do good and to share what you have,
for such sacrifices are pleasing to God.

17 Obey your leaders and submit to
them, for they are keeping watch over
your souls and will give an account.
Let them do this with joy and not with
sighing—for that would be harmful to
you.

18 Pray for us; we are sure that we
have a clear conscience, desiring to act
honourably in all things. 19I urge you all
the more to do this, so that I may be restored to you very soon.

BENEDICTION

20 Now may the God of peace, who
brought back from the dead our Lord
Jesus, the great shepherd of the sheep,
by the blood of the eternal covenant,
21make you complete in everything
good so that you may do his will, working among us[q] that which is pleasing in
his sight, through Jesus Christ, to whom
be the glory for ever and ever. Amen.

FINAL EXHORTATION AND GREETINGS

22 I appeal to you, brothers and sisters,[r] bear with my word of exhortation, for I have written to you briefly. 23I
want you to know that our brother Timothy has been set free; and if he comes
in time, he will be with me when I see
you. 24Greet all your leaders and all the
saints. Those from Italy send you greetings. 25Grace be with all of you.[s]

[n] 13.3 Gk *were in the body* [o] 13.9 Gk *not by foods* [p] 13.10 Or *tabernacle* [q] 13.21 Other ancient authorities read *you* [r] 13.22 Gk *brothers* [s] 13.25 Other ancient authorities add *Amen*

The Letter of

JAMES

The Letter of James is thought by some to have been written by Jesus' own brother (Gal 1.19), who became the leader of the church in Jerusalem (Acts 15.13; 21.18). It appears, however, that the Letter was written by a well-educated, Greek-speaking Christian and not by an Aramaic-speaking peasant. The Letter is addressed to "the twelve tribes in the Dispersion" (1.1), which, in a Jewish context, means the people of Israel living outside of Palestine. Here, however, it most likely represents the church as the new Israel and refers to Jewish Christian communities in Palestine, Syria, and elsewhere in the area. The Letter is an exhortation that offers many prescriptions about how to live in a morally responsible manner. The content is presented in a way that is similar to Proverbs and Sirach and corresponds to topics that also appear in the synoptic Gospels, especially in Matthew's Sermon on the Mount.

The Letter of James, with its emphasis on the importance of good works, is well known because of the concern it raised in the sixteenth century over whether it contradicts Paul's teaching. Paul states clearly in his Letter to the Romans: "A person is justified by faith apart from works prescribed by the law" (Rom 3.28). James states that without good works faith is dead (2.14–17). The two seem to offer very different points of view about salvation. The context in James is not concern about the works of circumcision or ritual requirements of the law of Moses as in Romans, but the works that correspond to mercy and justice that come from fulfilling the law of love, "You shall love your neighbour as yourself" (2.8).

In administering the Sacrament of Anointing of the Sick, the church always reads the well-known passage from the Letter of James that asks for the elders of the church to come and pray over the sick, anointing them with oil in the name of the Lord (5.13–15). This use of the Letter of James in the visitation of the sick is a fine example of the kind of application that resonates with the Letter's own call for the community to "be doers of the word, and not merely hearers who deceive themselves" (1.22).

SALUTATION

1 James, a servant[a] of God and of the Lord Jesus Christ,
To the twelve tribes in the Dispersion:
Greetings.

FAITH AND WISDOM

2 My brothers and sisters,[b] whenever you face trials of any kind, consider it nothing but joy, 3because you know that the testing of your faith produces endurance; 4and let endurance have its full effect, so that you may be mature and complete, lacking in nothing.

5 If any of you is lacking in wisdom, ask God, who gives to all generously and ungrudgingly, and it will be given you. 6But ask in faith, never doubting, for the one who doubts is like a wave of the sea, driven and tossed by the wind; 7,8for the doubter, being double-minded and unstable in every way, must not expect to receive anything from the Lord.

[a] 1.1 Gk *slave* [b] 1.2 Gk *brothers*

POVERTY AND RICHES

9 Let the believer[c] who is lowly boast in being raised up, 10and the rich in being brought low, because the rich will disappear like a flower in the field. 11For the sun rises with its scorching heat and withers the field; its flower falls, and its beauty perishes. It is the same with the rich; in the midst of a busy life, they will wither away.

TRIAL AND TEMPTATION

12 Blessed is anyone who endures temptation. Such a one has stood the test and will receive the crown of life that the Lord[d] has promised to those who love him. 13No one, when tempted, should say, 'I am being tempted by God'; for God cannot be tempted by evil and he himself tempts no one. 14But one is tempted by one's own desire, being lured and enticed by it; 15then, when that desire has conceived, it gives birth to sin, and that sin, when it is fully grown, gives birth to death. 16Do not be deceived, my beloved.[e]

17 Every generous act of giving, with every perfect gift, is from above, coming down from the Father of lights, with whom there is no variation or shadow due to change.[f] 18In fulfilment of his own purpose he gave us birth by the word of truth, so that we would become a kind of first fruits of his creatures.

HEARING AND DOING THE WORD

19 You must understand this, my beloved:[g] let everyone be quick to listen, slow to speak, slow to anger; 20for your anger does not produce God's righteousness. 21Therefore rid yourselves of all sordidness and rank growth of wickedness, and welcome with meekness the implanted word that has the power to save your souls.

22 But be doers of the word, and not merely hearers who deceive themselves. 23For if any are hearers of the word and not doers, they are like those who look at themselves[h] in a mirror; 24for they look at themselves and, on going away, immediately forget what they were like. 25But those who look into the perfect law, the law of liberty, and persevere, being not hearers who forget but doers who act—they will be blessed in their doing.

26 If any think they are religious, and do not bridle their tongues but deceive their hearts, their religion is worthless. 27Religion that is pure and undefiled before God, the Father, is this: to care for orphans and widows in their distress, and to keep oneself unstained by the world.

WARNING AGAINST PARTIALITY

2 My brothers and sisters,[i] do you with your acts of favouritism really believe in our glorious Lord Jesus Christ?[j] 2For if a person with gold rings and in fine clothes comes into your assembly, and if a poor person in dirty clothes also comes in, 3and if you take notice of the one wearing the fine clothes and say, 'Have a seat here, please', while to the one who is poor you say, 'Stand there', or, 'Sit at my feet',[k] 4have you not made distinctions among yourselves, and become judges with evil thoughts? 5Listen, my beloved brothers and sisters.[l] Has not God chosen the poor in the world to be rich in faith and to be heirs of the kingdom that he has promised to those who love him? 6But you have dishonoured the poor. Is it not the rich who oppress you? Is it not they who drag you into court? 7Is it not they who blaspheme the excellent name that was invoked over you?

8 You do well if you really fulfil the royal law according to the scripture, 'You shall love your neighbour as yourself.' 9But if you show partiality, you commit sin and are convicted by the law as transgressors. 10For whoever keeps the whole law but fails in one point has become accountable for all of it. 11For the one who said, 'You shall not commit adultery', also said, 'You shall not murder.' Now if you do not commit adultery but if you murder, you have become a transgressor of the law. 12So speak and so act as those who are to be judged by the law of liberty. 13For judgement will be without mercy to anyone who has shown no mercy; mercy triumphs over judgement.

FAITH WITHOUT WORKS IS DEAD

14 What good is it, my brothers and sisters,[m] if you say you have faith but do not have works? Can faith save you? 15If a brother or sister is naked and lacks

[c] **1.9** Gk *brother* [d] **1.12** Gk *he*; other ancient authorities read *God* [e] **1.16** Gk *my beloved brothers* [f] **1.17** Other ancient authorities read *variation due to a shadow of turning* [g] **1.19** Gk *my beloved brothers* [h] **1.23** Gk *at the face of his birth* [i] **2.1** Gk *My brothers* [j] **2.1** Or *hold the faith of our glorious Lord Jesus Christ without acts of favouritism* [k] **2.3** Gk *Sit under my footstool* [l] **2.5** Gk *brothers* [m] **2.14** Gk *brothers*

daily food, 16 and one of you says to them, 'Go in peace; keep warm and eat your fill', and yet you do not supply their bodily needs, what is the good of that? 17 So faith by itself, if it has no works, is dead.

18 But someone will say, 'You have faith and I have works.' Show me your faith without works, and I by my works will show you my faith. 19 You believe that God is one; you do well. Even the demons believe—and shudder. 20 Do you want to be shown, you senseless person, that faith without works is barren? 21 Was not our ancestor Abraham justified by works when he offered his son Isaac on the altar? 22 You see that faith was active along with his works, and faith was brought to completion by the works. 23 Thus the scripture was fulfilled that says, 'Abraham believed God, and it was reckoned to him as righteousness', and he was called the friend of God. 24 You see that a person is justified by works and not by faith alone. 25 Likewise, was not Rahab the prostitute also justified by works when she welcomed the messengers and sent them out by another road? 26 For just as the body without the spirit is dead, so faith without works is also dead.

TAMING THE TONGUE

3 Not many of you should become teachers, my brothers and sisters,[n] for you know that we who teach will be judged with greater strictness. 2 For all of us make many mistakes. Anyone who makes no mistakes in speaking is perfect, able to keep the whole body in check with a bridle. 3 If we put bits into the mouths of horses to make them obey us, we guide their whole bodies. 4 Or look at ships: though they are so large that it takes strong winds to drive them, yet they are guided by a very small rudder wherever the will of the pilot directs. 5 So also the tongue is a small member, yet it boasts of great exploits.

How great a forest is set ablaze by a small fire! 6 And the tongue is a fire. The tongue is placed among our members as a world of iniquity; it stains the whole body, sets on fire the cycle of nature,[o] and is itself set on fire by hell.[p] 7 For every species of beast and bird, of reptile and sea creature, can be tamed and has been tamed by the human species, 8 but no one can tame the tongue—a restless evil, full of deadly poison. 9 With it we bless the Lord and Father, and with it we curse those who are made in the likeness of God. 10 From the same mouth come blessing and cursing. My brothers and sisters,[q] this ought not to be so. 11 Does a spring pour forth from the same opening both fresh and brackish water? 12 Can a fig tree, my brothers and sisters,[r] yield olives, or a grapevine figs? No more can salt water yield fresh.

TWO KINDS OF WISDOM

13 Who is wise and understanding among you? Show by your good life that your works are done with gentleness born of wisdom. 14 But if you have bitter envy and selfish ambition in your hearts, do not be boastful and false to the truth. 15 Such wisdom does not come down from above, but is earthly, unspiritual, devilish. 16 For where there is envy and selfish ambition, there will also be disorder and wickedness of every kind. 17 But the wisdom from above is first pure, then peaceable, gentle, willing to yield, full of mercy and good fruits, without a trace of partiality or hypocrisy. 18 And a harvest of righteousness is sown in peace for[s] those who make peace.

FRIENDSHIP WITH THE WORLD

4 Those conflicts and disputes among you, where do they come from? Do they not come from your cravings that are at war within you? 2 You want something and do not have it; so you commit murder. And you covet[t] something and cannot obtain it; so you engage in disputes and conflicts. You do not have, because you do not ask. 3 You ask and do not receive, because you ask wrongly, in order to spend what you get on your pleasures. 4 Adulterers! Do you not know that friendship with the world is enmity with God? Therefore whoever wishes to be a friend of the world becomes an enemy of God. 5 Or do you suppose that it is for nothing that the scripture says, 'God[u] yearns jealously for the spirit that he has made to dwell in us'? 6 But he gives all the more grace; therefore it says,

'God opposes the proud,
  but gives grace to the humble.'

7 Submit yourselves therefore to God. Resist the devil, and he will flee from you. 8 Draw near to God, and he will draw near to you. Cleanse your hands, you sinners, and purify your hearts, you

[n] **3.1** Gk *brothers* [o] **3.6** Or *wheel of birth* [p] **3.6** Gk *Gehenna* [q] **3.10** Gk *My brothers* [r] **3.12** Gk *my brothers* [s] **3.18** Or *by* [t] **4.2** Or *you murder and you covet* [u] **4.5** Gk *He*

double-minded. 9Lament and mourn
and weep. Let your laughter be turned
into mourning and your joy into dejec-
tion. 10Humble yourselves before the
Lord, and he will exalt you.

WARNING AGAINST JUDGING ANOTHER

11 Do not speak evil against one another, brothers and sisters.[v] Whoever
speaks evil against another or judges
another, speaks evil against the law and
judges the law; but if you judge the law,
you are not a doer of the law but a judge.
12There is one lawgiver and judge who
is able to save and to destroy. So who,
then, are you to judge your neighbour?

BOASTING ABOUT TOMORROW

13 Come now, you who say, 'Today or
tomorrow we will go to such and such
a town and spend a year there, doing
business and making money.' 14Yet you
do not even know what tomorrow will
bring. What is your life? For you are a
mist that appears for a little while and
then vanishes. 15Instead you ought to
say, 'If the Lord wishes, we will live and
do this or that.' 16As it is, you boast in
your arrogance; all such boasting is evil.
17Anyone, then, who knows the right
thing to do and fails to do it, commits sin.

WARNING TO RICH OPPRESSORS

5 Come now, you rich people, weep
and wail for the miseries that are
coming to you. 2Your riches have rotted, and your clothes are moth-eaten.
3Your gold and silver have rusted, and
their rust will be evidence against you,
and it will eat your flesh like fire. You
have laid up treasure[w] for the last days.
4Listen! The wages of the labourers who
mowed your fields, which you kept back
by fraud, cry out, and the cries of the
harvesters have reached the ears of the
Lord of hosts. 5You have lived on the
earth in luxury and in pleasure; you
have fattened your hearts on a day of
slaughter. 6You have condemned and
murdered the righteous one, who does
not resist you.

PATIENCE IN SUFFERING

7 Be patient, therefore, beloved,[x] until the coming of the Lord. The farmer
waits for the precious crop from the
earth, being patient with it until it
receives the early and the late rains.
8You also must be patient. Strengthen
your hearts, for the coming of the Lord
is near.[y] 9Beloved,[z] do not grumble
against one another, so that you may
not be judged. See, the Judge is standing at the doors! 10As an example of suffering and patience, beloved,[a] take the
prophets who spoke in the name of the
Lord. 11Indeed we call blessed those who
showed endurance. You have heard of
the endurance of Job, and you have seen
the purpose of the Lord, how the Lord is
compassionate and merciful.

12 Above all, my beloved,[b] do not
swear, either by heaven or by earth or
by any other oath, but let your 'Yes' be
yes and your 'No' be no, so that you may
not fall under condemnation.

THE PRAYER OF FAITH

13 Are any among you suffering?
They should pray. Are any cheerful?
They should sing songs of praise. 14Are
any among you sick? They should call
for the elders of the church and have
them pray over them, anointing them
with oil in the name of the Lord. 15The
prayer of faith will save the sick, and
the Lord will raise them up; and anyone who has committed sins will be
forgiven. 16Therefore confess your sins
to one another, and pray for one another, so that you may be healed. The
prayer of the righteous is powerful and
effective. 17Elijah was a human being
like us, and he prayed fervently that it
might not rain, and for three years and
six months it did not rain on the earth.
18Then he prayed again, and the heaven
gave rain and the earth yielded its harvest.

19 My brothers and sisters,[c] if anyone among you wanders from the truth
and is brought back by another, 20you
should know that whoever brings back
a sinner from wandering will save the
sinner's[d] soul from death and will cover
a multitude of sins.

[v] **4.11** Gk *brothers* [w] **5.3** Or *will eat your flesh, since you have stored up fire* [x] **5.7** Gk *brothers*
[y] **5.8** Or *is at hand* [z] **5.9** Gk *Brothers*
[a] **5.10** Gk *brothers* [b] **5.12** Gk *brothers*
[c] **5.19** Gk *My brothers* [d] **5.20** Gk *his*

The First Letter of PETER

Traditionally, 1 Peter was thought to have been written by Peter the apostle (1.1). More recently, biblical scholars accept that the Letter was written pseudonymously, i.e., in Peter's name, but not by the apostle himself. Some propose Silvanus, his secretary, as the author (5.12). Peter was a lower-class fisherman from Galilee described to be "uneducated and ordinary" in the book of Acts (Acts 4.13). It is evident that this Letter was written by a well-educated and Greek-speaking Christian.

The Letter is directed to Christians living in Asia Minor (modern-day Turkey) who were experiencing suffering through persecution. The date of the Letter is uncertain, but allusions to widespread persecution would place the Letter in the late first or early second century. There was no widespread persecution of Christians until the time of Domitian (81–96 CE), although Nero seemed to single out Christians for persecution between 64 and 67 when Peter was martyred in Rome.

First Peter, more than any other book of the New Testament, deals with Christian suffering. The word "suffering" occurs more often in this short Letter than in any other writing of the New Testament. The author mentions "the fiery ordeal that is taking place among you" (4.12). The Letter attempts to console and encourage those in the community who are suffering by asserting that their persecution is a share in the sufferings of Christ (4.13).

At the same time, the Letter urges Christians not to create reasons for persecution by their own misbehavior, sabotaging authority or causing insubordination in family life (2.11—3.12). The Letter walks a fine line between accepting alienation for the sake of the gospel (2.11) and rejecting behaviors that oppose shared values of the pagan culture (2.13–17). In other words, the community members should not behave in a way that offends pagans unnecessarily. Instead, they should be prepared to explain why they are a people set apart as belonging to God alone (2.4–5, 9–10; 3.13–17).

Selections from 1 Peter are read during the Easter season of Year A. The texts remind the church over these Sundays and throughout the ages to recognize its distinctive call to be a people born anew destined for salvation, and also to be a people responsible to provide living testimony by doing good in the world.

SALUTATION

1 Peter, an apostle of Jesus Christ,
To the exiles of the Dispersion in
Pontus, Galatia, Cappadocia, Asia, and
Bithynia, 2who have been chosen and
destined by God the Father and sanc-
tified by the Spirit to be obedient to
Jesus Christ and to be sprinkled with
his blood:

May grace and peace be yours in abundance.

A LIVING HOPE

3 Blessed be the God and Father of our
Lord Jesus Christ! By his great mercy he
has given us a new birth into a living hope
through the resurrection of Jesus Christ
from the dead, 4and into an inheritance

that is imperishable, undefiled, and unfading, kept in heaven for you, 5who are
being protected by the power of God
through faith for a salvation ready to be
revealed in the last time. 6In this you rejoice,[a] even if now for a little while you
have had to suffer various trials, 7so that
the genuineness of your faith—being
more precious than gold that, though
perishable, is tested by fire—may be
found to result in praise and glory and
honour when Jesus Christ is revealed.
8Although you have not seen[b] him, you
love him; and even though you do not
see him now, you believe in him and rejoice with an indescribable and glorious
joy, 9for you are receiving the outcome of
your faith, the salvation of your souls.

10 Concerning this salvation, the
prophets who prophesied of the grace
that was to be yours made careful search
and inquiry, 11inquiring about the person or time that the Spirit of Christ
within them indicated, when it testified
in advance to the sufferings destined for
Christ and the subsequent glory. 12It
was revealed to them that they were
serving not themselves but you, in regard to the things that have now been
announced to you through those who
brought you good news by the Holy
Spirit sent from heaven—things into
which angels long to look!

A CALL TO HOLY LIVING

13 Therefore prepare your minds for
action;[c] discipline yourselves; set all
your hope on the grace that Jesus Christ
will bring you when he is revealed.
14Like obedient children, do not be conformed to the desires that you formerly
had in ignorance. 15Instead, as he who
called you is holy, be holy yourselves in
all your conduct; 16for it is written, 'You
shall be holy, for I am holy.'

17 If you invoke as Father the one
who judges all people impartially according to their deeds, live in reverent
fear during the time of your exile. 18You
know that you were ransomed from
the futile ways inherited from your ancestors, not with perishable things like
silver or gold, 19but with the precious
blood of Christ, like that of a lamb without defect or blemish. 20He was destined
before the foundation of the world, but
was revealed at the end of the ages for
your sake. 21Through him you have
come to trust in God, who raised him
from the dead and gave him glory, so
that your faith and hope are set on God.

22 Now that you have purified your
souls by your obedience to the truth[d]
so that you have genuine mutual love,
love one another deeply[e] from the
heart.[f] 23You have been born anew, not
of perishable but of imperishable seed,
through the living and enduring word
of God.[g] 24For

'All flesh is like grass
and all its glory like the
flower of grass.
The grass withers,
and the flower falls,
25 but the word of the Lord
endures for ever.'

That word is the good news that was announced to you.

THE LIVING STONE AND A CHOSEN PEOPLE

2 Rid yourselves, therefore, of all malice, and all guile, insincerity, envy,
and all slander. 2Like newborn infants,
long for the pure, spiritual milk, so that
by it you may grow into salvation— 3if
indeed you have tasted that the Lord is
good.

4 Come to him, a living stone, though
rejected by mortals yet chosen and precious in God's sight, and 5like living
stones, let yourselves be built[h] into a
spiritual house, to be a holy priesthood,
to offer spiritual sacrifices acceptable to
God through Jesus Christ. 6For it stands
in scripture:

'See, I am laying in Zion a stone,
a cornerstone chosen
and precious;
and whoever believes in him[i] will
not be put to shame.'

7To you then who believe, he is precious; but for those who do not believe,

'The stone that the builders rejected
has become the very head
of the corner',

8and

'A stone that makes them stumble,
and a rock that makes them fall.'

They stumble because they disobey the
word, as they were destined to do.

9 But you are a chosen race, a royal
priesthood, a holy nation, God's own
people,[j] in order that you may proclaim

[a] 1.6 Or *Rejoice in this* [b] 1.8 Other ancient authorities read *known* [c] 1.13 Gk *gird up the loins of your mind* [d] 1.22 Other ancient authorities add *through the Spirit* [e] 1.22 Or *constantly* [f] 1.22 Other ancient authorities read *a pure heart* [g] 1.23 Or *through the word of the living and enduring God* [h] 2.5 Or *you yourselves are being built* [i] 2.6 Or *it* [j] 2.9 Gk *a people for his possession*

the mighty acts of him who called you
out of darkness into his marvellous
light.

10 Once you were not a people,
but now you are God's people;
once you had not received mercy,
but now you have received mercy.

LIVE AS SERVANTS OF GOD

11 Beloved, I urge you as aliens and
exiles to abstain from the desires of
the flesh that wage war against the
soul. 12Conduct yourselves honourably
among the Gentiles, so that, though
they malign you as evildoers, they may
see your honourable deeds and glorify
God when he comes to judge.[k]

13 For the Lord's sake accept the authority of every human institution,[l]
whether of the emperor as supreme,
14or of governors, as sent by him to punish those who do wrong and to praise
those who do right. 15For it is God's will
that by doing right you should silence
the ignorance of the foolish. 16As servants[m] of God, live as free people, yet do
not use your freedom as a pretext for
evil. 17Honour everyone. Love the family of believers.[n] Fear God. Honour the
emperor.

THE EXAMPLE OF CHRIST'S SUFFERING

18 Slaves, accept the authority of
your masters with all deference, not
only those who are kind and gentle but
also those who are harsh. 19For it is to
your credit if, being aware of God, you
endure pain while suffering unjustly.
20If you endure when you are beaten
for doing wrong, where is the credit in
that? But if you endure when you do
right and suffer for it, you have God's
approval. 21For to this you have been
called, because Christ also suffered for
you, leaving you an example, so that
you should follow in his steps.

22 'He committed no sin,
and no deceit was found
in his mouth.'

23When he was abused, he did not return abuse; when he suffered, he did not
threaten; but he entrusted himself to
the one who judges justly. 24He himself
bore our sins in his body on the cross,[o]
so that, free from sins, we might live
for righteousness; by his wounds[p] you
have been healed. 25For you were going
astray like sheep, but now you have returned to the shepherd and guardian of
your souls.

WIVES AND HUSBANDS

3 Wives, in the same way, accept the
authority of your husbands, so that,
even if some of them do not obey the
word, they may be won over without
a word by their wives' conduct, 2when
they see the purity and reverence of
your lives. 3Do not adorn yourselves
outwardly by braiding your hair, and by
wearing gold ornaments or fine clothing; 4rather, let your adornment be the
inner self with the lasting beauty of a
gentle and quiet spirit, which is very
precious in God's sight. 5It was in this
way long ago that the holy women who
hoped in God used to adorn themselves
by accepting the authority of their husbands. 6Thus Sarah obeyed Abraham
and called him lord. You have become
her daughters as long as you do what is
good and never let fears alarm you.

7 Husbands, in the same way, show
consideration for your wives in your life
together, paying honour to the woman
as the weaker sex,[q] since they too are
also heirs of the gracious gift of life—so
that nothing may hinder your prayers.

SUFFERING FOR DOING RIGHT

8 Finally, all of you, have unity of
spirit, sympathy, love for one another,
a tender heart, and a humble mind. 9Do
not repay evil for evil or abuse for abuse;
but, on the contrary, repay with a blessing. It is for this that you were called—
that you might inherit a blessing. 10For

'Those who desire life
and desire to see good days,
let them keep their tongues from evil
and their lips from
speaking deceit;
11 let them turn away from
evil and do good;
let them seek peace and pursue it.
12 For the eyes of the Lord are
on the righteous,
and his ears are open to
their prayer.
But the face of the Lord is against
those who do evil.'

13 Now who will harm you if you are
eager to do what is good? 14But even if
you do suffer for doing what is right,
you are blessed. Do not fear what they
fear,[r] and do not be intimidated, 15but in

[k] 2.12 Gk *God on the day of visitation* [l] 2.13 Or *every institution ordained for human beings* [m] 2.16 Gk *slaves* [n] 2.17 Gk *Love the brotherhood* [o] 2.24 Or *carried up our sins in his body to the tree* [p] 2.24 Gk *bruise* [q] 3.7 Gk *vessel* [r] 3.14 Gk *their fear*

your hearts sanctify Christ as Lord. Always be ready to make your defence to
anyone who demands from you an account of the hope that is in you; 16yet do
it with gentleness and reverence.[s] Keep
your conscience clear, so that, when you
are maligned, those who abuse you for
your good conduct in Christ may be put
to shame. 17For it is better to suffer for
doing good, if suffering should be God's
will, than to suffer for doing evil. 18For
Christ also suffered[t] for sins once for all,
the righteous for the unrighteous, in
order to bring you[u] to God. He was put
to death in the flesh, but made alive in
the spirit, 19in which also he went and
made a proclamation to the spirits in
prison, 20who in former times did not
obey, when God waited patiently in the
days of Noah, during the building of the
ark, in which a few, that is, eight people, were saved through water. 21And
baptism, which this prefigured, now
saves you—not as a removal of dirt from
the body, but as an appeal to God for[v] a
good conscience, through the resurrection of Jesus Christ, 22who has gone into
heaven and is at the right hand of God,
with angels, authorities, and powers
made subject to him.

GOOD STEWARDS OF GOD'S GRACE

4 Since therefore Christ suffered in
the flesh,[w] arm yourselves also
with the same intention (for whoever
has suffered in the flesh has finished
with sin), 2so as to live for the rest of
your earthly life[x] no longer by human
desires but by the will of God. 3You have
already spent enough time in doing
what the Gentiles like to do, living in
licentiousness, passions, drunkenness,
revels, carousing, and lawless idolatry.
4They are surprised that you no longer
join them in the same excesses of dissipation, and so they blaspheme.[y] 5But
they will have to give an account to him
who stands ready to judge the living
and the dead. 6For this is the reason the
gospel was proclaimed even to the dead,
so that, though they had been judged
in the flesh as everyone is judged, they
might live in the spirit as God does.
7 The end of all things is near;[z] therefore be serious and discipline yourselves
for the sake of your prayers. 8Above all,
maintain constant love for one another,
for love covers a multitude of sins. 9Be
hospitable to one another without complaining. 10Like good stewards of the
manifold grace of God, serve one another with whatever gift each of you has
received. 11Whoever speaks must do so
as one speaking the very words of God;
whoever serves must do so with the
strength that God supplies, so that God
may be glorified in all things through
Jesus Christ. To him belong the glory
and the power for ever and ever. Amen.

SUFFERING AS A CHRISTIAN

12 Beloved, do not be surprised at
the fiery ordeal that is taking place
among you to test you, as though something strange were happening to you.
13But rejoice in so far as you are sharing
Christ's sufferings, so that you may also
be glad and shout for joy when his glory
is revealed. 14If you are reviled for the
name of Christ, you are blessed, because
the spirit of glory,[a] which is the Spirit
of God, is resting on you.[b] 15But let none
of you suffer as a murderer, a thief, a
criminal, or even as a mischief-maker.
16Yet if any of you suffers as a Christian, do not consider it a disgrace, but
glorify God because you bear this name.
17For the time has come for judgement
to begin with the household of God; if
it begins with us, what will be the end
for those who do not obey the gospel of
God? 18And

'If it is hard for the righteous
to be saved,
what will become of the ungodly
and the sinners?'

19Therefore, let those suffering in accordance with God's will entrust themselves to a faithful Creator, while continuing to do good.

TENDING THE FLOCK OF GOD

5 Now as an elder myself and a witness of the sufferings of Christ, as
well as one who shares in the glory to
be revealed, I exhort the elders among
you 2to tend the flock of God that is in
your charge, exercising the oversight,[c]
not under compulsion but willingly, as
God would have you do it[d]—not for sordid gain but eagerly. 3Do not lord it over

[s] 3.16 Or *respect* [t] 3.18 Other ancient authorities read *died* [u] 3.18 Other ancient authorities read *us* [v] 3.21 Or *a pledge to God from* [w] 4.1 Other ancient authorities add *for us*; others, *for you* [x] 4.2 Gk *rest of the time in the flesh* [y] 4.4 Or *they malign you* [z] 4.7 Or *is at hand* [a] 4.14 Other ancient authorities add *and of power* [b] 4.14 Other ancient authorities add *On their part he is blasphemed, but on your part he is glorified* [c] 5.2 Other ancient authorities lack *exercising the oversight* [d] 5.2 Other ancient authorities lack *as God would have you do it*

those in your charge, but be examples
to the flock. 4And when the chief shepherd appears, you will win the crown
of glory that never fades away. 5In the
same way, you who are younger must
accept the authority of the elders.[e] And
all of you must clothe yourselves with
humility in your dealings with one another, for

'God opposes the proud,
but gives grace to the humble.'

6 Humble yourselves therefore under the mighty hand of God, so that he
may exalt you in due time. 7Cast all your
anxiety on him, because he cares for
you. 8Discipline yourselves; keep alert.[f]
Like a roaring lion your adversary the
devil prowls around, looking for someone to devour. 9Resist him, steadfast
in your faith, for you know that your
brothers and sisters[g] throughout the
world are undergoing the same kinds of
suffering. 10And after you have suffered
for a little while, the God of all grace,
who has called you to his eternal glory
in Christ, will himself restore, support,
strengthen, and establish you. 11To him
be the power for ever and ever. Amen.

FINAL GREETINGS AND BENEDICTION

12 Through Silvanus, whom I consider a faithful brother, I have written
this short letter to encourage you, and
to testify that this is the true grace
of God. Stand fast in it. 13Your sister
church[h] in Babylon, chosen together
with you, sends you greetings; and so
does my son Mark. 14Greet one another
with a kiss of love.

Peace to all of you who are in Christ.[i]

[e] 5.5 Or *of those who are older* [f] 5.8 Or *be vigilant* [g] 5.9 Gk *your brotherhood* [h] 5.13 Gk *She who is* [i] 5.14 Other ancient authorities add *Amen*

The Second Letter of

PETER

If Peter had written 2 Peter, it would have been shortly before his martyrdom around 64/65 CE. The Letter, however, is a testament probably written in Peter's name to the church in Rome at a time when the apostolic teaching was being challenged. This document asserts the special importance of the teaching of the apostles for the church after the apostles' death.

The earliest Christian communities expected Christ's return in glory during their own lifetime. However, the first generation had to deal with the disappointment that Christ's second coming would be delayed. Second Peter confronts the skepticism about this delay and insists on continued patience (1.16–21; 3.3–10) and growth in the way of grace and knowledge of Jesus Christ (3.14–18). The Letter also articulates for the Christian community a way of transition from an apostolic to a postapostolic age (3.2).

The Letter provides an answer to the question about how Christians should live in the time between now and the final coming of Christ. The answer given is read at the liturgy during the Second Sunday of Advent in Year B: "Therefore, beloved, while you are waiting for these things, strive to be found by him at peace, without spot or blemish; and regard the patience of our Lord as salvation" (3.14–15).

SALUTATION

1 Simeon[a] Peter, a servant[b] and apostle of Jesus Christ,

To those who have received a faith as precious as ours through the righteousness of our God and Saviour Jesus Christ:[c]

2 May grace and peace be yours in abundance in the knowledge of God and of Jesus our Lord.

THE CHRISTIAN'S CALL AND ELECTION

3 His divine power has given us everything needed for life and godliness, through the knowledge of him who called us by[d] his own glory and goodness. 4Thus he has given us, through these things, his precious and very great promises, so that through them you may escape from the corruption that is in the world because of lust, and may become participants in the divine nature. 5For this very reason,
you must make every effort to support your faith with goodness, and goodness with knowledge, 6and knowledge with self-control, and self-control with endurance, and endurance with godliness, 7and godliness with mutual[e] affection, and mutual[f] affection with love.
8For if these things are yours and are increasing among you, they keep you from being ineffective and unfruitful in the knowledge of our Lord Jesus Christ.
9For anyone who lacks these things is short-sighted and blind, and is forgetful of the cleansing of past sins. 10Therefore, brothers and sisters,[g] be all the more eager to confirm your call and election, for if you do this, you will never stumble.
11For in this way, entry into the eternal

[a] 1.1 Other ancient authorities read *Simon* [b] 1.1 Gk *slave* [c] 1.1 Or *of our God and the Saviour Jesus Christ* [d] 1.3 Other ancient authorities read *through* [e] 1.7 Gk *brotherly* [f] 1.7 Gk *brotherly* [g] 1.10 Gk *brothers*

kingdom of our Lord and Saviour Jesus
Christ will be richly provided for you.
12 Therefore I intend to keep on reminding you of these things, though
you know them already and are established in the truth that has come to you.
13I think it right, as long as I am in this
body,[h] to refresh your memory, 14since I
know that my death[i] will come soon, as
indeed our Lord Jesus Christ has made
clear to me. 15And I will make every effort so that after my departure you may
be able at any time to recall these things.

EYEWITNESSES OF CHRIST'S GLORY

16 For we did not follow cleverly devised myths when we made known to
you the power and coming of our Lord
Jesus Christ, but we had been eyewitnesses of his majesty. 17For he received honour and glory from God the
Father when that voice was conveyed to
him by the Majestic Glory, saying, 'This
is my Son, my Beloved,[j] with whom I
am well pleased.' 18We ourselves heard
this voice come from heaven, while we
were with him on the holy mountain.
19 So we have the prophetic message
more fully confirmed. You will do well
to be attentive to this as to a lamp shining in a dark place, until the day dawns
and the morning star rises in your
hearts. 20First of all you must understand this, that no prophecy of scripture
is a matter of one's own interpretation,
21because no prophecy ever came by human will, but men and women moved
by the Holy Spirit spoke from God.[k]

FALSE PROPHETS AND THEIR PUNISHMENT

2 But false prophets also arose among
the people, just as there will be false
teachers among you, who will secretly
bring in destructive opinions. They
will even deny the Master who bought
them—bringing swift destruction on
themselves. 2Even so, many will follow
their licentious ways, and because of
these teachers[l] the way of truth will be
maligned. 3And in their greed they will
exploit you with deceptive words. Their
condemnation, pronounced against
them long ago, has not been idle, and
their destruction is not asleep.
4 For if God did not spare the angels
when they sinned, but cast them into
hell[m] and committed them to chains[n]
of deepest darkness to be kept until the
judgement; 5and if he did not spare the
ancient world, even though he saved
Noah, a herald of righteousness, with
seven others, when he brought a flood
on a world of the ungodly; 6and if by
turning the cities of Sodom and Gomorrah to ashes he condemned them
to extinction[o] and made them an example of what is coming to the ungodly;[p]
7and if he rescued Lot, a righteous man
greatly distressed by the licentiousness
of the lawless 8(for that righteous man,
living among them day after day, was
tormented in his righteous soul by their
lawless deeds that he saw and heard),
9then the Lord knows how to rescue the
godly from trial, and to keep the unrighteous under punishment until the day
of judgement 10—especially those who
indulge their flesh in depraved lust, and
who despise authority.
Bold and wilful, they are not afraid
to slander the glorious ones,[q] 11where-
as angels, though greater in might and
power, do not bring against them a
slanderous judgement from the Lord.[r]
12These people, however, are like irrational animals, mere creatures of instinct,
born to be caught and killed. They slander what they do not understand, and
when those creatures are destroyed,[s]
they also will be destroyed, 13suffering[t]
the penalty for doing wrong. They count
it a pleasure to revel in the daytime.
They are blots and blemishes, revelling
in their dissipation[u] while they feast
with you. 14They have eyes full of adultery, insatiable for sin. They entice unsteady souls. They have hearts trained
in greed. Accursed children! 15They have
left the straight road and have gone
astray, following the road of Balaam
son of Bosor,[v] who loved the wages of
doing wrong, 16but was rebuked for his
own transgression; a speechless donkey spoke with a human voice and restrained the prophet's madness.
17 These are waterless springs and
mists driven by a storm; for them the
deepest darkness has been reserved.

[h] 1.13 Gk *tent* [i] 1.14 Gk *the putting off of my tent* [j] 1.17 Other ancient authorities read *my beloved Son* [k] 1.21 Other ancient authorities read *but moved by the Holy Spirit saints of God spoke* [l] 2.2 Gk *because of them* [m] 2.4 Gk *Tartaros* [n] 2.4 Other ancient authorities read *pits* [o] 2.6 Other ancient authorities lack *to extinction* [p] 2.6 Other ancient authorities read *an example to those who were to be ungodly* [q] 2.10 Or *angels*; Gk *glories* [r] 2.11 Other ancient authorities read *before the Lord*; others lack the phrase [s] 2.12 Gk *in their destruction* [t] 2.13 Other ancient authorities read *receiving* [u] 2.13 Other ancient authorities read *love-feasts* [v] 2.15 Other ancient authorities read *Beor*

18 For they speak bombastic nonsense,
and with licentious desires of the flesh
they entice people who have just[w] escaped from those who live in error.
19 They promise them freedom, but they
themselves are slaves of corruption; for
people are slaves to whatever masters
them. 20 For if, after they have escaped
the defilements of the world through
the knowledge of our Lord and Saviour
Jesus Christ, they are again entangled
in them and overpowered, the last state
has become worse for them than the
first. 21 For it would have been better for
them never to have known the way of
righteousness than, after knowing it,
to turn back from the holy commandment that was passed on to them. 22 It
has happened to them according to the
true proverb,

'The dog turns back to its own vomit',
and,
'The sow is washed only to
wallow in the mud.'

THE PROMISE OF THE LORD'S COMING

3 This is now, beloved, the second
letter I am writing to you; in them
I am trying to arouse your sincere intention by reminding you 2 that you
should remember the words spoken in
the past by the holy prophets, and the
commandment of the Lord and Saviour
spoken through your apostles. 3 First of
all you must understand this, that in
the last days scoffers will come, scoffing
and indulging their own lusts 4 and saying, 'Where is the promise of his coming? For ever since our ancestors died,[x]
all things continue as they were from
the beginning of creation!' 5 They deliberately ignore this fact, that by the
word of God heavens existed long ago
and an earth was formed out of water
and by means of water, 6 through which
the world of that time was deluged with
water and perished. 7 But by the same
word the present heavens and earth
have been reserved for fire, being kept
until the day of judgement and destruction of the godless.

8 But do not ignore this one fact, beloved, that with the Lord one day is like
a thousand years, and a thousand years
are like one day. 9 The Lord is not slow
about his promise, as some think of
slowness, but is patient with you,[y] not
wanting any to perish, but all to come
to repentance. 10 But the day of the Lord
will come like a thief, and then the heavens will pass away with a loud noise,
and the elements will be dissolved with
fire, and the earth and everything that
is done on it will be disclosed.[z]

11 Since all these things are to be dissolved in this way, what sort of people
ought you to be in leading lives of holiness and godliness, 12 waiting for and
hastening[a] the coming of the day of
God, because of which the heavens will
be set ablaze and dissolved, and the elements will melt with fire? 13 But, in accordance with his promise, we wait for
new heavens and a new earth, where
righteousness is at home.

FINAL EXHORTATION AND DOXOLOGY

14 Therefore, beloved, while you are
waiting for these things, strive to be
found by him at peace, without spot or
blemish; 15 and regard the patience of our
Lord as salvation. So also our beloved
brother Paul wrote to you according to
the wisdom given to him, 16 speaking of
this as he does in all his letters. There
are some things in them hard to understand, which the ignorant and unstable
twist to their own destruction, as they
do the other scriptures. 17 You therefore,
beloved, since you are forewarned, beware that you are not carried away with
the error of the lawless and lose your
own stability. 18 But grow in the grace
and knowledge of our Lord and Saviour
Jesus Christ. To him be the glory both
now and to the day of eternity. Amen.[b]

[w] **2.18** Other ancient authorities read *actually*
[x] **3.4** Gk *our fathers fell asleep* [y] **3.9** Other ancient authorities read *on your account*
[z] **3.10** Other ancient authorities read *will be burned up* [a] **3.12** Or *earnestly desiring*
[b] **3.18** Other ancient authorities lack *Amen*

The First Letter of JOHN

The First Letter of John was probably written at the end of the first century or the beginning of the second. It is more like a theological essay than a letter. In terms of language and style, it seems to have been written by the same author as the Gospel of John. Although scholars do not believe that the Gospel or the Letters of John are from the actual hand of the apostle, most do believe that the Letter comes from the same early Christian community or "school" as the Gospel that bears the apostle's name.

First John seems to address those who oppose the traditional beliefs about Jesus that were held by the Johannine community (2.21–22; 4.1–2). Scholars suggest that false teachings influenced by docetism had infiltrated the community. These false teachings denied the humanity of Jesus and the value of his actual death. The ideas seemed to spiritualize Jesus' life and death and to separate Christ's divinity so it did not become tainted by his humanity. First John emphasizes the saving reality of the humanity of Christ and the connection between knowledge of God and the commandment to love one's neighbor. Readers of this Letter will recognize the contrasting images between light and darkness, truth and error, worldly life and eternal life so typical of John's Gospel.

Passages from 1 John are read during the seven Sunday liturgies of the Easter season during Year B of the liturgical calendar. The Letter's proclamation that "God is love" reverberates throughout the ages whenever it is read: "God is love, and those who abide in love abide in God, and God abides in them" (4.16).

THE WORD OF LIFE

1 We declare to you what was from
the beginning, what we have heard,
what we have seen with our eyes, what
we have looked at and touched with our
hands, concerning the word of life—
2this life was revealed, and we have
seen it and testify to it, and declare to
you the eternal life that was with the
Father and was revealed to us— 3we
declare to you what we have seen and
heard so that you also may have fellowship with us; and truly our fellowship is
with the Father and with his Son Jesus
Christ. 4We are writing these things so
that our[a] joy may be complete.

GOD IS LIGHT

5 This is the message we have heard
from him and proclaim to you, that
God is light and in him there is no
darkness at all. 6If we say that we have
fellowship with him while we are walking in darkness, we lie and do not do
what is true; 7but if we walk in the
light as he himself is in the light, we
have fellowship with one another, and
the blood of Jesus his Son cleanses us
from all sin. 8If we say that we have no
sin, we deceive ourselves, and the truth
is not in us. 9If we confess our sins, he
who is faithful and just will forgive us
our sins and cleanse us from all unrighteousness. 10If we say that we have not
sinned, we make him a liar, and his
word is not in us.

[a] 1.4 Other ancient authorities read *your*

CHRIST OUR ADVOCATE

2 My little children, I am writing
these things to you so that you
may not sin. But if anyone does sin, we
have an advocate with the Father, Jesus
Christ the righteous; 2and he is the
atoning sacrifice for our sins, and not
for ours only but also for the sins of the
whole world.
3 Now by this we may be sure that
we know him, if we obey his commandments. 4Whoever says, 'I have come to
know him', but does not obey his commandments, is a liar, and in such a person the truth does not exist; 5but whoever obeys his word, truly in this person
the love of God has reached perfection.
By this we may be sure that we are in
him: 6whoever says, 'I abide in him',
ought to walk just as he walked.

A NEW COMMANDMENT

7 Beloved, I am writing you no new
commandment, but an old commandment that you have had from the beginning; the old commandment is the word
that you have heard. 8Yet I am writing
you a new commandment that is true
in him and in you, because[b] the darkness is passing away and the true light
is already shining. 9Whoever says, 'I am
in the light', while hating a brother or
sister,[c] is still in the darkness. 10Who-
ever loves a brother or sister[d] lives in
the light, and in such a person[e] there is
no cause for stumbling. 11But whoever
hates another believer[f] is in the darkness, walks in the darkness, and does
not know the way to go, because the
darkness has brought on blindness.

12 I am writing to you, little children,
because your sins are forgiven
on account of his name.
13 I am writing to you, fathers,
because you know him who is
from the beginning.
I am writing to you, young people,
because you have conquered
the evil one.
14 I write to you, children,
because you know the Father.
I write to you, fathers,
because you know him who is
from the beginning.
I write to you, young people,
because you are strong
and the word of God abides in you,
and you have overcome
the evil one.

15 Do not love the world or the things
in the world. The love of the Father is
not in those who love the world; 16for all
that is in the world—the desire of the
flesh, the desire of the eyes, the pride in
riches—comes not from the Father but
from the world. 17And the world and its
desire[g] are passing away, but those who
do the will of God live for ever.

WARNING AGAINST ANTICHRISTS

18 Children, it is the last hour! As
you have heard that antichrist is coming, so now many antichrists have
come. From this we know that it is the
last hour. 19They went out from us, but
they did not belong to us; for if they
had belonged to us, they would have remained with us. But by going out they
made it plain that none of them belongs
to us. 20But you have been anointed by
the Holy One, and all of you have knowledge.[h] 21I write to you, not because you
do not know the truth, but because you
know it, and you know that no lie comes
from the truth. 22Who is the liar but the
one who denies that Jesus is the Christ?[i]
This is the antichrist, the one who denies the Father and the Son. 23No one
who denies the Son has the Father; everyone who confesses the Son has the
Father also. 24Let what you heard from
the beginning abide in you. If what you
heard from the beginning abides in
you, then you will abide in the Son and
in the Father. 25And this is what he has
promised us,[j] eternal life.
26 I write these things to you concerning those who would deceive you.
27As for you, the anointing that you received from him abides in you, and so
you do not need anyone to teach you.
But as his anointing teaches you about
all things, and is true and is not a lie,
and just as it has taught you, abide in
him.[k]
28 And now, little children, abide
in him, so that when he is revealed we
may have confidence and not be put to
shame before him at his coming.

CHILDREN OF GOD

29 If you know that he is righteous,
you may be sure that everyone who does
3 right has been born of him. 1See
what love the Father has given us,

[b] 2.8 Or *that* [c] 2.9 Gk *hating a brother* [d] 2.10 Gk *loves a brother* [e] 2.10 Or *in it* [f] 2.11 Gk *hates a brother* [g] 2.17 Or *the desire for it* [h] 2.20 Other ancient authorities read *you know all things* [i] 2.22 Or *the Messiah* [j] 2.25 Other ancient authorities read *you* [k] 2.27 Or *it*

that we should be called children of God;
and that is what we are. The reason the
world does not know us is that it did
not know him. 2Beloved, we are God's
children now; what we will be has not
yet been revealed. What we do know is
this: when he[l] is revealed, we will be like
him, for we will see him as he is. 3And
all who have this hope in him purify
themselves, just as he is pure.

4 Everyone who commits sin is
guilty of lawlessness; sin is lawlessness.
5You know that he was revealed to take
away sins, and in him there is no sin.
6No one who abides in him sins; no one
who sins has either seen him or known
him. 7Little children, let no one deceive
you. Everyone who does what is right is
righteous, just as he is righteous. 8Ev-
eryone who commits sin is a child of
the devil; for the devil has been sinning
from the beginning. The Son of God was
revealed for this purpose, to destroy the
works of the devil. 9Those who have
been born of God do not sin, because
God's seed abides in them;[m] they cannot
sin, because they have been born of God.
10The children of God and the children
of the devil are revealed in this way:
all who do not do what is right are not
from God, nor are those who do not love
their brothers and sisters.[n]

LOVE ONE ANOTHER

11 For this is the message you have
heard from the beginning, that we
should love one another. 12We must not
be like Cain who was from the evil one
and murdered his brother. And why
did he murder him? Because his own
deeds were evil and his brother's righteous. 13Do not be astonished, brothers
and sisters,[o] that the world hates you.
14We know that we have passed from
death to life because we love one another. Whoever does not love abides in
death. 15All who hate a brother or sister[p] are murderers, and you know that
murderers do not have eternal life abiding in them. 16We know love by this,
that he laid down his life for us—and
we ought to lay down our lives for one
another. 17How does God's love abide in
anyone who has the world's goods and
sees a brother or sister[q] in need and yet
refuses help?

18 Little children, let us love, not in
word or speech, but in truth and action. 19And by this we will know that
we are from the truth and will reassure
our hearts before him 20whenever our
hearts condemn us; for God is greater
than our hearts, and he knows everything. 21Beloved, if our hearts do not
condemn us, we have boldness before
God; 22and we receive from him whatever we ask, because we obey his commandments and do what pleases him.

23 And this is his commandment,
that we should believe in the name of his
Son Jesus Christ and love one another,
just as he has commanded us. 24All who
obey his commandments abide in him,
and he abides in them. And by this we
know that he abides in us, by the Spirit
that he has given us.

TESTING THE SPIRITS

4 Beloved, do not believe every spirit,
but test the spirits to see whether
they are from God; for many false prophets have gone out into the world. 2By
this you know the Spirit of God: every
spirit that confesses that Jesus Christ
has come in the flesh is from God, 3and
every spirit that does not confess Jesus[r]
is not from God. And this is the spirit of
the antichrist, of which you have heard
that it is coming; and now it is already
in the world. 4Little children, you are
from God, and have conquered them;
for the one who is in you is greater than
the one who is in the world. 5They are
from the world; therefore what they say
is from the world, and the world listens
to them. 6We are from God. Whoever
knows God listens to us, and whoever is
not from God does not listen to us. From
this we know the spirit of truth and the
spirit of error.

GOD IS LOVE

7 Beloved, let us love one another,
because love is from God; everyone who
loves is born of God and knows God.
8Whoever does not love does not know
God, for God is love. 9God's love was revealed among us in this way: God sent
his only Son into the world so that we
might live through him. 10In this is
love, not that we loved God but that he
loved us and sent his Son to be the atoning sacrifice for our sins. 11Beloved, since
God loved us so much, we also ought to
love one another. 12No one has ever seen
God; if we love one another, God lives in
us, and his love is perfected in us.

[l] **3.2** Or *it* [m] **3.9** Or *because the children of God abide in him* [n] **3.10** Gk *his brother* [o] **3.13** Gk *brothers* [p] **3.15** Gk *his brother* [q] **3.17** Gk *brother* [r] **4.3** Other ancient authorities read *does away with Jesus* (Gk *dissolves Jesus*)

13 By this we know that we abide in
him and he in us, because he has given
us of his Spirit. 14 And we have seen and
do testify that the Father has sent his
Son as the Saviour of the world. 15 God
abides in those who confess that Jesus is
the Son of God, and they abide in God.
16 So we have known and believe the
love that God has for us.

God is love, and those who abide in
love abide in God, and God abides in
them. 17 Love has been perfected among
us in this: that we may have boldness on
the day of judgement, because as he is,
so are we in this world. 18 There is no fear
in love, but perfect love casts out fear;
for fear has to do with punishment, and
whoever fears has not reached perfection in love. 19 We love[s] because he first
loved us. 20 Those who say, 'I love God',
and hate their brothers or sisters,[t] are liars; for those who do not love a brother
or sister[u] whom they have seen, cannot love God whom they have not seen.
21 The commandment we have from him
is this: those who love God must love
their brothers and sisters[v] also.

FAITH CONQUERS THE WORLD

5 Everyone who believes that Jesus
is the Christ[w] has been born of
God, and everyone who loves the parent loves the child. 2 By this we know
that we love the children of God, when
we love God and obey his commandments. 3 For the love of God is this, that
we obey his commandments. And his
commandments are not burdensome,
4 for whatever is born of God conquers
the world. And this is the victory that
conquers the world, our faith. 5 Who is
it that conquers the world but the one
who believes that Jesus is the Son of
God?

TESTIMONY CONCERNING THE SON OF GOD

6 This is the one who came by water
and blood, Jesus Christ, not with the
water only but with the water and the
blood. And the Spirit is the one that testifies, for the Spirit is the truth. 7 There
are three that testify:[x] 8 the Spirit and
the water and the blood, and these three
agree. 9 If we receive human testimony,
the testimony of God is greater; for this
is the testimony of God that he has testified to his Son. 10 Those who believe in
the Son of God have the testimony in
their hearts. Those who do not believe
in God[y] have made him a liar by not believing in the testimony that God has
given concerning his Son. 11 And this is
the testimony: God gave us eternal life,
and this life is in his Son. 12 Whoever has
the Son has life; whoever does not have
the Son of God does not have life.

EPILOGUE

13 I write these things to you who
believe in the name of the Son of God,
so that you may know that you have
eternal life.

14 And this is the boldness we have
in him, that if we ask anything according to his will, he hears us. 15 And if we
know that he hears us in whatever we
ask, we know that we have obtained
the requests made of him. 16 If you see
your brother or sister[z] committing
what is not a mortal sin, you will ask,
and God[a] will give life to such a one—to
those whose sin is not mortal. There is
sin that is mortal; I do not say that you
should pray about that. 17 All wrongdoing is sin, but there is sin that is not
mortal.

18 We know that those who are born
of God do not sin, but the one who was
born of God protects them, and the evil
one does not touch them. 19 We know
that we are God's children, and that the
whole world lies under the power of the
evil one. 20 And we know that the Son
of God has come and has given us understanding so that we may know him
who is true;[b] and we are in him who is
true, in his Son Jesus Christ. He is the
true God and eternal life.

21 Little children, keep yourselves
from idols.[c]

[s] **4.19** Other ancient authorities add *him*; others add *God* [t] **4.20** Gk *brothers* [u] **4.20** Gk *brother* [v] **4.21** Gk *brothers* [w] **5.1** Or *the Messiah* [x] **5.7** A few other authorities read (with variations) *7There are three that testify in heaven, the Father, the Word, and the Holy Spirit, and these three are one. 8And there are three that testify on earth:* [y] **5.10** Other ancient authorities read *in the Son* [z] **5.16** Gk *your brother* [a] **5.16** Gk *he* [b] **5.20** Other ancient authorities read *know the true God* [c] **5.21** Other ancient authorities add *Amen*

The Second Letter of

JOHN

The Second Letter of John has an opening salutation from the "elder" to the "elect lady," which is probably a metaphor for a local church community. It also contains a closing greeting and is similar to a more typical letter because of these formularies. This is the shortest of the New Testament writings, being only 13 verses in length. It too was written at the end of the first century like the other Letters of John. The author is a person of authority, but probably not the apostle John (see Introductions to the Gospel of John and 1 John).

The only passage from 2 John that is contained in the liturgical calendar is one that is read in Year II of the weekday lectionary on the Friday of the Thirty-Second Week of Ordinary Time. In that passage, the author makes a request: "Let us love one another. And this is love, that we walk according to his commandments; this is the commandment just as you heard it from the beginning—you must walk in it" (vv. 5–6). This emphasis on the commandment of love is characteristic of the writings in the New Testament that bear John's name.

SALUTATION

1 The elder to the elect lady and her
children, whom I love in the truth, and
not only I but also all who know the
truth, 2because of the truth that abides
in us and will be with us for ever:
3 Grace, mercy, and peace will be
with us from God the Father and from[a]
Jesus Christ, the Father's Son, in truth
and love.

TRUTH AND LOVE

4 I was overjoyed to find some of your
children walking in the truth, just as we
have been commanded by the Father.
5But now, dear lady, I ask you, not as
though I were writing you a new commandment, but one we have had from
the beginning, let us love one another.
6And this is love, that we walk according
to his commandments; this is the commandment just as you have heard it from
the beginning—you must walk in it.
7 Many deceivers have gone out
into the world, those who do not confess that Jesus Christ has come in the
flesh; any such person is the deceiver
and the antichrist! 8Be on your guard,
so that you do not lose what we[b] have
worked for, but may receive a full reward. 9Everyone who does not abide in
the teaching of Christ, but goes beyond
it, does not have God; whoever abides in
the teaching has both the Father and
the Son. 10Do not receive into the house
or welcome anyone who comes to you
and does not bring this teaching; 11for
to welcome is to participate in the evil
deeds of such a person.

FINAL GREETINGS

12 Although I have much to write to
you, I would rather not use paper and
ink; instead I hope to come to you and
talk with you face to face, so that our joy
may be complete.
13 The children of your elect sister
send you their greetings.[c]

[a] 3 Other ancient authorities add *the Lord*
[b] 8 Other ancient authorities read *you*
[c] 13 Other ancient authorities add *Amen*

The Third Letter of

JOHN

The Third Letter of John was addressed to a particular individual named Gaius. The purpose of this brief writing (a total of 15 verses) was to commend a person named Demetrius and his companions to the hospitality of Gaius. Gaius seems to be a trusted personal acquaintance of the author's. Apparently, another church leader, Diotrephes, is not so welcoming and is accused by the author of the Letter to be one "who likes to put himself first" and who resists the elder's authority (v. 9).

A passage from 3 John is read in Year II of the weekday lectionary on the Saturday of the Thirty-Second Week (vv. 5–8). Through the reading of this passage, hospitality and support of co-workers in the faith are encouraged throughout the church.

SALUTATION

1 The elder to the beloved Gaius, whom I love in truth.

GAIUS COMMENDED FOR HIS HOSPITALITY

2 Beloved, I pray that all may go well with you and that you may be in good health, just as it is well with your soul. 3I was overjoyed when some of the friends[a] arrived and testified to your faithfulness to the truth, namely, how you walk in the truth. 4I have no greater joy than this, to hear that my children are walking in the truth.

5 Beloved, you do faithfully whatever you do for the friends,[b] even though they are strangers to you; 6they have testified to your love before the church. You will do well to send them on in a manner worthy of God; 7for they began their journey for the sake of Christ,[c] accepting no support from non-believers.[d] 8Therefore we ought to support such people, so that we may become co-workers with the truth.

DIOTREPHES AND DEMETRIUS

9 I have written something to the church; but Diotrephes, who likes to put himself first, does not acknowledge our authority. 10So if I come, I will call attention to what he is doing in spreading false charges against us. And not content with those charges, he refuses to welcome the friends,[e] and even prevents those who want to do so and expels them from the church.

11 Beloved, do not imitate what is evil but imitate what is good. Whoever does good is from God; whoever does evil has not seen God. 12Everyone has testified favourably about Demetrius, and so has the truth itself. We also testify for him,[f] and you know that our testimony is true.

FINAL GREETINGS

13 I have much to write to you, but I would rather not write with pen and ink; 14instead I hope to see you soon, and we will talk together face to face.

15 Peace to you. The friends send you their greetings. Greet the friends there, each by name.

[a] 3 Gk *brothers* [b] 5 Gk *brothers* [c] 7 Gk *for the sake of the name* [d] 7 Gk *the Gentiles* [e] 10 Gk *brothers* [f] 12 Gk lacks *for him*

The Letter of JUDE

The author of the Letter of Jude may or may not have been one of the brothers of Jesus mentioned in Mark 6.3. Little is known about Jude, and the Letter attributed to him could have been composed while Jude was still alive. The precise date, place of composition, and actual author of the brief Letter (25 verses) cannot be determined with certainty.

The Letter warns against false teachers or "intruders" who are beginning to circulate among various Christian communities. There is no explicitly designated group or church community as the intended recipients of this Letter. Apparently, some who claimed to be spiritually enlightened also presented themselves to be above any moral authority and acted as they pleased (v. 4), even indulging in sexual immorality (v. 7). This Letter opposes them harshly (vv. 5–16). It exhorts the community members to keep themselves "in the love of God" (v. 21). Finally, it ends with an elaborate doxology (vv. 24–25).

A passage from the Letter of Jude is read during Year II on Saturday of the Eighth Week of the Year and offers this majestic concluding doxology: "Now to him who is able to keep you from falling, and to make you stand without blemish in the presence of his glory with rejoicing, to the only God our Saviour, through Jesus Christ our Lord, be glory, majesty, power, and authority, before all time and now and for ever. Amen" (vv. 24–25).

SALUTATION

1 Jude,[a] a servant[b] of Jesus Christ and brother of James,

To those who are called, who are beloved[c] in[d] God the Father and kept safe for[e] Jesus Christ:

2 May mercy, peace, and love be yours in abundance.

OCCASION OF THE LETTER

3 Beloved, while eagerly preparing to write to you about the salvation we share, I find it necessary to write and appeal to you to contend for the faith that was once for all entrusted to the saints. 4For certain intruders have stolen in among you, people who long ago were designated for this condemnation as ungodly, who pervert the grace of our God into licentiousness and deny our only Master and Lord, Jesus Christ.[f]

JUDGEMENT ON FALSE TEACHERS

5 Now I desire to remind you, though you are fully informed, that the Lord, who once for all saved[g] a people out of the land of Egypt, afterwards destroyed those who did not believe. 6And the angels who did not keep their own position, but left their proper dwelling, he has kept in eternal chains in deepest darkness for the judgement of the great day. 7Likewise, Sodom and Gomorrah and the surrounding cities, which, in the same manner as they, indulged in sexual immorality and pursued unnatural lust,[h] serve as an example by undergoing a punishment of eternal fire.

8 Yet in the same way these dreamers also defile the flesh, reject authority, and slander the glorious ones.[i] 9But when the archangel Michael contended with the devil and disputed about the

[a] 1 Gk *Judas* [b] 1 Gk *slave* [c] 1 Other ancient authorities read *sanctified* [d] 1 Or *by* [e] 1 Or *by*
[f] 4 Or *the only Master and our Lord Jesus Christ*
[g] 5 Other ancient authorities read *though you were once for all fully informed, that Jesus* (or *Joshua*) *who saved* [h] 7 Gk *went after other flesh*
[i] 8 Or *angels*; Gk *glories*

body of Moses, he did not dare to bring a condemnation of slander[j] against him, but said, 'The Lord rebuke you!' 10 But these people slander whatever they do not understand, and they are destroyed by those things that, like irrational animals, they know by instinct. 11 Woe to them! For they go the way of Cain, and abandon themselves to Balaam's error for the sake of gain, and perish in Korah's rebellion. 12 These are blemishes[k] on your love-feasts, while they feast with you without fear, feeding themselves.[l] They are waterless clouds carried along by the winds; autumn trees without fruit, twice dead, uprooted; 13 wild waves of the sea, casting up the foam of their own shame; wandering stars, for whom the deepest darkness has been reserved for ever.

14 It was also about these that Enoch, in the seventh generation from Adam, prophesied, saying, 'See, the Lord is coming[m] with tens of thousands of his holy ones, 15 to execute judgement on all, and to convict everyone of all the deeds of ungodliness that they have committed in such an ungodly way, and of all the harsh things that ungodly sinners have spoken against him.' 16 These are grumblers and malcontents; they indulge their own lusts; they are bombastic in speech, flattering people to their own advantage.

WARNINGS AND EXHORTATIONS

17 But you, beloved, must remember the predictions of the apostles of our Lord Jesus Christ; 18 for they said to you, 'In the last time there will be scoffers, indulging their own ungodly lusts.' 19 It is these worldly people, devoid of the Spirit, who are causing divisions. 20 But you, beloved, build yourselves up on your most holy faith; pray in the Holy Spirit; 21 keep yourselves in the love of God; look forward to the mercy of our Lord Jesus Christ that leads to[n] eternal life. 22 And have mercy on some who are wavering; 23 save others by snatching them out of the fire; and have mercy on still others with fear, hating even the tunic defiled by their bodies.[o]

BENEDICTION

24 Now to him who is able to keep you from falling, and to make you stand without blemish in the presence of his glory with rejoicing, 25 to the only God our Saviour, through Jesus Christ our Lord, be glory, majesty, power, and authority, before all time and now and for ever. Amen.

[j] **9** Or *condemnation for blasphemy* [k] **12** Or *reefs* [l] **12** Or *without fear. They are shepherds who care only for themselves* [m] **14** Gk *came* [n] **21** Gk *Christ to* [o] **23** Gk *by the flesh*. The Greek text of verses 22–23 is uncertain at several points

The
REVELATION
to John

The book of Revelation seems to have been written during a time of persecution of Christians such as that of Nero in 64 CE or as late as during the time of the reign of Domitian (81–96). The author is probably not John the Apostle, but a disciple of his or another Christian leader who claimed to be living in exile on the island of Patmos. This final book of the Bible is a specific kind of writing called apocalyptic literature and is the only book of the Old Testament or the New Testament that is totally written in this style. Other books of the Bible contain apocalyptic parts, such as Daniel 7–12 and Mark 13.

Apocalyptic writing is very imaginative, with strange stories of cosmic visions told through many wild symbols and allegories that seek to convey the meaning of present or future spiritual events. The book of Revelation speaks about the coming of a future age when present human history, with its conflict between good and evil, will come to an end in a decisive victory by God over evil. A new heaven and a new earth will be established, where God's faithful people will live with God forever (21.1–7).

The author of Revelation writes about a guided tour of the heavenly realm, where he sees visions of the future earth. In the context of the writing of this book, the author gives assurance to persecuted Christians that neither the Roman Empire, the evil empire of its age, nor the Roman emperor, the antichrist, will be victorious in the battle between good and evil. Instead, the message of the book of Revelation is that God ultimately will bring victory to those who remain faithful to Christ through the present time.

Selections from the book of Revelation are read during the Sundays following Easter in Year C. A passage is also read every year at the Chrism Mass on Holy Thursday, when the church gives praise to Christ and recalls its own identity in Christ: "To him who loves us and freed us from our sins by his blood, and made us to be a kingdom, priests serving his God and Father, to him be glory and dominion for ever and ever. Amen" (1.5–6). This same passage is also read in Year B on the last Sunday of Ordinary Time or the Feast of Christ the King.

INTRODUCTION AND SALUTATION

1 The revelation of Jesus Christ,
which God gave him to show his
servants[a] what must soon take place;
he made[b] it known by sending his angel to his servant[c] John, 2who testified
to the word of God and to the testimony
of Jesus Christ, even to all that he saw.
3 Blessed is the one who reads aloud
the words of the prophecy, and blessed
are those who hear and who keep what
is written in it; for the time is near.

4 John to the seven churches that are
in Asia:
Grace to you and peace from him who
is and who was and who is to come, and
from the seven spirits who are before
his throne, 5and from Jesus Christ, the
faithful witness, the firstborn of the
dead, and the ruler of the kings of the
earth.

[a] 1.1 Gk *slaves* [b] 1.1 Gk *and he made* [c] 1.1 Gk *slave*

To him who loves us and freed[d] us
from our sins by his blood, 6and made[e]
us to be a kingdom, priests serving[f] his
God and Father, to him be glory and dominion for ever and ever. Amen.

7 Look! He is coming with the clouds;
  every eye will see him,
even those who pierced him;
  and on his account all the tribes
    of the earth will wail.
So it is to be. Amen.

8 'I am the Alpha and the Omega',
says the Lord God, who is and who was
and who is to come, the Almighty.

A VISION OF CHRIST

9 I, John, your brother who share
with you in Jesus the persecution and
the kingdom and the patient endurance, was on the island called Patmos
because of the word of God and the testimony of Jesus.[g] 10I was in the spirit[h]
on the Lord's day, and I heard behind
me a loud voice like a trumpet 11saying,
'Write in a book what you see and send
it to the seven churches, to Ephesus, to
Smyrna, to Pergamum, to Thyatira, to
Sardis, to Philadelphia, and to Laodicea.'

12 Then I turned to see whose voice it
was that spoke to me, and on turning I
saw seven golden lampstands, 13and in
the midst of the lampstands I saw one
like the Son of Man, clothed with a long
robe and with a golden sash across his
chest. 14His head and his hair were white
as white wool, white as snow; his eyes
were like a flame of fire, 15his feet were
like burnished bronze, refined as in a furnace, and his voice was like the sound of
many waters. 16In his right hand he held
seven stars, and from his mouth came
a sharp, two-edged sword, and his face
was like the sun shining with full force.

17 When I saw him, I fell at his feet
as though dead. But he placed his right
hand on me, saying, 'Do not be afraid; I
am the first and the last, 18and the living one. I was dead, and see, I am alive
for ever and ever; and I have the keys of
Death and of Hades. 19Now write what
you have seen, what is, and what is to
take place after this. 20As for the mystery of the seven stars that you saw in
my right hand, and the seven golden
lampstands: the seven stars are the angels of the seven churches, and the seven
lampstands are the seven churches.

THE MESSAGE TO EPHESUS

2 'To the angel of the church in Ephesus write: These are the words of
him who holds the seven stars in his
right hand, who walks among the seven
golden lampstands:

2 'I know your works, your toil and
your patient endurance. I know that
you cannot tolerate evildoers; you have
tested those who claim to be apostles
but are not, and have found them to
be false. 3I also know that you are enduring patiently and bearing up for the
sake of my name, and that you have not
grown weary. 4But I have this against
you, that you have abandoned the love
you had at first. 5Remember then from
what you have fallen; repent, and do the
works you did at first. If not, I will come
to you and remove your lampstand from
its place, unless you repent. 6Yet this is
to your credit: you hate the works of the
Nicolaitans, which I also hate. 7Let anyone who has an ear listen to what the
Spirit is saying to the churches. To everyone who conquers, I will give permission to eat from the tree of life that
is in the paradise of God.

THE MESSAGE TO SMYRNA

8 'And to the angel of the church in
Smyrna write: These are the words of
the first and the last, who was dead and
came to life:

9 'I know your affliction and your
poverty, even though you are rich. I
know the slander on the part of those
who say that they are Jews and are not,
but are a synagogue of Satan. 10Do not
fear what you are about to suffer. Beware, the devil is about to throw some
of you into prison so that you may be
tested, and for ten days you will have
affliction. Be faithful until death, and I
will give you the crown of life. 11Let anyone who has an ear listen to what the
Spirit is saying to the churches. Whoever conquers will not be harmed by the
second death.

THE MESSAGE TO PERGAMUM

12 'And to the angel of the church in
Pergamum write: These are the words
of him who has the sharp two-edged
sword:

13 'I know where you are living,
where Satan's throne is. Yet you are
holding fast to my name, and you did not
deny your faith in me[i] even in the days
of Antipas my witness, my faithful one,

[d] 1.5 Other ancient authorities read *washed*
[e] 1.6 Gk *and he made* [f] 1.6 Gk *priests to*
[g] 1.9 Or *testimony to Jesus* [h] 1.10 Or *in the Spirit* [i] 2.13 Or *deny my faith*

who was killed among you, where Satan
lives. 14But I have a few things against
you: you have some there who hold to
the teaching of Balaam, who taught Balak to put a stumbling-block before the
people of Israel, so that they would eat
food sacrificed to idols and practise fornication. 15So you also have some who
hold to the teaching of the Nicolaitans.
16Repent then. If not, I will come to you
soon and make war against them with
the sword of my mouth. 17Let anyone
who has an ear listen to what the Spirit
is saying to the churches. To everyone
who conquers I will give some of the
hidden manna, and I will give a white
stone, and on the white stone is written
a new name that no one knows except
the one who receives it.

THE MESSAGE TO THYATIRA

18 'And to the angel of the church
in Thyatira write: These are the words
of the Son of God, who has eyes like a
flame of fire, and whose feet are like
burnished bronze:

19 'I know your works—your love,
faith, service, and patient endurance. I
know that your last works are greater
than the first. 20But I have this against
you: you tolerate that woman Jezebel,
who calls herself a prophet and is teaching and beguiling my servants[j] to practise fornication and to eat food sacrificed
to idols. 21I gave her time to repent, but
she refuses to repent of her fornication.
22Beware, I am throwing her on a bed,
and those who commit adultery with
her I am throwing into great distress,
unless they repent of her doings; 23and I
will strike her children dead. And all the
churches will know that I am the one
who searches minds and hearts, and I
will give to each of you as your works
deserve. 24But to the rest of you in Thyatira, who do not hold this teaching, who
have not learned what some call "the
deep things of Satan", to you I say, I do
not lay on you any other burden; 25only
hold fast to what you have until I come.
26To everyone who conquers and continues to do my works to the end,

I will give authority over
  the nations;
27 to rule[k] them with an iron rod,
  as when clay pots are shattered—

28even as I also received authority from
my Father. To the one who conquers I
will also give the morning star. 29Let
anyone who has an ear listen to what
the Spirit is saying to the churches.

THE MESSAGE TO SARDIS

3 'And to the angel of the church in
Sardis write: These are the words
of him who has the seven spirits of God
and the seven stars:

'I know your works; you have a name
for being alive, but you are dead. 2Wake
up, and strengthen what remains and
is at the point of death, for I have not
found your works perfect in the sight
of my God. 3Remember then what you
received and heard; obey it, and repent.
If you do not wake up, I will come like
a thief, and you will not know at what
hour I will come to you. 4Yet you have
still a few people in Sardis who have not
soiled their clothes; they will walk with
me, dressed in white, for they are worthy. 5If you conquer, you will be clothed
like them in white robes, and I will not
blot your name out of the book of life;
I will confess your name before my Father and before his angels. 6Let anyone
who has an ear listen to what the Spirit
is saying to the churches.

THE MESSAGE TO PHILADELPHIA

7 'And to the angel of the church in
Philadelphia write:

These are the words of the holy
  one, the true one,
who has the key of David,
who opens and no one will shut,
  who shuts and no one opens:

8 'I know your works. Look, I have set
before you an open door, which no one
is able to shut. I know that you have but
little power, and yet you have kept my
word and have not denied my name. 9I
will make those of the synagogue of Satan who say that they are Jews and are
not, but are lying—I will make them
come and bow down before your feet,
and they will learn that I have loved you.
10Because you have kept my word of patient endurance, I will keep you from the
hour of trial that is coming on the whole
world to test the inhabitants of the
earth. 11I am coming soon; hold fast to
what you have, so that no one may seize
your crown. 12If you conquer, I will make
you a pillar in the temple of my God; you
will never go out of it. I will write on you
the name of my God, and the name of
the city of my God, the new Jerusalem
that comes down from my God out of
heaven, and my own new name. 13Let
anyone who has an ear listen to what the
Spirit is saying to the churches.

[j] **2.20** Gk *slaves* [k] **2.27** Or *to shepherd*

THE MESSAGE TO LAODICEA

14 'And to the angel of the church in Laodicea write: The words of the Amen, the faithful and true witness, the origin[l] of God's creation:

15 'I know your works; you are neither cold nor hot. I wish that you were either cold or hot. 16 So, because you are lukewarm, and neither cold nor hot, I am about to spit you out of my mouth. 17 For you say, "I am rich, I have prospered, and I need nothing." You do not realize that you are wretched, pitiable, poor, blind, and naked. 18 Therefore I counsel you to buy from me gold refined by fire so that you may be rich; and white robes to clothe you and to keep the shame of your nakedness from being seen; and salve to anoint your eyes so that you may see. 19 I reprove and discipline those whom I love. Be earnest, therefore, and repent. 20 Listen! I am standing at the door, knocking; if you hear my voice and open the door, I will come in to you and eat with you, and you with me. 21 To the one who conquers I will give a place with me on my throne, just as I myself conquered and sat down with my Father on his throne. 22 Let anyone who has an ear listen to what the Spirit is saying to the churches.'

THE HEAVENLY WORSHIP

4 After this I looked, and there in heaven a door stood open! And the first voice, which I had heard speaking to me like a trumpet, said, 'Come up here, and I will show you what must take place after this.' 2 At once I was in the spirit,[m] and there in heaven stood a throne, with one seated on the throne! 3 And the one seated there looks like jasper and cornelian, and around the throne is a rainbow that looks like an emerald. 4 Around the throne are twenty-four thrones, and seated on the thrones are twenty-four elders, dressed in white robes, with golden crowns on their heads. 5 Coming from the throne are flashes of lightning, and rumblings and peals of thunder, and in front of the throne burn seven flaming torches, which are the seven spirits of God; 6 and in front of the throne there is something like a sea of glass, like crystal.

Around the throne, and on each side of the throne, are four living creatures, full of eyes in front and behind: 7 the first living creature like a lion, the second living creature like an ox, the third living creature with a face like a human face, and the fourth living creature like a flying eagle. 8 And the four living creatures, each of them with six wings, are full of eyes all around and inside. Day and night without ceasing they sing,

'Holy, holy, holy,
the Lord God the Almighty,
who was and is and is to come.'

9 And whenever the living creatures give glory and honour and thanks to the one who is seated on the throne, who lives for ever and ever, 10 the twenty-four elders fall before the one who is seated on the throne and worship the one who lives for ever and ever; they cast their crowns before the throne, singing,

11 'You are worthy, our Lord and God,
to receive glory and honour
and power,
for you created all things,
and by your will they existed
and were created.'

THE SCROLL AND THE LAMB

5 Then I saw in the right hand of the one seated on the throne a scroll written on the inside and on the back, sealed[n] with seven seals; 2 and I saw a mighty angel proclaiming with a loud voice, 'Who is worthy to open the scroll and break its seals?' 3 And no one in heaven or on earth or under the earth was able to open the scroll or to look into it. 4 And I began to weep bitterly because no one was found worthy to open the scroll or to look into it. 5 Then one of the elders said to me, 'Do not weep. See, the Lion of the tribe of Judah, the Root of David, has conquered, so that he can open the scroll and its seven seals.'

6 Then I saw between the throne and the four living creatures and among the elders a Lamb standing as if it had been slaughtered, having seven horns and seven eyes, which are the seven spirits of God sent out into all the earth. 7 He went and took the scroll from the right hand of the one who was seated on the throne. 8 When he had taken the scroll, the four living creatures and the twenty-four elders fell before the Lamb, each holding a harp and golden bowls full of incense, which are the prayers of the saints. 9 They sing a new song:

'You are worthy to take the scroll
and to open its seals,

[l] **3.14** Or *beginning* [m] **4.2** Or *in the Spirit*
[n] **5.1** Or *written on the inside, and sealed on the back*

for you were slaughtered and by your
blood you ransomed for God
saints from[o] every tribe
and language and
people and nation;
10 you have made them to be a
kingdom and priests
serving[p] our God,
and they will reign on earth.'
11 Then I looked, and I heard the
voice of many angels surrounding the
throne and the living creatures and the
elders; they numbered myriads of myriads and thousands of thousands, 12sing-
ing with full voice,
'Worthy is the Lamb that
was slaughtered
to receive power and wealth and
wisdom and might
and honour and glory and blessing!'
13Then I heard every creature in heaven
and on earth and under the earth and in
the sea, and all that is in them, singing,
'To the one seated on the throne
and to the Lamb
be blessing and honour and
glory and might
for ever and ever!'
14And the four living creatures said,
'Amen!' And the elders fell down and
worshipped.

THE SEVEN SEALS

6 Then I saw the Lamb open one of
the seven seals, and I heard one of
the four living creatures call out, as with
a voice of thunder, 'Come!'[q] 2I looked,
and there was a white horse! Its rider
had a bow; a crown was given to him,
and he came out conquering and to conquer.
3 When he opened the second seal,
I heard the second living creature call
out, 'Come!'[r] 4And out came[s] another
horse, bright red; its rider was permitted to take peace from the earth, so that
people would slaughter one another;
and he was given a great sword.
5 When he opened the third seal, I
heard the third living creature call out,
'Come!'[t] I looked, and there was a black
horse! Its rider held a pair of scales in
his hand, 6and I heard what seemed to
be a voice in the midst of the four living
creatures saying, 'A quart of wheat for a
day's pay,[u] and three quarts of barley for
a day's pay,[v] but do not damage the olive
oil and the wine!'
7 When he opened the fourth seal,
I heard the voice of the fourth living
creature call out, 'Come!'[w] 8I looked and
there was a pale green horse! Its rider's
name was Death, and Hades followed
with him; they were given authority
over a fourth of the earth, to kill with
sword, famine, and pestilence, and by
the wild animals of the earth.
9 When he opened the fifth seal, I
saw under the altar the souls of those
who had been slaughtered for the word
of God and for the testimony they had
given; 10they cried out with a loud
voice, 'Sovereign Lord, holy and true,
how long will it be before you judge and
avenge our blood on the inhabitants
of the earth?' 11They were each given a
white robe and told to rest a little longer, until the number would be complete
both of their fellow-servants[x] and of
their brothers and sisters,[y] who were
soon to be killed as they themselves had
been killed.
12 When he opened the sixth seal, I
looked, and there came a great earthquake; the sun became black as sackcloth, the full moon became like blood,
13and the stars of the sky fell to the
earth as the fig tree drops its winter
fruit when shaken by a gale. 14The sky
vanished like a scroll rolling itself up,
and every mountain and island was removed from its place. 15Then the kings
of the earth and the magnates and the
generals and the rich and the powerful, and everyone, slave and free, hid in
the caves and among the rocks of the
mountains, 16calling to the mountains
and rocks, 'Fall on us and hide us from
the face of the one seated on the throne
and from the wrath of the Lamb; 17for
the great day of their wrath has come,
and who is able to stand?'

THE 144,000 OF ISRAEL SEALED

7 After this I saw four angels standing at the four corners of the earth,
holding back the four winds of the earth
so that no wind could blow on earth or
sea or against any tree. 2I saw another
angel ascending from the rising of the
sun, having the seal of the living God,
and he called with a loud voice to the
four angels who had been given power to
damage earth and sea, 3saying, 'Do not
damage the earth or the sea or the trees,
until we have marked the servants[z]

[o] 5.9 Gk *ransomed for God from* [p] 5.10 Gk *priests to* [q] 6.1 Or *'Go!'* [r] 6.3 Or *'Go!'* [s] 6.4 Or *went* [t] 6.5 Or *'Go!'* [u] 6.6 Gk *a denarius* [v] 6.6 Gk *a denarius* [w] 6.7 Or *'Go!'* [x] 6.11 Gk *slaves* [y] 6.11 Gk *brothers* [z] 7.3 Gk *slaves*

of our God with a seal on their foreheads.'

4 And I heard the number of those
who were sealed, one hundred and
forty-four thousand, sealed out of every
tribe of the people of Israel:
5 From the tribe of Judah twelve thousand sealed,
from the tribe of Reuben twelve
thousand,
from the tribe of Gad twelve thousand,
6 from the tribe of Asher twelve thousand,
from the tribe of Naphtali twelve
thousand,
from the tribe of Manasseh twelve
thousand,
7 from the tribe of Simeon twelve
thousand,
from the tribe of Levi twelve thousand,
from the tribe of Issachar twelve
thousand,
8 from the tribe of Zebulun twelve
thousand,
from the tribe of Joseph twelve thousand,
from the tribe of Benjamin twelve
thousand sealed.

THE MULTITUDE FROM EVERY NATION

9 After this I looked, and there was
a great multitude that no one could
count, from every nation, from all tribes
and peoples and languages, standing
before the throne and before the Lamb,
robed in white, with palm branches in
their hands. 10 They cried out in a loud
voice, saying,
'Salvation belongs to our God who
is seated on the throne,
and to the Lamb!'
11 And all the angels stood around the
throne and around the elders and the
four living creatures, and they fell on
their faces before the throne and worshipped God, 12 singing,
'Amen! Blessing and glory
and wisdom
and thanksgiving and honour
and power and might
be to our God for ever and
ever! Amen.'

13 Then one of the elders addressed me,
saying, 'Who are these, robed in white,
and where have they come from?' 14 I said
to him, 'Sir, you are the one that knows.'
Then he said to me, 'These are they who
have come out of the great ordeal; they
have washed their robes and made them
white in the blood of the Lamb.
15 For this reason they are before
the throne of God,
and worship him day and night
within his temple,
and the one who is seated on the
throne will shelter them.
16 They will hunger no more,
and thirst no more;
the sun will not strike them,
nor any scorching heat;
17 for the Lamb at the centre
of the throne will be
their shepherd,
and he will guide them to springs
of the water of life,
and God will wipe away every
tear from their eyes.'

THE SEVENTH SEAL AND THE GOLDEN CENSER

8 When the Lamb opened the seventh
seal, there was silence in heaven
for about half an hour. 2 And I saw the
seven angels who stand before God, and
seven trumpets were given to them.

3 Another angel with a golden censer came and stood at the altar; he was
given a great quantity of incense to offer
with the prayers of all the saints on the
golden altar that is before the throne.
4 And the smoke of the incense, with the
prayers of the saints, rose before God
from the hand of the angel. 5 Then the
angel took the censer and filled it with
fire from the altar and threw it on the
earth; and there were peals of thunder,
rumblings, flashes of lightning, and an
earthquake.

THE SEVEN TRUMPETS

6 Now the seven angels who had the
seven trumpets made ready to blow
them.

7 The first angel blew his trumpet,
and there came hail and fire, mixed
with blood, and they were hurled to
the earth; and a third of the earth was
burned up, and a third of the trees were
burned up, and all green grass was
burned up.

8 The second angel blew his trumpet,
and something like a great mountain,
burning with fire, was thrown into the
sea. 9 A third of the sea became blood, a
third of the living creatures in the sea
died, and a third of the ships were destroyed.

10 The third angel blew his trumpet,
and a great star fell from heaven, blaz-

ing like a torch, and it fell on a third of
the rivers and on the springs of water.
11 The name of the star is Wormwood. A
third of the waters became wormwood,
and many died from the water, because
it was made bitter.

12 The fourth angel blew his trumpet,
and a third of the sun was struck, and
a third of the moon, and a third of the
stars, so that a third of their light was
darkened; a third of the day was kept
from shining, and likewise the night.

13 Then I looked, and I heard an eagle crying with a loud voice as it flew
in mid-heaven, 'Woe, woe, woe to the
inhabitants of the earth, at the blasts
of the other trumpets that the three angels are about to blow!'

9 And the fifth angel blew his trumpet, and I saw a star that had fallen
from heaven to earth, and he was given
the key to the shaft of the bottomless
pit; 2 he opened the shaft of the bottomless pit, and from the shaft rose smoke
like the smoke of a great furnace, and
the sun and the air were darkened with
the smoke from the shaft. 3 Then from
the smoke came locusts on the earth,
and they were given authority like the
authority of scorpions of the earth.
4 They were told not to damage the grass
of the earth or any green growth or any
tree, but only those people who do not
have the seal of God on their foreheads.
5 They were allowed to torture them for
five months, but not to kill them, and
their torture was like the torture of a
scorpion when it stings someone. 6 And
in those days people will seek death but
will not find it; they will long to die, but
death will flee from them.

7 In appearance the locusts were like
horses equipped for battle. On their
heads were what looked like crowns of
gold; their faces were like human faces,
8 their hair like women's hair, and their
teeth like lions' teeth; 9 they had scales
like iron breastplates, and the noise of
their wings was like the noise of many
chariots with horses rushing into battle. 10 They have tails like scorpions, with
stings, and in their tails is their power
to harm people for five months. 11 They
have as king over them the angel of the
bottomless pit; his name in Hebrew
is Abaddon,[a] and in Greek he is called
Apollyon.[b]

12 The first woe has passed. There are
still two woes to come.

13 Then the sixth angel blew his
trumpet, and I heard a voice from the
four[c] horns of the golden altar before
God, 14 saying to the sixth angel who
had the trumpet, 'Release the four angels who are bound at the great river
Euphrates.' 15 So the four angels were
released, who had been held ready for
the hour, the day, the month, and the
year, to kill a third of humankind. 16 The
number of the troops of cavalry was two
hundred million; I heard their number.
17 And this was how I saw the horses in
my vision: the riders wore breastplates
the colour of fire and of sapphire[d] and
of sulphur; the heads of the horses were
like lions' heads, and fire and smoke
and sulphur came out of their mouths.
18 By these three plagues a third of humankind was killed, by the fire and
smoke and sulphur coming out of their
mouths. 19 For the power of the horses is
in their mouths and in their tails; their
tails are like serpents, having heads; and
with them they inflict harm.

20 The rest of humankind, who were
not killed by these plagues, did not repent of the works of their hands or give
up worshipping demons and idols of
gold and silver and bronze and stone
and wood, which cannot see or hear or
walk. 21 And they did not repent of their
murders or their sorceries or their fornication or their thefts.

THE ANGEL WITH THE LITTLE SCROLL

10 And I saw another mighty angel coming down from heaven,
wrapped in a cloud, with a rainbow over
his head; his face was like the sun, and
his legs like pillars of fire. 2 He held a little scroll open in his hand. Setting his
right foot on the sea and his left foot on
the land, 3 he gave a great shout, like a
lion roaring. And when he shouted, the
seven thunders sounded. 4 And when
the seven thunders had sounded, I was
about to write, but I heard a voice from
heaven saying, 'Seal up what the seven
thunders have said, and do not write
it down.' 5 Then the angel whom I saw
standing on the sea and the land

raised his right hand to heaven
6 and swore by him who lives
for ever and ever,

who created heaven and what is in it,
the earth and what is in it, and the sea
and what is in it: 'There will be no more
delay, 7 but in the days when the seventh

[a] 9.11 That is, *Destruction* [b] 9.11 That is, *Destroyer* [c] 9.13 Other ancient authorities lack *four* [d] 9.17 Gk *hyacinth*

angel is to blow his trumpet, the mystery of God will be fulfilled, as he announced to his servants[e] the prophets.'

8 Then the voice that I had heard from heaven spoke to me again, saying, 'Go, take the scroll that is open in the hand of the angel who is standing on the sea and on the land.' 9 So I went to the angel and told him to give me the little scroll; and he said to me, 'Take it, and eat; it will be bitter to your stomach, but sweet as honey in your mouth.' 10 So I took the little scroll from the hand of the angel and ate it; it was sweet as honey in my mouth, but when I had eaten it, my stomach was made bitter.

11 Then they said to me, 'You must prophesy again about many peoples and nations and languages and kings.'

THE TWO WITNESSES

11 Then I was given a measuring rod like a staff, and I was told, 'Come and measure the temple of God and the altar and those who worship there, 2 but do not measure the court outside the temple; leave that out, for it is given over to the nations, and they will trample over the holy city for forty-two months. 3 And I will grant my two witnesses authority to prophesy for one thousand two hundred and sixty days, wearing sackcloth.'

4 These are the two olive trees and the two lampstands that stand before the Lord of the earth. 5 And if anyone wants to harm them, fire pours from their mouth and consumes their foes; anyone who wants to harm them must be killed in this manner. 6 They have authority to shut the sky, so that no rain may fall during the days of their prophesying, and they have authority over the waters to turn them into blood, and to strike the earth with every kind of plague, as often as they desire.

7 When they have finished their testimony, the beast that comes up from the bottomless pit will make war on them and conquer them and kill them, 8 and their dead bodies will lie in the street of the great city that is prophetically[f] called Sodom and Egypt, where also their Lord was crucified. 9 For three and a half days members of the peoples and tribes and languages and nations will gaze at their dead bodies and refuse to let them be placed in a tomb; 10 and the inhabitants of the earth will gloat over them and celebrate and exchange presents, because these two prophets had been a torment to the inhabitants of the earth.

11 But after the three and a half days, the breath[g] of life from God entered them, and they stood on their feet, and those who saw them were terrified. 12 Then they[h] heard a loud voice from heaven saying to them, 'Come up here!' And they went up to heaven in a cloud while their enemies watched them. 13 At that moment there was a great earthquake, and a tenth of the city fell; seven thousand people were killed in the earthquake, and the rest were terrified and gave glory to the God of heaven.

14 The second woe has passed. The third woe is coming very soon.

THE SEVENTH TRUMPET

15 Then the seventh angel blew his trumpet, and there were loud voices in heaven, saying,

'The kingdom of the world has
    become the kingdom
    of our Lord
  and of his Messiah,[i]
and he will reign for ever and ever.'

16 Then the twenty-four elders who sit on their thrones before God fell on their faces and worshipped God, 17 singing,

'We give you thanks, Lord
    God Almighty,
  who are and who were,
for you have taken your great power
  and begun to reign.
18 The nations raged,
  but your wrath has come,
  and the time for judging the dead,
for rewarding your servants,[j]
    the prophets
  and saints and all who
    fear your name,
  both small and great,
and for destroying those who
    destroy the earth.'

19 Then God's temple in heaven was opened, and the ark of his covenant was seen within his temple; and there were flashes of lightning, rumblings, peals of thunder, an earthquake, and heavy hail.

THE WOMAN AND THE DRAGON

12 A great portent appeared in heaven: a woman clothed with the sun, with the moon under her feet, and on her head a crown of twelve stars.

[e] 10.7 Gk *slaves* [f] 11.8 Or *allegorically*; Gk *spiritually* [g] 11.11 Or *the spirit* [h] 11.12 Other ancient authorities read *I* [i] 11.15 Gk *Christ* [j] 11.18 Gk *slaves*

2She was pregnant and was crying out
in birth pangs, in the agony of giving
birth. 3Then another portent appeared
in heaven: a great red dragon, with seven
heads and ten horns, and seven diadems
on his heads. 4His tail swept down a
third of the stars of heaven and threw
them to the earth. Then the dragon
stood before the woman who was about
to bear a child, so that he might devour
her child as soon as it was born. 5And she
gave birth to a son, a male child, who is
to rule[k] all the nations with a rod of iron.
But her child was snatched away and
taken to God and to his throne; 6and the
woman fled into the wilderness, where
she has a place prepared by God, so that
there she can be nourished for one thousand two hundred and sixty days.

MICHAEL DEFEATS THE DRAGON

7 And war broke out in heaven; Michael and his angels fought against
the dragon. The dragon and his angels
fought back, 8but they were defeated,
and there was no longer any place for
them in heaven. 9The great dragon was
thrown down, that ancient serpent,
who is called the Devil and Satan, the
deceiver of the whole world—he was
thrown down to the earth, and his angels were thrown down with him.
10 Then I heard a loud voice in
heaven, proclaiming,
'Now have come the salvation
    and the power
  and the kingdom of our God
  and the authority of his Messiah,[l]
for the accuser of our comrades[m]
    has been thrown down,
  who accuses them day and
    night before our God.
11 But they have conquered him by
    the blood of the Lamb
  and by the word of their
    testimony,
for they did not cling to life even
    in the face of death.
12 Rejoice then, you heavens
  and those who dwell in them!
But woe to the earth and the sea,
  for the devil has come down to you
with great wrath,
  because he knows that his
    time is short!'

THE DRAGON FIGHTS AGAIN ON EARTH

13 So when the dragon saw that he
had been thrown down to the earth,
he pursued[n] the woman who had
given birth to the male child. 14But the
woman was given the two wings of the
great eagle, so that she could fly from
the serpent into the wilderness, to her
place where she is nourished for a time,
and times, and half a time. 15Then from
his mouth the serpent poured water
like a river after the woman, to sweep
her away with the flood. 16But the
earth came to the help of the woman;
it opened its mouth and swallowed the
river that the dragon had poured from
his mouth. 17Then the dragon was angry with the woman, and went off to
make war on the rest of her children,
those who keep the commandments of
God and hold the testimony of Jesus.

THE FIRST BEAST

18 Then the dragon[o] took his stand
13 on the sand of the seashore. 1And
I saw a beast rising out of the
sea, having ten horns and seven heads;
and on its horns were ten diadems, and
on its heads were blasphemous names.
2And the beast that I saw was like a
leopard, its feet were like a bear's, and
its mouth was like a lion's mouth. And
the dragon gave it his power and his
throne and great authority. 3One of its
heads seemed to have received a death-
blow, but its mortal wound[p] had been
healed. In amazement the whole earth
followed the beast. 4They worshipped
the dragon, for he had given his authority to the beast, and they worshipped
the beast, saying, 'Who is like the beast,
and who can fight against it?'
5 The beast was given a mouth uttering haughty and blasphemous words,
and it was allowed to exercise authority for forty-two months. 6It opened
its mouth to utter blasphemies against
God, blaspheming his name and his
dwelling, that is, those who dwell in
heaven. 7Also, it was allowed to make
war on the saints and to conquer them.[q]
It was given authority over every tribe
and people and language and nation,
8and all the inhabitants of the earth will
worship it, everyone whose name has
not been written from the foundation of
the world in the book of life of the Lamb
that was slaughtered.[r]

[k] 12.5 Or *to shepherd* [l] 12.10 Gk *Christ*
[m] 12.10 Gk *brothers* [n] 12.13 Or *persecuted*
[o] 12.18 Gk *Then he*; other ancient authorities read *Then I stood* [p] 13.3 Gk *the plague of its death*
[q] 13.7 Other ancient authorities lack this sentence
[r] 13.8 Or *written in the book of life of the Lamb that was slaughtered from the foundation of the world*

9 Let anyone who has an ear listen:
10 If you are to be taken captive,
into captivity you go;
if you kill with the sword,
with the sword you
must be killed.
Here is a call for the endurance and faith
of the saints.

THE SECOND BEAST

11 Then I saw another beast that rose
out of the earth; it had two horns like a
lamb and it spoke like a dragon. 12 It exercises all the authority of the first beast
on its behalf, and it makes the earth and
its inhabitants worship the first beast,
whose mortal wound[s] had been healed.
13 It performs great signs, even making
fire come down from heaven to earth
in the sight of all; 14 and by the signs
that it is allowed to perform on behalf
of the beast, it deceives the inhabitants
of earth, telling them to make an image
for the beast that had been wounded by
the sword[t] and yet lived; 15 and it was
allowed to give breath[u] to the image
of the beast, so that the image of the
beast could even speak and cause those
who would not worship the image of
the beast to be killed. 16 Also it causes
all, both small and great, both rich and
poor, both free and slave, to be marked
on the right hand or the forehead, 17 so
that no one can buy or sell who does not
have the mark, that is, the name of the
beast or the number of its name. 18 This
calls for wisdom: let anyone with understanding calculate the number of the
beast, for it is the number of a person.
Its number is six hundred and sixty-
six.[v]

THE LAMB AND THE 144,000

14 Then I looked, and there was the
Lamb, standing on Mount Zion!
And with him were one hundred and
forty-four thousand who had his name
and his Father's name written on their
foreheads. 2 And I heard a voice from
heaven like the sound of many waters
and like the sound of loud thunder; the
voice I heard was like the sound of harpists playing on their harps, 3 and they
sing a new song before the throne and
before the four living creatures and before the elders. No one could learn that
song except the one hundred forty-four
thousand who have been redeemed
from the earth. 4 It is these who have
not defiled themselves with women, for
they are virgins; these follow the Lamb
wherever he goes. They have been redeemed from humankind as first fruits
for God and the Lamb, 5 and in their
mouth no lie was found; they are blameless.

THE MESSAGES OF THE THREE ANGELS

6 Then I saw another angel flying
in mid-heaven, with an eternal gospel
to proclaim to those who live[w] on the
earth—to every nation and tribe and
language and people. 7 He said in a loud
voice, 'Fear God and give him glory, for
the hour of his judgement has come;
and worship him who made heaven and
earth, the sea and the springs of water.'
8 Then another angel, a second, followed, saying, 'Fallen, fallen is Babylon
the great! She has made all nations
drink of the wine of the wrath of her
fornication.'
9 Then another angel, a third, followed them, crying with a loud voice,
'Those who worship the beast and its
image, and receive a mark on their foreheads or on their hands, 10 they will also
drink the wine of God's wrath, poured
unmixed into the cup of his anger, and
they will be tormented with fire and
sulphur in the presence of the holy angels and in the presence of the Lamb.
11 And the smoke of their torment goes
up for ever and ever. There is no rest
day or night for those who worship the
beast and its image and for anyone who
receives the mark of its name.'
12 Here is a call for the endurance
of the saints, those who keep the commandments of God and hold fast to the
faith of[x] Jesus.
13 And I heard a voice from heaven
saying, 'Write this: Blessed are the dead
who from now on die in the Lord.' 'Yes,'
says the Spirit, 'they will rest from their
labours, for their deeds follow them.'

REAPING THE EARTH'S HARVEST

14 Then I looked, and there was a
white cloud, and seated on the cloud was
one like the Son of Man, with a golden
crown on his head, and a sharp sickle in
his hand! 15 Another angel came out of
the temple, calling with a loud voice to
the one who sat on the cloud, 'Use your
sickle and reap, for the hour to reap has

[s] **13.12** Gk *whose plague of its death* [t] **13.14** Or *that had received the plague of the sword*
[u] **13.15** Or *spirit* [v] **13.18** Other ancient authorities read *six hundred and sixteen*
[w] **14.6** Gk *sit* [x] **14.12** Or *to their faith in*

come, because the harvest of the earth
is fully ripe.' 16 So the one who sat on the
cloud swung his sickle over the earth,
and the earth was reaped.

17 Then another angel came out of
the temple in heaven, and he too had a
sharp sickle. 18 Then another angel came
out from the altar, the angel who has
authority over fire, and he called with
a loud voice to him who had the sharp
sickle, 'Use your sharp sickle and gather
the clusters of the vine of the earth, for
its grapes are ripe.' 19 So the angel swung
his sickle over the earth and gathered
the vintage of the earth, and he threw it
into the great wine press of the wrath of
God. 20 And the wine press was trodden
outside the city, and blood flowed from
the wine press, as high as a horse's bridle, for a distance of about two hundred
miles.[y]

THE ANGELS WITH THE SEVEN LAST PLAGUES

15 Then I saw another portent in
heaven, great and amazing:
seven angels with seven plagues, which
are the last, for with them the wrath of
God is ended.

2 And I saw what appeared to be a sea
of glass mixed with fire, and those who
had conquered the beast and its image
and the number of its name standing
beside the sea of glass with harps of God
in their hands. 3 And they sing the song
of Moses, the servant[z] of God, and the
song of the Lamb:

'Great and amazing are your deeds,
Lord God the Almighty!
Just and true are your ways,
King of the nations![a]
4 Lord, who will not fear
and glorify your name?
For you alone are holy.
All nations will come
and worship before you,
for your judgements have
been revealed.'

5 After this I looked, and the temple of the tent[b] of witness in heaven
was opened, 6 and out of the temple
came the seven angels with the seven
plagues, robed in pure bright linen,[c]
with golden sashes across their chests.
7 Then one of the four living creatures
gave the seven angels seven golden
bowls full of the wrath of God, who lives
for ever and ever; 8 and the temple was
filled with smoke from the glory of God
and from his power, and no one could
enter the temple until the seven plagues
of the seven angels were ended.

THE BOWLS OF GOD'S WRATH

16 Then I heard a loud voice from
the temple telling the seven angels, 'Go and pour out on the earth the
seven bowls of the wrath of God.'

2 So the first angel went and poured
his bowl on the earth, and a foul and
painful sore came on those who had the
mark of the beast and who worshipped
its image.

3 The second angel poured his bowl
into the sea, and it became like the
blood of a corpse, and every living thing
in the sea died.

4 The third angel poured his bowl
into the rivers and the springs of water,
and they became blood. 5 And I heard
the angel of the waters say,

'You are just, O Holy One,
who are and were,
for you have judged these things;
6 because they shed the blood of
saints and prophets,
you have given them
blood to drink.
It is what they deserve!'

7 And I heard the altar respond,

'Yes, O Lord God, the Almighty,
your judgements are
true and just!'

8 The fourth angel poured his bowl
on the sun, and it was allowed to scorch
people with fire; 9 they were scorched
by the fierce heat, but they cursed the
name of God, who had authority over
these plagues, and they did not repent
and give him glory.

10 The fifth angel poured his bowl
on the throne of the beast, and its kingdom was plunged into darkness; people
gnawed their tongues in agony, 11 and
cursed the God of heaven because of
their pains and sores, and they did not
repent of their deeds.

12 The sixth angel poured his bowl
on the great river Euphrates, and its water was dried up in order to prepare the
way for the kings from the east. 13 And I
saw three foul spirits like frogs coming
from the mouth of the dragon, from the
mouth of the beast, and from the mouth
of the false prophet. 14 These are demon-
ic spirits, performing signs, who go
abroad to the kings of the whole world,

[y] 14.20 Gk *one thousand six hundred stadia*
[z] 15.3 Gk *slave* [a] 15.3 Other ancient authorities read *the ages* [b] 15.5 Or *tabernacle*
[c] 15.6 Other ancient authorities read *stone*

to assemble them for battle on the great day of God the Almighty. 15('See, I am coming like a thief! Blessed is the one who stays awake and is clothed,[d] not going about naked and exposed to shame.') 16And they assembled them at the place that in Hebrew is called Harmagedon.

17 The seventh angel poured his bowl into the air, and a loud voice came out of the temple, from the throne, saying, 'It is done!' 18And there came flashes of lightning, rumblings, peals of thunder, and a violent earthquake, such as had not occurred since people were upon the earth, so violent was that earthquake. 19The great city was split into three parts, and the cities of the nations fell. God remembered great Babylon and gave her the wine-cup of the fury of his wrath. 20And every island fled away, and no mountains were to be found; 21and huge hailstones, each weighing about a hundred pounds,[e] dropped from heaven on people, until they cursed God for the plague of the hail, so fearful was that plague.

THE GREAT WHORE AND THE BEAST

17 Then one of the seven angels who had the seven bowls came and said to me, 'Come, I will show you the judgement of the great whore who is seated on many waters, 2with whom the kings of the earth have committed fornication, and with the wine of whose fornication the inhabitants of the earth have become drunk.' 3So he carried me away in the spirit[f] into a wilderness, and I saw a woman sitting on a scarlet beast that was full of blasphemous names, and it had seven heads and ten horns. 4The woman was clothed in purple and scarlet, and adorned with gold and jewels and pearls, holding in her hand a golden cup full of abominations and the impurities of her fornication; 5and on her forehead was written a name, a mystery: 'Babylon the great, mother of whores and of earth's abominations.' 6And I saw that the woman was drunk with the blood of the saints and the blood of the witnesses to Jesus.

When I saw her, I was greatly amazed. 7But the angel said to me, 'Why are you so amazed? I will tell you the mystery of the woman, and of the beast with seven heads and ten horns that carries her. 8The beast that you saw was, and is not, and is about to ascend from the bottomless pit and go to destruction. And the inhabitants of the earth, whose names have not been written in the book of life from the foundation of the world, will be amazed when they see the beast, because it was and is not and is to come.

9 'This calls for a mind that has wisdom: the seven heads are seven mountains on which the woman is seated; also, they are seven kings, 10of whom five have fallen, one is living, and the other has not yet come; and when he comes, he must remain for only a little while. 11As for the beast that was and is not, it is an eighth but it belongs to the seven, and it goes to destruction. 12And the ten horns that you saw are ten kings who have not yet received a kingdom, but they are to receive authority as kings for one hour, together with the beast. 13These are united in yielding their power and authority to the beast; 14they will make war on the Lamb, and the Lamb will conquer them, for he is Lord of lords and King of kings, and those with him are called and chosen and faithful.'

15 And he said to me, 'The waters that you saw, where the whore is seated, are peoples and multitudes and nations and languages. 16And the ten horns that you saw, they and the beast will hate the whore; they will make her desolate and naked; they will devour her flesh and burn her up with fire. 17For God has put it into their hearts to carry out his purpose by agreeing to give their kingdom to the beast, until the words of God will be fulfilled. 18The woman you saw is the great city that rules over the kings of the earth.'

THE FALL OF BABYLON

18 After this I saw another angel coming down from heaven, having great authority; and the earth was made bright with his splendour. 2He called out with a mighty voice,

'Fallen, fallen is Babylon the great!
It has become a dwelling-place
of demons,
a haunt of every foul spirit,
a haunt of every foul bird,
a haunt of every foul and
hateful beast.[g]
3 For all the nations have drunk[h]
of the wine of the wrath of
her fornication,

[d] 16.15 Gk *and keeps his robes* [e] 16.21 Gk *weighing about a talent* [f] 17.3 Or *in the Spirit* [g] 18.2 Other ancient authorities lack the words *a haunt of every foul beast* and attach the words *and hateful* to the previous line so as to read *a haunt of every foul and hateful bird* [h] 18.3 Other ancient authorities read *She has made all nations drink*

and the kings of the earth
have committed
fornication with her,
and the merchants of the earth
have grown rich from the
power[i] of her luxury.'
4 Then I heard another voice from
heaven saying,
'Come out of her, my people,
so that you do not take
part in her sins,
and so that you do not share
in her plagues;
5 for her sins are heaped high
as heaven,
and God has remembered
her iniquities.
6 Render to her as she herself
has rendered,
and repay her double for her deeds;
mix a double draught for her
in the cup she mixed.
7 As she glorified herself and
lived luxuriously,
so give her a like measure of
torment and grief.
Since in her heart she says,
"I rule as a queen;
I am no widow,
and I will never see grief",
8 therefore her plagues will come
in a single day—
pestilence and mourning
and famine—
and she will be burned with fire;
for mighty is the Lord God
who judges her.'
9 And the kings of the earth, who
committed fornication and lived in luxury with her, will weep and wail over
her when they see the smoke of her
burning; 10 they will stand far off, in fear
of her torment, and say,
'Alas, alas, the great city,
Babylon, the mighty city!
For in one hour your judgement
has come.'
11 And the merchants of the earth
weep and mourn for her, since no one
buys their cargo any more, 12 cargo
of gold, silver, jewels and pearls, fine
linen, purple, silk and scarlet, all kinds
of scented wood, all articles of ivory,
all articles of costly wood, bronze, iron,
and marble, 13 cinnamon, spice, incense, myrrh, frankincense, wine, olive
oil, choice flour and wheat, cattle and
sheep, horses and chariots, slaves—and
human lives.[j]
14 'The fruit for which your soul longed
has gone from you,
and all your dainties and
your splendour
are lost to you,
never to be found again!'
15 The merchants of these wares, who
gained wealth from her, will stand far
off, in fear of her torment, weeping and
mourning aloud,
16 'Alas, alas, the great city,
clothed in fine linen,
in purple and scarlet,
adorned with gold,
with jewels, and with pearls!
17 For in one hour all this wealth
has been laid waste!'
And all shipmasters and seafarers,
sailors and all whose trade is on the sea,
stood far off 18 and cried out as they saw
the smoke of her burning,
'What city was like the great city?'
19 And they threw dust on their heads, as
they wept and mourned, crying out,
'Alas, alas, the great city,
where all who had ships at sea
grew rich by her wealth!
For in one hour she has been
laid waste.'
20 Rejoice over her, O heaven, you
saints and apostles and prophets! For
God has given judgement for you against
her.
21 Then a mighty angel took up a
stone like a great millstone and threw it
into the sea, saying,
'With such violence Babylon
the great city
will be thrown down,
and will be found no more;
22 and the sound of harpists and
minstrels and of flautists
and trumpeters
will be heard in you no more;
and an artisan of any trade
will be found in you no more;
and the sound of the millstone
will be heard in you no more;
23 and the light of a lamp
will shine in you no more;
and the voice of bridegroom and bride
will be heard in you no more;
for your merchants were the
magnates of the earth,
and all nations were deceived
by your sorcery.
24 And in you[k] was found the blood
of prophets and of saints,
and of all who have been
slaughtered on earth.'

[i] **18.3** Or *resources* [j] **18.13** Or *chariots, and human bodies and souls* [k] **18.24** Gk *her*

THE REJOICING IN HEAVEN

19 After this I heard what seemed
to be the loud voice of a great
multitude in heaven, saying,
'Hallelujah!
Salvation and glory and
power to our God,
2 for his judgements are true and just;
he has judged the great whore
who corrupted the earth
with her fornication,
and he has avenged on her the
blood of his servants.'[l]
3 Once more they said,
'Hallelujah!
The smoke goes up from her
for ever and ever.'
4 And the twenty-four elders and the four
living creatures fell down and worshipped
God who is seated on the throne, saying,
'Amen. Hallelujah!'
5 And from the throne came a voice
saying,
'Praise our God,
all you his servants,[m]
and all who fear him,
small and great.'
6 Then I heard what seemed to be the
voice of a great multitude, like the sound
of many waters and like the sound of
mighty thunder-peals, crying out,
'Hallelujah!
For the Lord our God
the Almighty reigns.
7 Let us rejoice and exult
and give him the glory,
for the marriage of the Lamb
has come,
and his bride has made
herself ready;
8 to her it has been granted to be clothed
with fine linen, bright and pure'—
for the fine linen is the righteous deeds
of the saints.
9 And the angel said[n] to me, 'Write
this: Blessed are those who are invited
to the marriage supper of the Lamb.'
And he said to me, 'These are true words
of God.' 10 Then I fell down at his feet to
worship him, but he said to me, 'You
must not do that! I am a fellow-servant[o]
with you and your comrades[p] who hold
the testimony of Jesus.[q] Worship God!
For the testimony of Jesus[r] is the spirit
of prophecy.'

THE RIDER ON THE WHITE HORSE

11 Then I saw heaven opened, and
there was a white horse! Its rider is
called Faithful and True, and in righteousness he judges and makes war.
12 His eyes are like a flame of fire, and
on his head are many diadems; and he
has a name inscribed that no one knows
but himself. 13 He is clothed in a robe
dipped in[s] blood, and his name is called
The Word of God. 14 And the armies of
heaven, wearing fine linen, white and
pure, were following him on white
horses. 15 From his mouth comes a sharp
sword with which to strike down the
nations, and he will rule[t] them with a
rod of iron; he will tread the wine press
of the fury of the wrath of God the Almighty. 16 On his robe and on his thigh
he has a name inscribed, 'King of kings
and Lord of lords'.

THE BEAST AND ITS ARMIES DEFEATED

17 Then I saw an angel standing in
the sun, and with a loud voice he called
to all the birds that fly in mid-heaven,
'Come, gather for the great supper of
God, 18 to eat the flesh of kings, the flesh
of captains, the flesh of the mighty, the
flesh of horses and their riders—flesh
of all, both free and slave, both small
and great.' 19 Then I saw the beast and
the kings of the earth with their armies gathered to make war against the
rider on the horse and against his army.
20 And the beast was captured, and with
it the false prophet who had performed
in its presence the signs by which he deceived those who had received the mark
of the beast and those who worshipped
its image. These two were thrown alive
into the lake of fire that burns with sulphur. 21 And the rest were killed by the
sword of the rider on the horse, the
sword that came from his mouth; and all
the birds were gorged with their flesh.

THE THOUSAND YEARS

20 Then I saw an angel coming
down from heaven, holding
in his hand the key to the bottomless
pit and a great chain. 2 He seized the
dragon, that ancient serpent, who is
the Devil and Satan, and bound him for
a thousand years, 3 and threw him into
the pit, and locked and sealed it over
him, so that he would deceive the nations no more, until the thousand years
were ended. After that he must be let
out for a little while.

[l] 19.2 Gk *slaves* [m] 19.5 Gk *slaves* [n] 19.9 Gk *he said* [o] 19.10 Gk *slave* [p] 19.10 Gk *brothers* [q] 19.10 Or *to Jesus* [r] 19.10 Or *to Jesus* [s] 19.13 Other ancient authorities read *sprinkled with* [t] 19.15 Or *will shepherd*

4 Then I saw thrones, and those seated
on them were given authority to judge. I
also saw the souls of those who had been
beheaded for their testimony to Jesus[u]
and for the word of God. They had not
worshipped the beast or its image and
had not received its mark on their foreheads or their hands. They came to life
and reigned with Christ for a thousand
years. 5(The rest of the dead did not come
to life until the thousand years were
ended.) This is the first resurrection.
6Blessed and holy are those who share in
the first resurrection. Over these the second death has no power, but they will be
priests of God and of Christ, and they will
reign with him for a thousand years.

SATAN'S DOOM

7 When the thousand years are ended,
Satan will be released from his prison
8and will come out to deceive the nations
at the four corners of the earth, Gog and
Magog, in order to gather them for battle; they are as numerous as the sands
of the sea. 9They marched up over the
breadth of the earth and surrounded the
camp of the saints and the beloved city.
And fire came down from heaven[v] and
consumed them. 10And the devil who
had deceived them was thrown into the
lake of fire and sulphur, where the beast
and the false prophet were, and they will
be tormented day and night for ever and
ever.

THE DEAD ARE JUDGED

11 Then I saw a great white throne
and the one who sat on it; the earth and
the heaven fled from his presence, and
no place was found for them. 12And I saw
the dead, great and small, standing before the throne, and books were opened.
Also another book was opened, the book
of life. And the dead were judged according to their works, as recorded in the
books. 13And the sea gave up the dead
that were in it, Death and Hades gave
up the dead that were in them, and all
were judged according to what they had
done. 14Then Death and Hades were
thrown into the lake of fire. This is the
second death, the lake of fire; 15and anyone whose name was not found written
in the book of life was thrown into the
lake of fire.

THE NEW HEAVEN AND
THE NEW EARTH

21 Then I saw a new heaven and a
new earth; for the first heaven
and the first earth had passed away,
and the sea was no more. 2And I saw
the holy city, the new Jerusalem, coming down out of heaven from God, prepared as a bride adorned for her husband. 3And I heard a loud voice from
the throne saying,

'See, the home[w] of God is
among mortals.
He will dwell[x] with them;
they will be his peoples,[y]
and God himself will be with them;[z]
4 he will wipe every tear from
their eyes.
Death will be no more;
mourning and crying and pain
will be no more,
for the first things have passed away.'

5 And the one who was seated on the
throne said, 'See, I am making all things
new.' Also he said, 'Write this, for these
words are trustworthy and true.' 6Then
he said to me, 'It is done! I am the Alpha and the Omega, the beginning and
the end. To the thirsty I will give water
as a gift from the spring of the water
of life. 7Those who conquer will inherit
these things, and I will be their God and
they will be my children. 8But as for the
cowardly, the faithless,[a] the polluted,
the murderers, the fornicators, the sorcerers, the idolaters, and all liars, their
place will be in the lake that burns with
fire and sulphur, which is the second
death.'

VISION OF THE NEW JERUSALEM

9 Then one of the seven angels who
had the seven bowls full of the seven last
plagues came and said to me, 'Come, I
will show you the bride, the wife of
the Lamb.' 10And in the spirit[b] he carried me away to a great, high mountain
and showed me the holy city Jerusalem
coming down out of heaven from God.
11It has the glory of God and a radiance
like a very rare jewel, like jasper, clear as
crystal. 12It has a great, high wall with
twelve gates, and at the gates twelve angels, and on the gates are inscribed the
names of the twelve tribes of the Israelites; 13on the east three gates, on the
north three gates, on the south three
gates, and on the west three gates.

[u] 20.4 Or *for the testimony of Jesus*
[v] 20.9 Other ancient authorities read *from God, out of heaven*, or *out of heaven from God*
[w] 21.3 Gk *the tabernacle* [x] 21.3 Gk *will tabernacle* [y] 21.3 Other ancient authorities read *people* [z] 21.3 Other ancient authorities add *and be their God* [a] 21.8 Or *the unbelieving*
[b] 21.10 Or *in the Spirit*

14 And the wall of the city has twelve
foundations, and on them are the
twelve names of the twelve apostles of
the Lamb.
15 The angel[c] who talked to me had
a measuring rod of gold to measure
the city and its gates and walls. 16 The
city lies foursquare, its length the same
as its width; and he measured the city
with his rod, fifteen hundred miles;[d]
its length and width and height are
equal. 17 He also measured its wall, one
hundred and forty-four cubits[e] by human measurement, which the angel
was using. 18 The wall is built of jasper,
while the city is pure gold, clear as glass.
19 The foundations of the wall of the city
are adorned with every jewel; the first
was jasper, the second sapphire, the
third agate, the fourth emerald, 20 the
fifth onyx, the sixth cornelian, the seventh chrysolite, the eighth beryl, the
ninth topaz, the tenth chrysoprase,
the eleventh jacinth, the twelfth amethyst. 21 And the twelve gates are twelve
pearls, each of the gates is a single pearl,
and the street of the city is pure gold,
transparent as glass.
22 I saw no temple in the city, for its
temple is the Lord God the Almighty
and the Lamb. 23 And the city has no
need of sun or moon to shine on it, for
the glory of God is its light, and its lamp
is the Lamb. 24 The nations will walk by
its light, and the kings of the earth will
bring their glory into it. 25 Its gates will
never be shut by day—and there will be
no night there. 26 People will bring into
it the glory and the honour of the nations. 27 But nothing unclean will enter
it, nor anyone who practises abomination or falsehood, but only those who
are written in the Lamb's book of life.

THE RIVER OF LIFE

22 Then the angel[f] showed me the
river of the water of life, bright
as crystal, flowing from the throne of
God and of the Lamb 2 through the middle of the street of the city. On either
side of the river is the tree of life[g] with
its twelve kinds of fruit, producing its
fruit each month; and the leaves of the
tree are for the healing of the nations.
3 Nothing accursed will be found there
any more. But the throne of God and of
the Lamb will be in it, and his servants[h]
will worship him; 4 they will see his face,
and his name will be on their foreheads.
5 And there will be no more night; they
need no light of lamp or sun, for the
Lord God will be their light, and they
will reign for ever and ever.
6 And he said to me, 'These words
are trustworthy and true, for the Lord,
the God of the spirits of the prophets,
has sent his angel to show his servants[i]
what must soon take place.'
7 'See, I am coming soon! Blessed
is the one who keeps the words of the
prophecy of this book.'

EPILOGUE AND BENEDICTION

8 I, John, am the one who heard and
saw these things. And when I heard and
saw them, I fell down to worship at the
feet of the angel who showed them to
me; 9 but he said to me, 'You must not
do that! I am a fellow-servant[j] with you
and your comrades[k] the prophets, and
with those who keep the words of this
book. Worship God!'
10 And he said to me, 'Do not seal up
the words of the prophecy of this book,
for the time is near. 11 Let the evildoer
still do evil, and the filthy still be filthy,
and the righteous still do right, and the
holy still be holy.'

12 'See, I am coming soon; my reward is with me, to repay according to
everyone's work. 13 I am the Alpha and
the Omega, the first and the last, the beginning and the end.'

14 Blessed are those who wash their
robes,[l] so that they will have the right
to the tree of life and may enter the city
by the gates. 15 Outside are the dogs and
sorcerers and fornicators and murderers
and idolaters, and everyone who loves
and practises falsehood.
16 'It is I, Jesus, who sent my angel to you with this testimony for the
churches. I am the root and the descendant of David, the bright morning star.'
17 The Spirit and the bride say, 'Come.'
And let everyone who hears
say, 'Come.'
And let everyone who is
thirsty come.
Let anyone who wishes take the
water of life as a gift.

18 I warn everyone who hears the
words of the prophecy of this book: if

[c] 21.15 Gk *He* [d] 21.16 Gk *twelve thousand stadia* [e] 21.17 That is, almost seventy-five yards [f] 22.1 Gk *he* [g] 22.2 Or *the Lamb. 2In the middle of the street of the city, and on either side of the river, is the tree of life* [h] 22.3 Gk *slaves* [i] 22.6 Gk *slaves* [j] 22.9 Gk *slave* [k] 22.9 Gk *brothers* [l] 22.14 Other ancient authorities read *do his commandments*

anyone adds to them, God will add to
that person the plagues described in
this book; 19 if anyone takes away from
the words of the book of this prophecy,
God will take away that person's share
in the tree of life and in the holy city,
which are described in this book.

20 The one who testifies to these
things says, 'Surely I am coming soon.'

Amen. Come, Lord Jesus!

21 The grace of the Lord Jesus be
with all the saints. Amen.[m]

[m] **22.21** Other ancient authorities lack *all*; others lack *the saints*; others lack *Amen*

PRAYING WITH THE BIBLE

Besides liturgical and devotional prayer Catholics also pray with the Bible. There are many different ways to use the Bible for Prayer.

MEDITATION

Lectio Divina is a slow, contemplative praying of the Scriptures which enables you to spend time with God through reading and meditating on the word in the Scriptures. It involves reading a passage of Scripture, listening quietly to what it is saying, meditating on what you have read and heard, praying or having a conversation with God about what you hear and how that applies to your life. And finally contemplating or just being in the presence of God. This form of prayer has no other goal than spending time with God through the medium of his Word. The amount of time we spend in any of the four steps of lectio divina, whether it is reading, meditation, praying or contemplation depends on God's Spirit.

IMAGINATION

Quiet your spirit in a comfortable place. Begin with a prayer that your time with the Scripture reading will draw you closer to God. Read the passage. Imagine yourself in the passage as one of the characters and observe what is happening. Notice your feelings, thoughts and insights as you read the story. Pause. For a few minutes allow your self to be quiet with your feelings, thoughts and insights then bring them into conversation with the Lord. End your time with a prayer to carry the message of your prayer with you during the day.

JOURNALING

Quiet your spirit in a comfortable place. Begin with a prayer that your time with the Scripture reading will draw you closer to God. Read the Scripture passage you have selected once. Pause and reflect. Write a dialogue with a person, word, event, or phrase that caught your attention as you read the passage.

PRAYING WITH THE PSALMS

Quiet your spirit in a comfortable place. Read one of the Psalms that describes images of God, such as Psalm 62. Reflect for a moment on these or similar questions: When has God been your rock and fortress? When have you stopped and waited for God to give you strength and refuge? Remembering God's trustworthiness, pray this psalm again, pausing after each image that touches your heart. Let each image lap over you as do the waves of the ocean. Continue to pray each verse of the psalm in this manner and at your own pace.

PRAY WITH BIBLICAL PRAYERS

1. David's prayer of thanks (2 Samuel 7.18–29)
2. Hannah's prayer (1 Samuel 2.10)
3. Mary's Magnificat (Luke 1.46–55)
4. Simeon's canticle (Luke 2.29–32)
5. Paul's Prayer for the Strengthening of Christians (Ephesians 3.14)
6. The "Shema" (Deuteronomy 6.4–5)

ANY OF THE PSALMS

Meditate on one of the Mysteries of the Rosary or Stations of the Cross.

PRAY WITH THE BIBLICAL WORDS

See the earlier section "Biblical Words" and choose a word. Follow the outline to pray and meditate.

PRAY WITH THE WITNESSES OF FAITH

See the earlier section "Witnesses of Faith" and choose a character. Follow the outline to read and pray over this person's story.

BIBLE READING PLANS

The main reading plan for Catholics is the lectionary, which assigns typically four readings each Sunday, special holiday, and celebrations, as well as each regular day of the year according to the Church Calendar. These lists of readings are readily available online and in many source books available to Catholics. We have also included more specialized reading plans for those interested in particular topics.

TWO-WEEK PLAN ON BIBLICAL PRAYERS

1. 1 Samuel 2.1–10 . . . . Hannah's Prayer
2. 2 Samuel 1.17–27 . . . . David's Lament
3. 2 Samuel 7.18–29. . . . . David's Prayer of Thanks
4. Ezra 9.5–15 . . . . Ezra's Prayer
5. Job 3.1–26 . . . . . Job complains to God
6. Psalm 57 . . . . Prayer for Help
7. Psalm 80. . . . . Prayer for a Nation
8. Sirach 39.16–35 . . . . . . Sirach's prayer of praise
9. Luke 1.46–55 . . . . Mary's Prayer
10. Luke 2.28–32 . . . . Canticle of Simeon
11. Luke 17.5. . . . . . . Prayer of the Apostles
12. Matthew 6.9–13. . . . . . . Lord's Prayer
13. John 17.1–26. . . . . Jesus' Prayer for his disciples
14. 2 Sam 7.18–29; Ephesians 3.14. . . . . . . Paul's Prayer of Thanks

ONE-WEEK PLAN ON COURAGE

1. Joshua 1 . . . . . . Call to be courageous
2. 1 Samuel 17.26–50 . . . David's courage
3. Esther 4–5 . . . . Esther's courage
4. Tobit 4–8 . . . . Story of Tobit
5. John 16 . . . . Jesus urges courage
6. Acts 4; 5.17–42 . . . . . Apostles' courage
7. 1 Corinthians 16.13 . . . . Have courage

TWO-WEEK PLAN ON SIN AND THE COVENANT

1. Genesis 3. . . . . . . The first sin and the promise of salvation
2. Genesis 6 . . . . Evil
3. Genesis 12.1–9 . . . . . The beginning of the Covenant
4. Exodus 6.1–9 . . God rescues the people
5. Leviticus 4 . . Sin offering for sacrifice
6. Psalm 51 . . . . . . A prayer of confession
7. John 3.1–21 . . God sends the promised savior
8. Mark 8.31–38 . . . . . . The sacrifice of a disciple
9. Matthew 26.26–28 . . . A new sacrifice and covenant
10. Romans 7 . . . Sin, freedom, and death
11. Romans 8 . . The experience of sin and the covenant
12. Galatians 3.23–29 . . . We are children of God
13. Hebrews 10.18–15 . . . . . . The sacrifice
14. 1 John . . . . Live in the Light

TWO-WEEK PLAN ON FAITH

1. Psalm 115 . . . . Keeping faith
2. Isaiah 26. . . . . Faith of a nation
3. Habakkuk 2 . . . . Justice and faith
4. Matthew 9 . . . Jesus' response to faith
5. Matthew 14 . . . . Doubt and faith
6. Matthew 17 . . . . . . How much faith?
7. Luke 12 . . . . Dependence on God
8. Luke 22.24–38 . . . . Faith in crisis
9. Acts 3 . . Acting in and preaching faith
10. Romans 1.1–17. . Exhortation to faith
11. Romans 4. . . . . . . Inheritance of faith
12. 1 Thessalonians. . . Witnesses of faith
13. 1 Timothy. . . . . Effects of faith
14. Hebrews 11. . . . . What is faith?

ONE-WEEK PLAN ON GOD AND NATURE

1. Genesis 1. . . . . . First story of creation
2. Genesis 2 . . . Second story of creation
3. Proverbs 8 . . . . Wisdom sees creation
4. Genesis 7. . . . God preserves creation
5. Job 38–40 . . God's conversation about creation
6. Isaiah 65. . . . . A New Earth
7. Psalm 8. . . . . Praise the Creator

ONE-WEEK PLAN ON GRATITUDE

1. Psalm 107 . . . . . Give thanks for God's goodness

2. Isaiah 38.10–20 . . The living give God thanks
3. Matthew 26.26–29; Mark 14.22–26; Luke 22.14–20; 1 Corinthians 11.23–26 Eucharist as thanksgiving
4. Ephesians 1.15–23 . . Paul gives thanks for the faith at Ephesus
5. Philippians 1.3–8. . . . . . Paul prays in thanksgiving for his dear friends
6. Colossians 3.5–17 . . . . . Be thankful for being called
7. Revelation 4.1–11 Do not cease giving thanks to God

TWO-WEEK PLAN ON THE HOLY SPIRIT

1. Judges 14 . . . . . The Spirit of the Lord comes upon Samuel
2. 1 Samuel 16.12–13 . David is anointed with the Spirit
3. Joel 3.1–5. . . The promise of the Spirit
4. Luke 1.26–38 . . . . The Holy Spirit and the Virgin birth
5. Matthew 3.1–4.10 . . . .The Holy Spirit and Jesus' Baptism and temptation
6. Luke 4.14–21 . . . . The Holy Spirit and Jesus' public ministry
7. John 14 . . The Holy Spirit as advocate
8. John 16 . . . . . The Holy Spirit as guide
9. Acts 2.1–41 . . The coming of the Holy Spirit at Pentecost
10. Acts 8.4–21. . . . . The power of the Holy Spirit
11. 1 Corinthians 12.1–27 . . . . The Gifts of the Spirit
12. Galatians 5.1–26 . . Living by the Spirit
13. Ephesians 4.25–32. . Do not grieve the Holy Spirit
14. 1 John 4.1–21 . . . . Discerning the Holy Spirit

ONE-WEEK PLAN ON HOPE

1. Psalm 11 . . . . Confidence in the presence of God
2. Psalm 33 . . . . Praise God's providence
3. Ezekiel 37.1–14 . . . Vision of dry bones
4. Romans 4.18–5.21 . . . . . Our hope is in Christ
5. Colossians 1.15–23. . Our hope is in the gospel
6. 1 Thessalonians 4.13–18 . . . . Hope for those who have died
7. 1 Peter 1.1–21 . . . . Living in hope

TWO-WEEK PLAN ON HEALING

1. Matthew 8.1–4 ; Mark 1.40–45; Luke 5.12–16 . . . . Cleansing of a leper
2. Matthew 8.5–13; Luke 4.38–41. . . . . . A centurion's servant
3. Matthew 8.14–17; Mark 1.29–34; Luke 4.38–41 . . . Peter's mother-in-law and others
4. Luke 5.17–16. . . . . The paralytic
5. Matthew 9.20–22; Mark 5.25–34; Luke 8.43–48 . . Woman with a hemorrhage
6. Matthew 9.27–31; Mark 10.46–52 . . . . . Two blind men
7. Matthew 12.9–14; Mark 3.1–6; Luke 6.6–11 . . . Man with a withered hand
8. Matthew 15.21–28; Mark 3.1–6 . . . The Canaanite woman
9. Matthew 15.29–31; Mark 7.31–37 . . The deaf man
10. Luke 13.10–17 . . . The crippled woman
11. Luke 14.1–6 . . . The man with dropsy
12. Luke 17.12–19 . . . . Ten lepers
13. John 5.1–9 . . . The cripple of 38 years
14. John 9.1–7 . . . . . The man born blind

TWO-WEEK PLAN ON LIFE AND TEACHINGS OF JESUS

1. Luke 1.5–56 Announcing the birth of Jesus
2. Luke 1.57; Matthew 3.4–7; Luke 3.21–22; 9.7–9 . . . . John the Baptizer
3. Luke 2.1–52. . . Birth and childhood of Jesus
4. Luke 3.21–4.12 . . . .Beginning of Jesus' public life: Baptism and temptation of Jesus
5. Luke 4.16–30 . . . . . . Jesus' rejection at Nazareth
6. Mark 1.16–20; Luke 5.2–11 . . . . . Call of the disciples
7. Mark 9.2–49. . Typical day in Jesus' life
8. Matthew 5.1–48. . . . . . Sermon on the Mount
9. Matthew 6.1–7.29 . . . . Sermon on the Mount
10. Luke 14.1–24; 15;1–32. . Parables of Jesus
11. Luke 22.14–38; John 13.1–17.26 . . Last Supper
12. Matthew 26.36–27.66 . . . Passion and Death of Jesus
13. Matthew 28.1–20 . .The Resurrection; commissioning of the disciples
14. Luke 24.13–35; John 21.15–19 . . . . . The Risen Christ

ONE-WEEK PLAN ON SOCIAL JUSTICE

1. Exodus 3.7–10 . . God hears the cry of the poor
2. Leviticus 25.1–53 . . . A Jubilee Year of rest, forgiveness and generosity
3. Psalm 82–83. . . . . Prayers for the justice of God
4. 1 Kings 21.1–29 . . . . Elijah speaks out against economic oppression
5. Micah 6.1–8 . . . . . What the Lord asks
6. Matthew 6.24–34 God is the source of riches
7. Matthew 25.14–45. . . . . . Judgment of justice

MIRACLES OF JESUS

Jesus did many miracles. He healed people, fed people, and even raised people from the dead. Acts 10.38 says, "God anointed Jesus of Nazareth with the Holy Spirit and with power; . . . he went about doing good and healing all who were oppressed by the devil, for God was with him." Each of Jesus' miracles showed God's glory and proved that Jesus was and is the Son of God. Here's where you can read about some of those miracles.

Changing water into wine . . . . John 2.1–11
Casting out demons . . . . Matthew 8.28–32; Mark 1.21–28
Healing Peter's mother-in-law . . . . Luke 4.38–39
Filling nets with fish . . . . Luke 5.3–11
Healing a man with a skin disease . . . . Matthew 8.1–3
Making the paralyzed man walk . . . . Mark 2.1–12
Healing the man with the crippled hand . . . . Luke 6.6–10
Healing the soldier's servant . . . . Matthew 8.5–13
Bringing the widow's son back to life . . . . Luke 7.11–17
Healing the son of the king's officer . . . . John 4.46–54
Calming the wind and the waves . . . . Matthew 8.23–27
Healing the bleeding woman . . . . Mark 5.25–34; Luke 8.43–48
Healing Jairus's daughter . . . . Luke 8.41–42, 49–56
Healing the sick man by the pool . . . . John 5.1–9
Feeding more than 5,000 people . . . . Mark 6.35–44
Walking on water . . . . John 6.16–21
Freeing a girl from a demon . . . . Matthew 15.21–28
Healing the man who could not hear or speak . . . . Mark 7.31–37
Healing everyone who came to him . . . . Matthew 15.29–31
Feeding more than 4,000 people . . . . Matthew 15.32–38
Healing the blind man in Bethsaida . . . . Mark 8.22–26
Freeing a boy from a demon . . . . Matthew 17.14–20
Catching a fish with a coin in its mouth . . . . Matthew 17.24–27
Healing the man who was born blind . . . . John 9.1–7
Healing ten men with a skin disease . . . . Luke 17.11–19
Bringing Lazarus back to life . . . . John 11.1–44
Healing blind Bartimaeus . . . . Mark 10.46–52
Drying up the fig tree . . . . Matthew 21.18–22
Healing the man whose ear was cut off . . . . Luke 22.47–51
Coming back to life himself . . . . Matthew 28.1–10; Mark 16.1–8; Luke 24.1–12; John 20.1–10
Filling nets with fish after his resurrection . . . . John 21.1–13

KIDS IN THE BIBLE

Children are very important to Jesus. One time his disciples thought the children in the crowd were getting in the way. They tried to make the children go away, but Jesus made the disciples stop. He said, "Let the little children come to me." And then, the Bible says, "He took them up in his arms, laid his hands on them, and blessed them" (Mark 10.14, 16).

First Timothy 4.12 says not to be embarrassed about being young. Even though you aren't grown up yet, you are still special. And God can do great things through you! Take a look at these children of the Bible. Read how their lives made a difference.

Samuel—As a boy, Samuel heard God's voice and then grew up to be a great prophet.

1 Samuel 3.1–19

David—As a young shepherd, David accepted the call to become the future king; he also played music that brought peace to King Saul, and he killed the giant Goliath.

1 Samuel 16–17

Naaman's servant girl—She told Naaman about a prophet who could heal him and change his life.

2 Kings 5.1–14

Joash—He became king when he was seven, and during his reign, he repaired God's temple.

2 Kings 11–12

Josiah—He was crowned king at age eight and later led the people of Israel to follow God.

2 Kings 22

Jesus—He listened and taught in the temple when he was only twelve years old.

Luke 2.42–52

Children coming to Jesus—Jesus gave them his blessing.

Matthew 19.13–15; Mark 10.13–16; Luke 18.15–17

Boy with five loaves and two fish—He shared his lunch and helped Jesus feed more than 5,000 people.

John 6.1–14

Rhoda—This servant girl opened the door for Peter and was among the first to hear how an angel had freed Peter from prison.

Acts 12.12–19

Timothy—He was raised by a godly mom and grandmother and grew up to love and serve God.

2 Timothy 1.5–8

BIBLE VERSES FOR MY LIFE

WHEN I NEED PEACE

Psalm 29.11
May the LORD give strength to his people! May the LORD bless his people with peace!

Isaiah 26.3
Those of steadfast mind you keep in peace—in peace because they trust in you.

John 14.27
Peace I leave with you; my peace I give to you. I do not give to you as the world gives. Do not let your hearts be troubled, and do not let them be afraid.

WHEN I NEED HEALING

Psalm 147.3
He heals the broken-hearted, and binds up their wounds.

Isaiah 53.5
But he was wounded for our transgressions, crushed for our iniquities; upon him was the punishment that made us whole, and by his bruises we are healed.

Matthew 9.35
Then Jesus went about all the cities and villages, teaching in their synagogues, and proclaiming the good news of the kingdom, and curing every disease and every sickness.

1 Peter 2.24
He himself bore our sins in his body on the cross, so that, free from sins, we might live for righteousness; by his wounds you have been healed.

WHEN I NEED HELP

Deuteronomy 31.6
Be strong and bold; have no fear or dread of them, because it is the LORD your God who goes with you; he will not fail you or forsake you.

Psalm 46.1
God is our refuge and strength, a very present help in trouble.

Psalm 54.4
But surely, God is my helper; the Lord is the upholder of my life.

John 14.26
But the Advocate, the Holy Spirit, whom the Father will send in my name, will teach you everything, and remind you of all that I have said to you.

WHEN I NEED HOPE

Psalm 145.9

The LORD is good to all, and his compassion is over all that he has made.

Sirach 39.33

All the works of the Lord are good, and he will supply every need in its time.

Jeremiah 29.11

For surely I know the plans I have for you, says the LORD, plans for your welfare and not for harm, to give you a future with hope.

Philippians 4.19

And my God will fully satisfy every need of yours according to his riches in glory in Christ Jesus.

James 1.17

Every generous act of giving, with every perfect gift, is from above, coming down from the Father of lights, with whom there is no variation or shadow due to change.

WHEN I NEED SOMEONE TO LISTEN

Matthew 7.7

Ask, and it will be given to you; search, and you will find; knock, and the door will be opened for you.

1 Peter 3.12

For the eyes of the Lord are on the righteous, and his ears are open to their prayer. But the face of the Lord is against those who do evil.

1 John 5.14–15

And this is the boldness we have in him, that if we ask anything according to his will, he hears us. And if we know that he hears us in whatever we ask, we know that we have obtained the requests made of him.

Psalm 91.14–15

Those who love me, I will deliver; I will protect those who know my name. When they call to me, I will answer them; I will be with them in trouble, I will rescue them and honour them.

WHEN I NEED TO FEEL LOVED

Zephaniah 3.17

The LORD, your God, is in your midst, a warrior who gives victory; he will rejoice over you with gladness, he will renew you in his love; he will exult over you with loud singing.

John 3.16

For God so loved the world that he gave his only Son, so that everyone who believes in him may not perish but may have eternal life.

1 John 3.1

See what love the Father has given us, that we should be called children of God; and that is what we are.

Romans 8.38–39

For I am convinced that neither death, nor life, nor angels, nor rulers, nor things present, nor things to come, nor powers, nor height, nor depth, nor anything else in all creation, will be able to separate us from the love of God in Christ Jesus our Lord.

WHEN I NEED STRENGTH

Isaiah 40.29

He gives power to the faint, and strengthens the powerless.

Isaiah 41.10

Do not fear, for I am with you, do not be afraid, for I am your God; I will strengthen you, I will help you, I will uphold you with my victorious right hand.

Philippians 4.13

I can do all things through him who strengthens me.

Ephesians 6.10

Finally, be strong in the Lord and in the strength of his power.

WHEN I NEED PROTECTION

Psalm 91.4–5

He will cover you with his pinions, and under his wings you will find refuge; his faithfulness is a shield and buckler. You will not fear the terror of the night, or the arrow that flies by day.

Nahum 1.7

The LORD is good, a stronghold on a day of trouble; he protects those who take refuge in him.

2 Thessalonians 3.3

But the Lord is faithful; he will strengthen you and guard you from the evil one.

WRITE

DRAW

WRITE

DRAW

WRITE

DRAW

WRITE

DRAW

WRITE

DRAW

A NOTE REGARDING THE TYPE

This Bible was set in the Zondervan NRSV Typeface, commissioned by Zondervan, a division of HarperCollins Christian Publishing, and designed in Aarhus, Denmark, by Klaus E. Krogh and Heidi Rand Sørensen of 2K/DENMARK. The design takes inspiration from the vision of the New Revised Standard Version (NRSV) to be a modern, ecumenical translation that serves the church in personal spiritual formation, in the liturgy, and in the academy. The designers of the Zondervan NRSV Typeface sought to reflect the rich heritage of the New Revised Standard Version and its tradition of being renowned for its beautiful balance of scholarship and readability. The result is a distinctive Bible typeface that is uncompromisingly beautiful, clear, and readable at any size, and will faithfully serve a broad range of Bible readers now and in years to come.